Quality of Life
and
Pharmacoeconomics
in
Clinical Trials

Second Edition

Quality of Life
and
Pharmacoeconomics
in
Clinical Trials

Second Edition

Editor

Bert Spilker, Ph.D., M.D.
President
Orphan Medical, Inc.
Minnetonka, Minnesota

Adjunct Professor of Medicine
Adjunct Professor of Pharmacology
Clinical Professor of Pharmacy
University of North Carolina Schools of Medicine and Pharmacy
Chapel Hill, North Carolina

Clinical Professor of Pharmacy Practice
University of Minnesota School of Pharmacy
Minneapolis, Minnesota

Lippincott - Raven
P U B L I S H E R S

Philadelphia • New York

Lippincott-Raven Publishers, 227 East Washington Square, Philadelphia, Pennsylvania 19106

Printed and bound in the United States of America

Library of Congress Cataloging-in-Publication Data

Quality of life and pharmacoeconomics in clinical trials / editor,
  Bert Spilker.—2nd ed.
     p.   cm.
  Rev. ed. of: Quality of life assessment in clinical trials. c1990.
  Includes bibliographical references and index.
  ISBN 0-7817-0332-8
  1. Clinical trials—Social aspects. 2. Quality of life—
Evaluation. I. Spilker, Bert. II. Quality of life assessment in
clinical trials.
  [DNLM: 1. Quality of life. 2. Clinical trials. 3. Drug Therapy—
economics. WA 30 Q1027 1996]
R853.C55Q35 1996
615.5—dc20
DNLM/DLC
for Library of Congress   95-17690

10 9 8 7 6 5 4 3 2 1

To all clinical researchers who are working
to improve the quality of life of patients.

Contents

I: Introduction to the Field of Quality of Life Trials

II: Standard Scales, Tests, and Approaches to Quality of Life Assessments

III: Specific Scales, Tests, and Measures

IV. Choosing and Administering Tests and Treatments

V: Analyzing, Interpreting, and Presenting Data

VI: Special Perspectives on Quality of Life Issues

VII: Cross-Cultural and Cross-National Issues

VIII: Health Policy Issues

IX: Special Populations to Assess Quality of Life

X: Specific Problems and Diseases

XI: Pharmacoeconomics

Contributors

Neil K. Aaronson, Ph.D.
Head
Division of Psychosocial Research and
  Epidemiology
The Netherlands Cancer Institute
Antoni van Leeuwenhoek Hospital
Plesmanlaan 121
1066 CX Amsterdam
The Netherlands

Linda N. Abetz, B.A.
Research Analyst
Child Health Assessment Project
The Health Institute, Box 345
New England Medical Center Hospital
750 Washington Street
Boston, Massachusetts 02111

Catherine Acquadro, M.D.
Associate Professor and
  Development Director
MAPI Research Institute
27 rue de la Villette
F-69003 Lyon
France

John P. Anderson, Ph.D.
Specialist
Division of Health Care Sciences, 0622
Department of Family and Preventive Medicine
School of Medicine
University of California, San Diego
9500 Gilman Drive
La Jolla, California 92093

Roger T. Anderson, Ph.D.
Assistant Professor
Social Sciences and Health Policy Section
Department of Public Health Science
Bowman Gray School of Medicine
Wake Forest University
Medical Center Boulevard
Winston-Salem, North Carolina 27157

Andrew M. Baker, M.P.A.
Director, Outcomes Research
U.S. Pharmaceuticals Group
Pfizer Inc
235 East 42nd Street
New York, New York 10017

Ivan Barofsky, M.A., Ph.D.
Associate Professor of Medical Psychology
Department of Psychiatry and Behavioral
  Sciences
The Johns Hopkins University School of
  Medicine
Division of Digestive Diseases
Johns Hopkins Bayview Medical Center
4940 Eastern Avenue
Baltimore, Maryland 21224

Judith T. Barr, Sc.D.
Director
National Education and Research Center for
  Outcomes Assessment in Healthcare
  (NERCOA)
Bouvé College of Pharmacy and Health Sciences
Northeastern University
105 Dockser Hall
Boston, Massachusetts 02115

Richard S. Beaser, M.D.
Assistant Clinical Professor of Medicine
Harvard Medical School
Assistant Section Head of Internal Medicine
  Section
Medical Director of the Diabetes Treatment Unit
Joslin Diabetes Center and New England
  Deaconess Hospital
One Joslin Place
Boston, Massachusetts 02215

C. Keith Beck, M.D.
Assistant Clinical Professor
Department of Medicine
Harbor-UCLA Medical Center
1000 West Carson Street
Torrance, California 90509

Thomas K. Beckett, B.S.
President
Langford Creek Associates, Ltd.
6920 Pentridge Lane
Chestertown, Maryland 21620

Kathryn J. Bennett, M.Sc.
Department of Clinical Epidemiology and
*   Biostatistics*
McMaster University
1200 Main Street West
Hamilton, Ontario L8N 3Z5
Canada

Jürg Bernhard, Ph.D.
Clinical Psychologist
International Breast Cancer Study Group
(IBCSG)
Coordinating Center
Konsumstraße 13
CH-3007 Bern
Switzerland

Richard A. Berzon, Dr.P.H.
Health Economics Research Scientist
Department of Economics Research
ISEER Division
Burroughs Wellcome Company
3030 Cornwallis Road
Research Triangle Park, North Carolina 27709

Stefan Björk, B.A., Ph.D.
Programme Manager
IHE-The Swedish Institute for Health Economics
Råbygatan 2, Box 2127
S-22002 Lund
Sweden

Amy E. Bonomi, B.S.
Operations Director
Department of Psychosocial Oncology
Rush-Presbyterian–St. Luke's Medical Center
1725 West Harrison Street, Suite 863
Chicago, Illinois 60302

Samuel A. Bozzette, M.D., Ph.D.
Associate Professor of Medicine
University of California, San Diego
Senior Scientist
Department of Social Policy
RAND Corporation–Health Sciences Program
1700 Main Street, (P.O. Box 2138)
Santa Monica, California 90407

Andrew L. Brickman, Ph.D.
Research Assistant Professor
Department of Psychiatry and Behavioral
*   Sciences*
University of Miami School of Medicine
1400 North West 10th Avenue, Room 704 (D-79)
Miami, Florida 33136

Dan Brock, Ph.D.
Department of Philosophy
Brown University
Providence, Rhode Island 02912

Meryl Brod, Ph.D.
Assistant Adjunct Professor
Division of Gerontology and Geriatric Medicine
Department of Medicine
Director
Center for Clinical and Aging Services Research
UCSF/Mount Zion Center on Aging
3330 Geary Boulevard, 2nd Floor
San Francisco, California 94118

Monika Bullinger, Ph.D.
Associate Professor
Institute for Medical Psychology
University of Munich
Goethestraße 31/1
FRG 80336 Munich
Germany

Gregory Burke, M.D., Ph.D.
Division of Oncology and Pulmonary Drug
*   Products*
Center for Drug Evaluation and Research
Food and Drug Administration
Rockville, Maryland 20857

Barbara J. Burns, Ph.D.
Professor of Medical Psychology
Department of Psychiatry and Behavioral
*   Sciences*
Duke University Medical Center
Suite 22B Brightleaf Square
905 West Main Street
Durham, North Carolina 27701

Kathleen A. Cagney, M.A.
Research Associate
Department of Medicine
School of Medicine
Health Services Research and Development
Center
Department of Health Policy and Management
School of Hygiene and Public Health
Johns Hopkins University
624 North Broadway, Room 633
Baltimore, Maryland 21205

Barrie R. Cassileth, Ph.D.
Adjunct Professor
Department of Medicine
University of North Carolina
Consulting Professor
Department of Community and Family Medicine
Duke University
8033 Old NC 86
Chapel Hill, North Carolina 27516

David F. Cella, Ph.D.
Associate Professor
Department of Psychology and Social Sciences
Rush Medical College
1725 West Harrison Street, Suite 863
Chicago, Illinois 60612

Larry W. Chambers, B.A. (Hons.), M.Sc., Ph.D.
Professor
Department of Clinical Epidemiology and
Biostatistics
McMaster University
Epidemiology Consultant, Hamilton-Wentworth
Department of Public Health Services
McMaster University Medical Centre
10 George Street, Suite 302
Hamilton, Ontario L8P 1C8
Canada

Christopher C. Chapman, B.A.
Research Assistant
8033 Old NC 86
Chapel Hill, North Carolina 27516

Paul D. Cleary, Ph.D.
Professor
Department of Health Care Policy
Harvard Medical School
25 Shattuck Street, Parcel B, 1st Floor
Boston, Massachusetts 02115

Jennifer J. Clinch, B.Sc. (Hons), M.A.
Co-Director, Research Analysis
World Health Organization Collaborating
Centre for Quality of Life in Cancer Care
St. Boniface General Hospital Research Centre
351 Tache Avenue
Winnipeg, Manitoba R2H 2A6
Canada

Alan Coates, M.D., F.R.A.C.P.
Associate Professor in Cancer Medicine
University of Sydney
Senior Medical Oncologist
Department of Medical Oncology
Royal Prince Alfred Hospital
Missendon Road
Camperdown NSW 2050
Australia

Bernard F. Cole, Ph.D.
Assistant Professor
Department of Community Health
Brown University
Box F, 182 George Street
Providence, Rhode Island 02912

John M. Conley, Ph.D.
William Rand Kenan, Jr. Professor of Law
School of Law
University of North Carolina at Chapel Hill
Campus Box 3380
Chapel Hill, North Carolina 27599

Carol E. Cornell, Ph.D.
Assistant Professor of Medicine
Behavioral Medicine Unit
Department of Medicine
Division of Preventive Medicine
University of Alabama at Birmingham
1717 11th Avenue South, Suite 401
Birmingham, Alabama 35205

Joyce A. Cramer, B.S.
Associate in Research
Yale University School of Medicine
New Haven, Connecticut
Project Coordinator
Health Services Research 116A
Veterans Affairs Medical Center
950 Campbell Avenue
West Haven, Connecticut 06516

Ann M. Cull, B.Sc., M.Phil., Ph.D.
Consultant Clinical Psychologist
ICRF Medical Oncology Unit
Western General Hospital
Edinburgh, EH4 2XU
Scotland

William E. Cunningham, M.D., M.P.H.
Assistant Professor of Public Health and
*   Medicine*
School of Public Health
University of California, Los Angeles
31-254A CHS
Los Angeles, California 90095

Susan M. Czajkowski, Ph.D.
Social Science Analyst
Division of Epidemiology and Clinical
*   Applications*
National Heart, Lung, and Blood Institute
National Institutes of Health
Bethesda, Maryland 20892

Anne M. Damiano, Sc.D.
Senior Associate
Health Technology Associates, Inc.
1100 New York Avenue, NW, Suite 200 East
Washington, D.C. 20005

Patricia M. Danzon, Ph.D.
Celia Moh Professor
Department of Health Care Systems and
*   Insurance and Risk Management*
The Wharton School
University of Pennsylvania
3641 Locust Walk
Philadelphia, Pennsylvania 19104

Richard F. Davis, Psy.D.
Center for Studies of Addiction
University of Pennsylvania
Department of Veterans Affairs Medical Center
3900 Chestnut Street
Philadelphia, Pennsylvania 19104

Atara Kaplan De-Nour, M.D.
Professor and Chairman
Department of Psychiatry
Hadassah University Hospital
P.O. Box 12000
91120 Jerusalem
Israel

Leonard R. Derogatis, Ph.D.
President
Clinical Psychometric Research, Inc.
100 West Pennsylvania Avenue, Suite 302
Towson, Maryland 21204

Maureen F. Derogatis, M.A.S.
Clinical Psychometric Research, Inc.
100 West Pennsylvania Avenue, Suite 302
Towson, Maryland 21204

Douglas A. Drossman, M.D.
Professor of Medicine and Psychiatry
Department of Medicine
University of North Carolina at Chapel Hill
420 Burnett-Womack Building, CB 7080
Chapel Hill, North Carolina 27599

Michael F. Drummond, B.Sc., M. Com.,
*   **D. Phil.***
Professor of Economics
Centre for Health Economics
University of York
Heslington, York YO1 5DD
England

David M. Eddy, M.D., Ph.D.
Senior Advisor for Health Policy and
*   Management*
Southern California Kaiser Permanente
Walnut Center
393 East Walnut Street
Pasadena, California 91188

Jan M. Ellerhorst-Ryan, R.N., M.S.N., C.S.
Oncology/HIV Clinical Nurse Specialist
Abbey Infusion Services
2327 Crowne Point Drive
Cincinnati, Ohio 45241

David Ellis, M.A.
Consultant in Linguistics
MAPI Research Institute
27 rue de la Villette
F-69003 Lyon
France

Robert S. Epstein, M.D., M.S.
Outcomes Research and Management
Merck & Company
P.O. Box 4, WP 39-1097
West Point, Pennsylvania 19486

Pennifer Erickson
Chief
Clearinghouse on Health Indexes
Office of Analysis, Epidemiology, and Health
* Promotion*
National Center for Health Statistics, Room 730
6525 Belcrest Road
Hyattsville, Maryland 20782

Margot K. Ettl, R.N., M.A.
Center for Clinical AIDS Research and
* Education (CARE)*
University of California, Los Angeles
BH-412 CHS
10833 Le Conte Avenue
Los Angeles, California 90095

Diane L. Fairclough, Dr.P.H.
Lecturer
Department of Biostatistics
Harvard School of Public Health
44 Binney Street
Boston, Massachusetts 02115

David H. Feeny, Ph.D.
Professor of Economics and Clinical
* Epidemiology and Biostatistics*
Centre for Health Economics and Policy
* Analysis*
Health Sciences Center, Room 3H3
Department of Clinical Epidemiology and
* Biostatistics*
McMaster University
1200 Main Street West
Hamilton, Ontario, L8N 3Z5
Canada

Betty R. Ferrell, Ph.D., F.A.A.N.
Associate Research Scientist
Department of Nursing Research and Education
City of Hope National Medical Center
1500 East Duarte Road
Duarte, California 91010

Megan P. Fleming, B.A., Ph.D. (Cand)
Department of Clinical and Health Psychology
Hahnemann University
12 Hamilton Circle
Philadelphia, Pennsylvania 19130

Floyd J. Fowler, Jr., Ph.D.
Senior Research Fellow
Center for Survey Research
University of Massachusetts at Boston
100 Morrissey Boulevard
Boston, Massachusetts 02125

Michael A. Fraumeni, B.A., B.Ed., M.L.S.
Librarian
Library Services
Hamilton Regional Cancer Centre
Ontario Cancer Treatment and Research
* Foundation*
699 Concession Street
Hamilton, Ontario L8V 5C2
Canada

Marsha D. Fretwell, M.D.
Medical Director
The Senior Wellness Clinic
714 Champ Davis Road
Wilmington, North Carolina 28405

Michael A. Friedman, M.D.
Cancer Therapy Evaluation Program
Division of Cancer Treatment
National Cancer Institute
Bethesda, Maryland 20892

James F. Fries, M.D.
Professor
Department of Medicine
Stanford University School of Medicine
1000 Welch Road, Suite 203
Palo Alto, California 94304

Curt D. Furberg, M.D., Ph.D.
Professor
Department of Public Health Sciences
Bowman Gray School of Medicine
Wake Forest University
Medical Center Boulevard
Winston-Salem, North Carolina 27157

William J. Furlong, B.Sc.
Researcher
Centre for Health Economics and Policy
* Analysis*
Department of Clinical Epidemiology and
* Biostatistics*
McMaster University
1200 Main Street West
Hamilton, Ontario L8N 3Z5
Canada

Barbara L. Gandek, M.S.
Senior Project Director
The Health Institute
New England Medical Center
750 Washington Street, Box 345
Boston, Massachusetts 02111

Sharon B. Garbus, B.P.S.
Consultant, Clinical Research
Department of Internal Medicine
Joslin Diabetes Center
One Joslin Place
Boston, Massachusetts 02215

Stanley B. Garbus, M.D., M.P.H.
Vice President, Medical Director
ClinMark Associates, Inc
800 Palisade Avenue, Suite 801
Fort Lee, New Jersey 07024

Richard D. Gelber, Ph.D.
Professor of Pediatrics (Biostatistics)
Harvard Medical School
Harvard School of Public Health
Dana-Farber Cancer Institute
44 Binney Street
Boston, Massachusetts 02115

Shari Gelber, M.S.W., M.Sc.
Biostatistician
Frontier Science and Technology Research
   Foundation
303 Boylston Street
Brookline, Massachusetts 02146

Paul P. Glasziou, M.B., B.S., Ph.D.
Senior Lecturer in Clinical Epidemiology
Department of Social and Preventive Medicine
Medical School
University of Queensland
Herston Road, Herston
Brisbane QLD 4006
Australia

Christopher G. Goetz, M.D.
Professor
Department of Neurological Sciences
Rush University/Rush-Presbyterian–St. Luke's
   Medical Center
1725 West Harrison Street, Suite 1106
Chicago, Illinois 60612

Aron Goldhirsch, M.D.
Professor
International Breast Center Study Group and
   Swiss Group for Clinical Research
Department of Medical Oncology
Ospedale Civico
6900 Lugano
Switzerland

**Michael D. E. Goodyear, B.Med. Sc.,
   M.B.B.S., F.R.A.C.P., F.R.C.P.(C),
   F.A.C.P.**
Medical Oncologist
Hamilton Regional Cancer Centre
McMaster University
699 Concession Street
Hamilton, Ontario L8V 5C2
Canada

Deborah R. Gordon, Ph.D.
Research Associate, Medical Anthropology
Department of Clinical Epidemiology
Center for the Study and Prevention of Cancer
Via di San Salvi, 12
50131 Florence
Italy

Carolyn Cook Gotay, Ph.D.
Associate Researcher
Cancer Research Center
University of Hawaii
1236 Lauhala Street, Room 406
Honolulu, Hawaii 96813

Henry G. Grabowski, Ph.D.
Professor
Department of Economics
Duke University
305 Social Sciences, Box 90097
Durham, North Carolina 27708

Marcia M. Grant, D.N.Sc., F.A.A.N.
Director and Associate Research Scientist
Department of Nursing Research and Education
City of Hope National Medical Center
1500 East Duarte Road
Duarte, California 91010

Edward Guadagnoli, Ph.D.
Assistant Professor
Department of Health Care Policy
Harvard Medical School
25 Shattuck Street
Parcel B, 1st Floor
Boston, Massachusetts 02115

Peter J. Guarnaccia, Ph.D.
Associate Professor
Department of Human Ecology
Cook College, Box 231
Associate Professor
Institute for Health, Health Care Policy, and
  Aging Research
Rutgers University
30 College Avenue
New Brunswick, New Jersey 08903

Harry A. Guess, M.D., Ph.D.
Adjunct Professor of Epidemiology and
  Biostatistics
Department of Epidemiology
University of North Carolina
CB 7400, McGavran-Greenberg Hall
Chapel Hill, North Carolina 27599
Merck Research Laboratories
10-Sentry Parkway
Blue Bell, Pennsylvania 19422

Gordon H. Guyatt, M.D., F.R.C.P.(C)., B.Sc.
Professor
Department of Medicine, Clinical
  Epidemiology, and Biostatistics
McMaster University
Health Sciences Centre
1200 Main Street West
Hamilton, Ontario L8N 3Z5
Canada

Ronald W. Hansen, Ph.D.
Associate Dean of Academic Affairs
William E. Simon Graduate School for
  Business Administration
University of Rochester
Dewey 203
Rochester, New York 14627

Ron D. Hays, Ph.D.
RAND
1700 Main Street
Santa Monica, California 90407
Adjunct Associate Professor
Department of Medicine
UCLA School of Medicine
10833 Le Conte Avenue
Los Angeles, California 90095

Susan C. Hedrick, Ph.D.
Associate Professor
Department of Health Services
University of Washington
Associate Research Career Scientist
Health Services Research and Development
  Field Program (152)
Department of Veterans Affairs Medical Center
1660 South Columbian Way
Seattle, Washington 98108

Alan L. Hillman, M.D., M.B.A.
Associate Professor
Departments of Medicine and Health Care
  Systems
The Wharton School
University of Pennsylvania
3641 Locust Walk
Philadelphia, Pennsylvania 19104

Pamela S. Hinds, Ph.D., R.N., C.S.
Coordinator of Nursing Research
Associate Director of Research for Behavioral
  Medicine
Departments of Nursing and Behavioral
  Medicine
St. Jude Children's Research Hospital
332 North Lauderdale, Box 318
Memphis, Tennessee 38101

Christoph D. T. Hürny, M.D.
Lecturer of Psychosocial Medicine
Medical Division Lory
University Hospital Insel
CH-3010 Bern
Switzerland

Janis F. Hutchinson, Ph.D.
Associate Professor
Department of Anthropology
University of Houston
1400 Calhoun Street
Houston, Texas 77204

Alan M. Jacobson, M.D.
Associate Professor in Psychiatry
Harvard Medical School
Chief, Psychiatry Service
Joslin Diabetes Center
One Joslin Place
Boston, Massachusetts 02215

Roman Jaeschke, M.D., M.Sc.
Associate Clinical Professor
Department of Medicine
McMaster University
301 James Street South
Hamilton, Ontario L8P 3B6
Canada

Bernard Jambon, M.A.(Law, Economics)
General Manager
MAPI Research Institute
27 rue de la Villette
F-69003 Lyon
France

Magnus Johannesson, Ph.D.
Associate Professor of Health Economics
Centre for Health Economics
Stockholm School of Economics
Box 6501
S-113 83 Stockholm
Sweden

Deborah J. Johnson, B.A.
Research Associate
The Dartmouth COOP Project
Department of Community and Family Medicine
Dartmouth Medical School
Hinman Box 7265
Hanover, New Hampshire 03755

Thomas M. Johnson, Ph.D.
Professor
Family Medicine Program
School of Primary Medical Care
The University of Alabama in Huntsville
201 Governor Drive Southwest
Huntsville, Alabama 35801

David A. Jones, M.Sc., C. Stat.
Department of Strategic Health Economics
The Wellcome Foundation, Ltd.
Langley Court, Beckenham
Kent BR3 3BS
England

Bengt G. Jönsson, Ph.D.
Professor of Health Economics
Centre for Health Economics
Stockholm School of Economics
Box 6501
S-113 83 Stockholm
Sweden

Elizabeth F. Juniper, M.C.S.P., M.Sc.
Associate Clinical Professor
Department of Clinical Epidemiology and
  Biostatistics
McMaster University
Faculty of Health Sciences Center
1200 Main Street West
Hamilton, Ontario L8N 3Z5
Canada

Stein Kaasa, M.D.
Professor of Palliative Medicine
Palliative Medicine Unit
Department of Oncology and Radiotherapy
Trondheim University Hospital
Olav Kyrress Gate 17
N-7006 Trondheim
Norway

Robert M. Kaplan, Ph.D.
Professor and Chief
Division of Health Care Sciences
Department of Family and Preventive Medicine
School of Medicine
University of California, San Diego
9500 Gilman Drive, Box 0622
La Jolla, California 92037

Elizabeth W. Karlson, M.D.
Instructor of Medicine
Department of Rheumatology/Immunology and
  Medicine
Brigham and Women's Hospital
75 Francis Street
Boston, Massachusetts 02115

Jeffrey N. Katz, M.D., M.S.
Assistant Professor of Medicine
Department of Rheumatology/Immunology and
  Medicine
Harvard Medical School
Brigham and Women's Hospital
Robert B. Brigham Multipurpose Arthritis and
  Musculoskeletal Diseases Center
75 Francis Street
Boston, Massachusetts 02115

Susan D. Keller, Ph.D.
Instructor
Harvard University
School of Public Health
The Health Institute
New England Medical Center
750 Washington Street, Box 345
Boston, Massachusetts 02111

Paul Kind, M.Sc., M.Phil.
Senior Research Fellow
Centre for Health Economics
University of York
York, YO1 5DD
England

Susan V. M. Kleinbeck, R.N., M.S.,
 C.N.O.R., Ph.D(Cand)
University of Kansas School of Nursing
3901 Rainbow Boulevard
Kansas City, Kansas 66160

Richard A. Krueger, Ph.D.
Professor
Minnesota Extension Service and
 Department of Vocational Technical
 Education
University of Minnesota
1954 Buford Avenue
St. Paul, Minnesota 55108

Roberta Labelle (Deceased)
Department of Clinical Epidemiology and
 Biostatistics
Center for Health Economics and Policy
 Analysis
Department of Management Science
McMaster University
Hamilton, Ontario L8N 325
Canada

Karen T. Labuhn, M.S.N., M.P.H., Ph.D.
Associate Professor
College of Nursing
Wayne State University
Cohn Building
5557 Cass Avenue
Detroit, Michigan 48202

Jeanne M. Landgraf, M.A.
Director, Child Health Assessment Project
The Health Institute
New England Medical Center
350 Washington Street, Box 345
Boston, Massachusetts 02111

Karen J. Lechter, J.D., Ph.D.
Social Science Analyst
Division of Drug Marketing, Advertising, and
 Communications
United States Food and Drug Administration
5600 Fishers Lane
Rockville, Maryland 20857

Paul P. Lee, M.D., J.D.
Assistant Professor
Department of Ophthalmology
University of Southern California School of
 Medicine
1450 San Pablo Street
Los Angeles, California 90033
Consultant
Health Sciences Program
RAND
1700 Main Street
Santa Monica, California 90407

Victor C. Lee, M.D.
Associate Professor
Department of Anesthesiology
University of Virginia Health Sciences Center
Box 238
Charlottesville, Virginia 22908

Anthony F. Lehman, M.D., M.S.P.H.
Professor
Department of Psychiatry
University of Maryland
645 West Redwood Street
Baltimore, Maryland 21201

Alain P. Leplège, M.D., Ph.D.
Health Science Researcher
INSERM, Unit 292
Hôpital de Bicêtre
Service de Santé Publique et d'Épidémiologie
78 rue du Général Leclerc
94275 Le Kremlin-Bicêtre Cédex
France

Joseph A. Leveque, M.D., M.B.A.
Vice President
Lash Group Healthcare Consultants
1400 Fashion Island Boulevard, Suite 810
San Mateo, California 94404

Robert J. Levine, M.D.
Professor of Medicine and Lecturer in
 Pharmacology
Department of Medicine
Yale University
333 Cedar Street, Room IE-48 SHM
New Haven, Connecticut 06520

Matthew H. Liang, M.D., M.P.H.
Professor
Department of Rheumatology/Immunology and
*   Medicine*
Brigham and Women's Hospital
75 Francis Street
Boston, Massachusetts 02115

Stephen R. Lloyd, Ph.D.
Assistant Professor of Psychology
Departments of Psychology and Social Science
Rush-Presbyterian–St. Luke's Medical Center
1725 West Harrison Street, Suite 863
Chicago, Illinois 60612

Brian Lovatt
Director, Business Economics
The Wellcome Foundation, Ltd.
Beckenham, Kent BR3 3BS
England

Thomas M. Lumley, M.Sc.
NHMRC Clinical Trials Centre
Edward Ford Building (A27)
The University of Sydney
Sydney NSW 2006
Australia

Eva G. Lydick, Ph.D.
Director, Pharmacoepidemiology
Worldwide Product Safety and Epidemiology
Merck Research Laboratories
P.O. Box 4, BLA-31
West Point, Pennsylvania 19486

Carol M. Mangione, M.D., M.S.P.H.
Assistant Professor
Department of Medicine
University of California, Los Angeles
10833 Le Conte Avenue
Los Angeles, California 90095

Patrick Marquis, M.D., M.B.A.
Study Director
MAPI Research Institute
27 rue de la Villette
F-69003 Lyon
France

Andrew J. Martin, B.A., M.A.
Senior Research Assistant
NHMRC Clinical Trials Centre
The University of Sydney
Sydney 2006
Australia

Josephine A. Mauskopf, Ph.D., M.H.A., M.A.
Department Head
International Economics Research
Burroughs Wellcome Company
3030 Cornwallis Road
Research Triangle Park, North Carolina 27709

Mary S. McCabe, R.N., C.T.E.P., D.C.T., N.C.I.
Clinical Trials Specialist
Cancer Therapy Evaluation Program–EPN
*   715A*
Division of Cancer Treatment
National Cancer Institute
Bethesda, Maryland 20892

Newell E. McElwee, Pharm.D., M.S.P.H.
Director, Pharmacoeconomics
Intergrated Therapeutics Group, Inc.
A Subsidiary of Schering-Plough Corporation
2000 Galloping Hill Road, K-6-2-D5
Kenilworth, New Jersey 07033

James McEwen, M.B.Ch.B., F.F.P.H.M., F.F.O.M., F.R.C.P.(Glasg)
Henry Mechan Professor of Public Health
Department of Public Health
University of Glasgow
2 Lilybank Gardens
Glasgow, G12 8RZ
Scotland

Mary S. McFarlane, M.A., Ph.D.
Assistant Professor of Biostatistics
Section of Biostatistics
Department of Public Health Sciences
Bowman Gray School of Medicine
Wake Forest University
Medical Center Boulevard
Winston-Salem, North Carolina 27157

William F. McGhan, Pharm.D., Ph.D.
Professor and Senior Researcher
Institute for Pharmaceutical Economics
Department of Pharmacy Practice and
*   Administration*
Philadelphia College of Pharmacy and Science
600 South 43rd Street
Philadelphia, Pennsylvania 19104

Stephen P. McKenna, B.A., Ph.D.
Director
Galen Research
137 Barlow Moor Road
West Didsbury
Manchester M20 2PW
England

Robin S. McLeod, M.D., F.R.C.S.(C).,
F.A.C.S.
Professor of Surgery
Departments of Surgery, Preventive Medicine,
*   and Biostatistics*
University of Toronto
Clinical Epidemiology Unit
Samuel Lunenfeld Research Institute
Mount Sinai Hospital
600 University Avenue, Room 449
Toronto, Ontario M5G 1X5
Canada

A. John McSweeny, Ph.D.
Professor of Psychiatry and Neurology
Department of Psychiatry
Medical College of Ohio
3000 Arlington Avenue
Toledo, Ohio 43699

Joseph Menzin, Ph.D.
Senior Economist
Policy Analysis, Inc.
Four Davis Court
Brookline, Massachusetts 02146

David S. Metzger, Ph.D.
Center for Studies of Addiction
University of Pennsylvania
Department of Veterans Affairs Medical Center
3900 Chestnut Street
Philadelphia, Pennsylvania 19104

Andrew S. Mitchell, B.Pharm., M.Med.Sci.
Director
Pharmaceutical Evaluation Section
Pharmaceutical Benefits Branch
Department of Human Services and Health
GPO Box 9848
Canberra ACT 2601
Australia

Vincent Mor, Ph.D.
Professor of Medical Science
Department of Community Health, Medical
*   School*
Director, Center for Gerontology and Health
*   Care Research*
Brown University
171 Meeting Streets, Box G-213
Providence, Rhode Island 02912

Louis A. Morris, Ph.D.
Division of Drug Marketing, Advertising, and
*   Communications (HFD-240)*
Food and Drug Administration
5600 Fishers Lane
Rockville, Maryland 20857

Michelle J. Naughton, Ph.D., M.P.H.
Assistant Professor
Section on Social Sciences and Health Policy
Department of Public Health Sciences
Bowman Gray School of Medicine
Wake Forest University
Medical Center Boulevard
Winston-Salem, North Carolina 27157

Susan G. Nayfield, M.D., M.Sc.
Medical Officer
Chemoprevention Branch, Cancer Prevention
*   Research Program*
Division of Cancer Prevention and Control
National Cancer Institute
National Institutes of Health
9000 Rockville Pike, Room 201A, EPN
Bethesda, Maryland 20892

Eugene C. Nelson, D.Sc., M.P.H.
Professor, Community and Family Medicine
Dartmouth Medical School
Director, Quality Education, Measurement,
*   and Research*
Lahey Hitchcock Clinic
One Medical Center Drive
Lebanon, New Hampshire 03756

Paul Nordberg, A.B.
Department of Health Policy and Management
Harvard School of Public Health
677 Huntington Avenue
Boston, Massachusetts 02115

Albert Oberman, M.D., M.P.H.
Professor, Department of Medicine
Director, Division of Preventive Medicine
University of Alabama at Birmingham
1717 11th Avenue South, Suite 731
Birmingham, Alabama 35205

Bernie J. O'Brien, B.A., M.Sc., Ph.D.
Associate Professor
Department of Clinical Epidemiology and
*   Biostatistics*
McMaster University
Centre for Evaluation of Medicines, H-329
St. Joseph's Hospital
50 Charlton Avenue East
Hamilton, Ontario L8N 4A6
Canada

Charles P. O'Brien, M.D., Ph.D.
Center for Studies of Addiction
University of Pennsylvania
Department of Veterans Affairs Medical Center
3900 Chestnut Street
Philadelphia, Pennsylvania 19104

Charles L. M. Olweny, M.B.Ch.B., M.Med.,
**   M.D., F.R.A.C.P.**
Professor
University of Manitoba
Department of Medicine
St. Boniface General Hospital
351 Tache Avenue
Winnipeg, Manitoba R2H 2A6
Canada

Flemming Ørnskov, M.D., M.B.A. (Cand.)
Associate Director
Department of Outcomes Research
Merck and Company, Inc.
One Merck Drive
P.O. Box 100, WS1B-75
Whitehouse Station, New Jersey 08889

Gerry Oster, Ph.D.
Vice President
Policy Analysis Inc.
Four Davis Court
Brookline, Massachusetts 02146

Eugenio Paci, M.D.
Epidemiologist
Center for the Study and Prevention of Cancer
Department of Clinical Epidemiology
Unit of Epidemiology
Via di San Salvi, 12
50131 Florence
Italy

Geraldine V. Padilla, Ph.D.
Professor
School of Nursing
University of California, Los Angeles
Factor Building, Room 2-244
10833 Le Conte Avenue
Los Angeles, California 90095

A. David Paltiel, Ph.D.
Assistant Professor
Department of Health Policy and Management
Harvard School of Public Health
718 Huntington Avenue
Boston, Massachusetts 02115

Donald L. Patrick, Ph.D., M.S.P.H.
Professor
Department of Health Services, SC-37
University of Washington
Box 357660
Seattle, Washington 98195

John E. Paul, Ph.D.
Director
Clinical Analytical Services
Disease Management Division
Glaxo Wellcome, Inc.
3030 Cornwallis Road
P.O. Box 12700
Research Triangle Park, North Carolina 27709

Michael J. Power, B.Sc., M.Sc., D.Phil.
Professor of Clinical Psychology
Department of Psychiatry
Royal Edinburgh Hospital
University of Edinburgh
Kennedy Tower
Morningside Park
Edinburgh EH10 5HF
Scotland

Cary A. Presant, M.D., F.A.C.P.
California Cancer Medical Center
1250 South Sunset Avenue, Suite 303
West Covina, California 91790

James M. Raczynski, Ph.D.
Professor
Behavioral Medicine Unit
Department of Medicine
Division of Preventive Medicine
University of Alabama at Birmingham
1717 11th Avenue South, Suite 401
Birmingham, Alabama 35205

Dena R. Ramey, B.A.
Senior Research Assistant
Outcome Assessment/Quality Control Director
Department of Medicine
Division of Immunology and Rheumatology
Stanford University
1000 Welch Road, Suite 203
Palo Alto, California 94304

Dennis A. Revicki, Ph.D.
Vice President
Health Outcomes Research
MEDTAP International
2101 Wilson Boulevard, Suite 802
Arlington, Virginia 22201
Professor
Department of Health Policy and Administration
School of Public Health
University of North Carolina at Chapel Hill
Chapel Hill, North Carolina 27599

Brian E. Rittenhouse, Ph.D.
Assistant Professor
Pharmaceutical Policy and Evaluative Sciences
University of North Carolina at Chapel Hill
CB7360, Beard Hall
Chapel Hill, North Carolina 27599

Peter L. Rosenbaum, M.D., F.R.C.P.(C).
Professor
Department of Pediatrics
McMaster University/Chedoke-McMaster
  Hospitals
Box 2000
Hamilton, Ontario L8N 3Z5
Canada

John C. Rowlingson, M.D.
Professor of Anesthesiology
Director, Pain Management Center
Department of Anesthesiology
University of Virginia Health Sciences Center
Jefferson Park Avenue
Charlottesville, Virginia 22908

Lisa V. Rubenstein, M.D., M.S.P.H.
Associate Clinical Professor
Department of Medicine
University of California, Los Angeles
Veterans Health Administration Medical
  Center (152)
16111 Plummer Street
Sepulveda, California 91343

Peter J. Rutigliano, B.A., Ph.D. (Cand)
School of Medicine
Department of Clinical and Health Psychology
Hahnemann University/M.S. 626
Broad and Vine Streets
Philadelphia, Pennsylvania 19102

Saroj Saigal, M.D., F.R.C.P.(C).
Neonatologist
Professor, Department of Pediatrics
Children's Hospital at Chedoke-McMaster
1200 Main Street West
HSC-3C20
Hamilton, Ontario L8N 3Z5
Canada

Harvey Schipper, B.A.Sc., M.D., F.R.C.P.(C)
Director
World Health Organization Collaborating
  Centre for Quality of Life in Cancer Care
R-2019
351 Tache Avenue
Winnipeg, Manitoba R2H 2A6
Canada

John R. Schoenfelder, Ph.D.
Director, Biostatistics
Pharmacia, Inc.
P.O. Box 16529
Columbus, Ohio 432167

Stephen W. Schondelmeyer, Pharm.D.,
  M.A.Pub.Adm., Ph.D.
Director, PRIME Institute
Department of Pharmacy Practice
University of Minnesota College of Pharmacy
Health Sciences Unit F, Room 7-159
308 Harvard Street South East
Minneapolis, Minnesota 55455

Gerald E. Schumacher, Pharm.D., Ph.D.
Professor of Pharmacy
Department of Pharmacy Practice
Northeastern University
360 Huntington Avenue, 105DK
Boston, Massachusetts 02115

Martin F. Shapiro, M.D., Ph.D.
Professor
Department of Medicine
University of California, Los Angeles
B558-173617
10833 Le Conte Avenue
Los Angeles, California 90095

Cathy D. Sherbourne, Ph.D.
Senior Health Policy Analyst
RAND–Health Sciences Program
1700 Main Street, P.O. Box 2138
Santa Monica, California 90407

Dale Shoemaker, Ph.D.
Chief, Regulatory Affairs Branch
Cancer Therapy Evaluation Program
Division of Cancer Treatment
National Cancer Institute
Bethesda, Maryland 20892

Sally A. Shumaker, Ph.D.
Professor and Section Head
Social Sciences and Health Policy
Department of Public Health Sciences
Bowman Gray School of Medicine
Wake Forest University
Medical Center Boulevard
Winston-Salem, North Carolina 27157

George P. Simeon, M.A.
Pharmacoeconomist
Ciba-Geigy Limited
Ph9, K-147.6.36
CH-4002 Basel
Switzerland

**R. John Simes, M.D., B.Sc. (Med), M.B., B.S
   (Harvard), F.R.A.C.P.**
Director
NHMRC Clinical Trials Centre
Edward Ford Building A27
The University of Sydney
Sydney NSW 2006
Australia

Gurkirpal Singh, M.D.
Clinical Instructor
Stanford University School of Medicine
Division of Immunology and Rheumatology
1000 Welch Road, Suite 203
Palo Alto, California 94304

Carol E. Smith, R.N., Ph.D.
Professor
School of Nursing
University of Kansas
5030 Taylor Building
3901 Rainbow Boulevard
Kansas City, Kansas 66160

William D. Spector, Ph.D.
Research Fellow
Division of Long Term Care Studies
Agency for Health Care Policy and Research
Center for Intramural Research
2101 East Jefferson Street, Suite 500
Rockville, Maryland 20852

Bert Spilker, Ph.D., M.D.
President
Orphan Medical, Inc.
13911 Ridgedale Drive, Suite 475
Minnetonka, Minnesota 55305

Mirjam A. G. Sprangers, Ph.D.
Division of Psychosocial Research and
   Epidemiology
The Netherlands Cancer Institute
Plesmanlaan 121
1066 CX Amsterdam
The Netherlands

Glenn T. Stebbins, Ph.D.
Assistant Professor
Department of Neurological Sciences
Rush-Presbyterian–St. Luke's Medical Center
1725 West Harrison, Suite 1106
Chicago, Illinois 60612

Donald M. Steinwachs, Ph.D.
Professor and Chair
Health Policy and Management
Johns Hopkins School of Hygiene and Public
   Health
624 North Broadway
Baltimore, Maryland 21205

Anita L. Stewart, Ph.D.
Associate Professor in Residence
Institute for Health and Aging
Department of Social and Behavioral Sciences
University of California, San Francisco
Box 0646 Laurel Heights
San Francisco, California 94143

Aaron A. Stinnett, M.S.P.H., Ph.D. (Cand.)
Department of Health Policy and Management
Harvard School of Public Health
718 Huntington Avenue
Boston, Massachusetts 02115

David S. Sugano, Dr.P.H.
Director, Pharmacoeconomics
Integrated Therapeutics Group, Inc.
A Subsidiary of Schering-Plough Corporation
2000 Galloping Hill Road, K-6-2-D5
Kenilworth, New Jersey 07033

Silvija Szabo, Ph.D.
Professor
Department of Psychology
Faculty of Philosophy
University of Zagreb
Salajeva 3
41000 Zagreb
Croatia

Richard C. Taeuber, Ph.D.
OLGA
28165 Bishops Court
Salisbury, Maryland 21801

Robert J. Temple, M.D.
Director, Office of Drug Evaluation I
Center for Drug Evaluation and Research
Food and Drug Administration
5600 Fishers Lane, HFD-100
Rockville, Maryland 20857

Hugh H. Tilson, M.D., Dr.P.H.
Worldwide Director and Vice President
Epidemiology, Surveillance, and Policy
* Research*
Glaxo Wellcome
3030 Cornwallis Road
Research Triangle Park, North Carolina 27709

George W. Torrance, B.A.Sc., M.B.A., Ph.D.
Professor
Department of Clinical Epidemiology and
* Biostatistics*
McMaster University
1200 Main Street West
Hamilton, Ontario L8N 3Z5
Canada

Ralph R. Turner, Ph.D.
Director
Department of Health Economics
Johnson & Johnson, Inc.
920 US 202, P.O. Box 300
Raritan, New Jersey 08869

Claudette G. Varricchio, D.S.N., R.N.,
** O.C.N., F.A.A.N.**
Program Director/Nurse Consultant
Community Oncology Rehabilitation Branch
Division of Cancer Prevention and Control
National Cancer Institute
9000 Rockville Pike, EPN 300
Bethesda, Maryland 20892

John E. Ware, Jr., Ph.D.
Senior Scientist
New England Medical Center
The Health Institute
Division of Health Improvement, Box 345
750 Washington Street
Boston, Massachusetts 02111

John H. Wasson, M.D.
Herman O. West Professor
Research Director, COOP Project
Department of Community and Family Medicine
Dartmouth Medical School
Hinman Box 7265
Hanover, New Hampshire 03755

Milton C. Weinstein, Ph.D.
Henry J. Kaiser Professor
Department of Health Policy and Management
Harvard School of Public Health
718 Huntington Avenue
Boston, Massachusetts 02115

Nanette K. Wenger, M.D.
Professor of Medicine (Cardiology)
Emory University School of Medicine
Grady Memorial Hospital
69 Butler Street, South East
Atlanta, Georgia 30303

Marie B. Whedon, M.S., R.N.
Clinical Nurse Specialist
Instructor, Departments of Medicine
* (Hematology/Oncology) and Psychiatry*
Dartmouth-Hitchcock Medical Center
One Medical Center Drive
Lebanon, New Hampshire, 03756

Ingela K. Wiklund, M.Sc., Ph.D.
Professor of Health Care Research
Department of Public Health
Bergen University
Bergen, Norway
Director
Department of Behavioral Medicine
Astra Hassle AB
Molndal S-431 83
Sweden

David Wilkin, B.Sc., M.Sc., Ph.D.
Professor of Health Services Research
National Primary Care Research and
* Development Centre*
University of Manchester
Oxford Road
Manchester, M13 9PL
England

Alan H. Williams, B.Com.
Professor of Economics
Centre for Health Economics
University of York
York, YO1 5DD
England

T. Franklin Williams, M.D.
Distinguished Physician
Veterans Affairs Medical Center
Canandaigua, New York
Professor of Medicine Emeritus
University of Rochester
Monroe Community Hospital
435 East Henrietta Road
Rochester, New York 14620

Robert S. Wilson, Ph.D.
Associate Professor
Department of Neurological Sciences
Rush University
Rush Alzheimer's Disease Center
Rush-Presbyterian–St. Luke's Medical Center
1645 West Jackson Boulevard
Chicago, Illinois 60612

Benjamin D. Wright, Ph.D.
Professor
Departments of Education and Psychology
MESA Psychometric Laboratory
University of Chicago
5835 South Kimbark Avenue
Chicago, Illinois 60637

James G. Wright, M.D., M.P.H., F.R.C.S.(C).
Assistant Professor
Preventive Medicine, Surgery, and Biostatistics
University of Toronto
Staff Orthopedic Surgeon
Department of Orthopaedic Surgery
The Hospital for Sick Children
555 University Avenue, Suite S107
Toronto, Ontario M5G 1X8
Canada

Albert W. Wu, M.D., M.P.H.
Assistant Professor
Health Services Research and Development
  Center
Department of Health Policy and Management
School of Hygiene and Public Health
Department of Medicine
School of Medicine
Johns Hopkins University
624 North Broadway
Baltimore, Maryland 21205

Preface to the First Edition

The impetus for this book arose because no comprehensive books exist for clinical investigators who conduct quality of life assessments. A few books focus on either a single therapeutic area (e.g., cardiology, oncology) or on selected therapeutic areas. A more comprehensive book which emphasizes the various perspectives both globally and in more detail was needed. This book was designed to meet those needs. It discusses the tests that are available to assess quality of life and the pros and cons of each test, and it also comments on the appropriateness of these tests. Authors were chosen who are acknowledged experts in their field to make this book as authoritative as possible.

The intended audience for this book is primarily the academic, government, or pharmaceutical investigator who is planning to conduct a quality of life trial or to include quality of life assessments as part of a larger trial. The contents of this book will also be of interest to others who plan, conduct, analyze, interpret, review, or otherwise use results of quality of life trials. This includes psychologists, sociologists, statisticians, research assistants, nurses, and numerous other health professionals. Readers are encouraged to review chapters outside their usual areas of interest, because many chapters make important points that are likely to stimulate creative ideas and approaches to those working in other areas.

This book addresses the following basic questions:

1. What are the available tests and methods to use in measuring quality of life?
2. Which tests and methods are validated for use and how may other scales be validated?
3. How does an investigator choose which specific tests to use in specific situations for specific purposes?
4. What is the state-of-the-art in various therapeutic areas' quality of life?

The first section provides an overall perspective on quality of life issues. Specific chapters describe definitions, concepts, appropriate approaches, and basic issues in this area. Section II presents standard scales, tests, and approaches by focusing on the individual component categories (i.e., domains) of quality of life: economics, social interactions, psychological well-being, and physical function. Section III focuses on a number of special perspectives that are pertinent for viewing this field: cultural aspects, marketing, drug industry, and regulatory considerations. The fourth section concerns special patient populations and approaches. These include pediatric, geriatric, drug abuse, rehabilitation, chronic pain, and surgery patients. The fifth and final section discusses specific problems and diseases in a wide variety of therapeutic areas.

There is a certain degree of overlap between chapters in the five sections. This is intentional, because it allows the reader to approach any specific question or situation in multiple ways (e.g., from the perspective of the disease, type of parameters measured, purpose of the study, nature of the patient). Thus, the separate sections are intended to create a whole that is greater than the sum of the individual components.

Bert Spilker

Preface to the Second Edition

Three major considerations prompted me to undertake this second edition of *Quality of Life and Pharmacoeconomics in Clinical Trials*.

First, progress in the area of quality of life has been rapid since the first edition appeared. Cross-national and cross-cultural considerations have exploded, and important progress has been made in these and other areas. I have become aware of different perspectives on health-related quality of life from professionals in areas such as anthropology, alternative treatments, social services, and nursing. Formulary Committee members and other decision-makers also have fueled new insights. This diverse thinking has expanded my views and opened new topics for exploration.

Second, the field of pharmacoeconomics has become far more important in assessing new medicines. The role this concept plays in our society's health care is expanding each year. In this new edition, the relationship, overlap, and interactions of pharmacoeconomics with more traditional quality of life issues are discussed to fully understand quality of life. Health policy issues, such as outcomes research, also play increasingly important roles in our decision-making and need to be part of our thinking in relation to both quality of life and pharmacoeconomics.

Third, it was apparent to me (and to many of you) that a number of issues addressed in the first edition required more detailed discussion. This edition meets that need and goes beyond by adding chapters on several new topics including philosophy, spirituality, phenomenology, and alternative/complementary medical treatments, as related to quality of life.

When is a book complete enough to be a comprehensive reference, and when is it too large? Are there too many chapters in this book to make the subject understandable and digestible? This was an issue raised by a reviewer of the second edition of *Multinational Pharmaceutical Companies: Principles and Practices* which, like this book, more than doubled its size in going from a first to a second edition. My reply is that this book is intended as a reference and therefore must reflect the information in the most comprehensive manner possible. Some chapters clearly overlap because they present different perspectives of the same issue. The subject index and chapter outlines are designed to help you locate information quickly and easily.

One comment I frequently hear about the first edition is that many chapters contain information useful to people in very different disciplines. These people found it valuable to browse through chapters they normally consider outside their realm of interest. We are indeed fortunate that many of the most respected authorities on quality of life issues have participated in this current project and have provided us with important information. I hope this edition will provide you with pleasant surprises, as well as pearls of wisdom and general assistance.

Bert Spilker

Acknowledgments for the First Edition

The editor wishes to acknowledge useful discussions with and help from Dr. Luigi Cubeddu in the early stages of this work. Most of the authors have also provided advice during the numerous stages of this book. Mrs. Joyce Carpunky provided technical assistance throughout this project and Mrs. Brenda Price assisted with typing. Their help is gratefully acknowledged.

Acknowledgments for the Second Edition

When Raven Press asked me to create a second edition of *Quality of Life Assessments in Clinical Trials,* I realized that it was impossible for me to complete this task without help. Raven agreed and asked Judy Hummel to work with me. Completion of this project is due in significant measure to her efforts, efficiency, and organizational skills. I owe her an enormous debt for her hard work, dedication, and cheerful disposition throughout.

In planning this volume, I discussed the concept with a number of people and received valuable advice. I am grateful to all of them for their help. Special thanks to Rick Berzon, David Feeny, Edward Guadagnoli, and Ralph Turner for their comments.

About The Editor

Bert Spilker, Ph.D., M.D., F.C.P., F.F.P.M. is the President of Orphan Medical, Inc. He holds faculty appointments as Adjunct Professor at the University of North Carolina in the Schools of Medicine (Departments of Medicine and Pharmacology) and as Clinical Professor of Pharmacy. He is also Clinical Professor of Pharmacy Practice at the University of Minnesota. Dr. Spilker has over 24 years experience in the pharmaceutical industry, having worked for Pfizer Ltd. (United Kingdom), Philips-Duphar B.V. (The Netherlands), Sterling Drug Inc. (Rensselaer, New York), and the Burroughs Wellcome Co. (Research Triangle Park, North Carolina). He has experience with a private consulting company in the Washington, DC area and has worked in the private practice of general medicine.

Bert Spilker received his Ph.D. in pharmacology from the State University of New York, Downstate Medical Center, and did post-doctoral research at the University of California Medical School in San Francisco. He received his M.D. from the University of Miami Ph.D. to M.D. Program and did a residency in internal medicine at Brown University Medical School. Bert Spilker is the author of over 100 publications plus thirteen books in a wide area of pharmacology, clinical medicine, and medicine development. He is the recipient of numerous honors including the FDA Commissioner's Special Citation for work on orphan medicines.

Dr. Spilker is married and has two grown children.

Other Books by Bert Spilker

Guide to Clinical Studies and Developing Protocols
  (Raven Press, 1984)

Guide to Clinical Interpretation of Data
  (Raven Press, 1986)

Guide to Planning and Managing Multiple Clinical Studies
  (Raven Press, 1987)

Multinational Drug Companies: Issues in Drug Discovery and Development
  (Raven Press, 1989)

Inside the Drug Industry
  (with Pedro Cuatrecasas, Prous Science Publishers, 1990)

Quality of Life Assessments in Clinical Trials
  (Edited, Raven Press, 1990)

Presentation of Clinical Data
  (with John Schoenfelder, Raven Press, 1990)

Patient Compliance in Medical Practice and Clinical Trials
  (Edited with Joyce A. Cramer, Raven Press, 1991)

Data Collection Forms in Clinical Trials
  (with John Schoenfelder, Raven Press, 1991)

Guide to Clinical Trials
  (Raven Press, 1991)

Patient Recruitment in Clinical Trials
  (with Joyce A. Cramer, Raven Press, 1992)

Multinational Pharmaceutical Companies: Principles and Practices (Second Edition)
  (Raven Press, 1994)

Medical Dictionary in Six Languages
  (Compiled in collaboration with DTS Language Services, Inc., Raven Press, 1995)

Selected List of Abbreviations Used in the Text

Many additional abbreviations are used in specific chapters and are identified when they are used.

SF at the end of an instrument's abbreviation usually denotes a short form of the instrument and are not generally listed below. SR at the end of an instrument's abbreviation usually denotes a self-report form of the instrument and is often not listed separately below.

ACE	Angiotensin Converting Enzyme
ACT	Adaptive Control of Thought
ACTG	AIDS Clinical Trial Group
ADL	Activities of Daily Living
ADR	Adverse Drug Reaction
ADVS	Activities of Daily Vision Scale
AHCPR	Agency for Health Care Policy and Research
AIDS	Acquired Immune Deficiency (or Immunodeficiency) Syndrome
AIMS	Arthritis Impact Measurement Scale
ANCOVA	Analysis of Covariance
ARAMIS	Arthritis Rheumatism and Aging Medical Information System
AUASI	American Urological Association Symptom Index
AUC	Area Under the Curve
BCQ	Breast Cancer Chemotherapy Questionnaire
BDI	Beck Depression Inventory
BMT	Bone Marrow Transplant
BPH	Benign Prostatic Hypertrophy
BPI	Brief Pain Inventory
BPRS	Brief Psychiatric Rating Scale
BSI	Brief Symptom Inventory
CABG	Coronary Artery Bypass Grafting
CARE	Care and Resource Evaluation
CARES	Cancer Rehabilitation Evaluation System
CAST	Cardiac Arrhythmia Suppression Trial
CBA	Cost-Benefit Analysis
CCOP	Community Clinical Oncology Program
CDAI	Crohn's Disease Activity Index

CDC	Centers for Disease Control
CEA	Cost-Effectiveness Analysis
CES-D	Centers for Epidemiologic Studies-Depression
cGVHD	Chronic Graft Versus Host Disease
CHAQ	Childhood Health Assessment Questionnaire
CHF	Congestive Heart Failure
CMA	Cost-Minimization Analysis
CMV	Cytomegalovirus
COI	Cost of Illness
COOP	Dartmouth Function Charts
COPD	Chronic Obstructive Pulmonary Disease
CR	Coefficients of Reproducibility
CRDQ	Chronic Respiratory Disease Questionnaire
CS	Coefficients of Scalability
CUA	Cost-Utility Analysis
DABS	Derogatis Affects Balance Scale
DCCT	Diabetes Control and Complications Trial
DHHS	Department of Health and Human Services
DNA	Deoxyribonucleic Acid
DPRS	Derogatis Psychiatric Rating Scale
DQO	Direct Questioning of Objectives
DQOL	Diabetes Quality of Life Measure
DRGs	Diagnostic Related Groups
DSM-IIIR	Diagnostic and Statistical Manual of Mental Disorders-Third Edition—Revised
DUHP	Duke-UNC Health Profile
DVT	Deep Vein Thrombosis
ECOG	Zubrod Scale
EORTC	European Organization for Research and Treatment of Cancer
ESI-55	Epilepsy Surgery Inventory
ESRD	End-Stage Renal Disease
EUROQOL	European Quality of Life Index
FACT	Functional Assessment of Cancer Therapy
FAHI	Functional Assessment of HIV Infection
FDA	Food and Drug Administration
FEV 1	Forced Expiratory Volume in One Second
FIM	Functional Independence Measure

FLIC	Functional Living Index—Cancer		NCI	National Cancer Institute
FLIE	Functional Living Index—Emesis		NLM	National Library of Medicine
FLP	Functional Limitations Profile (Anglicized SIP)		NHANES	National Health and Nutrition Examination Survey
FSI	Functional Status Instrument		NHP	Nottingham Health Profile
FSQ	Functional Status Questionnaire		NHRQL	Non-Health Related Quality of Life
GAO	General Accounting Office		NIH	National Institutes of Health
GDP	Gross Domestic Product		NOAA	National Oceanic and Atmospheric Administration
GHQ	General Health Questionnaire		NSAIDs	Non-Steroidal Antiinflammatory Drugs
GIQLI	Gastrointestinal Quality of Life Index		OLGA	On-Line Guide to Quality of Life Assessment
GRACI	Gastroesophageal Reflux Disease Activity Index		OTC	Over the Counter
GSRS	Gastrointestinal Symptom Rating Scale		PAIS	Psychosocial Adjustment to Illness Scale
GVHD	Graft Versus Host Disease		PASI	Patient-Specific Index
HAQ	Health Assessment Questionnaire		PBAC	Pharmaceutical Benefits Advisory Committee
HCFA	Health Care Financing Administration		PBM	Pharmacy Benefits Manager
HIE	Health Insurance Experiment		PBPA	Pharmaceutical Benefits Pricing Authority
HIV	Human Immunodeficiency Virus		PBS	Pharmaceutical Benefits Scheme
HMO	Health Maintenance Organization		PDAI	Perianal Disease Activity Index
HRQL	Health-Related Quality of Life		PDP	Parallel Distributed Processing
HSCL	Hopkins Symptom Checklist		PEDI	Pediatric Evaluation of Disability Inventory
HUI	Health Utility Index			
HYE	Healthy Years Equivalent		PES	Pharmaceutical Evaluation Section
IADL	Instrumental Activities of Daily Living		PGWB	Psychological General Well-Being Index
IBCSG	International Breast Cancer Study Group		POMS	Profile of Mood States
IBD	Inflammatory Bowel Disease		PORT	Patient Outcomes Research Team
IBDQ	Inflammatory Bowel Disease Questionnaire		PSE	Present State Examination
ICD-10	International Classification of Disease—Tenth Revision		PTCA	Percutaneous Transluminal Coronary Angioplasty
IMPS	Inpatient Multidimensional Psychiatric Scale		PTSD	Post-Traumatic Stress Disorder
IMS	International Monetary System		QALYs	Quality Adjusted Life Years
IPN	International Product Name		QLI	Quality of Life Index
I-PSS	International Prostate Symptom Score		QLQ-C36	EORTC First-Generation Core Questionnaire
IQOLA	International Quality of Life Assessment		QLQ-C30	EORTC Second-Generation Core Questionnaire
IRT	Item Response Theory			
IWB	Index of Well-Being		QOL	Quality of Life
KPS	Karnofsky's Performance Status		QOL-CA	Quality of Life—Cancer Scale
MACTAR	McMaster Toronto Arthritis Patient Function Preference Questionnaire		QOLIE	Quality of Life in Epilepsy
MANOVA	Multivariate Analysis of Variance		Q-TWiST	Quality Adjusted Time Without Symptoms and Toxicity
MAOI	Monoamine Oxidase Inhibitor		QWB	Quality of Well-Being Scale
MDS	Minimum Data Set		RCT	Randomized Clinical Trials
MHAQ	Modified Health Assessment Questionnaire		R&D	Research and Development
MHIQ	McMaster Health Index Questionnaire		RDC	Research Diagnostic Criteria
MHQ	Middlesex Hospital Questionnaire		REM	Rapid Eye Movements
MMPI	Minnesota Multiphasic Personality Inventory		SAHS	Self-Assessed Health Status
MMSE	Mini-Mental State Exam		SAT	Scholastic Aptitude Test
MOS	Medical Outcomes Study		SCI	Science Citation Index
MOS SF-36	MOS 36 Item Short-Form Health Survey		SCL-90	Hopkins Symptom Checklist
MOT	Medical Outcomes Trust		SD	Standard Deviation
MPAQ	Memorial Pain Assessment Card		SDS	Zung Self-Rating Depression Scale
MPQ	McGill Pain Questionnaire		SDRS	Socially Desirable Response Set
			SEM	Standard Error of the Mean

SF-36	Short Form 36 (of MOS Health Survey)	UDS	Uniform Data System for Medical Rehabilitation
SG	Standard Gamble	UTI	Urinary Tract Infection
SGA	Subjective Global Assessment	UK	United Kingdom
SIP	Sickness Impact Profile	US	United States
SRT	Symptom Rating Scale	VAS	Visual Analog Scale
SSA	Subjective Symptom Assessment Profile	VRS	Verbal Rating Scales
SSCI	Social Science Citation Index	WHO	World Health Organization
STAI	Spielberger State-Trait Anxiety Inventory	WHOQOL	World Health Organization Quality of Life Assessment Instrument
TPN	Total Parenteral Nutrition	WHYMPI	West Haven–Yale Multidimensional Pain Inventory
TTO	Time Trade-Off		
TURP	Transurethral Prostatectomy or Transurethral Resection of the Prostate	WOMAC	Western Ontario and McMaster University Osteoarthritis Index
TWiST	Time Without Symptoms and Toxicity		

Quality of Life
and
Pharmacoeconomics
in
Clinical Trials

Second Edition

Quality of Life and Pharmacoeconomics in Clinical Trials, Second Edition, edited by B. Spilker.
Lippincott-Raven Publishers, Philadelphia © 1996.

CHAPTER 1

Introduction

Bert Spilker

INTRODUCTION

Quality of life has become a relevant measure of efficacy in clinical trials. Its use is spreading, and its importance is growing as a valid indicator of whether or not a medical treatment is beneficial. Quality of life may be viewed in terms of an individual, group, or large population of patients. Each of these groups is discussed in this book, and increased attention is given to populations of patients in this edition.

One of the major reasons for confusion in this field is that different authors approach quality of life of pharmacoeconomic issues from totally different perspectives. While some of these differences may never be totally bridged, this introduction is intended to provide a frame of reference that may be used to approach both this book and literature in general.

TYPES OF QUALITY OF LIFE

While it is widely agreed that health-related quality of life is not the only type of quality of life, there is no agreement on the number or identity of other specific types. The most often described other type is non–health-related quality of

life. Health-related quality of life is the subject of this book and several authors use the broad definition of health proposed by the World Health Organization (WHO): "Health is a state of complete physical, mental and social well-being and not merely the absence of disease or infirmity." This broad definition, however, does not cover most nonhealth-type domains of quality of life. Chapter 3 proposes a model of quality of life, as well as levels of quality of life and the influences on them.

Life events that happen to an individual are often independent of one's health and have not been routinely assessed in clinical trials. The relationship of life events and quality of life is discussed in Chapter 49.

Personal life events often affect health through stress, anxiety, or various emotions. Because of the intimate connection between social relationships and health (as defined by the WHO) and also between spirituality and health, all domains should be assessed when health-related quality of life is measured. Therefore, descriptions of health-related quality of life domains include consideration of most personal issues, and they are usually discussed as a single entity.

DEFINITION OF QUALITY OF LIFE

In editing this book it was necessary to decide on whether or not to insist on a common definition of quality of life.

B. Spilker: Orphan Medical, Inc., Minnetonka, Minnesota 55305.

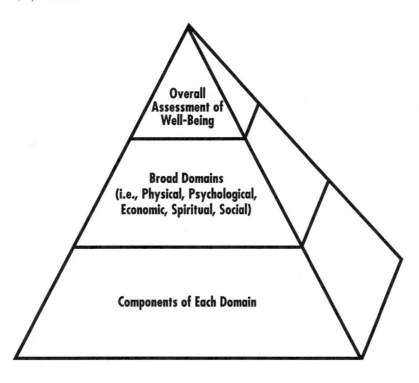

FIG. 1. Three levels of quality of life. In their totality these three levels constitute the scope (and definition) of quality of life.

An obvious alternative was for each author to define quality of life on his or her own terms. The problem with the first approach is that no single, clear, universally accepted definition exists. Moreover, because the field is diverse and changing, it would be unfair to limit the authors to a specific, narrow definition. Besides, a single definition would likely yield a stilted book that could not reflect the rich diversity in the field.

The problem with allowing each author carte blanche to use his or her own definition is that the book could lose the unity and cohesiveness desired. It would become merely a collection of loosely connected chapters. A compromise was reached where a general definition, based on that of Schipper et al. (see Chapter 2), was proposed to each author as a basis for his or her chapter. The fact that some authors adopted this definition while others used alternatives is viewed as a strength of the book. The definition of quality of life is illustrated schematically in Fig. 1 as consisting of three levels.

USES OF QUALITY OF LIFE DATA

One of the most important and basic questions about quality of life is why it should be studied and what data support its use? This question may be addressed from the perspective of a patient, physician, company, or country. The answer is most obvious for an individual patient: quality of life trials can help improve the quality of that patient's treatment and outcomes. In addition, quality of life trials may be used to differentiate between two therapies with marginal

differences in mortality or morbidity and to compare outcomes between two different treatment modalities, such as medicine versus surgery. Quality of life data may also be used to estimate the burden of specific diseases and to compare the impact of different diseases on functioning and well-being.

After quality of life trials are published, the data may be used for practical or commercial purposes. For example, important trials may influence prescribing. Companies developing medicines might decide to focus more efforts on finding medicines that improve patients' quality of life. This would be expected in areas such as cancer if differences in survival or even morbidity could not be demonstrated, but differences in quality of life could. Other commercial advantages for a company, such as getting a medicine onto a formulary, are described in other chapters. For a country's health planners, the most important use of quality of life data is to improve the allocation of health care resources.

DOMAINS OF QUALITY OF LIFE

The overall concept of quality of life consists of a number of distinct domains. The five major domains of quality of life generally referred to by most authors include the following categories:

1. Physical status and functional abilities
2. Psychological status and well-being
3. Social interactions
4. Economic and/or vocational status and factors
5. Religious and/or spiritual status

Some authors describe their research or clinical studies as dealing with quality of life issues when in fact they have studied only one or two of these broad domains. Clinical trials that evaluate only some domains should be distinguished from those that evaluate all domains, because the former group cannot be said to have investigated the full range of quality of life characteristics. The most common counterargument to this proposal is that not all domains are pertinent to study in every study—and that is true. The pitfalls of not studying all domains (except perhaps spiritual) are described in Chapter 7.

Spiritual Domain

The most direct approach to evaluate the spiritual domain is to interview a patient with a standard test or with a number of obvious questions: How important is religion to you? Are you a member of an organized religion? How do you practice your religion? How have your feelings about religion changed since you became ill? How have your religious beliefs changed since you became ill and also since you began treatment? I sought a more objective assessment (i.e., a validated test) that allowed many or most of these answers to be quantified. Several theologians and religious scholars intimately concerned with quality of life from a spiritual perspective told me that no such instrument exists. Fortunately, I learned that the nursing literature contains various measures and Jan Ellerhorst-Ryan has written extensively on this subject. This experience with theologians reinforces the need to expand our awareness of relevant literature in other disciplines.

The spiritual domain is discussed in this book because of the importance that it has in many people's lives and the fact that it is rarely assessed in clinical trials. There are many cases when its measurement would add value to a trial. One only has to think of young Hispanics who do not volunteer for clinical trials because their concept of body image is based on religious beliefs. There are also clinical trials that ask or require people to do things that go against their religious beliefs, such as adhere to a special diet.

Every person has a spiritual domain, whether one considers oneself a believer, agnostic, or atheist. Given the central nature of spirituality to each person's being it is less likely to be altered by disease than the other domains and is less likely to be changed by therapy. However, there are a number of instances where changes in this domain would be expected:

1. A chronically ill patient may "lose his faith" or gradually alter her spiritual beliefs over a long period of time. Successful medical treatment could indirectly restore a person's belief.
2. A sudden health crisis could lead to serious questioning of central spiritual beliefs.
3. A series of unexpected health problems among family or friends could lead to questioning, doubt, or rejection of certain beliefs—even if the patient was not directly affected himself or herself.

The concept of spirituality for an individual usually differs from religion and the psychosocial dimension. Religion is often discussed by people using words such as *systems, beliefs, organization, practices,* and *worship,* whereas spirituality is often discussed using words such as *life principle, being, quality, relationship, personal,* and *transcendent.* The difference is usually one of viewing religion as an organized external activity and spirituality as part of one's self. Clearly there is a large overlap for many people.

QUALITY OF LIFE FOR INDIVIDUAL PATIENTS AND GROUPS OF PATIENTS

Quality of life must be viewed on a number of levels. Although the exact number and definition of levels is likely to vary among authors, the three-level model shown in Fig. 1 provides a generally accepted basic approach.

The overall assessment of well-being is the top level and may be described as an individual's overall satisfaction with life and one's general sense of personal well-being. This overall assessment may be measured by summing the scores of an index test that evaluates each individual domain, or by simply asking patients, "On a scale of 1 to 10 (or a 1 to 100 or by descriptive categories), how would you assess your overall well-being?" In the clinical trial literature, this is referred to as a global quality of life assessment. Several variations of this question exist.

It is also important to establish through careful wording whether the patient is to consider the present moment, the last 24 hours, the week or time since their previous clinic visit, or other time period in answering the questions. Moreover, the question may ask the patient to compare the time period with their baseline state. This is particularly relevant in a trial. Given the highly personal way that patients judge their quality of life, it may readily be seen that this global quality of life assessment question is best answered by the patient and not by the physician. However, a global quality of life question that assesses disease severity is best answered by the physician because the assessment of disease severity involves clinical measures and clinical judgment and does not require an assessment of quality of life domains.

The middle level in Fig. 1 describes the broad domains discussed by most authors in this book. The exact number and identity of quality of life domains vary from three to six, depending on which authors are read. Nonetheless, both the number and general identity of these domains are similar; each cuts the overall pie (level 1) into different pieces of domains (level 2).

The lower or third level of Fig. 1 includes all components of each domain that are specifically assessed by quality of life tests and scales. Among the components of the psychological domain are anxiety, depression, and cognition. A single index or an entire battery of tests may be used to evaluate the components of just one or all domains. When a single clinical index is created to evaluate a single disease, widely differing parameters may be included, and each factor may be assigned a specific weight.

There is an important alternative to using tests to evaluate quality of life. One or more specific parameters or questions may be used in a clinical trial to evaluate a single or a few components of one or more domains. Those parameters or questions should be highly important measures of the particular component. Although these few questions do not represent a validated test of quality of life, their importance for assessing quality of life in a particular disease is often obvious. It may be appropriate to include pertinent quality of life questions in clinical trials rather than a standard (or new) test or scale, particularly in those diseases or conditions where a validated test does not exist.

QUALITY OF LIFE FOR POPULATIONS OF PATIENTS

The purpose of studying quality of life of large populations of patients is to learn what treatments have the optimal effects on large groups of patients and to understand the burden of different diseases. This information may be used to help government and managed care decision makers allocate funds to those treatments shown to elicit the best quality of life outcomes. This assumes that all major efficacy and safety parameters are approximately equal among the treatments compared for the same disease. This is rarely the case in practice.

Exceptions exist to virtually all generalizations and conclusions of population-based studies. Thus, every health care professional must be sensitive to the needs and responses of individual patients in the choice of treatment(s) as well as in the modification of those treatments.

The pyramidal hierarchy for overall assessment, domains, and components shown in Figure 1 for individual patients also applies to a population of patients. On the other hand, the implications of these levels for patients and populations are quite different.

The most specific and valuable data for determining optimal treatment for an individual patient arise from direct experience in the patient himself or herself. Next comes the total experience gained by the health professional, followed by case reports from colleagues or the literature, and finally from population-based studies. In most instances, the population-based studies should have the greatest influence on the specific treatment an individual patient receives. But, in the real world, most physicians rely primarily on their own experience.

The level of consensus achieved in population-based issues varies from (a) individual opinion at the bottom through (b) professional society endorsement to (c) national consensus agreements to (d) official guidelines promulgated by appropriate national or international groups.

Some of the major issues addressed by decision makers regarding the implications of a quality of life trial or report for another patient population are listed below. The major questions are:

1. To what degree
   —are patients similar in the test population and in the published report population?
   —are the conditions of use similar in the test population and in the published report population?
   —can the results in the published report be extrapolated to the test population?
   —is the treatment appropriate for the test population?
2. What other products in the formulary are used for the same treatment and how do they compare with the test treatment?
3. Is the price for the new treatment reasonable or acceptable?
4. If there are issues about price, can creative answers be found to address them?

COMBINING QUALITY OF LIFE DATA FROM MULTIPLE DOMAINS OR TESTS

A table could be created that lists the major domains and the specific instruments or tests that are used to evaluate them. Quality of life tests measure either specific or general aspects of the various domains. If a single test that measures each of the domains (and is validated for each of these domains) is used in a clinical trial, then an aggregate overall assessment of quality of life can be obtained. In this case, it should be relatively straightforward to compare different medicines or treatments. One problem with obtaining a single overall score for quality of life, however, is that different domains may yield different results (e.g., treatment A was better than treatment B in two domains, but the opposite result was obtained in the other two domains). Even within a single domain it is common for a specific component to yield different results to different treatments.

If a battery of validated tests is used to evaluate a single domain (or all domains), it is impossible to combine all test results into a single number. Individual test results may be aggregated, however, by presenting them in a comparative manner. Investigators must establish the relative importance of each individual test used to measure one or more aspects of quality of life before conducting the trial. This practice ensures that data obtained from tests defined as minor are not later used to claim that a certain treatment is more or less effective than another.

Different tests and scales may be required to measure specific aspects of each domain or component of a domain depending on the patients being evaluated and the interests of the investigators. Moreover, different weights may be assigned to each of the five broad domains, based on the patients' beliefs as influenced by the severity of the disease and other factors. Although, there is no *a priori* reason to state that each of these components must be measured and combined to understand changes in a patient's quality of life, failure to do so raises the question of whether important data were missed. Nonetheless, one domain or even a single component of a domain may reflect quality of life issues better than the combination of several or many separate measures.

Assessment of quality of life requires input from patients to ensure that the patients' perceptions are included and accurate. A study that compared physician and patient perceptions of quality of life using several different scales found that correlation between the two was poor (1). This supports the view that physicians cannot accurately assess a patient's quality of life in all, or perhaps most, situations. This may result from the fact that physicians usually judge patients' clinical responses rather than how clinical responses are filtered through a patient's values and beliefs.

RELATIONSHIP OF CLINICAL SAFETY AND EFFICACY DATA TO QUALITY OF LIFE: THE FILTERING PHENOMENON

To understand why patients who experience the same general benefits and adverse reactions as other patients assess their quality of life differently, it is necessary to ask how a medical treatment's benefits or adverse reactions affect quality of life.

On first consideration, it appears that adverse reactions diminish a patient's quality of life and beneficial effects enhance it. But both positive and negative clinical changes are generally judged in comparison with other benefits or problems of the treatment and with other treatments the patient has received. The patient's values and beliefs determine how different factors involved with treatment are perceived. The benefits and problems are, in a sense, filtered through a patient's values, beliefs, and judgments to determine whether the net change represents a positive or negative effect on overall quality of life. The major factors influencing the patients' values, beliefs, and judgments are their culture and, probably to a lesser degree, their genetic makeup.

The net result of a treatment on a patient's quality of life often cannot be predicted or assessed by the physician. In many cases, a spouse may not be fully aware of how the patient assesses changes in quality of life. Deciding whether the change in quality of life is positive or negative is often a complex judgment that can differ for each of the broad domains or for each component of a single domain. Moreover, within each domain some components may be more positive as a result of a specific treatment, while other components become more negative.

We generally assume that severe adverse reactions have a negative effect on quality of life and marked improvements in therapeutic response have a positive effect. But there are exceptions to both situations because of the patient's values. For example, severe adverse reactions accompanied by clinical improvement may result in a net improvement in quality of life as judged by one patient, but the opposite conclusion may be reached by another patient experiencing similar effects. These points are illustrated in the model shown in Fig. 2. A corollary of this model is that one cannot simply measure adverse reactions or assess clinical benefits of a medical treatment and reach any firm conclusions about how a patient's quality of life is affected.

It is generally necessary to measure most or all quality of life domains for a specific patient, or group of patients, to assess and document how the benefits or adverse reactions have been filtered through the patient's values, beliefs, and judgments. Some parameters of clinical efficacy or adverse reactions are very closely related to quality of life. For example, any improvement of pain in patients with chronic pain will be interpreted as an improvement in quality of life, but patients who have changes in mild to moderate headache may not have changes in their quality of life, and patients who reduce nonsymptomatic risk factors with medicines may view this as having an extremely weak association with quality of life.

Although only one direction of arrows has been used in Fig. 2, there is a bidirectional flow under certain circumstances. For example, changes in one or more quality of life domains, independent of medical treatment, may affect the patient's compliance with treatment and thereby influence its effectiveness. A person who loses a job or is hurt in an accident may not have enough money to purchase medical treatment.

An illustration similar to Fig. 2 could be constructed for a broad patient population or health care sector. In such a model, consideration of resource availability, allocation, and consumption would have to be included, as well as the impact of a patient's quality of life on the community. This information is of paramount importance to health care planners who allocate resources to those medical treatments that provide the greatest benefit in clinical terms and, it is hoped, in terms of quality of life.

CATEGORIES OF INSTRUMENTS USED TO MEASURE QUALITY OF LIFE

Of the many hundreds of instruments used to measure one or more aspects of quality of life, some focus on parameters universally agreed to be part of quality of life. In addition, some instruments are better validated than are others. The most frequently used and most well-validated instruments are referred to as core instruments. A more extensive discussion of this topic and one prototype list of 54 specific core instruments plus name and address of a contact person is given by Spilker et al. (2). This list was created by identifying those instruments cited at least seven times in two bibliographies, a highly imperfect means of creating a core list.

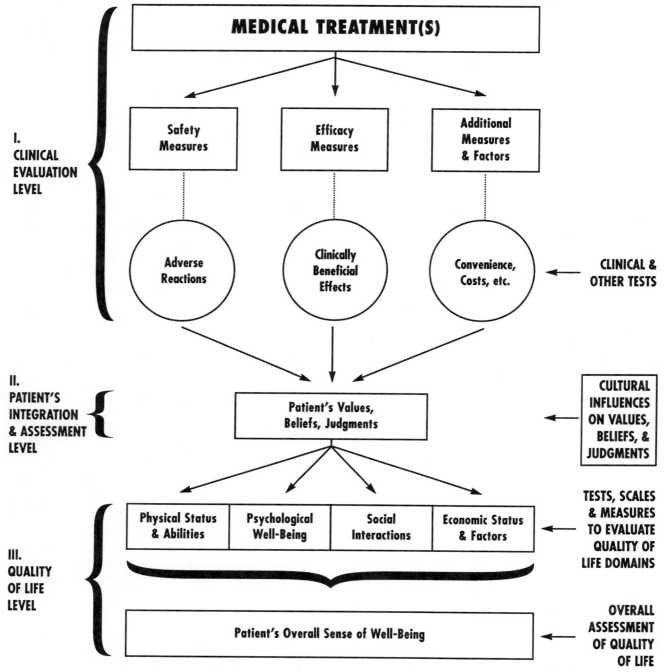

FIG. 2. Model of how clinical aspects of efficacy (i.e., benefits), safety (e.g., adverse reactions), or other factors are integrated and filter through the patient's values, beliefs, and judgments to influence his or her quality of life domains.

Instruments used to measure quality of life can be broadly categorized as follows:

I. Instruments that focus on parameters or functions universally agreed to be part of health-related quality of life for all people.

II. Instruments that focus on parameters or functions that many believe to be part of health-related quality of life for all people and are primarily used to evaluate quality of life.

III. Instruments that focus on parameters or functions most believe to be part of health-related quality of life for patients with a specific disease or particular characteristic (e.g., elderly) and are primarily used to evaluate quality of life.

IV. Instruments that focus on parameters or functions that

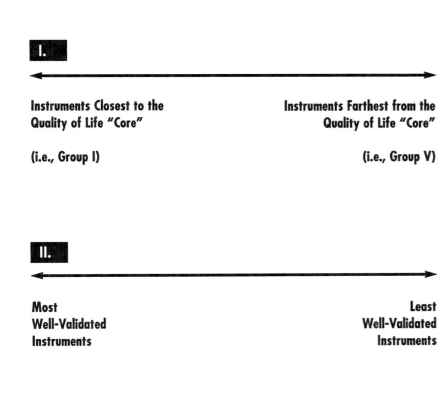

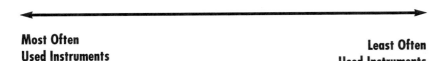

FIG. 3. Spectra that illustrate three characteristics of core instruments used to measure quality of life.

are sometimes part of quality of life but are usually viewed as clinical measures such as depression scales, pain scales, and tests of cognitive function.

V. Instruments that focus on tangential issues to quality of life but may be used on occasion to assess a component of quality of life (e.g., social functioning measure, personality test).

These categories move progressively from the heart of the core group of instruments to those on the periphery and may be visualized as moving through concentric rings. Another way of visualizing instruments is along the three spectra shown in Fig. 3. These spectra may serve as a basis for establishing future lists of core instruments.

PHARMACOECONOMICS

The field of pharmacoeconomics is rapidly expanding for a variety of reasons—regulations, competition, formularies—described in many chapters. The economics of medicines can be viewed at three levels:

Industry level—This level focuses on financial aspects of the many companies that make up the pharmaceutical industry. This level describes the financial forecasts, financial performances and related fiscal aspects of a company and is not discussed in this book. This area is not part of the field of pharmacoeconomics, but economics.

Specific medicine level—This level is the primary one referred to as pharmacoeconomics and includes studies to evaluate costs and benefits of specific medicines. The evaluation of these studies by a variety of decision makers on formulary committees, in government, and elsewhere is also discussed in this book. Studies usually compare a medicine with others or to other modalities but may evaluate a single treatment. The field of pharmacoeconomics identifies, measures, and compares the costs and outcomes of using treatments. Data at this level are used to make decisions on using medicines at all levels from international and national governments to specific patients.

Individual patient level—While assessments of individual patient costs and benefits are quantitatively evaluated as part of pharmacoeconomic studies at the medicine level, another economic aspect can be studied in clinical trials. This involves the attitudes of a person toward work and economic self-sufficiency as well as his or her abilities to perform work-related functions to be productive. An evaluation of how this changes as a result of treatment in a clinical trial is part of quality of life and is generally considered an independent domain. In addition to measuring patient attitudes, it is possible to assess actual parameters such as (a) Did the patient work? and (b) How many days did he or she work per month or year? This topic is discussed in the quality of life sections of this book.

Many perspectives may be applied when viewing the pharmacoeconomic level. Some of the important perspectives include those of the patient, health provider, hospital administration, payer, formulary committee, regulatory authority, academic scientist, vendor organization, and the overall society. Because these perspectives often involve either the payment or receipt of money, there is a strong tension and vested interests in the decisions made by various groups. Pharmaceutical companies have sometimes prospered or bankrupted themselves as a result of a single pharmacoeconomic decision.

The more one explores this topic, the more one uncovers a multitude of issues and complexities in what data are collected and how they are interpreted and used. These issues are discussed in various chapters, but one example is mentioned here as an indication of the issues involved.

Many hospital *charges* to patients (and indirectly to the insurance companies) for products or services do not relate closely to the actual *costs* of those products or services. The procedures for determining charges and the amounts charged for identical products or services vary widely, even within the same geographic location. While there are many explanations for such differences, they may greatly influence results of a pharmacoeconomic study.

The ramifications of pharmacoeconomics have become widespread in our society and will become even more so in the future. This occurs not only in establishing which pharmaceuticals enter formularies, but also in terms of prices, reimbursement, and promotional practices. While pricing is established as part of the regulatory approval process in some countries, this author hopes that pharmacoeconomic data are *not* more widely used as a part of the regulatory approval process in the future.

The actual economic methods used in pharmacoeconomics (e.g., cost-benefit, cost-effectiveness, cost-utility, cost of illness, cost minimization) are well validated (as opposed to many instruments used in quality of life studies). But these pharmacoeconomic methods may be used in many ways, a number of which are *not* scientifically (or ethically) acceptable (see the chapters discussing standards). Cost-benefit, cost-effectiveness, cost-utility, cost of illness, and cost-minimization methods have specific definitions and are discussed at length in the text. Each method is desirable under specific conditions. These methods (and the entire field of pharmacoeconomics) are valuable tools to provide important data

for many decision makers. Two of the most important principles in this field are to explain assumptions and to clarify what was done.

RELATIONSHIP OF PHARMACOECONOMICS AND QUALITY OF LIFE

The types of outcomes of a medical treatment for a specific patient include three broad areas:

1. *Clinical*—the changes in an individual patient's signs and symptoms of disease, as well as other directly measurable benefits. Health outcomes in medicine (as opposed to clinical trials) are assessed under the subject of outcomes research.
2. *Economic*—the costs of the patient's treatment, who is paying, and what limitations are being placed on the system because of economic factors. Health care costs are assessed under the subject of health economics.
3. *Personal*—the quality of life benefits the patient assesses himself or herself in terms of how treatment affects the broad domains and their components.

There is an overlap between pharmacoeconomic and quality of life assessments, depending on the specific situation. In the clinical area, certain measures are essential for assessing cost-effectiveness. Although cost-benefit analyses express clinical benefits in monetary terms, the clinical parameters must be measured. Cost-utility analyses usually require patient judgments, although these may be estimated, based on clinician or investigator judgments.

While quality of life may change as a result of an individual's clinical changes, these changes are often an indirect result of the clinical effect.

Economic parameters are clearly of paramount importance in pharmacoeconomics. Economics is also considered an independent domain in quality of life and usually focuses on vocational and work performance, although direct costs of treatment and its side effects are also critical in many cases for their impact on patients. Economics related to quality of life may overlap with, but generally differs greatly from, economic aspects of most pharmacoeconomic areas.

There are relatively few areas of overlap or interaction between pharmacoeconomics and quality of life in the personal area. The major exception relates to cost-utility analyses. Utility measures require patients to consider trade-offs they would make between quality of life and additional years of life. This differs from specifically assessing a patient's quality of life.

From a different perspective, there is a very important relationship between pharmacoeconomics and quality of life. That is the perspective of third-party payers, formularies, and health planners who ask the question, "Are the changes demonstrated for quality of life worth the cost of the treatment?" This economic issue is addressed by a pharmacoeconomic evaluation of the reported (or assumed) benefits in quality of life. This evaluation may be a comparative one where two or more products or therapies are compared or, alternatively, where a single product or therapy is evaluated.

HEALTH POLICY

Health policy, not pharmacoeconomics, wrestles with questions of whether the price for a particular treatment is appropriate or too high. To make this decision or to decide under which medical and social conditions an approved but expensive medicine should be used, it is essential to have meaningful clinical, economic, and quality of life data that are relatively complete and relatively free of bias. Paramount in this issue is the concept that the price of a new medicine may only represent the tip of the total treatment cost and may influence that substantially. It is imperative that the total clinical, economic, and quality of life value of the treatment be assessed in comparison with other alternative treatments.

By comparing the total costs and benefits of two or more treatments, the relative value of those treatments can be established. For example, a new medicine that costs twice as much as existing therapy for the same condition but decreases hospital stays by 50% (with all other factors equal) will likely have greater value and will save society money in the long term. Of course, all other factors are almost never equal.

Health policy also deals with data obtained from outcomes research. This area has expanded greatly in recent years as people have asked more questions about how treatments are working in the real world of patient practice as opposed to the more artificial environment of clinical trials. Health policy affects everyone, and it is important that the decision makers have the best data available to help them reach wise decisions.

OUTCOMES RESEARCH

Health care costs are discussed in terms of health economics by trained economists, whereas health outcomes are discussed as outcomes research by epidemiologists, psychologists, and others trained in this area.

The outcome of a medical intervention is the health state noticed by the patient. This includes satisfaction with care received, quality of life, morbidity, compliance measures, performance symptoms, patient performance, and other characteristics. If at least one treatment is a medicine, the outcomes may be viewed as pharmaceutical outcomes and may be measured in either efficacy or effectiveness studies. The latter incorporates the patient's perspective.

Outcome studies differ from traditional randomized trials in that outcomes research:

1. presents outcomes from the patient's perspective and not the health care professionals.

2. extrapolates results more broadly than is done with randomized trials.
3. focuses on costs more than dose-randomized trials.
4. often assesses usual care of patients.
5. sometimes uses data bases as their data source

The four parts of outcomes management as described by Ellwood (3) would focus on four techniques. "First, it would place greater reliance on standards and guidelines that physicians can use in selecting appropriate interventions. Second, it would routinely and systematically measure the functioning and well-being of patients, along with disease-specific clinical outcomes, at appropriate time intervals. Third, it would pool clinical and outcome data on a massive scale. Fourth, it would analyze and disseminate results from the segment of the data base most appropriate to the concerns of each decision maker." He goes on to say that "Outcome management's closest relative is the clinical trial," clearly relating the two in an important way that is relevant to this book.

FUTURE ISSUES TO ADDRESS

The quality of life field is a rapidly changing and developing medical arena. The standards developed over the next several years will probably have a major influence on this area for some time. It is premature to define golden rules for this field, although one of the most important is that only validated scales should be used in clinical trials. In addition, a few other major issues for discussion are worth mentioning here.

The question of disease-specific versus generic scales to evaluate quality of life had been widely debated, but there is now a general consensus to use generic measures supplemented with disease-specific measures for outcomes in quality of life trials.

Scales used to evaluate quality of life are not always disease-specific. Some are function-specific (e.g., sexual or emotional function) or population-specific (e.g., geriatric). Many disease-specific scales are fairly general in the type of information they elicit and therefore bridge the gap between general and disease-specific scales (e.g., Health Assessment Questionnaire for arthritis, Quality of Life Index for cancer). This topic is discussed in greater detail by Patrick and Deyo (4). The choice of using a single index test to evaluate two or more domains versus using a battery of tests may never be settled by consensus. A number of authors in this book discuss this issue and many of the trade-offs involved (e.g., see Chapter 15 by Naughton et al.).

The number of scales available for evaluating quality of life issues in clinical trials is huge. Many of these tests have been validated in one or more patient populations. A consensus is likely to be reached in the future on a few widely accepted scales being most credible to use for each domain. Other scales may be viewed as less credible, and many may eventually be rejected for quality of life assessments. Several authors in this book have already honed the large number of possible scales and tests to a small number that are reviewed in their chapters.

A related subject is obtaining better identification of specific conditions under which individual scales should be used. At a more detailed level, specific questions relate to whether tests should (a) quantitate events or assess how patients value those events; (b) measure what patients *actually do* (i.e., activities) versus what they *can do* (i.e., capabilities); (c) use concomitant control groups, or historical controls, or use the patient as his own control; and (d) assess the last 24 hours for evaluation versus considering the previous week (or other period).

If several people administer a test in one clinical trial, interrater reliability must be assessed. Some experts have also questioned whether it is necessary to train and certify individuals who administer various quality of life tests. If this is perceived to be a problem, then more attention will likely be paid to this issue. The qualifications and training of those who interpret test results is a related issue that should be discussed, especially for those scales involving subjective responses (e.g., given through interview methods).

A final issue concerns choosing which domains of quality of life should be measured in a clinical trial and choosing the tests to be used to assess these domains. This is an important issue because it is often possible to measure just those domains and components that are most likely (or even known) to show the changes desired. This is equivalent to ''stacking the deck'' before the game is played. This quasi-ethical approach to evaluating quality of life will be prevented when decision makers refuse to accept such data and journals refuse to publish data obtained in such studies.

CONCLUSIONS

It is hoped that this book will help advance the usefulness of quality of life assessments by (a) helping to standardize definitions and approaches to studying quality of life, (b) indicating which tests are validated for specific diseases and domains, (c) identifying state-of-the-art tools for measuring quality of life in many patient populations, (d) stimulating wider use of these measures in clinical trials, and (e) assisting the analysis and interpretation of quality of life data. This introduction presents a frame of reference to assist in reading many of the following chapters.

ACKNOWLEDGMENT

The author thanks Dr. Dennis Revicki for reading the manuscript and making numerous suggestions.

REFERENCES

1. Slevin MR, Plant H, Lynch D, Drinkwater J, Gregory WM. Who should measure quality of life, the doctor or the patient? *Br J Cancer* 1988;57: 109–112.
2. Spilker B, Simpson RL Jr, Tilson HH. Quality of life bibliography and indexes: 1991 update. *J Clin Res Pharmacoepidemiol* 1992;6:205–266.
3. Ellwood PM. Shattuck Lecture—outcomes management. *N Engl J Med* 1988;318:1549–1556.
4. Patrick DL, Deyo RA. Generic and disease-specific measures in assessing health status and quality of life. *Med Care* 1989;27:S217–S232.

Quality of Life and Pharmacoeconomics in Clinical Trials, Second Edition, edited by B. Spilker. Lippincott-Raven Publishers, Philadelphia © 1996.

CHAPTER 2

Quality of Life Studies: Definitions and Conceptual Issues

Harvey Schipper, Jennifer J. Clinch, and Charles L. M. Olweny

INTRODUCTION

Since the first edition of this book was published, *quality of life* has achieved respectability both as a matter of clinical concern, and as a focus of research and evaluation. Quality of life has become an expected measure of success in many clinical trials, a criterion for licensing new medicines in several jurisdictions, and the focus of a specific journal (*Quality of Life Research,* Rapid Communications, Oxford) (1). This interest follows on the recognition that it is necessary to describe the overall results of our diagnostic and treatment efforts in a way that makes sense to both patients and health professionals. In recent years substantial rigor has come to the field. Instrument development procedures have been refined, leading to an array of questionnaires, both general and specific. As was the case during the evolution of

the cancer clinical trials process a generation ago, pitfalls of this type of research have been identified, and techniques developed to circumvent the problems. Important clinical trials are under way, and specific, empirically derived data are beginning to influence patterns of research and health care delivery.

The quality of life concept has been approached from many perspectives, including physical well-being, the spiritual and psychological approaches, and the social, economic, and political. In the current clinical setting, the conceptual formulation that has emerged defines quality of life functionally by patients' perceptions of performance in four areas: physical and occupational, psychological, social interaction, and somatic sensation. However, the specific terminology differs among investigators. In this model the patient serves as his or her own control, the comparisons being made against expectation of function. Quality of life will fluctuate over time, the result of changes in any or all of its component parts. This is an intensely patient-centered approach. In some respects it is a departure from the more accustomed outcome measures, because the focus is on patient perception, rather than measured physiological values.

H. Schipper, J. J. Clinch, and C. L. M. Olweny: World Health Organization Collaborating Centre for Quality of Life in Cancer Care, Winnipeg, Manitoba R2H 2A6, Canada.

In the past physicians have generally viewed this "subjective" assessment of treatment outcome with suspicion. The reasons are multiple and include the belief that the process of medical research is and should be identical to that of the so-called "hard sciences" such as physics, requiring the rigorous application of the Scientific Method to the processes of clinical inquiry and treatment. Other reasons include the belief that psychosocial parameters are of secondary importance compared with the physiological mechanisms of illness, concern about the lack of a pragmatic definition, and unfamiliarity with psychosocial methodologies. The reductionist nature of contemporary medical analysis makes it difficult for some to accommodate to the interdependent, nonlinear, and time-variable properties of this broadened view of clinical outcome. Over the past decade many of these concerns have begun to recede, aided by the recognition that traditional medical science is not necessarily as precise as once assumed, and that a concept offering conceptual common ground between health professionals of different persuasions and patients had much to offer (2,3).

This chapter introduces the concept. We begin with discussion of a number of notional approaches that consider quality of life from different perspectives, leading to the emergence of the model as it is now understood. The discussion and debate about the conceptual roots of quality of life is not finished. Perhaps, what can be said now is that a range of different strategies, approaching the problem differently, seem to be converging toward a more defined, possibly common *gestalt*. The derived quality of life concept has operational properties that are unique and materially affect the design and interpretation of trials. These will be introduced and tactical suggestions for the conduct of quality of life studies will be offered.

Most early quality of life studies utilized this terminology without definition. The result was that the rubric became a catchall for inconsistently designed trials with unclear goals. For example, investigators may have focused on the rate of wound healing, or sexuality, or financial concerns, and correlated that directly with quality of life (4–8). While many of these individual issues may be significant contributors to quality of life, in the absence of a consistent definition it is not possible to draw other than the most limited conclusions about a patient's overall function when examining a single variable.

From an operational perspective, the quality of life we are discussing and seeking to measure is a multifactorial construct, whose component parts remain consistent, but whose individual significance within the overall model may vary over time. The ability to ride a bicycle may be very important to a younger person, but with increasing age or a change in habitus or social circumstance, the ability to perform that skill may take on a very different meaning. As we shall see later, examination of individual components of patient function may play a valuable role in elucidating the impact of a disease and its treatment on overall quality of life.

TOWARD A DEFINITION OF QUALITY OF LIFE

The conceptual formulation of quality of life is the result of a global consensual process, a brief review of which offers insight into the strengths and weaknesses as well as the future direction of the quality of life research effort.

Karnofsky and Burchenal (9) first proposed a nonphysiological outcome parameter for cancer in 1947. What it lacked in conceptual underpinnings, it made up for in the perforce logic and simplicity of its application. Although validated only much later (10), and clearly representative of physical function only, the Karnofsky Scale remains a hallmark of cancer therapy trials to this day. (The New York Heart Association and the American Rheumatism Association Functional Capacity Classifications have similar histories.) They are all designed for "third party" use, meaning they are intended to elicit health professionals' opinions rather than directly those of patients. After Priestman and Baum (11) published a more broadly based, although empirical, breast cancer quality of life index, researchers began to ask whether it might be possible to develop a conceptual definition of quality of life acceptable as the basis of a rigorous standard for the development and evaluation of useful measures of quality of life. At first the *gestalt* was considered too vague and too individual to be generalized. However, five concepts emerged that contribute to the evolution of our current understanding: the psychological approach, the time trade-off or utility concept, Ware's (12) community-centered concept, the reintegration concept, and Calman's (13) gap principle.

The Psychological View

Psychologically and anthropologically speaking, quality of life reflects the patient-perceived illness side of the distinction between illness and disease (14). Physicians concentrate upon the disease process (the pathophysiology) and attempt to resolve it, often paying less attention to patients' perceptions of the disease, which are the experience of illness. An example is hypertension, which is usually detected by the physician when the patient is asymptomatic. The physician has diagnosed a "disease" while the patient is "well." The treatment may make the patient feel sick. Many variables contribute to the illness experience: the perception of symptoms, the way in which the patient labels them and communicates the distress they cause, the experience of being unable to function normally, and the methods of coping used by patients and families to gain some control over the disorder. In the chronically ill, dealing strictly with the disease process may be inadequate because the disease problems are often amplified by the psychosocial response to symptoms. In recent years there has been an explosion of interest in this area. Medical school curricula are being revised to incorporate psychosocial material, and academic and clinical departments are being created. The treatment process now takes more than physiology into account.

Psychological variables have been shown to be a factor in some disease states, for example, the role of stress in the development of hypertension and the relative risk of developing heart disease in different personality types (15,16). This has led to a greater acceptance of the relevance of psychological variables in the etiology and treatment of disease, especially since a possible mechanism for this process has been discovered in the demonstration of the effect of certain psychological states on the function of the immune system (17).

Operationally, this means that physiological and psychological states are not independent. One may directly influence the other. Equally important, the apportioning of disability from the point of view of quality of life rests as much on a patient's perception as on some ''objective'' measure of psychological state. Early in their careers, clinicians experience the humbling lack of correlation between how such a patient should behave, based on a ''medical'' assessment, and his actual demonstrated ability to carry on in the community. The importance of this psychological approach is its dual emphasis: on patient perception and on the psyche as an overt contributor to physiological outcome.

''Utility''—The Trade-offs We Make

Related to the relevance of certain quality of life domains to subsets of individuals is the concept of trade-offs in quality and quantity of life. Some individuals may prefer survival at any cost, whereas others would not consider life to be worth living under certain circumstances. McNeil et al. (18) presented groups of normal individuals with two treatment alternatives for laryngeal cancer. The first was laryngectomy, which offers longer survival. The second was radiation therapy with the attendant risk of shorter survival, but with voice preservation. On average, individuals indicated that they would trade off 14% of their full life expectancy to avoid loss of speech. The two groups were executives and firefighters, and although there was no significant difference noted in the number of years they would be willing to trade off to retain normal speech, executives on average would have been willing to trade off 17% of their full life expectancy versus only 6% for firefighters. Obviously executives placed a higher value on retaining normal speech. A more recent study focused on treatment options for prostate cancer (19). The investigators reported an age-dependent response to a trade-off between longevity and preservation of sexual function. Younger subjects wanted to preserve sexual function. Not surprisingly, the choices we make depend on age as well as occupational circumstance. In these examples, the group differences might have been expected on common-sense grounds, but such preferences may not always be obvious, especially to researchers working in different cultural settings where different values apply.

There are numerous other examples of the utility concept. Most of the studies that have been done pose hypothetical trade-offs in an attempt to put some value on an organ or functional capability. At its most primitive, the utility concept is rather like an accident insurance policy—so much for one arm, a little more for an eye and a leg, and so on. Used with insight, they are an avenue to understanding how people accommodate to the impairment or loss of a part of themselves.

Working daily with quality of life data, one senses these utility trade-offs being made all the time, as patients seek to maximize quality of life. On one occasion, a patient in our palliative care unit observed that she could no longer work and that at intervals, the pain was terrible. However, she was also able to be with friends, to talk, reminisce, and. in her phrase, ''to consolidate.'' She knew nothing of our arcane quality of life construct. Involuntarily she had traded off occupational function for social interaction. When she went on to say that what she had lost in the ability to work she had more than made up by the opportunity to consolidate and to share, for us she epitomized the ceaseless trade-offs we make.

Toward a Broader View:
A Community-Centered Concept

Ware (12) proposed another way of organizing the variables that constitute health status and quality of life concepts, one that provides a sense of the impact illness has on the broader community. In his conceptualization, the variables can be grouped in concentric domains starting with the physiological parameters of disease at the core and diffusing in turn to personal functioning, psychological distress/well-being, general health perceptions, and finally social/role functioning.

As discussed previously, the variables that measure disease are physiological and highly specific to the disease in question. Personal functioning is defined as the performance or capacity to perform everyday tasks including self-care, mobility, and physical activities. Such measures of functional status are commonly used in the chronically ill, but are often insensitive to disease status and are only weakly related to emotional functioning. Therefore, they cannot be used alone to provide a comprehensive picture of the degree of health and well-being.

The third level of health status is psychological. It is important as a disease category both in its own right and because it interacts with physical disease and response to treatment. It is clear that it affects, and is affected by, both. Psychological well-being is included with psychological distress, because most existing measures concentrate on the distress end of the continuum and are not sensitive to changes that occur at the well-being end. It may be that reduction in psychological well-being rather than overt distress is more likely to reflect the response to physical disease or its treatment.

General health perception is in the fourth circle because it is felt to encompass the individual's evaluation of the three preceding concepts. However, the correspondence is far from perfect; there is clearly more involved in a general self-rating of health status, perhaps the personal values put upon each concept. The final circle is that of social/role functioning, which refers to an individual's capacity to perform activities associated with one's usual role, including employment, school, or homemaking.

Ware's concept emphasizes a hierarchy by placing physical illness at the center of the circle. Thus it opens the issue of weighting, apportioning relative values to the component parts of the quality of life construct. Also implicit in Ware's model is the effect of illness upon a community. More than a single patient's quality of life is affected by an illness. Thus, in measuring quality of life, how far must we extend our reach?

Reintegration to Normal Living

The concept of "reintegration to normal living" has been proposed as a proxy for quality of life (20). The definition offered was the reorganization of physical, psychological, and social characteristics of an individual into a harmonious whole, so that well-adjusted living can be resumed after an incapacitating illness or trauma. The domains discovered during the process of developing an index to measure this concept were mobility, self-care abilities, daily activities, recreational activities, social activities, family roles, personal relationships, presentation of self, and general coping skills. Although certain areas usually covered by quality of life measures were not included, such as symptoms and emotional functioning, they were thought to be subsumed under the more global items. Two subscales were developed and found to correlate to some extent with appropriate groupings of items from Spitzer's quality of life scale (21). Hence, this concept, although related to the quality of life concept, is by no means identical to it.

In spite of the differences in domain definition between reintegration to normal living and quality of life, the occasions on which it would be appropriate to measure either concept coincide. Reintegration means the ability to do what one has to do or wants to do, but it does not mean being free of disease or symptoms. Thus, it is an appropriate measure for treatment outcome in chronic diseases where no cure is expected and the patient has to learn to live with the disease. The extent to which this is achieved can be thought of either in terms of reintegration, or quality of life, or both. Rehabilitation as a focus of quality of life assessment forms

the conceptual basis of one widely used measure, the Cancer Rehabilitation Evaluation System (22).

Calman's Gap: Quality of Life Compared with What?

To this point, our conceptual discussion has focused on three issues: quality of life is multidimensional, each dimension changes over time, and it is a patient-perceived entity. The next question is that of scalar values. Against what standard do we measure quality of life?

Calman (13) defined quality of life as the gap between the patient's expectations and achievements. Thus the smaller the gap, the higher the quality of life. Conversely, the less the patient is able to realize his expectations, the poorer his quality of life. In his analysis, Calman showed that the gap between expectations and achievement may vary over time as the patient's health improves or regresses in relation to the effectiveness of treatment or progress of disease. He emphasized that the goals set by the patient must be realistic in order to thwart undue frustration. He noted that here the professional may temper the patient's expectations and prepare him for the changes and limitations that will ensue as the disease progresses. The "impact of illness" (Calman's term) may vary depending on the patient's perception of his quality of life when he is given a diagnosis. Thus, a person who had been losing weight and becoming fatigued during the months prior to diagnosis may have prepared himself psychologically and already reduced his expectations.

Another gap that reflects a further component of quality of life is that between the patient's actual achievements and his or her potential achievements (a third-person estimation) (23). Andrews and Stewart (24) showed, in day-hospital patients seen following inpatient care in a stroke unit, that there was an important difference between the patient's potential achievements, as shown in the objective day hospital activities of daily living (ADL) assessments, and the patient's actual achievements as measured by the same observers when assessing these patients at home. Channer (25) showed, in patients presenting with chest pain but found not to have any evidence of ischemic heart disease, that the explanation of this fact to the patient failed to prevent further chest pain in 70% of the subjects. Both these studies are examples of a gap between the patient's actual achievements (poor ADL function and persistent restricting chest pain, respectively) and the patient's potential achievements. Both led to a diminution of quality of life: in the first study, diminution according to the external observer; in the second study, diminution according to the subject's own experiences. By potential achievements, we do not mean those that are theoretically possible but those shown actually to occur, albeit under certain conditions. Wood (26) drew attention to the importance of increasing the patient's appraisal and coping skills to enhance quality of life rather than just aiming at increasing patient satisfaction and happiness.

Subjectivity and Objectivity

An issue that occasionally complicates discussion about quality of life assessment is the distinction between objective and subjective data. The classic definition of an objective measure is that which is externally observable and directly measurable along a physical dimension. Quality of life data deviate from both criteria, being perceptual and reported by the subject. Implicit in the discussion is concern that these subjective measures are less credible and intrinsically imprecise. The confusion comes in the assumption that something subjective cannot be measured appropriately, and hence cannot compete with the validity of physical measurements. The considerable emphasis on validation for instruments and procedures for the conduct and analysis of studies has alleviated these differences of view. For the purposes of this discussion, we take the distinction between objective and subjective to mean whether or not something is directly observable by a third party, but that observations of both types can be designed to meet scientific standards of reliability and validity. The essential third requirement is relevance to the question at hand.

THE CULTURAL DIMENSION

The first generation of quality of life measurement questionnaires were developed in English-speaking countries. Even then, there was an element of amazement expressed when the instruments designed on different continents and validated in different places seemed similar in content. Subsequently, the use of these techniques and tools has been extended both to different language groups within the broad Western cultural tradition and more recently to parts of the world where the social and cultural ethos is totally different (14,27–35). Although this issue is discussed at greater length in a subsequent chapter, it is important enough that the basic issues need to be introduced at this juncture, as they reflect upon the conceptual underpinnings of quality of life research.

As currently conceived and executed, the assessment of quality of life derives from Western concepts of illness, and of man's fate. In the West, illness is almost an external intervention, adversely affecting an otherwise self-determined life course. This is not true in many other cultures where fatalism, karma, and cultural predeterminism are essentials of the life cycle. The consequences of illness may not be perceived as distinct from other aspects of the life journey. The reductionism of modern Western medical science is quite foreign to many African and Asian cultures, which speak more of subtle balances, both within the body and between body and environment (36). Moreover, the types of medical interventions we consider routine may be considered profound violations of the sanctity of body and soul. The fact that the roles of healer and spiritual leader are merged in many societies makes this important distinction clear. Thus, when considering quality of life research in these very different settings, it is essential to understand that with the approach come the parameters and presuppositions of Western medicine. This may be perfectly appropriate under some circumstances, particularly in intensely westernized cities such as Bombay, Singapore, or Harare. However, even there this type of assessment only touches the diaphanous veneer of modernization. Yet, the study of quality of life is important in this context. Western medicine is becoming globalized. Our profoundly interventive therapies impose both physiological and cultural stresses. If only as a first approximation, we owe it to our culturally distinct neighbors to be as interested in and informed about the broader aspects of their illness as we are becoming about ours.

Anthropologists study the nuances of culture. From them we learn that language is an expression of culture, and further that translation is distinct from understanding. It is tempting to transpose quality of life methodologies from Western society because there are important questions to ask. There may be a highly prevalent disease in Africa [human immunodeficiency virus (HIV)-related Kaposi's sarcoma, for example], or an opportunity for intellectual collaboration. In the West, the methodologies have been well established, and it seems efficient to "use what we know." In working in another culture, there are three seminal questions to ask. First, are the concepts being explored compatible, and is the question of value of relevance to the subject? The familiar concept of coping may be incomprehensible to some communities. Second, is the study feasible, given the cultural and physical setting? Third, can a valid and understandable textual translation of measurement tools be made?

QUALITY OF LIFE: A DEFINITION

The quality of life rubric that has emerged from these conceptual discussions represents an attempt to quantitate, in scientifically analyzable terms, the net consequence of a disease and its treatment on the patient's perception of his ability to live a useful and fulfilling life. What emerges is a functional definition of quality of life, measurable and evaluable over time. The measurement is subjective in two senses. First, many of the dimensions being assessed are not directly physically measurable. Second, we are as much concerned with the patient's view of the importance of the dysfunction as with its existence. As Kaplan et al. (37) put it, the focus is on "the qualitative dimension of functioning."

For most models of quality of life, the patient serves as his own internal control. Thus the primary analytic strategy has been to look for change in quality of life across the illness (disease) trajectory, rather than toward some absolute value as a benchmark of disease or response. This circumvents two important limitations to the generality of the concept. The first is cultural, meaning the difference between socioeconomic or ethnic groupings. Comparing the quality of life of Kalahari bushmen with New York stockbrokers could be a problem. Nonetheless, there is recent evidence that the overall functional quality of life construct may be cross-culturally valid. Measurement tools have been validated not only across languages within related cultural groups (as in Europe), but also into Chinese, Malay, and subcontinental Indian and African languages such as Shona and Luganda, where the tools appear to perform well (34,38).

The second issue relates to baseline assessment. Unlike a disease, which often has a definable time of onset, quality of life is a lifelong continuous variable. Because it is multifactorial and encompassing, defining baseline norms can be difficult. Provided measurement tools are linear in their response properties (an as yet thoroughly unresolved question), using "change from time of intervention" rather than "return to normal" success measurement strategies circumvents the co-morbidities issue, and allows both group and individual data interpretation. That having been said, numerous investigators have identified measured quality of life as an important prognostic factor (39–44).

The questions that form the basis of assessment may be drawn from the experience of patients, relatives, and health care providers, but they are to be answered from the patient's perspective. This is not to deny the impact of disease on a patient's relatives or the community at large. This approach is accepted as a necessary pragmatic compromise in order that meaningful studies can reasonably be undertaken. We are generalizing from the specific physiological or biochemical parameters of a disease to an attempt to encompass the overall impact of the disease and its treatment on a particular patient. We want to know what happens to a patient in a functional way.

Intrinsic to this conceptualization is a definition of health. One possibility is to base our model on the World Health Organization (WHO) definition: "A state of complete physical, mental and social well-being and not merely the absence of disease or infirmity." This is commendable but includes elements that are beyond the purview of traditional, apolitical medicine. Opportunity, education, and social security are important overall issues in the development of community health, but they are beyond the immediate goal of this assessment, which is treating the sick. We have chosen instead a second pragmatic definition of quality of life, which emphasizes the day-to-day comings and goings of a free living individual. "Quality of life" in clinical medicine represents the functional effect of an illness and its consequent therapy upon a patient, as perceived by the patient. A fascination

over the years for this WHO Centre group has been to observe the crystallization of this concept (45). As reflected by many other contributors to this volume, the points of departure for the development process have been different, as have the theoretical constructs underlying the research. Nonetheless, a similar *gestalt* emerges. Terminologies for component factors vary somewhat, but the general theme is the same, close enough in fact that research is under way to develop an interconversion table linking the more widely used questionnaires (DF Cella, *personal communication*).

This definition is based on the premise that the goal of medicine is to make the morbidity and mortality of a particular disease disappear. What we seek to do is to take away the disease and its consequences and leave the patient thereafter as if untouched by the illness.

THE DOMAINS OF QUALITY OF LIFE

Although terminology may differ, there are four broad components of the quality of life construct: physical and occupational function, psychological state, social interaction, and somatic sensation (46–48). Some investigators, particularly those in the United States, add a separate financial component (49). We think it an inappropriate and possibly distorting addition. While the financial consequences of an illness are clearly important, their effect upon a patient, and the community as a whole, is dependent on the structure of community social support programs rather than the biology of the disease. The financial costs that are incurred in the course of an illness fall into two categories: the direct costs of medical supplies and services, and the employment-related opportunity costs. The former is a social policy issue, likely not comparable from one community to another, not to speak of across national boundaries. This latter component is reflected in the physical-function part of the quality of life measure.

If overall quality of life is somehow the combined effect of the four components, it may be that interventions specifically focused at one or more of the contributory factors will significantly change a patient's quality of life. We usually think in terms of radiotherapy or chemotherapy as therapeutic interventions for cancer. If we are looking for objective tumor response as measured traditionally, then these are the appropriate measures to consider. On the other hand, if we broaden our horizons to include overall quality of life, it may be that at a given point in the natural history of a particular disease or in a particular patient, a nonmedical intervention may make a more significant contribution to a patient's quality of life than would conventional medical therapy. Likewise, a treatment may offer benefit when measured according to one set of parameters, for example, survival or disease-free survival, but a disadvantage when viewed from the prospect of quality of life or even between its component parts.

Physical and Occupational Function

Physical and occupational function is the quality of life factor most nearly approximating the outcome measures physicians traditionally use. Questions about strength, energy, and the ability to carry on expected normal activities are typically asked. They correlate reasonably with physician estimates of patient well-being and function (50). To a certain extent, they follow objective measures of tumor response or physiology, but the correlation is not strong. Questions should elicit responses uninfluenced by age, sex, or geographical habitus. A question asking about difficulty climbing stairs is of little relevance in those parts of the world where there are no stairs. Likewise, questions in this domain must be answerable both by those who have traditional occupations, such as steelworkers and accountants, and by housewives who might interpret such questions as having something to do with employment.

One of the subtleties implicit in the design of such instruments is that they be constructed so as to provide a scalar representation of the severity of impairment. Psychometricians use the term *Guttman Scale* when referring to a series of questions exploring gradations of difficulty, effort, or impact of a particular dimension. The goal is to establish either a linear, or definably nonlinear, response spectrum. A difficulty often encountered, particularly when borrowing from other detailed evaluations of physical or occupational function, is the truncation artifact (50). Many of these measures are designed and validated in institutionalized populations. The top level on such scales often represents the minimum functional state required for self-care. If such measures are transposed to quality of life studies, particularly when examining ambulatory populations, everyone answers at the top of the scale, and discriminant function is seriously compromised. Analogous problems have also been encountered at the lower limits of such scales when they are applied in the terminal care setting (51).

Psychological Function

Psychological function is relatively comfortable territory for psychologists and psychometricians, but is frequently problematic for physicians. There are numerous studies that show that doctors involved in traditional medical care are poor estimators, compared with nurses, social workers, and psychologists, of a patient's psychological state (52,53). Operationally, this provides an important rationale for establishing a clinic environment where both the attending physician and the nurse have individual opportunities to speak with each patient.

Of the many psychological parameters that have an impact on quality of life, the ones most studied are anxiety, depression, and fear. From a number of studies there seems to be an underlying natural evolution of emotions encompassing depression and anxiety at the time of diagnosis, anxiety with each approaching reassessment, and fear at moments of diagnostic or therapeutic uncertainty (54–56). The psychometric measures employed in quality of life studies may be simple questions inquiring directly as to mood, anxiety, or depression, or they may be more sophisticated borrowings from the psychometric testing literature.

Of substantial concern, however, is the fact that the study population we are targeting, namely chronically ill patients, comes from neither of the populations for whom these tests were initially devised. Many tests draw norms from a healthy population. Other measures have been developed to assess persons with diagnosed mental or psychiatric disabilities. Their scalar properties are often adjusted to evaluate the severity of preexisting psychiatric conditions. Thus, the validity of the psychological component of quality of life measure tends to be held hostage to the developmental root of its questions, and is not readily transported to another use such as quality of life assessment. Our experience, and that of our colleagues at the European Organization for Research and Treatment of Cancer (EORTC), suggests that straightforward questioning, with a small number of items, provides quite reasonable correlation with more detailed psychological and psychometric examinations (50,57). However, analysis of this factor should not be extended to the making of specific psychological diagnoses but rather be limited, as a broad indicator of overall psychological function.

Social Interaction

Social interaction refers to a patient's ability to carry on the person-to-person interactions at the core of communal living. These interactions are traditionally thought of as forming a hierarchy: family, close friends, work and vocational associates, and the general community. The importance of this parameter has long been underestimated.

Somatic Sensation

Somatic sensation, or symptoms, encompasses unpleasant physical feelings that may detract from someone's quality of life. They include pain, nausea, and shortness of breath, among others. Of particular interest to an number of observers is the role that the attribution of discomfort has on overall quality of life. Although the data are not conclusive, many believe that unpleasant somatic sensations associated with therapy have a less deleterious effect on quality of life than similar sensations of like duration and intensity that must be attributed to the disease (58). Duration and intensity appear to interact, particularly for pain. Ventafridda et al. (59) suggest that multiplying the intensity of pain by its duration offers an accurate estimate of a patient's reserve. They further suggest that the relief of pain may directly prolong life (*personal communication*).

These four domains likely do not represent the total spectrum of quality of life. They appear to encompass a large proportion of the everyday concerns of free-living people. There is a broader conceptualization that has thus far eluded measurement. This may be described as the health trinity: body, mind, and spirit. The focus of contemporary quality of life measurement is largely on the first two components, where there seems to be a pragmatic consensus that the dimensions are measurable and that perhaps they are more broadly translatable between individuals and cultures than is spirituality. An important conceptual area to be explored is the relation between dimensions.

Aaronson et al. (60) state that a major conceptual weakness has been to adopt an ad hoc approach to measuring health-related quality of life and suggest that future research should be based on conceptual models that explain the interrelationships among quality of life domains throughout the stages of a disease and its treatment. The usefulness of such models will be in the hypotheses generated for investigating the links among the variables studied (e.g., antecedent, mediating, modifying) and specific quality of life outcomes. Hollen et al. (61) characterized 11 different conceptual models for quality of life while deriving their own conceptual model for evaluating quality of life during lung cancer. The more common dimensions of physical, functional, psychological, and social aspects of quality of life were represented in most of the 11 models; however, there were several dimensions unique to some of the models. In nine of the models, the dimensions were modeled as independent, and only two delineated interdependent dimensions with directional relationships amenable to testing. Thus there is a growing feeling that the hypothesized relationships between quality domains could lead to some very interesting outcome studies.

PROPERTIES OF THE QUALITY OF LIFE PARADIGM

Quality of life assessment measures are now relatively mature. They are in wide use in clinical trials settings, and as such are beginning to influence clinical practice. An important early outcome has been the repeated demonstration that quality of life is an independent prognostic indicator, whose influence is greater than measures of physical function such as Karnofsky and ECOG (Eastern Cooperative Oncology Group) scores. Further, from a policy perspective, the notion that a quality of life benefit may complement or even compete with more traditional response and survival data has gained considerable credence. The result is clinical trials groups are beginning to mandate quality of life assessment, and regulatory agencies will consider quality of life as a drug licensure criterion (1,62). Thus given the power and utility of the tool, it is necessary to understand its properties and limitations in order to use it appropriately.

The quality of life paradigm has a number of operational characteristics different from the usual clinical outcome measures (46). It is important to understand these differences in order to avoid pitfalls in clinical trials design. There are numerous examples of well-intentioned trials whose outcome and interpretation are suspect because the investigators were unfamiliar with these properties, methods of data analysis, the handling of missing data, as well as the limitations of the methodology. Four important properties of the quality of life parameter merit discussion: it is multifactorial, it is patient self-administered, its value is variable over time, and it is subjective.

Multifactoriality

It is apparent that the quality of life parameter measures more than one single aspect of a patient's overall function. Having operationally defined quality of life as the synthesis of four domains (physical/occupational function, psychological function, social interaction, and somatic sensation), one needs to be satisfied that enough of a patient's overall daily living is encompassed by these measures for the score to be truly representative of the whole process. This is analogous to determining how representative either the blood glucose or the hemoglobin A_{1C} is of the overall diabetic process.

The next question to ask is whether the brief inquiries into each domain of quality of life reflect their target adequately. It is clear one cannot make a detailed psychosocial or occupational evaluation based on four or five questions. However, correlation studies comparing quality of life, on a factor by factor basis, with much more detailed measures representing each factor provide reassurance about their validity. The factor analysis process is a standard for instrument validation (63). This is a multistage technique whose intent is to reveal the constructs that underlie responses to batteries of questions, although the technique can be used in other settings. In interpreting factor analyses, it is important to distinguish between the factors, which are the underlying concepts, and the scales, which represent the sum of questions that load most highly on each factor. Put in other terms, the formal calculation of a factor score means taking the weighted sum of scores of each item multiplied by the factor weighting for that item. In contrast, a scalar score means summing the scores of those items loading most heavily on each factor. In general, the factor analysis process gives confidence that the questions point to specific factors rather than being vague probes of well-being (64–73).

Numerous investigators have developed global, cancer-specific quality of life indices (50,66,74–78). These tools have many themes in common, the differences being relative emphasis of component factors, the method of index derivation, and questionnaire format (e.g., Likert, analogue, dichotomous responses). Cella et al. (67) have developed a "conversion" table linking the Functional Living Index–Cancer and the more recently developed Functional Assessment of Cancer Therapy index (*personal communication*). This and similar exercises currently in process provide further evidence of the rigor of the quality of life concept and of contemporary instrument development techniques.

In attempting to provide a compact index of broad applicability, repeatable at frequent intervals, some compromise has been made. In particular, the analysis of specific somatic disability has been abbreviated. It simply is not feasible to ask every patient, at every intervention, about a vast range of symptoms and side effects that may have little relevance to the particular clinical situation. In an attempt to resolve this difficulty, Aaronson et al. (57) have proposed a "core plus module" approach, which has been widely adapted. Its essence is that one administers both a global quality of life index and an additional smaller module that is disease specific. In principle this allows one to make consistent overall quality of life assessments, while at the same time dissecting the dysfunctions identified with measures specific to each disease. Many modules have been developed. What has yet to be determined is how much they add to the sensitivity of the measurement. It may be the module provides additional descriptive information explaining the quality of life state without adding precision.

The weighting problem is more vexing and largely unresolved. How does one weigh the individual domain scores so as to arrive at a reasonable overall quality of life score? At the present time, few studies are examining this issue. It may be that the relative weightings of quality of life domains are themselves time-variable. This means that before comparing quality of life outcomes of different trials, one is required to take into account differences in domain weightings between the quality of life measures used. A series of quality of life studies has applied the technique of judgment analysis to the development of the Schedule for the Evaluation of Individual Quality of Life (SEIQoL) (79–82). Judgment analysis is derived from social judgment theory and allows individual judgments to be modeled mathematically. The justification for applying this technique to quality of life assessments is that specific goals or behaviors important to individual quality of life are not represented adequately by broad questions about physical mobility or mental health; apparently similar behaviors do not have the same significance for all individuals; and they do not retain the same significance for a given individual with the passage of time or over the course of an illness.

The procedure allows the patient to select five areas of life considered most important in assessing overall quality of life, during a semistructured interview. Each cue is then rated on a vertical visual analog scale between the upper and lower extremes of "As good as it could possibly be" and "As bad as it could possibly be." In the second stage, the relative contribution of each elicited cue to the overall judgment of quality of life is determined for each individual. Thirty different hypothetical profiles using the elicited cues unique to each patient are presented for visual analog scale rating of overall quality of life, a procedure that takes 30 minutes. A computer program based on multiple regression analysis then uses these ratings to provide a weight for each cue. The final score is computed by multiplying each cue weight by the patient's current self-rating and summing across cues to obtain a total score. The same procedure can be used with provided cues representing standard quality of life dimensions. In a study of quality of life in patients undergoing hip replacement, the elicited SEIQoL scores showed significant improvement with surgery, whereas the *provided* SEIQoL scores showed no difference. This result provides support for the idea of allowing patients to choose and weight their quality of life domains in assessing overall quality of life in that greater sensitivity to treatment differences may result. There are two major drawbacks to this system: first, that the effect of treatment on a specific quality of life area can only be determined for the subset of patients that chose that area, and second, that the procedure is very time and resource intensive compared with other methods of quality of life assessment.

It may serve as an enlightening historical aside to note that when the Functional Living Index–Cancer was first devised, we tended to provide an overall quality of life score because we lacked confidence that the factor scores were representative (50). Many researchers are now more confident in the use of quality of life subscores as probes (not as diagnostics), and suggest that an assessment of quality of life may include both an overall score, as defined precisely for the instruments being used, as well as component subscores.

From an analytic point of view this makes it possible to begin to dissect out component factors of quality of life and the variable impact treatment may have on each. Implicit in this strategy is the large volume of data that flows from a quality of life study. Several variables are measured at each encounter and patients are followed for a considerable time. In addition to the usual clinical information, several items of quality of life data will be collected. This has clear workload implications.

Self-Administration

Most, but not all, quality of life indices are patient self-administered. Some, such as Spitzer's Quality of Life Index, are designed to be administered by third parties (21). As previously noted, the evidence suggests that physicians tend to focus on physiological data, whereas nurses, social workers, family, and patients tend to place more emphasis on psychosocial measures (53). This means that if one chooses an externally administered subjective measure, in addition to making the usual evaluation of its reliability and validity, one has to take into account who is doing the testing. Further, one must be consistent. It is not appropriate to have the physician do the measuring at one time, the psychologist at another time, and the social worker or family member at still another time. Likewise, one must not haphazardly adapt a test designed for patient self-administration to the externally administered format and vice versa. One interesting study came to grief in part because a tool designed for patient self-administration was used with a follow-up design that allowed an external observer to attempt to recover missing data by phoning the patient, reading the questionnaire over the telephone, and estimating a result (83).

There is another property of the quality of life measure, related to subjectivity and self-administration, that contributes greatly to its cross-cultural validity. It is designed to use patients as their own internal controls. It can be used without norms. With this approach, the critical quality of life value is not the score a patient provides, but rather the change in that patient's score over time. In other words when making comparisons of groups of patients, the central issue is not whether the overall score in one group is better than the other, but rather whether the change in scores observed over time is different in each group. In relatively homogeneous populations it is probably reasonable to look at differences in raw score, but many of the problems associated with comparing people of different social, economic, and cultural milieus are circumvented when change in score within patients becomes the focus of the examination. However, to employ this approach, timing of the initial quality of life assessment is critical. Insofar as it is possible, this first assessment must be done at the same time in the natural history of the investigation and treatment of the disease in every patient. Otherwise the baseline against which all comparisons are made will be inconsistent and the trial less evaluable.

Quality of Life Is Time-Variable

The quality of life parameter is variable over time. In that sense it is like a measure of blood sugar or tumor size. It is sharply different from the cancer clinical trials measures we use that record response, disease-free survival, and survival. Survival and disease-free survival curves are monotonically decreasing. Studies that select these as primary outcome measures derive a single data point from each patient entered in the study. That data point is acquired only when the patient either dies or fails therapy. Thus it is entirely possible to enter a patient into a study, lose all track of him for 15 years, and recover all the survival data, without compromise, by having the patient walk into the clinic alive after that long interval. This is not the case with quality of life data, which because of its fluctuating nature is not recoverable once lost. Thus meticulous follow-up and careful attention to the timing of measurement and consistency of measurement across treatments becomes important. Further, resources must be available to achieve the timely collection of data that is otherwise irretrievable. One trial, which compared continuous with intermittent treatment for an advanced malignant disease, was seriously flawed by the fact that quality of life was measured on a reasonably regular basis for those on continuous treatment, but was not measured in those patients on the intermittent therapy arm when they were off therapy (84). As the authors themselves point out,

the obtained result was contrary to their expectation. The data lost could not be recovered.

Quality of Life Is Subjective

The subjective nature of the quality of life measure is a source of some unease among investigators. Those of us raised in the Western basic science milieu tend to view medicine, at least in its research and development components, in Flexnerian terms, as a science amenable to the objectivity incumbent upon the scientific method. Since this model has as its basis a dispassionate molecular or biochemical understanding of disease, we believe that we will be distracted from our course by less precisely measurable concerns. What we have to keep in mind is that the heterogeneity of our patient populations and our inability to identify, let alone control, all variables that influence disease progression have forced us to accept broader measurement tolerances in clinical medicine than would reassure most basic scientists. We have difficulty probing our patients, so critical measurements are often significantly inaccurate (2). Most important, in clinical medicine the ultimate observer of the experiment is not a dispassionate third party but a most intimately involved patient. Further, there is increasing evidence that there are real links between basic physiological function and the broader psychosocial issues that are encompassed in the quality of life paradigm. To a certain extent what the psychosocial measure may lack in precision it may compensate for in relevance.

The goal of treatment is to make the manifest effects of an illness go away. In a sense the quality of life measure represents the final common pathway of all the physiological, psychological, and social inputs into the therapeutic process. Appropriate, rigorously designed and evaluated quality of life instruments can be used in carefully designed studies to provide objective representations of what we have until recently viewed as essentially intangible subjective processes. Further, the evaluable multidimensional nature of the construct provides a cross-disciplinary probe into the relationship between the clinic and the laboratory.

TACTICS FOR CONDUCTING QUALITY OF LIFE TRIALS

Following are some general tactics for the conduct of quality of life trials.

1. Choose a study in which you expect substantial differences in quality of life outcome. To conduct a study in which you expect only subtle differences will likely prove frustrating and counterproductive.
2. The ideal study measures quality of life and overall survival in addition to other clinical parameters, which may include disease-free survival as well as specific physiological data.

3. In calculating the number of patients required, a quality of life study will not necessarily increase the sample size requirement. In fact, since each patient contributes repeated measures of the same variables over time, you will need fewer patients than are required for estimation of survival or disease-free survival. (It is a well-known fact that repeated measures designs have an increased power to detect between group differences) (85).

4. Use quality of life instruments that are both reliable and valid. Do not reinvent the wheel. Understand the properties and limitations of the measurement tools selected.

5. Define precisely when the initial quality of life measurement is to be done and by whom. This serves as the key measurement against which subsequent results are compared.

6. Repeat the quality of life measurement at intervals frequent enough to track treatment and the natural history of the disease. Do not confound your study by measuring some patients when they are sick and other patients when you expect them to be well. Where possible, it is best to measure quality of life with the same pattern of measurement in each treatment arm.

7. The period of accurate recall for a psychological variable reflecting feeling states is somewhere between 2 and 4 weeks (86). It reflects an average of the time in question with some emphasis on either major events or more recent experiences. To emphasize the effect of an intervention, do the test shortly after. To minimize that effect, and possibly better sample the overall progression of the disease, do the test before the next treatment event. Whatever your choice, be consistent across treatment arms.

8. Follow all patients until the natural end point of their disease is reached or until all influence of treatment is likely to have passed. Failure to do so may create biases related to ''up-front'' treatments.

9. Do not analyze your data solely by simple averaging. Techniques such as time series analysis and multivariate analysis of variance take into account the pattern of quality of life response and are much more revealing of the social and biological effects of therapy. These techniques are standard approaches to handling multivariate, time-variable data. Techniques are being developed to alleviate problems such as missing data, nonlinearity, present versus future value, and loss of data due to patient death.

10. In addition to looking at overall quality of life outcome, it is reasonable to evaluate each of the component factors. However, one must be modest with extrapolations.

CONCLUSIONS

The first edition of this book introduced quality of life as a new scientific concept. At that time, authors suggested that the paradigm offered the potential for both patients and caregivers to use the same currency for evaluating the effectiveness of treatment. Over the past 10 years, we have progressed from serious doubts about whether the concept is definable to a broadly accepted concept (although without a unifying formal definition), an understanding of the properties of the paradigm, and a framework for doing meaningful studies. There is now solid clinical data relating to both instrument robustness and deriving from the outcome of clinical studies. Nonetheless, it is prudent to retain our previous concluding recommendation. We must remain cautious lest our enthusiasm outpace our rigor.

REFERENCES

1. Miller L, Vestal R, Dalton M, Atwood B, Perkins JG, Lyon G. Quality of life II. Oncology: regulatory/scientific aspects and the drug approval process. *J Clin Res Pharmacoepidemiol* 1990;4:39–53.
2. Warr D, McKinney S, Tannock I. Influence of measurement error on assessment of response to anticancer chemotherapy: proposal for new criteria of tumor response. *J Clin Oncol* 1984;2:1040–1046.
3. Schipper H. Why measure quality of life? *Can Med Assoc J* 1983;128:1367–1370.
4. Sichel MP. Quality of life and gynecological cancers. *Eur J Gynaecol Oncol* 1990;11:485–488.
5. Ammirati M, Vick N, Liao YL, Ciric I, Mikhael M. Effect of the extent of surgical resection on survival and quality of life in patients with supratentorial glioblastomas and anaplastic astrocytomas. *Neurosurgery* 1987;21:201–206.
6. Blake DJ, Maisiak R, Alarcon GS, Holley HL, Brown S. Sexual quality-of-life of patients with arthritis compared to arthritis-free controls. *J Rheumatol* 1987;14:570–576.
7. Sugimachi K, Maekawa S, Koga Y, Ueo H, Inokuchi K. The quality of life is sustained after operation for carcinoma of the esophagus. *Surg Gynecol Obstet* 1986;162:544–546.
8. Oakley JR, Jagelman DG, Fazio VW, et al. Complications and quality of life after ileorectal anastomosis for ulcerative colitis. *Am J Surg* 1985;149:23–30.
9. Karnofsky DA, Burchenal JH. The clinical evaluation of chemotherapeutic agents in cancer. In: Maclead CM, ed. *Evaluation of chemotherapeutic agents.* New York: Columbia University Press, 1947.
10. Yates JW, Chalmer B, McKegney FP. Evaluation of patients with advanced cancer using the Karnofsky Performance Status. *Cancer* 1980;45:2220–2224.
11. Priestman TJ, Baum M. Evaluation of quality of life in patients receiving treatment for advanced breast cancer. *Lancet* 1976;1:899–901.
12. Ware JE Jr. Conceptualizing disease impact and treatment outcomes. *Cancer* 1984;53:2316–2323.
13. Calman KC. Quality of life in cancer patients—an hypothesis. *J Med Ethics* 1984;10:124–127.
14. Kleinman A. Culture, the quality of life and cancer pain: anthropological and cross-cultural perspectives. In: Ventafridda V, ed. *Assessment of quality of life and cancer treatment.* Excerpt Medica International Congress Series 702. Amsterdam: Elsevier, 1986;43–50.
15. Dimsdale JE. A perspective on type A behavior and coronary disease (editorial). *N Engl J Med* 1988;318:110.
16. Patel C, Marmot MG. Stress management, blood pressure and quality of life. *J Hypertens Suppl* 1987;5:S21–S28.
17. Levy SM, Herberman RB, Maluish AM, Schlien B, Lippman M. Prognostic risk assessment in primary breast cancer by behavioral and immunological parameters. *Health Psychol* 1985;4:99–113.
18. McNeil BJ, Weichselbaum R, Pauker SG. Speech and survival: trade-offs between quality and quantity of life in laryngeal cancer. *N Engl J Med* 1981;305:982–987.
19. Singer PA, Tasch ES, Stocking C, Rubin S, Siegler M, Weichselbaum R. Sex or survival: trade-offs between quality and quantity of life. *J Clin Oncol* 1991;9:328–334.
20. Wood Dauphinee S, Williams JI. Reintegration to normal living as a proxy to quality of life. *J Chronic Dis* 1987;40:491–499.
21. Spitzer WO, Dobson AJ, Hall J, et al. Measuring the quality of life

of cancer patients: a concise Q/L index for use by physicians. *J Chronic Dis* 1981;34:585–597.

22. Schag CA, Ganz PA, Heinrich RL. Cancer Rehabilitation Evaluation System—Short Form (CARES-SF): a cancer specific rehabilitation and quality of life instrument. *Cancer* 1991;68:1406–1413.

23. Powell V, Powell C. Quality of life measurement (letter). *J Med Ethics* 1987;13:222.

24. Andrews K, Stewart J. He can but does he? *Rheumatol Rehabil* 1979;18:43–48.

25. Channer KS. Failure of a negative exercise test to reassure patients with chest pain. *Q J Med* 1987;63:315–322.

26. Wood C. Are happy people healthier? *J R Soc Med* 1987;80:354–356.

27. Marshall PA. Cultural influences on perceived quality of life. *Semin Oncol Nurs* 1990;6:278–284.

28. Chelvam P. Quality of life—Asian perspective—a personal view. *Scand J Gastroenterol Suppl* 1993;199:16–17.

29. Bullinger M, Anderson R, Cella D, Aaronson N. Developing and evaluating cross-cultural instruments from minimum requirements to optimal models. *Qual Life Res* 1993;2:451–459.

30. Leininger M. Quality of life from a transcultural nursing perspective. *Nurs Sci Q* 1994;7:22–28.

31. Guillemin F, Bombardier C, Beaton D. Cross-cultural adaptation of health-related quality of life measures: literature review and proposed guidelines. *J Clin Epidemiol* 1993;46:1417–1432.

32. Chaturvedi SK. What's important for quality of life to Indians—in relation to cancer. *Soc Sci Med* 1991;33:91–94.

33. Moller V, Schlemmer L. South African quality of life: a research note. *Soc Indicators Res* 1989;21:279–291.

34. Goh CR, Tan TC, Schipper H, et al. Cross-cultural validation of quality of life assessment tools: methodologies and results of English, Chinese and Malay translation of the Functional Living Index for Cancer (FLIC) in Singapore. *Proc Am Soc Clin Oncol* 1994;13:455(abstract).

35. Rankin SH, Galbraith ME, Johnson S. Reliability and validity data for a Chinese translation of the Center for Epidemiological Studies–Depression. *Psychol Rep* 1993;73:1291–1298.

36. Farquhar J. *Knowing practice: the clinical encounter of Chinese medicine.* Boulder, San Francisco & Oxford: Westview Press, 1994.

37. Kaplan RM, Anderson JP, Wu AW, Mathews WC, Kozin F, Orenstein D. The Quality of Well-being Scale. Applications in AIDS, cystic fibrosis, and arthritis. *Med Care* 1989;27:S27–S43.

38. Clinch J, Olweny CLM, Schipper H, et al. Cross-cultural validation of the Functional Living Index-Cancer (FLIC) using epidemic Kaposi's sarcoma (EKS) patients in Zimbabwe. *Proc Am Soc Clin Oncol* 1995 (abstract).

39. Ganz PA, Lee JJ, Siau J. Quality of life assessment. An independent prognostic variable for survival in lung cancer. *Cancer* 1991;67:3131–3135.

40. McClellan WM, Anson C, Birkeli K, Tuttle E. Functional status and quality of life: predictors of early mortality among patients entering treatment for end stage renal disease. *J Clin Epidemiol* 1991;44:83–89.

41. Buddeberg C, Riehl Emde A, Landont Ritter C, Steiner R, Sieber M, Richter D. [The significance of psychosocial factors for the course of breast cancer—results of a prospective follow-up study]. *Schweiz Arch Neurol Psychiatr* 1990;141:429–455.

42. Addington Hall JM, MacDonald LD, Anderson HR. Can the Spitzer Quality of Life Index help to reduce prognostic uncertainty in terminal care? *Br J Cancer* 1990;62:695–699.

43. Coates A, Thomson D, McLeod GR, et al. Prognostic value of quality of life scores in a trial of chemotherapy with or without interferon in patients with metastatic malignant melanoma. *Eur J Cancer* 1993;29A:1731–1734.

44. Coates A, Forbes J, Simes RJ. Prognostic value of performance status and quality-of-life scores during chemotherapy for advanced breast cancer. The Australian New Zealand Breast Cancer Trials Group (letter). *J Clin Oncol* 1993;11:2050.

45. Olweny CL. Quality of life in cancer care. *Med J Aust* 1993;158:429–432.

46. Schipper H, Clinch J. Assessment of treatment in cancer. In: Teeling-Smith G, ed. *Measuring health: a practical approach.* New York: Wiley, 1988;109–155.

47. Cella DF, Tulsky DS. Measuring quality of life today: methodological aspects. *Oncology Williston Park* 1990;4:29–38.

48. Strain JJ. The evolution of quality of life evaluations in cancer therapy. *Oncology Williston Park* 1990;4:22–26.

49. Padilla GV, Presant C, Grant MM, Metter G, Lipsett J, Heide F. Quality of life index for patients with cancer. *Res Nurs Health* 1983;6:117–126.

50. Schipper H, Clinch J, McMurray A, Levitt M. Measuring the quality of life of cancer patients: the functional living index-cancer: development and validation. *J Clin Oncol* 1984;2:472–483.

51. Morris JN, Suissa S, Sherwood S, Wright SM, Greer D. Last days: a study of the quality of life of terminally ill cancer patients. *J Chronic Dis* 1986;39:47–62.

52. Presant CA. Quality of life in cancer patients: Who measures what? *Am J Clin Oncol* 1984;7:571–573.

53. Stam HJ, Challis GB. Ratings of cancer chemotherapy toxicity by oncologists, nurses and pharmacists. *J Pain Symptom Management* 1989;4:7–12.

54. Morris JN, Sherwood S. Quality of life of cancer patients at different stages in the disease trajectory. *J Chronic Dis* 1987;40:545–556.

55. Mor V. Cancer patients' quality of life over the disease course: lessons from the real world. *J Chronic Dis* 1987;40:535–544.

56. Lasry JM, Margolese RG, Poisson R. Depression and body image following mastectomy and lumpectomy. *J Chronic Dis* 1987;40:529–534.

57. Aaronson NK, Bullinger M, Ahmedzai S. A modular approach to quality-of-life assessment in cancer clinical trials. *Recent Results Cancer Res* 1988;111:231–249.

58. Fishman B, Loscalzo M. Cognitive-behavioral intervention in pain management: principles in application. In: Payne R, Foley KM, eds. *Medical clinics North America.* Philadelphia: WB Saunders, 1987.

59. Ventafridda V, DeConno F, DiTrapani P, et al. A new method of pain quantification based on a weekly self-descriptive record of the intensity and duration of pain. In: Bonica J, ed. *Advances in pain research and therapy.* New York: Raven Press, 1983;891–895.

60. Aaronson NK, Meyerowitz BE, Bard M, et al. Quality of life research in oncology. Past achievements and future priorities. *Cancer* 1991;67:839–843.

61. Hollen PJ, Gralla RJ, Kris MG, Cox C. Quality of life during clinical trials: conceptual model for the Lung Cancer Symptom Scale. *Support Care Cancer* 1994;2:213–222.

62. Osoba D. Measuring quality of life. *Prog Clin Biol Res* 1990;354B:233–240.

63. Harman HH. *Modern factor analysis,* 3rd ed. Chicago: University of Chicago Press, 1976.

64. Jenkins CD, Jono RT, Stanton BA, Stroup Benham CA. The measurement of health-related quality of life: major dimensions identified by factor analysis. *Soc Sci Med* 1990;31:925–931.

65. Finkelstein DM, Cassileth BR, Bonomi PD, Ruckdeschel JC, Ezdinli EZ, Wolter JM. A pilot study of the Functional Living Index-Cancer (FLIC) Scale for the assessment of quality of life for metastatic lung cancer patients. An Eastern Cooperative Oncology Group study. *Am J Clin Oncol* 1988;11:630–633.

66. Kaasa S, Mastekaasa A, Stokke I, Naess S. Validation of a quality of life questionnaire for use in clinical trials for treatment of patients with inoperable lung cancer. *Eur J Cancer Clin Oncol* 1988;24:691–701.

67. Cella DF, Tulsky DS, Gray G, et al. The Functional Assessment of Cancer Therapy scale: development and validation of the general measure. *J Clin Oncol* 1993;11:570–579.

68. Ruckdeschel JC, Piantadosi S. Assessment of quality of life (ql) by the functional living index-cancer (flic) is superior to performance status for prediction of survival in patients with lung cancer (meeting abstract). *Proc Annu Meet Am Soc Clin Oncol* 1989;8:311.

69. Schipper H. Measuring quality of life: risks and benefits. *Cancer Treat Rep* 1985;69:1115–1125.

70. Ciampi A, Lockwood G, Sutherland HJ, Llewellyn-Thomas HA, et al. Assessment of health-related quality of life: factor scales for patients with breast cancer. *J Psychosoc Oncol* 1988;6:1–19.

71. Ringdal GI, Ringdal K. Testing the EORTC Quality of Life Questionnaire on cancer patients with heterogeneous diagnoses. *Qual Life Res* 1993;2:129–140.

72. McHorney CA, Ware JE Jr, Raczek AE. The MOS 36-Item Short-Form Health Survey (SF-36): II. Psychometric and clinical tests of validity in measuring physical and mental health constructs. *Med Care* 1993;31:247–263.

73. Ballatori E, Roila F, Basurto C, et al. Reliability and validity of a quality of life questionnaire in cancer patients. *Eur J Cancer* 1993;29A(suppl 1):S63–S69.

74. Churchill DN, Torrance GW, Taylor DW, et al. Measurement of quality

of life in end-stage renal disease: the time trade-off approach. *Clin Invest Med* 1987;10:14–20.

75. Sugarbaker PH, Barofsky I, Rosenberg SA, Gianola FJ. Quality of life assessment of patients in extremity sarcoma clinical trials. *Surgery* 1982;91:17–23.

76. Selby PJ, Chapman JAW, Etazadi-Amoli J, Dalley D, Boyd NF. The development of a method for assessing the quality of life of cancer patients. *Br J Cancer* 1984;50:13–22.

77. Gough IR, Furnival CM, Schilder L, Grove W. Assessment of the quality of life of patients with advanced cancer. *Eur J Cancer Clin Oncol* 1983;19:1161–1165.

78. Pezim ME, Nicholls RJ. Quality of life after restorative proctocolectomy with pelvic ileal reservoir. *Br J Surg* 1985;72:31–33.

79. O'Boyle CA, McGee H, Hickey A, O'Malley K, Joyce CR. Individual quality of life in patients undergoing hip replacement. *Lancet* 1992; 339:1088–1091.

80. McGee HM, O'Boyle CA, Hickey A, O'Malley K, Joyce CR. Assessing the quality of life of the individual: the SEIQoL with a healthy and a gastroenterology unit population. *Psychol Med* 1991;21:749–759.

81. O'Boyle CA, McGee H, Hickey A, O'Malley KM, Joyce CRB. Reliability and validity of judgement analysis (JA) as a method for assessing quality of life (QOL). *Proc BPS* 1989;155P.

82. Brown BP, O'Boyle CA, McGee H, et al. Individual quality of life in the healthy elderly. *Qual Life Res* 1994;4:235–244.

83. Ganz PA, Haskell CM, Figlin RA, La Soto N, Siau J. Estimating the quality of life in a clinical trial of patients with metastatic lung cancer using the Karnofsky performance status and the Functional Living Index–Cancer. *Cancer* 1988;61:849–856.

84. Coates A, Gebski V, Bishop JF, et al. Improving the quality of life during chemotherapy for advanced breast cancer. A comparison of intermittent and continuous treatment strategies. *N Engl J Med* 1987; 317:1490–1495.

85. Kirk RE. *Experimental design: procedures for the behavioral sciences.* Belmont, California: Brooks/Cole, 1968.

86. Nunnally JC. *Psychometric theory.* New York: McGraw-Hill, 1967.

Quality of Life and Pharmacoeconomics in Clinical Trials, Second Edition, edited by B. Spilker.
Lippincott-Raven Publishers, Philadelphia © 1996.

CHAPTER 3

Taxonomy of Quality of Life

Bert Spilker and Dennis A. Revicki

INTRODUCTION

Health-related quality of life (HRQL) is a subset of the overall concept of quality of life so that the two concepts are closely related (1–3). Environmental, economic, social, spiritual, and political variables often influence a person's quality of life, but these factors are not expected to be directly affected by most health care interventions. This chapter develops a taxonomy of quality of life to encourage further discussion and research into the influences of non–health-related factors on both HRQL and non–health-related quality of life (NHRQL), and to stimulate development of instruments to measure NHRQL factors more accurately.

The taxonomy proposed suggests that there are two main encompassing types of quality of life, health-related quality of life and non–health-related quality of life. HRQL represents those parts of quality of life that directly relate to an individual's health (4,5). Conceptually, HRQL includes the domains of physical, psychological, social, spiritual, and role functioning, as well as general well-being (6,7). Although various conceptualizations of HRQL exist, there is general consensus that these domains are necessary for any comprehensive definition of HRQL (3,4,6,7). Other chapters in this book provide detailed specification of HRQL, so that no further explanation is presented.

The relative influence of these two types of quality of

   B. Spilker: Orphan Medical, Inc., Minnetonka, Minnesota, 55305.
   D. Revicki: MEDTAP International, Arlington, Virginia 22201.

life on an individual varies depending on one's state of health as well as on many other factors. Figure 1 illustrates this phenomenon by showing the importance of various domains and their components for healthy and chronically ill individuals. The principle illustrated by Figure 1 is reminiscent of the utility concept described in several chapters in this book.

Wilson and Cleary (8) have recently offered a well thought out conceptual model for patient outcomes that includes biological and physiological variables, symptoms, function, health perceptions, and overall quality of life. The focus of their discussion is on HRQL. Most of the medical literature on quality of life discusses HRQL and focuses on the individual.

Although most medical discussions of quality of life refer to the individual patient, the concept of both HRQL and NHRQL may also be applied to larger groups of patients and to larger geographical units than a single person and his or her home. These themes are introduced in this chapter and a model is proposed that includes two types of levels as well as the two types of quality of life and their components.

NON–HEALTH-RELATED QUALITY OF LIFE

Many factors, both internal and external to an individual, may affect health perceptions, functioning, and well-being. For example, patient-specific characteristics such as motivation and personality may be important influences on HRQL (9,10). Social networks, including friends and family, may be instrumental in helping a person cope and adapt to a

A. Individuals in Good Health

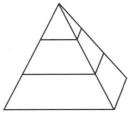

**Nonhealth Quality
of Life Factors**   **Health Quality
of Life Factors**

B. Individuals with a Chronic Illness

 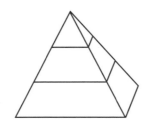

**Nonhealth Quality
of Life Factors**   **Health Quality
of Life Factors**

FIG. 1. Relative importance of the two types of quality of life for different individuals. The size of each pyramid is drawn relative to its importance to most healthy people (**A**) or those with a chronic illness (**B**). The top of each pyramid represents the overall quality of life level. The middle third represents the domains level, and the lowest third represents the components of the domains. Individual factors that make up the components are not illustrated.

TABLE 1. *Domains and selected components of non–health-related quality of life*

Personal-internal
   Values and beliefs
   Desires and goals
   Personality attributes
   Coping strategies
   Spiritual status
Personal-social
   Social networks
   Family structure
   Social groups
   Financial status
   Vocational status
External-natural environment
   Air, water, and land quality
   Weather
   Geographic characteristics
External-societal environment
   Cultural institutions and opportunities
   Religious institutions and opportunities
   Schools
   Shopping facilities and opportunities
   Medical facilities and services
   Government and political policies, institutions
   Personal safety in the environment
   Transportation and communication systems
   Social and recreational institutions and facilities
   Community spirit and demographics
   Business institutions

serious chronic disease, resulting in improved psychological well-being compared to others who may have limited social resources. Factors in the natural environment may also have an impact on HRQL, such as the impact of poor air quality on patients with asthma.

Our conceptualization of NHRQL includes four domains: (a) personal-internal, (b) personal-social, (c) external-natural environment, and (d) external-societal environment. Each of these domains consists of several components, and each component consists of individual factors. Thus, the organizational structure of NHRQL is similar to that of HRQL. Table 1 lists several components of these four domains and Table 2 illustrates some examples of factors of a few of these components.

Personal-Internal

This domain represents the facets within each person that may influence his or her perceptions of functioning and well-being. Personal-internal factors may also affect the person's interactions with the external social and natural environment. These factors consist of personality attributes, motivation, value and belief systems about health and other life areas, coping strategies, desires, and life goals. For example, elderly women with severe osteoarthritis treated with knee-replacement surgery may have different health outcomes depending on their level of motivation in rehabilitation and personality factors (e.g., need for self-sufficiency and independence, perceived control). A nursing-home patient study found that personal control and responsibility were associated with improved physical health and morale and lower mortality (11). Sometimes individuals can surmount and overcome severe disabilities and live very personally satisfying lives.

These internal characteristics influence the person's perceptions of and interactions within his or her social environment. Personality and other internal factors affect perceptions of life events and other life circumstances, including illness and disease. The experience of symptoms and disease, including uncertainty concerning diagnosis, effects of treatment, and prognosis, are colored by personality attributes and internal value systems. The individual's sense of personal control, self-efficacy, motivation, and other factors are associated with successful adaptation and coping with health problems and stressful life circumstances. These factors may also affect the person's health perceptions, mental health, and functioning.

TABLE 2. *Examples of factors of selected NHRQL components*

Air, water, or land quality
  Degree of pollution
  Quality of the air (e.g., humidity, pollen, temperature)
  Quality of the water or land (e.g., regulations and enforcement)
Personal safety
  Road safety
  Public transportation safety
  Ability to walk or travel in the environment
  Fear of crime in one's home, neighborhood, and community
Cultural events and institutions
  Facilities for holding events (e.g., condition, aesthetic qualities, distance)
  Quality of events that are held
  Availability of seats and affordability of seats
  Number of events that are held
Personality attributes
  Motivation
  Perceived control
  Self-sufficiency
  Ability to trust others
  Ability to delegate appropriately
Social status
  Scope of contacts among family, friends, others
  Number of contacts per week (or month)
  Quality of contacts

Personal-Social

All humans live and function within an immediate social environment. Although the characteristics of this social environment vary widely and different individuals have different needs for social contact and interaction, most individuals live in social environments. Basically, personal-social factors encompass the person's social network and immediate social environment. This includes family structures, social networks, religious groups, clubs, and other structural aspects of the social environment. The person's social environment has an important impact on his or her functioning and well-being. The individual's social network consists of family, friends, and neighbors with whom a person has social contact. Contact may be frequent or infrequent, as long as these social interactions provide satisfactory social resources for the person. For example, a person's psychological and physical health may be affected by family and or friends who are willing to provide socioemotional support (e.g., availability of a confidant) and instrumental support (e.g., transportation to social events or for grocery shopping). There is a considerable amount of research supporting the relationship between physical and psychological health status and quantitative and qualitative measures of social support (12–14).

External-Natural Environment

The quality and nature of the geographical and natural environment that an individual resides and works in may have significant impact on one's quality of life. External-environment components are those of the natural environment that the person usually does not have direct control over. These components include air and water quality, the weather, geographic characteristics, and natural wonders (e.g., mountains, forests, beaches).

Conditions in the natural environment have some influence over health and perceptions of quality of life. For example, countries and other geographic areas that have long, dark, and inclement winters also have higher rates of depression and suicide among their populations than many countries where there is more light and warmth. Seasonal affective disorder is a condition that affects some people and is related to light deprivation often occurring during the fall and winter months (15). Treatment of seasonal affective disorder may include light therapy to offset the effects of light deprivation.

Air and water quality are important factors in health status as well as in quality of life. For example, people with asthma and other chronic lung diseases may be adversely affected by environments with excessive pollution and dust.

Therefore, there may be either a direct or indirect impact of various environmental factors on both physical and psychological states. The natural environment provides an overarching ecological context to people's lives that may enhance their quality of life. For example, living in close proximity to beautiful natural environments, such as the mountains or seacoast, may actually contribute to psychological well-being and feelings of life satisfaction. People are remarkably adaptable to living in different environments, but sometimes movement from a familiar environment to one that is less familiar may have a negative impact on their NHRQL. Natural disasters, such as earthquakes, have an immediate, direct impact on both HRQL and NHRQL for large numbers of the population, sometimes for years.

External-Societal Environment

The external-societal environment includes society-created and -maintained organizations, structures, and institutions in the person's environment. These factors, in general, encompass social, political, and economic aspects that provide the larger context for people's everyday lives. Examples include neighborhoods, cities, shopping centers, art museums, and other cultural institutions, economic markets, political structures, government entities, employment and vocational opportunities, and crime and security issues. These factors can be differentiated from other external factors in that they are created by humans. They are distinguished from personal-social factors because of social distance and limited amount of personal control. Basically, these factors make up the external social world or context for the person's interactions with society as a whole as opposed to his or her immediate social network (e.g., family and friends).

Clearly, many aspects of the external-societal environment will affect an individual's NHRQL and some may affect one's health status as well. Concerns about crime and security may limit a person's social activities and sense of well-being. Disasters of human origin, such as Chernobyl or the war in Bosnia, have direct and sometimes long-term effects on the HRQL of the population as well as influencing their NHRQL. The impact of society and its institutions on an individual's global quality of life (i.e., both NHRQL and HRQL), may not be easily measured, but it seems that these factors provide the larger social ecological and environmental context needed by many people as a framework for conceptualizing their activities and relating to society.

Many distant environmental events may greatly influence an individual's quality of life. A few examples include wars, stock market changes, famines, recessions, and discoveries of new treatments for one's disease made in a foreign laboratory. In the sense that all people and events are interconnected at some level, all distant environment changes have the potential to influence any person's quality of life.

Measuring the Domains of NHRQL

Personal health aspects are assessed with traditional quality of life instruments. Although adequate instruments do not exist for comprehensively measuring the two environmental domains of NHRQL, there are means to assess their impact using current instruments. It may be important to specifically

assess one or more of these domains in certain clinical trials, in which case better definition of those states will be necessary.

Interactions Among the Four Domains of NHRQL

Domains of all four types may interact in numerous ways. The final result of these interactions is their impact on an individual in terms of one's HRQL or NHRQL. Some influences are related to life events that occur in a person's life and these events may occur in any of the four domains. Chapter 49 discusses life events in more detail and compares some of the similarities, relationships, and differences among life events and quality of life.

Another type of interaction is illustrated in Fig. 2. This figure shows that a person's disease and treatment affect one's clinical signs, symptoms, adverse experiences, and clinical benefits in a rather complex way to be integrated by the person in terms of how it is deemed to influence his or her physical and psychological domains of HRQL. These influences in turn then have an effect (i.e., an indirect effect) on the social and economic domains.

To more clearly understand how events in the environment influence an individual's quality of life, here are a few examples:

1. Water pollution may affect health, either acutely or chronically, in many ways.

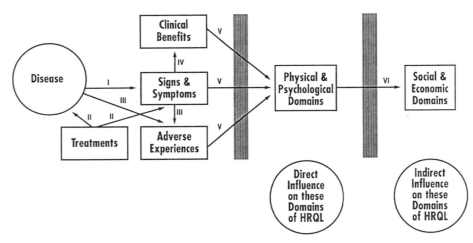

FIG. 2. The relationships among several factors influencing quality of life domains. I. Disease causes or leads to a constellation of clinical signs and symptoms. II. Medicine and other treatments are directed at the underlying disease and/or ameliorating or eliminating signs and symptoms. In some cases other treatments are directed to ameliorating adverse reactions. III. Treatments may elicit adverse experiences, either as a result of attempts to affect the underlying disease or the signs and symptoms resulting from the disease. IV. Treatments directed against clinical signs and symptoms may lead to clinical benefits. V. Signs and symptoms, benefits, and adverse experiences filter through the patient's beliefs, judgments, and values (see Chapter 1 for a description of this filtering phenomenon) to influence the physical and psychological domains. VI. Influences on the physical and/or psychological domain may in turn pass through the patient's beliefs, judgments, and values to influence the social and economic domain. For example, a patient who feels better physically or psychologically may then be able to interact socially or to work at his or her job. HRQL, health-related quality of life.

2. The fear of crime may lead to psychological distress and physical manifestations, such as sweating, rapid heart beats, and trembling.
3. Food that is tainted, covered with pesticide residues, or is otherwise unfit for human consumption may cause mild, moderate, or even severe food poisoning.
4. A person who receives a letter of praise from an unknown person in a distant place will generally feel good, and this may have a positive influence on one's life, at least temporarily.

GEOGRAPHICAL LEVELS OF QUALITY OF LIFE

Why Is Geography Important in Quality of Life?

The medical literature seldom deals with the overall quality of life of a specific community, nation, or the entire world. Nonetheless, the same HRQL and NHRQL domains relevant for an individual are also relevant for an entire community. These include its collective physical, psychological, social, economic, and spiritual status. Additional domains also come into play for larger geographical units, and these domains are the same as those for NHRQL (Table 1).

These same considerations apply to geographical levels beyond communities. The increasing awareness that everyone on the planet is connected in many important ways has contributed not only the concepts of ''global community'' and ''world neighborhood,'' but also to an understanding of a ''worldwide quality of life.'' Lewis Thomas has written eloquently on this topic in his book *Lives of a Cell* (16), as well as in his other writings. He discusses not only the desire for people to adopt a world view, but also the absolute necessity of our doing so.

If one accepts the concept that a community (or region, nation, or the world) can be considered a single organism, then it logically follows that that organism has a quality of life. The specific description of the quality of life for the major geographical levels (Fig. 3) will vary greatly in some cases, but the general terms used to measure and describe the findings will be the same.

A community represents much more than the sum of its inhabitants. Therefore, it is not sufficient to understand the statistical details of inhabitants or to measure the community's quality of life with the types of instruments described in this book. Additional levels may be relevant, particularly when there is a blending from one level to the next. Terms and measurements used for individuals are also relevant, although modifications are needed for evaluating specific geographical units.

Description of the Geographical Levels

A region may be viewed as a part of a nation that contains many communities, whether the region is a province, canton,

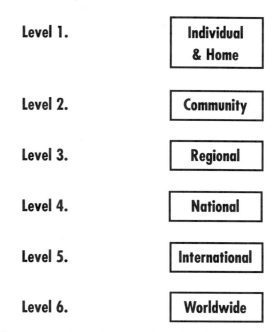

Level 1.	Individual & Home
Level 2.	Community
Level 3.	Regional
Level 4.	National
Level 5.	International
Level 6.	Worldwide

FIG. 3. Geographical levels of quality of life. Although six levels are shown, these could be combined or divided into more categories.

or other formal division with many communities. A whole series of progressively larger regions may be defined and studied when relevant. For example, progressively larger sections of a nation could be described as a home, neighborhood, section of a city, community, group of communities, county, province, part of a nation, or entire nation.

Groups of nations may be described as being on a spectrum ranging from total heterogeneity at one extreme to total homogeneity at the other extreme. Countries in Scandinavia or the Benelux countries are closer to the homogeneous end of the spectrum, although significant differences exist among individual countries in either group. The countries in the North Atlantic Treaty Organization (NATO) or those in the European Community are probably near the midpoint of the spectrum. Countries loosely tied by a treaty but with little else in common such as the Southeast Asia Treaty Organization (SEATO) countries of Japan, Philippines, Australia, and the United States (among others) would be more heterogeneous. In 1950, the British Commonwealth countries shared certain characteristics but had many significant differences as well. The position of the British Commonwealth along that spectrum would depend on the specific issue being addressed.

As the need for evaluating quality of life among nations becomes greater, the need for better scales to measure NHRQL in larger geographical areas will encourage researchers to develop such scales. HRQL is already being evaluated across national borders, as is described in other chapters of this book.

Measuring NHRQL Within Each Geographical Level

Not all aspects of quality of life have to be measured at all geographical levels when NHRQL is being assessed at one (or more) levels. Although six major geographical levels are described, not all of them are appropriate to measure in most circumstances.

For many decades, demographers and others have collected large volumes of statistics for each of the six major geographic levels. Quality of life at these levels has often been addressed by evaluating industrial production, human consumption, or other easy-to-quantitate material aspects of the area measured. Numbers per se do not really relate to quality of life for an area and only serve to quantitate some of the information that may or may not influence or describe specific aspects of quality of life.

A number of surveys by government agencies and other groups, such as the Rand Corporation and some academicians, have attempted to assess subjective characteristics related to satisfaction with both personal and environmental domains within specific geographical areas.

PATIENT-RELATED LEVELS OF QUALITY OF LIFE

In addition to considering progressively larger geographical units from a single home to the world, it is also possible to focus solely on patients in conceptualizing levels of quality of life. Figure 4 suggests groups ranging from a single patient to all patients with a specific disease. Other groupings of patients could be described as various levels, depending on the needs of the researcher and the circumstances of the situation.

Patients with a subtype of a disease are generally understood as being in a separate category from others with the disease, particularly when the categories of disease classification are widely understood and accepted. The different subtypes may be defined in terms of stages, cell type, clinical manifestations, or names of the causative agents (e.g., enzyme involved). Patients who have the same disease or the same disease subtype may not share many other characteristics useful for evaluating quality of life. Some examples of these characteristics are economic status, age, duration of disease, severity of disease, previous treatment, race, risk factors, and prognosis, among others.

The assessments of HRQL in levels of smaller numbers of patients are generally based on measurements in individual patients that are summed, averaged, and otherwise statistically analyzed. The data often come from a clinical trial. Assessment for larger numbers of patients usually involve a degree of extrapolation, often using data from a few patients studied in clinical trials.

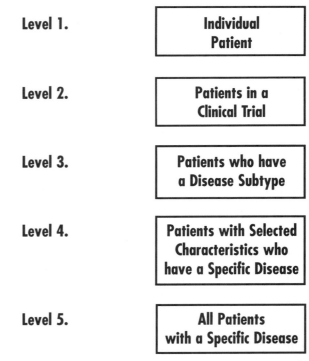

Level 1. Individual Patient

Level 2. Patients in a Clinical Trial

Level 3. Patients who have a Disease Subtype

Level 4. Patients with Selected Characteristics who have a Specific Disease

Level 5. All Patients with a Specific Disease

FIG. 4. Patient levels of quality of life. Although five levels are shown, these could be combined or divided into more categories.

MODEL OF TYPES OF QUALITY OF LIFE AND THEIR LEVELS

Figure 5 summarizes much of the discussion in this chapter by illustrating the two types of quality of life (HRQL and NHRQL), and the principle that each of them consists of domains (described in the text). Two levels for assessing HRQL and NHRQL are shown (described in the text).

CONCLUSIONS

This chapter presents a model of quality of life taxonomy. Two types of quality of life (HRQL and NHRQL), four domains of NHRQL, and two types of levels of viewing quality of life are included in the model. The four domains of NHRQL (each of which consists of multiple components) are personal-internal, personal-social, external-natural environment, and external-societal environment. The geographical levels described are home, community, region, nation, group of nations, and the world. The five patient levels described vary based on the number and type of patients with a single disease. Additional research on these topics will help create improved models to better understand the relationships among these factors and the best ways to measure quality of life in all its myriad forms.

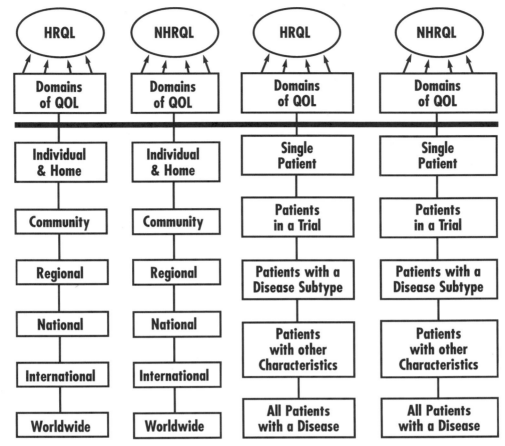

FIG. 5. A model of two types of quality of life, their domains, and two types of levels of quality of life.

REFERENCES

1. Andrews FM, Withey SB. *Social indicators of well-being: Americans' perceptions of life quality.* New York: Plenum Press, 1976.
2. Berg RL, Hallauer DS, Berk SN. Neglected aspects of the quality of life. *Health Serv Res* 1976;11:391–395.
3. Patrick DL, Erickson P. *Health status and health policy: allocating resources to health care.* New York: Oxford University Press, 1992.
4. Bergner M. Quality of life, health status and clinical research. *Med Care* 1989;27:S148–S156.
5. Patrick DL, Bergner M. Measurement of health status in the 1990s. *Annu Rev Public Health* 1990;11:165–183.
6. Revicki DA. Health care technology and health-related quality of life. In: HD Banta, BR Luce, eds. *Health care technology and its assessment: an international perspective.* New York: Oxford University Press, 1993:114–131.
7. Ware JE. Standards for validating health measures: definition and content. *J Chronic Dis* 1987;40:473–480.
8. Wilson IB, Cleary PD. Linking clinical variables with health-related quality of life: a conceptual model of patient outcomes. *JAMA* 1995; 273:59–65.
9. Greenfield S, Nelson EC. Recent developments and future issues in the use of health status assessment measures in clinical settings. *Med Care* 1992;30:MS23–MS41.
10. Patrick DL. Patient reports of health status as predictors of physiologic health in chronic disease. *J Chronic Dis* 1987;40:S37–S40.
11. Rodin J, Langer EJ. Long-term effects of a control-relevant intervention with institutionalized aged. *J Pers Soc Psychol* 1977;35:897–902.
12. Broadhead WE, Kaplan BH, James SA, et al. The epidemiologic evidence for a relationship between social support and health. *Am J Epidemiol* 1983;117:521–537.
13. Kaplan BH, Cassel JC, Gore S. Social support and health. *Med Care* 1977;15(suppl):47–58.
14. Kessler RC, McLeod JD. Social support and psychological distress in community surveys. In: S Cohen, SL Syme, eds. *Social support and health.* New York: Academic Press, 1985.
15. Rosenthal NE. Diagnosis and treatment of seasonal affective disorder. *JAMA* 1993;270:2717–2719.
16. Thomas L. *The lives of a cell.* New York: Bantam, 1974.

Quality of Life and Pharmacoeconomics in Clinical Trials, Second Edition, edited by B. Spilker.
Lippincott-Raven Publishers, Philadelphia © 1996.

CHAPTER 4

The Hierarchy of Patient Outcomes

James F. Fries and Gurkirpal Singh

INTRODUCTION

Quality of life is a term at once pejorative and vague. The term as often used offers hope and meaning but lacks focus and precision. In the context of clinical studies, we have a restricted concept of quality of life in mind. We do not mean happiness, satisfaction, living standard, climate, or environment. Rather, we are speaking topically of health-oriented quality of life—those aspects of life quality that relate to health.

The World Health Organization (WHO) definition of health is "not merely the absence of disease, but complete physical, psychological, and social well-being" (1). This broad and inclusive definition goes far beyond the medical model, which specifically seeks cure and palliation of disease. Essentially, it is this WHO definition of health that encompasses our restricted definition of quality of life. It is this increased breadth of mission that distinguishes quality of life studies from traditional clinical study of medical outcomes.

This chapter presents a hierarchical framework into which specific individual life quality assessments may fit, and describes the Health Assessment Questionnaire (HAQ) as an example of a set of instruments designed to address this framework. A hierarchical perspective allows the investigator flexibility in choice of instruments for particular purposes and is of critical overall importance.

J. F. Fries and G. Singh: Department of Medicine, Stanford University School of Medicine, Stanford, California 94305.

QUALITY OF LIFE, HEALTH STATUS, AND PATIENT OUTCOME

The terms *quality of life, health status,* and *patient outcome* as generally used have overlapping meanings. As indicated, quality of life has a restricted meaning close to the WHO definition of health. Health status is a measure of that life quality at a particular point in time. Patient outcome usually refers to a final health status measurement after the passage of time and the application of treatment. In the future, patient life quality outcomes will be increasingly described by a cumulative series of health status measurements.

It would be highly desirable to represent any of these terms by a single number. Thus, in clinical studies, one could conclude that the quality of life (or patient outcome) with treatment A was 86, whereas with treatment B it was 93; hence, treatment B was to be preferred. Unfortunately, there are major obstacles to calculation of a single index number that can serve as a primary dependent variable in clinical studies. Such an index would require, for example, face validity, reliability, and sensitivity in a clinical study situation.

There are two ways to develop a single index number. First, it can be obtained directly. For example, one could use an analog scale question with an appropriate stem that asks the subjects to make a mark that represents, broadly considered, their global health status at the moment. Such a simplistic approach can in fact be useful for validating more sophisticated approaches, but experience with such scales has shown them to be very insensitive and to fail to identify the specific positive and negative inputs that are included in the global judgment.

The second approach is to calculate a single index number indirectly, by combining numbers from different scales representing different facets of health status. Good measurement characteristics and sensitivity may be obtained by such an approach, but it involves an indefensible series of major value judgments by the investigator in the implicit or explicit weighting systems that must, of necessity, be employed. Detailed discussion of techniques for assigning weights and utilities is beyond the scope of this chapter and are discussed elsewhere, but, in summary, the value judgments that are required of individuals are known to vary substantially among individuals, in the same individual at different periods of life, and between patients with a particular illness and those without the illness (2,3).

Therefore, if attempts to develop single variable indexes are attempted, a clear exposition of techniques used to combine the component data are required. Not only should the required value judgments be defended as thoroughly as possible, but the index itself must be conceptually complete. All of the elements that make up the composite quality of life, health status, or patient outcome measure must be included and specified. Completeness of assessment is crucial, since otherwise an uncounted outcome can under some circumstances dominate a particular situation and reverse a conclusion. One cannot use just economic variables, or just physical ones. All relevant dimensions must be defined and measured.

THE DIMENSIONS OF HEALTH OUTCOMES

Implicit in the concept of patient outcome assessment is a shift from reliance on measures of medical process (such as antibody to DNA, erythrocyte sedimentation rate, cholesterol level, latex fixation titer, coronary arteriogram) toward those elements that are of direct importance to the patient (4). These are readily identified. Multiple surveys of patients or public, prompted or open-ended, have yielded similar outcome dimensions, although the rank order of importance of each dimension varies from survey to survey and situation to situation (5–7). Patients desire (a) to be alive as long as possible; (b) to function normally; (c) to be free of pain and other physical, psychological, or social symptoms; (d) to be free of iatrogenic problems from the treatment regimen; and (e) to remain in financial health after medical expenses. These five dimensions (death, disability, discomfort, drug side effects, and dollar cost) collectively define patient outcome and life quality (8). The dimensions must be considered mutually exclusive and collectively exhaustive. That is, the terms must be defined broadly so that any specific aspect of patient outcome may be categorized under one or another dimension.

These primary outcome dimensions separate rather naturally into subdimensions (9). Economic impact consists of direct medical costs and the indirect costs due to effects on productivity. Iatrogenic effects may be due to medication or to surgery. Discomfort may be physical or psychological. Disability can involve fine movements of the upper extremity or locomotor activities of the lower extremity. Death can

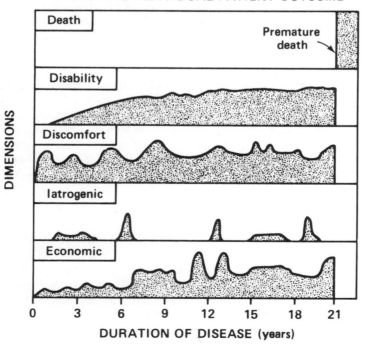

FIG. 1. The five primary dimensions of patient outcome. In this example, the health outcomes of a patient with rheumatoid arthritis are graphed over time. Over 21 years of illness, the patient suffers economic distress; iatrogenic difficulties; symptomatic physical, psychological, and social distress; becomes progressively disabled; and dies prematurely.

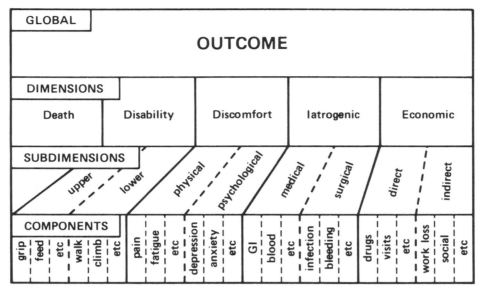

FIG. 2. The hierarchy of patient outcome.

be broken down by specific cause and quantitated in terms of expected time to death.

The subdimensions in turn can be considered to be made up of different components. The components in turn may be developed from particular questions and specific variables. Thus, a hierarchy may be developed that is conceptually complete and provides a location in the framework for all possible measures relevant to quality of life outcomes (Figs. 1 and 2).

PRACTICAL USE OF THE HIERARCHY OF OUTCOMES

Uniform agreements on specific assessment instruments and on assessment techniques that are suitable in all medical situations is unlikely. In particular situations, strong arguments can be made for using one instrument instead of another and for obtaining information by questionnaire, by interview, by telephone, by performance testing, or by other techniques. Indeed, uniform agreement is probably undesirable, since such agreement might stifle the growth of the field, discourage development of improved techniques, and ignore the particular strengths of those instruments not selected. General agreement on a hierarchical framework, however, is not only possible, it has already been implicitly accomplished to a considerable extent.

There are at least seven advantages to employing an outcome hierarchy. First, a hierarchy allows a variety of assessment techniques to be mixed as appropriate to the particular situation. Although it is crucial to measure the dimension of disability, in most cases it is much less important which of the available reliable and valid instruments is chosen for the assessment. Second, it allows elaboration in specific

areas where detailed and specific assessment is required for a particular task.

Third, the hierarchy provides a perspective on the role of a particular instrument. If one is particularly interested in, for example, patient satisfaction, this area can be readily conceived as a component of psychological discomfort and its position in the hierarchy identified. One can avoid exaggeration of the importance of a particular measure by noting its level in the hierarchy and its distance from the primary preferences expressed by patients.

Fourth, the hierarchy provides a minimum number (such as five) of summary indexes at the level of dimensions. One cannot determine if treatment A is better than treatment B by individually analyzing 100 different dependent variables; therefore, some level of aggregation is essential. Although the value-judgment problem involved in determining a single index variable may be insurmountable, the lesser value judgments required to develop indexes for individual outcome dimensions are more defensible.

Fifth, the hierarchy makes assumptions explicit. The upper levels of the hierarchy flow so naturally from patient desires that it is difficult to defend major changes in structure, but if an investigator desires to alter the explicit assumptions and present a different hierarchy, such a change may be argued on its merits.

Sixth, a structure, even loosely conceived, encourages longitudinal study and cumulative assessment of treatment impact. Long-term studies must maintain some degree of constancy between measures made in different years of the study, and the framework assists in this requirement (Fig. 2).

Finally, the hierarchy emphasizes and encourages completeness of assessment. Consider the necessity for such completeness with common examples. Quality of life assessment of total hip replacement cannot be completely assessed without consideration of the operative and perioperative mortality, the cost of the procedure and the source of those funds, the cost savings and side effect benefits of decreased medication requirements, the lessening of pain, and any changes in function that result. Coronary artery bypass surgery cannot be fully evaluated without counting both short-term and long-term death rates, the costs of one procedure versus another, the changes in pain and the duration of that effect, improvement or loss of function, and changes in future medication requirements. Treatment with antihypertensives cannot be completely assessed without counting all effects on morbidity and mortality, costs of alternative treatments, and presence of impotence or other side reactions.

Consideration of the five outcome dimensions provides a revealing way to compare alternative treatment regimens. The number of dimensions is small enough to be judged reasonably and large enough to allow identification of specific areas of clear superiority of one treatment over another.

Overall judgment of the superiority of a particular regimen may be made at three levels. First, one treatment might be superior over all five dimensions. Thus, a decision in its favor would be "value-independent" since any set of relative value judgments between the different dimensions would yield the same conclusions. Second, utility judgments relating the relative importance of the various dimensions can be developed, at the individual or group level. Typically, such value judgments will have wide confidence limits reflecting individual values and differences depending on the clinical situation of the respondent. Utilizing the 95% confidence limits of group utilities is a conservative way to handle this problem. Thus, one treatment might be superior to the other using any set of value judgments that are within the 95% confidence limits of a formal survey of value trade-offs. For example, a small increase in cost and in side effects might be more than offset by major changes in longevity, disability, and symptom level using "any reasonable" value system.

Finally, if neither of these tests yields a clearly superior treatment, combination of dimensions may be accomplished using standard utility theory constructs and the *mean* value trade-offs of a representative population. This test will be more sensitive to differences between regimens, but the results may not always apply given the value systems of particular reasonable individuals. Such situations should be clearly identified as "value-dependent" so that a reviewer may recalculate results using alternative value systems.

THE CONCEPT OF CUMULATIVE OUTCOME

Most serious illness is chronic illness. Chronic illness must be measured chronically. As noted, health status generally refers to a patient's status at a particular point in the course of illness and outcome to the most recent (or end of study) health status measurement.

Figure 1 shows the typical course of a patient with rheumatoid arthritis. Death occurs 4 to 12 years prematurely on average, disability increases through the disease course, pain and symptomatology vary at different points, side effects occur irregularly, and costs are generally progressive but are influenced strongly by particular events along the way. A health status measurement represents a vertical slice at a particular point in time. Conventional outcome assessment represents only the most recent of such measurements.

Obviously, a concept of cumulative outcome is far superior because the outcome actually desired by the patient is inversely related to the area under all of the curves rather than just to the value at some specific point in time. A treatment that reduces the area under the curve, even if the condition later returns to a similar point, represents a health benefit.

Cumulative outcome represents the most sensitive measure of the effect of a treatment in chronic illness (9). For example, it is relatively easy to demonstrate that methotrexate therapy in rheumatoid arthritis will decrease the area under the disability and pain curves, although when viewed from a cross-sectional analysis many years later this effect may not be ascertainable. Sequential health status measurements at regular intervals allow calculation of the approximate area under the curve. With this technique, the relevant dependent variables are measured in disability years, discomfort years, side-effect-index units recorded cumulatively, lifetime medical costs, and time to death as represented by life table determinations. The most sophisticated quality of life studies will utilize such measures.

It may be argued that happenings late in a disease course should be weighted less than those occurring earlier, that distant events should be "discounted." Such adjustment is usual in economic projection. Although such adjustment is unlikely to make a difference very often in comparisons of two treatments, we recommend that cumulative outcome results be presented with discounting at 0% per year, 5% per year, and 10% per year.

THE HEALTH ASSESSMENT QUESTIONNAIRE

The Health Assessment Questionnaire (HAQ), discussed in detail in a subsequent chapter, was designed with this hierarchical model in mind. The hierarchy was developed first, then the specific instruments for each dimension were developed and validated. The measurement technique has been validated for self-assessment by questionnaire, and Health Assessment Questionnaire instruments have been validated for use by mail, in the office, by telephone, by paraprofessional, and by physician (8). These instruments were designed to be efficient, were structured for time available during office medical visits, and were intended to be compatible with high return rates when administered by mail. Initial development of the Health Assessment Questionnaire was under the auspices of the Stanford Arthritis Center funded by the National Institutes of Health, and it has been subsequently widely used by many investigators including the Arthritis Rheumatism and Aging Medical Information System (ARAMIS), the National Health and Nutrition Survey (NHANES I follow-up), and other projects.

The instrument was designed for use in all illnesses and was designed to allow supplementation by additional measures for particular studies. The impact of illness varies markedly among different diseases; thus, the instrument allows comparison of the impact of such disparate processes. For example, in osteoarthritis, pain is dominant; in rheumatoid arthritis, disability; and in cancer, death.

The Health Assessment Questionnaire was developed by parsing questions and components from a variety of instruments previously used for similar purposes. Correlation matrices were constructed that allowed elimination of variables redundant to other variables or inconsistent with the dimension consisting of the mean of all remaining variables. It has been validated in over 100 studies, revised as required, and now has been administered over 200,000 times in various national and international settings.

DISABILITY

The disability section of the Health Assessment Questionnaire was constructed first and has received the widest attention and the most frequent use. It can be completed by a patient in less than 5 minutes and scored in less than 1 minute. It measures disability over the past week by asking a total of 20 questions in eight categories of function: arising, dressing, eating, walking, hygiene, reach, grip, and activities. There are at least two component questions in each of these categories that are representative of the universe of functional activities. Scoring is patterned after the American Rheumatism Association functional classes: normal, adequate, limited, or unable (10). For each component question the level of difficulty is scored from 0 to 3, with 0 equal to no difficulty and 3 equal to unable to do. The highest component score in each category determines the score for the category unless assistance is required. Dependence on equipment or physical assistance adjusts a lower category score to 2 (with much difficulty or limited). Category scores are averaged to give the Disability Index, a continuous scale ranging from 0 to 3.

PAIN

Extensive research activity on the pain dimension resulted in a return to simplicity. Attempts to elaborate pain activity by part of the body involved, times during the day that pain was felt, and severity of pain in different body parts failed to yield indexes that outperformed a simple analog scale (11–13). Returning to the basic principle that symptomatology is what the patient says it is, discomfort is measured by a double-anchored visual analog scale. It is scored from 0 (no discomfort) to 3 (severe discomfort).

Medications may have both positive and negative effects upon life quality, and it is essential, particularly in the clinical trial settings, to quantitate the magnitude of the adverse effects associated with each specific medication. The Health Assessment Questionnaire hierarchy highlighted this need, yet a search of the literature failed to identify any prior attempts to develop an overall index score for drug toxicity (14).

We surveyed patients and medical care providers to establish weights for the various symptoms, laboratory abnormalities, and hospital stays resulting from adverse drug reactions. Using these weights we constructed a Toxicity Index that combines the weights and their severity for the several categories of toxicity and can be computed from the Health Assessment Questionnaire. Standardized rules are used to attribute particular events to particular therapies. The index was validated and tested for sensitivity to differing weights and scoring systems, and found to be stable. Adjustment of the index statistically corrects for differences in patient characteristics on different medications (14,15).

Even in early use, many important insights have emerged from the Toxicity Index. Comparison of toxicity among the nonsteroidal antiinflammatory drugs (NSAIDs) demonstrated a large, two- to threefold difference in toxicity; these drugs had previously been considered to be of equivalent toxicity (16). Toxicity of the disease-modifying drugs for rheumatoid arthritis was found to be variable as well, but less than expected, and sometimes less than that of the supposedly more benign NSAIDs (17). Aspirin, in actual use, was found less toxic than generally expected, as a result of use of lower doses and use of coated preparations as contrasted with earlier clinical trials (18). The Toxicity Index methodology also permits quantification of drug toxicities related to a particular organ system. For example, the gastrointestinal (GI) toxicity index provides a comparison of the GI toxicity of various NSAIDs (19).

MEASUREMENT OF COSTS

Study of the costs of different medications is a major focus of the new science of pharmacoeconomics, and the important questions are more subtle than generally appreciated. Costs of a medication are not only those of the drug itself, but also include the costs of laboratory test monitoring for toxicity, additional visits to health providers for periodic assessment, and of hospitalizations for toxic reactions (20). The Health Assessment Questionnaire captures the necessary data for computation of and statistical adjustments to the total costs attributable to a medication. Insights here are important, too. Commonly, a drug with a higher shelf price may actually be less expensive than a lower-priced alternative when total costs attributable to the medication are tallied.

Economic impact is assessed both as direct costs and indirect costs. Costs are measured in terms of units of service required rather than charges or costs actually paid, allowing automatic adjustment for inflation and for different pricing structures in different regions. Standard costs for each service are developed from multiple sources, averaged, and applied to computations that cumulate variables such as doctor visit costs, hospitalization costs, and medication costs into a direct cost figure, and productivity losses into an indirect cost figure.

ASSESSMENT OF FATAL EVENTS

The fact of death is ascertained regularly by protocol and an audit is made of all deaths, including death certificate and clinical information, in order to identify cause of death and to allow attribution to specific therapy when appropriate. The National Death Index is used to complete ascertainment of all deaths.

VALIDATION

The Health Assessment Questionnaire has undergone repeated testing and revision and the psychometric properties of the scale have been, and continue to be evaluated (8,21). The disability scale is reliable. Two-week test-retest reliability was assessed on 37 rheumatoid arthritis and osteoarthritic patients who were enrolled in the arthritis self-management courses given by the Stanford Arthritis Center. There were no significant differences for the Disability Index using Student's paired t-test (D = 0.04, t = .78, df = 36). Spearman's rho was 0.87. Strong correlations were also reported by other groups. Pincus et al. (22) modified the Health Assessment Questionnaire to use only one question in each of the eight categories and added questions on satisfaction and change in activities and reported on the reliability properties of the disability scale. The correlation for 1-month test-retest on 28 rheumatoid arthritis patients was .78. Goeppinger et al. (23), in their study of the use of the Health Assessment Questionnaire disability scale in a rural, low-education population, reported a 1-week test-retest correlation of .95 on 30 rheumatoid arthritis patients and .93 on 30 osteoarthritis patients.

Principal component analysis of the 15 original questions identified two components (11). The first explained 65% of the variance, and the second, which had positive loadings on lower extremity activities involving large movements and negative loadings on upper extremity small movements, explained another 10% of the variance.

The initial validation studies were designed to assess the feasibility of the self-administered format and to test whether the scale actually measured functional ability (8). The comparison of patient-completed questionnaire responses with interview on a sample of 40 rheumatoid arthritis patients indicated that similar results were obtained using either for-

mat. Spearman's rho for the Disability Index was .85. On another sample of 50 rheumatoid arthritis patients, questionnaire responses were compared with activity performance. Spearman's rho was .88. Cathey et al. (24) compared the performance of five standardized work tasks using work simulator machinery with the patient-reported Disability Index in 26 rheumatoid arthritis patients. Correlations between the total work score and the index was .77.

Validation studies have been replicated, primarily in rheumatoid arthritis and osteoarthritis patients, usually following modifications or translations (25–28). Results have been consistent. Kirwan et al. (25) reported a correlation of .92 between self-administered questionnaires and rheumatologist interview on 33 British rheumatoid arthritis patients. Self-reported disability correlated well with interview in the Netherlands ($r = .94$, $N = 38$) and in Austria ($r = .86$, $N = 46$) (19,20). Sullivan et al. (28) completed home performance evaluations on 64 patients with rheumatoid arthritis, osteoarthritis, and gout. The mean difference between reported and observed disability was .18 (CI $-.8$, 1.2) and the correlation was .83. Our initial studies and those reported subsequently provided evidence that the disability scale is measuring what it purports to measure and that patient self-reports are a valid measure of disability.

Both convergent validity (agreement with another measure of the same attribute) and discriminate validity (weaker agreement with measures of different attributes) were examined in a study comparing the Health Assessment Questionnaire disability and pain scales with the Arthritis Impact Measurement Scale (AIMS) from the Boston University Multipurpose Arthritis Center (11). There was strong agreement between the two questionnaires. Spearman's rho was .91 for the disability-related scales; for the pain-related scales Spearman's rho was .64. In a combined factor analysis of the AIMS and HAQ scales, the factor loadings for physical disability and pain were quite close between measures: physical, .88 (AIMS) and .85 (HAQ); and pain, .87 (AIMS) and .84 (HAQ).

On the other hand, and fitting the hierarchical model, interdimensional correlations of HAQ disability and HAQ pain (rho = .30), AIMS pain (rho = .39), and AIMS psychological (rho = .23) were weak. Disability was also weakly correlated with the Beck Depression Inventory ($r = .37$) and the Hamilton Interviewer Rating Scale ($r = .24$) on 107 rheumatoid arthritis patients (29). Thus, disability, as measured by the Health Assessment Questionnaire, is an attribute distinct from pain or psychological distress.

USE OF THE TEST IN RESEARCH AND CLINICAL PRACTICE

The Disability Index is able to differentiate across patients. In a cross-sectional analysis, the Disability Index increased in morning stiffness, the number of involved joints, and latex positivity (14). Average Disability Index scores differ by diagnosis. The mean Disability Index was higher for rheumatoid arthritis (1.2) and progressive systemic sclerosis (.92) than for osteoarthritis (.4–.6) and systemic lupus erythematosus (.66), supporting the conventional wisdom that osteoarthritis and systemic lupus erythematosus are less-disabling diseases (21,30–32). Average disability in fibromyalgia is similar to that of systemic sclerosis, .9 (24).

Since the Health Assessment Questionnaire was designed, in part, to evaluate interventions, a useful disability measure must also be sensitive and able to detect clinically important changes in function among and within patients. Liang et al. (33) showed a change in disability in a study of 50 osteoarthritis patients who had hip or knee replacements. Bombardier et al. (34) used the Health Assessment Questionnaire in a 6-month multicenter clinical trial of auranofin and placebo. Their results showed statistically ($p < .01$) and clinically significant changes in function between the experimental group of 154 patients (change = $-.31$, SEM = .04) and the control group of 149 patients (change = $-.17$, SEM = .05). The magnitude of the differences in disability changes between the two groups was similar to the differences for the changes in clinical variables: number of swollen joints, number of tender joints, pain, and grip strength. The results of this randomized clinical trial demonstrate that the disability scale is able to detect meaningful changes in function.

In a study of risk factors for hospitalization and surgery, the Disability Index predicted an increase in admissions ($p < .01$) (35). The partial odds ratio for those with a Disability Index in the highest quartile was 9.4 for surgery and 27.2 for joint replacement. These analyses were adjusted for age, sex, and disease characteristics. The Disability Index is also a predictor of mortality. Wolfe et al. (36) reported a relative risk for mortality of 1.77 (95% CI: 1.02–3.06) for each unit increase in the Disability Index. They also found that the initial Disability Index was associated with increased utilization of both inpatient and outpatient services.

The Health Assessment Questionnaire has been in wide and increasing use both in research and clinical practice in many areas as noted above. It is proven sensitive to measuring the change in disability in a clinical study and the progression of disability with age in national probability samples (NHANES) (34,37). It has been modified for use in human immunodeficiency virus (HIV)-positive populations.

USE OF HEALTH ASSESSMENT QUESTIONNAIRE WITH OTHER TESTS

The Health Assessment Questionnaire is often supplemented for specific clinical projects, and such use is encouraged. We have been unhappy with available tools for efficient assessment of psychological impacts, although these are measured to a substantial degree by other parts of the Health Assessment Questionnaire. The disability section, as generally used, does not adequately pick up problems with the organs of special sense, and adaptations including questions on vision and hearing have been developed. The Health Assessment Questionnaire lacks questions on social networking and patient satisfaction, and when information on these outcomes is desired, supplementation is required. We have no present plans to develop instruments in these areas but continue to regularly survey available instruments (such as SF36) as appropriate supplements to the Health Assessment Questionnaire.

CONCLUSIONS

The quality of life can be measured accurately and validly. It can be related to the value systems of the patient and the public. An outcome hierarchy makes dimensions and components comprehensible and provides both perspective and focus. A treatment that does not affect at least one major dimension positively is unlikely to be a major contribution. Individual instruments may be judged on their ability to most optimally assess specific attributes. Far more importantly, the concept of an outcome hierarchy allows harmony among the many investigators seeking to improve this field and helps avoid self-serving arguments for particular instruments. The need for quality-of-life studies is increasingly perceived but is not yet dominant in health assessment. The combined efforts of the many investigative groups, working in concert, are required to persuade the unpersuaded of the merits and importance of this approach.

ACKNOWLEDGMENT

This work was supported in part by a grant from the National Institutes of Health to ARAMIS (AM21393).

REFERENCES

1. World Health Organization. *The first ten years of the World Health Organization.* Geneva: WHO, 1958.
2. Sox HC, Blatt MA, Higgin MC, Marton KI. *Medical decision making.* London: Butterworths, 1988.
3. Moskowitz AJ, Kuipers B, Kassirer JP. Academia and clinic: dealing with uncertainty, risks, and tradeoffs in clinical decisions: a cognitive science approach. *Ann Intern Med* 1988;108:435–449.
4. Fries JF. Toward an understanding of patient outcome measurement. *Arthritis Rheum* 1983;26:697–704.
5. White KL. Improved medical care: statistics and the health service system. *Public Health Rep* 1967;82:847–854.
6. Lorig K, Cox T, Cuevas Y, Kraines GH, Britton MC. Converging and diverging beliefs about arthritis: Caucasian patients, Spanish-speaking patients and physicians. *J Rheumatol* 1984;11:76–79.
7. Potts M, Mazzuca S, Brandt K. Views of patients and physicians regarding the importance of various aspects of arthritis treatment. Correlations with health status and patient satisfaction. *Patient Educ Couns* 1986;8:125–134.
8. Fries JF, Spitz PW, Kraines RG, Holman HR. Measurement of patient outcome in arthritis. *Arthritis Rheum* 1980;23:137–145.
9. Fries JF. The assessment of disability: from first to future principles. *Br J Rheumatol* 1983;22(suppl):48–58.
10. Steinbrocker O, Trager CH, Betterman RC. Therapeutic criteria in rheumatoid arthritis. *JAMA* 1949;140:659–662.

11. Brown JH, Kazis LE, Spitz PW, Gertman PM, Fries JF, Meenan RF. The dimensions of health outcomes: a cross-validated examination of health status measurement. *Am J Public Health* 1984;74:159–161.

12. Langley GB, Sheppeard H. Problems associated with pain measurement in arthritis: comparison of the visual analogue and verbal rating scales. *Clin Exp Rheumatol* 1984;2:231–234.

13. Anderson KO, Bradley LA, McDaniel LK, et al. The assessment of pain in rheumatoid arthritis: disease differentiation and temporal stability of a behavioral observation method. *J Rheumatol* 1987;14:700–704.

14. Fries JF, Spitz PW, Williams CA, Bloch DA, Singh G, Hubert HB. A toxicity index for comparison of side effects among different drugs. *Arthritis Rheum* 1990;33(1):121–130.

15. Fries JF. The hierarchy of Quality-of-Life Assessment, the Health Assessment Questionnaire, and issues mandating development of a Toxicity Index. *Controlled Clin Trials* 1991;12(4):106S–117S.

16. Fries JF, Williams CA, Bloch DA. The relative toxicity of non-steroidal anti-inflammatory drugs (NSAIDs). *Arthritis Rheum* 1991;34(11):1353–1360.

17. Fries JF, Williams CA, Ramey D, Bloch DA. The relative toxicity of disease modifying antirheumatic drugs (DMARDs). *Arthritis Rheum* 1993;36:297–306.

18. Fries JF, Ramey DR, Singh G, Morfeld D, Bloch DA, Raynauld JP. A reevaluation of aspirin therapy in rheumatoid arthritis (RA). *Arch Intern Med* 1993;153:2465–2471.

19. Singh G, Williams C, Ramey DR, Fries J. A toxicity index for comparison of the gastrointestinal toxicity of nonsteroidal antiinflammatory drugs (NSAIDs). *Arthritis Rheum* 1993;36:(suppl 9);S178.

20. Singh G, Ramey DR, Fries JF. The costs of immunosuppressive therapy for rheumatoid arthritis. *Arthritis Rheum* 1993;36(suppl 9);S178.

21. Fries JF, Spitz PW, Young DY. The dimensions of health outcomes: the Health Assessment Questionnaire, disability, and pain scales. *J Rheumatol* 1982;9:789–793.

22. Pincus T, Summey JA, Soraci SA, et al. Assessment of patient satisfaction in activities of daily living using a modified Stanford Health Assessment Questionnaire. *Arthritis Rheum* 1983;26:1346–1353.

23. Goeppinger J, Doyle M, Murdock B, et al. Self-administered function measures: the impossible dream? *Arthritis Rheum* 1985;28:S145 (abstract).

24. Cathey MA, Wolfe F, Kleinheksal SM. Functional ability and work status in patients with fibromyalgia. *Arthritis Care Res* 1988;1:85–98.

25. Kirwan JR, Reeback JS. Stanford Health Assessment Questionnaire modified to assess disability in British patients with rheumatoid arthritis. *Br J Rheumatol* 1986;25:206–209.

26. Siegert CEH, Vleming LV, VBan-Denbroucke JP, Cats A. Measurement of disability in Dutch rheumatoid arthritis patients. *Clin Rheumatol* 1984;3:305–309.

27. Singer F, Kolarz G, Mayrhofer F, Scherak O, Thumb N. The use of questionnaires in the evaluation of the functional capacity in rheumatoid arthritis. *Clin Rheumatol* 1982;1:251–261.

28. Sullivan FM, Eagers RC, Lynch K, Barber JH. Assessment of disability caused by rheumatic diseases in general practice. *Ann Rheum Dis* 1987;46:598–600.

29. Peck JF, Ward JR, Smith TW, et al. Convergent/discriminant validity of the HAQ disability index in rheumatoid arthritis using a multitrait-multimethod matrix. *Arthritis Rheum* 1987;30:S193(abstract).

30. Wolfe F, Kleinheksel SM, Spitz PW, Lubeck DP, Fries JF, Young DY, Mitchell DM, Roth SH. A multicenter study of hospitalization in rheumatoid arthritis: frequency, medical-surgical admissions, and charges. *Arthritis Rheum* 1986;29:614–619.

31. Poole J, Steen V. The use of the Health Assessment Questionnaire (HAQ) to determine physical disability in systemic sclerosis. *Arthritis Rheum* 1986;29:S152(abstract).

32. Hochberg MC, Sutton JD. Physical disability and psychosocial dysfunction in systemic lupus erythematosus (SLE). *J Rheumatol* 1988;15:959–964.

33. Liang MH, Larson MG, Cullen KE, Schwartz JA. Comparative measurement efficiency and sensitivity of five health status instruments for arthritis research. *Arthritis Rheum* 1985;28:542–547.

34. Bombardier C, Ware J, Russell IJ, et al. Auranofin therapy and quality of life in patients with arthritis, results of a multicenter trial. *Am J Med* 1986;81:565–578.

35. Nevitt MC, Yelin EH, Henke CJ, et al. Risk factors for hospitalization and surgery in patients with rheumatoid arthritis: implications for capitated medical payment. *Ann Intern Med* 1986;105:421–428.

36. Wolfe F, Kleinheksel SM, Cathey MA, et al. The clinical value of the HAQ disability index in patients with rheumatoid arthritis. *J Rheumatol* 1988;15:1480–1488.

37. Hubert HB, Bloch DA, Fries JF. Risk factors for physical disability in an aging cohort: The NHANES I Epidemiologic Followup Study. *J Rheumatol* 1993;20:480–488.

Quality of Life and Pharmacoeconomics in Clinical Trials, Second Edition, edited by B. Spilker.
Lippincott-Raven Publishers, Philadelphia © 1996.

CHAPTER 5

Measurements in Clinical Trials: Choosing the Right Approach

Gordon H. Guyatt, Roman Jaeschke, David H. Feeny, and Donald L. Patrick

INTRODUCTION

Perceived health status, functional status, and *quality of life* are three concepts often used interchangeably to refer to the same domain of "health" (1). The health domain ranges from negatively valued aspects of life, including death, to the more positively valued aspects such as role function or happiness. The boundaries of definition usually depend upon why one is assessing health and the particular concerns of patients, clinicians, and researchers. We use the term *health-related quality of life* (HRQL) because there are widely valued aspects of life that are not generally considered as "health" including income, freedom, and quality of

G. H. Guyatt: Department of Clinical Epidemiology and Biostatistics, Department of Medicine, McMaster University, Hamilton, Ontario L8N 3Z5, Canada.

R. Jaeschke: Department of Medicine, McMaster University, Hamilton, Ontario L8P 3B6, Canada.

D. H. Feeny: Department of Clinical Epidemiology and Biostatistics, Department of Economics, Centre for Health Economic and Policy Analysis, McMaster University, Hamilton, Ontario L8N 3Z5, Canada.

D. L. Patrick: Department of Health Services, School of Public Health and Community Medicine, University of Washington, Seattle, Washington 98195.

the environment. While low or unstable income, the lack of freedom, or a low quality environment may adversely affect health, these problems are often distant from a health or medical concern. For clinicians, HRQL is the appropriate focus, keeping in mind that when disease and illness are experienced by a patient, almost all aspects of life can become health-related.

This chapter reviews the possible approaches to measurement of HRQL in clinical studies and considers their relative merits. We focus the discussion on the empirical performance of HRQL measures in clinical trials, rather than on the theoretical framework on which the measures are based. Our discussion is based largely on previously published work (2).

Before applying any HRQL instrument in a clinical study one needs to address several issues. First, the purpose for which the instrument is being used must be clearly stated. Second, the instrument must have certain attributes, or *measurement properties,* that will determine its usefulness for a specific goal. Third, one needs to determine the general category of HRQL instruments required, from which a suitable questionnaire can be chosen. Finally, if alternative formats of the questionnaire are available, one must select the appropriate format for one's study. We will examine these four issues in turn.

POTENTIAL PURPOSES OF HRQL INSTRUMENTS

The potential applications of HRQL measures can be divided into three broad categories: discrimination, prediction, and evaluation.

Discriminative Index

A *discriminative index* is used to distinguish between individuals or groups with respect to an underlying dimension when no external criterion or "gold standard" is available for validating these measures. Intelligence tests, for example, are used to distinguish between children's learning abilities. Use of an instrument from this category in a clinical study can be illustrated by a following example: If one had a group of patients with a myocardial infarction and wanted to divide them into those with good and poor quality of life (with a view, for example, to intervening in the latter group), one would require a discriminative index.

Predictive Index

A *predictive index* is used to classify individuals into a set of predefined measurement categories when a gold standard is available, either at the time of initial measurement or some time in the future. This gold standard is subsequently used to determine whether individuals have been classified correctly. Although there is no gold standard available for measurement of HRQL, predictive instruments are still relevant. Let us assume that investigators had developed an HRQL instrument that one believed was definitive, but took over an hour to administer. Since an hour represents rather a long interview, it would be desirable to have a shorter version. One might choose a subsample of questions from the original and examine the performance of the new, shorter instrument, using the original as a gold standard.

Evaluative Index

An *evaluative index* is used to measure the magnitude of longitudinal change in an individual or group. Such instru-

ments are needed for quantitating the treatment benefit in clinical trials or investigating the impact of illness over time. In the next sections, concerned with what makes a good HRQL instrument, we list key measurement properties separately for discriminative and evaluative instruments. The properties that make useful discriminative and evaluative instruments are presented in Table 1.

NECESSARY ATTRIBUTES OF AN HRQL MEASUREMENT INSTRUMENT

Signal and Noise

HRQL instruments must do two things: they must be able to detect differences in HRQL (the signal) above the random error associated with any measurement (the noise), and they must really measure what they are intended to measure. For discriminative instruments the signal is the difference between patients at a point in time, and the noise is the differences observed in subjects whose HRQL is stable. The way of quantitating the signal-to-noise ratio is called *reliability*. If the variability in scores between subjects (the signal) is much greater than the variability within subjects (the noise) an instrument will be deemed reliable. Reliable instruments will generally demonstrate that stable subjects show more or less the same results on repeated administration.

For evaluative instruments, those designed to measure changes within individuals over time, the way of determining the signal-to-noise ratio is called *responsiveness*. Responsiveness refers to an instrument's ability to detect change. If a treatment results in an important difference in HRQL, investigators wish to be confident they will detect that difference, even if it is small. Responsiveness is directly related to the magnitude of the difference in score in patients who have improved or deteriorated (the signal) and the extent to which patients who have not changed obtain more or less the same scores (the noise).

The responsiveness of evaluative instruments may be compromised by *ceiling* effects, in which patients with the best score nevertheless have substantial HRQL impairment,

---

TABLE 1. *What makes a good HRQL measure?*

Instrument property	Evaluative instruments (measuring differences within subjects over time)	Discriminative instruments (measuring differences between subjects at a point in time)
High signal-to-noise ratio	Responsiveness	Reliability
Validity	Correlations of changes in measures over time consistent with theoretically derived predictions	Correlations between measures at a point in time consistent with theoretically derived predictions
Interpretability	Differences within subjects over time can be interpreted as trivial, small, moderate, or large	Differences between subjects at a point in time can be interpreted as trivial, small, moderate, or large

or *floor* effects, in which patients with the worst score may yet deteriorate further. Bindman and colleagues (3), for instance, found that of hospitalized patients who already had the lowest possible score on a generic measure, the Medical Outcome Study Short Form (MOS-20), many reported their health became worse in the subsequent year. Clearly, that deterioration could not be detected by the MOS-20—a floor effect. Ganiats and colleagues (4) found that patients who all had the highest possible score (representing the best possible function) on a physical functioning scale, the Functional Status Index, varied considerably on their score on a generic utility measure, the Quality of Well-Being. This implies that some patients with the best possible Functional Status Index could still improve on their health status—a ceiling effect.

Validity When There Is a Gold Standard

Validity has to do with whether the instrument is measuring what it is intended to measure. For a predictive instrument, one determines whether an instrument is measuring what is intended using *criterion validity,* according to which an instrument is valid insofar as its results correspond to those of the criterion standard. Criterion validity is applicable not only when a shorter version of an instrument (the test) is used to predict the results of the full-length index (the gold standard) but when an HRQL instrument is used to predict an outcome such as mortality. In this instance, to the extent that variability in survival between patients (the gold standard) is explained by the questionnaire results (the test), the instrument will be valid. Self-ratings of health, like more comprehensive and lengthy measures of general health perceptions, include an individual's evaluation of her or his physiological, physical, psychological, and social well-being. Perceived health, measured through self-ratings, are an important predictor of mortality (5).

Validity When There Is No Gold Standard

When there is no gold or criterion standard, HRQL investigators have borrowed validation strategies from clinical and experimental psychologists who have for many years been dealing with the problem of deciding whether questionnaires examining intelligence, attitudes, and emotional function are really measuring what they are supposed to measure. The types of validity that psychologists have introduced include content and construct validity. *Face validity* refers to whether an instrument appears to be measuring what it is intended to measure, and *content validity* refers to the extent to which the domain of interest is comprehensively sampled by the items, or questions, in the instrument. Quantitative testing of face and content validity are rarely attempted. Feinstein (6) has reformulated these aspects of validity by suggesting criteria for what he calls the *sensibility,* including

the applicability of the questionnaire, its clarity and simplicity, likelihood of bias, comprehensiveness, and whether redundant items have been included. Because of their specificity, Feinstein's criteria facilitate quantitative rating of an instrument's face and content validity (7).

The most rigorous approach to establishing validity is called *construct validity.* A construct is a theoretically derived notion of the domain(s) we wish to measure. An understanding of the construct will lead to expectations about how an instrument should behave if it is valid. Construct validity therefore involves comparisons between measures, and examination of the logical relationships that should exist between a measure and characteristics of patients and patient groups.

The first step in construct validation is to establish a "model" or theoretical framework, which represents an understanding of what investigators are trying to measure. That theoretical framework provides a basis for understanding how the system being studied behaves, and allows hypotheses or predictions about how the instrument being tested should relate to other measures. Investigators then administer a number of instruments to a population of interest and examine the data. Validity is strengthened or weakened according to the extent the hypotheses are confirmed or refuted.

For example, a discriminative HRQL instrument may be validated by comparing two groups of patients: those who have undergone a very toxic chemotherapeutic regimen and those who have undergone a much less toxic chemotherapeutic regimen. An HRQL instrument should distinguish between these two groups, and if it does not it is very likely that something has gone wrong. Alternatively, correlations between symptoms and functional status can be examined, the expectation being that those with a greater number and severity of symptoms will have lower functional status scores on an HRQL instrument. Another example is the validation of an instrument discriminating between people according to some aspect of emotional function. Results from such an instrument should show substantial correlations with existing measures of emotional function.

The principles of validation are identical for evaluative instruments, but their validity is demonstrated by showing that changes in the instrument being investigated correlate with changes in other related measures in the theoretically derived predicted direction and magnitude. For instance, the validity of an evaluative measure of HRQL for patients with chronic lung disease was supported by the finding of moderate correlations with changes in walk test scores (8).

Validation is not an all-or-nothing process. We may have varying degrees of confidence that an instrument is really measuring what it is supposed to measure. A priori predictions about the magnitude of correlations between the new instrument and other measures that one should find if the new instrument is really measuring what is intended strengthen the validation process. Without such predictions, it is too easy to rationalize whatever correlations between measures are observed. Validation does not end when the first study with data concerning validity is published, but continues with repeated use of an instrument. The more frequently an instrument is used, and the wider the situations in which it performs as we would expect if it were really doing its job, the greater our confidence in its validity. Perhaps we should never conclude that a questionnaire has "been validated"; the best we can do is to suggest that strong evidence for validity has been obtained in a number of different settings and studies.

Interpretability

A final key property of an HRQL measure is *interpretability*. For a discriminative instrument, we could ask whether a particular score signifies that a patient is functioning normally, or has mild, moderate, or severe impairment of HRQL. For an evaluative instrument we might ask whether a particular change in score represents a trivial, small but important, moderate, or large improvement or deterioration.

A number of strategies are available for trying to make HRQL scores interpretable (9). For an evaluative instrument, one might classify patients into those who had important improvement and those who did not and examine the changes in score in the two groups; interpret observed changes in HRQL measures in terms of elements of those measures that will be familiar to readers (for instance, descriptions of changes in mobility); or determine how scores in HRQL measures relate to marker states that are familiar and meaningful to clinicians. We now know that for instruments that present response options as seven-point scales, small, medium, and large effects correspond to average changes of approximately 0.5, 1.0, and greater than 1.0 per question (10,11). Investigators used this information to interpret a recent trial that showed that bronchodilators result in small but clinically important improvement in dyspnea, fatigue, and emotional function in patients with chronic airflow limitation (12). In a study of patients with arthritis, interpretation was aided by the estimate that a change of 0.02 points in the Quality of Well-Being utility instrument was equivalent to all treated patients improving from moving their own wheelchair without help to walking with physical limitations (13).

In its use as a discriminative instrument, we know how patients in various health states score on the Sickness Impact Profile: patients shortly after hip replacement have scores of 30, which decrease to less than 5 after full convalescence (14); scores in patients with chronic airflow limitation severe enough to require home oxygen are approximately 24 (15); scores in patients with chronic, stable angina are approximately 11.5 (16); scores in those with arthritis vary from 8.2 in patients with American Rheumatism Association arthritis class I to 25.8 in class IV (17). The availability of data that improves the interpretability of HRQL measures is likely to increase exponentially in the next decade.

CATEGORIES OF QUALITY OF LIFE MEASURES: A TAXONOMY

Generic Instruments—Health Profiles

Two basic approaches characterize the measurement of HRQL: *generic instruments* (including single indicators, health profiles, and utility measures) and *specific instruments* (Table 2) (18). *Health profiles* are instruments that attempt to measure all important aspects of HRQL. The Sickness Impact Profile is an example of a health profile, and includes a Physical dimension (with categories of ambulation, mobility, and body care and movement), a Psychosocial dimension (with categories including social interaction, alertness behavior, communication, and emotional behavior), and five independent categories (eating, work, home management, sleep and rest, and recreations and pastimes). Major advantages of health profiles are that they deal with a wide variety of areas and can be used in virtually any population, irrespective of the underlying condition. Because generic instruments apply to a wide variety of populations, they allow for broad comparisons of the relative impact of various health care programs. Generic profiles may, however, be less responsive to changes in specific conditions.

Generic Instruments—Utility Measures

The other type of generic instrument, *utility measures* of quality of life, are derived from economic and decision theory, and reflect the preferences of patients for different health states. The key elements of utility measures are that they incorporate preference measurements and relate health states to death. This allows them to be used in *cost-utility analyses* that combine duration and quality of life. In utility measures HRQL is summarized as a single number along a continuum that usually extends from death (0.0) to full health (1.0), although scores less than 0, representing states worse than death, are possible (19). Utility scores reflect both the health status and the *value* of that health status to the patient. The usefulness of utility measures in economic analysis is increasingly important in an era of cost constraints in which health care providers are being asked to justify the resources devoted to treatment.

Utility measures provide a single summary score of the net change in HRQL—the HRQL gains from the treatment effect minus the HRQL burdens of side effects. Utility measures are therefore useful for determining if patients are on the whole better off as the result of therapy, but may fail to reveal the dimensions of HRQL on which patients improved versus those on which they worsened. The simultaneous use of a health profile or specific instruments can complement the utility approach by providing this valuable information.

The preferences in utility measurements may come directly from individual patients who are asked to rate the value of their health state. Alternatively, patients can rate

TABLE 2. *Taxonomy of measures of HRQL*

Approach	Strengths	Weaknesses

Generic instruments
  Health profile
	Single instrument
	Detects differential effects on different
	  aspects of health status
	Comparison across interventions;
	  conditions possible
		May not focus adequately on area of
		  interest
		May not be responsive

Utility measurement	Single number representing net impact on
	  quantity and quality of life
	Cost-utility analysis possible
	Incorporates death
		Difficulty determining utility values
		Doesn't allow examination of effect on
		  different aspects of quality of life
		May not be responsive

Specific instruments
  Disease specific
  Population specific
  Function specific
  Condition or problem
    specific
	Clinically sensible
	May be more responsive
		Doesn't allow cross-condition
		  comparisons
		May be limited in terms of populations
		  and interventions
		Restricted to domains of relevance to
		  disease, population, function, or
		  problem; other domains that are
		  important to overall HRQL not
		  measured

their health status using a multiattribute health status classification system (such as the Quality of Well-Being scale or the Health Utilities Index). A previously estimated scoring function derived from results of preference measurements from groups of other patients, or from the community, is then used to convert health status to a utility score (20).

Specific Instruments

The second basic approach to quality-of-life measurement focuses on aspects of health status that are specific to the area of primary interest. The rationale for this approach lies in the potential for increased responsiveness that may result from including only important aspects of HRQL that are relevant to the patients being studied. The instrument may be specific to the disease (such as heart failure or asthma), to a population of patients (such as the frail elderly), to a certain function (such as sleep or sexual function), or to a problem (such as pain). In addition to the likelihood of improved responsiveness, specific measures have the advantage of relating closely to areas routinely explored by clinicians.

Choosing the Right HRQL Measure

Health Status Surveys

The choice of an HRQL measure depends very much on the purpose of the study (21). Generic measures may be particularly useful for surveys that attempt to document the range of disability in a general population or a patient group. In one survey, for instance, investigators used the Sickness Impact Profile to examine the extent of disability in patients with chronic airflow limitation (4). Their striking finding was that the effect of chronic airflow limitation in patients' lives was not restricted to areas such as ambulation and mobility, but was manifested in virtually every aspect of HRQL. This included social interaction, alertness behavior, emotional behavior, sleep and rest, and recreation and pastime activities. For surveys investigating the range of disability, specific measures are unlikely to be of much use and investigators will therefore rely on health profiles or the closely related multiattribute health status classification and utility function approaches.

Clinical Trials

Clinical investigators are, with increasing frequency, choosing HRQL measures as primary and secondary outcomes in clinical trials. In the initial stages of studying a new therapy—such as a new drug—investigators are likely to rely on a disease-specific measure. Disease-specific measures are clinically sensible in that patients and clinicians intuitively find the items directly relevant. Disease-specific measures' increased potential for responsiveness is particularly compelling in the clinical trial setting. Investigators will have additional reason for choosing a disease-specific measure if there are no other outcomes that are directly clinically relevant to the patient. A recent study in which a questionnaire designed specifically for patients with chronic renal failure was used to demonstrate that erythropoietin-induced increases in hemoglobin improved HRQL in renal-failure patients illustrates the important information that use of a disease-specific measure can provide (22). When carefully constructed, disease-specific HRQL measures can also be more responsive than traditional measures of patient experience, such as symptom diaries (23).

A number of specific measures can be used together in a battery to obtain a comprehensive picture of the impact of different interventions on HRQL. A wide variety of instruments including measures of well-being, physical function, emotional function, sleep, sexual function, and side effects were used to demonstrate that antihypertensive agents have a differential impact on many aspects of HRQL (24). This trial showed that an angiotensin-converting enzyme (ACE) inhibitor was not as effective in lowering blood pressure, when used alone, as a beta antagonist or methyldopa. The ACE inhibitor was, however, found to have substantially less adverse effects on HRQL. One would adduce substantially different treatment recommendations from this trial if one considered only the effect of medication on blood pressure rather than both the effects on blood pressure and HRQL. The potential disadvantages of this approach are that the multiple comparisons being made and the lack of a unified scoring system may lead to difficulties in interpretation. A study examining multiple outcomes runs the risk that, simply by chance, one or two will favor an experimental treatment. When this happens, there is a possibility that a useless or marginally effective treatment will be erroneously presented as demonstrating an important improvement in HRQL.

There are a number of situations in which generic measures are highly appropriate for clinical trials. If there is already a clinical outcome—such as myocardial infarction or stroke—of direct relevance to patients, a generic HRQL measure can provide complementary information about the range and magnitude of treatment effects on HRQL. Previously unrecognized adverse experiences may be detected. If the efficacy of an intervention is established, the purpose of a clinical trial may be to elucidate the full impact of a treatment. Utility measures are particularly relevant if the economic implications of an intervention are a major focus of investigation. In one randomized trial, for instance, investigators demonstrated that a compliance-enhancing maneuver for patients with chronic lung disease undergoing exercise rehabilitation improved HRQL, and the cost was approximately $25,000 per quality-adjusted life year gained (25).

Another instance in which generic measures may be particularly appropriate is when there may be a real trade-off between length of life, or length of remission, and quality of life. Such situations include chemotherapy for malignant disease and antiviral agents for patients with human immunodeficiency virus (HIV) infection. A trial of zidovudine for mildly symptomatic HIV infection demonstrated that the drug lengthened the period of progression-free survival by an average of 0.9 months. However, when the investigators used a technique called "quality-adjusted time without symptoms or toxicity" (Q-TWIST), which counts either disease progression or severe adverse events as negative outcomes, patients treated with zidovudine actually fared less well (26). In this instance, the HRQL perspective could reverse the treatment decision.

Having illustrated situations in which specific and generic measures are likely to be particularly appropriate, it is worth pointing out that use of multiple types of measures in clinical trials yields additional information that may prove important. For instance, a randomized trial of patients with severe rheumatoid arthritis showed not only that patients receiving oral gold were better off in terms of disease-specific functional measures, but also that they had higher utility scores than patients receiving placebo (27). The investigators were therefore able to demonstrate the impact of the treatment using measures of direct relevance to both patients and health workers and to provide the information necessary for an economic cost-utility analysis. An argument can be made for inclusion of a specific measure, a health profile, and a utility measure in any clinical trial in which the major focus is patient benefit. Because disease-specific measures are of greatest interest to the patients themselves and to the clinicians who treat them, while generic measures, because they permit comparisons across conditions and populations, may be of greatest interest to the policy or decision maker, use of both categories of measures will be most appropriate when the results could be of interest to both audiences. HRQL measures may also find a place in clinical practice, providing clinicians with information they might not otherwise obtain. Forms that can be self-administered and immediately scanned by computer can be used to provide rapid feedback of HRQL data to clinicians.

MODES OF ADMINISTRATION

The strengths and weaknesses of the different modes of administration are summarized in Table 3. HRQL questionnaires are either administered by trained interviewers or self-administered. The former method is resource intensive but ensures compliance and minimizes errors and missing items. The latter approach is much less expensive but increases the number of missing patients and missing responses. A compromise between the two approaches is to have the instrument completed under supervision. Another compromise is the telephone interview, which minimizes errors and missing data but dictates a relatively simple questionnaire structure. Investigators have conducted initial experiments with computer administration of HRQL measures, but this is not yet a common method of questionnaire administration.

Investigators may often consider using a *surrogate respondent* to predict results that one would get from the patient herself. For instance, McKusker and Stoddard (28) were interested in what patients might score on a general, comprehensive measure of HRQL, the Sickness Impact Profile, when they were too ill to complete the questionnaire. The investigators wished to use a surrogate to respond on behalf of the patient, but wanted assurance that surrogate responses would correspond to what patients would have said had they been capable of answering. They administered the Sickness Impact Profile to terminally ill patients who were still capable of completing the questionnaire and to

TABLE 3. *Modes of administration of HRQL measures*

Mode of administration	Strengths	Weaknesses
Interviewer-administered	Maximize response rate Few, if any, missing items Minimize errors of misunderstanding	Requires many resources, training of interviewers May reduce willingness to acknowledge problems
Telephone-administered	Few, if any, missing items Minimize errors of misunderstanding Less resource intensive than interviewer-administered	Limits format of instrument
Self-administered	Minimal resources required	Greater likelihood of low response rate, missing items, misunderstanding
Surrogate responders	Reduces stress for target group (very elderly or sick) Can include patients unable to respond for themselves (cognitively impaired, children, language barriers)	Perceptions of surrogate may differ from target group

close relatives of the respondents. The correlation between the two sets of responses was .55, and the difference between the two pairs of responses was greater than 6 on a 100-point scale in 50% of the cases. The results suggest that surrogate responses to the Sickness Impact Profile in this situation cannot substitute for the patients' response.

These results are consistent with other evaluations of ratings by patients and proxies. In general, the correspondence between respondent and proxy response to HRQL measures varies depending on the domain assessed and the choice of proxy. As might be expected, proxy reports of more observable domains such as physical functioning and cognition are more highly correlated with reports from the patients themselves. For functional limitations, proxy respondents tend to consider patients more impaired, i.e., overestimate patient dysfunction relative to the patients themselves. This is particularly characteristic of those proxies with the greatest contact with the respondent (29). For other sorts of morbidity, patients tend to report the most problems, followed by close relatives, and clinicians the least. These findings have important clinical implications in that they suggest that clinicians should concentrate on careful ascertainment of the reported behaviors and perceptions of patients themselves, limiting the inferences they make on the basis of the perceptions of the caregivers.

CONCLUSIONS

Choosing the appropriate approach to the use of HRQL measures will determine the accuracy of the conclusions obtained after clinical study is completed. Defining the precise goal of the study, and determining the relative merits of existing instruments should be done before a questionnaire is chosen. Investigators can access a large number of "proven" instruments, or refer to guidelines for construction of new, specific instruments.

REFERENCES

1. Patrick D, Bergner M. Measurement of health status in the 1990s. *Annu Rev Public Health* 1990;11:165–183.
2. Guyatt GH, Feeny DH, Patrick DL. Measuring health-related quality of life: basic sciences review. *Ann Intern Med* 1993;70:225–230.
3. Bindman AB, Keane D, Lurie N. Measuring health changes among severely ill patients. *Med Care* 1990;28:1142–1152.
4. Ganiats TG, Palinkas LA, Kaplan RM. Comparison of Well-Being Scale and Functional Status Index in patients with atrial fibrillation. *Med Care* 1992;30:958–964.
5. Mossey J, Shapiro E. Self-rated health: a predictor of mortality among the elderly. *Am J Public Health* 1982;72:800–809.
6. Feinstein AR. *Clinimetrics.* New Haven, CT: Yale University Press, 1987:141–166.
7. Oxman A, Guyatt GH. Validation of an index of the quality of review articles. *J Clin Epidemiol* 1991;44:1271–1278.
8. Guyatt GH, Berman LB, Townsend M, Pugsley SO, Chambers LW. A measure of quality of life for clinical trials in chronic lung disease. *Thorax* 1987;42:773–778.
9. Guyatt GH, Feeny D, Patrick D. Proceedings of the International Conference on the Measurement of Quality of Life as an Outcome in Clinical Trials: Postscript. *Controlled Clin Trials* 1991;12:266S–269S.
10. Jaeschke R, Guyatt G, Keller J, Singer J. Measurement of health status: ascertaining the meaning of a change in quality-of-life questionnaire score. *Controlled Clin Trials* 1989;10:407–415.
11. Juniper EF, Guyatt GH, Willan A, Griffith LE. Determining a minimal important change in a disease-specific quality of life instrument. *J Clin Epidemiol* 1994;47:81–87.
12. Guyatt GH, Townsend M, Pugsley SO, et al. Bronchodilators in chronic airflow limitation, effects on airway function, exercise capacity and quality of life. *Am Rev Respir Dis* 1987;135:1069–1074.
13. Thompson MS, Read JL, Hutchings HC, et al. The cost effectiveness of auranofin: results of a randomized clinical trial. *J Rheumatol* 1988;15:35–42.
14. Bergner M, Bobbitt RA, Carter WB, Gilson BS. The Sickness Impact Profile: development and final revision of a health status measure. *Med Care* 1981;19:787–805.

15. McSweeney AJ, Grant I, Heaton RK, et al. Life quality of patients with chronic obstructive pulmonary disease. *Arch Intern Med* 1982;142:473–478.

16. Fletcher A, McLoone P, Bulpitt C. Quality of life on angina therapy: a randomised controlled trial of transdermal glyceryl trinitate against placebo. *Lancet* 1988;2:4–7.

17. Deyo RA, Inui TS, Leininger JD, Overman SS. Measuring functional outcomes in chronic disease: a comparison of traditional scales and a self-administered health status questionnaire in patients with rheumatoid arthritis. *Med Care* 1983;21:180–192.

18. Patrick DL, Deyo RA. Generic and disease-specific measures in assessing health status and quality of life. *Med Care* 1989;27:F217–232.

19. Boyle MH, Torrance GW, Sinclair JC, Horwood SP. Economic evaluation of neonatal intensive care of very-low-birth-weight infants. *N Engl J Med* 1983;308:1330–1337.

20. Feeny D, Barr RD, Furlong W, et al. A comprehensive multiattribute system for classifying the health status of survivors of childhood cancer. *J Clin Oncol* 1992;10:923–928.

21. Patrick DL. Health-related quality of life in pharmaceutical evaluation. Forging progress and avoiding pitfalls. *Pharmacoeconomics* 1992;1:76–78.

22. Laupacis A. Changes in quality of life and functional capacity in hemodialysis patients treated with recombinant human erythropoietin. The Canadian Erythropoietin Study Group. *Semin Nephrol* 1990;10S:11–19.

23. Juniper EF, Guyatt GH, Ferrie PJ, King DR. Sodium cromoglycate eye drops: regular versus ''as needed'' use in the treatment of seasonal conjunctivitis. *J Allergy Clin Immunol* 1994;94:36–43.

24. Croog SH, Levine S, Testa MA, et al. The effects of antihypertensive therapy on the quality of life. *N Engl J Med* 1986;314:1657–1664.

25. Toevs CD, Kaplan RM, Atkins CJ. The costs and effects of behavioral programs in chronic obstructive pulmonary disease. *Med Care* 1984;22:1088–1100.

26. Gelber RD, Lenderking WR, Cotton DJ, et al. Quality-of-life evaluation in a clinical trial of zidovudine therapy in patients with mildly symptomatic HIV infection. *Ann Intern Med* 1992;116:961–966.

27. Bombardier C, Ware J, Russell IJ, Larson M, Chalmers A, Read JL. Auranofin therapy and quality of life in patients with rheumatoid arthritis. *Am J Med* 1986;81:565–578.

28. McCusker J, Stoddart AM. Use of a surrogate for the Sickness Impact Profile. *Med Care* 1984;22:789–795.

29. Rothman ML, Hedrick SC, Bulcroft KA, Hickam DH, Rubenstein LZ. The validity of proxy-generated scores as measures of patient health status. *Med Care* 1991;29:1151–1224.

Quality of Life and Pharmacoeconomics in Clinical Trials, Second Edition, edited by B. Spilker.
Lippincott-Raven Publishers, Philadelphia © 1996.

CHAPTER 6

How to Develop and Validate a New Health-Related Quality of Life Instrument

Elizabeth F. Juniper, Gordon H. Guyatt, and Roman Jaeschke

INTRODUCTION

The previous chapter has discussed in detail the different types of health-related quality of life (HRQL) instruments (generic health profiles, utilities, and specific instruments) and their strengths and weaknesses. It has explored the different uses of instruments (discriminative, predictive, and evaluative) and the measurement properties required. Using these concepts, in this chapter we describe methods for developing and testing new instruments.

There are a large number of generic health profiles available, including the Sickness Impact Profile (1), the Nottingham Health Profile (2), the SF-36 (3), and the McMaster Health Index Questionnaire (4). These instruments are widely used, and their measurement properties have been well established. A compelling case would have to be made to justify the development of yet another generic instrument. Therefore, this chapter focuses on the construction and testing of specific instruments. These may be specific for a disease, a function, an age group, or any other specific population of interest to the investigator. As a practical example, we will

use a questionnaire for asthma to which we will refer in each section. We will review the following steps in instrument development and testing (Table 1):

A. Development
   1. Specifying measurement goals
   2. Item generation
   3. Item reduction
   4. Questionnaire formatting
B. Testing
   5. Pretesting
   6. Reliability
   7. Responsiveness
   8. Validity
   9. Interpretability

INSTRUMENT DEVELOPMENT

Specifying Measurement Goals

Before embarking on the development of any new instrument, the investigator should define exactly what the instrument is to measure. This initial definition will help the investigator design appropriate development and testing protocols and will enable other users of the instrument to recog-

E. F. Juniper, G. H. Guyatt, and R. Jaeschke: Department of Clinical Epidemiology and Biostatistics, McMaster University Health Sciences Centre, Hamilton, Ontario L8N 3Z5, Canada.

TABLE 1. *Major issues in instrument development and validation*

	Discriminative	Predictive	Evaluative
Item generation	Identify all items of impairment that might be important to patients	Identify all items of impairment that might be important to patients	Identify all items of impairment that might be important to patients
Item reduction	Delete items common to all patients	Delete items common to all patients	Select the most frequent and important items; delete nonresponsive items
Response options	Response options adequate to achieve fine or coarse discrimination, depending on goals	Response options adequate to predict criterion standard	Response options with sufficient gradations to register within-patient change
Reliability	Large and stable interpatient variation	Large and stable interpatient variation	Not relevant
Responsiveness	Not relevant	Not relevant	Able to detect small within-patient change over time
Validity	Cross-sectional construct validity	Cross-sectional criterion validity	Longitudinal construct validity

nize its applicability to their own patients and studies. The investigator should consider at least the following criteria.

Patient Population

As in a clinical trial, there should be clear inclusion and exclusion criteria that identify the precise clinical diagnosis and basic patient characteristics. A detailed definition might include age, literacy level, language ability, and presence of other illnesses that might have impact on HRQL. An investigator may be thinking of a particular study in which the instrument is to be used, but constructing an instrument for too specific a population or function may limit its subsequent use. One can usually choose a patient population that is narrow enough to allow focus on important impairments in that disease or function but broad enough to be valid for use in other studies.

Primary Purpose

The investigator needs to decide whether the primary purpose of the instrument is going to be evaluative, discriminative, or predictive. Although some instruments may be capable of all three functions, it is difficult to achieve maximum efficiency in all three.

Patient Function

In most disease-specific instruments, investigators want to include all areas of dysfunction associated with that disease (physical, emotional, social, occupational). However, there are some instruments that are designed to focus on a particular function (e.g., emotional function, pain, sexual function) within a broader patient population. The investigator should

decide whether all or only specific functions are to be included.

Other Considerations

The investigator should also decide on the format of the instrument. Will it be interviewer and/or self-administered? Does it need to be suitable for telephone interviews? Approximately how many items will the instrument contain?

Example

We defined the following measurement goals for the Asthma Quality of Life Questionnaire (5): the instrument will assess health-related quality of life in adults (18 to 70 years) with non–oral steroid–dependent asthma, as defined by the American Thoracic Society (6), and minimal fixed airway obstruction [forced expiratory volume in one second (FEV_1) postbronchodilator >60% predicted]. Primarily, it will be an evaluative instrument for use in clinical trials. It will include both physical and emotional function, be suitable for both interviewer and self-administration, and have approximately 30 items.

Item Generation

The first task in instrument development is to generate a pool of all potentially relevant items. From this pool, the investigator will later select items for inclusion in the final questionnaire. The most frequently used methods of item generation include unstructured interviews with patients believed to have particular insight into their condition, patient focus group discussions, a review of the disease-specific literature, discussions with health care professionals who work closely with the patients, and a review of generic HRQL instruments.

Item Reduction

Reducing Items on the Basis of Their Frequency and Importance

Having generated a large item pool, the investigator must select the items that will be most suitable for the final instrument. HRQL instruments usually measure health status from the patients' perspective and so it is appropriate that patients themselves identify the items that are most important to them. Investigators should ensure that the patients selected represent the full spectrum of those identified in the patient population. If one is interested in checking that the final instrument is applicable to subgroups within that population (e.g., mild, moderate, and severe disease), then it is important to ensure that all of the subgroups are adequately represented.

One approach to item reduction is to ask patients to identify those items that they have experienced as a result of their illness. For each positively identified item, they rate the importance using a 5-point Likert type scale ("extremely important" to "not important"). Results are expressed as *frequency* (the proportion of patients experiencing a particular item), *importance* (the mean importance score attached to each item), and the *impact,* which is the product of frequency and importance.

Very occasionally, there are items that have absolutely no potential of changing over time either as a result of an intervention or through the natural course of the disease. If one is developing an evaluative instrument, one may consider excluding such unresponsive items because they will only add to the measurement noise and the time taken to complete the questionnaire. However, if such an item is considered very important by patients and therefore potentially a future target for therapy, exclusion because of apparent unresponsiveness to current therapies may be unwise.

Let us assume one has decided that the final questionnaire will ask subjects whether they have, or have not, experienced a problem (i.e., a dichotomous response) rather than providing an opportunity to grade the severity of the problem. If virtually all subjects experience the problem, then it will not be useful to include such an item in a discriminative instrument. On the other hand, if the final instrument will grade the extent to which a problem effects the respondents, items that the entire population finds a problem may still prove very useful in discrimination.

A comprehensive set of items will inevitably include some redundancies. How does one decide whether to include, for instance, both fatigue and tiredness, if the two items have a high impact score? One approach is to test whether the items are highly correlated. If Spearman rank order correlations are high (that is, patients who identify fatigue as a problem and rate its importance high are the same patients

who identify tiredness as a high-impact item, and the same patients who rate one item low in impact also rate the other item low) one can consider omitting one of the items. This strategy is particularly appropriate for a discriminative instrument, for highly correlated items will add little to one another in distinguishing those with mild and severe quality of life impairment from one another. It is somewhat riskier for evaluative instruments; just because items correlate with one another at the item reduction phase does not guarantee that they will change in parallel when measured serially over time.

Investigators can select the sample size for the item reduction process by deciding how precise they want their estimates of the impact of an item on the population. The widest confidence interval around a proportion (the frequency with which patients identify items) occurs when the proportion is 50%; any other value will yield narrower confidence intervals. If one recruits 25 subjects, and an item is identified by 50% of the population, the true prevalence of that item is somewhere between approximately 30% and 70% (that is, the 95% confidence interval around the proportion of .5 is approximately .3 to .7). If one recruits 50 subjects, the 95% confidence interval around a proportion of .5 will be approximately .14. For 100 subjects, the confidence interval will be from .4 to .6. We recommend recruitment of at least 100 subjects for this part of the questionnaire development process.

Individualized Items

Patients may identify that they experience limitation in their day-to-day activities and that these limitations are very important. However, because the types of activities undertaken by patients vary enormously, it is often difficult to find important activities that are common to all patients. A successful solution to this problem has been to include three to five "individualized" activity items (5,7,8). At the beginning of any study, each patient identifies activities that are limited by their condition, are important, and are done frequently. These are retained for the individual patient throughout the study. This strategy is applicable to evaluative, but not to discriminative instruments.

Factor Analysis

Some investigators use mathematical modeling (factor analysis) to determine which items should be included in HRQL instruments. In factor analysis, items that have high correlations with one another are grouped together. Items that are not strongly associated with one of the domains or factors that emerge from the factor analysis are excluded from the final questionnaire. The disadvantage of using factor analysis for item reduction is that the "orphan" items that are excluded from the factor analysis model may be important to patients. The issue is the relative importance one puts on the impact of an item and its relationship with other items. We believe the priority should be on the former and are therefore reluctant to use factor analysis for item reduction.

Deciding on Instrument Domains

At the end of the reduction phase, the investigator has the required number of items for the final questionnaire and usually wants to group them into domains or dimensions (e.g., symptoms, emotional function, activity limitation). The easiest method is to review the items and use common sense, clinical experience, and domains described in established instruments to group the items. If one has defined in the initial criteria that certain functions are to be included in the final questionnaire, it is important to ensure that these criteria are met.

Intuition has its limitations in grouping items. First, different people may have a different intuitive sense as to where an item may fit. Second, an investigator may be uncertain where an item should be placed. Third, people's intuition may agree, but they may be wrong (that is, not understand the underlying relation between items). Statistical strategies based on correlations between items offer an alternative approach to creating instrument domains, and factor analysis is the most popular of these strategies. The disadvantage of the factor analysis approach is that if one arrives at counter-intuitive groupings, how one should proceed is not self-evident. A compromise may be to place items in the domains that make intuitive sense and, if uncertainty remains about some items, examine the correlations of those items with items that clearly fall in particular domains.

Questionnaire Formatting

Selection of Response Options

Response options refer to the categories or scales that are available for responding to the questionnaire items. For example, one can ask whether the subject has difficulty climbing stairs; two response options, yes and no, are available. If the questionnaire asks about the degree of difficulty, a wide variety of response options are available.

An evaluative instrument must be responsive to important changes even if they are small. To ensure and enhance this measurement property, investigators usually choose scales with a number of options, such as a 7-point scale where responses may range from 1 = no impairment to 7 = total impairment or a continuous scale such as a 10-cm Visual Analog Scale (VAS). We use the 7-point Likert scale because although both yield similar data, the Likert scale has practical advantages over the VAS, being both easier to administer and easier to interpret (9).

Likert and VAS can be used for discriminative and predictive instruments, and are likely to yield optimal measure-

ment properties (5). However, Likert and VAS are more complex than a simple yes/no response and they are very difficult to use for telephone interviews. In health surveys, investigators requiring only satisfactory discriminative or predictive measurement properties of their instrument may choose a simple response option format.

Time Specification

A second feature of presentation is time specification: patients should be asked how they have been feeling over a well-defined period of time. We use 2 weeks in most of our instruments on the basis of our intuitive impression that this time frame is near the upper limit of what patients can accurately recall. Time specification can be modified according to the study, and other investigators may have different impressions of the limits of their population's memory.

Questionnaire Administration

In the traditional approach to questionnaire administration, patients are not permitted to see the responses they gave on previous occasions. We have found that showing patients their previous responses improves the validity of the questionnaire without adversely affecting the responsiveness (10,11). Therefore, we recommend that patients should see their previous responses when the questionnaires are being used for evaluative purposes.

Language Suitable for Translation

Very rarely will an instrument be used only in the country and culture in which it was developed. To make adaptation for use in a new country easier, it is wise to avoid jargon, idioms, or metaphors in a new instrument. Even within the English-speaking world, there are words and terms that are not common to all cultures and countries. For instance, *crook, down-in-the-dumps,* and *pooped* are used in some geographic areas and not in others. Therefore, it is best to use words that apply to the widest range of cultures and geographic areas.

INSTRUMENT TESTING

Pretesting

When a new questionnaire is first administered there are invariably some problems with patients not correctly understanding items and with the wording or format of the questionnaire. It is wise to pretest the instrument in a small number of patients to resolve these problems before embarking on a more costly and complex validation study. We administer the new questionnaire to approximately five patients, selected to represent as wide a spectrum as possible (disease severity, educational background, age, and gender). After an uninterrupted administration of the questionnaire, we ask patients to explain in their own words exactly how they understand each item. We note consistent problems in wording and understanding, make the necessary changes, and administer the revised instrument to another group of five patients. This process is repeated until no more changes are needed.

Reliability

The purpose of discriminative and predictive instruments is to measure differences between patients at a point in time. The measurement property required for this function is reliability, which expresses the relationship between the signal, in this case the difference between subjects, and the noise, the difference within a subject when the clinical state is stable (see previous chapter). In testing a new instrument, we need to estimate the noise of the instrument and determine whether it is sufficiently large to mask the various sizes of signal that we might be wanting to measure (Table 2).

Reliability is most commonly and appropriately expressed statistically as an intraclass correlation coefficient that relates the between-subject variance to the total variance. The instrument is administered on two or more occasions, and investigators use the results to estimate the reliability. The intraclass correlation will increase as the variability between subjects increases, and will decrease with either systematic or random differences between scores on the original and subsequent administrations.

If one wants to estimate the reliability of the instrument under optimum conditions, then it is important to keep all other sources of noise to a minimum, for example, ensuring that the patient's health state is stable, using only one interviewer, making sure the environment is quiet and free from interruptions or distractions, and interviewing the patient at the same time of day and, if possible, the same day of the week. However, if one wants to know the noise associated with administration under certain study conditions (e.g., more than one interviewer) then the testing environment should simulate that of the study.

The noise of the instrument is likely to be fairly constant across different levels of quality of life impairment but the magnitude of the signal (in this case, the variability in responses between different respondents) may vary considerably depending on the population one is studying. For instance, if the instrument is going to be asked to discriminate between patients with mild and severe disease, the signal to be detected is going to be much larger than if the instrument is to detect differences between patients with mild and very mild disease. To put this in numerical terms, let us say that the within-subject variance (noise) of the instrument is 2.0; if the true difference between mild and severe disease is a score of 5.0, then the ability of the instrument to detect this difference will be much better than if it is asked to detect a difference between mild and very mild disease of 0.5. The reliability of the instrument (signal-to-noise ratio) in the first instance will be high and in the second much lower.

For this reason, the patients selected to take part in the reliability testing of the instrument must be selected to represent the population in which the instrument is to be used. If the original or other investigators subsequently decide to use the questionnaire in a narrower range of patients, they can evaluate the reliability of the instrument in the new circumstances by first assuming that the within-subject standard deviation is constant and then generating an estimate of the between-subject standard deviation either intuitively or by actually measuring the mean and standard deviation in the new population.

Responsiveness

An evaluative instrument requires good responsiveness. When there is a change in the health state of the individual patient, the instrument must be able to detect this change even if it is small. The signal for an evaluative instrument is the true change occurring in a patient over a period of time. This change may occur spontaneously or as the result of an intervention. The noise that interferes with detection of the signal is the within-subject variance unrelated to the true within-subject change.

TABLE 2. *Necessary measurement properties for evaluative and discriminative instruments*

	Discriminative	Evaluative
Signal	Between-patient differences	Within-patient differences related to true within-patient change
Noise	Within-patient differences	Within-patient differences unrelated to true within-patient change
Signal-to-noise ratio: descriptive term	Reliability	Responsiveness
Example statistic	Reliability coefficient (ratio of between-patient to total variance)	Responsiveness index (ratio of minimal important difference to standard deviation of change)

There are a number of approaches to testing responsiveness. We usually use three strategies that address the following questions: In patients who truly change their health status, can we measure this change (using a paired t-test to compare baseline and follow-up scores)? Is the instrument able to distinguish between those patients who change and those who stay stable (using an unpaired t-test to determine if the magnitude of change in instrument score differs between stable subjects and those whose HRQL has changed). What is the magnitude of the instrument's responsiveness index (12)? This index is calculated from the minimal important difference ["the smallest difference in score in the domain of interest which patients perceive as beneficial and would mandate, in the absence of troublesome side effects and excessive cost, a change in the patient's management" (13)] and the pooled within-subject standard deviation of change in patients who remain stable and those who change. From the responsiveness index, it is very simple to calculate the sample sizes needed for both parallel group and crossover clinical study designs for various levels of type 1 (alpha) and type 2 (beta) error rates (5).

Validity

Part of the evaluation of any new instrument must be an assessment of whether the instrument is actually measuring what it is supposed to measure. The different approaches that can be used to evaluate validity when there is a gold standard (criterion validity) and when there is not (construct validity) have been extensively discussed in the previous chapter. Since the practical aspects of establishing criterion validity are fairly straightforward, this chapter focuses on how to establish the construct validity of a new specific instrument.

For discriminative instruments, one establishes construct validity by examining the relation between scores on the new instrument and other indices at a single point in time. These indices might include the conventional clinical outcomes and generic HRQL instruments. For evaluative instruments, one examines the relationship between changes in overall HRQL and in each of the domains of the new instrument and changes in other indices of impairment. Validation is far stronger if investigators have made a priori predictions about how the new instrument should relate to existing measures, if it is actually measuring what is intended. Additional, although somewhat weaker validation, can be obtained by seeing if the population behaves as it should if the HRQL measure is doing its job. For instance, does the mean score improve in a group of patients who receive a known efficacious treatment?

A Detailed Example of Construct Validation

The Asthma Quality of Life Questionnaire has 32 items in four domains (symptoms, emotional function, activity limitation, and problems associated with exposure environ-mental stimuli). The questionnaire was administered to 39 adults with asthma on three occasions each separated by 4 weeks. At each visit, patients also completed the Sickness Impact Profile (1) and a shortened version of the Rand general health survey (3); spirometry and airway responsiveness to methacholine were measured. For 1 week before each clinic visit, patients completed a daily diary in which they recorded morning peak expiratory flow rates, medication use, and asthma symptoms. At each follow-up clinic visit, patients completed five global rating of change questionnaires, one for overall HRQL and one for each of the domains of the Asthma Quality of Life Questionnaire. Prior to data analysis, the investigators and an experienced asthma clinician made predictions about how changes in each of the domains of the Asthma Quality of Life Questionnaire should relate to changes in the indices of clinical asthma severity and generic HRQL. There were three categories of a priori predictions: strongly correlated, $r > .5$; moderately correlated, $r = .35$ to $.5$; and poorly correlated, $r = .20$ to $.35$. These are some examples of the predictions:

1. Change in clinical asthma control should be strongly correlated ($r > .5$) with changes in the symptom domain of the Asthma Quality of Life Questionnaire. Observed correlation: $r = .67$.
2. Changes in FEV_1 will be only poorly correlated ($r = .20$ to $.35$) with changes in the activity limitation domain. Observed correlation: $r = .28$.
3. The global rating of change for emotional function will be moderately correlated ($r = .35$ to $.5$) with change in the emotional function domain. Observed correlation: $r = .52$.
4. Changes in the psychosocial domain of the Rand index will be moderately correlated ($r = .35$ to $.5$) with changes in the emotional function domain of the Asthma Quality of Life Questionnaire. Observed correlation: $r = .30$.

Of the 27 predictions made for the longitudinal validation, 13 agreed exactly with the observed results, 14 were off by one category, and none were off by more than one category. These data provided fairly good support for the validity of the questionnaire as an evaluative instrument. However, as discussed in the previous chapter, validation is not an all-or-nothing process; it does not end with the first study. The more frequently an instrument is used and the more situations in which it performs as expected, the greater our confidence in its validity.

Interpretability

Repeated experience with a wide variety of physiological measures allows clinicians to make meaningful interpretation of results. For instance, the experienced clinician will have little difficulty in interpreting a 10 mm Hg fall in diastolic blood pressure or a 0.5 litre increase in FEV_1. In contrast, the meaning of a change in score of 1.0 on an HRQL instrument is less intuitively obvious, not only because the units may be unfamiliar but also because health professionals seldom use HRQL measures in clinical practice.

Two fundamental approaches have been suggested for the interpretation of HRQL data (14). The first, distribution-based, is based entirely on the statistical distribution of the results of a particular study, the most commonly used being the effect size, which is derived from the magnitude of change and the variability in stable subjects. The problem with this approach is that there is still no indication as to whether the effect is trivial, of moderate magnitude, or large from the point of view of its impact on the patient. The second approach, which is the one we use, is referred to as anchor-based, where the changes in quality of life measures are compared, or anchored, to other clinically meaningful outcomes.

We have addressed the issue of interpretability by defining the minimal important difference (see above) (13). We have estimated the minimal important difference by examining the relation between global rating of change questionnaires that are administered to the patients at each follow-up visit during a validation study, and HRQL instrument scores. In brief, patients are asked whether they have experienced any change in the outcome of interest since the last clinical visit. Responses are given on a 15-point scale which ranges from -7 (a very great deal worse) to 0 (no change) to 7 (a very great deal better). Patients have indicated consistently that changes in scores less than -2 and greater than $+2$ are important to them. Therefore, patients who score -3, -2, $+2$, and $+3$ are considered to have experienced a minimal important change (15). The change in HRQL score between the initial and follow-up visit for these patients is considered to be the minimal important difference. Patients who score -5, -4, $+4$, and $+5$ are considered to have experienced a moderate change, and those scoring -7, -6, $+6$, and $+7$ to have had a large change. The magnitude of the change in HRQL score, both overall and for each of the domains of the instrument, associated with each of these categories, provides the information necessary for the full clinical, as opposed to statistical, interpretation of the data generated by the HRQL instrument. For example, we have shown that when using 7-point response options, a mean change in score, for both overall quality of life and for individual domains, of 0.5 per item represents a minimal clinically important difference, a change in score of 1.0 represents a moderate change in HRQL, and a change in score of about 1.5 represents a large change. These results have been consistent for patients with chronic lung disease, heart failure, and both adults and children with asthma (5,7,16,17).

Measuring Reliability and Responsiveness and Assessing Validity and Interpretability

Under ideal circumstances, there is the time and the money to carry out a full "stand alone" validation study. Sometimes circumstances are not so kind and one is forced to build a validation study into an existing clinical trial. With a little

ingenuity and a few additional questionnaires, this can be done quite satisfactorily.

In distinct validation studies patients are followed for a period of time with assessments at regular intervals. During this time, some patients will remain clinically stable while others will change either spontaneously or as a result of some intervention. One can ensure that some patients will fall into the "change" category by offering an intervention of known therapeutic benefit to those patients who have the potential to improve. For each time interval between evaluations, each patient is categorized either as having "stayed stable" (group A) or "changed" (group B) using a global rating of change or clinical indices. When using the global ratings, patients scoring -1, 0, and $+1$ are considered to have remained stable and are placed in group A. Patients responding between -7 and -2 and between $+2$ and $+7$ are considered to have experienced a change in their health status and are categorized as part of group B.

Data from the clinically stable patients who fall into group A are used for estimating the reliability of the instrument. Data from both groups are used for the three methods of assessing responsiveness. First, data from group B is used to evaluate the change in HRQL scores between consecutive assessments using a paired t-test. Second, change in HRQL scores between consecutive visits for the two groups are compared using an unpaired t-test. Third, the responsiveness index is derived from the minimal important difference (see Interpretability) and the pooled standard deviation of patients in both group A and group B.

To assess construct validity, outcomes that are predicted to be related to the new instrument should be measured at each clinic visit. A group of investigators and clinical specialists should make predictions as to where they would expect to find correlations before the analysis of the validity study data. Investigators can assess both cross-sectional validity for discriminative instruments and longitudinal validity for evaluative instruments.

CONCLUSIONS

We have presented an approach to instrument development and testing that we believe is robust and easily replicated. With care in choosing items that are important to patients, and careful structuring of the questionnaire, investigators can usually construct HRQL instruments with satisfactory measurement properties.

REFERENCES

1. Bergner M, Bobbitt RA, Carter WB, Gilson BS. The Sickness Impact Profile: development and final revision of a health status measure. *Med Care* 1981;19:787–805.
2. Hunt SM, McKenna SP, McEwen J, Backett EM, Williams J, Papp E. A quantitative approach to perceived health status: a validation study. *J Epidemiol Community Health* 1980;34:281–286.
3. Stewart AL, Hays R, Ware JE. The MOS short-form general health survey. Reliability and validity in a patient population. *Med Care* 1988;26:724–732.

4. Sackett DL, Chambers LW, MacPherson AS, Goldsmith CH, McAuley RG. The development and application of indices of health: general methods and summary of results. *Am J Public Health* 1977;67:423–428.

5. Juniper EF, Guyatt GH, Ferrie PJ, Griffith LE. Measuring quality of life in asthma. *Am Rev Respir Dis* 1993;147:832–838.

6. American Thoracic Society. Guidelines to the diagnosis and treatment of asthma. *Am Rev Respir Dis* 1987;136:225–244.

7. Guyatt GH, Berman LB, Townsend M, Pugsley SO, Chambers LW. A measure of quality of life for clinical trials in chronic lung disease. *Thorax* 1987;42:773–778.

8. Juniper EF, Guyatt GH. Development and testing of a new measure of health status for clinical trials in rhinoconjunctivitis. *Clin Exp Allergy* 1991;21:77–83.

9. Jaeschke R, Singer J, Guyatt GH. A comparison of seven-point and visual analogue scales: data from a randomized trial. *Controlled Clin Trials* 1990;11:43–51.

10. Guyatt GH, Berman LB, Townsend M, Taylor DW. Should study subjects see their previous responses? *J Chronic Dis* 1985;38:1003–1007.

11. Guyatt GH, Townsend M, Keller JL, Singer J. Should study subjects see their previous responses: data from a randomized control trial. *J Clin Epidemiol* 1989;42:913–920.

12. Guyatt GH, Walter S, Norman G. Measuring change over time: assessing the usefulness of evaluative instruments. *J Chronic Dis* 1987;40:171–178.

13. Jaeschke R, Singer J, Guyatt GH. Measurement of health status: ascertaining the minimal clinically important difference. *Controlled Clin Trials* 1989;10:407–415.

14. Lydick E, Epstein RS. Interpretation of quality of life changes. *Qual Life Res* 1993;2:221–226.

15. Juniper EF, Guyatt GH, Willan A, Griffith LE. Determining a minimal important change in a disease-specific quality of life questionnaire. *J Clin Epidemiol* 1994;47:81–87.

16. Guyatt GH, Norgradi S, Halcrow S, Singer J, Sullivan MJJ, Fallen EL. Development and testing of a new measure of health status in heart failure. *J Gen Intern Med* 1989;4:101–107.

17. Juniper EF, Guyatt GH, Feeny DH, Ferrie PJ, Griffith LE, Townsend M. Measuring quality of life in children with asthma. *J Allergy Clin Immunol* 1995;95:226.

Quality of Life and Pharmacoeconomics in Clinical Trials, Second Edition, edited by B. Spilker.
Lippincott-Raven Publishers, Philadelphia © 1996.

CHAPTER 7

Adopting Higher Standards for Quality of Life Trials

Bert Spilker

INTRODUCTION

Quality of life is increasingly becoming an accepted measure of the efficacy of a medicine in clinical trials. It is being added as an adjunct in many clinical trials and as a primary end point in others. Its growing importance may be observed through (a) increased awareness within pharmaceutical companies of the relevance and importance of quality of life data, (b) increased attention to developing and validating new instruments used to measure quality of life, (c) submission of quality of life data as supportive evidence for new medicine approval, (d) inclusion of medicines on formularies based on quality of life data, and (e) use of quality of life data to promote medicines to physicians. The reasons for conducting quality of life trials have been discussed (1) and are generally accepted. Typical industry-oriented questions relating to quality of life assessment are:

1. Should a company organize a group to address quality of life issues, and if so, how?
2. How may quality of life data be used in marketing a medicine?
3. Who wants and will use the data obtained?
4. For which medicines should quality of life data be evaluated?
5. How may a quality of life plan be initiated, coordinated, and reviewed?
6. At what phase of clinical development should quality of life trials be conducted?

7. How should quality of life data be presented to regulatory authorities?

Each of these questions has been discussed (1,2).

A MAJOR PROBLEM

The domains chosen for study (e.g., physical, psychological, social, economic) and the specific components of each domain evaluated in quality of life trials vary from a single component of a single domain to many components of all domains. At present, the choice of how many domains and components to study is generally based on the specific outcome that a researcher desires to demonstrate.

When most phase II and III clinical trials (not involving quality of life) are initiated, their outcome is usually unknown in terms of overall and/or specific results; the purpose of conducting most trials is indeed to determine the outcome and to obtain data. The data obtained are analyzed to ascertain if they support the hypothesis (objective) of the trial or not. The researchers may or may not have strong preconceived views about what type and magnitude of response they expect to find, but the trial is usually objectively designed to obtain a scientifically valid response. If the design is inappropriately chosen to obtain a predetermined result, the data and the trial itself would be strongly challenged.

With quality of life trials a different scenario generally unfolds. The researchers usually know in advance the type and often the magnitude of the end result they expect (or desire) to find. They work backward to choose the specific instrument(s) that will demonstrate the desired conclusion most convincingly. They often choose one or more compara-

B. Spilker: Orphan Medical, Inc., Minnetonka, Minnesota 55305.

tor medicines that are known to elicit worse results (e.g., more adverse reactions) in the specific domains they intend to evaluate. One or more areas are studied that the investigator or sponsor believes will show the superiority (in terms of quality of life) of the test medicine. This approach is motivated by the promotional use desired for the data obtained. For example, if a sponsor desires to claim that medicine A yields a better quality of life than medicine B, it is unlikely that the sponsor would choose to study a domain where their medicine was not known a priori to be superior. This approach to conducting quality of life trials is akin to stacking a deck of cards in favor of the treatment preferred by the company.

Specific comments of published studies are not presented because the practice described is extremely widespread. The majority of industry-sponsored quality of life trials appear to be guilty of some (or most) of these problems. Also, criticizing certain studies would not serve to foster healthy dialogue.

RECOMMENDED SOLUTION

Given this problem, can an objective approach be designed that would place all sponsors on a more equal basis? The answer is yes, and a fair solution is both simple to describe and easy to implement. That approach is to establish the standard that quality of life trials evaluating or comparing medicines will evaluate not one or two carefully selected domains or their components, but *all* domains as well as *multiple* components of each domain. Numerous advantages of this approach exist for all groups. Pharmaceutical companies will know that their competitors will not unfairly test and malign their medicines; formulary committees will know that quality of life data submitted are relatively objective and fair; physicians who read advertisements and are given reprints by company representatives will know that the data they assess are more balanced and credible than those from many previously conducted trials referred to as "quality of life trials"; patients will receive more appropriate treatment because of the better information received and rational decisions made by their physicians; and regulators will generally improved standards in this area, and the quality of life data they receive will be more objective.

The consequences for the pharmaceutical industry of not adhering to these higher standards are that quality of life trials will eventually obtain the reputation of being biased and unreliable. These trials will then not be valuable for the purposes to which they are currently put. This will undoubtedly occur as more and more individuals and groups become steadily more knowledgeable and sophisticated about the field of quality of life, and realize that data from purportedly objective trials may be misleading. If this tarnished reputa-

tion becomes attached to all quality of life trials, it will be difficult to restore them to their appropriate level of respectability.

The implementation of this recommendation should not be particularly difficult. The major groups that can apply pressure are:

1. Journal editors who refuse to publish results of trials that are not designed appropriately.
2. Formulary committees that refuse to place medicines onto their formulary if the quality of life data submitted are incomplete or biased.
3. Regulatory authorities who refuse to accept incomplete or inappropriate trials as providing evidence in support of an application.
4. Ethics committees and institutional review boards that require quality of life trials to adhere to higher standards.
5. Enlightened people at all pharmaceutical companies who promote the design of quality of life trials to an appropriate standard.

It will remain appropriate for academics to conduct quality of life trials that do not evaluate all domains. However, pharmaceutical companies should not commit the sin of omission and fail to examine all domains. No one will have to wonder if important results that could have been obtained by a more complete evaluation were missed or purposely avoided. Although the study of all domains is likely to yield primarily negative data (i.e., showing no effect), the method will provide assurances that no one is trying to avoid studying a potentially relevant area.

Quality of life trials are not a fad. They provide important data that rightfully influence many levels of medical decision making regarding the choice of therapy. The reputation of these trials is too important to allow them to be manipulated and seriously damaged by a number of people seeking an easy means of obtaining a competitive advantage.

CONCLUSION

Quality of life trials on medicines and other treatments should assess all domains and many components of each domain. While some exceptions to this principle exist, adherence will assure many audiences that no attempt is being made to avoid studying areas where different results are likely to occur.

REFERENCES

1. Henderson-James D, Spilker B. An industry perspective. In: Spilker B, ed. *Quality of life assessments in clinical trials.* New York: Raven Press, 1990.
2. Spilker B. *Guide to clinical trials.* New York: Raven Press, 1991.

Quality of Life and Pharmacoeconomics in Clinical Trials, Second Edition, edited by B. Spilker.
Lippincott-Raven Publishers, Philadelphia © 1996.

CHAPTER 8

On Learning and Understanding Quality of Life: A Guide to Information Sources

Susan C. Hedrick, Richard C. Taeuber, and Pennifer Erickson

INTRODUCTION

There is no universally applicable magic elixir, or "best" quality of life measure, and it is probably futile to think in such terms. Quality of life assessment is growing constantly in terms of acceptance, use, and expectation. Thus, it is important for researchers to be aware of the strengths and weaknesses of available measures and of the underlying theory and concepts, when setting out to study quality of life within a given study context.

The incorporation of health-related quality of life measures into a clinical investigation or a health services evaluation requires that everyone be cognizant of the state of the art and underlying concepts of outcomes assessment. Everyone with a role in quality of life research has a responsibility to oneself and to the project team to gain knowledge of quality of life sufficient to be able to

1. properly frame the questions to ask about the project,
2. make meaningful suggestions to address questions raised,
3. evaluate the completeness of proposals, and
4. track the progress of the overall project.

As learning, training, and research in quality of life continues expanding, information resources need to be as current as possible, and also readily accessible.

This chapter presents an overview of

1. selected books that describe the theory, findings, and realities of health-related quality of life research,
2. major journals to be considered for an operating library,
3. principal computerized bibliographic systems, and
4. a unique PC-based service that has been developed to provide information on quality of life instruments and their uses.

Any of these resources can serve as a portion of one's "library" and can provide a font of knowledge to build competence and awareness of essential elements in the areas of quality of life and health outcomes research.

PRINT MEDIA

Books

Recent years have seen the publication of a diversity of books that discuss concepts, specific measurements, and practical aspects of measuring quality of life. Some are edited volumes that highlight problems and promises of using quality of life assessment in particular applications (1–3). These books can be very useful if one is working in a particular area, such as cancer research and treatment. Other volumes focus on the philosophical or ethical aspects

S. C. Hedrick: Health Services Research and Development Field Program, Department of Veterans Affairs Medical Center, Seattle, Washington 98108.
R. C. Taeuber: OLGA (The On-Line Guide to Quality-of-Life Assessment), Salisbury, Maryland 21801.
P. Erickson: Clearinghouse on Health Indexes, OAEHP, National Center for Health Statistics, Hyattsville, Maryland 20782.

of the field such as those by Nussbaum and Sen (4) and Walter and Shannon (5).

Of broader use, however, are those books that cover a wide range of conceptual, methodological, and practical issues related to quality of life assessment. This section reviews a selection of key, measurement-oriented volumes.

The previous edition of this volume, *Quality of Life Assessments in Clinical Trials* (6), is a frequently cited guide to choosing existing measures and developing new ones. It contains reviews of instruments in economics, psychosocial status, and functional disability; presents ethical, cultural, marketing, industry, and regulatory perspectives; discusses special populations including pediatric, geriatric, and chronic pain patients; and has separate chapters on measurement of quality of life for eight specific conditions.

A classic text is *Assessing the Elderly: A Practical Guide to Measurement* by Rosalie and Robert Kane (7). This book contains an analysis of uses and abuses of measurement for various purposes followed by reviews of numerous assessment instruments divided into four categories: physical functioning, mental functioning, social functioning, and multidimensional measures. Most instruments are reprinted in the volume; tables present information on their administration, reliability, and validity; and the authors present conclusions regarding the instruments most suitable for specific uses.

Another very useful text is *Measuring Health: A Guide to Rating Scales and Questionnaires* by McDowell and Newell (8). This book reviews scales in six areas: functional disability, psychological well-being, social health, quality of life and life satisfaction, pain, and general health or multidimensional measures. At the beginning of each chapter, the authors provide a summary table presenting their assessment of a number of characteristics of the scales, checked for accuracy by the scale developers or other experts. The characteristics are level of measurement (nominal, ordinal, interval, ratio), number of items, application (clinical, research, or survey), method of administration (self, interviewer, expert rater), time required, the number of studies that have used the instrument, the thoroughness and results of reliability and validity testing, and, for the general health measures, the number of questions on various topics. The instruments are reprinted and the authors present a summary commentary on each.

Measuring Health: A Practical Approach (9) presents information on various approaches to health status measurement from British economists, social scientists, and clinicians. The book is designed to serve as a guide for the use of health status measurement in clinical trials, especially for pharmaceutical treatment, management, and clinical care. It includes chapters on assessment of treatments in Parkinson's disease, cancer, rheumatoid arthritis, heart disease, and irritable bowel syndrome.

Another British test, *The Quality of Life: Missing Measurement in Health Care* (10), contains discussions of philosophical and methodological issues in assessing quality of life in chronic diseases. The author reviews the relevant generic and disease-specific assessments for each of the

illnesses included in the book and reproduces part or all of some of the more frequently used assessments. Chapters are devoted to measuring quality of life among persons with cancer, cardiovascular disease, arthritis, and acquired immune deficiency syndrome (AIDS), as well as among elderly persons and among persons who are terminally ill.

Instruments in Clinical Nursing Research (11) contains 25 chapters by various authors discussing the assessment of commonly measured concepts such as functional and mental status and social support as well as less commonly measured concepts such as self-care activities, information-seeking behaviors, attitudes toward chronic illness, sleep, body image, spirituality, and hope. The chapters on specific clinical problems include pain, nausea and vomiting, skin integrity, and alterations in taste and smell. A new edition is in preparation that has additional chapters on concepts including adaptation of instruments for socioeconomically disadvantaged populations and instrument translations, special issues for the elderly and children, and the measurement of such concepts as compliance, family outcomes, outcomes of discharge planning, healthy lifestyle, and potential for falls.

Bech (12), in his book entitled *Rating Scales for Psychopathology, Health Status and Quality of Life: A Compendium on Documentation in Accordance With the DSM-III-R and WHO Systems,* presents extensive discussion of many of the commonly used scales, especially those that have been derived from the use of psychometric and clinimetric techniques. This compendium starts with a critical comparison of rating scales and two prominent, international classification systems, the ICD-10 and DSM-III-R. Subsequent chapters discuss rating scales for psychopathological states, mental disorders, somatic disorders, psychosocial stressors, social function, and coping. The last two chapters discuss scales for assessing health-related quality of life and adverse drug reactions. The extensive indexes assist the user of this compendium in readily accessing the detailed discussions of specific instruments, or identifying possible alternates to consider.

Quality of Life Assessment: Key Issues in the 1990s (13) is an edited volume with chapters on the major multidimensional health status measures such as the Quality of Well-Being Scale, Nottingham Health Profile, McMaster Health Index Questionnaire. Later chapters discuss the assessment of quality of life in major disease areas including cancer, rheumatoid arthritis, Parkinson's disease, chronic obstructive lung disease, hypertension, angina, psychiatry, and skin disease. The final section presents chapters on ethical questions; perspectives from industry, health care purchasers, and regulatory groups; pharmaceutical research; and policy research.

Health Status and Health Policy: Quality of Life in Health Care Evaluation and Resource Allocation (14) presents detailed information for the development and selection of health status measures as a part of a comprehensive guide to the use of such measures in health care policy. The book begins and ends with an examination of a suggested strategy for allocating health resources by comparing costs and outcomes of alternative health policies to identify those with the greatest benefit in relation to cost. The middle section provides an analysis of the theoretical background for health status measurement, techniques for assigning values to health status, guidelines for selection of measures, secondary data analysis strategies, estimation of prognosis and years of healthy life, and guidelines for the use of measurement in monitoring of health status, clinical trials, and health services research.

Finally, books are also available that provide guidance in the use of particular measures. For example, *Measuring Functioning and Well-Being: The Medical Outcomes Study Approach* (15) presents the development and application of the set of instruments developed for the Medical Outcomes Study. *The European Guide to the Nottingham Health Profile* (16) provides guidance for the English, Swedish, French, Italian, and Spanish versions of that instrument. *The Hippocratic Predicament: Affordability, Access, and Accountability in American Medicine* (17) discusses the Quality of Well-Being Scale and the General Health Policy Model in the context of allocating resources to health care.

Journals

In addition to these key books, selected journal titles are also important for keeping abreast of new developments in the field of quality of life assessment. This list is not considered to be exhaustive, but rather is intended to indicate the types of journals that increasingly are publishing measurement articles related to quality of life assessment.

American Journal of Public Health
Gerontologist
Health Economics
Health Policy
Health Psychology
International Journal of Technology Assessment in Health Care
Journal of Aging and Health
Journal of the American Geriatrics Society
Journal of Clinical Epidemiology
Journal of Epidemiology and Community Health
Journal of General Internal Medicine
Medical Care
Medical Decision Making
Milbank Quarterly
PharmacoEconomics
Quality of Life Research
Social Science and Medicine

In addition to these general journals, disease-specific or clinical journals are increasingly devoting space to coverage of health-related quality of life research. Thus, to keep up-to-date on new developments or applications within a particular field of interest, one needs to keep abreast of relevant disease-specific clinical journals. For example, since 1992, in

the area of arthritis and other rheumatic diseases, *Arthritis and Rheumatism* has published approximately 20 articles on health-related quality of life, the *Journal of Rheumatology* approximately 50, and the *British Journal of Rheumatology* approximately 40. Similar sets of journals exist for many of the more frequently studied diseases.

Occasionally the general journals will publish a bibliography or a review article that includes an extensive set of references. An example of the former is ''Quality of Life Bibliography and Indexes'' by Spilker et al. (18), which covered select literature published through 1989. The initial effort, and the series of updates, have been sponsored by Burroughs Wellcome Co. A series of updates has followed to cover highlights of the literature (19–22).

COMPUTERIZED BIBLIOGRAPHIC SYSTEMS

Specialized bibliographic systems and information services, especially those that maintain electronic data bases, are another source of information on quality of life measures and their uses. The principal systems are described briefly below, and contact information for each is provided.

The *National Library of Medicine* maintains a number of on-line data bases, the largest of which is MEDLINE. The output consists of bibliographic citations, keywords, and authors' abstracts for selected articles.

The *MEDLARS* system, developed by the U.S. Public Health Service's National Library of Medicine (NLM), was established in the late 1960s. Coverage has expanded from a select set of regional medical libraries to include almost all medical libraries in the United States as well as medical and health facilities throughout the world.

For quality-of-life researchers, the *MEDLINE* file is one of the two most relevant of NLM's data bases. Citations from over 2,000 medical and health journals from around the world are entered into a central data base. Each article is assigned 5 to 15 keywords, taken from a standard vocabulary, to be used for retrieval purposes. In addition, researchers can search for words in the title or abstract of the article. Researchers are able to identify applications of quality of life measures if the quality of life aspects have been included in the keywords or text of the author-provided abstracts. The other relevant data base is *HSTAR*, a new on-line data base that provides access to the published literature of health services research. Topics covered in HSTAR include planning, evaluation, quality assessment and assurance, health technology assessment, clinical practice guidelines development and use, and health services research methods. Contact the local reference librarian or National Library of Medicine, 8600 Rockville Pike, Bethesda, MD 20894, telephone (800) 272-4787.

Excerpta Medica is an on-line retrieval system with keyword and structured indexing vocabulary to identify articles on human medicine and related disciplines. Its output consists of bibliographic citations with or without abstracts as well as selected index fields. Data bases maintained by Excerpta Medica are other general-purpose systems that provide information similar to that provided by the National Library of Medicine. In addition to standard bibliographic and outcomes information, the Excerpta Medica data base, *EMBASE,* incorporates information on treatment modalities, including prescribed medicines and their manufacturers, as part of the standard output. Thus, this file is useful for identifying applications of quality of life assessments in pharmaceutical studies. Contact: Manager, North American Database Department, Elsevier Science Publishers, 52 Vanderbilt Avenue, New York, NY 10017, telephone (800) 457-3633 or (212) 633-3971 (voice), or (212) 633-3913 (fax). In Europe: Elsevier Science Publishers B.V., Excerpta Medica Publishing Group, Database Marketing Department, Molenwerf 1, 1014 AG Amsterdam, The Netherlands, telephone (31) 020-5803-507 (voice) (31) 020-5803-439 (fax).

The *Institute for Scientific Information* (ISI) offers an on-line retrieval system with text, keyword, and citation searching of Science Citation Index (SCI) and Social Science Citation Index (SSCI). The output consists of bibliographic citations and references. The SCI and SSCI are additional alternatives to the data bases available through the National Library of Medicine. Both SCI and SSCI contain references to the application of quality of life assessments in a wide range of health care and medical settings. Although there is some overlap between the two data bases, SCI is preferred when looking for information about the use of quality of life measures with particular indications. SSCI, on the other hand, is more useful for socioeconomic applications, including cost-effectiveness analysis and cost-utility analyses. Contact: ISI Technical Help Desk, Institute for Scientific Information, 3501 Market Street, Philadelphia, PA 19104, telephone (800) 336-4474 or (215) 386-0100 ext. 1591 (voice) or (215) 386-6362 (fax). In Europe: ISI Technical Help Desk, Institute for Scientific Information, 132 High Street, Uxbridge, Middlesex UB8 1DP, United Kingdom, telephone (44) 895-70016 (voice) (44) 895-56710 (fax).

The *Health and Psychosocial Instruments* (HAPI) offer an on-line retrieval system with text and keyword searching to identify survey instruments. They provide a brief abstract plus several references for each instrument. The computerized retrieval systems mentioned above provide information on articles that are published in professional journals and describe methodological, practical, and empirical studies about quality of life assessment. The HAPI file, on the other hand, is a computerized data base that allows the searcher to identify either general or disease-specific quality-of-life measures. The instruments indexed in this system have been identified from the psychological, nursing, and health services research literature. Each instrument is described in a brief abstract that is accompanied by a checklist that indicates availability of information about reliability and validity of the instrument. Up to ten references describing the assessment's development and application are also provided. Contact: Bibliographic Retrieval Service (BRS), Information

Technologies, 8000 Westpark Drive, McLean, VA 22102, telephone (703) 442-0900 or (800) 289-4277.

The *Clearinghouse on Health Indexes* is an information analysis center that promotes application of measures of health-related quality of life, and publishes the *Bibliography on Health Indexes,* an annotated bibliography that is disseminated quarterly. In addition, the clearinghouse serves as a communication channel between instrument developers and health services researchers on the one hand and medical and other health researchers who want to use their tools in clinical or population-based research. The *Bibliography on Health Indexes* serves to update researchers as to new health-related quality of life assessments and research. Contact: Clearinghouse on Health Indexes, Office of Analysis, Epidemiology, and Health Promotion, National Center for Health Statistics, 6525 Belcrest Road, Room 730, Hyattsville, MD 20782, telephone (301) 436-5975 (voice) (301) 436-8459 (fax).

A problem remains, however, with these information sources, especially books and retrieval systems, in that they may be of limited value for specific applications of quality of life assessments. Articles may be missed because relevant keywords may be excluded. Also, only published information is available. Furthermore, books of assessment are found to be quickly dated in a field that is growing as fast as quality of life assessment. These shortcomings coupled with advances in information technology led to the development of OLGA.

AN INFORMATION SERVICE

OLGA: The On-Line Guide to Quality of Life Assessment

Identifying and reviewing the extensive set of assessments[1] that have been developed and used, let alone reviewing the prior utilization of even a single measure or assessment, can be daunting. If an electronic bibliographic system is to be a true service, then

1. standardized terminology must be used, and standardized citations of the assessments, i.e., reduction to a single title, are needed for all developmental and research usages cited;
2. indexing must be proactive, rather than passive, because authors and editors often do not include quality of life–relevant terms and usages in the abstract or keyword listing; and

---

[1]An issue of terminology within the field is the lack of standardization in the use of the terms *instrument, assessment,* and *assessment strategy.* Questionnaires and rating scales that assess one or more concepts included in a definition of quality of life are generally referred to as instruments. Other forms of quality of life assessment are available, however. The most notable of the noninstrument approaches to assessing quality of life are the classification and valuation schemes that have been developed for use with socioeconomic or decision analyses. OLGA covers the complete range of approaches for assessing quality of life and not just a subset based on a particular format for data collection.

3. translating the interests of the searcher, whether for specific research interest or general learning purposes, into terminology and techniques for efficient retrieval requires aggressive assistance.

These concerns were addressed, as suggested by Bech (23), "from the very beginning of the quality of life epoch" in the development of OLGA as a pooled resource for the various quality of life research communities. At the present time access is limited to those research groups that obtain a site license for the service. As of today, access is primarily available to pharmaceutical company research staffs, although they are having discussions with other types of clients. The service is not broadly available to the research public as are the other systems discussed above.

OLGA includes summaries of existing assessments and their measurement properties, names and addresses of contact persons and consultants, and empirical evidence about each assessment's performance, all fully and functionally indexed and cross-referenced with guided intelligent access support. OLGA also provides an up-to-date synthesis of international information on assessments and on the use and findings of research reports as a support service to target the background efforts of those undertaking the selection or design of an assessment, or for those just wanting to gain an understanding of quality of life within a specific context.

The ASSESSMENT data base contains information on

over one thousand instruments that have been used in quality of life studies;
main concepts of quality of life that are included in the measure (e.g., depression, return to work, or sleep dysfunction), and measurement properties (reliability, validity, and responsiveness);
purpose of the assessment, whether for clinical research, outcomes management, screening or diagnosis, or for economic analysis;
practical aspects of each assessment, such as whether interviewer or self-administered, time to administer, and languages in which the assessment is available; and
copyright and instrument availability contacts, and citations to development references.

The REFERENCES data base contains citations to empirical research that has been conducted in which these assessments have been used, and research reports that are fully cross-indexed to the assessments used and the health conditions evaluated.

These data bases are based on published literature, unpublished manuscripts, abstracts of meeting presentations, and personal communications from contacts throughout the international research community. They are updated continuously, and are available as a PC-based system updated three times a year for their site-licensed clients.

In addition to the data bases, OLGA contains decision-theoretic computer programs. These "OLGArithms" assist with the design of a quality-of-life assessment strategy and are based on accepted guidelines for selecting assessments of health-related quality of life (14,24–27). The OLGArithms incorporate a multidimensional definition of quality of life, one that includes impairments, functional states of physical, social and psychological well-being, perceptions and potential. OLGA is thus able to assist the user in developing an assessment strategy, either one that is made up solely of a general health status measure or one that is a combination of general, disease- and/or treatment-specific measures (14,24,26,27). The OLGArithms also allow the user to examine each strategy for considerations that affect the cost of conducting each study, e.g., the mode of administration and the length of time to administer.

The references data base for the full range of prior usage of measures can provide (a) normative data for study groups based on medical condition and selected sociodemographic characteristics; (b) validation of one's findings with a given assessment by the comparison with others' results; (c) identification of indications, treatment benefits, and side effects for which specific assessments have been used; and (d) information about determinations of reliability, validity, and responsiveness.

OLGA also supports the novice who just wants to probe the quality of life field to get some feel for what has been done in the past or gain a deeper understanding of the concepts and realities of quality of life research activities. OLGA's ability to intelligently guide a user thus supports learning by permitting a focus on the literature on quality of life aspects of a disease or condition of specific interest to the individual researcher wanting familiarity with a demanding research challenge. Contact: Richard C. Taeuber, Ph.D., OLGA, 711 College Lane #1, Salisbury, MD 21801, telephone 410-860-2582 (voice and fax). In Europe contact: Bernard Jambon, MAPI, 27 rue de la Villette, 69003 Lyon, France, telephone (33) 72-33-00-48 (voice) (33) 78-53-67-61 (fax).

COST ISSUES

An important aspect of information retrieval and knowledge processing is that of the costs associated with information, either its acquisition or its inadequacy when decisions must be made. Cost issues, although an important reality in any research activity, have not been addressed in the above review because of their highly individualized nature; that is, some applications of quality of life assessments may be very straightforward and require minimal information resources to implement. Other applications may, however, be very innovative and thus require extensive evaluation of what has been tried before and of the results of those research efforts, so as to provide insight into what might be appropriate for the unique aspects of one's particular area of concern and research activity. Clearly this latter application will be more resource intensive.

CONCLUSIONS

This chapter has addressed the challenge of obtaining the knowledge of past quality of life assessment strategies and research activity results on a timely basis with minimal search staff efforts and costs, with the intent of providing guidance in the selection of a specific set of resources that can most efficiently supply the relevant information. This may be as simple as selecting a book from one's bookshelf. The most efficient and time-saving alternative may be to use a comprehensive service that can guide one through the review process.

REFERENCES

1. Osoba D, ed. *Effect of cancer on quality of life.* Boca Raton, FL: CRC Press, 1991.
2. Aaronson NK, Beckmann J, eds. *The quality of life of cancer patients.* New York: Raven Press, 1987.
3. Trimble MR, Dodson WE, eds. *Epilepsy and quality of life.* New York: Raven Press, 1994.
4. Nussbaum M, Sen A, eds. *Quality of life.* New York: Oxford University Press, 1993.
5. Walter JJ, Shannon TA, eds. *Quality of life: the new medical dilemma.* Malwah, NJ: Paulist Press, 1990.
6. Spilker B, ed. *Quality of life assessments in clinical trials.* New York: Raven Press, 1990.
7. Kane RA, Kane RL. *Assessing the elderly: a practical guide to measurement.* Lexington, MA: Lexington Books, 1981.
8. McDowell I, Newell C. *Measuring health: a guide to rating scales and questionnaires.* New York: Oxford University Press, 1987.
9. Smith GT, ed. *Measuring health: a practical approach.* New York: John Wiley, 1988.
10. Fallowfield L. *The quality of life: missing measurement in health care.* London: Souvenir Press, 1990.
11. Frank-Stromborg M. *Instruments in clinical nursing research.* Norwalk, CT: Appleton and Lange, 1988.
12. Bech P. *Rating scales for psychopathology, health status, and quality of life: a compendium on documentation in accordance with the DSM-III-R and WHO Systems.* Berlin: Springer-Verlag, 1993.
13. Walker SR, Rosser RM, eds. *Quality of life assessment: key issues in the 1990s.* Dordrecht, The Netherlands: Kluwer Academic, 1993.
14. Patrick DL, Erickson P. *Health status and health policy: quality of life in health care evaluation and resource allocation.* New York: Oxford University Press, 1993.
15. Stewart AL, Ware JE, eds. *Measuring functioning and well-being: The Medical Outcomes Study Approach.* Durham, NC: Duke University Press, 1992.
16. European Group for Quality of Life and Health Measurement. *The European Guide to Nottingham Health Profile.* Brookwood, Surrey, UK: Brookwood Medical, 1994.
17. Kaplan RM. *The Hippocratic predicament: affordability, access, and accountability in American medicine.* San Diego: Academic Press, 1993.
18. Spilker B, Molinek FR Jr, Johnston KA, Simpson RL Jr, Tilson HH. Quality of life bibliography and indexes. *Med Care* 1990;28(suppl 12).
19. Spilker B, White WSA, Simpson RL Jr, Tilson HH. Quality of life bibliography and indexes: 1990 update. *J Clin Res Pharmacoepidemiol* 1992;6:87–156.
20. Spilker B, Simpson RL Jr, Tilson HH. Quality of life bibliography and indexes: 1991 update. *J Clin Res Pharmacoepidemiol* 1992;6:205–266.
21. Berzon RA, Simeon GP, Simpson RL Jr, Tilson HH. Quality of life bibliography and indexes: 1992 update. *J Clin Res Drug Dev* 1993;7: 203–242.
22. Berzon RA, Simeon GP, Simpson RL Jr, Donnelly MA, Tilson HH. Quality of life bibliography and indexes: 1993 update. *Qual Life Res* 1995;4:53–74.
23. Bech P. Health-related quality of life. *Ann Med* 1993;25:103–104.
24. Bergner M, Rothman M. Health status measures: an overview and guide for selection. *Annu Rev Public Health* 1987;8:191–210.
25. Barofsky I, Cohen SJ, Sugarbaker PH. Selecting a quality of life assessment: standardized tests, clinical assessments, or custom-designed instruments. In: Wenger NK, Mattson ME, Furberg CD, et al., eds. *Assessment of quality of life in clinical trials of cardiovascular therapies.* New York: Le Jacq, 1984:239–249.
26. Erickson P, Patrick DL. Guidelines for selecting quality of life assessment: methodological and practical considerations. *J Drug Ther Res* 1988;13(5):159–163.
27. Ware JE. Methodological considerations in the selection of health status assessment procedures. In: Wenger NK, Mattson ME, Furberg CD, et al., eds. *Assessment of quality of life in clinical trials of cardiovascular therapies.* New York: Le Jacq, 1984:87–117.

Quality of Life and Pharmacoeconomics in Clinical Trials, Second Edition, edited by B. Spilker.
Lippincott-Raven Publishers, Philadelphia © 1996.

CHAPTER 9

Normalcy, Supernormalcy, and Subnormalcy

Bert Spilker

INTRODUCTION

Most people think of themselves as "normal." We assume we know what normal means, but in fact the entire concept of normalcy is vague and complex. This chapter explores various aspects of this concept from a general medical perspective and attempts to clarify a number of issues that arise in the planning, conduct, and interpretation of clinical trials. There is scant literature on the boundaries and interactions of normalcy with quality of life. Once a better understanding of normalcy is achieved, clinical research can better focus on studying the phenomenon and its relationship to medical treatments and to an individual's quality of life.

The literature on normalcy is extremely large in the fields of psychology, psychiatry, philosophy, sociology, and law. In fact, a discipline known as normatology has grown up that primarily attempts to distinguish between normal behavior and psychopathology in psychology and psychiatry (1). Offer and Sabshin (1) propose five axes of normalcy, two based on personality, one on physical health and personality, one on stress and personality, and one on global well-being. This chapter does not cover this perspective or discuss the psychology/psychiatric viewpoints on normalcy.

DEFINITIONS AND DESCRIPTIONS

Normal is defined differently, depending on the discipline involved. For example, the dictionary defines normal as "not deviating from an established norm or standard." In biology, normal generally means "unaffected by any partic-

B. Spilker: Orphan Medical, Inc., Minnetonka, Minnesota 55305.

ular infection or experimental treatment." Psychiatrists use normal to mean "free from mental disorders." An operational definition (used in this chapter) is "the usual state of how one feels and acts physically, psychologically, socially, spiritually, and economically when one is not ill, or when one has adjusted to one's illness."

This definition is consistent with those described by Koeslag (2), who concluded that "a quality of life instead of a length-of-life criterion should determine what is normal and what is not."

Normalcy is judged in relation to previous states of feeling and acting, and also in relation to what a person sees in other so-called normal people. In extreme cases, people may change their frame of reference about what is normal because of an external crisis such as war, famine, or being in a concentration camp.

Most people describe their own state as being either better or worse than normal at some times in their lives. These states are referred to as "supernormal" and "subnormal." Clearly, there is a gradient from supernormalcy to normalcy to subnormalcy, but these concepts are far more complex than a simple linear continuum would imply (Fig. 1).

The states of supernormalcy, normalcy, and subnormalcy may be visualized as a circle (Fig. 2). Illness, a subnormal state, may accompany either of the other states, and supernormalcy is not always free of the other two states. The obvious mixtures of normal and supernormal characteristics, and also that of normal and subnormal characteristics (or states), are not illustrated in Fig. 2. The characteristics of supernormalcy vary greatly among individuals, but some of the more common characteristics are listed in Table 1. A few of the methods used to approach or attain supernormalcy are listed in Table 2. Most people can define different states

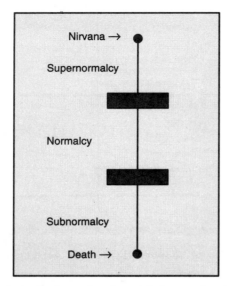

FIG. 1. A single-dimensional model of normalcy, supernormalcy and subnormalcy.

of being that fit each of the three states of normalcy. These states may overlap, and three selected examples are shown for normalcy, subnormalcy, and supernormalcy in Fig. 3.

People who gradually become subnormal may adjust to their new state, so that over time they begin to describe themselves as being normal and not subnormal. These con-

TABLE 1. *Characteristics often reported by people who view themselves as "supernormal"*

High energy level
Very alert
Positive self-image
Self-confident
Optimistic about the future
Low stress level

cepts are illustrated in Fig. 4. While quality of life measures indicate a worsening over time, each stage of subnormalcy is shown to be accompanied by an adjustment returning the patient to a level of normalcy. Similarly, individuals who have achieved a means of maintaining a supernormal state may adjust to it and perceive it as normal. The degree to which patients can adapt and adjust to changes in their disease (usually a worsening) determines the level of their quality of life.

In most situations, a person who sees himself or herself as normal is also viewed as normal by others because (a) there are very few objective signs of abnormality, (b) the abnormal signs observed are not far from a normal range and are not considered important, or (c) the abnormalities are not externally apparent. An individual with bizarre behavior or obvious physical problems may be called normal by others because the term *normal* may be used to mean

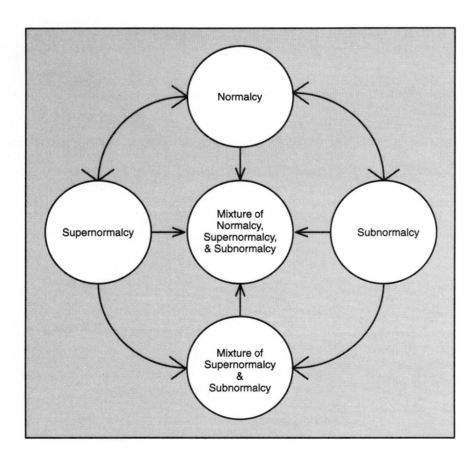

FIG. 2. An interactive model of normalcy, supernormalcy and subnormalcy.

TABLE 2. *Methods people use to move toward supernormalcy* [a]

Special foods and diets
Nutritional supplements
Spiritual exercises such as prayer or meditation
Physical exercise
Weight loss
Psychological exercises
Physical and spiritual lovemaking
Illicit drugs

[a] These methods are also used to move from subnormalcy to normalcy.

"normal for him or her." A physician who assesses a patient may describe normalcy in objective or subjective terms (Fig. 5). For instance, abnormal heart sounds may be described as 1+, 2+, 3+, or 4+ abnormal. Laboratory values may be described in terms of any arbitrary scale to illustrate the degree of abnormality. Subjective parameters such as affect may be described in Likert scale categories that indicate levels of abnormality (e.g., mildly abnormal, moderately abnormal, markedly abnormal).

Medical science has not explored the concept of normalcy in detail and there is no standardized global test to determine whether or not a person is normal. Medical disciplines have

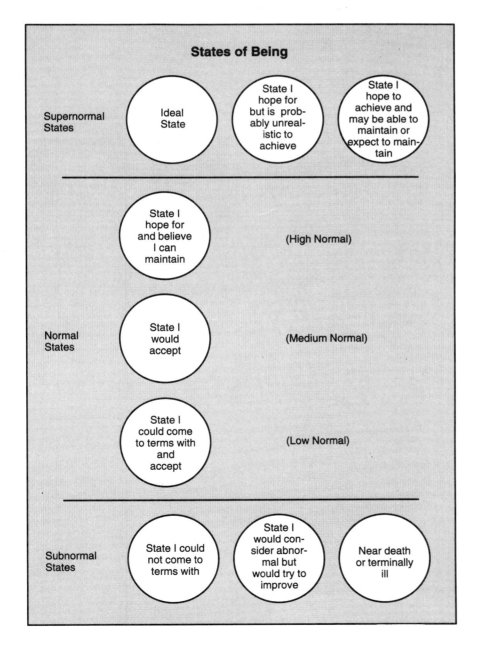

FIG. 3. States of being that a person may define for him- or herself. Each of the three examples of states shown for normalcy, subnormalcy, and supernormalcy may overlap, although this is not shown.

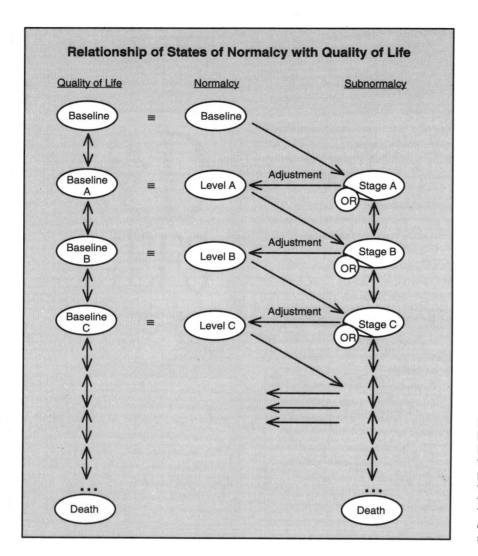

FIG. 4. Patients who deteriorate from a baseline state (level) of normalcy to a lower state of subnormalcy may adjust that state to a new level of normalcy. This process may occur many times. Patients who do not adjust and who deteriorate follow the progression shown on the right. The quality of life baseline (downward) is equivalent to the level of normalcy or subnormalcy.

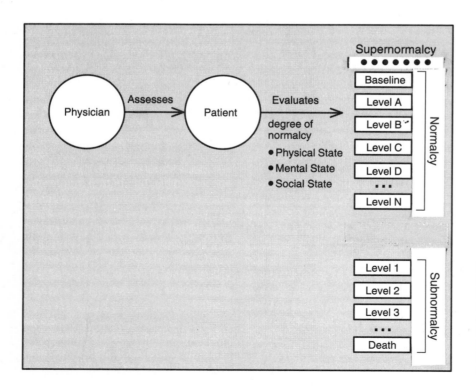

FIG. 5. Objective or subjective levels of normalcy. This figure illustrates that normal and subnormal states are often classified in multiple levels (e.g., staging of a cancer, degree of laboratory abnormality). Supernormal states (i.e., above the row of dots) are not generally described in different levels by physicians, except with adjectives.

TABLE 3. *Relationships and areas in which a patient functions*[a]

Spouse
Family
Friends
Other people
Work
Daily activities
Religion
Professional associations and groups
Social groups

[a]Physical, social, or psychological limitations of the patient in each of these areas vary from none to mild, moderate, strong, or extreme.

instead focused on the study and treatment of disease, illness, problems, syndromes, and other abnormal states. Clinical trials usually are designed to evaluate prevention, diagnosis, and treatment of these abnormal states. The primary goal of medical intervention is to bring patients from a state considered abnormal toward a state that achieves or approaches normalcy.

HOW IS NORMALCY ASSESSED?

For a clinical trial, a patient's normalcy may be evaluated by a single health professional or by a group of health professionals. The evaluation can be totally subjective, or it may use individual components of normalcy that can be measured. Quite often, the patient is simply asked whether or not he or she feels normal. Such a general question requires patients to evaluate the basic domains of physical, psychological, social, spiritual, and economic well-being and integrate their feelings about these domains. This integration usually involves a patient's consideration of other groups and activities (Table 3). People ascribe different values to normalcy and therefore assess it differently.

A quantitative assessment of normalcy in a clinical trial ideally should (a) include all domains, (b) determine which components of each domain are important to each patient, and (c) include an evaluation of clinical signs, symptoms, psychological evaluations, and laboratory tests. The data from each patient in a clinical trial should be compared with his or her own baseline values, and groups of patients may be compared with each other to assess treatment effects, if any. However, it is undesirable to compare the overall subjective changes from normalcy for any two or more patients because (a) their concept of normalcy will differ, (b) their method for assessing change will differ, and (c) the ability to measure subjective changes from normalcy is extremely difficult. Unless a person's basic concept of normalcy changes during a clinical trial (which may occur from time to time), individual deviations from a normal state will be more illuminating of treatment effects than will differences between the groups. While some clinical trials involve a single patient, most diseases or characteristics of a disease are studied in small or large groups of patients in clinical trials. Some of the categories that may be used to evaluate and describe normalcy in a clinical trial or in extrapolating data from a group of patients to all patients are shown in Fig. 6.

Clinical trial outcomes could be expressed by methods such as stating that 10 of 12 patients on treatment A moved toward a more normal state, whereas only 2 of 10 patients on placebo did so. Dose-response evaluations could also be used to present data on how perceptions or evaluations of normalcy changed during a clinical trial. An important issue is whether increased doses of a medicine led to a greater proportion of patients who moved to a more normal state.

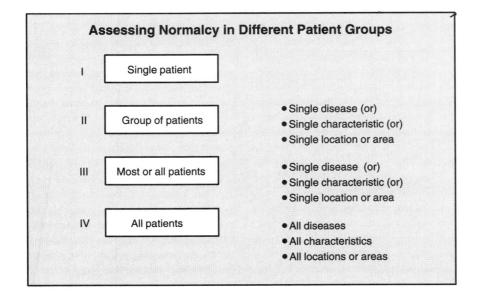

FIG. 6. Levels of patient groups used to assess and describe normalcy in a clinical trial or in extrapolating data.

HOW ABNORMAL MAY A STATE BE AND STILL BE DESCRIBED AS NORMAL?

Most normal people who develop an abnormal sign or symptom still consider themselves normal. At a certain point of physical or psychological deterioration, people begin to see themselves as abnormal or subnormal. The point at which this occurs varies greatly, depending on personality, pain tolerance, upbringing, personal values, and experiences, among other factors. While some people consider even a slight shift from normalcy as placing them in a subnormal state, others will describe themselves as normal despite major physical or mental deterioration. It is reminiscent of the degree of physical abnormality required before a person believes he or she should go to a hospital. Some stoic patients wait until they are near death, while others rush to an emergency room because of minor changes.

A person who admits he or she is abnormal but who subsequently recovers is more likely to recognize an abnormal state if the same symptoms arise in the future. Denial of a subnormal state may in itself be a medical abnormality, but this trait usually decreases with repeated episodes of an illness.

As a normal person becomes progressively subnormal from a disease, he or she may see many signs of illness in others. It is ironically rational for these people to deny that anyone is truly normal. This is generally based on a very narrow definition of normalcy. In fact, review of laboratory blood and urine values of so-called normal patients shows that extremely few have values entirely within the normal range. This phenomenon has been studied at length and is discussed in *Guide to Clinical Trials* (3). Therefore, it is inappropriate to specify in a clinical trial protocol that healthy volunteers must have all their laboratory values within the normal range.

CHARACTERIZING SUBNORMALCY VERSUS NORMALCY

Subnormalcy is best described and quantitated by identifying as many patient characteristics, functions, and values as appropriate in the most specific terms possible. For example:

1. A lesion of 2.5 × 5.0 mm is present at the upper right margin of the liver that is hard, and . . .
2. The BUN has been elevated for 4 months and is 124 mg/100 ml today. The trend of values shows a steady decrease from a maximum of 168 mg/100 ml 6 days ago. Other signs of renal status are . . .
3. The x-rays show that . . .
4. The patient has been treated with medicine X for 4 months at a dose of Y and the response is . . .

There is no simple way to describe normalcy or demonstrate its presence. In some ways normalcy is a diagnosis of exclusion. Patients cannot simply be asked if they are normal, with their answers accepted as valid. For example, many psychotic people consider themselves normal, and many mentally healthy people may be unaware of major physical abnormalities. In psychiatry and psychology, the establishment of normalcy begins with the question of whether the person is orientated to person, place, and time—does the person know who he is, where he is, and what the date is? Interview techniques and many written, verbal, or performance tests can be used to evaluate psychological abnormality. The standard physical examination and laboratory tests evaluate physical characteristics, and many abnormalities can be detected. The trained professional integrates all available data to reach a conclusion about the degree of normalcy or subnormalcy.

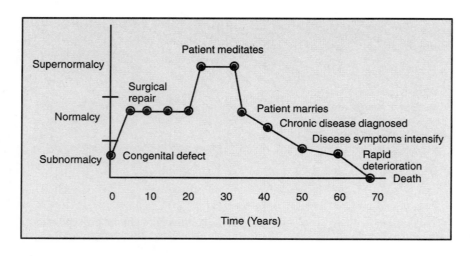

FIG. 7. A hypothetical patient's changing baseline of normalcy.

Whether a person can be characterized as normal is often viewed as a semantic argument because the physician must judge supernormal, normal, and subnormal aspects of each patient. One way of resolving this is to say the patient is normal except for *X*. It is also possible to state that the patient has a certain abnormality but is otherwise normal. This approach is appropriate for describing a complex combination of results. Another approach is to chronologically describe the changes in a person's life. This may also be visually drawn, as illustrated in Fig. 7.

QUALITY OF LIFE

Each of the three states described incorporates considerations of the basic domains of quality of life: physical, psychological, social, spiritual, and economic. The relative impor-

tance and, indeed, the components of each domain included in an individual's concept of normalcy vary greatly. A Tibetan monk is likely to ascribe far less importance to physical comfort and well-being in assessing his normal state than is a middle-class Westerner living in a highly developed country. Likewise, the components of the spiritual or psychological domain will be far more important to the monk than to many Westerners.

Severely debilitated patients may assess quality of life in terms of their ability to make small, positive improvements in their baseline condition. The ability to improve manual dexterity by a small degree may be much more important to a severely disabled arthritic patient than to someone with dementia or paraplegia. It is usually healthy for a severely debilitated person to describe him or herself as normal, but the term may be used by the patient to refer primarily to psychological rather than physical status. Alternatively, it

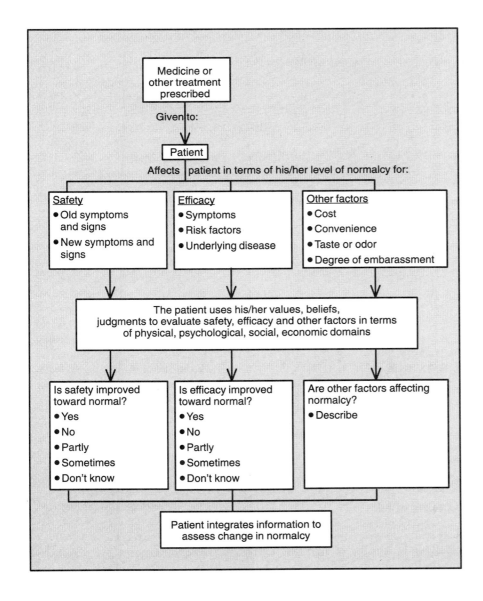

FIG. 8. Relationship of quality of life to assessment of normalcy. "Old symptoms and signs" in the upper left box refer to preexisting conditions.

may mean that this person has adjusted to his or her physical state.

Thus, the relationship of these three states of normalcy to quality of life must be assessed on a case-by-case basis. Figure 8 illustrates one model of the relationship of normalcy to quality of life. Note the relationship of this figure to Fig. 2 in Chapter 1. It would be interesting to know how people rate their state of normalcy or subnormalcy, in addition to quality of life, at the onset of a clinical trial and then to assess whether improvements or deterioration in one paradigm (i.e., quality of life or normalcy) parallel improvements or deterioration in the other. In many situations the two aspects would change in the same direction. However, a physician may note great improvement in an important clinical parameter of normalcy (such as tumor size or creatinine clearance) while the patient may actually feel the same or worse because of the treatment (e.g., chemotherapy). There are important differences between quality of life, which is a more subjective parameter, and normalcy, which may be based on more objective measures. Nonetheless, the definition of normalcy proposed as an operational definition is rooted in the domains of quality of life.

CONCLUSIONS

The concepts of normalcy, subnormalcy, and supernormalcy are used frequently by all people to describe themselves and their state of being, but there is little agreement as to exactly what is meant by these terms. In clinical trials, normalcy is seldom evaluated in a systematic way, if at all. Normalcy is operationally defined as "the usual state of how one feels and acts physically, psychologically, socially, spiritually, and economically when one is not ill, or when one has adjusted to one's illness." The relationship to the standard quality of life domains is clear and is also relevant for individuals who are either in supernormal or subnormal states. Research that helps clarify these concepts, even on an individual-patient basis, will benefit the design and interpretation of future clinical trials.

ACKNOWLEDGMENT

The author acknowledges and thanks Dr. Richard Gelber for stimulating the thinking that led to this chapter, as well as reviewing the manuscript. Dr. Ivan Barofsky is thanked for pointing out the area of normatology to the author.

REFERENCES

1. Offer D, Sabshin M. *The diversity of normal behavior—further contributions to normatology.* New York: Basic Books, 1991.
2. Kolslag JH. What is normal? *South African Med J* 1993;83:47–50.
3. Spilker B. *Guide to clinical trials.* New York: Raven Press, 1991.

Quality of Life and Pharmacoeconomics in Clinical Trials, Second Edition, edited by B. Spilker. Lippincott-Raven Publishers, Philadelphia © 1996.

CHAPTER 10

Future Directions of Quality of Life Research

Paul D. Cleary

INTRODUCTION

Until recently, health-related quality of life (HRQL) measures have been used relatively infrequently in clinical trials. There are several conceptual, methodologic, practical, and attitudinal explanations for why such measures have not been used more frequently (1,2). Many of these issues now have been resolved; there is a growing consensus about the importance of such measures in clinical trials (3–6), and the use of such measures is increasing rapidly (7–12).

It is impossible to make confident predictions about future directions in such a dynamic field, but in this chapter I review several general issues that I think will be major foci of research in the next few years. The first is the development and testing of more explicit theoretical models of the associations among the types of clinical variables and measures of HRQL that are used in clinical trials, as well as the associations among different components of HRQL measures. A second, and related, issue concerns the analysis and interpretation of multidimensional HRQL measures. A third issue concerns the analytic models used to develop and evaluate HRQL scales. A final area in which I think there will be a great deal of research in the next few years is the development of better ways of calibrating changes in HRQL scales that are more meaningful to patients, clinicians, and those responsible for evaluating the results of clinical trials (e.g., regulatory agencies).

THEORETICAL MODELS

To date, theoretical discussion of HRQL measures has focused primarily on the definition of HRQL, the dimensions that constitute HRQL (13–16), and taxonomies of HRQL scales (17, 18). Related theoretical issues are whether HRQL can be assessed with generic instruments, or whether there are ''condition-specific'' components that require special measures. A final, frequently debated, issue is the extent to which HRQL is a single global concept or is necessarily defined by multiple measures.

There has been relatively little discussion of the theoretical links among the components of HRQL or of the differential associations between HRQL measures and more traditional biomedical outcome measures. Several researchers (6,15,16, 19,20) have suggested that future research should focus on developing better theoretical models of the relationships among the specific components of HRQL, as well as the relationships between HRQL dimensions and other more traditional measures of health status, such as disease progression and mortality.

There are several conceptual models of the relationships among the components of HRQL (15,21–25). None of these models, however, includes the full range of variables that now typically are included in HRQL assessments, most do not include biological measures, and there are few empirical evaluations of these models.

The choice of primary end points in clinical trials should be based on knowledge of, or theory about, the mechanism of action of the drug or intervention being evaluated. That is, one should have a specific hypothesis about how a medical or surgical intervention will affect a biological end point. It also is important to know the mechanism of action linking the intervention to HRQL in order to select the most appropriate

P. D. Cleary: Department of Health Care Policy, Harvard Medical School, Boston, Massachusetts 02115.

HRQL measures. That is, it is necessary to have a theoretical model of the associations between the clinical intervention and different aspects of HRQL. Without a clear model of the associations between the biological process measured and different components of HRQL, or of the associations among different components of HRQL, it is difficult to select the HRQL measures that will best detect the effects of interest.

There are several reasons why we think there will be increasing use of more explicit theoretical frameworks for the development, selection, and analysis of HRQL scales to be used in clinical trials. In the absence of a clear theoretical model that can be used to select HRQL measures, it might be necessary to measure an extremely large number of HRQL constructs. This can result in unnecessary respondent burden and costs of data collection that often are critical factors in the design of clinical trials (26). In such a situation it also is difficult to determine what is the appropriate way to combine or evaluate the multiple measures.

A clear theoretical model would allow clinical researchers considering new or revised measures for inclusion in clinical trials to assess more critically both the validity and empirical utility of the new measures. Furthermore, a model of HRQL would allow researchers to test more refined hypotheses about clinical and other patient characteristics that might confound the associations between a clinical treatment and the measured outcomes.

A second reason we think there will be increasing use of explicit theoretical models in clinical trials is the increasing importance of, and scrutiny of, HRQL measures as end points. If HRQL measures are being used only to provide descriptive information that complements results from the primary end points, then it may be appropriate to include HRQL measures selected without attention to hypothesized links to the intervention being evaluated. When HRQL measures are used as primary end points or end points that will be used to make explicit claims, however, researchers will be required to develop more specific hypotheses about which dimensions are expected to show differential effects and to account for multiple statistical tests of related constructs (27). Thus, it will be increasingly important to have a model for selecting the measures that are most likely to reflect the anticipated benefits of treatment.

One of the most important practical advances in this field in the past decade is the development of very short, multidimensional instruments that have demonstrated reliability and validity, such as the RAND 36-Item Health Survey (28,29). Because of the extensive research that has been conducted using this and other generic scales, many researchers have a natural inclination to use them without thinking critically about the specific aspects of HRQL most likely to be affected by the intervention under investigation and the scale or scales that would best measure those dimensions. Any short generic scale designed for widespread use is unlikely to contain the best measures of specific components of interest in different clinical trials. Unfortunately, unless researchers think carefully about such issues it is difficult to ensure that the best measure is being used.

We have described a model that specifies the relationships among the determinants and measures of HRQL (19,20,30) that we think is more general and more applicable to clinical trials than other models that have been proposed (15,21–25). Many of the existing models were motivated by the observation that commonly used measures of HRQL frequently include conceptually distinct constructs of disease, functional limitations, and self-rated health. However, none of these models includes the full range of variables that now typically are included in HRQL assessments, most do not specify the links between biological and other types of measures, and generally, they have not been tested empirically (cf. 19,25).

We have proposed that measures of health be thought of as being on a continuum of increasing biological, social, and psychological complexity (20). At one end of the continuum are specific biological measures such as blood pressure and at the other are more complex and integrated measures such as physical functioning and general health perceptions. This model does not imply that there are not reciprocal relationships. Nor does it imply that there are not relationships between nonadjacent levels in the model. The main purpose of the model is to distinguish among conceptually distinct measures of HRQL and to make explicit what we think are the dominant causal associations. We have described this model in detail elsewhere (20) but the rationale and details are not critical for the discussion here. Irrespective of the specific model adopted, we think future research in this area will be stronger if it is based on this or other theoretical models that make explicit hypothesized links among variables when selecting and testing HRQL measures for clinical trials.

MULTIDIMENSIONAL MEASURES

Some of the earliest and most influential uses of HRQL measures in clinical trials involved studies in which the investigators used a large number of fairly long scales covering numerous dimensions of HRQL (7,8). In some of the first trials using HRQL batteries this was appropriate because the analyses often were exploratory rather than testing a focused hypothesis.

Because of concerns about patient burden, researchers have devoted substantial effort to developing shorter scales of specific constructs and to reducing the overall length of HRQL assessments (28,29,31–36). In addition, as HRQL measures become more prominent in evaluations of the effectiveness of medical treatments, researchers have become more concerned about the potential problems associated with the statistical testing of multiple HRQL end points.

When there are multiple end points that are substantively similar and empirically correlated, this raises two main issues: how to adjust for multiple tests of related constructs and how to summarize the impact of a treatment on HRQL if the treatment has differential or even opposite effects on different domains of HRQL. These issues are even more complicated when an intervention involves a trade-off between survival and HRQL (37).

There are several approaches to analyzing multiple end points in clinical trials (38). One approach is to adjust the significance level for rejecting the null hypothesis using a technique such as Bonferroni adjustment. Another approach is to develop a global statistic for the null hypothesis of no treatment effect versus the alternative hypothesis that one treatment is better than the other for HRQL as a whole (38,39). The problem with adjusting the significance level for multiple correlated measures is that such an approach may underestimate the significance of certain results. A related problem with developing a global statistic for multiple, related end points is that such a statistic may obscure important differences among the effects on different outcomes.

A third way to combine information about different aspects of HRQL is to use value measures or utilities to weight different aspects of HRQL or to use them as summary measures of HRQL. The term *utility* has both a general and a specific meaning (37). Broadly, it refers to the level of satisfaction or enjoyment experienced by a person in a particular state. Essentially, utilities are cardinal values representing preferences for health states on a scale on which 0 represents death and 1.0 represents perfect health. One can use either ratings or equivalence measures to establish utilities (40,41). Equivalence measures ask the respondent to compare a health state with an explicit metric such as time, money, another health state, or willingness to take risk (37).

Although the idea of using a single metric that incorporates information about utilities to summarize a person's HRQL has great appeal, it is fraught with difficulties. One problem is that utility measures undoubtedly are a function of both individual and situational factors, as well as health status (42). Probably partly because of this, several studies have found that health value measures tend to be less responsive to clinical change than health status measures (9,18, 43–47).

A fourth approach to HRQL assessment that obviates some of these potential problems is to specify more precisely the hypothesized relationships among measures, as described above, and delineate more clearly between primary and secondary end points. For example, if a drug for treating persons with AIDS is expected primarily to have a beneficial effect on fatigue, relative to another treatment, fatigue could be defined as a primary end point. In such a situation, it might be important to know how strongly fatigue was related to physical and social functioning and how strongly differences in fatigue levels were related in overall assessments of HRQL. These later questions could be specified as based on secondary end points. Thus, with a clearer theoretical formulation of HRQL hypotheses, investigators could use nominal significance levels for testing primary end points and retain the ability to examine the more diffuse impact of an intervention on multiple aspects of HRQL.

ANALYTIC MODELS

The vast majority of research on the development of HRQL scales has been based on the premises of, and used the analytic techniques of, classic test theory (48, cf. 49). Among the limitations of this approach are that it is difficult to distinguish between the influences of respondent and item characteristics on observed responses, and item characteristics are a function of the group within which they were developed. One consequence of this is that items or scales that are developed in one patient population may not perform the same way in dissimilar populations. For example, if the health state in two subject groups is different, the HRQL scores may have different amounts of measurement error in the two populations. Classical test theory cannot predict how individuals will respond to questions unless those items have previously been administered to similar individuals (50).

An alternative model for measure development is item response theory (IRT) (50). With respect to HRQL, the basic postulates of IRT are that responses to a scale item are a function of the underlying health state of the individual and that the relationship between patients' responses to a particular question and health state can be described by a monotonically increasing function called an item characteristic curve.

Analytic techniques based on item response theory can provide (a) item characteristics that are not group-dependent, (b) data describing respondent characteristics that are not scale dependent, (c) a model that is expressed at the item level rather than at the test level, (d) a model that does not require parallel tests for assessing reliability, and (e) a model that provides a measure of precision for each score.

These techniques can be extremely useful for developing scales that perform well in the target population and for avoiding problems sometimes encountered when using scales developed using classic test theory in new populations, such as ceiling and floor effects (51).

IRT techniques also can be used to test whether items function differently in different subsets of respondents (differential item functioning). A common criticism of clinical trials in recent years has been that clinical trial populations do not adequately represent the types of persons for whom the intervention being evaluated is applicable. Specifically, women and older persons (52) have not been represented adequately in certain types of evaluations, and there is increasing sensitivity to the need to include persons of different racial and ethnic backgrounds in clinical trials.

As the criteria for clinical trial enrollment become more inclusive, it will be increasingly important to ensure that HRQL scales "function" the same in different subsets of study populations. Most existing health status and quality of life patient questionnaires and interviews have been developed and standardized in the United States, and to a lesser extent in the United Kingdom (53,54). The vast majority of these studies have been conducted with English-speaking subjects and little attention has been devoted to the influence of native language or culture on the validity of scale responses.

There are technical, linguistic, and conceptual issues involved in translating quality of life instruments into different languages (53–56). A substantial amount of work has been conducted developing French, Spanish, Swedish, Catalan, and Italian versions of the Nottingham Health Profile (53,54, 57,58). Several investigators also have developed Spanish translations of the Sickness Impact Profile (59–61) and several research groups have investigated factors affecting the validity of health surveys in Hispanic populations (56,62,63). A five-country consortium currently is developing a generic instrument for describing and valuing HRQL (64).

Although some work that has been done in this area is reassuring, there is also evidence that there may be large, systematic differences in the ways different types of respondents interpret and respond to certain HRQL measures, and there may be important gaps in the spectrum of health states assessed by some widely used scales, even among English-speaking subjects (49).

Given these types of findings and the availability of software based on IRT, we expect that researchers will increasingly use IRT analytic techniques to ensure adequate and efficient coverage of the spectrum of underlying health states of interest, using items that function in comparable ways in different types of respondents.

INTERPRETING MEANINGFUL DIFFERENCES

In addition to the need for more widespread use of explicit theoretical models and improved analytic treatment of HRQL data, there also is a need to develop better methods for presenting the results of HRQL assessments in a way that is intuitively meaningful for patients, clinicians, and policy makers. The interpretation of the relative risk or relative odds of dying is often difficult and the interpretation of risk information is extremely complicated (65–67). Nevertheless, a reduction in the probability of death or a reduction in specific symptoms is relatively easy to explain. It is more difficult to quantify and explain an important or meaningful difference in HRQL (68–71).

There are several definitions of clinically important change that correspond to the perspective of the evaluator. Jaeschke et al. (68) have defined minimal important difference as the smallest difference that patients perceive and that would mandate a change in clinical management. This definition combines the perspective of the patient and clinician. It may be desirable to evaluate these separately.

It is possible to have clinicians provide judgments about scores that are clinically significant. For example, in a study using the Functional Status Questionnaire, the investigators showed clinicians different combinations of item responses that would result in specific scale scores and asked them to determine scores that they thought were clinically significant (72).

However, the patient's perspective often is different from the physician's perspective for a variety of reasons. There is substantial data showing that physicians frequently are inaccurate when they are asked to estimate patients' functional status, or other aspects of HRQL (73–75). A factor that may influence physicians' evaluation of the importance of changes in different dimensions of HRQL is the extent to which the dimension of HRQL under consideration is related to factors that can be modified by medical treatment (20).

Another perspective is that of a third party responsible for paying for medical care or a regulatory agency responsible for approving a medicine or treatment for reimbursement, e.g., the Federal Drug Administration (27). In this case, considerations such as the relationship between cost of care and degree of improvement may be critical, although numerous factors influence such decisions (76,77). Economic and regulatory considerations are discussed at length in other chapters in this volume so I will comment only on the patient and physician perspectives.

There are several ways of using information from patients to evaluate the significance of changes in HRQL scale scores. One is to describe a scale score change in terms of the typical change in component items. For example, scores on the Intermediate Activities of Daily Living (IADL) scale from the Functional Status Questionnaire (FSQ) are a function of responses to six questions about how much difficulty a person had doing different activities in the previous month (78). Often FSQ scores are scaled so that the possible range is 0 to 100. Such scores are useful because the potential range is apparent, but they are difficult to interpret in terms of the content of the questions.

One approach is to describe the likelihood of a particular question at different scores. For example, one could compute the proportion of persons with different scores (e.g., 60, 70, 80, etc.) who had a great deal of difficulty walking one block or climbing one flight of stairs. One problem with this approach is that such associations tend to be group specific. That is, different types of patients with comparable scores may have different types of limitations.

Another approach is to relate HRQL scores to an associated, clinically meaningful, symptom. For patients with cardiovascular disease, for example, it is possible to calculate the average IADL score for patients with different classes of angina.

Finally, it is possible to relate changes in HRQL scores to patients' perceptions of change. From the patient's perspective one can think of what psychologists refer to as a "just noticeable difference"; one can ask patients to evaluate the size of the change (e.g., not at all, somewhat, a lot), or ask patients to evaluate the importance or impact of the change. Guyatt and colleagues (68,70,79), for example, have related change scores in HRQL to patients' perception of improvement and suggested that a change score of 0.5 on a seven-point scale can be considered a minimal important difference.

If there were consensus among patients about what degree of change is important, this would greatly simplify the task of interpreting scale score changes. However, unpublished analyses by our group on this issue using HRQL data collected from patients treated for nine medical and surgical conditions suggest several reasons for caution. First, for each condition we find tremendous heterogeneity among subjects with respect to their subjective evaluation of comparable changes in HRQL scores. Furthermore, there appear to be large systematic differences among conditions in the way patients evaluate comparable changes in HRQL scale scores. Nevertheless, we think Guyatt and his colleagues have suggested a potentially important way of using patient perceptions to help calibrate the meaning of HRQL scale score changes. We think this will be an interesting area of research in coming years.

CONCLUSIONS

Many of the methodological and practical problems limiting the use of HRQL measures in clinical trials have been solved. As a result, their use is increasing rapidly. However, as such measures have become more accepted and widely used in clinical trials they also have become subject to greater scrutiny. It is impossible to predict the areas in which we will see the most interesting and important substantive and methodological advances in the coming years. We have outlined several areas we think researchers will focus on in the near future. These topics undoubtedly will account for only a small proportion of the research in this area, but they illustrate some of the challenges and opportunities in this exciting and growing field.

ACKNOWLEDGMENTS

Work on this chapter was supported in part by PORT Grant R01-HS06341 from the Agency for Health Care Policy and Research and the MacArthur Foundation Research Network on Successful Midlife Development.

REFERENCES

1. Deyo RA. Measuring functional outcomes in therapeutic trials for chronic disease. *Controlled Clin Trials* 1984;5:223–240.
2. Deyo RA, Patrick DL. Barriers to the use of health status measures in clinical investigation, patient care, and policy research. *Med Care* 1989;27:S254–S268.
3. Fayers PM, Jones DR. Measuring and analyzing quality of life in cancer clinical trials: a review. *Stat Med* 1983;2:429–446.
4. de Haes JCJM, van Knippenberg FCE. The quality of life of cancer patients: a review of the literature. *Soc Sci Med* 1985;20:809–817.
5. McMillen-Moinpour C, Feigl P, Metch B, Hayden KA, Meyskens FL, Crowley J. Quality of life end points in cancer clinical trials: review and recommendations. *J Natl Cancer Inst* 1989;81:485–495.
6. Aaronson NK, Meyerowitz BE, Bard M, et al. Quality of life research in oncology. Past achievements and future priorities. *Cancer* 1991;67:839–843.
7. Croog SH, Levine S, Testa MA, et al. The effects of antihypertensive therapy on the quality of life. *N Engl J Med* 1986;314:1657–1664.
8. Bombardier C, Ware J, Russell IJ, Larson M, Chalmers A, Read JL,

and the Auranofin Cooperating Group. Auranofin therapy and quality of life in patients with rheumatoid arthritis. *Am J Med* 1986;81:565–578.
9. Canadian Erythropoietin Study Group. Association between recombinant human erythropoietin and quality of life and exercise capacity of patients receiving haemodialysis. *Br Med J* 1990;300:573–578.
10. Cleary PD, Epstein AM, Oster G, et al. Health-related quality of life among patients undergoing percutaneous transluminal coronary angioplasty. *Med Care* 1991;29:939–950.
11. Dwosh IL, Giles AR, Ford PM, et al. Plasmapheresis therapy in rheumatoid arthritis. *N Engl J Med* 1983;308:1124–1129.
12. Meenan RM, Anderson JJ, Kazis LE, Egger MJ, Altz-Smith M, et al. Outcome assessment in clinical trials: evidence for the sensitivity of a health status measure. *Arthritis Rheum* 1984;27:1344–1351.
13. Ware JE Jr, Brook RH, Williams RN, et al. *Conceptualization and measurement of health for adults in the Health Insurance Study.* Model of health and methodology, vol 1. DHEW Publ No. R-1987/1. Santa Monica, CA: Rand Corp, 1981.
14. Guyatt GH, VanZanten SJOV, Feeney DH, Patrick DL. Measuring quality of life in clinical trials: a taxonomy and review. *Can Med Assoc J* 1989;140:1441–1448.
15. Patrick DL, Bergner M. Measurement of health status in the 1990's. *Annu Rev Public Health* 1990;11:165–183.
16. Greenfield S, Nelson EC. Recent developments and future issues in the use of health status assessment measures in clinical settings. *Med Care* 1992;30:MS23–MS41.
17. Guyatt GH, Van Zanten SJOV, Feeney DH, Patrick DL. Measuring quality of life in clinical trials: a taxonomy and review. *Can Med Assoc J* 1989;140:1441–1448.
18. Guyatt G, Feeny D, Patrick D. Issues in quality-of-life measurement in clinical trials. *Controlled Clin Trials* 1991;12:81S–90S.
19. Cleary PD, Wilson IB, Fowler FJ Jr. Health related quality of life in persons with AIDS: a conceptual model. In: Dimsdale JE, Baum A, eds. *Perspectives on behavioral medicine.* Northvale, NJ: Lawrence Erlbaum, 1995:191–204.
20. Wilson IB, Cleary PD. Linking clinical variables with health-related quality of life: a causal model of patient outcomes. *JAMA* 1995;273:59–65.
21. Bergner M. Measurement of health status. *Med Care* 1985;23:696–704.
22. Nagi S. Some conceptual issues in disability and rehabilitation. In: Sussman MB, ed. *Sociology and rehabilitation.* Washington, DC: American Sociological Association, 1965.
23. Read JL, Quinn RJ, Hoefer MA. Measuring overall health: an evaluation of three important approaches. *J Chronic Dis* 1987;40:7S–21S.
24. Verbrugge LM. Physical and social disability in adults. In: Hibbard H, Nutting PA, Grady ML, eds. *Primary care research: theory and methods.* Washington, DC: U.S. Dept. of Health and Human Services, 1991:31–53.
25. Johnson RJ, Wolinsky FD. The structure of health status among older adults: disease, disability, functional limitation, and perceived health. *J Health Soc Behav* 1993;34:105–121.
26. Elegant VA. Quality of life in multi-centre trials. *Respir Med* 1991;85:39–41.
27. Smith ND. Quality of life studies from the perspective of an FDA reviewing statistician. *Drug Info J* 1993;27:617–623.
28. McHorney CA, Ware JE Jr, Raczek AE. The MOS 36-item short-form health survey (SF-36): II. Psychometric and clinical tests of validity in measuring physical and mental health conditions. *Med Care* 1993;31:247–263.
29. McHorney CA, Ware JE, Lu JFR, Sherbourne CD. The MOS short-form health survey (SF-36): III. Tests of data quality, scaling assumptions, and reliability across diverse patient groups. *Med Care* 1994;32:40–66.
30. Cleary PD, Fowler FJ, Weissman J, et al. Health-related quality of life in persons with AIDS. *Med Care* 1993;31:569–580.
31. Parkerson GR, Broadhead WE, Tse CJ. The Duke Health Profile: a 17-item measure of health and dysfunction. *Med Care* 1990;28:1056–1072.
32. Hunt SM, McEwen J, McKenna SP. Measuring health status: a new tool for clinicians and epidemiologists. *J R Coll Gen Pract* 1985;35:185–188.
33. Nelson EC, Wasson JH, Krik JW. Assessment of function in routine clinical practice: description of the COOP chart method and preliminary findings. *J Chronic Dis* 1987;40(s1):55S–63S.
34. Stewart AL, Hays RD, Ware JE Jr. The MOS short-form General

Health Survey: reliability and validity in a patient population. *Med Care* 1988;26:724–735.

35. McHorney CA, Ware JE, Rogers W, Raczek AE, Lu JFR. The validity and relative precision of MOS short- and long-form health status scales and Dartmouth COOP charts. *Med Care* 1992;30:MS253–MS265.

36. Ware JE, Sherbourne CD. The MOS 36-item short-form health survey (SF-36): I. Conceptual framework and item selection. *Med Care* 1992;30:473–483.

37. Tsevat J, Weeks JC, Guadagnoli E, et al. Health-related quality of life information: clinical encounters, clinical trials, and health policy. *J Gen Intern Med* 1994;9:30–41.

38. Pocock SJ, Geller NL, Tsiatis AA. The analysis of multiple endpoints in clinical trials. *Biometrics* 1987;43:487–498.

39. Tandon PK. Applications of global statistics in analyzing quality of life data. *Stat Med* 1990;9:819–827.

40. Froberg DG, Kane RL. Methodology for measuring health-state preferences—I: Measurement strategies. *J Clin Epidemiol* 1989A;42:345–354.

41. Froberg DG, Kane RL. Methodology for measuring health-state preferences—IV: Progress and a research agenda. *J Clin Epidemiol* 1989B;42:675–685.

42. Fowler FJ Jr, Cleary PD, Massagli MP, Weissman J, Epstein A. The role of reluctance to give up life in the measurement of health status. *Med Decis Making* 1995. In press.

43. Tsevat J, Goldman L, Soukup JR, et al. Stability of time-tradeoff utilities in survivors of myocardial infarction. *Med Decis Making* 1993;13:161–165.

44. Llewellyn-Thomas HA, Sutherland HJ, Theil EC. Do patients' evaluations of a future health state change when they actually enter that state? *Med Care* 1993;31:1002–1012.

45. Llewellyn-Thomas HA, Sutherland HJ, Ciampi A, Etezadi-Amoli J, Boyd NF, Till JE. The assessment of values in laryngeal cancer: reliability of measurement methods. *J Chronic Dis* 1993;37:283–291.

46. O'Connor AM, Boyd NF, Warde P, Stolbach L, Till JE. Eliciting preferences of alternative drug therapies in oncology: influence of treatment outcome description, elicitation technique and treatment experience on preferences. *J Chronic Dis* 1987;40:811–818.

47. Katz JN, Phillips CB, Fossel AH, Liang MH. Stability and responsiveness of utility measures. *Med Care* 1994;32:183–188.

48. FM Lord, Novick MR. *Statistical theories of mental test scores.* Reading, MA: Addison-Wesley, 1968.

49. Haley SM, McHorney CA, Ware JE. Evaluation of the MOS SF-36 physical functioning scale (PF-10): I. Unidimensionality and reproducibility of the Rasch item scale. *J Clin Epidemiol* 1994;47:671–684.

50. Lord FM. *Applications of item response theory to practical testing problems.* Hillsdale, NJ: LawrenceErlbaum, 1980.

51. Bindman AB, Keane D, Lurie N. Measuring health changes among severely ill patients: the floor phenomenon. *Med Care* 1990;28:1142–1152.

52. Wenger NK, ed. *Inclusion of elderly individuals in clinical trials.* Kansas City: Marion Merrell Dow, 1993.

53. Hunt SM. Cross-cultural issues in the use of socio-medical indicators. *Health Policy* 1986;6:149–158.

54. Hunt SM, Alonso J, Bucquet D, Niero M, Wiklund I, McKenna S. Cross-cultural adaptation of health measures. *Health Policy* 1991;19:33–44.

55. Phililps HP. Problems of translation and meaning in field work. *Human Organization* 1959;18:184–192.

56. Aday LA, Chiu GY, Andersen R. Methodological issues in health care surveys of the Spanish heritage population. *Am J Public Health* 1980;70:367–374.

57. Alonso J, Anto JM, Moreno C. Spanish version of the Nottingham Health Profile: translation and preliminary validity. *Am J Public Health* 1990;80:704–708.

58. Bucquet D, Condon S, Ritchie K. The French version of the Nottingham Health Profile. A comparison of items weights with those of the source version. *Soc Sci Med* 1990;30:829–835.

59. Gilson BS, Erickson D, Chavez CT, Bobbitt RA, Bergner M, Carter WB. A Chicano version of the sickness impact profile (SIP). *Cult Med Psychiatry* 1980;4:137–150.

60. Deyo RA. Pitfalls in measuring the health status of Mexican Americans; comparative validity of the english and spanish sickness impact profile. *Am J Public Health* 1984;74:569–573.

61. Hendricson WD, Russell IJ, Prihoda TJ, Jacobson JM, Rogan A, Bishop GD. An approach to developing a valid Spanish language translation of a health-status questionnaire. *Med Care* 1989;27:959–966.

62. Berkanovic E. The effect of inadequate language translation on Hispanics' responses to health surveys. *Am J Public Health* 1980;70:1273–1276.

63. Howard CA, Samet JM, Buechley RW, Schrag SD, Key CR. Survey research in New Mexico Hispanics: some methodological issues. *Am J Epidemiol* 1983;117:27–34.

64. Brooks RG, Jendteg S, Lindgren B, Persson U, Bjork S. EuroQol: health-related quality of life measurement. Results of the Swedish questionnaire exercise. *Health Policy* 1991;18:37–48.

65. Weinstein ND. Optimistic biases about personal risk. *Science* 1989;246:1232–1234.

66. Slovic P. Perception of risk. *Science* 1987;236:280–285.

67. Zeckhauser RJ, Viscusi WK. Risk within reason. *Science* 1990;248:559–564.

68. Jaeschke R, Singer J, Guyatt GH. Measurement of health states. Ascertaining the minimal clinically important difference. *Controlled Clin Trials* 1989;10:407–415.

69. Jaeschke R, Guyatt GH, Keller J, Singer J. Interpreting changes in quality-of-life score in NN of 1 randomized trials. *Controlled Clin Trials* 1991;12:226S–233S.

70. Juniper EF, Guyatt GH, Willan A, Griffith LE. Determining a minimal important change in a disease-specific quality of life questionnaire. *J Clin Epidemiol* 1994;47:81–87.

71. Guadagnoli E, Nordberg P, Cleary PD. Interpreting change in health-related quality of life scores (unpublished manuscript). 1995.

72. Jette AM, Davies AR, Cleary PD, et al. The Functional Status Questionnaire: its reliability and validity when used in primary care. *J Gen Intern Med* 1986;1:143–149.

73. Calkins DR, Rubenstein LV, Cleary PD, et al. Failure of physicians to recognize functional disability in ambulatory patients. *Ann Intern Med* 1991;114:451–454.

74. Nelson EC, Conger B, Douglass R. Functional health status levels of primary care patients. *JAMA* 1983;249:3331–3338.

75. Wartman SA, Morlock LL, Malitz FE, Palm E. Impact of divergent evaluations of physicians and patients of patients' complaints. *Public Health Rep* 1983;98:141–145.

76. Mechanic D. Establishing mental health priorities. *Milbank Q* 1994;72:501–514.

77. Pollack DA, McFarland BH, George RA, Angell RH. Prioritization of mental health services in Oregon. *Milbank Q* 1994;72:515–550.

78. Cleary PD, Greenfield S, McNeil BJ. Assessing quality of life after surgery. *Controlled Clin Trials* 1991;12:189S–203S.

79. Guyatt GH, Nogradi S, Halcrow S, et al. Development and testing of a new measure of health status for clinical trials in heart failure. *J Gen Intern Med* 1989;4:101–107.

Quality of Life and Pharmacoeconomics in Clinical Trials, Second Edition, edited by B. Spilker.
Lippincott-Raven Publishers, Philadelphia © 1996.

CHAPTER 11

Economic Scales and Tests

Henry G. Grabowski and Ronald W. Hansen

INTRODUCTION

Just as medical decision makers must be concerned with assessing the merits of alternative therapeutic modalities, economists are involved with assessing the merits of alternative allocations of resources. Health care decisions involve both changes in health outcomes and in allocations of resources. It should not be surprising that there are considerable areas of health care in which the decision process is of interest to and affected by both medical professionals and economists. The development of quality of life indices and their application is one area of mutual concern. This chapter focuses on those indices that are linked to economic concerns even though their application does not necessarily require economic training.

To place the economic measures of quality of life assessments in perspective, one should consider the types of issues that are of concern to economists. Generally economists are concerned with the allocation of resources to alternative ends or objectives. Resources are broadly defined to include not only natural resources but also a wide variety of factors involved in the production of goods and services such as labor, capital equipment, knowledge, skills, and location. The objectives may be stated in terms of the production of goods and services but ultimately involve the satisfaction of individual wants and desires.

When considering the production of goods and services, economists are often concerned with the efficiency of the

production process, i.e., what is the least costly way of producing a given product or service? Economists also study consumer decisionmaking, frequently considering how individuals select varying combinations of goods and services to maximize their well-being. These two areas can be combined to address the question of how to allocate resources to the production of the set of goods and services that maximize consumer well-being or utility.

Although economists frequently use the terms *utility, individual well-being,* and *satisfaction,* there is no consensus on how to measure these domains. We can often identify changes that increase or decrease individual satisfaction, but attempts to quantify the level of satisfaction are fraught with many problems. Moreover, even if one were satisfied with a scale for a particular individual, it is impossible to make interpersonal comparisons of utility. The question "Has John reached a higher level of utility or satisfaction than Harry?" is not answerable.

Individuals can increase their utility by exchanging goods and services in the marketplace at prices expressed in monetary units such as dollars. We can compare individuals' income or wealth in dollar terms, and increases or decreases in income or wealth can be translated into increases or decreases in the utility levels achievable by individuals. Even though the ultimate objective may be expressed as improving the well-being of individuals, dollar values are used for the analytical purpose of assessing programs. Wherever possible economists tend to measure goods and services in common dollar units. However, this is difficult to do for many health-related issues since there is no explicit market for states of health. One cannot directly buy relief from pain or elimination of heart disease; one can only purchase medical services or products that may cure or alleviate health problems. Given

H. G. Grabowski: Department of Economics, Duke University, Durham, North Carolina 27708.
R. W. Hansen: Simon Graduate School of Business Administration, University of Rochester, Rochester, New York 14627.

the absence of market prices, economists have devised various methods to value health states. We will consider three such measures and describe how they can be incorporated into clinical trials.

One should note a caveat that applies to many other quality of life measures. For the purposes of many evaluations one is concerned with aggregate or average values. Thus, the empirical basis for estimation is a representative sample. However, when the question involves choices for a specific individual, in most instances the preferences and values of that individual should be given greater weight. Clearly, the basis for establishing values must be consistent with their eventual use. Where resources are provided through public sources and trade-offs are involved in their application to alternative programs, the issue of how to value the preferences of different individuals with stakes in the decision process must be explicitly faced by the decision maker (1).

PRODUCTIVITY OR HUMAN CAPITAL MODELS

The two major financial costs of disease are treatment costs and the loss in productivity during the course of the disease or subsequent disability. The productivity effects of death and disability have been incorporated in cost-benefit studies of health programs and in a variety of projects affecting public safety such as highway improvements and flood control projects. A review undertaken by the U.S. Congress of Technology Assessment (2) provides numerous examples of such approaches in the health area. In some applications market-based productivity changes have been the sole measure of the value of programs affecting death and disability.

One way of viewing this approach is to consider it as valuing individuals only for their productivity, much as one might value investment in industrial equipment. Loss of human capital, whether in the form of death or diminished capacity, reduces the ability of the economy to produce much like the destruction or impairment of capital equipment. However, such a narrow valuation of humans does not accord with values expressed in other contexts. Most defenders of the measure do not argue that productivity is the only measure of the value that should be placed on changes of an individual's well-being. They will generally claim that it is an important portion of the value and that it should be adjusted to reflect other less well defined and measured values. Although "quality of life" certainly implies more than lost workplace activity, work remains one of the major human activities and the impact of disease on work will be reflected in other aspects of an individual's life condition. Loss of income may have serious impact on the other dimensions of the life, including effects on one's family.

A practical reason for the reliance on lost productivity or human capital approaches is the ease with which these changes in human conditions can be translated into dollar values for inclusion in cost-benefit studies. Their status is further enhanced by their use in civil court cases as the basis for the economic losses suffered in death and disability cases. Despite the theoretical shortcomings, they are often an acceptable measure that can be an important component of cost-benefit analyses tied to clinical trials.

The methodology for calculating lost productivity is at once both extremely straightforward and potentially complex. The complexity is a function of the disease/disability and of the occupation of the individual. Some very simple cases will be examined here, then complexities will be introduced.

The easiest case to consider is an acute illness that before its appearance has no effect on the patient's ability to perform his occupational activities. At a definable point the disease incidence begins, therapy is administered, and following a recuperation period the patient is restored to his/her predisease state with no subsequent impact on the ability to perform occupational activities. In this event all the productivity effects are measurable within the period from disease onset to recovery.

When examining lost productivity, one should be careful to separate productivity from salary and wages. One of the basic premises of microeconomics is that in a well-functioning labor market, the employer pays the worker an amount that equals his/her marginal productivity. Hence the compensation of the employee equals the value of the employee's productivity. Compensation includes more than gross salary since the employer typically provides vacation pay, retirement (including employer's social security contribution), and health and disability insurance. Thus, should an individual be unable to work, the lost productivity is the full compensation, not just the net wage received by the employee.

Sick pay is often provided by employers and the income actually lost by the employee during the illness may be minimal. If one is concerned only with the employee perspective, then the effect of illness on his income will be reduced or possibly eliminated by sick pay or disability compensation. From a broader perspective, however, there is a loss equal to the employee's reduced productivity. If the employer is self-insured for sick pay or disability, then the lack of productivity, although not representing an income loss to the employee, will be a direct loss to the employer. Insurance merely affects the distribution of the loss. However, if the availability of insurance causes the worker to remain away from work beyond the period of full recovery, this is a productivity loss due to adverse insurance incentive effects. It is inappropriate to include this in the lost productivity associated with the illness, although these effects may be difficult to separate in actual practice.

In the simple case just constructed, information should be obtained on the extent of work loss over the duration of the illness and recovery period. Since the ability to return to work may be occupationally related, occupational information should be obtained. To translate the work days lost into a measure of lost productivity one requires an estimate of daily compensation, i.e., wages plus benefits.

It may be possible to obtain wage information from the individuals in a clinical trial, but this poses several problems.

First is the issue of data confidentiality. Most individuals are reluctant to share specific information about their income, and if participation in the clinical trials is voluntary, mandatory salary information may deter some individuals from participating. Second, if the objective of the economic portion of the study is to measure the impact on a general population, then the use of age and occupationally adjusted national average compensation information may be preferable. By using the income information from the study participants, one is in effect estimating general income levels from a sample that is small compared with other bases for income estimation.

The estimation process becomes more complex if the disease has produced a long-term impact on the individual's productivity. Individuals with the particular disability may be working at less than full normal capacity and may not be restored to full health. If one is analyzing two different treatments, in addition to determining work days lost, one needs to assess the level of productivity. For example, an individual whose normal occupation requires great manual dexterity may, as a result of arthritis, seek employment in an occupation requiring less dexterity. They may be fully employed but at a job that is less productive than the one for which they were originally trained, or the individual may remain in the same occupation but be less productive. Measuring days of work lost will not capture these reductions in productivity. The methods for measuring lost productivity through job switching will depend on the manner in which one expects the loss to manifest itself. The researcher may be required to collect information on job history with particular emphasis on job changes occasioned by the disease.

Many individuals are not members of the market labor force but are nevertheless productive in household or other activities. This productivity may also be impaired by disease or disability and the value of this lost productivity should be calculated. Since there is no specific market wage, alternative methods for valuing this productivity must be used. Since many of these activities are replicated in the marketplace, researchers have valued them by utilizing the rates charged for cleaning services, meal preparation, child care, etc. The average daily economic value of homemaker services is comparable to the average marketplace compensation for females according to some studies.[1] During the clinical investigation, information on the change in activities should be obtained and then later analyzed to see how sensitive the evaluation of the program is to variations in the methods of valuing time in nonmarket activities.

In collecting activity data, one may be able to specify particular days during which individuals not in the market labor force are unable to perform their normal activities. What is often the case, however, is that these individuals continue with some but not all of their daily activities. For example, the housewife may continue to perform some of her activities, but the remainder are either postponed, performed by other family members, or hired out. An analysis of the extent of lost productivity requires follow-up interviews.

For productivity effects that occur over lengthy periods of time, it is appropriate to adjust future values by a "discount rate." This reflects the time preference of individuals for present over future economic benefits, as well as the fact that economic resources can be productively invested for future gains. These factors provide the basis for a positive rate of interest in market economies. Although discounting is employed in economic analyses involving multiple time periods, no general consensus exists as to the specific discount or market interest rate that should be employed in cost-benefit analysis of health programs (7). In the absence of consensus, many researchers use a range of plausible values and then perform a sensitivity analysis on how the discount rate parameter influences the results. Sensitivity analyses are appropriately employed for all parameters subject to uncertainty and measurement error. One special group worth noting in this context is the case of children. For this group, the human capital approach focuses on how the economic present value of expected lifetime earnings is affected by long-term illness or disability. Given the long time horizons involved and the greater uncertainty involving in these economics calculations, a sensitivity analysis with respect to the discount factor and other economic parameters is generally undertaken as an integral part of the analysis.

Viscusi and Moore have used data from labor market experiences, where workers are making long-term decisions on job market risks, to compute a plausible range on the discount rate (8). Using a variety of economic techniques, they find discount rates that vary from 1% to 14%. This range encompasses normal market rates of interest. As a consequence, they suggest using prevailing market rates in discounting health effects in medical decisions. In fact, many cost-effectiveness studies use a discount rate of 5% as their baseline value (8).

The productivity or human capital approach to valuing the effect of disease on the quality of life admittedly captures only a portion of the effect on quality of life. It measures health and quality of life as though they are a unit of production, not as something of intrinsic value. As long as leisure and consumption have positive values, the human capital approach will provide lower bound estimates of quality of life (9). By its construction it also values the health of high earners more than of low wage earners, a feature that many individuals find objectionable. This may have program implications since some diseases are more prevalent among individuals in their high income working years, whereas other conditions are more prevalent among individuals who have retired from the labor force.

Despite these shortcomings, productivity effects may prove to be a useful proxy for quality of life effects in certain circumstances. For example, productivity may be useful when one is focusing on a homogeneous group of patients and where job market performance is an important component of well-being. Furthermore, it is often easier to collect data on this measure than on some of the theoretically preferable alternatives discussed below. For these reasons, the human capital model has gained a fair degree of usage in the benefit-cost studies as well as in the tort litigation process.

THE WILLINGNESS-TO-PAY CONCEPT

In assessing the value of goods and services to individuals, economists often employ the concept of willingness to pay. The act of market exchange is an expression of the willingness of individuals to give up some goods or services in exchange for other goods and services. In most instances, money acts as a medium of exchange, breaking the direct link between items sold and items purchased in exchange.

To assess the value of different health states or quality of life, it is natural to determine the values in the manner in which the marketplace determines other values, i.e., by the willingness to pay for improved health or quality of life. As noted earlier there are no explicit markets for health, so one must uncover ways to calculate willingness to pay. The approaches taken can be divided into questionnaire-based and revealed preference–based methods.

Questionnaire-Based Models

Questionnaire-based willingness to pay approaches basically attempt to have the respondent estimate the value placed on different health states or quality of life. Designing a willingness-to-pay survey demands considerations similar to those for other survey research including the quality of life measures discussed in greater detail in other chapters. One must be concerned with validity and reliability as well as ease of administration (10–12). The questions may ask for direct responses for the items to be valued, use some forms of paired comparisons, or seek to value the specific attributes of the item or state, and aggregate to produce a value for the total. Specific issues arising when dollar values are involved in a health survey should be addressed.

In most instances the survey questions elicit a response for willingness to pay for an improvement or to prevent a worsening of health status. In such instances the respondents' evaluation will be affected by their income or assets, i.e., we should expect on average that wealthy individuals will be willing to pay a larger dollar amount for a given improvement than will a poor individual (although the percentage of income or wealth may be similar). Thus the willingness-to-pay approach, like the human capital productivity approach, is also influenced by an individual's income.[2]

An alternative formulation reverses the question to ask how large a payment would be required for the individual to willingly accept a reduction in health state or to forgo an improvement. Since the response is not bounded by the individual's current assets, the values are likely to be larger and there is a presumption that there would be less of an income bias, although it is probably not eliminated.

A general criticism of questionnaire-based estimates is that they are not validated. Opinions are being solicited about hypothetical situations that may be far removed from the experience of the respondent. A healthy individual may have great difficulty imagining how his life would change were he partially paralyzed and hence have a hard time assessing his willingness to pay to avoid this condition. If the payment is hypothetical, i.e., he will not be charged based on his answer, his answer may be quite different than in a situation in which he actually had to pay. There is also the problem of the respondent's giving an answer that he thinks the interviewer wants, particularly in personal interview situations using hypothetical payments.

In evaluating disease states in a clinical situation, the respondents have either experienced the health states being evaluated or have given more thought to the potential impact of these states. However, there is another potential source of bias produced by their status as a patient. They may believe that their answers to the questions may affect the amount that they have to pay or the type of therapy they receive. Care should be taken in the design of the study to minimize these potential sources of bias.[3]

The standard gamble approach has been employed to construct health indices (16). As explained in Chapter 12, this approach confronts the respondent with a choice between a certain event and a gamble that will result in either a better or worse state than the certain event. By determining the probability level at which individuals are indifferent about the gamble and the certain state, the relative value assigned to each state can be estimated. By including a dollar value as part of one of these states it is possible to translate this model into one that estimates dollar values for death or disease risks, for example, if the choice is between perfect health or a gamble that, if won, results in $10,000 plus retaining perfect health and, if lost, results in partial paralysis. The probability of winning, which makes the respondent indifferent between accepting the gamble or the certainty of perfect health, can be used to construct the respondent's assessment of the cost of paralysis. The rationale for this opinion-based method is similar to the revealed preference–based model discussed below.

Revealed Preference–Based Models

One of the difficulties with opinion-based willingness-to-pay models is that they usually measure what individuals state they would be willing to pay rather than measure what individuals do in fact pay. Several attempts have been made to develop willingness-to-pay measures based on actual behavior affecting health or quality of life. However, since there is not a direct market for health, this must be inferred from other actions.

Individuals make many decisions that involve risks of death and/or disability. These decisions include job choice, purchase of safety equipment, recreational activities, and diet. In these decisions they trade off potential changes in health states for other attributes such as income or pleasure. By observing the choices people make that involve risk of death or disability, one may be able to calculate the value individuals place on their health. The basic premise behind revealed preference–based models is that the observed choices reflect the individual's relative valuation of health and other attributes given the expected outcome probabilities.

There are many variations of revealed preference–based models, but most are based on the following. An individual chooses between two activities, A and B, that differ in two dimensions: income (or some surrogate) and risk of death or disability. Individuals who accept the higher-risk activity have revealed a willingness to face a higher probability of death/disability in return for an increase in income. For example, these individuals may choose an activity that exposes them to a 1 in 1,000 higher probability of death but offers a $2,000 higher income. These individuals value the 1 in 1,000 risk of death at a maximum value of $2,000. In some studies, linearity is assumed such that the implied "value of life" is $2 million.

Studies of this nature are relatively recent but have sparked a lot of controversy. Some assert that it is wrong for individuals to place a monetary value on their lives or health. While one could argue the merits of this position on ethical grounds, the empirical observations suggest that people do in fact risk life and limb for other objectives, including monetary rewards. A somewhat more neutral phrasing recognizes that death appears to be inevitable and that the question is one of changing the time of death rather than saving a life in perpetuity. Whereas most of the original work in this area was expressed as valuing a "life," more recent work has focused on valuing a life-year (17,18).

Even among individuals who are willing to accept the basic design of these studies there are questions about the validity of the results. One source of concern is the extent to which the choices are being made by fully informed individuals.[4] Are the probabilities of death or disabilities known to the individuals making the choice? To the extent that individuals act on incorrect estimates but the researcher uses true probabilities, the empirical estimates will be in error. For many occupations this difference may be substantial; however, for others the risks may be well known. Those who accept risky jobs (e.g., coal mining) may also have a constrained choice set due to limited mobility as well as information.

There is some evidence that individuals have difficulty dealing with low probability, high value events (19). The difference between a 1 in a million and a 1 in 10 million chance is a 10 to 1 ratio but may both be essentially zero to the average individual. Yet the risk faced in some occupations on a weekly or monthly basis are of this order of magnitude. Individuals, particularly healthy persons, may be myopic in dealing with questions concerning their own death.[5] The "it won't happen to me" phenomenon calls into question the rational choice-making assumptions of these revealed-preference models.

The existing revealed-preference studies for valuing life-years or quality of life have produced a relatively wide range of estimates.[6] It is probably too soon to use the results of a single study as the definitive estimate. However, despite the criticism of the existing risk assessment/revealed-preference models, they are a promising line of research. Most studies have been conducted using labor force data and the results are often intended to be used as inputs to assessments involving death and disease outcomes. These values may be used to value therapeutic choices, but the clinical setting offers some interesting possibilities for extending this research. Choices that individuals make regarding their own therapy in the face of different estimated outcomes can be used to derive relative values. Whether these can be expressed in dollar terms depends on the nature of the choices available.

CONCLUSIONS

The productivity/human capital approach has been the most frequently employed of the economic models used in quality of life assessments in clinical studies. Data on the work activities of the patients can be gathered to assess the lost productivity in a variety of disease and treatment combinations. The major problem with this measure is that it does not address quality of life per se, but rather the ability to perform workplace activities.

Willingness-to-pay models have the virtue (or vice) of attempting to value changes in health states or quality of life from the same perspective used to determine individual values for other goods and services. The methods for obtaining willingness-to-pay estimates are problematic. Opinion-based estimates suffer from several potential sources of bias. Revealed-preference models treat individuals as though they make well-informed choices in decisions involving risk of death and disability. This assumption may be far from the truth in some of the situations studied. These models have been developed relatively recently and with further work may produce very valuable results. Not only may they provide values to use in assessing clinical outcomes, but it may be possible to construct clinical trials that will advance our understanding of individuals' willingness to pay for changes in quality of life.

ENDNOTES

1. See the analysis of homemaker time valuation by the Institute of Life Insurance (3). Further information on the allocation of time to homemaker services and their valuation in the market is provided in Gauger and Walker (4), Mushkin and Landefeld (5), and Juster and Stafford (6).
2. Appel et al. (13) constructed willingness-to-pay measures for the reduced risks of side effects from radiographic contrast media. They found a positive relation between willingness to pay and income, but most individuals also exhibited a higher value for the superior contrast media than its cost. For other examples of willingness-to-pay studies, see Pauly (14).
3. In a recent survey, Kaplan (15) suggests that there is considerable homogeneity in the preferences across health states of patients and the general population, as reflected in the responses of some recent research studies.

4. In addition to information issues, there may well be unique properties of the risk that cannot be early captured in a hedonic regression analysis, and mortality and mortality risks may interact in a complex way that is difficult to estimate (14).
5. The low voluntary utilization rate for automobile seat belts, despite their high potential effectiveness in preventing many potential deaths and serious injuries, can be explained in part on such grounds (20).
6. For a review of recent studies, see Viscusi (21). One major reason for the difference in estimated values across studies is the different sample populations employed. Those studies that focus on a more risky set of occupations generally have found lower values of life. This reflects a self-selection process in job market choice. In particular, individuals who choose jobs with above-average risks generally have a greater preference for assuming risk in exchange for monetary compensation. Hence, estimates based on their behavior cannot be utilized as representative of the general population without some adjustments.

REFERENCES

1. Williams A. Measuring quality of life. In: Teeling Smith GS, ed. *Health economics: prospects for the future*. London: Office of Health Economics, 1987:200–210.
2. Office of Technology Assessment of the U.S. Congress. *The implications of cost-effectiveness analyses of medical technology*. Background paper 1. *Methodological issues and literature review*. Washington, DC: Government Printing Office, 1980.
3. Institute of Life Insurance. *Do you know what a homemaker is worth?* Institute of Life Insurance, 1978.
4. Gauger WH, Walker KE. *The dollar value of household work*. Information Bulletin 60. Ithaca, NY: Cornell University, 1980.
5. Mushkin SJ, Landefeld JS. *Non-health sector costs of illness*. Report A7. Washington, DC: Public Services Laboratory, Georgetown University, 1980.
6. Juster FT, Stafford FP. *Time goods and well being*. Ann Arbor, MI: University of Michigan, 1985.
7. Warner KE, Luce BR. *Cost benefit effectiveness analysis in health care*. Ann Arbor, MI: Health Administration Press, 1982.
8. Viscusi WK. Discounting health effects for medical decisions. In: Sloan FA, ed. *Valuing health care: cost benefits and effectiveness of pharmaceuticals and other medical technologies*. Cambridge: Cambridge University Press, 1994;125–147.
9. Berger MC, Blomquist GC, Kenkel D, Tolley GS. Valuing changes in health risks: a comparison of alternative measures. *Southern Econom J* 1989;53(4):967–984.
10. Brooks RG. *The development and construction of health status measures: an overview of the literature*. Lund: The Swedish Institute for Health Economics, 1986.
11. Kaplan RM, Bush JW, Berry C. Health status: types of validity and the index of well-being. *Health Serv Res* 1976;11:478–507.
12. Read JL, Quinn RJ, Hoefer MA. Measuring overall health: an evaluation of three important approaches. In: Lohr KN, Ware JE Jr, eds. *Advances in health assessment conference proceedings. J Chronic Dis* 1987;40 (suppl 1):7S–21S.
13. Appel LJ, Steinbert EP, Powe NR, Anderson GF, Dwyer SA, Faden RR. Risk reduction from low osmolality contrast medic—what do patients think it is worth? *Med Care* 1990;28 pt. 1(4):324–337.
14. Pauly MV. Valuing health care benefits in money terms. In: Sloan FA, ed. *Valuing health care: cost benefits and effectiveness of pharmaceuticals and other medical technologies*. Cambridge: Cambridge University Press, 1994;99–124.
15. Kaplan RM. Utility assessment for estimating quality-adjusted life year. In: Sloan FA, ed. *Valuing health care: cost benefits and effectiveness of pharmaceuticals and other medical technologies*. Cambridge: Cambridge University Press, 1994;31–60.
16. Torrance GW. Measurement of health state utilities for economic appraisal: a review. *J Health Econom* 1986;5:1–30.
17. Thaler R, Rosen S. The value of saving a life: evidence from the labor market. *Household Production and Consumption* 1976;265–302.
18. Moore MJ, Viscusi WK. The quantity adjusted value of life. *Econom Inquiry* 1988;26:369–388.
19. Kunreuther H. Limited knowledge and insurance protection. *Public Policy* 1976;24:229–261.
20. Arnould R, Grabowski H. Auto safety regulation: an analysis of market failure. *Bell J Econom* 1981;12:27–48.
21. Viscusi WK. The value of risks to life and health. *J Econom Literature* 1993;31:1912–1946.

Quality of Life and Pharmacoeconomics in Clinical Trials, Second Edition, edited by B. Spilker.
Lippincott-Raven Publishers, Philadelphia © 1996.

CHAPTER 12

Integrating Economic Evaluations and Quality of Life Assessments

David H. Feeny, George W. Torrance, and Roberta Labelle†

INTRODUCTION

The essence of economic evaluation is a comparison of the costs and consequences of alternative health care programs. There are a variety of meaningful ways to measure consequences. During the past two decades health-related quality of life measures have been developed, providing new and highly relevant approaches to assessing the consequences of the use of health care resources.

This chapter examines the strategies and implications of combining traditional methods of economic evaluation with the newer techniques for health-related quality of life assessment.[1] The major forms of economic evaluation are briefly described. A taxonomy for health-related quality of life assessment measures is presented. Practical and conceptual considerations of combining these methods are then discussed. Finally, the advantages and disadvantages of incorporating economic and health-related quality of life outcome measures concurrently in clinical trials are considered briefly.

MAJOR STUDY DESIGNS FOR ECONOMIC EVALUATION OF HEALTH CARE SERVICES

Economic evaluation relies upon the estimation of the dollar costs of providing alternative forms of health care services, for instance surgical versus medical therapy for the same condition or one drug regimen versus another. The dollar (or *pecuniary* in the jargon of the economist) costs include direct costs (items such as professional fees, drugs, hospitalization, diagnostic tests) and indirect costs (earnings of patient forgone as a result of treatment). The basic study designs for three major forms of economic evaluation are summarized in Table 1. In each case the costs of treatment are compared with the outcomes of treatment. In cost-effectiveness analysis (CEA), outcomes are measured in natural units of clinical effects. These units are typically the ones employed in clinical studies. They may be as narrow as millimeters of mercury for reductions in blood pressure or as broad as life-years gained for reductions in mortality. The key feature of the CEA design is that the analyst need not assign a dollar value to the outcome. The analyst can also continue to rely on standard clinical measures.

In cost-utility analysis (CUA), the measure of clinical effects is adjusted to reflect the health-related quality of life of the outcome. In this approach life-years are converted into quality-adjusted life years (methods for estimating the quality adjustments are discussed below). As in CEA the analyst is not required to place a dollar value on the outcome.

D. Feeny, G. W. Torrance: Department of Clinical Epidemiology and Biostatistics, Centre for Health Economics and Policy Analysis, Department of Economics, McMaster University, Hamilton, Ontario L8N 3Z5, Canada.
†R. Labelle: Deceased.

TABLE 1. *Major study designs for economic evaluations*

Type of analysis	Compares	To
Cost-effectiveness	$ Value of resources used up	Clinical effects
Cost-utility	$ Value of resources used up	Quality of life produced by the clinical effects
Cost-benefit	$ Value of resources used up	$ Value of resources saved or created

Based on ref. 5.

Unlike the CEA approach, however, the approach does explicitly incorporate health-related quality of life information in the results.

In cost-benefit analysis (CBA) costs and consequences are all expressed in pecuniary terms. This technique was first applied to the evaluation of public expenditures in water resource development. In the context of health care, however, most analysts have found CBA to be less satisfactory than CEA or CUA for several reasons. In particular, many analysts are uncomfortable with the ethical judgments that appear to accompany assigning dollar values to peoples's lives and their suffering. The result has been that CEA studies have become the dominant study design in health care evaluation.[2] In recent years, however, there has been a resurgence in interest in cost-benefit analyses, relying on elicitations from patients of willingness to pay as the source for the estimation of benefits expressed in pecuniary terms.

The focus in the health care evaluation literature on cost-effectiveness analysis has, in concert with the growth in the breadth of outcome measures for clinical studies, shifted toward comparing pecuniary and health-related quality of life outcome measures. The trend reflects two factors. First, as health care interventions are increasingly focused less on reducing mortality, and more on reducing morbidity and improving health-related quality of life, it has become more important to measure these outcomes directly and accurately. Second, clinical managers and third-party payers have become increasingly interested in the evaluation of new and existing treatment alternatives and have demanded evidence on costs and effects both in pecuniary and nonpecuniary terms.

TAXONOMY OF HEALTH-RELATED QUALITY OF LIFE MEASURES

A wide variety of health-related quality of life measures have emerged. Such a diversity is both inevitable and appro-

priate. Health-related quality of life is a broad multidimensional concept. Different measures may tap different domains of health-related quality of life. Investigators also have a variety of objectives and thus may require a battery of instruments for different questions and situations. In the discussion that follows the focus is on the measurement of health-related quality of life. A variety of other factors including socioeconomic status also influence overall quality of life. In the context of clinical studies, the implicit assumption is that these other factors may be ignored for the purposes of making comparisons of the quality of life impact among alternative treatments, thus justifying the development of instruments focused on health-related quality of life.

There are a number of ways to classify health-related quality of life measures. One classification scheme is presented in Table 2. Specific instruments are developed for application to particular populations. Typically these measures focus on the dimensions of health-related quality of life relevant to a particular disease (or health problem) and its treatment. By including only those elements that are most important in the particular clinical situation, these measures can be constructed to include a wide range of effects (for instance, physical function, emotional function, characteristics that are of special concern to individual patients) without imposing a large burden on respondents. These measures have usually also been constructed to maximize their responsiveness to change. A good example of a specific instrument is the Chronic Respiratory Disease Questionnaire developed by Guyatt et al. (10).

Generic instruments are suitable for use with virtually any (adult) population. Therefore, generic measures typically include a number of dimensions of health-related quality of life including physical function, social and emotional function, pain, and self-care.

It is useful to distinguish at least two major subcategories

TABLE 2. *Taxonomy of health-related quality of life assessment measures: category and examples*

Specific instruments
　Chronic Respiratory Questionnaire
　Arthritis Categorical Scale
　Arthritis Impact Measurement Set
Generic instruments
　Health profiles
　　Sickness Impact Profile
　　Nottingham Health Profile
　Utility measures
　　Visual analog scale
　　Time trade-off
　　Standard gamble
　　Multiattribute health status classification systems in combination with multiattribute preference functions

Based on refs. 7, 8, and 9.

of generic instruments: health profiles and utility measures. Health profiles provide separate scores for a number of categories or dimensions of health status or health-related quality of life. The profile may or may not allow for aggregation into a single summary score. The Sickness Impact Profile developed by Bergner et al. (11) is a good example of a health profile measure that allows for a single summary score. The Nottingham Health Profile (see Chapter 29) is one that does not.

Utility measures share some characteristics with health profiles and specific instruments. Like health profiles, utility measures are widely applicable. Utility instruments give scores on a very generalizable 0 (death) to 1 (perfect health) scale, thus facilitating broad comparisons of the effects of alternative health care programs. The design of utility measures for specific applications, however, allows the analyst to incorporate, as with specific instruments, items of particular importance or relevance in that setting. Health-state descriptions used with utility instruments typically include physical mobility, vision, hearing, speech, emotion, cognition, dexterity, and pain. A good example of the application of utility analysis to the measurement of health-related quality of life is found in the evaluation of neonatal intensive care by Boyle et al. (12). The approach has also been applied in a major clinical trial designed to investigate the health-related quality of life impact of a new oral gold compound for the treatment of arthritis by Bombardier et al. (13).

The utility approach has an advantage relative to the specific approach in that the patient globally assesses the net effect of the treatment on his/her health-related quality of life. Thus the patient's response summarizes his/her evaluation both of the positive treatment effects and the negative side effects. With specific instruments, these are measured separately and therefore the analyst has little or no information on the patient's trade-offs among the therapeutic improvements and treatment side effects. The same point applies to health-profile instruments for which no single summary score is available.

statistical tools for the analysis of data drawn from experience, but a much less extensive set of tools for the direct measurement of utility.

The standard approach of inferring preferences for health states from health care expenditures is, however, flawed for several reasons. First, the standard analysis rests upon an assumption of well-informed consumers. Thus, to make reliable inferences of health-state utilities from the expenditures of consumers, one would have to assume that consumers are well aware of the efficacy and effectiveness of the treatment alternatives and their consequences, and are making well-informed choices on the basis of their preferences. Many analysts (15,16) find this assumption in the context of health care to be highly questionable. Instead it is assumed that consumers seek the advice of an expert, a health care professional, in deciding what health care technologies are available, what their effects are, and what the best treatment plan for that particular person is. Accordingly, the actual expenditures reflect not only the preferences of the patient but the advice of the professional. Thus, to infer the preferences of patients from behavior that is not solely determined by patients may be unreliable.[4] Second, in most settings (at least within developed countries) patients have access to some form of third-party payment (health insurance) and thus do not bear fully the monetary cost of their treatment. Because of this cost sharing, it is again unlikely that preferences may reliably be inferred from health care expenditures. Third, some have advocated that in the willingness-to-pay approach (as an indirect method for assessing preferences) elicitations should focus on ''insurance-type'' questions— the subject's willingness to pay for a reduction in the probability of contracting an illness in the future (18). Although conceptually appealing, the feasibility of this approach is questionable. Substantial evidence from psychology and decision science indicates that subjects typically have difficulty understanding complex probabilistic questions. Thus the usefulness of the empirical results of such approaches remains to be demonstrated.

THE UTILITY MEASUREMENT OF HEALTH-RELATED QUALITY OF LIFE

Utility, a concept used in economics and decision analysis, refers to the level of satisfaction or enjoyment experienced by the consumer of the good or service. Because many investigators are unfamiliar with the utility approach to assessing health-related quality of life, a brief review is provided. In general, economists do not attempt to measure utility (the preferences of consumers for various consumption alternatives) directly.[3] In the context of the analysis of behavior in most market settings, preferences may be inferred from observing the behavior of consumers. As a result, the discipline of economics has a well-developed set of

TABLE 3. *Example of health-state description*

Able to see, hear, and speak normally for age
Requires the help of another person to walk or get around; and requires mechanical equipment as well
Occasionally fretful, angry, irritable, anxious, depressed, or suffering ''night terrors''
Learns and remembers schoolwork normally for age
Eats, bathes, dresses, and uses toilet normally for age
Free of pain and discomfort
Able to have children with a healthy spouse

Note: This health state description is presented in a multiattribute health status system, namely the Health Utilities Index Mark II system. For more on these systems see Chapter 26. Based on ref. 22.

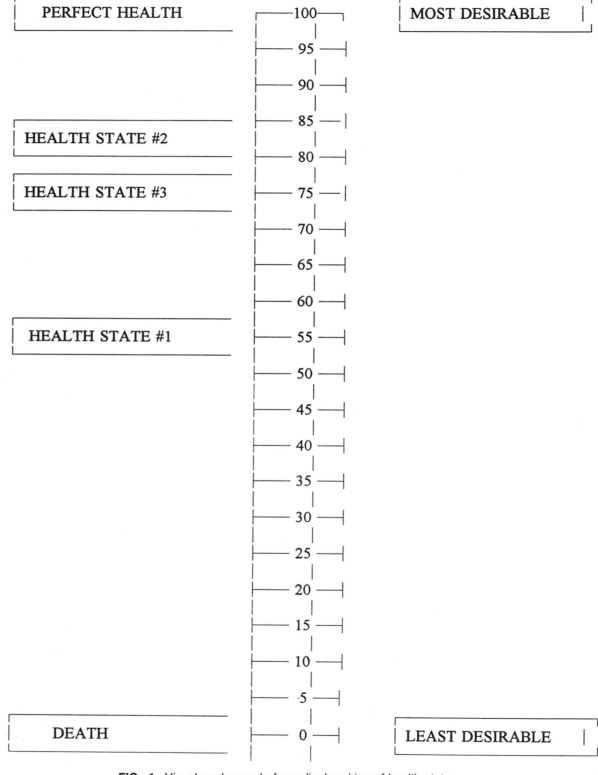

PERFECT HEALTH

MOST DESIRABLE

HEALTH STATE #2

HEALTH STATE #3

HEALTH STATE #1

DEATH

LEAST DESIRABLE

100
95
90
85
80
75
70
65
60
55
50
45
40
35
30
25
20
15
10
·5
0

FIG. 1. Visual analog scale for ordinal ranking of health states.

These considerations have led some investigators to search for methods for the direct measurement of the utility of various health states. A small family of reliable measurement approaches has been developed.[5]

Here is a brief outline of the practical steps of this approach. Typically a number of health-state scenarios are described, perhaps including the patient's subjectively defined current health state along with hypothetical health states relevant to the disease or condition of that class of patients. For instance, hypothetical health-state descriptions might include mild, moderate, and severe versions of the condition—the marker state approach (this approach is described more fully in Bennett and Torrance, Chapter 27). These scenarios cover a wide range of dimensions, including physical mobility, sensation, cognition, emotion, pain and discomfort, and any special features of the disease or its treatment (an example is provided in Table 3). Subjects are then asked to rank the health states, often with the assistance of a visual analog scale marked from 0 to 100, known as a feeling thermometer (Fig. 1). Scores on the feeling thermometer give the investigator a firm indication of the ordinal rankings of the health states (various treatment outcomes) and some information on the intensity of those preferences.

Although the feeling thermometer would appear to give interval-scale values, evidence to date indicates that while it does provide a good indication of ordinal rankings, it does not directly provide cardinal utility scores.

The measurement of cardinal scores for the utility of health states is performed using one of two techniques: standard gamble (SG) or time trade-off (TTO).[6] In the SG approach, the subject is offered a choice between two alternatives: living in the health state in choice B with certainty or taking a gamble on treatment, choice A, with an uncertain outcome (Fig. 2). The most straightforward approach to measurement is to suggest that treatment A leads to perfect health for a defined remaining lifetime with probability p and immediate death with probability $(1 - p)$, and that the health state in choice B also lasts for the same defined lifetime.[7]

The probability p is then varied until the subject is indifferent between choices A and B. The lower the indifference probability, the greater the risk of death the subject is willing to consider, and thus the lower the utility of the health state described under choice B. The utility scale is defined with 1.0 as perfect health and 0.0 as death.[8]

Because some respondents have experienced difficulty in understanding probabilities, an alternative technique, TTO,

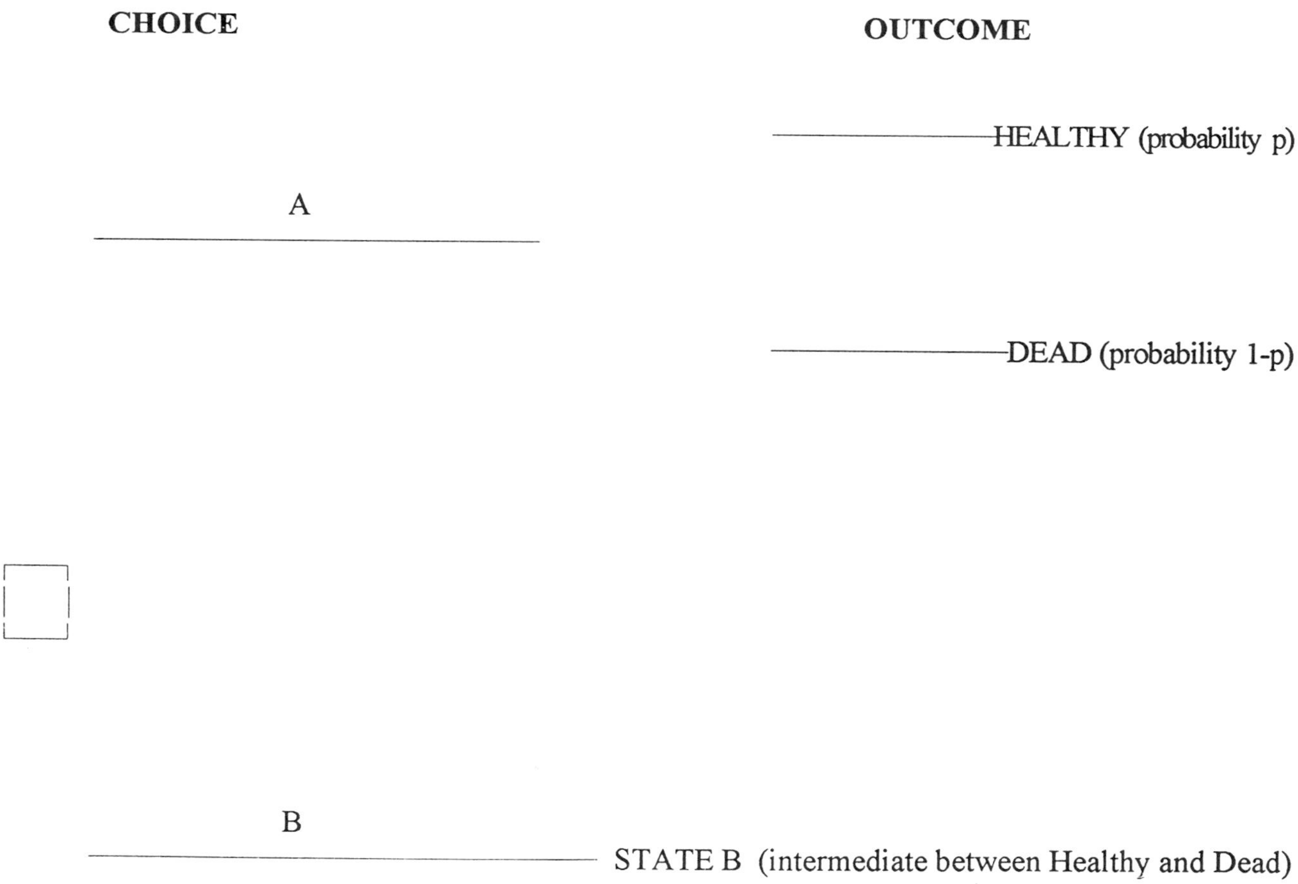

CHOICE

OUTCOME

A

————————HEALTHY (probability p)

————————DEAD (probability 1-p)

B

——————————————————— STATE B (intermediate between Healthy and Dead)

FIG. 2. Standard gamble approach for eliciting utility values.

has been developed (Fig. 3). In this technique the subject is first offered a choice of living for t years in perfect health or t years in some alternative health state that is less desirable (and the one for which the analyst wants the utility score). Obviously the subject will choose perfect health. The interviewer then reduces the period of perfect health, x, in a systematic fashion designed to minimize measurement biases, until the subject is indifferent between the shorter period in perfect health and the longer period in the less desirable state. The TTO preference score for the state then equals x/t.[9]

Using current preference-elicitation technology, the cognitive burden of the standard gamble only marginally exceeds that of the TTO technique. While most respondents can readily handle the feeling thermometer, a few (adult) respondents will not be able to handle the standard gamble, because of the need for short-term memory, concentration, and focus. Of those who cannot handle the SG, only a small minority will in fact be able to handle the TTO, which requires the same basic cognitive skills.

Standard gamble, time trade-off, and variations on these techniques provide reliable and valid methods for eliciting scores for health-state utilities. The prior use of the feeling thermometer appears to assist respondents in their introspection concerning their preferences for the health states being evaluated. The preference measurement interview assists respondents in their efforts to discover and construct their preferences for health states. The health states to be evaluated may include states the respondent has experienced or is now experiencing or has never experienced (hypothetical states). In this regard, the utility approach differs from the other

high-related quality of life measures. The utility approach, when it includes hypothetical states, allows the investigator to obtain important information from all patients on how they think they would feel if they experienced some of the infrequent outcomes. Evidence to date shows that evaluations by persons experiencing the state and by others for whom the state is hypothetical usually do not differ substantially (20). If there is a systematic difference it is that persons experiencing the state rate it marginally higher than those who have not experienced it, but this is not as yet conclusive. Thus the health-related quality of life of rare or infrequent outcomes may be assessed along with that of the frequent outcomes by combining actual and hypothetical states in the set of outcomes for evaluation.

COMBINING PECUNIARY AND HEALTH-RELATED QUALITY OF LIFE EVALUATIONS

The basic approach in cost-effectiveness analysis is to compare the pecuniary cost of treatment to its outcome, measured in broadly defined (e.g., life-years) or narrowly defined (e.g., weight loss) natural units. These comparisons are potentially useful for management decisions for individual patients, clinical departments, hospitals, and systems of health care delivery. (In practice cost-effectiveness studies are seldom used for individual patient management.)

The choice of outcome measure with which to compare data on cost depends on the objectives of the evaluation exercise. If the focus is on resource allocation among alternatives aimed at the same clinical problem, the outcome mea-

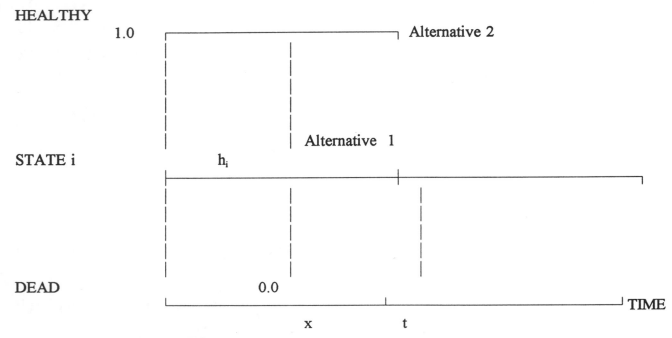

FIG. 3. Time trade-off approach for eliciting utility values.

sure can be narrow. This approach often has the advantage of clinical sensibility in that health care professionals can readily understand and appreciate how outcomes are measured. Thus a comparison of the cost per kilogram of weight loss among alternative treatment programs is likely to be meaningful to clinicians. Similarly, comparing the cost per change score in a specific health-related quality of life instrument among alternative therapies for the same disorder could be clinically sensible. Thus, the assessment of alternative drug regimens for the control of asthma in adult patients could be displayed in terms of a set of cost-effectiveness ratios of dollars per change in the Asthma Quality of Life Questionnaire score (8) for each drug regimen. Because, in this case, the measure of health-related quality of life is specific to a particular disease the cost-effectiveness ratio would be relevant only for comparisons among alternatives for the treatment of asthma for adult patients, and would not allow for broader comparison, say at the level of resource allocation among clinical departments or within a health care system. Thus, while the cost-effectiveness ratio using specific instruments as an outcome measure may be meaningful to clinicians, its narrow generalizability limits its usefulness to third-party payers, regulatory officials, and others.

Given that specific health-related quality of life instruments have been developed only recently, it is not surprising that few, if any, studies combining dollar cost with these health-related quality of life measures have appeared in the literature. One can speculate, however, that given the increasing popularity of the specific measures, such studies will be forthcoming. On the other hand, recent pharmacoeconomic guidelines [Canadian Coordinating Office for Health Technology Assessment (29); Ontario (30); see also Henry (31) and Detsky (32)] stress the usefulness of cost-utility analyses for making broad comparisons and thus may have reduced enthusiasm for using health-related quality of life as an outcome measure in cost-effectiveness analysis.

Broader comparisons can be made by combining pecuniary measures and more generalizable or generic health-profile measures of health-related quality of life, such as the Sickness Impact Profile (SIP) and others that provide for a single global score, as long as the score is on an interval scale. Given the wide applicability of these instruments, comparisons of cost-effectiveness of seemingly different programs, measured, for instance, as dollars per change in SIP score, could be made. Such comparisons come closer to the broadly formulated CEA in which cost per life-year gained is compared among a wide variety of alternative health care programs. The advantage in generalizability may, however, come at a cost in clinical sensibility. Clinicians may not readily understand changes in health-related quality of life as measured on such scales. Thus while the results of such a cost-effectiveness evaluation may be useful for clinical managers, hospital administrators, and third-party payers, they may not be especially meaningful to health care providers. Furthermore, the approach can provide useful information only if there are no differences in mortality among the

relevant treatment alternatives. If there are differences in mortality, then a framework capable of combining mortality and morbidity (such as quality adjusted life-years) is required.

The use of specific and health-profile measures in cost-effectiveness analysis will, however, not always be appropriate. The meaningfulness of CEA depends on comparing costs to a relevant and comprehensive measure of outcome or consequences (33). For specific health-profile instruments that do not provide a single score, the meaningfulness of CEAs that utilize them is dubious. For instruments for which single summary cardinal (interval scale) scores are available, the CEA is much more meaningful, but will still fall short of the potential available in cost-utility analysis in which mortality and morbidity effects may be combined.

Combining utility measures of health-related quality of life with pecuniary measures of cost converts CEA into cost-utility analysis. The outcome is a comparison of the cost to the gain in utility expressed as quality-adjusted life-years. At the pragmatic level the approach shares the advantages and disadvantages of combining pecuniary and health-profile measures; the procedure facilitates broad comparisons but comes at the expense of attenuated clinical sensibility.

At a more fundamental methodological level, however, CUA has an important advantage with respect to cost-effectiveness studies that employ health-profile or specific health-related quality of life measures. Both the family of economic evaluation approaches and the utility approach to the measurement of health-related quality of life are based on the same underlying economic theory.[10] The assumptions made in both approaches are consistent. Furthermore, the assumptions are explicit. Thus, the analyst knows precisely what is being assumed about the structure of human preferences. In general the same cannot be said for psychometrically based measures.

While few studies have combined pecuniary measures with health-related quality of life outcome measures based on the specific or health-profile measures, there are a number of studies that have employed CUA.[11] Given the number of such studies and growing use of CUA, it is likely that investigators using CUA will have a broad range of evaluations of health care interventions with which to compare the results of their evaluation. For some purposes, such as influencing third-party payers or regulatory officials, this is potentially an advantage.

The relatively large and increasing number of CUA studies provided Laupacis et al. (35) with an evidential basis for suggesting tentative guidelines for using CUA estimates in making resource allocation decisions. There are a number of important reservations that must be kept in mind in employing CUA estimates or decision rules derived from them to help formulate health care policy. These include the comparability of results across studies, the completeness of the CUA estimates themselves, the unbiasedness of the estimates, and the precision of the estimates. In addition, as typically constructed CUA estimates omit information on ethical and political considerations that may also be important in the formulation of policy.

The issues involving comparability among studies completeness of the estimates are well discussed in the literature.[12] One issue is the external validity or generalizability of the estimates. Well-constructed estimates often compare the incremental costs and consequences of one intervention versus another. The estimate, while valid in that neighborhood, may not be in another range. The degree of variability in study methods is often quite substantial. Some studies base the estimates of cost on the viewpoint of the health care system; others adopt the broader societal viewpoint. Discount rates used to translate future costs and effects into their present values often vary considerably. Different methods for estimating the utility scores for outcomes often provide substantially different answers. The choice of comparator program is also important. CUA studies compare the costs and consequences among relevant alternatives; the relative performance of an intervention depends crucially on the alternative to which it is compared.

The trade-offs among unbiasedness and precision in obtaining CUA estimates is also controversial. Laupacis et al. (35) stressed the importance of basing estimates on methodologically rigorous studies such as randomized controlled clinical trials, implicitly arguing that the unbiasedness of the estimates is, in general, the first priority. Naylor et al. (43) in their critique of Laupacis et al. appear to be arguing that precision is more important. They stress, quite appropriately, that variability of precision of the estimates of the numerator and denominator of a cost-utility ratio can lead to substantial variability in the estimate of the ratio itself.[13]

Clearly, there are substantive reasons to exercise care and caution in using the results of clinical, economic, health-related quality of life evaluations, and, in particular, cost-effectiveness and cost-utility ratios in helping to formulate resource allocation decisions in health care. Nonetheless if decision makers are aware of the limitations of the evidence and use them intelligently, there is a substantial potential for the results of such studies to assist decision makers in formulating policy on the adoption and utilization of health care technologies. Although even the best CUA studies are incomplete in that they do not reflect all of the considerations of relevance to the decision maker, good economic evaluative studies do help to reduce the scope of ignorance in decision making.

In summary, it makes sense to combine economic evaluations and health-related quality of life measures in cost-effectiveness and cost-utility studies. Cost estimates summarize important, but incomplete, information on treatment alternatives. Health-related quality of life is frequently the most important outcome. Thus cost-effectiveness ratios that reflect both sets of information provide a more complete assessment of the implications of treatment options. Specific, health-profile, and utility measures of health-related quality of life can all be appropriate for use in such cost-effectiveness studies. The utility approach has the advantages of generalizability, its ability to combine mortality and morbidity effects, and its inherent compatibility with pecuniary evaluations.

COMBINING PECUNIARY AND QUALITY OF LIFE MEASURES IN CLINICAL TRIALS

If pecuniary evaluations and health-related quality of life assessments of a particular drug or health care program are both deemed to be relevant and important, need they be done concurrently? Need they be incorporated in a clinical trial? There are a number of advantages to performing the evaluations together in the context of a prospective and rigorous clinical trial. First, a health-related quality of life measure may be included in a clinical trial because it is one of the relevant outcome measures, or the only one. Second, data collected within prospective studies with blinding as to outcome and appropriate baseline measurement is, in general, more reliable and valid. Third, there are important logistical advantages to collecting data on the costs of treatment, especially patient-borne costs, as part of an ongoing clinical study. For instance, the gathering of data on costs can be combined with the periodic administration of health-related quality of life instruments. In the common situations in which recall is unreliable, such prospective data collection can be especially important. Fourth, data on clinical efficacy and/or effectiveness derived from well-designed randomized clinical trials is more valid. The results of the cost estimates are therefore combined with higher quality data on clinical effects; no matter how precise the cost estimates in an economic evaluation, the results of a CEA, CUA, or CBA can be no better than clinical data on effectiveness. Finally, by combining clinical, economic, and health-related quality of life investigations into a single study, all of the results are available in a timely fashion to affect clinical and health care policy.

These potential advantages, however, are accompanied by disadvantages. First, already complex clinical evaluations are made more complex by adding additional measurement instruments. Furthermore, some clinical investigators will have little experience with or understanding of these instruments. Second, if the results of the clinical evaluation indicate that the new drug is not efficacious, the pecuniary evaluation may be redundant. Third, some clinicians who are consumers of such studies will find the pecuniary and health-related quality of life information to be foreign, thus reducing the acceptability of the results. Finally, there is an important issue about the extent of generalizability of the results of a pecuniary evaluation conducted within a clinical trial. Even management trials are not fully representative of ordinary clinical practice. For instance, trials typically include special compliance-enhancing strategies that both increase the costs of the care being provided, and potentially, the effectiveness of that care. There is no reason to believe that the percent increase in costs and percent increase in effectiveness will

TABLE 4. *Advantages and disadvantages of incorporating economic evaluations and health-related quality of life assessments in clinical trials*

Advantages
   Relevance of quality of life as an outcome measure
   Logistical advantages
   Quality of data on efficacy and/or effectiveness
   Timeliness of comprehensive results
Disadvantages
   Additional complexity
   Potential redundancy
   Acceptability of study results
   Generalizability of economic evaluations based on data
     obtained during a trial

Based on ref. 47.

be roughly equal, so that the cost-effectiveness ratio is left unbiased.

The advantages and disadvantages of including health-related quality of life and economic evaluation components in clinical trials will vary with the questions being asked, stage of development of the drug or clinical intervention, and other factors specific to the clinical study. The discussion is summarized in Table 4.[14]

CONCLUSIONS

Pecuniary and health-related quality of life evaluations complement each other by adding important information about the consequences of various health care interventions. Economic evaluation provides a framework for comparing the costs of care to its effects measured in both pecuniary and nonpecuniary terms. Health-related quality of life measures provide crucial information on the outcomes of the clinical intervention. In this way, the use of health-related quality of life assessment conforms to an underlying premise in the health and social sciences that health care is provided to improve the welfare of patients and, indirectly, their families. More traditional pecuniary measures, and the more recently developed health-related quality of life measures, provide a means for quantification of these goals. Such studies provide clinicians with information that is useful in their decisions concerning patient management. The studies also provide third-party payers, regulatory authorities, and others with important information on the costs and consequences, now measured in a more comprehensive fashion by including health-related quality of life measurement, of various uses of scarce health care resources.

The combination of pecuniary and specific and health-profile health-related quality of life measurement is still in its infancy. Although more fully developed, cost-utility analysis is less than three decades old. Health-related quality of life measurement is rapidly evolving at the conceptual, methodological, and pragmatic levels. It is, however, very likely that the incorporation of pecuniary measures, health-related quality of life measures, and combinations of the two approaches will become increasingly common. Cost-utility analysis is ideally suited for these purposes.

ACKNOWLEDGMENTS

The authors wish to thank William Furlong, Gordon Guyatt, Bert Spilker, and Marie Townsend for helpful comments on the 1990 version of this chapter.

ENDNOTES

1. For a review of the methods of economic evaluation, see Chapter 11 by Henry Grabowski and Ron Hansen. The issues discussed in this paper are also considered in Feeny (1), Feeny and Torrance (2), Torrance and Feeny (3), and Tsevat et al. (4).
2. Trends in economic evaluation of health care services are described in Udvarhelyi et al. (6). When cost-benefit analysis was first applied to the evaluation of health care services, estimates of the benefits of the delay of premature mortality were obtained by computing the present value of the lifetime earnings of survivors. This approach was labeled the human-capital approach. It has the advantage of providing a relatively straightforward procedure for estimating the benefits of reductions in mortality. It is not, however, consistent with the economic theory upon which CBA is based. Conceptually the proper measure of the benefits of reductions in mortality would be the willingness of patients to pay for reductions in their risk of premature mortality. Although some studies have asked this question of respondents in hypothetical situations, there are important reasons to question the reliability and validity of the responses. First, patients are often not well informed about the risk and reductions in risk that treatment will produce. Thus their answers are likely to be affected by any of their misperceptions of the clinical information on risks or the effectiveness of treatment. Their answers are also likely to be affected by what they have been told by their health care provider. Second, willingness to pay also depends on income, and like the human-capital approach, is therefore not free of the potential to overrepresent the preferences of the economically advantaged. (Because of this problem, many investigators also collect information on the ability to pay of respondents.) Third, individuals may be motivated to misrepresent their willingness to pay. For example, some may underestimate the value because of a concern that at a later date they may be expected to actually pay. Others may overstate their willingness in order to influence the priority assigned to their condition. These and other difficulties with inferring preferences from willingness to pay led some investigators to attempt to measure preferences directly, and in turn led to the development of cost-utility analysis. Many of these criticisms also apply to more recent attempts to apply willingness to pay in the evaluation of health care services.
3. See for instance Ellsberg (14). The direct measurement of utility is, however, a routine practice in the discipline of decision analysis.
4. This point also applies to applications of the willingness-to-pay approach that use responses from patients as the (or a portion of the) source for the estimation of the pecuniary benefits of treatment. An example of such a study is Johannesson and Jonsson (17).
5. Practical methods for designing and implementing direct utility measurements are described in Furlong et al. (19); see also Torrance (20,21). The underlying theory is described briefly in Torrance (20), Feeny and Torrance (2), and Torrance and Feeny (3).
6. Utility scores are cardinal in that they possess interval-scale properties. That is, the distance from 0.2 to 0.4 is the same as the distance from 0.4 to 0.6. The scores are not cardinal in the sense of a ratio scale; that is, 0.2 is not twice as good as 0.1. These interval-scale cardinal utilities should not be confused with the ratio-scale cardinal utilities of the utilitarian approach common among nineteenth-century economists. For more on this distinction see Torrance (20) and Torrance (23).

7. It is not, however, necessary to offer perfect health and death as the alternatives in choice A for each standard gamble. The standard gamble requires that the health state in choice B be a state that is ranked intermediately—that is, the outcomes in choice A include one state that is better than the one in B and one that is worse. (Thus it can be readily seen that it is important that the ordinal rankings of the health states be established before standard gamble questions are posed.) If it is undesirable to offer death as an option in the standard gamble, for instance because it upsets respondents or because it is not a relevant outcome in the clinical situation, another state (one for which the utility score is low) can be substituted for death in choice A. The utility of the state in Choice B may then be computed with respect to this state. Its utility in turn is determined separately by performing a standard gamble that includes death, thus providing the information to anchor B on the 0.0 (death) to 1.0 (perfect health) scale.

8. If the standard gamble included perfect health and death as the outcomes under choice A and remembering that perfect health = 1.0 and death = 0.0, the indifference probability is then a cardinal score of the utility of the health state in choice B. The indifference means that the expected utility of A equals the expected utility of B. (Expected utility is the sum of the utilities multiplied by their probabilities.) The expected utility of A is p (1.0) + (1 − p) (0.0), which equals p. [In general, if O_1 and O_2 are the outcomes of the lottery, choice A, and O_3 is the sure thing—the outcome in choice B, then the utility of O_3 equals p times the utility of O_1 plus (1 − p) times the utility of O_2.] The standard-gamble approach to measuring health-state utilities is based directly on the analysis of decision making under uncertainty developed by von Neumann and Morgenstern (24). The axioms upon which von Neumann–Morgenstern functions are based ensure that scores have interval-scale properties. These axioms, although closely related to the usual axioms of economic theory, are somewhat more restrictive [see for instance Baumol (25) and Luce and Raiffa (26)]. Methods for states considered to be worse than death are described in Drummond et al. (5), Boyle et al. (12), and Patrick et al. (26).

9. Although the scores derived from time trade-off provide a measure of the preference for a health state, they are not identical to those obtained using standard gamble. Conceptually, this difference, although not quantitatively large (see Ref. 20) is expected. In addition to tapping the subject's preferences for the health state and its duration, the standard-gamble score also reflects the subject's attitudes toward risk (the subject's risk preferences). Time trade-off scores do not reflect these risk attitudes. Furthermore, the standard-gamble technique has the conceptual advantage in that it is based directly on the von Neumann–Morgenstern (24) theory and does not require additional assumptions about the structure of preferences.

10. Economic analysis is, in general, based on the assumption that a person's preference ordering may be represented as an ordinal utility function (25). Informally, the axioms required for this type of analysis state that consumers have a complete and transitive ordering of preferences over all possible bundles of goods and services, that within the feasible choice set they will select the bundle that is most preferred to them, and that more is better than less. These axioms allow the analyst to represent preferences as an ordinal utility function and in turn legitimate the interpretation of the pecuniary evaluation of the value of resources used in producing health care services. The von Neumann–Morgenstern (24) utility function approach for decision making under uncertainty expands the set of axioms so that preferences may be represented by a utility function with interval-scale properties. The assumptions underlying these utility functions are therefore consistent with the assumptions underlying standard demand analysis in economic theory, the theory upon which the pecuniary evaluations are based.

11. Torrance and Feeny (3), p. 570, provide a table in which the results of a number of CUA studies are listed; see also Mason et al. (34).

12. Prominent contributions to this literature focus on the usefulness and validity of league tables—organized lists of CUA estimates. See for instance, Adams et al. (36), Birch and Gafni (37), CCOHTA (29), Drummond et al. (39), Drummond and Davies (40), Drummond et al. (41), Gerard and Mooney (42), Kamlet (33), Laupacis et al. (35), Mason et al. (33), Naylor et al. (43), and Ontario (30).

13. Issues concerning the statistical estimation of cost-utility and cost-effectiveness ratios are discussed by O'Brien et al. (44,45) and Drummond and O'Brien (46).

14. For a more detailed discussion of the issues, see Drummond and Stoddart (47) and O'Brien et al. (44,45).

REFERENCES

1. Feeny D. Can we use quality-of-life measures for economic evaluations? *Qual Life Cardiovasc Care* 1988;4(4):185–190.
2. Feeny D, Torrance GW. Incorporating utility-based quality of life assessment measures in clinical trials: two examples. *Med Care* 1989;27(3)(suppl):S190–S204.
3. Torrance W, Feeny D. Utilities and quality-adjusted life years. *Int J Technol Assess Health Care* 1989;5(4):559–575.
4. Tsevat J, Weeks JC, Guadagnoli E, et al. Using health-related quality of life information: clinical encounters, clinical trials, and health policy. *J Gen Intern Med* 1994;9(10):576–582.
5. Drummond MF, Stoddart GL, Torrance GW. *Methods for the economic evaluation of health care programmes.* Oxford: Oxford University Press, 1987.
6. Udvarhelyi S, Colditz GA, Rai A, Epstein AM. Cost-effectiveness and cost-benefit analyses in the medical literature. *Ann Intern Med* 1992;116(3):238–244.
7. Guyatt H, Veldhuyzen Van Zanten SJO, Feeny D, Patrick DL. Measuring quality of life in clinical trials: a taxonomy and review. *Can Med Assoc J* 1989;140:1441–1448.
8. Feeny D, Guyatt GH, Patrick DL, eds. Proceedings of the International Conference on the Measurement of Quality of Life as an Outcome in Clinical Trials. *Controlled Clin Trials* 1991;12(4)(suppl).
9. Guyatt GH, Feeny DH, Patrick DL. Measuring health-related quality of life. *Ann Intern Med* 1993;118(8):622–629.
10. Guyatt G, Townsend M, Pugsley O, Keller L, Short HD, Taylor DW, Newhouse MT. Bronchodilators in chronic air-flow limitation: effects on airway function, exercise capacity, and quality of life. *Am Rev Respir Dis* 1987;135:1069–1074.
11. Bergner M, Bobbit RA, Carter WB, Gilson BS. The sickness impact profile: development and final revision of a health status measure. *Med Care* 1981;19(8):787–805.
12. Boyle MH, Torrance GW, Sinclair JC, Horwood SP. Economic evaluation of neonatal intensive care of very-low-birthweight infants. *N Engl J Med* 1983;308:1330–1337.
13. Bombardier C, Ware J, John RI, Larson M, Chalmers A, Read J. Auranofin therapy and quality of life in patients with rheumatoid arthritis: results of a multicenter trial. *Am J Med* 1986;81:565–578.
14. Ellsberg D. Classic and current notions of ''measurable utility.'' *Econ J* 1954;64:528–556.
15. Arrow KJ. Uncertainty and the welfare economics of medical care. *Am Econ Rev* 1963;53(5):941–973.
16. Harris E. The internal organization of hospitals: some economic implications. *Bell J Econ* 1977;8(2):467–482.
17. Johannesson M, Jonsson B. Willingness to pay for antihypertensive therapy: results of a Swedish pilot study. *J Health Econ* 1991;10:461–474.
18. Gafni A. Willingness-to-pay as a measure of benefits. Relevant questions in the context of public decisionmaking about health care programs. *Med Care* 1991;29:1246–1252.
19. Furlong W, Feeny D, Torrance GW, Barr R, Horsman J. Guide to design and development of health-state utility instrumentation. McMaster University Centre for Health Economics and Policy Analysis Working Paper No 90-9, June 1990.
20. Torrance GW. Measurement of health state utilities for economic appraisal: a review article. *J Health Econ* 1986;5:1–30.
21. Torrance GW. Utility approach to measuring health-related quality of life. *J Chronic Dis* 1987;40(6):593–600.
22. Feeny D, Furlong W, Barr RD, Torrance GW, Rosenbaum P, Weitzman S. A comprehensive multiattribute system for classifying the health status of survivors of childhood cancer. *J Clin Oncol* 1992;10(6):923–928.
23. Torrance GW. Social preferences for health states. An empirical evaluation of three measurement techniques. *Socioeconomic Plan Sci* 1976;10:129–136.
24. von Neumann J, Morgenstern O. *Theory of games and economic behaviour,* 1st and 2nd eds. Princeton: Princeton University Press, 1944; 1947.
25. Baumol J. *Economic theory and operations analysis.* New York: W.W. Norton, 1965.
26. Luce RD, Raiffa H. *Games and decisions: introduction and critical survey.* New York: John Wiley, 1957.

27. Patrick L, Starks HE, Cain KC, Uhlmann RF, Pearlman RA. Measuring preferences for health states worse than death. *Med Decis Making* 1994;14(1):9–18.

28. Juniper E, Guyatt GH, Epstein RE, et al. Evaluation of impairment of health related quality of life in asthma: development of a questionnaire for use in clinical trials. *Thorax* 1992;47:76–83.

29. Canadian Coordinating Office for Health Technology Assessment. Guidelines for economic evaluation of pharmaceuticals: Canada, 1st ed. Ottawa: Canadian Coordinating Office for Health Technology Assessment, 1994.

30. Ministry of Health, Ontario. Ontario guidelines for economic analysis of pharmaceutical products. Toronto: Queens Printer for Ontario, 1994.

31. Henry D. Economic analysis as an aid to subsidisation decisions: the development of Australian guidelines for pharmaceuticals. Review article. *PharmacoEconomics* 1992;1(1):54–67.

32. Detsky AS. Guidelines for economic analysis of pharmaceutical products: a draft document for Ontario and Canada. *PharmacoEconomics* 1993;3(5):354–361.

33. Kamlet MS. *The comparative benefits modeling project. A framework for cost-utility analysis of government health care programs.* Public Health Service, U.S. Department of Health and Human Services, 1992.

34. Mason J, Drummond MF, Torrance GW. Some guidelines on the use of cost effectiveness league tables. *Br Med J* 1993;306:570–572.

35. Laupacis A, Feeny D, Detsky AS, Tugwell PX. How attractive does a new technology have to be to warrant adoption and utilization? Tentative guidelines for using clinical and economic evaluations. *Can Med Assoc J* 1992;146(4):473–481.

36. Adams ME, McCall NT, Gray DT, Orza MJ, Chalmers TC. Economic analysis in randomized control trials. *Med Care* 1992;30(3):231–243.

37. Birch S, Gafni A. Cost-effectiveness ratios: in a league of their own. *Health Policy* 1994;28:133–141.

38. Drummond M. Cost-effectiveness guidelines for reimbursement of pharmaceuticals: is economic evaluation ready for its enhanced status? *Health Economics* 1992;1:85–92.

39. Drummond M, Brandt A, Luce B, Rovira J. Standardizing methodologies for economic evaluation in health care: practice, problems, and potential. *Int J Technol Assess Health Care* 1993;9(1):26–36.

40. Drummond MF, Davies L. Economic analysis alongside clinical trials: revisiting the methodological issues. *Int J Technol Assess Health Care* 1991;7(4):561–573.

41. Drummond MF, Torrance GW, Mason J. Cost-effectiveness league tables: more harm than good? *Soc Sci Med* 1993;37:33–40.

42. Gerard K, Mooney G. QALY league tables: handle with care. *Health Economics* 1993;2:59–64.

43. Naylor C, Williams JI, Basinski A, et al. Technology assessment and cost-effectiveness: misguided guidelines? *Can Med Assoc J* 1993;148:921–929.

44. O'Brien BJ, Drummond MF. Statistical versus quantitative significance in the socioeconomic evaluation of medicines. *PharmacoEconomics* 1994;5(5):389–398.

45. O'Brien BJ, Drummond MF, Labelle RJ, Willan A. In search of power and significance: issues in the design and analysis of stochastic cost-effectiveness studies in health care. *Med Care* 1994;32(2):150–163.

46. Drummond MF, O'Brien B. Clinical importance, statistical significance and assessment of economic and quality-of-life outcomes. *Health Economics* 1993;2(3):205–212.

47. Drummond MF, Stoddart GL. Economic analysis and clinical trials. *Controlled Clin Trials* 1984;5:115–128.

Quality of Life and Pharmacoeconomics in Clinical Trials, Second Edition, edited by B. Spilker.
Lippincott-Raven Publishers, Philadelphia © 1996.

CHAPTER 13

Social Interaction Tests and Scales

Edward Guadagnoli, Paul Nordberg, and Vincent Mor

INTRODUCTION

Of the domains selected to represent the concept of quality of life as defined in this book, *social interaction* or *social participation* is the least well conceptualized. Our inability to fine-tune its operational definition makes the development of valid, reliable measurement scales a formidable task. The practical use of this concept as a measure of quality of life in clinical trials depends upon a definition that encompasses features of an individual's functioning that realistically can be influenced by the medical treatment or intervention under study. Conceptualizations and/or measures that include, for instance, the documentation of one's marital status are not relevant potential outcomes for medical clinical trials. Rarely, if ever, would a change in patients' marital status be an outcome of interest. The proper use of quality of life measures depends upon the basic assumption that we expect the intervention under study to differentially influence health-related quality of life across intervention levels. Unfortunately, many potential measures of social interaction suffer from the inclusion of items that are not relevant to the assessment of health status or quality of life and are, therefore, not viable outcomes of interest for assessment of a medical intervention.

In this chapter we attempt to provide a definition for social interaction within the context of health-related quality of life, and we review several scales that might be used to measure this concept. Given the practical considerations of clinical trials research (1) we selected for review brief measures that do not require administration by an expert (for example, a physician, social worker, or psychologist). For each measure selected we identify its underlying construct, if any, and the population for which it was developed, and we describe its psychometric properties, scoring, analysis, and interpretation. We do not review single-item measures of social interaction.

SOCIAL INTERACTION

Social interaction is a component of the broader concept, social well-being. Donald and Ware (2) suggest that social well-being is made up of social contact (social interaction) and social resource dimensions. Social interaction encompasses the activities of an individual and his/her involvement with others; social resources relate to the resources or reserves available to an individual (2). If we accept this broad definition for social well-being, the concept is not appropriate for use in clinical trials designs since improved social

   E. Guadagnoli: Department of Health Care Policy, Harvard Medical School, Boston, Massachusetts 02115.
   P. Nordberg: Department of Health Policy and Management, Harvard School of Public Health, Boston, Massachusetts 02115.
   V. Mor: Center for Gerontology and Health Care Research, Brown University, Providence, Rhode Island 02912.

resource availability is not likely to be an intended outcome of a medical intervention. An assessment of patients' activities with others and in social situations, however, is a potential outcome of interest.

Few measures have been designed specifically to measure social interaction. This construct is typically included as part of a more comprehensive health status battery [e.g., the Sickness Impact Profile (3)] or as a component of a social health or well-being scale [for example, the Rand Social Health Battery (2)].

Social interactions occur within several domains: family, friends, community, and work. Social interaction scales that include independent measures of each of these domains are rare. In fact, expectations that social interaction items will cluster statistically by domain have not been met (2). Typically, a total interaction score made up of responses to items spanning each of these domains is calculated. A problem arises when this approach is used because all individuals may not be able to respond to all items that make up the overall scale (for example, items dealing with employment).

Another potential problem in the measurement of social interaction is that individuals' preferences differ with respect to interactions with others. It is a safe assumption that maximum physical or emotional functioning is valued by all individuals. However, individuals' preferences with respect to the quantity and quality of social interactions is more variable. The solution typically has been to assess the quantity of social interactions and to operate under the assumption that more social interaction is better. Ware (4) argues that assessment of the quantity of social interactions should be a health outcome measure because society values social functioning.

Social interaction is sometimes confused with the concept of social support. Although social interaction can be conceived of as a component of social support, it is not synonymous with this construct. Social support is defined in a much broader manner and is used rarely, if ever, as an outcome measure in research designs. It is defined as "the emotional, instrumental, and financial aid that is obtained from one's social network" (5, p. 415). The role of social support is postulated as either a buffer effect, providing protection from the negative influences of stress, or as a main effect, enhancing health or well-being without reference to level of stress (6). In research designs, social support measures are typically independent variables included as potential correlates of physical and mental health indicators.

SOCIAL INTERACTION SCALES AS OUTCOME MEASURES

The use of social interaction instruments as outcome measures in clinical trials research may not be appropriate even when other components of health-related quality of life are included. The selection of any outcome measure should be dictated by the expectation that the intervention will effect it. Social interaction measures should be included in the design of trials that involve interventions expected to affect one's willingness or ability to deal with others. For example, one might include a social interaction measure in a trial comparing the efficacy of treatments whose aim is to relieve physical deformation (burns, dermatology problems, and so on). In addition to providing physical relief, such treatments are also likely to be judged successful if they are associated with an increase in social activity over the treatment course. Similarly when an intervention's side effects are expected to affect patients' body image, social interaction data may provide the information necessary to chose between two (or more) otherwise efficacious treatments. For example, clinical trial results often suggest little or no difference between nonsurgical, antineoplasm therapies. Nonetheless, patients report that side effects such as hair and weight loss affect their willingness to interact socially with others. In addition to direct measures of the side effects themselves, social interaction data can also be a useful indicator of a treatment's utility.

Social interaction measures have been included in research designs that do not directly involve medical interventions. For example, investigators who conducted the Health Insurance Experiment (7) initially included social health as a component of their overall model of health, and therefore assessed social interaction as an outcome measure in their study of the influence of health care financing mechanisms on health status. Other "social experiments" such as the National Hospice Study (8) and the National Long-Term Care Channeling Demonstration (9) have included social interaction as an outcome measure with the assumption that improved community functioning will enhance individuals' physical capacity to deal with others.

SOCIAL INTERACTION TESTS AND SCALES

Once the decision to measure social interaction is made, an instrument must be selected. Given the practical constraints of conducting clinical trials research (1), particularly patient and staff burden, brief instruments are desirable. Instruments that require expert raters are typically avoided because of increased time and expense requirements. Furthermore, desirable social interaction instruments should contain items that apply to all members of the population under study. Data analysis, missing data, and measurement standardization problems arise when all items cannot be answered by all respondents (2). Several instruments designed to measure social interaction are described below. In most cases, social activity is part of an overall battery of measurements that assess physical, emotional, and social aspects of health-related quality of life. The World Health Organization's definition of health as "a state of complete physical, mental and social well-being and not merely the absence of disease or infirmity" (10) has been influential in determining the dimensions of health assessed by these measures.

The Health Insurance Experiment Social Battery, the Medical Outcomes Study Health Measures, and the SF-36 (2)

The Health Insurance Experiment Social Battery

Following an extensive review of the literature (11), investigators at Rand generated an 11-item social well-being scale for use in the Health Insurance Experiment (HIE) (7). The battery was intended for use with the general population, although for the HIE, individuals aged 14 to 61 made up the population of interest. As indicated above, Rand's social well-being model incorporates two dimensions: social interaction and social ties. The operational definition of social well-being included "interpersonal interactions (for example, visits with friends) and activities indicative of social participation (for example, memberships in clubs)" (2, p. 132). All but one of the 11 items deal with the behavioral aspects of social activity. The remaining item involves a subjective evaluation of one's ability to get along with others.

From the original 11-item scale, five items met internal and external consistency criteria established by the investigators for the construction of two multi-item scales. Both of these scales, Social Contacts and Group Participation, relate directly to the concept of social interaction. The Social Contacts scale is made up of three items documenting visits with friends or relatives, home visits by friends, and visits to homes of friends. Potential responses are not identical across items. Items are rated along several scales that involve six or seven categories. The Group Participation scale is made up of two items detailing number of voluntary group memberships and level of group activity. Based on item analyses, an item-response recoding scheme has been generated for each item. The battery, original item responses, and recoding scheme are presented in (2).

Due to variance differences within each scale, Donald and Ware (2) suggest standardizing items to a mean of 0 and a standard deviation of 1 prior to summing to obtain scale scores. A high Social Contacts score is defined as "home visits by friends two or three times a month or more; visits with friends and relatives and visits to homes of friends once a week or more." (2, p. 106). The absence of visits indicate a low score on this scale. Five or more group memberships and very active group participation indicate high Group Participation while no memberships define a low score.

Both scales appear to be homogeneous and consistent. Internal consistency coefficients calculated across all HIE data collection sites were .72 for the Social Contacts scale and .84 for the Group Participation scale (2). One-year stability coefficients for the Social Contacts and Group Participation scales were .55 and .68, respectively (2).

The very low correlation between these measures ($r =$ .05) suggests that these scales measure different components of social well-being. Correlations with other health measures, positive well-being, emotional ties, and current health, although statistically significant, were low (.04 to .19). This suggests that these measures are not redundant with other health dimensions. Correlations with functional or physical measures of health, however, were not reported. We would expect that correlations between functional status measures and social interaction scales would be higher than those reported for well-being, emotional ties, and current health. Finally, Donald and Ware (2) examined the influence of socially desirable response set (SDRS) on each of these scales. Adjusting for SDRS did not result in changes among relationships between the two social interaction scales and other measures of health.

This scale was not developed from data collected exclusively from patient samples. However, the Social Contacts scale should be amenable for use by patients. Assuming that measuring frequency of contact is of value to the assessment of the intervention of interest, one can expect variability in patient responses if this measure is used. We feel that measuring Group Participation is less likely to be of use in clinical trials research and suggest employing this scale in the design only if group membership and participation can be linked meaningfully to the goals or effects of the intervention.

The data describing the development and interpretation of these scales is perhaps the most extensive available for any individual scale. We refer the reader to the Rand series on the *Conceptualization and Measurement of Health for Adults in the Health Insurance Study* (11–18) for further descriptions of social well-being items and scales.

The Medical Outcomes Study Health Measures

The concepts and measurements of the Medical Outcomes Study (MOS) health measures are derived from those associated with the Health Insurance Experiment. Because of the demands for efficiency in a study of over 20,000 patients, standard and compact instruments were a matter of necessity and the definitions, survey items, and rating scales of the HIE were carefully culled and refined. There are four sets of MOS measures (19). The fullest, the 149-question MOS Functioning and Well-Being Profile, includes 35 scales and eight summary indices. A smaller subset, the 113-item Core Subset, includes 20 scales and four summary indices. The extremely brief 20-item MOS-20 includes a single question on social interaction. The Short-Form 36 (SF-36) includes a Social Functioning scale based on two questions. The SF-36 is discussed in detail in Chapter 34.

The MOS investigators included social functioning as a component of their definition of health. "Social functioning is defined as the ability to develop, maintain, and nurture social relationships. . . . We do not consider social functioning per se as health. Instead, we view social functioning measures as being indicative of physical and mental health status" (20, p. 174). The MOS investigators studied three components of social functioning: changes due to health in social activities, quality of interaction in family functioning, and sexual function and dysfunction. Of these, emphasis has been on health-related limitations of the individual's normal social activities. This component is the defining concept of the Social Activity Limitations due to Health measure of the MOS Functioning and Well-Being Profile, the Core Subset, the MOS-20, and the SF-36. The Social Activity Limitations due to Health measure of the Functioning and Well-Being Profile has four questions that deal with limitations on social activities: frequency of interference, extent of interference, social activity compared to usual level, and social activity compared to others of similar age. Responses are graded on five-point ordinal scales appropriate to the particular question content. The response values are subsequently combined and transformed to a range from 0 (worst functioning) to 100 (best functioning) (20). The Social Activity scale included in the Core Subset is identical to that of the Functioning and Well-Being Profile. The SF-36 includes a two-question Social Function scale made up of two (frequency of interference and extent of interference with social interaction) of the same four items (21).

The internal consistency coefficient of the Social Limitations due to Health measure of the Well-Being Profile was .77 in the pilot study of 2,181 patients. The investigators evaluated the construct validity of the measure in reference to their overall conceptual framework for health. In an analysis of 1,980 patients, they postulated, and found, a two-factor solution to health measurement, with rotated components corresponding to physical and mental health. The Social Limitations scale was positively correlated, as predicted, with both physical and mental measures (22).

For the SF-36, various studies have found coefficient alphas for Social Function ranging from .63 to .80. Two studies, one of 235 diabetic patients and one of 187 British general-practice patients, have reported test-retest reliability correlations of .60 (21). The SF-36 has, however, been criticized for paying insufficient attention to demonstrating temporal stability (23). Validation analyses using the SF-36 hypothesized and verified that Social Function correlated moderately with physical health and strongly with mental health (21). In a comparison with the Nottingham Health Profile (24), the SF-36 Social Function scale correlated moderately ($r = -.41$) with the Nottingham Social Isolation scale and somewhat more strongly with the Nottingham Energy scale ($r = -.51$) (24). These results demonstrate that Social Function

is not independent of the physical and mental function aspects of health-related quality of life.

The family of Medical Outcomes Study instruments is notable for its careful development and the interest they have received. As the evolution has progressed toward shorter forms, notable features have been the rejection of social function as a useful health measurement by itself and the focus on measurement of health-related change and departures from an individual's normal pattern of activity.

The Functional Status Questionnaire

The Functional Status Questionnaire (FSQ) is a 34-item self-administered survey assessing physical, psychological, social, and role function. The FSQ shares some concepts and items with the MOS instruments, reflecting common adaptations by the developers from existing instruments. The FSQ was specifically designed to measure functional disability and change in function in a clinical context. Its scoring results in six summary scale measures and six single-item scores, generally covering activities in a one-month period. The time frame for both sets of questions is "during the past month." All scales are transformed to a range of 0 (lowest functioning) to 100 (highest) (25).

The instrument includes two social scales, Social Activity and Quality of Interaction, which the developers clearly differentiate from role function in work (25). There are three Social Activity questions: "Have you . . . —had difficulty visiting with relatives or friends? —had difficulty participating in community activities, such as religious services, social activities, or volunteer work? —had difficulty taking care of other people such as family members?" There are four graded responses and an explicit opportunity to report inapplicability: 4, usually did with no difficulty; 3, usually did with much difficulty; 2, usually did with some difficulty; 1, usually did not do because of health; and 0, usually did not do for other reasons. There are five Quality of Interaction questions: "Have you . . . —isolated yourself from people around you? —acted affectionate toward others? —acted irritable toward those around you? —made unreasonable demands on your family and friends? —gotten along well with other people?" Responses are graded on a scale of 1, all of the time, to 6, none of the time.

Reliability estimates for the scales exist in the form of internal consistency coefficients. In a primary care setting, coefficient alphas were .65 for the Social Activity scale, and .64 for Quality of Interaction. The authors suggest that although these values are somewhat less than optimal for evaluation of individual patients, they are reasonable for group comparisons, especially given the relatively low number of items that make up the scales (25). The authors hypothesized that valid measures of social function would be inversely related to age, number of bed-disability days, and role limitations, and positively associated with health satisfaction, number of close friends, and frequency of social contact. In a validation study of primary care patients, all of the expected relationships were observed except for the association with patient reports of the number of close friends. In a six-hospital study assessing quality of life after surgery, the Social Activities scale showed significant improvement after cholecystectomy, total hip replacement, and coronary artery bypass surgery, but not after transurethral prostate resection (26).

The Sickness Impact Profile (3)

The Sickness Impact Profile (SIP) is a behaviorally based measure of health status (3,27). It contains 136 items that deal with 12 areas of dysfunction. The instrument does not appear to be based upon a formal model of health. The SIP was specifically designed as a health care outcome measure. It was "developed to provide a measure of perceived health status that is sensitive enough to detect changes or differences in health status that occur over time or between groups" (3, p. 787) and, like the MOS instruments and the FSQ, it specifically sets out to discover limitations due to health.

In addition to generating items from a review of the literature, the instrument's developers acquired the original SIP item pool by asking individuals involved in sickness episodes to generate items. Among the 12 SIP categories is a 20-item Social Interaction scale and an 8-item Recreation and Pastimes scale. In addition to social activity items, the Social Interaction scale also contains items dealing with the quality of contact with others.

Respondents indicate whether an item describes their status today and is related to their health. Each item endorsed is assigned a standardized weight and items are summed to create scale and total scales. In addition to individual category scores and a total score, Physical and Psychosocial dimension scores can be calculated. The latter scores are not independent of individual category scores. Scores can range from 0 to 100 with higher scores indicating poorer health (28).

Much of the published work describing the final version of the SIP has not involved discussion of the psychometric properties of the instrument's individual scales. However, earlier studies describing scale level results from prior versions of the SIP are available (27,29). The overall SIP is reported to be internally consistent (Cronbach's alpha > .90), stable (24-hour reproducibility coefficient $\geq$ .50), and valid as demonstrated by the results of construct, convergent, and discriminant validity studies with other health status measures (3). Items making up each category were confirmed using a cluster analysis procedure (3). Interview and self-administration have worked well with patients. SIPs sent by mail, however, have not yielded data comparable to the other forms of administration (3).

The developers of the profile have recently tested and described a somewhat abbreviated instrument, the SIP68 (30). The instrument was constructed by selecting exactly half of the items from the original battery. It includes a 12-item Social Behavior scale evaluating the "possible consequences of a health deviation on a person's functioning in relation to other persons" (30, p. 864). In a study of 51 rheumatic patients, this scale was found to have good temporal stability in repeated measurements over 2 weeks (intraclass correlation coefficient = .94). The authors report that "the internal consistency of the SIP68 and its categories appeared to be approximately of the same level as that of the original instrument" (30).

Like the Rand Social Health Battery, the SIP has undergone extensive instrument development work. Examination of its item content suggests that the Social Behavior scale of the newer SIP68 is a potentially appropriate outcome measure. Further investigation, however, specifically dealing with the validity of this scale as a social interaction measure appears necessary.

The Psychosocial Adjustment to Illness Scale (24)

Seven dimensions of psychosocial adjustment underlie the construction of this 46-item instrument. The domains selected were deemed most germane to psychosocial adjustment to medical illness (31). Among the seven areas assessed are two that relate to social interaction: Extended Family Relationships (four items) and Social Environment (six items). Within the framework of typical family interactions the Extended Family Relationships scale assesses "negative impact of the illness upon communication, quality of relationships, interest in interacting with family, and other variables reflective of this life domain" (31, p. 78). Social Environment "reflects the patient's current social and leisure time activities, as well as the degree to which the patient has suffered impairment or constriction of these activities as a result of the current illness and/or its sequelae" (31, pp. 78–79). Items in this category focus both on interest and behavior. Respondents rate Psychosocial Adjustment to Illness Scale (PAIS) items relative to "the past thirty days including today."

The PAIS was initially designed as a semistructured interview. A self-report version (PAIS-SR), however, has been developed in the interest of feasibility and cost-effectiveness (32). Characteristics of the instrument described here relate to the semistructured interview version of the instrument. In acknowledgment of the fact that the effects of illnesses vary, the instrument's authors have decided to establish illness-specific norms for the PAIS and PAIS-SR (31). Normative data exist for lung cancer patients', renal dialysis patients', acute burn patients', and essential hypertensive patients' responses to the PAIS. PAIS-SR norms are available for cardiac bypass patients and for a sample of multisite cancer patients. Items are scored on an ordinal scale from 0 to 3. Values associated with each response vary by item. Poorer adjustment is associated with higher scale scores.

Reported internal consistency coefficients (Cronbach's alpha) for the Extended Family Relationships scale and the Social Environment scale are variable. Assessed with respect to the dialysis, lung cancer, and cardiac sample, coefficient alphas ranged from .78 to .90 for Social Environment. Coefficient alphas for the Extended Family Relationships scale were lower, .62 and .66, with a very low .12 in the lung cancer sample.

Correlations between the social interaction domains of the PAIS are moderately high, $r = .51$ among lung cancer patients and $r = .53$ among Hodgkin's patients (31), suggesting that each domain may not be a unique component of psychosocial adjustment to illness.

Kaplan De-Nour (33) in a study of chronic hemodialysis patients' psychosocial adjustment, observed that patients' Social Environment scores were among the scores indicating the poorest adjustment while patients reported few or no Extended Family Relationship adjustment problems. Scale scores do not appear to be redundant with measures assessing psychological functioning. Correlations of the Extended Family Relationships scale and the Social Environment scale with psychological measures were lower than correlations between PAIS scales tapping psychological content and these measures (31). Derogatis (31) tested the predictive ability of the PAIS by examining differences between patients screened positive and negative for lung cancer. Patients screened positive scored higher on the Social Environment scale. Extended Family Relationships scores did not differ between groups.

Compared to the Rand Social Health Battery and the SIP, the PAIS has undergone less instrument development work. The work performed thus far is impressive, however. The idea of establishing PAIS scale norms for separate illnesses should help researchers in the selection of social interaction scales. When selecting a potential scale for a clinical trials investigation, a researcher could review these norms to establish whether acceptable variability in scores has been observed for the particular illness of interest. In addition, scale scores would be available for comparison following data collection. The high correlations reported between Social Environment and Extended Family Relationship suggest that the use of both scales in a clinical trial design may not be necessary.

The Nottingham Health Profile

The Nottingham Health Profile (NHP) and its development are described in Chapter 29. The NHP is made up of two parts. Part I contains 38 items leading to six scales: Energy, Pain, Emotional Reactions, Sleep, Social Isolation, and Physical Mobility. Part II contains seven single-item statements relative to various aspects of life affected by

health, including social life, family relations, sex life, and hobbies and interests. In addition, there is a single general question about present health. For all items except the general health one, the respondent is asked to indicate yes or no in response to statements presented.

The developers intended to generate the social measurement concepts of the NHP through empirical study and screening of a large number of statements made by patients during interviews (the original set had 2,200 statements) rather than from a predetermined theoretical framework. The final set of Social Isolation questions of Part I has five yes-no items asking for respondents' subjective feelings about social relationships. Respondents receive a point for each yes response. The Item responses are summed and the score is converted to range from 0 (no problems) to 100 (all possible problems) (34).

Estimates of the reliability of the NHP have focused on stability over time. One study of test-retest reliability involved patients with arthritis who were administered the instrument 4 weeks apart and found Spearman's $r = .78$ for the Social Isolation scale of Part I (34). Another test-retest assessment involving patients with peripheral vascular disease found $r = .77$ for the Part I scale (34). Temporal stability appeared to be good across the spectrum of subject and age groups studied (34). It should be noted, however, that these reliability estimates were observed in subjects with relatively severe disease (34).

Validity studies have demonstrated that the Social Isolation scale is able to distinguish between patients with severe illness only and not between patients with less severe illness or disability. One study of 167 subjects compared two groups of elderly patients known to have frequent or diagnosed severe disability with two other groups from the general population. The Social Isolation scale was able to discriminate between the groups with recognized disability and the general population groups only (35). A small study found the Social Isolation scale useful in studying the effect of cardiac transplant in patients 70 or older (36). A specific analysis of the Nottingham Health Profile's ability to differentiate illness groups found that the scale did not distinguish between the level of disability experienced by inpatients with rheumatoid arthritis and that of outpatients at a migraine clinic (37).

The development of the Nottingham Health Profile was an unusually careful and thoughtful process, and its reliability and validity are highly satisfactory for its intended uses. As the instrument developers have pointed out, "The NHP is clearly tapping only the extreme end of perceived health problems" (38, p. 154). Because the measure is specific to the culture of the United Kingdom, it is not known whether it will perform well in other social contexts.

The Duke-UNC Health Profile and Duke Health Profile

The development of the Duke Health Profile (DUKE) and its longer forbear, the Duke-UNC Health Profile (DUHP) spanned a period of at least a dozen years, beginning in the late 1970s. The 63-question DUHP was designed to be a comprehensive self-administered health status instrument suitable for use in both research and primary clinical care assessment. Rather than focusing on severe illness, the DUHP set as its goal to be "sensitive to small changes in health status" and "oriented toward health rather than disease" (39). The DUHP measures physical function, emotional function, social function, and symptom status. A decade's experience with the instrument identified important problems with it, including its longer than ideal length and "sequestration of all symptom items into a symptom status dimension separate from the three major World Health Organization (WHO) dimensions of physical, mental, and social health . . . and [a] definition of social function restricted to social role performance" (40).

The 17-item DUKE was developed as a totally reconceptualized and shorter measure in response to these issues. It measures ten aspects of health, including the three dimensions of health defined by the WHO. Several items are scored on more than one scale. General Health is defined as the sum of all 15 items composing Physical Health, Mental Health, and Social Health. Two single questions ask about perceived basic health and disability events (40).

Under the parent DUHP formulation, "*Social function* is measured in terms of a person's ability to perform his or her usual role in society (39, p. 809)," a broadly inclusive definition. In the somewhat narrowed DUKE conceptualization, Social Health includes self-concepts about relationships with other people and frequency of social activities, but seems to remain more an empirical than a conceptual matter. Specifically, the survey asks for responses to five items: (1) "I am not an easy person to get along with"; (2) "I am happy with my family relationships"; (3) "I am comfortable being around people"; (4) I "socialize with other people (talk or visit with friends or relatives)"; (5) I "take part in social, religious, or recreational activities (meetings, church, sports, parties)." Response possibilities are "none," "some," and "a lot." The combined responses are scaled from 0 to 100, with high scores representing good health (40).

The reliability of the DUKE measures was evaluated by measurement of internal consistency and temporal stability. In a study of 683 ambulatory adult patients, the coefficient alpha of the Social Health scale was .55, a somewhat low value, perhaps because of the different notions included in "Social Health." Temporal stability during a 1- to 8-week time period, as measured by test-retest Spearman coefficients in a population of 55, was .57. The validity of the DUKE instrument was assessed by comparisons with existing measures, including the parent DUHP, the SIP, and the Tennessee Self-Concept Scale. For the DUHP comparison, the correlation between the social health scales was .61, with discriminant validity generally established with regard to the other scales of the DUHP. The Spearman rank-order correlation of the DUKE scale with the SIP (which reads in the opposite direction) was −.41. Finally, the Spearman rank-order correlation with the Tennessee measure was .60 (40).

The McMaster Health Index Questionnaire

The McMaster Health Index Questionnaire (MHIQ) has its roots in work done at the McMaster University Medical School in Ontario in 1970. An interdisciplinary team of scholars selected an initial pool of 172 items, following the WHO definition of health. The panel reviewed other instruments in use, but did not select any in particular as a basis for its work. The initial items went through a long screening process that involved assessing sensitivity to change in function of general hospital patients and ability to predict family physicians' global assessments of function. The MHIQ contains 59 items producing three scales. The Physical Function scale has 24 items, the Social Function scale has 25 items, and the Emotional Function scale has 25 items. There are six items common to both the social and emotional scales (41).

The Social Function scale encompasses general well-being, work/social role performance/material welfare, family support/participation, and global social function. Some of the questions are broad self-assessments, for instance, "How would you say your health is today?" Others probe the occurrence of particular social events within specified time frames, such as, "During the last year, have you had trouble getting along with friends/relatives?" and "Has a friend visited you in the last week?" Still others probe background issues such as church attendance or amount of television viewing. Scoring requires use of a key supplied by the authors. In the scoring key, the possible replies for each scale item are assigned a "good" function response weight of 1 or a "poor" function weight of 0. The Social Function Index is the sum of items assigned 1 divided by 25.

Given the disparate nature of the concepts included in the Social Function scale, no one seems to have set out to establish the internal consistency of the MHIQ. The reliability of the Social Function scale has been measured by test-retest reliability in physiotherapy patients (kappa = .48) and psychiatry patients (kappa = .66). The scale has been able to discriminate between populations with various illnesses, but work still needs to be performed to establish that the social and emotional scales are sensitive to change in persons whose functioning is known to have changed (41).

Since the MHIQ scales were derived empirically, there is not a preestablished definition of Social Function. Rather, measures of performance, subjective judgments, and demographic characteristics all contribute to the final scale value. Many items do not seem plausible as clinical outcomes, for instance, "Do you have a telephone?" For other items, the coding of the responses may produce an outcome measure inappropriate for particular contexts; for example, in response to the question of occupational status, "retired" or no answer are scored as "poor" responses. The MHIQ may, however, provide a useful general assessment of Social Function complementing that of more specific clinical measures.

Social Engagement Scale

In the most seriously impaired populations it is not always possible for the patient to describe his or her own state of being. This is particularly true of nursing home residents, over half of whom have varying levels of dementia (42). As in other fields of quality of life assessment, basic physical functioning dominates most measures of nursing home quality of life. Congress mandated the development of the Minimum Data Set (MDS) for resident assessment, which as of 1991 is completed periodically for all residents of nursing homes in the United States. The MDS includes other dimensions of quality of life more consistent with the premise that these facilities are *homes* to the residents.

In consultation with social workers, activities therapists, and other clinicians involved in improving the psychosocial aspects of residents' lives, six items assessing the social well-being of the resident were included in the instrument. The concepts addressed in these items focus on the extent to which the individual resident is engaged in the social life of the facility, including interacting with others, doing self-initiated activities or those initiated by others. Each item is scored dichotomously and staff are instructed to score a yes for any evidence of the behavior. Like the entire MDS, each of the six items is rooted in observable behaviors since the instrument is completed by staff members. Interrater reliability testing following training of facility staff yielded an average reliability coefficient (intraclass correlation) of .57 (43).

A summary scale measuring social engagement is created as a simple linear sum of the positive responses, and the internal consistency of this scale has been reported to be .79 (44). Analyses of the validity of the scale were undertaken in a random sample of 2,175 nursing home residents in 270 facilities in 10 states using structural equation modeling (44). Findings revealed that social engagement is strongly related to physical and cognitive functioning and that the structure of the interitem relations is comparable for the most and least severely physically and cognitively impaired. Furthermore, there was considerable variability in the measure in all but the most impaired residents and this variance was partially explained by facility characteristics, including the types of services available.

FUTURE RESEARCH

The highest priority in this area should be to establish a consensus as to the definition of social interaction. We feel the major conceptual issue to be addressed is the orientation of the definition. Should the concept be wholly defined in behavioral terms? If frequency of contacts is measured, should it be measured from the perspective of patient initia-

tion, initiation by others, or by both? Finally, what role does interest or desire to participate in social interactions play in this conceptualization? Answers to these questions should bring us closer to a more solid formalization of this concept and will provide the framework for the development and assessment of measurement instruments.

CONCLUSIONS

Compared with other components of quality of life, social interaction is the least well conceptualized. This construct does not relate solely to the individual assessed. Unlike physical and mental health, social interaction can be considered at least partially external to an individual's quality of life or health status (2). Difficulty dealing with this concept is exemplified by Ware and Donald's (2) revision of their health status model following analysis of their social health data. In deciding that social function should be considered external to an individual's health status (that is, as an independent variable rather than as an outcome variable), they concluded that this model "explains empirical results better than one that includes social function as an integral component of individual health" (2, p. 6).

We have taken the view here that social interaction is a potential outcome measure in clinical trials designs. The most important decision one makes in this regard is that social interaction is in fact an outcome measure of interest. Unless social interaction can be considered to be influenced, directly or indirectly, by the intervention under study, the concept should not be measured. We feel this rule should be followed when any quality of life domain is considered for assessment.

We selected brief, self-report measures for review. Several (for example, the SIP and the PAIS) were developed specifically for use in patient populations. Scales contained in these measures and in the Medical Outcome Study portfolio of instruments hold the most promise as social interaction measures. An impressive amount of instrument development work exists for these measures. Although other social interaction measures exist, we tried to select scales that assess features of social functioning appropriate to medical interventions and to all potential patients assessed. For example, we excluded from consideration social interaction measures whose content relates to issues such as marital satisfaction, employability, and the assessment of mental dysfunction. More extensive reviews of social health measures in general are presented in McDowell and Newell (45) and Mangen and Peterson (46).

ACKNOWLEDGMENTS

This research was supported in part by grants from the National Cancer Institute (CA59408 and CA57755) and from the Agency for Health Care Policy and Research (HS08071).

REFERENCES

1. Yancik R, Yates JW. Quality-of-life assessment of cancer patients: conceptual and methodological challenges and constraints. *Cancer Bull* 1986;38:217–222.
2. Donald CA, Ware JE. *The quantification of social contacts and resources.* Santa Monica: Rand, 1982.
3. Bergner M, Bobbitt RA, Carter WB, Gilson BS. The sickness impact profile: development and final revision of a health status measure. *Med Care* 1981;19:787–805.
4. Ware JE. The assessment of health status. In: Aiken LH, Mechanic D, eds. *Applications of social science to clinical medicine and health policy.* New Brunswick: Rutgers University Press, 1986:204–228.
5. Berkman L. Assessing the physical health effects of social networks and social support. *Annu Rev Public Health* 1984;5:412–432.
6. Cohen S, Syme SL. Issues in the study and application of social support. In: Cohen S, Syme SL, eds. *Social support and health.* Orlando: Academic Press, 1985:3–22.
7. Brook RB, Ware JE, Rogers WH, et al. Does free care improve adults' health? Results from a randomized controlled trial. *N Engl J Med* 1983;309:1426–1434.
8. Mor V, Greer OS, Kastenbaum R, eds. *The hospice experiment.* Baltimore: Johns Hopkins University Press, 1988.
9. Carcagno GJ, Kemper P. The evaluation of the national long term care demonstration: an overview of the channeling demonstration and its evaluation. *Health Serv Res* 1988;23:1–22.
10. World Health Organization. *The first ten years of the World Health Organization.* Geneva: WHO, 1958.
11. Ware JE, Brook RH, Williams KN, Stewart AL, Davies-Avery A. *Conceptualization and measurement of health for adults in the health insurance study; Vol I, Model of health and methodology.* Santa Monica: Rand, 1978.
12. Stewart AL, Ware JE Jr, Brook RH, Davies-Avery A. *Conceptualization and measurement of health for adults in the health insurance study: Vol II, Physical health in terms of functioning.* Santa Monica: Rand, 1978.
13. Johnston SA, Ware JE Jr, Davies-Avery A, Brook RH. *Conceptualization and measurement of health for adults in the health insurance study: Vol III, Mental health.* Santa Monica: Rand, 1978.
14. Donald CA, Ware JE, Brook RH, Davies-Avery A. *Conceptualization and measurement of health for adults in the health insurance study: Vol. IV, Social health.* Santa Monica: Rand, 1978.
15. Ware JE, Davies-Avery A, Donald CA. *Conceptualization and measurement of health for adults in the health insurance study: Vol V, General health perceptions.* Santa Monica: Rand, 1978.
16. Ware JE Jr, Brook RH, Davies-Avery A. *Conceptualization and measurement of health for adults in the health insurance study: Vol VI, Analysis of relationships among health status measures.* Santa Monica: Rand, 1978.
17. Rogers WH, Williams KN, Brook RH. *Conceptualization and measurement of health for adults in the health insurance study: Vol VII, Power analysis of health status measures.* Santa Monica: Rand, 1978.
18. Brook RH, Ware JE Jr, Davies-Avery A, Stewart AL, Johnston SA, Donald CA, Rogers WH, Williams KN. *Conceptualization and measurement of health for adults in the health insurance study: Vol VIII, Overview.* Santa Monica: Rand, 1978.
19. Stewart AL, Sherbourne CD, et al. Summary and discussion of MOS measures. In: Stewart AL, Ware JE, eds. *Measuring functioning and well-being: the Medical Outcomes Study approach.* Durham: Duke University Press, 1992.
20. Sherbourne CD. Social functioning: social activity limitations measure. In: Stewart AL, Ware JE, eds. *Measuring functioning and well-being: the Medical Outcomes Study approach.* Durham: Duke University Press, 1992.
21. Ware JE, et al. SF-36 Health Survey: manual and interpretation guide. Boston: The Health Institute, New England Medical Center, 1993.
22. Hays RD, Stewart AL. Construct validity of MOS health measures. In: Stewart AL, Ware JE, eds. *Measuring functioning and well-being: the Medical Outcomes Study approach.* Durham: Duke University Press, 1992.
23. Hunt SM, McKenna SP. Letter. *Br Med J* 1992;305:645.
24. Brazier JE, Harper R, Jones NM, et al. Validating the SF-36 health survey questionnaire: new outcome measure for primary care. *Br Med J* 1992;305:160–164.
25. Jette AM, Davies AR, Cleary PD, Calkins DR, Rubenstein LV, Fink A, et al. The Functional Status Questionnaire: reliability and validity when used in primary care. *J Gen Intern Med* 1986;1:143–149.
26. Cleary PD, Greenfield S, McNeil BJ. Assessing quality of life after surgery. *Controlled Clin Trials* 1991;12(4 suppl):189S–203S.
27. Bergner M, Bobbitt RA, Pollard WE, Martin DP, Gilson BS. The Sickness Impact Profile: validation of a health status measure. *Med Care* 1976:14:57–67.
28. Read JL, Quinn RJ, Hoefer MA. Measuring overall health: an evaluation of three important approaches. *J Chronic Dis* 1987;40:7S–21S.
29. Pollard WE, Bobbitt RA, Bergner M, Gilson BS. The sickness impact profile: reliability of a health status measure. *Med Care* 1976;14:146.
30. DeBruin AF, Buys M, DeWitte LP, Diederiks JP. The Sickness Impact Profile: SIP68, a short generic version. First evaluation and reproducibility. *J Clin Epidemiol* 1994;47:863–871.
31. Derogatis LR. The psychological adjustment to illness scale (PAIS). *J Psychosom Res* 1986;30:77–91.
32. Derogatis LR, Lopez M. *Psychological adjustment to illness scale (PAIS & PAIS-SR): scoring procedures & administration manual—I.* Baltimore: Clinical Psychometric Research, 1983.
33. Kaplan De-Nour AK. Psychological adjustment to illness scale (PAIS): a study of chronic hemodialysis patients. *J Psychosom Res* 1982;26:11–22.
34. McEwen J. The Nottingham Health Profile. In: Walker SR, Rosser RM, eds. *Quality of life assessment: key issues in the 1990's.* Lancaster, UK: Kluwer Academic, 1993.
35. Hunt SM, McKenna SP, McEwen J, Backett EM, Williams J, Papp E. A quantitative approach to perceived health status: a validation study. *J Epidemiol Community Health* 1980;34:281–286.
36. Aravot DJ, Banner NR, Khaghani A, et al. Cardiac transplantation in the seventh decade of life. *Am J Cardiol* 1989;63:90–93.
37. Jenkinson C, Fitzpatrick R, Argyle M. The Nottingham Health Profile: an analysis of its sensitivity in differentiating illness groups. *Soc Sci Med* 1988;12:1411–1414.
38. Hunt S, McEwen J, McKenna P. *Measuring health status.* London: Croon Helm, 1986.
39. Parkerson GR, Gehlbach SH, Wagner EH, et al. The Duke-UNC Health Profile: an adult health status instrument for primary care. *Med Care* 1981;19:806–828.
40. Parkerson GR Jr, Broadhead WE, Tse CK. The Duke Health Profile. A 17-item measure of health and. dysfunction. *Med Care* 1990;28:1056–1072.
41. Chambers LW. The McMaster Health Index Questionnaire: an update. In: Walker SR, Rosser RD, eds. *Quality of life assessment: key issues in the 1990's.* Boston: Kluwer Academic, 1993;131–149.
42. Sekscenski ES. Discharge from nursing homes: preliminary data from the 1985 National Nursing Home Survey. NCHS Advance data from Vital & Health Statistics of the National Center for Health Statistics, #142 September 1987 DHHS Publication Number (PHS) 87-1250. Hyattsville, MD: Public Health Service, 1987.
43. Hawes C, Morris JN, Phillips CD, Mor V, Fries BE, Nonemaker S. Reliability estimates for the minimum data set for nursing home resident assessment and care screening (MDS). *Gerontologist* 1995;35:172–178.
44. Mor V, Branco K. Fleishman J, Hawes C, Phillips C, Morris J, Fries B. The structure of social engagement among nursing home residents. *J Gerontol Psychol Sci* 1995;50:P1–P8.
45. McDowell I, Newell C. *Measuring health; a guide to rating scales and questionnaires.* New York: Oxford University Press, 1987.
46. Mangen DJ, Peterson W, eds. *Research instruments in social gerontology.* Minneapolis: University of Minnesota Press, 1982.

Quality of Life and Pharmacoeconomics in Clinical Trials, Second Edition, edited by B. Spilker. Lippincott-Raven Publishers, Philadelphia © 1996.

CHAPTER 14

Cognitive Aspects of Quality of Life Assessment

Ivan Barofsky

INTRODUCTION

When people respond to the questions on a quality of life assessment they use the same cognitive processes they would when responding to any type of question. For example, a person may be asked, "How are you?" This question is usually used as a greeting that also asks respondents to reflect about their status. It provides no direction on the content to include in a response, and in this sense leaves the respondents free to select aspects of their life that they consider determinants of their current status.

In contrast consider the self-assessed health status (SAHS) question, "In general, would you say your health is excellent, very good, good, fair, or poor?" This question is found in national health surveys and specific quality of life assessments (1–3). Here, too, respondents are to reflect on memories of past events, select those of importance to themselves, process this information, and use it to generate a response. What is different about the SAHS question compared with the previous question is that it refers to the more limited domain of a person's health status. Both questions, however, provide little insight into the elements actually used by a person to make a quality of life judgment. Multiattribute health status assessments (4,5), in contrast, provide a selected range of quality of life domains for the respondent to consider, such as physical performance, recreation, interpersonal relationships, and so on. In responding to items on a multiattribute questionnaire the person would still select material from a broad array of experiences, but now experiences associated with a specific domain.

The advantage of the multiattribute over the single-item assessment is that it offers the investigator greater analytical potential. It is limited in the sense that the person is asked to address a prescribed number of domains, independent of whether they are relevant to the person's life. The person could also determine (scale and value) the saliency of his or her response to a question dealing with a specific domain of quality of life (e.g., physical status). The scaling of items usually occurs along intensive dimensions but can also indicate the presence or absence of change in the domain.

Most multiattribute assessments do not offer the respondent the opportunity to indicate the relative importance (or value) of the domains surveyed in the quality of life assessment, although some do (6,7). As a consequence, the significance of a difference in patient responses, as indicated by a particular multiattribute assessment, is often left to persons other than the respondent.

Both types of assessments require aggregation, especially if the information retrieved is to be used for initiating behaviors or making policy. Aggregation occurs informally for the single indicator (as when a person selects several experiences and privately uses cognitive rules to combine them into a single quality of life index), and formally for the multiattribute assessment (which usually is determined by a scoring system). Both types of assessments can be presented as an index, although multiattribute assessments can also be presented as profiles. Aggregation can also occur for profiles but now within quality of life domains (see below). More recently, Joyce and his colleagues (8) have developed a methodology that permits individuals to select the domains that are most relevant to them to include in a quality of life assessment. By so doing they have provided another level of specificity, now at the individual patient level, in generating a quality of life assessment. Guyatt et al. (9) have devel-

I. Barofsky: Department of Psychiatry and Behavioral Sciences, Johns Hopkins University School of Medicine, Baltimore, Maryland 21224.

oped an intermediate strategy that allows patients to select a certain number of issues of particular relevance to themselves, but also asks the patients a standard set of items. Broadly sketched, then, the cognitive elements common to single-item or multiattribute quality of life assessments are retrieval from memory of past events, scaling of these events, valuations or statements of preferences for the indicated outcomes, and aggregation of these events into an index.

Why is it important to understand the cognitive model implicit in any quality of life assessment? It is important because the specific cognitive processes evoked by different types of questions may result in reports of different quality of life outcomes. Erickson et al. (10), for example, have found that depending on the type of question, the estimate of the number of persons free of limitations in major activities may vary as much as from 12% to 85%. It can also be shown that the assessments differ in terms of whether the implied cognitive activities are done formally or informally, who does them, and what cognitive rules, if any, are followed.

There are also differences in the relationship between aggregation rules and a cognitive process. Thus, the Index of Well-Being (IWB) (11) is based on a clear theoretical foundation, Norman Anderson's cognitive algebra (12), while the Health Utility Index (HUI) (13) is aggregated using an arbitrary set of rules (see below). The fundamental question here is whether these differences lead to differences in the information provided by the assessment. Investigators and policy makers may want to know this when they have to interpret the results of their assessment. Differences in the cognitive model could be created as a result of the question format (to what extent the question taps implicitly or explicitly learned events), the time frame of the question (which would have an impact on the accuracy of information recalled), the aggregation system (how diverse experiences are combined to provide an index), and so on. On the other hand, if the cognitive model underlying a multiattribute quality of life assessment can be shown to be similar to or simulate the cognitive processes that a person uses when generating, for example, a global quality of life assessment, then the information provided by the alternative assessments would reflect a high degree of internal consistency. This is discussed in this chapter, along with cognitive interviewing methods helpful in establishing the meaning of questions on any quality of life assessment. This discussion demonstrates that there are methods to reassure investigators that they are achieving their intent in designing their questionnaire.

COGNITION AND QUALITY OF LIFE ASSESSMENT: AN OVERVIEW

There are four basic methods for collecting quality of life data; self reports, direct one-to-one interviewing, surrogate responders, and telephone interviews (14). Each method would be expected to involve different cognitive processes. To simplify the discussion, this chapter deals only with quality of life assessments based on self-reports. Self-reports, how-

ever, are complex behaviors involving the respondents' interpretation of the question, retrieval from their memory, and even their editing of their response for reasons of social pressure or to ensure privacy.

Table 1 includes a number of questions on several generic quality of life assessments that ask about the pain experience of the respondents. Inspection of the table reveals that the items differ in terms of their time reference and scaling method. The EURQOL assessment asks the respondents to consider what is true for them today and the SF-36 asks what is true over the last month, while the Nottingham Health Profile has no particular time reference. Jobe et al. (15) summarize evidence suggesting that the time reference for a health survey question can be an important determinant of the accuracy of the response to the item. The Medical Outcomes Study and the EURQOL use intensity scaling, while the Nottingham Health Profile asks respondents to indicate the presence or absence of a pain condition. Only one item asks about the impact of pain on the person's functioning (SF-36 item #8). All the other items imply that the presence of intense pain would be disruptive of quality of life but do not provide any direct assessment of it (see Barofsky, Chapter 103).

Implicit in Table 1 is the assumption that questions that have a common reference, in this case pain, generate comparable information. The same question could be asked about different quality of life assessments. Studies in which several multiattribute quality of life assessments are administered to the same person do suggest that a reasonable degree of correlation exists between assessments (16–20). What does this observation mean? For one, it may simply mean that the several assessments overlap in the items included. For example, the SF-36 consists of items from the Health Interview Survey and Psychological General Well-Being Scale (21), and the Nottingham Health Profile (NHP) (22) and the Arthritis Impact Measurement Scale (AIMS) (23) both include items that were originally on the Sickness Impact Profile (SIP) (24). It would not be too surprising then to discover that the assessments appear related.

Liang et al. (19) suggest another approach to this task—the ability of different assessment instruments to monitor effect size. Thus, if instruments differ in their sensitivity to change then they are not providing the conditions necessary to generate the same level of information. Liang et al. compared the Functional Status Instrument (FSI) (25), the Health Assessment Questionnaire (HAQ) (26), the AIMS (23), the IWB (27), and SIP (24). What they found for global indexes was that the FSI and the HAQ were relatively insensitive. They found that other measures of change (28,29) are available to compare assessment instruments. Thus, while the number of studies in this area is not large, it is clear that an adequate methodology exists to permit at least a first approximation of the comparative informational content among quality of life assessments.

What about comparing information about domains within an assessment? Liang et al. (19), using the same methodology described above, found that the HAQ and the IWB were

TABLE 1. *Representative pain questions from various quality of life assessments*

The MOS-36:

7. How much bodily pain have you had during the <u>past 4 weeks</u>?

   None, mild, moderate, severe, very severe.

8. During the <u>past 4 weeks</u> how much did <u>pain</u> interfere with your normal work (including both work outside the home and housework)?

   Not at all, a little bit, moderately, quite a bit, extremely.

The Nottingham Health Profile:

   Listed below are some problems people have in their daily life. Please read each one carefully. If it is true, check off in the box under Yes. If it is not true, check off in the box under No. If you are not sure whether to answer yes or no to a problem, ask yourself whether it is true for you in general.

	YES	NO
I have pain at night.	_____	_____
I have unbearable pain.	_____	_____
I find it painful to change position.	_____	_____
I am in pain when I walk.	_____	_____
I am in pain when I am standing.	_____	_____
I am in constant pain.	_____	_____
I am in pain when going up and down stairs or steps.	_____	_____
I am in pain when I am sitting.	_____	_____

EURQOL:

   By placing a tick in one box in each group below, please indicate which statements best describe your health state today.

_____ I have no pain or discomfort.
_____ I have moderate pain or discomfort.
_____ I have extreme pain or discomfort.

---

least sensitive as measures of mobility, while the AIMS and IWB were least sensitive for measures of social functioning. All the measures had equal sensitivity to pain scales. Liang et al.'s study clearly indicates that not all quality of life assessments would be equally useful in providing information about specific quality of life domains. Parr et al. (30) compared the responses to a visual analog measure of pain and the eight items on the NHP (22). They found that while the visual analog measure of pain varied between drug treatments, the pain subscale of the NHP did not. This is just what would be expected if differences in question format and structure led to differences in cognitive processing, and therefore information generated by an assessment. Part of the problem here is that most quality of life assessments do not capture the complex nature of the phenomena being measured. For example, Salovey et al. (31) discuss the fact that the assessment of pain in surveys such as quality of life assessments can be expected to be a complex task involving several types of measures, including establishing a semantic space, scaling the intensity of the pain, defining pain in sensory, affective, and evaluative terms, distinguishing pain reports from pain behavior, and so on.

The above discussion supports the view that understanding the cognitive basis for responses to questions on a quality of life assessment would enhance the design, selection of assessment instruments, and interpretation of quality of life data. To gain some perspective on the role of cognition in quality of life assessment it will first be necessary to review some of the theories underlying cognitive processing. This should help investigators focus on the aspects of current cognitive research that would be most applicable to quality of life assessment.

Many theories of cognition are based on the *information processing* perspective that has evolved since the development of computers. These theories propose that there are cognitive structures and processes for transferring information between these structures (32). Classical information theory assumes that information received by the organism is first sensed and then analyzed by perceptual feature detectors and/or pattern recognizer. This information is then attended to and if relevant stored in short-term memory. Primary or short-term memory is where judgments, inferences, and problem solving occurs (32). Information stays in primary memory as long as it is rehearsed. If primary memory leads to action, then a memory trace occurs and the information is stored as long-term memory. If action does not occur then the memory decays.

An alternative information processing model called the Adaptive Control of Thought (ACT) (33) holds that memory is divisible into two types: declarative and procedural. Declarative memory can be further divided into episodic memory (memory for specific events that a person experiences) and semantic memory (memory that reflects abstract knowledge). Declarative memory is generally available to a person by introspection, while procedural information (how we do things) is not. Thus, declarative memory is a conscious process, while procedural memory is not. The acquisition of procedural memory occurs implicitly, without a person's awareness, whereas a person is aware of events leading to declarative memory. Another model, the parallel distributed processing (PDP) (34,35), assumes that a large number of personal computers are available, all of which are interconnected, permitting a very large number of simultaneous calculations. Transposed to the brain, this model assumes that a large number of central nervous system structures are interconnected and arranged so that a vast array of calculations are possible. This system is working all the time, rather than sequentially, as the other two theories assume. Consciousness in this theory is a matter of time, with the longer the calculations the more aware the person is of the events he is experiencing. Much of what is considered learned is assumed to be unconscious or implicitly learned.

What seems central to these models is an effort to account for two major methods whereby information is acquired and stored, one implicit and one explicit (36,37). Implicit learning, for example, is based on elementary learning processes and is more dependent on perceptual processes. Learning the grammatical foundation of a language without being aware of it would be an example of implicit learning. The PDP model, or variants of it (35), provides a conceptual foundation for implicit learning. Explicit learning is more likely to involve abstraction, and awareness of the learning.

Explicit memory involves a direct test of memory, such as when subjects are asked to freely recall an event, use cues to recall, or recognize the event after being presented with some information about the event. Each of these methods differs in the degree that subjects are provided with information about what it is they are to recall. For example, when SF-36 item #7 (Table 1) lists pain intensity as possibly varying from none to very severe the respondent is immediately told that pain can vary along this range. Thus, the item is an example of cued recall. In contrast, the items on the NHP would be an example of free recall; no information, other than presence or absence, is provided to help guide the person's response.

Implicit memory refers to any memory task that is tested without direct or specific reference to the event. The notion that past adverse experiences can affect a person's current mentation is an old one, and frequently encountered in the psychologist's clinic (36). Descartes (38) and Leibnitz (39) both speak of frightening and stressful experiences affecting a person's behavior without the person's being aware of the connection. A study reported by Zeitlin and McNally (40) illustrates the role of both implicit and explicit memory bias in posttraumatic stress disorder (PTSD) patients. They administered a cued recall (explicit memory) test and a word completion (implicit memory) test to a group of PTSD veterans and non-PTSD veterans. Each group was exposed to combat, threatening, positive, and neutral words. The results suggested that the PTSD veterans exhibited poor memory for all cued words except combat words, suggesting an explicit memory bias. In addition, the PTSD veterans exhibited a bias for combat words on the word completion test. The authors interpret the results of their study as support for the

notion that a "memory bias" underlies the reexperiencing of symptoms characteristic of PTSD, and that the bias could have been acquired both implicitedly and explicitly.

A study reported by Barofsky et al. (41) illustrates how implicit memory biases may play a role in quality of life assessment. They had developed a simple quality of life assessment that asked patients to check off domains impacted by gastrointestinal disturbances, as well as rate global visual analog scales. The patients were also administered the Symptom Check List-90 (42) questionnaire, a measure of psychological distress. What they found was that the global assessments were significantly correlated to measures of nine different dimensions of distress but not to the ten specific domains. It was also possible to identify persons who met the definition of "caseness" (persons whose score suggested that their type of distress was clinically significant), and repeat the correlational analysis without these persons in the sample. When this was done only five of the nine distress dimensions remained significantly correlated to the global assessments. These data, as well as others, suggest that the response to global indicators are more likely to be effected by the emotional characteristics of a person (43). How could emotional factors bias the response to one type of quality of life questionnaire and not another? The answer to this question is not provided by this study. However, as was evident from studies of the effect of implicit and explicit memory biases (40), the type of question used may tap different acquisition processes. Thus, it would be of interest to determine if the emotionality attached to global assessments was implicitedly acquired and more likely to be expressed with a global question, while the information surrounding domain-specific assessments was more explicated and consciously acquired.

Finally, it is necessary to return to the items in Table 1 and ask whether the information utilized in response to a question on pain was acquired implicitedly or explicitedly and whether the investigators took advantage of this information in the design of items on their quality of life questionnaire. There is very little evidence that such issues were considered when pain, or any other type of questionnaires were designed (68). To do so would imply that investigators recognize that the most reliable and valid method of assessment replicates the method whereby the experience was acquired.

COGNITIVE MODELS IN ESTABLISHED QUALITY OF LIFE ASSESSMENTS

Aggregation and the reduction of information into more discrete units is one of the most fundamental of cognitive processes. We do it as a part of our normal personal and social interchanges, and it is an essential part of making policy and clinical decisions. Tversky and Kahnman (44) and others have demonstrated that people use cognitive devices, such as heuristic ones, to help order information. How have quality of life researchers ordered the information they have gathered, and do they acknowledge the methods people use in ordering information in the design of their assessments? The simplest way to answer this question is to inspect the scoring systems used for the various quality of life assessments. The reader is referred to Chapter 6 in Patrick and Erickson (45) as a convenient way to be introduced to this literature. Patrick and Erickson identify two principal approaches to scoring quality of life assessments: the use of statistical procedures and preference systems. The virtues and limitations of each of these approaches were elegantly debated by Ware (46) and Bush (47). However, neither of these approaches necessarily reflects the cognitive processes people use.

It is important that the way an assessment instrument summarizes its observations is in concordance with the way a person thinks about and processes information. One only has to look at the continuing debate concerning the interpretation of intelligence testing (48,49) and its applicability to social policy to appreciate the importance of this concordance. IQ is an example of a psychometrically created construct whose existence is made secure more by its measurement than by its biology. Stated differently, there appears to be a good fit between the data and the model that proposes the existence of IQ, but there is less evidence that the IQ model is represented in reality (50).

The potential here for abuse is enormous, creating a clear threat to social policy. It is also true that there is a potential for the premature use of information based on such models. This is already occurring in the area of health status assessment; witness the current application of social preferences to prioritized health services in the state of Oregon (51). How can these dangers be avoided and the opportunity offered by the technology evolving in the area of quality of life assessment taken advantage of? The author's answer is, by ensuring that the formal quality of life assessment system created by investigators matches what respondents do when they informally generate a quality of life assessment. In this sense, quality of life assessment investigators have an advantage over those interested in intelligence testing; they have a standard with which they can compare their models.

Table 2 summarizes the scoring system used to assess the two questions on bodily pain on the SF-36. The scoring system used to aggregate the response to the two items in the index does not simply add the score of each item together, but rather makes the score for item #7 dependent on the score for item #8. In contrast, the scoring system of other

TABLE 2. *Bodily pain: verbatim items and scoring information*

Verbatim Items:

7. How much bodily pain have you had during the last 4 weeks?

8. During the past 4 weeks, how much did pain interfere with your normal work (including both work outside the home and housework)?

Precoded and Final Values for Item 7:

Response choices	Precoded item value	Final item value
None	1	6.0
Very mild	2	5.4
Mild	3	4.2
Moderate	4	3.1
Severe	5	2.2
Very severe	6	1.0

Scoring for Item 8—if both Items 7 and 8 are answered:

Response choices	If item 8 (precoded item value)	and	Item 7 (precoded item value)	then	Item 8 (final item value)
Not at all	1		1		6
Not at all	1		2 through 6		5
A little bit	2		1 through 6		4
Moderately	3		1 through 6		3
Quite a bit	4		1 through 6		2
Extremely	5		1 through 6		1

Scoring for Item 8—if Item 7 is not answered:

Response choices	Precoded item value	Final item value
Not at all	1	6.0
A little bit	2	4.75
Moderately	3	3.5
Quite a bit	4	2.25
Extremely	5	1.0

Adapted from ref. 52.

SF-36 domains do sum scores across items included in the domain (52). Note also that the differences in the scale values assigned to the response choices are not equal. This implies that the intervals between responses were adjusted by Ware (52) as a result of studies that indicated that respondents did not perceive the distance between intervals as equal. This is exactly what one would expect if an investigator were sensitive to the importance of how people process information and how this information affects their rating behavior. What the SF-36 does not do, however, is to provide a method whereby the eight domains assessed can be combined into a single index. Nor does it provide a means whereby individuals can indicate their preference for the outcomes measured by the assessment instrument. Both of these are cognitive activities that people do, especially when providing a global assessment, and would be expected to be in place for a comprehensive quality of life assessment instrument.

The scaling described in the SF-36 is based on a Likert scale (53). An alternative method was developed by Guttman (54) and has been referred to as cumulative scaling. It was adapted by Katz and his colleagues (55) for measuring activities of daily living. It is of interest here not so much because it presents an alternative scaling method but because it may reflect an alternative way people think about the scaling task. There is no evidence, however, that respondents organize their information according to the method of cumulative scaling.

Table 3 summarizes the scoring systems for the IWB (56) and HUI (57). Both measures provide single indexes that are preference weighted. Thus, both assessments provide a measure of the relative importance of the various health states a person may be in. Neither provides a description of the health states themselves and in this sense both have less analytical potential than, say, the SF-36. What they both can provide is an estimate of the benefit in a cost-benefit analysis. This the SF-36 cannot do, since it provides no rules for aggregation or preference estimates. Note also that the terms in the IWB are added together (Table 3), while they are multiplied in the HUI. Kaplan (58) has suggested that the addition in the model follows the rules of cognitive algebra described by Anderson (12). What is important about Anderson's cognitive algebra is that it permits a direct statistical testing of the judgment model inherent to the quality of life assessment. Analysis of variance methods can be used to determine if main, but not interaction, effects characterize the person's response. In this way it is possible to directly test if the judgment a person makes is based on an additive algebra model. No such direct test of the cognitive foundation underlying the HUI has been described. Torrance (57) is known to have done a study comparing time trade-off techniques, standard gambles, and category scaling. He advises that category scaling be avoided since it did not correlate as well with the results generated by use of the standard gamble. He is, in effect, arguing that a utility approach to preference estimation and the standard gamble be used as

TABLE 3. *Formulas for calculating preferences*

Health Utility Index:
$$U = 1.42 \, (P, R, S, H) - 0.42$$

P = Physical function
R = Role function
S = Socioemotional function
H = Health problems

Index of Well-Being:
$$W = 1 + (CPXwt) + (MOBwt) + (PACwt) + (SACwt)$$

CPXwt = Symptom Problem Complex × Weighting Factor
MOBwt = Mobility × Weighting Factor
PACwt = Physical Activity Scale × Weighting Factor
SACwt = Social Activity Scale × Weighting Factor

the benchmark measure since it evolved directly from von Neumann–Morgenstern theory (59).

It is also of interest to note that some of the earlier work of Ware's included a study with Clairice Veit who promoted applications of Anderson's cognitive algebra. She and her colleagues (60) reported a study with college students who were asked to judge which of two health states they preferred. She used Anderson's idea that all possible combinations of the variables be compared in a factorial design. They found that physical and mental health were additive, although individual differences were also noted.

Most of the theoretical work on the cognitive foundation of health status and quality of life measurements was done in the late 1970s and hasn't been revisited since. This is unfortunate, because much has been learned since then about cognitive processing, information that has yet to be integrated into the design and administration of quality of life assessments.

COGNITIVE INTERVIEWING METHODS AND QUALITY OF LIFE ASSESSMENTS

Most thoughtfully developed quality of life assessments include deliberate efforts to involve the persons to whom the assessment is to be applied in the development of the assessment. Guyatt et al. (61), for example, have developed a methodology that ensures that the items used in the questionnaire reflect the most important issues to the respondents. Other investigators have involved clinicians as well (24). These efforts would be expected since quality of life assessments should, by definition alone, reflect a person's perspective. There are, however, additional questions that need to be asked, such as what do a person's answers to these questions mean. To gain some insight into this issue it would be helpful if quality of life researchers would use some of the methodologies being developed by survey researchers who are developing cognitive models of the survey response process (62). Researchers at the National Center for Health Statistics, for example, have established a Questionnaire Design Research Laboratory (63), whose purpose is to design survey items whose meaning, and therefore, interpretation is clear. Willis (64) has provided a training manual that can be used to do cognitive interviewing when developing a questionnaire. He and his colleagues attempt to answer three questions as a result of their activities: First, do the respondents understand the question? Second, what cognitive processes are involved in their effort to retrieve memory or relevant information to answer the question? Third, how do the respondents use this information in making their response to the question?

To determine if the respondents understand the question, they are asked what they think the question is asking. They are also asked to specify what particular words or phrases mean. To determine the retrieval process the respondents are encouraged to reveal what information they would use when responding to the question, and also to describe how they would proceed in answering the question. For example, the answer to a biographical question may involve counting events or rating past experiences. In this case a single question may involve several cognitive processes. Also, the interviewer wants to get some sense of how committed the respondents are in answering the question. Are they giving an answer that is expected of them or an answer that reflects their true beliefs.

Willis (64) describes two cognitive interviewing techniques that can be used to obtain information about a person's response to a question: the think-aloud interviewing procedure and the use of probe techniques. In the think-aloud procedure, respondents are asked to think aloud as they answer their question. The advantage of this procedure is that it frees the respondents from biases that the interviewer may create by asking questions, but it has the disadvantage that respondents have to be trained to think aloud. There are many cognitive probes that can be used. Respondents can be asked what a word means, to paraphrase a question in their own words, to indicate how they remember what they recall, and so on. They can also be asked general questions, such as, how they arrived at their answer. The advantage of using probes is that it ensures that certain types of information will be generated by the interview, but it has the disadvantage of biasing the output of the interview.

Many quality of life researchers who have developed an assessment instrument fail to use cognitive interviewing techniques. There is even less discussion about the relationship between the type of item on a questionnaire and the cognitive process evoked. Some work has been reported recently applying cognitive interviewing techniques to the SAHS question found in various national health surveys and quality of life assessments (65). Davies and Ware (66) had previously reported a correlational analysis of responses to the SAHS question. Both the qualitative study of Krause and Jay (65) and the quantitative study of Davies and Ware (66) have shown that respondents are quite selective about the information they use when responding to an item such

as the SAHS question. For example, the most frequent first-mentioned response to the open-ended probes in the Krause and Jay study involved the presence of health problems, but the second most mentioned response was the absence of health problems. What was particularly revealing was the virtual absence of references to mental status as a basis for responding to the SAHS question. One implication of these findings is that models of quality of life assessment that are based, for example, on the WHO definition of health (which includes mental along with physical health status as a component of health) may not reflect a person's perception of what constitutes health.

Krause and Jay (65) also examined their data in terms of age. They found some suggestion of an age effect but this seemed dependent on the number of age categories they divided their data into. It is possible that they would be able to clarify this relationship if the sample size were larger. They also found that response to the open-ended questionnaire was related to the level of SAHS selected by respondents. For example, persons who first mentioned health problems in response to a probe concerning the basis for their response were most likely to rate SAHS as fair or poor. These data further verify the task ahead, which is to pursue the meaning of responses to questions on a quality of life assessment.

CONCLUSIONS

A quality of life assessment is something that a person does as they answer questions about themselves, their health, their pain, and so on. Its reality need not be inferred from the results of a multiattribute paper and pencil test. If a quality of life assessment is something that someone does, then the optimal design of any assessment would duplicate what people do. This is important not only to ensure the validity of any assessment task, but also to ensure the ethical character of the assessment. Intelligence testing lacks such an internal standard to compare itself to. As a result intelligence testing has been misapplied to social policy, a fate that does not necessarily have to befall quality of life assessment.

Several distinct cognitive activities are associated with generating a quality of life assessment: Recall from memory, scaling of the memories, valuating the importance of the memories, and aggregating the results of different memories into an index. Each of these activities reflects complex cognitive activities that people engage in. A review of current models of cognition suggests that implicit and explicit learning and memory should also be included in studies of quality of life. Implicit learning, for example, could account for a variety of phenomena including how emotional factors, stereotypes (67), and measures of self-esteem affect a quality of life assessment.

Data supports the notion that different types of quality of life assessments produce different types of information. The implication of these observations is that some assessments do a better job at measuring the effect of treatments on quality of life than others. Why this is so is not clear from the literature, but differences in the cognitive task inherent to each assessment could account for such differences. The data on this issue remain sparse.

There is a relationship between cognitive processes and aggregation and the scoring system used by various quality of life assessments. Some of the available assessments are based on testable cognitive models and others are not. Evaluating the significance of such differences remains to be determined.

Finally, there is a major focus on reviewing techniques that could help an investigator determine what responses to a quality of life assessment mean, and that the questions used in the assessment address the issues the investigator intended to study. Studies of this sort also provide information that confirms that persons recruit different memories when responding to the same question (the SAHS question). These data support the notion that the future development of quality of life assessments will increasingly incorporate the individual's perspective in generating an estimate of their qualitative state.

REFERENCES

1. National Center for Health Statistics (1973–91). Current estimates from the National Health Interview Survey: United States. *Vital and health statistics.* Washington, DC: U.S. Government Printing Office.
2. Stewart AL, Ware JE. *Functioning and well-being: the Medical Outcome Study approach.* Durham: Duke University Press, 1992.
3. Jacobson AM, Barofsky I, Cleary P, Rand L (DCCT Writing Committee). A diabetes quality of life measure: preliminary study of its reliability and validity. *Diabetes Care* 1988;11:725–732.
4. Torrance GW. Health status index models: the unified mathematical view. *Manage Sci* 1976;22:990–1001.
5. Cella DF, Tulsky T, Ulsky DS. Measuring quality of life today: methodological aspects. *Oncology* 1991;4:29–38, 209–232.
6. Boyle MH, Torrance GW. Developing multi-attribute health indices. *Med Care* 1984;22:1045—1057.
7. Bush JW. General health policy model/quality of well-being (QWB) scale. In: Wenger NK, Mattson ME, Furberg CD, Elinson J, eds. *Assessment of quality of life in clinical trials of cardiovascular therapies.* New York: LeJacq, 1984:189–199.
8. O'Boyle C, McGee H, Hickey A, Joyce CRB. Individual quality of life in patients undergoing hip replacement. *Lancet* 1992;339:1088–1091.
9. Guyatt G, Berman LB, Townsend M, Rugsley SO, Chambers LW. Measure of quality of life for clinical trials in chronic lung disease. *Thorax* 1987;42:773–778.
10. Erickson P, Kendall EA, Anderson JP, Kaplan RM. Using composite health status measures to assess the nation's health. *Med Care* 1989; 27(3-S):S66–S76.
11. Kaplan RM, Bush JW. Health-related quality of life measurement for evaluation, research, and policy analysis. *Health Psychol* 1982;1: 61–80.
12. Anderson NH. *Contributions to information integration theory,* vol 1–3. Hillsdale, NJ: Erlbaum, 1991.
13. Torrance GW, Boyle MH, Horwood SP. Application of multi-attribute utility theory to measure social preferences for health states. *Oper Res* 1982;30:1043–1069.
14. Guyatt GH, Fenny DH, Patrick DL. Measuring health-related quality of life. *Ann Intern Med* 1993;118:622–629.
15. Jobe JB, Tourangeau R, Smith AF. Contributions of survey research to the understanding of memory. *Appl Cognit Psych* 1993;7:567–584.
16. Bombardier C, Waire JE, Russell IJ, et al. Auranofin therapy and quality of life in patients with rheumatoid arthritis. *Am J Med* 1986;81:565.
17. Katz JM, Larson MG, Phillips CB, Fossel AH, Liang MH. Comparative measurement sensitivity of short and longer health status instruments. *Med Care* 1992;30:917–925.
18. Liang MH, Larson MG, Cullen KE, Schwartz JA. Comparative measurement efficiency and sensitivity of five health-status instruments for arthritic research. *Arthritis Rheum* 1985;28:542–547.
19. Liang MH, Fossel AH, Larson MG. Comparison of five health-status instruments for orthopedic evaluation. *Med Care* 1990;28:632–642.
20. Visser MC, Fletcher AE, Parr G, Simpson A, Bulpitt CJ. A comparison of three quality of life instruments in subjects with angina pectoris: the Sickness Impact Profile, the Nottingham Health Profile, and the Quality of Well-Being Scale. *J Clin Epidemiol* 1994;47:157–163.
21. Dupuy HJ. A psychological general well-being (PGWB) index. In: Wenger NK, Mattson ME, Furberg CD, Elinson J, eds. *Assessment of quality of life in clinical trials of cardiovascular therapies.* New York: LeJacq, 1984:170–193.
22. Hunt SM, McKenna SP, McEwen JA. A quantitative approach to perceived health status: a validation study. *J Epidemiol Community Health* 1980;34:281–285.
23. Meenan RF, Gertman PM, Mason JM. Measuring health status in arthritis: the Arthritis Impact Measurement Scale. *Arthritis Rheum* 1980;23:146–152.
24. Bergner M, Bobbitt RA, Carter WB, Gilson ES. Sickness Impact Profile: development and final revision of a health-status measure. *Med Care* 1981;19:787–805.
25. Jette AM, Deniston OL. Inter-observer reliability of a functional status assessment instrument. *J Chronic Dis* 1978;31:573–580.
26. Fries JR, Spitz P, Kraines RG, Holman HR. Measurement of patient outcome in arthritis. *Arthritis Rheum* 1980;23:137–145.
27. Kaplan RM, Bush JW, Berry CC. Health status: types of validity of an index of well-being. *Health Serv Res* 1976;11:478–507.
28. Guyatt G, Walter S, Norman G. Measuring change over time: assessing the usefulness of evaluative instruments. *J Chronic Dis* 1987;40: 171–178.
29. Cohen J. *Statistical power analysis for the behavioral sciences.* New York: Academic Press, 1977.
30. Parr G, Darekar B, Fletcher A, Bulpitt C. Joint pain and quality of life: results of a randomized trial. *Br J Clin Pharmacol* 1989;27:235–242.
31. Salovey T, Phil FM, Smith AF, Turk BC, Jobe JB, Willis GB. Reporting chronic pain episodes on health surveys. *Vital and health statistics,* series 6, Cognition and Survey Measurement no. 6. Washington DC: DHHS Publication #92-1081, 1992.
32. Kihlstrom JF. The cognitive unconscious. *Science* 1987;237:1445–1452.
33. Anderson JR. *Language, memory and thought.* Hillsdale, NJ: Erlbaum, 1976.
34. Hinton GE, Anderson JA, eds. *Parallel models of associated memory.* Hillsdale, NJ: Erlbaum, 1981.
35. Cleermans A. *Mechanisms of implicit learning: connectionistic models of sequential processing.* Cambridge, MA: MIT Press, 1993.
36. Parkin AJ. *Memory: phenomena, experiment, and theory.* Cambridge, England: Blackwell, 1993.
37. Reber AS. *Implicit learning and tact knowledge: an essay on the cognitive unconscious.* New York: Oxford University Press, 1993.
38. Descartes R. *Discours de la methode,* Gadoffre G, ed. Manchester, England: Manchester University Press, 1649/1941.
39. Leibnitz GW. *New essays concerning human understanding: Chicago* Open Court. 1916.
40. Zeitlin SV, McNally RJ. Implicit and explicit memory bias for threat and post-traumatic stress disorder. *Behav Res Ther* 1991;29:451–457.
41. Barofsky I, Schuster MM, Whitehead WE. The impact of psychological factors on quality of life assessment in the GI patient. *Gastroenterology* 1993;104:A473.
42. Derogatis LR, Lipman RS, Covi L. The SCL-90: an out-patient psychiatric rating scale, preliminary report. *Psychopharmacol Bull* 1973;9: 13–28.
43. Watson D, Pennebaker JW. Health complaints, stress, and distress: exploring the central role of negative affectivity. *Psychol Rev* 1989; 96:234–254.
44. Tversky A, Kahnman D. Judgment under uncertainty: uristics and biases. *Science* 1974;185:1124–1131.
45. Patrick DL, Erickson P. *Health status and health policy: quality of life and health care evaluation and resource allocation.* New York: Oxford University Press, 1993.

46. Ware JE. Methodological considerations in the selection of health-status assessment procedures. In: Winger NK, Mattson ME, Furberg CD, Elinson J, eds. *Assessments of quality of life in clinical trials of cardiovascular therapies.* New York: LeJacq, 1984:87–117.

47. Bush JW. Invited discussion: relative preference vs relative frequency in health-related quality of life evaluations. In: Winger NK, Mattson ME, Furberg CD, Elison J, eds. *Assessments of quality of life in clinical trials of cardiovascular therapies.* New York: LeJacq, 1984:118–139.

48. Herrnstein RJ, Murray C. *The bell curve: intelligence and class structure in American life.* New York, Simon & Schuster, 1994.

49. Sternberg RJ. Human intelligence: the model is the message. *Science* 1985;230:1111–1118.

50. Rothman KJ. *Modern epidemiology.* Boston: Little, Brown, 1986: 306–307.

51. Eddy DM. Oregon's plan: should it be approved? *JAMA* 1991; 266:2439–2445.

52. Ware JE. *SF-36 Health Survey: manual and interpretation guide.* Boston: Health Institute, 1993.

53. Likert R. A technique for the measurement of attitudes. *Arch Psychol* 1932:140:5–55.

54. Guttman LA. A basis for scaling qualitative data. *Am Soc Rev* 1944; 9:139–150.

55. Katz S, Ford AB, Moskowitz RW. The index of ADL: standardized measure of biological and psychosocial function. *JAMA* 1963;185: 914–919.

56. Kaplan RM, Anderson JP. A general health policy model: updated applications. *Health Serv Res* 1988;23:203–235.

57. Torrance GW. Social preferences to health states: an empirical evaluation of three measurement techniques. *Socio-Econ Plan Sci* 1976; 10:129–136.

58. Kaplan RM. Human preference measurements to help physicians in the evaluation of long-term care. In: Kane RL, Kane RA, eds. *Values of long-term care.* Lexington, MA: Lexington Books, 1982:157–188.

59. Von Neumann J, Morgenstern O. *Theory of gains and economic behavior.* New York: Wiley, 1944.

60. Viet CT, Rose BJ, Ware JE. Effects of physical and mental health on health state preferences. *Med Care* 1982;20:386–401.

61. Guyatt GH, Velzhuyzen ban Zanten S, Feeny DH, Patrick DL. Measuring quality of life in clinical trials: a taxonomyanel review. *Can Med Assoc J* 1989;140:1441–1448.

62. Tanur JM, ed. *Questions about questions: inquiries into the cognitive basis of surveys.* New York: Russell Sage Foundation, 1991.

63. Jobe JB, Mingay DJ. Cognitive and survey measurement history and overview. *Appl Cognit Psych* 1991;5:175–192.

64. Willis GB. *Cognitive interviewing and questionnaire design: a training manual.* Cognitive working paper series #7. Office of Research and Methodology, National Center for Health Statistics, March 19, 1994.

65. Krause NM, Jay GM. What do global self-rated health items measure? *Med Care* 1994;32:930–942.

66. Davies AR, Ware JE. *Measuring health perceptions in the health insurance experiment. H for health, I for insurance, E for experiment.* Santa Monica, CA: Rand Corporation, 1981, publication no. R-2711.

67. Greenwald AG, Banaji MR. Implicit social cognition: attitude, self-esteem, and stereotypes. *Psycho Rev* 1995;102:4–27.

68. McDowell I, Wewell C: Measuring health: a guide to rating scales and questionnaires. New York: Oxford, 1987.

Quality of Life and Pharmacoeconomics in Clinical Trials, Second Edition, edited by B. Spilker.
Lippincott-Raven Publishers, Philadelphia © 1996.

CHAPTER 15

Psychological Aspects of Health-Related Quality of Life Measurement: Tests and Scales

Michelle J. Naughton, Sally A. Shumaker, Roger T. Anderson, and Susan M. Czajkowski

INTRODUCTION

Over the past 20 years, there has been a rapidly growing interest in measuring the effects of medical treatments or other interventions on participants' health-related quality of life (HRQL) (1–5). Research in HRQL is now at a stage in which social scientists are frequently consulted to provide the most appropriate and psychometrically sophisticated measures of HRQL for a broad range of populations and circumstances. The current demand for reasonable HRQL assessments in clinical trials presents social scientists with a unique opportunity to demonstrate the important links between human behavior, social-psychological variables, and overall health status. However, with this opportunity comes the necessity of carefully assessing and evaluating conceptual models and research tools related to HRQL.

In this chapter, issues relevant to the measurement of HRQL in clinical studies are considered. First, one model of HRQL is presented, distinguishing between properties of the concept and factors that may influence HRQL. Next, methodological issues in conducting HRQL are discussed. Then important properties used to determine the value of a particular HRQL instrument are considered, and these properties are applied to psychologically based measures used in HRQL research. This chapter concludes with examples of how psychologically based HRQL measures have been applied in clinical trials.

A MODEL OF QUALITY OF LIFE

Definition

Regardless of how HRQL is measured in a specific study, it is critical that a clear model of the construct is used. Although HRQL has been measured for several decades, experts in the field of quality of life have held varying viewpoints on how to define the concept. Recent years, however, have brought greater convergence of opinion with respect to definitions of HRQL (6). Several definitions have been

M. J. Naughton, S. A. Shumaker, and R. T. Anderson: Department of Public Health Sciences, Bowman Gray School of Medicine of Wake Forest University. Winston-Salem, North Carolina 27157.

S. M. Czajkowski: Division of Epidemiology and Clinical Applications, National Heart, Lung, and Blood Institute, National Institutes of Health, Bethesda, Maryland 20892.

proposed, and these have ranged from very broad perspectives, reminiscent of the early definitions of quality of life, to narrower definitions that are more specific to HRQL (7). For the purposes of this chapter, we have adopted the definition that HRQL encompasses: "Those attributes valued by patients, including: their resultant comfort or sense of well-being; the extent to which they were able to maintain reasonable physical, emotional, and intellectual function; and the degree to which they retain their ability to participate in valued activities within the family, in the workplace, and in the community" (8).

Explicit within this definition is the multidimensional aspect of HRQL, and that actual functional status and the individuals' perceptions regarding "valued activities" are critical to identify. Although there has been some debate among experts, a recent consensus conference composed of an international group of HRQL experts reached agreement on the fundamental dimensions essential to any HRQL assessment (6). These fundamental or primary dimensions include physical functioning, psychological functioning, social functioning and role activities, and the individuals' overall life satisfaction and perceptions of their health status. Thus, experts agreed that in order for investigators to assert that they have measured HRQL in a particular study, at least these dimensions should be included. However, there are certainly instances in which fewer dimensions may be applicable to a specific intervention or population. For example, it is unlikely that, in the examination of the short-term effects of hormone therapy on perimenopausal symptoms, the physical functioning of the study participants (women in their mid-forties to early fifties) will be influenced. Thus, the inclusion of this dimension of HRQL in the trial would impart unnecessary patient burden. In such instances, investigators would report that they had included a *subset* of HRQL dimensions in their study design. In such cases, it is important for the investigators to defend their use of a subset of HRQL dimensions in order to avoid the perception of bias (e.g., deleting HRQL dimensions that might make the intervention under study "look bad").

Other commonly assessed dimensions of HRQL include cognitive or neuropsychological functioning, personal productivity, and intimacy and sexual functioning. Measures of sleep disturbance, pain, and other symptoms, which are associated with a condition or illness and the adverse effects of treatment, are also often assessed. The specific dimensions included in a given study, however, will depend on such factors as the study population, the type and severity of the condition or illness, and, in the case of clinical trials, the intervention being investigated.

Methodological Issues

The dimensions composing HRQL are influenced by a broad range of factors. It is important to maintain a distinction between these moderating factors and HRQL. Moderating factors can be divided into three categories: contextual, interpersonal, and intrapersonal (9). Contextual factors include such variables as the setting (for example, urban-rural, single-dwelling building versus high rise), the economic structure, and sociocultural variations. Interpersonal factors include such variables as the social support available to individuals, exposure to stress, economic pressures, and the occurrence of major life events, such as bereavement or sweepstakes wins. Intrapersonal factors include coping skills, personality traits, and physical health. This distinction between the dimensions that compose HRQL and the factors that moderate HRQL has implications for the selection of HRQL measures in specific studies, as well as for data analysis and interpretation.

In addition to these three categories of moderating factors, in clinical trials any intervention may induce changes, improvements as well as impairments, in a participant's well-being. Also, changes in the natural course of the disease or conditions must be considered, especially in trials of relatively long duration. Concomitant interventions or the regimen of care itself may also affect HRQL. This is particularly likely to happen in trials where the active intervention is considerably different from that for the control group. It is important to consider what effects the intervention will have on the participants' well-being before initiating the trial in order to be able to assess the potential impact of these factors on the HRQL of the participants.

The actual quality of life-related goals of a study often vary considerably and may include the following: (a) using quality of life as baseline data to predict morbidity and mortality; (b) assessing the effects of treatment on overall quality of life or on specific dimensions of quality of life in more detail; (c) where treatment is unlikely to influence quality of life, establishing detailed quality of life normative data on a particular population; (d) assessing patterns of a quality of life dimension over time; and (e) assessing the dimensions and moderators of quality of life most amenable to interventions with a more process-oriented approach. Each of these goals will lead to a different selection of appropriate HRQL instruments.

A variety of instruments and methods are used to assess HRQL. Measures of HRQL can be classified as either generic (that is, instruments designed to assess HRQL in a broad range of populations), or condition/population-specific (for example, instruments designed for specific diseases, conditions, age groups, or ethnic groups) (10). Within these two categories of measures are single questionnaire items; dimension-specific instruments, which assess a single aspect of HRQL; health profiles, which are single instruments measuring several different dimensions of HRQL and provide a score for each dimension of HRQL; and a battery or group of measures assessing both single and multiple dimensions of HRQL. In assessing HRQL, the trend in most studies has been to use either profiles or batteries of instruments.

The type of instruments selected for inclusion in a clinical trial will depend on the goals of the intervention. For example, within a given dimension of HRQL like physical functioning, one can assess the degree to which an individual is able to perform a particular task, his or her satisfaction with the level of performance, the importance to him or her of performing the task, or the frequency with which the task is performed. Thus, the aspects of HRQL measured in studies vary depending on the specific research questions to be investigated.

Based on the model discussed above as well as the methodological concerns considered, the authors' recommendation is to use a battery approach where the instruments selected for any given study correspond to the dimensions of quality of life most likely to be *either positively or negatively* affected by an intervention or the natural course of the condition, and to use the best available instruments to assess each of these dimensions. A major drawback to this approach is the possibility that investigators will select those dimensions of quality of life to be most positively affected by the treatment under study. More likely, investigators may inadvertently overlook an aspect of quality of life affected by treatment. Thus, use of a battery approach requires a thorough understanding of the population under study, the clinical course of the untreated condition, and all potential effects of the intervention(s) (11).

Although the dimensions of quality of life are not limited to psychological constructs (e.g., physical functioning), this chapter focuses on the psychological constructs relevant to quality of life. Before considering these, however, the criteria used to judge the comparative research value of various instruments are reviewed.

CRITICAL PROPERTIES OF RESEARCH INSTRUMENTS

Objectivity and Standardization

A central aim in most scientific endeavors is that observations should be free of subjective judgment. In psychological testing, clinicians and researchers must be assured that an individual will obtain, theoretically, the same score regardless of who is administering, scoring, or interpreting the data. Methods to interpret a test score objectivity depend on the type of assessment instrument used and the specific research goals. A raw score for a social or psychological construct generally has no inherent meaning, and the use of norms established for a specific instrument with regard to a specific population is required. Thus, for example, an individual's test score is meaningful by its location on a continuum of performance representative of an appropriate control sample or diagnostic standard. In some situations the individual case is a legitimate unit of analysis, and a total score will be interesting in its own right. For example, comparison of pre- and postintervention scores of anxiety may provide useful information on recovery independent of the magnitude of deviation from the norm.

A related function of standardization is to ensure that scores obtained by different persons are comparable. Having clinic or research staff trained in the proper administration and evaluation of psychological assessment is a requisite step in this process.

Psychometric Properties

Whether an instrument has utility as a diagnostic or predictive indicator of behavior depends on the proper construction of the instrument, as well as on careful selection of a measure suitable to the behavior under consideration. Psychometric evaluation of an assessment instrument begins with questions regarding its reliability and validity (12–14). The responsiveness of the instruments to clinically significant changes over time is also important.

Reliability

Reliability refers to the consistency of a measurement, and is usually determined by the extent to which a score can be replicated in identical or equivalent testing situations. Conceptually, a test score contains a "true-score" component and an "error" component. To the extent that random error is large, a test score will be unstable and, therefore, unreliable. There are three basic ways to evaluate the reliability of a given instrument.

Internal consistency reliability is the most frequently used estimate of a measure's reliability. Multiple responses are obtained in most HRQL assessments that are then summed or reduced to a single score. An implicit assumption in this approach is that the individual items measure the same thing, or that the items are consistent with each other. To the extent that this is true, a test can be held to measure the same attribute across subjects and time. Operationally, the higher the correlations of the items within the test, the higher is their multiple correlation with the single factor they measure in common. Thus, a measure of internal consistency is the average degree of association among the items on a test. Coefficient alphas are the basic formulas for determining the reliability of instruments based on internal consistency (15).

Test-retest reliability is the correlation between scores obtained by the same person on two separate occasions; the error variance corresponds to the random fluctuations of performance between the two observations. This interpretation is complicated by the fact that actual changes may have occurred in behavior or functional status during the time interval itself. Thus, low test-retest reliability does not necessarily reflect the psychometric properties of the test. For example, the stability coefficients for the State-Trait Anxiety Inventory range from .65 to .86, although its internal consistency has been reported to be in the .90s (16). Thus, test-retest is only useful when it appears that there are no changes in the person or the situation between test administrations.

This issue brings up a potential difficulty in HRQL assessment. Since some behavioral or psychological attributes may lack temporal stability, the usefulness of point prevalence estimates of the attribute is questioned. The researcher is compelled to show whether it is reasonable to expect that any changes in the attribute due to treatment can be detected, and whether data on duration and frequency are useful. Toward this end, the temporal stability of the behavior or attribute to be measured in the study should be examined. It must be decided whether strategies are needed to increase reliability (e.g., increasing the number of assessments, or using group estimates), or to use alternative assessment instruments, which are more sensitive to fluctuations in mood or behavior.

Equivalent-forms reliability refers to the agreement between an individual's score on two or more instruments designed to measure the same attribute. It insures that scores obtained on two administrations of the instruments are independent and measure the temporal stability of responses to the items between testing times. Important sources of error variance in this type of reliability assessment include fluctuations in time (e.g., intervening events and practice effects) and in the composition of the forms (e.g., number, content, order, range, and difficulty of items).

Validity

Demonstrating reliability in measurement is essentially providing the existence of a stable or generalizable concept. However, reliability says nothing about the nature of that concept. Thus, a set of items may yield a repeatable score that may be an invalid indicator of the construct under study. Validity is defined as the extent to which an instrument measures what it was intended to measure. Establishing validity in instrumentation is achieved by the extent of agreement between the measure and a designated ''gold standard'' or ''criterion.'' Some authors argue that validity is more important than reliability. However, both properties can seriously influence the correctness of inference and therefore should be viewed as equally important qualities. Both must be maximized in the selection or development of an instrument. Although it is true that validity in measurement is necessary to interpret what a test score means conceptually, it can be shown statistically that small decrements in reliability can result in large decrements in validity (17). The following kinds of evidence are generally used to infer validity of measurement.

Content validity is the extent to which an instrument measures a representative range of the attribute under study. In interpreting content validity, questions regarding item sufficiency for the proposed investigation and the nature of the patient sample should be addressed carefully. For example, the range of items needed to adequately assess physical functioning in arthritic patients would be too gross for application to many coronary heart disease samples. Similarly,

some depression questionnaires cover mainly one or two aspects of depression, e.g., subjective (18) and somatic complaints (19). A clear idea of what aspects of the behavioral or psychological attribute are of interest to the study is essential to judge the degree of content validity for a particular assessment instrument.

Construct validity refers to evidence that a measured construct behaves in a manner consistent with its referent theoretical or logical properties. Construct validity is established through a series of tests demonstrating that the variable, as measured (a) does not correlate positively with measures of related but different constructs (discriminant validity), (b) does correlate positively with related and similar constructs (convergent validity), (c) taps the measures of the construct intended, and (d) is not dominated by irrelevant factors (20). The process of assessing these aspects of validity is used to increase confidence that an observed effect pertains to the variable of interest. In HRQL research, one of the largest problems in establishing construct validity is the lack of agreement over the operational definition of dimensions of HRQL, as well as differences in population characteristics and the population-specific criteria used in many measures.

Criterion validity refers to the performance of the instrument against an external ''gold standard'' or actual outcome the test was developed to assess. Thus, one type of evidence of validity is prediction of future performance, events, or outcomes. Another type is agreement with clinical assessments or standards. Often a criterion will not exist for overall HRQL measures but only for dimensions of HRQL. All validation reports should describe the conditions under which the validation was conducted, including the demographic characteristics of the study population, and the range of illness or symptoms experienced in the sample. As with known-groups validity, estimates should be provided regarding the sensitivity and specificity of the instrument in detecting the criterion. This can provide a basis for comparing results across clinical samples and populations.

Predictive validity is the degree to which a test can predict how well an individual will do in a future situation. Predictive validity is determined by the degree of correspondence between the assessment instrument and the specific criterion used for future performance. Again, all validation reports for assessment instruments should describe the conditions under which the validation was conducted. It is crucial that these be considered before employing an instrument. *No test is inherently ''valid''; rather, a test is valid with regard to a specific purpose, range, and sample.*

Responsiveness

A final indicator of an instrument's validity, which is important in evaluation research such as in clinical trials, is the responsiveness of the instruments to clinically significant changes over time. While Guyatt et al. (21) have suggested that responsiveness is a separate and distinct psychometric property, Hays and Hadorn (22) purport that responsiveness is actually another type of validity that incorporates longitudinal information (change). Sensitivity to change should be reported for all HRQL instruments developed for use in evaluation research. However, this is not done commonly. Evidence of responsiveness can include pre- and posttest comparisons, but is strengthened when correlations with other indicators of the HRQL-related characteristics are included (e.g., clinically assessed change in status). Attention should be given to the phenomenon being measured and its expected responsiveness. Measures of psychological traits are less likely to change than psychological states in response to interventions.

HRQL ASSESSMENT:
MODES OF ADMINISTRATION

HRQL data can be collected in an interview format, either by telephone or in person, or from self-administered instruments, completed in person or through the mail (23). There is some debate regarding the relative merit of interviewer-administered versus self-administered instruments. Self-administered instruments are more cost-effective from a staffing perspective, and may yield more disclosure on the part of the participant, particularly with the collection of sensitive information. However, self-administered instruments tend to yield more missing and incomplete data and do not allow for clarification. In the long run, and with some populations, they may actually prove to be more expensive than interviewer-administered instruments.

Interviewer-administered instruments usually provide more complete data and allow for probes and clarification. However, there may be a reluctance on the part of some participants to openly discuss some HRQL issues (for example, depression or sexuality), whereas they may be willing to respond to questions about these same issues in a self-administered format. Given the relatively high proportion of functional illiteracy in groups within the United States, in-person interviewer administration may be required, depending upon the particular population under study. Interviewer administration may also be the best way to obtain information for culturally diverse populations. Finally, interviewer-administered instruments are subject to interviewer bias and require intensive interviewer training, certification, and repeat training, especially within the context of studies of long duration. Thus, they can be considerably more expensive than self-administered instruments and serious thought must be given at the planning phases of a study regarding the trade-offs between self-administered versus interviewer-administered measures.

In practice, studies that include measures of HRQL usually incorporate a combination of profiles augmented with either generic or population-specific measures of the dimensions most relevant to the study population and intervention (24). In addition, most HRQL measures are designed to be either interviewer- or self-administered, and both modes of administration can be used within single trials.

PSYCHOLOGICAL MEASURES
IN HRQL RESEARCH

Very few psychological or behavioral instruments have been developed exclusively for HRQL research. Instead, researchers often employ existing psychological instruments that measure specific dimensions of HRQL most relevant to the particular research investigation. Several of the more commonly used psychological measures are the General Health Questionnaire, the Psychological General Well-Being Index, the Profile of Mood States, the Beck Depression Inventory, the Centers for Epidemiologic Studies–Depression Scale, the Zung Self-Rating Depression Scale, and the Spielberger State-Trait Anxiety Inventory. The psychometric properties of these instruments are reviewed below. In addition, a detailed description of the psychometric properties and use of several of these instruments in other languages/cultures can be found in Chapter 69 of this volume.

The General Health Questionnaire

The General Health Questionnaire (GHQ) was designed to measure current psychiatric/affective disorders (25). It focuses on breaks in normal functioning rather than on life-long traits. It is chiefly concerned with identifying an "inability to carry out one's normal 'healthy' functions, and the appearance of new phenomena of a distressing nature" (26). The GHQ is not intended to detect serious illnesses, but is designed to identify individuals at risk who should then be examined using standard psychiatric interviews (25). The GHQ has been used extensively, however, to estimate the prevalence of affective disorders and to assess illness severity (27). The GHQ was developed to be used in primary medical care settings, in general population or community surveys, and among general medical outpatients.

The items included on the GHQ were selected from existing instruments and from clinical experience, and the measure contains statements covering four main areas: depression, anxiety, social impairment, and hypochondriasis (as indicated by organic symptoms) (25). Several versions of the GHQ have been developed. The original version of the GHQ contains 60 items and is generally recommended for use because of its superior validity. Shorter versions of the GHQ are available, however. These include 12- and 30-item scales, which exclude items most usually selected by physically ill individuals (25). A GHQ-28 was also developed using factor analysis, and contains four subscales: anxiety and insomnia, somatic symptoms, social dysfunction, and severe depression (26). There is only partial overlap between the GHQ-28 and GHQ-30, which share 14 items in common. A detailed guide on the different versions of the GHQ, and advice on their most appropriate uses in clinical practice and research, is available elsewhere (28).

Response categories on the GHQ are "better than usual," "same as usual," "worse than usual," and "much worse than usual." Respondents are asked to mark the items based on their experiences "over the past few weeks," emphasizing departures from their usual states. The GHQ was designed to be self-administered, and it takes approximately two minutes to complete the GHQ-12 and approximately 10 minutes to complete the GHQ-60. Items may be scored using a traditional Likert format of 0-1-2-3, or the responses may be scored as 0-0-1-1, which indicates the presence or absence of symptoms, ignoring frequency (29). Comparing the two scoring methods, Goldberg and Hillier (26) found the Likert method (0-1-2-3) to hold little advantage over the simpler method (0-0-1-1) in discriminating cases and non-cases.

Scores on the GHQ are interpreted to indicate the severity of psychological disturbance on a continuum, or as an initial screen in identifying cases applying cutoffs. There is no universally accepted cutoff point for each of the GHQ versions that identifies psychiatric cases. Instead, the cutoff points vary based on the purpose for which the GHQ is being used, and the characteristics of the population in which it is being applied. For the GHQ-60, cutoff points of 9/10, 10/11, and 11/12 have been used (29). Cutoff points for the other versions of the GHQ are 4/5 for the GHQ-30 and GHQ-28, 3/4 for the GHQ-20, and 2/3 for the GHQ-12 (30). An alternative method of scoring (C-GHQ) has also been developed and shown to produce a less-skewed distribution of scores (31). This method is thought to make it more likely to detect chronic disorders, and has an alternative way of scoring positive and negative items. Additional information on the scoring methods applied to the GHQ can be found in the *User's Guide to the General Health Questionnaire* (28).

The reliability of the GHQ has been evaluated in several studies. Split-half reliability was reported as .95 for the GHQ-60, with equivalent values for the GHQ-30, GHQ-20, GHQ-12 reported at .92, .90, and .83, respectively (29). Assessments of test-retest reliability have been somewhat problematic, since the GHQ focuses on conditions that may be transient (27). To address this issue, Goldberg (29) has assessed test-retest reliability only in cases showing essentially no changes in condition between two administrations. In one study, test-retest reliability after 6 months was .90, and in another study test-retest reliability was .75 (29). Results from both general population surveys (32) and clinical surveys (33), however, indicate that there may be a retest effect resulting in lower scores on repeat administrations.

Validity assessments of the GHQ have been conducted in a variety of settings and cultures, and extensive review of these studies can be found in the *User's Guide to the General Health Questionnaire* (28). In general, the GHQ-60 is the strongest psychometrically, while the GHQ-12 has shown comparatively lower validity. Criterion validity has most often been assessed by comparing the GHQ to standard clinical psychiatric interviews, and the results have indicated high correlations (.80 and above) between the GHQ and the clinical measures. Sensitivity and specificity of the GHQ have generally ranged from 0.73% to 0.96%, depending on the population studied and the version of the GHQ tested (28,34). The factor structure of the GHQ has also been examined, and up to 19 factors have been identified in the GHQ-60 and only two or three factors in the GHQ-12. The GHQ-28 contains four subscales (28). Studies have indicated that several of the GHQ factors are stable across settings (35,36).

Many of the criticisms of the GHQ reflect limitations imposed by the deliberate design of the instrument and not by the psychometric properties of the measure (34). The GHQ was designed to assess acute and not chronic conditions, and was not intended to be used to assess severity or changes in treatment effects over time, although it has been used for these purposes (27). The GHQ, however, has been proven to be useful as a screening tool for measuring psychological distress of a nonchronic nature.

Psychological General Well-Being Index

The Psychological General Well-Being Index (PGWB) was designed to measure subjective feelings of psychological well-being and distress (37). The instrument has been used with a variety of sociodemographic groups, such as rural and urban dwellers, inpatient populations, and community residents. It has also been used to assess changes in subjective well-being due to mental health treatments. The instrument includes both positive and negative affective states, and covers the following six dimensions: anxiety, depression, general health, positive well-being, self-control, and vitality. The PGWB was designed to be self-administered, but it can be used in an interview format. It has been used as a proxy for HRQL in a number of studies within the United States and Europe.

Twenty-two items are contained on the PGWB and respondents are asked to respond to each item as it has applied to them "during the last month." The response categories for each statement range from either 0 to 5 or 1 to 6, with lower values indicating more negative responses, and higher values indicating more positive responses. A total summated score is also calculated, which ranges from 0 to 110 using the 0 to 5 scoring method, and from 22 to 132, using the 1 to 6 scoring method. Each of the six dimension subscales can also be given a score. The mean value of the PGWB total score in non-patient populations is approximately 105.

Internal consistency reliability of the PGWB has been consistently high, with Cronbach's alpha correlations ranging from .90 to .94 (37). Individual responses to the items have also been found to be highly consistent. Test-retest coefficients have ranged from .50 to .86 for a median value of .66. Initial low scores on the PGWB tend to rise on retest, and very high scores tend to drop.

Concurrent validity of the PGWB has been investigated in a variety of studies. In the National Health and Nutrition Examination Survey (NHANES 1), the PGWB was significantly correlated with items assessing needs and utilization of mental health services, sociodemographic variables, and medical history items (38,39). Correlations of the PGWB with standardized mental indices have provided the following results: CES-D (−.72); Beck Depression Inventory (BDI) (−.68); Zung Depression Inventory (−.75); Langner Psychiatric Symptoms (−.77); Hopkins Symptom Checklist (SCL-90) (−.77); Minnesota Multiphasic Personality Inventory (MMPI) (−.55); Psychiatric Symptoms Scale–depression (−.76); College Health Questionnaire–current depression (−.80); and the Personal Feelings Inventory–depression (−.78) (38–40). The results of these investigations indicate the sensitivity of the PGWB, at least in the lower range of its scores, to psychoneurotic subjective distress (37). In addition, the PGWB has been found to be sensitive to an affective balance between subjective states of positive and negative feelings (41), and to distinguish mental health clients from community residents (37). Dupuy (37) reports that the generalizability of the PGWB index can be extended to population estimates of noninstitutionalized American adults aged 25 to 75 years through data collected by NHANES 1 (42), and from a community sample of persons aged 15 to 60 years and older (43).

In summary, the PGWB has been found to have a high degree of reliability and validity in both population-based and mental health samples, although the validity of the PGWB has been identified primarily through its relationships with negative conditions instead of conditions that indicate more positive life events (37). Data on the responsiveness of the instrument to changes in status is limited. Advantages of the PGWB over other standardized assessments of psychological health are that the PGWB contains aspects of positive well-being, avoids references to physical symptoms of emotional distress, is not condition specific, and is not oriented solely toward discriminating psychiatric cases from healthy individuals.

The Profile of Mood States

The Profile of Mood States (POMS) (44) was designed to assess mood states and transient changes in mood. Six identifiable moods or affective states are measured: tension-anxiety, depression-dejection, anger-hostility, vigor-activity, fatigue-inertia, and confusion-bewilderment. The scales for these mood states were determined from the results of factor analysis from several research studies. The POMS is self-administered and contains 65 adjectives relating to mood states during the past week, which are scored on a 5-point scale from 0 (not at all) to 4 (extremely). The time reference

may be eliminated to measure mood traits. A score for each factor is produced by simply adding responses. A summary measure of total distress can also be obtained by summing all scores.

In normative samples consisting of male college students, male psychiatric outpatients, and male patients at a university hospital outpatient clinic, internal consistency coefficients of the POMS factors were found to be near .90. Without a treatment intervention, test-retest coefficients in a sample accepted for psychiatric treatment ranged from $r = .65$ for vigor to $r = .74$ for depression for a median time of 20 days. Correlations of scores following 6 weeks of treatment were much lower.

In addition to factorial-based validity for the six POMS subscales, predictive and concurrent validities were established for the instrument in several studies (44). In the normative samples, the POMS factors were found to be moderately to highly correlated with three clinically derived distress scales on somatization, anxiety, and depression. Discriminative validities of the separate factors were not strong, especially anxiety (tension) and depression, where the intercorrelations ranged from $r = .56$ to .77. Of the 26 intercorrelations reported among the five factors, the median coefficient is $r = .60$. Validity data are not presented in the manual for the total measure of distress score. Studies in cancer patients, however, have found moderate correlations of the total measure of distress with the degree of physical impairment, extent of disease, and pain, suggesting its usefulness as an overall distress measure.

In general, the evidence from large standardization samples suggests that the POMS is a valid and reliable descriptive tool for assessing mood states in both psychiatric and nonpsychiatric populations. Despite its being developed to address several specific moods, the moderate to high intercorrelations among factor scores suggest that the POMS may be better suited to measuring general mood disturbance. Studies have shown that the strongest associations among the POMS's factor scores and extent of disease or prognostic factors have been for vigor and fatigue, and there is very little association with factors relevant to emotional distress. It is not clear to what extent disease affects emotional distress as measured by the POMS, but it is concluded that this instrument is a reasonably good measure of general mood disturbance in a wide range of populations, and may be a valuable test to include as the psychological component of a HRQL battery.

Beck Depression Inventory

The Beck Depression Inventory (BDI) is an instrument designed to measure the existence and severity of depression in both adolescents and adults (45). The BDI has been used in both clinical practice and research studies as a means to assess the intensity of depression in psychiatric patients (46), to detect possible depression in normal populations (47), and to monitor the effectiveness of interventions over time. The original version of the BDI was published in 1961 (48) but was subsequently revised and re-copyrighted in 1978 (49). It is the revised form of the BDI that has been marketed and used in clinical and research settings since 1972 (45).

The items for the BDI were generated based on clinical observations and descriptions of symptoms provided by depressed psychiatric patients, as contrasted with those given by nondepressed psychiatric patients (48). Those items that appeared specific to depression and consistent with research in the area were selected for inclusion in the inventory. By design, the selected items represent cognitive rather than somatic or affective symptoms of depression and include items that describe the manifestation of depression in relation to general life satisfaction, mood, relations with others, self-esteem, appetite, sleep, and libido (27).

The format of the BDI is distinctive in that it consists of 84 statements, grouped into 21 categories (four statements per category), and one statement is selected by the respondents for each category. Although the BDI was originally designed to be administered in an oral format, it can also be self-administered, and takes, on average, 10 to 15 minutes to complete. The items selected by the respondents are rated on a 4-point scale ranging from 0 to 3 in terms of severity. Total scores are calculated by adding the scores on each of the 21 items, resulting in total scores ranging from 0 to 63. There is no cutoff point for the BDI that universally classifies individuals as being depressed. It is recommended that cutoff scores for the BDI be based on clinical decisions or the research criteria for which the instrument is being used (50,51).

A 13-item short form of the BDI was developed by selecting the categories that had the highest correlations with the long form and with ratings of depression provided by clinicians (52). Internal consistency of the BDI–short form, as assessed by Cronbach's alphas, have ranged from .74 to .90, depending on the population being assessed (50,53–56). Principal components analysis of the short form have generally revealed two underlying factors (54–56).

A number of studies have reviewed the psychometric properties of the BDI with various samples of psychiatric patients and normal populations (50,57–59). Test-retest reliability of the BDI has generally been high, but has varied based on the time interval between the administration dates and the nature of the samples tested (i.e., psychiatric versus nonpsychiatric patients) (57). Nonpsychiatric samples have generally displayed more stable BDI scores than psychiatric samples (.60 to .83, nonpsychiatric samples; and .48 to .86, psychiatric samples) (57). In a review of 25 years of evaluation of the instrument, Beck et al. (57) examined the internal consistency of the BDI. For psychiatric populations, the Cronbach alphas were found to range from .76 to .95, with a mean value of .86. For nonpsychiatric samples, the mean alpha was .81 with a range from .73 to .92. The short form

of the BDI was shown to have a level of internal consistency similar to that of the long version (60).

Content validity of the BDI has generally been found to cover six of the nine *Diagnostic and Statistical Manual of Mental Disorders* (DSM-IV) criteria for depression (55,61). The BDI has been found to differentiate psychiatric patients from normal individuals, and can discriminate between different levels of severity of depression (59). The inventory has also been able to differentiate between psychiatric and normal populations of adolescents (62–65). The BDI appears to be sensitive to changes associated with clinical trials and other types of interventions, and to be predictive of outcome (59). In addition, the BDI has been found to correlate highly with existing measures of depression, such as the Hamilton Psychiatric Rating Scale for Depression and the Zung Self-Reported Depression Scale, across a variety of investigations (57). Also, in a variety of studies addressing the construct validity of the BDI, the measure has been significantly correlated, in the expected direction, with a variety of conditions, such as suicidal behaviors (66) and alcohol use (67).

The factor structure of the BDI has been examined with both clinical and nonclinical populations. Four or more extracted factors have been reported in various studies, although the replicability of the factor structures over time has not been demonstrated across independent samples. Recent studies suggest that the BDI measures depressive symptoms in a unidimensional, global fashion, relying predominantly on cognitive-affective factors, rather than tapping a variety of more specific constructs as suggested by previous researchers (68,69).

Centers for Epidemiologic Studies–Depression

The Centers for Epidemiologic Studies–Depression (CES-D) scale was designed to measure symptoms of depression in community populations (70–73). It is not intended to provide a diagnosis of depression, nor is it able to determine the cause of the depressive symptoms (e.g., physical illness, medication, psychiatric disorder, or a reaction to an event). The instrument consists of 20 items selected from previously developed scales. These questions are considered to be representative of the major symptoms in the clinical syndrome of depression, as identified by clinical judgment, frequency of use in other instruments for depression, and factor analytic studies (70). Where data were available, reliability and discriminatory power were also taken into account in designing the instrument. Major contributors to the CES-D scale were the Beck Depression Inventory (48), Zung's depression scale (74), a self-report inventory of depression by Raskin et al. (75), the depression scale of the Minnesota Multiphasic Personality Inventory (76), and a scale developed by Gardner (77).

The CES-D was designed to be a self-administered scale, although it has also been used in interview formats. The

20 items include questions on depressive symptomatology, depressed mood, feelings of guilt and loneliness, hopelessness, loss of appetite, sleep disturbance, and psychomotor retardation. Respondents are asked to rate the frequency of 20 symptoms over the past week by choosing one of four response categories ranging from 0, "rarely or none of the time," to 3, "most or all of the time." Each response category also has a number of days associated with it, in order to decrease the problems related to different interpretations of the responses to the items. Scores on the CES-D are calculated by a simple sum of the 20 items, and the scores have a potential range from 0 to 60. The score is equal to six symptoms for most of the previous week or to a majority of symptoms for shorter periods of time. High scores indicate both the presence and persistence of the symptoms represented by the scale. A cutoff score of 16 is generally used to distinguish individuals considered to be depressed from those classified as nondepressed (70,78).

A short version of the CES-D has also been developed for use in research studies (79). This instrument is composed of eight items, six of which were taken from the original CES-D to represent the six global categories measured by the instrument. The additional two items are summary questions that ask the respondents to report the presence of persistent depressive symptoms in their lifetime.

The reliability and validity of the CES-D have been tested on both clinic populations (71,80,81) and on probability samples of communities (71,73,82). Results of these investigations indicate that the CES-D has high internal consistency, as measured by Cronbach's alpha (range .83–.91), acceptable test-retest reliability, and good construct validity in both the clinical and community samples (71,81,83). Radloff (71) examined the factor structure of the CES-D, and identified four distinct components: depressed affect, positive affect, somatic and retarded activity, and interpersonal. The CES-D has also been sensitive to detecting changes in symptoms in psychiatric patients over time (73).

A major concern with using the CES-D in research investigations has been the specificity with which the instrument detects depressive disorders. The CES-D does not appear to measure only depressive symptoms but a combination of symptoms common to both major depression and generalized anxiety disorders (72,83,84). Roberts et al. (81) suggest that the CES-D is really measuring demoralization, which could be a precursor to the development of a depressive or anxiety disorder.

The CES-D has not always been able to correctly classify individuals as depressed or nondepressed. In a community sample of high school students, the CES-D had adequate internal consistency, and sensitivity and specificity for detecting current episodes of depression, but many false positives were generated (85). Similarly, in an adult community sample, the CES-D, when compared with the Schedule for Affective Disorders and Schizophrenic/Research Diagnostic Criteria, yielded a modest relationship between RDC diagnoses of depression and those cases identified by the CES-D (83). The instrument was also reasonably good at screening out the nondepressed (true negatives), but was not very efficient in identifying true positives. For these reasons, it has been suggested that the CES-D only be used as an initial screening tool and should not be relied on solely for ascertaining cases of depression.

Zung Self-Rating Depression Scale

The Zung Self-Rating Depression Scale (SDS) was designed to provide an objective, quantitative assessment of the subjective experience of depression (74). The SDS was not intended to be a substitute for clinical evaluation and diagnosis. The instrument has been used to measure depressive symptomatology in the general population, to distinguish depressed patients from other diagnostic groups, to monitor treatment effects, and in cross-cultural studies of patients with depressive disorders (27).

The content of the SDS was developed based on an analysis of statements collected during patient interviews (74). Twenty items are contained in the scale, statements concerning affective, cognitive, behavioral, and psychological symptoms of depression (86). The items are evenly divided between positive and negative phrasing. The response categories range from 1 "none or a little of the time," to 4, "most or all of the time." Respondents are asked to rate each item as to how it has applied to them during the past week (87). The instrument is usually self-administered and takes approximately 5 minutes to complete.

Scores on the SDS are calculated by summing the item scores. This summated score is then converted to an index by dividing the summated score by 80 and then multiplying that figure by 100. Scores below 50 reflect individuals in the normal range, scores of 50 to 59 indicate the presence of minimal to mild depression, 60 to 69 reflect marked depression, and a score of 70 or above indicates severe to extreme depressive symptoms (88). There are no agreed on cutoff points to define psychiatric cases. Scores of 50, 55, and 60 have been used in various studies (27).

There is little available data examining the reliability of the SDS. Split-half reliability in a psychiatric population was .73 (89), and tests of internal consistency have generated satisfactory results (90). Test-retest reliability has not been demonstrated adequately (27,86). Although there are problems in distinguishing between real change and error in test-retest correlations, such information would be useful in interpreting findings generated from the SDS and in selecting appropriate uses for the instrument in clinical and general populations (27).

A variety of studies have examined the validity of the SDS. Concurrent validity has been tested by comparing the SDS with other standardized scales, such as the Beck Depression Inventory, the Hamilton Rating for Depression, and the

Minnesota Multiphasic Personality Inventory (86). The SDS has also been correlated with interviewer-administered assessments of depression, but the results have been mixed (86). Examinations of the content validity of the SDS have suggested that the measure does not cover symptoms of depression adequately (91) and includes other items not necessarily related to the presence of mental illness (92).

Factor analyses of the SDS have extracted from two to seven factors, accounting for 33% to 75% of the variance. In a review of these studies, Hedlund and Vieweg (86) revealed four major factors in the SDS, involving affective, cognitive, behavioral, and physiological components. Factor profiles of the SDS have been used to discriminate between patient groups. In addition, the SDS has been used to measure treatment effects, but disagreements remain as to the responsiveness of the instrument to treatment-induced changes (27).

As has been found with other measures of psychological functioning, scores on the SDS have been shown to vary by the sample being evaluated. In normal, nonpatient populations, subjects 19 years of age or younger and those 65 years and older have shown higher baseline values than individuals in between these ages (88). With patient populations, however, there is no clear age effect (86), although elderly patient scores have been shown to have lower correlation with physicians' judgments than a rater-administered interview (93). Females have tended to score higher on the SDS than males in both patient and nonpatient populations, but this tendency is small and unstable (86). Less-educated subjects also tend to score higher on the SDS. In their review of the SDS, Hedlund and Vieweg (86) concluded that the evidence on validity supports the use of the instrument as a screening tool or as an adjunct to clinical evaluation, but not as a diagnostic measure of depression (27).

Spielberger State-Trait Anxiety Inventory

The Spielberger State-Trait Anxiety Inventory (STAI) (16) is the most widely used anxiety scale. Spielberger and his colleagues developed the STAI between 1964 and 1970, when the initial version was published, and later published a revised version in 1983 as Form Y. Items were taken from the Taylor Manifest Anxiety Scale, the Welsh Anxiety Scale, and the IPAT Anxiety Scale, and tested using different college student samples. Items for state-anxiety were selected for their ability to discriminate between stress and nonstress conditions; trait anxiety items were chosen for their stability over time. The State-Anxiety Scale (STAI Form Y-1) consists of 20 statements on a 4-point scale covering apprehension, tension, nervousness, and worry, which evaluate how the subject feels "at this moment." The Trait-Anxiety (STAI Form Y-2) consists of 20 statements on a 4-point scale pertaining to how the subject generally feels. Both scales were designed to contain an anxiety present and anxiety absent factor. The State-Trait Anxiety Inventory

was designed for high school and college students, and adults.

To score the instrument, the 20 responses for each scale are summed. High scores are interpreted as indicating more state or trait anxiety, and can be compared with normative data provided in the test manual. Alpha coefficients of internal consistency for the state anxiety scale range from .86 to .95, and for the trait anxiety scale range from .89 to .91. Median test-retest correlations for the trait scale have ranged from $r = .65$ to .86. Since state anxiety is by definition unstable, test-retest estimates are not informative.

Validation studies of Form Y indicate that discrimination between state and trait anxiety was achieved, yielding two separate factors (94). Convergent validity of the State-Trait Anxiety Inventory is established by high correlations with other self-report scales of emotional disturbance, such as the Minnesota Multiphasic Personality Inventory. Correlations between this trait-anxiety scale and other trait anxiety scales range from $r = .52$ to .80. The state-trait anxiety scale discriminates between military recruits beginning a stressful training program and high school students, and detects anxiety induced by stressful experimental conditions in college students (16). Both trait and state anxiety scales have shown moderate correlations with medical symptom indices, which indicates a possible organic bias; however, data on specificity and sensitivity are not provided by Spielberger.

In general, the State-Trait Anxiety Inventory is a good self-report instrument for the measurement of anxiety. However, the following shortcomings should be considered: in the State-Trait Anxiety Inventory there is a high correlation between state and trait anxiety, and there is also a high correlation between trait anxiety and psychological disturbance (e.g., depression). These problems suggest that at least trait-anxiety is a more general measure of psychological distress than was intended by its authors. The evidence for validity of the state-anxiety scale is stronger, however, and shows discrimination among levels of severity.

METHODOLOGICAL PROBLEMS IN ASSESSING HRQL

Studies that have assessed HRQL in the areas of cardiovascular disease are described here to illustrate methodological issues in accurately assessing HRQL in research investigations. First considered are several methodological flaws that are not limited to studies investigating HRQL, but have occurred in the HRQL area. Then, some of the methodological problems unique to assessing HRQL employing a battery approach (i.e., a group of instruments assessing both single and multiple dimensions of HRQL) are presented.

General Methodological Problems

Many studies on HRQL in the cardiovascular disease area contain methodological flaws that qualify the findings of the effects of various treatments on HRQL. The most serious of these problems are lack of double-blinding in clinical trials of cardiovascular therapies; use of inappropriate controls or reference groups; use of retrospective self-report data rather than inclusion of pretreatment data; and lack of standardized, well-validated, and reliable measures of HRQL.

An illustration of the problems inherent in the use of single- rather than double-blind design can be found in two prospective, multicenter, randomized clinical trials comparing the effects of several hypertensive medications (captopril versus methyldopa or oxprenolol) on HRQL (95). In these trials, quality of life was operationalized as rate of compliance, activity index, and depression. Patients taking captopril had a significantly lower symptom complaint rate than those taking methyldopa; however, the study was single-blind, and a number of HRQL questionnaires had to be discarded due to evidence that physicians "helped" their patients complete the instruments. Since the study was single-blind, the possibility that systematic bias was introduced limited the conclusions drawn regarding the effects of a treatment on HRQL.

Problems in interpreting data also occur when inappropriate control or reference groups are used for comparison purposes. Siegrist et al. (96) compared hypertensive patients who were being treated with those who refused treatment across several HRQL dimensions, including physical symptoms, mental alertness, emotional well-being, and work-role performance. The two groups were not comparable since individuals who refuse hypertensive treatment may differ in many respects from those who adopt and maintain a treatment regimen. Similarly, Wiklund et al. (97) compared the HRQL of 177 men at one year following a myocardial infarction with that of a random sample of 175 healthy men used as a reference group. The post–myocardial infarction group reported significantly more symptoms and emotional disturbances, and differed from the health controls in type of leisure activity. Again, the reference group used differed from the post–myocardial infarction group in ways other than the presence of cardiovascular disease (e.g., lifestyle factors predictive of cardiovascular disease and psychosocial factors).

Interventions also often include nonspecific components, such as increases in social support, that are not included in a control group. For example, Patel and Marmot (98) randomly assigned hypertensive subjects to a program involving weekly relaxation and stress management sessions, or to receive health-education leaflets concerning smoking and diet. The weekly relaxation sessions involved an increase in social support available to participants, but not to those in the control group. Therefore, the significant differences between the two groups found on the HRQL measures may have resulted from the greater support received by those assigned to the group. Naismith et al. (99) have similar interpretive problems in their study comparing the HRQL of post–myocardial infarction patients who received intensive psychological counseling versus information materials on risk factor reduction.

Lack of pretreatment data makes it impossible to compare patients' HRQL following treatment to their prior level of HRQL. LaMendola and Pellegrini (100) interviewed coronary artery bypass graft patients 6 months to 4 years following surgery. In addition to the lack of comparability in terms of amount of time following surgery (which was not controlled for in the analyses), HRQL was assessed following surgery only, and therefore it was impossible to compare the patients' changes in HRQL over time. Also, there is no way to know whether or not the two groups were comparable with respect to HRQL prior to surgery. Similar problems occurred for Flynn and Frantz (101) and for Raft et al. (102) in their studies of HRQL following coronary bypass surgery.

Finally, a problem with many early studies assessing HRQL and that persists today in spite of advances in HRQL measures, is the use of measures that are not well validated or reliable. Often, instruments used to measure HRQL components consist of a single item or a series of items that are created specifically for the study. Furthermore, attempts are rarely made to assess the reliabilities of scales used (see earlier discussion). Use of a single item to assess a HRQL domain such as social functioning is inadequate to reliably capture the complexity of the dimensions of HRQL. The use of sets of items that have inadequate internal consistency (and are thus insensitive measures of quality of life) can also impede the identification of important differences. More serious still, in terms of threats to internal validity, is the use of subjective open-ended items, rated post hoc, as measures of specific HRQL dimensions.

Examples of the use of interview data to rate patients' HRQL include two studies of HRQL following a myocardial infarction (103, 104). In both of these studies, patients were interviewed about such dimensions as work, leisure, sexual activity, family and social life, emotional state, and work status. Mayou et al. (103) used consensus ratings of change in activity and satisfaction with the change based on the interview data, but failed to specify how these consensus ratings were determined. Although these are extreme examples of the use of ad hoc measures in HRQL research, investigators continue to use measures that have not been validated, have inadequate reliability, and are not sensitive enough to reliably distinguish HRQL changes due to treatment over time.

Problems Specific to a Battery Approach to HRQL Measurement

Since this chapter focuses on psychological measures of HRQL, an explicit assumption is that a battery approach to measuring HRQL should be used. A characteristic of many HRQL studies that is problematic, in general, and a particular problem when a battery approach is employed, is the use of small sample sizes. Samples sizes of 20 to 30 patients are not unusual in the HRQL literature. Although a small sample may provide preliminary information about HRQL or be useful for relatively simple, exploratory analyses, the use of multiple HRQL measures and the resulting use of multivariate analytical procedures require relatively large sample sizes. Even when univariate procedures are employed, sample sizes of 30 or less may not provide the power necessary for testing specific hypotheses. An example of this problem is Gundle et al.'s study (105), in which a number of predictor variables, including preoperative symptoms, type A behavior, and preoperative employment status, were used to predict several HRQL variables (such as sexual functioning and postoperative work status), using a sample of 30 coronary bypass surgery patients.

Even when sample sizes are adequate, the study is generally well designed, and reliable and valid measures are used, several problems can occur. One such problem is the use of univariate statistical techniques to analyze multiple measures of HRQL. An example of this is the Jenkins et al. (106) prospective, observational study assessing HRQL in 318 coronary bypass surgery patients who were interviewed before and 6 months following surgery. HRQL was assessed across a broad range of dimensions, including cognitive, physical, social, emotional, and sexual functioning. Results showed improvement on many of the HRQL dimensions, especially for reports of angina, anxiety, depression, and sleep problems. However, no attempt was made to control for the increased chance of a type I error (i.e., rejection of a true hypothesis) since a large number of measures were used (e.g., 11 scales were used to assess the psychological functioning components). The use of paired *t*-tests for such a large number of comparisons is inappropriate; instead, a multivariate approach, or at least the use of multiple comparison procedures that minimize type I error are advisable when a battery of HRQL measures are used.

Another study that employed a comprehensive, multidimensional HRQL assessment with standardized, well-validated measures is the Croog et al. (107) double-blind, randomized clinical trial. This study compared the effects of three hypertensive medications on the quality of life of 626 hypertensive men. HRQL was defined as emotional well-being (including anxiety, depression, and vitality), physical symptoms, sexual functioning, cognitive functioning, work performance and satisfaction, and social participation. HRQL was measured prior to a 4-week placebo period and at 4, 8, and 24 weeks into active treatment. Multivariate procedures were used, and when univariate tests were performed on the basis of an overall significant multivariate statistic, multiple range procedures were employed to minimize type I error. Results showed that patients taking captopril had significantly more favorable scores on the quality of life measures than those on methyldopa or propranolol.

Another problematic area in HRQL research is the statistical methods used for data analysis. In the Croog et al. (107) study, for example, HRQL was assessed at multiple times (prior to placebo, following the 4-week placebo period, after 8 weeks of treatment, and after 24 weeks of treatment), but the only statistical comparisons reported were changes from the pretreatment (post-placebo) period to those at 24 weeks of therapy. This approach does not allow an assessment of patterns across time. However, an analysis of change across time is particularly difficult when multiple measures are used. Complex statistical techniques such as multivariate repeated measures analyses of variance are required, and problems occur when data are missing for some measurement periods. The handling of missing data is a controversial issue in HRQL research in general, particularly when attrition is due to death or major morbidity. It is extremely problematic with multivariate repeated measures designs, however, since equal sample sizes are needed at each measurement period.

Recently, attempts have been made to apply more sophisticated statistical methods to HRQL data in order to better characterize the impact of interventions or specific conditions on HRQL over time. One such technique has been to calibrate changes in HRQL scores to determine their clinical significance. In a double-blind, randomized clinical trial of two antihypertensive medications, Testa et al. (108) constructed a calibration model that related longitudinal changes in HRQL scores (e.g., overall quality of life, general perceived health, psychological well-being, and psychological distress) to longitudinal changes in scores for three objective indices: side effects and symptom distress, stress, and life events. Calibration with the life events index showed that drug-induced changes in HRQL were substantial and that the different effects of these two medications on HRQL had clinical meaning.

An additional issue in HRQL research is whether to assess HRQL comprehensively, with inclusion of measures that cover a broad range of dimensions, or only measure those domains that are relevant to the treatments or diseases under study. The former approach is more general HRQL measurement strategy, whereas the latter is more condition- and treatment-specific. The use of general measurement strategy may be more desirable when the effects of the treatment or condition on HRQL are largely unknown (e.g., when HRQL is being assessed for a new drug or category of drugs or for one whose effects are not well documented). However, when HRQL components that are not clearly linked to a specific treatment are included in a battery, they may add unnecessary complexity to the design and analysis. If a reasonable rationale is not provided for each dimension selected for inclusion, it may be preferable to use condition-specific HRQL measures with the hypothesized relationships between these measures and the treatments or disease process under study clearly stated.

CONCLUSIONS

The assessment of HRQL in clinical trials requires careful consideration of (a) the dimensions of HRQL most relevant to the clinical trial, (b) the best available instruments for the dimensions of HRQL to be measured, and (c) the analytical techniques required in multiple measure studies. In this chapter the basis for evaluating instruments that tap the psychologically oriented HRQL dimensions were considered and the psychometric properties of a few of the more frequently used psychological measures were described. This presentation is not an exhaustive review of psychological measures. Rather, it provides a guide to the criteria that should be used in selecting instruments for research studies evaluating HRQL.

Currently, there are instruments available to assess the various dimensions of HRQL; however, they vary considerably with respect to the psychometric properties reviewed in this chapter (27, 34). Furthermore, most of the available instruments were not designed to reliably discriminate between treatment effects in the homogeneous populations that are frequently sampled in clinical trials. (This latter point is also true of the indices specifically developed for HRQL assessment.)

Most "dimensions" of HRQL are composed of several components, each of which would require a separate instrument to evaluate. For example, emotional or affective functioning might include anxiety and depression (the most common constructs assessed), as well as variables such as hostility, anger, or happiness. Cognitive functioning can be assessed with a broad range of instruments that examine factors such as short- or long-term memory, visual reproduction, facial recognition, laterality, or confusion. Thus, in selecting instruments to assess HRQL, the relevant aspects of each dimension must be considered. For example, if a treatment may affect cognitive functioning, then the investigator must determine what specific aspects of cognitive functioning are most likely to be influenced by treatment, since a full neuropsychological battery would be impractical for most studies. Thus, a carefully selected subset of instruments are recommended for HRQL assessments of psychological well-being.

A battery approach to HRQL assessment of psychological well-being has the potential of providing rich data on this inherently multidimensional concept. Furthermore, a reliable measure of each dimension of HRQL recognizes the variable impact that any treatment has on various aspects of an individual's functioning and also allows for targeted interventions. Although there are instruments available to assess the various HRQL dimensions, a battery approach has its drawbacks. In most clinical trials, a separate instrument for each dimension of HRQL is impractical in terms of patient burden, staff time, and data analysis. Thus, a carefully selected subset of instruments are recommended for HRQL assessments of psychological well-being.

REFERENCES

1. Quality of Life Assessment in Cancer Clinical Trials. *Report of the Workshop on Quality of Life Research in Cancer Clinical Trials.* Bethesda, MD: USDHHS, 1991.
2. Wenger N, Mattson M, Furberg C, Elinson J, eds. *Assessment of quality of life in clinical trials of cardiovascular therapies.* Washington, DC: LeJacq, 1984.
3. Spilker B, ed. *Quality of life assessment in clinical trials.* New ork: Raven Press, 1990.
4. Spilker B, Molinek FR, Johnston KA, et al. Quality of life bibliography and indexes. *Med Care* 1990;28:DS1–DS77.
5. Spitzer WO, Dobson AJ, Jall J, et al. Measuring the quality of life of cancer patients. *J Chronic Dis* 1981;34:585–597.
6. Berzon R, Hays RD, Shumaker SA. International use, application and performance of health-related quality of life instruments. *Qual Life Res* 1993;2:367–368.
7. Stewart AL. Conceptual and methodological issues in defining quality of life: state of the art. *Prog Cardiovasc Nurs* 1992;7:3–11.
8. Wenger NK, Furberg CD. Cardiovascular disorders. In: Spilker B, ed. *Quality of life assessment in clinical trials.* New York: Raven Press, 1990.
9. Shumaker SA, Anderson R, Czajkowski SM. Psychological aspects of HRQL measurement: tests and scales. In; Spilker B, ed. *Quality of life assessment in clinical trials.* New York: Raven Press, 1990:95–113.
10. Schron EB, Shumaker SA. The integration of health quality of life in clinical research: experiences from cardiovascular clinical trials. *Prog Cardiovasc Nurs* 1992;7(2):21–28.
11. Cella DF, Wiklund I, Shumaker SA, Aaronson NK. Integrating health-related quality of life into cross-national clinical trials. *Quality Life Res* 1993;2:433–440.
12. Nunnally JC. *Psychometric theory.* New York: McGraw-Hill, 1967.
13. Hays RD, Anderson R, Revicki R. Psychometric considerations in evaluating health-related quality of life measures. *Qual Life Res* 1993;2:441–449.
14. Ghiselli EE, Campbell JK, Zedeck S. *Measurement theory for the behavioral sciences.* San Francisco: W. H. Freeman; 1981.
15. Cronbach LJ. Coefficient alpha and the internal structure of tests. *Psychometrika* 1951;16:297–334.
16. Spielberger CD. *Manual for the State-Trait Anxiety Inventory (Form Y).* Palo Alto, CA: Consulting Psychologists, 1983.
17. Heitzmann CA, Kaplan RM. Assessment of methods for measuring social support. *Health Psychol* 1988;7(1):75–109.
18. Gallagher D, Nies G, Thompson L. Reliability of the Beck Depression Inventory with older adults. *J Consult Clin Psychol* 1974;50:152–153.
19. Zung WW. A self-rating depression scale. *Arch Gen Psychiatry* 1970;12:63–70.
20. Cook TD, Campbell DT. *Quasi-experimentation: design and analysis issues for field settings.* Boston: Houghton Mifflin, 1976.
21. Guyatt G, Walter S, Norman G. Measuring change over time: assessing the usefulness of evaluative instruments. *J Chronic Dis* 1987;40:171–178.
22. Hays R, Hadorn D. Responsiveness to change: an aspect of validity, not a separate dimension. *Qual Life Res* 1992;1:73–75.
23. Babbie ER. *The practice of social research.* Belmont, CA: Wadsworth Publishing, 1975.
24. Aaronson NK. Quality of life: what is it? How should it be measured? *Oncology* 1988;2:69–74.
25. Goldberg DP. *The detection of psychiatric illness by questionnaire.* Maudsley Monogram #21. London: Oxford University Press, 1972.
26. Goldberg DP, Hillier VF. A scaled version of the General Health Questionnaire. *Psychol Med* 1979;9:139–145.
27. Wilkin D, Hallam L, Doggett M-A. *Measures of need and outcome for primary health care.* Oxford: Oxford University Press, 1992.
28. Goldberg DP, Williams P. *Users' guide to the general health questionnaire.* Windsor, England: NFER-Nelson, 1988.
29. Goldberg DP. *Manual of the General Health Questionnaire.* Windsor, England: NFER, 1978.
30. Worsley A, Gribbin CC. A factor analytic study of the twelve item General Health Questionnaire. *Aust NZ J Psychiatry* 1977;11:269–272.
31. Goodchild ME, Duncan-Jones P. Chronicity and the General Health Questionnaire. *Br J Psychiatry* 1985;146:56–61.
32. Henderson SH, Byrne DG, Duncan-Jones P. *Neurosis and the social environment.* Sydney: Academic Press, 1981.
33. Ormel J, Koeter MW, Van den Brink W. Measuring change with the General Health Questionnaire (GHQ). The problem of retest effects. *Soc Psychiatry Psychiatric Epidemiol* 1987;24:227–232.
34. McDowell I, Newell C. *Measuring health: a guide to rating scales and questionnaires.* New York: Oxford University Press, 1987.
35. Huppert F, Walters D, Day N, Elliott BJ. The factor structure of the

General Health Questionnaire (GHQ-30): a reliability study on 6317 community residents. *Br J Psychiatry* 1989;155:178–185.

36. Vazquez-Barquero J, Williams P, Manrique JF, et al. The factor structure of the GHQ-60 in a community sample. *Psychol Med* 1988; 18:211–218.

37. Dupuy HJ. The Psychological General Well-Being (PGWB) Index. In: Wenger NK, Mattson ME, Furberg CD, Elinson J, eds. *Assessment of quality of life in clinical trials of cardiovascular therapies.* New York: Le Jacq, 1984:170–183.

38. Dupuy HJ. The psychological section of the current health and nutrition examination survey. In: *The Proceedings of the Public Health Conference on Records and Statistics, Meeting Joining with the National Conference on Mental Health Statistics,* 14th National Meeting, June 12–15, 1972. U.S. Department of Health, Education and Welfare publication No. (HRA) 74–1214. Washington, DC: Government Printing Office, 1973.

39. Dupuy HJ. Utility of the National Center for Health Statistics' General Well-Being Schedule in the assessment of self-representations of subjective well-being and distress. In: *The National Conference on Evaluation in Alcohol, Drug Abuse, and Mental Health Programs.* Washington, DC: ADAMHA, 1974.

40. Fazio AF. *A concurrent validational study of the NCHS General Well-Being Schedule.* Vital and Health Statistics Series 2, No.73. DHEW Publication No. (HRA) 78–1347. Hyattsville, MD: National Center for Health Statistics, 1977.

41. Kammann R, Flett R. Affectometer 2: a scale to measure current level of general happiness. *Aust J Psychol* 1983;35:259–265.

42. Wan TTH, Livieratos B. Interpreting a general index of subjective well-being. *Milbank Memorial Fund Q* 1978;56:531–556.

43. Ware JE, Johnston SA, Davies-Avery A, Brook RH. *Conceptualization and measurement of health for adults in the Health Insurance Study, vol 3, Mental Health.* (Publication No. R-1987/3-HEW.) Santa Monica, CA: Rand Corporation, 1979.

44. McNair D, Lord M, Droppleman LF. *EITS manual for the Profile of Mood States.* San Diego, CA: Educational Testing Service, 1971.

45. Beck AT, Steer RA. *Beck Depression Inventory manual.* San Antonio: Harcourt Brace Jovanovich, 1987.

46. Piotrowski C, Sheer D, Keller JW. Psychodiagnostic test usage: a survey of the Society for Personality Assessment. *J Personal Assess* 1985;49:115–119.

47. Steer RA, Beck AT, Garrison B. Applications of the Beck Depression Inventory. In: Sartorius N, Ban TA, eds. *Assessment of depression.* New York: Springer-Verlag, 1986:121–142.

48. Beck AT, Ward CH, Mendelson M, Mock J, Erbaugh J. An inventory for measuring depression. *Arch Gen Psychiatry* 1961;4:561–571.

49. Beck AT, Rush AJ, Shaw BF, Emery G. *Cognitive therapy of depression.* New York: Guilford Press, 1979.

50. Beck AT, Beamesderfer A. Assessment of depression: The Depression Inventory. In: Pichot P, ed. *Modern problems in pharmacopsychiatry.* Basel, Switzerland: Karger, 1974:15–169.

51. Williamson HA, Williamson MT. The Beck Depression Inventory: normative data and problems with generalizability. *Family Med* 1989; 21(1):58–60.

52. Beck AT, Rial WY, Rickels K. Short form of depression inventory: cross validation. *Psychol Rep* 1974;34:1184–1186.

53. Gould J. A psychometric investigation of the standard and long-form Beck Depression Inventory. *Psychol Rep* 1982;51:1167–1170.

54. Foelker GA, Shewchuk RM, Niedereke G. Confirmatory factor analysis of the short form Beck Depression Inventory in elderly community samples. *J Clin Psychol* 1987;43:111–118.

55. Vredenburg K, Krames L, Flett GL. Reexamining the Beck Depression Inventory: the long and short of it. *Psychol Rep* 1985;57:767–778.

56. Leahy JM. Validity and reliability of the Beck Depression Inventory–Short Form in a group of adult bereaved females. *J Clin Psychol* 1992;48:64–68.

57. Beck AT, Steer RA, Garbin M. Psychometric properties of the Beck Depression Inventory: a review. *Clin Psychol Rev* 1988;8:77–100.

58. Boyle GJ. Self-report measures of depression: some psychometric considerations. *Br J Clin Psychol* 1985;24:45–59.

59. Steer RA, Beck AT, Riskind J, Brown G. Differentiation of depressive disorders from generalized anxiety by the Beck Depression Inventory. *J Clin Psychol* 1986;40:475–478.

60. Scogin F, Beutler L, Corbishley A, Hamblin D. Reliability and validity of the Short Form Beck Depression Inventory with older adults. *J Clin Psychol* 1988;44:853–857.

61. Moran PW, Lambert MJ. A review of current assessment tools for monitoring changes in depression. In: Lambert MS, Christensen ER, DeJulio SS, eds. *The assessment of psychotherapy outcome.* New York: Wiley, 1983:263–303.

62. Krauth MR, Zettle RD. Validation of depression measures in adolescent populations. *J Clin Psychol* 1990;46(3):291–295.

63. Barrera M, Garrison-Jones CV. Properties of the Beck Depression Inventory as a screening instrument for adolescent depression. *J Abnormal Child Psychol* 1988;16(3):263–273.

64. Kashani JH, Sherman DD, Parker DR, Reid JC. Utility of the Beck Depression Inventory with clinic-referred adolescents. *J Am Acad Child Adolesc Psychiatry* 1990;29(2):278–282.

65. Ambrosini PJ, Metz C, Bianchi MD, Rabinovich H, Undie A. Concurrent validity and psychometric properties of the Beck Depression Inventory in outpatient adolescents. *J Am Acad Child Adolesc Psychiatry* 1991;30(1):51–57.

66. Emery GD, Steer RA, Beck AT. Depression, hopelessness, and suicidal intent among heroin addicts. *Int J Addict* 1981;16:425–429.

67. Fine EW, Steer RA. The relationships between alcoholism and depression in black men. *Curr Alcoholism* 1977;2:35–43.

68. Louks J, Hayne C, Smith J. Replicated factor structure of the Beck Depression Inventory. *J Nerv Ment Dis* 1989;177(8):473–479.

69. Welch G, Hall A, Walkey F. The replicable dimensions of the Beck Depression Inventory. *J Clin Psychol* 1990;46:817–827.

70. Comstock GW, Helsing KJ. Symptoms of depression in two communities. *Psychol Med* 1976;6:551–563.

71. Radloff LS. The CES-D Scale: a self-report depression scale for research in the general population. *Appl Psychol Meas* 1977;1:385–401.

72. Myers JK, Weissman MM. Use of a self-report symptom scale to detect depression in a community sample. *Am J Psychiatry* 1980;137:1081.

73. Weissman MM, Sholomskas D, Pottenger M, et al. Assessing depressive symptoms in five psychiatric populations: a validation study. *Am J Epidemiol* 1977;106:203–214.

74. Zung WWK. A self-rating depression scale. *Arch Gen Psychiatry* 1965;12:63.

75. Raskin A, Schulterbrandt J, Reating N, McKeon J. Replication of factors of psychopathology in interview, ward behavior and self-report ratings of hospitalized depressives. *J Ner Ment Dis* 1969;198:87–96.

76. Dahlstrom WG, Welsh GS. *An MMPI handbook.* Minneapolis: University of Minnesota Press, 1960.

77. Gardner EA. *Development of a symptom checklist for the measurement of depression in a population.* Unpublished manuscript, 1968.

78. Weissman MM, Locke BZ. Comparison of a self-report symptom rating scale (CES-D) with standardized depression rating scales in psychiatric populations. *Am J Epidemiol* 1975;102:430–431.

79. Shumaker SA, Schron E, Ockene J, eds. *The handbook of health behavior change.* New York: Springer, 1990.

80. Craig TJ, Van Natta P. *Validation of the Community Mental Health Assessment Interview Instrument among psychiatric inpatients:* Working Paper B-27a. Rockville, MD: Center for Epidemiologic Studies, 1973.

81. Roberts RE, Vernon SW, Rhoades HM. Effects of language and ethnic status on reliability and validity of the Center for Epidemiologic Studies–Depression Scale with psychiatric patients. *J Nerv Ment Dis* 1989;177(10):581–592.

82. Roberts RE. Prevalence of psychological distress among Mexican Americans. *J Health Soc Behav* 1980;21:134–145.

83. Roberts RE, Vernon SW. The Center for Epidemiologic Studies Depression Scale: its use in a community sample. *Am J Psychiatry* 1983;140(1):41–46.

84. Breslau N. Depressive symptoms, major depression, and generalized anxiety: a comparison of self-reports on CES-D and results from diagnostic interviews. *Psychiatry Res* 1985;15:219–229.

85. Roberts RE, Lewinsohn PM, Seeley JR. Screening for adolescent depression: a comparison of depression scales. *J Am Acad Child Adolesc Psychiatry* 1991;30:58–66.

86. Hedlund JL, Vieweg BW. The Zung Self-Rating Depression Scale: a comprehensive review. *J Operational Psychiatry* 1979;10:51–64.

87. Zung WWK. Self-Rating Depression Scale and Depression Status Inventory. In: Sartorius N, Ban TA, eds. *Assessment of depression.* Heidelberg: Springer, 1986;221–231.

88. Zung WWK. The measurement of affects: depression and anxiety. In: Pichot P, ed. Psychological measurement in psychopharmacology.

Modern problems of pharmacopsychiatry. Basel: Karger, 1974;7: 170–188.

89. Zung WWK. The depression status inventory: an adjunct to the Self-Rating Depression Scale. *J Clin Psychol* 1972;28:539–543.

90. Giambria L. Independent dimensions of depression: a factor analysis of three self-report depression measures. *J Clin Psychol* 1977;33: 928–935.

91. Blumenthal M. Measuring depressive symptomatology in a general population. *Arch Gen Psychiatry* 1975;34:971–978.

92. Snaith RP. The concept of mild depression. *Br J Psychiatry* 1987; 150:387–393.

93. Toner J, Gurland B, Teresi J. Comparison of self-administered and rater-administered methods of assessing levels of severity of depression in elderly patients. *J Gerontol* 1988;43:136–140.

94. Vagg PR, Spielberger CD, O'Hearn TP. Is the State-Trait Anxiety Inventory multidimensional? *Pers Indiv Diff* 1980;1:207–214.

95. Hill JF, Bulpitt CJ, Fletcher AE. Angiotensin converting enzyme inhibitors and quality of life: the European trial. *J Hypertens* 1985;3(suppl 2):S91–S94.

96. Siegrist J, Matschinger H, Motz W. Untreated hypertensives and their quality of life. *J Hypertens* 1987;5(suppl 1):S15–S20.

97. Wiklund I, Sanne H, Vedin A, Wilhelmsson C. Psychosocial outcome one year after a first myocardial infarction. *J Psychosom Res* 1984; 28:309–321.

98. Patel C, Marmot MG. Stress management, blood pressure and quality of life. *J Hypertens* 1987;5(suppl 1):S21–S28.

99. Naismith LD, Robinson JF, Shaw GB, MacIntyre MM. Psychological rehabilitation after myocardial infarction. *Br Med J* 1979;1:439–442.

100. LaMendola W, Pellegrini R. Quality of life and coronary artery bypass surgery patients. *Soc Sci Med* 1979;13A:457–461.

101. Flynn MK, Frantz R. Coronary artery bypass surgery: quality of life during early convalescence. *Heart Lung* 1987;16:159–167.

102. Raft D, McKee DC, Popio KA, Haggerty JJ. Life adaptation after percutaneous transluminal coronary angioplasty and coronary artery bypass grafting. *Am J Cardiol* 1985;56:395–398.

103. Mayou R, Foster A, Williamson B. Psychosocial adjustment in patients one year after myocardial infarction. *J Psychosom Res* 1978; 22:447–453.

104. Trelawny-Ross C, Russell O. Social and psychological responses to myocardial infarction: multiple determinants of outcome at six months. *J Psychosom Med* 1987;31:125–130.

105. Gundle MD, Reeves BR, Tate S, Raft D, McLaurin L. Psychosocial outcome after coronary artery surgery. *Am J Psychiatry* 1980;137: 1591–1594.

106. Jenkins CD, Stanton B, Savageau JA, Denlinger P, Klein MD. Coronary artery bypass surgery: physical, psychological, social and economics outcomes six months later. *JAMA* 1983;250:782–788.

107. Croog SH, Levine S, Testa MA, Brown B, Bulpitt CJ, Jenkins CD, Klerman GL, Williams GH. The effects of antihypertensive therapy on the quality of life. *N Engl J Med* 1986;314:1657–1664.

108. Testa MA, Anderson RB, Nackley FN, Hollenberg NK, et al. Quality of life and antihypertensive therapy in men: A comparison of captopril and enalapril. *N Engl J Med* 1993;328(13):907–913.

Quality of Life and Pharmacoeconomics in Clinical Trials, Second Edition, edited by B. Spilker.
Lippincott-Raven Publishers, Philadelphia © 1996.

CHAPTER 16

Functional Disability Scales

William D. Spector

INTRODUCTION

The periodic assessment of disabilities has become an integral part of the standard medical evaluation of the elderly, supplementing diagnosis, history, laboratory tests, and physical findings. Goals of treatment for chronic diseases include measures that go beyond notions of cure and survival, to more sensitive measures of progress that relate to overall functioning. Interventions for chronic diseases are applied at any point along the disease-impairment-disability-handicap continuum (1,2). Increasingly, clinicians and researchers need reliable and validated measures of functional disability in order to measure clinical progress, evaluate programs, and establish appropriate eligibility criteria for government and insurance programs (3–5).

Considered here are a small number of functional disability scales for which reliability and validity have been studied

and which have gained some acceptance in the clinical and health services research fields. The scales included vary in terms of the scope of use and extensiveness of the validation work that has been published.

Most of the scales are not new. To a large extent this is because many of the newer scales have not been extensively evaluated. The chapter includes discussion of the Pfeffer Functional Activities Questionnaire, which is relatively new (less than 15 years old) compared with the other scales, which are as much as 40 years old. Although the newer scale has not gained large acceptance, the conceptual basis of the scale and the relatively extensive research on reliability and validity make it worthy of inclusion.

Functional disability measures can be grouped into generic and disease-specific scales. This chapter is concerned with generic measures including activities of daily living (ADL), instrumental activities of daily living (IADL), and mobility. The disease-specific scales are discussed elsewhere in this book. Scales specifically designed for children are also not discussed. Multidimensional scales that include functional disability items as one dimension are also not

W. D. Spector: Division of Long Term Care Studies, Agency for Health Care Policy and Research, Rockville, Maryland 20852.

discussed here. A number of articles have made a more comprehensive review of measures of disability (6–9). The reader may refer to these reviews for descriptions of other instruments.

This chapter focuses mainly on four scales and variations of these scales: the Index of Activities of Daily Living (10), the Barthel Index (12), the Instrumental Activities of Daily Living Scale (13), and the Functional Activities Questionnaire (14). Scales that combine IADL and ADL measures are also reviewed, mainly to discuss methodological issues.

DEFINING DISABILITY AND IMPAIRMENT

In this chapter we define terms following the World Health Organization's (WHO) International Classification of Impairments, Disabilities, and Handicaps. Using this approach impairments are defined as abnormalities of body structure and appearance and organ or system function, resulting from any cause. These include mental impairments and loss of limbs, and limitations in range of motion, for example. Disabilities are defined as ''restrictions or lack of ability to perform an activity in a manner or within the range considered normal for a human being'' (2). Impairments relate to performance of an organ or mechanism; disability relates to the performance of an activity by an individual. A person may be mentally impaired, have restricted range of motion, or be missing an arm, but not show any disabilities by being able to carry out all basic activities independently. In another example, limitations in eye function, referred to as visual impairment, may result in an inability to dress or wash oneself, which are examples of disabilities.

The disability definition used here contrasts with the broader definition that is often used in literature on disability associated with persons under 65 years of age. Disability in this literature usually refers to specific tasks associated with roles in society. Disability from this point of view includes concepts such as work disability (15–17). This broader definition of disability overlaps with the WHO definition of handicap, ''a disadvantage for a given individual resulting from an impairment or a disability, that limits or prevents the fulfillment of a role that is normal for that individual'' (2). Some researchers distinguish between work disability and disability in community living (18). To clarify this distinction the term *functional disability* is used in this chapter to refer to the narrower definition of disability that includes only activities related to community living (activities of daily living and instrumental activities of daily living), but not limitations in work roles.

Many of the scales that have been developed are based on unifying concepts other than disability, for example, self-care. Consequently they include measures other than disabilities. When this occurs note is made of it in our discussion, so constructs can be clarified.

METHODOLOGICAL CONSIDERATIONS

Kirshner and Guyatt (19) have suggested a framework for evaluating health indices. They divide scale development into six aspects: selection of item pool, item scaling, item reduction, reliability, validity, and responsiveness. A seventh aspect, the purpose of the scale, they treat as an overriding factor that affects all other aspects of the scale. This framework was used as a guide to compare and contrast the disability scales discussed in this chapter.

The description of each scale is divided into six sections: description, purpose and use, scale structure, reliability, validity, and responsiveness. The quality of research on disability scales for each of these topics varies. When results for a specific topic are sparse, general methodological concerns are discussed. The discussion of responsiveness is almost totally conceptual, because few studies are available that provide change information on standardized scales. This chapter reviews the two activities of daily living scales separately, discusses the instrumental activities of daily living scales, and concludes with a brief discussion of scales that involve both activities of daily living and instrumental activities of daily living measures.

ACTIVITIES OF DAILY LIVING SCALES: KATZ SCALE OF ACTIVITIES OF DAILY LIVING AND THE BARTHEL INDEX

Description

The Katz Index of Activities of Daily Living scale is based on six functions: bathing, dressing, going to the toilet, transferring (bed to chair), continence, and feeding. The scale includes basic self-care activities. One of the items, transfer, may be classified as a measure of mobility; incontinence may be classified as an impairment. The items in the scale and their respective definitions are conceptually based to reflect the organized locomotor and neurologic aspects of basic activities necessary for survival independent of cultural and social forces. In studies of recovery from chronic disease, the order of recovery using the Katz scale is similar to the progression of functional development of a child (10).

Each activity is divided into three levels, but these levels can be combined so that each activity can be dichotomized to independence and dependence. Patients who are independent do the activity without human assistance, but they may use a prosthesis. Human assistance includes supervision as well as hands-on help.

Using the dichotomies, an ordered unidimensional aggregate scale can be constructed. The aggregate scale consists of eight levels designated by letters A to G, plus ''other.'' The levels of disability are as follows: independent in all six functions; dependent in one function; dependent in bathing plus one other; dependent in bathing and dressing plus one other; dependent in bathing, dressing, and toileting plus one other; dependent in bathing, dressing, toileting, and transferring plus one other; dependent in all six functions; and other, which includes all patterns that do not fit into the above categories. These patterns are more independent than the G category, but more dependent than those classified in A or B. The scale is sometimes scored by counting the number of dysfunctions, thereby eliminating the "other" category. This approach relies heavily on the Guttman properties of the scale, which may vary depending on the specific implementation of the scale.

The scale was designed to be administered as an assessment completed by a professional, but experience by nonclinicians with knowledge of gerontology has been reported (10). Information is derived from direct observation of residents, discussion with primary caregiver, and from the medical record. For demented residents information is derived from the primary caregiver and the medical record only. The final score is based on judgment of the assessor after reviewing information from all sources.

The Katz scale is a measure of independence. Some scales, such as the Barthel Index, measure ability. The advantage of measuring independence is that it measures a real situation, whereas the second approach often assesses a hypothetical situation (e.g., if persons did this activity on their own without a device or human help). Psychological and personality characteristics of the individual may confound an assessment based on a hypothetical situation. The disadvantage is that a measure of independence is influenced by motivation, environmental factors, and access to help that may enable or inhibit a person from doing a set of activities or receive help. On the other hand, independence measures may better reflect the need for services than ability measures. One approach used in some large surveys has been to ask about receipt of help, but also determine when a person is dependent, if it is due to a physical or mental health problem. In addition, questions are often added to determine if there is unmet need, to account for situations where persons do not receive help, although they need help, and situations where the help does not fulfill all the need (11).

The Barthel Index includes 15 items: drinking, feeding, dressing upper body, dressing lower body, donning brace or prosthesis, grooming, washing and bathing, bladder control, bowel control, chair transfers, toilet transfers, tub/shower transfers, walking on level for 50 yards, climbing one flight of stairs, and maneuvering a wheelchair. The first nine activities may be classified as self-care items, whereas the next six items are measures of mobility (12). The Barthel Index includes a much more comprehensive assessment of mobility than the Katz scale. The Barthel Index has incontinence separated into bowel and bladder incontinence and provides more detail for dressing by distinguishing between upper body and lower body limitations. Each item is valued on three levels: can do by myself, can do with the help of someone else, and cannot do at all. In contrast to the Katz

scale, these items are measures of ability ("can do") and not independence ("do"). Arbitrary weights ranging from 0 to 15 are used to create an aggregate score. A score of 0 represents complete inability and a score of 100 represents complete ability on all items.

Purpose and Use

The Katz Activities of Daily Living (ADL) scale was developed as an evaluative tool to study the results of treatment and prognosis in the elderly and chronically ill, but it has been used for a number of purposes as originally designed or in modified forms. The Katz ADL scale was developed at the Benjamin Rose Hospital, a chronic care hospital and early research using the scale studied recovery from stroke, fracture of the hip, and rheumatoid arthritis (20–22). More recent studies have used the Katz ADL scale in nursing homes (23–28). For these populations the scale discriminates well, providing a good distribution of disability levels with few elders scoring either not disabled or disabled on all items. For nursing home residents, or a useful modification to improve discrimination, the final category divides into those who are dependent in five ADLs and need some help with feeding and those who are dependent in five ADLs and need total help with feeding (resident does not participate or is fed intravenously or with tubes) (27,28).

The scale has also been used in studies of elders in the community. For this population the scale does not discriminate well. Branch et al. (29), using a Katz Activities of Daily Living scale modified for personal interview rather than assessment (with only four items) found 7.6% dependent based on the scale. Adding grooming and walking across a small room increased the estimate of dependence to 15.9%.

The Katz scale has also been used to measure functional deterioration as a health status measure to evaluate effectiveness in major health services experiments. In the Continued Care Study (30) the effectiveness of regular home visits by a public health nurse after discharge from a rehabilitation hospital was evaluated. In the Chance for Change study (31) the effectiveness of home visits by health assistants working with an interdisciplinary team after discharge from an acute care hospital was evaluated. In an evaluation of the federal survey and certification process for nursing homes, 6-month ADL outcomes in facilities that received a new, more patient centered, regulatory process were compared with ADL outcomes in facilities that received the traditional survey (32). The scale has also been used to measure change in ADL function for nursing home residents as an outcome indicator of quality. In a study of all certified nursing homes in Rhode Island, resident and facility factors associated with 6-month functional improvement and decline were evaluated (25). In a study of nursing home quality using the National Medical Expenditure Survey data, Cohen and Spector (27) assessed the impact of Medicaid reimbursement methods on nursing homes resident outcomes including 6-month ADL change.

The Barthel Index was developed in a chronic hospital setting (12) and has become the instrument of choice for rehabilitation studies. In contrast to the Katz scale, it has not generally been adopted to study disabled elders in the community. The scale has been used to monitor progress for severely disabled person in comprehensive medical rehabilitation centers (33). Studies of stroke have shown a correlation between admission and discharge scores on the Barthel Index and discharge location and recovery. A higher likelihood of recovery was found for those with an admission score of 21 or greater and discharge scores of 41 or greater. A high proportion of those attaining a score of 61 or more returned home (34). Studies of functional change from stroke rehabilitation using the Barthel Index have demonstrated that motor persistence score and half-hour recall are the strongest psychological predictors of recovery (35). Urinary incontinence, arm motor deficit, sitting balance, hemianopia, and age are the greatest physical predictors of recovery (36).

Scale Structure

The Katz ADL scale is a semi-Guttman scale. A Guttman scale orders items with one pattern by degree of difficulty of items. For example, if a person is dependent in feeding, he would also be dependent in bathing, dressing, toileting, transferring and continence, for example. In the 1963 paper (10), 86% of persons were represented by the strict hierarchy.

Other researchers have presented coefficients of reproducibility (CR) and scalability (CS) for the Katz Activities of Daily Living scale. The coefficient of reproducibility, the percent of total possible errors that are not made by using the strict pattern, is reported with analyses of ordered scales. It is a measure of both reliability and reproducibility. The original article by Guttman sets a standard of .90 or greater for a reliable and reproducible scale (37). A second measure, the coefficient of scalability, measures the amount of improvement over the minimum coefficient of reproducibility. A minimum CR greater than 0 occurs when there are persons on the extremes of the scale (i.e., totally dependent or totally independent). A minimum standard for the coefficient of scalability is .60. Kane and Kane (7) report studies at the Hebrew Rehabilitation Center for Aged that found coefficients of reproducibility of greater than .94 for samples of home care recipients and a sheltered home sample. Spector and Takada (25), for a nursing home population, report a coefficient of reproducibility of .95 and a coefficient of scalability of .86. Researchers in Sweden, with patients in acute care settings, report CS's above .70 (38–40).

The Katz scale is a semi-Guttman scale because it does not strictly use the order of items as determined by the Guttman analysis, but includes levels defined, for example, as dependency in one ADL, or dependency in bathing plus one ADL.

Although the scale exceeds all minimum scaling standards for a Guttman scale, the researchers were not willing to consider all nonhierarchical patterns as error. Therefore, a number of patterns were combined in the scale and not all placed into the "other" category, which is the closest category the researchers have to represent error. The patterns that were grouped together were treated as representing equivalent degrees of disability.

Although hierarchical properties of the activities of daily living measure have been reported by Katz, it is important for users to test the scalability of their data to determine if their particular implementation of the scale meets the standards of scalability derived from other experiences. Differences in sample populations and modifications of the scales such as a different reference period, adding (e.g., grooming) or replacing items (e.g., walking for transferring), or variations in definitions (e.g., including cutting meat in eating dependency) may alter the scale properties and the ordered relationship of items.

The Barthel Index is not an ordered scale. Aggregation is based on a weighting scheme and as such does not guarantee that there is a uniform underlying dimension as is implied with the Katz scale. Interpretation of the Barthel is more difficult as a result, because it is not certain that a lower score on the Barthel, for example, implies more disability, unless one is confident that the arbitrary weights are correct. Also, the same score may result from a number of different profiles. If there is concern over loss of specific profile information when an aggregate scale is used, individual item scores may be retained and used to supplement the aggregate scores for completeness of information.

Reliability

Reliability is the proportion of the true variance to the total variance. There are three basic reliability measures: interperson reliability (consistency of scoring between different individuals), test-retest reliability (consistency of scoring over a short period of time when subjects have not changed), and internal reliability (the correlation of individual items to the total score). Internal reliability is usually measured with Cronbach's alpha (41). The coefficient of reproducibility is also a measure of reliability for ordered scales. Published reports of reliability using the Katz and Barthel scales are not extensive, however.

The coefficient of reproducibility as discussed above is a measure of the internal consistency of an ordered measure. These results have been discussed above for the Katz scale. Katz et al. (10) report an interperson reliability of .95 or better after training. Spector and Takada (25) report a similar experience. Test-retest reliability has not been reported.

The Barthel Index has been shown to have both high test-retest reliability and high interperson reliability. Granger et al. (33) report test-retest reliability of .89 and interperson reliability of .95. High internal reliability has also been found in studies at the Hebrew Rehabilitation Center for the Aged (alpha scores of between .953 and .965) (7). Shinar et al. (42) report high interperson reliability and test-retest reliability with stroke patients both at the individual item level and the aggregate level, comparing results from observers and administrators and among observers and among administrators. Individual Spearman's rho correlations ranged from .71 to 1.00. The lowest correlations were found for wash and bathe, bowel incontinence, and grooming. Overall Pearson r correlations for the aggregate scores were .99 or higher. The authors emphasize that these results are dependent on highly trained interviewers. They advise that telephone interviews should not be given to patients who may score differently on verbal responses versus performance.

Sensitivity to Setting

There is concern that the measurement of disability used in a clinical trial may be sensitive to the setting. Few comparisons have been made on the same persons over a short period of time in different settings (e.g., hospital–nursing home, hospital–home). Depending on how the measures are defined, the sensitivity to setting may differ. Katz et al. (10) warn that the Katz scale is sensitive to environment. As a measure of independence the assessment is affected by the environment as well as physical and mental abilities. These environmental influences may be because of physical impediments in the environment or organizational rules that influence how caregivers interact with residents. An analysis of the environment may indicate where modifications could improve ADL performance (43). In both hospitals and nursing homes, organizational rules (e.g., mandating that aides help all residents bathe), often established because of concerns for safety and cost, may affect the score on dressing, transferring, toileting, and bathing. Because the scale is based on independence, not ability, the Katz scale is particularly sensitive. The Barthel scale, which is an ability measure, should be less sensitive. Also the differential availability of prosthetic devices may affect the disability score in alternative settings. Comparisons of assessments in the hospital and in the home over a short period with a modified index of ADL have found more severe disability measured in the home. Presumably this results from the unavailability of many mechanical devices in the home (44,45). In some circumstances Katz et al. (10) recommend that ability as well as performance may need to be assessed to determine the impact of environmental artifacts on the disability score. One approach is to ask the resident to simulate the activity.

Validity

Three measures of validity are usually determined: criterion validity, content validity, and construct validity. *Crite-*

rion validity refers to the extent that the same results as a gold standard are produced. *Content validity* refers to the judgment that the items included in the scale are representative of the domain measured. *Construct validity* refers to the variation explained by other constructs or tests. A fourth aspect of validity, sometimes included with construct validity, is the ability to predict. Kane (46) argues that the ability of a scale to predict who will incur medical problems is the ultimate test of a scale.

There are no gold standards for disability measures. Therefore, validity testing for these scales is limited to content and construct validations. With respect to content validity, the Katz ADL includes measures of basic self-care. All measures would be classified as disability measures except incontinence, an impairment.

Some research has suggested that incontinence should not be included in the scale, but treated separately. Jagger et al. (47), with questions similar to those of the Katz scale and using principal component analysis, identified two components: physical activities and incontinence of feces and urine. Similarly, analysis of the structure of the Functional Independence Measure, a scale used for inpatient medical rehabilitation, found incontinence of feces and incontinence of urine not to fit with other ADL measures (48). Nevertheless, inclusion of incontinence for a population of nursing home residents improves discrimination for severely disabled residents. One solution may be to present the information with two scores for each person: a basic AOL score and a continence score.

With respect to construct validity of the Katz scale, Katz et al. (49) report moderate correlations for the index of ADL with measures of range of motion, intelligence, and orientation. Jackson et al. (26), using the Katz ADL, showed a positive relationship between more disability and the proportion of nursing home residents with at least one disruptive behavior. Spector and Kemper (11) and Spector (50) showed a strong correlation between the number of ADL deficits (based on five ADLs excluding incontinence) and hours of formal and informal care received per week in the community.

The Katz scale has been shown to have predictive validity also. Studies have demonstrated a positive relationship between ADL dependency level and mortality among nursing home residents (25,27). Studies have also showed a relationship between the Katz ADL and discharge status (28,51). Spector et al. (28) found this relationship weakened as length of stay increased.

The Barthel Index includes measures of self-care and mobility, as well as continence. Jette (52,53), in two articles examining the correlations of a number of self-care, instrumental, and basic activities of daily living, identified five dimensions. The dimensions varied slightly in the two studies. At issue was the combination of mobility transfers from chair to bed, and items such as attending meetings and driving a car. If transferring and mobility are combined as in the second study, the Barthel may be viewed as a two-dimensional scale including mobility and personal care items. Incontinence was not included in either of the Jette studies.

A number of construct validity results have been reported for the Barthel Index. The scale is highly correlated with both the Katz ADL and the Kenny Self-Care Evaluation (54) and the Pulses Profile (33). For patients in a comprehensive stroke program, the admission Barthel score discriminated between those that died and those that survived (mean score of 6.2 versus 41.9) (34). Other studies have found similar results (55,56). The scale also predicts the likelihood of discharge home (34,57).

For chronically ill persons living alone, the Barthel score was highly correlated with the number of personal care tasks performed independently. Low correlations were found with household tasks such as light housework and cooking meals, but no relationships were found for instrumental activities such as shopping, laundry, and heavy housecleaning. The Barthel Index was also shown to be negatively correlated with psychological measures and age. Those with more disability were less likely to make decisions easily, had decreased ability to fulfill usual roles, and were more likely to be disoriented or depressed. Those with more disability were likely to be older (58).

Using a modified ADL index (17 items that are similar to the Barthel Index), Sheikh et al. (44) compared scores on the ADL scale with the number of neurological deficits, a measure of the extent of cerebral lesions. Those scoring high on activities of daily living had a high number of neurological deficits ($r = .376$). A sensitivity of .70 and a specificity of .87 were found.

The Katz scale and the Barthel Index administered on the same patients produce a high degree of agreement. A Barthel score of between 0 and 49 is comparable to a Katz F or G, a Barthel score of between 50 and 79 is comparable to a D or E, a Barthel score of 80 to 99 is comparable to a B or C, and a Barthel score of 100 is comparable to an A on the Katz. The kappa coefficient of agreement, which adjusts for random chance of agreement, was .77. A score greater than .75 represents excellent agreement (54,59).

Responsiveness of Instruments to Medical Treatments

The study of functional change is in its infancy, with few published results that may serve as standards for comparison studies. To a large extent this is because change results are very sensitive to the exact formulation of the scale. Studies of change generally have used idiosyncratic versions of the original scales or are not population based. One exception is Verbrugge et al. (60), who studied the dynamics of functional change of persons aged 55 and over who were hospitalized over a year. They found that ADL status, as measured by the Katz scale, was stable over a 2-week period, but was very unstable over a 1-year period.

For a scale to be useful for clinical studies and health services evaluations, it must be responsive to change sufficient enough to detect clinically important changes. A study may show no effect on functional disability levels because the measure is not sensitive enough rather than the intervention not effective. Therefore, this is an important concern.

Scales may be made more sensitive by increasing the number of possible responses reflecting disability severity. For example, the minimum data set for nursing home residents includes five responses for each activity: independence, supervision, limited assistance, extensive assistance, and total dependence. In addition, the amount of support that is provided is assessed: no setup or physical help, setup help only, physical help from one person, and physical help from two or more (61). However, increase in the number of levels of an item is accompanied by reduction in reliability. In addition these distinctions need to be clinically meaningful. Although the ability to distinguish between measurement error and true change is important, disability studies generally have not made appropriate corrections for attenuation when evaluating correlations with change measures (62).

INSTRUMENTAL ACTIVITIES OF DAILY LIVING

Instrumental activities of daily living scales include activities that concern a person's ability to adapt to the environment. The activities include items such as shopping, getting around outside with transportation, preparing meals, and doing housework. Independence on these scales demonstrates an ability to live independently in the community. Residents in specialized housing may be able to remain although they are dependent in some of the items depending on the services provided in these settings. The scales are generally not appropriate for residents in nursing homes or other institutions, but would discriminate well in a community population and in a continuing care community environment, which generally include an assisted living level of care. Norms for residents in different settings have not been established.

In general instrumental activities of daily living measures are recommended to supplement activities of daily living as part of a geriatric assessment for a population of elders. These measures are also gaining popularity in assessments of nonelderly populations (63). Its use as a clinical tool in an institutional environment is limited, however, but may be useful in discharge planning from a hospital (3–5).

The Lawton Instrumental Activities of Daily Living Scale and the Older Americans Resources and Services Instrument

In the Lawton scale, the instrumental activities of daily living (13) include eight items: telephoning, shopping, food preparation, housekeeping, laundry, transportation, medications, and handling finances. All eight items are used for women but only five are used for men, with food preparation, housekeeping, and laundry eliminated. The scale measures performance in contrast to ability. Instrumental activities of daily living questions incorporated into multidimensional instruments are modifications of the Lawton scale using all items for men, but question if the inability is due to a disability or health problem (e.g., 1982 and 1984 National Long Term Care Surveys). The Duke Older Americans Resources and Services instrument asks all questions of both men and women but asks about ability, not performance (64).

The Pfeffer Functional Activity Questionnaire

The Pfeffer Functional Activities Questionnaire, a ten-item scale, expands on the Lawton Instrumental Activities of Daily Living Scale by including measures more directly tapping cognition: tracks current events; pays attention to, understands, and discusses plot of television programs, books, or magazines; remembers appointments, medicines, or other things; and plays skilled games or hobbies. The scale has items similar to the Lawton scale: shopping, simple financial activities, and meal preparation. In addition there is a more difficult financial activity than in the Lawton scale, and a preparation of tea or coffee item. Activities such as use of the telephone, housekeeping, or laundry are not included.

The scale is administered by a nonprofessional. Each item is divided into six levels: someone has recently taken over the activity; requires advice or assistance; does without assistance or advice but more difficult than used to, does without difficulty or advice; never did, and would find it difficult to start now; and never did, but can do if had to. The first four levels are scaled from 0 to 3 and the last two levels are scored 1 and 0, respectively.

Purpose and Use of Instrumental Activities of Daily Living

Lawton (65) states that the IADL scale was intended to identify independence on tasks instrumental to an independent life. It is recommended for use as a guide to help identify the optimum living situation for an elderly person. The instrumental activities of daily living are viewed as a set of activities on a continuum of complexity between physical self-maintenance (ADLs) and effectance behaviors: recreational and creative behaviors. Although a number of studies have used instrumental activities of daily living items, generally the Lawton scale has been modified and the ordered relationship of the items has been ignored.

The Functional Activity Questionnaire was designed to sample more complex activities than the Lawton scale, but activities that are universal. It was envisioned for use in retirement communities with the intent to tap mild dementia (14). It has not received wide acceptance, but its conceptual basis and psychometric properties indicate increased use in the future.

Scaling Instrumental Activities of Daily Living

The Lawton Instrumental Activities of Daily Living Scale is a Guttman scale. The CR for the IADL scale is reported as .96 for men and .93 for women in the original article (13). The scale items, in order of increasing difficulty, are the following: uses telephone, takes care of all shopping needs, plans and prepares and serves adequate meals independently, maintains light housework independently, does all laundry, travels by car or public transportation, takes medications with correct dosage at right time, and manages all financial tasks except major purchases or banking.

The Pfeffer scale aggregates six levels for each of the ten items by using arbitrary weights: dependent = 3, requires assistance = 2, has difficulty = 1, never did and would have difficulty = 1, didn't do but could do now = 0. Concern about arbitrary weights has been addressed above.

A concern with instrumental activities of daily living is that they provide a biased measure of disability comparing men with women due to the division of labor on household tasks along gender lines. A man with the same level of disability may be more likely to respond he is unable to cook, for example, than a woman. The Lawton scale includes fewer items for men than women because of this problem. This does not successfully solve the problem, because it becomes a scale that discriminates better for women than men. Modifications of the scale have asked about ability rather than performance or linked the disability to a health or impairment problem. Johnson and Wolinsky (66) found race-gender biases for both self-reported instrumental activities of daily living and activities of daily living in a national survey.

Reliability of Instrumental Activities of Daily Living Scales

For the Lawton scale, the high coefficients of reproducibility indicate strong internal reliability. Interperson reliability results show a correlation of .85 between total scores for two social workers who scored the same persons. Test-retest reliability results have not been published (13).

For the Pfeffer scale, internal reliability is strong with correlations among individual items on the Functional Activity Questionnaire and total score ranging from .81 to .90. Interrater reliability of a neurologist and nurse was high (Tau B = .802). Test-retest reliability results are not available (14).

Validity of Instrumental Activities of Daily Living Scales

For the Lawton scale, correlations with activities of daily living, mental status, physical health (based on history, physical findings, and laboratory tests), and a behavior and adjustment scale have been reported. Correlations are .77, .74, .50, and .36, respectively (13).

The correlation between a modified Lawton scale (using weights) and the Pfeffer scale was reported as .72 (14). Comparisons of correlations of a modified Lawton scale and measures of social and cognitive function found the Pfeffer scale to be more correlated than the modified Lawton Instrumental Activities of Daily Living Scale. The largest differences were for correlations with estimates of residual deficit by neurologists (−.83 and −.68, respectively), and the Mini-Mental State Examination (67) (−.71 and −.55, respectively). This is not surprising because of the larger number of activities in the Pfeffer scale that directly relate to cognition.

Combining Activities of Daily Living and Instrumental Activities of Daily Living

To further improve discrimination in healthy populations, the instrumental activities of daily living are often combined with the ADL to broaden the definition of disability (4,68). The appropriate method for combining activities of daily living and instrumental activities of daily living items has not been thoroughly studied, however. Some research indicates that instrumental activities of daily living and activities of daily living form one underlying dimension, justifying combining them into one additive scale, whereas other research indicates that there are separate dimensions. Many researchers use simple aggregation approaches. Often an arbitrary number of activities of daily living and instrumental activities of daily living items are combined by counting the total number of disabilities. For example, Jette and Branch (68) combine six activities with five instrumental activities in this manner. No evidence is provided that these items are a Guttman scale or that assigning a weight of one for each activity is appropriate. Nevertheless, scales of this type are interpreted as if more disabilities imply more severe disability.

Two scales that have received some interest in the research community and include both instrumental activities of daily living and activities of daily living items are the Rosow Scale and the Rapid Disability Scale. Rosow and Breslau (69) presented a Guttman scale that combines ADL and IADL items with more emphasis on instrumental activities of daily living. The scale had a CR of .91. The scale is rarely used in total, however, but some of the items have been incorporated in large surveys.

Linn and Linn (70) introduced a modified Rapid Disability Scale, which includes detailed activities of daily living, a general instrumental activities of daily living item, a number of impairments, and psychological items. It is a multidimensional scale going beyond activities of daily living and instrumental activities of daily living, but uses a simple scoring system that would be difficult to justify. Reliability results are strong, but validity testing has not been extensive. The scale has been gaining in popularity.

The Groningen Activities Restrictions Scale (71,72) has 11 activities, including standard activities of daily living items and mobility items (e.g., get around in the house, go up and down stairs and walk outdoors, and stand up from sitting in a chair) and seven instrumental activities of daily living covering aspects of shopping, laundry, meal preparation, and housework. Each item is scored with one of five response categories: can do fully independently, without any difficulty; fully independently with some difficulty; fully independently with great difficulty; cannot do fully independently, but can do only with someone's help; and cannot do at all, need complete help.

Using principal components factor analysis, the Groningen Activities Restrictions Scale has been shown to have one general factor indicating that both activities and instrumental activities of daily living form one underlying dimension of disability. The items range in difficulty from heavy cleaning (the most difficult) to washing face and hands (the least difficult). Interestingly the instrumental activities of daily living items overlap with the activities of daily living items. Light cleaning and preparing breakfast/lunch were less difficult than some activities of daily living. Only making beds, shopping, and heavy cleaning were more difficult than any of the activities of daily living. These findings indicate that some instrumental activities of daily living may be helpful in measuring functional disability at levels of severity previously attributed only to activities of daily living deficits. Other instrumental activities of daily living items provide a measure of disability for persons with no activities of daily living deficits and thereby help discriminate among persons with milder deficits. The scale correlates highly with the Karnofsky Performance Status Scale (.68) and the Physical Mobility subscale of the Nottingham Health Profile (.78).

In contrast, Wolinsky and Johnson (73), Johnson and Wolinsky (74), and Fitzgerald et al. (75) have identified three correlated dimensions using factor analyses. Although these studies do not exactly replicate the items in these dimensions, they have consistently found two instrumental activities of daily living dimensions and one activities of daily living dimension.

Spector et al. (76) analyzed the scalability of four activities of daily living (bathing, dressing, transferring, and feeding) with two instrumental activities of daily living (shopping and transportation). CRs from secondary analysis of data from three studies (Cleveland-GAO study, Georgia-Medicaid study, and the Homemaker–Day Care study) were all above .94. CSs were all above .74. Correlation analyses of individual items indicated that a strict hierarchical relationship between shopping and transportation was not apparent. A number of persons were dependent in shopping and bathing but independent in transportation, whereas another group was dependent only in transportation. Nevertheless, persons dependent in activities of daily living were also dependent in both instrumental activities of daily living; a number of persons were dependent in instrumental activities of daily living only. In the three data sets, few persons were dependent in activities of daily living only (less than 1% in the Georgia-Medicaid and Homemaker–Day Care study, and 2% in the GAO-Cleveland study). The authors suggested that the activities of daily living and instrumental activities of daily living could be combined into the following scale: independent in instrumental activities of daily living and activities of daily living; dependent in shopping or transportation; shopping and transportation; shopping, transportation, plus one activity of daily living; shopping, transportation, bathing, plus one activity of daily living; shopping, transportation, bathing, dressing, plus one activity of daily living; and six activities. For this scale, in the three studies, the frequency of the ''other'' category ranged from 2.2% to 4.8%.

Validation of the instrumental activities of daily living–activities of daily living hierarchy was based on the three aggregated categories: independent in instrumental activities of daily living and activities of daily living, dependent in instrumental activities of daily living only, and dependent in instrumental activities of daily living and activities of daily living. The level of disability was correlated with age. The independent proportion decreased with age, and the proportion only dependent in instrumental activities of daily living increased with age, as did the proportion dependent in both instrumental activities of daily living and activities of daily living. Those dependent in instrumental activities of daily living were more likely to die in a year than those independent, but less likely to die than those dependent in both instrumental activities of daily living and activities of daily living. The proportion hospitalized in a year increased with level of disability.

CONCLUSIONS

The chapter reviewed a small number of functional disability scales, emphasizing scales that include one type of disability measure, either activities of daily living or instrumental activities of daily living, and did not review disability scales that were part of multidimensional instruments including psychological and social dimensions. Scales that have received acceptance in the clinical and research arenas and that had sufficient reliability and validity results were reviewed in detail, although scales varied in terms of the quality and extent of their reliability and validity results as

well as in the number of studies that have included the scales. Important differences were highlighted and conceptual concerns were discussed.

In general any of the scales discussed in detail here would be worthy of strong consideration. No scale is best for all purposes, however. The scale should be chosen based on the specific purpose for its use. Moreover, the properties of the scale should be carefully studied after implementation to assure that expected relationships between items exist. This is particularly important if the scale is applied to a new population or if modifications have been made. Researchers should be cautious about constructing new scales or using scales that have not been validated. They should be equally cautious about combining items in simplistic ways without doing appropriate scalability and validity analyses. The interpretation that a higher score (or lower score) implies more severe disability may be incorrect. Finally, researchers should be encouraged to publish reliability and validity results of scales used in evaluative and population studies to help further understanding of the usefulness of these instruments.

REFERENCES

1. Besdine RW. The educational utility of comprehensive functional assessment in the elderly. *J Am Geriatr Soc* 1983;31:651–656.
2. World Health Organization. *International classification of impairments, disabilities, and handicaps.* Geneva: World Health Organization, 1980.
3. Williams TF. Comprehensive assessment of frail elderly in relation to needs for long-term care. In: Calkins E, Davis PJ, Ford AB, eds. *The practice of geriatrics.* Philadelphia: WB Saunders, 1986.
4. Kane RL, Ouslander JG, Abrass IB. *Essentials of clinical geriatrics.* New York: McGraw-Hill, 1984.
5. Rubenstein LZ, Abrass IB. Geriatric assessment. In: Exton-Smith AN, Weksler ME, eds. *Practical geriatric medicine.* Edinburgh: Churchill Livingstone, 1985.
6. Ernst M, Ernst NS. Functional capacity. In: Mangen DJ, Peterson WA, eds. *Health, program evaluation, and demography,* vol 3. Minneapolis: University of Minnesota Press, 1984.
7. Kane RA, Kane RL. *Assessing the elderly.* Lexington, MA: DC Heath, 1981.
8. Deyo RA. Measuring functional outcomes in therapeutic trials for chronic disease. *Controlled Clin Trials* 1984;5:223–240.
9. Hedrick SC, Katz S, Stroud MW. Patient assessment in long-term care: is there a common language? *Aged Care Services Rev* 1981;2:1–19.
10. Katz S, Ford AB, Moskowitz RW, Jackson BA, Jaffe MW. Studies of illness in the aged: the index of ADL: a standardized measure of biological and psychosocial function. *JAMA* 1963;185(12):914–919.
11. Spector WD, Kemper P. Disability and cognitive impairment criteria: targeting those who need the most home care. *Gerontologist* 1994;34(5):640–651.
12. Mahoney FI, Barthel DW. Functional evaluation: the Barthel Index. *Maryland State Med J* 1965;14:61–65.
13. Lawton MP, Brody EM. Assessment of older people: self-maintaining and instrumental activities of daily living. *Gerontologist* 1969;9:179–186.
14. Pfeffer RI, Kurosaki MS, Harrah CH, Chance JM, Filos S. Measurement of functional activities in older adults in the community. *J Gerontology* 1982;37(3):323–329.
15. Luft H. *Poverty and health.* Cambridge, MA: Ballinger, 1878.
16. Nagi SZ. Some conceptual issues in disability and rehabilitation. In: Sussman MB, ed. American Sociological Association, Washington, DC. *Sociology and rehabilitation.* 1965:100–113.

17. Wolfe BL. Measuring disability and health. *J Health Econ* 1984;3: 187–193.
18. Nagi SZ. An epidemiology of disability among adults in the United States. *Milbank Memorial Fund Q* 1976;54(4):439–467.
19. Kirshner B, Guyatt G. A methodological framework for assessing health indices. *J Chronic Dis* 1985;38(1):27–36.
20. Staff of the Benjamin Rose Hospital. Multidisciplinary studies of illness in aged persons: III. Prognostic indices in fracture of hip. *J Chronic Dis* 1960;11:445–455.
21. Katz S, Jackson BA, Jaffe MW, Littell AS, Turk CE. Multidisciplinary studies of illness in aged persons: VI. Comparison study of rehabilitated and nonrehabilitated patients with fracture of the hip. *J Chronic Dis* 1962;15:979–984.
22. Katz S, Vignos PJ, Moskowitz RW, Thompson HM, Sveck KH. Comprehensive outpatient care in rheumatoid arthritis: a controlled study. *J Am Med Soc* 1968;206:1249–1254.
23. Spector WD, Kapp MC, Tucker RJ, Sternberg J. Factors associated with presence of decubitus ulcers at admission to nursing homes. *Gerontologist* 1988;28(6):830–834.
24. Sternberg J, Spector WD, Fretwell MD, Jackson ME, Drugovich ML. Use of psychoactive drugs in nursing homes: prevalence and residents' characteristics. *J Geriatr Drug Ther* 1990;4(3):47–60.
25. Spector WD, Takada HA. Characteristics of nursing homes that affect resident outcomes. *J Aging Health* 1991;3(4):427–454.
26. Jackson ME, Drugovich ML, Fretwell MD, Spector WD, Sternberg J, Rosenstein RB. Prevalence and correlates of disruptive behavior in the nursing home. *J Aging Health* 1989;1(3):349–369.
27. Cohen JW, Spector WD. The effect of Medicaid reimbursement on quality of care in nursing homes. *J Health Econ* forthcoming.
28. Spector WD, Kapp MC, Eichorn AM, Tucker RJ, Rosenstein RB, Katz S. *Case-mix outcomes and resource use in nursing homes.* Final report prepared for the Health Care Financing Administration. HCFA, cooperative agreement no. 18-C-98719/1. Providence, RI: Center for Gerontology and Health Care Research, Brown University, 1988.
29. Branch LG, Katz S, Kniepmann K, Papsidero JA. A prospective study of functional status among community elders. *Am J Public Health* 1984;74(3):266–268.
30. Katz S, Ford AB, Downs TD, Adams M, Rusby DI. *Effects of continued care: a study of chronic illness in the home.* Washington DC: US Government Printing Office, 1972.
31. Papsidero J, Katz S, Kroger MH, Akpom CA. *Chance for change.* East Lansing: Michigan State University Press, 1979.
32. Spector WD, Drugovich ML. Reforming nursing home quality regulation: impact on cited deficiencies and nursing home outcomes. *Med Care* 1989;27(8):789–801.
33. Granger CV, Albrecht GL, Hamilton BB. Outcome of comprehensive medical rehabilitation: measurement by Pulses Profile and the Barthel Index. *Arch Phys Med Rehabil* 1979;60:145–154.
34. Granger CV, Sherwood CC, Greer DS. Functional status measures in a comprehensive stroke care program. *Arch Phys Med Rehabil* 1977;58: 555–561.
35. Novack TA, Haban G, Graham K, Satterfield WT. Prediction of stroke rehabilitation outcome from psychologic screening. *Arch Phys Med Rehabil* 1987;68:729–734.
36. Wade DT, Skilbeck CE, Hewer RL. Predicting Barthel ADL score at 6 months after an acute stroke. *Arch Phys Med Rehabil* 1983;64:24–28.
37. Guttman L. A basis for scaling qualitative data. *Am Soc Rev* 1944;9: 139–150.
38. Brorsson B, Asberg KH. Katz index of independence in ADL: reliability and validity in short-term care. *Scand J Rehabil Med* 1984;16:125–132.
39. Asberg KH. Assessment of ADL in home care for elderly: change in ADL and use of short-term hospital care. *Scand J Soc Med* 1986;14: 105–111.
40. Asberg KH. Disability as a predictor of outcome for the elderly in a department of internal medicine. *Scand J Soc Med* 1987;15:261–265.
41. Cronbach LJ. Coefficient alpha in the internal structure of tests. *Psychometrika* 1951;16:297–334.
42. Shinar D, Gross CR, Bronstein KS, Licata-Gehr EE, Eden DT, Cabrera AR, Fishman IG, Roth AA, Barwick JA, Kunitz SC. Reliability of the activities of daily living scale and its use in telephone interview. *Arch Phys Med Rehabil* 1987;68:723–728.
43. Clark MC, Czaja SJ, Weber RA. Older adults and daily living task profiles. *Hum Factors* 1990;32(5):537–549.
44. Sheikh K, Smith DS, Meade TW, Goldenberg E, Brennan PJ, Kinsella G. Repeatability and validity of a modified activities of daily living (ADL) index in studies of chronic disability. *Int Rehabil Med* 1979;1: 51–58.
45. Haworth RJ, Hollings EM. Are hospital assessments of daily living activities valid? *Int Rehabil Med* 1979;1:59–62.
46. Kane RL. Commentary: functional assessment questionnaire for geriatrics patients—or the clinical Swiss army knife. *J Chronic Dis* 1987;40 (suppl 1):95S–98S.
47. Jagger C, Clarke M, Davies RA. The elderly at home: indices of disability. *J Epidemiol Community Health* 1986;40:139–142.
48. Linacre JM, Heinemann AW, Wright BD, Granger CV, Hamilton BB. The structure and stability of the functional independence measure. *Arch Phys Med Rehabil* 1994;75:127–132.
49. Katz S, Downs TD, Cash HR, Grotz RC. Progress in development of the index of ADL. *Gerontologist* 1970;10:20–30.
50. Spector WD. Cognitive impairment and functional disability: implications for home care eligibility for the elderly. Paper presented at the 47th annual meeting of the Gerontological Society of America, November 1994.
51. Densen PM, Jones EW, McNitt BJ. *An approach to the assessment of long term care.* Final report, research grant No. HS-01162. Boston: Harvard Center for Community Health and Medical Care, 1976.
52. Jette AM. Functional status index: Reliability of a chronic disease evaluation instrument. *Arch Phys Med Rehabil* 1980;61:395–401.
53. Jette AM. Functional capacity evaluation: an empirical approach. *Arch Phys Med Rehabil* 1980;61:85–89.
54. Gresham GE, Phillips TF, Labi MLC. ADL status in stroke: relative merits of three standard indexes. *Arch Phys Med Rehabil* 1980;61: 355–358.
55. Wylie CM. Measuring end results of rehabilitation of patients with stroke. *Public Health Rep* 1967;82:893–898.
56. Carroll D. Disability in hemiplegia caused by cerebrovascular disease: serial studies of 98 cases. *J Chronic Dis* 1962;15:179–188.
57. Granger CV, Greer DS. Functional status measurement and medical rehabilitation outcomes. *Arch Phys Med Rehabil* 1976;57:103–108.
58. Fortinsky RH, Granger CV, Seltzer GB. The use of functional assessment in understanding home care needs. *Med Care* 1981;19(5):489–497.
59. Sheik K. Disability scales: assessment of reliability. *Arch Phys Med Rehabil* 1986;67:245–249.
60. Verbrugge LM, Reoma JM, Gruber-Baldini AL. Short-term dynamics of disability and well-being. *J Health Soc Behav* 1994;35:97–117.
61. Morris JN, Hawes C, Murphy K, Nonemaker S, Phillips C, Fries BE, Mor V. *Resident assessment instrument training manual and resource guide.* Natick, MA: Eliot Press, 1991.
62. Lord FM. Elementry models for measuring change. In: Harris CW, ed. *Problems in measuring change.* Madison, WI: The University of Wisconsin Press, 1963:21–37.
63. Reardon M, Hitzing W. *The Ohio eligibility determination instrument user manual.* Ohio Department of Metal Retardation and Developmental Disabilities, Columbus, Ohio, 1992.
64. Center for the Study of Aging and Human Development. *Multidimensional assessment: the OARS methodology.* Durham, NC: The Center for Study of Aging and Human Development, Duke University, 1978.
65. Lawton MP. Assessment, integration, and environments for older people. *Gerontologist* 1970;10:38–46.
66. Johnson RJ, Wolinsky FD. Gender, race, and health: the structure of health status among older adults. *Gerontologist* 1994;34(1):24–35.
67. Folstein M, Anthony JC, Parhad I, Duffy B, Gruenberg EM. The meaning of cognitive impairment in the elderly. *J Am Geriatr Soc* 1985;33(4):228–235.
68. Jette AM, Branch LG. Impairment and disability in the aged. *J Chronic Dis* 1985;38(1):59–65.
69. Rosow I, Breslau N. A Guttman health scale for the aged. *J Gerontol* 1966;21:556–559.
70. Linn MW, Linn BS. The rapid disability rating scale–2. *J Am Geriatr Soc* 1982;30:378–382.
71. Kempen GI, Suurmeijer TP. The development of a hierarchical polychotomous ADL-IADL scale for noninstitutional elders. *Gerontologist* 1990;30(4):497–502.

72. Suurmeijer TP, Doeglas DM, Mourn T, Briancon S, Krol B, Sanderman R, Guillemin F, Bjelle A, Van-den-Heuvel WJ. The Groningen Activity Restriction Scale for measuring disability: its utility in international comparisons. *Am J Public Health* 1994;84(8):1270–3.

73. Wolinsky FD, Johnson RJ. The use of health services by older adults. *J Gerontol Soc Sci* 1991;46:S345–S357.

74. Johnson RJ, Wolinsky FD. The structure of health status among older adults: disease, disability, functional limitation, and perceived health. *J Health Soc Behav* 1993;34:105–121.

75. Fitzgerald JF, Smith DM, Martin DK, Freedman JA, Wolinsky FD. Replication of the multidimensionality of activities of daily living. *J Gerontol Soc Sci* 1993;48(1):S28–S31.

76. Spector WD, Katz S, Murphy JB, Fulton JP. The hierarchical relationship between activities of daily living and instrumental activities of daily living. *J Chronic Dis* 1987;40(6):481–489.

Quality of Life and Pharmacoeconomics in Clinical Trials, Second Edition, edited by B. Spilker.
Lippincott-Raven Publishers, Philadelphia © 1996.

CHAPTER 17

Instruments to Measure Spiritual Status

Jan M. Ellerhorst-Ryan

INTRODUCTION

Commitment to viewing health care in a comprehensive manner must include the client's spiritual concerns. High-field and Cason (1) stated, "We cannot abdicate our responsibility for treating a person's spiritual needs to the chaplain, any more than we can abdicate our responsibility for man's physical needs to the physician, or his psychosocial needs to the psychologist and social worker" (p. 191).

Historically, research on spirituality has focused on religiosity. Moberg and Brusek (2), in comparing religiosity and spiritual well-being, associate the former with institutional goals and behaviors. Measures of religious practice are not always reliable indicators of spirituality.

Spirituality is more than the sum of the client's religious preference, religious beliefs, and religious practices. It relates to "the totality of man's inner resources, the ultimate concerns around which all other values are focused, the central philosophy of life that guides conduct, and the meaning-giving center of human life which influences all individual and social behavior" (3, p. 2). It encompasses man's need to find satisfactory answers to questions about the meaning of life, illness, and death.

The Third National Conference on Classification of Nursing Diagnoses recognized the importance of spirituality by including "spiritual concerns," "spiritual distress," and "spir-

itual despair" in the list of approved nursing diagnoses. In 1980, the Fourth National Conference combined these three diagnoses into one, "spiritual distress," defined as "a disruption in the life principle which pervades a person's entire being and which integrates and transcends one's biological and psychosocial nature" (4). This definition, although a beginning, is vague and does not lend itself easily to research.

Spiritual concepts apply to persons who are religious, nonreligious, or anti-religious. Given that both a religious component and a psychosocial component are involved in spiritual concerns, both should be addressed in a tool designed to assess aspects of spirituality.

The concept of "God" does not easily conform to a universal definition. It is, therefore, important to consider ways of eliciting information about the subject's perception of God. Persons holding traditional views of God characterize Him as the ultimate Deity. For others, particularly the nonreligious or anti-religious, "God" may be whatever s/he values most, the focal point of life—work, family, community service, and so on.

In view of the significant influence that the Judeo-Christian philosophy has had on the development of Western culture, the instruments discussed most often reflect that perspective. Information regarding applicability to persons who have other religious orientations are included when it is available for those instruments presented.

INSTRUMENTS

Before selecting a measurement tool, the researcher must first decide which aspect of spirituality is to be investigated.

J. M. Ellerhorst-Ryan: Abbey Infusion Services, Cincinnati, Ohio 45241.

Originally published in Frank-Stromborg Instruments for Clinical Research. Boston: Jones & Bartlett, 1995. Reprinted with permission.

Spiritual needs in general may be studied, or the focus may be limited to a specific spiritual need. Four commonly identified spiritual needs are (a) hope, (b) forgiveness, (c) love and relatedness, and (d) meaning and purpose in life. Other related concepts for which measurement tools are available include spiritual well-being, spiritual coping, and religious orientation.

Consideration must also be given to the population under study (e.g., adults vs. children, nurses vs. patients) to assure appropriate measurement tool selection.

Spiritual Needs: Quantitative Tools

The *Spiritual Health Inventory* (5) is a 31-item self-report instrument worded in the first person. Respondents rank how often they have experienced the feeling or behavior described on a 1 to 5 Likert scale. Content of the Spiritual Health Inventory is consistent with the author's definition of spiritual health, having satisfactorily met spiritual needs for self-acceptance; a trusting relationship with self based on a sense of meaning and purpose in life (e.g., "I feel valuable as a person even when I cannot do as much as before"); relationships with others and/or a supreme other characterized by unconditional love, trust, and forgiveness (e.g., "I believe my nurses and doctors care about me," "I feel a need to be forgiven for some of my thoughts and feelings"); and hope (e.g., "I worry about life after death") (5). A ranking of 5 indicates frequent occurrence, while a ranking of 1 indicates infrequent occurrence.

Scores are determined by reversing subject-recorded ratings of each negative indicator of spiritual health, then summing ratings for all items. Higher scores are associated with higher levels of spiritual health.

The content and construct validity of the Spiritual Health Inventory are based on a review of the literature, input from an expert panel, and factor analysis. Three factors, representing the spiritual needs for self-acceptance, relationships, and hope, account for 71.5% of variance. Analysis using 23 subjects produced a Cronbach's alpha of $r = .77$ (5).

The *Spiritual Perspective Scale,* formerly titled the Religious Perspective Scale, contains ten items that measure the subjects' "perspectives on the extent to which spirituality permeates their lives and (their degree of engagement) in spiritually related interactions" (6, p. 337). The Spiritual Perspective Scale can be administered either as a structured interview or questionnaire. Responses are ranked on a scale of 1 to 6. Scores are determined by calculating the arithmetic mean across all items, with higher scores indicating greater spiritual perspective. Examples of items include:

In talking with your family or friends, how often do you mention spiritual matters?

1. Not at all
2. Less than once a year
3. About once a year
4. About once a month
5. About once a week
6. About once a day

My spirituality is especially important to me because it answers many questions about the meaning of life.

1. Strongly disagree
2. Disagree
3. Disagree more than agree
4. Agree more than disagree
5. Agree
6. Strongly agree

Reliability and validity for the Spiritual Perspective Scale have been demonstrated in both healthy and terminally ill adult populations. Internal consistency was measured by Cronbach's alpha, with alpha coefficients ranging from .93 to .95. Interitem analysis revealed average correlations between .57 to .68. The fact that subjects who reported having a religious background scored higher on the Spiritual Perspective Scale provided evidence for construct validity (6,7).

The 40-item *Serenity Scale* is designed to measure serenity, "a spiritual experience of inner peace that is independent of external events" (8). Although related to peace of mind, serenity goes further, bringing comfort to those confronted by harsh circumstances that are difficult and sometimes impossible to change. Attributes of serenity, as discussed by the authors of the scale, include hope, forgiveness, love and relatedness, and meaning and purpose in life (8).

Items are scored using a Likert scale, with subjects rating frequencies of personal experiences from "never" (rated 1) to "always" (rated 5). Thirteen of the 40 items are negatively stated and require reverse scoring. Higher scores indicate greater levels of serenity. Examples of test items include "I experience an inner calm even when under pressure" and "I experience an inner quiet that does not depend upon events."

Content validity of the Serenity Scale was established by an expert panel analysis during instrument development. Internal consistency was established by Cronbach's alpha, reported as .92. Factor analysis revealed nine factors that explained 58.2% of the variance: Inner Haven, Acceptance, Belonging, Trust, Perspective, Contentment, Present Centered, Beneficence, and Cognitive Restructuring (8). The authors acknowledge questionable validity with low-literacy subjects.

Serenity transcends formal religious dogma; therefore, the *Serenity Scale* can be used with subjects holding a variety of religious views, including atheism. Participants in field studies represent a wide range of age and socioeconomic status from both rural and urban areas. The authors note, however, that the scale has been tested on primarily white and well-educated adults (8).

Spiritual Needs: Qualitative Tools

Interview schedules using open-ended questions may be a more useful tool for qualitative spiritual research. The interview tools described here can be utilized in populations of individuals with diverse religious beliefs and orientations.

Stallwood (9), Hess (10), and Stoll (11), well known for their interest in spiritual concerns of patients, have defined spiritual needs as "any factors necessary to establish and/or maintain a dynamic personal relationship with God (as defined by the individual) and out of that relationship to experience forgiveness, love and relatedness, hope, trust and meaning and purpose in life" (9). Each author has developed an assessment tool useful for interviewing and data collection.

Hess's *Spiritual Needs Survey* was designed for use in hospitals or extended care facilities, but could be easily modified for use in other settings (10). Five questions focus on the patient's awareness of his/her spiritual needs and efforts to address them:

Were you aware of having a spiritual need at any time during your hospitalization?
Are you able to describe it? Can you tell me about it?
With whom did you discuss this need?
How did you feel about the assistance you received?
Has your need been met to any degree or is it still present?

Although Stoll's *Guidelines for Spiritual Assessment* were not designed for use as a research tool, they have been used in conjunction with other measurement scales to evaluate the ability of hospitalized patients to have their spiritual needs met (11–13). Stoll's guidelines include 13 questions addressing the person's concept of God, sources of hope and strength, religious practices, and the relationship between spiritual beliefs and health. Sample items include (12):

To whom do you turn when you need help?
Has being sick made any difference in your feelings toward God? toward yourself? toward others?

Fish and Shelly (14) modified Stoll's guidelines to organize the questions into four categories: understanding a person's beliefs about and involvement with God and religious practice, determining the extent to which a person's religious practices serve as a resource for faith and life, assessing whether resources for hope and strength are founded in reality, and extending an opportunity to accept spiritual help. Excluding the fourth category, which is an invitation for intervention by the interviewer, the remaining three categories make up 11 open-ended questions. As with any instrument using open-ended questions for data collection, interviewers must be instructed in the use of the instrument and appropriate measures taken to assure interrater reliability.

The *Reed Interview Schedule* is designed to elicit information regarding patient preferences for spiritually related nursing interventions (15). The schedule consists of one structured item and one open-ended item. The structured item—"In what ways could hospital nurses help you in your spiritual needs?"—is followed by descriptions of seven spiritually related interventions identified in a review of current nursing literature. Interventions included reading to/with the patient; allowing time for personal prayer or meditation; talking with the patient about beliefs and concerns; providing time for the patient to talk or pray with family members; arranging a visit with a minister, priest, or rabbi; and helping the patient attend the hospital chapel. Participants may select more than one intervention in response to the question. The open-ended item invites participants to describe other interventions important to them but not listed in the first item. Usefulness of the Reed Interview Schedule is limited to descriptive studies investigating health care interventions to address spiritual needs.

Singular Concepts of Spiritual Needs

An alternative to investigating spiritual needs is to limit the scope of the study to one or more specific spiritual needs. The concepts of hope, meaning and purpose in life, forgiveness, and love and relatedness are briefly reviewed here with one corresponding measurement tool highlighted.

Hope

Dufault and Martocchio (16) have defined hope as "a multidimensional life force characterized by a confident yet uncertain expectation of achieving a future good which . . . is realistically possible and personally significant." These characteristics are clearly demonstrated in the *Nowotny Hope Scale* (17), a 29-item questionnaire that assesses six components of hope: confidence in outcome, relationships with others, belief in the possibility of a future, spiritual beliefs, active involvement, and inner readiness. Responses are recorded using a four-point scale (strongly agree, agree, disagree, strongly disagree). Nowotny Hope Scale items include:

I can take whatever happens and make the best of it.
Sometimes I feel I am all alone.

Reliability analysis of the Nowotny Hope Scale using Cronbach's alpha yielded a coefficient of .90. Concurrent validity was established by comparing participant scores on the Nowotny Hope Scale with scores on the Beck Hopelessness Scale. Pearson product moment correlation produced $r = -.47$ ($p < .001$) (17).

Meaning and Purpose in Life

Crumbaugh's *Purpose in Life Test* is designed to measure the degree to which a person experiences a sense of meaning and purpose in life (18). The tool was developed based on Frankl's concepts of noogenic neurosis, which occurs in response to an absence of purpose in life, manifested by "existential frustration" and boredom (19).

The Purpose in Life Test consists of 20 items to which respondents reply on a seven-point scale:

I am usually

1	2	3	4	5	6	7
completely bored			(neutral)			exuberant, enthusiastic

Construct validity was established by comparing scores of healthy subjects with clients undergoing psychiatric therapy. Differences reported were significant and in the direction predicted. Concurrent validity was demonstrated by correlating Purpose in Life Test scores with therapists' ratings for psychiatric clients and ministers' ratings of healthy subjects. Correlations were .37 ($n = 50$) and .47 ($n = 120$), respectively. Reliability testing, using split-half correlation ($n = 120$) yielded a coefficient of .85, corrected to .92 by the Spearman-Brown formula (20).

Love and Relatedness

While the definitions of social support vary, factors consistently identified include the perception that one is cared about, loved, esteemed, and valued, and the perception that support is readily available when needed. These elements of love and relatedness are not only essential components of relationships with other people, but are also present to varying degrees in a person's relationship with God (21).

Maton's *Spiritual Support Scale* employs three items to assess perceived support from God. Responses are recorded using a five-point scale, ranging from "not at all accurate" to "completely accurate." The first two items, "I experience God's love and caring on a regular basis" and "I experience a close personal relationship with God," were found in a prior study to predict well-being in a congregational sample and to correlate positively with other measures of intrinsic religion (22). A third item, "My religious faith helps me cope during times of difficulty," elicits faith aspects of perceived spiritual support. Cronbach's alpha produced a reliability coefficient of .92, with test-retest reliability yielding $r = .81$ ($n = 66$) (21).

The Spiritual Support Scale has been used to evaluate the relationship between perceived levels of spiritual support and well-being among two groups of high-stress and low-stress individuals (21). Among recently bereaved parents and adolescents experiencing three or more uncontrollable life events, perceived spiritual support correlated significantly with multiple measures of well-being in the direction predicted. No significant relationships were found between spiritual support and well-being in low-stress populations. Limitations acknowledged by the author in testing the Spiritual Support Scale include small sample size and inadequate minority representation (21).

Forgiveness

Studzinski (23) has defined forgiveness as "a response to suffering which an individual has incurred at the hands of someone else. . . . the choice presented to the sufferer is between harbouring resentment or allowing the healing of forgiveness to take place." Two scales measuring forgiveness were developed by Mauger et al. (24) as part of a project to produce an objective personality inventory that would examine multiple dimensions of behavior related to personality disorders. The scales, Forgiveness of Self and Forgiveness of Others, are actually subscales of the Behavior Assessment System 1, an inventory consisting of 301 true-false items (25,26). Each of the Forgiveness scales is composed of 15 statements. Items on the Forgiveness of Others scale focus on taking revenge, justifying retaliation, and holding grudges: "I would secretly enjoy hearing that someone I dislike had gotten into trouble" and "It is not right to take revenge on a person who tries to take advantage of you." The Forgiveness of Self scale assesses feelings of guilt over past mistakes, perception of oneself as sinful, and having a variety of negative attitudes toward self: "I am often angry at myself for the stupid things I do" and "It is easy for me to admit that I am wrong" (24).

Test-retest reliability was calculated with 21 graduate students who completed the scales with a 2-week interval between administrations. Reliability for Forgiveness of Others was reported at .94, for Forgiveness of Self .67. In reviewing these differences, the authors suggest that "forgiveness of others is a stable characteristic across time, but our attitude toward ourselves, as reflected in feelings of guilt, anger at ourselves, and having a negative evaluation of ourselves, fluctuates over time" (24).

Further testing of validity and reliability on the Forgiveness of Self and Forgiveness of Others scales was performed using data from 237 outpatient counseling clients from Christian counseling centers. Clients completed both the Behavior Assessment System and the Minnesota Multiphasic Personality Inventory as part of the initial intake process. The authors noted a correlation of .37 between scores on Forgiveness of Others and Forgiveness of Self, indicating that the scales measure two related but different phenomena. In addition, factor analysis reveals different loading patterns for the two forgiveness scales. The Forgiveness of Others scale loads significantly on a factor labeled Alienation From Others, which includes other scales such as Cynicism, Negative Attitudes Toward Others, and Passive Aggressive Behavior; the Forgiveness of Self scale loads primarily on the factor Neurotic Immaturity, along with Negative Self-Image, Self-Control Deficit, and Motivation Deficit scales. Correlations between the forgiveness scales and scales of the Minnesota Multiphasic Personality Inventory indicate an association between problems with forgiveness and some types of psychopathology, including depression, anxiety, anger, distrust, and negative self-esteem (24).

Information regarding demographics of subjects involved in validity and reliability testing for Forgiveness of Self and Forgiveness of Others is limited to age, sex, and education, with sex being the only variable with clinical significance.

Women tended to report slightly more difficulty in forgiving themselves than did men. There are no references in either scale to religious beliefs, which would appear to make the Forgiveness scales useful regardless of religious orientation.

Spiritual Well-Being

An alternative approach to assessing spiritual needs is the evaluation of spiritual well-being, which has been defined by the National Interfaith Coalition on Aging as "the affirmation of life in a relationship with God, self, community, and environment that nurtures and celebrates wholeness" (27). The universality of spiritual well-being was summarized by Moberg (28):

> A central concern of the Christian faith, if not also of Islam, Judaism, Hinduism, and Buddhism, is to enhance the spiritual well-being of people. Although the semantics and theology of this concern vary from one group to another, it is located at the very core of many religious goals. It also is central to the ultimate values of Soviet Marxism, which hopes to shape "the new man" who combines "spiritual richness" with "moral purity." (p. 351)

The *Spiritual Well-Being Scale*, a 20-item Likert-type tool authored by Ellison and Paloutzian, reflects the belief that spiritual well-being involves a vertical and a horizontal dimension. The vertical dimension refers to the sense of well-being in the relationship with God, while the horizontal refers to sense of purpose in and satisfaction with life (27,29). These two dimensions can be addressed separately using one of the two subscales comprising the Spiritual Well-Being Scale. The Religious Well-Being subscale measures the vertical component, while the Existential Well-Being subscale focuses on the horizontal. For example, the statement "I have a personally meaningful relationship with God" refers to religious well-being; "I believe that there is some purpose for my life" refers to existential well-being (27). Responses to each item range from "strongly agree" to "strongly disagree."

Factor analysis of the Spiritual Well-Being Scale using Varimax rotation was performed on data obtained from 206 students at three colleges having a religious orientation. The items clustered together as expected, with existential items loading into two subfactors, life direction and life satisfaction (27,29).

The scale was then administered to 100 student volunteers at the University of Idaho. Test-retest reliability coefficients were .93 (spiritual well-being), .96 (religious well-being), and .86 (existential well-being). Internal consistency was evaluated using coefficient alpha, yielding .89 (spiritual well-being), .87 (religious well-being), and .78 (existential well-being) (27).

Examination of item content supports the face validity of the scale. In addition, the Spiritual Well-Being Scale scores have correlated in predicted ways with other theoretically related measures, including the Purpose in Life Test and Intrinsic Religious Orientation (27).

The authors of the Spiritual Well-Being Scale acknowledge that the tool arises from the Judeo-Christian perception of religious well-being in which God is viewed in personal terms. However, they note that "it is . . . possible that those from Eastern religions such as Hinduism and Buddhism may be able to use the scale if they can meaningfully interpret the statements about relationship with God" (27).

Moberg's *Indexes of Spiritual Well-Being,* a 45-item questionnaire, includes a variety of factors that may influence Spiritual Well-Being: social attitudes; self-perceptions; theological orientation; activities serving others in charitable, political, and religious contexts; and religious beliefs, opinions, experiences, preferences, and affiliation (28). Seven indexes identified through factor analysis include Christian faith, self-satisfaction, personal piety, subjective spiritual well-being, optimism, religious cynicism, and elitism.

Response categories for most items range from "strongly agree" to "strongly disagree." Items in the personal piety index differ in that they require a response that indicates how frequently the subject participates in a particular activity. Examples from this tool include:

> My faith helps me to make decisions. (Christian faith)
> How often do you pray privately? (personal piety)
> Organized religion has hindered or harmed my own spiritual well-being more than it has helped. (religious cynicism)

The indexes of Spiritual Well-Being is believed to have face validity, as the items were based upon information gained through multiple earlier studies performed by the tool's author (28). Preliminary data support criterion validity of the indexes. When scores for evangelical Christians were compared with those of other Christians, differences were in the expected direction. Likewise, scores for Christians were higher than scores for persons professing to be agnostic or atheist (28). Additional testing with other criterion groups is needed to further establish the tool's validity. Further analysis of the validity of the indexes has demonstrated coefficients ranging from .60 to .86 when scores were correlated with the Spiritual Well-Being Scale.

Moberg's Indexes of Spiritual Well-Being represents a major attempt to demonstrate the multifaceted nature of spiritual well-being. It has two characteristics that may limit its usefulness in clinical research: in its present form it is somewhat lengthy and may not be practical for use with populations that have extensive disease and, as a result, would tire easily; and the indexes are specific to Christianity and could not be used in its present form with patients of Jewish or Eastern orientations.

Spiritual Coping

The importance of religious faith is often overlooked by health care professionals when routinely assessing how a person copes with disease. Investigation of spiritual coping may appear, on the surface, to document the performance of religious activities. In reality, spiritual coping looks beyond the actual behavior to the meaning or significance the behavior holds for the individual.

The *Patient Spiritual Coping Interview* was developed by McCorkle and Benoliel (30) and adapted for use in a "one-time" interview format by Sodestrom and Martinson (31). This semistructured interview contains 30 items that investigate relationship with God or a "higher being," use of spiritual behaviors and/or resource persons, expressions of spiritual needs, and perception of the nurse's role in spiritual care (31). Questions include "Do you ever watch religious TV or listen to religious radio?" "Have you spoken about your spiritual thoughts or concerns to someone?" "How do you think nurses can assist you with your spiritual needs?"

Content validity of the interview was established by its consistency with the current literature, and an expert panel of judges, three in oncology nursing research and two in theology, agreed that the items included were adequate and appropriate. Reliability was inferred by the assumption that subjects are reliable sources of information pertaining to the use of spiritual coping strategies (31). Although this instrument was designed for use by and for nurses, it can be easily modified for use by other health care professionals.

Religious Orientation

The importance of spirituality in a person's life can also be evaluated by the *Intrinsic Religious Motivation Scale* developed by Hoge (32). An intrinsically motivated person is one whose most central and ultimate motive in life can be found in his/her religious faith. The extrinsically motivated person views his/her religion as subservient to other aspects of life, such as economic or social status (33). The scale consists of ten statements to which the participant answers yes or no. "One should seek God's guidance when making every important decision" indicates intrinsic motivation. "It doesn't matter what I believe as long as I lead a moral life" is consistent with extrinsic motivation (32).

The Intrinsic Religious Motivation Scale was administered to 42 adult Protestants, 21 of whom were judged by their ministers as intrinsically motivated and 21 judged as extrinsically motivated. The initial scale included 30 items. The final scale is composed of the ten items having highest validity, reliability, item-to-item correlations, and item-to-scale correlations.

All ten items correlated with the ministers' predictions in the direction predicted beyond the .03 level of significance. The reliability of the scale, measured by the Kuder-Richardson formula 20, was .901. Item-to-item correlations ranged from .132 to .716, with 22 of 45 item-to-item correlations greater than .5 (32).

The shorter version of the Intrinsic Religious Motivation Scale may be easier to use when compared with the Patient Spiritual Coping Interview. However, the Intrinsic Religious Motivation Scale fails to identify specific behaviors that provide a source of comfort or strength to the subject.

Another potential problem with the Intrinsic Religious Motivation Scale lies in the classification of items. Seven of the items are indicative of intrinsic motivation, while only three reflect external motivation. The author has acknowledged this limitation and suggests deletion of the intrinsic item "My faith sometimes restricts my actions." With this change, the Kuder-Richardson score becomes .902 (32).

Spiritual Needs of Children

The potential difficulties in obtaining spiritual data from children are summarized by Shelly (34):

> If sound assessment is crucial to caring for adults, it is even more important in the pediatric setting. Children, especially young children, have a limited ability to communicate, particularly about abstract concepts. (p. 88)

A study of adolescents reported by Elkind (35) used only two questions: "When do you feel closest to God?" and "Have you ever had a particular experience when you felt especially close to God?" Responses from 144 ninth-grade students to these items indicated differences between males and females and between honor students and "average" students ($p < .05$). Differences were also noted between Protestants, Catholics, and Jews; however, the uncertainty about exact numbers in each denomination precluded statistical analysis.

A Nurses Christian Fellowship task force developed a seven-question assessment tool to obtain information about the spiritual needs of children: "How do you feel when you're in trouble?" "Do you know who God is? What is He like?" (34).

Additional information can be obtained from young children by asking them to draw pictures of God and themselves and/or with significant others. Using this technique requires special skill in interpretation in order to obtain meaningful data.

Nurse Recognition of Spiritual Needs of Patients

Several tools measure nurses' awareness of and appropriate interventions for spiritual needs. Although designed to be used for and by nurses, other health care professionals seeking similar types of information could easily adapt them for their use.

Chadwick (36) devised a seven-item multiple choice questionnaire to investigate "awareness and preparedness of nurses to meet spiritual needs.'' Sample questions include: ''How long has it been since you last recognized a spiritual need in your patients?'' ''Have you ever read the Bible or prayed with a patient?''

Sodestrom and Martinson (31) developed a Nurse Interview schedule to correspond to the one discussed above for patients (30). Seventeen items were selected from the patient interview and modified to evaluate nurses' awareness of the spiritual strategies used by patients in coping with disease. Nurse participants answer ''yes,'' ''no,'' or ''don't know'' to questions such as ''Do you know if your patient has spoken to a clergyman?'' ''Do you know if s/he has read the Bible?'' and ''Does your patient make reference to guilt feelings related to God?'' Reliability and validity for the Nurse Interview are based on the same data as the Patient Spiritual Coping Interview.

Highfield and Cason (1) developed a 49-item questionnaire for their study of nurses' ability to identify behaviors and conditions expressive of spiritual health or spiritual need. Nurse participants are instructed to note whether the behavior or condition described is related to either the spiritual or psychosocial dimension. They are also to rate on a scale of 1 to 5 how frequently each behavior or condition is noted in their patients. Finally, participants are to note each item considered to be a patient problem.

The items contained in the Highfield-Cason questionnaire were identified from the nursing and pastoral care literature and were submitted to a review panel of theology and psychology experts. Although many items in the questionnaire are legitimately a part of the spiritual domain (e.g., ''expresses resentment toward God,'' ''expresses despair''), several are less clear (e.g., ''expresses fear of tests and diagnosis,'' ''is unable to pursue creative outlets''). The less-specific items could easily represent a psychosocial problem rather than or in addition to a spiritual problem. This ambiguity needs to be addressed by researchers who choose to use the Highfield-Cason questionnaire.

CONCLUSIONS

Clinical research related to spiritual issues has been hampered by a variety of factors including discomfort among health professionals who believe that spirituality and spiritual needs are a private matter, difficulty in distinguishing psychosocial needs from spiritual needs, lack of valid and reliable measurement tools that address spiritual concerns, and confusion about differences between spiritual concerns and religiosity.

The tools described here represent a heightened awareness of different aspects of spirituality. The development of new measures and further refinement of tools currently available will enable us to expand our understanding of this underresearched area.

RESEARCH REVIEW

Carson V, Loeken KL, Shanty J, Terry L. Hope and spiritual well-being: essentials for living with AIDS. *Perspectives in Psychiatric Care* 1990;26:28–34.

The purpose of the study was to evaluate levels of hope and spiritual well-being among HIV-positive men. Sixty-five subjects were recruited, 25 of whom had been diagnosed with AIDS. Participants completed the Beck Hopelessness Scale and the Spiritual Well-Being Scale while waiting in an outpatient clinic to be seen by the physician. Only four subjects had scores consistent with hopelessness, with half scoring in the range of no or minimal pessimism. Persons with AIDS were found to be significantly more hopeful than those with AIDS-related complex (ARC) ($p < .05$). Spiritual Well-Being scores were determined for overall spiritual well-being, existential well-being, and religious well-being. Participants were found to have positive levels of spiritual well-being; those with higher spiritual well-being scores tended to be more hopeful. A similar pattern was seen with existential well-being and religious well-being scores; however, the relationship between hope and existential well-being was significantly stronger than between hope and religious well-being.

The authors note that existential well-being enables individuals to respond to a crisis as a challenge and as an opportunity for personal growth. They suggest that the greater contribution of existential well-being to overall spiritual well-being reflects feelings of alienation and abandonment experienced from society and from organized religion.

The study is important in that it examines the spiritual health of a group of gay men who are HIV-infected. The findings support those of other studies demonstrating a direct relationship between spiritual well-being and hope (37,38). Moreover, the results are consistent with subjective observations that homosexual men are often poorly accepted in organized religion. Denying homosexual men access to religious participation (i.e., opportunities to experience religious well-being) may compromise overall spiritual well-being for some, although the population studied may have offset its religious well-being losses to some degree through enhancement of existential well-being.

COMPENDIUM

For additional information about the research instruments reviewed, including permission for use:

Title: Forgiveness of Others Scale
Generic Name/Abbr.: FO
Purpose: Evaluates subject's ability to forgive wrongs committed by others
Contact Person: P. A. Mauger, PhD, Psychological Studies Institute, 2055 Mt. Paran Rd., N.W., Atlanta, GA 30327

Title: Forgiveness of Self Scale
Generic Name/Abbr.: FS
Purpose: Assesses feelings of guilt over past mistakes
Contact Person: P. A. Mauger, PhD, Psychological Studies Institute, 2055 Mt. Paran Rd., N.W., Atlanta, GA 30327

Title: Guidelines for Spiritual Assessment
Generic Name/Abbr.: none
Purpose: Evaluates subject's ability to have spiritual needs met
Contact Person: R. I. Stoll, DNSc, RN, Prof. Dept. of Nursing, Messiah College, Grantham, PA

Title: Indexes of Spiritual Well-Being
Generic Name/Abbr.: none
Purpose: Measures factors that influence spiritual well-being
Contact Person: D. O. Moberg, PhD, Professor of Sociology, Marquette University, Milwaukee, WI 53233

Title: Intrinsic Religious Motivation Scale
Generic Name/Abbr.: none
Purpose: Evaluates the importance of spirituality in subject's life
Contact Person: Dean R. Hoge, PhD, Dept. of Sociology, Catholic University, 620 Michigan Ave. NE, Washington, DC 20064

Title: Nowotny Hope Scale
Generic Name/Abbr.: NHS
Purpose: Measures hope experienced while facing stressful event
Contact Person: M. L. Nowotny, PhD, RN, Assoc. Dean for Academic Affairs, Baylor University School of Nursing, Dallas, TX

Title: Purpose in Life Test
Generic Name/Abbr.: PIL
Purpose: Measures the degree to which subject experiences a sense of meaning and purpose in life
Contact Person: Psychometric Affiliates, Box 3167, Munster, IN 46301

Title: Reed Interview Schedule
Generic Name/Abbr.: none
Purpose: Elicits information about preferences for spiritually related nursing interventions
Contact Person: P. G. Reed, PhD, College of Nursing, University of Arizona, Tucson, AZ 85721

Title: Serenity Scale
Generic Name/Abbr.: SS
Purpose: Measures spiritual experience of inner peace that is independent of external events
Contact Person: K. T. Roberts, EdD, RN, C, Assoc. Prof. of Nursing, University of Louisville, Louisville, KY 40292

Title: Spiritual Coping Interview
Generic Name/Abbr.: SCI
Purpose: Investigates relationship with God or higher being, use of spiritual behaviors and/or resource persons, expressions of spiritual needs, and nurse's role in spiritual care
Contact Person: R. McCorkle, PhD, RN, FAAN, University of Pennsylvania, School of Nursing, 420 Guardian Rd., Philadelphia, PA 19104

Title: Spiritual Health Inventory
Generic Name/Abbr.: SHI
Purpose: Identifies attitudes and behaviors that are either positive or negative expressions of spiritual health
Contact Person: M. F. Highfield, PhD, RN, Assoc. Chief, Nursing Service/Education, Wadsworth Division, VA Medical Center-West Los Angeles, Los Angeles, CA 90073

Title: Spiritual Needs Survey
Generic Name/Abbr.: none
Purpose: Elicits information about subject's awareness of spiritual needs and efforts to address them
Contact Person: J. Hess, RN, 740 N. Compton Rd., Farmington, UT 84025

Title: Spiritual Perspective Scale
Generic Name/Abbr.: SPS
Purpose: Measures extent to which spirituality permeates life and degree of engagement in spiritually related interactions
Contact Person: P. G. Reed, PhD, College of Nursing, University of Arizona, Tucson, AZ 85721

Title: Spiritual Support Scale
Generic Name/Abbr.: none
Purpose: Assesses subject's perceived support from God
Contact Person: K. I. Maton, Asst. Professor, Dept. of Psychology, University of Maryland, Baltimore, MD

Title: Spiritual Well-Being Scale
Generic Name/Abbr.: SWBS
Purpose: Measures religious and existential well-being
Contact Person: C. W. Ellison, PhD, Life Advance, Inc., 81 Front St., Nyack, NY 10960

Title: Highfield-Cason Spiritual Need Questionnaire
Generic Name/Abbr.: none
Purpose: Determine nurses' ability to identify behaviors and conditions expressive of spiritual health or spiritual need
Contact Person: M. F. Highfield, PhD, RN, Assoc. Chief, Nursing Service/Education, Wadsworth Division, VA Medical Center–West Los Angeles, Los Angeles, CA 90073

REFERENCES

1. Highfield M, Cason C. Spiritual needs of patients—are they being recognized? *Cancer Nurs* 1983;6(3):187–192.
2. Moberg D, Brusek P. Spiritual well-being: a neglected subject in quality of life research. *Soc Indicators Res* 1978;5(3):303–323.
3. Moberg DO. Development of social indicators of spiritual well-being for quality of life research. In: Moberg DO, ed. *Spiritual well-being: sociological perspectives.* Washington: University Press of America, 1979:1–13.
4. Kim M, Moritz D. *Classification of nursing diagnoses: Proceedings of the Third and Fourth National Conferences.* New York: McGraw-Hill, 1980.
5. Highfield MF. Spiritual health of oncology patients. *Cancer Nurs* 1992;15(1):1–8.
6. Reed PG. Spirituality and well-being in terminally ill hospitalized adults. *Res Nurs Health* 1987;10:335–344.
7. Reed PG. Religiousness in terminally and healthy adults. *Res Nurs Health* 1986;9:35–41.
8. Roberts KT, Aspy C. Development of the serenity scale. *J Nurs Meas* in press.
9. Stallwood J. Spiritual dimensions of nursing practice. In: Beland I, Passos J, eds. *Clinical nursing.* New York: Macmillan, 1975:1086–1098.
10. Hess JS. Spiritual needs survey. In: Fish S, Shelly JA, eds. *Spiritual care: the nurse's role.* Downers Grove, IL: Intervarsity Press, 1988:157–159.
11. Stoll R. Guidelines for spiritual assessment. *Am J Nurs* 1979;79(9):1574–1577.
12. Stoll R. Spiritual assessment: a nursing perspective. Presented at Spirituality in Nursing workshop. Marquette University, Milwaukee, WI, August, 1984.
13. Fordyce E. An investigation of television's potential for meeting the spiritual needs of hospitalized persons (doctoral dissertation, Catholic University of America, 1981). *Dissertation Abstracts International,* 1982.
14. Fish S, Shelly JA. *Spiritual care: the nurse's role.* Downers Grove, IL: Intervarsity Press, 1988.
15. Reed PG. Preferences for spiritually related nursing interventions among terminally ill and nonterminally ill hospitalized adults and well adults. *Appl Nurs Res* 1991;4(3):122–128.
16. Dufault K, Martocchio BC. Hope: its spheres and dimensions. *Nurs Clin North Am* 1986;20(2):379–391.
17. Nowotny ML. Assessment of hope in patients with cancer: development of an instrument. *Oncol Nurs Forum* 1989;16(1):57–61.
18. Crumbaugh JC, Maholick LT. An experimental study in existentialism: the psychometric approach to Frankl's concept of noogenic neurosis. *J Clin Psychol* 1964;20:200–207.
19. Frankl V. *Man's search for meaning.* New York: Washington Square Press, 1984.
20. Crumbaugh JC. Cross-validation of purpose in life test based on Frankl's concepts. *J Individual Psychol* 1968;24:74–81.
21. Maton KI. Stress-buffering role of spiritual support: cross-sectional and prospective investigations. *J Sci Study Religion* 1989;28(3):310–323.
22. Maton KI. *Empowerment in a religious setting: an exploratory study.* Unpublished master's thesis, University of Illinois at Urbana-Champaign, 1984.
23. Studzinski R. Remember and forgive: psychological dimensions of forgiveness. In: Floristan C, Duquoc C, eds. *Forgiveness.* Edinburgh: T & T Clark, 1986:12–21.
24. Mauger PA, Perry JE, Freeman T, et al. Measurement of forgiveness: preliminary research. *J Psychol Christianity* 1992;11(2):170–180.
25. Mauger PA, Webb JH, Davis R, et al. Development of a multi-dimensional inventory for the diagnosis of personality disorders. Paper presented at the annual meeting of the Southeastern Psychological Assn., Atlanta, GA, 1985.
26. Mauger PA. *Behavior assessment system I, preliminary manual,* version 2.1. Atlanta: Automated Assessment, 1991.
27. Ellison CW. Spiritual well-being: conceptualization and measurement. *J Psychol Theol* 1983;11(4):330–340.
28. Moberg D. Subjective measures of spiritual well-being. *Rev Relig Res* 1984;25(4):351–364.
29. Paloutzian R, Ellison CW. Loneliness, spiritual well-being, and the quality of life. In: Peplau A, Perlman D, eds. *Loneliness: a sourcebook of current theory, research, and therapy.* New York: Wiley Interscience, 1982:224–237.
30. McCorkle R, Benoliel JQ. *Manual of data collection instruments.* Unpublished manual, University of Washington, 1981.
31. Sodestrom KE, Martinson I. Patients' spiritual coping strategies: a study of nurse and patient perspectives. *Oncol Nurs Forum* 1987;14(2):41–46.
32. Hoge DR. Validated intrinsic religious motivation scale. *J Sci Study Religion* 1972;11:369–376.
33. Soderstrom D, Wright EW. Religious orientation and meaning in life. *J Clin Psychol* 1977;33(1):65–68.
34. Shelly JA. *Spiritual needs of children.* Downers Grove, IL: Intervarsity Press, 1982.
35. Elkind D, Elkind S. Varieties of religious experience in young adolescents. *J Sci Study Religion* 1962;2(1):102.
36. Chadwick R. Awareness and preparedness of nurses to meet spiritual needs. In: Fish S, Shelly JA, eds. *Spiritual care: the nurse's role.* Downers Grove, IL: Intervarsity Press, 1988:177–178.
37. Carson V, Soeken KL, Grimm PM. Hope and its relationship to spiritual well-being. *J Psychol Theol* 1988;16(2):159–167.
38. Mickley JR, Soeken K, Belcher A. Spiritual well-being, religiousness, and hope among women with breast cancer. *Image* 1992;24(4):267.

Quality of Life and Pharmacoeconomics in Clinical Trials, Second Edition, edited by B. Spilker.
Lippincott-Raven Publishers, Philadelphia © 1996.

CHAPTER 18

Pharmacoeconomics and Quality of Life Research Beyond the Randomized Clinical Trial

Ron D. Hays, Cathy D. Sherbourne, and Samuel A. Bozzette

INTRODUCTION

Randomized clinical trials (RCTs) yield essential information about potential therapeutic interventions when the optimal treatment for a condition is unknown. RCTs provide a strong basis for causal inference about the effects of medication on quality of life (i.e., internal validity) by virtue of their rigorous experimental design. With this design, variables other than the randomized factor(s) that can affect quality of life are controlled by the randomization of patients to control or treatment(s) conditions. Although RCTs could in theory be only minimally intrusive, most RCTs distort clinical practice in a number of ways, including effects on both the population under treatment and on the care provided. Therefore, despite the obvious strengths of RCTs, in most implementations they can only suggest what is possible (i.e., efficacy) rather than what will actually happen when a medicine is tested beyond the confines of the trial. Thus, findings from RCTs might not generalize to care as typically given.

The goal of effectiveness research is to observe what takes place under existing circumstances. To accomplish this, it is necessary to avoid impacting on events taking place. In effectiveness research, the investigator tries to document variations in real world forces and effects that are not under his or her control to provide a basis for plausible inferences about underlying mechanisms. Effectiveness studies are essential to evaluate the impact of medication and other interventions in naturalistic settings (1).

There are a variety of ways in which the emphasis of effectiveness studies differ from that of a typical RCT. Three important differences we discuss here are (a) selection of participants, (b) assessment of study variables, and (c) analyses of outcomes data.

SELECTION OF PARTICIPANTS

RCTs often exclude participants who might complicate the interpretation of intervention effects. For example, RCTs of the efficacy of a particular medication often exclude patients with specific comorbidities who might eventually be treated with the agent after approval. As a result, participants tend to be more homogeneous and less diverse than otherwise, and even may be atypical. In contrast, effectiveness studies are often designed to capture diversity and ensure adequate representation of underrepresented populations.

A comparison of participants in a effectiveness study of the quality of life impact of treatment for human immunodeficiency virus (HIV) symptoms with participants in multicenter clinical trials of therapies for advanced HIV disease revealed that the former scored about a standard deviation below the latter on standardized measures of health-related quality of life (2). This one example does not demonstrate that such large differences in participants is universal, but

R. D. Hays and C. D. Sherbourne: RAND, Santa Monica, California 90407.

S. A. Bozzette: RAND, Santa Monica, California 90407 and University of California–San Diego and the San Diego Veterans' Affairs Medical Center, La Jolla, California 92161.

it does emphasize the importance of caution in generalizing results from RCTs.

Another example of an effectiveness study is the Medical Outcomes Study (MOS). The MOS was designed to examine variations in physician practice styles and patient outcomes in three different systems of care (3,4). Patients with hypertension, diabetes, coronary heart disease, and/or depression visiting providers in four general medical specialties (internal medicine, family practice, endocrinology, and cardiology) or mental health practitioners were studied. Unlike most RCTs, the MOS included patients with multiple comorbidities, and MOS depressed patients had an average of two medical comorbidities. Clinical trials of treatment for depression that exclude patients with other major medical or psychiatric disorders may not generalize to patients with comorbidities.

Because of the fundamental difference in those targeted for investigation, greater resources may be needed for collecting quality of life data in effectiveness studies than in RCTs. Data collection is more expensive when respondents are not excluded for literacy, health, or other problems, because more extensive efforts are required to obtain data of satisfactory psychometric quality (5). In addition, paying respondents to complete questionnaires is often necessary to ensure an acceptable response rate in effectiveness studies, whereas access to investigational medicines is often sufficient motivation in RCTs. In the MOS, a check was enclosed with mailed questionnaires at longitudinal follow-ups. Participants often expressed their gratitude for these payments, including thank-you notes along with their returned questionnaires (6). In a study of HIV patients receiving care at public hospitals, a refusal rate of 17% was observed in initial follow-up attempts (5). After a $20 cash incentive was offered for completion of the intake interview, participating rates improved significantly (refusal rate dropped to 12%).

The increased complexity of field work is not only costly monetarily, it also requires greater demands on project staff, as alternatives to self-administered questionnaires, such as interviews and proxy reports, are more likely to be needed to collect quality of life data for sicker, more disadvantaged populations. For example, in a study of elderly, chronically ill patients suffering from a variety of illnesses (cancer, stroke, degenerative neurological diseases), a special card containing response options was designed that was handed to patients so they could point to their response (7). Similarly, 27% of the 165 individuals with kidney disease administered a quality of life questionnaire at outpatient dialysis centers reported receiving assistance in completing it (8). In addition, the investigators used a half-inch, three-hole binder so patients could place the questionnaire on their lap while they were being dialyzed. Although some RCTs are targeted at the elderly and sicker populations, effectiveness studies are characterized by a greater emphasis on disadvantaged populations, who have poorer access and are less likely to avail themselves of RCTs.

The design of RCTs often requires that participants attend a number of regularly scheduled sessions at the site where care is delivered or at a separate trial venue. Thus, study participants are generally accessible for quality of life assessments. Effectiveness-study participants are observed receiving care as usual and are less likely to be regulated by a visit schedule imposed by the research team. In addition, effectiveness study sites are generally not set up to collect data efficiently as are RCT sites, as collecting data is the purpose of the latter.

It can be especially difficult to obtain follow-up data in effectiveness studies because of the imperative to minimize interference with the natural course of events. Thus, for example, it may be necessary to mail follow-up questionnaires to participants rather than scheduling visits for the sole purpose of collecting data. In contrast, ethical considerations mandate that RCTs be conducted only if the procedures for performing monitoring and assessment on a regular basis are assured.

ASSESSMENT OF STUDY VARIABLES

Randomization in experimental research usually insures that people assigned to different groups have equivalent baseline characteristics. Because of the lack of control over confounding factors in effectiveness studies, comprehensive assessment of preexisting differences that may explain variation in outcomes between participants is essential. Thus, substantial resources need to be devoted to measuring covariates in effectiveness studies. However, covariate adjustment is limited by the fact that many of the potential confounding variables are unknown and unmeasured.

Clinical trials are designed to provide specific tests of circumscribed hypotheses about the effects of key independent variables on outcomes. In contrast, effectiveness studies tend to be more exploratory with multiple, more-or-less clearly specified, hypotheses. As a result, the range and variety of independent and outcome variables in effectiveness studies can be greater than in clinical trials.

The MOS included an extensive battery of 149 quality of life items (9–17). In comparison, many clinical trials include a much more abbreviated battery of quality of life items. For example, the core AIDS Clinical Trial Group quality of life battery now consists of 21 items (18,19). Despite the brevity of this instrument, eight subscales are represented, each with multiple items: physical functioning (4 items), role functioning (2 items), pain (2 items), current health perceptions (3 items), emotional well-being (3 items), cognitive functioning/distress (2 items), energy/fatigue (2 items), and social functioning (2 items). The reliabilities of these scales were adequate and they correlated with corresponding long-form scales at .93 or higher (19). In addition, these scales were as efficient in detecting differences between HIV treatments as long-form scales (19).

A large battery of other self-report measures were also part of the MOS including patient sociodemographic characteristics (age, gender, education, income, race/ethnicity, marital status), patient adherence to medical recommendations (20), exercise (21), alcohol use (22), other health-related behaviors (e.g., smoking, overweight), social support (23), and coping (24). In addition, the MOS chronic conditions required a separate set of questions specific to each of them.

In effectiveness studies it is critical to gather as much data as possible on structure and process of care to explain variation in outcomes. The MOS also assessed system of care in terms of organization characteristics (fee-for-service, HMO, multispecialty group) and provider specialty (4). Process-of-care variables included technical and interpersonal quality of care (25–27), counseling and detection of depression (28,29), medication prescribing (30), continuity of care, and utilization (4).

ANALYSES OF OUTCOMES DATA

Because of the complexity of the natural world, inferences about the effects of provider interventions, such as prescribing medications on quality of life, are much more difficult in effectiveness research than in RCTs, and these nonexperimental studies need to be interpreted very cautiously. Observed quality of life differences in effectiveness studies are the result of an unknown combination of disease state, drug effect, and patient and provider behavior. For example, an effectiveness study of treatment for localized prostate cancer found that patients treated with surgery or radiation scored worse in some prostate-targeted quality of life domains than patients being managed with observation alone, but the conclusions of the study were tempered by the fact that patients were not randomized to treatment groups (31). A comparison of results from RCTs versus nonrandomized studies for six medical therapies revealed support for therapy over the control group in 79% of the nonrandomized studies, in contrast to only 20% of the RCTs (32).

Adjusting for covariates is especially important in analyzing effectiveness studies. Because patients self-select into different health care plans (e.g., healthier patients enroll in prepaid plans) and sicker patients may be more likely to be prescribed medication, quality of life differences may be due to factors other than quality of care or access. Adjusting for case-mix differences can help to compensate for preexisting differences.

However, if selection biases are strong, adjusting for these differences is problematic. In the MOS, for example, we found that depressed patients in the mental health specialty sector tended to be sicker at the baseline of the study, but they improved more in functioning and well-being over time than did similar patients in the medical sector (33). These relative improvements might be due to greater recognition of depression (29) and the more appropriate and intensive mental health care delivered in the mental health specialty sector. However, we could not directly study treatment effects on the course of depression because we observed low rates of treatment and such strong selection biases (30). Detection of depression was not significantly related to outcomes in the MOS. Because detection probably does not make people worse off, this nonsignificant result was in part due to the fact that detection was high when doctors encountered very sick patients and the MOS measures of sickness failed to capture this.

Analysis of change from baseline to a single follow-up time point is the most common analysis performed in longitudinal effectiveness studies. In RCTs, precision is enhanced by regressing follow-up quality of life on group assignment (intervention versus control), controlling for baseline quality of life (34). Because of nonrandom assignment of participants to intervention and control groups, adjustment for baseline level of the outcome measure can lead to biased estimates of regression parameters in nonexperimental studies (35), and analysis of difference scores without including baseline status has been advocated (36).

As an example of how improper analysis of nonexperimental data can lead to biased estimates, assume one is interested in the effect of a diet pill on weight loss in a nonexperimental study of nine women and nine men. An extreme example of selection bias would exist if the females all ended up in one group and the males in another. That is, let's assume that all those electing to take the diet pill are women and all those who choose not to are men. One might then find the baseline and follow-up weights shown in Table 1. Inspection of the weights reveals that those for the males are equal to the female weights plus a constant (20 pounds). The average weight for females is 116.67 pounds at baseline and 120 pounds at follow-up; for males the average weight is 136.67 pounds at baseline and 140 pounds at follow-up. Thus, on average, both groups (diet pill users versus nonusers) gain 3.33 pounds. If follow-up weight is regressed on group (dummy variable: 1 = diet pill user,

TABLE 1. *Hypothetical weights for 18 individuals in nonexperimental study*

Baseline		Followup	
Females	Males	Females	Males
090	110	110	130
100	120	110	130
110	130	110	130
110	130	120	140
120	140	120	140
130	150	120	140
120	140	130	150
130	150	130	150
140	160	130	150

Note—Weight is reported to the nearest pound.

0 = nonuser), controlling for baseline weight, the resulting prediction equation is as follows:

$$\hat{Y} = 78.50 + (0.45 * \text{baseline weight}) - (11.0 * \text{diet pill group})$$

Both the regression coefficients for baseline weight and for group (diet pill users vs. nonusers) are statistically significant ($p < .05$). A naive interpretation would lead to the conclusion that, controlling for baseline status, those in the diet pill group lost an average of 11 pounds. This is the major problem with analysis of covariance (ANCOVA) adjustment for baseline status in nonexperimental studies, referred to as Lord's paradox in the literature (37,38).

Despite these caveats, ANCOVA models are commonly reported in nonexperimental studies. Practical experience with analyses of nonexperimental data suggests that change score models may be too conservative and ANCOVA models too liberal (21,39). Change scores remove constant individual-specific factors, but initial sickness may also affect the rate of change in health status. We need, therefore, to test a variety of models (sensitivity analyses) when analyzing outcomes in nonexperimental studies. The distinction between the ANCOVA and difference score models is as follows:

$$\text{ANCOVA: } T2 = a + (b * T1) + \text{covariates} + \text{error}$$
$$\text{Difference score: } (T2 - T1) = a + \text{covariates} + \text{error}$$
$$\text{or } T2 = a + (1 * T1) + \text{covariates} + \text{error}$$

Thus, difference score and ANCOVA models yield similar results as b approaches 1 (baseline status is a good predictor of follow-up status), but dissimilar results when b is different from 1.

FUTURE RESEARCH

In practice, patients selected into RCTs fit particular clinical characteristics and are likely to comply with treatment recommendations. Clinicians conducting RCTs are likely to be expert in the disease under study, to provide high quality care, and to closely monitor patients (e.g., tightly control medications). When evaluations of efficacy and effectiveness of a medical procedure differ, it is common to try to understand this in terms of process of care (40). For example, surgery may be efficacious if performed by the most skilled surgeon, but ineffective when performed by the average surgeon.

In pharmacoeconomic interventions, the difference between efficacy and effectiveness may not be due so much to process of care as to patient adherence. RCTs "typically include special compliance-enhancing strategies that increase both the costs of the care being provided and, potentially, the effectiveness of that care" (41, p. 81). It is estimated that at least a third of all patients do not adhere to their medical treatment regimens (42), and that long-term adherence to prescribed medical therapy is 50% or lower (43). In addition, clinicians in everyday practice may have different incentives than clinicians in RCTs, the latter being perhaps less concerned about costs. Patients also may not comply with prescribed medications, because of barriers such as the cost of medications.

CONCLUSIONS

RCTs and carefully conducted effectiveness studies in tandem are essential in establishing the impact of medicines on quality of life. RCTs establish the potential therapeutic value, and effectiveness studies can show whether this potential is realized. In addition, information on the cost-effectiveness of care as practiced is needed for policymaking. Specifically, comparisons across very different interventions in terms of cost-effectiveness are needed for developing health care policy priorities.

Documentation of both the efficacy and effectiveness in terms of quality of life outcomes will continue to be important in future studies. When efficacy and effectiveness studies concur, the strongest case is made for the product. When divergence occurs, it is important to understand the underlying reasons and use this information to enhance the beneficial impact of medicines on quality of life in the future.

ACKNOWLEDGMENTS

The opinions expressed are those of the authors and do not necessarily reflect the views of RAND, UCLA, UCSD, or the San Diego VA. Thanks are due to Craig Barela for secretarial support. Preparation of this chapter was supported in part by RAND from its internal funds. Dr. Bozzette is an HSR&D Senior Research Associate of the Department of Veteran's Affairs.

REFERENCES

1. Ellwood P. Shattuck lecture—Outcomes management: a technology of patient experience. *N Engl J Med* 1988;318:1549–1556.
2. Cunningham WE, Bozzette SA, Hays RD, Kanouse DE, Shapiro, MF. Comparison of health-related quality of life in clinical trial and nonclinical trial HIV infected cohorts. *Med Care* 1995;33:AS15–AS25.
3. Rogers W, McGlynn E, Berry W, et al. Methods of sampling. In: Stewart AL, Ware JE, eds. *Measuring functional status and well-being: The Medical Outcomes Study approach.* Durham, NC: Duke University Press, 1992:27–47.
4. Tarlov AR, Ware JE, Greenfield S, Nelson EC, Perrin E, Zubkoff M. The Medical Outcomes Study: an application of methods for monitoring the results of medical care. *JAMA* 1989;262:925–930.
5. Ettl M, Hays RD, Cunningham W, Shapiro MF. Assessing health-related quality of life in disadvantaged populations. In: Spilker B, ed. *Quality of life and pharmacoeconomics in clinical trials,* 2nd ed. New York: Raven Press, 1995.
6. Berry SH. Methods of collecting health data. In: Stewart AL, Ware JE, eds. *Measuring functioning and well-being: The Medical Outcomes Study approach.* Durham, NC: Duke University Press, 1992:48–64.
7. McCusker J. Development of scales to measure satisfaction and prefer-

ences regarding long-term and terminal care. *Med Care* 1984;22:476–493.

8. Hays RD, Kallich JD, Mapes DL, Coons SJ, Carter WB. Development of the Kidney Disease Quality of Life (KDQOL) instrument. *Qual Life Res* 1994;3:329–338.

9. Hays RD, Stewart AL. Sleep measures. In: Stewart AL, Ware JE, eds. *Measuring functioning and well-being: The Medical Outcomes Study approach.* Durham, NC: Duke University Press, 1992:235–259.

10. Sherbourne CD. Social functioning: social activity limitations measures. In: Stewart AL, Ware JE, eds. *Measuring functioning and well-being: The Medical Outcomes Study approach.* Durham, NC: Duke University Press, 1992:173–181.

11. Sherbourne CD. Pain measures. In: Stewart AL, Ware JE, eds. *Measuring functioning and well-being: The Medical Outcomes Study approach.* Durham, NC: Duke University Press, 1992:220–234.

12. Sherbourne CD, Allen H, Kamberg C, Wells KB. Physical/psychophysiologic symptoms measure. In: Stewart AL, Ware JE, eds. *Measuring functioning and well-being: The Medical Outcomes Study approach.* Durham, NC: Duke University Press, 1992:260–276.

13. Sherbourne CD, Stewart AL, Wells KB. Role functioning measures. In: Stewart AL, Ware JE, eds. *Measuring functioning and well-being: The Medical Outcomes Study approach.* Durham, NC: Duke University Press, 1992:205–219.

14. Stewart AL, Kamberg C. Physical functioning. In: Stewart AL, Ware JE, eds. *Measuring functioning and well-being: The Medical Outcomes Study approach.* Durham, NC: Duke University Press, 1992:86–101.

15. Stewart AL, Sherbourne CD, Hays RD, et al. Summary and discussion of MOS measures. In: Stewart AL, Ware JE, eds. *Measuring functioning and well-being: The Medical Outcomes Study approach.* Durham, NC: Duke University Press, 1992:345–371.

16. Stewart AL, Ware JE, Sherbourne CD, Wells KB. Psychological distress/well-being and cognitive functioning measures. In: Stewart AL, Ware JE, eds. *Measuring functioning and well-being: The Medical Outcomes Study approach.* Durham, NC: Duke University Press, 1992.

17. Stewart AL, Hays RD, Ware JE. Health perceptions, energy/fatigue, and health distress measures. In: Stewart AL, Ware JE, eds. *Measuring functioning and well-being: The Medical Outcomes Study approach.* Durham, NC: Duke University Press, 1992:143–172.

18. Bozzette SA, Hays RD, Berry S, Kanouse D. A perceived health index for use in persons with advanced HIV disease: derivation, reliability, and validity. *Med Care* 1994;32:716–731.

19. Bozzette SA, Hays RD, Wu AW, Berry SH, Kanouse D. Derivation and psychometric properties of a brief health-related quality of life instrument for HIV disease. *J Acquired Immunodeficiency Synd* in press.

20. Kravitz R, Hays RD, Sherbourne CD, DiMatteo MR, Rogers WH, Ordway L, Greenfield S. Recall of recommendations and adherence to advice among patients with chronic medical conditions: results from the Medical Outcomes Study. *Arch Intern Med* 1993;153:1869–1878.

21. Stewart AL, Hays RD, Wells KB, Rogers WH, Spritzer KL, Greenfield S. Long-term functioning and well-being outcomes associated with physical activity and exercise in patients with chronic conditions in the Medical Outcomes Study. *J Clin Epidemiol* 1994;47:719–730.

22. Sherbourne CD, Hays RD, Wells KB, Rogers W, Burnam MA. Prevalence of comorbid alcohol disorder and consumption in depressed and medically ill patients. *Arch Family Med* 1993;2:1142–1149.

23. Sherbourne CD, Hays RD. Marital status, social support and health transitions in chronic disease patients. *J Health Soc Behav* 1990;31:328–343.

24. Sherbourne CD, Hays RD, Ordway L, DiMatteo MR, Kravitz R. Antecedents of adherence to medical recommendations: results from the Medical Outcomes Study. *J Behav Med* 1992;15:447–468.

25. Marshall GN, Hays RD. *The Patient Satisfaction Questionnaire Short-Form (PSQ-18).* Santa Monica, CA: RAND, P-7865, 1994.

26. Marshall GN, Hays RD, Sherbourne CD, Well KB. The structure of patient ratings of outpatient medical care. *Psychol Assess* 1993;5:477–483.

27. Ware JE, Hays RD. Methods for measuring patient satisfaction with specific medical encounters. *Med Care* 1988;26:393–402.

28. DiMatteo MR, Sherbourne CD, Hays RD, Ordway L, Kravitz RL, McGlynn EA, Kaplan S, Rogers WH. Physicians' characteristics influence patients' adherence to medical treatment: results from the Medical Outcomes Study. *Health Psychol* 1993;12:93–103.

29. Wells KB, Hays RD, Burnam A, et al. Detection of depressive disorders for patients receiving prepaid or fee-for-service care. *JAMA* 1989;262:3298–3302.

30. Wells KB, Katon W, Rogers B, Camp P. Use of minor tranquilizers and anti-depressant medications by depressed outpatients: results from the Medical Outcomes Study. *Am J Psychiatry* 1994;151:694–700.

31. Litwin M, Hays RD, Fink A, Ganz PA, Leake B, Leach GE, Brook RH. Quality of life outcomes in men treated for localized prostate cancer. *JAMA* 1995;273:129–135.

32. Sacks H, Chalmers TC, Smith H. Randomized versus historical controls for clinical trials. *Am J Med* 1982;72:233–240.

33. Hays RD, Wells KB, Sherbourne CB, Rogers WH, Spritzer K. Functioning and well-being outcomes of patients with depression compared to chronic medical illness. *Arch Gen Psychiatry* 1995;52:11–19.

34. Frigon J.-Y, Laurencelle L. Analysis of covariance: a proposed algorithm. *Educ Psychol Meas* 1993;53:1–18.

35. Kaplan RM, Berry CC. Adjusting for confounding variables. In: Sechrest L, Perrin E, Bunker J, eds. *Research methodology: strengthening causal interpretations of nonexperimental data.* Rockville, MD: U.S. Department of Health and Human Services, 1990:105–114.

36. Allison PD. Change scores as dependent variables in regression analysis. *Sociol Methodol* 1990;20:93–114.

37. Lord FM. A paradox in the interpretation of group comparisons. *Psychol Bull* 1967;68:304–305.

38. Lord FM. Statistical adjustments when comparing pre-existing groups. *Psychol Bull* 1969;72:336–337.

39. Hays RD, Kravitz RL, Mazel RB, Sherbourne CD, DiMatteo MR, Rogers WH, Greenfield S. The impact of patient adherence on health outcomes for chronic disease patients in the Medical Outcomes Study. *J Behav Med* 1994;17:347–358.

40. Brook RH, Lohr KN. Efficacy, effectiveness, variations, and quality: boundary-crossing research. *Med Care* 1985;23:710–722.

41. Feeny D, Labelle R, Torrance GW. Integrating economic evaluations and quality of life assessments. In: Spilker B, ed. *Quality of life assessments in clinical trials.* New York: Raven Press, 1990:71–83.

42. Haynes RB, Taylor DW, Sackett DL, eds. *Compliance in health care.* Baltimore: Johns Hopkins University Press, 1979.

43. Rainwater N. Adherence to the diabetes medical regimen: assessment and treatment strategies. *Pediatr Ann* 1983;12:658–661.

Quality of Life and Pharmacoeconomics in Clinical Trials, Second Edition, edited by B. Spilker.
Lippincott-Raven Publishers, Philadelphia © 1996.

CHAPTER 19

Dartmouth COOP Functional Health Assessment Charts: Brief Measures for Clinical Practice

Eugene C. Nelson, John H. Wasson, Deborah J. Johnson, and Ron D. Hays

INTRODUCTION

The Dartmouth Primary Care Cooperative Information Project (COOP) chart system has been developed and refined for over a decade for the purpose of making a brief, practical, and valid method to assess the functional status of adults and adolescents. The system was developed by the Dartmouth COOP Project, a network of community medical practices that cooperate on primary care research activities.

The charts are similar to Snellen charts, which are used medically to measure visual acuity quickly in busy clinical practices. Each chart consists of a title, a question referring to the status of the patient over the past 2 to 4 weeks, and five response choices. Each response is illustrated by a drawing that depicts a level of functioning or well-being along a 5-point ordinal scale (1,2). The illustration makes the charts appear "user-friendly" without seeming to bias the responses (3).

In accordance with clinical convention, high scores (i.e., patient ratings of 4 or 5) represent unfavorable levels of health (life quality or social support) on each chart. For example, Physical Chart responses range from 1 to 5 with a score of 5 representing major limitations.

The charts are a simple, easily administered, self-scoring system for screening, assessing, monitoring, and maintaining patient function. This system has been tested in many different practices, in both North America and elsewhere, to evaluate and establish its reliability, validity, and acceptability. One set of the charts—the WONCA version for adults (Fig. 1)—has been developed as the international standard for classifying the functional status of adult medical patients in primary care settings (4). The COOP/WONCA version of the charts differs somewhat from the original COOP charts by asking about function in the previous 2 weeks (rather than 4 weeks). The dimensions of health status measured by the health charts are Physical, Emotional, Daily Activities, Social Activities, Social Support, Pain, and Overall Health. The adult charts have been used widely (5–22).

BACKGROUND

The methods used to evaluate the reliability and validity of the charts are comparable to those that other researchers have used to assess their health status measures. For example, the techniques we used to check reliability and validity are similar to those used to evaluate the RAND health status measures (23), the Sickness Impact Profile (24), and the Duke-UNC Health Profile (25). Therefore, it is possible to compare the reliability and validity of the charts with those other multidimensional measures, and the reliability and validity coefficients of the charts are similar to those observed for these other measures.

E. C. Nelson, J. H. Wasson, and D. J. Johnson: The Dartmouth COOP Project, Department of Community and Family Medicine. Dartmouth Medical School, Hanover, New Hampshire 03755.

R. D. Hays: RAND, 1700 Main Street, Santa Monica, California 90407.

PHYSICAL FITNESS

During the past 4 weeks . . .
What was the hardest physical activity
you could do for at least 2 minutes ?

Very heavy, (for example) •Run, fast pace •Carry a heavy load upstairs or uphill (25 lbs/10 kgs)		1
Heavy, (for example) •Jog, slow pace •Climb stairs or a hill moderate pace		2
Moderate, (for example) •Walk, medium pace •Carry a heavy load level ground (25 lbs/10 kgs)		3
Light, (for example) •Walk, medium pace •Carry light load on level ground (10 lbs/5kgs)		4
Very light, (for example) •Walk, slow pace •Wash dishes		5

A

FEELINGS

During the past 4 weeks . . .
How much have you been bothered by
emotional problems such as feeling anxious,
depressed, irritable or downhearted and blue ?

Not at all		1
Slightly		2
Moderately		3
Quite a bit		4
Extremely		5

B

DAILY ACTIVITIES

During the past 4 weeks . . .
How much difficulty have you had doing your usual
activities or task, both inside and outside the house
because of your physical and emotional health ?

No difficulty at all		1
A little bit of difficulty		2
Some difficulty		3
Much difficulty		4
Could not do		5

C

SOCIAL ACTIVITIES

During the past 4 weeks . . .
Has your physical and emotional health limited
your social activities with family, friends,
neighbors or groups ?

Not at all		1
Slightly		2
Moderately		3
Quite a bit		4
Extremely		5

D

FIG. 1. COOP adult charts. (© Trustees of Dartmouth College/COOP Project 1995. Permission to use the COOP charts specifically excludes the right to distribute, reproduce or share the charts in any form for commercial purposes or sale.)

CHANGE IN HEALTH

How would you rate your overall health now compared to 4 weeks ago ?

Much better	▲▲ ++	1
A little better	▲ +	2
About the same	◀▶ =	3
A little worse	▼ —	4
Much worse	▼▼ ——	5

E

OVERALL HEALTH

During the past 4 weeks . . .
   How would you rate your health in general ?

Excellent		1
Very good		2
Good		3
Fair		4
Poor		5

F

SOCIAL SUPPORT

During the past 4 weeks . . .
   Was someone available to help you if you
   needed and wanted help? For example if you
   — felt very nervous, lonely, or blue
   — got sick and had to stay in bed
   — needed someone to talk to
   — needed help with daily chores
   — needed help just taking care of yourself

Yes, as much as I wanted		1
Yes, quite a bit		2
Yes, some		3
Yes, a little		4
No, not at all		5

G

QUALITY OF LIFE

How have things been going for you during the past 4 weeks?

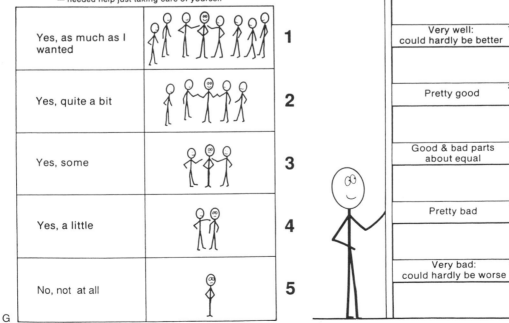

Very well: could hardly be better 1

Pretty good 2

Good & bad parts about equal 3

Pretty bad 4

Very bad: could hardly be worse 5

H

FIG. 1. *Continued*

PAIN

During the past 4 weeks . . .
How much bodily pain have you
generally had ?

No pain		1
Very mild pain		2
Mild pain		3
Moderate pain		4
Severe pain		5

FIG. 1. *Continued*

Studies to assess the charts' reliability, validity, acceptability, and clinical utility were conducted on over 2,000 patients in four diverse clinical settings. One-hour test-retest intraclass correlations for elderly patients ranged from .78 to .98 and from .73 to .98 for low-income patients. The average Pearson product-moment correlation between the charts and previously validated measures of function was .62 (Table 1), and the charts were as capable of detecting the association between disease and functioning as were longer, standard measures. Most clinicians and patients re-ported that the charts are easy to use and provide a valuable tool to measure overall function in a busy office practice (2,26). Tables 2 and 3 illustrate how the charts scores generally parallel RAND measures of function in the Medical Outcomes Study (MOS).

The adolescent charts (Fig. 2) have been used in doctors' offices and school classrooms for both English- and Spanish-speaking youths (27,28). Six charts were determined to be the most effective in measuring mutually exclusive dimensions of health and social problems: Physical Fitness, Emotional Feelings, School Work, Social Support, Family Communication, and Health Habits (Table 19-4). The average correlation between charts and longer sets of questions measuring the same health dimension was .62; for noncorresponding correlations the average was .32. Average test-retest intraclass correlations for six charts was .77. Compared with multi-item questionnaires, respondents found the charts easier to understand and less likely to induce dishonest replies.

Adolescent girls generally score worse than boys on the Physical Fitness and Emotional Feelings charts but better on the (at-risk) Health Habits charts. The scores of teenagers known to have behavioral problems are worse on the Health Habits chart. Simplified versions of the adolescent charts suitable for administration to children, aged 8 to 12, have somewhat less reliability and validity.

CLINICAL USE OF THE COOP CHARTS

The clinical advantages of the charts are ease of administration and scoring. However, compared to longer multi-item instruments, single-item charts are likely to have less precision (29). Clinicians argue that this loss of precision is not critical (30) for medical decision-making.

Practicing clinicians typically ask three questions about health status assessment:

Why do you measure functional status?
How do you fit functional measurement into a patient encounter of limited duration?
What do you do with the information from the assessment?

TABLE 1. *Correlation of adult COOP charts with adult Rand measures*

MOS scales	COOP charts						
	Physical function	Emotional status	Role function	Social function	Pain	Overall health	Social support
Physical function	0.59[a]	0.12	0.52	0.34	0.36	0.43	0.15
Emotional status	0.01	0.69[a]	0.41	0.53	0.25	0.48	0.44
Role function	0.40	0.29	0.60[a]	0.47	0.40	0.50	0.27
Social function	0.20	0.44	0.53	0.62[a]	0.33	0.52	0.36
Pain	0.28	0.30	0.50	0.43	0.60[a]	0.41	0.27
Overall health	0.37	0.33	0.51	0.44	0.38	0.61[a]	0.30
Social support	0.05	0.41	0.24	0.34	0.17	0.32	0.61[a]

[a]Convergent correlations.

TABLE 2. *Comparison of MOS SF-36 multi-item scale score with COOP chart scores for patients with hypertension and diabetes*

Domain	Hypertension		Diabetes		Depressive symptoms	
	COOP score	MOS score	COOP score	MOS score	COOP score	MOS score
Physical	49	49	48	48	49	50
Emotional	52	52	52	53	42	43
Daily activities	51	50	51	50	47	46
Social activities	52	52	51	50	44	45
Pain	50	50	51	50	47	47
Overall health	51	51	51	48	47	45

Why?

The "why" question has been addressed by many authoritative sources in medicine. For example, the American College of Physicians (31) has listed these potential benefits of health status assessment:

Detecting, quantifying, and identifying the source(s) of decreased functional capacity

Guiding management decisions

Guiding the efficient use of resources

Improving the prediction of the course of chronic disease

Improving patient outcomes: symptoms, mortality, satisfaction with care, function, and quality of life.

How?

The COOP charts were designed to fit into the standard data collection routine of busy ambulatory practices. The charts can be administered via two modes: (a) clinician administered (physician, nurse, medical assistant) or (b) patient self-administered. The charts' major positive feature for the clinician and office staff is their user-friendliness. This instrument is easy to administer and score, and requires

TABLE 3. *Formula for translation of COOP chart average scores to an estimated score for the SF-36 or its derivatives*

MOS score to be predicted	Translation	COOP chart item
Physical	105.6 minus (Physical times 13.5)	Physical
Mental Health	98.2 minus (Emotional times 12.1)	Feelings
Social Activities	104.1 minus (Social times 14.4)	Social Activities
Pain	98.5 minus (Pain times 11.4)	Pain
Role Physical	88.7 minus (Daily Activities times 18.5)	Daily Activities
Role Emotional	94.6 minus (Daily Activities times 14.3)	Daily Activities
Overall Health	90.9 minus (Overall times 11.8)	Overall Health

few consumable supplies. The scores can be easily recorded in the medical record using a patient data flow sheet.

What?

For practical purposes, a chart score of 4 or 5 should always be considered abnormal. Once a clinician knows that a patient's score is "abnormal," the critical step is to verify the score and make a specific functional diagnosis. Once the specific cause for the dysfunction(s) is recognized, the clinician then has to determine the need for special resources to manage the problem.

The ease of administering the COOP charts has also made them helpful for efficiently evaluating care that patients have received, delivering patient education, and rapidly measuring patient opinion of care received to manage a functional problem (32). Patient-based information about the patients' health and their experiences with the health care system can be used to improve care in two ways: (a) to immediately improve patient care during the office visit, and (b) to feed back into the redesign of care for future patients (Fig. 3).

The COOP chart–based questionnaire titled "Improve Your Medical Care" illustrates these two approaches. The questionnaire asks about function, clinical symptoms, and health risk. It also asks about the patient's perception of the doctor's awareness of problems, as well as perceptions of treatment benefit and doctor explanations about the problems. *In short, the questionnaire allows the doctor to see through the patient's eyes.*

Many practices use bar-code scanning of the "Improve Your Medical Care" questionnaire to generate automatically a patient health report letter. Using computer-based algorithms, the letter immediately informs patients of health problems that could be addressed and accordingly tailors the prescription to treat the patient's problems. A computer-generated flow sheet is included in the medical record.

Individual patient feedback stimulates physicians and prompts them to discuss unmet needs and prescribe applicable and educational self-care "homework." When aggregated responses are examined, physicians are encouraged to focus on areas where improvements in the process of care

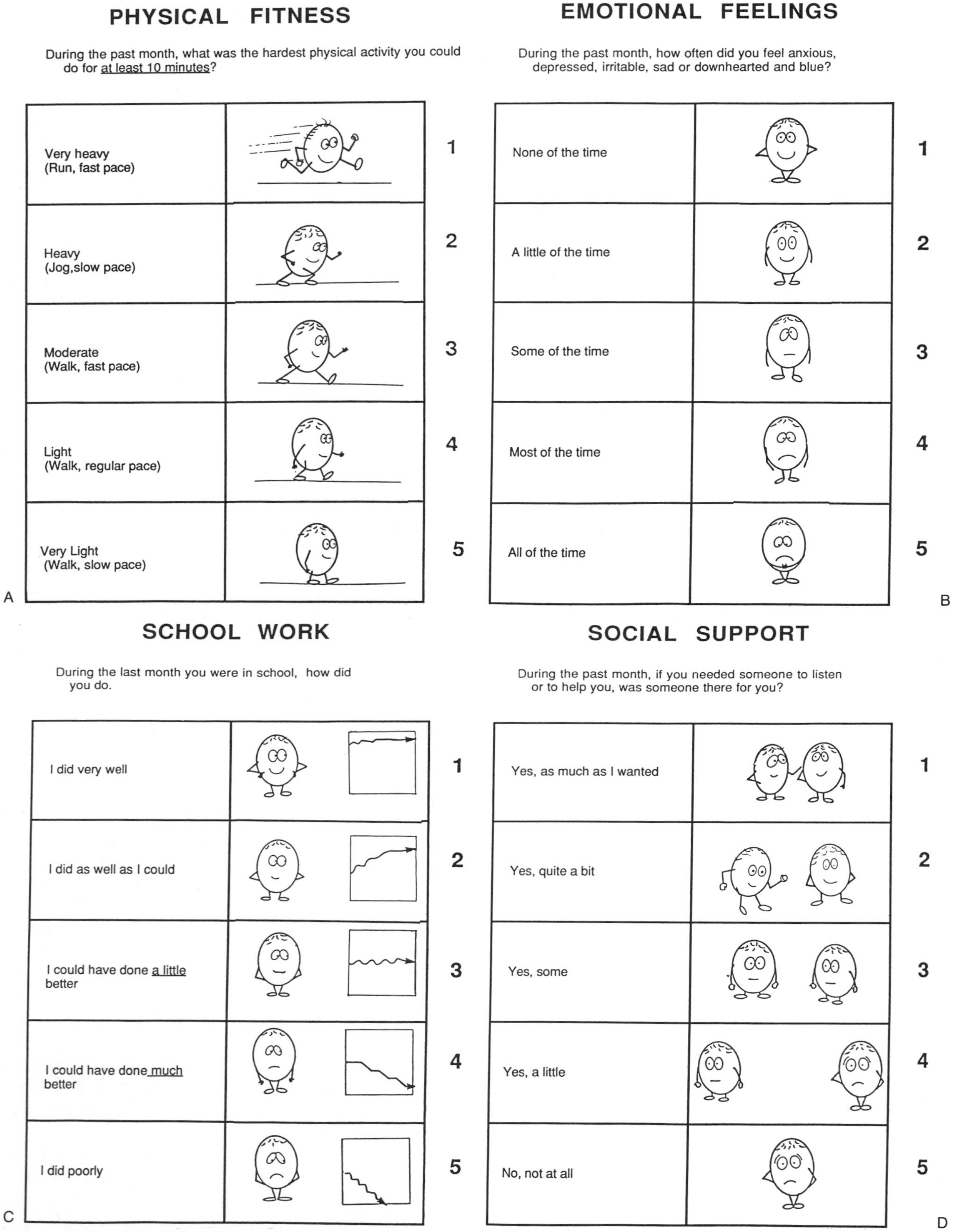

PHYSICAL FITNESS

During the past month, what was the hardest physical activity you could do for at least 10 minutes?

Very heavy (Run, fast pace)		1
Heavy (Jog, slow pace)		2
Moderate (Walk, fast pace)		3
Light (Walk, regular pace)		4
Very Light (Walk, slow pace)		5

A

EMOTIONAL FEELINGS

During the past month, how often did you feel anxious, depressed, irritable, sad or downhearted and blue?

None of the time		1
A little of the time		2
Some of the time		3
Most of the time		4
All of the time		5

B

SCHOOL WORK

During the last month you were in school, how did you do.

I did very well		1
I did as well as I could		2
I could have done a little better		3
I could have done much better		4
I did poorly		5

C

SOCIAL SUPPORT

During the past month, if you needed someone to listen or to help you, was someone there for you?

Yes, as much as I wanted		1
Yes, quite a bit		2
Yes, some		3
Yes, a little		4
No, not at all		5

D

FIG. 2. COOP adolescent charts. (© Trustees of Dartmouth College/COOP Project 1995. Permission to use the COOP charts specifically excludes the right to distribute, reproduce or share the charts in any form for commercial purposes or sale.)

FAMILY

During the past month, how often did you talk about your problems, feelings or opinions with someone in your family?

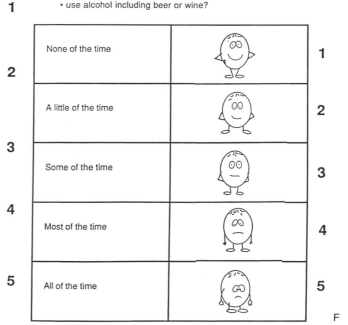

All of the time		1
Most of the time		2
Some of the time		3
A little of the time		4
None of the time		5

E

HEALTH HABITS I

During the past month, how often did you do things that are harmful to your health such as:
- smoke cigarettes or chew tobacco
- have unprotected sex
- use alcohol including beer or wine?

None of the time		1
A little of the time		2
Some of the time		3
Most of the time		4
All of the time		5

F

FIG. 2. *Continued*

TABLE 4. *Correlations of adolescent COOP charts with long-form measures of function*

Multi-item questionnaire scales	COOP charts					
	Physical fitness	Emotional feelings	School work	Social support	Family communication	Health habits
Physical	0.52[a]	0.50	0.25	0.35	0.23	0.31
Emotional	0.34	0.74[a]	0.16	0.65	0.45	0.31
School work	0.35	0.06	0.66[a]	0.27	0.50	0.49
Social support	0.04	0.45	0.17	0.68[a]	0.43	0.25
Family communication	0.22	0.40	0.31	0.67	0.72[a]	0.16
Health habits	0.36	0.43	0.38	0.44	0.28	0.71[a]

[a]Convergent correlations.

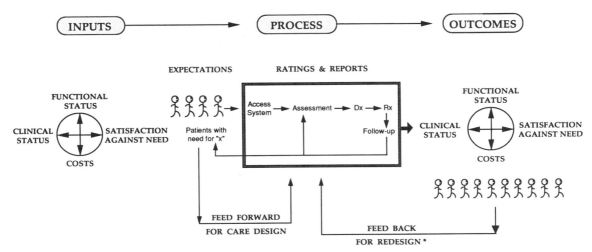

FIG. 3. Using patient-based information to redesign care for individual patients.

will generate the greatest impact for future patients. Ongoing monitoring of patient-based information produces a constant stream of ideas for changing the delivery process to get better results.

CONCLUSIONS

Integration of functional assessment in clinical practice has hardly begun, but it promises to be a useful means to improve care quality and provider/patient communication. The cost of implementing the approaches described above is small. Patient and provider appreciation of the information is immediate.

REFERENCES

1. Nelson EC, Wasson, J, Kirk J, et al. Assessment of function in routine clinical practice: description of the COOP chart method and preliminary findings. *J Chronic Dis* 1987;40(S1):55S–63S.
2. Nelson EC, Landgraf JM, Hays RD, et al. The functional status of patients: how can it be measured in physician's offices? *Med Care* 1990;28(12):1111–1126.
3. Larson CO, Hays RD, Nelson EC. Do the pictures influence scores on the Dartmouth COOP charts? *Qual Life Res* 1992;1:247–249.
4. Scholten JHG, Van Weel C. *Functional status assessment in family practice: the Dartmouth COOP functional health assessment charts/WONCA.* Lelystad, Netherlands: MEDITekst, 1992.
5. Nelson EC, Landgraf JM, Hays RD, et al. The COOP function charts: a system to measure patient function in physicians' offices. In: Lipkin M Jr, ed. *Functional status measurement in primary care: frontiers of primary care.* New York: Springer-Verlag, 1990:97–131.
6. Meyboom-De Jong B, Smith RJA. Studies with the Dartmouth COOP charts in general practice: comparison with the Nottingham Health Profile and the General Health Questionnaire. In: Lipkin M Jr, ed. *Functional status measurement in primary care: frontiers of primary care.* New York: Springer-Verlag, 1990:132–149.
7. Landgraf JM, Nelson EC, Hays RD, et al. Assessing function: does it really make a difference? A preliminary evaluation of the acceptability and utility of the COOP function charts. In: Lipkin M Jr, ed. *Functional status measurement in primary care: frontiers of primary care.* New York: Springer-Verlag, 1990:150–165.
8. Westbury RC. Use of the Dartmouth COOP charts in a Calgary practice. In: Lipkin M Jr, ed. *Functional status measurement in primary care: frontiers of primary care.* New York: Springer-Verlag, 1990:166–180.
9. Shigemoto H. A trial of the Dartmouth COOP charts in Japan. In: Lipkin M Jr, ed. *Functional status measurement in primary care: frontiers of primary care.* New York: Springer-Verlag, 1990:181–187.
10. Hickey ME, Carter JS, Davis SM. Adaptation of Dartmouth COOP charts for a Pueblo Native American population. *J Gen Intern Med* 1994;9(2):105.
11. Goertz CMH. Measuring functional health status in the chiropractic office using self-report questionnaires. *Topics Clin Chiropract* 1994;1(1):51–59.
12. Froom J, Schlager DS, Steneker S, Jaffe A. Detection of major depressive disorder in primary care patients. *J Am Board Fam Pract* 1993;6(1):5–11.
13. Wong-Chung D, Mateijsen N, West R, et al. Assessing the functional status during an asthma attack with Dartmouth COOP charts. Validity with respect to the change in asthma. *Fam Pract* 1991;8(4):404–408.
14. Krousel-Wood MA, McCune TW, Abdoh A. Predicting work status for patients in an occupational medicine setting who report back pain. *Arch Fam Med* 1994;3(4):349–355.
15. Siu AL, Reuben DB, Ouslander JG, Osterweil D. Using multidimensional health measures in older persons to identify risk of hospitalization and skilled nursing placement. *Qual Life Res* 1993;2(4):253–261.
16. Hays RD, Shapiro MF. An overview of generic health-related quality of life measures for HIV research. *Qual Life Res* 1992;1(2):91–97.
17. Siu AL, Ouslander JG, Osterweil D, et al. Change in self-reported functioning in older persons entering a residential care facility. *J Clin Epidemiol* 1993;46(10):1093–1101.
18. Bruusgaard D, Nessioy I, Rutle O, et al. Measuring functional status in a population survey. The Dartmouth COOP functional health assessment charts/WONCA used in an epidemiological study. *Fam Pract* 1993;10(2):212–218.
19. de Haan R, Aaronson N, Limburg M, et al. Measuring quality of life in stroke. *Stroke* 1993;24(2):320–327.
20. Bass MJ. Assessing functional status in family practice. *Fam Med* 1992;24(2):134–135.
21. Meyboom-de Jong BM, Smith RJ. How do we classify functional status? *Fam Med* 1992;24(2):128–133.
22. Landgraf JM, Nelson EC. Summary of the WONCA/COOP international health assessment field trial. *Aust Fam Physician* 1992;21(3):255–257, 260–262, 266–269.
23. Ware JE, Brook RH, Davies-Avery A, et al. *Conceptualization and measurement of health for adults in the Health Insurance Study: Vol 1, Model of health and methodology.* Santa Monica, CA: Rand (R-1987/1-HEW), 1980.
24. Bergner M, Bobbitt RA, Carter WB, et al. The Sickness Impact Profile: conceptual formulation and methodology for the development of a health status measure. *Int J Health Serv* 1976;6:393.
25. Parkerson GR, Gehlbach SH, Wagner EH, et al. The Duke-UNC health profile: an adult health status instrument for primary care. *Med Care* 1981;19:806.
26. Ware JE, Nelson EC, Sherbourne CD, et al. Preliminary tests of a 6-item general health survey: a patient application. In: Stewart A, Ware JE, eds. *Measuring functioning and well-being: the Medical Outcomes Study Approach.* Durham and London: Duke University Press, 1992:291–303.
27. Wasson JH, Kairys SW, Nelson EC, et al. A short survey for assessing health and social problems of adolescents. *J Fam Pract* 1994;38(5):489–494.
28. Wasson JH, Kairys SW, Nelson EC, et al. Adolescent health and social problems: a method for detection and early management. *Archives Fam Med* 1995;4:51–56.
29. McHorney CA, Ware JE, Rogers W, et al. The validity and relative precision of MOS short- and long-form Health Status Scales and Dartmouth COOP charts: results from the Medical Outcomes Study. *Med Care* 1992;30(5):MS253–MS265.
30. Wasson J, Keller A, Rubenstein L, Hays R, et al. Benefits and obstacles of health status assessment in ambulatory settings: the clinician's point of view. *Med Care* 1992;30(5):MS42–MS49.
31. American College of Physicians, Health and Public Policy Committee. Comprehensive functional assessment for elderly patients. *Ann Intern Med* 1988;10:1111.
32. Nelson EC, Wasson JH. Using patient-based information to rapidly redesign care. *Health Care Forum* 1994; July–August:25–29.

Quality of Life and Pharmacoeconomics in Clinical Trials, Second Edition, edited by B. Spilker.
Lippincott-Raven Publishers, Philadelphia © 1996.

CHAPTER 20

Derogatis Affects Balance Scale: DABS

Leonard R. Derogatis and Peter J. Rutigliano

INTRODUCTION

Extensive research in behavioral medicine and psychopathology has related affective or mood status to both psychological and physical health and well-being. For many years such studies concentrated almost exclusively on the relationships between negative or dysphoric affects and mental and physical health. More recently, a discernible body of research has emerged concerned with *positive affect states* and their relationships to various indicators of health status, and with the importance of *affects balance* as a valid indicator of well-being.

Although arising from disparate fields, research on the relationship between positive affects, affects balance, and health has suggested that positive mood states are a valid predictor of both physical and mental health status. Mechanic and Hansell (1) studied over 1,000 high school students and demonstrated a significant relationship between psychological well-being and academic performance, perceived quality of health, and participation in exercise and athletic programs. Similarly, Clark and Watson (2) intensively studied a sample of young adults and observed that high levels of positive affects were strongly related to levels of social interaction and physical activity, and inversely related to numbers of health complaints. James and his colleagues (3), using young adults in a laboratory measurement paradigm, demonstrated that scores on a measure of happiness were inversely related to blood pressure levels, while anxiety scores were directly related to elevations in blood pressure.

L. R. Derogatis and P. J. Rutigliano: Department of Clinical and Health Psychology, Hahnemann University, Philadelphia, Pennsylvania 19102.

Also using blood pressure as an outcome criterion in a study of high-risk adolescents, Derogatis and his associates (4) demonstrated significant inverse correlations between Derogatis Affects Balance Scale measures of positive affectivity and both systolic and diastolic blood pressures, while relationships with negative affects measures were minimal. Similarly, Wetzler and Ursano (5) demonstrated a significant association between positive affects, overall feelings of well-being, and seven major physical health practices (e.g., alcohol consumption, exercise, smoking) in a sample of over 6,600 Air Force personnel.

Based on a systematic series of studies relating affectivity to health outcomes and well-being, Watson and his associates (6) have developed a theoretical basis for the relationship of positive and negative affectivity. These investigators conceptualize positive affect and negative affect as two fundamental, essentially independent, constructs that make up the cardinal dimensions of emotional experience. They further distinguish *state* and *trait* versions of positive affect and negative affect (6). Positive affect is described as being associated with feelings of high energy, enthusiasm, and activity, with the capacity for high concentration, and pleasurable engagement with the environment. Its relative absence or reduction is characterized by lethargy and sadness. Negative affect is delineated as a dimension of general psychological distress subsuming the common dysphoric mood states (e.g., anxiety, anger, depression). At the trait level, positive affect and negative affect are conceived of as corresponding approximately to the personality dimensions of *extroversion* and *neuroticism* (7), respectively. Trait negative affect is described as a broadly based persistent tendency to experience life events in the context of a dysphoric emotional coloring that progressively extends to negatively influence cognitive style and self-concept. Trait positive affect is characterized as a persistent tendency to respond to the environment with an active, enabling posture, reflecting a general sense of competence, mastery, and personal well-being. As part of this program of studies, Watson (8) has done research showing significant relationships between positive affects and social activity and exercise, and has shown positive affects levels to be a reliable discriminator between depressive disorders (where positive affect is significantly reduced) and anxiety states (where positive affect is relatively unaffected) (9).

DEROGATIS AFFECTS BALANCE SCALE

Development

Development of the Derogatis Affects Balance Scale (DABS) was initiated in the early 1970s, and derived from two major origins: a persuasive series of studies that demonstrated that positive and negative affectivity were essentially uncorrelated (10–13), and a somewhat serendipitous clinical observation made by the author. During a therapeutic trial with depressed outpatients, it was noted that ultimate therapeutic response was more substantially correlated with levels of positive affectivity than with negative affectivity, a finding recently convincingly affirmed (14). A review of then current clinical mood and affects scales revealed that few if any measures addressed positive affectivity systematically, and none was designed to rigorously measure *affects balance*. These events led to the initial studies on the DABS which was completed in 1975 and originally named the Affects Balance Scale (15). The instrument's name was later changed to avoid confusion with a popular 10-item survey instrument of the same name developed by Bradburn (10).

Descriptive Profile

The DABS is a multidimensional mood and affects inventory composed of 40 adjective items that measures affectivity and affects balance via eight primary affect dimensions and five global scores. The *positive* affects dimensions are labeled *joy, contentment, vigor,* and *affection*. The *negative* affects dimensions are *anxiety, depression, guilt,* and *hostility*. The DABS global scores consist of the Positive Total score, Negative Total score, and the Affects Balance Index. Recently, two additional global measures, the Affects Expressiveness Index and the Positive Affects Ratio have been created for the DABS, and a brief form of the scale, the DABS-SF, has been normed and introduced.

The Positive Affects Total (PTOT) is defined as the sum of all scores on the four positive affects dimensions of joy, contentment, vigor, and affection, while the Negative Affects Total (NTOT) is represented as the sum of scores on the four negative dimensions of anxiety, depression, guilt and

hostility. The Affects Balance Index is defined as PTOT − NTOT/20. The Affects Expressiveness Index is defined as the sum total of affective expression, regardless of valance (i.e., regardless of positive or negative direction). It represents an attempt to measure the individual's affective "charge" or total affectivity. The Positive Affects Ratio illustrates a different approach to measuring global affectivity, in that it is designed to communicate the proportion of total affective expression that is positive. It is defined as the ratio of *positive affectivity* to *total affectivity* (i.e., positive plus negative affectivity) on the DABS and reflects the proportion of affective expression due to positive emotions. The DABS currently has a single norm developed for it based on approximately 500 community respondents. Although slight gender differences exist on several DABS measures, they are minimal, and clinically insignificant so that gender-keyed norms have not been developed for the inventory.

Reliability and Validity

As has been pointed out numerous times in the excellent collection on measurement in this volume, *reliability* has to do with the precision or accuracy of measurement, while *validity* addresses the essence of what is being measured. Demonstrations of the former are usually achieved through one or more very specific sets of operations, while confirmation of the latter is highly programmatic, requiring multiple experiments and research studies. Viewed from one perspective, the validation process is unending, since the limits of generalizability (i.e., valid application) of a substantive psychological measuring instrument are constantly being tested, expanded and redefined.

Reliability

In the case of self-report inventories, there are usually two forms of reliability that are important: *internal consistency* and *test-retest*. Internal consistency reliability is a measure of homogeneity or consistency of item selection; it reflects the degree to which the items chosen to operationalize the test or subtest in question are drawn from the same population of items. Test-retest reliability is a measure of temporal stability; it demonstrates the degree to which scores achieved at a particular time of assessment correlate with scores achieved on subsequent assessment occasions. In general, the longer the period between assessments, the lower the test-retest reliability will be.

In Table 1 both internal consistency and test-retest coefficients are provided for the dimensions and globals of the DABS. The coefficients alpha (a) were based on a sample of 355 psychiatric inpatients, while the test-retest coefficients (r_{tt}) were developed from a small sample of 16 primary breast cancer patients, with one week separating the two assessment occasions. Both sets of coefficients are well

TABLE 1. *DABS internal consistency and test-retest reliability coefficients*

DABS measure	Coefficient α (n = 355)	Test-Retest r_{tt} (n = 16)
Positive affects		
Joy	.92	.84
Contentment	.85	.80
Vigor	.85	.83
Affection	.84	.81
Negative affects		
Anxiety	.79	.78
Depression	.85	.82
Guilt	.82	.79
Hostility	.84	.80
Global scores		
PosTot	.94	.84
NegTot	.93	.81

within the acceptable range and suggest that the DABS is a reliable measure of mood and affects.

Convergent-Discriminant Validation

Of the many forms of validation required in the development of a psychological test one of the most fundamental is *convergent-discriminant* validity. First proposed by Campbell and Fiske (16) as a minimal validation maneuver, this type of validity study has over the past 25 years become a standard validation exercise. The fundamental idea in convergent-discriminant validity is to demonstrate that the operational definition(s) of the test construct(s) in question correlate positively with like measures of the construct, and negatively or neutrally with measures of dissimilar constructs.

In the validation of the DABS, a good demonstration of convergent-discriminant validity has been provided by a study exploring the relationships between the DABS positive and negative affect total scores (i.e., Positive Affects Total score and Negative Affects Total score) and scores on the Global Severity Index of the SCL-90-R, a symptom self-report inventory. The convergent-discriminant characteristics of the study arise from the fact that symptomatic distress and negative affectivity are anticipated as demonstrating a direct, convergent relationship, while positive affectivity is anticipated as showing a strong inverse or discriminative relationship with symptomatic distress. This study, which has not been reported elsewhere, involved dichotomizing the PTOT and NTOT scores at the normative medians to develop four distinct affective subtypes: (a) *high affective charge* = high positive/high negative, (b) *positive affective charge* = high positive/low negative, (c) *negative affective charge* = low positive/high negative, and (d) *low affective charge* = low positive/low negative.

Measurements of affectivity and symptomatic distress were recorded from three distinct samples: (a) *normals,*

a sample of 200 continuing education students from the community; (b) *sexual dysfunctions,* a sample of 88 outpatients presenting to a sexual medicine clinic with a primary complaint of sexual dysfunction; and (c) *psychiatric inpatients,* a sample of 50 patients from the inpatient services of a psychiatric hospital. Respondents in each sample were characterized as to their affective subtype patterns according to this paradigm, and results of the characterization are presented in Table 2.

Concerning positive affectivity, the ordinal ranking of the three cohorts was hypothesized to progress from a low among psychiatric outpatients, through a moderate position among the sexual dysfunctions, to its highest level in the normal cohort. This is in fact what was observed, with a positive affective charge being revealed in only 8% of psychiatric patients, 27.3% of sexual dysfunctions, and 56.0% of normals. A converse relationship was anticipated with negative affectivity and was also confirmed, with the ordinal relationship progressing from a low of 14.5% among normals, through 39.8% among the sexual dysfunctions, to 70.0% in our psychiatric inpatient sample.

A similar validation demonstration is provided by the data summarized in Table 3. In this analysis the Affects Balance Index was employed as the global affectivity measure, and scores from the normative distribution of the test were trichotomized into "low," "medium," and "high" subgroups. Individuals were then assigned to low, medium, or high well-being groups on the basis of their scores. Seventy-eight percent of the normals, but only 18% of the psychiatric inpatients, were assigned to the high well-being group. Conversely, 56% of psychiatric inpatients, but only 2.5% of normals, achieved low well-being status. Sexually dysfunctional outpatients revealed proportions that fell between the other two samples.

Validation of Dimensional Structure

An important demonstration in the construct validation of a multidimensional psychological test involves the verifi-

TABLE 2. *DABS affective subtype patterns in normals, sexual dysfunctions, and psychiatric inpatients*

Sample	Affective subtype			
	High charge n (%)	Positive charge n (%)	Negative charge n (%)	Low charge n (%)
Normals (n = 200)	32 (16.0)	112 (56.0)	29 (14.5)	27 (13.5)
Sexual dysfunctions (n = 88)	13 (14.8)	24 (27.3)	35 (39.8)	16 (18.2)
Psychiatric inpatients (n = 50)	5 (10.0)	4 (8.0)	35 (70.0)	6 (12.0)

TABLE 3. *Proportions with low, moderate, and high DABS affects balance indices (ABI) in samples of normals, sexually dysfunctional, and psychiatric inpatients*

Sample	Low ABI n (%)	Moderate ABI n (%)	High ABI n (%)
Normals (n = 200)	5 (2.5)	38 (19.0)	157 (78.5)
Sexual dysfunctions (n = 88)	16 (18.2)	34 (38.6)	38 (43.2)
Psychiatric inpatients (n = 50)	28 (56.0)	13 (26.0)	9 (18.0)

$\chi^2 = 119.4$; $p < .00001$.

TABLE 4. *Factor loading coefficients describing two higher-order dimensions of positive and negative affectivity underlying DABS subscales*

DABS dimension	Factor I	Factor II
Joy	.851	−.340
Contentment	.767	−.426
Vigor	.869	−.037
Affection	.798	−.081
Anxiety	−.210	.793
Depression	−.430	.672
Guilt	−.195	.817
Hostility	−.003	.844

cation of dimensional structure. The operational definitions (i.e., dimensions) of the primary hypothesized constructs measured by the test must be confirmed in terms of real-world clinical data. In the case of the DABS, validation requires verification at two distinct levels of structure. At the most fundamental level, the eight hypothesized primary affects dimensions of the test require confirmation. At a broader conceptual level, the overarching constructs of positive and negative affectivity require corroboration.

To achieve a verification of dimensional structure, admissions DABS from 355 psychiatric inpatients at a private psychiatric hospital were scored and subjected to principal components analysis with an orthogonal varimax rotation. Six factors or dimensions were recovered that met the Scree criterion (17), and accounted for approximately 70% of the variance in the correlation matrix. Three factors emerged that clearly reflected positive affects dimensions: a combined *joy/contentment* dimension, an *affection* dimension, and a *vigor* dimension. On the negative side, the largest factor represented a combined *depression/guilt* factor, with two additional components clearly reflecting *anxiety* and *hostility*. Although this analysis did not achieve a perfect recovery of the hypothesized eight-factor structure, it did confirm the majority of the constructs hypothesized. The fusing of the joy and contentment dimensions on the positive side, and the negative affect dimensions of depression and guilt cannot be considered totally unexpected, considering the fact that the respondents in this instance were seriously ill psychiatric patients who were assessed during the first week of their admission to hospital. In such a situation, affect and mood states would almost certainly have a tendency to be blurred, and in a manner not inconsistent with these findings.

To verify the higher-order factors of positive and negative affectivity, the primary dimension correlation matrix was also subjected to principal components analysis with orthogonal varimax rotation. Two principal components were identified that accounted for 72.2% of the variance. The factor structure derived from this analysis is reproduced in Table 4, and is represented graphically in Fig. 1.

Predictive Validity: The Practical Utility of a Test

When clinicians and investigators speak about the validity of a psychological test they are referring to its *predictive* validity. Predictive validity addresses the practical utility of the test: how well, for example, it identifies positive cases, discriminates effective from ineffective treatments, distinguishes treatment responders from nonresponders, or correlates with other independent measures of outcome. In this section we review applications of the DABS as a primary outcome measure in a broad variety of clinical research contexts.

Psychosocial oncology is a division of medicine in which the DABS has been used frequently over the years. Numerous investigators have utilized the DABS to evaluate the affective and emotional dimensions of cancer illnesses and the effectiveness of various coping and adjustment strategies. One of the earliest published studies using the DABS was reported by Derogatis et al. (18), in their research on coping styles and length of survival with metastatic breast patients. This was an early study that explored the role of psychological factors in morbidity and mortality from cancer. Although assays of the immune system were not done in this early trial, findings showed that DABS negative affect measures significantly discriminated ''long'' from ''short'' survivors in this sample. In a related study, Levy and her associates (19) evaluated survival hazards across a 7-year follow-up interval in a sample of first recurrent breast cancer patients. Using a Cox proportional hazards model, these investigators found that disease-free interval, the DABS joy scale, physician's prognosis, and number of metastatic sites were significant predictors of length of survival. Using other prediction models, the investigators found in general that longer survival was associated with positive mood states, and concluded that such states represented a measure of resilience or hardiness. In a somewhat analogous study, Edwards et al. (20) used the DABS within a battery of psychological measures in hopes of identifying a pretreatment survival marker for patients with testicular cancer. Twenty-six patients participated in the study, with 19 (long survivors) living to 7 years postassessment, and 7 (short survivors) dying during the first year. In a manner analogous to the

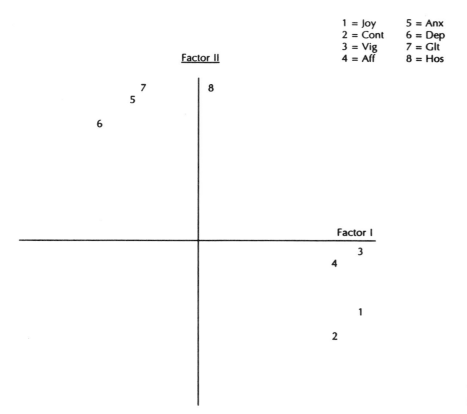

1 = Joy   5 = Anx
2 = Cont   6 = Dep
3 = Vig   7 = Glt
4 = Aff   8 = Hos

FIG. 1. Rotated principal components from analysis of DABS primary affects dimensions.

Derogatis et al. study, analysis of DABS profiles revealed that long survivors had significantly higher levels of anxiety, hostility, and depression than did the short survivors. The authors interpreted the high levels of negative affectivity as indicators of a successful coping style relative to the disease and its treatment.

Also working with breast cancer patients, Ayres and her colleagues (21) evaluated the factors involved in predicting compliance with chemotherapy regimen. High scores on DABS measures of vigor, anxiety, and depression, and the "fighting spirit" scale of the Mental Adjustment to Cancer Scale, predicted adherence, while high DABS guilt and hostility scores predicted poor compliance. A discriminant function analysis correctly assigned 86% of the sample relative to compliance using the above measures. Northouse and Swain (22) applied the DABS to primary breast cancer patients, as well as their spouses, immediately after mastectomy and subsequently one month postsurgery. They found a consonance of affect status between husbands and wives. Both patients and spouses showed a significant decrement in positive affect status immediately postsurgery, which returned to normative levels 1 month later. There were no significant differences between spouse and patient Affects Balance Index scores at either time of assessment. Carter et al. (23) also recently reported a study contrasting breast cancer patients and their spouses on the DABS. Consistent with Northouse and Swain, these investigators also found few differences between husbands and wives in affective

status, with both scoring within normative limits. DABS scores were further utilized in the study to establish whether or not different patterns of emotional expression might characterize different personality types. Analyses revealed significant differences in affective expression as measured by the DABS across five personality/gender types.

Several research groups have used the DABS in research focused on coping with loss. Rabins and his associates (24) used the DABS among other measures to contrast the coping effectiveness of a sample of caregivers working with Alzheimer's patients with the coping of caregivers involved with cancer patients. No noteworthy differences between the two groups were observed; however, they identified correlates of positive and negative adjustment for both sets of caregivers. The DABS Positive Total score correlated significantly with number of social contacts, family cohesiveness, extroversion, and strength of religious faith. Quinn and Strelkauskas (25) completed a trial in which they employed the DABS with a small sample of recently bereaved individuals who were being treated with Therapeutic Touch. Very substantial changes were noted on all DABS measures from baseline to posttreatment. Positive affectivity was significantly enhanced and negative affectivity was substantially reduced across the treatment period.

A number of studies with the DABS have focused on what might broadly be referred to as stress or stress-related states. Taking contemporary stress theory as their theoretical foundation, Wolf et al. (26) used the DABS to establish the affective status of a sample of freshman medical students. The purpose of the study was to investigate the relationship between hassles, uplifts, life events, and psychological well-being across a 9-month period. Findings indicated that while the hassles measure was found to be a better predictor of concurrent and subsequent negative affective states (i.e., NTOT), life stress was found to be a better predictor of subsequent positive affectivity and well-being (i.e., Positive Affects Total score, Affects Balance Index). These investigators have recently reported further research on this topic, in which psychological changes during the first year of medical school were determined (27). They observed consistent significant reductions in positive affectivity over the interval and elevations in negative affectivity. During the same period, hassles were significantly increased while uplifts and self-esteem fell significantly. Correlations among measures, both at baseline and terminal assessment, indicated significant correlations between DABS global affectivity scores and both self-esteem and health locus of control scores. Although less clearly a stress study per se, Derogatis and his colleagues (28) recently utilized the DABS in an interesting study of the relationship between androgens and depression in hirsute women. Among six androgens evaluated for their relationship to clinical depression, only unbound fractions of testosterone (i.e., biologically active and free testosterone) were found to correlate very significantly with the DABS depression score ($r = .60$; $p < .01$). The unbound fractions also showed significant inverse correlations with measures of positive affectivity ($r = -.51$; p, $<.05$) and the Affects Balance Index ($r = -.49$; p, $<.05$). Results were interpreted as suggesting that depression among hirsute women may be more etiologically related to a deranged neuroendocrine mechanism than to psychological causes.

Treatment outcome has become an increasingly important area of application for the DABS since affectivity and affects balance are such sensitive indicators of emotional status and well-being. Hoehn-Saric and his associates (29) utilized the DABS in a trial of clonidine versus placebo in a heterogeneous group of patients suffering from anxiety disorders. Overall, there was some support for clonidine's efficacy with these patients; however, few differences were significant. Specifically on the DABS, the depression score was marginally lowered, and the Affects Balance Index showed a marginally significant elevation. Interestingly, a significant increase in the hostility score was observed in the clonidine group during the second week of the trial.

Hoehn-Saric (30) also utilized the DABS within a battery of psychological measures to profile the affective status of chronically anxious patients. In general, results of the study showed that patients with mixed anxiety-depression had more negatively balanced affect profiles than patients suffering from anxiety disorders alone. The poor affects balance was due to both reductions in positive affects and enhancements or elevations in negative affectivity. The author further compared the DABS profiles of patients suffering from gen-

eralized anxiety disorder with those of a "mixed" group of anxiety patients suffering from panic disorder, agoraphobia, and obsessive-compulsive disorder. Profiles were generally comparable, with the exception that the generalized anxiety disorder group had significantly higher scores on the DABS anxiety dimension. This study also compared the affective profiles of patients scoring high on introversion versus those with high extroversion scores. As would be predicted from theory, the extroverted subgroup revealed significantly higher scores on positive affects and significantly lower negative affectivity.

Sangal and his associates (31) also utilized the DABS in a drug trial with anxiety disorders, in this instance in an attempt to characterize improved versus unimproved patients. Those judged improved by independent criteria demonstrated both reduced negative affectivity on the DABS and increased positive mood states. Holland and her research group (32) compared alprazolam to progressive relaxation in the treatment of anxious and depressive symptoms in cancer patients in a multicenter trial at three different centers. Results indicated that DABS measures of depression and anxiety showed significant reductions across the course of treatment for both drug and behavioral interventions. However, findings revealed a significant advantage for alprazolam over relaxation in both rapidity and magnitude of therapeutic effects.

Particularly as it defines the relationship between normal cognitive functioning and psychopathology, Garamoni and his colleagues (33) have developed a theoretical model referred to as the States of Mind model. The central thesis of this model is that healthy functioning is characterized by an optimal balance between positivity and negativity of cognitions and/or affects. Specific mental disorders are then characterized by deviations in direction, magnitude, duration, and frequency from the optimal balance. The model operationally defines five states of mind by distinct positivity/negativity ratios: positive monologue = >.70; positive dialogue = .56–.69; conflicted dialogue = .45–.55; negative dialogue = .30–.44; negative monologue = <.30. Although initial research focused on cognitions, in the majority of their recent research on affects balance this group has used the DABS to define positive and negative affectivity.

Garamoni et al. (33) reported a study on approximately 40 depressed outpatients and an approximately equal number of healthy controls in which they tested the validity of the States of Mind model using the DABS. The primary hypothesis of the study predicted that the outpatient sample would show an affects balance in the negative dialogue range, while healthy controls would demonstrate a balance characterized as positive dialogue. Results showed the patients' affects balance to be precisely in the range predicted (mean = .35; SD = .14), while controls showed a somewhat higher balance than anticipated (mean = .78; SD = .10). The difference between group means was highly significant statistically ($p < .0001$) and there was almost no overlap between distributions of scores between the two samples. As predicted, affects balance values were negatively correlated with measures of symptomatic distress.

This research group also reported another study (14) in which depressed outpatients participated in a 20- to 24-session trial of cognitive behavior therapy. Upon completion, patients were categorized as either "responders" or "nonresponders" on the basis of independent clinical ratings of depression severity. Predictions based on States of Mind theory were upheld in that responders shifted their affects balance into the optimal range by the completion of treatment, while nonresponders remained in the negative dialogue range. As a corollary hypothesis the authors postulated that responders would achieve their therapeutic movement primarily by reducing negative affectivity, with little alteration in positive affectivity. Results of the study clearly contradicted this hypothesis, in that responders clearly increased positive affectivity significantly over the course of treatment at a rate significantly more dramatic than the rate of reduction of negative affects. The authors caution, however, that this effect may be specific to depressed patients, since research on cognitive balance using anxious patients clearly supported their original hypothesis (34).

In another innovative study with depressed patients (35), this same group of researchers used the DABS to examine the relationship between affects intensity and phasic REM sleep, pre- and posttreatment with cognitive behavior therapy. Forty-five depressed males and 43 healthy male controls were evaluated with regard to the relationship between measures of affectivity and measures of REM sleep. Among depressed patients, there was a significant correlation ($r = .42$; $p < .005$) between REM latency and REM density and the affective expression index (which these investigators refer to as "affective intensity"), both prior to and subsequent to treatment. No such relationship was observed in the group of healthy male controls. The authors suggest that the persistence of the relationship between measures of affectivity and REM sleep, even after effective therapy, may be a signal of persistent vulnerability in certain depressed individuals for disturbed affective processing.

Research in sexual medicine is another area where the DABS has been used extensively, in part because it is a formal subtest of the Derogatis Sexual Functioning Inventory (36). Derogatis and his colleagues have over the years profiled a number of the major sexual diagnostic subgroups with the DABS. These characterizations began with a study of the affective profiles of the common sexual dysfunctions in men and women (37). Individuals suffering from these disorders (i.e., premature ejaculation and male erectile disorder in men; hypoactive sexual desire and female orgasmic disorder in women) demonstrated affects balances a full standard deviation below the normative mean. DABS profiles of the common sexual dysfunctions showed substantial elevations of negative affectivity ($p < .001$), with concomitant significant suppression of positive affectivity ($p < .001$)

compared with healthy controls. DABS profiles have also been established on gender dysphoric patients, i.e., both male (38) and female (39) transsexuals, and males suffering from retarded ejaculation (40). Male gender dysphorics presented with dramatically negative affects balances; positive affectivity was profoundly suppressed compared with the healthy controls ($p < .001$), and elevations in negative affectivity were also statistically significant. The authors characterized the male gender dysphorics as suffering from a "pervasive anhedonia." In the cohort of female gender dysphorics profiled (39), affectivity was not as dramatically disturbed. Significant suppression of positive affects was observed; however, only modest elevations on depression and anxiety were in evidence concerning negative affect measures.

A further application of the DABS in patients with sexual dysfunction occurred in a study that sought to identify distinct subtypes of women suffering from female orgasmic disorder or "anorgasmia" (41). Hierarchical cluster analysis was utilized with case history and Derogatis Sexual Functioning Inventory data from 76 women to create a mathematical taxonomy of women suffering from anorgasmia. Four subtypes were identified through cluster analysis: low desire, histrionic, psychiatric disorder, and constitutional. Affects profiles for the constitutional and low-desire subtypes revealed modest positive affects suppression, but were essentially clinically unremarkable. However, histrionic and pyschiatric-disordered subtypes revealed dramatically negative affects balances, clearly in the clinical range, with significant loss of positive affectivity and elevation of negative affects.

The data reviewed above focus on the relationship between affectivity and sexual functioning among individuals with diagnosed sexual disorders. We have recently completed analyses in a study investigating the relationship between affectivity and quality of sexual functioning in healthy community normals (42). Approximately 250 community men and women from various professions agreed to participate in a brief anonymous survey of quality of sexual functioning and feelings of well-being. Quality of sexual functioning was assessed via the Derogatis Interview for Sexual Functioning (43,44) and affectivity and well-being were measured via the DABS. Although details of the study will be reported elsewhere, we observed significant correlations between all positive affects measures of the DABS, including PTOT and the Affects Balance Index, and all domain and global scores of the Derogatis Interview for Sexual Functioning. Similar findings were not in evidence regarding negative affectivity. Significant inverse correlations between negative affects measures and the Derogatis Interview for Sexual Functioning were observed only on the *orgasm* scale. These findings were interpreted as providing additional support for the premise that positive affectivity is a more sensitive indicator of well-being and functional status than negative affectivity, particularly in nonpsychiatric populations.

Recently, empirical evidence has mounted in support of the concept of heritability of personality traits. Henderson's (45) comprehensive review of twin research attests to prominent heritability for the personality characteristics of extraversion and neuroticism. More recently, Plomin et al. (46) cite an impressive body of research affirming heritability across a wide variety of personality characteristics. More specific to affectivity, Tellegen and his associates (47) utilized co-twin and adoption methodologies to assess heritability of a variety of personality features in fraternal versus identical twins. General sense of well-being was found to correlate approximately .50 among identical twins whether reared together or apart. The accumulated evidence from these and other research trials convey the impression that there is an explicit genetic component to affectivity, one that may eventually be demonstrated to be quite substantial.

A central question in interpreting findings such as these concerns the distinction between cause and effect. Do high levels of positive affects reflect a constitutional characteristic, equivalent to Meehl's (48) concept of "hedonic capacity," or are positive affects more accurately represented as responses, "effects", determined by and indicative of more fundamental biological and psychosocial processes? A definitive answer to this question awaits further study.

CONCLUSIONS

Whichever posture one takes concerning the basic nature of the relationship between positive affectivity and health and well-being, affects balance has clearly been shown to have substantial associations with multiple health indicators. Just as certain personality constellations are believed to represent markers for the "disease-prone personality" (49), it is equally possible that positive affects balance represents a reliable marker for disease-resistance. The DABS is designed to be a brief, reliable, and valid measure of the primary constructs of affectivity and affects balance, and should help to address these questions in a valid and cost-effective manner.

ACKNOWLEDGMENT

The publisher of the DABS and DABS-SF is Clinical Psychometric Research of Towson, Maryland.

REFERENCES

1. Mechanic D, Hansell S. Adolescent competence, psychological well-being and self-assessed physical health. *J Health Soc Behav* 1987; 28:364–374.
2. Clark LE, Watson D. Mood and the mundane: relations between daily life events and self-reported mood. *J Pers Soc Psychol* 1988; 54:296–308.
3. James SA, Hartnett SA, Kalsbeek WD. John Henryism and blood pressure differences among black men. *J Behav Med* 1983;6:259–278.
4. Derogatis LR, Falkner B, Kareken DA, Graber C. Psychosocial features and elevated blood pressure in adolescents. Presented at the 11th Annual Meeting of the Society of Behavioral Medicine, Chicago, IL, April 19, 1990.
5. Wetzler HP, Ursano RJ. A positive association between physical health practices and psychological well-being. *J Nerv Ment Dis* 1988; 171:280–283.
6. Watson D, Tellegen A. Toward a consensual structure of mood. *Psychol Bull* 1985;98:219–235.
7. Eysenck HJ, Eysenck SBG. *Eysenck personality inventory.* San Diego, CA: Educational and Industrial Testing Service, 1968.
8. Watson D. Intraindividual and interindividual analyses of positive and negative affect: their relation to health complaints, perceived stress and daily activities. *J Pers Soc Psychol* 1988;54:1020–1030.
9. Watson D, Clark LA. Positive and negative affectivity and their relation to anxiety and depressive disorders. *J Abnorm Psychol* 1988;97: 346–353.
10. Bradburn NM. *The structure of well-being.* Chicago: Aldine, 1969.
11. Beiser M, Feldman JJ, Egelhoff CS. Assets and affects: a study of positive mental health. *Arch Gen Psychiatry* 1972;27:545–549.
12. Gaitz CM, Scott J. Age and the measurement of mental health. *J Health Soc Behav* 1972;13:55–67.
13. Ware P, Wall T. *Work and well-being.* Hammandsworth, England: Penguin, 1975.
14. Garamoni GL, Reynolds CF, Thase ME, Frank E, Fasiczka AL. Shifts in affective balance during therapy of major depression. *J Consult Clin Psychol* 1992;60:260–266.
15. Derogatis LR. *The Affects Balance Scale.* Baltimore: Clinical Psychometric Research, 1975.
16. Campbell DT, Fiske DW. Convergent and discriminant validation by the multitrait-multimethod matrix. *Psychol Bull* 1959;56:81–105.
17. Cattell RB. The Scree test for number of factors. *Mult Behav Res* 1966;1:245.
18. Derogatis LR, Abeloff MD, Melisaratos N. Psychological coping mechanisms and survival time in metastatic breast cancer. *JAMA* 1979;242:1504–1508.
19. Levy SM, Lee J, Bagley C, Lippman M. Survival hazards analysis in first recurrent breast cancer patients: seven-year follow-up. *Psychosom Med* 1988;50:520–528.
20. Edwards J, DiClemente C, Samuels ML. Psychological characteristics: a pretreatment survival marker of patients with testicular cancer. *J Psychosoc Oncol* 1985;3(1):79–94.
21. Ayres A, Hoon PW, Franzoni JP, Matheny KB, Cotanch PH, Takayanagi S. Influence of mood and adjustment to cancer on compliance with chemotherapy among breast cancer patients. *J Psychosom Res* 1994;38(5):393–402.
22. Northouse LL, Swain MA. Adjustment of patients and husbands to initial impact of breast cancer. *Nurs Res* 1987;36(4):221–225.
23. Carter RE, Carter CA, Prosen HA. Emotional and personality types of breast cancer patients and spouses. *Am J Fam Ther* 1992; 20(4):300–309.
24. Rabins PV, Fitting MD, Eastham J, Fetting J. The emotional impact of caring for the chronically ill. *Psychosomatics* 1990;31(3):331–336.
25. Quinn JF, Strelkauskas AJ. Psychoimmunologic effects of therapeutic touch on practitioners and recently bereaved recipients: a pilot study. *Adv Nurs Sci* 1993;15(4):13–26.
26. Wolf TM, Elston RC, Kissling GE. Relationship of hassles, uplifts and life events to psychological well-being of freshman medical students. *Behav Med* 1989; Spring:37–45.
27. Wolf TM, von Almen TK, Faucett JM, Randall HM, Franklin FA. Psychological changes during the first year of medical school. *Med Ed* 1991;25:174–181.
28. Derogatis LR, Rose LI, Shulman LH, Lazarus LA. Serum androgens and psychopathology in hirsute women. *J Psychosom Obstet Gynecol* 1993;14:269–282.
29. Hoehn-Saric R, Merchant AF, Keyser ML, Smith VK. Effects of clonidine on anxiety disorders. *Arch Gen Psychiatry* 1981;38:1278–1282.
30. Hoehn-Saric R. Affective profiles of chronically anxious patients. *Hillside J Clin Psychol* 1983;5(1):43–56.
31. Sangal R, Coyle G, Hoehn-Saric R. Chronic anxiety and social adjustment. *Compr Psychiatry* 1983;24(1):75–78.
32. Holland JC, Morrow GR, Schmale A, Derogatis LR, Stefanek M, Berenson S, Carpenter PJ, Breitbart W, Feldstein M. A randomized clinical trial of alprazolam versus progressive muscle relaxation in

cancer patients with anxiety and depressive symptoms. *J Clin Oncol* 1991;9(6):1004–1011.

33. Garamoni GL, Reynolds CF, Thase ME, Frank E, Berman SR, Fasiczka AL. The balance of positive and negative affects in major depression: a further test of the states of mind model. *Psychiatry Res* 1991; 39:99–108.

34. Schwartz RM. The internal dialogue: on asymmetry between positive and negative coping thoughts. *Cog Ther Res* 1986;10(59):591–605.

35. Nofzinger EA, Schwartz RM, Reynolds CF, Thase ME, Jennings JR, Frank E, Fasiczka AL, Garamoni GL, Kupfer DJ. Affect intensity and phasic REM sleep in depressed men before and after treatment with cognitive-behavior therapy. *J Consult Clin Psychol* 1994;62(1):83–91.

36. Derogatis LR, Melisaratos N. The DSFI: a multidimensional measure of sexual function. *J Sex Marital Ther* 1979;5:244–281.

37. Derogatis LR, Meyer JK. A psychological profile of the sexual dysfunctions. *Arch Sex Behav* 1979;8(3):201–223.

38. Derogatis LR, Meyer JK, Vazquez N. A psychological profile of the transsexual—I. The male. *J Nerv Ment Dis* 1978;166(4):234–254.

39. Derogatis LR, Meyer JK, Boland P. A psychological profile of the transsexual—II. The female. *J Nerv Ment Dis* 1981;169(3):167–168.

40. Derogatis LR. Retarded ejaculation. In: JK Meyer, CW Schmidt, TN Wise, eds. *Clinical management of sexual disorders,* 2nd ed. Baltimore: Williams & Wilkins, 1983.

41. Derogatis LR, Schmidt CW, Fagan PJ, Wise TN. Subtypes of anorgasmia via mathematical taxonomy. *Psychosomatics* 1989;30(2): 166–173.

42. Sudler N, Applegate C, Fleming M, Derogatis LR. The relationship between affectivity and quality of sexual functioning in a community population. (submitted for publication, 1994)

43. Derogatis LR. *Derogatis Interview for Sexual Functioning (DISF).* Baltimore, MD: Clinical Psychometric Research, 1987.

44. Zinreich ES, Derogatis LR, Herpst J, Auvil G, Piantadosi S, Order SE. Pre and posttreatment evaluation of sexual functioning in patients with adenocarcinoma of the prostate. *Int J Radiat Oncol Biol Phys* 1991;20:729–732.

45. Henderson ND. Human behavior genetics. *Annu Rev Psychol* 1982; 33:403–440.

46. Plomin R, DeFries JC, McClearn GE. *Behavioral genetics,* 2nd ed. New York: W.H. Freeman, 1990.

47. Tellegen A, Lykken DT, Bouchard TS, Wilcox K, Segal N, Rich S. Personality similarity in twins reared apart and together. *J Pers Soc Psychol* 1988;54:1031–1039.

48. Meehl PE. Hedonic capacity: some conjectures. *Bull Mennin Ger Clin* 1975;39:295–307.

49. Friedman HS, Booth-Kewley S. The disease-prone personality. *Am Psychol* 1987;42:539–558.

Quality of Life and Pharmacoeconomics in Clinical Trials, Second Edition, edited by B. Spilker.
Lippincott-Raven Publishers, Philadelphia © 1996.

CHAPTER 21

The European Organization for Research and Treatment of Cancer (EORTC) Modular Approach to Quality of Life Assessment in Oncology: An Update

Neil K. Aaronson, Ann M. Cull, Stein Kaasa, and Mirjam A. G. Sprangers

INTRODUCTION

Historically, the evaluation of new cancer therapies has focused on such biomedical outcomes as tumor response, disease-free and overall survival, and treatment-related toxicity. While these broad outcome parameters remain central in the evaluation process, there is increasing recognition of the need to assess more formally and systematically the impact of cancer and its treatment on the functional, psycho-

logical, and social health of the individual. Support for such "quality of life" investigations has been voiced by prominent clinical trial groups in North America (1–4) and Europe (5–7), national and international cancer institutes and societies (8–10), regulatory agencies responsible for the approval of new antineoplastic agents (11), and the pharmaceutical industry (12).

Increasingly, clinical research in oncology is characterized by close international cooperation and collaboration. The establishment of strong international links among clinical investigators carries with it a number of important advantages. Such international networks can facilitate the rapid exchange of information, minimize redundancy of effort, encourage the standardization of research methods, and accelerate the rate of patient accrual into clinical trials.

Although multinational research can add complexity to the clinical trial process, particularly in terms of organization and quality control, the geographic and cultural background of patients and investigators do not influence the definition or measurement of the biologic end points of primary interest (e.g., tumor response, survival).

N. K. Aaronson: Division of Psychosocial Research and Epidemiology, The Netherlands Cancer Institute, 1066 CX Amsterdam, The Netherlands.

A. M. Cull: ICRF Medical Oncology Unit, Western General Hospital, Edinburgh, EH4 2XU Scotland.

S. Kaasa: Palliative Medicine Unit, Department of Oncology and Radiotherapy, University Hospital of Trondheim, N-7006 Trondheim, Norway.

M. A. G. Sprangers: Division of Psychosocial Research and Epidemiology, The Netherlands Cancer Institute, 1066 CX Amsterdam, The Netherlands.

Such a culture-free research environment cannot be assumed, however, when one is interested in assessing more subjective outcomes such as symptoms, psychological well-being, and social functioning. On the contrary, the ways in which individuals define, recognize, and report their illness experience, whether expressed in terms of symptoms or levels of functioning, can be highly influenced by such factors as gender, culture, and socioeconomic status (13–15).

In this chapter we describe the ongoing efforts of a multinational clinical trials group—the European Organization for Research and Treatment of Cancer (EORTC)—to develop an integrated system for assessing the quality of life of patients participating in international clinical trials. Although the focus is on cancer, many of the conceptual, methodological, and cross-cultural issues addressed may be of interest and relevance to those working in the broader field of chronic disease research.

THE EUROPEAN ORGANIZATION FOR RESEARCH AND TREATMENT OF CANCER

The EORTC is one of the oldest and largest clinical trials groups in Europe. With its data center and coordinating office in Brussels, the EORTC is organized into a series of tumor-oriented (e.g., breast cancer, lung cancer, etc.) "cooperative groups," each of which is responsible for developing and implementing its clinical trials program. All of the countries of Western Europe, and an increasing number from Eastern Europe, are represented within the EORTC. There is close cooperation with other clinical trials groups within Europe, as well as with the U.S. National Cancer Institute.

In 1980, in response to an expressed need within the EORTC for a coherent policy on quality of life research, the Study Group on Quality of Life was created to advise the data center and the various cooperative groups on the design, implementation, and analysis of quality of life studies within selective phase III clinical trials. Currently, 16 European countries are represented within the study group, as well as Australia, Canada, and the United States. From its inception, the study group has included a broad range of professionals, including oncologists, radiotherapists, surgeons, psychiatrists, psychologists, social workers, and research methodologists. This cultural mix defined as much in terms of professional background as language and geography, has proven invaluable in shaping the study group's approach to quality of life assessment.

EARLY DEVELOPMENTAL ACTIVITIES

An early goal of the study group was to achieve consensus on how quality of life should be defined and measured. Much of the early discussion within the group was very basic, and often quite philosophical in nature. What was quality of life? Could it be quantified? If so, could it be measured with standardized instruments, or were in-depth interviews necessary?

A wide range of viewpoints was represented in these discussions. At one extreme were those who believed that quality of life is a highly personal construct that does not lend itself easily, if at all, to standardized measurement. At the other extreme were those who preferred to ignore entirely the epistemologic issues, focusing instead on the technical "nuts and bolts" of psychometrics and research design.

Ultimately, the more pragmatically oriented members of the group prevailed. While acknowledging the difficulties inherent in defining quality of life in its broadest sense, they argued that, by focusing on *health-related* issues, one could identify a limited set of life domains most likely to be affected by cancer and its treatment.

Much less controversial, at least within the study group, was the question of who should assess patients' quality of life. Given its inherently subjective nature, consensus was quickly reached that quality of life ratings should, whenever possible, be elicited directly from patients themselves. This conclusion, however, was not entirely self-evident to the clinicians directly responsible for conducting EORTC clinical trials.

Historically, it had most often been the treating physician who had provided such ratings, albeit in a limited way. That is, in most EORTC clinical trials, the clinicians are asked to assess both the patients' performance status (e.g., using the Karnofsky or ECOG scales) and the degree of toxicity (based on laboratory values and subjective judgment) associated with the treatment. Why then, was it necessary to introduce an additional layer of complexity to these trials by requiring that patients complete questionnaires?

Fortunately, at the time these discussions were taking place, sufficient empirical data had become available to provide more than an ideological response to this question. A number of studies had documented low levels of reliability in physicians' performance status ratings and, perhaps more importantly, low levels of agreement between ratings provided by physicians and those of their patients (16,17). If substantial measurement error was found in ratings of the more observable, functionally oriented aspects of quality of life, one could logically anticipate even greater problems in assessing such highly subjective experiences as pain, fatigue, and psychological distress (16). Thus, albeit with some initial reluctance, the study group's recommendation to employ patient self-report questionnaires was endorsed by the EORTC cooperative groups interested in incorporating quality of life outcomes into their clinical trial program.

Of course, these discussions were not carried out in a vacuum. An important influence in shaping the thinking of the study group was the measurement strategy employed by John Ware, Jr., Anita Stewart, and their colleagues at the RAND Corporation in the Health Insurance Experiment (18) and later in the Medical Outcomes Study (19). Of particular value was their conceptual framework, which placed signs and symptoms of disease at the core of health status (or health-related quality of life) assessment, followed by personal functioning, psychological distress, general health perceptions, and social role functioning. Equally influential was the battery of self-report questionnaires developed at RAND to operationalize each of these domains with a high degree of reliability and validity (19).

Within the cancer field, preliminary work carried out by individual members of the study group, as well as the efforts of Priestman and Baum (20) in the United Kingdom and Schipper and coworkers (21) in Canada were influential in demonstrating the feasibility of employing brief questionnaires to evaluate the quality of life of patients participating in clinical studies. The practical constraints operating within EORTC clinical trials necessitated the use of such abbreviated instruments.

A MODULAR APPROACH TO QUALITY OF LIFE ASSESSMENT

An important issue for the EORTC was to determine the optimal level of instrument specificity. Quality of life measures were placed on a continuum reflecting their intended spectrum of application: (a) generic instruments designed for both the general population and for a wide range of chronic disease populations; (b) disease-specific measures designed for use with cancer patients, in general; (c) diagnosis-specific measures (e.g., for use with breast cancer patients only); and (d) ad hoc, study-specific measures.

A major advantage associated with the most generic class of quality of life measures is that it allows for comparison of results across studies of different patient populations. This is particularly relevant if one is primarily interested in larger health policy and resource allocation issues. However, within the EORTC, the central research focus is on comparing treatments within well-defined, relatively homogeneous patient populations, rather than across populations. Serious concerns were raised about the ability of generic instruments to detect small, yet clinically meaningful group differences in quality of life, or in detecting changes in quality of life over time. At the opposite end of the spectrum, a measurement strategy based on study-specific quality of life instruments was viewed as both impractical and inefficient. Although such instruments can be designed to address very specific research questions, there is seldom time to assure that they meet even minimal standards of validity and reliability. Additionally, such measures rule out any possibility of cross-study comparisons, even within a single diagnostic group.

Rather than forcing a choice between the two remaining measurement strategies (disease-specific versus diagnostic-specific), a compromise was adopted that incorporated positive features of both. The intent was to generate a *core* questionnaire incorporating a range of physical, emotional,

and social health issues relevant to a broad spectrum of cancer patients, irrespective of specific diagnosis. This core instrument could then be supplemented by diagnosis-specific (e.g., for lung cancer or breast cancer) and/or treatment-specific questionnaire modules. This *modular* approach was intended to reconcile two principal requirements of quality of life assessment in the EORTC clinical trials program: (a) a sufficient degree of generalizability to allow for cross-study comparisons; and (b) a level of specificity adequate for addressing those research questions of particular relevance in a given clinical trial (22).

DEVELOPMENT OF THE EORTC CORE QUALITY OF LIFE QUESTIONNAIRE

While several cancer-specific questionnaires were available by the early 1980s, few had yet undergone sufficient field testing to recommend them for general use. Two instruments that had been submitted to preliminary psychometric evaluation—the Functional Living Index–Cancer (21) and the questionnaire developed by Selby and his colleagues (23)—were rejected as candidate measures for use in EORTC trials owing to anticipated problems with data reduction and interpretation: the first yields a single, overall score reflecting the sum of the individual items, while the second treats each item separately. In the former case, the total quality of life score was considered too coarse for meaningful interpretation. In the latter case, there was concern that the absence of subscales summarizing the individual items would yield unreliable data and would result in information overload.

Given the absence of other well-validated, cancer-specific questionnaires, the study group elected to embark on the long-term process of instrument development and testing. Within the overall framework of the "core plus module" assessment strategy outlined above, a number of criteria were established for constructing the EORTC questionnaire. General agreement was reached that the questionnaire should be (a) specific to cancer; (b) designed primarily for patient self-completion; (c) multidimensional in structure, covering at least four basic quality of life domains—physical symptoms, physical and role functioning, psychological functioning, and social functioning; (d) composed primarily of multi-item scales; and (e) relatively brief. Additionally, the instrument had to meet standards set for reliability, validity, and responsiveness to clinical changes in patients' health status over time. Finally, given the international context of EORTC clinical trials, the questionnaire had to be amenable for use across national and cultural boundaries (i.e., to exhibit cross-cultural as well as statistical validity).

For each substantive quality of life domain considered for inclusion in the core questionnaire, a position paper was prepared that summarized the relevant literature and identified potential items and/or subscales that might be adopted, with or without revision. These position papers were circulated among the study group members for comment, and then were discussed in a series of plenary meetings. These meetings were particularly valuable in ensuring the clinical relevance of proposed content areas and the cross-cultural appropriateness of candidate items. For example, compared with other quality of life measures, the EORTC core questionnaire contains a relatively large number of items assessing disease-related symptoms and treatment-related side effects. This was done primarily at the insistence of the clinicians within the study group who argued that physical symptoms are of central concern when assessing the quality of life of cancer patients under active treatment. They also predicted that their clinical colleagues would be more apt to accept the more psychosocially oriented components of the questionnaire if physical symptoms were first adequately addressed. In practice, this indeed proved to be the case.

The multicultural composition of the study group had fewer consequences for the selection of content areas to be covered by the core questionnaire than some might perhaps expect. In large part, this may be attributed to the fact that the quality of life domains considered for inclusion in the questionnaire were quite broad, reflecting basic issues of physical, psychological, and social health and functioning. Additionally, the decision to employ an *unweighted* scoring system avoided the need for eliciting patients' preferences for different health states. Such preferences (e.g., the relative value placed on physical versus psychological well-being) are more likely to be affected by cultural values and norms than is the choice of relevant domains per se.

The involvement of individuals representing a broad range of cultures and languages was, however, quite important in assuring that the wording of questionnaire items remained relatively simple, straightforward, and free of jargon. Idiomatic expressions such as ''walking a block'' or ''feeling down in the dumps'' were studiously avoided, as were culture-specific examples employed to clarify the meaning of specific items (e.g., ''playing tennis or bowling'' to illustrate a rigorous level of physical activity). Careful attention to such issues during the initial phase of questionnaire development resulted in an original source document (in English) that could be translated with relative ease into other languages.

TWO GENERATIONS OF CORE QUESTIONNAIRES

The EORTC QLQ-C36

The first generation core questionnaire, the QLQ-C36 (24), consisted of 36 items organized into four functional scales (physical, role, emotional, and social functioning), two symptom scales (fatigue and nausea/vomiting), and a global perceived health status/quality of life scale.

Additional single items assessed other common symptoms (e.g., pain, dyspnea, sleep problems), as well as the perceived financial impact of the disease and its treatment (Table 1).

Standard forward-backward translation procedures were employed to generate each language version of the questionnaire. Typically, four or more individuals were involved in the translation process, all of whom were bilingual (some with English as their native tongue, others with the target language). This was an iterative process, involving several rounds of forward and backward translation before a satisfactory, provisional translation could be achieved. Documentation of the translation process, including copies of all forward and backward translations, was forwarded to a central coordinator for review.

The provisional translations were then pretested in each participating country. A small sample of patients (typically 10 to 15) was asked to complete the questionnaire, as well as a number of ''debriefing questions'' regarding (a) the time it took to complete the questionnaire, (b) whether any assistance was required, (c) whether there were any questions that were either confusing or upsetting, and (d) any additional comments on the questionnaire's content or layout.

Problems encountered with the questionnaire in either the translation or the pretesting phase were reviewed in plenary session. In some cases this resulted in only minor modifications in question wording. In other cases more substantive changes were made in the content of the questionnaire. For example, an early version of the QLQ-C36 contained several questions intended to assess future health perspective (e.g., whether patients expected their health to improve as a result of treatment). However, because many patients were reluctant to answer such questions (either because they felt that

TABLE 1. *Content areas of the EORTC QLQ-C36 and the QLQ-C30*

Quality of life domains	QLQ-C36	QLQ-C30
Functioning scales/items		
Physical	7	5
Role	2	2
Emotional	8	4
Cognitive	1	2
Social	2	2
Global quality of life	2	2
Symptom scales/items		
Fatigue	5	3
Nausea and vomiting	2	2
Pain	1	2
Dyspnea	1	1
Sleep disturbance	1	1
Appetite loss	1	1
Constipation	1	1
Diarrhea	1	1
Financial impact	1	1
Total	36	30

they were not in a position to do so or because they found them to be too upsetting) they were subsequently deleted from the questionnaire.

Following the pretest phase, the QLQ-C36 was field tested in a large sample of lung cancer patients ($n = 537$) drawn from 15 countries, including most Western European countries, Australia, Canada, and Japan. Although the overall psychometric results were promising (24), they also indicated the need for further developmental work on selected items and scales. Most of the revisions involved only minor changes in the wording of items. A few noninformative items were discarded. The only scale requiring substantial revision, due to inadequate reliability, was the eight-item emotional functioning scale.

The EORTC QLQ-C30

The second generation core questionnaire, the QLQ-C30 (25), employs the same basic structure as the QLQ-C36. The QLQ-C30 includes five functional scales (physical, role, emotional, social, and cognitive functioning), three symptom scales (fatigue, pain, and nausea and vomiting), a global health status/quality of life scale, and a number of single items assessing additional symptoms (dyspnea, sleep disturbance, constipation, and diarrhea) and perceived financial impact (Table 1). The principal changes in the QLQ-C30 from the QLQ-C36 include replacement of the eight-item emotional functioning scale with a shorter four-item scale, inclusion of an additional pain item (thus creating a two-item scale), and separating out memory and concentration problems, yielding a two-item cognitive functioning scale (see Appendix for the item content of the QLQ-C30).

For the majority of the QLQ-C30 items a four-point Likert-type response scale is used. Exceptions include the physical and role functioning scales (employing dichotomous response choices) and the global health status/quality of life scale (where a seven-point scale is used). For ease of presentation and interpretation, all subscale and individual item responses are linearly converted to a 0 to 100 scale. For the functional and global quality of life scales, a higher score represents a better level of functioning. For the symptom scales and items, a higher score reflects a greater degree of symptomatology.

As with the QLQ-C36, the QLQ-C30 was submitted to international field-testing in a sample of lung cancer patients ($n = 305$) drawn from 12 countries: Australia, Belgium, Canada, Denmark, France, Germany, Italy, the Netherlands, Norway, Sweden, the United Kingdom, and the United States. Detailed results of the study are reported elsewhere (25). The following discussion provides a brief summary of the key findings of this study, as well as of a number of additional studies that have generated data relevant to examining the reliability and validity of the QLQ-C30 in a wide range of patient populations and treatment settings. These latter studies included patients with head-and-neck cancer (26,27), patients with acquired immune deficiency syndrome (AIDS) or a human immunodeficiency virus (HIV) infection (28), and heterogeneous patient samples (including breast, ovarian, lung, gastrointestinal, prostate and testicular cancer, melanoma, and lymphoma) (29–34).

Reliability

Table 2 summarizes the findings from seven published studies (including the original, international field study) in which the reliability (i.e., internal consistency) of the multi-item scales of the QLQ-C30 has been assessed. In the original field study, internal consistency coefficients for the QLQ-C30 scales ranged from .52 (for the role functioning scale) to .89 (for the global health status/quality of life scale). The .70 reliability criterion recommended for group comparisons was met for eight of the nine scales at one or both of the assessment points.

Evaluation of the reliability of the QLQ-C30 across languages and cultures was an essential element of this study. While a country-by-country or language-by-language analysis would have been preferable, the sample size requirements for such an analysis were prohibitively large. As a more feasible alternative, reliability tests were repeated for three subgroups of patients, organized into those from English-speaking countries, those from Northern Europe, and those from Southern Europe. With one exception, the scale reliability estimates were very similar across these three broad cultural subgroups. The reliability of the nausea and vomiting scale was substantially lower for the Southern European patients. This could be explained largely by the fact that these patients were significantly less likely to have received emesis-inducing treatment than were those from Northern Europe or from English-speaking countries (i.e., the lack of score variance in the Southern European sample resulted in a low internal consistency estimate for this scale).

Across all seven studies reviewed, the scales exhibiting the most consistently high internal consistency include the overall quality of life scale (range = .80 to .94), the fatigue scale (range = .80 to .91), the emotional functioning scale (range = .73 to .85), and the pain scale (range = .70 to .86). The remaining scales yield lower, and generally less consistent, reliability estimates.

Results from the three studies that employed a longitudinal design (25,28,31) indicate that the reliability of the QLQ-C30 scales improves with repeated measurement. This may reflect the fact that the distribution of scores is often narrower at baseline assessment (i.e., prior to the start of treatment) than at later assessment points (i.e., during treatment).

To date, no published data are available on the test-retest reliability or stability of the QLQ-C30 scales. Studies are currently being performed in Canada, Norway, and the Netherlands that will yield this type of reliability data.

TABLE 2. *Internal consistency (Cronbach's alpha) of the QLQ-C30 scales*

Author	n	Sample	Design		PF	RF	EF	CF	SF	FA	PA	NV	QL
Aaronson et al. (25)	305	Lung cancer	Longitudinal	T1	.68	.54	.73	.56	.68	.80	.82	.65	.86
				T2	.71	.52	.80	.73	.77	.85	.76	.73	.89
Bjordal and Kaasa (26)	126	Head and neck cancer	Cross-sectional		.74	.74	.83	.28	.77	.84	.70	.82	.90
Bjordal et al. (27)	204	Head and neck cancer (long-term survivors)	Cross-sectional		.74	.74	.85	.73	.77	.88	.79	.56	.93
de Boer et al. (28)	156	HIV/AIDS	Longitudinal	T1	.64	.31	.82	.69	.40	.83	.81	.55	.80
				T2	.76	.43	.85	.69	.73	.91	.85	.66	.86
Fosså (29)	177	Heterogeneous cancer diagnoses	Cross-sectional		.61	.53	.75	.69	.72	.83	.85	.84	.91
Osoba et al. (30)	535	Ovarian cancer, breast cancer, lung cancer	Longitudinal	T1	.68	.54	.73	.56	.68	.80	.82	.65	.86
				T2	.75	.53	.84	.58	.83	.90	.83	.78	.94
Ringdal & Ringdal (31)	177	Heterogeneous cancer diagnoses	Cross-sectional		.75	.55	.85	.65	.72	.83	.86	.84	.85

PF, physical functioning; RF, role functioning; EF, emotional functioning; CF, cognitive functioning; SF, social functioning; FA, fatigue; PA, pain; NV, nausea/vomiting; QL, quality of life; T1, first measurement; T2, second measurement.

Validity

Table 3 summarizes the available published data relevant to assessing the validity of the QLQ-C30. In all of the studies reviewed, validity has been examined in terms of the ability of the QLQ-C30 scales to distinguish between subgroups of patients formed on the basis of their clinical or treatment status (i.e., clinical validity, known-groups comparisons). The grouping variables employed in these analyses have included primary diagnosis (30), stage of disease (28,30), performance status (25,28), weight loss (25), treatment status (26,27,29), treatment toxicity (25), and prognosis (32).

Across studies, the physical functioning, role functioning, fatigue, and overall quality of life scales have exhibited consistently high levels of known-groups validity. This is not unexpected in that the grouping variables used in these analyses tend to reflect physical rather than psychosocial attributes of the disease and its treatment.

Moderate evidence of scale validity was found for the pain, emotional functioning, and social functioning scales. The two scales that performed least well in distinguishing between patient subgroups were those assessing cognitive functioning and nausea/vomiting. In the case of the nausea and vomiting scale, both the internal consistency and validity estimates are higher when the analysis includes a substantial number of patients receiving emesis-inducing therapy (data not shown).

Two studies (26,33) have investigated the construct validity of the QLQ-C30 emotional functioning scale by correlating it with the General Health Questionnaire, a widely used

TABLE 3. *Known-groups validity of the QLQ-C30 functional and symptom scales*

Author	Grouping variable	PF	RF	EF	CF	SF	FA	PA	NV	QL
Aaronson et al. (25)	Pretreatment ECOG performance status	●	●	●	●	○	●	●	●	●
	On-treatment ECOG performance status	●	●	●	●	●	●	●	●	●
	Pretreatment weight loss	●	●	○	○	○	●	○	○	●
	Treatment toxicity	○	●	●	●	●	●	●	●	●
Bjordal and Kaasa (26)	Acute/subacute treatment toxicity	○	○	○	○	●	●	●	○	●
Bjordal et al. (27)	Conventional vs. hypofractionated radiotherapy	○	●	●	○	●	●	○	○	●
de Boer et al. (28)	AIDS vs. symptomatic HIV	●	○	●	○	○	○	○	○	○
	Karnofsky performance status	●	●	○	○	●	●	○	○	●
Fosså (29)	Treatment status (on versus off)	●	●	●	○	●	●	●	●	●
Osoba et al. (30)	Local vs. metastatic disease	●	●	○	○	●	●	●	○	●
	Primary tumor site	●	●	○	○	●	●	●	○	●
Ringdal et al. (32)	Prognosis	●[a]	●[a]	○	○	○	●	●	●[b]	●

[a]The physical and role functioning scales were combined to form a single, personal functioning scale.
[b]The nausea/vomiting scale was combined with the single item on appetite loss.
PF, physical functioning; RF, role functioning; EF, emotional functioning; CF, cognitive functioning; SF, social functioning; FA, fatigue; PA, pain; NV, nausea/vomiting; QL, quality of life; ●, a statistically significant (p < .05) between-group difference in mean scores; ○, no statistically significant between-group difference in mean scores was found.

measure of psychological distress. In both studies, the two measures were found to be significantly correlated ($r = .70$ and $.61$, respectively). Niezgoda and Pater (33) also found moderate support for the construct validity of the QLQ-C30 pain scale, which correlated significantly with the sensory affective ($r = .57$) and the pain intensity ($r = .53$) subscales of the McGill Pain Questionnaire.

Current and Planned Research

A number of single-country studies are currently being conducted or are being planned to test proposed refinements in the content and scale structure of the QLQ-C30. These include (a) an alternative role functioning scale that incorporates a broader spectrum of role activities (i.e., not only work and household jobs, but also hobbies and leisure time activities) and a wider range of response categories (i.e., a four-point Likert-type response scale rather than dichotomous response choices); (b) a revised physical functioning scale that employs four-point, rather than dichotomous, response choices; (c) a revised overall health status/quality of life scale in which less weight is placed on the physical aspects of health; and (d) the use of structural equation models and confirmatory factor analysis to construct higher-order physical and psychosocial component scores. Additionally, two large scale, international field studies will be initiated by the study group in 1995 to test the psychometric and cross-cultural performance of the QLQ-C30 (incorporating the revisions noted above) in patients with breast cancer and with head-and-neck cancer.

Perhaps the most efficient means of generating additional psychometric data on the QLQ-C30 is to employ it in prospective clinical trials. According to records kept by the EORTC data center in Brussels, there are currently 27 EORTC phase II or phase III clinical trials that are employing the QLQ-C30. Additionally, the questionnaire is being used in over 100 clinical investigations being carried out by other clinical trial groups (e.g., the National Cancer Institute–Canada, the U.S.–based Cancer and Leukemia Group B, the U.K.–based Medical Research Council), by individual institutions, or by the pharmaceutical industry. As these studies mature, a wealth of data should become available relating to the performance of the questionnaire in the research setting for which it was primarily designed.

THE DEVELOPMENT OF SUPPLEMENTARY QUESTIONNAIRE MODULES

An essential component of the EORTC measurement strategy involves the use of supplementary questionnaire modules that, when employed in conjunction with the QLQ-C30, can provide more detailed information relevant to evaluating the quality of life of specific patient populations. A module may be developed to assess (a) disease symptoms related to a specific tumor site (e.g., urinary symptoms in prostate cancer); (b) side effects associated with a given treatment (e.g., chemotherapy-induced neuropathy); or (c) additional quality of life domains affected by the disease or treatment (e.g., sexuality, body image, fear of disease recurrence). In some cases, the content of a module is intended to expand on issues touched on only briefly within the core instrument (e.g., dyspnea or pain). In other cases, entirely new subject matter may be covered (e.g., alopecia, sexuality).

The Lung Cancer Module

The first questionnaire module developed within the EORTC was designed to address specific symptoms associated with lung cancer and its treatment. This 13-item questionnaire was developed primarily on the basis of expert advice from chest physicians involved in the study group and the Lung Cancer Cooperative Group. It incorporated two multiple-item scales to assess dyspnea and pain, and a series of single items assessing coughing, sore mouth, peripheral neuropathy, alopecia, and hemoptysis. The format of the questions and the response categories parallel those employed with the core questionnaire.

The lung cancer module was employed in the initial international field studies of both the QLQ-C36 and the QLQ-C30, yielding a data base with over 700 patients. While the hypothesized scale structure could be only partially confirmed, all of the symptom measures (both scales and individual items) were able to discriminate clearly between patients differing in performance status. Additionally, all symptom and toxicity scores changed significantly over time, with disease symptoms declining and treatment toxicities increasing during the treatment period. The observed pattern of self-reported, treatment-related symptoms was consistent with expectations, with those patients undergoing chemotherapy reporting problems with hair loss and peripheral neuropathy, and patients receiving radiotherapy reporting increased difficulties with swallowing (34).

Guidelines for Module Development

The lung cancer module represented the first attempt within the study group to develop supplemental questionnaires for use in combination with the core instrument. Because this module was constructed in parallel with the core instrument, full advantage could be taken of the existing research infrastructure in carrying out the requisite tasks (e.g., item generation, translation, and pretesting). It was recognized, however, that future work on module development would require a somewhat modified research infrastructure and a revised set of procedures. In particular, greater reliance would have to be placed on smaller subgroups of investigators within the study group, each with interest, expertise, and experience in a specific field (e.g., breast cancer, palliative care, sexuality research). While such decentralization of effort brings with it a greater degree of flexibility and increased efficiency, it also necessitates the development of clear guidelines to ensure consistently high standards of work and optimal coordination of activities.

Formal guidelines for the development of EORTC questionnaire modules have recently been published (35). These guidelines outline four phases in the module development process: (a) generation of relevant quality of life issues; (b) development of questionnaire items and scales (c) module pretesting; and (d) large scale, international field-testing. Each of these phases will be described briefly, in turn.

To generate an exhaustive list of quality of life issues to be considered for inclusion in a new module, three sources of information are drawn upon consecutively. First, literature searches are conducted to identify relevant issues, as well as any available instruments designed to address those issues. A small sample (e.g., 5–10) of health care professionals is then asked to evaluate the comprehensiveness of the resulting list (in combination with the core instrument), to rate the relative importance of each issue to the target patient population of interest, and to suggest any additions or deletions. Finally, this amended list, together with the core instrument, is administered to a small (e.g., 10–15) sample of patients representative of those to whom the module is targeted. The patients are asked to report the extent to which they have experienced the physical and/or psychosocial problems enumerated, and to indicate any significant omissions in the list.

In the second phase, the resulting list of quality of life issues is operationalized into specific questionnaire items. These items may be adapted from existing instruments (with the explicit permission of the instrument's authors), or may be newly generated. Whenever possible, the same format and time frame as that of the QLQ-C30 is employed.

In the third phase of module development a new sample of patients (e.g., 10–15) drawn from the target population is asked to complete the core questionnaire, the provisional module, and the series of "debriefing" questions described earlier. Based on the results of the pretest, the provisional questionnaire may require further adaptation (e.g., deletions, additions, or rewording of items).

Finally, the questionnaire module is ready for larger scale, international field-testing. Since the number of patients consulted during phase I (generation of quality of life issues) and phase III (pretesting) is limited, the basis on which to eliminate (or add) issues and/or items is relatively narrow. The module to be field-tested may therefore contain a larger pool of items than is actually necessary for reliable assessment, and the field-testing allows for further refinement of the module based on standard psychometric analyses. For purpose of external validation of the module, additional sociodemographic and clinical data are collected, and other instruments intended to measure the same or similar quality of life issues may be administered (for purposes of concurrent validation). Additionally, repeated administrations of the module permits the evaluation of its responsiveness to changes over time.

Ideally, each step of the module development process should be carried out simultaneously in a wide range of languages and countries. This approach, however, may not always be possible. A more feasible alternative is to involve a more limited number of countries, each representing a broadly defined geographic and cultural category (e.g., Anglo-Saxon countries, Northern Europe, and Southern Europe), in the three initial phases of module development. A less desirable, but still acceptable, option is to limit the module construction process to at least two countries, one representing Anglo-Saxon cultures, and one non–Anglo-Saxon cultures. In practice, a reasonable degree of flexibility is necessary in the rules governing the composition of module development teams. Ultimately, one is dependent on the interest and initiative of individual investigators to get the developmental process going. However, the sooner one can achieve true international collaboration, the greater is the likelihood that the resulting questionnaire module will be appropriate for use in a cross-cultural research context.

Prior to initiating international field-testing of a module, high-quality translations need to be generated in *all* relevant languages. Thus, even if a particular country is not involved directly in the early stages of module development, potential cross-cultural problems may still be detected during the translation and within-country pretesting phase. If these problems are of a serious-enough nature, they can necessitate further refinements in the module's item content or wording.

Since different subsets of the study group's members are involved in module construction, quality control and coordination of activities are of critical importance. To ensure uniformly high quality in questionnaire modules, the entire developmental process is subject to internal peer review. A committee composed of study group members not involved directly in the development of a given module is asked to evaluate each step of the process on the basis of a written report. The module's developers may be requested to provide additional explanatory information to justify any deviations from the standard procedures and, in the case of serious deviations, may be asked to repeat one or more of the steps in the process.

As a means of facilitating coordination of activities within the study group, all documents relating to modules that have been developed or that are under construction are housed in a central data base. The purpose of maintaining this data base is to facilitate communication and retrieval of information about available modules, to avoid duplication of effort, and to optimize compatibility in module construction.

Questionnaire modules currently under development within the study group include those for (a) breast cancer, (b) head-and-neck cancer (36), (c) colorectal cancer, (d) oesophageal cancer, (e) use in palliative care settings, and (f) assessing patient satisfaction with medical care. We are also aware of efforts outside of the EORTC to develop modules for primary brain cancer, testicular cancer, prostate cancer, and for assessing body image whereby the investigators are adhering, at least in part, to the EORTC guidelines.

CONCLUSIONS

In this chapter we have described a modular approach to assessing the quality of life of cancer patients developed by the EORTC Study Group on Quality of Life. This approach involves two principal elements: (a) a ''core'' questionnaire designed for use across a broad range of cancer patient populations, irrespective of diagnosis; and (b) diagnostic-specific and/or treatment-specific questionnaire modules intended to supplement the core instrument. The current core questionnaire, the QLQ-C30, is the product of more than a decade of collaborative research. While some minor fine-tuning of the questionnaire may still be forthcoming, it has been judged sufficiently mature to justify its adoption as the standard quality of life instrument for use in EORTC clinical trials.

Following its release for general use in the spring of 1993, the QLQ-C30 has been introduced into a wide range of non-EORTC, university- and industry-based clinical trials as well. The multinational nature of many of these studies has necessitated translating the questionnaire into a large number of languages. Currently, translations of the QLQ-C30 are available or are pending in 24 languages. All of these translations have been generated according to standard guidelines, have been accompanied by written documentation of the translation process, and have been submitted to a centralized review process.

The substantive focus of the study group has now shifted to the construction of supplementary questionnaire modules. In generating these modules, advantage can be taken of the many lessons learned during the development of the core instrument. At the same time, however, the module development process brings with it a new set of challenges. In particular, the need to decentralize responsibility for module construction, while maintaining high scientific standards, calls for a flexible research infrastructure. The availability of standard guidelines for module development, as outlined briefly in this chapter, is intended to facilitate the work of semi-independent teams of investigators on the one hand, and efficient overall project management and coordination on the other.

The EORTC, with its clinical focus, its multidisciplinary membership, and its multicultural orientation, provides a rather unique context for developing and testing quality of life questionnaires. Key decisions regarding the form and content of such questionnaires are, in large part, guided by the substantive research questions being addressed by the clinical cooperative groups, and by the practical constraints operating within these groups. By encouraging a balanced representation of professional disciplines—including oncologists, social scientists, research methodologists, and statisticians—in the instrument development process, it is possible to assure that issues relating to clinical relevance and methodologic rigor receive equal attention. Additionally, the cultural diversity of the EORTC membership facilitates the construction of questionnaires whose content and style of presentation are appropriate for use among patients recruited from a wide range of countries.

Finally, it is important to emphasize that the process of generating cross-culturally appropriate quality of life measures is an iterative one, necessitating a willingness to incorporate changes in research procedures and revisions in research products as new information becomes available. During the early phases of questionnaire construction, it is expected that decisions regarding the form and content of a questionnaire will be of a provisional nature. Yet, experience suggests that the need for additional revisions is often recognized only after a questionnaire has entered into wider circulation. For example, in the translations of the QLQ-C30 released for general use, no consideration had been given to the need for gender-specific versions of the questionnaire. In large part, this could be attributed to the fact that the validation studies carried out within the EORTC had employed samples with a predominance of male patients (e.g., lung cancer). Only when the questionnaire was introduced into multinational studies in breast cancer did the need for a female-gender version of the questionnaire become apparent (e.g., in French, Italian, Spanish, and Polish).

In the short term, the need to respond flexibly to feedback regarding the performance of a questionnaire will understandably be met with some resistance. Every suggestion for revision, however minor, implies many weeks, if not months, of additional work. Yet, in the long run, attention to such detail can only increase the validity, both psychometric and cross-cultural, of the instruments that we are increasingly coming to rely upon to evaluate the impact of cancer and its treatment on the quality of life of our patients.

ACKNOWLEDGMENTS

The current members of the EORTC Study Group on Quality of Life are, in alphabetical order: N. Aaronson, The Netherlands Cancer Institute, Amsterdam, The Netherlands; S. Achard, Hôtel-Dieu de Paris, Paris, France; M. Ahiner-Elmqvist, Malmö General Hospital, Malmö, Sweden; S. Ahmedzai, The Leicestershire Hospice, Leicester, United Kingdom; N. Ambler, Frenchay Hospital, Bristol, United Kingdom; F. Anagnostopoulos, Oncological Hospital "Sts Anargyri," Athens, Greece; J. J. Arraras, Clinica Universitaria, Pamplona, Spain; A. Barbosa, Lisbon, Portugal; B. Bergman, Renströmska Hospital, Götenborg, Sweden; J. Bernhard, Swiss Group for Clinical Cancer Research, Bern, Switzerland; K. Bjordal, The Norwegian Radium Hospital, Oslo, Norway; J. Blazeby, Bristol Royal Infirmary, Bristol, United Kingdom; C. Bolund, Karolinska Hospital, Stockholm, Sweden; G. Borghede, Sahlgrenska Hospital, Götenborg, Sweden; A. Brédart, Institut Jules Bordet, Brussels, Belgium; M. Bullinger, Biometric Center for Therapeutic Studies, Munich, Federal Republic of Germany; P. Csepe,

Semmelweis University of Medicine, Budapest, Hungary; A. Cull, Imperial Cancer Research Fund (ICRF) Medical Oncology Unit, Edinburgh, United Kingdom; F. van Dam, The Netherlands Cancer Institute, Amsterdam, The Netherlands; R. Dunlop, St Christopher's Hospice, London, United Kingdom; M. Eisemann, Umea University, Umea, Sweden; P. Erbil, University of Istanbul, Istanbul, Turkey; P. Fayers, MRC Cancer Trials Office, Cambridge, United Kingdom; A. Filiberti, Instituto Nazionale Tumori, Milan, Italy; H. Flechtner, University of Cologne, Cologne, Federal Republic of Germany; J. Franklin, MD Anderson Cancer Center, Houston, Texas; H. Funaki, London, United Kingdom; K. Gamble, Royal Marsden Hospital, London, United Kingdom; F. Gil, Memorial Sloan-Kettering Cancer Center, New York, New York; M. Groenvold, University of Copenhagen, Copenhagen, Denmark; H. de Haes, Academic Medical Center, Amsterdam, The Netherlands; P. Hopwood, CRC Psychological Medicine Group, Manchester, United Kingdom; C. Hürny, Swiss Group for Clinical Cancer Research, Bern, Switzerland; S. Kaasa, Trondheim University Hospital, Trondheim, Norway; D. Kissane, Monash Medical Centre, Clayton, Victoria, Australia; M. Klee, Rigshospitalet, Copenhagen, Denmark; M. Koller, Phillips University Marburg, Marburg, Federal Republic of Germany; T. Küchler, University Hospital Eppendorf, Hamburg, Federal Republic of Germany; G. Lavrentiadis, Psychiatric Hospital Thessaloniki, Thessaloniki, Greece; D. Machin, MRC Cancer Trials Office, Cambridge, United Kingdom; J. Maher, Mount Vernon Hospital, Northwood, United Kingdom; J. Meyza, The Maria Sklodowska-Curie Memorial Cancer Center, Warsaw, Poland; C. Morris, Lasaretts Ansluten Hemsjukvård, Motala, Sweden; C. Moynihan, Royal Marsden Hospital, Sutton, United Kingdom; M. Nordenstam, Axlagarden Hospice, Umea, Sweden; D. Osoba, British Columbia Cancer Agency, Vancouver, Canada; R. Paridaens, Universitaire Ziekenhuizen, Leuven, Belgium; M. Peetermans, Universiteit Antwerpen, Gravenwezel, Belgium; A. Piga, Ospedale Torrette, Ancona, Italy; F. Porzsolt, Tumor Center Ulm, Ulm, Federal Republic of Germany; D. Razavi, Institut Jules Bordet, Brussels, Belgium; P. Rofe, Royal Adelaide Hospital, Adelaide, South Australia; S. Schraub, Centre Hospitalier Regional de Besançon, Besançon, France; R. Schwarz, University of Heidelberg, Heidelberg, Federal Republic of Germany; S. Serbouti, EORTC Data Center, Brussels, Belgium; M. Sprangers, The Netherlands Cancer Institute, Amsterdam, The Netherlands; R. Stephens, MRC Cancer Trials Office, Cambridge, United Kingdom; F. Takeda, Saitama Cancer Centre, Saitama, Japan; E. Tollesson, Sahlgrenska Hospital, Göteborg, Sweden; M. Watson, Royal Marsden Hospital, Sutton, United Kingdom; S. Wright, Leicester General Hospital, Leicester, United Kingdom; and R. Zittoun, Hôtel-Dieu de Paris, Paris, France.

The authors would also like to thank J. Beckmann, J. Bernheim, S. Bindemann, D. Crabeels, N. Duez, U. Frick, M. Kerekjarto, K. Sneeuw, and A. Stewart for their earlier contributions to the work of the study group.

REFERENCES

1. McMillen Moinpour C, Feigl P, Metch B, Hayden KA, Meyskens FL Jr, Crowley J. Quality of life end points in cancer clinical trials: review and recommendations. *J Natl Cancer Inst* 1989;81:485–495.
2. Kornblith AB, Anderson J, Cella DF, et al. Quality of life assessment of Hodgkin's disease survivors: a model for cooperative clinical trials. *Oncology* (Williston Park) 1990;4:93–101.
3. Finkelstein DM, Cassileth BR, Bonomi PD, Ruckdeschel JC, Ezdinli EZ, Wolter JM. A pilot study of the Functional Living Index–Cancer (FLIC) Scale for the assessment of quality of life for metastatic lung cancer patients. *Am J Clin Oncol* 1988;11:630–633.
4. Osoba D. The quality of life committee of the clinical trials group of the National Cancer Institute of Canada: organization and functions. *Qual Life Res* 1992;1:203–211.
5. Aaronson NK, Beckmann J, eds. *The quality of life of cancer patients.* EORTC Monograph Series, vol 17. New York: Raven Press, 1987.
6. Aaronson NK, van Dam FSAM, Polak CE, Zittoun R. Prospects and problems in European psychosocial oncology: a survey of the EORTC Study Group on Quality of Life. *J Psychosoc Oncol* 1986; 4:43–53.
7. Ganz PA, Bernhard J, Hürny C. Quality of life and psychosocial oncology research in Europe: state of the art. *J Psychosoc Oncol* 1991; 9:1–22.
8. Nayfield SG, Hailey BJ, eds. *Quality of life assessment in cancer clinical trials.* Bethesda, MD: Division of Cancer Prevention and Control, National Cancer Institute, U.S. Department of Health and Human Services, 1991.
9. American Cancer Society. American Cancer Society's second workshop on methodology in behavioral and psychosocial cancer research. *Cancer* 1991;67(suppl).
10. Stjernswärd J, Teoh N. Perspectives on quality of life and the global cancer problem. In: Osoba D, ed. *Effect of cancer on quality of life.* Boca Raton: CRC Press, 1991:1–5.
11. Johnson JR, Temple R. Food and Drug Administration requirements for approval of new anticancer drugs. *Cancer Treat Rep* 1985;69: 1155–1159.
12. Henderson-James D, Spilker B. An industry perspective. In: Spilker B, ed. *Quality of life assessment in clinical trials.* New York: Raven Press, 1990:183–192.
13. Kleinman A, Eisenberg L, Good B. Culture, illness and care: clinical lessons from anthropologic and cross-cultural research. *Ann Intern Med* 1978;88:251–258.
14. Payer L. *Medicine and culture.* New York: Henry Holt, 1988.
15. Bullinger M, Anderson R, Cella D, Aaronson NK. Developing and evaluating cross-cultural instruments: from minimum requirements to optimal models. *Qual Life Res* 1993;2:451–459.
16. Sprangers MAG, Aaronson NK. The role of health care providers and significant others in evaluating the quality of life of patients with chronic disease: a review. *J Clin Epidemiol* 1992;45:743–760.
17. Slevin ML, Plant H, Lynch D, et al. Who should measure quality of life, the doctor or the patient? *Br J Cancer* 1988;57:287–295.
18. Ware JE, Brook RH, Davies-Avery A, et al. *Conceptualization and measurement of health of adults in the health insurance study, Vol 1: Model of health and methodology.* Santa Monica, CA: Rand Corporation, 1980.
19. Stewart Al, Ware JE, eds. *Measuring functioning and well-being: the medical outcomes study approach.* Durham, NC: Duke University Press, 1992.
20. Priestman TJ, Baum M. Evaluation of quality of life in patients receiving treatment for advanced breast cancer. *Lancet* 1976;1:899–901.
21. Schipper H, Clinch J, McMurray A, Levitt M. Measuring the quality of life of cancer patients: The Functional Living Index-Cancer: development and validation. *J Clin Oncol* 1984;2:472–483.
22. Aaronson NK, Bullinger M, Ahmedzai S. A modular approach to quality of life assessment in cancer clinical trials. *Recent Results Cancer Res* 1988;111:231–249.
23. Selby PJ, Chapman JAW, Etazadi-Amoli J, Dalley D, Boyd NF. The development of a method of assessing the quality of life of cancer patients. *Br J Cancer* 1984;50:13–20.
24. Aaronson NK, Ahmedzai S, Bullinger M, et al. The EORTC core quality of life questionnaire: interim results of an international field

study. In: Osoba D, ed. *Effect of cancer on quality of life.* Boca Raton: CRC Press, 1991:185–203.

25. Aaronson NK, Ahmedzai S, Bergman B, et al. The European Organization for Research and Treatment of Cancer QLQ-C30: a quality-of-life instrument for use in international clinical trials in oncology. *J Natl Cancer Inst* 1993;85:365–376.

26. Bjordal K, Kaasa S. Psychometric validation of the EORTC core quality of life questionnaire, 30-item version and a diagnosis-specific module for head and neck cancer patients. *Acta Oncol* 1992;31:311–321.

27. Bjordal K, Kaasa S, Mastekaasa A. Quality of life in patients treated for head and neck cancer: a follow-up study 7 to 11 years after radiotherapy. *Int J Radiat Oncol Biol Phys* 1994;28:847–856.

28. de Boer JB, Sprangers MAG, Aaronson NK, Lange JMA, van Dam FSAM. The feasibility, reliability and validity of the EORTC QLQ-C30 in assessing the quality of life of patients with a symptomatic HIV infection or AIDS (CVC IV). *Psychol Health* 1994;9:65–77.

29. Fosså S. Quality of life assessment in unselected oncologic out-patients: a pilot study. *Int J Oncol* 1994;4:1393–1397.

30. Osoba D, Zee B, Warr D, Kaizer L, Latreille J. Psychometric properties and responsiveness of the EORTC quality of life questionnaire (QLQ-C30) in patients with breast, ovarian and lung cancer. *Qual Life Res* 1994;3:353–364.

31. Ringdal GI, Ringdal K. Testing the EORTC quality of life questionnaire on cancer patients with heterogenous diagnoses. *Qual Life Res* 1993; 2:129–140.

32. Ringdal GI, Ringdal K, Kvinnsland S, Götestam KG. Quality of life of cancer patients with different prognoses. *Qual Life Res* 1994; 3:143–154.

33. Niezgoda HE, Pater JL. A validation study of the domains of the core EORTC quality of life questionnaire. *Qual Life Res* 1993;2:319–325.

34. Bergman B, Aaronson NK, Ahmedzai S, Kaasa S, Sullivan M. The EORTC QLQ-LC13: a modular supplement to the EOLRTC core quality of life questionnaire (QLQ-C30) for use in lung cancer clinical trials. *Eur J Cancer* 1994;30a:635–642.

35. Sprangers MAG, Cull A, Bjordal K, Groenvold M, Aaronson NK. The European Organization for Research and Treatment of Cancer approach to quality of life assessment: guidelines for developing questionnaire modules. *Qual Life Res* 1993;2:287–295.

36. Bjordal K, Ahlner-Elmqvist M, Tollesson E, Jensen AB, Razavi D, Maher EJ, Kaasa S. Development of a European Organization for Research and Treatment of Cancer (EORTC) questionnaire module to be used in quality of life assessments in head and neck cancer patients. *Acta Oncol* 1994;33:879–885.

APPENDIX: ITEM CONTENT OF THE EORTC QLQ-C30

1. Do you have any trouble doing strenuous activities, like carrying a heavy shopping bag or a suitcase?
2. Do you have any trouble taking a *long* walk?
3. Do you have any trouble taking a *short* walk outside of the house?
4. Do you have to stay in a bed or a chair for most of the day?
5. Do you need help with eating, dressing, washing yourself, or using the toilet?
6. Are you limited in any way in doing either your work or doing household jobs?
7. Are you completely unable to work at a job or to do household jobs?
8. Were you short of breath?
9. Have you had pain?
10. Did you need to rest?
11. Have you had trouble sleeping?
12. Have you felt weak?
13. Have you lacked appetite?
14. Have you felt nauseated?
15. Have you vomited?
16. Have you been constipated?
17. Have you had diarrhea?
18. Were you tired?
19. Did pain interfere with your daily activities?
20. Have you had difficulty in concentrating on things, like reading a newspaper or watching television?
21. Did you feel tense?
22. Did you worry?
23. Did you feel irritable?
24. Did you feel depressed?
25. Have you had difficulty remembering things?
26. Has your physical condition or medical treatment interfered with your *family* life?
27. Has your physical condition or medical treatment interfered with your *social* activities?
28. Has your physical condition or medical treatment caused you financial difficulties?
29. How would you rate your overall *physical condition* during the past week?
30. How would you rate your overall *quality of life* during the past week?

Note: The EORTC QLQ-C30 is a copyrighted questionnaire. Requests for permission to use the questionnaire and for scoring instructions should be addressed to the Quality of Life Unit, EORTC Data Center, Avenue E. Mounier 83, Bte 11, 1200 Brussels, Belgium.

Quality of Life and Pharmacoeconomics in Clinical Trials, Second Edition, edited by B. Spilker. Lippincott-Raven Publishers, Philadelphia © 1996.

CHAPTER 22

The EuroQoL Instrument:
An Index of Health-Related Quality of Life

Paul Kind

INTRODUCTION

There can be little doubt that the measurement of outcome forms an essential component in the evaluation of health care. While there may be general support for the principle of measuring health status, and hence for deriving quantitative data on health outcomes, there is no corresponding consensus regarding the means of executing such measurement. An ever-growing number of studies incorporate measures of health status, but the task of comparing their results is complicated by the use of different (and oftentimes incompatible) instruments. In this field of inquiry there are no standard units of measure; indeed it seems improbable that a "gold standard" could be defined. But given the proliferation of new instruments there does seem to be a niche for a simple device that could be used *alongside* other measures, to enable the comparison of results obtained in different disease groups, in different care settings, and in different countries.

It was against this broad background, therefore, that a multidisciplinary group of researchers from England, Finland, the Netherlands, Norway, and Sweden came together early in 1987 to discuss common problems arising from their experience of developing and applying measures of health status, and to investigate practical solutions. This initial meeting led ultimately to the development of the EuroQoL—a multidimensional measure of health-related quality of life, capable of being expressed as a single index value.

This chapter does not give a definitive account of the genesis of the EuroQoL, but rather an abbreviated and partial history, which should suffice to provide the reader with evidence of a serious research project that continues to address a series of long-standing issues of interest to those committed to the clinical and economic evaluation of health care.

DESIGNING THE EuroQoL

The design of any measure of health status must take account of the areas of application for which it is intended, since these will influence the properties of the measure and the way in which it is constructed. For example, measures intended for use with a well-defined condition should be designed so as to detect important clinical stages, and to respond to changes in a patient's clinical state. By contrast, such sensitivity may not be required in a general-purpose instrument designed for use as an adjunct to such condition-specific measures, or for use in population health surveys. Several generic instruments capable of being used in this way have been developed, but they mostly suffer from limitations that undermine their potential—notably in the absence of any social preferences indicating the values to be attached to different aspects of health status, and in their inability to represent health status as an aggregated index.

P. Kind: Centre for Health Economics, University of York, York, Y01 5DD, England.

In considering the descriptive content of a new measure, a degree of compromise has to be expected in trading off its complexity and comprehensiveness, against practical considerations of ease of administration. An exhaustive list of items covering large tracts of personal health experience may be descriptively interesting, but can also be tiring for the respondent or interviewer administering it. The multidimensional nature of health status has led some researchers to the view that it can only be measured by simultaneously observing a large set of independent dimensions. While this "profile" approach has clear resonance for those who wish to have detailed information on individual patients, it proves to be less useful as such information passes through the decision-making hierarchy, where considerations are centered on the evaluation of programs of care rather than on interventions for specific patients.

Several related design features were established by the EuroQoL group from the outset. It was universally agreed that irrespective of any other consideration, the group required a measure that was capable of representing health status as a single index value. The group recognized explicitly that only a small number of health-related dimensions could be tapped, since wider coverage would impose greater costs on respondents and researchers alike. Within each dimension it would be possible to create subdivisions, but as the number of such levels increases, there is an exponential rise in the number of composite health states that can be defined. For example, six dimensions each with two levels yields a total of $2^6 = 64$ states. By expanding the number of levels within dimensions from two to three, the number of possible health states increases from 2^6 to 3^6, or 729—an 11-fold increase. The number of dimensions/levels, and consequently health states, has a direct bearing on the type of scaling method that can be utilized in order to derive valuations, and here too the group determined that a simple, self-administered method was required. Such methods again, are most readily applicable to relatively small descriptive systems. Finally, it was envisaged that the new instrument would be completed by respondents themselves, avoiding the need for interviewers. Since it was expected that this task would be *additional* to other measures of health status, it was accepted that this too would require simplicity (1).

DESCRIBING HEALTH STATUS

Any indicator of health status requires a means of systematically *describing* health. As previously remarked, a central requirement in the design of the EuroQoL was simplicity of completion, which in turn indicated that only a small number of dimensions of health status could be included. Given that there is a far larger set of dimensions that could be potentially used, some means of determining the descriptive content had to be decided. The choice of descriptive content could be informed through empirical study, for example using semistructured interviews (2). This approach gener-

ates a considerable volume of information, which although grounded in the perception of individual respondents, has still to be "coerced" into a more-structured form suitable for the purposes of constructing a health status measure. An alternative strategy was adopted by the EuroQoL group, in which researchers principally drew on their own expertise and the evidence available from the literature in order to determine the dimensions of interest. Dimensions were selected following a detailed review of the descriptive content of the extant health status measures, including the Quality of Well-Being Scale (3), the Rosser Index (4), the Sickness Impact Profile (5), and the Nottingham Health Profile (6). Other measures then in use by the group were also reviewed, including the 15-D (7) and the Health Measurement Questionnaire (8).

The original descriptive system resulted from extensive discussion within the group, which included substantial time devoted to issues relating to the acceptability of concepts in different national settings. Although English was the common language adopted by the group for these discussions, and it is this language that constitutes the standard form of the measure, language variants were simultaneously developed for all countries represented by the original researchers. The initial descriptive system was based on six dimensions, each being divided into two or three categories. This generated a total of 216 health states, formed by combining discrete levels from each dimension. The dimensions were

EuroQoL descriptive system

- **Mobility**
  1 .. No problems in walking about
  2 .. Some problems in walking about
  3 .. Confined to bed

- **Self-care**
  1 .. No problems with self-care
  2 .. Some problems washing or dressing self
  3 .. Unable to wash or dress self

- **Usual activity** *
  1 .. No problems with usual activity
  2 .. Some problems with usual activity
  3 .. Unable to perform usual activity

- **Pain / discomfort**
  1 .. No pain or discomfort
  2 .. Moderate pain or discomfort
  3 .. Extreme pain or discomfort

- **Anxiety / depression**
  1 .. Not anxious or depressed
  2 .. Moderately anxious or depressed
  3 .. Extremely anxious or depressed

FIG. 1. Classification of health states.

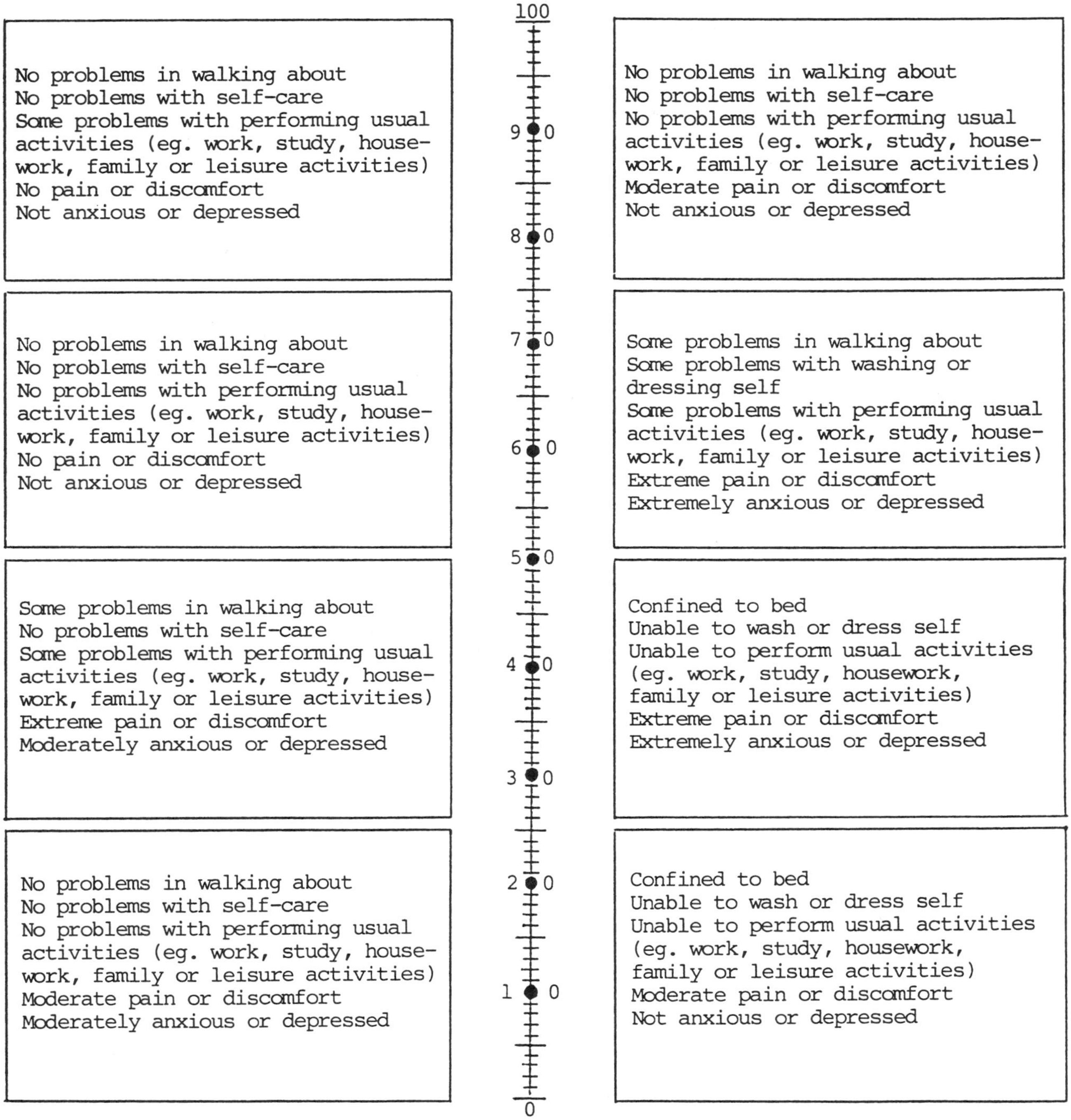

Best
imaginable
health state

100

No problems in walking about
No problems with self-care
Some problems with performing usual
activities (eg. work, study, house-
work, family or leisure activities)
No pain or discomfort
Not anxious or depressed

No problems in walking about
No problems with self-care
No problems with performing usual
activities (eg. work, study, house-
work, family or leisure activities)
Moderate pain or discomfort
Not anxious or depressed

9 0

8 0

No problems in walking about
No problems with self-care
No problems with performing usual
activities (eg. work, study, house-
work, family or leisure activities)
No pain or discomfort
Not anxious or depressed

7 0

Some problems in walking about
Some problems with washing or
dressing self
Some problems with performing usual
activities (eg. work, study, house-
work, family or leisure activities)
Extreme pain or discomfort
Extremely anxious or depressed

6 0

5 0

Some problems in walking about
No problems with self-care
Some problems with performing usual
activities (eg. work, study, house-
work, family or leisure activities)
Extreme pain or discomfort
Moderately anxious or depressed

Confined to bed
Unable to wash or dress self
Unable to perform usual activities
(eg. work, study, housework,
family or leisure activities)
Extreme pain or discomfort
Extremely anxious or depressed

4 0

3 0

No problems in walking about
No problems with self-care
No problems with performing usual
activities (eg. work, study, house-
work, family or leisure activities)
Moderate pain or discomfort
Moderately anxious or depressed

2 0

Confined to bed
Unable to wash or dress self
Unable to perform usual activities
(eg. work, study, housework,
family or leisure activities)
Moderate pain or discomfort
Not anxious or depressed

1 0

0

Worst
imaginable
health state

PLEASE CHECK THAT YOU HAVE DRAWN ONE LINE FROM EACH BOX
(that is, 8 lines in all)

FIG. 2. Standardized questionnaire for valuing EuroQoL health states.

reviewed after several feasibility studies conducted concurrently in England, Netherlands, Sweden, Norway and Finland, which examined, *inter alia,* valuations for standard sets of EuroQoL health states. Two important changes were introduced as a consequence. Analysis of the separate contribution of each dimension revealed that social relationships played little part in determining health state valuations. The number of dimensions was consequently reduced from six to five, with social relationships being incorporated within the "usual activities" dimension, which encompasses work, study, housework, family, and leisure activities. A further modification involved dividing all dimensions into three, indicating "no problem," "some problem," and "extreme problem." This introduced a more balanced structure for each dimension, giving equal salience to each component in the resulting composite health states. The current descriptive system, shown in Fig. 1, is made up of five dimensions each of three levels, defining 243 health states. In addition to these states defined in terms of the five dimensions of the EuroQoL descriptive system, two further states have been specified—death and unconscious—so that the final tally rises to 245 states.

Valuing Health States

In the same way that opinion is divided on the issue of the form and descriptive content of health status measures, so too opinion divides on the means by which valuations for health states are obtained. A wide range of techniques have been deployed in pursuit of this objective, including magnitude estimation (9), category scaling (10), and utility scaling methods such as standard gamble (11) and time trade-off (12). For the EuroQoL group, the choice of scaling method was largely driven by practical considerations. Methods were excluded if they were considered likely to impose a significant experimental burden, in terms of either the resource costs of collecting data or the complexity facing individual respondents. A graphical rating system, based on a vertical 20-cm visual analog scale that had previously been used by one of the original EuroQoL group (7), was selected as the standard means of capturing valuations for health states. The end points of the scale are labeled "best imaginable health state" and "worst imaginable health state," and have numeric values of 100 and 0, respectively. Although it was agreed that all researchers would include this valuation method in their own local studies, several other scaling methods at one time or another have been used alongside the standard "thermometer," including paired comparisons, equivalence scaling, several variants of category rating, standard gamble, time trade-off, and a form of multiattribute scaling.

A standardized questionnaire has been evolved for the collection of health state values. Descriptions of 16 health states, in two groups of eight, are presented over two consecutive pages. Each of these pages has a common format, as shown in Fig. 2. Four states are printed on either side of the "thermometer" rating scale. Respondents are asked to draw a line from each state to the thermometer, indicating how good or bad that state is. The logically best health state (with no problem on any dimension), and the logically worst state (with extreme problems on all dimensions) are reproduced on *both* pages of the questionnaire. Although originally included as a test of consistency, this duplication has been maintained so as to provide a constant perceptual framework. As well as recording values for nonfatal health states, respondents are also requested to indicate a value for death by marking the visual analog scale accordingly.

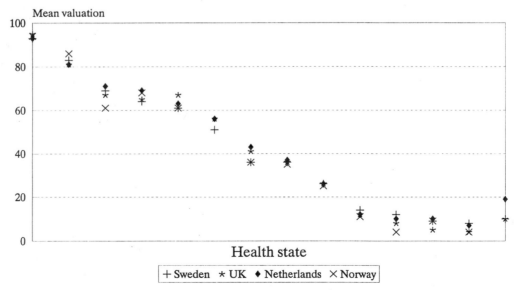

FIG. 3. Valuations for EuroQoL health states.

Values for EuroQoL Health States

The EuroQoL classification defines a fixed number of health states, but leaves open the issue of what value should be assigned to each of those states. Valuations for EuroQoL health states have been obtained in several population studies, in the Netherlands (13), Sweden (14), Norway (15), and the UK (16). These early results indicated that valuations for a standard set of EuroQoL health states were broadly similar, as can be seen in Fig. 3, which plots the mean values from these four countries.

More recently, valuations for EuroQoL states have been obtained in several other European and Nordic countries, including Spain, France, Germany, and Finland, as well as in non-European countries such as Thailand and Australia. As might have been anticipated, the initial pattern of similarity in valuations seen between studies conducted in different countries has given way to one of diversity. The most recent study, conducted in the UK, elicited valuations from over 3,330 individuals in face-to-face interviews. As is standard practice within the EuroQoL Group, all surveys incorporate the basic valuation method shown in Fig. 2, as well as such additional valuation tasks as are required by the local research group. In the case of the UK national survey, this involved both the thermometer and time trade-off methods. The test-retest reliability of health state valuations was investigated as part of a large population survey conducted in the Netherlands (17).

THE EuroQoL INSTRUMENT

It is important to distinguish between the classification of health states defined by the EuroQoL descriptive system and its associated set of health state valuations, and the method by which individuals describe and rate their current health status. Figure 4 shows the full EuroQoL instrument used for this second purpose.

Information generated by these six items of data can be used in four distinct ways. First, for individual respondents or groups of respondents, a *profile* of health status can be formed, containing information on the level of reported problems. Figure 5 reports on data from a series of postal surveys conducted in the UK with members of the general public, together with similar data obtained from a survey in the Netherlands (18). For each of the five EuroQoL dimensions it gives the proportions of respondents indicating any problem. Almost a third of respondents reported a problem with pain and about one in six indicated a problem with anxiety or depression. There appears to be a marked difference in the frequency of reported problem with usual activity. Individual self-reported health status described in this way can be used to distinguish between significant subgroups, for example in demonstrating variations associated with age, as shown in Fig. 6, which gives the percentage of reported problem in two groups—respondents aged 60 and under, and respondents aged over 60. It might be expected that older respondents would report significantly more problems than younger respondents, and indeed this proves to be the case for all dimensions except anxiety and depression. Presented separately, these data provided a qualitative picture of reported problems described in terms of the EuroQoL dimensions.

The second descriptive form in which these self-report data can be represented is achieved by converting the original responses for each respondent, into one of the 243 unique EuroQoL states. For example, a respondent indicating levels 2 on mobility, 2 on self-care, 3 on usual activity, 1 on pain/discomfort, and 2 on anxiety/depression would be categorized as being in state 22312. The majority of respondents in UK general population surveys appear to report problems with pain and discomfort, and/or anxiety and depression. Results from a 1993 postal survey are typical, as shown in Table 1. A third of respondents had a problem with either pain or mood, or both.

For each EuroQoL state there exists a corresponding valuation. Hence, the third form in which these self-report data can be represented is an index, in which the appropriate valuation replaces the classified state. Had the state 11121 been given a value of, say 0.85, then this would be the weighted health status given to a respondent who indicated some problem with pain (level 2 on dimension 4). Repeated observation using this index form of the EuroQoL provides cardinal data on changes in health status, and thus on health outcomes.

The second page of the EuroQoL instrument asks respondents to mark a point on the standard 20-cm thermometer, indicating their rating of their own health status on a scale bounded by 0 and 100. This generates a fourth form of self-reported health status. Figure 7 shows the mean values of self-rated health status recorded in a series of postal surveys conducted in the UK. The mean values for adjacent age groups are for the most part statistically significant.

While the responses on the first page shown in Fig. 2 can be converted into one of the EuroQoL health states, the corresponding valuation for that state is imported from a previously determined tariff of values generated by third parties, for example, from surveys of the general public. The self-rated visual analog scale scores, by contrast, give an indication of the respondent's personal value for that health state. That value may, or may not, accord with the valuations arising from a general population tariff. Both forms of weighted index value might be used in evaluating changes in health status, with one set being expressed in terms of community preferences and the second in terms of the values held by the beneficiaries of care.

Methodological and Design Issues

Since its inception, the EuroQoL classification and methods of obtaining values for defined health states have been

By placing a tick (thus ☑) in one box in each group below, please indicate which statements best describe your own health state today.

Mobility

- : I have no problems in walking about
- : I have some problems in walking about
- : I am confined to bed

Self-Care

- : I have no problems with self-care
- : I have some problems washing or dressing myself
- : I am unable to wash or dress myself

Usual Activities

- : I have no problems with performing my usual activities (e.g. work, study, housework, family or leisure activities)
- : I have some problems with performing my usual activities
- : I am unable to perform my usual activities

Pain/Discomfort

- : I have no pain or discomfort
- : I have moderate pain or discomfort
- : I have extreme pain or discomfort

Anxiety/Depression

- : I am not anxious or depressed
- : I am moderately anxious or depressed
- : I am extremely anxious or depressed

Compared with my general level of health over the past 12 months, my health state today is

PLEASE TICK ONE BOX

- : Better
- : Much the same
- : Worse

A

FIG. 4. The EuroQoL instrument for self-rated health status.

To help people say how good or bad a health state is, we have drawn a scale (rather like a thermometer) on which the best state you can imagine is marked by 100 and the worst state you can imagine is marked by 0.

We would like you to indicate on this scale how good or bad is your own health today, in your opinion. Please do this by drawing a line from the box below to whichever point on the scale indicates how good or bad your current health state is.

```
┌─────────────────────────────┐
│                             │
│      Your own health        │
│       state today           │
│                             │
└─────────────────────────────┘
```

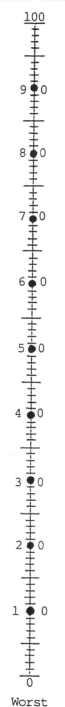

FIG. 4. *Continued.*

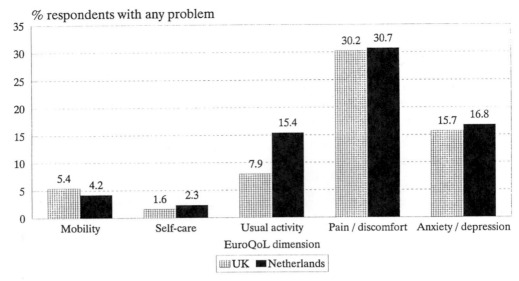

FIG. 5. Self-reported health-status (postal survey results).

the subject of systematic inquiry by the group. As well as pursuing an agreed-upon research agenda, individual researchers have followed their own particular lines of inquiry, exposing a wide range of additional issues to critical review. It is to be expected that these endeavors will be reported personally in peer-reviewed journals by individuals concerned. Some of the issues that have been investigated over the past years continue to be unresolved, either in the context of the EuroQoL system, or more generally with respect to any index of health status. For example, no single method of health state valuation has yet been recognized as standard, although so far as the valuation of EuroQoL health states is concerned, all participant research groups incorporate visual

analog scaling alongside any other method that they are using.

Layout and Presentational Issues

At a practical level, there are questions related to the construction of a health status measure that are open to empirical study, and several such subjects have received attention. The presentation of health state descriptions has been one such topic. Composite health states defined by the EuroQoL descriptive system consist of a series of phrases, each drawn from one of the corresponding dimensions, and

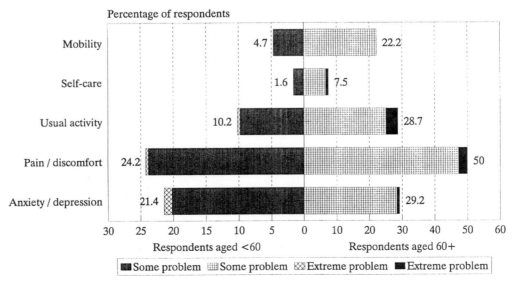

FIG. 6. Variation in self-reported health status, discriminating by age.

TABLE 1. *Results from postal survey*

EuroQoL state	Respondents (%)
1 1 1 2 1	11.5
1 1 1 1 2	10.4
1 1 1 2 2	5.4
1 1 2 2 1	3.4
1 1 2 2 2	2.2
1 1 2 1 1	1.7
2 1 2 2 1	1.7

the textual description of these health states is presented within a rectangular box. The number of health states presented on each page of the questionnaire was determined in the first instance simply by the space available on a sheet of paper. Given 16 states (including two duplicated states used for test-retest purposes), the standard layout required two pages, with eight states being presented on each. Alternative formats, which varied the number of states per page and the length and orientation of the visual analog scale, were tested.

Results suggested that the number of health state descriptions that are presented on a page does appear to influence the values given to those states. A single health state when judged in the context of four such states has a different value to that which results when that same state is presented as one among eight states. Valuations obtained from vertical and horizontal thermometers were not significantly different. The performance of the vertical thermometer was further examined by halving its length to 10 cm. This shortened version was used to value groups of four states as opposed to the eight states in the standard EuroQoL layout. Valuations obtained using a shorter scale differed significantly for some states, but it was unclear whether this resulted from the reduced length of the thermometer and the consequent compression of the valuation scale, or from other contextual effects.

Perceptual Set

In any study that involves the use of practical or conceptual material that is unfamiliar, it is difficult to control completely for the respondents' interpretation of the task they are asked to undertake. Some direction can be achieved through an introductory statement. In the case of the EuroQoL the standard preamble directs respondents to judge health states with respect to "people like you." The influence of this preamble on valuations for health states was explored in a postal survey. Half the questionnaires mailed out contained a modified introductory text that encouraged respondents to consider the difficulties in making decisions in allocating the health service's scarce resources. Respondents were reminded that the information they gave would be used to help determine health priorities. This policy-oriented version of the questionnaire yielded somewhat higher scores for the more severe EuroQoL states than resulted from the standard version.

Consistency in Judging Health State Values

Each of the EuroQoL dimensions can be regarded as an ordinal scale in which level 2 is worse than level 1, and level 3 is worse than level 2. It follows, therefore, that for some health states there is an expected ordinal relationship based on the logical structure of its components. For example, if states A and B are respectively 13221 and 12221, then it follows that state A is logically worse than state B,

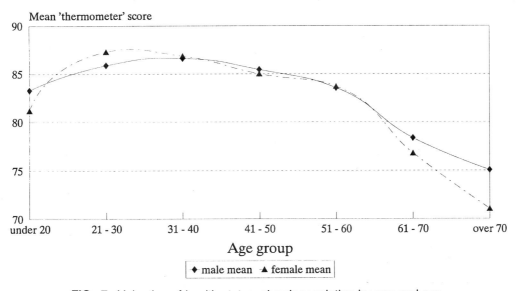

FIG. 7. Valuation of health status, showing variation by age and sex.

since for each dimension in state A the level is equal to or worse than the corresponding level for state B. A respondent who gave a value for state A that was *better* than that given to state B would be valuing the states in a way that violated the underlying logical structure, and in that narrow respect might be labeled as inconsistent. There is clear evidence that older respondents display higher levels of logical inconsistency, as do respondents with lower levels of education. Modifying the number of states presented for valuation on each page also appears to adversely affect individual respondent's consistency.

Valuation of Death

In its original format, the EuroQoL questionnaire contained a box labeled ''being dead'' as one of the standard set of health states to be rated. However, significant numbers of respondents failed to record a value for death. Such respondents tended to be older than those who supplied such a value. Write-in comments on returned questionnaires suggested that some respondents were reluctant to place any value on death, and that for others, ''death'' was not considered to be a state of health. Some respondents gave scores indicating that death was close to the ''best imaginable health state.'' Other techniques for eliciting a value for death have been used, including the paired comparisons judgments in which respondents are asked to indicate whether a health state is better or worse than death. However, the issue of identifying a value for death using questionnaire-based visual analog scale methods remains problematic.

Other Factors Affecting Valuations

Information on respondents' self-reported current health status, together with data on their experience of serious illness in themselves, their family or others, has been used to test the impact of these variables on valuations for EuroQoL health states. Respondents who report a problem on any EuroQoL dimension, tend to give higher valuations to all health states than were recorded by respondents who indicate no problem on any of the EuroQoL dimensions. A slightly different result is obtained if current health status is measured using the self-rated thermometer scores. Those who score their own health below the median for the general population, give higher valuations to the poorer health states, indicating that these states are not so severe. However, these same respondents give *lower* valuations to the mild states, producing a compression effect with responses tending to occupy the mid-range of the thermometer scale.

THE CONTINUING RESEARCH AGENDA

The EuroQoL-based research outline here only partially describes the extent of work of the group as a whole. Several substantial issues remain to be tackled, including the improvement of response rates in postal surveys, and the investigation of any response bias. We know little about the personal characteristics of nonresponders and their health state valuations. Some reassurance can be taken from the knowledge that values obtained in face-to-face interviews (with a high compliance rate) do not differ substantially from those obtained from postal surveys.

The measurement characteristics of visual analog scale ratings has still to be thoroughly investigated, although there is evidence that categorical scaling models applied to such data yield results that are similar to health state valuations based directly upon the thermometer scores. If personal preferences are to be incorporated within a system of health state valuations, then accessible methods are required to capture that information. Adopting such an approach confers significant advantage on health status measures that can then truly be said to represent the patient's point of view.

CONCLUSIONS

Given the considerable lead time and resource costs of developing a new measure, it would seem prudent to pause and take stock. While several generic measures exist, as profiles or indexes, little is known about the relationship between them. Comparisons have been made between the EuroQoL and other generic measures, such as the SF-36 (19), but more systematic inquiry is needed to establish the ways in which information generated on one measure can be mapped into another. This exercise is by no means limited to comparison with generic measures, and the nature of links between the EuroQoL and clinically specific measures has to be investigated, too. Here the problem is one of information management. Its low-cost profile and high information yield have led to a surge of interest in the EuroQoL, with consequent difficulty in tracking the wide range of clinical studies that now incorporate it.

Finally, the progress that has been achieved in developing the EuroQoL has been made possible by a working practice based on a quite remarkable openness and willingness to exchange material that has characterized the group since its very beginning. This powerful scientific tradition of unqualified collaboration indicates that progress will continue to be made in the future.

REFERENCES

1. EuroQoL Group. EuroQoL—a new facility for the measurement of health-related quality of life. *Health Policy* 1990;16:199–208.
2. van Dalen H, Williams A, Gudex C. Lay people's evaluation of health: are there variations between different subgroups? *J Epidemiol Community Health* 1994;48:248–253.
3. Patrick DL, Bush JW, Chen MM. Methods for measuring levels of well-being for a health status index. *Health Services Res* 1973;8:228–245.
4. Rosser RM, Watts VC. The measurement of hospital output. *Int J Epidemiol* 1972;1:361–368.

5. Bergner M, Bobbitt RA, et al. The Sickness Impact Profile: conceptual formulation and methodology for the development of a health status measure. *Int J Health Services* 1976;6(2):393–415.

6. Hunt S, McEwen J. The development of a subjective health indicator. *Soc Health Illness* 1980;2:231–246.

7. Sintonen H. An approach to measuring and valuing health states. *Soc Sci Med* 1981;15c:55–65.

8. Gudex C, Kind P. The HMQ: measuring health status in the community. Discussion Paper #93. Centre for Health Economics, 1991.

9. Rosser RM, Kind P. A scale of valuations of states of illness: is there a social consensus? *Int J Epidemiol* 1978;7:347–358.

10. Kaplan RM, Bush JW, Berry CC. Category rating versus magnitude estimation for measuring levels of well-being. *Med Care* 1979;18(5):501–518.

11. McNeil BJ, Weichselbaum R, Pauker SG. Trade-offs between quality of life and quantity of life in laryngeal cancer. *N Engl J Med* 1981;305(17):982–987.

12. Sackett DL, Torrance GW. The utility of different health states as perceived by the general public. *J Chronic Dis* 1978;31:697–704.

13. Essink-Bot ML, Bonsel GJ, van der Maas PJ. Valuations of health states by the general public: feasibility of a standardized measurement procedure. *Soc Sci Med* 1990;31(11):1201–1206.

14. Brooks RG, Jendteg S, Lindgren B, Persson U, Bjork S. EuroQoL: health-related quality of life measurement. Results of the Swedish questionnaire exercise. *Health Policy* 1991;18:25–36.

15. Nord E. EuroQoL: health-related quality of life measurement. Valuations of health states by the general public in Norway. *Health Policy* 1991;18:25–36.

16. Kind P. Measuring valuations for health states: a survey of patients in general practice. Discussion Paper #76. Centre for Health Economics, 1990.

17. van Agt H, Essink-Bot M, Krabbe PFM, Bonsel GJ. Test-retest reliability of health state valuations collected with the EuroQoL questionnaire. *Soc Sci Med* 1994;39(11):1537–1544.

18. Stouthard MEA, Essink-Bot M. EuroQoL 1991—the Rotterdam survey: results in *EuroQoL Conference Proceedings,* Working Paper #2. Institute for Health Economics, University of Lund, 1992.

19. Brazier J, Jones N, Kind P. Testing the validity of the EuroQoL and comparing it with the SF-36 health survey questionnaire. *Qual Life Res* 1993;2:169–180.

Quality of Life and Pharmacoeconomics in Clinical Trials, Second Edition, edited by B. Spilker.
Lippincott-Raven Publishers, Philadelphia © 1996.

CHAPTER **23**

The Functional Assessment of Cancer Therapy (FACT) and Functional Assessment of HIV Infection (FAHI) Quality of Life Measurement System

David F. Cella and Amy E. Bonomi

INTRODUCTION

The *Functional Assessment of Cancer Therapy* (FACT) and the *Functional Assessment of HIV Infection* (FAHI) measurement systems are collections of self-report scales of quality of life for people with cancer and HIV infection. The general version of the instrument (FACT-G) has been validated in English (1–6) and is being used extensively in North America. Because item wording avoids specific terms such as *cancer* and *HIV infection,* they have also been used for people with other chronic medical conditions, such as kidney failure, liver disease, benign urinary incontinence, and multiple sclerosis. Specific modifications in the FACT are under way for these and other conditions. All of the subscales of the FACT measurement system were first developed in the English language, and have subsequently been translated into Spanish, primarily for use among Spanish-speaking people in the United States health care system. More recently, the FACT has been translated into six other languages in preparation for its use in European clinical trials. Nearly all patients with a sixth grade reading level can easily complete the FACT without assistance. There are

currently 14 scales available in English, 10 of which are disease-specific extensions of the 29-item general version (FACT-G) and include items relevant to a particular form of cancer. Nine of the 14 scales have been translated into Spanish. The first round of the six-language translation project (Dutch, French, German, Italian, Norwegian, and Swedish) was completed in September 1994. Currently available versions of the FACT are listed below (an asterisk indicates versions that are available in *English only*):

FACT-G:	A *g*eneral version of the scale, which can be used with patients of any tumor type and constitutes the core of the following disease, treatment, or symptom-specific subscales
*FAACT:	For patients with *a*norexia/*c*achexia related to cancer or HIV infection
FACT-A/F:	For patients with cancer-related *a*nemia or *f*atigue
FACT-B:	For patients with *b*reast cancer
*FACT-Bl:	For patients with *bl*adder cancer
FACT-BMT:	For patients undergoing *b*one *m*arrow *t*ransplant
*FACT-Br:	For patients with primary *br*ain tumors
FACT-C:	For patients with *c*olorectal cancer
*FACT-Cx:	For patients with *c*ervi*x* cancer

D. F. Cella and A. E. Bonomi: Rush-Presbyterian–St. Luke's Medical Center, Chicago, Illinois 60612.

FACT-H&N: For patients with *head* and *neck* cancer
FACT-L: For patients with *lung* cancer
FACT-O: For patients with *ovarian* cancer
FACT-P: For patients with *prostate* cancer
FAHI: For patients with *HIV infection*

A copy of version 3 of the FACT-G (English version) is in the Appendix.

THE GENERAL VERSION (FACT-G)

There are 29 Likert-type items that make up five general subscales common across all 14 scales. The number of scored items specific to the disease, treatment, or symptom making up the sixth subscale varies from 9 to 21. For every instrument, the five general (FACT-G) subscales are (a) Physical Well-Being, (b) Social/Family Well-Being, (c) Relationship with Doctor, (d) Emotional Well-Being, and (e) Functional Well-Being. A total score can also be obtained by summing each of the subscales. A summary of each scale, and the currently available additional subscales, is presented in Table 1. Although the FACT-G (version 3) is composed of 29 items, only 28 are scored in version 3. Thus, the numbers included in Table 1 reflect the total possible score for 28 items of the FACT-G.

There are *experimental items* (8,16,19,26,34 and the last item of "Additional Concerns") on the FACT-G. One additional item at the end of each subscale asks respondents to rate how much that particular aspect of life (e.g., physical well-being, social/family well-being) affects his or her quality of life. These ratings are made on a 0 to 10 scale, where a "0" corresponds with "not at all" and a "10" corresponds with "very much so." These items are currently experimental and may ultimately be used to weight subscale scores. For now, unweighted scores are used, so experimental items are not used in subscale or total quality of life scores. Ultimately, however, it is hoped that these experimental questions will allow patients to provide individualized weights. These weights can be applied to each subscale, enabling people to place emphasis upon quality of life dimensions that reflect their personal values or preferences.

Administration

The FACT scales are designed for patient self-administration, but can also be administered in an interview. For self-administration, patients should be instructed to read the brief directions at the top of the page. After the patient's correct understanding has been confirmed, he/she should be encouraged to complete every item in order without skipping any, except where directed (e.g., item 15). For interview administration, it is helpful to have the patient hold a card on which the response options have been printed.

TABLE 1. *FACT scale descriptions*[a]

Scale/subscale	No. of items	No. of items scored	Range of scores
Physical well-being	8	7	0–28
Social/family well-being	8	7	0–28
Relationship with doctor	3	2	0–8
Emotional well-being	7	5	0–20
Functional well-being	8	7	0–28
FACT-G total	34	28	0–112
Additional subscales			
Anorexia/cachexia (FAACT)	19	18	0–72
Cancer-related anemia or fatigue (FACT-A/F)	22	21	0–84
Breast cancer (FACT-B)	10	9	0–36
Bladder cancer (FACT-Bl)	13	12	0–48
Bone marrow transplant (FACT-BMT)	13	12	0–48
Brain tumor (FACT-Br)	20	19	0–76
Colon cancer (FACT-C)	10	9	0–60
Cervix cancer (FACT-Cx)	16	15	0–36
Head and neck cancer (FACT-H&N)	12	11	0–44
Lung cancer (FACT-L)	10	9,7[b]	0–36; 0–28
Ovarian cancer (FACT-O)	13	12	0–48
Prostate cancer (FACT-P)	13	12	0–48
Human immunodeficiency virus (HIV) infection (FAHI)	10	9	0–36

[a]Composition of these subscales is current as of June 1995. Number of items and score ranges are subject to change pending further study.
[b]As a result of psychometric analysis, the lung cancer subscale can be scored as a 9-item or 7-item index. Similar refinements are anticipated over time with other additional subscales.

Scoring

A scoring guide is provided in the FACT (version 3) manual (2). The scoring guide identifies those items that must be reversed before being added to obtain subscale totals. Items are reversed by subtracting the response from 4. After reversing proper items, all subscale items are summed to a total subscale score.

Handling Missing Items

If there are missing items, subscales scores can be prorated. This is done by multiplying the sum of subscale by the number of items in the subscale, then dividing by the number of items actually answered. This can be done on the manual scoring guide (2) or by using the formula below:

$$\text{Prorated score} = (\text{Sum of Item Scores}) \times (n \text{ of Items in Subscale}) \div (n \text{ of Items Answered})$$

When there are missing data, prorating by subscale in this way is acceptable as long as *more than* 50% of the items were answered (e.g., a minimum of 4 of 7 items, 2 of 2 items, 3 of 5 items, etc.). The total score is then calculated as the sum of the unweighted subscale scores. The FACT scale is considered to be an acceptable indicator of patient quality of life as long as *overall item response rate* is greater than 80% (i.e., at least 23 of 28 scored FACT-G items completed). This should not be confused with individual subscale item response rate, which allows a subscale score to be prorated for missing items if greater than 50% of items are answered.

Scoring the Specific Scales

The specific scales are FACT-A/F, B, Bl, BMT, Br, C, Cx, H&N, L, O, P, FAACT, and FAHI. The total score for the specific FACT subscales is the sum of the FACT-G (the first five subscales common to all scales) plus the "Additional Concerns" subscale. Again, over 50% of the items (e.g., 5 of 9 items, 7 of 12 items) must be completed in order to consider the subscale to be valid. For the "Additional Concerns" subscale (i.e., disease-specific questions), a scoring guide is available in the manual (2). The procedure for scoring is the same as described above for the FACT-G. The user scores only those items that apply to the specific scale completed (e.g., FACT-L; FACT-B). By following this scoring guide and transcribing the FACT-G score, the two totals can be summed to derive the *total fact score*. The foreign language versions can be scored on the English-language scoring guides (2).

Selecting Scores for Analysis

The FACT scoring templates allow one to obtain two different total scores in addition to each individual subscale score (2). The FACT-G total score provides a useful summary of overall quality of life across a diverse group of patients. The disease-specific questionnaire total scores (i.e., FACT-G plus disease-specific subscale score) may further refine the FACT-G summary score. Two alternative approaches are noteworthy, however. One is to separately analyze the FACT-G total score and the disease-specific subscale score. Another is to select subscales of the FACT that are most likely to be changed by an intervention being tested. For example, the Physical, Functional, and Disease-specific subscales would be most likely to change in a chemotherapy clinical trial. One could also consider creating a separate a priori index that sums two or three subscales. This has been done with the FACT-L, combining the Physical, Functional,

and seven-item Lung Cancer subscales into a 21-item Trial Outcome Index (7). On the other hand, the Emotional or Social Well-Being subscales would be expected to change most when evaluating a psychosocial intervention. This has been demonstrated, for example, with the FAHI by McCain and colleagues (8,9).

Development and Initial Validation Studies

Development and initial validation of the FACT instrument took place in four phases: item generation, item reduction, scale construction, and psychometric evaluation. Illustration of the first three phases can be found in descriptions of the development of the FACT-G (1) and of the FAACT (10). The last (fourth) phase resulted in the creation of the current version of the scale (version 3). Each of these phases will be described briefly.

Phase I: Item Generation

The purpose of this initial phase was to generate an exhaustive list of possible items that would later be systematically reduced. The largest possible starting list of items was generated by assembling expert panels of patients and oncology specialists. Patients with common solid tumors were selected as a starting point from which to generate items generic to most forms of cancer and items specific to each tumor type. To increase the likelihood that patients in this phase would have had sufficient experience with cancer symptoms and treatment side effects, eligibility was restricted to patients currently receiving treatment (including hormone therapy) for advanced (stage III or IV) cancer. It was also required that patients be able to read and speak English and that they have no known evidence of brain metastasis, delirium, psychosis, or severe depression.

Patients currently receiving treatment for advanced breast ($n = 15$), lung ($n = 15$), and colorectal ($n = 15$) cancer were approached to participate in a brief interview "to help develop a measure of quality of life for people with your illness." All agreed to participate in the 30-minute interview while they waited to see their oncologist or nurse. Median age of the patients was 60 (range, 27 to 76). Overall quality of life ratings were similar across groups. In cases where they differed, lung cancer patients reported the poorest quality of life and colorectal patients reported the best quality of life (3,6).

After gathering demographic and treatment information, patients were asked to complete a brief version of the Profile of Mood States (11) and two quality of life measures: the Functional Living Index–Cancer (FLIC) (12) and Spitzer et al.'s (13) Quality of Life Index (QLI), modified for self-administration. After completing the questionnaires, patients were asked to report as many "quality of life items" as they could imagine, given their experience with their disease and treatment. Patients were advised to use the existing scales they had just completed as guides, but were encouraged not to feel limited by them. After recording all patient responses to the open-ended prompt, the interview was slowly closed by asking increasingly specific questions about possible quality of life items related to their disease, their treatment, their physical, emotional, family, and social functioning, coping challenges, sexuality/intimacy, work, and future orientation.[1]

Oncology specialists had to meet the following qualifications to be eligible: (a) M.D. or R.N. degree, and (b) minimum 3 years' experience treating at least 100 patients having the tumor type in question. These 15 specialists (8 physicians and 7 nurses) were given samples of existing quality of life measures (FLIC, QLI) to review prior to and during the open-ended item generation interview. The specialists were asked to review the standardized test items from the perspective of "the typical patient with [*specified site*] receiving chemotherapy for advanced disease." The specialists were then asked to name any quality of life issues that did not receive adequate coverage in the existing set of questions. Their responses were combined with those of the patients. Three independent judges reviewed these tabulated items and rated them independently for overlap and/or irrelevance to quality of life. The judges then met to combine their ratings of each item and derive lists of quality of life items for each of the disease sites. After completing this process, the initial item pool for patients with breast cancer was 137; for those with colorectal cancer, 126; for those with lung cancer, 107. Subsequent review of item content by three independent raters revealed approximately 40% overlap across disease sites.

Phase II: Item Reduction

After all potential items were identified, the total number of items was reduced based on data obtained from a new sample of 90 patients receiving chemotherapy (30 lung, 30 breast, 30 colorectal). To incorporate input about patient values/preferences, each patient was asked to evaluate items for their relative importance to quality of life while they receive chemotherapy. The items were ranked by patients on a four-point Likert scale (1 = of little or no importance, 2 = somewhat important, 3 = very important, 4 = extremely important). Items that were generally rated as very and extremely important (median or mean greater than 3) were retained. While there were some items rated as important only to patients with one or two of the three cancer types, the majority of the items retained were common to patients across all three disease sites. The items that were common across disease sites were reviewed for redundancy by an independent panel of oncologists, oncology nurses, and social scientists, and similar items were eliminated. The remaining items were then reviewed for content. It was noted that the retained items were lacking in two domains (physical and sexual). To ensure adequate content validity, items emphasizing overall physical well-being, and intimacy/sexuality were re-added to form a final core of 38 "general" items. These items constituted version 1 of the Functional Assessment of Cancer Therapy–General (FACT-G).

In addition to these 38 items, a number of items surfaced as important only to patients with one or two of the original three cancer types. To accommodate these differences across sites, nine disease-specific items were included with the FACT-G to form the site-specific scales for lung cancer (FACT-L), colon cancer (FACT-C), and breast cancer (FACT-B). The specific items were selected based on a combination of the patients' and health professionals' responses. After gaining some experience with the FACT-G, FACT-L, FACT-B, and FACT-C, site-specific items were generated for the FACT-Bl, FACT-Br, FACT-Cx, FACT-H&N, FACT-O, FACT-P, and FAHI by combining expert-provided items with input from selected patients with each of these diseases. The FACT-BMT items were developed using a similar combination of 15 patients who had undergone bone marrow transplantation and six expert professionals. Finally, the FAACT and FACT-A/F were developed with expert input combined with that of patients who were currently symptomatic.

Phase III: Scale Construction

There are three versions of each FACT scale. There are two key differences between versions 1 and 2. The first is that version 2 omitted 10 items of the 38 original general items, due to their "fit" statistics, as described later. The second difference is that version 2 omitted the second response option regarding patient expectation for each item. This omission came from a desire to make the scale feasible in a clinical trial setting, *not* because any validity problem had been found with the second response option. A number of minor differences exist between versions 2 and 3. For example, item #3 has been slightly modified and now reads, "Because of my physical condition, I have trouble meeting the needs of my family." Also, item #25, "I worry that my condition will get worse," has been added to the Emotional Well-Being subscale of version 3, thus lengthening each of the scales by one item (so that now the FACT-G comprises the first 34 items of each instrument). Despite the addition of one item (#25) to the Emotional Well-Being subscale, scoring the FACT-G (version 3) remains unchanged from version 2 since the added question (#25) is not included in the current scoring.

Format of Version 1

The item presentation format for version 1 of the FACT was derived from the investigators' definition of quality of life, which included a comparison between *actual* and *expected* function and well-being (14). To ensure that the theoretical underpinnings of the investigators' definition were captured by the FACT measures, the format for item

---

[1]The item-generation interview guide is available on request.

presentation was presented to the 90 participants in phase II. Each patient was asked to comment on whether the distinction between *actual* and *expected* function can be made. Most (79 of 90) had little difficulty conceptualizing this distinction. Patients understood that *current expectation* is fluid and dependent upon a variety of personal, disease, and treatment considerations. They did not rate previous or preexisting expectations as fixed; rather they reported their expectations as analogous to aspirations for the future.

Piloting versions of the FACT format during the item-reduction phase of the study showed that patients prefer simultaneous reporting of actual and expected status. After deriving the 47 items (38 generic, 9 site-specific), ten new patients were presented with two versions of the same scale, using different formats. Nine of them preferred a ''Better, Worse, As expected'' format for the expectation ratings, to a dual-Likert format. As a result, the format used in version 1 was Likert for the rating of actual functioning and categorical (better, worse, as expected) for the expectation rating. Version 1 of the FACT scales can be found in Tchekmedyian and Cella (15,16).

In a sample of 425 mixed cancer patients, the correlation coefficient between logit scores for the total FACT and logit scores for the expectation rating on the FACT was .41, suggesting that while the two responses are moderately related to one another, there is unique information provided by asking patients about their expectations independent of their actual functioning. Further study of the two response formats will shed more light upon their relationship.

Format of Version 2

The 28 preserved items from FACT-G (version 1) and the site-specific items are formatted precisely the same as the actual functioning items of version 1. In addition to these items, there are six (five on the FACT-G) experimental items at the end of each subscale that assess patient appraisal of the extent to which each domain affects quality of life. These items are rated on a 0 to 10 numerical analogue scale. Version 2 of the FACT-G can be found in Cella et al. (1).

Format of Version 3

The FACT-G is now composed of 29 items due to the addition of one item to the Emotional Well-Being subscale. However, this item is not scored in FACT version 3. All other items, including the additional six experimental items, have been retained. (Version 3 of the FACT-G is presented in the Appendix.)

Phase IV: Psychometric Information on the FACT-G

The 38-item version 1 of the FACT-G was administered to 630 patients as part of a larger validation packet that included the following: The Functional Living Index-Cancer (FLIC) (12), a patient-completed version of the Quality of Life Index (QLI) (13), the Eastern Cooperative Oncology Group (ECOG) ''0–4'' performance status rating (PSR) (17), and shortened forms of the Profile of Mood States (Brief POMS) (11), the Taylor Manifest Anxiety Scale (TMAS) (18), and the Marlowe-Crowne Social Desirability Scale (M-CSDS) (19).

Basic psychometric information on the FACT-G is presented in Table 2. The 28-item FACT-G total score derived from the above administration is able to distinguish metastatic ($M = 79.6$) from nonmetastatic disease ($M = 83.7$), $F(1,334) = 5.38$, $p < .05$. It also distinguishes between stage I, II, III, and IV disease, $F(3,308) = 2.94$, $p < .05$. On the FACT-G, sensitivity to disease status was restricted to the Physical ($p < .01$) and Functional ($p < .01$) subscales. Concurrent validity is supported by strong correlations with the FLIC (.80) and the patient completed version of the QLI (.74). Initial evidence for construct validity is supported by (a) moderate to high correlations with mood state as measured by the shortened TMAS (.57) and the Brief POMS (.69), (b) moderate correlation with activity level as measured by the ECOG five-point PSR (.56), and (c) no correlation with social desirability as measured by the shortened M-CSDS (.03). More detail is provided elsewhere (1).

Table 2 presents subscale and FACT-G means and standard deviations on the standardization sample. Table 2 also

TABLE 2. *FACT-G psychometric information (n = 466 mixed cancer patients)*

Subscale	Scored items	Range of scores	Mean	Standard deviation	Alpha	Percent of variance[a]
Physical (P)	7	0–28	20.49	5.45	.82	22
Social (S)	7	0–28	21.93	4.77	.69	9
Emotional (E)	5	0–20	14.82	3.88	.74	6
Functional (F)	7	0–28	17.96	6.10	.80	9
Relationship with doctor (R)	2	0–8	6.85	1.51	.65	5
Total (P+S+E+F+R)	28	0–112	82.05	15.86	.89	51

[a]Percent of variance accounted for by the factor composed of items from each subscale in the oblique-rotated factor analysis.

provides information on internal consistency of each subscale and the total FACT-G score, as well as the percent of variance accounted for by each of the subscales in the factor analysis, which is explained briefly below and in more detail elsewhere (1,2). Internal consistency (coefficient alpha) of the 28-item FACT-G is .89, indicating that the multidimensional items also measure a central underlying factor. Alpha reliability was also uniformly high on the five subscales, even the two-item "Relationship with Physician" subscale (see Table 4).

Item Analysis

In addition to other approaches to data analysis, it was decided to use a Rasch Model rating scale analysis to examine the properties of the resulting scale. Using a procedure described by Wright and Linacre (20), single-person scores were produced in log odds units, and log odds difficulty scores were produced for each item. Fit statistics for each item are reported as mean square residuals. Inspection of item characteristic curves and outfit statistics led to a reduction in the number of FACT-G items from 38 to 28. These 28 items were then subjected to a factor analysis.

Factor Analysis

Because factor analysis requires interval scaling, a log-odds transformation was performed on each item to ensure that equal intervals existed across the five levels of each item. Because of conceptual, clinical, and empirical evidence supporting the fact that quality of life domains are modestly but significantly intercorrelated (21–23), it was decided to subject the factors to an oblique rotation so as to make them more interpretable. Factor-analysis was conducted on a sample of 545 patients with mixed cancer diagnoses. Six factors with eigenvalues greater than 1 were extracted, accounting for 51% of the total variance. A scree plot (24) supported the inclusion of all six factors. (See Table 2 for a breakdown of accounted variance by subscale.)

Studies Subsequent to Initial Validation Study

After creating version 2 of the FACT as described above, it became important to address three additional parameters with subsequent studies on new (i.e., previously untested with the FACT) groups of patients: test-retest reliability, sensitivity to change, and cross-cultural validation within the Spanish-speaking population.

Test-Retest Reliability

The FACT-G was administered to a previously untested sample of 70 outpatients with mixed cancer diagnoses. A second administration was planned within 3 to 7 days. Timing was prearranged to avoid chemotherapy administration between administration 1 and administration 2 of the FACT-G. Of the 70 patients who completed administration 1, 60 (86%) completed administration 2 within 3 to 7 days. Test-retest correlation coefficients for these 60 patients were as follows: Physical Well-Being, (.88); Functional Well-Being, (.84); Social Well-Being, (.82); Emotional Well-Being, (.82); Relationship with Doctor, (.83); and Total Score, (.92).

Sensitivity to Change

Sensitivity to change is an important capability of any quality of life instrument that is proposed to evaluate treatment or illness-related differences in a clinical trial. To a great extent, the performance of an instrument "in the field" will document its sensitivity. However, it was decided to obtain an early indication of whether subtests and the overall score would fluctuate as expected in patient groups that are known to change over time. A common (albeit global) parameter of change is performance status, and it was predicted that the physical and functional subtests would show the most significant sensitivity to change in this parameter, whereas other subtests might show marginal sensitivity to the related-but-distinct construct of performance status. The FACT was administered to an additional previously untested sample of 104 patients currently receiving chemotherapy for advanced breast, lung, or colon cancer. A second administration occurred 2 months later. Patient-reported performance status ratings (17) were also generated in an interview conducted before completion of the FACT. Patients were then categorized into three groups, according to change in performance status over time: those whose performance status declined ($n = 27$), those whose performance status improved ($n = 17$), and those whose performance status remained unchanged ($n = 60$). One-way analyses of variance then tested the ability of the subtests and the total score to distinguish the three groups. Results are presented in Table 3.

Cross-Cultural Validation

While it would be ideal to have an evaluation that could be applied to people who speak all languages, we have first chosen to translate the FACT scales into Spanish because, after English, Spanish is the most common language spoken in the United States. In order to demonstrate that the FACT scales are unbiased when they are applied to the Hispanic population, a very thorough "double (back)" translation procedure was used (25). The double (back) translation method employed two independent translators in sequence, with the first translation from English to Spanish, and then the Spanish version back into English. Comparisons were then made between the two versions in the original (English) language, to identify inconsistencies and loss or change of meaning. These inconsistencies were then resolved by the study team, in conjunction with a bilingual expert in linguis-

TABLE 3. *Preliminary evaluation of sensitivity to change in performance status: 2-month change score in FACT-G*

	n	Physical	Functional	Social	Emotional	Relationship with doctor	Total
Declined PSR	27	−2.7	−2.3	−1.0	−0.8	−.1	−6.8
No change in PSR	60	0.7	.3	.5	.5	.0	2.0
Improved PSR	17	3.2	1.6	−0.8	1.1	−.2	5.4
		$F = 12.6^{***}$	$F = 5.1^{**}$	$F = 2.6^{*}$	$F = 3.9^{*}$	$F = .4$	$F = 11.9^{**}$

Note: Overall multivariate $F(12,190) = 2.67$ ($p < .05$).
$^{*}p < .05$; $^{**}p < .01$; $^{***}p < .001$.

tics, and returned to the translators for discussion. The translated documents were then tested, and subsequent revisions to both the source (English) and target (Spanish) documents were made. The specific procedure was as follows: The FACT-G plus five site-specific subscales (FACT-B, FACT-C, FACT-H&N, FACT-L, and FAHI) were translated from English to Spanish by an independent professional Puerto Rican translator. The translated instruments were then given to an expert advisory committee that consisted of seven bilingual medical oncology specialists from Puerto Rico. They compared the Spanish translation to the original English version and selected the format that best matched the intent of the items. Each member received at least two of the original and translated sections of the FACT, and discrepancies were identified and discussed in an open meeting. Parallel to this activity, a bilingual/bicultural Central/South American expert advisory committee composed of nine medical oncology specialists from the United States also reviewed the English and Spanish translations. In addition, one member back-translated the Spanish instrument into English and submitted the responses to the coordinator of the expert advisory committee in Puerto Rico. With the goal of deriving a single, universal Spanish version of the FACT scales, the coordinator in Puerto Rico submitted tabulations, comments, and translations of both expert advisory committees to a linguist. The linguist then compared input from both committees with the initial forward translation. Item-by-item, whenever ambiguity arose, the linguist proposed a change in the Spanish version that would not alter the semantic and content equivalency of forms. The linguist then compiled a list that included each problem item in English along with several Spanish alternative translations for each item. The list was sent to all members of the Puerto Rican and Central/South American committees, each of whom independently rated which alternative he/she considered to be the most linguistically appropriate and culturally relevant. These individual evaluations were tabulated by the linguist, and the result was a second Spanish version of the FACT.

The second Spanish version was tested in a pilot study with 92 Spanish-speaking patients across five disease sites (breast, colorectal, head and neck, lung, and HIV-related malignancies) from the mainland United States and Puerto Rico. Eighteen patients per disease site (with the exception of 20 HIV patients) completed the corresponding disease-specific subscales. In addition, patients were asked to rate on a four-point Likert scale, ranging from 0 = not at all to 4 = extremely relevant, how relevant each item was to their quality of life. Patients were also asked to indicate whether there were any items on the Spanish FACT scales that were difficult to understand. Finally, patients were asked about what things they consider to contribute to a good quality of life. Analysis of the pilot data showed that there was only one item on the FACT-G and a total of five items across all disease-specific subscales that had median relevance scores below 3.0. The problematic FACT-G item was #24 ("I worry about dying") for which the median was 1.0. Although a decision was made to retain this item, an additional item ("I worry that my condition will get worse") was added to the Emotional Well-Being subscale. This item was added to retain the capability of assessing concern about disease progression without necessarily tapping concern about dying. It is likely that this new item will replace or be added to the concern over dying item. However, until this can be evaluated in future studies, we recommend continuing to score the Emotional Well-Being subscale using the original dying item (#24) and not the condition getting worse item (#25).

A few of the original (source) English questions required minor modification/improvement in order to create linguistically equivalent Spanish and English documents. These changes were made at the completion of the pilot study ($n = 92$) using a decentering approach and paying careful attention to responsiveness to patients with lower educational level. These changes are summarized in the next section of the chapter and are reflected in the appended English FACT (version 3). Table 4 presents initial psychometric data using the Spanish translation of the FACT on the cross-cultural validation ($n = 92$) sample.

The inclusion of a multinational, multicultural expert advisory committee and linguistic input contributed to the generation of a FACT scale that reflects a single Spanish language. Moreover, preliminary testing with mainland United States and Puerto Rican patients revealed no significant problems in the administration or interpretation of this universal Spanish measure. The existence of a single-language version permits comparisons across subgroups of Hispanic patients. Copies of the Spanish versions of the FACT are available in the manual (2). The Spanish versions of three additional FACT

TABLE 4. *FACT-G psychometric information (n = 92 Spanish-speaking mixed cancer patients)*

Subscale	No. of items	Range of scores	Mean	Standard deviation	Alpha
Physical (P)	7	4–28	18.9	6.4	.81
Social (S)	7 (6)*	4–28 (4–24)*	18.7 (16.9)*	4.9 (5.1)*	.58 (.73)*
Emotional (E)	5	1–20	15.6	3.9	.66
Functional (F)	7	2–28	18.2	6.6	.84
Relationship with Doctor (R)	2	1–8	6.4	1.7	.75
Total	28 (27)*	28–112 (0–108)*	77.8 (76.0)*	16.8 (17.0)*	.87 (88)*

*Internal consistency of the Social Well-Being subscale improved from .58 to .73 by dropping item 13, which showed negative correlations with all other items, due to translation error. Adjusted data for total (FACT-G) scores are also presented in parentheses. A corrected (retranslated) item 13 is shown in this manual (see Appendix).

scales (FACT-BMT, FACT-O, and FACT-P) have been professionally translated and are available for use, but have not yet undergone rigorous validation studies.

Reading Level of the English Version of the FACT

The Fog Index (26) of reading level was calculated by an independent investigator (D. Bruner, R.N., M.S.N.). The FACT scales were found to read at the 7.2 grade level. To further evaluate this, we conducted analyses on existing data sets from Rush-Presbyterian–St. Luke's Medical Center (n = 446) and Cook County Hospital (n = 85). In both studies that produced these data sets, patients were asked to complete the FACT on their own. Interviewer assistance was provided upon request. We recorded whether the scale was self- or interview-administered, and educational level. Although educational level does not perfectly predict reading level, we used it as a proxy in order to explore the capability of people who could complete the FACT by themselves. The median educational level of those patients who completed the FACT by self-administration was 12 years (range, 3–18 years, with four patients reporting less than eighth grade education) for the Cook County sample, and 14 years (range, 2–25 years, with 27 patients reporting less than eighth grade education) for the Rush-Presbyterian–St. Luke's sample. This suggests that many patients with limited educational background (and presumably relatively low literacy) can complete the English FACT. We have compared FACT scores of patients who require or request interview assistance with those of patients who complete the FACT on their own. In the original validation sample, there was not a significant total score difference between self (n = 333, M = 82.0; SD = 16.3) and interview (n = 127; M = 82.5; SD = 14.9) administration data, F (1,451) = 0.09, p = .77. For a second (minority) sample from Cook County Hospital, there was also no difference: Self (n = 46; M = 76.1; SD = 16.8) versus interview (n = 39; M = 78.4; SD = 15.7), F (1,83) = 0.42, p =

.52. Although these data are not from randomly assigned groups, they support the notion that there is technical equivalence across mode of administration.

In the course of our validation studies, we have administered the FACT scales, along with other instruments, to over 2,000 patients at Rush-Presbyterian–St. Luke's Medical Center and Cook County Hospital. Many of these patients have low literacy skills, as evidenced by their educational level and difficulty completing the form without assistance, even in the absence of other known barriers to self-administration. No matter how simple a self-report form is made, some patients will always require assistance. We are therefore currently conducting a systematic study to determine the extent to which providing such assistance might bias responses.

The FACT scales have been administered in English to over 500 black non-Hispanic patients and in Spanish to over 600 Hispanic patients without difficulty. Internal consistency reliability (alpha) coefficients on a subsample of 85 minority patients were computed and are quite acceptable: Physical Well-Being, .69; Social Well-Being, .69; Relationship with Doctor, .76; Emotional Well-Being, .73; Functional Well-Being, .80; and total score, .86.

Experience with HIV Patients—The Functional Assessment of HIV Infection (FAHI)

The FACT-G is the core of the FAHI scale. The HIV-specific items were developed using the same methodology as the FACT site-specific items, including interviews with five HIV specialists and 15 patients. The FAHI was then administered in a pilot study to 85 volunteers of the ACT-UP organization (New York City). The FAHI was rated as very relevant and easy to complete by these respondents. It has been selected by the ECOG as its measure to evaluate quality of life in all HIV-related malignancy trials. Preliminary data have been collected at Rush-Presbyterian–St. Luke's Medical Center with 53 men with HIV infection

The Questionnaire: FACT-G (Version 3)

Below is a list of statements that other people with your illness have said are important. By circling one number per line, please indicate how true each statement has been for you during the past 7 days.

PHYSICAL WELL-BEING

During the past 7 days:	not at all	a little bit	some-what	quite a bit	very much
1. I have a lack of energy	0	1	2	3	4
2. I have nausea	0	1	2	3	4
3. Because of my physical condition, I have trouble meeting the needs of my family	0	1	2	3	4
4. I have pain	0	1	2	3	4
5. I am bothered by side effects of treatment	0	1	2	3	4
6. I feel sick	0	1	2	3	4
7. I am forced to spend time in bed	0	1	2	3	4

8. Looking at the above 7 questions, how much would you say your **PHYSICAL WELL-BEING** affects your quality of life? (circle one number)

0 1 2 3 4 5 6 7 8 9 10
Not at all　　　　　**Very much so**

SOCIAL/FAMILY WELL-BEING

During the past 7 days:	not at all	a little bit	some-what	quite a bit	very much
9. I feel distant from my friends	0	1	2	3	4
10. I get emotional support from my family	0	1	2	3	4
11. I get support from my friends and neighbors	0	1	2	3	4
12. My family has accepted my illness	0	1	2	3	4
13. Family communication about my illness is poor	0	1	2	3	4
14. I feel close to my partner (or the person who is my main support)	0	1	2	3	4
15. Have you been sexually active during the past year? No ___ Yes ___ If yes: I am satisfied with my sex life	0	1	2	3	4

16. Looking at the above 7 questions, how much would you say your **SOCIAL/ FAMILY WELL-BEING** affects your quality of life? (circle one number)

0 1 2 3 4 5 6 7 8 9 10
Not at all　　　　　**Very much so**

RELATIONSHIP WITH DOCTOR

During the past 7 days:	not at all	a little bit	some-what	quite a bit	very much
17. I have confidence in my doctor(s)	0	1	2	3	4
18. My doctor is available to answer my questions	0	1	2	3	4

19. Looking at the above 2 questions, how much would you say your **RELATIONSHIP WITH THE DOCTOR** affects your quality of life? (circle one number)

0 1 2 3 4 5 6 7 8 9 10
Not at all　　　　　**Very much so**

EMOTIONAL WELL-BEING

During the past 7 days:	not at all	a little bit	some-what	quite a bit	very much
20. I feel sad	0	1	2	3	4
21. I am proud of how I'm coping with my illness	0	1	2	3	4
22. I am losing hope in the fight against my illness	0	1	2	3	4
23. I feel nervous	0	1	2	3	4
24. I worry about dying	0	1	2	3	4
25. I worry that my condition will get worse	0	1	2	3	4

26. Looking at the above 6 questions, how much would you say your **EMOTIONAL WELL-BEING** affects your quality of life? (circle one number)

0 1 2 3 4 5 6 7 8 9 10
Not at all　　　　　**Very much so**

FUNCTIONAL WELL-BEING	not at all	a little bit	some-what	quite a bit	very much
During the past 7 days:					
27. I am able to work (include work in home)	0	1	2	3	4
28. My work (include work in home) is fulfilling	0	1	2	3	4
29. I am able to enjoy life	0	1	2	3	4
30. I have accepted my illness	0	1	2	3	4
31. I am sleeping well	0	1	2	3	4
32. I am enjoying the things I usually do for fun	0	1	2	3	4
33. I am content with the quality of my life right now	0	1	2	3	4

34. Looking at the above 7 questions, how much would you say your **FUNCTIONAL WELL-BEING** affects your quality of life?

(circle one number)

0 1 2 3 4 5 6 7 8 9 10
Not at all   Very much so

of varying severity (8). For example, the mean and (more importantly) standard deviation of the subtest and overall scores on the FAHI are closely matched to those of mixed cancer patients on the FACT-G. Internal consistency of each of the subscales is high (range = .68–.92). The pattern of correlations between FAHI subscales (including the HIV-specific questions) and the other measures used in the pilot study to assess mood (Profile of Mood States), coping style (Dealing with Illness Scale, Impact of Event Scale), and activity level (ECOG performance status) are all in the expected direction, supporting the differential sensitivity of FAHI subtests previously demonstrated in FACT-G subtests. Subsequent study with the FAHI have found it to be responsive to the benefits of a stress management training group (9).

Examination of the correlation matrix of our available data sets, which include the FACT scales (combined $n > 2000$), showed consistent and *predicted* associations between performance status and Physical Well-Being (.65–.73), Functional Well-Being (.48–.53), Emotional Well-Being (.22–.35), Social Well-Being (.13–.24), Relationship with Doctor (.03–.14), and total score (.52–.57). Relationships with socioeconomic status, age, and gender were weaker, with the 18 coefficients ranging from .00 to.22. Performance status, socioeconomic status, age, and gender were entered step-wise, enabling us to evaluate effects of mode of administration and race/ethnicity after controlling for the explanatory variables. Results across each subscale and the total score generally showed the expected non-difference, with some exceptions (e.g., Physical and Social Well-Being scores differed across mode of administration).

CONCLUSIONS

The FACT scales are currently being used within several United States and international cooperative group and industry-sponsored clinical trials. Currently it is estimated that the FACT measurement system is included in over 80 multicenter trials. It has also been employed in approximately 100 single institution studies. Significant expansion into international trials is anticipated with the recent availability of multiple translations. The translation procedure for the Dutch, French, German, Italian, Norwegian, and Swedish versions was built on the success of the Spanish translation project. The nature of quality of life instrument development is such that there is expected to be continual addition and refinement over the next decade. By contacting the authors of this chapter, interested investigators may obtain the most up-to-date versions of any of the FACT scales in any of the available languages. This includes provision of updated psychometric data as they become available. It is expected that in exchange for this, investigators will provide the authors with periodic updates regarding their experience with the FACT measurement system. This will result in the most efficient scientific progress in the area of quality of life or health status measurement in clinical trials and clinical practice.

ACKNOWLEDGMENTS

The writing of this chapter was supported by U.S. Public Health Service Grant numbers R29 CA51926 and R01 CA61679, from the National Cancer Institute. We acknowledge the following collaborators for their essential contributions: N. S. Tchekmedyian (FAACT), D. Bruner (FACT-Bl), M. Weitzner (FACT-Br), M. McNamara (FACT-Cx), J. Eriksson (FACT-O), and P. Esper/K. Pienta (FACT-P).

REFERENCES

1. Cella DF, Tulsky DS, Gray G, et al. The Functional Assessment of Cancer Therapy Scale: development and validation of the general measure. *J Clin Oncol* 1993;11(3):570–579.
2. Cella DF. *Manual for the Functional Assessment of Cancer Therapy (FACT) and Functional Assessment of HIV Infection (FAHI) quality of life scales,* 3rd ed. Chicago: Rush-Presbyterian–St. Luke's Medical Center, 1994.
3. Cella DF, Lee-Riordan D, Silberman M, Andrianopoulos G, Gray G, Purl S, Tulsky D. Quality of life in advanced cancer: three new disease-specific measures. *Proc Am Soc Clin Oncol* 1989;8:315 (#1225).
4. Cella DF, Tulsky DS, Bonomi A, Lee-Riordan D, Silberman M, Purl S. The Functional Assessment of Cancer Therapy (FACT) scales: incor-

porating disease-specificity and subjectivity into quality of life (QL) assessment. *Proc Am Soc Clin Oncol* 1990;9:307 (#1190).

5. Tulsky DS, Cella DF, Bonomi A, Lee-Riordan D, Silberman M. Development and validation of new quality of life measures for patients with cancer. *Proc Soc Beh Med 11th Ann Meeting* 1990;11:45–46.

6. Tulsky DS, Cella DF, Sarafian B. The Functional Assessment of Cancer Treatment: three new site-specific measures. *J Cancer Res Clin Oncol* 1990;116(suppl):54(#A1.241.03).

7. Cella DF, Bonomi AE, Lloyd S, Tulsky D, Bonomi P, Kaplan E. Reliability and validity of the Functional Assessment of Cancer Therapy-Lung (FACT-L) quality of life instrument. *Lung Cancer* 1994; 11(suppl 1):89(abstract #336).

8. McCain NL, Cella DF. Correlates of stress in HIV disease. *West J Nurs Res* 1995;17(2):141–155.

9. McCain NL, Zeller JM, Cella DF, Urbanski PA, Novak RM. The influence of stress management training in HIV disease. *Nurs Res*, in press.

10. Cella DF, Bonomi AE, Leslie WT, Von Roenn J, Tcheckmedyian NS. Quality of life and nutritional well-being: measurement and relationship. *Oncology* 1993;7(suppl 11):105–111.

11. Cella DF, Jacobsen PB, Orav EJ, Holland JC, Silberfarb PM, Rafla S. A brief POMS measure of distress for cancer patients. *J Chronic Dis* 1987;40:939–942.

12. Schipper H, Clinch J, McMurray A, Levitt M. Measuring the quality of life of cancer patients: the Functional Living Index-Cancer: development and validation. *J Clin Oncol* 1984;2:472–483.

13. Spitzer WO, Dobson AJ, Hall J, Chesterman E, Levi J, Shepherd R, Battista RN, Catchlove BR. Measuring the quality of life of cancer patients: a concise QL-Index for use by physicians. *J Chronic Dis* 1981;34:585–597.

14. Cella DF, Cherin EA. Quality of life during and after cancer treatment. *Compr Ther* 1988;14(5):69–75.

15. Tchekmedyian NS, Cella DF, eds. Quality of life in current oncology practice and research. *Oncology* 1990;4(5).

16. Tchekmedyian NS, Cella DF, eds. *Quality of life in current oncology practice and research.* Williston Park, NY: Dominus, 1991.

17. Zubrod CG, Schneiderman M, Frei E, et al. Appraisal of methods for the study of chemotherapy of cancer in man: comparative therapeutic trial of nitrogen mustard and triethylene thiophosphoramide. *J Chronic Dis* 1960;11:7–33.

18. Taylor JA. A personality scale for manifest anxiety. *J Abnormal Social Psychol* 1953;48(2):285–290.

19. Strahan R, Gerbasi KL. Short homogeneous versions of the Marlowe-Crowne Social Desirability Scale. *J Clin Psychol* 1972;28:191–193.

20. Wright BD, Linacre JM. *A User's Guide to the BIGSTEPS Rasch Model Computer Program, version 2.1.* Chicago: Mesa, 1991.

21. Cella DF, Orofiamma B, Holland JC, et al. Relationship of psychological distress, extent of disease, and performance status in patients with lung cancer. *Cancer* 1987;60:239–245.

22. Cella DF, Tulsky D. Measuring quality of life today: methodological aspects. *Oncology* 1990;4(5):29–38.

23. Hays RD, Stewart AL. The structure of self-reported health in chronic disease patients. *Psychological Assessment Am J Consult Clin Psychol* 1990;2(1):22–30.

24. Cattell RB. The meaning and strategic use of factor analysis. In: Cattell RB, ed. *Handbook of multivariate experimental psychology.* Chicago: Rand-McNally, 1966.

25. Brislin R. Back-translation for cross-cultural research. *J Cross Cultural Psychol* 1970;1:185–216.

26. Gunning R. The Fog Index after twenty years. *J Business Communication* 1968;6:3–13.

APPENDIX: FACT-G (VERSION 3)

Summary of Changes from Version 2

Several relatively minor changes were made to version 2 of the FACT in June 1994, producing the current version

3. Version 3 is scored the same as version 2 (2). Changes made to version 2 of the FACT are summarized below:

1. One question has been added to the Emotional Well-Being subscale. This question, item 25 of FACT version 3 ("I worry that my condition will get worse"), was added for two reasons. First, a pilot study with 92 Spanish-speaking cancer patients from the mainland United States and Puerto Rico resulted in a strong cross-cultural endorsement of every FACT-G (version 2) item except #24 ("I worry about dying"). Second, parallel studies using the FACT-G (version 2) in patients with non–life-threatening conditions have shown that they too perceive all but this question to be relevant to their condition. To solve this issue in the parallel studies with non–life-threatening conditions, the question "I worry about dying" was *replaced* by "I worry that my condition will get worse." Rather than replace the question about dying in the cancer version of the FACT, it was decided to *add* the question relating to concern about one's condition worsening to the Emotional Well-Being subscale. This will allow users to continue to compare their version 3 Emotional Well-Being scores to those of version 2, and yet will permit more culture-fair/relevant questioning. This new question (#25) is *not* included in the scoring template at this time.

2. Item #3 ("I have trouble meeting the needs of my family") in the Physical Well-Being subscale of version 2 of the FACT was reworded to clarify its meaning. The wording of item #3 now reads, "Because of my physical condition, I have trouble meeting the needs of my family." Adding the introductory phrase should reduce ambiguity when patients interpret the meaning of the question. No changes in scoring accompany this item.

3. The experimental items, which appear at the end of each of the five subscales of the FACT-G and also at the end of each of the additional subscales of the FACT, have been reworded. FACT version 2 experimental questions were not specific enough to ensure patients were providing weights rather than secondary evaluations of each subscale. To reduce ambiguity, it was decided to add an additional phrase. These items are now worded so as to explicitly request that patients consider their responses to the set of questions in the subscale before providing a weight. This rewording should increase the likelihood that patients weigh their previous responses in light of their personal values.

4. Items #6, "I feel sick" (formerly, "In general, I feel sick"), #29, "I am able to enjoy life" (formerly item #28, "I am able to enjoy life in the moment") and #32, "I am enjoying the things I usually do for fun" (formerly item #31, "I am enjoying my usual leisure pursuits") were reworded based on a decentering translation approach.

5. A "skip option" has been added explicitly into question #15 and removed for question #14. This allows one to

more accurately separate patients who are not sexually active from those who are uncomfortable with the question.

6. An explicit "skip option" has been added to the FACT-C disease-specific subscale ("Do you have an ostomy appliance?").

7. An explicit "skip option" has been added to the FACT-L disease-specific subscale ("Have you ever smoked?").

8. An alternative (7-item) scoring for the FACT-L subscale is provided in addition to the original (9-item) scoring template (2). This is provided because psychometric analyses ($n = 58$ lung cancer patients) showed that the dropping of two questions produced a substantially improved internal consistency coefficient (.52 up to .66) and increased the sensitivity of the subscale to change in performance status over time (7). The two items that were dropped from the 9-item version to generate a new 7-item subscale are (a) version 2 item #38 (#39 in version 3): "I have been bothered by hair loss," and (b) version 2 item #42 (#43 in version 3): "I regret my smoking." Regardless of whether one uses the 9-item or 7-item score, the 9-item subscale should be administered. Other existing subscales of the FACT are undergoing similar analyses and may likewise see future scoring refinements.

9. Finally, there are many additional disease-, treatment-, and symptom-specific FACT scales under development that are not described in this chapter. These are (a) FACT-CNS (central nervous system disease), (b) FACT-Ntx (Neurotoxicity subscale), (c) FACT-Sp (spiritual concerns), (d) FAIT (Functional Assessment of Incontinence Therapy), (e) FANLT (Functional Assessment of Non–Life-Threatening conditions), (f) FAMS (Functional Assessment of Multiple Sclerosis), (g) FACT-E (Esophageal cancer), and (h) FACT-RT (Radiation Therapy).

Quality of Life and Pharmacoeconomics in Clinical Trials, Second Edition, edited by B. Spilker.
Lippincott-Raven Publishers, Philadelphia © 1996.

CHAPTER 24

The Functional Living Index–Cancer: Ten Years Later

Jennifer J. Clinch

INTRODUCTION

The Functional Living Index–Cancer (FLIC) was developed in the context of a research project to test the safety and efficacy of a cancer chemotherapy outreach program in the Canadian province of Manitoba. It was thought that the delivery of chemotherapy at rural sites would improve the quality of life of rural cancer patients who would otherwise have to deal with the inconvenience of receiving their treatment at the centralized facilities in the city of Winnipeg. In the late 1970s there was no accepted measure of quality of life suitable for cancer patients at all stages of disease that covered all areas of life that might be affected by the symptoms and treatment of cancer. There were many questionnaires that covered separate aspects of physical, emotional, and social well-being. However, combining several questionnaires into one would have resulted in a battery that would have been burdensome to patients, especially to those who were very debilitated. Consequently, we embarked on the journey toward developing a questionnaire that was reliable, valid, short, repeatable at regular intervals, sensitive to treatment effects, sensitive to change over time, sen-

sitive to stage of disease, and that covered the multidimensional universe of content applicable to cancer patients at all stages of disease and treatment. Some of these goals were achieved immediately and others have had to await the test of time.

DEVELOPMENT

The development of the FLIC has been described elsewhere (1) and the process will be summarized here. Initially a panel was convened to determine the areas of concern to patients at all stages of disease. Since quality of life in disease states is a very broad-based concept, the composition of such a panel should reflect as many perspectives on cancer and its treatment as possible. Consequently, the panel was composed of a male patient, a female patient, spouses of two patients representing both the urban and rural populations, two physicians, a psychology methodologist, an oncology nurse, a clinical psychologist, a public health nurse assessor, and a clergyman. The panel was given the mandate of developing a questionnaire representing *functional* quality of life. In other words, what was important was the effect of the symptoms of cancer and its treatment on functional ability in all areas of life and not simply the degree of symptomatology. The role of the panel was to reach a consensus on the specific areas of concern (domains) that would

   J. J. Clinch: WHO Collaborating Centre for Quality of Life Studies in Cancer, St. Boniface General Hospital, University of Manitoba, Winnipeg, Manitoba R2H 2AG, Canada.

TABLE 1. *Steps in the development of the FLIC*

Version	Subjects	Items	Purpose
I	175	92	Determination of: clarity / general applicability
II	312	42	Factor analysis / Item reduction
III	175	20	Factor analysis / Concurrent validation
IV	175	26	Testing new items / Stability of the factors / Further concurrent validation / Social desirability
V		22	Final version

define the universe of content for the questionnaire and independently to develop questions to cover these domains approximately equally.

The initial item pool comprised approximately 250 questions and the final goal was a questionnaire of approximately 20 items. From this point the questionnaire went through four versions before the fifth and final version. At each step

TABLE 2. *Sociodemographic data - versions III and IV*

	Winnipeg n = 174	Edmonton n = 173
Sex		
Male	31.6	28.9
Female	68.4	71.1
Marital status		
Single	13.2	7.5
Married/common-law	71.2	78.0
Separated/divorced	6.9	6.9
Widowed	8.6	7.5
Age		
<20	0.6	0.0
20–29	10.3	1.8
30–39	7.5	6.5
40–49	14.4	24.2
50–59	28.1	27.3
60–69	29.9	27.8
70–79	8.6	11.2
80–89	0.0	1.2
90–99	0.6	0.0
Children		
No	23.0	17.1
Yes	77.0	82.9
Children living at home		
No	60.5	60.8
Yes	39.5	39.2
Employment status		
? Housework	74.1	86.3
Employed at diagnosis	51.8	65.7
Employed	29.5	40.7
On leave of absence	11.2	8.0
Retired	33.1	33.1
Student at diagnosis	3.7	2.5
Student now	0.0	0.6

TABLE 3. *Types of cancer and treatment: version III*

Current treatment	
Chemotherapy	59.0
Radiotherapy	3.6
No therapy	37.2
Previous treatment	
Chemotherapy	76.3
Radiotherapy	37.9
Surgery	54.4
Type of cancer	
Breast	43.7
Lymphoma	15.6
Gastrointestinal	12.0
Leukemia/myeloma	7.8
Lung	7.2
Gynecologic	6.0
Hodgkin's	4.8
Testis	3.6
Other	5.4

of the way the questionnaire was progressively refined and validated. Table 1 summarizes each step and its purpose.

Patient Population Characteristics

Several authors have commented on the absence of sociodemographic and disease site information in the original publication on the FLIC, and consequently this previously unpublished information will be presented here. The patient population for versions I, II, and III were both inpatients and outpatients at the Manitoba Cancer Treatment and Research Foundation (MCTRF) in Winnipeg, whereas the patient population for version IV were outpatients at the W. W. Cross Cancer Institute in Edmonton. The patient characteristics for the Winnipeg version III and Edmonton version IV questionnaires are shown in Table 2. There are sociodemographic differences between the two samples in that there is a larger proportion of patients in their twenties and a smaller proportion in their forties in the Winnipeg sample. Consistent with this is the higher proportion of single as opposed to married patients in the Winnipeg sample. Employment is higher at diagnosis and at the time of questionnaire completion in the Edmonton sample, a finding consistent with there being no inpatients in this sample. The distribution of cancer diagnoses in the Winnipeg sample was obtained from the Manitoba Cancer Registry and is shown in Table 3 with some treatment information. Similar information was not available in Edmonton.

CHARACTERISTICS OF THE INSTRUMENT

The characteristic that differentiates this instrument from other available instruments is the emphasis on the extent to which patients' normal function is affected by cancer and its treatment. Questions regarding symptoms such as pain and nausea concern not only the extent of such symptoms but also the extent to which these symptoms interfere with normal life. This is in contrast to many instruments that focus on the extent of symptoms without asking if they are disturbing.

Patients answer the questions using a linear analog scale divided into six segments giving seven numbered points on the line. Respondents are instructed to place a vertical line through the scale at the point that applies to them. The scales have verbal anchors at each end describing the extremes of possible answers. For some questions good quality of life is represented by the right-hand scale anchor and for others the left. The polarity of the answer scales was reversed at random in order to avoid the development of a response set (the tendency to mark all answers at the same point on the line). Since these reversals may lead to incorrect responses, it is important to check the answers to similar questions against each other in order to determine if an error has been made.

Despite careful instructions some patients do not grasp immediately the conceptual basis of the linear analog scale. Some patients will circle the verbal anchors at the ends of the scale and some the numbers on the line. Others, while placing a vertical slash through the line will always do so at one of the division marks and never in between. Such incorrect responses are in the minority. A simple training exercise will usually correct these inappropriate uses of the scale [see for example Guyatt et al. (2)].

A sine qua non for obtaining valid and reliable information from questionnaires is readability. This is usually determined by various formulas that are now calculated by most computer word-processing programs. The answer provided is a grade level indicating that individuals who have completed this grade of schooling in North America, or its equivalent in other countries, should be able to comprehend the analyzed text. The Flesch-Kincaid grade level is based upon the average number of syllables per word and the average number of words per sentence, whereas the Coleman-Liau grade level is based upon the average word length in characters and the average number of words per sentence (3). The numbers, linear analog scales, scale anchors, and title were removed from the questionnaire before determination of grade level since their presence may have artificially reduced the calculated values. Consequently, the questions and instruction regarding the time frame for answering were the only parts analyzed. Using Microsoft Word for Windows version 6.0, the Flesch-Kincaid grade level and the Coleman-Liau grade level of the questions were found to be 6.0 and 8.3, respectively. Standard writing averages seventh to eighth grade; therefore, the FLIC has an appropriate level of readability.

As is frequently noted, there are large numbers of individuals in North America today who are functionally illiterate. Although self-administration would be precluded in such persons, they might easily comprehend the questionnaire if it were read to them, but problems would still exist with the answer format. In anticipation of there being a substantial portion of such individuals in some of the populations investigated in our projects, an answering method was developed for illiterate individuals. It is similar in design to an abacus and consists of a plastic ring on a wire that is held horizontally in a wooden frame. Patients are told which end of the wire represents good quality of life and which end poor, and are instructed to move the plastic ring to a point consistent with how they are feeling regarding the specific question asked. A research nurse asks each question verbally, indicates which end of the wire is which, asks the patient to move the plastic ring, and records the position. The position is read from a ruler that faces the nurse and this is facilitated by a pointer that hangs from the plastic ring. Interestingly some patients have opted for this response format even when they are able to read and understand how to use the linear analog scale.

SCORING

The original scoring instructions were to score to the nearest integer. In the event that a mark is exactly halfway between two of the numbered scale dividers, the nearest *even* integer should be used. However, Juniper et al. (4) have shown that the minimal important difference on seven-point scale response options is 0.5. Therefore we are currently investigating whether an exact measuring of the scale might provide greater discriminatory power. In either event the score must be reversed for those items where poor quality of life provides a high score. For example, question 11—"How uncomfortable do you feel today?"—has the scale anchors of "Not at all" on the left and "Very uncomfortable" on the right and a high score on this question is associated with poor quality of life. The score should be reversed by subtracting the actual score from 7 and adding 1 (because the scales start at 1 rather than 0). Thus, for example, a score of 6 becomes $7 - 6 + 1$ or 2. The questions can be summed to obtain an overall score, though some would dispute the usefulness of such an index. Clearly more information can be gained by calculating subscale scores, since some elements of the overall questionnaire could improve while others deteriorate, and this would not be reflected in the overall score.

If a few items are missing on the questionnaire, it makes sense to prorate the total score for the answered questions to obtain an appropriate score for the patient and eliminate the problem of a missing time of measurement. Since the questionnaire is multifactorial, the subscales should be prorated rather than the whole questionnaire. If a total score is required the prorated subscale scores should be added together. Prorating is equivalent to assigning the mean score for the answered questions to the missing answer. Clearly it makes more sense to make this assignment based on similar questions, i.e., those belonging to the same subscale. For example the psychological subscale is composed of six questions (see below). Suppose that only five were answered and the total score for those five was 25 out of a possible 35. The highest possible score for the fully answered scale is 42. Prorating the score for the five answered questions to that which would have been obtained if all six questions had been answered is done by the following calculation:

$$\text{Total for the answered questions} \times \frac{\text{Total questions in the scale}}{\text{Total questions answered}} = \text{Prorated score}$$

In this specific example the answer is 30. The whole area of imputing missing values is receiving considerable attention currently, not only for missing items but also when a time of assessment is missed. Imputation should be done with caution especially in the latter situation but also when there are missing items. This method of prorating subscale scores is not recommended unless more than 50% of the items are answered.

TRANSLATIONS

As a result of a desire to conduct clinical trials in a number of non–English-speaking countries or cultural groups, the FLIC has been translated into 19 different languages including most of the European languages and some Asian and African languages.[1] The majority of these translations were conducted by the World Health Organization Collaborating Centre for Quality of Life in Cancer Care. In all these cases careful translation and back-translation procedures were used. Several iterations of the process were usually necessary before a satisfactory conceptual identity was achieved between the original and the translation. To date only three of these translated versions have gone through the validation process. Two versions were studied in Singapore, a Malay and a Chinese version, and one was studied in Zimbabwe, the Shona version. In both locations the factor analysis showed remarkable similarity to the original.

COMPLETION BY CAREGIVERS

Ideally, the index should always be completed by the patient, but in the advanced disease setting patients may become too debilitated to complete the questionnaire as they approach death. Consequently a caregiver version of the index was developed. Caregivers are instructed to complete the questionnaire to reflect how they perceive the patient to be feeling. The questions were reworded so that the word *you* was replaced by *the patient*. In a pilot study of needs

---

[1]The FLIC has been translated into Afrikaans, Chinese, Danish, Dutch, Flemish, two French versions one each for France and Canada, two German versions one each for Germany and Austria, Greek, Italian, Japanese, Luganda, Malay, Ndebele, Portuguese, Shona, Spanish, and Swedish.

and quality of life in those with advanced cancer (5), patient-caregiver pairs completed the FLIC on two occasions. On the first occasion data was available for 35 pairs and on the second only 17, since half the patients could no longer complete the questionnaire or had died. It was predicted that the correlation between the patient and caregiver might increase on the second occasion due to dialogue between the patient and caregiver regarding their responses to the questionnaire, although they were required to complete them independently. The correlations at time 1 and 2 were .77 and .82, respectively. However, correlations can be high in the presence of substantial mean differences. Hospitalized patients rated their quality of life significantly higher (7.1 ± 2.5 points) than did their caregiver, but there were no significant differences between the patients' and caregivers' mean scores for those at home. It is our hope that the patient and caregiver assessments will converge in the continuing study as numbers of assessment times accumulate.

A similar study was conducted on cancer patients in the ambulatory setting. Differences between the patient's and their significant other's perceptions of the patient's quality of life were found for only three FLIC questions—the items on physical appearance, nausea, and time spent dwelling on illness (6). In another study of psychosocial adjustment after bone marrow transplant, the quality of life of patients and their significant other were compared using the FLIC. One month after hospital discharge the patients had significantly lower physical well-being and activities and significantly higher personal/family hardship than their significant other, but no difference in emotional adjustment as measured by the Profile of Mood States (7).

PSYCHOMETRIC PROPERTIES

Factor Analyses and Subscales

The initial factor analyses of the FLIC were done on versions II, III, and IV of the instrument having 42, 20, and 26 items, respectively. In each case the factors were similar even though the item content changed for each version. The five factors were described as physical well-being and ability, emotional state (psychological well-being), sociability, family situational (hardship due to cancer), and nausea. Two factor analyses of the final 22-item version by other authors are now available. Ruckdeschel and Piantadosi (8) report results obtained on 438 patients entered into all Lung Cancer Study Group trials active in 1985. A factor analysis was done on the baseline FLIC scores (in some trials this was after surgery but was always prior to chemotherapy). Their analytic method was a principal components analysis followed by a Promax rotation. Use of this oblique rotation method allowed the factors to be correlated with each other but no pair-wise factor correlation was above .4. The same factors emerged with the same questions loading on each factor as in the factor analysis on the 26-item questionnaire tested in Edmonton. Subscales of the FLIC derived from this factor analysis are shown in Table 4.

Morrow et al. (9) used the FLIC on a mixed group of cancer patients at the time of their fourth chemotherapy treatment. Their analytic method was a principal components analysis followed by a varimax rotation. In their five-factor

TABLE 4. *Subscales of the FLIC*[a]

Question no.	Question
	Physical well-being and ability
7.	Do you feel well enough to make a meal or do minor household repairs today?
15.	How much of your usual household tasks are you able to complete?
13.	How much is pain interfering with your daily activities?
4.	Rate your ability to maintain your usual recreation or leisure activities?
20.	How much of your pain or discomfort over the past 2 weeks was related to your cancer?
11.	How uncomfortable do you feel today?
22.	How well do you appear today?
10.	Rate your satisfaction with your work and your jobs around the house in the past month.
6.	How well do you feel today?
	Psychological well-being
18.	Rate the degree to which you are frightened of the future.
9.	Rate how often you feel discouraged about your life.
3.	How much time do you spend thinking about your illness?
2.	How well are you coping with your everyday stress?
1.	Most people experience some feelings of depression at times. Rate how often you feel these feelings.
21.	Rate your confidence in your prescribed course of treatment.
	Hardship due to cancer
12.	Rate in your opinion, how disruptive your cancer has been to those closest to you in the past 2 weeks.
8.	Rate the degree to which your cancer has imposed a hardship on those closest to you in the past 2 weeks.
14.	Rate the degree to which your cancer has imposed a hardship on you (personally) in the past 2 weeks.
	Social well-being
16.	Rate how willing you were to see and spend time with those closest to you, in the past 2 weeks.
19.	Rate how willing you were to see and spend time with friends, in the past 2 weeks.
	Nausea
5.	Has nausea affected your daily functioning?
17.	How much nausea have you had in the past 2 weeks?

[a]Items are listed in order of the factors extracted and the factor loadings.

solution the physical factor separated into two—physical ability and current well-being. The psychological functioning (emotional state), gastrointestinal symptoms (nausea), and social functioning factors were similar to the other analyses. However, the questions making up the original family situational/hardship factor appeared to load on several factors. Morrow et al. noted that these items had in common the use of the word *cancer*. Our recent preliminary findings from a factor analysis of the baseline scores (before treatment) for a group of patients with epidemic Kaposi's sarcoma showed a six-factor solution in which the original five factors emerged. The additional factor was due to the separation of the physical area into physical functioning and current well-being, as with the data of Morrow et al. If a five-factor solution was imposed on the data, the result was almost identical to Morrow et al.'s in that the cancer-related items loaded on the physical function factor. Morrow et al. suggested that the FLIC might be more psychometrically sound with these items eliminated. However, we would be reluctant to remove them because they seem to be sensitive to changes over time (see below).

Morrow et al. investigated the subscales suggested by their factor analytic solution. The results showed internal consistencies, as measured by Cronbach's alpha, of over 0.8 for the physical functioning, psychological functioning, and gastrointestinal symptoms subscales and over 0.6 for the current well-being and social functioning subscales (9). This suggests that the use of FLIC subscales is feasible.

Reliability

As indicated above, the internal consistency reliability of three of the five subscales identified by Morrow et al. is in the acceptable range. A recent estimate of Cronbach's alpha for the entire 22-item scale was found to be .89 on the baseline data for a group of patients about to start chemotherapy (our group's unpublished data). Test-retest reliabilities at 1-month intervals for the same group of patients after starting chemotherapy ranged from .68 to .81. As expected these reliability coefficients dropped as the time between assessments increased. A 2-month interval produced values ranging from .62 to .68, values for 3-month intervals ranged from .59 to .64, values for 4-month intervals were .57 and .60, and the single value for a 5-month interval was .48. With increasing time between assessments the correlations become less because real changes are occurring to different extents and in different directions for different individuals. Cronbach's alpha is probably the best indicator of reliability because there is no time delay involved.

Validity

If the questionnaire measures what it is intended to measure, then it is valid. The evaluation of validity is difficult because it is not easy to define internal states such as perceptions of quality of life. Objective indicators are much easier to define but they are not necessarily good indicators of how patients are feeling. There are numerous conceptual definitions of quality of life and each implies a different type of questionnaire and different content. The construct behind the development of a questionnaire must have a precise definition or validation is not possible. Concurrent validity is determined by simultaneously administering other questionnaires that are expected to correlate with the index to be validated—either the entire index or portions of it. Construct validity accrues as the instrument is used to discriminate groups that may theoretically be expected to show differences in quality of life or to show changes over time that reflect the natural history of disease and/or its treatment.

The definition of quality of life used in the development of the FLIC was pragmatic and simply that the quality of various aspects of life contributed to overall quality of life in proportion to the number of questions developed for each domain. The original concurrent validation of the instrument was against a variety of well-recognized existing tests: Speilberger's State Trait Anxiety Inventory (STAI) (10), Goldberg's General Health Questionnaire (11), Beck's Depression Inventory (12), The McGill Pain Questionnaire (13), Katz's Activities of Daily Living Scale (14), Karnofsky's Performance Status (KPS) Index (15), and the social desirability scale from Jackson's Personality Inventory (16). These tests were chosen because of their preeminence and because they reflected the various domains defined by the panel who developed the questionnaire. With the exception of the Katz scale, all correlations were in the range of .55 to .77. Correlations with the Katz scale were low because this scale is designed for individuals who are much more incapacitated than the populations used in the validation studies. There was a very restricted range of scores on the Katz and consequently low correlations with the FLIC. Correlations of the physical and emotional factor scores with the validation tests demonstrated convergent and discriminant validity of these two factors. Correlations of the physical factor were high with validation tests measuring physical function and low with tests measuring psychological function, and vice versa for the emotional factor. Morrow et al. (9) confirmed these findings for the STAI. They also showed that correlations of post-nausea and post-vomiting severity correlated with the nausea scale, whereas correlations with the other scales were close to 0.

In the original study (1), the FLIC was shown to discriminate between groups of patients according to the expected severity of their condition. The sample was divided according to whether patients were on follow-up, adjuvant therapy, active treatment for recurrent disease, or hospitalized. There was a progressive decline in total FLIC scores across these groups. Morrow et al. were able to show that the FLIC discriminated various patient groups categorized by clinical state and demographic and psychological variables (9).

As a measure of the acceptance of the FLIC, it has itself been used to validate other quality of life questionnaires developed subsequent to its introduction in 1984. The Cancer Rehabilitation Evaluation System–Short Form (CARES-SF) was developed from its parent instrument the CARES in 1991 (17). In a sample of newly diagnosed breast cancer patients the CARES-SF scales and total score were all found to correlate significantly with the FLIC. Of particular interest are the correlations, albeit small, with the marital and sexual scales of −.31 and −.18, respectively. The FLIC does not have any questions pertaining specifically to these two areas but the correlations indicate that these areas must be reflected to some extent in overall quality of life. Indeed Schag et al. (17) found correlations of .40 and .38 between the sexual scale and the physical and psychosocial scales, respectively, of the CARES-SF. However, the FLIC may not be sensitive enough to sexual issues in some groups of patients and additional measures should be used if this is a critical area of interest. A study of soft tissue sarcoma patients undergoing multimodality therapy (including limb-sparing surgery) showed significant decreases in sexual function from baseline at both 6 and 12 months after surgery but no changes in FLIC scores (18).

Cella et al. (19) have developed a new general quality of life measure for cancer patients called the Functional Assessment of Cancer Therapy (FACT) scale. Several instruments were administered to a mixed group of cancer patients during the validation process. The pattern of correlations of the FLIC with the other validation tests was almost identical to that for the FACT and, as expected, the correlation between the FLIC and FACT was high (.79). Correlations were reported for the Profile of Mood States (−.66), the Taylor Manifest Anxiety Scale (−.58), and the Eastern Cooperative Oncology Group performance status rating (−.60).

Monahan (20) investigated the relationship of the FLIC to Spitzer's Quality of Life Index (QLI) on a sample of 40 patients attending a medical oncology outpatient clinic and receiving varying cycles of a first course of chemotherapy. Correlation of the QLI with the KPS was higher (.73) than its correlation with the FLIC (.49). This is to be expected since both the KPS and the QLI were physician completed and the FLIC is a patient self-report instrument. In another study on the patient-completed version of the QLI (21) the correlation with the FLIC was .67. In general, then, the FLIC correlates more highly with other patient-reported measures of quality of life than it does with those measures assessed by a physician.

A number of more specific outcome measures in oncology populations have been validated using the FLIC. These include several pain measures, one of which is the Memorial Pain Assessment Card (MPAC). In two studies of cancer-associated pain, one on ovarian (22) and the other on pancreatic cancer patients (23), the FLIC scores for patients with and without pain were significantly different. The FLIC also correlated significantly with visual analog scales of pain intensity ($r = -.3$) and mood ($r = .55$) as measured by the MPAC. The West Haven–Yale Multidimensional Pain Inventory has also been validated using the FLIC (24).

Fatigue is another frequent side effect of cancer and its therapy. In an investigation of interferon-induced fatigue the FLIC correlated $-.74$ with a specific measure of fatigue, the Pearson-Byars fatigue feeling checklist (25). On the other hand, an ergonomically derived self-report physical activity scale had a relatively low but significant correlation (.29) with the FLIC in newly diagnosed breast cancer patients (26).

An instrument known as the Functional Living Index–Emesis (FLIE) and based on the FLIC has been developed by Lindley et al. (27) to assess the effect of chemotherapy-induced nausea and vomiting on quality of life. It is composed of two subscales containing identical questions except that the word *nausea* appears in one subscale and *vomiting* in the other. Lindley et al. found that the nausea subscale of the FLIE correlated .83 with the nausea subscale of the FLIC in a mixed group of medical and surgical adult oncology outpatients receiving bolus combination chemotherapy. A factor analysis of the FLIC in this population reproduced the factors identified in the original validation study. A marked, statistically significant drop in both FLIC and FLIE scores was observed from baseline to 3 days after the start of chemotherapy in those who experienced emesis. It would appear from the change in mean scores in this group that the FLIE was more sensitive than the FLIC to the emetogenic effect of chemotherapy. The larger change in mean FLIE scores from 115 to 85 as opposed to the change in FLIC scores from 119 to 101 supports the use of the FLIE as a specific measure of the quality of life effects of chemotherapy-induced emesis. Since its development, a number of investigators have used the FLIE to assess the effectiveness of various medications in controlling chemotherapy-induced nausea and emesis (28–31).

REVIEW OF USE OF THE FLIC AS AN OUTCOME MEASURE

Sensitivity to Treatment Effects and Change Over Time

Ultimately the most useful aspect of quality of life assessment is to follow the natural history of a disease and its treatment. This provides a longitudinal picture of the quality of life impact of a disease and its treatment in the short and long term so that the immediate and late effects of toxic therapies can be evaluated along with the extent of survival. It may also be important to separate out the components of quality of life since each may follow a different time course. Where different treatments are included, the time curve may well be different for each, leading to a statistical hypothesis of interaction between treatment groups and time. In situations where the groups are self-selected there may be baseline differences in quality of life. This necessitates the use

of the baseline scores to adjust subsequent scores so as to eliminate the bias due to starting differences in quality of life.

The short-term effects of chemotherapy were demonstrated in a group of 13 women receiving intravenous chemotherapy containing cisplatin for gynecological cancers (32). The FLIC was administered the evening before chemotherapy, the next morning before chemotherapy, and in the afternoon following chemotherapy. There was no significant difference between the total FLIC score means for first and second administrations, 128 versus 126, but the difference between the second and third administrations was significant, the mean declining from 126 to 111. This result indicates the sensitivity of the FLIC to treatment and emphasizes the importance of accurate and consistent timing of quality of life assessments.

A second study indicating the deleterious effects of chemotherapy on mean FLIC scores was over a longer time period. Patients with metastatic sigmoid or rectal carcinoma, randomly assigned to chemotherapy with either epirubicin or 5-fluorouracil were evaluated at baseline and exit from the study. Significant deterioration occurred in both groups but was significantly greater with epirubicin than 5-fluorouracil for the total FLIC score and its physical and emotional subscales (33).

Another study of advanced epithelial ovarian cancer patients receiving intensive versus nonintensive cyclophosphamide and cisplatin showed a marked disparity on the nausea subscale of the FLIC, with those on the intensive regimen showing more frequent and severe nausea. The authors concluded that the intensive regimen may not be worthwhile if it were to prove only marginally better for response and survival (34).

Schag and Ganz and their coworkers (17,35) followed a group of newly diagnosed breast cancer patients for 1 year to determine if their rehabilitation needs, as measured by the CARES, decreased over time. Both the CARES and the FLIC were administered at 1, 4, 7, and 13 months after surgery. Parallel significant improvement in both the CARES, FLIC, and KPS was noted over the year of study. One of the goals of the study was to determine whether there were any differences in psychological adjustment or quality of life between patients who had a modified radical mastectomy versus a segmental mastectomy. Although mood and quality of life improved over time there was no difference between the surgical groups and no interaction of surgery and time.

Kornblith et al. (36) investigated the effect of three different dosages of megestrol acetate on the quality of life of noncachectic advanced breast cancer patients at baseline and at 1 and 3 months. It was predicted that quality of life would be less in the highest dosage group due to weight gain. Between baseline and 1 month, total FLIC scores improved for all three dose groups (160 mg/d, 800 mg/d, and 1,600 mg/d) but subsequently quality of life continued to improve only for the lowest dose. Quality of life was maintained for the intermediate dose and fell back to the baseline value for the highest dose fulfilling the prediction. Significant predictors of the 3-month FLIC score in a multiple regression were baseline FLIC, pain, dose group, feeling bloated, weight gain, and no insurance.

In another study of metastatic breast cancer patients treated with high-dose chemotherapy and autologous bone marrow support (HDC/ABMT), quality of life as measured by the FLIC was assessed on four occasions—during the first cycle (two to four cycles) of doxorubicin, methotrexate, and 5-fluorouracil; in the week prior to HDC; and 6 weeks and 6 months after hospital discharge (37). FLIC scores fell 6 weeks after HDC from 115 at baseline to 109 and rose to 124 at 6 months post-HDC. Baseline FLIC scores were significantly higher in 25 patients with a good outcome (completion of protocol therapy with a complete or partial response) than in 15 patients who had a poor outcome (progressive disease during treatment, toxicity precluding completion of protocol therapy, death)—115 versus 94.

The long-term effects of treatment with HDC-ABMT on quality of life were evaluated in a group of patients surviving at least 12 months posttherapy (38). Half were treated for metastatic disease and half in the adjuvant setting ($\geq$ 10 positive nodes). Their mean FLIC score was 130 and did not correlate with time elapsed since HDC-ABMT, initial stage of disease, income, education, age, or spirituality. The mean FLIC score of 119 was significantly lower in 14 patients who have developed recurrent disease versus the mean score of 134 for those who were disease free.

Andrykowski et al. (39) have investigated the long-term effect of ABMT on quality of life for a 2-year period from 1 year post-ABMT. No change over time was noted in three annual assessments using the FLIC. There was considerable variation in the actual time post-ABMT for each of the annual assessments: time 1 was 8 to 52 months, time 2 was 12 to 57 months, and time 3 was 26 to 71 months post-ABMT, which may make it difficult to observe a time effect. The sample size was very small—16—and consequently power was low. In another report on long-term survivors of ABMT (40) there was a differential FLIC outcome according to age at ABMT, with those under 30 at ABMT having a better outcome than those over 30. Again no effect of time since ABMT was observed. The graphs presented suggest an interaction between age at ABMT and time since ABMT but this was not significant. Again sample size was small. Andrykowski et al. (41) also compared the FLIC scores of adult survivors of ABMT with those of renal transplant recipients (matched for age, sex, and time since transplant) and found little difference. Neither were found to have normal quality of life. In contrast Peters et al. (42) found that high-risk primary breast cancer patients, who were more than 1 year post–high-dose chemotherapy followed by autologous bone marrow support, had an essentially normal quality of life as measured by the FLIC.

Cassileth et al. (43) investigated the response to treatment of two groups of stage D prostate cancer patients who chose either surgical or medical castration (using goserelin acetate) as treatment for their disease. The assessments including the FLIC were done at baseline, 3, and 6 months. Mean FLIC scores improved from baseline to 3 months in both groups. However, whereas quality of life continued to improve in the medically treated group, it fell back to baseline in the group treated with orchiectomy. A question by question analysis of the change from baseline to 6 months indicated that there had been an improvement of greater than 0.5 on the seven-point scale for 11 of the 22 questions in the goserelin acetate group. No question showed a greater than 0.5 deterioration. For the orchiectomy group four questions showed a greater than 0.5 improvement and six showed a greater than 0.5 deterioration. None of the questions that showed deterioration in the orchiectomy group had shown improvement in the goserelin acetate group. Thus, it would appear that the subscales on the instrument had been differentially affected by the two treatments.

A study recently completed in Manitoba and in preparation for publication has looked at the differential behavior of the FLIC subscales over time for different therapeutic groups. A repeated-measures analysis of variance using a chemotherapy groups by scales by time design (scales and time are repeated factors) revealed two significant two-way interactions between scales and time and between scales and chemotherapy type. Graphical representation (Fig. 1) indicated that in this population of cancer patients (largely gynecological malignancies) the social and nausea subscales remained relatively stable from baseline over cycles of chemotherapy, while the physical, psychological, and hardship scales showed improvement. The second interaction is a reflection of the fact that while the social and nausea scales were the same for each type of chemotherapy, the physical, psychologic, and hardship scales were lower in the induction chemotherapy group than in the adjuvant and salvage chemotherapy groups.

A different approach to analyzing change over time was taken in a group of patients with metastatic non–small-cell lung cancer receiving various types of chemotherapy (44). Noting that there was a strong correlation between the FLIC and physical status rather than time on therapy, the authors measured time in reverse as months prior to death rather than months since therapy began. This is a common procedure in research on populations of terminally ill patients. Graphic representation of FLIC scores against time before death showed a dramatic decline in quality of life from 12 months to 1 month before death of 110 to 97. Additionally, this study showed that decline in quality of life from baseline to after completion of one cycle of chemotherapy was associated with a decline in performance status, poor baseline performance status, and a decrease in weight of at least 5%.

In addition to the studies described above, several other authors have reported that they have used the FLIC in their investigations but as yet either have no data available or only preliminary information, or insufficient information was given to enable interpretation of the results (45–58).

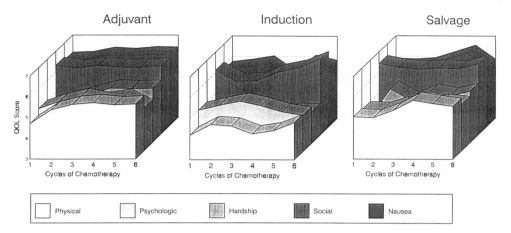

FIG. 1. Quality of Life Scale scores over the course of chemotherapy.

Some other studies have not been described because they did not include either group comparisons or changes over time (59–61).

Prognostic Value

Traditionally variables such as performance status and extent of disease have been used to predict survival and response to therapy. Although the primary intent of quality of life assessment was to compare the well-being of patients on various therapies for specific types of cancers, it should come as no surprise that baseline quality of life is a strong predictor of survival in advanced disease settings. Coates and his coworkers (62,63) have shown that quality of life is a predictor of survival in advanced breast cancer and in metastatic malignant melanoma. Neither of these studies used the FLIC.

The Lung Cancer Study Group has used the FLIC in eight different trials for patients with various extents of disease at the start of therapy. The FLIC was administered at baseline and then at regular intervals just prior to a course of therapy. Quality of life, KPS, weight loss, and several stage- and study-related items were all individually predictive of both survival and time to recurrence. Using a multivariate proportional hazards model, quality of life, tumor size, nodal status, and KPS were all significantly predictive of survival as well as small-cell histology. When patients were stratified for small-cell histology quality of life was the strongest prognostic factor and independent of KPS. In four phase-III trials the initial quality of life score and change in quality of life over time were significantly prognostic for survival even after correcting for initial PS and stage. Subscales and individual items were also assessed for their prognostic value but the total score was superior to any item or scale.

Ganz et al. (64) also investigated the prognostic value of baseline FLIC scores for survival in advanced metastatic lung cancer. They found no relationship to survival of treatment group assignment, cell type, KPS, weight loss, number of metastatic sites, ages, or gender. Both the baseline FLIC and marital status were predictive of survival when an interaction term between these two variables was included in the model (which also approached significance). In both these studies the FLIC was clearly superior to the KPS in predicting survival.

A contrary result was obtained in a group of 18 patients with AIDS-related non-Hodgkin's lymphoma (65). Several clinical factors but none of the quality of life indicators, including the FLIC, were significantly predictive of survival. However, several quality of life indicators were prognostic for response to treatment.

CONCLUSIONS

When designing a self-report assessment instrument, one starts out with an individual definition of what it is that one wants to measure and each member of a research team will have their own. The challenge is to arrive at a consensual definition of the construct being measured. Much of the problem is in the description of individual perceptions that do not have an external referent. Thus we can never be sure that we all mean the same thing by quality of life. It is because of this that a particular instrument comes to define what is being measured. Quality of life as measured by the CARES, EORTC-QLQ-C30, FACT, or FLIC is slightly different for each instrument. The results obtained from different instruments when used to determine group differences, changes over time, and prognosis will be slightly different. This will depend on what groups of patients are being assessed and the relative representation of the domains of interest. We would argue that the FLIC provides a useful definition of quality of life in that it has shown the anticipated effects of time and treatment.

Eventually it is hoped that quality of life assessment will be used on a regular basis to direct individual patient management during cancer treatment and follow-up. This requires that the standard error of measurement be low and correspondingly that the reliability be high. The reliabilities of the entire scale and subscales are quite sufficient for use of the FLIC as a research instrument, but for assessing individual changes over time the reliabilities of the subscales are not high enough. As with all existing short quality of life scales more items need to be added especially to the shorter subscales to improve their reliability. Only then will it be feasible to use all subscales to assist in patient management.

REFERENCES

1. Schipper H, Clinch JJ, McMurray A, Levitt M. Measuring the quality of life of cancer patients: The Functional Living Index–Cancer: development and validation. *J Clin Oncol* 1984;2:472–483.
2. Guyatt GH, Townsend M, Berman LB, Keller JL. A comparison of Likert and visual analogue scales for measuring change in function. *J Chronic Dis* 1987;40:1129–1133.
3. Miller LR. Predictive powers of multiple-choice and Cloze-derived readability formulas. *Reading Improvement* 1975;5:52–58.
4. Juniper EF, Guyatt GH, Willan A, Griffith LE. Determining a minimal important change in a disease-specific quality of life questionnaire. *J Clin Epidemiol* 1994;47:81–87.
5. Dudgeon D, Clinch J. A longitudinal study of needs and quality of life in advanced cancer patients. *Proc Annu Meet Am Soc Clin Oncol* 1994;13:437.
6. Gilyon K. Quality of life. Perceptions of cancer patients and significant others. *Oncol Nurs Forum* 1988;15:108.
7. Magid DM, Barker C, Browning A, Williams S, Bitran J. Psychosocial adjustment (PA) of patients (PTS) and their significant others (SO) to high dose chemotherapy and autologous bone marrow reinfusion (HDC-ABMR). *Proc Annu Meet Am Soc Clin Oncol* 1988;7:A1042.
8. Ruckdeschel JC, Piantadosi S, for the Lung Cancer Study Group. Quality of life in lung cancer surgical adjuvant trials. *Chest* 1994;106(suppl):324–328.
9. Morrow GR, Lindke J, Black P. Measurement of quality of life in patients: psychometric analyses of the Functional Living Index Cancer (FLIC). *Qual Life Res* 1992;1:287–296.
10. Speilberger CD, Gorsuch RL, Lushene RA. *STAI Manual for the State-Trait Anxiety Inventory*. Palo Alto, CA: Consulting Psychologists Press, 1970.
11. Goldberg DP, Hellier VF. A scaled version of the General Health Questionnaire. *Psychol Med* 1979;9:139–145.
12. Beck AT, Ward CH, Mendolson M, Mock J, Erbaugh J. An inventory for measuring depression. *Arch Gen Psychiatry* 1961;4:561–571.
13. Melzack R. The McGill Pain Questionnaire: major properties and scoring methods. *Pain* 1975;1:277–299.
14. Katz S, Akpom CA. A measure of primary sociobiological functions. *Int J Health Services* 1976;6:493–508.
15. Karnofsky DA, Burchenal JH. The clinical evaluation of chemotherapeutic agents in cancer. In: Macleod CM, ed. *Evaluation of Chemotherapeutic Agents*. New York: Columbia University Press, 1949:191–205.
16. Jackson DN. *Personality Research Form Manual*, rev. ed. Port Huron, MI: Research Psychologists Press, 1974.
17. Schag CAC, Ganz PA, Heinrich RL. CAncer Rehabilitation Evaluation System–Short Form (CARES-SF): a cancer specific rehabilitation and quality of life instrument. *Cancer* 1991;68:1406–1413.
18. Chang A, Culnane M, Lampert M, Simpson C, Steinberg S, White D, Hicks J, Rosenberg SA. Quality of life (QOL) changes in soft tissue sarcoma patients (STSP) undergoing multimodality treatment. *Proc Annu Meet Am Soc Clin Oncol* 1987;6:A1000.
19. Cella DF, Tulsky DS, Gray G, Sarafian B, Linn E, Bonomi A, Silberman M, Yellen SB, Winicour P, Brannon J, Eckberg K, Lloyd S, Purl S, Blandowski C, Goodman M, Barnicle M, Stewart I, McHale M, Bonomi P, Kaplan E, Taylor S, Thomas CR, Harris J. The Functional Assessment of Cancer Therapy scale: development and validation of the general measure. *J Clin Oncol* 1993;11:570–579.
20. Monahan ML. Quality of life of adults receiving chemotherapy: a comparison of instruments. *Oncol Nurs Forum* 1988;15:795–798.
21. Foltz A, Gilyon K. Comparison of two quality of life (QOL) measures. *Oncol Nurs Forum* 1988;15:119.
22. Portenoy RK, Kornblith AB, Wong G, Vlamis V, McCarthy Lepore J, Loseth DB, Hakes T, Foley KM, Hoskins WJ. Pain in ovarian cancer patients: prevalence, characteristics, and associated symptoms. *Cancer* 1994;74:907–915.
23. Christman K, Kelsen D, Niedzwiecki D, Portenoy R, Banks W, Tao Y, Brennan M, Foley K. Progression of pain and psychosocial distress (PD) over time in patients with pancreas cancer (PC). *Proc Annu Meet Am Soc Clin Oncol* 1992;11:A1441.
24. Thompson M. Investigation into the reliability and validity of a multidimensional pain inventory in an oncology population. *Oncol Nurs Forum* 1990;17:160.
25. Trahan PA. Interferon-induced fatigue: a study of fatigue measurement. *Oncol Nurs Forum* 1987;14:97.
26. Ganz PA, Polinsky ML, Cheng H, Bloom J. Validation of a physical activity scale (PAS) in a sample of breast cancer patients. *Proc Annu Meet Am Soc Clin Oncol* 1989;8:A205.
27. Lindley CM, Hirsch JD, O'Neill CV, Transau MC, Gilbert CS, Osterhaus JT. Quality of life consequences of chemotherapy-induced emesis. *Qual Life Res* 1992;1:331–340.
28. O'Brien BJ, Rusthoven J, Rocchi A, Latreille J, Fine S, Vandenberg T, Laberge F. Impact of chemotherapy-associated nausea and vomiting on patients' functional status and on costs: survey of five Canadian centres. *Can Med Assoc J* 1993;149:296–302.
29. Berry WR, House KW, Lee JT, Plagge PB, Meshad MW, Grapski R. Results of a compassionate-use program using intravenous ondansetron to prevent nausea and vomiting in patients receiving emetogenic cancer chemotherapy. *Semin Oncol* 1992;19(suppl 15):33–37.
30. Clavel M, Soukop M, Greenstreet YLA. Improved control of emesis and quality of life with ondansetron in breast cancer. *Oncology* 1993;50:180–185.
31. Bonneterre J, Clavel M. Comparison between ondansetron tablet and alizapride injection in the prevention of emesis induced by cytotoxic regimens in breast cancer. *Ann Oncol* 1992;3(suppl 5):183.
32. Bow EJ, Clinch J, Schipper H, Kilpatrick M. The short term effects of chemotherapy on quality of life (Q/L). *Proc Annu Meet Am Soc Clin Oncol* 1992;11:A1419.
33. Blum R, Lafleur F, Green MD, Dubin N, Shemano I, and the Rectal Study Group. Feasibility of prospective quality of life assessment (QLA) in phase III trial of epirubicin (E) vs 5-flourouracil (F) in sigmoid and rectal carcinoma. *Proc Annu Meet Am Soc Clin Oncol* 1986;5:951.
34. Walczak JR, Brady M, The Johns Hopkins Oncology Center, and Gynecologic Oncology Group, Buffalo. Comparison of quality of life (QOL) in ovarian cancer patients (PTS) participating in a national cooperative group phase III randomized trial. *Proc Annu Meet Am Soc Clin Oncol* 1991;10:A122.
35. Ganz PA, Schag CAC, Lee J, Polinsky ML. Breast conservation versus mastectomy: is there a difference in psychological adjustment or quality of life in the year after surgery? *Cancer* 1992;69:1729–1738.
36. Kornblith AB, Hollis DR, Zuckerman E, Lyss AP, Canellos GP, Cooper MR, Herndon JE, Phillips CA, Abrams J, Aisner J, Norton L, Henderson C, Holland JC for the Cancer and Leukemia Group B. Effect of megestrol acetate on quality of life in a dose-response trial in women with advanced breast cancer. *J Clin Oncol* 1993;11:2081–2089.
37. Winer E, Gold D, Lees J, Affronti M, Westlund R, Ross M, Vredenburgh J, Jones R, Shpall E, Trump DL, Peters WP, Cohen HJ. Quality of life (QL) following high dose chemotherapy with autologous bone marrow support (HDC) in patients with metastatic breast cancer. *Proc Annu Meet Am Soc Clin Oncol* 1991;9:A122.
38. Winer E, Lindley C, Hardee M, Brunatti C, Sutton L, Lees J, Gold D, Sawyer W, Peters WP. Quality of life (QL) assessment in patients with breast cancer surviving 12 months or more following high dose chemotherapy with autologous bone marrow transplant (HDC-ABMT). *Proc Annu Meet Am Soc Clin Oncol* 1992;11:A1328.
39. Andrykowski MA, Henslee PJ, Barnett RL. Longitudinal assessment of psychosocial functioning of adult survivors of allogeneic bone marrow transplantation. *Bone Marrow Transplant* 1989;4:505–509.
40. Andrykowski MA, Henslee PJ, Farrall MG. Physical and psychosocial functioning of adult survivors of allogeneic bone marrow transplantation. *Bone Marrow Transplant* 1989;4:75–81.

41. Andrykowski MA, Altmaier EM, Barnett RL, Otis ML, Gingrich R, Henslee-Downey PJ. The quality of life in adult survivors of allogeneic bone marrow transplantation: correlates and comparison with matched renal transplant recipients. *Transplantation* 1990;50:399–406.

42. Peters WP, Ross M, Vrendenburgh JJ, Meisenberg B, Marks LB, Winer E, Kurtzberg J, Bast RC, Jones R, Shpall E, Wu K, Rosner G, Gilbert C, Mathias B, Coniglio D, Petros W, Henderson IC, Norton L, Weiss RB, Budman D, Hurd D. High-dose chemotherapy and autologous bone marrow support as consolidation after standard-dose adjuvant therapy for high-risk primary breast cancer. *J Clin Oncol* 1993; 11:1132–1143.

43. Cassileth BR, Soloway MS, Vogelzang NJ, Chou JM, Schellhammer PD, Seidman EJ, Kennealey GT. Quality of life and psychosocial status in stage D prostate cancer. Zoladex Prostate Cancer Study Group. *Qual Life Res* 1992;1:323–329.

44. Finkelstein DM, Cassileth BR, Bonomi PD, Ruckdeschel JC, Ezdinli EZ, Wolter JM. A pilot study of the Functional Living Index–Cancer (FLIC) scale for the assessment of quality of life for metastatic lung cancer patients. *Am J Clin Oncol (CCT)* 1988;11:630–633.

45. Ahlgren JD, Leming PD, Fryer D. Protracted infusion 5-FU (PIF) +α2b-interferon (α-IFN): a well-tolerated regimen for palliation of advanced carcinoid. A Mid-Atlantic Oncology Program (MAOP) study. *Proc Annu Meet Am Soc Clin Oncol* 1993;12:A661.

46. Brenckman WD, Laufman LR, Adamkiewicz BB, Collier MA, Sullivan BA and the NW Colorectal Cancer Cooperative Group. Is fluorouracil (FU) plus placebo (P) as effective as equitoxic doses of FU plus high dose oral leucovorin (LV) in colorectal cancer? *Proc Annu Meet Am Soc Clin Oncol* 1990;9:A421.

47. Curley T, Scher H, Thaler H, Yeh S, Friedlander-Klar H, O'Dell M, Larson S, Foley K, Portenoy R. Rhenium [Re-186-HEDP] for palliation of painful bone metastases from prostatic cancer (PC). *Proc Annu Meet Am Soc Clin Oncol* 1991;10:A1231.

48. Foltz A, Gilyon K, Monahan M. Quality of life among 127 ambulatory cancer patients. *Oncol Nurs Forum* 1989;16:162.

49. Herbst LH, Strause LG. Transdermal fentanyl use in hospice home-care patients with chronic cancer pain. *J Pain Symptom Manage* 1992;7:S54–S57.

50. Higgs D, Jassaud J, Miller M. Quality of life as an outcome variable in clients receiving chemotherapy for lung cancer. *Oncol Nurs Forum* 1989;16:138.

51. Kavanagh JJ, Morris M, Smalldone L, Kwan J, Ammerman MB. A randomized trial of carboplatin versus variably timed continuous infusion etoposide (VP16) in refractory epithelial ovarian cancer. *Proc Annu Meet Am Soc Clin Oncol* 1989;8:A637.

52. Levy MH, Rosen SM, Kedziera P. Transdermal fentanyl: seeding trial in patients with chronic cancer pain. *J Pain Symptom Manage* 1992; 7:S48–S50.

53. Loprinzi CL, Goldberg RG, Su JQ, Mailliard J, Maksymiuk A, Kugler J, Ghosh C, Pfeifle D, Wender D, Burch P, Jett J. Randomized double-blind, placebo-controlled trial evaluating hydrazine sulfate (HS) in patients with newly diagnosed non-small cell lung cancer. A North Central Cancer Treatment Group Trial. *Proc Annu Meet Am Soc Clin Oncol* 1993;12:A1124.

54. Magid DM, Vogelzang N, Richards J, Barker E, Ramming K. A randomized study of psychosocial adjustment (PA) of patients (PTS) receiving interleukin-2 (IL-2) alone vs. IL-2 and lymphokine-activated killer cells (LAK). *Proc Annu Meet Am Soc Clin Oncol* 1989;8:A1207.

55. Maves TJ, Barcellos WA. Management of cancer pain with transdermal fentanyl: phase IV trial, University of Iowa. *J Pain Symptom Manage* 1992;7:S58–S62.

56. Scheithauer W, Rosen H, Kornek GV, Sebesta C, Depisch D. Randomised comparison of combination chemotherapy plus supportive care with supportive care alone in patients with metastatic colorectal cancer. *Br Med J* 1993;306:752–755.

57. Scialla SJ. A clinimetric process of care in geriatric oncology. *Proc Annu Meet Am Soc Clin Oncol* 1990;9:A1186.

58. Slover R. Transdermal fentanyl: clinical trial at the University of Colorado Health Sciences Center. *J Pain Symptom Manage* 1992;7: S45–S47.

59. Arzouman JMR, Dudas S, Ferrans CE, Holm K. Quality of life patients with sarcoma postchemotherapy. *Oncol Nurs Forum* 1991;18:889–894.

60. Hagle ME. Cancer patients' experiences with portable chemotherapy pumps. *Dissertation Abstr Int B* 1990;50:5547.

61. Roberts CS, Rossetti K, Cone D, Cavanagh D. Psychosocial impact of gynecologic cancer: a descriptive study. *J Psychosoc Oncol* 1992;10:99–109.

62. Coates A, Gebski V, Signorini D, Murray P, McNeil D, Byrne M, Forbes JF for the Australian New Zealand Breast Cancer Trials Group. Prognostic value of quality-of-life scores during chemotherapy for advanced breast cancer. *J Clin Oncol* 1992;10:1833–1838.

63. Coates A, Thomson D, McLeod GR, Hersey P, Gill PG, Olver IN, Kefford R, Lowenthal RM, Beadle G, Walpole E. Prognostic value of quality of life scores in a trial of chemotherapy with or without interferon in patients with metastatic malignant melanoma. *Eur J Cancer* 1993;29A:1731–1734.

64. Ganz PA, Lee JJ, Siau J. Quality of life assessment: an independent prognostic variable for survival in lung cancer. *Cancer* 1991;67: 3131–3135.

65. Remick SC, McSharry JJ, Wolf BC, Blanchard CG, Eastman AY, Wagner H, Portuese E, Wighton T, Powell D, Pearce T, Horton J, Ruckdeschel JC. Novel oral combination chemotherapy in the treatment of intermediate-grade and high-grade AIDS-related non-Hodgkin's lymphoma. *J Clin Oncol* 1993;11:1691–1702.

Quality of Life and Pharmacoeconomics in Clinical Trials, Second Edition, edited by B. Spilker. Lippincott-Raven Publishers, Philadelphia © 1996.

CHAPTER 25

The Health Assessment Questionnaire 1995 — Status and Review

Dena R. Ramey, James F. Fries, and Gurkirpal Singh

INTRODUCTION

The measurement of patient outcomes in clinical trials requires instruments that are comprehensive, valid, and reliable. This is particularly imperative in the study of chronic diseases where short-term survival is not the primary outcome of interest. To represent the full spectrum of patient outcomes, measures of patients' functional status, quality of life, psychological status, and the costs of medical care are needed along with clinical, laboratory, and radiographic data. Over the past 15 years since its development, the Stanford Health Assessment Questionnaire (HAQ) has become one of the most widely used measures of functional status in studies of patients with rheumatic diseases and human immunodeficiency virus (HIV) as well as studies of the development of musculoskeletal disability with age.

Since 1980, the HAQ has been administered over 125,000 times in various national and international settings. In 1992 we published a review article (1) that included 109 references to the HAQ published between 1980 and 1991. In the past 2 1/2 years, nearly 80 additional articles have been published describing and utilizing the HAQ. This major explosion in the number of articles using the HAQ reflects its increased utilization in clinical practice and clinical trials and the availability of versions in more than 15 languages. The HAQ has also been increasingly applied to patients with a wider variety of diseases. We have also noted an increase in the number of studies of patients early in their disease course and more studies correlating the HAQ with various other self-report measures of health status and psychosocial constructs.

This chapter provides an overview of the HAQ and a guide to the accumulated literature through mid-1994 (2–197) so that researchers can more easily find references related to particular topics of interest. This chapter consists primarily of a series of tables that categorize all of the HAQ references as to language, applications to patients with various diagnoses, studies relating the HAQ to various other types of measures, randomized clinical trials, and so on. Although we have tried to be reasonably complete, the included references are not exhaustive of all research with the HAQ. Except in a few instances, we have not included papers that are available only in abstract form.

THE DIMENSIONS OF HEALTH OUTCOMES

Over the past several years, there has been a shift in emphasis in research studies from reliance on measures of

D. R. Ramey, J. F. Fries, and G. Singh: Division of Immunology and Rheumatology, Department of Medicine, Stanford University School of Medicine, Palo Alto, California 94304.

medical process (e.g., erythrocyte sedimentation rate or joint count) to measures of outcomes of direct importance to patients. These elements have been identified by multiple surveys of both patients and the general population (198–201). Patients desire to be alive as long as possible, to function normally, to be free of pain and other physical, psychological, and social symptoms, to be free of iatrogenic problems from the treatment regimen, and to incur as few costs for medical care as possible. These five dimensions (death, disability, discomfort, drug side effects, and dollar costs), broadly construed, constitute a comprehensive set of domains of patient outcomes.

These primary outcome dimensions may be further separated into their natural subdimensions. Economic impact consists of direct medical costs and indirect medical costs due to effects on productivity. Iatrogenic effects may be due to medication(s) or to surgery. Discomfort may be physical, psychological, or social. Disability may involve fine movements of the upper extremities or locomotor activities of the lower extremities. Death can be broken down by specific cause and quantitated in terms of expected time to death. Each subdimension can in turn be subdivided into components comprised of specific individual questions or variables. Thus, a hierarchy of patient outcomes may be developed that is conceptually complete and provides a location in the framework for all possible measures (see Fig. 2 in Chapter 4).

There are distinct advantages to the employment of a hierarchy of patient outcomes. A hierarchy allows a variety of assessment instruments and techniques to be mixed as appropriate to the particular situation and encourages assessment of the full spectrum of patient outcomes. The full HAQ (as opposed to the HAQ disability index) was designed using this hierarchical model. The hierarchy was developed first, then the specific items for each dimension were developed and validated. The HAQ was designed to be used in a variety of illnesses rather than only rheumatic disease and was designed to be supplemented with additional measures for particular studies for which detailed and specific assessment of particular dimensions is required.

The impact of illnesses varies markedly among different diseases; thus a comprehensive instrument based on the outcome hierarchy allows comparison of the impact of the different diseases across the full spectrum of patient outcomes. For example, in osteoarthritis, pain is more dominant; in rheumatoid arthritis, disability, and in pancreatic cancer, death. Reliance on a single outcome may provide a biased view of the impact of a disease or treatment. For example, one medication may reduce pain significantly more than another medication, but that information is not adequate to decide between the two medications. It may be that the second medication reduces disability significantly more than the first. The relative efficacy in both these areas needs to be taken into account along with the relative cost and toxicity of the medications to properly evaluate the relative "worth" of the two drugs and decide on the optimal drug to use

for a given patient or group of patients under a given set of circumstances.

DEVELOPMENT OF THE HAQ

The HAQ was developed by culling questions and components from a variety of instruments previously used for similar purposes. We then performed a complete validation of each set of items including reviewing intercorrelations, item-total correlations, correlations with "gold standards" (e.g., performance of activities of daily living, clinical and laboratory measures, chart review). Questions that were too highly correlated with each other (≥.9) indicated redundancy and permitted elimination of some questions. Other items were eliminated based on low item-total correlations (<.5), which indicated that these items were not measuring the same construct as the other items in that section. The HAQ was developed to address the above-mentioned five dimensions:

1. The disability section was the first section to be constructed and validated. It has been widely used in the United States and internationally and is the primary focus of this chapter. The HAQ disability index is a self-report functional status instrument that can be completed by a patient in less than 5 minutes and can be scored in less than 1 minute. It measures disability over the past week by asking a total of 20 questions in eight categories of function: dressing, arising, eating, walking, hygiene, reach, grip, and activities. There are at least two component questions in each category and the eight categories represent the universe of functional activities. Scoring is patterned after the American Rheumatology Association/American College of Rheumatology functional classes; normal, adequate, limited, or unable (125,202). For each component question, the level of difficulty is scored from 0 to 3, with 0 equal to no difficulty, 1 equal to some difficulty, 2 equal to much difficulty, and 3 equal to unable to do. The highest component score in each category determines the score for the category unless aids or assistance are required. Dependence on equipment or physical assistance adjusts a lower category score to 2 (with much difficulty or limited). Category scores are averaged to give the disability index, a continuous scale ranging from 0 to 3. An alternative scoring method ignores the aids and devices when computing the category scores. The disability index is based on the number of categories answered and is not computed if the patient does not have scores for at least six categories.

2. Although the discomfort dimension includes physical, psychological, and social subdimensions, the HAQ is primarily concerned with the measurement of physical pain. The development of a pain scale for the HAQ initially involved extensive examination of other pain scales

(11,203,204). Attempts to elaborate pain activity by part of body involved, times during the day that were painful, and severity of pain in different body parts failed to yield indexes that outperformed a simple analog scale. Returning to the basic principle that symptomatology is what the patient says it is, pain is measured by a double-anchored visual analog scale. It is scored from 0 (no pain) to 3 (severe pain). Visual analog pain scales have been used extensively in studies using the HAQ (2,3, 5,8,11,15–19,21,22,24,26,27,30–32,35,40–42,44,46, 48–50,52,53,55–61,66–69,72,80,84,93,97,101,104, 107,110,114–116,122,123,127,131,132,134,140,143, 150,154,155,159,163,165,171,173,175–177,186,187, 191,196,197).

3. Iatrogenic events are measured using both self-report and audit of hospital records and death certificates. Patients are asked to report on all adverse drug reactions including the side effect, the drug responsible, the severity of the side effect, and whether the drug was discontinued as a result of the side effect. Patients are also asked to report on all hospitalizations. Several studies have been done using the HAQ side-effect data (2,5,15,16,29,46,56,66, 78,89,95,97,98,109,147,148,169,193). A toxicity index (TI) to quantify the total toxicity experienced by a patient or attributed to a particular drug has been validated (78,98,147,148,193). The TI includes three components: side effects, laboratory abnormalities, and hospitalizations attributed to particular drugs. Weights have been established for different side effects after rating by physicians, patients, and health professionals. Standardized rules are used to attribute particular events to particular therapies based on known toxicities of particular drugs as reported in the literature.

4. Economic impact is assessed as both direct and indirect costs. Costs are measured in terms of units of service required rather than charges or costs actually paid, allowing automatic adjustment for inflation and for different pricing structures in different regions. Standard costs for each service are developed from multiple sources (e.g., Physicians' Fee Reference, Medicare reimbursements, surveys of providers, insurance company data, American Hospital Association data, and pharmaceutical industry sources) and applied to computations that cumulate such variables as doctor visits, hospital days, and medication costs into a direct cost figure, and productivity losses into an indirect cost figure. There have been 15 studies using cost data from the HAQ (2,12,15, 18,19,27,29,48,52,58,59,81,113,141,159).

5. The fact of death is ascertained regularly by protocol and an audit is made of all deaths, including acquisition of death certificates and clinical information, in order to identify cause of death and to allow attribution to specific therapy when appropriate. The National Death Index is searched regularly to ascertain patient status. Several mortality studies have been published using data from these sources (15,52,56,66,78,97,104,179,197).

This description of the HAQ has been, by necessity, brief. Many of the publications referenced in this chapter can provide more information on the history and development of the HAQ and its utility in various situations. The remainder of this chapter outlines and categorizes the references to the HAQ disability index.

RELIABILITY AND VALIDITY

The HAQ disability index has been shown to be reliable and valid in a number of different languages and contexts (2,14,25,38,44,47,75,84,99,121,131,139,142,145,149,163, 167). Test-retest correlations have ranged from .87 to .99 (2,44,47,75,99,121,131,139,145,163,167), and correlations between interview and questionnaire formats have ranged from .85 to .95 (2,14,25,131). Validity has been demonstrated in numerous studies. There is consensus that the HAQ disability scale possesses face and content validity, and correlations between questionnaire or interview scores and task performance have ranged from .71 to .95 demonstrating criterion validity (2,38,44,145,167). The construct/convergent validity, predictive validity, and sensitivity to change have also been established in numerous observational studies and clinical trials (17,88,91,108,123,149,153). In one key study (11) the correlation between the HAQ disability index and Arthritis Impact Measurement Scales physical ability scales was .91 and between the corresponding pain scales

TABLE 1. *Applications of the HAQ disability scale in various rheumatic diseases*

Disease	References
Rheumatoid arthritis	2–5, 10–15, 17, 18, 20, 21, 24–30, 32, 35, 36, 38–40, 42–44, 46–48, 52–61, 63–70, 73–76, 78, 80, 84, 85, 87–92, 94, 95, 97–104, 109–116, 118–125, 127, 128, 131, 133–135, 137–140, 142–146, 149–151, 153–155, 157–159, 164–176, 178, 180–182, 186–188, 190, 191, 192, 194–197
Osteoarthritis	3, 17, 19, 26, 31, 35, 38, 39, 47, 57–60, 64, 67, 71, 84, 87, 93, 101, 122, 124, 130, 159, 162, 164, 168, 169, 177, 187, 191
System lupus erythematosus	50, 163, 168
Scleroderma	106, 168
Ankylosing spondylitis	72, 79, 87, 122, 152, 183, 184
Fibromyalgia	16, 22, 42, 49, 101, 107, 124, 132, 156
Juvenile rheumatoid arthritis	86, 108, 136
Other rheumatic diseases	38, 67, 87, 101, 118, 164, 168
HIV infection	105, 129, 160, 161, 189
Normal aging	33, 82, 179, 185
National sample	126

was .64. The patterns of factor loadings in both separate and combined factor analyses were also quite comparable. The HAQ disability index has also demonstrated a high level of convergent validity based on the pattern of correlations with other measures. Correlations with physical measures tend to be high and correlations with other measures are in the expected direction and of the expected magnitude.

APPLICATIONS TO VARIOUS DISEASES

Most studies using the HAQ have involved patients with rheumatoid arthritis, but over the past 13 years there have been an increasing number of applications of the HAQ in other diseases. The HAQ disability scale has now been used in studies of osteoarthritis, juvenile rheumatoid arthritis, systemic lupus erythematosus, scleroderma, ankylosing spondylitis, fibromyalgia, and other rheumatic diseases, as well as HIV infection and normal aging (Table 1).

LANGUAGE ADAPTATIONS

The HAQ disability scale was originally developed in U.S. English and was validated in United States and Canadian

TABLE 2. *Language adaptations of the HAQ*

Country/language	References
British versions	
England	25, 38, 51, 55, 67, 87, 110, 118, 119, 120, 122, 130, 134, 140, 149–151, 156, 162, 164, 169, 180, 187, 190, 192
Scotland	165, 188
Australia	178, 182
Spanish versions	
Spain	145
Mexico	139
United States	62 (MHAQ), Lorig, Russell
Portuguese versions	
Brazil	75, 76
Portugal	DeQueiroz
Scandinavian versions	
The Netherlands	14, 88, 111, 152, 153, 155, 166, 170–172, 183, 184, 195
Sweden	43, 44, 73, 74, 92, 136–138, 142–144, 194
Norway	102
Finland	181
Scandinavia, multiple languages	40
French versions	
France	79, 99, 121
French Canadian	131
Other versions	
Italy	133, 167
Austria	4
Russia (based on MHAQ)	68, 69

English-speaking populations. To utilize the HAQ disability scale in non–English-speaking populations in the United States and in other countries, it has been translated into numerous languages (Table 2). To adapt the disability index to cultural differences, modifications of the individual items were sometimes necessary (e.g., cartons of milk are not widespread in some countries). Back translations were used in the development of many of the translations. In most instances, the language-modified HAQ has been fully validated including such procedures as test-retest reliability, internal reliability (item-total correlations), convergent validity, interviewer vs. self-administered formats, factor analysis, and so on. There are also versions of the HAQ currently being developed in Portugal (V. De Queiroz, Faculdade de Medinina de Lisboa, Lisbon, Portugal) and for Spanish-speaking U.S. populations (K. Lorig, Stanford Arthritis Center; I. J. Russell, University of Texas, San Antonio).

MODIFICATIONS AND DERIVATIVE SCALES

In addition to the translations and cultural adjustments discussed above, various researchers have made adaptations to the content, format, and/or scoring of the HAQ to meet their needs. For example, there have been several studies of ankylosing spondylitis patients using two versions of the HAQ that have added additional items designed to assess disability specifically due to problems with the spine (72, 79,152,183,184). An abridged instrument, the modified Health Assessment Questionnaire (MHAQ) has been derived from the HAQ disability scale. The MHAQ, developed by Pincus and his colleagues, measures patients' difficulty, satisfaction, and pain in activities of daily living using 8 of the 20 HAQ disability items (9,32,41,53,63,71,81). There is some concern about whether a single question can reliably measure each functional category. This is reflected in the psychometric properties of this instrument (71).

APPLICABILITY OF THE HAQ

Childhood Populations

The Childhood HAQ (CHAQ) developed by Singh and his colleagues (86) is a parent- and/or self-administered questionnaire designed to measure health status in children as young as 1 year of age. Singh et al. added several new questions and modified many existing ones so that for each functional area, there is at least one question that is relevant to children of all ages. The Childhood HAQ has been validated in patients with juvenile rheumatoid arthritis and dermatomyositis; it has also been translated into several languages (Italian, Dutch, Norwegian, Swedish, Portuguese).

Clinical Practice

Over the past several years, the HAQ disability scale has increasingly been used in routine clinical practice in both private practices and in university clinic settings for patients with various rheumatic diseases. The physicians who have implemented the HAQ in their clinical practice have found that it can be easily completed by most patients without assistance in a few minutes before being seen by the physician. Scoring takes only a minute and the results can be displayed numerically in a flow chart or graphically to illustrate changes in disability over time. The HAQ correlates well with various clinical and laboratory parameters and provides useful current and predictive information regarding disease status, utilization of services, and mortality (52,117).

Clinical Trials

Several studies have shown the HAQ disability index to be sensitive to change over time and useful as a measure of functional status for clinical trials. The American College of Rheumatology Committee on Outcome Measures in Rheumatoid Arthritis Clinical Trials has recently recommended a preliminary core set of disease activity measures for rheumatoid arthritis clinical trials that includes seven disease activity measures including a measure of the patient's assessment of physical function (146). They recommend the use of "any patient self-assessment instrument which has been validated, has reliability, has been proven in RA trials to be sensitive to change, and which measures physical function in RA patients" (146). They indicate that the HAQ disability index meets these criteria.

The HAQ disability index has served as an outcome variable, predictor, stratifying variable, covariate, and standard

TABLE 4. *Studies correlating HAQ disability with self-reported health status scales*

Scale	References
Arthritis Impact Measurement Scales (AIMS)	3, 11, 17, 47, 48, 52, 68, 80, 114, 116, 133, 175, 181
Arthritis Self-efficacy	57, 159, 194
Beck Depression Scale	61
Degree of Adjustment	144
Dutch Personality Inventory (neuroticism, social inadequacy, and self-esteem)	183
Exercise of Self-Care Agency Instrument	135
Global Health Status	11, 17, 42, 49, 63, 114, 116, 127, 131, 171, 173, 196
Hospital Anxiety and Depression Scale	156
Modified HAQ	134
Patient Rating of Change	145
Patient Rating of Severity	145
Psychosocial Adjustment to Illness Scale (PAIS)	50
Quality of Life Status and Change Instrument	138
Sense of Coherence Questionnaire	124
Short Geriatric Depression Scale	154, 186
Sickness Impact Profile (SIP)	138, 183
Symptom Check List–Psychological Distress (anxiety and depression subscales of SCL-90)	143
Visual Analog Pain Scale	2, 10, 32, 41, 44, 50, 52, 53, 55, 61, 68, 69, 114, 116, 127, 131, 133, 136, 145, 171, 173, 181, 196
Zung Depression Inventory	133

TABLE 3. *Randomized intervention studies using the HAQ*

Disease	Intervention	References
Rheumatoid arthritis	Auranofin vs. placebo	21, 40, 91
	Day patient vs. inpatient management	188
	Fasting and vegetarian diet vs. control	102
	Goal setting vs. pain attention with home exercise	194
	Health Status Report	81
	IM gold + OH chloroquine vs. IM gold + placebo in patients with suboptimal response to IM gold	165
	IM methylprednisolone vs. pulse oral methylprednisolone during induction of chrysotherapy	140, 182
	Sulfasalazine vs. OH-chloroquine	88, 171
Rheumatoid arthritis and osteoarthritis	Arthritis Self-Management Program	18, 26, 58–60
Osteoarthritis	Acetaminophen vs. ibuprofen	93
	S-adenosylmethione (SAM) vs. placebo	177
Fibromyalgia	Ibuprofen and alprazolam vs. ibuprofen and placebo vs. alprazolam and placebo vs. double placebo	132
Ankylosing spondylitis	Group physical therapy vs. individualized therapy	152, 184

of comparison for validation of other instruments in many studies. Table 3 lists the randomized controlled trials of interventions (including medications and patient education) that have used changes in HAQ disability scores as an outcome variable. In all these studies, the disability index was sensitive to change and changes in disability scores were consistent with, and often more sensitive than other outcome variables, particularly on a long-term basis.

CORRELATIONS OF THE HAQ DISABILITY SCALE WITH OTHER MEASURES

There have been numerous studies that have correlated the HAQ with various health status, laboratory, physical, and psychosocial measures. Table 4 lists studies correlating the HAQ disability index with various self-report measures including the Arthritis Impact Measurement Scales. visual analog pain scale, and measures of psychological functioning (anxiety, depression). The HAQ disability index has also often been used in conjunction with other, more traditional ways of evaluating both the short- and long-term impact of the rheumatic diseases. Table 5 lists studies in which the disability index was correlated with clinical and laboratory measures.

The HAQ disability index has been used in a wide variety of descriptive and observational studies as a predictor variable or correlate. Some examples of variables that have been related to HAQ disability scores include work-related measures [work capacity (68), household work performance (90), work task performance (42), work disability (143), and occupation (126)], measures of costs [direct costs (27,52), hospital admission (30), length of hospital stay (85), post-surgery delirium (64), use of aids and devices (170)], and miscellaneous other measures [specialty care (93,113), patient satisfaction with health care workers (137), and health care system (19)].

FUTURE DIRECTIONS

Over the next few years, the trend toward increasing numbers of studies utilizing the HAQ disability index should continue. There will also likely be an increase in the number of studies using the other components of the complete HAQ. The American College of Rheumatology guidelines for disease activity measures for rheumatoid arthritis clinical trials will result in increasing use of the HAQ in clinical trials including trials of new biological therapies. This will probably necessitate translations of the HAQ into additional languages. The current health care reform climate will result in an increase in cost-identification and cost-effectiveness studies of various therapies. Related studies of primary care versus rheumatology subspecialty care and the care provided under various types of insurance programs will also be possible using HAQ data.

As the HAQ is used over longer time frames in a variety of different populations and diseases, researchers will be able to take greater advantage of time series and other analytic methods for longitudinal data. Researchers will increasingly be able to examine the development of disability at different stages of a disease and for groups of patients with different disability curves. As data sets mature, researchers will also

TABLE 5. *Studies correlating HAQ disability with clinical and laboratory variables*

Variable	References
Body mass index	82, 185
Button test	63, 68, 69
C-reactive protein	99, 121, 145, 171
Excretion of pyridinium cross-links	180
Flexibility and mobility	43, 44, 71, 72, 76, 106
GALS locomotor screen	164
Grip strength	10, 28, 31, 36, 43, 44, 52, 55, 63, 68, 69, 71, 77, 114, 145, 171, 181
Health habits (e.g., exercise, smoking, diet)	185
Hemoglobin	145, 171
HLA type	65, 111, 142, 172
Keitel function test	181
Morning stiffness	3, 13, 36, 43, 55, 68, 69, 114, 131, 136, 145, 171, 181
Muscle function	74, 162
Physician rating of disease activity/severity	119, 131, 136, 139, 145, 151, 171, 172, 196
Radiology and bone density	28, 31, 36, 63, 82, 88, 99, 121, 130, 150, 155, 172, 181, 192
Rheumatoid factor	3, 8, 13, 28, 36, 52, 63, 88, 103, 114
Sedimentation rate	10, 28, 36, 43, 44, 52, 55, 63, 99, 103, 114, 121, 145, 171, 181, 196
Serotonin levels	107
Sex hormones	120
Steinbrocker/ARA/ACR functional class	10, 25, 28, 36, 43, 55, 63, 75, 125, 131, 136, 139, 145, 167, 172
Swelling, joint count	3, 10, 28, 36, 52, 63, 68, 69, 79, 103, 114, 127, 131, 145, 166, 171, 181
Tenderness, Ritchie Index	4, 13, 31, 43, 44, 55, 63, 68, 69, 106, 121, 145, 166, 171, 172, 181
Total hip replacement/total knee replacement	187, 190
Walking time	10, 36, 63, 68, 69, 71

ACR, American College of Rheumatology; ARA, American Rheumatology Association; HLA, human leukocyte antigen.

be able to analyze cumulative outcomes (the total disability, pain, toxicity, and so on, experienced by a patient over the disease course), to compare the overall impact of various treatment strategies over time.

The next few years will also see the maturation of several data sets that look at the development of disability in a general aging population (rather than a population of patients with a particular disease). These data sets will also allow studies of the compression of morbidity. Over the next several years the routine collection of HAQ data at clinic visits will likely increase and various technologies will facilitate entry and utilization of this data for clinical and research purposes. This will also promote more pooling of HAQ and clinical data from various sources and will encourage collaborative research studies of larger, more representative data sets.

CONCLUSIONS

In the 14 years since the original HAQ paper was published (2), the HAQ has been shown to be a valuable tool for the measurement of health status in clinical trials and observational studies. Applications of the HAQ are expanding beyond the rheumatic diseases and into at least 15 other languages. From only two papers using the HAQ in 1982, it has grown to over 40 papers published in 1993. We hope this review will prove useful as a guide to the accumulated literature and provide ideas for further research and collaborations.

For further information, or to obtain a copy of the HAQ, please write to Dr. James F. Fries, Division of Immunology and Rheumatology, 1000 Welch Road, Suite 203, Palo Alto, CA 94304.

REFERENCES

1. Ramey DR, Raynauld JP, Fries JF. The Health Assessment Questionnaire 1992: status and review. *Arthritis Care Res* 1992;5:119–129.
2. Fries JF, Spitz PW, Kraines RG, Holman HR. Measurement of patient outcome in arthritis. *Arthritis Rheum* 1980;23:137–145.
3. Fries JF, Spitz PW, Young DY. The dimensions of health outcomes: the Health Assessment Questionnaire, disability and pain scales. *J Rheumatol* 1982;9:789–793.
4. Singer F, Kolarz G, Mayrhofer F, Scherak O, Thumb N. The use of questionnaires in the evaluation of the functional capacity in rheumatoid arthritis. *Clin Rheumatol* 1982;1:251–261.
5. Coles LS, Fries JF, Kraines RG, Roth SH. From experiment to experience: side effects of nonsteroidal anti-inflammatory drugs. *Am J Med* 1983;74:820–828.
6. Fries JF. The assessment of disability: from first to future principles. *Br J Rheumatol* 1983;22(suppl):48–58.
7. Fries JF. Toward an understanding of patient outcome measurement. *Arthritis Rheum* 1983;26:697–704.
8. Liang MH, Cullen KE, Larson MG. Measuring function and health status in rheumatic disease clinical trials. *Clin Rheum Dis* 1983;9:531–539.
9. Pincus T, Summey JA, Soraci SA Jr, Wallston KA, Hummon NP. Assessment of patient satisfaction in activities of daily living using a modified Stanford Health Assessment Questionnaire. *Arthritis Rheum* 1983;26:1346–1353.
10. Wolfe F. Effect of age, disease duration and disease activity on disability in rheumatoid arthritis [abstr]. *Arthritis Rheum* 1983;26:S55.
11. Brown JH, Kazis LE, Spitz PW, Gertman P, Fries JF, Meenan RF. The dimensions of health outcomes: a cross-validated examination of health status measurement. *Am J Public Health* 1984;74:159–161.
12. Lubeck DP, Spitz PW, Fries JF. The Health Assessment Questionnaire (HAQ): assessment of personal economic costs [abstr]. *Arthritis Rheum* 1984;25:S24.
13. Reeback J, Silman A. Predictors of outcome at two years in patients with rheumatoid arthritis. *J R Soc Med* 1984;77:1002–1005.
14. Siegert CE, Vleming LJ, Vandenbroucke JP, Cats A. Measurement of disability in Dutch rheumatoid arthritis patients. *Clin Rheumatol* 1984;3:305–309.
15. Spitz PW. The medical, personal, and social costs of rheumatoid arthritis. *Nurs Clin North Am* 1984;19:575–582.
16. Wolfe F, Cathey MA, Kleinheksel SM. Fibrositis (Fibromyalgia) in rheumatoid arthritis. *J Rheumatol* 1984;11:814–818.
17. Liang MH, Larson MG, Cullen KE, Schwartz JA. Comparative measurement efficiency and sensitivity of five health status instruments for arthritis research. *Arthritis Rheum* 1985;28:542–547.
18. Lorig K, Lubeck DP, Kraines RG, Seleznick M, Holman HR. Outcomes of self-help education for patients with arthritis. *Arthritis Rheum* 1985;28:680–685.
19. Lubeck DP, Brown BW, Holman HR. Chronic disease and health system performance: care of osteoarthritis across three health services. *Med Care* 1985;23:266–279.
20. Reeback JS, Silman AJ, Holborow EJ, Maini RN, Hay FC. Circulating immune complexes and rheumatoid arthritis: a comparison of different assay methods and their early predictive value for disease activity and outcome. *Ann Rheum Dis* 1985;44:79–82.
21. Bombardier C, Ware J, Russell IJ, Larson M, Chalmers A, Read JL, et al. Auranofin therapy and quality of life in patients with rheumatoid arthritis. Results of a multicenter trial. *Am J Med* 1986;81:565–578.
22. Cathey MA, Wolfe F, Kleinheksel SM, Hawley DJ. Socioeconomic impact of fibrositis: a study of 81 patients with primary fibrositis. *Am J Med* 1986;81:78–84.
23. Fries JF. Measuring the quality of life: the new science of patient-outcome assessment. *Mediguide Inflammatory Dis* 1986;4:1–6.
24. Fries JF, Spitz PW, Mitchell DM, Roth SH, Wolfe F, Bloch DA. Impact of specific therapy upon rheumatoid arthritis. *Arthritis Rheum* 1986;29:620–627.
25. Kirwan JR, Reeback JS. Stanford Health Assessment Questionnaire modified to assess disability in British patients with rheumatoid arthritis. *Br J Rheumatol* 1986;25:206–209.
26. Lorig K, Feigenbaum P, Regan C, Ung E, Chastain RL, Holman HR. A comparison of lay-taught and professional-taught arthritis self-management courses. *J Rheumatol* 1986;13:763–767.
27. Lubeck DP, Spitz PW, Fries JF, Wolfe F, Mitchell DM, Roth SH. A multicenter study of annual health service utilization and costs in rheumatoid arthritis. *Arthritis Rheum* 1986;29:488–493.
28. Sherrer YS, Bloch DA, Mitchell DM, Young DY, Fries JF. The development of disability in rheumatoid arthritis. *Arthritis Rheum* 1986;29:494–500.
29. Wolfe F, Kleinheksel S, Spitz PW, et al. A multicenter study of hospitalization in rheumatoid arthritis. Frequency, medical-surgical admissions, and charges. *Arthritis Rheum* 1986;29:614–619.
30. Wolfe F, Kleinheksel SM, Spitz PW, Lubeck DP, Fries JF, Young DY, Mitchell DM, Roth SH. A multicenter study of hospitalization in rheumatoid arthritis: effect of health care system, severity, and regional difference. *J Rheumatol* 1986;13:277–284.
31. Baron M, Dutil E, Berkson L, Lander P, Becker R. Hand function in the elderly: relation to osteoarthritis. *J Rheumatol* 1987;14:815–819.
32. Callahan LF, Brooks RH, Summey JA, Pincus T. Quantitative pain assessment for routine care of rheumatoid arthritis patients, using a pain scale based on activities of daily living and a visual analog pain scale. *Arthritis Rheum* 1987;30:630–636.
33. Lane NE, Bloch DA, Wood PD, Fries JF. Aging, long-distance running, and the development of musculoskeletal disability. *Am J Med* 1987;82:772–780.
34. Meenan RF, Pincus T. The status of patient status measures. *J Rheumatol* 1987;14:411–414.
35. Mullen PD, Laville E, Biddle AK, Lorig K. Efficacy of psycho-

educational interventions on pain, depression, and disability with arthritic adults: a meta-analysis. *J Rheumatol* 1987;14:33–39.

36. Sherrer YS, Bloch DA, Mitchell DM, Roth SH, Wolfe F, Fries JF. Disability in rheumatoid arthritis: comparison of prognostic factors across three populations. *J Rheumatol* 1987;14:705–709.

37. Spitz PW, Fries JF. The present and future of comprehensive outcome measures for rheumatic diseases. *Clin Rheumatol* 1987;6(suppl 2):105–111.

38. Sullivan M, Eagers RC, Lynch K, Barber JH. Assessment of disability caused by rheumatic disease in general practice. *Ann Rheum Dis* 1987;46:598–600.

39. Yelin E, Lubeck DP, Holman H, Epstein W. The impact of rheumatoid arthritis and osteoarthritis: the activities of patients with rheumatoid arthritis and osteoarthritis compared to controls. *J Rheumatol* 1987;14:710–717.

40. Borg G, Allander E, Lund B, et al. Auranofin improves outcome in early rheumatoid arthritis. Results from a 2-year, double blind, placebo controlled study. *J Rheumatol* 1988;15:1747–1754.

41. Brooks RH, Callahan LF, Pincus T. Use of self-report activities of daily living questionnaires in osteoarthritis. *Arthritis Care Res* 1988;1:23–32.

42. Cathey MA, Wolfe F, Kleinheksel S. Functional ability and work status in patients with fibromyalgia. *Arthritis Care Res* 1988;1:85–98.

43. Eberhardt KB, Svensson B, Mortiz U. Functional assessment of early rheumatoid arthritis. *Br J Rheumatol* 1988;27:364–371.

44. Ekdahl C, Eberhardt K, Andersson SI, Svensson B. Assessing disability in patients with rheumatoid arthritis—use of Swedish version of the Stanford Health Assessment Questionnaire. *Scand J Rheumatol* 1988;17:263–271.

45. Fries JF. *Milestones in rheumatologic patient care.* Syntex Puerto Rico, San Juan, Puerto Rico, 1988.

46. Fries JF, Bloch DA, Segal MR, Spitz PW, Williams CA, Lane NE. Postmarketing surveillance in rheumatology: analysis of purpura and upper abdominal pain. *J Rheumatol* 1988;15:348–355.

47. Goeppinger J, Doyle MA, Charlton SL, Lorig K. A nursing perspective on the assessment of function in persons with arthritis. *Res Nurs Health* 1988;11:321–331.

48. Hawley DJ, Wolfe F. Anxiety and depression in patients with rheumatoid arthritis: a prospective study of 400 patients. *J Rheumatol* 1988;15:932–941.

49. Hawley DJ, Wolfe F, Cathey MA. Pain, functional disability, and psychological status: a 12-month study of severity in fibromyalgia. *J Rheumatol* 1988;15:1551–1556.

50. Hochberg MC, Sutton JD. Physical disability and psychosocial dysfunction in systemic lupus erythematosus. *J Rheumatol* 1988;15:959–964.

51. Thompson PW. Functional outcome in rheumatoid arthritis. *Br J Rheumatol* 1988;27(suppl 1):37–43.

52. Wolfe F, Kleinheksel SM, Cathey MA, Hawley DJ, Spitz PW, Fries JF. The clinical value of the Stanford Health Assessment Questionnaire functional disability index in patients with rheumatoid arthritis. *J Rheumatol* 1988;15:1480–1488.

53. Callahan LF, Smith WJ, Pincus T. Self-report questionnaires in five rheumatic diseases: comparisons of health status constructs and associations with formal educational level. *Arthritis Care Res* 1989;2:122–131.

54. Ferraz MB, Atra E. Rheumatoid arthritis and the measurement properties of the physical ability dimension of the Stanford Health Assessment Quesitonnaire. *Clin Exp Rheum* 1989;7:341–344.

55. Fitzpatrick R, Newman S, Lamb R, Shipley M. A comparison of measures of health status in rheumatoid arthritis. *Br J Rheumatol* 1989;28:201–206.

56. Fries JF, Miller SR, Spitz PW, Williams CA, Hubert HB, Bloch DA. Toward an epidemiology of gastropathy associated with nonsteroidal antiinflammatory drug use. *Gastroenterology* 1989;96:647–655.

57. Lorig K, Chastain RI, Ung E, Shoor S, Holman HR. Development and evaluation of a scale to measure perceived self-efficacy in people with arthritis. *Arthritis Rheum* 1989;32:37–44.

58. Holman HR, Mazonson P, Lorig K. Health education for self-management has significant early and sustained benefits in chronic arthritis. *Trans Assoc Am Physicians* 1989;102:204–208.

59. Lorig K, Holman HR. Long-term outcomes of an arthritis self-management study: effects of reinforcement efforts. *Soc Sci Med* 1989;29:221–224.

60. Lorig K, Seleznick M, Lubeck DP, Ung E, Chastain RL, Holman HR. The beneficial outcomes of the Arthritis Self-Management Course are inadequately explained by behavior change. *Arthritis Rheum* 1989;32:91–95.

61. Peck JR, Smith TW, Ward JR, Milano R. Disability and depression in rheumatoid arthritis. A multi-trait, multi-method investigation. *Arthritis Rheum* 1989;32:1100–1106.

62. Perez ER, Mackenzie CR, Ryan C. Development of a Spanish version of the modified Health Assessment Questionnaire [abstr]. *Arthritis Rheum* 1989;32:S100.

63. Pincus T, Callahan LF, Brooks RH, Fuchs HA, Olsen NJ, Kaye JJ. Self-report questionnaire scores in rheumatoid arthritis compared with traditional physical, radiographic, and laboratory measures. *Ann Intern Med* 1989;110:259–266.

64. Rogers MP, Liang MH, Daltroy LH, Eaton H, Peteet J, Wright E, Albert M. Delirium after elective orthopedic surgery: risk factors and natural history. *Int J Psychiatry Med* 1989;19:109–121.

65. Sansom DM, Amin SN, Bidwell JL, Louda PT, Bradley BA, Eviswon G, Goulding NJ, Hall ND, Maddison PJ. HLA-DQ-related restriction fragment length polymorphism in rheumatoid arthritis: evidence for a link with disease expression. *Br J Rheumatol* 1989;28:374–378.

66. Singh G, Fries JF, Spitz P, Williams CA. Toxic effects of azathioprine in rheumatoid arthritis. A national post-marketing perspective. *Arthritis Rheum* 1989;32:837–843.

67. Walker DJ, Usher K, O'Morchoe M, Sandles L, Griffiths ID, Pinder IM. Outcome from multiple joint replacement surgery to the lower limbs. *Br J Rheumatol* 1989;28:139–142.

68. Amirdzhanova VN, Folomeeva OM, Tsvetkova ES, Loginova Elu. Otsenka i prognozirovanie trudosposobnosti pri revmatoid artrite. [Evaluation and prognosis of work capacity in rheumatoid arthritis.] *Revmatologiia (USSR)* 1990:41–46.

69. Amirdzhanova VN, Folomeeva OM, Tsvetkova ES, et al. Primenenie modifitsirovannoi ankety otsenki zdorov'ia dlia otsenki effektivnosti terapii v usloviiakh statsionara. [The use of a modified Health Assessment Questionnaire for evaluating the effectiveness of therapy at a hospital.] *Ter Arkh (USSR)* 1990;62:103–106.

70. Bell MJ, Bombardier C, Tugwell P. Measurement of functional status, quality of life, and utility in rheumatoid arthritis. *Arthritis Rheum* 1990;33:591–601.

71. Blalock SJ, Sauter SVH, DeVellis RF. The Modified Health Assessment Questionnaire difficulty scale. A health status measure revisited. *Arthritis Care Res* 1990;3:182–188.

72. Daltroy LH, Larson MG, Roberts NW, Liang MH. A modification of the Health Assessment Questionnaire for the spondyloarthropathies. *J Rheumatol* 1990;17:946–950.

73. Eberhardt KB, Rydgren LC, Pettersson H, Wollheim FA. Early rheumatoid arthritis—onset, course, and outcome over 2 years. *Rheumatol Int* 1990;10:135–142.

74. Ekdahl C. Muscle function in rheumatoid arthritis. Assessment and training. *Scand J Rheumatol* 1990;86:9–61.

75. Ferraz MB, Oliveira LM, Araujo PM, Atra E, Tugwell P. Crosscultural reliability of the physical ability dimension of the Health Assessment Questionnaire. *J Rheumatol* 1990;17:813–817.

76. Ferraz MB, Oliveira LM, Araujo PM, Atra E, Walter SD, EPM-ROM scale: an evaluative instrument to be used in rheumatoid arthritis. *Clin Exp Rheumatol* 1990;8:491–494.

77. Fries JF, Spitz PW. The hierarchy of patient outcomes. In: Spilker B, ed. *Quality of life assessment for clinical trials.* New York: Raven Press, 1990.

78. Fries JF, Spitz PW, Williams CA, Singh G, Bloch DA, Hubert HB. A toxicity index for comparison of side effects among different drugs. *Arthritis Rheum* 1990;33:121–130.

79. Guillemin F, Briancon S, Pourel J, Gaucher A. Long-term disability and prolonged sick leaves as outcome measurements in ankylosing spondylitis. Possible predictive factors. *Arthritis Rheum* 1990;33:1001–1006.

80. Hill J, Bird HA, Lawton CW, Wright V. The arthritis impact measurement scales: an anglicized version to assess the outcome of British patients with rheumatoid arthritis. *Br J Rheumatol* 1990;29:193–196.

81. Kazis LE, Callahan LF, Meenan RF, Pincus T. Health status reports in the care of patients with rheumatoid arthritis. *J Clin Epidemiol* 1990;43:1243–1253.

82. Lane NE, Bloch DA, Hubert HB, Jones HH, Simpson U, Fries JF.

Running, osteoarthritis, and bone density: initial two-year longitudinal study. *Am J Med* 1990;88:452–459.

83. Lequesne M. Methodology issues in the evaluation of NSAID in inflammatory arthritis. *J Rheumatol Suppl* 1990;20:25–28.

84. Liang MH, Fossel AH, Larson MG. Comparisons of five health status instruments for orthopedic evaluation. *Med Care* 1990;28:632–642.

85. Sibley J, Blocka K, Haga M, Martin W, et al. Clinical course and predictors of length of stay in hospitalized patients with rheumatoid arthritis. *J Rheumatol* 1990;17:1623–1627.

86. Singh G, Athreya B, Fries J, Goldsmith D. Measurement of health status in children with juvenile rheumatoid arthritis. *Arthritis Rheum* 1994;37:1761–1769.

87. Sullivan FM, Barber JH, Sturrock RD. Rheumatology at the general practitioner/hospital interface: a study of prevalence and access to specialist care. *Ann Rheum Dis* 1990;49:983–985.

88. van der Heijde DM, van Riel PL, van de Putte LB. Sensitivity of a Dutch Health Assessment Questionnaire in a trial comparing hydroxychloroquine vs. sulphasalazine. *Scand J Rheumatol* 1990;19:407–412.

89. Wolfe F, Hawley DJ, Cathey MA. Termination of slow acting antirheumatic therapy in rheumatoid arthritis: a 14-year prospective evaluation of 1017 consecutive starts. *J Rheumatol* 1990;17:994–1002.

90. Allaire SH, Meenan RF, Anderson JJ. The impact of rheumatoid arthritis on the household work performance of women. *Arthritis Rheum* 1991;34:669–678.

91. Bombardier C, Raboud J, The Auranofin Cooperating Group. A comparison of health-related quality-of-life measure for rheumatoid arthritis research. *Control Clin Trials* 1991;12(suppl):243S–256S.

92. Bostrom C, Harms-Ringdahl K, Nordemar R. Clinical reliability of shoulder function assessment in patients with rheumatoid arthritis. *Scand J Rheumatol* 1991;20:36–48.

93. Bradley JD, Brandt KD, Katz BP, Kalasinski LA, Ryan SI. Comparison of an antiinflammatory dose of ibuprofen, an analgesic dose of ibuprofen, and acetaminophen in the treatment of patients with osteoarthritis of the knee. *N Engl J Med* 1991;325:87–91.

94. Epstein WV, Henke CJ, Yelin EH, Katz PP. Effect of parenterally administered gold therapy on the course of adult rheumatoid arthritis. *Ann Intern Med* 1991;114:437–444.

95. Felson DT, Anderson JJ, Meenan RF. Use of short-term efficacy/toxicity trade offs to select second-line drugs in rheumatoid arthritis. *Arthritis Rheum* 1992;35:1117–1125.

96. Fries JF. The hierarchy of quality of life assessment, the Health Assessment Questionnaire (HAQ), and issues mandating development of toxicity index. *Controlled Clin Trials* 1991;12:106S–117S.

97. Fries JF, Spitz PW, Bloch DA, Williams CA. Factors in the duration and discontinuation of treatment with nonsteroidal anti-inflammatory medications. *Clin Ther* 1991;13(A):51–62.

98. Fries JF, Williams CA, Bloch DA. The relative toxicity of nonsteroidal anti-inflammatory drugs. *Arthritis Rheum* 1991;34:1353–1360.

99. Guillemin F, Briancon S, Pourel J. Mesure de la capacite fonctionnelle dans la polyarthrite rhumatoide: Adaptation Francaise du Health Assessment Questionnaire (HAQ). [Measurement of functional capacity in rheumatoid arthritis: French adaptation of the Health Assessment Questionnaire (HAQ).] *Revue Rhuma* 1991;58:459–465.

100. Hawley DJ, Wolfe F. Are the results of controlled clinical trials and observational studies in rheumatoid arthritis valid and generalizable as measures of rheumatoid arthritis outcome: an analysis of 70 published reports. *J Rheumatol* 1991;18:1008–1014.

101. Hawley DJ, Wolfe F. Pain, disability, and pain/disability relationships in seven rheumatic disorders: a study of 1522 patients. *J Rheumatol* 1991;18:1552–1557.

102. Kjeldsen-Kragh J, Haugen M, Borchgrevink CF, et al. Controlled trial of fasting and one-year vegetarian diet in rheumatoid arthritis. *Lancet* 1991;338:899–902.

103. Leigh JP, Fries JF. Education level and rheumatoid arthritis: evidence from five data centers. *J Rheumatol* 1991;18:24–34.

104. Leigh JP, Fries JF. Mortality predictors among 263 patients with rheumatoid arthritis. *J Rheumatol* 1991;18:1307–1312.

105. Lubeck DP, Fries JF, McShane DJ. Health status among persons with HIV infection: a community-based study. *Med Care* 1993;31:269–276.

106. Poole J, Steen VD. The use of the Health Assessment Questionnaire (HAQ) to determine physical disability in systemic sclerosis. *Arthritis Care Res* 1991;4:27–31.

107. Russell IJ, Fletcher EM, Michaleck JE, Hester GG. Treatment of primary fibrositis/fibromyalgia syndrome with ibuprofen and alprazolam. A double-blind, placebo-controlled study. *Arthritis Rheum* 1991;34:552–560.

108. Singh G, Brown B, Athreya B, Goldsmith D, Rettig P, Bloch D, Fries J. Functional status in juvenile rheumatoid arthritis: sensitivity to change of the Childhood Health Assessment Questionnaire [abstr]. *Arthritis Rheum* 1991;34:S81.

109. Singh G, Fries JF, Williams CA, Zatarain E, et al. Toxicity profiles of disease-modifying anti-rheumatic drugs in rheumatoid arthritis. *J Rheumatol* 1991;18:188–194.

110. Thompson PW, Pegley FS. A comparison of disability measured by the Stanford Health Assessment Questionnaire disability scales (HAQ) in male and female rheumatoid arthritis outpatients. *Br J Rheumatol* 1991;30:298–300.

111. van Zeben D, Hazes JM, Zwinderman AH, Cats A, Schreuder GM, D'Amaro J, Breedveld FC. Association of HLA-DR4 with a more progressive disease course in patients with rheumatoid arthritis. Results of a followup study. *Arthritis Rheum* 1991;34:822–830.

112. Ward MM, Leigh JP. Marital status and the progression of functional disability in patients with rheumatoid arthritis. *Arthritis Rheum* 1993;36:581–588.

113. Ward MM, Leigh JP, Fries JF. Progression of functional disability in patients with rheumatoid arthritis: associations with rheumatology subspecialty care. *Arch Intern Med* 1993;153:2229–2237.

114. Wolfe F, Cathey MA. The assessment and prediction of functional disability in rheumatoid arthritis. *J Rheumatol* 1991;18:1298–1306.

115. Wolfe F, Cathey MA. The effect of age on methotrexate efficacy and toxicity. *J Rheumatol* 1991;18:974–977.

116. Wolfe F, Hawley DJ, Cathey MA. Clinical and health status measures over time: prognosis and outcome assessment in rheumatoid arthritis. *J Rheumatol* 1991;18:1290–1297.

117. Wolfe F, Pincus T. Standard self-report questionnaries in routine clinical and research practice: an opportunity for patients and rheumatologists (editorial). *J Rheumatol* 1991;18:643–646.

118. Woolf AD, Hall ND, Goulding NJ, et al. Predictors of the long-term outcome of early synovitis: a 5-year follow-up study. *Br J Rheumatol* 1991;30:251–254.

119. Deighton CM, Surtees D, Walker DJ. Influence of the severity of rheumatoid arthritis on sex differences in Health Assessment Questionnaire scores. *Ann Rheum Dis* 1992;51:473–475.

120. Deighton CM, Watson MJ, Walker DJ. Sex hormones in postmenopausal HLA-identical rheumatoid arthritis discordant sibling pairs. *J Rheumatol* 1992;19:1663–1667.

121. Guillemin F, Briancon S, Pourel J. Validity and discriminant ability of the HAQ functional index in early rheumatoid arthritis. *Disabil Rehabil* 1992;51:972–973.

122. Hardo PG, Wasti SA, Tennant A. Night pain in arthritis: patients at risk from prescribed night sedation. *Ann Rheum Dis* 1992;51:972–973.

123. Hawley DJ, Wolfe F. Sensitivity to change of the Health Assessment Questionnaire (HAQ) and other clinical and health status measures in rheumatoid arthritis: results of short-term clinical trials and observational studies versus long-term observational studies. *Arthritis Care Res* 1992;5:130–136.

124. Hawley DJ, Wolfe F, Cathey MA. The Sense of Coherence Questionnaire in patients with rheumatic disorders. *J Rheumatol* 1992;19:1912–1918.

125. Hochberg MC, Change RW, Dwosh I, Lindsey S, Pincus T, Wolfe F. The American College of Rheumatology 1991 revised criteria for the classification of global functional status in rheumatoid arthritis. *Arthritis Rheum* 1992;35:498–502.

126. Leigh JP, Fries JF. Disability in occupations in a national sample. *Am J Public Health* 1992;82:1517–1524.

127. Leigh JP, Fries JF. Predictors of disability in a longitudinal sample of rheumatoid arthritis patients. *Ann Rheum Dis* 1992;51(5):581–587.

128. Leigh JP, Fries JF, Parikh N. Severity of disability and duration of disease in a sample of rheumatoid arthritis patients followed for eight years. *J Rheumatol* 1992;19:1906–1911.

129. Lubeck DP, Fries JF. Changes in quality of life among persons with HIV infection. *Qual Life Res* 1992;1:359–366.

130. McAlindon TE, Snow S, Cooper C, Dieppe PA. Radiographic patterns

of osteoarthritis of the knee joint in the community: the importance of the patellofemoral joint. *Ann Rheum Dis* 1992;51:844–849.

131. Raynauld JP, Singh G, Shiroky JB, et al. A French-Canadian version of the Health Assessment Questionnaire. *Arthritis Rheum* 1992;35:S125.

132. Russell IJ, Michalek JE, Vipraio GA, Fletcher EM, Javors MA, Bowden CA. Platelet 3H-imipramine uptake receptor density and serum serotonin levels in patients with fibromyalgia fibrositis syndrome. *J Rheumatol* 1992;19:104–109.

133. Salaffi F, Ferracciloi GF, Carotti M, Blasetti P, Cervini C. Disability in rheumatoid arthritis: the predictive value of age and depression. *Recenti Prog Med* 1992;83:675–679.

134. Ziebland S, Fitzpatrick R, Jenkinson C, Mowat A. Comparison of two approaches to measuring change in health status in rheumatoid arthritis: the Health Assessment Questionnaire (HAQ) and modified HAQ. *Ann Rheum Dis* 1992;51:1202–1505.

135. Ailinger RL. Self-care agency in persons with rheumatoid arthritis. *Arthritis Care Res* 1993;6:134–140.

136. Andersson Gare B, Fasth A, Wiklund I. Measurement of functional status in juvenile chronic arthritis: evaluation of a Swedish version of the Childhood Health Assessment Questionnaire. *Clin Exp Rheumatol* 1993;11:569–576.

137. Bendtsen P, Bjurulf P. Perceived needs and patient satisfaction in relation to care provided in individuals with rheumatoid arthritis. *Qual Assur Health Care* 1993;5:243–253.

138. Bendtsen P, Hornquist JO. Severity of rheumatoid arthritis, function and quality of life: subgroup comparisons. *Clin Exp Rheumatol* 1993;11:495–502.

139. Cardiel MH, Abello-Banfi M, Ruiz-Mercado R, Alarcon-Segovia D. How to measure health status in rheumatoid arthritis in non-English speaking patients: validation of Spanish version of the Health Assessment Questionnaire Disability Index. *Clin Exp Rheumatol* 1993;11:117–121.

140. Choy EH, Kingsley GH, Corkill MM, Panayi GS. Intramuscular methylprednisolone is superior to pulse oral methylprednisolone during the induction phase of chrysotherapy. *Br J Rheumatol* 1993;32:734–739.

141. Clarke AE, Bloch DA, Lacaille D, Danoff DS, Fries JF. A Canadian study of total medical costs for patients with systemic lupus erythematosus and the predictors of costs. *Arthritis Rheum* 1993;36:1548–1559.

142. Eberhardt K, Grubb R, Johnson U, Pettersson H. HLA-DR antigens, GM allotypes and antiallotypes in early rheumatoid arthritis—their relation to disease progression. *J Rheumatol* 1993;20:1825–1829.

143. Eberhardt K, Larsson BM, Nived K. Early rheumatoid arthritis—some social, economical, and psychological aspects. *Scand J Rheumatol* 1993;22:119–123.

144. Eberhardt K, Larsson BM, Nived K. Psychological reactions in patients with early rheumatoid arthritis. *Patient Educ Counsel* 1993; 20:93–100.

145. Esteve-Vives J, Batlle-Gualda E, Reig A. Spanish version of the Health Assessment Questionnaire: reliability, validity and transcultural equivalency. Grupo para la Adaptacion del HAQ a la Poblacion Espanola. *J Rheumatol* 1993;20:2116–2122.

146. Felson DT, Anderson JJ, Boers M, et al. The American College of Rheumatology preliminary core set of disease activity measures for rheumatoid arthritis clinical trials. The Committee on Outcome Measures in Rheumatoid Arthritis Clinical Trials. *Arthritis Rheum* 1993; 36:729–740.

147. Fries JF, Ramey DR, Singh G, Morfeld D, Bloch DA, Raynauld JP. A reevaluation of aspirin therapy in rheumatoid arthritis (RA). *Arch Intern Med* 1993;153:2465–2471.

148. Fries JF, Williams CA, Ramey DR, Bloch DA. The relative toxicity of disease modifying antirheumatic drugs (DMARDs). *Arthritis Rheum* 1993;36:297–306.

149. Gardiner PV, Sykes HR, Hassey GA, Walker DJ. An evaluation of the Health Assessment Questionnaire in long-term longitudinal follow-up of disability in rheumatoid arthritis. *Br J Rheumatol* 1993;32:724–728.

150. Hall GM, Spector TD, Griffin AJ, Jawad AS, Hall ML, Doyle DV. The effect of rheumatoid arthritis and steroid therapy on bone density in postmenopausal women. *Arthritis Rheum* 1993;36:1510–1516.

151. Hassell AB, Davis MJ, Fowler PD, et al. The relationship between serial measures of disease activity and outcome in rheumatoid arthritis. *Q J Med* 1993;86:601–607.

152. Hidding A, van der Linden S, Boers M, et al. Is group physical therapy superior to individualized therapy in ankylosing spondylitis? A randomized controlled trial. *Arthritis Care Res* 1993;6:117–125.

153. Jacobs JW, van der Heide A, Rasker JJ, Bijlsma JW. Measurement of functional ability and health status in the arthritic patient. *Patient Educ Counsel* 1993;20:121–132.

154. Katz PP, Yelin EH. Prevalence and correlates of depressive symptoms among persons with rheumatoid arthritis. *J Rheumatol* 1993;20: 790–796.

155. Laan RF, Buijs WC, Verbeek AL, et al. Bone mineral density in patients with recent onset rheumatoid arthritis: influence of disease activity and functional capacity. *Ann Rheum Dis* 1993;52:21–26.

156. Ledingham J, Doherty S, Doherty M. Primary fibromyalgia syndrome—an outcome study. *Br J Rheumatol* 1993;32:139–142.

157. Leigh JP, Fries JF. Tobit, fixed effects, and cohort analyses of the relationship between severity and duration of rheumatoid arthritis. *Soc Sci Med* 1993;36:1495–1502.

158. Leigh JP, Ward MM, Fries JF. Reducing attrition bias with an instrumental variable in a regression model: results from a panel of rheumatoid arthritis patients. *Stat Med* 1993;12:1005–1018.

159. Lorig KR, Mazonson PD, Holman HR. Evidence suggesting that health education for self-management in patients with chronic arthritis has sustained health benefits while reducing health care costs. *Arthritis Rheum* 1993;36:439–446.

160. Lubeck DP, Bennett CL, Mazonson PD, Fifer SK, Fries JF. Quality of life and health service use among HIV-infected patients with chronic diarrhea. *J Acquir Immune Defic Syndr* 1993;6:478–484.

161. Lubeck DP, Fries JF. Health status among persons with HIV infection: a community-based study. *Med Care* 1993;31:269–276.

162. McAlindon TE, Cooper C, Kirwan JR, Dieppe PA. Determinants of disability in osteoarthritis of the knee. *Ann Rheum Dis* 1993;52: 258–262.

163. Milligan SE, Hom DL, Ballou SP, Persse LJ, Svilar GM, Boulton CJ. An asessment of the Health Assessment Questionnaire functional ability index among women with systemic lupus erythematosus. *J Rheumatol* 1993;20:972–976.

164. Plant MJ, Linton S, Dodd E, Jones PW, Dawes PT. The GALS locomotor screen and disability. *Ann Rheum Dis* 1993;52:886–890.

165. Porter DR, Capell HA, Hunter J. Combination therapy in rheumatoid arthritis—no benefit of addition of hydroxychlorquine to patients with a suboptimal response to intramuscular gold therapy. *J Rheumatol* 1993;20:645–649.

166. Prevoo MLL, Van Reil PLCM, van'T Hof MH, et al. Validity and reliability of joint indices. A longitudinal study in patients with recent onset rheumatoid arthritis. *Br J Rheumatol* 1993;32:589–594.

167. Ranza R, Marchesoni A, Calori G, et al. The Italian version of the functional disability index of the Health Assessment Questionnaire. A reliable instrument for multicenter studies on rheumatoid arthritis. *Clin Exp Rheumatol* 1993;11:123–128.

168. Redelmeier DA, Lorig K. Assessing the clinical importance of symptomatic improvements. An illustration in rheumatology. *Arch Intern Med* 1993;153:1337–1342.

169. Taha AS, Morran C, Sturrock RD, Russell RI. The Health Assessment Questionnaire as a predictor of non-steroidal peptic ulceration. *Br J Rheumatol* 1993;32:135–138.

170. van der Heide A, Jacobs JW, van Albada-Kuipers GA, Kraaimaat FW, Geenen R, Bijlsma JW. Self report functional disability scores and the use of devices: two distinct aspects of physical function in rheumatoid arthritis. *Ann Rheum Dis* 1993;52:497–502.

171. van der Heijde DMFM, van'T Hof M, van Riel PLCM, van de Putte LBA. Validity of single variables and indices to measure disease activity in rheumatoid arthritis. *J Rheumatol* 1993;20:538–541.

172. van Zeben D, Hazes JM, Zwinderman AH, Vandenbroucke JP, Breedveld FC. Factors predicting outcome of rheumatoid arthritis: results of a followup study. *J Rheumatol* 1993;20:1288–1296.

173. Ward MM, Leigh JP. The relative importance of pain and functional disability to patients with rheumatoid arthritis. *J Rheumatol* 1993; 20:1494–1499.

174. Wells GA, Tugwell P, Kraag GR, Baker PR, Groh J, Redelmeier DA. Minimum important difference between patients with rheumatoid arthritis: the patient's perspective. *J Rheumatol* 1993;20:557–560.

175. Wolfe F, Hawley DJ. The relationship between clinical activity and depression in rheumatoid arthritis. *J Rheumatol* 1993;20:2032–2037.

176. Wolfe F, Hawley DJ, Cathey MA. Measurement of gold treatment effect in clinical practice: evidence for effectiveness of intramuscular gold therapy. *J Rheumatol* 1993;20:797–802.

177. Bradley JD, Flusser D, Katz BP, et al. A randomized, double blind,

placebo controlled trial of intravenous loading with S-adenosylmethionine (SAM) followed by oral SAM therapy in patients with knee osteoarthritis. *J Rheumatol* 1994;21:905–911.

178. Crotty M, McFarlane AC, Brooks PM, Hopper JL, Bieri D, Taylor SJ. The psychosocial and clinical status of younger women with early rheumatoid arthritis: a longitudinal study with frequent measures. *Br J Rheumatol* 1994;33:754–760.

179. Fries JF, Singh G, Morfeld D, Hubert HB, Lane NE, Brown BW. Running and the development of disability with age. *Ann Intern Med* 1994;121:502–509.

180. Gough AK, Peel NF, Eastell R, Holder RL, Lilley J, Emery P. Excretion of pyridinium crosslinks correlates with disease activity and appendicular bone loss in early rheumatoid arthritis. *Ann Rheum Dis* 1994;53:14–17.

181. Hakala M, Nieminen P, Manelius J. Joint impairment is strongly correlated with disability measured by self-report questionnaires. Functional status assessment of individuals with rheumatoid arthritis in a population based series. *J Rheumatol* 1994;21:64–69.

182. Heytman M, Ahern MH, Smith MD, Roberts-Thompson PJ. The long-term effect of pulsed corticosteroids on the efficacy and toxicity of chrysotherapy in rheumatoid arthritis. *J Rheumatol* 1994;21:435–441.

183. Hidding A, de Witte L, van der Linden S. Determinants of self-reported health status in ankylosing spondylitis. *J Rheumatol* 1994;21:275–278.

184. Hidding A, van der Linden S, Gielen X, de Witte L, Dijkmans B, Moolenburgh D. Continuation of group physical therapy is necessary in ankylosing spondylitis. *Arthritis Care Res* 1994;7:90–96.

185. Hubert HB, Fries JF. Predictors of physical disability after age 50. Six-year longitudinal study in a runners club and a university population. *Ann Epidemiol* 1994;4:285–294.

186. Katz PP, Yelin EH. Life activities of persons with rheumatoid arthritis with and without depressive symptoms. *Arthritis Care Res* 1994;7:69–77.

187. Kirwan JR, Currey HL, Freeman MA, Snow S, Young PJ. Overall long-term impact of total hip and knee joint replacement surgery on patients with osteoarthritis and rheumatoid arthritis. *Br J Rheumatol* 1994;33:357–360.

188. Lambert CM, Hurst NP, Lochhead A, McGregor K, Hunter M, Forbes J. A pilot study of the economic cost and clinical outcome of day patient vs inpatient management of active rheumatoid arthritis. *Br J Rheumatol* 1994;33:383–388.

189. Lubeck DP, Fries JF. Changes in health status after one year for persons at-risk for and with HIV infections. *Psychol Health* 1994;9:79–92.

190. McDonagh JE, Ledingham J, Deighton CM, Griffiths ID, Pinder IM, Walker DJ. Six-year follow-up of multiple joint replacement surgery to the lower limbs. *Br J Rheumatol* 1994;33:85–89.

191. Meyer CL, Hawley DJ. Characteristics of participants in water exercise programs compared to patients seen in a rheumatic disease clinic. *Arthritis Care Res* 1994;7:85–89.

192. Shenstone BD, Mahmoud A, Woodward R, Elvins D, Palmer R, Ring EF, Bhalla AK. Longitudinal bone mineral density changes in early rheumatoid arthritis. *Br J Rheumatol* 1994;33:541–545.

193. Singh G, Ramey DR, Morfeld D, Fries JF. Comparative toxicity of non-steroidal anti-inflammatory agents. *Pharmacol Ther* 1994;62:175–191.

194. Stenstrom CH. Home exercise in rheumatoid arthritis functional class II: goal setting versus pain attention. *J Rheumatol* 1994;21:627–634.

195. van Leeuwen MA, van der Heijde DM, van Rijswijk MH, et al. Interrelationship of outcome measures and process variables in early rheumatoid arthritis. A comparison of radiologic damage, physical disability, joint counts, and acute phase reactants. *J Rheumatol* 1994;21:425–429.

196. Ward MM. Clinical measures in rheumatoid arthritis: which are most useful in assessing patients? *J Rheumatol* 1994;21:17–27.

197. Wolfe F, Mitchell DM, Sibley JT, et al. The mortality of rheumatoid arthritis. *Arthritis Rheum* 1994;37:481–494.

198. White KL. Improved medical care: statistics and the health service system. *Public Health Rep* 1967;82:847–854.

199. McNeil BJ, Pauker SG, Sox HC, Tversky A. On the elicitation of preferences for alternative therapies. *N Engl J Med* 1982;306:1259–1262.

200. Lorig K, Cox T, Cuevas Y, et al. Converging and diverging beliefs about arthritis: Caucasian patients, Spanish-speaking patients and physicians. *J Rheumatol* 1984;11:76–79.

201. Potts M, Mazzuca S, Brandt K. Views of patients and physicians regarding the importance of various aspects of arthritis treatment. Correlations with health status and patient satisfaction. *Patient Educ Couns* 1986;8:125–134.

202. Steinbrocker O, Trager CH, Betterman RC. Therapeutic criteria in rheumatoid arthritis. *JAMA* 1949;140:659–662.

203. Langley GB, Sheppeard H. Problems associated with pain measurement in arthritis: comparison of the visual analogue and verbal rating scales. *Clin Exp Rheumatol* 1984;2:231–234.

204. Anderson KO, Bradley LA, McDaniel LK, et al. The assessment of pain in rheumatoid arthritis: disease differentiation and temporal stability of a behavioral observation method. *J Rheumatol* 1987;14:700–704.

Quality of Life and Pharmacoeconomics in Clinical Trials, Second Edition, edited by B. Spilker.
Lippincott-Raven Publishers, Philadelphia © 1996.

CHAPTER 26

Health Utilities Index

David H. Feeny, George W. Torrance, and William J. Furlong

INTRODUCTION

The Health Utilities Index (HUI) is a generic approach to the measurement of health status and assessment of health-related quality of life (HRQL). The HUI provides a comprehensive framework within which to measure health status and calculate HRQL scores. The HUI is comprised of two complementary components. The first component is a multiattribute health status classification system that is used to describe health status. The second component is a multiattribute utility function that is used to value health status as measured within the corresponding multiattribute health status classification system.

The focus of the chapter is on two recently developed systems, the Health Utilities Index Mark II and III systems. The chapter discusses the definition of health status, the evolution of the HUI systems, and the assessment of health status in the HUI. Examples of the use of the HUI to describe

health status are provided. The conceptual foundations of utility theory and multiattribute utility functions are then discussed. The use of HUI utility scores is illustrated. Finally, additional methodological issues are considered and conclusions are drawn.

DEFINITION AND MEASUREMENT OF HEALTH STATUS

Health status is a multidimensional concept. To capture this, a multiattribute approach is used in the HUI system. In the HUI a number of aspects of health status are specified using a comprehensive and compact classification system. In the language of decision analysis these aspects are referred to as *attributes;* in the language of sociology and psychology the terms *dimensions* or *domains* could be substituted for attributes. Examples of attributes include mobility, cognition, emotion, and pain (1–6). In the context of assessing health status, the HUI is conceptually similar to a number of traditional multidimensional systems. In the context of the valuation of health status, however, the HUI, by exploiting multiattribute utility theory, differs importantly from traditional multidimensional systems.

D. H. Feeny, G. W. Torrance, and W. J. Furlong: Department of Clinical Epidemiology and Biostatistics, Centre for Health Economics and Policy Analysis, Department of Economics, McMaster University, Hamilton, Ontario L8N 3Z5, Canada.

In the HUI, the health status of a person at a point in time is assessed in terms of his/her ability to function on each attribute of health status. The ability to function on each attribute is described by levels that vary from severely impaired to normal. The HUI is an example of the generic approach to the assessment of health-related quality of life (7,8).

Measures of health status are often used for one of three major purposes: discrimination, evaluation, or prediction (7,9). Discriminative measures are used to distinguish differences in health status within and among populations. Evaluative measures focus on the assessment of changes in health status within an individual over time. Predictive measures are used for prognostic purposes. It is not uncommon for an investigator to be interested in more than one of these purposes. Nonetheless in the context of clinical trials and pharmacoeconomics, evaluative and discriminative applications are usually the most relevant.

There are a wide variety of definitions of health status. (A useful review is found in ref. 10, Chapter 4; see also refs. 11 and 12.) The definition that is chosen for any particular study should be compatible with the study objectives and nature of the health status information that is available.

Some multidimensional systems such as the Sickness Impact Profile have adopted relatively inclusive definitions of health status with a broad array of dimensions including social interaction. Other approaches such as the HUI Mark II and III systems to be described below have adopted a relatively more narrow "within the skin" approach to health status that focuses on physical and emotional dimensions of health status and excludes social interaction because it takes place "outside the skin" (13). This focus was chosen in part because it facilitates the development of quantitative preference functions for the assessment of health-related quality of life. The "within the skin" definition also facilitates a focus on health-related quality of life as opposed to more general concepts of quality of life or well-being that are implicated when social interaction and other "outside the skin" phenomenon are included.

EVOLUTION OF HEALTH UTILITIES INDEX SYSTEM

Fanshel and Bush (14) (see also 15–19) devised one of the first multiattribute systems, comprised of four attributes:

TABLE 1. Mark II health status classification system

Attribute	Level	Level description
Sensation	1	Ability to see, hear, and speak normally for age
	2	Requires equipment to see or hear or speak
	3	Sees, hears, or speaks with limitations even with equipment
	4	Blind, deaf, or mute
Mobility	1	Able to walk, bend, lift, jump, and run normally for age
	2	Walks, bends, lifts, jumps, or runs with some limitations but does not require help
	3	Requires mechanical equipment (such as canes, crutches, braces, or wheelchair) to walk or get around independently
	4	Requires the help of another person to walk or get around and requires mechanical equipment as well
	5	Unable to control or use arms and legs
Emotion	1	Generally happy and free from worry
	2	Occasionally fretful, angry, irritable, anxious, depressed, or suffering night terrors
	3	Often fretful, angry, irritable, anxious, depressed, or suffering night terrors
	4	Almost always fretful, angry, irritable, anxious, depressed
	5	Extremely fretful, angry, irritable, or depressed usually requiring hospitalization or psychiatric institutional care
Cognition	1	Learns and remembers schoolwork normally for age
	2	Learns and remembers schoolwork more slowly than classmates as judged by parents and/or teachers
	3	Learns and remembers very slowly and usually requires special educational assistance
	4	Unable to learn and remember
Self-care	1	Eats, bathes, dresses, and uses the toilet normally for age
	2	Eats, bathes, dresses, or uses the toilet independently with difficulty
	3	Requires mechanical equipment to eat, bathe, dress, or use the toilet independently
	4	Requires the help of another person to eat, bathe, dress, or use the toilet
Pain	1	Free of pain and discomfort
	2	Occasional pain; discomfort relieved by nonprescription drugs or self-control activity without disruption of normal activities
	3	Frequent pain; discomfort relieved by oral medicines with occasional disruption of normal activities
	4	Frequent pain, frequent disruption of normal activities; discomfort requires prescription narcotics for relief
	5	Severe pain; pain not relieved by drugs and constantly disrupts normal activities
Fertility	1	Ability to have children with a fertile spouse
	2	Difficulty in having children with a fertile spouse
	3	Unable to have children with a fertile spouse

From ref. 5.

mobility, physical activity, social activity, and symptom-problem complex. A number of other systems have been developed (20) including a system by Rosser and Watts (21) (see also 22–26).

Torrance and colleagues (6,27–29) extended the multi-attribute framework developed by Bush and colleagues for use in evaluating outcomes for very low birth weight infants. The system is comprised of four attributes—physical function, role function, social-emotional function, and health problem—with four to eight levels of function for each. The system describes 960 unique health states. Subsequently this system has been labeled as the Health Utilities Index Mark I system (10, pp. 381–389).

The Mark I system devised by Torrance and colleagues for neonatal intensive care was further extended for pediatric application by Cadman and colleagues (1). Their study elicited preference judgments both from parents and children to determine the core set of attributes considered to be most important. A careful review of the literature produced the following set of potential attributes: physical activity, mobility, self-care, school performance, play, learning ability, happiness, pain or discomfort, sight, hearing, speech, use of limbs, cause of health problem, age of onset of health problem, and name of disease or disorder. Eighty-four parent and child pairs evaluated the set of 15 potential attributes to determine which were most important. The six attributes rated as most important were sensory and communication ability (comprised of vision, hearing, and speech), happiness, self-care, pain or discomfort, learning and school ability, and physical activity ability.

The results of the Cadman et al. (1–3) study formed the basis for the Mark II (Table 1) seven-attribute system (5,30). The system was initially conceived as a tool to assess health status in survivors of childhood cancer. Subsequently the Mark II system was adapted for use in population health surveys (31). The resulting Mark III system is presented in Table 2.

A number of other multiattribute systems have recently been developed. the EuroQoL system is an example (32–34).

CONTENT OF HEALTH UTILITIES INDEX MARK II AND III SYSTEMS

As outlined above, the Mark II system was based both on the Mark I system and the work of Cadman and colleagues. To the six attributes identified by Cadman et al. (1), fertility was added as a seventh attribute in order to capture the subfertility and infertility sequelae of many forms of childhood cancer. The Mark II system describes 24,000 unique health states.

The Mark II seven-attribute system was subsequently modified for use in general population health surveys (31). One problem discovered in the application of the Mark II system was an overlap (lack of structural independence) among self-care and other attributes. An important ramification of the lack of structural independence was that some

of the health states defined by the system, for instance having level 1 (normal) self-care while also having level 5 mobility (unable to control arms and legs), were virtually impossible to imagine—thus complicating the estimation of the preference function. Furthermore, problems in self-care could be due to a variety of causes, including impairments in mobility, vision, cognition, or emotion. In revising the Mark II system, one potential cause of problems with self-care that was not covered by the other attributes was identified, namely problems with fine motor skills and dexterity. Therefore, to enhance the structural independence among attributes, self-care was replaced with dexterity. In addition, to increase the precision of health status measurement, sensation was divided into its three distinct components: vision, hearing, and speech. Finally, fertility was eliminated. The resulting eight attribute Mark III system (see Table 2) has been used in the 1990 Ontario Health Survey (35) and 1991 Statistics Canada General Social Survey (36–38) and is being used in the National Population Health Survey and National Longitudinal Health Survey of Children in Canada.

The Mark III system specifies five or six levels per attribute and describes 972,000 unique health states. In addition to its use in population health surveys (and thus the availability of data on population norms), it has also been incorporated into a number of clinical and program evaluation studies. Questionnaires for the collection of Mark III health-status classification data are currently available in English and French Canadian, in child and adult versions, and for three modes of administration (self report, face-to-face interview, and telephone interview).

The HUI Mark II and III systems are based on concepts of functional capacity rather than performance. The intent is to document the extent to which deficits in health status for each attribute inhibit or prohibit normal functioning rather than to report the level at which an individual chooses to function, as would be reflected in a measure of performance. Ordinarily, the focus is on one's usual capacity, although in an evaluative context one can instead focus on capacity during some recent and explicitly specified time period. Although the conceptual focus is on capacity, for the purpose of measurement it may be necessary to use observations about performance as proxy for information on capacity. For instance, the levels of capacity for speech in the Mark III system (see Table 2) are defined in terms of performance.

The focus on capacity in the Mark II and III systems reflects in part the choice of a "within the skin" definition of health status described above. The choice also reflects the two-step approach to the assessment of health-related quality of life within the HUI system. In the HUI system the first step is to assess health status, defined as capacity, and (at least conceptually) independently of the value that the subject attaches to that health status. In the second step, a multiattribute utility function is used to value health status as defined in the first step.

Approaches that rely on performance rather than capacity as the conceptual basis for assessing health status tend to

TABLE 2. *Mark III health status classification system*

Attribute	Level	Level description
Vision	1	Able to see well enough to read ordinary newsprint and recognize a friend on the other side of the street, without glasses or contact lenses
	2	Able to see well enough to read ordinary newsprint and recognize a friend on the other side of the street, but with glasses
	3	Able to read ordinary newsprint with or without glasses but unable to recognize a friend on the other side of the street, even with glasses
	4	Able to recognize a friend on the other side of the street with or without glasses but unable to read ordinary newsprint, even with glasses
	5	Unable to read ordinary newsprint and unable to recognize a friend on the other side of the street, even with glasses
	6	Unable to see at all
Hearing	1	Able to hear what is said in a group conversation with at least three other people, without a hearing aid
	2	Able to hear what is said in a conversation with one other person in a quiet room without a hearing aid, but requires a hearing aid to hear what is said in a group conversation with at least three other people
	3	Able to hear what is said in a conversation with one other person in a quiet room with a hearing aid, and able to hear what is said in a group conversation with at least three other people with a hearing aid
	4	Able to hear what is said in a conversation with one other person in a quiet room without a hearing aid, but unable to hear what is said in a group conversation with at least three other people even with a hearing aid
	5	Able to hear what is said in a conversation with one other person in a quiet room with a hearing aid, but unable to hear what is said in a group conversation with at least three other people even with a hearing aid
	6	Unable to hear at all
Speech	1	Able to be understood completely when speaking with strangers or friends
	2	Able to be understood partially when speaking with strangers but able to be understood completely when speaking with people who know the respondent well
	3	Able to be understood partially when speaking with strangers or people who know the respondent well
	4	Unable to be understood when speaking with strangers but able to be understood partially by people who know the respondent well
	5	Unable to be understood when speaking to other people (or unable to speak at all)
Ambulation	1	Able to walk around the neighborhood without difficulty, and without walking equipment
	2	Able to walk around the neighborhood with difficulty, but does not require walking equipment or the help of another person
	3	Able to walk around the neighborhood with walking equipment, but without the help of another person
	4	Able to walk only short distances with walking equipment, and requires a wheelchair to get around the neighborhood
	5	Unable to walk alone, even with walking equipment; able to walk short distances with the help of another person, and requires a wheelchair to get around the neighborhood
	6	Cannot walk at all
Dexterity	1	Full use of two hands and ten fingers
	2	Limitations in the use of hands or fingers, but does not require special tools or help of another person
	3	Limitations in the use of hands or fingers, is independent with use of special tools (does not require the help of another person)
	4	Limitations in the use of hands or fingers, requires the help of another person for some tasks (not independent even with use of special tools)
	5	Limitations in use of hands or fingers, requires the help of another person for most tasks (not independent even with use of special tools)
	6	Limitations in use of hands or fingers, requires the help of another person for all tasks (not independent even with use of special tools)
Emotion	1	Happy and interested in life
	2	Somewhat happy
	3	Somewhat unhappy
	4	Very unhappy
	5	So unhappy that life is not worthwhile
Cognition	1	Able to remember most things, think clearly and solve day to day problems
	2	Able to remember most things, but have a little difficulty when trying to think and solve day to day problems
	3	Somewhat forgetful, but able to think clearly and solve day to day problems
	4	Somewhat forgetful, and have a little difficulty when trying to think or solve day to day problems
	5	Very forgetful, and have great difficulty when trying to think or solve day to day problems
	6	Unable to remember anything at all, and unable to think or solve day to day problems
Pain	1	Free of pain and discomfort
	2	Mild to moderate pain that prevents no activities
	3	Moderate pain that prevents a few activities
	4	Moderate to severe pain that prevents some activities
	5	Severe pain that prevents most activities

From ref. 80.

collapse health status assessment and valuation into a single step. By assessing health status on the basis of performance, that is, on what people choose to do, the measure of health status reflects information on three related concepts: the person's underlying capacity, the opportunities and choices they face, and their preferences. Thus, people with the same underlying capacity who face different opportunity sets or have different preferences may be assessed as having different health status in a system that relies on performance but the same health status in a system that relies on capacity. Either or both of these concepts are potentially valid or useful, depending on the intended uses of the measure.

HEALTH STATUS ASSESSMENT IN THE HUI MARK II AND III SYSTEMS

The health status of a person at a particular point in time is described by the Mark II system as a seven-element vector $(x_1, x_2, x_3, x_4, x_5, x_6, x_7)$, in which x_i describes the level (1 to 3, 1 to 4, or 1 to 5) for attribute i. Changes in health status are assessed by serial application. The precision of the health state descriptions in the Mark II system, derived from the large number of combinations of levels among the attributes, provides a framework for capturing important changes in health status over time. Similarly health status at a point in time is described by an eight-element vector in the Mark III system with five to six levels per attribute.

Levels in the Mark II and III systems were chosen to span the range of functioning from severely impaired to normal. Levels were constructed to provide descriptive categories that people recognize as being important and distinct from each other. The levels are not an interval scale; they are simply categories. The importance of a change from level 1 function to level 2 function is not, in general, equal to the importance of a movement from level 2 to level 3. Similarly, the importance of a change from level 1 to level 2 is not "equal" among attributes.

Both the Mark II and III systems may be subject to ceiling effects but are unlikely to be vulnerable to floor effects. That is, many individuals in the context of population health surveys may fall in the highest level of an attribute (normal), but very few, in either clinical or population health studies, are likely to be worse than the lowest level (the most severely impaired). Ceiling effects are unlikely to be important in most clinical studies, although they may be apparent among special clinical populations.

The potential for ceiling effects is perhaps especially relevant for ambulation and emotion. The Mark III system will not distinguish between the person who is very physically fit (supranormal ambulation) and a person with normal capacity for ambulation. The importance of this omission when one defines health status in capacity terms is not obvious. When instead one uses a concept of performance to define health status, the omission does imply a loss of descriptive completeness. There is some evidence indicating that su-

pranormal ambulation or emotion has prognostic value. Thus in the context of predictive uses (as opposed to discriminative or evaluative uses) the omission of supranormal may have nontrivial implications. If the intended use of the measure requires an ability to distinguish normal from supranormal individuals, one can add supranormal levels for descriptive purposes.

In spite of the comprehensiveness of the Mark III system, there may be some impairments that may escape measurement. For instance, musculoskeletal problems that are not associated with the lower limbs or hands and fingers but that nonetheless represent a burden of morbidity, may not be captured.

EXAMPLES OF APPLICATIONS OF HUI SYSTEMS

The Mark II and III systems have been used in a number of clinical evaluative and population health survey studies. The Mark II system has been used to describe the health status of survivors of childhood cancer (5,30,39–41). It is also being used to describe the health status of survivors of neonatal intensive care for very low birth weight and patients in pediatric intensive care (42,43). The descriptions of the levels in the Mark II system have been rewritten for use among adult populations and the system is being used to describe health status for head injury and cardiac surgery patients.

Examples of results from the use of the Mark II system in a clinical study is given in Tables 3 and 4. The Mark II system was used to classify the health status of survivors of high-risk acute lymphoblastic leukemia. In Table 3 patients are classified according to the number of attributes with less than full (level 1) function. The results highlight the importance of multiple sequelae; 26% of survivors experienced impairments in two or more attributes. The complete enumeration of the health outcomes for the 69 survivors is given in Table 4. There are 25 distinct health states. Again, the results highlight the varying levels of severity of deficits and multiple sequelae, especially combinations of cognition

TABLE 3. *Frequencies of Mark II attributes affected in survivors of high-risk acute lymphoblastic leukemia (ALL)*

Number of attributes affected	Number of patients reported (%)
0	29 (42.0)
1	22 (31.9)
2	12 (17.4)
3	4 (5.8)
4	2 (2.9)
Total	69 (100.0)

From ref. 30.
Note: Because fertility is in most cases unknown, it is excluded from the enumeration of the number of attributes affected.

TABLE 4. *Frequencies of Mark II health states reported for survivors of high-risk ALL*

| Health states defined by attribute levels | | | | | | | Frequency (%) of health states |
Sens	Mob	Emot	Cog	S-C	Pain	Fert[b]	
1	1	1	1	1	1	Unknown	28 (40.6)
1	1	1	2	1	1	Unknown	12 (17.4)
1	1	2	1	1	1	Unknown	3 (4.3)
1	1	1	1	1	1	1	1 (1.4)
1	1	1	1	1	1	3	2 (3.0)
1	1	1	2	1	1	3	2 (3.0)
1	1	4	1	1	1	Unknown	2 (3.0)
1	1	3	2	1	1	Unknown	2 (3.0)
2	1	1	1	1	1	3	1 (1.4)
2	1	1	2	1	1	3	1 (1.4)
3	1	2	1	1	1	Unknown	1 (1.4)
3	2	2–3	3	1	1	Unknown	1 (1.4)
4	3	Unknown	3	1	1	Unknown	1 (1.4)
1	1	1	1	1	Unknown	1	(1.4)
1	2	1	1	1	2	Unknown	1 (1.4)
1	1	2–3	2	1	1	Unknown	1 (1.4)
1	1	2	1	1	1	1	1 (1.4)
1	1	2	2	1	1	3	1 (1.4)
1	1	3	3	1	1	Unknown	1 (1.4)
1	1	3–4	2	1	1	Unknown	1 (1.4)
1	1	3	2	1	2	Unknown	1 (1.4)
1	1	4	1	1	2	3	1 (1.4)
1	1	4	2	1	1	Unknown	1 (1.4)
1	1	4	3–4	1	1	Unknown	1 (1.4)
1	1	1	2	1	1	1	1 (1.4)
Total							69 (99.6)[a]

From ref. 30.
[a]Should be 100.0 (difference due to rounding errors).
[b]Fertility is unknown in 58 cases and known in 11 cases.
Sens, sensation; Mob, mobility; Emot, emotion; Cog, cognition; S-C, self-care; Fert, fertility.

and emotion deficits. (Health-related quality of life scores for these health states are presented below in Table 7.)

Similarly, it took 61 health states to describe the health status of 156 survivors of neonatal intensive care evaluated at age 8 as compared with only 19 health states to describe the health status of 145 children drawn from a random sample of 8-year-old children attending school (42,43). Again the Mark II system was able to capture multiple sequelae and varying levels of severity of impairments experienced by survivors of neonatal intensive care. In these applications, the Mark II system proved to be useful in distinguishing the burden of morbidity both among individuals and between groups. The system is useful for discriminative purposes.

The Mark III system has been used in two major population health surveys in Canada: the 1990 Ontario Health Survey (35) and the 1991 Statistics Canada General Social Survey (37,38). In the Ontario Health Survey there were 1,755 distinct health states reported for 68,394 subjects; the 129 most prevalent states accounted for 94.8% of the sample. In the General Social Survey, 950 health states were reported for 11,567 subjects. Only 12 states had a prevalence greater than 1% of the sample. These 12 states accounted for 75.4%

of the sample. Both surveys were of the noninstitutionalized population; thus additional health states would likely be identified among clinical populations. Nonetheless, although all combinations of health states were not observed, all of the levels for each attribute were in fact utilized to describe the health status of at least one individual in the population samples.

Although the number of states reported in the Ontario Health Survey and the General Social Survey is only a small fraction of the number that can be represented by the Mark III system, it is interesting to note that the number of distinct health states reported exceeds the descriptive power of several other multiattribute systems, including Rosser and Kind (25) and EuroQoL (34).

Theoretical Foundations of Multiattribute Utility Theory

An important advantage of the multiattribute approach utilized in the HUI is its complementarity with multiattribute utility theory. Multiattribute utility theory provides the intellectual foundation for estimating a scoring function that is used to value health status as described in the multiattribute system. Thus the basis for the valuation of health status—the source for health-related quality of life scores—is both explicit and based on a rigorous normative theory.

Von Neumann-Morgenstern utility theory, first postulated in the 1940s, continues to be the dominant normative paradigm for decision making under uncertainty (44–49). In the 1970s the theory was extended to the class of problems in which the outcomes are described by multiple attributes (50–55). The extension is known as multiattribute utility theory. Multiattribute utility theory is the basis for scoring the HUI Mark II and Mark III classification systems.

TYPES OF PREFERENCES

The fundamental underlying principle for the HUI is that individuals have preferences for alternative health outcomes, they can express them, and their preferences should count. Preferences may be ordinal or cardinal. Ordinal preferences are simply a rank order of alternative health outcomes from most preferred to least preferred. Cardinal preferences are interval scale measurements such that the numbers associated with the health outcomes represent the strength of preference for the outcome. More precisely, because an interval scale is unique up to a positive linear transformation (for example, like temperature in degrees Celsius), ratios have no meaning while intervals do. For example, if on an interval scale of preference A = 0.60, B = 0.30, and C = 0.15, it is inappropriate to state that A is twice as preferred as B, but it is appropriate to state that the difference in preference between A and B is twice as much as the difference between B and C.

There are two types of cardinal preferences: values and utilities. Values are cardinal preferences measured under certainty and for use in situations of certainty. That is, there are no probabilities involved in performing the measurement and there are no probabilities in the problem to which the resulting scores are applied. Value measurements are based on value theory (56,57). In contrast, utilities are preferences measured under uncertainty, and for use in problems with uncertainty. Utility measurements are founded on von Neumann–Morgenstern (44) utility theory.

Values and utilities for health states differ empirically. Because risk (uncertainty) is a factor in the measurement of utilities but not values, the difference can be attributed to the risk attitudes of the respondents. In general, the utility score for a health state exceeds the value score for the same health state (6,58–63).

MEASUREMENT INSTRUMENTS

The three most widely used instruments to measure preferences for health states are the visual analog scale, the time trade-off, and the standard gamble (64). It is important to note that, because no probabilities are involved in the measurement task, the visual analog scale and time trade-off techniques produce value scores, not utilities. The standard gamble is the only technique that produces von Neumann–Morgenstern utilities.

Multiattribute utility theory is a technique to determine a mathematical formula that will allow the estimation of preference scores for a large number of health states defined in a multiattribute framework based on the measurement of preference scores for a small, carefully selected subset of those states. Multiattribute utility theory can be used with either value measurements or utility measurements as the underlying metric. To differentiate these two alternatives, multiattribute value function and multiattribute utility function will be used for the value and utility cases, respectively.

APPLICATIONS OF PREFERENCE SCORES

Preference scores are widely used as quality weights for quality adjusting life years in undertaking cost-effectiveness analyses or cost-utility analyses (65–70). There are a number of reasons why utilities are appropriate scores for use as quality weights in these applications. The weights should be based on individuals' preferences and utilities measure preferences. Future health is uncertain and utilities are preferences measured under conditions of uncertainty. Utility measurements are based on an explicit, well-established theory and measurement methodology, so the resulting utility scores have a clear unambiguous interpretation.

Utility scores can also be used as quality weights for calculating health expectancy in population health studies. Health expectancy represents a relatively new concept for measuring, monitoring, and comparing the health of populations (6,71–75). An age- and sex-adjusted health expectancy table captures in an integrated way both the quantity of life (life expectancy) and the quality of life of the population. Unfortunately, terminology in this field has not yet been standardized. Health expectancy is also called quality-adjusted life expectancy, health-adjusted life expectancy (75), disability-adjusted life expectancy (76), and years of healthy life (77,78). All of these concepts are identical; all use quality weights to adjust life years in calculating life expectancy results.

UTILITY INDEPENDENCE AND MULTIATTRIBUTE UTILITY THEORY

Multiattribute utility theory applies to the measurement of preferences for health states that are defined according to a multiattribute health status classification system. To extend traditional von Neumann–Morgenstern utility theory to the case of multiattribute outcomes, one additional assumption is required, which is that the utility independence among the attributes can be represented by at least order-one utility independence, and perhaps by even stronger utility independence (mutual utility independence, additive independence). These three types of utility independence going from the least restrictive to most restrictive cases are described below.

Order-One Utility Independence (Multilinear Utility Function)

Order-one utility independence implies there is no interaction (synergy) between preferences for levels on any *one* attribute and the fixed levels for the other attributes. This characteristic must hold for each attribute. This is a weaker condition than mutual utility independence and as a result requires the fitting of a relatively complex utility function known as the multilinear model.

An example of order-one utility independence would be the case where level 3 mobility has a utility of 0.6 on the mobility subscale, regardless of the health status of the individual on the other attributes. (The mobility subscale is the single attribute utility function for mobility, scaled such that the best level of mobility is 1.0 and the worst level of mobility is 0.0.) Note that the overall weight for mobility could change based on the health status on the other attributes, and thus the overall impact of changes in mobility could change without violating order-one utility independence. For example, a change from level 1 mobility to level 3 mobility could reduce overall utility by 0.2 if that were the only health status deficit, but by less than 0.2 if the individual already had other major health status deficits. All that is required for order-one utility independence is that the relative scaling *within* the mobility subscale stays constant.

Mutual Utility Independence (Multiplicative Utility Function)

Mutual utility independence implies there is no interaction (synergy) between preferences for levels on *some* attributes and the fixed levels for other attributes. It requires the fitting of a multiplicative utility model that is less complex than the multilinear one. This characteristic must hold for all possible subsets of attributes. An example of mutual utility independence would be the case where level 2 on sensation coupled with level 3 on mobility has a utility of 0.7 on the sensation-mobility subscale, regardless of the health status of the individual on the other attributes. (The sensation-mobility subscale is the subscale for these two attributes combined, such that the worst level on sensation coupled with the worst level on mobility is 0.0 and the best level on sensation coupled with the best level on mobility is 1.0). Note that the weight of this subscale for sensation and mobility could change given different health status on other attributes, so that the overall impact of changes within sensation and mobility could differ without violating mutual utility independence. For example, a change from level 1 on sensation and level 1 on mobility to level 2 on sensation and level 3 on mobility could reduce overall utility by 0.25 if that

were the only deficit, but by less than 0.25 if the individual already had other major deficits. What is required for mutual utility independence is that the relative scaling *within* the sensation-mobility subscale stays constant.

Additive Utility Independence (Additive Utility Function)

Additive independence implies there is no preference interaction (synergy) among attributes at all. That is, the overall preference score depends only on the individual levels of the attributes and not on the manner in which the levels of the different attributes are combined. Additive independence requires the fitting of the least complicated of the three utility function models, the additive function. An example of additive independence would be the case where a change from level 1 mobility to level 3 mobility would reduce the overall utility by 0.2 *regardless* of the health status on the other attributes.

The three independence assumptions lead to three different multiattribute functions, presented in order of increasing model complexity (but decreasing restrictiveness of the assumptions about the structure of preferences among attributes): additive, multiplicative, and multilinear. If additive independence holds, the function is additive. If mutual utility independence holds, the function is multiplicative. If only order-one utility independence holds, the function is multilinear. These three functions are shown in Table 5. If

TABLE 5. *Types of multiattribute utility theory models*

Additive:

$$u(x) = \sum_{j=1}^{n} k_j u_j(x_j)$$

$$\text{where } \sum_{j=1}^{n} k_j = 1$$

Multiplicative[a]

$$u(x) = (1/k) \left[\prod_{j=1}^{n} (1 + k k_j u_j(x_j)) - 1 \right]$$

$$\text{where } (1 + k) = \prod_{j=1}^{n} (1 + k k_j)$$

Multilinear:

$$u(x) = k_1 u_1(x_1) + k_2 u_2(x_2) + \ldots$$
$$+ k_{12} u_1(x_1) u_2(x_2) + k_{13} u_1(x_1) u_3(x_3) + \ldots$$
$$+ k_{123} u_1(x_1) u_2(x_2) u_3(x_3) + \ldots$$
$$+ \ldots$$
where Σ All k's = 1

Hybrid:
Various hybrid models are possible, based on hierarchically nested subsets of attributes.

[a]The multiplicative model contains the additive model as a special case. In fitting the multiplicative model, if the measured k_j sum to 1.0, then $k = 0$ and the additive model holds.

Notation: $u_j(x_j)$ = the single attribute utility function for attribute j. $u(x)$ is the utility for health state x represented by an n-element vector. k and k_j are model parameters. Π is the multiplication sign with $j = 1$ through n.

none of these three independence assumptions holds, multi-attribute utility theory cannot be used.

In practice the assumptions of the additive versus multiplicative forms can be tested directly from the measurements taken to fit the model. The degree to which the multiattribute utility theory model predicts the utility of independent directly measured states not used in the fitting of the model (predictive validity) is taken as an indication of the extent to which the functional form of the estimated utility function is a reasonable approximation of the utility structure of the respondents.

Applications of Multiattribute Utility Theory

Health Utilities Index—Mark I

The multiplicative multiattribute utility function was used for the HUI Mark I. Measurements were collected from a random sample of parents of school children ($n = 87$) in Hamilton, Ontario (6,28). The measurement instruments consisted of visual analog scale and time trade-off. The visual analog scale value scores were converted to utilities using a power curve taken from a previous study (58). (A power curve converts values (v) to utilities (u) by using an empirically derived power function of the type $(1 - u) = (1 - v)^\alpha$, where α is estimated from measurements of v and u on the same health states.) Time trade-off scores were not converted through a power curve, based on previous work (58), which had indicated that time trade-off results were a reasonable approximation for standard gamble results. (It should be noted that more recent findings have rejected this conclusion.) The multiplicative multiattribute utility function for the HUI Mark I is available in simplified format in the book by Drummond et al. (65, pp. 121–124).

Health Utilities Index—Mark II

Preference measurements were collected from a random sample of parents of schoolchildren ($n = 293$) in Hamilton, Ontario. The measurement instruments were visual analog scale and standard gamble. The visual analog scale was used to measure the seven single-attribute value functions, and to measure the value for 14 multiattribute states. The standard gamble was used to measure the utility of four multiattribute states, a subset of the 14 states measured using the visual analog scale. Multiattribute functions were fitted for each individual and aggregated. A multiattribute function was also fitted for person mean, the mean preference scores for each health-state description across all respondents. There was little difference in the results of these two approaches, and the person-mean approach was selected as the primary modeling strategy to represent the general public preference function.

The visual analog value scores were converted to utilities using a power curve estimate based on data from the four

multiattribute health states that had been measured both with the visual analog and the standard gamble. Thus, preference data was available from all respondents both as values and as utilities. Accordingly, two multiattribute preference functions were fitted: a multiattribute value function and a multiattribute utility function. As with the HUI Mark I the data strongly rejected the additive model; therefore the multiplicative model was fitted.

Two multiplicative multiattribute models were fitted: a multiplicative multiattribute value function and a multiplicative multiattribute utility function. Both are available in standard format and in simplified format in the technical report from the project (78). The multiplicative multiattribute utility function in simplified format is shown in Table 6. The table includes the formula and all numerical figures required to calculate utility scores for the 24,000 health states defined by the HUI Mark II health status classification system.

The predictive validity of these models was tested by determining the accuracy with which they were able to predict the directly measured scores for four health states not used in the model construction. The performance of the multiattribute utility function was particularly encouraging, with the standard deviation of the prediction error equal to 0.06. In addition, the multiattribute utility function was an unbiased predictor of directly measured scores, whereas the multiattribute value function exhibited a negative bias (79).

Health Utilities Index—Mark III

The Mark III multiattribute health status classification system defines 972,000 states using five or six functional levels for eight attributes. The attributes were deliberately selected to be structurally independent. That is, being in a particular level on one attribute does not preclude being in any particular level on other attributes; or equivalently, there are no combinations of levels on different attributes that are mutually exclusive. The plans to develop the scoring algorithm for this version have been described in detail elsewhere (80,81). The field work is completed, the analysis is under way, and the scoring functions are expected to be available in 1995. Briefly, the measurements have been collected from a random sample of 504 adults from Hamilton, Ontario, using a combination of visual analog scale and standard gamble. Visual analog value scores will be converted to utilities using the estimated relationship from the study itself. A new and more complicated measurement strategy is being used such that additional results will be available. In addition to the ability to estimate the additive and the multiplicative models, the data will also allow for the first time the estimation of the full multilinear model. This is accomplished by using a fractional factorial experimental design as part of the measurement strategy (82). In addition, we have obtained direct measurements on 70 health states that were reported by Statistics Canada (38) to be prevalent among respondents to the 1991 Canadian General

TABLE 6. *Multiattribute utility function on dead-healthy scale for HUI Mark II system*

Sensation		Mobility		Emotion		Cognition		Self-Care		Pain		Fertility	
x_1	b_1	x_2	b_2	x_3	b_3	x_4	b_4	x_5	b_5	x_6	b_6	x_7	b_7
1	1.00	1	1.00	1	1.00	1	1.00	1	1.00	1	1.00	1	1.00
2	0.95	2	0.97	2	0.93	2	0.95	2	0.97	2	0.97	2	0.97
3	0.86	3	0.84	3	0.81	3	0.88	3	0.91	3	0.85	3	0.88
4	0.61	4	0.73	4	0.70	4	0.65	4	0.80	4	0.64		n.a.
	n.a.	5	0.58	5	0.53		n.a.		n.a.	5	0.38		n.a.

Formula:

$$u^* = 1.06(b_1 \times b_2 \times b_3 \times b_4 \times b_5 \times b_6 \times b_7) - 0.06$$

where u^* is the utility of the health state on a utility scale where dead has a utility of 0.00 and healthy has a utility of 1.00. Because the worst possible health state was judged by respondents as worse than death, it has a negative utility of -0.03. The standard error of u* is 0.015 for measurement error and sampling error, and 0.06 if model error is also included.

x_i is attribute level code for attribute i; b_i is level score for attribute i.

Social Survey. These will be useful particularly in estimating the health-related quality of life and the health expectancy for the Canadian population, and also will provide a much larger set of health states for testing the validity of preference models than has been available in the past.

Methodological Issues

Four important methodological issues regarding the applications of multiattribute utility theory are model appropriateness, the choice of utilities versus values, reliability, and validity.

Model Appropriateness

In our experience with multiattribute utility functions, the additive model has always been rejected by the data. On the other hand, the Quality of Well-Being Scale uses an additive model. Although it is likely that the different structure of the two classification systems leads to this difference in the model, the question still remains whether the additional precision we obtain with a nonadditive model is worth the additional complexity. If the underlying structure of preferences is indeed one that involves quantitatively important interactions for preferences among attributes, then reliance on the additive model might provide reasonable estimates in the middle of the multiattribute space while providing quite distorted scores around the extremes of the space. Although further investigation of the suitability of the additive versus more complicated models is required, tentatively the evidence appears to favor the more complicated functional forms.

Utilities versus Values

Selected health states are shown in Table 7, with utilities and value scores calculated from the HUI Mark II multiattri-

bute preference functions. The reader can use Table 6 to verify the utility scores to ensure a complete understanding of the calculation method.

The HUI Mark II application of multiattribute utility theory produced two scoring formulae, utility and value, and, as an inspection of Table 7 reveals, the difference is substantial. We recommend that users select utility as the primary measure, for two reasons. First, the theory indicates that utility is the appropriate construct for problems that involve uncertainties. Virtually all applications in health fall in this category; that is, the future health for all of us is uncertain. Second, we note that the utility formula performed better in the predictive validation test. While we do not recommend values as the primary measure, they are useful, in part, because some of the other preference-based multiattribute systems available, Quality of Well-Being and some versions of EuroQoL, are based on visual analog scale instruments and therefore are value scored. If comparisons are being made to results from these systems, the HUI value scores may be useful in exploring differences.

Although the difference between utility scores and value scores is substantial, as demonstrated in Table 7, the important question in program evaluation applications is whether this difference translates into different priority rankings or different resource allocations. Some might argue that, because economic evaluation methods use incremental differences between the program and the comparator, it does not matter that utilities are greater than values as long as one system is used consistently. The reasoning would be that values are lower for both the program and the comparator, and that this would cancel out in calculating the incremental difference. Even if it did not entirely cancel out, it might be argued that the program rankings would still be the same with either set of weights, and thus the final policy recommendations would be the same.

This line of reasoning is incorrect. Although it might hold in certain selected cases, the reasoning does not hold in general, as is evident in Table 7, because values give much greater relative weight to preventing or curing minor disabili-

TABLE 7. *Utility and value scores in HUI Mark II system for selected health states* [a]

Health state	Defined by attribute levels							Preference score		
	Sensation	Mobility	Emotion	Cognition	Self-care	Pain	Fertility	Utility (U)	Value (V)	Difference (U−V)
1	1	1	1	1	1	1	1	1.00	1.00	0.00
2	1	1	1	1	2	1	1	0.97	0.88	0.09
3	1	1	1	2	1	1	1	0.95	0.71	0.24
4	1	1	2	1	1	1	1	0.93	0.68	0.25
5	1	1	1	1	1	1	3	0.87	0.60	0.27
6	1	1	2	2	1	1	3	0.76	0.29	0.47
7	1	1	4	1	1	2	3	0.57	0.17	0.40
8	1	1	4	3–4[b]	1	1	unknown[c]	0.51	0.17	0.34
9	1	1	4	3–4[b]	1	1	unknown[d]	0.44	0.10	0.44
10	3	3	3	3	3	3	3	0.31	0.01	0.30
11	4	4	4	4	4	4	3	0.04	−0.02	0.06
12	4	5	5	4	4	5	3	−0.03	−0.02	−0.01

[a]Many of the health states are selected from those reported for survivors of high-risk acute lymphoblastic leukemia (see Table 4).
[b]Cognition assumed at level 3.5, scored as 0.5 level 3 + 0.5 level 4 = (0.88 + 0.65)/2 = 0.765.
[c]Fertility assumed at level 1.
[d]Fertility assumed at level 3.

ties, compared with major disabilities, than do utilities. For example, consider health state 4 in Table 7 (utility = 0.93, value = 0.68), a minor disability, and health state 9 (utility = 0.44, value = 0.10), a major disability. On the utility scale preventing the minor disability produces a gain of 0.07 which is 12.5% of the gain from preventing the major disability, 0.56. On the value scale preventing the minor disability produces a gain of 0.32 which is 35.6% of the gain from preventing the major disability, 0.90. Thus, the value scale gives substantially greater emphasis to preventing or curing minor disabilities than does the utility scale. In a policy application, this could lead to the kinds of anomalies seen in the first priority lists from the Oregon project, which used a value scale, the Quality of Well-Being (83). Thus, the question of whether to use a value scale or a utility scale is important and does have important policy consequences, and we would argue that the utility scale is the better choice.

Reliability

Reliability of a preference-based multiattribute system requires reliability of the questionnaire and the health status classification process, and reliability of the scoring formula. With regard to the former, we have studied the test-retest reliability of the HUI Mark III used in the Canadian General Social Survey 1991 (84). A stratified random sample of individuals ($n = 506$) completing the General Social Survey telephone interviews were reinterviewed a month later. The results indicate that the individual questions, algorithms for determining attribute levels, and a provisional HUI index formula generally provided reliable (reproducible) information about the health status of subjects in the General Social

Survey. Using provisional HUI index scores to quantify overall health status, the test-retest reliability was estimated to be .767, as measured by the intraclass correlation coefficient. Further evidence on validity and reproducibility of the HUI Mark III system is found in Grootendorst (85,86).

To measure the reliability of the scoring formula itself one would have to redevelop the formula on an entirely new population. In the HUI Mark II this was done. The same procedures that were used in the main sample of the general public were used in a second sample of parents of childhood cancer patients. In part, these subjects were selected to determine if their experience with life-threatening disease would lead to different scores. In fact, the scores and the overall multiattribute formulae are almost identical.

Validity

Validity of the system requires both validity of the classification system and validity of the scoring. The face validity of the system is empirically supported by the fact that, although there are numerous levels on each attribute, all levels on every attribute appeared at least once in the population health surveys. That is, there are no attribute levels that represent nonexisting outcomes. Criterion validity of the multiattribute utility function was established by determining the ability of the model to predict directly measured scores not used to create the system (the criteria). Further evidence about the predictive ability of the system is provided by the findings in the National Health and Nutrition Examination Survey (NHANES-1) study that the utility score is a strong predictor of future health outcomes (87). There is also evidence that these systems can be used to distinguish between groups known to have clinically important differences in health status. Saigal et al. (42,43) reported differences in health status between extremely low birth weight and control children at age 8. The mean score for the extremely low birth weight children of 0.82 was significantly lower than that for the reference children, 0.95. The variability of scores was greater among the extremely low birth weight children. The distribution of the scores was such that 50% of extremely low birth weight children, but only 10% of reference children had scores less than 0.89. Only 17% of extremely low birth weight children were assigned scores of 1.00, compared with 50% of reference subjects.

CONCLUSIONS

The HUI provides a comprehensive but compact method for describing health status in both clinical studies and population health surveys. Thus the HUI allows for comparison of clinical populations and population norms. The HUI provides detail on an attribute by attribute basis and the ability to represent combinations of problems with varying levels of severity.

The HUI health status classification approach can be used serially in the context of clinical trials as a method for assessing health status at points in time and changes in health status over time. It is a generic approach to assessing health status. In general its use should be supplemented with specific measures (7).

The HUI system is also an efficient method of determining a general public–based utility score for a health outcome or for the health status of an individual. The utility score is based on von Neumann–Morgenstern utility theory, and in particular, on the extension into multiattribute utility theory. The HUI utility scores have three related uses: in clinical populations to provide a single summary measure of health-related quality of life, in cost-utility analyses as quality weights in calculating quality-adjusted life years, and in population health studies as quality weights for calculating quality-adjusted life expectancy and a population health index.

ACKNOWLEDGMENTS

The authors acknowledge the contributions of Dr. Ronald D. Barr, Nancy Bishop, Dr. David Cadman, Gary Catlin, Shelley Chambers, Dr. Margaret Denton, Paul Grootendorst, John Horsman, Dr. Sargent Horwood, Dr. Alison Leiper, Robin Roberts, Dr. Peter Rosenbaum, Lori Scapinello, Carol Siksay, Dr. John Sinclair, Dr. David Streiner, Dr. Qinan Wang, Dr. Sheila Weitzman, Dr. Michael Wolfson, Yueming Zhang, and Dr. Alvin Zipursky to the research reported in the chapter. The financial support of the Ontario Ministry of Health (01386 and 04020), Statistics Canada, the Natural Sciences and Engineering Research Council of Canada, the Merck Foundation, and Ortho-McNeil and CILAG International is gratefully acknowledged.

REFERENCES

1. Cadman D, Goldsmith C, Torrance GW, et al. *Development of a health status index for Ontario children*. Final report to the Ontario Ministry of Health on Research Grant DM648 (00633). Hamilton: McMaster University, 1986.
2. Cadman D, Goldsmith C, Bashim P. Values, preferences, and decisions in the care of children with developmental disabilities. *Dev Behav Pediatr* 1984;5:60–64.
3. Cadman D, Goldsmith C. Construction of social value or utility-based health indices: the usefulness of factorial experimental design plans. *J Chronic Dis* 1986;39:643–651.
4. Rosenbaum P, Cadman D, Kirpalani H. Pediatrics: assessing quality of life. In: Spilker B, ed. *Quality of life assessment in clinical trials*. New York: Raven Press, 1990:205–215.
5. Feeny DH, Furlong W, Barr RD, et al. A comprehensive multi-attribute system for classifying the health status of survivors of childhood cancer. *J Clin Oncol* 1992;10:923–928.
6. Torrance GW, Boyle MH, Horwood SP. Application of multi-attribute utility theory to measure social preferences for health states. *Operations Res* 1982;30:1043–1069.
7. Guyatt GH, Feeny DH, Patrick DL. Measuring health-related quality of life. *Ann Intern Med* 1993;118:622–629.
8. Torrance GW, Furlong W, Feeny D, et al. Multi-attribute preference functions: Health Utilities Index. *Pharmacoeconomics* 1995;7:503–520.
9. Kirshner B, Guyatt G. A methodological framework for assessing health indices. *J Chronic Dis* 1985;38:27–36.
10. Patrick DL, Erickson P. *Health status and health policy: quality of life in health care evaluation and resource allocation*. New York: Oxford University Press, 1993.
11. Ware JE, Sherbourne CD. The MOS 36-Item Short Form Health Survey (SF-36). *Med Care* 1992;30:473–483.
12. World Health Organization. Measuring quality of life: the development of the World Health Organization Quality of Life Instrument (WHO-QOL). Geneva: World Health Organization, 1992.
13. Ware JE, Brook RH, Davies AR, et al. Choosing measures of health status for individuals in general populations. *Am J Public Health* 1981;71:620–625.
14. Fanshel S, Bush JW. A health status index and its application to health services outcomes. *Operations Res* 1970;18:1021–1066.
15. Bush JW, Chen MM, Patrick DL. Social indicators of health based on function status and prognosis. *Proceedings of the American Statistical Association, Social Statistics Section*. Washington, DC: American Statistical Association, 1972.
16. Kaplan RM, Bush JW, Berry CC. The reliability, stability and generalizability of a health status index. *Proceedings of the Social Statistics Section*. Washington, DC: American Statistical Association, 1978:704–709.
17. Kaplan RM, Bush JW. Health related quality of life measurement for evaluation research and policy analysis. *Health Psychol* 1982;1:61–80.
18. Patrick DL, Bush JW, Chen MM. Methods for measuring levels of well-being for a health status index. *Health Serv Res* 1973;8:228–245.
19. Patrick DL, Bush JW, Chen MM. Toward an operational definition of health. *J Health Soc Behav* 1973;14:6–23.
20. Patrick DL, Bergner M. Measurement of health status in the 1990s. *Annu Rev Public Health* 1990;11:165–183.
21. Rosser RM, Watts V. The sanative output of a health care system. Paper presented at the Conference of the Operations Research Society of America, Dallas, Texas, May 5–7, 1971.
22. Rosser RM. Recent studies using a global approach to measuring illness. *Med Care* 1976;14(suppl 5):138–147.
23. Kind P, Rosser R. The quantification of health. *Eur J Soc Psychol* 1988;18:63–77.
24. Rosser R, Watts V. The measurement of illness. *J Oper Res Soc* 1978;29:529–540.
25. Rosser R, Kind P. A scale of valuations of states of illness: is there a social consensus? *Int J Epidemiol* 1978;7:347–358.
26. Rosser RM, Watts V. A clinical classification of disability and distress and its application to the awards made by the courts in personal injury cases. *New Law J* 1975;125:323–326.
27. Feeny D, Furlong W, Boyle M, Torrance GW. Multi-attribute health status classification systems: Health Utilities Index. *Pharmacoeconomics* 1995;7:490–502.
28. Boyle MH, Torrance GW, Sinclair JC, et al. Economic evaluation of

neonatal intensive care of very-low-birth-weight infants. *N Engl J Med* 1983;308:1330–1337.

29. Boyle MH, Torrance GW. Developing multi-attribute health indexes. *Med Care* 1984;22:1045–1057.

30. Feeny DH, Leiper A, Barr RD, et al. The comprehensive assessment of health status in survivors of childhood cancer: application to high-risk acute lymphoblastic leukaemia. *Br J Cancer* 1993;67:1047–1052.

31. Furlong W, Feeny D, Torrance G, et al. *Design and pilot testing of comprehensive health-status measurement system for the Ontario Health Survey.* Final Report for Ontario Ministry of Health, 1989.

32. EuroQol Group. EuroQol—a new facility for the measurement of health-related quality of life. *Health Policy* 1990;16:199–208.

33. Nord E. EuroQol: health-related quality of life measurement. Valuations of health states by the general public in Norway. *Health Policy* 1991;18:25–36.

34. Essink-Bot ML, Stouthard MEA, Bonsel GJ. Generalizability of valuations on health states collected with the EuroQol questionnaire. *Health Econ* 1993;2:237–246.

35. Ministry of Health, Ontario. *Ontario Health Survey 1990. User's Guide, Vol 1: Documentation.* Toronto: Ministry of Health, Ontario and Premiers Council on Health, Well-Being and Social Justice, 1993.

36. Strike C. Overview of 1991 General Social Survey on Health (GSS-6). Statistics Canada General Social Survey Working Paper No. 1, July, 1991.

37. Statistics Canada. *The 1991 General Social Survey—Cycle 6: Health—Public Use Microdata File Documentation and User's Guide.* Ottawa: Statistics Canada, June, 1992.

38. Statistics Canada. *Health Status of Canadians: Report of the 1991 General Social Survey.* Ottawa: Statistics Canada, March, 1994.

39. Barr RD, Furlong W, Dawson S, et al. An assessment of global health status in survivors of acute lymphoblastic leukemia in childhood. *Am J Pediatr Hematol Oncol* 1993;15:284–290.

40. Barr RD, Pai MKR, Weitzman S, et al. A multi-attribute approach to health status measurement and clinical management—illustrated by an application to brain tumors in childhood. *Int J Oncol* 1994;4:639–648.

41. Barr RD, Feeny DH, Furlong W, et al. Health-related quality of life in children with cancer. *Int J Pediatr Hematol Oncol* forthcoming.

42. Saigal S, Rosenbaum P, Stoskopf B, et al. Comprehensive assessment of the health status of extremely low birthweight children at eight years of age: comparison with a reference group. *J Pediatr* 1994; 125:411–417.

43. Saigal S, Feeny D, Furlong W, et al. Comparison of the health-related quality of life of extremely low birthweight children and a reference group of children at eight years of age. *J Pediatr* 1994;125:418–425.

44. Von Neumann J, Morgenstern O. *Theory of games and economic behaviour.* Princeton, NJ: Princeton University Press, 1944.

45. Luce RD, Raiffa H. *Games and decisions.* New York: Wiley 1957.

46. Raiffa H. *Decision analysis: introductory lectures on choices under uncertainty.* Reading, MA: Addison-Wesley, 1968.

47. Bell DE, Raiffa H, Tversky A. Descriptive, normative, and prescriptive interactions in decision making. In: Bell DE, Raiffa H, Tversky A, eds. *Decision making: descriptive, normative, and prescriptive interactions.* NY: Cambridge University Press, 1988:9–30.

48. Howard RA. Decision analysis: practice and promise. *Mgmt Sci* 1988;34(6):679–695.

49. Luce RD, Von Winterfeldt D. What common ground exists for descriptive, prescriptive, and normative utility theories? *Mgmt Sci* 1994; 40(2):263–279.

50. Keeney RL. Utility functions for multiattributed consequences. *Mgmt Sci* 1972;18(5):276–287.

51. Keeney RL. Building models of values. *Eur J Operational Res* 1988;37:149–157.

52. Farquhar PH. A fractional hypercube decomposition theorem for multi-attribute utility functions. *Oper Res* 1975;23(5):941–967.

53. Farquhar PH. Pyramid and semicube decompositions of multiattribute utility functions. *Oper Res* 1976;24(2):256–271.

54. Farquhar PH. A survey of multiattribute utility theory and applications. *TIMS Studies Mgmt Sci* 1977;6:59–89.

55. Keeney RL, Raiffa H. *Decisions with multiple objectives: preferences and value tradeoffs.* New York: Wiley, 1976.

56. Von Winterfeldt D, Edwards W. Value and utility measurement. In: *Decision analysis and behavioral research.* Cambridge: Cambridge University Press, 1986:205–241.

57. Krantz DH, Luce RD, Suppes P, Tversky A. Difference measurement.

In: *Foundations of measurement.* New York and London: Academic Press, 1971:136–198.

58. Torrance GW. Social preferences for health states: an empirical evaluation of three measurement techniques. *Socioecon Planning Sci* 1976; 10(3):129–136.

59. Read JL, Quinn RJ, Berwick DM, Fineberg HV, Weinstein MC. Preferences for health outcomes—comparisons of assessment methods. *Med Decis Making* 1984;4(3):315–329.

60. Elstein AS, Holzman GB, Ravitch MM, et al. Comparison of physicians' decisions regarding estrogen replacement therapy for menopausal women and decisions derived from a decision analytic model. *Am J Med* 1986;80:246–258.

61. Boyd NF, Sutherland HJ, Heasman KZ, et al. Whose utilities for decision analysis? *Med Decision Making* 1990;10(1):58–67.

62. Bass EB, Bergner M, Pitt HA, et al. Comparison of patient utilities for gallstone treatments and related outcomes by rating scale and standard gamble techniques. *Med Decis Making* 1991;11(4):333(abstr).

63. Patrick DL, Starks HE, Cain KC, Uhlmann RF, Pearlman RA. Measuring preferences for health states worse than death. *Med Decis Making* 1994;14(1):9–18.

64. Furlong W, Feeny D, Torrance GW, Barr R, Horsman J. Guide to design and development of health-state utility instrumentation. McMaster University Centre for Health Economics and Policy Analysis Working Paper No. 90-9, June 1990.

65. Drummond MF, Stoddart GL, Torrance GW. *Methods for the economic evaluation of health care programmes.* Oxford: Oxford University Press, 1987.

66. Eisenberg JM. Clinical economics—a guide to the economic analysis of clinical practices. *JAMA* 1989;262(20):2879–2886.

67. Torrance GW, Feeny D. Utilities and quality-adjusted life years. *Int J Tech Assess Health Care* 1989;5(4):559–575.

68. Weinstein MC. Principles of cost-effective resource allocation in health care organizations. *Int J Tech Assess Health Care* 1990;6:93–103.

69. Laupacis A, Feeny DH, Detsky AS, Tugwell P. How attractive does a new technology have to be to warrant adoption and utilization? Tentative guidelines for using clinical and economic evaluations. *Can Med Assoc J* 1992;146(4):473–481.

70. Kaplan RM, Feeny DH, Revicki DA. Methods for assessing relative importance in preference based outcome measures. *Qual Life Res* 1993;2(6):467–475.

71. Wilkins R, Adams O. Measuring health. *Policy Options* 1983; 4(5):28–31.

72. Wilkins R, Adams OB. Health expectancy in Canada, late 1970's: demographic, regional and social dimensions. *Am J Public Health* 1983;73(9):1073–1080.

73. Wilkins R, Adams O. *Healthfulness of life.* Montreal: The Institute for Research on Public Policy, 1983.

74. Wolfson MC. A system of health statistics: toward a new conceptual framework for integrating health data. In: *CIAR Population Health Working Paper No. 1.* Toronto: The Canadian Institute for Advanced Research, August 1989.

75. Berthelot JM, Roberge R, Wolfson MC. The calculation of health-adjusted life expectancy for a Canadian province using a multi-attribute utility function: a first attempt. In: Robine JM, Mathers CD, Bone MR, Romieu I, eds. *Calculation of health expectancies: harmonization, consensus and future perspectives.* vol. 226. Montrouge, France: John Libbey Eurotext, 1993:161–172.

76. World Bank. *World development report, 1993: investing in health.* New York: Oxford University Press, 1993.

77. Gold MR, Franks P, McCoy K. Condition weights for chronic diseases from a nationally representative sample. Office of Disease Prevention, Washington, D.C. Abstract presented at the Society for Medical Decision Making, Cleveland, October 1994.

78. Erickson P, Wilson R, Shannon I. *Years of healthy life, statistical notes,* Number 7. Hyattsville, MD: National Center for Health Statistics, 1994.

79. Torrance GW, Zhang Y, Feeny D, Furlong W, Barr R. Multi-attribute preference functions for a comprehensive health status classification system, Hamilton, Ontario: McMaster University, Centre for Health Economics and Policy Analysis, Working Paper No. 92-18, 1992.

80. Feeny DH, Torrance GW, Goldsmith CH, et al. A multi-attribute approach to population health status. *Proceedings of the 153rd Annual Meeting of the American Statistical Association,* 1993:161–166.

81. Feeny D, Torrance GW, Goldsmith C, Furlong W, Boyle M. A multi-attribute approach to population health status. McMaster University,

Centre for Health Economics and Policy Analysis Working Paper 94-5, 1994.

82. Kirk RE. *Experimental design: procedures for the behavioural sciences.* Belmont, CA: Brooks/Cole, 1968.

83. Hadorn DC. Setting health care priorities in Oregon: cost-effectiveness meets the rule of rescue. *JAMA* 1991;265(17):2218–2225.

84. Boyle MH, Furlong W, Torrance GW, et al. Reliability of the health utilities index–Mark III used in the 1991 cycle 6 General Social Survey Health Questionnaire. McMaster University Centre for Health Economics and Policy Analysis Working Paper 94-07, March, 1994.

85. Grootendorst P. Results of an investigation into the integrity of the Ontario Health Survey. McMaster University Centre for Health Economics and Policy Analysis Working Paper 94-5, 1994.

86. Grootendorst P, Feeny D, Furlong W. Does it matter whom and how you ask? A technical report on inter- and intra-rater agreement in the Ontario Health Survey. McMaster University Centre for Health Economics and Policy Analysis Working Paper 94-12, June, 1994.

87. Franks P, Gold M, Erickson P. Do utility-based measures of health-related quality of life predict future health states? Longitudinal evidence from a nationally representative cohort. Presented at the Society of Medical Decision Making, Portland, 1992. University of Rochester, Department of Family Medicine, Technical Report.

Quality of Life and Pharmacoeconomics in Clinical Trials, Second Edition, edited by B. Spilker.
Lippincott-Raven Publishers, Philadelphia © 1996.

CHAPTER 27

Measuring Health State Preferences and Utilities: Rating Scale, Time Trade-Off, and Standard Gamble Techniques

Kathryn J. Bennett and George W. Torrance

INTRODUCTION

The purpose of this chapter is to assist readers who are contemplating the assessment of health state preferences and utilities in evaluations of clinical and health care interventions. The chapter focuses on instruments that use rating scale, time trade-off, or standard gamble preference measurement techniques. Preference values and utilities derived indirectly from preference-scored, multiattribute health status classification systems, such as the Health Utilities Index, are described in Chapter 26.

The chapter is divided into five sections. The first section provides an introduction to the measurement of health state preferences and the concept of utility. The second section presents a methodological framework for developing and

validating health state preference instruments. The framework describes the steps involved in instrument development and identifies the reliability and validity issues that must be addressed. The third section presents special issues in instrument development including the choice of the utility scale anchor(s), estimating utility scores from rating scale values, temporary and chronic health states, and states worse than death. The fourth section presents a critical review of published studies that have applied rating scale, time trade-off, and standard gamble techniques to determine health state preferences and utilities. The advantages and disadvantages of the various applications are discussed, and the trade-offs between practicality and methodological sophistication are highlighted. The chapter concludes with a discussion of future directions and methodologic challenges.

HEALTH STATE PREFERENCES AND UTILITY MEASURES

This section begins with a discussion of health state preferences and utility measures within the context of health-

K. J. Bennett: Department of Clinical Epidemiology and Biostatistics, McMaster University, Hamilton, Ontario L8N 3Z5, Canada.
G. W. Torrance: Centre for Health Economics and Policy Analysis, Department of Clinical Epidemiology and Biostatistics, Department of Management Science, McMaster University, Hamilton, Ontario L8N 3Z5, Canada.

related quality of life (HRQL) assessment. This is followed by a discussion of (a) the "utility" concept and utility measurement (What is utility and what are utility measures?); (b) a review of its theoretical foundations (Where did utility measures come from?); and (c) the application of the utility approach in clinical and health care evaluations (How are utility measures used?).

Health-Related Quality of Life, Health State Preferences, and Utility Measurement

HRQL measures are self- or interviewer-administered questionnaires about health, functional status, and quality of life. This type of measure is complementary to physician and laboratory assessments of health status, disease activity, and improvement following a clinical or health care intervention. A taxonomy has been derived that identifies three classes of HRQL measures, namely generic health indices and profiles, specific measures (disease, condition, population), and preference-based measures (1,2; also see Chapters 12,26). Utility measurement is a preference-based approach.

Health state preferences and utility measures differ from generic and specific measures in important ways. First, preference-based measures assess the preferences of individuals for alternative health states or outcomes, whereas generic and disease-specific HRQL approaches concentrate on identifying the presence, absence, severity, frequency, and/or duration of specific symptoms, impairments, or disabilities. Second, preference-based measures provide a comprehensive measure of HRQL in which the respondent combines the positive and negative dimensions of a particular health state into a single number. This number reflects the trade-off, that is, it represents the net effect of the positive and negative aspects of the health state as seen by the respondent. Third, in contrast to specific HRQL measures, preference-based measures provide a common unit of analysis and thereby allow the outcomes of different types of programs to be compared on the same scale.

Measurement of Health State Preferences and Utilities

Preference and utility measurement is concerned with quantifying preferences for health states or outcomes. As will be described in the next section, the measurement process consists of a set of health state descriptions that are usually presented to respondents by a trained interviewer in a structured interview. The interview questions are constructed using specialized preference measurement techniques that include the standard gamble, time trade-off, and rating scale. Respondents can be asked about their own self-health state and about other hypothetical health states that they may or may not have experienced in the past. The feasibility, reliability, and validity of preference and utility measurement has been shown in a range of chronic diseases (3).

Most recently, we have applied utility measures to assess mental health states.

Traditionally, the preference or utility scale in health extends from 1, perfect health, to 0, death, and possibly beyond. The objective of the measurement process is to determine the score (desirability or preference) for specific health states (or outcomes) on this scale. Several investigators have reported health states that are considered to be worse than death. However, the appropriate method of scaling for these states is not yet established (4–6).

To this point in the discussion the terms *preference, preference value, preference-based,* and *utility* have been used without precise definition. Unfortunately, terminology in this field is not entirely standardized. The following taxonomy is one that we find useful to distinguish among the concepts. *Preference* is the umbrella term that refers to preferences, no matter how they are measured. Under this umbrella term there are two main types of preferences; values and utilities. Values are preferences measured under certainty; that is, there is no risk or uncertainty in the preference measurement question. Rating scale and time trade-off approaches are preference measurement instruments that produce values. Utilities, on the other hand, are preferences measured under uncertainty; that is, there is risk or probabilities involved in the preference measurement question. Standard gamble is the preference measurement instrument that produces utilities.

The distinction between values and utilities is important. They come from different scientific paradigms; value measurement is founded on psychological scaling (7), while utility measurement is founded on von Neumann–Morgenstern (8) utility theory. Empirically, the differences are systematic (utilities exceed values for health states), and can be quite large (see Chapter 114).

Von Neumann–Morgenstern (8) utility theory is the dominant normative theory of decision making under uncertainty (9,10). The theory is based on a small number of simple axioms that collectively define the primitive notions of what it means to make rational decisions when faced with uncertainty (11). The strength of the theory lies in the face validity of the simple primitive notions embedded in the axioms. If a decision maker wishes decisions to be consistent with these fundamental axioms, and if the decision maker wishes to use a "divide and conquer" strategy in tackling the problem, then it follows that utilities for final outcomes should be measured using the standard gamble method and the decision that maximizes utility should be selected. It should be noted that the theory only applies to decision making by a single individual or a single decision-making unit, in the sense that the individual's or the unit's utilities can be measured. The original theory does not extend to multiperson decision making, and additional axioms are needed for such an extension.

Because von Neumann–Morgenstern is a theory of decision making in the face of uncertainty, and because health care decisions frequently involve quite large uncertainties, utilities are more appropriate than values for use in health applications.

Not everyone uses the terminology in the way it has been defined above. The other convention is for writers to use the term *utility* as the broad umbrella term covering all types of preferences. In this convention, von Neumann–Morgenstern utilities are specifically labeled vNM utilities for differentiation.

Preference and utility measures are not "off the shelf" HRQL instruments like generic and specific measures. Rather, the approach consists of a set of measurement techniques that can be applied by the researcher to develop a preference or utility questionnaire. The use of utility measures has increased steadily over the past two decades. Utility measures have been developed to assess acute and chronic physical health states and mental health states. However, despite the growing use only a few researchers will be fortunate enough to find a preexisting utility instrument that is appropriate for their research purposes. Instead they will need to develop their own instrument using the measurement techniques available. This chapter should assist those who wish to embark on this task.

Uses of Utility Measures

Utility measures can be used in at least four types of evaluations. First, they can be used in studies of clinical and health care interventions to determine the incremental gain in utility due to the experimental treatment compared with no treatment or the standard treatment. These results can be used to draw conclusions about the gain in HRQL associated with the intervention under study. Second, utility measures can be applied in economic evaluations to analyze the cost-utility of alternative programs and to make recommendations regarding the allocation of resources. In these types of studies utility weights are applied to calculate the quality adjusted life years gained as a result of the intervention or program under study. Third, utility measures are needed for medical decision-making models that explore possible courses of action and express the associated outcomes in terms of probability of occurrence and utility. Finally, utility measures can be used as a method of combining morbidity and mortality in the measurement and monitoring of population health (12).

DEVELOPMENT AND VALIDATION OF UTILITY MEASURES

This section presents a framework for the development and validation of utility measures. The framework identifies five steps in the construction of a reliable and valid health state preference instrument, and highlights the reliability and validity issues the investigator must address (Fig. 1). Steps one through three focus on the identification, development,

and validation of the health state descriptions: step one concerns the identification of the health states for which utility scores are required; step two concerns establishing a method to describe the health states; and step three focuses on the validity of the health state descriptions (face and content validity). Steps four and five concern instrument development and validation: step four involves the selection of utility measurement techniques, the development of the utility interview schedule, interviewer training, and quality control and pilot testing to evaluate the clarity of the script and health state descriptions, and the length of the interview; and step five concerns the psychometric properties of the instrument when administered to appropriate samples of respondents (reliability and validity).

Health State Identification

The first task is to identify the health states that are relevant to the research objectives. Once the health states are identified, the investigator can proceed to the second step of health state description. There are two types of health states: the self-health state of the respondent during a specified period of time, and hypothetical health states that the respondent may or may not have experienced.

Self-Health State

In evaluations of the effectiveness of clinical and health care interventions all investigators will be interested in the self-health state of the respondent, specifically whether clinically important changes occur as a result of the intervention. The study of the effectiveness of auranofin treatment in rheumatoid arthritis is an example (13). Studies of the HRQL of a specific population such as caregivers of the demented elderly (14) or of individuals suffering from a specific disease, such as end-stage renal disease (15), will also focus on the self-health state.

Clinical Marker Health States

In addition to the self-health state, investigators may want to include additional, hypothetical health states that the respondent may or may not have experienced. Clinical marker health states are a particular type of hypothetical state that have been found useful in a variety of studies. There are two main reasons to include clinical marker health states. The first is to provide an empirical base for interpreting the importance of changes in self-health utility due to treatment or disease progression. The clinical markers define milestones or benchmarks along the preference assessment scale between perfect health and death (16). Interpreting self-health utility change scores in this framework avoids arbitrary definitions of the minimum clinically important change.

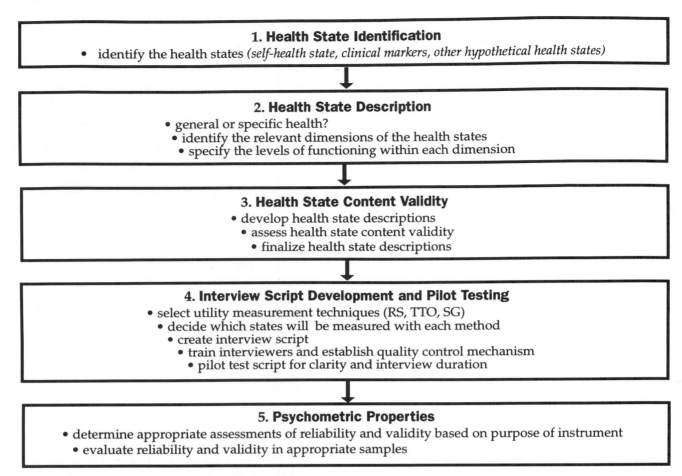

FIG. 1. Development and validation of utility measures.

For example, if the investigator includes clinically valid descriptions of mild, moderate, and severe levels of rheumatoid arthritis in the interview, the mean pre- and post-treatment self-health utility values can be interpreted with reference to the mean values for the clinical markers. It may be concluded (again for example) that on average the treatment under study moves patients from moderate to mild levels of rheumatoid arthritis.

Second, the clinical marker states act as a task comprehension aid for respondents (14). The markers assist respondents to think about the specific aspects of HRQL that are affected by the target disorder and the different ways that the disorder might affect an individual (for example, from a little to a great deal). Respondents can then think about their own health situation in the context of the marker health states. In addition, correct ranking of the health states gives assurance to the investigator that the respondent has understood the task.

Mohide and colleagues (14) at McMaster University defined three marker states (mild, moderate, and severe) for the health status of caregivers caring for disabled relatives at home, as an aid to task comprehension. The mild, moder-

ate, and severe marker state approach has also been applied at McMaster in a number of other clinical areas including pediatric asthma, hypertension, and rheumatoid arthritis (16).

Additional Hypothetical States

Other hypothetical states will be derived directly from the research questions under study. For example, the research question may call for the inclusion of health states that focus on side effects such as nausea, dizziness, pruritus, or anxiety. Or it may call for the inclusion of rare but important events such as a therapeutic abortion triggered by a false-positive genetic screening test (17). Temporary health states associated with the treatment itself are often important and require utility scores (17,18). Some investigators (particularly in the context of decision analysis) may be interested in health states that represent the goals of treatment or components of the decision analysis model, such as the occurrence of endometrial cancer, hip fracture, and menopausal symptoms in estrogen replacement therapy (19). Other researchers may wish to assess health states associated with specific interventions such as open cholecystectomy (20) or the preferences of defined populations, for example those of parents and children in the general population for various child health outcomes (21).

Health State Descriptions

Health state descriptions provide an explicit, objective statement of the HRQL associated with a specific health problem or outcome. A variety of approaches have appeared in the literature including (a) a label for the health state, but no standardized description; (b) holistic health states that describe more than one attribute of HRQL and are expressed in terms of levels of functioning (these health states may be written in narrative or point form and they may describe general or specific health); and (c) single attribute descriptions of one component of HRQL, such as emotion (decomposed).

The discussion that follows focuses on the development and application of a health state classification system to describe general and specific health states. Compared with the other approaches that have been used, the health state classification system approach has a number of advantages. First, health states composed of labels with no description leave open to question what it was that respondents were thinking about when they made their response. Health states derived from a health state classification scheme provide explicit, standardized descriptions. Second, compared with narrative approaches, descriptions based on health state classification systems are presented in point form and therefore should reduce respondent burden. Finally, a health state classification system is based on an explicit model of the dimensions of health; both the system and the resulting health states can be assessed easily for face and content validity by potential users.

Health State Classification Systems

This approach requires the investigator to identify the dimensions (or attributes) of health relevant to the disorder under study and the levels of functioning associated with each dimension. The dimensions and levels form the basis for describing the self-health state and for developing other hypothetical health state descriptions. The full set of dimensions and levels is referred to as a health state classification system. A comprehensive health state classification system includes all the dimensions of general health functioning. Alternatively, a disease-specific system focuses on the subset of dimensions that characterize the impact of the target disorder. The Health Utilities Index (4,22–24; also see Chapter 26) is an example of a system to describe general levels of health functioning. The Health Utilities Index was developed for use in general populations and provides a system to describe and classify functional health status using eight dimensions of health: vision, hearing, speech, ambulation,

dexterity, emotion, cognition, and pain. Each dimension is defined by levels of functioning that describe full ability through to no ability.

The advantage of using the Health Utilities Index is that it provides a comprehensive approach to describing overall functional health status and is consistent with the current literature with respect to the relevant dimensions of health status (22). A possible disadvantage of using the Health Utilities Index could be a lack of sensitivity to change. That is, clinically important changes may occur that may not be detected by the levels of health status reflected within the Health Utilities Index dimensions.

In contrast, the depression health state classification system is an example of a disorder-specific system of dimensions and levels of functioning. It consists of six dimensions of depression based on the American Psychiatric Association *Diagnostic and Statistical Manual* (DSM-III-R) (25) criteria for the diagnosis of major, unipolar depression: emotion, self-appraisal, cognition, physiology, behavior, and role function.[1] Each dimension is operationalized by a number of components that capture the essence of the dimension in depression. For example, the components of emotion are mood and ability to experience pleasure. Four levels of functioning are defined for each dimension: no depression, mild, moderate, and severe depression. The levels for emotion are as follows: 1. Mood is normal. Life is generally enjoyable with the usual ups and downs. 2. Feels more down (or sad, blue, depressed) than usual and unable to enjoy (or less interested in) things as usual. 3. Mood is quite low most of the time. Unable to enjoy much these days and has little interest in most things. 4. Feel terribly depressed (or sad) all the time. Unable to enjoy anything and feels desperate (or it is painful).

Self-Health State

The health state classification system can be used by the respondents to describe their own health situation during a specified period of time (usually 7 days prior to the interview). The dimensions and levels can be presented as a HRQL checklist within the interview, prior to self-health rating scale, time trade-off, or standard gamble questions.

Clinical Marker Health States and Other Hypothetical States

The health state classification system can be used to develop descriptions of the clinical marker health states and other hypothetical states relevant to the research objectives. As is discussed in the next section, the method used to develop the descriptions should include strategies to assess face and content validity. Empirical assessments of the frequency of occurrence of the marker health states in appropriate samples of respondents can also be conducted.

SALLY

Able to see close-up and at a distance, but **with** glasses.

No trouble hearing (without a hearing aid).

Speech understood by both strangers and friends.

Unable to walk alone, even with walking equipment. Able to walk short distances with a helper, and requires a wheelchair to get around the neighbourhood.

Limited use of hands and fingers, but doesn't need tools or help from others.

Somewhat happy.

Able to remember most things, think clearly and solve day to day problems.

Severe pain that prevents most activities.

SYDNEY

Feels terribly down or sad all the time. Doesn't enjoy anything and feels desperate (or it is painful).

Feels worthless and sees absolutely no hope for himself, and/or doesn't know why people even care about him, and/or feels very guilty about the past and sees no future for himself.

Feels like his mind is shut down, overloaded or racing. Can't read or watch T.V. and can't make even little decisions.

Sleep is terrible these days and doesn't feel rested. Has absolutely no energy and feels constantly tired. Has no interest in food, and has lost a lot of weight over the last month (greater than 5% of body weight).

Can't do anything. Completely shut down, and/or is extremely agitated, and/or thinks of suicide constantly and has thoughts of plans to end his life.

Had to stop work and/or **do nothing at home,** and/or has completely withdrawn from everything.

FIG. 2. Clinical marker health states.

Figure 2 provides two examples of clinical marker health states, specifically severe disability due to knee disease (Sally) and severe depression (Sydney). Both states were developed by the authors using the health state classification systems described above and the face and content validity procedures described in the following section. In our approach, the marker states are given names in the interview.

Validation of Health State Descriptions

Face and content validity are key components of the validity of instruments designed to assess health state preferences and utilities. As is discussed below, health state face and content validity are aspects of instrument design that have not received much attention in the literature. A few studies have used interviews with patients to guide the development of health state descriptions, but for the most part states have been derived based on investigator judgments.

We have developed an explicit, structured approach to address the content validity of health state descriptions,

which incorporates both empirical and judgmental techniques. Our approach grew out of the need to establish the clinical credibility of the clinical marker health states, in order to justify their use in the interpretation of self-health utility. The approach consists of four elements: the first is the use of a health state classification system to derive health state descriptions; the second is the establishment of a consultant expert group; the third is the development of structured exercises that involve both empirical and judgmental tasks; and the fourth is the empirical assessment of the content validity of hypothetical health states, through comparisons with the self-health states observed in appropriate samples of individuals with the disorder of interest.

The health state classification approach requires the investigator to identify the attributes or dimensions that define the health or disease problem(s) of interest. The result is an explicit, comprehensive statement of the dimensions and levels of functioning that describe the problem under study. The dimensions and levels can be scrutinized by others and can be applied to describe health states. Under ideal circumstances the health state classification system would be developed in conjunction with an empirical study of patients with the condition of interest. For example, an investigator might develop a health state classification system for rheumatoid arthritis in collaboration with rheumatologists and other clinicians who work with this patient group and then test it by asking a consecutive series of patients with rheumatoid arthritis to (a) rate their self-health state on the dimensions and levels and (b) identify any aspects of their health state not covered. The results would then be examined to determine whether the health state classification system was working (that is, whether patients could rate themselves on each dimension and whether good discrimination was seen on the levels of functioning) and whether the patients identified important dimensions of their rheumatoid arthritis health state that were not covered by the health state classification system. The results would also guide the development of clinical marker health states and other hypothetical states relevant to the research objectives. For example, the clinical marker health states could be derived from natural clustering observed in the data.

In most cases the investigator will not have the luxury of this type of pretesting and fine-tuning prior to using the health state classification system to describe health states. We found ourselves in this situation and, as a result, derived a strategy that comprises the second and third elements of our approach to content validity, specifically the establishment of a consultant expert group and the development of structured exercises. The consultant expert group can consist of clinicians (such as physicians, nurses, physiotherapists, occupational therapists social workers), patients[2] or others with experience that is relevant to the development of the hypothetical states, such as family members or caregivers. The structured exercises are designed to be completed by the consultant expert group. They test the face and content validity of the health state classification system and the health state descriptions derived from it. The exercises are completed independently and then reviewed with the consultant expert group in two to three hour-long workshops, using an iterative process of individual response collation, followed by discussion, followed by additional independent exercises, response collation, and further discussion. The points of agreement and disagreement are highlighted; major disagreements between responses are resolved through group discussion. The workshop process can lead to the final version of the health state classification system and specific health states. However, in some cases the investigative team may need to make final decisions (using explicit decision rules) based on the workshop results. We have used consultant expert groups and structured exercises to develop health state classification systems and health states for rheumatoid arthritis, knee replacements, and depression, and found the approach to be feasible, enjoyable, and, most importantly, to produce useful results.

The fourth element concerns empirical assessments in appropriate samples of patients. As discussed above, the validity of the clinical markers and other hypothetical health states can be assessed by comparing them with the self-health states observed (using the health state classification system as a checklist) in a group of patients with the target disorder. For example, if the health states observed in patients prior to receiving treatment in a clinical trial are consistent with the clinical marker health states, the validity of the marker health states as benchmarks for the assessment of clinically important change is supported.

Interview Schedule Development and Pilot Testing

The development of the interview schedule requires two main decisions by the investigator. The first concerns selecting the preference measurement techniques (rating scale, time trade-off, and standard gamble) and the second concerns selecting the health states to be measured with each.

Selection of Preference Measurement Techniques

The three most widely used approaches to measure health state preferences are rating scale, time trade-off, and standard gamble. The standard gamble technique is the classical approach to utility measurement derived directly from the fundamental axioms of utility theory (3,8,11). The rating scale provides an approximation to the standard gamble, but the results cannot be directly interpreted as utilities because the technique does not incorporate risk or uncertainty. Values for health states obtained using this method must be transformed through a conversion curve to allow their interpretation as utilities. Empirically, a power curve has been found to fit the data well and has been used as the conversion curve (4,11,15; see below). The time trade-off technique also does not incorporate uncertainty and thus provides value scores not utility scores. Nevertheless, early empirical work sug-

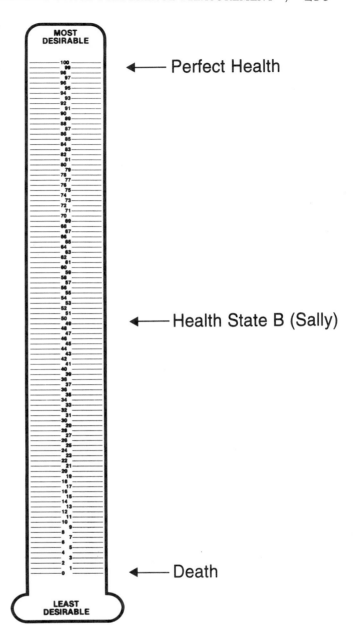

gested that time trade-off scores without any conversion were a reasonable approximation to standard gamble scores (3,4,26). Subsequent work suggests that the approximation is not so good, and that time trade-off scores, like rating scale scores, require adjustment before they can be used as utilities (27).

The rating scale is presented as a feeling thermometer (Fig. 3). The top of the thermometer, corresponding to a value of 100, is defined as the most preferred health state (perfect health). The bottom of the thermometer, corresponding to a value of 0, is defined as the least preferred health state. The subject selects the least preferred state, which may be death (if death is included in the set of states to be rated) or may be some other state. In some cases it may be desirable to omit death at this stage of the ratings, and to use the worst health state as the bottom anchor of the feeling thermometer. This may be especially appropriate when the health states are relatively mild, and constant comparisons to death would seem inappropriate, and when there is one health state that is unambiguously worse than all the others. In such a case, the strategy of omitting death from the rating scale could facilitate the interviews while also maximizing the use of the full range of the scale. However, when death is omitted at this stage, the rating scale values must be subsequently converted to the perfect health–death scale. Methods are available for doing so as described below.

In the rating scale task the respondent is asked to imagine that they would have to live in the designated state (for example, Sally), without change, for the designated time, often a specified lifetime, with the same outcome at the end of all states. The task for the respondent is to preference rank the states relative to each other and relative to the anchor states, and to place the states on the scale in their preference order and spaced relative to each other such that the intervals (distances) between the states match the strength of preference difference that the subject feels for these states. For example, states that are almost equally preferable would be placed very close together, while states that are very different in their desirability would be placed far apart, and all the distances would be adjusted relative to each other to reflect the differences in desirability.

The time trade-off method asks the respondent to choose between two possibilities. One possibility is to live in health state A for time x while the other possibility is to live in health state B for time t. At the end of the time, x or t, both possibilities have the same final outcome. Time x or t is varied in a systematic fashion to identify the point at which the subject is just indifferent between the two possibilities. Props are normally used as visual aids to enhance task comprehension, and the method of varying the time offered is designed to minimize measurement biases. The specifics of the method differ depending upon whether the health states being assessed are chronic lifetime states, or are temporary states, and in the case of chronic states, whether the state is considered better than death or worse than death (2; see also Chapter 12 by Feeny, Torrance, and Labelle). Figure 4 shows a graphic of the time trade-off question for the most common application, a chronic state (Sally) considered better than death. The subject would be offered two choices: health state B for a normal (age-specific for the subject) life expectancy of t years, or health state A (in this case, perfect health) for a shorter life expectancy of x years. Time x would be varied systematically to find that value of x at which the subject is just indifferent between the two possibilities. Then, the time trade-off score for health state B is x/t.

The standard gamble is a lottery in which the respondent is presented with two choices. Figure 5 displays the standard gamble choices for a chronic health state (Sally) considered

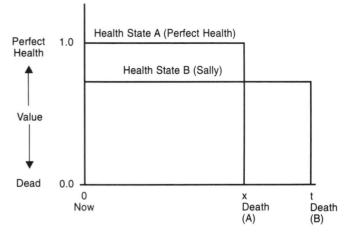

FIG. 4. Time trade-off.

better than death. Choice A is the uncertain choice and contains two possible health state outcomes: each health state is associated with a probability of occurring, p and $1 - p$. Choice B is the certain choice and includes only one possible health state or outcome, with 100% probability of occurring. The two living health states would be specified as lasting the same length of time, usually an age-specific normal life expectancy for the subject, and terminating in death. For clarity, it is useful to think of the two states in choice A as the anchors of the standard gamble scale: the state with p probability is the most preferred state and the state with $1 - p$ probability is the least preferred state. The state in choice B falls somewhere between the two. The probability p in choice A is varied systematically until the respondent is indifferent between the uncertain (choice A) and the certain choice (choice B). The probability p at the indifference point is the vNM utility of the health

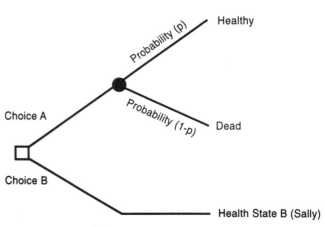

FIG. 5. Standard gamble.

state in choice B for the duration specified, on a scale where the utility of perfect health for the same duration is 1.0 and the utility of immediate death is 0.0.

The rating scale is often selected for part one of the interview because it is a useful introductory exercise that serves a number of purposes. It familiarizes the respondent with the objective of the interview and the notion of preferences. It allows the respondent to question and understand each health state, as they are introduced one by one. It initially poses the easiest preference task for the respondent—rank ordering the states according to preference. It is an efficient method to obtain a large number of cardinal preferences, although they are values, not utilities.

We typically select the standard gamble for part two of the interview because it is the only method that gives true vNM utilities. True utilities have major advantages in applications of health state preferences. They are the only measures consistent with von Neumann–Morgenstern utility theory, the dominant normative paradigm for decision making under uncertainty. Given the uncertainties and risks associated with health decisions, this is certainly the appropriate normative paradigm. Thus, vNM utilities are the appropriate measure for clinical decision analyses, are the preferred measure for cost-utility analyses using quality-adjusted life years (see Chapter 114 by Torrance), and are a suitable measure for population health (12). If used in all three levels of application, utilities can represent a unifying outcome measurement scheme for clinical decision analysis, technology assessment, and population health.

Selecting the States for the Standard Gamble Section

It may not be feasible to ask the respondent to rate all of the health states on both the rating scale and standard gamble due to the length of time needed. In this case, given the investigator includes all states on the feeling thermometer, the number assessed on the standard gamble can be reduced to a subset of the total. The states that are not assessed on the standard gamble can be converted to the perfect health (1) to death (0) utility scale using the transformation procedure to be outlined below. It is important that the selection of the subset includes the state(s) expected to fall in the mid-range of the scale to enhance the calculation of the power curve coefficient.

Interviewer Training and Quality Control

Once the interview schedule has been developed, the investigator can then proceed to interviewer training, quality control, and pilot testing. A detailed training manual and program must be developed to prepare interviewers to administer the structured utility interview. The manual serves as a basis for the training program, and consists of an overview to the interview, a description of the materials required to conduct an interview (feeling thermometer, chance board, and health state cards), and specific instructions for conducting the assessment. A complete interview script is also included. The training program consists of three phases: (a) a one on one session between the trainer and trainee to review the interview content and procedures; (b) independent practice interviews by the trainee with volunteers; and (c) an evaluation by the trainer of a formal interview with a patient by the trainee. A list of criteria is used by the trainer to assess performance and provide constructive feedback.

Interviewer performance should be monitored throughout the study by the research coordinator/trainer. Each interview should be tape recorded; the tape is submitted with the completed case report forms. Tapes and case report forms should be reviewed regularly to ensure completeness and consistency, thus providing quality control.

Pilot Test

Before embarking on the main study, the utility interview should be pilot tested in a convenience sample of patients. The objective is to assess the clarity of wording of the health states and utility interview script and to determine the duration of the interview. Five to ten patients should be interviewed and the results reviewed. Adjustments should be made and then at least five more patients should be interviewed.

Assessment of Instrument Psychometric Properties

The fifth step focuses on the psychometric properties of the instrument when administered to appropriate groups of respondents. Reliability concerns observer agreement and test-retest reliability. Observer agreement is difficult to assess because of the nature of the interview process. It is generally accepted that some error will be introduced due to the interviewer. Strategies to minimize interviewer effects include balancing the number of interviews done by each interviewer between comparison groups. In addition, the scores of interviewers can be examined to see if there are any systematic differences, such as one interviewer consistently obtaining higher scores than other interviewers or terminating interviews more often. Test-retest reliability can be assessed for both the self-state and hypothetical health states. Two to four weeks is the usual period of time between assessments. The interpretation of test-retest data must take into account the influence of random measurement error and real changes in preferences. Very little data is available on the stability of preferences over time.

Assessments of instrument validity include comparisons with other measures of HRQL (convergent validity), comparisons with measures not associated with HRQL (discriminant validity), and responsiveness to change.

SPECIAL ISSUES IN INSTRUMENT DESIGN

Choice of Utility Scale Anchor

In some cases the investigator may choose not to use death as the bottom anchor of the scale in order to maximize the use of the full range of the scale and to minimize the number of comparisons against death. The choice of the least-preferred health state can be decided by the investigator, or alternatively, the investigator may allow the respondent to choose the least-preferred state from among the full set. The advantage of allowing the respondent to choose is that no assumptions are made about the preferences of the respondent. When the least-preferred health state is used as the anchor for the rating scale, time trade-off or standard gamble, all respondents must be asked to rate this state against death. This allows the conversion of all rating scale states to the perfect health–death scale.

Estimating Utilities from Rating Scale Values

Empirically, utilities (u) tend to exceed rating scale values (v) in a systematic way that can be approximated by the power curve $(1 - u) = (1 - v)^b$ (23,24,29). Here, v is the rating scale value on the dead-healthy (0–1) scale, b is the exponent for the power curve, and u is the estimated utility on the dead-healthy (0–1) scale. The exponent b can be estimated from the subset of states that have been measured on both the rating scale and the standard gamble. The conversion curve approach can be applied at the individual level or at the group mean level. At the individual level, b can be determined for each subject, that subject's rating scale scores can be converted into utilities using the subject's individual b, and the mean utility for each health state for the group can be computed. Alternatively, for each health state a group mean v can be computed, and converted into a group u, using the group value for b. These two approaches have been compared in one study, and the latter approach is both better and easier (24).

The group value for b for the conversion curve is determined from the states that were measured on both rating scale and standard gamble. The first step is to calculate for these states the mean rating scale scores on the dead-healthy (0–1) scale (v) and the mean standard gamble score on the dead-healthy (0–1) scale. The value of b is estimated from these data by transforming $(1 - u) = (1 - v)^b$ to $\ln(1 - u) = b \ln(1 - v)$ and using linear regression on the transformed variables with the intercept suppressed (24).

Temporary and Chronic Health States

The preference measurement instruments described in this chapter (rating scale, time trade-off, and standard gamble) can be used to measure preferences for either temporary or chronic health states, and the detailed procedures have been described elsewhere (3,28). However, most of the applications to date have been undertaken on chronic health states. This has probably occurred for two reasons. First, chronic outcomes often dominate the analysis in the sense that they have a much greater influence on the results of the study than do the temporary outcomes. Second, it is easier to measure preferences on chronic outcomes. Some of the problems in measuring preferences for temporary outcomes are the following: (a) Temporary outcomes may have widely varying durations, and yet for the purpose of preference measurement health states must be batched in sets with a common duration for each set. (b) Preferences for temporary states may be confounded by preferences for an inferred prognosis, despite the researchers' best efforts to dissuade this line of thinking by the subject. For example, a subject might decide that the temporary pain and discomfort associated with a treatment should have a higher preference score because it will lead to an improved long-term outcome. This, of course, is confounding the utility of the temporary state with that of the long-term chronic outcome. (c) It is difficult to link the preferences for temporary states onto the dead-healthy (0–1) scale, which is necessary for calculating quality-adjusted life years. This difficulty arises because, to make this link, the health state of "death" must be in the set of temporary health states being measured, or at least be linked to the set being measured. Because a state of "temporary death" does not exist, the problem has to be solved some other way. One approach is to measure separately the preference of the least preferred temporary state against healthy and dead using the same time duration as the temporary state, but assuming death occurs at the end of the time regardless of the state (2). Essentially this converts the temporary state into a short-term chronic state. An alternative is to create a proxy for "temporary death" such as "a health state as bad as being dead" or "unwanted sleep/coma."

States Worse than Death

Several investigators have reported that respondents may rate health states as worse than death (4,6). In the standard gamble a negative utility can be obtained for a state rated worse than death by exchanging the death anchor in choice A with the state considered worse than death and continuing to alter the probabilities in choice A in the normal fashion until the respondent is indifferent. The result is a negative utility for the state, using the equation $u = -p/(1 - p)$ where p is the indifference probability. Negative utilities measured in this way give rise to two scaling problems. First, the resulting utility scale is asymmetric with a maximum score in the positive direction of 1.00; the lower limit is dependent on the instrument itself. The lower limit depends upon the maximum indifference probability available in the instrument; for example, if the maximum indifference probability is .95, the lowest utility is -19.0, while if the maximum probability is .975 the lowest utility is -39.0.

Second, the data are highly negatively skewed; that is, there is a very long tail in the negative direction.

Because of these scaling problems, transformations of the negative utilities have been proposed. Torrance and colleagues (4) used a linear transformation that eliminated the asymmetry but not the skewness. However, it did have the advantage that the transformed scores were still utilities, although no longer on the same scale as the positive utilities. Patrick and colleagues (6) used a nonlinear transformation that eliminated both the asymmetry and the skewness, but the resulting transformed scores are no longer utilities, and must be interpreted only as measures of HRQL. Other statistical techniques, such as the Windsorized mean and the trimmed mean, are also possibilities, but have not been attempted in previous studies.

REVIEW OF STUDIES OF HEALTH PREFERENCES AND UTILITIES

As part of another project, more than 50 studies have been located by the authors[3] wherein one, or a combination of, rating scale, time trade-off, or standard gamble techniques(s) were used to assess health state preferences. The applications cover a broad range of disease groups and populations including bowel, breast, and laryngeal cancer, gallstones, musculoskeletal disease (hip and knee replacement, rheumatoid arthritis, and low back pain), renal disease, total parenteral nutrition, deep vein thrombosis, estrogen replacement therapy, child health, adult health, dental health, and caregiver well-being. Most studies have focused on preferences for specific rather than general health states and about equal numbers have used narrative or point-form descriptions derived from a health state classification system; very few have used labels with no descriptions.

Study objectives have included assessments of clinical effectiveness and cost-utility analysis, decision analysis, and evaluations of the HRQL of specific populations. Almost half of the studies have included investigations of methodological questions. Examples of the methodologic issues investigated include comparisons of the results of the rating scale, time trade-off, and standard gamble (20,30), the influence of framing effects on preferences (31), differences in preferences between different types of raters (32), comparisons between alternative measures of HRQL (33), the influence of health state duration on preference scores, and comparisons of health paths composed of more than one health state with utility weighted, quality-adjusted life years (34).

Formal assessments of the face and content validity of the health states are rare. Most health states are derived from the judgments of the investigators; in a few instances interviews of patients suffering from the disease have been used as a basis for the descriptions (34). In fact, many studies provide very little information on the development of the

health states or instrument; often examples of the health states are not even included in the publication.

Most studies have used either the time trade-off or standard gamble and provide scores on the perfect health to death scale. Only a few studies used the rating scale alone. Most studies report good respondent acceptability with low rates of refusals or terminated interviews. Respondent comprehension is also reported to be good, but the method of assessing comprehension is not usually described.

Almost all studies used instruments administered by a trained interviewer. However, very few studies provided information on interviewer characteristics, training, or quality control. One study applied the time trade-off by telephone (35). This approach resulted in a brief and inexpensive survey process, but, unfortunately, telephone administration has not yet been validated against interviews conducted by a trained interviewer. Another study tested U-titer, a computer-assisted approach (36). The approach was feasible and satisfactory agreement was demonstrated between U-titer and person-to-person interviews.

Only a handful of studies have assessed the psychometric properties of their preference instrument, for example test-retest reliability and construct validity. Some authors have reported high levels of test-retest reliability using the intraclass correlation coefficient (15). Other authors have reported only modest correlations between repeated individual assessments, but good results for the reproducibility of group means (3). Two studies provide evidence of responsiveness to change (13,14). Assessment of the psychometric properties of preference measurement instruments is an area that needs further attention, particularly with respect to the added information value of including preference assessments in evaluations of the effectiveness of clinical and health care.

Finally, two studies were found that addressed the cross-cultural adaptation of rating scale, time trade-off, or standard gamble techniques (37,38). Methodologic standards are available to guide the translation and adaptation of measures of HRQL (39). Experience in adapting measures of functional status is available (40), but very little work has been done with rating scale, time trade-off, and standard gamble techniques.

FUTURE DIRECTIONS

Substantial experience with the use of rating scale, time trade-off, and standard gamble preference measurement techniques has been gained in a wide variety of disease populations and types of evaluations. The techniques are acceptable to respondents and comprehension appears to be good. Although most investigators will need to develop their own instrument, many will find an application in the literature relevant to their research question and patient population. Clinical marker health states should aid in interpreting the clinical importance of instrument scores.

However, a number of challenges confront the field and should be considered in further applications of these techniques. Further work is needed to address the measurement characteristics of preference-based HRQL instruments. For example, the stability of preferences is not well understood, and the relationship between specific changes in clinical status and changes in preference needs to be investigated. Increased attention should be given to the use of preference measures in evaluations of treatment effectiveness. This will improve our understanding of when to include these approaches in randomized trials of treatment effectiveness. Further work is also needed on the factors that influence health state preferences such as age, sex, education, respondent's health status, and health state duration. Cross-cultural adaptation of health state preference measurement techniques is a new area that is just beginning to be addressed.

Another challenge concerns the interpretation and application of utilities in calculating quality-adjusted life years. For example, when the health path over which the quality-adjusted life year must be calculated consists of a path of changing health states going out over time, there are two ways that quality-adjusted life years can be calculated. The conventional way, and the easy way, is to use utility weights for each health state on the path, to compute quality-adjusted life years, and to sum up the quality-adjusted life years over time, with or without discounting. An alternative method, which is much more demanding, is to measure the utility for the entire path all at once, if possible, and to calculate the quality-adjusted life years for the entire path treating the path as one giant chronic state. Again, this calculation can be done with and without discounting. The conventional method is more consistent with the quality-adjusted life years paradigm. The alternative method is more consistent with the utility paradigm. Little is known about the feasibility of the alternative approach or the extent to which it produces different results.

CONCLUSIONS

The importance of assessing health state preferences and utilities is now well recognized in the clinical and health care evaluation literature. Significant progress has been made in the development of acceptable and feasible instruments using rating scale, time trade-off, and standard gamble approaches. The experience to date is a useful guide to those who wish to apply preference measurement techniques in their research and provides stimulating conceptual and methodological challenges to those who wish to advance the field.

ENDNOTES

1. Further information is available from the authors.
2. To date, we do not have experience with including patients or other nonclinicians in the development of marker health states.
3. Bibliography available from the authors.

REFERENCES

1. Guyatt GH, Patrick DH, Patrick DL. Measuring health-related quality of life. *Ann Intern Med* 1993;118:622–629.
2. Canadian Coordinating Office for Health Technology Assessment. *Guidelines for economic evaluation of pharmaceuticals: Canada,* 1st ed. Ottawa: CCOHTA, 1994.
3. Torrance GW. Measurement of health state utilities for economic appraisal. A review. *J Health Econ* 1986;5:1–30.
4. Torrance GW, Boyle MH, Horwood SP. Application of multi-attribute utility theory to measure social preferences for health states. *Oper Res* 1982;30:1043–1069.
5. Torrance GW. Health states worse than death. In: van Eimeren W, Engelbert R, Flagle CD, eds. *Third International Conference on System Science in Health Care.* Berlin: Springer, 1984:1085–1089.
6. Patrick DL, Starks HE, Cain KC, Ullmann RF, Pearlman RA. Measuring preferences for health states worse than death. *Med Decis Making* 1994;14(1):9–18.
7. von Winterfeldt D, Edwards W. *Decision analysis and behavioural research.* Cambridge: Cambridge University Press, 1986.
8. Neumann J von, Morgenstern O. *Theory of games and economic behaviour.* Princeton, NJ: Princeton University Press, 1944.
9. Keeney RL, Raiffa H. *Decisions with multiple objectives: preferences and value trade-offs.* New York: Wiley, 1976.
10. Holloway CA. *Decision making under uncertainty: models and choices.* Englewood Cliffs, NJ: Prentice-Hall, 1979.
11. Torrance GW, Feeny D. Utilities and quality-adjusted life years. *Int J Tech Assess Health Care* 1989;5:559–575.
12. Berthelot JM, Roberge R, Wolfson MC. The calculation of health-adjusted life expectancy for a Canadian province using a multi-attribute utility function: a first attempt. In: Robine JM, Mathers CD, Bone MR, Romieu I, eds. *Calculation of health expectancies: harmonization, consensus and future perspectives,* vol 226. John Libbey Eurotext, 1993:161–172.
13. Bombardier C, Ware J, Russell J, Larson M, Chalmers A, Read L. Auranofin therapy and quality of life in patients with rheumatoid arthritis. *Am J Med* 1986;81:565–578.
14. Mohide EA, Torrance GW, Streiner DL, Pringle DM, Gilbert R. Measuring the well-being of family care-givers using the time trade-off technique. *J Clin Epidemiol* 1988;41:475–482.
15. Churchill DN, Torrance GW, Taylor DW, Barnes CC, Ludwin D, Shimizu A, Smith EKM. Measurement of quality of life in end-stage renal disease: the time trade-off approach. *Clin Invest Med* 1987;10:14–20.
16. Bennett KJ, Torrance GW, Tugwell P. Methodologic challenges in the development of utility measures of health related quality of life in rheumatoid arthritis. *Controlled Clin Trials* 1991;12(suppl):118S–128S.
17. Feeny DH, Torrance GW. Incorporating utility-based quality-of-life assessment measures in clinical trials: two examples. *Med Care* 1989;27(3)(suppl):S190–S204.
18. Feeny D, Barr R, Furlong W, Torrance GW, Weitzman S. Quality of life of the treatment process in pediatric oncology: an approach to measurement. In: Osobo D, ed. *Effect of cancer on quality of life.* Boca Raton: CRC Press, 1991:73–88.
19. Elstein AS, Holzman GB, Ravitch MM, Metheny WA, Holmes MM, Hoppe RB, Rothert ML, Rovner DR. Comparison of physicians decisions regarding estrogen replacement therapy for menopausal women and decisions derived from a decision analytic model. *Am J Med* 1986;80:246–258.
20. Bass EB, Steinberg EP, Pitt HA, Griffiths RI, Lillemoe KD, Saba GP, Johns C. Comparison of the rating scale and standard gamble in measuring patient preferences for outcomes of gallstone disease. *Med Decis Making* 1994;14:307–314.
21. Cadman D, Goldsmith CH, Torrance GW, Boyle MH, Furlong W. Development of a health status index for Ontario children. Report to the Ontario Ministry of Health, 1986.
22. Feeny DH, Torrance GW, Goldsmith CH, Furlong W, Boyle M. *A multi-attribute approach to population health status.* 1993 Proceedings of the Social Statistics Section. Alexandria, VA: American Statistical Association, 1994:161–166.
23. Furlong WH, Torrance GW, Feeny D, Boyle MH. McMaster Health Utilities Index of health-related quality of life. *Qual Life Res* 1994;3:76.

24. Torrance GW, Zhang Y, Feeny D, Furlong W, Barr W. Multi-attribute preference functions for a comprehensive health status classification system. Centre for Health Economics and Policy Analysis Working Paper 92-18, McMaster University, 1992.

25. *Diagnostic and Statistical Manual of Mental Disorders* (DSM-III-R). Washington, DC: American Psychiatric Association, 1987.

26. Torrance GW. Social preferences for health states: an empirical evaluation of three measurement techniques. *Socioecon Planning Sci* 1976;10(3):129–136.

27. Read JL, Quinn RJ, Berwick DM, Fineberg HV, Weinstein MC. Preferences for health outcomes: comparisons of assessment methods. *Med Decis Making* 1984;4(3):315–329.

28. Furlong W, Feeny DF, Torrance GW, Barr R, Horsman J. Guide to design and development of health-state utility instrumentation. Centre for Health Economics and Policy Analysis Working Paper 90-9, McMaster University, 1990.

29. Torrance GW, Furlong W, Feeny D, Boyle M. Multi-attribute preference functions: health utilities index. *Pharmacoeconomics* 1995; 7:503–520.

30. Sackett DL, Torrance GW. The utility of different health states as perceived by the general public. *J Chronic Dis* 1978;31:697–704.

31. Llewellyn-Thomas HA, Sutherland HJ, Tibshsirani R, Ciampi A, Till JE, Boyd NF. Describing health states: methodologic issues in obtaining values for health states. *Med Care* 1984;22:543–552.

32. Boyd NF, Sutherland HJ, Keasman KZ, Tritchler DL, Cummings BJ. Whose utilities for decision analysis? *Med Decis Making* 1990; 10:58–67.

33. Hornberger JC, Redelmeier DA, Petersen J. Variability among methods to assess patients well-being and consequent effect on a cost-effectiveness analysis. *J Clin Epidemiol* 1992;32:183–188.

34. Hall J, Gerard K, Salkeld G, Richardson J. A cost-utility analysis of mammography screening in Australia. *Soc Sci Med* 1992;34:903–1004.

35. Katz J, Phillips CB, Fossel AH, Liang MH. Stability and responsiveness of utility measures. *Med Care* 1994;32:183–188.

36. Sanders GD, Owens DK, Padian N, Cardinalli AB, Sullivan AN, Nease RF. A computer-based interview to identify HIV risk behaviours and to assess patient preferences for HIV related health states. In: *Proceedings of the Eighteenth Annual Symposium on Computer Applications in Medical Care.* Washington, DC, 1994.

37. Bakker C, Rutten E, van Doorslaer E, Bennett K, van der Linden S. Feasibility of utility assessment by rating scale and standard gamble in patients with ankylosing spondylitis and fibromyalgia. *J Rheumatol* 1994;21:269–275.

38. Ferraz MB, Quaresma MR, Goldsmith CH, Bennett KJ, Atra E. Corticosteroids in patients with rheumatoid arthritis: utility measurements for evaluating risks and benefits. *Rev Rhum (Engl Ed)* 1994;61:240–244.

39. Guillemin F, Bombardier C, Beaton D. Cross-cultural adaptation of health-related quality of life measures: literature review and proposed guidelines. *J Clin Epidemiol* 1994;46:1417–1432.

40. Bennett KJ, Cardiel M, Ferraz M, Riedemann P, Goldsmith CH, Tugwell P. Community screening for rheumatic disease: cross-cultural adaptation and validation of the ILAR-COPCORD questionnaire in Brazil, Chile and Mexico. (Submitted)

Quality of Life and Pharmacoeconomics in Clinical Trials, Second Edition, edited by B. Spilker.
Lippincott-Raven Publishers, Philadelphia © 1996.

CHAPTER **28**

The McMaster Health Index Questionnaire

Larry W. Chambers

INTRODUCTION

Many health care interventions are designed to improve the quality of, rather than extend the duration of, the patient's life. Since 1970, when work on the initial version of the McMaster Health Index Questionnaire (MHIQ) began, there has been increasing recognition of the need for direct measures of quality of life/health status to assess the benefit of such interventions as evidenced by a conference and workshops (1,2) devoted to this topic. Quality of life and health status cover a range of diverse components such as the patient's capacity for work, hobbies, and psychosocial relationships, as well as the performance of essential acts of daily living in personal hygiene and ambulation. The importance of systematic measurement of these components presents challenges to clinicians and researchers, unlike measurement of inanimate substances and technology used in laboratory measurements. The assessment of quality of life/ health status is affected by all the human reactions and variations that can occur when individual persons are the observers and the observed. Guyatt and his colleagues (3) have outlined the several stages in the development and testing of a quality of life/health status measure:

selecting an initial item pool,
choosing the best items from that pool,

deciding on questionnaire format,
pretesting the instrument,
demonstrating the responsiveness and validity of the instrument.

They go on to point out that at each stage, the investigator must choose between a rigorous, time-consuming approach to questionnaire construction that will establish clinical relevance, responsiveness, and validity of the instrument and a more efficient, less costly strategy that leaves reproducibility, responsiveness, and validity untested.

This chapter describes the development of the MHIQ and its application in a number of clinical settings. The general approach to development of the MHIQ has been of a rigorous and time-consuming nature; hence, the ability to report major findings with the instrument more than 25 years after it was initially conceived. However, a modified MHIQ or alternative instruments must be developed to address newly identified methodological issues related to such instruments. A later section of this chapter outlines the strengths and limitations of the MHIQ and identifies methodological issues that should be considered by potential users of the MHIQ.

DEVELOPMENT OF THE QUESTIONNAIRE

Selection of the Initial Item Pool

Selection of the initial pool of 172 items for the MHIQ was conducted by multidisciplinary teams consisting of ex-

L. W. Chambers: Department of Clinical Epidemiology and Biostatistics, McMaster University, Hamilton, Ontario L8P 1C8, Canada.

perts in internal medicine, family medicine, psychiatry, epidemiology, biostatistics, and social science. The 1958 World Health Organization (WHO) (4) definition of health was used as the conceptual basis for defining health status:

> A state of complete physical, mental, and social well-being and not merely the absence of disease or infirmity.

The original selection of questionnaire items for inclusion in the MHIQ resulted from a number of different approaches: (a) external consultants, e.g., the St. Thomas Hospital Health Survey in England (5), and the East York Project in Toronto, Ontario (6; Allodi, *personal communication*); (b) brainstorming sessions with faculty and community representatives (physicians and health administrators); and (c) internal consultants from psychiatry, sociology and anthropology, geriatrics, social work, and psychiatry.

Items in the St. Thomas Health Survey Questionnaire (5) and the Katz Activities of Daily Living scale (7) were adapted for use as MHIQ items that tapped the physical function area. No single scale was used to develop MHIQ social function items; however, a description of the review process has been reported (8). MHIQ emotional function items were adapted, and in some instances taken verbatim, from the Social Readjustment Rating Scale (9), the FIRO-B Interpersonal Behavior scale (10), and instruments presented in Measures of Social Psychological Attitudes (11). The original draft version of the MHIQ consisted of 172 items.

Choosing the Best Items from that Pool

The original 172 items, although only a sample of all possible physical, emotional, and social function items, took approximately one hour to administer by interview. Also, after numerous occasions of field testing, the wording of some of the original items has been slightly altered.

The best 59 items were identified by assessing their responsiveness to change in function (in before/after interviews of general hospital patients) and their ability to predict family physician global assessments of physical function, emotional function, and social function (8). Linear chisquare trend analyses and multivariate discriminant function analyses were used to identify the best items, using family physician global assessments as the criterion variable. Physicians' assessments are important because the physician is a key decision maker about what health-system resources should be brought to bear, and indeed whether any response will be made to problems the patient presents.

Instrument Description

The three dimensions of health assessed by the MHIQ are physical, social, and emotional function. The 24 physical function items cover physical activities, mobility, self-care activities, communication (sight and hearing), and global physical function. The 25 social function items are concerned

with general well-being, work/social role performance/material welfare, family support/participation, friends support/participation, and global social function. The 25 emotional function items are concerned with feelings of self-esteem, attitudes toward personal relationships, thoughts about the future, critical life events, and global emotional function. In total, the MHIQ contains only 59 items, since some of the items address both social and emotional function (see Appendix).

All the physical function items are designed to evaluate the patient's functional level on the day the MHIQ is administered. The social function items are explicitly concerned with a specific time period (usually the present). Agree–disagree emotional function items do not refer to a specific time period, but are phrased in the present tense. Other emotional function items refer to the recent past, as specifically defined (e.g., within the last year). None of the items asks the respondent to report changes in physical, social, or emotional function.

An attempt was made to phrase all items in the performance mode in order to elicit only information on activities that can actually be observed at the time the MHIQ is completed. The aim of this approach is to avoid the ambiguity of the capacity mode, which may imply either ability or willingness on the part of the respondent. An example of this distinction between the capacity and the performance mode is the difference between the question "*Can* you dress yourself?" (capacity mode) and the question "*Did* you dress yourself?" (performance mode). The extent to which MHIQ items reflect the performance mode is reported in the validity section, below.

Deciding on the Questionnaire Format

The self-completed version of the MHIQ takes 20 minutes for administration. A validity study estimated the degree to which the mode of administration affects the responsiveness of the MHIQ to changes in health status or quality of life (12). The MHIQ was given to 96 physiotherapy outpatients, who were randomly assigned to one of three methods of administration (self-completion, telephone interview, or in-person interview) on four occasions including when clinically significant changes in health status had occurred. Social and emotional function scores were not affected by the mode of administration, and as predicted, these scores did not show changes in the study group. Clinically significant change accounted for up to 30% of variation in physical function, indicating that the mode of administration had little effect and that the physical function component of the MHIQ is responsive to change in any of these three modes.

Pretesting the Instrument

Whenever the MHIQ is used in clinical drug trials, it should be pretested with a group of patients with similar characteristics to those who will be included in the trial. This will assist the investigator in determining the length of time for the MHIQ to be completed, acceptability of the questionnaire to patients, and how the MHIQ fits in with other measures also being used in the trial. Other measures used in a trial than the more general MHIQ will focus on specific aspects of quality of life of subjects directly related to their health problem. For example, trials of medications for subjects with cancer would focus on pain.

Reliability

Reliability was assessed by asking 30 physiotherapy and 40 psychiatry outpatients to complete the MHIQ at their first visit to their respective clinics and again within one week of the first visit (13). Patients were not expected to change their functional status in this short period, an observation confirmed by independent assessments by the physiotherapists. Retest reliability coefficients of .53, .70, and .48 (intraclass correlation) for the MHIQ physical, emotional, and social function scores, respectively, were observed in the physiotherapy patients. In the psychiatry patients, the coefficients were .95 for physical function scores, .77 for emotional function scores, and .66 for social function scores. In a rehabilitation clinic (14) test-retest physical function scores were reported to be .80 (Kappa). An acceptable level of retest reliability of MHIQ physical function change scores was demonstrated for all three methods of administration.

Validity

Validity of the MHIQ has been assessed in a wide variety of populations and studies. Validity was assessed by comparison of MHIQ scores with global measures of health status, observed performance, clinical-biological indicators, and MHIQ scores in different patient groups.

Global Measures

The MHIQ physical function, emotional function, and social function scores have been shown to correlate with global assessments made by health professionals (8,13–15).

Observed Performance

The ability of the MHIQ physical function scores to reflect actual patient performance was examined with 40 patients who first completed the MHIQ and then, immediately after, were observed performing physical functions from areas covered in the Lee Index (16). A subset of ten patients was assessed independently by two occupational therapists. A substantial Kappa score of .86 was achieved between the two therapists. For the 40 patients, the MHIQ physical function index scores ranged from 0 to 0.76. The MHIQ physical

function index correlated with observed patient performance as assessed by the occupational therapists who used the Lee Index (Fig. 1) (17).

Clinical/Biological Indicators

The 40 rheumatoid arthritis patients who had completed the MHIQ were examined by their rheumatologists, who reported the following clinical/biological indicators: active joint count (the Ritchie Articular Index) (18), duration of morning stiffness and the erythrocyte sedimentation test (17). Table 1 gives summary statistics for the three MHIQ indices for different levels on each of the clinical/biological indicators. A gradient is present with the MHIQ physical function index only. The MHIQ scores in Table 1 should be useful for estimating sample size requirements for clinical trials.

Different Patient Groups

Figure 2 shows the mean scores for the three MHIQ indexes obtained in the physiotherapy clinic (96 patients) and in the psychiatry outpatient clinic (40 patients) (13). The mean MHIQ physical function score in the physiotherapy outpatient clinic was 0.59, whereas the mean physical function score in the psychiatry clinic was 0.89. This difference was statistically significant ($p < .01$, unpaired t-test), indicating relatively poorer physical function among the physiotherapy patients. Conversely, as predicted, the mean MHIQ emotional function scores were 0.66 in the physiotherapy clinic and 0.44 in the psychiatry clinic, a difference that was statistically significant, and the mean MHIQ social function score was also significantly higher in the physiotherapy clinic (0.71).

Further evidence of clinical and biological validity is summarized in Figs. 3, 4, and 5. These figures show the MHIQ

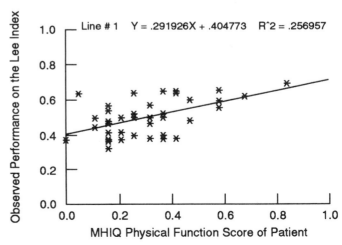

FIG. 1. Physical function scores of patients with rheumatoid arthritis versus observed performance on Lee Index.

TABLE 1. *MHIQ physical, emotional, social function association with clinical/biological indicators of rheumatoid arthritis (n = 40)*

Clinical/ biological indicator		n	MHIQ physical function index			MHIQ emotional function index			MHIQ social function index		
			Median	Mean	SD	Median	Mean	SD	Median	Mean	SD
Ritchie Articulator Index[a]	0–19	11	0.37	0.42	0.21	0.54	0.56	0.15	0.61	0.65	0.14
	20–29	12	0.37	0.29	0.19	0.56	0.57	0.14	0.63	0.64	0.10
	30–39	12	0.24	0.25	0.13	0.52	0.53	0.15	0.64	0.62	0.05
	40–59	5	0.17	0.23	0.13	0.48	0.48	0.10	0.63	0.62	0.05
Age (years)	15–29	1	0.74	0.74	0.00	0.46	0.46	0.00	0.64	0.64	0.00
	30–49	9	0.41	0.37	0.26	0.65	0.60	0.17	0.64	0.64	0.08
	50–64	17	0.29	0.32	0.14	0.52	0.12	0.62	0.62	0.62	0.14
	65+	13	0.32	0.29	0.15	0.51	0.53	0.15	0.64	0.65	0.09
Patient experiences morning stiffness	No	6	0.34	0.39	0.29	0.48	0.49	0.20	0.62	0.65	0.08
	Slight	8	0.29	0.34	0.22	0.48	0.50	0.16	0.64	0.62	0.10
	Moderate	8	0.34	0.36	0.14	0.54	0.56	0.09	0.64	0.66	0.10
	Severe	10	0.24	0.25	0.12	0.51	0.50	0.09	0.56	0.56	0.08
	Very severe	4	0.18	0.21	0.09	0.58	0.60	0.13	0.66	0.71	0.12
Duration of morning stiffness	30 min	9	0.42	0.41	0.23	0.49	0.52	0.18	0.67	0.67	0.09
	>30 min	31	0.28	0.31	0.17	0.53	0.55	0.13	0.62	0.62	0.11
Erythrocyte sedimentation rate (mm/h)	3–17	3	0.42	0.38	0.11	0.62	0.62	0.12	0.58	0.59	0.05
	18–40	12	0.29	0.35	0.24	0.61	0.55	0.20	0.64	0.65	0.08
	41–70	8	0.34	0.35	0.17	0.52	0.55	0.10	0.66	0.67	0.12
	71–120	11	0.31	0.32	0.19	0.49	0.50	0.09	0.57	0.56	0.10

[a]Good articular function = 0, poor = 78.
From ref. 17, with permission.

physical function, emotional function, and social function index scores for four different groups of patients: outpatient physiotherapy clinic patients, chronic respiratory disease patients at home, long-term insulin-dependent diabetic patients at home, and family practice patients (13).

The family practice patients were hypothesized to have better physical function than the other four groups because

these were ambulatory patients presenting with a wide range of complaints. Figure 3 shows the distribution of physical function scores with more of the family practice patients having good MHIQ physical function scores than the other three patient groups.

The emotional function of family practice patients was hypothesized to be poorer than the other three patient groups,

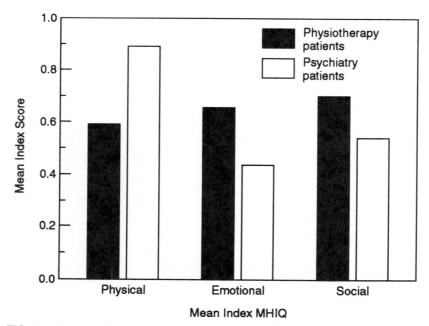

FIG. 2. Comparison of mean index score on MHIQ indexes by patient group.

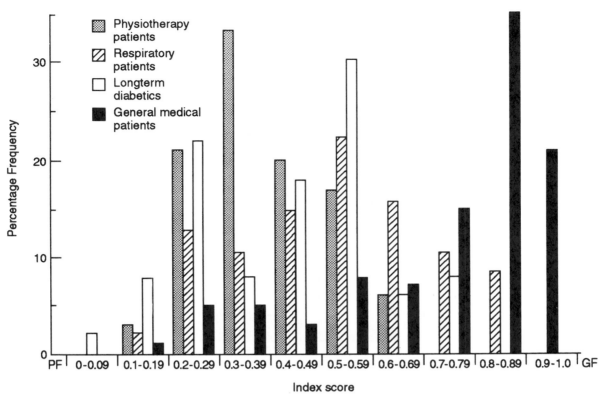

FIG. 3. Physical function status of selected populations.

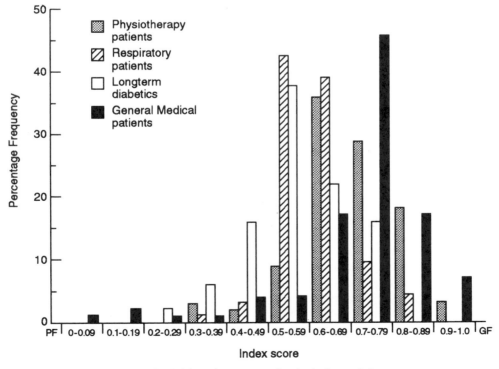

FIG. 4. Social function status of selected populations.

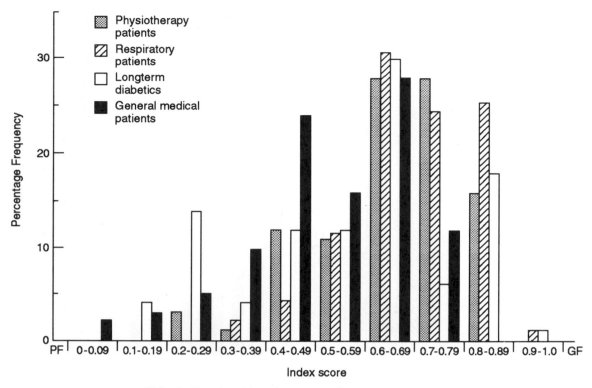

FIG. 5. Emotional function status of selected populations.

based on reports from Last and White (19) that approximately 50% of family practice patients present with emotional problems. This trend was found and Fig. 4 shows the family practice patients have poorer MHIQ emotional function scores than the other three groups.

The patients being cared for at home, who included the respiratory disease patients and the long-term diabetic patients, were hypothesized to have poorer social function than the other two groups of patients. Figure 5 shows the respiratory disease patients and the long-term diabetic patients had poor MHIQ social function scores compared with the other two patient groups.

Responsiveness (Sensitivity to Change in Health Status)

Figure 6 shows the MHIQ physical function index mean and standard error scores for four administration times in the study of physiotherapy outpatients (12). A one-week no-change interval occurred between times I and II and between times III and IV. Patients entered the clinic at time I and were discharged from the clinic at time III. Thus the time II to time III interval was expected to show change on the MHIQ. The results confirmed this did occur, with no change, as expected, between times I and II and times III and IV. As reported above in the questionnaire format section, the MHIQ scores were responsive to change regardless of the

mode of administration of the MHIQ. Future studies need to be conducted with persons whose social and emotional functioning are known to change to determine the responsiveness to change of the MHIQ social and emotional function scores.

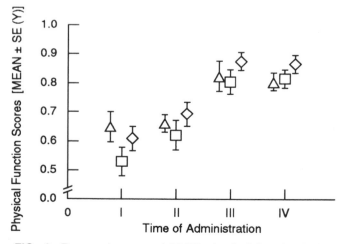

FIG. 6. Responsiveness of MHIQ physical function index scores to change in health status. Physiotherapy outpatients were assessed on four occasions by either self-assessment (△); telephone interview (□); or personal interview (◇).

ASSESSMENT OF THE QUESTIONNAIRE

Applications

The MHIQ has been used in the following patient populations: physiotherapy outpatients (12), psychiatry outpatients (13), insulin-dependent diabetic patients receiving home nursing care (13), chronic respiratory disease patients living at home (13), family practice patients (15), patients with rheumatoid arthritis (13), multiple sclerosis patients living at home (20), elderly patients under acute care in a hospital (21), elderly patients discharged from a home care program by public health nurses (22), patients at a rehabilitation center (14), and patients with acute myocardial infarction (23).

Strengths and Limitations

Feinstein and his colleagues (24) outline six main clinical and scientific issues related to the assessment and application of indexes of quality of life/health status (functional disability) such as the MHIQ: the omission of attention to personal collaboration, the role of personal preferences, the measurement of change, the selection and aggregation of components, the strategies used in justifying an index, and the unsatisfactory application of "established" indexes. Each of these issues will be briefly outlined and used to describe the strengths and weaknesses of the MHIQ.

Patient's Collaboration

> When a patient's collaboration is needed to perform a task, the index will be inadequate if it describes only the magnitude of the task while omitting such crucial concomitant factors as the patient's effort or support in the performance. An improved index would appropriately modify the ratings according to these additional factors (24).

As Guyatt et al. (3) have shown in a randomized controlled trial, the distance covered in a timed walking test can be substantially increased if a technician walks alongside the patient offering encouragement. The MHIQ adequately taps the magnitude of the task or performance, as outlined above (Instrument Description) but it does not include items on the patient's effort or support in performance. Feinstein et al. (24) suggest that instruments such as the MHIQ should be supplemented with a single question about the availability of a person who is willing and ready to give support if needed, or, instead of trying to estimate patient's "motivation" in working at rehabilitative exercises, nurses or other therapists could be asked to rate the observed effort and cooperation. The MHIQ should also recognize certain non-human sources of support, such as including a question about the use of ramps or elevators for someone who is wheelchair bound, that can also make important distinctions in a patient's ability to function. Inclusion of one or more of these

additions to the MHIQ would address this important issue of patient collaboration and result in an instrument that measures more than just the magnitude of the task alone.

Patient's Preferences

> If an index refers to multiple disabilities, the focus of the index may become blurred in the combination of ratings for important and unimportant problems. By determining the patient's preferences about the relative importance of the disabilities, and by adjusting the focus of the index accordingly, investigators can aim at clearer targets in planning and evaluating therapeutic interventions (24).

In a recent study of patients with chronic respiratory disease (25), patients were asked to select quality of care/health status items that were important to them and only these were included in a new instrument to measure quality of life for such patients. This study showed that using only items viewed by patients as important can decrease the sample size required in clinical trials, as these items were more sensitive to change when compared with general measures of quality of life/health status such as the MHIQ. Thus, there is now documentary evidence to support the point that unselected items (global measures) create problems of distinguishing changes (24). In contrast to this new instrument, items in the MHIQ are preselected for the patients and therefore may not include quality of life/health status items that are important to specific patients with specific diseases. The MHIQ is a global measure of physical, emotional, and social function. Consequently, it should be supplemented with items that have a specific bearing on the study questions in order to improve the validity of the results in studies that evaluate health care interventions or describe or predict health status/quality of life (26).

Measurement of Changes

> Indexes that have been constructed to describe a patient's single state in time may not always be suitable for discriminating changes. The changes may be either poorly discerned if the rating scale has too few categories, or obscured if too many extraneous variables are included in the index. The problem can often be solved by developing indexes that are specifically concerned with transitions and that concentrate on the main attributes of interest (24).

The MHIQ physical function scores have been shown to reflect clinically important change, such as discharge from hospital or an outpatient physiotherapy clinic (12,15). Also, the single state in time items used to calculate MHIQ physical function scores were found to be correlated with the transition ratings (for example, "Since [time of first visit] has the patient's physical function changed?—better, same, worse") of a physiotherapist (12). This responsiveness is presumably because the MHIQ physical function scores consist of items that cover a range of quality of life/health status categories, and few extraneous items contribute to the MHIQ physical function score.

In a randomized trial evaluating the effects of a drug prescribed to patients with rheumatoid arthritis, the responsiveness of the MHIQ physical, social, and emotional function scores to small, clinically significant changes were compared with other instruments including the MACTAR (McMaster Toronto Arthritis) Patient Function Preference Questionnaire (27). With the MACTAR, it was possible for an interviewer to ask each patient to identify activities related to mobility, self-care, work, and social and leisure activity. Patients were then asked to rank these activities in the order in which they would most prefer to have them improved. At the end of the study (18 weeks) or at the time of dropout, all patients were asked if there had been improvement in the ranked disabilities specified by them at the beginning of the study. The MACTAR outperformed the three MHIQ indexes in reflecting clinically significant changes when compared with physician assessments and patient self-report measures of change. Again, the MHIQ physical function scores outperformed the social function and emotional function scores in reflecting change.

The usefulness of the MHIQ score to detect change, therefore, will depend on the MHIQ's applicability to the study question and analysis of individual item changes to determine which items contributed to the changed MHIQ score. The MHIQ could be supplemented with transition items for the patient to complete in these studies designed to detect change in the quality of life/health status of the patient.

Hierarchical Aggregations

When multiple variables are aggregated, the resulting scale of categories can be arranged as a summation or as a hierarchy. The summations are easier to organize but may be ambiguous because the same summary score can be produced by many different variations in scores of the components. The hierarchical arrangements provide clearer ideas of what is contained in each score but are difficult to construct because the combinations of different components must be ranked for relative importance. The hierarchical decisions can be eased if the ''importance'' of individual variables or combinations is determined from patients' preferences, clinical judgements, or documentary correlations (24).

The responses to MHIQ items are dichotomized and weights of one for a good health response and zero for a poor health response are assigned to each item, then added to calculate an MHIQ physical function score, an MHIQ social function score, and a MHIQ emotional function score (see Appendix). Function scores are standardized to index values ranging from 0 (extremely poor function) to 1.0 (extremely good function).

The use of other weights for good and poor responses was assessed with a group of chronic obstructive lung disease patients at home (13). In this study, 12 respirologists based in the Hamilton area identified 94 chronic obstructive lung

disease patients in their practices. All patients were experiencing shortness of breath and were over 40 years of age. Trained interviewers administered the MHIQ to these patients in their homes. Some wording of the MHIQ items was altered slightly to refer specifically to chronic respiratory disease. In addition, health professionals working with chronic respiratory disease patients were approached to assist in developing preference weights for scoring the MHIQ. Each was asked to assign to each item in the MHIQ a score between 1 and 10, according to what they thought was most important for a typical chronic respiratory disease patient's overall social, emotional, and physical functioning. Each function area was weighted separately. These scores were averaged and the mean score for each question was used as a weight given to that question in a second analysis, following the analyses using the 0 and 1 arbitrary weights.

The unweighted (0–1 weights) physical and emotional function scores slightly underestimated the function of patients. The results for physical function are shown in Fig. 7. No systematic differences were found between the weighted and unweighted social function scores. The psychology literature (28) provides evidence that little difference in total explained variance will occur between weighting schemes. However, the ranking of individuals with the MHIQ may differ using different weights and the total explained variance may increase if new health status items are included in addition to MHIQ items.

Early in the development of the MHIQ, a decision was made to report disaggregated physical, social, and emotional MHIQ scores and a single MHIQ score was not calculated. Thus, in a clinical trial, an MHIQ profile can be reported showing the separate physical, social, and emotional function scores in the experimental and control groups. This profile also leaves it to the investigator or reader of the study results to decide on the relative importance of each of the three components of the MHIQ. As Feinstein et al. (24)

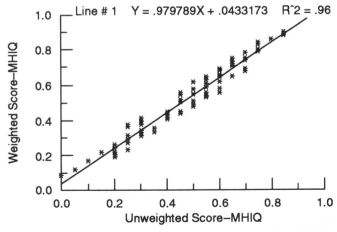

FIG. 7. A comparison of weighted versus unweighted MHIQ physical function scores in patients with chronic obstructive lung disease.

APPENDIX: MHIQ ITEMS

Method of Scoring the MHIQ Physical Function Index

	Item scoring	
Physical function items	"Good" function response weight of "1"	"Poor" function response weight of "0"
Today, are you physically able to run a short distance, say 300 feet, if you are in a hurry? (This is about the length of a football field or soccer pitch).	YES	NO, NO ANSWER
Today, are you physically able to take part in any sports (hockey, swimming, bowling, glob, and so forth) or exercise regularly?	YES	NO, NO ANSWER
At present, are you physically able to walk out-of-doors *by yourself* when the weather is good?	YES } *This combination SCORES ONE*	NO, NO ANSWER
What is the farthest you can walk?	ONE MILE OR MORE }	LESS THAN 1 MILE BUT MORE THAN 30 FEET, LESS THAN 30 FEET, BETWEEN ROOMS, WITHIN ROOMS, CAN'T WALK AT ALL
Today, do you (or would you) have any physical difficulty at all with walking, as far as a mile?	NO	YES, NO ANSWER
Today, do you (or would you) have any physical difficulty at all with climbing up 2 flights of stairs?	NO	YES, NO ANSWER
Today, do you (or would you) have any physical difficulty at all with standing up from, and/or sitting down in a chair?	NO	YES, NO ANSWER
Today, do you (or would you) have any physical difficulty at all with dusting and/or light housework?	NO	YES, NO ANSWER
Today, do you (or would you) have any physical difficulty at all with cleaning floors?	NO	YES, NO ANSWER
Today, do you (or would you) have any physical difficulty at all traveling by bus whenever necessary?	NO	YES, NO ANSWER
Today, do you have any physical difficulty at all traveling by car whenever necessary?	NO	YES, NO ANSWER
Today do you have any physical difficulty driving a car?	NO or DO NOT HAVE LICENSE	YES, NO ANSWER
Today, do you (or would you) have any physical difficulty at all feeding yourself?	NO	YES, NO ANSWER
Today, do you (or would you) have any physical difficulty at all with undressing?	NO	YES, NO ANSWER
Today, do you (or would you) have any physical difficulty at all with washing (face and hands), shaving (men) and/or combing hair?	NO	YES, NO ANSWER
Today, do you (or would you) have any physical difficulty at all with shopping?	NO	YES, NO ANSWER
Today, do you (or would you) have any physical difficulty at all with cooking?	NO	YES, NO ANSWER
Do you wear glasses?	YES or NO and	YES SOMETIMES YES ALWAYS, NO ANSWER
Do you have any trouble reading ordinary newsprint?	NO, NEVER and } *SCORE ONE*	
Do you have a headache after watching television or reading?	NO, NEVER	
Do you wear a hearing aid?	YES or NO and	YES, SOMETIMES YES ALWAYS, NO ANSWER
Do you have trouble hearing in a normal conversation with several other persons?	NO, NEVER and } *SCORE ONE*	
Do you have trouble hearing the radio or television?	NO, NEVER	
How would you say your *physical* function is today? (By this we mean the ability to move around, see, hear and so forth)	YES	NO, NO ANSWER

$$\text{PHYSICAL FUNCTION INDEX} = \frac{\text{SUM OF ITEMS ASSIGNED "1"}}{19}$$

Method of Scoring the MHIQ Social Function Index

Social function items	Item scoring	
	"Good" function response weight of "1"	"Poor" function response weight of "0"
How would you say your health is today?	VERY GOOD, PRETTY GOOD	NOT TOO GOOD, NO ANSWER
Taking all things together, how would you say things are today?	VERY HAPPY, PRETTY HAPPY	NOT TOO HAPPY, NO ANSWER
In general, how satisfying do you find the way you're spending your life today?	VERY SATISFYING, PRETTY SATISFYING	NOT TOO SATISFYING, NO ANSWER
What is your occupational status?	WORK FULL-TIME, WORK PART-TIME, ON VACATION, A STUDENT, A HOUSEWIFE	RETIRED, ON SICK LEAVE, NO ANSWER
How long has it been since you last had a holiday?	LESS THAN OR EQUAL TO 12 MONTHS	GREATER THAN 12 MONTHS
During the last year, have you gone on welfare (or received monies from unemployment insurance, workmen's compensation, or mother's allowance)?	NO	YES, NO ANSWER
During the last year, have you retired from work?	NO	YES, NO ANSWER
Which of the following describe your usual social and recreational activities? going to a relative's home?	YES	NO, NO ANSWER
Has a relative visited you in the last week?	YES	NO, NO ANSWER
During the last year, have you separated from your spouse?	NO	YES, NO ANSWER
During the last year, have you divorced?	NO	YES, NO ANSWER
During the last year, have you had trouble getting along with friends/relatives?	NO	YES, NO ANSWER
During the last year, have you had some other problem or change in your life?	NO	YES, NO ANSWER
How much time in a one-week period do you usually spend watching television?	NONE, LESS THAN 3 HOURS A WEEK, LESS THAN 1 HOUR PER DAY BUT MORE THAN 3 HOURS A WEEK	TWO HOURS OR MORE PER DAY, LESS THAN TWO HOURS PER DAY BUT MORE THAN ONE HOUR A DAY
Which of the following describe your usual social and recreational activities? going to church?	YES	NO, NO ANSWER
Which of the following describe your usual social and recreational activities? any other activities? (please specify)	YES, SOME ACTIVITIES	NONE, NO ANSWER
Has a friend visited you in the last week?	YES	NO, NO ANSWER
Has a religious group member visited you in the last week?	YES	NO, NO ANSWER
Has a social agency representative visited you in the last week? (for example, welfare, mother's allowance, workmen's compensation board, Victorian Order of Nurses)	NO	YES, NO ANSWER
Have you used your telephone in the last week to call a friend?	YES	NO, NO ANSWER
Have you used your telephone in the last week to call a religious group member?	YES	NO, NO ANSWER
Have you used your telephone in the last week to call a social agency representative? (for example, welfare, mother's allowance, workmen's compensation board, Victorian Order of Nurses)	NO	YES, NO ANSWER
Have you been called in the last week by a social agency representative?	NO	YES, NO ANSWER
Do you have a telephone?	YES	NO, NO ANSWER
How would you say your social functioning is today? (By this we mean working with others, getting along with friends or family)	GOOD, GOOD TO FAIR	FAIR, FAIR TO POOR, NO ANSWER

$$\text{SOCIAL FUNCTION INDEX} = \frac{\text{SUM OF ITEMS ASSIGNED "1"}}{25}$$

Method of Scoring the MHIQ Emotional Function Index

Emotional function items	Item scoring	
	"Good" function response weight of "1"	"Poor" function response weight of "0"
I sometimes feel that my life is not very useful.	STRONGLY DISAGREE, DISAGREE	STRONGLY AGREE, AGREE, NEUTRAL, NO ANSWER
I am a useful person to have around.	STRONGLY AGREE, AGREE	STRONGLY DISAGREE, DISAGREE, NEUTRAL, NO ANSWER
I am inclined to feel I am a failure.	STRONGLY DISAGREE, DISAGREE	STRONGLY AGREE, AGREE, NEUTRAL, NO ANSWER
Many people are unhappy because they do not know what they want out of life.	STRONGLY DISAGREE, DISAGREE	STRONGLY AGREE, AGREE, NEUTRAL, NO ANSWER
I am a quick thinker.	STRONGLY AGREE, AGREE	STRONGLY DISAGREE, DISAGREE, NEUTRAL, NO ANSWER
Some people feel that they run their lives pretty much the way they want to and that is the case with me.	STRONGLY AGREE, AGREE	STRONGLY DISAGREE, DISAGREE, NEUTRAL, NO ANSWER
I am usually alert.	STRONGLY AGREE, AGREE	STRONGLY DISAGREE, DISAGREE, NEUTRAL, NO ANSWER
Everyone should have someone in his/her life whose happiness means as much to him/her as his/her own.	STRONGLY AGREE, AGREE	STRONGLY DISAGREE, DISAGREE, NEUTRAL, NO ANSWER
In a society where almost everyone is out for himself/herself, people soon come to distrust each other.	STRONGLY DISAGREE, DISAGREE	STRONGLY AGREE, AGREE, NEUTRAL, NO ANSWER
There are many people who don't know what to do with their lives.	STRONGLY DISAGREE, DISAGREE	STRONGLY AGREE, AGREE, NEUTRAL, NO ANSWER
Most people don't realize how much their lives are controlled by plots hatched in a secret by others.	STRONGLY DISAGREE, DISAGREE	STRONGLY AGREE, AGREE, NEUTRAL, NO ANSWER
People feel affectionate toward me.	STRONGLY AGREE, AGREE	STRONGLY DISAGREE, DISAGREE, NEUTRAL, NO ANSWER
I think most married people lead trapped (frustrated or miserable) lives.	STRONGLY DISAGREE, DISAGREE	STRONGLY AGREE, AGREE, NEUTRAL, NO ANSWER
Some people feel as if other people push them around a good bit and I feel this way too.	STRONGLY DISAGREE, DISAGREE	STRONGLY AGREE, AGREE, NEUTRAL, NO ANSWER
I would say I nearly always finish things once I start them.	STRONGLY AGREE, AGREE	STRONGLY DISAGREE, DISAGREE, NEUTRAL, NO ANSWER
When I make plans ahead, I usually get to carry things out the way I expected.	STRONGLY AGREE, AGREE	STRONGLY DISAGREE, DISAGREE, NEUTRAL, NO ANSWER
It's hardly fair to bring children into the world the way things look for the future.	STRONGLY DISAGREE, DISAGREE	STRONGLY AGREE, AGREE, NEUTRAL, NO ANSWER
Nowadays a person has to live pretty much for today and let tomorrow take care of itself.	STRONGLY DISAGREE, DISAGREE	STRONGLY AGREE, AGREE, NEUTRAL, NO ANSWER

	Item scoring	
Emotional function items	"Good" function response weight of "1"	"Poor" function response weight of "0"
During the last year, have you separated from your spouse?	NO	YES, NO ANSWER
During the last year, have you divorced?	NO	YES, NO ANSWER
During the last year, have you gone on welfare (or received monies from unemployment insurance, workmen's compensation, or mother's allowance)?	NO	YES, NO ANSWER
During the last year, have you had trouble getting along with friends/relatives?	NO	YES, NO ANSWER
During the last year, have you retired from work?	NO	YES, NO ANSWER
During the last year, have you had some other problem or change in your life?	NO	YES, NO ANSWER
How would you say your *emotional* functioning is today? (By this we mean your ability to remain in good spirits most of the time, and to be usually happy and satisfied with your life.)	GOOD, GOOD TO FAIR	FAIR, FAIR TO POOR, POOR

$$\text{EMOTIONAL FUNCTION INDEX} = \frac{\text{SUM OF ITEMS ASSIGNED "ONE"}}{25}$$

point out, the relative importance of components could also be decided by the patients themselves. They also suggest that the importance of different components could be determined from their statistical correlation with a selected external variable, such as hours of daily care needed, costs of care, or some other relevant attribute such as the patient's subsequent need for placement in a nursing home. For example, among recently discharged clients from home (public health) nursing care, better MHIQ physical and social function scores were more likely in older persons who received and were given more aid by their social network, but this did not hold for MHIQ emotional function scores (22). In summary, as documentary evidence accumulates about MHIQ scores, the implications of the method of hierarchical aggregation used in MHIQ scoring will be clarified.

Documentary Justification

Although an index may be reported with an account of its conceptual justification, most indexes have not been accompanied by documentary evidence showing how well they do their job, particularly in comparison with appropriate existing indexes. The absence of such documentation—a striking feature of the published literature—can be remedied by appropriate attention from investigators and editors (24).

As outlined in the Validity section, the MHIQ physical function, emotional function and social function scores correlate with global assessments made by health professionals, and by relatives or friends, with other questionnaires such as the Bradburn Scale of Psychological Well-Being and with biological parameters of severity of disease. The MHIQ was designed to be flexible enough to use in different settings, easily communicable to health professionals, clear in its direc-

tion of improvement, and amenable to mathematical index construction. If instruments that the MHIQ was designed to replace did not meet one or more of these prerequisites, they were not compared with the MHIQ. However, future uses of the MHIQ will be better justified if further documentary evidence is accumulated about how it compares with other general measures of quality of life/health status.

Suitability of Established Indexes

When investigators choose indexes that have shown good statistical coefficients in tests of "reliability" and "validity," the subsequent results may be unsatisfactory because the established indexes are too complex or are not aimed at the specific goal of the study. This problem can be solved by adding "sensibility" as a criterion for choosing indexes or by creating new indexes as needed (24).

The MHIQ has been widely used because it is simple to use and has proved to be substantially useful as a general measure of quality of life to supplement more specific clinically relevant indicators in clinical trials and health evaluations. As the first part of this chapter demonstrates, the MHIQ has been around long enough to have been applied in a number of settings and this has resulted in the accumulation of evidence regarding its validity and reliability. Future users of the MHIQ must however very carefully assess these data and the usefulness of the MHIQ in addressing the questions they are proposing for their study.

CONCLUSIONS

On the basis of a review of a number of studies, the accumulated evidence of the validity and reliability of the MHIQ was presented. Application of the Feinstein et al. (24) issues related to scientific and clinical problems with indexes of quality of life/health status have shown that the MHIQ:

does a poor job of tapping patient effort and patient preferences,

is a fair measure of change,

adequately deals with the hierarchical aggregation of the components of quality of life/health status,

has above average documentation that can be used to justify its use,

receives high marks on ''sensibility'' as it actually has been used for research studies.

Future use of the MHIQ will depend on the resources available to develop alternative better instruments and the applicability of the MHIQ to the purpose of the study.

REFERENCES

1. Buchanan WW, Tugwell P, Bombardier C (eds.). Proceedings of the Conference on Outcome Measures in Rheumatological Clinical Trials, December 7–8, 1981, Hamilton, Ontario, Canada. *J Rheumatol* 1982; 9:749–806.
2. Wenger NK, Mattson ME, Furberg CD, et al. (eds). *Assessment of quality of life in clinical trials of cardiovascular therapies.* New York: Le Jacq, 1984.
3. Guyatt GH, Bombardier C, Tugwell PX. Measuring disease-specific quality of life in clinical trials. *Can Med Assoc J* 1986;134:889–895.
4. World Health Organization. *The first ten years of the World Health Organization.* Geneva: World Health Organization, 1958.
5. Bennett AE, Garrad J, Halil T. Chronic disease and disability in the community: a prevalence study. *Br Med J* 1970;3:762–764.
6. Allodi FA, Coates DB. Social stress, psychiatric symptoms and help seeking patterns. *Can Psychiat Assoc J* 1973;15:153–158.
7. The Staff of the Benjamin Rose Hospital. Multidisciplinary study of illness in aged persons. I. Methods and preliminary results. *J Chronic Dis* 1958;7:332–345.
8. Chambers LW, Sackett DL, Goldsmith CH, et al. Development and application of an index of social function. *Health Serv Res* 1976;11: 430–441.
9. Holmes TH, Rahe RH. The social readjustment rating scale. *J Psychosom Res* 1967;11:213.
10. Schultz, WC. *The Firo Scales.* Palo Alto, CA: Consulting Psychologists Press, 1967.
11. Robinson JP, Shaver PR. Measures of social psychological attitudes. Ann Arbor Survey Research Center, Institute for Social Research, University of Michigan, 1973.
12. Chambers LW, Haight M, Norman G, et al. Measurement of health status: sensitivity to change and the effect of mode of administration on health status measurement. *Med Care* 1987.
13. Chambers LW. *The McMaster Health Index Questionnaire (MHIQ): methodologic documentation and report of the second generation of investigations.* Department of Clinical Epidemiology and Biostatistics. Hamilton: McMaster University, 1982.
14. Fortin F, Kerouac S. Validation of questionnaires on physical function. *Nurs Res* 1977;26:128–135.
15. Sackett DL, Chambers LW, Macpherson AS, et al. The development and application of indexes of public health: general methods and a summary of results. *Am J Public Health* 1977;67:423–428.
16. Lee P, Jasani MK, Dick WC, et al. Evaluation of a functional index in rheumatoid arthritis. *Scand J Rheumatol* 1973;2:71–77.
17. Chambers LW, MacDonald LA, Tugwell P, et al. The McMaster Health Index Questionnaire as a measurement of quality of life for patients with rheumatoid disease. *J Rheumatol* 1982;9:780–784.
18. Ritchie DM, Boyle JA, McInnes JM, et al. Clinical studies with an articular index for the assessment of joint tenderness in patients with rheumatoid arthritis. *O J Med NS* 1968;37:393–406.
19. Last JM, White KL. The content of medical care in primary practice. *Med Care* 1969;7(2):41–48.
20. Harper AC, Harper DA, Chambers LW, et al. Physical and psychosocial disability in multiple sclerosis: an epidemiological survey of patients in a regional clinic. *J Chronic Dis* 1986;39:305–310.
21. Gibbon M, Tugwell P, Chambers LW, et al. Measurement of health status in the evaluation of coordinated home health care. Presented at the 111th Annual Meeting of the American Public Health Association, Dallas, November 1983.
22. Black M. Health and social support of older adults in the community. *Can J Aging* 1985;4:213–226.
23. Tugwell P, Sackett DL, Goldsmith CH, et al. Quality of care in acute myocardial infarction. Final Report, US National Center for Health Services Research Grant No. R01 HS 03239, October 1983.
24. Feinstein AR, Josephy BR, Wells CK. Scientific and clinical problems in indexes of functional disability. *Ann Intern Med* 1986;105:413–420.
25. Guyatt GH, Berman LB, Townsend M, et al. A new measure of quality of life for clinical trials in chronic lung disease. *Thorax* 1987.
26. Kirshner B, Guyatt G. A methodological framework for assessing health indices. *J Chronic Dis* 1985;38:27–36.
27. Tugwell P, Bombardier C, Buchanan WW, et al. Methotrexate in rheumatoid arthritis: impact on quality of life assessed by traditional standard-item and individualized patient preference health status questionnaires. *Arch Intern Med* 1990;150:59–82.
28. Wainer H. Estimating coefficients in linear models: it don't make no never mind. *Psychol Bull* 1976;83:213–217.

Quality of Life and Pharmacoeconomics in Clinical Trials, Second Edition, edited by B. Spilker.
Lippincott-Raven Publishers, Philadelphia © 1996.

CHAPTER 29

Nottingham Health Profile

James McEwen and Stephen P. McKenna

INTRODUCTION

During the 1970s there was considerable interest in the factors other than the disease process that contributed to health and ill health and internationally there was considerable research commitment into the production of measures that would be more sensitive to such variations in states of health. Thus, although one of the prime aims of the Nottingham Health Profile (NHP) was to produce an instrument that would be used in epidemiological studies of health and disease, it soon became evident that there was a demand for measures that could be used to evaluate different forms of intervention, either in prevention or treatment, and that would not only provide a more sensitive and detailed measure of health, but would reflect the views of the patient.

No measure escapes criticism when it is used widely. Many of the limitations of the NHP were recognized at the design stage and indeed decisions were made as to its scope and applicability. Since it was first used by the authors in early studies, many new measures in the wider field of "quality of life" have been developed. There is always a debate about the relative merits of retaining a measure unchanged over the years to allow comparability or to develop and refine it.

    J. McEwen: Department of Public Health, University of Glasgow, Glasgow G12 8RZ, Scotland.
    S. P. McKenna: Galen Research, West Didsbury, Manchester M20 2PW, England.

DEVELOPMENT OF THE NHP

When it was first published, the Nottingham Health Profile was a two-part self-completion questionnaire providing a health profile on a number of different parameters. Part I of the profile consists of statements about how people feel or function, while part II inquires about the effect of ill health on seven areas of daily life. Part II, which was always considered to be less rigorous, is structurally different and is currently less frequently used.

A full account of the development of the NHP is given by Hunt et al. (1). Two key issues lay behind all the research and debate about measures of self-rated or perceived health. Was a person's own assessment of the health state something that was worth assessing, and could a measure be devised for such vague or diffused feelings that was valid and reliable?

In the 1970s, there was a great debate over the terms *objective data* and *subjective data,* and clinicians in particular were reluctant to accept that a subjective impression produced by a patient could be a valid measure. It was, however, accepted that patient feelings were of major importance in the decision to seek medical care. The NHP was designed to allow patients to assess their health status and, as such, was as valid a way of measuring health as any of the more objective medical criteria. It was, however, recognized that self-assessed need and other-assessed need (usually by a health professional) may not agree (2). Thus it became accepted gradually that at least the two aspects of self-assessment and professional assessment could be regarded as two different but equally essential contributions to our understanding of health and ill health.

Again, during the 1970s there were research developments that assisted with the second problem, that of devising a valid and reliable instrument. Psychological and other social sciences were making a considerable impact both on the understanding of health and disease and in the study of the process of health care, and their expertise in questionnaire design could now be applied to the measurement of health states. The idea behind the Nottingham Health Profile was that a measure should be developed that derived its parameters of health status from the perceptions of the lay public and used lay person's modes of expression to describe them. The aim was to devise a measure of perceived health state via self-report.

Following earlier work by McDowell and Martini (3) on factors contributing to outcomes of care, work began on the NHP in 1975, with the aim of developing an indicator that could:

1. provide some assessment of a person's need for care that was not based on purely medical criteria;
2. enable the subsequent evaluation of care provided for persons in need;
3. make a start on the development of an indicator that could be used for the survey of population health status.

By 1978 Martini and McDowell (4) had shown that an index of subjective well-being was feasible, acceptable, and potentially sensitive to different states of health. The possible direction of the work was reviewed and research proceeded on the development of a perceived health indicator that was required to fulfill the following criteria:

1. It must be short and simple enough to be self-administered.
2. Response categories must be unambiguous.
3. The level of expression should be compatible with that of a vast majority of the population.
4. Scoring must be relatively easy.
5. It must be reliable.
6. It must have face validity and biological validity.
7. It must be sensitive to change in the same individuals over time and to differences in the consequences of different pathological states.

From initial interviews with 768 patients with a variety of acute and chronic conditions, a total of 2,200 statements were generated describing the effects of ill health. These were grouped and reduced by excluding statements that were found to be redundant, ambiguous, or not easily understood, that required a reading age greater than 11 years, that were negative, or that could not be answered by a simple yes or no. Finally, these statements were tested on a group of patients and nonpatients for clarity, consensus of meaning, and ease of answering. This left a total of 38 statements in six sections: energy level, emotional reactions, physical mobility, pain, social isolation, and sleep. As it was considered that it would be meaningless to combine the scores for these

disparate sections into a single index, each section had to be scored separately. Thurstone's (5) method of paired comparisons was used to rate the severity of each statement in each particular section. This resulted in part I of the Nottingham Health Profile.

The second part of the Nottingham Health Profile was intended to reflect how perceived health problems were affecting a respondent's daily life. An item analysis of the original set of statements found that seven activities were most often reported to be affected by health problems: work, personal activities, social life, family life, sex, spare time activities, and holidays and travel. It was not found to be possible to devise and weight questions within each section, but only to identify by yes or no whether a particular area had been affected by the person's health. Thus part II of the Nottingham Health Profile simply consisted of seven questions.

There are a number of problems in testing the validity of a measure of perceived health since there is no obvious "gold standard." Extensive studies were carried out in the development stage, but it was acknowledged at the time that the testing was inevitably limited and that further work would be required (1). Although objective standards were generally used, the emphasis was on the ability of the NHP to distinguish between various groups with different medical conditions, different degrees of fitness, users and nonusers of health service, and people progressing through a stage of life such as pregnancy or recovery from fractures. Patterns of the NHP for these groups and by age, sex, and social class were obtained.

These initial studies and two subsequent larger population studies, one from general practice and one from an industrial work force, were considered to have established the face, content, criterion, and discriminant validity of the NHP as a measure of physical, social, and emotional distress and the degree to which such distress is disruptive of daily activities. They also confirmed that the questionnaire was suitable for use with a wide range of people and could be used as a self-completion instrument.

Subsequent studies by other researchers, while primarily applying the Nottingham Health Profile in different clinical settings or population groups, have also used it in conjunction with other health status measures. However, this raises exactly the same issues as those faced by the authors, that these other measures tap into different aspects of the parameters of quality of life. Jenkinson et al. (6) used both the Nottingham Health Profile and Goldberg's General Health Questionnaire, while more recently there has been a study comparing the NHP with the SF-36 (7). When agreement or differences are found, it results in explanation either that one instrument is superior or more sensitive than the other, that they are testing different things, or that there is no obvious explanation. Although any researcher seeks to develop or to apply a well-validated and reliable instrument, it is recognized that with limited staff and funding, full and complete testing may be both impractical and indeed impossible to achieve. Equally, those wishing to use developed instruments in this area of research have to accept that the perfect, all-purpose quality of life measure does not exist. All current generic instruments, while they have their own strengths, also have limitations, and are designed for particular types of measurement—a specific age group, a particular aspect of health status, or for administration in a particular format.

STRENGTHS AND WEAKNESSES OF THE NHP

Strengths

As indicated earlier, there was a clear understanding in the development stage of the purposes of the proposed instrument and strict criteria were applied. Potential users of any measure should be familiar both with the stated aims of the authors and with the cumulative experiences of use by researchers since initial development. The present position is summarized as follows:

The NHP is the only generic health status measure derived entirely from lay people. As such, it reflects the values and concerns of the people who are required to complete the measure. Consequently, patients find the measure relevant and highly acceptable. Because the items are expressed in the words of ordinary people, biases associated with social class are minimized. The lack of artificial items aids translation into other languages.

The measure is easy to complete and score. It has a required reading age of 9 years and a simple response format—essential in countries where form-filling is uncommon. Respondents are asked to indicate whether or not each item applies to them. As a consequence of the simple items and response format, very few missing answers result. Where the measure is used in postal surveys, high response rates are achieved.

The measure is available in a large number of languages. The adaptations that have been developed are of a high quality, allowing clinical trial data to be combined from different countries. Other language versions of the NHP are described below.

The NHP is the most widely used measure of perceived health status in Europe. The measure is also becoming more common in North America and other English-speaking countries. As a consequence of this usage, many clinicians are familiar with the measure and interpretation of scores. NHP data are also acceptable to authorities evaluating clinical trial results (8).

The measure is administered from one center, whichever language versions are required. This minimizes administration for the users.

Manuals are available for each language version of the measure, as well as a Euroguide. Reference values are also available for some of the language versions, based on large-scale population studies using the NHP.

Weaknesses

Like all the generic measures of health status, the NHP lacks sensitivity. The measure works best with chronic, disabling illnesses, and with elderly populations.

Again, with the other generic measures, the content of the NHP is aging. This will be further discussed later in the chapter.

New measures of quality of life are now available with superior reliability and sensitivity. However, these measures are specific to the illness being studied.

Again, like the other generic measures, the NHP was not designed to be used in clinical trials. In fact the measure does work well in such situations because of its simplicity. However, a profile (NHP, Sickness Impact Profile) like the components of the SF-36 makes change more difficult to evaluate as improvements in some sections can be associated with worse scores in others. Furthermore, it is not possible to compare the importance of the different sections. Pharmacoeconomic analyses also demand an index of quality of life.

Like all the generic measures, the NHP cannot be validly used with hospitalized patients. This limits the number of clinical trials for which the measure is appropriate.

The attractiveness of the NHP to both respondents and researchers has led to its overuse. Furthermore, because it is the only health status measure available in a large number of European languages it has become the measure of choice in multinational clinical trials in Europe—even where it is not particularly suitable for the illness studied. This attractiveness has led to the development of many pirated versions of the measure. Such versions are in breach of copyright and lack the quality of the official measures. Problems have arisen where researchers have translated and used the measure without adequate care and retesting, leading to a lack of conceptual equivalence with the original NHP. Other researchers have changed the format of the measure, also making comparison with the original impossible. It is essential that the official versions are used, if the quality of the data is to be relied on. Pirated versions have also been produced for many Asian and African countries. It is unlikely that measures developed in the West will be appropriate for such different cultures. Rather than copy existing instruments, researchers in these countries should develop more relevant instruments of their own.

OTHER LANGUAGE VERSIONS

The widespread use of the NHP soon led to requests from other countries for their own language versions. Initially NHPs were developed for France, Spain, Italy, Sweden, and North America. More recently NHPs for Germany, the Netherlands, Denmark, Finland, and Norway have been produced. Various pirated versions of the measure have been produced for the Asian countries and also for Eastern and Western Europe. These versions have not used approved methods of adaptation and their use is in breach of copyright. As the measure is becoming more widely used in international clinical trials, a number of new versions are in preparation.

Each new language version has been carefully adapted and shown to be reliable and valid. Care has been taken to ensure the conceptual equivalence of items, rather than linguistic equivalence. The rather dated and imprecise method of back translation has been avoided by the use of translation panels. The final selection of items is made by nonprofessional individuals in each country, thereby maintaining the ethos of the measure (9).

One of the advantages of the NHP is that it is relatively easy to adapt. This is a result of the method by which the items were derived. The experience of illness has many commonalities between countries. In contrast, function-based measures, such as the SF-36, have proved rather difficult to adapt as the content is more culture-specific.

Because the different language versions of the NHP are conceptually equivalent, it is acceptable to combine data from different countries in clinical trials. This is particularly important with relatively rare conditions that have few cases in each country. For example, the NHP has been used in several international trials of growth hormone for growth hormone–deficient adults (10).

A Euroguide (European Group for Quality of Life Assessment and Health Measurement, 1993) has been produced for the measure (11). This includes the manuals for the UK, French, Italian, Spanish, and Swedish measures.

USES OF THE NHP IN CLINICAL STUDIES

As with a number of other measures of health status that were developed about the same time, the primary intention was that the measure should be used in community studies, normally based on epidemiological principles, to compare health states between different populations; to examine the link between health and various social, personal or environmental factors; and to identify areas of unmet health need. Although a number of such studies have been carried out, the main demand has been for outcome measures in health care. In the early days of the use of the NHP, the main application was in large clinical studies such as the heart transplant evaluation, or as an additional assessment in planned research programs examining different conditions such as arthritis or particular types of treatment such as antihypertensive therapy. Over the years, the pattern of requests for use of the NHP has extended to individual researchers often carrying out small projects, who apparently believe that no study is complete without the inclusion of a health status measure. Frequently, there is little understanding of the im-

portance of study design, population size, length of treatment, choice of measure, or analysis.

While clearly NHP can be used in clinical trials for selected groups of patients, it can also be of value in other clinical settings such as monitoring changes in health of chronically ill patients, as an adjunct to the clinical interview, and in evaluating other forms of clinical intervention.

In the choice of instrument or the package of instruments that are required for a particular study, there are now several general texts on quality of life measures that provide clear accounts of the approaches that can be adopted, and the decisions that have to be made. Jonsson (12) suggested that it is often "advisable to use one general instrument, one disease-specific instrument and one study-specific instrument." However, it has also been argued that wherever possible only one measure should be employed in clinical studies (13), as often too little attention is paid to the burden placed on patients in clinical trials. The choice can be related back to the purpose of the study. Is it to measure outcome in terms of general health, measure reduction in one or more particular symptoms, measure adverse effects, or to examine the wider perceived psychological or sociological aspects of either the condition or the treatment? Although the ideal approach in clinical studies is the randomized clinical trial, frequently there may have to be acceptance of less rigorous designs.

One of the earlier studies using the Nottingham Health Profile was the Department of Health study in 1985 on the heart transplant program (14). While randomization was not possible, data were collected before and after transplant and the dramatic improvement in health status of survivors was clearly recognized. In a later study of liver transplantation (15), because of sometimes acute onset of liver failure and the administrative difficulties associated with patients coming from different centers, pretransplantation data were not always available and NHP reference values from general population studies provided a useful comparison. These types of study illustrate perhaps the simplest use of the NHP—a serious illness, a dramatic intervention, and a need to monitor health for a prolonged period. Although it might be argued that detailed measurement is not required, survival in itself being a sufficient indicator of success, the arguments over costs and benefits and the uncertainty over the long-term quality of life in such survivors, justified the use of instruments like the NHP, which demonstrated that there is a return to normality, or near normal functioning, over a wide range of parameters within the profile, and that this is maintained over a prolonged period.

THE USE OF THE NHP IN CLINICAL TRIALS

A recent review of the medical literature found over 140 studies in which the NHP had been used. Of these 15 were

TABLE 1. *Clinical trials employing the NHP*

Condition	Number of trials
Hormone deficiencies	5
Cardiovascular	3
Pulmonary	2
Neurological	2
Joint pain	1
Surgical procedures	1
Fatigue syndrome	1

placebo-controlled clinical trials. Table 1 shows the clinical conditions in which the measure has been used.

In the recent few years, there has been a dramatic increase in the number of requests to use the NHP in clinical trials. Of the trials reported, the NHP was found to be particularly effective in studies of rheumatic conditions, hypertension, menopausal symptoms, growth hormone deficiency in adults, stroke, and asthma.

Detailed examinations of the papers, however, highlighted poor technique in the use of the NHP. Unfortunately, misuse of patient-completed measures is not uncommon in the clinical literature. These problems included:

use of inadequate sample sizes,
omission of parts of the measure,
adding together different sections to provide an overall score,
use of inappropriate statistical tests and poor interpretation
    of statistical findings,
use of the measure with hospitalized patients, and
use of pirated (and hence, untested) versions of the measure.

It is not unusual for authors to claim that the NHP lacks sensitivity in studies where it was not an appropriate measure or where the sample sizes were inadequate.

There is a clear need for clinical researchers to become more familiar with patient-completed measures and their use before introducing them into clinical trials.

FUTURE DEVELOPMENT

A number of researchers have attempted to adapt the NHP to provide a single score (14,16). However, the methods used have been arbitrary and of questionable validity. A 24-item version of the measure has been produced for use with hospitalized patients. The new measure provides an index of distress with good reliability and has been shown to distinguish between groups of differing health status (17).

The widely used measures of health status have provided valuable service over the years. However, it is clear that they have a limited future, particularly in clinical trials, for the following reasons:

The commonly used measures (NHP, General Health Questionnaire, Sickness Impact Profile, SF-36) contain items

generated 20 or more years ago. Health perceptions change with time and a new generation of measures is required.

Advances are being made in our understanding of constructs such as quality of life, and it is clear that none of the generic measures assesses this construct. There has been a tendency in recent years to construct measures from older instruments in an atheoretical components–type approach. The best example of this is the SF-36, which is the latest form of a measure developed from the original RAND studies (18). New theories of quality of life are being produced and these should form the basis of the new measures.

One such theory (19) argues that quality of life is the extent to which illness prevents needs being met. This model has formed the basis of a number of illness-specific quality of life measures (10,13,20). These new measures have levels of reliability, sensitivity, and validity far superior to the generic measures, such that they can be used to assess progress in individual patients.

The value of generic measures in clinical trials is questionable. Because only part of their content is relevant to the illness, they lack sensitivity and, on occasions, offend the respondents. They also miss out on aspects of the experience of illness that are important to the patients. The new specific measures, when carefully developed, contain only relevant items and cover all the important aspects.

Since the 1970s, the factors that influence the direction of research have changed. There is now a much greater understanding of the necessity of a theoretical base and clarification of concepts such as *health status* and *quality of life*. To continue to rely on generic health status measures to evaluate the effectiveness of interventions on quality of life is equivalent to assessing clinical effectiveness with a thermometer.

In the production of a relatively short and simple instrument designed for self-completion, it is necessary to reduce any particular section to a minimum. During the development of the NHP, interest was shown in examining in greater detail the particular domains that formed part I of the profile. Recently the subject of pain, which is one of the specific domains, has been explored by a team in Glasgow that was concerned about the lack of general epidemiological studies on pain, and that this was associated with the absence of a comprehensive and effective instrument for measuring pain.

Existing measures of pain, designed for use in clinical practice, tend to focus on pain intensity and relief, and although a number of general measures of health status do contain questions on pain and a few such as the NHP have a separate section, none of these seemed to provide a comprehensive measure of pain from the individual's perspective. It was decided to explore pain using a similar approach to that outlined above in development of the NHP, to see if a new measure could be derived that could be used both in clinical and population studies. The first papers on this have been submitted for publication (21,22). The work has produced an instrument that has been called the Glasgow Pain Questionnaire, which measures self-rated pain in five categories: pain frequency, intensity, emotional reaction, ability to cope, and restriction of daily living. Preliminary testing indicates its validity, reliability, and potential in assessing pain in different groups.

CONCLUSIONS

The NHP is still being used in its original form and is being found to be of value because of the strengths it has been shown to possess. In addition, there have been direct developments from it, and further work is in progress on specific applications that go some way to addressing the long-recognized issue of what aspects of health and ill health are of particular importance to individual patients.

Researchers wishing to use the NHP or purchase copies of the User's Manual or Euroguide should apply to Dr. McKenna, Galen Research, Southern Hey, 137 Barlow Moor Road, West Didsbury, Manchester, M20 2PW, England.

REFERENCES

1. Hunt SM, McEwen J, McKenna SP. *Measuring health status.* London: Croom Helm, 1986.
2. Magi M, Allander E. Towards a theory of perceived and mentally defined need. *Sociol Health Illness* 1981;3:49–71.
3. McDowell I, Martini CJM. Problems and new directions in the evaluation of primary care. *Int J Epidemiol* 1976;5:247–250.
4. Martini CJM, McDowell I. Health status; patient and physician judgements. *Health Serv Res* 1978;11:505–515.
5. Thurstone LL. *The measurement of values.* Chicago: University of Chicago Press, 1959.
6. Jenkinson C, Fitzpatrick R, Argyle M. The Nottingham Health Profile. An analysis of its sensitivity in differentiating illness groups. *Soc Sci Med* 1988;27:1411–1414.
7. Brazier JE, Harper K, Jones NHB, et al. Validating the SF-36 health survey questionnaire: new outcome measures for primary care. *Br Med J* 1992;305:160–164.
8. McKenna SP. Commonly used measures of health status in European clinical trials. *Br J Med Econ* 1993;6C:3–15.9.
9. Hunt SM, Alonso J, Bucquet D, Niero M, Wiklund I, McKenna SP. Cross-cultural adaptation of health measures. *Health Policy* 1992;19:33–44.
10. Hunt SM, McKenna SP, Doward LC. Preliminary report on the development of a disease-specific instrument for assessing quality of life of adults with growth hormone deficiency. *Acta Endocrinol* 1993;128(suppl 2):37–40.
11. European Group for Quality of Life Assessment and Health Measurement. *European guide to the Nottingham Health Profile.* Surrey: Brookwood Medical Publications, 1993.
12. Jonsson B. Assessment of quality of life in chronic diseases. *Acta Paediatr Scand* 1987(suppl 337):164–165.
13. McKenna SP, Hunt SM. A new measure of quality of life in depression: testing the reliability and construct validity of the QLDS. *Health Policy* 1992;22:321–330.
14. Buxton MJ, Acheson R, Caine N, Gibson S, O'Brien BJ. *Costs and benefits of the heart transplant programmes at Harefield and Papworth Hospitals.* DHSS Research Report No 12. London: HMSO, 1985.
15. Lowe D, O'Grady J, McEwen J, Williams R. The quality of life following liver transplantation—a preliminary report. *J R Coll Phys Lond* 1990;24:43–46.
16. Ebrahim S, Barer D, Nouri F. The use of the Nottingham Health Profile with patients after a stroke. *J Epidemiol Community Health* 1986;40:166–169.
17. McKenna SP, Hunt SM, Tennant A. The development of a patient-completed index of distress from the Nottingham Health Profile: a new measure for use in cost-utility studies. *Br J Med Econ* 1993;6:13–24.
18. Stewart AL, Ware JE, Brook RH, Davies-Avery A. *Conceptualization and measurement of health for adults in the health insurance study, vol 2, Physical health in terms of functioning.* Publication no R-1987/2-HEW. Santa Monica, CA: RAND, 1978.
19. Hunt SM, McKenna SP. The QLDS: a scale for the measurement of quality of life in depression. *Health Policy* 1992;22:307–319.
20. Doward LC. Developing a measure of quality of life for patients with recurrent genital herpes. *Drug Info J* 1994;28:19–25.
21. Thomas RJ, McEwen J, Asbury AJ. The Glasgow Pain Questionnaire: a new generic measure of pain. Development and testing. (submitted for publication)
22. Thomas RJ, Asbury AJ, McEwen J. The Glasgow Pain Questionnaire. A pilot study of pain problems in general practice. (submitted for publication)

Quality of Life and Pharmacoeconomics in Clinical Trials, Second Edition, edited by B. Spilker. Lippincott-Raven Publishers, Philadelphia © 1996.

CHAPTER 30

Psychological Adjustment to Illness Scale: PAIS and PAIS-SR

Leonard R. Derogatis and Megan P. Fleming

INTRODUCTION

In recent years, there has been a greatly intensified interest in the concept of *psychosocial adjustment*. This has been evident not only in psychological medicine, but in more traditional medical disciplines as well. In psychiatry, increased concern for the social reintegration of patients has derived from the increased emphasis on community care of psychiatric patients during recent decades (1). In other areas of health care, technologic and treatment advances have resulted in expanded numbers of individuals suffering from chronic conditions, many of whom would have previously succumbed to acute phases of the disorder. The enhanced demands made by such illnesses on the coping skills, psychological integrity, and social support systems of these individuals has dramatically enhanced the importance of psychosocial adjustment.

The first formal attempts at measuring psychosocial adjustment date back to the 1950s, when professionals desired

a quantitative mechanism to assess the differential adjustment of psychiatric patients being returned to the community on a variety of therapeutic regimens. Few of the prototype adjustment scales are still in use; however, experiences with these early approaches laid the groundwork for more contemporary measurement instruments that have demonstrated high utility in the assessment of the adjustment of psychiatric patients. In several reviews on the topic, Weissman (1,2) has identified approximately two dozen instruments developed to assess the psychosocial functioning of diverse groups of psychiatric patients. In terms of global characteristics, these measures extend from highly structured interviews taking up to 2 hours to administer, to self-report inventories requiring 20 minutes to complete. For a number of years, the psychiatric investigator or clinician seeking to assess the psychosocial adjustment of his or her patients has had an extensive range of instruments to select from.

When concern is directed to the psychosocial adjustment of patients from traditional medical specialties, rigorous assessment methods have been extremely scarce; few formal psychometric instruments have been developed to evaluate the psychosocial adjustment of medical patients. This is so even though a strong psychosocial component is characteris-

L. R. Derogatis and M. P. Fleming: Department of Clinical and Health Psychology, Hahnemann University, Philadelphia, Pennsylvania 19102.

tic of many chronic medical conditions (e.g., heart and vascular disorders, cancers, diabetes), and may have a role not only in the etiology of the disease, but also in the course or outcome of the illness. This observation served as the primary impetus that led ultimately to the development of the Psychological Adjustment to Illness Scale (PAIS) and the self-report version (PAIS-SR).

THE CONCEPT OF PSYCHOSOCIAL ADJUSTMENT AND ITS MEASUREMENT

Since psychosocial adjustment tends to be defined somewhat differently from one context to the next, it is worthwhile examining the construct in some detail. It is obvious from the term *psychosocial* that more than just intrapsychic processes are involved; it is also evident that the concept embraces interactions between individuals and the prominent institutions of the respondent's social and cultural environment. Such interactions are usually achieved through loosely prescribed behavioral patterns termed *roles*.

How functionally efficient an individual's role behaviors (e.g., spouse, parent, professional) are judged to be tend to be highly correlated with judgments concerning his or her levels of psychosocial adjustment. Further, it has been consistently observed within the contexts of numerous major diseases (3–5) that the nature of the patient's psychosocial adjustment can be as meaningful as the status of his/her physical disease in determining the quality of an illness experience.

Like many complex hypothetical constructs in psychological medicine, psychosocial adjustment is typically conceived of as an overarching multidimensional construct arising from multiple domains. Many of the principal domains of psychosocial adjustment are composed of, or strongly associated with, salient role behaviors. The vocational role as worker, domestic roles of spouse and parent, and social-leisure roles all represent significant aspects of psychosocial functioning. It follows from this observation that realistic measurement of psychosocial adjustment should represent it as *multidimensional* and *generic* in nature.

Choices concerning the domains to be represented in an instrument designed to measure psychosocial adjustment are intrinsically difficult. Ultimately, the dimensions included are determined by domain relevance, construct and predictive validity, measurability, time constraints, and cost-efficiency. All of the domains that possess conceptual appeal or predictive relevance for adjustment cannot be included, some because they are tangential to the major measurement construct, and others, although highly relevant, because they do not easily lend themselves to psychometric operational definition. In addition, the time window for assessment is highly constrained by competition from other medical evaluative procedures, by the patient's tolerance and motivation to endure prolonged evaluative sessions, and by the realiza-

tion that after the first few domains, each additional domain will contribute substantially decreasing increments to the cumulative sensitivity of the test battery.

In practical terms, this means that only the most central and salient domains can be designed into an instrument. Consistent with this realization, the PAIS and PAIS-SR were designed to represent adjustment as the linear combination of measures of seven principal psychosocial domains. PAIS domains have been repeatedly demonstrated to have high relevance for global adjustment to illness, both in our own clinical research and in the experience of other investigators. These facets of the patient's experience are evaluated by means of either a semistructured interview, i.e., the PAIS, or a self-report inventory, the PAIS-SR, and when scored and normatively interpreted, provide a comprehensive evaluation of the individual's adjustment to his/her illness.

A DESCRIPTIVE PROFILE OF THE PAIS AND PAIS-SR

The Psychosocial Adjustment to Illness Scale (PAIS) is a semistructured interview designed to assess the quality of a patient's psychosocial adjustment to a current medical illness or its residual effects. With minor alterations in format, the PAIS may also be used to measure the quality of spouses', parents', or other relatives' adjustment to a patient's illness, or their perceptions of the patient's adjustment.

The PAIS is designed to be completed in conjunction with a personal interview with the respondent, conducted by a trained health professional or interviewer. The PAIS interview requires approximately 20 to 25 minutes to complete. When conducted within a broader interview, PAIS items should be presented consecutively without the interjection of external items or queries. The PAIS is typically made available in reusable booklets with separate answer and score/profile forms.

In addition to the PAIS interview, there is also a self-report version of the scale, the PAIS-SR. The PAIS-SR is designed to be completed directly by the respondent, with instructions printed in a consumable booklet. The PAIS-SR also requires from 20 to 25 minutes to complete, with separate answer and score/profile forms available.

The PAIS and PAIS-SR reflect psychosocial adjustment to illness via seven primary domains of adjustment:

   I. Health Care Orientation
  II. Vocational Environment
 III. Domestic Environment
 IV. Sexual Relationships
  V. Extended Family Relationships
 VI. Social Environment
VII. Psychological Distress

Interview questions are designed to assess the quality of adjustment in each of these primary adjustment areas. A total of 46 items are completed concerning the respondent in a PAIS interview, with each item being rated on a four-point (0–3) scale of adjustment. Higher ratings indicate poorer adjustment. There is an equivalent item for each of the 46 PAIS items on the PAIS-SR, rewritten or modified for a self-report format. A four-point scale of distress (0–3) is also used with the PAIS-SR but scale direction is alternated on every other item to reduce position response biases.

Definition of PAIS Domains

The seven principal measurement domains of the PAIS were developed through a combination of rational-deductive and empirical-analytic procedures. The domains represent constructs that have repeatedly been identified as having high predictive relevance for adjustment to illness. Each domain is operationally defined by a series of questions or items that are relatively homogeneous in the measurement of that specific construct. In developing the PAIS, the instrument was designed so that all domain subscores correlate substantially with the total adjustment score (PAIS Total Score) but have minimal intercorrelations among themselves. Such a strategy reduces redundancy in measurement and enhances sensitivity by having each subdomain contribute relatively unique variance to measurement of the superordinate construct, *adjustment to illness*.

Health Care Orientation

The domain of Health Care Orientation (eight items) addresses the nature of the respondent's health care posture, and whether it will function to promote a positive or negative adjustment to the condition or illness and its treatment. Patient attitudes, quality of information, and the nature of the patient's expectancies about his/her disorder and its treatment are all assessed in this domain. The major thrust of this section of the instrument is to evaluate the respondent's health care posture and whether it will facilitate or impede adjustment to the disorder and its sequelae.

Vocational Environment

This section (six items) is designed to reflect the impact that the condition or disorder may have on vocational adjustment, where "vocational" is flexibly defined to indicate work, school, or home, whichever is most appropriate. The six items sample perceived quality of job performance, job satisfaction, lost time, job interest, and a number of other variables that are associated with the nature of vocational adjustment. The Vocational Environment section is designed to tap disruption in job performance, satisfaction, and adjustment that is attributable to the present illness or disability. It is important to note that students and housewives are

evaluated in terms of functions specific to their current circumstances and roles.

Domestic Environment

The Domestic Environment domain (eight items) is oriented toward illness-induced difficulties that arise in the home or family environment. It is designed to assess problems in adjustment experienced by the patient and the patient's family in response to the patient's illness or condition. The eight items measure a number of aspects of family living, including financial impact of the illness, quality of relationships, family communications, and effects of physical disabilities. If the patient is not presently living with his/her family but elsewhere (e.g., rooming house, relatives) then relationships in the most current domicile are taken as the domestic referent. The same adjustment is made when the patient has no family.

Sexual Relationships

This section on sexual relationships (six items) is designed to provide a measure of any changes in the quality of sexual functioning or relationship associated with the patient's illness or sequelae of the illness. Items are designed to be presented in a progressive sequence, beginning with a focus on quality of interpersonal relationship, and moving toward more specific issues of sexual functioning. Items assessing sexual interest, frequency, quality of performance, and level of satisfaction are included in the measurement of this domain. This section is designed to assess any changes in the quality of sexual behavior or relationship that are attributable to the present illness or its aftermath. The questions in this section are progressive in that they start with a focus on the general quality of interpersonal relationship with a significant other, and progress into specifically sexual behavior. After an initial question on interpersonal relationships, subsequent items deal with alterations in sexual interest, frequency, and satisfaction. If formal responses to any of these queries are positive, then additional questions further explore the possibility of sexual dysfunction being present.

Extended Family Relationships

This section (five items) is devoted to measuring any disruption or derangement in relationships with the extended family constellation that arises associated with the illness experience. The framework of typical interactions with extended family is used to assess any negative impact of the illness upon communication, quality of relationships, interest in interacting with family, and other variables reflective of this domain. This domain of behavior is a component of the PAIS interview designed to reflect any difficulties in relationships within the extended family constellation that arise directly or indirectly as a result of the illness. Because there is great variability in the extent to which individuals interact with extended family members (e.g., brothers, sisters, aunts, cousins), some respondents have little relationship with these family members normally, while others have frequent interactions with large numbers of relatives. Assessments should be made in terms of *typical patterns of interaction* rather than in any absolute sense.

Social Environment

This domain (six items) reflects the status of the patient's current social and leisure time activities, and the degree to which the patient has suffered impairment or constriction of these activities as a result of the current condition and/or its residual effects. Activities are partitioned into "individual," "family," and "social" categories with domain items sampling interest and actual behavior in each category. The purpose of this domain is to determine the degree to which the patient has suffered incursions due to illness into his/her typical social and leisure activities. Physical debilitation or other difficulties may prevent the individual from carrying out normal leisure time activities but may have less effect on interest in them. A different positive adaptive posture may find the individual showing a significant diminution of interest in leisure time activities as well as being impaired in his/her ability to perform them.

To adequately conduct this portion of the interview, it is necessary to have information on the respondent's normal leisure time pattern of behavior (e.g., hobbies, sports). This information may be more easily obtained early in the interview, although the interviewer may wish to wait until reaching this section specifically before asking about these activities.

Psychological Distress

The final section of the PAIS covers psychological distress (seven items), and is designed to measure dysphoric thoughts and feelings that accompany the patient's disorder or are a direct result of the illness and its sequelae. Major indicators of psychological distress such as anxiety, depression, and anger, as well as reduced self-esteem, body image problems, and inappropriate guilt make up the substance of this domain. The intention of this portion of the interview is to measure the degree to which the respondent experiences dysphoric thoughts and feelings as a result of his/her illness or condition. The format of this domain is distinct from the other sections in that in addition to a suggested question to the patient for each item, there is also a question to the interviewer that must be answered. The suggested question is intended to serve as a means of eliciting the information necessary for the interviewer to make the appropriate judgment.

Item Applicability

There are occasions when a specific item or even a series of items do not apply to a particular patient. For example, if the patient is a member of certain religious orders, questions about sexual relationships and queries concerning the financial impact of the illness are not appropriate. For single individuals living alone, questions #1 and #2 of section III (Domestic Environment) are problematic. For the individual without living relatives, a number of items have no meaning, or must be redefined as outlined in the administration manual for the PAIS/PAIS-SR (6).

ADMINISTRATION

Although this section provides a brief review of the procedures associated with the administration of the PAIS and PAIS-SR, detailed instructions, essential to the valid administration of these instruments, are presented with particulars in the tests' administration manual (6).

PAIS

The PAIS interview is semistructured in that the suggested order of the PAIS items is as presented in the PAIS booklet, but it is *not* essential that this precise order be utilized. To conduct the interview adequately, the interviewer should determine the nature of the present illness or condition, age, sex, and occupation of the respondent, his or her household and extended family composition, and typical social and leisure time activities. If the respondent is a relative of the patient, the interviewer must remember to focus questions on the *relative's* rather than the patient's adjustment. In the event the format of the interview is designed to elicit a *relative's perception* of the patient's adjustment to illness, the interviewer must address the respondent's best judgments concerning the patient's acclimation to the limitations of his/her condition. In any format, the interviewer should make every effort to keep the interview focused on the particular domain he/she is currently exploring. If, however, the patient begins to address an issue that is out of sequence, it should be explored, and when convenient, a return to sequence should be accomplished. There are no designated "probes" in the PAIS interview; additional questions are left to the discretion of the interviewer. Such a design provides additional flexibility and allows the interview to be conducted in a more "natural" fashion.

The PAIS interview gains added elasticity from the fact that the interview question designated for each item is merely the *recommended* form of the query. The interviewer may use any form of the question that is felt to be appropriate as long as the *answer to the designated question is obtained*. The exception to this rule occurs in section VII on Psychological Distress, where each item is provided with both a "required" question and a "recommended" question, the latter designed to elicit an accurate response to the former.

PAIS-SR (Self-Report)

Instructions for administration of the self-report PAIS-SR are printed on the inside front cover of each consumable booklet containing the instrument. Although every effort was made to compose articulate instructions that clearly communicate what the respondent is to do, it is very helpful to have an institutional staff member (e.g., nurse, social worker, secretary) review the instructions with the respondent. Upon completion, the PAIS-SR should be reviewed again by the person responsible for administration to confirm that the respondent clearly understood directions. The respondent should also be asked at that time if he/she has any questions about the assessment, or if anything about the PAIS-SR was unclear.

If the PAIS-SR is administered by mail, then it is recommended that a separate page of instructions be included with the test. The instructions should reiterate to a certain extent the instructions in the booklet, and in addition, indicate that the instrument should be completed by the respondent *alone* in a quiet, non-distracting environment. The additional instructions should encourage the patient to avoid skipping any items, and to write any questions he/she may have about the scale in the space provided. During typical administration of the PAIS-SR, the staff member administering the test should remain in close proximity to the respondent and be available to answer any questions the respondent may have.

Time Reference

The general time frame for both the PAIS and the PAIS-SR is the *most recent 30 days*. A minor exception to this rule is provided in questions #1 and #3 of section 1, Health Care Orientation, which ask about the respondent's *typical* attitudes about health and quality of medical care. All other items are to be responded to in terms of the "past 30 days including today." In the event that the respondent is currently hospitalized, then the time frame for responding should be modified slightly. In such instances the referent time period should be the *30 days immediately prior to entering the hospital.* If the PAIS (or PAIS-SR) is administered during the first few days of hospitalization, such a modification is probably unnecessary. If assessment is done one week or more after hospitalization then such an adjustment in time set should be made.

When the PAIS or PAIS-SR are administered to patients who have undergone a prolonged hospitalization (i.e., who are hospitalized for longer than 30 days) establishing an appropriate time referent can become problematic. Use of the standard time referent of "the past 30 days" will, of course, reflect the limitations imposed by hospitalization, and almost certainly result in a somewhat biased (poorer)

adjustment picture. If hospitalization has not been for longer than 45 days, then an acceptable rule of thumb is to make reference to the 30 days immediately preceding hospitalization. If duration of hospitalization has progressed beyond 45 days, *forgetting* can result in systematic biases, the exact size and nature of which are difficult to estimate. Also, as duration of hospitalization becomes extended, assessments aimed at the patient's status prior to hospitalization can less validly be treated as "current" or "baseline." For truly prolonged hospitalizations it is probably best to use the standard time referent of "the past 30 days," and where possible interpret scores in terms of norms for similar patients. When the PAIS respondent is a patient's *relative* the standard referent should always be used. Respondents who are intermittently hospitalized over the most recent 30-day period should also be instructed to use the standard time frame for their responses.

APPROPRIATE APPLICATIONS AND RESPONDENTS

The PAIS and PAIS-SR are designed to enable the user to assess a very broad range of the illness/disorder continuum, from conditions that are considered minor inconveniences to diseases that have the potential to result in mortality. The nature of psychosocial adjustment is such that the most productive applications of the instrument are found in the assessment of more chronic or protracted conditions. Acute disorders and trauma, by their nature, tend to have a less significant psychosocial, and more compelling medical, components. Once the acute phase of a disorder has passed, however, the PAIS is quite appropriate for the assessment of adjustment to rehabilitative regimens, or enduring residual effects of the original acute condition.

For measurement with the PAIS or PAIS-SR to be valid the respondent must be capable of understanding the questions being put to him/her and accurately communicating a response. This requirement poses fewer problems for the PAIS interview where there are no reading demands. Nonetheless, care must be exercised concerning the patient's level of cognitive functioning, since more subtle states of delirium or dementia can compromise the reliability and validity of responses.

In using the PAIS-SR one inherits all the strengths and weaknesses of self-report measurement. As has been pointed out previously (7,8), the self-report modality of psychological measurement has many positive features to recommend it, but also possesses some potential liabilities. Principal problems with self-report stem from the fact that one must tacitly assume the validity of the "inventory premise" (9), that the respondent *can* and *will* respond to questions accurately and without distortions arising from conscious or unconscious motives, personality characteristics, or impaired states of cognitive functioning. Difficulties can arise from manifest constraints the respondent brings to the assessment situation, such as delirium, illiteracy, or poor vision, or they may develop from motivated distortions in responding. Fortunately, the former difficulties can usually be adjusted to by careful screening, and the interview (PAIS) version of the instrument may be an alternative in situations where reading or vision present limitations.

Alternatively, self-report has many positive attributes to recommend it. *Economy of professional effort* is a major asset of self-report assessment, since nonprofessional personnel can be trained to administer self-report inventories. Because of the relatively low levels of technology typically required, self-report inventories are *highly transportable* across a broad range of evaluation contexts. Such scales also tend to be *brief, cost-efficient,* and, as a consequence, *cost-beneficial* as well. Probably, the most compelling positive feature of self-report arises from the fact that the basic data of measurement are derived from a unique source—*the test respondent himself.* All other observers are limited to reporting "apparent" versions of the phenomena under study, construed from interpretations of the patient's behavior or its absence. Although this feature provides the basis for response biases, clinical observer and interviewer are certainly not free of biases, and the patient does provide a singular perspective on his/her adjustment.

In general, the PAIS is appropriate for the assessment of adjustment of any medical condition that has an identifiable psychosocial component and that is of sufficient severity to impact measurably on the psychological and interpersonal integrity of the patient. To achieve a valid PAIS or PAIS-SR assessment, the respondent should be alert, favorably motivated to participate in the assessment, and intellectually unimpaired.

Both the PAIS and the PAIS-SR are well suited for sequential measurement over time. Clinical trials with repeated measures, follow-up evaluations, and routine (e.g., monthly, semiannual) evaluations may be validly accomplished with these methods. The PAIS and the PAIS-SR may be utilized to accomplish current, point-in-time assessment of adjustment as well as to document sequential trends in psychosocial integrity. In addition, with slight alterations in format, the scales may be used to evaluate caregiver adjustment to patient conditions and relative estimates of patient adjustment. Reliability and validity studies (see below) suggest excellent sensitivity across an extensive range of illness and respondent contexts.

SCORING AND NORMS

Scoring the PAIS or the PAIS-SR is a relatively uncomplicated procedure. In both cases, seven domain totals and the PAIS Total Score must be calculated. In addition, when scoring the PAIS-SR, the *even position* items (i.e., position #2 through position #46) must be "reflected" (i.e., the score must be subtracted from 3) before being added to the do-

main sums. The seven domain sums are then converted to standardized area T-scores (by identifying the correct T-score equivalents in the appropriate normative tables), and summed to generate the PAIS Total Score. Scoring the PAIS or PAIS-SR requires only the arithmetic operations of addition and subtraction.

Scoring is greatly facilitated by using one of the several score profile forms available from the instrument's publisher, Clinical Psychometric Research. Each published norm for the PAIS (i.e., A—lung cancer patients; B—renal dialysis patients; C—burn patients; D—essential hypertension patients) and PAIS-SR (AA—cardiac patients; BB—mixed cancer patients; CC—diabetic patients) is profiled on one side of these forms with the standard PAIS (or PAIS-SR) scoring template on the opposite side. There is also a non-normed scoring form available for users who are assessing patients who are not easily compared to the available normative groups. Scoring is further facilitated through the use of SCORPAIS, a PC-based computerized scoring program. SCORPAIS may be obtained from the publisher with all currently available norms. All PAIS and PAIS-SR norms are developed in terms of standardized area T-scores, so that true centile equivalents may be assigned to respondent's levels of adjustment.

RELIABILITY

Reliability essentially concerns the consistency of measurement, or the accuracy with which an instrument measures the characteristic(s) under observation. This is true of both the physical and the behavioral sciences. In the former, because of the relatively sophisticated instrumentation available, errors of measurement are small and the detailed operations of reliability are rarely explicitly stated. In the behavioral sciences, since we are almost always attempting to measure hypothetical constructs, scales of measurement rarely achieve even interval levels of sophistication. Consequently, errors of measurement may be relatively substantial. For these reasons, the operations essential to estimating the reliability of a psychological measure should be presented in detail, in clear quantifiable terms.

In perfectly reliable measurement systems all sources of error or "unreliability" are eliminated and measurements are exactly repeatable or reproducible. In the actual world of measurement, it is impossible to abolish all sources of error, with the result that each score or measurement has two distinct determinants: true score variation, and error variance. To the extent that the ratio of true score variation to total variation in measurement is large (i.e., approaches 1.00) errors are minimized, and we have reliable measurement. If this ratio is small, then measurement is unreliable and precision is attenuated.

Since there are multiple potential sources of error in psychological measurement several different forms of estimat-

TABLE 1. *Internal consistency reliability coefficients (α) for the PAIS and PAIS-SR*

PAIS measure	Renal dialysis (PAIS: n = 269)	Lung cancer (PAIS: n = 89)	Cardiac (PAIS: n = 69)	Burns[a] (n = 260)	Pain[b] (n = 222)	Cardiac[c] (n = 96)
I. Health Care Orientation	.63	.83	.47	–	–	–
II. Vocational Environment	.81	.87	.76	–	–	–
III. Domestic Environment	.67	.68	.77	–	–	–
IV. Sexual Relationship	.80	.93	.83	–	–	–
V. Extended Family	.66	.12	.62	–	–	–
VI. Social Environment	.78	.93	.80	–	–	–
VII. Psychological Distress	.80	.81	.85	–	–	–
PAIS Total Score	–	–	–	.94	.81	.91

[a]From ref. 11.
[b]From ref. 12.
[c]From ref. 13.

ing reliability have evolved. One of the most basic reliability estimates is termed *internal consistency reliability*. Internal consistency reliability derives from the domain sampling model (10), and relates to the consistency (in terms of average intercorrelations) with which items composing a particular scale measure the construct in question. Internal consistency reliability coefficients for the PAIS and PAIS-SR are given in Table 1. These estimates of reliability derive from our own work with three of the instruments' normative samples, and the published work of several independent investigators.

As the coefficients alpha suggest, the subscales (domains) of the PAIS and PAIS-SR generally show high internal consistency, a characteristic that appears particularly uniform among the large sample of renal dialysis patients. Coefficients are also very substantial in the lung cancer sample, although the alpha for the Extended Family scale was reduced to .12. The coefficients for the lung cancer sample were derived based on an early version of the Extended Family subscale that included only four items. The scale has since been revised, with one item being rewritten and an additional new item added. Three independent investigators (11–13) have also published data on the internal consistency

reliability of the scale. Coefficients alpha for the PAIS Total Score were quite acceptable in all three studies. Unfortunately, investigators did not publish estimates for the separate PAIS domains.

When instruments are designed to elicit clinical judgments and ratings from clinical observers (e.g., psychologists, physicians, nurses, social workers) reliability may be estimated in another fashion, i.e., through interrater agreement. Such *interrater reliability* reflects the degree of concordance or consistency shown between separate clinical observers in judging the status of a common cohort of patients. Two estimates of interrater reliability from our own work are given for the PAIS in Table 2 based upon distinct sets of patients and clinical observers. Again, an independent estimate of interrater reliability for the PAIS Total Score is also provided (12).

As is evident from the sizes of the coefficients, agreement between clinical judges on most PAIS domains was well into the acceptable range, and in most instances very good. A clinical psychologist and a nurse were the observers for the breast cancer sample, while a mixed group of interviewers, including physicians, psychologists, and social workers, were involved in the ratings of the Hodgkin's patients.

TABLE 2. *Estimates of interrater reliabilities for the PAIS*

PAIS domain	Breast cancer (n = 17)	Hodgkin's disease (n = 37)	Pain patients[a] (n = 222)
I. Health Care Orientation	.74	.70	–
II. Vocational Environment	.68	.62	–
III. Domestic Environment	.61	.52	–
IV. Sexual Relationship	.86	.81	–
V. Extended Family	.56	.33	–
VI. Social Environment	.82	.72	–
VII. Psychological Distress	.84	.82	–
PAIS Total Score	.86	.83	.86

[a]From ref. 12.

VALIDITY

Although a number of authorities such as Nunnally (14) have suggested that newer developments in psychometrics make it difficult to use older terms (e.g., ''reliability'' or ''validity'') with precision, when we speak about the validity of measurement, we are basically concerned with the *essence* of what is being measured. The most comprehensive and demanding form of validity is *construct validation,* which is highly programmatic and requires input from numerous studies of the predictive and convergent/discriminative types. The set of operations inherent in construct validation may be best appreciated as equivalent to the steps involved in adequately testing a scientific theory (15). Nunnally (14) describes construct validity as representing an expanding network of ''circumstantial evidence'' supporting the idea that the operational definition of the construct (i.e., the test) truly measures the attribute(s) being considered.

Confirmation of Structure

Particularly in the case of multidimensional tests, an important step in construct validation involves the confirmation of the hypothesized dimensional structure of the instrument, i.e., domain-item relationships. Typically, this step involves a factor analysis of a representative set of individuals' responses to the test and a comparison of the empirical factor (dimensional) structure with the *a priori* rational-hypothesized structure of the test. The degree of agreement between the rational and empirical structures provides a measure of the consonance between the theoretic and actual dimensions or domains of measurement, and thereby of construct validity.

Such a factor analysis of the PAIS, based upon the assessments of the 120 patients making up the lung cancer cohort was accomplished and reported by Derogatis and Derogatis (6). An initial principal components analysis was subsequently rotated to a normalized varimax solution. The orthogonal rotated factor matrix resulted in seven substantive dimensions being identified, accounting for approximately 63% of the variance in the matrix. Factor I accounted for 18% of the variance, with the remaining dimensions being associated with 10%, 9%, 8%, 7%, 7%, and 5%, respectively. The hypothesized dimensional structure of the PAIS was strongly confirmed by this analysis in that each of the seven postulated dimensions was clearly revealed in the empirical factor structure.

Interrelationships Among Domains and the Total Score

One ideal of multidimensional measurement is to identify domains of a particular construct of interest in such a manner that they are relatively specific and unique in their contribution to the definition of the construct, i.e., are relatively orthogonal (uncorrelated) components of the attribute in

question. The appeal of such a configuration rests in the fact that subscales of a test derived in such a manner will tend to be relatively uncorrelated with each other, but will correlate well with the total score of the test. Such a strategy reduces redundancy and acts to increase the breadth and sensitivity of construct measurement.

In the clinical situation it is extremely difficult to develop tests that reveal such a pattern of relationship. In spite of being able to identify constructs that are considered orthogonal it is very unusual to find test subscales that do not show at least moderate correlations in terms of actual test scores.

In developing the PAIS and PAIS-SR, a great deal of attention was devoted to first identifying domains of adjustment that were felt to be relatively specific, and subsequently constructing items that would retain that same level of specificity in empirical measurement. That we have been reasonably successful in this endeavor is borne out by the data given in Table 3. The coefficients in Table 3 represent correlations among the seven domain scores of the PAIS and PAIS-SR, and also between the domain scores and the PAIS Total Score. Three separate sets of coefficients are given in the table (two for the PAIS, one for the PAIS-SR) developed from three distinct study cohorts. Samples *a* and *b* represent two PAIS normative groups, while sample *c* was derived from an earlier pilot study with the PAIS (16). The coefficients demonstrate a consistent pattern of low intercorrelations among domain scores with concomitant high correlations with the PAIS Total Score. This is true for both the PAIS, where the average intercorrelation among domains was .33 among lung cancer patients and .10 among Hodgkin's patients, and the PAIS-SR where the average domain intercorrelation was .29. In almost every instance, domain total correlations were substantial and in the moderate to high range. This pattern of relationship between components of the tests begin to approach an optimal configuration, and suggests that the PAIS and the PAIS-SR possess promising measurement conformations.

Convergent Validation

A number of investigators have reported good convergent relationships for the PAIS. In an early pilot project with the scale (16) a series of significant correlations with external criteria for the PAIS Domain Scores were established. De-Nour (17) also reported significant convergent relationships between the PAIS-SR Total Score and the Multiple Affects Adjective Checklist and between physicians' ratings for psychological impairment and the Psychological Distress Score on the PAIS-SR. In a study of 70 cardiac transplantation patients, Freeman and his colleagues (18) demonstrated high correlations between convergent PAIS scores and both the Zung Depression Scale and the State-Trait Anxiety Inventory across a postoperative period of 2 years. Similarly, Hochberg and Sutton (19) showed very significant correlations between all dimensions of the PAIS-SR and the Dis-

TABLE 3. *Correlations among domain scores and total score for the PAIS and PAIS-SR based on three clinical samples[a]*

		II			III			IV			V			VI			VII			PAIS Total		
		a	b	c	a	b	c	a	b	c	a	b	c	a	b	c	a	b	c	a	b	.c
I.	Health Care Orientation	.15	.01	.03	.32	.27	.05	.16	.14	.19	.30	.31	.24	.39	.28	.14	.22	.31	.05	.56	.53	.46
II.	Vocational Environment				.47	.03	.01	.24	.03	.05	.05	.11	.01	.45	.05	.04	.35	.01	.18	.60	.12	.22
III.	Domestic Environment							.34	.39	.03	.50	.59	.00	.70	.52	.08	.55	.58	.16	.83	.79	.43
IV.	Sexual Relationship										.04	.23	.33	.26	.41	.10	.26	.30	.04	.53	.60	.47
V.	Extended Family													.51	.53	.22	.25	.48	.01	.47	.70	.08
VI.	Social Environment																.55	.47	.09	.83	.77	.34
VII.	Psychological Distress																			.75	.76	.44

[a]Sample *a* = 120 lung cancer patients—PAIS; sample *b* = 148 kidney patients; sample *c* = 37 patients with Hodgkin's disease (PAIS).

ability Index, Pain Score, and Global Assessment Rating of the Stanford Health Assessment Questionnaire in a sample of 106 ambulatory patients with systemic lupus erythematosus. Moguliner et al. (20), investigating the adjustment of children and their parents to the latter's chronic hemodialysis, showed consistently high correlations between the parents' PAIS scores and a variety of measures of child adjustment, including the Tennessee Self-Concept Scale and the Thematic Apperception Test. An investigation into the psychological status of polio survivors (21) correlated the domain scores of the PAIS with the global scores of the SCL-90-R (a popular self-report symptom inventory). Findings revealed highly significant correlations between all measures of the PAIS and the Global Severity Index of the SCL-90-R, with the highest coefficient ($r = .72$) being on the Psychological Distress domain.

Predictive Validity: The Practical Utility of the PAIS/PAIS-SR

As has been noted previously (22), when most investigators and practitioners make reference to the validity of a psychological test, they are most frequently referring to the *predictive* validity of the instrument. Predictive validity references the capacity of a test to predict or discriminate among outcomes, and defines the utility of the instrument for various classes of predictive applications. The prefix *pre* implies that the direction of relationship between assessment and outcome must be oriented toward the future; however, the predictive capacity of the test may be focused on current status in time, or may even be postdictive in its orientation.

An important characteristic of predictive validity is its *high specificity*. The general questions, "Is this test valid?" has no scientific meaning, unless the conditional interrogatory, "For what purpose?" is addressed. Measurement

specificity is conspicuous in the physical sciences, but less obvious in psychological measurement. A test may have high predictive validity (i.e., sensitivity and specificity) as a screen for depressive disorder but be of little value in screening for thought disorder (23). A cognitive screening test may be highly sensitive in identifying current frontal lobe lesions, but be highly *in*sensitive to brain stem damage. An indication of specific criteria and purposes should accompany predictive validity statements about a test so that users will appreciate its range of valid application as well as its limitations.

Concerning the predictive validity of the PAIS and the PAIS-SR, the instruments have been utilized in numerous clinical research protocols and outcome trials that have confirmed their predictive capacities relative to numerous external criteria of interest. In this section we catalogue in synopsis form the results of these investigations.

In an interesting investigation dealing with physicians' perceptions of their patients' psychological status, DeNour (24) contrasted the PAIS-SR scores of dialysis patients rated as "good" and "bad" adjusters by their treating physicians. Statistically significant differences between groups were observed on the PAIS-SR total and PAIS-SR domain scores. Working with a similar cohort of patients Murphy (25) used the PAIS to observe consistent predictive relationships between PAIS domain scores and external measures of adjustment. Also studying patients with renal disorders, Kaye and her colleagues (26) evaluated the impact of dialysis on the adjustment using patients from multiple centers. Pre-post assessments with the PAIS revealed significant improvements on Health Care Orientation, Vocational Environment, and Extended Family Domains. Lamping (27) has also reported research with dialysis patients that supports the predictive validity of the PAIS. Her study demonstrated significant correlations between PAIS measures and medical compliance, as well as appropriate scales from the Profile of Mood States and the Minnesota Multiphasic Personality

Inventory. In addition, she was able to show discrimination between patients in terms of life events, stress, work status, severity of illness, and coping styles on the basis of PAIS scores.

More recently, Oldenberg et al. (28) utilized the PAIS and the SCL-90-R with a cohort of end-stage renal disease patients, and found the PAIS to be quite accurate in predicting adjustment to disease. Similarly, Moguliner (20) demonstrated high correlations between patients and spouses on the PAIS in a chronic hemodialysis sample, and further showed that adult adjustment scores on the PAIS correlated well with independent adjustment measures of the patients' children.

The PAIS and PAIS-SR have also been used a great deal with cancer populations. Evans et al. (29) employed the PAIS to demonstrate clear differences in levels of adjustment between cancer patients suffering from clinical depression and treated appropriately, and similar patients who did not receive appropriate treatment. Gilbar and DeNour (30) used the PAIS and the Brief Symptom Inventory to demonstrate marked differences between 53 patients who dropped out of chemotherapy and a matched control group who remained in treatment. Principal differences were observed on the Health Care Orientation and Vocational, Domestic, and Social Environment scales. In an innovative study Friedman and her colleagues (31) related PAIS dimension scores to measures of family type, cohesion, and satisfaction in a sample of 57 women with breast cancer. PAIS scores significantly discriminated between family types and levels of cohesion and showed significant correlations with measures of family satisfaction and adjustment.

In a related study with breast cancer patients, Wolberg et al. (32) contrasted three groups of women with breast disease—benign, unconfirmed malignancy, and confirmed malignancy—at time of initial evaluation. These investigators found that the PAIS successfully discriminated the benign sample from the two cohorts with cancer. Subsequently, those women with neoplasia were offered either mastectomy or surgery with breast conservation procedures. PAIS measures continued to discriminate the benign biopsy sample from the mastectomy and breast conservation samples for up to 16 months postsurgery. Gilbar (33) used the PAIS to evaluate 70 cancer patients who refused treatment with chemotherapy, and compared them with 70 matched patients who participated in the prescribed regimen. Results showed significantly poorer adjustment on six of seven of the PAIS measures among the cohort who refused treatment, with only the Extended Family domain failing to discriminate the groups. In a recent study evaluating the impact of quality of interpersonal communication on adjustment in cancer patients, Gotcher (34) used the PAIS to define adjustment. Discriminant function analyses determined that frequency of interpersonal interaction and level of emotional support were the significant discriminators between those who made "good" versus "poor" adjustments. Also working with cancer patients, both Andrykowski et al. (35) and Jenkins and his colleagues (36) have recently used the PAIS to

evaluate levels of psychosocial morbidity among bone marrow transplant recipients.

Probably, the broadest application of the PAIS and PAIS-SR has come in research on the psychosocial adjustment of cardiac patients. In an innovative study with 410 coronary bypass patients, Folks and his associates (37) demonstrated high predictive validity for the PAIS Sexual Functioning score in predicting postsurgical levels of clinical depression. Using both the Zung and Center for Epidemiologic Studies– Depression scales as measures of depression, this research group demonstrated mean correlations of .30, .45, .53, and .57 between preoperative PAIS Sexual Functioning scores, and depression scores at pre-, 3, 6, and 12 months postbypass. These investigators concluded that they could predict with "80% accuracy who will be at risk for a 'poor' outcome as defined by a PAIS score of <55 preoperatively." The same team of researchers (38) have also used the PAIS to predict adjustment in 19 patients who underwent cardiac transplant. In this study, the PAIS was able to document significant improvements in psychosocial adjustment at both 6 and 12 month posttransplant periods.

Langeluddecke et al. (39) also used the PAIS to evaluate adjustment in 89 Australian coronary artery bypass patients. The study patients were prospectively followed for 1 year following surgery. All seven PAIS domain scores and the PAIS Total Score showed significant improvements in psychosocial adjustment at both 6 and 12 months postsurgery. Reductions in distress were of such a magnitude to carry patients from the clinical range into normative levels of adjustment. In a companion study, Langeluddecke and her colleagues (40) used the PAIS-SR along with other psychological measures to evaluate the adjustment of spouses of coronary artery bypass patients to the index patient's illness. Preoperative evaluations revealed high levels of Psychological Distress and disturbances in Social Environment, with slightly smaller but significant decrements in adjustment on Vocational and Domestic Environment scores, as well as on Sexual Functioning. At 12 months postoperative, significant or near-significant reductions in almost all PAIS domain scores were observed, as was true of independent measures of anxiety and depression.

Hegelson (13,41,42) has used the PAIS extensively to study factors having impact on the adjustment of patients and their spouses experiencing first cardiac events. In an initial study (41), perceived control on the part of patients was evaluated as to its impact on psychosocial adjustment. Results indicated that perceived lack of personal control facilitated adjustment only in instances where the patient underwent invasive procedures. This study also showed that perceived control generally enhanced adjustment under conditions of severe threat (e.g., poor prognosis). In a second study (13) Hegelson evaluated the personality profiles of patient-spouse pairs and how patterns of relationship affected adjustment to a first cardiac event. The PAIS was utilized as the primary measure of psychosocial adjustment. In a third investigation (42), the author studied the influence of perceived social support on adjustment to a first cardiac event. Findings indicated that perceived support was more important than received support in promoting adjustment, and that negative social interactions were a powerful predictor of poor subsequent adjustment.

Shifting focus somewhat from cardiac patients, Powers and Jalowiec (43) used the PAIS in a prediction paradigm related to blood pressure control in a sample of 450 hypertensives. The PAIS was also utilized as a dependent measure of adjustment to illness. Using discriminant function analysis to distinguish controlled from uncontrolled hypertensives, the PAIS Health Care Orientation score demonstrated the highest standardized coefficient in the discrimination. The study boasted an 80% rate of correct classification using the derived predictor variable set.

As mentioned in the previous discussion of convergent validity, Conrady et al. (21) accomplished a unique study with the PAIS-SR and the SCL-90-R concerned with the long-term psychosocial adjustment status of polio survivors. The study evaluated levels of psychological distress and psychosocial adjustment years after the acute illness. Interestingly, high psychological morbidity was demonstrated on the Somatization, Depression, and Anxiety subscales of the SCL-90-R, concomitant with poor adjustment scores on PAIS measures of Health Care Orientation, Social Environment, and Extended Family Relations. Several investigators have used the PAIS to study the postdischarge adjustment of burn patients. Roberts and her colleagues (11) used the PAIS to evaluate relationships between quality of adjustment and coping styles in a sample of 260 burn patients. The PAIS Total Score and the Psychological Distress score were used as dependent criterion variables in multiple regression models that fit various sets of coping variables as predictors. Roca et al. (44) also used the PAIS as a primary outcome criterion with burn patients at a 4-month follow-up assessment. These authors found significant relationships between PAIS scores and a number of injury-specific, treatment, and patient personality variables. Facial and significant genital involvement in the burns were significantly related to decrements on the Social Environment and Sexual Functioning domain scores. Delirium during treatment was a significant determinant of poorer scores in both Domestic and Vocational domains, and length of hospitalization correlated substantially ($r = .63$ and $r = .73$, respectively) with these two PAIS measures.

In an interesting clinical study with pain patients, Crook et al. (45) used the PAIS to contrast pain sufferers from a family practice clinic with those from a specialty pain clinic and evaluate the impact of differential coping styles. With the exception of Sexual Functioning, all PAIS measures showed significantly higher scores for the specialty clinic patients (i.e., poorer psychosocial adjustment) than for the family practice patients, while there were no significant differences between the samples on coping measures. Weir and her associates (12) also studied specialty pain clinic patients using the PAIS, and did extremely comprehensive analyses

of utilization patterns and costs associated with varying levels of adjustment. Using sophisticated analytic algorithms, these investigators showed that the 80% of the patients in the "fair" and "poor" adjustment groups account for 90% of the costs of total health care use. Compared with other chronic illness groups, however, the chronic pain group evidenced three to five times lower direct and indirect costs.

Diabetes is another chronic illness in which psychological and social adjustment play an extremely key role in determining the patient's quality of life, sometimes over very long periods. Proliferative diabetic retinopathy (PDR) is one of the very difficult complications of the disease that can greatly tax adjustment. Derogatis et al. (46) evaluated psychological adjustment in diabetic patients with and without evidence of advanced PDR and observed significant differences across a number of domains of adjustment. More recently, Wulsin et al. (47) also evaluated the specific adjustment problems associated with advanced PDR. They reported this patient group to have significant elevations on all PAIS measures in comparison to the diabetes normative group, with particular problems in the area of Health Care Orientation. They also observed significant correlations between PAIS Total Score, four of seven PAIS domain scores, and visual acuity in the best eye.

Other illness groups in which the PAIS or PAIS-SR have been reported as sensitive outcome measures include gastrointestinal disorders, in which the PAIS was shown to discriminate between a group with functional dyspepsia versus a duodenal ulcer group (48), and adult cystic fibrosis (49) patients, where the instrument clearly discriminated between "good" and "poor" copers. Individual items of the Psychological Distress scale were particularly effective in this regard.

The breadth and scope of the diverse body of research reviewed here provides strong confirmation of the validity of the PAIS and PAIS-SR. Studies showing the instruments' sensitivity to an impressive array of personal, illness-induced, and treatment-related effects, across a variety of distinct disorders, tends to promote confidence in the PAIS and PAIS-SR measurement system. As the PAIS/PAIS-SR are utilized with more diverse illness groups, it is hoped such demonstrations will continue to expand the network of valid predictive relationships and their generalizability and enable more investigators to utilize them. The research alluded to above has progressed well beyond the initial phases of validation and now represents a substantive body of empirical data supporting the sensitivity and construct validity of the instruments.

INTERPRETATION

The PAIS and PAIS-SR are designed to be interpreted at three distinct but related levels: the *global* level, the *domain* level, and the *discrete item* level. Ideally, data from each of the three levels of interpretation should converge to deliver an integrated picture of the respondent's adjustment to the illness or condition of note. The PAIS Total Score, particularly when evaluated in terms of a relevant normative group, often provides a good indicator of the level of the patient's overall adjustment. Domain scores contribute a profile of areas of relative strength and vulnerability in the patient's adjustment. Discrete items from the test often communicate important specifics about coping with the illness experience that can serve to highlight unique aspects of the patient's adjustment to illness.

The PAIS and PAIS-SR are equally applicable as point-in-time measures, or sequential assessments of a patient's continuing course of adjustment. We hope to soon provide *change norms* for the instruments that will standardize increments of change in adjustment status for major illness groups. The fact that slight alterations in format enable the assessment of not only a respondent's perception of his/her adjustment but also the perceptions of spouses, parents, and other relatives concerning the respondent's adjustment, as well as their own adjustments to the respondent's illness, makes for an extremely flexible system of measurement. In addition, the PAIS/PAIS-SR are available in a number of foreign language translations. Specifically, one or another of the instruments are published in Italian, Spanish, Portuguese, Hebrew, Danish, Norwegian, French, Japanese, Chinese, and Korean. Evidence accrued so far suggests that the PAIS/PAIS-SR can be a valid and extremely useful means of defining and quantifying adjustment to illness. As our research and the research of other investigators in this area continue we believe the validation and development of the PAIS/PAIS-SR will see further gains and improvements.

CONCLUSIONS

The PAIS/PAIS-SR represents a multidimensional psychometric definition of the construct of adjustment to illness that ties the construct very closely to the functional efficiencies of primary social role behaviors. The guiding philosophy behind the development of the PAIS/PAIS-SR treats illnesses as distinct and specific entities each of which calls for its own distinct norms. Ultimately, particularly in the case of many chronic illnesses, norms by stage or phase of disease will be available. The PAIS/PAIS-SR system is designed to allow assessment based on either clinical judgment or self-report, and is sufficiently flexible to enable multiple respondents. Because of its design, not only can the nature of the index patient's adjustment be established from multiple perspectives, but the adjustment of significant others (e.g., spouses, children, caregivers) to the index patient's illness may also be assessed. With a systematic expansion of foreign translations, further development of computer administration and scoring software, and a vigorous ongoing program of validation studies, the PAIS/PAIS-SR promises to be an even more useful system in the future for the assessment of adjustment to illness.

ACKNOWLEDGMENT

The publisher of the PAIS & PAIS-SR is Clinical Psychometric Research, 100 West Pennsylvania Ave., Suite 302, Towson MD, 21204.

REFERENCES

1. Weissman MM. The assessment of social adjustment: a review of techniques. *Arch Gen Psychiatry* 1975;32:357–365.
2. Weissman MM, Sholomskas D, John K. The assessment of social adjustment: an update. *Arch Gen Psychiatry* 1981;38:1250–1258.
3. DeNour AK. Psychosocial Adjustment to Illness Scale (PAIS): a study of chronic hemodialysis patients. *J Psychosom Res* 1982;26(1):11–22.
4. Murawski BJ, Penman D, Schmitt M. Social support in health and illness: the concept and its measurement. *Cancer Nurs* 1978;1:365–371.
5. Zysanski SJ, Stanton BA, Kahn MD. Medical and social outcome in survivors of major heart surgery. *J Psychosom Res* 1981;23:213–221.
6. Derogatis LR, Derogatis MF. *The psychosocial adjustment to illness scale (PAIS) & (PAIS-SR): administration, scoring & procedures manual-II, 2nd ed.* Baltimore: Clinical Psychometric Research, 1992.
7. Derogatis LR, Lipman RS, Rickell K, Uhlenjuth EH, Covi L. The Hopkins Symptom Checklist (HSCL): a self-report symptom inventory. *Behav Sci* 1974;19:1–15.
8. Derogatis LR. Self-report measures of stress. In: Goldberger L, Breznitz S, eds. *Handbook of stress.* New York: Free Press, 1982.
9. Wilde GTS. Trait description and measurement by personality questionnaires. In: Cattell RB, ed. *Handbook of modern personality theory.* Chicago: Aldine, 1972.
10. Nunnally JC. *Psychometric theory,* 2nd ed. New York: McGraw-Hill, 1978.
11. Roberts JG, Browne G, Streiner D, Byrne C, Brown B, Love B. Analyses of coping responses and adjustment: stability of conclusions. *Nurs Res* 1978;36(2):94–97.
12. Weir R, Browne GB, Tunks E, Gafni A, Roberts J. A profile of users of specialty pain clinic services: predictors of use and cost estimates. *J Clin Epidemiol* 1992;45(12):1399–1415.
13. Helgeson VS. Implications of agency and communion for patient and spouse adjustment to a first coronary event. *J Pers Soc Psychol* 1993;64(5):807–816.
14. Nunnally JC. An overview of psychological measurement. In: Wolman B, ed. *Clinical diagnosis of mental disorders: a handbook.* New York: Plenum Press, 1978.
15. Messick S. Constructs and their vicissitudes in educational and psychological measurement. *Psychol Bull* 1981;89:575–588.
16. Morrow GR, Chiarello RJ, Derogatis LR. A new scale for assessing patient's psychosocial adjustment to medical illness. *Psychol Med* 1978;8:605–610.
17. DeNour AK. Social adjustment of chronic dialysis patients. *Am J Psychiatry* 1982;139(1):97–99.
18. Freeman AM, Fahs JJ, Kolks DG, Sokol RS. Cardiac transplantation: clinical correlates of psychiatric outcome. *Psychosomatics* 1988;29(1):47–54.
19. Hochberg MC, Sutton JD. Physical disability and psycho-social dysfunction in systemic lupus erythematosus. *J Rheumatol* 1988;15:959–964.
20. Moguliner ME, Bauman A, DeNour AK. The adjustment of children and parents to chronic hemodialysis. *Psychosomatics* 1988;29(3):289–294.
21. Conrady LJ, Wish JR, Agre JC, Rodriguez AA, Sperlin G, Keith BS. Psychological characteristics of polio survivors: a preliminary report. *Arch Phys Med Rehabil* 1989;70:458.
22. Derogatis LR, Spencer PM. Psychometric issues in the psychological assessment of the cancer patient. *Cancer* 1984;53:2228–2234.
23. Derogatis LR, DellaPietra L. Psychological tests in screening for psychiatric disorder. In: Maruish M, ed. *Psychological testing, treatment planning and outcome assessment.* New York: Lawrence Erlbaum, 1994.

24. DeNour AK. Psychosocial adjustment to illness scale (PAIS): a study of chronic hemodialysis patients. *J Psychosomatic Res* 1982;26(1):11–22.
25. Murphy SP. Factors influencing adjustment and quality of life: a multivariate approach. Doctoral Dissertation, University of Illinois Medical Center, Chicago, 1982.
26. Kaye J, Bray S, Gracely EJ, Levison S. Psychosocial adjustment to illness and family environment in dialysis patients. *Fam Sys Med* 1989;7(1):77–89.
27. Lamping DL. Psychosocial adaptation and adjustment to the stress of chronic illness. Doctoral Dissertation. Harvard University, Cambridge, 1981.
28. Oldenberg B, MacDonald GJ, Perkins RJ. Prediction of quality of life in a cohort of end-stage renal disease patients. *J Clin Epidemiol* 1988;41(60):555–564.
29. Evans DL, McCartney CF, Haggerty JJ, Nemeroff C, Golden RN, Simon JB, Quade D, Holmes V, Droba M, Mason GA, Fowler C, Raft D. Treatment of depression in cancer patients is associated with better life adaptation: a pilot study. *Psychosom Med* 1988;50:72–76.
30. Gilbar O, DeNour AK. Adjustment to illness and dropout of chemotherapy. *J Psychosom Res* 1989;33(1):1–5.
31. Friedman LC, Baer PE, Nelson DV, Lane M, Smith FE, Dworkin RJ. Women with breast cancer: perception of family functioning and adjustment to illness. *Psychosom Med* 1988;50(3):529–540.
32. Wolberg WH, Tanner MA, Malec JF, Tomsaas EP. Psychosexual adaptation to breast-cancer surgery. *Cancer* 1989;63(8):1645–1655.
33. Gilbar O. Who refuses chemotherapy? a profile. *Psychol Rep* 1989;64:1291–1297.
34. Gotcher JM. Interpersonal communication and psychosocial adjustment. *J Psychosoc Oncol* 1992;10(3):21–39.
35. Andrykowski MA, Altmaier EM, Barnett RL, Burnish TG, Gingrich R, Henslee-Downey PJ. Cognitive dysfunction in adult survivors of allogenic marrow transportation: relationship to dose of total body irradiation. *Bone Marrow Transplant* 1990;6:269–276.
36. Jenkins PL, Lester H, Alexander J, Whittaker J. A prospective study of psychological morbidity in adult bone marrow transplant recipients. *Psychosomatics* 1994;35(4):361–367.
37. Folks DG, Baker DM, Blake DJ, Freeman AM, Sokol RS. Persistent depression in coronary-bypass patients reporting sexual maladjustment. *Psychosomatics* 1988;29(4):387–391.
38. Folks DG, Blake DJ, Fleece L, Sokol RS, Freeman AM. Quality of life six months after coronary artery bypass surgery; a preliminary report. *South Med J* 1986;79:397.
39. Langeluddecke P, Baird D, Hughes C, Tennant C, Fulcher G. A perspective evaluation of the psychosocial effects of coronary artery bypass-surgery. *J Psychosom Res* 1989;33(1):37–45.
40. Langeluddecke P, Tennant C, Fulcher G, Baird D, Hughes C. Coronary artery bypass surgery: impact upon the patient's spouse. *J Psychosom Res* 1989;33(2):155–159.
41. Helgeson VS, Vicki S. Moderators of the relation between perceived control and adjustment to chronic illness. *J Pers Soc Psychol* 1992;63(4):656–666.
42. Helgeson VS. Two important distinctions in social support: kind of support and perceived versus received. *J Appl Soc Psychol* 1993;23(10):825–845.
43. Powers MJ, Jalowec A. A profile of the well-controlled well-adjusted hypertensive patient. *Nurs Res* 1987;36(2):106.
44. Roca RP, Spence RJ, Munster AM. Posttraumatic adaptation and distress among adult burn survivors. *Am J Psychiatry* 1992;149(9):1234–1228.
45. Crook J, Kalaher S, Roberts J, Tunks E. Coping with persistent pain: a comparison of persistent pain sufferers in specialty pain clinics and in a family practice. *Pain* 1988;34(2):175–184.
46. Derogatis LR, Georgopolous A, Saudek CD. Psychological factors predictive of glycemic control in diabetics on insulin pump therapy. Presented at the 46th Annual Meeting and Scientific Session of the American Diabetes Association, Anaheim, CA, June 22–24, 1986.
47. Wulsin LR, Jacobson AM, Rand LI. Psychosocial adjustment to advanced proliferative diabetic retinopathy. *Diabetes Care* 1993;16(8):1061–1066.
48. Haug TT, Svebak S, Wilhelmsen I, Berstad A, Ursin H. Psychological factors and somatic symptoms in functional dyspepsia. A comparison with duodenal ulcer and healthy controls. *J Psychosom Res* 1994;38(4):281–291.
49. Pinkerton P, Duncan F, Trauewr T, Hodson ME, Batten JC. Cystic fibrosis in adult life: a study of coping patterns. *Lancet* 1985;2:761–763.

Quality of Life and Pharmacoeconomics in Clinical Trials, Second Edition, edited by B. Spilker. Lippincott-Raven Publishers, Philadelphia © 1996.

CHAPTER 31

Quality of Life–Cancer

Geraldine V. Padilla, Marcia M. Grant, Betty R. Ferrell, and Cary A. Presant

INTRODUCTION AND DEFINITIONS OF QUALITY OF LIFE

The multidimensional Quality of Life (QOL) scale evolved from a need for a single, short, easy to administer, reliable, and valid graphic measure of well-being in persons with cancer. The authors conceptualize quality of life as "a personal statement of the positivity or negativity of attributes that characterize one's life" (1,2). This definition indicates that quality of life is a subjective, multidimensional construct that likely includes health as a relevant construct at some point in a person's life. For example, some people in very good health may not consider health when evaluating their quality of life; rather, they may focus on friendships, financial success, and their feeling of satisfaction with their life. Others, confronted by acute or chronic illness, will likely attribute certain dimensions of life quality to health-related outcomes.

Based on this definition of quality of life, the authors further clarify health-related quality of life (HRQL) as a four-dimensional construct of well-being. The model includes physical well-being and associated symptom distress, and psychological, social, and existential/spiritual well-being (3–7).

G. V. Padilla: School of Nursing, University of California at Los Angeles, Los Angeles, California 90095.

M. M. Grant and B. R. Ferrel: Department of Nursing Research and Education, City of Hope National Medical Center, Duarte, California 91010.

C. A. Presant: California Cancer Medical Center, West Covina, California 91790.

Existential/spiritual well-being refers to the meaning that disease and treatment impart to one's life, feelings of hope/despair, personal beliefs, religiosity, and inner strength (7).

Quality of life is viewed as a dynamic construct affected by one's ability to adapt in the face of discrepancies between expected and experienced well-being. HRQL is determined by the manner in which changes in health, particularly disease severity, comorbid conditions, and treatment-related symptoms affect the similarity or discrepancy between expectations and experiences surrounding the four dimensions of well-being (8). Based on past conceptualizations (1–9), the authors currently define HRQL as a personal, evaluative statement summarizing the positivity or negativity of attributes that characterize one's psychological, physical, social, and spiritual well-being at a point in time when health, illness, and treatment conditions are relevant.

This view of HRQL as a subjective, multidimensional experience is supported by other investigators. For example, Gill and Feinstein (10) describe quality of life as "a uniquely personal perception, denoting the way that individual patients feel about their health status and/or nonmedical aspects of their lives." The Division of Mental Health of the World Health Organization (11) defined quality of life as "an individual's perception of their position in life in the context of the culture and value systems in which they live and in relation to their goals, expectations, standards and concerns." Further efforts to develop an operational definition of quality of life that reflect health concerns led to this definition: "Health-related quality of life is the value assigned to duration of life as modified by the impairments, functional states, perceptions and social opportunities influenced by disease, injury, treatment or policy" (12).

THE QUALITY OF LIFE SCALE

The Quality of Life (QOL) scale derived from pilot experiments performed between 1979 and 1981 (13). It was originally termed the *Quality of Life Index* (QLI) when it was published in 1983 (14). Ferrell and colleagues (15) then used the name *City of Hope Medical Center Quality of Life Survey*. Padilla and colleagues (8) changed the name to the *Multidimensional Quality of Life Scale* (MQOLS) to differentiate the instrument from Ferrans and Powers' (16) QLI published in 1985 and Spitzer et al's. (17) QL-Index published in 1981. Recently, the name was simplified to the QOL scale. The QLI/MQOLS/QOL has undergone a number of revisions. It is available in generic versions (14,15,18–20) and population-specific versions for persons with colostomies (21,22), persons receiving radiation for cancers of the pelvis (23,24) and head and neck area (9,24), persons with gynecological cancer (8,9), survivors of bone marrow transplantation (3), and family caregivers of persons with cancer pain (4,5,25). Versions of the QOL focusing on breast cancer and cancer survivors are being tested.

The generic version of the multidimensional QOL scale used to measure HRQL in persons with a variety of cancer diagnoses undergoing different types of treatments is called the Quality of Life–Cancer Scale (QOL scale). This chapter describes the development of the basic 30-item QOL-CA instrument into its two current versions: the QOL (19) and QOL-CA (20).

CONCEPT AND THEORY DEVELOPMENT STUDIES BEHIND THE QOL SCALE

In-depth face-to-face interviews with 41 cancer patients with pain revealed the following dynamics about the meaning of quality of life and the impact of pain on activities to maintain or improve it. Patients adjust their quality of life expectations based on perceived health and function (1). For example, patients talk about making the best of life, refocusing life, planning one day at a time, and being active during good days. Patients readjust their definition of enjoying life to include those activities that still offer pleasure and happiness such as being alive, appreciating surroundings, doing what one wants to do. Patients also tend to narrow their focus of concern to currently relevant attributes of quality of life. For the 41 patients with cancer-related pain, controlling pain was critical to improving their quality of life (1). This study supports a three-dimensional model of HRQL (physical well-being including symptom distress, psychological well-being including spiritual and existential aspects of quality of life, and interpersonal well-being). The study also suggested that people perceive the discrepancies that mark the quality of their lives, identify the sources of these discrepancies, and engage in adaptive activities to reduce discrepancies.

A second study of 119 bone marrow transplant survivors asked six open-ended questions about the meaning of quality of life and how the bone marrow transplant procedure affected quality of life (6,7). Content analysis of the responses yielded nine themes in relation to the meaning of quality of life: being physically, mentally, and spiritually healthy; having a heightened appreciation for life; having family and relationships; being normal; being satisfied and fulfilled with life; being able to work/financial success; being independent; being alive; and having self-esteem and self-respect. In response to the query about how the bone marrow transplant procedure affected quality of life, nine themes emerged: second chance given; opportunity to improve quality of life given; increased appreciation of life and relationships; numerous side effects; spirituality increased; strength and stamina decreased; work/activities limited; infertility resulted; and fear of relapse present. In answer to the question what makes quality of life better, six themes were apparent: having good health; having family and friends; being alive and appreciating life; having a positive attitude/peace of mind; having a job/money; having goals and being productive. The things that made life worse were described as: experiencing physical losses, losing relationships, having unfulfilled goals, and being financially (job, money) distressed (6,7). This second study validated the themes found in the previous investigation (1) and reinforced a four-dimensional model of HRQL (physical, psychological, social, spiritual well-being).

A study of 100 women with gynecological cancer yielded some support for conceptualizing health-related quality of life as the outcome of an adaptation process explained by the uncertainty in illness theory (8). Mishel (26) describes uncertainty as the inability to determine the meaning of illness-related events. However, since uncertainty in illness explained only 56% of the variance in the total quality of life score, additional work is required. The view of quality of life as the result of the degree of discrepancy between expectations and experiences concerning quality of life attributes may be a useful framework for predicting HRQL outcomes with greater accuracy when combined with the uncertainty in illness theory. By identifying the cognitive, adaptive mechanisms at work to close a perceived gap in an attribute of quality of life that is relevant to the individual, one should be able to predict or improve HRQL in a systematic manner.

RESPONSE SCALES AND SCORING SCHEMES

A variety of response scales have been used to measure quality of life. The Karnofsky scale measures performance on a scale from 100 = normal to 0 = dead in increments of 10 (27,28). Flanagan (29) used the critical incident technique. Kaplan et al. (30,31) use mortality and morbidity data to express health status as equivalents of well-years of life. Picture charts have been used to measure functional status

(32,33). Stewart and Ware (34), Ferrans and Powers (35), Schag and colleagues (36), Stewart et al. (37), and Cella and colleagues (38), to name a few, use the popular Likert scale. Linear analog scales are useful because they provide graphic representations of subjective states on continuous scales, responses may be normally distributed, and scales are usually reliable and valid (39).

The QLI/MQOLS/QOL uses linear analog scales as the basis for respondents to rate their own, or someone else's, quality of life. Originally, the instrument used unnumbered, 100-mm lines anchored at each end with an extreme positive or negative rating as the response mode for questions about physical, psychological, and social well-being or symptom distress. Existential/spiritual well-being items were not included in the early questionnaires. Example:

How good is your quality of life?
Extremely poor 0 _____ (100 mm) _____ 100 Excellent

The 0 end of the scale indicates poorest outcome, while the 100 end indicates the best outcome. Some items are scored from left to right and some, in reverse, from right to left depending on which end indicates the poorest outcome. An alternative scheme is to score all items from left to right and then subtract from 100 the score for items with the poor quality of life response on the right. QOL total or subscale scores are obtained by adding item scores and dividing by the total number of items in the scale. The range of scores possible for both the total and subscale scores is 0 (poorest quality of life–related outcome) to 100 (best quality of life–related outcome).

One recent version focusing on ostomy patients uses a linear scale with numbers from 0 to 5 appearing along the line at equal intervals (22). This instrument has a French translation. Another tool, addressing bone marrow transplant survivors, uses the numbers 1 and 10 to anchor a line notched at equal intervals (3). Example:

How good is your quality of life?
Extremely poor 0 _| | | | | | |_ 10 Excellent

RELIABILITY AND VALIDITY STUDIES

It is not possible to provide information about all the studies that have tested the QLI/MQOLS/QOL in its various diagnosis-specific forms. Table 1 summarizes the work on the most generic versions that would be applicable to a wide variety of cancer diagnoses (40). Presant and his colleagues (13) developed the original quality of life questionnaire using linear scales. The second version expanded the number of items to 14 linear scales measuring three facets of QOL: psychological well-being (general quality of life, fun, satisfaction with life, usefulness, sleep), physical well-being (strength, appetite, work, eating, sex), and symptom distress (pain, nausea, vomiting) (14,21). Subsequent versions utilized between 21 to 30 items (Table 1).

The information in Table 1 indicates that each of the different versions yielded an instrument with satisfactory levels of internal consistency for the total scale and for the major subscales identified: physical, psychological, social, spiritual/existential, and/or symptom-related subscales. Factor analytic, multitrait-multimethod, and contrasting groups construct validity as well as criterion-related concurrent validity were found for the various questionnaires. A word of caution: The number of items and wording of some items differs across the assorted versions of the scale. Likewise, the subscales in the different studies contain some similar and some dissimilar items. Therefore, subscales are not strictly comparable. Item by item comparisons may be more accurate.

The QOL and QOL-CA are two recent versions of the scale. They differ in two items. The QOL-CA includes items concerning "discouraged . . . life not worthwhile" and "hopeful things will improve." The QOL incorporates items that asked about "sufficient support from others" and "feel in control of things." The 30-item QOL instrument was used in a recently completed intervention study on the management of cancer pain in 80 subjects receiving care at home (19). The QOL-CA scale was used in a study of a heterogeneous group of 227 cancer patients discharged to home care (20). Both instruments use 100-mm linear scales anchored at each end with a descriptor that indicates the poorest quality of life outcome (0), and the best outcome (100). Items 1, 2, 5, 6, 7, 9, 12, 13, 14, 16, 17, 18, 20, 21, 22, 23, 28, and 29 are scored from left (0) to right (100), while items 3R, 4R, 8R, 10R, 11R, 15R, 19R, 24R, 25R, 26R, 27R, and 30R are scored in reverse from right (0) to left (100).

Table 2 lists each QOL-CA subscale, the items in each subscale, and the item loading on the factor that defines the subscale. The QOL is not included in Table 2 since factor loadings are not available (19). As in other studies (9), a principal component, varimax rotation factor analytic strategy was used for the QOL-CA scores. A comparison of the factor loadings for the QOL-CA data (20) and studies of the other versions of the scale (QLI/MQOLS) (6) reveal some variation in factor definition across studies, as well as some highly consistent structural patterns.

Factor f1 is consistently defined by four psychological well-being items: enjoy life (fun), feel happy, have a satisfying life, and have a good quality of life. In addition, the QOL-CA data show the first factor to be a complex one. It includes psychosocial items (adjust to disease/treatment, sufficient affection given/received, disease/treatment interferes with personal relationships), and existential items (discouraged . . . life not worth living, worried about outcome of disease/treatment, hopeful things will improve). Hence, the Psychosocial-Existential subscale for the QOL-CA consists of 11 items including the question of sleep (numbers 1, 2, 6, 7, 8R, 9, 10R, 11R, 16, 17, and 20). This factor is the most important in defining HRQL. The item concerning

TABLE 1. *Development of the Quality of Life–Cancer Scale (QOL-CA) (aka QLI/MQOLS/QOL)*

Scales, items, measurement times, sample	Reliability	Validity
QLI-Ca (9,14) 14 items; QLI measured once; total $n = 255$; (48 chemo inpts, 43 chemo outpts, 39 RT outpts, 48 nonpts with varied Dx, 77 diabetic females)	*Test-retest r's* for 14 items from .11 to .97 with 52 of 56 item r's ≥ .60 *Internal consistency:* alpha .88 for total scale	*Factor analytic construct validity:* four factors (psychological, physical, symptoms, financial) *Contrasting groups construct validity:* Nonpts have significantly better scores than chemo inpts for 12 of 14 items; than chemo and RT outpts for 9 of 14 items; and chemo outpts have significantly better scores than RT outpts for 4 of 14 items; chemo inpts and RT outpts taking no pain drugs have better symptom control than those taking pain drugs; diabetic outpts score better than cancer inpts and poorer than nonpts on three subscales and total QLI-Ca score *Concurrent validity:* significant r (.36, .49, .40) between MD ratings of patients' quality of life and patients' QLI-Ca physical well-being subscale score
QLI-RT (9,23,24) 21 items; QLI measured 3 times: $n = 186$ RT week 1; $n = 174$ RT week 3; $n = 146$ RT 1st FU; Factor analysis $n = 85$ at RT week 1; regression analysis $N = 101$ (sample of patients with CA pelvic area)	*Internal consistency:* thetas for total scale: RT week 1 = .86 RT week 3 = .90 RT FU week = .92 *Internal consistency:* alphas at RT FU; subscales: psychol .87, physical .87, symptoms .86, sex .97, worry over cost .42	*Factor analytic construct validity:* five factors (psychological, physical, symptoms, sexual activity, worry over weight and cost of RT) *Concurrent validity:* Significant r's of .58 between tension-anxiety and psychological well-being subscale; and .60 between fatigue and physical well-being subscale
QLI-RT (9,24) 21 items; QLI measured 6 times: $n = 181$ RT week 1; $n = 176$ RT week 3; $n = 156$ end of RT; $n = 129$ RT 1st FU; $n = 109$ 3 mo. FU; $N = 82$ 18 mo. FU; factor analysis $n = 110$ at RT week 1 (sample of pts. CA of head and neck)	*Internal consistency:* theta .88 total scale	*Factor analytic construct validity:* six factors (psychological, physical, nutrition and pain distress, other symptom distress, sleep and worry over cost, treatment anxiety-adjustment)
QLI-Pain (9,15) 28 items: QLI measured once: $n = 150$ (3 groups 50 each: Ca + pain, Ca + no pain, no Ca + no pain)	*Internal consistency:* alphas total scale .88; subscales: psychol .69, physical .74, symptoms .75, social .65	*Content validity* index from panel of experts .90 *Factor analytic construct validity:* nine factors (psychological, worry, nutrition, pain, mobility, esteem, strength, finance, fatigue) *Contrasting groups construct validity:* Ca pts with pain had significantly lower total and subscale scores than the other two groups, $p < .006$. *Concurrent validity:* the total QLI-Pain score correlated significantly with the McGill Present Pain Intensity scale (.54) and the Karnofsky scale (.59); individual QLI-pain distress and amount items correlated significantly with McGill Present Pain Intensity scale (.62, .73) and the Karnofsky scale (.64, .63).
QLI-Pain (46) 28 items; QLI measured 4 times: $n = 83$ (random assignment of 41 to short-acting, 42 to controlled release analgesia)	*Internal consistency:* alphas total scale .82; subscales: psychol .62, physical .72, symptoms .63, social .68; *test-retest r* .60	*Factor analytic construct validity* confirmed previous study findings (15): nine factors (psychological, worry, nutrition, pain, mobility, esteem, strength, finance, fatigue)
QLI/MQOLS-CA (8,9) 24 items: QOL measured once: $n = 100$ Gyn Ca; Dx <12 mos	*Internal consistency:* theta .88 total scale	*Factor analytic construct validity:* five factors (psychological, physical, symptoms-side effects, nutrition, social-financial)
QOL (6,7,19) 30-item pt version $n = 80$ (elderly Ca pts with pain)	*Internal Consistency:* alphas total scale = .82; subscales: psychol .82, physical .62, social .53, spiritual .49	*Content Validity:* four subscales based on content analysis of patient responses to questions about the meaning of quality of life, impact of disease on quality of life, what makes quality of life better or worse (1,6,7); subscales identified are psychological, physical, social, and spiritual well-being
QOL-CA (20) 30 items; QOL measured once: total $n = 227$ (CA patients receiving home care)	*Internal consistency:* alphas total scale .91; subscales: psychosocial-existential .88, physical function .80, symptom distress (combined) .77; nutrition .77; pain/bowel pattern .68; worry .52	*Content validity:* items supported by content analysis of patient responses to questions about quality of life (1) *Factor analytic construct validity:* five factors [psychosocial-existential well-being, physical function well-being, symptom distress—nutrition, symptom distress—pain/fatigue (two factors combined to form one subscale), worry attitude *Multitrait-multimethod construct validity:* highest, significant correlations found between patient/nurse ratings on the OARS Multidimensional Functional Assessment Questionnaire (OMFAQ) (47,48) and similar concepts on the QOL-CA2 subscale scores, while lower r's found between unlike concepts in the two instruments: (a) OMFAQ pts rated social resources, interference of health problems with activities, and poorness of general health r highest with QOL-CA2 psychosocial-existential well-being (.32, −.23, −.49); (b) pt rated ADL r highest with pt rated QOL-CA2 physical function (.33); (c) OMFAQ RN ratings of patients' social resources r highest with pt rated QOL-CA2 psychosocial-existential well-being (.20); (d) OMFAQ RN ratings of poorness of physical health r highest with QOL

From ref. 40.

Ca, cancer; Dx, diagnosis; chemo, chemotherapy; RT, radiation therapy; pt(s), patient(s); inpts, inpatients; outpts, outpatients; ADL, Activities of Daily Living; FU, follow-up.

TABLE 2. *Factor loadings for the QOL-CA scale in a home care sample*

Scales and items[a]	QOL-CA home care (*n* = 227)
Factor 1: Psychosocial-Existential Well-Being	
1. Adjust to disease/treatment?	.61
2. Enjoy life (fun)?	.74
6. Feel happy?	.74
7. Have satisfying life?	.76
8R. Discouraged . . . life not worthwhile?	−.62
9. Sufficient affection given/received?	.61
10R. Disease interferes with personal relationships?	−.52
11R. Worried about outcome of disease?	−.61
16. Sufficient sleep?	.48
17. Good quality of life?	.66
20. Hopeful things will improve?	.53
Factor 2: Physical-Functional Well-Being	
5. Feel useful	.52
12. Do things you like	.49
13. Able to pay attention	.48
14. Strength	.42
15R. Tire easily	−.22
18. Able to care for personal needs?	.72
28. Able to get around?	.65
29. Satisfied with appearance?	.49
Factor 3/4: Symptom Distress: Nutrition, Pain/Fatigue	
4R. Distress from pain	.66 f4
19R. How much pain?	.80 f4
21. Appetite?	−.51 f3
22. Bowel pattern	−.40 f4
23. Eat sufficient?	−.48 f3
25R. Nausea (distress)?	.85 f3
26R. Vomit (distress)?	.78 f3
27R. Taste changes?	.69 f3
Factor 5: Attitude of Worry	
3R. Worry about cost?	.65
24R. Worry about weight?	.63
30R. Worry about unfinished business	.49

From ref. 40.

[a]Item numbers correspond to numbers as they appear in the QOL-CA scale (20). Numbers with "R" mean the item is scored in reverse.

sufficient sleep may need to be reworded or deleted since it sometimes defines psychological well-being and other times loads on other factors.

Factor f2 is most consistently defined by items concerned with physical-functional well-being: feel useful, do things you like, able to pay attention, strength, and tire easily. While strength and tire easily did not load highly on factor 2 for the QOL-CA study (Table 2), it did so for other studies (9). Additionally, the QOL-CA data include new items related to function: able to care for personal needs, able to get around, satisfied with appearance. The QOL-CA physical-functional well-being subscale consists of eight items (numbers 5, 12, 13, 14, 15R, 18, 28, and 29).

Factors f3 and f4 consistently define aspects of symptom distress. These symptoms focus on nutrition (appetite, eat sufficient, nausea distress, vomiting distress), and pain distress. Furthermore, QOL-CA data include items pertaining to taste changes, amount of pain, and bowel patterns. These two factors are collapsed into one eight-item symptom distress scale (numbers 4R, 19R, 21, 22, 23, 25R, 26R, and 27R).

After factor f4, there is poor consistency in factor structure across studies. Only worry about cost consistently appears in factor 5. Items containing the word *worry* may need to be reworded, since these conceptually different items cluster together. Insofar as the QOL-CA factor loadings are concerned, the items that define the attitude of worry subscale are worry about cost (3R), weight (24R), and unfinished business (30R).

The factors achieved with the orthogonal rotation method do not strictly support the four-dimensional model of HRQL espoused by the investigators. (Oblique rotations may have supported the four-dimensional model, but they were not pursued in an effort to maintain independence between factors.) Nevertheless, the original model of psychological, physical, social, and spiritual well-being is useful for generating items, assessing patient needs, and planning clinical interventions. Health care providers are accustomed to addressing patient needs in these familiar clusters. For this reason, subscale scores that reflect the four-dimensional model are recommended if they are reliable and valid using other forms of construct and concurrent validity.

There is support for a simpler three-dimensional model. The first dimension embraces the nonphysical attributes of perceived well-being, namely the psychosocial-existential dimension. The second dimension encompasses the physical-functional attributes of HRQL, and the third dimension addresses disease/treatment specific symptom distress. The three-dimensional model may be useful for testing interventions that examine the effect of the physical function and symptom distress areas of HRQL on the nonphysical aspects of HRQL. Since nutrition items consistently cluster together, while pain, fatigue, and other side effects cluster together, investigators who are specifically interested in nutrition may want to split the third subscale into two: nutrition (items 21, 23, 25R, 26R, and 27R) and pain/other symptoms (items 4R, 19R, and 22).

SCORES ON THE QOL-CA AND OTHER QOL SCALES

Data from the studies listed in Table 1 show that subjects use the whole 100-mm scale for most items. However, the majority of responses fall between the 25- to 75-mm range for persons with cancer. This could indicate (a) a reluctance to use the lower and upper ends of the scale; (b) biased samples of patients whose quality of life was not poor enough or good enough to be scored in the extremes; (c) accidental exclusion of patients with the poorest quality of life who may have been too sick to participate in the studies, and those with the best quality of life who do not have cancer; and/or (d) a tendency for some patients to "save" the poor quality of life end of the scales for later use when they expect things will be worse. It is important to investigate this occurrence, particularly in light of the fact that some of the poorest scores are consistently due to the items "tire easily" and "strength," common reasons for not participating in the studies, for missing data collection sessions, or for dropping out of the studies.

Table 3 lists the mean scores for items that are very similar or exactly the same in more than one version of the instrument, i.e., the QOL-CA, QOL, QLI-RT, MQOLS. The item concerning sleep is not included because of its failure to fit well with any one subscale. Only the item about emesis elicited a mean score over 80. All other scores were under 80, with most scores falling between 50 and 80. The poorest scores across groups, ranging from 31 to 58, concerned fatigue—"tire easily" and "strength." Moderately low scores were also revealed for "working at usual tasks," "feeling useful," "worrying about cost," "enjoying life," "worrying about the outcome of disease/treatment," and "experiencing distress from pain." Items with mean score ranges greater than 20 mm concern "satisfying life," "sufficient sexual activity," "good quality of life," "appetite," and "distress from pain." Items with narrow mean score ranges are "work at usual tasks," "nausea," and "worry about cost." Not surprisingly, elderly patients with pain report the poorest quality of life across all the items (19). In addition, patients receiving radiation to the pelvic area score the poorest in having "sufficient sexual activity." Those receiving radiation therapy to the head and neck area also score poorly in "appetite" and "eating sufficiently." The gynecological cancer group, with about a fourth of the sample on chemotherapy, also report poor scores for "nausea and vomiting."

SERIAL EVALUATION OF QOL—IMPACT OF INTERVENTIONS

The QOL-CA has been used in serial evaluations of the impact of therapy (41,42). Based on this experience, criteria have been suggested for significant responses in quality of

TABLE 3. *Mean scores for selected items common to QOL-CA, QOL, QLI-RT, MQOLS-CA*

Scales and items	QOL-CA2[a]	QOL[b]	QLI-RT[c]	QLI-RT[d]	MQOLS-CA[e]
Psychosocial well-being					
Enjoy life (fun)?	59	47	63	58	66
Feel happy?	61	51	70	64	70
Have satisfying life?	61	46	69	64	69
Sufficient affection given/received?	78	65	n/a	n/a	n/a
Sufficient sexual activity?	n/a	n/a	41	59	68
Worried about outcome of disease (treatment)?	61	51	64	65	63
Good quality of life?	68	49	71	67	73
Functional well-being					
Feel useful?	55	44	63	60	61
Able to work at usual tasks?	n/a	n/a	58	55	54
Symptom distress: nutrition					
Appetite?	59	46	72	56	68
Eat sufficient?	73	63	78	65	76
Nausea?	73	69	76	72	66
Vomit?	83	71	78	73	67
Symptom distress: pain/fatigue					
Distress from pain?	63	41	60	60	65
Strength?	56	40	58	57	56
Tire easily?	44	31	41	44	44
Attitude of worry					
Worry about cost?	62	57	59	58	57

From ref. 40.
[a]Home care 4th week, n = 177–181 (20).
[b]Elderly, CA pain, 1st home visit, n = 80 (19).
[c]Pelvic 1st FU visit n = 101–146, n's generally range from 139 to 146 with the exception of items concerning sufficient sex, which is 101 (40).
[d]Head and neck, 1st FU visit, n = 95–129 (40).
[e]Gyn ≤ 12 mo. dx, n = 100 (40).
n/a, not applicable because the item was not part of the instrument; RT, radiation treatment; 1st FU, first outpatient visit following the end of radiation treatment; Dx, diagnosis.

life (43). These criteria have been applied in recent studies of liposomal chemotherapy in symptomatic AIDS patients with Kaposi's sarcoma (44). Serial evaluations of post–head and neck radiation therapy over an 18-month period revealed distinct quality of life response patterns, i.e. stable high, stable low, declining, improving, and U-shaped HRQL responses over time. Personal characteristics such as outlook, mood, and optimism differentiated significantly among HRQL response patterns more so than other characteristics (45).

FUTURE DEVELOPMENT OF THE QOL-CA

Future development of the instrument will focus on changing the response mode to a 0 to 10 scale with a notched line, each notch indicating a different number. The notched and numbered line will replace the current smooth 100-mm line anchored by 0 and 100. This change is required to facilitate mailed questionnaire and telephone interview data collection strategies, which are more cost- and time-effective. Grant and colleagues (3) experienced a 96% return rate of mailed questionnaires. Ferrell et al. (49), in a recently completed survey of cancer survivors, obtained a >50% return rate. Future studies need to determine if these return rates are indicative of feelings of indebtedness toward health care providers or of a bias toward not reporting negative outcomes because survivors are just happy to be alive. Future research will also be directed at producing more independent, robust, and reliable existential/spiritual well-being and social well-being subscales.

CONCLUSIONS

Based on past conceptualizations, the authors currently define HRQL as a personal, evaluative statement summarizing the positivity or negativity of attributes that characterize one's psychological, physical, social, and spiritual well-being at a point in time when health, illness, and treatment conditions are relevant (1–9). The QLI/MQOLS/QOL has undergone several name changes, a number of revisions, and is available in different versions. From concept and theory development studies, the authors propose a four-dimensional model of HRQL that includes psychological, physical, social, and spiritual well-being. This model is partially supported by current validity studies. Two current 30-item versions, the QOL and QOL-CA (19,20) include questions that address these four dimensions of HRQL. Both versions have good internal consistency of subscales. Validity and reliability have been supported for the different versions of the instruments. A comparison of items that are the same across the different versions of the instrument indicate that responses across different groups are similar, except where they are expected to be different, e.g., most distress from pain in elderly patients with cancer-related pain (19). Serial evaluations of HRQL have led to the development of

criteria for significant responses in quality of life related to the impact of medical treatment (41–44), and the identification of patterns of change in quality of life. Evaluations of HRQL are based on uncertainties about illness and the gap perceived between experiences and expectations about HRQL attributes. Maintenance or change in HRQL is effected by adaptive behaviors that close the perceived gap.

ACKNOWLEDGMENTS

The authors wish to acknowledge Paula R. Anderson, R.N., M.S.N., Frances Heidi, R.N., M.S., James Lipsett, M.D., Gerald Metter, Ph.D., Michelle Rhiner, R.N., M.S., Judith Saunders, D.N.Sc., Elfriede Greimel, Ph.D., and numerous other staff and patients who generously contributed their time, ideas, and energy to the development of the Quality of Life–Cancer instrument and other treatment-specific versions of the instrument. The development and testing of the instrument was supported, in part, by grants from various United States Public Health Service agencies: Division of Nursing, NU00849, NU01042, NU011304; National Cancer Institute, CA31164; National Center for Nursing Research, NR01042. Some studies were supported by grants from private agencies: American Cancer Society, American Nurses' Foundation, Purdue Frederick Company.

REFERENCES

1. Padilla GV, Ferrell BR, Grant MM, Rhiner M. Defining the content domain of quality of life for cancer patients with pain. *Cancer Nurs* 1990;13(2):108–115.
2. Grant MM, Padilla GV, Ferrell BR, Rhiner M. Assessment of quality of life with a single instrument. *Semin Oncol Nurs* 1990;6:260–270.
3. Grant M, Ferrell B, Schmidt GM, Fonbuena P, Niland JC, Forman SJ. Measurement of quality of life in bone marrow transplant survivors. *Qual Life Res* 1992;1(6):375–384.
4. Ferrell BR, Rhiner M, Cohen M, Grant M. Pain as a metaphor for illness. Part I: Impact of cancer pain on family caregivers. *Oncol Nurs Forum* 1991;18(8):1303–1309.
5. Ferrell BR, Cohen M, Rhiner M, Rozak A. Pain as a metaphor for illness. Part II: Family caregivers' management of pain. *Oncol Nurs Forum* 1991;18(8):1315–1321.
6. Ferrell B, Grant M, Schmidt GM, Rhiner M, Whitehead C, Fonbuena P, Forman SJ. The meaning of quality of life for bone marrow transplant survivors. Part 2. Improving quality of life for bone marrow transplant survivors. *Cancer Nurs* 1992;15(4):247–253.
7. Ferrell B, Grant M, Schmidt GM, Whitehead C, Fonbuena P, Forman SJ. The meaning of quality of life for bone marrow transplant survivors. Part 1. The impact of bone marrow transplant on quality of life. *Cancer Nurs* 1992;15(3):153–160.
8. Padilla GV, Mishel MH, Grant MM. Uncertainty, appraisal and quality of life. *Qual Life Res* 1992;1(3):155–165.
9. Padilla GV. Validity of health-related quality of life subscales. *Prog Cardiovasc Nurs* 1992;7(1):13–20.
10. Gill TM, Feinstein AR. A critical appraisal of the quality of quality-of-life measurements. *JAMA* 1994;272:619–626.
11. World Health Organization. *WHOQOL study protocol: the development of the World Health Organization quality of life assessment instrument*, MNH/PSF/93.9. Geneva, Switzerland: Division of Mental Health, World Health Organization, 1993.
12. Patrick DL, Erickson P. *Health status and health policy: quality of life in health care evaluation and resource allocation*. New York: Oxford University Press, 1993.

13. Presant CA, Klahr C, Hogan L. Evaluating quality-of-life in oncology patients: pilot observations. *Oncol Nurs Forum* 1981;8(3):26–30.

14. Padilla GV, Presant C, Grant MM, Metter G, Lipsett J, Heide F. Quality of life index for patients with cancer. *Res Nurs Health* 1983;6(2):117–126.

15. Ferrell BR, Wisdom C, Wenzl C. Quality of life as an outcome variable in the management of cancer pain. *Cancer* 1989;63(11 suppl):2321–2327.

16. Ferrans CE, Powers MJ. Quality of life index: development and psychometric properties. *Adv Nurs Sci* 1985;8(1):15–24.

17. Spitzer WO, Dobson AJ, Hall J, Chesterman E, Levi J, Shepherd R, Battista RN, Catchlove BR. Measuring the quality of life of cancer patients: a concise QL-index for use by physicians. *J Chronic Dis* 1981;34(12):585.

18. Ferrell BR, Wisdom C, Wenzl C, Brown J. Controlled release vs short acting analgesia: effects on pain and quality of life. *Oncol Nurs Forum* 1989;16(4):521–526.

19. Ferrell BR, Ferrell BA, Ahu C, Tran K. Pain management for elderly cancer patients at home. *Cancer* 1994;74(7):2139–2146.

20. Padilla GP, Grant MG, Saunders J, Greimel E. Hospital-home continuity of care and quality of life measurement. 1994; submitted.

21. Padilla GV, Grant MM. Quality of life as a cancer nursing outcome variable. *Adv Nur Sci* 1985;8(1):45–60.

22. Mapi Values. *Quality of life in ostomy patients—psychometric results of a cross-sectional study*. Final report for Convatec Europe. Bollington, UK: Mapi Values Limited, unpublished.

23. Padilla GV. Gastrointestinal side effects and quality of life in patients receiving radiation therapy. *Nutrition* 1990;6(5):367–370.

24. Padilla GV, Grant MM, Lipsett J, Anderson PR, Rhiner M, Bogen C. Health quality of life and colorectal cancer. *Cancer* 1992;70(5 suppl):1450–1456.

25. Ferrell BR, Ferrell BA, Rhiner M, Grant M. Family factors influencing cancer pain. *Post Grad Med J* 1991;67(suppl 2):S64–S69.

26. Mishel MH. Uncertainty in illness. *Image J Nurs Scholar* 1988;20:225–232.

27. Karnofsky D, Burchenal J. *The clinical evaluation of chemotherapeutic agents in cancer*. New York: Columbia Press, 1949.

28. Karnofsky DA, Abelman WH, Craver LF, Burchenal JH. The use of the nitrogen mustard in the palliative treatment of carcinoma. *Cancer* 1948;1(4):634–656.

29. Flanagan J. Measurement of quality of life: current state of the art. *Arch Phys Med Rehabil* 1982;63(2):56–59.

30. Kaplan RM, Anderson JP, Wu AW, Mathews WMC, Kozin F. The quality of well-being scale: applications in AIDS, cystic fibrosis, and arthritis. *Med Care* 1989;27(3 suppl):S27–S43.

31. Kaplan RM, Anderson JP. A general health policy model: update and applications. *Health Serv Res* 1988;23(2):203–235.

32. Nelson EC, Landgraf JM, Hays RD, Wasson JH, Kirk JW. The functional status of patients: how can it be measured in physicians' offices? *Med Care* 1990;28(12):1111–1126.

33. Nelson EC, Landgraf JM, Hays RD, et al. The Coop function charts: a system to measure patient function in physician's offices. In: Lipkin M Jr, ed. *Functional status measurement in primary care*. New York: Springer-Verlag, 1990:97–131.

34. Stewart AL, Ware JE. *Measuring functioning and well-being: the medical outcomes study approach*. Durham, NC: Duke University Press, 1992.

35. Ferrans C, Powers M. Psychometric assessment of the quality of life index. *Res Nurs Health* 1992;15(1):29–38.

36. Schag CAC, Ganz PA, Heinrich RL. Cancer Rehabilitation Evaluation System–Short Form (CARES-SF). *Cancer* 1991;68(6):1406–1413.

37. Stewart AL, Hays RD, Ware JE. The MOS short-form general health survey: reliability and validity in a patient population. *Med Care* 1988;26(7):724–735.

38. Cella DF, Tulsky DS, Gray G, Sarafian B, Linn E, Bonomi A, Silberman M, Winicour P, Brannon J, Eckberg K, Lloyd S, Purl S, Blendowski C, Goodman M, Barnicle M, Stewart I, Mchale M, Bonomi P, Kaplan E, Taylor S, Thomas IV, Charles R Jr, Harris J. The functional assessment of cancer therapy scale: development and validation of the general measure. *J Clin Oncol* 1993;11(3):570–579.

39. Bond A, Lader M. The use of analogue scales in rating subjective feelings. *Br J Med Psychol* 1974;47:211–218.

40. Grant MG, Padilla GP, Ferrell BR. *Manual of the Quality of Life Scale (QOL)*. Duarte, CA: City of Hope Medical Center, 1994.

41. Presant CA, Soloway MS, Klioze SS, Kosola JW, Yakabow AL, Mendez RG, Kennedy PS, Wyres MR, Naessig VL, Ford KS, et al. Buserelin as primary therapy in advanced prostatic carcinoma. *Cancer* 1985;56:2416–2419.

42. Presant CA, Soloway MS, Klioze SS, Yakabow A, Presant SN, Mendez RG, Kennedy PS, Wyres MR, Naessig VL, Todd B, et al. Buserelin treatment of advanced prostatic carcinoma—long term follow-up of antitumor responses and improved quality of life. *Cancer* 1987;59(10):1713–1716.

43. Presant CA, Wiseman C, Blayney D, Kennedy P, Gala K, King M. Proposed criterion for serial evaluation of quality of life in cancer patients. *J Natl Cancer Inst* 1990;82(9):322–323, 796.

44. Presant CA, Scolaro M, Kennedy P, Blayney DW, Flanagan B, Lisak J, Presant J. Liposomal daunorubicin treatment of HIV-associated Kaposi's sarcoma. *Lancet* 1993;341(8855):1242–1243.

45. Brecht ML, Padilla GV, Grant MM. Patterns of change in health-related quality of life. Paper presented at the International Society for Quality of Life Conference, Brussels, February 1994.

46. Ferrell BR, Wisdom C, Wenzl C, Brown J. Effects of controlled-release morphine on quality of life cancer pain. *Oncol Nurs Forum* 1989;16:521–526.

47. Multidimensional functional assessment. *The OARS methodology, a manual*, 2nd ed. Center for the Study of Aging and Human Development. Durham, NC: Duke University, 1978.

48. Fillenbaum GG, Smyer MA. The development, validity, and reliability of the OARS Multidimensional Functional Assessment Questionnaires. *J Gerontol*. 1981;36(4):428–434.

49. Ferrell BR, Hassey-Dow K, Leigh S. Quality of life in cancer survivors. *Oncol Nurs Forum* 1995;22(7);In Press.

Quality of Life and Pharmacoeconomics in Clinical Trials, Second Edition, edited by B. Spilker. Lippincott-Raven Publishers, Philadelphia © 1996.

CHAPTER 32

The General Health Policy Model: An Integrated Approach

Robert M. Kaplan and John P. Anderson

INTRODUCTION

Quality of life data are becoming increasingly important for evaluating the cost-utility and cost-effectiveness of health care programs. Such analyses require the evaluation of very different types of health care interventions using the same outcome unit. This chapter highlights some of the strengths and weaknesses of general health outcome measures. The value of general versus disease-specific measures within clinical populations is also addressed. In addition, we consider the boundaries of the quality of life concept.

QUALITY OF LIFE MEASUREMENT

Why Measure Quality of Life?

The conceptualization and measurement of health status has interested scholars for many decades. Following the Eisenhower administration, the President's Commission on National Goals identified health status measurement as an

important objective. In *The Affluent Society,* Galbraith described the need to measure the effect of the health care system on "quality of life." Within the last two decades, many groups have attempted to define and measure health status (1–3). Before considering any specific approach, it is worth noting that traditional indicators of "health" have well-identified problems that need to be addressed before they can be considered part of an adequate measure of quality of life.

Mortality

Mortality remains the major outcome measure in many epidemiologic studies and some clinical trials. Typically, mortality is expressed in a unit of time and the rates are often age-adjusted. Case fatality rates express the proportion of persons who died of a particular disease divided by the total number with the disease (including those who die and those who live). Mortality rates have many benefits as health outcome measures. They are "hard" data, despite some misclassification bias (4), and the meaning of the outcome is not difficult to comprehend. Despite their many advantages, mortality outcomes have some obvious limitations. Mortality rates consider only the dead and ignore the living. Many important treatments or programs might have little or no impact

R. M. Kaplan and J. P. Anderson: Division of Health Care Sciences, Department of Family and Preventive Medicine, University of California, San Diego, La Jolla, California 92093.

on mortality rates and many frequently occurring illnesses, such as arthritis, have relatively little impact on mortality. Thus, there has been an incentive to define and measure nonfatal outcomes.

Morbidity

The most common approach to health status assessment is to measure morbidity in terms of function or role performance. For example, morbidity estimates often include workdays missed or bed-disability days. Many different approaches to health status assessment using morbidity indicators have been introduced. These include, for example, the Sickness Impact Profile (5), which represents the effect of disease or disability on a variety of categories of behavioral function, and the Medical Outcomes Study measures, which have separate categories for the effects of disease or health states on physical function, social function, and mental function (3). These measures are important quantitative expressions of health outcome. However, they do not integrate morbidity and mortality, although as each birth cohort ages, mortality cases accrue.

Death is a health outcome, and it is important that this outcome not be excluded from any expression of health status. For example, suppose we are evaluating the effect of program A, which integrates support and treatment, for randomly assigned groups of very ill, elderly, nursing home residents against the effect of program B, which offers no support or treatment. Let us suppose that program A maintains patients at a very low level of function throughout the year, but that in the comparison group (program B), the sickest 10% died. Looking just at the living in the follow-up, one finds program B patients to be healthier, since the sickest have been removed by death. By this standard, the program of no supportive treatment might be put forth as the better alternative. With a measure that combines morbidity and mortality the outcome will be very different, because mortality effects will reduce the overall health of program B to a very low level.

Behavioral Dysfunction

When Sullivan (6) reviewed the literature on health measurement nearly 30 years ago, he emphasized the importance of behavioral outcomes. Behavioral indicators such as absenteeism, bed-disability days, and institutional confinement were identified as the most important consequences of disease and disability. Ability to perform activities at different ages could be compared with societal standards for these behaviors. Restrictions in usual activity were seen as *prima facie* evidence of deviation from well-being. Many other investigators have focused on point-in-time measures of dysfunction as measures of health (3,7,8).

Prognosis

The problem with measures of behavioral dysfunction is that they often neglect what will happen in the future. The spectrum of medical care ranges from primary prevention to rehabilitation. Many programs affect the probability of occurrence of future dysfunction (e.g., vaccines), rather than alter present functional status. In many aspects of preventive care, for example, the benefit of the treatment cannot be seen until many years after the intervention. A supportive family that instills proper health habits in its children, for example, may also promote better health in the future, yet the benefit may not be realized for years. The concept of health must consider not only the present ability to function, but also the probability of future changes in function. A person who is functional and asymptomatic today may harbor a disease with a poor prognosis. Thus, many individuals are at high risk of dying from heart disease even though they are perfectly functional today. Should we call them "healthy"? We hold that the term *severity of illness* should take into consideration both dysfunction and prognosis (or probability of future dysfunction and mortality).

Many medical treatments may cause near-term dysfunction to prevent future dysfunction. For example, coronary artery bypass surgery causes severe dysfunction for a short period of time, yet the surgery is presumed to enhance function or decrease mortality at a later time. Patients may be incapacitated and restricted to coronary care units following myocardial infarction. Yet, the treatment is designed to help them achieve better future outcomes. Pap smears and hysterectomies are performed in order to decrease the probability of future deaths due to cancer. Much of health care involves looking into the future to enhance outcomes over the life span. Therefore, it is essential to divide health into current and future components. We prefer the term *prognosis* to describe the probability of transition among health states over the course of time (9).

IS QUALITY OF LIFE DIFFERENT FROM HEALTH STATUS?

In the preceding section, we have described some common elements in existing measures of health status. However, there is considerable variability in the definition of quality of life. Some authors define quality of life as health outcomes that are different from traditional health outcomes. Using these definitions, quality of life measures are typically limited to psychological and social attributes (10). By contrast, our definition of health-related quality of life focuses on the qualitative dimension of functioning. It also incorporates duration of stay in various health states. We will return to this definition later in the chapter; in this section, however, we review the value dimension, which is an important aspect of quality of life.

The Value Dimension

Scholars have debated the components of "health" for many centuries (11). Most concepts of morbidity involve three types of evidence: clinical, subjective, and behavioral (6). *Clinical* outcomes include clinical judgment, physical findings, laboratory tests, or results of invasive procedures. Clinical evidence is valuable if, and only if, it is clearly related to well-defined behavioral health outcomes. For example, significant abnormalities in certain blood proteins are of concern only if these deviations correlate with morbidity or early mortality. The burden of proof is on the scientist to demonstrate these associations.

Subjective evidence includes symptoms and complaints that are also very important in health care. Symptoms are a major correlate of health care utilization, but not all symptoms should be given equal weight because neither the type nor the number of symptoms necessarily depicts the severity of disease. For example, an adult with an acute 24-hour flu may have an enormous number of symptoms. Although these can include nausea, headache, cough, sneezing, aches and pains, vomiting, and diarrhea, it is not clear that this condition is more severe than the single symptom of a very severe headache.

Several factors need to be considered. First, we must determine the degree to which the symptoms limit functioning. Consider an individual with five symptoms—an itchy eye, runny nose, coughing, fatigue, and headache—but who still feels well enough to work and to perform all usual activities. Another person with the single symptom of a severe headache may be limited to bed. Would we want to call the person with five symptoms less well? Another dimension is the duration of the symptoms. A year in pain is certainly worse than a day in pain. The final, and perhaps the most often neglected, factor is the value or preference associated with different types of dysfunction.

Biomedical investigators often avoid reference to values or preferences because these constructs are not considered "scientific." However, the value dimension in health status is inescapable. Fishburn (11) defined value as the quantification of the concept of worth, importance, or desirability. Ultimately, our judgments of the value of health states, and whether one level of functioning is "better" than another level of functioning, depend on subjective evaluations. If we advise individuals to change their diet to avoid heart disease, we inherently assume that the reduced probability of heart disease later in life is valued more than the immediate but enduring mild displeasure of dietary change. The phrase *quality of life* necessarily presumes a qualitative judgment.

As noted earlier, Sullivan (6) emphasized *behavioral dysfunction* as the third type of evidence for morbidity. Behavioral dysfunction includes disruption in role performance, confinement to hospitals, or work loss.

SHOULD QUALITY OF LIFE BE LIMITED TO PSYCHOLOGICAL AND SOCIAL ATTRIBUTES?

Some authors use the term *quality of life* as a limited descriptor of psychological and social health (10). We believe that most psychological and social dimensions can be incorporated into a general health status measure. However, some concepts of social health are correlates of health outcomes rather than outcomes themselves. We have addressed these issues elsewhere (12–14) but will summarize them here.

Social Health

For nearly 35 years, physicians, psychologists, sociologists, and epidemiologists have been attempting to include social support and social function in a definition of health status. Despite relentless efforts, it has been difficult to meaningfully define social support as a component of health. The term *social health* was included in the World Health Organization definition of health that accompanied their charter document in 1948 (15). They defined health as "a state of complete physical, mental, and social well-being and not merely the absence of infirmity." In identifying the dimensions of health, the World Health Organization neglected to provide any operational definitions. Thus, different investigators have taken different approaches in their attempts to capture physical, mental, and social dimensions. Since the publication of the World Health Organization statement, many investigators have tried to develop measures to operationalize the three components of health status. With surprising consistency, authors quote the World Health Organization definition and then present their methods for measuring the three components. So prevalent is the notion that health status must include these three components that many reviews now negatively evaluate any measure that does not conform to the World Health Organization definition. For example, Meenan (16) disapproved of several health measures because, "these approaches fall short of conceptualizing or measuring health in the World Health Organization sense of a physical, psychological, and social state."

With the command of the World Health Organization so plainly set forth, many investigators have struggled to develop their measures of social health. Yet there have been consistent problems. For example, Kane and Kane (17) devoted a substantial section of their monograph to describing problems in the quantification of social health. These problems included vague concepts, lack of norms, the interactive nature of variables, difficulty in construction of a continuum, and the subjective nature of social health.

Only Ware and colleagues (18,19) have begun to question the meaning of social health. In one paper, Ware and Donald (19) reviewed 70 studies relevant to social health. From these they selected 11 studies for more detailed analysis. The great majority of these studies focused on what we now call social support. Yet there were at least two separate components being assessed by the many investigators contributing to this literature. One component is social contacts, or the performance of social role. The other component is social resources, which is more analogous to the concept of social support. This distinction is very important. Social contacts might include participation in work, attendance at school, and other aspects of functioning. Social resources are relevant to social life, friendships, and family relationships.

In a series of analyses, it has been demonstrated that social support may be a predictor for health outcomes (13,19), but the direction is not always clear. For example, Heitzmann and Kaplan (20) have demonstrated that social support may predict positive outcomes for women but negative outcomes for men. Social support is not an outcome that can serve as the target of health care. On the other hand, social functioning is a component of health status. Diseases and disabilities affect social function. Social function is a central component in the concept of quality of life (21). Optimizing social health raises issues of social control and public policy. Considering the example of function, there is strong consensus that function is desirable. Thus, it seems reasonable to devote public resources to maximize the level of function and quality of life within a community.

Optimized health status might be considered a common goal, as is national defense, a strong educational system, and so on. Many current methods of health measurement do include a social functioning component. On the other hand, including social support in the definition of health status would imply that community resources should be used to obtain some defined level of social support. We might expect considerable public disagreement about what the social support objective might be. For example, would we want to develop a public policy that requires people to have friends?

Excluding social support from the definition of health makes policy analysis relatively straightforward. There is little disagreement about what levels of functioning are desirable (22). When people agree on what is desirable, the objective of health care can be directed toward achieving the desired states. A major issue is in defining a mix of programs that most efficiently and effectively achieve these objectives. Programs that enhance social support might be considered in this mix, but we believe that including social support in the definition of health only confuses the definition of these objectives.

Mental Health

The separate category for mental health in the World Health Organization definition prompted many investigators to develop separate measures of mental health functioning. Perhaps the best known effort in this area is the work by Ware and his associates (23). These investigators adapted

Dupuy's (24) General Well-Being Index and administered it to large numbers of people as part of the RAND Health Insurance Experiment. Ware et al. (25) argue that the correlation between psychological distress and physical functioning is only .25 and suggested that this confirmed that mental health was a separate dimension. In addition, they offered comparisons between those with no physical limitations but with differences on items about psychological distress. For this high physically functioning group, those with higher scores on mental distress used three times as many mental health services as those low in distress.

The separate measurement of mental health remains a major issue in the conceptualization of general health status. Although our position is against the norm, we believe mental health can be conceptualized as a portion of general health status and that there is considerable disadvantage to attempting separate measurement and specification of mental function. We do understand that some investigators are interested in specific subcomponents of mental health, such as cognitive functioning. In these cases, more detailed measures might be considered additions to (but not replacements for) the general measures. We will return to this argument later.

We argue that the World Health Organization conceptualization of health status promotes an artificial dichotomy between mental and physical function. To understand this argument, it is important to think about the impact of mental illness, anxiety, or poor social adjustment on functioning. Mental health affects longevity (26) and quality of life. In other words, the impact of mental health on general health status is expressed through its impact on life expectancy, functioning, and symptoms. However, many individuals with perfect physical functioning experience symptoms. For example, an individual experiencing anxiety at work might report a symptom describing anxiety. This anxiety might effect quality of life in a manner similar to a physical symptom such as shortness of breath. Severe anxieties, such as phobias, may disrupt role performance. Thus, individuals may be limited to their homes because they are afraid to go outside. Many individuals experience symptomatic depression that does not disrupt their activities of daily living. At the other extreme, anxiety and depression can be so severe that they result in hospitalization. Thus, the impact of the condition on functioning is very much the same as the impact of a physical malady.

As in physical health, the duration of mental health conditions must also be considered. For example, depression may last 3 days, 3 weeks, or 1 year. The total impact needs to be expressed as a function of its duration. More importantly, mental health status may effect differential transition among functional states over the course of time. The term *positive health* is used typically to describe some aspect of lifestyle or mental outlook that is associated with better future health. Or people with positive health have lower probabilities of transition to poor health over the course of time. An individual who can cope with stress may seem no different from individuals without such coping skills. However, given certain epidemiologic linkages, they may have a higher probability of better functioning at future points in time.

Much of the confusion about mental health has been generated by a very refined technology for assessing mental states. Often, detailed questionnaire methods have been factor analyzed to describe different dimensions of mental health. Nevertheless, these very different levels of functioning may ultimately have impact on the general well-being. This may be analogous to the many available measures of blood chemistry. For example, indicators of kidney function (creatinine, BUN, and so on) may be identified as separate factors, yet the importance of these measures is their relationship to longevity and to function at particular points in time. We might not be concerned about elevated creatinine, for example, if these blood levels were not correlated with death or dysfunction due to kidney disease.

There are some justifications for not separating mental and physical function. The growing literature on psychoneuroimmunology (27) clearly demonstrates the intertwining nature of physical and mental health outcomes. In addition, experiments have demonstrated that general health status can be improved in medical patients even though physical functioning is unaffected. For example, patients with chronic obstructive pulmonary disease do not achieve changes in lung function following rehabilitation. However, they may reach higher levels of activity and reduced symptoms (28). The rehabilitation programs are not necessarily medical and may depend on physical or respiratory therapists. Indeed, the changes in outcome may result from improved attitude or from the enhanced ability to cope with symptoms. Ultimately, we are interested in patient function and quality of life. It may not matter if this is achieved through enhanced lung function or improved coping skills. The most important point is that all providers in health care are attempting to improve quality of life and extend the duration of life. It may be worthwhile to allow mental health providers and physical health providers to compare the benefits of their services using a common unit.

Health-Related Quality of Life

The objectives of health care are twofold. First, health care and health policy should increase life expectancy. Second, the health care system should improve the quality of life during the years that people are alive. It is instructive to consider various measures in health care in light of these two objectives. Traditional biomedical indicators and diagnoses are important to us because they may be related to mortality or to quality of life. We prefer the term *health-related quality of life* to refer to the impact of health conditions on function. Thus, health-related quality of life may be independent of quality of life relevant to work setting, housing, air pollution, or similar factors (29).

Numerous quality of life measurement systems have evolved during the last 30 years. These systems are based primarily on two different conceptual approaches. The first approach grows out of the tradition of health status measurement. In the late 1960s and early 1970s, the National Center for Health Services Research funded several major projects to develop general measures of health status. Those projects resulted in the Sickness Impact Profile (5), the Quality of Well-Being Scale (30,31), and the General Health Rating Index. The latter measure, originally developed at Southern Illinois University, was adapted by the RAND Corporation under Health and Human Service grants and has become known as the RAND Health Status Measure (8). This measure evolved into the SF-36. These efforts usually involved extensive multidisciplinary collaboration between behavioral scientists and physicians. Most of the measures are focused on the impact of disease and disability on function and observable behaviors, such as performance of social role, ability to get around the community, and physical functioning. Some systems include separate components for the measurement of social and mental health. All were guided by the World Health Organization's above-mentioned definition of health status.

The second conceptual approach is based on quality of life as something independent of health status. Some investigators now use traditional psychological measures and call them quality of life outcomes. For instance, Follick et al. (10) suggest that quality of life represents psychological status in addition to symptoms and mortality. Croog et al. (32) used a wide variety of outcome measures and collectively referred to them as "quality of life." These measures included the patients' subjective evaluation of well-being, physical symptoms, sexual function, work performance and satisfaction, emotional status, cognitive function, social participation, and life satisfaction. Yet mortality is not part of the concept. Other investigators, including Hunt and McEwen (33), regard quality of life as subjective appraisals of life satisfaction. In summary, a wide variety of different dimensions have all been described as quality of life. Although agreement is lacking on which dimensions should be considered the standard for assessing quality of life in research studies, recurrent themes in the methodological literature can assist in the evaluation of existing instruments. As will be shown, our approach to quality of life measurement focuses on health-related outcomes of mortality, morbidity, symptoms, and prognosis. We believe that many definitions of quality of life are poorly operationalized. Before addressing our definition of health-related quality of life, it is also important to clarify some economic terms that are often used in the literature.

Cost-Utility versus Cost-Benefit

The terms *cost-utility, cost-effectiveness,* and *cost-benefit* are used inconsistently in the medical literature (34). Some economists have favored the assessment of cost-benefit. These approaches measure both program costs and treatment outcomes in dollar units. For example, treatment outcomes are evaluated in relation to changes in use of medical services and economic productivity. Treatments are cost-beneficial if the economic return exceeds treatment costs. Diabetic patients who are aggressively treated, for example, may need fewer medical services. The savings associated with decreased services might exceed treatment costs. As Kaplan and Davis (35) have argued, there is relatively little strong empirical evidence that patient education or behavioral treatments are actually cost-beneficial. In addition, as suggested by Russell (36), the requirement that health care treatments reduce costs may be unrealistic. Patients are willing to pay for improvements in health status just as they are willing to pay for other desirable goods and services. We do not treat cancer in order to save money. Instead, treatments are given in order to achieve better health outcomes.

Cost-effectiveness is an alternative approach in which the unit of outcome is a reflection of treatment effect. In recent years, cost-effectiveness has gained considerable attention. Some approaches emphasize simple, treatment-specific outcomes. For example, the cost per pound lost has been used as a measure of cost-effectiveness of weight loss programs (37). Public competitions, for example, achieve a lower cost-per-pound loss ratio than do traditional clinical interventions. The major difficulty with cost-effectiveness methodologies is that they do not allow for comparison across very different treatment interventions. For example, health care administrators often need to choose between investments in very different alternatives. They may need to decide between supporting liver transplantation for a few patients versus prenatal counseling for a large number of patients. For the same cost, they may achieve a large effect for a few people or a small effect for a large number of people. The treatment-specific outcomes used in cost-effectiveness studies do not permit these comparisons.

Cost-utility approaches use the expressed preference or utility of a treatment effect as the unit of outcome. As noted in World Health Organization documents (38), the goals of health care are to add years to life and to add life to years. In other words, health care is designed to make people live longer (increase the life expectancy) and to live a higher quality of life in the years prior to death. Cost-utility studies use outcome measures that combine mortality outcomes with quality of life measurements. The utilities are the expressed preferences for observable states of function on a continuum bounded by 0 for death to 1.0 for optimum function (39–41). In the next section, we outline a model that combines utilities with measures of mortality, morbidity, symptoms, and prognosis. The system can be used as either a health-related quality of life measure or an instrument in cost-utility analysis.

A COMPREHENSIVE SYSTEM—THE GENERAL HEALTH POLICY MODEL

Our approach is to express the benefits of medical care, behavioral intervention, or preventive programs in terms of

well-years. Others have chosen to describe the same outcome as quality-adjusted life-years (42). Well-years integrate mortality and morbidity to express health status in terms of equivalents of well-years of life. If a cigarette smoker died of heart disease at age 50 and we would have expected him to live to age 75, it might be concluded that the disease cost him 25 life-years. If 100 cigarette smokers died at age 50 (and also had life expectancies of 75 years), we might conclude that 2,500 (100 people × 25 years) life-years had been lost.

Death is not the only outcome of concern in heart disease. Many adults suffer myocardial infarctions that leave them somewhat disabled over a longer period of time. Although they are still alive, the quality of their lives has diminished. Our model permits all degrees of disability to be compared with one another. A disease that reduces the quality of life by one-half will take away 0.5 well-years over the course of 1 year. If it effects two people, it will take away 1.0 well-year (equal to 2 × 0.5) over a 1-year period. A medical treatment that improves the quality of life by 0.2 for each of five individuals will result in a production of 1 well-year if the benefit is maintained over a 1-year period. Using this system, it is possible to express the benefits of various programs by showing how many equivalents of well-years they produce (39–41). Yet not all programs have equivalent costs. In periods of scarce resources, it is necessary to find the most efficient use of limited funds. Our approach provides a framework within which to make policy decisions that require selection from competing alternatives. Preventive services may in this way compete with traditional medical services for the scarce health care dollar. Performing such comparisons requires the use of a general health decision model. In the next section the general model of health status assessment and benefit-cost-utility analysis is presented.

The General Model

Building a Health Decision Model

The Health Decision Model grew out of substantive theories in economics, psychology, medicine, and public health. These theoretical linkages have been presented in several previous papers (43–45). Building a health decision model requires at least five distinct steps.

Step 1: Define a Function Status Classification

During the early phases of our work, a set of mutually exclusive and collectively exhaustive levels of functioning were defined. After an extensive, specialty-by-specialty review of medical reference works, we listed all of the ways that disease and injuries can affect behavior and role performance. Without considering etiology, it was possible to match a finite number of conditions to items appearing on standard health surveys, such as the Health Interview Survey (National Center for Health Statistics), the Survey of the

Disabled (Social Security Administration), and several rehabilitation scales and ongoing community surveys. These items fit conceptually into three scales representing related but distinct aspects of daily functioning: Mobility, Physical Activity, and Social Activity. The Mobility and Physical Activity scales have three levels, whereas Social Activity has five distinct levels. Table 1 shows the steps from the three scales. Several investigators have used this function status classification (or a modified version of it) as an outcome measure for health program evaluation (46,47). However, the development of a truly comprehensive health status indicator requires several more steps.

Step 2: Classify Symptoms and Problems

There are many reasons a person may not be functioning at the optimum level. Subjective complaints are an important component of a general health measure because they relate dysfunction to a specific problem. Thus, in addition to function level classifications, an exhaustive list of symptoms and problems has been generated. Included in the list are 25 complexes of symptoms and problems representing all of the possible symptomatic complaints that might inhibit function. These symptoms and problems are shown in Table 2.

Step 3: Preference Weights to Integrate the Quality of Well-Being Scale

We now have described the three scales of function and 25 symptom/problem complexes. With these, all we can do is compare populations in terms of frequencies of each scale step (and, if necessary, Symptom/Problem Complex). Although comparisons of frequencies are common in health services research, our system offers a strategy for integrating the frequencies into a single comprehensive expression. If our intent is to say which of these distributions is "better off" and which "worse," simple frequency distributions may not be able to help much. For example, is a group with 80 people able to travel but limited in their mobility and 5 restricted to their homes worse off than a group in which 85 can travel freely, but 10 are restricted to their homes? Obviously comparing frequency distributions is complex. Further, the example involves frequencies for only one scale. How can one make decisions when there are three scales and Symptom/Problem Complexes to consider?

Another step is necessary to integrate the three scales and the Symptom/Problem Complexes in a manner that will allow a single numerical expression to represent each combination of steps on the scales and Symptom/Problem Complexes. The empirical means of accomplishing this is measured preferences for the health states. These might be regarded as "quality" judgments. As we noted earlier, the General Health Policy Model includes the impact of health conditions on the quality of life. This requires that the desirability of health situations be evaluated on a continuum from

TABLE 1. *Quality of Well-Being/General Health Policy Model: elements and calculating formulas (function scales, with step definitions and calculating weights)*

Step no.	Step definition	Weight
	Mobility Scale (MOB)	
5	No limitations for health reasons	−.000
4	Did not drive a car, health related; did not ride in a car as usual for age (younger than 15 yr), health related, and/or did not use public transportation, health related; or had or would have used more help than usual for age to use public transportation, health related	−.062
2	In hospital, health related	−.090
	Physical Activity Scale (PAC)	
4	No limitations for health reasons	−.000
3	In wheelchair, moved or controlled movement of wheelchair without help from someone else; or had trouble or did no try to lift, stoop, bend over, or use stairs or inclines, health related; and/or limped, used a cane, crutches, or walker, health related; and/or had any other physical limitation in walking, or did not try to walk as far or as fast as other the same age are able, health related	−.060
1	In wheelchair, did not move or control the movement of wheelchair without help from someone else, or in bed, chair, or couch for most or all of the day, health related	−.077
	Social Activity Scale (SAC)	
5	No limitations for health reasons	−.000
4	Limited in other (e.g., recreational) role activity, health related	−.061
3	Limited in major (primary) role activity, health related	−.061
2	Performed no major role activity, health related, but did perform self-care activities	−.061
1	Performed no major role activity, health related, and did not perform or had more help than usual in performance of one or more self-care activities, health related	−.106
	Calculating formulas	
	Formula 1. Point-in-time well-being score for an individual (*W*): $W = 1 + (CPXwt) + (MOBwt) + (PACwt) + (SACwt)$ where *wt* is the preference-weighted measure for each factor and CPX is symptom/problem complex. For example, the *W* score for a person with the following description profile may be calculated for one day as:	
CPX-11	Cough, wheezing, or shortness of breath, with or without fever, chills, or aching all over	−.257
MOB-5	No limitations	−.000

TABLE 1. *(Continued)*

Step no.	Step definition	Weight
PAC-1	In bed, chair, or couch for most or all of the day, health related	−.077
SAC-2	Performed no major role activity, health related, but did perform self-care	−.061
	$W = 1 + (−.257) + (−.000) + (−.077) + (−.061) = .605$	
	Formula 2. Well-years (*WY*) as an output measure:	
	$WY = [\text{No. of persons} \times (CPXwt + MOBwt + PACwt + SACwt) \times \text{Time}]$	

death to completely well. An evaluation such as this is a matter of utility or preference; thus, combinations of behavioral dysfunction and symptom/problem complexes are scaled to represent degrees of relative importance.

Human judgment studies are used to determine weights for the different states. We have asked random samples of citizens from the community to evaluate the relative desirability of a good number of health conditions. Random sample surveys were conducted in the San Diego community during 2 consecutive years. The probability sample included 866 respondents ethnically representative of the population. When necessary, interviews were conducted in Spanish. From a listing of all possible combinations of the scale (Mobility, Physical Activity, Social Activity, and Symptom/Problem Complexes), we drew a stratified random sample of 343 case descriptions (items) and divided them into eight sets of computer-generated booklets. All respondents were assigned randomly to one of the eight booklets, creating eight subgroups of approximately 100 respondents each. In a series of studies, a mathematical model was developed to describe the consumer decision process. The validity of the model has been cross validated with an *r* of .94 (10). These weights, then, describe the relative desirability of all of the function states on a scale from 0 (for death) to 1.0 (for asymptomatic optimum function). Thus, a state with a weight of .50 is viewed by the members of the community as being about one-half as desirable as optimum function or about halfway between optimum function and death.

Some critics have expressed concern that community, rather than specific population weights are used. The advantage of community weights is that they are general (like the model) and do not bias policy analysis toward any interest group. More important, however, is that empirical studies consistently fail to show systematic differences between demographic groups (21), providers, students and administrators (20), and Americans versus British (48). Relevant to the general versus disease-specific issue, Balaban and colleagues (49) found that weights provided by rheumatoid arthritis patients are remarkably similar to those we obtained from members of the general population.

TABLE 2. *Quality of Well-Being/General Health Policy Model: symptom/problem complexes (CPX) with calculating weights*

CPX no.	CPX description	Weights
1	Death (not on respondent's card)	−.727
2	Loss of consciousness such as seizure (fits), fainting, or coma (out cold or knocked out)	−.407
3	Burn over large areas of face, body, arms, or legs	−.387
4	Pain, bleeding, itching, or discharge (drainage) from sexual organs—does not include normal menstrual (monthly) bleeding	−.349
5	Trouble learning, remembering, or thinking clearly	−.340
6	Any combination of one or more hands, feet, arms, or legs either missing, deformed (crooked), paralyzed (unable to move), or broken—includes wearing artificial limbs or braces	−.333
7	Pain, stiffness, weakness, numbness, or other discomfort in chest, stomach (including hernia or rupture), side, neck, back, hips, or any joints or hands, feet, arms, or legs	−.299
8	Pain, burning, bleeding, itching, or other difficulty with rectum, bowel movements, or urination (passing water)	−.292
9	Sick or upset stomach, vomiting or loose bowel movement, with or without chills, or aching all over	−.290
10	General tiredness, weakness, or weight loss	−.259
11	Cough, wheezing, or shortness of breath, with or without fever, chills, or aching all over	−.257
12	Spells of feeling, upset, being depressed, or of crying	−.257
13	Headache, or dizziness, or ringing in ears, or spells of feeling hot, nervous, or shaky	−.244
14	Burning or itching rash on large areas of face, body, arms, or legs	−.240
15	Trouble talking, such as lisp, stuttering, hoarseness, or being unable to speak	−.237
16	Pain or discomfort in one or both eyes (such as burning or itching) or any trouble seeing after correction	−.230
17	Overweight for age and height or skin defect of face, body, arms, or legs, such as scars, pimples, warts, bruises, or changes in color	−.188
18	Pain in ear, tooth, jaw, throat, lips, tongue; several missing or crooked permanent teeth—includes wearing bridges or false teeth; stuffy, runny nose; or any trouble hearing—includes wearing a hearing aid	−.170
19	Taking medication or staying on a prescribed diet for health reasons	−.144
20	Wore eyeglasses or contact lenses	−.101
21	Breathing smog or unpleasant air	−.101
22	No symptoms or problem (not on respondent's card)	−.000
23	Standard symptom/problem	−.257
X24	Trouble sleeping	−.257
X25	Intoxication	−.257
X26	Problems with sexual interest or performance	−.257
X27	Excessive worry or anxiety	−.257

Note: x indicates that a standardized weight is used.

Using preference weights, one component of the general model of health is defined. This is the Quality of Well-Being Scale, which is the point-in-time component of the General Health Policy Model (50,51). The quality of well-being score for any individual can be obtained from preferences or "quality" judgments associated with his/her function level, adjusted for symptom or problem.

The example in Table 1 describes a person classified on the three scales of observable function and on a symptom/problem. The table shows the adjustments for each of these components. Using these, a weight of .605 is obtained. By including symptom/problem adjustments, the index becomes very sensitive to minor "top end" variations in health status. The adjustments for particular symptom/problems are shown in Table 2. For example, there are Symptom/Problem complexes for wearing eyeglasses, having a runny nose, or breathing polluted air. These symptom adjustments apply even if a person is in the top step in the other three scales. For example, a person with a runny nose receives a score of .83 on the Quality of Well-Being Scale when he is at the highest level of behavioral function (i.e., the top step on each scale shown in Table 1). Thus, the index can make fine as well as gross distinctions.

Step 4: Estimate Transitions among Health States

The Quality of Well-Being (QWB) Scale is the point-in-time component of the model. A comprehensive measure of health status also requires an expression of prognosis or the probability of moving between health states over time. People who are well now want to remain well. Those who are at suboptimal levels want to become well, or at least not get worse. A general health policy model must consider both current functioning and probability of transition to other function levels over the course of time. When transition is considered and documented in empirical studies, the consideration of a particular diagnosis is no longer needed. We fear diseases because they affect our current functioning or the probability that there will be a limitation in our functioning some time in the future. A person at high risk for heart disease may be functioning very well at present, but may have a high probability of transition to a lower level (or death) in the future. Cancer would not be a concern if the disease did not affect current functioning or the probability that functioning would be affected at some future time.

When weights have been properly determined, health status can be expressed precisely as the expected value (product) of the preferences associated with the states of function at a point in time and the probabilities of transition to other states over the remainder of the life expectancy. Quality of Well-being (W) is a static or time-specific measure of function, whereas the well-life expectancy (E) also includes the dynamic or prognostic dimension. The well-life expectancy is the product of quality of well-being times the expected duration of stay in each function level over a standard life period. The equation for the well-life expectancy is

$$E = \Sigma\ W_K Y_K$$

where E is the symptom-standardized well-life expectancy in equivalents of completely well-years, W_K is the Quality of Well-Being score, and Y_K is the expected duration of stay in each function level or case type estimated with an appropriate statistical (preferably stochastic) model.

A sample computation of the well-life expectancy is shown in Table 3. Suppose that a group of individuals was in a well state for 65.2 years, in a state of non-bed disability for 4.5 years and in a state of bed disability for 1.9 years before their deaths at the average age of 71.6 calendar years. To make adjustments for the diminished quality of life they suffered in the disability states, the duration of stay in each state is multiplied by the preference associated with the state. Thus, the 4.5 years of non-bed disability become 2.7 equivalents of well-years when we adjust for the preferences associated with inhabiting that state. Overall, the well-life expectancy for this group is 68.5 years. In other words, disability has reduced the quality of their lives by an estimated 3.1 years.

Step 5: Estimating the Benefit-Cost/Utility Ratio

The San Diego Group has shown in a variety of publications how the concept of a well or weighted life expectancy can be used to evaluate the effectiveness of programs and health interventions. The output of a program has been described in a variety of publications as quality-adjusted life-years (43,52,53), well-years, equivalents of well-years, or discounted well-years (20,51,54). Weinstein et al. (55,56) call the same output quality-adjusted life-years (QALYs), and this has been adopted by the Congressional Office of Technology Assessment (57). It is worth noting that the quality-adjusted life-years terminology was originally introduced by Bush et al. (43), but later abandoned because it has surplus meaning. The term *wellness* or *well-years* implies a more direct linkage to health conditions. Whatever the term, the number shows the output of a program in years of life adjusted by the quality of life that has been lost because of diseases or disability.

TABLE 3. *Illustrative computation of the well-life expectancy*

State	k	Y_k	W	WY_k
Well	A	65.2	1.00	65.2
Non-bed disability	B	4.5	.59	2.7
Bed disability	C	1.9	.34	.6
Total		71.6		68.5

Current life expectancy ΣY_k: 71.6 life-years.
Well-life expectancy ΣWY_k: 68.5 well-years.
From ref. 51.

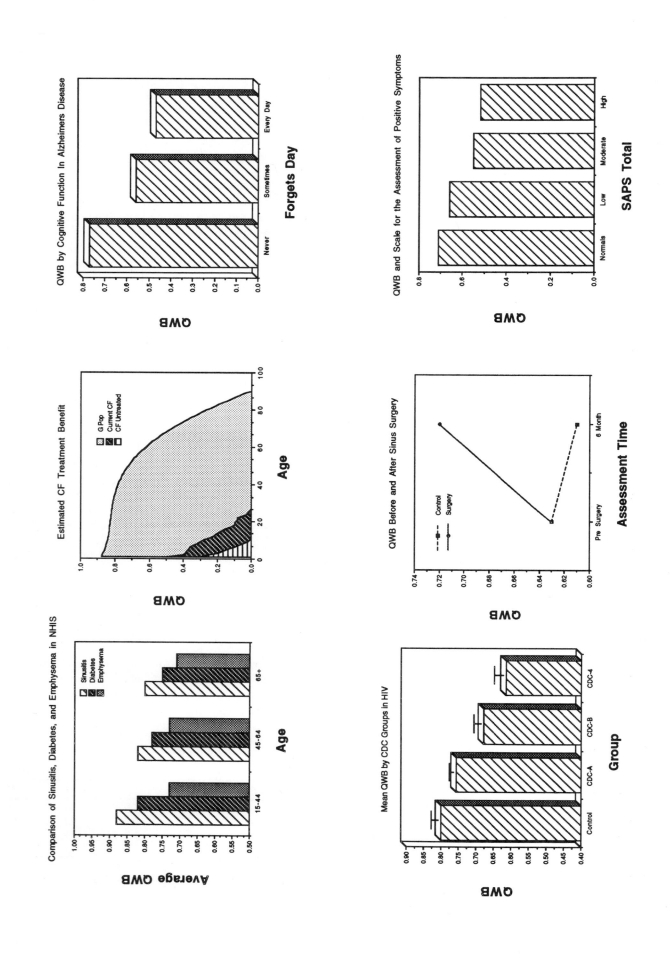

Validity of the Quality of Well-Being Scale

The QWB has now been used in a wide variety of different studies. The validity evidence will be reviewed briefly and the reader is referred to the specific papers. The upper left panel of Fig. 1 summarizes QWB scores, estimated from the U.S. National Health Interview Survey, in relation to three problems: sinusitis, diabetes, and chronic lung disease. In each of three age groups, sinus disease is shown to be a less serious problem than diabetes, which, in turn, has less impact than emphysema (58). The upper center panel of Fig. 1 shows how the method might be used to estimate the impact of an illness such as cystic fibrosis. According to this analysis, cystic fibrosis causes the loss of about 52 QALYs each year. The total area under the curve shows estimates of the total QALYs for the U.S. population. The area under the second curve shows life expectancy for people with cystic fibrosis. The third curve shows the quality-adjusted life expectancy for people with cystic fibrosis 25 years ago. The area between the second and third curves shows the advances in cystic fibrosis treatment within the last quarter century. The area between the first and second curves describes the distance we must travel in order to reduce the impact of this disease (59).

The upper right panel of Fig. 1 summarizes the relationship between the QWB and measures of cognitive impairment for patients with Alzheimer's disease. Patients at the San Diego Alzheimer's Disease Research Center were evaluated and classified according to whether they forget what day it is every day, sometimes, or never. These cognitive impairments were systematically related to QWB scores (60). The lower left panel summarizes the relationships between the QWB and stage of human immunodeficiency virus (HIV) disease. The Centers for Disease Control (CDC) IV group (full AIDS) was significantly lower (.661) than the CDC II/III groups (asymptomatic HIV infected) (.755) and a control group matched for age, sex, and lifestyle (.802) (61).

The General Health Policy Model has been used in a wide variety of population studies (58–62). In addition, the methods have been used in clinical trials and studies to evaluate therapeutic interventions in a wide range of medical and surgical conditions. These include chronic obstructive pulmonary disease (63), AIDS (64), cystic fibrosis (65), diabetes mellitus (66), atrial fibrillation (67), kidney disease (39), lung transplantation (68), arthritis (69), cancer (70), and several other conditions (71). The lower middle section of Figure 1 shows how the measure defects change in a clinical trial of sinus surgery (72). Further, the method has been used for health resource allocation modeling and has served as the basis for an innovative experiment on rationing of health care by the state of Oregon (73,74).

Studies have also demonstrated that the QWB is responsive to clinical change in a variety of conditions. The lower center section of Fig. 1 compares QWB scores for patients undergoing sinus surgery with those for a control group that did not receive surgery. Patients who undergo this difficult surgery achieve significant QWB benefits (72). The QWB also has shown small but significant improvements for patients using a new drug (auranofin) for the treatment of rheumatoid arthritis (75) and has been shown to be responsive to changes resulting from use of zidovudine for AIDS (64).

Despite widespread interest in the model among practitioners in many different specialties, the concept of a quality-adjusted life-year has received very little attention in the mental health fields. In several studies we have shown that the QWB is indeed related to measures of mental health status. One of these studies is summarized in the lower right panel of Fig. 1. The QWB was shown to be systematically related to level of the Assessment of Positive Symptoms for adults with schizophrenia (SAPS) (76). In summary, we believe that the QWB has validity for measuring a wide variety of health outcomes.

CONCLUSIONS

The term *quality of life* has been used inconsistently in the health services research literature. The definitions range from descriptions of functioning, to qualitative judgments of functioning, to measures typically unrelated to traditional health outcomes. Several dimensions of quality of life emerge across different discussions. These include mortality, functioning and role performance, symptoms, prognosis, and preference weights. We have proposed a system that combines these dimensions into a single number.

The objectives of health care include the extension of the life expectancy and the maximization of quality of life during years people are alive. In other words, health care should add years to life and also add life to years. All activities in the system should be evaluated by estimating their contribution toward these goals. The General Health Policy Model attempts to quantify the contributions from various providers

FIG. 1. *Top left:* Comparison of estimated QWB for patients with sinusitis, diabetes mellitus, and emphysema at different ages. (Data from the National Health Interview Survey, adapted from ref. 58.) *Top center:* Area under curve in cystic fibrosis. Top curve is the estimated U.S. quality adjusted life expectancy. Middle curve is the estimate for patients with cystic fibrosis. The bottom curve is the estimate for cystic fibrosis 25 years age. (Adapted from ref. 59.) *Top right:* QWB scores by levels of cognitive impairment for patients with Alzheimer's disease. (From ref. 60.) *Bottom left:* Comparison of mean QWB by CDC class in HIV disease. (From ref. 61.) *Bottom center:* QWB scores for those undergoing sinus surgery in comparison to controls. (Adapted from ref. 74.) *Bottom right:* QWB scores for schizophrenic patients rated on the scale for the assessment of positive symptoms as normal, low impairment, moderate impairment, an high impairment. (From ref. 76.)

and interventions so that the outcomes can be compared across very different interventions. These broad comparisons require an aggregate measure of health outcome. Profiles that have different dimensions for different components of outcome have little value for these comparisons. For example, many investigators suggest mental health outcomes cannot be evaluated using the same systems as used to measure physical health outcomes. However, we ultimately must make decisions about the comparative value of programs aimed at mental or physical health problems. Further, we must evaluate products that may have some benefits in one domain and side effects in another. A comprehensive system is required for these evaluations.

The General Health Policy Model has been used to evaluate outcomes in a variety of settings. Although we cannot review each of these applications in detail, different investigators have estimated the expected well-year benefits of

competing interventions. Table 4 summarizes many of these studies with adjustments to 1993 dollars. As the table suggests, some interventions, such as aerosolized pentamidine for prophylaxis of *Pneumocystis carinii* pneumonia in HIV disease, cost nearly one-half million dollars to produce the equivalent of a life-year. Traditional medical interventions in prevention, such as cholesterol and blood pressure reduction, may be much less expensive to produce the equivalent of a year of life. However, some nontraditional interventions including programs of smoking cessation counseling are even more cost-effective. Interestingly, our estimate suggests that the most cost-effective program has nothing to do with traditional health care: it involves passing laws that require the use of seat belts.

The use of the General Health Policy Model requires many heroic assumptions. The data for Table 4 come from a variety of different studies. In many of these cases, the

TABLE 4. *Summary of cost/well-year estimates for selected medical, surgical, and preventive interventions*[a]

Program	Reference	Cost/well-year
Seat belt laws	Kaplan (1988)	0
Antepartum and anti-D injection[b]	Torrance and Zipursky (1984)	1,543
Pneumonococcal vaccine for the elderly	OTA (1979)	1,765
Postpartum and anti-D injection[b]	Torrance and Zipursky (1977)	2,109
Coronary artery bypass surgery for left main coronary	Weinstein (1982)	4,922
Neonatal intensive care, 1,000–14,999 g	Boyle et al. (1983)	5,473
Smoking cessation counseling	Shulman (1991)	6,463
T4 (thyroid) screening	Epstein et al. (1981)	7,595
PKU screening	Bush et al. (1973)	8,498
Treatment of severe hypertension (diastolic > 105 mm Hg) in males age 40	Stason and Weinstein (1977)	10,896
Oral gold in rheumatoid arthritis	Thompson et al. (1987)	12,059
Dapsone for prophylaxis for PCP pneumonia	Freedberg (1991)	13,400
Treatment of mild hypertension (diastolic 95–104 mm Hg) in males age 40	Weinstein and Stason (1976)	22,197
Oat bran for high cholesterol	Kinosian et al. (1988)	22,910
Rehabilitation in COPD	Toevs et al. (1984)	28,320
Estrogen therapy for postmenopausal symptoms in women without a prior hysterectomy	Weinstein (1980)	32,057
Neonatal intensive care, 500–999 g	Boyle et al. (1983)	38,531
CABG (surgery) 2-vessel disease	Weinstein and Stason (1982)	39,770
Hospital hemodialysis	Churchill et al. (1984)	40,200
Coronary artery bypass surgery for single-vessel disease with moderately severe occlusion	Weinstein (1981)	42,195
School tuberculin testing program	Bush et al. (1972)	43,250
Continuous ambulatory peritoneal dialysis	Churchill et al. (1984)	54,460
Cholestipol for high cholesterol	Kinosian et al. (1988)	92,467
Cholestyramine for high cholesterol	Kinosian et al. (1988)	153,105
Screening mammography	Eddy (1990)	167,850
Total hip replacement	Liang (1987)	293,029
CABG (surgery) 1-vessel heart disease	Weinstein and Stason (1982)	662,835
Aerosolized pentamidine for prophylaxis of PCP pneumonia	Freedberg (1991)	756,000

[a]All estimates adjusted to 1993 U.S. dollars.
[b]Treatment for Rh immunization.
PKU, phenylketonuria; PCP, Pneumocystis carinii pneumonia; COPD, chronic obstructive pulmonary disease; CABG, coronary artery bypass graft.

health benefits were estimated using expert judgment. The accuracy of many of these estimates is unknown because they are based on judgments and not empirical studies. Furthermore, there are important assumptions in the application of the model that include the discount rate and the reliability of the estimate of treatment effectiveness. Despite these limitations, we believe the General Health Policy Model provides a unique new way of thinking about alternatives in health care. We hope to see more systematic experimental trials that employ structured measures such as the Quality of Well-Being Scale. As more data accumulate, we hope to provide a stronger data base for comparing different alternatives in health care.

ACKNOWLEDGMENT

This work was supported in part by grant PO 1-AR-40423 from the National Institute of Arthritis, Musculoskeletal, and Skin Disorders of the National Institutes of Health.

REFERENCES

1. Walker S, Rosser R, eds. *Quality of life assessment: key issues in the 1990s*. Dordrecht, Boston: Kluwer Academic, 1993.
2. Patrick DL, Erickson P. *Health status and health policy: quality of life in health care evaluation and resource allocation*. New York: Oxford University Press, 1993.
3. Ware JE, Sherbourne CD. The MOS 36-item short-form health survey (SF-36): conceptual framework and items selection. *Med Care* 1992; 30:473–483.
4. National Institutes of Health. *Epidemiology at Respiratory Diseases Task Force*. NIH Publication. Washington, DC: U.S. Government Printing Office, 1979;81:2019.
5. Bergner M, Babbitt RA, Carter WB, Gilson BS. The sickness impact profile: development and final revision of a health status measure. *Med Care* 1981;19:786–787.
6. Sullivan DF. Conceptual problems in developing an index of health. Office of Health Statistics. National Center for Health Statistics. Monograph Series II. No. 17. 1966.
7. Katz ST, Downs H, Cash H, Grotz R. Progress and development of an index of ADL. *Gerontologist* 1970;10:20–30.
8. Stewart AL, Ware JE, Brook RH, Davies-Avery A. *Conceptualization and measurement of health for adults: Vol II. Physical health in terms of functioning*. Santa Monica: RAND, 1978.
9. Fanshel S, Bush JW. A health status index and its applications to health-services outcomes. *Operations Res* 1970;18:1021–1066.
10. Follick MJ, Gorkin L, Smith T, et al. Quality of life post-myocardial infarction: the effects of a transtelephonic coronary intervention system. *Health Psychol* 1988;7:169–182.
11. Fishburn P. *Decision and value theory*. New York: Wiley, 1964.
12. Kaplan RM, Anderson JP. A general health policy model: update and applications. *Health Serv Res* 1988;23:203–235.
13. Kaplan RM. Social support and social health: Is it time to rethink the WHO definition of health? In: Sarason IG, Sarason BR, eds. *Social support: theory, research, and applications*. The Hague: Martinus Nijhoff, 1985:95–112.
14. Kaplan RM. Human preference measurement for health decisions and the evaluation of long-term care. In: Kane RL, Kane RA, eds. *Values and long-term care*. Lexington, MA: Lexington Books, 1982:157–188.
15. World Health Organization. *Constitution of the World Health Organization*. Geneva: WHO Basic Documents, 1948.
16. Meenan RF. AIMS approach to health status measurement: conceptual background and measurement properties. *J Rheumatol* 1982;9:785–788.
17. Kane RA, Kane RL. *Assessing the Elderly*. Boston: D.C. Heath, 1985.
18. Donald CA, Ware JE Jr, Brook RH, Davies-Avery A. Conceptualization and measurement of health for adults in the health insurance study. In: *Social health (R-198714-HEW) (vol IV)*. Santa Monica: RAND, 1980.
19. Ware JE Jr, Donald CA. *Social well-being: its meaning and measurement*. Santa Monica: RAND, 1980.
20. Heitzmann C, Kaplan RM. Interaction between sex and social support in the control of type II diabetes mellitus. *J Consult Clin Psychol* 1984;52(6):1087–1089.
21. Kaplan RM. Measures of health outcome in social support research. In Shumaker S, Czajkowski SM, eds. *Social support in cardiovascular disease*. New York: Plenum, 1994:65–94.
22. Kaplan RM. Value judgment in the Oregon Medicaid Experiment. *Med Care* 1994;32(10):975–988.
23. Ware JE Jr, Johnston SA, Davies-Avery A, Brook RH. Conceptualization and measurement of health for adults. In: *The Health Insurance Study, Vol 111. Mental Health*. Santa Monica: RAND, 1979.
24. Dupuy H. Utility of the national center for health statistics general well-being schedule in the assessment of self-representation of subjective well-being and distress. *National Conference on Education in Alcohol and Drug Abuse and Mental Health Programs*, Washington, D.C., 1974.
25. Ware JE Jr, Manning WG, Duan N, et al. Health status and the use of outpatient mental health services. *Am Psychol* 1984;30:1090–1100.
26. Wells KB. *Depression as a tracer condition for the national study of medical care outcomes*. Santa Monica: RAND, 1985.
27. Andersen BL, Kiecolt-Glaser JK, Glaser R. A biobehavioral model of cancer stress and disease course. *Am Psychol* 1994;49(5):389–404.
28. Atkins CJ, Kaplan RM, Timms RM, Reinsch S, Lofback K. Behavioral programs for exercise compliance in chronic obstructive pulmonary disease. *J Consult Clin Psychol* 1984;52:591–603.
29. Rice RM. Organizational work and the overall quality of life. In: Oscamp S, ed. *Applied social psychology annual: applications in organizational settings*, vol 5. Beverly Hills, CA: Sage, 1984:155–178.
30. Kaplan RM. An outcomes-based model for directing decisions in women's health care. *Clin Obstet Gynecol* 1994;37(1):192–206.
31. Kaplan RM, Feeny D, Revicki DA. Methods for assessing relative importance in preference based outcome measures. *Qual Life Res* 1993; 2:467–475.
32. Croog SH, Levine S, Testa MA, Brown D, Bulpitt CJ, Jenkins CD, Klerman GL, Williams GH. The effects of anti-hypertensive therapy on quality of life. *N Engl J Med* 1986;314:1657–1664.
33. Hunt SM, McEwen J. The development of a subjective health indicator. *Sociol Health Illness* 1983;2:231–245.
34. Doubilet P, Weinstein MC, McNeil BJ. Use and misuse of the term "cost-effectiveness" in medicine. *N Engl J Med* 1986;314:253–256.
35. Kaplan RM, Davis WK. Evaluating the costs and benefits of outpatient diabetes education and nutritional counseling. *Diabetes Care* 1986;9: 81–86.
36. Russell L. *Is prevention better than cure?* Washington, D.C.: Brookings Institution, 1986.
37. Yates BT, DeMuth NM. Alternative funding and incentive mechanisms for health systems. In: Broskowski A, Marks E, Budman SH, eds. *Linking health and mental health*. Beverly Hills, CA: Sage, 1981:77–99.
38. World Health Organization. *Health promotion: a discussion document on the concept and principles*. Copenhagen:WHO Regional Office for Europe, 1984.
39. Kaplan RM, Mehta R. Outcome measurement in kidney disease. *Blood Purification* 1994;12:20–29.
40. Kaplan RM. Using quality of life information to set priorities in health policy. *Soc Indicators Res* 1994; in press.
41. Kaplan RM, Anderson JP, Ganiats TG. The quality of well-being scale: rationale for a single quality of life index. In: Walker SR, Rosser RM, eds. *Quality of life assessment: key issues in the 1990s*. London: Kluwer Academic, 1993:65–94.
42. Weinstein MC, Stason WB. *Hypertension: a policy perspective*. Cambridge, MA: Harvard University Press, 1976.
43. Bush JW, Chen MM, Patrick DL. Cost-effectiveness using a health status index: analysis of the New York State PKU screening program. In: Berg R, ed. *Health Status Index*. Chicago: Hospital Research and Educational Trust, 1973:172–208.
44. Chen MM, Bush JW, Patrick DL. Social indicators for health planning and policy analysis. *Policy Sci* 1975;6:71–89.
45. Fanshel S, Bush JW. A health status index and its application to health-services outcomes. *Operations Res* 1970;18:1021–1066.

46. Reynolds WJ, Rushing WA, Miles DL. The validation of a function status index. *J Health Soc Behav* 1974;15:271.

47. Stewart AL, Ware JE Jr, Brook RH, Davies-Avery A. *Conceptualization and measurement of health for adults: Vol 2. Physical health in terms of functioning.* Santa Monica: RAND, 1978.

48. Patrick D, Sittanpalam Y, Somerville S, et al. A cross-cultural comparison of health status values. *Am J Public Health* 1985;75(12):1402–1407.

49. Balaban DJ, Fagi PC, Goldfarb NI, Nettler S. Weights for scoring the quality of well-being instrument among rheumatoid arthritic patients. *Med Care* 1986;24(11):973–980.

50. Kaplan RM, Bush JW. Health-related quality of life measurement for evaluation research and policy analysis. *Health Psychol* 1982;1:61–80.

51. Kaplan RM, Bush JW, Berry CC. Health Status: types of validity for an index of well-being. *Health Serv Res* 1976;11:478–507.

52. Anderson JP, Kaplan RM, Berry CC, Bush JW, Rumbaut RG. Interday reliability of function assessment for a health status measure: the quality of well-being scale. *Med Care* 1989;27(11):1076–1084.

53. Bush JW, Fanshel S, Chen MM. Analysis of a tuberculin testing program using a health status index. *Soc Econ Planning Sci* 1972;6:49–69.

54. Patrick DL, Bush JW, Chen MM. Toward an operational definition of health. *J Health Soc Behav* 1973;14:6–23.

55. Weinstein MC, Feinherg H. *Clinical decision analysis.* Philadelphia: WB Saunders, 1980.

56. Weinstein MC, Stason WB. *Cost-effectiveness of coronary artery bypass surgery.* Cambridge, MA: Harvard University Center for Analysis of Health Practice, 1983.

57. Office of Technology Assessment. U.S. Congress. *A review of selected federal vaccine and immunization policies: based on case studies of pneumococcal vaccine.* Washington, D.C.: U.S. Government Printing Office, 1979.

58. Erickson P, Kendall EA, Anderson JP, Kaplan RM. Using composite health status measures to assess the nation's health. *Med Care* 1989;27(suppl 3):S66–S76.

59. Orenstein DM, Kaplan RM. Measuring the quality of well-being in cystic fibrosis and lung transplantation. The importance of the area under the curve. *Chest* 1991;100:1016–1018.

60. Kerner D, Patterson TL, Kaplan RM. Validity of the Quality of Well-Being Scale in Alzheimer's disease. 1994; in preparation.

61. Kaplan RM, Anderson JP, Patterson TL, McCutchan JA, Weinrich JD, Heaton RH, Atkinson JH, Thal L, Chandler J, Grant I. Validity of the Quality of Well-Being Scale for persons with HIV infection. *Psychosom Med* 1995; in press.

62. Anderson JP, Kaplan RM, DeBon M. Comparison of responses to similar questions in health surveys. In: Fowler F, ed. *Health survey research methods.* Washington, D.C.: National Center For Health Statistics, 1989:13–21.

63. Kaplan RM, Atkins CJ, Timms R. Validity of a quality of well-being scale as an outcome measure in chronic obstructive pulmonary disease. *J Chronic Dis* 1984;37(2):85–95.

64. Kaplan RM, Anderson JP, Wu AW, Mathews WC, Kozin F, Orenstein D. The Quality of Well-Being Scale: applications in AIDS, cystic fibrosis, and arthritis. *Med Care* 1989;27(suppl 3):S27–S43.

65. Kaplan RM, Hartwell SL, Wilson DK, Wallace JP. Effects of diet and exercise interventions on control and quality of life in non-insulin-dependent diabetes mellitus. *J Gen Intern Med* 1987;2:220–228.

66. Orenstein DM, Nixon PA, Ross EA, Kaplan RM. The quality of well-being in cystic fibrosis. *Chest* 1989;95:344–347.

67. Ganiats TG, Palinkas LA, Kaplan RM. Comparison of Quality of Well-Being Scale and functional status index in patients with atrial fibrillation. *Med Care* 1992;30(10):958–964.

68. Squier H, Kaplan RM, Ries AL, et al. Quality of Well-Being predicts survival in lung transplantation. 1994; *Am J Respir Crit Care Med*; In press.

69. Kaplan RM, Kozin F, Anderson JP. Measuring quality of life in arthritis patients (including discussion of a general health-decision model). *Qual Life Cardiovasc Care* 1988;4:131–139.

70. Kaplan RM. Quality of life assessment for cost/utility studies in cancer. *Cancer Treat Rev* 1993;19(suppl A):85–96.

71. Kaplan, RM. The Ziggy Theorem: towards an outcome focused health psychology. *Health Psychol* 13;457–460.

72. Hodgkin PS. Health impact of endoscopic sinus surgery assessed by the Quality of Well-Being (QWB) Scale. Unpublished paper, University of California, San Diego, 1994.

73. Kaplan RM. Application of a general health policy model in the American health care crisis. *J R Soc Med* 1993;86:277–281.

74. Kaplan RM. *Hippocratic predicament: affordability, access, and accountability in health care.* San Diego: Academic Press, 1993.

75. Bombardier C, Ware J, Russell IJ, et al. Auranofin therapy and quality of life for patients with rheumatoid arthritis: results of a multicenter trial. *Am J Med* 1986;81:565–578.

76. Patterson TL, Kaplan RM, Grant I, Semple SJ, Moscona S, Koch WL, Harris MJ, Jeste DV. Quality of well-being in late-life psychosis. 1994; submitted.

Quality of Life and Pharmacoeconomics in Clinical Trials, Second Edition, edited by B. Spilker.
Lippincott-Raven Publishers, Philadelphia © 1996.

CHAPTER 33

SCL-90-R and the BSI

Leonard R. Derogatis and Maureen F. Derogatis

INTRODUCTION

The SCL-90-R, the Brief Symptom Inventory (BSI), and the matching clinical observer's scales of the Psychopathology Rating Scale series have their psychometric origins in some of the earliest scientific instruments designed to measure psychopathology and psychological distress (1,2).[1] The most immediate predecessor to the current series was the Hopkins Symptom Checklist (HSCL) (3,4), which itself represented a continuation of earlier psychometric efforts in self-report clinical assessment, most notably the Cornell Medical Index (5). Although the HSCL received favorable review in general (6,7), it also possessed a number of limitations that rendered it problematic. The HSCL was designed exclusively as a research instrument, and was never formally normed. In addition, the five dimensions of the HSCL were not sufficiently comprehensive in their coverage of the range of contemporary psychopathology. Also, a number of items were not factorially "pure" measures of the five primary symptom constructs, which further acted to introduce "noise" into measurement. Finally, an analogous clinical observer's scale, designed to provide a comparable clinician's assessment of the patient's status, was never developed for the HSCL.

L. R. Derogatis: Department of Clinical and Health Psychology, Hahnemann University, Philadelphia, Pennsylvania 19102.
M. F. Derogatis: Clinical Psychometric Research, Inc., Towson, Maryland 21204.

In response to these concerns, an organized psychometric development program was embarked upon during the 1970s that ultimately resulted in the SCL-90-R, the BSI, and the other instruments of the Psychopathology Rating Scale series. In developing the SCL-90-R, the core items of the five primary symptom dimensions of the HSCL as defined by Derogatis and his colleagues (8,9) were retained, and 45 new items, subsumed under four new symptom dimensions, were added. Revisions in the distress continuum, the administrative format, and the instructions were also introduced, and three related global measures of distress were designed into the instrument. The results of this program of research resulted in the SCL-90-R, a 90-item symptom self-report inventory; the BSI, a 53-item brief form of the scale; and two matching clinical observer's scales, the Derogatis Psychiatric Rating Scale (DPRS) and the SCL-90 Analogue. This is the series reviewed in this chapter.

A DESCRIPTIVE PROFILE OF THE SCL-90-R AND THE BSI

SCL-90-R

The SCL-90-R is a 90-item self-report symptom inventory designed to reflect the psychological symptom patterns of respondents in community, medical, and psychiatric settings. A prototype version of the scale was introduced by Derogatis and his associates (10) and, based on extensive clinical and psychometric evaluation, was amended and validated in the present revised form (11). The items of the SCL-90-R are rated on a five-point distress scale (0–4), ranging from "not-at-all" to "extremely." The inventory is scored and interpreted in terms of nine primary symptom dimensions and three global indices of distress. The primary symptom dimensions and globals are labeled as follows:

  I. Somatization
 II. Obsessive-compulsive
III. Interpersonal sensitivity
 IV. Depression
  V. Anxiety
 VI. Hostility
VII. Phobic Anxiety
VIII. Paranoid Ideation
 IX. Psychoticism
     Global Severity Index (GSI)
     Positive Symptom Distress Index (PSDI)
     Positive Symptom Total (PST)

The global indices have been developed to provide more flexibility in overall assessment of the patient's psychological distress status and to provide summary indices of levels of symptomatology and psychological distress. Previous research using analogs of these measures has confirmed that, although related, the three indicators reflect distinct aspects of psychological disorder (12).

Brief Symptom Inventory (BSI)

The BSI (13) is composed of 53 items and represents the brief form of the SCL-90-R. Completed subsequently to the SCL-90-R, it reflects psychopathology and psychological distress in terms of the same nine symptom dimensions and three global indices as the SCL-90-R. The BSI was designed specifically for the clinical assessment situation where time is a critical factor. It achieves reliable and valid measurement of the same symptom constructs as its longer companion through an item selection algorithm that retained items with the most "saturated" loadings on the nine primary symptom dimensions of the longer test. Correlations between the BSI and the SCL-90-R are very high (1,13), which has led some clinicians and investigators to employ the test even when time constraints are not an issue.

ADMINISTRATION

The SCL-90-R and the BSI are measures of current psychological symptom status and are not personality measures, except indirectly, in that certain personality types and *Diagnostic and Statistical Manual* (DSM) axis II disorders may tend to manifest characteristic profile on the primary symptom dimensions when distressed. In spite of their brevity, the SCL-90-R and the BSI do require a brief introduction

and a minimal amount of instruction is required to assure measurement validity. The test administrator's attitude concerning the value of the assessment is also extremely important. The instruments should always be introduced to the respondent in a professional and informed manner, which communicates the relevance of the psychological assessment to the individual's health status and potential treatment decisions.

Typically, the SCL-90-R requires between 12 and 15 minutes to complete, while the BSI usually requires 8 to 10 minutes. Typical time for administrative instruction is 2 to 5 minutes. The standard time reference for both tests is "7 days including today," although the tests are designed to be flexible so that evaluations over other specific periods of time can be made. A more detailed discussion of variations in assessment time reference can be found in the administration manuals for the two tests (1,13).

Appropriate Applications and Samples

The SCL-90-R and the BSI are designed to measure and quantify the psychological symptom status of patients with psychiatric disorder, medical patients, and community individuals who are not currently patients. They may be used appropriately with any respondents from these broad populations, since they represent the principal normative groups for both tests. The tests may also be utilized with adolescents (as young as 13) since separate norms for adolescents have been developed for both the SCL-90-R and the BSI.

Patients who fail to conform to the "inventory premise" (e.g., delirious, retarded, or floridly psychotic individuals) are usually considered to be poor candidates for administration of these inventories, as they would be for any self-report inventory. Similarly, individuals motivated to distort their answers (either minimizing or exaggerating distress), by virtue of the context in which they were being tested, are also poor candidates.

The SCL-90-R and the BSI may be used as a single, one-time assessments of the patient's clinical status, or they may be utilized repeatedly, to document formal outcomes, establish response trends, or quantify pre- to posttreatment evaluations. Test-retest reliabilities are superior for both tests (1,13), and significant "practice" effects that might bias results of repeated administration appear absent.

MATCHING CLINICAL RATING SCALES

A unique feature of both the SCL-90-R and the BSI derives from the fact that two matching clinical observer's rating scales, measuring the same psychopathologic constructs as the self-report scales, are available to quantify clinician judgments concerning patient psychological distress levels. The Derogatis Psychiatric Rating Scale (DPRS) and the SCL-90 Analogue Scale between them enable a broad range of clinical observers (e.g., psychiatrists, psychologists, physicians, nurses, social workers) to record systematic judgments concerning patient status.

The Derogatis Psychiatric Rating Scale

The DPRS is a multidimensional psychiatric rating scale designed to be a clinician's version of the SCL-90-R. The first nine symptom dimensions of the DPRS were constructed to match the nine primary symptom dimensions of the ''90.'' The DPRS also contains eight additional dimensions felt to be important to accurate clinical assessment, but not amenable to accurate patient self-report. The DPRS also contains a global rating scale termed the Global Pathology Index.

The DPRS is designed to be used by clinicians formally trained in psychopathology and familiar with contemporary models of psychiatric disorder (e.g., psychiatrists, psychologists, psychiatric nurses). Each dimension of the DPRS has been assigned a fundamental definition and represented on a seven-point scale (0–6) ranging from ''none'' to ''extreme.'' In addition to the normal adjectival and numerical definitions for scale points, three of the seven points on each dimension are further defined by brief clinical descriptors. The clinical descriptors were arrived at through the judgments of a panel of psychiatrists who utilized the psychophysical method of direct magnitude estimation to assign numerical values to over 12 descriptors per dimension.

A brief form of the DPRS, the Brief Derogatis Psychiatric Rating Scale (BDPRS) has also been developed. It differs from the parent instrument only in that the additional eight dimensions (non–SCL-90-R/BSI dimensions) are not represented on the brief form.

The SCL-90 Analogue Scale

The SCL-90 Analogue is a clinical observer's scale designed for the health professional without detailed psychiatric training or experience with psychopathology (e.g., physicians, nurses, clinical technicians). It is a graphic or analog scale in that each of the nine primary symptom dimensions of the SCL-90-R is represented on a 100-mm line, extending from ''not-at-all'' at one pole to ''extremely'' at the other.

In completing the SCL-90 Analogue, the clinical observer simply places a mark on each dimension line that he/she judges to be proportional to the degree the patient currently manifests that syndrome. Brief definitional paragraphs for each dimension are provided for easy reference and explanation. The SCL-90 Analogue is brief and uncomplicated to use, and usually requires less than 5 minutes to complete. In addition to the nine symptom dimensions, the SCL-90 Analogue also contains a Global Distress Scale. Psychometric data and information on clinical research done with both

the DPRS and the SCL-90 Analogue have recently been summarized elsewhere (1).

SCORING AND NORMS

Scoring for the SCL-90-R or the BSI is a straightforward procedure. It can be accomplished by using either SCL-90-R/BSI scoring templates and worksheets or a computerized scoring service available from the tests' publisher, National Computer Systems. Operationally, once calculated, raw scores for the nine symptom dimensions and three global indices are then converted to standardized T scores and plotted on the appropriate profile (according to norm group).

The use of standardized scales (e.g., area T scores) enables comparisons of the status or performance of an individual with that of a relevant reference group of interest. Standardized scales also enable meaningful comparisons of an individual's performance or status in one domain to that in another (e.g., relative levels of anxiety and depression, verbal versus quantitative abilities). There are a number of standardized scales currently in use; however, we chose the *area T score* for our instruments. The area T score represents a normalizing transformation that carries with it interpretable centile equivalents; linear T scores do so only when the basic raw score distribution is normal.

An added refinement inherent in the norms of the SCL-90-R and the BSI concerns the fact that they are *gender-keyed*; that is, separate norms are available for males and females. The development of gender-appropriate norms is based on the consistent observation that females in our culture routinely report significantly more psychological symptoms than males do, and they also express greater levels of distress associated with emotional conflicts. Regardless of the ultimate basis for this observation, gender-keyed norms are essential psychometric adjustment mechanisms that introduce increased precision and meaning into the interpretation of test scores. Currently there are four formal norm groups for the two inventories: adult psychiatric outpatients (norm A), adult community nonpatients (norm B), adult psychiatric inpatients (norm C), and adolescent community nonpatients (norm E). Detailed normative data is provided in the respective administration manuals of the two tests (1,13).

VALIDATION STUDIES

Two issues essential to an informed appreciation of validity relative to psychological test instruments are an understanding of (a) the *programmatic* nature of the validation process, and (b) the highly *specific* nature of validity. The former refers to the fact that recent psychometric theorists have strongly emphasized construct validity as the central criterion for ascribing validity and meaning to psychological tests (14). We are reminded that the validation process is comprised of a systematic program of experiments and analyses that are analogous to the sequence of research activities necessary to prove a scientific theory. Validation is not accomplished through a single definitive experiment; rather, it is achieved through a systematic series of rational operations and empirical procedures that converge to establish and redefine the limits of meaning of the measured construct(s). Construct validity represents the degree to which there is correlation between the operations of measurement and the theoretical constructs that they purport to measure. Data from predictive, content, convergent-discriminant, and other types of validation studies contribute to the ultimate validation of the hypothetical construct(s) that our tests serve to operationalize. Validation is a programmatic process; one that is dynamic and ongoing rather than one that is represented by a static, point-in-time achievement.

The issue concerning specificity on the other hand refers to the fact that the frequently asked question "Is this test valid?" has no scientific meaning, unless the question "For what purpose?" is simultaneously addressed. Psychological tests are not "valid" in general, but like all other scientific measures, they are valid for certain specific assessments and invalid for most others. Validity, relative to psychological test instruments, takes on practical meaning only in regard to specific objectives or criteria.

In the years since the original introduction of the SCL-90-R and BSI, the tests have been widely employed as self-report symptom inventories. They have been utilized as screening tests, treatment planning aids and outcome measures across a broad spectrum of clinical and research contexts. Although this chapter does not comprehensively review these applications, in the sections that follow we attempt to review and briefly describe outstanding studies that reveal the tests' outcome sensitivity and make a significant contribution to construct validation.

Convergent-discriminant validation is a fundamental form of validity that demonstrates that the measure under evaluation displays substantial correlations with independent measures of the same construct and shows minimal correlation with measures of dissimilar constructs. A number of studies have been reported that contrast the SCL-90-R and the BSI with other established multidimensional measures of psychopathology in an effort to determine the instruments' convergent-discriminant validity. Derogatis et al. (15) used 119 "symptomatic volunteers" to contrast the dimension scores of the SCL-90-R with scores from the Minnesota Multiphasic Personality Inventory (MMPI). In addition to scoring for the standard clinical scales, the MMPI was also scored for Wiggins (16) content scales, and Tryon's (17) cluster scales. Results showed very acceptable levels of convergent-discriminant validity. An analogous study was completed utilizing the three sets of MMPI scores with the BSI (13), which also showed high levels of appropriate convergence and discrimination.

A similar analysis (18) was reported comparing the SCL-90-R with the dimensions of the Middlesex Hospital Questionnaire (MHQ). In the majority of instances there was very good convergence between like dimensions, as well as good discrimination between dissimilar constructs. Other investigators have shown high correlations between specific dimensions of the SCL-90-R and various unidimensional tests. Featuring the Depression dimension as an example, reports have been published demonstrating high convergence with the Center for Epidemiologic Studies–Depression scale and the Hamilton Depression Rating Scale (19), the Raskin Depression Screen (20), and the Beck Depression Scale (21).

In addition, two recent studies compared the performance of the SCL-90-R with the General Health Questionnaire (GHQ). Koeter (22) evaluated the convergent and discriminant validity of the two instruments with particular emphasis on anxiety and depression, and concluded that both scales show good convergent and discriminant validity. He further recommended the SCL-90-R as a superior multidimensional measure of psychopathology, and concluded that it possessed a preferable Anxiety dimension. In a second comparison, Wiznitzer et al. (23) used Receiver Operating Characteristic (ROC) analysis to contrast the performance of the SCL-90-R, the GHQ-28, and the Young Adult Self-Report (YASR) scale in screening for psychopathology in samples of young adults. The SCL-90-R and the YASR essentially performed at an equivalent level, with both outperforming the GHQ-28 across the range of the ROC screening curve.

In a very rigorous and systematic effort, Peveler and Fairburn (24) published an integrated series of validation studies with the SCL-90-R that reflect elements of concurrent, predictive, and construct validity. These investigators correlated scores from the SCL-90-R with those from the Present State Examination (PSE) (25), a clinician-administered structured interview. They utilized two distinct samples: a chronic medical disease group comprised of 102 diabetic patients, and a psychologically distressed cohort represented by 71 patients suffering from bulimia. Three distinct validation experiments were included in the study. The first investigation assessed the case finding power of the SCL-90-R via ROC analysis and logistic regression. This study evaluated the proficiency with which the SCL-90-R detected PSE-defined psychiatric disorders in the two samples. Results demonstrated high efficiency for the SCL-90-R with both groups, in that the area under the curve was .90 + .03 in both samples. Among diabetics sensitivity was 88% with a specificity of 80%; in the bulimic sample, sensitivity was 76% with a specificity of 92%. Logistic regression analysis, which related the GSI scores from the SCL-90-R to the probability of being a PSE-defined case also portrayed the SCL-90-R favorably. Sensitivity among diabetics was 72%, whereas specificity was 87%. In the bulimic group, coefficients were 77% and 91%, respectively.

The study also evaluated the validity of the global indices of the SCL-90-R as general psychopathology measures by virtue of the magnitude of their correlations with the global indices of the PSE. Across both samples, all correlations were statistically significant and ranged from a low of approximately .60 to a high of .82. Peveler and Fairburn (24) further employed discriminant function analysis to test the validities of the SCL-90-R primary symptom dimensions to predict convergent PSE syndromes. Appropriate subscales were identified in 12 of 14 instances in the diabetic sample and 11 of 14 cases in the bulimic cohort. A further test of concurrent validity was conducted with the depression dimension of the SCL-90-R by correlating its scores with two unidimensional depression instruments, the Beck Depression Inventory and the Asberg Rating Scale. Correlations were .80 and .81, respectively. This series of validation experiments, accomplished across two distinct types of patient samples, makes a substantial contribution to the construct validity of the instrument.

Predictive Validity: The SCL-90-R as an Outcome Measure

The form of validation that has the highest practical appeal in most clinical and research contexts is *predictive validity.* The more extensive and integrated the network of evidence of predictive validity for a psychological test, the greater the potential utility of that instrument. The most recent edition of *The SCL-90-R Bibliography* (26) includes approximately 800 published reports on research using the SCL-90-R, while the comparable *BSI Bibliography* (27) lists over 200 published studies with the BSI. This accumulation of research, which includes numerous predictive validity studies, demonstrates in compelling fashion the breadth of validation of the two inventories.

This chapter cannot comprehensively review this body of research. Nonetheless, in the sections that follow, we document the instruments' sensitivity to psychological distress and psychopathologic states across an extensive range of medical and psychiatric cohorts. We will also examine their sensitivity to change and outcome in a spectrum of therapeutic intervention studies that range from meditation (28), to multicenter psychotherapy studies (29), to pharmacotherapeutic drug trials (30). Mental health outcomes take place over varying periods of time, from weeks to months, and in some cases, years. Test-retest reliabilities for the SCL-90-R and the BSI show them to have good temporal stability, and studies documented here show them to be sensitive to therapeutic effects many weeks and months subsequent to baseline.

Screening Studies

As the magnitude of the additional costs associated with undiagnosed psychiatric illness in medical populations has become better recognized (31–33), the application of formal screening paradigms to enhance the identification of occult psychiatric disorders in primary care has become more widespread (34). Probably because of its relative brevity, the BSI has been used in such applications more frequently than the SCL-90-R.

As early as 1980, Boughsty and Marshal (35) used the BSI in a community screening study in which between 25% and 33% of the population were found to be experiencing high distress levels. More recently (36), the BSI was employed in a screening paradigm developed on an orthopedic service. Of the patients referred for consultation, approximately 80% were identified as positive for psychiatric disorder by the BSI, with an 87% confirmation rate coming from formal psychiatric diagnosis.

Working in an oncology setting, Zabora and his associates (37) utilized the BSI to identify newly diagnosed cancer patients who were likely to manifest clinical levels of psychological distress, both at the time of diagnosis and in the future. The BSI correctly identified 84% of patients as potentially problematic, who were in fact judged to be clinically distressed one year later. Their research also showed the BSI to have high cost-benefit relative to alternative approaches. Also in the context of an oncology population, Derogatis et al. (38) used the SCL-90-R in a multicenter trial examining the prevalence of psychiatric disorder among newly diagnosed cancer patients. The screening test also showed high agreement with DSM-III psychiatric diagnostic interviews across study centers.

In a somewhat nontraditional application of screening methodology, Royse and Drude (39) used the BSI in an effort to identify clients at an outpatient drug treatment agency with differential levels of drug abuse. They found very strong associations between distress levels on the BSI and levels of drug use, as well as between BSI scores and ultimate case disposition.

Suicide Risk

A perennially important issue in psychological assessment concerns the reliable early identification of the suicidal patient. A number of recent studies have addressed this question using the SCL-90-R or the BSI. Bulik et al. (40) compared 67 patients suffering from recurrent major depression and a history of attempted suicide with 163 recurrent depressives negative for a history of suicidal behavior. Four subscales (Somatization, Interpersonal Sensitivity, Paranoid Ideation, and Psychoticism) and the global scores significantly discriminated positive from negative suicide attempters. A logistic regression analysis including these SCL-90-R subscales and additional variables enabled a 77% accurate prediction of cases.

In an comparable evaluation of panic patients who were positive and negative for attempted suicide, Noyes and his colleagues (41) reported findings similar to those of Bulik and her colleagues (40). Seven of the nine SCL-90-R symptom dimensions and the GSI successfully discriminated suicide attempters from those who did not make attempts. Just as the previous investigators, these researchers found that patients who made suicide attempts had greater severity of distress in general, with particular elevations on measures of inferiority feelings and self-deprecation.

Swedo and her associates (42) recently extended the predictive validity of the SCL-90-R regarding suicidal behavior to an adolescent population. This group compared adolescents with a history of attempted suicide to adolescents judged to be at risk for suicide for a variety of reasons, and an adolescent control group. All SCL-90-R subscales successfully discriminated suicide attempters from controls, while the majority of scales differentiated those at risk from controls. The Obsessive-Compulsive score and the PSDI significantly discriminated suicide attempters from those at risk. As is true of their adult counterparts, adolescents who actually attempt suicide tend to perceive themselves as more highly distressed and hopeless than adolescents who are merely at risk. In a more general review of the utility of the SCL-90-R with depressed and conduct disordered adolescents, McGough and Curry (43) demonstrated convergent and discriminant validity for the test. They further showed that several SCL-90-R subscales had diagnostic specificity for major depression and conduct disorders. In an interesting study with a schizophrenic cohort in a community treatment center, Cohen et al. (44) used the BSI to demonstrate that the 10% of patients who eventually committed suicide had significantly higher distress profiles at the time of admission.

Psychotherapy Outcome Research

The efficacy of psychotherapeutic interventions in patients suffering from psychological distress and psychiatric disorder is obviously an issue of major interest in modern health care. Crits-Christoph (45) recently completed a meta-analysis of almost one dozen contemporary studies evaluating the efficacy of brief dynamic psychotherapy (BDP). The outcome measure chosen to record the "general level of psychiatric symptoms" in the meta-analysis was the SCL-90-R. Using Cohen's (46) *d-statistic,* the SCL-90-R demonstrated large treatment effects for brief dynamic psychotherapy when compared to waiting list control ($d = .82$), small effects ($d = .20$) when contrasted with nonpsychiatric interventions, and equivalent effects when compared to alternative psychotherapeutic approaches ($d = .05$). Based on these data Crits-Christoph concluded that efficacy does not differ significantly across therapies.

Horowitz et al. (47) also studied the efficacy of BDP using the SCL-90-R in their research with bereaved individuals. They found SCL-90-R Anxiety and Depression subscales and globals were highly sensitive to treatment-induced improvement. Further, they observed that magnitude of distress reduction was significantly correlated with baseline distress levels. Garner et al. (48) also evaluated the efficacy of BDP, contrasting it with supportive-expressive therapy in a sample of 151 bulimic patients. These investigators found that both therapies significantly reduced eating disturbances and psychological distress; however, the cognitive behavior approach was significantly more efficacious in reducing Depression, Interpersonal Sensitivity, and general psychological distress.

In yet another evaluation of brief dynamic psychotherapy, Horowitz and associates (49) employed the SCL-90-R to assess symptomatic distress during a 10-week waiting period followed by 20 sessions of active treatment. Analysis showed a small but reliable reduction in distress levels during the waiting period, followed by a dramatic reduction in distress during the first 10 psychotherapy sessions. Further reductions in distress were minimal after session 20, probably because distress levels had been reduced to the margins of the normal range by session 10 with little likelihood of further decline. These investigators concluded that symptomatic improvement tends to occur disproportionately during earlier phases of treatment.

A number of recent studies have used the SCL-90-R to evaluate alternatives to dynamic psychotherapies. Fairburn et al. (50) compared two variations of cognitive behavior therapy and interpersonal therapy in a cohort of bulimic patients. The SCL-90-R revealed significant efficacy for all three interventions from baseline to treatment termination; however, no significant differential treatment effects were observed across any of the three treatments. Kabat-Zinn et al. (51) demonstrated significant efficacy for a meditation-based group stress reduction program with patients suffering from generalized anxiety disorder and panic disorder. Those patients whose GSI scores were above the 70th centile on the SCL-90-R community nonpatient norm demonstrated disproportionate benefit from this therapeutic intervention. Also working with panic patients, Beck et al. (52) compared relaxation training with cognitive therapy and a minimal contact condition in a small group format across a 10-week period. The Phobic Anxiety dimension of the SCL-90-R revealed significant mean differences across the three groups, with the cognitive therapy group having significantly lower levels than the other two groups, and relaxation therapy also showing better scores than minimal contact. Shear (53) compared cognitive behavioral treatment with nonprescriptive reflective treatment with patients diagnosed with panic disorder over 12 treatment sessions. Assessments were done at pre- and posttreatment and 6 months follow-up. The SCL-90-R showed both treatments to be essentially equivalent in reducing symptomatic distress across the 12 treatment sessions, a finding shared by the other measures in use. At 6 months follow-up, however, scores on the "90" showed continued improvement differentially for the nonprescriptive reflective treatment group, a finding not observed with other study measures. Finally, in an extension of the Sheffield Psychotherapy Project, Shapiro and his colleagues (54) recently reported on a comparison of cognitive behavior therapy and psychodynamic interpersonal therapy with depressed patients. The study design called for randomization into either 8-week or 16-week treatment groups and three levels of depression (high, moderate, low) severity. The two treatments were found to be equally effective in general, with no overall advantage associated with the longer treatment regimen. They did observe an interactive effect between depression severity and treatment duration, however, in that those patients with the most severe depressions responded significantly better to 16-week treatment.

Using a unique patient sample, Kleinhauz (55) applied the inventory in a dentally phobic population treated via behavior modification. They observed significantly higher scores on Somatization, Psychoticism, and the PSDI among treatment successes compared to treatment failures. The predictive value of the selected SCL-90-R scales was 71%.

Although not as extensively utilized as the SCL-90-R, the BSI has also been employed frequently as an outcome measure in psychotherapy trials. For example, Thompson et al. (56) contrasted behavioral, cognitive, and psychodynamically oriented group therapies in depressed geriatric patients. Although the BSI did not reveal noteworthy differences across treatments, it showed very significant differences from pre- to posttreatment in all three groups. Johnson and Thorn (57) used the BSI to compare group versus individual therapy in chronic headache patients over a 10-week period. They also found no significant therapeutic differences across treatments, but substantial differences from baseline to posttreatment. Baider et al. (58) reported similar findings for postmastectomy patients treated via different time-limited thematic groups. Nezu et al. (59) extended the application of the BSI to dually diagnosed, mentally retarded individuals in a study contrasting assertiveness training versus problem-solving training. Substantial differences were observed for both techniques, both during treatment and at 3-month follow-up. Beutler et al. (60) also used the BSI to compare the relative efficacy of group cognitive therapy, focused expressive therapy, and supportive self-directed therapy in patients with major depressive disorder. Patient coping style was employed as a major mediating variable. Results of the study revealed very significant interactive effects between reduction in distress, type of treatment, and patient coping style.

Psychopharmacology Outcome Trials

Drug treatment represents one of the foundations of contemporary therapeutic approaches to psychiatric disorders, both as a sole intervention in mental conditions, and in combination with various forms of psychotherapy. In the design of drug trials, comparisons between active drugs from the same therapeutic class place stringent demands on the psychometric sensitivity of outcome measures (61). However, to be minimally acceptable as an outcome measure in psychotropic drug trials, an instrument must at least demonstrate sensitivity to drug versus placebo differences. The selective review that follows attests to the fact that the SCL-90-R and the BSI have been employed as primary outcome measures in psychotropic drug trials for almost 20 years, and have displayed substantial utility and predictive validity in this capacity.

Ravaris and his associates (62) utilized the SCL-90-R in a study that represents the first definitive double-blind controlled comparison of a monoamine oxidase inhibitor (MAOI) with a tricyclic antidepressant in the treatment of depression. These investigators compared the tricyclic amitriptyline to the MAOI phenelzine and demonstrated both drugs to have significant efficacy beyond placebo in reducing symptomatic distress of depressed outpatients over a period of 6 weeks. More impressively, in drug-drug comparisons the SCL-90-R showed phenelzine to be significantly more efficacious than amitriptyline in reducing anxiety. In comparisons with SCL-90-R adult community norms, analyses revealed that although distress was significantly reduced after 6 weeks of treatment, symptoms remained elevated beyond normal levels. More recently, several trials have been reported in which the SCL-90-R has documented the differential efficacy of phenelzine. Soloff et al. (63) contrasted phenelzine with haloperidol and placebo in a randomized double-blind trial with 108 hospitalized patients suffering from borderline personality disorder. The MAOI was found to be differentially effective over haloperidol on the SCL-90-R obsessive-compulsive, depression, anxiety, and GSI measures. McGrath et al. (64) also recently reported a double-blind crossover trial of phenelzine against imipramine in the treatment of outpatients with treatment-refractory depression. Sixty-seven percent of the patients who were initially clinically unresponsive to imipramine improved on phenelzine.

In a somewhat specialized patient setting, Levine et al. (65) used the SCL-90-R with a small sample of HIV patients suffering from major depressive syndrome who were treated with fluoxetine. They observed significant improvement on almost all SCL-90-R dimensions over the 4 weeks of active treatment, gains that were sustained at 2-month follow-up. Walsh et al. (66) also used the SCL-90-R in a three-phase evaluation of the efficacy of desipramine in the treatment of depressed bulimics. Four SCL-90-R primary dimension scores and the GSI revealed significant efficacy for the active drug over placebo.

Turning to the pharmacotherapy of anxiety disorders, the SCL-90-R served as one of the principal outcome measures in a large multicenter trial evaluating the efficacy of alprazolam in the treatment of panic disorder and agoraphobia (30). In this trial the scale demonstrated substantial efficacy for alprazolam compared with placebo. In an analogous study, Schweizer et al. (67) used the SCL-90-R in a comparison of alprazolam with imipramine over 8 weeks of acute treatment followed by an additional 6 months of maintenance treatment. Results showed both compounds effective in eliminating and maintaining freedom from panic; however, side effect and attrition rates clearly favored alprazolam. In treating a related condition, Noyes et al. (68) reported a double-blind crossover study of diazepam versus the beta-blocker propranolol in the treatment of panic-driven agoraphobia. SCL-90-R measures of Anxiety, Phobic Anxiety, and the GSI showed very impressive efficacy for diazepam over propranolol in this study in which no placebo group was utilized. Although the BSI is not utilized as frequently in drug trials, Woodman and Noyes (69) reported on a trial very recently in which the scale was used to document the treatment efficacy of divalproex sodium in the treatment of panic disorder. The design involved a 6-week open trial with flexible dose design in which patients were evaluated weekly with the BSI and at 6 months follow-up. Very significant reductions were noted on the BSI dimensions of Somatization, Anxiety, and Phobic Anxiety that were sustained throughout the 6 weeks of treatment and at 6 months follow-up.

Although clomipramine is primarily noted for its therapeutic effects in obsessive compulsive disorder, Judd et al. (70) utilized the drug with patients suffering from panic disorder. In an 8-week treatment trial, the SCL-90-R showed significant reductions in distress on most subscales, particularly on the Anxiety dimension. Similarly, Kahn et al. (71) contrasted clomipramine with 5-hydroxytryptophan in an 8-week double-blind, placebo-controlled trial with mixed anxiety disorders. Results showed both drugs significantly superior to placebo, with clomipramine demonstrating significantly greater efficacy in reducing depressive symptoms. A comparable study comparing clomipramine with fluvoxamine in this population (72) revealed both drugs to be superior to placebo; however, drug-drug comparisons showed clomipramine to be superior to fluvoxamine on several SCL-90-R subscales.

In another interesting trial, Perse et al. (73) employed the SCL-90-R to assess the efficacy of fluvoxamine in the treatment of obsessive-compulsive disorder in a 20-week, double-blind, crossover design against placebo. Eighty-one percent of the patients on the active drug, versus 19% on placebo, improved on multiple SCL-90-R scales. In particular the obsessive-compulsive dimension revealed significant change, demonstrating clear efficacy for the drug, and validity and outcome sensitivity for the SCL-90-R. Kim and Dysken (74) also used the SCL-90-R as an outcome assessment with obsessive-compulsive patients in a 12-week open trial with fluoxetine. Focusing on the obsessive-compulsive subscale, these investigators reported significant reductions from baseline to treatment completion.

Recently, psychopharmacologists have increasingly attempted to intervene in axis II personality disorders with pharmacologic agents. For example, Teicher et al. (75) reported on an open trial of low-dose thioridazine in the treatment of borderline personality disorder. The SCL-90-R was utilized as a self-report measure of psychopathology. Results showed significant reductions in distress on many SCL-90-R subscales, particularly for the subgroup who completed the full 12 weeks of treatment. Similarly, Cornelius et al. (76), postulating that borderline personality disorder has its etiology based in deranged serotonin regulation, utilized the SCL-90-R as an outcome measure in an 8-week trial of the seroto-

nin uptake inhibitor fluoxetine. The majority of SCL-90-R dimensions were sensitive to a therapeutic effect for the drug over the 8-week period.

Taken together this selected review of studies not only demonstrates the requisite sensitivity to drug-placebo comparisons essential in a psychopharmacologic outcome measure, but discloses the much more demanding capacity of the SCL-90-R to identify differences between active pharmacotherapeutic drugs of the same functional class.

Somatization Disorders

There is consistent evidence of a strong association between manifestations of somatization and psychiatric disorders in primary care populations (77,78). Additionally, recent evidence suggests that individuals suffering from various somatization disorders utilize health care services at a rate as high as *nine* times that of the general population (79). These observations have resulted in enhanced interest in this class of disorders, and given impetus to a substantial amount of new research. Since the SCL-90-R is multidimensional in nature, and contains a Somatization dimension, it has been viewed as a very appropriate outcome measure in studies on patients suffering from a variety of somatic complaints.

Katon and his colleagues (80) used the SCL-90-R to operationally define a group of "high distressed high utilizers" within two large primary care practices. The group was further divided into four subgroups on the basis of numbers of self-reported, unexplained somatic symptoms. The investigators observed linear increases in SCL-90-R scores on Somatization, Depression, and Anxiety as they moved from low to high across the somatic symptom subgroups. In addition, several independent indicators of the prevalence of psychiatric disorder also showed linear increases across the four subgroups.

Also investigating somatizing patients, Kellner et al. (81) used the SCL-90-R to relate different dimensions of psychopathology to distinct aspects of hypochondriasis. They found that self-rated Somatization and Anxiety were predictive of hypochondriacal fears and beliefs, but Depression was not. Further, they reported that fear of disease correlated highest with Anxiety, while a false conviction of having a disease was more highly associated with Somatization. Dickson and his associates (82) also evaluated somatizing patients in a university medical clinic setting. They found that high somaticizers had the highest prevalence of psychiatric disorders and substance abuse, and demonstrated the highest mean SCL-90-R symptom distress profile.

Chiles et al. (83) recently reported a very interesting study with the BSI. Although not a study of somatization disorder per se, the results seem to have relevance for this area of research. These investigators surveyed over 800 members of a state bar association, evaluating smoking, alcohol consumption, and medical status, as well as levels of psychological distress using the BSI. Among male lawyers, scores on the Somatization, Anxiety, and Depression dimensions discriminated markedly between smokers and nonsmokers. Discriminant function analysis demonstrated that smoking was also disproportionately associated with greater alcohol use.

Outcomes in Anxiety and Depressive Disorders

A series of reliably derived estimates indicate that anxiety and depressive disorders account for approximately 75% to 80% of the psychiatric conditions seen in either the community or primary care practice (34). A number of authorities estimate that depressive disorder is *the* most prevalent clinical problem in primary care (33). For these reasons, we review recent research with the SCL-90-R and BSI specific to the anxiety and depressive disorders.

In a confirming demonstration of differential sensitivity for the SCL-90-R, Rosenberg et al. (84) used the test to discriminate various categories of panic patients with and without comorbid clinical depression. The SCL-90-R profile was substantially different between patients diagnosed with concomitant major depression, minor depression, and absence of mood disorder based on the Hamilton Rating Scale for Depression. In addition, the SCL-90-R also effectively discriminated between diagnostic categories of current major depressive episode, other mood disorder, and no mood disorder based on the Standardized Clinical Interview for Diagnosis of DSM-III Disorders. The authors concluded that the findings support the theory of a common diathesis for panic and mood disorders, with more severe variants of the condition being characterized by symptoms of *both* anxiety and depression. Vollrath et al. (85) have also recently reported on comparisons of patients with panic disorder versus those with panic and comorbid depression using the SCL-90-R. These investigators reported similar findings in that the Phobic Anxiety dimension, and to a lesser degree, the Anxiety dimension clearly discriminated the subgroups, with the panic/depression group displaying greater general severity and the indication of a more specific nosology. Going a step further in assessing the significance of comorbidity, Andreoli et al. (86) evaluated pairs of subjects suffering from major depressive episode with and without comorbid panic disorder. Depressives were contrasted with matched controls to determine whether T-lymphocyte abnormalities were associated with panic disorder comorbidity. Results showed patients with comorbid panic disorder had greater numbers of T lymphocytes and significantly higher scores on the SCL-90-R Anxiety dimension.

The SCL-90-R has been used as a frequent outcome measure in studies focused on depression. Weissman et al. (87) used the instrument to characterize primary versus secondary depressions, and further, used the scale in an epidemiologic study of depression in five psychiatric populations. Wetzler et al. (88) profiled depressed versus panic patients using the SCL-90-R; Stewart et al. (89) contrasted atypical depressions with seasonal affective disorders using the test; and Cameron

and colleagues (90) evaluated the exacerbating potential of exercise using the test. Bryer et al. (91) used the SCL-90-R to predict suppressors versus nonsuppressors on the dexamethasone suppression test (DST). Employing discriminant function analysis, they correctly predicted DST status in 73% of cases. In another prospective study, Robinson et al. (92) found that during the second trimester of pregnancy, elevated scores on the SCL-90-R predicted those women who would have difficulties adjusting 1-year postpartum. Katon and Sullivan (33) recently reviewed studies of depression occurring in chronic medical patients, and examined a number of studies done with the SCL-90-R.

The BSI has also been utilized in clinical research on depression. Amenson and Lewinsohn (93) reported on a longitudinal prevalence study of depression in the community. They observed that the prevalence of depression was persistently higher for women than for men, regardless of the measures they utilized to operationally define depression. In addition, women with a prior history of depression were much more likely to experience recurrences than were their male counterparts with such histories. Buckner and Mandell (94) also used the BSI in a prospective design with young adults using psychoactive drugs to establish risk of developing depressive symptoms. Detailed analysis of the data identified the drug methaqualone as being a significant predictor of increased risk, with low self-esteem and negative life events also having predictive significance.

The inventories have also been frequently used in research on the anxiety disorders. Cameron et al. (95) used the SCL-90-R to profile patients with different DSM-III anxiety disorders. The same research team also employed the instrument to evaluate the influence of exercise on levels of anxiety in patients diagnosed with anxiety disorders (96). Findings revealed that 31% of patients with panic attacks were exercise sensitive, compared with only 7% of other anxiety disordered patients. The SCL-90-R Anxiety and Phobic Anxiety subscales were particularly effective in making this discrimination.

Ae Lee and Cameron (96) used the SCL-90-R to assess the relationship between type-A behavior, symptom distress patterns, and family history of coronary heart disease among anxiety-disordered subjects. Significant correlations between SCL-90-R Anxiety and Hostility scores and Jenkins Activity Scale type-A scores were observed among males, but not among female patients. The same research group (97) also used the instrument to evaluate the relationship between caffeine consumption and the experience of anxiety in anxious patients. They discovered that levels of anxiety were unrelated to overall amount of caffeine consumed, but that the subset of patients who reported becoming anxious in response to coffee had higher SCL-90-R Somatization and Phobic Anxiety scores than those who did not, even though their daily caffeine consumption was equivalent.

In an interesting discriminative study Noyes et al. (98) contrasted SCL-90-R individual symptom and dimension profiles across samples of patients diagnosed with generalized anxiety disorder (GAD) and those with a panic disorder (PD) diagnosis. Patients diagnosed with GAD had symptom patterns indicative of CNS hyperarousal, while patients with PD diagnoses manifested symptoms more indicative of autonomic hyperactivity. The GAD sample evidenced much lower scores on dimensions of Anxiety, Depression, and Phobic Anxiety, and appeared to have less overall psychological morbidity.

In their recent extensive review, Katon and Roy-Byrne (32) proposed the existence of a pervasive subclinical, mixed anxiety-depression syndrome. They cite compelling evidence to substantiate the existence of this subdiagnostic syndrome, with studies involving the SCL-90-R contributing confirmatory data for their hypothesis. Individuals afflicted with the condition are found to have a high incidence of medically unexplained problems, and utilize health care resources to a proportionally greater degree. They are also observed to be at increased risk for more severe anxiety and mood disorders. Taking a somewhat different theoretical position, Clark and Watson (99) developed a tripartite model of anxiety and depression. Based on a meta-analysis of psychometric data, they propose that at the clinical level, anxiety and depressive phenomena may be explained by a general distress factor and two additional specific factors of anxiety and depression. The authors present a substantial body of data in support of their position, in particular noting the explicit presence of this pattern in numerous studies with the SCL-90-R.

Applications in Medicine

From their inception, the SCL-90-R and the BSI were designed for use in primary care and other medical populations. An early application of the SCL-90-R in a medical environment was reported by Snyder et al. (100). In a family practice setting, these investigators showed that those patients who revealed significant communication problems with their physicians also had significantly higher distress scores on the SCL-90-R. More recently, as part of the Family Heart Study, Weidner et al. (101) demonstrated significant reductions in SCL-90-R Depression and Hostility scores over a 5-year dietary intervention program designed to reduce plasma cholesterol. In a different chronic disease context, Irvine et al. (102) demonstrated that worry concerning hypoglycemia and behavior focused on avoiding this condition were clearly correlated with multiple SCL-90-R dimension scores among a cohort of insulin-dependent diabetics.

Within medicine, the SCL-90-R has had particularly broad application in the area of oncology. Craig and Abeloff (103) used the test to demonstrate clinical levels of psychological distress among cancer patients, and Abeloff and Derogatis (104) employed the SCL-90-R to characterize the specific symptom picture of breast cancer patients. In a further study in the series, Derogatis et al. (105) employed the SCL-90-R in research showing that length of survival with metastatic breast cancer was distinctly related to coping style, a conclusion also reached by Rogentine et al. (106) using the SCL-90-R with malignant melanoma patients.

In other areas of medicine, Hendler and his coworkers (107) showed the SCL-90-R to be sensitive to biofeedback-induced changes in a chronic pain population, while Harper and Steger (108) demonstrated a significant relationship between chronic tension headache and the SCL-90-R profile. Subsequent work (109–111) continues to support the validity of the SCL-90-R as a sensitive psychological distress measure with patients suffering from chronic pain.

The SCL-90-R has also been utilized effectively in studies focused on treatment planning and those with a health care systems orientation. Saravay et al. (112) used the scale to evaluate the impact of psychological morbidity and length of stay in the general hospital. SCL-90-R Depression, Anxiety, and global scores were significantly correlated with length of stay, although psychiatric diagnosis was not. Similarly, Katon et al. (80) used the test to define "highly distressed" patients among 767 high health care utilizers in a large HMO. Fifty-one percent of the sample fit the criterion. These patients not only made disproportionate uses of health care facilities, they also revealed a high prevalence of chronic medical problems, experienced significant limitation of activities associated with their illnesses, and had substantially elevated rates of major depressive disorder, dysthymia, and anxiety disorders. From a somewhat analogous perspective, Drossman et al. (113) evaluated the nature of health care behavior in a sample of almost 1,000 patients with inflammatory bowel disease. The SCL-90-R was one of the measures of psychological status employed, and was found to have significant predictive value in a regression model predicting number of physician visits during the previous 6 months. Malec and Neimeyer (114) also used the SCL-90-R in a cohort of spinal cord injured patients, with the anticipation of predicting length of inpatient rehabilitation and quality of performance of self-care at discharge. Results of the study showed the Depression subscale to be the best predictor of length of stay, while the GSI had the highest (inverse) correlation with a discharge self-care rating. The authors concluded that brief psychological measures such as the SCL-90-R have substantial utility for treatment planning with these patients.

CONCLUSION

This review of the SCL-90-R and the BSI, of necessity, omits a great deal of excellent work done with these inventories. Specifically, research in the areas of substance and alcohol abuse, sexual abuse, sexual dysfunction, stress, post-traumatic stress disorder, HIV, student mental health, and general psychopathology was not included in the present commentary. More detailed reviews of research in these areas may be found elsewhere (1,13).

ENDNOTE

[1]SCL-90-R and BSI are registered trademarks owned by Leonard R. Derogatis, Ph.D. The SCL-90-R and the BSI have been translated into approximately two dozen foreign languages and a considerable amount of research with the instruments has appeared in foreign journals (1,13). At present, the SCL-90-R and the BSI are available from their publisher, National Computer Systems (NCS) of Minneapolis, MN in Spanish, Portuguese, German, Italian, Dutch, French, Japanese, Korean, Chinese, Vietnamese, Swedish, Hebrew, Arabic, Danish, Norwegian, and a substantial number of other languages.

REFERENCES

1. Derogatis LR. *SCL-90-R: Administration, scoring and procedures manual,* 3rd ed. Minneapolis: National Computer Systems, 1994.
2. Derogatis LR, Lazarus L. SCL-90-R, Brief Symptom Inventory, and matching clinical rating scales. In: Maruish M, ed. *Psychological testing treatment planning, and outcome assessment.* New York: Lawrence Erlbaum, 1994.
3. Derogatis LR, Lipman RS, Rickels K, Uhlenhuth EH, Covi L. The Hopkins Symptom Checklist (HSCL). A measure of primary symptom dimensions. In: Pichot P, ed. *Psychological measurements in psychopharmacology.* Basel: Karger, 1974.
4. Derogatis LR, Lipman RS, Rickels K, Uhlenhuth EH, Covi L. The Hopkins Symptom Checklist (HSCL): a self-report symptom inventory. *Behav Sci* 1974;19:1–15.
5. Wider A. *The Cornell Medical Index.* New York: Psychological Corporation, 1948.
6. Waskow I, Parloff M. *Psychotherapy change measures.* Rockville, MD: NIMH, 1975.
7. McNair D. Self-evaluations of anti-depressants. *Psychopharmacologia* 1974;37:281–302.
8. Derogatis LR, Lipman RS, Covi L, Rickels K. Neurotic symptom dimensions as perceived by psychiatrists and patients of various social classes. *Arch Gen Psychiatry* 1971;24:454–464.
9. Derogatis LR, Lipman RS, Covi L, Rickels K. Factorial invariance of symptom dimensions in anxious and depressive neuroses. *Arch Gen Psychiatry* 1972;27:659–665.
10. Derogatis LR, Lipman RS, Covi L. SCL-90: an outpatient psychiatric rating scale—preliminary report. *Psychopharmacol Bull* 1973;9(1):13–27.
11. Derogatis LR. *The SCL-90-R.* Baltimore: Clinical Psychometric Research, 1975.
12. Derogatis LR, Yevzeroff H, Wittelsberger B. Social class, psychological disorder, and the nature of the psychopathologic indicator. *J Consult Clin* 1975;43:183–191.
13. Derogatis LR. *Brief Symptom Inventory (BSI): administration scoring and procedures manual,* 3rd ed. Minneapolis: National Computer Systems, 1993.
14. Messick S. Constructs and their vicissitudes in educational and psychological measurement. *Psychol Bull* 1981;89:575–588.
15. Derogatis LR, Rickels K, Rock A. The SCL-90 and the MMPI: a step in the validation of a new self-report scale. *Br J Psychiatry* 1976;128:280–289.
16. Wiggins JS. Content dimensions in the MMPI. In: Butcher JN, ed. *MMPI: Research developments and clinical applications.* New York: McGraw-Hill, 1969.
17. Tryon RC. Unrestricted cluster and factor analysis with application to the MMPI and Holzinger-Harman problems. *Multivar Behav Res* 1966;1:229–244.
18. Boleloucky Z, Horvath M. The SCL-90 rating scale: first experience with the Czech version in healthy male scientific workers. *Act Nerv Super* 1974;16:115–116.
19. Weissman MM, Sholomskas D, Pottenger M, Prusoff BA, Locke BZ. Assessing depressive symptoms in five psychiatric populations: a validation study. *Am J Epidemiol* 1977;106:203–214.
20. Weissman MM, Prusoff BA, Thompson WD, Harding PS, Meyers JK. Social adjustment by self-report in a community sample and in psychiatric outpatients. *J Nerv Ment Dis* 1978;166:317–326.
21. Moffett LA, Radenhausen RA. Assessing depression in substance abusers: Beck Depression Inventory and SCL-90-R. *Addict Behav* 1990;15:179–181.
22. Koeter MW. Validity of the GHQ and SCL-90-R anxiety and depression scales. A comparative study. *J Affect Disorders* 1992;24:271–279.
23. Wiznitzer M, Verhulst FC, Van den Brink W, Koeter M, van der Enoe J, Giel R, Koot HM. Detecting psychopathology in young adults: the Young Adult Self-Report, The General Health Questionnaire, and the Symptom Checklist as screening instruments. *Acta Psychiatr Scand* 1992;86:32–37.
24. Peveler RC, Fairburn CG. Measurement of neurotic symptoms by self-report questionnaire: validity of the SCL-90-R. *Psychol Med* 1990;20:873–879.
25. Wing JK. A standard form of psychiatric present state examination and a method for standardizing the classification of symptoms. In: Hare EH, Wing JK, eds. *Psychiatric Epidemiology.* London: Oxford University Press, 1970.
26. Derogatis LR. *The SCL-90-R bibliography.* Minneapolis: National Computer Systems, 1994.
27. Derogatis LR. *The BSI bibliography.* Minneapolis: National Computer Systems, 1994.
28. Carrington P, Collings GH, Benson H, Robinson H, Wood LW, Lehrer PM, Woolfolk RL, Cole J. The use of meditation-relaxation techniques for the management of stress in a working population. *J Occup Med* 1980;22(4):221–231.
29. Shapiro DA, Firth J. Prescriptive vs. exploratory psychotherapy: outcomes of the Sheffield Psychotherapy Project. *Br J Psychiatry* 1987;151:790–799.
30. Ballenger JC, Burrows GD, Dupont RL, Lesser IM, Noyes R, Pecknold JC, Rifkin A, Swinson RP. Alprazolam in panic disorder and agoraphobia—results from a multicenter trial. I. Efficacy in short-term treatment. *Arch Gen Psychiatry* 1988;45(5):413–422.
31. Derogatis LR, Wise TN. *Anxiety and depressive disorders in the medical patient.* Washington, DC: American Psychiatric Press, 1989.
32. Katon W, Roy-Byrne PP. Mixed anxiety and depression. *J Abnorm Psychol* 1991;100:337–345.
33. Katon W, Sullivan MD. Depression and chronic medical illness. *J Clin Psychiatry* 1990;15:3–11.
34. Derogatis LR, DellaPietra L. Psychological tests in screening for psychiatric disorder. In: Maruish M, ed. *Psychological testing: treatment planning and outcome assessment.* New York: Lawrence Erlbaum, 1994.
35. Bougsty T, Marshal P. Prevention and remediation of social/psychological problems in energy impacted communities. Paper presented at the International Symposium on the Human Side of Energy, Laramie, WY, 1980.
36. Kuhn WF, Bell RA, Seligson D, Laufer ST, Lindner JE. The tip of the iceberg. Psychiatric consultations on an orthopedic service. *Int J Psychiatry Med* 1988;18:375–382.
37. Zabora JR, Smith-Wilson R, Fetting JH, Enterline JP. An efficient method for psychosocial screening of cancer patients. *Psychosomatics* 1990;31:1992–1996.
38. Derogatis LR, Morrow G, Fetting J, et al. The prevalence of psychiatric disorders among cancer patients. *JAMA* 1983;249:751–757.
39. Royse D, Drude K. Screening drug abuse clients with the Brief Symptom Inventory. *Int J Addict* 1984;19:849–857.
40. Bulik CM, Carpenter LL, Kupfer DJ, Frank E. Features associated with suicide attempts in recurrent major depression. *J Affect Dis* 1990;18:27–29.
41. Noyes R, Christiansen J, Clancy J, Garvey MJ, Suelzer M, Anderson DJ. Predictors of serious suicide attempts among patients with panic disorder. *Compr Psychiatry* 1991;32:261–267.
42. Swedo SE, Rettew DC, Kuppenheimer M, Lum D, Dolan S, Goldberger E. Can adolescent suicide attempters be distinguished from at-risk adolescents? *Pediatrics* 1991;88:620–629.
43. McGough J, Curry JF. Utility of the SCL-90-R with depressed and conduct disordered adolescent inpatients. *J Personal Assess* 1992;59:552–563.
44. Cohen LJ, Test MA, Brown RL. Suicide and schizophrenia: data from a prospective community treatment study. *Am J Psychiatry* 1990;47:602–607.

45. Crits-Christoph P. The efficacy of brief dynamic psychotherapy: a meta-analysis. *Am J Psychiatry* 1992;149(2):151–158.

46. Cohen J. *Statistical power analysis for the behavioral sciences.* New York: Academic Press, 1977.

47. Horowitz MJ, Krupnick J, Kaltreider N, Wilner N, Leong A, Marmar C. Initial psychological response to parental death. *Arch Gen Psychiatry* 1981;38:316–328.

48. Garner DM, Rockert W, Davis R, Garner MV, Olmstead MP, Eagle M. Comparison of cognitive behavioral and supportive expressive therapy for bulimia nervosa. *Am J Psychiatry* 1993;150:37–46.

49. Horowitz MJ, Marmar C, Weiss DS, DeWitt KN, Rosenbaum R. Brief psychotherapy of bereavement reactions. *Arch Gen Psychiatry* 1984;41:438–448.

50. Fairburn CG, Jones R, Peveler RC, et al. Three psychological treatments for bulimia nervosa: a comparative trial. *Arch Gen Psychiatry* 1991;48:463–469.

51. Kabat-Zinn J, Massion AO, Kristeller J, et al. Effectiveness of meditation-based stress reduction program in the treatment of anxiety disorders. *Am J Psychiatry* 1992;149:936–943.

52. Beck JG, Stanley MA, Baldwin LE, Deagle EA, Averill PM. Comparison of cognitive therapy and relaxation training for panic disorder. *J Consult Clin Psychol* 1994;62:818–826.

53. Shear MK, Pilkonis PA, Cloitre M, Leon AC. Cognitive behavioral treatment compared with nonprescriptive treatment of panic disorder. *Arch Gen Psychiatry* 1994;51:395–401.

54. Shapiro DA, Barkham M, Reese A, Hardy GE, Reynolds S, Startup M. Effects of treatment duration and severity of depression on the effectiveness of cognitive behavioral and psychodynamic interpersonal psychotherapy. *J Consult Clin Psychol* 1994;62:522–534.

55. Kleinhauz M, Eli I, Baht R, Shamay D. Correlates of success and failure in behavior therapy for dental fear. *J Dent Res* 1992;71:1832–1835.

56. Thompson LW, Gallagher D, Breckenridge J. Comparative effectiveness of psychotherapy for depressed elders. *J Consult Clin Psychol* 1987;55:385–390.

57. Johnson PR, Thorn BE. Cognitive behavioral treatment of chronic headache: group versus individual treatment format. *Headache* 1989;29:358–390.

58. Baider L, Amikam JC, DeNour AK. Time-limited thematic group with post mastectomy patients. *J Psychosom Res* 1984;28:323–330.

59. Nezu CM, Nezu A, Arean P. Assertiveness and problem solving training for mildly mentally retarded individuals with dual diagnoses. *Res Dev Disabil* 1991;12:371–386.

60. Beutler LE, Engle D, Mohr D, Daldrup RJ, Bergen J, Meredith K, Merry W. Predictors of differential response to cognitive experiential, and self-directed psychotherapeutic procedures. *J Consult Clin Psychol* 1991;59:333–340.

61. Derogatis LR, Bonato RR, Yang KC. The power of the IMPS in psychiatric drug research: as a function of sample size, number of raters, and choice of treatment comparison. *Arch Gen Psychiatry* 1968;19:689–699.

62. Ravaris CL, Robinson DS, Ives JO, Nies A, Bartlett D. Phenelzine and amitriptyline in the treatment of depression. *Arch Gen Psychiatry* 1980;37:1075–1080.

63. Soloff PH, Cornelius J, Anselm G, Swami N, Perel JM, Ulrich RS. Efficacy of haloperidol and phenelzine in borderline personality disorder. *Arch Gen Psychiatry* 1993;50:377–385.

64. McGrath PS, Stewart JW, Nunes EV, et al. A double-blind crossover trial of imipramine and phenelzine for outpatients with treatment-refractory depression. *Am J Psychiatry* 1993;150:118–123.

65. Levine S, Anderson D, Bystritsky A, Baron D. A report of eight HIV-seropositive patients with major depression responding to fluoxetine. *J Acquir Immun Defic Synd* 1990;3:1074–1077.

66. Walsh TB, Hadigan CM, Devlin MJ, Gladis M, Roose SP. Long-term outcome of antidepressant treatment for bulimia nervosa. *Am J Psychiatry* 1991;148:1206–1212.

67. Schweizer E, Rickels K, Weiss S, Zavodnick S. Maintenance drug treatment of panic disorder. I. Results of a prospective, placebo-controlled comparison of alprazolam and imipramine. *Arch Gen Psychiatry* 1993;50:51–60.

68. Noyes R, Anderson DJ, Clancy J, Crowe RR, Slymen DJ, Ghoneim MM, Hinrichs JV. Diazepam and propranolol in panic disorder and agoraphobia. *Arch Gen Psychiatry* 1984;41:287–292.

69. Woodman CL, Noyes R. Panic disorder: treatment with valproate. *J Clin Psychiatry* 1994;55:134–136.

70. Judd FK, Burrow GD, Marriott PF, Farnbach P, Blair-West S. A short-term open trial of clomipramine in the treatment of patients with panic attacks. *Hum Psychopharmacol* 1990;6:53–60.

71. Kahn RS, Westenberg HG, Verhoeven WM, Gispen-De Wied CC, Kamerbeek DW. Effect of a serotonin precursor and uptake inhibitor in anxiety disorders; a double-blind comparison of 5-hydroxytryptophan, clomipramine and placebo. *Int Clin Psychopharmacol* 1987;2:33–45.

72. Den Boer JA, Westenberg GM, Kamerbeer DJ, Verhoeven MA, Kahn RS. Effect of serotonin uptake inhibitors in anxiety disorders: a double-blind comparison of clomipramine and fluvoxamine. *Int J Clin Psychopharmacol* 1987;3:21–32.

73. Perse TL, Greist JH, Jefferson JW, Rosenfeld R, Dar R. Fluvoxamine treatment of obsessive-compulsive disorder. *Am J Psychiatry* 1987;144:1543–1548.

74. Kim SW, Dysken WW. Open fixed dose trial of fluoxetine in the treatment of obsessive compulsive disorder. *Drug Dev Res* 1990;19:315–319.

75. Teicher MH, Glod CA, Aaronson ST, Gunter PA, Schatzberg AF, Cole JO. Open assessment of the safety and efficacy of thioridazine in the treatment of patients with borderline personality disorder. *Psychopharmacol Bull* 1989;25:535.

76. Cornelius JR, Soloff PH, Perel JM, Ulrich RF. Fluoxetine trial in borderline personality disorder. *Psychopharmacol Bull* 1990;26:151–154.

77. Kirmayer LJ, Robbins JM, Dworkind M, Yaffe MJ. Somatization and the recognition of depression and anxiety in primary care. *Am J Psychiatry* 1993;150:734–741.

78. Simon GE, VonKorf M. Somatization and psychiatric disorder in the NIMH epidemiologic catchment area study. *Am J Psychiatry* 1991;148:1491–1500.

79. Smith GR. The course of somatization and its effects on utilization of health care resources. *Psychosomatics* 1994;35:263–267.

80. Katon W, Von Korff M, Lin E, Lipscomb P, Russo J, Wagner E, Polk E. Distressed high utilizers of medical care DSM-III-R diagnoses and treatment needs. *Gen Hosp Psychiatry* 1990;12:355–362.

81. Kellner R, Hernandez J, Pathak D. Hypochondriacal fears and beliefs, anxiety and somatization. *Br J Psychiatry* 1992;160:525–532.

82. Dickson LR, Hays LR, Kaplan C, Scherl E, Abbott S, Schmitt F. Psychological profile of somatizing patients attending the integrative clinic. *Int J Psychiatry Med* 1992;22:141–153.

83. Chiles JA, Benjamine AH, Cahn TS. Who smokes? Why? Psychiatric aspects of continued cigarette use among lawyers in Washington state. *Compr Psychiatry* 1990;31:176–184.

84. Rosenberg R, Bech P, Mellergard M, Ottoson JO. Secondary depression in panic disorder; an indicator of severity with a weak effect on outcome in alprazolam and imipramine treatment. *Acta Psychiatr Scand* 1991;365:39–45.

85. Vollrath M, Koch R, Angst J. The Zurich Study: IX. Panic disorder and sporadic panic: symptoms, diagnosis, prevalence and overlap with depression. *Eur Arch Psychiatry Neurol Sci* 1990;239:221–230.

86. Andreoli A, Keller SE, Rabahus M, Zaugg L, Garrone G, Taban C. Immunity, major depression, and panic comorbidity. *Biol Psychiatry* 1992;31:896–908.

87. Weissman MM, Pottenger M, Kleber H, Ruben HL, Williams D, Thompson WD. Symptom patterns in primary and secondary depression: a comparison of primary depressives and depressed opiate addicts, alcoholics, and schizophrenics. *Arch Gen Psychiatry* 1977;34:854–862.

88. Wetzler S, Kahn RS, Cahn W, van Praag HM, Asnis GM. Psychological test characteristics of depressed and panic patients. *Psychiatry Res* 1990;31:179–192.

89. Stewart JW, Quitkin FM, Terman M, Terman JS. Is seasonal affective disorder a variant of atypical depression? Differential response to light therapy. *Psychiatry Res* 1990;33:121–128.

90. Cameron OG, Hudson CJ. Influence of exercise on anxiety level in patients with anxiety disorders. *Psychosomatics* 1986;27(10):720–723.

91. Bryer JB, Borrelli DJ, Matthews EJ, Kornetsky C. The psychological correlates of the DST in depressed patients. *Psychopharmacol Bull* 1983;19(4):633–637.

92. Robinson GE, Olmsted MP, Garner DM. Predictors of postpartum adjustment. *Acta Psychiatr Scand* 1989;80:561–565.

93. Amenson CS, Lewinsohn PM. An investigation into the observed sex difference in prevalence of unipolar depression. *J Abnorm Psychol* 1981;90:1–13.
94. Buckner CJ, Mandell W. Risk factors for depressive symptomatology in a drug-using population. *Am J Public Health* 1990;80:580–585.
95. Cameron OG, Thyer BA, Nesse RM, Curtis GC. Symptom profiles of patients with DSM-III anxiety disorders. *Am J Psychiatry* 1986; 143:1132–1137.
96. Ae Lee M, Cameron G. Anxiety, type A behavior and cardiovascular disease. *Int J Psychiatry Med* 1986;16(2):123–129.
97. Ae Lee M, Cameron OG, Greden JF. Anxiety and caffeine consumption in people with anxiety disorders. *Psychiatry Res* 1985;15:211–217.
98. Noyes R Jr, Woodman C, Garvey MJ, Cook BL, Suelzer M, Clancy J, Anderson DJ. Generalized anxiety disorder vs. panic disorder. Distinguishing characteristics and patterns of comorbidity. *J Nerv Ment Dis* 1992;180:369–379.
99. Clark LA, Watson D. Tripartite model of anxiety and depression: psychometric evidence and taxonomic implications. *J Abnorm Psychol* 1991;100:316–336.
100. Snyder D, Lynch J, Derogatis LR, Gruss L. Psychopathology and communication problems in a family practice. *Psychosomatics* 1980; 21:661–670.
101. Weidner G, Connor SL, Hollis JF, Conor WE. Improvements in hostility and depression in relation to dietary change and cholesterol lowering. The Family Heart Study. *Ann Intern Med* 1992;117: 820–823.
102. Irvine AA, Cox D, Gonder-Fredrick L. Fear of hypoglycemia: relation to physical and psychological symptoms in patients with insulin-dependent diabetes mellitus. *Health Psychol* 1992;11:135–138.
103. Craig TJ, Abeloff M. Psychiatric symptomatology among hospitalized cancer patients. *Am J Psychiatry* 1974;131:1323–1327.
104. Abeloff MD, Derogatis LR. Psychologic aspects of the management of primary and metastatic breast cancer. In: Stonesifer GL Jr, Montague ACW, Lewison EF, eds. *Breast cancer.* Baltimore: Johns Hopkins University Press; 1977:506–516.
105. Derogatis LR, Abeloff MD, Melisaratos N. Psychological coping mechanisms and survival time in metastatic breast cancer. *JAMA* 1979;242:1504–1508.
106. Rogentine DS, VanKammen DP, Fox BH, Docherty JP, Rosenblatt JE, Boyd SC, Bunney WE. Psychological factors in the prognosis of malignant melanoma: a prospective study. *Psychosom Med* 1979;41: 647–655.
107. Hendler N, Derogatis LR, Avella J, Long D. EMG biofeedback in patients with chronic pain. *Dis Nerv Syst* 1977;38:505–509.
108. Harper RG, Steger JC. Psychological correlates of frontalis EMG and pain in tension headaches. *Headache J* 1978;18:215–218.
109. Hendler N, Viernstein MD, Guler P, Long DA. Preoperative screening test for chronic back pain patients. *Psychosomatics* 1979;20:801–808.
110. Viernstein MD. Psychological testing for chronic pain patients. In: Hendler NH, Long DM, Wise TN, eds. *Diagnosis and treatment of chronic pain,* vol 19. Boston: John Wright, PSG, Inc., 1982:383–388.
111. Pelz M, Merskey H. A description of the psychological effects of chronic painful lesions. *Pain* 1982;14:293–301.
112. Saravay SM, Steinberg MD, Weinschel B, Pollack S, Alovis N. Psychological comorbidity and length of stay in the general hospital. *Am J Psychiatry* 1991;148:324–329.
113. Drossman DA, Leserman J, Mitchell CM, Zhiming M, Zagami EA, Patrick DL. Health status and health care use in persons with inflammatory bowel disease: a national sample. *Dig Dis Sci* 1991;36:1746–1755.
114. Malec J, Neimeyer R. Psychologic prediction of duration of inpatient spinal cord injury rehabilitation and performance of self-care. *Arch Phys Med Rehabil* 1983;64:359–363.

Quality of Life and Pharmacoeconomics in Clinical Trials, Second Edition, edited by B. Spilker.
Lippincott-Raven Publishers, Philadelphia © 1996.

CHAPTER 34

The SF-36 Health Survey

John E. Ware, Jr.

INTRODUCTION

The SF-36—a short-form with 36 items—is a multipurpose survey of general health status (1,2). It was constructed to fill the gap between much more lengthy surveys and relatively coarse single-item measures. SF-36 multi-item scales yield a profile of eight concepts as well as summary physical and mental health measures. These summary measures are scored by aggregating the most highly related scales (3,4). The SF-36 also includes a self-evaluation of change in health during the past year. Both standard (4-week) and acute (1-week) recall versions have been published. The SF-36 has proven useful in comparisons of the relative burden of different diseases and preliminary results suggest that it may also be useful in estimating the relative benefits of different treatments.

CONSTRUCTION OF THE SF-36

The SF-36 was constructed to satisfy minimum psychometric standards necessary for group comparisons involving generic health concepts—that is, concepts that are not specific to any age, disease, or treatment group. The eight health concepts were selected from 40 included in the Medical Outcomes Study (MOS) (5) to represent those hypothesized

J. E. Ware, Jr.: Division of Health Improvement, The Health Institute, New England Medical Center, Boston, Massachusetts 02111.

to be most frequently measured in widely used health surveys and those most affected by disease and treatment (2,6). They also represent multiple operational definitions of health, including function and dysfunction, distress and well-being, objective reports and subjective ratings, and both favorable and unfavorable self-evaluations of general health status (2). Most items have their roots in instruments that have been in use for more than 20 years (5), including the General Psychological Well-Being Inventory (7), various physical and role functioning measures (8–11), the Health Perceptions Questionnaire (12), and other measures that proved to be useful during the Health Insurance Experiment (HIE) (13). MOS researchers selected and adapted questionnaire items from these and other sources and developed new measures to construct the 149-item Functioning and Well-Being Profile (5), which was the source for SF-36 items.

SF-36 MEASUREMENT MODEL

Figure 1 illustrates the measurement model underlying the construction of the SF-36 scales and summary measures. This model has three levels: (a) items, (b) eight scales that aggregate two to ten items each, and (c) two summary measures that aggregate scales. All but one of the 36 items (self-reported health transition) are used to score the eight SF-36 scales. Each item is used in scoring only one scale. The eight scales are hypothesized to form two distinct higher-ordered clusters due to the physical and mental health variance that they have in common. Factor analytic studies have

Items   Scales   Summary Measures

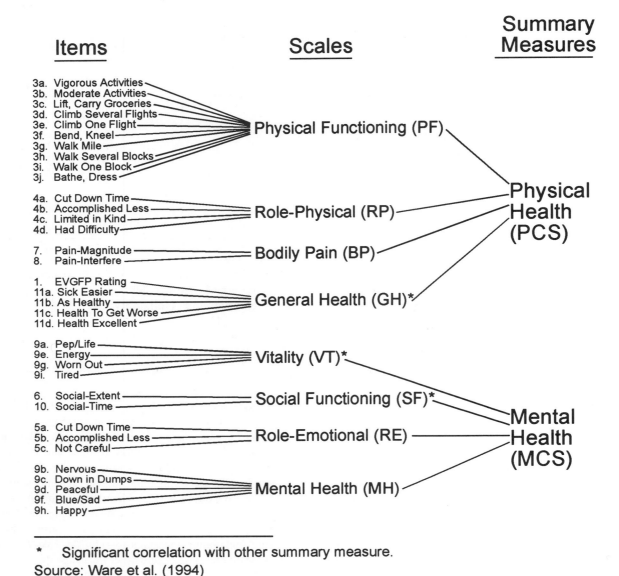

*   Significant correlation with other summary measure.
Source: Ware et al. (1994)

FIG. 1. SF-36 measurement model.

confirmed physical and mental health factors that account for 80% to 85% of the reliable variance in the eight scales in the United States general population (3), among MOS patients (14), and in general populations in Sweden (15) and the United Kingdom (3). Three scales (Physical Functioning, Role-Physical, Bodily Pain) correlate most highly with the physical component and contribute most to the scoring of the Physical Component Summary (PCS) measure (3). The mental component correlates most highly with the Mental Health, Role-Emotional, and Social Functioning scales, which also contribute most to the scoring of the Mental Component Summary (MCS) measure. Three of the scales (Vitality, General Health, and Social Functioning) have noteworthy correlations with both components.

ADMINISTRATION METHODS AND DATA QUALITY

The SF-36 is suitable for self-administration, computerized administration, or administration by a trained interviewer in person or by telephone, to persons age 14 and older. The SF-36 has been administered successfully in general population surveys in the United States and other countries (16) as well as to young and old adult patients with specific diseases (2,17). It can be administered in 5 to 10 minutes with a high degree of acceptability and data quality (2). Indicators of data quality that have yielded satisfactory results in studies to date include very high item completion rates and favorable results for a response consistency index based on 15 pairs of SF-36 items, which is scored at the individual level (2). Computer-administered and telephone voice recognition interactive systems of administration are currently being evaluated.

SCALING AND SCORING ASSUMPTIONS

A major objective in constructing the SF-36 was achievement of high psychometric standards. Guidelines for testing were derived from those recommended for use in validating psychological and educational measures by the American Psychological Association, the American Educational Research Association, and the National Council on Measurement in Education (18). Extensive psychometric testing has been conducted on the SF-36 in the United States (2,3,17), the United Kingdom (19–22), and in numerous other countries (15,23–26).

On the strength of favorable results from tests to date, nearly all studies have used the method of summated ratings and standardized SF-36 scoring algorithms documented elsewhere (2,27). This method assumes that items shown in the same scale in Fig. 1 can be aggregated without score standardization or item weighing. Standardization of items within a scale was avoided by selecting or constructing items with roughly equivalent means and standard deviations. Weighing was avoided by using equally representative items (that is, items with roughly equivalent relationships to the underlying scale dimension). All items have been shown to correlate substantially (greater than .40, corrected for overlap) with their hypothesized scales with rare exceptions (2,17). These results support analysis as interval-level measurement scales.

RELIABILITY AND CONFIDENCE INTERVALS

The reliability of the eight scales and two summary measures has been estimated using both internal consistency and test-retest methods. With rare exceptions, published reliability statistics have exceeded the minimum standard of .70 recommended for measures used in group comparisons; most have exceeded .80 (2,17). Reliability estimates for physical and mental summary scores usually exceed .90 (3). One review of 15 published studies revealed that the median reliability coefficients for each of the eight scales was equal or greater than .80 except Social Functioning, which had a median reliability across studies of .76 (2). In addition, a reliability of .93 has been reported for the Mental Health scale using the alternate forms method, suggesting that the internal-consistency method underestimated the reliability of that scale by about 3% (28).

The trends in reliability coefficients for the SF-36 scales and summary measures summarized above have also been replicated across 24 patient groups differing in sociodemographic characteristics and diagnoses (2,3,17). While studies of subgroups indicate slight declines in reliability for more disadvantaged respondents, reliability coefficients consistently exceeded recommended standards for group level analysis.

Standard errors of measurement, 95% confidence intervals for individual scores, and distributions of change scores from test-retest and one-year stability studies have been published (2,3,19). Confidence intervals around individual scores are much smaller for the two summary measures than for the eight scales (6–7 points versus 13–32 points, respectively) (3). Estimates of sample sizes required to detect differences in average scores of various magnitudes have been documented for five different study designs for each of the eight scales and for the two summary measures (2,3).

NORMS FOR GENERAL AND SPECIFIC POPULATIONS

The SF-36 has been normed in the general U.S. population and for representative samples from Denmark, Germany, Sweden, and the United Kingdom using common translation and norming protocols developed by the International Quality of Life Assessment (IQOLA) Project (15,25,29). Other norming studies, which are under way in Australia, Denmark, France, Italy, and The Netherlands, will be completed in 1995. From the general U.S. population, norms for age and sex groups and for 14 chronic diseases have been published along with estimates of the effect of telephone-administered relative to self-administered versions (2,3,30).

For patients with chronic conditions participating in the MOS, cross-sectional norms and average changes over a one-year follow-up period have been published for congestive heart failure, diabetes (type II), hypertension, myocardial infarction (recent survivors), and depressive disorders (2,3). In addition, norms have been published for uncomplicated hypertensive patients with the following comorbid conditions: angina (recent), chronic obstructive pulmonary disease, back pain/sciatica, osteoarthritis, musculoskeletal complaints, benign prostatic hypertrophy, varicosities, and dermatitis.

VALIDITY

Studies of validity are about the meaning of scores and whether or not they have their intended interpretations. Because of the widespread use of the SF-36 across a variety of applications, evidence of all types of validity is relevant. Studies to date have addressed content, concurrent, criterion, construct, and predictive validity.

The content validity of the SF-36 has been compared with that of other widely used generic health surveys (2,6). Systematic comparisons indicate that the SF-36 includes eight of the most frequently represented health concepts. Among the content areas included in widely used surveys, but not included in the SF-36, are sleep adequacy, cognitive functioning, sexual functioning, health distress, family functioning, self-esteem, eating, recreation/hobbies, communication, and symptoms/problems that are specific to one condition. Symptoms and problems that are specific to a particular condition are not included in the SF-36 because the SF-36 is a generic measure. To facilitate the consideration of concepts not included, the SF-36 users' manual includes tables of correlations between the eight scales and the two summary measures and 32 measures of other general concepts (2,3) and 19 specific symptoms. SF-36 scales correlate substantially ($r = .40$ or greater) with most of the omitted general health concepts and with the frequency and severity of many specific symptoms and problems. A noteworthy exception is sexual functioning, which correlates relatively weakly with SF-36 scales and is a good candidate for inclusion in questionnaires that supplement the SF-36.

Because most SF-36 scales were constructed to reproduce longer scales, much attention has been given to how well the short-form versions perform in empirical tests relative to the full-length versions. Compared with the longer MOS measures they were constructed to reproduce, SF-36 scales have been shown to perform with about 80% to 90% empirical validity in studies involving physical and mental health "criteria" (31).

The validity of each of the eight scales and the two summary measures has been shown to differ markedly as would be expected from factor analytic studies of construct validity (3,14,16). Specifically, the Mental Health, Role-Emotional, and Social Functioning scales and the MCS summary measure have been shown to be the most valid mental health measures in both cross-cultural and longitudinal tests using the method of known-groups validity. The Physical Functioning, Role-Physical, and Bodily Pain scales and the PCS have been shown to be the most valid physical health measures. Criteria used in the known-groups validation of the SF-36, which include accepted clinical indicators of diagnosis and severity of depression, heart disease, and other conditions, are well documented in peer-reviewed publications and in the two users' manuals (2–4,14,32).

The Mental Health scale has been shown to be useful in screening for psychiatric disorders (3,33), as has the MCS summary measure (3). For example, using a cutoff score of 42, the MCS had a sensitivity of 74% and a specificity of 81% in detecting patients diagnosed with depressive disorder (3).

Relative to other published measures, SF-36 scales have performed well in most tests published to date (19,34–37). Predictive validity studies have linked SF-36 scales and summary measures to utilization of health care services (3), the clinical course of depression (38), loss of job within 1 year (3), and 5-year survival (3).

Results from clinical studies comparing scores for patients before and after treatment have largely supported hypotheses about the validity of SF-36 scales based on factor analytic studies. For example, clinical studies have shown that the three most valid physical scales (Physical Functioning, Role-Physical, and Bodily Pain) tend to be most responsive to the benefits of knee replacement (35), hip replacement (39,40), and heart valve surgery (41). Likewise, the three most valid mental health scales (Mental Health, Role-Emotional, and Social Functioning) in factor analytic studies have been shown to be most responsive in comparisons of patients before and after recovery from depression (4).

The discovery that 80% to 85% of the reliable variance in the eight SF-36 scales was explained by two components led to the construction of psychometrically based physical and mental health summary measures. It was hoped that they would make it possible to reduce the number of statistical comparisons involved in analyzing the SF-36 (from eight to two) without substantial loss of information. In both cross-sectional and longitudinal studies reported to date, this appears to be the case (3,4). The advantages and disadvantages of analyzing the eight-scale SF-36 profile versus the two summary measures are illustrated and discussed elsewhere (3,4).

Finally, the SF-36 self-evaluated health transition item (five levels from "much better" to "much worse"), which is not used in scoring the scales or summary measures, has been shown to be useful in estimating average changes in health status during the year prior to its administration. In the MOS, measured changes in health status during a one-year follow-up period corresponded substantially, on average, to self-evaluated transitions at the end of the year. Using the 0–100 GHRI (General Health Rating Index) scale (42) as a "criterion," those who evaluated their health as "much better" improved an average of 13.2 points. The average change was 5.8 points for those who reported that they were "somewhat better." An average decline of -10.8 was observed for those who reported that their health was "somewhat worse" and -34.4 for those reporting "much worse." (It should be noted that the latter category had only 29 patients.) Change scores for those choosing the "about the same" category averaged 1.6 points. These results are encouraging with regard to the use and interpretation of self-evaluated transitions at the *group* level. However, these items should be interpreted with caution at the individual level, pending results from ongoing studies of the reliability of responses. Additional results and their implications are discussed elsewhere (2,3).

SUMMARY OF INFORMATION ABOUT SF-36 SCALES AND SUMMARY MEASURES

Table 1 summarizes information about the eight SF-36 scales and two summary measures that is important in their use and interpretation. The eight scales are ordered in terms of their factor content (i.e., construct validity), as they are in the SF-36 profile, to facilitate interpretation. The first scale is Physical Functioning (PF), which has been shown to be the best all-around measure of physical health; the last scale, Mental Health (MH) is the most valid measure of

TABLE 1. *Summary of information about SF-36 scales and physical and mental component summary measures*

| Scales | Correlations | | Number of | | | | | | Definitions (% observed) | |
	PCS	MCS	Items	Levels	Mean	SD	Reliability	CI[a]	Lowest possible score—floor	Highest possible score—ceiling
Physical functioning (PF)	.85	.12	10	21	84.2	23.3	.93	12.3	Very limited in performing all physical activities including bathing or dressing (0.8%)	Performs all types of physical activities including the most vigorous without limitations due to health (38.8%)
Role—physical (RP)	.81	.27	4	5	80.9	34.0	.89	22.6	Problems with work or other daily activities as a result of physical health (10.3%)	No problems with work or other daily activities (70.9%)
Bodily pain (BP)	.76	.28	2	11	75.2	23.7	.90	15.0	Very severe and extremely limiting pain (0.6%)	No pain or limitations due to pain (31.9%)
General health (GH)	.69	.37	5	21	71.9	20.3	.81	17.6	Evaluates personal health as poor and believes it is likely to get worse (0.0%)	Evaluates personal health as excellent (7.4%)
Vitality (VT)	.47	.65	4	21	60.9	20.9	.86	15.6	Feels tired and worn out all of the time (0.5%)	Feels full of pep and energy all of the time (1.5%)
Social functioning (SF)	.42	.67	2	9	83.3	22.7	.68	25.7	Extreme and frequent interference with normal social activities due to physical and emotional problems (0.6%)	Performs normal social activities without interference due to physical or emotional problems (52.3%)
Role-emotional (RE)	.16	.78	3	4	81.3	33.0	.82	28.0	Problems with work or other daily activities as a result of emotional problems (9.6%)	No problems with work or other daily activities (71.0%)
Mental health (MH)	.17	.87	5	26	74.7	18.1	.84	14.0	Feelings of nervousness and depression all of the time (0.0%)	Feels peaceful, happy, and calm all of the time (0.2%)
Physical component summary (PCS)			35	567[b]	50.0	10.0	.92	5.7	Limitations in self-care, physical, social, and role activities, severe bodily pain, frequent tiredness, health rated "poor" (0.0%)	No physical limitations, disabilities, or decrements in well-being, high energy level, health rated "excellent" (0.0%)
Mental component summary (MCS)			35	493[b]	50.0	10.0	.88	6.3	Frequent psychological distress, social and role disability due to emotional problems, health rated "poor" (0.0%)	Frequent positive affect, absence of psychological distress and limitations in usual social/role activities due to emotional problems, health rated "excellent" (0.0%)

From ref. 4.
[a]CI = 95% confidence interval.
[b]Number of levels observed at baseline; scores rounded to the first decimal place (*n* = 2,474).

mental health in studies to date (2,3,14). Interestingly, MH and PF are the poorest measures of the physical and mental components, respectively. Scales in between are ordered according to their validity in measuring physical and mental health. The Vitality (VT) and General Health (GH) scales have substantial or moderate validity for both components of health status and should be interpreted accordingly.

The number of items and levels and the range of states defined by each scale are also shown in Table 1. These attributes have been linked to their empirical validity (31). The most precise (least coarse) scales are those with 20 or more levels (PF, GH, VT, and MH). They also define the widest range of health states and, therefore, usually produce the least skewed score distributions. The relatively coarse role disability scales (Role-physical [RP] and Role-emotional [RE]) each measure only four or five levels across a restricted range and, therefore, usually have the most problems with ceiling and floor effects.

Means and standard deviations for each of the eight scales in the general U.S. adult population are also presented. These can be used to determine whether a group or individual in question scores above or below the U.S. average. Detailed normative data including frequency distributions of scores and percentile ranks are documented in the two users' manuals (2,3). Reliability estimates and 95% confidence intervals for individual scores are also presented. These estimates are based on internal-consistency reliability coefficients and standard deviations from the general U.S. population, as documented elsewhere (2,3).

Table 1 illustrates the practical implications of a number of theoretical advantages of the PCS and MCS summary measures as compared with the eight SF-36 scales. These advantages include a very large increase in the number of levels defined, much smaller confidence intervals for individual scores relative to each of the eight scales, as well as the elimination of both floor and ceiling effects. The implications for the use of the PCS and MCS in clinical practice and research are currently being evaluated; preliminary results are encouraging (3).

DOCUMENTATION AND AVAILABILITY

The scoring of the eight SF-36 scales and two summary measures and detailed interpretation guidelines (content-based, norm-based, and criterion-based), are documented in two users' manuals (2,3). A third manual documents English-language adaptations and scoring algorithms for use in Australia, Canada, and the UK (43), and a fourth manual documents the Swedish translation and related norms and validations (44). Others are forthcoming from the IQOLA Project.

Permission to use and reproduce the SF-36 is routinely granted by the Medical Outcomes Trust (MOT) without charge (27). The trust is a nonprofit clearinghouse for widely used, patient-based measures. Permission to reproduce the SF-36 items and scoring algorithms has also been granted to computer software vendors and dozens of commercial survey and data processing firms offering a wide range of services based on standard SF-36 scoring algorithms and interpretation guidelines. The SF-36 Scoring Exercise, available from the MOT includes a computer diskette with scoring algorithms and a test data set (45); the summary measures manual also includes the SF-36 scoring diskette (3).

DISCUSSION

The widespread adoption of the SF-36 in general population surveys, clinical trials, and clinical practice is evidence that more practical measurement tools are more likely to be used. The standardization of measurement across studies is producing considerable information about norms and benchmarks useful in comparing "well" and "sick" populations and for estimating the burden of specific conditions. At the time of this writing, 86 publications reporting results for the SF-36 had been identified. (Following the references, there is a list of 38 additional publications using the SF-36 health survey. Studies reporting results for one or more of the SF-36 scales are starred in the reference lists.)

The brevity of the SF-36 was achieved by focusing on only eight of 40 health concepts studied in the MOS and by measuring each concept with a short-form scale. The scales chosen (other than General Health) have been shown to explain about two-thirds of the reliable variance in individual evaluations of current health status in the United Kingdom, United States, and Sweden (16). In the U.S., addition of 14 multi-item measures (e.g., sleep problems, family and sexual functioning) added only about 5% to the variance explained.

Although many studies appear to rely on the SF-36 as the principal measure of health outcome, it may be best to rely upon it as a "generic core," pending further research. A generic core battery of measures serves the purpose of comparing results across studies and populations and greatly expands the interpretation guidelines that are essential to determining the clinical, economic, and human relevance of results. Because it is short, the SF-36 can be reproduced in a questionnaire with ample room for other more precise general and specific measures. Numerous studies in progress and some that have been published (22,35,46) adopted this strategy and have illustrated the advantages of using the SF-36 as a generic core and the advantages of supplementing it.

How useful is the SF-36 for purposes of comparing general and specific population groups, relative to longer surveys? Some SF-36 scales have been shown to have 10% to 20% less precision than the long-form MOS measures they were constructed to reproduce (31). This disadvantage of the SF-36 should be weighed against the fact that some of these long-form measures require five to ten times greater respondent burden. Empirical studies of this tradeoff suggest that the SF-36 provides a practical alternative to longer measures and that the eight scales and two summary scales rarely miss a noteworthy difference in physical or mental health status in group-level comparisons (2,3,39). Regardless, the fact that the SF-36 represents a documented compromise in measurement precision (relative to longer MOS measures) leading to a reduction in the statistical power of hypothesis testing should be taken into account in planning clinical trials and other studies. To facilitate such planning, five tables of sample size estimates for differences in scores of various amounts for conventional statistical tests are published in the two SF-36 users' manuals (2,3). In relation to longer non-MOS measures, such as the Sickness Impact Profile, the SF-36 has performed equally well or better in detecting average group differences or changes over time (39,47).

The value of general and specific population norms, which was demonstrated well for the Sickness Impact Profile (48) and later for the MOS SF-20 (49) and other measures, has also been demonstrated for the SF-36. In addition to the 20 medical conditions described in the MOS and 14 conditions described in the U.S. population norming survey (3), other publications have reported descriptive data for patients with cardiac disease (50), epilepsy (22,51), diabetes mellitus (46,52), migraine headache (53), heart transplant patients (54), ischemic heart disease (41), and ischemic stroke (55), low back pain (20,40), lung disease (56), menorrhagia (20), orthopedic conditions leading to knee replacement (35), knee surgery (57), and hip replacement (39,40), and for renal disease (58–60). Whereas some of the initial descriptive studies using the SF-36 were performed primarily to validate scale scores (31), on the strength of validation studies to date, SF-36 scales appear to be increasingly accepted as valid health measures for purposes of documenting disease burden.

Relatively little is known about population health in comprehensive terms, the relative burden of disease, or the relative benefits of alternative treatments. One reason has been the lack of practical measurement tools appropriate for widespread use across diverse populations. The SF-36 was constructed to provide a basis for such comparisons of results.

CONCLUSIONS

As predicted when it was first published (1), the SF-36 has been widely adopted because of its brevity and its comprehensiveness. Although these two measurement goals are competing, the SF-36 appears to have achieved a psychometrically sound compromise between them. Population and large-group descriptive studies and clinical trials to date suggest that the SF-36 will prove very useful for descriptive purposes such as documenting differences between sick and well patients and for estimating the relative burden of different medical conditions. Experience to date, however limited, suggests that the SF-36 may also have potential in evaluating

the benefits of alternative treatments. Additional research is necessary before that potential and the features of study designs essential to success can be well understood.

ACKNOWLEDGMENTS

Development and validation of the SF-36 Health Survey was supported by a grant from the Henry J. Kaiser Family Foundation to The Health Institute, New England Medical Center (J. E. Ware, Jr., Principal Investigator). Development of the SF-36 PCS and MCS summary measures was supported by unrestricted research grants for the International Quality of Life Assessment (IQOLA) Project from the Glaxo Research Institute, Research Triangle Park, North Carolina and Schering-Plough Corporation, Kenilworth, New Jersey (J. E. Ware, Jr., Principal Investigator).

REFERENCES[1]

NOTE: Following the chapter citation list is an additional list of references not cited in the chapter but included in the *SF-36 Bibliography* compiled by Ware et al. at The Health Institute, New England Medical Center, Boston, Massachusetts. These are presented to provide the interested reader with references to the SF-36 in addition to those cited in the chapter. All references with asterisks from the chapter citation list are also included in the *SF-36 Bibliography*.

1. Ware JE, Sherbourne CD. The MOS 36-Item Short-Form Health Status Survey (SF-36): 1. Conceptual framework and item selection. *Med Care* 1992;30(6):473–483.
*2. Ware JE, Snow KK, Kosinski M, Gandek B. *SF-36 Health Survey manual and interpretation guide.* Boston: New England Medical Center, The Health Institute, 1993.
*3. Ware JE, Kosinski M, Keller SD. *SF-36 physical and mental component summary measures—a users' manual.* Boston: The Health Institute, 1994.
*4. Ware JE, Kosinski M, Bayliss MS, et al. Comparison of methods for the scoring and statistical analysis of the SF-36 health profile and summary measures: results from the Medical Outcomes Study. *Med Care* 1995;33:A5264-A5279.
5. Stewart AL, Ware JE, eds. *Measuring functioning and well-being: the Medical Outcomes Study approach.* Durham, NC: Duke University Press, 1992.
6. Ware JE. The status of health assessment 1994. *Annu Rev Public Health* 1995;16:327–354.
7. Dupuy HJ. The Psychological General Well-Being (PGWB) Index. In: Wenger NK, Mattson ME, Furberg CD, Elinson J, eds. *Assessment of quality of life in clinical trials of cardiovascular therapies.* New York: Le Jacq, 1984.
8. Patrick DL, Bush JW, Chen MM. Toward an operational definition of health. *J Health Soc Behav* 1973;14:6–24.
9. Hulka BS, Cassell JC. The AAFP-UNC study of the organization, utilization, and assessment of primary medical care. *Am J Public Health* 1973;63:494–501.
10. Reynolds WJ, Rushing WA, Miles DL. The validation of a function status index. *J Health Social Behav* 1974;15:271–288.
11. Stewart AL, Ware JE, Brook RH. Advances in the measurement of functional status: construction of aggregate indexes. *Med Care* 1981;19:473–488.
12. Ware JE. Scales for measuring general health perceptions. *Health Serv Res* 1976;11:396–415.

---

[1]Entries preceded by an asterisk report results for SF-36 scales.

13. Brook RH, Ware JE, Davies-Avery A, et al. Overview of adult health status measures fielded in RAND's Health Insurance Study. *Med Care* 1979;17(7 suppl).

*14. McHorney CA, Ware JE, Raczek AE. The MOS 36-Item Short-Form Health Status Survey (SF-36): II. Psychometric and clinical tests of validity in measuring physical and mental health constructs. *Med Care* 1993;31(3):247–263.

*15. Sullivan M, Karlsson J, Ware JE. The Swedish SF-36 Health Survey: I. Evaluation of data quality, scaling assumptions, reliability, and construct validity across several populations. *Soc Sci Med* 1995; in press.

*16. Ware JE, Keller SD, Gandek B, and the IQOLA Project team. Evaluating translations of health status surveys: lessons from the IQOLA project. *Int J Technol Assess Health Care* 1995; in press.

*17. McHorney CA, Ware JE, Lu JFR, Sherbourne CD. The MOS 36-item Short-Form Health Survey (SF-36): III. Tests of data quality, scaling assumptions and reliability across diverse patient groups. *Med Care* 1994;32(4):40–66.

18. American Psychological Association. *Standards for education and psychological testing.* Washington, DC: American Psychological Association, 1985.

*19. Brazier JE, Harper R, Jones NMB, et al. Validating the SF-36 Health Survey Questionnaire: new outcome measure for primary care. *Br J Med* 1992;305:160–164.

*20. Garratt AM, Ruta DA, Abdela MI, Buckingham JK, Russell IT. The SF-36 Health Survey Questionnaire: an outcome measure suitable for routine use within the NHS? *Br Med J* 1993;306:1440–1444.

*21. Jenkinson C, Coulter A, Wright L. Short Form 36 (SF-36) Health Survey Questionnaire: normative data for adults of working age. *Br Med J* 1993;306:1437–1440.

*22. Wagner AK, Keller SD, Kosinski M, et al. Advances in methods for assessing the impact of epilepsy and antiepileptic drug therapy on patients' health-related quality of life. *Qual Life Res* 1995; in press.

*23. Sullivan M. LIVSKVALITESMÄTNING. Nytt generellt och nytt tumörspecifikt formulär för utvärdering och planering. *Lakartidningen* 1994;91(13):1340–1342.

*24. Rampal R, Martin C, Marquis P, Ware JE, Bonfils S. A quality of life study in five hundred and eighty-one duodenal ulcer patients. *Scand J Gastroenterol* 1994;29(206):44–51.

*25. Bullinger M. German translation and psychometric testing of the SF-36 health survey: preliminary results from the IQOLA project. *Soc Sci Med* 1995; in press.

*26. McCallum J. *The new "SF-36" health status measure: Australian validity tests.* National Centre for Epidemiology and Population Health, The Australian National University, 1994 (Record Linkage Pilot Study).

27. Medical Outcomes Trust. *How to score the SF-36 Short-Form Health Survey.* Boston: The Health Institute, 1992.

*28. McHorney CA, Ware JE. Construction and validation of an alternate form general mental health scale for the Medical Outcomes Study short-form 36-item health survey. *Med Care* 1995;33(1):15–18.

*29. Ware JE, Gandek B, the IQOLA Project Group. The SF-36 health survey: development and use in mental health research and the IQOLA project. *Int J Mental Health* 1994;23:49–73.

*30. McHorney CA, Kosinski M, Ware JE. Comparisons of the costs and quality of norms for the SF-36 survey collected by mail versus telephone interview: results from a national survey. *Med Care* 1994;32:551–567.

*31. McHorney CA, Ware JE, Rogers W, et al. The validity and relative precision of MOS short- and long-form health status scales and Dartmouth COOP Charts: results from the Medical Outcomes Study. *Med Care* 1992;30(5):MS253–MS265.

*32. Kravitz RL, Greenfield S, Rogers WH, et al. Differences in the mix of patients among medical specialties and systems of care: results from the Medical Outcomes Study. *JAMA* 1992;267:1617–1623.

*33. Berwick DM, Murphy JA, Goldman PA, et al. Performance of a five-item mental health screening test. *Med Care* 1991;29(2):169–176.

*34. Weinberger M, Samsa GP, Hanlon JT, et al. An evaluation of a brief health status measure in elderly veterans. *J Am Geriat Soc* 1991;39(7):691–694.

*35. Kantz ME, Harris WJ, Levitsky K, et al. Methods for assessing condition-specific and generic functional status outcomes after total knee replacement. *Med Care* 1992;30(5):MS240–MS252.

*36. Krousel-Wood MA, McCune TW, Abdoh A, Re RN. Predicting work status for patients in an occupational medicine setting who report back pain. *Arch Family Med* 1994;3(4):349–355.

*37. Krousel-Wood MA, Re RN. Health status assessment in a hypertension section of an internal medicine clinic. *Am J Med Sci* 1994;308(4):211–217.

*38. Wells KB, Burnam MA, Rogers W, et al. The course of depression in adult outpatients: results from the Medical Outcomes Study. *Arch Gen Psychiatry* 1992;49:788–794.

*39. Katz JN, Larson MG, Phillips CB, et al. Comparative measurement sensitivity of short and longer health status instruments. *Med Care* 1992;30(10):917–925.

*40. Lansky D, Butler JBV, Waller FT. Using health status measures in the hospital setting: from acute care to outcomes management. *Med Care* 1992;30(5):MS57–MS73.

*41. Phillips RC, Lansky DJ. Outcomes management in heart valve replacement surgery: early experience. *J Heart Valve Dis* 1992;1(1):42–50.

42. Davies AR, Ware JE. *Measuring health perceptions in the Health Insurance Experiment,* publication no. R-2711-HHS. Santa Monica, CA: RAND, 1981.

43. Medical Outcomes Trust. *SF-36 Health Survey scoring manual for English language adaptations: Australia/New Zealand, Canada, United Kingdom.* Boston: The Health Institute, 1994.

*44. Sullivan M, Karlsson J. *SF-36 Hälsoenkät: Svensk manual och tolkningsguide (Swedish manual and interpretation guide).* Gothenburg: Sahlgrenska University Hospital, 1994.

45. Medical Outcomes Trust. *Scoring exercise for the MOS SF-36 health survey,* 2nd ed. Boston: The Health Institute, 1994.

*46. Nerenz DR, Repasky DP, Whitehouse MD, et al. Ongoing assessment of health status in patients with diabetes mellitus using the SF-36 and Diabetes TYPE Scale. *Med Care* 1992;30(5):MS124.

*47. Beaton DE, Bombardier C, Hogg-Johnson S. Choose your tool: a comparison of the psychometric properties of five generic health status instruments in workers with soft tissue injuries. *Qual Life Res* 1994; 3:50.

48. Bergner M, Bobbitt RA, Carter WB, Golson BS. The Sickness Impact Profile: development and final revision of a health status measure. *Med Care* 1981;19:787–805.

49. Stewart AL, Greenfield S, Hays RD, et al. Functional status and well-being of patients with chronic conditions: results from the Medical Outcomes Study. *JAMA* 1989;262:907–913.

*50. Jette DU, Downing J. Health status of individuals entering a cardiac rehabilitation program as measured by the Medical Outcomes Study 36-item short-form survey (SF-36). *Phys Ther* 1994;74(6):521–527.

*51. Vickrey BG, Hays RD, Graber J, et al. A health-related quality of life instrument for patients evaluated for epilepsy surgery. *Med Care* 1992;30(4):299–319.

*52. Jacobson AM, de Groot M, Samson JA. The evaluation of two measures of quality of life in patients with type I and type II diabetes mellitus. *Diabetes Care* 1994;17(4):267–274.

*53. Osterhaus JT, Townsend RJ, Gandek B, Ware JE. Measuring the functional status and well-being of patients with migraine headache. *Headache* 1994;34(6):337–343.

*54. Rector TS, Ormaza SM, Kubo SM. Health status of heart transplant recipients versus patients awaiting heart transplantation: a preliminary evaluation of the SF-36 questionnaire. *J Heart Lung Transplant* 1993;12(6 pt 1):983–986.

*55. Kappelle LJ, Adams HP, Heffner ML, Torner JC, Gomez F, Biller J. Prognosis of young adults with ischemic stroke: a long-term follow-up study assessing recurrent vascular events and functional outcome in the Iowa registry of stroke in young adults. *Stroke* 1994;25(7):1360–1365.

*56. Viramontes JL, O'Brien B. Relationship between symptoms and health-related quality of life in chronic lung disease. *J Gen Intern Med* 1994;9(1):46–48.

*57. Katz JN, Harris TM, Larson MG, et al. Predictors of functional outcomes after arthroscopic partial meniscectomy. *J Rheumatol* 1992; 19(12):1938–1942.

*58. Kurtin PS, Davies AR, Meyer KB, et al. Patient-based health status measurements in outpatient dialysis: early experiences in developing an outcomes assessment program. *Med Care* 1992;30(5):MS136–MS149.

*59. Meyer KB, Espindle DM, DeGiacomo JM, Jenuleson CS, Kurtin PS, Davies AR. Monitoring dialysis patients' health status. *Am J Kidney Dis* 1994;24:267–279.

*60. Benedetti E, Matos AJH, Hakim N, Fasela C, et al. Renal transplantation for patients 60 years or older: a single-institution experience. *Ann Surg* 1994;220(4):445–458.

SF-36 BIBLIOGRAPHY RECOMMENDED FOR FURTHER READING

*Aaronson NK, Acquadro C, Alonso J, et al. International Quality of Life Assessment (IQOLA) project. *Qual Life Res* 1992;1:349–351.

*Bonfils S. Les questionnaires de qualité de view: irremplaçables instruments d'approximation. In: *Impertinente psychosomatique.* Montrouge: John Libbey Eurotext, 1993:293–300.

*Bousquet J, Knani J, Dhivert H, Richard A, Chicoye A, Ware JE, Michel FB. Quality of life in asthma. I. Internal consistency and validity of the SF-36 questionnaire. *Am J Respir Crit Care Med* 1994;149:371–375.

*Brazier J. The SF-36 health survey questionnaire—a tool for economists. *Health Econ* 1993;2:213–215.

*Brazier J, Jones N, Kind P. Testing the validity of the Euroqol and comparing it with the SF-36 health survey questionnaire. *Qual Life Res* 1993;2:169–180.

*Dixon P, Heaton J, Long A, et al. Reviewing and applying the SF-36. *Outcomes Briefing* 1994;4:3–25.

*Fryback DG, Dasbach EJ, Klein R, et al. The Beaver Dam Health Outcomes Study: initial catalog of health state quality factors. *Med Decis Making* 1993;13(2):89–102.

*Garratt AM, MacDonald LM, Ruta DA, et al. Towards measurement of outcome for patients with varicose veins. *Qual Health Care* 1993;2:5–10.

*Garratt AM, Ruta DA, Abdalla MI, Russell IT. The SF-36 health survey questionnaire: II. Responsiveness to changes in health status for patients with four common conditions. *Qual Health Care* 1995; in press.

*Haley SM, McHorney CA, Ware JE. Evaluation of the MOS SF-36 physical functioning scale (PF-10): I. Unidimensionality and reproducibility of the Rasch item scale. *J Clin Epidemiol* 1994;47:671–684.

*Hays RD, Sherbourne CD, Mazel RM. The RAND 36-item health survey 1.0. *Health Econ* 1993;2:217–227.

*Hill S, Harries U. Assessing the outcome of health care for the older person in community settings: should we use the SF-36. *Outcomes Briefing* 1994;4:26–27.

*Jenkinson C, Wright L. The SF-36 health survey questionnaire. *Auditorium* 1993;2:7–12.

*Jenkinson C, Wright L, Coulter A. *Quality of life measurement in health care: a review of measures and population norms for the UK SF-36.* Oxford, England: Health Services Research Unit, Department of Public Health and Primary Care, University of Oxford, 1993.

*Jenkinson C, Wright L, Coulter A. Criterion validity and reliability of the SF-36 in a population sample. *Qual Life Res* 1994;3(1)7–12.

*Kutner NG, Schechtman KB, Ory MG, Baker DI. Older adult's perceptions of their health and functioning in relation to sleep disturbance, falling, and urinary incontinence. *J Am Geriatr Soc* 1994;42(7):757–762.

*Lancaster TR, Singer DE, Sheehan MA, et al. The impact of long-term warfarin therapy on quality of life. *Arch Internal Med* 1991;151(10):1944–1949.

*Lerner DJ, Levine S, Malspeis S, et al. Job strain and health-related quality of life in a national sample. *Am J Public Health* 1994;84:1580–1585.

*Levin NW, Lazarus JM, Nissenson AR. National Cooperative rHu Erythropoietin Study in patients with chronic renal failure—an interim report. *Am J Kidney Dis* 1993;22(2, suppl 1):3–12.

*Lyons RA, Perry HM, Littlepage BN. Evidence for the validity of the Short-Form 36 questionnaire (SF-36) in an elderly population. *Age Ageing* 1994;23(3):182–184.

*Mangione CM, Marcantonio ER, Goldman L, et al. Influence of age on measurement of health status in patients undergoing elective surgery. *J Am Geriatr Soc* 1993;41(4):377–383.

*Martin C, Marquis P, Bonfils S. A "quality of life questionnaire" adapted to duodenal ulcer therapeutic trials. *Scand J Gastroenterol* 1994;206 (29 suppl):40–43.

*Martin C, Marquis P, Ware JE, Bonfils S. A quality of life study of nizatidine in 581 DU patients: maintenance treatment versus intermittent treatment. *Gastroenterology* 1993;104:A141.

*Orley J, Kuyken W. *Quality of life assessment: international perspectives.* Berlin, Heidelberg: Springer-Verlag, 1994.

*Park Nicollet Medical Foundation. *Final report: a comparison of alternative approaches to risk management.* Minneapolis, MN: Physical Payment Review Commission, 1994.

*Ruta DA, Abdalla MI, Garratt AM, et al. The SF-36 health survey questionnaire: I. Reliability in two patient-based studies. *Qual Health Care* 1995; in press.

Ruta DA, Garratt AM, Teng M, et al. A new approach to the measurement of quality of life: The Patient-Generated Index. *Med Care* 1994;32(11):1109–1126.

*Ruta DA, Garratt AM, Wardlaw D, Russell IT. Developing a valid and reliable measure of health outcome for patients with low back pain. *Spine* 1994;19(17):1887–1896.

*Siu AL, Hays RD, Ouslander JG, et al. Measuring functioning and health in the very old. *J Gerontol* 1993;48(1):M10–M14.

*Street RL, Gold WR, McDowell T. Using health status surveys in medical consultations. *Med Care* 1994;32(7):732–744.

*Usherwood T, Jones N. Self-perceived health status of hostel residents: use of the SF-36D health survey questionnaire. *J Public Health Med* 1994;25(4):311–314.

*vanTulder MW, Aaronson NK, Bruning PF. The quality of life of long-term survivors of Hodgkin's disease. *Ann Oncology* 1994;5:152–158.

*Ware JE. *How to score the revised MOS Short Form Health Scale (SF-36).* Boston, MA: The Health Institute, New England Medical Center Hospitals, 1988.

*Ware JE. Captopril, enalapril, and quality of life (letter to the editor). *N Engl J Med* 1993;329(7):506–507.

*Ware JE. Evaluation measures of general health concepts for use in clinical trials. In: Furberg CD, Schuttinga JA, eds. *Quality of life assessment: practice, problems, and promise,* October 15–17, 1990, (NIH Publication No. 93-3503). Washington, DC: U.S. Department of Health and Human Services, Public Health Service, National Institutes of Health, pp. 51–63.

*Ware JE. Measuring patients'views: the optimum outcome measure. *Br Med J* 1993;306:1429–1430.

*Ware JE. The MOS 36-Item Short-Form Health Survey (SF-36). In: Sederer LI, Dickey B. *Outcomes assessment in clinical practice.* Baltimore, MD: Williams and Wilkins, 1995; in press.

*Ware JE, Keller SD. Interpreting general health measures. In: Spilker B, ed. *Quality of Life and Pharmacoeconomics in Clinical Trials, Second Edition.* New York: Raven Press, 1995; in press.

*Weinberger M, Kirkman MS, Samsa GP, et al. The relationship between glycemic control and health-related quality of life in patients with non–insulin-dependent diabetes mellitus. *Med Care* 1994;32(12):1173–1181.

Quality of Life and Pharmacoeconomics in Clinical Trials, Second Edition, edited by B. Spilker.
Lippincott-Raven Publishers, Philadelphia © 1996.

CHAPTER **35**

The Sickness Impact Profile

Anne M. Damiano

INTRODUCTION

The Sickness Impact Profile (SIP) is a behaviorally based health status measure. It has been used extensively in clinical trials since its development in the 1970s by the late Marilyn Bergner and an interdisciplinary team at the University of Washington. The SIP was one of the first measures of overall health available to researchers, and it continues to be a reliable and valid measure that discriminates among groups with different levels of health and is sensitive to changes in health over time. This chapter describes the instrument and demonstrates its utility in clinical trials.

DESCRIPTION OF THE SICKNESS IMPACT PROFILE

Development of the SIP was prompted by the observation that frequently used clinical measures were not always sensitive to patient reports of progress (1). It was hypothesized that individual behavior would be a more useful measure for assessing new treatments, evaluating health care programs, and measuring the health levels of a population. Thus, the SIP was developed to supplement clinical measures of health.

The instrument consists of 136 items that describe activities associated with everyday living (Table 1). Each item is written in the first person case and the present tense. The SIP can be either interview- or self-administered. Respondents are asked to endorse (i.e., say ''Yes'' to if interview-administered or place a check by if self-administered) those items that they are sure describe them on that day and that are related to their health. For example, a respondent is instructed to endorse an item such as ''I sit during much of the day'' only if he sits for much of that day and if the reason for sitting so much is attributable to his health. If the respondent sits much of the day because he has a sedentary job, then the respondent would not endorse this item.

The SIP is scored according to the number and type of items that are endorsed. Each item has a numeric scale value that reflects its degree of dysfunction. Higher scale values indicate greater dysfunction. An individual's total SIP score is computed by summing the scale values for the items that he endorses, dividing by the total possible score (if all items were endorsed), and multiplying by 100. The score is expressed as a percent and can range from 0 to 100 where 0 represents no dysfunction and 100 represents maximal dysfunction.

Scoring is also possible at the level of categories and dimensions. The 136 items are aggregated into 12 categories that represent specific areas of activity (Table 2). To score an individual category, the scale values for all endorsed items in that category are divided by the total possible score for the category and multiplied by 100. Four categories,

A. M. Damiano: Health Technology Associates, Inc., Washington, D.C. 20005.

TABLE 1. *Sample SIP items*

Category	Sample item
Sleep and Rest	I sit during much of the day
Emotional Behavior	I act nervous or restless
Body Care and Movement	I change position frequently
Home Management	I am not doing any of the clothes washing that I usually do
Mobility	I am not going into town
Social Interaction	I am going out less to visit people
Ambulation	I walk more slowly
Alertness Behavior	I do not keep my attention on any activity for long
Communication	I don't write except to sign my name
Work	I am not working at all
Recreation and Pastimes	I am doing fewer community activities
Eating	I am eating much less than usual

Emotional Behavior, Social Interaction, Alertness Behavior, and Communication, can be further aggregated into a Psychosocial dimension. Three categories, Body Care and Movement, Mobility, and Ambulation, define a Physical dimension. Dimension scores are computed in the same manner as category and total scores.

CONCEPTUAL FRAMEWORK

The developers of the SIP chose to measure sickness-related behavior for several reasons (2). First, behaviors can be directly reported by the individual or they can be observed and reported by another respondent referring to the individual. Second, medical treatment can affect behavior independent of effects on the disease itself. Third, behaviors can be measured whether or not the individual seeks medical care. Finally, the effects of sickness as manifested in behavioral changes is a concept that is familiar and accepted by both consumers and providers of health care.

The relationship between health and sickness and behavior provides the conceptual foundation of the instrument and is

TABLE 2. *Categories and dimensions of the Sickness Impact Profile*

Dimension	Category
Physical	Ambulation
	Mobility
	Body Care and Movement
Psychosocial	Communication
	Alertness Behavior
	Emotional Behavior
	Social Interaction
Independent Categories	Sleep and Rest
	Eating
	Work
	Home Management
	Recreation and Pastimes

defined on a continuum (2). At one end of the continuum, the individual is healthy and behaves without limitation. At the other end, the individual is sick, experiences limitation(s), and, therefore, exhibits dysfunction. A behavior defined as dysfunctional can be a modification or impairment in the degree or manner of carrying out an activity, the cessation of an activity, or the initiation of an activity that interferes with or replaces a usual activity.

These dysfunctions serve as the measurable end points in a model of sickness behavior (2) that begins with signs or symptoms. The individual observes signs or symptoms and perceives them as related to sickness. Based on his perceptions, he may or may not seek medical care. If he does not seek care and the sickness persists, the individual nonetheless experiences the impacts of sickness. If he does seek care, the medical care process, in addition to his own perceptions, affects the impacts of sickness that he experiences. Impacts of sickness are manifested in the individual's behavior and, therefore, serve as the basis for response to SIP items.

DEVELOPMENT OF THE SICKNESS IMPACT PROFILE

Development of the SIP spanned a 5-year period and is well documented (2–6). The development strategy was based on the desire to produce an instrument that is reliable and valid in a variety of settings, discriminates groups with varying levels of dysfunction, and provides a unique contribution as a measure of outcome. The first step was to establish the content of the instrument. Then, three field trials were conducted during which the properties of the SIP were assessed and revisions made.

An exhaustive list of statements that describe health-related changes in behavior that range from minimal to maximal dysfunction was obtained through a large survey of health care professionals, patients, individuals caring for patients, and the apparently healthy. More than 1,100 survey participants provided statements describing health-related dysfunctions on open-ended request forms. Additional potential SIP items were obtained from existing catalogs of illness-related behavior dysfunction. Statements from both sources were evaluated and considered for the SIP if they described a behavior and the nature of the dysfunction. To avoid redundancy, each statement had to be unique either in the behavior it described, in the nature of the dysfunction it described, or in the degree of dysfunction it described. Potential items were sorted by the investigators into categories that describe a common activity. This data gathering, sorting, and grouping process produced the initial version of the SIP, which consisted of 312 items in 14 categories (2).

The objectives of the 1973 field trial were to provide scale values for the SIP items so that the instrument could be scored, to assess feasibility of administration, to provide preliminary assessments of reliability and validity, and to review and revise the content of the instrument (2). For the first objective, a group of 25 health care professionals and students participated in a two-part scaling exercise that yielded scale values for the SIP items (2,3). They were asked to rate the degree of dysfunction of the items. First, the 25 judges rated items within each category on equal-interval, 11-point scales. In the second part of the exercise, judges rated the least and most dysfunctional items from each category (identified by the within-category average ratings) on an equal-interval, 15-point scale so that items across all categories could be evaluated on a single scale. The two sets of judgments provided scale values that were then used to score the SIP.

To assess feasibility and to review the content of the instrument, 246 outpatients, inpatients, home care patients, walk-in clinic patients, and nonpatients participated in this field trial by responding to the SIP (2). Based on reports from the field, subjects found the instrument and the interview process acceptable. A content analysis, principally based on multiple regression models of category scores as a function of individual item values, produced a shortened (189 items) and revised instrument.

Finally, results from the 1973 field trial were used for a preliminary validation of the scale values derived from the 25 judges (2). An independent group of judges rated un-scored SIP profiles of the 246 subjects. SIP scores using the scale values were highly correlated with these independent ratings of unscored SIPs ($r \geq .85$). This latter observation provides evidence for the validity of the scale values as well as for the validity of the dysfunction construct.

The second field trial, in 1974, was designed to assess the reliability of the SIP and to provide preliminary assessments of validity (4,5). Purposive samples were selected to address the applicability and sensitivity of subsets of SIP items. The total sample ($n = 278$) was made up of rehabilitation inpatients and outpatients, speech pathology inpatients, chronic disease outpatients, and enrollees in a large, prepaid, group health plan who were not ill at the time. Test-retest reliability was high and was not significantly affected by different interviewers ($r = .73$ to $.96$), modes of administration ($r = .85$ to $.95$), and the patients' level or type of dysfunction ($r = .64$ to $.92$) (4). Correlations between SIP scores and criterion variables were moderate (5). The criterion variables included patient self-assessments of sickness ($r = .54$) and dysfunction ($r = .52$), clinician assessments of sickness ($r = .27$) and dysfunction ($r = .49$), the Katz Activities of Daily Living Index ($r = .46$) (7), and selected questions from the National Health Interview Survey that assess restricted activity ($r = .61$) (8). Further, SIP scores discriminated among the patient subsamples in the trial (5). Thus, the conceptual validity and discriminative capacity of the SIP were confirmed.

Data from the 1974 field trial also resulted in the second revision of the SIP (6,9). The interrelationships among items, the relationship of items to category and overall scores, and the relationship of items to the criterion variables were examined and used to revise or eliminate items. These analy-

ses suggested that a shorter version might be adequate to provide a sensitive instrument. Since data had been collected from purposive samples, field testing on a broader sample was necessary before finalizing a shortened version.

A third field trial was conducted in 1976 (6). In this trial, 696 members of a prepaid group practice and 199 "sick" patients from a family medicine clinic were interviewed. A small subset of participants ($n = 53$) was interviewed on two occasions so that test-retest reliability could be reviewed. The primary objectives of this trial, however, were to evaluate different modes of administration, discriminant validity, convergent validity, and clinical validity of the instrument.

Three modes of administration were evaluated: interviewer-administered (I), interviewer-delivered but self-administered (ID), and mail-delivered and self-administered (MD). Test-retest reliability was high for both the I ($r = .97$) and ID ($r = .87$) modes of administration; test-retest reliability could not be assessed for the MD mode. Internal consistency reliability was high for all three modes of administration but was lower for the MD mode ($\alpha = .81$) relative to the I and ID modes ($\alpha = .94$). Correlations between criterion variables (as defined above) and the MD SIP scores ($r = .05$ to $.48$) were lower than those for the I ($r = .55$ to $.64$) and ID ($r = .60$ to $.74$) SIP scores as well. These data suggest that self-administered SIPs, if not accompanied by verbal instructions, may not be as reliable or provide the same information as interviewer-administered or interviewer-delivered, self-administered SIPs (6).

SIP scores were more highly correlated with those criterion measures that were hypothesized, *a priori,* to reflect the sickness/dysfunction construct of the SIP. Briefly, SIP scores were hypothesized to be most related to self-assessments of dysfunction. The next highest relationship was hypothesized between SIP scores and self-assessments of sickness. Then, in order of descending strength of relationship, SIP scores were hypothesized to be less related to the National Health Interview Survey index, clinician ratings of dysfunction, and clinician ratings of sickness. The correlations between overall SIP scores and these criterion variables are displayed in Table 3 (6). Multi-trait, multi-method analyses of SIP scores and the criterion variables confirmed this relationship and were used to further assess the convergent and discriminant validity of the SIP. Finally, multiple regression models of criterion variables on SIP category scores provided additional evidence for the convergent and discriminant validity of the SIP (6).

Three groups of patients were selected to assess the clinical validity of the SIP: patients with total hip replacement, patients with hyperthyroidism, and patients with rheumatoid arthritis. These patient groups were selected because of the availability of reliable clinical measures known to parallel patient functional health status. Correlations between SIP scores and clinical indicators in the three groups were moderate to high ($r = .41$ to $.91$). Profiles of SIP category scores confirmed, as well as enlightened, hypothesized clinical pictures of each disease (6).

TABLE 3. *Correlations between overall SIP scores and criterion measures, 1976 field trial*

Criterion measure[a]	Correlation with overall SIP score
Self-Assessment of Dysfunction	.69
Self-Assessment of Sickness	.63
National Health Interview Survey Index	.55
Clinician Assessment of Dysfunction	.50
Clinician Assessment of Sickness	.40

[a]Listed in order of hypothesized strength of association from greatest to least.

TABLE 4. *Internal consistency reliability (alpha coefficients) by category for the SIP*

Category	Alpha[a]
Social Interaction	.81
Ambulation	.84
Sleep/Rest	.84
Eating	.63
Work	.78
Home Management	.88
Mobility	.84
Body Care and Movement	.90
Communication	.89
Recreational Pastimes	.87
Alertness Behavior	.88
Emotional Behavior	.84
Overall	.96[b]

[a]Alpha that would be obtained if each category had 20 items.
[b]Not adjusted for number of items.

Combined data from all three field trials was used to develop the final version of the SIP (6). In examining the relationship among categories, the high correlation between Movement of Body and Personal Hygiene resulted in a single Body Care and Movement category. Regression analyses suggested that similarly worded items in the Family Interaction and Social Interaction categories did not uniquely explain subject variance in the Psychosocial dimension score. Therefore, the two categories were combined into the single Social Interaction category. Item analyses (cluster analyses, frequency of item endorsement by demographic characteristics, reliability of items, interitem correlations, correlations between items, and criterion variables) resulted in deletions and combinations of items. The end result was the final, 136-item instrument.

Scale values, methods of scoring the SIP, and degree of aggregation were evaluated and finalized (3,9). Data from the 1973 and 1976 field trials indicated that the scale values provided by the 25 health care professionals and students were comparable to those provided by health care consumers (108 enrollees from a prepaid group practice) and that the scaling metric was, as intended, equal-interval. To ensure that the scale values represented a broad social consensus, the final scale values were based on ratings obtained from both the professional and consumer samples (3). Percent scores had substantially higher correlations with patient self-assessments of dysfunction than did an alternative, categorical scoring method (9). Stepwise multiple regression models, correlations between the hypothesized Physical and Psychosocial dimension scores, correlations between the dimension and overall scores, and cluster analyses confirmed the aggregation of scores: an overall score, two dimension scores (Physical and Psychosocial), and 12 category scores (9).

PROPERTIES OF THE FINAL VERSION

This developmental process produced the final, 136-item, 12-category instrument. Where possible, the properties of this final version were evaluated using field trial data (9). In general, the properties of the final version were consistent with earlier, longer versions of the instrument. Internal consistency of the 136-item SIP is .96, well beyond the minimum level of .80 considered appropriate for the description or comparison of populations (10). Internal consistency of categories ranges from .63 for Eating to .90 for Body Care and Movement (Table 4) (9).

Correlations of category and overall SIP scores with the criterion variables indicate that no category in the final version lost a significant amount of its discriminative capacity. The overall SIP score has correlations of .73, .68, and .49 with patient self-assessments of dysfunction, the National Health Interview Survey index, and clinician assessments of dysfunction, respectively. Regression models of criterion variables indicate that the 136-item SIP accounts for approximately the same amount of variance as did an earlier, 189-item version. The SIP explains 59% of the variance in both patient self-assessments and the National Health Interview Survey index and 31% of the variance in clinician assessments. Thus, reliability of the SIP is good and validity, with respect to the criterion measures used in the field trials, has been demonstrated. Since the completion of its development in the late 1970s, the value of the SIP as a reliable and valid health status measure has been demonstrated repeatedly in clinical trials, epidemiological studies, and program evaluations.

EXAMPLES OF THE SICKNESS IMPACT PROFILE IN CLINICAL TRIALS

Researchers have used the SIP to assess the burden of illness associated with different diseases or conditions. Because the SIP has been used so extensively, published scores are available for several diseases or conditions. In a review of generic health status measures, Patrick and Deyo (11) reported published overall SIP scores for 18 different disease conditions or population groups. Scores range from less than

5 for the group health enrollees who participated in the development of the SIP, survivors of cardiac arrest, and another general population sample to between 30 and 35 for chronic pain and amyotrophic lateral sclerosis patients.

The examples cited in this section are drawn from early, well-known applications of the SIP and some more recent applications. They are not representative of an extensive literature review. Rather, they were selected to illustrate particular uses or features of the instrument. Further, they were selected from several disciplines, such as nursing, surgery, physical therapy, health services research, and epidemiology, to illustrate the variety of SIP applications in the medical field. Finally, they do not include examples of the use of the SIP in numerous clinical trials conducted by pharmaceutical and medical device companies. Most of these latter studies are not available in the medical literature because of proprietary interests in the new medications or products studied.

Prospective Studies

Lower Extremity Fracture

Recently, MacKenzie et al. (12) used the SIP in a prospective study to examine the functional outcomes and general health status of 444 individuals sustaining lower extremity fractures. The SIP was administered to patients before discharge from the hospital and again 6 months following discharge. Before discharge, patients were asked to complete the SIP based on their functional status immediately prior to injury so that a preinjury baseline was established. Mean 6-month overall SIP scores were significantly higher than preinjury scores (9.8 versus 2.5; $p < .01$). Comparing the overall 6-month mean SIP score with those of other diseases and conditions reported by Patrick and Deyo (11), individuals sustaining lower extremity fractures exhibit moderate levels of dysfunction comparable to patients with Crohn's disease.

To further assess the burden of illness experienced by individuals sustaining lower extremity fracture, MacKenzie et al. (12) analyzed SIP categories and items. With the exception of Eating and Communication, all 6-month category scores were significantly higher than preinjury scores. Areas of activity with notably higher mean postinjury scores were Ambulation (16.2 versus 1.1), Household Management (14.5 versus 2.6), Sleep and Rest (13.1 versus 5.1), Recreational Pastimes (17.6 versus 4.2), Emotional Well-Being (9.9 versus 2.1), and Work (33.2 versus 8.8). Twenty-five of the 136 SIP items were endorsed by at least 20% of the patients 6 months following injury. Those items represented 9 of the 12 SIP categories and those items endorsed most frequently were, as expected, related to limitations in ambulation. However, the authors concluded that the most important finding was the wide scope of problems reported by these patients.

Not only were they limited in ambulation, but they were still experiencing dysfunction in several major areas of everyday living 6 months after their injury.

Further, MacKenzie et al. reported that the SIP was relatively easy to administer, the response rate was high (96%), and the SIP was sensitive to differences in the type and severity of the lower extremity fracture. With respect to the latter, the mean overall SIP score was significantly associated with the number of fractures such that higher mean scores were reported by patients with three or more fractures (16.1) compared to those with one or two fractures (9.1). Among patients with only one fracture, mean overall SIP scores reported by patients with high-energy fractures (10.5) were significantly higher than those reported by patients with low-energy fractures (7.3). Thus, by providing a profile of the health status of the study patients and by virtue of its feasibility and sensitivity, the utility of the SIP in clinical trials was confirmed for a lower extremity fracture population.

Hyperthyroidism

In one of the earliest clinical trials using the SIP, Rockey and Griep (13) assessed the behavioral dysfunction reported by patients with hyperthyroidism before, during, and after treatment with propranolol hydrochloride, propylthiouracil, and/or radioactive iodine. The SIP was administered to 14 patients at the time of diagnosis, at 4- to 8-week intervals during treatment, and again after they are euthyroid. In addition to patient assessments, a biochemical marker, adjusted serum thyroxine (T_4) level, was measured and recorded during the study period.

Prior to treatment, the mean overall SIP score for the hyperthyroid patients was about 12. Patients primarily reported dysfunctions in the Sleep and Rest, Home Management, and Recreational Pastimes categories. A review of frequently endorsed items suggested that hyperthyroid patients were less active during the day, spending much of the day sitting or lying down to rest, sleeping or napping during the day, or doing more inactive pastimes rather than usual activities. These patients also indicated that they were irritable, critical, and demanding in their family and social interactions. Half of the patients reported that they were clumsy.

During treatment, patients reported less dysfunction. At the first assessment during treatment, the mean overall SIP score dropped to about 6. At the second assessment, the mean dropped to about 4. Patient-reported dysfunction resolved as patients became euthyroid. Further, there was a strong positive correlation between T_4 and SIP scores. SIP scores fell toward zero as T_4 levels returned to normal. Thus, the SIP was useful in demonstrating the effectiveness of a treatment in terms of restoring patient function and for establishing a physiological basis for dysfunction in patients with hyperthyroidism.

Cataract

In a larger, recent trial, the SIP was used as a measure of general health status for 426 patients undergoing cataract surgery in one eye (14). The SIP was administered prior to surgery and at 4 and 12 months following surgery. The mean (SD) presurgery overall SIP score was 7.1 (9.3). After 1 year, the mean (SD) SIP score change was an improvement of 2.0 (5.7) points. While the cataract patients had moderately low SIP scores and were fairly stable over time, the SIP was sensitive to changes in general health status when they occurred. Changes in SIP score were significantly associated with changes in patient global ratings of overall health ($p < .01$). For patients reporting an improvement in their overall health status ($n = 116$), the mean change in overall SIP score was a three-point improvement.

The cataract study suggests that a difference in SIP score as small as three points may be clinically significant. Clinically significant SIP score changes were defined as three points in a previous study of back pain (15). Others, however, have more conservatively defined differences in SIP scores of five points as clinically meaningful (16,17).

Randomized Controlled Trials

Chronic Lung Disease

The SIP was used in a randomized controlled trial to evaluate sustained home nursing care for patients with chronic obstructive pulmonary disease (COPD) (17). The trial was designed to assess the cost and efficacy of a specialized home care program requiring trained respiratory nurses relative to standard home care and to standard office care. Three hundred and one patients were randomized to either respiratory home care (RHC), standard home care (SHC), or standard office care (OC). Patients were followed for 1 year. The SIP was administered upon entry to the study and again at 1 year following entry.

The mean overall SIP score for the entire sample at study entry was 16.2. Physical dimension and Psychosocial dimension mean scores were 11.8 and 13.5, respectively. These scores are comparable to scores reported for patients with end-stage renal disease (11).

At 1 year, mean overall SIP scores for the RHC, SHC, and OC groups were 16.2, 15.3, and 13.5, respectively. These scores were comparable to baseline scores and similar across treatment groups. Only SIP Mobility scores were significantly different across treatment groups with patients in the OC group reporting less dysfunction in Mobility (14.4 for RHC, 17.0 for SHC, and 9.7 for OC).

The results indicate that COPD patients receiving sustained home care over a 1-year period do not report improved functional status. Additional cost analyses suggested that patients in the RHC group incurred higher health care costs than patients in either the SHC or OC groups, although the observed differences were not statistically significant. Therefore, the investigators concluded that home care services for unselected COPD patients do not result in either improved functional status or reduced health care costs.

Soft Tissue Sarcoma

In a smaller, randomized controlled trial, Sugarbaker et al. (18) randomized 26 patients with lower extremity, soft tissue sarcoma to either amputation and chemotherapy or limb-sparing surgery with radiation and chemotherapy. The SIP was administered to patients 1 to 3 years following surgery. The investigators hypothesized, *a priori,* that patients in the limb-sparing surgery group would report fewer dysfunctions than those in the amputation group since the effects of high-dose radiation therapy would be less severe than the impact of amputation. The amputees, however, reported significantly better ($p < .05$) SIP scores for Emotional Behavior (3.6 versus 11.2) and Body Care and Movement (2.5 versus 24.5). Mean overall SIP scores and the other ten category scores were not significantly different between the two groups. The initial hypothesis was rejected and the investigators concluded that limb-sparing surgery with multiple treatments, relative to amputation, did not lead to a better quality of life for extremity sarcoma patients. They further noted the value of this information to both physicians and patients involved in treatment decisions.

Fibromyalgia

A final illustration of the utility of the SIP in clinical trials was reported by Nichols et al. (19). Nineteen patients with fibromyalgia were randomized to either an aerobic walking program or to a sedentary control group. The SIP was administered before and after the 8-week program. Patients in the aerobic walking group had significantly higher ($p < .05$) mean Physical dimension scores (9.2 versus 5.7) and lower, but nonsignificant, mean Psychosocial dimension scores (16.2 versus 21.1) than patients in the sedentary control group after controlling for differences in SIP scores before the program. The authors concluded that the exercise program may have increased levels of perceived muscle stiffness or fatigue and, therefore, resulted in higher Physical SIP scores. On the other hand, the regular meetings of the exercise group may have promoted new social and emotional ties and, therefore, resulted in lower Psychosocial SIP scores. The trends suggest that an aerobic exercise program may have some beneficial effects. However, given the lack of statistical significance, further study was recommended.

SUMMARY

In each of these examples, the SIP provided a profile of patient-reported, health-related dysfunction and contributed to the assessment of the effectiveness of various treatment and rehabilitation strategies. In some cases, SIP findings were unexpected and generated new hypotheses. Bergner et al. (17) showed that, contrary to earlier studies and beliefs, home care services do not improve functional outcomes for COPD patients. Sugarbaker et al. (18) found that, contrary to their *a priori* hypothesis, limb-sparing surgery with radiation and chemotherapy does not lead to better functioning than amputation for patients with lower extremity soft tissue sarcoma. In other cases, SIP findings confirmed previously hypothesized relationships. Rockey and Griep (13) confirmed the physiological basis for behavioral dysfunction in patients with hyperthyroidism.

Finally, in these examples, the SIP was instrumental in assessing the burden of illness of a population, such as the lower extremity fracture population (12). The burden of illness relative to other conditions or diseases is possible because of the wealth of published SIP scores for different populations. By virtue of its multidimensionality, the SIP identifies specific types of dysfunction experienced by a population. Knowledge of both level and type of dysfunction are critical for the development of effective treatment and rehabilitation strategies.

GUIDELINES FOR USE

Copies of the SIP are available from the Johns Hopkins University, which holds the copyright for the instrument. Interested researchers should write to The Health Services Research and Development Center, The Johns Hopkins University School of Hygiene and Public Health, 624 North Broadway, Baltimore, Maryland 21205, Attn: Elizabeth Ann Skinner, MSW.

The SIP is designed to be either interview- or self-administered. For interview-administration, all interviewers should receive standardized training outlined in the "Administration Procedures and Interviewer Training for the Sickness Impact Profile" manual, which is also available from the Johns Hopkins University. All interviews should be standardized and structured according to the manual. Special attention should be paid to instructions for administration of the SIP by telephone since telephone interviews lack the visual cues present during in-person interviews. Also, administration by telephone has not been thoroughly evaluated to determine if the SIP retains its reliability and validity.

Self-administration has been tested in two ways. The first method requires an interviewer to deliver the SIP, provide verbal instructions and answer questions, and then leave the SIP to be self-administered. The second method is a mail-delivered SIP with written instructions. Mail-delivered SIPs have demonstrated lower, although acceptable, levels of internal consistency, reliability, and validity than interviewer-delivered SIPs. Thus, it is recommended that self-admin-

istration be accompanied by verbal instructions whenever possible.

The length of an interview ranges from 20 to 30 minutes depending on the severity of illness of the patient. While some researchers have been reluctant to use the SIP because of its length, patients rarely complain about the length and interviewers report that the instrument is feasible. Researchers sometimes ask if the SIP can be shortened by deleting items or categories that they believe are not relevant to the population under study. Items should not be deleted from the instrument because the reliability and validity of category, dimension, and overall scores would be unknown. While individual categories are reliable and valid, selective administration of categories is strongly discouraged because the discriminative capacity of the SIP will be decreased and because categories have demonstrated differential importance in accounting for the variance in overall SIP score for different patient groups. The total length of time required for an interview is not substantially reduced by shortening the instrument. For example, during the field trials, the difference in time between a 189-item and a 138-item version was only about 5 minutes.

A current demonstration of the feasibility of the SIP is in a large, randomized trial to evaluate the impact of prognostic information for critically ill adults (20). The SIP was administered by telephone 2 months following an episode of care. Reports from the field indicate that telephone interviews are feasible, even with seriously ill and primarily elderly patients. It was observed, however, that a standardized and structured format, particularly with respect to pauses after reading each item, is critical for a successful telephone interview. The functional outcome of these study patients, in terms of the SIP, was recently published (21).

CONCLUSIONS

The Sickness Impact Profile is an established, well-validated health status instrument. It is based on a conceptual model of sickness as manifested in changes in behavior. The model is familiar and acceptable to both health care professionals and patients. Development of the SIP was carefully planned, methodologically rigorous, and well documented. The instrument is comprehensive, assessing functioning across 12 distinct domains of everyday living: Ambulation, Mobility, Body Care and Movement, Communication, Alertness Behavior, Emotional Behavior, Social Interaction, Sleep and Rest, Eating, Work, Home Management, and Recreation and Pastimes. However, dysfunction can also be characterized overall with a single total SIP score and in two dimensions with the Physical and Psychosocial scores. The availability of published SIP scores for numerous samples representing healthy and various disease populations is, perhaps, the most compelling evidence of its feasibility and utility in a variety of settings.

ACKNOWLEDGMENT

The author acknowledges the late Marilyn Bergner, a mentor, a colleague, and a friend. This chapter is dedicated to her memory.

REFERENCES

1. Bergner M. Development, testing, and use of the Sickness Impact Profile. In: Walker SR, Rosser RM, eds. *Quality of life: assessment and application.* Lancaster: MTP Press, 1987:79–94.
2. Bergner M, Bobbit RA, Kressel S, Pollard WE, Gilson BS, Morris JR. The Sickness Impact Profile: conceptual formulation and methodology for the development of a health status measure. *Int J Health Services* 1976;6:393–415.
3. Carter WB, Bobbit RA, Bergner M, Gilson BS. Validation of an interval scaling: the Sickness Impact Profile. *Health Serv Res* 1976;11:516–528.
4. Pollard WE, Bobbit RA, Bergner M, Martin DP, Gilson BS. The Sickness Impact Profile: reliability of a health status measure. *Med Care* 1976;14:146–155.
5. Bergner M, Bobbit RA, Pollard WE, Martin DP, Gilson BS. The Sickness Impact Profile: validation of a health status measure. *Med Care* 1976;14:57–67.
6. Bergner M, Bobbit RA, Carter WB, Gilson BS. The Sickness Impact Profile: development and final revision of a health status measure. *Med Care* 1981;19:787–805.
7. Katz S, Ford A, Moskovitz RW, Jackson BA, Jaffe MW. Studies of illness in the aged. The Index of ADL: a standardized measure of biological and psychosocial function. *JAMA* 1963;185:914–919.
8. U.S. Department of Health, Education, and Welfare. Interviewing methods in the health interview survey. Vital and Health Statistics Series 2, No. 48, Washington, DC, 1972.
9. Gilson BS, Bergner M, Bobbit RA, Carter WB. *The Sickness Impact Profile: final development and testing, 1975–1978.* Seattle: Department of Health Services, School of Public Health and Community Medicine, 1979.
10. Nunnally J. *Psychometric theory.* New York: McGraw-Hill, 1978.
11. Patrick DL, Deyo RA. Generic and disease-specific measures in assessing health status and quality of life. *Med Care* 1989;27:S217–S232.
12. MacKenzie EJ, Burgess AR, McAndrew MP, et al. Patient-oriented functional outcome after unilateral lower extremity fracture. *J Orthop Trauma* 1993;7:393–401.
13. Rockey PH, Griep RJ. Behavioral dysfunction in hyperthyroidism. *Arch Intern Med* 1980;140:1194–1197.
14. Damiano AM, Steinberg EP, Cassard SD, et al. Comparison of generic versus disease-specific measures of functional impairment in patients with cataract. *Med Care* 1995;33:AS120–AS130.
15. Deyo RA, Diehl AK, Rosenthal M. How many days of bed rest for acute low back pain? A randomized clinical trial. *N Engl J Med* 1986;315:1064–1070.
16. Bergner L, Hallstrom AP, Bergner M, Eisenberg MS, Cobb LA. Health status of survivors of cardiac arrest and of myocardial infarction controls. *Am J Public Health* 1985;75:1321–1323.
17. Bergner M, Hudson LD, Conrad DA, Patmont CM, McDonald GJ, Perrin EB, Gilson BS. The cost and efficacy of home care for patients with chronic lung disease. *Med Care* 1988;26:566–579.
18. Sugarbaker PH, Barofsky I, Rosenberg SA, Gianola FJ. Quality of life assessment of patients in extremity sarcoma clinical trials. *Surgery* 1982;91:17–23.
19. Nichols DS, Glenn TM. Effects of aerobic exercise on pain perception, affect, and level of disability in individuals with fibromyalgia. *Phys Ther* 1994;74:327–332.
20. Murphy DJ, Cluff LE. SUPPORT: Study to Understand Prognoses and Preferences for Outcomes and Risks of Treatment—study design. *J Clin Epidemiol* 1990;43:1S–124S.
21. Wu AW, Damiano AM, Lynn J, et al. Predicting future functional status for seriously ill hospitalized adults: the SUPPORT model. *Ann Intern Med* 1995;15:170–179.

Quality of Life and Pharmacoeconomics in Clinical Trials, Second Edition, edited by B. Spilker.
Lippincott-Raven Publishers, Philadelphia © 1996.

CHAPTER 36

The World Health Organization Quality of Life (WHOQOL) Assessment Instrument

Silvija Szabo (on behalf of the WHOQOL Group)

INTRODUCTION

The World Health Organization Quality of Life (WHOQOL) assessment instrument inquires into the respondent's perception and subjective evaluation of various aspects of his/her life. It is designed to measure quality of life related to health and health care. The instrument is being developed within a cross-cultural multicenter project. A distinctive feature of the course of its development is an iterative feedback of information and data between the centers participating in its development. Experts and lay health care users in each center are involved in this process. Thus it may be assumed that the final instrument will allow a cross-cultural comparison of quality of life research data.

The World Health Organization's (WHO) initiative to develop a quality of life assessment arose for several reasons. First, in recent years there has been a broadening in focus in the measurement of health beyond traditional health indicators, such as mortality and morbidity (1,2), to include measures of the impact of disease and impairment on daily activities and behavior (e.g., Sickness Impact Profile; 3), perceived health measures (e.g., Nottingham Health Profile; 4), and disability/functional status measures. These mea-

sures, while beginning to provide a measure of the impact of disease, do not assess quality of life per se, which has been aptly described as the "missing measurement in health" (5). Second, most measures of health status have been developed in a single cultural setting, and the translation of these measures for use in other settings is time-consuming and unsatisfactory for a number of reasons (6). Third, the increasingly mechanistic model of medicine, concerned only with the eradication of disease and symptoms, reinforces the need for the introduction of a humanistic element into health care. Health care is essentially a humanistic transaction where the patient's well-being is a primary aim. WHO's initiative to develop a quality of life assessment arises, therefore, both from a need for a genuinely international measure of quality of life, and WHO's commitment to the continued promotion of a holistic approach to health and health care.

The WHOQOL is being developed, according to a standardized protocol (7), simultaneously in a wide range of languages and cultures. Field centers were selected to provide differences in level of industrialization, health service organization, and other culture-specific determinants affecting quality of life (e.g., role of family, perception of time, perception of self, dominant religion, etc.). Table 1 lists the field centers that participated in the development and testing of the WHOQOL pilot instrument.

The methodology of the WHOQOL's development comprises several stages that are outlined in this chapter.

S. Szabo: The WHOQOL Group, Division of Mental Health, World Health Organization, 1211 Geneva 27, Switzerland.

TABLE 1. *Field centers involved in the development of the WHOQOL pilot instrument*

Melbourne, Australia
Zagreb, Croatia
Paris, France
Delhi, India
Madras, India
Beer-Sheva, Israel
Tokyo, Japan
Tilburg, the Netherlands
Panama City, Panama
St. Petersburg, Russia
Barcelona, Spain
Bangkok, Thailand
Bath, United Kingdom
Seattle, Washington, United States
Harare, Zimbabwe

CONCEPTUALIZATION AND OPERATION OF QUALITY OF LIFE

Due to the lack of a universally agreed upon definition of quality of life, the first step in the development of the WHOQOL was to define the concept and make some assumptions about its measurement that would warrant cross-cultural comparison of data.

Quality of life is defined as individuals' perceptions of their position in life in the context of the culture and value systems in which they live, and in relation to their goals, expectations, standards, and concerns (8). It is a broad-ranging concept, incorporating in a complex way the persons' physical health, psychological state, level of independence, social relationships, personal beliefs, and relationship to salient features of the environment. This definition highlights the view that quality of life refers to a subjective evaluation, which includes both positive and negative dimensions, and which is embedded in a cultural, social, and environmental context.

Given that quality of life is a multidimensional construct to be amenable to measurement, it is necessary to identify its various component parts. Consultants and investigators from field centers proposed several broad domains assumed to contribute to an individual's quality of life (9,10). Each domain was further divided into a series of specific areas (facets) summarizing each particular domain.

The proposed hierarchical structure of quality of life allows for the development of an instrument that will produce a quality of life profile of the respondent with (a) an overall quality of life score, (b) domain scores, and (c) facet scores.

Focus groups were run in several field centers (Bangkok, Bath, Madras, Melbourne, Panama, St. Petersburg, Seattle, Tilburg, Zagreb) in order to (a) examine the meaning, variation, and perceptual experience of the quality of life construct in each of the WHOQOL field centers; and (b) test the face validity and comprehensiveness of the proposed WHOQOL domains and facets.

Participants of these groups were mostly individuals from the general population in contact with health care (11). A standardized interview schedule for use in the focus groups was provided by WHO Geneva. Some of the questions included in the schedule were:

1. What are the words or phrases that describe quality of life? (Objective: to arrive at a communal meaning of what is meant by the term *quality of life*.)
2. What are the things that affect people's quality of life? (Objective: to arrive at a list of areas/facets that the participants feel affect people's quality of life.)
3. Are there more general labels that include some of the things you have mentioned that affect quality of life? (Objective: to come up with broad areas (domains) that contribute to quality of life.)

In addition, participants classified the facets, proposed by the members of the group, as "not so important," "important," or "very important."

The data from the focus group discussions revealed the following:

1. Both within each cultural setting and between cultural settings quality of life cannot be easily described in terms of one or several words or phrases, but instead it is the breadth and content of quality of life issues that define it.
2. The issues that participants raised in discussion groups broadly reflected the issues covered in the WHOQOL domain and facet structure previously proposed by experts, but some modifications proved to be necessary.

The next step was to provide a definition for each facet. This consisted of a conceptual definition, a description of various dimensions along which a rating can be made for that facet, and a listing of some example situations or conditions that might significantly affect that facet at various levels of intensity. Facets describe behaviors (e.g., activities), states of being (e.g., fatigue), capacities (e.g., ability to move around), or subjective perceptions of experiences (e.g., pain). For example, the facet "positive feelings" was defined in the following way (12):

> "The facet examines how much a person experiences positive feelings of contentment, balance, peace, happiness, hopefulness, joy, and enjoyment of the good things in life. A person's view and feelings about the future are seen as an important part of this facet. For many respondents this facet may be regarded as synonymous with quality of life.
>
> (Negative feelings are not included as these are covered elsewhere.)
> Examples:
> A Buddhist monk, who has attained balance/contentment.

Facet definitions were translated into the language of the field centers following a standardized WHOQOL translation method (6). In brief, a process of forward and backward translation complemented by a review process by monolingual and bilingual groups was used to ensure meaningful translation of concepts.

The translated facet definitions were the basis for further focus group work in the field centers (12). This work had three aims: (a) to check further on the existing facet structure, (b) to generate items/questions for the WHOQOL pilot instrument, and (c) to obtain importance ratings of facets from participants.

Focus group participants from the following populations were sampled at each field center: (a) persons in contact with health services (both inpatients and outpatients with acute and chronic disorders), (b) persons from the general population (including some who were informal caregivers), and (c) health personnel. A minimum of two focus groups was conducted for each of the three population groups. However, where the data from any of these two groups were dissimilar, extra focus groups were conducted until the data showed a marked pattern and further focus groups added nothing new. In addition, in some centers further focus groups were run to sample individuals from very different populations (e.g., rural and urban, young and old).

The focus groups were, wherever possible, made up of a sample of individuals representative of the population of the field center. For the patient and ''well'' groups this applied to the demographic features: gender, age, educational background, socioeconomic group, marital status, and ethnic group. For the health personnel group this applied to professional role in the representative health care team in the country of the field center.

A standardized and detailed focus group protocol was used according to which the work in the groups was run. In order to standardize focus group moderation as far as possible, all primary focus group moderators were trained at WHO in Geneva. Two questions formed the basis for the discussion of each of the facets: (1) ''How does [facet] affect your (your patient's) quality of life?'' and (2) ''How would you ask about [facet]?'' After all facets had been discussed, participants were asked whether they considered any further issues to be important to quality of life.

To obtain a preliminary indication of the importance attached to each of the facets universally, and in a given field center, focus group participants were asked to rate the importance of each facet on a five-point rating scale.

On the basis of the focus group data some revisions of the WHOQOL facet structure, as well as of the definitions of some facets, were carried out. Table 2 displays the domain and facet structure adopted for the WHOQOL pilot instrument.

As can be seen from Table 2, the WHOQOL provides a balanced and holistic assessment of a person's quality of life, where positive and negative aspects are assessed. The coverage of quality of life that results ensures a conceptual coherence, or a gestalt, which is missing from many other measures of quality of life.

TABLE 2. *WHOQOL domains and facets*

Domain I—Physical domain	
1	Pain and discomfort
2	Energy and fatigue
3	Sexual activity
4	Sleep and rest
5	Sensory functions
Domain II—Psychological domain	
6	Positive feelings
7	Thinking, learning, memory, and concentration
8	Self-esteem
9	Bodily image and appearance
10	Negative feelings
Domain III—Level of independence	
11	Mobility
12	Activities of daily living
13	Dependence on medicinal substances and medical aids
14	Dependence on nonmedical substances (alcohol, tobacco, drugs)
15	Communication capacity
16	Work capacity
Domain IV—Social relationships	
17	Personal relationships
18	Practical social support
19	Activities as provider/supporter
Domain V—Environment	
20	Freedom, physical safety, and security
21	Home environment
22	Work satisfaction
23	Financial resources
24	Health and social care: accessibility and quality
25	Opportunities for acquiring new information and skills
26	Participation in and opportunities for recreation/leisure activities
27	Physical environment: (pollution/noise/traffic/climate)
28	Transport
Domain VI—Spirituality/religion/personal beliefs	

QUESTION GENERATION

Focus group data, as well as previous discussions of WHOQOL study group experts, indicated that questions addressing quality of life, as conceptualized in the WHOQOL, may be divided into two groups: (a) questions inquiring into the person's perception of his/her state, behavior, or capacity, and (b) questions inquiring into his/her subjective evaluation of these aspects of life. Among the latter, questions addressing the person's satisfaction with various components contributing to quality of life are prominent. The WHOQOL question typology and example questions are given in Table 3.

An additional aspect that may be of interest in the assessment of quality of life is the importance attributed by the respondent to various aspects of his/her life. Data from questions addressing importance of facets may be used to weight scores for each facet.

TABLE 3. *WHOQOL question typology*

Question type	Description	Sample
Perceived objective	Questions refer to a person's assessments of his/her behaviors, states, or capacities; inform about the individual's perception of his/her physical and psychological health, level of independence, social relationships, and environmental conditions	How well do you sleep? How is your memory? Do you feel hopeless? How dependent are you on medication? Are you able to work?
Self-report subjective	Questions refer to a person's subjective evaluation of his/her behaviors, states, or capacities; inform about the individual's satisfaction with or concerns about his/her physical and psychological health, level of independence, social relationships, and environmental conditions	How satisfied are you with your sight? How much do you worry about how you look? How much of a burden to you is caring for others?

TABLE 4. *Criteria for the WHOQOL questions*

Questions should:
- be based as far as possible on the suggestions of patients and health personnel participating in the focus groups
- give rise to answers that are illuminating about respondents' quality of life, as defined in the project
- be amenable to a rating scale
- reflect the meaning conveyed in the facet definition
- cover in combination with other questions for a given facet, the key aspects of that facet as outlined in the facet definition
- avoid any explicit reference point in terms of time or in terms of comparison point(s) (e.g., the ideal, or before I was ill)
- be applicable to patients with a range of impairment
- be phrased as questions rather than as statements
- be shorter rather than longer
- avoid double negatives
- avoid any ambiguities in terms of wording or phrasing

A question-writing panel was assembled in each of the field centers. The panel included the principal investigator, the main focus group moderator, a person with good interviewing skills, and a lay person to ensure that the questions were framed in a natural and comprehensive language.

Starting from the suggestions of participants in the focus groups, the panel framed a maximum of six questions per facet at each of the two levels of questioning (''perceived objective'' and ''self-report subjective'') according to the criteria outlined in Table 4. In addition, several questions addressing quality of life and health in general were framed.

Naturally questions were framed in the language of the field center (e.g., Croatian, English, or Hindi). However, as the working language of the WHOQOL project is English, for the purposes of combining these questions into a global question pool each center translated their proposed questions into English.

Questions from all centers were assembled in a global question pool of about 1,800 questions. After identifying semantically equivalent questions and deleting those that did not fully meet the criteria for WHOQOL questions (Table 4), the global pool was reduced to around 1,000 questions.

Given that a number of facets have several aspects addressed by the proposed questions (e.g., for the facet ''positive feelings,'' questions could be grouped into those addressing ''happiness and enjoyment of life,'' ''content-

ment,'' and ''hopefulness and optimism''), the next step was to form conceptual clusters within facets and within levels of questioning. Investigators in each field center then rank-ordered within each facet (a) the conceptual clusters according to their importance for quality of life in the culture of the center, and (b) the questions within each conceptual cluster according to how much the question tells about the respondent's quality of life in that particular culture. In the ranking process the investigators took into account data from focus group work.

From the combined rankings from all centers 231 questions addressing facets and five addressing overall quality of life and general health were selected for the WHOQOL pilot instrument. On average there were four questions for each of the two levels of questioning for each facet. The conceptual clusters ensured that the selected questions covered all the relevant aspects of a facet. Table 5 displays the number of questions in the WHOQOL pilot instrument derived in each of the field centers. To these questions 41 standardized questions were added to assess the importance attributed by the respondents to the selected WHOQOL facets.

Since this process of ranking by all centers may favor more global questions, some that address important but culture-specific features of facets may have been omitted. Some field centers opted to include several culture-specific questions to their national version of the pilot WHOQOL instrument. For example, in Thailand, where the vast majority of the population are Buddhists, the national version of the instrument included the following question for the facet of negative feelings: ''How well are you able to rid yourself of negative feelings through meditation?'' This question would clearly be inappropriate to most respondents in other settings, but addresses an important aspect of psychological well-being in Thailand. The inclusion of a limited number of culture-specific questions acknowledged that particular aspects of certain facets of quality of life are not universal,

TABLE 5. *Number of questions selected for the WHOQOL pilot instrument from each of the main study field centers*[a]

Field center	Number (percentage) of questions
Bangkok, Thailand	33 (14%)
Bath, United Kingdom	31 (13%)
Harare, Zimbabwe	33 (14%)
Madras, India	41 (17%)
Melbourne, Australia	49 (21%)
Panama City, Panama	48 (20%)
Paris, France	36 (15%)
St. Petersburg, Russia	22 (9%)
Seattle, Washington, United States	46 (20%)
Tilburg, Netherlands	50 (21%)
Zagreb, Croatia	63 (27%)
Questions proposed by coordinating group	7 (3%)

[a]Because a number of questions were proposed in identical or semantically equivalent forms the sum of all questions comes to more that the 236 questions in the pilot instrument. The seven questions proposed by the WHO coordinating group were proposed where existing questions inadequately covered the key areas of the facet.

and hence enhanced the ability of the WHOQOL to address these aspects. These questions were additional to the agreed upon core questions, but to be retained, these "national" questions had to compete with the "global" questions in the analysis of the pilot data.

RESPONSE SCALE GENERATION

Responses to questions in the WHOQOL are given on five-point Likert-type response scales. According to the differences in the content of questions, five different response scales were needed. The scales addressed (a) Intensity (not at all–extremely), (b) Capacity (not at all–completely), (c) Frequency (never–always), (d) Evaluation (very dissatisfied–very satisfied; very poor–very good), (e) Importance (not important–extremely important).

There were no difficulties in translating the end points (anchor points) of the scales, but adequate translation of descriptors of the three categories between the anchor points was difficult given that the descriptors should have covered equidistant magnitudes on the scale.

To ensure equidistance of descriptor magnitude across field centers the following procedure was used:

1. Anchor points were translated into the language of the field center using the WHOQOL translation methodology.
2. For each scale, about 15 descriptors were selected, covering the range of magnitudes between the anchor points.
3. For each response scale 20 lay subjects, representative of the health care users in the field center, were asked to place each descriptor on a 100-mm line, according to where they thought the descriptor lay in relation to the anchor points. The series of descriptors for a given response scale were presented in random order, and a new line was used for each descriptor.
4. For each scale the mean and standard deviation of estimates for each descriptor were calculated. The three intermediate descriptors were selected from the descriptors the means of which fell in the following ranges: (a) 20mm–30mm, (b) 45mm–55mm, (c) 70mm–80mm.

To check on the ordinality of response scales, each center asked a small group of respondents to rank order descriptors for each response scale. To check on the comparability of the derived descriptors between centers a bilingual review was used.

Table 6 shows the descriptors for the Frequency scale selected in a number of field centers.

TABLE 6. *Frequency response scales derived in some of the field centers*

	0 Anchor ("Never" for all centers)	25 Descriptor	50 Descriptor	75 Descriptor	100 Anchor ("Always" for all centers)
Bath		Seldom	Quite often	Very often	
Delhi		Occasionally	Often	Very often	
Harare		Occasionally	From time to time	Many times	
Madras		Not most of the time	Generally	Many times	
Melbourne		Infrequently	Sometimes	Frequently	
St. Petersburg		Rather rarely	Neither rarely nor often	Rather often	
Seattle		Rarely	Sometimes	Usually	
Tilburg		Seldom	Now and then	Reasonably often	
Zagreb		Sometimes	Usually	Quite often	

Following the described procedure, Intensity, Capacity, Frequency, and Evaluation scales were generated. The Importance scale was developed earlier in the course of focus group work.

PILOT TESTING OF THE WHOQOL PILOT INSTRUMENT

The WHOQOL pilot instrument was standardized across field centers with regard to formatting, instructions, and administration. Field centers pretested the questionnaire on a small sample of health users. On the basis of the data of the pretesting, some minor changes in the instructions and wording of some questions were made. Subsequently the instrument was administered in each field center on a sample of 300 respondents.

The sample of respondents in each field center to whom the pilot instrument was administered were adults, with "adult" being culturally defined. A sampling quota was applied with regard to health status (250 persons with a disease or impairment; 50 "well" persons), age ($\leq$45 years, 50%; $\geq$44 years, 50%), and gender (female, 50%; male, 50%). In selecting the respondents an attempt was made to recruit people with varied levels of quality of life. One way to achieve this was to include some people with quite severe and disabling chronic diseases, some people in contact with health facilities for more transient conditions, and others who were in contact with the health service for reasons that were not likely to impinge upon their quality of life to any greater extent.

The instrument was mainly self-administered. In some cases (e.g., poor vision, illiteracy) interviewers assisted respondents in completing the questionnaire. When answering the questions respondents were asked to take into account their life in the previous 2 weeks.

Analysis of data from the pilot testing of the WHOQOL pilot instrument, which is now under way, focuses on refining the facet structure and reducing the number of questions within facets, while maintaining a common core domain and facet structure across all centers. The ideal is to strike a balance between a minimum number of facets and questions and adequate coverage of the key areas contributing to respondents' quality of life in the various cultures included in this phase of work. In the analysis of the pilot data, a mapping procedure that focuses on representativeness and discriminatory power is used, whereby the association of domains to global questions about quality of life, of facets to domains, and facets to other facets can be examined (see Chapter 69 by Bullinger et al. in this volume for further details). Based on this data the facet structure is refined and reduced. The pooled data also enables an examination of the possibility that there are several core or primary facets that best summarize quality of life in all centers, and certain questions for each of these facets that are reliable and valid in all field centers. A strategy for question selection reflecting "representativeness" (high question–total correlations in the case of the specific facet) and discriminatory power (low question–total correlations in the case of other facets) is used to select questions that might be present in all national versions of the WHOQOL.

Preliminary analyses indicate that for the pooled data for all items from all centers, all but one facet (Activity as Provider facet 19) have high internal consistency, with Cronbach alphas ranging from .82 to .95. The analyses also indicate that all facets are fairly independent of each other. The ability of the facets to distinguish between the patient group and a well sample (this latter accounting for some 16% of the total), has also been examined, using all 236 items in the pilot instrument. Preliminary analysis indicates that all domains and all but four of the facets individually are able to significantly distinguish at the .05 level or better between the well and the ill. The four facets that failed to distinguish all came from the environmental domain, which contained nine facets in all. These preliminary analyses suggest therefore that the WHOQOL will have good reliability and validity.

The data for each of the project's field centers will then be analyzed separately, and the "best" questions, which define each facet most effectively, will be selected for that center. These analyses will also include national questions, which will have to compete with the core questions to be retained. In this way, it can be seen whether the various centers generate different sets of questions for each facet, or whether a common core of questions can be selected with high validity for all centers (see chapter by Bullinger et al.).

It is assumed, however, that even if the national instruments do contain questions that are idiosyncratic for that center, having been selected in the described way, the instrument will still yield cross-culturally comparable data. The comparability is based on:

1. simultaneous development of the instrument in numerous cultural settings,
2. a common set of agreed upon facet definitions,
3. a common methodology for question development and selection,
4. a "global" pool of questions with which any "national" questions have to compete.

ESTABLISHING THE WHOQOL'S PSYCHOMETRIC PROPERTIES

A version of the WHOQOL for further field testing will be developed on the basis of data from the administration of its pilot form. This will be tested to establish its psychometric properties (see chapter by Bullinger et al.). In each field center, studies will be conducted involving the following:

1. clear and homogeneous population(s),
2. longitudinal design,
3. specific intervention(s), and

4. parallel use of other national and international instruments with established psychometric properties to assess convergent validity.

From this, the following will be calculated: test-retest reliability; responsiveness to change; and test validation, specifically with regard to convergent, discriminant, and predictive validity.

FURTHER WORK ON THE WHOQOL

Different Forms

The present form of the WHOQOL, which allows for a comprehensive inquiry into quality of life, is envisaged as having some 100 items. Therefore, a shorter version will be developed that might address only the primary facets of quality of life or may utilize only the highest loading item for each facet. The short form could be used for screening, in clinical trials, repeated measures research design, or for clinical purposes where only a few minutes are available for its administration.

In addition interviewer-assisted and interviewer-administered forms of the instrument will be developed for respondents who cannot, for health or education reasons, read or write. Research using a multitrait, multimethod approach will be directed at establishing the correspondence between these different forms of the instrument. Different versions of the WHOQOL will ensure its high "application potential" (13).

New Centers

It is expected that further centers will want to develop a quality of life instrument besides those included in the original WHOQOL study. A protocol has been developed (14) that outlines the procedure to be used by new centers wishing to develop the WHOQOL for their own culture.

Population-Specific Modules

It is acknowledged that there are groups of persons whose quality of life might not be sufficiently or appropriately assessed with the described form of the WHOQOL instrument (core instrument or core module). For such groups of people, specific WHOQOL modules will be developed. A module will be a special set of facets/subfacets/questions that complement the core instrument for a particular group.

WHO has identified five priority areas for module development: (a) persons suffering from chronic diseases (e.g., epilepsy, arthritis, cancer, AIDS, diabetes), (b) caregivers of the ill or disabled (e.g., a person taking care of a terminally sick patient), (c) persons living in highly stressful situations (e.g., elderly people living in poorly run institutions, refugees in camps), (d) persons with difficulty communicating (e.g.,

persons with severe learning disabilities), and (e) children. The WHOQOL Study Protocol (7) provides an outline of how this might be done in the case of cancer.

CONCLUSIONS

WHO's commitment to the development of an international quality of life assessment arises from the lack of any genuinely international instruments that can be meaningfully used in both developed and developing world countries to measure the individual's view of the impact of disease and impairment on his/her life. The WHOQOL has been designed as a generic instrument for the assessment of both positive and negative aspects of quality of life. It provides instruments in a broad range of languages, each of which is closely comparable and yet each of which can retain features that might be unique to a particular language and culture. It yields a multidimensional profile with quality of life scores in six domains, encompassing over 20 facets of quality of life.

This chapter outlines WHO's work to date on the development of the WHOQOL. This has involved establishing an approach to quality of life assessment, developing an agreed upon and detailed study protocol, and following a series of steps leading to a reliable, valid, and responsive quality of life measure. The steps were as follows: (a) operationalizing the domains and facets of quality of life; (b) question and response scale generation; (c) extensive international piloting work with a preliminary version of the instrument; (d) development of the field trial WHOQOL instrument on the basis of this data; and (e) a further series of reliability, validity, and responsiveness studies. A key feature of this methodology is the use of an iterative process of input from health professionals and from lay groups from many countries around the world, through the use of focus groups as well as international expert review. Preliminary data arising from the extensive international piloting work attests to the considerable reliability, cross-cultural validity, discriminant validity, and construct validity of the WHOQOL. At the time of writing the field trial WHOQOL is being prepared for the final series of validity and responsiveness studies.

The work of the WHOQOL group serves to restate WHO's commitment to a holistic conception of health and the need for a humanistic element in health care that goes beyond the eradication of symptoms and disease.

ACKNOWLEDGMENTS

The WHOQOL group comprises a coordinating group, collaborating investigators in each of the field centers and a panel of consultants. Dr. J. Orley directs the project. He has been assisted by Dr. W. Kuyken, Dr. N. Sartorius, and Dr. M. Power. In the field centers collaborating investigators are Professor H. Herrman, Dr. H. Schofield, and Ms. B. Murphy, University of Melbourne, Australia; Professor Z.

Metelko, Professor S. Szabo, and Mrs. M. Pibernik-Okanovic, Institute of Diabetes, Endocrinology and Metabolic Diseases and Department of Psychology, Faculty of Philosophy, University of Zagreb, Croatia; Dr. N. Quemada and Dr. A. Caria, INSERM, Paris, France; Dr. S. Rajkumar and Mrs. Shuba Kumar, Madras Medical College, India; Dr. S. Saxena, All India Institute of Medical Sciences, New Delhi, India; Dr. D. Bar-On and Dr. M. Amir, Ben-Gurion University, Beer-Sheeva, Israel; Dr. Miyako Tazaki, Department of Science, Science University of Tokyo, Japan and Dr. Ariko Noji, Department of Community Health Nursing, St Luke's College of Nursing, Japan; Dr. G. van Heck and Mrs. J. De Vries, Tilburg University, The Netherlands; Professor J. Arroyo Sucre and Professor L. Picard-Ami, University of Panama, Panama; Professor M. Kabanov, Dr. A. Lomachenkov, and Dr. G. Burkovsky, Bekhterev Psychoneurological Research Institute, St. Petersburg, Russia; Dr. R. Lucas Carrasco, Barcelona, Spain; Dr. Yooth Bodharamik and Mr. Kitikorn Meesapya, Institute of Mental Health, Bangkok, Thailand; Dr. S. Skevington, University of Bath, United Kingdom; Dr. D. Patrick, Ms. M. Martin, and Ms. D. Wild, University of Washington, Seattle; and Professor W. Acuda, Dr. J. Mutambirwa, University of Zimbabwe, Harare, Zimbabwe.

An international panel of consultants includes Dr. N. K. Aaronson, Dr. P. Bech, Dr. M. Bullinger, Dr. He-Nian Chen, Dr. J. Fox-Rushby, Dr. C. Moinpour, and Dr. R. Rosser. Consultants who have advised WHO at various stages of the development of the project have included Dr. D. Buesching, Dr. D. Bucquet, Dr. L. W. Chambers, Dr. B. Jambon, Dr. C. D. Jenkins, Dr. D. De Leo, Dr. L. Fallowfield, Dr. P. Gerin, Dr. P. Graham, Dr. O. Gureje, Dr. K. Kalumba, Dr. Kerr-Correa, Dr. C. Mercier, Mr. J. Oliver, Dr. Y. H. Poortinga, Dr. R. Trotter, and Dr. F. van Dam.

Further information can be obtained from the WHOQOL Group, Division of Mental Health, World Health Organization, CH-1211 Geneva 27, Switzerland.

REFERENCES

1. World Bank. *World development report: investing in health.* New York: Oxford University Press, 1993.
2. World Health Organization. *World health statistics annual.* Geneva: WHO, 1991.
3. Bergner M, Bobbitt RA, Carter WB, Gilson BS. The Sickness Impact Profile: development of and final revision of a health status measure. *Med Care* 1981;19:797–805.
4. Hunt SM, McEwan J, McKenna SP. *Measuring health status.* London: Croom Helm, 1986.
5. Fallowfield L. *The quality of life: the missing measurement in health care.* London: Souvenir Press, 1990.
6. Sartorius N, Kuyken W. Translation of health status instruments. In: Orley J, Kuyken W, eds. *Quality of life assessment: international perspectives.* Heidelberg: Springer-Verlag, 1994:1–18.
7. World Health Organization. *WHOQOL study protocol.* Geneva: WHO (MNH/PSF/93.9), 1993.
8. World Health Organization. *WHO meeting on the assessment of quality of life in health care.* Geneva: WHO (MNH/PSF/91.4), 1991.
9. World Health Organization. *Meeting on quality of life.* Geneva: WHO (MNH/PSF/92.2), 1992.
10. World Health Organization. *Report of the meeting of investigators on quality of life.* Geneva: WHO (MNH/PSF/92.6), 1992.
11. World Health Organization. *WHOQOL focus group moderator training.* Geneva: WHO (MNH/PSF/92.9), 1992.
12. World Health Organization. *Report of WHOQOL focus group work.* Geneva: WHO (MNH/PSF/93.4), 1993.
13. Bullinger M. Indices versus profiles—advantages and disadvantages. In: Walker SR, Rosser RM, eds. *Quality of life assessment: key issues in the 1990's.* Lancaster, UK: Kluwer Academic, 1993:209–220.
14. World Health Organization. *WHOQOL protocol for new centres.* Geneva: WHO (MNH/PSF/94.4), 1994.

Quality of Life and Pharmacoeconomics in Clinical Trials, Second Edition, edited by B. Spilker. Lippincott-Raven Publishers, Philadelphia © 1996.

CHAPTER 37

Using Quality of Life Tests for Patient Diagnosis or Screening, or to Evaluate Treatment

Lisa V. Rubenstein

INTRODUCTION

Quality of life is most often measured to assess the outcomes of medical care. But it can also be measured for clinical evaluation and management purposes. This chapter discusses strategies for clinical use of quality of life measures, including when they are most useful, which types of measures are appropriate, and how to apply the information gained to a patient's clinical management. The strategies proposed are commonly used in geriatric practice but can apply to the assessment and management of any patient with chronic disease.

DEFINING QUALITY OF LIFE FOR CLINICIANS

When quality of life measures are used for evaluating clinical outcomes among groups of people, they should be

L. V. Rubenstein: Department of Medicine, Veterans Health Administration Medical Center, Sepulveda, California 91343; University of California, Los Angeles, California 90095; Health Services Program, RAND, Santa Monica, California 90407.

capable of reliably distinguishing those with better and worse quality of life. They need not provide clinically coherent information. But for use in clinical care for individuals, these measures must make sense within the framework of clinical disease and its management; for clinical decision making, clinicians must understand the relationships between clinical pathology and the patient's subjective experience of that pathology in daily life.

Figure 1 provides a framework that links quality of life and its components to the World Health Organization (WHO) model of the process of disablement (1–3). The WHO model can be viewed as describing the mechanisms by which diseases affect quality of life. All quality of life components within the framework are measurable or potentially measurable; in some cases, valid and reliable measures currently exist, while in others (e.g., measures for screening for impairments causing difficulty walking), tools have not been developed. While diseases can cause impairments, disabilities, and handicaps, medical management (e.g., medications, assistive devices), social support (e.g., transportation, household help, advocacy), and the individual's ability to adapt (e.g., adhere to medical regimens,

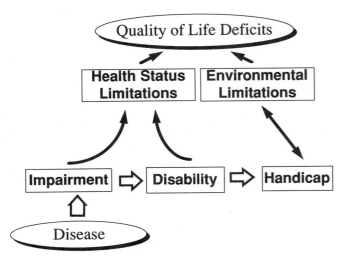

FIG. 1. Understanding the relationship between disease and quality of life.

change jobs, invent alternative methods for accomplishing tasks) all substantially modify the relationships among the severity of the disease, impairment, disability, and handicap. For example, a very compliant asthmatic patient who devises creative strategies for avoiding allergens and for adhering to a complex medical regimen may have a normal functional status, despite severe disease, while the less compliant individual with equally severe disease is completely disabled.

Overall quality of life is a summary measure of an individual's ability to participate fully in and enjoy life. It can be viewed as including two major components—health-related quality of life (health status) and non–health-related quality of life (environment). Quality of life and mortality rates are the two major outcome measures of medical care.

Environment is a summary measure of the external conditions within which the individual lives. It includes the physical, social, economic, and cultural factors affecting an individual's life, such as financial security, availability of food, and quality or appropriateness of housing. While these factors are less directly related to health than are clinical factors such as disease and disability, complex interactions link health status and environment. For example, a toxic waste dump can cause disease and disability. More commonly, as represented by the double-headed arrow linking environmental limitations and handicap, disease can cause worsening of the individual's environment due to disablement, job loss, and impoverishment. In some types of institutions, such as nursing homes, medical and social care providers have direct effects on the individual's environment; in these settings, measures of the quality of the environment may be especially relevant to health care professionals. Environmental factors can also affect the appropriate design and the likelihood of success of medical treatment.

Health status reflects an individual's perceptions of his or her physical, mental, and social health. It is a summary measure of the effects of impairments, disabilities, and handicaps on quality of life. As such, it also reflects the extent to which both medical management and an individual's adaptations to disease modify the natural progression from disease to impairment to disability to handicap. The effects of disease on self-perceived health status and quality of life are largely mediated by their effects on functional status (disability).

Risk indicators do not directly measure quality of life but may indicate a higher likelihood of current or future quality of life impairment; the most clinically useful risk factors can be modified through behavioral and medical interventions. Thus, measures of falls or risk factors for falls (4) do not directly indicate disability but may indicate impairments that are likely to result in disability. Recent hospitalization, needing more assistance to support daily functioning, and new or worsening chronic disease are examples of risk indicators for worsened functioning.

Diseases are pathological processes that produce changes in organ structure or function, and hence affect quality of life and mortality. The same disease may have very different effects on health status and quality of life from one individual to another depending upon life circumstances. For example, most individuals would suffer from anxiety (a symptom) if diagnosed with an otherwise asymptomatic disease. In one individual, the anxiety might be minimal and have little effect on health status, while in another the anxiety might cause significant disability.

Impairments are the mechanisms by which disease affects functional status; they can be physical or mental. Symptoms such as pain and incontinence and signs such as joint deformity can be considered to be impairments. For example, the disease of rheumatoid arthritis typically causes the symptom of joint pain and the sign of joint deformity. The pain directly reduces quality of life but also can cause inability to perform household chores, even in the absence of significant joint deformity. Joint deformity, likewise, can cause inability to do household chores, even in the absence of pain.

Functional status reflects the effects of impairments and adaptations to them on an individual's ability to perform physical, mental, and social activities in daily life. Measures of functioning thus focus on common, important, observable behaviors as they occur in a person's home and community life, such as eating, dressing, bathing, walking, handling finances, or visiting friends and relatives.

Handicaps reflect the effects of disability and adaptations to disability on an individual's ability to perform social roles (e.g., work, parenthood), and thus the degree of social disadvantage conferred by the disability. The degree of disadvantage incurred reflects interactions between the external environment and the disability; mild arthritis may have little effect on most people's lives but may terminate the career of a concert pianist.

PURPOSES OF QUALITY OF LIFE SCREENING AND ASSESSMENT

In theory, reliable and valid quality of life measures should be very useful to clinicians. Most other medical diagnosis and management tools and priorities are oriented more toward reducing risk of mortality than toward enhancing quality of life. In the absence of quality of life evaluation, the sign or symptom associated with a remote probability of death may be given much more attention than the sign or symptom indicating disability. Yet patients value quality of life highly (5,6), sometimes more than quantity of life. Quality of life screening using standardized tests provides an efficient way for clinicians to take into account the effects of diseases and treatments on patients' daily lives, and can be used to ensure that these effects are priorities in designing a clinical management plan. It can also be used to detect otherwise unrecognized onset or worsening of disease for which treatment can be instituted. In either case, if screening for quality of life deficits is to be effective, it must be linked to comprehensive, often interdisciplinary assessment that determines the causes and suggests solutions for the prob-

lems identified, followed by implementation of a comprehensive management plan (Fig. 2).

Detection of Disease

Quality of life screening and assessment may result in the detection of new or worsening diseases or complications of therapy that are otherwise undetected by clinicians. Diseases detected can then be managed with medications (7), therapeutic procedures (e.g., surgery, joint injections) (8), and counseling (including health habit counseling, patient education, and psychological counseling). Sometimes these diseases are important causes of mortality, and sometimes their only importance is due to their detrimental effects on quality of life. Depression is an example of a common, treatable, and frequently undetected disease that causes disability out of proportion to its much smaller effects on mortality (8). Undiagnosed foot pain that ultimately proves to be due to severe fungal infection may be non–life-threatening, but can cause major health status impairment when chronic foot pain causes decreased ambulation, inability to

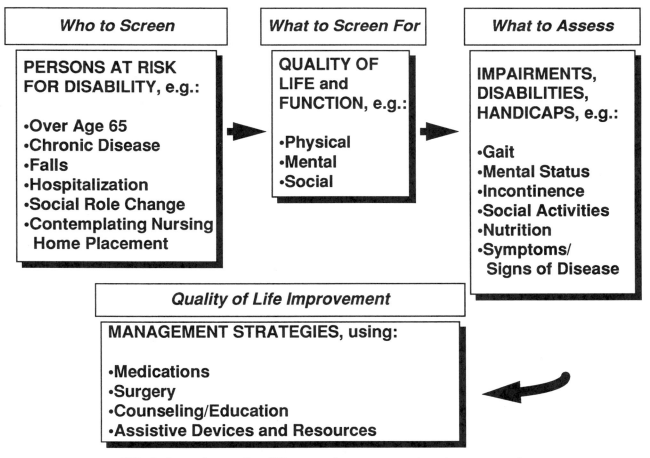

FIG. 2. Improving quality of life: screening, assessment, and management.

concentrate, and job loss. Medication side effects that do not cause increased mortality, and hence are not routinely screened for, can have major effects on quality of life (10). Diseases and complications like these whose consequences are more strongly related to quality of life than to mortality are particularly likely to be overlooked in many health care settings because their costs or consequences are borne outside of the medical care system. For example, uncontrolled angina will cause hospital admissions, and the costs of admission will tend to be recognized and avoided by managed care providers through better medical management. For depression, in contrast, the highest costs will be borne by employers, family members, and others, and may be given priority only when these groups actively demand improvements (11).

A close relationship often does exist between health-related quality of life and diseases commonly responsible for mortality. For example, poor or worsening of physical functioning (e.g., walking several blocks, using transportation) predicts significantly increased hospitalization, nursing home placement, and mortality over the succeeding 1 to 3 years (12,13). Thus, worsening of quality of life can be an early sign of mortality risk due to the progression of disease or complications of therapy, often at a stage when improvements in management can be undertaken.

Assessing the Need for Procedures

A newer but related use of quality of life screening is in assessing need for surgical procedures whose goal is to improve functioning. Individuals with cataracts who have no difficulty performing visual functions such as reading or driving are unlikely to benefit from cataract removal (8). Likewise, individuals who are able to perform all but the most advanced activities of daily living (running, lifting heavy objects. active sports) may not benefit from joint replacement, because surgery may be unlikely to restore advanced athletic ability. There is usually a limited range of function or life quality within which a given medical or surgical procedure can effectuate change.

Improving Adaptations to Impairments and Disabilities

Even if it is not possible to reverse impairments and disabilities through better management of diseases, it is often both possible and necessary to intervene directly to improve the patient's adaptation to these deficits. Strategies for improving adaptation include counseling patients, recommending appropriate assistive devices, and involving community resources such as home care and nursing homes (14,15). *Counseling* can involve education about diseases, disabilities, and body mechanics, strategies to engage patients in active problem solving or to improve patient adherence to the medical regimen, and psychological counseling. *Assistive devices* include canes, walkers, visual aids, reach extenders,

wide-handled utensils, raised toilet seats, and many others. *Community resources* include self-help groups, societies, and centers (e.g., senior centers, Braille Institute, Multiple Sclerosis Society), financial and work programs, home help, sheltered housing, and nursing homes. In some cases, the appropriate action may be to reverse or avoid another intervention, such as removal of a medication or avoidance of nursing home placement. In some cases, the patient, family, and medical care team may decide that the patient needs long-term care, once the full extent of the patient's disabilities has been identified (for example, irreversible, severely impaired mental status with incontinence and impaired ambulation). Considerable ingenuity can be used to devise ways around irremediable functional deficits. For example, if a patient has difficulty eating, changing the diet or the dentures might improve nutrition. If a patient is unable to cook, a meal service may provide the solution. Reminder systems can improve compliance with medication regimens.

Selecting Treatments

Medical decisions often require compromises between alternative therapeutic goals. Treatment can decrease mortality and increase quality of life, decrease mortality and decrease quality of life, and increase quality of life but also increase mortality. An antihypertensive medication that controls blood pressure optimally but compromises quality of life significantly may be less appropriate than one that provides less optimal blood pressure control but better quality of life. A nonsteroidal anti-inflammatory drug that produces no significant change in functional status may not be worthwhile when weighed against the risk of increased morbidity and mortality. Extended life support may be beneficial when baseline (pre-acute problem) quality of life was evaluated and was good and the acute problem (e.g., pneumonia) is reversible, but harmful when baseline quality of life was very poor. Patient values and preferences may differ in terms of the relative priorities of quality of life and avoidance of mortality in selecting treatments. But measurement of quality of life has the potential of getting an informed conversation started.

CLINICAL ASSESSMENT AND MANAGEMENT OF QUALITY OF LIFE DEFICITS

Developing comprehensive management strategies depends upon an understanding of the complex relationships between diseases, impairments, disabilities, and handicaps. Clinicians seeking to improve quality of life based on quality of life screening and assessment results must understand the theoretical relationships among these factors and must use clinical tools and knowledge to understand the unique set of relationships pertaining to an individual.

The first step in designing a management plan based on the findings of quality of life screening is to perform a

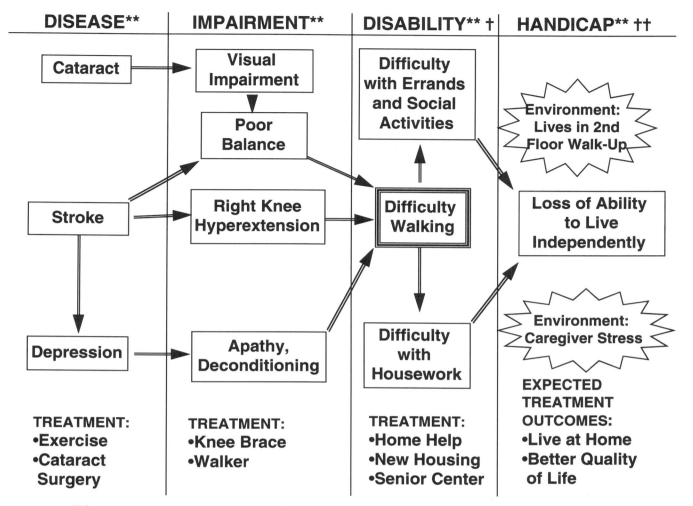

DISEASE** | **IMPAIRMENT**** | **DISABILITY** †** | **HANDICAP** ††**

Cataract → Visual Impairment

Visual Impairment → Poor Balance

Stroke → Poor Balance

Stroke → Right Knee Hyperextension

Stroke → Depression

Depression → Apathy, Deconditioning

Poor Balance → Difficulty Walking

Right Knee Hyperextension → Difficulty Walking

Apathy, Deconditioning → Difficulty Walking

Difficulty Walking ↔ Difficulty with Errands and Social Activities

Difficulty Walking ↔ Difficulty with Housework

Difficulty Walking → Loss of Ability to Live Independently

Environment: Lives in 2nd Floor Walk-Up

Environment: Caregiver Stress

TREATMENT:
•Exercise
•Cataract Surgery

TREATMENT:
•Knee Brace
•Walker

TREATMENT:
•Home Help
•New Housing
•Senior Center

EXPECTED TREATMENT OUTCOMES:
•Live at Home
•Better Quality of Life

FIG. 3. A clinical assessment and management map of the results of a quality of life assessment. This map shows the results of assessment of quality of life impairments detected on screening of an elderly man. Assessment involved a physician interview and examination as well as laboratory testing and examinations by a physical therapist, an occupational therapist, and a social worker. Assessment identifies the highest priority quality of life deficits and their clinical etiologies. The column headings indicate the type of information listed below them. For example, column one lists three diseases that are responsible for significant functional impairment in this patient—cataract, stroke, and depression. At the bottom of each column are listed the management plans that the physician and interdisciplinary team will implement to improve quality of life. Management is directed at diseases, impairment, disabilities, and handicaps.

+ In this column, difficulty walking is indicated as the key disability from which the patient's other problems stem. The physician believes that if the patient's mobility can be improved, many of his other problems would be ameliorated.

++ In this column, the result of the patient's disability that requires most attention is his ability to live independently (role functioning). Because of his social and environmental circumstances, the patient's difficulty walking is threatening to force him to move into a protected environment such as a nursing home. The physician thinks that nursing home placement is not necessary if treatment of the patient's disease, impairment, disability, and handicap are undertaken along with some later environmental modifiers (e.g., moving to the first floor). The remaining environmental stressor is his wife's level of caregiver stress, which can be expected to improve as the patient becomes more mobile. The expected outcome toward which management is directed is therefore maintaining independent living status.

comprehensive assessment that aims to determine the key diseases, impairments, disabilities, and handicaps that are limiting the individual's quality of life (16) (Fig. 2). While quality of life *screening* provides an overview of key aspects of the individual's daily life, quality of life *assessment* ensures that findings are confirmed and explained clinically. Interdisciplinary input is often necessary for full assessment; for example, the psychiatrist may be needed to comment on mental health, the social worker on the home situation, and the physical therapist on strength and gait. Administration of more detailed or comprehensive quality of life screening tools may also be part of the assessment process.

Because almost any acute or chronic disease can cause worsening in functioning, a key component of assessment involves evaluating the status of known diseases and searching for any new diseases suggested by the patient's signs or symptoms. Common but easily overlooked causes of disability include impaired cognition, impaired special senses (vision, hearing, balance), unstable gait and mobility, poor health habits (alcohol, smoking, lack of exercise), poor nutrition, polypharmacy, incontinence, psychosocial stress, and depression. To determine which diseases and impairments are most responsible for the disability, the physician must perform a focused history and physical examination guided by the functional disabilities detected and their differential diagnoses. Laboratory testing will usually also be necessary.

For example, the family of a 70-year-old man, Mr. Smith, was considering nursing home placement. Mr. Smith fell into the "At Risk" category in Fig. 2, and quality of life screening was indicated. He consulted his physician, who suggested an office visit and administered a brief, comprehensive functional status questionnaire (Quality of Life and Function Screening, Fig. 2). The questionnaire revealed that he was becoming markedly physically disabled and had decreased social activities and increased depressive symptoms as well. After reviewing questionnaire results, the physician decided that the disabilities required assessment and clinical intervention (Quality of Life Impairment, Disability and Handicap Assessment, Fig. 2). After discussing questionnaire results with the patient and performing a brief physical examination, the physician concluded that the patient's most critical disability as revealed by the questionnaire was difficulty walking one block. The physician then scheduled a full assessment with careful examination of gait and musculoskeletal and neurological functioning. She also scheduled consultations with physical therapy and social work services. After the assessment and discussion with consultants, the physician created a comprehensive management plan (Quality of Life Improvement, Fig. 2).

The assessment and management map in Fig. 3 represents the key results of the screening, assessment, and management process for this patient. He had three major diseases (stroke, depression, and cataracts) that interacted to worsen his functioning. Because balance in patients with stroke is often particularly dependent upon visual compensation for lost sensory input from other organs, visual loss can result in marked worsening of gait. Both direct neurohumoral ef-

fects of stroke and the effects of personal loss due to stroke can contribute to post-stroke depression, which in turn causes psychomotor retardation and apathy. These symptoms in turn further retard recovery. The patient's disabilities were responsible for deterioration in his social situation, with increasing caregiver burnout on the part of his wife. To avoid unnecessary nursing home placement, this patient's physician implemented a comprehensive management plan that included home help, environmental improvements, exercise, and adaptive devices. The physician decided not to initiate medication therapy for depression at this time because prior attempts at treatment with medications had been unsuccessful due to poor adherence. By beginning with physical disability–oriented strategies, the situational component of the depression might be ameliorated and strategies for improving adherence more easily instituted. Six months later, the patient had reduced difficulty walking, improved social activities, and a marked reduction in marital stress. Nursing home placement was successfully avoided.

COMPREHENSIVE GERIATRIC ASSESSMENT

The above description of quality of life assessment and management closely follows the geriatric assessment model. Geriatric assessment is a multidimensional, often interdisciplinary, diagnostic process intended to determine a frail elderly person's medical, psychosocial, and functional capabilities and problems, with the objective of developing an overall plan for treatment and long-term follow-up. A growing literature supports the efficacy of geriatric assessment in a variety of specialized settings (17). Many randomized trials have demonstrated major reductions in mortality and nursing home placement, as well as improvement in a number of quality of life indicators such as functional status, affect, and cognition. A recent meta-analysis of the findings from 28 trials of geriatric assessment with concurrent control groups showed a statistically significant 36% reduction in the odds of death at 6 months (18). Impacts from geriatric assessment programs tend to be highest when the programs are well targeted (patients are significantly disabled, but not end stage), the assessment program is involved in implementation of its recommendations and provision of follow-up, and the intervention is more intense, involving interdisciplinary team members.

IS STANDARDIZED MEASUREMENT OF QUALITY OF LIFE NECESSARY?

Studies have shown that measurement of quality of life is necessary if clinicians are to be made aware of the effects of illness on patients' daily lives. Even experienced clinicians markedly underestimate or overestimate some aspects of function for many of their patients (19). Some patients mask or understate their disabilities or feel reticent about discussing them with physicians. Some patients who appear disabled can actually perform all important daily activities.

Quality of life cannot be inferred from appearances; systematic screening seems to be required.

WHO SHOULD BE EVALUATED FOR QUALITY OF LIFE?

Because most medical interventions for improving quality of life involve treatment or palliation of impairments and disabilities, quality of life screening is particularly useful for evaluating individuals with poor functioning or who are at risk of functional deterioration. This includes elderly individuals, people with chronic diseases, and people who present with signs or symptoms of worsening disease or worsening functioning. Community-based screening of home-dwelling elderly individuals, followed by appropriate referrals, has reduced disability and mortality (20). Screening of hospitalized elderly patients for whom nursing home placement is contemplated, followed by geriatric assessment, has also reduced mortality (21). Screening of elderly individuals who have fallen has resulted in reduced hospitalization (22).

There is less evidence that quality of life screening of general medical populations is successful. Several studies have evaluated the effects of providing physicians in practice with information on the functional status of their ambulatory patients, and none of these has been successful in improving physical function (23–25). There is some evidence that mental health and social activities can be improved when feedback to physicians includes resource and management suggestions in addition to functional status results (26,27). In relatively healthy, younger clinic populations, typical of health maintenance organizations, symptoms of anxiety or depression are the most common quality of life deficits. There is little evidence that measuring quality of life, other than possibly measuring depressive symptoms (28–31), improves outcomes in low-risk populations, even when accompanied by resource and management suggestions.

In addition to selecting populations with relatively high prevalence of disability, we have seen that the most successful interventions involve referring patients with quality of life deficits for more detailed interdisciplinary assessment aimed at discovering the sources of functional deterioration. Thus, the availability of key resources for assessing the disabilities and impairments discovered may be important in deciding whom to screen.

WHAT TYPES OF QUALITY OF LIFE MEASURES FIT CLINICAL NEEDS?

Quality of life and its components can be measured using a variety of different types of measures. Instruments vary in the depth and specificity of the information they provide from brief screening instruments that seek to identify individuals with quality of life deficits to more detailed or focused instruments designed to indicate what the specific impairments, disabilities, and handicaps are. Available measures include self- or interviewer-administered surveys, targeted physical examination, performance testing, laboratory testing, and observation of daily life. The relevance of different types of measures and the availability of valid and reliable instruments varies depending upon the quality of life dimension being assessed, the setting, and the target population. Some types of measures are most useful for screening populations or case finding among people who come to physicians for other reasons, while others are most useful as part of the assessment of individuals already identified as having quality of life deficits. For example, self-administered or interviewer-administered surveys tend to be the most practical and accurate methods for screening for the common impairments and disabilities that affect people's daily lives at home and at work, while performance-based measures are particularly helpful in designing and evaluating clinical interventions for disability.

Advantages and Disadvantages of Surveys, Performance-Based Measures, and Direct Observation for Clinical Care

Surveys gather data by asking standardized questions and recording responses in a structured format. Performance-based measures gather data by asking people to perform structured tasks and judging their performance based on preset criteria. Direct observation of daily life uses timed sampling by trained observers or videotaping to document behaviors and activities. Each has advantages and disadvantages. For example, direct observation is impractical for most purposes. A possible exception, however, is in evaluating quality of life in nursing home patients (32). Performance measures can be more precise than either surveys or direct observation in localizing and quantitating specific impairments and disabilities. For example, a survey may indicate that an individual has difficulty with household chores, but a performance-based measure may be necessary to establish that upper arm reach and hand grip are the key causes of this difficulty. Surveys can ask patients about the causes of their disabilities, but the information patients can provide reliably may not be specific enough to use for medical management purposes. On the other hand, compared with performance-based measures, surveys have the advantages of summarizing daily functioning outside the clinic rather than in an artificial situation such as a doctor's or physical therapist's office; even if the performance test is carried out at home, test results may not reflect what the individual usually does on his or her own. Surveys generally require less data collector training than do performance-based tests, and cost less to administer. In addition, surveys can measure emotional and social aspects of quality of life, while performance-based measures are limited to measuring physical functions and impairments.

Rather than using one type of test, clinicians can benefit from becoming familiar with a variety of types of tests.

Performance-based measures, in conjunction with surveys, clinical history, physical examination, and laboratory tests, may be very useful in identifying the causes of disabilities and impairments. For example, a normal result on performance-based evaluation of gait and balance in an individual who has difficulty walking one block might indicate that the problem is less likely to be neurological, muscular, or skeletal but more likely to be due to cardiovascular or pulmonary disease. Such suspicions can be confirmed using standard clinical diagnostic techniques. Although the ability to function better at home or in the community is a more definitive outcome of care than is the ability to perform better on a test, performance-based measures may have advantages as intermediate outcomes for interventions to improve physical functioning. For example, it may be useful to know that physical therapy succeeded in reducing the amount of time it took an individual to walk 50 feet (50-foot walk time), even though this reduction did not result in improved functioning at home. Finally, performance-based measures may be useful in confirming or identifying disability in high-risk populations. For example, hospitalized patients may have difficulty answering many survey questions, since standard quality of life surveys often refer to performance of activities that are not applicable to hospital life or to a time frame (e.g., one month) during which the individual has experienced major changes in functioning. Patients with language barriers or mental impairment may be unable to answer surveys, or may answer them inaccurately. Patients with severe disability may fall below the range within which survey instruments can distinguish levels of disability, yet they may be amenable to clinical intervention. Use of performance-based measures can ameliorate these detection problems.

Clinical Examination

The clinical history and physical examination are critical in the full assessment of quality of life and share important features of survey and performance-based measures. The history and physical are somewhat standardized and are recorded in somewhat standard ways. These clinical examinations, however, are tailored to the individual patient using complex clinical reasoning. While individual components of the examination lack the reliability of standardized tests (33,34), the examination as a whole incorporates multiple confirmatory steps that would be virtually impossible to build into standardized tests.

ROUTINE EVALUATION OF QUALITY OF LIFE IN OFFICE PRACTICE

Table 1 depicts a strategy for incorporating routine and symptom-responsive or -triggered screening into office practice. In this table, we indicate the types of patients to consider for screening, what types of measures might be most appropriate given the patient's characteristics, and examples of measurement tools to consider. The specific tools we suggest are only examples; many other tools are reviewed elsewhere in this book and in the literature (35). The strategy we propose is not empirically validated, but combines clinical geriatric and general internal medicine experience with principles from the literature. The table is not intended for formal implementation by policy makers, for example, but rather for use by clinicians with special interest in quality of life. Clinicians who are committed to taking action based on screening results and who have access to appropriate resources to assist them will make the most effective use of the strategies proposed.

The first type of patient to consider for screening is the adult under age 65 who does not have known chronic diseases. In such individuals, an impaired sense of mental well-being, such as occurs with anxiety and depression, is a common cause of reduced quality of life (24). Very brief screens, such as a three-question lifetime depression measure (36), can indicate depression risk; individuals who are at risk can be further evaluated. The five-item Mental Health Index (37) is a complete component scale of two brief comprehensive health status measures [the Functional Status Questionnaire (38) and the RAND/Medical Outcome Study Short Form 36, or SF-36 (37)]. The General Health Questionnaire (31) is longer, but has been used extensively in primary care practices. Social and role function impairments are also relatively common. The RAND/Medical Outcome Study Social and Role Function Scales are brief, complete component scales of the SF-36, and can be used to screen for these problems (39). An alternative strategy to screening for well-being and social and role function would be to use a brief, comprehensive health status measure like the SF-36 or COOP Charts (25,40), but this strategy would require more patient time to take (e.g., 10 minutes) and clinician time to interpret.

In adults under age 65 with chronic diseases, physical functioning deficits are more likely than among those without chronic diseases. The brief, comprehensive screens listed in Table 1 for this group of patients cover multiple domains of functioning, including physical functioning, and take 5 to 30 minutes to complete. Individuals with poor reading skills or less education may require assistance or encouragement to complete these screens.

Adults 65 years of age or older and healthy can, in general, be screened similarly to the under 65 and chronically ill group. It should be remembered that mental status assessment and incontinence/toileting are omitted from the brief, comprehensive measures, and may need to be addressed separately. Addition of the Get Up and Go test (41,42) to the evaluation ensures that the clinician will pay particular attention to walking ability, since gait disorders are common in this group and may be detectable on clinical examination before they have marked effects on functioning in daily life.

Adults 65 years of age and older who have chronic diseases require a greater focus on physical functioning and

TABLE 1. *Recommendations for incorporating routine and symptom-responsive quality of life screening into office practice*

Patient type and screening activity	Types of screening quality of life measures to use and examples of measurement tools				
	Brief, comprehensive health status measures	Depression, anxiety, well-being, and mental status	Physical functioning and independence measures	Social activities, social support, and role function measures	Disease or impairment-specific measures
Routine screening					
1. Adult *under 65 years* and healthy: screen every 3 years	—	5-item Mental Health Index (37) Lifetime depression screen (36) General Health Questionnaire (31)	—	RAND/Medical Outcome Study Role Function (39)	—
2. Adult *under 65 years* and chronically ill: screen every year	RAND/Medical Outcome Study Short Form 36 (37) Sickness Impact Profile Short Form (46,47) Beth Israel/UCLA Functional Status Questionnaire (38) Nottingham Health Profile (48) McMaster Health Index (49) Quality of Well-Being (50) COOP Charts (25,40)	—	—	—	—
3. Adult *65 years or over* and healthy: screen every year	Use *same* measurement tools as for adults under 65 years and chronically ill	—	Get up and Go (41,42)	—	—
4. Adult *65 years or over* and chronically ill: screen every year	—	CES-D (56) Hamilton (57,58) Yesavage (51) Zung SDS (60,61) Folstein Mini Mental State (59)	Katz Basic Activities of Daily Living (43) Lawton/Brody Instrumental Activities of Daily Living (44) Barthel Index (52)	Beth Israel/UCLA Social Activities (38) MOS Social Support and Role Functioning (39) Sarasan Social Support Questionnaire (53)	McGill Pain Questionnaire (54,55) MOS Pain Measure (37)
Triggered screening					
5. Adult *65 years or over* and hospitalized: screen during admission and in 6 months	—	Use *same* measurement tools as for adults 65 years or over and chronically ill	Use *same* measurement tools as for adults 65 years or over and chronically ill	—	Use *same* measurement tool as for adults 65 years or over and chronically ill
6. *Adult* admitted to a nursing home: screen on admission and every 6 months thereafter	MDS (45)	—	—	—	—
7. *Adult* with increased need for assistance: screen urgently and in 6 months	—	Use *same* measurement tools as for adults 65 years or over and chronically ill	Use *same* measurement tools as for adults 65 years or over and chronically ill	—	Use *same* measurement tools as for adults 65 years or over and chronically ill
8. *Adult* requiring close monitoring for chronic disease: screen every 3–6 months with *either* disease—specific *or* brief, comprehensive measure	—	—	—	—	Arthritis Impact Measurement Scale (AIMS) (63) Spitzer Quality of Life Index (64)
9. *Adult,* falling or with difficulty walking: screen urgently	—	—	Use *same* measurement tools as for adults 65 years or over and chronically ill	—	Tinetti balance and gait evaluation (65)
10. *Adult* with signs or symptoms of depression: screen urgently	If under 65 years use *same* measurement tools as for adults under 65 years and chronically ill	CES-D (56) Beck Depression Inventory (62) Hamilton A (58) Hamilton D (57)	If over 65 years use *same* measurement tools as for adults 65 years or over and chronically ill	—	—

need for assistance than do other groups. The approach of using brief, comprehensive measures could be considered, particularly among those with a lower burden of disease. Most geriatric groups, however, who work with a more disabled elderly group of patients, rely on measures such as the Katz Activities of Daily Living (ADLs) (43) and the Lawton-Brody Instrumental Activities of Daily Living (IADLs) (44). These instruments focus on the kinds of activities that are necessary for independent living (IADLs) or for living without 24-hour care (ADLs). Use of these measures alone, however, omits consideration of depression, mental status impairment, social or role functioning, and pain, all of which can be critical in this type of patient, and we have suggested supplemental measures for these problems.

The final six categories in the table illustrate the use of quality of life measurement for evaluation of signs and symptoms. Technically, this kind of use of the measures is not screening at all, but rather part of the workup of identified problems. Individuals who are hospitalized, require more assistance at home, are admitted to a nursing home, fall, or have signs or symptoms of depression require immediate evaluation of quality of life, followed by assessment and management as depicted in Fig. 3. For many nursing home patients, the Minimum Data Set (MDS) (45) must be administered on admission and every 6 months as required by law. The information contained in the MDS includes data on functional status, mood, and other quality of life issues. Patients with chronic diseases who are facing therapeutic choices, such as an arthritis patient scheduled to receive gold or patients whose diseases are rapidly evolving, may benefit from disease specific screening using instruments such as those listed in the table for adults requiring close monitoring for chronic disease. Individuals who were screened routinely and were found to have disabilities such as depression, falls, or difficulty walking fall into the category of patients requiring evaluation for specific signs and symptoms.

One final aspect of quality of life measurement that should be considered, although not included in Table 1, is that of screening for health habits. Lack of exercise, alcohol abuse, and smoking in particular may have dramatic effects on functioning and quality of life, and are accessible to measurement by standard questionnaires.

Once basic screening is complete, patients found to have disabilities can be assessed using standard clinical methods. By using standard instruments as the basis for assessment, clinicians can take advantage of reliable and valid measures to identify problems, and focus on carrying out assessment and management activities that will maximize quality of life.

BARRIERS TO CLINICAL EVALUATION OF QUALITY OF LIFE

It is important to acknowledge that, while quality of life assessment is noninvasive and well accepted by patients, it is not without a price. Patients, families, and nonphysician medical personnel can administer questionnaires at relatively low cost. Expert time is required, however, to interpret the results and to use them to actually improve health. Most quality of life instruments require scoring either by hand or by computer. Physicians may need to spend extra, nonreimbursed cognitive time assessing quality of life deficits. Physicians may also lack the skills, particularly in terms of the musculoskeletal and neurological examinations, to assess impairments adequately. Finally, successful management of disabilities may depend upon the availability of an interdisciplinary team.

CONCLUSIONS AND RECOMMENDATIONS

1. Clinicians should become more aware of the quality of life effects of diseases and their treatments through systematic quality of life screening.
2. Younger patients generally require routine screening for mental health and social or role functioning; older individuals (over 65 years) and those with chronic diseases require more comprehensive screening on a routine basis.
3. All patients consulting with clinicians for signs or symptoms of new or worsening disabilities, including patients considering nursing home placement, require comprehensive screening for quality of life deficits followed by clinical assessment that identifies the key diseases, impairments, disabilities, and handicaps that are worsening the patient's quality of life.
4. Comprehensive clinical management plans for elderly patients with severe or worsening disability should be developed and implemented with input from all key members of the interdisciplinary team.

REFERENCES

1. Verbrugge LM. Physical and social disability in adults in primary care research: theory and methods. In: Hibbard H, Nutting PA, Grady MC, eds. *Primary care research.* Washington, DC: U.S. Department of Health and Human Services, Public Health Service Agency for Health Care Policy and Research, 1991:31–58.
2. Verbrugge LM. Disability. *Rheum Dis Clin North Am* 1990;16: 741–761.
3. *International classification of impairments, disabilities and handicaps: a manual of classifications relating to the consequences of disease.* Geneva, Switzerland: World Health Organization, 1990.
4. Tinetti ME, Williams TF, Mayewski R. Fall risk index for elderly patients based on number of chronic disabilities. *Am J Med* 1986;80: 429.
5. Kaplan RM, Bush JW, Berry CC. Health status: types of validity and the index of well-being. *Health Serv Res* 1976;Winter:478–507.
6. Patrick DL, Bush JW, Chen MM. Toward an operational definition of health. *J Health Soc Behav* 1973;14:6–23.
7. Siscovick DS, Strogatz DS, Fletcher SW, et al. The association between hypertension treatment, control, and functional status. *J Gen Intern Med* 1987;11:406–410.
8. Applegate WB, Miller ST, Elam JT, et al. Impact of cataract surgery with lens implantation on vision and physical function in elderly patients. *JAMA* 1987;257(8):1064–1066.

9. Wells KB, Stewart A, Hays RD, Burnam MA, Rogers W, Daniels M, Berry S, Greenfield S, Ware J. The functioning and well-being of depressed patients: results from the medical outcomes study. *JAMA* 1989;262:914–919.

10. Croog SH, Levine S, Testa MA, et al. The effects of anti-hypertensive therapy on the quality of life. *N Engl J Med* 1986;314:1657–1664.

11. Sturm R, Wells K. How can care for depression become more cost-effective? *JAMA* 1995;273:51–58.

12. Reuben DB, Rubenstein LV, Hirsch SH, Hays RD. Functional status as a predictor of health status and mortality: results of a prospective study. *Am J Med* 1992;93(6):663–670.

13. Siu AL, Reuben DB, Ouslander JG, Osterweil D. Using multidimensional health measures in older persons to identify risk of hospitalization and skilled nursing placement. *Qual Life Res* 1993;2:253–261.

14. Hoenig H, Mayer-Oakes A, Siebens H, Fink A, Brummel-Smith K, Rubenstein LV. Geriatric rehabilitation: what do physicians know about it and how should they use it? *J Am Geriatr* 1994;42:341–347.

15. Fortinsky RH, Granger CV, Seltzer GB. The use of functional assessment in understanding homecare needs. *Med Care* 1981;19(5):489–497.

16. Rubenstein LZ. Geriatric assessment: an overview of its impacts. *Clin Geriatr Med* 1987;3(1):1–15.

17. Rubenstein LZ, Rubenstein LV. Multidimensional assessment of elderly patients. *Adv Intern Med* 1990;36:81–107.

18. Stuck AE, Siu AL, Wieland GD, Adams J, Rubenstein LZ. Effects of comprehensive geriatric assessment on survival, residence, and function: a meta-analysis of controlled trials. *Lancet* 1993;342:1032–1036.

19. Calkins DR, Rubenstein LV, Cleary PD, Davies AR, Jette AM, Fink AR, Kosecoff J, Yong RT, Brook RH, Delbanco TL. Failure of physicians to recognize functional disability in ambulatory patients. *Ann Intern Med* 1991;114:451–454.

20. Vetter NJ, Jones DA, Victor CR. Effects of health visitors working with elderly patients in general practice: a randomized controlled trial. *Br Med J* 1984;288:369–372.

21. Rubenstein LZ, Josephson KR, Wieland GD, English PA, Sayre JA, Kane RL. Effectiveness of a geriatric evaluation unit: a randomized clinical trial. *N Engl J Med* 1984;311:1664–1670.

22. Rubenstein LZ, Josephson KR, Robbins AS. Falls in the nursing home. *Ann Intern Med* 1994;121(6):442–451.

23. Rubenstein LV, Calkins DR, Young RT, et al. Improving patient function: a randomized trial of functional disability screening. *Ann Intern Med* 1989;111(10):836–842.

24. Wasson J, Hays R, Rubenstein L, Nelson E, Leaning J, Johnson D, Keller A, Landgraf J, Rosenkrans C. The short-term effect of patient health status assessment in a health maintenance organization. *Qual Life Res* 1992;1:99–106.

25. Wasson J, Keller A, Rubenstein L, Hays R, Nelson E, Johnson D, The Dartmouth Primary Care COOP Project. Benefits and obstacles of health status assessment in ambulatory settings: the clinician's point of view. *Med Care* 1992;30(5 suppl):42–50.

26. Rubenstein LV, McCoy JM, Cope DW, Barrett PA, Hirsch SH, Messer KS, Young RT. Improving patient functional status: a randomized trial of computer-generated resource and management suggestions. *Clin Res* 1989;37(2):801A.

27. McCoy JM, Rubenstein LV, Barrett PA, et al. *A feedforward system for functional status information.* Washington, DC: Symposium on Computer Applications in Medical Care, 1988;63:283–287.

28. Hoeper EW, Nycz GR, Kessler LG, et al. The usefulness of screening for mental illness. *Lancet* 1984;1:33–35.

29. Rand EH, Badger LW, Coggins DR. Recognition of mental disorders by family practice residents: the effect of GHQ feedback in mental disorders in general health care settings. Research Conference, Seattle, Washington, 1987:164–166.

30. Linn L, Yager J. Screening of depression in relationship to subsequent patient and physician behavior. *Med Care* 1982;20:1233–1240.

31. Goldberg DP. Identifying psychiatric illness among general medical patients. *Br Med J* 1985;291:161–163.

32. Weiland D, Rubenstein LV, Hirsch SH. Quality of life in nursing homes: an emerging focus of research and practice. In: Katz P, Kane RL, Mezey M, eds. *Advances in long-term care,* vol 3. New York: Springer, 1995; in press.

33. Koran LM. The reliability of clinical methods, data and judgments, I. *N Engl J Med* 1975;293:642–646.

34. Koran LM. The reliability of clinical methods, data and judgments, II. *N Engl J Med* 1975;293:695–701.

35. Bowling A. *Measuring health: a review of QOL measurement scales.* Washington, DC: Open University Press, Taylor and Francis, 1991.

36. Burnam MA, Wells KB, Leake B, et al. Development of a brief screening instrument for detecting depressive disorders. *Med Care* 1988;26:775–789.

37. Stewart AL, Hays RD, Ware JE. Communication: the MOS short-form general health survey: reliability and validity in a patient population. *Med Care* 1988;26(7):724–735.

38. Jette AM. The functional status questionnaire: reliability and validity when used in primary care. *J Gen Intern Med* 1986;1:143.

39. Sherbourne CD, Stewart AL. The MOS social support survey. *Soc Sci Med* 1991;32(6):701–714.

40. Nelson E, Wasson J, Kirk J, et al. Assessment of function in routine clinical practice: description of the COOP chart method and preliminary findings. *J Chronic Dis* 1987;40(1):55S.

41. Wasson JH, Gall V, McDonald R, et al. The prescription of assistive devices for the elderly: practical considerations. *Rev J Gen Intern Med* 1990;5:46–54.

42. Mathias S, Nayak USL, Isaacs B. Balance in elderly patients: the ''get up and go'' test. *Arch Phys Med Rehabil* 1986;67:387–389.

43. Katz S, Akpom CA. Index of ADL. *Med Care* 1976;14:116–118.

44. Lawton MP, Brody EM. Assessment of older people: self-maintaining and instrumental activities of daily living. *Gerontologist* 1969;9:179.

45. Morris J, Hawes C, Fries BE, et al. Designing the National Resident Assessment Instrument for nursing homes. *Gerontologist* 1990;30:293–307.

46. Bergner M, Bobbit R, Pollard W, et al. The Sickness Impact Profile: validation of a health status measure. *Med Care* 1976;14:57.

47. de Bruin AF, de Witte LP, Stevens F, Diederiks JP. Sickness Impact Profile: the state of the art of a generic functional status measure. Review. *Soc Sci Med* 1992;35:1003–1014.

48. Jenkinson C, Fitzpatrick R, Argyle M. The Nottingham Health Profile: an analysis of its sensitivity in differentiating illness groups. *Soc Sci Med* 1988;27:1411–1414.

49. Chambers LW, MacDonald LA, Tugwell P, et al. The McMaster Health Index Questionnaire as a measure of quality of life for patients with rheumatoid disease. *J Rheumatol* 1992;9:780–784.

50. Kaplan, RM, Bush JW, Berry CC. Health status: types of validity and the index of well-being. *Health Serv Res* 1976;Winter:478–507.

51. Yesavage J, Brink T, Rose T, et al. Development and validation of a geriatric screening scale: a preliminary report. *J Psychiatr Res* 1983;17:37–49.

52. Collin C, Wade DT, Davies D, et al. The Barthel ADL Index: a reliability study. *Int Disabil Studies* 1988;10:61–63.

53. Sarason IG, Levine HM, Rasham RB, et al. Assessing social support: the social support questionnaire. *J Pers Soc Psychol* 1983;44:127–139.

54. Graham C, Bond SS, Gerkovich MM, et al. Use of the McGill pain questionnaire in the assessment of cancer pain: reliability and consistency. *Pain* 1980;6:377.

55. Melzack R. The short-form McGill Pain Questionnaire. *Pain* 1987;30:191–197.

56. Radloff LS. The CES-D scale: a self-report depression scale for research in the general population. *Appl Psychol Meas* 1977;1:385–401.

57. Hamilton M. Clinical evaluation of depression: clinical criteria and rating scales, including a Guttman scale. In: Gallant DM, Simpson GM, eds. *Depression: behavioral, biochemical, diagnostic and treatment concepts.* New York: Spectrum; Halsted Press Distributors, 1976.

58. Hamilton M. The assessment of anxiety states by rating. *Br J Med Psychol* 1959;32:50–55.

59. Folstein MF, Folstein SE, McHugh PR. Mini-mental state—a practical method for grading the cognitive state of patients for the clinician. *J Psychiatr Res* 1975;12:189.

60. Zung WWK, Richards CB, Short MJ. Self rating depression scale in an out-patient clinic: further validation of the SDS. *Arch Gen Psychiatry* 1965;13:508–515.

61. Zung WWK. A self-rating depression scale. *Arch Gen Psychiatry* 1965;12:63–70.

62. Beck AT, Steer RA, Garbin MG. Psychometric properties of the Beck Depression Inventory: twenty-five years of evaluation. *Clin Psychol Rev* 1988;8:77–100.

63. Meenan RF. New approaches to outcome assessment: the AIMS questionnaire for arthritis. In: Stollerman GH, ed. *Advances in internal medicine,* vol 31. New York: Year Book Medical Publishers, 1985.

64. Spitzer WO, Dobson AJ, Hall J, et al. Measuring quality of life of cancer patients: a concise Q1 index for use by physicians. *J Chronic Dis* 1981;34:585–597.

65. Tinetti ME, Williams TF, Mayewski R. Fall risk index for elderly patients based on number of chronic disabilities. *Am J Med* 1986; 80:429.

Quality of Life and Pharmacoeconomics in Clinical Trials, Second Edition, edited by B. Spilker. Lippincott-Raven Publishers, Philadelphia © 1995.

CHAPTER 38

Choosing a Health Profile (Descriptive) and/or a Patient-Preference (Utility) Measure for a Clinical Trial

Richard A. Berzon, Josephine A. Mauskopf, and George P. Simeon

INTRODUCTION

This chapter explores the selection and use of health-related quality of life (HRQL) questionnaires for clinical trial research within the context of satisfying the information needs of diverse audiences. We identify relevant decision makers and the problems they face, and, in so doing, we differentiate between the information derived from two distinct types of HRQL instruments: health profile (descriptive) measures and patient-preference (utility) measures.

The selection of either a health profile or a patient-preference questionnaire for a clinical trial depends upon the information needs of the particular audience(s) to whom the research is directed. In addition, selection and use of an instrument depends on the focus of the research, specifically on whether the focus is on the individual patient or on society as a whole.

Health profile measures group questions reflective of *individual* patient and provider disease concerns and/or intervention effects into separate domains or dimensions of patient function and satisfaction. These descriptive questionnaires provide disaggregated measures of changes in patient func-

tional status and satisfaction attributable to the intervention—throughout this chapter, a pharmacologic drug(s)—being assessed. In contrast, where decisions for groups of patients are required for program administrators, health policy makers, and regulators, the focus is on *society* as a whole and the societal allocation of health care resources. In this case, preference-weighted measures, which assign a single aggregated score for changes in health status based on patient relative preferences, allow comparison of the impact of the drug on HRQL to other treatments for the same condition and/or to other treatments for different conditions.

Important information for health care decisions are provided by both types of HRQL questionnaires, and, within a clinical trial, a case can often be made to collect such data in both aggregated and disaggregated forms (1). The development of HRQL instruments that have the capability to address the needs of patients, providers, health care administrators, and policy makers would be a meaningful methodological development.

HEALTH-RELATED QUALITY OF LIFE CONSTRUCT

The following definition reflects a growing consensus about the HRQL concept: ''Quality of life refers to patients' appraisal of and satisfaction with their current level of functioning as compared to what they perceive to be possible or

R. A. Berzon: Outcomes Research Bristol-Myers Squibb Pharmaceutical Research Institute, Wallingford, Connecticut 06492.

J. A. Mauskopf: ISEER Division, Burroughs Wellcome Co., Research Triangle Park, North Carolina 27709.

G. P. Simeon: Ciba-Geigy Limited, Basel, Switzerland.

ideal'' (2). The purpose of an HRQL instrument is not merely to measure the presence and severity of symptoms of disease, but also to show how the manifestations of an illness or treatment are experienced by an individual, whether this experience is descriptive or in terms of relative preferences for various health states. Therefore, the definition selected emphasizes the subjectivity of HRQL assessment as well as the preference or value given to an individual's current health state.

Evaluations of health care treatments using HRQL questionnaires are conducted within clinical trials for decision makers who want to assess an intervention's clinical efficacy, its economic value, or both. The need for specific information by the decision maker(s) often determines the type of instrument(s) required. In the next section, we consider—within the context of a changing health care environment—the needs of those who might require HRQL information to make various health care decisions.

PROBLEMS CONFRONTING DECISION MAKERS

Health Profile Measures for Physicians and Patients

A new pharmacologic treatment will be evaluated within a clinical trial, and results from the trial will determine whether a physician recommends its use to a patient to control or eliminate the particular medical condition. Because information about the intervention's impact upon the individual patient will be used by both clinicians and patients to make a decision regarding its use, there is nothing more relevant to making the decision than the patient's own quality of life assessment (3). Circumstances such as these, involving physician and patient decision making, favor use of health profile measures because they reflect the individual patient's multidimensional, disaggregated concerns exclusively, that is, without consideration of the preferences of others. This situation permits each individual patient to weight each dimension separately.

Experts in the field agree upon the fundamental dimensions that are essential to a generic health profile measure (4–7). These include physical, mental/psychological, and social health, as well as global perceptions of function and well-being. Examples of popular health profile measures include the Sickness Impact Profile, the Nottingham Health Profile, and the MOS questionnaires (the SF-20 and the SF-36 in particular).

Individual treatment decisions are often made jointly by physicians and patients who consider both the disease and the intervention effects upon the patient's quality of life. When the side effects (toxicities) of a medication are important for the patient—as they are with cancer, for example—not only a listing of adverse events (such as on a product label) but also a description of their impact upon HRQL would be important information to physician and patient decision makers.

Until recently, there have been no standardized means available to physicians and patients for the evaluation of quality of life impacts of treatment. An example of this circumstance is antidepressant medication, where potential side effects, such as sexual dysfunction, are known, but not the precise nature of their influence upon such HRQL domains as emotional well-being, interpersonal relationships, cognitive ability, and sexual satisfaction. Information on the HRQL impact in these domains could be used to inform patients about the nature of drug therapy, encourage them to adopt practices that would minimize side effects, and adopt necessary coping strategies.

In some cases, standard clinical morbidity and mortality outcomes in clinical trials of therapies are not the best indicators of the efficacy of an intervention (8,9). Such situations arise when clinical measures are not reliable, valid, or available. In such cases, the patient's perceptions of his health status, as revealed by a descriptive HRQL assessment, may be the best method available to measure severity of illness and determine selection of treatment. An example is migraine headache where the condition manifests itself in various forms and at different levels of severity. While measures of pain severity, intensity, and quality are meaningful, the disorder's role in the patient's daily life—particularly between migraine episodes—would be important to consider with respect to selection of treatment. The disorder could manifest itself not only through pain, but also through poor mental health (through an increase in anxiety) or role functioning at work or in social situations. The patient's self-assessed HRQL may be the best indicator of disease severity or appropriate course of treatment for migraine.

In cases where treatments are thought to be of similar efficacy and result in no clinical differences, the collection of HRQL descriptive data can provide additional important information. If salient HRQL differences are found to exist, patient compliance with the prescribed medication can be affected. For example, it was recently found that two angiotensin-converting enzyme inhibitors were indistinguishable with respect to clinical assessment but had different effects on HRQL (10). It can be inferred that patient compliance with a prescribed medication may be at risk if the medication's clinical and side-effect profile affect patient satisfaction and well-being.

Situations may arise wherein the comfort of the patient is the dominant therapeutic consideration. One such example is with respect to analgesics that are designed to relieve pain in chronic diseases. In a review of research in quality of life patients with inflammatory bowel disease, Kunsebeck et al. (11) found that HRQL measurements were better reflections of a patient's concerns, such as pain, than clinical measures. Other chronic conditions wherein health profile measures would provide necessary information about treatment with respect to supportive care include cancer and acquired immune deficiency syndrome (AIDS).

The identification of high-risk patients with respect to noncompliance, morbidity, and mortality would be an important tool for physicians. In describing HRQL experiences from cardiovascular clinical trials, Schron and Schumaker (12) found that in certain instances health profile domains could be used to predict mortality and compliance. If such findings are accurate, clinical trial and epidemiologic data could be used to target high-risk groups for more thorough follow-up and additional or alternate treatment strategies.

Results from health profile instruments typically serve as the best means to provide important information about impacts of disease and intervention upon HRQL. Generic measures were designed to be applicable across many diseases and states of functioning. As they have been validated in many populations, they are useful for cross-disease comparisons but may yield less detailed information about the particular nature of a disease or intervention.

Specific measures contain questions that are pertinent only to the area they have been designed to evaluate. The number of domains that they cover may be limited. The main strength of specific measures is that they allow the investigator to focus only upon areas that are relevant to the particular condition; measures are then better able to identify changes in the disease condition being studied. The danger in this approach is the loss of information from unexpected changes in the omitted domains and the possibility of designing an instrument that deliberately avoids certain areas that investigators might wish to ignore. However, because focus groups are generally used to create condition-specific instruments, the questions selected for the questionnaires reflect areas of life affected by the disease that patients believe are important, and therefore the potential for deliberate investigator bias is minimized (13).

Preference-Weighted Measures for Program Administrators and Health Policy Makers

Patient-preference (utility-weighted) measures differ from health profile measures in their intended approach and utilization. Health profile measures are, for the most part, developed by psychometricians to measure areas of behavior, function, or experience; neither the individual questions nor the domains are weighted. The importance that a patient may attach to a specific dimension(s) is considered relevant only insofar as its impact upon that desired construct. The result is that each domain's score must be interpreted individually; a five-point change in one domain does not necessarily mean the same thing in another domain. Decision makers who require a single summary score of the net change in HRQL—for example, HRQL treatment gains minus HRQL side-effect burdens—would find interpreting health profiles difficult.

Utility measures of quality of life are derived from economic and decision theory and reflect the preferences of groups of persons for particular treatment outcomes and disease states (13,14). These types of questionnaires incorporate preference measurements where HRQL is summarized as a single number along a continuum that extends from death (0.0) to optimal health (1.0). The preference values for states of health (often called "utilities") reflect both the health status and the value of that status to the patient. Since changes in health status are captured in a single number, the effect is unambiguous and more easily interpretable to program administrators, health policy makers, and others whose primary focus is society as a whole.

While preference-weighted measures are useful for determining if patients improve overall, they do not reveal in which domains the improvement or deterioration occurs. Essentially, the measures lack the ability to distinguish specific effects upon quality of life and may have limited use in the evaluation of specific treatment effects over time. Their primary advantage in *economic* analysis is important to decision makers who must justify the societal allocation of health care resources. And, as the cost variable becomes increasingly important in the health care equation, discrimination between interventions by administrators and regulators will no longer focus solely upon improvements in clinical efficacy, especially when such effects are found to be marginal.

Another reason to consider a preference-weighted measure for a clinical study is that the preference values derived can be combined with survival data to estimate the quality-adjusted life years (QALYs) gained by treatment. Once determined, an economic evaluation comparing treatments in terms of their cost per QALY gained is one form of cost-utility analysis that will be useful to conduct for the societal decision-making audience (1).

The ability of HRQL instruments to discriminate between interventions, across diseases, and between disease therapies is becoming increasingly important as the rationing of health care resources becomes a means of fiscal restraint. Preference-weighted measures are likely to play an important role in these kinds of public sector decision making because preference values for states of health ("utilities") represent the general population's preferences for treatment outcomes and health states.

An example of this type of health policy initiative occurred recently in the state of Oregon, where, in an attempt to ensure access to basic health care, the state's government adopted a priority-setting process based upon cost and outcome of all health services delivered by the state under its Medicaid health insurance program. Outcomes were evaluated using a set of health and functional states described by the Quality of Well-Being Scale. Panels of physicians were consulted to establish norms from the literature and clinical experience (15). While this initial experiment was generally considered a failure—for technical rather than conceptual reasons—further attempts by policy makers to employ patient-weighted measures within the public policy process are likely once methods by which utilities are determined are improved.

Within the private sector, health care managers and insurance company administrators are requesting additional types of information about new drug therapies that transcend traditional drug efficacy data. Short-term benefits and comparisons to placebo groups will no longer convince formulary committees to add new products. Long-term benefits, comparisons with commonly available therapies, and cost justification will necessitate the use of HRQL instruments with versatile discriminative and economic properties. Because cost is increasingly a concern among all types of health care decision makers, preference-weighted measures can be used by both private business and government agencies (such as health care financing and drug regulatory agencies) to more efficiently allocate to society health care resources. Cost information combined with QALYs, for example, can provide decision makers with a means to evaluate the relative impact of treatments; this cannot be accomplished with health profile measures.

League tables have been created to rank interventions in terms of their cost per quality-adjusted life year. Dissimilar interventions can thus be compared using a common framework, for example, value for money. Gudex (16), for example, estimated that given a life expectancy of 10 years and a 4% discount rate, the cost per QALY for a kidney transplant would be £1,342 ($2,300) but only £599 ($950) for a shoulder joint replacement. Using league tables, administrators are thus able to select between programs competing for resources on the basis of a synthesis of cost and health benefit. The attractiveness of league tables notwithstanding, however, a lack of data on many interventions, ethical objections to the use of QALYs, and unresolved methodological controversies with respect to cost-effectiveness analysis has checked their widespread acceptance by societal decision makers.

Another methodologic issue associated with the use of QALYs has to do with whether these preference values for states of health represent true utilities (and, therefore, whether a subsequent cost-utility analysis has validity for societal decision makers requiring such information). Those who believe that QALYs do not represent true utilities have developed an alternate measure, the healthy years equivalent (HYE), to address this concern (17). Proponents of HYE measurement argue that QALYs assume that the value of a health state is independent of the time spent in that state and that QALYs lack the ability to quantify the coping capability or increasing burden that patients likely experience over time. HYE estimation presents respondents with full information about the disease and time spent in each state; however, given the complexity of this approach, it may also impose a higher respondent and staff burden. More research is needed to determine whether the results of these competing approaches differ in practice (1).

DISCUSSION

While health profile (descriptive) and patient preference (utility) HRQL questionnaires can both be used within the context of a clinical trial, they serve the needs of distinct audiences. Where information about the nature of a particular treatment and its effects on the individual is important, a health profile measure will typically be used. When discrimination between various procedures for the purposes of health care resource allocation and economic analysis is of prime concern, preference-weighted instruments are customarily used.

Clinical investigators face several practical constraints when making decisions about which instruments to include in a study. They must consider the cost of including and analyzing the results of additional instruments as well as the burden that would be placed upon the patients. Researchers must ensure that relevant instruments have been culturally adapted for international trials. Given the number of instruments available, an appropriate selection may prove to be a difficult task.

HRQL instruments that both could provide descriptive scores for multiple domains and could be aggregated into a single preference-weighted score would give decision makers both an increased capacity to interpret results and the capability of using this information for individual treatment and societal allocation of resources. Cross-disease comparisons could be readily accomplished with generic instruments of this type (e.g., EuroQol or McMasters Health Utilities Index), while specific instruments would provide the best information for discrimination between interventions within a disease group.

CONCLUSIONS

The use of HRQL results from clinical studies can serve two purposes: to aid in individual clinical decision making and to aid in societal health care resource allocation. When differentiating the impact of pharmaceutical agents upon HRQL compared with other treatments, utility-weighted instruments provide the basis for societal allocation of health care resources. Health profile instruments are useful when the focus is upon important HRQL changes associated with a particular disease for an individual. The decision to include a particular type of instrument will depend upon the objective of the study and the needs of the audience.

REFERENCES

1. Drummond M. Quality of life measurement within economic evaluations. Paper presented at the ESRC/SHHD workshop on Quality of Life, Edinburgh, April 27–28, 1993.
2. Cella DF, Tulsky DS. Measuring quality of life today: methodological aspects. *Oncology* 1990;5(4):29–38.
3. Ganz PA. Quality of life measures in cancer chemotherapy. *Pharmacoeconomics* 1994;5(5):376–388.
4. Aaronson NK. Quantitative issues in health-related quality of life assessment. *Health Policy* 1988;10:217–230.
5. Berzon RA, Simeon GP, Simpson RL, Tislon HH. Quality of life bibliography and indexes: 1992 update. *J Clin Res Drug Dev* 1993;7(4): 203–242.
6. Schipper H, Levitt M. Measuring QOL. *Cancer Treat Rep* 1985;69 (10):1115–1125.
7. Ware JE. The general health rating index. In: Wenger NK, Mattson ME, Furberg CD, Elinson J, eds. *Assessment of quality of life in clinical trials of cardiovascular therapies*. New York: Le Jacq, 1984.

8. Pocock SJ. A perspective on the role of quality of life assessment in clinical trials. *Controlled Clin Trials* 1991;12:257S–265S.

9. Smith M. Medication, quality of life and compliance: the role of the pharmacist. *Pharmacoeconomics* 1992;1(4):225–230.

10. Testa MA, Anderson RB, Nackley JF, Hollenberg NK. Quality of life and antihypertensive therapy in men. *N Engl J Med* 1993;328(13):907–913.

11. Kunsebeck HW, Korber J, Jurgen H. Quality of life in patients with inflammatory bowel disease. *Psychother Psychosom* 1990;54:110–116.

12. Schron EB, Schumaker SA. The integration of health-related quality of life in clinical research: experiences from cardiovascular clinical trials. *Prog Cardiovasc Nurs* 1992;7(2):21–28.

13. Jaeschke R, Guyatt GH, Cook D. Quality of life instruments in the evaluation of new drugs. *Pharmacoeconomics* 1992;1(2):84–94.

14. Guyatt GH, Feeny DH, Patrick DL. Measuring health-related quality of life. *Ann Intern Med* 1993;118(8):622–629.

15. Eddy DM. Oregon's methods: did cost-effectiveness fail? *JAMA* 1991;166(15).

16. Gudex C. QALYs and their use by health service. Discussion Paper 20. Centre for Health Economics, University of York, York, UK, 1986.

SUGGESTED READINGS

Mehrez A, Gafni A. Quality-adjusted life years, utility theory, and healthy-years equivalents. *Med Decis Making* 1989;9:142–149.

Aaronson NK. Quality of life assessment in clinical trials: methodologic issues. *Controlled Clin Trials* 1989;10:195S–208S.

Bagne CA, Lewis RF. Evaluating the effects of drugs on behavior and quality of life: an alternative strategy for clinical trials. *J Consult Clin Psychol* 1992;(60)2:225–239.

Bech P. Quality of life in psychosomatic research. *Psychopathology* 1987;20:169–179.

Berzon R, Shumaker S. A critical review of cross national health-related HRQL instruments. *MAPI Qual Life Newsletter* 1993;5(Oct 1992–Jan 1993):1–2.

Billings AG, Moos RH, Miller III JJ, Gottlieb JE. Psychosocial adaptation in juvenile rheumatic disease: a controlled evaluation. *Health Psychol* 1987;6(4):343–359.

Bradlyn AS, Harris CV, Warner JE, Richey AK, Zaboy K. An investigation of the validity of the Quality of Well-Being scale with pediatric oncology patients. *Health Psychol* 1993;12(3):246–250.

Bullinger M, Hasford J. Evaluating quality of life measures for clinical trials in Germany. *Controlled Clin Trials* 1991;12:91S–105S.

Burckhardt CS, Woods SL, Schultz AA, Ziebarth DM. Quality of life in adults with chronic illness: a psychometric study. *Res Nurse Health* 1989;12:347–354.

Butler RN. Quality of life: can it be an endpoint? How can it be measured? *Am J Clin Nutr* 1992;(55):1267S–1270S.

Cunny KA, Perry M. Single-item vs multiple-item measures of health-related quality of life. *Psychol Rep* 1991;69:127–130.

Deyo R, Diehr P, Patrick D. Reproducibility and responsiveness of health status measures: statistics and strategies for evaluation. *Controlled Clin Trials* 1991;12:142S–158S.

Deyo RA, Centor RM. Assessing the responsiveness of functional scales to clinical change: an analogy to diagnostic test performance. *J Chronic Dis* 1986;(39)11:897–906.

Faden R, Leplege A. Assessing quality of life: moral implications for clinical practice. *Med Care* 1992;30(5;suppl):MS166–MS175.

Feinstein AR. *Clinimetrics*. New Haven: Yale University Press, 1987.

Feinstein C, Kaminer Y, Barrett RP, Tylenda B. The assessment of mood and affect in developmentally disabled children and adolescents: the Emotional Disorders scale. *Res Dev Disabil* 1988;9:109–121.

Fries JF. The hierarchy of quality of life assessment: the Health Assessment Questionnaire (HAQ) and issues mandating development of a toxicity index. *Controlled Clin Trials* 1991;12:106S–117S.

Gafni A. The quality of QALYs (quality-adjusted-life-years): do QALYs measure what they at least intend to measure? *Health Policy* 1989;13:81–83.

Goldberg DO, Hillier VF. A scales version of the General Health Questionnaire. *Psychol Med* 1979;9:139–145.

Greenwald HP. The specificity of quality of life measures among the seriously ill. *Med Care* 1987;(25)7:642–651.

Guyatt GH, Townsend M, Berman LB, Keller JL. A comparison of Likert and visual analogue scales for measuring change in function. *J Chronic Dis* 1987;40(12):1129–1133.

Guyatt G, Walter S, Norman G. Measuring change over time: assessing the usefulness of evaluative instruments. *J Chronic Dis* 1987;40(2):171–178.

Guyatt GH, Deyo RA, Charlson M, Levine MN, Mitchell A. Responsiveness and validity in health status measurement: a clarification. *J Clin Epidemiol* 1989;42(5):403–408.

Guyatt G, Feeny D, Patrick D. Issues in quality of life measurement in clinical trials. *Controlled Clin Trials* 1991;12:81S–90S.

Guyatt GH, Kieshner B, Jaeschke R. Measuring health status: what are the necessary measurement properties? *J Clin Epidemiol* 1992;45(12):1341–1345.

Katz JN, Larson MG, Phillips CB, Fossel AH, Liang MH. Comparative measurement and sensitivity of short and longer health status measurement instruments. *Med Care* 1992;(30)10:917–925.

Kempen GIJM. The MOS short-form general health survey: single item vs multiple measures of health-related quality of life: some nuances. *Psychol Rep* 1992;70:608–610.

Kirshner B, Guyatt G. A methodological framework for assessing health indices. *J Chronic Dis* 1985;39(1):27–36.

Kleinbaum DG, Kupper LL, Muller KE. *Applied regression analysis and other multivariable methods*. Boston: PWS-Kent, 1988.

Lane DA. Utility, decision, and quality of life. *J Chronic Dis* 1987;40(6):585–591.

Lester L, et al. Towards the development of a play performance scale for children. *Cancer* 1985;56:1837–1840.

Linstrom B, Eriksson B. Quality of life among children in the Nordic countries. *Qual Life Res* 1993;2:23–32.

Loomes G, McKenzie L. The use of QALYs in health care decision making. *Soc Sci Med* 1989;(28)4:299–308.

Lydick E, Epstein RS. Interpretation of quality and life changes. *Qual Life Res* 1993;June.

MacKeigan LD, Pathak DS. Overview of health-related quality-of-life measures. *Am J Hosp Pharm* 1992;49:23236–2245.

Mangione CM, Marcantonio ER, Goldman L, Cook EF, Donaldson MC, Sugarbaker DI, Poss R, Lee TH. Influence of age on measurement of health status in patients undergoing elective surgery. *J Am Geriatr Soc* 1993;41:337–383.

Mansfield E. *Statistics for business and economics*. New York: W.W. Norton, 1987.

Maylath NS. Development of the Children's Health Rating scale. *Health Educ Q* 1990;17(1):89–97.

McCauley C, Bremier BA. Subjective quality of life measures for evaluating medical intervention. *Eval Health Prof* 1991;14(4):371–387.

Milsten JM, Cohen ME, Sinks LF. The influence and reliability of neurologic assessment and Karnofsky performance score on prognosis. *Cancer* 1985;56:1834–1936.

Neff EJA, Dale JC. Assessment of quality of life in school aged children: a method—phase I. *Matern Child Nurs J* 1990;19(4):314–320.

Packer RJ, et al. Quality of life in children with primitive neurodermal tumors (medulloblastoma) of the posterior fossa. *Pediatr Neurosci* 1987;12:169–175.

Rating scales and assessment instruments for use in pediatric psychopharmacology research. *Psychopharmacol Bull* 1985;21(4).

Testa MA, Lenderking WR. Interpreting pharmacoeconomic and quality-of-life clinical trial data for use in therapeutics. *Pharmacoeconomics* 1992;2(2):107–117.

Torrance GW, Feeny D. Utilities and quality-adjusted life years. *Int J Tech Assess* 1989;5:559–575.

Tugwell P, et al. Current quality of life research challenges in arthritis relevant to the issue of clinical significance. *Controlled Clin Trials* 1991;12:217S–225S.

van Knippenberg FCE, Haes JCJM. Measuring the quality of life of cancer patients: psychometric properties of instruments. *J Clin Epidemiol* 41(11):1043–1053.

Wagstaff A. QALYs and the equity-efficiency trade-off. *J Health Econ* 1991;10:21–41.

Ware JE. Standards for validating health measures: definition and content. *J Chronic Dis* 1987;40(6):473–480.

Weissman MM, Orvaschel H, Padian N. Children's symptom and social functioning self-report scales. *J Nerv Ment Dis* 1980;168(12):735–740.

Wu AW, Rubin HR. Measuring health status and quality of life in HIV and AIDS. *Psychol Health* 1992;6:251–264.

Zwinderman AH. The measurement of change of quality of life in clinical trials. *Stat Med* 1990;9:931–942.

Quality of Life and Pharmacoeconomics in Clinical Trials, Second Edition, edited by B. Spilker. Lippincott-Raven Publishers, Philadelphia © 1996.

CHAPTER 39

Data Collection Methods

Floyd J. Fowler, Jr.

INTRODUCTION

A central component of most clinical studies is collecting data from subjects by asking them questions. Certain kinds of information can never be reliably gathered from clinical records or from examinations; only subjects themselves can provide the answers. Among the topics most commonly covered are:

Demographic characteristics.
History of medical treatments and conditions.
Symptoms experienced as a result of conditions or treatments.
Patient perceptions of health, psychological well-being, and functioning.

When data such as these are to be collected from patients, researchers have to decide how the question-and-answer process is going to be handled. There are three key decisions that define data collection procedures:

1. Will respondents read questions and record answers themselves, or will an interviewer ask the questions and record the answers?

F. J. Fowler, Jr.: Center for Survey Research, University of Massachusetts at Boston, Boston, Massachusetts 02125.

2. If it is self-administered, will there be someone present to explain things and answer questions or not? If interviewer-administered, will the interview be done in person or on the telephone?
3. Will the data collection instrument be paper and pencil, or will it be assisted by computer and/or audio technology?

The choice of data collection methods has many implications. Each of the approaches to data collection implied by the list above has the potential to solve problems, as well as to pose challenges. This chapter describes the advantages and disadvantages associated with each option, the procedures needed to develop and test data collection strategies, and the procedures needed to ensure quality control of data collection.

CHOOSING A METHOD OF DATA COLLECTION

The total data collection protocol will be driven by practical considerations, as well as by concerns about data quality. Thus, how patients will be recruited, how long and how often follow-up data are to be collected, and whether or not the protocol calls for subjects to return to the clinical site for other reasons all will affect the choice of data collection strategy. However, regardless of other aspects of the protocol, researchers must choose whether or not to use interviewers and whether or not to use various technologic aids in the collection of their data.

Whether or Not to Use an Interviewer

For most studies, it is easier for the investigator to have respondents fill out questionnaires than it is to use interviewers. The very fact of having to hire, train, and supervise interviewers introduces an element into the study that may be difficult to accomplish well and typically increases the cost of data collection. On the other hand, interviewers can be a great aid in the data collection process. Interviewers can follow a complex protocol of questions that is difficult to design for a self-administered form. When respondents misunderstand questions, interviewers are there to clarify and probe. Interviewers help ensure that questions are answered adequately and fully. This is particularly helpful if respondents are being asked questions to be answered in narrative form. If an interviewer is involved, the answers can be probed and clarified to make sure that the data are specific enough to be understood and used. However, for all kinds of questions, surveys using interviewers have less missing data than self-administered surveys.

From the point of view of the kind of questions that are asked, questions that are to be answered in narrative form are almost impossible to use in self-administered forms. Respondents will not write lengthy answers, and the answers they do write will often prove to be uncodable. In contrast, interviewer administration makes such questions quite feasible.

Interviewers also offer a clear advantage for those respondents who have difficulty with reading and writing. There are many people for whom an oral interview is easier than self-administration, such as those who lack good reading and writing skills, whose first language is not English, or who have difficulty seeing.

Having cited the various advantages of interviewers, three advantages of self-administration should also be noted. First, there is a growing body of evidence that people are more willing to report socially undesirable facts about themselves in a self-administered form than they are to report them to an interviewer. Thus, if obtaining an accurate reporting of such sensitive events as use of illegal drugs or having an abortion is important to a research project, serious consideration should be given to self-administration (1,2). Second, in a more general way, self-administration can give respondents more time to think carefully about their answers. The interview process tends to be a relatively quick question-and-answer process, with pressure on respondents to answer quickly. Although this pressure can be mitigated with proper interviewer training and procedures, there may be some advantage in data quality to letting respondents proceed at their own pace. Finally, and probably most important, poor-quality interviewing can be a significant source of error. If data collection can be self-administered, it obviates the need to provide good interviewers.

Mixing Modes

Sometimes an attractive option is to mix modes of data collection, with some data being collected via self-administration and others being collected by an interviewer. There are two different ways in which this is done.

As noted above, there are some kinds of questions that benefit from having an interviewer involved in the data collection. Alternatively, there are some kinds of questions that people seem to answer more accurately via self-administration. Thus, one attractive option is to have interviewers ask the questions for which they can be helpful, but let respondents who are able fill out a self-administered questionnaire for those questions that may benefit from self-administration.

Another way in which modes have been combined is to have respondents who are able fill out a self-administered form, while those who are unable to fill out such forms are interviewed. Such an option may be necessary so that those who do not speak English well, or who cannot read for other reasons, are not excluded from a study. Combining data collected by different modes rests on the assumption that the mode of data collection will not affect the results.

There have been numerous studies that have compared data collected by self-administration and by interviewer. Most such comparisons show that the majority of answers are not affected by the mode of data collection (2–5). However, most such studies also show that some answers are affected by mode of data collection. It was already mentioned that socially undesirable behaviors or facts are more likely to be reported in self-administered forms. Moreover, two recent studies have shown that people seem to use response scales somewhat differently depending on the mode. On all of the eight indices that are part of the 36-item short-form instrument Ware and associates developed to measure health states (6), it was found that the average scores were higher when the data were collected by telephone interviewer than when they were collected by self-administration (7). In a similar way, Fowler et al. (8) found that respondents consistently reported more problems related to treatment of prostate cancer in self-administration than to a telephone interviewer. It also should be noted that by psychometric standards, such as internal consistency and test-retest reliability, these studies showed no discernible differences in data quality by how the data were collected.

These results suggest that if multiple modes are necessary in order to ensure a high rate of participation in a project, and if change over time (or lack thereof) is a primary measure of interest, it might be best to keep the same data collection mode for any given subject. In addition, if there is concern about the effect of data collection mode on any particular estimates, it is wise to assign a representative subset of subjects to each alternative strategy for data collection, so that the effect of mode on distributions and estimates can, in fact, be estimated.

Supervised Versus Unsupervised Self-Administration

If data are being collected via self-administration at a clinical site, or in combination with an interview, there will be someone present to answer respondent questions and possibly to check for skipped questions and missing data. In contrast, if respondents are mailed a questionnaire, respondents are on their own. Probably the greatest challenge of collecting data by mail is motivating the respondents to complete the instrument. How easy or hard that is will depend on the subject matter, the interest of respondents in the project, and what kind of prior contact has been had with respondents. Almost certainly, a mail procedure will require some kind of follow-up and reminder process. In addition, there almost certainly will be more missing data when data are collected by mail. On the other hand, once subjects have been enrolled in a study, periodic mail follow-ups can often be a very effective way to collect data.

Telephone Versus In-Person Interviews

If subjects are being seen in a clinical setting and an interviewer is to be used, then the interviews are in person. However, there frequently is a choice about how follow-up data over time will be collected; interviews can be conducted on the telephone, in the clinical setting, or interviewers can visit respondents in their homes.

There are several advantages to telephone interviews. First, although the cost in interviewer time of interviewing people in the clinical setting will vary with the circumstances, it almost always is less expensive to interview people on the telephone than to send an interviewer to a subject's home. Second, telephone interviews can be conducted from a centralized setting, in which interviewer supervision can be maximized, possibly improving standardization and the quality of interviewing. Third, interviewers do not have to be proximate to the subjects. Widely scattered respondents can be interviewed by a small number of interviewers in a central place. Finally, providing computer assistance to telephone interviewers in a central location is particularly easy.

So should telephone interviewing always be the strategy of choice? Obviously, that approach only works for those who have telephone service. In the United States, 95% of households are served by a telephone, and an even higher percentage of households with residents over 65 (9). Hence, that is not much of a limiting factor, although it may be for some populations. However, there are people who do not use a telephone very well. For example, those who are hard of hearing or who are not fluent in English can be more easily interviewed in person than by telephone. A practical consideration is that there are some data collection activities that cannot be performed on the telephone. Those questions that require visual aids or involve lists of response alternatives are difficult to do on the telephone. In addition, if the

protocol requires a patient to sign a consent form, a telephone data collection poses problems.

Finally, with respect to data quality, most comparisons suggest that data collected by telephone are very similar to those collected by personal interviewers (10,11). When differences in response have been detected, they often have been in the direction of suggesting people report fewer problems and less socially undesirable facts over the telephone than they do a personal interviewer. However, it should be emphasized that for most questions, the data collected in person and by telephone interviewers have been indistinguishable. Thus, telephone data collection is a realistic and appropriate option for many study designs.

Computer-Assisted Data Collection

The first application of computers to data collection was computer-assisted telephone interviewing. When interviewers are working from a centralized facility, the questions appear on a screen to be read by interviewers, and interviewers record answers directly into the computer.

There were two main contributions that this methodology made to data collection. First, the computer was able to follow complex instructions for question order. In particular, it was possible to design sequences of questions dependent on previous answers, or even data from other sources, that would be very difficult to implement with a standard paper and pencil instrument. Second, by virtue of having the data entered directly into a computer, researchers could ensure that interviewers did not enter any answer that was logically inconsistent or outside the field of legal answers. In addition, because the data were entered into a computer, data files were quickly created (12,13).

Although computer-assisted telephone interviewing has been used since the 1970s, the use of computers in connection with personal interviews and self-administered data collection only started to develop in the late 1980s and early 1990s. However, as computers became more portable and more powerful, it became feasible to give personal interviewers, even those interviewing in homes, computer-assisted interviewing capability. The same virtues associated with computer-assisted telephone interviewing can be associated with computer-assisted personal interviewing. Computers can be used for self-administered data collection as well. Questions can pop up on a screen, and respondents can enter their answers in a computer. The limit of this technology is that respondents vary in how comfortable they are in working with a computer.

Self-administered data collection using computers has to be supervised. If technical assistance is available, people who are able to fill out self-administered questionnaires should be able to answer questions via computer. The task can be simplified, moreover, if respondents are not required to use a standard keyboard but can use some other kind of entry system that is easier and has fewer options.

One of the intriguing applications of this technology has been to combine it with computer-assisted personal interviewing. An interviewer conducts a portion of an interview using a computer. Then, for certain sections of data collection that deal with particularly sensitive topics, interviewers turn the computer around, instruct respondents in its use, and allow respondents to enter answers to questions in the computer without the answers being monitored by the interviewer.

There are disadvantages to computer-assisted data collection. One of the most important issues is that the programs need to be error free, which often means a considerable lead time to design and test them. Computers can reduce flexibility; for example, it often is difficult or impossible to go back in a program and correct a previously given answer. Data entry cannot be checked or verified; once an answer is entered, there is no other record of the response. Interviewers using computers need special training and need to have access to technical assistance. Narrative answers require special handling, thus limiting the interviews to questions with fixed response alternatives.

Audio-Assisted Interviewing

Another way in which technology can be used to assist in the data collection process is audio-assisted interviewing. Questions are read out loud to respondents, who are asked to enter their answers either in a computer or on paper. Some computers have audio capabilities. Questions can also be recorded on tapes, which can be played with a portable tape player and a headset (14).

There are three striking advances that are possible with audio-assisted data collection. First, people who have difficulty reading can participate in essentially a self-administered data collection process. Second, people who do not speak English can participate. Audio-assisted data collection enables researchers to make an audiotape in the respondents' language. Thus it is not necessary to recruit, hire, and train bilingual interviewers. Third, playing the set of questions on headphones allows the question-and-answer process to be confidential.

This technology was used recently to do surveys of teenagers about health-related activities. The interviews were conducted in the teenagers' homes. However, in order to enable the teenagers to participate freely without concern that their parents would monitor their answers, the questions were tape recorded. Teenagers listened to them through headphones and then answered on a self-administered form.

In the mid 1990s, computer-assisted telephone interviewing is standard operating procedure, while computer-assisted personal interviewing and other technical assistance is more experimental. However, it is quite clear that computers and audio assistance can provide important options to data collectors to solve some problems that they may confront and will be an increasingly common part of data collection protocols.

TESTING THE QUALITY OF THE DATA COLLECTION INSTRUMENT

Survey questions have to meet at least two standards:

1. They have to be understood consistently.
2. They have to be questions people can answer.

One requirement of good research practice is to evaluate the questions that are asked to make sure they meet those standards. In the past, survey instruments were "pretested" in one of two ways. If they were self-administered forms, respondents were asked to complete the questionnaire, then provide researchers with feedback about whether questions were hard to understand or answer. If data collection was interviewer-administered, interviewers would conduct some pretest interviews, then report back any problems they had. Unfortunately, neither of these strategies is well designed to evaluate how well questions meet the above standards. To do that, it is necessary to do cognitive testing or cognitive evaluation (15,16).

Cognitive Evaluation of Questions

Cognitive evaluation of questions is done orally, even if questions eventually will be self-administered. Usually, the testing is done with volunteer respondents who are paid for their time. Interviewers administer the questions, then use one of several techniques to get information about how the questions were understood and answered. The most common strategy for assessment is to ask respondents several follow-up questions after they answer the test question. Typical follow-up questions will ask respondents to define key terms, describe in their own words what the question is asking for, and describe how they arrived at their answers. This kind of narrative response from respondents enables the researcher to see whether, in fact, the questions mean to people what the researcher intended and whether the answers actually meet the question objectives.

Researchers have found that it does not take very many such tests to identify common problems with questions; often fewer than ten interviews are done to evaluate questions (17). Such testing can make a major contribution to improving the quality of measurement and should be a standard part of any survey that is relying on data collection from patients.

Evaluating an Interview Schedule

Just because questions can be understood and answered in a laboratory setting does not mean that they will work in practice. If data collection is interviewer-administered, the data collection instrument is a script for the interviewer as well as a set of questions. If the instrument is to work well, the interview schedule must be one that interviewers can administer exactly as worded. Moreover, when interviewers read the question as written, respondents should be able to answer them readily. To find out how well the instrument works from that perspective, a field pretest under realistic conditions is necessary.

As one part of the evaluation, it is appropriate to have interviewers report back on any problems they had with reading the questions, following the protocol, or having respondents answer in ways that meet question objectives. In addition, it is increasingly standard practice to tape record pretest interviews. These tape recordings are then coded to describe systematically the question-and-answer process. Specifically, coders tabulate the rates at which interviewers read questions exactly as worded, respondents ask for clarification of questions, and respondents fail initially to give adequate answers to questions. It has been found that when these behaviors occur in 15% or more of interviews, it usually reflects a genuine problem with the question (18,19). Behavior coding offers a systematic, objective way to evaluate how well survey interview schedules work in practice. It, too, should be a standard part of the question evaluation process.

Evaluating Self-Administered Procedures

Whether the respondent is going to be asked to fill out a paper-and-pencil questionnaire or to answer questions on a computer, it is necessary to evaluate the forms and procedures to see if people can actually perform the tasks required of them. The only way to do this is to pretest the instruments. By observing respondents, as well as talking with them afterward about problems they had, investigators can identify problems with their data collection instruments and procedures. It is particularly valuable to include in the pretest experience respondents with low educational attainment or who have other characteristics that may make the data collection task more difficult. Although such pretests are not infallible, the more pretesting that is done, the better the data collection. When data collection is to be self-administered, with no one around to help respondents, it is particularly important to design forms and data collection procedures that are as foolproof as possible.

QUALITY CONTROL OF DATA COLLECTION

Self-Administration

The primary mechanism for quality control of self-administered data collection is to review completed questionnaires to make sure respondents are answering all the questions and they are following instructions. One common issue is whether or not respondents should be recontacted in the event that they fail to answer a question. If a question is factual in nature and it is critical to the study, researchers may think it is worth the expense to do that. However, in general, missing data are fairly infrequent. A more important

strategy is to review early returns to make sure that there are no questions that are systemically being skipped because instructions are unclear. If such a problem is found, the most important thing to do is to change the data collection instrument to solve the problem.

If respondents are working with computer-assisted self-administration, it usually is hard for them to inappropriately skip questions; that is one of the strengths of computer-assisted data collection. Probably the key to quality control is to have someone monitor early respondents, keep track of questions they ask, and identify any difficulties respondents have in using the machine. Again, the goal at the early stages is to identify problems and solve them, so the remainder of the data collection goes more smoothly.

Quality Control of Interviewers

If data are to be collected by an interviewer, it is critical that interviewers behave as standardized data collectors. Specifically, that means:

1. Asking questions exactly as worded.
2. Probing inadequate answers in nondirective ways.
3. Training respondents in their role in a consistent way.
4. Maintaining a neutral, nonbiasing relationship with respondents.

Particularly in clinical studies, it is tempting to use nurses, receptionists, or other staff in clinical settings as interviewers. Although that may be convenient, the risk is that people who are not primarily interviewers are being asked to do a very important job that they may not want to do or may not think is important. When possible, there probably are real advantages to using interviewers for whom interviewing is the main job.

No matter who is the interviewer, interviewers must be properly trained and supervised. Simply explaining to a would-be interviewer how to behave is not enough. Studies have shown that training that includes a reasonable amount of supervised role-playing is essential to producing interviewers who can meet reasonable standards. In addition, interviewers must be supervised (20, 21). If interviewers are working on telephones, one approach is to have a supervisor systematically monitor a sample of each interviewer's work. At a minimum, all of the early interviews should be monitored, until an interviewer has proven to be acceptable, and then monitor a sample of interviews. Continuing to monitor, even after interviewers have demonstrated that they can interview appropriately, is essential in order to maintain high quality data collection (22).

If interviewers are doing interviews in person, or even if they are working on the telephone and a supervisor cannot be present at all times, tape recording interviews is an alternative way of monitoring the question-and-answer process. Again, early interviews plus a sample of subsequent interviews can be reviewed by a supervisor, systematically evaluated, and the results used to provide feedback and additional training as needed (20).

It is very tempting to think that a professional, such as a nurse, would be well qualified to carry out an interview. However, unless a person is properly trained and supervised, he or she will not be a good interviewer, no matter what other kinds of training that person has received.

Finally, as with self-administered forms, reviewing a sample of completed interviews may help to identify questions with which interviewers and respondents are having difficulty. Changes in interviewing instructions, or even restructuring questions, may be the solution to produce better data collection throughout the study. However, for interviewer-administered data collections, the key is to monitor the process of the data collection.

CONCLUSIONS

There is no single right way to collect data. All of the strategies discussed in this chapter are appropriate for some projects, depending upon the constraints, the data requirements, and the design of the study. However, regardless of strategies used for data collection, it is essential that all aspects of the protocol be carefully evaluated prior to the onset of full-scale data collection. In the past, evaluation of questions has been a weak area. Although psychometric evaluation after data collection is common, presurvey evaluation of comprehension and difficulty in answering questions has been neglected, to the detriment of the research. Also, too little attention has been given to the importance of interviewer training and supervision and of testing survey instruments to make sure they can be administered in a standardized way.

The improvement of techniques and standards for evaluating these aspects of data collection procedures is one of the major advances that has occurred over the past decade. While no doubt further advances will be made as more attention is given to quality control, the steps outlined in this chapter will make a major contribution to the quality of the data collection and the quality of the resulting data.

REFERENCES

1. Turner CF, Lessler JT, Gfroerer JC. *Survey measurement of drug use: methodological studies.* Washington, DC: U.S. Government Printing Office, 1992.

2. Fowler FJ. *Survey research methods,* 2nd ed. Newbury Park, CA: Sage, 1993.

3. Hochstim J. A critical comparison of three strategies of collecting data from households. *J Am Stat Assoc* 1967;62:976–989.

4. Mangione T, Hingson R, Barret J. Collecting sensitive data: a comparison of three survey strategies. *Sociol Methods Res* 1982;10(3):337–346.

5. Groves RM. *Survey errors and survey costs.* New York: John Wiley, 1989.

6. Ware JE, Sherbourne CD. The MOS 36-Item Short-Form Health Survey (SF-36): I. Conceptual framework and item selection. *Med Care* 1992; 30(6):473–483.

7. McHorney C, Kosinski M, Ware JE. Comparisons of the costs and quality of norms for the SF-36 Health Survey collected by mail versus telephone interview: results from national survey. *Med Care* 1994;32 (6):551–567.

8. Fowler FJ, Roman AM, Zhu XD. Mode effects in a survey of Medicare prostate surgery patients. *Proceedings, Survey Methods Section, American Sociological Association* 1993:730–735.

9. Thornberry OT, Massey JT. Trends in United States telephone coverage across time and subgroups. In: Groves RM, Biemer PN, Lyberg LE, Massey ML, Nichols WL II, Waksberg J. *Telephone survey methodology.* New York: John Wiley, 1988:25–50.

10. Groves RM, Kahn RL. *Surveys by telephone.* New York: Academic Press, 1979.

11. Cannell C, Groves R, Magilary L, Mathiowetz N, Miller P. An experimental comparison of telephone and personal health interview surveys. In: *Vital and Health Statistics,* Series 2, 106. Washington, DC: Government Printing Office, 1987.

12. Saris W. *Computer-assisted interviewing.* Newbury Park, CA: Sage, 1991.

13. Weeks MF. Computer-assisted survey information collection: a review of CASIC methods and their implications for survey operation. *J Official Stat* 1992;8(4):445–465.

14. O'Reily JM, Hubbard M, Lessler J, Biemer P, Turner C. Audio and video computer assisted self-interviewing: preliminary tests of new technologies for data collection. *J Official Stat* 1994;10(2):197–214.

15. Lessler J, Tourangeau R. Questionnaire design in the cognitive research laboratory. In: *Vital and Health Statistics,* Series 6, 1. Washington, DC: Government Printing Office, 1989.

16. Forsyth BH, Lessler JT. Cognitive laboratory methods: a taxonomy. In: Biemer, PN, Groves RM, Lyberg LE, Mathiowetz NA, Sudman S, eds. *Measurement errors in surveys.* New York: John Wiley, 1992: 393–418.

17. Royston PN. Using intensive interviews to evaluate questions. In: Fowler FJ, ed. *Conference proceedings: health survey research methods.* Washington, DC: National Center for Health Services Research, 1989:3–8.

18. Oksenberg L, Cannell C, Kalton G. New strategies of pretesting survey questions. *J Official Stat* 1991;7:349–366.

19. Fowler FJ. How unclear terms affect survey data. *Public Opinion Q* 1992;56(2):218–231.

20. Fowler FJ, Mangione TW. *Standardized survey interviewing: minimizing interviewer related error.* Newbury Park, CA: Sage, 1990.

21. Billiet J, Loosveldt G. Interviewer training and quality of responses. *Public Opinion Q* 1988;52(2):190–211.

22. Cannell CF, Oksenberg L. Observation of behaviour in telephone interviewers. In: Groves RM, Biemer PN, Lyberg LE, Massey JT, Nichols WL II, Waksberg J, eds. *Telephone survey methodology.* New York: John Wiley, 1988:475–495.

Quality of Life and Pharmacoeconomics in Clinical Trials, Second Edition, edited by B. Spilker.
Lippincott-Raven Publishers, Philadelphia © 1996.

CHAPTER 40

Narrative and Quality of Life

Deborah R. Gordon and Eugenio Paci

INTRODUCTION

Narratives, or stories, are naturally at home around illness. People tell stories of their illness and learn about their illness through the stories of others. They, together with others, construct stories of their own illness. "Stories are habitations. We live in and through stories. They conjure worlds. We do not know the world other than as story world" (1). But perhaps more fundamentally, people live their illness and their therapies, much as they live their lives, through stories. And they evaluate their illnesses much as they evaluate their lives in terms of stories they are living or trying to create.

Narrative also has a natural though perhaps less acknowledged home among health professionals. Therapists not only talk about patients through stories, they reason about what to do through them. They also construct stories, not only stories of disease but also therapy stories, that solicit the patient's participation and set out a particular path for the patient to follow (2).

When we speak about narrative in this chapter, then, we have more in mind than qualitative research or open-ended or even semi-structured interviews. We refer to narrative in two main ways. First, we use it as a concept, roughly

synonymous to "story" that encompasses not only storytelling but also story making (2), not only the life story of a person but narratives of illness, therapy, recovery, and death. Second, we use the term to refer to both a general research approach that offers more space to respondents to speak in their own words, as well as a more specific approach that solicits and analyzes accounts as "stories" or narratives.

We propose the use of narrative to the following ends: (a) to improve theoretical understanding, as a means for understanding what is quality of life, how is it lived, and how it is evaluated; (b) to generate quality of life outcomes that are closer to actual experience; (c) to describe and evaluate the quality of life of particular individuals, groups, and subgroups; (d) to identify and evaluate how narrative influences quality of life and reaction to therapy—the extent to which everyday, personal, and life narratives are affected by illness and how this affects the quality of life experienced, how different narrative responses to illness influence quality of life, and what therapeutic narratives are constructed and emplotted for patients; (e) to understand and interpret individual and group contexts of quality of life evaluations; and (f) to contribute to the evaluation of medical technologies in clinical trials and clinical decisions for individuals.

Consensus is growing that quality of life studies should present the patient's perspective, be multidimensional, include an overall global component, and be internationally appropriate (3). Here we will first consider some current problems in quality of life studies that narrative theory and research may be able to help address.

D. R. Gordon and E. Paci: Centre for the Study and Prevention of Cancer, Department of Clinical Epidemiology, Unit of Epidemiology, Firenze 50135, Italy.

PROBLEMS WITH QUALITY OF LIFE STUDIES IN CLINICAL RESEARCH

Quality of life is obviously not a simple reflection of biological definitions of disease and illness. Disease is not lived as "brute data," but through interpretation, expectation, meaning, past experiences and future intentions (4,5). In the social sciences, this distinction has been embodied in the words *disease* and *illness,* the latter referring to the patients' experience of biological alterations that physicians label "disease" (6).

Similarly, symptoms are rarely experienced as mere physical sensations, but are lived through their meaning, both in and of themselves and as part of whole meanings or stories. To take an obvious example, nausea due to pregnancy and nausea due to chemotherapy can be experienced very differently. Similarly, the lack of decreased quality of life among some patients taking chemotherapy may be due to the positive meanings they may attribute to it (5). In fact, patients want to know what their symptoms mean—is the symptom part of the illness, part of the therapy, normal, abnormal?—and these meanings in turn affect how symptoms are experienced (4) and structure the patients' attention to them.

Yet almost no attempt is made in quality of life studies to solicit patients' understanding of and meanings associated with their medical story—their disease, their symptoms, their treatment—or their own sense of their health—of being healed or cured, deformed, or disabled—or to explore what counter-stories they construct around, through, or parallel to the biological story. In fact, patients' reports of their health status strongly predict prognosis (7).

This silence belies the enduring strength of a Cartesian separation of mind and body (7) and the assumption of a docile, mindless body. Studies that evaluate the effect of illness or a therapy on a person's quality of life assume almost a direct interaction between the technology or the illness and quality of life.

While attention has been given to developing culturally sensitive translations of quality of life questionnaires, the cultural question does not end there (8–10) (also see Chapter 55 by Guarnaccia). Quality of life, the experience of illness and symptoms, and their evaluation are all deeply embedded in culture. And so are the traditional tests for quality of life, which clearly reflect the research culture based in North America and Europe (Guarnaccia).

Illness touches who we are, our existential being, not just our bodies (1). Traditional indicators, however, tend to be superficial, as if many researchers have accepted the limitations of their instruments and do not even attempt to measure the "immeasurable," to grasp the complex depths and breadths of experience. As a result, these fundamental dimensions are often missed: "Despite their global sound, evaluation of quality of life more generally stays on the surface, while the disease and the treatments involve the whole person, with h/her complexity" (11, p. 3). This may also contribute to the apparent insensitivity of many studies,

such as those that show that women with mastectomies and women with conservative operations have the same quality of life (12). Translating evaluations into quantifiable terms strips them of their meaning, and in so doing eliminates their quality.

Beyond one or two single questions that address overall quality of life, the whole picture in traditional studies is usually calculated by adding up the component dimensions. Such scores flatten out meaning and hierarchy, essentially putting all components of one's life on equal footing (13). Further, in many cases, a global sense or way of being determines the evaluation of individual items. For example, as Gordon (14) observed in her ethnographic study of women with breast cancer, how much someone is bothered by a symptom, as determined, for example, by the Rotterdam Symptom Check List (15), may be determined by a number of global features, such as how much one feels to still be among the living, how novel a symptom is, and what one's reference group is at the time. Pain also tends to become a global feature that affects all the parts (16).

This whole-as-the-sum-of-the-parts approach constructs a hyphenated, fractioned view of a person's life and experiences, the sum of which can never equal the whole. It leaves most questionnaires insensitive to experiences of fragmentation or wholeness that are so much a part of illness and so important to recovery and health in general. But more profoundly, most questionnaires lack as a fundamental whole: the "I" who is doing the evaluating, for example, or the story or stories in which traits such as symptoms or limitations acquire their meaning.

It is with these problems in mind that we turn to narrative. First we look at what narrative is, then at what illness, recovery, therapy, and quality of life look like in narrative terms. Finally, we consider the role of narrative in studies of quality of life in clinical and experimental research.

WHAT IS NARRATIVE?

Narrative is pervasive in our lives: "We dream in narrative, day-dream in narrative, remember, anticipate, hope, despair, believe, doubt, plan, revise, criticise, construct, gossip, learn, hate and love by narrative" (17, p. 5). While defined and used in many ways, from loose definitions to more precise, narrow ones, narratives are "meaning-making structures" (18–20) in which the meaning is in the sequence of events in time. Peter Brooks (21) writes, "Narrative is one of the large systems of understanding that we use in our negotiations with reality, specifically, in the case of narrative, with the problems of temporality" (p. xi). Narratives are "inherently sequential" (19) and ordered in terms of a plot: "Plot as I conceive it is the design and intention of narrative, what shapes a story and gives it a certain direction or intent of meaning" (21, p. xi). Plot makes events into a story (22).

Bruner contrasts narrative and narrative thinking with what he calls paradigmatic, logico-scientific thinking, characterized by universal, abstract terms, general causes, and logical deduction (18).

Some of the outstanding characteristics of narratives—using a loose interpretation for the moment—may be synthesized as follows:

narratives are about time, not linear time of isolated events, but time and events unified by configuration; narratives have direction—they lead somewhere, often where we don't know and have to figure out; narratives have a point, a telos, or plot (23);

narratives give shape to disorderly experiences, they connect the exceptional with the ordinary (19) and construct coherence; narratives are about order, disorder and making sense;

narratives are about becoming and unbecoming (2), about the "vicissitudes of human intention" (18, p. 16); narratives are about change;

narratives are positioned and partial, always in the eye of the protagonists (18); they grab us, pull us in, make us identify with one, hate another; stories "call" us (24); narratives are about the "feltness" of life (25), about events as experienced (2);

narratives are where the real and the imaginary have equal voice (19), where the "as if" is;

narratives are about the indeterminate, about possibilities, not certainties, narratives are about the "subjunctive" and multiple perspectives (18,26,27);

narratives are about obstacles and plight (2,18), surprise, and suspense; narrative is drama (2,18,19);

narratives are about conflict and breach (20)—between ideal/real, self/society, expected/encountered—about crisis and redemption; narratives are about suffering and its transcendence (4);

narratives are about morals (4,19,28), about the good and the bad (29), heroes and antiheroes; narratives are about what matters and what's at stake (30); narratives select the essential;

narratives are social and cultural (1,4,19,26,27,31,32), about power (20) and community; narratives link the individual to the cultural.

While stories are particular by their very nature, they are concrete generalizations (2,33). Their generalizability comes not through elements that can be taken out of context and compared, but rather through resemblance as a whole picture, as a whole story or exemplar (34,35). Generalization comes from analogy, i.e., drawing parallels to other situations (2).

Relationships Between Narrative, Reality, and Experience

A frequent question posed around narrative is what is its relationship to reality and truth? And perhaps of more relevance to quality of life issues, what are the relationships between narrative and experience? Following Mattingly (2)

we distinguish three types of relationships between narrative, on the one hand, and truth and experience on the other:

1. Narratives as "imitating" or "referring" to reality and experience: The traditional approach operating within science holds to a correspondence view of language, such that the truth of language and narrative is in its correspondence to reality. Here narrative is considered in reference to an objective account of "what happened," and its truthfulness is judged in terms of how accurately it represents reality. Similarly, illness or life stories were traditionally read as documents of what happened more than as constructions.

2. Narrative as rhetoric, as transforming or distorting reality and experience: Narratives, however, are not just neutral mirrors that reflect back what happened in "real life." Narratives like language cannot mirror but inevitably transform. Narrative is discourse leading to action or not (36–38), used to persuade and transform (39), to evoke experiences.

Example: Narrative as Self-Presentation—

Reissman, a sociologist, soliciting narratives of a sample of divorced people, analyzes how the respondents construct a positive self through retelling events in their biography, focusing in particular on the strategic ways they guide the impressions we form of them (39).

3. Narrative as shaping reality and experience: In this relationship, narrative is understood not just to follow or reflect reality, but to actively constitute it. We make phenomena real through storytelling (20,39). Putting something out into social space creates a new reality. Language here is understood not so much as expressing an inner state, but as constituting it (26,40,42). When one describes having a certain feeling, such as shame, the experience of the feeling and the articulation of it are one (41).

But it is not only through storytelling that we actually constitute the realities that language refers to. Narrative is also a powerful force for story making (2,43). Rosaldo (43), an anthropologist, noted this double function when analyzing hunting stories told by Ilongot men in the Phillipines: "The stories these Ilongot men tell about themselves both reflect what actually happened and define the kinds of experiences they seek out on future hunts. . . . the story informs the experience of hunting at least as much as the reverse." In other words, the stories we tell define the kinds of experiences we seek (2). This is of relevance when considering the stories in which therapies are embedded, including the story of a clinical trial.

Even more, "stories are lived before they are told" (17). We create stories that in turn structure our experience, not only in directing us toward a future, a goal; plot or telos give prospective meaning to something (2,44). We act in this way at this moment in order to reach that place. We act within a vision (45). Its meaning is in terms of its goal, its telos. This is called "emplotment" (2,23,44,46). Therapists, for example, construct narratives in order to persuade patients to participate. They "emplot" therapy (44). Emplotment "involves making a configuration in time, creating a whole out of a succession of events" (22,23). A story is the rendering and ordering of a sequence of events into parts that belong to a larger temporal whole (44). Particular actions take their meaning by belonging and contributing to the story.

Example: Storymaking—Therapeutic Emplotment

Mattingly (2), in her study of occupational therapists, analyzes how these therapists create meaningful stories and plots for patients in order to solicit their much needed participation in the therapy. A tour of the hospital for patients with severe head injuries, for example, emplots a new narrative of hard work in rehabilitation that leads to a return home and a life with new meaning. Mattingly argues for a dialogical, almost confrontational, relationship between narrative and experience: "Prospective narratives are being projected, unravelled, and remade in the course of trying to live them out" (2).

Stories structure experience in another fundamental way: we inhabit stories (1), we live in them, often many of them, and they provide a type of dwelling, an emotional house.

Example: Stories as Habitations

Mrs. Teresa was diagnosed very late with advanced breast cancer. She had always kept herself informed of her situation and insisted on being told what she had. After several metastases had developed, including to the lung, she became sicker and sicker, bothered most by a continuous cough. She was given radiation treatment for symptom relief. More than a month after she finished the radiotherapy, her cough still constant, she said that her doctor still attributed it to the radiotherapy. This was of course farfetched, and she said very wearily, "I don't know if he is telling me the truth or not, whether in fact this is from the illness, but for the moment it makes me feel a little better to believe him" (48). Living in the narrative that it was the therapy that caused her coughing instead of the metastases to her lung seemed to serve as a resting place for Mrs. Teresa, a place to dwell in for a moment that gave some relief.

In this way, narratives not only operate as goals for action, but they also define a person's actual situation. In both ways they function as selective frames of attention that allow certain things to show up and others to recede in the background or be taken for granted. The world is grasped through concerns and intentions (35,50) in part structured by narrative.

Strong and Weak Interpretations of Narrative

There are both strong and weak interpretations of the role of narrative in human experience. The first and more common approach sees stories as superimposed on human experience, which has no real narrative structure—no real beginnings, middles, ends—to speak of. Time tends to be understood as inhuman homogeneous time (36,37). Narrative and reality, in other words, are discontinuous (45). We construct order and coherence where there is none.

A stronger reading of narrative is as social action. This version distinguishes between the nature of "reality" and "lived human reality" and maintains that narrative, i.e., configuration, is already inherent in human experience and action, that we actually live through narrative, that our actions are structured in narrative terms (2,34,42,44–46,49, 50). Narrative and everyday reality are continuous. Hardy (51), in fact, argues that "it's nature, not art, that makes us all storytellers."

Narrative then refers not only to the more traditional understanding of stories, such as patient accounts of their illnesses or people's life stories. Narrative also refers to little stories in action, to little plots, such as placing a person within an illness narrative through communicating the diagnosis of cancer, or soliciting participation in an experimental drug trial for advanced cancer. These stories are often not explicit or conscious, but embodied and taken for granted. Nonetheless, they powerfully structure our behavior and experience.

HEALTH, ILLNESS, RECOVERY, THERAPY, DYING AND QUALITY OF LIFE IN NARRATIVE TERMS

What do health, illness, recovery, healing look like in narrative terms? What does a narrative reading of quality of life offer us? And finally, what do we see if we shine a narrative light on therapy and treatment?

Disease inhabits not just a person's body but his or her life and social world as well (4,26). Illness enters and disrupts biographies (52), breaking down or diverting narratives, as the title of a recent article puts it: "My story is broken, can you help me fix it?" (53). Patients can suffer "narrative loss" (2), what is sometimes called "loss of self," a self that is much defined through narrative. "I used to be Gilda Radner," is how the famous comedian put it (54).

On a deeper experiential level another narrative is often broken with the threat of a serious illness, the narrative of forever, of immortality, challenged by a new narrative of precariousness or finitude. The existential crisis this can trigger is well known, well captured by an Italian woman newly diagnosed with a tumor:

> Woman: "When I returned for the exam and this man who I don't know says, 'Signora, where will you be operated on?' I fell down from the clouds. . . . That was a blow, it was."

Interviewer: "How did you feel?"
Woman: "I don't know. Like someone with wings, who flies. . . . I didn't feel like a person, I seemed to be raised above the ground. . . . Remembering that day, naturally after that phrase, the atmosphere was icy, squalid, . . . darkness, winter, rain, cold, and this man who gives me this sentence . . . death . . ." (55).

In fact, one of the gradings of the impact of illness or therapy is the degree to which everyday and life narratives are broken, destroyed, lost, maintained, reconstructed. For example, Gordon met Mrs. Teresa as she was being diagnosed for breast cancer. She repeatedly mentioned how she had never been sick, how she was always the healthy one, had never gone to the doctor. The full meaning of this was truly brought home when Gordon asked Mrs. Teresa to tell the story of her illness. In fact, she began with the statement, "I had always been very healthy, even when others around were always getting sick."

The diagnosis of illness not only breaks down old narratives, it presents the person with a new illness narrative. Specific illness narratives are constructed through an ongoing process with a number of inputs (4,26): cultural narratives and meanings associated with a particular illness personal illness narratives; biomedical narratives; family narratives; and popular narratives. For example, most women's typical first association to hearing they have a tumor is to think of another significant person they know who had one. This narrative association colors their experience:

At the moment when the doctor told me, "You need an operation," in that moment there I thought of my mamma who had begun like that, and that inside this thing they call "fibroma" there is all the rest. It was the first impact with the illness and I said to myself, "It's over, you'll finish like your mother." I saw myself already dead, not right away, but within 12 years, having had to suffer a bunch of problems in the interim. This was perhaps the worst thing. [woman in her 60s with breast cancer (55)].

A person's illness narrative influences their sense of cure, healing, health, and even prognosis. For example, narratives of 80 patients with hip injuries were compared in terms of the patients' explanation of their injury, their sense of disability, of their future, and prognosis (56). Those who understood the injury as an external, mechanical problem had a better prognosis, i.e., began to ambulate sooner, than those who felt it was due to an organic and internal problem.

Patients deal with illness and its effects by constructing and telling stories. Stories, as Broyard (57) found, offer a sense of control:

My initial experience of illness was as a series of disconnected shocks, and my first instinct was to try to bring it under control by turning it into a narrative. Always in emergencies we invent narratives. We describe what is happening, as if to confine the catastrophe. . . . Storytelling seems to be a natural reaction to illness. People bleed stories. . . . Stories are antibodies against illness and pain. [pp. 19–20]

Stories provide a map (57), a way of making sense (32), a way of sharing experience and tying it to larger cultural

models (31,32), a way of placing illness experiences within the context of a life. Williams (58) found within patient stories of the genesis of illness efforts at "narrative reconstruction" to repair the ruptures between self and society caused by their illness or efforts to "remake" a world "unmade" by illness or pain (26).

Accommodating or Opposing Illness

An important issue affecting quality of life is whether or not an illness is absorbed within an old self-narrative or whether a new narrative is created. For how people experience symptoms is affected by what narrative they live within. Radley (59), for example, identified two types of responses to cardiac illness among the 42 men he interviewed. One group of men affirmed their initial identity and stood opposed to their illness, constructed metaphorically as an entity with whom to fight. Symptoms and flare-ups were lived as breakdowns and minimized or fought. The other group saw the illness metaphorically as a "crossroads" and worked to carve out a new narrative that not only offered positive meaning, but incorporated the illness and the accompanying symptoms.

Similarly, Benner and colleagues (60) identified two main types of relationships to one's illness through a combined quantitative/qualitative study of 96 people with asthma: an adversarial, oppositional relationship and an accepting caring relationship, almost always acquired through experience with the illness. In both studies, those with an oppositional relationship had more extreme mood swings than those who had learned to accept and incorporate—rather than fight and control—the illness as part of their life narrative.

The illness and life narratives people live out or try to actualize embody morality, i.e., notions of the good and bad, the worthy, the unworthy. In turn, people experience illness and its implications through moral emotions such as feeling good, bad, guilty, shameful, blameworthy, illegitimate, punished, "soiled," or courageous, redeemed, and honorable. Benner and colleagues found, for example, that asthma sufferers whose life narratives were guided by the values of autonomy and self-control felt responsible for not being able to "control" their illness, and in turn suffered the additional burden of feeling shameful, guilty, and blameworthy when they could not (60).

Narratives shape, in other words, the very powerful and often hidden moral dimension of illness experiences (4, 60–62). Often this morality is socially forced upon people. The stigma around certain conditions, such as cancer, often forces people into new narratives by excluding them from the "normal": "We're uncomfortable people," "they want to throw us to the sea," is the way two Italian women with breast cancer put it (63). Similarly many chronic pain patients are denied a legitimate illness narrative of physical illness and are offered instead an illegitimate one of mental illness (61,64).

Therapy, recovery, cure, and healing can be read in narrative terms as the mending, healing, or reconstruction of personal life narratives. As Charon (65) writes, "A narratively competent medical care . . . contributes to health by helping patients and care-givers to reestablish narrative order and thereby to restore intelligibility to otherwise meaningless events."

Despite the common medical narrative, "After the _____, you'll be your old self again," this is rarely the case. Rather than feel "recovered," many people feel changed in who they are, feel they are reborn, or redeemed (66), or have simply survived. Arthur Frank (54), a sociologist and survivor of cancer, identifies four types of self-change narratives appearing in today's autobiographical accounts: discovering "what I always have been"; discovering "who I might become"; discovering "what the illness has made me into"; and those feeling little or no change.

Therapy, Dying, and Narrative

Narrative plays a fundamental role in actualizing therapy and shaping patients' experience of it, underscoring how treatment is not just a physiological event but a meaningful one (2). Therapy is presented, planned, and "sold" to patients in terms of "therapeutic narratives" (2,44,67). Patients must see something at stake for them in the therapy (2), especially difficult therapies like anti-tumoral therapies (67) or rehabilitation therapies that require patient participation and motivation. A clinical trial, for example, presents a patient with a narrative of being on the cutting edge of science (67) and possibly helping others as well as oneself. Therapists must create a therapeutic plot that compels a patient to see therapy as integral to healing (2,44).

Example: A physician presenting a difficult chemotherapy treatment plan to a newly operated patient warned the patient: "Now you are euphoric. But 6 weeks down the road you will be fed up and want to quit this therapy. But it is essential that you see this therapy to the end. It is like putting money in the bank" (unpublished data from video study in Florence, Italy).

Therapeutic narratives set up expectations that in turn shape feelings when these expectations are met or not met. One common narrative presented to patients with breast cancer in Florence, Italy, for example, was: "You find it [the unnamed tumor], you remove it, and then it's all over" (55):

> When I woke up and the professor told me, "Signora, thank Heaven that you no longer have the illness upon you . . . that it could be removed!" They told me they had removed the breast, and little by little, I was happy, . . . they have removed the illness from me.

In fact the organization for women previously operated on for breast cancer is called "Women as Before." Similarly, some women with benign breast disease at very high risk for breast cancer constructed a plot in which prophylactic mastectomy would remove the problems (68). Many, however, discovered that the operation was the beginning of a new set of problems and another story rather than the end of one. The great disappointment, frustration, and anger this caused can be in part attributed to the therapeutic narrative that was constructed.

Therapists actively shape patients' sense of time by creating vague time horizons or bringing in the time frame to focus on the present and small progress, as a means of constructing hope and possibility in the face of limitations, such as terminal or incurable illness (67). They participate in constructing endings to patients' lives (67) that can mean the difference between a good death and a bad one. Especially where therapy can no longer cure, meaning becomes paramount in importance. Suffering is relieved, notes Cassell (69), most often by changing the meaning of the experience for the sufferer and by restoring a sense of connectedness (70).

Narrative and Quality of Life: Some Connections

A number of reasons then support the inclusion of narrative research in quality of life research. We will summarize them, beginning first by reviewing some of the ways narrative influences patient experience of illness and therapy, and in turn, evaluation of quality of life:

1. Narratives set up expectations of what to look for. Experience is in part a result of the confrontation of these expectations and reality. Patients often speak of an experience as being "worse than I expected," "not as bad as I expected."
2. Narratives embody goals and desires, the "ends" toward which a person is striving. People evaluate their situation in terms of these desired ends. For example, for a stroke patient for whom recovery was symbolized by a return to fishing, each development was evaluated in its relationship to realizing that goal (71).
3. Personal narratives embody notions of the good and the bad (28,60), prescribing particular behaviors and prohibiting others. How morally sustained or degraded a person feels in confronting many of the experiences that illness presents depends in part on the moral dimensions embodied in guiding narratives and how much these are adapted to the new situation.
4. Narratives set up salience, drawing some things forward into the foreground of importance and moving others to the background. They thus operate as frames for selective attention, which in turn affects how much symptoms and capacities are attended to and experienced. A person who does not incorporate his illness into his life narrative, for example, may attend less to symptoms and try and minimize them, as Radley (59) found.
5. Narratives can solicit healing behavior and participation by offering and creating new meaningful "ends" or goals for people whose illness may preclude the realization of old ones.
6. Narratives can construct a sense of continuity or positive meaning to counter negative medical narratives. For ex-

ample, stories of uphill progress or spiritual or psychological development can help counterbalance a downward cycle of physical health.

Beyond the powerful influence of narrative on experience, other characteristics of narrative research make it particularly able to compensate for some of the problems of traditional quality of life research cited at the beginning of the chapter:

1. Narrative is natural discourse. People tend naturally and frequently to communicate about their illness through stories. Narrative research offers a relational context more conducive to soliciting more complex, profound, personal accounts of elusive yet powerful feelings.
2. Narrative captures "how protagonists interpret things" (19, p. 51), the experiential terms through which people understand their lives, the meaning of events for a person (19,62). Narrative allows patients to define or describe in their own words, stories, images what quality of life means to them. It provides a context for soliciting patient understanding of and meanings associated with their illness, symptoms, therapy, and the narrative frameworks through which they experience them. It helps understand what is at stake for patients in their illness and therapy (30).
3. Narrative is well suited to track the complicated flow of experience over time, making connections that are unexplorable and inarticulatable in terms of an algorithm.
4. Narrative offers an avenue to hear or detect fragmentation and efforts of integration and reconstruction.
5. Narrative provides access to understanding the whole that determines the part, the perspective of the "I" who is evaluating. Is it the same "I" that was evaluating before an illness or a person fundamentally changed and in a "different place"?
6. Narrative offers access to the moral dimension of illness (62) so often inaccessible in medical accounts.
7. Narrative can help identify central meanings for people that orient them in their recovery and provide the frame of evaluation.
8. Narrative offers a means of understanding the life world and social context of the evaluator, what illness or symptoms means in terms of a life. Further it allows greater access to understanding how the social world influences and is influenced by the illness (64).
9. Narrative offers a means to understanding the cycle of exacerbation and attenuation of symptoms and illness (4).
10. Narrative allows room to elicit what stories patients are living out, what stories are they in, what stories they want to be in, and how this affects their experience of their illness or symptoms.
11. Narrative allows us to understand how a person's biography and past experiences enter in and mix with present ones, thus providing access to the historical dimension of illness experience (72).

In the next section we shall briefly consider some of the ways that narrative research can be integrated and used in clinical and experimental research.

NARRATIVE, QUALITY OF LIFE, AND CLINICAL RESEARCH

Narrative methods can be used independently, complementarily, or comparatively with traditional quantitative methods in clinical and experimental research. Similarly, their timing—before, during, or after traditional studies—will depend on this use. A narrative/ethnographic study of the context of a proposed clinical research would be the first step toward integrating narrative into clinical research. Such studies (e.g., 73), would explore not only the experiences of the patient but also how these are related to patients' understanding the effects of treatment, including side effects, of the illness, and other physical problems, and how these distinctions are handled and how symptoms are explained and emplotted by caregivers regarding long-term and short-term effects. It would include attention to what experiences the technology entails: Physically, how is it lived? What emotions and sensations patients experience using it? How do patients think it works? How much do they think it works?

From these exploratory narratives and ethnography could be developed interview schedules for larger samples of less in-depth interviews.

These interviews in turn could be analyzed to produce outcome variables that are closer to experience and trial-sensitive to include in quality of life questionnaires themselves. These could be in the form of traditional questions, but could also entail brief scenarios of actual cases, of narrative story lines, or of small stories.

These three levels of evaluation—in-depth narrative/ethnographic study of the local context focusing on a small sample; a larger sample narrative study; and experience-near, context-relevant outcome variables included in a questionnaire—would be added and evaluated together with the clinical research or clinical trial.

The two kinds of studies (quantitative and qualitative) should be designed while planning the clinical research. Narrative would be directed to provide sound knowledge of the context and considered as part of the evaluation of a clinical practice. The experience of patients, reported as narrative, could be compared with more traditional instruments (e.g., 74) and an expert panel could be asked to evaluate the individual trajectories of the illness, given all the available information. This kind of approach could be especially relevant, for example, in palliative care studies.

We propose the following uses of narrative in studies of quality of life in the context of clinical research:

1. Pre-research/trial use;
   (a) as an exploratory study to be used as a baseline for understanding the phenomenon and its context to be studied:

(b) as a basis for generating sensitive outcome variables to be incorporated in quality of life questionnaires for clinical trials;

(c) as a basis for generating more experience-near outcome measures for quality of life.

2. Simultaneous/complementary use:

(a) to describe and evaluate the clinical research or trial as a particular context (control for clinical trial);

(b) to evaluate the particular local world as context (control for local world, particularly relevant in cross-cultural work);

(c) to compare (with a limited sample) patients' assessment of quality of life via questionnaire with patient narratives on quality of life (control for method of evaluation);

(d) to have patients elaborate/explain/contextualize their responses to the questionnaire (complementary to questionnaire);

(e) to provide additional data for how a particular therapy is lived and what it means (complementary to questionnaire);

(f) to compare whether the mode in which a therapy is presented and "emplotted" makes a difference in outcome (control for therapeutic narrative);

(g) to explore patient perceptions of the therapies, e.g., what therapy they think they received, how they feel about therapies and how they work (control for therapeutic narrative and patient expectations).

3. Post-research/trial to help interpret results from standard questionnaire (7), to help identify and understand subgroups (post-questionnaire).

CONCLUSIONS

The proposal of narrative as concept and method is a proposal for extending what we consider to be essential and optimal research and our criteria of what authorizes our decisions. Each research tradition offers a perspective on a complicated, multidimensional, changing story. We cannot allow ourselves to be monopolized by quantification when dealing with profound human issues with powerful human consequences.

The profound and complex dimensions of illness cannot be bracketed out of our research because they are "immeasurable." We will not be able to humanize patient care without also humanizing our research methods.

Narrative studies can help insert both "quality" and "life" into quality of life studies and technological evaluations, and in so doing, help realize our attempt to put the person, not the disease, at the center of our concern.

Illness transforms. One dies along the way. One may be reborn. It is how these experiences are interpreted and configured, unraveled, resewn that constitutes the illness experience and, in turn, quality of life. Quality of life is about meaning, and meaning among other things is grasped and dwelled on through narrative. Evaluation of quality of life that excludes terms of significance will fail not only to grasp the experience of symptoms, but what even counts as a symptom. "Stories," writes Charon (75), a physician, "are instruments that allow us to see within patients' lives with a clarity equal to that achieved by medical instruments that allow physicians to see within their patients' bodies" (cited in 76). In many ways, narratives are to people's experience of quality of life and illness what disease is to the physician in his interpretation of symptoms. Physicians do not listen to the body, add up the symptoms, and arrive at a disease. Rather they listen and configure through disease concepts. Patients configure all the time, in part through narratives. What and how they and their family and the health care team configure will have much to do with what quality of life means to them and how they experience it.

ACKNOWLEDGMENTS

We are grateful to Stef Solum and Lucas Bergmann for their research assistance and to the Italian National Research Council, Project ACRO (CNR 94.01322.PF 39) and A.I.R.C. for their financial support.

REFERENCES

1. Mair M. Psychology as storytelling. *Int J Personal Construct Psychol* 1988;1:125–138.
2. Mattingly C. *Story and experience: narrative shapes in clinical time.* Cambridge: Cambridge University Press, in press.
3. Ganz PA. Quality of life and the patient with cancer: individual and policy implications. *Cancer* 1994;74(suppl):1445–1452.
4. Kleinman A. *The illness narratives: suffering, healing and the human condition.* New York: Basic Books, 1988.
5. Good BJ, Good M-JD. The meaning of symptoms: a cultural hermeneutic model for clinical practice. In: Eisenberg L, Kleinman A, eds. *The relevance of social science for medicine.* Norwell, MA: D. Reidel, 1980.
6. Eisenberg L. Disease and illness: distinctions between professional and popular ideas of sickness. *Cult Med Psychiatry* 1977;1:9–23.
7. Holman HR. Qualitative inquiry in medical research. *J Clin Epidemiol* 1993;46:29–36.
8. Kleinman A. Culture, the quality of life, and cancer pain: anthropological and cross-cultural perspectives. In: Ventafridda V, van Dam FSAM, Yancik R, Tamburini M, eds. *Assessment of quality of life and cancer treatment.* Amsterdam: Elsevier Science, 1986:43–50.
9. Campos SS, Johnson TM. Cultural considerations. In: Spilker B, ed. *Quality of life assessments in clinical trials.* New York: Raven Press, 1990:163–171.
10. Marshall P. Cultural influences on perceived quality of life. *Semin Oncol Nurs* 1990;6:278–284.
11. Zittoun R. Introduction. In: Zittoun R, ed. *Quality of life of cancer patients: a review.* Levallois-Perret, France: Editorial Assistance, 1992:1–3.
12. Fallowfield L. *Quality of life: the missing measurement in health care.* London: Souvenir Press, 1990.
13. Ganz PA, Coscarelli Schag CA, Cheng H-L. Assessing the quality of life: a study in newly-diagnosed breast cancer patients. *J Clin Epidemiol* 1990;43:75–86.
14. Gordon DR. *More quality for quality of life studies.* Paper presented at Study Day on Quality of Life, Florence, Italy, October, 1991.
15. de Haas JCJM, Raatgever JW, van der Burg MEL, Hamersma E, Neijt JP. Evaluation of the quality of life of patients with advanced ovarian cancer treated with combination chemotherapy. In: Aaronson NK, Beckmann J, eds. *The quality of life of cancer patients.* New York: Raven Press, 1987:215–226.
16. Ferrell B, et al. The experience of pain and perceptions of quality of life: validation of a conceptual model. *Hospice J* 1991;7:9–24.

17. Hardy B. Towards a poetics of fiction: an approach through narrative. *Novel* 1968;2:5–14.

18. Bruner J. *Actual minds, possible worlds.* Cambridge, MA: Harvard University Press, 1986.

19. Bruner J. *Acts of meaning.* Cambridge, MA: Harvard University Press, 1990.

20. Reissman CK. *Narrative analysis.* Thousand Oaks, CA: Sage, 1993.

21. Brooks P. *Reading for the plot: design and intention in narrative.* Cambridge, MA: Harvard University Press, 1984.

22. Ricoeur P. Narrative time. In: Mitchell WT, ed. *On narrative.* Chicago: University of Chicago Press, 1981:165–186.

23. Ricoeur P. *Time and narrative,* vol 1. Chicago: University of Chicago Press, 1984.

24. Coles R. *The call of stories: teaching and the moral imagination.* Boston: Houghton Mifflin, 1989.

25. Burke K. *Counter statement.* Berkeley: University of California Press, 1931.

26. Good BJ. *Medicine, rationality and experience: anthropological perspectives.* Cambridge: Cambridge University Press, 1993.

27. Good BJ, Good M-JD. In the subjunctive mode: epilepsy narratives in Turkey. *Soc Sci Med* 1994;38:835–842.

28. MacIntyre A. *After virtue.* Notre Dame, IN: University of Notre Dame Press, 1981.

29. Benner P. The role of experience, narrative, and community in skilled ethical comportment. *Adv Nurs Sci* 1991;14:1–21.

30. Kleinman A, Kleinman J. Suffering and its professional transformation: toward an ethnography of interpersonal experience. *Cult Med Psychiatry* 1991;15:275–302.

31. Price L. Ecquadorian illness stories: cultural knowledge in natural discourse. In: Holland D, Quinn N, eds. *Cultural models in language and thought.* Cambridge: Cambridge University Press, 1987:313–142.

32. Early EA. The logic of well being: therapeutic narratives in Cairo, Egypt. *Soc Sci Med* 1982;16:1491.

33. Burke K. *Language as symbolic action: essays on life, literature, and method.* Berkeley: University of California Press, 1966.

34. Benner P. *From novice to expert: excellence and power in clinical nursing practice.* Reading, MA: Addison-Wesley, 1984.

35. Benner P. Quality of life: a phenomenological perspective on explanation, prediction and understanding in nursing research. *Adv Nurs Sci* 1985;8:1–14.

36. Aristotle. *Poetics,* translated by F. Else. Ann Arbor, MI: University of Michigan Press, 1970.

37. Godzich W. Forward. In: Coste D, *Narrative as communication.* Minneapolis, MN: University of Minneapolis Press, 1989:ix–xvii.

38. Coste D. *Narrative as communication.* Minneapolis, MN: University of Minnesota Press, 1989.

39. Reissman CK. Strategic uses of narrative in the presentation of self and illness: a research note. *Soc Sci Med* 1990;30:1195–1200.

40. Young K. *Taleworlds and storyrealms: the phenomenology of narrative.* Boston: Martinus Nijhoff, 1987.

41. Taylor C. *Philosophical papers,* vol I. Cambridge: Cambridge University Press, 1985.

42. Heidegger M. *Being and time,* translated by E. Robinson and J. Macquarrie. New York: Harper and Row, 1962.

43. Rosaldo R. *Ilongot Headhunting: 1883–1974.* Stanford, CA: Stanford University Press, 1980:134.

44. Mattingly C. The concept of therapeutic "emplotment." *Soc Sci Med* 1994;38:811–822.

45. Carr D. *Time, narrative and history.* Bloomington, IN: Indiana University Press, 1986.

46. Ricoeur P. The narrative function. In: Thompson JB, ed. *Paul Ricoeur: hermeneutics and the human sciences.* Cambridge: Cambridge University Press, 1982:274–296.

47. Sacks O. *The man who mistook his wife for a hat.* New York: Picador, 1985.

48. Gordon DR. The ethics of ambiguity and concealment around cancer: interpretations through a local Italian world. In: Benner P, ed. *Interpretive phenomenology.* Thousand Oaks, CA: Sage, 1994:279–322.

49. Arendt H. *The human condition.* Chicago: University of Chicago Press, 1958.

50. Dreyfus HL. *What computers can't do,* Rev. ed. New York: Harper and Row, 1979.

51. Hardy B. *Tellers and listeners: the narrative imagination.* London: Athlone Press, 1975:vii.

52. Bury MR. Chronic illness as biographical disruption. *Sociol Health Illness* 1982;4:167–182.

53. Brody H. "My story is broken, can you help me fix it?" Medical ethics and the joint construction of narrative. *Lit Med* 1994;13:79–92.

54. Frank A. The rhetoric of self change. *Sociol Q* 1993;34:39–52.

55. Gordon DR. Embodying illness, embodying cancer. *Cult Med Psychiatry* 1990;14:275–298.

56. Borkan JM, Quirk M, Sullivan M. Finding meaning after the fall: injury narratives from elderly hip fracture patients. *Soc Sci Med* 1991;33:947–957.

57. Broyard A. *Intoxicated by my illness and other writings on life and death.* New York: Fawcett Columbine, 1992.

58. Williams G. The analysis of chronic illness: narrative reconstruction. *Social Health Illness* 1984;6:175–200.

59. Radley A. The role of metaphor in adjustment to chronic illness. In: Radley A, ed. *Worlds of illness: biographical and cultural perspectives on health and disease.* London: Routledge, 1993:108–122.

60. Benner P, Janson-Bjerklie S, Ferketich S, Becker G. Moral dimensions of living with a chronic illness: autonomy, responsibility and the limits of control. In: Benner P, ed. *Interpretive phenomenology.* Thousand Oaks, CA: Sage, 1994:225–254.

61. Good M-JD, Brodwin PE, Good BJ, Kleinman A. *Pain as human experience: an anthropological perspective.* Berkeley: University of California Press, 1992.

62. Churchill LR, Churchill SW. Storytelling in medical arenas. *Lit Med* 1982;1:73–79.

63. Paci E, Venturini A, eds. *Dall'esperienza di malattia una nuova cultura.* Firenze: Lega Italiana Contro i Tumori, 1989.

64. Kleinman A. Pain and resistance: the delegitimation and relegitimation of local worlds. In: Good M-JD, Brodwin PE, Good BJ, Kleinman A, eds. *Pain as human experience: an anthropological perspective.* Berkeley: University of California Press, 1992:198–207.

65. Charon R. Medical interpretation: implications of literary theory of narrative for clinical work. *J Narr Life His* 1991;3:79–97.

66. Sacks O. *Awakenings.* New York: Picador, 1982.

67. Good M-JD, Munakata T, Kobayashi Y, Mattingly C, Good BJ. Oncology and narrative time. *Soc Sci Med* 1994;38:855–862.

68. Gifford S. The meaning of lumps. In: Janes C, Stall R, Gifford S, eds. *Epidemiology and anthropology.* Dordrecht, Holland: D. Reidel, 1986.

69. Cassell EJ. *The nature of suffering and the goals of medicine.* New York: Oxford University Press, 1991.

70. Brody H. *Stories of sickness.* New Haven: Yale University Press, 1987.

71. Doolittle ND. A clinical ethnography of stroke recovery. In: Benner P, ed. *Interpretive phenomenology.* Thousand Oaks, CA: Sage, 1994:211–224.

72. Pandolfi M. Boundaries inside the body: women's sufferings in southern peasant Italy. *Cult Med Psychiatry* 1990;14:255–275.

73. Plough AL. *Borrowed time: artificial organs and the politics of extending lives.* Philadelphia: Temple University Press, 1986.

74. Heyink JW, Tymstra TJ. The function of qualitative research. *Soc Indicators Res* 1993;29:291–305.

75. Charon R. Commencement address, State University of New York, Stony Brook School of Medicine, June, 1985, unpublished (cited in ref. 76).

76. Mishler E. *Research interviewing: context and narrative.* Cambridge, MA: Harvard University Press, 1986.

Quality of Life and Pharmacoeconomics in Clinical Trials, Second Edition, edited by B. Spilker.
Lippincott-Raven Publishers, Philadelphia © 1996.

CHAPTER 41

Group Dynamics and Focus Groups

Richard A. Krueger

INTRODUCTION

The first edition of this book shared the work, wisdom, and insights of professionals struggling to assess the quality of life of people participating in clinical trials. Much of the discussion centered on how to quantify and objectively assess quality of life. This chapter offers an approach that relies on qualitative data, the focus group interview, that can complement and strengthen existing assessment approaches.

The focus group interview is a group interview process developed during World War II to gain insights and perceptions of soldiers that could be used to assess their psychological standing. Over time, the process has been adapted and used widely within the market research field to develop and promote consumer products. During the last 15 years the process has been gaining acceptance among nonprofit groups as a way to gain information to improve the design, implementation, and promotion of programs and services.

The purposes of this chapter are to (a) distinguish focus groups from other group processes used to gain information or input, (b) describe the history and characteristics of focus groups, and (c) provide examples of how focus group interviewing might be used by quality of life researchers to enhance their understanding of quality of life from the patients' perspective.

GROUP PROCESSES

In spite of our considerable experience and cumulative wisdom about groups, we often struggle with both the purpose and process of group interactions. Sometimes the purpose of the group is clearly understood, such as that of a nominating committee where the end result is a slate of officer candidates. Other times the purpose of the group is vaguely understood or perceived differently by participants. Too often we engage in group experiences without being clear about the purpose. Indeed, considerable misunderstanding can develop when the participants or planners are unclear about the group's purpose. It is important that the researcher be clear about the purpose of the group and inform the participants so everyone can contribute in the most useful way.

There are a variety of groups processes used by researchers and practitioners to gain insights and information. Among these are the nominal group process, Delphic groups, brainstorming, hearings, and focus groups. Each of these has a different purpose and group process procedure. We have all been involved in one or more of these group events. To clarify what a focus group is and isn't it may be helpful to

R. A. Krueger: Minnesota Extension Service and Department of Vocational Technical Education, University of Minnesota, St. Paul, Minnesota 55108.

contrast these various groups processes. The focus group differs in both purpose and process from the other group experiences.

The nominal group technique seeks to identify differing points of view and then to arrive at a mutually agreed upon solution or common ground. The processes used in the nominal technique help ensure that individual views are articulated and honored, and then that the most preferred solutions are collectively identified.

The Delphic technique also seeks to arrive at consensus, but through a set of stages that provide feedback and shift the level of understanding to progressively higher levels.

Brainstorming differs substantially in that it does not seek consensus but instead attempts to use the group to generate ideas to discover new, different, or creative solutions.

Public hearings are regularly used in democratic societies. The hearing has multiple purposes of fostering a sense of participation among those affected by future regulation or legislation and it attempts to help decision makers understand the critical arguments on either side of the issue.

When compared with these commonly used group procedures, the focus group has some similarities but also major differences that make it distinctive.

THE DISTINCTIVE ROLE FOR FOCUS GROUP RESEARCH

To a casual observer a focus group may resemble informal group discussions familiar to any of us. The conversation is, however, deliberately structured and carefully moderated to maximize opportunity for interaction in a permissive, nonthreatening environment. The purpose of the focus group is typically to hear the range of perceptions, insights, and points of view and from these to discover what themes reoccur, what ideas or arguments are persuasive, or how different groups of people see an issue or idea differently. Statistics are not used. People are usually not asked to vote. And participants can leave feeling okay that their perspective was different.

Participants have opportunities to hear opinions of others and are encouraged to present their views. A dynamic that often occurs in focus groups is that one idea triggers another and a seemingly simple topic is then discussed in considerable detail. A 2-minute response in an individual interview may become a 20-minute discussion in a focus group.

Focus group participants are selected based on the presence or absence of characteristics (e.g., gender, job, age, level of experience with the subject) that are expected to influence the way they see or experience an idea or situation. Focus groups provide an environment where disclosure is encouraged. The moderator's role is to gently guide the group through a predetermined set of open-ended questions.

Too often professionals (in education, medicine, public health) assume that they know the motivations and circumstances that guide the lives of those they serve. Often profes-

sionals have different values or beliefs than customers, which in turn bring different colors to how they react to, experience, or bring meaning to situations. We all filter experiences through values derived from our backgrounds, and we often assume that others would feel or think the same if only they really understood the issue. Focus groups respect differing values and experiences. By having people share in group settings, we as researchers either begin to get a glimmer of others' understandings or we advance our understanding of their experiences.

Focus group research is premised on the belief that wisdom is obtained not only from professionals but also from the target audience. Focus group participants may hold seemingly irrational views or illogical opinions. Nevertheless, the researcher treats each point of view with patience and respect. Nothing less will suffice. This approach is difficult for professionals who have spent a career finding and defending a particular truth—and then find that focus group participants with absolutely no formal training completely disregard scientific evidence.

THE EVOLUTION OF FOCUS GROUP RESEARCH

Much of the pioneering work in focus group research began with Robert Merton and his colleagues. Many procedures that have come to be accepted as common practice in focus group interviews were set forth in the classic work by Robert K. Merton, Marjorie Fiske, and Patricia L. Kendall, *The Focused Interview* (1). During the decades after World War II group interviewing was regarded with suspicion within the academic community. The prevailing norm was to interview people individually to avoid contamination and then researchers would consolidate the information into central themes. Market researchers were less troubled about dangers of contamination and through experimentation and practical experience found that carefully formed groups guided by a skillful interviewer could yield insights that were not emerging from individual, in-depth interviews. When conducted in a permissive environment these market research groups exhibited a candor that sanctioned divergent and opposing views and produced valuable information that guided product development.

It wasn't until the 1970s that social scientists began to rethink the benefits of group interviewing. The previous hesitation about contamination was reconsidered and the realization grew that individuals are often influenced in their decision making by people around them. It was also learned that the information obtained through focus groups was richer than that of individual interviews because people built on previous comments of others that led to greater depth of information. The focus group was considered to be a laboratory where one could observe emergence of opinions and learn about thought processes that guided consumer behavior. By the late 1970s and early 1980s a number of social scientists were using focus groups to gain information for needs assessment, program development, and program evaluation.

As applied social scientists renewed their interest in group interviewing they also adapted the focus group technique to fit a wider range of audiences. Market research focus groups targeted products used by consumers (often Caucasian) with purchasing power. Groups were conducted in special focus group rooms with one-way mirrors. The social scientists, however, sought out a broader range of participants, introduced topics of increased complexity and sought out meeting places that were comfortable and natural to participants. Social scientists also placed greater emphasis on systematic analysis strategies and applied traditional qualitative research analysis procedures to the focus group environment.

In the past two decades focus groups have expanded beyond the marketing research environment and have been applied to a host of concerns in nonprofit and public organizations. This acceptance by the social science community is an acknowledgment that focus group interviewing is a powerful research tool that can and should be adapted to fit changing needs, audiences, and environments.

ESSENTIAL FEATURES OF FOCUS GROUP RESEARCH

What Is a Focus Group?

In the past decade focus group interviewing has gained so much popularity that the term is often used inappropriately. It is not unusual to see the term *focus group* applied to group discussions (e.g., study groups, community hearings) that are considerably different from core principles that have historically been the hallmark of focus group interviews. Focus group interviews typically have five characteristics: (a) they involve a limited number of people, who (b) possess certain characteristics, who (c) provide data (d) of a qualitative nature (e) in a focused discussion.

Focus Groups Involve People

Focus groups are typically composed of five to ten people, but the size can range from as few as four to as many as 12. The size is conditioned by two factors: it must be small enough for everyone to have an opportunity to share insights and yet large enough to provide diversity. A rule of thumb is that the more expertise participants have on the subject the lower the number of participants in the group.

Focus Group Participants Are Similar

Focus groups are composed of people who are similar to each other. The nature of this homogeneity is determined by the purpose of the study. This similarity is a basis for recruitment, and participants are typically informed of these common factors at the beginning of the discussion. Traditionally focus groups had been composed of people who did not know each other, but more recent focus groups have been very successful with people acquainted with each other. However, power differentials between participants should be avoided. For example, mixing health providers and health recipients may be unwise because of the tendency for customers to be intimidated and defer to those who supposedly have more insight about the topic. Likewise, mixing different kinds or levels of health professionals in the same group may limit open communication.

Typically three groups are conducted of each participant category so the analyst can look for patterns of themes across the groups. It is dangerous to rely on the comments of one group. For example, in a recent study of rehabilitation services in Minnesota, at least three groups were conducted with each of the following types of people to obtain perspectives on mental health services: service providers, customers, mental health advocates, and government officials.

Focus Groups Are a Data Collection Procedure

Focus groups produce data of interest to researchers. This purpose differs from other group interactions where the goal is to reach consensus, provide recommendations, or make decisions. Focus groups work particularly well within a rather narrow purpose—to determine perceptions, feelings, and thinking of respondents to ideas, products, services, or opportunities.

Focus Groups Make Use of Qualitative Data

Focus groups produce qualitative data solicited primarily through open-ended questions but also through observations of respondents in a group discussion. Generally focus groups are audiotaped to capture ideas in the participants' words. An assistant moderator also usually takes notes. Quantitative data is not a product of focus groups. The limited number of participants and the method of selection of participants makes quantitative presentation of data inappropriate.

Focus Groups Have a Focused Discussion

Discussion topics or questions in a focus group are carefully predetermined, sequenced, and targeted to provide answers on critical aspects of the study. Two different strategies of asking questions are regularly used in focus groups. One style is the topic guide where the moderator will have a list of key words or short phrases that are used to ask conversational questions. The second style is the questioning route where questions are prepared word-for-word. The topic guide style, which is regularly used by professional moderators, is not recommended for novice moderators because it demands consistency in phrasing questions. The questioning route ensures that the questions are asked in a uniform manner and allows for greater comparability across different focus groups.

A distinctive characteristic of focus groups is the sequencing of questions. Questions at the beginning of the focus group are typically more general and designed to help participants gather their thoughts, reflect on their experiences, and hear about experiences of others. The most important questions in the focus group usually occur in the last half of the discussion period after participants have had the benefit of reflection and comparing their views to that of others in the group.

CRITICAL FACTORS IN SUCCESSFUL FOCUS GROUPS

Skillful Moderating

One of the essential features of successful focus groups is the moderating strategy of the researcher. Quality questions are important, but results can be jeopardized by the moderator. Beginning moderators have difficulty listening and curtailing their desire to inject their own opinions, answers, or values. Moderators are neither teachers providing instruction nor participants in an engaging conversation, but more like sponges soaking up the insights of the participants. Moderators are not judges deciding appropriate and inappropriate responses but rather sympathetic listeners creating an environment where people feel free to share.

The moderator establishes a permissive and open environment, guides the group in the beginning questions, and encourages participants to talk to each other about the topic. An assistant moderator helps with the logistics (tape recording, note taking, refreshments) but does not participate in the group discussion. The moderator guides the group discussion using questions, pauses, probes, and eye contact. A more complete discussion of moderating skills is found in Chapter 4 of *Focus Groups* by R. A. Krueger (2).

Asking Good Questions in a Focus Group

Questions are the heart of the focus group interview. Researchers need to think carefully about the wording and sequencing of questions. Good questions appear to be spontaneous, but have been carefully selected and phrased in advance to elicit the maximum amount of information. Questions used in a focused interview look deceptively simple. Usually a focused interview will include fewer than a dozen questions and often around eight to ten total. If these questions were asked in an individual interview, the respondent would probably fully answer them in a few minutes. However, when these questions are used in a group environment the discussion can last for several hours. As participants answer questions the responses spark new ideas or connections from others.

When selecting questions consider these pointers:

1. Use open-ended questions. Open-ended questions allow respondents to answer from a variety of dimensions. In open-ended questions the answer is not implied nor is the manner of response suggested. The major advantage of the open-ended question is that it reveals what is on the respondent's mind as opposed to what the interviewer suspects is on the respondent's mind.
2. Avoid dichotomous questions. Dichotomous questions are those that can be answered with a simple "yes" or "no" response. The yes-no question usually does not evoke the desired group discussion. They also tend to elicit ambiguous responses, which can muddy the discussion.
3. Avoid asking "Why?" Why questions present difficulties for several reasons. First, they imply a rational answer, one developed by thought and reflection. In reality, a number of decisions result from impulse, habit, tradition, or in a manner using limited rationality. When asked why, respondents often attempt to provide answers that seem rational or appropriate to the situation. Second, why questions are imprecise. When asked why, respondents typically comment in a variety of ways. They may describe the influences that prompted them to attend ("My boss told me to come!"), or desirable attributes of training ("The instructor was an expert in the topic"). Instead of asking why, a preferred option is to ask about factors that influence behavior or positive attributes of the training.

Analysis of Focus Group Results

Analysis can be the "black hole" of focus group interviewing. It can be time-consuming and frustrating, and results are vulnerable to criticism. Analysis must be systematic and verifiable. It is systematic in that there is a systematic procedure of data collection and analysis followed by the researcher. Data gathering is not arbitrary or accidental; it follows a prescribed set of procedures. Furthermore, the analysis process is verifiable in that another researcher can follow the trail of evidence and replicate or audit the analysis. A lengthy description of these protocols is included in *Focus Groups* (2).

Analysis begins immediately after the first interview, when the moderator and assistant moderator spend time reflecting on what was said and how it was stated. Later the analyst (usually the moderator) examines the data (tape recording or transcript or field notes) and highlights the themes or patterns that emerge from similar groups.

POTENTIAL USES OF FOCUS GROUPS IN QUALITY OF LIFE ASSESSMENTS

The focus group interview has potential for assisting researchers explore the issues and interrelationships in quality of life assessment. Here are some examples of how focus groups might be used to enhance the study of quality of life:

Focus groups can be used to gain understanding of quality of life from the perspective of different populations. What does quality of life mean to different people? What are the ingredients of quality of life? How do specific ingredients fit into a larger whole? How do different categories of people view quality of life, such as healthy people, or people of differing ages, ethnicity or race, gender, income, occupation, or geographic location? Learning how different people view quality of life will provide a greater understanding of the concept and how it might be assessed. It also can help to support the predictive power of other studies.

Focus groups can be used to help generate ideas related to the design of scales or tests. For example, health care professionals, patients, or family members could be asked to talk about the kinds of things that might be important to examine when measuring quality of life of AIDS patients. This general discussion creates an opportunity for participants to talk about what first comes to their mind or what is most important to them. Ideas are often generated that the research team may not have considered. If no new ideas are generated, the discussions can provide affirmation to the research team that they are on the right track.

Focus groups can be used to help refine a test instrument and the process for administration. Focus groups with health professionals and patients can help answer the following types of questions: Are quality of life indicators used within a particular scale or test complete and comprehensive? Are indicators missing, redundant, or inappropriate? Are questions understandable? Do the questions have face validity? Do questions have the same meaning to different types of people? What pitfalls might be experienced in administering the test? How can these be avoided?

Getting people's reactions to instruments, questions, and protocols early in a process can save time, resources, backtracking, and costly mistakes. Several years ago public health researchers in Florida were concerned about the lack of participation in a low-income health clinic. Mail surveys of current and potential clientele revealed that limiting factors were cost and distance to the clinic. Serious consideration was given to further reducing patient cost and building additional clinics. But before these steps were taken researchers conducted a series of focus group interviews. The focus groups confirmed that cost and distance were important, but a new and unforeseen barrier emerged as even more important. Participants said they were not treated with respect at the clinics and that even if new clinics were built and costs further reduced they would still be reluctant to use the services. Unfortunately, when researchers designed the mail-out survey with closed-ended questions they failed to include a response choice on treatment of patients or a blank line for other comments.

Researchers assumed that patients were treated with respect but patients felt differently. General discussions about the barriers and incentives for attending public health clinics revealed the problem.

An advantage of focus group research is that the researcher doesn't need to know all possible response categories. The genius of focus group research lies in asking the right open-ended question and then letting participants offer answers.

Focus groups can be used to help examine priorities among varying quality of life indicators. For example: What priorities should be given to various quality of life indicators and are these priorities consistent over time? How do priorities change as patients progress in treatment? Are those indicators that are considered priorities early in treatment the same over time? What about priorities prior to treatment, versus during or after?

Focus groups can be used to help interpret data collected through other tests and approaches. At times researchers obtain information that is counterintuitive, surprising, and/or difficult to explain. Focus groups can help shed new light on confusing data. In the group, researchers can describe the situation, share the data, and ask for ideas about what is happening. Patients or health professionals may be quickly able to provide insight into the situation.

Focus groups can be used to help tell the story—to report findings. When reporting findings the golden rule is to keep your audience in mind and write for that audience. Often our problem is that we don't know the audience very well and we don't know how they would talk about the issue. Focus groups with a particular group can give us ideas about how to present information to that audience: Who would be a credible spokesperson? What kind of information is most important to share? What are the key messages to be sent? What images should be shared? What media should be used? What distribution channels are these people tapped into?

For example, to help tell the story of the advantages of breast-feeding, low income mothers were asked to review materials to be used in WIC clinics. The mothers said the women pictured in the brochures weren't low income mothers. Their image was that wealthy women breast-fed, and the pictures in the materials reinforced this belief for them. The women were asked to help select images that were more appropriate and the materials were then revised using new images and quotes obtained from them during the focus groups. The revised materials were retested and have been used very successfully in the southeastern United States.

The focus group interview has potential for use before, during, and after quality of life tests. Focus groups can be used before implementing quality of life indicators. The researcher can determine which tests are appropriate and meaningful and how they might be best implemented. Focus groups during the assessment period serve as a formative evaluation to determine if modifications or changes are needed in the ongoing measurement to ensure quality of results. They can also supply a complementary source of data that can be used to make reporting more accessible to a variety of audiences. Finally, focus group interviews can be conducted after other quality of life assessments to provide additional interpretation of results.

CONCLUSIONS

The focus group interview provides researchers with information that typically cannot be obtained by other methodological procedures. Focus groups are unique in that they allow researchers to listen and observe a target audience discuss the topic of concern in a permissive and nonthreatening environment. When the purpose of research is to gain insight into complex human activity the focus group interview can be indispensable. Focus group interviews can provide a valuable complement to quality of life indicators. They enable the researcher to bridge the gap between the patient and the health professional. Focus groups can be helpful in gaining understanding of the patient's point of view. This understanding can be of particular benefit in refining quality of life tests, determining priorities in those instruments, interpreting results, and reporting findings.

REFERENCES

1. Merton RK, Fiske M, Kendall PL. *The focused interview,* 2nd ed. Glencoe, IL: Free Press, 1956.
2. Krueger RA. *Focus groups: a practical guide for applied research.* Thousand Oaks, CA: Sage, 1994.

Quality of Life and Pharmacoeconomics in Clinical
Trials, Second Edition, edited by B. Spilker.
Lippincott-Raven Publishers, Philadelphia © 1996.

CHAPTER 42

Incorporating Trade-Offs in Quality of Life Assessment

Andrew J. Martin, Thomas S. Lumley, and R. John Simes

INTRODUCTION

Quality of life is an important factor in the evaluation of many medical therapies and treatment decisions, as is information on survival benefits (or risks) and economic costs. These data may be difficult to interpret when trade-offs arise between aspects of quality of life, or between overall quality of life and other outcomes. In such cases, the relative value of treatment benefits versus costs (both economic and otherwise) will be important in decision making. For example, adjuvant chemotherapy for breast cancer may be considered beneficial only if the poorer quality of life associated with side effects of therapy is outweighed by the longer survival benefit anticipated. Similarly, chemotherapy for advanced cancer may be preferred provided improvements in quality of life (associated with better cancer control) outweigh any side effects of treatment. A patient with significant disability from ischemic chest pain may be willing to undergo surgery, and thereby accept some risk of operative mortality, if it provides long-term improvements in quality of life by reliev-

ing chest pain. In each of these examples, a value judgment is needed on the relative importance of the possible benefits and costs of treatment in order to make a treatment choice.

While value judgments should be viewed from the patient's perspective, it is important to distinguish the average value of a group of patients for a particular outcome (useful in making policy decisions) from the sometimes considerably different perspective of individual patients (needed for individualized treatment choice). For policy decisions, information collected in clinical trials on different aspects of quality of life, as well as the relative value or utility of each component, will be particularly valuable. For individual treatment decisions, simply combining individual quality of life information into a summary score will be often inappropriate. Methods for applying an individual's preferences to data collected in the clinical trials are needed.

This chapter reviews some approaches to assessing quality of life information in clinical trials where trade-offs in treatment choice are involved. Some of these approaches employ formal methodologies, such as decision analysis (1), to systematically incorporate large amounts of information into the trade-off assessment. In these cases information from clinical trials may assist in providing more accurate estimates of risks or probabilities for different health outcomes where the synthesis of the information is then done explicitly in the decision analysis. Alternatively the components of quality of

A. J. Martin, T. S. Lumley, and R. J. Simes: NHMRC Clinical Trials Centre and the Statistical Centre for the Australian-New Zealand Breast Cancer Trials Group, University of Sydney, NSW 2006, Australia.

life may be combined within the trial itself into global quality of life scores or other combined measures. The utility of different outcomes is implicit in these combined scores. Approaches that allow the use of individual preferences to be applied to data from clinical trials are also presented.

TYPES OF TRADE-OFFS

Trade-Offs Between Aspects of Quality of Life

Information on quality of life is often collected in clinical trials and used in treatment evaluations, and plays a substantial role in treatment decisions (2–14). Quality of life outcomes may be critical in many treatment choices, dominating survival or financial issues. For some situations the impact of treatment on quality of life may be clear-cut with a benefit of one treatment over another in terms of each aspect of quality of life measured. More often, however, each therapy will be associated with some advantages and some disadvantages. How the components of quality of life are then combined will be very important in determining which approach appears to be preferred. In these circumstances, while it is often desirable to collapse these data into a single summary measure to facilitate treatment comparisons, it can be difficult or even inappropriate to do so without additional information on the subjective importance that patients place on the various components.

Example 1

The Australian-New Zealand Breast Cancer Trials Group (15) has been undertaking a trial comparing two chemotherapy strategies for patients with advanced breast cancer. The study has been designed to test whether a less toxic but less active treatment, mitozantrone, compared with a standard combination chemotherapy, CMFP (cyclophosphamide, methotrexate, 5-fluorouracil, and prednisone), could be given as initial therapy and result in better quality of life without compromising survival. If no significant differences in survival are found, then treatment choice will depend principally on the impact of each treatment on quality of life. Patients have been asked to complete a set of linear analog scales on 13 health-related factors, with the plan to compare treatment differences in quality of life over the first 13 weeks of treatment. Since the trial is not yet complete, hypothetical differences generated from an interim data set are shown in Table 1. One treatment (A) was associated with significantly better quality of life in terms of less hair loss and less tiredness but worse quality of life in terms of other factors such as pain, mood, nausea and vomiting, and appetite/taste. A single overall measure of quality of life (16) did not differ significantly (statistically) but tended to favor treatment B slightly.

In this example trade-offs among aspects of quality of life can make the treatment comparison difficult. An unweighted combination of the patient's separate scores as recommended

TABLE 1. *Quality of life comparisons in the ANZ8614 advanced breast cancer trial: hypothetical differences averaged over 13 weeks of treatment and relative weights for 11 of the 13 quality of life scales*[a]

Quality of life component	Weight	Comparison favors	Degree
Scales of Preistman and Baum			
Physical well-being	15.5	B	+
Mood	5.5	B	++
Pain	4.2	B	++
Nausea and vomiting	0.55	B	++
Appetite	5.1	B	+
GLQ-8 questionnaire			
Feeling anxious/ depressed	6.65	B	+
Feeling sick/nausea	–	B	++
Numbness/pins and needles	0.25	–	
Hair loss	1[b]	A	++++
Tiredness	3.9	A	+
Appetite/sense of taste	–	B	++
Sexual interest/ ability	1.15	B	+
Thought of having treatment	2.9	B	+

[a]The feeling sick/nausea and appetite/sense of taste scales of the GLQ-8 were very similar to two scales of the Preistman and Baum questionnaire, and so their weights were set to 0.
[b]Weights are relative to hair loss = 1.
+, Not statistically significant ($p > .05$); ++, $p < .05$; +++, $p < .01$; ++++, $p < .001$.

by Cox et al. (17) has the merit of simplicity but may give too much or too little emphasis to certain aspects by assuming that patients place an equal subjective weight on each aspect of quality of life measured. A single global measure provides an implicit weighting of each component from the patient perspective but may be less precise. A weighted combination of quality of life components according to averaged or individual patient preferences seems desirable.

Trade-Offs Between Quality of Life and Quantity of Life

Quality and quantity of life are clearly both important treatment outcomes, and ideally a treatment should enhance the two. Sometimes treatment may provide gains in survival at the expense of worse quality of life due to side effects or as a consequence of major surgery. For example, adjuvant chemotherapy can result in modest survival gains (e.g., 10% increase in the 5-year survival rate for premenopausal patients with node positive breast cancer) (18) while inducing a number of unpleasant side effects such as nausea, vomiting, and hair loss. Here, patients opting to have chemotherapy should feel that the increased chance for longer survival justifies the toxicity of treatment. In contrast, some treatment decisions may be dominated by concerns to improve quality of life rather than survival. For example, some patients with coronary heart disease may have better quality of life following coronary artery bypass surgery due to the alleviation of ischemic chest pain, yet run a small risk of operative mortality without necessarily prolonging long-term survival (19). Surgery will still be a valued therapy in this setting provided patients are willing to take a small risk of early death in return for the long-term symptomatic relief. In each of these two cases, the impact of trade-offs between quality of life and survival need to be evaluated to assess the net value of each treatment. Such an evaluation must incorporate the subjective importance patients place on quality of life outcomes relative to survival outcomes.

Early Versus Later Treatment Benefits and Costs

In addition to weighing up the relative importance of different outcomes, the timing of benefits and costs may also be critical in treatment choice. A therapy that improves life expectancy or 5-year survival rates will not necessarily be preferred if the immediate mortality risk is too high, such as with some radical surgery. McNeil et al. (20) have illustrated this issue well several years ago when comparing the relative merits of surgery versus radiotherapy for lung cancer. Although surgery was likely to lead to greater long-term survival, on average, it placed patients at immediate risk of operative mortality. Hence surgery was not automatically the preferred treatment. A smoking cessation intervention may ultimately lead to substantial improvements in future quality of life and survival but at the expense of more immediate unpleasant withdrawal symptoms. The poor compliance rates in some programs are consistent with people placing more value on their immediate well-being relative to future health benefits. In these and other cases, evidence suggests that people tend to discount the value of future outcomes. Gafni and Torrance (21) detail several reasons why people's preferences for treatment outcomes may be affected by the timing of benefits and costs including the concepts of risk-aversion, time preference, and decreasing marginal value. It may therefore be important that future health benefits are discounted at an appropriate rate or, even better, that utilities on treatment outcomes incorporate patient preferences based on the timing of those outcomes.

Trade-Offs Between Treatment Benefits and Their Financial Costs

For many treatment decisions, after consideration of the above trade-offs there may be a clear net clinical benefit for one treatment over the other for the individual patient. Yet difficult decisions may still need to be made from the community perspective as to which health care programs to finance in order to best use limited health care resources. If the health gain for individual patients is small and at considerable expense to health care resources, then alternative uses of the funds may provide greater health benefit to the community. Health care policy makers must therefore weigh up the therapeutic benefits of a treatment against its economic cost to ensure that health care resources are used efficiently.

Recently, a large trial evaluating thrombolytic regimens for acute myocardial infarction has demonstrated a reduction in mortality and net clinical benefit for patients receiving a more expensive regimen using tissue plasminogen activator compared with previous standard therapy using streptokinase (22). While this trial suggested a modest net clinical benefit for individual patients, the decision to use this treatment more widely in the coronary care setting is dependent on the health gains that might be obtained by alternative use of such funds (23). Trade-offs between treatment efficacy and their financial cost are unavoidable and must be assessed. Methods for assessing such trade-offs, in particular using cost-effectiveness analysis and cost-utility analysis are described in detail elsewhere (24–29) and in Chapter 114 of this book.

GENERAL APPROACHES IN ASSESSING TRADE-OFFS

Three general steps are suggested to optimally assess trade-offs involving quality of life outcomes in clinical trials. First, accurate and detailed information on quality of life and other treatment outcomes should be collected. Second, the relative importance of these outcomes, from the patient's perspective, must be assessed so that a treatment recommendation can be made. Third, the robustness of such recommendations to individual patient preferences or values should be subjected to a sensitivity or threshold analysis.

Measuring Quality of Life and Other Outcomes

Methods for measuring quality of life (30–37), for obtaining other treatment outcome information in clinical trials (38), and for assessing the economic costs of therapies (24–29) have been reviewed elsewhere. In particular, methods for quality of life assessment are covered in detail in Chapters 11 to 36 of this book. It is important that the quality of life measures used in an assessment have been previously shown to be reliable, valid, and sensitive to anticipated changes in quality of life for the treatments in question. Further, it is helpful that measures of quality of life are used from which utility data can be derived (see below).

Evaluating the Importance of Benefits and Costs

In weighing up the relative benefits and costs of each treatment, a value judgment is needed on the importance of each outcome. This may be undertaken *implicitly* by the decision maker by considering all relevant information simultaneously and subconsciously applying value judgments to trade-offs in the different outcomes. However, trade-off evaluations quickly become an overwhelming task to handle implicitly when the volume of information that needs to be considered is large, when there are uncertainties relating to benefits, costs or their relative importance, and/or when the evaluation incorporates the preferences of more than one individual. In these situations it is often desirable to estimate the relative importance of the separate components of an assessment along a value or utility scale and combine these data more *explicitly* using methods such as decision analysis.

Value and Utility Scales

The distinction between value and utility scales is subtle, though important. *Value* scales can be thought of as reflecting preference for certain or sure outcomes, whereas *utility* scales reflect strength of preference of uncertain outcomes. The utility of 5 years' symptom-free survival may differ, for example, from the utility of an uncertain outcome that on average results in the same 5 years symptom-free survival, but with some probability of a longer or shorter time. Utility assessments provide a means of comparing the importance of a therapy that offers a good chance of a mediocre outcome and a therapy that offers a slim chance of an especially valued outcome. Utility-based measures are therefore useful for assessing preferences for therapies since treatment outcomes are always uncertain to some extent. Utility-based data has the advantage of allowing decision making to be based on the principles of expected utility theory (39,40). Although this approach can provide a sound basis for prescriptive decision making, some have raised concerns about its validity (40–43), as well as problems in the measurement of utilities (44–48).

Combining Outcome Data

Two broad strategies can be adopted when combining outcomes and incorporating trade-offs in quality of life assessment. The first involves asking individuals themselves to make a trade-off evaluation based on the information for the separate component outcomes. The second involves combining data on quality of life and/or other outcomes from a clinical trial to form a summary measure that reflects averaged or group preferences.

Group preferences need to be considered whenever a treatment evaluation or decision has the potential to affect more than one individual, but combining *individual preferences* has given rise to controversy and may violate conditions of individual rankings (49) or individual utilities (50). In practice there are various reasonable methods of assigning utilities to outcomes when decisions must be based on the preferences of a group of people, yet different methods may give different results. The theoretical difficulties involved

mean that the rationale for using group utility data is less compelling than in the individual case.

For this reason the robustness of treatment recommendations based on average preferences should be reviewed further by varying utilities across a plausible range, to judge the potential impact a trade-off evaluation will have on individual treatment decisions.

SPECIFIC APPROACHES TO TRADE-OFF EVALUATIONS

Trade-Offs Between Aspects of Quality of Life

Single Direct Measures

The simplest way of assessing trade-offs between aspects of quality of life is to ask individuals to rate the value or utility of their overall quality of life as a single measure. Here patients implicitly weigh up the relative importance of different aspects of quality of life. The average quality of life score for the trial will then reflect averaged individual, or group, preferences. An example of a value-based global quality of life measure is the GLQ-Uniscale (16), on which the patients rate their quality of life on a single linear analog scale. An example of a utility-based global quality of life measure is the standard gamble (51), where the patients rate their current quality of life against taking a gamble with a chance of full health and a risk of death. The utility assigned to their overall quality of life is obtained by varying the probabilities of the gamble until it is considered of equivalent value to present quality of life. The time trade-off method, devised by Torrance et al. (52), is a simpler alternative to the standard gamble and produces scores that are similar to, but usually lower than, those elicited using standard gambles (53,54). These questions ask for the shorter time period in full health considered equivalent to a longer period of survival with current quality of life. Time trade-off questions are a theoretically less attractive means of assessing utility than standard gamble questions, but in practice are generally easier to administer. Standard gamble questions are more complicated and need to be administered in a face-to-face interview. In contrast, even self-administered time trade-off questions are feasible. However, irrespective of whether these three methods provide a true utility measure or not, they each enable any trade-offs between different components of quality of life to be reflected in the summary measure.

Example 2

Modifications of the self-administered time trade-off question in Fig. 1 have been used successfully as a global quality of life assessment in a number of clinical trials being conducted in association with the National Health and Medical Research Council (NHMRC) Clinical Trials Centre. One of these, the Australian arm of the International tPA/SK

If you consider yourself in less than full health, please help us determine how important quality of life versus length of life is to you by answering the following hypothetical question.

Imagine a friend who is expected to live for 15 years with the same quality of life as you have now. Suppose treatment could restore them to full health, but would shorten their life. At most, how much time would you advise giving up out of 15 years?

I would advise giving up at most ____ years and/or ____ months in order to return to full health.

FIG. 1. Self-administered time trade-off.

(tissue plasminogen activator/streptokinase) Mortality Trial, comparing two thrombolytic therapies for acute myocardial infarction, evaluated quality of life in 776 patients by means of a questionnaire that included a self-administered time trade-off question (55).

The time trade-off data shown by dyspnea grades in Table 2 indicate that patients would on average be willing to give up more time to return to full health if suffering from more significant symptoms of dyspnea ($p < .001$). For example, patients with dyspnea present only on strenuous exertion were prepared, on average, to give up 0.9 years out of 15 to be restored to full health whereas the four patients with dyspnea at rest were prepared to trade 5.0 years to be restored to full health.

Combined Measures

A disadvantage of single-item quality of life assessments, be they value- or utility-based, is that they provide no descriptive information on the components comprising quality of life. This makes it more difficult to explicitly state what

trade-offs are involved (if any) in the summary measure and whether there is a need to tailor treatment choice to individual preferences. A number of multidimensional instruments with value-based (56,57) and (quasi) utility-based scoring systems (2,58,59) exist. One problem common to several of these instruments is that their scoring systems are based on the preferences of population samples, and so do not necessarily reflect the preferences of the patient. Studies have shown that different population groups assign different utilities to health states [see Froberg and Kane (60) for a review]. One method for ensuring that the quality of life information obtained using multidimensional instruments is summarized in such a way as to reflect the preferences of the patients filling them in is to use a self-calibrating scoring approach.

If both a multidimensional instrument and a simple overall quality of life measure are administered to the same group of subjects, it is possible to produce a self-calibrating measure of overall quality of life, where the relationship between the dimensions of quality of life is estimated by linear regression and the resulting weights are applied to calculate an overall score. The effect of this is to produce a single score that measures the same overall quality of life as the original unidimensional measure but has substantially less test-retest variability due to the incorporation of information from the multidimensional questionnaire. The weights derived by this procedure also indicate the relative importance of quality of life dimensions and it is possible to calculate the extent to which the unidimensional measure contains information from unmeasured dimensions of quality of life.

This method, described in detail by Lumley et al. (61), creates two unidimensional measures, one that combines only the aspects of quality of life measured in the multidimensional questionnaire (a subset estimate) and one that also includes the original unidimensional measure (a global estimate). The former has greater reliability and may be easier to interpret, but only measures aspects of quality of life included in the multidimensional questionnaire; the latter always measures the same quantity as the original unidimensional questionnaire, but more accurately. The level of agreement between the two indicates the extent to which the multidimensional questionnaire measures all aspects of quality of life affected by the treatments.

TABLE 2. Time trade-off data from tPA/SK trial

	Completed time trade-off	Time trade-off (years traded)[a]
Functional status[b]		
No dyspnea	344 (48%)	0.5
1 On strenuous exertion	261 (37%)	0.9
2 On normal exertion	66 (9%)	2.3
3 On mild exertion	38 (5%)	2.3
4 At rest	4 (1%)	5.0
Karnofsky category (66)		
A: Normal activity	571 (80%)	0.5
B: Unable to work	140 (20%)	2.4
C: Unable to care for self	3 (0%)	9.6
Total	714	

[a]Average number of years patients were willing to trade out of 15 years in order to be restored to full health.
[b]Dyspnea grades 1–4 are based on New York Heart Association (67) classification. No grade was given for 1 patient.

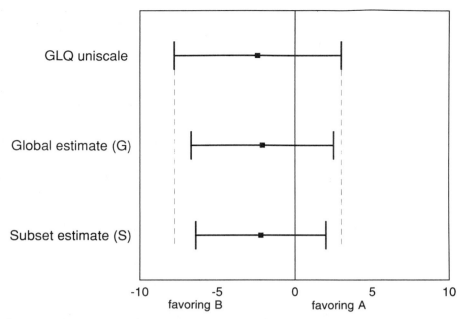

FIG. 2. Summaries of quality of life differences and 95% confidence intervals in ANZ8614 breast cancer trial. For three summary measures of overall quality of life over the first 13 weeks of treatment based on the data described in Table 1. The GLQ (General Life Quality) uniscale is a single linear analog scale and the global and subset estimates are weighted combinations of 13 separate dimensions of quality of life. The global estimate also includes the uniscale quality of life measure; the subset estimate does not.

Example 1 (Continued)

This approach was applied to the data set from the ANZ8614 advanced breast cancer trial described in Table 1. Figure 2 shows 95% confidence intervals for the difference between mean quality of life changes over the first 13 weeks of treatment with CMFP or mitozantrone as measured by the original unidimensional measure [the GLQ uniscale (16)] and the two combined assessments. The subset estimate provides a summary measure of the 13 quality of life items weighted according to the relative importance of each measure in predicting the GLQ uniscale. The global estimate also captures other aspects of quality of life judged important by the patient but not reflected in the 13 items by including a weight for the uniscale as well. The figure shows an increase in precision resulting from the combined measures. To increase the precision of comparison based on the GLQ uniscale to that of the global combined estimate it would have been necessary to recruit 37% more patients to the trial.

Table 1 shows the weights derived for the quality of life questions administered in this trial [the GLQ-8 and five linear analog self-assessment scales of Priestman and Baum (16)] for this group of patients. It shows that some of the commonly reported adverse effects of chemotherapy such as nausea and hair loss were less important in this group of patients with advanced disease than other items such as physical well-being and mood. Broadly similar weights were found in another advanced cancer trial but different weights might well arise from an adjuvant chemotherapy trial where

there is no alleviation of symptoms to balance the toxic effects of the treatment.

Assessing Trade-Offs Between Quality of Life and Quantity of Life

Time Trade-off Questions

In addition to being useful as a method for estimating the utility of various levels of quality of life, time trade-off questions may also be used to explore an individual's preference for trade-offs between quality of life and survival outcomes. The following example of this approach comes from Coates and Simes (62).

Example 3

To assess whether patients with early breast cancer felt the increased chance of longer survival justified the toxicity of adjuvant chemotherapy, a series of time trade-off questions were administered by interview in a study with 104 cancer patients who had previously received adjuvant chemotherapy. The time trade-off questions involved asking patients to express a preference between living for 5 years (or 15 years) without any adjuvant chemotherapy or living for a longer period of time following an initial 6-month course of CMF chemotherapy.

The results (Table 3) showed that most patients felt even modest survival benefits of an additional 1 to 2 years out-

TABLE 3. *Preferences for CMF*

Hypothetical survival benefit of CMF	Proportion of patients preferring CMF given...	
	a 5-year life expectancy without CMF	a 15-year life expectancy without CMF
Additional 1 year survival	77%	61%
Additional 2 year survival	89%	74%
Additional 5 year survival	98%	91%

weighed the side effects of adjuvant chemotherapy. Such benefits are within the survival gains estimated from an overview of adjuvant chemotherapy trials (18). Although the majority of patients rated a benefit of one year survival as worthwhile, there was a small group that indicated that even very large benefits would not be enough to justify the side effects.

Interestingly, the results also revealed that the utility of survival benefits with chemotherapy were relative to expected survival without chemotherapy. The additional benefit of 1 year on top of 5 years life expectancy was more attractive (77% answered that chemotherapy was worthwhile) than 1 year on top of 15 (only 61% answered that chemotherapy was worthwhile). The timing of the benefit associated with treatment appeared to have been important and suggests that the patients interviewed tended to discount future benefits.

Quality-Adjusted Survival

Trade-off preferences can also be assessed using data collected in clinical trials by evaluating quality of life and survival data along a common index such as quality-adjusted survival time. The quality-adjusted survival model involves translating a treatment outcome (e.g., 5 years survival with mild side effects) into an equally preferable amount of time spent in full health (e.g., as 4.5 years with full health). The quality-adjusted survival associated with a particular treatment regimen can be calculated by weighting survival curves or by partitioning survival curves into time spent in various health states and calculating a weighted sum of these components.

If quality of life data are regularly collected in a clinical trial, an estimate of quality of life can be produced for individuals (or treatment arms) at any given time post-baseline by interpolating between assessments. This information can be used to estimate quality-adjusted survival or quality-adjusted life years by applying it to the group's survival data.

Unfortunately if the survival times are censored this method is biased. The difficulty is somewhat subtle, but is a consequence of the fact that people censored with a small number of accumulated quality-adjusted life years (QALYs) tend to have low quality of life and so will have accumulated few extra QALYs when they die. As the accumulated QALYs

at censoring predict the QALYs accumulated after censoring, the censoring process is informative and standard survival analysis techniques give biased results (63). The partitioned survival analysis approach (63,64) avoids the problem of informative censoring by partitioning the survival curve from baseline into time spent in discrete health states. With cancer, these states may be toxicity (TOX), time without symptom or toxicity (TWiST), time spent with symptoms (SYM), and time spent in relapse (REL).

Example 4

Figure 3 illustrates this approach comparing two of the arms of the Ludwig III trial: adjuvant chemo-endocrine therapy (CMFpT) and no adjuvant therapy (observation) in patients with postmenopausal breast cancer. Patients receiving adjuvant chemotherapy had a longer time without symptoms

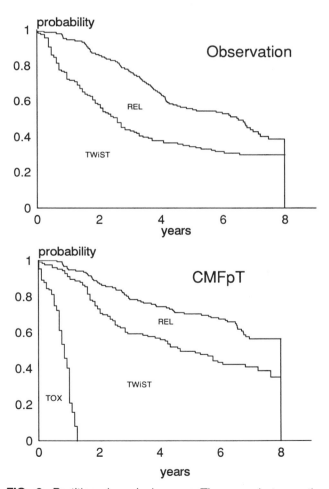

FIG. 3. Partitioned survival curves. The areas between the curves indicate the time spent in each health state for the two treatment arms (CMFpT and Observation). The area is multiplied by the utility weight for the health state and summed to give a quality-adjusted survival estimate. This chart is an updated version of a previously published analysis (63).

and toxicity (TWiST) than the control arm but at the expense of an initial period with toxicity (TOX). The total quality adjusted survival (Q-TWiST) was based on the total time in each of the states weighted by the utility of each health state. This generally resulted in more Q-TWiST for adjuvant therapy.

One of the greatest advantages of the Q-TWiST method is that is lends itself nicely to threshold analyses (discussed below), where the results are presented as a graph or table of the weights for which the two treatments are equally preferred. These weights can then be compared with preferences elicited from an individual patient and a simple decision reached.

The main disadvantage of the Q-TWiST method is that it is restricted to a small number of discrete states, each of which must be assigned a single, constant weight. This is reasonable in many adjuvant cancer therapy trials but is difficult in many other situations. If too few states are used, the assumption of a constant weight becomes untenable; if too many are used, it becomes difficult to track all the transitions between them.

SENSITIVITY AND THRESHOLD ANALYSIS

Many of the methods discussed so far for evaluating trade-offs between treatment benefits and costs are based upon the preferences of groups of individuals, that is, on averaged data from clinical trials. This sort of information is important in terms of providing overall treatment recommendations and for making policy decisions. Nevertheless, it is important to realize that group-based preferences do not necessarily reflect the opinions of individual patients faced with a treatment decision. Sensitivity and threshold analyses provide a means of exploring the impact of a range of different perspectives on treatment decisions or evaluations (65). If conclusions are especially sensitive to differences in individual patient preferences then the universal adoption of a therapy cannot be recommended. Consequently, the threshold analysis can help identify and simplify what information on patient preferences is needed for treatment recommendations.

A sensitivity analysis applied to trade-off assessment involves repeating the original analysis with different utility values for treatment outcomes, or using a different choice of statistical model. If these analyses give results within a close interval, greater confidence can be given to recommendations remaining stable for different patient utilities.

In some simple situations when there are only two or three uncertain parameters, it may be possible to go further than a sensitivity analysis and consider all possible values of the parameters. For example, in the Q-TWiST analysis described earlier (Example 4), the results depend on the two weights assigned to the TOX (toxicity) and REL (symptomatic relapse) health states. These two quantities can be plotted on a graph (Fig. 4) with an individual patient's preferences corresponding to a point on the graph. The lines on the graph

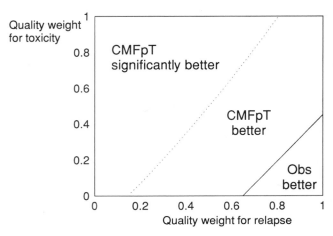

FIG. 4. Threshold analysis based on quality-adjusted survival accumulated over 6 years. A point on this chart indicates the values attached to time in toxicity and time in relapse by an individual. The *solid line* indicates the threshold at which the two treatments appear equally preferable. The *dotted line* is a 95% confidence limit for this threshold and indicates where a test comparing the quality-adjusted survival times would give a *p* value of .05. The three regions indicate values for which Observation is preferred, CMFpT is preferred, and CMFpT is preferred with 95% confidence. This chart is based on that presented by Glasziou et al. (63).

divide it into regions where no treatment (observation) is preferred, chemotherapy is preferred, and where chemotherapy is preferred with 95% confidence. The graph indicates that for most weights where the utility of TOX is greater than for REL, chemotherapy is the preferred option. For individuals where this amount is known on preferences, more detailed preference assessment is not needed.

The only drawback of threshold analysis is that it becomes impractical when more than three or four quantities are involved. It may be possible to simplify a problem if the values for all but a few of the quantities do not affect the decision. For example, in the ANZ8614 example discussed earlier the weight for numbness will not affect the treatment decision as there is no difference between treatments in this aspect of quality of life.

CONCLUSIONS

Trade-offs between aspects of quality of life, and between quality of life and other treatment outcomes and costs regularly arise in the evaluation of therapies and in medical decision making. Because of this, it is important to collect not only descriptive information on aspects of quality of life in clinical trials, but also data on the relative importance or utility patients place on the quality of life components measured, relative to survival and other treatment outcomes. These data enable policy decisions or general recommendations to be made in the presence of trade-offs, yet does not necessarily facilitate individual treatment decisions because individual preferences may differ substantially from averaged or group preferences. Sensitivity and threshold analysis, however, provides a method for utilizing averaged data from clinical trials to reach such personalized treatment decisions.

While none of the assessment procedures presented in this chapter is perfect, they allow many unavoidable trade-off decisions to be addressed in a clear and open manner, taking into account all the available evidence on patient preferences and treatment outcomes.

ACKNOWLEDGMENTS

We wish to thank the International Breast Cancer Study Group and the Australian-New Zealand Breast Cancer Trials Group for providing breast cancer data from the Ludwig III trial and the ANZ8614 trial.

REFERENCES

1. Weinstein MC, Fineberg HV, Elstein AS, Frazier HS, Neuhauser D, Neutra RR, McNeil BJ. *Clinical decision analysis*. Philadelphia: WB Saunders, 1980.
2. Kaplan RM, Anderson JP, Wu AW, Mathews C, Kozin F, Orernstein D. The Quality of Well-Being Scale: applications in AIDS, cystic fibrosis, and arthritis. *Med Care* 1989;27:S27–S43.
3. Croog SH, Levin S, Testa MA, Brown B, Bulpitt CJ, Jenkins CD, Klerman GL, Williams GH. The effects of antihypertensive therapy on the quality of life. *N Engl J Med* 1986;314:1657–1664.
4. Bombadier C, Ware J, Russell IJ, Larson M, Chalmers A, Read JL. Auranofin therapy and quality of life in patients with rheumatoid arthritis: results of a multicenter trial. *Am J Med* 1986;81:565–578.
5. Troidl H, Kusche J, Vestweber K, Eypasch E, Koeppen L, Bouillon B. Quality of life: an important endpoint both in surgical practice and research. *J Chronic Dis* 1987;40:523–528.
6. O'Young J, McPeek B. Quality of life variables in surgical trials. *J Chronic Dis* 1987;40:513–522.
7. Fletcher AE, Hunt BM, Bulpitt CJ. Evaluation of quality of life in clinical trials of cardiovascular disease. *J Chronic Dis* 1987;40:557–566.
8. Coates A, Gebski V, Bishop JF, Jeal PN, Woods RL, Snyder R, Tattersall MHN, Byrne M, Harvey V, Gill G, Simpson J, Drummond M, Browne J, van Cooten R, Forbes JF, for the Australian-New Zealand Breast Cancer Trials Group. Improving the quality of life during chemotherapy for advanced breast cancer. A comparison of intermittent and continuous treatment strategies. *N Engl J Med* 1987;317:1490–1495.
9. Gelber RD, Lenderking WR, Cotton DJ, Cole BF, Fischl MA, Goldhirsch A, Testa MA. Quality-of-life evaluation in a clinical trial of zidovudine therapy in patients with mildly symptomatic HIV infection. *Ann Intern Med* 1992;116:961–966.
10. Allen-Mersh TG, Earlam S, Fordy C, Abrams K, Houghton J. Quality of life and survival with continuous hepatic-artery floxuridine infusion for colorectal liver metastases. *Lancet* 1994;344:1255–1259.
11. McKenna KT, McEniery PT, Maas R, Aroney CN, Bett JHN, Cameron J, Holt G, Hossack KF. Percutaneous transluminal coronary angioplasty: clinical and quality of life outcomes one year later. *Aust N Z J Med* 1994;24:15–21.
12. Kornblith AB, Hollis DR, Zukerman E, Lyss AP, Canellas GP, Cooper MR, Herndon JE, Phillips CA, Abrams J, Aisner J, Norton L, Henderson C, Holland JC, for the Cancer and Leukemia Group B. Effect of megestrol acetate on quality of life in a dose-response trial in women with advanced breast cancer. *J Clin Oncol* 1993;11:2081–2089.
13. Testa MA, Anderson RB, Nackley JF, Hollenberg NK, The Quality of Life Hypertension Group. Quality of life and antihypertensive therapy in men: a comparison of captopril with enalapril. *N Engl J Med* 1993;328:907–913.
14. Churchill DN, Morgan J, Torrance GW. Quality of life in end-stage renal disease. *Peritoneal Dialysis Bull* 1984;4:20–23.
15. Coates A, Forbes J for the ANZ Breast Cancer Trials Group. Clinical Trials in breast cancer in Australia and New Zealand. *Med J Aust* 1990;152:601–606.
16. Coates A, Glasziou P, McNeil D. On the receiving end—III: measurement of quality of life during cancer chemotherapy. *Ann Oncol* 1990;1:213–217.
17. Cox DR, Fitzpatrick R, Fletcher AE, Gore SM, Spiegelhalter DJ, Jones DR. Quality-of-life assessment: can we keep it simple? *J R Stat Soc A* 1992;155:353–393.
18. Early Breast Cancer Trialist's Collaborative Group. Effects of adjuvant tamoxifen and of cytotoxic therapy on mortality in early breast cancer. An overview of 61 randomized trials among 28,896 women. *N Engl J Med* 1988;319:1681–1692.
19. Hamptom JR. Coronary artery bypass grafting for the reduction of mortality: an analysis of the trials. *Br Med J* 1984;289:1166–1170.
20. McNeil BJ, Weichselbaum R, Pauker SG. Fallacy of the five-year survival in lung cancer. *N Engl J Med* 1978;299:1397–1401.
21. Gafni A, Torrance GW. Risk attitude and time preference in health. *Manage Sci* 1984;30:440–451.
22. The GUSTO Investigators. An international randomized trial comparing four thrombolytic strategies for acute myocardial infarction. *N Engl J Med* 1993;329:673–682.
23. Mark DB, Hlatky MA, Califf RM, Naylor CD, Lee KL, Armstrong P, Barbash G, White H, Simoons ML, Nelson CL, Clapp-Channing N, Knight JD, Harrell FE, Simes J, Topol EJ. Cost effectiveness of thrombolytic therapy with tissue plasminogen activator versus streptokinase for acute myocardial infarction: results from the GUSTO randomized trial. *N Engl J Med* 1995; in press.
24. Bulpitt CJ, Fletcher AE. Measuring costs and financial benefits in randomized controlled trials. *Am Heart J* 1990;119:766–771.
25. Weinstein MC, Stason WB. Foundations of cost-effectiveness analysis for health and medical practices. *N Engl J Med* 1977;296:716–721.
26. Kamlet MS. *The comparative benefits modeling project: a framework for cost-utility analysis of government health care programs*. Washington, DC: U.S. Department of Health and Human Services; Public Health Service, 1992.
27. Shepard DS, Thompson MS. First principles of cost-effectiveness analysis in health. *Public Health Rep* 1979;94:535–543.
28. Drummond MF, Stoddart GL, Torrance GW. *Methods for the economic evaluation of health care programmes*. Oxford: Oxford Medical, 1987.
29. Drummond MF. *Principles of economic appraisal in health care*. Oxford: Oxford Medical, 1980.
30. Guyatt GH, Feeny DH, Patrick DL. Measuring health-related quality of life. *Ann Intern Med* 1993;118:622–629.
31. Patrick DL, Deyo RA. Generic and disease-specific measures in assessing health status and quality of life. *Med Care* 1989;27:S217–S232.
32. Fitzpatrick R, Fletcher A, Gore S, Jones D, Spiegelhalter D, Cox D. Quality of life measures in health care. I: applications and issues in assessment. *Br Med J* 1992;305:1074–1077.
33. Guyatt GH, Veldhuyzen Van Zanten SJO, Feeny DH, Patrick DL. Measuring quality of life in clinical trials: a taxonomy and review. *Can Med Assoc J* 1989;140:1441–1448.
34. McDowell I, Newell C. *Measuring health: a guide to rating scales and questionnaires*. Oxford: Oxford University Press, 1987.
35. Walker SR, Rosser RM, eds. *Quality of life: assessment and application*. Lancaster: MTP Press, 1988.
36. Spilker B, ed. *Quality of life assessments in clinical trials*. New York: Raven Press, 1990.
37. Walker SR, Rosser RM, eds. *Quality of life assessment: key issues in the 1990s*. Dordrecht, Boston, London: Kluwer Academic, 1993.
38. Spilker B. *Guide to clinical trials*. New York: Raven Press, 1991.
39. Keeney RL, Raiffa H. *Decisions with multiple objectives: preferences and value tradeoffs*. New York: John Wiley, 1976.
40. Schoemaker PJH. The expected utility model: its variants, purposes, evidence and limitations. *J Econ Lit* 1982;20:529–563.
41. Tversky A. A critique of expected utility theory: descriptive and normative considerations. *Erkenntnis* 1975;9:163–173.
42. Fischer GW. Utility models for multiple objective decisions: do they accurately represent human preferences? *Decis Sci* 1979;10:451–479.
43. Hansson B. The appropriateness of the expected utility model. *Erkenntnis* 1975;9:175–193.
44. Hershey JC, Kunreuther HC, Schoemaker PJH. Sources of bias in

assessment procedures for utility functions. *Manage Sci* 1982;28:936–954.

45. Tversky A, Kahneman D. The framing of decisions and the psychology of choice. *Science* 1981;211:453–458.

46. Ciampi A, Silberfeld M, Till JE. Measurement of individual preferences: the importance of "situation-specific" variables. *Med Decis Making* 1982;2:483–495.

47. McNeil BJ, Pauker SG, Sox HC, Tversky A. On the elicitation of preference for alternative therapies. *N Engl J Med* 1982;306:1259–1262.

48. Hilden J, Glaziou PP, Habbema JDF. A pitfall in utility assessment—patients' undisclosed investment decisions. *Med Decis Making* 1992;12:39–43.

49. Arrow KJ. *Social choice and individual values.* New York: John Wiley, 1963.

50. Hilden J. The nonexistence of interpersonal utility scales: a missing link in medical decision theory? *Med Decis Making* 1985;5:215–228.

51. Torrance GW, Feeny D. Utilities and quality-adjusted life years. *Int J Technol Assess Health Care* 1989;5:559–575.

52. Torrance GW, Thomas WH, Sackett DL. A utility maximization model for evaluation of health care programs. *Health Serv Res* 1972;7:118–133.

53. Read JL, Quinn RJ, Berwick DM, Fineberg HV, Weinstein MC. Preferences for health outcomes: comparison of assessment methods. *Med Decis Making* 1984;4:315–329.

54. Stiggelbout AM, Kiebert GM, Kievit J, Leer JWH, Stoter G, de Haes JCJM. Utility assessment in cancer patients: adjustment of time tradeoff scores for the utility of life years and comparison with standard gamble scores. *Med Decis Making* 1994;14:82–90.

55. Glasziou PP, Bromwich S, Simes RJ. Quality of life six months after myocardial infarction treated with thrombolytic therapy. *Med J Aust* 1994;161:532–536.

56. Bergner M, Bobbitt RA, Carter WB, Gilson BS. The Sickness Impact Profile: development and final revision of a health status measure. *Med Care* 1981;19:787–805.

57. Chambers LW. The McMaster Health Index Questionnaire: an update. In: Walker SR, Rosser RM, eds. *Quality of life assessment: key issues in the 1990s.* Dordrecht, Boston, London: Kluwer Academic, 1993: 131–150.

58. Torrance GW, Boyle MH, Horwood SP. Application of multi-attribute utility theory to measure social preferences for health-states. *Operations Res* 1982;30:1043–1069.

59. Gudex C, Kind P. *The QALY toolkit,* discussion paper number 38. Centre for Health Economics, York: University of York, 1988.

60. Froberg DG, Kane RL. Methodology for measuring health-state preferences—III: population and context effects. *J Clin Epidemiol* 1989;42: 585–592.

61. Lumley TS, Simes RJ, Gebski V. Combining quality of life measurements to increase precision and evaluate trade-offs NHMRC Clinical Centre Technical Report 9501. Sydney 1995.

62. Coates A, Simes RJ. In: Williams CJ, ed. *Introducing new treatments for cancer: practical, ethical and legal problems.* Chichester: John Wiley, 1963.

63. Glasziou PP, Simes RJ, Gleber RD. Quality adjusted survival analysis. *Stat Med* 1990;9:1259–1276.

64. Goldhirsch A, Gelber RD, Simes RJ, Glasziou P, Coates AS, for the Ludwig Breast Cancer Study Group. Costs and benefits of adjuvant therapy in breast cancer: a quality-adjusted survival analysis. *J Clin Oncol* 1989;7:36–44.

65. Simes RJ. Application of statistical decision theory to treatment choices: implications for design and analysis of clinical trials. *Stat Med* 1986;5:411–420.

66. Orr ST, Aisner J. Performance status assessment among oncology patients: a review. *Cancer Treat Rep* 1986;70:1423–1429.

67. New York Heart Association Criteria Committee. *Nomenclature and criteria for diagnosis of diseases of the heart and blood vessels.* Boston: Little, Brown, 1979.

Quality of Life and Pharmacoeconomics in Clinical Trials, Second Edition, edited by B. Spilker. Lippincott-Raven Publishers, Philadelphia © 1996.

CHAPTER 43

Patient-Reported Assessments Versus Performance-Based Tests

Carolyn C. Gotay

INTRODUCTION

Information about the impact of treatment on a patient's ability to fulfill basic human functions (e.g., ambulation, communication, emotional stability), and carry out day-to-day activities (e.g., self-care, roles in the family, workplace, and community) is fundamental to evaluating the impact of clinical trials on quality of life. When it comes to assessing patient performance, the researcher or clinician has two basic choices: to ask the patient to provide subjective information, or to obtain performance ratings from another source. Each of these approaches is subject to different potential biases and sources of error. This chapter reviews major approaches to subjective and performance-based assessments of functioning, discusses the strengths and weaknesses of different strategies, and provides concrete suggestions for investigators and future research. We consider a number of strategies that, while they are well established in other fields, have been used infrequently in health-related quality of life research. It is hoped that investigators will be stimulated to consider and develop creative approaches to measuring quality of life in clinical trials.

PATIENT-RATED ASSESSMENTS

Approaches to Obtaining Ratings from Patients

Among the copious numbers of measures used to assess health-related quality of life (1–3), those relying on patient self-reports are by far the most common. There are several different ways that this information can be obtained (Table 1). We will briefly discuss each technique before evaluating different methods. The reader is referred to detailed discussions of specific self-report instruments elsewhere in this text.

Interviews

Interviews can be structured, including a set list of questions, or unstructured. Unstructured interviews generally begin with a broad question (e.g., "How would you describe your quality of life?"), with subsequent queries based on patient responses. Specific questions can be closed-ended (in which respondents are provided with specified response options from which they may choose), or open-ended (where respondents reply in their own words). In practice, many interviews follow a semi-structured protocol, including a mixture of standard questions and free responses. There are not many tools designed explicitly to be interviewer-administered. One notable exception is the Quality of Well-

C. C. Gotay: University of Hawaii Cancer Research Center, Honolulu, Hawaii 96813.

TABLE 1. *Methods for obtaining patient self-reports of quality of life*

Interviews
Questionnaires
Diaries
Personal narratives
Projective techniques

Being (QWB) Scale (4). This measure uses a structured interview to obtain information about functional level, symptoms, and medical problems. The interviewer then classifies the respondents' answers within a preexisting matrix.

Questionnaires

Questionnaires are by far the most frequent patient-rated quality of life assessment technique, as the contents of this book amply demonstrate. The reader is also referred to other discussions of questionnaire design (5–7). Questionnaires are characterized by a series of items; the patient is asked to choose the most appropriate response for him or her. Respondents may indicate their answers by placing a slash on a line (e.g., linear analog scales), indicating a unit on a scale (e.g., Likert scales, semantic differentials), checking a response with a predetermined score (e.g., Guttman scales), among other formats. Questionnaires can be self-administered (in a research setting or via mail), interviewer-administered (in person or over the telephone), or computer assisted (8). Many quality of life questionnaires can be administered in several modes (e.g., by interview or self-administered) with equivalent results (9). The Sickness Impact Profile (SIP) (10) is the most frequently used instrument in the quality of life field (1–3). The SIP consists of 136 items that cover 12 different dimensions; each question asks patients if they have engaged in a specified behavior that day.

Diaries

Diaries represent a form of self-monitoring, which has been used extensively by behavior therapists both to record data and to effect behavior change (11). In the context of quality of life assessment, diaries have been used by asking patients to describe aspects of their life, generally on an ongoing, prospective basis. For example, Fraser et al. (12,13) used the "Qualitator," a daily diary card, in a study of chemotherapy. With this tool, patients selected their five most important questions from four quality of life domains. They then recorded their own experience on five-point scales daily for up to 6 months. Diaries may be particularly useful for outcomes that may vary considerably from day to day and where charting patient experience over time is important, e.g., treatment-related symptoms and pain.

Personal Narratives

Personal narratives represent a qualitative approach to quality of life assessment. Personal narratives may be written or utilize other recording techniques, such as tape recorders. Patients describe significant aspects of quality of life in their own words. Transcripts of the data are prepared and meaningful "units" of information can be abstracted, summarized, and compared (see Chapter 40 by Gordon and Paci).

Projective Techniques

The underlying assumption of projective techniques is that an individual's concerns can be expressed indirectly and symbolically. In clinical psychology, tests such as the Rorschach, in which individuals are asked to provide an interpretation of abstract designs, are useful in assessing personality traits that underly patient conflicts and psychopathology. Standard projective tests have been used only rarely in health-related quality of life assessment (14), and are unlikely to be widely useful in this field. However, as a methodology, projective techniques might make a useful contribution in addressing the issue of patient biases discussed below; this is an empirical question for future research. For example, patients could be shown a picture of a person similar to themselves and asked to describe how that person is likely to be functioning. Or patients could be given stick figures representing themselves, family members, and the health care team and asked to place them on a board; the distance between the figures could be used as an indication of interpersonal distance or perceived support.

Strengths and Weaknesses of Different Self-Report Methods

Strengths

The strengths of patient-reported assessments are well known. In some cases, the patient is the only source of data, or the source that may be easiest to tap. Patient reports, questionnaires in particular, are a relatively low-cost and efficient way to collect information. Most patients are well acquainted with completing forms, and questionnaires following standard formats are likely to be well accepted. Diaries require careful training (both initially and on follow-up) to ensure complete and consistent recording. No staff is needed to administer self-administered questionnaires, personal narratives, or patient diaries, although as Cella and Tulsky (15) point out, the value of information from self-administered forms can be enhanced by the participation of an interviewer who can check the questionnaire for accuracy and completeness, follow up on particular responses, and provide clarification or answer questions. Even when interviewers are required to collect information, they generally can be trained for the study and need not have a particular educational background. Finally, the value of patient self-reports can be supported empirically. In recent years, increased attention has focused on developing self-report instruments that meet accepted scientific standards for methodological rigor; at this point, many questionnaires have demonstrated impressive levels of validity, reliability, and responsiveness and have provided information that is important in clinical decision making (16).

Weaknesses

There are a number of potential weaknesses to self-reports (Table 2), some of which are relatively more common with different self-report methods. Many of the weaknesses can be addressed if they are considered in the design of the measure.

Form-Based Response Biases

Response biases occur when respondents are affected not only by their true response to a question, but also by how the question is worded or by their own motivations. These biases can add error to findings and, at their worst, could render findings useless. Response biases in questionnaires or interviews may include yea-saying (the tendency to always agree with items), end aversion (the tendency to use middle values rather than the end points of a scale), halo (in which an overall evaluation affects ratings in different domains), and framing (in which the manner of describing a question, e.g., whether one's prognosis is described in terms of probability of living or dying, affects responses). Many response biases can be prevented through appropriate instrument design; for example, yea-saying can be addressed by ensuring that the wording of items is balanced so that there are both negative and positive items in the questionnaire or interview. Additional suggestions are given elsewhere (7).

Personal narratives and projective techniques offer potential strengths against response bias, since patients can express themselves in their own words (through personal narratives) or indirectly (in projective techniques).

Patient-Based Response Biases

Additional response biases in health-related quality of life assessment include social desirability and response shifts. These biases are not necessarily conscious or recognized by the respondents. Patients, especially if they are interviewed by a member of the health care team, may be influenced by a number of factors: e.g., they want to be seen as "good patients," they don't want to complain, they don't want to seem ungrateful for the care they have received, they are embarrassed to admit they have certain problems. Several investigators have shown that social desirability imparts a considerable impact on questionnaire-obtained quality of life ratings (17,18). In anonymous questionnaires and diaries, and especially in personal narratives and projective techniques, these socially desirable tendencies should be less of a problem. However, in questionnaires, Breetvelt and Van Dam (19) suggest that a different bias may be operative. Their review indicated that patients tend to underreport the problems they face; these authors hypothesize that patients who face a life-threatening disease modify their internal standards of evaluation, so that lower levels of functioning are seen as relatively better. Patients could also be motivated to respond that they are experiencing more problems, in order to obtain, or not to lose, services or benefits. For example, the clinical form of the Cancer Rehabilitation Evaluation System (CARES) (20) includes a column in which the patient is asked to indicate if s/he needs assistance (and presumably, patients would expect to receive some kind of follow-up to their response). Individuals' responses may be affected by whether they want (or do not want) help for certain problems, in addition to their actual experience. Memory also poses limitations, especially when questions use a long time frame and in patients who have cognitive deficits. As well, literacy level may affect patient response.

Leading the Patient

Another drawback to most questionnaires and interviews and many diaries is that the questions themselves may change the way the patients assess their quality of life, a kind of psychological Heisenberg's uncertainty principle. Asking a patient to respond to questions about quality of life may raise issues that s/he had not considered previously. As such, the questionnaire itself may trigger new concerns or evoke a different evaluation than the one the patient started with. Monitoring one's experiences with a diary may lead to much greater scrutiny of experience than would normally be the case, thus resulting in data that diverge from the patient's "normal" experience. Narratives, by allowing

TABLE 2. *Potential biases in self-reports*

Form-based response biases
Yea-saying or acquiescence
End-aversion, positive skew, and halo
Framing
Patient-based response biases
Social desirability and faking good
Deviation and faking bad
Memory
Literacy
"Leading" the patient

patients to select their own focus, may render a more natural account of life quality. Projective techniques may offer an advantage, in theory at least, since they rely on indirect and unconscious processes.

Interpretation

Additional research is needed to elucidate the meaning of questionnaire scores (21); e.g., what significance does a change of three units on a scale have—does it have predictive value or clinical usefulness? Possible cultural differences in the meaning of quality of life (22,23) and test scores may also make it difficult to interpret to make intergroup comparisons. If anything, the interpretation of data from personal narratives and projective approaches is an even more difficult challenge and may limit the use of such techniques in clinical trials until more basic research has demonstrated their interpretability.

PERFORMANCE-BASED EVALUATIONS

Performance-based evaluations are reported frequently in research. In fact, some studies that draw conclusions about quality of life do not obtain any direct information from the patients themselves (24). Although observer ratings are by far the most frequently used approach to rating performance, there are several other ways that performance can be evaluated, including direct measurement of patient performance and physiological indicators (Table 3). A common thread that distinguishes performance-based evaluations is that they are based on observable, and potentially repeatable and verifiable, information. It is also important to document the context in which a given behavior occurs, if at all possible. Technologies such as tape or video recording can provide a performance record that can be analyzed by multiple raters. Although behavioral ratings may seem to have the most applicability for physical functioning, patient performance is relevant in many other areas as well (e.g., psychological and social functioning).

TABLE 3. *Methods for obtaining performance-based reports of quality of life*

Patient behaviors
Participant observer ratings
Naturalistic observation
Analog observation
Measures of activity
Tests of performance
Product-of-behavior measures
Psychophysiological measures

Patient Behaviors

Participant Observer Ratings

A number of observer-based tools are available, most being "participant observer" approaches, since the individual making the observations is generally someone who is interacting with the patient. For the most part, such ratings are made in a hospital or physician's office. Ratings reflect clinical judgments based on interaction with the patient: information from verbal, nonverbal, and physical cues that may include direct questions. Participant observation includes most scales of activities of daily living and instrumental activities of daily living (which focus on independence in self-care and daily life), which are also a frequent aspect of quality of life assessment, especially for elderly or institutionalized populations (5,6).

The Karnofsky Performance Index (KPI) (25) is an example of an observer measure that is widely used in clinical trials research [the most often-cited behaviorally based scale cited in Spilker et al.'s reviews (1–3)]. In cancer research, it has been used as an eligibility criterion for trial participation, as a patient stratification factor, and as an outcome measure for both treatment efficacy and quality of life (26). The KPI assigns a rating from 0 (dead) to 100 (no evidence of disease, able to carry out normal activity and to work); as such, the rating reflects a combination of disease status, independence, and role functioning. Spitzer et. al.'s (27) Quality of Life Index (QLI) is one of the few multidimensional observer scales. (A self-report version is also available.) Observers assign one of three ratings in five different areas: activity, daily living, health, support, and outlook. Both the KPS and QLI have been used among health care providers, research workers, and family members (and patients as well).

Naturalistic Observation

It is obvious that the behaviors required in hospitals differ from those at home, and a more accurate observation of day-to-day activities could be made in the home. Related to this strategy is obtaining information from *analog observation.* This strategy involves setting up a situation as much like the real world as possible, but under conditions that facilitate the systematic collection of data. For example, one could evaluate family functioning by asking the patient and family to engage in discussion and observing their behaviors from a one-way mirror. Other possible applications of these approaches are numerous but not common in quality of life assessment. One scale that comes close to naturalistic observation (combined with self-report) is Lansky's performance status scale for head and neck cancer patients (28). This instrument requires the interviewer to rate patient performance regarding normalcy of diet, eating in public, and understandability of speech. The eating behaviors ratings are based on patient self-reports regarding specific aspects of their diet and dining patterns, while the speech component is based on the interviewer's experience communicating with the patient during the interview.

Tests of Performance

Standard physical, psychological, or neurological tests can be used to measure patient abilities that are important aspects of quality of life. Appropriate tests depend on the disease, treatment, patient population, and study question, and some tests may even be administered in the context of patient care. For example, cognitive functioning is an important aspect of quality of life in survivors of childhood cancer. Studies of pediatric cancer survivors frequently include data from neuropsychological tests such as the Trail-Making Test (to measure cognitive flexibility), the Continuous Performance Test (to assess vigilance), and the Halsted-Reitan Neuropsychological Battery, which were used to complement other quality of life information (29). It is somewhat surprising that quality of life research with adults seldom includes neuropsychological test results. For example, cancer incidence increases with age, as does chronic brain syndrome, implying that some proportion of cancer patients are likely to manifest at least some impairment of cognitive function. However, cancer-related quality of life studies rarely report patient performance on tests such as the Mental Status Examination (30), a brief screening test for chronic brain syndrome. It is not clear if researchers routinely exclude such patients from quality of life studies, limiting generalizability of the findings, or if this aspect of life quality is overlooked.

Direct Measures of Activity

Precise measurements of activity can be made with electronic and mechanical methods (31). Mason and Redeker (32) have identified three approaches: (a) nonmemory frequency counters that are sensitive only to the total number of movements over a given time; (b) frequency counters that record movement as a time series; and (c) intensity recorders that include time series information as well as force or intensity. Many different kinds of recorders are available, including wristwatch-like devices that patients can wear, or motion detectors that can be attached to a bed or crib. These devices can provide data on activities such as mobility, immobility, restlessness, fatigue, sleep, and rhythmic patterning (32), and have proved useful in clinical research and practice, including studies of pain, arthritis, coronary heart disease, dementia, and cancer (31). However, activity measures have rarely been used in clinical trials; Williams et al. (33) attempted to use a self-report instrument, a diary, and an activity monitor to measure activity levels in college students and had considerable logistic problems with the monitors. They concluded that activity monitors

need additional feasibility testing before widespread research use can be advocated.

Product-of-Behavior Measures

According to Haynes (34), product-of-behavior measures are temporary or permanent records that reflect specific, targeted behaviors. A concrete example is weight: if appetite is an important aspect of quality of life in a particular trial, one could monitor weight gain or loss in addition to or instead of asking the patient, "How is your appetite?" Similarly, absenteeism from school or work could provide information about energy or role status. Such indicators have their weaknesses (e.g., behaviors such as weight change are multiply determined and reflect other factors beyond appetite, such as concurrent medications). However, these kinds of data are frequently available and accessible at low cost to collect.

Psychophysiological Measures

A number of physical measures in addition to studying end points, e.g., heart rate, galvanic skin response, oxygen consumption, have the potential to add additional information about patient well-being. Numerous possible outcomes and assessment techniques are possible (35). In a study of diabetics and hypertensives, Kaplan (36) found that laboratory test values complemented findings from self-report health status measures.

Strengths

Behavior-based measures have a number of strengths. The various biases that affect self-reports are less likely to play a role, especially when behavior is observed or measured in a naturalistic context. Focusing on specific behaviors and their environmental contingencies may guide the way to intervention: if better quality of life is manifested under some conditions than others, one has potentially identified a confounder to interpreting findings, or a potential way to improve well-being. Observer responses offer a particularly efficient and economical way of collecting data; for some patients (e.g., those who are very ill), observer ratings may offer the only way to obtain information. Based on studies of the KPI, observers can be trained to achieve acceptable levels of interrater reliability (37,38). Conditions that can interfere with one's ability to complete questionnaires, such as problems with vision, literacy, or language, are to a large degree removed in performance measures. Behavioral measures reflect the current situation; as such, they are not subject to selective memory, recall failure, or rapid changes in outcomes, an issue in a number of self-report measures; for example, the Nottingham Health Profile (39) self-report questionnaire asks patients to consider the preceding month in their responses, an interval that may pose difficulties for debilitated patients. However, by the same token, behavioral measures are limited in the scope reflected by any one assessment and must be conducted repeatedly to obtain a perspective on changes over time.

Weaknesses

Probably the biggest problem with behavioral measures of quality of life is that many such measures (observer ratings excepted) have not been included traditionally in quality of life assessments, particularly in the clinical trials context. As such, individuals skilled in collecting these measures are not available in many settings, and specialized training is needed to ensure reliable assessments. Training protocols may need to be tailored to the individual observer: e.g., physicians vs. researchers vs. significant others. While psychophysiological measures seem to offer precision in measurement, they are frequently nonspecific; e.g., an increased heart rate may signify more than one possible quality of life domain. In addition, information about validity and interpretation of findings, especially with respect to specific populations, is not available for many measures. For certain aspects of quality of life, it may be difficult to develop behavioral indicators that adequately reflect the phenomenon of interest; however, clinical psychologists have well-established behavioral assessment techniques for psychological constructs like anxiety (40) and depression (41), which have potential application in quality of life research. Since collecting behavioral data may take considerable time and effort, it may not be a cost-effective way of gathering information in clinical trials. However, not all behavioral measures are costly. And if behavioral information is key in therapy evaluation, collecting and analyzing such data may represent resources well spent.

HOW DO PATIENT SELF-REPORTS COMPARE WITH PERFORMANCE-BASED RATINGS?

While additional head-to-head comparisons of many different approaches to quality of life assessment are needed, there is considerable information available comparing patient self-reports with observer ratings. Sprangers and Aaronson (42) provided a comprehensive analysis of this literature. They reviewed 48 studies that compared patient quality of life ratings to those of health care providers and/or significant others. Their overall conclusions were as follows: (a) there is far from perfect concordance between patients and observers; (b) the more concrete and observable a phenomenon, the more agreement; (c) both providers and significant others give lower estimates of quality of life than do patients; (d) there is more agreement between patients and significant others who live in close proximity to one another.

Sprangers and Aaronson (42) took the perspective that the patient's rating was the "gold standard," and that observers provided more or less accurate ratings to the degree that they agreed with the patients. However, as we have discussed, patients' ratings themselves are subject to biases. Perhaps a more useful question might be "To what degree do patient and observer ratings provide useful information?" A recent study by Coates and colleagues (43) provides an interesting perspective on this question, since it is one of the few studies that looked at survival as a function of both patient and physician quality of life ratings (as opposed to solely physician KPI ratings). Over 240 breast cancer patients participating in a clinical trial of chemotherapy completed a quality of life questionnaire (including physical well-being, mood, pain, nausea and vomiting, appetite, and an overall rating), and their physicians also completed the QLI (27), a multidimensional quality of life assessment and a performance status measure. A survival analysis revealed that both patient- and physician-rated quality of life were significant and independent predictors of length of survival; survival was linked with physicians' multidimensional ratings, but only with the patient ratings of physical well-being. In an editorial about this study, Weeks (44) commented, "Further work will be needed to determine whether this finding reflects differences in the way physicians and patients rate physical well-being, each providing important information not appreciated by the other, or whether some feature of physicians' assessments of other aspects of quality of life renders them better predictors than patients' assessments" (p. 1828). This study points out the value of performance-based observer ratings. Whether other behavioral measures of performance would add further explanatory power remains to be seen.

Are Patient Self-Reports or Performance-Based Measures Preferable?

The researcher is left with a dilemma: given that there are drawbacks and merits to any single approach to quality of life assessment, how does one choose an appropriate approach to measurement? A number of researchers have offered helpful guides for how to select instruments to assess quality of life (45–48), and the comments below are intended to supplement their suggestions.

The specific question that drives the study is the most important factor in selecting a measurement strategy. With respect to assessment of patient performance, there are at least four possible queries that might be posed: (a) Can the patient enact a particular behavior? (b) Does the patient perform the behavior? (c) Does the patient have problems in carrying out the behavior? and (d) How does the patient feel about his or her performance level?

The first question relates to capacity: could someone perform a behavior? Patient self-reports could be biased by hypothetical judgments, whereas a direct measure of behavior (through observer reports, tests, or other methods) would provide more clear-cut evidence. The second question relates to actual behavior, and self-reports, observations, or direct measures of behavior could provide valid data. The SIP (10) is among the self-report questionnaires that focuses specifically on performance: respondents indicate if they engage in specified behaviors. Observers who are trained to monitor concrete patient activities, per Sprangers and Aaronson's (42) suggestions, would seem able to provide useful information relative to this question. The third question does not focus on what a patient does, but rather on difficulties experienced. A number of self-report questionnaires rely heavily or exclusively on questions about problems. For example, typical questions on the CARES (20) include, ''I find it difficult to swallow'' and ''My partner and I have difficulty talking about our fears.'' Since this question relies on a subjective definition of what is a problem or difficulty, patient self-reports may be the best way to gather such information. However, if concrete, observable manifestations of problems can be identified, observers and other behavioral approaches could be used as well.

Finally, the fourth question relates to patient satisfaction: does the patient feel upset or satisfied with his/her functioning in specified areas? This is one area where probably the only meaningful, patient-specific data can be obtained from the patients themselves. Many self-report instruments concentrate heavily on the subjective satisfaction domain; for example, the Ferrans and Powers Quality of Life Index (49) asks patients how satisfied they are with a number of domains, including health, stress, or worries in their lives, and family happiness, as well as the importance of each area. The importance of asking individual patients their subjective appraisals cannot be denied; in particular, at the clinical level, decision making for an individual needs to be made in the context of that person's evaluations, values, and desires. There are also many other purposes for asking patients about their quality of life. However, to view this component of life quality as synonymous with quality of life (cf. 24) is limiting (50,51), especially in the context of clinical trials research. Not many therapeutic clinical trials are undertaken with the primary goal of increasing patient satisfaction; while this may be one component of evaluating the efficacy of a new medicine or treatment, it should not be the sole outcome assessment. Questionnaires that include both patient self-reports of performance and self-appraisals have the potential for providing the greatest amount of important information. For example, the European Organization for Research and Treatment of Cancer (EORTC's) quality of life questionnaire (52) asks both about performance (e.g., ''Do you have to stay in bed or a chair for most of the day?'') and its perceived impact (e.g., ''Has your physical condition or medical treatment interfered with your social activities?''). Additional research is needed to understand the relative contributions of different kinds of questions to overall quality of life ratings as well as to other outcomes including survival.

The preferred approach to assessment is the multimethod, multitrait approach (53): by obtaining data in a number of different ways, the biases and error variance inherent in any one method can be compensated for by data from another. Wherever possible, investigators should seek to include data from different sources. While this can be prohibitively difficult or costly, there may in fact be efficient approaches to data collection available, e.g., developing a checklist at the top of a patient chart that reflects judgments that nurses are already making but not recording, incorporating data from the patient record in quality of life analyses. It is important for future studies to build on available measurement tools and implementation guidelines wherever possible, especially when these tools have already demonstrated psychometric soundness and have contributed to the interpretation of clinical results. Newly developed psychophysiological measures may hold particular potential for quality of life research. For example, Fawzy et al. (54,55) included the Profile of Mood States (POMS; 56), a measure of the affective domain of quality of life and a panel of immunological assessments in their study of short-term psychiatric group in cancer patients. They found that scores on the POMS and immune functioning were well correlated. This represents an exciting integration of assessment methods. New techniques can be used to supplement existing approaches and provide additional data to validate or refine these techniques.

CONCLUSIONS

This chapter has provided an overview of contrasting approaches to collecting data to assess health-related quality of life. There are many reasonable approaches to measurement, both measures based in patient self-reports and in measures of behavior. The particular approach recommended in a given study depends on the research question. In many quality of life clinical trials, measures that incorporate both patient performance and patient satisfaction offer the most potential. Creativity in quality of life assessment is encouraged, especially in consideration of difficult-to-avoid patient biases. However, innovative measures should be evaluated side by side with available tools, in order that the contributions of each are appropriately recognized.

ACKNOWLEDGMENTS

The preparation of this paper was supported in part by grants from the National Cancer Institute (CA61711 and CA01642).

REFERENCES

1. Spilker B, Molinek FR, Johnston KA, Simpson RL Jr, Tilson HH. Quality of life bibliography and indexes. *Med Care* 1990;28(suppl): DS1–DS77.
2. Spilker B, White WSA, Simpson RL Jr, Tilson HH. Quality of life bibliography and indexes, 1990 update. *J Clin Res Pharmacoepidemiol* 1992;6:87–156.

3. Spilker B, Simpson RL Jr, Tilson HH. Quality of life bibliography and indexes, 1991 update. *J Clin Res Pharmacoepidemiol* 1992;6:205–266.

4. Kaplan RM, Bush JW, Berry CC. Health status: types of validity and the Index of Well-Being. *Health Serv Res* 1976;11:478–507.

5. Kane RA, Kane RL. *Assessing the elderly: a practical guide to measurement.* Lexington, Massachusetts: Lexington Books, 1981.

6. McDowell I, Newell C. *Measuring health: a guide to rating scales and questionnaires.* New York: Oxford University Press, 1987.

7. Streiner DL, Norman GR. *Health measurement scales: a practical guide to their development and use.* New York: Oxford University Press, 1989.

8. Siegel K, Mesagno FP, Chen J-Y, et al. Computerized telephone assessment of the "concrete" needs of chemotherapy outpatients: a feasibility study. *J Clin Oncol* 1988;6:1760–1767.

9. Kornblith AB, Anderson J, Cella DF, et al. Quality-of-life assessment of Hodgkin's disease survivors: a model for cooperative clinical trials. *Oncology* 1990;4:93–101.

10. Bergner M, Bobbitt RA, Carter WB, Gilson BS. The Sickness Impact Profile: development and final revision of a health status measure. *Med Care* 1981;14:57–61.

11. Bornstein PH, Hamilton SB, Bornstein MT. Self-monitoring procedures. In: Ciminero AR, Calhoun KS, Adams HE, eds. *Handbook of behavioral assessment.* New York: John Wiley, 1986:176–222.

12. Fraser SCA, Ramirez AJ, Ebbs SR, et al. A daily diary for quality of life measurement in advanced breast cancer trials. *Br J Cancer* 1993;67:340–346.

13. Fraser SCA, Dobbs H, Ebbs SR, Fallowfield LJ, Bates T, Baum M. Combination of mild single agent chemotherapy for advanced breast cancer? CMF vs epirubicin measuring quality of life. *Br J Cancer* 1993;67:402–406.

14. Spunberg JJ, Chang CH, Goldman M, Auricchio E, Bell JJ. Quality of long-term survival following irradiation for intracranial tumors in children under the age of two. *Int J Radiat Oncol Biol Phys* 1981;7:727–736.

15. Cella DR, Tulsky DS. Quality of life in cancer: definition, purpose, and method of measurement. *Cancer Invest* 1993;11:327–336.

16. Osoba D. Lessons learned from measuring health-related quality of life in oncology. *J Clin Oncol* 1994;12:608–616.

17. Mastekaasa A, Kaasa S. Measurement error and research design: a note on the utility of panel data in quality of life research. *Soc Indicators Res* 1989;21:315–335.

18. Ward SE, Leventhal H, Love R. Repression revisited: tactics used in coping with a severe health threat. *Pers Soc Psychol Bull* 1988;14:735–746.

19. Breetvelt IS, Van Dam FSAM. Underreporting by cancer patients: the case of response-shift. *Soc Sci Med* 1991;32:981–987.

20. Ganz PA, Schag CA, Lee JJ, Sim MS. The CARES: a generic measure of health-related quality of life for patients with cancer. *Qual Life Res* 1992;1:19–29.

21. Juniper EF, Guyatt GH, Willan A, Griffith LE. Determining a minimal important change in a disease-specific quality of life questionnaire. *J Clin Epidemiol* 1994;47:81–87.

22. Chaturvedi SK. What's important for quality of life to Indians—in relation to cancer. *Soc Sci Med* 1991;33:91–94.

23. Marshall PA. Cultural influences on perceived quality of life. *Semin Oncol Nurs* 1990;6:278–284.

24. Gill TM, Feinstein AR. A critical appraisal of the quality of quality-of-life measurements. *JAMA* 1994;272:619–626.

25. Karnofsky DA, Burchenal JH. The clinical evaluation of chemotherapeutic agents in cancer. In: Macleod CM, ed. *Evaluation of chemotherapeutic agents in cancer.* New York: Columbia University Press, 1949:191–205.

26. Orr ST, Aisner J. Performance status assessment among oncology patients: a review. *Cancer Treat Rep* 1986;70:1423–1429.

27. Spitzer WO, Dobson AJ, Hall J, et al. Measuring the quality of life of cancer patients: a concise QL-index for use by physicians. *J Chronic Dis* 1981;34:585–597.

28. List MA, Ritter-Sterr C, Lansky SB. A performance status scale for head and neck cancer patients. *Cancer* 1990;66:564–569.

29. Mulhern RK. Neuropsychological late effects. In: Bearison DJ, Mulhern RK, eds. *Pediatric psychooncology.* New York: Oxford University Press, 1994:99–121.

30. Kahn RL, Goldfarb AI, Pollack M, Peck A. Brief objective measures for the determination of mental status in the aged. *Am J Psychol* 1960;117:326–328.

31. Tryon WW. *Activity measurement in psychology and medicine.* New York: Plenum Press, 1991.

32. Mason DJ, Redeker N. Measurement of activity. *Nurs Res* 1993;42:87–92.

33. Williams E, Klesges RC, Hanson CL, Eck LH. A prospective study of the reliability and convergent validity of three physical activity measures in a field of research trial. *Epidemiology* 1989;42:1161–1170.

34. Haynes SN. Behavioral assessment of adults. In: Goldstein G, Hersen M, eds. *Handbook of psychological assessment.* Elmford, NY: Pergamon Press, 1990:423–463.

35. Rugh JD, Gable RS, Lemke RR. Instrumentation for behavioral assessment. In: Ciminero AR, Calhoun KS, Adams HE, eds. *Handbook of behavioral assessment.* New York: John Wiley, 1986:79–108.

36. Kaplan SH. Patient reports of health status as predictors of physiologic health measures in chronic disease. *J Chronic Dis* 1987;40(suppl 1):27S–35S.

37. Mor V, Laliberte L, Morris JN, Weimann M. The Karnofsky Performance Status scale: an examination of its reliability and validity in a research setting. *Cancer* 1984;53:2002–2007.

38. Schag CC, Heinrich RL, Ganz PA. Karnofsky Performance Status revisited: reliability, validity, and guidelines. *J Clin Oncol* 1984;2:187–193.

39. Hunt S, McKenna SP, McEwan J, Williams J, Papp E. The Nottingham Health Profile: subjective health status and medical consultations. *Soc Sci Med* 1981;15A:221–229.

40. Bernstein DA, Borkovec TD, Coles MGH. Assessment of anxiety. In: Ciminero AR, Calhoun KS, Adams HE, eds. *Handbook of behavioral assessment.* New York: John Wiley, 1986:353–403.

41. Carson TP. Assessment of depression. In: Ciminero AR, Calhoun KS, Adams HE, eds. *Handbook of behavioral assessment.* New York: John Wiley, 1986:404–445.

42. Sprangers MAG, Aaronson NK. The role of health care providers and significant others in evaluating the quality of life of patients with chronic disease: a review. *J Clin Epidemiol* 1992;45:743–760.

43. Coates A, Gebski V, Signorini D, et al. Prognostic value of quality-of-life scores during chemotherapy for advanced breast cancer. *J Clin Oncol* 1992;10:1833–1838.

44. Weeks J. Quality-of-life assessment: performance status upstaged? *J Clin Oncol* 1992;10:1827–1829.

45. Aaronson NK. Methodologic issues in assessing the quality of life of cancer patients. *Cancer* 1991;67(suppl):844–850.

46. Cella DF, Tulsky DS. Measuring quality of life today: methodological aspects. *Oncology* 1990;4:29–38.

47. Patrick DL, Erickson P. *Health status and health policy.* New York: Oxford University Press, 1993.

48. Till JE. Quality of life measurements in cancer treatment. In: DeVita VT, Hellman S, Rosenberg SA, eds. *Important advances in oncology.* Philadelphia: JB Lippincott, 1992:189–204.

49. Ferrans CE, Powers MJ. Quality of Life Index: development and psychometric properties. *Adv Nurs Sci* 1985;8:15–24.

50. Guyatt GH, Cook DJ. Commentary: health status, quality of life, and the individual. *JAMA* 1994;272:630–631.

51. Spitzer WO. State of science 1986: quality of life and functional status as target variables for research. *J Chronic Dis* 1987;40:465–471.

52. Aaronson NK, Ahmedzai S, Bergman B, et al. The European Organization for Research and Treatment of Cancer QLQ-C30: a quality-of-life instrument for use in international trials in oncology. *J Natl Cancer Inst* 1993;85:365–376.

53. Campbell DT, Fiske DW. Convergent and discriminant validation by the multitrait-multimethod matrix. *Psychol Bull* 1959;56:81–105.

54. Fawzy FI, Cousins N, Fawzy NW, Kemeny ME, Elashoff R, Morton D. A structured psychiatric intervention for cancer patients: I. Changes over time in methods of coping and affective disturbance. *Arch Gen Psychiatry* 1990;47:720–725.

55. Fawzy FI, Kemeny ME, Fawzy NW, Elashoff R, Morton D, Cousins N, Fahey JL. A structured psychiatric intervention for cancer patients: II. Changes over time in immunological measures. *Arch Gen Psychiatry* 1990;47:729–735.

56. McNair DM, Lorr M, Droppelman LF. *EITS manual for the profile of mood states.* San Diego, CA: Educational and Industrial Testing Service, 1981.

Quality of Life and Pharmacoeconomics in Clinical Trials, Second Edition, edited by B. Spilker.
Lippincott-Raven Publishers, Philadelphia © 1996.

CHAPTER 44

Alternative and Complementary Treatments

Barrie R. Cassileth and Christopher C. Chapman

INTRODUCTION

Alternative and complementary treatments lend themselves especially well to quality of life evaluation. *Complementary* therapies are used to enhance the well-being of patients under conventional treatment and therefore aim by definition to improve quality of life. Because it appears unlikely that cures for major illnesses are hidden among *alternative* remedies, successes among such therapies also are likely to enhance quality of life rather than cure disease. This chapter describes alternative and complementary treatments and discusses the challenges associated with evaluating these treatments for quality of life benefits.

DEFINITION AND TERMINOLOGY

Although it is often a misnomer, *alternative medicine* has become the umbrella phrase used in the United States to describe a wide array of unproven remedies and techniques. Whether unproven, disproved, or currently under study, these are popular remedies, endorsed by proponents and used with enthusiasm. The term encompasses a heterogeneous array of treatments, illnesses, and practitioner involvement. Alternative medicine includes five medical spectra: (a) ranges of therapeutic goals from symptom control to cure; (b) types of treatment from those geared to deal with highly targeted

clinical problems to "whole being" therapies; (c) degrees of technicality from home remedies to complex, manufactured products; (d) practitioner involvement extending from none through peer to highly skilled; and (e) efficacy that ranges from extremely effective to no activity or even harmful effects.

Similarly, the term *alternative medicine* often is applied to self-limiting problems, to potentially fatal illnesses, and to the vast array of ailments in between. Perhaps of greatest relevance to this chapter, alternative approaches are applied not only to heal or prevent illness, but also to maintain well-being and enhance quality of life. The commonality among these varied approaches is that they are both popular and unproven.

Many terms are used synonymously for alternative and complementary medicine. The profusion and confusion of terminology perhaps is symbolic of events in this area of medicine. What used to be a relatively simple and understandable dichotomy—quackery versus conventional medicine—has become a complex array of points on a continuum. These include *complementary medicine,* the term preferred in Britain and elsewhere to define therapies used in conjunction with, rather than instead of, conventional treatments; unproven conventional therapies, which are as-yet-undocumented regimens under investigation by the National Institutes of Health (NIH) or in medical center clinical trials; unproven, unorthodox, or questionable methods; self-help or non–physician-based help such as home remedies or group support; and quackery, which entails treatments that were studied and found to be worthless or that are patently fraudulent.

Other variations on the general theme exist, and yet other terms are applied as well. Compounding the confusion is

B. R. Cassileth: Department of Medicine, University of North Carolina; Department of Community and Family Medicine, Duke University, Chapel Hill, North Carolina 27576.

C. C. Chapman: University of North Carolina, Chapel Hill, North Carolina 27576.

the fact that the phrase *alternative medicine* is applied to encompass the terms noted above, masking the often profound differences that exist among these various expressions of unconventional and adjunctive medicine. A further and important point is that an approach is alternative not necessarily because of what it is, but rather according to the intent behind its use. Muscle massage or relaxation therapy, for example, can be extremely beneficial. When applied with the intention of helping patients feel relaxed and comfortable, they are valuable adjunctive or complementary techniques. When offered as cures to be used instead of conventional medical treatment, however, these therapies shift to the questionable or unproven category. The NIH Office of Alternative Medicine defines alternative medicine as therapies that are unproven.

THE SHIFTING POPULARITY OF ALTERNATIVE THERAPIES

Several years ago, Laetrile reigned as a prominent alternative, especially for cancer. This "treatment," derived from apricot kernels, was superseded in popularity by others (1), including special diets, "metabolic" therapy with its emphasis on internal detoxification, mental imagery and a wide assortment of lesser, commonly used, unproven methods (2). Natural products and self-care trends predominated. Alternative medicine is characterized by fads and rapid changeover (3), so that today's list of in-vogue alternative therapies looks quite different, and categorizations of alternatives change with the shifting emphases that occur over time.

The Office of Alternative Medicine categorizes today's popular unproven methods as mind/body interventions, bioelectromagnetics, manual healing, traditional and folk healing systems, pharmacologic and biologic treatments, herbal medicine, and diet and nutrition. Because the classification of unproven methods is largely arbitrary, it varies from one organization to another.

However they may be categorized, acupuncture, traditional Chinese and Indian medicine, homeopathy, herbal remedies, and hands-on structural therapies now capture the public imagination (4). Vials of pastel homeopathic cures line supermarket shelves, and acupressure clinics can be found in small towns as well as major cities. Americans are fascinated with mind-body routes to well-being and with ancient belief systems. "Natural" preventive and healing remedies of many types are widely available through local practitioners, health food and grocery stores, and for purchase by mail. The yellow pages and the abundance of television specials and best-selling books on these topics speak to their wide appeal. Although this varied collection includes some disproved or outright quack remedies, most alternative remedies appear to be offered by well-meaning people who believe in their efficacy.

THE APPLICATION OF ALTERNATIVE MEDICINE

Alternatives are used by patients with serious, chronic illnesses such as cancer, diabetes, and AIDS, by people with self-limiting illnesses such as sore throats and colds, and as preventives or routes to emotional or spiritual well-being by those who are physically healthy. Thus, alternative remedies are applied in some instances in efforts to effect cure, in others to achieve symptom relief, and in yet others to enhance psychological or metaphysical comfort. Often the same alternative is applied by different people for each of these purposes. It is the last two of the three goals noted above that are concerned with quality of life.

Numerous symposia, workshops, newsletters, books, and articles are available to educate the public about the merits and specifics of alternative medicine. Many advertised programs are lifestyle oriented, encouraging health diets, spirituality, and other goals that should be helpful to most people whether they are sick or healthy. Practitioners often combine parts of several different types of alternative therapies, sometimes adding their own ingredients or applications.

ALTERNATIVE CONCEPTS AND RATIONALE

Conceptually, the diverse expressions of unconventional or alternative medicine have little in common. With the exception of themes of balance and vital energy, the various expressions of alternative medicine today are not linked by an overriding rationale, set of hypotheses, basic principles, or even a shared fundamental understanding of health, illness, and human physiology. The notable exception is the belief in a vital force or life energy that flows through the human body and the related importance of balance. The vital force may be described as chemical, bioelectric, or currently unexplainable. In some belief systems, it may be transferred from one individual to another. An illustrative expression of this concept appears in a talk given at a recent national symposium on alternative medicine, later published in an alternative newsletter. Entitled "Toxemia—Degenerative Conditions and the Lymphatic System," the presentation states: "Stagnant energy flow . . . creates a poisonous environment in the body, creating the prime cause of malignant, viral, bacterial and allergic diseases. . . . The most important causes underlying disease . . . are . . . obstruction and congestion of the lymphatic system. . . . Technological advances are now able to measure an individual's core energy vibrations as well as the energy vibrations of our different organs."

Different expressions of that concept, perhaps better known, are the "Qi" energy of traditional Chinese medicine and the belief that gifted healers can transmit their own life energy to others. The rationales behind alternative therapies may differ from one another, but typically they also are inconsistent with the tenets and principles of traditional science. Just as scientists use this nonconformity to nullify the logic and value of alternative concepts, so proponents of alternative medicine attack science for its limitations and the medical establishment for its narrowmindedness.

Homeopathy illustrates both the public appeal and the inconsistency with science's basic postulates that characterize much of contemporary alternative medicine. Homeopathy was founded by an early 19th century German physician, Samuel Hahnemann, who refined the much older view that cure of disease lies in taking minute doses of a substance that, in larger quantities, produces in healthy volunteers the same symptoms suffered by the patient. This small dose, like-cures-like notion apparently holds universal and timeless appeal. It dates back to 16th century Germany where Paracelcus treated plague by giving patients a droplet of their own excrement, to Hippocrates who wrote in 400 B.C. that disease can be cured through "application of the like," to even earlier Hindu physicians who described what is still known in homeopathy as the Law of Similars (5).

A concept of physical energy (some would view this as a variation of the vital energy force) is used to explain the effectiveness of homeopathic remedies, which are said to become increasingly powerful the more they are diluted. This belief that the higher dilution, the stronger the remedy, is fundamental to homeopathic preparations. Shaken vigorously between each of thousands of dilutions, the resultant remedy contains less than one molecule of the original substance.

From the homeopaths' perspective, this is neither unreasonable nor unprecedented, because, they claim, similarly diluted physiologic substances routinely effect important changes in the body (6). From the perspective of conventional science, homeopathic remedies exceed Avogadro's limit (5,7) and thus contain nothing but water.

Theoretically, how can homeopathic therapies work? Homeopathic practitioners believe that the imprint or trace memory of the substance remains to produce effective, nontoxic therapy with no side effects (5,6). Two of the major difficulties with this explanatory concept are worthy of consideration. One is that the concept of water having a memory does not conform to known laws of physics and chemistry. A second is that most water today is recycled. Trace memories of many substances, some unpleasant and most unrelated to the cure, should be present in the substance if the homeopathic trace memory concept were valid. Proponents offer no explanation for how a particular (homeopathic) imprint affects the individual while all of the other memory traces do not.

Homeopathic practitioners rarely if ever treat cancer or other potentially fatal illnesses with homeopathic remedies. Instead, they focus on lesser ailments such as asthma, skin conditions, low back pain, and colds (8). Those of a more conventional persuasion, including professionals who view homeopathy as the baldest of quackeries, might attribute any benefit perceived for homeopathic remedies to the body's capacity for self-repair, or to a placebo effect. The latter is a powerful mechanism (5) that may in many instances enhance quality of life. It is of interest to note that many if not most homeopathic practitioners in the United States as elsewhere are M.D.s, and that organizations of homeopathic physicians exist in this and other countries (8).

BELIEF IN THE CURATIVE POWER OF THE MIND

A very different alternative approach with similarly broad appeal involves mind-body interaction. The well-known former Yale surgeon Dr. Bernie Siegel brought this area to widespread attention through best-selling books such as *Love, Medicine, and Miracles* and numerous media appearances. Promoting the idea that cancer cures are facilitated by positive attitudes and patients' assumptions of responsibility for their own health, Dr. Siegel claims success for his "exceptional cancer patients" (E-CaP) support groups (9,10).

Following more than a decade of such claims, a study that evaluated the success of the E-CaP groups was conducted. Published in a major medical journal with Dr. Siegel as an author, it received virtually no public attention. The study showed that E-CaP patients lived no longer than clinically similar patients who did not attend the support sessions (11), thus directly contradicting the public claims. The results of this investigation failed to alter claims made by E-CaP proponents.

Belief in the mind's ability to control physiologic function and dysfunction—to cause or cure disease—has strong roots in American culture. The power and supremacy of the individual and of the will of the individual are quintessentially American beliefs, born of our frontier society. This is the conviction that the individual can beat insurmountable odds, and single-handedly conquer any enemy. This theme is apparent in our popular movies, in which a Stallone or Eastwood or Bronson tackles an overwhelming enemy alone, and is victorious. The folk belief is that the individual's determination and will can conquer an entire army, or triumph equally well over biologic forces—disease—that threaten destruction (12).

Of the various types of alternative and complementary therapies, mind-body techniques probably are most geared to quality of life. Although some practitioners tout mental attitude, imagery, and other mind-body therapies as cures that should be used independent and in lieu of conventional treatment, most aim to induce relaxation, comfort, tranquility, symptom control, and other facets of quality of life. Used in this way they are not "alternative" practices, but therapies applied in conventional settings to help patients cope with symptoms and the stress of illness.

THE ALLURE OF ALTERNATIVE PRACTICES

Unconventional medicine clearly shares broadly appealing characteristics, and these tend to be quality of life oriented. Unproven methods treat with equivalent concern diagnosable disease, spiritual disquiet, and trivial or self-limiting medical problems. And alternative practitioners do so with an emphasis on all aspects of the individual, including worries, aches and pains, emotional status and existential malaise, as well as disease and illnesses with or without conventionally demonstrable cause. This multifaceted, whole-person emphasis is highly valued by the public.

EVALUATING ALTERNATIVE THERAPIES

Unproven methods in medicine are not new to the 1980s and 1990s. They have been with us for centuries (3). Despite their longevity, alternative therapies rarely have been subjected to investigation. If properly studied and found to be effective, an alternative remedy automatically would become recategorized as conventional treatment, a new addition to establishment medicine's armamentarium. Patients and proponents, however, along with the thousands of M.D.s whose names fill the directories of homeopaths, chelation therapists, anthroposophically extended medicine, mind-body specialists, acupuncturists, holistic physicians, and so on, believe in the efficacy of alternative remedies and find neither the time nor the need for documentation beyond that provided by their own practice and beliefs.

Belief in the efficacy of particular regimens stems from experience and anecdote, for few alternative or complementary therapies have been studied in a conventional scientific fashion (13). The general public and many alternative practitioners, however, seem marginally if at all concerned with hard data on alternative practices and often react with hostility to research that fails to confirm anecdotal reports or long-held beliefs (14,15).

The dearth of research is primarily a function of philosophical differences between alternative and conventional medicine. Science is based in facts and data determined by investigations using approved methods. The alternative medicine worldview often is hostile toward science, its clinical practices, and methodologies (16), citing blind rigidity and the historic reluctance of establishment medicine to entertain new ideas. Semmelweiss is a frequently noted example in this regard (17).

In general, alternative practitioners and proponents prefer to rely on the personal experience of patients who say they were helped by a particular approach, on practitioners' clinical experience, and on the longevity of a practice. The latter is especially relevant to today's very popular Chinese and Indian (Ayer Vedic) traditional healing approaches. For many practitioners and users, these medical systems attain de facto respectability and merit because they have been in use for thousands of years. Left unnoted is the fact that binding the feet of baby girls and burying the emperor's concubines in his tomb, customs as ancient as traditional Chinese medicine, are not deemed meritorious despite their antiquity.

Although their efficacy remains largely unverified, many alternative approaches have become well-established components of health care in North America and Europe. In addition to its broad public availability, alternative medicine has achieved a remarkable degree not only of visibility and acceptance in recent years, but also of respectability. The latter is evident in three international circumstances: the increasing involvement of physicians in the practice of alternative medicine and of prominent academic centers in its teaching and study; the growing use of alternatives by an educated general public; and the establishment of organizations to mount, assist, and oversee studies of the value of popular unproven methods.

In the United States, many prominent universities offer courses in alternative medicine. Similar situations exist in other countries. Since 1992, a passing grade in a natural healing procedures course has been required of all M.D. candidates in Germany, and a regional hospital there has a Model Clinic for Integrated Medicine. This prototypic 176-bed facility contains traditional departments of medicine, cardiology, and so on, along with equivalent, integrated departments of various complementary (the preferred European alternative to "alternative") medical practices. Diagnoses and treatment plans are organized jointly by an internist, a complementary doctor, and a psychosocial practitioner.

Homeopathy, used by the royal family, is widely available in Britain. Medical societies in Canada have offered official recognition to alternative medicine, which in that country leans toward acupuncture and electroacupuncture, traditional Chinese and other herbal remedies, ozone therapy, homeopathy, chelation, and nutritional approaches.

It is of interest to note that components of traditional Chinese medicine such as acupuncture and herbal remedies, so much in vogue in the Western world, are applied in urban medical centers in the Orient to complement rather than supplant more technologic interventions. Their use as primary agents in Eastern countries predominates among those with limited access to modern technology.

The growing international acceptance of alternative and complementary medicine and its substantial popularity in the United States (4) probably contributed to the federal action that established the Office of Alternative Medicine (OAM), created by Congressional mandate in 1992 and placed under the Office of the Director of the National Institutes of Health with a 1994 budget of $6 million. OAM's major stated goal is to study popular alternatives.

Amid continuing controversy, that office funded 30 pilot grants at $30,000 each. The funded studies range from evaluation of therapeutic touch to light treatment, from intercessory prayer to anti-oxidizing agents. Some of these currently active studies may find enhanced quality of life and similar benefits for the alternative therapy under investigation. Major therapeutic breakthroughs are not anticipated by most observers, but improved quality of life is a logical expectation for many researched alternatives. Positive pilot results will be pursued with more substantive studies involving, as appropriate, control groups, placebo interventions, prospective longitudinal designs, and so on.

Appropriate methodologies for the study of alternative medicine are no different than for analogous conventional trials. Quality of life measures selected should be consistent with the illness or expected outcome under study. Of greatest importance, sound methodology must be applied in studying an alternative techniques's ability to cure disease or improve quality of life.

The lack of research training or experience among practitioners of alternative medicine, their frequent antipathy to "conventional" methodologic techniques, and the view that because alternative medicine is fundamentally different it should not follow conventional medicine's research methods and indeed should develop its own special techniques, represent the most challenging problem facing alternative research today. It is a difficult political problem faced by the Office of Alternative Medicine because the official council that guides OAM activity as well as unofficial outside pressures often insist on investigative approaches that are unacceptable to science.

CONCLUSIONS

Because unproven methods may yield proven benefits if tested properly and because its widespread use alone confers substantial importance, alternative medicine warrants no less than conclusive, well-designed research. Most individuals who use unproven methods are healthy people striving to enhance their general well-being or hoping to reduce the symptoms of self-limiting or relatively minor ailments. Among the seriously ill, some patients try unproven routes to cure, but the majority use complementary techniques to calm symptoms and to participate in the management of their illness—in short, to enhance quality of life. Although most alternative and complementary regimens aim to improve quality of life, few studies address quality of life specifically (13). However, there are few methodologically sound studies in alternative medicine generally. Most reports are anecdotal; most studies lack rudimentary components of clinical investigation such as controls, attention to placebo effects, or even documentation of the illness against which the method is applied.

As alternative medicine becomes increasingly a subject of clinical investigation, more and better studies will be conducted. Quality of life most certainly will become an important and explicitly stated outcome measure. Complementary and alternative approaches, exalted by adherents as panaceas and damned by many scientists as quackery, will begin to provide the data that, finally, will support their efficacy or document their inability to enhance quality of life. Society and medical care will benefit from research results regardless of their outcome.

REFERENCES

1. Cassileth BR. After Laetrile, what? *N Engl J Med* 1982;306:1482–1484.
2. Cassileth BR, Lusk EJ, Strouse TB, Bodenheimer BJ. Contemporary unorthodox treatments in cancer medicine: a study of patients, treatments and practitioners. *Ann Intern Med* 1984;101:105–112.
3. Cassileth BR, Brown H. Unorthodox cancer medicine. *CA* 1988;38: 176–186.
4. Eisenberg DM, Kessler RC, Foster C, Norlock FE, Calkins DR, Delbanco TL. Unconventional medicine in the United States. *N Engl J Med* 1993;328:246–252.
5. Buckman RB, Sabbagh K. *Magic or medicine?* Toronto: Key Porter Books, 1993.
6. Weil A. *Health and healing.* Boston: Houghton Mifflin, 1988.
7. Zwicky JF, Hafner AW, Barrett S, Jarvis WT. *Reader's guide to alternative health methods.* Milwaukee: American Medical Association, 1993.
8. The Burton Goldberg Group. *Alternative medicine: the definitive guide.* Puyallup, WA: Future Medicine, 1993.
9. Siegel BS. *Love, medicine, and miracles: lessons learned about self-healing from a surgeon's experience with exceptional patients.* New York: Harper and Row, 1986.
10. Siegel BS. *Peace, love, and healing: body-mind communication and the path to self-healing: an exploration.* New York: Harper and Row, 1989.
11. Gellert GA, Maxwell RM, Siegel BS. Survival of breast cancer patients receiving adjunctive psychosocial support therapy: a 10-year follow-up study. *J Clin Oncol* 1993;11:66–69.
12. Cassileth BR. The social implications of mind-body cancer research. *Cancer Invest* 1989;7:361–364.
13. Cassileth BR, Lusk EJ, Guerry D, Blake AD, Walsh WP, Kascius L, Schultz DJ. Survival and quality of life among patients on unproven versus conventional cancer therapy. *N Engl J Med* 1991;324:1180–1185.
14. Moertel CG, Fleming TR, Rubin J, Kvols LK, Sarna G, Koch R, Currie VE, Young CW, Jones SE, Davignon. A clinical trial of amygdalin (Laetrile) in the treatment of human cancer. *N Engl J Med* 1982; 306:201–206.
15. Moertel CG, Fleming TR, Creagan ET, Rubin J, O'Connell MJ, Ames MM. High-dose vitamin C versus placebo in the treatment of patients with advanced cancer who have had no prior chemotherapy: a randomized double-blind comparison. *N Engl J Med* 1979;312: 137–141.
16. Coulter HL. *The controlled clinical trial: an analysis.* Washington, DC: Center for Empirical Medicine, 1991.
17. Inglis B. *A history of medicine.* Cleveland, OH: World Publishing, 1965.

Quality of Life and Pharmacoeconomics in Clinical Trials, Second Edition, edited by B. Spilker.
Lippincott-Raven Publishers, Philadelphia © 1996.

CHAPTER **45**

Quality of Life: Statistical Issues and Analysis

Diane L. Fairclough and Richard D. Gelber

INTRODUCTION

Most clinical trials have focused traditionally on end points of efficacy such as survival. However, there has been a shift that is reflected by the World Health Organization (WHO) definition of health: "Health is not only the absence of infirmity and disease but also a state of physical, mental and social well-being." Thus health is a composite of related outcomes that reflect functional, cognitive, and social well-being, as well as survival and disease-specific physiological responses. If there are minimal differences in the efficacy of particular therapies, the issue of toxicity and the general impact of therapy on quality of life (QOL) become particularly relevant. Even when there are significant differences in the effectiveness of different therapies, the impact of severe and/or chronic toxicity on QOL may be relevant to clinical practice. Thus, the desirability for QOL assessment in clinical trials has increased with the awareness that comparisons of therapeutic regimens should not be based solely on efficacy outcomes such as survival.

Although the characteristics and validation of QOL instruments have been extensively discussed, issues of statistical analysis have not been adequately addressed. In this chapter we discuss various aspects of the design and analysis of clinical trials involving QOL assessments with special emphasis on three specific issues: multiple comparisons, missing data, and integrating QOL and time. In most clinical trials, QOL end points have been incorporated by administering questionnaires at multiple points in time before, during, and after the intervention, with the goal of characterizing the patients' QOL in a longitudinal fashion. This, combined with the multidimensional QOL scales, results in a high-dimensional repeated measures design with the associated problem of multiple comparisons. The second issue is the likelihood of missing data in a study with long-term follow-up and possibly significant mortality. The possibility that QOL scores might be missing for reasons that reflect a systematically poor or favorable overall outcome is of particular concern. The third issue is the simultaneous presentation of efficacy and QOL results in a way that is clinically meaningful and easily interpretable.

PRIMARY STATISTICAL ISSUES

Multiple Comparisons

Analysis of QOL data differs from the analysis of other clinical end points for several reasons. First, there are often

D. L. Fairclough and R. D. Gelber: Department of Biostatistics, Harvard School of Public Health and Division of Biostatistics, Dana-Farber Cancer Institute, Boston, Massachusetts 02115.

428 / Chapter 45

a large number of measures resulting from both multiple dimensions of QOL (multiple instruments and/or subscales) and repeated assessments over time. The resulting problem of multiple comparisons was the primary analytic consideration identified by the Statistical Working Group during the 1990 National Cancer Institute (NCI) Workshop on Quality of Life Research in Clinical Trials (1). Univariate tests for each subscale and time point can seriously inflate the type I (false positive) error rate for the overall trial such that the investigator is unable to distinguish between the true and false positive differences. Furthermore, it is often impossible to determine the number of tests performed at the end of analysis and adjust post hoc. Methods that allow summarization of multiple outcomes both simplify the interpretation of the results and often improve the statistical power to detect clinically relevant differences, especially when small but consistent differences in QOL occur over time or across multiple domains. On the other hand, significant differences at a particular time or within a particular domain may be blurred by aggregation.

Missing Data

Missing data refers to missing items in scales and missed and/or mistimed assessments. If the assessment is missing for reasons that are unrelated to the patient's QOL, the data are classified as "missing at random" (2). Examples might be staff forgetting to administer the assessment, a missed appointment due to inclement weather, or the patient moved out of the area. Data that are administratively missing because the patient has not been on-study long enough to reach the assessment time point (i.e., the data are censored or incomplete) are also considered missing at random. Assessments may be mistimed if they are actually given but the exact timing does not correspond to the planned schedule of assessments for reasons unrelated to the patient's QOL. While these types of missing/mistimed data make analyses more complex and may reduce the power to detect differences, the estimates of QOL are unbiased even if they are based only on the observed QOL assessments.

Nonrandomly missing or informatively censored data present a much more difficult problem. One example of this type of missing data is that due to death, disease progression, or toxicity where the QOL would generally be poorer in the patients who were not observed than in those who were observed. In the chronic disease setting, this relationship between QOL and missing data might manifest itself as study dropout due to lack of relief, presence of side effects, or, conversely, improvement in the condition. The difficulty occurs because analyses that inappropriately assume the data are randomly missing will result in biased estimates of QOL reflecting only the more limited population of patients who were assessed rather than the entire sample or population under study. One possibility is to limit the analysis, and

thereby the inference, to patients with complete data. In most cases, however, this strategy is not acceptable to achieve the goal of comparing QOL assessments for all patients. Unless careful prospective documentation of the reasons for missing assessments is available in a clinical trial, it is generally impossible to know definitively whether the reason for the missing assessment is related to the patient's condition and/or QOL.

Integration of QOL and Time

In clinical trials with significant disease-related mortality there is a need to integrate survival with QOL. This was identified by the participants in the 1990 NCI QOL workshop who "acknowledged that the use of QOL data in clinical decision-making will not routinely occur until a larger body of QOL data is available and models for integrating medical and QOL information are available" (1). In studies where both QOL (or toxicity) and clinical end points indicate the superiority of one treatment over another, the choice of the best treatment is clear. Similarly, if either QOL or the efficacy outcome demonstrate a benefit and there is no difference in the other, the choice of treatment is straightforward. The dilemma occurs when there is a conflict in the QOL and efficacy outcomes; this is often the case when there is significant toxicity associated with the more effective treatment.

DESIGN ISSUES

Study Objectives

Clear study goals are prerequisites to developing appropriate design and analysis strategies that answer clinically relevant questions. Overly general objectives, such as "Describe the QOL . . ." don't adequately address whether the focus is the comparison of the two treatment arms, whether the comparisons are limited to the period of therapy or extend across time within treatment group. Without a focused objective, unnecessary assessments are often included in protocol designs. This increases the multiple comparisons and missing data problems and increases the possibility that critical assessments will be omitted.

QOL Instruments

QOL assessments should be limited to the briefest and least complicated instrument or combination of instruments that adequately address the primary question (e.g., 30 vs. 150 questions). Adding scales/instruments to obtain data that are not necessary to the primary objective will increase both the multiple comparisons problem and the likelihood that data will be incomplete. This will potentially compromise the ability of the trial to achieve the primary objective.

Timing of Assessments

The timing of the QOL assessments must also be specified to achieve the study goals. Baseline measures that precede therapy allow for assessment of treatment-related changes within an individual. Depending on the goals of the study, it is also important to have a sufficiently long period of follow-up after therapy to allow for assessment of the long-term treatment effect and potential late sequelae. In the phase III treatment comparison setting, it is critical that QOL should be assessed regardless of treatment and disease status. Patients who have changes in status or who have discontinued treatment should not stop their assessment of QOL, as the biggest differences in QOL may be in these patients. Without these measurements it will be difficult to derive summary measures and impossible to make unbiased comparisons of the effects of different therapeutic regimens on QOL. Procedures for obtaining assessments for patients who have changed status or discontinued therapy should be explicitly stated in protocols.

The timing of assessments should be chosen to minimize missing data. It is generally recommended that the frequency of assessments be minimized for patient and staff considerations. However, in some cases more frequent administration linked to the clinical routine (e.g., at the beginning of every treatment cycle) may result in more complete data because the pattern of assessment is established as part of the clinical routine.

Sample Size and Power

The sample size and power to detect meaningful differences for primary QOL hypotheses is critical to any study in which QOL is an important end point. In addition to the usual estimates of variation and correlations, the sensitivity of the QOL instrument to detect clinically significant changes is the most useful information that can be provided during the validation of a QOL instrument. For example, Cella et al. (3) shows that the Functional Assessment of Cancer Therapy Scale is sensitive to changes in performance status. Specific estimates of the changes in subscales and global scales related to clinical status give the statistician and the clinician a clear and familiar reference point for defining differences that are clinically relevant. This is critical for insuring an adequate sample size for the study. It should be noted that because end points may involve both repeated measurements at different times and/or combinations of subscales, both test-retest correlations and among-subscale correlations are useful and should be reported for validated instruments.

If the sample size requirements for the QOL component are substantially less than for the entire study, an unbiased strategy for selection of a subset of patients in which QOL will be assessed should be identified. For example, the first 500 patients enrolled in the study might be included in the QOL substudy. This may have an additional advantage in studies with a long duration of QOL follow-up. This strategy is being used in the design of an Eastern Cooperative Oncology Group (ECOG) study (4), in which patient entry is expected to take 5 years, an additional follow-up of 2.5 years is planned for the survival end point, and the desired duration of QOL assessments is 5 years. By limiting the patients in which QOL is assessed to those enrolled in the first 2.5 years, the QOL study is expected to be complete at the same time as the final analysis of the primary survival end points.

ANALYSIS FROM THE QOL MEASUREMENT PERSPECTIVE

In general, statistical methods for QOL data analysis can be classified in two major groups. In the first group the statistical analysis is expressed in the metric of the QOL scales (as discussed in this section), whereas in the second group the outcome is expressed in terms of time (discussed in the following section).

Dealing with Missing Items in QOL Scales

In scales based on multiple items, missing information results in a serious missing data problem. If only 0.1% of items are randomly missing for a 50-item instrument, 18% ($[1 - .999^{4 \times 50}] * 100\%$) of the subjects will have one or more items missing over four assessments. If the missing rate is 0.5% (1 in 200 items), then only 37% ($[.995^{4 \times 50}] * 100\%$) of subjects will have complete data. Deletion of the entire case when there are missing items results in loss of power and potential bias if subjects with poorer QOL are more or less likely to skip an item. Individuals with high levels of nonresponse (> 50%) should be dealt with on a case-by-case basis. Careful selection of a method for imputing missing items for an individual who has answered most questions would, in general, be preferable to deletion of the entire case or observation. A simple method based solely on the patient's own data would use the mean of all nonmissing items for the entire scale or the specific subscale. Methods based on other patients would include the mean of that item in individuals who had responded. Another method utilizing data from other subjects is based on the high correlation of items within a scale or subscale and utilizes information about the individual's tendency to score correlated items high or low and the tendency of a particular item to be scored high or low relative to other items. The procedure is to regress the missing item on the nonmissing items using data from individuals with complete data, and to then predict the value of the missing item using the information from the completed items in the individual with the missing item (5).

Univariate Methods

One approach to the reporting of QOL data has been descriptive univariate statistics such as means and proportions at each specific point in time. These descriptive statistics may be accompanied by simple parametric or nonparametric tests such as t-tests or Wilcoxon tests. While these methods are easy to implement and often used (6), they do not address any of the three previously identified issues. One recommended solution to the multiple comparisons problem is to limit the number of a priori end points in the design of the trial to three or less (7). The analyses of the remaining scales and/or time points can be presented descriptively or graphically (1). While theoretically improving the overall type I error rate for the study, in practice investigators are reluctant to ignore the remaining data and may receive requests from reviewers to provide results from secondary analyses with the corresponding significance levels.

An alternative method of addressing the multiple comparisons problem is to apply a Bonferroni correction, which adjusts the test statistics on k end points so that the overall type I error is preserved for the smallest p value. The procedure is to accept as statistically significant only those tests with p values that are less than α/k, where α is the overall type I error usually set equal to .05. However, this results in a focus on the smallest p value and may yield conclusions that are counterintuitive. For example, Fig. 1A illustrates an analysis of $k = 4$ end points (either four different time points or four QOL dimensions) all with test statistics corresponding to $p = .02$ and effects in the same direction. Using the Bonferroni adjustment, the differences displayed in the figure would not be considered statistically significant because all p values are greater than .0125. In contrast, the result displayed in Fig. 1B would be considered statistically

significant because the test statistic at the first end point reached $p = .01$.

Multivariate Methods

Multivariate analysis techniques include approaches such as repeated measures of analysis of variance (ANOVA) or multivariate ANOVA (MANOVA) (8). These techniques require complete data, which limits their use to settings where there is a low risk of mortality and very high compliance with QOL assessment. If the data are not complete, the inferences are restricted to a very select and generally nonrepresentative group of patients. Multivariate statistics such as Hotelling's T are frequently used to control for type I error. These statistics, however, answer global questions such as "Are any of the dimensions of QOL different?" or "Are there differences in QOL at any point in time?" without regard to whether the differences are in consistent directions. In general, the multivariate test statistics are not sensitive to differences in the same direction across the multiple end points.

The requirement for complete data can be relaxed by using repeated measures or mixed effects model with structured covariance (9). These methods assume that the data are missing for reasons unrelated to the patients QOL, such as staff forgetting to administer the assessment. If the missing assessments can reasonably be assumed to be missing at random, a likelihood-based analysis approach, such as a mixed-effects models or EM (Estimation-Maximization) algorithm for repeated measures models, enables incorporating all patients with at least one assessment in the analysis (9,10). This approach has the additional advantages of estimation of within- and between-subject variation, inclusion of time-

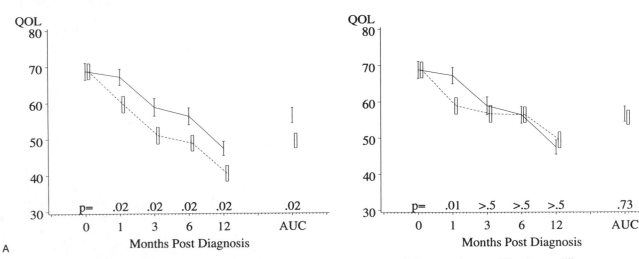

FIG. 1. Hypothetical studies with (**A**) consistent differences in QOL over time or (**B**) a large difference at a single point in time. *Boxes* indicate interquartile ranges and *vertical lines* indicates interdecile ranges. Medians are joined by *horizontal line*. P values correspond to unadjusted Wilcoxon rank sum test statistics.

varying covariates, and testing of changes over time. Software for these methods is available in some of the major packages (SAS, Proc Mixed; BMDP, 5V).

However, in most settings where QOL is of interest, the causes of missing assessments are likely to be related to the patients' illness and thus to their QOL. There are a number of suggested approaches for longitudinal studies that are interested in change over time and where the change is expected to be linear over time. The simplest approach is an unweighted average of individual least-squares slopes. Alternative approaches include modeling of the censoring process (11) or use of a conditional linear model (12). Both methods are based on a growth curve model approach with the individual slope parameter(s) related to censoring of later observations (right censoring) either through a linear random effects model with a probit model for the censoring process or a conditional linear model. Mori et al. (13) propose empirical Bayes estimates, which adjust for informative right censoring.

When the change over time is not expected to be linear or the censoring times vary across patients, an alternative approach needs to be considered. Schluchter (14) and De-Gruttola and Tu (15) have proposed extensions of the two-stage mixed-effects model, in which the time of censoring (or death) is incorporated into the second-stage model of the population parameters.

A nonparametric approach to nonrandom missing data would involve ranking the data at each time point with the lowest ranks assigned for missing assessments due to death, disease progression, or severe toxicity. The assumption is that the QOL values for these nonrandomly missing observa-

tions are lower than the observed data. Group differences could be examined at each time point with nonparametric tests such as the two-sample Wilcoxon rank sum test. These statistics can be combined across time points using a procedure such as that described by Wei and Johnson (16) for combining two-sample Wilcoxon tests.

The influence of missing data on the statistical analysis of QOL data is illustrated in the results displayed in Fig. 2. A total of 1,475 premenopausal women with operable node-positive breast cancer were included in a randomized clinical trial of adjuvant chemotherapy conducted by the International Breast Cancer Study Group (IBCSG Trial VI; see Chapter 72 by Bernhard et al.). Figure 2A shows the median and interquartile ranges for the physical well-being linear analog self-assessment scores at 1 year after randomization for 961 patients with one to three positive nodes compared with 514 patients with four or more positive nodes (high scores represent better QOL). At 1 year, QOL assessments were missing due to relapse or death for 5% of patients, due to short follow-up (administrative censoring) for 5%, and due to other reasons for 26%. Missing assessments due to early relapse or death differed between the two groups (2% for the first group and 9% for the second group). Three methods of handling missing data are illustrated in Fig. 2 and p values are calculated using the nonparametric Wilcoxon statistic. The ''ignore'' method ignores all missing assessments; patients with four or more positive nodes report significantly higher scores (better QOL) than patients with one to three positive nodes ($p = .013$). The last value carried forward method replaces the missing values with the last

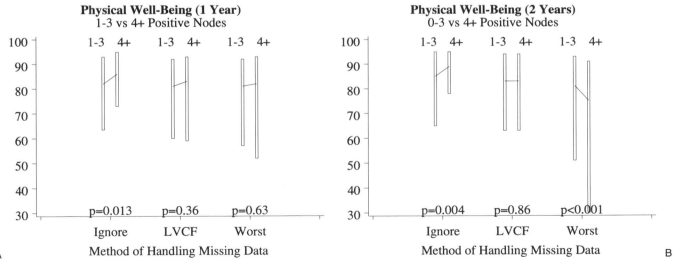

FIG. 2. Average scores from the physical well-being linear analog self-assessment (LASA) scale for 1,475 premenopausal breast cancer patients who received adjuvant chemotherapy in International Breast Cancer Study Group (IBCSG) Trial VI. Scores for patients with one to three positive nodes are compared with scores for patients with four or more positive nodes using three different policies for handling missing data. Results are shown at (**A**) 1 year and (**B**) 2 years from randomization. The *vertical boxes* show the interquartile ranges of the distributions of scores and the *horizontal lines* connect the median scores for the two patient groups. Higher scores indicate better physical well-being.

reported value; the difference is no longer statistically significant as the patients with four or more positive nodes who were missing data tended to have worse QOL prior to the 1-year assessment. Finally, the "worst" method replaces the values that are missing due to prior relapse or death with the worst QOL scores possible; because more patients with four or more positive nodes are missing due to this reason, the comparison of QOL between the groups is even less significant. Figure 2B shows the same set of analyses performed at 2 years after randomization when data were missing due to prior relapse or death for 8% of the patients with one to three positive nodes and for 27% of patients with four or more positive nodes. In this case patients with four or more positive nodes either have a significantly better QOL, no difference, or a significantly worse QOL compared with the one to three positive node group depending on the method chosen to handle missing data.

Summary of Global Statistics

One limitation of the multivariate methods is that they do not directly provide a summary measure that would facilitate the interpretation of longitudinal data such as when early toxicity may be balanced by later QOL advantages (relapse-free, survival). In settings where QOL is expected to improve or decline over time, it may be possible to summarize the data as the slope of QOL versus time. If the trend in QOL is expected to be linear over time, unweighted analysis of

individual slopes is a commonly recommended method. This has several advantages. First, it provides a single easy to interpret summary of multiple measurements obtained over time. Second, if there are at least two measurements, randomly missing and/or mistimed observations are not a problem. Finally, when the censoring is informative (e.g., patients who die earlier have more negative slopes than those who survive), unweighted analyses of the slopes are not biased as long as all subjects have at least two measurements.

Change from baseline to the last QOL assessment is a form of last-observation-carried-forward (17). The drawback of this approach is that if QOL is declining over time, the rate of change will be underestimated for patients with earlier final measurements.

Figure 3 illustrates two different approaches to the graphical presentation of multidimensional QOL data. Both are from randomized studies designed to evaluate combination chemotherapy for patients with breast cancer. In one study (Fig. 3A), a summary QOL score derived from the 30-item Breast Cancer Chemotherapy Questionnaire (BCQ) (18) was obtained at multiple time points during and following completion of chemotherapy. The figure illustrates that the summary QOL scores are lower for a longer period of time among patients who received 36 weeks of adjuvant chemotherapy compared with 12 weeks of treatment. This might reflect the fact that the BCQ measure was designed to be sensitive to specific chemotherapy side effects. In contrast, the presentation of data from the second study highlights treatment comparisons in terms of the change in scores for

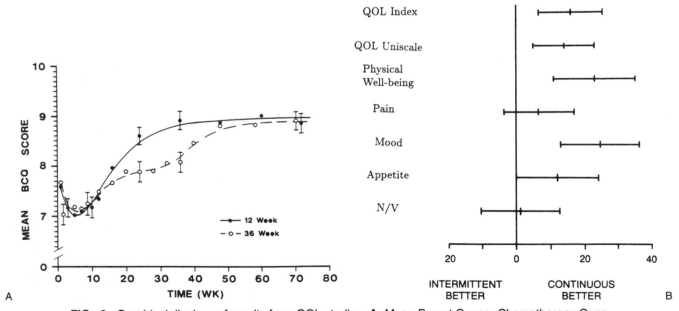

FIG. 3. Graphical displays of results from QOL studies. **A:** Mean Breast Cancer Chemotherapy Questionnaire (BCQ) scores over time for two adjuvant chemotherapy programs of different duration. (From ref. 18, with permission.) **B:** Comparison between continuous and intermittent chemotherapy programs (after the programs diverged at 3 months but before disease progression) using a QOL-index questionnaire, a global uniscale, and LASA scales for individual domains. (From ref. 19, with permission.)

separate domains of QOL (19). In this study the randomized comparison was between intermittent chemotherapy (discontinuation of treatment if disease was stable after three cycles) and continuous chemotherapy (administration of treatment continuously until disease progression) for patients with metastatic breast cancer. The separate domains were measured using linear analog self-assessment scales, a global uniscale for overall QOL completed by the patient and a QOL-index questionnaire completed by the physician. Patients on the continuous chemotherapy regimen reported better physical well-being, mood, and overall QOL (uniscale and index) than those who received the intermittent treatment. In both cases, by graphically presenting the multiplicity of data either across time (Fig. 3A) or across QOL domains (Fig. 3B), the reader can informally synthesize a global QOL treatment comparison without performing a formal multivariate analysis.

O'Brien (20) and Pocock et al. (21) suggest summary statistics that are sensitive to consistent trends in the same direction across multiple end points and control the type I error rate for multiple outcomes. O'Brien (20) proposes a weighted average of the individual t-statistics for the k end points. The weights are based on the correlations between the k end points, such that end points that are more highly correlated are down-weighted. If the multiple end points are subscales of a QOL instrument, this weighted average of the subscale scores would be an alternative to a total score generated by the sum of the item scores. Another application would be the combination of t-statistics generated at different points in time. Pocock et al. (21) suggest the potential extension of this strategy to the combination of any asymptotically normal test statistics, which would include t-statistics for QOL scores and log-rank statistics for survival. The advantage is that the weights do not have to be prespecified. The corresponding disadvantage is that the weights will vary from study to study, thus limiting the generalizability and making it difficult to interpret from a clinical standpoint (22).

Cox et al. (22) suggest an approach that provides a summary measure of QOL over time and accounts for missing data resulting from death or censoring where follow-up is not complete at the time of analysis. The summary statistic is the area under the curve (AUC) of QOL scores (Y_i) plotted versus time (t_i). Scores for assessment times after death would have a value of 0 or some arbitrarily specified low QOL value:

$$AUC = \sum_{i=1}^{I} (t_i - t_{i-1}) * (Y_i + Y_{i-1})/2$$

Note that this can also be expressed as a weighted function of the QOL scores:

$$AUC = (t_1 - t_0)/2 * Y_0 + \sum_{i=2}^{I-1} (t_{i+1} - t_{i-1})/2 * Y_i + (t_I - t_{I-1})/2 * Y_I.$$

As shown for the hypothetical data of Fig. 1, this summary statistic is most sensitive to differences between treatments that are consistent over time.

Korn (23) suggests presenting these AUC values for groups of patients, as one would present survival data. This approach has the advantage of both displaying more information about the distribution of the AUC values and accommodating administrative censoring. Unfortunately, the administrative censoring is informative on the QOL scale (24,25) and the usual Kaplan-Meier estimate will be biased. Specifically, if the censoring mechanism due to staggered entry and incomplete follow-up is identical for two groups, the group with poorer QOL will have lower values of the AUC and will be censored earlier on the AUC scale. Korn (23) suggests a procedure to reduce the bias of the Kaplan-Meier estimator by assuming that the probability of administrative censoring in short intervals is independent of the QOL measures prior to that time. This assumption is probably not true. The violation, however, may be small enough that the estimator will not be badly biased, especially if QOL is measured frequently and the relationship of QOL AUC and censoring is weak.

ANALYSIS FROM THE TIME PERSPECTIVE

Time to a Prespecified QOL End Point

A simple univariate statistic incorporating time and QOL is the proportion of patients experiencing some QOL event. For example, the proportion of patients who drop more than ten points from baseline during 6 months of therapy or the proportion of patients improving to within five points of baseline after a particularly toxic therapy. In both cases, since the baseline measurement plays such a critical role in the end point, it would be advisable to obtain multiple assessments of baseline whenever feasible.

Time can be incorporated into this concept by graphically displaying the time to the QOL event in the form of a familiar Kaplan-Meier plot. This type of presentation was used by Rosenman and Choi (26) in which the QOL end point was the duration of time with Karnofsky Index > 60 (Fig. 4). The analysis and interpretation are generally straightforward. However, interesting differences between treatment groups may not be reflected by the time to reach a specific level of QOL. For example, two patients might both decline to a Karnofsky score of 60 at 6 months (thus being considered equivalent in the analysis), while one maintained a consistent Karnofsky score of 70 and the other maintained a score of 90 for the entire 6 months prior to dropping to 60.

Quality-Adjusted Life Years (QALY)

An intuitive method of incorporating QOL and time would be to adjust life years by down-weighting time spent in periods of poor quality of life. However, what would seem to be a simple idea has many methodologic challenges. The first is the determination of weights. Torrance (27) describes several techniques for eliciting weights for states of health

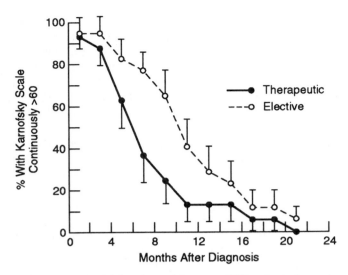

FIG. 4. Kaplan-Meier plots of time to a QOL-oriented event. (From ref. 26, with permission.)

including direct ratings, time trade-offs, and standard gambles. In addition to the difficulties of administering some of these techniques in clinical trials, weights elicited by the different techniques or from different respondents may not result in equivalent measures (28). The choice of anchor points and content validity may mean that weights that are appropriate in one setting may be inappropriate in another. The other methodologic difficulty occurs in trials with censored data. Although it might seem appropriate to undertake a standard survival analysis of individual quality-adjusted survival times, the usual product limit estimator of the survival function is biased because censoring is related by the future outcome (24,25). For example, if two groups have the same censoring times due to death, the group with the poorer QOL will be censored earlier on the QALY scale. This latter problem can be addressed by estimating the average time spent in each health state and then computing a weighted average of the time as is done in the Q-TWiST approach.

Q-TWiST

The objective of the Q-TWiST method is to evaluate therapies based on both quantity and quality of life. Q-TWiST stands for *Q*uality-adjusted *T*ime *Wi*thout *S*ymptoms of disease and *T*oxicity of treatment (25,29). It is based on the concept of quality-adjusted life years (QALYs) (30) and represents a utility-based approach to QOL assessment in clinical trials (31). The starting point is to define QOL-oriented clinical health states, one of which represents relatively good health with minimal symptoms of disease or treatment associated toxicity (TWiST). Patients will progress through or skip these clinical health states, but will not backtrack. The next step is to partition the area under the overall

Kaplan-Meier survival curve and calculate the average time a patient spends in each clinical health state. The final step is to compare the treatment regimens using weighted sums of the mean duration of each health state, where the weights are utility based. If these utility weight are unknown, as is generally the case, treatment comparisons can be made using sensitivity analyses, also called threshold utility analyses. More details are provided in Chapter 46 by Gelber et al.

Markov and Semi-Markov Models

Markov and semi-Markov models have been used to compare treatments based on estimates of the time spent in different health states and the probabilities of transitions between these states. The relevant health states must be identified and then each is weighted to reflect the relative value of a health state compared to perfect health. The treatments are then compared in terms of the total quality-adjusted time, the weighted sum of the health state durations. In general, to calculate the transition probabilities an underlying model must be assumed. The most commonly used model is the Markov chain, which assumes that the transitions from one QOL state to another are independent and continuous and only depend upon the previous state (32). This requires that the assessments are made at time points independent of the patients' treatment schedule or health state. Discrete-time transient semi-Markov processes were used to model the health state transition probabilities corresponding to the prolongation of life, while a simple recurrent Markov process was used to derive the QOL state transition probabilities. In a semi-Markov process, the state changes from an embedded Markov chain and the times spent in different health state are mutually independent and depend only on the adjoining states (33).

CONCLUSIONS

We have identified three characteristics of QOL studies that present challenges for analysis and interpretation. The first is the occurrence of both randomly and nonrandomly missing data. The analysis of randomly missing data is generally well defined with enough experience to have addressed both practical and theoretical issues. In contrast, development of methods for the analysis of nonrandomly missing data is in its infancy, and we will need more experience to determine which methods are most practical and appropriate.

The second issue is the multivariate nature of QOL studies. Not only is QOL a multidimensional concept measured by multiple scales, but most studies are longitudinal. Separate analyses of each domain at multiple time points may make it difficult to communicate the results in a manner that is meaningful for clinicians and patients. Summary measures may reduce the multidimensionality of the problem but may not make the interpretation much easier. The issue of weights that vary by technique and study also adds to the complexity of interpretation. In general, it would be advisable to perform the analyses under various assumptions to verify that the results were not sensitive to small changes in the assumptions.

The third issue is the integration of survival data with QOL measures. This can be addressed from either the perspective of QOL or time. From a research perspective both approaches can be informative; however, currently time is a dimension with which both clinicians and biostatisticians are most familiar. The existence of multiple QOL instruments with different relationships of scores with clinical impressions contributes to the difficulty of interpretation. Finally, interpretation of clinical trials may not always be helpful in guiding individual patient decisions. In theory, individual patients could utilize the threshold utility analysis of Q-TWiST, but this may require extensive patient education.

There are a number of statistical methodologies that can be employed in the analysis of QOL data, each of which is based on specific assumptions, yields a different summary measure, and thus emphasizes different aspects of QOL. When there are more than one analysis strategies that will answer the primary QOL questions, the strategy that best anticipates the above issues should be considered. Analyses should be clearly and concisely reportable so that the relevant differences can be readily understood by those who will use the results.

ACKNOWLEDGMENTS

We thank the International Breast Cancer Study Group for allowing us to use the QOL data appearing in Fig. 2. This investigation was supported by grants CA06516, CA23318 awarded by the National Cancer Institute, DHHS, and PBR-53 from the American Cancer Society.

REFERENCES

1. Korn EL, O'Fallon J. Statistical considerations, statistics working group. *Quality of life assessment in cancer clinical trials, report on Workshop on Quality of Life Research in Cancer Clinical Trials, Division of Cancer Prevention and Control.* Bethesda, MD: National Cancer Institute, 1990.
2. Little RJ, Rubin DB. *Statistical analysis with missing data.* New York: John Wiley, 1987:14–17.
3. Cella DF, Tulsky DS, Gray G, et al. The Functional Assessment of Cancer Therapy Scale: development and validation of the general measure. *J Clin Oncol* 1993;11:570–579.
4. Eastern Cooperative Oncology Group. E7892: a phase III randomized double blind trial of adjuvant hormonal therapy for surgically-treated pathologic stage C carcinoma of the prostate, 1994.
5. Buck SF. A method of estimation of missing values in multivariate data suitable for use with electronic computer. *J R Stat Soc B* 1960;22:303–306.
6. Schumacher M, Olschewski M, Schulgen G. Assessment of quality of life in clinical trials. *Stat Med* 1991;10:1915–1930.
7. Gotay CC, Korn EL, McCabe MS, Moore TD, Cheson BD. Building quality of life assessment into cancer treatment studies. *Oncology* 1992;6:25–28.
8. Zee B, Pater J. Statistical analysis of trials assessing quality of life. In: Osoba D, ed. *Effect of cancer on quality of life.* Boston: CRC Press, 1991:113–124.
9. Jennrich R, Schluchter M. Unbalanced repeated-measures models with structured covariance matrices. *Biometrics* 1986;42:805–820.
10. Dempster AP, Laird NM, Rubin DB. Maximum likelihood from incomplete data via the EM algorithm (with discussion). *J R Stat Soc B* 1972;39:1–38.
11. Wu MC, Carroll RJ. Estimation and comparison of changes in the presence of informative right censoring by modeling the censoring process. *Biometrics* 1988;44:175–188.
12. Wu MC, Bailey KR. Estimation and comparison of changes in the presence of informative right censoring: conditional linear model. *Biometrics* 1989;45:939–955.
13. Mori M, Woodworth GG, Woolson RF. Application of empirical Bayes inference to estimation of rate of change in the presence of informative right censoring. *Stat Med* 1992;11:621–631.
14. Schluchter MD. Methods for the analysis of informatively censored longitudinal data. *Stat Med* 1992;11:1861–1870.
15. DeGruttola V, Tu XM. *Modeling progression of CD4-lymphocyte count and its relationship to survival time.* Technical Report, Biostatistics, Harvard School of Public Health, 1992.
16. Wei LJ, Johnson WE. Combining dependent tests with incomplete repeated measurements. *Biometrika* 1985;72:359–364.
17. Tandon PK. Application of global statistics in analyzing quality of life data. *Stat Med* 1990;9:819–827.
18. Levine MN, Guyatt GH, Gent M, et al. Quality of life in stage II breast cancer: an instrument for clinical trials. *J Clin Oncol* 1988;6:1798–1810.
19. Coates A, Gebski V, Bishop JF, et al. Improving the quality of life during chemotherapy for advanced breast cancer: a comparison of intermittent and continuous treatment strategies. *N Engl J Med* 1987;317:1490–1495.
20. O'Brien PC. Procedures for comparing samples with multiple endpoints. *Biometrics* 1984;40:1079–1087.
21. Pocock SJ, Geller NL, Tsiatis AA. The analysis of multiple endpoints in clinical trials. *Biometrics* 1987;43:487–498.
22. Cox DR, Fitzpatrick R, Fletcher AI, Gore SM, Spiegelhalter DJ, Jones DR. Quality-of-life assessment: can we keep it simple? (with discussion). *J R Stat Soc A* 1992;155:353–393.
23. Korn EL. On estimating the distribution function for quality of life in cancer clinical trials. *Biometrika* 1993;80:535–542.
24. Gelber RD, Gelman RS, Goldhirsh A. A quality of life oriented endpoint for comparing therapies. *Biometrics* 1989;45:781–795.
25. Glasziou PP, Simes RJ, Gelber RD. Quality adjusted survival analysis. *Stat Med* 1990;9:1259–1276.
26. Rosenman J, Choi NC. Improved quality of life of patients with small-cell carcinoma of the lung by elective irradiation of the brain. *Int J Radiat Oncol Biol Phys* 1982;8:1041–1043.
27. Torrance GW. Measurement of health state utilities for economic appraisal: a review. *J Health Econ* 1986;5:1–30.
28. Froberg D, Kane R. Methodology for measuring health-state preferences: II. Scaling methods. *J Clin Epidemiol* 1989;42:459–471.
29. Goldhirsch A, Gelber RD, Simes RJ, et al., for Ludwig Breast Cancer Study Group. Costs and benefits of adjuvant therapy in breast cancer: a quality-adjusted survival analysis. *J Clin Oncol* 1989;7:36–44.
30. Weinstein MC, Stason WB. Foundations of cost-effective analysis for health and medical practices. *N Engl J Med* 1977;296:716–721.
31. Feeny DH, Torrance GW. Incorporating utility-based quality-of-life assessment measures in clinical trials. *Med Care* 1989;27:S190–S204.
32. Gore S. Integrated reporting of quality and length of life—a statistician's perspective. *Eur Heart J* 1988;9:228–234.
33. Loewy JW, Kapadia AS, Hsi B, Davis BR. Statistical methods that distinguish between attributes of assessment: prolongation of life versus quality of life. *Med Decis Making* 1992;12:83–92.

Quality of Life and Pharmacoeconomics in Clinical Trials, Second Edition, edited by B. Spilker.
Lippincott-Raven Publishers, Philadelphia © 1996.

CHAPTER 46

The Q-TWiST Method

Richard D. Gelber, Bernard F. Cole, Shari Gelber, and Aron Goldhirsch

INTRODUCTION

The evaluation of quality of life (QOL) concepts has become increasingly important in clinical research (1–3). Investigators must utilize appropriate methods for incorporating QOL information when comparing treatment options. Such methods are especially useful when there is a trade-off between increased treatment toxicity and improved response. For example, a new therapeutic regimen may significantly delay disease recurrence or progression but may also have undesirable side effects as compared with a standard treatment. It is important that the evaluation of QOL is made within the context of clinical outcomes related to the disease and its treatment.

First attempts at assessing the impact of treatments on QOL were made by identifying and grading the side effects

of therapies. Subsequent efforts beginning with Priestman and Baum (4) measured patients' perceptions of these side effects and the symptoms of their disease. These efforts have resulted in the development of numerous QOL assessment instruments that have been reviewed for their psychometric properties and value for eliciting patient perceptions (5–7). Further efforts focused on the integration of both quality and quantity of life into a single analysis to be used for treatment comparisons. This led to the development of the TWiST method (8) and its extension into Q-TWiST, Quality-adjusted Time Without Symptoms of disease and Toxicity of treatment. This method was originally designed to incorporate aspects of QOL into adjuvant chemotherapy and endocrine therapy comparisons for the treatment of breast cancer (9–11); however, the methodology has also been useful in other disease settings such as acquired immune deficiency syndrome (AIDS) (12,13).

This chapter explains the Q-TWiST method and demonstrates how it can be used to compare treatments simultaneously in terms of survival and QOL outcomes. First the three steps for conducting a standard Q-TWiST analysis are described. Then the procedure is illustrated in an analysis of a clinical trial comparing treatments for human immunodeficiency virus (HIV) infection. Next several recent extensions of the standard methodology are presented, including new applications of Q-TWiST. Finally, guidelines for applying the Q-TWiST method are outlined.

R. D. Gelber: Department of Pediatrics (Biostatistics), Harvard Medical School, Harvard School of Public Health, and Dana-Farber Cancer Institute, Boston, Massachusetts 02115.

B. F. Cole: Department of Community Health and Division of Applied Mathematics, Brown University, Providence, Rhode Island 02912.

S. Gelber: Department of Biostatistics, Frontier Science and Technology Research Foundation, Brookline, Massachusetts 02146.

A. Goldhirsch: International Breast Cancer Study Group and Swiss Group for Clinical Cancer Research, Department of Oncology, Ospedale Civico, Servizio Oncologico, 6900 Lugano, Switzerland.

THE Q-TWiST METHOD

The Q-TWiST method performs treatment comparisons in terms of quality and quantity of life by penalizing treatments that have negative QOL effects and rewarding those that increase survival and have other positive QOL effects. As in an ordinary survival analysis, the focus of the method is on time, but instead of using a single outcome such as overall survival or disease-free survival, multiple outcomes corresponding to changes in QOL are considered. The objective is to include both survival and QOL in an analysis highlighting specific trade-offs using defined clinical events of interest. Thus Q-TWiST links aspects of QOL with the clinical outcomes (disease and treatment related) that are ordinarily used to separately evaluate the efficacy and toxicity of treatments. A Q-TWiST analysis can also be used to assist with treatment decision making when there is a trade-off between side effects and a possible future benefit. It can demonstrate to a patient what the benefit might be depending on his or her tolerance for the treatment toxicities; this might improve patient compliance.

The multiple outcomes partition the overall survival time into clinical health states that differ in QOL. These clinical health states are selected to be relevant to the clinicians and patients. Each clinical health state is assigned a weight that corresponds to its value in terms of QOL relative to a state of perfect health. A weight of 0 indicates that the health state is as bad as death, and a weight of 1 indicates perfect health. Weights between 0 and 1 indicate degrees between these extremes. These weights are called utility scores. The Q-TWiST outcome is obtained by summing the weighted clinical health state durations. Thus the method highlights trade-offs that result from different weightings of the clinically relevant health states. Glasziou et al. (14) provide a more detailed description of the statistical methodology of Q-TWiST. The application of the method proceeds according to the three steps described below.

THE THREE STEPS OF A Q-TWiST ANALYSIS

Defining Clinical Health States

The first step in the analysis is to define QOL-oriented health states that are relevant for the disease setting under study. These should highlight specific differences between the treatments being compared (see Fig. 1 for an example from an HIV study). Usually included among these states is TWiST, a period of relatively uncompromised QOL, representing the best QOL available for the study patients. Each clinical health state is then assigned a utility score, which may be unknown. The utility score for TWiST is usually assumed to be unity because it characterizes a period of relatively perfect health. In some treatment comparisons TWiST might be assigned a value of less than unity such as when one therapeutic regimen might return patients to a

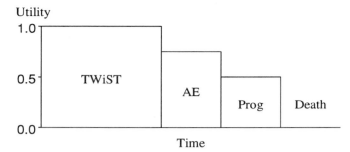

FIG. 1. Health states for a Quality-adjusted Time Without Symptoms and Toxicity (Q-TWiST) analysis of zidovudine for asymptomatic HIV-infected patients. Illustration of the division of overall survival time into TWiST, AE (time after a severe symptomatic adverse event), and Prog (time after HIV disease progression), and the weighting of these time periods using utility scores u_{AE} and u_{Prog}.

better state of TWiST (relatively good health) than another. The other clinical health states are generally associated with diminished QOL. Patients progress through the health states chronologically, possibly skipping one or more states, but never backtracking. This allows for a patient dying prematurely or not experiencing treatment toxicity. These states can be defined retrospectively at the time of data analysis or can be specified prospectively in the protocol document in anticipation of performing a Q-TWiST analysis.

Partitioning the Overall Survival

In the second step, Kaplan-Meier curves for the times to events that signal transitions between the clinical health states are used to partition the area under the overall survival curve separately for each treatment (see Fig. 2 for an example from an HIV study). The areas between the curves are estimates of the mean health state durations (15). For example, the area between the overall survival curve and the progression-free survival curve is an estimate of the mean duration of time following progression. In practice, censoring often precludes one from estimating the entire survival curve. In this case the average clinical health state durations (i.e., the areas between the Kaplan-Meier curves) are calculated within the follow-up interval of the study cohort. The resulting estimates are called restricted means (15) because they represent the mean health state durations restricted to the length of the follow-up interval. For example, if the median follow-up of patients in a breast cancer study was 7 years, then it would be reasonable to calculate estimates of time spent in each clinical health state within 7 years from randomization (i.e., average times restricted to 7 years). Covariation among these restricted means can be estimated using a resampling procedure such as the bootstrap method (14). As a useful visual display, the transitional survival curves corresponding to the multiple outcomes for one treatment can be plotted on the same graph. Separate graphs can

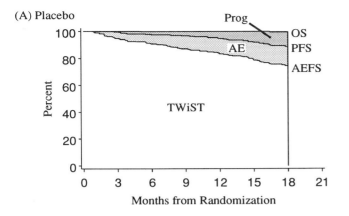

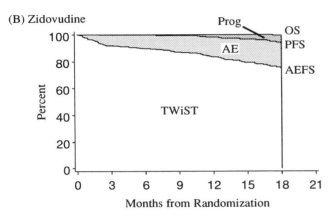

FIG. 2. Partitioned survival plots for the placebo group (**A**) and for the 500 mg zidovudine group (**B**). In each graph, the area under the overall survival curve (OS) is partitioned by the Kaplan-Meier curves for HIV progression-free survival (PFS) and adverse event-free survival (AEFS). The areas between the Kaplan-Meier curves up to 18 months of follow-up give the restricted mean times in the clinical health states TWiST, AE and Prog. (From ref. 13, with permission.)

be produced for each treatment group. These are called partitioned survival plots (14).

Comparing Treatments Using Q-TWiST

The third step is to compare the treatment regimens using the weighted sum of the mean durations of each clinical health state as calculated in the second step. For example, in a disease setting involving TWiST and two other clinical health states,

$$Q\text{-}TWiST = TWiST + u_1 \times State\ 1 + u_2 \times State\ 2,$$

where TWiST, State 1, and State 2 represent the average amounts of time spent in each state as estimated in the second step, and u_1 and u_2 represent the utility scores.

Q-TWiST is calculated separately for each treatment group, and treatment effects are estimated by computing the differences in mean Q-TWiST. Statistical inferences on the Q-TWiST treatment effects are conducted using the large sample theory for restricted means estimated from the Kaplan-Meier curves (14). This quality-adjusted survival comparison offers the opportunity to include the utility weights to reflect the relative value to the patient of the different clinical health states. Treatment comparisons are made using a sensitivity analysis, called threshold utility analysis, which displays the treatment comparison for varying values of the utility scores (14). Thus, Q-TWiST is not dependent on the inclusion of patient-derived preference measures.

The methodology for generating patient-derived utility scores is still in development. There is debate about which methods (time trade-off, standard gamble, and multiattribute techniques) to use for eliciting the utilities [see Torrance (16) for a discussion of these techniques]. There is also concern regarding whose perspective should be measured—patients, family members, general public, or clinicians. If patient-derived utility data are available, these can be incorporated into a Q-TWiST analysis; however, a threshold utility analysis well illustrates the treatment comparison for all possible combinations of utility scores.

AN AIDS CLINICAL TRIAL EXAMPLE

Lenderking et al. (13) recently published a Q-TWiST analysis evaluating the QOL associated with zidovudine treatment in asymptomatic HIV infected patients. The original study performed by the AIDS Clinical Trials Group (ACTG Study 019) was a double-blind, randomized, placebo-controlled clinical trial designed to study the efficacy and safety of two different doses of zidovudine (1,500 mg and 500 mg daily) as compared with placebo in 1,338 asymptomatic HIV-infected patients (17). In this example the 500 mg dose group (453 patients) is compared with placebo group (428 patients) in a Q-TWiST analysis. This analysis evaluated the trade-off between the potential delay in disease progression and the toxicities associated with the use of zidovudine in patients who were experiencing little or no disease-related symptoms at the time of study entry. The QOL evaluation is especially important in this comparison because of the very similar survival experiences among the three arms of the study. The progression-free survival was significantly better for the low-dose zidovudine group (94% 18-month progression-free survival) compared with the placebo group (89% progression-free survival; $p < .01$).

In step one of the Q-TWiST analysis the following three clinical health states were defined: (a) TWiST, the number of months preceding the development of a grade 3 or worse symptomatic adverse event or HIV disease progression, whichever occurred first; (b) AE, the period after the first occurrence of a severe symptomatic adverse event (e.g., gastrointestinal symptoms, headache, psychiatric disorders, fatigue); and (c) Prog, the period after the progression of HIV disease. These definitions allow for an evaluation of the trade-off between increased adverse events and delayed disease progression, which are both characteristic of zidovudine therapy.

The Q-TWiST model used the utility scores u_{AE} and u_{Prog} to reflect the diminished QOL of the clinical health states AE and Prog, respectively. TWiST was assigned a weight of 1.0 and death a weight of 0.0. Thus the QOL-adjusted survival was calculated as:

$$Q\text{-}TWiST = TWiST + u_{AE} \times AE + u_{Prog} \times Prog,$$

where TWiST, AE, and Prog denote the clinical health state durations. Figure 1 shows an example of the different time periods with arbitrary utility coefficients of 0.75 for AE and 0.5 for Prog.

Step two used the clinical trial data to calculate separate Kaplan-Meier curves for the adverse event-free survival, progression-free survival, and overall survival. The first two curves partition the overall survival time into periods of time in TWiST, AE, and Prog. This is illustrated in the partitioned survival analyses for the standard-dose zidovudine group (500 mg daily) and for the placebo group shown in Fig. 2. The results were restricted to the first 18 months of follow-up corresponding to the median follow-up duration of the study cohort at the time of analysis. On average, patients treated with zidovudine therapy spent less time in Prog but more time in AE than patients in the placebo group (Table 1). The two groups had approximately equal amounts of TWiST shown by the areas representing the clinical health state durations in Fig. 2.

In the third step, the two treatment groups (zidovudine 500 mg daily versus placebo) were compared using a threshold utility analysis for all possible combinations of values of u_{AE} and u_{Prog} (ranging from 0.0 to 1.0). This is shown in Fig. 3. The threshold line (solid line) is obtained by finding

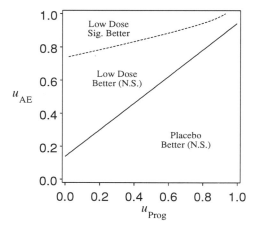

FIG. 3. Threshold utility analysis comparing the 500 mg dose of zidovudine with placebo within 18 months of follow-up. The vertical axis shows the value of the time after an adverse symptomatic event (u_{AE}) and the horizontal axis shows the value of the time after disease progression (u_{Prog}). The values for both range from 0.0 to 1.0, with a value of 1.0 indicating that time is worth the same as TWiST, and a value of 0.0 indicating that the time is worth nothing. The *solid line* is the threshold (based on values of u_{AE} and u_{Prog}) for which the zidovudine and placebo groups have equal amounts of Q-TWiST. The *dashed line* shows the upper 95% confidence boundary for threshold line (the lower confidence boundary is out of the possible range of utility values and hence is not shown). The lines divide the plot into three areas showing the utility values for which Q-TWiST was significantly longer in the zidovudine group (*upper left*), the values for which Q-TWiST was longer, but not significantly so, for the zidovudine group (*middle region*), and the values for which Q-TWiST was longer, but not significantly so, in the placebo group (*lower right*). (From ref. 13, with permission.)

the unknown utility values for which the treatments have equal Q-TWiST. Pairs of utility scores above this line correspond to values of u_{AE} and u_{Prog} for which mean Q-TWiST was greater for the zidovudine group. Pairs of values below the line favor placebo. A confidence region for the threshold line can also be included. This is obtained by finding the pairs of utility score values for which the confidence interval for the treatment effect captures zero. The 95% confidence interval for the threshold line is shown as a dashed line in Fig. 3 and was calculated using the bootstrap method.

Subjective patient judgments provide the weights for the components of Q-TWiST influencing treatment comparisons. A traditional efficacy analysis would consider the delay of disease progression as the main end point. This is equivalent to assigning a value of 1.0 to the coefficient u_{AE} and 0.0 to the coefficient u_{Prog}. For these extreme utility values the zidovudine treatment yielded the better result (0.5 additional months for zidovudine). In fact, zidovudine provided significantly ($p < .05$) more Q-TWiST than placebo for all patients with utility scores in the upper left corner of Fig. 3, those above the dashed line. The advantage shifted away from zidovudine for patients who value Prog greater than AE.

TABLE 1. *Average months in the clinical health states TWiST, AE, and Prog within 18 months of follow-up for the AIDS Clinical Trials Group Study 019*

End point	Treatment		Treatment difference (95% confidence interval)
	Zidovudine	Placebo	
TWiST	15.6	15.7	−0.08 (−0.8 to 0.6)
AE	2.1	1.6	0.6 (−0.03 to 1.2)
Prog	0.3	0.7	−0.5 (−0.8 to −0.2)
Overall survival	18.0	18.0	0.03 (−0.03 to 0.09)
Progression-free survival	17.7	17.2	0.5 (0.2 to 0.8)

Modified from ref. 13.

EXTENSIONS OF THE Q-TWiST METHOD

In this section, several recent extensions of the basic Q-TWiST methodology are described. These extensions allow (a) patient-derived preferences to be incorporated into the analysis, (b) changes over time of the treatment comparison to be illustrated graphically, (c) covariates to be included in the analysis by proportional hazards regression, (d) parametric models to predict long-term treatment effects, (e) the Q-TWiST method to be used in meta-analyses, and (f) in economic considerations.

Incorporating Patient-Derived Preferences

A clinical trial comparing adjuvant therapies for breast cancer, being conducted by the International Breast Cancer Study Group, is the first trial to collect patient-derived QOL scores for incorporation into a Q-TWiST analysis. QOL measurements have been collected from over 2,000 patients. An ongoing intergroup study comparing surgical procedures for colon cancer has begun administering the Quality of Life Index, which will be converted to utilities for a Q-TWiST analysis (18). In addition a protocol has been developed to obtain utility scores from the Health Utility Indexes (19–21) to evaluate treatment regimens for childhood acute lymphoblastic leukemia.

The Gain Function

In practice, the restriction time is taken to be the median length of follow-up. However, by restricting the Q-TWiST analysis to regular intervals leading up to median follow-up, it is possible to see how the Q-TWiST treatment effects unfold over time. The estimated treatment effect (i.e., Q-TWiST for treatment A minus Q-TWiST for treatment B) can be plotted on a time axis in order to display the results (22). A single curve can be plotted for any specific utility score values, and a shaded region can be used to display the range of the treatment effect as the utility scores range between zero and unity. This is called the Q-TWiST gain function because it illustrates the amount of quality-adjusted survival time gained for one treatment compared with another.

Figure 4 illustrates a Q-TWiST gain function comparing two adjuvant breast cancer treatment regimens (10,23), one of long duration, thus incurring more toxicities, and the other of short duration. The three clinical health states in this example are TWiST, the period of treatment toxicities (TOX) and the time following relapse (REL). The solid line in Fig. 4 corresponds to utility coefficient values of 0.5 for both TOX and REL. The shaded region illustrates the range of results for the Q-TWiST gain function as the utility score values for TOX and REL range between 0 and 1. Early in the course of follow-up, the toxic effects of the long-duration treatment result in an initial loss in Q-TWiST compared

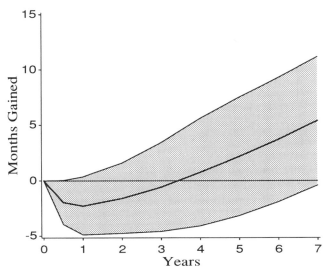

FIG. 4. Q-TWiST gain function for the breast cancer example. The *solid curved line* gives the average months of Q-TWiST ($u_{TOX} = u_{REL} = 0.5$) gained for the long duration treatment compared with the short duration treatment in IBCSG Trial V as a function of years from randomization. The *shaded region* surrounding the *solid curved line* shows the ranges for the Q-TWiST gain function as the utility scores vary between 0.0 and 1.0. TOX, toxicity; REL, relapse. (From ref. 22, with permission.)

with the short-duration treatment. This is because the advantages of the long-duration treatment (i.e., increased disease-free survival and overall survival) do not appear until later in time. As the benefits are realized with additional follow-up, the Q-TWiST gain function begins to increase and will continue to increase provided the disease-free survival curves for the two treatments remain separated.

Incorporating Prognostic Factors

The Q-TWiST method has recently been extended to incorporate prognostic factors using proportional hazards regression models (24). These models are used to predict the curves for the times to transitions between the clinical health states for various patient profiles, allowing one to look at how the prognostic situation affects the treatment evaluation in terms of Q-TWiST. In particular, separate threshold utility analyses are performed according to each patient profile.

As in the standard approach, the first step in the prognostic factor analysis involves defining the QOL-oriented clinical health states such as TOX, AE, and Prog. It is also important at this time to define the patient profiles that are of interest. Typically, these will range from a good prognostic situation to a poor prognostic situation. For example, in HIV disease various values of CD4$^+$ cell counts would be appropriate.

In the second step of the analysis, appropriate proportional hazards models are estimated for each of the transition times between health states. It is not necessary to use a proportional hazards model for all of the outcomes. For outcomes that are not related to any of the covariates considered, the Kaplan-Meier method can be used (for example duration of treatment toxicity). Each transition model is used to predict the transitional survival curves for each patient profile of interest. The predicted curves are then used to partition the overall survival time and provide profile-specific estimates of the mean clinical health state durations restricted to the follow-up interval. As in a standard Q-TWiST analysis, the bootstrap method is used to estimate covariation among the restricted means.

The third step proceeds as in the general method, except that the threshold plot treatment comparisons are performed for each patient profile. This analysis illustrates how the gain in Q-TWiST might differ with respect to prognostic factors.

Forecasting Treatment Benefits

In the previous sections, treatment benefits were expressed as the amount of Q-TWiST gained within the follow-up period using restricted means. In some instances, however, it may be possible to forecast the future treatment benefit based on the available data. This has recently been done using parametric models to predict the tails of the Kaplan-Meier curves for times to transitions between the clinical health states (25,26). The projected Kaplan-Meier curves can be used to increase the restriction time placed on the Q-TWiST analysis.

Meta-analysis

During the last decade, the meta-analysis, or overview, has become an increasingly popular method for making treatment comparisons. This method involves combining results of several randomized trials with similar treatment arms in order to increase the statistical power to detect treatment effects. The Q-TWiST method has been extended to incorporate aspects of QOL into meta-analysis.

In collaboration with the Early Breast Cancer Trialists' Collaborative Group (27), a Q-TWiST meta-analysis of adjuvant chemotherapy for premenopausal breast cancer was performed (28). Data were analyzed from 1,229 node-positive breast cancer patients randomized in eight clinical trials comparing chemotherapy versus no adjuvant systemic therapy. The individual trial data were combined to produce an overall threshold utility plot and an overall gain function.

Economic Considerations

Financial costs can be important considerations for treatment choice, especially when overall survival differences have not been demonstrated. The different clinical health states defined for a Q-TWiST analysis may be associated with different economic costs. An Eco-TWiST analysis weights the duration of each clinical health state according to its financial impact. In an Eco-TWiST analysis for the AIDS example, the utility scores u_{AE} and u_{Prog} would be replaced by weights reflecting dollars per unit of time spent in AE or Prog relative to the dollar per unit of time spent in TWiST. The estimation of these weights requires averaging the economic costs of living in the specific health states. The Eco-TWiST analysis highlights the cost differences between the treatment regimens being compared. Furthermore, it incorporates costs for clinical health states during the entire survival time of the patient. Specifically costs arising as a consequence of disease progression are included. The threshold utility analysis for Eco-TWiST illustrates how the various cost estimates might influence treatment decision making.

Q-TWiST APPLICATIONS

The Q-TWiST method has been incorporated in research proposals in a variety of disease settings. In each situation the definitions of the appropriate health states has posed interesting challenges. Close collaboration with clinicians treating the disease is necessary to assure the identification of the trade-offs that are most relevant.

For instance, in a recently designed protocol evaluating treatment regimens for childhood acute lymphoblastic leukemia (ALL), the major concern is the late adverse effects of the toxic treatments. Although prior to the 1960s ALL was almost always lethal, it currently has a 70% to 75% cure rate (29). Unfortunately long-term survival has been associated with numerous late sequelae. These included cardiac late effects (30), cognitive impairment (31), growth abnormalities (32), and second malignancies (33). Thus the Q-TWiST analysis had to incorporate the reduced QOL for those children who were afflicted with one or more late toxicities. These late sequelae have been clinically identified, but the extent to which they have an impact on patients' QOL has not yet been determined. Thus the selection of which late events to include in a Q-TWiST evaluation had to be done prospectively.

While the consequences of late effects in ALL are chronic, many affecting the child for the remainder of life, treatments for colorectal cancer can be associated with late toxicity (34), which is severe but might be improved by specific intervention. In this case, the late effects clinical health state could be followed by a resumption of TWiST.

Small cell lung cancer presents different issues for a quality-adjusted survival analysis. The short survival time characteristic of this disease focuses extra concern on the acute treatment toxicities and associated decrease in QOL (35). Since the treatments being evaluated may not return patients to relatively good health, this may be a situation where TWiST should be valued at less than 1.

Another disease setting in which a Q-TWiST analysis has been planned is multiple sclerosis (36). This chronic illness is characterized by progressive debilitation. A recent therapeutic intervention, betaseron, has demonstrated some impact on the disease progression (37,38); however, it is important to evaluate the effect of this drug on the overall QOL of the patient.

GUIDELINES FOR PERFORMING A Q-TWiST ANALYSIS

As illustrated by the AIDS example, a Q-TWiST analysis may be performed retrospectively after the completion of a clinical trial. In this case data must be available for partitioning overall survival into the clinically relevant health states. These are often broadly defined, for example using the entire treatment period to represent toxicity.

Alternatively, a Q-TWiST analysis can be planned prospectively as described above in the leukemia example. This enables a more precise definition of the clinical health states and provides the opportunity to collect the specific end points required to partition the overall survival time. Patient-derived utilities can also be obtained during the trial. Even when estimates for utility scores are available within a trial, we recommend that the threshold utility analysis be performed to allow the trial results to be interpreted for individual patient preferences.

In practice, the most challenging component to define is toxicity. Typically it is preferable to use criteria that focus on symptomatic rather than on laboratory events, as the former most directly influence patients' QOL. It may be difficult to precisely accommodate intermittent toxicities because the clinical health states are progressive. It is possible, however, to define toxicity as the time period from initial treatment until all toxicity has resolved. If there are long periods of time captured in this definition that are actually free of toxicity, this will be reflected by having a higher value for the average toxicity utility score.

CONCLUSIONS

The main advantage of the Q-TWiST method is that it incorporates time into the analysis of QOL by using restricted survival means. This can be very important in clinical trials, because the QOL experienced depends on the amount of time spent with toxicity or adverse events and the time following disease recurrence or progression. Often these are directly affected by the treatment. Other QOL measures, which do not account for time, only indirectly reflect benefits of delayed disease recurrence or progression. Furthermore, Q-TWiST does not aggregate QOL results for an entire population; instead, it allows individual patients and physicians to determine the preferred treatment according to individual preferences. This advantage is derived from the threshold utility analysis, which gives the preferred treatment according to all combinations of the utility scores. Q-TWiST can also accommodate patient-derived utility scores. In addi-

tion, prognostic factors can be included in the analysis by proportional hazards regression, allowing the prediction of treatment effects according to different prognostic situations. Longer-term treatment effects can be approximated using parametric models. Finally, Q-TWiST can be incorporated into meta-analyses and, using Eco-TWiST, can evaluate cost considerations in treatment comparisons.

By defining the clinical health states to reflect specific trade-offs of concern to health professionals and patients, Q-TWiST provides a framework for treatment decision making. In the AIDS example the attention was focused on the trade-off between increased adverse events and delayed disease progression associated with zidovudine therapy. A Q-TWiST analysis of the efficacy of treatments designed to prolong event-free survival can highlight the influence of late sequelae by defining a clinical health state to capture the occurrence of late events as previously described in the setting of ALL. Thus Q-TWiST can emphasize those aspects of a disease and its treatment that are the most relevant in making treatment decisions. By relying on the threshold utility analysis, Q-TWiST presents the implications that various choices for patient preference have on the treatment decision process. Q-TWiST provides a broad evaluation of treatment outcomes and costs considering the entire survival experience of patients.

ACKNOWLEDGMENTS

We thank the International Breast Cancer Study Group (IBCSG) and the AIDS Clinical Trials Group (ACTG) for their permission to use their clinical trial data in the examples. Partial support for this work was provided by grant PBR-53 from the American Cancer Society, grant CA06516 from the National Cancer Institute, DHHS, contract AI95030 from the National Institute of Allergy and Infectious Diseases, DHHS, and a grant from Frontier Science and Technology Research Foundation.

REFERENCES

1. Schumacher M, Olschewski M, Schulgen G. Assessment of quality of life in clinical trials. *Stat Med* 1991;10:1915–1930.
2. Cox DR, Fitzpatrick R, Fletcher AE, Gore SM, Spiegelhalter DJ, Jones DJ. Quality of life assessment: Can we keep it simple? *J R Stat Soc A* 1992;155:353–393.
3. Gelber RD, Goldhirsch A, Hürny C, Bernhard J, Simes RJ, for the International Breast Cancer Study Group. Quality of life in clinical trials of adjuvant therapies. *J Natl Cancer Inst Monogr* 1992;11:127–135.
4. Priestman TJ, Baum M. Evaluation of quality of life in patients receiving treatments for advanced breast cancer. *Lancet* 1976;1:899–900.
5. Maguire P, Selby P, on behalf of the Medical Research Council's Cancer Therapy Committee Working Party on Quality of Life. Assessing quality of life in cancer patients. *Br J Cancer* 1989;60:437–440.
6. Donovan K, Sanson-Fisher RW, Redman S. Measuring quality of life in cancer patients. *J Clin Oncol* 1989;7:959–968.
7. Moinpour CM, Feigl P, Metch B, Hayden KA, Meyskens FL Jr, Crowley J. Quality of life end points in cancer clinical trials: review and recommendations. *J Natl Cancer Inst* 1989;81:485–495.
8. Gelber RD, Goldhirsh A. A new endpoint for the assessment of adjuvant

therapy in postmenopausal women with operable breast cancer. *J Clin Oncol* 1986;4:1772–1779.

9. Goldhirsch A, Gelber RD, Simes RJ, Glasziou P, Coates A, for the Ludwig Breast Cancer Study Group. Costs and benefits of adjuvant therapy in breast cancer: a quality adjusted survival analysis. *J Clin Oncol* 1989;7:36–44.

10. Gelber RD, Goldhirsch A, Cavalli F, for the International Breast Cancer Study group. Quality-of-life-adjusted evaluation of a randomized trial comparing adjuvant therapies for operable breast cancer. *Ann Intern Med* 1991;114:621–628.

11. Gelber RD, Gelman RS, Goldhirsch A. A quality-of-life oriented endpoint for comparing therapies. *Biometrics* 1989;45:781–795.

12. Gelber RD, Lenderking WR, Cotton DJ, Cole BF, Fischl MA, Goldhirsch A, Testa M, for the AIDS Clinical Trials Group. Quality-of-life evaluation in a clinical trial of zidovudine therapy in patients with mildly symptomatic HIV infection. *Ann Intern Med* 1992;116:961–966.

13. Lenderking WR, Gelber RD, Cotton DJ, Cole BF, Goldhirsch A, Volberding PA, for the AIDS Clinical Trials Group. Evaluation of the quality of life associated with zidovudine treatment in asymptomatic human immunodeficiency virus infection. *N Engl J Med* 1994;330:738–743.

14. Glasziou PP, Simes RJ, Gelber RD. Quality adjusted survival analysis. *Stat Med* 1990;9:1259–1276.

15. Kaplan EL, Meier P. Nonparametric estimation from incomplete observations. *J Am Stat Assoc* 1958;54:457–481.

16. Torrance GW. Measurement of health state utilities for economic appraisal: a review. *J Health Econ* 1986;5:1–30.

17. Volberding PA, Lagakos SW, Koch MA, et al. Zidovudine in asymptomatic human immunodeficiency virus infection: a controlled trial in persons with fewer than 500 CD-4 positive cells per cubic millimeter. *N Engl J Med* 1990;322:941–949.

18. Weeks JC, O'Leary J, Fairclough D, Paltiel D, Weinstein M. The "Q-tility index": a new tool for assessing health-related quality of life and utilities in clinical trials and clinical practice. *Proc ASCO* 1994;13:436.

19. Feeny DH, Torrance GW, Goldsmith CH, Furlong W, Boyle M. A multi-attribute approach to population health status. Alexandria, VA: *Proceedings of the 153rd Annual Meeting of the American Statistical Association* 1993;161–166.

20. Feeny D, Furlong W, Barr RD, Torrance GW, Rosenbaum P, Weitzman S. A comprehensive multi-attribute system for classifying the health status of childhood cancer. *J Clin Oncol* 1992;10:923–928.

21. Torrance GW, Zhang Y, Feeny DH, Furlong WJ, Barr RD. Multi-attribute preference functions for a comprehensive health status classification system. *McMaster University Centre for Health Economics and Policy Analysis Working Paper #92-18,* 1992.

22. Gelber RD, Cole BF, Goldhirsch A, for the International Breast Cancer Study Group. Evaluation of effectiveness: Q-TWiST. *Cancer Treat Rev* 1993;19:73–84.

23. The Ludwig Breast Cancer Study Group. Combination adjuvant chemotherapy for node-positive breast cancer: inadequacy of a single perioperative cycle. *N Engl J Med* 1988;319:677–683.

24. Cole BF, Gelber RD, Goldhirsch A, for the International Breast Cancer Study Group. Cox regression models for quality adjusted survival analysis. *Stat Med* 1993;12:975–987.

25. Gelber RD, Goldhirsch A, Cole BF. Parametric extrapolation of survival estimates with applications to quality of life evaluation of treatments. *Controlled Clin Trials* 1993;14:485–499.

26. Cole BF, Gelber RD, Anderson KM, for the International Breast Cancer Study Group. Parametric approaches to quality adjusted survival analysis. *Biometrics* 1994;50:621–631.

27. Early Breast Cancer Trialists' Collaborative Group. Systemic treatment of early breast cancer by hormonal, cytotoxic, or immunotherapy: 133 randomized trials involving 31,000 recurrences and 24,000 deaths among 75,000 women. *Lancet* 1992;339:1–15, 71–85.

28. Cole BF, Gelber RD, Goldhirsch A. A quality-adjusted survival meta-analysis of adjuvant chemotherapy for premenopausal breast cancer. *Stat Med* 1995;14:1771–1784.

29. Barr RD, DeVeber LL, Pai KM, et al. Management of children with ALL by the Dana-Farber Cancer Institute protocols—an update of the Ontario experience. *Am J Pediatr Oncol* 1992;14:136–139.

30. Lipschultz SE, Colan SD, Gelber RD, Perez-Atayde AR, Sallan SE, Sanders SP. Late cardiac effects of doxorubicin therapy for acute lymphoblastic leukemia in childhood. *N Engl J Med* 1991;324:808–815.

31. Waber DP, Bernstein JH, Kammerer BL, Tarbell NJ, Sallan SE. Neuropsychological diagnostic profiles of children who received CNS treatment for acute lymphoblastic leukemia: the systemic approach to assessment. *Dev Neuropsych* 1992;8:1–28.

32. Schriock EA, Schell MJ, Carter M, Hustu O, Ochs JJ. Abnormal growth patterns and adult short stature in 115 long-term survivors of childhood leukemia. *J Clin Oncol* 1991;9:400–405.

33. Kreissman SG, Gelber RD, Cohen HJ, Clavel LA, Leavitt P, Sallan SE. Incidence of secondary acute myelogenous leukemia after treatment of childhood acute lymphoblastic leukemia. *Cancer* 1992;70:2208–2213.

34. Krook JE, Moertel CG, Gunderson LL, et al. Effective surgical adjuvant therapy for high-risk rectal carcinoma. *N Engl J Med* 1991;324:709–715.

35. Grilli R, Oxman AD, Julian JA. Chemotherapy for advanced non-small-cell lung cancer: How much benefit is enough? *J Clin Oncol* 1993;11:1866–1872.

36. Lechtenberg R. *Multiple sclerosis fact book.* Philadelphia: F.A. Davis, 1988.

37. The IFNB Multiple Sclerosis Study Group. Interferon beta-1b is effective in relapsing-remitting multiple sclerosis. I. Clinical results of a multicenter, randomized, double-blind, placebo-controlled trial. *Neurology* 1993;43:655–667.

38. Paty DW, Li DKB, the UBC MS/MRI Study Group, and the IFNB Multiple Sclerosis Study Group. Interferon beta 1b is effective in relapsing-remitting multiple sclerosis. II. MRI analysis results of a multicenter, randomized, double-blind, placebo-controlled trial. *Neurology* 1993;43:662–667.

Quality of Life and Pharmacoeconomics in Clinical Trials, Second Edition, edited by B. Spilker.
Lippincott-Raven Publishers, Philadelphia © 1996.

CHAPTER 47

Interpreting General Health Measures

John E. Ware, Jr. and Susan D. Keller

INTRODUCTION

Among the questions most frequently asked about results from widely used health status surveys are: What do the numbers mean? What is a high score? What is a low score? While a three-point difference on a health scale may be statistically significant, is it clinically relevant? Is it important to society? Can scores be used to determine the need for treatment? Can the same interpretation guidelines used in group-level analyses be applied to individual patients?

Answering the above questions is a challenge of moving from the abstract to the more concrete. Health status scores, like most measures, are abstractions. The numbers provided by measures are a kind of shorthand used to facilitate description and communication regarding complex phenomena. However, to the extent that something is abstract, it lacks the contextual details that provide meaning in any particular instance. The meaning of a score is understood through our experience of how it relates to other variables.

The gathering of information used in the interpretation of scores is a process that is ongoing for the life of a questionnaire. With the accumulation of experience, the understanding of the meaning of scores increases. This process of interpretation can be illustrated by considering the example of a thermometer. A thermometer can be a reliable and valid measure of temperature, but the numbers it yields are meaningless until they are linked to meaningful experiences. For example, 32° Fahrenheit comes to mean something when

it is associated with a chilly feeling outside, frost on the windshield, and rain turning to snow.

THE RELATIONSHIP BETWEEN INTERPRETATION AND VALIDATION

Interpretation requires the assignment of meaning to health status scores, usually by studying their relationships to other variables. Interpretation guidelines include the results of validity analyses, but they also include other types of analyses and a different display of results than is typical of validity analyses. Validity is the extent to which a score measures what it is supposed to measure (1). Validity is supported when hypotheses about the relationship between scale scores and particular criteria are confirmed. Tests of these hypotheses usually include estimates of the statistical significance of results. By contrast, evidence useful in the interpretation of scale scores requires more than the establishment of statistical significance; namely, it requires demonstration of a clinically or socially relevant relationship between two variables. In addition, the display of results for validity and interpretation analyses differ. In validity analyses, the expression of relationships between scale scores and criteria are summarized in terms of statistical estimates of the strength of association. For example, the commonly used product moment correlation expresses the strength of a linear association in standard units (2). Yet, standard units are rarely as meaningful to people as are raw scores; moreover, the correlation coefficient does not express the fact that, as illustrated below, the relationship of scale scores to criteria is often nonlinear across a range of scores. Interpreta-

J. E. Ware, Jr. and S. D. Keller: New England Medical Center, The Health Institute, Boston, Massachusetts 02111.

tion is facilitated most when differences in scale scores at a particular scale level are linked to units of the criteria in specific amounts that make sense.

Some strategies for interpreting scores overlap with strategies for validating scores. For example, the analysis of questionnaire content, construct, and criterion relationships can be used both for validation and interpretation (3). However, interpretation research goes a step further and includes a greater range of approaches than those used by validity studies. The difference between validation and interpretation might best be expressed by considering the purposes for which the two types of information are used. Validity information is used to indicate that a questionnaire has been shown to measure what it was designed to measure. Interpretation guidelines indicate the meaning of scale scores to a particular audience. Like validity, the interpretation of scale scores is not something that is established; it is something about which evidence is accumulated within and across specific applications.

This chapter describes the interpretation strategies that we have found most useful and illustrates three types of strategies with examples. Although many of the examples come from studies of the SF-36 Health Survey (SF-36) profile and summary measures, the examples have much broader applicability, because SF-36 concepts and questionnaire items have their roots in or are reproduced in other widely used surveys including the Sickness Impact Profile (SIP), the Psychological General Well-Being Index, the Functional Status Questionnaire, the Health Perceptions Questionnaire, the Medical Outcomes Study (MOS) SF-20 Health Survey, and the Dartmouth COOP Charts. Further, the strategies illustrated here should prove useful regardless of the content of the health measure in question.

ATTRIBUTES OF SCALE SCORES THAT AFFECT INTERPRETATION

While there are many attributes of scale scores that affect interpretation, the importance of three attributes—reliability, range of measurement, and the number of levels of measurement—is often not well understood. We discuss other attributes elsewhere (4).

Reliability has to do with how confident we can be that a particular score is the true score (2). Scale score reliability is a precondition for interpretation. It would be an inefficient use of resources to try to understand the meaning of a number that did not represent a true value. Reliability is an issue of repeatability. We can be confident that a score is the true score if we would obtain the same score again and again upon repeated assessments of an unchanging respondent. There are several methods to estimate the repeatability of a scale score. The most common among them are (a) to treat the questions (items) in a scale as repeated measures of the same concept and estimate reliability from the relationships among them (internal consistency method) (2), (b) to deter-

mine the association between scores collected from a clinically stable sample at two points in time (test-retest correlation) (5), and (c) to assess the percentage of scores at time two that are statistically different from scores at time one (the confidence interval method) (6).

The range of measurement is important because it determines the levels of health for which the questionnaire is useful in describing differences in health status and changes in health over time. Health status measures cover health states ranging from very poor, including disability and dysfunction, to very good, including high levels of functioning and well-being. The range of measurement determines how many people are concentrated at the top (ceiling) and at the bottom (floor) of the scale score distribution, which, in turn, determines whether distinctions can be made among people and whether changes can be described over time. Because many health status measures focus on the lower levels of health, they often produce large "ceiling" effects in scale score distributions (6,7). This is similar to attempting to obtain the weight of adults with a scale that ends at 100 pounds. Everyone who steps on that scale who weighs 100 pounds or more is assigned the heaviest weight. Such a scale is not useful in describing differences in weight among those who weigh more than 100 pounds, nor is it useful in measuring an increase in weight among those people. Conversely, if a disabled population were given a health status measure designed for athletes, we would expect to find most respondents at the bottom of the scale score distribution ("floor" effect).

The number of levels of measurement in a scale is also important in interpreting scale scores because the ability of a scale to describe differences among people and changes within people over time increases with increased levels of measurement. For example, consider a walking scale with only two levels of measurement: 1) I can walk, and 2) I cannot walk. This is a very "coarse" scale because it contains only two gross categories of response. The great majority of people in the general population would endorse the first statement. Therefore, most people would receive the same score on this scale, and it would not be possible to describe differences in walking ability among these people. The only change that could be detected among this group of people would be if someone became unable to walk. In contrast, consider the example of a scale with four levels of measurement: 1) I walk with no difficulty; 2) I walk, but with some difficulty; 3) I walk, but with a great deal of difficulty; and 4) I cannot walk. The group of people who endorsed the first response on the coarser scale would now be divided between responses 1, 2, and 3 on this finer scale. There is a greater possibility of distinguishing among people in terms of their walking ability and in describing change in people over time. The scale score has greater meaning or interpretability.

The coarseness of a scale refers to how large the differences are between scale levels that define categories into which people are classified; that is, how many different kinds of people are grouped together into one category as a result of using this scale? Range and levels of measurement determine the coarseness of a scale and the coarseness of a scale affects the reliability of the measure, as well as the ability of the measure to describe people. Figure 1 illustrates all three attributes (range of measurement, levels of measurement, and reliability) depicting the relationship between a global (one-item, five-level) measure of physical limitations and a multi-item (35-item, 100-plus level) Physical Component Summary (PCS) measure using data from patients in the MOS (8). The correlation between the two measures is .75, suggesting that the global item captures substantial information in the multi-item scale (2,9). However, the scatter plot shows three ways in which the global single-item measure misses much of the information contained in the multi-item summary measure. First, the restricted range of the five levels, as defined by the global item, is apparent, particularly for the top level. The scatter plot shows a large "ceiling effect" for the global item in that a substantial proportion of respondents score at the highest level. The highest level of the global item is just slightly above the mean of the PCS (the PCS mean is 45), a scale that extends the range of measurement into higher levels of functioning and well-being than limitation and disability. This demon-

strates that the global physical functioning item is primarily a measure of disability and, thus, will not describe the health of those who are not disabled. Second, there are large gaps in measurement between the five levels on the global measure, relative to those on the PCS. The global measure defines only five levels of measurement in comparison with hundreds for the PCS (10). The restricted range and few levels of measurement (i.e., the coarseness of the scale), lead to a lack of reliability in measurement. At each of five levels on the global item, there is a wide range of PCS scores. The fact that each level of the global item includes nearly the full range of levels on the multi-item scale shows that the global item lacks precision relative to the multi-item scale.

SPECIFIC METHODS OF SCALE SCORE INTERPRETATION

The ways of generating information useful in scale score interpretation can be as varied as the many different ways in which health status scores are used. We describe below three different strategies that we have found very useful and illustrate each with examples from the literature.

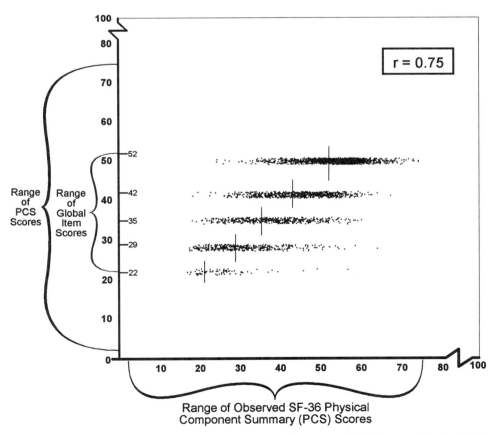

FIG. 1. Plot of global item and SF-36 Physical Component Summary (PCS) Scores, Medical Outcomes Study (N = 2,833).

Content-Based Interpretation

Characterization of Content of General Health Status Surveys

Table 1 summarizes the content of ten of the most commonly used "generic" health status measures (11). Most of these measures address the concepts of physical functioning, mental health, role functioning, pain, and general health perceptions. Other concepts not included in all measures are energy, cognitive functioning, and sleep. Measures that yield scores for a specific concept usually have a more direct interpretation in relation to criteria that are relevant to that concept. For example, role-functioning measures would have a more direct interpretation in terms of work behavior than would mental health measures.

Content-based interpretation should also consider the *type* of information sought about each health concept. For example, some scale items ask for reports of behavior, whereas others ask for a more subjective rating or evaluation. Another attribute of content is range of health states described, as discussed above. For the SIP, the Quality of Well-Being Scale (QWB), and the Nottingham Health Profile (NHP), the "best" or highest level of health measured is the absence of functional limitations and/or specific symptoms and problems. Other surveys in Table 1 also measure these levels, but they extend the measurement range into higher levels of health. For example, four surveys (the Health Insurance Experiment battery, the Duke, the MOS Functioning and Well-Being Profile (FWBP), and the MOS SF-36) extend measurement of mental health well into the psychological well-being range, with proven advantages in interpretation and prediction (12). The range of health content sampled by a measure will determine the degree of floor and ceiling effects typically observed in "sick" and "well" populations.

Single-Item Scales

Content-based interpretation for a single item scale, such as one of the COOP charts (9) is based on the content of the question and the response choices (Fig. 2). That content determines what the respondent thinks about in replying to the question and, therefore, provides excellent clues as to what his or her answers mean. For example, a choice of "Heavy" on the chart in Fig. 2 defines the most strenuous activity that could be performed in the past week as jogging at a slow pace or climbing stairs at a moderate pace. As defined in Fig. 2, going from level 2 to level 1 is an improvement from being able to jog at a slow pace to being able to run at a fast pace.

TABLE 1. *Summary of content of widely used general health surveys*

Concepts[a]	QWB	SIP	HIE	NHP	QLI	COOP	EUROQOL	DUKE	MOS FWBP	MOS SF-36
Physical functioning	●	●	●	●	●	●	●	●	●	●
Social functioning	●	●	●	●	●	●	●	●	●	●
Role functioning	●	●	●	●	●	●	●	●	●	●
Psychological distress		●	●	●	●	●	●	●	●	●
Health perceptions (general)			●	●	●	●	●	●	●	●
Pain (bodily)		●	●	●		●	●	●	●	●
Energy/fatigue	●		●	●				●	●	●
Psychological well-being			●					●	●	●
Sleep		●		●				●	●	
Cognitive functioning		●						●	●	
Quality of life			●			●			●	
Reported health transition						●			●	●

[a]Rows are ordered in terms of how frequently concepts are represented; only concepts represented in two or more surveys are listed. Analyses of content were based on published definitions. Columns are roughly ordered in terms of date of first publication.

QWB, Quality of Well-Being Scale (1973); SIP, Sickness Impact Profile (1976); HIE, Health Insurance Experiment Surveys (1979); NHP, Nottingham Health Profile (1980); QLI, Quality of Life Index (1981); COOP, Dartmouth Function Charts (1987); EUROQOL, European Quality of Life Index (1990); DUKE, Duke Health Profile (1990); MOS FWBP, MOS Functioning and Well-Being Profile (1992); MOS SF-36, MOS 36-Item Short-Form Health Survey (1992).

PHYSICAL CONDITION

During the past 4 weeks . . .
  * What was the most strenuous level
of physical activity you could do for at
least 2 minutes?

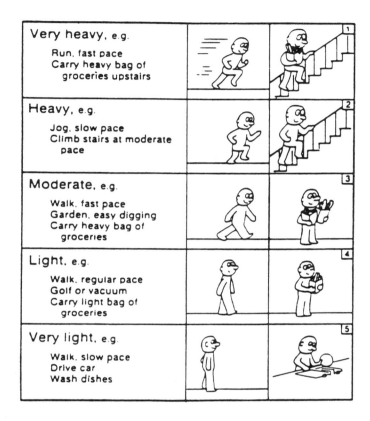

Very heavy, e.g.		
Run. fast pace		
Carry heavy bag of groceries upstairs		
Heavy, e.g.		
Jog. slow pace		
Climb stairs at moderate pace		
Moderate, e.g.		
Walk. fast pace		
Garden, easy digging		
Carry heavy bag of groceries		
Light, e.g.		
Walk. regular pace		
Golf or vacuum		
Carry light bag of groceries		
Very light, e.g.		
Walk. slow pace		
Drive car		
Wash dishes		

FIG. 2. COOP Chart to measure physical functioning. Reprinted with permission from COOP/WONCA Charts Copyright © Trustees of Dartmouth College/COOP Project 1989.

Multi-Item Scales

While multi-item scales have the potential to provide a more comprehensive sample of the universe of content, more levels of measurement, and greater reliability relative to single-item scales (2), content-based interpretation of the scores they yield can be more complex. Scores for people who score at that top or bottom of the scale are easy to interpret by looking at the items and response choices necessary to earn those scores. For example, the top score of the SF-36 Physical Functioning scale (13) is earned only by being able to perform all physical activities measured, including vigorous activities, without limitations due to health. Conversely, the bottom score is assigned only to those limited a lot by their health in performing all physical activities, including bathing or dressing.

How are intermediate scale levels interpreted using the content method? A useful method is to use responses to a single item from the scale to interpret scores across scale levels. This approach involves several steps. First, an item

that describes important, common, or easily understood health behavior is chosen. Second, responses to the item are dichotomized in a way that is meaningful and that reveals differences across levels of the scale in the score range of interest. Third, the percentage endorsing the item is plotted for each level of the scale being interpreted. For example, what does it mean to improve from a score of 40 to 50 on the PF-10, the Physical Functioning (PF) scale used in the MOS FWBP and SF-36? To address this question, responses to the "walk one block" item from the PF scale were dichotomized to indicate that people either could or could not walk one block without limitation. The percentage of people who responded that they could walk a block without difficulty was calculated for each of ten levels of the PF scale (Fig. 3). As the PF scale scores increase from 40 to 50 points, 18% more people indicate that they can walk one block without limitations. Therefore, a ten-point improvement at this level of the scale results in nearly a 55% increase in the percentage of people who are likely to report that they can walk a block without difficulty. In addition, most people

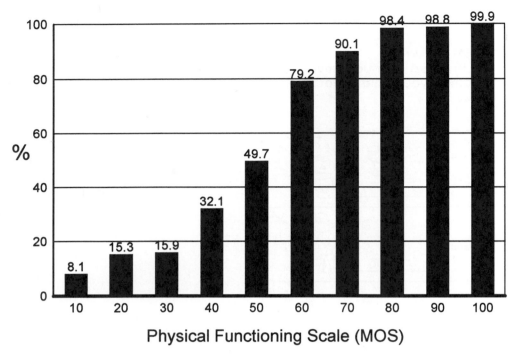

FIG. 3. Percentage that can walk one block or more at each scale level.

who reach a score of 70 on the PF can walk a block without limitation. Thus, one meaning of a PF score of 70 is that the vast majority of people with this score can walk a block without difficulty. Other examples of content-based interpretation are presented elsewhere (4,10).

Weighting Questionnaire Content for Interpretation

Several widely used health status surveys weight items according to evaluations of item content (14). To form weights, item content is interpreted by judges either in terms of the degree of disability expressed (e.g., the SIP, the NHP) or in terms of the desirability of the health state expressed [e.g., the QWB, the European Quality of Life Index (Euro-Qol)]. These weights are then averaged across the items endorsed by the respondent. The SIP (15) weights were formulated by asking 133 judges (including enrollees in a prepaid health plan, health professionals, and preprofessional students) to rate the degree of severity of dysfunction expressed by each item. These item weights are then summed and the total SIP score for a dimension is expressed as a percentage of the highest possible score (15). The SIP scores are, thus, directly interpretable as reflecting the subjective evaluations of the relative degree of disability as judged by patients and clinicians.

Weights for items in the QWB (16–18) and EuroQol scales (19) were derived from judgments regarding the desirability of the different health states described in the items. For example, the QWB scale produces a single score that is "simply an average of the relative desirability scores assigned to a group of persons for a particular day or a defined interval of time" (17, p. 704). Scale levels are the "weights, social preferences, or measures of relative importance that members of society associate with each of the Function Levels and Symptom/Problem Complexes" (17, p. 704). The weights for these levels were obtained through a series of preference studies wherein subjects rated case descriptions on a scale (17,18). In the development of the EuroQol, weights for health states were identified by asking subjects to describe "how good or bad each of these states would be for a person like you" (19, p. 204).

Construct-Based Interpretation

The meaning of scale scores can also be understood on the basis of how the scales relate to one another, to the dimensions of health they were designed to represent, and to other conceptually related measures. Constructs are unmeasured variables thought to be responsible for the relationship between measured variables. They are called constructs because they are "constructed" based on the relationships between measured variables (2). Construct-based interpretation answers questions such as: What do health scale scores reveal about underlying health concepts? Where do these scales fit into a general model of health? How are they likely to relate to other questionnaires in a battery? Will they provide new information or are they likely to be redundant?

The Relationships Among Health Status Scores from Different Questionnaires

Interpretation of health status scores can be accomplished by assessing the relationship of health status scores from one questionnaire to another. Scales that measure similar concepts will be highly related to one another and those that measure dissimilar concepts will have weaker relationships. A strong empirical relationship between scales indicates that they measure common concepts and therefore have overlapping interpretations. Table 2 shows correlations among MOS SF-20 and Duke Health Profile scales (20) and among NHP and SF-36 scales (6). These correlations demonstrate substantial relationships between scales that were designed to measure similar health constructs. The mental health scales from the MOS SF-20 and the Duke were highly correlated, as were the perceived health and pain scales. The correlations between the physical morbidity, pain, mental health, and vitality scales from the SF-36 and the NHP were also very high. These high correlations mean that these scales can be interpreted as measuring similar concepts. While these correlational analyses tell us something about the meaning of the scale, they do not provide interpretations for specific scores on that scale. Correlational analyses do not calibrate scores on one scale to those of another. This type of calibration requires the use of other methods such as test equating procedures (21). It is also important to keep in mind that high correlations between measures, such as those illustrated above, can mask important differences in the range and coarseness of measures as illustrated in Fig. 1.

The Relationships Among Scales Within the Same Questionnaire

Examining the relationship among scales within a questionnaire is another way of interpreting the meaning of scales. For example, the SF-36 Physical Functioning, Bodily Pain, and Role Physical scales have high correlations with each other, as do the Mental Health, Role Emotional, and Social Functioning scales; and the correlation between the Mental Health and Physical Functioning scales is low (4,22). We might hypothesize that the pattern of relationships among these scales is due to some scales targeting physical health while others target mental health.

This hypothesis can be formally tested by performing a factor analysis of the matrix of correlations to identify a smaller set of dimensions that explain relationships among those scales (23,24). Such analyses have revealed that two components predict over 80% of the reliable variance in the eight SF-36 scale scores (10,25,26) and that each scale has a very different interpretation in relation to these physical and mental health concepts (Fig. 4). Those scales that have the largest relationship to the first component (Physical Functioning, Role Physical, Bodily Pain) suggest that this component measures physical health, while those scales that have the largest relationship to the second component (Mental Health, Role Emotional, Social Functioning) suggest that this component measures mental health. The two scales that measure physical and mental health about equally (Vitality and General Health Perceptions) may be interpreted as general health measures. As shown in Fig. 4, these analyses

TABLE 2. *Correlations between health status scales*

SF-20 Scales MOS Short-form	Duke Health Profile					
	Physical health[a]	Mental health[a]	Social health[a]	Perceived health[a]	Disability[b]	Pain[b]
Physical functioning[a]	.18	.08	−.03	.07	−.20	−.22
Mental health[a]	.27	.51	.22	.22	.05	.00
Social functioning[a]	.32	.13	.07	.18	−.38	−.27
Health perceptions[a]	.28	.49	.29	.42	−.12	−.28
Role functioning[a]	.10	.17	.10	.24	−.32	−.00
Pain[b]	−.40	−.20	−.10	−.09	.03	.60

Nottingham Health Profile	SF-36 scales				
	Physical functioning[a]	Social functioning[a]	Pain[a]	Mental health[a]	Vitality[a]
Physical morbidity[b]	−.52	−.35	−.45	−.19	−.36
Social isolation[b]	−.20	−.41	−.18	−.47	−.36
Pain[b]	−.47	−.35	−.55	−.21	−.33
Emotional reactions[b]	−.18	−.53	−.28	−.67	−.55
Energy[b]	−.37	−.51	−.37	−.47	−.68

[a]High scores = good health.
[b]High scores = poor health.
Shaded correlations are between the most similar scales from the two measures. The top table is adapted with permission from ref. (20). The bottom table is adapted with permission from ref. (6).

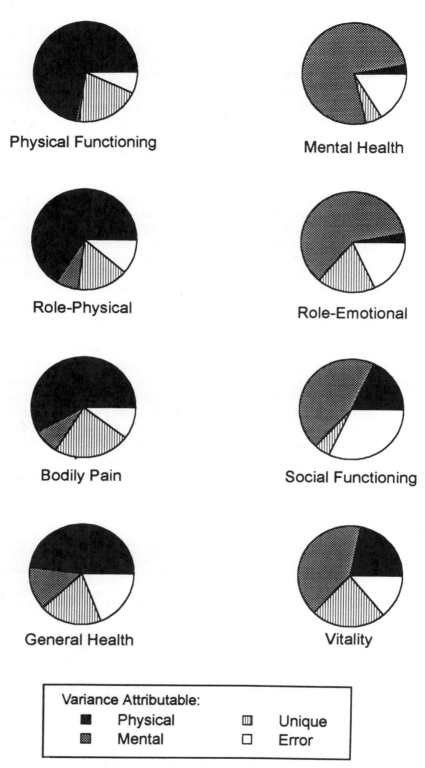

Physical Functioning

Mental Health

Role-Physical

Role-Emotional

Bodily Pain

Social Functioning

General Health

Vitality

Variance Attributable:
■ Physical   ▦ Unique
▧ Mental   ☐ Error

FIG. 4. Relationship of SF-36 scales to physical and mental components.

also provide other information useful in interpretation, including the amount of unique reliable variance in each score.

Factor analysis has also been applied to SIP scores to identify summary health constructs (15). These findings were useful in scoring and interpreting summary measures and in interpreting each SIP scale (15). One study of hospitalized patients (27), for example, identified dimensions of psychosocial health (Social Interaction, Emotional Behavior, Alertness Behavior and Communication) and physical health (Ambulation, Bodycare and Movement).

A practical advantage of interpreting scale scores based on relationships internal to the questionnaire is that such interpretations are not dependent on the definition or measurement of external variables. A theoretical advantage is that factor analytic results will predict how scale scores will be related to other measures. For example, research with the SF-36 has demonstrated that the three scales that best represent physical health, according to factor analytic evidence, tend to do best in detecting the impact of clinical changes in physical health (28–30). Similarly, those scales that best represent mental health do best in detecting the impact of clinical changes in mental health (25,26).

Criterion-Based Interpretation

Criterion-based analyses use information about how scale scores relate to external variables to determine their meaning or interpretation. Scale scores are studied in relation to criterion variables retrospectively, concurrently, or prospectively. These analyses answer questions such as: What is the clinical relevance of scores on a particular measure in relation to other measures (such as a concurrent measure of disease severity)? Can these scores predict socially relevant outcomes such as work productivity or the cost of subsequent medical services?

There are different ways of assessing the clinical and social relevance of scores. This can be done by looking at the relationship between scale scores and other life events (31,32), such as loss of a job (33,34), probability of clinical diagnoses (35,36), or death (37–40). Other types of criterion-related analyses include calculating the relationship between health status and role strain (41) or work behavior. These benchmarks address the social significance of scale scores. For example, Hunt et al. (42) found a significant association between scores on the NHP and absence from work. After controlling for the effects of chronic illness, sociodemographics (age, race/ethnicity, gender, and education), and psychosocial variables (social supports, life satisfaction), Lerner et al. (41) found a significant relationship between job strain and five SF-36 scales (Physical Functioning, Role Physical, Vitality, Social Functioning, and Mental Health).

Beyond Correlational Analyses

Interpretation of specific differences in scale scores requires taking correlational analyses a step further. To assign meaning to scores, we must estimate the criterion values across particular scale scores or ranges of scores. For example, we may know that scores for the SF-36 Physical Component Summary (PCS) are correlated with job loss in the future; however, this does not tell us the meaning of any particular range of scores on the PCS scale in these terms. To answer this question, results such as those depicted in Fig. 5 must be displayed. The figure illustrates the relationship between job loss due to health problems at one-year follow-up and baseline scores on the SF-36 PCS scale. The data show that a difference in PCS scores from 50 to 40 (the midpoints of the second and third scale levels) is predictive of an 80% increase in health-related job loss (from 10% to 17.9%) (10).

Another example of an analysis that goes beyond correlational evidence is that linking specific amounts of change in mental health to specific stressful events. For example, a three-point difference in the 38-item Mental Health Index was found to be equivalent to the stress of being fired or laid off from work (43). Table 3 summarizes the relationships between scores on the SF-36 five-item Mental Health (MH) scale to other criteria. The rows of the table show the percentage of people who were dissatisfied with life, had depressive symptoms, were diagnosed with depression, had suicidal ideation, or used mental health care at each of the scale score levels. The table also illustrates that these differences are greater at some MH score levels than others. For example, the percent of people reporting suicidal ideation changes from 14.4 to 29.6 when MH scores change from 40 to 20. Thus, between these scale levels, a two-point difference in the MH scale is associated with a 1.5% increase in reports of suicidal ideation. By contrast, each two-point difference at the top of the scale (from 100 to 80) is associated with only a 0.14% increase in suicidal ideation. Thus, the interpretation of differences in MH scores, in terms of suicidal ideation and other criteria illustrated in Table 3, must take into account the level at which the change occurred.

Utilization of Health Care Services

Because of the cost implications, the rates at which patients visit their physicians, are prescribed drugs, and are hospitalized are important interpretation guidelines (44). Evaluations of poor health are associated with more doctor visits, greater rates of prescriptions, and greater hospitalization (44). Table 3 also demonstrates the interpretation of changes in MH scores in terms of percentage of people using mental health services. For example, across the range of scores from 100 to 60, each two-point decrease in mental

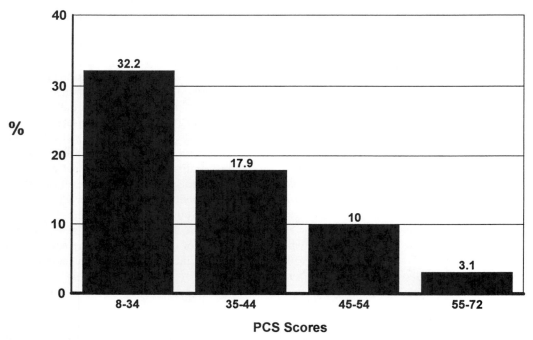

FIG. 5. Percentage of working MOS patients who lost their job one year later, four levels of the baseline PCS scale.

health is associated with a 1.5% increase in the amount of people seeing a mental health specialist.

Mortality

Death rates are also useful in interpreting general health status scores (37). General perceptions of health have been shown to be predictive of mortality over and above the effects of age or physical status (38–40). Fig. 6 provides 5-year mortality rates for five levels of the PCS. While less than 2% of MOS patients with PCS scores of 55 and greater died within 5 years, nearly 22% with scores at or below 24 died within 5 years. Age-adjusted odds-ratio analyses indicated that individuals with PCS scores in the range of

8 to 24 were nearly seven times more likely to die within 5 years than those with PCS scores 55 or greater (10).

Known-Groups Interpretation

Another example of criterion-based interpretation is based on "known-groups" comparisons. The meaning of scale scores can be understood by looking at scores that are typical of individuals known to differ in health (45–47). For example, Hunt et. al. (42) compared NHP scores of those who consulted a doctor for medical reasons (consulters) to those who did not consult a doctor (nonconsulters). It was hypothesized that scores for consulters would indicate higher disability than scores of nonconsulters, since the decision to consult

TABLE 3. *Percentages scoring positive on independent criterion scores for six levels of the Mental Health (MH) scale (n = 2,988)*

Independent criteria	Scale levels					
	(0)	(20)	(40)	(60)	(80)	(100)
Dissatisfaction with life	70.8	42.4	29.1	12.4	4.5	1.0
Depressive symptoms	78.8	78.7	68.6	50.3	30.0	12.5
Diagnosis of depression	54.9	46.2	30.9	18.4	7.6	2.2
Suicide ideation	43.1	29.6	14.4	5.6	1.9	.5
Mental health care:						
Outpatient (past 6 months)	51.6	45.8	37.4	25.8	13.2	4.6
Specialist (current)	72.0	66.8	60.5	47.0	32.1	17.0
Inpatient (past 12 months)	39.3	27.2	16.6	12.2	6.9	3.1

Sample includes MOS patients with one or more chronic conditions and complete data for the MHI-5 (*n* = 2,988).

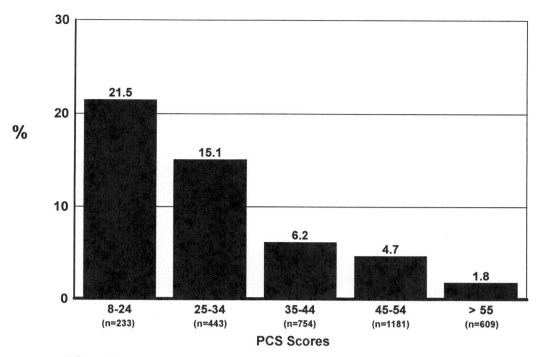

FIG. 6. Five-year mortality rates for MOS patients, four levels of PCS scores.

a doctor suggested that the patient perceived a health problem. Results confirmed the hypothesis: for every scale (i.e., Physical Mobility, Pain, Sleep, Emotional Reactions, Social Isolation, and Energy), the mean rank of consulters was significantly ($p < .01$) higher (indicating worse health) than that of nonconsulters. Brooks et al. (27) interpreted the severity of the SIP total scores for patients hospitalized for combined medical and psychiatric problems. According to total SIP scores, study patients (mean total SIP = 23.8) were more severely disabled (higher scores indicate more disability) than those with severe rheumatoid arthritis (mean total SIP = 15.6), about as compromised as those with severe pulmonary disease (mean total SIP = 24.0), and not quite as disabled as those with amyotrophic lateral sclerosis (mean total SIP = 30.0).

Known groups comparisons are used to interpret the *size* of differences in scale scores. The difference in scale scores between two groups of individuals who should have vast differences in health will indicate what a large difference in scores is likely to be. For example, the difference in scores between hypertension and congestive heart failure (CHF) patients should be large because CHF is a much more debilitating condition than hypertension. Thus, differences in scale scores that are equivalent to the differences in scores between hypertension and CHF patients could be considered large. To determine the size of small differences in health status scores, comparisons may involve looking within a disease at groups of individuals who differ according to some measure of disease severity. For example, the scores of individu-

als with a mild asthma condition could be compared to those with no asthma symptoms to get a sense of what a small difference in scale scores would be.

Norm-Based Interpretation

Norm-based comparisons are a popular method of interpreting scale scores (45,48–50). Scores are understood as departures from expected or typical scores; these expected or typical scores are called *norms*. Norms can be computed at the individual or group level. At the individual level, norms are the scores that are typical of the individual under stable conditions. At the group level, norms are the average values for the group and can be calculated based on a sample of the general population. Norm-based interpretation answers questions of whether or not an observed score is typical: Is this the score one would expect to see for this individual or group of individuals? Is there anything remarkable or out of the ordinary about this score?

Among the earliest comprehensive use of norms was for the interpretation of SIP scale scores (51). SIP estimates were also among the first to be adjusted for sociodemographic characteristics (52). Bergner et al. (52) presented the average SIP scores for cardiac arrest survivors as compared to a well norm (group health plan enrollees who were not ill) (Fig. 7). Besides norm-based interpretation, this SIP study illustrated other methods (for example, the use of confidence intervals in the display of results and the use of summary scores to

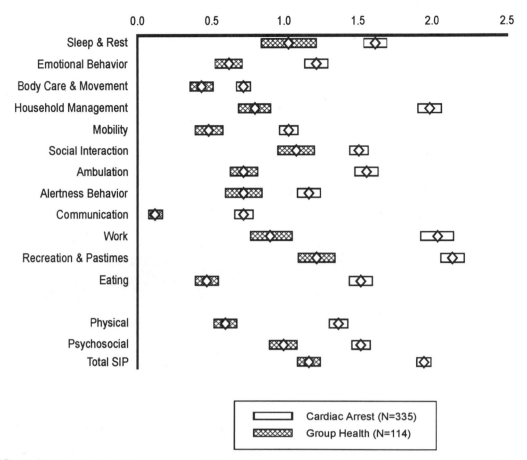

FIG. 7. Mean adjusted SIP scores and 95% confidence intervals for cardiac arrest patients and group health enrollees.

address the problem of multicollinearity among scale scores), and other issues (such as the impact of age and gender on scale scores), that affect the interpretability of scale scores. As illustrated by the nonoverlapping confidence intervals, those with heart disease had significantly higher scores (indicating more disability) than well individuals on the Sleep and Rest, Emotional Behavior, Body Care and Movement, Household Management, Mobility, Social Interaction, Ambulation, Alertness Behavior, Communication, Work, Recreation and Pastimes, Eating scales, SIP Psychosocial and Physical Dimensions, and SIP Total score. Due to multicollinearity among the 12 scales, the authors recommended focusing on the Physical and Psychosocial dimension scores and the SIP Total score as a better estimate of the real difference between those with heart disease and those who are well.

Scale scores can be put on an equivalent metric by expressing them as deviations from a norm (53). In this method, the mean of a score is subtracted from the mean of the norm and divided by the standard deviation for the norm. This facilitates comparisons between scale scores that may have different average values and different standard deviations. For example, SF-36 scales that primarily measure disabil-

ity (Physical Functioning, Role Physical, Role Emotional, Bodily Pain, and Social Functioning) have higher scores in most samples than those scales that extend measurement into high levels of functioning and well-being (General Health Perceptions, Vitality, and Mental Health). Because scores have different average values, the scores cannot be compared across scales. Scale scores vary also in the amount of error they have about the mean. For example, scales such as the SF-36 role-functioning measures have larger standard errors than other scales in the questionnaire. Thus, a large change in role functioning may actually be small when converted to standard deviation units.

The effect on interpretation of differences between scale scores in mean values and standard deviations is illustrated by the following example. Osterhaus et al. (54) used norm-based comparisons to interpret the impact of migraine on SF-36 scores. In Fig. 8, we display the data reported by Osterhaus et al. in two ways to illustrate (a) the value of norm-based comparisons, and (b) the additional information offered by standardizing scores to the norm. Fig. 8 shows two graphs: A (to the left) is a plot of raw, unstandardized scores, and B (to the right) is a plot of scores standardized to the mean and variance of the general United States well

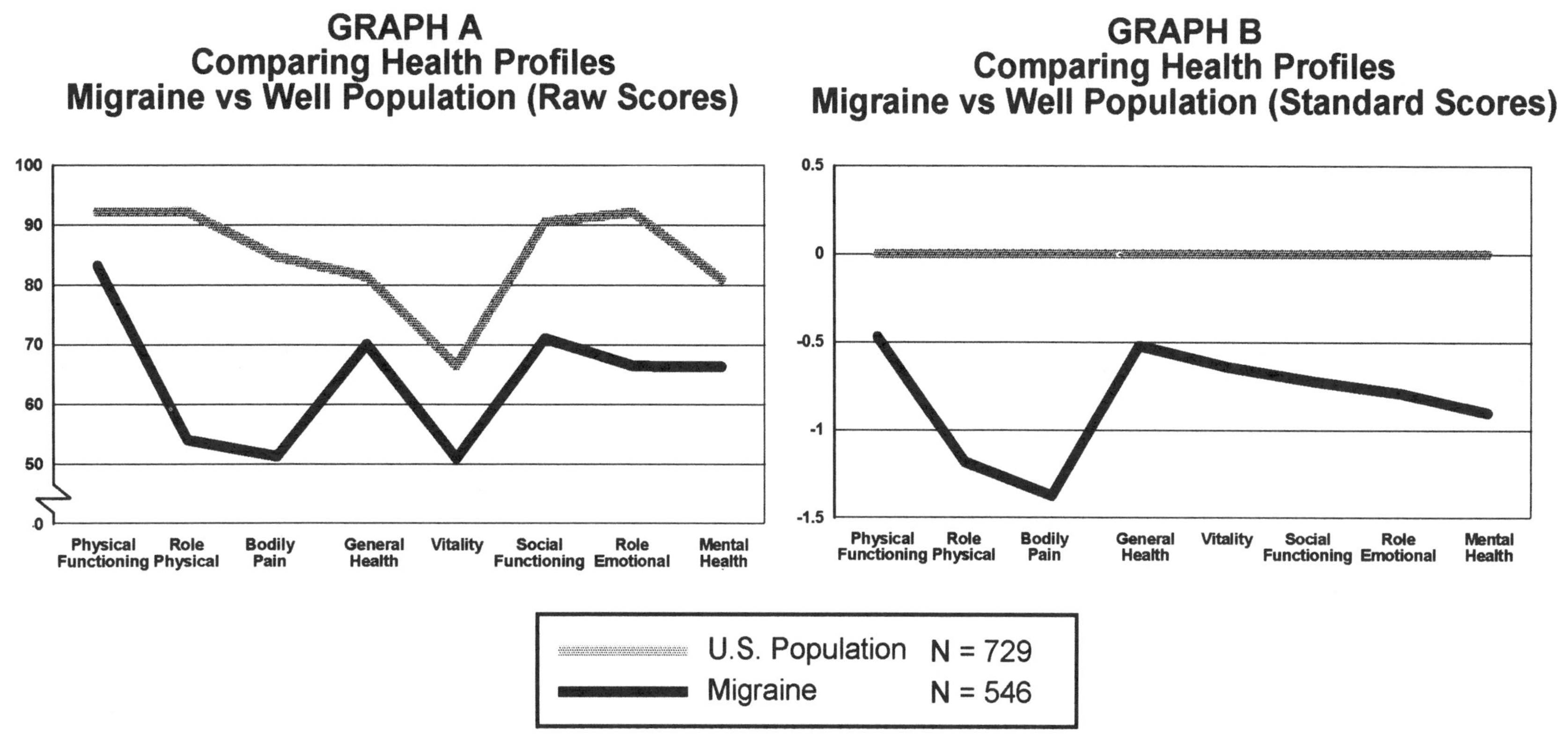

GRAPH A
Comparing Health Profiles
Migraine vs Well Population (Raw Scores)

GRAPH B
Comparing Health Profiles
Migraine vs Well Population (Standard Scores)

U.S. Population   N = 729
Migraine   N = 546

Note: The U.S. General population scores were adjusted to the age and sex distribution of the migraine sample. The U.S. General population sample included only those with no reported medical conditions. The scores of the migraine sample were adjusted for the effect of comorbid conditions.

FIG. 8. The health burden of migraine.

population. Both graphs illustrate the significant health burden of migraine; however, it is easier to identify the particular health concepts that are affected by looking at B rather than A. Graph A seems to indicate that Vitality scores are as low as Bodily Pain scores. However, the average U.S. population value for Vitality is much lower than that for Bodily Pain so, in fact (as illustrated by graph B), migraineurs are much less impaired in terms of Vitality than they are in terms of Bodily Pain. Also, in graph A, the burden of migraine on Role Emotional seems to be larger than the burden on Mental Health. However, the error around scores on Role Emotional is much larger than that around scores on Mental Health, and when that is taken into account, as it is in graph B, the burden of migraine on Mental Health is shown to be actually larger than it is on Role Emotional.

Because it has been shown that the health status of individuals is influenced by variables such as age and gender (4,52), normative values are often calculated separately for males and females and for different age groups. There is a great need for normative values of change over time for well and chronically ill persons. For example, in assessing the effect of a treatment over time for individuals with progressive neuromuscular disease, one would need to know what to expect in terms of a decline in health status for untreated individuals. The interpretation of change scores within diseases will be greatly facilitated by such longitudinal norms.

SUMMARY

The scores that health status questionnaires yield, like those of any other measure, can be understood by examination of their content and their relationships to other well-understood indicators or meaningful outcomes. Score interpretation is limited by score reliability, the range of scale measurement, and the number of levels measured. We have illustrated several strategies that have proved useful in interpreting health status scores, including content-, construct-, criterion-, norm-, and known groups-based strategies. It is important to end this chapter with a brief warning about sources of misinterpretation and the role of standardization in guarding against bias in measurement.

SOURCES OF MISINTERPRETATION

Misinterpretation of health status scores can occur when there is a lack of standardization across comparisons made within groups over time or among groups at one point in time, with regard to types of respondents surveyed or methods used to collect the health status information. It is very important to standardize mode of data collection, questionnaire format (including instructions), and to take into account differences in sociodemographics of respondents. Research indicates that how data are collected, whether by face-to-face interview, telephone, or mail, will affect scale scores (55). Instructions, such as the recall period, also have been

shown to influence scale scores (56). Every effort should be made to make questionnaire administration procedures, such as mode of administration and the format of the questionnaire, invariant across longitudinal and cross-sectional comparisons. The type of respondent also has an effect of scale scores. Proxy responses to health status surveys typically differ from personal responses (57). Thus, if proxy data are used, they should be used consistently throughout a study. Sociodemographic variables such as gender, age, education, income, and race/ethnicity (58–60) have been shown to be associated with health status, so comparisons should be restricted to groups that are equivalent in terms of these background variables or statistical controls for these variables should be implemented.

CONCLUSIONS

Interpretation guidelines are most useful when they go beyond correlational validity to express scale scores in terms of specific quantities along a criterion of interest. It is not enough to know that there is a strong or statistically significant relationship between the scores and a criteria; what is important is to know how that relationship is expressed in terms of a specific scale score or range of scores. In this way, scale scores are translated into meaningful units. The meaningfulness of the criterion used to interpret scale scores will depend on the audience. Different constituencies will benefit from different expressions of health status scores in different types of "currencies." Demographers may be most interested in expressing scores relative to the rest of the population. Economists may be interested in the dollar implication of health status scores. Employers may be interested in what scores mean in terms of absenteeism, productivity, and satisfaction with health care benefits.

In addition, interpretation requires determining the specific health concepts and the specific range of scores that yield the most information about the criterion of interest. Different dimensions of health have completely different relationships to criteria. For example, measures of physical health are more predictive of death than are measures of mental health. Consistent with those who favor a negative definition of health (perfect health is the absence of disability), we have found that the numbers yielded by health status scores are probably more important at the negative end of the continuum; that is, changes in health status scores relative to many criteria are larger in the disability than in the well-being range. However, there are social consequences of differences at the top of the scale as well; for example, the probability of hospitalization increases nearly 30% (from 27 to 35/1,000), going from "excellent" to "very good" health (44).

The field of health status assessment will take a giant leap forward as evidence for the interpretation of scores of widely used health status measures is documented in user-friendly terms. We hope that the examples presented in this chapter will facilitate much-needed progress toward that objective.

ACKNOWLEDGMENTS

The authors would like to acknowledge Mark Kosinski for his help with the data analysis, Barbara Gandek for her edits of an earlier version of the chapter, Rebecca Voris for production of figures, and Sharon Ployer for text preparation.

REFERENCES

1. Anatasi A. *Psychological testing.* New York: Macmillan, 1976.
2. Nunnally JC, Bernstein IR. *Psychometric theory,* 3rd ed. New York: McGraw-Hill, 1994.
3. Stewart AL, Hays RD, Ware JE. Methods of validating MOS health measures. In: Stewart AL, Ware JE, eds. *Measuring functioning and well-being: The Medical Outcomes Study approach.* Durham, NC: Duke University Press, 1992:325–344.
4. Ware JE, Snow KK, Kosinski M, Gandek B. *SF-36 Health Survey manual and interpretation guide.* Boston, MA: New England Medical Center, The Health Institute, 1993.
5. Ghiselli EE, Campbell JP, Zedeck S. *Measurement theory for the behavioral sciences.* San Francisco: Freeman, 1981.
6. Brazier JE, Harper R, Jones NMB, O'Cathain A, Thomas KJ, Usherwood T, Westlake L. Validating the SF-36 health survey questionnaire: new outcome measure for primary care. *Br Med J* 1992;305: 160–164.
7. Anderson RT, Aaronson NK, Wilkin D. Critical review of the international assessments of health-related quality of life. *Qual Life Res* 1993;2:369–395.
8. Tarlov AR, Ware JE, Greenfield S, Nelson EC, Perrin E, Zubkoff M. The Medical Outcomes Study: an application of methods for monitoring the results of medical care. *JAMA* 1989;262:925–930.
9. Nelson EC, Landgraf JM, Hays RD, et al. The COOP function charts: a system to measure patient function in physicians' offices. In: Lipkin M, ed. *Functional status measurement in primary care.* New York: Springer-Verlag, 1990.
10. Ware JE, Kosinski M, Keller SD. *SF-36 physical and mental component summary measures—a user's manual.* Boston, MA: The Health Institute, 1994.
11. Ware JE. The status of health assessment. *Annu Rev Public Health* 1995;16:327–354.
12. Ware JE, Manning WG, Duan N, Wells KB, Newhouse JP. Health status and the use of outpatient mental health services. *Am Psychol* 1984;39(10):1090–1100.
13. Ware JE, Sherbourne CD. The MOS 36-item short-form health survey (S-36): I. Conceptual framework and item selection. *Med Care* 1992;30:473–483.
14. Patrick DL, Erickson P. *Health status and health policy: allocating resources to health care.* New York: Oxford University Press, 1993.
15. Bergner M. Development, testing, and use of the Sickness Impact Profile. In: Walker SR, Rosser RM, eds. *Quality of life: assessment and application.* Lancaster: MTP Press, 1988:79–94.
16. Patrick DL, Bush JW, Chen MM. Methods for measuring levels of well-being for a health status index. *Health Serv Res* 1973;8:224–229.
17. Kaplan RM, Bush JW, Berry CC. *The reliability, stability, and generalizability of a health status index. Proceedings of the American Statistical Association, Social Statistics Section.* Washington, DC: ASA, 1978: 704–709.
18. Kaplan RM, Anderson JP. A general health policy model: update and applications. *Health Serv Res* 1988;23:203–235.
19. EuroQOL Group. EuroQOL—a new facility for the measurement of health-related quality of life. *Health Policy* 1990;16:199–208.
20. Parkerson GR, Broadhead WE, Tse CJ. Comparison of the Duke Health Profile and the MOS short-form in healthy young adults. *Med Care* 1991;29:679–683.
21. Crocker L, Algina J. *Introduction to classical and modern test theory.* New York: Harcourt Brace Jovanovich, 1986.
22. Ware JE, Keller SD, Gandek B, and the IQOLA Project Group. Evaluating translations of health status questionnaires: methods from the IQOLA Project. *Int J Technol Assess Health Care* 1995;11(3).
23. Kim J, Mueller CW. *Factor analysis: statistical methods and practical issues.* Beverly Hills, CA: Sage, 1978.
24. Stevens J. *Applied multivariate statistics for the social sciences,* 2nd ed. Hillsdale, NJ: Lawrence Erlbaum, 1992.
25. Ware JE, Kosinski M, Bayliss MS, McHorney CA, Rogers WH, Raczek A. Comparison of methods for scoring and statistical analysis of SF-36 health profile and summary measures: summary of results from the Medical Outcomes Study. *Med Care* 1994;33(Suppl 4):AS264–AS279.
26. McHorney CA, Ware JE, Raczek AE. The MOS 36-Item Short-Form Health Survey (SF-36): II. Psychometric and clinical tests of validity in measuring physical and mental health constructs. *Med Care* 1993;31:247–263.
27. Brooks WB, Jordan JS, Divine GW, Smith KS, Neelon FA. The impact of psychologic factors on measurement of functional status: assessment of the Sickness Impact Profile. *Med Care* 1990;28:793–804.
28. Phillips RC, Lansky DJ. Outcomes management in heart valve replacement surgery: early experience. *J Heart Valve Dis* 1992;1:42–50.
29. Katz JN, Larson MG, Phillips CB, Fossel AH, Liang MH. Comparative measurement sensitivity of short and longer health status instruments. *Med Care* 1992;30:917–925.
30. Kantz ME, Harris WJ, Levitsky K, Ware JE, Davies AR. Methods for assessing condition-specific and generic functional status outcomes after total knee replacement. *Med Care* 1992;30(Suppl 5):MS240–MS252.
31. Sherbourne CD, Hays RD, Meredith L, Mazel RM. Life events as benchmarks for quality of life changes in the MOS SF-36[abstract]. *Qual Life Res* 1994;3:55.
32. Williams AW, Ware JE, Donald CA. A model of mental health, life events, and social supports applicable to general populations. *J Health Soc Behav* 1981;22:324–336.
33. Brook RH, Ware JE, Rogers WH, et al. Does free care improve adults' health? Results from a randomized controlled trial. *N Engl J Med* 1983;309:1426–1434.
34. Ware JE, Brook RH, Rogers WH, et al. Comparison of health outcomes at a health maintenance organization with those of fee-for-service care. *Lancet* 1986;1:1017–1022.
35. Berwick DM, Murphy JM, Goldman PA, Ware JE, Barsky AJ, Weinstein MC. Performance of a five-item mental health screening test. *Med Care* 1991;29:169–176.
36. Weinstein MC, Berwick DM, Goldman PA, Murphy JM, Barsky A. A comparison of three psychiatric screening tests using Receiver Operating Characteristic (ROC) analysis. *Med Care* 1989;27:593–607.
37. Ware JE. Evaluating measures of general health concepts for use in clinical trials. In: Furberg CD and Schuttinga JA, eds. *Quality of life assessment: practice, problems, and promise.* Proceedings of a Workshop Sponsored by the Office of the Director, National Institutes of Health. (NIH Publication No. 93-3503). Washington, DC: U.S. Department of Health and Human Services, 1993:51–63.
38. Idler EL, Kasl S. Health perceptions and survival: do global evaluations of health status really predict mortality? *J Gerontol* 1990;46:S55–S65.
39. Kaplan G, Barell V, Lusky A. Subjective state of health and survival in elderly adults. *J Gerontol* 1988;43:S114–S120.
40. Kazis LE, Anderson JJ, Meenan RF. Health status as a predictor of mortality in rheumatoid arthritis: a five-year study. *J Rheumatol* 1990: 17.
41. Lerner DJ, Levine S, Malspeis S, D'Agostino RB. Job strain and health-related quality of life in a national sample. *Am J Public Health* 1994;84:1580–1585.
42. Hunt SM, McKenna SP, McEwen J, Williams J, Papp E. The Nottingham Health Profile: subjective health status and medical consultations. *Soc Sci Med* 1981;15a:221–229.
43. Brook RH, Ware JE, Rogers WH, et al. Does free care improve adults' health? Results from a randomized controlled trial. *N Engl J Med* 1983;309:1426–1434.
44. Kravitz RL, Greenfield S, Rogers WH, et al. Differences in the mix of patients among medical specialties and systems of care: results from the Medical Outcomes Study. *JAMA* 1992;267:1617–1623.
45. Stewart AL, Greenfield S, Hays RD, et al. Functional status and well-being of patients with chronic conditions: results from the Medical Outcomes Study. *JAMA* 1989;262:907–913.
46. Cassileth BR, Lusk EJ, Strouse TB, Miller DS, Brown LL, Cross PA, Tenaglia AN. Psychosocial status in chronic illness: a comparative analysis of six diagnostic groups. *N Engl J Med* 1984;311:506–511.
47. Jenkinson C, Fitzpatrick R, Argyle M. The Nottingham Health Profile: an analysis of its sensitivity in differentiating illness groups. *Soc Sci Med* 1988;27:1411–1414.

48. Follick MJ, Smith TW, Ahern DK. The Sickness Impact Profile: a global measure of disability in chronic low back pain. *Pain* 1985;21: 67–76.

49. Wells KB, Stewart A, Hays RD, et al. The functioning and well-being of depressed patients: results from the Medical Outcomes Study. *JAMA* 1989;262:914–919.

50. Deyo RA, Inui TS, Leininger J, Overman, S. Physical and psychosocial function in rheumatoid arthritis: clinical use of a self-administered health status instrument. *Arch Intern Med* 1982;142:879–882.

51. Bergner M, Bobbitt RA, Pollard WE, Martin DP, Gilson BS. The Sickness Impact Profile: validation of a health status measure. *Med Care* 1976;14:57–67.

52. Bergner L, Bergner M, Hallstrom AP, Eisenberg M, Cobb L. Health status of survivors of out-of-hospital cardiac arrest six months later. *Am J Public Health* 1984;74:508–510.

53. Garratt AM, Ruta DA, Abdalla MI, Buckingham JK, Russell IT. The SF-36 Health survey questionnaire: an outcome measure suitable for routine use within the NHS? *Br Med J* 1993;306:1440–1444.

54. Osterhaus JT, Townsend RJ, Gandek B, Ware JE. Measuring the functional status and well-being of patients with migraine headaches. *Headache* 1994;34(6):337–343.

55. McHorney CA, Kosinski M, Ware JE. Comparisons of the costs and quality of norms for the SF-36 Health Survey collected by mail versus telephone interview: results from a national survey. *Med Care* 1994; 32:551–567.

56. Keller SD, Bayliss MB, Damiano A, Goss T, Hsu MA, Ware JE. Comparison of responses to SF-36 health survey questions with one-week and four-week recall periods. *Health Serv Res* 1995.

57. Sprangers MAG, Aaronson NK. The role of health care providers and significant others in evaluating the quality of life of patients with chronic disease: a review. *J Clin Epidemiol* 1992;45:743–760.

58. Mossey JM, Shapiro E. Self-rated health: a predictor of mortality among the elderly. *Am J Public Health* 1982;72:800–808.

59. Ren XS, Amick BC. Racial/ethnic disparities in self-assessed health status: evidence from the National Survey of Families and Households. *Ethnicity and Disease* 1995 (in press).

60. Singer E, Garfinkel R, Cohen SM, Srole L. Mortality and mental health: evidence from the midtown Manhattan study. *Soc Sci Med* 1976; 10:517–525.

Quality of Life and Pharmacoeconomics in Clinical Trials, Second Edition, edited by B. Spilker.
Lippincott-Raven Publishers, Philadelphia © 1996.

CHAPTER 48

Clinical Significance of Quality of Life Data

Eva G. Lydick and Robert S. Epstein

INTRODUCTION

Small quality of life (QOL) changes may be statistically significant, especially with large studies, but the clinical relevance of these changes may be difficult to interpret. While numerous books and papers have been published pertaining to the correct calculation and expression of statistical significance, a clear understanding of the concept of clinical significance and its application to study results has not received the same degree of attention.

This necessity of defining clinical meaningfulness is certainly not unique to QOL research. However, the definition of a clinically significant change is often under greater scrutiny in QOL research partly due to a general lack of familiarity with QOL measurement on the part of many clinicians and policy makers. Since practitioners have only recently been confronted with QOL results, they have not yet acquired the same level of intuition about the relevance of changes in these measures that they have about the relevance of clinical measures such as blood pressure, hemoglobin, or serum creatinine. Additionally, as QOL measures are perceptual and not physiological, they are viewed skeptically as "soft" or subjective, thus often believed to be less meaningful, clinical or otherwise, than are physiological measures. Finally, QOL scores have arbitrary units that vary with the instrument, as opposed to laboratory tests. The latter, for example, may measure serum levels by chromatography,

immunoassay, or bioassay, and, regardless of the test, report the results in a universally understood unit. Confusion also arises in that QOL results are compared to laboratory test results or other indications of progression of the underlying disease state. However, quality of life may be viewed as an outcome, not a measure of pathology or underlying disease state. Thus, it may be argued that any change in a QOL measure should be considered as clinically significant, as any change represents a patient's perception of a diminished or improved health outcome. Few would question whether a fracture is clinically significant. Yet a report of diminished quality of life due to a fracture is expected to be accompanied by an additional measure of clinical relevance.

Because the question will arise, an investigator must be prepared to describe how changes or differences seen with QOL instruments can be translated into clinically meaningful terms.

CLINICAL TRIALS

The issue of clinical significance in non-QOL end points has received the most comprehensive attention from researchers involved in the design and analysis of clinical trials. Estimation of sample size is an essential element of the design of any clinical trial. For continuous measures, sample size estimates are based on the level of type I error, the acceptability of a type II error, the variance of the measurement, and the minimal difference considered clinically important. This clinical difference has often been chosen because of practical or economic concerns of accruing and following a large number of subjects. However, economic principles can be used to quantitatively derive the "clinically

E. G. Lydick: Department of Epidemiology, Merck Research Laboratories, West Point, Pennsylvania 19486.
R. S. Epstein: Department of Outcomes Research and Management, Merck Research Laboratories, West Point, Pennsylvania 19486.

important'' difference by balancing the cost of an increasingly large clinical trial capable of detecting increasingly small differences in risk reduction with the overall improvement in health status of the population that could occur as the result of adopting a truly effective therapy (1). More commonly, this difference is determined as (a) the amount of difference on a proxy that relates to a significant outcome difference; (b) previous experience, that is, a new intervention should be as good or better than the old; and (c) natural history and change in measures of the disease over time.

Thus, it would seem that a clinically important difference has traditionally been in the eye of the beholder. This is not to say that there is no commonly recognized threshold for a given test or result. Clinicians may ''know'' clinical significance when they see it and they may agree fairly well on what constitutes clinical significance (2), but they may not realize that their understanding of clinical significance of objective measures is based on their experience (or the experience of their teachers) with a large number of patients followed over time. Unfortunately, this experience is not available with QOL measures for most clinicians at this time.

Recently it has been suggested that patients or other members of the public be given an active role in determining the magnitude of a clinically important treatment effect for trial planning (3). Using probability trade-offs, patients or healthy volunteers could be asked to indicate the degree of benefit they would want from a new treatment, given the potential side effects. Thus we have come full circle from being asked as QOL researchers to justify our subjective results in terms of objective measures to having trialists request subjective assessment from patients of proposed objective trial results.

POPULATION VERSUS INDIVIDUAL PERSPECTIVE

As is often the case, clinical relevance depends on the perspective taken. Results can be interpreted from the viewpoint of the patient under care, of the clinician treating the patient, of the patient's family or caregiver, of the political or economic body paying for the care, or of society as a whole evaluating the care in epidemiologic or public health terms (4). These different viewpoints can, in a rough sense, be divided into those that measure relevance to an individual (that is, patient or someone else evaluating the patient's condition) and those that measure relevance to a population.

Reports of clinical significance for QOL, as with objective measures, include both those related to the individual and those related to population. For example, differences seen in a study can be applied to a much larger population (population attributable risk), as in this example from Testa et al. (5):

20% of the patients receiving methyldopa and 15% of patients receiving propranolol would have remained stable or improved had they been treated with captopril. Given an average hypertensive clinical practice of size 500, this means that 100 individual patients receiving treatment with methyldopa could have maintained their quality of life on medication rather than experiencing a worsening. Of those 100, 45 could have been spared substantial worsening in their levels of positive well-being, vitality, depression and anxiety. This model extended to a population of 1 million hypertensive patients translates into 90,000 individuals spared substantial decreases in their general well-being.

Another form of expressing population-level clinical significance may relate changes in QOL to other population-level measures such as resource utilization, thus employing the construct of medical care resources to benchmark the QOL change:

Mental health status, as measured by the MHI, is a major predictor of the use of outpatient mental health services. The average patient scoring in the lowest tertile of the MHI score distribution spent over three times more per year for mental health care than the average person in the highest tertile (6).

Contrast these population perspectives with that of an individual perspective such as reported by Brook et al. (7):

A 5-point difference on a standardized health perception scale = the effect of having been diagnosed as having hypertension. A 10-point difference on a standardized physical functioning scale = the effect of having chronic, mild osteoarthritis.

While the reader is usually aware of the perspective by the context, this distinction is rarely stated in reporting clinical significance. However, the shifting perspective (from individual to population) when talking about clinical significance has added to the misunderstanding surrounding interpretation for both QOL and non-QOL measures alike.

This confusion is exacerbated by the emphasis of reporting clinical trial results in terms of mean difference of the change from baseline between treated and control groups. Often the mean change is within the test variance for an individual patient. This mean difference has little relevance to an individual patient. For illustration, if the Scholastic Aptitude Test (SAT) score of a student seeking admission to Harvard improves by ten points on repeat examination, it is unlikely that this would warrant comment. If, however, a new statewide school program results in an improvement of ten points on mean SAT scores for all students in the state, it is likely that the teachers and developers of this new program would be congratulated and rewarded (8). Thus a mean difference may have great relevance when assessing the impact of an intervention in a population and less relevance in understanding individual changes.

A useful way of presenting trial results for both QOL and non-QOL end points would be to describe the distribution of change; for example, how many patients benefit, how many show no change, and how many worsen. Even on a population basis, the greatest impact of an intervention is often in the tails of the distribution. Statistics that describe the tails or a cumulative distribution function would more clearly indicate how many patients are likely to have a significant benefit than the mean or median. It would be easier to judge the likely significance of the therapy to an individual patient and the number of patients likely to benefit.

DEFINING CLINICAL SIGNIFICANCE FOR AN OBJECTIVE TEST

When faced with a completely new test and new units, interpretation of objective measures is no easier than interpretation of QOL results. Clinical trials of a new therapy for benign prostatic hyperplasia used urine flow as an outcome measure (9). Following one year of treatment, the urine flow in individuals who received the active treatment improved on average by 3 cc/sec over those who received placebo. Clinicians found it very difficult to judge whether an improvement of 3 cc/sec was clinically meaningful. A subsequently published epidemiologic study in untreated men ages 40 to 79 found that urine flow rates decline by an average of approximately 0.2 to 0.3 cc/sec per year of life (10). A 3 cc/sec improvement in urine flow could be interpreted as roughly equivalent to restoring an individual's urinary status to what it was approximately 10 to 15 years earlier. Thus, the clinical trial results were not clear until put into context with the findings of the epidemiologic study.

CLINICAL SIGNIFICANCE IN QOL STUDIES

Likewise, QOL results require some contextual relationship in order to understand their relevance. Jaeschke et al. (11) define "minimal clinically important difference" as the smallest difference in a score in a domain of interest that patients perceive as beneficial and that would mandate, in the absence of troublesome side effects and excessive cost, a change in the patient's management. This definition incorporates several important concepts. It focuses attention on the patient's perception of benefit from therapy. Also, it suggests that this benefit would prompt a change in management which emphasizes the clinical aspect. Finally, it incorporates the risk/benefit equation of costs and side effects. While this is an excellent definition, it does not directly suggest an operational method for defining clinical meaningfulness. After a literature search and discussions with colleagues regarding the various ways in which QOL researchers have operationally defined clinical meaningfulness, we previously proposed a taxonomy of these attempts based on two broad categories that we termed distribution-based and anchor-based interpretations (12).

Distribution-Based Interpretation

Distribution-based interpretations are those based on the statistical distributions of the results obtained from a given study. Most of these interpretations involve permutations of the means and standard deviations of changes seen in a particular study or comparisons of study results to the means or standard deviations of some reference population.

The most commonly cited of these measures is the effect size in which the importance of the change is scaled by comparing the magnitude of the change to the variability in stable subjects, for example on baseline or among untreated individuals (13). Guyatt et al. (14) believe that effect size is more a measure of responsiveness and, at best, an underestimate of the minimal clinically important difference. Nevertheless, this measure has been used in a number of publications as an estimate or as evidence of clinical significance (15). While the most common, effect size is certainly not the only measure of clinical significance built on distributions.

Even though based on means, distribution-based interpretation may clearly be intended to relate QOL results to the individual. For example, consider these two definitions from Jacobson and Truax (16), of *proximity to the mean*

> The level of functioning subsequent to therapy places the individual closer to the mean of the functional population than it does to the mean of the dysfunctional population.

and *normative level of functioning*

> The level of functioning subsequent to therapy should fall within the range of the functional or normal population, where range is defined as within two standard deviations of the mean of that population.

Another example uses within-individual variation (5):

> The monitoring of a single patient requires that the physician be familiar with the within-individual variance of the QOL instrument. A single shift in the negative direction of 16 General-Well-Being units or more would have a probability of less than 0.05 and should immediately raise a flag to the practising clinician.

Clinically important difference is clearly related to magnitude of the difference. Burnand et al. (17) reviewed the levels at which investigators tended to view their results as quantitatively significant in evaluating (a) the ratio of two means, (b) odds ratios, (c) differences between two rates, and (d) correlation coefficients. In a survey of 142 published reports, they found that investigators do appear to use certain standards regularly for decisions of when to emphasize a clinical finding. For example, irrespective of statistical significance, investigators tended to report their results as "significant," "impressive," a "dramatic increase," or an "important difference"

in about 90% of the occurrences of a ratio ≥ 1.5 in two means,
in 80% to 100% of occurrences of an odds ratio ≥ 3.0,
in 90% to 100% of standardized increments ≥ 0.6 for two rates,
in all occurrences of a correlation coefficient that is ≥ 0.6.

Anchor-Based Interpretation

Alternatively, QOL measures may be compared, or anchored, to other clinical changes or results. Thus, our second broad taxonomic grouping is that of anchor-based interpretations of clinical meaningfulness. Normative data at first glance appears to be a distribution-based measure of clinical significance, but it goes further than just restate a statistical change and "anchors" such changes to the population as a whole. For example, using population norms, Guess et al. (18) could conclude

> Treatment with finasteride for 36 months reduced symptoms [scores] from about the 86th population percentile to the 64th population percentile, while treatment for TURP [transurethral prostatectomy] at Mayo Clinic reduced symptoms from the 97th population percentile to the 49th population percentile. This comparison is likely to be more understandable to clinicians and patients than simply describing the finasteride results as having reduced mean symptoms scores by 3.5 points on a scale of 0 to 36.

Fortunately, population norms are becoming available for the more commonly used instruments (19,20). With the availability of normative data, comparisons can be made between treated and untreated patients, ill and well populations, and, in some instances, patients with different diseases.

The most commonly reported anchor-based interpretation is that suggested by Jaeschke et al. (11) and is based on a patient and/or clinician global rating question. To use these authors' example, they looked at changes in a global assessment question over time and compared changes seen on their disease-specific questionnaire between four groups of patients defined as (a) those having no change in their global health status, (b) those having small changes in function (absolute changes of one to three response items on the global question), (c) those having moderate changes in function (absolute changes of four or five response items), and (d) those having large changes in function (absolute changes of six or seven on the global question). Thus, the changes seen in a disease-specific questionnaire are "anchored" to reported changes in overall health status.

Other anchors may be time, as in the non-QOL example of urine flow or in this example from the QOL literature:

> Disability in rheumatoid arthritis appears to increase by approximately 0.1 units on Health Assessment Questionnaire each year for the first few years of disease and then rises more slowly, at a rate of approximately 0.02 units per year after that (21).

An additional anchor may be changes with therapy, for example:

> The heart failure score, as measured by Chronic Heart Failure Questionnaire, improved by a mean of 2.1 points, when patients received digoxin. In another study, the heart failure score improved 1.6 points when patients received digoxin (11).

Thus changes seen with other therapies can be tied to the clinician's understanding of the efficacy of digoxin.

In addition to the examples previously quoted from Brook et al. (7) correlating diagnosis or impact of living with a specific condition, there is also an example anchoring changes on a QOL questionnaire to observed life events:

> a three-point difference on standardized mental health scale = the impact of being fired or laid off from a job.

Being able to predict future outcomes is an obvious anchor that has not been as commonly used as one would expect. Marder et al. (22) describe levels at which changes on the Brief Psychiatric Rating Scale are shown to be predictive of a psychotic exacerbation within 4 weeks. Thus, a clinician may judge the level of change at which to institute a change in the patient's management. Deyo and Inui (23) correlated changes in the Sickness Impact Profile with changes in more traditional measures of functional status in patients with arthritis.

Ideally, an attempt should be made to describe QOL values or changes in a way that will convey meaning to a clinician. These anchor-based interpretations of clinical significance all relate the change in QOL not to the distribution of scores but to some outside measure that is more clearly understood or familiar to their audience than the QOL scores themselves. This strategy was put forth by Brook and Kamberg (24) in 1987:

> 1. All clinical trials should include at least one readily understandable "non-traditional" measure of outcome that is of primary interest to clinicians. Work-loss days, days not confined to bed or chair, days out of hospital, and other similar measures are potential candidates.
> 2. Where possible, clinical trials should include one general health status measure, although it would not be used as the trial's primary outcome. . . . At least at the beginning of this endeavor, we should be satisfied with learning more about the meaning and interpretation of these general health status measures.

We believe that expressing changes in relation to an external anchor is of more value than the tautalogic reference of clinical importance back to statistical significance. In time, as our audience becomes more familiar with QOL measures and their scores, anchoring to other conditions and results may no longer be necessary; however, the need to consider clinical significance along with statistical significance will not disappear.

The relevant anchor, or the amount of change judged clinically significant, may differ with different populations and one may need to estimate clinical significance in different patient groups, just as one needs to validate the same questionnaire in each different patient group. This is particularly true as many scales are not completely linear. Scales may contain both a floor and ceiling in their relationship to an anchor (25), or it may be that smaller differences in the extremes may be substantially more important than the same level of change in mid-range (26).

CONCLUSIONS

We hope that by summarizing efforts to date, we provide a framework from which investigators can further refine means of assessing changes seen with QOL instruments. The need for defining clinically meaningful changes is likely to receive increased attention from clinicians, patients, policy makers, public health personnel, and quality of life researchers in the future. Results from objective tests are seen to be clinically meaningful only because of historical context. The problem with defining clinical significance of quality of life changes has nothing to do with any innate inferiority in QOL as a type of measure. It is merely a reflection on the newness of these measures and our inexperience with them. As all parties involved gain increased familiarity with these measures, their clinical significance will become more obvious and less problematic.

In the meantime, quality of life researchers should be as clear as possible when speaking of clinically significant differences. We should not use the term loosely without some framework for justifying why we believe our results are clinically significant. We should not confuse statistical significance with clinical significance.

With both QOL and non-QOL results, the perspective of the researcher needs to be clear. If we are speaking about the impact of an intervention on a population, perhaps we should not talk of clinical significance, but of public health significance or economic significance. A change in a measure that has been calibrated to be meaningful in population terms would not be expected to have the same relevance on an individual basis.

REFERENCES

1. Detsky AS. Using economic analysis to determine the resource consequences of choices made in planning clinical trials. *J Chronic Dis* 1985;38:753–765.
2. Bellamy N, Buchanan WW, Esdaile JM, Fam AG, Kean WF, Thompson JM, Wells GA, Campbell J. Ankylosing spondylitis antirheumatic drug trials. III. Setting the delta for clinical trials of antirheumatic drugs—results of a consensus development (Delphi) exercise. *J Rheumatol* 1991;18:1716–1722.
3. Naylor CD, Lleywellyn-Thomas HA. Can there be a more patient-centered approach to determining clinically important effect sizes for randomized treatment trials? *Pharmacoeconomics* 1994;47:787–795.
4. Spilker B. *Guide to clinical trials.* New York: Raven Press, 1991.
5. Testa MA. Interpreting quality-of-life clinical trial data for use in the clinical practice of antihypertensive therapy. *J Hypertens* 1987; 5(suppl 1):S9–S13.
6. Ware JE Jr, Manning WG Jr, Duan N, Wells KB, Newhouse JP. Health status and the use of outpatient mental health services. *Am Psychol* 1984;39:1090–1100.
7. Brook RH, Ware JE Jr, Rogers WH, Keeler EB, Davies AR, Donald CA, Goldberg GA, Lohr KN, Masthay PC, Newhouse JP. Does free care improve adults' health? Results from a randomized controlled trial. *N Engl J Med* 1983;309:1426–1434.
8. Example suggested by Dr Harry Guess, Epidemiology, Merck Research Laboratories.
9. Gormley GJ, Stoner E, Bruskewitz RC, et al. The effect of finasteride in men with benign prostatic hyperplasia. *N Engl J Med* 1992;327:1185–1191.
10. Girman CJ, Panser LA, Chute CG, Osterling JE, Barrett DM, Chen CC, Arrighi HM, Guess HA, Lieber MM. Natural history of prostatism: urinary flow rates in a community-based study. *J Urol* 1993;150:887–892.
11. Jaeschke R, Singer J, Guyatt GH. Measurement of health status: ascertaining the minimal clinically important difference. *Controlled Clin Trials* 1989;10:407–415.
12. Lydick E, Epstein RS. Interpretation of quality of life changes. *Qual Life Res* 1993;2:221–226.
13. Kazis LE, Anderson JJ, Meenan RF. Effect sizes for interpreting changes in health status. *Med Care* 1989;27:S178–S189.
14. Guyatt G, Walter S, Norman G. Measuring change over time: assessing the usefulness of evaluative instruments. *J Chronic Dis* 1987;40:171–178.
15. Fletcher A, Gore S, Jones D, Fitzpatrick R, Spiegelhalter D, Cox D. Quality of life measures in health care. II. Design, analysis, and interpretation. *Br Med J* 1992;305:1145–1148.
16. Jacobson NS, Truax P. Clinical significance: a statistical approach to defining meaningful change in psychotherapy research. *J Consult Clin Psychol* 1991;59:12–19.
17. Burnand B, Kernan WN, Feinstein AR. Indexes and boundaries for "quantitative significance" in statistical decisions. *J Clin Epidemiol* 1990;66:1273–1284.
18. Guess HA, Jacobsen SJ, Girman CJ, Osterling JE, Chute CG, Panser LA, Lieber MM. The role of community-based longitudinal studies in evaluating treatment effects—Example: benign prostatic hyperplasia. *Med Care* 1995;33:AS26–AS35.
19. Ware JE, Snow KK, Kosinski M, Gandek B. *SF-36 health survey manual and interpretation guide.* Boston, MA: Health Institute, New England Medical Center, 1993.
20. Fryback DG, Dasbach EJ, Klein R, Klein BED, Dorn N, Peterson K, Martin PA. The Beaver Dam Health Outcomes Study: initial catalog of health-state quality factors. *Med Decis Making* 1993;13:89–102.
21. Spitz PW, Fries JF. The present and future comprehensive outcome measures for rheumatic diseases. *Clin Rheumatol* 1987;6(suppl 2):105–111.
22. Marder SR, Mintz J, Van Putten R, Lebell M, Wirshing WC, Johnston-Cronk K. Early prediction of relapse in schizophrenia: an application of receiver operating characteristics (ROC) methods. *Psychopharmacol Bull* 1991;27:79–82.
23. Deyo RA, Inui TS. Toward clinical applications of health status measures: sensitivity of scales to clinical important changes. *Health Serv Res* 1984;19:275–289.
24. Brook RH, Kamberg CJ. General health status measures and outcome measurement: a commentary on measuring functional status. *J Chronic Dis* 1987;40(suppl1):131S–136S.
25. Ware JE Jr. Content-based interpretation of health status scores. *Med Outcomes Trust Bull* 1994;2:3.
26. Gold D. Statistical tests and substantive significance. *Am Sociol* 1969;4:42–46.

Quality of Life and Pharmacoeconomics in Clinical Trials, Second Edition, edited by B. Spilker. Lippincott-Raven Publishers, Philadelphia © 1996.

CHAPTER 49

Evaluating and Comparing Life Events Data with Quality of Life Data

Bert Spilker

INTRODUCTION

Life events such as a marriage, pregnancy, change in job, change in personal relationships, new residence, and death in the family are seldom recorded in clinical trials of medicines or therapy regimens. Nonetheless, there is a growing awareness that these events may influence the clinical interpretation of the data or may confound the trial's results, particularly in regard to quality of life assessments. For example, most significant life events would be expected to have a greater impact on a patient's quality of life than on their hematocrit or other laboratory parameters.

Life events may affect patients positively, negatively, or neutrally. A disproportionate number of positive events in patients receiving a test medicine may weight the outcome on the side of efficacy. On the other hand, if these events occur in patients receiving placebo, the result may show no difference between treatments. Ultimately this could prevent a good therapy from being used. Likewise, a disproportionate number of negative events in patients receiving a test medicine could lead to rejection of an effective therapy.

This chapter primarily focuses on life events data and presents a number of approaches for systematically collecting, quantitating, and interpreting life events data in clinical trials. The chapter also compares life events with quality of life. No presentations or details are included of the rich literature of life events in sociology, psychology, and psychiatry, because those papers focus on stressful life events leading to psychological or behavioral symptoms and illness, which is a different perspective than that presented here. Moreover, as described later, this literature describes weighting symptoms and statistically analyzing scores of life events to determine the overall seriousness of life events in terms of mental health. This highly quantitative approach is not supported in this chapter.

BACKGROUND

Why Measure Life Events?

The process of patient randomization to treatment groups should result in an even distribution of life events in each treatment group. Unfortunately, there are many cases where randomization results in an unequal distribution in one or

B. Spilker: Orphan Medical, Inc., Minnetonka, Minnesota 55305.

more characteristic; if life events are of interest, it is difficult to collect these data after a trial is complete.

In clinical trials that take place over a period of 4 or more months, external events in patients' lives may influence responses to treatment, preventive measures, or interventions. To assess whether this has occurred and how life events may have influenced patients, it is necessary to collect data on such events and their significance. Of course, life events may influence trials of shorter durations and even a trial of 4 days could be affected.

Collecting life events data should always be considered in long-term trials (4 months or longer for each patient); the longer the trial, the more likely it is that life events data are worthwhile to collect. It is particularly relevant to collect this information in quality of life trials because of the potential for life events affecting quality of life independent of the effects of the test treatment.

Evaluating the relationship of stress to psychological and psychiatric symptoms and illness was the primary stimulus for the development of a large field of life events papers starting in the 1970s. Weights were assigned to different life events to quantify the research and the total scores for a patient were summed—under the assumption that stress is cumulative and may be summed. This enabled statistical analyses to be conducted on the data. So many life events weighting procedures were used that Ross and Mirowsky (1) were able to compare 23 different methods in their study.

It is not necessary to collect life events data in most clinical trials, even in those over 4 months' duration. Only when there is a specific reason to evaluate such data or to confirm the lack of influence on the trial's results should they be collected.

Can Life Events Occur as the Result of Clinical Benefits, Adverse Reactions, or the Clinical Trial Process Itself?

Most life events (Table 1) that occur during a clinical trial are independent of both the treatment received and the process involved. Nonetheless, there is sometimes a direct or indirect connection. For example, a patient whose symptoms improve may, as a result, be able to find a job, earn a promotion, take an important trip, get married, or interact better with important people in his or her life.

The opposite can also occur. For example, a patient may have exacerbated or new problems that lead to major negative life changes. If the symptoms of the disease worsen as a result of treatment, then the deterioration is classified as an adverse event causally related to treatment. New symptoms, clinical signs, or laboratory-determined abnormalities are also classified as adverse events. The relationship of all adverse events to the test medicine must be assessed.

Both positive and negative life experiences can result indirectly or directly from participation in a clinical trial and have nothing to do with the treatment received. For example,

TABLE 1. *Examples of life events*

A. Family
 1. Pregnancy, abortion, miscarriage, birth
 2. Marriage, separation, divorce, reconciliation
 3. Quarrels or fights (increases or decreases in number or intensity)
 4. Death of friend, relative, or acquaintance
 5. Illness (self, child, or relative)
 6. Important changes in children's lives that influence their parents
B. Work
 1. New job, new responsibilities
 2. Resigned, fired, or other major change
 3. New hours, conditions, or coworkers
 4. Quarrels with coworkers or superiors
 5. Longer hours
C. Social
 1. Personal habits are altered
 2. Social interactions change in number or frequency
 3. Vacation taken
 4. Eating, sleeping, or other regular patterns are altered
 5. Change in time spent on recreation, hobbies, sports
 6. Move to a new home
D. Economics
 1. New loans taken out (or repaid)
 2. Bankruptcy
 3. Major change in status
 4. Major purchase made

a patient may meet someone at a clinic visit and develop a romantic relationship, be robbed or attacked in the clinic parking lot, or have an automobile accident while driving to the clinic. Many other positive or negative life experiences may have a connection with a patient's participation in a clinical trial and not with the treatment involved.

COLLECTING LIFE EVENTS DATA

Collecting Life Events Data Prospectively

A separate data collection form can be used as a life events questionnaire. The data could be collected either as written responses or as a checklist that captures most possibilities.

Significant life events also can be documented by an open-ended question posed by an investigator, study coordinator, or other individual during the trial. The question may be: "Have any events occurred during the last x weeks or months that have had an influence on your life?" This question may also be presented as a specific checklist or group of categories given to the patient to consider and complete.

In addition to identifying events, it is essential to capture the significance of each event for the patient. This may be accomplished with (a) a visual analog scale using two or more anchors (e.g., extremely positive and extremely negative) to identify end points, (b) an open question, (c) a Likert scale, or (d) a numerical scale (Tables 2 and 3). The preferred

TABLE 2. *Example of a form that may be used to collect data on life events in a clinical trial*

Patient number: _____

Visit: _____ _____ (Date)

Interviewer: _____

Life events since last visit:

	−5 to 0; 0 to +5 (a) (+5 is most positive, −5 is most negative)	Related to trial (yes/no*)	Previous report (yes/no)
_____	_____	_____	_____
_____	_____	_____	_____
_____	_____	_____	_____
_____	_____	_____	_____
_____	_____	_____	_____

(a) Based on your interview, rate the effect of each event on the patient.
Although these events may be in different directions, what was their overall effect on the patient (use the same scoring system).
The patient must supply this integrated number.

Overall effect= _____ (Rate from +5 to −5)

*Describe any yes answers:

---

approach in most trials is to use a Likert scale or a numerical scale. Likert scales such as that in Table 3 provide appropriate labels that are relevant for patients, physicians, or study coordinators. Measures of significance should be placed next to the descriptors of the life events so significance data are collected at the same time.

If life events were collected without capturing data on the significance of the event for the individual patient, the patient could be asked for this assessment at the next visit. But if data on the life event relevance were not collected during the trial, another approach must be considered, such as a telephone interview or an additional clinic visit.

Collecting Life Events Data Retrospectively

If life events constitute a primary end point of a clinical trial, then the failure to obtain data on their significance constitutes a major study flaw. For example, a treatment may be compared with placebo to evaluate whether socially withdrawn patients increase the number and quality of their social interactions as a result of treatment. It is doubtful that any retrospective collection of data will convince readers and reviewers of the validity of the trial. In most trials,

TABLE 3. *Possible categories to use on a data collection form to assess the significance of life events[a]*

A. 1. Strongly positive
   2. Mildly positive
   3. Neutral
   4. Mildly negative
   5. Strongly negative
B. 1. One of the most positive events I've experienced
   2. Strongly positive
   3. Moderately positive
   4. Mildly positive
   5. Neutral
   6. Mildly negative
   7. Moderately negative
   8. Strongly negative
   9. One of the most negative events I've experienced
C. 1. Very good and/or happy event
   2. A little good and/or happy event
   3. A so-so event of not much consequence
   4. A little bad and/or unhappy event
   5. A very bad and/or unhappy event

[a]These are examples of Likert scales. Many variations are possible.

however, life events data are a relatively minor parameter and a retrospective collection of life events data should be possible without a major compromise of their value.

The same data collection forms can be used to collect either prospective or retrospective data. Interviews or filling out of questionnaires should always take place in a quiet area set aside for this purpose during the clinic visit. This helps ensure that the patient does not feel rushed and stress is kept to a minimum. While life events data could be collected by telephone interview, this method should only be considered in a prospective trial. Even then it is less desirable than a face-to-face meeting at the clinic site. Whatever methods are used, the same methods must be applied to all patients. It is inappropriate for some patients to be interviewed and others to be given questionnaires. It is also important for the same interviewer to interact with the patient whenever possible. For patient-completed questionnaires, it is desirable for the health care professional who collects the data to briefly review patient responses just after the form is filled out to ensure that all questions have been answered appropriately. If any questions arise, the patient can clarify the responses.

Designing Life Events Questionnaires and Data Collection Forms

Life events questionnaires do not have to be validated before inclusion in a clinical trial in the same way that quality of life instruments require validation. This is because life events questionnaires are merely collecting information that is later tabulated in a straightforward manner. Although patients must use judgments in their responses as to which events to mention, each patient reads the same instructions or hears the same question. The establishment of significance levels is also relatively straightforward.

Some of the questions to consider in creating a data collection form for life events data are:

1. Is it desirable to collect data cumulatively? If so, it is likely that the number of events will grow from visit to visit. But some events that were extremely important for a patient during one period may have lost importance by the following visit. Thus, creating a cumulative list of life events over the course of a trial can be counterproductive. Nonetheless, some important life events are likely to remain important. Therefore, each data collection should only focus on the time since the previous visit.

2. What is the time period a patient should be told to consider in answering a question? This could be the time since their last clinic visit, the last month, or any other specified time. If there is a 6-month period between clinic visits, it may be desirable to focus on the previous month since that is freshest in the patient's mind. The disadvantage of this approach is that events during the first part

of the period may have had the greatest impact on the patient.

3. Can a patient be expected to differentiate between a life event, a disease-related event, and a medicine-related event? Many times this will be difficult. For example, if a patient's health gradually deteriorates, it may be related to the medicine (i.e., an adverse event), the disease being treated (i.e., a disease-related event), a life event such as the death of a spouse, or aspects of the trial such as having to undergo many difficult tests. But regardless of the actual cause, each of these is an important life event. The implications of this example suggest that if patient-completed questionnaires are used, the investigator or another qualified person should review the answers with the patient to assure that they reasonably reflect the facts and the significance of those events to the patient. Any relationship to the trial itself or to the patient's disease can then be discussed and assessed.

4. Does the patient view a life event as positive or negative? The investigator must never assume he or she understands the significance of any life event. For example, the patient may lose a job, but perhaps he or she hated that job. The opportunity to find a better position could be a positive event. Perhaps the patient wanted to leave that job but did not have the courage to quit. In extreme cases, the death of a family member or someone else could be felt as a liberating experience.

If standardized questionnaires are desired for assessing life events, the sociology and psychology literature is a rich resource (2–5).

What Specific Data Should be Collected?

The process of collecting and interpreting life events data would be easier if each event could be associated with a predetermined degree of significance. The level of significance could be judged along a numerical scale (e.g., from 1 to 100) or categorized in Likert categories. I believe it is impossible to create and use a standard reference list of significance values to associate with specific events. For example, a standard list would ascribe the death of a parent with a certain significance, the death of a sibling with another, the death of a cousin with a third, and so forth. The death of a cousin may have little significance for many people but may be a major calamity for a specific patient. Understanding the relationship between the patient and a cousin is not enough information to be confident in ascribing a certain level of significance to the event. Even if the patient is extremely close to a cousin, the impact of the death may not be felt for many months, if at all. Alternatively, the death of a distant cousin that the patient has had little contact with may affect the patient very strongly. Clearly, the significance of life events depends on many factors and is often extremely difficult, if not impossible, to predict with any accuracy.

A simple list of life events may be used to stimulate recollections rather than as a checklist. While it is impossible to identify all possible life events, the major categories can be outlined. Such a list might include:

1. Family and friends (death, divorce, quarrels)
2. Social activities (change in one's social life, holiday)
3. Work (new position, new responsibilities)
4. Economic status (loans, mortgages)
5. Personal (new illnesses, psychological stresses, moving, change in personal habits)

Whether these or other categories are used to elicit recollections in a clinical trial, and regardless of the specific events described by the patient, the degree to which events are accurately described is less important than is their collective impact on the patient.

One patient may describe five life events, whereas another patient who had the same experiences may describe them as a single event. Likewise, a physician who has interviewed a patient may integrate five reported life events as a single event when describing them. Another physician who interviews the same patient may describe these same experiences as five events. This issue of lumping or splitting life events should not be a problem; the most essential question is what is their collective significance or impact on the patient? It is also necessary to evaluate whether or not there is any relationship to the clinical trial.

The data collection form should indicate the importance of each individual event to the patient, as well as the overall importance. The importance may be assessed using the scales shown in Tables 2 or 4 or with the Likert-type scale shown in Table 3. It is also important for the interviewer to assess whether there is any relationship of the life events reported to the procedures or conduct of the clinical trial and to describe any such relationship.

After the data are collected for a patient at a clinic visit, the investigator must determine whether life events had an influence on that patient's clinical response since his or her last visit. The investigator must address the following question and record the answer: "To what degree do you believe life events reported by this patient today have influenced the clinical response over the period covered by the life events?" Replies could include 1) not applicable (because no life events were reported); 2) none; 3) very slight degree; 4) mild degree; 5) moderate degree; 6) fairly marked; 7) strong; 8) extremely strong. If desired, the reason for the investigator's opinion can be included, but this greatly increases the amount of nonquantitative data and can slow the analysis.

It is important that this question be addressed at each visit where life events data are collected. At a later date, it will be difficult to accurately establish the importance of life events as related to individual clinic visits, even as an opinion.

TABLE 4. *Example of a form that may be used by a patient to identify and assess the relevance of life events*[a]

Patient: Date: 01.02.99

Please identify all significant events that have affected your life since your last clinic visit and identify their relative importance in your life on the right as *positive* (0, +1, +2, +3, +4, or +5, with +5 the most positive) or as *negative* (0, −1, −2, −3, −4, or −5, with −5 the most negative).

1.

2.

3.

4.

5.

6.

7.

8.

Please circle the number that best describes the *overall* impact of *all these events* on your life since your last visit.   −5 −4 −3 −2 −1 0 +1 +2 +3 +4 +5

[a]Various formats can be used for the patient's responses, such as ruled columns, boxes, blank lines, etc.

If the investigator does not collect the life events data, it must be determined whether the person interviewing the patient is qualified to answer this question. This could be a major issue if the person answering the question has not interviewed and observed the patient directly. Ideally, the person interviewing the patient should be professionally qualified to form a judgment on the association between life events reports and clinical responses. Of course, someone else can provide the patient with questionnaires and collect the data, as long as the patient is interviewed and the data are reviewed by a health professional qualified to evaluate the significance of life events.

Who Collects Life Events Data and How Often Should They be Collected?

The best person to collect life events data is the one who knows the patient best, whether physician, nurse, or trial coordinator. More accurate data can generally be collected if the patient has had a long-term relationship with a health care professional or group.

There is no *a priori* answer to the question of how often to collect life events data. Nonetheless, a few guidelines should be kept in mind. First, the data requested must be relatively fresh in a patient's mind. If patients are asked once a year in a two-year trial to describe life events, they usually recall only the few most important events and tend to forget others, even though they may have had an important influence on the patient's life at the time. This may or may not be a major problem for interpreting results of the clinical trial, but data on significant events should be collected more frequently than on an annual basis. On the other hand, weekly data collection is probably too frequent. An appropriate time interval in most clinical trials is from once a month to once every 6 months, depending in part on whether minor and major events are being collected, or only major ones.

QUANTITATING LIFE EVENTS DATA

Two approaches to quantitate life events data are (a) to assign (before the trial) a set of relative values to all possible events or (b) to have the patient, spouse, or health professional assign relative values to actual events that occurred. The former approach has been widely used in the sociology and psychology literature and standardizes how individual life events are to be viewed. This type of list could theoretically be created after a significant amount of research has been conducted. Such research will undoubtedly show that the significance of most life events for a specific person depends on social, environmental, cultural, historical, and many other factors. Moreover, the data collected probably will be incorrect in many situations, because major life events may have little impact on a patient for many months (if ever) and minor life events may have a disproportionately great effect on a patient. These issues provide strong incentive not to utilize this approach in clinical trials.

The other approach of having patients rate their own life events allows for patient-to-patient differences in rating the

(a) Differences in magnitude of positive life events for a single patient

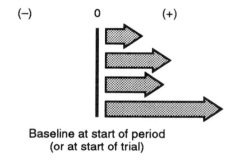

Baseline at start of period
(or at start of trial)

(b) Two patients with the same net score but different intensities and relevance of life events

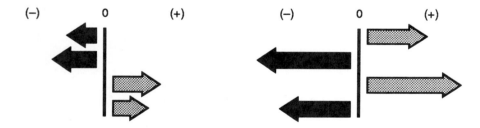

(c) Expressing a separate overall score for positive and negative life events

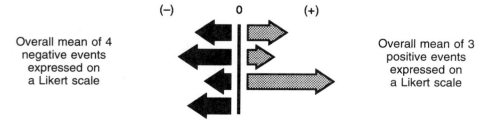

Overall mean of 4 negative events expressed on a Likert scale

Overall mean of 3 positive events expressed on a Likert scale

FIG. 1. Conceptualizing changes in life events where each *arrow* represents a separate event. In approach C, each patient expresses the influence of life events as a single Likert category for positive events and a single one for negative events.

impact of a single event. Patients may be asked to either complete their own life event questionnaires or to provide life event information to a professional interviewer who completes the forms. I prefer the former method and believe the most reliable data will be obtained if all completed questionnaires are carefully reviewed with the patient after they are completed.

The simplest approach for a professional to collect data on the overall relevance of life events is to ask the global question, "Overall, how have these events you've mentioned affected you over the last *x* weeks (months)?" This question asks the patient to integrate all of the positive and negative life experiences into a global assessment. Even if a patient is mentally able to do this easily and to provide an answer on a numerical or Likert scale, important data may still be lost if individual assessments of each life event are not also made. For example, a highly positive and a highly negative life event may cancel each other out, and a patient may state that their collective impact was nil. In actuality, both events may have had a major impact on the patient, and the magnitude of their impact in terms of stress or other emotions should be measured and assessed further. The magnitude of each event may be more important to assess than the identity of each specific event or even the overall net result of all life events on the patient. If this aspect is eventually shown to have the greatest impact on a clinical trial, then it would be desirable to interpret data in terms of the maximal significance of each event for the patient rather than the overall significance. Figure 1 illustrates some of these considerations. It is likely to be many years before it is known whether this theory is valid.

Expressing and Analyzing Results

Data collected in one format may be converted to another for ease of analysis. For example, data may be converted from Likert scale B shown in Table 3 to a numerical scale of 0 to plus 4 for positive effects and 0 to minus 4 for negative efforts. If the data analyst prefers a unidirectional scale, then a 9- (or other number) point scale may be used (e.g., 1 to 7, 0 to 6). A table may be created to present the data and also to compare two or more treatment groups (Table 5). Any statistical comparisons between groups should be conducted with great caution and after thorough discussion among relevant personnel. This is because it is easy to see these numbers as being measures of comparable qualities and therefore combinable. In reality, however, the numbers represent concepts and emotions that are often unrelated among individuals in the same treatment group or even among different events reported by the same person.

Nonetheless, it is possible to analyze life events data statistically in some clinical trials. If there are two or more treatment groups, it will generally be useful to consider comparisons both within treatment groups and between treatment groups. It is possible, though almost certainly not

TABLE 5. *Life events data from three groups studied in a clinical trial[a]*

Overall scores of patients in treatment group[b]:		
Active control	Test medicine	Placebo
+2	−1	0
+4	−2	0
−1	0	+1
0	0	+1
0	0	−2
+3	+2	−3
−2	−3	+2
+1	+4	0

Average:
±SD

[a]This type of table could be created for each treatment period (e.g., three blocks of 4 months each in a one-year clinical trial), as well as for the sum of all treatment periods.
[b]Group headings are examples only.

meaningful, to compare the number of life events between groups, or the number of patients who report life events.

Most life events that occur during a clinical trial are not directly related to the medicine used or to the underlying disease being treated, although these possibilities must be assessed. The range of intensities reported for life events may also be compared between groups.

A table listing and summarizing all life event data obtained in a clinical trial would be a useful tool for illustrating the findings obtained within each group. Statistical variance within each group, as well as the magnitude of change from baseline plus the direction of change, would be important to assess. Further analyses should be discussed with a statistician to determine the appropriateness of their use.

INTERPRETING LIFE EVENTS DATA

The investigator must evaluate the influence of all of a patient's life events on his or her overall clinical response to treatment. This must be done before the double-blind is broken and after the investigator has reviewed all of the patient's data. The investigator's conclusion may use a Likert scale (e.g., scale A in Table 3) to address the question, "To what degree do you believe life events reported by the patient influenced his or her clinical response over the entire course of the trial?" The investigator should support all conclusions with data.

The investigator must also evaluate the collective influence of all patients' life events in each treatment group before breaking the trial's blind. This can be done in the same way individual data are assessed, as described above. Illness-related life events experienced by patients should be captured on separate data collection forms and not confounded with non–trial-related life events.

The *number* of life events reported for a clinical trial per patient, per treatment period, or per treatment group is obviously unimportant. The *significance* life events have on a patient may have importance for a patient's response. Whether differences between test groups are due to chance or to the treatment itself must be assessed. Life events, just as disease-related events, may either positively or negatively influence the perceived benefits or toxicity of a medicine.

Differences in total life event scores between treatment groups should be interpreted in respect to:

1. *Outliers.* Have the values of one or a small number of patients influenced the total score? If so, how relevant are they in deriving the interpretation?
2. *Quality of life scales and tests.* How consistent are the results obtained on life events with results in quality of life tests? This comparison can be assessed for both groups and individuals.
3. *Clinical trial.* How consistent are the life events results with results in the overall clinical trial? Does there seem to be any relationship? If necessary, the efficacy and safety results of individual patients may be evaluated in comparison to their life event results.
4. *Adverse reactions.* What is the relationship between the adverse reactions observed in the clinical trial and those of the life events? This is one area where investigators have often looked for life events to explain clinical results. For example, an epileptic patient or one with migraine or asthma may have an attack triggered by a romantic breakup, a sudden cold or illness, or another life event.

Most assessments of life events in a clinical trial will confirm that no clinically significant difference existed between groups of patients. After all, most life events should be independent of the clinical trial and should be generally balanced between groups. Thus, the statistician and clinician involved with the analysis and interpretation of data should be cautioned about conducting more statistical tests, interpretations, or extrapolations of the data than warranted. It is possible, of course, that the trial stratified patients to treatment groups on the basis of previous life events and that this parameter is of great importance for assessing the trial's objectives. In that case, extensive discussions should be held before the trial to create the optimal trial design, data collection forms, and plans for data analysis.

The interpretation of life events should be presented in the text of a report or article describing the data, even if the description is limited to a single sentence. Any relevant differences should be supported by appropriate analyses.

COMPARISON OF LIFE EVENTS AND QUALITY OF LIFE DATA

Life events and quality of life data are compared below using a number of parameters. The purposes of collecting life events data are to confirm that the two (or more) treatment groups were equal and that any differences resulting from treatment were not caused by differences in the distribution of life events. Under rare circumstances, evaluation of life events may represent the primary objective of the clinical trial. Quality of life scales and tests are evaluated in clinical trials to see if there are differences between groups that are related to differences in their treatment.

Life events data may be viewed as biological "noise" that may influence either safety or efficacy data. Understanding life events and their influence on the trial is viewed as an additional control element. Quality of life data are one type of efficacy data and may be necessary to evaluate as part of addressing the primary objective of a clinical trial.

Domains of quality of life are widely discussed in this book and the author's view is that the entire sum of all domains is divided differently by different authors, but that it is nonetheless generally the same whole. Life events may occur in any of the quality of life domains.

Validation is one of the most critical aspects of quality of life instruments. A large literature has developed on the types of validation, and each instrument is evaluated for its degree and type. Life events questionnaires do not require validation. They represent a survey of information obtained from patients.

Life events data are collected from patients either by an interviewer or by the patient completing a questionnaire. While specific events are listed in some formal questionnaires used in sociology and psychology research, I favor a more open format of patients listing their own events. Quality of life data are collected using specific instruments. While a patient's answers to questions may be based on or influenced by life events, the events themselves are usually not captured by the instrument. Quality of life tests sometimes take an hour or more to complete, whereas life events data are usually collected within a few minutes.

Life events data are not particularly robust from a statistical perspective, and few (if any) statistical tests should be conducted on them. Quality of life data vary in their robustness, but many tests yield data that are robust and should, or even must, be analyzed statistically.

Finally, the interpretation of these two types of data should be considered by clinical investigators. The significance of life events and quality of life are assessed by patients. The data from both are assessed by professional investigators. No qualitative differences in approaches to the data are apparent between life events and quality of life assessments.

CONCLUSIONS

Life event data are sometimes relevant to collect in clinical trials, particularly quality of life trials where such events may be a confounding factor, or in long-term trials. These data can play a valuable function as an additional control, even if they only show the life events had no clinically significant impact on the trial's results. Appropriate methods to collect, present, and analyze data are described, as well as a comparison with quality of life data.

ACKNOWLEDGMENTS

The author acknowledges and thanks Dr. Sigrid Jensen of Novo Nordisk (Denmark) for her valuable insights, and Dr. Dennis Revicki of Battelle for his critical review of the manuscript. This article was modified from an article published by the author in *Applied Clinical Trials* (1994;3:45–52) and is reprinted in part by kind permission of the publisher (Advanstar).

REFERENCES

1. Ross CE, Mirowsky J II. A comparison of life-event weighting schemes: change, undesirability, and effect-proportional indices. *J Health Soc Behav* 1979;20:166–177.
2. Holmes TH, Rohe RH. The social readjustment rating scale. *Psychosom Med* 1967;11:213–218.
3. Dohrenwend BS, Krasnoff L, Askenasy AR, Dohrenwend BP. Exemplification of a method for scaling life events: the PERI life events scale. *J Health Soc Behav* 1978;19:205–229.
4. Horowitz M, Schaefer C, Hiroto D, Wilner N, Levin B. Life events questionnaires for measuring presumptive stress. *Psychosom Med* 1977;39:413–431.
5. Horowitz M, Wilner BA, Alvarez W. Impact of event scale: a measure of subjective stress. *Psychosom Med* 1979;41:209–218.

Quality of Life and Pharmacoeconomics in Clinical Trials, Second Edition, edited by B. Spilker.
Lippincott-Raven Publishers, Philadelphia © 1996.

CHAPTER 50

Presentation of Quality of Life Data

John R. Schoenfelder and Bert Spilker

INTRODUCTION

Quality of life variables are generally analyzed and displayed similarly to other efficacy variables. Although this chapter is primarily directed toward the display, i.e., the presentation, of quality of life data, it is important first to describe briefly the analysis of those variables. Although most scales used in assessing quality of life are intuitively "reasonable," many have not been validated or well-validated. Even those scales that have been well validated are often used in therapeutic situations in which they have not been validated.

Analytic considerations include the selection of an appropriate quality of life scale, the collection of all necessary data (i.e., ensuring that the selected scale is used at the appropriate times during the study), and the selection of appropriate data transformations for statistical analysis. The latter issue is important because it will often be necessary to analyze more than just the initial and final scores of the scale. Reader interest will also focus on such values as the best on-treatment score, the worst on-treatment score, the average on-treatment score, the change from baseline value, the proportion of patients demonstrating a prespecified amount of improvement, and other data transformations. Care must be taken to ensure that all transformations are scientifically valid and capable of conveying meaningful information. The

"output" and interpretation of all analysis results must be easily understandable by the physicians who will be the principal users of the treatments studied.

Regardless of the specific scales chosen for assessing quality of life and the specific data transformations actually employed, the statistical considerations associated with the analysis and presentation of those variables are similar to the corresponding considerations relating to the analysis and presentation of other efficacy data. Major statistical considerations include ensuring that displays intended for categorical variables (e.g., yes/no variables) are not inappropriately used to display numerical variables, and ensuring that sufficient information be included in the display so that the presented result can be properly interpreted. For example, it is important to indicate if statistical tests used were one-sided or two-sided. Since a medicine or other treatment may be detrimental to some areas of a patient's quality of life and yet still be beneficial overall because of benefit to risk considerations, it is usually (if not always) appropriate to perform two-sided tests. This is true even if the efficacy of a new investigational medicine is being compared to a placebo—a situation where many clinicians and statisticians generally support the use of one-sided tests.

Quality of life data should usually be presented in a manner intended to mimic a clinician's way of thinking about a patient or group of patients. As discussed by Spilker and Schoenfelder (1), this is usually in terms of (a) the patient's current state versus previous state(s) before treatment, (b) the patient's current state versus previous state(s) while on treatment, (c) the patient's degree of improvement observed versus degree desired as a goal, or (d) observed trends.

   J. R. Schoenfelder: Biostatistics Pharmacia, Inc., Columbus, Ohio 43216.
   B. Spilker: Orphan Medical, Inc., Minnetonka, Minnesota 55305.

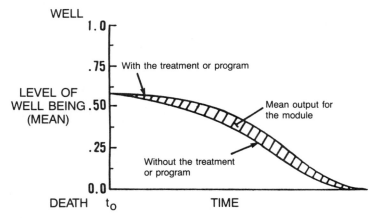

FIG. 1. Level of well being over time with and without a program. The axes are both clearly labeled. Note that the label for the *vertical axis* is rotated so that it can be easily read. The range of the potential values of the scale (0.0 to 1.0) is clearly indicated. It is also immediately evident that high values of the scale are better than lower values. This figure clearly presents both the baseline and "end of program" values for both comparison groups (with and without a treatment program). The *shading* of the area between the two lines (i.e., with and without the treatment program) provides a dramatic demonstration of the impact of the treatment program. Even though the difference may or may not be significant at any individual assessment point, the overall impact is dramatically emphasized by this display.

Since all patients contributing data clearly die by the end of the study, it is most likely the case that the sample size is not constant along the time axis. Some indication of the decline in sample size is necessary in order for the curves to be properly interpreted. As the figure is currently constructed, in both groups the observed decrease in well-being over time is most likely a combination of a true decrease and also the fact that the sample size is changing. The addition of error bars at various points along the time axis (i.e., the *x* axis) would help to interpret the graphs and to quantify the effects of the changing sample size. Alternatively, that information could be summarized in a footnote, described in the text, or presented in a table. The smooth nature of the lines leads one to believe that the presented lines are from a curve-fitting procedure, such as Kaplan-Meier graphs. If that is the case, then the curve-fitting technique used should be indicated. (From ref. 6, with permission.)

RELEVANT CONSIDERATIONS

Before creating the details of a presentation, an individual usually considers several issues to guide choices of presentation format (e.g., figure or table) and the structure of the selected format. There are five basic considerations:

1. *What is the objective of the display?* Is it to present data from a single group of patients, or is it to present data comparing two or more groups? Assuming the latter, is the objective to show a comparison with respect to change from baseline (either improvement or deterioration) or with respect to the ability to reach a prespecified level of improvement? In either case, if there is a "minimally acceptable" (in terms of general well-being) level of the scale, then that level should be clearly indicated on the display.

2. *Is the display descriptive only, or will it also include statistical information?* If the latter, is the comparison being made with respect to change from baseline and/or final value? In either case, the display should also allow for a formal or an informal comparison of the groups with respect to status as baseline.

3. *Is the quality of life scale used in the study well known to the target audience?* If not, then extra attention must be given to ensure that the display includes sufficient information (e.g., range of attainable values, explicit indication as to whether high or low values are good) to allow a reader to properly interpret the results. One may not need to include as much information about well-known scales.

4. *Should the data be displayed via a table or a graph?* Although more quantitative information can be displayed in a table, a more demonstrative visual effect may be obtained by using a figure. A table is often chosen for conveying information, and a figure is used to display information. The choice should be dictated by the major point(s) one wishes to communicate, and both tables and figures are often used.

5. *Are the values to be displayed categorical or numerical?* Bar graphs (e.g., histograms) are often useful for presenting categorical data, and line graphs are more appropriate for numerical data.

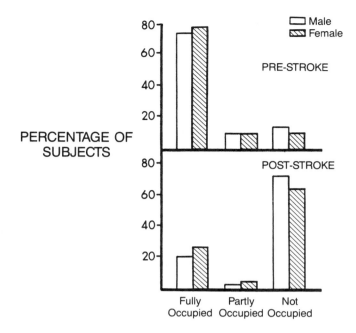

FIG. 2. Distribution of occupational status before stroke, as compared with the situation 3 years after the event in 45 patients. "Fully occupied" includes housework for a family, in the case of women; "not occupied" includes those people capable of self-care but with no responsibility outside self-care. Separate displays (i.e., "bars") for males and females readily show that there are no differences between the sexes. Note that the *heavier, filled-in bars* (in this case, the females) catch the eye much "stronger" than the *empty bars* (in this case, the males). Thus, if one wants to emphasize one group over the other, one should chose a heavier "fill" for the group to be emphasized. Presenting the prestroke data immediately over the poststroke data vividly emphasizes the effect of the stroke. It is important that the vertical scale be the same for both the prestroke and the poststroke displays. If the scales were different, then the reader's eye would most probably be led to an incorrect conclusion, unless the difference was obvious and stressed. The logical ordering of the occupational groups—fully occupied to partly occupied to not occupied—is clearly appropriate. (From ref. 7, with permission.)

PRESENTATION GUIDELINES

Guidelines for choosing tables, graphs, or figures for presenting clinical data, as well as guidelines for deciding which of those formats to use in particular instances, are presented and discussed by Spilker and Schoenfelder (1). Selected guidelines for creating quality of life tables, graphs, and figures are given below.

General Guidelines for Preparing Tables to Present Data from Quality of Life Variables

1. The title of the table should be concise, yet convey sufficient information so that the reader immediately knows what data are being presented. If necessary, a footnote may be used to expand or to discuss the title.
2. The table should be self-contained. The body of the table and, if necessary, one or more footnotes should contain all information necessary for the reader to understand the table. A reader should not be asked to refer to either the text of the document or to another table in order to understand the contents of a given table. Nonetheless, reference to the text or another table is appropriate if it enables the reader to expand the table's contents in a new way.
3. The tables must be arranged in a logical order in the text. Determine what information readers already have when they approach the table, and what information

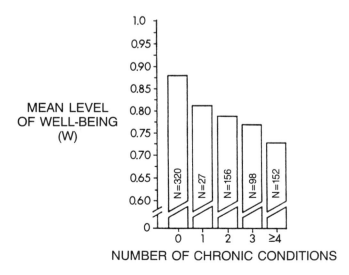

FIG. 3. Mean symptom-standardized level of well-being (W) for groups of persons reporting specific numbers of chronic conditions (weighted Pearson's $r = -0.96$). The *vertical axis* does not start with zero. This is indicated by a "broken" axis. The corresponding break in the bars of the histogram adds emphasis to that break. This emphasis is very helpful to the reader's correct interpretation of the presented information. The histogram bars could equally well have been broken with a horizontal or a zigzag line, rather than a diagonal line. The use of the diagonal line, however, is aesthetically pleasing. Placing the sample size within the bars is somewhat novel. Including the value of the correlation coefficient in the title aids in interpreting the strength of the relationship. It would have made a stronger (visual) effect, however, if the value of that correlation coefficient had been printed in the space above the right of most bars of the histogram (i.e., in the space that is empty as a result of that negative correlation. The label for the *y* axis is very easy to read. (From ref. 8, with permission.)

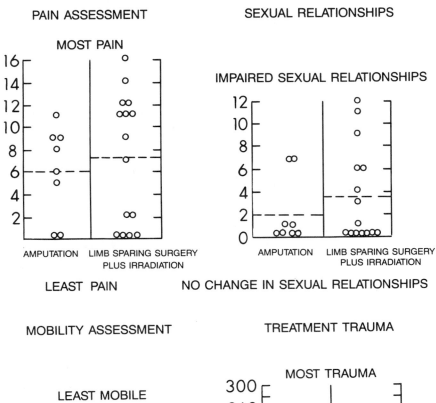

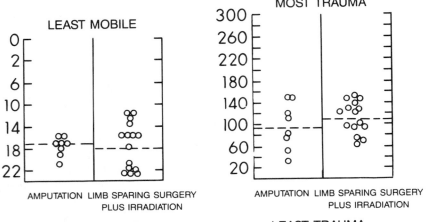

FIG. 4. Clinical tests to specifically link treatment consequences with quality of life. Illustrates grouping several scattergrams together to compare the effect of an intervention of various components of quality of life. Each "plot" has a horizontal reference line. Unfortunately, it is unclear what that reference is—a mean score, a median score, a prespecified "acceptable" level, or something else. Although it is most likely mentioned in the text, a self-contained figure should also indicate this information. The *vertical axis* is labeled by text directly under and directly above each scattergram and also by the scales along the axes. This is somewhat confusing since the group labels for the *horizontal axis* ("amputation" and "limb sparing surgery plus irradiation") lie between the *horizontal axis* and the *vertical axis* labels, and the scores are not described. (From ref. 9, with permission.)

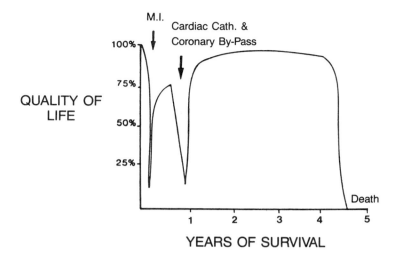

QUALITY OF LIFE

"Vitagram" showing quality of life in patient who had coronary artery bypass grafts following myocardial infarction (MI). Cath., catheterization. Length of life for this patient afer MI was 4.5 years. This display effectively illustrates the impact of both negative and positive medical events on an individual patient's quality of life. The basis for the value on the y axis should be explained. This approach is easy to understand and has dramatic visual appeal, partly because it describes a single patient and is easy to relate to. A series of graphs would illustrate differing medical histories in a dramatic fashion. (From ref. 10, with permission.)

they will be seeking. The logic used should be explained if it is not totally clear to any reader.

4. Row and column headings should relate to information that the readers already have, and the body of the table should contain the information that they are seeking. If the table's layout is not clear or if it is aesthetically challenging, consider reversing the rows and columns.

5. Information within a table should be presented in a sequence that makes sense to the reader (e.g., from left to right and from top to bottom). Do not make the reader work hard in order to understand the data in the table.

6. Data that are related should be grouped together within a table. The spacing between rows and/or columns of related data should be less than the spacing between rows and/or columns of less-related data within the same table. Such an arrangement allows the readers' eyes to immediately make the desired groupings. Lines may sometimes be used to achieve the same effect as spacings.

7. When readers are asked to compare items within a table, it is usually easier for them to scan vertically than horizontally.

8. Scanning along a row is facilitated by including sufficient space above and below the row. Scanning along a column is facilitated by including sufficient space to its right and left. If it is not possible to include sufficient space, then consider techniques such as adding thin lines or using bold type for alternate rows and columns.

9. When listing data from individual patients, a blank line between patients may not be necessary if the display is a "one row per patient" table. If, however, the data from some (or all) patients require more than one row, then a blank line between patients (not between rows) is desirable.

10. Tables should never contain columns of identical or nearly identical numbers. For example, a column listing the number of patients assessed may have the same (or

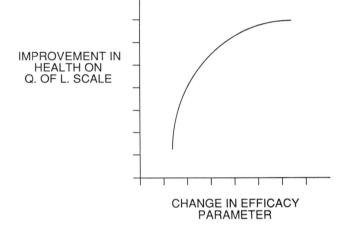

IMPROVEMENT IN HEALTH ON Q. OF L. SCALE

CHANGE IN EFFICACY PARAMETER

Improvement in health as a function of change in efficacy parameters. Q. of L., quality of life. The format visually relates data on a quality of life scale to data obtained with another efficacy parameter. If both the quality of life and efficacy scales are ratio variables, then a correlation coefficient could be printed to indicate the strength of any observed trend. Separate lines could be included for various groups of patients (e.g., a line for males and another for females). The area between the lines could then be shaded to indicate the differences between the patient groups. Individual patient data could be displayed by incorporating a separate line for each patient (if that is practical). An overall "mean" line could then be plotted in a different color or thickness from the individual patient lines. Separate lines could also be used to display the results using several different quality of life scales, one line for each scale used. This can only be accomplished if each of the included quality of life scales has the same range of collected values, and if high (or low) values are good (or bad) for each of those scales. A good example would be when the data were obtained using visual analog scales. Alternatively, data could be normalized or two sets could be compared using two y axes (i.e., both right and left sides) for two scales. (From ref. 1, with permission.)

TABLE 1. *Measures used to assess quality of life*

1. The General Well-Being Adjustment Scale
2. The Physical Symptoms Distress Index
3. The Sleep Dysfunction Scale
4. The Sexual Symptoms Distress Index
5. The Positive Symptoms Index
6. The Wechsler Memory Scale
7. The Reitan Trail Making Test
8. The Life Satisfaction Index

A table such as this is appropriate when presenting data from studies where multiple instruments are used to assess quality of life. The table allows the reader to learn immediately what tools are used in the assessment. If there are intrinsic groupings among the quality of life scales used, then the table could be improved by indicating that grouping via subheadings and/or blank rows between the groups. A footnote should state if the scales are listed in order of importance, order of administration, alphabetically, or in no particular order. Each of these scales are generally further described in the text. Footnotes could indicate whether high scores are good or bad. If a table as this is used, then all scales used in the clinical trial should be included in the list. (From ref. 2, with permission.)

nearly the same) entry in each row, and thus could possibly focus a reader's attention on relatively unimportant sample size information. The common sample size (N) and relevant exceptions may be incorporated into a footnote. Additionally, such uninformative information uses up valuable space in the table that would be better used to present more informative data.

11. It is best to avoid vertical lines, unless they are necessary for clarity. They generally interfere with horizontal scanning.

12. The visual impact of a table has a role to play in determining how many readers will approach it, and how deeply they will delve into it.

General Guidelines for Preparing Graphs and Figures to Present Data from Quality of Life Variables

1. The title of the graph or figure should be as concise as possible, yet it must convey sufficient information that the reader will immediately know what data are being presented. If necessary, consider adding a footnote to expand upon the title.

2. Adopt and follow the "less is more" principle so that each graph makes a single major point. It is preferable that both the layout of the graph and the illustrated data are simple rather than complex. This often requires two or more graphs to illustrate material that could be presented in a single display. Remember, the purpose of the display is to communicate information, not to impress the reader with one's ability to present the maximum amount of data in a single format.

3. Avoid extraneous data and unnecessary information. Details and ancillary information may be incorporated in the legend or in the text.

4. The number of separate curves that can be appropriately displayed on a graph depends on how close the curves are to each other, how many times they cross each other, and what other information (e.g., error bars) is to be included. Since clarity is a primary concern, it is always better to create more graphs rather than crowd curves.

5. Artistic emphasis should be placed on the data presented, rather than on the axes of the display. This may be done by making curves or other lines on a graph thicker, or in some way more pronounced, than the lines used for the axes.

6. Label the vertical axis (i.e., ordinate) so that the page does not need to be rotated to be read. This can be accomplished either by having the type rotated so that it is perpendicular to the axis, or by ensuring that the print is sufficiently legible that it can be read vertically with a minimum of effort. It is important to minimize the effort needed to understand the display.

7. Labels on the axes should be complete and explanatory. Labels must clearly identify the variables graphed and the associated units of measurement.

8. Directly label curves and data points, and avoid using a key whenever possible. If a key is necessary, then place it within the graph or as close to the data as possible. Try to facilitate the reader's understanding of your message.

9. A modest proportion of the population is color blind. In addition, photocopies of color rarely have the distinction (i.e., resolution) of the original. Thus, one should not rely on color as the only mechanism for differentiating among data curves.

The guidelines presented above clearly apply to displays of all types of data, not just to quality of life variables. Strict, or reasonably strict, adherence to these guidelines will assist one in constructing a clear and unambiguous presentation of data. Before those guidelines can be used, however, one must first decide what specific information is to be included in the presentation.

General Guidelines for Determining What Information to Include in a Presentation of Quality of Life Data

The following list identifies considerations that need to be addressed when determining what quality of life data to present. For the most part, these considerations are independent of what specific quality of life scales are used in the quality of life assessment(s), and also of what methods of statistical analysis are employed to test the relevance of the information contained in the collected data.

1. Review the literature to determine if there are commonly utilized formats for the specific variables you desire to

TABLE 2. *Comparison of performance status*

	Visit 1					
	Drug A		Drug B		Drug C	
All patients treated	# Pts.	(%)	# Pts.	(%)	# Pts.	(%)
Score						
0	35	(25%)	49	(35%)	34	(26%)
1	58	(42%)	48	(35%)	62	(47%)
2	38	(27%)	34	(24%	28	(21%)
3	2	(1%)	7	(5%)	7	(5%)
4	6	(4%)	1	(1%)	1	(1%)
Unknown	7		7		8	
No. patients treated	146		146		140	
Mean	1.2		1.0		1.1	
Median	1.0		1.0		1.0	
S.D.	1.0		0.9		0.9	
Comparison with Drug C Wilcoxon Rank Sum Test						
p value	0.49		0.45			
Improvement from baseline						
3	0	(0%)	0	(0%)	0	(0%)
2	0	(0%)	8	(0%)	1	(1%)
1	7	(5%)	10	(7%)	12	(9%)
0	103	(74%)	100	(72%)	94	(71%)
−1	20	(14%)	21	(15%)	23	(17%)
−2	6	(4%)	6	(4%)	2	(2%)
−3	3	(2%)	1	(1%)	0	(0%)
−4	0	(0%)	0	(0%)	0	(0%)
Unknown	7		8		8	
No. patients treated	146		146		140	
Mean	−0.2		−0.2		−0.1	
Median	0.0		0.0		0.0	
S.D.	0.7		0.7		0.6	
Comparison with Drug C Wilcoxon Rank Sum Test						
p value	0.23		0.47			

Actual distribution of scores, in addition to the mean and median values, at the evaluation visit is displayed. This allows the reader to more fully comprehend both the collected scores and those scores displayed as improvement from baseline. The alignment of the percentages allows readers to more easily identify "single digit" and "double digit" percentages. Note that when giving the distribution of the scores the column heading for the columns presenting percentages is labeled "(%)", and also a percentage sign is attached to each entry in those columns. Either one of those labeling options would be sufficient by itself. The spacing between the data columns allows the reader to easily identify that there are three pairs of columns rather than six columns. If the columns had been evenly spaced, then the reader would have had to work to form those groupings. It would be better to label the bottom half of the table as "Improvement/ Deterioration" in order to emphasize that the negative values represent deterioration. Alternatively, the label could be changed to "Improvement(+) or deterioration(−)." The bottom half of the table, change from baseline, is probably the most important comparison illustrated. It would be difficult, however, to properly interpret it without the top half of the table, which gives reference values. (Alternatively, baseline values could be given as reference.) The statistical tests utilized are clearly identified. It would also be informative to perform and present a statistical comparison of all three treatment groups, as well as the two pairwise treatment comparisons presented. The layout would be somewhat improved by adding an additional two or three blank lines between the top half and the bottom half of the display. Note that the presenter is somewhat "tricky" in that the second title line (All patients treated) clearly implies an intent-to-treat analysis. However, the use of a "no data" line, which clearly does not contribute to the percentages making up the distribution of observed values, effectively turns the display into an "evaluable patients" or "all patients with data" analysis.

TABLE 3. *Changes in quality of life measures in the three treatment groups*

Quality of life measure	Percent of patients			p value[a]
	Improvement	None	Worsening	
General well-being				
Captopril (N = 181)	51.4	17.7	30.9	
Methyldopa (N = 143)[b]	39.2	9.8	51.0	p<.01
Propranolol (N = 161)[b]	39.1	15.5	45.4	
Physical symptoms				
Captopril (N = 181)	29.3	45.3	25.4	
Methyldopa (N = 142)[b]	19.7	43.4	36.6	p<.05
Propranolol (N = 160)[b]	17.5	45.6	36.9	
Sexual dysfunction				
Captopril (N = 181)	18.2	63.0	18.8	
Methyldopa (N = 141)[b]	9.2	66.7	24.1	p<.05
Propranolol (N = 160)[b]	8.8	65.6	25.6	

[a]P value based on chi-square test (3 × 3) for independence with 4 degrees of freedom.
[b]Variations in the numbers of patients in the methyldopa and propranolol treatment groups are due to incomplete responses to the assessment measures.

This display is arranged so that the reader must scan vertically down the columns when comparing treatment groups. Changes from baseline are presented without any information of baseline value or final value for reference. This makes inferences very difficult. Data presented is proportion of patients improved, unchanged, or worsened. No consideration is given of magnitude. Thus, the display could be inadvertently concealing an important difference. Footnotes are used to provide information necessary for a complete understanding of the table: the identification of the statistical test used, and an explanation of the changes in sample sizes. Because the treatment group names have been indented, the reader's eye immediately makes the desired grouping of the important rows. Since sample size information has been incorporated into the treatment group name, no sample size column is necessary. Changes in sample size are adequately explained in a footnote. (From ref. 2, with permission.)

display. If there are, then it is generally advisable to use them. The reading audience will be familiar with the formats.

2. Unless the quality of life scale is extremely well known, the range of values that it may attain should be indicated either within the display or in a footnote. Additionally, the display should indicate if high (or low) values of the scale are good (or bad). This may also be stated in a footnote.

3. The display should include the baseline value (or summary statistics) of the scale. In quality of life assessments, it is extremely important to know where the patient was at the beginning of the trial. It is imperative that one "set the stage" that existed at the time of patient enrollment so that observed improvement (or deterioration) can be readily assessed.

4. The display should also include the final value (or summary statistics) of the scale. It is important to know where, on the scale, the patient was when he or she completed the trial. This is true whether or not the patient completed the trial as scheduled.

5. It is insufficient to present change from baseline without also displaying the final value. Even if an investigational medicine had a highly significant advantage over "no treatment" with respect to a quality of life variable, that

information would be of little importance if the final value of that scale was still indicative of an unacceptable level of well-being.

6. Never present percent change or percent of baseline without indicating the original value to provide a necessary reference point.

7. If statistical tests were made, then the display should include the results of those tests. Those results should indicate the test employed, (possibly) the value of the test statistic, and the corresponding p value or confidence limits. The statistical information, however, should not be the primary focus of the display. The presentation of the actual data should be primary, with the statistical information added as a complement to assist interpretation.

8. If you are illustrating data collected over time, then all collected points should be included in the graph. One should not generally plot a subset of the data points, unless sample size considerations dictate otherwise, a complete discussion is provided, or all data are placed in the appendix.

The examples in Figs. 1–6 and Tables 1–7 are displays of quality of life data that are taken from the current literature. They are included because they illustrate one or more

TABLE 4. *Changes in clinical and health status measures and composite scores between baseline and sixth month by treatment group (N = 303)*

	Possible range (worst to best)	Change from baseline		Treatment effect (p value)[a]
		Placebo (N = 149)	Auranofin (N = 154)	
Clinical measures				
Number of tender joints		−4.5 ± 0.9[b]	−7.3 ± 1.0	0.01
Number of swollen joints		−3.6 ± 0.7	−5.5 ± 0.7	0.01
50-foot walk time (sec)		+0.61 ± 0.66	−0.74 ± 0.40	0.11
Duration of morning stiffness (min)		−2 ± 13	−28 ± 12	0.1
Grip strength adjusted (mm Hg)		−2 ± 8	+13 ± 8	0.02
Composite score		0.16 ± 0.05	0.35 ± 0.05	0.003
Function measures				
Health Assessment Questionnaire	3–0	−0.17 ± 0.04	−0.31 ± 0.05	0.01
Keitel Assessment	98–0	+1.7 ± 1.0	−1.5 ± 0.9	0.003
Quality of Well-Being Questionnaire	0–1	−0.0001 ± 0.0007	+0.023 ± 0.007	0.005
Composite score		0.05 ± 0.05	0.28 ± 0.28	0.001
Pain measures				
McGill Pain Questionnaire	78–0	−5.6 ± 1.0	−8.0 ± 1.1	0.02
Pain ladder scale (6-day mean)	0–10	+0.61 ± 0.13	+0.96 ± 0.18	0.09
10-centimeter pain line	10–0	−0.91 ± 0.18	−1.44 ± 0.17	0.01
Composite score		0.48 ± 0.07	0.74 ± 0.08	0.021
Global impression measures				
Arthritis				
Categorical scale	1–5	+0.31 ± 0.07	+0.65 ± 0.08	<0.001
Ladder scale (6-day mean)	0–10	+0.59 ± 0.14	+0.98 ± 0.18	0.11
Overall health				
Ladder scale, current	0–10	+0.39 ± 0.14	+0.65 ± 0.15	0.19
Ladder scale, 6-day mean	0–10	+0.35 ± 0.12	+0.87 ± 0.15	0.007
RAND Current Health Assessment	9–45	+0.51 ± 0.47	+1.82 ± 0.49	0.01
10-centimeter line, by patient	0–10	+0.51 ± 0.13	+0.89 ± 0.16	0.1
10-centimeter line, by physician	0–10	+0.46 ± 0.12	+0.58 ± 0.13	0.2
Composite score		0.27 ± 0.05	0.50 ± 0.07	0.007

[a]Significance level of the treatment effect determined by analysis of covariance adjusting for baseline values of age, sex, clinic, functional class, and the variable tested.
[b]Mean changes ± SE.

Inclusion of a column providing the range for the scales is extremely helpful. The footnote identifying the "±" values as standard errors is informative. Too often, tables fail to identify whether those "±" values are standard errors or standard deviations. Even though that information can often be deduced from the scale of those values to the presented means, one should not require readers to make such deductions. The footnote associated with the p value column is informative. The spacing of the columns allows for the reader's eye to easily make desired groupings. The presented scales are grouped well. Because the names of the scales have been indented, the reader's eye is able to immediately "pick up" those groupings. Unfortunately, only the change from baseline is presented. Even though the analysis can be based on changes from baseline, quality of life displays should include at least baseline or "final" values so that the impact of the changes can be properly assessed and interpreted. Sample size information has been incorporated into the column heading, rather than added as separate columns. (Presumably, meaningful deviations from those sample sizes would have been expressed in a footnote.) (From ref. 3, with permission.)

TABLE 5. *Quality of life scales at baseline and during active therapy (24 weeks) for patients with complete 24-week follow-up who were receiving captopril (N = 181), methyldopa (N = 143), or propranolol (N = 162); means + SE*

Scale[a]	Baseline[b]			24 Weeks[b]			Comparisons between groups in changes from baseline[c]
	Captopril (A)	Methyldopa (B)	Propranolol (C)	Captopril (A)	Methyldopa (B)	Propranolol (C)	
General well-being (+)	103.4 ± 1.0	105.0 ± 1.1	104.0 ± 1.1	105.6 ± 1.1[d]	103.4 ± 1.2	103.7 ± 1.1	AB[d]AC[d]
Physical symptoms (−)	5.0 ± 1.0	4.9 ± 0.4	4.9 ± 0.4	4.8 ± 0.3	5.8 ± 0.4[e]	5.5 ± 0.4[e]	AB[e]AC[e]
Sexual dysfunction (−)	2.3 ± 0.3	2.3 ± 0.3	1.9 ± 0.3	2.5 ± 0.3	2.93 ± 0.3[e]	2.7 ± 0.3[e]	AC[e]
Work performance (−)	16.8 ± 0.5	17.2 ± 0.6	17.8 ± 0.5	15.9 ± 0.5[e]	18.2 ± 0.7	17.6 ± 0.6	AB[d]BC[e,f]
Sleep dysfunction (−)	7.9 ± 0.3	7.7 ± 0.3	7.5 ± 0.3	7.7 ± 0.3	7.5 ± 0.3	7.6 ± 0.3	
Cognitive function (−) (Trail making B)	97.4 ± 3.5	93.8 ± 4.0	97.1 ± 3.7	78.4 ± 2.3	82.9 ± 3.3[d]	80.2 ± 2.7[d]	AB[e]
Life satisfaction (−)	28.4 ± 0.3	28.2 ± 0.4	28.1 ± 0.4	28.9 ± 0.4	29.5 ± 0.4[d]	28.8 ± 0.4[e]	AB[e]
Social participation (−)	11.9 ± 0.2	12.1 ± 0.2	12.5 ± 0.2	11.6 ± 0.2	11.9 ± 0.2[d]	11.9 ± 0.2[d]	

[a]Plus sign denotes improvement with an increasing score, and minus signs denote improvement with a decreasing score.

[b]Symbols in the body of the table indicate p values comparing 24-week levels with baseline levels, based on the mean difference and t-statistic.

[c]Univariate contrasts of rates of change between groups within pairs, determined with the F-statistic.

[d]p of difference <.01.

[e]p of difference <.05.

[f]A univariate contrast is reported, although in overall multivariate analysis. B versus C was not significant.

Sample size information, and explanation of table entries, are included in the title. Usually it would be better to keep the title concise and to include such information in footnotes. However, since this table already uses a relatively large number of footnotes, it is reasonable to include the explanatory material in the title. The use of small letters, as opposed to small numbers, to identify footnotes allows easy differentiation from numerical entries in the table. The use of plus and minus signs in the row labels to indicate whether increases or decreases represent improvement in quality of life is useful. If possible, it would have been better to have the rows equally spaced. When looking at the table, a reader initially feels that there are five "groups" of scales (rows 1, 2, 3, 4–6, and 7–8). On closer examination, however, it appears that no such groupings are present. The columns spacings generate the proper "eye groupings." It would, however, be nicer if an additional space or two (i.e., one or two blank columns) could be inserted between the baseline and Week 24 results to set them apart. The footnotes explaining the statistical analysis methodologies are very helpful. The use of footnote designations in order to report both within group and between group comparisons is an excellent approach. Presumably the final column only indicates the comparisons that were statistically significant. Although somewhat obvious, it would be better if the fact were explicitly stated. (From ref. 2, with permission.)

TABLE 6. *Effect of age on quality of life*

	ICU patients		Non-ICU patients		
	Age 65–75 (N = 39)	Age ≥76 (N = 20)	Age 65–75 (N = 43)	Age 76–85 (N = 44)	Age ≥86 (N = 22)
Sickness Impact Profile (SIP)					
Physical score	3.6 ± 0.8	8.7 ± 2.6	1.5 ± 0.4[a]	5.3 ± 1.0[a]	12.3 ± 2.7[a]
Psychosocial score	5.3 ± 1.3	8.3 ± 2.1	2.9 ± 1.0	5.4 ± 0.8	8.7 ± 2.4
Total SIP score	5.6 ± 1.1[a]	11.0 ± 2.0[a]	2.3 ± 0.6[a]	4.9 ± 0.8[a]	9.4 ± 2.0[a]
Adjusted SIP score[b]	4.8 ± 1.0[a]	9.1 ± 2.0	2.2 ± 0.5[a]	4.8 ± 0.8	9.3 ± 2.0[a]
Uniscale	8.13 ± 0.45[a]	8.00 ± 0.57	9.05 ± 0.24[a]	8.25 ± 0.31	

[a]Group differs significantly (p <.05) from all other groups.

[b]Does not include work category.

This table illustrates a way of incorporating the effect of a third variable (in this case age) on quality of life assessments. It would be helpful to incorporate a blank line between the Adjusted SIP score and the Uniscale score. That line (or a space) would help the reader's eye make the appropriate grouping. It would be helpful to include the range of the scales in the display. Also, it is not stated if the tabulated values are means or medians, nor is it stated if the "±" values are standard errors or standard deviations. It is also unclear as to what groups are statistically compared (using unspecified statistical methodology). It could be all five groups together, or the two groups of ICU patients together and the three groups of non-ICU patients together. Since the reader does not know if large values are good or bad, it is not possible to evaluate the effect of age using only information presented in the table. It would be useful if appropriate information would be added so that the table itself would be self-contained. (From ref. 4, with permission.)

TABLE 7. *Measuring change over time*

Instrument A	Time 1	Time 2	Intervention	Time 3	Difference score	Exercise test result
Subject 1	8	9		15	+6	Much improved
Subject 2	9	8		15	+7	Much improved
Subject 3	8	9		15	+6	Much improved
Subject 4	9	8		15	+7	Much improved
Subject 5	8	9		8	−1	Unchanged
Subject 6	9	8		9	+1	Unchanged
Subject 7	8	9		8	−1	Unchanged
Subject 8	9	8		9	+1	Unchanged

Instrument B	Time 1	Time 2	Intervention	Time 3	Difference score	Exercise test result
Subject 1	5	5		5	0	Much improved
Subject 2	9	9		9	0	Much improved
Subject 3	13	13		13	0	Much improved
Subject 4	17	17		17	0	Much improved
Subject 5	5	5		5	0	Unchanged
Subject 6	9	9		9	0	Unchanged
Subject 7	13	13		13	0	Unchanged
Subject 8	17	17		17	0	Unchanged

Illustrates a way of presenting individual patient data. A summary row giving the mean values for each time point, as well as an overall assessment, would be helpful. Presumably the exercise test result reported in the final column is not an assessment based on the tabulated difference scores. A footnote should indicate what it is based on. (From ref. 5, with permission.)

of the considerations discussed above. Each included display is accompanied by notes that state why the example was selected. Although critical comments are also included for some of the displays, none of the displays were selected because they were "bad" examples.

CONCLUSIONS

By adhering to generally accepted principles of data presentation, investigators will be able to best communicate quality of life data to their readers. No particular methods are necessary to utilize for presenting quality of life data beyond those used for other efficacy parameters.

REFERENCES

1. Spilker B, Schoenfelder J. *Presentation of clinical data.* New York: Raven Press, 1990.
2. Croog SH, Levine S, Testa MA, Brown B, Bulpitt CJ, Jenkins CD, Klerman GL, Williams GH. The effects of antihypertensive therapy on the quality of life. *N Engl J Med* 1986;314:1657–1664.
3. Bombardier C, Ware J, Russell IJ, Larson M, Chalmers A, Read JL. Auranofin therapy and quality of life in patients with rheumatoid arthritis: results of a multicenter trial. *Am J Med* 1986;81:565–578.
4. Sage WM, Hurst CR, Silverman JF, Bortz WM II. Intensive care for the elderly: outcomes of elective and nonelective admissions. *J Am Geriatr Soc* 1987;35:312–318.
5. Jaeschke R, Guyatt GH. How to develop and validate a new quality of life instrument. In: Spilker B, ed. *Quality of life assessments in clinical trials.* New York: Raven Press, 1990:47–57.
6. Kaplan RM. *Human preference measurement for health decision and the evaluation of long-term care.* Lexington, MA: D.C. Heath, 1982.
7. Lawrence L, Christie D. Quality of life after stroke: a three-year follow-up. *Age Ageing* 1979;8:167–172.
8. Kaplan RM, Bush JW, Berry CC. Health status: types of validity and the index of well-being. *Health Serv Res* 1976;11:478–507.
9. Sugarbaker PH, Barofsky I, Rosenberg SA, Gianola FJ. Quality of life assessment of patients in extremity carcinoma clinical trials. *Surgery* 1982;91:17–23.
10. Eiseman B. The second dimension (Editorial). *Arch Surg* 1981;116:11–13.

Quality of Life and Pharmacoeconomics in Clinical Trials, Second Edition, edited by B. Spilker.
Lippincott-Raven Publishers, Philadelphia © 1996.

CHAPTER 51

Quality of Life Assessments in Clinical Trials: An Ethical Perspective

Robert J. Levine

INTRODUCTION

One should not introduce new therapies into the practice of medicine without having first conducted appropriate research to establish their safety and efficacy. There is a broad social consensus that such research is required ethically; for some classes of therapies it is also required by law. What is not clear is whether the ethical obligation to conduct such research entails a requirement to assess the effects of a new therapy on quality of life. It is not because there are irreconcilable controversies in the field that we have this lack of clarity; rather it is because the controversial issues remain to be identified and controverted to the point that a broad social consensus could begin to emerge.

It is against this backdrop that in this chapter I consider the ethical obligation to conduct quality of life assessments during the course of development of new therapies. This consideration begins with identification and discussion of the major ethical principles and norms that have become part of the broad social consensus in the fields of therapeutic innovation and medical therapy focusing on those that are most germane to the problem at hand. I then explain why I conclude that if these principles and norms are applied consistently, there is an ethical obligation to conduct quality of life assessments in connection with some but not all projects designed to develop new therapies. This conclusion is presented in the form of this guideline: In general, quality of life assessments are required when there are good

R. J. Levine: Departments of Medicine and Pharmacology, Yale University School of Medicine, New Haven, Connecticut 06510.

reasons to predict that their results will yield information that will be of practical utility to doctors and patients in making choices about whether to use the new therapy and when the importance of such information justifies the costs and risks of developing it. The chapter ends with a discussion of criteria for determining the applicability of this guideline.

OBLIGATIONS TO CONDUCT RESEARCH

Before considering whether there is an ethical obligation to assess the effects on quality of life of new (or, for that matter, old) medical therapies, it is a good idea to reflect on an even more fundamental question: Is there an ethical obligation to do any biomedical research at all? Does society[1] have an obligation to conduct or finance research having as its ultimate purpose the development of improved means to accomplish the purposes of the medical profession?

If society has such an obligation—and I shall soon explain why I think it does—it is not among the strongest of its obligations. To illustrate this point, Hans Jonas (1) contrasts and compares the obligation to conduct biomedical research with some of the more fundamental obligations of society such as protecting its members from harm and securing the conditions of its preservation. Such objectives necessarily have the highest priority. Unless society can, for example, secure the conditions of its preservation, it is impossible for its members to live meaningful lives; they cannot live according to plans grounded in reasonable expectations regarding the consequences of their actions (2).

Biomedical research is usually directed not at preserving society but rather at improving it. Only in the most extreme circumstances could biomedical research be said to be directed toward preserving society. For example, if we were faced with an epidemic having the proportions of the Black Death of the Middle Ages but caused by an infectious agent refractory to all known curative or preventive measures, then biomedical research could play a role in preserving society. Society's obligation to conduct research designed to end such an epidemic would assume a very high priority indeed. In such circumstances, one could claim that there was a strict obligation to conduct biomedical research, the goal of which was to preserve society. Otherwise, the improvement of society through the conduct of biomedical research may be considered an ethically optional goal.

Jonas (1) helps us put the nature of this obligation in perspective (p. 14):

> Unless the present state [conditions of life in our society] is intolerable, the melioristic goal [of biomedical research] is in a sense gratuitous, and this is not only from the vantage point of the present. Our descendants have a right to be left an unplundered planet; they do not have a right to new miracle cures. We have sinned against them if by our doing we have destroyed their inheritance . . . not . . . if by the time they come around arthritis has not yet been conquered (unless by sheer neglect).

Ours is a society that has a commitment to progress. As citizens we expect more of society than the fundamental obligations discussed so far. We are committed to a vigorous and persistent effort to improve the conditions of life in our society. In the domain of our concern, we expect that through biomedical research we will continue to develop improved methods and modalities with which we can combat or prevent diseases and their attendant disability, pain, suffering, and premature death. Our perception of ourselves as a society committed to progress is reflected in the way we have shaped our society in the twentieth century. As a people we have charged our government with responsibility for conducting and supporting biomedical research and for encouraging and regulating such research in the private sector. To the extent that the government is charged with this responsibility and to the extent it has accepted this charge, one may say that the government has assumed on behalf of society an obligation to conduct biomedical research.

Government's acceptance of this charge is manifested in its creation and continued operation of such agencies as the National Institutes of Health and the National Science Foundation. It supports additional biomedical research outside its own agencies by means of grants and contracts. Further, it encourages biomedical research in the private sector by protecting economic incentives for the development of safe and effective new remedies. By accepting the charge of the people, by responding in these ways to their expectations, government has created a set of expectations regarding its future activities. As a people we rightfully expect that the government will continue to conduct, support,

and encourage biomedical research. Failure to do so would be morally blameworthy in the sense that it is morally wrong not to honor one's commitments; one is bound to honor commitments in the absence of good reasons to do otherwise. Thus, in the ordinary course of events in our society—e.g., in the absence of crises that threaten the integrity of the society—our government can be regarded as having assumed an ethical obligation to conduct, support, and encourage biomedical research.

Regarding the obligations of other agents and agencies in our society, it seems clear that none have a strict obligation to conduct biomedical research unless they are voluntarily engaged in some specific activity that necessarily entails such an obligation. Most conspicuously included among such agents are those who wish to develop and market a new drug or device designed to cure, diagnose, or prevent human diseases or to alleviate their manifestations. Such persons are required ethically and legally to substantiate their claims of safety and efficacy for their new products through the conduct of what the Food, Drug, and Cosmetic Act calls "adequate and well-controlled" studies. Others may be bound ethically and legally to conduct biomedical research through accepting funds to conduct such research from either the government or private philanthropies. I could argue also that in our society any person who wishes to make a public claim that anything has an effect on the health of persons has an ethical obligation to back up such a claim with appropriate evidence.

So far we may conclude that in our society there are no persons or agencies who have a strict ethical obligation to conduct biomedical research. Some, however, have assumed or may assume such an obligation by virtue of various sorts of commitments they have made. The government, for example, has accepted the mandate of society to conduct, support, and encourage biomedical research. Others, for example those who wish to introduce new therapies for diseases, assume an obligation to conduct research designed to demonstrate their safety and efficacy.

OBLIGATIONS TO ASSESS QUALITY OF LIFE

Does the acceptance of such an obligation entail or encompass an obligation to assess quality of life? Let us consider a more sharply focused question: When one's obligation to conduct biomedical research arises by virtue of one's intention to develop a new therapy, does one assume an obligation to assess its effects on the quality of life of patients for whom it will be prescribed or to whom it will be recommended?

To begin to answer this question it is necessary to reflect on the purpose of this class of biomedical research. There is a general consensus in our society that biomedical research cannot be justified unless it is designed sufficiently well so that there will be a reasonable expectation that it will accomplish its purpose. The National Commission for the Protection of Human Subjects of Biomedical and Behavioral

Research (National Commission) (3) articulated this consensus in these words: "Subjects should not be exposed to risk in research that is so inadequately designed that its stated purposes cannot be achieved" (p. 22).

In the field of therapeutic innovation the central purpose is to develop therapies that will accomplish the goals of curing or preventing diseases or of ameliorating their manifestations. This purpose is related to the basic ethical principle of beneficence which, as interpreted by the National Commission (4), embodies two general rules: "Do no harm, and maximize possible benefits and minimize possible harms" (p. 6).

In the context of medical practice, considerations of beneficence are expressed in such familiar maxims as *primum non nocere* (first do no harm) and the Hippocratic oath's "I will use treatment to help the sick according to my ability and judgment." In biomedical research, the leading ethical codes such as the World Medical Association's Declaration of Helsinki enjoin the physician-investigator not only to secure the well-being of individuals (research subjects and patients) but also to develop information that will form the basis of being better able to do so in the future (5). According to the Nuremberg Code, the risks of research must be justified by "the humanitarian importance of the problem to be solved by the experiment."[2]

Research in the field of therapeutic innovation has a tendency to focus on "outcome measures or endpoints which are considered objective in so far as they are based on external observation of the patient" (6, p. 115). In the field of oncology, for example, one measures how many patients have substantial reductions in the size of their tumors and how long these "remissions" last. Research on antihypertensive agents reflects a principal concern with the magnitude of reduction of diastolic blood pressure. In the course of these studies one also records and reports the adverse effects experienced by the patient-subjects.

Based upon the results of such research, the physician may have reasonable confidence that a chemotherapeutic regimen is likely to reduce the size of a cancer or that an antihypertensive agent is likely to lower blood pressure. Such information is important, of course, but there is much more to medical practice than that. Patients do not consult physicians because they are offended by sphygmomanometer readings. They have a much broader view of what it means to secure their well-being now and in their personal futures. What they really want to know is this: "What is my life likely to be like if I take these drugs? What will I be able to do? How will I feel? And what if I don't?" These are, of course, questions about not only the quantity but also the quality of their lives.

Such questions lead us to a consideration of another basic ethical principle, respect for persons. This principle, as interpreted by the National Commission (4),

incorporates at least two basic ethical convictions: First, that individuals should be treated as autonomous agents, and second, that persons with diminished autonomy are entitled to protection. . . .

An autonomous person is an individual capable of deliberation about personal goals and of acting under the direction of such deliberation. To respect autonomy is to give weight to autonomous persons' considered opinions and choices while refraining from obstructing their actions unless they are clearly detrimental to others. To show a lack of respect for an autonomous agent is to repudiate that person's considered judgments, to deny an individual the freedom to act on those considered judgments, or *to withhold information* necessary to make a considered judgment, when there are no compelling reasons to do so. [pp. 4–5, emphasis supplied]

The most widely recognized instrumentality through which doctors show respect for the persons who are patients is informed consent. Informed consent, as envisioned in both law and ethics, includes (among other things) a presentation of information to the patient (5); the essential categories of information are commonly referred to as "elements." The elements that are most germane to the present discussion are disclosure of (a) risks, (b) benefits, and (c) alternatives. Such disclosure must not only be in a language that the patient can understand, it should convey meanings that are relevant to the patient's concerns. It should be responsive to such questions as those mentioned earlier: "What is my life likely to be like if I take these drugs? What will I be able to do? How will I feel? And what if I don't?"

Meaningful answers to such questions are often (not always) required by the patient to enable him or her to make considered judgments about therapies. Autonomous persons live according to life plans that reflect their personal conceptions of what it means to lead a good life. The usually unanticipated contingency of disease often forces persons to reconsider and reevaluate their life plans.[3] Faced with a disease that is almost certain to cause death within five years, for example, the patient may wish to reconsider a life plan that included graduate education. Similarly, the same patient might accept or reject therapy designed to postpone the fatal outcome based upon an assessment of the expected effects of therapy on his or her life plan. The patient may decide, for example, that there is a better chance of completing and enjoying graduate school without repeated episodes of severe nausea and vomiting and frequent threats of bone marrow depression with all of its ramifications.

Thus, underlying the questions I have put in the mouth of the patient are concerns about his or her life plan. The questions can be restated, "If I take these medicines (or undergo that surgery) am I more or less likely to be able to live according to my life plan (to lead what I consider a good life) than if I pursue another course of therapy?" To show respect for autonomous persons who are patients, doctors must attempt to be responsive to such questions.

During the course of development of a new therapy, it is usually possible to foresee when such questions will be relevant after the new therapy is introduced into the practice of medicine (*vide infra*). Research that neglects to develop information upon which answers to such questions may be based, when the relevance of such questions can be foreseen, must be regarded as inadequate. It is not adequately responsive to the ethical requirement that research be designed sufficiently well that there will be a reasonable expectation that it will accomplish its purposes: (a) to develop therapies that will enhance the well-being of patients as such well-being is envisioned by particular patients, and (b) to develop information that will enable patients to make satisfactory choices regarding the use of such therapies.

Schipper and Clinch (6) expressed in somewhat different terms a conclusion that is substantively the same: "In the end, the carefully designed, well-conducted randomized clinical trial may provide statistical evidence of an outcome difference. However, the evidence is mathematical. It remains the obligation of the researcher to assure that the 'significance' has biological and human importance" (p. 116).

Let us consider briefly the obligations of the researcher. The development of a new therapy is generally a complex enterprise involving the cooperation of multiple individuals and institutions. The responsibility for coordinating the activities of all of the participants resides with the individual or institution that intends to make a public claim regarding the safety and efficacy of the new therapy. In the case of drugs, devices, and other articles regulated by the Food and Drug Administration (FDA), the responsible agent is called the "sponsor," who requests of the FDA permission to make the public claim by filing a New Drug Application. It is the sponsor's obligation to see to it that all of the required activities are performed satisfactorily during the development of a new therapy. Therapeutic innovation in fields such as surgery in which there is no traditional way to identify an agent having responsibilities analogous to those of the sponsor may be problematic. I believe that there would be fewer problems in such fields if some individual or institution regularly assumed the responsibilities of the sponsor. Drawing on the model provided by FDA-regulated activities, I suggest that such responsibilities are or should be assumed by those who intend to make a public claim regarding the safety and efficacy of a new therapy.

CRITERIA FOR DETERMINING THE NEED FOR QUALITY OF LIFE ASSESSMENTS

As already noted, quality of life assessments are required only for some but not all new therapies. I propose this *guideline* for determining when in the course of developing a new therapy there is a requirement for such assessments: In general, quality of life assessments are required when there are good reasons to predict that their results will yield information that will be of practical utility to doctors and patients in making choices about whether to use the new therapy and when the importance of such information justifies the costs and risks of developing it.

The proposed guideline presents the obligation to conduct quality of life assessments in the form of a *prima facie* rule.

A *prima facie* rule is ethically binding unless it is in conflict with other stronger rules or unless in a specific situation there is ethical justification for overriding the rule's requirements. In this case, the requirement for quality of life assessment does not apply if the importance of the anticipated information does not justify either the costs to the sponsor of the new therapy or the risks to the research subjects.

Under what circumstances might it be claimed that there are good reasons to predict that quality of life studies will yield information that will be of practical utility? Suggestive evidence is provided by a finding that the new therapy has an effect that is likely to impair quality of life. It may produce, for example, nausea, exercise intolerance, or dumping syndrome. To the extent that the patient must necessarily experience this effect for a long time, the need for quality of life assessment is increased proportionately. Patients who have chronic diseases, for example, may have to receive the therapy for the remainder of their lives or, for another example, the effects of a single intervention, such as gastrectomy, may be irreversible (7,8).

The criterion of "practical utility" is closely related to the concept of "material risk" in the law of informed consent. Legally, any risk of a proposed medical intervention that is "material" must be disclosed to the patient. In a leading informed consent case, *Canterbury v. Spence* (9), the court held: "A risk is thus material when a reasonable person, in what the physician knows or should know to be the patient's position, would be likely to attach significance to the risks or cluster of risks in deciding whether or not to forego the proposed therapy."[4] Thus a risk is "material" if information about it has practical utility in reaching a decision about whether to accept or reject a proposed therapy. The legal formulation does not determine the ethical obligation to develop data about quality of life. It does, however, provide some perspective on the purpose of such information.

Terms such as *practical utility, importance,* and *justifies* do not have precise, inelastic meanings. Deciding what is important or justified in particular cases cannot be accomplished according to an ethical algorithm. As in most such matters, there is a need for informed and sensitive judgments.

Let us consider some examples of situations in which information about quality of life might have great practical utility. In these three examples quality of life considerations are likely to be very important; for many patients they will be more important than any other. These examples illustrate the types of situations in which the obligation to do quality of life assessments seems most compelling.

1. Therapy is to be administered to patients who feel well for the purpose of achieving a slight reduction in the probability of a serious morbid event in the distant future; this is exemplified by drug therapy of patients with mild essential hypertension (10).
2. In some cases, highly toxic chemotherapy may offer a small chance of a remission to patients with highly resistant cancers, e.g., hypernephroma. This small chance not-

withstanding, the average patient who accepts chemotherapy is likely to experience decreases in both quality and quantity of life (6,11).

3. In some cases, two therapies may yield the same results when expressed in such terms as overall survival or disease-free survival. However, there are substantial differences in the quality of life of patients who choose to receive these therapies. This situation is exemplified by the use of either radical mastectomy or simple mastectomy in the treatment of some patients with breast cancer (12).

According to Spilker (13), quality of life assessments are "generally not necessary ... when a drug is life saving" (pp. 266–267). Let us consider this criterion in some detail. When a drug or any other therapy is very likely to save a patient's life and to restore the patient promptly to his or her premorbid state of "normal living" (14), there is no requirement for quality of life evaluation. No reasonable patient would refuse an appendectomy for acute appendicitis or antibiotic therapy for meningococcal meningitis because he or she is unwilling to accept the transient detriments to quality of life expected of such therapeutic interventions.

There are, however, lifesaving therapies that many reasonable people reject because they would find the quality of life during or following their administration unacceptable. Prominent examples include cardiopulmonary resuscitation, ventilators, and nasogastric tube feeding in certain patients who are near death (15). On similar grounds, many reasonable persons are likely to refuse to accept a totally implantable artificial heart at its current state of development (16).

What if a therapy is more likely than another to cure a lethal disease? We cannot assume that all or even most persons will opt for such a therapy if it is likely to create an important detriment to the quality of their lives. This is illustrated in the work of McNeil and her colleagues (17), who asked healthy volunteers to imagine that they had cancer of the larynx in order to determine how much longevity they would exchange for voice preservation. The volunteers were 37 middle and upper management executives and 12 firefighters, each group averaging age 40. Using principles of expected utility theory to develop a method for sharpening decisions, they found that to avoid artificial speech the firefighters would trade off about 6% of their full life expectancy. Although executives would trade off more, an average of 17%, the difference was nonsignificant. "Although most subjects were willing to accept some decrease in long-term survival to maintain normal speech, virtually none would ever accept any decrease below 5 years."

Subjects were informed that with surgery 60% could expect to survive 3 years and with radiation, 30% to 40%. The subjects reacted as follows: If radiation offered only a 30% chance of survival for 3 years, practically none would decline surgery. By contrast, if the chance of survival for 3 years were 40%, 19% of the subjects would choose radiation therapy alone and 24% would choose radiation followed by delayed laryngectomy if necessary. The authors conclude that "treatment choices should be made on the basis of patients' attitudes toward the quality as well as the quantity of survival."

On the basis of the foregoing considerations I conclude that even if a therapy is designed to be lifesaving, the need for quality of life assessment should be determined according to the criterion specified earlier—viz., when there are good reasons to predict that their results will yield information that will be of practical utility to doctors and patients in making choices about therapies and when the importance of such information justifies the costs and risks of developing it.

Spilker (13) proposes one additional criterion for determining the necessity for quality of life studies; that is, when a treatment is "extremely expensive" (p. 267). This proposition raises issues that have not been addressed so far in this chapter. These issues are related to the third of the three ethical principles identified by the National Commission (4)—justice. Justice requires that the burdens and benefits of society be distributed fairly or equitably.

In March 1983, the President's Commission for the Study of Ethical Problems in Medicine and Biomedical and Behavioral Research (President's Commission) (18) addressed the problems of equitable distribution of health services (benefits) in its report, *Securing Access to Health Care;* in this report it made these recommendations:

> The Commission concludes that society has an ethical obligation to ensure equitable access to health care for all. ...
> Equitable access to health care requires that all citizens be able to secure an adequate level of health care without excessive burdens. [pp. 4–5]

In its commentary on the latter recommendation, the President's Commission elaborated as follows:

> A determination of this level will take into account the *value* of various types of health care in relation to each other as well as the *value* of health care in relation to other important goods for which societal resources are needed. Consequently, changes in the availability of resources, in the effectiveness of different forms of health care, or in society's priorities may result in a revision of what is considered "adequate." [p. 5, emphasis added]

In recent years the costs of health care in the United States have been increasing at a rate that exceeds substantially that of inflation (19). Eventually, if they have not already, the costs of health care will become unacceptably high in that they will deny us the ability to finance "other important goods for which societal resources are needed."

To make informed choices in the public policy arena, decision makers must have access to relevant information regarding the expected consequences of their choices.[5] Relevant information about new medical modalities, for reasons I have already discussed, must take into account effects on both quantity and quality of life. In choosing among alternative therapies designed to accomplish the same health objective, the prudent decision maker in the policy area should generally select the one shown to be superior in cost-utility analysis; for example, the therapy that secures the largest number of quality-adjusted years of life expectancy for each dollar spent (20).

I do not mean to suggest that cost utility is the only relevant consideration in making policy decisions. There are many other factors that must be taken into account (18); a discussion of these factors is beyond the scope of this chapter. However, since information about quality of life will often be relevant to, and sometimes decisive in, making policy decisions regarding expensive new technologies, the cost of a new therapy should be taken into account in determining the necessity for quality of life assessments.

In cases in which the prime consideration is to develop data designed to facilitate decision making in the policy arena rather than in the context of the doctor-patient relationship, our guideline should be restated: In general, quality of life assessments are required when there are good reasons to predict that their results will yield information that will be of practical utility to decision makers in the policy arena in choosing whether to finance the new therapy and when the importance of such information justifies the costs and risks of developing it.

Further work is required to determine who should bear the responsibility of conducting and financing research having as its aim the enhancement of decision making in the policy arena. The grounds for assigning this responsibility to the sponsor of the new therapy are not as clear as they were for research designed to enhance decision making in the context of the treatment of individual patients.

ACKNOWLEDGMENTS

I am grateful to Harvey Schipper and Bert Spilker for their helpful criticisms of a draft of this chapter.

ENDNOTES

1. The term *society* in this chapter follows the usage of the President's Commission (18): "In speaking of society, the Commission uses the term in its broadest sense to mean the collective American community. The community is made up of individuals who are in turn members of many other, overlapping groups, both public and private: local, state, regional, and national units; professional and workplace organizations; religious, educational, and charitable institutions; and family, kinship and ethnic groups. All these entities play a role in discharging societal obligations" (p. 4).

2. The Declaration of Helsinki and the Nuremberg Code are reprinted in *Ethics and Regulation of Clinical Research* (5).

3. For an excellent discussion of the concept of "life plan," the central role it plays in living a meaningful life, and the interplay between sickness and life plans, see *Stories of Sickness* (2).

4. For further discussion of the various standards for determining the materiality of risks, see *Ethics and Regulation of Clinical Research* (5, pp. 103–105).

5. This discussion addresses the need for information in the public policy arena because it is public (governmental) officials who are responsible for distributing the benefits of society equitably. A consideration of the needs of others who require similar information is beyond the scope of this chapter. Such others include those who make decisions regarding hospital formularies, the scope of coverage by private insurance companies and health maintenance organizations, and the like.

REFERENCES

1. Jonas H. Philosophical reflections on experimenting with human subjects. In: Freund PA, ed. *Experimentation with human subjects.* New York: George Braziller, 1970:1–31.
2. Brody H. *Stories of sickness.* New Haven and London: Yale University Press, 1987.
3. The National Commission for the Protection of Human Subjects of Biomedical and Behavioral Research. *Institutional review boards: report and recommendations.* Washington, DC: DHEW Publication No. (OS) 79-008, 1978.
4. The National Commission for the Protection of Human Subjects of Biomedical and Behavioral Research: *The Belmont report: ethical principles and guidelines for the protection of human subjects of research.* Washington, DC: DHEW Publication No. (OS) 78-0012, 1978.
5. Levine RJ. *Ethics and regulation of clinical research,* 2nd ed. Baltimore: Urban & Schwarzenberg, 1986.
6. Schipper H, Clinch J. Assessment of treatment in cancer. In: Smith GT, ed. *Measuring health: a practical approach.* New York: John Wiley, 1988:109–155.
7. Troidl H, Kusche J, Vestweber KH, et al. Quality of life: an important endpoint both in surgical practice and research. *J Chronic Dis* 1987;40:523–528.
8. O'Young J, McPeek B. Quality of life variables in surgical trials. *J Chronic Dis* 1987;40:513–522.
9. *Canterbury v. Spence,* 464 F 2d 72, CA DC 1972.
10. Fletcher AE, Hunt BM, Bulpitt CJ. Evaluation of quality of life in clinical trials and cardiovascular disease. *J Chronic Dis* 1987;40:557–566.
11. Levine RJ. Uncertainty in clinical research. *Law Med Health Care* 1988;16:174–182.
12. Lasry JCM, Margolese RG, Poisson R, et al. Depression and body image following mastectomy and lumpectomy. *J Chronic Dis* 1987;40:529–534.
13. Spilker B. *Guide to clinical interpretation of data.* New York: Raven Press, 1984.
14. Wood-Dauphinee S, Williams JI. Reintegration to normal living as a proxy to quality of life. *J Chronic Dis* 1987;40:491–499.
15. President's Commission for the Study of Ethical Problems in Medicine and Biomedical and Behavioral Research. *Deciding to forego life-sustaining treatment: ethical, medical and legal issues in treatment decisions.* Washington, DC: U.S. Government Printing Office, Stock No. 040-000-00470-0, 1983.
16. The Working Group on Mechanical Circulatory Support of the National Heart, Lung and Blood Institute. *Artificial heart and assist devices: directions, needs, costs, societal and ethical issues.* Bethesda, MD: National Heart, Lung and Blood Institute, 1985.
17. McNeil BJ, Weichselbaum R, Pauker SG. Speech and survival: trade-offs between quality and quantity of life in laryngeal cancer. *N Engl J Med* 1981;305:982–987.

18. President's Commission for the Study of Ethical Problems in Medicine and Biomedical and Behavioral Research. *Securing access to health care: the ethical implications of differences in the availability of health services.* Washington, DC: U.S. Government Printing Office, Stock No. 0-401-553-QL3, 1983.

19. Ginzberg E. A hard look at cost containment. *N Engl J Med* 1987; 316:1151–1154.

20. Drummond MF. Resource allocation decisions in health care: a role for quality of life assessments? *J Chronic Dis* 1987;40:605–616.

Quality of Life and Pharmacoeconomics in Clinical Trials, Second Edition, edited by B. Spilker.
Lippincott-Raven Publishers, Philadelphia © 1996.

CHAPTER 52

Quality of Life Measures in Health Care and Medical Ethics

Dan Brock

INTRODUCTION

There has been considerable philosophical work during the last two decades, especially in the United States but not limited to there, in a relatively new field called medical ethics. My aim in this chapter is to explore what illumination that body of work might offer to our understanding of the quality of life. If one looks only to the medical ethics literature explicitly addressing the notion of the quality of life, there are few sustained analyses of it and of its role in various medical and health care contexts. Consequently, it is necessary to look more broadly to issues and areas of research that often do not explicitly address the quality of life, but that nevertheless have an important bearing on it. I believe there are two main areas of work in medical ethics that fit this criterion. The first is work on ethical frameworks for medical treatment decision making in a clinical context, including accounts of informed consent and life-sustaining treatment decisions. The second is the development of valuational measures of outcomes of health care treatments and programs; these outcome measures are designed to guide health policy and so must be able to be applied to substantial numbers of people, including across or even between whole societies. The two main parts of this chapter will address these two main bodies of work. Before doing so, however, several preliminary issues need to be briefly addressed.

I have mentioned that the literature that I will be summarizing and drawing on often does not explicitly address the concept of quality of life, but instead uses other notions that are either closely related or roughly equivalent in the context. Sometimes a notion of "health" is employed, particularly in its broader interpretations, as exemplified in the World Health Organization definition of health as a state of complete physical, mental, and social well-being (1). The notion of patient well-being, independent of its use within a definition of health, is also often employed for evaluation of outcomes in health care. Another conceptual framework commonly employed for evaluating health care outcomes is the assessment of the benefits and burdens of that care for the patient (and sometimes for others as well). Still another common conceptual framework often employed looks to the effects of health care on patients' interests, with a best interests standard particularly prominent for patients whose preferences cannot be determined. These and other conceptual schemes are not fully interchangeable in health care, much less in broader contexts. Nevertheless, they all have in common their use in evaluating health care outcomes for patients and their employment as at least part of a comprehensive account of a good life for persons. I shall freely draw here on each of these conceptual frameworks, and others, though indicating where differences between them become important.

Quality of life can be given a number of more or less broad interpretations, depending on the scope of the evaluative factors concerning a person's life that it is taken to include. Medicine and health care often affect a person's life in only some limited areas or respects. Nevertheless, my concern will be with the broadest conception of, in Derek Parfit's (2) words, "what makes a life go best," and I shall try to show that medicine and health care may affect and

D. Brock: Department of Philosophy, Brown University, Providence, Rhode Island 02912.

illuminate more aspects of that question than might at first be thought. No concept is entirely apt or widely accepted in either philosophical or common usage for this broad role, but I shall use the concept of a ''good life'' to refer to the quality of life of persons in its broadest interpretation.

It is common in much philosophical work on theories of the good for persons or of a good life to distinguish three broad kinds of theory. While this classification misses some distinctions important for my purposes here, it provides a natural starting point. These three alternative theories I will call the hedonist, preference satisfaction, and ideal theories of a good life. Much of the philosophical work on these theories has been in the service of developing an account of ''utility,'' broadly construed for employment in consequentialist moral theories (3,4). What is common to hedonist theories, as I will understand them here, is that they take the ultimate good for persons to be the undergoing of certain kinds of conscious experience. The particular kinds of conscious experience are variously characterized as pleasure, happiness, or the satisfaction or enjoyment that typically accompanies the successful pursuit of our desires. Particular states of the person that do not make reference to conscious experience, such as having diseased or healthy lungs, and particular activities, such as studying philosophy or playing tennis, are part of a good life on this view only to the extent that they produce the valuable conscious experience.

Preference satisfaction theories take a good life to consist in the satisfaction of people's desires or preferences. I here understand desires or preferences as taking states of affairs as their objects: for example, my desire to be in Boston on Tuesday is satisfied just when the state of affairs of my being in Boston on Tuesday obtains. This is to be distinguished from any feelings of satisfaction, understood as a conscious experience of mine, that I may experience if I am in Boston on Tuesday. The difference is clearest in cases in which my desire is satisfied, but I either do not or could not know that it is and so receive no satisfaction from getting what I desire, for example, my desire that my children should have long and fulfilling lives, a state of affairs that will only fully obtain after my death. For preference satisfaction theories of a good life to be at all plausible, they must allow for some correcting or ''laundering'' of a person's actual preferences. Virtually all discussions of desire or preference satisfaction theories of the good contain some provision for correcting preferences. One of the better treatments, with extensive references to the literature, is Goodin (5). The most obvious example is the need to correct for misinformed preferences, for example, my desire to eat the sandwich before me not knowing that its ingredients are bad and will make me ill. Other corrections of preferences have also been supported by proponents of the preference satisfaction theory that are compatible with its underlying idea that ultimately what is good for persons is that they should get what they most want or prefer.

The third kind of theory holds that at least part of a good life consists neither of any conscious experience of a broadly

hedonist sort nor of the satisfaction of the person's corrected preferences or desires, but of the realization of specific, explicitly normative ideals.[1] For example, many have held that one component of a good life consists in being a self-determined or autonomous agent, and that this is part of a good life for a person even if he or she is no happier as a result and has no desire to be autonomous. Ideal theories will differ both in the specific ideals the theories endorse and in the place they give to happiness and preference satisfaction in their full account of the good for persons. There is a strong tendency in much of the philosophical literature to seek a simple, comprehensive theory, such as the hedonist or preference satisfaction theories; proponents of ideal theories commonly acknowledge a plurality of component ideals that place constraints on and/or supplement the extent to which happiness and/or preference satisfaction serves a person's good. The account I will develop of quality of life judgments in health care strongly suggests that it is a mistake to let the attractions of a simple, unified theory of a good life force a choice between the hedonist and preference satisfaction theories. Instead, these quality of life judgments suggest the importance of giving independent place to the considerations singled out by each of the three main alternative theories, as ideal theories do, in any adequate overall account of the quality of life or of a good life for persons. The quality of life judgments made in medicine and health care also help to fill in the content of a theory of a good life.

A major issue concerning ethical judgments generally, and judgments concerning a good life in particular, is the sense and extent to which such judgments are objective or subjective. A number of different senses have been given to the notions of ''objectivity'' and ''subjectivity'' in these contexts. I will not attempt an extended analysis of this general theoretical issue here. Nevertheless, one sense in which what constitutes a good life for a particular person is believed to be subjective or objective mirrors the distinction between hedonist and preference satisfaction theories on the one hand, and ideal theories on the other. Hedonist and preference theories are both subjective in the sense that both hold that what is good for a particular person depends on what in fact makes that person happy or what that person in fact (with appropriate corrections) desires. (This is compatible, of course, with acknowledging that what will make a particular person happy or satisfy his or her preferences is an ''objective matter of fact,'' even if often an extremely difficult one to determine.)

Ideal theories are objective, or at least contain objective components, in the sense that they hold a good life for a person is, at least in part, objectively determined by the correct or justified ideals of the good life, and does not in those respects depend either on what makes that person happy or on what that person's (even corrected) preferences happen to be. The question of whether accounts of a good life are objective or subjective is, then, an explicitly normative issue about what is the correct or most justified substantive theory of a good life. This sense of the objective-subjective dispute has been a central concern in the debates in medical ethics and health care about the quality of life. Interestingly, I believe that medicine and health care provide some of the most persuasive instances for both the objective and the subjective components of a good life, and so point the way toward a theory that incorporates hedonist, preference, and ideal components.

Haavi Morreim (6) has distinguished a different sense in which quality of life judgments in medicine are either objective or subjective. In her account, objective quality of life judgments are made on the basis of intersubjectively observable, material facts about a person (facts concerning his or her body, mind, functional capabilities, and environment), together with a socially shared evaluation of those facts, specifically of how those facts determine the person's quality of life. Subjective quality of life judgments also appeal to material facts about a person and his or her condition (though these may also include facts about the person's private psychological states), together with that person's value judgments about how those facts affect his or her quality of life. According to this account, the essential issue that determines whether a quality of life judgment is objective or subjective is whether the evaluative judgments concerning a particular individual's quality of life are and must be shared by some wider group or are, instead, only the individual's own. Since there are many possible wider social groups, one respect in which one could make sense of degrees of this kind of objectivity is in terms of the size, breadth, or nature of the wider social group; important variants include an individual's community or larger society, and a maximally wide group might be all humans or rational agents. It should be obvious that my and Morreim's senses of the objective-subjective distinction are independent; the individual whose quality of life is in question might hold any of the three substantive theories of the good for persons distinguished above, as might any wider social group.

A full conception of a good life for a person that does not reduce to a single property like happiness or preference satisfaction must assign a weight to the various components that contribute to that life's being good, though there may not be full comparability between different components and so in turn only partial comparability between different possible life courses for a person. Amartya Sen (7–10) has suggested the formal device of understanding these different components as independent vectors, each of which contributes to an overall assessment of the degree to which a person has a good life. There are several benefits to an analysis of what constitutes a good life into a number of independent vectors. First, it allows us to accept part of what proponents of each of the three traditional theories of a good life have wanted to insist on, namely the theoretical independence of those components. The three components of happiness, preference satisfaction, and ideals of a good life can each be represented by their individual vectors, or subdivided further into distinct vectors within each compo-

nent, having independent weight within an overall account of a good life. Second, the vector approach quite naturally yields the possibility of two senses of partial comparability of the quality of different lives. For a single individual, alternative possible lives may be only partially commensurable if one alternative life provides a greater value on one vector, but a lesser value on another vector, than another possible life. But for two different persons it is important that at least partial comparability between their lives may be possible, contrary to the dogma about the impossibility of interpersonal comparisons of utility, by comparing common vectors or by comparing different changes in common vectors making up a good life for each. Medicine and health care provide strong grounds for insisting on these independent vectors and, perhaps more importantly, also suggest a content and structure to the ideals along the lines proposed by Sen in his work on agency and capabilities, which drew on settings largely outside of health care.

We also need to distinguish between the relative importance of a particular feature or condition, say as represented by a specific vector, in its contribution to a person having a good life, compared with what I shall call its broader moral importance. A simple example will suffice. One condition that may plausibly contribute to a person's quality of life or good life is his or her physical mobility. It may be possible to specify roughly a normal level of physical mobility for persons of a similar age at a particular historical stage and in a particular society, and then to specify roughly levels of mobility say 25% below and 25% above the norm, such that the effect on a person's quality of life in moving from 25% below the norm up to the norm is quantitatively roughly the same as moving from the norm to 25% above it. While the degree or importance of the two changes in a person's quality of life or good life may be roughly the same, it can nonetheless be consistently held that these two comparable effects on the person's quality of life have different *moral* importance or priority. It might be held, for example, that on grounds of equality of opportunity bringing a person's mobility from 25% below the norm up to the norm has greater moral priority than increasing his mobility from the norm to 25% above it. The general point is that aspects of a person's quality of life may play a role not only in judgments about his quality of life or about how good a life he has, but also in other distinct moral and political judgments, or in the application of independent moral principles such as a principle of equal opportunity. This is, of course, a thoroughly familiar point in moral and political philosophy generally, and concerning consequentialist moralities in particular, against which it is often objected that they ignore the moral importance of whether the good is fairly or justly distributed. In the present context its importance is in reminding us to distinguish judgments concerning the improvement or reduction of people's quality of life from other independent moral evaluations of those same changes so as not to confuse needlessly the nature of quality of life judgments in health care.

ETHICAL FRAMEWORKS FOR HEALTH CARE TREATMENT DECISION MAKING

The first broad area of work within medical ethics bearing on the concept of the quality of life concerns the aims of medicine and the account of medical treatment decision making appropriate to those aims. It may be helpful to begin with a natural objection to thinking that these issues in medical ethics will illuminate any broad notion of the good life. On the contrary, as Leon Kass (11) has argued, medicine's proper end is the much narrower one of health, or the healthy human being, and other goals such as happiness and gratifying patient desires are false goals for medicine. Kass understands health to be a naturalistically defined property of individual biological organisms, organisms that must be understood as organic wholes, and whose parts

> have specific functions that define their nature as parts: the bone marrow for making red blood cells; the lungs for exchange of oxygen and carbon dioxide; the heart for pumping the blood. Even at a biochemical level, every molecule can be characterized in terms of its function. The parts, both macroscopic and microscopic, contribute to the maintenance and functioning, of the other parts, and make possible the maintenance and functioning of the whole. [p. 171]

What constitutes well-functioning varies with the particular biological species in question, but Kass is at pains to argue that "health is a natural standard or norm—not a moral norm, not a 'value' as opposed to a 'fact,' not an obligation—a state of being that reveals itself in activity as a standard of bodily excellence or fitness" (p. 173).[2]

Kass's work constitutes one of the more ambitious attempts to justify two common-sense beliefs about the "objectivity" of medicine, that the aim of medicine is and should be the patient's health, and that health is a biologically determined, objective matter of fact. If so, then physicians, with their impressive body of scientific knowledge concerning human biological functioning and the impact of therapeutic interventions on diseases and their natural courses, would seem to be the proper judges of whether we are healthy and, if we are not, what therapeutic interventions will be likely to make us more so. This hardly begins to do justice to the subtlety of Kass's view—though it is a view that I believe to be fundamentally mistaken—but it does bring out why one might think medicine, properly aimed only at human health defined in terms of biological functioning, has little to teach us regarding broader social issues about the quality of life. I believe it is fair to say that the main body of work in medical ethics within the last two decades has rejected Kass's view that the sole proper aim of medicine is health, defined in naturalistic, biological terms, and the ethical framework for medical treatment decision making that it would seem to imply. We need to see how the alternative, broader view of the aims of medicine that should guide medical treatment decision making bears on an understanding of the quality of life.

It has become a commonplace, at least in the developed countries, that medicine has achieved the capacity commonly to offer to patients suffering from particular diseases a number of alternative treatments, and to extend patients' lives in circumstances in which the benefit to the patient of doing so is increasingly problematic. In the United States this has led to patients pursuing various means of gaining control over decisions about their treatment. In the case of competent patients, a broad consensus has developed that such patients have the right to decide about their care in a process of shared decision making with their physicians and to reject any preferred treatment. In the case of incompetent patients, an analogous consensus has been developing that an incompetent patient's surrogate, seeking to decide as the patient would have decided in the circumstances if competent, is likewise entitled to decide about the patient's care with the patient's physician and to reject any care the patient would not have wanted—though the consensus concerning incompetent patients is less broad and more ringed with qualifications. Each consensus is reflected in a large medical ethics literature, a growing body of legal decisions, legal mechanisms such as living wills and durable powers of attorney for health care, whose purpose is to ensure patients' control over their care, pronouncements and studies of anthoritative bodies and commissions, policies of health care institutions, and the practice of health care professionals.[3]

The common view is now that health care decision making should be a process of shared decision making between patient (or the patient's surrogate in the case of an incompetent patient) and physician.[4] Each is seen as indispensable to sound decision making. The physician brings his or her training, knowledge, and expertise to bear for the diagnosis of the patient's condition, the estimation of the patient's prognosis with different alternative treatments, including the alternative of no treatment, and a recommendation regarding treatment. The patient brings the knowledge of his or her aims, ends, and values that are likely to be affected by different courses of treatment, and this enables a comparative evaluation of different possible outcomes to be made. As alternative treatments have multiplied and become possible in circumstances promising increasingly marginal or questionable benefits, both physicians and patients are called upon to make increasingly difficult judgments about the effects of treatment on patients' quality of life. It is worth noting that proponents of shared decision making need not reject the functional account of health as a biological norm defended by Kass and others. What they can reject is the claim that the only proper goal of medicine is health. Instead, medicine's goal should be to provide treatment that best enables patients to pursue successfully their overall aims and ends, or life plans. It is the relative value of health, and of different aspects of health, as compared with other ends, that varies for different persons and circumstances.

Most patients' decisions about life-sustaining treatment will be based on their judgment of the benefits and burdens of the proposed treatment and the life it sustains, though in some instances patients may give significant weight to other factors such as religious obligations, the emotional burdens and financial costs for their families, and so forth. Except for patients who hold a form of vitalism according to which human life should or must be sustained at all costs and whatever its quality, these decisions by competent patients must inevitably involve an assessment of their expected quality of life if life-sustaining treatment is employed, though, as I shall note shortly, of only a very restricted sort.

Some have rejected the acceptability of quality of life judgments in the case of incompetent patients unable to decide for themselves, for whom others must therefore make treatment decisions (25). One version of the objection is that no one should decide for another whether that other's quality of life is such that it is not worth continuing it. More specifically, the objection is that it is unacceptable to judge that the quality of another person's life is so poor that it is not worth the cost and effort to others to sustain that person's life. This objection, however, is not to making quality of life judgments in this context generally, but only to concluding that a person's life is not worth sustaining because its poor quality makes it not of value, but instead a burden, to *others*. The sound point that this objection confusingly makes is that quality of life judgments concerning a particular person should address how the conditions of a person's life affect its quality or value to *that person,* and not its value to others. Moreover, persons might judge their quality of life to be low and nevertheless value their lives as precious. In economic and policy analysis one version of the so-called human capital method of valuing human life, which values a person's life at a given point in time by his or her expected future earnings minus personal consumption, in effect values a person's life in terms of its economic value to others (26). But there is no reason to reject the soundness of any evaluation by one person of another's quality of life simply because some might draw a further unjustified conclusion that if its quality is sufficiently low to make it on balance a burden to others, it ought not to be sustained.

The quality of life judgment appropriate to life-sustaining treatment decisions, whether made by a competent patient or an incompetent patient's surrogate, should thus assess how the conditions of the patient's life affect the value of that life to that patient. Nevertheless, even properly focused in this way, the role of quality of life judgments in decisions about whether to withhold or withdraw life-sustaining treatment is extremely limited. This quality of life judgment focuses only on which side of a *single threshold* a person's quality of life lies. The threshold question is, Is the quality of the patient's life so poor that for that person continued life is worse than no further life at all? Or, in the language of benefits and burdens commonly employed in this context, Is the patient's quality of life so poor that the use of life-sustaining treatment is unduly burdensome, that is, such that the burdens to the patient of the treatment and/or the life

that it sustains are sufficiently great and the benefits to the patient of the life that is sustained sufficiently limited, to make continued life on balance no longer a benefit or good to the patient?[5] The only discrimination in quality of life required here is whether the quality of the life is on balance sufficiently poor to make it worse than nonexistence to the person whose life it is.

There have been attempts to formulate some general substantive standards to determine when an incompetent patient's quality of life is so poor that withholding or withdrawing further life-sustaining treatment is justified. Nicholas Rango (27), for example, has proposed standards for nursing home patients with dementia. He emphasizes the importance of being clear about the purposes for which care is provided and distinguishes three forms of care: (1) palliative care aimed at relieving physical pain and psychological distress; (2) rehabilitative care aimed at identifying and treating "excess disabilities, the gap between actual level of physical, psychological or social functioning and potential functioning capacity" (EM Brody, quoted in ref. 27); and (3) medical care aimed at reducing the risk of mortality or morbidity. He emphasizes the importance of therapeutic caution because a seriously demented patient will not be able to understand the purposes of painful or invasive interventions, and so presumably cannot choose to undergo and bear burdensome treatment for the sake of promised benefits. The importance of this factor was stressed in a widely publicized legal decision (28) concerning the use of painful chemotherapy for a man suffering from cancer who had been severely retarded from birth.

Rango (27) proposes two conditions, either of which is sufficient to justify forgoing further treatment of a chronic medical condition or a superimposed acute illness: (a) when the patient is burdened by great suffering despite palliative and rehabilitative efforts; (b) when the dementia progresses "to a stuporous state of consciousness in which the person lives with a negligible awareness of self, other, and the world" (p. 838). Even within the relatively narrow focus of life-sustaining treatment decisions for demented patients, Rango's proposal can be seen to include three different kinds of components of quality of life assessments. The first, covered by treatment aim (1) and patient conditions (a) and (b), concerns the quality of the patient's conscious experience. The second, covered especially by treatment aim (2) and patient condition (b), concerns the patient's broad functional capacities. The third, covered especially by patient condition (b) and by the patient's ability to understand the purpose of treatment and in turn to choose to undergo it, concerns the centrality to quality of life of the capacity to exercise choice in forming and pursuing an integrated and coherent life plan. Each of these three kinds of condition is an essential component of an adequate account of the quality of life.

What is the relation between these two values of patient self-determination and well-being, commonly taken as underlying the informed consent doctrine, and the broad concept of a good life? The conventional view, I believe, is that the patient's well-being is roughly equivalent to the patient's good and that individual self-determination is a value independent of the patient's well-being or good. Respecting the patient's right to self-determination, then, at least sometimes justifies respecting treatment choices that are contrary to the patient's well-being or good. Respecting self-determination is commonly held to be what is required by recognizing the individual as a person, capable of forming a conception of the good life for him or herself. If personal self-determination is a fundamental value—fundamental in that it is what is involved in respecting persons—however, then I suggest that our broadest conception of a good life should be capable of encompassing it rather than setting it off as separate from and in potential conflict with a person's well-being or good, as in the conventional account of informed consent. What we need is a distinction between a good life for a person in the broadest sense and a person's personal well-being, such that only personal well-being is independent of and potentially in conflict with individual self-determination.

In the usual case in which an incompetent patient has left no formal advance directive, two principles for the guidance of those who must decide about treatment for the patient have been supported—the *substituted judgment* principle and the *best interests* principle. The substituted judgment principle requires the surrogate to decide as the patient would have decided if competent and in the circumstances that currently obtain. The best interests principle requires the surrogate to make the treatment decision that best serves the patient's interests. This has the appearance of a dispute between what I earlier called normatively subjective and normatively objective accounts of a good life, since the only point of the best interests principle as an alternative to substituted judgment might seem to be that it employs a normatively objective standard of the person's good that does not depend on his or her particular subjective preferences and values. However, this appearance is misleading. These two principles of surrogate decision making are properly understood, in my view, not as competing alternative principles to be used for the same cases, but instead as an ordered pair of principles to cover all cases of surrogate decision making for incompetent patients in which an advance directive does not exist, with each of the two principles to apply in a different subset of these cases. (This is not to say that these two principles are always in fact understood in medical ethics, the law, or health care practice as applying to distinct groups of cases; the treatment of these two principles is rife with confusion.)

The two groups of cases are differentiated with regard to the information available or obtainable concerning the patient's general preferences and values that has some bearing on the treatment choice at hand. The two principles are an ordered pair in the sense that when sufficient information is available about the relevant preferences and values of the patient to permit a reasonably well-grounded application of the substituted judgment principle, then surrogate decision makers for the patient are to use that information and that principle to infer what the patient's decision would have been in the circumstances if he or she were competent. In the absence of such information, and only then, surrogate decision makers for the patient are to select the alternative that is in the best interests of the patient, which is usually interpreted to mean the alternative that most reasonable and informed persons would select in the circumstances. Thus, these two principles are not competing principles for application in the same cases, but alternative principles to be applied in different cases.

Nevertheless, it might seem that the best interests standard remains a normatively objective account when it is employed. However, this need not be so. If the best interests standard is understood as appealing to what most informed and reasonable persons would choose in the circumstances, it employs the normatively subjective preference standard. And it applies the choice of most persons to the patient in question because in the absence of any information to establish that the patient's relevant preferences and values are different than most people's, the most reasonable presumption is that the patient is like most others in the relevant respects and would choose like those others. Thus, the best interests standard, like the two other standards of choice for incompetent patients—the advance directive and substituted judgment standards—can be understood as requiring the selection of the alternative the patient would most likely have selected, with the variations in the standards suited to the different levels of information about the patient that is available. Just as with the informed consent doctrine that applies to competent patients, so these three principles—advance directives, substituted judgment, and best interests—guiding surrogate choice for incompetent patients can all be understood as supported and justified by the values of patient well-being and self-determination. Thus, each of these three principles implicitly employs an account of a good life that is a life of choice and self-determination concerning one's aims, values, and life plan.

HEALTH POLICY MEASURES OF THE QUALITY OF LIFE

I want now to shift attention from the account of the quality of life presupposed by ethical frameworks for medical treatment decision making to more explicit measures used to assess health levels and the quality of life as it is affected by health and disease within larger population groups. Early measurement attempts focused on morbidity and mortality rates in different populations and societies. These yield only extremely crude comparisons, since they often employ only such statistics as life expectancy, infant mortality, and reported rates of specific diseases in a population. Nevertheless, they will show gross differences between countries, especially between economically developed and underdeveloped countries, and between different historical periods, in both length and quality of life as it is affected by disease. Major changes in these measures during this century, as is well known, have been due principally to public health measures such as improved water supplies, sewage treatment, and other sanitation programs and to the effects of economic development in improving nutrition, housing, and education; improvements in the quality of and access to medical care have been less important. In recent decades, health policy researchers have developed a variety of measures that go substantially beyond crude morbidity and mortality measures. Before shifting our attention to them, however, it is worth underlining the importance of mortality measures to the broad concept of a good life.

When quality and quantity of life are distinguished, both are relevant to the degree to which a person has a good life. People whose lives are of high quality, by whatever measure of quality, but whose lives are cut short well before reaching the normal life span in their society, have had lives that have gone substantially less well, because of their premature death, than reasonably might have been expected. People typically develop, at least by adolescence, more or less articulated and detailed plans for their lives; commonly, the further into the future those plans stretch, the less detailed, more general, and more open-ended they are. Our life plans undergo continuous revision, both minor and substantial, over the course of our lives, but at any point in time within a life people's plans for their lives will be based in part on assumptions about what they can reasonably expect in the way of a normal life span (29,30). When their lives are cut short prematurely by illness and disease they lose not just the experiences, happiness, and satisfactions that they would otherwise have had in those lost years, but they often lose as well the opportunity to complete long-term projects and to achieve and live out the full shape, coherence, and conclusion that they had planned for their lives. It is this rounding out and completion of a life plan and a life that helps enable many elderly people, when near death, to feel that they have lived a full and complete life and so to accept their approaching death with equanimity and dignity. The loss from premature death is thus not simply the loss of a unit of a good thing, so many desired and expected-to-be-happy life-years, but the cutting short of the as yet incompletely realized life plan that gave meaning and coherence to the person's life.

There is a voluminous medical and health policy literature focused on the evaluation of people's quality of life as it is affected by various disease states and/or treatments to ameliorate or cure those diseases (31–59). The dominant conception of the appropriate aims of medicine focuses on medicine as an intervention aimed at preventing, ameliorating, or curing disease and its associated effects of suffering and disability, and thereby restoring, or preventing the loss of, normal function or of life. Whether the norm be that of the particular individual, or that typical in the particular society or species, the aim of raising people's function to *above* the norm is not commonly accepted as an aim of medicine of equal importance to restoring function *up to* the norm. Problematic though the distinction may be, quality of life measures in medicine and health care consequently tend to focus on individuals' or patients' *dysfunction* and its relation to some such norm. At a deep level, medicine views bodily parts and organs, individual human bodies, and people from a functional perspective. Both health policy analysts and other social scientists have done considerable work constructing and employing measures of health and quality of life for use with large and relatively diverse populations. Sometimes these measures explicitly address only part of an overall evaluation of people's quality of life, while in other instances they address something like overall quality of life as it is affected by disease. A closely related body of work focuses somewhat more narrowly on an evaluation of the effect on quality of life of specific modes of treatment for specific disease states. This research is more clinically oriented, though the breadth of impact on quality of life researchers seek to measure does vary to some extent, depending often on the usual breadth of impact on the person of the disease being treated. Generally speaking, the population-wide measures tend to be less sensitive to individual differences as regards both the manner and the degree to which a particular factor affects people's quality of life. It will be helpful to have before us two representative examples of the evaluative frameworks employed.

The Sickness Impact Profile (SIP) was developed by Marilyn Bergner and colleagues (60) to measure the impact of a wide variety of forms of ill health on the quality of people's lives (Table 1).

A second example of an evaluative framework is the Quality of Life Index (QLI) developed by Walter O. Spitzer and colleagues (61) to measure the quality of life of cancer patients (Table 2).

It would be a mistake to attempt to infer precise and comprehensive philosophical theories of the quality of life or of a good life from measures such as these. The people who develop them are social scientists and health care researchers who are often not philosophically sophisticated or concerned with the issues that divide competing philosophical accounts of a good life. The practical and theoretical difficulties in constructing valid measures that are feasible for large and varied populations require compromises with and simplifications of—or simply passing over—issues of philosophical importance. Nevertheless, several features of these measures are significant in showing the complexity of the quality of life measures employed in health care and, I believe, of any adequate account of the quality of life or of a good life.

First, the principal emphasis in each of the three measures of quality of life is on function, and functions of the whole person as opposed to body parts and organ systems. In each case the functions are broadly characterized so as to be relevant not simply to a relatively limited and narrow class of life plans, but to virtually any life plan common in modern

TABLE 1. *Sickness Impact Profile categories and selected items*

Dimension	Category	Items describing behavior related to:	Selected items
Independent categories	SR	Sleep and rest	I sit during much of the day
			I sleep or nap during the day
	E	Eating	I am eating no food at all, nutrition is taken through tubes or intravenous fluids
			I am eating special or different food
	W	Work	I am not working at all
			I often act irritable towards my work associates
	HM	Home management	I am not doing any of the maintenance or repair work around the house that I usually do
			I am not doing heavy work around the house
	RP	Recreation and pastimes	I am going out for entertainment less
			I am not doing any of my usual physical recreation or activities
I. Physical	A	Ambulation	I walk shorter distances or stop to rest often
			I do not walk at all
	M	Mobility	I stay within one room
			I stay away from home only for brief periods of time
	BCM	Body care and movement	I do not bathe myself at all, but am bathed by someone else
			I am very clumsy in my body movements
II. Psychosocial	SI	Social interaction	I am doing fewer social activities with groups of people
			I isolate myself as much as I can from the rest of the family
	AB	Alertness behavior	I have difficulty reasoning and solving problems, e.g. making plans, making decisions, learning new things
			I sometimes behave as if I were confused or disoriented in place or time, e.g. where I am, who is around, directions, what day it is
	EB	Emotional behavior	I laugh or cry suddenly
			I act irritable and impatient with myself, e.g. talk badly about myself, swear at myself, blame myself for things that happen
	C	Communication	I am having trouble writing or typing
			I do not speak clearly when I am under stress

societies. Following the lead of Rawls's (30) notion of "primary good," I shall call these "primary functions." In the SIP, the categories of sleep and rest, and eating are necessary for biological function. The categories of work, home management, and recreation and pastimes are central activities common in virtually all lives, though the relative importance they have in a particular life can be adjusted for by making the measure relative to what had been the individual's normal level of activity in each of these areas prior to sickness. The two broad groups of functions, physical and psychosocial, are each broken down into several distinct components. For each primary function, the SIP measures the impact of sickness by eliciting information concerning whether activities typical in the exercise of that function continue to be performed, or have become limited. Even for primary functions, about which it is plausible to claim that they have a place in virtually any life, the different functions can have a different *relative* value or importance within different lives, and the SIP makes no attempt to measure those differences. The

QLI likewise addresses a person's levels of activity in daily living, specifically measuring the presence of related behaviors in the relevant areas. In measuring health and outlook, the primary concern is with subjective feeling states of the person, though here too there is concern with relevant behavior. The category of support addresses both the social behavior of the individual and the availability of people in the individual's environment to provide such relationships. This category illustrates the important point that most primary functional capacities require both behavioral capacities in the individual and relevant resources in the individual's external environment. It is noteworthy that neither the SIP nor QLI measures the presence or absence of disease, as one might expect given common understandings of "health" as the absence of disease; they measure levels of very broad primary functions.

A second important feature of these measures is best displayed in the "outlook" category of the QLI, though it is also at least partly captured in the "emotional behavior"

TABLE 2. *Quality of Life Index: formal final version adopted*

Study No _____

Age _____ □□
See M₁ F₂ (Ring appropriate letter) _____ □
Primary Problems or Diagnosis _____
_____ □□□
Secondary Problem or Diagnosis, or complication (if appropriate) _____ □□□
Scorer's Speciality _____ □□□

Scoring Form

Score each Reading 2, 1 or 0 according to your most recent assessment of the patient.

ACTIVITY   *During the last week, the patient*
- has been working or studying full time, or nearly so, in usual occupation; or managing own household, or participating in unpaid or voluntary activities, whether retired or not 2
- has been working or studying in usual occupation or managing own household or participating in unpaid or voluntary activities, but requiring major assistance or a significant reduction in hours worked or a sheltered situation or was on sick leave 1   □
- has not been working or studying in any capacity and not managing own household 0

DAILY LIVING   *During the last week, the patient*
- has been self-reliant in eating, washing, toileting, and dressing: using public transport or driving own car... 2
- has been requiring assistance (another person or special equipment) for daily activities and transport but performing light tasks.. 1   □
- has not been managing personal care or light tasks and/or not leaving own home or institution at all... 0

HEALTH   *During the last week, the patient*
- has been appearing to feel well or reporting feeling "great" most of the time 2
- has been lacking energy or not feeling entirely "up to par" more than just occasionally 1   □
- has been feeling very ill or "lousy," seeming weak and washed out most of the time, or was unconscious 0

SUPPORT   *During the last week*
- the patient has been having good relationships with others and receiving strong support from at least one family member and/or friend.. 2
- support received or perceived has been limited from family and friends and/or by the patient's condition 1   □
- support from family and friends occurred infrequently or only when absolutely necessary or patient was unconscious 0

OUTLOOK   *During the past week the patient*
- has usually been appearing calm and positive in outlook, accepting and in control of personal circumstances, including surroundings 2
- has sometimes been troubled because not fully in control of personal circumstances or has been having periods of obvious anxiety or depression 1   □
- has been seriously confused or very frightened or consistently anxious and depressed or unconscious 0

QL INDEX TOTAL □□

How confident are you that your scoring of the preceding dimensions is accurate? Please ring the appropriate category.

Absolutely Confident	Very Confident	Quite Confident	Not Very Confident	Very Doubtful	Not at all Confident	
1	2	3	4	5	6	□

category of the SIP. Both these categories can be understood as attempts to capture people's subjective response to their objective physical condition and level of function, or, in short, their level of happiness or satisfaction with their lives, though the actual measures are far too crude to measure happiness with much sensitivity. The important point is that the use of these categories represents a recognition that *part* of what makes a good life is that the person in question is happy or pleased with how it is going; that is, subjectively experiences it as going well, as fulfilling his or her major aims, and as satisfying. This subjective happiness component is not unrelated to how well the person's life is going as measured by the level of the other objective primary functions. How happy we are with our lives is significantly determined by how well our lives are in fact going in other objective respects. Nevertheless, medicine provides many examples that show it is a mistake to assume that the subjective happiness component correlates closely and invariably with other objective functional measures. In one study, for example, researchers found a substantial relation between different objective function variables and also between different subjective response or outlook variables, but only a very limited relation between objective and subjective variables (62). These data reinforce the importance of including both objective function and subjective response categories in a full conception of the quality of life, since neither is a reliable surrogate for the other. Given this at least partial independence between happiness and function variables, what is their relative weight in an overall assessment of a good life? Here, too, medicine brings out forcefully that there can be no uniform answer to this question. In the face of seriously debilitating injuries, one patient will adjust her aspirations and expectations to her newly limited functional capacities and place great value on achieving happiness despite these limitations. Faced with similar debilitating injuries, another patient will assign little value to adjusting to the disabilities in order to achieve happiness in spite of them, stating that she "does not want to become the kind of person who is happy in that debilitated and dependent state."[6]

There are other important qualifications of the generally positive relation between this happiness component of a good life and both the other primary function components and the overall assessment of how good a life it is. These qualifications are not all special to health care and the quality of life, but some are perhaps more evident and important in the area of health care than elsewhere. The first qualification concerns people's adjustments to limitations of the other primary functions. Sometimes the limitation in function, or potential limitation, is due to congenital abnormalities or other handicaps present from birth. For example, *60 Minutes* reported (February 21, 1988) on a follow-up of some of the children, now young adults, born to pregnant women who had taken the drug thalidomide in the late 1950s. The people reported on had suffered no brain damage but had been born with serious physical deformities, including lacking some or any arms and legs. While this placed many impairments in the way of carrying out primary functions such as eating,

working, home management, physical mobility, and ambulation in the manner of normal adults, these people had made remarkable adjustments to compensate for their physical limitations: one was able to perform all the normal functions of eating using his foot in place of missing arms and hands; another made his living as an artist painting with a brush held between his teeth; another without legs was able to drive in a specially equipped car; and a mother of three without legs had adapted so as to be able to perform virtually all the normal tasks of managing a family and home.

These were cases where physical limitations that commonly restrict and impair people's primary functional capacities and overall quality of life had been so well compensated for as to enable them to perform the same primary functions, though in different ways, as well as normal, unimpaired persons do. While a few life plans possible for others remained impossible for them because of their limitations (for example, being professional athletes), their essentially unimpaired level of primary functions as a result of the compensations they had made left them with choice from among a sufficiently wide array of life plans that it is probably a mistake to believe that their quality of life had been lowered much or at all by their impairments. These cases illustrate that even serious physical limitations do not always lower quality of life if the disabled persons have been able or helped sufficiently to compensate for their disabilities so that their level of primary functional capacity remains essentially unimpaired; in such cases it becomes problematic even to characterize those affected as disabled.

In other cases, compensating for functional disabilities, particularly when they arise later in life, may require adjustments involving substantial changes in the kind of work performed, social and recreational activities pursued, and so forth. When these disabilities significantly restrict the activities that had been and would otherwise have been available to and pursued by the person, they will, all other things being equal, constitute reductions in the person's quality of life. If they do so, however, it will be because they significantly restrict the choices, or what Norman Daniels (63) has called the normal opportunity range, available to the persons, and not because the compensating paths chosen need be, once entered on, any less desirable or satisfying. The opportunity for choice from among a reasonable array of life plans is an important and independent component of quality of life; it is insufficient to measure only the quality of the life plan the disabled person now pursues and his or her satisfaction with it. Adjustments to impairments that leave primary functions undiminished or that redirect one's life plan into areas where function will be better—both central aims of rehabilitative medicine—can, however, enhance quality of life even in the face of a diminished opportunity range.

In his theory of just health care Daniels uses the notion of an age-adjusted normal opportunity range, which is important for the relation between opportunity and quality of life or a good life. Some impairments in primary functions occur as common features of even the normal aging process, for example, limitations in previous levels of physical activity. Choosing to adjust the nature and level of our planned activities to such impairments in function is usually considered a healthy adjustment to the aging process. This adjustment can substantially diminish the reduction in the person's quality of life from the limitations of normal aging. Nevertheless, even under the best of circumstances, the normal aging process (especially, say, beyond the age of 80), does produce limitations in primary functions that will reduce quality of life. Thus, while quality of life must always be measured against normal, primary functional capacities for humans, it can be diminished by reductions both in individual function below the age-adjusted norm and by reductions in normal function for humans as they age.

I have suggested above that adjustments in chosen pursuits as a result of impairments in primary, or previously pursued individual, functions can compensate substantially (fully, in the effects on happiness) for impaired function, but will often not compensate fully for significant reductions in the range of opportunities available for choice, and so will not leave quality of life undiminished. In some cases, however, a patient's response and adjustment to the limitations of illness or injury may be so complete, as regards his commitment to and happiness from the new chosen life path, that there is reason to hold that his quality of life is as high as before, particularly as he gets further away in time from the onset of the limiting illness or injury and as the new life becomes more securely and authentically the person's own. An undiminished or even increased level of happiness and satisfaction, together with an increased commitment to the new life, often seem the primary relevant factors when they are present. But we must also distinguish different reasons why the affective or subjective component of quality of life, which I have lumped under the notion of happiness, may remain undiminished, since this is important for an evaluation of the effect on quality of life.

A person's happiness is to some significant extent a function of the degree to which his or her major aims are being at least reasonably successfully pursued. Serious illness or injury resulting in serious functional impairment often requires a major reevaluation of one's plan of life and one's major aims and expectations. Over time, such reevaluations can result in undiminished or even increased levels of happiness, despite decreased function, because the person's aspirations and expectations have likewise been revised and reduced. The common cases in medicine in which, following serious illness, people come to be satisfied with much less in the way of hopes and accomplishments illustrate clearly the incompleteness of happiness as a full account of the quality of life. To be satisfied or happy with getting much less from life, because one has come to expect much less, is still to get less from life or to have a less good life. (The converse of this effect is when rising levels of affluence and of other objective primary functions in periods of economic development lead to even more rapidly rising aspirations and expectations, and in turn to an increasing gap between accomplishments and expectations). Moreover, whether the

relation of the person's choices to his aspirations and expectations reflects his exercise of self-determination in response to changed circumstances is important in an overall assessment of his quality of life and shows another aspect of the importance of self-determination to quality of life.

Illness and injury resulting in serious limitations of primary functions often strike individuals without warning and seemingly at random, and are then seen by them and others as a piece of bad luck or misfortune. Every life is ended by death, and few people reach death after a normal life span without some serious illness and attendant decline in function. This is simply an inevitable part of the human condition. Individual character strengths and social support services enable people unfortunately impaired by disease or injury to adjust their aims and expectations realistically to their adversity, and then to get on with their lives, instead of responding to their misfortune with despair and self-pity. Circumstances beyond individuals' control may have dealt them a cruel blow, but they can retain dignity as self-determining agents capable of responsible choice in directing and retaining control over their lives within the limits that their new circumstances permit. We generally admire people who make the best of their lot in this way, and achieve happiness and accomplishment despite what seems a cruel fate. This reduction in aims and expectations, with its resultant reduction in the gap between accomplishments and aims, and the [in turn] resultant increase in happiness, is an outcome of the continued exercise of self-determination. It constitutes an increase in the happiness and self-determination components of quality of life though, of course, only in response to an earlier decrease in the person's level of primary functions.

Other ways of reducing this gap between accomplishments and expectations bypass the person's self-determination and are more problematic as regards their desirability and their effect on a person's quality of life. Jon Elster (64) has written, for example, outside of the medical context, of different kinds of nonautonomous preferences and preference change. Precisely characterizing the difference between what Elster calls nonautonomous preferences and what I have called the exercise of self-determination in adjusting to the impact of illness and injury raises deep and difficult issues that I cannot pursue here. Nevertheless, I believe that response to illness through the exercise of self-determined choice, in the service of protecting or restoring quality of life, is one of the most important practical examples of the significance for overall assessments of the quality of life of *how* to achieve the reasonable accord between aims and accomplishments that happiness requires.

CONCLUSIONS

Let us tie together some of the main themes in accounts of the quality of life or of a good life suggested by the literature in medical ethics and health policy. While that literature provides little in the way of well-developed, philosophically sophisticated accounts of the quality of life or of a good life, it is a rich body of analysis, data, and experience on which philosophical accounts of a good life can draw. I have presented here at least the main outlines of a general account of a good life suggested by that work. The account will be a complex one that, among the main philosophical theories distinguished earlier, probably most comfortably fits within ideal theories. I have suggested that we can employ Sen's construction of a plurality of independent vectors, each of which is an independent component of a full assessment of the degree to which a person has a good life.

The ethical frameworks for medical treatment decision making bring out the centrality of a person's capacity as a valuing agent, or what I have called self-determination, in a good life. The capacity for and exercise of self-determination can be taken to be a—or I believe *the*—fundamental ideal of the person within medical ethics. The exercise of self-determination in constructing a relatively full human life will require in an individual four broad types of primary functions: biological, including, for example, well-functioning organs; physical, including, for example, ambulation; social, including, for example, capacities to communicate; mental, including, for example, a variety of reasoning and emotional capabilities. There are no sharp boundaries between these broad types of primary function, and for different purposes they can be specified in more or less detail and in a variety of different bundles. The idea is to pick out human functions that are necessary for, or at least valuable in, the pursuit of nearly all relatively full and complete human life plans. These different functions can be represented on different vectors and they will be normatively objective components of a good life, though their relative weight within any particular life may be subjectively determined.

There are in turn what we can call agent-specific functions, again specifiable at varying levels of generality or detail, which are necessary for a person to pursue successfully the particular purposes and life plan he or she has chosen: examples are functional capacities to do highly abstract reasoning of the sort required in mathematics or philosophy and the physical dexterity needed for success as a musician, surgeon, or athlete. Once again, these functions can be represented on independent vectors, though their place in the good life for a particular person is determined on more normatively subjective grounds depending on the particular life plan chosen. The relative weight assigned to agent-specific functions and, to a substantially lesser degree, to primary functions, will ultimately be determined by the valuations of the self-determining agent, together with factual determinations of what functions are necessary in the pursuit of different specific life plans. The centrality of the valuing and choosing agent in this account of a good life gives both primary and, to a lesser extent, agent-specific functional capacities a central place in the good life because of their necessary role in making possible a significant range of opportunities and alternatives for choice.

At a more agent-specific level still are the particular desires pursued by people on particular occasions in the course of pursuing their valued aims and activities. Different desires and the degree to which they can be successfully satisfied can also be represented using the vector approach. It bears repeating that the level of a person's primary functional capacities, agent-specific functional capacities, and satisfaction of specific desires will all depend both on properties of the agent and on features of his or her environment that affect those functional capacities and desire pursuits. The inclusion of primary functions, agent-specific functions, and the satisfaction of specific desires all within an account of the good life allows us to recognize both its normatively objective and normatively subjective components. Analogously, these various components show why we can expect partial, but only partial, interpersonal comparability of the quality of life or of good lives—comparability will require interpersonal overlapping of similarly weighted primary functions, agent-specific functions, and specific desires. The importance of functional capacities at these different levels of generality reflects the centrality of personal choice in a good life and the necessity for a choice of alternatives and opportunities.

Finally, there will be the hedonic or happiness component of a good life, that aspect that represents a person's subjective, conscious response in terms of enjoyments and satisfactions to the life he or she has chosen and the activities and achievements it contains. These may be representable on a single vector or on a number of distinct vectors if the person has distinct and incommensurable satisfactions and enjoyments. Happiness will usually be only partially dependent on the person's relative success in satisfying his or her desires and broader aims and projects. Once again, it is the valuations of the specific person in question that will determine the relative weight the happiness vector receives in the overall account of a good life for that person.

Needless to say, in drawing together these features of an account of the quality of life or of a good life from the medical ethics and health policy literatures, I have done no more than sketch a few of the barest bones of a full account of a good life. However, even these few bones suggest the need for more complex accounts of the quality of life than are often employed in programs designed to improve the quality of life of real people.

ENDNOTES

1. What I call ideal theories are what Parfit (2) calls "objective list" theories. I prefer the label "ideal theories," because what is usually distinctive about this kind of theory is its proposal of specific, normative ideals of the person.

2. For a more philosophically sophisticated analysis of the concept of health that also construes it in functional terms as a natural, biological norm not involving value judgments, see Boorse (12,13). One of the most useful collections of papers on concepts of health is Caplan et al. (14).

3. I make no attempt here to provide any more than a few representative references to this very large literature. Probably the single best source for the medical ethics literature in this area is the *Hastings Center Report*. In the medical literature, see Wanzer et al. (15) and Ruark et al. (16). For a good review of most of the principal legal decisions in the United States concerning life-sustaining treatment, see Annas and Glantz (17). The most influential treatment of these issues by a governmental body in the United States is the report of the President's Commission for the Study of Ethical Problems in Medicine and Biomedical and Behavioral Research (18). See also the recent report by the Hastings Center (19). For discussions of living wills and durable powers of attorney see Steinbrook and Lo (20), and Schneiderman and Arras (21). An application to clinical practice of the consensus that patients should have rights to decide about their care is given in Jonsen et al. (22).

4. An influential statement of the shared decision-making view is another report of the President's Commission for the Study of Ethical Problems in Medicine and Biomedical and Behavioral Research (23). A sensitive discussion of the difficulties of achieving shared decision-making in clinical practice is found in Katz (24).

5. It has been argued that this is the proper understanding of the distinction between "ordinary" and "extraordinary" treatment. That is, extraordinary treatment is treatment that for the patient in question and in the circumstances that obtain is unduly burdensome (18).

6. The main character in the popular play and subsequent film *Whose Life is it Anyway?,* having become paralyzed from the neck down, displayed this attitude of not wanting to become a person who had adjusted to his condition.

REFERENCES

1. Breslow L. A quantitative approach to the World Health Organization definition of health: physical, mental and social well-being. *Int J Epidemiol* 1972;1:347–355.
2. Parfit D. *Reason and persons.* Oxford: Oxford University Press, 1984.
3. Brock DW. Recent work in utilitarianism. *Am Philos Q* 1973;10:241–376.
4. Griffin J. *Well-being.* Oxford: Oxford University Press, 1986.
5. Goodin R. Laundering preferences. In: Elster J, Hylland A, eds. *Foundations of social choice theory.* Cambridge: Cambridge University Press, 1986.
6. Morreim EH. Computing the quality of life. In: Agich GJ, Begley CE, eds. *The price of health.* Dordrecht: D. Reidel, 1986.
7. Sen A. Plural utility. *Proc Aristotelian Soc* 1980;81:193–218.
8. Sen A. *Commodities and capabilities.* Amsterdam: Elsevier Science, 1985.
9. Sen A. Well-being, agency and freedom: The Dewey Lectures. *J Philos* 1985;82:169–221.
10. Sen A. *The standard of living.* Cambridge: Cambridge University Press, 1987.
11. Kass L. *Toward a more natural science.* New York: Free Press, 1985.
12. Boorse C. On the distinction between disease and illness. *Philos Public Affairs* 1975;5:49–68.
13. Boorse C. Health as a theoretical concept. *Philos Sci* 1977;44.
14. Caplan, AL, et al. *Concepts of health and disease: interdisciplinary perspectives.* Reading, MA: Addison-Wesley, 1981.
15. Wanzer SH, et al. The physicians' responsibility toward hopelessly ill patients. *N Engl J Med* 1984;310:955–959.
16. Ruark JE, et al. Initiating and withdrawing life support. *N Engl J Med* 1988;318:25–30.
17. Annas G, Glantz L. The right of elderly patients to refuse life-sustaining treatment. *Milbank Q* 1986;64(suppl 2):95–162.
18. President's Commission for the Sutdy of Ethical Problems in Medicine and Biomedical and Behavioral Research. *Deciding to forgo life-sustaining treatment.* Washington: US Government Printing Office, 1983.
19. Hastings Center. *Guidelines on the termination of treatment and the care of the dying.* Briarcliff Manor, NY: Hastings Center, 1987.
20. Steinbrook R, Lo B. Decision-making for incompetent patients by designated proxy: California's new law. *N Engl J Med* 1984;310:1598–1601.
21. Schneiderman L, Arras J. Counseling patients to counsel physicians on future care in the event of patients incompetence. *Ann Intern Med* 1985;102:693–698.
22. Jonsen AR, Segler M, Winslade WJ. *Clinical ethics.* New York: Macmillan, 1982.
23. President's Commission for the Study of Ethical Problems in Medicine and Biomedical and Behavioral Research. *Making health care decisions.* Washington: US Government Printing Office, 1982.
24. Katz J. *The silent world of doctor and patient.* New York: Free Press, 1981.
25. Ramsey P. *Ethics at the edge of life.* New Haven: Yale University Press, 1978.
26. Brock DW. The value of prolonging human life. *Philos Studies* 1986;50:401–428.
27. Rango N. The nursing home resident with dementia. *Ann Intern Med* 1985;102:835–841.
28. *Superintendant of Belchertown State School v. Saikewicz.* 1977;370 N.E. 2d 417.
29. Fried C. *An anatomy of values.* Cambridge, MA: Harvard University Press, 1970.
30. Rawls J. *A theory of justice.* Cambridge, MA: Harvard University Press, 1971.
31. Anderson JP, et al. Classifying function for health outcome and quality-of-life evaluation. *Med Care* 1986;24:454–471.
32. Berg RL. Neglected aspects of the quality of life. *Health Serv Res* 1986;21:391–395.
33. Bergner M, et al. The Sickness Impact Profile: conceptual formulation and methodology for the development of a health status measure. *Int J Health Serv* 1976;6:393–415.
34. Calman KC. Quality of life in cancer patients: an hypothesis. *J Med Ethics* 1984;10:124–127.
35. Cohen C. On the quality of life: some philosophical reflections. *Circulation* 1982;66(suppl 3):29–33.
36. Cribb A. Quality of life: a response to K.C. Calman. *J Med Ethics* 1985;11:142–145.
37. Editorial. Assessment of quality of life in clinical trials. *Acta Med Scand* 1986;220:1–3.
38. Edlund M, Tancredi L. Quality of life: an ideological critique. *Perspect Biol Med* 1985;28:591–607.
39. Flanagan JC. Measurement of quality of life: current state of the art. *Arch Phys Rehabil Med* 1982;63:56–59.
40. Gehrmann F. "Valid" empirical measurement of quality of life. *Soc Ind Res* 1978;5:73–109.
41. Gillingham R, Reece WS. Analytical problems in the measurement of the quality of life. *Soc Ind Res* 1980;7:91–101.
42. Grogono AW. Index for measuring health. *Lancet* 1971;2:1024–1026.
43. Guyatt GH, et al. Measuring disease-specific quality of life in clinical trials. *Can Med Assoc J* 1986;134:889–895.
44. Hunt S, McEwen J. The development of a subjective health indicator. *Sociol Health Illness* 1980;2:203–231.
45. Katz S, et al. Studies of illness in the aged. The Index of ADL: a standardized measure of biological and psychosocial function. *JAMA* 1963;185:914–919.
46. Klotkem FJ. Philosophic considerations of quality of life for the disabled. *Arch Phys Rehabil Med* 1982;63:59–63.
47. Kornfeld DS, et al. Psychological and behavioral responses after coronary artery bypass surgery. *Circulation* 1982;66(suppl 3):24–28.
48. Liang M, et al. In search of a more perfect mousetrap (health status or quality of life instrument). *J Rheumatol* 1982;9:775–779.
49. Najman J, Levine S. Evaluating the impact of medical care and techno-

logies on the quality of life: a review and critique. *Soc Sci Med* 1981;15F:107–115.

50. Pearlman R, Speer J. Quality of life considerations in geriatric care. *J Am Geriatr Soc* 1983;31:113–120.

51. Presant CA. Quality of life in cancer patients. *Am J Clin Oncol* 1984;7:571–573.

52. The 1984 Report of the Joint National Committee on Detection, Evaluation, and Treatment of High Blood Pressure. *Arch Intern Med* 1984;144:1045–1057.

53. Starr TJ, et al. Quality of life and resuscitation decisions in elderly patients. *J Gen Intern Med* 1986;1:373–379.

54. Sullivan DF. Conceptual problems in developing an index of health. *Vital Health Stat* 1966;2:1–18.

55. Thomasma, DC. Ethical judgment of quality of life in the care of the aged. *J Am Geriatr Soc* 1984;32:525–527.

56. Thomasma DC. Quality of life, treatment decisions, and medical ethics. *Clin Geriatr Med* 1986;2:17–27.

57. Torrance GW. Social preferences for health states: an empirical evalua-

tion of three measurement techniques. *Socioecon Planning Sci* 1972;10:129–136.

58. Torrance GW. Toward a utility theory foundation for health status index models. *Health Serv Res* 1976;10:129–136.

59. Torrance GW, et al. A utility maximization model for evaluation of health care programs. *Health Serv Res* 1976;6:118–133.

60. Bergner M, et al. The Sickness Impact Profile: development and final revision of a health status measure. *Med Care* 1981;19:787–805.

61. Spitzer WO, et al. Measuring the quality of life of cancer patients: a concise QL-index for use by physicians. *J Chronic Dis* 1981;34:585–597.

62. Evans RW. The quality of life of patients with end stage renal disease. *N Engl J Med* 1985;312:553–559.

63. Daniels N. *Just health care.* Cambridge: Cambridge University Press, 1985.

64. Elster J. Sour grapes: utilitarianism and the genesis of wants. In Sen A, Williams B, eds. *Utilitarianism and beyond.* Cambridge: Cambridge University Press, 1982.

Quality of Life and Pharmacoeconomics in Clinical Trials, Second Edition, edited by B. Spilker.
Lippincott-Raven Publishers, Philadelphia © 1996.

CHAPTER 53

Cultural Considerations

Thomas M. Johnson

INTRODUCTION

The 1980s saw a rapid growth in the area of quality of life research. Studies encompassing a multitude of cultures currently are being conducted by developmental aid agencies, health care facilities, and university scholars, among others. These studies focus on issues having an impact on quality of life, such as overpopulation, poverty, disaster relief, urbanization, industrialization, migration, and immunization campaigns. Publications like the *Journal of Social Indicators Research* and the *Quality of Life Newsletter* reflect increased interest in quality of life, and provide a common forum for cross-cultural exchange of ideas about all aspects of quality of life research.

Due to developing global interests in this area of research, the need for culturally sensitive methods to assess quality of life has never been greater. Researchers are increasingly asking whether a method used to assess quality of life in culture A can also be used in culture B. Although some researchers may desire a scale or similar instrument for global assessment of cultures, permitting comparison of the "nature" of one culture with another (or the views of an individual from one culture with someone from another), no such scale exists. In fact, given the multiplicity of variables or domains comprising a culture, that goal is unrealistic, both theoretically and methodologically.

This does not mean, however, that researchers should abandon attempts to include cultural variables in quality of life assessments. In fact, greater effort should be expended in considering cultural issues. Before culturally sensitive methods can be developed, however, the relationship between culture and quality of life must be understood. This chapter (a) introduces concepts necessary to understand the relationship between quality of life and culture, (b) discusses the advantages and disadvantages of different types of quality of life measures, and (c) proposes an approach that includes the cultural considerations essential when developing or modifying quality of life assessment instruments for effective use in multicultural settings.

ANTHROPOLOGICAL VIEWS OF CULTURE

The term *culture* is used as a scientific concept by all of the social sciences. There is still no single accepted definition of culture. In cultural anthropology, culture is generally defined as a shared conception and perception of reality that is socially transmitted to succeeding generations. Culture also includes norms that regulate behavior and result in distinctive roles that define *society* as the organization and interaction of people. In short, culture includes learned and shared ways of interpreting the world and interacting in society, and thereby provides all individuals with ideas about what is relevant or irrelevant, valued or devalued, in life.

Each member of society has multiple social roles. The sum total of these roles makes up an individual's status in society. An example of an individual's social roles may include husband, father, accountant, parishioner, and friend. In each role, individuals have expectations placed on them as to how to act toward others. Roles are prescribed by society, thus social interaction is based on a culture-specific

T. M. Johnson: Family Medicine Program, School of Primary Medical Care, University of Alabama, Huntsville, Alabama 35801.

consensus concerning the appropriateness of actions, ideals, or expectations of a person in a given status.

Contemporary societies are very diverse. That is to say, even though the members of a society share the same culture, they still may have radically different experiences and beliefs concerning quality of life. A society may appear to be an identifiable homogeneous group when viewed superficially from outside, yet when examined systematically from within, actually appears to be quite heterogeneous. Such ''plural'' societies consist of smaller groups that are recognized as distinctive by members of the society. Examples of smaller groups are individuals with common occupation, wealth, religious affiliation, ethnic background, age, geographic location, and ideology. These groups sometimes are so distinctive in relation to the rest of society (e.g., cults, youth gangs, ethnic communities) that they are considered to be outside the larger group or society, although many of their views and values may be similar to the larger group. This complex cultural ecology challenges researchers both theoretically and methodologically (1).

Quality of life perceptions by any group or individual are to a large extent ''culture bound.'' In other words, standards for evaluating quality of life vary dramatically from society to society or within a society depending on their particular culture. Unwary or unskilled researchers studying quality of life cross-culturally may be victims of *ethnocentrism*—the interpretation of the behavior of others in terms of one's own personal feelings, which likewise are powerfully shaped by cultural values. In terms of quality of life, ethnocentrism is the enemy of understanding. To assess quality of life in a culturally sensitive way, researchers must adopt the tenet of cultural relativism, the practice of analyzing beliefs and behaviors in the context of the culture in which they belong. Cultural relativism would suggest that although there are values that are universally accorded recognition (such as food and shelter), there are no absolute standards of quality of life that can be indiscriminately applied to all cultures.

QUALITY OF LIFE ASSESSMENT

There are two approaches a researcher can use to assess quality of life: objective and subjective. The differences between the two are substantial, and choosing one over the other has important implications for the research conducted. Before one approach is chosen the researcher must be aware explicitly of the scope of the project and its goals for measuring quality of life. All research efforts are constrained by logistics and funding, but a project's goals should determine which approach to quality of life assessment is chosen.

The objective approach assumes that health, physical environment, income, housing, and other observable and quantifiable indicators are valid measures of quality of life and that there are absolute standards for assessing these variables that are used to determine or define quality of life. On the surface, an objective method for assessing quality of life

seems logical. After all, there are dimensions of life that people require and/or value, such as food, shelter, mobility, and good health.

Certainly there are minimal levels of nutrition compatible with life, and there are evaluation technologies (at the individual level, such as dietary intake logs, and at the group level such as per capita food production) to assess nutritional levels as one facet of quality of life. In addition, it is possible to assess amount of square feet of living space per person, presence of running water and plumbing, and the like as measures of adequacy of shelter. It is also possible to determine the amount of migration through census data, case studies, and other techniques. Looking at job, income, and housing changes may be used to assess social mobility. There are also standard data sources for health care utilization and surveys can glean data about the type of health care available and/or accessible for given populations.

Many of these objective measures may be misleading, however. Stability and predictability of food supply may be far more important for quality of life than absolute per capita protein/caloric intake. Cultures vary widely in the type of housing that is available and desirable, and the extent to which privacy is a salient dimension of quality of life. In many parts of the world population density is very high, yet privacy is also high due to both the nature of housing construction and the norms of interaction within living spaces; conversely, in other cultures population density is low, yet normal patterns of interaction preclude privacy. For many people in other cultures, privacy is not even a meaningful concept. To be sure, running water and adequate sanitation have been associated with reduced morbidity and mortality around the world, yet the social consequences of, for example, closing centralized water wells and discouraging communal use of natural waterways for bathing or washing clothes may be perceived as reducing quality of life because of disrupted traditional patterns of social interaction. Although migration is now a ubiquitous feature of life in many cultures, and many may assume that migration is uniformly disruptive in quality of life terms, it is clear that forced migration is more deleterious than voluntary migration. Social mobility may also be used as a measure of quality of life, but upward social mobility may not be uniformly positive. Studies indicate that the first generation of upwardly mobile people suffers more adverse health consequences, and family disruption is common. On the other hand, in the face of so-called blocked mobility, where a group that may be relatively affluent by world standards is excluded from opportunities for social and economic advancement, the group may perceive that its quality of life is suboptimal. The freedom to practice religion may be considered indicative of high quality of life, but religious pluralism or totalitarianism, particularly when it is associated with systematic social discrimination (such as in Northern Ireland) can have very adverse effects on quality of life.

Clearly, objective quality of life criteria such as nutrition, population density, housing, sanitation, migration, social mobility, and religious practices, will be different in different cultures because they are inextricably linked to less objective aspects of culture such as values, attitudes, and ideology. Without an understanding of the values and beliefs of a population, and of how those values and beliefs are manifested in individual people, the weighting and priority attached to any life area is arbitrary. Consequently any naive assertion as to the quality of life of a group or individual based on the above criteria alone is of questionable validity. Criteria such as income, health, food, and shelter as evaluated in one cultural context cannot necessarily be relied on to measure quality of life in another culture.

In the literature using objective approaches to quality of life assessment, there have been several problems involving disagreement about which indicators are relevant, and lack of understanding of the association between objective conditions of life and the subjective perception of these conditions (2). Inconsistencies occur between and even within studies. For example, in one study of the quality of life in different United States cities, little correlation exists among the variables used to assess the quality of life of these areas. Thus a city could score high in living conditions and low in measures such as racial discrimination, crime rate, and cost of living. The failure to find highly correlated variables suggests that the measures employed are not addressing a common, underlying dimension of life experience.

Finally, a number of studies have already demonstrated that objective conditions of life are only tenuously related to the subjective experience of quality of life (3–7). One such study indicates that people who are disabled because of an accident may report happiness levels that are surprisingly high and even comparable to people who are not disabled (8,9). Similarly, Campbell et al. (7) found that older blacks in the United States report higher levels of happiness than older whites despite their inferior objective living conditions. Further, it has been shown that women express a greater fear of violent assault compared with men despite the objective reality that men are more likely to be victims of violent assaults (10).

These studies and many others raise substantial doubt about the utility of objective quality of life indicators. Studies that use only objective quality of life measures simply project researchers' own values and priorities onto their subjects, contributing little to understanding of quality of life experience. Stated another way, objective measures do not assess the quality of life, but rather the quantity of life.

Subjective Approaches

Subjective approaches attempt to assess people's qualitative perceptions of life experiences. Such approaches must consider more idiosyncratic evaluations on the part of people, and do not link quality of life to absolute or standard variables; rather, they assess people's feelings regarding quality of life. Subjective studies have identified a number of existential dimensions that seem to be linked to a high quality of life, including (a) positive social relationships, (b) stability and conformity to a set of role expectations, and (c) minimal disparity between expectations and achievements.

As an example of positive social relationships affecting quality of life, numerous studies have found that positive subjective descriptions of marital and familial relationships are the best predictors of high quality of life assessment (4,6,7,11). Conversely, people who are widowed, divorced, and separated express lower life satisfaction (12–15). As an example of the effect of stability of role expectations on quality of life, another study found that American women who were brought up earlier in this century, and therefore who have more traditional views, express levels of satisfaction with their roles as homemakers comparable to that of men in respect to their occupations. However, younger women whose socialization and role expectations differ from the older cohort express less satisfaction with housekeeping activities (16). A related study indicates that younger women who now are able to choose between homemaking roles and outside work are happier than those who feel that they have no choice (12). Still other studies have shown that level of life satisfaction is related to disparity between one's goals and achievements (17). To the extent that people are successful in achieving the goals they set for themselves at different life stages, they will more likely report higher quality of life.

Quality of Life Assessment in Medical Research

Quality of life assessment is now becoming more important in the evaluation of medical care, particularly since medical interventions increasingly are designed to help people cope with chronic health problems and diminished functional capacity, rather than simply to cure acute conditions and restore people to their prior level of functioning. This is also true in the case of mental health care where deinstitutionalization has placed many people with diminished adaptive capacity in community settings. In either case, it is clear that the presence or absence of disease (measurable biophysiological abnormality) is not as important in predicting quality of life as is illness (the subjective psychological and social distress caused by symptoms) (18). In fact, approximately 50% of patients with symptom complaints in primary health care settings have no demonstrable physical disease, and are often referred to as the "worried well" (19–22). Conversely, people with hypertension may have disease, yet have no subjective sense of being sick; in fact, the problem with treating hypertension is that in curing the disease (through use of medications), subjective quality of life often suffers because patients feel worse than when they were "diseased." Health care workers and quality of life researchers alike need to be aware of this distinction between objective (disease) and subjective (illness) dimensions of sickness.

In short, by utilizing subjective measures to assess quality of life, individual, social, and cultural factors are automatically included in the analysis, since individuals' subjective experiences result from complex interaction of variables at all three levels. Unfortunately, a review published in 1988 indicated that 41% of the quality of life studies analyzed used only objective measures, despite the fact that subjective measures have produced more consistent findings than did the objective measures (23). Although 41% may appear high, it represents an important increase in utilization of subjective measures, because a 1981 review in the same journal found that 87% of the studies used only objective assessment techniques (2). Guidelines for developing cross-cultural instruments have proliferated recently (24,25).

CANTRIL SELF-ANCHORING STRIVING SCALE

The most accurate manner in which to assess quality of life is subjective because objective categories, which reflect bias on the part of the researcher, are not valid measures cross-culturally or between social groups. Ironically, as we have discussed above, measures that are purported to be objective are actually based on the subjective opinions of the researchers. The process of translating instruments for use in cross-national quality of life investigations is, itself, problematic (26–28). There is a great need, especially in medical research and practice, for a method to assess quality of life that collects comparable and quantifiable data without imposing culture-specific standards. Such a method must also have a high degree of flexibility, being adaptable for use in many different situations. A quality of life approach is needed that can be applied in highly diverse areas of medicine. It is necessary to measure a person's response and progress in therapy, whether treatment is psychological, pharmacological, somatic, or a combination of these. The Cantril Self-Anchoring Striving Scale can be used as a quality of life assessment method that is capable of fulfilling the above criteria. This scale is a simple, widely applicable method for tapping the unique ''reality'' of each individual, that has been translated into 26 different languages and found to have a reliability coefficient of .95 (13). It is extremely versatile, and can be used to assess global perceptions of quality of life. This scale can also be used to elicit subjective assessments of very specific aspects of life, such as housing, nutrition, health care, treatment outcomes, and the like.

The Cantril Self-Anchoring Striving Scale is based on a model of a ladder with ten rungs (Fig. 1), with the top rung representing ''the best possible _____'' and the bottom representing ''the worst possible _____'' for the research subject or patient. To do a global quality of life assessment, the blank should be completed to form general statements such as, ''the best possible life for you,'' or ''the most successful outcome for you.'' For assessment of more specific variables, the blanks should be completed to form statements like ''the best possible housing situation,'' ''the best

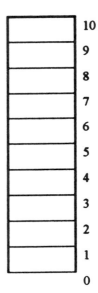

FIG. 1. Cantril Self-Anchoring Striving Scale.

possible treatment outcome,'' or ''the most satisfactory diet.'' The quality of life researcher simply asks patients to rate ''where you are on the ladder currently'' and ''where you were [some period of time ago],'' and may also choose to ask ''where you think you will be [some period of time in the future].'' Then the researcher simply asks, ''What reasons do you have for putting yourself on [whatever rung]?'' In this ''self-anchoring'' approach, each individual defines quality of life based on his or her own assumptions, perceptions, aspirations, and values relative to the two extremes, or anchoring points. This self-defined continuum is then used as the measuring device. The scale can be used as either a pre–post or retrospective assessment of a clinical or community-level intervention.

In analyzing data from the Cantril Self-Anchoring Striving Scale, quantitative change scores can be computed to evaluate the impact of any interventions on quality of life. Mean quality of life levels can also be computed, although this is of less value. Qualitatively, it is then necessary to conduct content, cluster, or domain analysis of responses to the reasons people give for putting themselves on certain rungs of the ladder.

It must be stressed that the Cantril Self-Anchoring Striving Scale is a technique used to elicit information and a scale used to record and quantify it. It is not an index with a set of *a priori* criteria used to evaluate an individual. To utilize the scale, only one question needs to be designed to elicit information on each quality of life issue to be assessed. The questions used to qualify the numerical responses from the scale are extremely important. It is not enough for clinicians to conduct research on a particular area, for example, aphasia, and to devise questions. Open-ended questions must be used when asking patients to discuss why they gave their numerical responses (rungs on the ladder); only this type of question can elicit patient concerns about aphasia, which may be quite different from clinician concerns. One study found that when three groups (one of rehabilitation clinicians and two of aphasic patients) generated separate lists of situations in which communication problems occur, the patient groups' lists were much more similar to each other's than to the clinicians' lists (29). Moreover, the clinicians vastly underestimated the patient's focus on social concerns. In addition, the patients generated more concrete situations, which are useful to quality of life research. This study suggests that previous quality of life measures that have relied solely on clinical judgment for determination of their content may inadequately represent patient, and therefore cultural, values.

The benefits of using quality of life as both a measurement and a rehabilitation tool in clinical therapy are enormous, as long as the patients' subjective assessments are considered. It is theoretically possible for a clinician-generated index that assesses an aphasic patient's quality of life to reflect a response to therapy, while an index using the Cantril Self-Anchoring Striving Scale may show a reduced or unimproved quality of life. This is because clinicians typically rate quality of life improvement in aphasia based on ability to speak, whereas patients are more concerned with the perceived social benefits of being better able to speak.

CONCLUSIONS

A subjective approach should be used in any quality of life research project and, when applicable, objective measures should also be employed. It is only through the use of a subjective measure of quality of life that a patient's implicit cultural and personal values can be included in the assessment. Objective measures are often purported to be cross-culturally valid; however, they are only valid in the most general sense. Objective measures do not account for subcultural differences in perceptions of quality of life. In addition, although a certain group shares the same culture, the individuals of the group still have widely varying personal beliefs and values. Thus, while an objective assessment instrument may be valuable for assessing general quality of life issues for the cultural group, it is unable to assess the feelings and concerns regarding quality of life for a particular patient. With the subjective Cantril Self-Anchoring Striving Scale approach described, it is possible to account both for the broader values of the group and also for the idiosyncratic concerns and values of the individual.

ACKNOWLEDGMENT

I would like to acknowledge the research, typing, and editing skills of Melodie Drewyor, Research Assistant in the University of Alabama in Huntsville's School of Primary Medical Care, Family Medicine Department, in the preparation of this chapter.

REFERENCES

1. Sasao T, Sue S. Toward a culturally anchored ecological framework of research in ethnic-cultural communities. *Am J Community Psychol* 1993;21:705–727.
2. Najman JM, Levine S. Evaluating the impact of medical care and technologies on the quality of life: a review and critique. *Soc Sci Med* 1981;15F:107–115.
3. Palmore E, Luikart C. Health and social factors related to life satisfaction. *J Health Soc Behav* 1972;13:68–80.
4. Bharadwaj L, Wilening EA. The prediction of perceived well-being. *Soc Indicat Res* 1977;4.
5. Larson R. Thirty years of research on the subjective well-being of older Americans. *J Gerontol* 1978;33(1):109–25.
6. Wilkening EA, McGranahan D. Correlates of subjective well-being in Northern Wisconsin. *Soc Indicat Res* 1978;5.
7. Campbell A, Converse PE, Rodgers WL. *The quality of American life.* New York: Russell Sage, 1976.
8. Bulman RJ, Wortman CB. Attributions of blame and coping in the "real world": severe accident victims react to their lot. *J Pers Soc Psychol* 1977;35(5):357–363.
9. Brickman P, Coates D, Janoff-Bulman R. Lottery winners and accident victims: Is happiness relative? *J Pers Soc Psychol* 1978;36(8):917—927.
10. Mason R, Faulkenberry GD. Aspirations, achievements and life satisfaction. *Soc Indicat Res* 1978;5.
11. Weaver CN. Job satisfaction as a component of happiness among males and females. *Pers Psychol* 1978;31(4):831–840.
12. Orden SR, Blackburn NM. Dimensions of marriage happiness. *Am J Sociol* 1968;73:715–731.
13. Bradburn NM, Caplovitz D. *Reports on happiness.* Chicago: Aldine, 1965.
14. Glenn ND. The contribution of marriage to the psychological well-being of males and females. *J Marr Fam* 1975;37(3):594–600.
15. Near JP, Rice RW, Hunt RG. Work and extra-work correlates of life and job satisfaction. *Acad Manage J* 1978;21(2):248–264.
16. Rodgers WL. Work status and the quality of life. *Soc Indicat Res* 1977;4.
17. Cantril H. *The patterns of human concerns.* New York: University Press, 1966.
18. Kleinman A, Eisenberg L, Good B. Culture, illness, and care: clinical lessons from anthropologic and cross-cultural research. *Ann Intern Med* 1978;88:251–258.
19. Hilkevitch A. Psychiatric disturbances in outpatients of a general medical outpatient clinic. *Int J Neuropsych* 1965;1.
20. Lipsitt DR. Psychodynamic considerations of hypochondrias. *Psychother Psychosom* 1974;88.
21. Katon W, Ries R, Kleinman A. The prevalence of somatization in primary care. *Compr Psychiatry* 1984;25(3):309–314.
22. Cummings NA. The dismantling of our health system: strategies for survival of psychological practice. *Am Psychol* 1986;41(4):426–431.
23. Hollandsworth JG. Evaluating the impact of medical treatment on the quality of life: a 5-year update. *Soc Sci Med* 1988;26:425–434.
24. Bullinger M, Anderson R, Cella D, Aaronson N. Developing and evaluating cross-cultural instruments from minimum requirements to optimal models. *Qual Life Res* 1993;2:451–459.
25. Cella DF, Wiklund I, Shumaker SA, Aaronson NK. Integrating health-related quality of life into cross-national clinical trials. *Qual Life Res* 1993;2:433–440.
26. Guillemin F, Bombardier C, Beaton D. Cross-cultural adaptation of health-related quality of life measures: literature review and proposed guidelines. *J Clin Epidemiol* 1993;46:1417–1432.
27. Guyatt GH. The philosophy of health-related quality of life translation. *Qual Life Res* 1993;2:461–465.
28. Naughton MJ, Wiklund I. A critical review of dimension-specific measures of health-related quality of life in cross-cultural research. *Qual Life Res* 1993;2:397–432.
29. Lomas J, Pickard L, Mohide A. Patient versus clinician item generation for quality-of-life measures. *Med Care* 1987;25.

Quality of Life and Pharmacoeconomics in Clinical Trials, Second Edition, edited by B. Spilker.
Lippincott-Raven Publishers, Philadelphia © 1996.

CHAPTER 54

The Role of Quality of Life Assessments in Medical Practice

Albert W. Wu and Kathleen A. Cagney

INTRODUCTION

Current medical practice is largely disease and problem focused, concentrating on the diagnosis and treatment of anatomic and physiologic abnormalities. Underlying this approach is the assumption that physiologic parameters most accurately reflect the patient's health, and that when a patient's disease is "better," his or her quality of life will also be better. However, physiologic measures are imperfect surrogates for good outcomes. The poor correlation between physiologic tests and patient-reported outcomes has been demonstrated repeatedly (1,2). Two patients with comparable disease states may differ greatly in how they are able to function, and improvements in physiologic findings may not be accompanied by improvements in functional status or emotional state.

The desire to gain understanding not only into what treatment regimes increase longevity but also provide for a better and more manageable existence has led researchers to develop a variety of measures to capture quality of life information. Health-related quality of life, encompassing dimensions of health status that are directly experienced by the person, such as physical functioning, mental health, social and role functioning, and symptoms, has enjoyed increased attention in clinical research and policy making. Health status measures play an increasingly important role in defining the effectiveness of treatments in outcomes research and clinical trials.

Practicing physicians know that it is not enough to monitor biologic parameters, and implicitly assess general psychological and social well-being. However, data on functional problems or emotional status are not systematically collected. This traditional emphasis may cause the clinician to overlook problems with function and other aspects of quality of life. For example, physicians often fail to recognize functional disability in ambulatory patients (3–5), and frequently fail to recognize depression (6,7). In managing a patient, a physician may prescribe an appropriate dose of insulin for a patient with diabetes, but fail to recognize that the patient is unable to prepare his own meals.

Incomplete knowledge about the effectiveness of treatments or practices can lead to uncertainty about the best course of action in a given clinical situation. Although increasingly studies of efficacy (how a treatment works in ideal circumstances) and effectiveness (how a treatment works under ordinary conditions) include quality of life outcomes, many important studies have often omitted quality of life outcomes. For example, in a recent clinical trial comparing foscarnet to ganciclovir in the treatment of cytomegalovirus retinitis, quality of life was not included as an outcome variable, making it harder to judge which treatment is preferable.

Less is known about the efficacy of common diagnostic tests, such as endoscopy versus upper gastrointestinal series for patients with dyspepsia. Still less is known about the

A. W. Wu and K. A. Cagney: Health Services Research and Development Center, Johns Hopkins University, Baltimore, Maryland 21205.

use of these tests in combination or used repeatedly, such as the efficacy of repeated magnetic resonance imaging scans for patients with persistent headache. Almost nothing is known about the efficacy of cognitive and interpersonal services such as listening to or reassuring patients. Since less is known about effectiveness than efficacy, it is not surprising that practicing physicians face considerable uncertainty. Practicing physicians receive little feedback about the kinds of outcomes they achieve, and how these outcomes compare to those of practitioners. Widespread adoption of a model of shared decision making, in which patients actively participate in the choice of treatment, has also increased the emphasis on patient preferences for risks and outcomes.

In this chapter, we examine whether and how patient-reported measures can be used by the clinician to answer questions about health-related quality of life and explore methods to help the clinician identify and effectively manage important functional and emotional problems.

Specifically, this chapter addresses the following issues:

current applications of health status measures in clinical practice;
barriers to the use of these measures in patient management and clinical care;
implications for use of these measures in clinical practice; and
potential for future work in the field.

APPLICATIONS OF HEALTH STATUS MEASURES

To some extent, health status measures have been integrated in the clinical practice of psychiatry, rheumatology, geriatrics, and in nursing, where they are often referred to as scores, indexes, stages, classes, systems, or criteria. Clinicians commonly use the Apgar score to rate the clinical condition of a newborn baby (8). Primary care physicians may use the CAGE (9) questionnaire to screen for alcohol dependency, or the mini–mental status examination (10) to screen for dementia. Cardiologists and other physicians may use the New York Heart Association Functional Classification (11), but most often only use it if the patient is the worst class (IV). Oncologists frequently use the Karnofsky Performance Status (12) in studies to stratify and select patients, and as an outcome variable to describe the patient's ability to work, to carry out normal activities without assistance, and to care for personal needs. Clinicians often ask patients to describe the intensity of their pain on a unidimensional 1–10 scale. Nurses use scales of Activities of Daily Living (13) to report the functional ability or actual performance of the patient, while occupational and physical therapists assess functional capacity or potential performance of a patient.

In the above applications, health status measures are rarely central to evaluation and treatment. However, as Table 1 illustrates, health status measures have the potential to be

TABLE 1. *Health status measures used in medical applications*

Applications	Examples
Screening/detection of unrecognized disease	The Dartmouth COOP Charts
Planning of treatment/ decision making	Decision analysis Shared decision-making program SUPPORT prognostic model for functional status
Longitudinal monitoring of individual patients	SF-36 in end-stage renal disease
Quality of care	Managed Health Care Association Outcomes Management Project

used in screening, planning patient care, monitoring progress and outcomes of management, and describing the health of groups of patients in evaluating the quality of care.

Screening/Detection of Unrecognized Disease

An important deficiency in current medical practice is an incomplete data base in areas that lie outside the realm of biomedicine. A major strength of health status assessment is the potential to bring to the health care data base precise information not currently there (14)—in a sense extending the current review of systems.

Health status measures may be used in clinical practice as the first step in a multistage diagnostic screening process. They can act as flags both for functional and emotional problems or limitations that might necessitate further exploration.

One example of this role is being tested in the Dartmouth COOP Project (15). The Dartmouth COOP charts are single items consisting of a simple title, a question asking about status over the past 4 weeks, and five ordinal response choices, illustrated by a drawing. In one study, the COOP charts are self-administered as part of the data collection routine of ambulatory practices and, along with additional vital signs, are placed in the patient's chart at the time of the visit (5). In one arm of the assessment, physicians are given a resource book suggesting action to take when scores are low. For example, if a patient reports a low physical functioning score, the resource book might suggest a physical therapy evaluation. Preliminary results suggest that of the 25% of patients in whom the charts uncovered new information, changes in clinical management were initiated in 40% of them (5).

In an international feasibility study of the COOP charts in primary care practices, most practitioners felt the charts were clinically useful, often had a positive effect on patient-physician communication, and were easy for the patient to understand and complete (16). One physician reported that a patient was able to "admit to mild depression" which he had not mentioned before the encounter.

Planning of Treatment/Decision Making

Physicians and patients are often faced with choices among different treatment options for a given condition: weighing the benefit of surgery versus more palliative approaches, deciding whether to act or wait when embarking upon a new treatment path, choosing the appropriate medication, or making end-of-life decisions. Collection of data on health status and preferences, and interpretation of the resulting scores, can help both patient and clinician lay out and understand the implications of treatment alternatives. Examples of applications include formal decision analysis, shared decision-making programs, and prognostic modeling of functional status.

Decision Analysis

To make an informed choice among possible treatments, a patient who wishes to be involved in decision making should have information about the likely outcomes of each strategy (17). Relevant outcomes may include both survival and aspects of health status. Given information about the likelihood of different outcomes, the patient can decide on the preferred set of outcomes. The choice of medication or the option of surgery can often be communicated to a patient via the probability of complications, side effects, and the chance of recovery. In some cases a formal exercise such as a decision analysis can help the patient express his or her values (18). The innovation is that this process is formalized, with a rigorous determination of patient preferences and the subsequent recording of these findings.

Shared Decision-Making Programs

The shared decision-making programs are based on twin objectives for outcomes research: finding what works and then finding what patients want. The programs use an interactive personal computer–based/laser disk multimedia format to present patient-specific probabilities of possible outcomes of the treatment alternatives to improve understanding of the patient's preference.

Before viewing, the patient completes a questionnaire detailing symptom levels, functional status, quality of life, and general health. This information is entered into the computer to configure the program which provides data specific to the patient's symptom levels and health status. The program incorporates data from outcome studies to calculate probabilities of outcomes. Vicarious understanding of what these outcomes mean in real terms is improved by video interviews with patients who have experienced the benefits or harms of treatment.

The first program dealt with treatment alternatives for benign prostatic hyperplasia, including surgical techniques, medical treatment, and watchful waiting, and was based in part on data from the prostate PORT (Patient Outcomes

Research Team) (19). Programs are now available for low back pain, mild hypertension, breast cancer treatment (the surgery decision and adjuvant therapy (20)).

The SUPPORT Prognostic Model for Functional Status

In recent years, accurate prognostic models have been developed (21) that could help clinicians, patients, and families make decisions for the critically ill. Prognostic information about functional status would help people weigh the merits of life-sustaining therapy and plan for supportive care. In SUPPORT (the Study to Understand Prognoses and Preferences for Outcomes and Risks of Treatments), a large multicenter study of outcomes and decision making for seriously ill hospitalized adults, investigators developed a model using admission data (chart and interview based) to estimate the probability of severe functional limitation 2 months after hospitalization (22). The intervention phase of SUPPORT evaluated the impact of prognostic information and enhanced communication. Patients whose physicians were assigned to the intervention group were provided with prognostic data on survival and future functional status.

Longitudinal Monitoring of Individual Patients

Collection of health status and quality of life measures over time can provide the opportunity to track both changes and rates of changes in patient outcomes. Health status instruments can provide a mechanism to collect these data at regular intervals. Automated health status assessment offers the opportunity to summarize, store, and retrieve information that previously only existed in fragmentary, usually handwritten, notes.

SF-36 in End-Stage Renal Disease

Over the past 3 years, a group of nephrologists have used the SF-36 Health Survey (23) to assess the self-reported health of patients on chronic hemodialysis. They are attempting to use the data as a screen for problems, and to understand the patient's clinical course (24).

Preliminary results suggest that regular administration in the hemodialysis unit is feasible and that interpretations enhance the collective understanding of the dialysis team. Changes in patterns sometimes suggest that the patient was either more or less impaired than the team would otherwise have thought. Serial measurements of health status allow recognition of patterns of individual response, with changes that frequently exceed the 95% confidence intervals for group level scores.

Patients have commented that they describe their health more fully on the SF-36 than in conversations with dialysis staff. The investigators also commented that in retrospect they had overestimated their ability to assess functional status implicitly in the course of the routine clinical encounter.

They noted that scores have also been useful for screening. For example, in one patient, SF-36 scores brought hip pain to the team's attention for the first time. In addition, mental health scores have come to be regarded as data to be considered in approach to possible depression.

Quality of Care

Health status measures can be used to evaluate the quality of care for a particular condition across population groups. This information can then be used to provide data about where variations in practice exist, and where there are opportunities to improve practice. Monitoring patient outcomes also has the potential to help physicians learn what kind of outcomes they are achieving.

Managed Health Care Association Outcomes Management Project

An attempt to collect and share comparable data using a standardized protocol is being conducted by the Managed Health Care Association's Outcomes Management Project, a consortium of major employers and their managed care organizations. A pilot test to determine the feasibility of measuring meaningful outcomes was initiated for two patient populations: (a) individuals with asthma, and (b) patients undergoing coronary angiography. Patients completed a questionnaire on current health status, past health events, and ratings of care. Three months later the patient was again asked to complete a questionnaire to obtain information on changes in health status, service utilization, and satisfaction with care. Preliminary results suggested that patient questionnaires appeared to provide reliable and valid assessments of aspects of patients' health, and that these data could be used to provide risk-adjusted outcomes. A current, larger scale study of asthma is beginning to provide useful data to evaluate the quality of care within and across managed care organizations, which should spur future quality improvement efforts (25).

BARRIERS TO USE

While there may be both the need for health status measures in clinical practice and the existing tools necessary to complete such a task, adoption by providers is hindered by both theoretical and practical concerns.

In general, clinicians believe that they have always evaluated the health status of their patients on an ongoing basis (26). They may not be convinced that formalizing data collection for health status will measurably improve outcomes nor that collection of health-related quality of life data will provide information that they are trained to act upon. Even

if they are willing to consider use of health status measures in practice, the current lack of standardization may frustrate some providers both in selecting measures and acting on the results. Information, particularly information not tailored to a particular practice environment, will not by itself change physician behavior (4,6,27).

Conceptually, differences from traditional modes of clinical data collection and interpretation may make health status assessment methods seem unappealing. Health status measures include some concepts that physicians may consider to be outside the bounds of clinical care. The subjective nature of this data may inspire skepticism and unfamiliar data collection instruments may cause concern. Structured questions may seem inflexible, questions within particular scales may seem redundant, and specific questions may appear intrusive or inappropriate for the condition at hand.

Further, physicians are trained to think dichotomously. Findings are generally labeled as normal or abnormal and there are algorithms that specify appropriate steps to take. The lack of clearly defined thresholds for health status and the limited guidelines for action available with health status measures leave clinicians frustrated. As Meyer et al. (24) state, "We know what to do about a high serum phosphorus, however textbooks do not teach the differential diagnosis or appropriate evaluation of a declining social function score."

Practically, the use of quality of life measures raises concerns regarding the burden of data collection, both in terms of both time and capital costs. In some instances, the clinic must be willing to make the investment in the software and/or hardware necessary to support such data collection, along with the staff to manage and complete the operation.

IMPLICATIONS FOR USE OF HEALTH STATUS MEASURES IN CLINICAL PRACTICE

There are a number of issues that need to be addressed before health status measures are likely to come into widespread clinical use. First, application of quality of life measures would be facilitated if clinicians had a better understanding of the principles of measurement and the methods of health status assessment, and a greater appreciation of the value of patient-reported data. Education of physicians about these issues should begin in medical school.

Second, clinically relevant disease-specific measures are available for relatively few conditions. Further development and refinement of generic and disease-specific measures of health-related quality of life are needed to increase their relevance to clinicians and their responsiveness to clinically important changes in condition.

Third, and closely related to this is better explanation of the meaning of scores to both clinicians and patients. Both groups need to understand the content of the measure and need to grasp what questions these measures can answer and what questions they cannot. Practically oriented research is needed into how to present health status information to physicians and patients in the most user-friendly manner. For generic measures it will be important to establish norms analogous to the normal ranges for laboratory parameters. For applications in quality of care assessment, models will be needed to adjust for case mix and severity of illness so that fair comparisons can be made.

Fourth, testing of quality of life instruments is needed in the clinical setting. As researchers continue to assess the reliability and validity of measures of health-related quality of life, they must work to ensure that instruments can be practically administered in a clinical setting and that the results are rapidly available and easily interpretable. Work is needed to refine and streamline applications and improve and automate administration. Measures need to be tested in more diverse populations, incorporating variations of language, age, race, and education level. Feasibility tests must be conducted, and standard methodological procedures should be used regarding the best time to administer a follow-up questionnaire and the choice of self-administered versus interviewer-administered questionnaires. Studies are needed to determine which measures add useful information and in which clinical situations they add the most.

Finally, it is crucial to link assessments to suggested action. Most clinicians have well-developed routines for responding to abnormal laboratory or imaging results. If a hemoglobin is low, physicians have learned to consider a differential diagnosis, and to order a battery of tests to rule out the various items in the differential. Similar differential diagnoses, diagnostic steps, and therapeutic prescriptions need to be developed for less familiar problems such as low energy. Analogous routines could be established, e.g., referral to rehabilitation, a mental health provider, a social worker, or home health aide, that become standard practice. The information, to some degree, should be considered like a laboratory test. It should be viewed in the context of a threshold for action and the clinician needs to know that the test is sensitive and specific. Clinical trials are needed to examine the effectiveness of treatments and practice in terms of health-related quality of life. The results of these studies should eventually lead to practice guidelines for problems expressed in terms of health status.

CONCLUSIONS

There is a clear need for improvements in medical practice. Health status measurement may be able to play a useful role in broadening the scope of screening, decision making, and evaluation.

Routine application of health status assessments in clinical practice may lead to a more appropriate focus on the goals of care. For a patient hospitalized with diabetic ketoacidosis, it is legitimate that much of the focus in the hospital is on correcting physiologic abnormalities. However, when the patient is discharged, the focus should be on her and on optimizing her life, rather than on her diabetes and optimizing glycemic control.

An explicit focus on improving various aspects of patients' health-related quality of life represents a paradigm shift to optimizing various kind of outcomes. In the long-term, the choice of health indicator tends to affect the health of the population. Thus, in the same way that choosing the infant mortality rate as a health indicator may contribute to a decrease in infant deaths, choosing social functioning as an indicator may result in improved social health. However, health status is but one of many potentially important indicators, and its value for various applications still needs to be assessed.

Clinicians should keep in mind the patient's needs and concerns and base treatment decisions on this information. The aim of medical care is to prolong life, eliminate or reduce deviations in biologic function, relieve pain and suffering, ease fear and anxiety through compassionate interactions and acts of caring, and improve general functioning and well-being (28). Clinical application of health status measures may allow a more systematic focus on quality of life that is satisfying to both patients and clinicians alike.

REFERENCES

1. Steinberg EP, Tielsch JM, Schein OD, et al. The VF-14: an index of functional impairment in patients with cataract. *Arch Ophthalmol* 1994;112:630–638.
2. Kaplan RM, Atkins CJ, Timms R. Validity of a quality of well-being scale as an outcome measure in chronic obstructive pulmonary disease. *J Chronic Dis* 1984;37(2):85–95.
3. Deyo RA, Carter WB. Strategies for improving and expanding the application of health status measures in clinical settings: a researcher-developer viewpoint. *Med Care* 1992;30(5):MS176–MS186.
4. Calkins DR, Rubenstein LV, Cleary PD, et al. Failure of physicians to recognize functional disability in ambulatory patients. *Ann Intern Med* 1991;114:451.
5. Nelson EC, Landgraf JM, Hayes RD, et al. The functional status of patients: how can it be measured in physicians' offices? *Med Care* 1990;28:1111.
6. German PS, Shapiro S, Skinner EA, et al. Detection and management of mental health problems of older patients by primary care providers. *JAMA* 1987;257:489.
7. Wells KB, Hays RD, Burnham A, et al. Detection of depressive disorder for patients receiving prepaid or fee-for-service care: results from the Medical Outcomes Study. *JAMA* 1989;262:3298.
8. Apgar V. The newborn (Apgar) scoring system: reflections and advice. *Pediatr Clin North Am* 1966;13:645.
9. Ewing JA. Detecting alcoholism: the CAGE questionnaire. *JAMA* 1984;252:1905.
10. Folstein MF, Folstein SE, McHugh PR. "Mini-mental state": a practical method for grading the cognitive state of patients for the clinician. *J Psychiatr Res* 1975;12:189.
11. The Criteria Committee of the New York Heart Association. *Diseases of the heart and blood vessels: nomenclature and criteria for diagnosis,* 6th ed. Boston: Little, Brown, 1964.
12. Karnofsky DA, Abelman WH, Craver LF, Burcheneal JH. The use of nitrogen mustards in the palliative treatment of carcinoma. *Cancer* 1948;1:634–656.
13. Katz S, Ford AB, Moskowitz RW, Jackson BA, Jaffee MW. Studies of illness in the aged: the index of ADL: a standardized measure of biological and psychosocial function. *JAMA* 1963;185:914–919.
14. Ware JE. Comments on the use of health status assessment in clinical settings. *Med Care* 1992;30(5):MS205–MS209.
15. Nelson EC, Wasson JH, Kirk JW. Assessment of function in routine

clinical practice: description of the COOP chart method and preliminary findings. *J Chronic Dis* 1987;40(suppl 1):55S.

16. Landgraf JM, Nelson EC, and the Dartmouth COOP Primary Care Project. Summary of the WONCA/COOP International Health Assessment Field Trial. *Aust Fam Physician* 1992;21:255–269.

17. Tsevat J, Weeks JC, Guadagnoli E, Tosteson ANA, Mangione CM, Pliskin JS, Weinstein MC, Cleary PD. Using health-related quality-of-life information: clinical encounters, clinical trials, and health policy. *J Gen Intern Med* 1994;9:576–582.

18. Levine MN, Gafni A, Markham B, MacFarlane D. A bedside decision instrument to elicit a patient's preferences concerning adjuvant chemotherapy for breast cancer. *Ann Intern Med* 1992;117:53–58.

19. Wennberg JE. On the status of the prostate disease assessment team. *Health Serv Res* 1990;25(5):709–716.

20. Kasper JF, Mulley AG, Wennberg JE. Developing shared decision making programs to improve the quality of health care. QRB 1992;18(6):183–190.

21. Knaus WA, Wagner DP, Draper EA, et al. The APACHE III prognostic system. Risk prediction of hospital morality for critically ill hospitalized adults. *Chest* 1991;100(6):1619–36.

22. Wu AW, Damiano A, Lynn J, Alzola CF, Teno J, Landefeld CS, et al. Predicting future functional status for seriously ill hospitalized adults. *Ann Intern Med* 1995;122:342–350.

23. Ware JE, Sherbourne CD. The MOS 36-item short form healthy survey (SF-36): I. conceptual framework and item selection. *Medical Care* 1992;30:473–483.

24. Meyer KB, Espindle DM, DeGiacomo JM, et al. Monitoring dialysis patients' health status. *Am J Kidney Dis* 1994;24(2):267–279.

25. Steinwachs DM, Wu AW, Skinner EA. How will outcomes management work? *Health Affairs* 1994;13:153–162.

26. Blim RD. Strategies for improving and expanding the application of health status measures in clinical settings: discussion. *Med Care* 1992;30(5):MS196–MS197.

27. Greenfield S, Nelson EC. Recent developments and future issues in the use of health status assessment measures in clinical settings. *Med Care* 1992;30(5):MS23–MS41.

28. Faden R, Leplege A. Assessing quality of life: moral implications for clinical practice. *Med Care* 1992;30(5):MS166–MS175.

Quality of Life and Pharmacoeconomics in Clinical Trials, Second Edition, edited by B. Spilker.
Lippincott-Raven Publishers, Philadelphia © 1996.

CHAPTER **55**

Anthropological Perspectives: The Importance of Culture in the Assessment of Quality of Life

Peter J. Guarnaccia

INTRODUCTION

There have been recent initiatives to make quality of life assessments more sensitive to multicultural populations (1). This is an important process that will make participation in clinical trials more accessible to minority and other special populations, and ultimately should lead to improvements in outcome for people with cancer and other serious diseases. From an anthropological perspective, three key problems have emerged in adapting quality of life instruments to culturally diverse populations: (a) researchers are starting with an underdeveloped notion of culture and its impact on quality of life assessments; (b) in focusing on particular ethnic populations, there is a lack of attention to inter- and intracultural diversity (2) among study populations; and (c) inadequate approaches are employed to the adaptation and translation of quality of life instruments.

The central tenet of the anthropological perspective is that quality of life is inherently shaped by and embedded in culture (3). There is no such thing as a culture-free measure of quality of life. At the same time, it should be possible to develop scales that measure quality of life across cultures along similar metrics, although the specific content of those scales may differ. That is, one can develop scales with different items that would still yield high, medium, and low levels of quality of life across cultural groups being treated in clinical settings.

P. J. Guarnaccia: Institute for Health, Health Care Policy & Aging Research, Rutgers University, New Brunswick, New Jersey 08903.

This chapter (a) discusses how anthropologists view culture, (b) further explores my contention that quality of life is unavoidably a culture-laden concept, (c) examines issues of cultural diversity and its effect on quality of life measures and their development, and (d) identifies issues in translation of quality of life instruments for different cultures that need more development in future work.

DEFINITIONS OF CULTURE

While *multiculturalism* and *cultural sensitivity* have become popular concepts in the health field, most uses of the concept of *culture* in the health literature are overly simplified. Many health writers have turned to earlier writings by anthropologists to present a definition of culture. In general, these definitions have reflected a static view of culture as the distinctive set of beliefs, values, morals, customs, and institutions that people inherit through growing up in a culture. More recent approaches to culture in anthropology provide a more dynamic perspective of this key concept (4,5). Recent views of culture, while not discarding the importance of a person's cultural inheritance of ideas, values, feelings, ways of relating, and behaviors, have focused equally on the importance of viewing culture as a process in which views and practices are dynamically affected by social transformations, social conflicts, power relationships, and migrations. Culture is a product of group values, norms, and experiences, and of individual innovations and life histories.

There is no such thing as a culture as a static phenomenon. Rather, most social settings involve multiple cultures in interaction—influencing, changing, and conflicting with each other. Culture is as much a process as a thing, and thus attempts to freeze culture into a set of generalized value orientations or behaviors will constantly misrepresent what culture is. Culture is a dynamic and creative phenomenon, some aspects of which are shared by large groups of people and other aspects of which are the creations of small groups and individuals.

Culture serves as the web that structures human thought, emotion, and interaction. Culture provides a variety of resources for dealing with major life changes and challenges, including serious illness and hospitalization. Culture is continually being shaped by social processes such as migration and acculturation that bring people from different cultures into interaction in settings where translation between cultures is required and where one group may have more control of the situation than the other. Cultures vary not only by national, regional, or ethnic background, but by age, gender, and social class. Much of culture is embedded in and communicated by language; language cannot be understood or used outside of its cultural context. Thus the very processes of quality of life research—developing questions, carrying out interviews, interpreting answers—are all culturally laden processes.

IMPACT OF CULTURE ON ASSESSMENTS OF QUALITY OF LIFE

Schipper et al. (6) have defined quality of life as "the functional effect of an illness and its consequent therapy upon a patient, as perceived by the patient." They go on to highlight four broad domains as part of this concept: physical and occupational function, psychological state, social interaction, and somatic sensation. Cella (7) identifies two key dimensions of the quality of life construct: subjectivity and multidimensionality. The focus on subjectivity, that is the perception and report of the patient/person, of their assessment of their quality of life, places the entire study of quality of life within the domain of culture. Given the understanding of culture presented above, it becomes nonsensical to think that a person can give an assessment of his or her quality of life outside of a cultural context or that we can aspire to a "culture-free" assessment. In focusing on each of the multidimensional domains of quality of life, the profound influence of culture becomes even more apparent.

The medical anthropological literature (8,9) provides considerable data on the cultural shaping of the major domains of quality of life: physical and occupational function, psychological state (depression), somatic sensation (pain), and social interaction (6). The whole notion of disability, the negative aspect of physical and occupational function, is highly culturally and socially determined (10–12). At a clini-

cal level, it is a commonplace for most providers that individuals with the same diagnosis and similar lesion may experience quite different levels of impairment in activities of daily living and occupational participation. Research has also shown that across cultures and historical time, different diseases have been more highly marked in terms of fear, stigma, and disability, for example, cancer in Japan and chronic fatigue syndrome in the United States (13,14). In terms of psychological state, there is a wealth of anthropological writing that has demonstrated that emotions are differently expressed and experienced across cultures. Given the focus on depression in work on quality of life and serious disease, a key collection is that of Kleinman and Good on *Culture and Depression* (15). Many of the articles in this collection point to the prominent somatic dimension of depression across cultures, making the separation of physical and psychological states in serious disease an unrealistic dichotomy. Ever since the classic work of Zborowski (16,17) on ethnic differences in the expression of pain, researchers have found that both individual experience and group culture greatly shape the experience and expression of pain (18). The source and extent of social support an ill individual receives is highly culturally determined, and research, particularly in the area of serious mental illness, has shown the differing effects of culturally mediated social responses to disease on course and outcome (19–21).

Through this brief summary I have suggested a variety of ways in which quality of life is a culturally shaped construct. A corollary of these assertions is that the methods for developing quality of life instruments have also resulted in "culture-dependent" instruments. Since most quality of life instruments have been developed by European and American clinicians and researchers working with a largely European and American client population in tertiary care settings, the resulting instruments have embedded the cultural orientations of these groups both in the language used and in the domains measured. The cultural dependence of these instruments is not apparent because to a large extent clinicians/researchers and patients/clients share the same culture. This is not a criticism of these instruments in general; rather, it is a specific reflection on the instruments using the notion of culture presented in the first section of this chapter. Taking the concept of culture presented earlier seriously, quality of life instruments could not have been developed in any other way. The problem occurs in trying to use these instruments with culturally different populations and assuming either (a) that the instruments, because they have passed several psychometric tests, are cross-culturally applicable or (b) that to make them culturally appropriate requires only minor adjustments of content and language.

Developing quality of life measures for cross-cultural use requires the same depth of knowledge and similar detailed research process as was involved in developing the original instruments for European and American populations. That is, the instruments available for quality of life assessment are the products of a long research process. Clinician/researchers often start with the concerns about the quality of life impacts of disease and therapy of their patients/clients and then generate items to operationalize those concerns. Often, extensive literature reviews are carried out to identify relevant issues from other studies and specific items to include from other instruments. Then extensive batteries of items are tested and reduced using a variety of qualitative and quantitative methods. When instruments are used with new populations, a similar process needs to be followed to develop items; it is a naive and inaccurate assumption that all that is needed to adapt an existing instrument is some minor modifications of vocabulary and language while the content of items and domains remains essentially unaltered.

The critique I have outlined flows from taking seriously the understanding of culture and its role in health briefly described above. I would argue that these developmental tasks across cultural groups are essential for the development of valid and reliable quality of life instruments. Some may criticize this approach because it will result in highly noncomparable instruments at the level of items. My response is that one would expect item content to differ for culturally different populations. The comparative potential comes not at the level of specific items, from this perspective, but rather from the overall and specific dimensional assessments of quality of life. It should be quite feasible to rate people as low, moderate, or high in levels of physical function, pain, or overall quality of life across cultural groups even if the specific items are different. Within a cultural group, specific responses should indicate these different levels of quality of life. This is certainly the case for different diseases where different items have been developed for cancer or arthritis quality of life instruments and should be equally so across cultural groups.

The National Cancer Institute took a significant step toward supporting the development of culturally appropriate quality of life assessments starting in 1992 in funding a program on quality of life assessment in special populations (1). The request for applications specifically ruled out "simple translation of standardized instruments" as an adequate approach and called on researchers "to develop or adapt existing methods for assessing aspects of quality of life in cancer patients from special populations that are sensitive to (a) language and dialect; (b) customs, beliefs, and traditions; and (c) education and socioeconomic status" (1). As one of the anthropological reviewers for the proposals submitted in response to this request for applications, I was both heartened by the cultural sophistication of the program officers, reviewers, and proposers and concerned by some of the consistent misunderstandings of issues of culture in developing the studies. The rest of this chapter addresses two issues that repeatedly emerged in the proposals: a misuse of ethnic categories resulting from lack of attention to inter- and intraethnic differences, and inadequate approaches to translation of instruments.

ISSUES OF INTER- AND INTRAETHNIC DIVERSITY

There is a complex debate occurring in American social science (and society) about the definition and meaning of ethnicity (22,23). For purposes of this chapter, I am going to define ethnic groups as cultural groups interacting in a multicultural context. Ethnic groups arise out of a need to define oneself and one's group in comparison to other cultural groups who may be co-residing, cooperating, and/or competing within a particular social and political context. Ethnic groups share not only cultural features, but also histories, migrations, and political and economic processes that define them both to themselves and to others.

Returning to the issue of developing quality of life measures for different ethnic groups, the focus of development is often on too large a social group to meaningfully reflect the culture of that group. Often, researchers refer to developing quality of life instruments for Hispanic Americans or Asian Americans or African Americans. These broad ethnic categories subsume cultural groups with different languages and dialects, countries of origin, histories of migration, and social and economic statuses.

The first level of attention is to interethnic differences. For example, there are profound differences in history, language, migration, and social status among the different Hispanic groups in the United States—Mexicans, Puerto Ricans, Cubans, Dominicans, Salvadorans, Colombians. In thinking about developing quality of life instruments, researchers need to define more culturally similar populations. In this sense a Hispanic sample of 100 patients—45 Mexican origin, 25 Puerto Rican, 10 Cuban, 10 Colombian, and 10 Salvadoran—would be inappropriate. Rather, depending on what part of the country one is working in, it makes sense to draw your sample of 100 from one of the Hispanic groups. A research enterprise that incorporated researchers from around the country who independently developed quality of life measures on several Hispanic groups and then compared them would inform the research and clinical community considerably both about Hispanic cultures and quality of life.

Even within specific ethnic groupings, researchers need to pay more attention to intracultural diversity. For example, some Mexican Americans have been living in what is now the United States for approximately 400 years; others have arrived from rural areas of central and southern Mexico in the last year. Some Mexican Americans speak only English, others only Spanish, and still others move fluidly between Spanish and English depending on the social context. Many Mexican Americans are Catholic; large groups of Mexican Americans have joined various Protestant groups, some of which see prayer and belief in God as the primary means of coping with serious illness. These brief examples illustrate a few of the dimensions of diversity.

My focus on a more careful, detailed, and thoughtful definition of ethnicity in developing quality of life measures and selecting samples for the testing of the validity and reliability of measures may at first seem dauntingly complex, making cross-cultural instrument development and clinical research impossible. Again, I draw the parallel to discussions in the quality of life field about the value of disease-specific or general measures of quality of life. Great care has been taken in selecting samples for development of disease-specific measures that people have the same kinds of cancers and/or are undergoing similar types of treatments (i.e., radiation or chemotherapy) (24). I choose this analogy purposefully to make the point that these kinds of decisions are made in quality of life research regularly in other areas and apply in a parallel way to selecting cultural groups for instrument development and clinical assessment. I also choose this analogy to highlight the issue that these kinds of research decisions involve judgments for which there is no ultimately "perfect" answer; rather, the answer is contextualized in each research setting and clinical problem. There is no perfect solution to the selection of the specificity of ethnic/cultural group to study; the definition of ethnic group should have some cultural coherence and should respond to the major ethnic groups in the community and affected by the disease problem.

TRANSLATION OF RESEARCH INSTRUMENTS

The centrality of language to understanding and researching culture makes translation issues central from an anthropological perspective. In developing quality of life assessment methods for culturally diverse populations, the issue of translation of items and instruments into different languages looms large. Translation is critical both for items that already exist in English and need to be used with other groups and to make instruments developed in another language accessible to bilingual or English-dominant members of that cultural group.

The broad process of translation has been described in detail by Brislin and colleagues (25) and the notion of "equivalence" of an original and translated instrument has been elaborated by Flaherty (26). Some of the most detailed discussions of the translation of research instruments from English to Spanish have been written by the research group at the Behavioral Sciences Research Institute of the University of Puerto Rico Medical Sciences Campus (27,28).

I will briefly review the key steps of translation, as other chapters will address this issue in more detail. The first step in translation is often referred to as "de-centering" the original version of the instrument. This refers to rewriting items in simple, direct, and noncolloquial language to make it possible to be translated. Given my contention earlier about the extent that culture is embedded in the development and writing of quality of life measures, the process of de-centering itself begins to highlight issues of making items and instruments applicable to different cultural groups. An oft-cited example of this issue is the common item in scales of psychologic state: "I felt down or blue." The de-centering process would involve rewriting this item in a form such as "I felt sad" and then finding the appropriate word for sad or another relevant construct in the second language.

In general, translation proceeds through an iterative process of translation and back-translation. Ideally, a bilingual person whose native language is the one to be translated into takes the original version and writes it into the second language. This usually requires a highly experienced translator who can capture the meaning of the item as well as the words. Often, bilingual clinicians without translating experience find this difficult. The next step is to have a bilingual person native in the original language take the translated version and back-translate it into the original language. The two original language versions are then compared and any discrepancies adjusted.

Two committee processes should be involved that are often left out of the process. One is to have a committee of native speakers review the translated version to be sure that it captures the meaning of the original, is grammatically and colloquially correct, and is at a level of literacy appropriate for the study population. Another committee involves the investigators and translation consultants discussing the reasons for discrepancies between the original and back-translated versions. Several decisions may be made to resolve discrepancies: (a) the original item may be retranslated; (b) the original item may be revised in the original language to make its intent clearer and then translated again, which involves changing both versions of the instrument; or (c) an item may be divided into a few items in both or one version where concepts are not equivalent. This last decision raises the issue of dimensions of equivalence between an original and translated instrument.

Following Brislin and colleagues (25), researchers have used the notion of multiple dimensions of equivalence to test the adequacy of their translations (26–28). The first level is semantic equivalence, which involves assessing that the words used in the items mean the same thing in both languages. The processes of translation, back-translation, and committee review have a primary focus on assessing semantic equivalence. Content equivalence refers to whether the content of the item is relevant in both cultures. For example, in assessing physical function, one would want to know if the types of activities mentioned are relevant across cultural contexts (golf or tennis vs. bocce or soccer). The content equivalence is best assessed in the committee process and in pretests of the interview with the cultural group to be studied. The technical equivalence of the instrument involves whether the measuring techniques, such as interview approaches (self-administer, computer-administered, etc.) and answer scales (Likert scales, Cantrill ladder, etc.) are equally understandable, interpreted in the same way, and part of the sociocultural experience of the group being studied. Issues of literacy and educational level are important dimensions of assessing technical equivalence. Criterion equivalence focuses on whether the item and instrument's criterial structure function similarly across cultures. For example, I have argued that different case criteria should be used with the Center for Epidemiological Studies—Depression Scale in different cultural groups because different groups have different responses to and styles of answering this symptom-based scale of psychological function (29). The final level of equivalence is conceptual equivalence, that the construct being measured by the method or instrument is similar in the two cultural groups. This, in essence, has been the focus of this chapter—how do we know that what we mean by quality of life is being similarly assessed across cultural groups.

FUTURE RESEARCH

The future research agenda for work on cross-cultural assessment of quality of life from an anthropologically informed perspective is still ahead of us. The studies initiated by the National Cancer Institute (1) are a major start in this process. The results of these studies should not only provide clinicians and researchers with new methods for assessing quality of life in multicultural populations, but should also provide new insights into the meaning of quality of life in clinical work and research more broadly.

The future research process can be briefly summarized into the following steps:

1. Identification of key cultural/ethnic populations for research both in relation to their representation in the overall population and their representation in specific groups with critical diseases (e.g., African-American women with cervical cancer; Puerto Ricans with asthma).
2. Identification of the relevant domains of quality of life for these groups. While the four domains identified by Schipper and colleagues (6) are broadly applicable, more sense of the relative weights of different aspects of those domains (the meaning of work, employment, and career; the centrality of family contact and support and the definition of family) across and within ethnic groups needs elucidation. In addition, some domains may need to be added that are not obviously part of these four; one of the most often discussed is the domain of spirituality.
3. Development of specific, culturally relevant measures of these quality of life domains.
4. Development of appropriate linguistic adaptations of quality of life measures.
5. Design of comparable scoring approaches so that quality of life assessments can be compared across cultural groups in evaluating treatment outcomes in clinical trials.

CONCLUSIONS

Quality of life is inherently a cultural construct. Recognition of this should aid in the development and refinement of quality of life assessment for all clinical populations. In

developing quality of life assessments, more attention to the cultural dimensions of the domains of physical functioning, psychological state, somatic sensation, and social interaction will aid in assessing these areas across cultural/ethnic groups. Detailed attention to the language used in developing quality of life measures and the translation of those instruments will improve both the reliability and validity of those measures. More careful delineation of the cultural groups to be studied will improve the sensitivity of those instruments, both in a cultural and epidemiological sense. Through careful attention to the role of culture in structuring quality of life assessments, researchers will gain an enriched understanding of the experience of chronic and serious illness and of the impact of treatment on people's lives and on the dimensions of quality of life that are central to well-being in the face of the challenges of disease.

REFERENCES

1. National Cancer Institute. *Quality of life assessment in special populations.* RFA Number CA/NR-92-27. Bethesda, MD: National Institutes of Health, 1992.
2. Pelto PJ, Pelto GH. Intracultural diversity: some theoretical issues. *Am Ethnol* 1975;2:1–17.
3. Campos SS, Johnson TM. Cultural considerations. In: Spilker B, ed. *Quality of life assessment in clinical trials.* New York: Raven Press, 1990:163–170.
4. Geertz C. Thick description: toward an interpretive theory of culture. In: Geertz C, ed. *The interpretation of cultures.* New York: Basic Books, 1973:3–30.
5. Good BJ. *Medicine, rationality and experience: an anthropological perspective.* Cambridge: Cambridge University Press, 1994.
6. Schipper H, Clinch J, Powell V. Definitions and conceptual issues. In: Spilker B, ed. *Quality of life assessment in clinical trials.* New York: Raven Press, 1990:11–24.
7. Cella DF. Quality of life: the concept. *J Palliat Care* 1992;8:8–13.
8. Johnson TM, Sargent CF, eds. *Medical anthropology: contemporary theory and method.* New York: Praeger, 1990.
9. Lindenbaum S, Lock M, eds. *Knowledge, power and practice: the anthropology of medicine and everyday life.* Berkeley: University of California Press, 1993.
10. Kleinman A. *The illness narratives.* New York: Basic, 1988.
11. Murphy RF. *The body silent.* New York: Norton, 1990.
12. Kaufman SR. Toward a phenomenology of boundaries in medicine: illness experience in the case of stroke. *Med Anthropol Q* 1988;2:338–354.
13. Payer L. *Medicine and culture: varieties of treatment in the United States, England, West Germany and France.* New York: Henry Holt, 1988.
14. Sontag S. *Illness as metaphor.* New York: Farrar, Strauss, & Giroux, 1978.
15. Kleinman A, Good B. *Culture and depression: studies in the anthropology and cross-cultural psychiatry of affect and disorder.* Berkeley: University of California Press, 1985.
16. Zborowski M. Cultural components in the response to pain. *J Soc Issues* 1952;8(4):16–31.
17. Zborowski M. *People in pain.* San Francisco: Jossey-Bass, 1969.
18. Good MJD, Brodwin PE, Good BJ, Kleinman A. *Pain as human experience: an anthropological perspective.* Berkeley: University of California Press, 1992.
19. WHO. *The International Pilot Study of Schizophrenia.* Geneva: WHO, 1973.
20. WHO. *Schizophrenia: an international follow-up study.* Chichester: John Wiley, 1979.
21. Jenkins J, Karno M. The meaning of expressed emotion: theoretical issues raised by cross-cultural research. *Am J Psychiatry* 1992;149:9–21.

22. Alba RD. *Ethnic identity: the transformation of white America.* New Haven: Yale University Press, 1990.

23. Waters MC. *Ethnic options: choosing identities in America.* Berkeley: University of California Press, 1990.

24. Guyatt GH, Jaeschke R. Measurements in clinical trials: choosing the appropriate approach. In: Spilker B, ed. *Quality of life assessment in clinical trials.* New York: Raven Press, 1990:37–46.

25. Brislin RW, Lonner WJ, Thorndike RM. *Cross-cultural research methods.* New York: John Wiley, 1973.

26. Flaherty JA. Appropriate and inappropriate research methodologies for Hispanic mental health. In: Gaviria M, ed. *Health and behavior: research agenda for Hispanics.* Chicago: University of Illinois Press, 1987:177–186.

27. Bravo M, Rubio-Stipec M, Woodbury-Fariña M. A cross-cultural adaptation of a research instrument: the DIS adaptation in Puerto Rico. *Cult Med Psychiatry* 1991;15:1–18.

28. Bravo M, Woodbury-Fariña N, Canino GJ, Rubio-Stipec M. The Spanish translation and cultural adaptation of the Diagnostic Interview for Children (DISC) in Puerto Rico. *Cult Med Psychiatry* 1993;17:329–344.

29. Guarnaccia PJ, Good BJ, Kleinman A. A critical review of epidemiological studies of Puerto Rican mental health. *Am J Psychiatry* 1990;147:1449–1456.

Quality of Life and Pharmacoeconomics in Clinical Trials, Second Edition, edited by B. Spilker.
Lippincott-Raven Publishers, Philadelphia © 1996.

CHAPTER 56

Quality of Life: The Nursing Perspective

Pamela S. Hinds and Claudette G. Varricchio

INTRODUCTION: NURSES, PATIENTS, AND QUALITY OF LIFE

Nurses have a long-standing tradition of learning as much as possible about what patients and their families find meaningful in life and how health fits in with their personal perspective. This person-specific knowledge is considered essential for providing nursing care that will contribute to improved health for the patient. Sensitive efforts to obtain and apply this information directly represent what nurses consider to be the essence of good nursing care: a therapeutic nurse-patient relationship (1,2). The intent of this relationship is to keep the focus of the care efforts on the patient. Because of this intent, nurses often pose variations of the following questions:

Are we listening to the patient?
Do we know how the patient is feeling about this situation and what is important to him/her?
Are we taking the actions that the patient would have us take, or are we initiating well-intentioned actions that may adversely affect the patient and his/her life situation?
Are we making decisions about the patient's care that could be better made by the patient?

These questions have been addressed most satisfactorily for nurses in clinical care and clinical research with the construct of quality of life. Nurses' intense interest in quality of life is based on the desire for valid knowledge about a patient throughout his/her care experience that could be used to make a positive difference for that patient. Because of this strong interest, the discipline of nursing has committed considerable resources to developing conceptual descriptions that could aid nurses in determining quality of life from the patient perspective and to devising ways to measure quality of life that are accurate and acceptable to the patient.

This chapter describes nurses' efforts to conceptually analyze the term *quality of life* and the domains and characteristics that have been identified to date, reviews the approaches most often used to measure quality of life, presents dilemmas that nurses have identified in studying and applying research findings, and discusses planned future efforts to study quality of life and to integrate findings into nursing practice.

NURSING'S EFFORTS TO DEFINE QUALITY OF LIFE

Quality of life is mentioned frequently in the nursing literature, particularly in the nursing oncology, cardiovascular, and transplantation literature. Most studies have focused on adult patients (3–11). Only rarely is quality of life mentioned in the pediatric or family nursing literature (12–16). Related concepts such as coping and adaptation, patient decision making, and patient autonomy are frequently cited but the elusiveness of the meaning of quality of life and the resulting difficulties in defining it are readily apparent in the nursing literature. Clinical experiences and anecdotes are valuable sources of information that have revealed the ever-changing nature of individual patient's quality of life. These clinical observations convincingly demonstrate that (a) knowledge of a patient's perceived quality of life at a single point in time is insufficient to fully grasp what is of

P. S. Hinds: Departments of Nursing Administration and Behavioral Medicine, St. Jude Children's Research Hospital, Memphis, Tennessee 38101.
C. G. Varricchio: CORB/DCPC, National Cancer Institute, National Institutes of Health, Bethesda, Maryland 20892.

greatest meaning to that patient, (b) determination of the quality of life for an individual patient or a well-described group of patients does not allow for a nurse or other health care provider to estimate the quality of life for other individual or groups of patients without seeking the patients' personal reports, and (c) application of the information from a single point in time or from another individual or group could result in suboptimal outcomes for a specific patient. The current interest in more precisely defining quality of life has evolved from these clinical observations.

Formal methods of concept analysis have been applied by nurses to the term *quality of life*. Observation and interview data from well and ill individuals, patients and their family members, and health care providers have been incorporated into the analysis (17–19). This diversity of information sources reflects nursing's assumptions that quality of life is (a) influenced by state of health, and (b) often perceived and reported differently by patients, their family members, and health care providers. A consensus on the exact domains and characteristics of quality of life does not yet exist in nursing (18,20), but there is similarity among most published reports in the nursing literature.

The most commonly identified domains of quality of life for adults are physical health, psychological/spiritual health, family relationships, and socioeconomic resources. Components of those domains, respectively, include symptoms and health conditions, satisfaction with self and life satisfaction (including achievement of personal goals), family functioning and health, and financial support and employment status (3–5, 20–24).

In the pediatric nursing literature, the more commonly identified domains (and their components) include physical health (symptom and health conditions), psychological/spiritual health (satisfaction with self and orientation toward the future), and family relationships (coping abilities of parents and siblings) (12–14). These domains and components reflect nursing's interest in knowing what is meaningful to patients in the context of their health and in identifying areas of meaning that could be amenable to nursing interventions, such as assisting a patient in (a) adapting to health-related situations, (b) limiting treatment-related toxicity, (c) understanding self and others, or (d) reducing personal vulnerability to specific or general health threats. Indeed, quality of life is viewed by some nurses as an outcome variable that can be influenced both directly and indirectly by specific nursing care actions (4,12).

Within the domains of quality of life, there are certain characteristics that are repeatedly reported in the nursing literature. These characteristics include the dynamic nature of quality of life, even within the same individual across time, situations, and health states; the subjective and personal nature of quality of life; sensitivity to input from others; multidimensionality; and relatedness to the agreement between hopes and actual conditions. These characteristics are reflected in the definitions and descriptions of quality of life used by nurses in their clinical and research efforts (Table

TABLE 1. *Frequently cited definitions and descriptions of 'quality of life' developed by nurses*

Source	Definition/description
Ferrans and Powers (27)	An individual's perceptions of well-being that stem from satisfaction or dissatisfaction with dimensions of life that are important to the individual
Grant et al. (31)	A personal statement of the positivity or negativity of attributes that characterize one's life
Young and Longman (25)	The degree of satisfaction with perceived present life circumstances
Hinds (12)	Children's and adolescents' subjective and changeable sense of well-being that reflects how closely their desires and hopes match what is actually happening and their orientation toward the future, both their own and that of others
Lewis (16)	The degree to which one has self-esteem, a purpose in life, and minimal anxiety
McDaniel and Bach (18)	The congruence or lack of congruence between actual life conditions and one's hopes and expectations

1) and provide a convincing explanation for the uniqueness of quality of life to each individual. Although the domains, components, and characteristics of quality of life now identified in the nursing literature represent significant progress in developing useful working definitions of this construct, the current definitions and descriptive statements contain abstract terms. This lack of precise, concrete definitions needs to be considered when changes in nursing care for patients based on quality of life reports are being contemplated. Additionally, because of the wide scope reflected in the domains of quality of life in the nursing literature, it is important that nurses focus primarily on the domains that are most directly related to health and are amenable to nursing interventions.

QUALITY OF LIFE MEASURES DEVELOPED BY NURSES

Three different approaches to measuring quality of life have been used by nurses: single-item scales to measure general quality of life; single-scale, multidimensional approaches; and multiple scales. The latter two approaches tend to be disease-specific measures. Examples of the single-item approach are represented in the studies of Young and Longman (25) and Graham and Longman (26), who worked with adult cancer patients. The first 23 patients enrolled in the pilot study were asked to respond to a six-point Likert scale item (where 1 indicates ''poor'' and 6 ''excellent'') regarding their quality of life. The nurse investigators then decided that greater discrimination was needed, so the final 37 patients in the study were asked to rate their quality of life on a ten-point scale. The scale was found to have concurrent validity, in that it was positively correlated with an indicator of patients' behavior-morale and negatively associated with indicators of disease- and treatment-related symptoms and social dependency. Although this study was well regarded by nurses, they infrequently use a single-item scale, as it yields inadequate information about the accepted domains of quality of life. Without information about the individual domains, it is unlikely that a focused nursing intervention could be developed for a particular patient or patient group.

Currently, the most frequently used approach in nursing is that of the multidimensional, disease-specific, patient-report, single scale. This approach is best exemplified in the work by Ferrans and Powers (27) to develop and test their quality of life index and by Grant and colleagues to develop and test their quality of life index. The Ferrans and Powers Quality of Life Index was originally developed as a 31-item, six-point Likert Scale to measure quality of life in well or ill adults (27). A cancer-specific version with 34 items is also available (3). The index has two sections that allow the respondents to rate the same items in two different dimensions: satisfaction (1 "very dissatisfied" to 6 "very satisfied") and importance (1 "very unimportant" and 6 "very important"). Both versions have been reported to have stability (test-retest coefficients of .80 or better), and to have strong internal consistency (Cronbach alpha coefficients of greater than .90), and moderate to strong concurrent and construct validity estimates (3,8–11,28). Recently, the original version of the index was found to be content-valid for use with the elderly (29). The Ferrans and Powers Quality of Life Index is available in English, Japanese, Korean, Mandarin Chinese, Mexican-Spanish, Romanian, and Swedish.

The Quality of Life Index developed by Grant et al. includes 14 items that assess physical health, personal attitudes, and normal activities. It was derived from a scale developed by Presant et al. (30) to evaluate quality of life in adult oncology patients, but differs from that scale in the number of items, the wording and sequence of the items, and in the wording of the general instructions. This index is a linear, visual analog scale in which 100-mm lines have anchors describing extremes in perceptions or sensations. The anchors differ somewhat across the items, e.g., "none" and "excruciating" for the item on pain; "none" and "constant nausea" for the nausea item. The index has moderate test-retest reliability (coefficients of at least .60), and strong internal consistency (Cronbach coefficients of .80 and higher), and moderate estimates of concurrent and construct validity (31). It has been adapted by Grant and colleagues (23) for use with adults who have a colostomy, and by Ferrell and colleagues (6) to form a pain-specific quality of life measure (28 items to reflect the dimensions of physical well-being, psychological well-being, general symptom control, specific symptom control, and social support).

The third approach, multiple instruments, reflects nursing's attempt to measure the multidimensionality of quality of life and the factors in a health-related situation that can influence quality of life. A nursing intervention that changed a patient's quality of life could indirectly affect other life factors. By measuring the factors that indirectly influence quality of life in addition to quality of life itself, it may be possible to determine the true impact of a nursing intervention or treatment, or to better understand the measured change. The multiple-instrument approach also makes possible collecting subjective and objective reports of quality of life, qualitative and quantitative data, and the perspectives of patients, their family members, and their health care providers (32,33). An example of this approach is a current longitudinal study of adolescents with newly diagnosed cancers. This study includes four data collection points in the first 6 months of treatment and incorporates observation, self-report, and laboratory data (34). The adolescents respond to a set of six interview questions regarding their hopefulness and their self-care coping activities and complete five questionnaires that index their psychological well-being and symptoms. Laboratory data for impact of treatment on all organ systems and clinical reports of disease state obtained at each data collection point will eventually be compared with the self-report data. Although this study is producing valuable findings regarding the domains of quality of life and the factors that may alter quality of life in these adolescents, it also suffers the inherent difficulties of a multiple-instrument approach. Specifically, feasibility is a problem in a clinical setting with patients who do not feel well. It takes 18 to 37 minutes to complete the instruments, which can be burdensome for a fatigued or ill patient. The burden for the patients may be reflected in the participation refusal rate for this study (21%), which is two to five times higher than rates for previous nursing studies done in the same setting and with the same population that did not require the extensive self-report data at multiple time points (35). Additionally, the time necessary to complete multiple instruments stresses a busy health care system that needs to conserve space and staff time.

Nursing has not used the unidimensional approach used by some other disciplines. Nurses find this approach insufficient, as they believe that quality of life is multidimensional and that one domain affects all other domains. Quality of life assessments need to provide well-grounded direction for nursing interventions. A patient's rating on one health-related domain of quality of life does not sufficiently predict that patient's overall quality of life.

NURSING DILEMMAS REGARDING QUALITY OF LIFE

The challenges that nurses have encountered in their research and clinical work with quality of life (such as developing and testing psychometrically sound measures) are similar to those experienced by other disciplines. But the dilemmas reported by nurses in their work with quality of life reflect their focus on clinical care directed at improving patient outcomes. It is this focus and its accompanying dilemmas that distinguish the work of nurses from that of other disciplines that are attempting to establish parameters for certain populations (such as participants in phase I clinical trials) or to provide the basis for health policy (such as resource utilization).

One dilemma nurses encounter is whether to use a multidimensional or multiple-instrument approach when measuring the quality of life of patients as opposed to choosing an abbreviated instrument (i.e., one with fewer items representing each domain) (36). The first option presumably would yield more comprehensive information that could offer direction for subsequent nursing interventions. The second option is less burdensome for patients and thus may result in more valid responses. The abbreviated instrument results in less inconvenience and expense for the health care system because it requires less space and staff time. The dilemma highlights the need for a quality of life measure that is feasible for use in a clinical setting, sensitive to the energy level of the target population, and yields accurate and detailed information that will assist in clinical decision making.

A related dilemma is whether to measure quality of life at multiple time points using a preestablished, research- or clinician-determined standard of comparison (such as current quality of life scores compared with what patients recall as their pre-illness quality of life) (37) or to measure quality of life at multiple points without a preestablished standard, allowing patients to identify their personal standards of comparison at each measurement point. The former approach is expected to yield quality of life scores that can be meaningfully compared and to identify patterns of actual change in those scores. The latter choice may result in more valid estimates of patients' health-related quality of life at each measurement point. This choice reveals additional information about what the patients consider to be meaningful standards at each measurement point that could contribute to good clinical care. However, it does not permit meaningful comparisons of scores across measurement points and may not be suitable for use by disciplines that conduct clinical trials research, where comparable scores are essential. This dilemma stems from the phenomenon of "shifting standards," which occurs when the basis of comparison used by patients is fluid and changes between measurement points. For example, at measurement points that occur shortly after a diagnosis, patients tend to identify the difference between their perceptions on the day of measurement and their recall of their pre-diagnosis quality of life as their personal standard of comparison. Later in the continuum of care, these same patients typically compare how they feel on the day of measurement with how they felt at a particularly difficult and earlier point in treatment (34). This dilemma points out the need to have measurement approaches that allow patients to identify their current personal standard of comparison and that obtain a rating that is directly comparable to their previously obtained scores of quality of life. This could be accomplished by adding an item to the quality of life measure that directly asks patients how their current ratings compare with their previous ratings.

Another dilemma is whether to base nursing interventions upon the total scale score or the subscale scores from a quality of life measure. The total score provides a single, overall quotient that represents health-related quality of life. The subscale scores reflect how the domains compare with each other and how each domain compares with itself across measurement points. This dilemma emphasizes the need to have a quality of life assessment that is clinically feasible and that provides sufficient information to alert nurses to a change in the patient's quality of life and to enable them to identify the source of that change.

A final dilemma is whether to invest nursing resources in establishing normative scores of quality of life for specific patient populations that reflect the entire spectrum of health state or to use existing measures of quality of life and combine the resulting estimates with other clinically derived impressions. The former would provide relevant comparison standards and the latter, more individualized information. Either approach will ultimately involve nursing judgment regarding the extent of change in quality of life and its meaning and the nursing intervention indicated. This and the other dilemmas strongly reflect nursing's acceptance of the relevance of the construct of quality of life and nursing's intent to use quality of life both as a basis for initiating nursing interventions that are designed to improve patient health states and as an outcome measure of the effectiveness of those interventions.

FUTURE NURSING EFFORTS

Future nursing efforts with quality of life will focus both on clinical research and clinical care. The research focus will include continued efforts to refine existing quality of life scales so that resulting scores will accurately reflect the culture, ethnicity, and developmental stage of patients. A strong example of this focus is the recently initiated effort by Ferrans (38) to develop two versions of the Ferrans and Powers Quality of Life Index that will be appropriate for use with adult African-American and Mexican-American cancer patients who have low education levels. The future clinical care focus includes identifying critical time points on the health care continuum for measuring patients' quality of life and establishing which quality of life scales are most feasible to use in clinical settings. The clinical care focus will also include determining what constitutes a quality of life nursing intervention and what nursing interventions are effective for each domain of quality of life. Nursing research efforts will help to evaluate the effectiveness of the quality of life nursing interventions.

Perhaps the greatest challenge will be for nurses to determine how to use quality of life data in the context of other patient data sources when attempting to determine if an intervention is needed and what type of nursing intervention would be most beneficial for the patients' unique health situations. Guidelines for such decision making, assisted by research, will need to be developed for a variety of clinical situations. This future development also has implications for nursing education, as curricula will need added content on how nurses can incorporate quality of life data into the information they use to form the basis of their nursing care decisions.

CONCLUSIONS

Nursing is remarkably comfortable with considerable weight in clinical decision making being given to patients' reports of their quality of life. In the future, both research and clinical care efforts by nurses will greatly assist our discipline in its plans to use quality of life data to help in establishing goals of nursing care with patients and in evaluating the outcomes of that care.

REFERENCES

1. Henderson VA. *The nature of nursing: reflections after 25 years.* New York: National League for Nursing Press, 1991.
2. Meister SB. The family's agents: policy and nursing. In: Freetham S, Meister S, Bell J, Gillis C, eds. *The nursing of families: theory/research/education/practice.* Newbury Park, CA: Sage, 1993:3–10.
3. Ferrans C. Development of a quality of life index for patients with cancer. *Oncol Nursing Forum* 1990;17(3)(suppl):15–19.
4. Padilla GV, Grant MM. Quality of life as a cancer nursing outcome variable. *ANS* 1985;8(1):45–60.
5. Grant MM, Ferrell BR, Schmidt GM, Fonbuena P, Niland JC, Forman SJ. Measurement of quality of life in bone marrow transplantation survivors. *Qual Life Res* 1992;1:375–384.
6. Ferrell BR, Wisdom C, Wenzl C. Quality of life as an outcome variable in the management of cancer pain. *Cancer* 1989;63:2321–2327.
7. Whedon M, Ferrell BR. Quality of life in adult bone marrow transplant patients: beyond the first year. *Semin Oncol Nurs* 1994;10(1):42–57.
8. Hicks F, Larson J, Ferrans C. Quality of life after liver transplantation. *Res Nurs Health* 1992;15:111–119.
9. Hughes KK. Psychosocial and functional status of breast cancer patients. *Cancer Nurs* 1993;16(3):222–229.
10. Bliley AV, Ferrans C. Quality of life after angioplasty. *Heart Lung* 1993;7(1):18–28.
11. Cowan M, Young-Graham K, Cochrane B. Comparison of a theory of quality of life between myocardial infarction and malignant melanoma: a pilot study. *Prog Cardiovasc Nurs* 1992;7(1):18–28.
12. Hinds PS. Quality of life in children and adolescents with cancer. *Semin Oncol Nurs* 1990;6:285–291.
13. Weaver-McClure LL, Venzon DJ, Horowitz ME. A comparison of distress levels in pediatric/young adult cancer patients and their significant others. *Qual Life Nurs Challenge* 1993;2:11–16.
14. Weaver-McClure LL, Venzon DJ, Horowitz ME. A comparison of young cancer patients and nurses' perceptions of patient quality of life (Abstract). Paper presented at the 17th Annual Conference of the Association of Pediatric Oncology Nurses, Reno, NV, October 1993.
15. Jassak PF, Knafl KA. Quality of family life: exploration of a concept. *Semin Oncol Nurs* 1990;6(4):298–302.
16. Lewis FM. Experienced personal control and quality of life in late stage cancer patients. *Nurs Res* 1982;6:219–225.
17. Goodinson SM, Singleton J. Quality of life: a critical review of current concepts, measures and their clinical implications. *Int J Nurs Stud* 1989;26(4):327–341.
18. McDaniel RW, Bach CA. Quality of life: a concept analysis. *Rehabil Nurs Res* 1994;3(1):18–22.
19. Padilla GV, Ferrell BR, Grant MM, Rhiner M. Defining the content domain of quality of life for cancer patients with pain. *Cancer Nurs* 1990;13(2):108–115.
20. Ferrans CE. Quality of life: conceptual issues. *Semin Oncol Nurs* 1990;6:248–254.
21. Ferrell BR. Overview of psychological well-being and quality of life. *Qual Life Nurs Challenge* 1993;1(2):1–3.
22. Grant MM, Ferrell BR, Schmidt G, Fonbuena P, Nilandm J, Forman S. Researching quality of life indicators: their impact on the daily life of bone marrow transplant patients. In: *Proceedings of the Seventh International Conference on Cancer Nursing.* Vienna; 1992:80–84.
23. Grant MM, Padilla G, Presant C, Upsett J, Runa PL. Cancer patients and quality of life. In: *American Cancer Society Proceedings of the Fourth National Conference on Cancer Nursing.* Atlanta, American Cancer Society, 1984:2–11.
24. Ferrell BR, Rivera LM. Measurement of physical well-being as a dimension of quality of life. *Qual Life Nurs Challenge* 1993;1(1):45–51.
25. Young KJ, Longman AJ. Quality of life and persons with melanoma: a pilot study. *Cancer Nurs* 1983;6:219–225.
26. Graham KJY, Longman AJ. Quality of life in persons with melanoma. *Cancer Nurs* 1987;10:338–346.
27. Ferrans C, Powers M. Quality of life index: development and psychometric properties. *Adv Nurs Sci* 1985;8:15–24.
28. Ferrans C, Powers M. Psychometric assessment of the quality of life index. *Res Nurs Health* 1992;15:29–38.
29. Oleson M. Content validity of the quality of life index. *Appl Nurs Res* 1990;3(3):126–127.
30. Presant CA, Klahr C, Hogan L. Evaluating quality of life in oncology patients: pilot observations. *Oncol Nurs Forum* 1981;8(3):26–30.
31. Grant MM, Padilla GV, Ferrell BR, Rhiner M. Assessment of quality of life with a single instrument. *Semin Oncol Nurs* 1990;6(4):260–270.
32. Dean H. Choosing multiple instruments to measure quality of life. *Oncol Nurs Forum* 1985;12:96–100.
33. Jalowiec A. Issues in using multiple measures of quality of life. *Semin Oncol Nurs* 1990;6(4):271–277.
34. Hinds PS. Self care outcomes in adolescents with cancer. R01CA48432, National Cancer Institute, 1990–1995.
35. Hinds PS, Quargnenti A, Madison J. Refusal to participate in clinical nursing research. *West J Nurs Res* 1995;17(2):232–236.
36. Varricchio C. Relevance of quality of life to clinical nursing practice. *Semin Oncol Nurs* 1990;6(4):255–259.
37. Wright P. Parents' perceptions of their quality of life. *J Pediatr Oncol Nurs* 1993;10:139–145.
38. Ferrans C. Quality of life index for Black and Hispanic patients. 1R01CA61698-01, National Cancer Institute, 1994.

Quality of Life and Pharmacoeconomics in Clinical Trials, Second Edition, edited by B. Spilker. Lippincott-Raven Publishers, Philadelphia © 1996.

CHAPTER 57

An Industry Perspective

Bert Spilker and Stanley B. Garbus

INTRODUCTION

Quality of life issues in clinical trials are important to pharmaceutical companies because of their applications to medical practice, regulatory approval, marketing efforts, and outcomes-based health policy. The first major quality of life study on a pharmaceutical product published in the *New England Journal of Medicine* occurred in 1986 (1). Journal editors felt the subject was of sufficient importance to the medical community to make it that issue's lead article. This event sent a clear message to the entire pharmaceutical industry about quality of life data. This message was confirmed when subsequent sales of the product described increased.

In the 5-year period since the first edition of this book was published, the pharmaceutical industry has undergone major changes, and quality of life studies have become increasingly important to companies. The following current trends often influence the design and/or the application of quality of life trials:

B. Spilker: Orphan Medical, Inc., Minnetonka, Minnesota 55305.
S. B. Garbus: ClinMark Associates, Inc., Fort Lee, New Jersey 07204.

–More knowledgeable and sophisticated customers
–Increased product competition
–Increased price sensitivity
–Lower introductory product prices
–Smaller price increases
–More large purchasers of medicines
–Increased cost awareness by private and government third-party payers
–Increased importance of managed health care groups
–Increased need for product differentiation
–Corporate restructuring, realignment, and alliances
–Increased costs of research and development
–Increased need for global research and development plans
–Therapeutic research networks (e.g., Joslin TrialNet for diabetes, Preferred Oncology Network of America, NIH AIDS Clinical Trial Group)
–Aging populations and increasing number of patients with chronic diseases and cancers

This chapter explores corporate, marketing, medical, and regulatory perspectives of quality of life issues. From a corporate view, the major quality of life issues are organizational and conceptual. The essential goals a marketing unit seeks from quality of life data are a strong marketing position and competitive advantage. Medical groups focus on defining a product profile that they hope will enhance clinical benefits for patients, and regulatory groups seek information that increases the chances of approval and acceptance for the company's products by regulatory authorities.

CORPORATE PERSPECTIVE

What Are the Corporate Issues?

The expanding inclusion of quality of life studies (as well as pharmacoeconomic studies) as part of pharmaceutical company-sponsored clinical trials is the result of the industry's recognition that traditional safety and efficacy data plus strong marketing may not be sufficient to ensure a product's success. Pharmaceutical executives therefore need to know what quality of life studies are, why they are necessary, when they should be conducted, how they can be used to enhance the approval process, how they can be used for product positioning and marketing, and how the company's resources should be organized to conduct these studies most effectively.

Why Conduct Quality of Life Studies?

Five general reasons support the conduct of quality of life studies. Each of these reasons has important commercial implications for the company, and several reasons have important medical implications for physicians who prescribe medicines and for patients who take them.

First, improved quality of life benefits over traditional therapies may assist regulatory strategies. For example, the data may increase the pressure within regulatory agencies in some countries for a medicine to be approved more rapidly. In some cases, a new medicine or a new indication for a marketed medicine may be approved based primarily or secondarily on quality of life data. These data may enable medicines to be differentiated that are otherwise similar in terms of conventional efficacy and safety parameters. Quality of life studies may also be used to modify and improve the labeling of a marketed medicine.

Second, quality of life studies can assist in pricing products. If a company can demonstrate increased quality of life benefits to patients with a new medicine, they may charge patients more than for existing medicines and still maintain the same or better cost-to-benefit relationship. These data are therefore important in addition to pharmacoeconomic data.

Third, quality of life studies provide customers with complete product information. Advertising and other promotional vehicles as well as professional publications are important for disseminating information to customers. The degree to which these efforts are pursued depends on the company's culture and goals. Advances in life-prolonging technologies and increased public awareness of quality of life issues are focusing public attention on the risks as well as benefits of medicines. If an anticancer medicine prolongs the life of a patient who is severely ill but reduces his or her quality of life, what is the medical, economic, or societal wisdom for its use? This major ethical question is being discussed without adequate information about the effects of most medicine regimens on quality of life. This inadequacy must be addressed by the pharmaceutical industry to protect the future of its medicines.

Fourth, quality of life considerations help determine which types of information are most useful for specific audiences (e.g., to obtain formulary acceptance for a medicine). This information can be used to design appropriate pre- or post-marketing studies to evaluate the medicine.

Finally, in situations of therapeutic substitution, quality of life evaluations might show differences that help a company counter substitution practices. Differences might be as subtle as taste distinctions that lead to decreased patient compliance with the other medicine or as obvious as decreased medical benefits with other medicines. Quality of life trials should be used to evaluate possible differences.

How Should a Company Organize a Group to Address Quality of Life Issues?

Several organizational issues should be addressed before a company's resources are allocated to quality of life trials:

1. Which division or department in the company should be responsible for conducting quality of life trials?
2. How should marketing and medical groups, the groups primarily concerned with quality of life issues, interact to best serve the company's interest?
3. Should quality of life activities be assigned to existing groups or should an independent organizational structure be created?

The usual contenders for organizational control of quality of life studies are marketing and medical units, although a current trend is to establish an independent outcomes research group that serves as in-house consultants to all departments responsible for these trials. The traditional location of clinical trials suggests that a medical group is the more logical site for controlling quality of life trials. Medical groups determine the efficacy and safety of a product; however, the impetus for quality of life trials usually comes from marketing groups, and some companies have placed quality of life trials under the direction of marketing. A strong case may be made, however, to create an independent outcomes group that has responsibility for both pharmacoeconomics and quality of life. This department should report to a very high level within the company.

The allocation of human resources to quality of life trials depends on how clinical medicine is organized within the company and on how senior executives view the importance of quality of life data. A single medical advisor well versed in quality of life methodology may serve as a consultant to all medical groups conducting these trials. Alternatively, a separate group may be established within the medical unit to pursue the planning and initiation of quality of life trials. This group should have strong organizational ties to the other medical groups that conduct phase 1 to 4 trials, as well as strong ties to marketing personnel who are knowledgeable about quality of life needs within marketing groups.

As the economics of health care delivery have changed and cost containment issues have become dominant, a more competitive marketplace has been created. Hospitals, health maintenance organizations, government programs, and some traditional insurance programs have established restricted formularies to control dispensing patterns. A restrictive formulary limits the number of medicines available for physicians to use for the same condition. Absence of a medicine from a formulary limits its sale. Placement on many formularies requires additional information beyond the usual efficacy and safety data available for a medicine. Quality of life information becomes an important marketing tool to help medicines achieve formulary approval and thus enhance sales. An improved product profile obtained through quality of life advantages provides the competitive advantage that marketing constantly seeks.

Information developed independently of a specific customer's needs may make it much more difficult to convince that customer to use the medicine. For example, marketing groups usually respond to specific needs of health marketing organizations, hospitals, and other providers whose decisions may be influenced by quality of life data. Quality of life trials that include these provider groups as research sites will make the results of the trial more compelling to those groups.

MARKETING PERSPECTIVE

How May Quality of Life Data be Used in Marketing?

Quality of life trials can provide information to help a company determine a marketing strategy and establish the comparative advantage of one product over another. Information obtained in quality of life trials can help select the niche in which a medicine should compete. Data from such trials can help determine which attributes of a product to emphasize in positioning the product. Lastly, the data obtained can address the question of how to approach the different customers that marketing must reach.

Quality of life trials can provide information to enhance the medicine's efficacy and safety profile. These additional data allow a better comparison of a medicine's benefits (efficacy) to risks (adverse reactions) than using efficacy and safety data alone. These trials may demonstrate important advantages of one product over another in terms of benefits viewed by patients. Benefits might include aspects of psychological well-being such as reduced worry or increased

happiness, improved physical status such as greater comfort, and increased social interactions.

How Will Data Obtained in Trials be Used?

Among today's customers for the products of the pharmaceutical industry are those who make economic decisions affecting medical care. These groups include national, state or provincial, and local governments; managed care systems (including health maintenance and preferred provider organizations); buying groups; and insurance companies. These groups are using numerous mechanisms to control medical practice through controlling expenditures. The ability to demonstrate improved quality of life or cost savings versus another therapy increases the probability that these agencies will encourage the product's use.

Medical and marketing goals are not necessarily the same. To be successful, marketing must respond to the needs of its various audiences. Marketers would like information about a medicine that is individualized to specific customers (e.g., health maintenance organizations or state Medicaid programs). On the other hand, medical groups want to define the profile of a medicine that will be used by all of marketing's audiences.

For decision makers in a health maintenance organization, data from trials conducted in most fee-for-service settings are less meaningful than data from trials in a health maintenance organization. Likewise, Medicaid or Medicare trials that focus on their particular patient populations will be accepted more readily by decision makers within those groups than data from trials conducted with other populations. Although it is not possible to conduct a single quality of life trial to please everybody, study site selection criteria should consider the identity of the groups that will eventually review the data.

Quality of life data can be used to promote customer and physician loyalty. Another benefit is to provide advantages for specific patient populations, for example, home care parenteral therapy.

The outlook for quality of life data to be used for decisions about reimbursement is not clear. Neither Medicare nor Medicaid requires quality of life information for reimbursement of hospitals or patients who are using specific medicines. However, quality of life data can help persuade Medicaid administrators to include specific medicines in formularies or can support pricing decisions.

When Should Quality of Life Data be Obtained?

Ideally, quality of life information on a new medicine should be available at the time of product launch. However, this raises two major issues about conducting quality of life trials. First, quality of life studies conducted before regulatory approval generates data that are not based on real-world behavior. The controlled nature of clinical trials, the close supervision of medical practice and patient behavior, and the use of traditional clinical sites produces results that are sometimes difficult to reproduce in physicians' offices, hospitals, or health maintenance organizations after a medicine is launched. Benefits demonstrated in controlled settings may diminish or even disappear when physicians are less intensive in their medical treatment. The opposite phenomenon also occurs; some medicines are more effective in practice than in clinical trials.

Clinical studies conducted after marketing approval allow for evaluation of medicines under more realistic conditions. Usage on the market may subjectively demonstrate significant quality of life benefits to patients and physicians. These benefits can be most clearly demonstrated in well-controlled, randomized clinical trials. Waiting for regulatory approval before initiating well-designed and -controlled trials, however, delays the availability of the information and may reduce the eventual usefulness and profitability of the product.

Which Medicines Should be Evaluated?

Not all medicines need quality of life trials. First, acute therapies are inappropriate to test because of their short use. Second, the perceived medical advantage of a new product may be so significant that there would be little or no benefit derived from documenting quality of life improvements. Medicines without competition do not generally require these trials, unless cost is a major factor. Cost issues may be so insignificant that trial results could not add to the medicine's commercial value.

Other factors may also influence the decision for or against conducting a quality of life trial. For example, how important is the commercial value of the medicine to the pharmaceutical company? How important is it to demonstrate quality of life benefits to physicians, patients, and to those who pay for the therapy?

Medicines that are not profitable or not expected to be profitable do not require quality of life trials. Because a product with limited sales potential is less likely to be a candidate for quality of life trials, it is better to place research resources where they will achieve the greatest results. If potential advantages of a medicine product have little or no meaning to those who will prescribe, use, or pay for the product, there is little reason to conduct such trials. Though quality of life trials may initially appear to be relevant for all products, a company must be selective in its use of resources for these trials.

The selection of medicines to compare with a company's medicine depends on reaching a consensus between medical and marketing interests. Products perceived as competitors from medical's point of view may not be the products that marketing primarily wants to compete against. Marketing may want to reposition a product, to change a product from one market to another, or to find a more suitable niche in the existing market. Medical personnel may feel that marketing's desire for repositioning a product weakens the clinical significance of the product. Joint discussions are often required to resolve differences.

In summary, from a marketing perspective, the specific types of medicines for which quality of life trials should be conducted include (a) medicines in intense competition, (b) "me-too" medicines, (c) medicines in certain therapeutic areas (e.g., cancer, cardiology) where the data may help speed the regulatory approval process, and (d) medicines for palliative treatment (e.g., AIDS, cancer). In each of these cases, the costs of conducting quality of life trials must be justified in terms of anticipated commercial benefits.

MEDICAL PERSPECTIVE

For certain medicines, quality of life trials represent an integral component of the comprehensive product profile. These trials provide additional data on the medicine's effectiveness and sometimes data on the economic and medical consequences of its adverse experiences. The impact of a new medicine on the emotional, social, and physical well-being of a patient offers many professionals (e.g., physician, regulatory authority, policy planner, formulary committee) a more comprehensive assessment of a medicine and its effect on treatment outcomes than merely measuring clinical signs and symptoms. The value of this information may be assessed in terms of the corporate resources needed to conduct these trials and the likelihood of eventual market success.

How May a Quality of Life Plan be Initiated, Coordinated, and Reviewed?

The responsibility for raising questions about quality of life issues on a new investigational medicine generally belongs with the project team involved in its development. This group usually has both medical and marketing members. If this group is not involved (or is only indirectly involved) in quality of life trials, then the quality of life and/or pharmacoeconomic group within marketing or medical should contact the project group to discuss this issue.

Quality of life trials require well-designed protocols, clear end points, and attention to study conduct. Both marketing and medical involvement are needed to assist a sponsor in the choice of (a) appropriate end points that will meet the trial's objectives, (b) site selection, and (c) protocol design. Medical personnel must monitor the trial and analyze the results. Although quality of life trials must be conducted by medical groups, those groups may be directed or controlled by marketing interests, if not by marketing personnel.

What Elements Should be Considered in the Development of a Quality of Life Plan?

The development of useful quality of life information for physicians depends primarily on two issues: which product(s) and which attributes are to be compared. Product comparisons should cover five areas: physical status, physical ability, psychological well-being, social interactions, and economic profiles. The clinical efficacy and safety profiles of new medicines are most often compared with standard medicines in phase 3 and 4 clinical trials. Data obtained may influence medicine labeling. In addition to basic efficacy and safety data on how medicines compare with others, it is important for physicians to understand differences in how medicines affect quality of life. Improvement in overall quality of life measures is not yet an accepted basis for medicine approval, especially if safety and efficacy do not meet the standards of existing therapy.

Several issues about quality of life trials should be addressed before the actual trials are initiated. Is a pilot study required? Should quality of life measures be included as part of other clinical trials or should they be conducted on their own? During what phase of development should these trials be conducted? What measurement tools should be used? Before decisions are made about what parameters to evaluate in a quality of life trial, it is necessary to determine the goals of the trial, plus (a) indications to analyze, (b) patient populations to enroll, and (c) type or nature of sites to use in the trial(s).

If quality of life trials are conducted on their own and not as part of other clinical trials, then factors such as cost, personnel, and timing should be explored. A separate trial usually costs more than adding a few questions or tests to an existing trial. Determining differences between medicines when measuring them on quality of life issues may require large populations. The larger the trial, the larger the commitment of both company personnel and capital. A third factor in the cost equation is the duration of quality of life trials. Often the most important end point of a quality of life trial is the long-term outcome of medicine therapy. Patient enrollment in such trials could range from one to several years. The trial, from time of protocol development to medical report summarization, could last 1 to 2 years longer than the length of enrollment of any one patient.

Providing necessary resources to conduct a major trial of this type may affect development of other medicines within the company. However, scarce human resources may be augmented by using outside clinical trial vendors. Company culture, capable vendors, importance of rapidly completed trials, and available company resources necessary to manage the contract are the major elements to consider in reaching a decision to use outside contractors.

At What Phase of Clinical Development Should Quality of Life Trials be Conducted?

Most of the reasons for conducting quality of life trials relate to a medicine's marketing. This suggests that at least some quality of life trials should be conducted before regulatory approval so information is available when the medicine is initially marketed. Following this reasoning, quality of life considerations could begin as early as phase 2 during the conduct of well-controlled trials. Phase 2 trials could be used to identify which parameters and populations of patients (e.g., severely ill versus mildly ill) should be more completely evaluated in later trials. For example, if a product is thought capable of reducing length of stay in an intensive care unit, then collection of such data in phase 2 could determine if the supposition is warranted, give a sense of how much the stay is reduced, or determine at what levels of medicine dosing the best efficacy and stay reduction is achieved. Such information will allow for the design for phase 3 trials that produce data necessary to test the hypothesis. Another approach is to use observational method studies to identify parameters.

Three general approaches are described for deciding the most appropriate timing for quality of life trials. The first is to conduct trials during phases 2b and 3a if data are likely to enhance the speed of regulatory approval. For chemotherapy products there is a growing acceptance in the industry and regulatory agencies that approval could be based, at least in part, on quality of life data. These data should be gathered in studies conducted during phases 2b and 3a, before New Drug Application (NDA) submission. Medicines in a number of other therapeutic areas (e.g., cardiology) may also be candidates for early clinical trials on quality of life.

A second approach to the question of when to conduct quality of life trials is to wait until the NDA has been filed. These trials would be conducted during the regulatory review (phase 3b). This approach does not delay the submission of the NDA and has the possibility of having quality of life information available at the time of product launch. It does require submission of appropriate information to the regulatory authority before final medicine approval, and this could potentially slow the regulatory review of the medicine.

A third approach is to wait until the medicine is approved before conducting quality of life trials. Neither the submission nor the regulatory review is delayed. However, if the medicine is launched without sufficient quality of life information, the potential impact of this information is diminished.

What Methods Should be Used and What Data Should be Obtained?

Quality of life trials must use the same rigorous statistical and protocol design standards used in clinical research. The well-controlled, randomized clinical trial should be used whenever possible. In certain situations observational methods may be used, but findings from such trials should be confirmed through more rigorous clinical trial methods.

Quality of life trials evaluating or comparing medicines should assess all quality of life domains and multiple components of each, rather than potentially biasing a trial by selecting only one or two domains. Adhering to these standards will provide credible data.

The specific data to collect depends on what is important to patients and to customers, plus the ability to collect and analyze valid data. If a product is being developed for a disease where the only current therapy is surgery, then the ability to avoid surgery becomes an important economic variable to assess in a quality of life trial. If the product under development is going to compete with other medicines, then the economics of concomitant medicine usage, length of therapy, and necessity of monitoring medicine usage are often important.

In selecting a scale to use in a quality of life trial, avoid unvalidated scales whenever possible. Confirm that scales to be used have been validated for the population to be studied. Quality of life scales are often validated only for specific populations or for a specific means of administration (self-administered, telephone, mail, physician interviewer).

REGULATORY PERSPECTIVE

Results of quality of life trials may sometimes support corporate regulatory strategies. Regulatory authorities may use quality of life assessments as a basis for granting marketing approval, either as the principal basis of such approval or as supportive evidence. To date, no medicine has received approval for its initial indication based primarily on quality of life data. In addition to assisting the approval of a new medicine, quality of life data may be used when applying for an expanded indication or labeling change of a marketed product.

How Should Quality of Life Data be Presented to Regulatory Authorities?

Neither regulation nor law currently requires quality of life information for regulatory authority approval or government reimbursement. Therefore, the decision to provide this information to an agency is based on answers to these questions: What will the agency do with the information? How will the information help the approval process? What resources are needed to obtain the data? And how long will it take to obtain the data?

As part of the review process for ''life-threatening conditions,'' the Food and Drug Administration will consider risk-benefit information in its decision making. Although risk-benefit analysis does not have to include quality of life information, it does allow for such data. Quality of life factors could therefore be used by regulatory authorities in their current review and approval process. While such information could in theory be requested either before approval or in post-marketing studies, it is hoped that the regulatory pendulum does not swing to that extreme position.

CONCLUSIONS

The changing health care environment has resulted in a growing interest in the additional product information produced by quality of life trials. Although quality of life data are not generally the primary basis for new medicine approval or reimbursement, the role of these data is being expanded and will have increased value in future regulatory considerations.

Quality of life trials need to be well-designed, well-controlled, and randomized. They need to use validated measurement instruments. These studies provide important information to assist medical decisions regarding improved patient care, choice of therapy, and clinical guidelines. Trials will be most valuable if they incorporate the perspectives of the customers for whom they are developed and include all quality of life domains and appropriate components of the domains.

Joint corporate medical and marketing efforts in studying new or existing products are critical in the more competitive and customer-oriented marketplace. A detailed company strategy for planning quality of life trials should be developed. Quality of life trials, along with other outcomes research, will assist innovative product development and sales and, most importantly, improve the quality of patient care.

ACKNOWLEDGMENT

The authors gratefully acknowledge the contributions of Mr. Doug Henderson-James to the first edition of this chapter.

REFERENCE

1. Croog SH, Levine S, Testa MA, et al. The effects of antihypertensive therapy on the quality of life. N Engl J Med 1986;314:1657–1664.

Quality of Life and Pharmacoeconomics in Clinical Trials, Second Edition, edited by B. Spilker. Lippincott-Raven Publishers, Philadelphia © 1996.

CHAPTER 58

A Marketing Perspective: Theoretical Underpinnings

Louis A. Morris,* Thomas K. Beckett, and Karen J. Lechter*

INTRODUCTION

During the past three decades, the marketing of pharmaceuticals has shifted from a producer- to a consumer-driven activity. At one time, physicians looked forward to the latest offerings of pharmaceutical companies and eagerly prescribed new products. Not only were products selected that represented clear advantages over existing products, but the latest member of a class of drugs could look forward to trial prescribing by a sizable group of physicians regardless of any real benefits in efficacy and safety compared with the competition. Physicians paid little heed to the price of these new innovations and purchasers (mostly patients with the assistance of a passive insurer) paid the asking price. As long as expenses remained small (relative to other health care costs), this financial system worked well to provide for the delivery of pharmaceutical products and services while sustaining a generous profit margin for the pharmaceutical industry.

Beginning in the 1980s, the marketing environment began to change. During the 1970s and early 1980s, the pharmaceutical industry did not raise prices as rapidly as other industries did despite relatively high overall inflation. Toward the end of this period, the expiration of major patents accelerated; legislation and regulatory activity provided rapid availability of generic products, and therapeutically similar products became much more conspicuous in certain product categories. At the same time, research and development costs increased. As these pressures threatened industry margins, companies sought to maintain income levels by aggressively increasing their prices (during a period of relatively low inflation). Not only were the prices of existing products raised, but for certain high-tech/small-market products, prices were set at noticeably high levels (attracting attention from both press and politicians).

By the late 1980s, insurers and payers began to notice the increased costs of pharmaceuticals as they sought ways to reduce their health care outlays. Adapting techniques and technologies from hospital pharmacies, institutional purchasers began to exert much greater pressure on pharmaceutical companies to lower prices. Since the late 1980s there has been a near revolution in the distribution channel for pharmaceuticals. Pharmaceutical decision making, which had been the almost exclusive role of the fiercely independent physician, has changed in two dramatic ways.

First, as competition among physicians has risen, physicians have had to become more conscious of their patients' needs and desires. This has led physicians to become increas-

   L. A. Morris and K. J. Lechter: Division of Drug Marketing, Advertising, and Communications, United States Food and Drug Administration, Rockville, Maryland 20857.
   T. K. Beckett: Langford Creek Associates, Ltd., Chestertown, Maryland 21620.
   *The views expressed are solely those of the authors and do not reflect the policies of the U.S. Food and Drug Administration.

ingly sensitive to claims about pharmaceuticals that would influence patient satisfaction. Thus, changes in how drugs influence patient perceptions of health status, functioning, and the value of pharmaceuticals, along with greater knowledge of the cost of the drug to the patient, have become more influential in physicians' selection of pharmaceutical products.

Second, the rise in managed care and the introduction of restricted formularies administered by pharmaceutical benefit managers have increased "institutional control" over a large percentage of drug purchasing. The placement of brands or generic versions of drug products on formularies has limited the physician's ability to select specific brands of pharmaceuticals. The selective purchasing within pharmaceutical classes has also increased competition within the drug industry, as broad pharmacologic or therapeutic classes of drugs now compete for limited slots on a formulary. To qualify for a position on the formulary, companies must price their product below the competition or persuade formulary managers of the unique value of their products, either by demonstrating the advantages of their product over competing products or by convincing buyers of the cost-effectiveness of their product.

This power shift in the distribution channel for pharmaceuticals has forced drug companies to market their products in new ways. One effect of the emphasis on demonstrating value has been an increased interest in quality of life assessment in the evaluation of pharmaceutical products. Quality of life measures are seen as important signals of the patient's perspective of the impact of pharmaceutical therapy as well as an important element in the evaluation of the cost-effectiveness of pharmaceuticals. While the assessment of the risks and benefits of pharmaceuticals has traditionally been at the core of the drug development process, quality of life evaluation has enlarged the sphere of evaluative criteria for drugs and focused assessment on parameters that are perceived to be important to patients.

In this chapter we review the role of quality of life in the marketing of pharmaceuticals. We review the conceptual underpinnings of pharmaceutical marketing and the role of quality of life assessment in the interaction between marketers, decision makers, and users of pharmaceuticals. We focus on the role of quality of life in pharmaceutical decisions made by prescribers and formulary decision makers in selecting drug products for their patients.

Quality of life assessment can inform physicians about how the products they prescribe influence patients' health status on a range of dimensions. A wide variety of general and disease-specific multidimensional scales have been developed to perform these assessments. Quality of life can also be a part of the evaluation of the cost-effectiveness of pharmaceuticals, as a unitary econometric measure that permits the simultaneous comparison of a range of diverse therapies along a single dimension. In this form, quality of life measures can be used to adjust assessments of the years of life saved by a therapy to take into account the value that

patients (or other observers) place on that general health state. The use of a unitary scale to measure a diverse set of diseases and their consequences is fraught with measurement and interpretation ambiguities, and these concerns influence acceptance of these forms of quality of life assessment.

In this chapter, we describe three categories of quality of life research and its application to marketing as a basis for (a) promotion of a better product, (b) promotion of a different product, and (c) patient segmentation.

Throughout this discussion, questions about the validity and interpretability of quality of life measurements will be raised. As a still-developing concept, quality of life assessment remains a potentially important concept in the selection and prescribing of pharmaceuticals. However, as the "Peanuts" character Charlie Brown has suggested, great potential is a heavy burden. Incorporation of quality of life into routine therapeutic decisions remains an unrealized goal of quality of life advocates. The necessary and sufficient conditions for quality of life to serve reliably as an accepted measure of the functional impact or as an indicator incorporated into cost-effectiveness evaluations of a therapy remain to be illustrated.

THE MARKETING CONCEPT

Most people view marketing and selling as analogous concepts. In each case, the producer transfers goods and services for which the consumer transfers a payment. Over the years, however, the marketing concept has evolved and changed its focus away from the selling of commodities and toward the "exchange" process between two social units (1). Several important implications flow from this change in focus.

Rather than emphasizing goods and services, consumer needs are the nucleus of the marketing function. Rather than accrue profits through sales volume, modern marketers view consumer satisfaction as the route to repeat business, consumer loyalty, and ultimately to increased profits. Rather than viewing the selling function as a one-way flow of goods and services, marketing is accomplished through a two-way flow between producer and consumer.

To the extent that a product or service enhances the quality of life of an individual, one would expect that the individual would be motivated to seek to obtain that product compared with another product that does not improve quality of life outcomes to as great an extent. However, this analysis is based upon the assumption that products have similar costs and actually produce differential effects, and that the consumer notices changes in health status, cognitively appraises these effects, attributes changes to the therapeutic intervention, and positively evaluates these changes in health status. Unfortunately, in its current state, there are several limitations to the direct application of quality of life research to the improvement of marketing exchanges.

First, to our knowledge, there has been little research on the extent to which quality of life improvements correlate with consumer satisfaction measures. Models of consumer satisfaction are based primarily on the extent to which observed product performance meets expectations (2). Thus, even if health status is improved, a consumer may remain dissatisfied if the rate or extent of improvement is below expected levels. For the most part, quality of life measurement is based upon descriptive measures of health status rather than comparisons of expected and achieved health status. The failure to take into account health status expectations suggests that quality of life measurement may not provide sufficient "contextual" information to understand fully its impact on patients' health status appraisal and satisfaction with treatment. Health care providers must project their own expectations to estimate the extent to which a quality of life outcome would result in patient satisfaction with treatment. Measurement of patient expectations and other parameters may help to improve our understanding of the extent to which consumers' quality of life assessments translate to perceived satisfaction improvements.

Second, quality of life research has concentrated almost exclusively on assessment of health status as opposed to understanding the appraisal process underlying quality of life judgments (3). Thus, quality of life research has concentrated on the development of scales that seek to measure health outcomes validly. This process assumes that quality of life assessment is based upon the patient's review of a fixed number of factors (presumably sampled by questionnaire items) to assess a functional domain. Tversky et al. (4) have suggested that while the review of a fixed number of factors may validly describe the processes underlying consumer choice, other types of consumer judgments (such as health status evaluations) may be better represented by a more dynamic process in which extreme outcomes on any of a large number of attribute dimensions could influence overall judgments. Applying this logic, for example, if an arthritic treatment caused extreme fatigue, this effect may not be measured by scales that assess ability to perform routine physical tasks (e.g., walking stairs, moving without pain). However, this side effect may be highly salient and weighted heavily when patients make overall evaluations of the product's performance in achieving expected results and their own satisfaction with treatment. Without a better understanding of how patients make quality of life judgments, it is unclear if therapies selected on the basis of their impact on quality of life assessment would be evaluated positively by patients when broader (satisfaction) judgments are made.

Third, the multidimensional nature of quality of life measurement suggests that competing products (especially those from different pharmacological classes) may have variable quality of life profiles that are differentially valued by patients. Thus, even if prescribers attempt to use quality of life measurements as input into decision making, selecting which product is best suited for which patient may be difficult if quality of life profiles differ among products and no product is superior on all relevant dimensions. Even if a product has some distinct advantages over another product, it may not be positively judged by patients who do not have a value system compatible with its profile. It may be difficult for prescribers to apply judgments successfully based upon the patient's value system because values may be difficult for patients to communicate and prescribers may not fully understand how patients would make trade-offs among various risk/benefit outcome strategies (5). The use of quality of life indices in prescribing decisions may be quite limited if the physician's choice is narrowed to selecting brands within a therapeutic class. Even if quality of life differences exist, it may be quite difficult to detect quality of life differences among similar pharmacologic products.

Given these difficulties in directly applying quality of life outcomes, it is clear that much more work is needed for quality of life research to contribute to our understanding of mechanisms that would improve marketing exchanges. However, even in its present state, there are important roles for quality of life research in facilitating marketing exchanges. Two marketing principles, market segmentation and product positioning, can be used to help integrate quality of life assessment into pharmaceutical marketing.

Market Segmentation

The first principle, marketing segmentation, is based on the premise that consumers can be clustered into homogeneous but distinctive groups or market segments. Rather than mass market a therapy (i.e., develop one therapy and communications program suited for all potential consumers), more carefully targeted therapies can be created by grouping consumers (e.g., based on age or lifestyle preferences) and developing therapies and communications programs more specifically suited for these smaller groups.

Market segmentation is a common practice in medical marketing when, for example, different dosage forms are used by pediatric and geriatric patients or when marketers create different advertising campaigns for family physicians and specialists. However, the "basis" or variable used to segment a market need not be a demographic category such as age or profession. Any variable that reliably measures a consumer trait or characteristic can potentially be used as a basis for market segmentation.

One of the popular bases for segmenting markets is by virtue of the particular benefits that consumers seek from different products (i.e., benefit segmentation) (6). Thus, it is possible that quality of life data could be used to group patients into homogeneous but distinct segments on the basis of similarity in the quality of life preferences for therapeutic outcomes. To the extent to which therapies can be shown to have reliable quality of life profiles, it is reasonable to assume that patients (or physicians who serve as their agents) could identify patient groups that value particular outcomes. One advantage to marketers of knowing the benefits sought by different groups is that marketers could better understand associated characteristics of such patients. This information could be used to help select and use different therapies. For example, if certain candidates for a pain medication value improved social role functioning while other candidates value physical functioning, medications that avoid encumbering side effects that would inhibit social interaction (e.g., running nose) would be best used by the social role segment while other medications that do not cause sedation would be applied to the physical functioning segment.

Once these segments are identified, markets could also seek to understand how medication adherence and information search patterns vary among segments. This information could aid in supplying patients with information that may help improve utilization and adherence.

Product Positioning

The second principle, product positioning, is based on the premise that within a competitive marketing environment, each product must maintain a distinct image in the consumer's mind. In the case of a drug product, the consumer may be the patient, the prescriber, or a decision maker choosing products for inclusion in the formulary or for reimbursement. The meaning that a consumer attributes to a product is based on the consumer's assessment of the product's attributes. Attributes may be physical descriptions of the product (e.g., a white-colored tablet), effects produced by the product (e.g., the drug causes drowsiness and decreases ability to drive a car), or symbolic elements (e.g., one must be quite sick to take such a serious medication). Marketers can "position" their product by changing (a) the product itself (e.g., dosage form, packaging, labeling, or even the product's name), (b) the promotion, (c) the distribution system (e.g., through physicians' offices, hospitals, pharmacies), and (d) the pricing structure (price and quality are often assumed to be positively correlated). In addition, factors outside the marketer's control can influence the product image; for example, the press may publicize stories about the product's risks or benefits.

An important lesson from marketing is that product positioning must be clear and meaningful. Emphasizing too many attributes will lead to unclear positioning, as consumers will have difficulty understanding how one product is different from its competitors. Marketers must choose which attributes to emphasize (so the product will be perceived as distinct from the other products in the class) and how to communicate those distinctions. Thus, some nonsteroidal anti-inflammatory drugs may be positioned as "pain receivers" and others as "arthritis treatments," although a product could potentially treat both conditions. A superior marketing position is obtained to the extent that a product is beneficial to the target market compared with competing products. Thus, choosing a product position (i.e., creating a theme that characterizes the product) is a function of (a) assessing the com-

petition to understand existing product positions and finding a unique "niche" or a preferred position, and (b) understanding the needs and values of the target market to find a theme that will clearly emphasize the perceived benefits of the product for the target market.

In marketing pharmaceuticals, the drug decision maker and the drug user are different. Prescribers typically seek to select the therapy that most benefits patients. It is not clear, however, how accurately prescribers can make these judgments, especially when there is a mixture of benefits and adverse effects that may be differentially valued by individuals. Institutional decision makers also have difficulties with individual judgments and are sensitive to cost issues as well. Quality of life, as a descriptor of patient functioning on a series of scales, can potentially provide prescribers with information about the effects of medicines on parameters viewed as (seemingly) important to the patient. However, this potential is dependent upon the extent to which scales can detect what may be small differences in quality of life parameters between similar drugs within a class. While disease-specific quality of life scales apparently have greater likelihood of assessing these differences because of increased sensitivity, questions may arise about the validity of such scales, especially if the scales are new and do not have a long track record that can be used to assess their validity. General scales, which measure functioning along broad categories, may have a longer track record but are unlikely to have sufficient sensitivity to distinguish between similar drugs. Although general scales may be able to demonstrate "pre-post" differences in patients after treatment, conclusions drawn from these types of assessments cannot reliably differentiate among products because people may draw the conclusion that the quality of life outcomes apply to an entire class of drugs and that competing products would be likely to demonstrate similar quality of life outcomes.

The use of quality of life as a unitary utility measure is appealing because it potentially provides prescribers and institutions constructing formularies with information about the value of a pharmaceutical product. As cost-consciousness increases, demonstrating value in meaningful and believable ways is becoming an important prerequisite to the adoption of pharmaceuticals. Unfortunately, there must be considerable reservations about the quality and usefulness of such measures. Attempting to reduce the impact of a therapy to a single holistic subjective measure is fraught with methodological obstacles. Measurement biases can be caused by minor variations in question phrasing, ordering of questions, and any number of factors. Interpretation of the meaning of such responses is similarly highly problematic.

QUALITY OF LIFE AND MARKETING

With this primer on marketing as background, one can see how quality of life measures would appeal to marketers. Quality of life data hold the potential for translating physical and biological effects to psychological and behavioral effects that have special value to patients. In an age in which "consumerism" in medicine is increasing, prescribers and institutional decision makers are likely to be responsive to claims made about a therapy's impact on patients' quality of life. If therapies can be credibly portrayed as having a positive impact on quality of life, they may be evaluated positively by physicians (7). Therapies that are perceived to have quality of life advantages over other treatments, especially if they have little or no increased cost, may be favored by institutional decision makers over therapies with less favorable quality of life profiles. Critical to the use of quality of life in marketing is whether studies can be successful in reliably differentiating competing products along quality of life dimensions.

Quality of life data are still relatively new to marketing and how these data will be used to characterize products is still evolving. It is possible to describe three ways in which marketers have used, are currently using, or may use quality of life measurement in the future.

Category 1: A Better Product

During the early stages of interest in quality of life, drug advertisers sometimes made broad claims that their products improved quality of life or used words suggestive of quality of life. For example, claims that Ridura (Smith, Kline, and Beckman's arthritis therapy) or Procardia (Pfizer's antianginal medicine) "improves quality of life" or that Transderm-Nitro (Ciba-Geigy's nitroglycerine patch) "helps angina patients get more out of life" suggested superiority of the product on some quality of life measure. These claims were often based on a logical analysis that people felt better about their condition when treated by medication.

In these cases, the marketer capitalized on the prescriber's initial interest in quality of life by translating demonstrated clinical effects into language that used the "quality of life" buzzword to reflect benefits that might be derived by patients. For example, makers of Zofran (Cerenex's antinausant for chemotherapy-induced nausea) used quality of life wording to describe patient benefits from the decreased nausea and vomiting demonstrated by clinical trials. Although the Food and Drug Administration (FDA) initially accepted this analysis, the FDA later objected to this broad claim because it implied more than had been studied or shown. Companies that wished to use such claims were asked to substantiate these claims with data from adequate and well-controlled studies that utilized validated quality of life scales.

The FDA also objected to the misuse of quality of life claims, especially claims that communicated therapeutic benefits that were not consistent with the therapeutic effects of the advertised products. Some manufacturers advertised that their drug "improved" quality of life when the data indicated that the drug merely had a less disruptive side effect profile. Those data would support claims that the drug

"maintained" quality of life but they would not support claims of improvement.

Generally, the FDA has objected to vague and overly broad claims of quality of life. Drug marketers have responded by narrowing quality of life claims by adding qualifying language. For example, the FDA objected to the claim that Tenex (A. H. Robbins's antihypertensive) was "patient friendly" and requested that additional specific information about side effects be added to explain what was so "friendly" about the medicine.

The usefulness of broad quality of life claims has decreased as competitors have made similar broad claims and as the FDA has begun to require greater substantiation. A once-differentiated product becomes undifferentiated as the competition begins to make identical or highly similar claims. The trend toward more specific quality of life claims has already begun, with claims being based on individual domains, such as mobility, cognitive processes, and dexterity. The trend is important because overuse of unqualified quality of life claims would likely lead to trivialization of the quality of life concept and would diminish its value in signifying unique product benefits. If these broad claims are reserved for marketers who have demonstrated real quality of life benefits, a quality of life claim can remain an important "signal" to prescribers about patient benefits of pharmaceutical products.

For institutional purchasing, the use of quality of life data integrated into cost-effectiveness analyses may serve as an indicator of the value of individual products. To the extent that institutions selecting therapies utilize measures of economic value over the long course of treatment, quality of life measures can help provide insight into the effects of therapy as moderated by patients' "utilities" for the general health states that result from treatment.

The use of quality of life data in pharmacoeconomic analyses is also important to the pharmaceutical industry. With the large increase in institutional purchasing and the increase in the power of formularies to control product selection, pharmaceutical companies are being increasingly asked by purchasing and approving boards to justify their product's selection. These institutional decision makers can determine whether large segments of the population will have access to particular drugs. Marketers are asked to demonstrate the superiority of their products or to justify charged prices. Quality of life research may be one way to help do this.

The use of quality of life utility measures [e.g., quality adjusted life years (QALYs)] in cost-effectiveness analyses is not without debate (8). Critics have questioned the degree to which such broad measures can be meaningfully interpreted. Other psychometric qualities, such as validity, reliability, and sensitivity of the instruments, can also be questioned. Further, the incorporation of QALY measures in studies may be based upon subjective reports by samples of patients who may not represent the population for whom the drug is being considered, using survey instruments and data collection methodologies with varying degrees of care and rigor.

Direct promotional claims using QALY measures have not yet become common in drug advertising. It is likely that such claims would focus on cost-effectiveness as opposed to quality of life outcomes (assuming cost-effectiveness was demonstrated). Convincing institutional purchasers, prescribers, and the FDA about the meaning of economic-based quality of life measurement remains a challenge.

Use of quality of life measures as support for the value of pharmaceuticals is a developing discipline. These data have the potential to demonstrate direct benefits of a pharmaceutical product on patients' lives that may not be obvious by a simple extrapolation based on review of the drug safety and efficacy profile. The frequency with which these unanticipated benefits can be demonstrated is unknown. However, if successful at demonstrating these unique contributions, quality of life data can help justify a drug's inclusion in formularies or support the outlay of higher payment levels by purchasing organizations.

Category 2: A Different Product

As quality of life measurement becomes more psychometrically sophisticated, it is possible that marketers could utilize the information from quality of life studies to differentiate their products. The multidimensionality of psychometrically based quality of life measurement suggests the potential for new benefits to be discovered and new claims to be made.

As long as promotional materials are truthful and fairly balanced, marketers could selectively emphasize certain quality of life scale outcomes where a particular product outperforms others. Thus, if a product performs better on a cognitive functioning scale than competing products but is no different on other scales, the marketer could use cognitive functioning as a major positioning variable. Promotional materials could be geared to emphasize cognitive functioning (e.g., a theme of "when alertness counts" might be used) and pictures of patients in tasks requiring alertness can be shown (e.g., an air traffic controller). A competitor whose product is outperformed on the cognitive functioning scale but which performs better on a physical functioning scale would logically emphasize this advantage when positioning the product. The promotional materials for this product might emphasize physical performance (e.g., when "endurance" counts) and display pictures of patients in tasks or roles requiring physical stamina (e.g., a fireman). Not only would promotion be geared to reinforce this positioning, but the name of the product and any collateral materials developed (e.g., patient education materials, desktop media), public relations efforts, and associated activities could emphasize this theme.

Quality of life data have been used to position products. For example in the area of hypertension therapy, Hytrin (Abbott/Wellcome) was claimed to maintain physical, mental, and sexual performance; Prinivil (Merck) was promoted as letting active patients stay active; Trandate (Glaxo) was promoted as preserving vitality and exercise tolerance; and Capoten (Squibb) was promoted as contributing to the patient's feeling of well-being.

When selecting drug therapy, the prescriber must decide which product is best for each patient. Given an equivalence of medical and diagnostic criteria, if plausible, the prescriber might attempt to match the quality of life theme emphasized for the drug to the prescriber's perception of the importance of the theme to the individual patient.

The extent to which quality of life data are used as part of the prescriber's evaluation criteria when selecting drug products is unclear. Studies of physician prescribing indicate that efficacy, side effects, and cost are the most important criteria influencing selection of drug products (9,10). However, these studies may be dated, and the use of quality of life data in prescribers' decisions regarding drug product selection has not been adequately addressed in the scientific literature.

A more likely interpretation of the value of quality of life claims in advertising is that these claims do not represent wholly new claims for product performance. Nonetheless, as prescribers become more interested in satisfying their patients, they may perceive quality of life claims as indicative of the effects of drugs on patients' lifestyle and performance. Thus, quality of life information may not be perceived as a unique contribution to drug effects assessment, but as a means of translating physiological effects to patient performance measures.

Category 3: A Basis for Patient Segmentation

Even if the prescriber is aware of the advantages of different therapies, how is the prescriber to know which therapy an individual patient would prefer? There are three possible ways for the prescriber to learn about a patient's preferences and use that information as a basis for decision making.

First, the prescriber could make a determination about patient preferences based on gross observations of the patient, background data in the chart, and as the result of simple questions posed to the patient about lifestyle and preferred activities. Using this approach, the prescriber can make broad assumptions based on general characteristics of the patient. Thus, a prescriber may presume that cognitive functioning is important for a college professor, whereas physical performance is important for a laborer. Gross observation of the patient and simple, indirect questions may not provide enough information for the prescriber to reach a valid conclusion about patient preferences. In addition, there is no guarantee that the prescriber's perceptions are representative of the patient's. A laborer may value cognitive functioning (e.g., alertness) more than physical function (e.g., ambulation), whereas a college professor may hold the opposite set of values.

Formal quality of life assessment may provide a more objective and complete set of parameters on which to evaluate outcomes. Most quality of life variables are based upon patient assessments of dimensions that may not be immediately evident to an observer. For example, the Sickness Impact Profile contains 12 subscales measuring factors such as home management, body care and movement, ambulation, recreation and pastimes, social interaction, and alertness (11). The Activities of Daily Living Scale and the Instrumental Activities of Daily Living Scale contain subscales representing bathing, dressing, feeding, shopping, and housekeeping, among others (12). While a prescriber can engage in personal and insightful qualitative review of the patient's preferences, the availability of an objective and qualitative set of dimensions to evaluate therapies can add to this discussion.

Second, the prescriber could integrate the quality of life preferences of the patient into clinical decision making by questioning the patient in depth and soliciting feedback along a number of critical dimensions. This is the optimum solution to the problem of how to build patient utilities into the process. Unfortunately, the prospect of soliciting and obtaining such precise feedback is likely to require enormous time and patience by the prescriber (13). There may be a large number of quality of life variables measured and the prescriber would have to discuss all potential quality of life outcomes, or at least those on which therapies differed significantly. The prescriber would have to guard against framing effects (14) and other sources of bias, to insure that the patient's stated preferences were forthright and reflective of personal values.

Unfortunately, the complexity of the data confronting the patient may be overwhelming. In the face of this potential for information overload, the prescriber either would have to simplify the discussion (perhaps by summarizing or ignoring certain variables), which could prove biasing, or guard against confronting the patient with such a complex set of decisions that the patient abdicates his/her role in the decision-making process and leaves the therapy decision totally to the prescriber. Thus, while in-depth discussion of quality of life trade-offs among different therapies is the preferred method of obtaining patient feedback, it may be difficult to implement.

Third, it may be possible to use quality of life data, along with other data, to segment patients into meaningful subgroups. If patients can be grouped on the basis of consistencies in the values they assign to various quality of life outcomes and the resultant groups may be described along various demographic, psychographic, lifestyle, and prescriber-patient interaction proclivities, therapies could be assigned according to these preferences. Once the market segments are defined and described, both marketers and prescribers would have a more precise schema by which patients may be assigned to therapeutic options.

To develop these groupings, broad-scale segmentation studies would need to be performed. Preferences for quality of life outcomes would need to be the primary questions posed to a large sample of patients. These data would serve as input into cluster analyses that sought to define homogeneous but distinct subgroups. Further, a large number of additional variables would need to be added to the study questionnaire to permit prescribers to identify patients. These variables would include demographics, preferences for therapies and outcomes, lifestyle characteristics, information search proclivities, and other variables that would help identify segments and communicate more clearly to the defined groups. The inclusion of questions about enduring values preferences would aid in maintaining stability of the defined segments (15).

To utilize a value-based segmentational strategy, an implementation system would need to be developed. Prescribers would need to learn how to assign patients to groups correctly. It may be necessary to develop a short checklist to serve as an assignment guide. A brief questionnaire for prescribers to administer to patients may also be necessary. For example, Hatcher et al. (16) have demonstrated that "triaging" rules can be successfully established and followed to assign hypertensive patients to various health education interventions.

Would prescribers use this type of system? Prescribers would need to believe in the efficacy of such a system, so evaluation studies would be essential. Although some successes have been reported when patients are assigned to treatments based on their desires and coping skills, one review of the literature on matching patients to specific therapies on the basis of their "aptitude" indicated disappointing results (17). This review concentrated on psychological therapies for anxiety, depression, obesity, pain, and tobacco dependence, so it is unclear how drug treatments would be affected by assignments based on patient preferences and characteristics.

While quality of life preferences may serve as a basis for segmentation by prescribers, quality of life outcomes of treatment can serve as a basis for segmentation for institutional decision makers. For example, antihypertensives have varying side effect profiles and may differ significantly in cost. If drugs are comparable in effectiveness, it is reasonable to choose the least costly alternatives for inclusion in formularies and for reimbursement. However, there may be segments of the patient population for whom the quality of life is substantially reduced by the lower-cost drugs. A reasonable institutional decision would be to authorize the use of the higher-cost drugs for the patient subgroup that has a diminished quality of life using the less-expensive medications. The use of descriptive quality of life research to determine the extent of the patient population that should be taking the more costly drugs that produce fewer side effects would help institutional decision makers in planning their drug coverage and in estimating their costs. Descriptive quality of life studies to support such decisions should be based on populations similar to those served by the institutional decision makers, but they need not be based on feedback from the actual individuals who would be affected by the decision. Only when the choice must be made for an individual patient would it be necessary to assess that person's quality of life.

CONCLUSIONS

Quality of life data have the potential for helping pharmaceutical marketers to describe their products along dimensions that are meaningful to the patient. In addition to justifying the benefits of different medication to institutional purchasers and decision makers, quality of life data could help makers of pharmaceutical products be more responsive to the needs of the ultimate users of their products. For quality of life to exert its most profound effects, however, data from quality of life studies need to be part of the decision making process underlying therapeutic choice. We are only beginning to learn how to incorporate quality of life data into these decisions and much theoretical and empirical work lies ahead.

We have begun to see marketers utilize quality of life data to position their products. It is uncertain if such positioning is leading to therapeutic decisions that maximize patient preferences for obtaining therapeutic benefits and avoiding adverse effects, or whether it is contributing to better decisions about formularies. In the long run, however, there could be gains in patient satisfaction and in medicine as a whole if we can find ways of building the patient's preferences for drug therapy directly into the prescriber's decision process.

However, for quality of life to achieve these potentials, considerably more research must be devoted to understanding and applying quality of life to routine therapeutic decision making practices. We need to learn how well disease-specific measures capture quality of life changes and how they relate to global measurement. We also need to learn about the relationship of quality of life and other conceptually important marketing variables, such as patient satisfaction.

Although the research needs seem vast, the quest for these conceptual linkages is important. If we can select the best therapies to meet patients' needs, desires, and values, we can approach a new stage in patient-driven therapeutics. This seems a proper goal as we approach the next century.

REFERENCES

1. Kotler P. A generic concept of marketing. *J Marketing* 1972;36:46–54.
2. Oliver RL. Cognitive, affective, and attribute bases of the satisfaction response. *J Cons Res* 1993;20:418–430.
3. Barofsky I. *Quality of life measurement.* Paper presented at the meeting of the Drug Information Association, Washington, D.C., January, 1994.
4. Tversky A, Sattath S, Slovic P. Contingent weighting in judgment and choice. *Psychol Rev* 1988;95:371–384.
5. Redelmeier DA, Rozin P, Kahneman D. Understanding patients' decisions: cognitive and emotional perspectives. *JAMA* 1993;270:72–76.
6. Pernia J. The second generation of market segmentation studies: an audit of buying motivation. In: Wells W, ed. *Lifestyle and psychographics.* Chicago: American Marketing Association, 1974:287–324.
7. Linn LS, Dimatteo MR, Cope DW, et al. Measuring physicians' humanistic attitudes, values and behaviors. *Med Care* 1987;25:504–515.
8. Schwartz S, Richardson J, Glasziou PP. Quality-adjusted life years: origins, measurements, applications, objections. *Aust J Public Health* 1993;17:272–278.
9. Lilja J. How physicians choose their drugs. *Soc Sci Med* 1976;10: 363–365.
10. Miller RR. Prescribing habits of physicians (parts I–III). *Drug Intell Clin Pharm* 1973;7:492–500.
11. Bergner M, Bobbitt RA, Carter WB, et al. The Sickness Impact Profile: development and final revision of a health status measure. *Med Care* 1981;19:787–805.
12. Spector WD, Katz S, Murphy JB, et al. The hierarchical relationship between activities of daily living and instrumental activities of daily living. *J Chronic Dis* 1981;40:481–489.
13. Earker SA, Sox HC. An assessment of patient preferences for therapeutic outcomes. *Med Decis Making* 1981;1:29–39.
14. McNeil BJ, Weichselboom R, Pauker SG. Fallacy of the five-year survival rate in lung cancer. *N Engl J Med* 1978;299:1397–1401.
15. Mitchell A. *The nine American lifestyles.* New York: Macmillan, 1983.
16. Hatcher ME, Green LW, Levine DL, Flagle C. Validation of a decision model for triaging hypertensive patients to alternate health education interventions. *Soc Sci Med* 1986;22:813–819.
17. Dance KA, Neufeld RW. Aptitude-treatment interaction research in the clinical setting: a review of attempts to dispel the "patient uniformity" myth. *Psychol Res* 1988;104:192–213.

Quality of Life and Pharmacoeconomics in Clinical Trials, Second Edition, edited by B. Spilker.
Lippincott-Raven Publishers, Philadelphia © 1996.

CHAPTER 59

A Marketing Perspective: Practical Applications

Thomas K. Beckett

INTRODUCTION

As noted in the previous chapter, "A Marketing Perspective: Theoretical Underpinnings," the prescription pharmaceutical market is changing dramatically owing to the emerging influence of managed care and the patient on the physician's decision-making process. These new influences serve to increase the interest in quality of life and related cost-effectiveness themes in the creation of product positioning and market segmentation strategies, in spite of the fact that significant questions remain regarding how to assure the accuracy and objectivity of such strategies and whether in the final analysis most such approaches provide real value to the payer, the provider, and the patient.

This chapter addresses specific aspects of communicating quality of life information to those who influence product choice. These aspects include (a) understanding the marketing value of quality of life strategies, (b) structuring quality of life studies to provide credible evidence to back up promotional claims in marketing communications, (c) developing the marketing and communication plan, (d) judging the quality of the creative product, and (e) evaluating the results of the communication program.

Before we get into these specifics, however, it is important to describe and review the role of marketing communication in the exchange process between the marketer and those who purchase, prescribe, and use the marketer's product. For the purposes of this chapter, marketing communication includes any and all forms of organized, large-scale communi-

nication between the marketer and those who use or influence the use of the product. The purpose of communications can range from providing objective information to persuading health practitioners to specify the product. It obviously includes the most widely recognized forms of persuasive (promotional) communications such as detailing, mail and journal advertising, video and broadcast television advertising, and desktop media (anatomic models, calendars, pens, notepads, etc.). It also includes communications intended to inform and influence consumers and family caregivers such as print and television paid advertising, video news releases, talk show appearances, and grants to patient support groups in areas of marketing interest to the pharmaceutical company. And finally, it includes forms of informational communications such as sponsored symposia and conferences, publication of clinical evaluations in the peer-reviewed medical press, discussion panels, and other forms of sponsored peer-to-peer communication. These latter forms of communication must meet specific regulatory requirements if they are presented as independent scientific efforts.

In our culture, it is fashionable to deride promotional communications of any sort. Pharmaceutical promotion has been specifically singled out for harsh criticism. Regardless of whether these criticisms are warranted, marketing communication, including informational as well as persuasive communications, is an essential part of the exchange process between the marketer and the customer, particularly for a pharmaceutical product.

Unlike most consumer products, the value of a pharmaceutical product resides in the "informational envelope" that surrounds the product, not just the product itself. For example, with only a small amount of information, a consumer can determine the use for and value of consumer products

T. K. Beckett: Langford Creek Associates, Ltd., Chestertown, Maryland 21620.

such as a can opener or mousetrap or even a VCR or personal computer. In contrast, the use for and value of a pharmaceutical product cannot even remotely be determined by its appearance or even by an analysis of its contents. The user is dependent upon the informational envelope for the product even if he or she knows the chemical composition of the product. Particularly for an innovative product in the early stages of marketing, the commercial sponsor largely determines the content of that envelope and the nature of its dissemination. Furthermore, the sponsor's promotional communications play an important role in helping to ensure that health professionals (and occasionally patients) are aware of new information and understand its implications.

One can question the amount of communication necessary and debate whether the informational content of a communication program is complete and objective, but it should be recognized that marketing communication is an essential activity that possesses high social value when done appropriately. This chapter describes how marketing communication about quality of life evaluations can be accomplished appropriately and therefore possess high value to payers, providers, patients, and to the commercial sponsor.

THE MARKETING VALUE OF QUALITY OF LIFE THEMES

To understand the marketing value of quality of life themes, the marketer must first appreciate the essential difference between a quality of life study and a more traditional medical study related to the safety and efficacy of a pharmaceutical product.

Traditional medical studies reflect the effects of a drug on the patient's disease (efficacy) and on the patient's normal biological processes (safety). While these evaluations may include objective measures of improvement of subjective symptoms, such as improvement of mood in depression or reduction of pain in arthritis, these measures are generally based on the evaluation of someone other than the patient, using criteria that reflect medical values of success or failure, not necessarily the patient's values.

In contrast, a well-designed quality of life study measures the impact of a drug's efficacy and safety profile on the patient's quality of life based on psychometric measurements of the patient's, not the investigator's, point of view.

To illustrate the difference, consider a hypothetical example involving an antidepressant. A medical study might reveal that the drug improves mood but causes dry mouth and a sense of urinary urgency. A quality of life study of the same drug might demonstrate that the improvement in mood improves the patient's ability to perform activities of daily living but reduces social interaction because the adverse effects cause discomfort, bad breath, and the embarrassment of frequent, unproductive trips to the bathroom. A comparative trial might demonstrate that many patients place a high value on social interaction and therefore experience a better overall result with a different, somewhat less effective drug that does not cause severe dry mouth and urinary symptoms.

From a marketing point of view, quality of life studies are quite appealing because they afford an opportunity to differentiate the sponsor's product on the basis of patient values, which may or may not reflect traditional medical values. It is not inconceivable, as our hypothetical example suggests, that a well-designed quality of life study can restore market viability to a product that suffers in a traditional comparative medical trial.

This is not to suggest that quality of life studies can solve most marketing problems. In the most common competitive situation, involving therapeutically similar products, it may not be possible to demonstrate a comparative quality of life advantage simply because the products are so similar that no study is apt to show a difference. Even when it is possible to demonstrate a difference, health professionals (not to mention formulary committee influentials) may be reluctant to accept findings that appear counterintuitive.

It may be possible to demonstrate a quality of life benefit compared with therapy with a different class of drugs (e.g., an ACE inhibitor versus a beta blocker in hypertension), but it is unlikely that health professionals will attribute the benefit to a specific agent. Rather, they will attribute the benefit to a class effect.

Finally, most health professionals lack the familiarity and training necessary to understand and to critically evaluate quality of life studies. Since these studies involve psychometric rather than medical measurements, quality of life studies are more likely to be greeted with skepticism by medical professionals, unless the studies seem intuitively valid based on their clinical observations.

These problems with quality of life studies notwithstanding, the marketer ignores quality of life studies at some peril. As noted in the previous chapter, medical institutions and practitioners must now compete for patients as they never have had to before. To survive and thrive, they are learning to become patient focused. Quality of life studies address patient values and perspectives, and we should expect these types of studies soon to become essential to any pharmaceutical marketing program that is driven by the needs of its "customers."

CONSIDERATIONS IN STUDY DESIGN

To assure the effectiveness of a quality of life communication program, the marketing staff should work closely with those responsible for study design to ensure that marketing communication needs will be met. This must occur before the quality of life study is approved and implemented.

Marketing needs to ask two fundamental questions about the research protocol: First, given the known effects of the product, what specific quality of life claims can be supported? Second, will the proposed protocol provide sufficient evidence to support these claims? The evidence necessary to support advertising claims must meet rigorous scientific and regulatory standards. In addition to examining the methodology and design of studies used to support advertising claims, the Food and Drug Administration (FDA) will also ask for evidence of the validity and reliability of the measures used to assess quality of life. The sensitivity of quality of life measures is also of concern because it has impact on other study design considerations (such as sample size). Thus, in addition to general concerns regarding the design of adequate and well-controlled studies evident for all marketing claims, marketers must exhibit additional concerns about the psychometric quality of quality of life measures. The following is a list of some of the important criteria that marketers should consider in the development of quality of life claims in promotion:

- Do the quality of life measurement tools used in this study have sufficient evidence of validity? That is, do these tools measure what they purport to measure in the target population?
- Is the study of sufficient size and scope to demonstrate a significant difference between treatment arms? Have the results been duplicated in other studies? Are there any contradictory studies?
- Have sufficient safeguards been employed to minimize the potential for bias? Is it a prospective study? Is there a control as well as a treatment group? Is there randomization? Have patients and evaluators been sufficiently blinded to ensure objectivity?
- Are the conclusions consistent with and not contrary to current product labeling? Is there anything about this information that might lead a prescriber to use the product for an unproved or inappropriate use?
- Are specific promotional statements supported by the data? Has the sponsor generalized the promotional claim beyond that supported by the evidence?
- Are there any relevant negative findings disclosed by the study that are not reflected in the promotional campaign?

It is apparent that these criteria are almost identical to those used to evaluate promotion based on a more traditional clinical evaluation. The operative difference between a quality of life study and a clinical efficacy study is the measurement of the patient's assessment of the impact of therapy on his or her quality of life. As noted elsewhere in this volume, there are a number of well-validated tools to measure quality of life. If these ''off-the-shelf'' tools measure what providers and patients would benefit from knowing about quality of life, if the patient population parallels the labeled indication for the product, and if the study measures up to scientific standards for objectivity and rigor, then there should be few problems with the communication program. On the other hand, if the quality of life study requires a unique or modified measurement tool, it is important that the new tool be validated to ensure that it is measuring what it purports to measure before conducting the study.

The marketer is also cautioned to be wary of measurement tools that rely on the assessment of the impact on quality of life of anyone other than the patient or an evaluator who is specifically trained to elicit information objectively from the patient. Be particularly wary of measurements based on the prescriber's impression of the impact on the patient's quality of life. Prescribers may or may not possess the same value system as patients, and they may misjudge patients' perceptions about the quality of life impact of therapies.

If possible before conducting a quality of life study, prepare prototype communication materials that reflect probable outcomes and conduct a qualitative evaluation of the message with a limited but suitable number of intended recipients of the campaign. This will help ferret out possible problems in communicating information and provide some measure of how important and believable the recipients will consider the information. This will also help in developing the necessary contextual information that will be needed to qualify the claims so they will not be considered overly general or otherwise misleading by regulatory reviewers.

DEVELOPING THE MARKETING AND COMMUNICATION PLAN

Well in advance of the launch of a communication program, it is advisable to prepare a specific marketing and communication plan or to update existing plans to reflect the quality of life theme. The marketing and communication plan should address overall strategic marketing issues, not just quality of life promotion. In the process of developing the plan, the relative importance and therefore weight that quality of life themes will carry should become apparent. Marketing and communication plans should provide the following information:

- *Market analysis:* a discussion of market trends, competitive actions, company and product strengths and weaknesses, and customer attitudes, opinions, needs, and wants related to the company's product.
- *Statement of overall marketing objectives:* a good statement of a marketing objective, which is quantifiable; that is, it should provide a measurable outcome of the marketing program. An example of a good statement of a marketing objective might be: ''Extend overall market share by 3 percentage points to 27% by year's end. Expand formulary acceptance among managed health care plans from 22% to 45%.''
- *Statement of marketing strategy:* a clear statement of the strategic direction toward which the company's product marketing effort will be focused in order to achieve the objectives. The statement may describe a product positioning, market segmentation, packaging, distribution or pricing strategy, or perhaps some combination of these approaches. Traditionally, prescription pharmaceutical marketing strategies have centered on product positioning strategies. However, with the influence of managed care

and patients on product specification, segmentation, distribution, and pricing strategies may become as important as positioning strategies for many products. In today's market, a good statement of strategy reflecting a quality of life theme might read something like this: "Position [product] as an antihistamine that provides demonstrably less interference with mental acuity in patients with seasonal respiratory allergies. Enhance competitiveness within the managed care segment of the market by funding co-promotion programs to consumers highlighting health plan focus on quality of life."

• *Communication objectives:* a brief statement of the objectives for the communication program, expressed in quantifiable terms if possible. These objectives may be segmented by audience if appropriate. A typical objective might be: "Obtain a score of 36% for aided and unaided recall of the primary product positioning message among the top 50% of primary care prescribers of the market segment." A common mistake is to confuse marketing and communication objectives. A communication objective should describe and measure only that which communication can accomplish, specifically to build awareness and recall of messages communicated by advertising and promotion. Customer attitude and behavior, or product sales and market share, can be influenced by factors other than communication, such as pricing, packaging, product failure, or a new competitive product. If the advertising objectives encompass these other factors, the marketer will have trouble diagnosing deviations from the marketing objectives. Many effective advertising programs have been abandoned because the pricing was wrong. And many an advertising agency has taken the credit for an unexpected favorable sales outcome that owes more to a competitor's misadventure than to the effectiveness of the agency's ad campaign.

• *Promotional strategy:* a brief statement of the overall strategy that will be reflected in promotion. A good way to establish the statement of strategy is to capture the idea the audience should provide feedback after exposure to the promotional campaign. The promotion strategy statement may or may not be similar to the statement of marketing strategy. If the marketing strategy is essentially a positioning strategy, the promotional strategy is likely to be similar. If the marketing strategy reflects segmentation, pricing, packaging, or distribution strategies, the strategies should not be similar.

• *Audiences, messages, and media:* to whom promotional communications will be directed, with what messages, and in what media. It may be helpful in this section to weight the allocation of resources by target audience. The information might include the following:

Primary care physicians and allergists:
    Primary message: Less impairment of mental acuity.
    Secondary message: Notice of launch of co-op ads with regional health plans.
    Weighting: Approximately 50% of promotional resources.
    Media: Detailing, journals, mail, conferences.
Retail pharmacists:
    Primary message: Less impairment of mental acuity.
    Secondary message: Notice of launch of co-op ads with regional health plans.
    Weighting: 5% of promotional resources.
    Media: Mail.
Managed care executives and pharmacy benefit managers:
    Primary message: Availability of co-op consumer quality of life promotion program.
    Secondary message: Less impairment of mental acuity.
    Weighting: 5% of promotional resources.
    Media: National accounts staff.
Consumers:
    Primary message: [Health plan] and [company] work together to bring a better quality of life to [health plan] enrollees.
    Weighting: 40% of promotional resources.
    Media: Regional print, radio, and television spot ads.

As one can imagine from this hypothetical example, the decisions about audience, message, media, and weighting are interdependent and subjective. For example, in spite of the changing dynamics of the marketplace, physicians remain the most important audience for marketing communication programs, for without a knowledgeable health practitioner to initiate the prescription, the product will not be used. However, promotion to physicians remains expensive, because there are large numbers of physicians in the specialties that account for the bulk of medications used in primary care medicine and because personal calls by sales representatives remain the most effective means of communicating with physicians.

Health plan administrators and pharmacy benefits managers are also quite important to the success of any communication program because if the product is not available in the managed care plan, the prescription may not be filled even if it is written. However, communication to these influential individuals is relatively inexpensive. There are only a few hundred such individuals in the United States, and a relatively small national or regional account marketing staff can contact the most influential of these efficiently and quickly. Except for broad corporate or institutional positioning themes, there is little need for nonpersonal media promotion to these people.

Retail pharmacists have rather modest influence on choices of products. However, they need to be kept up to date with information about the product since they often field questions from local practitioners. Mailings and pharmacy journal advertisements easily meet the informational needs of retail pharmacists.

In absolute terms the cost of advertising to the consumer is high, particularly television spot advertising. However, the cost of an ad message per consumer is quite low, typically only a few cents per exposure. Therefore, the efficiency of consumer advertising can be quite good if large numbers of consumers can relate to the message or quite poor if the message applies only to a small proportion of the consumer universe.

The marketer of a product for a small market might choose instead to use a direct marketing approach to develop a list of patients with the condition. This could be accomplished by providing physicians and pharmacists with samples, brochures, or "point of purchase" displays with a business reply card enrolling the patient to receive a newsletter for patients with the disease.

Direct-to-consumer advertising by prescription drug marketers will necessarily be limited by market and financial realities. Most prescription products do not lend themselves to direct-to-consumer mass marketing approaches. This is certainly the case when patient candidates are symptomatic and likely to visit a health care professional. However, in instances in which patients may not be in regular contact with a health care professional, advertising can encourage consumers to visit the doctor to ask about new therapies. Most consumer campaigns for prescription products are driven by such a strategy.

Because quality of life is relevant to patients as well as to health care providers, the marketer will want to consider direct to consumer communications for quality of life marketing programs. Also, managed health plans compete for enrollees, and the marketer should not overlook the potential value of quality of life themes to the managed care organization. Advertising that the managed care formulary includes products that demonstrate quality of life advantages could be a competitive advantage for the managed care organization.

- *Program, budget, and timetable:* a list of each item planned for the communication program, described with sufficient detail to permit the staff responsible for design and production to create and produce each element with little further direction. A typical entry could look like this: "Detail brochure. 12 saddle-stitched pages. 8″ × 10″ with 2–4 color process photos. Theme: Provides less interference with mental acuity in patients with seasonal respiratory allergies. Quantity: 12,000. Unit cost: $0.95. Total budget: $11,400. Timing: 3d quarter."

CREATIVE ESSENTIALS

To assure clarity of communication, responsibility for creative development of copy and design for the campaign elements should be assigned to professionals skilled in the development of marketing communications materials. The communication quality of the materials can be evaluated by asking the following five questions:

1. *Is the media suited to the message?* Communication media vary considerably in what they can be expected to accomplish. Journal ads and television spots are best suited for simple, succinctly expressed ideas. These are

poor media to try to communicate complex information. These media are best suited for persuasive messages intended to motivate the prescriber to seek additional information or to remind prescribers of a theme or brand name. In contrast, direct mail letters, monographs, symposia, and their published proceedings are better suited for complex and lengthy messages. Detailing works best when the communication challenges require an interaction between the marketer and the health care professional. Peer-to-peer programs such as focus panel discussions and symposia serve a valuable role when the marketing challenge calls for an interaction between health professionals. A good communication program will employ a variety of media, each with a message that takes advantage of the attributes of each medium. For example, the marketer might use a print or television ad to build awareness of a new quality of life study and use a personalized mailing from the research department to describe the study fundamentals and to provide a synopsis of key findings. Reprints, a paper symposium, and a monograph could be provided on request to those who want full details of the study.

2. *Is the message suited to the medium?* Print advertisements work only if something in the ad headlines or artwork attracts and holds the interest of a reader. On the other hand, it is not necessary to use provocative artwork and headlines in a monograph. Video presentations provide an opportunity to animate findings or capture the human, emotional content of an idea. Visual aids for detailing are intended to support an oral presentation. They should avoid small type and long paragraphs and use bullet points and large type to capture the essential points and let the presenter fill in the nuances. Leave-behind sales brochures are an excellent way to provide more detailed information that the health professional may want to review later.

3. *Is the message focused and clearly stated?* Is there a single main point? Is the main point captured in the principal headline and subheadline? Does the artwork reinforce the main point? Is the main point clear to someone who is not involved? (Test this by asking a spouse, a friend, or administrative assistant what he or she thinks the ad says.) Does the main point address a perceived need of the intended recipient? The point to remember is that readers will not spend much time reading an advertisement that they do not understand or cannot relate to. If they don't get the point within a moment or two, they will turn the page.

4. *Are the copy points specific and accurately expressed?* This principle is particularly critical for quality of life themes. *Quality of life* is an all-encompassing term that is subject to widely different interpretations depending on the reader's values and perspectives. To some patients taking an antihypertensive, quality of life means no effect on sexual function. To others, it means no interference

with cognitive skills or exercise tolerance. Particularly in terms of quality of life, expectations are formed by experiences. Therefore, it is not a good idea to focus on an undefined quality of life benefit as the principal theme in an advertisement, simply because the phrase means so many different things to the audience. Being specific may narrow the appeal, but the advertisement will communicate far more powerfully to those who do value the particular attribute of the product.

5. *Does the communication provide access to the essential data needed to evaluate the validity of the quality of life claim?* As with any promotion of a scientific study, it is important to provide the reader with certain essential data, or access to the data, that they will need to assess the validity of the promoted claims. As a minimum, an advertisement should provide a literature citation to the original clinical report or an offer to provide a synopsis of the essential information upon request. In more elaborate materials, such as monographs (and perhaps even in leave-behind sales brochures), it is advisable to include a précis with at least this information:

Type of study
Principal investigators and their affiliations
Patient selection criteria
Criteria for assignment to treatments
Blinding techniques
Description of control and treatment groups
Number of patients in each group
Summary of favorable and unfavorable results, including measures of statistical reliability
References

EVALUATING RESULTS

Marketers may use message testing to evaluate the effectiveness of individual advertisements or to evaluate the effect of the total communications program over time. It is worthwhile to test individual advertisements for diagnostic purposes, to ensure that each advertisement is communicating as intended. There are several useful methodologies to measure the communications effectiveness of individual ads. These typically measure unaided and aided message recall and brand identification with a specific message. Some also measure message believability and persuasiveness. A typical evaluation will involve exposing a representative group of the intended audience to a specific advertisement in a portfolio of advertisements and then probing for recall. This will provide an "unaided" recall score ("What advertisements do you recall seeing in the portfolio?") and an "aided" recall score ("Do you recall seeing an advertisement for this specific product?"). Further probing of panelists to determine what message they received and whether any ele-

ments of the message were unbelievable will provide a wealth of diagnostic information to help improve the performance of an ad campaign. It is also a good idea to measure general perceptions after a campaign is well established, perhaps at the end of the first year of a program.

As noted previously, it is important to establish a clear and measurable communication objective during the planning process for the communications program. The process of evaluating the program involves measuring whether the audience has perceived the intended message to the extent anticipated by the communication objective.

The methodology for evaluating the effect of a campaign over time may involve a wide range of methods, such as ongoing portfolio testing to determine unaided and aided recall, or a simple questionnaire designed to test the extent to which the audience identifies the communication theme with the correct brand. One of the more useful techniques involves perceptual mapping of audience opinions regarding various products that participate in a therapeutic class. In this type of testing, target recipients are asked to rank various products on scales such as potential for adverse effects, efficacy, cost, convenience, or any other dimension of product performance that is relevant to the marketing program. Successful communications programs will usually result in a strengthening of the perceptual positioning that the sponsor's brand promotion has focused on over time.

CONCLUSIONS

Quality of life studies and promotion should be considered whenever there is a reasonable basis for believing that a well-designed quality of life study will contribute to an improved understanding of who will and who will not perceive a benefit from a particular therapy. By enhancing the likelihood of perceptively favorable outcomes, any information of this nature will result in better long-term product market performance. A competent marketing staff will address the need for quality of life studies at least annually and undertake these studies proactively based on customer needs rather than in response to competitive product threats. In the long run, this strategy will result in better studies, better promotion, and fewer competitive surprises. In marketing as in football, a good offense is the best defense.

ACKNOWLEDGMENTS

The author would like to acknowledge the invaluable assistance of Lou Morris, Ph.D. and Karen Lechter, J.D., Ph.D. of the Food and Drug Administration for their help in reviewing the information in this chapter that pertains to FDA regulation of prescription drug advertising.

Quality of Life and Pharmacoeconomics in Clinical Trials, Second Edition, edited by B. Spilker.
Lippincott-Raven Publishers, Philadelphia © 1996.

CHAPTER 60

An Epidemiologic Perspective

David S. Sugano and Newell E. McElwee

INTRODUCTION—EPIDEMIOLOGY AND QUALITY OF LIFE: ARE THEY RELATED?

The question of how "hard" or "soft" quality of life (QOL) data may be will likely be debated for some time. Perhaps a more specific question that is particularly relevant to QOL instruments that are included in randomized clinical trials is whether or not such information represents experimental or nonexperimental data. Information bias alone provides an argument that even under the most controlled circumstances QOL data might be considered more nonexperimental in nature than most other types of clinical data. If this is true, then an appreciation of some specific epidemiologic concepts and perspectives may be important to consider. A few of these issues are described from an epidemiologic

perspective in this chapter in the hope that they will stimulate more thinking in these areas.

QOL END POINTS AS POSSIBLE EPIDEMIOLOGIC VARIABLES

Kirschner and Guyatt (1) have noted that quality of life scales may be used for at least three major objectives: (a) discriminating between persons at a single point in time (similar to psychological measures of traits such as intelligence or personality); (b) predicting some future outcome or results of a more costly criterion measure or "gold standard"; and (c) measuring change over time, as is typically done in a randomized trial. In some ways the evolution of quality of life instruments in the past 50 years has followed the changing purposes for these new data as they have moved from these three different types of epidemiologic variables, i.e., from static means of classifying or discriminating between persons, to risk factors or prognostic variables, to actual outcome or response measurements.

D. S. Sugano and N. E. McElwee: Department of Pharmacoeconomics, Integrated Therapeutics Group, Inc., a subsidiary of Schering Plough Corporation, Kenilworth, New Jersey 07033.

QOL as Classification Variables

Early QOL scales were developed first to enable rapid characterization of patients into specific categories rather than to evaluate changes in functional status or other domains of quality of life. Although limited in many ways (e.g., it only measures physical performance and dependency), early scales such as the Karnofsky Performance Status (KPS) Scale (2) have served clinical research well because, unlike newer, multidimensional instruments of today, they were anchored in clinical health states that were reasonably well understood by researchers in the specific fields for which they were developed. For this reason, some of these scales are still being used today as baseline classification or discriminant variables for selecting patients for clinical trials.

QOL as Prognostic Variables

Over time, it became apparent that QOL scales not only could be useful as discriminant variables, but could also be important predictive variables for significant clinical outcomes, such as death. As such, they began to be used as stratification variables in the analysis and interpretation of clinical studies. Some, like the KPS, are often used in the pre-randomization stratification of patients for clinical trials because they are thought to be of such prognostic importance in specific diseases.

As newer, multidimensional quality of life instruments based upon theoretical constructs rather than specific clinical health states were developed, specific prognostic issues began to be explicitly addressed by, for example, eliciting patient assessments of their own predictions for future health events. Separate from other mathematical methods for modeling or estimating prognosis, such self-ratings of change can provide potentially useful qualitative data that may be of particular interest when long-term clinical outcomes may not be observable during the period of a trial or study.

QOL as Descriptive Outcome or Response Variables

In contrast to older QOL scales that were anchored in specific health states, the newer multidimensional instruments are based upon more theoretical ideas or concepts (e.g., emotional functioning) that cannot be measured directly. Like concepts or ideas are grouped into ''domains'' and the given instrument results in a set of indicators of these constructs that note the presence, absence, or degree of QOL (3). These new instruments are based upon explicit conceptual models of health, have been more extensively evaluated for reliability and validity, and have begun to be used as outcome or response variables in clinical studies.

Since these new QOL instruments can provide multidimensional information on patient functioning and status that is not always captured in traditional clinical trial end points, this new information is often useful as descriptive secondary information that can support the major findings of such studies. For example, if a new cancer therapy is shown to extend the time to progression in a clinical trial, quality of life data may demonstrate the importance of this clinical end point to the many dimensions of a patient's life. In cancer treatment in particular, since the two main objectives of therapy are prolongation of life and improvement in quality of life, one can argue that all other efficacy end points (i.e., tumor response, response duration, time to progression) are only possible surrogates for these two primary end points (4).

It is precisely on these grounds, i.e., that the critical goal of health care is improving the quantity and quality of life, that some have argued that the primary clinical end points in clinical studies should not be physiologic measurements such as blood pressure reading and biopsy, but rather the direct measurement of patient benefit in terms of quantity and quality of life. Although there is merit to this perspective, one should also note that while the need for measuring quantity of life is fairly clear-cut, any gold standard for proper measurement of quality of life has yet to be identified. Thus, the use of quality of life end points as ''secondary'' descriptive outcomes has not automatically led to their acceptance as ''primary'' clinical outcomes for trials.

QOL as Primary Outcome Variables: Some Issues

Accompanying the growing importance of quality of life measurement in clinical studies have been the issues associated with attempting to use these variables as primary end points. A few of these issues should be addressed briefly.

First, if quality of life is to be a primary outcome under study, then the emphasis in this effort should be on identifying in advance those specific scales of importance and then ensuring adequate responsiveness of the instrument to measure changes over time (5). This leads to the development of disease-specific or study-specific instruments that may be acceptable with respect to internal validity but weak in terms of external validity, i.e., interpreting the true impact of differences in a larger context than just the patients in the study. If only those scales that will be responsive to change over time between treatments are included in a study, then the real benefits of a multidimensional and overall assessment of quality of life are missing unless more generic and overall QOL or utilities are somehow also measured and reported.

Second, even if new quality of life instruments can be shown to measure accurately minimal changes in scores over time in specific domains, it is not always clear what the clinical significance of such changes may be. For example, scale scores may be sensitive, but not very specific to clinical change (e.g., scores may change even for clinically stable patients). Since newer instruments are based upon theoretical constructs of health, many of which (e.g., behavioral or perceptual issues) lack any ''gold standards'' defining these concepts, several specific problems are encountered. Criterion validity (i.e., the ability to show the relationship to accepted clinical measures) is often not possible to establish. Thus, one must depend primarily upon construct validity (empiric evidence based upon psychometric concepts such as convergent and discriminant validity) to demonstrate the coherence of the relationships between the various QOL concepts or domains being compared, rather than a direct validation against clinical standards. This dependence upon logical empiric data rather than "gold standards" in clinical practice raises major issues in terms of being able to properly interpret "statistically significant" changes in QOL scores and the entire issue of what "effect sizes" may mean. Deyo and Centor (6) have noted that instruments included in therapeutic trials not only must show sensitivity to change, but also must be able to discriminate between those patients who improve and those who do not. In specific physical functioning domains this will be much easier to demonstrate than in psychological or behavioral domains where the question of who is improving or not is harder to define with certainty.

Ultimately, the problem of interpreting "significant" QOL changes over time for clinical audiences is difficult if the scales themselves are not based upon clinically meaningful health states. As Johnson (4) points out, a clinically anchored scale such as the KPS is easy to interpret simply because it runs from 0 to 100 in ten-point increments with 0 being dead and 100 being normal. Each ten-point increment is defined on the basis of clinically meaningful health states; thus, if a patient's score improves from 50 (Requires considerable assistance and frequent medical care) to 80 (Normal activity with effort; some signs of symptoms and disease) the meaning of such an improvement is readily apparent. On a 100-point linear analog self-assessment scale, on the other hand, the intervals along the scale are not defined in clinically meaningful terms except at each end. Thus, an improvement from 50 to 80 on this scale may be statistically significant, but not clinically interpretable.

STRIVING FOR COMPARABILITY IN QOL DATA: LESSONS FROM EPIDEMIOLOGY ON ASSESSING AND CONTROLLING POTENTIAL BIASES

Most epidemiologic research is nonexperimental; techniques used to control bias in clinical trials such as randomization and blinding are not typically used in epidemiologic studies. Therefore, one of the central issues in epidemiologic research is the rigorous assessment and control of potential biases that could affect the validity of comparisons between groups. Conversely, there is often complacency about these issues when interpreting results from randomized trials because of the naive assumption that bias is always controlled by randomization and blinding. Epidemiologic approaches can be valuable in the assessment and control of potential biases in randomized clinical trials (7). Although the study end points of particular interest are quality of life, the issues discussed below also apply to clinical end points.

Randomization and Confounding Bias

When a third factor interferes with an exposure-outcome relationship, the outcome is said to be confounded (8). To confound the relationship, the third factor must be associated with both the exposure and the outcome (in the untreated group). There are many factors that might be associated with the outcome, for example, baseline factors related to prognostic risk, such as age and disease severity. However, if these factors are not associated with the exposure, that is, if their distributions are the same between exposure groups, then the outcome is not confounded. Randomization is used to help ensure that the distributions of these potential confounding variables, known and unknown, are evenly distributed between the exposure groups.

Published randomized clinical trials often report the distribution of baseline demographic and prognostic factors for the treatment groups to demonstrate whether the randomization was "effective." The two factors that determine if randomization was effective or whether "treatment imbalances" exist are the variability of the patients entered into the trial and sample size of the study (9). Patient variability can be decreased by restricting the study eligibility criteria to patients with similar prognostic risk, e.g., similar ages or disease severity categories. Of course, eligibility restrictions limit the inferences that can be made from the target population (patients meeting study eligibility criteria) to external populations (external generalizability is discussed below). The effect of sample size on the probability of a treatment imbalance between two treatment groups is shown in Fig. 1 for imbalances of .55, .60, and .70 (10). There is less than 5% probability of a treatment imbalance of .70 or more if the sample size is 30 or more. As the degree of imbalance approaches .50, e.g., evenly distributed groups, the sample size required to maintain a probability of less than 5% increases—more than 100 subjects are required for a treatment imbalance of .60 and more than 400 for a treatment imbalance of .55.

In summary, confounding bias should always be considered as a possible alternative explanation of quality of life results even in randomized trials. The likelihood of confounding bias is decreased when the study sample size is large and patient variability in factors related to quality of life is small.

Blinding and Observer Bias

Outcome assessments, including quality of life, may be biased by knowledge of the treatment assignment; consequently, many randomized trials are "double-blind." Under ideal conditions, double-blind implies that neither the investigator nor the patient knows which treatment the patient is

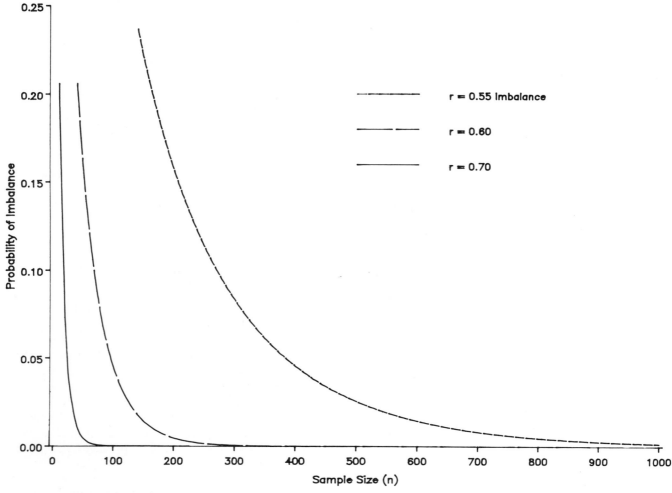

FIG. 1. Probability of treatment imbalances for complete randomization as a function of sample size (*n*), for imbalances max (*na, nb*) / *n* ≥ *r* and *r* = .55, .60, and .70. (From ref. 10, with permission.)

receiving. However, there is substantial evidence that both investigators and patients can accurately guess which treatment has been assigned (11). This occurs because of the recognition of characteristic side effects or, in the case of a placebo assignment, the lack of efficacy or side effects. This is particularly troublesome for quality of life studies because many of the assessments are subjective responses from the patient. Unfortunately, few quality of life studies report a post hoc assessment of how effective the blinding was. However, this phenomenon has been studied in psychotropic drug trials where the primary clinical end points are measured by patient and physician assessments of feelings and behavior, a situation somewhat analogous to quality of life endpoints. Fisher and Greenberg (12) reviewed all randomized, double-blind psychotropic drug trials where the effectiveness of blinding was evaluated; 23 of 26 trials reported that both patients and physicians could differentiate between an active drug and placebo at level significantly greater than chance.

This raises fundamental questions about observer bias in quality of life research that should be addressed in future studies.

APPROPRIATE COMPARISON GROUPS

Randomized clinical trials of medicines often use a placebo control because of regulatory requirements (13). This practice has been recently criticized in circumstances where an effective treatment exists because, according to the authors, it violates the Declaration of Helsinki (14). From a more pragmatic view, clinicians are more interested in whether quality of life is improved over standard therapy, not whether quality of life is improved over no therapy. However, in the case of medicines, treatment effects are usually small and will be more likely to be detected with a placebo control than an active control. Therefore, quality of life investigators often face a serious dilemma when choosing a control group. Active controls provide more useful information for decision makers but in many cases the treatment effect will be too small to be detected with a quality of life end point.

RELEVANCE OF EPIDEMIOLOGIC CONCEPTS IN INTERPRETATION OF QOL DATA

Whether one views QOL as being prognostic variables or outcome variables, given the multidimensional nature of these data and the difficulties in collecting this information in a truly experimental fashion, the possibility of false associations with other variables is not insignificant. Evaluating if such apparent associations represent true cause-effect relationships is relatively familiar territory for epidemiologists. Austin Bradford Hill (15) and others involved in this area have proposed specific criteria for evaluating evidence for and against causality of apparent associations. Strictly speaking, temporality is the only criterion that is ''necessary'' for a causal relationship, i.e., if temporality is not present, the relationship cannot be causal; however, other criteria help strengthen the argument for a causal association and provide a conceptual framework for evaluating causality (16). A brief review of these criteria and their potential relevance to QOL associations is useful.

Temporality (Causes Should Precede Effects)

This fundamental principle seems self-evident but may be overlooked, especially when both variables in question are measured at the same point in time. In an oncology study, for example, an apparent association between psychological status and tumor response would seem quite reasonable if a patient has knowledge of his treatment response status while completing his QOL assessment. In this case, the tumor response information is most likely the cause and the psychological status assessment the effect. If, however, patients have been blinded to tumor response information, and the changes in this QOL domain appear to precede any objective changes in tumor response, then another possible cause-effect relationship must be postulated.

Strength of Association (High Relative Risk)

Although the size of an association alone cannot be considered as proof positive of a causal relationship, strong associations are in general less likely to be due to unrecognized bias such as confounding factors than a relatively weak association. Odds ratios are often used in QOL studies to measure relative risk, and the size of these odds ratios would indicate the strength of the association between QOL domains and other variables.

Reversible Associations

A variable associated with another is more likely to be a cause of the other if its removal results in a commensurate change in the other. In evaluating the QOL of patients undergoing treatment such as chemotherapy, for example, one might find an association between fatigue/malaise and the introduction of a certain drug. This association is more likely to be a cause-effect relationship if the termination of this specific therapy results in a corresponding increase in the fatigue/malaise scale.

Dose-Response Relationship

Dose-response relationships (i.e., the higher the dose, the higher the response) obviously strengthen the argument for a cause-effect relationship. If, for example, a clinical study includes patients with a wide spectrum of disease severity, and quality of life is measured at baseline, then a possible association between certain QOL scales and disease severity would seem more likely to be causal if the QOL scale scores corresponded closely to the disease burden categories.

Consistency

A consistent association is one that is seen in a variety of settings. While a lack of consistency does not necessarily mean that the results of a particular study are invalid, when different studies all lead to the same result evidence for causality is obviously strengthened. In the area of quality of life research establishing consistency of associations across several studies between QOL end points and other outcomes or prognostic variables would seem particularly important as evidence for causality.

Biological Plausibility

Biological plausibility or coherence is the presence of some known biological mechanism to explain the purported association. The existence of known mechanisms to explain relationships between cause and effect is an important aspect of science and strengthens the case for causality. However, since biologically plausibility depends upon our current knowledge of disease mechanisms (which may be incomplete), the lack of coherence may simply indicate limitations of our medical knowledge rather than the lack of a causal relationship. Given the state of the art in measuring ''nonphysical'' factors or outcomes using quality of life or other instruments, biological plausibility may be one of the criteria that is more difficult to establish when relating QOL scores to other variables.

Statistical Significance

Different from strength of association, statistical significance simply means that a purported relationship is one that is based upon sufficient data to exhibit some degree of stability. To the extent that quality of life data are collected in clinical studies in a totally experimental fashion (e.g., double-blinded), statistical significance should bear a close relationship to the probability of random error. However, to the extent that these data are collected in a nonexperimental fashion (e.g., not blinded to treatment), any associations, even if statistically significant, should be interpreted with caution.

Specificity

Specificity, i.e., one cause, one effect, argues for causality if it is present. However, the absence of specificity does not necessarily rule out a possible cause-effect relationship. Given the multidimensional and somewhat overlapping nature of quality of life measurements, most associations probably will not have specificity. Unless a particular scale is developed to measure a specific clinical variable (say nausea and vomiting), specificity between an QOL domain and some other clinical variable is not likely to be observed.

POSSIBLE EPIDEMIOLOGIC APPROACHES TO EXTENDING INFERENCES FOR QUALITY OF LIFE DATA

Limitations of Quality of Life Data from Randomized Clinical Trials

The ultimate goal of quality of life research is to be able to extend the results of a particular clinical trial to a larger population. Initially, statistical inferences must be made from the study population (patients randomized) to the "randomizable" population, the latter consisting of the study population plus the population screened and eligible for enrollment but not randomized. Next, causal inferences must be made from the randomizable population to the target population, that is, patients who would have met eligibility criteria but were not screened for the study. And finally, it is often desirable to make causal inferences from the target population to the external population consisting of patients who may later use the medicine being investigated but who would not necessarily fit the study inclusion and exclusion criteria. Sampling and non-coverage bias should be considered at each step of the cascade of inferences from the study population to the randomizable population to the target population and finally to the external population.

The study population is often 50% or less of the randomizable population (17–19) and may be as low as 10% (20). In some cases, patients refuse informed consent and in others, physicians elect not to enroll the patient (17).

Whether sampling bias is introduced depends on whether randomized patients differ in some important way from patients who are randomizable but not enrolled. The characteristics of patients who are randomizable but not enrolled are rarely reported with a few exceptions. In an oncology study, patients who were randomized had a lower stage of cancer than those who were eligible but not randomized, resulting in potential bias of longer survival and better quality of life than might have been observed in the entire randomizable population (17). In the coronary artery surgery study (CASS), patients who were randomized were more likely to be cigarette smokers and have diabetes or hypertension than patients who were eligible but not randomized (18).

The CASS investigators then assessed whether these potential biases actually resulted in survival differences. Both randomized and randomizable but not enrolled patients were followed-up using a comprehensive cohort design and no differences were found in 10 year survival (18,20). The investigators concluded that inferences from the study could appropriately be made to the randomizable and target populations. Not surprisingly, quality of life was measured only in the randomized group; thus, the impact of sampling bias on quality of life responses could not be assessed. While this type of rigorous assessment of sampling bias is not feasible for all quality of life trials, it should be considered if problems with sampling bias are anticipated. Without this type of assessment, one should be cautious when extending inferences about quality of life data beyond the study population.

Another potential bias related to the study population and the randomizable population is whether participation in a trial changes QOL responses. For example, do patients once enrolled become more compliant and have subsequent increases in QOL? This bias would affect each treatment group and would represent overall QOL improvements not related to the study intervention. A lead-in phase is often used in randomized trials to control for this effect but there are no guidelines on whether the baseline QOL referent period should include the lead-in time or the time period prior to that. For example, in a trial with a placebo lead-in starting at week −4 and an instrument with a 4 week recall, should the referent period for the baseline QOL assessment be the week −8 to −4 time period or the week −4 to week 0 time period? The former would provide prior information without "trial effects" and is more appropriate for most situations.

Inferences made from the target population to an external population depend on how restrictive the inclusion and exclusion criteria were in the study protocol, that is, on how closely the target population reflects the external population ultimately of interest. Herein lies the dilemma. There is a trade-off between homogeneity of the target population and external generalizability (21). Investigators often desire a homogeneous study population so that between-patient variability is minimized and efficiencies can be gained in sample size. As eligibility criteria become more restrictive and the target population more homogeneous, the ability to make inferences from the study population to the external population is diminished and the potential for non-coverage bias is increased. Unfortunately, at least in the case of medicines, clinical trial eligibility criteria are highly restrictive, and at the time medicines are approved for use in the population at large predictions about how the drug will perform in the external population must be made. In these situations, inferences to the external population must be done cautiously and with guidance, for example, from criteria developed to make causal inferences from epidemiologic studies (see above) or other similar approaches. The primary issue that must be addressed is whether, based on knowledge of the disease and treatment, the treatment effect of the intervention on the *external* population would result in different quality of life responses from the treatment effect in the *target* population. In some circumstances this can be done with more certainty than others, but it still remains highly speculative.

Possible Methods to Determine Differences in Quality of Life Responses Between the Target Population and the External Population

Epidemiologic designs can be used to determine how demographic and disease-related differences between the target population and the external population impact quality of life responses. For example, cross-sectional studies of external patient populations can be done to determine whether patients on the medicine or intervention differ in quality of life responses by age or disease severity. Other factors, either restricted in the eligibility criteria or included but with insufficient statistical power, can also be evaluated using this approach. An even more compelling design would be to evaluate these variables for changes over time in quality of life responses using a cohort design. While the cohort would be useful for evaluating differences between the target population from clinical trials and the external population in patients taking the study medicine (or intervention), differences between treatment groups should not typically be compared because of potential confounding by indication or other factors.

CONCLUSIONS

Quality of life assessment is a relatively new discipline in applied research that, like other disciplines in applied research, can benefit from a multidisciplinary approach. Epi-

demiologic ideas contribute to the development of quality of life research in terms of the conceptualization of QOL measures as study end points, assessment of potential biases (both internal and external), and considerations for interpreting QOL causality.

REFERENCES

1. Kirschner B, Guyatt G. A methodologic framework for assessing health indices. *J Chronic Dis* 1985;38:27–36.
2. Karnofsky DA, Burchenal JH. The clinical evaluation of chemotherapeutic agents against cancer. In: McLeod CM, ed. *Evaluation of chemotherapeutic agents.* New York: Columbia University Press, 1949.
3. Patrick DL, Erickson P. *Health status and health policy: quality of life in health care evaluation and resource allocation.* New York: Oxford University Press, 1993.
4. Johnson JR. A regulatory view. In: Walker SR, Rosser RM, eds. *Quality of life assessment: key issues in the 1990s.* Boston: Kluwer Academic, 1993.
5. Guyatt G, Walter S, Norman G. Measuring change over time: assessing the usefulness of evaluative instruments. *J Chronic Dis* 1987;40:171–178.
6. Deyo RA, Centor RM. Assessing the responsiveness of functional scales to clinical change: an analogy to diagnostic test performance. *J Chronic Dis* 1986;39:879–906.
7. Rothman KJ. Epidemiologic methods in clinical trials. *Cancer* 1977;39:1771–1775.
8. Rothman KJ. *Modern epidemiology.* Boston: Little, Brown, 1985.
9. Hill AB. The clinical trial. *N Engl J Med* 1952;247:113–119.
10. Lachin JM. Properties of simple randomization in clinical trials. *Controlled Clin Trials* 1988;9:312–326.
11. Greenberg RP, Fisher S. Seeing through the double-masked design: a commentary. *Controlled Clin Trials* 1994;15:244–246.
12. Fisher S, Greenberg RP. How sound is the double blind design for evaluating psychotropic drugs? *J Nerv Ment Dis* 1993;181:345–350.
13. Temple R. Government viewpoint of clinical trials of cardiovascular drugs. *Med Clin North Am* 1989;73:495–509.
14. Rothman KJ, Michels KB. The continuing unethical use of placebo controls. *N Engl J Med* 1994;331:394–398.
15. Hill AB. *Principles of medical statistics.* New York: Oxford University Press, 1966.
16. Weed DL. Causal criteria and Popperian refutation. In: Rothman KJ, ed. *Causal inference.* Chestnut Hill, MA: Epidemiology Resources, 1988:15–32.
17. Antman K, Amato D, Wood W, et al. Selection bias in clinical trials. *J Clin Oncol* 1985;3:1142–1147.
18. Chaitman BR, Ryan TJ, Kronmal RA, Foster ED, Frommer PL, Killip T, et al. Coronary artery surgery study (CASS): comparability of 10 year survival in randomized and randomizable patients. *J Am Coll Cardiol* 1990;16:1071–1078.
19. Hampton JR. Presentation and analysis of the results of clinical trials in cardiovascular disease. *Br Med J* 1981;282:1371–1373.
20. Olschewski M, Schumacher M, Davis KB. Analysis of randomized and nonrandomized patients in clinical trials using the comprehensive cohort follow-up study design. *Controlled Clin Trials* 1992;13:226–239.
21. Coulter HL. *The controlled clinical trial.* Washington, DC: Center for Empirical Medicine, Project Cure, 1991.

Quality of Life and Pharmacoeconomics in Clinical Trials, Second Edition, edited by B. Spilker.
Lippincott-Raven Publishers, Philadelphia © 1996.

CHAPTER 61

Legal Considerations in the Development and Use of HRQL Measures for National and International Clinical Trial Research

Richard A. Berzon and John M. Conley

INTRODUCTION

Health-related quality of life (HRQL) measures can be seen as technological improvements over the clinician's time-honored question, "How are you?" (1). Their ultimate success will depend on a variety of factors, including their meaningfulness, that is, whether information made available from the use of the instruments is intelligible; their acceptability, that is, whether the scientific community will employ the measures to help evaluate patients' treatments; and their credibility, that is, whether positive findings of improved quality of life identified through the use of these measures in clinical trials are also observed when the new treatment is used in general practice.

The desirability of health-related quality of life assessments that incorporate the consumer's perspective during the development of new therapies is not in question. It is likely that a broad social consensus would endorse Robert Levine's (2) principle that, in general, quality of life assessments are required (a) when there are good reasons to predict that their results will yield information that will be of practi-

cal use to doctors and patients making choices about whether to use the new therapy, and (b) when the importance of such information justifies the costs and risks of developing it. Despite such a consensus, a variety of legal and ethical issues are being debated by those who work in the quality of life field as a result of the expanded use of these measures in clinical trial research (3).

While the issues under discussion overlap, there appear to be three fundamental questions: (a) Should access to HRQL measures be restricted at any point during or subsequent to development and, if so, how can such restriction be effected? (b) Is it appropriate for the developers of HRQL measures to assert intellectual property rights to limit use of their instruments and, if so, how can they accomplish this objective? (c) Under what circumstances is it legally and socially appropriate for an individual or institution who develops an HRQL measure to profit financially from the sale or use of that measure? We explore these questions in this chapter.

ACCESS TO AND USE OF HRQL INSTRUMENTS

It is essential for researchers to have access to HRQL instruments so that the integrity of the field can be maintained. For the purposes of this chapter, access is defined

R. A. Berzon: Outcomes Research, Bristol-Myers Squibb Pharmaceutical Research Institute, Wallingford, Connecticut 06492.

J. M. Conley: School of Law, University of North Carolina, Chapel Hill, North Carolina 27599.

as the degree to which an HRQL measure and the data supporting its psychometric properties are made available, either during or subsequent to the instrument's development. The key descriptor is degree, for access can be either broad or narrow. Having broad or completely unrestricted access to an HRQL measure denotes that data by which to evaluate it are freely available. Furthermore, there is the implication that even during the measure's development—should it appear, for example, in a peer reviewed journal as a work in progress in association with a particular intervention—data supporting its reliability, validity, and responsiveness will be made available upon request.

An instance in which such information is required occurs when an existing measure developed in the United States is adapted for authorized use in a non–English-speaking country. In such a circumstance, it is not sufficient for those responsible for the adaptation to write, simply, that the instrument was culturally adapted for use in the country in question. The precise nature of the cultural validation must be identified and the methodology clearly characterized so that the conceptual equivalence of the measure can be adequately assessed by those who are considering its use. Similarly, it is necessary to have access to data in support of a newly developed HRQL measure so that its psychometric properties can be reviewed prior to the measure's selection for use in a clinical trial. There is general agreement on the processes by which multi-item scales are evaluated for reliability, validity, and responsiveness (4,5). Data confirming the integrity of these processes must not be restricted if a critical evaluation of the measure is to occur.

Notwithstanding the scientific desirability of free exchange of HRQL instruments and data supporting their psychometric properties, the law of intellectual property provides several options for developers who choose to limit access to and use of their instruments. Legally, access and use are separate questions; gaining lawful access to an instrument does not confer an automatic right to use it. There is also a critical distinction between, on the one hand, the form of a particular instrument and, on the other, the information and ideas that the instrument embodies and the data that support it. Thus, one may have the right to use certain ideas that can be discerned from examining an instrument but may be barred from implementing those ideas in a form that resembles the original instrument.

RESTRICTING ACCESS THROUGH TRADE SECRET LAW

The only truly effective way to control access to an HRQL instrument and its supporting data is to treat these materials and the information they embody as proprietary trade secrets. In the United States, trade secret protection is a matter of state law. Thus, rights and responsibilities may vary from state to state, and there are often disputes over which state's

law will apply to a given controversy. Nonetheless, the general principles are nearly universal.

The basic orientation of American trade secret law is pragmatic; the proprietor of a trade secret must take reasonable steps to insure that it is disclosed only to those with a need to know, and that all such disclosures are accompanied by warnings of confidentiality. Ideally, those warnings will take the form of an explicit written contract that binds the recipient of the disclosure to secrecy. Even in the absence of a written contract, however, the law may find that the circumstances of the disclosures are sufficient to impose an implied duty of confidentiality on the recipient, for example, where a prospective investor is allowed to inspect a secret industrial process. Significantly, once a third party gains lawful, unrestricted access to the trade secret, the protection is lost and the information can be freely used and disseminated, irrespective of the wishes of the proprietor. (As it is sometimes stated, such information enters the public domain.) Thus, the publication of confidential data will vitiate trade secret protection, as will the unrestricted sale of a computer program from which proprietary algorithms can be discovered (6).

The international regime is much more complicated. The American principles set forth above also apply, more or less, in England, English-speaking Canada, Australia, New Zealand, and some other former British colonies. Trade secret law is less clearly demarcated in most of the rest of the world, including, notably, the countries of Continental Europe and their former colonies and the Asian-Pacific nations. Protections equivalent to those in the Anglo-American world are often available, but it is all but impossible to generalize (7).

In applying these principles to a U.S. HRQL developer who desires to limit access to an instrument and supporting data, the fundamental rule is that the developing company, group, or academic center must take reasonable steps to ensure that the protected material and the information it embodies are not disclosed outside of the circle of those participating in the development. At the outset of the project, all those within this circle should agree in writing to respect the confidentiality of the research as a condition of their participation (if they have not already signed general confidentiality agreements as a condition of employment). If disclosure outside the circle is necessary (to prospective joint venturers, for example), each recipient should be required to sign a similar agreement. Physical security is also important; documents containing confidential information should be so marked, for example, and both examination and copying should be carefully controlled.

When the development phase is substantially complete, it is difficult, but not impossible, to market an HRQL instrument (or any other product, for that matter) without waiving trade secret protection. The unrestricted sale or publication of the instrument itself will cause any information it embodies to enter the public domain, freely accessible to all comers.

Therefore, in order simultaneously to market the instrument and protect the information it embodies, the developer must avoid outright sales and instead require users to sign license agreements that grant them limited rights of use and bind them to confidentiality (much like the licenses under which software is marketed). Publication, of course, is out of the question.

The same rules apply to supporting data. Publication or unrestricted distribution to evaluators or others will cause the information to enter the public domain. Accordingly, publication must be avoided and evaluators must be required to sign confidentiality agreements.

In view of current practices in the HRQL field, it is unlikely that even a diligent developer will be able to maintain trade secret protection much beyond the initial development stage. Unrestricted dissemination of instruments and supporting data for evaluation purposes is commonplace, and the software licensing model described above has no precedent in the HRQL market. Accordingly, it is almost inevitable that there will be unrestricted public access to an instrument and its supporting data at or prior to the point it goes on the market.

LIMITING USE THROUGH COPYRIGHT LAW

Access, as stated earlier, does not necessarily imply a right of use. With respect to the supporting data and the facts and information that can be gleaned from inspection of the instrument, access is equivalent to the right of use in most cases. But with respect to the particular form of the instrument, "use" in the sense of the right to copy, adapt, or translate will still be prohibited even to those who have gained lawful access.

Under U.S. federal copyright law, a copyright in a "work of authorship"—a category that clearly includes HRQL measures and may include data bases—comes into being at the moment of creation, without the necessity of any formal action by the author (8). Readers are deemed to be on notice of the copyright, and it is waived only if the author takes affirmative steps to commit the work to the public domain (9). Absent such a commitment, others can reproduce, adapt, improve, translate the work, or prepare derivative works based upon it, only with the permission of the author (10).

Copyright protection is subject to two related limitations. First, the copyright protects only the expression contained in a work and not the underlying ideas (11). Second, copyright law forbids only actual copying, adaptation, or modification of the protected work's expression; the independent development of another work that turns out to be similar to the original is legal. Accordingly, a competitor is free to borrow the ideas contained in an HRQL measure and use them to develop a new instrument, provided that the competitor does not appropriate the original author's expression. Establishing the boundary between protected expression and unprotected ideas is the most contentious and frequently litigated issue in copyright law (12,13). Cases dealing with standardized test scoring sheets and other kinds of printed forms suggest that HRQL authors will be given copyright protection for even rudimentary expression in their instruments (14). Those who would adapt an HRQL measure should therefore assume that most of its verbal content will be protected, excepting only the most routine sorts of instructions. Even brief survey questions and simple scales that are presented to subjects should be assumed to be protected.

Copyright protection is also limited by the doctrine of fair use, which may excuse conduct that would otherwise constitute infringement. Whether a particular use of a copyrighted work is "fair," and thus non-infringing, is decided on a case-by-case basis and depends on such factors as the nature and purpose of the use, the proportion of the copyrighted work that has been used, and the effect on the market value of the copyrighted work. Although use for "nonprofit educational purposes" is favored, there is no blanket exemption for research (15). A 1985 Supreme Court decision denying fair use protection to a political journal that printed purloined excerpts from President Ford's soon-to-be-published memoirs persuaded many observers that the fair use doctrine was all but dead (16). However, several recent lower court decisions have permitted the unauthorized copying of copyrighted computer programs where the copying was essential to understanding unprotected ideas that the programs embodied (17). There is thus reason to believe that the unauthorized copying or adaptation of HRQL measures for research purposes might be treated as fair use, but there is currently no clear judicial precedent.

A regime of international treaties ensures U.S.-level copyright protection for American authors throughout much of the world. Most countries are parties to either or both of two major treaties whereby they guarantee each others' citizens "reciprocal national treatment"; for example, an American author seeking to assert a copyright in Germany would be allowed the same protection as a German author, and vice versa (18). The countries of Western Europe tend to provide authors even more protection than is available in the United States. In particular, these countries grant authors "moral rights" to prevent changes in their works that might damage their reputations, even after they have transferred the copyright to another. Moreover, Western European courts have been vigorous in enforcing authors' rights.

In the highly developed countries of Asia, by contrast, protection is theoretically comparable to that afforded here, but even in Japan American copyright holders find enforcement difficult. In countries such as Thailand and Malaysia, American authors and publishers have long complained of wholesale piracy, although the situation may be improving.

In the developing world, the problem facing American authors is twofold. First, some countries, recognizing their status as needy consumers of intellectual property rather than producers, do not have protective copyright laws on the books. Second, even those that do are often unwilling or unable to enforce them.

PATENT PROTECTION FOR HRQL MEASURES

The law of patent is tangentially relevant to HRQL instruments. Under United States patent law, an inventor may obtain a 17-year monopoly on any "new and useful process, machine, manufacture, or composition of matter, or any new and useful improvement thereof" (19). The word *new* does not have its ordinary meaning; novelty is determined according to a set of highly technical rules (20). An HRQL measure would not constitute a patentable machine or manufacture. Nonetheless, it is possible, though unlikely, that the administration and interpretation of a HRQL instrument could be held to constitute a patentable process. If so, the developer could prevent others from administering and interpreting equivalent measures, whether copied or independently developed. The authors are aware of no instances in which process patents have been obtained on HRQL measures.

THE INTELLECTUAL PROPERTY POLICY OF THE U.S. CONSTITUTION

It is clear from the foregoing discussion that the law of trade secret, copyright, and perhaps even patent can be used to control access to and use of HRQL measures. Whether an instrument's developer should assert intellectual property rights is a separate question. In evaluating this question, it is useful to consider the policy that underlies the law of intellectual property. According to the U.S. Constitution (Article 1, section 8), the purpose of intellectual property law is "To promote the Progress of Science and useful Arts, by securing for limited Times to Authors and Inventors the exclusive Right to their respective Writings and Discoveries." The constitutional theory is thus primarily an economic one; authors and inventors are encouraged to invest their time and capital in the scientific enterprise not by moral exhortation, but by the promise of a period of monopoly profits.

The intellectual property regime outlined in the Constitution seeks to balance competing short- and long-term interests. If one takes a short-term perspective on a given item of intellectual property, whether a copyright in an HRQL instrument or a drug patent, it can be argued that the scientific process will be best advanced by immediate disclosure and an unrestricted right of use. In the case of an HRQL instrument, critical assessment of the instrument's strengths and weaknesses requires access to the questionnaire and a meaningful exchange of supporting data between developers and evaluators. Those in the quality of life field who use HRQL instruments in clinical research must be able to ask hard questions and receive candid answers. Anything less can fairly be characterized as an impediment to the scientific

process. Individual scientists are also legitimately motivated by such concerns as tenure and professional development, which are usually advanced by prompt publication.

Nonetheless, it is also important to keep in mind the long-term needs of the scientific process. Although a given instrument may benefit from immediate and unrestricted circulation among the scientific community, that instrument's sponsor may be dissuaded from investing in future projects if he sees the fruits of his research passing directly into the public domain. In such circumstances, the short-term benefit may be obliterated by the long-term detriment to "the Progress of Science."

The constitutional compromise is to protect the inventor by granting a monopoly on certain kinds of intellectual property, but to protect the scientific enterprise and the public by limiting both the scope and length of that monopoly. The copyright monopoly, although it extends for the life of the author plus 50 years, protects only expression and not ideas (21); the patent monopoly, although it prohibits both copying and innocent reproduction, is conditioned on full disclosure of the knowledge underlying the invention, protects only against duplication of the specific invention, and is limited to 17 years (22). A fair-minded look at the scientific accomplishments of American private enterprise suggests that this compromise has been reasonably successful.

THE TRADE-OFFS OF RESTRICTED ACCESS

Deciding whether to allow access to and utilization of HRQL measures is a specific instance of the broader policy dilemma just discussed. Sharing HRQL measures during or subsequent to development aids the progress of knowledge; instruments are regularly circulated among trusted colleagues for comment, review, and suggestions on fine-tuning. (However, those who gain access to an instrument before rigorous psychometric evaluation has been conducted should either refrain from use of the instrument, or build such evaluation into their studies.) From this perspective, using trade secret protection to control access or copyright law to prevent duplication or modification impedes scientific progress. From the perspective of an instrument's developer, enforcing the copyright in a completed work is defensible, both scientifically and economically. Giving free rein to those who would modify the instrument—by substantially altering the wording or deleting questions, for example—and then using the modified version in research protocols can result in the validity of the original questionnaire being compromised. The more egregious case would be of the competitor who modifies the instrument, renames it, and then claims it as his or her own; this would represent obvious scientific plagiarism as well as clear economic injustice.

The balance is a delicate one. On the one hand, enforcing the copyright in an instrument protects the originator from abuses and ensures the integrity of the measure. On the other, it can also prevent the work from being improved.

Absent a commitment to the public domain or case-by-case permission from the originator, others cannot revise a copyrighted instrument. Consequently, newly discovered information, no matter how relevant or beneficial, cannot be incorporated into the original measure except by the progenitor.

Another consideration is that industry frequently gives financial support to the development of HRQL measures for special diseases, conditions, and populations. The pros and cons of whether to enforce the copyright of a measure that a private company has funded may be debated within the organization with a vested interest in the outcome. From a short-term financial perspective, it may make sense to assert the copyright and condition use of the instrument on the payment of user fees. Current user fee receipts can also be viewed as a source of funding for future projects. Moreover, as discussed earlier, the very fact that compensation is available may serve as a long-term incentive to the developers as well as to other businesses in the field.

However, there are also a number of long-term advantages to the company to making the measure widely available. Unrestricted access will allow the measure to be critically evaluated in the HRQL marketplace. Assuming that reevaluation confirms the psychometric robustness of the measure, it reinforces whatever benefits were found to be attributed to the company's product (for which the measure may have been originally developed). The credibility of the measure is thereby increased and the reputation of the institution is enhanced.

PROPRIETARY VERSUS PUBLIC OWNERSHIP

Another issue with respect to copyright is whether there are circumstances under which private interests should be allowed to claim the copyright in a measure that has been developed entirely with public money and market it for commercial gain. (Legally, the terms of the government grant or contract will determine whether any private party is entitled to assert a copyright; many such contracts require that research products be committed to the public domain. This discussion assumes a legal entitlement to a copyright and addresses the moral and economic question of whether the copyright holder should assert it.) Such a situation might arise, for example, if a measure that has been developed with U.S. government funds and is in the public domain is then culturally adapted for use outside the U.S. Under such circumstances, the developer could claim a copyright in what has been added to the public domain version. But, while remuneration for work performed to increase a measure's accessibility is appropriate, should the developer base his royalty charges on the entire value of the adapted instrument, or only on development and distribution costs?

This question raises the broader one of the extent to which HRQL measures are of value to society. In the present era of health care delivery, it is understood that society demands value for money, but what does that mean? From society's perspective, value is the collective judgment of what happens to a patient during and after a medical intervention. As a consequence of patients playing increasingly larger roles in their own care, they especially want to be able to understand, on a very personal level, the comprehensive effect of medical interventions. HRQL instruments facilitate that understanding by measuring these effects in a way to which people can relate.

From the perspective of society, therefore, it appears reasonable for HRQL assessments to play a vital role in the conduct of clinical research. It is also reasonable that society should support the conduct of clinical research because it is in its own interest to do so. When society supports research, it generally does so through taxes to the government, which assumes, on behalf of society, an obligation to conduct the research and to develop safe and effective technologies. If the result of this support is an HRQL measure for the public good developed with public monies, it seems inappropriate for any single individual or institution to profit from original work paid for by all, except to the extent of a return on a coinvestment that adds specifically identifiable value to the work.

To promote the public good, one option is for the governmental sponsor to dedicate the research product to the public domain, thereby foreclosing the assertion of intellectual property rights. Alternatively, the governmental sponsor can claim the applicable intellectual property rights and manage them for the public benefit. The National Institutes of Health (NIH), for example, has obtained patents on health-related inventions. Through a licensing program, the NIH attempts to maximize the ultimate utility of the patented technologies and also to generate income to support its mission.

There are some countervailing considerations, however, that may argue for private rights. First, when the government funds research, it does not write on a blank slate. The most important components of any research project are the researchers, who bring to bear their own skills, training, and ideas. In the case of public-private research partnerships, those skills, training, and ideas may owe a part of their existence to a private concern. That concern would seem to have a defensible claim for compensation. If private funding is used to enhance an existing HRQL measure or make it more widely accessible for use, a proprietary claim on the added value may be appropriate.

Second, government-funded basic research often depends on the private sector for its application. If private concerns see no economic incentive to participate in a research endeavor, the public may never see any benefit. "Orphan drugs" that never make the journey from the laboratory to the pharmacy are an example of this problem.

The ultimate objective must always be to balance public and proprietary ownership in such a way to maximize scientific productivity while treating all parties fairly. This is far easier said than done; the questions come more easily than the answers. Those who develop HRQL measures—or any tools for the public good—are entitled to compensation for work done; but at what point is instrument development perceived to be an entrepreneurial venture? How might that perception effect this field? Costs to oversee and fine-tune HRQL instruments should be recovered by those who create them, but at what point do those charges become a barrier to access? These are difficult questions and, even now, such queries are under intense discussion by health-related quality of life researchers and by others (3). These and related issues may become even more difficult if deficit reduction shrinks the pool of public research money and forces a fundamental rethinking of the nature of public-private research partnerships.

CONCLUSIONS

Several of the practical legal and ethical controversies that are currently being debated by researchers within the HRQL field have been discussed. Those cited are by no means exhaustive, nor are their solutions clear-cut. Access to HRQL research, whether in progress or ongoing, is to be encouraged since this is necessary for the quality of life field to progress. However, the need for protection from misuse of ongoing work is real and may, in certain circumstances, require that work be copyrighted. Such decisions ought to be made on a case-by-case basis.

HRQL measures developed entirely with public monies should remain in the public domain, or at least be managed for the public good, as the NIH patent model illustrates. Instruments developed with private funds should be treated in a manner that reflects a fair balance between the rights of the private developer and those of the scientific community and the public. HRQL questionnaires are regularly being refined; such work is costly. Investigators continuing research directly related to instrument refinement might rea-

sonably ask for compensation from those who wish to use their questionnaires.

REFERENCES

1. Faden R, Leplege A. Assessing quality of life: moral implications for clinical practice. *Med Care* 1992;30:MS166–MS175.
2. Levine RJ. An ethical perspective. In: Spilker B, ed. *Quality of life assessments in clinical trials.* New York: Raven Press, 1990:153–162.
3. Shapiro MF, et al. Is the spirit of capitalism undermining the ethics of health services research? *Health Serv Res* 1994;28(6):661–687.
4. Stewart AL, Hays RD, Ware JE Jr. Methods of validating MOS health measures. In: Stewart AL, Ware JE Jr, eds. *Measuring functioning and well-being.* Durham, NC: Duke University Press, 1992:309–324.
5. Guyatt GH, Walter S, Norman G. Measuring change over time: assessing the usefulness of evaluative instruments. *J Chronic Dis* 1987;40:171–178.
6. Nimmer RT, Krauthaus PA. Information as property—databases and commercial property. *Int J Law Information Technol* 1993;1:3–34.
7. Milgrim RM. *Milgrim on trade secrets.* New York: Matthew Bender, 1993:9-118–9-120.
8. Copyright Act of 1976, Title 17, United States Code, S102 (a).
9. Copyright Act of 1976, Title 17, United States Code, SS401–409.
10. Copyright Act of 1976, Title 17, United States Code, S106.
11. Copyright Act of 1976, Title 17, United States Code, S102 (b).
12. Nimmer RT. *The law of computer technology.* Boston: Warren Gorham Lamont, 1992:1-18–1-21.
13. Nimmer MB, Nimmer RT. *Nimmer on copyright.* New York: Matthew Bender, 1993:13-65–13-81, 16-2–16-4.
14. United States District Court for the Southern District of New York. *Harcourt, Brace, & World, Inc. v. Graphic Controls Corp.* Federal Supplement 1971;329:517–530.
15. Copyright Act of 1976, Title 17, United States Code, S107.
16. United States Supreme Court. *Harper & Row, Inc. v. Nation Enterprises.* United States Reports 1985;471:539–605.
17. Samuelson P. Fair use for computer programs and other copyrightable works in digital form. *J Intellectual Property Law* 1993;1:49–118.
18. Berne Convention for the Protection of Literary and Artistic Works, art. 5; Universal Copyright Convention, art. II.
19. Patent Act, Title 35, United States Code, S101.
20. Patent Act, Title 35, United States Code, S102.
21. Copyright Act of 1976, Title 17, United States Code, SS 102 (b).
22. Patent Act, Title 17, United States Code, SS 112, 154.

Quality of Life and Pharmacoeconomics in Clinical Trials, Second Edition, edited by B. Spilker.
Lippincott-Raven Publishers, Philadelphia © 1996.

CHAPTER **62**

Regulatory Perspectives on Quality of Life Issues

Mary S. McCabe, Dale Shoemaker, Robert J. Temple, Gregory Burke, and
Michael A. Friedman

INTRODUCTION

Clinical trials to determine the efficacy of new investigational agents in cancer patients present special challenges. Placebo-controlled trials are generally not appropriate for cancer patients, and in comparative trials crossover of patients progressing on investigational anticancer agents to salvage therapy may confound survival analysis. There is, therefore, growing interest in measures of clinical benefit that can be used, together with evidence of objective tumor response, as a basis for new drug approval. The use of quality of life outcome information is a method of demonstrating clinical benefit that has been gaining support in drug development research. Indeed, the Oncologic Drugs Advisory Committee (ODAC) of the Food and Drug Administration (FDA) has recommended survival and quality of life as the primary efficacy parameters for consideration in approving new anticancer agents (1).

In experience to date, most emphasis has been placed on quality of life data in the evaluation of palliative therapies, but these data can also be important for judging curative therapies, especially when such curative approaches employ analogs of approved active agents and aim to reduce toxicities. In this chapter we describe important issues for consideration as efforts expand to use quality of life evaluation in the development of new investigational anticancer agents and provide a list of the current National Cancer Institute (NCI) trials utilizing quality of life measurements. In addition, we present recent experience with quality of life measurement in new drug approval.

    M. S. McCabe, D. Shoemaker, and M. A. Friedman: Cancer Therapy Evaluation Program, Division of Cancer Treatment, National Cancer Institute, Bethesda, Maryland 20892.
    R. J. Temple: Office of Drug Evaluation I, Center for Drug Evaluation and Research, Food and Drug Administration, Rockville, Maryland 20857.
    G. Burke: Division of Oncology and Pulmonary Drug Products, Center for Drug Evaluation and Research, Food and Drug Administration, Rockville, Maryland 20857.

EXPANDING EFFORT OF THE QUALITY OF LIFE EVALUATION IN THE DEVELOPMENT OF NEW INVESTIGATIONAL ANTICANCER AGENTS

The number of clinical trials sponsored by the NCI that include a quality of life component has steadily increased in recent years. A list of current trials are presented in Table 1. Although different instruments have been devised to collect these data, there are several important aspects that must be considered in all trials in which quality of life is included: (a) administration of the questionnaire, (b) overall quality of life improvement due to treatment, (c) quality of life changes related to objective response, (d) symptom reduction, and (e) decreased toxicity.

Administration of the Questionnaire

A NCI workshop on quality of life research in cancer clinical trials in July 1990 (2) concluded that the patient self-report provided the best scientific and clinically relevant data for evaluating the impact of cancer treatments on the patient's quality of life. Substitution of proxy measures was generally not recommended. Neither physician nor family member measures have demonstrated good agreement with the patient report. There are, however, instances where proxy measures may be considered:

1. When the physician report provides a useful supplement to the patient report of quality of life, especially regarding physician-observed toxicities or performance status.
2. If the cognitive or physical function of the patient is expected to deteriorate significantly during the study, it may be helpful for the investigator to include spouse or family members in the ratings.
3. It may be useful to include in the validation of new quality of life instruments an examination of the degree of differences and agreement in the patient and proxy reports.
4. When the purpose of the trial is to assess the impact of therapy on individuals other than the patient, it would be useful to document the degree of burden experienced by the family during the patient's treatment. A family member may contribute to the evaluation by assessing his or her own quality of life.

There are situations identified in which proxy measures of patient quality of life should not be used:

1. A proxy rating is not considered appropriate when the patient is non–English-speaking and there is no translation of the quality of life measure or culturally sensitive instrument that meets accepted standards for translated instruments.
2. A proxy should not provide a report on a patient's quality of life if the patient refuses to participate in the quality of life portion of the clinical trial.

Overall Quality of Life Improvement Due to Treatment

Overall quality of life assessments can be used to compare the impact of treatment toxicities of different regimens on quality of life. They can also be used to measure the beneficial impact of tumor responses on the patient's life and the impact of the long-term effects of treatment (e.g., effects on neurologic, reproductive, and cognitive functioning) especially in patients cured of their cancer. Such assessments over time can be critical in determining an overall long-term improvement in quality of life that may be attainable despite short-term decrements due to treatment toxicity. A quality of life evaluation can also be important in adjuvant trials in which patients are relatively asymptomatic at baseline. The goal in this case is to determine whether quality of life is adversely affected by the therapy. For the most part, these types of evaluation have not been widely utilized in providing supportive information in cancer clinical trials.

Quality of Life Changes Related to Objective Response

Correlation of quality of life improvement with tumor response is a potentially important determination but has not yet been carefully evaluated in clinical trials. While there is some documentation that complete responses result in patient benefit, the importance of partial responses is not well established.

Symptom Reduction

The improvement of symptoms related to the tumor can be an important surrogate for evaluating improvement in the patient's overall quality of life. This improvement can be demonstrated in multiple ways, and is intended to target specific problems the patient actually has so that improvement in these areas can be specifically determined and not lost among other confounding patient parameters. In selected studies, it may be useful to focus on tumor-related symptoms that are unequivocally problems for the patient such as relief of an obstructed viscus (e.g., esophagus or bronchus), healing of malignant skin ulcers, resolution of paraneoplastic endocrine syndromes, relief of pruritus, resolution of bone pain at a site of metastasis (which can be signaled by decreases in analgesic requirements), a change in appetite accompanied by an increase in lean body weight in a previously cachectic patient, or an improvement in pulmonary function in a patient who had an identified pulmonary metastases but no pulmonary infection. If the response of such symptoms is to be a study end point, decisions should be made prospectively as to what symptoms are to be evaluated, the frequency of evaluation, and the type of questionnaire or other measurement to be used to provide quantitative data.

TABLE 1. *National Cancer Institute–sponsored phase III clinical trials with quality of life end points*

Title	Treatment	QOL instrument
Breast cancer		
Quality of life and psychosocial adjustment of patients with stage II and III breast cancer randomized to high-dose CPA/CDDP/BCNU with autologous bone marrow support vs. standard dose CPA/CDDP/BCNU as consolidation to adjuvant CAF	CAF ABMT	Functional Living Index–Cancer, Psychosocial Adjustment of Illness Scale, Symptom Distress Scale
A phase III study of Taxol® at three dose levels in the treatment of patients with metastatic breast cancer	G-CSF, Taxol®	Functional Living Index–Cancer, Symptom Distress Scale, CALGB sociodemographic background sheet
Phase III trial of adriamycin vs. Taxol® vs. Taxol® plus adriamycin plus G-CSF in metastatic breast cancer	G-CSF (A), doxorubicin, Taxol®	Functional Assessment of Cancer—Breast Cancer
Phase III comparison of tamoxifen vs. tamoxifen with ovarian ablation in premenopausal women with axillary node-negative receptor-positive breast cancer < 2 cm	Tamoxifen, Zoladex	Functional Assessment of Cancer Therapy–Breast, ECOG Menopausal Symptom Form
Central nervous system cancers		
Low-grade glioma phase III: surgery and immediate radiotherapy vs. surgery and delayed radiotherapy	Radiation Rx, surgery	Mini-mental state examination
Treatment of children with low-stage medulloblastoma: standard-dose craniospinal irradiation vs. reduced-dose craniospinal irradiation plus adjuvant chemotherapy with cisplatin, cyclophosphamide, and vincristine	Cisplatin, cyclophosphamide, Mesna, G-CSF, radiation Rx, vincristine	POG QOL questionnaire
Phase III intergroup randomized comparison of radiation alone vs. preradiation chemotherapy for pure and mixed anaplastic oligodendrogliomas	Procarbazine, lomustine, vincristine, radiation Rx	Karnofsky performance scale, mini-mental state examination
A phase III trial comparing the use of radiosurgery followed by conventional radiotherapy with BCNU to conventional radiotherapy with BCNU for supratentorial glioblastoma multiforme	BCNU, radiation Rx	Mini-mental state examination, spitzer QOL index
Postoperative radiotherapy for single brain metastases	Dexamethasone, radiation Rx, surgery	Mini-mental state examination
Gastrointestinal cancers		
A phase III prospective randomized trial comparing laparoscopic-assisted colectomy vs. open colectomy for colon cancer	Surgery	Symptom Distress Scale, QOL index, Q-TWiST
Phase III intergroup randomized trial of preoperative vs. postoperative combined modality therapy for resectable rectal cancer	Radiation Rx, surgery, 5-fluorouracil, CA leucovorin	Anorectal function assessment tool, Functional Assessment of Therapy–Cancer
Genitourinary cancers		
Randomized comparison of low dose steroids and mitoxantrone vs. low dose steroids in patients with "hormone refractory" stage D2 carcinoma of the prostate	Hydrocortisone, mitoxantrone	Functional Living Index–Cancer, Symptom Distress Scale, Sexual and Urologic Functioning Questionnaire, problems in daily activities

TABLE 1. *Continued.*

Title	Treatment	QOL instrument
Genitourinary cancers		
A phase III trial of the study of endocrine therapy used as a cytoreductive and cytostatic agent prior to radiation therapy in good prognosis locally confined adenocarcinoma of the prostate	Zoladex, flutamide, radiation Rx	Sexual Adjustment Questionnaire
Evaluation of quality of life in patients with stage C adenocarcinoma of the prostate enrolled on SWOG-8794	Radiotherapy	MOS-SF-20, Symptom Distress Scale, LASA
Evaluation of quality of life in patients with stage D2 prostate cancer enrolled on SWOG-8894	Flutamide, surgery	MOS-SF-20, Symptom Distress Scale, LASA
Gynecologic cancers		
A randomized study of surgery vs. surgery plus vulvar radiation in the management of poor prognosis primary vulvar cancer and of radiation vs. radiation and chemotherapy for positive inguinal nodes	5-Fluorouracil, cisplatin, surgery, radiation Rx	Functional Assessment of Cancer Therapy–General, GOG Symptom Inventory, Groningen Arousability Scale, Groningen Body Image Scale
A quality of life companion study to GOG-122—whole abdominal radiotherapy vs. combination doxorubicin-cisplatin chemotherapy in advanced endometrial carcinoma	Doxorubicin, cisplatin, surgery, radiation Rx	Functional Assessment of Cancer Therapy–cancer, assessment of peripheral neuropathy, functional alterations due to changes in elimination, fatigue
A phase III randomized study of cisplatin (NSC #119875) and Taxol® (paclitaxel) (NSC #125973) with interval secondary cytoreduction vs. cisplatin and paclitaxel in patients with suboptimal stage III & IV epithelial ovarian carcinoma	Cisplatin, Taxol®, surgery, G-CSF (A)	Functional Assessment of Cancer Therapy–Ovarian
Head and neck cancer		
Phase III trial to preserve the larynx: induction chemotherapy and radiation therapy vs. concomitant chemotherapy and radiation therapy versus radiation therapy	5-Fluorouracil, cisplatin, radiation Rx, surgery	Functional Assessment of Cancer–Head and Neck, Symptom Scale
Lung cancer		
Cisplatin plus etoposide vs. daily oral etoposide in elderly patients with extensive-stage small cell lung cancer	Cisplatin, etoposide	Functional Assessment of Cancer Therapy–Lung, ECOG Neurotoxicity-Related QOL Questionnaire
Phase III trial comparing etoposide/ cisplatin vs. Taxol®/cisplatin-G-CSF vs. Taxol®/cisplatin in advanced non–small cell lung cancer	Cisplatin, G-CSF, etoposide, Taxol®	Functional Assessment of Cancer–Lung
Cisplatin plus etoposide vs. cisplatin plus etoposide followed by topotecan in extensive-stage small cell lung cancer	Cisplatin, G-CSF, etoposide, topotecan	Functional Assessment of Cancer Therapy–Lung
A randomized phase III study of CODE plus thoracic irradiation vs. alternating CAV and EP for extensive stage small cell lung cancer	Cisplatin, cyclophosphamide, doxorubicin, etoposide, radiation Rx, vincristine	EORTC Quality of Life Questionnaire

TABLE 1. *Continued.*

Title	Treatment	QOL instrument
Lymphoma		
Randomized trial of subtotal nodal irradiation vs. doxorubicin, vinblastine and subtotal nodal irradiation for stage I-IIA Hodgkin's disease	Allopurinol, doxorubicin, radiation Rx, vinblastine	CARES-SF, Symptom Distress Scale, MOS SF-36 (Health Perception Scale and Vitality Scale)
Health status and quality of life in patients with early stage Hodgkin's disease	Doxorubicin, vinblastine, radiation, allopurinol	Symptom Distress Scale, CARES-SF, MOS SF-36
Myelodysplastic syndrome		
A randomized phase II controlled trial of subcutaneous 5-azacytidine (NSC #102815) vs. observation in myelodysplastic syndromes	5-Azacytidine	EORTIC QOL Questionnaire, Revised Rand General Well-Being Scale

BCNU, carmustine; CAF ABMT, cyclophosphamide, doxorubicin, 5-fluorouracil, autologous bone marrow transplant; CDDP, cisplatin; CPA, cyclophosphamide; CALGB, cancer and leukemia group B; ECOG, Eastern Cooperative Oncology Group; GOG, Gynecologic Oncology Group; POG, Pediatric Oncology Group; SWOG, Southwest Oncology Group; MOS-SF-20, Medical Outcomes Study–Short Form 20; MOS-SF-36, Medical Outcomes Study-Short Form-36; LASA, linear analogue self–assessment scale; CAV, cyclophosphamide, doxorubicin, vincristine; EP, etoposide, cisplatin; EORTC, European Organization for Research and Treatment of Cancer; CARES-SF, Cancer Rehabilitation Evaluation System–Short Form.

Decreased Toxicity

Clinical trials can be identified in which the choice of treatments with approximately equal efficacy could be influenced by their effects on the quality of life. In these trials, the use of concurrent medications (antiemetics, analgesics, stool softeners) and concurrent radiotherapy, and blindedness of the observer should be considered prospectively because they can easily confound comparisons. An example of such an evaluation is the comparison of a compound and its analog in which efficacy is equivalent but the analog is thought to have a more favorable toxicity profile. Another example is that of a trial comparing two treatment modalities in which the efficacy is equal but there is a differential effect in quality of life.

CURRENT ISSUES

In designing clinical trials that include a quality of life component, there are several issues that should be considered: (a) appropriate utilization of quality of life assessments in trials, (b) trial design and analysis considerations, and (c) issues associated with the instruments themselves.

Appropriate Utilization of Quality of Life Assessments in Trials

When quality of life evaluations are considered for inclusion in cancer clinical trials, they should be designed as an integral component of the research question (i.e., objective) and not as an appended companion evaluation. There should be a trial hypothesis and an expectation that the quality of life instrument will provide information that is additive to the traditional drug development objectives. The instruments chosen should be selected to answer a specific research question that cannot be answered with simple performance status or traditional toxicity rating.

Trial Design and Analysis Considerations

In developing the quality of life component of the trial, this evaluation should be carefully designed to complement the other major end points of the trial. Then, based on the trial goals, appropriate quality of life instruments can be chosen and the timing of administration of the questionnaires determined. For example, a trial evaluating the short-term effects of a chemotherapy regimen would choose an instrument very different from the instrument needed for evaluation of the long-term neurologic consequences in the successfully treated pediatric patient. It is also essential that the analytic plan be prospectively developed so that the necessary number of patients are included and the major planned analyses identified. This is a particularly important matter as many quality of life instruments have subsets and individual items to be analyzed, creating serious multiple comparison issues.

Issues Associated with the Instruments Themselves

Some general questions that should be considered prior to using a quality of life measure in clinical trials include:

1. Has the instrument been validated? Is the instrument known to be linear over the range of measurement and

is it sensitive to changes occurring in the patient? What is the clinical meaning of a given change in an instrument at each end of the scale? Does each instrument measure the same thing in patients with different cancers and in the same patient at different stages of disease? If quality of life is to be used to support effectiveness, there must be a distinction made between cancer-related and drug-related effects on the scores. Which statistical tests should be used to demonstrate significance?

2. Is improvement expected or is the best hope a change in rate of deterioration? When all the patients entered into a trial have good performance status or are asymptomatic, it may not be possible to demonstrate improvement. Instead, time to deterioration, probably using life table methods, may be the appropriate measure.

3. At what time points should assessment be made and how often should measurements be made? Should evaluations continue after the treatment is finished? If so, for how long? Should dropouts be censored?

4. Should results be adjusted using baseline scores on the instrument?

5. Should the observer and the patient be blinded as to treatment and whether or not there has been an objective response to treatment?

6. How much training of the patient and observer is necessary? What quality control measures of documentation should be used?

7. Should non–English-speaking patients be included? Is there a culturally relevant non-English questionnaire available?

This daunting list of issues needing consideration reflects the need for continued refinement of the role of quality of life instruments in general, and of particular in cancer trials.

USE OF QUALITY OF LIFE DATA BY REGULATORY AGENCIES

Quality of life measurements are potentially important end points for clinical trials with anticancer agents. The design of these measurements for use in pivotal trials is critically important. In 1985 Temple (3) proposed that more attention be paid to resolution of unequivocal cancer symptoms (pain over involved bone, extreme anorexia, decreased pulmonary function) as potential end points that might be used to demonstrate clinical benefit even when response rates are low. Wittes (4) further proposed that if such symptoms and signs (elements relevant to quality of life) could be shown to improve, then nonrandomized phase 2 trials could be persuasive in determining the benefit of an investigational agent. These controlled phase 2 trials would probably be larger and more complex than conventional phase 2 trials. It would be particularly important to include patients with unequivocal disease-related symptoms or signs at the start of therapy and to specify exactly how changes in these would be measured at various intervals throughout the course of treatment. Despite the fact that this approach was suggested almost a decade ago, and a general interest in quality of life as an end point in cancer trials was expressed in FDA guidelines, changes in cancer-related symptoms or quality of life have to date had little role in cancer drug approvals.

Nevertheless, the FDA continues to encourage the use of quality of life measurements in the clinical studies of investigational anticancer agents and continues to support measurement of cancer-related symptoms as outlined above as the role of quality of life evaluations in drug development trials continues to evolve.

CONCLUSIONS

Although improved symptom status has been part of the basis for the approval of anticancer agents, quality of life evaluations have not yet been a basis for approval. Many future applications for drug approval are likely to include symptom assessment and quality of life assessment information from both phase 2 and phase 3 clinical trials.

REFERENCES

1. Johnson JR, Temple R. Food and Drug Administration requirements for approval of new anticancer drugs. *Cancer Treat Rep* 1985;69: 1155–1157.
2. Nayfield SG, Hailey BT, McCabe M. Quality of life assessment in cancer clinical trials. Report of the Workshop on Quality of Life Research in Cancer Clinical Trials. National Cancer Institute, Bethesda, Maryland, July 1990.
3. Temple R. Transcript of the Oncologic Drugs Advisory Committee meeting, June 28, 1985.
4. Wittes RE. Antineoplastic agents and FDA regulations; square pegs for round holes? *Cancer Treat Rep* 1987;71:795–806.

Quality of Life and Pharmacoeconomics in Clinical Trials, Second Edition, edited by B. Spilker.
Lippincott-Raven Publishers, Philadelphia © 1996.

CHAPTER 63

Language and Translation Issues

Catherine Acquadro, Bernard Jambon, David Ellis, and Patrick Marquis

INTRODUCTION

What is language? What is translation? Why translate health-related quality of life (HRQL) instruments, and how should one proceed? What is involved in the translation into one or several target languages of an HRQL instrument developed in one country only? Without claiming to exhaust the subject, this chapter sets out to answer these questions.

But first we must place language and translation issues within the special context of HRQL assessment in multinational clinical trials. The last 20 years have seen the development of a large number of HRQL questionnaires (1–6), and these instruments are being used increasingly in clinical trials with a growing emphasis on multinational applications (7–9).

The principle of using the same questionnaire in different countries is based on two major arguments:

1. By analogy with other medical data, a common international interpretation and analysis of the results is only possible if the data come from the same instrument. Moreover, multinational operations are presented by pharmaceutical companies as a cost-effective strategy (10), the ideal being to aggregate data from international studies.
2. All new data acquired about an instrument advance knowledge of its psychometric qualities and hence its validity and reputation. Assessment of HRQL should be seen as a science under development. To date, few instruments have reached a maturity phase, especially disease-specific questionnaires.

As a result, the need for cross-nationally and cross-culturally valid, reliable, and responsive HRQL instruments has never been so great.

The strategies required to develop HRQL questionnaires that can be used cross-nationally are fully described in the chapter by Monika Bullinger et al. We will simply note that three strategies can be observed at present:

1. Translation into one or several other languages of instruments which are developed essentially for and within one country only (11). This is the most frequently used method, although certain authors (12,13) criticize the lack of intercultural appropriateness of these questionnaires and the risk of producing texts translated without conceptual equivalence.
2. Translation of instruments of which conception and development in a source language have been the subject of a consensus between several international teams in order to ensure their intercultural relevance and their conceptual equivalence (14).
3. The World Health Organization (WHO) Quality of Life (QOL) Group approach aims to create an instrument applicable to a large variety of cultures, with equivalent versions developed simultaneously in several languages. The questions developed in each dimension or domain may be different from one country to another (15). Such is not the case with the other two strategies.

All three cases involve the translation process. The guidelines and criteria required to choose the appropriate HRQL instrument applicable cross-nationally and cross-culturally have been presented elsewhere (16,17). They will not be developed here.

C. Acquadro, B. Jambon, D. Ellis, and P. Marquis: MAPI Research Institute, F-69003 Lyon, France.

Before addressing the methods used to translate HRQL instruments, we present certain essential general ideas on language and the translation process. While any generalizations on language require qualification, as exceptions can be found to any broad statements, the conclusions presented here are taken from the literature on the subject and are based on our experience at MAPI.

LANGUAGE

Language, which is an acquired and not an inborn characteristic,[1] is one of the components of culture: languages belong to the societies who speak them and are part of the definition of these societies (19). Many writers since Von Humboldt have stressed the interaction between the external world and language, between the concept man has of the world and the way he expresses it in language (19–21). This is what Sapir and Whorf formulated into the so-called Whorf hypothesis: every language reflects and transmits a *weltanschauung,* a vision of the world peculiar to itself; language is a prism through which its speakers are condemned to view the world[2] (22).

While there is a certain truth in this hypothesis, interpreted literally it would imply that any translation is impossible. Fortunately this is not the case, as our mentality is not totally trapped in the spirit of our language (20). Nevertheless, we will illustrate the link between language and a particular vision of the world by comparing and contrasting the differences between two Indo-European languages, one representing the Germanic languages, i.e., English, and the other, the Romance languages, i.e., French. Many other types of differences (e.g., alphabetical, lexical, grammatical, syntactic, and ''philosophical'') can be described when Germanic or Romance languages are compared with either Slavic (e.g., Russian), Semitic (e.g., Hebrew), or Asiatic (e.g., Chinese) languages. These differences need to be borne in mind and overcome in any translation process and particularly in the one that we define below.

Comparison of English and French

The differences between these two languages[3] can be grouped into four categories (23):

1. The vocabularies of English and French do not coincide.
2. English is more synthetic, French more analytic.
3. English is more concrete, French more abstract.
4. English is more dynamic, French more static.

These differences are discussed in the following subsections.

English Vocabulary Is Richer

English calls upon Latin and Germanic roots; English is capable of numerous word formations that are not so common in French (adjectival function of the noun and verbal forms). In many domains a greater number of synonyms is available originating from the English speaker's mental reaction to reality. Accustomed to simply recognizing this reality, the English speaker tends to accumulate the precise terms used to express the countless tangible aspects of the real world and in particular all sensory perceptions.

English Is More Synthetic

The English original is invariably shorter. Statistical studies on this (24) show that translation from English into French lengthens the text by an average of 16%. This is partly due to the nature of the language itself, English preferring to leave certain things vague or understood, whereas French demands more clarity and is more explicit. Moreover, French requires more connecting words to mark its path of reasoning.

English Is More Concrete

The English mind, which favors a certain objectivity in the face of facts and reality, limits itself to their external aspects, capturing the concrete, perceptible, tangible details observable to everyone. The existence of things is recognized without a precise cause being attributed to them, and therefore things are often expressed more simply in English. French tends much more toward the subjective interpretation of reality. The French mind prefers to commit itself, making judgments, decisions, taking a position. It is interested in the internal rather than the external aspect of things, the why and the wherefore, Neglecting detail, it maps out the main lines, the final result. The words used, therefore, have a more abstract quality than in English.

English Is More Dynamic

In the face of the same reality, French analyzes, judges, comments; English acts, participates, describes. As the language of reason, French tends to produce ''finished states,'' fixed forms indicating an adopted position. Hence the preference for the substantive and the static use of certain verbs of movement. English, closer to reality, tends to follow an action as it takes place, concentrating on the active process. It does so by orienting its sentences around the verb, and the progressive form (the ''-ing'' form) is the clearest example.

TRANSLATION

Translation Actors

Translation, which is an act of bilingual communication, is made possible not because of parallelisms in expressions, but because of parallelisms in thoughts and situations

(20,25). It can be seen as a transcoding operation in which the main problems originate from the different ways representation of reality is coded in different languages. Therefore, its main aim is to ensure that the information content remains unchanged despite the change of code at the level of expression (26). Furthermore, within a code itself, the speaker's idiolect might be different from the receiver's idiolect, as for a determined content each language offers many different ways of communicating a message (21). In other words, languages are able to give the same meaning to formally different statements. And, as a result, the formal expression of the translation is not absolute, but represents only one among several possibilities (27).

Translation involves three specific elements (24,26,28). The first is subjective, and the other two objective. The subjective element is represented by the communication triad: the author, the translator, and the user of the translation (26,28). The importance of each will be seen in the description of the methods used to translate HRQL questionnaires. The two objective elements are (a) reality as the subject of communication, and consequently as the context of the situation in its broadest sense; and (b) language as a means of communication, and consequently as the projection of a linguistic competence onto this situation. These two objective elements are to some extent colored with subjectivity. Linguistic competence as well as knowledge and interpretation of the situation when dealing with a foreign culture depend on the translator.

Therefore, we would not be overanticipating if we say that any intercultural project depends in part on the authority of a competent bilingual informant, the translator-interpreter, one of the key elements essential for its success (25,29).

Translation Techniques

At this point, it is useful to recall the range of translation techniques available. All translation techniques have the same aim: to remove the difficulties barring the optimal transfer of the informational, emotional, and stylistic content of the original message. Traditionally, they have been divided into two categories: direct and indirect translation (23). These techniques are extensively applicable when languages have dissimilar roots, e.g., Romance and Germanic roots (30). However, when roots are similar, e.g., French and Italian (31), some of these methods are less useful.

Direct Translation

Direct translation comprises borrowings, calques (loan translations), and word-for-word and literal translation.[4] A borrowing occurs when there is a gap in the target language and a word has to be imported directly from the source language. Strictly speaking, this is only a translation process to the extent that the translator takes the initiative in carrying over the word from the language translated. Otherwise, bor-

rowings that occur regularly can be considered features of the language in question. Classical borrowings (in this latter sense) most quoted are, from French into English, *fuselage* and, from English into French, *bulldozer* (this now rejected by the French Language Commission in favor of *bouteur*).

Borrowings have operated in both directions and continue to do so; English has borrowed heavily from French in the field of politics, diplomacy, and the fine arts; French has borrowed from English in the fields of sport, technology, and media (32). It is amusing to note that English uses a calque to render *calque* itself: *loan word* may be borrowed from the German *Lehnwort* (33).

Word-for-word and literal translation, often taken as synonyms, carried the same pejorative connotations until linguists classified word-for-word translation as the most elementary process of direct translation, thereby terminating the age-old false opposition between free and literal translation (34). In fact, any discussion should be about accurate translation exclusively (35).

Indirect Translation

Indirect translation processes are defined as transposition, modulation, equivalence, and adaptation.

Transposition operates on grammatical elements substituting one part of speech for another without changing anything in the global meaning. Examples abound and this process operates not only between languages but also within a given language (32).

Modulation operates on thought and not grammatical categories. (Example: modulation from the concrete to the abstract or from popular to learned terms: thus "on bare skin" can be rendered *à même la peau* in French and *hand-written, manuscrit*). In simple terms modulation is a change in the point of view of the author and can operate at the word, phrase, or sentence level. It is applied in many of the clichés or fixed expressions of everyday language translated from one language to another. Modulation encompasses the whole world of metaphor and metonymy.

Equivalence allows one to describe a given situation using different structural and stylistic means. Once more, this process can operate at all levels of the language and involves the total message. "You're welcome" becomes *De rien* in French or, by translation in British English, "Don't mention it."

In contrast to equivalence, *adaptation* seeks a recognizable correspondence between two situations. The process often has to be applied if the situation described in the original message is not common or does not exist in the language of translation. And this process is what most concerns us here as it falls into the sociocultural domain.

Chuquet and Paillard (32) assimilate equivalence into the process of modulation (they consider it nothing more than a lexical modulation) and relegate adaptation to the sociocultural domain, excluding it as a translation (linguistic) process. As a result they reduce translation processes to the two major categories of transposition and modulation.

Caution should be exercised in any attempt to classify into rigid categories, as examples can be found of translations representing one or more techniques: Vinay and Darbelnet (23), for instance, quote the translation of English "Private" by *Défense d'entrer* in French as an example of a transposition, modulation, and equivalence rolled into one.

TRANSLATION OF HRQL INSTRUMENTS

Apart from a few exceptions (36–38), most questionnaires have been developed in English (for the most part American English, sometimes British English). Although there are many examples in the literature of translation of HRQL questionnaires (39,40), there are few publications describing the guidelines to be followed (41–43). In fact, originally it is to the social psychologists involved in intercultural research (29,35,44–48) that we owe the conceptualization and elaboration of intercultural research methods leading to the use of questionnaires cross-nationally. These methods were then used and experimented with by health status researchers.

Cross-Cultural Equivalence

Comparable observations can be obtained only if the original instrument and the translation are equivalent (48,49). Several authors have proposed a taxonomy of equivalence in cross-cultural measurement (29,48,50–52). The fullest, in that it covers all of the phenomena to be taken into account when using questionnaires cross-culturally, is that produced by Hui and Triandis (48). They postulate four levels of equivalence (see Endnote 5), each level being the prerequisite of the next: (a) conceptual/functional equivalence, (b) equivalence in construct operationalization, (c) item equivalence, (d) scalar (or metric) equivalence. As a result of this postulate, they propose several strategies (among which, performing an adequate translation is quoted), allowing these four levels of equivalence to be checked in the measure concerned. From their work, it can be concluded that the cultural adaptation of an instrument in a target language involves two stages: translation, followed by evaluation of the instrument (i.e., psychometric tests).

All the authors quoted above agree on one essential point: if one wishes to carry out cross-culturally comparable assessments, conceptual equivalence of the construct to be measured between the cultures concerned is a necessary prerequisite, semantic or linguistic equivalence on its own not guaranteeing intercultural relevance of the questionnaires.

Bice and Kalimo (50) interestingly distinguish between conceptual and semantic equivalence. According to them, semantic equivalence refers to an equivalence of meaning and formulation (question wording). It can be achieved through translation techniques. As for conceptual equiva-

lence, this is achieved when answers to the same questions reflect the same concept. In other words, a construct is recognized as being conceptually equivalent cross-culturally if it can be meaningfully discussed in each of the cultures concerned (48).

According to Bice and Kalimo (50), when items of a questionnaire developed in a given language are translated into another language, the distinction between semantic and conceptual equivalence yields four types of items (Fig. 1):

Identical indicators are those that are both semantically and conceptually equivalent.

Equivalent indicators are those that are conceptually equivalent but semantically dissimilar.

"Culture-linked" items are semantically equivalent but do not measure the same concept in different settings.

"Unrelated" items are those that are neither conceptually nor semantically equivalent across nations or cultures.

Questionnaires made up of unrelated or culture-linked items cannot be used to carry out cross-culturally comparable measurements. It is these problems of conceptual equivalence and therefore of intercultural relevance that have led certain authors (12,13) to criticize and refute the adaptation for use in several countries of questionnaires developed in a single country.

Methodology

As mentioned above, the cross-cultural adaptation of an HRQL questionnaire takes place in two principal stages: translation, and evaluation of its psychometric properties, i.e., validity, reliability, responsiveness to change. (Which psychometric tests to use will be briefly addressed in this chapter. For a fuller development of the question, see Chapter 69 by Bullinger et al.). An intermediary step can be added: weighting of translated items when the original is weighted itself, as for example the Sickness Impact Profile (53) or the Nottingham Health Profile (54). In fact, it is rather artificial to separate translation from psychometric tests or weighting because these two processes can be considered as a means of quality control and as a check on the accuracy of the translation (49,55).

According to Guillemin et al. (43), translating a questionnaire developed in a specific (or so-called source) language and culture does not constitute a univocal process. It depends on the foreign (or target) language and culture concerned. The translation methods involved will slightly differ if one translates a questionnaire (developed for instance in American English) for people speaking similar languages in another country (e.g., English spoken by British people, Australians, South Africans, etc.), speaking dissimilar languages in another country (e.g., German, Italian, Arabic, Hebrew, Greek, Japanese, etc.), or speaking dissimilar languages in the same country (e.g., immigrants). The methodology that

Conceptually equivalent items

		Yes	No
Semantically equivalent items	**Yes**	"Identical indicators"	"Culture-linked items"
	No	"Equivalent indicators"	"Unrelated items"

FIG. 1. Typology of items for comparative research. (Reprinted from ref. 50, with permission.)

we describe below is applicable to the latter two cases, the first case requiring less involvement most of the time.

Translation Process

Taking into account the data in the literature (29,33,41, 43–46,50–52,56) and our experience in this field, one can summarize the translation of an HRQL questionnaire into one or more target languages by a combination of techniques, i.e., four interrelated headings or steps that may be iterative:

1. Forward step;
2. Quality control;
3. Pretest;
4. International harmonization.

As suggested elsewhere (43), the aim of each step is to add quality to the preceding one in terms of conceptual equivalence between source and target versions, in order to produce a relevant final translated version.

The famous communication triad of author, translator, and user intervenes at different points throughout the four steps. Consequently, the translation process is the result of a multidisciplinary team effort and, in order to ensure some consistency, has to be headed by one team leader taking responsibility for the project throughout its realization.

Forward Step (Source to Target)

Forward translation is the translation of a questionnaire (originally developed in a source language) into one or more target languages. This step, which is crucial to the whole process, is not simple and is not merely the production of a single target version. It is in fact the creation of a commonly agreed-on version built up through various stages:

contact with the author—conceptual definition; production of several forward translations; consensus meeting—production of an agreed-on forward version.

Contact with the Author—Conceptual Definition. As soon as an HRQL questionnaire has been chosen for inclusion in a multinational clinical trial and before any translation work is undertaken, we consider it essential to respect the following rule: make contact with the author(s). There are two reasons for this:

1. to secure authorization for use and translation of the questionnaire (rules of copyright, fees, etc.);
2. to define carefully the underlying concepts for each item and dimension in the questionnaire.

This step of conceptual clarification allows one to (a) respect the intentions of the author and avoid misinterpretations, (b) avoid a lack of conceptual equivalence in the target versions, (c) find acceptable equivalents, and (d) save time wasted in idle and unnecessary discussions.

Certain teams have successfully had recourse to this approach (42,56,57). During the adaptation into French of the Respiratory Illness Questionnaire developed in Dutch (38), we had to contact the author in order to find a satisfactory French equivalent of *fietsen* (to cycle) in item 3 of the Daily Activities Scale. It is a fact that cycling is much more common in Netherlands than it is in France, and, the country being flat, it is also much less of a sport in people's minds. We finally chose an equivalent of "to go for a walk or to climb a hill" as being the most adequate item, in this context, to describe a physical activity that does not require excessive physical strength (*unpublished report*).

Contact with the author should not be limited to this preliminary step; the author should be associated with the whole translation process and consulted whenever necessary, such as for clarification of remaining ambiguities.

Production of Several Forward Translations. As we have seen, translation is a subjective process and this is why, in order to ensure a final target version of quality, it is advisable (42,43) to produce several preliminary forward versions of a given questionnaire. Generally these multiple versions are produced independently by members of a translating team, which, for certain authors, should be exclusively made up of native speakers of the target language (43) and for others (41) of natives from both countries concerned.

Choice of translators. The translator(s), the second element in the communication triad defined above, is one of the key agents in the translation process and should therefore be chosen with care. Our experience dictates that these translations be carried out by local teams (e.g., Spanish translators living in Spain, Germans living in Germany) and not by teams transplanted into the country of the source language (e.g., Spanish or German translators living in the United States). Such translators lack daily practice in their mother tongue under the conditions of their home country, and are therefore not always competent to produce appropriate translations.

Too often we have experienced translations carried out in the country of the source language (frequently for time or financial considerations) that proved to be unusable either because they contained gross errors of syntax or because they were inadequate on the conceptual level.

Translators may be professionals or representatives from several horizons (medicine, health research, sociology) (41) or both.

Means available. Translators have at their disposal direct or indirect translation techniques described earlier. To ensure translations of quality, the author's intentions (concepts and dimensions of the instrument) are generally transmitted to them. Interestingly, Guillemin et al. (43) note that failure to do so can lead to detection of unexpected meanings in the original questionnaire. Translators are instructed to produce colloquial versions that are easily understood by a lay public. Experience shows that translations produced by highly educated individuals were sometimes judged to be too complicated and therefore difficult to understand for people of lesser education or lay panels (41,58).

Consensus Meeting—Production of an Agreed-on Forward Version (or First Version). Starting from the forward versions elaborated during the preceding phase, the purpose of this meeting is to produce an agreed-on forward version of which the quality (i.e., linguistic and conceptual equivalence with the source version) will be checked at a later stage. This meeting, chaired by the project team leader, is attended by a panel of experts (five to eight people), for example the forward translators, at least one expert in the pathology concerned (in the case of disease-specific questionnaires), and at least one expert from other fields (sociology, epidemiology), to whom lay persons can be added (41). Without being perfectly bilingual, all should have a knowledge of the two languages concerned (35). During this consensus meeting, each part of the questionnaire (the instructions, the items, the answer choices) should be carefully discussed.

Instructions. These are often neglected but they must be carefully translated to respect the replicability of the questionnaire (59). Guillemin et al. (43) suggest that the principle of redundancy described by Brislin (45) should be applied to the instructions in order to limit errors of comprehension.

Items. Benefiting from the data provided by the author, the panel examines the conceptual equivalence of each forward version (produced at the previous stage) with the original, the purpose being to obtain for each item a commonly agreed-on forward version that is satisfactory on the linguistic and conceptual levels. However, the translation of certain items often remains problematic and in this case it is advisable to propose alternatives (11,55) that will be checked and tested later. The author of the questionnaire may also be contacted at this point.

Hunt (41) suggests an interesting method of grading (from A: acceptable, to D: unsatisfactory) that allows one to categorize the items and to detect the problematical items in each country concerned. According to the literature and to our experience, there are several types of items giving rise to some difficulties or to some *a priori* unexpected solutions:

1. Items related to psychological and emotional states (52, 56,60).
2. Items related to social functioning (35). For instance, during the International Quality of Life Assessment (IQOLA) project (11), there were a lot of concerns about the translation of "social activities" in items 6 and 10 of the SF-36 (61). How should one translate "social activities" in each country concerned, knowing that in the United States it includes all kinds of activities with different types of people, for example family, friends, colleagues, which is not necessarily the case in other countries? In Russia, for instance, it means literally "to participate in political meetings or to act like a trade union leader." It was therefore adapted and translated by "to associate actively with people" (*unpublished report*).
3. Items related to physical or daily activities. For instance, the word "hobbies" is diversely rendered; in the Russian version of the EORTC QLQC-30, it was translated by its Russian calque Хобби (*unpublished report*). Butcher and Garcia (62) note that in the Spanish version of the Minnesota Multiphasic Personality Inventory "hobbies" was borrowed from the English since it is commonly used in Spain.

Answer choices. To evaluate the measurement equivalence between the source and target questionnaires, it is advisable (15,57) to examine the ordinality (Are answer choices in the same rank order in each country?) and interval score properties (Are the distances between answer choices identical between countries?) of the Likert-type answer choice scales, using a Thurstone scaling exercise (63). If the answer choices of each Likert-type scale of the source questionnaire are equidistant, the target answer choices should respect this equidistance, in order for the source and target questionnaires to be equivalent. During the meeting, therefore, the panel members should produce as many translation alternatives as possible for each answer choice on each scale. Those that are as equidistant as possible between each other will then be chosen.

Frequently, it is at this type of consensus meeting that weaknesses in the wording of the source questionnaire are revealed. The quality of the source versions may be improved at the construction phase by referring to the 12 guidelines developed by Brislin (46) (see Endnote 6):

1. use short, simple sentences;
2. employ the active rather than the passive voice;
3. repeat nouns instead of using pronouns;
4. avoid metaphors and colloquialisms;
5. avoid the subjunctive;
6. add sentences to provide context for key ideas;
7. avoid adverbs and prepositions telling "where" or "when";
8. avoid possessive forms where possible;
9. use specific rather than general terms;
10. avoid words indicating vagueness regarding some event or thing;
11. use wording familiar to the translators;
12. avoid sentences with two different verbs if the verbs suggest two different actions.

Although these guidelines have been developed to write translatable English, some of them are also applicable to other languages like Spanish or French (46).

To conclude, the consensus meeting should draw out the translation difficulties, elaborate a forward version [instructions, items, answer choices (if not Likert type)] and program an ordinality and equidistance test for the Likert-type answer choices.

Quality Control

We have insisted on the need to produce a target version that is equivalent to the source version both conceptually and linguistically. However, despite their competence and due to the subjective nature of their task, a panel of experts cannot, on their own, guarantee this equivalence (45). This is why quality controls have to be carried out. Generally they are of two types: (a) quality ratings, and (b) back-translation.

Quality Ratings. This method was developed by the IQOLA team (11). The agreed-on forward version is given to at least two reviewers (professional translators or otherwise), who are native speakers of the target language, for a qualitative evaluation. This is made on the basis of three criteria—conceptual equivalence with the original, clarity, and use of a familiar or colloquial register—each criterion being marked on a three-point scale. The results of this evaluation are then discussed between the reviewers and the project team leader; all items judged to be unsatisfactory, especially on the conceptual level, have to be retranslated and reevaluated (iterative process). It can be objected that this exercise is subjective and depends on the quality of the reviewers.

Back-Translation. This is defined as the retranslation into the source language of the target forward version. It is done either on the agreed-on version (11) or on the multiple preliminary forward versions as recommended by Guillemin et al. (43). Generally, the back-translation is made by a translator who is a native speaker of the source language and who has no knowledge of the source version. The aim of the back-translation is to detect errors of meaning in the target version from a comparison with the source version. All discrepancies with the original have to be discussed and analyzed and can possibly lead to modifications and improvements of the target version. This exercise is only valid if iterative (the modified target version having to be checked by a backward version). Recommended by certain authors (29,44) as a quality control method and a check on translation accuracy by persons totally ignorant of the target language (especially if the latter is non–Indo-European—Hebrew, for example), the back-translation method has been severely criticized by others (42,64, and *personal communications*), and has been abandoned by some (42).

This method has advantages and disadvantages. The major advantage is that it acts as a filter through which nonequivalent wordings have difficulty in passing and are therefore immediately detectable (51). It is also a means for the author of checking the translation. The major disadvantage is that it relies essentially on the back-translator who may produce an apparently satisfactory backward version from a forward version that sounds awkward and unnatural to the target language speaker (and is therefore inadequate) simply because he has glossed over the inadequacies by improving it in the translation; or a backward version that seems awkward to the source-language speaker without the forward version being necessarily inappropriate (indeed the forward version may seem perfectly natural for the target language speaker); or a backward version that will be questioned simply because, from all the source equivalents of a target word, he may have chosen not the same word as the original but rather another that contains shades of meaning not reflecting the author's intentions (whereas the target word is correct). In all these cases, the back-translation is a misleading guide as it creates false problems each time.

An equivalent of the back-translation, as described by Werner and Campbell (29), is the de-centering process, in which the source version is open to revision; this is not always the case with HRQL questionnaires. Although this method is of interest, it is not easy to apply when several target language versions of the source questionnaire are planned.

Pretest

Having checked the quality of the agreed-on forward version (that is, having evaluated its degree of conceptual and semantic equivalence with the source questionnaire), testing of the translated questionnaire on a sample of the population is generally recommended (42,43,45). Therefore, it is at this stage that the third partner of the communication triad mentioned previously, i.e., the user of the translation, intervenes. This test has several aims:

to measure the comprehensibility level of the translation (i.e., Is the questionnaire correctly understood?) and therefore correct any overcomplicated or sophisticated wording;

to test the translation alternatives and therefore the choice of the most suitable wording (when the translators have been unable to agree on a wording and have suggested several translation alternatives for the same item);

to highlight any unexpected translation errors and difficulties;

to reveal items that may be inappropriate on the conceptual level.

There are two types of test techniques that involve the participation on the one hand of monolingual subjects and on the other of bilinguals (45). Both enable one to explore the translated questionnaire's face validity. In all cases the population sample must be heterogeneous, that is to say made up of individuals from different socioeconomic and educational level backgrounds; the purpose is to produce an appropriate translation that will be understood by everyone (42). Recruitment according to age and sex follows, depending on the type of population addressed by the questionnaire (children, menopausal women, etc.). Similarly, healthy subjects or patients are recruited (if the questionnaire is disease-specific).

At this stage of the translation process, we usually recommend that gendered versions (i.e., male, female, or gender-mixed) of the translations be produced in each of the languages concerned. We have indeed often had comments from women who were offended by the use of male versions.

Monolingual Lay Panel. Generally the translation is tested either during in-depth face-to-face interviews (when the subject is alone with the interviewer) or in focus groups. The choice of method is often influenced by financial considerations or time constraints. Although more time-consuming and expensive, in-depth interviews are our preference as, in our experience, they enable one to make a more complete study. When the questionnaire is self-administered, each subject is asked to fill it in alone and unaided before the interview.

With the underlying concept of each item in mind, a trained interviewer reviews the questionnaire and for each item and each response asks: "Have you understood? What do you mean?" Each respondent is invited to express himself freely. Generally speaking, this type of test gives good results. It is often at this stage of the process that the major

translation difficulties are resolved or that misinterpretations are detected. It is also at this point that the author is contacted once more, often to clarify remaining obscure points. Badia and Alonso (65) mention that, as a result of a lay panel, they had to add an example to item 1 of the mobility scale of the Sickness Impact Profile (53), since the item was not understood by 20% of the respondents. On the Respiratory Illness Questionnaire (38), patients were a little taken aback by item 3 of the Daily Activities Scale, as they did not see any similarity between the physical activity mentioned and the heading of the scale. After much discussion, it was decided to produce the following adaptation: "To walk at a fast pace for a certain distance" (*unpublished report*).

Bilingual Lay Panel. The source and the target versions of the questionnaire are administered to a panel of bilinguals. So as to avoid a strong source-target reliability caused by a memorization factor, the bilinguals are split up randomly into two groups: one group responds to the first half of the questions in the source language and to the second half in the target language; the order is reversed for the second group. With this method, the translation of items eliciting discrepant response frequencies should be considered suspect and should be discussed. Although used (55) or recommended (45) by certain authors, tests with bilinguals are difficult to carry out and are therefore time-consuming and expensive. Very often it is difficult to find a sufficient number of bilinguals, especially in Latin countries.

International Harmonization Meeting

Generally speaking the pretest marks the end of the translation process: forward step, quality control, pretest. But when a questionnaire has to be translated simultaneously into several languages, our experience of linguistic validations as well as our participation in the IQOLA project have led us to add an extra step in the translation process: the international harmonization meeting. During this meeting the various translations of the questionnaire developed during the pretest are compared with each other as well as with the original. The meeting brings together as many professional translators as there are target languages, each of them being a native speaker of one of the target languages and bilingual in English. The aim is to detect any remaining errors that may not have been identified during the preceding steps. It is also an appropriate method for highlighting the differences in expressions and sometimes in concepts between the countries concerned. Finally, it is a further safety measure that ensures the quality of the final target versions.

During the international harmonization of the Psychological General Well-Being Index (66) in 11 languages, we realized that "personal life" (item 9) was diversely rendered:

with a linguistic equivalent of "life" in Germany and Sweden;

with a linguistic equivalent of "private life" in the Netherlands, Flanders, France, and Norway;

and with a literal equivalent of "personal life" in French Canada, Italy, Portugal, Israel, and the UK.

We had to recontact the author, who rejected the equivalents of private life since, according to him, they do not render the underlying concept of "life as a person."

Should there be discrepancies with the original and between target languages, the translators are asked to suggest alternative wordings that will later be discussed with the local teams in each country concerned. It is then up to the local teams to produce the final version of the questionnaire. If the changes are too far-reaching, a further pretest is recommended.

The Need to Document the Translation Process

To ensure the best results and correct analysis in the later stages of the cultural adaptation process (e.g., weighting and psychometric evaluation), we recommend, along with Butcher and Clark (67), that the entire translation process be documented, i.e., that a series of validation reports be kept. These reports should record, step by step and item by item, the solutions adopted as well as all the intermediary translations. Among other things the following will be noted:

what items are difficult to translate and why;
what items are easy to translate and why;
what items need cultural modification;
what are the idiomatic items that have been translated in an unidiomatic way and why.

Weighting and Psychometric Evaluation

Translation is only the first step of a process leading to an instrument of HRQL measurement that can be used in a different culture. An instrument is usually defined by a set of questions (i.e., the questionnaire), a scoring method, and psychometric properties. The scoring method is based upon a weighting that is either implicit (i.e., equi-weighting of the items through simple summing-up) or explicit (i.e., score calculation through coefficients). It seems reasonable to consider explicit weighting as a step of the cultural adaptation of an HRQL instrument, since it depends on each culture concerned. Indeed, it seems quite irrelevant to claim that a questionnaire is culturally adapted to a specific country when one uses a weighting developed in another country to calculate its scores. This calls for the production of item weights specific to each country concerned, following the same procedure as the one used by the author of the source questionnaire. To date, few data concerning cross-cultural weighting are available (68–70).

The linguistic validation (or cultural adaptation) of an HRQL questionnaire is only achieved when the psychometric properties of the translated questionnaire are documented. In some cases, the psychometric evaluation may lead to the retranslation of certain items. In other words, translation and conceptual equivalence are finally validated (or not) through psychometric testing. Criteria for decision making in psychometric testing should include the control of

the adequacy of the translated version with respect to the measurement model elaborated by the author, through the study of its factorial structure and scaling assumption;
its reliability (i.e., reproducibility, internal consistency and interrater reliability, if needed);
its validity (focusing on clinical validating, i.e., known-groups comparison);
its responsiveness over time.

Recent reviews of the literature (39,40) show that few data concerning cross-cultural psychometrics are available at this time. In the perspective of an international study, it is of great importance to have this type of data before pooling the results from different countries and performing a common analysis. Indeed, one should keep in mind that the interpretation and exploitation of the results rely essentially on the data (i.e., scores) provided by the instrument.

CONCLUSIONS

The translation of an HRQL questionnaire is not a simple operation as it is subject to one overriding requirement—equivalence between the source and target version(s), and subject to two constraints—of time and cost. All the techniques described in this chapter have one essential aim: to enable one to obtain equivalent source and target questionnaires. Choice of technique will be partly guided and limited by the constraints mentioned. However, it must be remembered that the translation conditions the results of future clinical trials. If certain items are badly worded or not understood correctly, the execution of the study and the interpretation of results will be adversely affected and distorted. For this reason we believe it essential to respect a minimum number of basic rules:

produce a meaningful forward version while following these guidelines: contact the author, produce several preliminary forward versions, work with local teams and in committee;
check the quality of this forward version;
test the forward version;
if several target translations are developed simultaneously, check their relative appropriacy by international harmonization.

Cultural adaptation will be complete when the psychometric qualities of the target translation(s) are studied. In the specific case of already existing questionnaires and in order to prevent the existence of more than one translation in the same language (and thus the use of inadequate forms), we urge authors or developers and teams interested in translation issues to join their efforts. In the specific case of questionnaires under development, the entire process of cultural adaptation would be considerably facilitated if instruments were developed with an international perspective. This is why it seems essential to us that teams presently developing new instruments for measuring HRQL should include in their development methodology tests of translatability, which would evaluate, for each item and each response scale in the future questionnaire, its potential linguistic and conceptual equivalence in the target language(s).

ENDNOTES

1. The nature and origins of language have long been debated and the discussion has been highly active this century, notably on the inborn/acquired issue. Of modern contributors, Noam Chomsky (18), with his "black box" theory (tending to stress the inborn potential for language), stands out.

2. The Whorf hypothesis has also been much discussed and in certain cases refuted by subsequent scholars. The least that can be said is that it has served as a stimulant to debate in linguistic circles and that the basic tenet still has a certain validity. The influence of language on thought patterns has marked much of contemporary philosophy in the English-speaking academic world.

3. These differences, quoted in the literature, do not apply across the board without qualification. While it is true that English has a much larger vocabulary in several distinct areas (to describe sounds, for example), it bows to French in such domains as cooking and the fine arts; a clear indication of this is the large number of borrowings that English has made from French in these areas. In any language there are domains that are more fully covered, the most often quoted example being that of the wide range of terms available to Eskimos in describing snow. It need hardly be said that this illustrates the indissociable sociocultural aspects of language.

4. Compared to word-for-word, literal translation is translation that takes into account the linguistic phenomena (grammatical, syntactical) essential for the production of a correct structure starting from a word-for-word version.

5. The four levels of equivalence in cross-cultural measurement postulated by Hui and Triandis (48) were reprinted from the Journal of Cross-Cultural Psychology with permission of Sage Publications, Inc. © 1985 by Sage Publications, Inc.

6. The 12 guidelines developed by Brislin (46) were reprinted from Field Methods in Cross-Cultural Research with permission of Sage Publications, Inc. © 1986 by Sage Publications, Inc.

REFERENCES

1. McDowell I, Newell C. *Measuring health: a guide to rating scales and questionnaires.* New York: Oxford University Press, 1987.
2. Spilker B, ed. *Quality of life assessments in clinical trials.* New York: Raven Press, 1990.
3. Wilkin D, Hallam L, Doggett MA. *Measures of need and outcome for primary health care.* New York: Oxford University Press, 1992.
4. Walker SR, Rosser RM, eds. *Quality of life assessment: key issues in the 1990s.* Dordrecht: Kluwer Academic, 1993.
5. Spilker B, Simpson RL, Tilson HH. Quality of life bibliography and indexes—1991 update. *J Clin Res Pharmacoepidemiol* 1992;6: 205–266.
6. Division of Mental Health, World Health Organization, eds. *Quality of life assessment—an annotated bibliography.* Geneva: WHO, 1993.
7. Fletcher AE, Bulpitt CJ, Chase DM, et al. Quality of life with three antihypertensive treatments: cilazapril, atenolol, nifedipine. *Hypertension* 1992;19:499–507.
8. Goldenberg F, Hindmarch I, Joyce CRB, et al. Zopiclone, sleep and health-related quality of life. *Hum Psychopharmacol* 1994;9:245–251.
9. Jacoby A, Baker G. A European study of people with epilepsy. *Qual Life Newsletter* 1994;10–11:3.
10. Irvine SH, Wright DE, Recchia GG, De Carli G. Measuring quality of life across cultures: some cautions and prescriptions. *Drug Info J* 1994;28:55–62.
11. Aaronson NK, Acquadro C, Alonso J, et al. International quality of life assessment (IQOLA) project. *Qual Life Res* 1992;1(5):349–351.
12. Hunt SM. Cross cultural comparability of quality of life measures. *Drug Info J* 1993;27:395–400.
13. Guyatt GH. The philosophy of health-related quality of life translation. *Qual Life Res* 1993;2:461–465.
14. Aaronson NK, Ahmedzai S, Bergman B, et al. The European Organization for Research and Treatment of Cancer QLQ-C30: a quality of life instrument for use in international clinical trials in oncology. *J Natl Cancer Inst* 1993;85(5):365–376.
15. Sartorius N. A WHO method for the assessment of health-related quality of life (WHOQoL). In: Walker SR, Rosser RM, eds. *Quality of life assessment: key issues in the 1990's.* Dordrecht: Kluwer Academic, 1993:201–207.
16. Cella DF, Wiklund I, Shumaker SA, Aaronson NK. Integrating health-related quality of life into cross-national clinical trials. *Qual Life Res* 1993;2:433–440.
17. Berzon R, Shumaker S. Evaluating health-related quality of life measures for cross-national research. *Drug Info J* 1994;28:63–67.
18. Chomsky N. *Aspects of the theory of syntax.* Cambridge, MA: MIT Press, 1965.
19. Hagège CL. *L'homme de paroles.* Paris: Fayard, 1985.
20. Mounin G. *Les problèmes théoriques de la traduction.* Paris: Gallimard, 1963.
21. Nida EA, Taber CR. *Theory and practice of translation.* Leiden: Brill, 1969.
22. Whorf BL. A linguistic consideration of thinking in primitive communities. In: Carroll JB, ed. *Language, thought and reality: selected writings of Benjamin Lee Whorf.* Cambridge, MA: MIT Press, 1956:65–86.
23. Vinay JP, Darbelnet J. *Stylistique comparée de l'anglais et du français.* Paris: Didier, 1958.
24. Van Hoof H. *Traduire l'anglais—Théorie et pratique.* Paris: Duculot, 1989.
25. Catford JC. *A linguistic theory of translation.* London: Oxford University Press, 1965.
26. Kade O. *Zufall und Gesetzmässigkeit in der Uebersetzung.* Leipzig: VEB Enzyklopädie, 1968.
27. Levy J. *Die literarische Uebersetzung. Theorie einer Kunstgattung.* Frankfurt: Athenäum Verlag, 1969.
28. Savory TH. *The art of translation.* London: Jonathan Cape, 1957.
29. Werner O, Campbell DT. Translating, working through interpreters and the problem of decentering. In: Narrol R, Cohen R, eds. *A handbook of method in cultural anthropology.* New York: American Museum of Natural History, 1970:398–420.
30. Malblanc A. *Stylistique comparée du français et de l'allemand.* Paris: Didier, 1968.
31. Scavée P, Intravaia P. *Traité de stylistique comparée. Analyse comparative de l'italien et du français.* Bruxelles Didier-Mons: Centre international de phonétique appliquée, 1984.
32. Chuquet H, Paillard M. *Approche linguistique des problèmes de traduction,* revised ed. Paris: Ophrys, 1989.
33. Yule G. *The study of language.* Cambridge: Cambridge University Press, 1985.
34. Newmark P. *Approaches to translation.* Oxford: Pergamon Press, 1981.
35. Deutscher I. Asking questions cross-culturally: some problems of linguistic comparability. In: Becker HS, Geer B, Riesman D, Weiss RS,

eds. *Institutions and the persons: papers presented to Everett C. Hughes.* Chicago: Adline, 1968:318–341.

36. Wiklund I. Mätning av livskavalitet vid kardiovaskulära sjukdomar. *Scand J Behav Ther* 1988;17(suppl 18):87–98.

37. Gerin P, Dazord A, Boissel JP, Hanauer MTh, Moleur P, Chauvin F. L'évaluation de la qualité de vie dans les essais thérapeutiques—aspects conceptuels et présentation d'un questionnaire. *Thérapie* 1989;44: 355–364.

38. Maillé AR, Koning CJM, Kaptein AA. Developing a quality of life questionnaire for patients with respiratory illness. *Qual Life Newsletter* 1992;5:5.

39. Anderson RT, Aaronson NK, Wilkin D. Critical review of the international assessments of health-related qualtiy of life. *Qual Life Res* 1993;2:369–395.

40. Naughton MJ, Wiklund I. A critical review of dimension specific measures of health-related quality of life in cross-cultural research. *Qual Life Res* 1993;2:397–432.

41. Hunt SM. *A methodology for the translation of health measures. Working paper no. 22.* Manchester: Galen Research and Consultancy, 1988:1–8.

42. Hunt S, McKenna S. The Nottingham Health Profile—English source version. In: The European group for quality of life and health measurement, eds. *European guide to the Nottingham Health Profile.* Manchester: Galen Research and Consultancy, 1992:1–75.

43. Guillemin F, Bombardier C, Beaton D. Cross-cultural adaptation of health-related quality of life measures: literature review and proposed guidelines. *J Clin Epidemiol* 1993;46(12):1417–1432.

44. Brislin RW. Backtranslation for cross-cultural research. *J Cross-Cultural Psychol* 1970;1(3):185–216.

45. Brislin RW. Questionnaire wording and translation. In: Lonner WJ, Thorndike RM, eds. *Cultural research methods.* New York: John Wiley, 1973:32–58.

46. Brislin RW. The wording and translation of research instruments. In: Lonner WJ, Berry JW, eds. *Field methods in cross-cultural research.* Beverly Hills: Sage, 1986:137–164.

47. Hofstede G. *Culture's consequences—International differences in work-related values,* abridged ed. Newbury Park: Sage, 1984.

48. Hui C, Triandis HC. Measurement in cross-cultural psychology: a review and comparison of strategies. *J Cross-Cultural Psychol* 1985; 16(2):131–152.

49. Alonso J, Antó JM, Prieto L. El Perfil de Salud de Nottingham—Spanish version. In: The European group for quality of life and health measurement, eds. *European guide to the Nottingham Health Profile.* Manchester: Galen Research and Consultancy, 1992:225–303.

50. Bice TW, Kalimo E. Comparisons of health-related attitudes—a cross national factor analytic study. *Soc Sci Med* 1971;5:283–318.

51. Sechrest L, Fay TL, Hafeez Zaidi SM. Problems of translations in cross-cultural research. *J Cross-Cultural Psychol* 1972;3(1):41–56.

52. Flaherty JA, Gaviria FM, Pathak D. Developing instruments for cross-cultural psychiatric research. *J Nerv Ment Dis* 1988;176(5):257–263.

53. Bergner M, Bobbitt R, Carter W, Gilson B. The Sickness Impact Profile: development and final revision of a health status measure. *Med Care* 1981;19:787–805.

54. McKenna SP, Hunt SM, McEwen J. Weighting the seriousness of perceived health problems using Thurstone's method of paired comparisons. *Int J Epidemiol* 1981;10:93–97.

55. Bucquet D, Condon S. L'Indicateur de Santé Perceptuelle de Nottingham—French version. In: The European group for quality of life and health measurement, eds. *European guide to the Nottingham Health Profile.* Manchester: Galen Research and Consultancy, 1992:105–182.

56. Spielberger CD, Sharma S. Cross-cultural measurement of anxiety. In: Spielberger CD, Diaz-Guerrero R, eds. *Cross-cultural anxiety.* Washington: Hemisphere, 1976:13–28.

57. Ware JE, Gandek B, the IQOLA project group. The SF-36 health survey: development and use in mental health research and the IQOLA project. *Int J Mental Health* 1994;23(2):49–73.

58. Deyo R. Pitfalls in measuring the health status of Mexican-Americans: comparative validity of the English and Spanish Sickness Impact Profile. *Am J Public Health* 1984;74:569–573.

59. Feinstein AR. The theory and evaluation of sensibility. In: Feinstein AR, ed. *Clinimetrics.* New Haven: Yale University Press, 1987:141–166.

60. Hunt SM. Cross-cultural issues in the use of socio-medical indicators. *Health Policy* 1986;6:149–158.

61. Ware JE, Sherbourne CD. The MOS 36-Item Short Form Health Survey (SF-36). I. Conceptual framework and item selection. *Med Care* 1992;30:473–483.

62. Butcher JN, Garcia R. Cross-national application of psychological tests. *Personnel and Guidance* 1978;56:472–475.

63. Thurstone LL, Chave EJ. *The measurement of attitude.* Chicago: Chicago University Press, 1928.

64. Leplège A, Verdier A. The adaptation of health status measures: methodological aspects of the translation procedure. In: Shumaker SA, Berzon RA, eds. *The international assessment of health-related quality of life: theory, translation, measurement and analysis.* Oxford: Rapid Communications; 1995:93–102.

65. Badia X, Alonso J. Adaptacion de una medida de la disfuncion relacionada con la enfermedad: la version espanola del Sickness Impact Profile. *Med Clin (Barc)* 1994;102(3):90–95.

66. Dupuy HJ. The Psychological General Well-Being Index. In: Wenger NK, ed. *Assessment of quality of life in clinical trials of cardiovascular therapies.* New York: Le Jacq, 1984:170–183.

67. Butcher JN, Clark LA. Recent trends in cross-cultural MMPI research and application. In: Butcher JN, ed. *New developments in the use of the MMPI.* Minneapolis: University of Minnesota Press, 1979.

68. Patrick DL, Sittampalam Y, Somerville SM, Carter WB, Bergner M. A cross-cultural comparison of health status values. *Am J Public Health* 1985;75(12):1402–1407.

69. Hunt SM, Wiklund I. Cross-cultural variation in the weighting of health statements: a comparison of English and Swedish valuations. *Health Policy* 1987;8:227–235.

70. Bucquet D, Condon S, Ritchie K. The French version of the Nottingham Health Profile—a comparison of items weights with those of the source version. *Soc Sci Med* 1990;30(7):829–835.

Quality of Life and Pharmacoeconomics in Clinical Trials, Second Edition, edited by B. Spilker.
Lippincott-Raven Publishers, Philadelphia © 1996.

CHAPTER **64**

Quality of Life in Ethnic Groups

Janis F. Hutchinson

INTRODUCTION: HEALTH AND ETHNICITY

Throughout the 19th and early 20th century health was viewed as the absence of disease. Dubos (1) stated that ''modern dictionaries define disease as any departure from the state of health and health as a state of normalcy free from disease or pain.'' From a biomedical perspective disease is defined as a ''deviation from clinical norms, an organic pathology or abnormality'' (2). Disease, then, is a biological process which can be treated and cured once the causative pathology is known.

This perspective provided the basis for Western medicine and led to the development of the doctrine of specific etiology. That is, for every symptomatically identifiable disease, there is a single cause that destroys the equilibrium of health (3). With the importance of microbial diseases in the 19th century, Koch, Pasteur, and others further developed the doctrine in the one germ–one disease theory. The germ theory is the foundation for much of modern medical and public health practices (4).

The background for the germ theory was a belief in the Cartesian model of mind-body dualism. The body was considered a physical entity separate from emotional and social attributes. It reduced patients with disease to a set of abnormal physiological parameters (5). Even today, Western medicine separates the training and clinical practices of those who treat the physical body versus those who treat emotional and social states.

J. F. Hutchinson: Department of Anthropology, University of Houston, Houston, Texas 77204.

In 1946 medical experts of the World Health Organization defined health as a state of complete physical, mental, and social well-being and not merely the absence of disease and infirmity (6). With this perspective, more medical professionals focused on emotional and social contributors to unhealthy conditions in their patients.

With the aid of new drugs, and a variety of preventive and therapeutic treatments, people are living longer. It is apparent, however that sustained life or the removal of disease does not necessarily mean that quality of life is maintained. Today, medical practitioners are concerned not only with removing pathogens and prolonging life, but also with maintaining quality of life. This chapter examines health-related measures of quality of life in ethnic groups.

Ethnicity is not the same parameter as race, although the two may overlap. Race is a biological phenomenon. It is a collection of physical characteristics that a group shares because of common ancestry (7). Ethnicity is a cultural category. Members of an ethnic group share certain norms, values, beliefs, and habits because of a common background. This common background may be historical experiences, geographic isolation, religion, language, or race. Ethnicity means that they have an identification with an ethnic group and exclude themselves from cultural affiliation with other groups (8). Studies of quality of life should focus on ethnicity and cultural perceptions of disease, not race.

ILLNESS VERSUS DISEASE

Schipper et al. (9) defined quality of life as ''the functional effect of an illness and its consequent therapy upon a patient, as perceived by the patient.'' Perception of illness varies on an individual and ethnic level. This is not to say that cultural background determines how its members perceive illness, but that it forms the foundation for defining and responding to illness. While disease is a universal fact of life, groups define disease based upon beliefs, cognition, and perceptions consistent with their cultural pattern (10).

Illness is a cultural category that an individual uses to interpret his or her experiences. Illness is the patient's perspective of disease and response to disease. This is how patients view the physical, mental, or social disequilibrium they are experiencing. Foster and Anderson (11) argued that illness ''is the social recognition that a person is unable to fulfill his normal roles adequately, and that something must be done about the situation.''

Cassell (12) argued that illness is what patients feel when they go to the doctor and disease is what they have on the way home from the doctor's office. Disease is physical and biological while illness is subjective and human. Helman (5) said:

> Illness is the subjective response of the patient, and of those around him, to his being unwell; particularly how he, and they, interpret the origin and significance of this event; how it effects his behavior, and his relationship with other people; and the various steps he takes to remedy the situation. It not only includes his experience of ill-health, but also the *meaning* he gives to that experience.

The *meaning* given to symptoms and the *emotional response* are influenced by individual background and personality as well as the cultural, social, and economic context in which they appear (13). The same disease, such as polio, may be interpreted differently by members of different cultures. In turn, this will affect their behavior and the kind of treatment they will seek (5). For example, the Mano of Liberia do not consider malaria and yaws to be illnesses since many adults suffer from them (11).

Determination of illness and response to illness are based upon (are a part of) the cosmology of the ethnic group. Within a culture, the major institutions (political, economic, religious, and medical) are interrelated and fulfill specific functions in relation to each other. Medical beliefs are part of the total cultural pattern. In non-Western societies health is considered a balanced relationship between humans, humans and nature, and humans and the supernatural world. Disharmony in any of these areas may produce abnormal physical and emotional symptoms. For example, in the Mexican mestizo village of Tzintzuntzan, health is a balance between ''hot'' and ''cold'' forces inherent in the body and surrounding environment. This is one view from a broader perspective of life, in which the healthy community prevails when there is a balance of goods of all kinds (economics, justice, power, etc.) (11).

In Western societies, illness is not so inclusive but involves physical, psychological, and behavioral aspects (5). Cultures, and therefore ethnic groups, differ in terms of their

definition of illness and how they respond to illness. For example, Guttmacher and Elinson (14) found that Puerto Ricans did not consider certain forms of social deviancy (homosexuality or getting into fights) as evidence of illness. Blacks, Jews, Italians, and the Irish were more likely to define these behaviors as expressions of illness. The response to illness varies among cultures because of differing cosmologies.

Defining oneself as ill can be based on one's own perception, the perception of others, or both. Illness is a social process that involves the patient and the people (ethnic group) around him. For a person to be defined as ill there must be agreement between the person's perception of impairment and the perception of those around him. This agreement is needed for the individual to adopt the sick role, ''the socially acceptable role of an ill person'' (5). People defined as sick are able to relinquish their obligations to social groups to which they belong, such as family, friends, workmates, etc. Fox (13) said that the sick role provides a legitimate avenue for withdrawal from responsibilities and a basis of eligibility for care by others. This role is usually legitimated by health professionals. Illness for some may be a coping mechanism and may not be viewed negatively.

Lewis (15) pointed out that in every society there are standards of behavior when people are ill. The presentation of illness and the response to illness by the patient and those around him are largely determined by sociocultural factors. Each culture has a language to bridge the gap between subjective experiences of illness and social acknowledgement of them. Culture determines which symptoms are perceived as abnormal and ''they also help to shape these diffuse emotional and physical changes into a pattern which is recognizable to both the sufferer and those around him'' (5).

DOMAINS OF QUALITY OF LIFE

Schipper et al. (9) defined four broad domains of quality of life: (a) physical and occupational function, (b) psychologic state, (c) social interaction, and (d) somatic sensation. Figure 1 shows the relationship between these variables using the patients' perception of illness as the core or integrating component in determining quality of life. McElroy and Townsend (2) pointed out that while the immediate clinical symptom of disease may be a virus, vitamin deficiency, or intestinal parasite, disease is due to a chain of factors related to ecosystemic imbalance. Quality of life is determined by the perception of this imbalance by the patient. Figure 1 indicates the relationship between the domains, perception of illness, and perception of quality of life. It is the perception of a ''quality life'' that results of surveys attempt to define and identify for patients and ethnic groups. A quality life is not determined by socioeconomic status or occupation. Rather, the perception of a quality life is conditioned by cultural norms that underlie personal experiences.

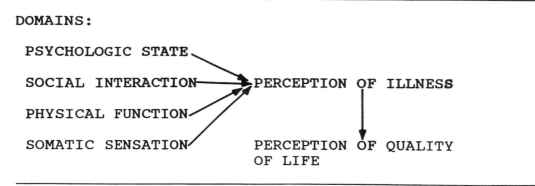

FIG. 1. Diagram of the relationship between quality of life domains and perception of illness.

Physical and Occupational Function

Physical function and occupational function are the traditional outcome measures of physicians. They include measures that examine response or physiology (9). The manner in which individuals respond to physical abnormalities and disabilities varies among ethnic groups. Individual and group response to physical disability are influenced by their belief system. For example, in rural Greece, measles, mumps, whooping cough, and chicken pox are not considered diseases but are thought to be a normal part of the process of growing up (16). Overnutrition is a health problem in Western societies; however, in West African societies, and to some extent among African Americans, obesity is not considered a negative attribute among women.

How ethnic groups respond to physiological malfunctions is related to cultural beliefs about causation. Disease causation can be divided into two categories: personalistic and naturalistic. In the former, disease is caused by the purposeful intervention of a sensate agent, supernatural being (deity or a god), nonhuman being (ghost, ancestor, or evil spirit), or human being (witch or sorcerer). The patient is a victim of aggression or punishment directed specifically against him (11). For example, among the Abron of the Ivory Coast, ghosts, bush devils, and witches may all cause disease (17). Among the Melanesian Dobuans all illness is attributed to agents, especially their envy. There are no accidents in these societies. Falling from trees is due to sensate agents as are other illnesses (18). Many African and Asian societies include this pattern within their medical system. Here, the maintenance of quality of life is impossible without assistance from a shaman and possibly the entire community.

The naturalistic causation is an imbalance or disequilibrium in the body or in the community. Health prevails when the insensate elements in the body—the cold, the heat, the humors, the yin and yang—are in balance for the age and condition of the individual in his natural and social environment (11). This type of causation is found in Asia, Latin America, and in Western societies.

Skultans (19) examined beliefs about menstruation among women in a mining village in South Wales. They believe that menstrual blood is "bad blood" and that menstruation is a way to purge the body of this badness or excess. They wanted a heavy flow each month so they could maintain a healthy equilibrium. These women were pessimistic about menopause but were not concerned about menorrhagia or an exceptionally heavy bleeding.

Psychological State

Schipper et al. (9) noted that the most studied psychological parameters of quality of life are anxiety, depression, and fear. Stress from functional impairment, life experiences, and/or pain from disease can affect one's psychological state and perception of disease. Stress is defined as a process of responding to environmental demands that threaten the well-being or stability of the individual (2). Tolerance of stress varies individually and culturally. Our childhood environment provides a basis for learning to enjoy or cope with levels of stimulation. For instance, Inuit infants are rarely alone. They sleep through constant noise, and adults complain that they feel nervous and cannot sleep when it is too quiet. For the Inuit, silence is sensory deprivation while for other non-Inuit Americans excessive noise creates sensory overload and problems sleeping (2). The perception of noise, comforting or distressing, depends upon child-rearing practices that are culturally based.

Folk illnesses are syndromes that members of an ethnic group claim to suffer and for which their culture provides an etiology, diagnosis, preventive treatment, and curing process (20). Folk illnesses include susto, a depressive-anxiety condition found in Latin America; koro in China, where men fear that their penis will withdraw into their body; windigo, a cannibalistic obsession found among Native Americans in the northeastern United States; and high blood, found in low-income blacks and whites in the United States. High blood is based on the belief that blood volume goes up or down depending on what one eats or drinks. Each of these is a unique disorder that is recognized mainly by members of a certain ethnic group. These illnesses have a range of symbolic meaning for the sufferer. They may link the sufferer to changes in the natural environment or to supernatural forces. In some cases, it provides a culturally appropriate way for the sufferer to express social conflict with family or friends (5,11). For instance, *narahatiye galb* or "heart distress," is found among the Maragheh in Iran. It manifests itself by physical symptoms such as trembling, fluttering, or pounding of the heart and with feelings of anxiety. The abnormal heartbeat is linked with experiences of social stress. It is most prevalent among Iranian women and often follows quarrels or conflict within the family, pregnancy, childbirth, and infertility (5).

Somatic Sensation

Somatic sensation includes all unpleasant feelings that detract from quality of life (9). Pain sensation is a universal human experience. Except those with genetically or congenital nerve ending insensitivity, even embryos respond to noxious stimuli. It is well established that there are individual differences in response to pain. It is also clear that there are differences in the perception of pain based upon worldview, values, and perceptions. Whether or not an ethnic group is sensitive to some degree of pain or expresses a pained response depends on many factors, among them, whether its culture values or disvalues the display of emotional expression and response to dysfunction (21).

Studies show that ethnicity influences pain response (22–26). For example, Sternback and Tursky (24) examined women in four ethnic groups: Protestants of British ancestry, the Irish, Jews, and Italians. They were all in the same social middle class. There were significant differences between the groups at pain tolerance level. Protestants had the highest mean scores, followed by Jews and the Irish. Italians had the lowest mean score. Sternbach and Tursky concluded that attitudinal differences among the ethnic groups accounted for the psychophysical and autonomic differences.

Zborowski (25) studied what he terms spontaneous pain (from disease or injury) among old Americans, Irish, Italians, and Jews. Among old Americans pain is reported, but they are not emotional about it, while the Irish denied pain. Italians wanted immediate pain relief and were content when pain was alleviated. Jews wanted pain relief also but tended to continue complaining after their pain diminished. Zborowski (25) suggested that Italians are present oriented while Jews are future oriented and when in pain present future-oriented anxiety. Old Americans are also future oriented but tend to be optimistic. Old Americans tended to withdraw socially when in pain while Jews and Italians wanted social interaction with family.

Opler (26) suggested that the excessive response to pain among Italians may be due to a general preoccupation with body image. The stoicism of the Irish may be, in part, from a tendency to disregard the physical self. Zborowski (25) concluded that similar reactions to pain do not necessarily indicate similar attitudes to pain, and reactive patterns to pain may have different function in various cultures. Wolff and Langley (21) stated that "any attempt to delineate cultural factors in the pain response should be made within the wider context of cultural attitudes toward sickness and health."

Zborowski (25) noted that whether or not a culture considers pain a normal part of life will determine if it is considered a problem. For example, he pointed out that in Poland labor pains are both expected and accepted and therefore it is not reported to health professionals. In the United States, on the other hand, labor pain is not accepted and analgesia is frequently demanded. Attitudes such as these are acquired early in life and are part of an ethnic group's child-rearing practices.

Social Interaction

Maintenance of social interactions after the onset of illness is partly determined by cultural background. As noted earlier, when in pain old Americans socially withdraw while Jews and Italians want to maintain interactions with family members (25).

The sick role is a semi-legitimate way to withdraw. If a person is defined as sick, he is exempt from performing normal roles and has a right to care (27). In Western societies, illness may represent a way to cope with failure. One can justify failure in terms of one's inability to perform as a result of illness (28).

EXAMPLES OF QUALITY OF LIFE STUDIES IN ETHNIC GROUPS

A computer search of quality of life studies in ethnic groups revealed four types of literature on this topic: (a) objective social indicators of quality of life, (b) subjective social indicators of quality of life, (c) the aged, and (d) institutional racism. Objective social indicators of quality of life are sociodemographic variables (29–38). For example, Mariante (38) examined sociodemographic indicators of quality of life among ethnic groups in Hawaii. He found differences in the income of various groups, with Caucasian, Chinese, Japanese, and Koreans enjoying incomes above the state median, while Puerto Ricans, Samoans, part-Hawaiians, Hawaiians, and Filipinos were all significantly below the median.

Other studies used subjective social indicators of quality of life, e.g., various items dealing with perceptions of well-being (35,39–43). Campbell (44) argued that:

If we believe that the quality of life lies in objective circumstances of life, these (objective) measures will tell us all we need to know; but if we believe . . . that the quality of life lies in the experience of life, then these are surrogate indicators. They describe the conditions of life that might be assumed to influence life experience, but they do not assess that experience directly.

Subjective social indicators describe the way individuals evaluate their perceived conditions of life. There are various individual measures of quality of life that assess well-being from different perspectives. In any study assessing quality of life, it is necessary to include a range of well-being domains to ensure that various dimensions of well-being are evaluated. It appears that a relatively small set of general well-being measures within domains is sufficient to evaluate quality of life (41). Bharadwaj and Wilkening (45) said that most life satisfaction measures can be derived from well-being domains that are broad in scope, personal, and central to the individual. They reported that domains of health, community, family, work, standard of living, and leisure activities were the most important domains for respondents in most groups. It was noted that different groups place different values on the various domains. For instance Chamberlain (41) said, "It may not matter, in terms of affecting overall well-being, if a person reports dissatisfaction with leisure activities or marriage provided that these domains are regarded as unimportant." In terms of cultural differences in values and the quality of life, Rokeach (46) argued that:

> Differences between cultures, social classes, occupations, religions, or political orientations are all translatable into questions concerning differences in underlying values and value systems. Differences between the generations, black and white Americans, and the rich and poor are all amenable to analysis in terms of value differences.

Chamberlain (41) reported that there is a large body of evidence to show that there are value differences and life-quality differences between groups classified in various ways (47–49). If there are differences in value systems between groups, then these differences exist between ethnic groups.

An example of this approach is Penning's (35) study of respondents' perceptions of their quality of life, personal values, feelings of alienation and policy attitudes for individuals aged 18 years of age or older. Penning measured the dimension labeled quality of life using one objective and three subjective indicators: income, perceived economic security, self-assessed health status, and perceived overall well-being. Perceived health status was the single most important predictor of quality of life for all age groups except 30 to 49 years, where economic security was more important. Health evaluations were lower among those from Poland, Russia, and East Germany and highest among those born in the United States and those from northern and southern Europe.

Quality of life among ethnic aged is another area reported in the literature (36,50–52). Vener et al. (51) reported the results of in-depth interviews with elderly Mexican-Americans with respect to quality of life. Degree of satisfaction

with quality of life was determined by respondents indicating their satisfaction with the current stage of their life; expectations for the future; life enjoyment opportunities; physical health; educational achievement; relations with the opposite sex; family life; relations with spouse, children, and friends; residence; purchasing power; physical mobility; and dealings with government officials. Overall they expressed little dissatisfaction with their lives. Mexican-Americans reported half as many dissatisfactions with their quality of life components compared with Anglos. The authors suggested that this difference was related to a *crisis of rising expectations* among Anglos, who felt deprived given their high expectations for adequate social security benefits and pensions upon retirement. These respondents believe that the government is responsible for high inflation and their anxiety. Mexican-Americans, on the other hand, may not have such high expectations and therefore experiences less deprivation.

MacLean and Sakadakis (50) report that ethnic minorities inevitably experience the natural physical and social stresses of aging when they grow old in a "second homeland." Such stresses are intensified by problems in coping with personal and cultural age-related changes in a country different from their birth country. Wilson (53) stated, "People come to a new country, they start a new life, but the past they can't forget it. They bring it with them—memories, attitudes and relationships." Aged ethnics may come into contact with social services for the first time and need assistance in bridging the gap between their culture and the dominant culture's methods of coping with stressors (52).

Ethnic aged encounter problems in economic, social, and psychological pressures of living in a society where there is racial intolerance (52). They suffer from racism, ageism, and sexism (54,55). Besides these problems, aged ethnics must deal with poverty.

Some assessments of quality of life focused on measures dealing with institutional racism (32,39,40,56). For instance, Thomas and Hughes (40) noted that over the past 25 years, blacks in the United States experienced changes in social status. For example, laws were established to outlaw most forms of discrimination, new doors of opportunities opened, and there has been a decline in the expression of racist attitudes toward blacks (57). However, despite these changes, blacks are still a disadvantaged group. Thomas and Hughes used the General Social Survey for 1972–1985 to examine quality of life among blacks and whites. They created items from the survey to measure a general life satisfaction, trust in people, anomie, general happiness, marital happiness, and physical health. For all of the variables whites reported better psychological well-being and quality of life than blacks. After controlling for social class, age, and marital status, none of the measures of psychological well-being indicated that the condition of blacks improved or declined significantly relative to whites between 1972 and 1985. This suggests the continuing significance of ethnicity in determining well-being.

APPLICATION OF QUALITY OF LIFE STUDIES IN CLINICAL TRIALS

All human beings belong to an ethnic group. While individuals in the United States may think of themselves as "Americans," they grew up in households with cultural traditions. These households dealt with illness according to health traditions held by family members and individual experiences. Both factors, health tradition and experiences, must be considered when determining quality of life in clinical trials.

Two basic approaches to clinical trials are possible when considering quality of life in ethnic groups. A generalized approach could be used for clinic populations of varied ethnicity or American populations. Quality of life (QOL) questionnaires would focus on the four domains outlined by Schipper et al. (9), but within each domain items would be weighted according to the value individuals placed on single items within domains and/or the overall domain. This approach would also take into consideration individual experiences with health and illness. A generic approach such as this would be a subjective social indicator of quality of life since it emphasizes the importance of items to the individual.

A second approach would be the development of a QOL instrument specific to a particular ethnic group. To accomplish this, the culture of the group would have to be understood. Using information from the literature and/or surveys on health beliefs in the target population, one could develop items that correspond to the health belief pattern of the group in the clinical trial. This data should be developed using the four domains of Schipper et al. (9) as a guide. Gender differences within ethnic groups should be included in these assessments. Since individual experiences (such as degree of assimilation) overlay ethnicity, items/domains should be weighted accordingly.

Extrapolation of QOL surveys to groups that they were not intended for may not be valid. As shown throughout this chapter, different cultures define disease based upon beliefs, cognition, and perceptions consistent with their cultural pattern. These perceptions vary from one group to another. Researchers cannot assume that groups outside the intended population will weight items on the questionnaire in the same manner. One can, on the other hand, use the same questionnaire when, in addition to responding to the item, clients place a value beside individual items and domains. This would reduce individual and cultural variation. However, with this approach, one cannot be sure that the appropriate questions are asked.

Quality of life surveys are used to provide a quantitative measure of patient's perception of their life. Such a number or numerical range should be contextualized with a range of client responses that summarize their attitudes about the quality of their life. For example, responses to an item like "Provide one example of the way that you feel about your life" may give a limited range of responses for various categories of quality of life. This would provide more than a number that indicates good, bad, or okay.

CONCLUSIONS

Greeley and McCready (58) stated that "many scholars consider religious, linguistic, ethnic and regional diversity to be so peripheral to our understanding of social processes that they seldom consider these forms of diversity worthy of serious investigation." Given concerns with quality of life, ethnic responses to illness must be examined. That is, learned ways of coping with illness vary across cultures and therefore across ethnicities.

Glazer and Moynihan (59) said, "Ethnicity is more than an influence on events: it is commonly the source of events." Individuals learn, through their culture, how to respond to problems in the environment, including health problems. Mechanic (60) argued that very young children learn how to respond to various symptoms and feelings in terms of reactions of others to their behavior and social expectations. With maturation, age and sex patterns become apparent and children become clearly differentiated in the way they respond to pain, their readiness to express hurts, and their risk-taking activities (61). Learning influences how we respond to symptoms. This learning takes place within cultural groups, which we call ethnicities.

Based on the literature, it is clear that more than ethnicity must be considered when examining quality of life. One cannot assume that all individuals belonging to a particular ethnic group will respond to illness in the same way. Besides life experiences, there are differences in perception of illness related to age, gender, and class. Length of residence in the United States may alter the perception of illness. Therefore, degree of acculturation may need to be examined before quality of life measures can be assessed.

With the influx of immigrants and refugees from around the world into the United States, ethnicity must be considered in quality of life studies. This is not to say that a different scale must be created for each ethnic group. However, the value the group places on quality of life domains must be known.

Lastly, present concern with quality of life rather than simply "surviving" the procedure or treatment is a major change in biomedical research and clinical trials. If quality of life is the focus, part of the treatment protocol must address access to a quality life for patients. As part of the treatment protocol, health care providers and administrators must be political advocates for equal access to a quality life for their clients. Treatment involves the whole person, not just the immediate physiological condition. Political advocacy for a quality life for patients is a form of prevention.

REFERENCES

1. Dubos R. *Man adapting.* New Haven: Yale University Press, 1980.
2. McElroy A, Townsend PK. *Medical anthropology in ecological perspective.* Boulder, CO: Westview Press, 1989.
3. Cohn H. The evolution of the concept of disease. In: Lush B, ed. *Concepts of medicine.* Oxford: Oxford University Press, 1960.

4. Armelagos GJ, Goodman A, Jacobs KH. The ecological perspective in disease. In: Logan M, Hunt EE, eds. *Health and the human condition.* Belmont, CA: Wadsworth, 1978.

5. Helman CG. *Culture, health and illness.* Boston: Wright, 1990.

6. World Health Organization. *Constitution of the World Health Organization.* Geneva: WHO, 1946.

7. Molnar S. *Human variation: races, types and ethnic groups.* Englewood Cliffs, NJ: Prentice Hall, 1992.

8. Kottak CP. *Anthropology: the exploration of human diversity.* San Francisco: McGraw-Hill, 1994.

9. Schipper H, Clinch J, Powell V. Definitions and conceptual issues. In: Spilker B, ed. *Quality of life assessments in clinical trials.* New York: Raven Press, 1990.

10. Wellin E. Theoretical orientations in medical anthropology: change and continuity over the past half-century. In: Logan M, Hunt EE, eds. *Health and the human condition.* Belmont, CA: Wadsworth, 1978.

11. Foster GM, Anderson BG. *Medical anthropology.* New York: John Wiley, 1978.

12. Cassell EJ. *The healer's art: a new approach to the doctor-patient relationship.* New York: Lippincott, 1976.

13. Fox RC. Illness. In: Wills D, ed. *International encyclopedia of the social sciences.* New York: Free Press, 1968.

14. Guttmacher S, Elinson J. Ethno-religious variations in perceptions of illness. *Soc Sci Med* 1971;5:117–125.

15. Lewis G. Cultural influences on illness behavior. In: Eisenberg L, Kleinman A, eds. *The relevance of social science for medicine.* Dordrecht, The Netherlands: Reidel, 1981.

16. Blum R, Blum E. *Health and healing in rural Greece: a study of three communities.* Stanford, CA: Stanford University Press, 1965.

17. Alland A. *Adaptation in cultural evolution: an approach to medical anthropology.* New York: Columbia University Press, 1970.

18. Fortune RF. *Sorcerers of Dobu: the social anthropology of the Dobu Islanders of the Western Pacific.* London: George Routledge, 1932.

19. Skultans V. The symbolic significance of menstruation and the menopause. *MAN* 1970;5:639–651.

20. Rubel AJ. The epidemiology of a folk illness: Susto in Hispanic America. In: Landy D, ed. *Culture, disease, and healing: studies in medical anthropology.* New York: Macmillan, 1977.

21. Wolff BB, Langley S. Cultural factors and response to pain: a review. *Am Anthropol* 1968;70:494–501.

22. Wolff BB, Krasnegor NA, Farr RS. Effects of suggestion upon experimental pain response parameters. *Percept Motor Skills* 1965;21:675–683.

23. Wolff BB, Horland AA. Effect of suggestion upon experimental pain: a validation study. *J Abnorm Psychol* 1967;72:402–407.

24. Sternback RA, Tursky B. Ethnic differences among housewives in psychophysical and skin potential responses to electric shock. *Psychophysiology* 1965;1:241–246.

25. Zborowski M. Cultural components in responses to pain. *J Soc Issues* 1952;8:16–30.

26. Opler MK. Ethnic differences in behavior and health practices. In: Galdson I, ed. *The family: a focal point for health education.* New York: New York Academy of Medicine, 1961.

27. Parsons T, Fox R. Illness, therapy and the modern urban American family. *J Soc Issues* 1952;8(4):31–44.

28. Shuval JT, Antonovsky A, Davies AM. Illness: a mechanism for coping with failure. *Soc Sci Med* 1973;7:259–265.

29. Maynard C. *Blacks in the coronary artery surgery study.* Dissertation, University of Washington, 1986..

30. Williamson JB. Social security and physical quality of life in developing nations: a cross-national analysis. *Soc Ind Res* 1987;19:205–227.

31. Mokuau N. The impoverishment of native Hawaiians and the social work challenge. *Health Soc Work* 1990;15:235–242.

32. Lieske J. The correlates of life quality in U.S. metropolitan areas. *Publius* 1990;20:43–54.

33. Ostroot NM, Snyder WW. Measuring cultural bias in a cross-national study. *Soc Ind Res* 1985;17:243–251.

34. Farley R. The quality of life for black Americans twenty years after the civil rights revolution. *Milbank Q* 1987;65(suppl 1):9–34.

35. Penning MJ. Multiple jeopardy: age, sex, and ethnic variations. *Canadian Ethnic Studies* 1983;15(3):81–105.

36. Gerber LM. Ethnicity still matters: socio-demographic profiles of the ethnic elderly in Ontario. *Canadian Ethnic Studies* 1983;15(3):60–80.

37. Zambrana RE. A research agenda on issues affecting poor and minority women: a model for understanding their health needs. *Women and Health* 1988;12(3–4):137–160.

38. Mariante BR. How have they fared in paradise? A reconnaissance of life-style indicators among Hawaiian ethnic groups. *Ethnic Groups* 1984;5:227–253.

39. Thomas ME. *Race, class and the quality of life of black people.* Dissertation, Virginia Polytechnic Institute, 1986.

40. Thomas ME, Hughes M. The continuing significance of race: a study of race, class, and quality of life in America, 1972–1985. *Am Sociol Rev* 1986;51:830–841.

41. Chamberlain K. Value dimensions, cultural differences, and the prediction of perceived quality of life. *Soc Ind Res* 1985;17:345–401.

42. Fazel MK, Young DM. Life quality of Tibetans and Hindus: a function of religion. *J Sci Study Rel* 1988;27(2):229–242.

43. Fine MA, McKenry PC, Chung H. Post-divorce adjustment of black and white single parents. *J Divorce and Remarriage* 1992;17(3/4):121–134.

44. Campbell A. Subjective measures of well-being. *Am Psychol* 1976;31:117–124.

45. Bharadwaj L, Wilkening EA. The prediction of perceived well-being. *Soc Ind Res* 1977;4:421–439.

46. Rokeach M. *The nature of human values.* New York: Free Press, 1973.

47. Andrews FM, Withey S. *Social indicators of well-being.* New York: Plenum, 1976.

48. Campbell A, Converse PE, Rodgers WL. *The quality of American life.* New York: Sage, 1976.

49. Campbell A. *The sense of well-being in America.* New York: McGraw-Hill, 1981.

50. MacLean MJ, Sakadakis V. Quality of life in terminal care with institutionalized ethnic elderly people. *Intern Social Work* 1989;32:209–221.

51. Vener AM, Krupka LR, Climo JJ. Drug usage and health characteristics in non-institutionalized Mexican-American elderly. *J Drug Educ* 1980;10(4):343–353.

52. Boneham MA. Ageing and ethnicity in Britain: the case of elderly Sikh women in a Midlands town. *New Community* 1989;15(3):447–459.

53. Wilson A. *Finding a voice, Asian women in Britain.* London: Virago, 1978.

54. National Urban League. *Double jeopardy: the older Negro in America today.* New York: NUL, 1964.

55. Palmore E, Manton K. Ageism compared to racism and sexism. *J Gerontol* 1973;28(3):363–369.

56. Bullard RD, Wright BH. Blacks and the environment. *Humboldt J Soc Rel* 1986/87;14(1/2):165–184.

57. Schuman H, Steeh C, Bobo L. *Racial attitudes in America: trends and interpretations.* Cambridge, MA: Harvard University Press, 1985.

58. Greeley AM, McCready WC. *Ethnicity in the United States: a preliminary reconnaissance.* New York: John Wiley, 1974.

59. Glazer N, Moynihan DP. *Beyond the melting pot.* Cambridge, MA: MIT Press, 1963.

60. Mechanic D. Social psychologic factors affecting the presentation of bodily complaints. *N Engl J Med* 1972;286(21):1132–1139.

61. Mechanic D. The influence of mothers on their children's health attitudes and behavior. *Pediatrics* 1964;33:444–453.

Quality of Life and Pharmacoeconomics in Clinical Trials, Second Edition, edited by B. Spilker.
Lippincott-Raven Publishers, Philadelphia © 1996.

CHAPTER 65

Assessing Health-Related Quality of Life in Disadvantaged and Very Ill Populations

Margot K. Ettl, Ron D. Hays, William E. Cunningham, Martin F. Shapiro, and C. Keith Beck

INTRODUCTION

The available literature provides few solutions to the problems faced by studies of health-related quality of life (HRQL) in disadvantaged, very ill populations. Clinical trials minimize these problems because they frequently use selection criteria that may differentially exclude minorities and sicker patients. We conducted an observational study of the effectiveness of clinical evaluation in the real-world settings of public clinics that treat patients with human immunodeficiency virus (HIV) disease. Clinically ill, poor, and minority patients were heavily represented. Because of the dearth of relevant literature, we use this study to illustrate the methodological problems presented by this population and provide recommendations from our experience.

Generic methodologic problems associated with studies of disadvantaged, very ill populations include (a) assuring the acceptability of personnel and methods to the target population; (b) anticipating and addressing difficult field realities by adapting methods as the project evolves; (c) motivating patients to participate when social and survival needs compete for the time and energy to participate in research; (d) allocating substantial resources to data collec-

tion; (e) assuring follow-up with a group that may have high residential mobility; (f) attending to the data quality and the problems of generalizing results from more affluent, less ill clinical populations to this understudied group; and (g) responding to the emotional toll on field staff resulting from work with the very ill and the poor. As health care delivery and demographic shifts increase the size of the population we targeted, methods for studying HRQL in these groups must be developed. To illuminate the methodologic approaches to effectiveness studies among poor, clinically ill populations, we suggest strategies we used in our study design.

Between 1991 and 1994, we conducted a longitudinal survey of HRQL among people with HIV infection. Patients were selected because they were receiving diagnostic evaluations for three difficult-to-diagnose symptoms: fever of unknown origin, persistent diarrhea, and unexplained weight loss. The purpose was to evaluate whether an invasive workup to determine a cause for these symptoms was worth it in terms of HRQL outcomes. HIV is a chronic, disabling, fatal illness that is spreading fastest among the groups we were targeting. The patients were very ill, poor, and in some cases had limited proficiency with English.

The characteristics of study personnel may also influence the success of data collection. Our research team included physicians involved in HIV care and/or health services research, an epidemiologist, biostatistician, a psychologist, an anthropologist/nurse as project director, and three bilingual research assistants. Latino, African American, and gay re-

M. K. Ettl, W. E. Cunningham, and M. F. Shapiro: University of California, Los Angeles, California 90095.
R. D. Hays: RAND, Santa Monica, California 90407.
C. Keith Beck: Harbor-UCLA Medical Center, Torrance, California 90509.

search team members were assembled to provide cultural sensitivity to those we studied. This diverse group was challenged to develop special methods for the research in response to an evolving set of field realities. For example, poverty, language barriers, poor education, crowded facilities, overburdened clinical staff, and acutely ill patients presented a challenge to the application of traditional survey methods.

STUDY SITE AND SAMPLE

We collected data on 301 HIV-infected patients at two public hospitals. To date, self-report data have been analyzed for 205 of these: 170 at the Los Angeles County–run facility, Harbor–UCLA Medical Center (HUMC), and 35 from the Veterans Administration Medical Center of West Los Angeles (VAMC). We included patients with HIV infection who were 21 years of age or older and who presented with at least one of the following clinical syndromes: sustained fever, involuntary weight loss of a least two pounds per week, and sustained unexplained diarrhea. Those with known or suspected etiologies, such as opportunistic infections, were excluded. Of the first 308 consecutive patients who met our inclusion criteria, 205 (67%) were enrolled in the study, 43 (14%) refused, and the remainder (19%) could not be enrolled for logistic reasons. Forty-three percent met the criteria for sustained fever, 7% for weight loss, and 50% for diarrhea.

Demographically, the sample was 93% male and 7% female. Twenty-six percent were non-Hispanic black, 28% were Latino, 38% were non-Hispanic white, and 8% were of other ethnicity. Seventeen percent of the HUMC sample were interviewed in Spanish. (None of the 35 patients enrolled at VAMC preferred a Spanish interview to an English one.) Forty-one percent were uninsured, 49% had public insurance (either VA or Medi-Cal), and 8% had other coverage. Mode of HIV transmission was 11% intravenous drug use, 56% male homosexual contact, 14% heterosexual contact, 5% blood transfusion, and 14% other exposure. Median annual incomes were 63% between $5,000 and $10,000, 26% between $10,001 and $30,000, and 11% between $30,001 and $100,000. Regarding education, 58% were high school graduates and 42% had not completed high school. Initially, we began enrolling patients at HUMC, but when accrual was slower than needed, we devised several strategies before adding a second site. Methodologic problems are discussed below, but we ultimately added the VAMC, thereby increasing the subset of English-speakers and veterans. All 35 veterans at the VAMC were English-speakers (Table 1).

Our survey design involved administering a 27-page baseline questionnaire at the time respondents were being evaluated for qualifying symptoms. Follow-up interviews were planned at 1, 3, and 6 months after baseline. The project director and the senior research assistant completed an extensive clinical data form for each patient at the 6-month inter-

TABLE 1. *Selected patient characteristics (n = 205[a])*

	n	%	Mean or median	SD
Gender				
Male	193	94		
Female	12	6		
Race/ethnicity				
Black	54	26		
Latino	57	28		
White	79	38		
Other	15	8		
Insurance				
Uninsured	84	41		
Medi-Cal	70	34		
VA	35	17		
Other	16	8		
HIV transmission				
Intravenous drug use	22	11		
Homosexual contact (male)	116	56		
Heterosexual contact	27	14		
Blood transfusion	11	5		
Other	29	14		
Enrollment site				
HUMC	170	83		
VAMC	35	17		
Other characteristics				
Spanish interview[b]	29	17		
Education[c]			9	(3)
Age[c]			36	(8)
Annual income[d]			$5K–$10K	
CD4 count[e]			144	(192)
Antiretroviral treatment	123	60		
PCP prophylaxis	63	31		
"Alternative" therapy[f]	29	14		

[a]Data are from the first 205 of 301 patients enrolled.
[b]Spanish interviews were done only at HUMC. No VAMC patients preferred a Spanish interview to an English one.
[c]Mean (SD).
[d]Median household.
[e]Mean $\times 10^3$ (SD). For the 49 patients who did not have CD4 counts at entry, but did have them within 7 months of study, the count at entry was estimated using ordinary least squares regression.
[f]Patients who received medications of which their provider was not aware or who received any holistic therapy, macrobiotic diets, herbal or folk medicine treatments.

view, at 9 months out from baseline if there was no 6-month interview, or at death.

QUESTIONNAIRE DEVELOPMENT

To maximize the acceptability and validity of questionnaire items, we first organized a focus group of people with acquired immune deficiency syndrome (AIDS), community activists, and health care providers. We used information obtained in focus groups in the development of our interview instruments. Although we invited twice the number of participants we needed (totaling 20), provided food, and met in the early evening, the turnout was disappointing. Only one community activist and four health care providers attended.

Focus groups provide critical insider opinions on what an HRQL agenda for the group might entail. The purpose of focus groups is to bring together members of the target study group to discuss feelings, attitudes, and perceptions, to "learn the vocabulary and thinking patterns of patients," (1) and to benefit from the group synergy that individual interviews may lack. In retrospect, it would have been better if we had targeted two separate groups: an expert group and a population-targeted group. Because of the diversity of the HIV population we studied, the latter would optimally have been divided into at least three groups: intravenous drug users, uninsured gay men, and Spanish-speaking women. People with AIDS who were community activists could have been included in the expert panel. From what we learned from our focus group, we expanded the questionnaire to include measures of loneliness, hopefulness, and social support.

Thorough pretesting of questionnaires may improve the quality of the collected data. We pretested the questionnaire as it was being finalized. We also piloted the questionnaire four times with a total of 16 patients. We modified it after each piloting as we identified various changes needed to improve the logical flow of the instrument, such as skip patterns. Interviews for pretesting and piloting were conducted with outpatients in the waiting room of the HUMC HIV clinic.

Attention to limiting respondent burden is also important. We estimated that administration of the intake interview would take 45 minutes to an hour. Items were eliminated because of concern about the difficulty of acutely ill patients completing such a lengthy interview. In piloting the questionnaire, we found it was feasible to conduct the interview in this time span. In actual practice, however, the questionnaire took from 45 minutes to 1 hour and 45 minutes. The actual population was more ill than the pilot population, and that fact accounted for the increased time requirement. However, even though the patients were acutely ill, they continued to tolerate and even enjoy being interviewed. Sheatsley (3) has observed that the psychological length of an interview is more important that the actual number of minutes it requires. "A 20-minute interview can seem insufferable if the content of the questionnaire is difficult or boring or makes the respondent feel uneasy. On the other hand, a 2-hour interview might be quite a pleasurable experience if respondents perceive the survey to be of value, recognize their own importance to it, and have been prepared for the length of time it actually required." Our participants seemed to like the detailed inquiry into quality of life issues and a bond was frequently established between them and the one who read the questionnaire to them. They also reported more self-awareness and more perspective on their health and happiness as a result of repeating the questionnaire at follow-up interviews.

Inability to speak and read English may also present problems. We anticipated a large number of patients would have limited English proficiency in this setting, which serves uninsured, low-income people. In addition, low literacy would present problems with written materials. We decided that all written material would be read aloud to respondents by our study staff. We planned oral interviews in the respondents' preferred language (Spanish or English) to minimize nonresponse bias. Seventeen percent of our patients were interviewed in Spanish.

When respondents include non–English speakers, careful attention to translation issues is required. We double translated the Spanish-language version of the questionnaire (4). First, the English instrument was translated by a professional medical translation service. For this initial translation, we decided to use an outside translation service that had no familiarity with the questionnaire. Second, it was back-translated by our two Latina research assistants: one from El Salvador and one from Puerto Rico. Because the translation service staff were primarily of Mexican and Mexican-American descent, we had a confluence of Spanish language culture. This diverse input was helpful when seeking a language style that would be acceptable to Los Angeles's diverse Latino community. Colloquial expressions and some word choice differed between the two translations. To resolve such differences, our research assistants made stylistic decisions and compromises. One had done health-services research in Puerto Rico and had a master's degree from there. She knew Spanish medical nomenclature, as well as university-level grammar. Our other research assistant was born in El Salvador but had grown up in Los Angeles. She had an ear for local expression and could match the tone of the English-language questionnaire because she had spoken English in school but Spanish at home.

PERSONNEL RECRUITMENT

The characteristics of data collection personnel may aid in eliciting respondents' participation. We hired native Spanish speakers who were also fluent in English as research assistants. In addition, they had health care experience and/or experience with HIV patients. The project director had moderate fluency and literacy in university Spanish, which aided in supervision. However, to assure standardized data collection, we had Spanish-speaking patients interviewed by fully fluent Spanish speakers.

All personnel conducting interviews were also chosen for their comfort with persons with HIV and with diverse lifestyles. Three of our interviewing staff were Latina, and two were Anglo nurses. Accuracy and meticulous attention to detail were important.

PATIENT ENROLLMENT AND FOLLOW-UP

We attempted to contact 100% of eligible patients at our study sites. Of the 308 consecutive patients who met our criteria for inclusion from September 1991 to October 1992, 205 (67%) were enrolled in the study (145 presenting to the outpatient clinic, and 60 hospitalized patients). Of the 103 patients not enrolled (56 outpatient and 47 inpatient), 43 refused, 27 were excluded because they were too ill, 15 could not be interviewed because of staff or patient scheduling problems, 14 left the site before they could be interviewed, and 4 were judged by their primary care provider to be too psychologically unstable to conduct the interview. Compared with enrolled patients, those eligible but not enrolled were significantly ($p <.05$) older (mean age 40 versus 36), and more likely to be hospitalized (46% of those not enrolled versus 29% of those enrolled).

Substantial data were necessary to determine eligibility. Each patient was screened at the time their vital signs and weight were done. We reviewed vital signs for fevers or weight loss and we asked if the patient was having any diarrhea. If they appeared eligible, we briefly described the study and invited them to participate. After their clinician had seen them, we reviewed the medical record to determine whether they met the inclusion criteria. If they were eligible, the clinician was asked to perform a specific set of diagnostic tests on that patient. Because this was a nonintervention study, algorithms were developed by advisory panels of national and local medical experts in order to create a set of tests that would be universally done by a prudent clinician. Our goal was to require no extra tests for the patients beyond what would usually be done.

Patient accrual was too slow in the first 2 months of the field season to meet our timetable, so the study team began ongoing, weekly discussions of what strategies we could use to increase enrollment. We had already realized that the outpatient population was contiguous with the inpatient population. Most patients were admitted through the emergency room, so we tried to track them through there. We found no effective way to identify eligible patients at the time they were seen in the emergency room. To identify and recruit eligible patients from the emergency room, we would have had to place staff there full-time. Such staffing would have been prohibitively expensive. Instead, we made arrangements for the immunology service fellows to evaluate new inpatients and notify us if they were possibly eligible and were willing to speak with us. Patients who were seen in the emergency room and then sent home were either missed or picked up at subsequent clinic appointments, if they remained eligible.

Originally, we planned to give respondent fees of $18 after the first follow-up interview and place $2 in a fund to create a lottery of several hundred dollars. This jackpot was awarded by drawing the name of a patient from among those who completed the 6-month interview cycle. In the first 5 months of the study we had a very high refusal rate of 17% (18 refusals out of 108 eligible patients). Because of the effort required for patients to participate in this information-gathering study that offered them no direct benefit, we added an additional $20 at the completion of the intake interview. Ongoing commitment to study participation was fostered by both these increased fees and the lottery. Some patients

stayed in contact with us primarily to find out when the jackpot would be awarded. (At the VAMC, no lottery was set up due to a Human Subjects Protection Committee decision. Rather, patients were paid a second sum of $20 after the 6-month follow-up.)

Consistent with other research (18), these fees did improve patient participation. Our refusal rate dropped to 13% (25 refusals out of 200 eligible patients) after fees were added. We were also creative when confronted with a patient refusal, trying to address and resolve any obstacles patients might be encountering. For instance, if they were too tired, we tried to a get a consent signed and an interview scheduled within the next 3 days. If they were hesitant due to confidentiality issues (e.g., their HIV status, financial status, immigrant status, or sexual orientation), we described our procedures for protecting their privacy, and when possible, asked their clinician to assure them as well.

Follow-up interviews present special challenges with this population. Lower income groups may have high residential mobility. At enrollment, we asked patients for phone numbers and addresses for themselves and at least one contact person. We systematically and aggressively tried to set dates for follow-up interviews by making phone or clinic contact in advance. We attempted to coordinate times with clinic appointments or other necessary hospital visits. If it was not possible to arrange interviews within the re-interview window (plus or minus 5 days), we did interviews over the phone. Phone interviews, like the face-to-face ones, involved reading the questionnaire verbatim to the respondent. At least one completed follow-up was obtained from 79% of the first 205 patients enrolled; another 17% died before a follow-up interview could be completed, and 4% were lost to follow-up.

For those who were lost to follow-up, we mailed packets to the last known address via "Addressee Only, Return Receipt Requested." Only three out of nine mailed were actually delivered. There was a potential for breach of confidence because in these three cases the mail was given to and signed for by someone other than the addressee. Only one follow-up interview resulted from these efforts.

One advantage our study sites afforded us was that these hospitals tended to be the "venues of last recourse" for their patients, which meant that patients had to return for care and stay in the system because they had few other health care options. Therefore, we found that the patients we had enrolled stayed in the system, and, even if they declined to complete all the follow-up interviews, we were able to track their clinical course and mortality.

Mortality was tracked by using medical records and requesting death certificates from Los Angeles County records. However, HUMC and VAMC draw from a six-county area, so the latter was not a thorough process. The National Death Index was not useful for our early analysis because its data lagged 2 years behind. The computer at the VAMC was a national network that enabled us to track mortality on patients there. There was a natural history of HIV study at UCLA that thoroughly tracked mortality, and most of our population at HUMC was subsumed in theirs. We also used patient contact phone numbers to determine whereabouts of study participants. People at those numbers would frequently volunteer that a patient had died, if we called asking to see how the patient was doing. Mortality was tracked at least 9 months out from baseline for every patient.

The fact that we got to know participants quite well over a 6-month period combined with their high degree of morbidity and mortality took an emotional toll on the field staff. Fifty percent of patients we enrolled died during the 3 years we were gathering data. We remained sensitive to this stress among the staff and devoted frequent time to debriefing and ventilating feelings with each other.

INTERVIEW PROCESS

Once patients were identified as eligible, the consent was reviewed with them, explaining that four interviews would be done over a 6-month follow-up period. We stressed that after the first interview, we would endeavor to interview them while they were waiting to be seen, so as not to add time to their usual appointment. After the consent, we performed an objective assessment of mental ability using the Mini-Mental State Exam (MMSE) (5), with a score of 23 or higher out of 30 being acceptable. We wanted defined criteria for determining ability to participate, rather than relying solely on clinical judgment. In practice, this way of screening prevented us from excluding a sizable number of patients. We often incorrectly anticipated that a patient would fail the MMSE, when in fact they passed with points to spare. Only two out of the first 308 consecutive patients who met the inclusion criteria failed the MMSE. After the patient passed the MMSE, we read the questionnaire to him or her.

Psychiatric problems caused some difficulties during interviews. Depression and weariness were also common among the patients. We interviewed people with paranoia, histrionics, bipolar illness (manic-depression), and schizophrenia, to name a few of the more challenging ones. As long as they were able to pass the MMSE, we enrolled them. On two occasions we were in the position of responding to actively suicidal patients. The first time, the patient was on the phone with a research assistant, who made a short-term no-harm contract with him, contacted his significant other, and notified the police. The second time, the patient was interviewed in the clinic by the project director, who obtained a psychiatric referral and accompanied the patient to the psychiatric emergency room.

Due to patients' circumstances, interviews sometimes took several sessions. We attempted to finish interviews within 3 days of consent, so that the patients would still be experiencing the symptomatic episode that had made them eligible. There were several circumstances that resulted in interrupted interviews. In some instances the patients were too ill to tolerate an unbroken one-hour interview. Medical treatments were given priority in interactions with both inpatients and outpatients. Visitors for inpatients and transportation schedules for outpatients also interrupted many interviews. Our goal was to accommodate the patient's schedule as much as possible, but to complete the interview without fail. Completed interview forms were reviewed by the project director or the senior research assistant for omissions or errors. When possible, the patient was recontacted within 3 days to complete any missing or erroneous data.

Interviews sometimes took several hours of staff time over a 3-day period to complete. This extended process was also found to be necessary with people with AIDS interviewed in a study by Fowler et al. (6). Although interviewing patients with other debilitating chronic diseases might require extra time, one feature common in the HIV-infected population is dementia. We found that most patients diagnosed with AIDS dementia who were able to be consented, successfully passed the Mini-Mental State Exam. Although they were extremely slow to interview, they were able to respond to all the items on the questionnaire. Their main impairment was their slowness. They were also willing respondents and represented an important element of our study population.

We feel these requirements may also have special applicability to research with a very ill population in general, as well as with the poor and those with limited English proficiency. The first group obviously has physical limitations that may diminish their motivation and stamina to participate in an interview. The poor frequently have competing survival needs such as transportation difficulties. Many are reliant on public transportation, which in the Los Angeles area runs relatively infrequently—typically every 30 to 60 minutes. Los Angeles is a sprawling low-rise city where it is common for bus stops to be spaced one mile apart. The hospital catchment area reaches a radius of 10 miles for HUMC, and up to 100 miles for the VAMC. Taxis are not financially feasible for even middle-income residents of Los Angeles, with 5-mile rides averaging $20 plus tip. Patients may also be trying to maintain jobs, lack help with child care, or feel general frustration and exhaustion from the time-consuming nature of health care received in public hospitals. Those with limited English proficiency, due to either being foreign born or their low education or ability level, may be less motivated to participate in research than better-educated groups because they may have less confidence in its relevance.

We sincerely believed that participating could be a rewarding experience for the patient, because we offered genuine interest and caring. For instance, we tried to be helpful to patients and clinicians in ways not necessarily related to the study. We tried to facilitate patients' attempts to maneuver through the hospital system. We acted as go-betweens for them and hospital personnel. We placed bins in the hospital conference room to collect food, toys, and clothes from staff to give to some of the mothers enrolled in the study. Our senior research assistant, who was particularly generous with her time, took the children of one patient shopping for groceries and layette supplies when there was no other way to provision the household for the impending birth of a grandchild. While these interventions might have had some impact, it is highly unlikely that these distorted our view of patients' HRQL.

Given the difficulties inherent in enrolling these patients, our efforts to accommodate their non–study-related needs were not only humanitarian but also practical. Patients were acutely ill and we wanted to assure completion of a lengthy interview. Visiting hours for family and friends were limited. Because we did not want to interfere with activities that might be contributing to their quality of life, interviews were scheduled around personal visits. The questionnaire was demanding. It probed emotional and intimate issues such as hopelessness and attitudes toward death, as well as potentially embarrassing topics of sexual satisfaction and detailed bowel habits. We needed to make the interview feasible by any means we could. We went to great lengths: following the patient to other appointments, seeing inpatients on weekends, interviewing over a meal in the cafeteria, or bringing snacks and magazines to inpatients. While our work essentially occurred between 8:00 A.M. and 7:30 P.M. on weekdays, extended hours were worked about two or three times a month when there was no other way to assure the completion of an interview.

PSYCHOMETRIC QUALITY OF DATA

It is important to examine the data quality and psychometric performance of HRQL measures in such populations. Our HRQL instrument includes 64 items hypothesized to assess general health, physical health, and mental health concepts. General health measures include current health perceptions (5 items), social function (2 items), and energy/fatigue (5 items); physical health measures include physical function (6 items), role function (2 items), freedom from pain (2 items), and disability days (1 item); mental health measures include overall quality of life (3 items), emotional well-being (5 items), hopefulness (11 items), freedom from loneliness (8 items), will to function (4 items), and cognitive function/distress (6 items). We also asked patients to rate directly the quality of their life in four specific life domains: leisure and social activities, sex life, family life, and friendships.

Most of the measures were adapted from the HIV-PARSE (HIV–Patient-Reported Status and Experience) (7), but we also included items tapping several other aspects of HRQL not included in previous HIV studies. The loneliness items were selected from the revised UCLA Loneliness Scale (8), and the hopefulness items were adapted from the Beck Hopelessness Scale (9), and supplemented with new items. We used five-point response options (*all of the time, most of the time, some of the time, a little of the time, none of the time*) rather than the original six-point options (excluding *a good*

bit of the time) for certain scales (e.g., cognitive function/distress, emotional well-being). For most of these items, we asked patients to report on their status during the preceding 4 weeks. Other items inquired about current status with the time frame left unspecified. All multi-item measures were scored as simple summated scores and transformed linearly to a 0 to 100 possible range so that higher scores represent better health. Internal consistency reliability estimates (10) were generally adequate for the multiple-item HRQL scales (Table 2). Reliabilities equaled or exceeded .70 for 10 of the 12 scales. Multitrait scaling analyses (11) provided strong support for item discrimination across scales. For the majority of items in the analysis, the largest item-scale correlation was observed for the hypothesized scale.

We also included measures of perceived access to medical care, social support, coping response, social disengagement, and symptoms. The access measures were derived from the Medical Outcomes Study (12) and included nine items designed to assess problems in several areas: affordability, availability, and convenience. Each item was measured on a five-point Likert-type scale ranging from strongly agree to strongly disagree. We used two items to measure problems with affordability of care, three items to measure availability of care, three items to measure convenience of care, and one item to measure access to specialists. These nine items were combined into a scale of overall perceived access (alpha = .73) using simple summated scores that gave equal weight to each item.

Social support was assessed using five items adapted from Sherbourne and Stewart (13) that tapped the availability of tangible, informational, and emotional support when needed (alpha = .88). Items adapted from Billings and Moss's (14) coping measure were supplemented with new items to develop a ten-item measure of coping response to HIV infection (alpha = .80). Based on focus group work suggesting that some patients with HIV reject social interaction, we developed a new four-item measure of social disengagement for the study (alpha = .53). All psychosocial measures were scored so that higher values represent better psychosocial functioning.

Because of the clinical importance of medical symptoms and their strong associations with HRQL measures (15,16), we assessed myalgias, loss of appetite (anorexia, nausea, and vomiting), night sweats, exhaustion, weight loss, fever, diarrhea severity, discomfort, and other complications. We assessed the frequency and severity of myalgia, amount of appetite loss, and frequency of nausea, vomiting, night sweats, and fatigue/exhaustion during the last 4 weeks. For weight loss, each patient reported how much they weighed at the time of the interview, 4 weeks earlier, 3 months earlier, and 6 months earlier as well as their usual or normal weight prior to getting HIV disease. For fever, patients were asked if they had ''felt feverish'' in the past 14 days. We also assessed diarrhea severity (both the frequency and consistency of stools), discomfort (abdominal pain with bowel movements, abdominal pain without bowel movements, te-

TABLE 2. *Reliability and descriptive statistics for multiple-item health-related quality of life scales*[a]

Scale	Number of items	Alpha	Mean	SD	Kurtosis	Skewness
General health						
Current health	5	.79	24.9	21.3	0.69	1.06
Social function	2	.71	48.6	28.8	−0.79	−0.07
Energy/fatigue	5	.86	36.6	22.9	−0.43	0.32
Physical health						
Physical function	6	.84	53.0	27.1	−0.82	−0.22
Role function	2	.73	39.5	30.6	−0.64	0.34
Freedom from pain	2	.64	53.5	25.9	−0.71	−0.06
Mental health						
Overall quality of life	3	.80	52.1	22.1	−0.36	0.13
Emotional well-being	5	.82	54.8	24.1	−0.66	−0.15
Hopefulness	11	.86	64.5	22.6	−0.19	−0.63
Not lonely	8	.84	60.0	25.6	−1.09	−0.14
Will to function	4	.49	56.5	21.6	−0.13	−0.32
Cognitive function/distress	6	.85	65.6	24.4	−0.51	−0.46

[a]All scales were scored on a 0–100 score range, with higher scores representing better health-related quality of life.

nesmus, and urgency without defecation), and other complications (night diarrhea and fecal incontinence). These measures are described in greater detail elsewhere (16,17).

Particularly in HIV disease, the results of clinical trials are applied broadly to populations, despite limited representation of minorities and disadvantaged groups. In a comparison of our nonclinical trial study group with an AIDS Clinical Trial Group cohort, the former group was low income, mostly minority, and served by public hospitals. The latter was middle income, mostly white, and served by a variety of public and private providers. Both groups were administered 30 HRQL items developed in the Medical Outcomes Study (MOS). HRQL measures such as those from the MOS are useful for assessing the similarity of different groups (1). As shown in Table 3, our nonclinical group scored about a standard deviation below that of the clinical trial group on the HRQL scales. We also found that the relationships of individual variables with HRQL differed between trial and nontrial samples, suggesting problems generalizing results from HIV clinical trials to important target populations.

CLINICAL DATA COLLECTION

At the end of the 6-month follow-up period, extensive clinical data were collected. Using medical records, clinic charts, computer data bases, and nurses' logs, we completed clinical data forms created by our research team. Clinical data collection was a labor-intensive, ongoing process for the field staff. Each form required 8 to 24 hours to complete, plus an additional 30 to 90 minutes for physician review. Because we had a population that was treated in public facilities due to a lack of other health care options, we frequently had access to continuous longitudinal data on the respondents. The acuteness and severity of their HIV-related symptoms increased the likelihood of their contact with the clinical facility.

TABLE 3. *Quality of life measures for clinical trial (n = 1193) and non-clinical trial (n = 180*[a]*) samples: summary statistics and internal consistency reliability estimates (alpha)*

Measure	Number of items	Clinical trial		Nonclinical trial	
		Mean (SD)	Alpha	Mean (SD)	Alpha
Current health	5	52 (26)	.88	24 (21)	.79***
Energy/fatigue	4	57 (24)	.89	36 (23)	.85*
Physical function	6	79 (22)	.87	53 (38)	.84
Physical pain	1	72 (25)	−	50 (29)	−
Role function	2	76 (30)	.86	39 (31)	.74***
Social function	1	75 (28)	−	48 (35)	−
Emotional well-being	5	67 (20)	.86	54 (24)	.82
Cognitive function	6	82 (18)	.90	66 (24)	.84**

*$p < .05$; **$p < .01$; ***$p < .001$.
−, Not applicable.
[a]Data are from first 180 of 301 patients enrolled.

The institutions themselves presented challenges for clinical data collection. Chart abstraction in hospitals was especially difficult. We experienced problems with chart retrieval, lassitude or resentment on the part of staff when asked for help on non–patient care activities such as research, delays in getting clinical documentation in the chart, and lost documentation. Also there was a variety of access obstacles (such as computers being down, hospital departments being closed or slow to respond, inability of medical records department to locate multiple volumes of patient charts, and archiving and purging of hospital computer data bases at irregular intervals, which made those data sources sometimes inaccessible). Aliases and multiple hospital numbers for some patients had to be dealt with to assure the collection of all clinical data available.

ADDRESSING PROBLEMS WITH STUDY IMPLEMENTATION

It is essential to allocate sufficient resources to data collection in studies of poor, clinically ill, limited English-proficiency groups. A study with this population is very labor intensive and, therefore, very expensive. We increased the proportion of funds used for data collection activities and extended time frames to obtain an extensive data base. We share the experience of Fowler et al. (6) that "despite the extensive experience of the investigators, every facet of this study has posed challenges and required problem solving that was not fully anticipated at the time this project was designed" (p.1065).

We had initially planned to use direct data entry with laptop computers, but this proved to be too slow and inflexible. The primary limitation was the program we used. We used PerForm Pro and found that it could not handle the complexity of the interview instrument efficiently. Faster laptop computers (ours were 386 microprocessors operating at 20 MHz) would have helped. However, the research environment made using laptops difficult because there was limited space for conducting interviews and there was no reliable electrical outlet when batteries were depleted. We ultimately returned to using pen and paper for all data collection.

In full-time equivalents, 3.25 field staff were required to enroll 301 patients from 1991 to 1994. If we had had one additional full-time clerical person, we could have completed the non–survey-related data collection in a more timely manner. Instead, we had to defer virtually all medical records abstraction until the interviews were complete. Without the level of staffing we did have, it would have been impossible to have assembled the high quality of data we did.

The first 6 months of the study we had only the project director and the senior research assistant on board. As we began enrolling patients, we added another full-time research assistant. When she moved on to another position 8 months later, we had already added the second site. We divided that position into two part-time positions, so that we could simultaneously staff both sites. One of these positions was half time and lasted 1 year. The other started out as half time and was increased to full time after 3 months. That research assistant remained with the project for a total of 15 months. The senior research assistant stayed on full time until 4 months after the last follow-up interview was due. The project director continued full time for another 3 months after that. We do not feel we would have maintained as high a level of rigor and consistency in the data collection had we employed more people for shorter terms.

As it was, there was a heavy concentration of diverse tasks on the project director and the senior research assistant, because of the early reallocation of the budget to the ultimately abandoned direct data entry approach. Prior to that, more clerical and secretarial support was planned. One advantageous result of this redistribution of funds was that we hired fewer staff (thinking the computers would reduce the need for clerical support) and hired much more experienced (and relatively expensive) field personnel. Although this approach meant the relatively expensive labor of the project director and her senior research assistant was applied to all aspects of the field work, in the long run it may have been cost-efficient. We feel that the high caliber of ability, training, commitment to research, and interpersonal skills of our field staff contributed immeasurably to the consistency and completeness of our interview and clinical data.

Neither hospital had telephones at the patients' bedside, so screening and interviewing of inpatients was a hit-and-miss proposition. On the dedicated HIV unit at the VAMC, we were able to make regular rounds. At HUMC, there was no dedicated unit and we relied on the fellows covering the inpatient service to identify potential patients for us. Multiple daily drop-in visits Monday through Friday were necessary to cover both areas for enrollment and follow-up.

We attended all HIV clinics, a total of five days per week between the two sites. We kept visible during the clinic period and stayed alert to any clues about new or follow-up patients. It was not possible to perform other research activities (such as clerical tasks) during clinic hours because of the sporadic flurries of activity we needed to monitor. At times this appeared to be an inefficient use of research staff time, but we found no way around it. Being in all the HIV clinics full-time was essential to getting our enrollments and follow-ups done.

We helped both patients and clinicians by conveying pertinent health-related information in either direction. Patients became more aware of significant information about their needs and care and learned ways to communicate this to clinicians. Thus, the interview process, at times, had educational value for the patients, and contributed to better patient histories for clinicians.

Patient confidentiality was vigilantly guarded, as promised in the Human Subjects Protection Committee consent. Study identification numbers were assigned at enrollment and names were linked to this number only in locked cabinets and encrypted computer data bases. When we reach a time when we no longer anticipate the need to return to the patients' medical records for data verification, all these linking files will be destroyed. In the interim, materials identifying patients are shredded when they have served their purpose. To assure confidentiality on the phone, we never identified ourselves except by first name and "Harbor" (HUMC) or "the Veterans Hospital" (VAMC). Words such as *research, study,* and *interview* were avoided to protect patient confidentiality with those who answered the phone. We referred to the study as the "outcomes study," omitting reference to HIV.

We interviewed patients wherever there was privacy available: in the halls, in the corners of the waiting room, and sometimes outdoors. We always checked with the respondent as to whether they were comfortable with any persons who might overhear us, such as partners, friends, or family. We did have an on-site study office at HUMC, but we usually did not interview there because the patient needed to stay within earshot of the clinic.

Research may impose extra work on hospital staff. We tried to make our study worth any extra effort it might entail for them. Usually it was possible to find ways to help them in their tasks while carrying on our work. At the minimum, we maintained an amiable and easygoing attitude, and greeted and thanked hospital staff by name. We provided help with Spanish translation when we were in the clinic or hospital. We created forms and flyers on our project computers, using WordPerfect and Harvard Graphics. We organized hospital staff birthday and farewell parties five or six times per year, and one year coordinated the annual outing to the Hollywood Bowl.

We had a unique position at VAMC and HUMC because we were not hospital employees but visiting researchers present for a 3-year period. While we worked side by side with hospital personnel, we had little involvement in workplace politics. This outsider-in-the-know status made us a safe haven for those needing a sounding board or confidant. We developed friendly relationships with virtually all hospital staff and they were generous with their help. There were a few crucial gatekeepers who never softened toward us. However, invariably we were able to find ways around these individuals by dealing with other staff, seeking help during their off hours, or going to their supervisors through one of the study physicians associated with the hospital.

CONCLUSIONS

Underrepresentation of demographic groups, which include the disadvantaged and the very ill, should be a major concern. They are likely to have a poorer HRQL and are also a fast-growing segment of the United States population. If we are to get the best information for the management of these target populations, a sizable investment of research is necessary to insure their participation. Good HRQL data can be gathered from these groups. However, collecting these data is expensive and the quality of data is proportional to the amount of effort expended on fieldwork.

Challenging field realities include poverty, language barriers, poor education, crowded facilities, overburdened hospital staff, and acutely ill patients. Good longitudinal data is available under these conditions as long as the research effort is well accepted by the patients and the hospital staff. We found the following approaches effective. First, we selected a research team that could produce an acceptable, valid methodology through scientific expertise and cultural sensitivity. Second, we developed a questionnaire tailored to our target population by conducting a focus group, pretesting, piloting, and double translating it. Third, we focused on building interpersonal relationships with patients and hospital staff to overcome obstacles to study participation. Fourth, we gathered data on differences between our population and more affluent, less ill HIV patients tested with the same measures. Fifth, we tracked our enrollment process closely so that we could identify ways to maximize study participation. Sixth, we reallocated funds as necessary to cover the higher-than-anticipated costs of data collection. Seventh, we were systematic and tireless in our interview efforts, including attending all clinics and devoting our efforts there solely to enrollment and follow-up. Lastly, the research staff took care of each other so that, despite the many demands of the project, job satisfaction for the field staff was very high.

REFERENCES

1. Cunningham WE, Bozzette SA, Hays RD, Kanouse DE, Shapiro MF. Comparison of health-related quality of life in clinical trial and non-clinical trial HIV infected cohorts. *Med Care* 1995;33-4:AS15–AS25.
2. Krueger RA. *Focus groups: a practical guide for applied research.* Newbury Park: Sage, 1988:39.
3. Sheatsley PB. Questionnaire construction and item writing. In: Russi PH, Wright J, Anderson AB, eds. *Handbook of survey research.* New York: Academic Press, 1983:195–230.
4. Marin G, Marin BV. *Research with Hispanic populations.* Newbury Park: Sage Publications, 1991:84–100.
5. Folstein MF, Folstein SE, McHugh PR. "Mini Mental State": a practical method for grading the cognitive state of patients for clinicians. *J Psychiatr Res* 1975;12:189–198.
6. Fowler FE, Massagli MP, Weissman J, Seage III GR, Cleary PD, Epstein A. Some methodological lessons for surveys of persons with AIDS. *Med Care* 1992;30(11):1059–1065.
7. Bozzette SA, Hays RD, Berry S, Kanouse D. A perceived health index for use in persons with advanced HIV disease: derivation, reliability, and validity. *Med Care* 1994;32:716–731.
8. Hays RD, DiMatteo MR. A short-form measure of loneliness. *J Pers Assess* 1987;51:69–81.
9. Beck AT, Steer RA. *Beck Hopelessness Scale.* San Antonio: Harcourt Brace Jovanovich, 1988.
10. Cronbach LJ. Coefficient alpha and the internal structure of tests. *Psychometrika* 1951;16:297–334.
11. Hays RD, Hayashi T. Beyond internal consistency reliability: rationale and user's guide for Multitrait Scaling Analysis Program on the microcomputer. *Behav Res Methods Instruments Computers* 1990;22:167–175.
12. Marshall GN, Hays RD, Sherbourne C, Wells KB. The structure of patient ratings of outpatient medical care. *Psychol Assess* 1993;5:477–483.

13. Sherbourne CD, Stewart AL. The MOS social support survey. *Soc Sci Med* 1991;32:705–714.
14. Billings AB, Moss RH. The role of coping responses and social resources in attenuating the stress of life events. *J Behav Med* 1988;4: 139–158.
15. Cleary PD, Fowler FJ, Weissman J, Massagli MP, Wilson I, Seage GR, Gatsonis C, Epstein A. Health-related quality of life in persons with acquired immune deficiency syndrome. *Med Care* 1993;31:569–580.
16. Shapiro MF, Hays RD, Dixon WJ, Visscher BR, Cunningham WE, George WL, Ettl MK, Beck K. Constitutional symptoms and quality of life in symptomatic HIV disease. (Manuscript).
17. Mertz H, Beck K, Dixon W, Esquivel A, Hays RD, Shapiro M. Validation of a new measure of diarrhea. *Digest Dis Sci* (in press).
18. Dillman DA. The design and administration of mail surveys. *Annu Rev Sociol* 1991;17:225–249.

Quality of Life and Pharmacoeconomics in Clinical Trials, Second Edition, edited by B. Spilker.
Lippincott-Raven Publishers, Philadelphia © 1996.

CHAPTER **66**

Conceptual Issues and Considerations in Cross-Cultural Validation of Generic Health-Related Quality of Life Instruments

Roger T. Anderson, Mary McFarlane, Michelle J. Naughton, and Sally A. Shumaker

INTRODUCTION

Determining whether health-related quality of life (HRQL) instruments may be used cross-culturally is a multifaceted problem, prone to frustrations especially from oversimplified methodology in cultural adaptation, incomplete psychometric evidence gathered, and the sometimes differing conceptualizations of HRQL among investigators.

The chapters by Bullinger et al. and Anderson et al. in this volume describe some of the technical complexities that must be considered when developing or adapting HRQL measures for multinational research studies such as clinical trials. These involve item meaning or content, construct validity, reliability, and the metric of the scale. Each is an aspect of measurement equivalence in cross-cultural research (1,2).

Although there is general agreement among investigators on the need to empirically demonstrate cross-cultural mea-

surement equivalence, there are differing views on how HRQL should be assessed. The latter is important as different conceptual models of HRQL include different assumptions about how the measures should perform. This chapter provides an overview of two assessment approaches of HRQL: functional-states and personal value judgments. It culminates with a review of several psychometric analytic methods that may be used to investigate cross-cultural validity relevant to either assessment approach.

GENERALITY OF THE CONSTRUCT HEALTH-RELATED QUALITY OF LIFE

There is general agreement among researchers advocating very different approaches to measuring HRQL that health-related quality of life includes at least broad dimensions of physical, social, and emotional well-being (3–5). Partly, this is based on the belief that improving or maintaining well-being in these areas is valued by all persons, and is rooted in general societal norms encouraging goal attainment, personal productivity, and self-fulfillment. These common dimensions of HRQL are also broadly based on a universal

   R. T. Anderson, M. McFarlane, M. J. Naughton, and S. A. Shumaker: Department of Public Health Sciences, Bowman Gray School of Medicine, Wake Forest University, Winston-Salem, North Carolina 27157.

definition of "health" developed by the World Health Organization (WHO) "as a state of complete physical, mental and social well-being and not merely the absence of disease or infirmity" (6). Whereas health may be assessed objectively through clinical indicators, biological samples, and diagnostic testing, the primary indicators of HRQL are centered on the *patient's point of view* or self-appraisal.

A fundamental assumption in assessing HRQL cross-culturally is the existence of a "universal" construct. That is, if a particular HRQL instrument is to be adapted or developed for use in two or more cultures, then it is assumed that HRQL is an underlying universal construct, assigned the same relevant attributes across cultures. We refer to this as an assumption of *generality of the construct*. A second common assumption is that this universal construct can be appropriately measured by a common set of indicators. This is an assumption of *generality of indicators*. A final common assumption is a *generality of scaling* in terms of the relationship of the response categories to the underlying dimension measured. Scaling assumptions in a cross-cultural context specify what is meant by metric equivalence, that is, whether the meanings of the response categories are the same across cultures or groups (e.g., "a little bit," "somewhat," "a lot").

Regardless of the conceptual model of HRQL undertaken, these assumptions of generality are logically the foundation for valid measurement cross-culturally. On an empirical level, the attributes or content of the indicators used to represent HRQL are substantially different according to whether a functional states or personal value judgment approach is taken to assessing HRQL.

THE FUNCTIONAL-STATES APPROACH TO MEASURING HRQL

In the functional-states approach, generic HRQL is conceptualized as a set of indicators representing functional states in the core dimensions of physical, social, and emotional health. Assessments typically include role performance, independence, quality of affective state, and pursuit of valued activities such as work, leisure, and recreation. Aspects of functioning assessed may include level of functioning or performance; frequency with which the function, state, or activity is experienced or performed; level of difficulty in daily functioning; and recent changes from usual level of functioning. These indicators of functional states are conceptually distinct from biomechanical or physiological measures because they reflect the patients' own experience or assessment of functioning. Some HRQL batteries may include objective measures of functional performance that are reasonably relevant to the respondent's daily functioning (e.g., the 6-minute walk); however, measures of biological processes (e.g., blood pressure) are not included in HRQL measures because they are not conceptualized as related to

the individual's perceptions of his or her physical, social, or emotional functioning.

Although the functional-states approach to HRQL may be characterized as impersonal in that normative standards are applied to the evaluation of HRQL, a functional-states approach does preserve the individual respondent's point of view by relying on self-appraised functioning and behaviors in life domains that generally are highly valued by most people. Moreover, many of the items in functional-states measures originated from interviews with patients and lay persons. A typical item in this approach might ask whether the respondent has "cut down on the amount of time spent on work." In this example, the impact of work reduction on lifestyle may be variously viewed by the respondent as inevitable or even favorable (e.g., those who desire retirement), or as a considerable inconvenience with a sense of role loss. It is simply whether a health condition has affected a major role activity that is the criterion used to appraise HRQL. This assumption is a hallmark of the functional-states approach to HRQL assessment, which, in turn, determines the nature of the variables used to examine content and criterion validity.

Another type of item often found in functional-states HRQL measures looks at breaks or changes from usual functioning. Items tapping change in functioning may avoid the problem of inferring an impact on the respondents' lifestyles by using the individuals' own usual levels as the standard. But the assumption is still made that a certain amount of absolute change in functioning constitutes a certain decrease or increase in HRQL.

Consistent with these views on HRQL, a scaling assumption in the functional-states approach is that individuals' ratings of health impacts on functional states (i.e., a little, some, or a lot of difficulty) are linearly related to some relevant physical or objective parameter, such as actual behavior.

In the context of cross-cultural assessments, the functional-states approach extends assumptions about the validity of the indicators and scales to situations in which diversity in lifestyles and norms for functioning among individuals is potentially great. This represents a "culture common" assumption in dealing with known cultural diversity in measurement, and is quite similar to approaches taken in psychological assessments (7). Specifically, the rationale of this approach is that while it may be futile to attempt a "culture-free" measurement of HRQL, it is possible to measure this construct by assessing its common dimensions across cultures.

It is the assumption of generality of a certain set of functional states as relevant attributes of HRQL and their scaling across cultures that must be tested explicitly. Irrespective of whether the functional-states indicators (e.g., "less time spent on work") may be valued differently among individuals, they should have equivalent validity across cultural settings in measuring behaviors that may be affected by health, and which are generally held to be important among members of each cultural group considered. In terms of scaling, a central assumption in the functional-states model is that the distance between response categories across cultures, judged by the respondent, represents the same amount of an attribute of functioning or performance. Examples of such attributes are time spent working or distance walked.

Although the data are limited, the literature indicates that indicators used to measure HRQL and the response format of the indicators may differ in important ways across cultures and across demographic groups (8–10). For example, gender and race differences in predictive and concurrent validities of scales measuring depressive affect have been found (11,12). The data suggest that the general dimension "emotional distress" cannot be measured with identical precision across these two groups. Likewise, in a review of the cross-cultural use of measures of depression, Naughton and Wiklund (8) reported some differences in factor structure among populations for the Center for Epidemiologic Studies–Depression Scale (CES-D), although many similarities were also found among countries.

Functional-states' indicators of physical and social role functioning may need to include different activities across cultures to capture the same level of well-being. Forms of physical activity that include sustained strenuous activity (e.g., aerobic exercise or athletic sports) may be broadly relevant only to persons in environments that encourage adopting such health behaviors, support maintaining an active lifestyle with illness, or as therapy. In a discussion of cross-cultural assessments in older adults, Herzog (10) described several examples of cultural influences that may invalidate the assumption of generality of functional-states indicators. These include laws or customs that regulate employment or retirement; and the influence of geography, architecture, economy, and customs on both the frequency and modes of interpersonal contacts and physical activity. In the International Quality of Life Assessment (IQOLA) project (13), which is currently adapting the SF-36 Health Survey for use in several countries, investigators found that some indicators of physical activity developed for United States populations, such as playing golf, were not appropriate in other cultural settings (14). In Sweden, for example, "picking berries" was viewed as the equivalent, while in France the equivalent was *jouer aux boules*. Findings reported from the IQOLA indicate that even something as "objective" as physical distance can be problematic. A city block was translated as 100 meters in some of the European versions; similarly, 1 mile was translated as 1 kilometer, except for the Swedish version where 2 kilometers was settled upon.

Because these distances are not physical equivalents of the original, it is uncertain whether they refer to the same level of physical functioning and well-being. For example, in Sweden, does the ability to walk 2 kilometers relate to physical well-being in the same way as the ability to walk 1 kilometer in France? Several examples of difficult item translations have also been reported for language adaptations of the Nottingham Health Profile (15).

An exploration of the assumptions of generality of indicators in the functional-states approach requires criteria that directly relate to functioning in each of the broad dimensions of HRQL. Because the construct HRQL is meaningful only to the extent that it reflects the respondents' life, cross-cultural validation should also compare the sensitivity of the instrument for actual performance of valued activities, and the respondents' feelings toward their ability to perform certain tasks. These criteria are valuable because they emphasize productivity and health, rather than limitations and disability, which are emphasized in many of the existing functional status measures. Thus, these criteria better reflect the WHO definition of health as "not just the absence of disease or infirmity."

Finally, the functional-states approach makes the assumption that the activities and tasks measured are highly valued across cultural settings, and can be interpreted in the same way in describing HRQL. However, it may be that a different HRQL emphasis is placed on specific activities across cultures. Techniques that could be used to weight HRQL scale scores in order to adjust for such cultural differences are discussed later in this chapter.

THE PERSONAL VALUE JUDGMENTS APPROACH

A contrasting conceptualization of HRQL relies on personal values as indicators of HRQL. These include appraisals (ratings) of health impacts in various life domains. Aspects of value judgments assessed include satisfaction, well-being, personal relationships, and outlook on life. This approach is consistent with the view of HRQL articulated by Calman (16) as "the extent to which our hopes and ambitions are matched by experience." The personal value judgments can be operationalized as the gap between a patient's hopes or expectations and what actually occurs. This conceptual model recognizes that satisfaction, valuations, and other forms of appraisal of life are based, in part, on people's general beliefs about the kinds of things their life should hold. As framed in this approach, an individual's HRQL is determined by the respondent's assumptions about normative functioning relative to age, illness or morbidity, and expectations for gains from treatment or amelioration of symptoms. A standard set of functional states and behavioral criteria would not capture the idiosyncratic nature of HRQL among respondents (17–19).

Cantril (17) conducted perhaps the most extensive study of the cross-cultural differences in subjective ratings of life satisfaction performed to date. In this study, a self-anchoring ladder scale, similar in form to those found in some HRQL batteries today (e.g., the Ladder of Life), was administered to general population samples in 14 Western and non-Western countries, and involved nearly 20,000 interviews. Although not a study of HRQL, the results showed that some basic properties were important to life satisfaction across cultures (e.g., health, functioning, providing for family, and security), although the indicators for these dimensions were often different.

The personal value judgments approach is more dynamic than the functional-states approach. The focus of the personal value judgments approach automatically includes assumptions that respondents may adapt to loss of function or achieve satisfaction through new routines for behaviors, and that the capabilities or activities that people use to define their HRQL may change over stages of treatment and recovery processes. Thus, the strength of the value judgments approach is the self-anchoring of evaluations used to construct HRQL scores. However, indicators that respond to adaptation may be insensitive to subsequent improvement in functioning, or movement toward ideal health. As with the functional-states approach, views on potential advantages and disadvantages are largely related to the conceptual model of HRQL.

In practice, while many HRQL instruments or batteries include items on life satisfaction, such as those based on the ladder scales, e.g., the Ladder of Life (21), the personal value judgments approach as a mainstay to assessing HRQL is uncommon. Likewise, there is very little work comparing this approach with functional states or subscales representing physical, social, and emotional functioning (22). Recently, some multidimensional HRQL instruments have been developed using the personal value judgments approach. Examples of these include the Multiple Index of Life Quality (23), the Patient-Generated Index (18), the Perceived Quality of Life Scale (20), and the Schedule for the Evaluation of Individual Quality of Life (24). Since the focus on this approach to assessing HRQL is relatively recent, little cross-cultural validation work has been performed on these measures as compared with the validation work conducted on the functional-states approach (25).

The personal value judgments approach does not impose criteria of specific behavior or functions in determining level of HRQL. Thus, measures of concepts other than functional states are needed to assess construct validity. While for research purposes value judgments have to be capable of distinguishing among patient groups known to have different levels of functioning, they measure a different aspect of HRQL than functional-states indicators (22).

An assumption of generality of indicators in the personal value judgments approach is that appraisals of satisfaction in indicators of physical, social, and emotional well-being are relevant and important to HRQL across cultures. For example, satisfaction in the indicators ''working life'' and ''relationships with coworkers'' would be assumed to be equally important in measuring social role functioning across cultural groups. Related to this is the assumption that treatment, including amelioration of symptoms and potential adverse effects, is a common determinant of satisfaction across cultures or population groups. Hunt and colleagues (15) have

emphasized that the subjective nature of HRQL is rooted inevitably in culture through socialization and the meanings attached to health and illness. There are currently few data to appraise the magnitude of potential biases in this regard. In Cantril's (17) study, common determinants of satisfaction were found, but the weights given these dimensions differed substantially across cultures. In the Nottingham Health Profile, a widely used HRQL measure, rankings given to symptom states were quite similar across Western European cultures (26). Since the item weighting in the latter study was not anchored in terms of an individual's ideal best and worst possible health states, it is unclear as to whether the absolute importance given the various states varied cross-culturally.

A central scaling assumption for ranking level of satisfaction or other appraisals is that the intervals between rankings reflect equivalent differences between present life situation and expected life situation, or subjective appraisals. If differences are obtained with respect to well-being or health, the investigator must determine whether this is a problem of insensitivity of the indicators to the underlying dimension of HRQL, or whether genuine differences exist between cultures with regard to appraisals of the impact of a specific health condition on HRQL. Related to this is the assumption that the same component or dimension of the appraisal is being measured. For example, ranking life satisfaction may reflect various qualities such as the importance of the life domain assigned by the respondent to HRQL, or satisfaction with performance or life situation.

The criterion variables for cross-cultural validation of HRQL instruments developed from the personal value judgments approach are different than the functional-states approach. With the former, the nature of HRQL is viewed as subjective. Thus, measures of affect and mood that possess adequate cross-cultural validity could be used for testing the equivalence of convergent validity of the personal value judgments across cultures. More direct measures that are sensitive to level of satisfaction would also be needed. Unfortunately, many of the instruments assessing psychological attributes or qualities that have been validated or compared across cultures are screens for depression or anxiety disorders (see Chapter 68 by Naughton et al.), and thus are not external criteria for validating life satisfaction measures. Cantril's (17) approach of using self-anchoring global satisfaction scales with a continuous response scale may be an alternative. Here, indicator scores for the HRQL dimensions could be compared with global appraisals.

Another issue is whether assumptions are made with respect to the generality of the stability of the value judgment scales across cultures. Ruta and colleagues (18) found evidence of changes in preference weights assigned by patients to life domains chosen as composing HRQL even among patients who reported no change in health. Because the personal value judgments model of HRQL may allow item or scale weights to change, it is important to state, *a priori,* any assumptions in this regard.

ASSESSING THE EMPIRICAL VALIDITY OF ASSUMPTIONS OF CROSS-CULTURAL GENERALITY IN HRQL MEASUREMENT

The content of the assumptions of generality of indicators and scaling of the functional-states and personal value judgments approaches affect which criteria are used for validation. This section discusses several methods for examining assumptions about cross-cultural validity that in theory are not bound to a particular view of HRQL. Also, methods that are possible within the research design and analysis when the assumptions of generality across cultures are untenable are discussed.

Cross-cultural validation of HRQL instruments should include key psychometric properties of *item equivalence*—the degree to which the items composing the instrument are identical across cultures; *scalar equivalence*—when a given rating or response is equated to the same degree of the construct across cultures (e.g., a rating of 5 on a life satisfaction item must refer to the same degree of satisfaction across cultures); and *internal structure congruence*—when a construct has the same dimensions and the same interrelations among the dimensions across cultures (2).

Item equivalence is heavily dependent upon proper translation of the instrument. Leplege and Verdier (27) and Brislin and colleagues (28) outline several methodological issues that should be considered in designing an item translation project. Scalar equivalence and internal structure congruence pertain to construct validity. We suggest four methods for examining these assumptions: multidimensional scaling, multigroup factor analysis, hierarchical linear modeling, and differential item functioning. Although our discussion is nontechnical we assume that the reader is familiar with general concepts of statistics, including some knowledge of factor analysis.

Multidimensional Scaling

As described above, there has been little systematic evaluation of the meaning or the relative importance of the various dimensions across cultures. One method of assessing the manner in which members of various cultures define and attach importance to the concept of HRQL involves multidimensional scaling (2). In a multidimensional scaling analysis, members of the various cultures are asked to rate the degree of similarity or dissimilarity between pairs of HRQL-related words, phrases, or concepts (e.g., "unable to dress myself," and "feeling useless"). The goal is to place the words or phrases in a multidimensional space such that the distances between them (i.e., the interpoint distance) accurately reflect the ratings of similarity provided by the members of the cultures. Thus, HRQL-related concepts that are judged to be very similar should lie close together in the multidimensional scaling solution. The dimensions of the space created by the multidimensional scaling analysis

may then be interpreted as the dimensions along which people make judgments of similarity between the HRQL-related concepts. For example, it is possible that task-related HRQL concepts (e.g., "unable to dress myself") may cluster together, and lie at one end of a particular dimension. Simultaneously, some concepts tapping an affective component of HRQL (e.g., "feeling useless") may cluster together, and lie at the other end of the same dimension. That dimension may then be considered a *functional-emotional* dimension, with positive values reflecting functional items and negative values reflecting more affective or emotional items.

An examination of the solution space created by each multidimensional scaling analysis reveals information about which concepts cluster together or remain separated on various dimensions. By examining multidimensional scaling solutions created in different cultures, researchers may be better able to understand the definitions and importance attached to each dimension in each culture in both functional-states and personal value judgments approaches.

Individual difference scaling (29) is useful in determining dimensional differences between cultures. This type of analysis addresses the issue of conceptual equivalence by allowing a direct visualization of the conceptualization of the construct across cultures. The results of the multidimensional scaling analysis reveal the importance of the dimensions of HRQL in the various cultures. If the dimensions are similarly defined across cultures, and if each dimension is given similar weight across cultures, then there is evidence that HRQL is defined similarly, or conceptually equivalent across cultures. If the construct is not conceptually equivalent, then it will be necessary to use multigroup factor analysis to determine and adjust for the specific differences between cultures.

Multigroup Factor Analysis

Multigroup factor analysis may be used to test a variety of hypotheses regarding equivalence of a construct across cultures. Briefly, a single-group factor analysis is used to determine the nature of the factors, or latent variables underlying a set of correlated, measured variables. For example, the composition of the subscales underlying the correlated items of an HRQL questionnaire are explored, as well as the interrelations among the subscales. In a multigroup factor analysis, hypotheses regarding the similarity of the number of factors, form and degree of the interrelations among the factors and measured variables, and the levels of the factors across groups are tested. The basic procedure is conceptually simple: independent, random samples of persons are obtained from each culture and administered an identical questionnaire. The goal is to determine whether the responses to the questionnaire may be modeled similarly across cultures. It should be emphasized that it will not be possible to prove definitively that the underlying construct is the same across cultures. However, to the degree that it is expected that the instrument measures the underlying construct, and to the degree that the responses may be similarly modeled across cultures, evidence is obtained that supports the hypothesis that the construct is equivalent across cultures.

One approach to examining the similarities of the factor-analytic solutions across cultures is to begin by hypothesizing a low level of invariance across cultures, and proceed by testing hypotheses regarding increasing levels of invariance. Each level of the hypothesis-testing hierarchy presupposes that equivalence was revealed at the previous level. That is, the process begins by testing whether the form of the factor structure, described below, is the same across cultures. Assuming that equivalence is shown at each level of invariance, the process ends by testing whether the levels of the factors are similar across cultures. A brief example follows.

Suppose that we administer a 40-item HRQL questionnaire, representing either assessment approach, to people in France, England, and the United States. The first test of invariance concerns the number of underlying factors (i.e., subscales), and the items that are related to (i.e., load on) those factors. Here, we are not concerned with the actual values of the parameters to be estimated; rather, we are interested in whether the form of the factor structure is the same across groups. If we find that the form of the factor structure is different (e.g., if there are only three subscales or factors in the French group and four in the British group), then there is not much sense in testing more restricted hypotheses. In such a case, it is likely that the instrument either measures different constructs across cultures, or the construct cannot be assessed adequately using this instrument in all cultures. However, if we find that the numbers of factors and the patterns of variables relating to the factors are the same across groups, then we have reason to test further hypotheses regarding equivalence.

At the next level, we test for similarity of the parameter values across the cultural groups. The first group of parameters to be tested is the factor loadings (i.e., the degree to which each factor is related to each measured variable). If these parameters are equivalent across groups, then we have evidence that the measured variables are related to the latent variables similarly across cultures, addressing the issues of conceptual and operational equivalence described above. We may further test whether the errors in measurement are similar across groups, and whether the interrelations among the latent variables are equivalent across cultures. If the factors are interrelated similarly across groups, and if they are related to the measured variables similarly, then we have evidence for internal structure congruence described above.

Finally, some factor analyses test the similarity of levels of the latent variable across groups. For example, our 40-item questionnaire may contain a subscale that, based on the variables composing it, we call Satisfaction with Relationships. We may be interested in determining whether the level of this latent variable is similar across groups. To answer this question, we may test whether the means of the latent variables are equivalent across cultures. Furthermore,

we may test whether the relationship between the means of the measured variables and the means of the latent variables is the same across groups, addressing the issue of scalar equivalence discussed above.

Adjusting the Analysis for Cultural Differences

When any of the above analyses (except the test of similarity of factor levels, or means) reveals group differences, a question arises as to how best to analyze the data. In such situations, the data should not be pooled; there is evidence that the data are distributed differently across groups, and there is evidence that the construct underlying the data may not behave in the same way across groups. One way to approach the analysis of such data is to compute factor scores. For example, we may discover that the same form of the factor structure for a given questionnaire exists in England, France, and the United States; that is, the same items are related to the same subscales across cultures. However, the items composing those subscales are related to the latent variable to radically different degrees across cultures; thus, it is inappropriate to simply sum the items representing a subscale and compare those sums across cultures. Instead, it is reasonable to combine the responses to those items according to the weights that appear in the factor pattern. The resultant factor scores have statistical properties that allow for comparisons across groups. In interpreting such scores, it is reasonable to assume that the same construct underlies the subscales. However, it is necessary to bear in mind that various items are related to the construct across cultures differentially.

Multigroup factor analysis can reveal a variety of differences in the responses to a questionnaire by members of different cultures. These differences may be found at a number of different levels in the analysis. To some extent, these differences may be adjusted for using factor scores. However, it is important to note that the differences themselves should be explored. The investigator would want to demonstrate that any differences found were not a result of inequivalence in item meanings across cultures. It is advisable to closely examine the differences between cultures and determine whether a covariate might account for differences in factor scores. For example, a questionnaire that measures the effect of an intervention on HRQL might differ across two cultures because of socioeconomic differences. If these differences can be revealed, then it is possible to adjust for them in further analyses of the questionnaire using analysis of covariance or other techniques. For these reasons, it is critical to examine both the similarities and the differences in the factor structures across cultures.

Hierarchical Models and Cross-Cultural Equivalence

As discussed previously, the notion of cross-cultural equivalence of HRQL relies on the fact that HRQL is internally equivalent across cultural groups, that is, the construct comprises the same elements in all cultures. Another important step in establishing cross-cultural equivalence is to determine whether HRQL is related to other relevant variables similarly across cultures. If it is assumed that HRQL can be captured appropriately in a questionnaire, then establishing functional equivalence involves establishing the questionnaire's external, predictive, concurrent, or construct validity in each culture. If the construct validity (as well as the internal structure) is similar across cultures, there is further evidence that this measure is appropriate for cross-cultural use. The examination of construct validity across cultures is easily performed using hierarchical models.

Hierarchical models are appropriate when variables are measured at more than one level of a hierarchy. For example, in an HRQL analysis in which the HRQL measure is known to correlate with disability, the relation between the HRQL questionnaire and a disability variable within cultures is measured. This relation is a measure of the construct validity of the questionnaire. Then, the difference between these relations across cultures is examined. Thus, the levels of the hierarchy may be called *within culture* and *between culture*. The goal of the analysis is to determine whether there are significant, statistical differences in the construct validity of the HRQL questionnaire (represented by the relation between HRQL and the disability variable) between cultures.

A hierarchical analysis may be conceptualized as follows: for each culture, we obtain a correlation coefficient that represents the correlation between the HRQL questionnaire and disability. Then an analysis of variance is performed using the correlation coefficient as the dependent variable and the cultural group as the grouping variable. The result is an estimate of the degree to which the construct validity varies across cultures.

An extension of this logic will allow the examination of the effect of specific cultural differences on construct validity. For example, if we administer an HRQL questionnaire and a health status questionnaire to people in different cultures, we might find that they are correlated differently across cultures. We may include covariates in the between-cultures level of the analysis, just as we include covariates in a typical analysis of covariance. In this way, we may account for differences in the correlation across cultures by including other variables in the analysis. Thus, hierarchical models provide an excellent framework for the examination of functional equivalence of the HRQL construct.

Differential Item Functioning: Analysis at the Item Level

After analyzing a questionnaire using factor-analytic and other techniques, it may become apparent that some items on the questionnaire are suspect, that is, these items are not performing similarly across cultures. It may be necessary to closely examine these items to determine whether they must be reworded or removed from the questionnaire. One method of determining whether an item is performing differently across cultures involves differential item functioning (DIF).

DIF is an extension of a field of psychometrics called item-response theory. The goal of a DIF analysis is to determine whether two people (from different cultural groups) with similar levels of the underlying, latent variable representing the construct HRQL have the same probability of responding positively to the item. If the two matched people have different probabilities of answering the question positively, then the item is said to exhibit DIF. If the DIF is large enough (as determined by technical criteria not described here), then the item should be reworded or removed from the questionnaire.

CONCLUSIONS

While a variety of psychosocial measures in anthropology, psychology, and sociology (2,28,30,31) have received rigorous psychometric investigation with respect to cross-cultural validation, for many outcome measures in medical and public health research this has not been the case. In HRQL research, it has been all too common to accept either that assumptions of generality of psychometric properties across cultural groups are met, or are inherent in the construct itself. As Leplege and Verdier (27) have noted, it is not unusual to find cross-cultural adaptation limited to rudimentary methods of translation to a target language.

In the last few years the growing need for HRQL measures to support multinational clinical trials in which data can be aggregated across sites has stimulated efforts to perform more extensive cross-cultural validation of HRQL instruments. The recent IQOLA project methodology (27,32) describes an exemplary approach to comprehensive cross-cultural development and validation of an HRQL instrument, which largely represents the functional-states approach. We are not aware of a comparable level of cross-cultural adaptation for measures using the personal value judgments approach.

The assumptions of generality of the construct HRQL and of its indicators and scale are necessary if data are to be aggregated across countries or cultural groups. However, the fundamental views of the construct HRQL in the functional-states and personal value judgments approaches lead to different specifications about these assumptions and how they are evidenced. This is an important aspect to note in reviewing or conducting cross-national validation studies of HRQL instruments. We must note, however, that a formal theoretical framework describing the implicit and explicit assumptions in the functional-states and personal value judgments approaches has not been developed in the literature. The assumptions we have listed for each HRQL assessment approach are our conclusions. They are synthesized from the rationale and objectives stated by the developers of some of the HRQL measures, and, de facto, from the way HRQL instruments' scores are interpreted. An evaluation of the feasibility of the cross-cultural use of HRQL instruments requires the use of both HRQL theory and statistical models of cross-cultural equivalence.

While the choice of criterion or comparison variables for validating HRQL instruments and the specific analyses necessary may vary according to the conceptual view of HRQL, the forms of evidence regarding measurement equivalence needed are the same. This chapter reviewed several psychometric methods by which the various assumptions of cross-cultural generality of the construct HRQL can be formally tested. In this regard, a key issue is that results from statistical models on cross-cultural validity are meaningful only when they can be related to the underlying theoretical model of HRQL chosen or developed.

It may be all too tempting to adopt a singular view of HRQL and exclude from consideration competing assessment approaches. However, it is unlikely that reliance on one assessment strategy will be adequate. Instead, the emphasis of one approach augments the other: personal value judgments are vital to assessing HRQL by providing unique information not collected by the more traditional functional states approach. Indeed, many studies have incorporated HRQL instruments or batteries that include measures from both approaches; it is only the cross-validation of the two approaches within a single analytical framework that seems to have lagged behind. Finally, the goal of adapting an HRQL instrument for cross-cultural use should not be to eliminate or obscure real differences in HRQL among cultures, but to accurately measure HRQL across cultural groups. Such systematic differences are valuable toward furthering our understanding of the undoubtedly large contribution of culture to HRQL.

REFERENCES

1. Kohlmann T. Aggregation of quality of life data from different countries and interpretation of results. *Br J Med Econ* 1993;6C:35–44.
2. Hui C, Triandis HC. Measurement in cross-cultural psychology: a review and comparison of strategies. *Cross Cultural Psychol* 1985;16: 131–152.
3. Berzon R, Shumaker S. A critical review of cross national health-related quality of life instruments. *QOL Newsletter* 1993;92(5):2.
4. Avis NE, Smith KW. Conceptual and methodological issues in selecting and developing quality of life measures. In: Albrecht G, Fitzpatrick R, eds. *Advances in medical sociology, vol V: Quality of life in health care.* Greenwich, CT: JAI Press, 1994.
5. Shumaker SA, Anderson RT, Czjkowski SM. Psychological tests and scales. In: Spilker B, ed. *Quality of life assessment in clinical trials.* New York: Raven Press, 1990.
6. World Health Organization. *Constitution of the World Health Organization.* Geneva: Who Basic Documents, 1978.
7. Anastasi A. *Psychological testing,* 5th ed. New York: Macmillan, 1964:343–349.
8. Naughton MJ, Wiklund I. A critical review of dimension-specific measures of health-related quality of life in cross cultural research. *Qual Life Res* 1993;2:397–432.
9. Shumaker SA, Anderson RT. The selection of health-related quality of life measures for older adults with cardiovascular disease. In: Walter P, ed. *Coronary bypass surgery in the elderly: ethical economical and quality of life aspects.* Dordrecht, The Netherlands: Kluwer Academic, 1995.
10. Herzog RA. Measurement of vitality in the Americans' changing lives study. In: Feirleib M, ed. Proceedings of 1988 International Symposium on Data on Aging. Vital and Health Statistics, Series 5 (6). Washington, DC: DHHS, Publication No. (PHS) 91-1482, 1991:223–234.
11. Callahan CM, Wolinsky F. The effect of gender and race on the measurement properties of the CES-D in older adults. *Med Care* 1994;32(4):341–356.
12. Kessler RC, McLeod J. Social support and psychological distress in community surveys. In: Cohen S, Syme L, eds. *Social support and health.* New York: Academic Press, 1984.
13. Aaronson NK, Acquadro C, Alonso J, et al. International Quality of Life Assessment (IQOLA) Project. *Qual Life Res* 1992;1:349–351.
14. Leplege A, Verdier A. Adaptation of health status measures—a discussion of mean approaches with special attention to the IQOLA methodology. Paper presented at the International Society of Behavioral Medicine, Amsterdam, The Netherlands, July 9, 1994.
15. Hunt SM, Alonso J, Bucquet D, Niero M, Wiklund I, McKenna S. Cross-cultural adaptation of health measures. *Health Policy* 1991;19: 33–44.
16. Calman KC. Quality of life in cancer patients—a hypothesis. *J Med Ethics* 1984;10:24.
17. Cantril H. *The pattern of human concerns.* New Jersey: Rutgers University Press, 1965.
18. Ruta DA, Garratt AM, Leng M, et al. A new approach to the measurement of quality of life: The Patient Generated Index. *Med Care* 1994; 32(11):1109–1126.
19. Guyatt GH. The philosophy of health-related quality of life translation. *Qual Life Res* 1993;2(6):461–465.
20. Patrick DL, Danis M, Southerland L, et al. Quality of life following intensive care. *J Gen Intern Med* 1988;3:218–223.
21. Andrews FM, Witley SB. Social indicators of well-being: Americans' perceptions of life quality. New York: Plenum, 1976.
22. Hays RD, Anderson R, Revicki D. Psychometric considerations in evaluating health-related quality of life measures. *Qual Life Res* 1993;2:441–450.
23. Avis NE, Smith KW, Feldman H. *Multidimensional Index of Life Quality* (MILQ). New England Research Institute, 1994.
24. O'Boyle CA, McGee H, Hickey A, et al. Individual quality of life in patients undergoing hip replacement. *Lancet* 1993;339:1088.
25. Anderson RT, Aaronson NK, Wilkin D. Critical review of international assessment of health related quality of life. *Qual Life Res* 1993;2:369–397.
26. Hunt SM, Wicklund I. Cross-cultural variation in the weighing of health statements: a comparison of English and Swedish valuations. *Health Policy* 1987;8:227–235.
27. Leplege A, Verdier A. The adaptation of health status measures: methodological aspects of the translation procedure. In: Shumaker S, Berzon R, eds. *The international assessment of health-related quality of life.* Oxford, England: Rapid Communications of Oxford, 1995.
28. Brislin R, Louner W, Thorndike R. *Cross cultural research methods.* New York: Wiley, 1993.
29. Carol JD, Chang J. Analysis of individual differences in multidimension scaling via an analysis of N-way generalization of "Eckant-Young" decomposition. *Psychometrica* 1970;35:283–319.
30. Cattell RB. Comparing factor trait and state scores across age and cultures. *J Gerontol* 1969;24:348–360.
31. Finifter B. The robustness of cross-cultural findings. *Ann NY Acad Sci* 1977;285:151–184.
32. Ware JE, Gandek B, and the IQOLA Project Group. The SF-36 Health Survey: development and use in mental health research and the IQOLA project. *Int J Mental Health* 1994;23:49–73.

Quality of Life and Pharmacoeconomics in Clinical Trials, Second Edition, edited by B. Spilker.
Lippincott-Raven Publishers, Philadelphia © 1996.

CHAPTER **67**

International Use and Application of Generic Health-Related Quality of Life Instruments

Roger T. Anderson, Neil K. Aaronson, Alain P. Leplège, and David Wilkin

INTRODUCTION

The goal of having health-related quality of life (HRQL) instruments that may be used cross-nationally in research stems, in part, from the need to pool data from multinational studies in a single analytical structure in clinical trials, and to compare and summarize results across independently conducted studies. While progress toward this goal has recently accelerated, the development of cross-culturally comparable and sensitive HRQL measures is a continual process of validation, and a matter of degree rather than an absolute property.

This chapter describes research conducted in adapting or developing generic HRQL instruments for cross-national use, and reviews the psychometric evidence relating to these instruments. Our evaluations include an assessment of the level of cross-cultural development a given measure appears to have reached. The scope of this review covers several generic health quality of life measures including the Nottingham Health Profile (NHP) (1), the Sickness Impact Profile (SIP) (2), the Medical Outcomes Study Short Form–36 (MOS SF-36) (3), the EuroQol (4), and the Dartmouth/ COOP Charts (5). These instruments are presented below according to their date of original publication. One generic HRQL instrument, the World Health Organization Quality of Life (WHOQOL) (6), is still in the preliminary stages of its development and hence psychometric data were not available for evaluation at the time this chapter was prepared.

At the same time that generic instruments have been developed for international use, disease-specific measures have been developed and adapted. The reader is referred to Chapter 21 for a prominent example of this genre of HRQL instrument, the European Research and Treatment of Cancer (EORTC) Quality of Life Questionnaire (QLQ) (7).

This chapter relied on published research and descriptive materials placed in the public domain. While the literature search was broad based over time (1980 through August 1994), geography, and content, some international studies or reports on HRQL measures were undoubtedly excluded from this review. For the most part this will have occurred where the material was wholly published in a language other than English, or where the research was conducted in countries outside of Western Europe or North America. To supplement the coverage of HRQL material accessed, published bibliographies of HRQL studies were used (8,9), and assistance was sought from HRQL researchers outside the United States.

R. T. Anderson: Department of Public Health Sciences, Bowman Gray School of Medicine, Wake Forest University, Winston-Salem, North Carolina 27157.

N. K. Aaronson: Division of Psychosocial Research and Epidemiology, The Netherlands Cancer Institute, 1066 CX Amsterdam, The Netherlands.

A. P. Leplège: Institut National de la Santé et de la Recherche Medical, Hospital de Bicetre, 94275 LKB Cedex, France.

D. Wilkin: Centre for Primary Care Research and Development, University of Manchester, Manchester M13 9PL, England.

The instruments reviewed below are judged mainly in terms relevant to cross-cultural development. In selecting instruments for cross-cultural use, researchers need to consider the development and psychometric properties of the parent or source instrument. Appropriate use of an HRQL instrument is conditional upon such issues as the range of severity of illness or nature of the patient population to be studied, the conceptualization and operationalization of the concept health-related quality of life, and whether transitory or chronic diseases or symptoms are to be measured. In-depth, critical reviews of most of the major HRQL instruments reviewed here can be found in books by McDowell and Newell (10), Wilkin et al. (11), and Wenger et al. (12).

CROSS-CULTURAL MEASUREMENT EQUIVALENCE

Evaluations of whether a measure can be used cross-culturally are qualified by specific issues involving the intended use of the measure, the population or sample, country, study design, and goals of the project. We have taken the more limited approach of describing the general cross-cultural achievements of each measure reviewed. This includes an assessment of the level of measurement equivalence that has been achieved supporting cross-cultural use, and the types of information needed for a more definitive assessment of comparability. Along another axis, a distinction must be made between evidence collected on an instrument's conceptual and psychometric properties within various cultures, versus between cultures where data has been aggregated in a multinational (or cultural) study and analyzed. While an ability to replicate an instrument's conceptual and psychometric properties within different countries is essential for conducting cross-cultural research, it does not of itself demonstrate validity for cross-cultural comparisons. We have noted this distinction in this review.

Four types of equivalence that may be evaluated across research settings are (a) conceptual equivalence, (b) operational equivalence, (c) scale equivalence, and (d) metric equivalence (5). These are the major sources that affect reliability and validity across culturally adapted or language-adapted versions of an instrument.

Conceptual equivalence has to do with whether the items in the target language version of a scale are similar in meaning to the source version. This form of equivalence goes beyond mere literal equivalence of how items are worded or described.

Operational equivalence refers to the adapted instrument's relative performance using various modes of questionnaire administration supported by the instrument (e.g., self-administered, telephone, and postal versions). This property can be evaluated by comparisons of psychometric performance (reliability and validity) and response distributions of items, as well as the quality of data obtained (e.g., missing data) for the different methods supported.

Scale or *construct equivalence* concerns how similarly the culturally adapted or translated versions perform psychometrically across versions. Key attributes on which the various language versions of the instrument are tested include reliability, validity, and responsiveness to change.

Finally, *metric equivalence* is the extent to which the adapted measures place individuals who are similar with regard to the HRQL states being measured on the same point in the continuum of scores. Investigating this property is difficult because an obvious "gold standard" is lacking. Calibrating scores using patient groups, clinical status outcomes, or population norms are some of the approaches taken to evaluating metric equivalence.

MODELS FOR DEVELOPING CROSS-CULTURAL INSTRUMENTS

Of the generic HRQL instruments identified in the literature for which cultural or language adaptations have been generated, several distinct strategies or models of adaptation can be identified. These underlying models are important to consider because they may affect, to some extent, the comparisons made across the language versions. Various models of instrument development are discussed in detail in the chapter by Bullinger et al.

The most common model for developing cross-national HRQL measures is the sequential model. This is exemplified by the Nottingham Health Profile (NHP) (1) and the Sickness Impact Profile (SIP) (2). These are existing measures that have been adapted to various language groups after substantial use in research in the country of origin. Newer instruments, such as the SF-36 (3), have taken a fast-track to international use with international adaptation beginning shortly after the original was developed, validated, and published. While it is not expected in the sequential model that the original source instrument would be revised on the basis of experience gained from cross-cultural applications, a universal version could be developed.

Another model for developing cross-national measures seeks to establish a basis for cross-national comparability in the original development and validation stages of the instrument. This model is referred to as parallel development. The WONCA (World Organization of General Practitioners and Family Physicians) developed version of the Dartmouth COOP charts (5) and the EuroQol group generic instrument (4) are examples. A common set of items is identified that is relevant to all countries or cultures specified. In this way, the goal of universal item content is inherent in the early stages of the instrument's development.

Simultaneous development of national HRQL versions of an instrument is the final model discussed. This approach seeks to build in cultural diversity in content for the various HRQL dimensions across national versions. This is a relatively new approach, and is currently being used by the World Health Organization in developing its quality of life instrument, the WHOQOL (6). Here, the item content and question format is allowed to differ across language versions according to cultural and normative experiences of each country. This approach may be necessary where sharp differences between lifestyle and culture are expected, such as in contrasts between Western European and Asian or African cultures.

Depending on the approach taken, there may be some important differences in the type of evidence needed to demonstrate equivalence. The sequential model holds the original version as a ''gold standard'' and seeks to examine the degree of universality of the measure in other cultures. Here, there is no *a priori* basis or assurance that the items' meanings and concepts will adequately translate in the target culture. Thus, comparability of a given language version will initially be influenced by whether the content of the original version is indeed universal to the culture or language group tested, and the quality of the translation. In contrast, instruments that were originally developed for multinational use have already undergone considerable testing and item selection to ensure universality of content. In the simultaneous model, equivalence of item meaning and content are allowed to differ by setting, and the focus instead would be on whether a common set of core measures exists across countries.

A TYPOLOGY FOR ASSESSING THE CROSS-CULTURAL DEVELOPMENT OF INSTRUMENTS

As stated above, cross-cultural equivalence in measurement is a matter of degree rather than being an absolute. A general typology of the level of cross-cultural equivalence for which an instrument version has been tested corresponds, roughly, to the methods and level of psychometric testing undertaken. An outline of a general typology of instrument development is shown in Table 1.

A first or *preliminary level* of measurement equivalence (level 1) that instruments may demonstrate is whether they appear to be qualitatively similar between cultures (13). The hallmark of this level is achieving similar face or content validity among versions. Generally, this means that translation has been methodically performed so that the general meaning of the items has been preserved across language versions. Ideally the methods of translation should be similar for all versions considered.

TABLE 1. *Categorization of HRQL instrument development by level and type of measurement equivalence*

Measurement features	Level		
	1	2	3
Conceptual equivalence	+	++	++
Scale or construct equivalence	−	+	++
Metric equivalence	−	−	+

−, insufficient or no evidence; +, satisfactory basic testing; ++, well established, comprehensive testing.

For instruments that were developed sequentially, face validity achieved at this stage rests upon the assumption of universality of HRQL indicators selected for the original source instrument. This should be assessed as part of the translation process (e.g., common word usage, conceptual equivalence, and difficulty of translation). Instruments developed with either parallel or simultaneous approaches have empirically established face validity as they were originally developed to contain indicators of health concepts that are reproduced in several cultures.

Level 1 instrument development may also include rudimentary psychometric testing of the translated instrument (reliability and criterion or construct validity). Similarity in performance across versions would provide preliminary evidence that these versions are measuring the same property or aspects of HRQL. This information is preliminary at this level, since both differences in research designs and materials across studies (e.g., patient population and demographics, protocol, inclusion and exclusion criteria), and the preliminary level of psychometric testing make it impossible to determine more precisely the nature and extent of conceptual equivalence between versions. As such, level 1 studies fall short of meeting the measurement requirements for pooling data across international sites, or studying between site differences.

Whereas level 1 development lacks both depth in psychometric testing and coordinated or systematic comparisons of instrument versions, an *intermediate level* (level 2) of cross-cultural development occurs when one of these two conditions has, in addition, been met. In this case, considerably more information is available about cross-cultural equivalence. This level largely represents a transition stage, where level 1 development has been advanced either by more extensive psychometric testing or by replicating validation methods used with the original source or standard version. At this level of development, direct assessment of cross-cultural equivalence between national versions still awaits comprehensive psychometric testing (e.g., formal tests of item and scale measurement models) systematically across versions (e.g., using common data collection protocols and clinical criterion variables).

Level 2 development may include replication studies of basic types of validity (e.g., known groups validity) and reliability using similar research designs and protocols across versions. This removes variability from noncultural sources such as differences in research methods, sampling, treatment, and protocol between studies. Alternatively, level 2 development can include instances where a language version has had fairly extensive psychometric testing (e.g., item analysis, factor analysis, and scaling analysis), but where considerable differences exist between versions in research methods and materials, confounding exact comparisons. This can occur, for example, when a language-adapted version of an HRQL instrument has received substantially more psychometric testing than the original. In this event, thorough testing may reveal the suitability of the instrument for use within a specific culture or country, but not for its cross-cultural use.

In summary, level 2 instrument development provides substantially more insight on cross-cultural equivalence by assessing scale or construct equivalence. Thus, this level would provide greater assurance of an instrument's ability to measure a construct reliably across cultural settings. Practical uses of instruments with level 2 development include independent research to corroborate evidence found in other cultures using the same measurement technology, or to generate research results that may be generalized across settings. By extension, studies using level 2 instruments could be included in meta-analyses of international studies to explore apparent trends or patterns associated with a treatment or manipulation.

At the far end of the continuum of instrument development is full or complete *cross-cultural validation* (level 3). At this level, validation has gone beyond that normally achieved with instruments used within cultures (10,11) to include a common set of statistical analysis of item performance, scale validity and calibration of scores systematically, and benchmarks or criteria among instrument versions (14). Differences attributable to sample composition such as age, gender, or illness severity can be accounted for, either statistically or by design. Thus, the hallmark of this level is that scale and metric equivalence of the developed versions can be formally tested and compared. This level of measurement equivalence has been considered necessary for pooling data across studies or versions (15).

A REVIEW OF GENERIC HRQL INSTRUMENTS

In this section we report on the features and level of cross-cultural development achieved for some of the major generic HRQL instruments. The continuum of development described above is used as a guide to summarization, although it should be noted that within each level important differences may be found between instruments. A complete description of the psychometric properties of the original, nonadapted, versions of these instruments can be found elsewhere in this volume.

Nottingham Health Profile

Purpose and Description

The Nottingham Health Profile (NHP) (1) is a self-administered measure of perceived distress relating to severe or potentially disabling health conditions. There are two separate measures within the NHP; completion of the entire NHP is reported to take 10 to 15 minutes (1). Only Part I, the major and most often used component of the NHP, is reviewed below.

The NHP (Part I) contains 38 items organized into six domains of distress: energy level, pain, emotional reactions, sleep, social isolation, and physical abilities (1). Summated scores are obtained for each NHP domain; an overall score is not provided. Items are scored 0 for a ''no'' response and 1 for a ''yes'' response, affirming the distress condition. Item weights are used to reflect varying levels of perceived distress among the items in the scale, using Thurstone scaling methods (16). They are transformed to yield scores ranging from 0 (no items checked) to 100 (all items checked) per scale.

Overview of Psychometric Properties in Country of Origin

The NHP has been used widely in England in patient populations with severe and moderately severe illnesses (17–26). Test-retest reliability reported for the six NHP domains appears adequate, with correlation coefficients between .77 (energy) and .85 (physical mobility and sleep) in patient samples with chronic illness or severe disability (1,27). Internal consistency of the NHP items and scales has not been reported.

Construct validity of the NHP is affirmed in the pattern of correlations among its scales, which, like other generic instruments (e.g., the Sickness Impact Profile, and the MOS SF-36), have shown general dimensions of emotional and physical health status underlying the various health states measured. Construct validity has been examined largely with known group comparisons of moderate to severe illness with well or mild-illness groups, or both. These studies indicate that the NHP can separate the extremes of severe from nonsevere illness or well groups, or groups using community health services (1,18).

An important consideration in evaluating the NHP is the range of distress from health impairment it was developed to measure. The developers of the NHP state explicitly that the NHP was *not* intended to measure HRQL in general population samples, or mildly affected patient groups (1,28). In fact, somewhat less precision is found in the NHP when used for minor or less than major disabling conditions (29,30). For example, the NHP pain score in patients with chronic migraine approximated that found for general patient samples (14.9 versus 15.9) (21), suggesting lower precision in detecting moderate differences in NHP pain severity not involving motion and mobility. Although the NHP emotional distress scale correlated moderately with the General Health Questionnaire (GHQ) ($r = .49$), it did not detect a more than twofold increase in prevalence of GHQ emotional distress found in a migraine patient group relative to an arthritic patient group. Additionally, while the NHP subscales have been shown to be responsive to changes associated with a variety of treatments such as heart/lung transplant (31) and recovery from limb fracture (32), they did not detect impacts of minor surgery (29) or mild levels of pain, emotional distress, and general health perceptions as identified with the MOS 20-item health status measure (33).

International Versions

The reported psychometric qualities of the NHP and acceptability demonstrated by its wide use has led to considerable international use of this measure. The literature shows the latter has consisted of independently conducted single site studies; none of these reports included multinational clinical trial designs.

The international adaptation of the NHP has been guided by the developers of the original NHP, and includes versions in French, Dutch, Swedish, Spanish, and Italian. In addition, work on versions in German, Finnish, and Danish is ongoing (34).

Adaptation procedures have been similar, but not identical for each of the four language versions currently available. The core translation methodology includes an independent item translation by a panel of 8 to 12 experts representing community medicine, sociology, health research, and medical specialties. Items are translated by bilinguals to attempt to replicate the underlying concept in the original, and graded by consensus of the panel whereby the highest-rated translation per item is selected. Item face validity of the draft version is evaluated by a lay panel with regard to naturalness, comprehensibility, and acceptability of the items. This is followed by a field test of face validity conducted in patient samples, leading to additional revisions. Back-translations are conducted to review conceptual equivalence based on lay samples.

The composition of the panel and lay samples was not replicated across studies, and may have differed in important ways (i.e., level of education, age, gender, and impairment) (34). Further, the sample composition and protocol used to obtain the item weights in the adapted versions cannot be compared directly to the original as a detailed description of the latter study was not located in the literature.

Language Versions

Research reporting on the psychometric properties of language-adapted NHP versions has appeared for French, Dutch, Spanish, and Swedish versions.

French

Bucquet et al. (35) published results pertaining to translation and adaptation of a French version of the NHP. Thurstone scaling was carried out using 625 hospital outpatients and nonpatients from a wide range of social backgrounds. Recruitment of the sample was similar to the general methods described above, but relied on population quota sampling. Spearman rank correlations of item ranks between the French and source versions were above .90 for the mobility, sleep, social isolation, and energy dimensions; the pain dimension and emotional reaction dimensions were less highly correlated (Spearman's $r = .76$, and $r = .58$ respectively) with the source instrument. Some item ranks were found to be discordant with the original weights, particularly in the Emotional Reaction scale. However, these weights were generally within a few scale points of the original. Variations in perceived severity of items by sociodemographic characteristics of the judges were found for all of the NHP dimensions. In this regard, significant discordance between ranks occurred on 31 of the 115 item pairs across sociodemographic groups, with most disagreement in the NHP physical mobility subscale.

Reliability. Data on reliability were not reported in the literature.

Validity. Data on construct and/or criterion validity were not reported in the literature.

Dutch

Van Schayck and colleagues (36) administered a Dutch version of the NHP in a randomized controlled clinical study of bronchodilator treatment involving 223 patients with chronic obstructive pulmonary disease or asthma with a mild to moderate airflow obstruction.

Reliability. Data on reliability were not reported in the literature.

Validity. The Dutch NHP Sleep and Pain scales discriminated between asthma and chronic obstructive pulmonary disease patients and general population norms like those found in an English study (37). However, the domain scales were generally not responsive to declines in lung function. Other measures of recent or acute changes in HRQL by which the performance of the NHP could be assessed were not included in the study.

Spanish

Alonso and colleagues (38,39) reported on the use of a Spanish version of the NHP. Item weights for the Spanish NHP were not produced prior to the validation, and are reported to be under development (38).

Reliability. Data on reliability were not reported in the literature.

Validity. Construct validity of the NHP has been tested against self-reported health, use of primary health services, and clinical status indicators (38,39). The Spanish version was correlated with levels of self-reported health, number of chronic conditions, recent use of health services (yes/no), and clinically assessed disease severity. The Spanish NHP scales, with the exception of the Social Isolation scale, discriminated levels of functional status and health in chronic obstructive pulmonary disease patients as measured by the Dyspnea Grade scale. Further, the NHP Energy and Physical Mobility scales discriminated among quartiles in the 6-minute walk performance in which lower performance related to higher levels of NHP distress. It is uncertain whether the HRQL dimensions not responding to performance or Dyspnea Grade levels either did not vary significantly, or whether the effects were below the threshold for detection in NHP scales. General population NHP scores obtained in Barcelona do not appear to be highly similar to those found in general population samples in England (36,37).

The Spanish NHP scores on energy and pain were also reported to correlate with duration of an exercise test in a sample of male cardiac patients with stable angina or recent coronary artery bypass graft surgery (38). The NHP did not discriminate between groups classified by the number of diseased vessels or functional class in symptomatic patients. Since exercise performance may achieve a wider separation of patients by severity of symptoms than clinical status, these results are consistent with the general performance of the NHP in detecting distress associated with physical health or disability.

Swedish

Of all international NHP versions, the Swedish NHP appears to be the most widely used and psychometrically evaluated. Most of this work has been conducted by Wiklund and colleagues (23,40–43), who have used this instrument to study HRQL in patients with arthritis of the hip joint, post-menopausal disorders, hypertension, and asthma.

Weights for the Swedish version were obtained, like the original, using Thurstone's method of paired comparisons in a study involving 202 outpatients, nonpatients, and their relatives (40). Rank correlation coefficients for item weights between the original and Swedish NHP ranged from 0.5 (energy) to 1.0 (sleep, and social isolation), with the coefficient for most scales in the high .80s. The low correlation observed for the energy scale resulted from one of three items being discordant with the original by one rank. The largest discordance was the emotional reactions scale, in which only one of the nine items in the scale was ranked identically to the source version. The overall assessment provided by the investigators (42) is that valuations placed on health problems in the NHP were quite similar in both cultures.

Reliability. In patients with arthritis of the hip joint, high test-retest reliability (4-week time interval) in the overall NHP score (Spearman's $r = .92$) was obtained for 69 (95%) patients completing the NHP at both baseline and at 4 weeks. The results for the separate dimensions ranged from .77 (social isolation) to .94 (sleep). These results are similar to the 4-week test-retest coefficients of the original NHP based on a sample of English arthritic patients (27).

The Swedish arthritis study provides the only report in the literature on internal consistency of the NHP scales. Results showed adequate internal consistency in Part I of the overall instrument ($r = .87$) (although the NHP is not an index measure) and in the NHP scales on Pain and Emotional Reactions ($r = .72$ and .81), but low internal consistency in the Social Isolation (.34), Mobility (.39), and Energy (.57) scales.

Validity. Validity of the Swedish version of the NHP was indicated by its ability to discriminate normotensives from hypertensives (23) in a pattern similar to that evidenced by comparable scales of the Subjective Symptoms Assessment Profile (emotional distress subscale) and the Minor Symptoms Evaluation Profile. Construct validity of the NHP in arthritic patients was assessed with clinically derived pre-operative scores for pain and mobility (Charnley-D'Aubignet Score (40). Results showed moderate correspondence ($r = .41$) with pain, but low correspondence with the mobility measure ($r = .22$).

The performance of the Swedish NHP in intervention studies is also consistent with the original. The NHP detected large improvements in changes in sleep, emotions, energy, and social isolation in a clinical trial of estrogen therapy involving 59 patients with postmenopausal disorders (including complaints of sweating, insomnia, depression, headache, and hot flashes) (41). Importantly, these changes were corroborated by other HRQL measures in the study. Conversely, in a randomized study of patient education for asthma (43), the NHP did not detect significant moderate improvements in emotional status, life satisfaction, and somatic problems in the education group found with specific HRQL-related measures.

Summary and Issues

Overall, the psychometric evidence reported for the NHP, based on qualitative comparisons of the data, indicate that the sequentially developed versions appear to reproduce the features of the original NHP. The cross-cultural evidence reported on the NHP does not represent a level at which formal testing of cross-cultural equivalence is complete. Continued development of the NHP would entail (a) additional benchmarks for the original NHP for comparison, including clinical significance of NHP scores, precision and responsiveness of its subscales, reliability of its item weights, a description of the relationships among subscales, and item-to-total correlations; (b) coordinated validation studies of national versions with the original, either concurrently or nonconcurrently using similar protocols, sample recruitment, and study designs; and (c) evidence of the responsiveness of the NHP across versions. Although there is no gold standard to assess HRQL measures, illness severity and functional impairment have been shown to be major determinants of NHP scores, and should be considered for international comparisons.

Some strengths in the cross-cultural development of the NHP include the systematic approach to item translations across versions, which included forward and backward translation and an iterative review of the quality of the linguistic and semantic translation. This attention to methodology supports the assumption of semantic equivalence across language versions. Qualitatively, the validity of language-adapted versions of the NHP appears to be comparable to the original. First is the evidence of similarity in the item weights of the French and Swedish versions to the original. This suggests that the underlying dimension of distress in functioning assessed by the NHP was reproduced in the language versions examined (42). Although some discordance in weights was found between versions in the Pain and Emotional Reactions scales, for many items affected the difference in ranking often was very small (i.e., one percentile point or less). Further, the discrepant items were located at the extremes of the scale where intervals between adjacent items may be unstable (17). In any case, data on the reliability of the weights in the original NHP are needed to more fully assess the significance of the dissimilarity in ranks between adapted and original versions of the NHP.

Second, the empirical data reported by which construct and criterion-related validity of the international versions can be assessed show performance consistent with the original in discriminating between major medical conditions, and symptomatic versus nonsymptomatic illness (44). This is especially true for the Swedish NHP, which, like the original, also displayed an insensitivity to moderate levels of symptom reduction or illness management (43). A more comprehensive assessment of the cross-national comparability of the NHP could include analyses of factor structure, item-discriminant validity, internal consistency of the subscale items, and the precision of the NHP scales in detecting clinically important effects and responsiveness to change.

Since item weights are used to score the NHP, preliminary evidence of metric equivalence is provided from the generally high reproducibility of item ranks. Patient norms for the various NHP subscales, floor and ceiling thresholds, reproducibility of item weights and intervals between items, and calibration studies using clinically relevant criterion measures or well-validated, accepted self-report instruments are needed for a more substantive appraisal of this feature of the NHP.

Finally, in terms of the question of overall operational equivalence in the language-adapted versions, data have not been reported comparing telephone, self-administered, and postal data collection methods.

Sickness Impact Profile

Purpose and Description

The Sickness Impact Profile (SIP) (2) was developed in the United States as a behaviorally based assessment of the impact of illness on everyday life. It covers a wide range of functioning in different areas of activity and, with its focus on behavior rather than subjective expressions, is intended to be broadly applicable across diverse demographic groups. The SIP consists of 136 yes/no statements describing limitations or recent change in 12 clinically distinguishable aspects of functioning: social interactions, communication, alertness, emotional behavior, body care, mobility, ambulation, work, eating, sleep, home management, and recreation. Respondents endorse items that apply to them on a given day due to ill health. An overall score, as well as scores for each category, are obtained by summing the items. Higher scores indicate less desirable outcomes. Equal-interval scaling of severity of health impacts covered by the items was used to determine item weights.

Validation studies have demonstrated that the SIP measures two underlying dimensions: the first four categories listed above describe psychosocial function, the next three physical function, and the remaining five are independent categories (45). Interviewer-administered, self-administered, and postal versions of the SIP are available.

Psychometric Properties in Country of Origin

A detailed review of the SIP is presented in Chapter 35 (A. Damiano) of this volume. The SIP has been widely used to assess HRQL in numerous patient populations including mild to severe health conditions (10,11,46). The instrument contains two general dimensions of psychosocial and physical functioning, consistent with other major generic HRQL measures studied (e.g., NHP, MOS). The SIP has demonstrated a high level of internal consistency and test-retest reliability (.90 and higher) with a variety of chronic disease conditions (47–51). Validity has been examined from correspondence with self-reports of dysfunction and severity of illness, clinical measures of illness, and dysfunction in chronic disease. Perhaps because of its broad scope, and the lack of validity of many traditional clinical measures, correlations between SIP total score and clinical status measures have been in the moderate range (11) (i.e., .40 to .60). However, correlations of the SIP total score and clinical measures of patients' functioning have generally been above .80. In some cases, the SIP has shown greater sensitivity to modest-sized differences in functional status due to chronic illness than some traditional clinical measures (52–55). Finally, while the independence of the 12 SIP functional dimensions has high face validity, the internal factor structure has not been empirically tested.

International Use

Due, in large part, to its comprehensive HRQL domain coverage, including subscales not available in many instruments measuring functioning, the SIP has been used widely in the United States and has seen considerable international use. Its theoretical approach of relying on behavioral impacts of health states was intended to achieve a measure of universal patterns of limitation due to illness, avoiding clinical bias expected with indicators describing feeling states (2). This feature of the SIP, combined with its generally solid psychometric properties, makes it an excellent candidate for cross-cultural development.

Language Versions

Seven translations of the SIP have been reported in Europe, including Anglican, Swedish, German, French, Danish, Norwegian, and Dutch versions (56). None of the reports on international use of the SIP involved multinational clinical trials designs.

The English-language literature contains reports of the Anglican, Swedish, Norwegian, French, and Dutch SIP versions; thus only these measures are presented below. Among these, the development of the Anglican and Dutch versions appears to have closely approximated the methods used for the original. Unlike other long-established HRQL measures, the adaptation of the SIP has included some studies replicating the conditions (e.g., procedures design and sample) under which the original was validated.

British

Patrick and colleagues (57–59) adapted and tested a British version of the SIP, designated the Functional Limitations Profile, for use in a longitudinal health survey of disability. Adaptation of the SIP to British English was conducted using British research staff to translate the statements. Further editing was carried out to preserve comparison in behavioral orientation and objectives with the source version. The statements were field tested among members of the local community (Lambeth) for further revision, and were adapted to the local dialect. A final conference was held to review the wording of each statement, and the results were sent to the developers of the SIP for final confirmation of its correspondence with the original version (57). One methodological change was reported in the format. In the original SIP, respondents endorse statements on the health-related impact on their level of functioning, whereas in the Functional Limitations Profile respondents first endorse statements on functioning and then are probed about health-relatedness.

A partial replication study was conducted to compare the relative weighting of Functional Limitations Profile statements with that of the source instrument, using equal-interval scaling methods similar to those used during the original development of the SIP (58). Two samples of judges were employed, consisting of nurses and general medical patients in Lambeth. Items were rated on a 15-point scale based on severity of dysfunction with regard to the Functional Limitations Profile category. Judges were trained in equal interval scaling, and were evaluated for proficiency. The Lambeth and Seattle mean SIP/Functional Limitations Pro-

file scale values were highly correlated at $r = .91$, but not identical. There was close agreement on items rated as severely dysfunctional, but less agreement among a few items at the least-severe end of the scale.

Reliability. Reliability of the Functional Limitations Profile scale scores over 2 days was tested in a sample of 30 disabled patients and was reported to be moderate (59), based on a review of scale score changes. However, correlation coefficients were not reported.

Validity. Validity of the Functional Limitations Profile was shown with the level of disability for self-rated health and number of medical conditions increasing with higher scores for the 12 SIP/Functional Limitations Profile categories. However, the Functional Limitations Profile global score and category scores performed poorly in discriminating level of medical service use. This perhaps reflects the SIP focus on the impact of illness on activity rather than perceived distress as in the NHP, which has shown stronger correlations with health service use. The Functional Limitations Profile global psychosocial and physical dimensions identified using cluster analysis were similar to the SIP, although some differences were noted in categories that clustered. Also similar to the SIP were the structures of the Functional Limitations Profile's eating, communication, and work categories.

French

A French version of the SIP was developed and validated in a sample of patients seeking routine medical care (60). Forward and backward translation was conducted using both professional and bilingual lay translators. Difficulty with item translations was assessed from moderate-sized differences in item ranks, compared with the original SIP under similar methodology, in a pretest of 40 patients. Problems in reproducing item valuations and/or content were reported for 28 SIP items, mostly involving the body care and movement, and social interaction subscales. Translated SIP items were further modified where problems in replicating meaning were found. It was also reported that many items remained dissimilar in ranking in the final version.

Reliability. Data on the reliability of the French language SIP were not located in the literature.

Validity. Data on the validity of the French version were not located in the literature.

Dutch

Several studies using Dutch versions of the SIP appear in the literature (61,62). A description of the validation and adaptation procedures (or its reference), however, was located only for the version developed and tested by Jacobs (61) at the University of Utrecht. Beyond testing the psychometric properties of the instrument in Dutch patient populations, the research team directly compared the translated version to the original SIP. Of all international versions of the

SIP identified, the Dutch SIP has been the most extensively studied. Content and semantic equivalence was examined using translation and back-translation methods. Difficulty encountered in finding an acceptable translation was monitored, and consultation with the developers of the original SIP guided suitable translations. All 136 SIP items were reported to be relevant to HRQL in the Dutch samples, although, initially, some difficulty was reported in translating the conceptual content of some of the emotional distress items. Item weights for the Dutch version of the SIP subscales were obtained and were reported to be strongly correlated with the original SIP weights (ranging from .80 to .97); the description of the weighting study was not available in the English language.

Reliability. Reliability of the Dutch SIP has been reported to be high in several studies. Internal consistency coefficients have been reported between .86 and .91 for total SIP scores, and of a similar magnitude for the dimension scores (61).

Validity. In addition to the close similarity in item weights found between the Dutch and original SIP, the adapted instrument was found to have behaved psychometrically in a manner consistent with the original. First, Dutch SIP scores in the physical functioning–related subscales increased (more disability) with increasing prevalence of health complaints. In addition, the psychosocial scale discriminated psychosocial from physical illnesses as has the original SIP in the U.S. samples. Second, there was evidence that general population SIP scores were highly correlated between American and Dutch samples (61). Intraclass correlations were used to examine the discriminative power of the Dutch SIP in patient samples ranging from self-limiting to serious disorders as ascertained 6 months post-baseline. SIP scores at baseline discriminated between patient groups, and after 6 months reflected the pattern in scores based on patient status in terms of transitory versus chronic illness and self-limiting versus serious illness. In another application, Schuling et al. (63) studied HRQL impact of stroke on older adults. Total SIP scores discriminated between stroke patients and patients seeking general medical care. Additionally, the specific SIP life domains affected by stroke were similar to those found in the Swedish study (64).

Results reported by Hulsebos and colleagues (65) indicate that this favorable comparison of the Dutch SIP with the original does not necessarily generalize to other methods of administration. In 221 former patients of an intensive care unit, comparing interviewer and self-administered methods of administration, a lower overall SIP score for the self-administered group compared with those interviewer administered (10.2 versus 16.3) was found. The original SIP (50) demonstrated score differences attributable to method of administration, but in the opposite direction. However, subjects were not randomized to SIP administration groups and thus the composition of the groups may have differed.

Because of the often cited concerns over the length of the SIP and lack of relevance of some items to a variety of patients, a Dutch investigative team has developed a short form of the SIP for research purposes (66). This instrument

version is currently found only in the Dutch language. This instrument, referred to as the SIP68, has 68 items divided over six functional domains: somatic autonomy, mobility, psychological autonomy and communication, social behavior, emotional stability, and mobility range. The final set of factors in the SIP68 was identified from results of a principal components analysis of a Dutch-translated version of the SIP in 835 patients representing ten different diagnostic groups (chronic conditions). Items were selected that demonstrated high factor loadings in the principal components analysis (greater than .40) and that did not yield highly skewed response patterns in the sample (affirmed by between 10% and 90% of the sample). Reliability of the SIP68 was assessed in a convenience sample of 51 outpatients of a rheumatology clinic. Test-retest reliability for subscale scores for two 48-hour periods over 18 days was high, ranging from .90 (mobility) to .97 (somatic autonomy). These coefficients are as high as those obtained for the original SIP (47–51). Internal consistency of the SIP68 was also similar to what has been found for the original SIP (approximately .90).

It is of interest that the initial analyses of the Dutch version of the SIP did not replicate 12 homogeneous factors among the original 136 SIP items as theorized. Instead, the items of functionally related SIP subscales were clustered as broader dimensions of functioning. There are no similar analyses reported of the original SIP in U.S. samples by which a cross-cultural comparison of the SIP's internal structure can be made. The finding that more than one-third of the original SIP items did not load on any factor at the specified eigenvalue level may indicate that the SIP structure of health-related functional status is not universal. However, a conclusion cannot be made without evidence of the conceptual equivalence of the translated SIP items. The items describing health impacts on work were deleted because of their cultural specificity (to the U.S.), although whether culturally equivalent translations were possible for these items is not evident from the report. It is impressive that the SIP emotional behavior factor was not replicated, and suggests that perhaps behavioral manifestations of emotional stress may differ substantially between cultures. The multidiagnostic population used in this study, combined with the methods of item selection (i.e., removal of skewed items and moderate factors loadings) likely resulted in identifying items and general factors that exist in common across very different patient groups. Arguably, many of the items dropped, such as those involving sleep and rest, communication, and dysphagia, have important health impacts to subsets of patients. Such streamlining, however, is consistent with the goals of developing a short-form.

Norwegian

Although a Norwegian translation of the SIP has been used in several clinical settings, only one report was identified in the English-language literature. HRQL was assessed with the SIP in a sample of community-living women reporting urinary incontinence (67).

Reliability. Data on the reliability of the Norwegian SIP were not located in the literature.

Validity. The Norwegian SIP was found to discriminate stress incontinence from detrusor instability in terms of the Sleep and Rest, Emotional Behavior, Mobility, Social Interaction, and Recreation and Pastimes subscales. Moreover, SIP scores were moderately correlated with amount of incontinence, largely reflecting the sensitivity of the Body Care and Movement, Sleep and Rest, and Recreation and Pastimes subscales. These results are consistent with general findings from other reports that HRQL is more strongly related to having episodes of incontinence than degree of incontinence (68).

Swedish

Sullivan and colleagues (69) have reported on the recent adaptation of a Swedish version of the SIP, which is now being used in a variety of clinical studies (69–71). The methods for adaptation included independent translations into the Swedish language by multiple evaluators. The translated forms were pooled to select the simplest phrasing, back-translated into English, and compared. Item weights developed for the original SIP were used, precluding an evaluation of conceptual equivalence of the underlying HRQL continuum in the SIP scores. The investigators state that the instrument was pilot tested and revised once, but no details are provided in the published report.

Reliability. The Swedish SIP was found to have high test-retest reliability ($r = .95$) for the overall score, and physical ($r = .92$) and psychosocial dimension ($r = .87$) scores in a sample of women with rheumatic disorders (71). These results are comparable to the original version.

Validity. The Swedish version of the SIP has performed quite well with rheumatic disorders. It has discriminated between patients with rheumatoid arthritis and with stroke from the general population, and between clinically defined degrees of disability (70,71). Multitrait-multimethod analysis of the SIP with measures of disease activity, physical function, and emotional functioning confirmed the validity of the physical and psychosocial dimensions in rheumatoid arthritis patients. The SIP was responsive to clinically meaningful 1-year changes (improvements as well as deteriorations) in assessments of physical function and disease activity (69,70).

Summary and Issues

Overall, the literature indicates that the SIP has translated well into other languages. The close relationship found in item rankings between the international versions and the original SIP provides evidence of a high degree of conceptual agreement on behavioral health states across countries. Overall, the performance of the language-adapted versions in separating chronic versus acute health conditions, and levels of illness severity indicate that the adoptions (for some versions) have been largely successful. In addition, the SIP's underlying physical and psychosocial behavioral dimensions have been reproduced (i.e., for the British and Swedish versions).

The cross-cultural evidence reported on the SIP does not represent a level at which formal testing of cross-cultural equivalence is complete. However, an international collaborative project is now under way that is designed to adapt the SIP for cross-cultural and international use; thus more extensive evidence of the SIP's measurement equivalence between cultures should be available in future years.

For the current literature on the SIP, the psychometric evaluations of the Dutch and Swedish versions of the SIP have been extensive, and are beyond what may be considered an early or preliminary stage. Moreover, several of the international validations studies used analyses and methods similar to the original SIP, and these show similar findings. In the absence of a coordinated international validation effort, such as for the SF-36 and NHP, many language versions of the SIP have been developed with often cursory translation or unspecified methodology. Questions about conceptual equivalence of the translated items preclude an evaluation of either their qualitative or quantitative similarity across cultures.

Some benchmarks needed for the original SIP for cross-cultural comparisons include (a) precision, and the responsiveness of SIP subscales and patient group norms; (b) item analyses; and (c) a more detailed description of the internal structure of the subscales.

Areas of measurement equivalence not widely examined in the SIP language versions include method of administration (operational equivalence), and metric equivalence, which has been examined solely from the standpoint of item weights.

Whether the reliance in the SIP on objective behavioral indicators of HRQL states has lessened the potential difficulties in adapting it to other cultures by avoiding references to health perceptions and appraisals of emotional states is unknown. Although objectively based, the SIP may contain several sources of cultural bias: correspondence of subjective states to behaviors, respondents' attributions of behavioral limitations to health, and behavioral norms that prevail in a culture. For example, Deyo (72) has raised the important general issue of whether different cultural groups may have very different norms for activity restrictions with medical illness. He found poor construct validity for a version of the SIP adapted to Mexican-American samples with clinical measures of low back pain severity, which he attributed to cultural biases in the concept of disablement. However, it is important to note that this version of the SIP was translated using Hispanics residing in Washington State but administered to Hispanics residing in Texas, who may have a sufficiently different dialect to invalidate the results.

The SIP's precision and sensitivity to clinically important changes in patient functioning (both positive and negative changes in performance) should be empirically tested. The sensitivity of the SIP in detecting small changes in functioning has been questioned, as some of the multiple functional activities referenced within the same statement may be performed at different levels of function (73).

MOS 36-Item Short Form Health Survey

Purpose and Description

The items included in the MOS 36-Item Short Form Health Survey (SF-36) (3) were developed by a team of RAND investigators in the Medical Outcomes Study (MOS). Recently, an identical form has been released by RAND entitled the RAND 36-Item Health Survey (74), which has minor differences in scoring from the MOS SF-36.

The SF-36 represents the latest addition to a series of short general health forms from the MOS, synthesizing both brevity (approximately 10 minutes administration time) and precision in a comprehensive HRQL measure (3). The central strategy in this regard was to develop a parsimonious set of items from the lengthier, original MOS form that incorporate eight health domains: physical functioning (ten items); role limitations due to physical (four items) and emotional problems (three items); pain (two items); general health perceptions (five items); vitality (four items); social functioning (two items); emotional well-being (five items); and a single item on change in health. These items have been selected or adapted from the MOS 20-item short form and the full-length MOS form.

The original SF-36 can be self-administered, or interviewer-administered in either telephone or face-to-face modes. The SF-36, like its predecessor MOS health survey variants, uses a four-week recall period. An alternative form using a 1-week recall period (acute version) is also available.

Psychometric Properties

The MOS SF-36 was recently published, and is reportedly already in use in a large number of clinical trials (75,76).

The validity of the subscales of the 36-item form has been largely established against clinically defined criterion groups (known group validity) and the long-form versions of MOS scales of proven validity (77). These analyses have demonstrated that the abbreviated scales perform favorably in separating psychiatric and physical illness populations and in discriminating severe major medical illness groups from moderately ill and healthy groups. Further, the physical and mental health scales each appropriately discriminate at least moderate levels of burden in patient groups due to physical or psychiatric illness. Results from several recently reported clinical studies are consistent with these validation reports, showing that the MOS SF-36 discriminates between symptomatic and asymptomatic patient groups, stages, and severity of disease, and moderate-sized treatment effects (78–83).

The MOS SF-36, like other generic HRQL instruments, was constructed to represent two distinct underlying dimensions of physical and mental health. Clinical tests of validity and factor analyses of the SF-36 have confirmed that some of the SF-36 subscales clearly differentiate mental morbidity from physical morbidity (76). Summary measures for these dimensions of health have recently been developed for the SF-36 (84) to measure overall impact on HRQL, and to reduce the number of statistical comparisons necessary. As with the other generic HRQL instruments reviewed, there are additional data needed on the precision and responsiveness of the SF-36 to change in major dimensions of HRQL. However, the SF-36 has demonstrated responsiveness to changes in physical functioning following hip arthroplasty (85), health of patients undergoing heart valve replacement (86), and changes in mental health and role disability following recovery from major depression (87). Clinical investigations have found floor effects in the role functioning scales in a severely ill patient population, where 25% to 50% of the sample obtained the lowest score possible (78), and 63% in a human immunodeficiency virus (HIV) population (80). Similar patterns for the role functioning scales are also noted in validation work (76).

Internal-consistency reliability coefficients reported for the SF-36 are high, generally between .80 and .90 or better (74,88). Similar results have been obtained in clinical studies of knee replacement (80), and in patients with end-stage renal disease (78).

Prior to formal publication of the "standard" version of the SF-36 by the Medical Outcomes Trust, a developmental version had been in use. Scoring algorithms are provided in the users' manual (76) to maximize comparability between versions; the potential for substantial differences in Bodily Pain Scale scores between versions has led the developers to caution against such comparisons between studies.

International Use and Development

The SF-36 has taken a "fast-track" to international adaptation, beginning around the time of publication of the validated instrument. In this regard, the instrument's developers have launched an extensive international validation effort, entitled the International Quality of Life Assessment Project (IQOLA) (89,90), whose objectives are to translate, validate, and establish norms for the MOS SF-36 in 15 countries. A more detailed description of the IQOLA project and results are presented in Chapter 71 (Ware, Gardek, Keller, and the IQOLA Project Group), of this volume.

International adaptations are being conducted using forward and backward translation, review by representative focus groups, and formal evaluation of the conceptual equivalence of the adapted form.

Currently, the original SF-36 has been the most extensively validated; however, cross-cultural validation studies are under way in Canada (French-Canadian), France, Germany, Italy, Japan, the Netherlands, Spain, the UK, and Sweden. At the time of this review, the British version of the SF-36 has been published and is available from the Medical Outcomes Trust (76); reports describing the translation and validation of the German and Swedish versions of the SF-36 have been recently published. Additional translations are planned for Australia, Belgium, Japan, and possibly other countries (90).

Goals for these national versions of the SF-36 include translation, confirmation of scaling assumptions, validation, and norming in relation to clinical status and change (91,92). Forms of validity to be assessed will include item discriminant and convergent validity, construct validity, empirical tests of validity in relation to clinical status, and formal tests of precision (91). In addition, formal tests of item and scale measurement models are being replicated in each country.

Measurement equivalence in the adapted versions of the MOS SF-36 will be evaluated in terms of standard psychometric properties, with common clinical criterion variables. On this basis the cross-cultural versions can be refined to closely approximate the performance of the original SF-36. In addition to the eight-scale MOS SF-36 profile, the IQOLA project also seeks to validate physical and mental health summary scores, and develop health utility indexes incorporating SF-36 scales for use in cost-utility studies (90).

Language Versions

British

There are several published reports on use of the developmental version of the Anglicized SF-36. These include a study in Scotland of patients with symptoms or complaints of low back pain, peptic ulcer, varicose veins, or menorrhagia (93); a postal survey (SF-36 and NHP) administered to 1,980 patients aged 16 to 74 years randomly selected from two general practices in Sheffield (94); and a large community sample drawn from four family health service areas (95).

The UK adaptation of the SF-36 required changes in 5 of the 36 items, including restating "block" as a distance measure, "pep" as "life," feeling "blue" as "low," and "sick a little easier" as "ill more easily." Analyses using the IQOLA core methodology (see above) including quantitative and qualitative evaluation of translation, and comprehensive testing of scaling assumptions, responsiveness, and formal tests of item and scale measurement models has not yet been reported for the British version.

Reliability. In these studies, internal consistency coefficients for subscales in the SF-36, measured by Cronbach's alpha, were high and exceeded .80 (range .80 to .93), except for the Social Functioning scale, which was less than .80 (.74 and .79) in two of the reports (94,95). Comparisons with data obtained from approximately similar populations in the U.S. show similar patterns of alpha coefficient above .80 for all but the Social Functioning scale. Test-retest reliability was found to be moderate to high with a range from

.60 to .80 (94). Data on test-retest for the original SF-36 are too sparse for comparison.

Validity. Consistent with the original SF-36, the Anglican SF-36 produced different profiles for each of the four patient groups recruited, and distinguished them from community controls. In the Scottish study involving a multidiagnostic patient group (93), factor analysis of the items revealed five independent HRQL factors rather than eight in the original. A similar factor analysis has not been reported for the original SF-36; however, in comparison with results from a principal components analysis (77), some differences appear to exist between versions in the clustering of SF-36 scales on underlying physical and psychological dimensions. In the Scottish study (93), social functioning, pain, and role limitations due to physical functioning were aggregated on a single factor; whereas in the original MOS SF-36, social functioning was most strongly associated with the principal component (mental) that had only low associations with pain and role limitations attributed to physical health. It is uncertain whether this difference results from cultural bias in attributions made toward role limitations along a physical-psychological axis, different patient populations, or from the somewhat different analytical methods used.

Evidence of construct validity of the Anglican version was demonstrated by confirming the expected distribution of scores by sociodemographic characteristics, medical care consultation, use of hospital services, and diagnosis of chronic illness (94,95).

A comparison of norms for random samples of the general population for the United States (76) and England (95) reveal that older adults (55 to 64 years old) in the United States score lower than the English sample on five of the eight subscales, but younger persons in both samples (25 to 34 years old) score similarly. It is uncertain whether this response difference represents potential differences in distributions of sociodemographic status, cohort effects reflecting cultural differences in item meanings, or real differences in lifestyle between American and English cultures with older age.

German

A report describing the preliminary results of the adaptation and validation of the German version of the SF-36 using IQOLA methodology has been completed (96). This is substantial in that it also represents one of the first detailed reports on the IQOLA protocol for instrument adaptation.

Forward translation of the form and its instructions was completed independently by two native German speakers; quality control of the translation was implemented by a rating (0 to 100) of item difficulty and quality. The conceptual equivalence and clarity of the consensus version with the U.S. original SF-36 was then rated by two additional native German speakers. Backward translation of the most developed version was subsequently performed, which in turn was rated for conceptual equivalence by English-speaking raters. A review of problematic translations was conducted. Results for the backward translation indicated that most items received high ratings for clarity, common language, and conceptual equivalence (seven items had low to moderate scores for the latter).

Scaling of the SF-36 response choices was examined using Thurstone scaling techniques, and observed to be similar but not identical in ordinal ranking and equidistance to American ratings. A statistical test of the differences in ratings obtained between cultures was not reported.

Reliability. Preliminary psychometric testing included subscale reliability, which ranged from .73 (social functioning) to .92 (physical functioning) in a migraine sample. These levels are comparable to results published for American samples. Test-retest reliability was not described.

Validity. For convergent validity, the German SF-36 subscales were correlated with the NHP (the source and translation of the NHP was not specified); these results showed moderate to strong correlations between like subscales of the two instruments (.40 to .78) in back-pain patients, and low to moderate correlations (.39 to .51) in healthy students. Construct validity was affirmed from the pattern of subscale score discriminating between healthy and ill populations; this version also demonstrated responsiveness to a pain intervention. Population norms for the German SF-36 were not available at the time of this review. However, substantial differences in means and percent of scores at the scale ceiling were observed for the Role-Physical and Bodily Pain subscales with the U.S. norms for a healthy population (males and females 18 to 24 years old). Additionally there were noticeable differences in scale scores and ceilings between German respondents and American back-pain patients (76). Confidence intervals for mean scores were not provided.

Swedish

This version of the SF-36 was translated prior to development of the IQOLA project. However, tests of translation and scaling assumptions follow IQOLA methods outlined above. The preliminary report of the Swedish SF-36 (97) did not include an examination of its ratings of the conceptual equivalence and quality of the translation, or on tests of its scaling assumptions.

Community studies of broadly representative samples of urban, suburban, and rural populations (97) were conducted for psychometric testing and to develop norms. Results for completeness of data indicate high percentages of complete items with the Swedish version, similar to a U.S. patient data base. However, a larger number of missing data was noted for the Swedish version Physical Functioning scale.

Reliability. Internal-consistency reliability estimates for the eight Swedish SF-36 subscales were high, ranging from .79 (Role-Emotional) to .93 (Bodily Pain); analyses of subgroups revealed somewhat lower internal-consistency relia-

bility (e.g., .70) in younger persons. Test-retest reliability was not reported.

Validity. Item and scale score distributions followed expected patterns for general populations, being skewed toward more favorable response choices. Item discrimination (item-scale correlations) replicated the structure observed for the U.S. version. Floor and ceiling effects resemble those reported for the U.S.

Summary and Issues

The SF-36 is the only generic HRQL instrument reviewed that is currently undergoing simultaneous, comprehensive development and evaluation for use outside the country and culture of its origin, using common clinical protocols. Outside of IQOLA project studies, there are very few published reports in the literature of international use of the SF-36.

The goals in the IQOLA project to examine relative precision, construct validity, and criterion-related validity in coordinated studies represent level 3 in our typology of instrument development. Whether, or which of, the national versions of the SF-36 will achieve this level of cross-cultural equivalence, and thus can be recommended for use in multinational clinical trials, remains to be seen. Preliminary evidence for the British, Swedish, and German versions suggests that the conceptual content and scoring system of the SF-36 is relevant and reproducible in European cultures.

Some difficulties have been encountered in item translation of the Physical Functioning scale in several of the international versions. A mile was translated as 1 kilometer in all versions except the Swedish version, which lists 2 kilometers as an equivalent. The descriptor "playing golf" to signify moderate physical activity was an uncommon descriptor in most European countries; it was translated differently in the target languages, for example as "picking berries" in Swedish, and *jouer aux boules* in French. More generally, there is some question whether performance of strenuous activity is a universal indicator of positive health.

With regard to validation, one concern is that the NHP, used to determine convergent validity for the Anglican and German versions of the SF-36, may not be a sensitive standard for general populations and some of the patient populations studied (i.e., back pain) (96). More advanced validation of the national versions of the SF-36 described above, and other versions currently under development, is eagerly awaited (96,97).

Establishing patient group norms, and a unified set of psychometric data for the national versions represents an important step forward in adapting existing HRQL instruments for cross-national use. It also provides the means to explore metric equivalence among the international versions, including between-country comparisons. It will be particularly important to observe whether the relationship among the eight scales, indicated by a pattern of scores that discriminate an illness condition along a continuum of physical-psychological impairment (77), has been successfully preserved in the adapted versions of this instrument.

EuroQol

Purpose and Description

EuroQol (4) is a generic multidimensional HRQL profile currently being developed and standardized for use in England, the Netherlands, Norway, Finland, and Sweden. The EuroQol contains two parts: a health status profile and a visual analog scale to rate global HRQL. The profile includes 16 items covering six health domains: mobility, self-care, main activity, social relationships, pain, and mood. The items were chosen from a pool of 216 items assembled from a review of the Quality of Well-Being Scale, SIP, NHP, and Rosser Index. A single score is generated for each health state. Scores on the visual analog scale range from 0 to 100. The EuroQol was designed to be self-completed, and short enough to be suitable for use as part of a battery of HRQL measures.

Psychometric Properties

There are few reports on the validity of the EuroQol in the published literature. The psychometric performance of the EuroQol was examined and compared to an Anglicized version of the SF-36 (98) in a general population sample (98). Results indicated that the EuroQol discriminated between persons with recent use and nonuse of medical services, while only the pain/discomfort score discriminated chronicity of medical problems. The EuroQol responses were highly skewed, with a median response of "no problem" for all of the functional scales, and more than 97% of respondents placed at the ceiling of the physical functioning measure (indicating good functioning). These effects are larger than those found for the SF-36. More extensive reports of the psychometric performance of the EuroQol are noted as forthcoming in the literature.

From a psychometric perspective, the large ceiling effect apparent in many of the EuroQol scales may necessitate supplementing the instrument in assessments of patient groups with less than major morbidity, or where small to moderate clinically significant changes (deterioration or improvement) in health and functional status are expected. Used in a battery approach with other HRQL instruments, the EuroQol may serve as a core measure of gross deficits in physical and psychosocial functioning.

International Development

The EuroQol is designed as a multinational measure, and is being piloted in five international collaborating centers. Validation work reported to date includes an investigation of

cross-cultural comparability of weighting of items in general population samples using a visual analog scale. The preliminary evidence gathered for this instrument, in its present form, does not provide a solid basis for assessing its feasibility for multinational research. It was shown that respondents in England, The Netherlands, Sweden (99), and Norway (100) similarly rank the EuroQol items in terms of severity for the same health states. It should be noted that in the Norwegian study only 8 of the 16 items were evaluated, and thus the results cannot be directly compared to those of the other centers. Further, the published reports described quite low response rates (about 26% to 40%) for most centers, introducing uncertainty about the external validity of the findings. Nonetheless, there is at least preliminary support for the comparability of health valuations across the countries considered.

Summary and Issues

The EuroQol has been developed as a core generic HRQL instrument for use with other dimension-specific measures. Given the range and item content it seems well suited for this purpose. As a generic HRQL measure based on a single set of items common to all settings (countries) it may likely possess conceptual equivalence; however, more research is needed to test this assumption. Although the literature indicates that no major problems have been encountered in adapting this measure internationally, little has been published on the methods of adaptation, leaving uncertainty about the quality of the translations. Conclusions about its psychometric performance between cultures (e.g., item and scale analysis, and construct validation) also await further validation.

Dartmouth COOP Function Charts

Purpose and Description

The Dartmouth COOP Charts (5) were developed by a cooperative group of community medical practices to fill the need for a brief tool for assessing patients' overall functioning that could be easily completed during a doctor–patient interview. There are a total of nine charts to screen and monitor patient functioning: three focus on specific dimensions of functioning (social, physical, and role functioning), two on symptoms (pain and emotional condition), three on perceptions (change in health, overall health, and quality of life), and one on social support. Each chart consists of a descriptive title, an item referring to an aspect of the patient's HRQL during the past 4 weeks, and five Likert-scaled response choices. The response format also includes pictorial representations for each of the five levels of health or functioning. Patients respond to one chart at a time, and the number of charts administered is variable and unstructured. Most patients can complete all nine charts in approximately

5 minutes. For each chart the range of scores is 1 to 5, with 5 indicating worst functioning. The developers have emphasized that each chart represents a distinct HRQL dimension, and scores should not be pooled to reflect an overall functioning score (101,102).

The COOP chart system is the only generic HRQL instrument reviewed that was specifically designed to be administered in daily clinical practice. The charts can be administered by a health care provider or self-administered. The suitability of the Physical Condition Chart for screening and monitoring purposes has been questioned (11) because of its truncated range, which excludes disability. In addition, it does not indicate functioning in major daily activities, which is of relevance in assessing the patient's level of functional independence. Unlike the subscales in other generic HRQL instruments, some of the COOP function charts are not criterion-based in terms of level of performance, but rely on a person-based approach that measures current functioning in comparison to the patient's usual level of functioning. Thus, the primary approach to screening and monitoring in the COOP charts is the detection of changes in functioning from previous levels.

Psychometric Evidence in Country of Origin

The COOP chart system was evaluated using over 1,400 patient-completed forms from four medical centers in the United States under different protocols (5). Patient samples included adults reporting common acute and chronic diseases; elderly patients under medical care for chronic conditions; low-income patients with hypertension or diabetes; and patients with cancer, hypertension, or depression.

Test-retest reliability was assessed at two of the study sites (102). Correlation coefficients for a 1-hour retest using the same test administrator ranged from $r = .74$ to .99. Two-week retests yielded substantially lower test-retest correlations ($r = .42$ to .88). In comparison to retests conducted by the same administrator, 1-hour test-retest coefficients using different test administrators resulted in somewhat lower correlation coefficients, ranging from $r = .60$ (role functioning) to $r = .92$ (emotional status). The reliability of self-administered forms was not tested.

The validity of the COOP charts has been studied using clinical status and diagnostic measures, and existing HRQL profiles and dimension-specific measures (102–104). The COOP charts have demonstrated low to moderate correlations with clinical status indicators (symptoms and chronic disease states), ranging from $r = .11$ (health change) to .34 (pain). These correlations are lower than those generally found for other generic HRQL measures. Correlations between COOP charts and other measures of functional status have been higher. For example, correlations in a Veterans Administration hospital sample ranged from $r = .51$ (Overall Health) to .70 (Emotional Condition).

Multitrait-multimethod analyses (104) revealed that the Physical and Role Functioning charts were as highly correlated with each other (trait) as with their paired measure (method), suggesting a global physical activity/role capability measure. In contrast, a clear pattern of independence was found for emotional status and social support charts, which appeared to measure different aspects of functional status. The COOP charts have been shown to distinguish between levels of function not detected by other generic measures of functional status. In a comparison of the COOP and NHP measures of physical fitness, emotional status, and pain (105), many patients (47% to 71%) who showed optimum functioning on the NHP had less than full functioning on the COOP chart measures.

Known groups validity of the COOP charts has been demonstrated to be high, and comparable to the MOS short-form measures (106); however, the single-item charts have less relative precision in detecting differences in functional status as compared to multi-item functional subscales. Potential gains in sensitivity by including illustrations in the response format to represent health states is uncertain. In a study comparing chart systems, McHorney and colleagues (103) reported that the illustration format may inadvertently increase sensitivity of the pain chart to concomitantly experienced emotional distress.

Calibration of the COOP charts to clinically meaningful or relevant events and determination of the size of the intervals in the response levels are reportedly among the objectives of future work with this measurement system (102).

International Use and Development

The Dartmouth COOP Charts system has seen international use in the Netherlands (106), Canada (107), and Japan (108); additionally, a French version is currently under development. In 1988, based on existing psychometric evidence available for the COOP charts, the World Organization of General Practitioners/Family Physicians (WONCA) selected this instrument as the basis to develop an international system for functional status measurement.

An international feasibility trial to explore the ease of administering the original COOP charts was conducted by WONCA in seven countries (109). Clinician-assessed usefulness of the charts and patient-assessed clarity of the chart contents were found to vary considerably by country. Since then, WONCA has revised the original instrument with the goal of making it applicable to international research settings. The original chart titles were renamed: Physical Fitness, Feelings, Daily Activities, Social Activities, Change in Health, and Overall Health (110). The Pain, Quality of Life, and Social Support charts were not included in the COOP/WONCA revision; however, the Pain chart may be used optionally. The content of the Physical Fitness chart response levels was changed to reflect one dimension, the ability to walk; and the response continuum was lowered to include "not able to walk." Other changes included rewording the lead question in the charts, changing the time reference to the past 2 weeks, and reducing the drawings to one drawing per response category incorporating internationally recognized symbols. A detailed report of the preliminary studies that guided these modifications was not found in the literature, but was reported to include 14 countries involving approximately 1,300 patients (111).

The COOP/WONCA charts are presently available in nine languages other than English: Danish, Dutch, Finnish, German, Hebrew, Japanese, Norwegian, Spanish (three major dialect variants), and Urdu (110). The translations were reported to have been carried out by WONCA clinicians, although no details of the procedures were provided.

Some operational changes from the original Dartmouth COOP system were also implemented. Under the old system, the three functional charts composed the "core" assessment package, with the remaining six charts used optionally. In the WONCA revision, all six charts retained are standard and an order of presentation has been specified. A preference has been stated for patient self-administration of the forms with a brief instruction session. The revised instrument was renamed the Dartmouth COOP Functional Health Assessment Charts/WONCA (COOP/WONCA). The current literature pertinent to this international version of the instrument is reviewed below.

WONCA

A summary report of the studies using the revised COOP charts has been published in a proceedings of a workshop held by WONCA (111). Only limited data and details on research design and study protocol have been provided.

Reliability. Four-week test-retest correlations in a German study were found to range from $r = .42$ to .62 (112). The lower retest correlations found for some charts is consistent with test-retest reliability reported for the original Dartmouth COOP charts under retest periods of several weeks and the Dutch version of the original unmodified COOP chart system (106).

Validity. A criterion validity study of the COOP/WONCA was carried out in patients with stroke (113). The COOP/WONCA charts correlated with other measures in an expected pattern based on physical and emotional dimensions of functional impacts. The functioning charts (Physical Fitness, Daily Activities, and Social Activities) were significantly correlated with Barthel Index scores during the follow-up period, whereas the Feelings chart was strongly correlated with the Zung Depression Scale. The sensitivity of the COOP/WONCA charts was examined in a Scottish study against a clinical assessment of severity of asthma (114). A change in peak expiratory flow of 10% corresponded to significant changes in the Physical Fitness, Daily Activities, and Social Activities, as predicted. There was no improvement in Feelings chart scores, providing additional evidence that the COOP charts can discriminate between physical and emotional components of general functioning. Similar findings have been reported in a Dutch study of asthmatic patients experiencing an exacerbation of symptoms (115).

Summary and Issues

The international development of the COOP/WONCA instrument, with the planned, or ongoing, testing of its reliability, validity, and sensitivity to change (111) is consistent with a preliminary level of development. The work conducted thus far with the revised COOP charts indicates that this instrument appears to detect moderate effects in physical and emotional functioning due to medical illness or health status. Evidence demonstrating cultural equivalence in construct and scale across national versions using a common set of procedures and methodology would be a next step in its development.

Studies on cross-cultural equivalence in terms of acceptability, relevance, and meaning of the verbal response levels and symbols in the WONCA-modified COOP chart system across language versions were not located in the literature. It would be valuable to know the extent to which the symbolic representations of level of functional state introduce cultural bias in measurement in some or any of the COOP/WONCA language versions. Finally, the Daily Activities and Social Activities charts combine physical and emotional health attributions with regard to current level of functioning in these categories. Unfortunately, this format prevents an investigation of potential systematic cultural effects in the relationships between physical and emotional functioning, and role activities, and in assessing clinical validity for various levels of physical and mental morbidities.

DISCUSSION

The international literature on HRQL research is large and expanding. This trend reflects a transition taking place in health outcomes research from focusing narrowly on morbidity and mortality to include an evaluation of the impact of illness and treatment on functioning using the patient's point of view. In recent years, the progress made toward developing cross-culturally equivalent HRQL measures has advanced from simplistic translations to thorough and objective methods that can substantially enhance the degree of conceptual equivalence achieved between versions.

Another positive trend has been the development of new HRQL measures (e.g., WHOQOL) that, from their inception, are designed to be internationally relevant and acceptable. This offers a valuable alternative from exporting HRQL indicators developed, in most instances, from the United States to other cultures. Together, these recent developments should provide information of a much higher technical level on cross-cultural assessment than has accumulated, to date, in the literature.

Even when adequately performed, language translations are superficial with respect to underlying cultural differences that may exist in the valuations and impacts of illness on functional status and well-being. However, the current psychometric evidence, albeit preliminary, suggests that despite the potential for differences in broader conceptualizations of health and well-being between cultures, cross-cultural assessment of the effects of illness and its treatment in an individual's physical, social, and psychological functioning appears feasible. The limits and qualifications of cross-cultural comparability in HRQL assessment will require painstaking investigation, and cannot be appraised within the current literature.

The current literature review also revealed some areas of HRQL instrument development for which there has been, as yet, little work performed. Emphasis on national and linguistic adaptation to some extent sidesteps broader issues of cultural differences. Hence, in addition to cross-national work in developing language versions of major HRQL instruments, more attention is needed on culture and ethnicity within nations and language groups. This may be important since cultural differences found in HRQL measurement between levels of social class, urban versus suburban or rural populations, and race or ethnicity may be as large or larger than differences found between representative population samples between countries. Some work in this area has been conducted (or is under way) with the SIP and SF-36 in the United States, but this scope of investigation has not been a standard one in HRQL instrument validation.

Another issue concerns the grounding of the concept of HRQL as a subjective experience versus an objective functional state; the latter has predominated in existing HRQL measures. Thus, another frontier in international HRQL instrument development is to examine the correspondence of various functional states with the respondent's valuations and appraisal (i.e., global and domain-specific measures of satisfaction). It would be interesting to know whether there are cultural differences in life satisfaction in the generic HRQL scales for varying health conditions. None of the studies reviewed above specifically addressed this topic. Further, there has been very little work performed on cultural differences in the personal and social referents used in self-appraisals of HRQL. By gaining a better understanding of the impact of culture on health valuations, we will be in a better position to evaluate the appropriateness of employing HRQL instruments in international health care settings.

Finally, the state of the science of cross-cultural aspects of health and illness is still in its early stages, and basic research is essential to future development of HRQL instruments for cross-cultural use. The myriad of effects of health conditions on life suggest a broader philosophical view of HRQL than is found in the existing HRQL measures. Thus,

it seems reasonable to suggest that the achievements made in adapting or developing cross-cultural HRQL instruments described above represent only an early milestone. Nearer the goal of investigating HRQL cross-culturally, both the differences and similarities, the current instruments are likely to be far from perfect. As a future direction, the validity of cross-cultural HRQL assessments should be assessed from broadly based multidisciplinary research programs involving sociologists, anthropologists, psychologists, economists, and clinicians using a variety of qualitative and quantitative methods.

CONCLUSIONS

Core categories of information reviewed to assess measurement equivalence are translation methods and general psychometric properties, including metric equivalence. Along these dimensions, while none of the instruments reviewed was judged to have data available for all aspects of measurement equivalence, a preliminary level of cross-cultural instrument development has been accomplished for at least some of the versions of the generic HRQL instruments reviewed in this chapter.

Assessment of scale equivalence, or the comparability in validity and reliability between instrument versions, has been limited by a lack of common study designs, protocol, and psychometric analyses across studies, and by less than complete psychometric testing. The latter shortcoming is not unique to international use and testing of HRQL measures, but is also sometimes the case with research reported on the original instrument. For example, limited data is available for the NHP, SIP, and SF-36 on sensitivity to change and the clinical significance of such change. A final category of equivalence has to do with the metric properties of the scales. Two versions of the same measure can be equally sensitive to a given change in functional status yet assign different numbers to the same amount of change or level of distress. In addition to assurances of scale or construct equivalence, pooling scores across language versions requires that various versions have been calibrated to give identical scores under identical circumstances, as the original. Currently this property has not been widely assessed in versions of generic HRQL measures studied. However, it is an evaluation goal in the IQOLA project and presumably in other instrument development projects as well.

With several international projects now under way, future years will bring more advanced development of major HRQL measures. It is likely that some of the major generic HRQL instruments will be found suitable for use in multinational clinical trials. More extensive validation and replication studies have been performed for some versions of the SIP, NHP, and SF-36, and this trend is continuing toward coordinated multinational studies using common validation protocols and quantitative assessments of cross-cultural equivalence. In this regard, the IQOLA project is exemplary of an advanced level of research and development strategies. As a future direction, it will be especially important to distinguish between psychometric evidence that an adapted HRQL instrument may be used in other cultures (levels 1 and 2 development in our typology) and evidence that it may be used in truly cross-cultural research, involving multinational study designs (level 3 development).

REFERENCES

1. Hunt SM, McEwen J, McKenna SP. *The Nottingham Health Profile user's manual*, 1981.
2. Bergner M, Bobbitt RA, Kressel S, et al. The Sickness Impact Profile: conceptual foundation and methodology for the development of a health status measure. *Int J Health Serv* 1976;6:393–415.
3. Ware JE, Sherbourne CD. A 36-item Short-Form Health Survey (SF-36): conceptual framework and item selection. *Med Care* 1992;30: 473–483.
4. The EuroQol Group. EuroQol—a new facility for the measurement of health-related quality of life. *Health Policy* 1990;16:199–208.
5. Nelson E, Wasson J, Kirk J, Keller A, Clark D, Dietrich A, Stewart A, Zubkoff M. Assessment of function in routine clinical practice: description of the COOP chart method and preliminary findings. *J Chronic Dis* 1987;40:55S–63S.
6. WHOQOL Group. Study protocol for the World Health Organization project to develop a quality of life assessment instrument (WHOQOL). *Qual Life Res* 1993;2:153–159.
7. Aaronson NK, Bullinger M, Ahmedzai S. A modular approach to quality-of-life assessment in cancer clinical trials. *Recent Results Cancer Res* 1988;111:231–249.
8. Spilker B, Molinek FR, Johnston KA, et al. Quality of life bibliography and indexes. *Med Care* 1990;28(suppl 12).
9. Spilker B, Simpson R, Tilson H. Quality of life bibliography and indexes: 1991 update. *J Clin Res Pharmacoepidemiol* 1992;6:205–266.
10. McDowell I, Newell C. *Measuring health: a guide to rating scales and questionnaires.* New York: Oxford University Press, 1987.
11. Wilkin D, Hallam L, Doggett M. *Measures of need and outcome for primary health care.* New York: Oxford Medical Publications, 1992.
12. Wenger NK, Mattson ME, Furberg CD, Elinson J, eds. *Assessment of quality of life in clinical trials of cardiovascular therapies.* Le Jacq, 1984.
13. Bullinger M, Anderson R, Cella D, Aaronson N. Developing and evaluating cross-cultural instruments from minimum requirements to optimal models. *Qual Life Res* 1993;2:451–459.
14. Ware JE, Keller S, Bentler P, Sullivan M, Brazier J, Gandek B. Comparison of health status measurement models and the validity of SF-36 in Great Britain, Sweden and the USA. *Qual Life Res* 1994; 3(1):68.
15. Kohlmann T. Aggregation of quality of life data from different countries and interpretation of results. *Br J Med Econ* 1993;6C:35–44.
16. McKenna SP, Hunt SM, McEwen J. Weighting the seriousness of perceived health problems using Thurstone's method of paired comparisons. *Int J Epidemiol* 1981;10(1):93–97.
17. Jenkinson C. Why are we weighting? A critical examination of the use of item weights in a health status measure. *Soc Sci Med* 1991; 32(12):1413–1416.
18. Hunt SM, McKenna SP, McEwen J. A quantitative approach to perceived health. *J Epidemiol Community Health* 1980;34:281–285.
19. Hunt SM, McKenna SP, McEwen J, et al. Subjective health status of patients with peripheral vascular disease. *Practitioner* 1982;226: 133–136.
20. McKenna SP, Hunt SM, McEwen J, et al. Changes in perceived health of patients recovering from fractures. *Public Health* 1984;98:97–102.
21. Jenkinson C, Fitzpatrick R, Argyle M. The Nottingham Health Profile: an analysis of its sensitivity in differentiating illness groups. *Soc Sci Med* 1988;27(12):1411–1414.
22. Permanyer-Miralda G, Alonso J, Anto JM, et al. Comparison of perceived health status and conventional functional evaluation in sta-

ble patients with coronary heart disease. *J Clin Epidemiol* 1991;44(8): 779–786.
23. Dimenas E, Wiklund I, Dahlof C, et al. Differences in the subjective well-being and symptoms of normotensives, borderline hypertensives and hypertensives. *J Hypertens* 1989;7:885–890.
24. Hunt SM, McEwen J, McKenna SP, Backett EM, Pope C. Subjective health assessments and the perceived outcome of minor surgery. *J Psychosom Res* 1984;28:105–114.
25. Mays N. Relative costs and cost-effectiveness of extracorporeal shock-wave lithotripsy versus percutaneous nephrolithotomy in the treatment of renal and ureteric stones. *Soc Sci Med* 1991;32(12):1401–1412.
26. Wallender M, Palmer L. A monitoring system for adverse drug experiences in a pharmaceutical company: the integration of pre- and post-marketing data. *Drug Information J* 1986;20:225–235.
27. Hunt SM, McKenna SP, Williams J. Reliability of a population survey tool for measuring perceived health problems: a study of patients with osteoarthrosis. *J Epidemiol Community Health* 1981;35:185–188.
28. Hunt SM. Nottingham Health Profile. In: Wenger NK, Mattson ME, Furberg CD, Elinson J, eds. *Assessment of quality of life in clinical trials of cardiovascular therapies.* Le Jacq, 1984.
29. Hunt SM, McEwen J, McKenna SP, Backett EM, Pope C. Subjective health assessments and the perceived outcome of minor surgery. *J Psychom Res* 1984;28(4):105–114.
30. Kind P, Carr-Hill R. The Nottingham Health Profile: a useful tool for epidemiologists. *Soc Sci Med* 1987;25:905–910.
31. O'Brien BJ, Banner NR, Gibson S, Yaucob M. The Nottingham Health Profile as a measure of quality of life following heart and lung transplantation. *J Epidemiol Community Health* 1988;42:232–234.
32. McKenna SP, Hunt SM, McEwen J, Pope C. Changes in the perceived health of patients recovering from fractures. *Public Health* 1984;98: 97.
33. Anderson JS, Sullivan F, Usherwood TP. The Medical Outcomes Study Instrument (MOSI)—use of a new health status measure in Britain. *Fam Pract* 1990;7(3):205–218.
34. Hunt SM, Alonso J, Bacquet D, Niero M, Wiklund I, McKenna S. Cross-cultural adaptation of health measures. *Health Policy* 1991;19: 33–44.
35. Bucquet D, Condor S, Ritchie K. The French version of the Nottingham Health Profile: a comparison of item weights with those of the source version. *Soc Sci Med* 1990;30(7):809–835.
36. van Schayck CP, Rutten-van Molken MP, van Dooslaer EK, Folgering H, van Weel C. Two-year bronchodilator treatment in patients with mild airflow obstruction. *Chest* 1992;102:1384–1391.
37. Hunt SM, McEwen J, McKenna SP. *Measuring health status*, 1st ed. London: Croom Helm, 1986.
38. Alonso J, Auto J, Moreno C. Spanish version of the Nottingham Health Profile: translation and preliminary validity. *Am J Public Health* 1990;80:704–708.
39. Alonso J, Anto J, Gonzalez M, Fiz J, Izquirdo J, Morera J. Measurement of general health status of non-oxygen dependent chronic obstructive pulmonary disease patients. *Med Care* 1992;30(5 suppl): MS125–135.
40. Wiklund I, Romanus B, Hunt S. Self-assessed disability in patients with arthosis of the hip joint. *Int Disabil Studies* 1988;10:159–163.
41. Wiklund I, Karlberg J. Evaluation of quality of life in clinical trials: selecting quality of life measures. *Controlled Clin Trials* 1991;12: 2045–2165.
42. Hunt SM, Wiklund I. Cross-cultural variation in the weighting of health statements: a comparison of English and Swedish valuations. *Health Policy* 1987;8:227–235.
43. Ringsberg KC, Wiklund I, Wilhelmsen L. Education of adult patients at an "asthma school": effects on quality of life, knowledge and need for nursing. *Eur Respir J* 1990;3:33–37.
44. Wiklund I. The Nottingham Health Profile—a measure of health-related quality of life. *Scand J Prim Health Care* 1990;suppl 1:15–18.
45. Bergner M, Bobbitt RA, Carter WB, Gilson BS. The Sickness Impact Profile: development and final revision of a health status measure. *Med Care* 1981;19:787–805.
46. Anderson R, Aaronson N, Wilkin D. Critical review of the international assessments of health-related quality of life. *Qual Life Res* 1993;2:369–395.
47. Rothman M, Hedrick S, Invi T. The Sickness Impact Profile as a

measure of the health status of noncognitively impaired nursing home residents. *Med Care* 1989;27(3):5157–5167.

48. Finlay AY, Khan GK, Luscombe D, Salek M. Validation of the Sickness Impact Profile and Psoriasis Disability Index in psoriasis. *Br J Dermatol* 1990;123:751–756.

49. Jones P, Baveystock C, Littlejohns P. Relationships between general health measured with the Sickness Impact Profile and respiratory symptoms, physiological measures and mood in patients with chronic airflow limitation. *Am Rev Respir Dis* 1989;140:1538–1543.

50. Deyo R, Invi T, Lenninger J, Overman S. Measuring functional outcomes in chronic disease: a comparison of traditional scales and a self-administered health status questionnaire in patients with rheumatoid arthritis. *Med Care* 1983;21(2):180–192.

51. Pollard WE, Bobbitt RA, Bergner M, et al. The Sickness Impact Profile: reliability of a health status measure. *Med Care* 1976;14: 146–155.

52. Sano M, Stern Y, Marder K, et al. A controlled trial of Piracetam in intellectually impaired patients with Parkinson's disease. *Mov Disord* 1990;5(3):230–234.

53. Rothman M, Hedrick S, Inui T. The Sickness Impact Profile as a measure of health status of noncognitively impaired nursing home residents. *Med Care* 1989;27:S157–S167.

54. Liang MH, Fossel AH, Larson MG. Comparisons of five health status instruments for orthopedic evaluation. *Med Care* 1990;28:632–642.

55. Bergner L, Hallstrom A, Bergner M, et al. Health status of survivors cardiac arrest and of myocardial infarction controls. *Am J Public Health* 1985;75(11):1321–1323.

56. DeBruin AF, De Witte LP, Diederiks JP. Sickness Impact Profile: the state of the art of a generic functional status measure. *Soc Sci Med* 1992;8:1003–1014.

57. Patrick DL. Standardization of comparative health status measures: using scales developed in America in an English speaking country. Third Health Survey Research Methods Biennial Conference, 1976. Reston, VA. Dept. Health and Human Services Pub. No. (PHS)80-3268.

58. Patrick D, Sittampalam Y, Sommerville S, et al. A cross-cultural comparison of health status values. *Am J Public Health* 1985;75: 1402–1407.

59. Charlton JR, Patrick DL, Peach H. Use of multi-variate measures of disability in health surveys. *J Epidemiol Community Health* 1983;37: 296–304.

60. Chwalow AJ, Lurie A, Bean K, Parent du Chatelet I, et al. A French version of the Sickness Impact Profile (SIP): stages in the cross cultural validation of a generic quality of life scale. *Fundam Clin Pharmacol* 1992;6:319–326.

61. Jacobs HM. *Health status measurement in family medicine research: the Sickness Impact Profile and its application in a follow-up study in patients with non-specific abdominal complaints.* Utrecht, the Netherlands: University of Utrecht Press, 1993.

62. deBruin AF, Diederiks JPM, deWitte LP, Stevens FCJ, Philipsen H. The development of a short generic version of the Sickness Impact Profile. *J Clin Epidemiol* 1994;47(4):407–418.

63. Schuling J, Greidanus J, Meyboom-De Jong B. Measuring functional status of stroke patients with the Sickness Impact Profile. *Disabil Rehab* 1993;15(1):19–23.

64. Nydevik I, Hulter-Asberg K. Sickness Impact after stroke: a 3-year follow-up. *Scand J Prim Care* 1992;10:284–289.

65. Hulsebos RG, Beltman F, Miranda D, et al. Measuring quality of life with the Sickness Impact Profile: a pilot study. *Intensive Care Med* 1991;17:285–288.

66. deBruin AF, Buys M, deWitte LP, Diederiks JPM. The Sickness Impact Profile: SIP68, a short generic version. First evaluation of the reliability and reproducibility. *J Clin Epidemiol* 1994;47(8):863–871.

67. Hunskaar S, Vinsnes A. The quality of life in women with urinary incontinence as measured by the Sickness Impact Profile. *J Am Geriatr Soc* 1991;39:378–382.

68. Norton C. The effects of urinary incontinence in women. *Int Rehab Med* 1982;4:9.

69. Sullivan M, Ahlmen M, Bjelle A. Health status assessment in rheumatoid arthritis: 1. Further work on the validity of the Sickness Impact Profile. *J Rheumatol* 1990;17:439–447.

70. Sullivan M, Ahlmen M, Archenholtz B, et al. Measuring health in rheumatic disorders by means of a Swedish version of the Sickness Impact Profile: results from a population study. *Scand J Rheumatol* 1986;15:193–200.

71. Ahlmen EM, Bengtsson CB, Sullivan M, Bjelle A. A comparison of overall health between patients with rheumatoid arthritis and a population with and without rheumatoid arthritis. *Scand J Rheumatol* 1990;19:413–421.

72. Deyo R. Pitfalls in measuring the health status of Mexican Americans: comparative validity of the English and Spanish Sickness Impact Profile. *Am J Public Health* 1984;74:569–573.

73. Jette AM. Health status indicators: their utility in chronic-disease evaluation research. *J Chronic Dis* 1980;33:567–579.

74. Hays RD, Sherbourne CD, Mazel RM. *Health economics.* 1993;2: 217–227.

75. The MOS 36-Item Short Form Health Survey (SF-36) Update: July 1992. The MOS Trust, Boston, 1992.

76. Ware J, Snow KK, Kosinski M, Gandek B. *SF-36 Health Survey: manual and interpretation guide.* Boston, MA: The Health Institute, New England Medical Center Hospitals, 1993.

77. McHorney CA, Ware JE Jr, Raczek AE. The MOS 36-item short-form health survey (SF-36): II. Psychometric and clinical tests of validity in measuring physical and mental health constructs. *Med Care* 1993;31:247–263.

78. Kurtin PS, Davies AR, Meyer KB, et al. Patient-based health status measurements in outpatient dialysis: early experiences in developing an outcomes assessment program. *Med Care* 1992;30(5)MS136–149.

79. Nerenz D, Repasky D, Whitehouse F, et al. Ongoing assessment of health status in patients with diabetes mellitus. *Med Care* 1992;30(5): MS112–MS124.

80. Kantz M, Harris W, Leguitsky K, et al. Methods for assessing condition-specific and generic functional status outcomes after total knee replacement. *Med Care* 1992;30:MS240–MS252.

81. Lansky D, Butler B, Waller F. Using health status measures in the hospital setting: from acute care to "outcomes management." *Med Care* 1992;30(5):M557–M573.

82. Wachtel T, Piette J, Mor V, Stein M, Fleishman J, Carpenter C. Quality of life in persons with human immunodeficiency virus infection: measurement by the medical outcomes study instrument. *Ann Intern Med* 1992;116:129–137.

83. Wu AW, Rubin HR, Mathews WC, Ware JE Jr, Brysk LT, Hardy WD, Bozzette SA, Spector SA, Richman DD. A health status questionnaire using 30 items from the medical outcomes study. *Med Care* 1991; 29:786–798.

84. Ware JE, Kosinski M, Keller SD. *SF-36 physical and mental health summary scales—a user's manual.* Boston, MA: The Health Institute, 1994.

85. Katz JN, Larson MG, Phillips CB, Fossel AH, Liang MH. Comparative measurement sensitivity of short and longer health status instruments. *Med Care* 1992;30:917.

86. Phillips RC, Lansky DJ. Outcomes management in heart valve replacement surgery: early experience. *J Heart Valve Dis* 1992;1:42.

87. Ware JE, Kosinski M, Bayliss MS, et al. Comparison of methods for the scoring and statistical analysis of the SF-36 health profile and summary measures: results from the Medical Outcomes Study. *Med Care* 1995 (in press).

88. Stewart A, Hays R, Ware J. The MOS short-form general health survey: reliability and validity in a patient population. *Med Care* 1988;26:724–735.

89. Ware J. Project summary: International Quality of Life Assessment (IQOLA) project. Unpublished document, October 22, 1991.

90. Aaronson NK, Acquadro C, Alonso J, Apolone G, et al. International quality of life assessment (IQOLA) project. *Qual Life Res* 1992;1: 349–351.

91. Ware JE Jr. Translating health: the International Quality of Life Assessment (IQOLA) project. Assessing health-related quality of life measures in international clinical trials. Burroughs-Wellcome Inc., Proceedings of a Workshop (Video tape), August 1992.

92. Ware JE, Gandek B, the IQOLA Project Group. The SF-36 Health Survey: development and use in mental health research and the IQOLA project. *Int J Mental Health* 1994;23:49–73.

93. Garratt AM, Rutta DA, Abdalla MI, et al. The SF-36 health profile: an outcome measure suitable for routine use within the NHS? *Br Med J* 1993;306:1440–1444.

94. Jenkinson C, Coulter A, Wright L. Short Form 36 (SF-36) Health Survey Questionnaire: normative data for adults of working age. *Br Med J* 1993;306:1437–1440.

95. Brazier JE, Harper R, Jones NMB, O'Cathain A, Thomas KJ, Ush-

erwood T, Westlake L. Validating the SF-36 Health Survey Questionnaire: new outcome measure for primary care. *Br Med J* 1992;305: 160–164.

96. Bullinger M. German translation and psychometric testing of the SF-36 Health Survey: preliminary results from the IQOLA Project. *Soc Sci Med* (in press).

97. Sullivan M, Karlsson J, Ware JE. The Swedish SF-36 Health Survey: I. Evaluation of data quality, scaling assumptions, reliability, and construct validity across general populations in Sweden. *Soc Sci Med* (in press).

98. Brazier J, Jones N, Kind P. Testing the validity of the EuroQol and comparing it with the SF-36 health survey questionnaire. *Qual Life Res* 1993;2:169–180.

99. Brooks R, Jendteg S, Lindgren B, Persson V, Bjonk S. EuroQol: health related quality of life measurement. Results from the Swedish questionnaire exercise. *Health Policy* 1991;18:37–48.

100. Nord E. EuroQol: health related quality of life measurement. Valuations of health states by the general public in Norway. *Health Policy* 1991;18:25–36.

101. Nelson EC, Landgraf JM, Hays RD, Wasson JH, Kirk JW. The functional status of patients—how can it be measured in physicians' offices? *Med Care* 1990;28:1111–1126.

102. Nelson EC, Landgraf JM, Hays RD, Kirk JW, Wasson JH, Keller A, Zubkoff M. The COOP function charts: a system to measure patient function in physicians' offices. In: Lipkin M Jr, ed. *Functional status measurement in primary care.* New York: Springer-Verlag, 1990: 97–131.

103. McHorney CA, Ware JE Jr, Rogers W, Raczek AE, Lu JFR. The validity and relative precision of MOS short- and long-form health status scales and Dartmouth COOP charts. *Med Care* 1992;30: MS253–MS265.

104. Landgraf JM, Nelson EC, Hays RD, Wasson JH, Kirk JW. Assessing function: does it really make a difference: A preliminary evaluation of the acceptability and utility of the COOP function charts. In: Lipkin M Jr, ed. *Functional status measurement in primary care.* New York: Springer-Verlag, 1990:150–165.

105. Coates AK, Wilkin D. Comparing the Nottingham Health Profile with the Dartmouth COOP charts. In: Scholten JHG, ed. *Functional status assessment in family practice.* Lelystad: Meditekst, 1992:81–86.

106. Meyboom-de Jong B, Smith RJA. Studies with the Dartmouth COOP charts in general practice: comparison with the Nottingham Health Profile and the General Health Questionnaire. In: Lipkin M Jr, ed. *Functional status measurement in primary care.* New York: Springer-Verlag, 1990:132–149.

107. Westbury RC. Use of the Dartmouth COOP charts in a Calgary practice. In: Lipkin M Jr, ed. *Functional status measurement in primary care.* New York: Springer-Verlag, 1990:166–181.

108. Shigemoto H. A trial of the Dartmouth COOP charts in Japan. In: Lipkin M Jr, ed. *Functional status measurement in primary care.* New York: Springer-Verlag, 1990:181–187.

109. Landgraf JM, Nelson EC, Dartmouth COOP Primary Care Network. Summary of the WONCA/COOP international health assessment field trial. *Aust Fam Physician* 1992;21:255–269.

110. Scholten JHG, Van Weel C. Manual for the use of the Dartmouth COOP Functional Health Assessment Charts/WONCA in measuring functional status in family practice. Part I. In: Scholten JH, Van Weel C, eds. *Functional status assessment in family practice.* Lelystad: Meditekst, 1992:17–50.

111. van Weel C, Scholten JHG. Report of an international workshop of the WONCA Research and Classification Committee. In: Scholten JHG, ed. *Functional status assessment in family practice.* Lelystad: Meditekst, 1992:5–51.

112. van de Lisdonk EH, van Weel C. Cataract and functional status. In: Scholten JHG, ed. *Functional status assessment in family practice.* Lelystad: Meditekst, 1992:70.

113. Schuling J, Meyboom-deJong B. Change in clinical status in patients with stroke. In: Scholten JHG, ed. *Functional status assessment in family practice.* Lelystad: Meditekst, 1992:73.

114. Patterson WM. Peak expiratory flow rates and functional status in asthma. In: Scholten JHG, ed. *Functional status assessment in family practice.* Lelystad: Meditekst, 1992:74.

115. van Weel C, Matteysen N, Wong Chung D, et al. Change in functional status following an asthma exacerbation. In: Scholten JHG, ed. *Functional status assessment in family practice.* Lelystad: Meditekst, 1992:74.

Quality of Life and Pharmacoeconomics in Clinical Trials, Second Edition, edited by B. Spilker.
Lippincott-Raven Publishers, Philadelphia © 1996.

CHAPTER 68

Dimension-Specific Instruments That May Be Used Across Cultures

Michelle J. Naughton and Ingela K. Wiklund

INTRODUCTION

The assessment of health-related quality of life (HRQL) in clinical trials and medical research has become more prominent in recent years. This chapter examines several dimension-specific HRQL measures that have been used cross-culturally.

In preparing for this review, computer literature searches were conducted on the following broad topic areas: depression; anxiety; pain; symptoms; physical, social, and cognitive functioning; emotionality; psychological distress; and sexuality. In addition, literature searches were completed on well-known dimension-specific instruments. Over 1,400 research articles, representing 35 countries outside of the United States, were identified. Although many of these references assessed dimensions of HRQL, such as physical or

M. J. Naughton: Department of Public Health Sciences, Bowman Gray School of Medicine, Wake Forest University, Winston-Salem, North Carolina 27157.
I. K. Wiklund: Department of Behavioural Medicine, Astra Hassle AB, S-431 83 Molndal, Sweden, and Ostra Hospital, S-416 85 Gothenburg, Sweden.

social functioning, few standardized instruments were found to be used across countries in the measurement of these constructs. For example, many investigators measured anxiety as an outcome in their HRQL research, but a majority of instruments or items used in these studies were newly developed by the researchers or had been validated only in their country of study. We encountered the additional problem of identifying several dimension-specific instruments, primarily in the area of physical functioning, that were widely used cross-culturally, but for which there was very limited published information on the psychometric properties of the instruments internationally.

As a result of our literature searches, we identified six scales that have been widely used in a variety of countries, and for which information on the psychometric properties of the non-English translations has been reported. These measures are the Beck Depression Inventory (BDI), the McGill Pain Questionnaire (MPQ), the Center for Epidemiologic Studies–Depression (CES-D), the Zung Self-Rating Depression Scale (SDS), the General Health Questionnaire (GHQ), and the Psychological General Well-Being Index (PGWB). These instruments primarily represent the psychological or emotional dimension of HRQL, and are scales that were developed and validated in either the United States, Canada, or Great Britain. The review of specific studies for each of the six instruments is not meant to be exhaustive, but rather to give an indication of the ways in which the instrument has been assessed or used in various countries. The focus throughout this chapter is on the psychometric properties (reliability, validity, and responsiveness) of these scales in different cultures, as well as the processes used to translate the instruments from English into another language.

A weakness in our methodology of obtaining appropriate literature citations is that the articles or books identified from the computer searches were for the most part, those published in English in internationally available journals. We realize that there could be material on cross-cultural HRQL measures published in languages other than English that were not included in the data bases available to us. Attempts were made, however, to obtain published literature on dimension-specific HRQL instruments by contacting colleagues in other countries and asking for their assistance in obtaining appropriate published or unpublished work in this area.

BECK DEPRESSION INVENTORY

Description

The Beck Depression Inventory (BDI) is an instrument designed to measure the existence and severity of depression in both adolescents and adults (1,2). The BDI has been used in both clinical practice and research studies as a means to assess the intensity of depression in psychiatric patients (3), to detect possible depression in normal populations (4), and to monitor the effectiveness of interventions over time. Questions on the BDI represent cognitive rather than somatic or affective symptoms of depression, and include items that describe the manifestation of depression in relation to general life satisfaction, mood, relations with others, self-esteem, appetite, sleep, and libido (5).

The format of the BDI is distinctive in that it consists of 84 statements, grouped into 21 categories (four statements per category), and one statement is selected by the respondents for each category. The items selected by the respondents are rated on a four-point scale ranging from 0 to 3 in terms of severity. Total scores are calculated by adding the scores on each of the 21 items, resulting in total scores ranging from 0 to 63.

A 13-item short form of the BDI is also available. This questionnaire was developed by selecting the categories that had the highest correlations with the long form and with ratings of depression provided by clinicians (6). Although the short form of the BDI has been used in several studies (7), it is not widely used, and therefore comments in this section will focus primarily on the 21-item version of the BDI.

The psychometric properties of the BDI with various samples of psychiatric patients and normal populations have been described elsewhere (8–14).

Cross-Cultural Versions

The BDI has been translated into a variety of languages including Chinese, Canadian-French, German, Dutch, Swedish, Turkish, Korean, and Finnish.

Chinese

Preliminary research on the reliability and validity of a Chinese version of the BDI have been reported. In work by Zheng et al. (15), the BDI was semantically translated into Chinese by a senior psychiatrist in the Department of Psychiatry, Hunan Medical University, and then backward translation was completed.

This instrument, named the Chinese Beck Depression Inventory (CBDI), was given to a sample of 329 clinically depressed adults to assess the reliability and validity of the instrument. The item-scale consistency was evaluated by correlating the item scores to the total scale score. All items, except loss of libido, had a correlation coefficient above .30. The internal consistency of the entire measure, as assessed by Cronbach's alpha, was .85. Test-retest reliability was not investigated in this study.

Concurrent validity was tested by correlating the scores on the CBDI with scores on the Chinese version of the Hamilton Depression Rating Scale. The correlation between these two measures was .56. Construct validity was assessed by factor analysis. This procedure extracted six factors, three of which were found to be uninterpretable in terms of clinical features of depression. The researchers concluded that although the BDI had been translated into the Chinese language semantically, the items on the inventory did not fit well with the cultural background of the Chinese, making the CBDI less sensitive when used with Chinese depressed patients.

In separate studies reported from Hong Kong, the use of another CBDI has produced more positive results in adolescent populations. Research by Shek (16) reported estimates of reliability and validity of a CBDI with 2,150 secondary school students aged 13 to 20 years of age. The overall reliability of the CBDI in this sample was .86, with a split half reliability of .77. The item-total correlations were also above .30 for all but two of the items. Factor analysis was used to assess construct validity. In this sample, a two-factor solution was employed, which resulted in a general depression, and a somatic disturbance factor. These factors were replicated by splitting the total sample into two subsamples. Further analysis of the reliability of these factors indicated that they were internally consistent. The reliability and validity estimates produced in this study by Shek are consistent with results found previously by Chan and Tsoi (17) in a small sample of junior college students. Discriminant or predictive validity was not examined in either of the studies by Shek or Chan and Tsoi. However, separate research examining the depressive symptoms of Chinese medical and nonmedical students indicated that the scores on the CBDI were not significantly different between those two groups of students, although the mean score for the Chinese medical students was higher than that typically reported for U.S. medical students (18).

Canadian-French

Bourque and Beaudette (19) reported the findings of a French translation of the BDI with university students. Early work on a French translation was completed in the mid-1960s (20,21), but modification of the American version of the BDI in the early 1970s (2) necessitated further refinement of a Canadian-French inventory.

The version of the BDI reported by Bourque and Beaudette (called the QDB) was translated at the Université de Moncton in New Brunswick, Canada. The instrument was administered to 498 university students across a variety of different programs of study. The internal consistency of the QDB was .92 for the standard 21-item form, and .90 for the 13-item short form. Test-retest reliability over a 4-month period indicated a moderate degree of stability ($r = .62$, $p < .001$). Factor analysis of the items revealed three factors, accounting for 76% of the variance. The norms obtained from this sample correspond well with those obtained with American college students (22), suggesting the validity of the QDB for use in college populations.

German

Kammer (23) examined the reliability and validity of a German version of the Beck Depression Inventory in a sample of 264 university students. Measures of internal consistency for the German translations were .82 for the full scale and .80 for the 13-item short form. Factor analyses delineated two factors for the short form (cognitive/affective and somatic/behavioral), and four factors for the full scale (guilt, self-punitiveness, somatic disturbances, and sadness). Construct validity of the full form of the German BDI was investigated by correlating the full instrument with three other measures of depression. The German BDI was found to be moderately correlated with the Hamburger Depressionsskala (.48) (24), the Depressivitatsskala des Freiburger Personlichkeits—inventors (.62) (25), and the Minnesota Multiphasic Personality Inventory (MMPI) depression scale (.61) (26).

Further investigation of the short and long forms of the German BDI are reportedly under way.

Dutch

A Dutch version of the BDI has been in use in the Netherlands, but few studies have examined the reliability and validity of the translation in Dutch populations. Bosscher et al. (27) examined the standard 21-item form of the BDI among a sample of 85 female and 118 male university students. No information was provided about the translation process used to construct the Dutch BDI. Internal consistency, as measured by Cronbach's alpha, was .82. Concurrent validity was assessed by correlating the scores on the Dutch BDI with the Dutch version of the Zung Self-Rating Depression Scale ($r = .69$) (28). No gender differences in the students' responses to the questionnaire items were found. The results of this study indicated the usefulness of the Dutch BDI with university students, although these results were not suggested to be generalizable to clinically depressed populations.

Swedish

A Swedish translation of the BDI has been employed in a study of adolescents (29). The translation was reportedly checked by three bilingual translators, and item 21 on the original BDI was changed from interest "in the opposite sex" to "interest in boys/girls." In addition, two items were also added to the instrument. These questions asked students to rate, on a 10-cm visual analog scale, their level of social activity, and to what extent they had felt depressed recently.

Twenty classrooms of students, representing 547 adolescents, were selected from a junior high school and an upper secondary school. Two classes were also randomly selected to participate in an examination of test-retest reliability, which was assessed at 2-week and 2-month intervals. The results indicated no significant differences in total scores on the BDI with respect to the ages of the students, school, or site, but the mean score for the girls ($\bar{x} = 8.5$) was twice that for the boys ($\bar{x} = 4.2$).

Reliability of the translated instrument was assessed in several ways. Total item correlations ranged from .44 to .68, and all were significant except for poor appetite, weight loss, worry about one's own health, and reduced interest in boys/girls. Correlations between the total score on the BDI and the single items ranged from .24 to .68. Interitem correlations ranged from $-.02$ to .57, with an average value of .25. Internal consistency, as measured by Cronbach's alpha, was .87. Test-retest reliability within 2 weeks was .86, and was .88 at 2 months. The mean scores on the BDI were found to decrease between the two testing times, however.

The factor-based structure of the Swedish version was examined using principal components analysis. Four factors were extracted, representing dysphoric mood, social activity, relationships, and food-related components. Discriminant validity of the translated measure was assessed using discriminant function analysis. Using this procedure, 88% of the adolescents were appropriately classified into nondepressed (mean score <15) or depressed categories (mean score of 16 or greater). Concurrent validity was not assessed in this investigation.

Turkish

A translation of the 1978 version of the BDI has been adapted for use in the Turkish culture. Measures of internal consistency for this instrument have ranged from .74 to .86 (30–32). Split-half reliability has been reported at .80 (30). Concurrent validity of the Turkish BDI has been assessed through correlating this instrument with the Turkish version of the MMPI–depression. Results indicated the correlation between the Turkish BDI and the Turkish MMPI to be .63 for a sample of medical students, and .50 for psychiatric samples (30). Cutoff points for the Turkish BDI have also been proposed for use with Turkish university students (BDI < 9 are asymptomatic; BDI > 17 are considered to be symptomatic) (33).

Korean

One study was identified from our literature search, which used a Korean translation of the BDI to validate the Korean Youth Depression Adjective Checklist (34). Lee (35) is reported to have translated the BDI into Korean, and found internal consistency reliability scores of .88 for college students and .84 for a nonclinical adult population. Lee's results are unpublished, but are provided for the interested reader.

Finnish

Several studies were obtained that used a Finnish version of the BDI in assessments of coronary artery bypass graft patients (36,37). No information was provided to the reader, however, regarding the process employed in translating the items into Finnish or the psychometric properties of the new instrument.

McGILL PAIN QUESTIONNAIRE

Description

The McGill Pain Questionnaire (MPQ) was designed to provide a quantitative profile of clinical pain (38). It was originally intended as a means to evaluate different pain therapies, but it has also been used as a diagnostic tool (39). The instrument is widely used both clinically and in pain research.

Melzack (40) approached the development of the MPQ on a theoretical basis, hypothesizing that there were three major psychological dimensions of pain: sensory-discriminative,

motivational-affective, and cognitive-evaluative. Melzack and Torgerson (41) selected 102 descriptive words relating to pain from existing literature and questionnaires. These words were sorted into categories assessing sensory qualities of pain (e.g., temporal, thermal); affective qualities of pain (e.g., tension, fear); and evaluative words that described the intensity of the pain experience. Words that were qualitatively similar were then sorted into subgroups within the three major categories, and the intensity of pain represented by the words in each subclass were rated using a numerical scale from least to worst by groups of patients, students, and doctors.

In the long form of the questionnaire, respondents are asked to select one word from each of the subgroups that best describes their pain. If none of the words in a subclass is appropriate, the item is left blank. Aside from the list of pain descriptor words, additional questions are also included in the MPQ, but are not used in scoring. These items are the patients' diagnosis, pain medical history, medications, present pain pattern and accompanying symptoms and modifying factors, and the effects of the patients' pain on their lives. Patients are also asked to indicate the location of their pain using a body figure printed on the questionnaire (42).

Scoring of the MPQ can be calculated in several different ways. Separate pain rating indices (PRI) can be obtained for the sensory, affective, miscellaneous, and evaluative subcategories of pain. A total PRI can be calculated by adding the four subscores. A pain intensity score is also calculated from the pain description section of the questionnaire. In addition, a quality score can be calculated by counting the total number of words chosen by a respondent. Weighted rank scores can also be calculated. The ranks applied to the items are obtained by the original work by Melzack and Torgerson (41).

A short form of the MPQ has also been developed, which takes approximately 5 minutes to complete (43). Respondents are asked to select one word each from 15 subclasses, representing the sensory and affective dimensions of pain (38). The short form is scored by summing the intensity scores for the affective and sensory components, as well as obtaining a total score for all items of the questionnaire (43).

The psychometric properties of the MPQ have been assessed in terms of test-retest reliability (38,44,45); construct, predictive, and concurrent validity (45–48); its factor structure (45,47,49,50); and its responsiveness to change (5).

Cross-Cultural Versions

The MPQ is widely used in the United States and other English-speaking countries, such as Great Britain, Canada, and Australia. In general, the MPQ has been found to have similar levels of reliability and validity within these countries. In addition to the English versions of the instrument, however, the MPQ has been translated into several other languages including Dutch, Finnish, Norwegian, German, Italian, French and Canadian-French, Arabic, and Spanish.

The psychometric properties of these versions of the MPQ are described below.

Dutch

Several versions of a pain scale based on the MPQ have been developed for use with Dutch-speaking populations. Van der Meij et al. (51) completed an earlier version of the MPQ, and Belgium researchers Vanderiet and colleagues (52) later developed a Flemish Dutch version of the MPQ, which closely followed the methodology outlined by Melzack. In the initial development of the Vanderiet et al. version, a wide inventory of pain descriptors was generated using descriptions obtained from patients and from preexisting lists of words used to describe pain. One hundred and twenty-four terms for pain resulted from this inventory, and were classified by students and experts into sensory, affective, and evaluative categories. The pain descriptors were rated for intensity of distress by pain experts, patients, and students.

The internal consistency of the Vanderiet et al. version was assessed for the component parts of the questionnaire as well as the scale as a whole, and showed results similar to those reported by Melzack for the original version. Test-retest validity was not assessed in this investigation. The sensitivity of the instrument to change was assessed by 20 pain patients who were given the instrument before and after a nerve block session. In this sample, pain scores decreased significantly after treatment, suggesting that the instrument was sensitive to treatment effects.

Another Dutch version of the MPQ was developed by Verkes and associates (53) in the Netherlands. In investigating the question of whether different cultures discriminate pain words in the same manner, this team of researchers examined the underlying semantic structure and dimensions of 176 common Dutch words used to describe pain. The list of pain descriptors was generated from patients, physicians, medical-psychological textbooks, and adjectives employed by Melzack and Torgerson. Fifty-three subjects sorted the words for similarity in meaning, and an additional 64 physiotherapy students rated the intensity of each of the words. A computer program for multiple correspondence analysis was used to generate a three-dimensional configuration differentiating evaluative/affective, sensory, temporal, and spatial aspects of pain. Intensity of pain was shown to be the main criteria for similarity within the affective/evaluative group, whereas intensity was not related to the similarities among the sensory words. Cluster analysis yielded 32 clusters of words among which the subscales of both the original MPQ and the Dutch version by Vanderiet et al. could be identified. Verkes et al. concluded that since these results were obtained in a different country and with different methods of data collection, they strongly indicated a cross-cultural and cross-methodological generality of the structure of pain descriptions.

Extensive testing of the reliability and validity of the Verkes et al. version of the MPQ has not been reported in the literature to date. In one study of rheumatoid arthritis patients, the instrument provided useful information on the sensory experience of pain, although the measure was only weakly related to the medical outcome variables (54).

A joint Dutch language version of the MPQ (the MPQ-DLV) has also been constructed recently. The Verkes et al. and the Vanderiet et al. groups cooperated together to produce this new version of the MPQ (55). Detailed information on the reliability and validity of the MPQ-DLV has not been presented as yet.

Finnish

Ketovouri and Pontinen (56) reported on the development of a Finnish version of the MPQ. Words describing pain were collected by students and patients who were asked to create a list by free association. These subjects were then given a dictionary-derived Finnish version of the MPQ, with the words arranged in alphabetical order, and were asked to place their own words for pain among the dictionary-derived words. Subjects also were asked to rate the intensity of each word by means of a visual analog scale. These words were placed into categories of pain, and another group of university students rated whether each word belonged to the category to which it had been assigned. Following this procedure, the words were arranged by order of intensity using a visual analog scale. The final 56 words chosen for the inventory were those that were most often selected by the students and that reflected a statistically significant change in intensity, as assessed by t-tests. Information on the reliability and validity of the instrument was not provided in this article.

Gronblad and colleagues (57) studied the intercorrelation of repeated measures for pain and disability in a study of low back patients using a Finnish translation of the MPQ short form, the Visual Analog Scale (VAS), and the Pain Disability Index (PDI). In this investigation, the total number of words chosen on the short form of the MPQ, and the worst pain during the preceding 2 weeks, as assessed by the VAS, were found to be the most stable indicators of pain under repeated measurements. The total number of markings on the pain drawing and the sensory word scale of the MPQ short form showed very little test-retest variability. The sensory word score of the MPQ short form was also found to be significantly correlated with present pain (VAS) and the PDI. The total number of markings on the pain diagram of the MPQ was seen to be a useful clinical tool, concurring with the findings of Vden and colleagues (58).

Norwegian

A simplified and standardized Norwegian form of the MPQ for use with lumbago/sciatica patients was published in 1983 (59). However, the development of a more comprehensive Norwegian pain questionnaire, to be applied to many different types of clinical populations, was later undertaken by Strand and Wisnes (60) using the MPQ as a model.

Several steps were taken to develop the pain instrument by Strand and Wisnes. To obtain descriptors of pain, 95 subjects, both patients and health professionals, were asked to list adjectives that could be used to describe pain. This resulted in 333 different adjectives, which were pared down to 110 words, and grouped by 10 subjects into 18 separate categories: 12 sensory, 5 affective, and 1 evaluative. The validity of this categorization was evaluated by 36 subjects who agreed on the classification of 106 of the 110 pain descriptors. The four words not agreed upon were deleted from the scale. The intensity of the descriptors was rated by 96 pain patients, by means of a visual analog scale.

Preliminary testing of the instrument indicated high internal reliability (Kuder-Richardson .60–.80 and above) for all 18 categories of pain, and high item-total correlations. Further testing of the inventory is needed, however, to investigate the reliability, validity, and sensitivity of this instrument in clinical and research studies.

German

Several German translations of the MPQ have been described in the published literature. Kiss and colleagues (61) produced a translated version of the MPQ and tested its validity on a population of cancer patients. The German translation was completed with the assistance of language teachers, physicians, interpreters, medical students, and lay persons. Information on the reliability and validity of the translated instrument was not provided in the published article. The sensitivity of the translated MPQ to treatment effects, however, was evaluated in the population of cancer patients.

Another German translation of the MPQ has been offered by Radvila and associates (62). The adjectives employed in the MPQ were translated into German by seven individuals fluent in both German and English. Nine of the English adjectives could not be translated, and consequently ten new German adjectives were added. The list of German adjectives were assigned to 20 groups, and 80 subjects rated the intensity of the words in each group on a visual analog scale. Three of the 20 groups of adjectives were eliminated from the translated version of the MPQ because they showed almost no differences in intensity along the visual analog scale. For the remaining 17 groups, the list of adjectives per group was reduced to three by eliminating the least discriminating words of each group. The three words retained in each category were then reassessed for intensity by 82 subjects. It was reported that considerable disagreements were found between the raters in their ranking of the three adjectives in nine of the categories.

The validity of the Radvila et al. translation was assessed in a clinical setting with a pain-provoking, intraarterial injection of contrast media. This instrument was able to differentiate between the intensity of two kinds of short-lasting acute pain, but not the qualitative aspects of these two types of pain. Additional information on the reliability and validity of this translation of the MPQ was not provided.

A third German version of the MPQ was developed by Stein and Mendl (63). This translation is distinct from those developed by Kiss et al. and Radvila et al. in that it was developed by adhering strictly to the original methodology outlined by Melzack and Torgerson. One group of 40 subjects was used to define five anchor words for the intensity scale. The 78 descriptors of the MPQ were then translated into German with the assistance of language teachers, psychologists, physicians, and laypersons. A second group of 42 subjects assigned an intensity rating (1–5) to each of the 78 adjectives. The mean ratings of each of the descriptors were then compared to those obtained in the original version of the MPQ. Fourteen descriptors whose mean intensity ratings differed markedly from those of the original version were resubmitted to a different group of 40 subjects, along with three or four synonyms, to reassign an intensity rating to each of the descriptors. The adjectives whose ratings corresponded closest to those in the English original were then selected for inclusion in the translated version. The resultant translation is reported to retain the original grouping of adjectives, the identical number of words per group, as well as their rank positions with the categories, making more direct comparisons between the German and English versions possible.

The Stein and Mendl version has been used in several published studies. Scores on the MPQ were found to vary by four morphine treatment conditions in patients immediately following arthroscopic knee surgery (64). No significant differences in MPQ scores were obtained, however, across two groups of patients in a study assessing the effect of interpleural morphine on postoperative pain and pulmonary function after thoracotomy (65). Scores on the MPQ were also not shown to differ across three shock-wave systems in a study investigating pain sensations experienced during extracorporeal shock-wave applications (66).

No additional information on the validity, sensitivity, or reliability of the Stein and Mendl version of the MPQ was found for this review.

Italian

An Italian version of the MPQ was developed by Maiani and Sanavio (67). This translation followed the methodology developed by Melzack, except that nonpatient subjects were used to provide rank and scale scores within each of the pain categories. Physicians, other health professionals, and patients suffering from chronic pain were excluded from this process. The 78 descriptors of the MPQ were translated into Italian, and Melzack's division of the descriptors into classes and subclasses was retained. Tests of the reliability and validity of this instrument were reported to be under way, and were not provided in the original article.

Several published studies were found that utilized the Maiani and Sanavio version of the MPQ in rheumatology studies. Work by researchers in a clinical setting showed the pain rating index of the Italian MPQ to distinguish between patients with rheumatoid arthritis, fibromyalgin syndrome, and osteoarthritis (68). Analyses of the words chosen by patients indicated a thermal sensory descriptor for fibromyalgia, suggesting that the pain rating index might be useful for the clinical assessment of fibromyalgic pain and in patient follow-up. In a study of women with knee osteoarthritis, the translated MPQ correlated with the Italian version of the Arthritis Impact Measurement Scale (69). In addition, pain and disability were found to be positively related to the levels of anxiety and depression experienced by the patients.

A second version of the MPQ was developed by Italian researchers De Benedittis and colleagues (70). To overcome the cross-cultural semantic barriers to literal translation of the MPQ, these researchers developed an Italian Pain Questionnaire based on the three factorial structures proposed by Melzack and Torgerson (i.e., sensory, affective, and evaluative). A group of physicians and university students were used to define five anchor words for the intensity scale by means of a visual analog scale. Another group of patients, students, and physicians were asked to sort 203 descriptors, generated by the researchers from patients and clinical literature, into four major categories: sensory, affective, evaluative, and miscellaneous. Subjects were asked to eliminate words that they did not consider to be adequate descriptors of pain. Fifty-six of the 203 descriptors were retained for subsequent intensity ratings and were divided into 23 subclasses. Statistical analyses further pared down the number of descriptors and subclasses, so that the final version of the Italian Pain Questionnaire contained 42 pain descriptors distributed into three major classes (sensory, affective, evaluative) and 16 subclasses. The subclasses differ somewhat from the original MPQ due to idiomatic and cultural differences in the way in which pain is perceived.

Information on the reliability and validity of the De Benedittis et al. version of the MPQ was not found in our review of the published literature.

French and Canadian-French

A French adaptation of the McGill Pain Questionnaire, the Questionnaire Douleau St. Antoine (QDSA), has been developed by Boureau and colleagues (71–73). It consists of 61 descriptors and 17 subclasses. Rank and mean values on a five-point intensity scale have been calculated for each descriptor. A sensory score (QDSA-S), an affective score (QDSA-A), and a total score (QDSA-T) can be calculated for the QDSA. Three different scoring procedures can be used: (a) the sum of the rank order value of the descriptor chosen in a subclass, (b) the sum of the means of the descrip-

tors chosen in a subclass, and (c) the sum of the patients' values assigned to the chosen descriptors.

The QDSA has been used in a published study of heterotopic chronic pain (74). The QDSA was not seen to distinguish between chronic pain patients and pain-free control groups, or between patient subgroups, on pain threshold, pain tolerance, and lower limb vociceptive reflex. Also, no significant correlation was found between the level of experimentally induced pain and clinical pain, anxiety, and depression scores. The chronic pain patients, however, had a higher threshold for unpleasantness, and judged the suprathreshold stimuli significantly less intense and unpleasant.

A Canadian-French translation of the MPQ was completed by Viguie (75) and was called the Questionnaire Algie (QA). The QA differs from the QDSA in that it consists of 77 descriptors in four major categories (affective, sensory, evaluative, and miscellaneous), and 20 subclasses. Thirty-three descriptors are common to the QA and QDSA questionnaires. The intensity of the QA descriptors was rated by 20 French physicians on a five-point intensity scale. The QA provides quantitative measures of pain similar to those in the original MPQ (i.e., the number of words chosen, pain rating index, and present pain intensity). Three scoring procedures are considered for the QA scores, and are identical to those described above for the QDSA. Five pain rating indices can be calculated from the QA: a total score (QA-T), a sensory score (QA-S), and affective score (QA-A), an evaluative score (QA-E), and a miscellaneous score (QA-M).

A study by Boureau and Paquette (76) compared the QA and the QDSA. One hundred chronic pain patients were administered both the QA and the QDSA in random order. The subjects also completed the Visual Analog Scale (VAS), the Beck Depression Inventory (BDI), the Spielberger State-Trait Anxiety Inventory (STAI), and the Binois-Pichot Vocabulary Aptitude Test (BPT). The results indicated a high correlation (.87) between QA-T and QDSA-T scores. The correlation was .83 between QDSA-S and QA-S, and .81 between QDSA-A and QA-A scores. The correlation was .50 between QDSA-S and QDSA-A, and .44 between QA-S and QA-A.

The QDSA and QA correlated similarly with the VAS (.34 between the QDSA-T and the VAS, .37 between the QA and VAS), the BDI (.52 between the QDSA-A and the BDI, .45 between the BDI and QA-A, .31 between the BDI and QDSA-S, and .28 between the BDI and QA-S), and the STAI (.53 between the QDSA-A and the STAI-S, .58 between the STAI-T and the QDSA-A, .36 between the QA-A and STAI-S, and .51 between the QA-A and the STAI-T).

Principal components analysis was used to examine the factor-based structure of both the QDSA and the QA. Five factors, accounting for 61.4% of the variance, were extracted from the 16 QDSA subclasses. Factor 1 represented the anxiodepressive component of pain. Factor 2 reflected an affective-evaluative component of the pain experience, and factors 3 to 5 were all sensory components of the pain experience. Principal components analysis examining the QA produced five factors, accounting for 59.9% of the variance, from the 20 subclasses. Factor 1 reflected an affective component of pain, and factors 2 to 5 reflected sensory components of pain. The results of these analyses supported the multidimensional structure of the QA and QDSA, even though a two-dimensional model (sensory and affective) was found in contrast to the three-dimensional model proposed by Melzack (i.e., sensory, affective, and evaluative).

No information on the reliability of the QDSA or QA was reported.

Arabic

The initial stages in the development of an Arabic pain inventory have been described (77). In stage I of this development, 279 Kuwaiti adults, composed of housewives, soldiers, teachers, and policemen were used to generate pain descriptors. Any word proposed by more than one subject was retained. After this task had been completed, the subjects were given a dictionary translation of the MPQ, and asked to indicate one of the following categories for each term: (a) unfamiliar with the word, (b) word appropriate for describing pain, and (c) word not appropriate for describing pain. Any translated items that the majority had rated as not understood or inappropriate were dropped, and a new translation of the item was substituted.

In stage II, 67 Kuwaiti undergraduates were asked to classify the words generated from stage I into sensory, affective, and evaluative categories. The students also rated the intensity of pain connoted with each descriptor on a visual analog scale. After this process was completed, the words were reorganized into the MPQ format. Words were rank ordered within each category based on their pain intensity score.

Over 100 terms were generated, which captured the multidimensional nature of the pain experience. Good correspondence in the intensity rank ordering of items in English and Arabic were found, although there was less agreement in the classification of words into the affective, sensory, and evaluative categories. Further development of the instrument is under way, with particular emphasis being placed on grouping pain terms into meaningful categories for Arabic patients.

Spanish

A Spanish translation of the MPQ was developed by Lahuerta et al. (78). Limited information was provided in the published article describing the process used to translate the instrument. The authors reported that when possible, literal translation of the terms was completed. Otherwise, synonyms or equivalent expressions were used. The original structure of the word descriptor subclasses was maintained.

No information on the reliability or validity of the Spanish translation of the MPQ was found in the published literature.

Other Translations

Translations of the MPQ have been reported in Sweden, Hungary, and Israel (79), but no detailed information regarding these translations was available for this review.

CENTERS FOR EPIDEMIOLOGIC STUDIES–DEPRESSION

Description

The Centers for Epidemiologic Studies–Depression (CES-D) scale was designed to measure symptoms of depression in community populations (80–83). It is not intended to provide a diagnosis of depression, nor is it able to determine the cause of the depressive symptoms (i.e., physical illness, medication, psychiatric disorder, or a reaction to an event). The instrument consists of 20 items selected from previously developed scales (1,84–87). These questions are considered to be representative of the major symptoms in the clinical syndrome of depression, as identified by clinical judgment, frequency of use in other instruments for depression, and factor analytic studies (80).

The 20 items on the CES-D include questions on depressive symptomatology, depressed mood, feelings of guilt and loneliness, hopelessness, loss of appetite, sleep disturbance, and psychomotor retardation. Respondents are asked to rate the frequency of 20 symptoms over the past week by choosing one of four response categories ranging from 0, ''rarely or none of the time,'' to 3, ''most or all of the time.'' Each response category also has a number of days associated with it, in order to decrease the problems related to different interpretations of the responses to the items. Scores on the CES-D are calculated by a simple sum of the 20 items, and the scores have a potential range from 0 to 60. High scores indicate both the presence and persistence of the symptoms represented by the scale. A cutoff score of 16 is generally used to distinguish individuals considered to be depressed from those classified as nondepressed (80,88).

A short version of the CES-D has also been developed for use in research studies (89). This instrument is composed of eight items, six of which were taken from the original CES-D to represent the six global categories measured by the instrument. The additional two items are summary questions that ask the respondents to report the presence of persistent depressive symptoms in their lifetime.

The long version of the CES-D is more widely used cross-culturally, and therefore the remarks in this section are limited primarily to the original and not the short form of the CES-D.

Information on the psychometric properties of the short and long forms of the CES-D can be found elsewhere (81, 82,90–95).

Cross-Cultural Versions

The CES-D is one of the few instruments in this review that has undergone reliability and validity testing in several ethnic groups within the United States, as well as internationally. Results are provided here for Black, Hispanic, and Asian-American samples; and Greek, French, Japanese, and Yugoslavian populations.

Black and Hispanic U.S. Studies

Radloff (81) examined the factor structure of the CES-D, and identified four distinct components: depressed affect, positive affect, somatic and retarded activity, and interpersonal. This factor structure was replicated by Roberts (92) in a confirmatory factor analysis of the scale in Anglo (whites of non-Hispanic origin), black, and Mexican-American samples. Roberts also found no differences among these three groups in terms of missing data or internal consistency reliability (96). A similar investigation examining the CES-D in the Hispanic Health and Nutrition Examination Survey data, however, failed to replicate the four factors (97). In this study, data from Mexican-Americans, Cuban-Americans, and Puerto Ricans yielded a three-factor solution with a combined affective and somatic factor. Intragroup differences were observed in the factor structures, and were strongly influenced by the gender of the respondent and whether the individual completed the CES-D interview in English or Spanish. In studies of psychiatric patients, Roberts et al. (91) found no systematic variation in either internal consistency, test-retest reliability, dimensionality, or ability of the CES-D scale to detect clinical depression among Anglos or persons of Mexican origin, classified according to language use as Spanish dominant. In related work, however, scores on the CES-D were found to be associated with generalized anxiety disorder in Anglos and English-speaking Mexican-Americans, but not Spanish-speaking Mexican-Americans. The agreement of the CES-D with the Diagnostic Interview Schedule was also poor, although the CES-D was positively associated with major depressive disorder in all three ethnic groups (98).

Responses to items on the CES-D have also been examined in relation to the social demographic factors of the respondents (99–105). In studies of both Hispanics and blacks, depressive symptoms were higher among those individuals who had not adapted to mainstream American society: women, the elderly, those with low educational achievement or low incomes, and those with low language skills. These results suggest that the low socioeconomic status experienced by many minorities may be an important determinant of higher rates of reported depression among blacks and Hispanics.

Asian-Americans

Kuo (106) examined the use of the CES-D with Asian-Americans in a sample of residents of Seattle, Washington. The ethnic groups included in this study were Chinese, Filipino, Japanese, and Korean Americans. The CES-D was administered through personal interviewers, who were matched to the respondents in ethnic background and language ability.

The factor structure of the CES-D was examined, and the four extracted factors were labeled: depressed and somatic, interpersonal, positive, and pessimistic. These four factors accounted for 53% of the variance on the scale items, and this percentage is similar to the figure of 48% reported by Radloff (81) in her examination of the factor-based structure of the CES-D discussed above. The factor structure of the CES-D with the Asian-Americans was not found to be substantially different from that of the white population. However, the scale items of depressive affect and somatic complaints tended to cluster together in Asian respondents, whereas they did not in studies completed in white populations. Among the four Asian groups examined in this investigation, the factor analysis revealed some common and overlapping patterns in the Chinese-, Korean-, and Japanese-American samples. The Filipino-American sample, however, had a unique factor in terms of its component items, which was not found in the other Asian-American groups. This result was believed to indicate that the expression of depressive symptoms in Filipinos may differ from those of the other East Asian groups due to the heavy impact of Spanish colonization and teaching of Confucian ethics not present in the three other groups.

The mean scores on the CES-D were found to be higher for the Asian-American samples than the means found in white samples (81,105). However, the means were lower than those found previously in Hispanic and black samples (105). In addition, 19.1% of the Asian samples had a CES-D score of 16 or above. In terms of differences among the four Asian-American groups studied, the Koreans had the highest mean score on the CES-D, followed by the Filipinos, then the Japanese and Chinese. In addition, foreign-born Asians were found to experience more depressive symptoms than the American-born Asians, except in the Chinese sample.

In terms of demographic characteristics, married individuals had lower CES-D scores than those who had never married. Among the Chinese and Filipinos, females reported more depressive symptoms than males, but among the Japanese and Koreans, the women reported fewer symptoms than their male counterparts. In general, the CES-D scores were highest among persons under 30 years of age, those unemployed or working part-time, those with incomes under $25,000 per year, those with lower educational attainment, and those whose religious beliefs made them a minority within their own group (e.g., Catholics among the Chinese and Koreans). No significant interactions were found between these demographic characteristics and the four ethnic groups.

Measures of reliability or concurrent validity were not assessed in this study.

In a more recent investigation, Ying (107) reported on the use of CES-D in a community sample of 360 Chinese-Americans in the San Francisco, California area. The CES-D was translated into Chinese by two translators who worked independently. The measure was then back-translated into English by two other independent translators. The back-translated versions were found to be similar to the original version and to each other. Minor differences in colloquial expressions in Mandarin and Cantonese Chinese were addressed in the revised version.

The translated version of the CES-D was administered in a telephone interview, and respondents were asked to indicate whether they had experienced each questionnaire item during the past week. The CES-D was administered in either English or Chinese (Cantonese or Mandarin), depending on the preference of the respondent.

Internal consistency of this version of the CES-D, as measured by Cronbach's alpha, was .77. The Guttman split-half and Spearman-Brown coefficients were also both .77. The factor structure of the instrument was examined and revealed three factors: depressed and somatic, positive affect, and interpersonal. The amount of variance accounted for by these three factors was 43.2%. These results are similar to those found by Kuo in that there was no distinction between the somatization and depressed factors as identified by Radloff (81) in her original sample described above. A LISREL (Linear Structural Relations) analysis comparing the Ying factors with the factors identified by Radloff indicated a poor goodness of fit between the Radloff and the Ying models.

The mean CES-D score in the Ying sample was 11.55, which was significantly higher than the mean scores of 7.94 to 8.58 identified by Radloff (81) in her predominantly white sample, and the mean of 6.93 reported by Kuo (106) in his sample of Chinese-Americans in Seattle. Using the cutoff score of 16, 24.2% of the Chinese-American respondents were found to have higher levels of depressive symptomatology in the Ying study. Mean CES-D scores were found to be higher among foreign-born Chinese-Americans, those who had resided in the United States for a shorter period of time, and those with lower status jobs and lower educational attainment. Marital status did not significantly affect the scores on the CES-D in this group. In general, persons of higher socioeconomic status, as measured by education and occupation, reported fewer depressive symptoms than persons of lower socioeconomic status.

From the results of this study, Ying (107) concluded that adequate internal consistency of the CES-D had been demonstrated with Chinese-Americans, but that further investiga-

tion of the conceptual and construct validity of the items for this population was warranted.

Greek

A Greek version of the CES-D has been reported by Madianos and colleagues (108). Several published articles were located that utilized the translated CES-D. However, limited information is available about the translation process used in developing the Greek version.

In a community sample of elderly Greek residents, test-retest reliability of the Greek CES-D was .76 (109,110). The internal consistency of the instrument was not examined in this population. The scores on the Greek CES-D were validated against a diagnosis of depression (depressed versus non-depressed) using the *Diagnostic and Statistical Manual* (DSM-III) criteria. A cutoff score of greater than 16 provided moderately high sensitivity (83.4%) and specificity rates (85.9%) (109). A cutoff point of greater than 20 produced a sensitivity and specificity of 85.7% and 84.6%, respectively (110). Twenty-seven percent of the elderly respondents were identified as depressed cases using a cutoff score of 16. However, only 9.5% of those individuals were diagnosed as suffering from clinical types of depression using the Psychiatric Evaluation Form supplemented with the DSM-III criteria. Depressive psychopathology was found to be higher among women, those of lower socioeconomic status, and those widowed, living alone, or experiencing stressful life events.

To further evaluate the use of the CES-D in identifying cases of depression, Madianos and Stefanis (111) examined the usefulness of the instrument in a nationwide probability sample of 4,292 respondents. Using the traditional cutoff point of 16, 29% of the respondents were identified as having a high degree of depressive symptomatology. To identify true depressed cases, Madianos and Stefanis developed a total of nine criteria, including the individual's score on the CES-D. Using these criteria, lower proportions of the sample were identified as probable (7.2%) and definite (8.0%) psychiatric cases. These results suggest the usefulness of a multidimensional approach in order to produce more valid and reliable estimates of mental disorders in community samples.

French

A French version of the CES-D was developed by Fuhrer and Rouillon (112). The number of items retained in the French CES-D is 20, with all possible scores ranging from 0 to 60. In comparing scores on the French CES-D with both clinical rating scales and clinical diagnoses based on DSM-III criteria, the recommended cutoff scores for the French instrument were determined to be 17 for males and 23 for females. These cutoff points are in contrast to the common cutoff score of 16.

The French CES-D has been used in a 5-year prospective, epidemiological survey of normal and pathological aging (113). This study involved a community sample of 2,792 noninstitutionalized persons, aged 65 and older, living in southwest France. The internal consistency reliability of the French CES-D in this sample was .89. Overall, 13.4% of the elderly individuals reported depressive symptoms. Scores on the CES-D were found to vary by the age, gender, educational level, and marital status of the respondents. Persons with no functional limitations also reported fewer depressive symptoms, but as the limitations increased, the mean scores on the French CES-D increased for both men and women. More symptoms were reported by the functionally impaired men than the functionally impaired women, however. A significant relationship was found between cognitive functioning, as assessed by the Mini-Mental State Examination and the CES-D scores, but after adjusting for age, living arrangements, and functional limitations, the relationship remained strong only for women.

Japanese

A Japanese version of the CES-D was developed by Shima and associates (114) in 1985. No detailed information was provided regarding the process used to translate the items into Japanese. This version of the CES-D was found to discriminate between depressed patients and normal controls, and the standard cutoff point of 16 was judged to be appropriate for use with this population.

Iwata and Saito (115,116) have used the Japanese CES-D in several investigations of Japanese workers. In these samples, the Japanese CES-D has been found to have acceptable reliability and good concurrent validity with other indices of psychological distress and depression. In a study of Japanese men and women tax office workers, the mean scales were found to be higher than those reported in the U.S. population (117). After controlling for age and marital status, depressive symptoms were found in 15.2% of the males and 10.6% of the females. Men over the age of 50, in particular, had more depressive symptoms than men in other age groups.

More detailed information on the reliability and validity of the Japanese translation of the CES-D was not found in the published literature.

Yugoslavian

Serbo and Jajic (118) reported on the use of the CES-D in Yugoslavian patients with rheumatoid arthritis. No information was provided in the article about the process used to translate the items. The results indicated that the means scores on the CES-D were higher for patients with rheumatoid arthritis than for a group of healthy controls, 13.05 versus 9.45, respectively. The CES-D was found to

have a significant, though modest correlation (.346) with a visual analog scale that measured the severity of the patients' arthritis pain in the past week from ''no pain'' to ''unbearable pain.'' Scores on the CES-D, however, were not found to be significantly different among rheumatoid arthritis patients when the duration of the patients' disease was examined in groups of 1 to 5 years and 15 to 24 years. No additional information on the validity or the reliability of the CES-D was provided in this study.

ZUNG SELF-RATING DEPRESSION SCALE

Description

The Zung Self-Rating Depression Scale (SDS) was designed to provide an objective, quantitative assessment of the subjective experience of depression (84). The SDS was not intended to be a substitute for clinical evaluation and diagnosis. The instrument has been used to measure depressive symptomatology in the general population, to distinguish depressed patients from other diagnostic groups, to monitor treatment effects, and in cross-cultural studies of patients with depressive disorders (5).

The content of the SDS was developed based on an analysis of statements collected during patient interviews (84). Twenty items are contained in the scale, and include statements concerning affective, cognitive, behavioral, and psychological symptoms of depression (119). The items are evenly divided between positive and negative phrasing. The response categories range from 1, ''none or a little of the time,'' to 4, ''most or all of the time.'' (120).

Scores on the SDS are calculated by summing the item scores. This summated score is then converted to an index by dividing the summated score by 80 and then multiplying that figure by 100. Scores below 50 reflect individuals in the normal range, scores between 50 and 59 indicate the presence of minimal to mild depression, scores between 60 and 69 reflect marked depression, and a score of 70 or more indicates severe to extreme depressive symptoms (121). There are no agreed on cutoff points to define psychiatric cases. Scores of 50, 55, and 60 have been used in various studies (6).

Information on the reliability (5,119,122,123), validity (119,124,125), factor structure (119), and responsiveness of the SDS to changes in clinical status (5) can be found elsewhere.

Cross-Cultural Versions

The SDS has been used cross-culturally in a variety of countries. In this section, non-English translations of the SDS are reviewed for cross-cultural studies and for Finnish, Dutch, Hmong, and Japanese investigations.

Cross-Cultural Validation Studies

Zung (126) examined the performance of the SDS in six countries in the late-1960s. Countries participating in this investigation were Japan, Australia, Czechoslovakia, England, Germany, and Switzerland. In each country, the SDS was translated by the study investigators, but the process used to perform the translations was not described in detail. The instrument was found to discriminate between depressed and nondepressed patient groups in all countries. Correlations between scores on the SDS and clinician ratings of depression were .43 for Japan, .52 for Australia, .50 for Czechoslovakia, .65 for England, .51 for Germany, and .45 for the Swiss sample. Correlation coefficients for the nondepressed patient groups were lower: .06 Japan, .09 Australia, .14 Czechoslovakia, .08 England, and −.14 Germany. (No correlation coefficient was calculated for the Swiss sample.)

Concurrent validity of the SDS was examined in the English and German samples. In the English sample, the SDS was significantly correlated with two specific depression rating scales, the Hamilton Rating Scale for Depression ($r = .56$), and the Beck Depression Inventory ($r = .76$). The SDS was less highly correlated with two nonspecific psychiatric scales, the Lubin scale ($r = .29$), and the Eysenck Personality Inventory ($r = .08$). The German translation of the SDS correlated at .72 with the Beck Depression Inventory.

Reliability of the SDS in the six countries was not reported.

Finnish

Kivela and associates (127–129) have examined the Zung Self-Rating Depression Scale in several studies of a Finnish elderly population. In one investigation, 1,358 individuals, aged 60 years and above, living in the Ahtari commune in middle-western Finland, completed a mailed survey (127). The results indicated that the SDS scores were higher for persons aged 75 and above than for those aged 60 to 74. Significant differences were also found between men and women in the mean scores of some of the individual SDS items. Factor analyses of the SDS showed a varying factor structure by the age and gender of the respondents. Four factors were identified for young-old men (60–74 years), three for old-old men (75+ years), three for young-old women (60–74 years), and four factors for old-old women (75+ years). The four factors for young-old men and old-old women were loss of self-esteem, agitated mood with somatic symptoms, psychomotor retardation, and somatic symptoms. For old-old men the three factors were loss of self-esteem, agitated mood with somatic symptoms, and somatic symptoms. For young-old women the three factors were loss of self-esteem, agitated mood with somatic symptoms, and depressed mood.

Internal consistency reliability of the instrument as assessed by Cronbach's alpha was .72 for persons aged 60 to 74 years and .77 for persons aged 75 years and over. Guttman's split-half coefficients were .63 for persons aged 60 to 74 years, and .70 for individuals aged 75 years and above. There were no significant differences in these reliability coefficients by gender in either of the age categories.

A similar study by Kivela and colleagues (128) examined the reliability and factor structure of the SDS in 321 elderly men (ages 65 to 84 years) living in eastern Finland, and 395 elderly men living in southwestern Finland. Reliability of the SDS in the eastern sample, as assessed by Cronbach's alpha, was .80 for the young-old (65–74), and .82 for the old-old (ages 75+). In the southwestern sample, reliability of the SDS was .80 for the young-old, and .815 for the old-old. Factor analyses of the SDS revealed three factors for the young-old men in the East and Southwest, and also for the old-old men in the Southwest. Four factors were identified for the old-old men in the eastern sample. The factor patterns of the first two factors were similar in both regions, but their order was different. Loss of self-esteem accounted for more of the common variance in the East, but agitated mood accounted for more of the variance in the Southwest.

Information on the process used to translate the SDS into the Finnish language was not provided in any of the articles referenced.

Dutch

Dijkstra (130) translated the SDS into Dutch, and reported satisfactory reliability and validity results in a diverse clinical sample. In a subsequent study, Gabrys and Peters (131) found that the SDS was able to discriminate between depressed and nondepressed patients. DeJonghe and Baneke (132) replicated the study by Gabrys and Peters with 113 Dutch patients attending a day clinic. In this investigation, internal consistency reliability was .82, with a split-half reliability (corrected for test-length) of .79. Not all items had an item-total correlation higher than .20, however. Women were found to have higher mean scores on the SDS than men, but no effects by the age of the respondents (range: 19–59 years) were noted. The instrument was able to discriminate between depressed and nondepressed patients (i.e., total scores were 53.47, SD = 8.15 and 46.82, SD = 88.97 for the depressed and nondepressed groups, respectively), although the rate of false positives was high in this study.

Several investigations of the validity of the Dutch SDS have been conducted with college students. College women scored higher on the SDS in one study; however, the mean scores between the men and women were not found to be statistically significant (27). Concurrent validity of the SDS has been assessed most frequently by correlating mean scores on the SDS with mean scores on the Beck Depression Inventory. Significant correlations between the two measures have been reported at .42 (133), .54 (134), .78 (135), and .69 (27) in college populations.

The psychometric properties of the Dutch SDS was also investigated in a sample of elderly individuals (ages 75 to 90 years) (136). Cronbach's alpha of reliability in this population was .83. Factor analysis of the SDS revealed six factors, although the majority of the variance in the instrument was explained by the first factor. No systematic biases were found in the scores by the respondents' physical vulnerability. In general, women scored higher on the SDS than men, and only a slight relationship was found between SDS scores and age. Frail elderly living alone and residents of retirement homes had significantly more depressive symptoms than frail elderly living with others or independently.

Hmong

Two samples of Hmong refugees living in the state of Minnesota in the United States were administered the SDS and the 90-item Symptom Checklist (SCL-90) (137). The first sample ($N = 86$) consisted of a field survey of all Hmong residing in Minnesota, and the second sample included 51 Hmong psychiatric outpatients. Translation of the SDS was completed by a former Hmong native, and back-translation of the instrument was completed by several Hmong people who spoke and read English. Both a Hmong (Latinized script) and a Hmong-dialect Lao (Sanskritic script) version were constructed.

In the Hmong field survey sample, the SDS and the SCL-90 were moderately correlated with one another ($r = .67$). In the psychiatric patient sample, the correlation between the two scales was $r = .65$. Both the SDS and the SCL-90 were also correlated with increased symptom reporting on nine of the SCL-90 subscales (e.g., anxiety, somatization). Item analyses also showed agreement between similar Zung and SCL-90 depression statements. The SDS was not found to be significantly correlated to the Hamilton Depression Scale, the Depressive Mood and Depression scales on the Brief Psychiatric Rating Scale (BPRS), the Anxious-Intrapunitiveness scale on the Inpatient Multidimensional Psychiatric Scale (IMPS), or the Depression scale of the Nurse's Observation Scale for Inpatient Evaluation. The SCL-90 was significantly correlated with the IMPS and the BPRS mood and depression scales.

The SDS was able to distinguish between depressed and nondepressed cases in the general population sample. Most of the single SDS and SCL-90 depression items also indicated significantly higher symptom levels in the depressed patients.

Internal consistency reliability or split-half reliability was not reported in this study.

Japanese

Several studies have been conducted in Japan using a translated version of the SDS. The instrument has been used in studies of Japanese elderly (138,139), and in stroke patients (140). The SDS has also been used in studies of Japanese workers. Kawakami and colleagues (141) investigated the effects of perceived job stress on depressive symptoms among male, blue-collar workers in a 3-year prospective study, and Kawada and Suzuki (142) examined the factor structure of the SDS in night shift workers of a railway company. In the latter study, internal consistency of the SDS, based on 1,274 male workers, was .835, and the reliability of the measure in a control group of daytime railway workers was .848. Factor analysis of the SDS items revealed two factors. Factor 1 consisted of eight items representing a positive domain, and factor 2 consisted of eight depression items. The four remaining items consisted of behavioral and somatic characteristics. This factor structure was similar in both the night shift and day shift workers. Mean scores on the SDS also did not differ significantly between the night shift and day shift employees.

Japanese and United States college undergraduates were studied in one investigation to examine the relationship between self-enhancement and depression (143). In the Japanese sample, 226 students were obtained from two universities in Tokyo, and 231 U.S. students were drawn from a university in the midwestern United States. Internal consistency reliability of the SDS was .83 in the Japanese sample, and .84 in the U.S. sample. Japanese students had significantly higher scores on the SDS, indicating a greater level of depressive symptoms in the Japanese group. Validity of the SDS in these two samples was not assessed.

Other Translations

Translated versions of the SDS have also been used in recent studies in Austria (144), Czechoslovakia (145), France (146), Germany (147–149), Iran (150), Italy (151–155), Poland (156), Sweden (157), and Venezuela (158). Detailed information regarding the psychometric properties of the SDS in these countries was not provided in the reporting of these investigations, however.

GENERAL HEALTH QUESTIONNAIRE

Description

The General Health Questionnaire (GHQ) is designed to measure current psychiatric/affective disorders (159). It focuses on breaks in normal functioning rather than on lifelong traits. It is chiefly concerned with identifying an "inability to carry out one's normal 'healthy' functions, and the appearance of new phenomena of a distressing nature" (160). The GHQ is not intended to detect serious illness, but is designed to identify potential patients who should then be examined using standard psychiatric interviews (159). The GHQ has been used extensively, however, to estimate the prevalence of affective disorders and to assess illness severity (5). The GHQ was developed to be used in primary medical care settings, in general population or community surveys, and among general medical outpatients.

The items included on the GHQ were selected from existing instruments and from clinical experience, and the measure contains statements covering four main areas: depression, anxiety, social impairment, and hypochondriasis (as indicated by organic symptoms) (159). Several versions of the GHQ have been developed. The original version of the GHQ contains 60 items and is generally recommended for use because of its superior validity. Shorter versions of the GHQ are available, however. These include 12- and 30-item scales, which exclude items most usually selected by physically ill individuals (159). A GHQ-28 was also developed using factor analysis, and contains four subscales: anxiety and insomnia, somatic symptoms, social dysfunction, and severe depression (160). There is only partial overlap between the GHQ-28 and GHQ-30, which share 14 items in common. A detailed guide on the different versions of the GHQ, and advice on their most appropriate uses in clinical practice and research, is available for the interested reader (161).

Response categories on the GHQ are "better than usual," "same as usual," "worse than usual," and "much worse than usual." Respondents are asked to mark the items based on their experiences "over the past few weeks," emphasizing departures from their usual states. Items may be scored using a traditional Likert format of 0-1-2-3, or the responses may be scored as 0-0-1-1, which indicates the presence or absence of symptoms, ignoring frequency (162). Comparing the two scoring methods, Goldberg and Hillier (160) found the Likert method (0-1-2-3) to hold little advantage over the simpler method (0-0-1-1) in discriminating cases and non-cases.

Scores on the GHQ are interpreted to indicate the severity of psychological disturbance on a continuum, or as an initial screen to identify cases. There is no universally accepted cutoff point for each of the GHQ versions that identifies psychiatric cases. For the GHQ-60, cutoff points of 9/10, 10/11, and 11/12 have been used (162). Cutoff points for the other versions of the GHQ are 4/5 for the GHQ-30 and GHQ-28, 3/4 for the GHQ-20, and 2/3 for the GHQ-12 (163). An alternative method of scoring (C-GHQ) has also been developed and shown to produce a less-skewed distribution of scores (164). This method is thought to make it more likely to detect chronic disorders, and has an alternative way of scoring positive and negative items. Additional information on the scoring methods applied to the GHQ can be found in the *Users' Guide to the General Health Questionnaire* (161).

Reliability of the GHQ has been evaluated in several studies in terms of split-half reliability (162), and test-retest reliability (5,162,165,166). Validity assessments of the GHQ have been conducted in a variety of settings and cultures, and extensive review of these studies can be found in the users' guide (161).

Cross-Cultural Versions

The GHQ was developed for use in England, but has been widely used in many different countries. A North American version (United States and Canada) of the instrument has been validated, which closely resembles the British version, although minor adjustments in idiomatic phrases and the wording of questionnaire items have been made to adapt the instrument for American use (43,159,162). A variety of psychometric studies have been conducted on the English versions of the GHQ in England, Scotland, Ireland, Australia, Canada, and the United States. In general, the GHQ has been found to have similar psychometric properties, across these countries, in studies of patient and nonpatient samples (161).

In this section, the review of the GHQ is limited to non-English versions of the instrument. Due to the high number of GHQ translations, the versions selected for inclusion represent those for which there were at least several published articles reporting on the psychometric properties of the instrument. The translated versions of the GHQ discussed in this section are French, Italian, Spanish, Norwegian, Dutch, Japanese, Chinese, Yoruba (Nigeria), and multinational studies.

French

Bolognini and colleagues (167) reported on the validity of a French-language version of the GHQ-28 in a population-based sample of 20-year-olds residing in a French-speaking region of Switzerland. No information was provided in the article about the translation process used to construct the instrument. The translated version was compared to the PSYDIS scale (Psychic Distress) (168) and the FLORES psychiatric interview (in French): *F*ormation, *LO*isirs, *RE*lations, *S*ante). While this version of the GHQ was found to compare favorably with the PSYDIS, it showed only a moderate correlation (.44) with the FLORES. The GHQ misclassified 18.5% of the respondents at the cutoff point of 5/6, with a specificity of 91.1% and a sensitivity of 49.1%. The C-GHQ method of scoring and simple Likert scoring improved the sensitivity of the French GHQ, although these scoring methods were less effective with males. The lower validity found in this study may be due, in part, to the lower morbidity rate found in population studies as compared with clinical settings, and may also reflect differences in the periods of assessment covered by the FLORES (i.e., difficulties in the past year) and the French GHQ (i.e., in the past few weeks). Bolognin et al. concluded that due to the lability of troubles/symptoms in young adults, and men's less expressiveness at this age as compared with women's, the GHQ should be used cautiously for epidemiological purposes.

Factor composition of the French version was not examined in this study, nor were either internal consistency or test-retest reliability.

In a subsequent study, Pariente and colleagues (169) used a back-translated version of the GHQ-28 in a sample of 158 French psychiatric patients. The patients were assessed simultaneously by psychiatrists with a list of DSM-III-R criteria for affective and anxiety disorders. The GHQ-28 items were rated according to the Likert scoring method (1 to 4), and a global score was calculated as the sum of all of the item scores. Mean scores between men and women were not found to differ significantly. Internal consistency of the instrument was .91. Principal components analysis provided a four-factor solution, which closely resembled that proposed by Goldberg and Hillier (160), except for some differences in how the insomnia items loaded during the procedure. Overall sensitivity and specificity of the translated version in classifying depression cases was 72% and 74%, respectively, although there were some differences in the distribution of psychiatric cases across the four medical centers participating in the study. The results of this investigation suggested the usefulness of the translated version of the GHQ in psychiatric patients in conjunction with a diagnostic set of criteria, such as the DSM-III-R.

Italian

Fontanesi and colleagues (170) conducted the first Italian application of the GHQ-30. The GHQ was translated into Italian, and the accuracy of the translation was checked independently by two Italian psychiatrists familiar with the British English version. The translated instrument was administered to 120 general practice patients, along with an Italian translation of the Clinical Interview Schedule (171), which was used as a validation measure to identify cases of psychiatric illness. Exploring variable cutoff points for caseness, the optimal combination of sensitivity and specificity on the translated GHQ was found to be 75.4% and 50.8%, respectively, using a cutoff score of 4/5. These values are lower than those that have been reported in other studies. The proportion of high GHQ scorers in this Italian sample was also larger than is typical in general patient populations.

The factor structure of the Italian translated version and estimates of reliability were not assessed in this study.

Spanish

Lobo and colleagues (173–174) have investigated the use of Spanish translations of the GHQ in several populations. The GHQ-30 was examined in studies of cancer patients, and the GHQ-28 was validated in internal medicine outpatients without severe pathology (175), and in endocrine patients (176). In the latter study, 100 Spanish inpatients admitted with an endocrine disorder and 30 hospital controls were examined. Endocrine cases manifesting severe psychiatric symptoms were identified using the Clinical Interview Schedule (CIS) (171). The Spanish GHQ-28 scores were highly correlated with CIS severity ratings in both groups of pa-

tients. The GHQ-28 total scores were also found to be significantly correlated with endocrine blood measures for diabetes and Addison's disease, but not for Cushing's disease, hyperprolactinemia, or hyperthyroidism. Using a 5/6 cutoff score, the instrument was found to have a sensitivity of 92.3% and a specificity of 77.7%, with a 9% misclassification rate. The questionnaire's efficacy was similarly high at the time of medical discharge, when the rate of psychiatric disorder in the patients was markedly lower.

The factor structure of the Spanish GHQ-60 has been examined by Vazquez-Barquero and colleagues (172). Participants in this investigation were drawn from a two-stage screening survey of a random sample of adults from a rural community in Spain. Six principal components were identified from the data analysis, which were similar to results found in previous studies (162). The two most important components represented disturbances of mood (general dysphoria) and social performance (social functional/optimism). While four of the six factors discriminated well between cases and noncases, as identified by the Present State Examination, only one factor, depressive thoughts, was found to be a good discriminator between depressed and nondepressed cases.

A Spanish translation of the GHQ-60 has also been examined in a study by Munoz and colleagues (177). The translated version was judged to have validity in medical outpatients experiencing a low frequency of somatic symptoms.

Reliability assessments were not reported in any of these studies examining the Spanish versions of the GHQ.

Norwegian

Several research articles were found for this review that used versions of the GHQ in Norwegian samples. Laerum and colleagues (178) employed a Norwegian version of the GHQ-20 to assess psychological and lifestyle changes in post–acute myocardial infarction patients. Malt (179) also used the GHQ-20 to assess the trauma experienced by patients injured in accidents. In this study, participants were administered the GHQ-20 during their hospital stay, and then twice during a 28-month follow-up period. All patients also completed a semistructured psychiatric interview in-hospital and at the final follow-up point. Split-half reliability was computed by correlating the sum score of the first ten items with the sum score for the last ten items. In the acute phase, the coefficient was $r = .81$; at the first follow-up point the coefficient was $r = .86$; and at the final follow-up evaluation, the coefficient was $r = .81$. The internal consistency for the GHQ-20 at the three data collection points was .81, .86, and .91, respectively. The sensitivity and specificity was calculated using three different scoring methods across a variety of different cutoff scores for the GHQ-20. Sensitivity and specificity were found to be moderate at the in-hospital assessment (62% sensitivity, 83% specificity with a cutoff score of 2/3), and at the final follow-up point (73% sensitivity, 79% specificity with a cutoff score of 3/4).

A Norwegian translation of the GHQ-28 was used, among other instruments, to assess changes in health and reemployment in a 2-year follow-up of long-term unemployed men and women (180). High scores on the GHQ-28 were found to be significantly associated with a reduction in the chances of obtaining a job. Individuals who indicated normal performance on psychometric testing showed a two to three times increased chance of being reemployed as compared with those individuals who indicated higher levels of psychological distress and psychiatric disorders. Reliability and validity assessments of the GHQ-28 were not a focal point of this article.

Dutch

A variety of published studies from the Netherlands have reported on the use of the GHQ in Dutch-speaking populations. None of the articles to be discussed in this section, however, provided detailed information about the processes used to translate the GHQ into the Dutch language.

The correlation between GHQ scores and psychiatric and somatic complaints of patients has been investigated in several Dutch studies. An investigation by Verhaak and colleagues (181) found only a moderate relationship between self-reported psychological symptoms and psychiatric cases, as identified by the GHQ-30, in a sample of 476 patients seen by general practitioners. Many patients who presented to their physicians with psychosocial problems had low GHQ-30 scores, while many patients with high GHQ-30 scores presented with somatic complaints. Only 39% self-identified ''cases'' presenting with psychological complaints were detected by the GHQ-30 using a cutoff score of 4/5, in contrast to the detection of a larger number of patients presenting with somatic complaints. The large number of false negatives among patients with psychological complaints is difficult to evaluate since patient reports are not a standard for caseness. Patients reporting one or several mild psychological symptoms may have been appropriately classified by the GHQ as either subthreshold for psychiatric disturbance or as stable. Results from a follow-up study by Verhaak and Tijhuis (182) provided similar results indicating that many patients with a probable mental illness list only physical symptoms to their general practitioner. In this sample, however, the severity of these patients' distress appeared to be less than that of patients with a probable mental illness who did express their psychological distress in overt ways.

Koeter et al. (183) investigated the sensitivity of the GHQ-28 in assessing chronic psychiatric complaints of 175 outpatients. Although the mean level of severity of chronic symptoms between patient groups with and without chronic complaints was not significantly different, patients with chronic complaints showed a significantly lower mean GHQ-28 score than patients without chronic complaints. These results concur with other researchers who have suggested that false negatives largely result from the insensitivity of the GHQ in detecting chronic disorders (164). The use of the revised scoring procedure, the C-GHQ, was able to decrease the number of false negatives generated by the original scoring procedure, but the largest reduction in false negatives occurred by using a combination of the original and C-GHQ scoring procedures.

Wilmink and Snijders (184) examined the sensitivity and specificity of the GHQ-30 in a primary care patient sample. These researchers used logistic regression models to predict psychiatric cases from GHQ-30 scores. The sensitivity of the GHQ-30 for detecting cases, as identified by the Present State Examination, was 91% and its specificity was 62%. These results closely resembled models derived for other general population samples in both Australia and the Netherlands.

Concurrent validity of the GHQ-28 has been examined in studies contrasting the performance of the GHQ-28 against other screening measures of psychopathology. Wiznitzer and colleagues (185) compared the use of the GHQ-28 with the Symptom Checklist-90 (SCL-90) and the Young Adult Self Report (YASR) in a sample of young adults. Using receiver operating characteristic analysis, the overall performance of the YASR and the SCL-90 was found to be better than the overall performance of the GHQ-28 in detecting psychopathology as indicated by referral status. The relatively poor performance of the GHQ-28 could not be attributed to the characteristics of the instrument or to the use of referral status as an indicator of psychopathology. It was suggested that an age-adjusted child-oriented instrument might be a better alternative to existing adult-oriented instruments in assessing psychopathology in young adult populations, particularly in studies following children into adulthood.

An additional study was found that also compared the GHQ-28 to the SCL-90. In this investigation, Koeter (186) compared the anxiety/insomnia and several depression subscales of the GHQ-28 to the anxiety, phobic anxiety, and depression scales of the SCL-90. The GHQ-28 depression scale and the SCL-90 anxiety and depression scales showed good convergent and divergent validity; however, the GHQ-28 anxiety/insomnia scale showed neither divergent or convergent validity. It was concluded that the SCL-90 is the preferred measure for a multidimensional measure of psychopathology, particularly for studies in which anxiety is of interest. As a screening instrument, however, the relative shortness of the GHQ-28 or the GHQ-12 may make these appropriate measures to employ in research investigations.

Estimates of reliability were not provided in any of these Dutch studies.

Japanese

Investigations of the validity of the GHQ in Japanese populations have been conducted in recent years (187). The

Japanese version of the GHQ-60 was translated by researchers at the National Institute of Mental Health of Japan. This process was included as part of the first project of the institute as a World Health Organization (WHO) collaborating center in psychiatry (188). The original GHQ-60 was translated into Japanese, and then retranslated back into English by individuals who were blind to the original version. Professor S. Hirsch of the Institute of Psychiatry in London was then asked to compare the Japanese version with the original version to confirm its content (187).

Several studies have examined the validity of various Japanese versions of the GHQ. Nakagawa and Daibo (188) found good levels of sensitivity and specificity in the Japanese GHQ-60 in a clinical validation study comparing psychiatric patients with nonpsychiatric normal volunteers. Kitamura and colleagues (189) examined the discriminant validity of the Japanese GHQ-30 in a study of first trimester pregnant women attending an antenatal clinic at a general hospital. In this study, psychiatric cases were identified in this study using the Schedule for Affective Disorders and Schizophrenia and the Research Diagnostic Criteria (190,191). The sensitivity and specificity of the GHQ-30 using the total score were 83.3% and 71.1%, respectively, using a cutoff point of 7/8 instead of the standard cutoff score of 4/5. Discriminant function analysis of the GHQ-30 indicated that only 13 items contributed to the discriminatory power of the instrument. The use of the discriminant function scores of these 13 items in an alternative scoring method provided higher levels of sensitivity and specificity than the simple summation of the GHQ-30 items. The lack of discriminatory power of the remaining 17 GHQ-30 items was hypothesized to be due to cultural differences, linguistic idiosyncracies, or confounding somatic and social factors.

In a similar study, Furukawa (192) used the Japanese GHQ-30 in a study of adolescent students. Using the cutoff point of 4/5, 51% of the students were identified as suffering from minor psychiatric disorders. Applying the cutoff point of 6.7, 28.5% of the students were judged to be psychologically disturbed. These figures were found to be comparable to the rate of Japanese high school students (45%) scoring above the cutoff point on the Japanese GHQ-60 (193).

Iwata et al. (194) have examined the use of the GHQ-28 in several investigations. In a study of concurrent validity, these researchers found that of the five GHQ versions, the GHQ-28 correlated most strongly with neurosis (115). A recent investigation by Iwata and Saito (187) examined the factor structure of the GHQ-28 in early adolescent Japanese students and adult employees. Principal components analysis restricting the number of factors to four, produced a similar factor structure across the adolescent and adult samples, although a slightly different factor structure emerged for employees between the ages of 40 and 49 years. Internal consistency reliability for the adolescent sample was .85 for each gender, and .86 for the adult sample.

In the same study, further analyses were conducted comparing the factor analysis results from the adolescent sample with data collected on European and Turkish samples of adolescent girls (195) and adolescent boys (196). The results indicated that the factor structure was similar across the various cultural groups for both the adolescent boys and girls.

Chinese

Several studies were identified that employed the GHQ-30 in Chinese samples (197). Chan and Chan (198) used the English version of the GHQ-30 in Chinese students who were bilingual. The internal consistency of the English version of the GHQ-30 with the Chinese students was .85. The measure correlated significantly with the Self Reporting Questionnaire and had sensitivity and specificity of greater than 70%. In subsequent work, Chan (199) utilized the translated Chinese version of the GHQ-30, and found a high degree of comparability between the English and Chinese versions. Factor analysis of this instrument produced five factors (anxiety, depression, interpersonal problems with anhedonia, sleep disturbance with dysphoria, and social dysfunctioning with dysphoria). Shek (200) further examined the reliability and factor structure of the Chinese GHQ-30 in a sample of secondary school students. The scale was found to have a high degree of internal consistency (Cronbach's alpha = .88), and five factor-based scales were also identified (anxiety, depression, inadequate functioning, social dysfunctioning, and insomnia).

Concurrent validity of the Chinese GHQ-30 has been assessed by Shek (197). The Chinese GHQ-30 was administered to 2,150 secondary school students aged 11 to 20, along with a battery of measures assessing different areas of psychopathology. The Chinese GHQ-30 was significantly correlated with the other measures of psychopathology, although the instrument was correlated more highly with scales that measured acute rather than chronic symptoms. The GHQ-30 was highly correlated with measures of anxiety and depression (e.g., Spielberger's State-Trait Anxiety Inventory, Beck Depression Inventory), than with scales that assessed non-anxiety or depression-related states. In addition, further analysis of the factor structure of the Chinese GHQ-30 indicated that the anxiety measures correlated most highly with factor 1 of the GHQ-30 (anxiety), and that the depression scales correlated most highly with factor 2 of the GHQ-30 (depression). Information on the reliability of the GHQ-30 was not provided in this article.

Yoruba

Research has been conducted in Nigeria on several versions of the GHQ translated into the Yoruba language. Oduwolfe and Ogunyemi (201) examined the validity of the GHQ-30 among 80 medical outpatients. The GHQ-30 underwent a forward-backward translation into the Yoruba language. Fifty-nine patients completed the English version, and 21 patients completed the Yoruba GHQ-30. Mean scores of the two versions of the questionnaire were not found to differ significantly from one another. Thirty-one patients randomly selected from the sample of 80 outpatients also completed a semistructured psychiatric interview to validate the translated version. Results indicated that using a cutoff score of 4/5 on the Yoruba GHQ-30, the instrument was able to correctly identify 67.2% or 21 psychiatric cases. The sensitivity and specificity of the translated version were 72.7% and 65.0%, respectively, with a positive predictive value of 53.3%. These findings were lower than the figures reported in Western studies examining the use of the GHQ-30, although the results were similar to the findings of Morakinyo (202) in a study of the validity of the GHQ-60 in a sample of university students. Reasons suggested for the lower sensitivity and specificity of the Yoruba GHQ-30 were cultural differences in how people perceive illness and respond to questions about illnesses, difficulties in completing a cross-culturally meaningful translation of questionnaire items (i.e., the Yoruba culture is one that expressed emotions in somatic terms), the criterion measure employed in the study, and the nature of the study sample (i.e., small number of persons, the inclusion of patients with more chronic than acute disorders).

Gureje (203) utilized a Yoruba version of the GHQ-12 in several investigations. Gureje examined the factor structure of the measure in a study of 787 medical outpatients. In this sample, internal consistency reliability of the Yoruba GHQ-12 was .82. Factor analytic procedures revealed two factors (social dysfunctioning/coping ability and psychic distress/dysphoria), which accounted for 45.6% of the variance. This two-factor structure was found to be stable across age and gender subgroups, even though the order in which the items loading on each factor and a few component items were sometimes different. These results were similar to findings of an investigation in a Spanish community (172). Increasing age was associated with higher scores on the two factors for both men and women, with men between the ages of 50 and 59 years particularly affected. Criterion validity of the Yoruba GHQ-12 was also assessed by use of the DSM-III-R diagnostic criteria to identify psychiatric cases. The two factors identified in the translated GHQ-12 were found to discriminate between psychiatric cases (with and without depressive disorders) and noncases. Most of the discriminative ability, however, came from the social dysfunctioning/coping factor and not the dysphoria factor. The author suggested that based on this finding, it is important to consider the item content of the responses and not only the respondents' total score on the GHQ-12.

Gureje and Obikoya (204) have also used the GHQ-12 as a screening instrument in studies of 787 outpatients at the Adeoyo State Hospital, Ibadan. Based on their scores on the GHQ-12 applying the C-GHQ scoring method (164), patients were interviewed with the Composite International Diagnostic Interview (CIDI) (205). One study examined somatic symptoms in the outpatients (206), and another examined alcohol use and dependence (207). Sensitivity and specificity of the Yoruba GHQ-12, as compared with the CIDI, was not examined in these studies, however.

A translated version of the GHQ-12 was also employed by Abiodun (208) in a study of psychiatric morbidity among primary care patients in Kwara. This back-translated version of the Yoruba GHQ-12 and the Present State Examination (PSE) schedule was administered to 272 outpatients. Sensitivity and specificity of the GHQ-12, using the PSE to identify psychiatric cases, was 83.7% and 79.8%, respectively, with a minimum misclassification rate of 19.4%. These figures were comparable to the results found in a Nigerian community sample (209). The reliability of the GHQ-12 was not assessed in this study.

A validation of the GHQ-28 was conducted by Aberibigbe and Gureje (210) in a study of psychiatric disorders associated with childbirth among 277 Nigerian women attending an antenatal clinic. A Yoruba version of the GHQ-28 was validated against the Psychiatric Assessment Schedule. Using the C-GHQ scoring method (164), the sensitivity and specificity of the GHQ-28 in this population was 82% and 85%, respectively. This revised scoring method performed better in distinguishing cases from noncases than the conventional scoring method, which produced values for sensitivity and specificity at 75% and 83%. A discriminant function analysis was also performed, and indicated that only three of the four subscales of the GHQ-28 contributed to the discriminative power of the instrument. Based on these results, the translated GHQ-28 was judged to be a valid tool for the detection of psychiatric morbidity in this population. Assessments of reliability were not performed in this study.

Multinational Studies

Several investigations have examined the use of the GHQ in cross-national studies of adolescents (195,196). Elton and colleagues (195) conducted a comparative investigation of the factor structure of the GHQ-28 using data from studies of anorexia nervosa involving adolescent female samples from England, Greece, Turkey, and West Germany. Factor analysis produced different numbers of components for the samples across the four countries, but restricting the number of components to four produced similar component structures across a subset of the groups investigated (i.e., Turkish, Greek, and a heterogeneous non-British group in London). The results from the group of British girls more closely resembled the factor structure of the GHQ-28 reported in other studies.

Analysis of variance of the factor scores of a combined principal components analysis produced significant overall differences by country for all components, as well as specific differences for anxiety and insomnia, social dysfunction, and severe depression. Across the four countries, somatic symptoms, and anxiety and insomnia subscales, either alone or in combination with other subscales, were found to contribute more frequently to the morbid status of the adolescent girls. Goldberg's hypothesis that there is a common language of psychological distress that cuts across cultural barriers was not supported in this investigation.

The reliability of the GHQ-28 and the translation processes employed in the four countries were not discussed in this article.

PSYCHOLOGICAL GENERAL WELL-BEING INDEX

Description

The Psychological General Well-Being Index (PGWB) was designed to measure subjective feelings of psychological well-being and distress (211). The instrument has been used with a variety of sociodemographic groups, such as rural and urban dwellers, in patient populations, and with community residents. It has also been used to assess changes in subjective well-being due to mental health treatments. The instrument includes both positive and negative affective states, and covers the following six dimensions: anxiety, depression, general health, positive well-being, self-control, and vitality.

Twenty-two items are contained on the PGWB and respondents are asked to respond to each item as it has applied to them "during the last month." The response categories for each statement range from either 0 to 5 or 1 to 6, with lower values indicating more negative responses, and higher values indicating more positive responses. A total summated score is also calculated, which ranges from 0 to 110 using the 0 to 5 scoring method, and from 22 to 132, using the 1 to 6 scoring method. Each of the six dimension subscales can also be given a score. The mean value of the PGWB total score in nonpatient populations is approximately 105.

Information on the reliability (211) and validity (211–217) of the PGWB can be found elsewhere.

Cross-Cultural Comparisons

The PGWB index has been used in a variety of research investigations, particularly clinical trials. In this section, we review some of the uses of the PGWB in the United States, Sweden, Norway, Germany, and Great Britain.

United States

The PGWB has been used in several clinical trials within the United States to assess the impact of antihypertensive drugs on patients' general well-being. Croog and colleagues (218) found that the PGWB was able to distinguish between treatment groups (captopril, methyldopa, propranolol) in a study of 626 men with mild to moderate hypertension. A similar study by Steiner et al. (219) examined the effects of two different beta blockers (atenolol and propranolol), and

two ACE inhibitors (captopril and enalapril) on the quality of life of 360 male patients with mild-to-moderate essential hypertension. After 4 weeks of maintenance therapy, atenolol, captopril and enalapril generally had equivalent effects on health-related quality of life as assessed by the PGWB and the Hopkins Symptom Checklist. For the propranolol group, the only significant effect of treatment was a reduction in the patients' ratings on the anxiety subscale of the PGWB. Analysis of covariance on the subscales of the PGWB also indicated differences in treatment on the mean scores of the vitality and depression dimensions of the PGWB.

The PGWB has also been used to assess changes in antihypertensive therapy in a multicenter clinical trial involving 306 black men and women with mild to moderate hypertension (220). No significant differences were found in mean scores of the PGWB from baseline to 8 weeks of active therapy between either male or female patients assigned to any of the three treatment groups (atenolol, captopril, or verapamil therapy). Within-group comparisons indicated that male patients showed improved 8-week scores on the PGWB in the atenolol and captopril treatment groups, whereas the female patients showed significant improvement in all three treatment conditions. In a study by Applegate and colleagues (221), the effect of atenolol, enalapril, and diltiazem on the blood pressure of 240 women aged 65 and older was examined. No significant differences in the patients' scores on the PGWB were found as a result of treatment.

In other hypertension studies employing the PGWB index, Chang and colleagues (222) compared diuretic medications with placebo in 176 hypertensive patients over an 8-week period. No adverse impact on well-being was observed in any of the treatment groups. Testa et al. (223) compared captopril and enalapril in more than 379 hypertensive male patients during a 6-month interval. In terms of the total PGWB score, no differences were observed by treatment condition.

No information on the reliability of the PGWB in these patient populations was provided in any of the studies described above.

Sweden

Wiklund and Karlberg (224) have reported on a Swedish version of the PGWB. Translation of the instrument was completed using backward-forward techniques. Internal consistency of the six subscales of the PGWB, as assessed by Cronbach's alpha, were anxiety, .82; depression, .89; well-being, .88; self-control, .76; general health, .61; and vitality, .85. The Cronbach alpha for the entire PGWB scale was > .90. Concurrent validity of the Swedish translation was completed by correlating the instrument with the Mood Adjective Checklist (MACL) and the Swedish version of the Nottingham Health Profile (NHP). Product moment correlations ranged from .65 to .80 between the anxiety, depression, and well-being dimensions of the PGWB index and the MACL subscales depicting tension, deactivation, and unpleasantness. The PGWB vitality subscale correlated at .70 with the NHP energy dimension.

The responsiveness of the Swedish PGWB to change has been assessed in several investigations examining transdermal estrogen replacement therapy in women experiencing menopausal complaints (225–227). In all of these studies, women showed improved scores on the PGWB following the instigation of treatment. Discriminant validity of the Swedish translation has also been assessed. In a descriptive study of adult patients with growth hormone deficiency, patients' mean scores on the PGWB were significantly lower on the vitality and well-being scales than the mean scores of a healthy control group matched for age and gender (228). Dimenas and colleagues (229) also found in a study of 1,600 patients presenting in general practice with gastrointestinal symptoms, that irrespective of whether endoscopic evidence of ulcers was found, patients experiencing gastrointestinal complaints generally had lower levels of well-being than those patients who were not experiencing such symptoms.

Norway

Omvik and colleagues (230) examined changes in health-related quality of life as part of a Norwegian clinical trial assessing the effects of treatment with amlodipine or enalapril in mild or moderate hypertensive patients. Patients' baseline scores on the total PGWB index as well as its subscales were compared with normative data from the RAND Health Insurance Study (211). The PGWB anxiety subscale scores were significantly higher for both the amlodipine and enalapril patient groups as compared with the RAND sample. The general health subscale scores were also significantly lower in both treatment groups than in the RAND sample.

Differences in PGWB total scores and subscale scores were found within the two treatment groups during the duration of the study. However, there was no significance between therapy group differences in the PGWB total score or subscale scores.

No information was provided about the process used to translate the PGWB into Norwegian or about the reliability of the PGWB in this sample.

Germany

Bullinger and colleagues (231) have reported on a German translation of the PGWB. The instrument was translated using a forward-backward translation method, and was given to 143 university students. A factor analysis of the PGWB was completed, and only four of the original six subscale factors were extracted. In addition, the factor structure of the well-being, anxiety, self-control, and vitality scales showed considerable overlap. Internal consistency reliability of the four subscales ranged from .76 to .85. Concurrent validity of the PGWB index was approximately .60 with both the German Life Satisfaction Scale and the Affect Balance Scale.

Intercorrelations between Profile of Mood States and PGWB subscales also averaged around .49. Further validation of the German PGWB index is reportedly under way with different samples of healthy and chronically ill individuals. It was expected that the PGWB would perform better in ill patients, assuming there was a higher variance in PGWB responses for these populations as compared with young, healthy adults.

England

The original American English version of the PGWB has been used in several research studies in the United Kingdom. The PGWB has been used in studies of hypertension (232), and in a clinical trial comparing the effect of growth hormone therapy and placebo on HRQL in 23 adult patients (233). These investigations indicate that the PGWB is sensitive to treatment effects in these patient populations.

Hunt and McKenna (234) have reported on an adaptation and retesting of a British English version of the PGWB. The adapted version of the PGWB index, called the AGWBI, was constructed following analysis of the PGWB questionnaire items by a panel of lay persons, and through pilot testing with 25 individuals. As a result of these investigations, minor changes in the wording of the questionnaire items were made, and all response categories were shortened from six to five alternatives, reportedly to simplify completion of the measure and to minimize response errors.

The AGWBI was tested on 215 patients receiving drug treatment for depression. The pattern and severity of their depression was assessed at three time points (i.e., at baseline, and after 3 and 6 weeks of treatment) by psychiatrists using the Montgomery-Asberg Depression Rating Scale (MADRS) On completion of each clinical interview, the patients were asked to complete the AGWBI, either that same day or the next day, and return it in the mail. Mean scores on both the MADRS and the AGWBI showed significant improvement with treatment at each of the three visits (i.e., increases in well-being with reductions in depressive symptomatology). The correlations between the AGWBI and the MADRS at each of the three visits were .49, .60, and .76, respectively. The correlations between the change scores on the AGWBI and the MADRS at each time point were .55 between visits 1 and 2, .56 between visits 2 and 3, and .70 between visits 1 and 3.

Test-retest reliability was assessed on 41 patients whose rating on the MADRS changed by 10% or less over the 3-week treatment period. The correlation between the AGWBI scores assessed on clinic visits 1 and 2 was .87. Internal consistency of the AGWBI in the sample was .92 at visit 1, .95 at visit 2, and .96 at visit 3.

Multinational Study

A multinational, randomized double-blind study of 6 months' duration was performed in 540 male and female patients with mild to moderate hypertension to determine the relative effects on quality of life of cilazapril, atenolol, and nifedipine retard (232). The study was conducted in 31 centers, primarily from general practices in ten European countries (Austria, Belgium, Denmark, Finland, France, Germany, Holland, Italy, Sweden, and the United Kingdom). Questionnaires were translated from English into seven other languages (Danish, Dutch, Finnish, French, German, Italian, and Swedish). The instruments were then back-translated into English by persons unfamiliar with the original English version. The original English and back-translated versions were then compared for consistency of meaning, and alterations were made in the translated questionnaires as required. The translated versions were further refined at a 3-day pre-study training session for the interviewers. Information on the reliability or validity of the PGWB in the various countries was not provided.

The results of the trial showed no significant differences among the hypertensive treatment groups on the total PGWB score or on any of the six subscale PGWB scores at either week 12 or week 24. Other quality of life measures used in the study (Health Status Index; assessment of work satisfaction; Profile of Mood States scales: tension, depression, anger, vigor, and confusion; Reitan Trail Making Test B; and life satisfaction) also did not differ significantly among the treatment groups.

CONCLUSIONS

This chapter examined the use of six dimension-specific HRQL instruments. In general, information on the psychometric properties of the original versions of the measures was well documented, although there were few data available on the responsiveness of these scales to changes in functional or clinical status. There was a lack of documentation, however, on the psychometric properties of many of the non-English translations of the instruments. Unlike studies of the older generic HRQL measures, such as the Nottingham Health Profile and the Sickness Impact Profile, there have been relatively few coordinated efforts to translate dimension-specific instruments cross-culturally. Very limited information was provided in most of the articles regarding the processes employed in translating the items from English into another language. Also, investigations of the translated instruments were often limited to evaluating the validity of the measures in specific populations or subgroups instead of also measuring the reliability of the instruments.

Similar to psychometric studies of the original versions of the questionnaires, the responsiveness of the translated instruments to change was not a primary focus in research investigations. This may be due, in part, to the fact that many of the reviewed questionnaires were originally designed for descriptive purposes rather than to assess changes in patient populations over time and/or to assess treatment efficacy in clinical trials. Moreover, the interpretation of significant change scores also remains unclear for many of the reviewed instruments.

Information was obtained from this investigation, however, on the cultural differences in the conceptualization of dimensions of HRQL. For example, similarities in perceptions of depression were clearly seen in the United States and European countries across the instruments reviewed. For the CES-D, in particular, differences in depressive symptomatology appeared to be attributed more to the socioeconomic and demographic characteristics of the populations studied, rather than to differences in the way in which depression was conceptualized by members of ethnic or cultural groups. Differences in the performance of the scales in Asian samples were observed, however, which suggests that the perception of depressive symptomatology may be somewhat distinct in Asian populations.

Of the six dimension-specific instruments reviewed, the non-English translations of the McGill Pain Questionnaire proved to be the most difficult to compare. This was due primarily to cross-cultural differences in the way in which pain is perceived and verbalized. This led to the development in several countries (e.g., Italy, Germany) of pain instruments that do not correspond directly to the methodology employed in the development of the original MPQ, but that attempt to adhere to the theoretical basis on which the MPQ was developed. Perceived pain is a difficult concept to measure, and innovative ways to assess pain in cross-national studies will need to be developed and evaluated.

Another important issue involves the methods used to score the translated versions of instruments cross-culturally. Whenever possible, uniform scoring systems need to be instituted across translated versions to enable more direct comparisons of study findings. This means that the metric properties of the scales need to be equivalent cross-culturally in similar populations of respondents. Although normative data on the performance of the instruments was provided in many of the studies reviewed, further research is also needed to identify normative scores on various subpopulations both within and between cultures. These normative data will be useful in defining conceptually equivalent cutoff points/scores for several of the psychological functioning scales, making comparisons between cultures more meaningful.

Despite the availability of a range of standard questionnaires that have been found to have acceptable reliability and validity in various cultures, or to hold promise of usefulness in cross-cultural studies, some investigators still continue to develop new measures for every research study. The development of new dimension-specific instruments, instead of further refining established measures, limits our ability to compare study results across cultures. This is particularly an important issue in cross-national clinical trials, where precision in instrumentation is essential.

In summary, the review of several dimension-specific HRQL instruments indicates that many standardized measures have been used in research investigations in a variety of countries and ethnic groups. Further documentation is needed in the published literature, however, on the processes used to translate the original instruments, and on the psychometric properties of the non-English translations, particularly the responsiveness of these measures to changes in functional or clinical status.

ACKNOWLEDGMENTS

This chapter is a modified version of an article published previously in Quality of Life Research 1933;2:397–432 and is reproduced by permission of Rapid Communications of Oxford Ltd., Oxford, England.

REFERENCES

1. Beck AT, Steer RA. *Beck Depression Inventory manual*. San Antonio: Harcourt Brace Jovanovich, 1987.
2. Beck AT, Rush AJ, Shaw BF, Emery G. *Cognitive therapy of depression*. New York: Guilford, 1979.
3. Piotrowski C, Sheer D, Keller JW. Psychodiagnostic test usage: a survey of the Society for Personality Assessment. *J Pers Assess* 1985;49:115–119.
4. Steer RA, Beck AT, Garrison B. Applications of the Beck Depression Inventory. In: Sartorius N, Ban TA, eds. *Assessment of depression*. New York: Springer-Verlag, 1986:121–142.
5. Wilkin D, Hallam L, Doggett M-A. *Measures of need and outcome for primary health care*. Oxford: Oxford University Press, 1992.
6. Beck AT, Rial WY, Rickels K. Short form of depression inventory: cross validation. *Psychol Rep* 1974;34:1184–1186.
7. Scogin F, Beutler L, Corbishley A, Hamblin D. Reliability and validity of the Short Form Beck Depression Inventory with older adults. *J Clin Psychol* 1988;44:853–857.
8. Beck AT, Beamesderfer A. Assessment of depression: The Depression Inventory. In: Pichot P, ed. *Modern problems in pharmacopsychiatry*. Basel, Switzerland: Karger, 1974:15–169.
9. Beck AT, Steer RA, Garbin M. Psychometric properties of the Beck Depression Inventory: a review. *Clin Psychol Rev* 1988;8:77–100.
10. Boyle GJ. Self-report measures of depression: some psychometric considerations. *Br J Clin Psychol* 1985;24:45–59.
11. Steer RA, Beck AT, Riskind J, Brown G. Differentiation of depressive disorders from generalized anxiety by the Beck Depression Inventory. *J Clin Psychol* 1986;40:475–478.
12. Moran PW, Lambert MJ. A review of current assessment tools for monitoring changes in depression. In: Lambert MS, Christensen ER, DeJulio SS, eds. *The assessment of psychotherapy outcome*. New York: Wiley, 1983:263–303.
13. Louks J, Hayne C, Smith J. Replicated factor structure of the Beck Depression Inventory. *J Nerv Ment Dis* 1989;177(8):473–479.
14. Welch G, Hall A, Walkey F. The replicable dimensions of the Beck Depression Inventory. *J Clin Psychol* 1990;46:817–827.
15. Zheng Y, Wei L, Lianggue G, Guochen Z, Chenggue W. Applicability of the Chinese Beck Depression Inventory. *Compr Psychiatry* 1988;29(5):484–489.
16. Shek DTL. Reliability and factorial structure of the Chinese version of the Beck Depression Inventory. *J Clin Psychol* 1990;46(1):35–43.
17. Chan CM, Tsoi MM. The BDI and stimulus determinants of cognitive-related depression among Chinese college students. *Cogn Ther Res* 1984;8:501–508.
18. Chan D. Depressive symptoms and depressed mood among Chinese medical students in Hong Kong. *Compr Psychiatry* 1991;32(2):170–180.
19. Bourque P, Beaudette D. Psychometric study of the Beck Depression Inventory in a sample of French-speaking university students. *Can J Behav Sci* 1982;14:211–218.
20. Delay J, Pichot P, Lemperiere T, Mirouze R. La nosologie des étas dépressifs. rapport entre l'étiologie et la sémiologic II. résultats du Questionnaire de Beck. *Encephale* 1963;52:497–505.
21. Pichot P, Lemperiere T. Analyse factorielle d'un quesionnaire d'auto-évaluation des symptomes dépressifs. *Rev Psychol Appl* 1964;14: 15–29.
22. Oliver JM, Burkham A. Depression in university students: duration, relation to calendar time, prevalence, and demographic correlates. *J Abnorm Psychol* 1979;88:667–670.
23. Kammer D. A study of the psychometric properties of the German Beck Depression Inventory. *Diagnostica* 1983;24:48–60.
24. Kerekjarto MV. Die hamburger depressionsskala. In: Hippius H, Selbach H, eds. *Das Depressive Syndrom*. Munchen: Urban and Schwarzenberg, 1969.
25. Fahrenberg J, Selg H, Hampel R. *Das Freiburger Personlichkeits-Inventar FPI*. Gottingen: Hogrefe, 1978.
26. Spreen O. *MMPI Saarbrucken Hardbuch*. Bern: Huber, 1963.
27. Bosscher R, Koning H, Van Meurs R. Reliability and validity of the Beck Depression Inventory in a Dutch college population. *Psychol Rep* 1986;58:696–698.
28. Dijkstra P. De zelfbeoardelingsschaal voor depressie van Zung: The Zung Self-Rating Depression Scale. In: van Praag HM, Rooymans HMG, eds. *Stemming en Ontstemming*. Amsterdam: Erven Bohn, 1974:98–121.
29. Larsson B, Melin L. Depressive symptoms in Swedish adolescents. *J Abnorm Child Psychol* 1990;18(1):91–103.
30. Hesli N. Beck Depresyon Envanterinin gecerligi uzerine bir calisma. [A study on the validity of the Beck Depression Inventory]. *Psikoloji Dergisi* 1988;6:118–126.
31. Karanci AN. Patterns of depression in medical patients and their relationship with causal attributes for illness. *Psychother Psychosom* 1988;50(4):207–215.
32. Boyocioglu G, Karanci AN. The relationship of employment status, social support, and life events with depressive symptomatology among married Turkish women. *Int J Psychol* 1992;27(1):61–71.
33. Sahin NH, Sahin N. Reliability and validity of the Turkish version of the automatic thoughts questionnaires. *J Clin Psychol* 1992;48: 334–340.
34. Sung H, Luben B, Yi J. Reliability and validity of the Korean Youth Depression Adjective Checklist (Y-DACL). *Adolescence* 1992;27(107): 527–533.
35. Lee Y. *A study on the reliability and validity of the self-report style depression scales*. Unpublished manuscript. Seoul, Korea: Seoul National University, 1989.
36. Engblom E, Hamalainen H, Lind J, et al. Quality of life during rehabilitation after coronary artery bypass surgery. *Qual Life Res* 1992;1:167–175.
37. Eriksson J. Psychosomatic aspects of coronary artery bypass graft surgery: a prospective study of 101 male patients. *Acta Psychiatr Scand* 1988;77(3405).
38. Melzack R. The McGill Pain Questionnaire: major properties and scoring methods. *Pain* 1975;1:277–299.
39. Melzack R. Psychologic aspects of pain. *Pain* 1980;8:143–154.
40. Melzack R. *The puzzle of pain*. New York: Basic Books, 1973.
41. Melzack R, Torgerson WS. On the language of pain. *Anesthesiology* 1971;34:50–59.
42. McDowell I, Newell C. *Measuring health: a guide to rating scales and questionnaires*. New York: Oxford University Press, 1987.
43. Melzack R. The Short-Form McGill Pain Questionnaire. *Pain* 1987; 30:191–197.
44. Graham C, Band SS, Gerkovich MM, Cook MR. Use of the McGill Pain Questionnaire in the assessment of cancer pain: replicability and consistency. *Pain* 1980;8:377–387.
45. Reading AE. The McGill Pain Questionnaire: an appraisal. In: Melzack R, ed. *Pain measurement and assessment*. New York: Raven, 1983:55–61.
46. Dubuisson D, Melzack R. Classification of clinical pain descriptions by multiple group discriminant analysis. *Exp Neurol* 1976;51:480–487.
47. Prieto EJ, Geisinger KF. Factor-analytic studies of the McGill Pain Questionnaire. In: Melzack R, ed. *Pain measurement and assessment*. New York: Raven Press, 1983:85–93.
48. Monks R, Taenzer P. A comprehensive pain questionnaire. In: Melzack R, ed. *Pain Measurement and Assessment*. New York: Raven Press, 1983:233–237.
49. Holroyd KA, Lukinman A, Konttinen YT. Chronic low back pain: intercorrelation of reported measures for pain and disability. *Scand J Rehab Med* 1990;22:73–77.
50. Lowe NK, Walker SN, MacCollum RC. Confirming the theoretical structure of the McGill Pain Questionnaire in acute clinical pain. *Pain* 1991;46:53–60.
51. Van der Meij J, Riezebos C, Tromp J. Het ontwikkelen van een pijnvragenlijst: een replica-onderzoek van de MPQ binnen het Nederlandse taalgebied. *Haags Tijdschr Fysiother* 1985;3:81–92.

52. Vanderiet K, Adriaensen H, Carton H, Vertommen H. The McGill Pain Questionnaire constructed for the Dutch language (MPQ-DV). Preliminary data concerning reliability and validity. *Pain* 1987;30: 395–408.

53. Verkes R-J, Van der Kloot WA, Van der Meij J. The perceived structure of 176 pain descriptive words. *Pain* 1989;38:219–229.

54. van Lankveld W, van't Pad Bosch P, van de Putte L, et al. Pain in rheumatoid arthritis measured with the visual analogue scale and the Dutch version of the McGill Pain Questionnaire. *Ned Tijdschr Geneesk* 1992;136(94):1166–1170.

55. Verkes RJ, Vanderiet K, Vertommen H, Van der Kloot WA, Van der Meij J. De MPQ-DLV, een standaard Nederlandstalige versie van de McGill Pain Questionnaire voor Belgie en Nederland. In: Van Der Kloot WA, Vertommen H, eds. *Een Standaard Nederlandstalige Versie van de McGill Pain Questionnaire: Achtergronden en Handleiding van de MPQ-DLV.* Swets and Zeitlinger: Lisse, 1990.

56. Ketovuori H, Pontinen PJ. A pain vocabulary in Finnish—the Finnish Pain Questionnaire. *Pain* 1981;11:247–253.

57. Gronblad M, Lukinman A, Konttinen YT. Chronic low back pain: intercorrelation of repeated measures for pain and disability. *Scand J Rehab Med* 1990;22:73–77.

58. Vden A, Astrom M, Bergenudd H. Pain drawings in chronic back pain. *Spine* 1988;13:389.

59. Ljunggren AE. Descriptions of pain and other sensory modalities in patients with lumbago-sciatica and herniated intervertebral discs. Interview administration of an adapted McGill Pain Questionnaire. *Pain* 1983;16:265–276.

60. Strand LI, Wisnes AR. The development of a Norwegian pain questionnaire. *Pain* 1991;46:61–66.

61. Kiss I, Muller H, Abel M. The McGill Pain Questionnaire—German version. A study on cancer pain. *Pain* 1987;29:195–207.

62. Radvila A, Adler RH, Galeazzi RL, Vorkfauf H. The development of a German language (Berne) pain questionnaire and its application in a situation causing acute pain. *Pain* 1987;28:185–195.

63. Stein C, Mendl G. The German counterpart to McGill Pain Questionnaire. *Pain* 1988;32:251–255.

64. Stein C, Comesel K, Haimerl E. Analgesic effect of intra-articular morphine after arthroscopic knee surgery. *N Engl J Med* 1991;325 (16):1123–1126.

65. Welte M, Haimerl E, Groh J. Effect of intrapleural morphine on postoperative pain and pulmonary function after thoracotomy. *Br J Anesth* 1992;69:637–639.

66. Schneider HT, Hummel T, Jarowitz P, et al. Pain in extracorporeal shock-wave lithotripsy: a comparison of different lithotripters in volunteers. *Gastroenterology* 1992;102:640–646.

67. Maiani G, Sanavio E. Semantics of pain in Italy: the Italian version of the McGill Pain Questionnaire. *Pain* 1985;22:399–405.

68. Nolli M, Gbirelli L, Ferraccioli FG. Pain language in fibromyalgia, rheumatoid arthritis, and osteoarthritis. *Clin Exp Rheumatol* 1988;6: 27–33.

69. Ferraccioli G, Cavalieri F, Salaffi F, et al. Neuroendocrinologic findings in primary fibromyalgia (soft tissue chronic pain syndrome) and in other chronic rheumatic conditions (rheumatoid arthritis, low back pain). *J Rheumatol* 1990;17:869–873.

70. De Benedittis G, Massei R, Nobili R, Pieri A. The Italian pain questionnaire. *Pain* 1988;33:53–62.

71. Boureau F, Luu M, Doubrere JF. Qualitative and quantitative study of a French pain McGill adapted questionnaire in experimental and clinical conditions. *Pain* 1984;(DB suppl 2):S422.

72. Boureau F, Luu M, Doubrere JF, Gay C. Elaboration d'ren questionnaire d'auto-evaluation de la douleur par liste de qualificatifs. Comparison avec le McGill Pain Questionnaire de Melzack. *Therapie* 1984; 39:119–139.

73. Boureau F, Doubrere JF, Luu M, Combes A, Paquette C. Chronic pain symptomatology assessment. In: Scherpereel P, et al., eds. *The pain clinic II: Proceedings of the Second International Symposium.* Utretch, The Netherlands: VNU Science Press, 1987:119–139.

74. Boureau F, Luu M, Doubrere JF. Study of experimental pain measures and vociceptive reflex in chronic pain patients and normal subjects. *Pain* 1991;44:131–138.

75. Viguie F. Questionnaire Algie. In: Melzack R, Wall PD, eds. *La Defi de la Douleur.* Paris: Maloine, 1982:46.

76. Boureau F, Paquette C. Translated versus reconstructed McGill Pain Questionnaires: a comparative study of two French forms. In: Dubner R, Gebhart FG, Bond MR, eds. *Proceedings of the Vth World Congress on Pain.* Amsterdam: Elsevier, 1988:395–402.

77. Harrison A. Arabic pain words. *Pain* 1988;32:239–250.

78. Lahuerta J, Smith BA, Martinez-Lage RJ. An adaptation of the McGill Pain Questionnaire in the Spanish language. *Schmerz* 1981;3:132–134.

79. Stelian J, Gil I, Habot B, et al. Improvement of pain and disability in elderly patients with degenerative osteoarthritis of the knee treated with narrow-band light therapy. *J Am Geriatr Soc* 1992;40:23–26.

80. Comstock GW, Helsing KJ. Symptoms of depression in two communities. *Psychol Med* 1976;6:551–563.

81. Radloff LS. The CES-D Scale: a self-report depression scale for research in the general population. *Appl Psychol Meas* 1977;1:385–401.

82. Myers JK, Weissman MM. Use of a self-report symptom scale to detect depression in a community sample. *Am J Psychiatry* 1980;137:1081.

83. Weissman MM, Sholomskas D, Pottenger M, et al. Assessing depressive symptoms in five psychiatric populations: a validation study. *Am J Epidemiol* 1977;106:203–214.

84. Zung WWK. A self-rating depression scale. *Arch Gen Psychiatry* 1965;12:63–70.

85. Raskin A, Schulterbrandt J, Reating N, McKeon J. Replication of factors of psychopathology in interview, ward behavior and self-report ratings of hospitalized depressives. *J Nerv Ment Dis* 1969;198:87–96.

86. Dahlstrom WG, Welsh GS. *An MMPI handbook.* Minneapolis: University of Minnesota Press, 1960.

87. Gardner EA. *Development of a symptom checklist for the measurement of depression in a population.* Unpublished manuscript, 1968.

88. Weissman MM, Locke BZ. Comparison of a self-report symptom rating scale (CES-D) with standarized depression rating scales in psychiatric populations. *Am J Epidemiol* 1975;102:430–431.

89. Burnam MA, Wells KB, Leake B, Landsverk J. Development of a brief screening instrument for detecting depressive disorders. *Med Care* 1988;26(8):775–789.

90. Craig TJ, Van Natta P. *Validation of the Community Mental Health Assessment Interview Instrument among psychiatric inpatients: working paper B-27a.* Rockville, MD: Center for Epidemiologic Studies, 1973.

91. Roberts RE, Vernon SW, Rhoades HM. Effects of language and ethnic status on reliability and validity of the Center for Epidemiologic Studies-Depression Scale with psychiatric patients. *J Nerv Ment Dis* 1989;177(10):581–592.

92. Roberts RE. Prevalence of psychological distress among Mexican Americans. *J Health Soc Behav* 1980;21:134–145.

93. Roberts RE, Vernon SW. The Center for Epidemiologic Studies Depression Scale: its use in a community sample. *Am J Psychiatry* 1983;140(1):41–46.

94. Breslau N. Depressive symptoms, major depression, and generalized anxiety: a comparison of self-reports on CES-D and results from diagnostic interviews. *Psychiatry Res* 1985;15:219–229.

95. Roberts RE, Lewinsohn PM, Seeley JR. Screening for adolescent depression: a comparison of depression scales. *J Am Acad Child Adolesc Psychiatry* 1991;30:58–66.

96. Roberts RE. Reliability of the CES-D Scale in different ethnic contexts. *Psychiatry Res* 1980;2:125–134.

97. Guarnaccia PJ, Angel R, Worobey JL. The factor structure of the CES-D in the Hispanic Health and Nutrition Examination Survey: the influences of ethnicity, gender, and language. *Soc Sci Med* 1989;29(1):85–94.

98. Roberts RE, Rhoades HM, Vernon SW. Using the CES-D scale to screen for depression and anxiety: effects of language and ethnic status. *Psychiatry Res* 1989;31:69–83.

99. Clark VA, Aneshensel CS, Frerichs RR, Morgan TM. Analysis of effects of sex and age in response to items on the CES-D scale. *Psychiatry Res* 1981;5:171–181.

100. Liang J, Van Tran T, Krause N, Markides KS. Generational differences in the structure of the CES-D Scale in Mexican Americans. *J Gerontol* 1989;44(3):S110–S120.

101. Garcia M, Marks G. Depressive symptomatology among Mexican-American adults: an examination with the CES-D Scale. *Psychiatry Res* 1989;27:137–148.

102. Mahard RE. The CES-D as a measure of depressive mood in the elderly Puerto Rican population. *J Gerontol* 1988;43(1):24–25.

103. Vega W, Warheit G, Buhl-Auth J, Meinhardt K. The prevalence of

depressive symptoms among Mexican Americans and Anglos. *Am J Epidemiol* 1984;120(4):592–607.

104. Gary LE. Correlated of depressive symptoms among a select population of black men. *Am J Public Health* 1985;75(10):1220–1222.

105. Frerichs RR, Aneshensel CS, Clark VA. Prevalence of depression in Los Angeles County. *Am J Epidemiol* 1981;113(6):691–699.

106. Kuo WH. Prevalence of depression among Asian-Americans. *J Nerv Ment Dis* 1984;172(8):449–457.

107. Ying Y. Depressive symptomatology among Chinese-Americans as measured by the CES-D. *J Clin Psychol* 1988;44(5):739–746.

108. Madianos M, Vaidakis N, Tomaras V, Kapsali A. The prevalence of depressive symptoms in the general population with the CES-D scale. *Encephalos* 1983;20:24–28.

109. Madianos MG, Gournas G, Stefanis CN. Depressive symptoms and depression among elderly people in Athens. *Acta Psychiatr Scand* 1992;86:320–326.

110. Gournas G, Madianos MG, Stefanis CN. Psychological functioning and psychiatric morbidity in an elderly urban population in Greece. *Eur Arch Psychiatry Clin Neurosci* 1992;242:127–134.

111. Madianos MG, Stefanis CN. Who needs treatment? A nationwide psychiatric case identification study. *Psychopathology* 1992;25:212–217.

112. Fuhrer R, Rouillon F. La Version Francaise de L'Echelle CES-D (Center for Epidemiologic Studies–Depression Scale). Description et traduction de l'Echelle d'Autoevaluation. *Psychiatr Psychobiol* 1989; 4:163–166.

113. Fuhrer R, Antonucci TC, Gagnon M, et al. Depressive symptomatology and cognitive functioning: an epidemiological survey in an elderly community sample in France. *Psychol Med* 1992;22:159–172.

114. Shima S, Shikano T, Kitamura T, et al. New self-rating scales for depression. *Clin Psychiatry* 1985;27:717–723.

115. Iwata N, Saito K. Relationships of the Todai Health Index to the General Health Questionnaire and the Center for Epidemiologic Studies Depression Scale. *Jpn J Hyg* 1987;42:865–873.

116. Iwata N, Saito K. Psychometric properties of the Center for Epidemiologic Studies Depression Scale for Japanese workers. *Jpn J Ind Health* 1989;31:20–21.

117. Iwata N, Okuyama Y, Kawakami Y, Saito K. Prevalence of depressive symptoms in a Japanese occupational setting: a preliminary study. *Am J Public Health* 1989;79(11):1486–1489.

118. Serbo B, Jajic I. Relationship of the functional status, duration of the disease and pain intensity and some psychological variables in patients with rheumatoid arthritis. *Clin Rheumatol* 1991;10(4):419–422.

119. Hedlund JL, Vieweg BW. The Zung Self-Rating Depression Scale: a comprehensive review. *J Operational Psychiatry* 1979;10:51–64.

120. Zung WWK. Self-Rating Depression Scale and Depression Status Inventory. In: Sartorius N, Ban TA, eds. *Assessment of depression.* Heidelberg: Springer, 1986:221–231.

121. Zung WWK. The measurement of affects: depression and anxiety. In: Pichot P, ed. *Psychological measurement in psychopharmacology. Modern problems of pharmacopsychiatry.* Basel: Karger, 1974;7: 170–188.

122. Zung WWK. The depression status inventory: an adjunct to the Self-Rating Depression Scale. *J Clin Psychol* 1972;28:539–543.

123. Giambria L. Independent dimensions of depression: a factor analysis of three self-report depression measures. *J Clin Psychol* 1977;33: 928–935.

124. Blumenthal M. Measuring depressive symptomatology in a general population. *Arch Gen Psychiatry* 1975;34:971–978.

125. Toner J, Gurland B, Teresi J. Comparison of self-administered and rater-administered methods of assessing levels of severity of depression in elderly patients. *J Gerontol* 1988;43:136–140.

126. Zung WWK. A cross-cultural survey of symptoms in depression. *Am J Psychiatry* 1969;126:116–121.

127. Kivela S-L, Pahkala K. Sex and age differences in the factor pattern and reliability of the Zung Self-Rating Depression Scale in a Finnish elderly population. *Psychol Rep* 1986;59:587–597.

128. Kivela S-L, Nissinen A, Punsar S, Puska P. Age and regional differences in reliability and factor structure of the Zung Self-Rating Scale in elderly Finnish men. *J Clin Psychol* 1987;43:318–327.

129. Lammi U-K, Kivela S-L, Nissinen A, Punsar S, Puska P, Karvonen M. Mental disability among elderly men in Finland: prevalence, predictors, and correlates. *Acta Psychiatr Scand* 1989;80:459–468.

130. Dijkstra P. De Zelfbeoordelingsschaal voor Depressie van Zung: The Zung Self-Rating Depression Scale. In: Van Praag HM, Rooymans

131. Gabrys JB, Peters K. Reliability, discriminant and predictive validity of the Zung Self-Rating Depression Scale. *Psychol Rep* 1985;57: 1091–1096.

132. deJonghe JFM, Baneke JJ. The Zung Self-Rating Depression Scale: a replication study on reliability, validity and prediction. *Psychol Rep* 1989;64:833–834.

133. Gould J. A psychometric investigation of the standard and short form Beck Depression Inventory. *Psychol Rep* 1982;51:1167–1170.

134. Kerner SA, Jacobs KW. Correlation between scores on the Beck Depression Inventory and the Zung Self-Rating Depression Scale. *Psychol Rep* 1983;53:969–970.

135. Hatzenbuehler LC, Parpal M, Matthews L. Classifying college students as depressed or nondepressed using the Beck Depression Inventory: an empirical analysis. *J Consult Clin Psychol* 1983;51:360–366.

136. Schrijnemaekers VJ, Haveman MJ. Depressive symptoms in physically frail elderly. *Tijdschr Gerontol Geriatr* 1992;23:217–224.

137. Westermeyer J. Two self-rating scales for depression in Hmong refugees: assessment in clinical and nonclinical samples. *J Psychiatr Res* 1986;20:103–113.

138. Horiguchi J, Inami Y. A survey of the living conditions and psychological states of elderly people admitted to nursing homes in Japan. *Acta Psychiatr Scand* 1991;83:338–341.

139. Yamashita K, Kobayashi S, Tsunematsu T. Depressed mood and subjective sensation well-being in the elderly living alone on Oki island in Shimane prefecture. *Nippon Ronen Igakkai Zasshi* 1992; 20:179–184.

140. Kikumoto O. Clinical study on depressive state following stroke. *Seishin Shinkeigaku Zasshi* 1990;92:411–434.

141. Kawakami N, Haratani T, Araki S. Effects of perceived job stress on depressive symptoms in blue-collar workers of an electrical factory in Japan. *Scand J Work Environ Health* 1992;18:195–200.

142. Kawada T, Suzuki S. Factor structure of self-rating depression scale by Zung and prevalence of depressive state of night shift workers. *Sangyo Igaku* 1992;34:131–136.

143. Hymes RW, Akiyama MM. Depression and self-enhancement among Japanese and American students. *J Soc Psychol* 1991;131:321–334.

144. Auff E, Doppelbauer A, Fertl E. Essential tremor: functional disability vs. subjective impairment. *J Neural Transm Suppl* 1991;33:105–110.

145. Hoschl C, Kozeny J. Verapamil in affective disorders: a controlled, double-blind study. *Biol Psychiatry* 1989;25:128–140.

146. Chapuy P, Cuny G, Delomier Y, et al. Depression in elderly patients. Value of tianeptine in 140 patients treated for 1 year. *Presse Med* 1991;20:1844–1852.

147. Przuntek H, Welzel D, Blumner E, et al. Bromocriptine lessens the incidence of mortality in L-Dopa-treated parkinsonian patients: Prado-study discontinued. *Eur J Clin Pharmacol* 1992;43:357–363.

148. Steiner B, Wolfersdorf M, Keller F, Straub R, Hole G. Psychopathologic and psychophysiologic follow-up of inpatient depressed patients with standardized treatment with clomipramine and oxaprotiline. *Schweiz Arch Neurol Psychiatr* 1991;142:259–269.

149. Zerfass R, Kretzschmar K, Forstl H. Depressive disorders after cerebral infarct. Relations to infarct site, brain atrophy and cognitive deficits. *Nervenartz* 1992;63:163–168.

150. Makaremi A. Sex differences in depression of Iranian adolescents. *Psychol Rep* 1992;71:939–943.

151. Indaco A, Carrieri PB. Amitriptyline in the treatment of headache in patients with Parkinson's disease: a double-blind placebo-controlled study. *Neurology* 1988;38:1720–1722.

152. Ardizzone A, Novi RF, Lamberto M, et al. Psychometric evaluations in a group of obese patients. *Minerva Endocrinol* 1990;15:135–139.

153. Comazzi AM, Nielsen NP, Zizolfi S, Dioguardi N. Neurotic and depressive status related to organic pathology in patients in thermal therapy. *Minerva Med* 1991;83:463–475.

154. Salaffi F, Ferraccioli GF, Carotti M, Blasetti P, Cervini C. Disability in rheumatoid arthritis: the predictive value of age and depression. *Recenti Prog Med* 1992;83:675–679.

155. Pintor PP, Torta R, Bartolozzi S, et al. Clinical outcome and emotional-behavioural status after isolated coronary surgery. *Qual Life Res* 1992;1:177–185.

156. Tyra TL. Personality features of spouses married to depressive partners. *Psychiatr Pol* 1992;26:66–70.

157. Widerstrom EG, Aslund PG, Gustafsson L-E, Mannheimer C, Carlson SG, Andersson SA. Relations between experimentally induced

HMG, eds. *Stemming en Ontstemming.* Amsterdam: Erven Bohn, 1974:98–121.

total pain threshold changes, psychometrics and clinical pain relief following TENS. A retrospective study in patients with long-lasting pain. *Pain* 1992;51:281–287.

158. Eblen A, Vivas V, Garcia J. Prevalence of depressive syndrome and its relationship with socioeconomic factors in a population of Valencia City, Carabobo state, Venezuela. *Acta Cient Venez* 1990;41:250–254.

159. Goldberg DP. *The detection of psychiatric illness by questionnaire.* Maudsley Monogram #21. London: Oxford University Press, 1972.

160. Goldberg DP, Hillier VF. A scaled version of the General Health Questionnaire. *Psychol Med* 1979;9:139–145.

161. Goldberg DP, Williams P. *Users' guide to the General Health Questionnaire.* Windsor: NFER-Nelson, 1988.

162. Goldberg DP. *Manual of the General Health Questionnaire.* Windsor: NFER, 1978.

163. Worsley A, Gribbin CC. A factor analytic study of the twelve item General Health Questionnaire. *Aust NZ J Psychiatry* 1977;11:269–272.

164. Goodchild ME, Duncan-Jones P. Chronicity and the General Health Questionnaire. *Br J Psychiatry* 1985;146:56–61.

165. Henderson SH, Byrne DG, Duncan-Jones P. *Neurosis and the social environment.* Sydney: Academic Press, 1981.

166. Ormel J, Koeter MW, Van den Brink W. Measuring change with the General Health Questionnaire (GHQ). The problem of retest effects. *Soc Psychiatry Psychiatr Epidemiol* 1987;24:227–232.

167. Bolognini M, Bettschart W, Zehnder-Guber M, Rossier L. The validity of the French version of the GHQ-28 and PSYDIS in a community sample of 20-year-olds in Switzerland. *Eur Arch Psychiatr Neurol Sci* 1989;238:161–168.

168. Uhlenhuth EH, Balter MG, Mellinger GD, Gisin IH, Clinthorne J. Symptom checklist syndromes in the general population: correlations with psychotherapeutic drug use. *Arch Gen Psychiatry* 1983;40:1167–1173.

169. Pariente PD, Challita H, Mesbah M, Guelfi JD. The GHQ-28 questionnaire in French: a validation survey in a panel of 158 general psychiatric patients. *Eur Psychiatry* 1992;7:15–20.

170. Fontanesi F, Gobetti C, Zimmerman-Tansella C, et al. Validation of the Italian version of the GHQ in a general practice setting. *Psychol Med* 1985;15:411–415.

171. Goldberg DP, Cooper B, Eastwood MR, Kedward HR, Shepherd M. A standardised psychiatric interview suitable for use in community surveys. *Br J Prevent Soc Med* 1970;24:18–23.

172. Vazquez-Barquero J, Williams P, Manrique JF, et al. The factor structure of the GHQ-60 in a community sample. *Psychol Med* 1988;18:211–218.

173. Lobo A, Folstein MF, Beloff MD. Incidencia, prevalencia y deteccion de morbilidad psiquiatrica en un hospital encologico. *Folia Neuropsiq* 1979;14:260–269.

174. Lobo A, Folstein MF, Escolar V, Morera B, Dia JL. Screening instruments and diagnostic criteria for psychiatric epidemiological studies in oncological patients. In: Lobo A, Tres A, eds. *Biobehavioral oncology.* Madrid: Ministerio de Sanidad, 1988.

175. Lobo A, Perez-Echeverria MJ, Artal J. Validity of the scaled version of the General Health Questionnaire (GHQ-28) in a Spanish population. *Psychol Med* 1986;16:135–140.

176. Lobo A, Perez-Echeverria M, Jimenez-Aznorez A, Sancho M. Emotional disturbance in endocrine patients: validity of the scaled version of the General Health Questionnaire (GHQ-28). *Br J Psychiatry* 1988;152:807–812.

177. Munoz P, Vazquez J, Dastrana E, et al. Study of the validity of Goldberg's 60-item GHQ in its Spanish version. *Soc Psychiatry* 1978;13:99–104.

178. Laerum E, Johnsen N, Smith P, Arnesen H. Positive psychological and lifestyle changes after myocardial infarction: a follow-up study after 2–4 years. *Fam Pract* 1991;8(3):229–233.

179. Malt VF. The validity of the GHQ in a sample of accidentally injured adults. *Acta Psychiatr Scand* 1989;80(suppl 355):103–112.

180. Claussen B, Bjorndal A, Hjort PF. Health and re-employment in a two-year follow-up of long term unemployed. *J Epidemiol Community Health* 1993;47:14–18.

181. Verhaak PF, Wennink H, Tijhuis M. The importance of the GHQ in general practice. *Fam Pract* 1990;7:319–324.

182. Verhaak PFM, Tijhuis MAR. Psychosocial problems in primary care: some results from the Dutch national study of morbidity and interventions in general practice. *Soc Sci Med* 1992;35(2):105–110.

183. Koeter MWF, Van Den Brink W, Ormel J. Chronic psychiatric complaints and the General Health Questionnaire. *Br J Psychiatry* 1989; 155:186–190.

184. Wilmink FW, Snijders TA. Polytomous logistic regression analysis of the General Health Questionnaire and the Present State Examination. *Psychol Med* 1989;19:755–764.

185. Wiznitzer M, Verhulst FC, van den Brink W, van der Ende J, Giel R, Koot HM. Detecting psychopathology in young adults: the Young Adult Self Report, the General Health Questionnaire, and the Symptom Checklist as screening instruments. *Acta Psychiatr Scand* 1992; 86:32–27.

186. Koeter MWJ. Validity of the GHQ and SCL anxiety and depression scales: a comparative study. *J Affect Dis* 1991;24:271–280.

187. Iwata N, Saito K. The factor structure of the 28-item General Health Questionnaire when used in Japanese early adolescents and adult employees: age and cross-cultural comparisons. *Eur Arch Psychiatry Clin Neurosci* 1992;242:172–178.

188. Nakagawa Y, Daibo I. Tests of the validity and reliability of the Japanese version General Health Questionnaire and its clinical applications. In: Nakagawa Y, ed. *The theory behind understanding psychiatric and neurotic symptoms using a questionnaire and its clinical applications.* Monograph of National Institute of Mental Health, Japan, Part 2, NIMH. Japan: Ichikawa, 1982:110–197. [In Japanese]

189. Kitamura T, Sugawara M, Aoki M, Shimi S. Validity of the Japanese version of the GHQ among antenatal clinic attendants. *Psychol Med* 1989;19:507–511.

190. Spitzer RL, Endicott J. *Schedule for affective disorders and schizophrenia,* 3rd ed. New York: New York State Psychiatric Institute, Biometrics Research, 1978.

191. Spitzer RL, Endicott J, Robins E. *Research Diagnostic Criteria (RDC) for a selected group of functional disorders,* 3rd ed. New York: New York State Psychiatric Institute, Biometrics Research, 1978.

192. Furukawa T. Perceived parental rearing, personality and mental status in Japanese adolescents. *J Adolesc* 1992;15:317–322.

193. Kitamura T, Suzuki T. Japanese versions of the Social Desirability Scale. *Jpn J Soc Psychiatry* 1986;9:173–180.

194. Iwata N, Suzuki K, Saito K, Abe K. Type A personality, work stress and psychological distress in Japanese adult employees. *Stress Med* 1992;8:11–21.

195. Elton M, Patton G, Weyerer S, et al. A comparative investigation of the principal component structure of the 28-item version of the General Health Questionnaire. *Acta Psychiatr Scand* 1988;77:124–132.

196. Weyerer S, Elton M, Diallina M, Fichter MM. The principal component structure of the General Health Questionnaire among Greek and Turkish adolescents. *Eur Arch Psychiatr Neurol Sci* 1986;236: 75–82.

197. Shek DTL. Validity of the Chinese version of the General Health Questionnaire. *J Clin Psychol* 1989;45:890–897.

198. Chan DW, Chan TS. Reliability, validity and the structure of the General Health Questionnaire in a Chinese context. *Psychol Med* 1983;15:147–155.

199. Chan DW. The Chinese version of the General Health Questionnaire: does language make a difference? *Psychol Med* 1985;15:147–155.

200. Shek DTL. Reliability and factorial structure of the Chinese version of the General Health Questionnaire. *J Clin Psychol* 1987;57:683–691.

201. Oduwolfe OO, Ogunyemi AO. Validity of the GHQ-30 in a Nigerian medical outpatient clinic. *Can J Psychiatry* 1989;34:20–23.

202. Morakinyo O. The sensitivity and validity of the Cornwall Medical Index and the General Health Questionnaire in an African population. *Afr J Psychiatry* 1979;1:1–8.

203. Gureje O. Reliability and the factor structure of the Yoruba version of the 12-item General Health Questionnaire. *Acta Psychiatr Scand* 1991;84:125–129.

204. Gureje O, Obikoya B. The GHQ-12 as a screening tool in a primary care setting. *Soc Psychiatry Psychiatr Epidemiol* 1990;25:276–280.

205. WHO/ADAMHA. *Composite International Diagnostic Interview.* Geneva: World Health Organization, 1987.

206. Gureje O, Obikoya B. Somatization in primary care: pattern and correlates in a clinic in Nigeria. *Acta Psychiatr Scand* 1992;86:223–227.

207. Gureje O, Obikoya B, Ikuesan BA. Alcohol abuse and dependence in an urban primary care clinic in Nigeria. *Drug Alcohol Depend* 1992;30:163–167.

208. Abiodun OA. A study of mental morbidity among primary care patients in Nigeria. *Compr Psychiatry* 1993;34:10–13.

209. Abiodun OA, Parakoyi DB. Psychiatric morbidity in a rural community in Nigeria. *Int J Mental Health* 1992;21:23–35.

210. Aberibigbe YA, Gureje O. The validity of the 28-item General Health Questionnaire in a Nigerian antenatal clinic. *Soc Psychiatry Psychiatr Epidemiol* 1992;27:280–283.

211. Dupuy HJ. The Psychological General Well-Being (PGWB) Index. In: Wenger NK, Mattson ME, Furberg CD, Elinson J, eds. *Assessment of quality of life in clinical trials of cardiovascular therapies.* New York: Le Jacq, 1984:170–183.

212. Dupuy HJ. The psychological section of the current health and nutrition examination survey. In: *The Proceedings of the Public Health Conference on Records and Statistics, Meeting Jointing with the National Conference on Mental Health Statistics,* 14th National Meeting, June 12–15, 1972, Publication No. (HRA) 74-1214. Washington, DC: U.S. Department of Health, Education, and Welfare, 1973.

213. Dupuy HJ. Utility of the National Center for Health Statistics' General Well-Being Schedule in the assessment of self-representations of subjective well-being and distress. In: *The National Conference on Evaluation in Alcohol, Drug Abuse, and Mental Health Programs.* Washington, DC: ADAMHA, 1974.

214. Fazio AF. *A concurrent validational study of the NCHS General Well-Being Schedule.* Vital and Health Statistics Series 2, No. 73. DHEW Publication No. (HRA) 78-1347. Hyattsville, MD: National Center for Health Statistics, 1977.

215. Kammann R, Flett R. Affectometer 2: a scale to measure current level of general happiness. *Aust J Psychol* 1983;35:259–265.

216. Wan TTH, Livieratos B. Interpreting a general index of subjective well-being. *Milbank Memorial Fund Q* 1978;56:531-556.

217. Ware JE, Johnston SA, Davies-Avery A, Brook RH. *Conceptualization and measurement of health for adults in the Health Insurance Study.* Vol 3, Mental Health. (Publication No. R-1987/3-HEW.) Santa Monica, CA: Rand Corporation, 1979.

218. Croog SH, Levine S, Testa MA, Brown B, et al. The effects of antihypertensive therapy on the quality of life. *N Engl J Med* 1986; 314(26):1657–1664.

219. Steiner SS, Friedhoff AJ, Wilson BL, Wecker JR, Santo JP. Antihypertensive therapy and quality of life: a comparison of atenolol, captopril, enalapril and propranolol. *J Hum Hypertens* 1990;4:217–225.

220. Croog SH, Kong W, Levine S, Weir MR, Baume RM, Saunders E. Hypertensive black men and women. *Arch Intern Med* 1990;150: 1773–1741.

221. Applegate WB, Phillips HL, Schnaper H, et al. A randomized controlled trial of the effects of three antihypertensive agents on blood pressure control and quality of life in older women. *Arch Intern Med* 1991;151:1817–1823.

222. Chang SW, Fine R, Siegel D, Chesney M, Black D, Hulley SB. The impact of diuretic therapy on reported sexual function. *Arch Intern Med* 1991;151:2402–2408.

223. Testa MA, Anderson RB, Nackely JF, Hollenberg NK. Quality of life and antihypertensive therapy in men. *N Engl J Med* 1993;328: 907–913.

224. Wiklund I, Karlberg J. Evaluation of quality of life in clinical trials: selecting quality of life measures. *Controlled Clin Trials* 1991;12: S204–S216.

225. Wiklund I, Holst J, Karlberg J, et al. A new methodological approach to the evaluation of quality of life in postmenopausal women. *Maturitas* 1992;14:211–224.

226. Wiklund I, Berg G, Hammar M, Karlberg J, Lindgren R, Sandin K. Long-term effect of transdermal hormonal therapy on aspects of quality of life in postmenopausal women. *Maturitas* 1992;14:225–236.

227. Wiklund I, Karlberg J, Mattsson L-A. Quality of life of postmenopausal women on a regimen of transdermal estradiol therapy: a double-blind placebo-controlled study. *Am J Obstet Gynecol* 1993;168(3): 824–830.

228. Bjorck S, Jonsson B, Westphal O, Levin J-E. Quality of life of adults with growth hormone deficiency: a controlled study. *Acta Paediatr Scand* 1983;356(suppl):55–59.

229. Dimenas E, Glise H, Hallerback G, Hernqvist H, Svedlund J, Wiklund I. Quality of life in patients with upper gastrointestinal disease. Improved possibility of evaluation of treatment regimens? *Scand J Gastroenterol* 1993;28(8):681–687.

230. Omvik P, Thaulow E, Herlan OB, Eide I, Midha R, Turner RR. Double-blind, parallel, comparative study on quality of life during treatment with amlodipine or enalapril in mild or moderate hypertensive patients: a multicentre study. *J Hypertens* 1993;11:103–113.

231. Bullinger M, Heinisch M, Ludwig M, Geier S. Skalen zur Erfassung des Wohlbefindens. Psychometrische uberprufung des Profile of Mood States (POMS) und des Psychological General Well-Being Index (PGWB). *Z Differentielle Diagn Psychol* 1990;11:53–61.

232. Fletcher AE, Bulpitt CJ, Chase DM, et al. Quality of life with three antihypertensive treatments. *Hypertension* 1992;19:499–507.

233. McGauley GA. Quality of life assessments before and after growth hormone treatment in adults with growth hormone deficiency. *Acta Paediatr Scand* 1989;356(suppl):70–72.

234. Hunt SM, McKenna SP. British adaptation of the General Well-Being Index: a new tool for clinical research. *Br J Med Econ* 1992;2:49–60.

Quality of Life and Pharmacoeconomics in Clinical Trials, Second Edition, edited by B. Spilker.
Lippincott-Raven Publishers, Philadelphia © 1996.

CHAPTER 69

Creating and Evaluating Cross-Cultural Instruments

Monika Bullinger, Michael J. Power, Neil K. Aaronson, David F. Cella, and Roger T. Anderson

INTRODUCTION

The Challenge of Cross-Cultural Quality of Life Assessment

The increasing international collaboration in quality of life research, accelerated, for example, in Europe by efforts toward formal political unification, has created a need for cross-culturally valid instruments for outcome assessment (1). International construction and evaluation of health status measures, however, is difficult and raises similar problems to those encountered in any scientific endeavor attempting to work cross-culturally with a standard measurement system

M. Bullinger: Institute for Medical Psychology, University of Munich, FRG 80336 Munich, Germany.

M. J. Power: Department of Psychiatry, Royal Edinburgh Hospital, University of Edinburgh, Edinburgh EH10 5HF, United Kingdom.

N. K. Aaronson: Division of Psychosocial Research and Epidemiology, Netherlands Cancer Institute, 1066 CX Amsterdam, The Netherlands.

D. F. Cella: Department of Psychology and Social Sciences, Rush Medical College, Chicago, Illinois 60612.

R. T. Anderson: Department of Public Health Science, Bowman Gray School of Medicine, Wake Forest University, Winston-Salem, North Carolina 27157.

(2,3). Contrary to the majority of outcome assessments in the life sciences, the relative cross-cultural stability or invariance of a measurement system cannot be assumed in the social and behavioral sciences. The end points relevant to this latter type of research often pertain to attitudinal orientations, cognitive evaluations, or emotional states of the respondents that are assumed to be culturally diverse (4).

The conduct of health-related quality of life (HRQL) investigations in a given country requires addressing three key issues. First, there are the conceptual issues pertaining to "What is health-related quality of life?" in a given cultural context. The second set of issues pertains to the methodological questions of "How are HRQL questions asked?" The third set of issues refers to the analytical question of "What do changes in HRQL mean and imply?" within a given culture. As the broad literature from social anthropology demonstrates, concepts, assessments, and relevance statements about constructs such as "happiness" or "quality of life" may vary dramatically by culture or national context (5). In HRQL research, these definitional components may determine which indicators are needed to refer to the various dimensions of health status and functioning states being measured, and what thresholds demarcate perceived normal levels of functioning from impairment.

Even though HRQL is generally taken to refer to impacts of a health state on an individual's general functioning, different approaches in eliciting information are possible that carry different assumptions about the universality of the underlying construct. One approach is to elicit an appraisal of global HRQL that reflects an individual's perception and overall assessment of an ideal or optimal health state. With this method there are no implicit assumptions of universality of the concept of HRQL as the ever-contextual factors that affect opinions about HRQL (e.g., personal resources, roles, social expectations, and views of health and well-being) are allowed to vary in the measure, and will vary by culture.

However, on an abstract level, there may be cultural universality in what it means to have a good quality of life. This universality could pertain to the assumption that, independent of national or cultural origins and actual living conditions, it is important for people to feel psychologically well, physically fit, socially integrated, and functionally competent (6). This general model does not imply that all cultures place the same weight on each dimension. Nevertheless, independent of specific behaviors and norms within a culture, approaching the above positive experiences would constitute a good quality of life. In fact, such a minimal definition of components relevant to assessing quality of life has often been expressed in the literature (7). If adopted, this would imply that a generic approach to conceptualizing quality of life internationally is worthwhile and that the minimal common denominators of the psychological, physical, social, and functional components should be addressed.

In addition to the cultural or national effects attributable to the approach used to classify HRQL states, there might be high cultural variability in the acceptability or appropriateness of the tools used to elicit and collect the information sought. While people in the North American culture may be more accustomed to providing written responses, for example, this might not be true for other parts of the world. Other cultural differences include norms for self-disclosure and privacy issues related to the subjective experiences queried. Thus, in addition to the difference between self-rated questionnaires and interviews, the type of information gathered (i.e., qualitative versus quantitative) matters. Finally, the significance placed on quality of life information might vary culturally. For example, the relevance of the concept of "happiness" as a part of psychological well-being may vary significantly across cultural or national contexts.

Available Instruments

Since the beginning of international quality of life research almost 20 years ago, a variety of quality of life instruments has been developed (8–10). These instruments are available primarily from Anglo-Saxon countries in which assessment of health status has a long history in public health and epidemiological research. The majority of currently available instruments tends to focus on generic quality of life assessments pertaining to dimensions of quality of life relevant to all persons, independent of health state. More recently a multitude of disease-specific instruments has been developed (11).

Generally, generic quality of life scales are applicable to a wide range of health conditions, assess main dimensions of well-being and function, are oriented toward diagnosis and screening, can be used to compare different patient populations, and have health-economic potential. Therefore, they can be included in research (a) to describe the quality of life of healthy and ill populations (which is necessary to identify quality of life problem areas and potential needs for interventions), (b) for the evaluation of interventions (including routine outcome assessments and quality of care), as well as (c) for health-economic evaluations (including comparing costs and benefits of treatments and allocating resources). Most of these generic instruments are patient-based and reflect the multidimensional nature of the quality of life construct. Examples of generic quality of life measures are the Sickness Impact Profile (12), the Nottingham Health Profile (13), the Psychological General Well-Being Index (14), the Quality of Well-Being Scale (15), the Short Form 36 (SF-36) Health Survey (16).

Only recently international efforts have been directed toward constructing cross-cultural quality of life measures. Three approaches to international scale development can be identified (17). The *sequential* approach refers to translations of an original source instrument into other languages (e.g., translating the American SF-36, see Chapter 34) (18). The *parallel* approach efforts are focused on identifying a common set of quality of life dimensions, making use of appropriate existing scales or newly constructed scales on the basis of international consensus building, e.g., as in the approach taken by the (EORTC) Quality of Life Study Group (see Chapter 21) (19). The third approach is a *simultaneous* one in that identification and wording of items are done at the same time in different countries, the results of which are then pooled and translated into one source version from which again back-translations into different languages are performed. An example of this approach is the development of the World Health Organization (WHO) Quality of Life Questionnaire (20) (see Chapter 36).

In all three approaches the conversion of the measure from one culture to another is necessary. The question here is how to transfer measures from one culture or language to another. The following sections of this chapter address standards and guidelines for producing quality of life instruments appropriate for cross-cultural use, and provide a brief overview over international quality of life measures currently available.

Approaches to Cross-Cultural Comparability

Interestingly, despite the growing literature on the use of quality of life questionnaires internationally, there are very few papers that address directly the methodological criteria for developing and evaluating quality of life measures in a cross-cultural context (3,21). A fruitful approach, although not specific to quality of life measures, has been presented by Hui and Triandis (22), who have postulated four dimensions of equivalence when attempting to internationally measure a construct such as quality of life. These dimensions are (a) *functional equivalence,* the extent to which the items of a questionnare in the translated version have a meaning similar to those in the source version, (b) *scale equivalence,* the extent to which individuals in different cultural groups respond to similar items in a similar way, (c) *operational equivalence,* the comparability of the procedures used in obtaining information needed, and (d) *metric equivalence,* the psychometric question of whether a measure orders individuals along a continuum in a comparable way across cultures. Along the lines of the Hui and Triandis approach described above, four problems are encountered in the international work with quality of life instruments: the adequacy of translation, the comparability of response scales, the standardization of psychometric testing procedures, and the transferability of scoring results from one culture to another. The above problems denote two steps in the approach to national application of internationally available instruments. These involve the creation (i.e., translation of items and responses) and evaluation (i.e., psychometric testing and norming) of an instrument.

While literature is available on the conduct of the translation process itself, relatively little was written on how to ensure the quality of translations and their cross-cultural comparability (21–23). Likewise, psychometric testing procedures for health status measures are well described (24,25), but guidelines for conducting instrument validations cross-nationally are rare (26,27). Yet is essential that a system for comparative evaluations of the quality of international translation as well as psychometric testing and norming be developed because only then the cross-cultural comparability of these results produced by the instrument can be ensured (28).

CREATING INSTRUMENTS

Of the different approaches available for translating measures the one that has been employed most commonly involves a forward/backward translation process of an original source language document into the target language. In addition, focus groups are often used for critical evaluation of the translation.

The Sequential Approach

Various examples can be found in the literature of the sequential approach to translation and psychometric testing of instruments such as the Nottingham Health Profile, the Sickness Impact Profile, and the Quality of Well-Being Scale (28,29). Most recently, the International Quality of Life Assessment (IQOLA) Project has established a set of procedures for the translation, validation, and norming of the Medical Outcomes Study Short-Form SF-36 Health Survey. The SF-36 Health Survey is a 36-item instrument developed in the Medical Outcomes Study and measures eight dimensions of subjective health that can be associated to two main dimensions—physical function and mental health (30). The

SF-36 is available and psychometrically well established in five languages, with ten other language versions currently being prepared. In Germany, for example, the SF-36 has been translated and psychometrically tested in healthy and patient populations, totaling almost 8,000 respondents (31). The process involves generating two forward translations of the original source instrument into the first target language, with two independent translators meeting to agree on a common version. The resulting target language version is then translated back into English by two other translators who also meet to agree on their version. These agreed-upon versions are quality rated according to "conceptual equivalence," "colloquial language use," and "clarity" of the translations by a set of reviewers, so that the quality of the translation is explicitly assessed. Finally, the English retranslation is compared to the original by one of the persons who originally developed the instrument. A second step involves a piloting phase by applying the translated instrument to a convenient sample of people from the target nations who are then interviewed about the comprehensibility, feasibility, and acceptability of the instrument. The information from the forward/backward translation process, the quality ratings, and the focus group results are then brought into an international discussion of translations produced within different languages so as to ensure the comparability not only between source and target languages, but also across target languages. To ensure metric equivalence of the SF-36 translations, a Thurstone scaling exercise (32) is used. In each country, response choices are presented in random order on visual analog scales so that the assumption of an equidistance interval scale can be tested and compared across nations.

The Parallel Approach

The second approach was adopted for example by the EORTC Quality of Life Study Group, founded in 1980. The EORTC Quality of Life Questionnaire QLQ-C30 (20) is a patient-based instrument reflecting eight dimensions of quality of life mainly relevant to cancer patients but possibly also to other patient populations. The group set out to develop an instrument for quality of life assessment in cancer care and clinical trials that has both generic aspects (core questionnaire) as well as specific supplements (e.g., for lung cancer, breast cancer, etc.) to assess the quality of life of cancer patients. This modular approach to quality of life assessment is, to date, unique (33). The international diversity of the group in terms of professional and cultural backgrounds assured that culturally relevant input was present throughout the questionnaire construction process. A highlight of this approach is that international discussions of each item are relied upon to help ensure that a single set of items is developed that is applicable, in terms of meaning and relevance, across national contexts. The resulting 36-item version of the questionnaire (EORTC QLQ-C36) was translated according to a forward-backward method, pilot tested in each participating country to determine the appropriateness of the content and wording, and applied in an international field study of 537 lung cancer patients, using a pretreatment and one treatment-related assessment (34). The group developed a procedure for evaluating quality of life measures cross-culturally by grouping patient information from all countries according to language groups and assessing the performance of scales in terms of psychometric criteria. This analysis resulted in a modified version of the questionnaire (EORTC QLQ-C30), which was additionally field tested for its performance in 305 patients with lung cancer (35). Within the EORTC study group the EORTC QLQ-C30 is now available in translated and psychometrically tested versions in various countries (32–35).

The Simultaneous Approach to Creating Instruments

The third approach is unique to HRQL research. It has been developed and carried out by the WHO Quality of Life group and is based on the assumption that, although cultural universality of quality of life dimensions may exist, culture-specific quality of life assessments are necessary (27). The WHO Quality of Life group is unique in its attempt to develop a quality of life questionnaire applicable worldwide. After reaching consensus on cross-culturally relevant domains of quality of life, each participating country is free to formulate its own items according to a standard set of procedures. In its preliminary form the WHO instrument (WHOQOL) includes more than 300 items that were reduced to form a common core applicable to different countries. In addition, country-specific modules will be considered based on information from two sources: first, the global questionnaire items that will not be included in the subsequent core instrument; and, second, a set of national questions that centers may want to include in addition to the global items. The Quality of Life Questionnaire has been tested to date in almost 5,000 individuals from 15 different centers worldwide. Results of psychometric field testing of the reduced version of the Quality of Life Questionnaire is currently under way (36). In summary, the group decided to develop internationally an overall set of components for quality of life, operationalize them, and establish working groups in specific cultures to formulate the relevant questions. An example of this is a question for depression that in Europe, might read, "Last week, did you feel depressed?" and in an African language might read, "Recently, have you felt like a branch hanging from a tree?" Thus, the item development process is less standardized than in the other two approaches. The items are then translated from one language to another with the goal of establishing a common pool of items, but the focus is on each nation being independent in having at hand its own quality of life instrument that can be compared to the instrument developed by another nation within the same project (37).

TESTING INSTRUMENTS

Response Choice Evaluation

To assess whether the response choices of an instrument are ordinal and equidistant, each response can be rated on a visual analog scale ranging from the item representing the lowest scale limit (0 mm) to the item representing the highest scale limit (100 mm). All responses are assembled on a page in random order and are presented to group of at least 50 persons per country. Since the ordinality and the interval character of response scales are prerequisites for scaling in each nation, a Thurstone scaling exercise (32) can be performed in each country. Using the extreme (lowest/highest response possibilities) on Likert-scaled items as anchors of 100-mm visual analog scales, each response can be placed on the line according to the degree of intensity or frequency it reflects. The respondent's task is to place a mark between 0 and 100 reflecting the relative position of the response to be rated in relation to the scale extremes. Examination of group means of these ratings per country and reconversion to the original order of the responses, e.g., 1,2,3,4,5 on a five-point Likert scale, then follows. Assembling this information per country and across all countries facilitates examining (a) the *ordinality of responses* in a country, i.e., whether the rank order of the original answer scale is reproduced, and pairwise comparisons indicating the number of violations of that order per country are examined; and (b) the *equidistance of responses,* i.e., whether the country means have equal intervals and deviations from the original. This approach was followed by the IQOLA group (for the SF-36) and the WHO group (for the WHOQOL). This approach to response scaling can be supplemented by log transformations of responses to a scale with interval properties (logit scores) that can then be tested for cross-cultural bias, using an extended Rasch model approach (38).

Evaluation

Psychometric Testing on the National Level

An important set of test criteria pertains to the psychometric properties of an instrument. These criteria and particularly those for reliability and validity have been repeatedly described in detail in the context of psychological test theory (24–26,39). However, certain aspects of validity involving responsiveness or sensitivity to change are less clearly defined (40). Criteria for psychometric testing concern the item and the scale level. At the *item level* it has been suggested that missing data in up to 20% of the items to be responded to per scale can be processed by mean substitution. Thus, missing data beyond 20% of the scale leads to drop out of the case. If means and standard deviations do not approach normal distribution, log transformed (logit) scores can be derived and analyzed as distribution-free standardizations (see Chapter 73 by Cella et al.). In general it should be noted that measures of kurtosis and skew easily return significant values for large sample sizes, so extremely conservative levels need to be set (e.g., $p < .001$) if these measures are considered. Perhaps more useful are the frequencies for the distributions for each item. With dichotomous (e.g., Yes-No) items, the recommended acceptable extremes are in the region of 80–20 or, at most, 90–10. It should be noted, however, that some of the rarely endorsed items may be the most important for distinguishing between a target group and a group of controls. With polychtomous response scales such as used for the WHOQOL, a 10% cutoff can be adopted for any two consecutive response points in order to ensure at least some screening of response distribution problems.

On the *scale level,* ceiling and floor effects should be less than 20% in order to assume that the scale is capturing the full range of potential responses in the population. In addition, the correlations between an item and its scale should be above $r = .40$ and each item should correlate significantly higher with its own scale than with other scales (scale fit with an optimum of 100%). In terms of reliability, an internal consistency for subscales of alpha $= .70$ or better is usually regarded as sufficient for group comparisons as is the test-retest correlation of at least $r = .70$ for measures administered at a one-week interval. Validity can be inferred by construct, criterion-based, and clinical validity techniques. While construct validity is not widely used in the health field, criterion-based validity, e.g., convergent validation, is. Convergent validation is sufficient if the correlation between the instrument tested and a comparable instrument yields correlation coefficients of about $r = .50$. Clinical validity refers to the ability of the instrument to significantly differentiate clinically known patient groups in terms of quality of life scores. More sophisticated validation strategies on the conceptual level include factor analysis (41) and structural equation modeling (42). Responsiveness pertains to the examination of change over time of subscales as related to specific criteria such as before and after intervention or as related to the individual change in comparison to the aggregated change of the group over time (40).

Psychometric Testing on the International Level

International examination of psychometric performance is more complicated than the examination of psychometrics at a single-nation level. The question is which set of criteria should be employed to infer the international validity and reliability of an instrument. One approach toward establishing international psychometric quality is to simply assemble for each country all the information on reliability, validity, and responsiveness of an instrument and use the classical cutoff points for instrument performance obtained from that country. If an instrument continues to show excellent psy-chometric properties under such diverse conditions, it can be assumed to be culturally acceptable. Thus by assembling information from different nations, international comparability could be inferred.

There are pitfalls, however, in the comparison of apples and oranges, because studies often have not been designed to be internationally comparable with regard to patient population, study design, and intervention. A minimum requirement, therefore, is to have one or two patient groups and study designs over different countries of sufficient comparability that psychometric performance criteria can be tied to specific populations and trial designs across cultures. The most elegant approach, however, is an *a priori* design of an international validation study in which patient populations, the study design employed, and the measures taken are equivalent. Such a study design would mimic the design of a multinational clinical trial including a well-written study protocol with a clear procedural section and a comprehensive set of planned statistical analyses.

To flesh out some of these recommendations, a number of the procedures used in the development of the field trial version of the WHOQOL will be outlined (see Chapter 36). The pilot data for the WHOQOL provided the rare possibility of devising an instrument from data that had been collected from 15 centers worldwide, rather than the usual procedure of basing item selection from the pilot version of an instrument on one set of culturally homogeneous data.

The procedures used for the selection of items from a large pool are iterative in that, for example, subscale reliabilities and item-discrimination correlations need to be recalculated each time groups of items are eliminated. This gradual filtering of scale items needs to take account not only of the performance of the items at a national level, but also their performance in a global data set that is obtained by combining the data from all centers. In the case of the WHOQOL, therefore, the national analyses were carried out on 15 data sets, each of approximately 300 respondents, which gave a total of over 4,500 respondents when all national data sets were combined.

In the development of the WHOQOL, the item analyses were effectively carried out at three levels: at the individual national level, at the level of a combined meta-analysis of item performance collated across the 15 centers, and at a global level with respondents from all centers pooled to form a single data set. Three sets of item analyses were then summarized, as shown in Table 1.

The first group of analyses summarizes the response frequency distributions for each item, analyzed at national and at global levels. A consistent pattern of frequency distributions at the national and at global levels would make that particular item a candidate for either selection or elimination, depending on whether or not the specified criteria had been met. Similarly, the internal consistency analyses provide item-subscale correlations together with the Cronbach alpha values at both the national and the global levels. If the alpha values for a proposed subscale consistently fall below the

TABLE 1. *Summary of sets of item analyses for response frequencies, sub-scale reliabilities, and item-discrimination ("MAP") analyses*

Item/ scale	Frequency analyses			Reliability analyses			Map analyses		
	(1)	(2)	(3)	(1)	(2)	(3)	(1)	(2)	(3)
1									
2									
3									
.									
.									
.									
.									
n									

The analyses are presented at each of three levels: (1) at the level of individual centers; (2) summarized across centers; and (3) at the level of pooled global data.

minimum value of .70 at the national and global levels, then such a subscale requires serious review; it may be considered for elimination altogether unless the exclusion of one or two poorer items improved the alpha to above the criterion. An alternative outcome is that the item-subscale correlations and alpha values are above criterion for some centers but below criterion for other centers. The more common such a pattern is across the subscales, the greater the likelihood that different national instruments need to be developed, and the lower the likelihood that a scale could be developed common to all cultures. A further possibility is that some subscales may perform consistently well across all centers, whereas others are more inconsistent; such a pattern would be indicative of the possibility of a core instrument common to all cultures, but that required specific add-on national modules for different centers. To date, the analyses of the WHOQOL suggest the possibility of a common instrument across all cultures, in that the subscales in the pilot form seem to perform either consistently badly, and so can be eliminated, or consistently well, and so can be included for all cultures.

To return to the question of preliminary item selection and elimination, Table 1 also shows a third set of analyses that summarize item-discriminability, that is, the degree to which an item correlates more highly with another subscale than it does with its own intended subscale; these analyses have been referred to as MAP analyses following the so-called Multitrait Analysis Program developed by Hays and his colleagues (43), although it is perfectly feasible to set up the equivalent analyses on widely available statistical packages such as SPSS (Statistical Program for the Social Sciences). Clearly, if an item correlates at <.4 with its intended subscale and >.4 with another subscale, then it should be considered for inclusion with the other subscale. In the case of the WHOQOL, however, out of the initial set of 236 items in the pilot version, *none* of the items matched this

pattern. Instead, a variant on this pattern was sometimes obtained in which an item loaded >.4 on both the intended subscale and one or more other subscales. In such cases an item was considered for elimination if it loaded more highly on the other subscales, but was still considered for selection if the highest loading was on the intended subscale. The problem with an item correlating with a number of subscales (and, indeed, of subscales correlating with each other) is a variant on a familiar psychometric problem of the desirable level for interitem correlations within a single scale. Although Cattell (44) argued that, in theory, the perfect scale should show zero interitem correlations together with high item to total scale correlations, this is particularly difficult to attain when attempting to develop brief scales due to the strong effect of scale lengths on internal consistency. Rather, most scales include items that correlate with each other, not only with the scale total. In the case of the WHOQOL, therefore, it was considered acceptable that items related to, for example, psychological well-being and energy level should also correlate with a number of other subscales as long as the highest correlation was with the intended subscale.

The analyses in Table 1 present a first step that allows the elimination of poor performing items and subscales. However, the analyses do not provide enough information for the final selection of items in cases where an excess number of items remain even after the elimination of other items. The pilot form of the WHOQOL contained approximately 8 to 10 items for each subscale, the plan being to reduce the number to four items in order to obtain an acceptable overall length of the scale while allowing further psychometric testing of subscale reliabilities. To carry out this further item reduction, a second series of analyses and questions were addressed. These additional steps for the WHOQOL are summarized in Table 2.

The first set of analyses shown in Table 2 are the revised reliability analyses repeated following the initial item elimination. Again, these analyses need to be considered at the

TABLE 2. *A summary of the final analyses for the selection of items for the WHOQOL*

Item/ scale	Revised reliability analysis			Validity analyses			Conceptual analyses		
	(1)	(2)	(3)	(1)	(2)	(3)	(1)	(2)	(3)
1									
2									
3									
.									
.									
.									
.									
n									

The analyses are presented at each of three levels: (1) at the level of individual centers; (2) summarized across centers; and (3) at the level of pooled global data.

individual national level, in summary form across national analyses, and at the global level. The exact thresholds for further elimination of items will vary according to the number of items available per subscale together with the appropriate subscale psychometrics, although clearly an item that correlated <.4 for the global data and failed to obtain a significant item-subscale correlation for one or more centers should be considered for elimination.

The second set of analyses shown in Table 2 have been referred to as validity analyses. In the case of the pilot WHOQOL, these data primarily referred to the results of a discriminant groups validity analysis, that is, whether or not an item successfully distinguished ill respondents from well respondents. Additional data that could be used, if available, are responsiveness data, such as whether an item's scores improved following a successful therapeutic intervention for a particular condition. But responsiveness data are not yet available for the WHOQOL, so it was decided that an item that failed the between-groups comparison and did not significantly distinguish ill from well groups would be unlikely to produce a significant within-group comparison if measuring illness status across time. Nevertheless, for item selection, the use of a discriminant groups validity analysis outcome is preferable to the reliability-based strategy of selecting high versus low scorers on the scale, in that reliability-type information is being inappropriately taken into account later.

The third set of analyses referred to in Table 2 has been labeled ''conceptual analyses.'' On the assumption that more than the minimum number of items survive the sequence of filters outlined so far, the final selection of items may have to be carried out in part conceptually. That is, where there is a choice of items, an attempt should be made to include items that reflect different aspects of a subscale rather than items that are merely rewordings of each other. For example, the WHOQOL subscale ''Thinking, Learning, Memory, and Concentration'' left the choice of items shown in Table 3. Although two of the high loading items referred to memory problems, only one of these items was selected because the choice of an alternative item that referred to decision making gave greater conceptual diversity to the subscale. In addition, where there is a suitable choice of items, other factors such as positive versus negative wording and the type of question being asked should be taken into account.

There are also a number of more complex analyses than those presented in Tables 1 and 2 that can be carried out on the data. For example, multidimensional scaling (MDS) analyses can provide a useful graphical representation to test the structure of the subscales within a center and, in the form of replicated MDS, can be carried out across centers to see if one or more centers are significantly different from the pattern common to the remainder. Traditional exploratory factor analysis can also be used, although the degree of *a priori* structure within scales such as the WHOQOL means that the more modern confirmatory factor analytic methods are preferable, especially when subsequent data sets

TABLE 3. *Items chosen for the WHOQOL subscale "Thinking, Learning, Memory, and Concentration"*

Item	Item-total correlation	Items chosen
F713: How would you rate your memory?	.68	–
F716: How well are you able to concentrate?	.53	–
F721: How satisfied are you with your ability to learn new information?	.61	3
F722: How satisfied are you with your memory?	.74	1
F723: How satisfied are you with your ability to make decisions?	.61	4
F725: How satisfied are you with your concentration?	.73	2

This table illustrates the importance of obtaining conceptual diversity through the choice of item F723 instead of the higher loading F713. Five items had been previously deleted from this subscale through the application of filters summarized in the text.

become available, rather than overanalyzing the data set that is used to derive the initial structure of an instrument (see ref. 41 for an excellent overview of these issues). Another innovative method to examine metric equivalence where a common set or subset of items are being used across nations is the Rasch technique of psychometric item analysis (item response theory) that transforms scores to log-odd units, creating an interval measure for each respondent on each item per scale referenced to each country or culture studied. However, because the Rasch approach was developed for scales that assess ''ability,'' e.g., cognitive skills of increasing complexity rather than scales in which, *a priori,* items are expected to be of equivalent difficulty, its application to quality of life scales will be useful only if the items of the scale can be ordered in terms of their likelihood of endorsement, i.e., their ''difficulty.'' This has been documented with the Functional Assessment of Cancer Therapy (45).

One additional concern is the question of the degree to which a scale is universally applicable or whether each culture requires its own culture-specific scales. For example, as noted earlier, the outcome of the WHOQOL pilot and field trial data analyses could be:

1. an instrument that is universally applicable across all cultures,
2. a core instrument that is universally applicable together with specific add-on national modules,
3. a series of national instruments specific to each culture.

In addition, modules that assessed specific populations (e.g., the elderly, those with cancer, etc.) could be added to any of these three possibilities. A further complexity of the WHOQOL procedure is that each center is able to include a set of specific national questions for each subscale in addition to the agreed-upon general questions asked across all centers (see Chapter 36). In theory, therefore, possibilities 2 and 3 above could be based on a culture-specific selection of *general* questions, on a selection of specific national questions, or on some combination of the two. It is a testament therefore to some of the universal problems of *la condition humaine* that, to date, the analyses of the WHOQOL seem to point to possibility 1 above, because there appears to be an instrument that is generally applicable across all cultures.

Norming

The development of norms involves the application of a scale to a representative sample of the national population or at least a sample that can ex post facto be related to representativeness criteria. The reasons for applying a scale in a large patient population are threefold. First, the influence of social factors and sociodemographic variables on quality of life can be assessed in a large patient population. There are many potential confounding variables to be taken into account in clinical studies applying quality of life measures descriptively or evaluatively over the course of treatment. Second, the application to a representative sample is the only procedure that allows norming of an instrument. The norming process refers to the possibility of obtaining age, sex, and other criterion-related information about a scale that can then be taken into account when comparing different patient populations with their respective reference group in the general population. Norming thus enables the researcher to adjust observed quality of life information in reference to a specified peer group. Third, only through a norming procedure performed in different countries is it possible to compare scale values obtained with a certain patient population in one country with a patient population in another country. Here the scale scores of the general population serve as a standard according to which international comparisons can be critically examined and adjusted in statistical comparisons, if necessary. The development of norms nationally and internationally requires a specific protocol that denotes the specific variables to be collected and stratification criteria to be included in a norming process. Without this strict standardization it is not possible to use norms comparatively and cross-culturally. Placing, for example, two individuals from different countries with identical scores on the scale assumes that the scale reflects the same degree of impairment in both countries. Before making this assumption, it is necessary to ascertain that the scores in fact represent an identical degree of impairment. This can be tested by including the questionnaire in a representative study that yields norms for the measure and that is carried out after the instrument development and aims at obtaining reference data from a representative population sample.

On a national level, the psychometric steps outlined for both testing and norming require observation of the suggested criteria. However, the development of cross-cultur-

ally comparable forms is more complicated and involves, after the creation of adequate translations, (a) homogeneous patient samples for psychometric testing in terms of diagnosis and sociodemographic information from each county (e.g., patients from a multinational trial), and (b) a standardized study protocol for data collection and an analysis plan defined *a priori* for the development of norms. Comparability of these data makes meta-analyses possible.

The possibility of comparability across cultures depends on how an instrument is developed; thus, both the sequential and the parallel approaches outlined earlier may be limited by the fact that one culture dominates a scale's development and thereby provides a Procrustean bed into which forms for other cultures are forced. The simultaneous approach, as used in the development of the WHOQOL, finesses the possibility of such cultural hegemony, because of the range of centers with equal levels of involvement in the production of the pilot instrument. The risk with such an approach, however, is that the data may reveal that there are no universal characteristics of quality of life, but that in theory each culture could value a different set of items or subscales, whether reflected in different subsets of items most relevant for a particular culture or in the need to include specific national questions for each culture. In such a case, with different cultures requiring different forms of an instrument, the only way forward would be to collect population norms that can be used to transform an individual's score to a standardized score. However, one may still be left with a conceptual problem of whether one is comparing like with like when such possibly diverse comparisons are being made. Similar issues have of course bedeviled the area of intelligence and intelligence testing for many decades because of the debate about whether there can be culture-free[1] tests or whether all tests are inherently culturally biased. One can only hope that the invidious comparisons of IQ across different cultures and ethnic groups will not be repeated with possible comparisons of "QI" (QOL index) across cultures and ethnic groups. By analogy with IQ, the best use of quality of life comparisons may be in the form of profiles across different domains (see Chapter 36 for a summary of the domains) rather than a global "QI" score.

CONCLUSIONS

The interest in the assessment of quality of life and subjective health is increasing internationally. In spite of a lack of profound theoretical elaborations of the quality of life concept, a consensus appears to have been reached about the main components of quality of life and possible methods of assessment. Although these methods of assessment stem historically from the Anglo-American literature, recent de-

---

[1] In fact it has been suggested that demand for culture-free measures is unrealistic (see chapter by Cella et al.).

velopments also pertain to the genuine international construction of quality of life measures as well as the development of generic and disease-specific instruments within single nations. The question, however, is how these instruments can be internationally tested for their performance.

This chapter has attempted to give an overview of guidelines to be followed for the adaptation of measures from one cultural context to another. These guidelines pertain to basic problems in ensuring cross-cultural comparability of measures as outlined by Hui and Triandis (22) and consist of a number of procedures relevant to the creation and evaluation of acceptable instruments. Interestingly, although criteria for the national work with instruments pertaining to these steps are available and, in particular, have been formulated for psychometric testing of questionnaires, criteria for international cross-cultural work are rarely found (23,46). In the age of increased multinational cooperation it is not enough to ensure the adequacy of the transformation of an instrument from its source language to a target language. Instead, it is necessary to employ meta-analytical methods appropriate to the psychometric testing of data sets stemming from different countries (47). The same is true for the development of norms, which requires common sets of norming criteria and standard information to be collected in all participating countries; however, due to cross-cultural diversity, this information is not easily obtained.

Finally, it must be noted that it is necessary to include quality of life measures in prospective studies. Potential areas of inclusion range from epidemiological studies of the state of quality of life in specific patients to clinical trials in which quality of life is used as an end point. Without the application of the already existing measures in research, it will not be possible to judge the benefit associated with the use of quality of life instruments in specific research contexts. It is hoped the empirical performance of the instruments within specific studies will yield enough information to assess their use within a particular country and within specific patient populations.

REFERENCES

1. Bullinger M, Hasford J. Evaluating quality of life measures in German clinical trials. *Controlled Clin Trials* 1991;12:915–1055.
2. Brislin RW, Lonner W, Thorndike RM. *Cross cultural research methods.* New York: John Wiley, 1973:51.
3. Sartorius N. Cross-cultural and international collaboration in mental health research and action. *Acta Scand Psychol* 1988;78(334 suppl): 71–74.
4. Dressler WW, Vieteri FE, Chavez A. Comparative research in social epidemiology: measurement issues. *Ethnicity Dis* 1991;1:379–393.
5. Kleinman A, Eisenberg L, Good B. Culture, illness and care: clinical lessons from anthropologic and cross-cultural research. *Ann Intern Med* 1978;88:251–258.
6. Bullinger M. Quality of life-definition, conceptualization and implications. The methodologist perspective. *Theor Surg* 1991;6:123–137.
7. Wenger NK, Mattson ME, Fürberg CJD, Ellison J. Assessment of quality of life in clinical trials of cardiovascular therapies. *Am J Cardiol* 1984;54:908–913.
8. McDowell I, Newell C. *Measuring health: a guide to rating scales and questionnaires.* New York: Oxford University Press, 1987.
9. Walker SR, Rosser RH. *Quality of life assessment.* New York: Kluwer Academic, 1992.
10. Spilker B. *Quality of life assessment in clinical trials.* New York: Raven Press, 1990.
11. Shumaker S, Anderson R, Aaronson N. Generic instruments for quality of life assessment. *Qual Life Res* 1993;2:61–74.
12. Bergner M, Bobbit RA, Carter WB, Gilson BS. The Sickness Impact Profile development and final revision of a health status measure. *Med Care* 1981;19:787–805.
13. Hunt SM, McKenna SP, McEwen J, Williams J, Papp E. The Nottingham Health Profile: subjective health status and medical consultations. *Soc Sci Med* 1981;15A:221–229.
14. Dupuy HJ. The Psychological General Well-Being (PGWB) Index. In: Wenger N, Attson M, Furberg C, Ellison J, eds. *Assessment of quality of life in clinical trials of cardiovascular therapies.* New York: Lejacq, 1984:170–183.
15. Kaplan RM, Bush JW, Berry CC. Health status: types of validity and the index of Wellbeing. *Health Serv Res* 1976;11:478–507.
16. Ware JE, Sherbourne C. The MOS 36-item short-form health survey (SF-36): international conceptual framework and item selection. *Med Care* 1992;30:473.
17. Bullinger M, Anderson R, Cella D, Aaronson N. Developing and evaluating cross-cultural instruments from minimum requirements to optional models. *Qual Life Res* 1993;2:451–459.
18. Aaronson NK, Acquadro C, Alonso J, Apolone G, et al. International quality of life assessment (IQOLA) project. *Qual Life Res* 1992; 1:349–351.
19. Aaronson NK, Cull A, Kaasa S, Sprangers MAG. The EORTC modular approach to quality of life assessment in oncology. *Int J Ment Health* 1994;23(2):75–96.
20. Sartorius N. A WHO method for the assessment of health-related quality of life (WHOQOL). In: Walker SR, Rosser RM, eds. *Quality of life assessment: key issues in the 1990's.* Boston: Kluwer Academic, 1993:201–207.
21. Hunt SM. Cross-cultural comparability of quality of life measures. *Drug Info J* 1993;27:395–400.
22. Hui C, Triandis HC. Measurement in cross-cultural psychology: a review and comparison of strategies. *Cross Cultural Psychol* 1985; 16:131–152.
23. Patrick DL. Cross-cultural validation of QOL measures. In: Orley W, Kuikken N, Sartorius N, eds. *Measurement of quality of life in health care settings—a WHO conference.* Berlin: Springer, 1994.
24. Ware JE. Standards for validating health measures: definition and content. *J Chronic Dis* 1987;40(6):473–480.
25. Nunnally JC. *Psychometric theory,* 2nd ed. New York: McGraw-Hill, 1987.
26. Guyatt GH. The philosophy of health related quality of life translation. *Qual Life Res* 1993;2:461–467.
27. Hunt SM, Wicklund I. Cross-cultural variation in the weighting of health statements: a comparison of English and Swedish valuations. *Health Policy* 1987;8:227–235.
28. Spilker B, Molinek FR, Johnston KA, et al. Quality of life bibliography and indexes. *Med Care* 1990;28(suppl 12).
29. Anderson RT, Aaronson NK, Wilkin D. Critical review of international assessments of health related quality of life. *Qual Life Res* 1993; 2:369–397.
30. Stewart AL, Ware JE, eds. *Measuring functioning and well-being: the Medical Outcomes Study approach.* Durham and London: Duke University Press, 1992.
31. Bullinger M. German translation and psychometric testing of the SF-36 Health Survey: preliminary results from the IQOLA Project. *Soc Sci Med* (in press).
32. Thurstone LL, Chave EJ. *The measurement of attitude.* Chicago: University of Chicago Press, 1928.
33. Aaronson NK, Bullinger M. A modular approach to quality of life assessment in cancer clinical trials. *Recent Results Cancer Res* 1988;111:231–248.
34. Aaronson NK, Ahmedzai S, Bullinger M, et al. The EORTC score quality-of-life questionnaire: interim results of an international field study. In: Osoba D, ed. *Effect of cancer on quality of life.* Boca Raton, FL: CRC Press, 1991:185–203.

35. Aaronson NK, Ahmedzai S, Bergman B, et al. The European Organization for Research and Treatment of Cancer QLQ-C30: a quality-of-life instrument for use in international clinical trials in oncology. *J Natl Cancer Inst* 1993;85:365–376.
36. Orley W, Kuyken N, Sartorius N. *Measurement of quality of life in health care settings—a WHO conference.* Berlin: Springer, 1994.
37. Kuyken W, Orley J, Hudelson P, Sartorius N. Quality of life assessment across cultures. *Int J Ment Health* 1994;23(2):5–28.
38. Rasch G. *Probabilistic models for some intelligence and attainment tests.* Copenhagen: Danish Institute for Educational Research, 1960.
39. DeVellis RF. Scale development: theory and application. *Applied social research methods series,* vol 26. Newbury Park, London, New Delhi: Sage, 1991.
40. Guyatt GH, Walter S, Norman G. Measuring change over time: assessing the usefulness of evaluative instruments. *J Chronic Dis* 1985; 40(2):171–178.
41. Kline P. *An easy guide to factor analysis.* London: Routledge, 1994.
42. Bentler PM. Multivariate analysis with latent variables: causal modelling. *Annu Rev Psychol* 1980;31:419–456.
43. Hays RD, Hayashi T, Carson S, Ware JE. *Users' guide for the Multitrait Analysis Program (MAP)* Rand, Santa Monica, CA: Cooperation Press, 1988.
44. Cattell RB. *Handbook of modern personality theory.* New York: Academic Press, 1971.
45. Cella DF, Tulsky DS, Gray G, et al. The Functional Assessment of Cancer Therapy (FACT) Scale. Development and validation of the general measure. *J Clin Oncol* 1993;11(3):570–579.
46. Guillemin F, Bombardier C, Beaton D. Cross-cultural adaption of health-related quality of life measures—a literature review and proposed guidelines. *J Clin Epidemiol* 1993;3:121–133.
47. Ware JE, Gandek B, and the IQOLA Project Group. The SF-36 Health Survey: development and use in mental health research and the IQOLA project. *Int J Ment Health* 1994;23(2):49–74.

Quality of Life and Pharmacoeconomics in Clinical Trials, Second Edition, edited by B. Spilker.
Lippincott-Raven Publishers, Philadelphia © 1996.

CHAPTER 70

A Mini-Handbook for Conducting Small-Scale Clinical Trials in Developing Countries

Harvey Schipper, Charles L. M. Olweny, and Jennifer J. Clinch

INTRODUCTION

Modern clinical trials methodology, and in particular the quality of life scientific ethos, takes its root in the English-speaking countries. More recently, there has been extensive activity in Europe (led principally by the European Organization for Research and Treatment in Cancer) and in Asia. Those who work in these settings usually find sufficient common ground in the culture and working environment that the conduct of research takes place against a seemingly transparent infrastructure.

Things are very different when working in developing and emerging countries. Many of the fundamentals, such as reliability of electric power, stability of government, trained personnel, and a reliable supply of drugs and materials, may not be assured. Moreover, the outside scientist/clinician, seeking to establish a project and a long-term working relationship, may not even be aware of the cultural, logistic, or jurisdictional maelstrom into which the project may plunge.

While data are hard to come by, one gets the impression that project failure rates are high and lead times are long. Research that pays meticulous attention to experimental design and cross-cultural sensitivity can be gutted by the unbelievable, the unexpected, and the invisibly obvious. What follows is an empiric, perhaps idiosyncratic, checklist that we have found useful in establishing and operating our

World Health Organization (WHO) Quality of Life Center research activities.[1] It derives from our experience in developing countries, but the process may equally have application closer to home, among aboriginal communities. The intent is to help the investigator get on with the science. The reader is referred to other chapters in this book for discussion of the principles and techniques of cross-cultural translation of instruments. It is our experience that good research can be done in developing countries, particularly when the ''translation'' logistics are carefully managed.

The projects under discussion are generally small. Large-scale intervention projects, such as those undertaken by the World Bank, involve layers of diplomatic and economic negotiation beyond the scope of this chapter. For further information in this area, refer to documents such as the World Bank Project Cycle document (1).

WHY UNDERTAKE RESEARCH IN EMERGING COUNTRIES?

Undertaking research or development projects is challenging and occasionally frustrating. Beyond wanderlust and

H. Schipper, C. L. M. Olweny, and J. J. Clinch: WHO Collaborating Centre for Quality of Life in Cancer Care, Winnipeg, Manitoba R2H 2A6, Canada.

---

[1] Readers may note the paucity of literature related to this topic, at least as available to the authors. In addition to conventional literature searchers, we consulted with a number of international assistance and research agencies. It appears that no similar documents exist. We hope, therefore, that this chapter begins to meet a widely expressed need. If readers are aware of other relevant literature, or wish to offer suggestions for later versions, please correspond with the authors.

pure humanitarianism, any project requires justification. What is the specific goal?, why there?, and why these collaborators? Giving thought to these types of questions, *a priori*, provides a framework for assessing both the specific research question, and the collaborative process. There are numerous justifications, some blatantly self-serving. Below are a number of "reasons" that make sense:

1. *The venue is a site of disease prevalence.* Examples would be schistosomiasis in the Nile basin, nasopharyngeal carcinoma in South East China, and polycythemia in Bolivia. It is possible to accrue patients more easily in areas of disease prevalence. The case is strengthened if the results of the inquiry have global implications (e.g., treatment of advanced cancer of the uterine cervix).
2. *The cost of doing the research is modest.* This may be due to lower professional and labor costs, cheaper drugs, and so on.
3. *Drugs are more available.* This may be the case where generic equivalent drugs are locally manufactured or more readily available because of differences in marketing or regulatory approval processes, or when an "indigenous" remedy is being evaluated.
4. *There is a strong collaborator on site* who wishes to advance a research and development initiative.
5. *There is a specific technology transfer mandate.*
6. The study is intended to *influence local patterns of practice* or policy.
7. The project is *of benefit to the local population.*

Conversely, there are reasons that are not appropriate and should not be used to justify projects, such as:

1. A captive population, but otherwise unwilling to cooperate,
2. Less stringent or altogether absent ethical review, and
3. Less likelihood of litigation.

THE OVERALL STRATEGY

From the germ of a research idea, the investigator must develop an operational plan for the conduct of the work. Since a new venue is part of the study, in addition to the science, it is essential to ascertain that the site is viable. Put simply, are the human, physical, fiscal, and institutional resources available to get the job done? There is no sure-fire way to guarantee the success of a collaboration across cultures and at a distance. However, there are ways to minimize the risks of failure. They can be summarized in three general principles:

1. The project must be of value to all the collaborating parties.
2. The project must be compatible with the resources and energies of all collaborators.
3. The project must not affront or circumvent the ethical

and moral standards of the collaborators, and in particular those of the experimental subjects (2).

We have employed a three-step strategy to establishing offshore, technology transfer projects:

Step One: Assessment at a Distance

The goal is to define the broad structure and process of the project, what the major impediments might be, and set the stage for a feasibility site visit. The visit only takes place if:

1. There are satisfactory answers to an operational checklist relating to project design, partnership, and infrastructure support.
2. There are no fundamental impediments that cannot be resolved.
3. There are funds and prospects for both site visit and study.

Step Two: The Feasibility Site Visit

The purpose of the site visit is to:

1. Confirm the assessment at a distance.
2. Make appropriate local contacts, at the political and scientific levels.
3. Check out infrastructure support.
4. Establish the partnership by:
    a. jointly designing the study
    b. defining roles
    c. setting up a pilot trial
    d. establishing follow-up plans.

Step Three: Running the Project

The goal is to initiate and run the project with focus on four areas:

1. Smooth operations
2. Quality control
3. Data acquisition and reporting
4. Next stage planning.

THE OPERATIONAL CHECKLIST

Over the years we have developed a checklist of items that we consider important to the success of projects in developing countries (Table 1). This checklist is written from the perspective of the industrialized country partner. However, the themes will be useful to both (all) partners in the project. This is not to suggest that the same issues are unimportant anywhere else. On the contrary. However, because the culture and the place tend to be so different, and these differences can lead to project failure if not recognized,

TABLE 1. *Checklist for conduct of small-scale clinical trials in developing countries*

Is there a genuine and compelling reason for undertaking your research in an emerging country?

If yes, then:
    Undertake "at a distance" assessment.
    If convinced of need, then follow through with feasibility site visit.
    If structure appears in place, then initiate and run the project.

"At a distance" assessment
    Define type of collaborative personnel and institutional relationship.
    Define the scientific question(s): Is the study and/or project relevant to the host country? Is it sensitive to the cultural mores?
    Identify and carefully select a reliable, credible working partner.
    Assess and be assured of institutional resources.
    Determine jurisdictional issues.
    Settle home base issues.

Feasibility site visit
    Aim to make contacts and establish credibility.
    Get to know partners, collaborators, colleagues.
    Confirm initial off-site assessment.
    Refine scientific question and design the study together with collaborators.
    Construct a budget.
    Clearly define collaborators' roles.
    Share the hiring process.
    Discuss quality control mechanisms.
    Make arrangements and test mechanisms for transmission of information and data.
    Define benchmarks.

Running the project
    On-going contact and communication essential.
    Sample, check, verify data at intervals.
    Site visits crucial to troubleshoot on the spot.
    Formal report at conclusion should be shared by all partners.
    Reporting first at local setting reassures the collaborating nature.

we find the checklist particularly useful to our mission. The checklist serves as the administrative background document for the project.

Step One: Assessment at a Distance

Whatever the genesis of a project, it is wise to take a critical first look at the intended partnership from a distance. Does the idea make sense? Is it logistically, scientifically, and politically feasible? How will it relate to ongoing activities at home and in the host setting? Background work on the country and specific institution, progressively more detailed correspondence with prospective partners, and local planning can provide clues to problem areas that may emerge, as well as to the likelihood that the project, as a whole, will succeed. Only if there is reasonable confidence that all the components are there should one venture further. Bluntly put, a high degree of objectivity saves money, avoids embarrassment, and, by defining the issues, allows the scientist to focus on impediments that may prevent otherwise promising studies from succeeding. If the results of the initial assessment justify a site visit, this assessment provides a framework for establishing the on-site collaboration and identifying problems to resolve. The process is meant to be transparent and open to the collaborators, in short a framework for the science. It can take months to complete.

Defining the Administrative Context: What Is the Nature of the Relationship?

The first question to ask is, What type of project relationship is to be established? There are a number of models to consider:

1. *Consultation (technical assistance):* Experts are called upon to give advice, but have no direct investment in the project. This process works best when there are a limited number of defined issues to resolve. The consultant relationship can run into trouble over the long-term as issues of ownership arise. The paradox is that from a technical standpoint, the more closely the consultant identifies with the project, the better the advice, but the more compromised the ownership issue.
2. *Contracting out:* Here a specific component of a project is assigned. It could be sample testing, data analysis, or even quality assurance. The contractee may have little involvement in the overall project. From the perspective of the developing country, this avenue is expensive, and there is little transmission of expertise.
3. *The joint venture:* This model implies an "equal partner" collaboration. The goal is to pool resources to complete a task. Each partner is assumed expert in a given discipline and the challenge is to identify compatible partners whose combined expertise and resources are sufficient to undertake the project. This is the common form of academic research working relationship in North America, Japan, and Europe.
4. *Direct investment (bootstrapping):* This model attempts to build a nascent research capability, where infrastructure and projects develop in parallel as the evolving local expertise permits. There are numerous examples of this model. It can be highly effective, provided both the outside experts and investors make sure that something is left when the initial capital investment (possibly a training period) is complete.
5. *The technology transfer model:* This is the model most familiar to this WHO centre. In some respects it is the most challenging, because in addition to conducting the research, the goal is to develop or substantively enhance a new area of expertise. The assumptions inherent in this model are that both parties share a common interest in

a problem, that each can contribute substantially from the outset, and that a planned continual transfer of expertise and project responsibility/leadership is explicit. It is the latter characteristic that defines a technology transfer project. The relationship may evolve over time, perhaps to a joint venture or to continued transfer in a different sphere or change to a higher level. The major challenges in this type of relationship are anticipating and planning for different (and shifting) levels of expectation in performance, evaluating the expertise transfer, and accommodating and maintaining a high level of common interest. Considerable patience is required of all participants, and longer proposed initiation and completion times are likely. However, sophisticated projects can be undertaken that form the basis of a sustainable expertise.

None of the models is necessarily preferable to another, although the expectations implicit in each are different. It is therefore important to select that model most appropriate to the project at hand, and to ensure that all the parties understand and agree.

Defining the Scientific Question

In any scientific inquiry, the more precisely the question is posed, the more likely the research will produce a useful result. For studies in developing countries, a critical further question must be asked: Assuming the disease process to be studied is prevalent enough, will the clinical material be accessible? For example, blood sampling to establish criteria for early diagnosis of some process may be impossible if cultural impediments to venipuncture exist. Photodocumentation projects have encountered analogous difficulties, since in many cultures the photograph touches on issues both of privacy and spirituality.

The questions to ask are:

1. What is the incidence and how reliable are the data?
2. What is the prevalence and how reliable are the data?
3. Are there cultural or geographic (logistic) impediments to accessing the clinical material?
4. Is the study relevant to the host institution/country?

The project must have value to all partners. However initially conceived, it must be fine-tuned locally. Many agencies (the Canadian International Development Agency being an example) require that the initiative come from the developing country partner, precisely to avoid externally imposed projects.

Identifying a Partner

Unless the investigator is planning to do all the work locally and has the local support mechanisms in place, a local partner is required. Collectively, the skill, interest, and resources to handle the science, politics, administration, and hands-on day-to-day work must be there. Partnerships can be forged through advertisements in journals or in the press, informal searches, or by assignment via an institution-to-institution agreement. Whatever the route, there are several important questions to ask:

1. Who is the partner? What training and/or credentials does s/he possess, and what position is currently held? The more secure and respected the person, and the positions, the more likely local management will be smooth.
2. Why is this person interested? Is it an area of personal curiosity or achievement? Is it a means of augmenting stature in the workplace, or securing funds and equipment? Could it be seen as an avenue to relocation abroad? A sense of these questions will provide insight into the likely effectiveness of the collaboration. To the extent the partners share common ground, the project will be enhanced. On the other hand, a local partner with only a short-term interest (because, perhaps, another job beckons), is a poor choice for a long-term project, unless a successor mechanism is provided.
3. Is the candidate knowledgeable in the area (e.g., clinical oncology)? A senior official with no expertise may be an excellent administrative or "political" partner, but there has to be someone who can run the project on a daily basis. To do that, solid knowledge and experience in the discipline is required to provide general project supervision.
4. Knowledge in the specific project methodology may be a part of the technology transfer exercise. Our experience is that specific techniques (data collection, data analysis, questionnaire design and testing, chromatography) can be taught on site. However, providing comprehensive training to a scientist or clinician is quite another matter. Determine the level of methodological skill vis-à-vis the project requirement. This allows one to estimate and plan for (a) start up training (cost and time), (b) quality assurance/evaluation, and (c) the scope and complexity of the project.
5. How much time and what resources can the partner reasonably commit? The question is what they *can* commit, not what they hope to. If a project requires 25% of a physician's or a research partner's time, make sure that this or compensating resources are indeed available. In developing countries, academic institutions frequently expect or require international projects to "buy" their faculty's time. This should be clarified and resolved.
6. Can the local partner "work the system"? Sometimes a well-conceived, relevant project fails, despite a qualified and motivated local partner, because the partner cannot "make it happen." There may be problems with interpersonal relationships, territorial disputes within the institution, or poor organizational skills. We encountered one circumstance where a very prevalent disease (gynecological malignancy), could not be studied, despite the institution's adequate resources and infrastructure, because the

highly motivated, well-qualified partner was, in her words, "[the] wrong sex, wrong religion, and [belonged to the] wrong political party"!

Once these issues have been addressed, and one is satisfied that the potential partnership is viable, the terms of the relationship should be mutually understood. Projects frequently fall apart because of misunderstood expectations.

Institutional Issues

Most projects take place within some institution. It may be visible and formal, such as a hospital, or more subtle, as in the case of an extended family. Whatever the format, there are some questions to ask:

1. How stable is the institution? How likely is it that a project will be aborted, because the host institution either disappears or is radically restructured?
2. What are the physical resources? The stability of electrical power is critical for some projects (a cell culture laboratory, for instance). Is there secure physical space for documents and equipment (computers and documents can be ruined in months by tropical humidity)? It is even fair to ask if the roof leaks. What level of telephone/fax, or modem communication is possible? Are there physical security concerns—vandalism, hacking, curiosity?; and if so, what can be done to minimize the risk? Each project will require particular physical resources, none of which should be assumed. One sophisticated project came to grief for lack of a source of carbon dioxide. When that was overcome, there was no source of dry ice for shipping. Then, when these issues were resolved, there were no airline links that would allow samples to be transported to the distant laboratory before they degraded. Each link in the process must be checked.
3. What are the human resources? This is one of the background questions most often taken for granted. A certain level of technical support is always required. Equipment fails, a relatively simple printing job needs to be done or blood pressure needs to be measured in 500 patients. While it is impossible to anticipate every problem, the investigator can get a sense of what is possible by exploring the range and sophistication of activity already taking place. The researcher accustomed to being at the technological cutting edge must be prepared to be highly self-sufficient at the partner site, or have both patience and resources to import help at inopportune moments. An example is the importation of three $-80°C$ freezers into a clinical research center in China. The power supply was adequate, space was available, and the project well conceived. But the high tech compressor motors failed and no one was available to repair them, resulting in lost samples. The project failed for lack of a refrigerator repairman! The inoperative freezers are now used to store old clinical records. An ill-defined critical mass of people

is required to support such ventures. Some of the skills can be acquired during the project, provided time and money have been budgeted for. The trick is to keep it simple, and where a critical piece of technology is required, think of redundancy (i.e., two computers).

4. Does the institution have the administrative authority to support the project? For example, can the host institution receive foreign currency and on what conditions (charges, overheads, etc.)? Is the institution able and willing to provide access to patients, libraries, and staff? Do the terms of the project compromise the relationship between your collaborator and his/her institution?
5. Defining the institutional relationship is important. Foreigners coming in and running projects can be a major problem for hospitals and universities. The same can be said of aboriginal communities, which are often the focus of research. The so-called Western expert walks in and expects gratitude for *noblesse* and interest. Yet, even small projects can cause major distortion in the day-to-day operation of stressed facilities. A quality of life study of a new HIV drug may cause a rush on crowded facilities, or draw into question patterns of operation in advance of the data. The visiting investigator is well advised to make the project known at the institutional level, clearly identifying the local participants, and who is responsible for what. Often it is helpful to define a position or title (such as senior fellow or visiting scientist), which carries with it established rights and responsibilities. A good project may be terminated because a visiting "expert" inadvertently offends a patient or experimental subject, who then complains to an administration which knows nothing about the project. In addition to securing permission to do the work, define who contributes what, what are the points of control, and who is administratively responsible.
6. Local approvals. Several levels of approval should be achieved:
   a. Project approval: The institution is aware of the work and supports it. This should be confirmed in writing, both administratively and politically, and from the scientific perspective.
   b. Fiscal: The means of financing and handling of funds are in place.
   c. Ethics: This is a complex issue. In general, ethical approval of both partner institutions is required. The problem arises where the ethical requirements of institutions are incompatible. For example, in a community where there are limited medical resources, a randomized trial comparing pain relief to systemic chemotherapy may be more ethically appropriate than *ad hoc* allocation of drug treatment by virtue of wealth, position, or influence, provided that the experimental question is based on the principle of equipoise, meaning that there is uncertainty as to the likely outcome. There are legitimate reasons why a trial may be ethical in one setting and not in an-

other. In fact, certain elements of the informed consent process commonly used in North America may not be acceptable elsewhere. The fundamental premise is that the issues of risks, benefits and confidentiality will be addressed. This will usually not be a problem, but a few basic concepts may be useful. First, there must be some process, at each site. Second, the process must be culturally sensitive, but also comprehensible to all parties. It is unfair to impose the nuances of the North American informed consent process in a different culture. It is also wrong to impose an ethically reprehensible study, approved abroad, on another center. The abiding principle is that the cultural ethos of the place where the experimental subjects reside should represent the dominant, but not exclusive, ethic.

Jurisdictional Issues

Every country (state/province) has laws, policies, and traditions that may affect even small projects. Among the issues to consider are:

1. What are the visa or entry requirements for project partners (both directions)?
2. Is some form of local licensure required for the outside investigator to fulfill his/her role in the project?
3. If drugs are required, what is the means of supply and what is the importation process? Will there be drug access after the study? Try to avoid the difficult situation in which a new treatment is locally established by a study (perhaps with free drugs from a pharmaceutical house), but will not be available subsequently, off study.
4. Are there restrictions in the transmittal of information? Certain areas of research may be socially and politically sensitive. The host country may not want the research done, or having permitted the process, may consider the data confidential to the state. Social science information, including quality of life, may be particularly sensitive. A graduate student at an American university encountered extraordinary problems when he reported on certain aspects of Chinese birth control policy. We are also aware of social welfare studies that required years of negotiation over issues of access, data control, and reporting. Many countries require government clearance prior to publication of locally conducted research. This requires clarification.
5. The political and social stability of the host country must be considered. In the corporate sector, "political risk analysis" has almost become an expert discipline. The scale of assessment may not need to be as intensive with small projects. In some instances, the social instability may provide the impetus for the research. Even in this instance, there are several questions to ask:
   a. Is the country (jurisdiction) politically unstable

to the point where a project is likely to be caught up in the turmoil?
   b. What are the daily safety and logistic concerns? Are subjects, researchers, or outside consultants vulnerable to petty violence or inconvenience?
   c. Are there health issues to consider? (See Appendix).

Home Base Issues

Being a partner in an offshore project raises issues at home base. Except possibly in institutions whose focus is development or offshore activity, these activities tend to make people uneasy. We have had the experience of returning exhausted and exhilarated from a site visit, only to be asked if we had a good holiday and were ready to work! Particularly where investigators have major clinical and teaching responsibilities, it is important to establish some local worth for the work, and to arrange that colleagues do not feel an undue burden as a result of absence.

From the project perspective, we offer the following suggestions:

1. The project should have local institutional review board (IRB) or ethics committee approval.
2. Depending on the time and travel commitment, there should be some documentation of the project and its home base workload responsibilities.
3. Clarify mechanisms for personnel exchange.
4. Clarify the rules and procedures for home base reporting of shared data.

It may not be possible to complete all items of this initial assessment before making the decision to invest in a site visit. However, by the time a substantial portion of the step one checklist is done, it is likely to provide an information base from which to make a reasonable guess as to what can and cannot be accomplished at a particular site, at a given time. Those areas that cannot be addressed form matters of first priority for the initial site visit. One of the clues to later project success is the ease with which information regarding these checklist items is exchanged.

Step Two: The Feasibility Site Visit

Establishing a collaborative project takes time and requires a considerable "up front" investment. Usually, one undertakes this sort of venture because, intuitively, it seems likely to work. The goal of step one was broad, focusing on project outline and paying particular attention to major impediments to be dealt with *before* investing in a site visit. Having committed to a site visit, the focus shifts perceptibly to a more precise definition of project and environment, while still keeping a watchful eye for trouble. By the end of the site visit, the investigator should have a good sense of the details of the project, the partner, and the physical and human infrastructure. In short, the collaboration should be coming together. The site visit has an agenda, part of which is political and part of which focuses on the science.

Making Contacts

The most important purpose of the site visit is making contacts and establishing personal credibility—yours, and that of your partner.

1. Get to know your partner. What is his/her role? Who are the work associates and how do they relate? Get a sense of where the project fits in your partner's priorities. Is this a priority, just another one of many projects, or a substantial effort that may stress overburdened professionals? Is your partner the one who is going to do the work or will it be delegated, and are his/her management capabilities appropriate to the task? Time spent coming to understand your partner, both professionally and socially, will form the basis of the relationship. Understanding the personality, as well as the work role, will make subsequent discussions about specific roles and expectations more realistic and fruitful.

   Handled appropriately, you and your partner are mutual assets. The outside colleague is in a position to offer ''face,'' stature, and respect among local colleagues, especially if willing to be shared, and introduced as a colleague, not just an ''outside expert.''

   Your partner must also know your home situation. What is required by your institution? How much can you provide, and what are your institutional limits? Perhaps the most demoralizing experience a developing country partner can have is to mobilize resources and credibility in a project only to have the outside ''expert'' disappear into the sunset leaving behind a trail of dashed hopes and Christmas cards. The better partners know one another and understand their respective limits, the less likely this is to happen. Parenthetically, sabbatical arrangements can be particularly perilous. On sabbatical, you are there full-time and politically unthreatening. Yet the project may carry on beyond the length of the sabbatical year, except you are now doing something else, usually overwhelmed at home doing academic penance. In this circumstance, careful continuity planning becomes very important.

2. Get to know the colleagues at the project site. What do they do? Where do they fit within the scheme of things? This is a chance to be mutually helpful. Set aside time to give a talk or seminar, or assist in solving a problem. Equally, ask for help and information. Are there skills or interests that can augment the project or form the basis of another one? Are there people who have doubts or concerns? Are the concerns real; can they be addressed?

3. Meet the ''higher ups'' such as university and hospital executives, the minister of health, deputy, or permanent secretary. Assess the welcome. Find out who has influence and who can be helpful. Learn a little about the broader institution and give the local partner credit and recognition. In addition to the scientific partner, the project needs local political and administrative partners. The more broadly based the team, the more likely problems that arise in any sphere will be easily and informally solved.

Confirm and Complete Initial Assessment

The step one assessment is fairly comprehensive, but the data will not likely be complete. There is a balance to be met between seeking all the necessary information prior to the site visit, and getting it on site, presumably more easily.

Having arrived for the site visit, the foremost ''technical'' obligation is to complete, compulsively, the ''at a distance'' assessment. This is the last chance to identify major impediments, come to know the local rules, and see if the whole idea is feasible.

1. Check out the physical plant. Is there appropriate space?
2. Are there adequate numbers of subjects to fulfill the study requirements? Are those persons with whom you will be working as familiar with the area as you thought? In the clinical setting, an excellent way to sample the waters is to make rounds and participate in an outpatient clinic. You will quickly get a spot census of the patient population, and see who the working staff are and how they relate to one another.

Try to get a sense of how your project fits into the existing level of technology. An example from China illustrates the principle. Medical schools and major hospitals in the People's Republic face the same pressures as encountered in North America, to utilize the most modern technology. Some years ago, an acute leukemia treatment unit with reverse laminar air flow isolation was set up in one school to treat about 20 patients per year (about 10% of the anticipated incidence). Unlike Western units, patients were two or three in a room. Much of the intravenous equipment was reusable, but sterilization procedures seemed reasonable. Down the corridor, however, on the same clinical service, the only sink and wash-up area was clogged with dirt. The juxtaposition was jarring. When the program director was asked why the unit was established, since it could only accommodate a tiny proportion of the target population, he said, absolutely seriously, ''We want to train medical staff to wash their hands!'' In this instance, the local partner was hoping to introduce a major behavioral change in a large institution, using the project as a lever. Try to intuit where your project fits, and imagine what it will look like.

Refine the Study with Your Local Colleagues

The best way to establish a working relationship is to design a study together. The idea is to define a project that interests the group, and is relevant to their experience. If a proposal was written in advance, set aside time with the principals and thoroughly review it. It should not be a surprise if the original study is substantially transformed. In this process one gains first-hand knowledge of the local clinical environment, as well as your partners' skills and aptitudes. They will learn the same about you. Some mental notes to make:

1. Do you understand their clinical setting?
2. Are the concepts and experimental design well understood? Most physicians are not trained as scientists, and basic principles such as randomization, types of design, consent, and expected difference may be unfamiliar. Moreover, unless broached in a convivial working session (a little local food helps!), the mutual ignorance can be embarrassing.
3. Consider a series of projects that build on one another. The first one ideally should be easy to manage, give a short-term answer, and serve as both a confidence builder and as a means to cement mutual respect and institutional credibility. Remember also that the randomized trial is not the only study format. Observational studies may form the solid foundation for more complex comparative experiments that are to follow.

For the first study, focus on question definition, accrual, explanation to subjects, follow-up, basic data handling and quality assurance, and training. Later you can consider analysis, reporting, and other issues.

The Budget

One of the most revealing exercises is constructing the budget. We have found it a useful exercise to ask each side to independently draft an overall budget. This usually facilitates detailed discussion of each step in the study. As a result, specific tasks are delineated and responsibility allocated (more about responsibility later). In particular, this is a good time to detail in-kind contributions, identify hidden overheads, and sort out record keeping and disbursement procedures.

An embarrassing pitfall is to estimate the contribution of the industrialized country partner in terms of North American dollars. Presenting such figures within the local project budget can lead to misunderstandings and jealousies. At the small project level, there are usually immense salary disparities between developed and developing countries, although not necessarily so when expressed in terms of purchasing power. It is much better to estimate time equivalents and replacement at local cost. We know of one example where an offshore project nearly upset years of negotiations over remuneration rates for medical specialists.

It is possible that the project you design will require local travel. Many developing world projects seem to center around acquiring a project vehicle (computers are becoming another favorite). If travel is required, define the logistics carefully and sort out what is the anticipated ultimate fate of the vehicle. Contrary to some expectations, it is possible to achieve excellent long-term follow-up in developing countries. Despite the fact that the research was conducted in the midst of major political unrest, the Uganda Cancer Centre achieved an almost perfect 10-year follow-up by providing rural patients with bus tickets and/or taxi fare to Kampala for follow-up appointments.

Define Roles

Each participant's role should be clearly defined. Where responsibilities are shared, one person should be the point of contact. A sample allocation might be as follows:

1. Offshore partner: overall project design, training, production of final grant proposals and papers, data repository and quality assurance, extramural fundraising, home ethics and other approvals, data analysis, and site visit initiation.
2. Site partner: accrual, local quality assurance, data entry, interim reporting, local site arrangements/visits, local site authorization, local fundraising, and contributions to grants/reports.

Share the Hiring Process

Where people are being recruited (i.e., lab, data input, etc.), a site visit is a good opportunity to define job descriptions and, if possible, share in the interviewing. This provides another chance for the partners to find common ground and clarify mutual expectations. It also allows one to get to know the project staff, who, in turn, know you as something more than a distant gray eminence.

Establish Data Control

Ownership, security, control, and transmission of data are fundamental to the research endeavors. Issues surrounding data frequently cause difficulty. It is common for data to be lost, unverifiable, or perhaps most frustrating of all, confiscated or "edited" by various authorities.

This discussion has four components: ownership, control, procedures, and security.

Ownership

Ownership of the data needs to be clarified from the outset. As a general principle, the data belong to the population under study, and if taken out there should be a "return" of results in a meaningful way. A functioning collaboration usually escapes data ownership problems because the partners share common cause, and have been participants at each step in the process. As part of the ownership discussion, investigators should establish an understanding of how the data is to be used and presented, especially to outside audiences. The issue is broader than simply crediting investigators in publications; it is also sharing findings internally in advance of publication or presentation.

Control

Clinical data has two components. The first is the raw data, which may come from established sources such as registries, clinical records, or trial-specific data sets. Particularly if data are taken from established sources, such as registries or government statistics, it is essential to have *a priori* authorization to access and use the data for each project. In North America we are less sensitive about reporting aggregated health data than most emerging countries. However, health data runs close to the core of government social policy. As a result, seemingly innocuous, humanitarian requests for data can be denied because they may have the potential to embarrass government. Initially it was very difficult to access AIDS data because the authorities feared the stigma of the disease. More recently, we are aware of instances where more than one year was required to gain partial access to national health expenditures data, without which an internationally sponsored study could not be undertaken.

To avoid difficulty, define the data requirement as precisely as possible, identify the responsible authority, and then with your partner jointly acquire the level of access and reporting, and confirm it in writing. If either source or interpretive data is to be taken out of the country, make sure it is legal to do so and that there are duplicate records, in the event of the unexpected. It is reasonable to assume that, as the outside investigator, you will not own the source data.

Results of the study, the interpreted data, is another matter. Ideally partners will share data and acknowledge its collaborative origins. It seems to us a good general principle that local data should have first exposure to a local audience. Local scientists will have to contend with the impact of the study. The specific feedback may improve the study and avoid the risk of ''washing someone else's laundry in public.''

Control of the data is distinct from where data are stored. As a general principle, the master data set should be located where the analysis is to be conducted, but that is to be balanced against ease of verification. Electronic data can easily be stored in more than one place.

Procedures

Identify the local data manager and go over procedures in detail. It is a good idea that the local partner participate in this process. The local manager has to understand why the data is being collected, how to use the forms, and the means of storage and transmittal. Providing a small simple library of reference material will likely prove useful and be appreciated.

Orderly, interpretable data collection is the core of the research effort. In any multicenter study, consistent forms and procedures greatly enhance the project. The clinical trials experience is now rich in guidelines and procedures. In addition, the researcher in a developing country should consider a few extra precautions.

1. *Collection:* Make sure the procedures, schedule, and setting for collection are very clear. Certain data may be particularly time sensitive (e.g., pre-chemotherapy quality of life data), others less so (e.g., routine liver function tests). Make sure the data collectors know why each item is being collected and the degree of leeway permitted. A short, very explicit procedure document can be a lifesaver. Data forms also tend to be cryptic, so an explanation form is also useful in this case.

2. *Entry:* The best way to assure the quality of the data collection is to conduct a dry run with a feasibility sample of subjects or volunteers. This is an excellent activity to schedule into a site visit. A common problem, namely incorrect data collection because people did not understand what was required, can usually be alleviated this way.

   Make sure that data are entered as soon as it is received. Lengthy backlogs risk loss and encourage shoddy entry and data collection procedures.

3. *Verification:* Verification means confirming that what was entered into the data base was the same as what was collected. With numeric data, the classic technique is double entry, whereby each datum is entered twice and directly compared, preferably electronically. There are numerous software programs that do this kind of thing and should be seriously considered if a computer is available.

   A more cumbersome alternative requires manually checking the entire data set or a sample, commonly by one person reading the data while another compares them to the data base.

   Particularly if collected data come from scattered sources, making a copy of the source document and filing it by category and date in the data file speeds up verification and limits the risk of loss. However, this can be costly.

4. *Checking:* Checking means assuring that the data collected make sense. A simple example in quality of life research is making sure questionnaire respondents understand what they are being asked. Especially if the polarity of individual items changes (as in the Functional Living Index for Cancer, for example), data managers check that answers to similar questions are logical and similar. If data entry and checking are prompt, errors and misunderstandings can be corrected, if necessary, before the subject leaves, and no later than the subject's next visit.

   It is critical to identify time-sensitive data. A serum chemistry value can be entered at a later date. Quality of life data must be collected at the appointed time, because they are by nature time variable.

Even if the data are being analyzed off-site, the local partner and data manager should review data on a regular, scheduled basis.

5. *Transmittal and confirmation:* We believe in redundancy. This extends to both paper and electronic files. We ask that copies of records be made at regular intervals (more or less monthly, depending upon the level of trial activity) and sent to the offshore site for storage and analysis. We ask the local site to define and implement good backup procedures.

   The offshore site should confirm receipt and check the data for integrity and completeness. Any apparent deficiencies should be addressed promptly and positively.

Security

At the best of times, researchers tend to be careless about data security. This is especially the case in new clinical research settings. Simple procedures go a long way toward preserving the integrity and confidentiality of data.

1. Assume that any computers on which the data are stored will be used for other purposes, and by other people. It is all but impossible and, from a human relations perspective, probably undesirable to act otherwise. Therefore:
   a. Put the computer in a secure, dry place.
   b. Where confidentiality is an issue, separate names from data and secure the correspondence table.
   c. Use passwords.
   d. Make copies of data at each session and store in a different, safe place.
2. Often the physical climate leads to deterioration of records and equipment. To minimize the damage:
   a. Keep good paper records, in a filing cabinet.
   b. Maintain the offshore update schedule.
   c. In the tropics, limit ambient humidity and direct exposure to the elements.
   d. If you are using a computer, find the best maintenance procedure from a local expert. Failing that, a major computer supplier may be able to provide advice.

Check Communication Links

The mechanics of communications can be a source of great frustration. Two general principles should be clarified: Who should communicate with whom? and Are there any legal or administrative barriers to consider?

Who Should Communicate?

The project partners should arrange a regular (not burdensome) plan to keep in touch. E-mail on Internet, FAX, mail, and telephone are the usual routes. Keep up-to-date ad-dresses, telephone, and FAX numbers. Note time zone differences and preferred contact times. Especially when more than four time zones separate the partners, be prepared to make or receive telephone calls at home.

Each communication mode has certain advantages to consider:

1. E-mail using the Internet: This used to be a preferred means. It is inexpensive (often free through university or government linkages) and easy to access. Although it requires a computer and some software, it is possible to message, network, and send complex files. Transmission time ranges from instantaneous to several weeks. Access has recently become a problem, because what was originally an academic research network is being commercialized and becoming overloaded. It is worth noting that Internet files are not particularly secure, so identifiable patient data should not be transferred in this way.
2. FAX: Facsimile transmission can be a cost-efficient way to transmit paper copy, but availability and confidentiality become the issues. If the line quality is poor, the document can be garbled and/or transmission rates can be slow and hence more expensive than expected. Although the technology is increasingly available, it is still unavailable in many smaller health care/research facilities. We once bypassed a communications logjam by approaching a large local private organization and asking if they were prepared to contribute facsimile communications through their equipment. They agreed, and the linkage led to broader collaboration.
3. Mail/courier: This is the preferred means for hard copy when time is not an issue. Large packages tend to be opened by the authorities. Do not mail the only copy of anything that is irreplaceable. Register important documents and let the recipient know they are coming. Complete the international customs declaration form. Although $3^{1}/_{2}$-inch computer disks usually travel well, $5^{1}/_{4}$-inch disks are less robust. In many countries overseas mail goes by boat unless otherwise specified. Your valuable data can ''age'' to oblivion in the hold of a freighter.
4. Telephone
   a. Voice: Nothing beats voice communication, but it is very expensive and vulnerable to problems with line quality and security. Keep in mind that the data on a one-page fax often cannot be conveyed in a 20 minute call. If you must use voice, consider sending an agenda in advance by fax or mail.
   b. Computer: Provided you can set up and maintain compatible software at both ends, this is a good way to transmit data. However, there has to be someone at each end who can keep the system going. Modems are still a rarity in much of the developing world and telephone access and line quality can be a major problem.

Define Benchmarks

Projects conducted at a distance tend to fall behind schedule. For each participant, a part of the venture is out of sight, and hence potentially out of mind. Particularly for technology transfer–based projects, the focus on the data tends to further obscure the goal of advancing the technology in the host institution. Therefore, in addition to establishing schedules for data exchange, write-up, project reports, and site and exchange visits define logical benchmarks for the technology transfer. If knowledge transfer is the goal, a series of tests might be constructed. If an apparatus (e.g., a chromatograph) is the focus, define a timeline for setup, calibration, and a progressive series of applications, ideally within the framework of the overall study.

By the end of the site visit, the project should be largely formulated, the partnership and its responsibilities defined, and a timetable and benchmarks established. As the project progresses, the issue of future site visits will be raised.

Step Three: Running the Project

Once established, studies conducted in emerging countries face problems similar to those undertaken in major centers. Assuming steps one and two have been completed, the issues will be maintaining timetables, assuring quality, and sustaining the prioritization of the study. Readers should consult reviews of ongoing data management and quality assurance techniques (3). In addition there are a few considerations specific to developing country research.

The first is ongoing communications. Even if things are going smoothly, regular progress communication keeps each party abreast of their partner's sector of the project. If there are regular project meetings at each site, they should be at least briefly minuted and circulated. Data should be sampled, checked, and verified at regular intervals. The derived experience should set the stage for formulating the next project so there is continuity rather than a large hiatus between studies. The timetable and benchmarks established during the first site visit form the basis of regular information exchange. They also provide the basis of in-process site visits.

Site Visits in Process

The purposes of in-process site visits are to:

1. monitor progress,
2. solve problems,
3. anticipate new problems,
4. plan future activities,
5. define relationships.

Frequency

The frequency of such visits depends on project activity levels, problems identified, the requirement for future planning, and cost. In general, one site visit per year is adequate, provided the project is well staffed locally.

The site visit should have a timetable and an agenda. That allows people to prepare and set aside time. It is a good idea to develop the agenda jointly and allow for debriefing at the end.

The agenda should include the following:

1. A check of the status of institution and partners.
2. A review of accrual, data collection, verification, checking, problems, budget.
3. An opportunity for the visitors to be locally useful—talks, rounds, consultations.
4. A local presentation of work in progress.
5. Future planning.

The atmosphere should be collaborative and the discussion bidirectional. If technology transfer is one of the project goals, one should assess progress against a series of benchmarks. These should be part of the site-visit agenda, as reflected in the overall project plan.

Who Should Go?

Generally speaking, one person serves as principal contact in a collaborative project, although there should be clear communication links for particular areas of expertise. The designated principal partners should make the trip, but depending upon the agenda, the technical requirements may require others on site. For our projects in Africa, the principal, who is medically trained and knows Africa well, and the project research and design expert make the trip. On occasion the presence of senior titular personnel facilitates a site visit. Senior staff in the WHO Centre have director or co-director titles, in part because this offers both credibility and status should more formal negotiations be required.

Reporting

At the conclusion of a trip a report should be provided, addressing all agenda items and any further developments. It should be shared among the partners. The format of the report may be a minute of the agenda or a more elaborate itemized report form.

Consider taking an updated copy of the data set and interval paperwork back to the center as part of the site visit.

Reporting Collaborative Study Results

Beyond the general principles of authorship, data interpretation, and targeting of reports, there are a few suggestions that are particular to this setting:

1. Where possible, report first in the local setting. Encourage local participants to take a major role in shaping any presentations. The format and content may be different than for a North American audience.
2. Broader reporting should make clear the collaborative nature of the project, by virtue of authorship and institutional designation.
3. Substantive write-up may be a good time for exchange visits. They can be very useful if there is a specific skill or technology to be transferred. Augmented library or writing resources may be at hand and the exchange may provide an opportunity for high-caliber outside input. This can be a good time to invite the outside collaborator to come as an expert on his/her own terms. The visit also raises the local profile of the project.

CONCLUSIONS

Much research is conducted in developing countries. There is a large anthropology literature in relation to specific activities in field research. Major agencies have project development and application criteria. Yet surprisingly there is little guidance for the small trial researcher who sets out to do clinical research (e.g., quality of life) in a developing country, or anywhere for that matter where the culture and technology of research are either vastly different or unformed.

As researchers, we know our science. We are becoming increasingly sensitive to and skilled in approaching issues of cultural nuance and difference. This is a separate subject of considerable scope.

Our goal in this chapter has been to set a framework for undertaking the science. The commonest problems arise because we are unaware of the context of our own work, and so are unfamiliar with the important things to check when beginning in a new place. In broad measures, there are four questions to ask:

1. Is the question of mutual value?
2. What is the nature of the place?
3. Who will be working together?
4. Is the work feasible?

Answering these questions before venturing off can avoid disappointment, project failure, and misunderstanding. There are skilled, motivated colleagues out there and important work to do. The joy of discovery can be twofold—the science and the new partnerships.

REFERENCES

1. Baum WC. *The project cycle*. Washington, DC: International Bank for Reconstruction and Development/The World Bank, 1982.
2. Olweny C. The ethics and conduct of cross-cultural research in developing countries. *Psycho-Oncology* 1994;3:11–20.
3. Spilker B. *Guide to clinical trials*. New York: Raven Press, 1991.

APPENDIX: HEALTH AND LOGISTIC CONSIDERATIONS FOR INDIVIDUALS

Travel to most emerging countries is not the perilous adventure it once was. True, anthropological research is often done in remote locations, days from anywhere. However, the type of research considered in this book is not likely to be that remotely sited. Having said that, one general principle for personal conduct holds true: The more remote you are, the more self-sufficient you must be.

There are numerous books and brochures about travel preparation that the investigator should seek out well in advance. The subject is wide, and recommendations tend to be specific to both place and person. However, a few comments may set that search into a clearer perspective:

1. Prepare passports and travel documents well in advance. Check on visa requirements for the type of work you are doing. In general, it is easier to travel on a tourist visa, as often business or research travelers encounter delays and prolonged questioning. Make copies of all essential documents (airline tickets, passport, visa, travelers' checks, itinerary, credit cards, identity cards, and list of contact phone numbers). Keep a copy with you, separate from the originals, and leave another copy at home where someone can find it quickly should it be needed.
2. Know the local rules and respect them. In particular, there may be religious, gender-specific, or other kinds of peculiarities that may limit an individual's role. Think about that as the project is being designed.
3. Health is a significant concern. Be properly immunized. Take precautions regarding sun, temperature and humidity, water supply, and insects and parasites. HIV, malaria, hepatitis, and trauma are common, largely controllable risks that should not be ignored. It is a good idea to take along a personal medical kit. Names and formulations of common medications are different abroad, and some things are not readily obtained. A very sophisticated kit can fit into a $20 \times 15 \times 6$ cm. zipper case. It is not a good idea to carry potent narcotics in such kits!
4. Pack lightly, selecting durable, easily washable, multipurpose clothing. In many parts of the world airport security is lax. While no suitcase defies all intruders, hard-sided luggage with built-in locks offers the best protection against rifled cases, and more frightening, protection against those who like to plant items, like drugs, for you to transport. Don't leave your belongings unattended. Carry valuable documents, essential medications, your camera, and perhaps a change of clothing in your hand luggage.
5. Know who to contact in the event of problems and have the phone numbers on your person. Make sure someone at each end of the trip knows your itinerary.

Quality of Life and Pharmacoeconomics in Clinical Trials, Second Edition, edited by B. Spilker.
Lippincott-Raven Publishers, Philadelphia © 1996.

CHAPTER 71

Evaluating Instruments Used Cross-Nationally: Methods from the IQOLA Project

John E. Ware, Jr., Barbara L. Gandek, Susan D. Keller, and the IQOLA Project Group

INTRODUCTION

As interest has grown in evaluating health status across countries, particularly in multinational clinical trials, increased attention has been paid to assessment methods (1–7). This effort has benefited from the fields of cross-cultural psychology and sociology, which have a long tradition of developing criteria for the adaptation, translation, and psychometric testing of measures across languages and cultures (8–16). Two objectives must be addressed simultaneously (17). On the one hand, to make comparisons across countries, questionnaires and scoring methods must be standardized and there must be proof that the same health attributes are being measured in each country (1,18). On the other hand, questionnaires must be meaningful within each country's culture. As others have noted, the International Quality of Life Assessment (IQOLA) Project is one of the few cross-cultural

efforts distinguished by a comprehensive methodological approach to meet both objectives (2).

The IQOLA project began in 1991 to translate and adapt the SF-36 Health Survey and to validate, norm, and document the new translations as needed for their proper use (19–25). The SF-36 contains 36 items that can be scored as eight scales (26,27) or as physical and mental health summary measures (28–30). It was chosen for the IQOLA project because it was a comprehensive measure of generic health status and could be supplemented with other measures in a clinical trial, due to its relatively short length. A number of studies had documented the acceptability, reliability, and validity of SF-36 scales (31–35), and research had indicated that it was applicable across heterogeneous populations in the United States (36). In addition, research in several countries using preliminary SF-36 translations and a translated "parent" questionnaire (37) suggested that the SF-36 could be translated successfully. Further information on the SF-36, including an updated list of studies, is provided in the chapter by Ware.

Since the inception of the project, interest in the SF-36 has grown worldwide. The IQOLA project now includes

J. E. Ware, Jr., B. L. Gandek, S. D. Keller, and the IQOLA Project Group: New England Medical Center, The Health Institute, Boston, Massachusetts 02111.

TABLE 1. *IQOLA project methodology: steps and products*

Steps	Products
I. Translation	Survey form
II. Scale construction	Scoring algorithms
III. Validation and norming	Interpretation
IV. Publication of results	User-friendly guidelines

sponsored investigators from 14 countries: Australia, Belgium, Canada, Denmark, France, Germany, Italy, Japan, The Netherlands, Norway, Spain, Sweden, the United Kingdom (English version), and the United States (English and Spanish versions). In addition, researchers from more than 15 other countries are translating the SF-36 using IQOLA project methods; as of the fall of 1994 these countries included Argentina, Brazil, China, Croatia, Finland, Hungary, Israel, Mexico, Poland, Portugal, Romania, Russia, South Africa, Tanzania, the United Kingdom (Welsh), and the United States (Chinese, Japanese, and Vietnamese).

This chapter summarizes the research methods used in the IQOLA project, which can be categorized into three broad stages: (a) rigorous translation and evaluation procedures to ensure conceptual equivalence and respondent acceptance, (b) formal psychometric tests of the assumptions underlying item scoring and construction of multi-item scales, and (c) validation and norming studies to evaluate the equivalence of interpretations across countries. As noted in Table 1, the products of these three research stages are (a) questionnaires that can be used in data collection, (b) scoring algorithms that can be used to make standardized comparisons, and (c) validation and norming studies that provide a basis for interpretation. To promote the standardization of the administration, scoring, and interpretation of the SF-36, IQOLA researchers are preparing user-friendly manuals and other publications.

IQOLA project translations are being evaluated using data from randomized clinical trials, observational studies of specific diseases, and general population surveys. Data from general population samples in three countries [Sweden, the United Kingdom, and the United States (22,23,38–40)] are used to illustrate the application of IQOLA project methods in this chapter.

Because IQOLA is an ongoing research effort, IQOLA project methods are described in the present tense throughout the chapter. However, results from several IQOLA project countries are published or in press (20–23). A more extensive account of IQOLA project methods is provided elsewhere (25).

STAGE 1: REPRODUCTION OF THE ORIGINAL SURVEY

Reproduction of the SF-36 is pursued through an iterative process of forward and backward translation or English-language adaptation of the form and by testing within small convenience samples of the lay public (4,8,9). Quantitative evaluations (e.g., conceptual equivalence, common word usage) are used to determine how well the underlying health concepts have been reproduced. IQOLA researchers also conducted a cross-cultural comparison of the face validity of the translations. The goal of the translation process is not to achieve literal or syntactic equivalence, but to establish functional or conceptual equivalence.

Iterative Translation Process

The translation process is iterative in nature. In the first step, at least two translators who are native speakers of the target language produce independent translations of each SF-36 item and each set of response choices. Translators also rate the difficulty of translating each item and response choice on a scale ranging from 0 (not at all difficult) to 100 (extremely difficult). The translators and the national principal investigator meet to develop one agreed-upon preliminary translation of the items and response choices. Selection of response choices also is informed by results from a Thurstone scaling exercise (41).

In this scaling exercise, convenience samples of adults are asked to position the set of response choices for each SF-36 scale using the Thurstone method of equal-appearing intervals (41). Raters are asked to mark the position of response choices (e.g., "very good," "good," or "fair") on a 10-cm line labeled on either end by the extreme responses for that response continuum (e.g., "excellent" and "poor") (Fig. 1). Descriptive statistics, such as the mean and median, are calculated for each possible response choice. Response choices are selected to have similar values as those for the original instrument, while also taking into account other criteria (e.g., common language use).

The quality of the preliminary forward translation is rated by two additional translators, using three criteria: clarity, use of common language, and conceptual equivalence to the original questionnaire. Ratings are made on a scale from 0 (low quality) to 100 (high quality). In addition, translators provide an overall rating of the acceptability of the translation. Based on the results of this evaluation, items or response choices that are rated unacceptable reenter the translation process until a suitable translation is found.

Two independent translators who are native speakers of English then translate the preliminary forward translation into English. The backwards translations are rated for equivalence to the original form by researchers associated with the development of the U.S. questionnaire, and reasons for discrepancies are reviewed with the national principal investigator. Discrepancies are resolved and a final forward translation is agreed upon.

Because bilinguals may differ from the lay public in their use and understanding of language, input from the lay public is important to address any bias that may result from the translation process (12,42,43). The translation is given to at least 50 individuals of varying sociodemographic characteristics who are asked if they found any questions confusing,

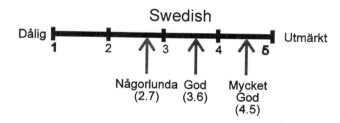

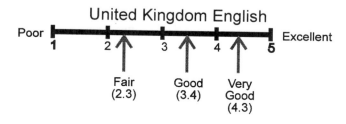

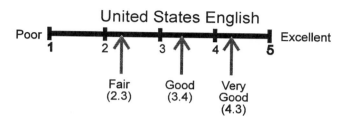

FIG. 1. Comparability of scale values for health ratings in three countries.

difficult to answer, or upsetting, using a modification of the European Organization for Research and Treatment of Cancer (EORTC) debriefing questionnaire (44).

Cross-Cultural Analyses of Quantitative Evaluations

Preliminary analyses of difficulty and quality ratings included the calculation of descriptive statistics across raters within a country, mean values across countries, and indices of agreement across raters within countries (25). Ratings of clarity, common language usage, and conceptual equivalence were uniformly high across countries. Difficulty ratings highlighted some parts of the SF-36 that generally were problematic for translators. In general, items that were difficult to translate also tended to be unfamiliar (e.g., "full of pep," "downhearted and blue") or ambiguous ("one block") to some respondents in the U.S., suggesting that minor rewording also would make the original form more culture-free. Some items required modifications to be culturally appropriate when translated. For example, the U.S. form used bowling and golf as examples of moderate activities; these examples were changed to activities such as gardening, berry picking, or cycling in some countries. In addition, the questionnaire's instructions often were more difficult to translate than the items themselves, suggesting that the instructions could be simplified.

Results of the Thurstone scaling exercise are currently being analyzed across countries for ordinality (Did respondents in each country place the translated response choices in the same order?) and interval score properties (Were the rated distances between response choices similar across countries?) (25). While most questionnaires do not have strictly equal intervals between response choices (45,46), departures from equal intervals that vary greatly across countries should be taken into account. Analyses confirmed that the response choices had ordinal properties. While distances between responses approximated equal intervals for some response sets, intervals were not equal for other response sets. These trends generally were apparent across countries (25) and are consistent with previous research conducted in the Health Insurance Experiment and the Medical Outcomes Study (47,48).

Results from three countries are presented in Fig. 1 for the first general health item EVGFP (representing the response choices "excellent," "very good," "good," "fair," and "poor"). This item is of particular importance because it is widely used in general population surveys and clinical studies, it has a different set of response choices from the true-false items it is combined with in the SF-36 General Health scale, and it is often used as a criterion of self-perceived health in evaluations of other measures. As shown, the interval between "poor" and "fair" is approximately twice as large as that between "very good" and "excellent" in all three countries and the item is scored accordingly (49).

Data Completeness

Evaluation of the extent and pattern of missing data also is used to diagnose potential translation problems. A high number of missing values for an item or scale may indicate that people find the question(s) confusing, offensive, inapplicable, or easy to overlook on the questionnaire. A high percentage of missing data throughout the questionnaire may indicate that respondents are not familiar with questionnaires, that there are cultural norms against self-disclosure, or that there is a greater prevalence of illiteracy in the country (5,50). In addition, the "grid" format used throughout the U.S. SF-36 (e.g., in items 3a–3j) may be confusing to some respondents, who may not understand that all items within a grid should be answered. Some respondents may require a version of the SF-36 with questions printed singly. Alternative layouts of the SF-36, such as a form in which all response choices are printed from left to right, also may reduce potential respondent confusion.

Summary

In summary, the overall goal of the translation process is to assure that differences in item and scale scores between countries are due to differences in health status and not to translation problems. Qualitative and quantitative methods are used to maximize the conceptual equivalence of questionnaires across countries, while maintaining cultural sensitivity. However, these results are not accepted as sole evidence of the conceptual equivalence of the questionnaires. Further proof of equivalence is sought through empirical tests of the item and scale properties of the translated questionnaires and evaluation of the questionnaires' validity.

STAGE 2: PSYCHOMETRIC TESTING OF SCORING ALGORITHMS

The second research stage of the IQOLA project tests the assumptions underlying item scoring and the construction of multi-item scales. The goal of this stage is to arrive at item and scale scoring algorithms that satisfy scaling assumptions and achieve comparable scale scores across countries. When scaling assumptions are not met, evidence is sought to determine if this is due to translation problems or to country-specific differences. Results from studies using translated forms are compared with those from previous studies, to gain insight into the extent to which equivalence of meaning has been achieved across countries (13).

Summated Rating Scale Assumptions

SF-36 scales are scored using the method of summated ratings. Assumptions made under this method must be tested prior to scale construction. The method of summated ratings assumes that items in the same scale can be aggregated without standardization of variances or weighting (51). To avoid standardization, items within a scale should have roughly equivalent means and standard deviations. To avoid weighting, items should be equally representative of the underlying scale dimension, as measured by the correlation between each item and the sum of the remaining items in the scale. In addition, items should correlate substantially [.40 or more (52), corrected for overlap (53)] with their hypothesized scale, to establish a linear relationship between each item and the underlying concept being measured. Higher linear correlations also are indicative of interval-level measurement scales (54). Tests of item-scale correlations for the three general population samples are summarized in Table 2 (row 1) and indicate that all correlations exceeded the .40 criterion.

These assumptions, which allow for simple summation of items into scales, have been supported by research in the U.S. and other IQOLA countries for most SF-36 items (20,23,36,38). Exceptions to this include two scales in which the response choices are not identical for all items (bodily pain and general health). In both scales, one item each is recalibrated to better meet the assumption of a linear relationship between the item and the underlying construct (49).

Item Discriminant Validity

In addition to testing the strength of the association between each item and its hypothesized scale, the strength of the association between each item and other scales also must be examined to determine if an item is a strong measure of concepts other than the one that it is hypothesized to measure. Item discriminant validity is supported when the correlation between an item and its hypothesized scale is larger than that item's correlation with other scales. These tests are summarized into item scaling success rates, which are the percentage of times in which items correlate higher with their hypothesized scales than with other scales (55,56).

Results of item discriminant validity tests in the three general population samples are presented in Table 2 (row 2). Because items correlated significantly higher with their hypothesized scale than with other SF-36 scales in virtually all tests, these results support the hypothesized grouping of items into scales in all three countries. Analyses of Swedish data also supported the SF-36 item groupings across samples differing by region, age, gender, education, employment status, and marital status (23). The eight scale grouping also has been supported across samples differing in age, education, and other characteristics in the U.S. (36).

Hypotheses Regarding Item Values

While an average item value is expected to vary with the level of health in a country and with the population sampled, the ordering of item means and the rough difference between

TABLE 2. *Summary of psychometric tests for the SF-36 in three countries*

	SF-36 scales							
	PF	RP	BP	GH	VT	SF	RE	MH
Range of item/scale correlations								
Sweden	.58–.80	.69–.77	.88	.57–.79	.60–.75	.71	.61–.66	.66–.75
U.K.	.56–.83	.68–.75	.87	.46–.76	.72–.73	.61	.66–.74	.59–.73
U.S.	.56–.82	.72–.80	.82	.46–.72	.70–.73	.52	.65–.71	.56–.69
% scaling success								
Sweden	100.0	100.0	100.0	100.0	100.0	100.0	100.0	100.0
U.K.	100.0	100.0	100.0	100.0	100.0	93.8	100.0	100.0
U.S.	99.0	100.0	100.0	100.0	100.0	100.0	100.0	100.0
Internal consistency reliability								
Sweden	0.91	0.88	0.93	0.84	0.85	0.83	0.79	0.87
U.K.	0.93	0.88	0.84	0.80	0.87	0.74	0.79	0.91
U.S.	0.93	0.89	0.90	0.81	0.86	0.68	0.82	0.84
% ceiling								
Sweden	45.9	72.2	39.1	13.5	7.3	66.1	76.6	16.1
U.K.	38.3	71.9	37.7	5.6	1.5	60.2	72.6	2.5
U.S.	32.5	65.8	29.6	6.5	1.4	53.1	69.9	4.4
% floor								
Sweden	0.3	8.9	1.0	0.2	0.8	0.6	6.6	0.2
U.K.	0.7	8.4	0.4	0.2	0.5	0.5	9.8	0.1
U.S.	1.1	12.7	0.9	0.0	0.8	0.8	10.9	0.0

Note: Number of respondents in each country: Sweden (*n*=8,930), UK (*n*=1,582), US (*n*=2,474).
PF, physical functioning; RP, role physical; BP, bodily pain; GH, general health; VT, vitality; SF, social functioning; RE, role emotional; MH, mental health.

them should not vary, if items are spaced along the health continuum consistently across countries. For example, physical functioning items that measure limitations in performing easier activities (e.g., "bathing or dressing," "walking one block") are expected to have higher mean scores (fewer reports of limitations) than items measuring more difficult activities (e.g., "vigorous activities," "walking more than a mile"). (All SF-36 items are scored so a higher value indicates a better health state.) Items measuring well-being (e.g., "happy person," "calm and peaceful") generally should have lower mean scores than items measuring distress (e.g., "downhearted and blue," "nervous person"), because the former are endorsed less often than the latter. If the translation process changes the meaning of an item, and thus the item is more or less frequently endorsed, the ordering of item means would be expected to vary substantially across countries.

Table 3 presents an example of item means (favorably scored) for two SF-36 scales, using data from the general population samples in three countries. Items are ordered in terms of their hypothesized mean scores, ranging from item clusters (noted by dotted lines) expected to have low mean scores (items measuring the well-being range of health) to those expected to have the highest mean scores (items measuring dysfunction). These results support the hypothesized ordering of item clusters. For example, the "vigorous activities" item had the lowest mean score in all three countries and the "bathing and dressing" item had the highest or second highest mean score, within the Physical Functioning scale. The two mental health items measuring levels of positive well-being had lower mean scores than those items

measuring anxiety and depression. An empirical test of the item clusters across all eight SF-36 scales supported their hypothesized ordering in the three countries (13,25).

The mean item values for physical functioning items in one Japanese sample, however, showed an atypical pattern. This was traced to a translation problem; respondents interpreted the instructions and response choices to indicate that they should report limitations only if a physician had told them to restrict their activities. Retranslation of this portion of the questionnaire corrected this problem and resulted in a pattern of mean item values consistent with that seen in other countries (25).

Item Response Theory

Item response theory (IRT) (57) is a more precise method for testing the equivalence of item values across translations (58–61). These methods take into account where both respondents and items are located on a scale and thus are sample free (57,62). Rasch IRT methods are used in the IQOLA project to estimate the equivalence of item response probabilities across countries, providing further evidence of the equivalence of translations (62–65). A Rasch IRT analysis of the Physical Functioning scale across four countries demonstrated substantial convergence of Germany, Swedish, and U.K. item values with those of the U.S. (25,66). These results also indicated that many respondents (33% to 43% across countries) had a higher level of physical functioning than that defined by the Physical Functioning scale, suggesting that items that measure even higher levels

TABLE 3. *Means for selected SF-36 items in three countries*[a]

Scale	SF-36 item[b]	Mean Sweden (*n*=8,930)	Mean UK (*n*=1,582)	Mean US (*n*=2,474)
Physical Functioning (PF)	Vigorous activities	2.32	2.23	2.17
	Climb several flights	2.73	2.58	2.54
	Bend, kneel	2.72	2.67	2.59
	Walk mile	2.76	2.70	2.55
	Moderate activities	2.74	2.78	2.65
	Lift, carry groceries	2.74	2.73	2.72
	Walk several blocks	2.89	2.82	2.69
	Climb one flight	2.88	2.84	2.78
	Walk one block	2.92	2.90	2.82
	Bathe, dress	2.90	2.92	2.88
Mental Health (MH)	Peaceful	4.59	3.74	4.06
	Happy	4.38	4.34	4.43
	Nervous	5.44	5.03	4.85
	Down in dumps	5.60	5.21	5.33
	Blue/sad	5.23	4.79	4.98

[a]Means for each item were based on all available responses.
[b]Abbreviated item content in U.S. questionnaire.

of functioning might be added when the SF-36 is used in general and healthy populations. Rasch IRT models also are being used to examine whether gains in precision with Rasch IRT-based scoring are worthwhile; preliminary results from the U.S. indicate this is likely (64).

Features of Scale Score Distributions

After item-level analyses have established that the assumptions underlying construction of summated rating scales have been met, SF-36 scales are scored and the properties of the scales are examined for comparability across countries. Scale means and standard deviations indicate where along a scale continuum the majority of individuals within a population are likely to be found. Large differences in mean scale scores across countries, within general population samples or clinically comparable samples, could indicate lack of equivalence in translation or a difference in health across countries.

Additionally, the SF-36 profile of mean scale scores is expected to have roughly the same shape across general population samples. This can be seen in the characteristic SF-36 profile for the three general population samples (Fig. 2). The five scales that primarily measure health-related disability (dark gray bars) have the highest mean scale scores, while lower mean scores are found for the three scales that extend measurement to the well-being range (white and gray bars). (All SF-36 scales are scored so a higher value indicates a better health state.) These results support the equivalence of the SF-36 scales across these countries.

Had substantial differences been found in mean scale scores across countries, within comparable samples, further evaluation would be needed to determine if the differences were due to translation problems or to country-specific differences in health. Examination of the pattern of country-specific differences across scales is useful in this regard. For example, if the mean Physical Functioning scale score was substantially lower in a general population sample from one country, and scores for scales known to be correlated with the Physical Functioning scale (e.g., Role Physical, Bodily Pain) also were lower in that country, a country-specific difference in health is supported. Conversely, if country-specific differences were not seen in other scales known to primarily measure physical health, a problem in the translation of the Physical Functioning scale could be indicated.

In addition to evaluating the mean and standard deviation, the percentage of people scoring at the floor (lowest level) and ceiling (highest level) are used to evaluate the skewness of scale scores. If a high percentage of people score at the top (or bottom) of a scale, it is impossible to detect an improvement (or decline) in health for that group. Within the U.S. general population, floor effects are minimal for most scales but several scales have notable ceiling effects (27,36,40). Other health status measures have greater ceiling effects among healthy adults (2,38). Within the three general population samples, floor and ceiling effects were largely comparable (Table 2, rows 4 and 5).

Reliability of Scale Scores

Reliability indicates the confidence with which the same or similar responses could be expected if a questionnaire was administered again to the same sample. Within the

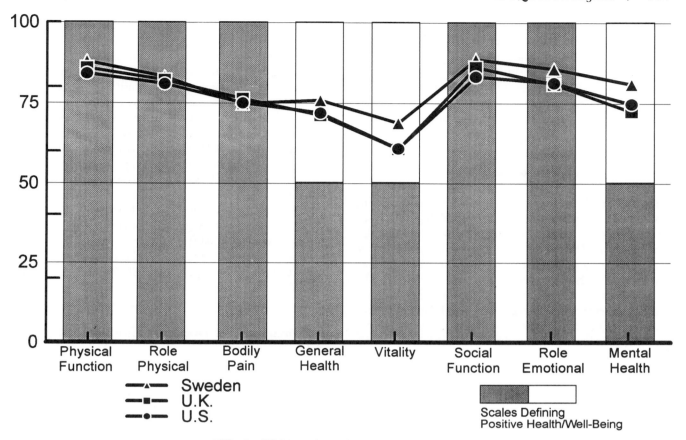

FIG. 2. SF-36 scale profiles in three countries.

IQOLA project, the reliability of scale scores is estimated with the internal consistency method, using Cronbach's alpha coefficient (67), and the test-retest method across repeated administrations. Test-retest reliability is assessed by comparing product moment and intraclass correlation coefficients, and by calculating the percentage of people whose retest scores fall within a 95% confidence interval of the first administration. Scale reliabilities of .70 or greater have been suggested for group-level analyses, while reliabilities of .90 or greater have been suggested for individual-level analyses (54). The reliability of SF-36 scales is generally well above .70 in U.S. studies (27,36).

Low internal consistency reliability estimates can be due to a number of factors. An uncharacteristically low reliability could be due to low correlations among items within a scale, which could indicate a problem with the translation of one or more items. Low reliability also could result from a lack of item score variation, which might be due to translation problems or other factors. In addition, some respondents may find the response format, particularly the "grid" layout of some SF-36 items, confusing and may give inconsistent responses. This problem would be particularly apparent for those scales in which higher values are sometimes paired with positive responses and sometimes with negative responses, to correct for response set bias (68).

Internal consistency reliabilities were high across the three general population samples for all eight SF-36 scales (Table 2, row 3). Analyses of population subgroups within Sweden and from other U.K. samples support the generalizability of these results (23,69–72).

STAGE 3: REPRODUCTION OF INTERPRETATIONS

A cross-cultural psychometric research tradition maintains that the degree to which universal concepts are captured by a measure can be evaluated by examining the extent to which measurement and structural models are replicated cross-culturally (13,73–79). Measurement models concentrate on questions, response choices, hypothesized item groupings, and scoring algorithms, as described previously (stage 2). Structural models (examined in stage 3) provide the theoretical basis underlying scale interpretation. To the extent that an SF-36 scale has the same relationship with other scales and external variables across countries, the meaning of scores for that scale will be consistent across countries.

Structural models focus on the relationship of SF-36 items and scales to each other, including the pattern of correlations among SF-36 scales and the relationship of scales to underlying factors. In addition, these models explore the relationship of SF-36 scale scores to external criteria, including sociodemographic variables, clinical measures, and scales from other health status questionnaires. These relationships provide further information for the interpretation of SF-36 scales and are illustrated in this chapter with examples of the "known groups" method of validity and norm-based interpretation.

Correlations Among SF-36 Scales

Scale reliability (described in stage 2) indicates the extent to which items within a scale correlate highly with each other, and thus the extent to which a scale has a high correlation with itself. The reliability of a scale should be greater than its correlations with other scales, if the SF-36 scales measure distinct health concepts. However, because all SF-36 scales measure health status, correlations among all pairs of scales are expected to be positive. These hypotheses were confirmed in the three general population samples (25). All interscale correlations were positive but were lower than the corresponding reliability coefficients. Furthermore, scales (see Table 1 for scale names) previously shown to primarily measure mental health (MH, RE, SF) generally had higher correlations with each other than with other SF-36 scales. Similarly, scales previously shown to primarily measure physical health (PF, RP, BP) generally correlated higher with each other than with other scales. In comparison, correlations between physical and mental scales were lower. The pattern of correlations among scales and their relationship to reliability coefficients is evidence of the construct validity of the SF-36 scales.

Factor Analysis of SF-36 Structure

Factor analytic studies of the SF-36 in U.S. general and patient populations have revealed a higher-order structure, corresponding to hypothesized physical and mental health dimensions (27–30). These components were also observed in Sweden and the U.K., using the same method of factor extraction and rotation as in the U.S. (28,30,80). As shown

in Table 4, the magnitude of the correlations between scales and components was largely equivalent across countries. For example, the Physical Functioning scale correlated the highest and the Mental Health scale correlated the lowest with the physical component; similarly, the Mental Health scale correlated highest and the Physical Functioning scale correlated lowest with the mental component. These results support the interpretation of each scale as a measure of physical and/or mental health in each country and the scoring of physical and mental summary components in Sweden and the U.K., as in the U.S. (29,30). The summary measures account for 82% to 84% of the reliable variance in SF-36 scale scores across countries, and thus make it possible to reduce the number of statistical comparisons without substantial loss of information.

Structural equation modeling also is being used to further explore the relationships among SF-36 items and scales within the U.S. and other countries (81).

Interpretation in Relation to Known Differences Between Groups

Validation of scales based on comparisons between groups known to differ in the characteristic being measured is called "known groups" validity (82). For example, previous U.S. research has demonstrated that scale scores for measures sensitive to changes in physical health (PF, RP, BP, and GH) differ by age, particularly after 65 years (27,40). If a similar pattern of results is observed in other countries, support is provided for interpretation of these four scales as measures of physical health in these countries as well. A different pattern of results may be due to cultural differences, translation problems, or both.

Figure 3 demonstrates that the age differences in scale scores seen in the U.S. also are evident in Sweden and the U.K. Based on more extensive data reported elsewhere (22,23,27,38), these graphs compare SF-36 profiles for those 18 to 34 and 65 to 74 years old. The greater health burden of old age, particularly in measures most associated with physical health, is confirmed in all three countries.

TABLE 4. *Correlations between SF-36 scales and physical (PCS) and mental (MCS) component summary measures in three countries*

Country	SF-36 scales							
	PF	RP	BG	GH	VT	SF	RE	MH
PCS								
Sweden (n=8,930)	.84	.78	.76	.66	.43	.32	.25	.15
U.K. (n=1,582)	.83	.79	.79	.62	.42	.49	.17	.10
U.S. (n=2,474)	.85	.81	.76	.70	.47	.42	.17	.17
MCS								
Sweden (n=8,930)	.15	.30	.28	.49	.74	.78	.71	.90
U.K. (n=1,582)	.10	.27	.23	.47	.72	.66	.78	.90
U.S. (n=2,474)	.12	.27	.28	.37	.65	.67	.78	.87

Shaded box indicates substantial correlations ($r > .40$).

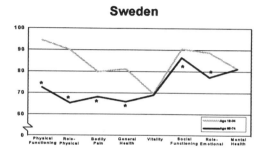

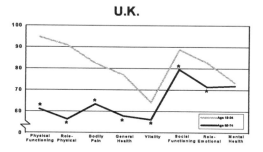

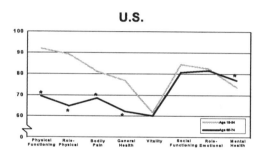

Note: Mean scores adjusted for gender   * p < 0.01

FIG. 3. SF-36 scale profiles for adults age 18 to 34 (thin line) and 65 to 74 (thick line) in three countries.

Conclusions about the equivalence of interpretations across countries should be based on the convergence of evidence from numerous tests, such as comparisons of scale scores for different chronic diseases or different severity levels within a disease, using the same definitions across countries. Cross-cultural comparisons using data from multinational studies, with common data collection protocols and common clinical "criterion" variables, will be analyzed to further evaluate the comparability of scores and interpretations across countries. More than 50 multinational clinical trials and clinical descriptive studies using IQOLA project SF-36 translations currently are under way, including studies of cancer, cardiovascular disease, central nervous system disorders, diabetes, gastrointestinal disorders, orthopedic disorders, psychiatric disorders, and respiratory diseases. These studies will provide useful information about the inter-

pretation of SF-36 scale scores in relation to clinical measures.

Interpretation in Relation to General Population Norms

Data from general population samples are useful in determining how SF-36 scale scores from individuals and populations (e.g., patients with a particular disease) compare to a reference standard. Because average health status scores differ by age and other sociodemographic variables (83–85), normative values often are presented separately by age, gender, and other classifications (27). Many studies have illustrated the usefulness of norms in interpreting the burden of chronic disease (29,69,86,87). General population norms for the SF-36 have been published for Sweden (22,23), the U.K. (38,71), and the U.S. (27,30,40). In addition, eight other IQOLA countries—Australia, Denmark, France, Germany, Italy, Japan, the Netherlands, and Norway—are implementing or planning to implement a common normative data collection protocol, which establishes standards for sample size, sampling methods used to achieve representativeness, data collection procedures, and collection of supplemental data for validation and norming.

CONCLUSIONS

We have described the methods used by the IQOLA project to adapt the SF-36 Health Survey for use in multinational studies. Experience to date suggests that the SF-36, which was originally developed and validated in the U.S., can be successfully translated, validated, and normed for use in other countries (20–23,38,69–72,88–91). Research in progress will determine the extent to which initial successes in Germany and Sweden can be generalized across countries, particularly beyond Western European cultures. However, findings to date from France (92) and the Netherlands (93), as well as research in progress, provide reason for optimism. In addition, a 14-country World Health Organization (WHO) study that included items from the MOS SF-20, which preceded the SF-36, also was successful (94).

At each stage, qualitative and quantitative methods have been used to evaluate and improve the translations. Experience to date underscores that all three stages of the IQOLA project methodology are important. Satisfactory reproduction of the SF-36 during the translation phase (stage 1) does not guarantee that data from translated questionnaires can be analyzed. Establishing that the translated scales meet psychometric standards (stage 2) is a necessary but insufficient prerequisite for their analytic use, although it is more likely that scales can be used in quantitative analyses when such scaling assumptions are satisfied. Equally important is stage 3, in which the validity and comparability of the scales is tested across cultures, in ways that closely approximate the intended use of the SF-36.

The IQOLA project has followed what might be called a deductive approach to developing valid cross-cultural questionnaires. Using an instrument first developed and tested in one country, IQOLA is studying the extent and nature of changes needed to achieve acceptable translations. This method also has been used with the Nottingham Health Profile and the Sickness Impact Profile (2). One risk of this approach is that a questionnaire developed in one country may require such extensive changes when used in another country that the resulting translation bears little similarity to the original instrument, for a number of reasons (17,77–79,95–99). An alternative, more inductive approach is to develop country-specific questionnaires and then identify common elements among them to form the core of a cross-cultural instrument. This approach is currently being tested by the WHO Quality of Life project (6) and assumes that cultural differences in health concepts are substantial enough to prevent a more deductive method.

The more deductive approach has a number of strengths. First, many of the issues addressed when translating an existing measure are the same as those addressed when the measure was developed, and the new research can be informed by the original research. Second, to the extent that the original measure can be used successfully across heterogeneous populations within one country (differing in characteristics such as ethnic background or mother tongue), further success can be expected in other countries. Third, tests of the measurement and structural models in other countries can be informed by results from the source country, if the assumption that these models are correct and generalizable across countries holds. Finally, use of country-specific questionnaires to develop a standard measure does not eliminate the need to address the same issues being faced in the IQOLA project: how to equate translations of a common pool of questions, to assure the quality of the translations, and to evaluate the equivalence of the translated forms.

The choice between these two approaches will depend on the extent and nature of the changes required to be made to the original form. If these changes are few in number and not extensive, the IQOLA approach is supported. If the translated forms have little or no recognizable similarity to the original instrument, a more inductive approach is supported. However, in this case the ability to make meaningful comparisons across countries also is limited (100). Experience to date in the IQOLA project suggests that the SF-36 can be adapted for use in other countries with relatively minor changes to the content of the form, providing support for the use of these translations in multinational clinical trials and other studies.

Standardization and Dissemination of SF-36 Translations

Standardization of the content, scoring, and labeling of the original U.S.-English SF-36 and its translations is necessary to ensure their scientific validity and the comparability of SF-36 results across studies and countries. To assure that the SF-36 translations and scoring documentation are standardized and widely available, published IQOLA project translations and scoring documentation are being placed in the Medical Outcomes Trust (49). The trust is a non-profit public service organization created in 1992 to insure the royalty-free distribution of the original SF-36 and many other patient-based health outcomes measures (101). As of the fall of 1994, the trust distributed the U.S.-English SF-36, English-language adaptations for Australia/New Zealand, Canada, and the U.K. (102), and the German and Swedish SF-36 translations. Announcement of the publication of IQOLA project translations will be made through the Medical Outcomes Trust Bulletin, published six times per year. For more information about the trust, published IQOLA project translations, and the availability of other questionnaires, contact the Medical Outcomes Trust, 20 Park Plaza, Suite 1014, Boston, MA 02116-4313, U.S.A. For information about the availability of IQOLA project translations, or to request permission to translate the SF-36 in other countries, contact the IQOLA project, The Health Institute, NEMCH-345, 750 Washington Street, Boston, MA 02111, U.S.A.

ACKNOWLEDGMENTS

The International Quality of Life Assessment (IQOLA) Project is sponsored by Glaxo Research Institute, Research Triangle Park, North Carolina, and Schering-Plough Corporation, Kenilworth, New Jersey. Additional support is provided by Procter & Gamble Pharmaceuticals, Solvay Duphar B.V., Laboratoires Synthélabo France, Parke-Davis, The Upjohn Company, and 14 other pharmaceutical companies.

In addition to the named authors, the IQOLA Project Group includes Neil K. Aaronson, Ph.D., The Netherlands Cancer Institute, The Netherlands; Catherine Acquadro, M.D., MAPI, France; Jordi Alonso, M.D., Ph.D., Institut Municipal d'Investigació Mèdica, Spain; Giovanni Apolone, M.D., Istituto Di Ricerche Farmacologiche "Mario Negri," Italy; Per Bech, M.D., Fredriksborg General Hospital, Denmark; John Brazier, M.Sc., University of Sheffield, United Kingdom; Monika Bullinger, Ph.D., Ludwig Maximilians Universität, Germany; Shunichi Fukuhara, M.D., M.Sc., University of Tokyo, Japan; Stein Kaasa, M.D., Ph.D., Trondheim University Hospital, Norway; Alain Leplège, M.D., Ph.D., INSERM Unité 292, France; Darius Razavi, M.D., Institut Jules Bordet, Belgium; Rob Sanson-Fisher, Ph.D., University of Newcastle, Australia; Marianne Sullivan, Ph.D., University of Göteborg, Sweden; Anita Wagner, Pharm.D., NEMC, USA; and Sharon Wood-Dauphinee, Ph.D., McGill University, Canada.

We gratefully acknowledge the substantial contributions of our colleague, Denis Bucquet, Ph.D., who guided the research on the SF-36 in France until his death in 1993.

REFERENCES

1. Anderson GF, Alonso J, Kohn LT, Black C. Analyzing health outcomes through international comparisons. *Med Care* 1994;32:526–634.

2. Anderson RT, Aaronson NK, Wilkin D. Critical review of the international assessments of health-related quality of life. *Qual Life Res* 1993;2:369–395.

3. Bullinger M, Anderson R, Cella D, Aaronson N. Developing and evaluating cross-cultural instruments from minimum requirements to optimal models. *Qual Life Res* 1993;2:451–459.

4. Guillemin F, Bombardier C, Beaton D. Cross-cultural adaptation of health-related quality of life measures: literature review and proposed guidelines. *J Clin Epidemiol* 1993;46:1417–1432.

5. Hunt SM, Alonso J, Bucquet D, Niero M, Wiklund I, McKenna S. Cross-cultural adaptation of health measures. *Health Policy* 1991;19:33–44.

6. WHOQOL Group, Division of Mental Health, World Health Organization. Study protocol for the World Health Organization project to develop a Quality of Life assessment instrument (WHOQOL). *Qual Life Res* 1993;2:153–159.

7. Berzon R, Hays RD, Shumaker SA. International use, application and performance of health-related quality of life instruments. *Qual Life Res* 1993;2:367–368.

8. Bracken BA, Barona A. State of the art procedures for translating, validating and using psychoeducational tests in cross-cultural assessment. *School Psychol Int* 1991;12:119–132.

9. Brislin RW. Back-translation for cross-cultural research. *J Cross-Cultural Res* 1970;1:185–216.

10. Brislin RW, Lonner WJ, Thorndike RM, eds. Introduction. In: *Cross-cultural research methods*. New York: Wiley, 1973.

11. Chapman DW, Carter JF. Translation procedures for the cross cultural use of measurement instruments. *Educ Eval Policy Anal* 1978;1:71–76.

12. de Figueiredo JM, Lemkau PV. Psychiatric interviewing across cultures: some problems and prospects. *Soc Psychiatry* 1980;15:117–121.

13. Hui CH, Triandis HC. Measurement in cross-cultural psychology: a review and comparison of strategies. *J Cross-Cultural Psychol* 1985;16:131–152.

14. Sechrest L, Fay TL, Zaidi SMH. Problems of translation in cross-cultural research. *J Cross-Cultural Psychol* 1972;3:41–56.

15. Straus MA. Phenomenal identity and conceptual equivalence of measurement in cross-national comparative research. *J Marriage Family* 1969;31:233–239.

16. Triandis HC, Brislin RW. Cross-cultural psychology. *Am Psychol* 1984;39:1006–1016.

17. Kuyken W, Orley J, Hudelson P, Sartorius N. Quality of life assessment across cultures. *Int J Ment Health* 1994;23:5–27.

18. U.S. Congress, Office of Technology Assessment. *International Health Statistics: What the numbers mean for the United States—background paper* (OTA-BP-H-116). Washington, DC: U.S. Government Printing Office, 1993.

19. Aaronson NK, Acquadro C, Alonso J, et al. International quality of life assessment (IQOLA) project. *Qual Life Res* 1992;1:349–351.

20. Bullinger M. German translation and psychometric testing of the SF-36 Health Survey: preliminary results from the IQOLA Project. *Soc Sci Med* (in press).

21. Sullivan M. Livskvalitetsmätning. Nytt generellt och nytt tumörspecifikt formulär för utvärdering och planering. *Lakartidningen* 1994;91:1340–1341.

22. Sullivan M, Karlsson J, Ware JE. *SF-36 Hälsoenkät: Svensk manual och tolkningsguide. (Swedish manual and interpretation guide.)* Gothenburg: Sahlgrenska University Hospital, 1994.

23. Sullivan M, Karlsson J, Ware JE. The Swedish SF-36 Health Survey: I. Evaluation of data quality, scaling assumptions, reliability, and construct validity across general populations in Sweden. *Soc Sci Med* (in press).

24. Ware JE, Gandek B, and the IQOLA Project Group. The SF-36 Health Survey: development and use in mental health research and the IQOLA project. *Int J Mental Health* 1994;23:49–73.

25. Ware JE, Keller SD, Gandek B, Brazier JE, Sullivan M, and the IQOLA Project Group. Evaluating translations of health status questionnaires: methods from the IQOLA project. *Int J Technol Assess Health Care* 1995;11(3) (in press).

26. Ware JE, Sherbourne CD. The MOS 36-Item Short-Form Health Survey (SF-36): I. Conceptual framework and item selection. *Med Care* 1992;30:473–483.

27. Ware JE, Snow KK, Kosinski M, Gandek B. *SF-36 Health Survey manual and interpretation guide.* Boston, MA: New England Medical Center, The Health Institute, 1993.

28. McHorney CA, Ware JE, Raczek AE. The MOS 36-Item Short-Form Health Survey (SF-36): II. Psychometric and clinical tests of validity in measuring physical and mental health constructs. *Med Care* 1993;31:247–263.

29. Ware JE, Kosinski M, Bayliss MS, McHorney CA, Rogers WH, Raczek A. Comparison of methods for scoring and statistical analysis of SF-36 health profiles and summary measures: summary of results from the Medical Outcomes Study. *Med Care* 1995;33(Suppl 4) AS264–AS279.

30. Ware JE, Kosinski M, Keller SD. *SF-36 physical and mental health summary scales—a users' manual.* Boston, MA: New England Medical Center, The Health Institute, 1994.

31. Berwick DM, Murphy JM, Goldman PA, Ware JE, Barsky AJ, Weinstein MC. Performance of a five-item mental health screening test. *Med Care* 1991;29:169–176.

32. Cleary PD, Greenfield S, McNeil BJ. Assessing quality of life after surgery. *Controlled Clin Trials* 1991;12:189S–203S.

33. Gelberg L, Linn LS. Psychological distress among homeless adults. *J Nerv Ment Dis* 1989;177:291–295.

34. Lancaster TR, Singer DE, Sheehan MA, et al. The impact of long-term warfarin therapy on quality of life: evidence from a randomized trial. *Arch Intern Med* 1991;151:1944–1949.

35. Weinberger M, Samsa GP, Hanlon JT, et al. An evaluation of a brief health status measure in elderly veterans. *J Am Geriatr Soc* 1991;39:691–694.

36. McHorney CA, Ware JE, Lu JFR, Sherbourne CD. The MOS 36-Item Short-Form Health Survey (SF-36): III. Tests of data quality, scaling assumptions and reliability across diverse patient groups. *Med Care* 1994;32:40–66.

37. Liang J, Wu SC, Krause NM, Chiang TL, Wu HY. The structure of the mental health inventory among Chinese in Taiwan. *Med Care* 1992;30:659–676.

38. Brazier JE, Harper R, Jones NMB, et al. Validating the SF-36 health survey questionnaire: new outcome measure for primary care. *Br Med J* 1992;305:160–164.

39. Thalji L, Haggerty CC, Rubin R, Berckmans TR, Pardee, BL. *1990 National Survey of Functional Health Status: Final Report.* Chicago, IL: National Opinion Research Center, 1991.

40. McHorney CA, Kosinski M, Ware JE. Comparisons of the costs and quality of norms for the SF-36 Health Survey collected by mail versus telephone interview: results from a national survey. *Med Care* 1994;32:551–567.

41. Thurstone LL, Chave EJ. *The measurement of attitude.* Chicago: University of Chicago Press, 1929.

42. Marshall PA. Cultural influences on perceived quality of life. *Semin Oncol Nurs* 1990;6:278–284.

43. Zambrana RE. Cross-cultural methodologic strategies in the study of low income racial ethnic populations. In: Hibbard H, Nutting PA, Grady ML, eds. *Primary care research: theory and methods.* Rockville, MD: U.S. Department of Health and Human Services, 1991:221–227.

44. Aaronson NK, Ahmedzai S, Bergman B, et al. The European Organization for Research and Treatment of Cancer QLQ-C30: a quality-of-life instrument for use in international clinical trials in oncology. *J Natl Cancer Inst* 1993;85:365–376.

45. Gardner PL. Scales and statistics. *Rev Educ Res* 1975;45:43–57.

46. Pedhazur EJ, Schmelkin LP. *Measurement, design, and analysis: an integrated approach.* Hillsdale, NJ: Lawrence Erlbaum, 1991.

47. Davies AR, Ware JE. *Measuring health perceptions in the Health Insurance Experiment* (R-2711-HHS). Santa Monica, CA: Rand Corporation, 1981.

48. Stewart AL, Ware JE, eds. *Measuring functioning and well-being: The Medical Outcomes Study approach.* Durham, NC: Duke University Press, 1993.

49. Medical Outcomes Trust. *How to score the SF-36 Health Survey.* Boston: Medical Outcomes Trust, 1992.

50. Kleinman A, Eisenberg L, Good B. Culture, illness, and care: clinical lessons from anthropologic and cross-cultural research. *Ann Intern Med* 1978;88:251–258.
51. Likert R. A technique for the measurement of attitudes. *Arch Psychol* 1932;140:5–55.
52. Helmstadter GC. *Principles of psychological measurement.* New York: Appleton-Century-Crofts, 1964.
53. Howard KI, Forehand GG. A method for correcting item-total correlations for the effect of relevant item inclusion. *Educ Psychol Meas* 1962;22:731–735.
54. Nunnally JC, Bernstein IR. *Psychometric theory*, 3rd ed. New York: McGraw-Hill, 1994.
55. Campbell DT, Fiske DW. Convergent and discriminant validation by the multitrait-multimethod matrix. *Psychol Bull* 1959;56:81–105.
56. Stewart AL, Hays RD, Ware JE. *Methods of constructing health measures.* In: Stewart AL, Ware JE, eds. *Measuring functioning and well-being: The Medical Outcomes Study approach.* Durham, NC: Duke University Press, 1992:67–85.
57. Crocker L, Algina J. *Introduction to classical and modern test theory.* New York: Harcourt Brace Jovanovich, 1986.
58. Candell GL, Hulin CL. Cross-language and cross-cultural comparisons in scale translations: independent sources of information about item nonequivalence. *J Cross-Cultural Psychol* 1986;17:417–440.
59. Ellis BB, Kimmel HD. Identification of unique cultural response patterns by means of item response theory. *J Appl Psychol* 1992;77:177–184.
60. Hulin CL. A psychometric theory of evaluations of item and scale translations: fidelity across languages. *J Cross-Cultural Psychol* 1987;18:115–142.
61. Hulin CL, Drasgow F, Komocar J. Applications of item response theory to analysis of attitude scale translations. *J Appl Psychol* 1982;67:818–825.
62. Andrich D. *Rasch models for measurement.* Newbury Park, CA: Sage, 1988.
63. Haley SM, McHorney CA, Ware JE. Evaluation of the MOS SF-36 Physical Functioning scale (PF-10): I. Unidimensionality and reproducibility of the Rasch item scale. *J Clin Epidemiol* 1994;47:671–684.
64. Haley SM, McHorney CA, Ware JE. Evaluation of the MOS SF-36 Physical Functioning scale (PF-10): II. Comparison of relative precision using Likert and Rasch scoring methods. *J Clin Epidemiol* (in review).
65. Rasch BG. An item analysis which takes individual differences into account. *Br J Math Stat Psychol* 1966;19:49–57.
66. Raczek A, Haley SM, Brazier J, et al. Tests of scaling assumptions and improved scoring algorithms for the SF-36 Physical Functioning scales in seven countries: results from the IQOLA project. *J Clin Epidemiol* (Special Issue). (forthcoming).
67. Cronbach LJ. Coefficient alpha and the internal structure of tests. *Psychometrika* 1951;16:297–334.
68. Ware JE, Davies-Avery A, Donald CA. *Conceptualization and measurement of health for adults in the Health Insurance Study: Vol. V, General health perceptions* (R-1987/5-HEW). Santa Monica, CA: RAND Corporation, 1978.
69. Garratt AM, Ruta DA, Abdalla MI, Buckingham JK, Russell IT. The SF-36 health survey questionnaire: an outcome measure suitable for routine use within the NHS? *Br Med J* 1993;306:1440–1444.
70. Jenkinson C, Coulter A, Wright L. Short form 36 (SF-36) Health Survey Questionnaire: normative data for adults of working age. *Br Med J* 1993;306:1437–1440.
71. Jenkinson C, Wright L, Coulter A. *Quality of life measurement in health care: a review of measures and population norms for the UK SF-36.* Oxford, England: Health Services Research Unit, Department of Public Health and Primary Care, University of Oxford, 1993.
72. Jenkinson C, Wright L, Coulter A. Criterion validity and reliability of the SF-36 in a population sample. *Qual Life Res* 1994;3:7–12.
73. Almagor M, Ben-Porath YS. The two-factor model of self-reported mood: a cross-cultural replication. *J Pers Assess* 1989;53:10–21.
74. Bice TW, Kalimo E. Comparisons of health-related attitudes: a cross-national, factor analytic study. *Soc Sci Med* 1971;5:283–318.
75. Buss AR, Royce JR. Detecting cross-cultural commonalities and differences: intergroup factor analysis. *Psychol Bull* 1975;82:128–136.

76. Cattell RB. Comparing factor trait and state scores across ages and cultures. *J Gerontol* 1989;24:348–360.
77. Davidson AR, Jaccard JJ, Triandis HC, Morales ML, Diaz-Guerrero R. Cross-cultural model testing: toward a solution of the emic-etic dilemma. *Int J Psychol* 1976;11:1–13.
78. Dressler WW, Viteri FE, Chavez A, Grell GAC, Dos Santos JE. Comparative research in social epidemiology: measurement issues. *Ethnicity Dis* 1991;1:379–393.
79. Irvine SH. Adapting tests to the cultural setting: a comment. *Occup Psychol* 1965;39:13–23.
80. Harman HH. *Modern factor analysis.* Chicago: University of Chicago Press, 1976.
81. Ware JE, Keller S, Bentler PM, Sullivan M, Brazier J, Gandek B. Comparisons of health status measurement models and the validity of SF-36 in Great Britain, Sweden and the USA. *Qual Life Res* 1994;3:68.
82. Kerlinger FN. *Foundations of behavioral research.* New York: Holt, Rinehart and Winston, 1964.
83. Idler EL, Angel R. Self-rated health and mortality in the NHANES-I epidemiologic follow-up study. *Am J Public Health* 1990;80:446–452.
84. Idler EL, Kasl SV, Lemke JH. Self-evaluated health and mortality among the elderly in New Haven, Connecticut and Iowa and Washington counties, Iowa, 1982–1986. *Am J Epidemiol* 1990;13:91–103.
85. Stoller EP. Self-assessments of health by the elderly: the impact of informal assistance. *J Health Soc Behav* 1984;25:260–270.
86. Osterhaus JT, Townsend RJ, Gandek B, Ware JE. Measuring the functional status and well-being of patients with migraine headache. *Headache* 1994;34:337–343.
87. Phillips RC, Lansky DJ. Outcomes management in heart valve replacement surgery: early experience. *J Heart Valve Dis* 1992;1:42–50.
88. Brazier J, Jones N, Kind P. Testing the validity of the Euroqol and comparing it with the SF-36 Health Survey Questionnaire. *Qual Life Res* 1993;2:169–180.
89. Garratt AM, Macdonald LM, Ruta DA, Russell IT, Buckingham JK, Krukowski ZH. Towards measurement of outcome for patients with varicose veins. *Quality Health Care* 1993;2:5–10.
90. Garratt AM, Ruta DA, Abdalla MI, Russell IT. The SF-36 Health Survey Questionnaire: II. Responsiveness to changes in health status for patients with four common conditions. *Qual Health Care* 1994;3:186–192.
91. Jenkinson C, Wright L. The SF-36 Health Survey Questionnaire. *Auditorium* 1993;2:7–12.
92. Bousquet J, Knani J, Dhivert H, et al. Quality-of-life in asthma: I. Internal consistency and validity of the SF-36 questionnaire. *Am J Respir Crit Care Med* 1994;149:371–375.
93. vanTulder MW, Aaronson NK, Bruning PF. The quality of life of long-term survivors of Hodgkin's Disease. *Ann Oncol* 1994;5:152–158.
94. Ormel J, VonKorff M, Ustun TB, Pini S, Korten A, Oldehinkel T. Common mental disorders and disability across cultures: Results from the who collaborative study on psychological problems in general health care. *JAMA* 1994;272:1741–1748.
95. Angel R, Cleary PD. The effects of social structure and culture on reported health. *Soc Sci Q* 1984;65:814–828.
96. Angel R, Thoits P. The impact of culture on the cognitive structure of illness. *Cult Med Psychiatry* 1987;11:465–494.
97. Blanc H. Multilingual interviewing in Israel. *Am J Sociol* 1956;62:205–209.
98. Guyatt GH. The philosophy of health-related quality of life translation. *Qual Life Res* 1993;2:461–465.
99. Hunt WL, Crane WW, Wahlke JC. Interviewing political elites in cross-cultural comparative research. *Am J Sociol* 1964;70:59–68.
100. Hunt SM, McKenna S. Cross-cultural comparability of quality of life measures. *Br J Med Econ* 1992;4:17–23.
101. Medical Outcomes Trust. *Medical Outcomes Trust: improving medical outcomes from the patient's point of view.* Boston, MA: Medical Outcomes Trust, 1991.
102. Medical Outcomes Trust. *SF-36 Health Survey scoring manual for English language adaptations: Australia/New Zealand, Canada, United Kingdom.* Boston, MA: Medical Outcomes Trust, 1994.

Quality of Life and Pharmacoeconomics in Clinical Trials, Second Edition, edited by B. Spilker.
Lippincott-Raven Publishers, Philadelphia © 1996.

CHAPTER **72**

Applying Quality of Life Principles in International Cancer Clinical Trials

Jürg Bernhard, Christoph D. T. Hürny, Alan Coates, and Richard D. Gelber

INTRODUCTION

In recent years, quality of life has become recognized as an important end point in cancer clinical trials. Principles for measuring quality of life have been established, mostly as a secondary criterion in evaluating clinical trial outcomes. Most studies have been regional or national. Studying quality of life in international trials presents additional complexities.

Controlled clinical trials (phase III) require large sample sizes because clinical outcome differences among the treatment regimens are generally expected to be small. Therefore, patients are often enrolled from multiple institutions (1). In such trials, the demonstration of a relatively small benefit by the experimental treatment can have a major impact on health care. For example, the demonstration that adjuvant systemic therapy can prolong the disease-free interval and

improve overall survival in breast cancer patients has substantially changed treatment policy worldwide (2).

International collaboration has emerged in the past two decades in order to accrue sufficient numbers of patients to answer this type of research question in reasonable time periods. The methodology and logistics of these trials are constantly being improved and adapted to the evolution of clinical questions. In the past few years, risk/benefit evaluations in terms of treatment toxicity and survival time have been recognized as crucially important in studying questions of cancer treatment policy. One such approach has been applied in cancer clinical trials internationally (3). Patient-rated quality of life measures are important as additional end points for treatment comparison and provide a further complementary step in this development. Few quality of life data from international cancer clinical trials have been published. The question of cultural differences to be considered in this setting has just begun to receive attention (4).

The conventional biomedical end points for comparing cancer treatments (response of the tumor, disease-free and overall survival, toxicity) are well defined and relatively easy to assess. They can be applied in international trials without being adjusted for local logistics and resources, or for cultural differences in patients' perception of their disease and treatment. In contrast, quality of life measures in cancer clinical trials are usually applied from a broader perspective, in that they include a multidimensional concept

J. Bernhard: International Breast Cancer Study Group (IBCSG) Coordinating Center, CH-3007 Bern, Switzerland.

C. D. T. Hürny: Medical Division Lory, University Hospital Insel, CH-3010 Bern, Switzerland.

A. Coates: Department of Cancer Medicine, University of Sidney; Department of Medical Oncology, Royal Prince Alfred Hospital, Camperdown, NSW 2050 Australia.

R. D. Gelber: Department of Biostatistics, Harvard School of Public Health, Department of Pediatrics, Harvard Medical School, Dana-Farber Cancer Institute, Boston, Massachusetts 02115.

of patient functioning and subjective experience of disease and treatment. In an international setting, both cultural factors and feasibility issues are important in developing and selecting quality of life measures for clinical trials. Correspondingly, cultural factors need to be considered in data analysis and interpretation.

CONCEPTS, METHODS, AND FEASIBILITY

Quality of Life End Points from a Cross-Cultural Perspective

The term *quality* implies both a description and a valuation of an outcome. In applying any definition or operationalization of quality of life, cultural characteristics of the responding subjects need to be considered. Both *quality of life* and *culture* are intuitively understandable constructs for which a single standard definition is neither available nor desirable. In practical assessment of quality of life in clinical trials, it is appropriate to focus instead on a series of narrower, operational definitions for each particular application.

Quality of life end points used in cancer clinical trials have been focused on *health-related* concepts and definitions. Cultural factors such as language and race have been considered only insofar as they are expected to interfere with the measurement of quality of life. However, few data have been published comparing the subjective impact of cancer diseases and treatments among patients from different cultures. As is known from cross-cultural psychology and psychiatry, the perception of a chronic disease may vary considerably among different countries and cultures. In cancer patients, there is overwhelming clinical evidence that race, ethnicity, and other cultural factors have a substantial influence on the subjective impact of physical and psychological symptoms and on treatment decisions (5). Cultural differences are closely associated with key quality of life domains, such as family function. Similarly, cultural factors are an integral part of the way patients cope with disease and treatment sequelae, as seen in attitudes toward illness and health practices (5).

Pain is an informative example of a symptom that has been well studied cross-culturally. There is no convincing experimental evidence to suggest a physiologic basis for cultural differences in pain response. However, the perception of the pain threshold and the related behavior does vary across cultures. Thus, in a comparison of cancer pain in United States and Vietnamese patients, the latter reported higher pain severity but not more interference with general activities and other quality of life issues because of the pain (6).

Although patients from different cultures may record comparable quality of life scores, this similarity may hide differences based on facets of culturally different perceptions, attitudes, and habits. An isolated interpretation of symptoms or any aspect of quality of life without regard to their social and cultural context can therefore be misleading.

Subtle differences in perception are inherent in differences in the semantic structures of the languages involved. Implicit values and attitudes are part of any verbal language and therefore inextricably mingled with the language itself. In studying health-related quality of life across language and cultural barriers, the association between health and quality of life needs special attention. Factors constituting "health" are generally more difficult to define cross-culturally than those constituting "illness" (7).

A classic example for the *cultural relativity* of quality of life concepts is Maslow's (8) hierarchy of human needs. Maslow's theory has served as a model for many Western approaches in quality of life research in healthy individuals. His theory has had a clear impact in focusing on the disparity between personal needs or goals and actual achievements in defining quality of life and its basic domains. It may have served as an implicit model for quality of life in the medical setting. However, it reflects individualistic values based on typical U.S. middle class views from the 1950s and its value in an international context is uncertain (9).

Changes across time also need to be considered. Accrual and follow-up in international cancer clinical trials usually takes years. Within this time, there may be major changes in cultural values and socio-environmental factors within particular trial populations. Immigration and economic instability are well-known examples. For example, in comparing work-related values in countries throughout the world, shifts on dominant patterns were documented over a 4-year period; a consistent increase in individualism was observed after an increase in wealth (9,10). Such processes on the social level may be reflected in individual patients' perception of disease and treatment-related sequelae, such as impaired role functioning.

Culturally sensitive methods are needed when studying quality of life in international cancer trials. This prerequisite is not unique for the international setting. Significant racial, ethnic, and socio-enviornmental diversity can be a factor even within local cancer clinical trials, an issue that has not received sufficient attention in the past.

From a theoretical point of view, a quality of life instrument that compares quality of life "culture-free," or investigates cultural factors contributing to health-related quality of life systematically and in depth, may be unachievable, given the inherent interdependence between an observer's cultural background and theoretical orientation and his or her perception of the "object" involved. From a practical and economical point of view, achieving a high standard cross-culturally is extremely demanding. Such an approach is needed in comprehensive health surveys.

However, for cancer clinical trials a more pragmatic approach is appropriate. We need to develop simple measures that can be applied across cultures while keeping in mind each measure's cultural background and limitations. Most accurately, such an approach is based on *subjective measures* where the responder's individual, social, and cultural factors form part of any estimation or judgment (11). These factors may be investigated and controlled for as required when comparing cancer treatments. They will help to answer the question about how a particular quality of life approach is perceived in the different cultures.

Selecting and Developing Quality of Life Measures

The basic assumption is that it is possible to develop psychometrically sound measures for quality of life end points in large-scale international cancer clinical trials. Patient-rated questionnaires based on a multidimensional concept of patient functioning and subjective experience of disease and treatment have become a standard for quality of life assessment in cancer clinical trials. They include distinct domains on the physical, mental, emotional, and social levels. From an international perspective, there are three questions that need to be addressed: (a) Which quality of life approach should be selected to answer the study question? (b) What measurement standard needs to be met? (c) How can this measurement standard be met cross-culturally? The specific conceptual, methodological, and feasibility issues in assessing quality of life in international cancer clinical trials are summarized in Table 1.

Which Quality of Life Approach Should be Selected to Answer the Study Question?

In selecting a quality of life approach and particular quality of life domains the main purpose of a large-scale international cancer clinical trial needs to be considered: In a comparative clinical trial, of primary interest is the difference in quality of life between treatments. Quality of life is usually not comprehensively described; rather treatments are compared with regard to their impact on patients' quality of life. This distinction has two theoretical implications for the choice of the measurement approach. First, the measurement can be focused on those domains that are thought from previous, usually smaller, investigations to be of clinical relevance in the target population for differentiating treatments to be compared. Second, for comparing treatments a limited set of indices and global estimations reflecting the basic quality of life domains is more appropriate than comparing numerous facets of quality of life in full detail.

In practice, this distinction is handled less stringently for two reasons. First, extra information in addition to the key domains is necessary to interpret outcome data of a specific trial with a specific question. In estimating the risk/benefit of a treatment, clinicians are interested in the relative impact of the symptoms of disease versus the side effects of treatment on patients' quality of life. Assessing disease and treatment-related symptoms, both general and specific, is complementary to more global measures of well-being and functioning. Studying their association over time and in relation to the biomedical variables can give insight into underlying interactions (12). In an international setting such a "modular" approach is useful to investigate the *culture-specific perception* of disease and treatment-related sequelae.

Second, the more pragmatic question of selecting the key domains is closely related to the task of choosing the appropriate measurement instrument. An instrument is both from its conceptualization and its methodology to be seen as an entity and in general has to be used as a whole. A study-specific adjustment by selecting or omitting particular subscales or items is only appropriate under specific circumstances. This is particularly important in cross-cultural trials where the original version of an instrument serves as reference for the culturally adapted versions. Another approach would be to assemble a battery of instruments or particular components of various instruments that are specifically fo-

TABLE 1. *Specific conceptual, methodological, and feasibility issues in assessing quality of life in large-scale international cancer clinical trials*

Selection of a quality of life approach and particular domains
    Potential cultural variation in perception of disease and treatment related sequelae
    Relevance to treatment comparison (based on previous smaller investigations)
    Simplicity in consideration of the logistic complexities within an international setting
Development and cross-cultural adaptation of instruments
    Trade-off between measurement precision and cross-cultural commonality
    Cross-cultural equivalence regarding conceptual, linguistic, and scaling issues
    Potential cultural variation in responsiveness
Implementation of the instruments
    Feasibility study of data collection procedures within an international setting
    Documentation of differences in procedures and events unique to particular countries and institutions, especially timing of assessments, antiemetic investigations and supportive care interventions
Data analysis
    Investigation of degree of cross-cultural equivalence in measurement instruments
    Investigation of culture-dependent nonresponse bias (i.e., biomedical, sociodemographic, and baseline quality of life data)
    Stratification of treatment outcome analysis according to language/cultural groups to obtain an overall effect measure

cused on the question of the trial. However, the properties of the resulting instrument would require investigation. The methodological limitations of this approach have been discussed elsewhere (13).

In addition, the possibilities to interpret outcome differences are substantially expanded if a measure is sensitive to comparisons across interventions or conditions. Within cancer diagnoses and therapies this might be the case in most of the cancer-specific quality of life instruments, but a cross-cultural data base may not yet be accessible. For some study questions, such as in prevention trials, it is of particular value to compare outcome differences in quality of life across other chronic diseases or with normative data from healthy individuals. A generic instrument is required for this purpose, but few of these are available with cross-cultural normative data.

What Measurement Standard Needs to be Met?

Cross-cultural equivalence—the key criterion in cross-cultural research—applies to all phases of carrying out a trial, from designing and conducting the trial to analyzing and interpreting the results (14). It is especially critical in instrument development.

Precision and *commonality* are two basic issues that need to be considered (15), as displayed in Fig.1: There is a negative relationship between precison and level of abstraction in assessing a given construct. For example, frequency of vomiting reflects a concrete treatment side effect that can be assessed relatively precisely and may result in an outcome difference in an international chemotherapy trial. However, it is not known to what extent an effect on this measure actually reflects the subjective impact of vomiting on quality of life in the different cultures involved. To answer this question, "commonality" among the cultures needs to be established. Commonality is defined as the subjective equivalence of a construct among cultures. It can be achieved by moving up to a higher abstraction level. There is a positive relationship between commonality and level of abstraction of a given construct. Asking about the *burden* related to vomiting would help to answer the question but at the expense of precision. Similarly, in some cultures "vomiting" may be perceived as more closely associated to "nausea" and related physical discomfort than in others; asking globally about "physical well-being" (a relatively abstract construct) would capture this information cross-culturally, but again at the expense of measurement precision. Thus, the aim of psychometric testing in the development of cross-cultural instruments is to maximize meaningfulness by

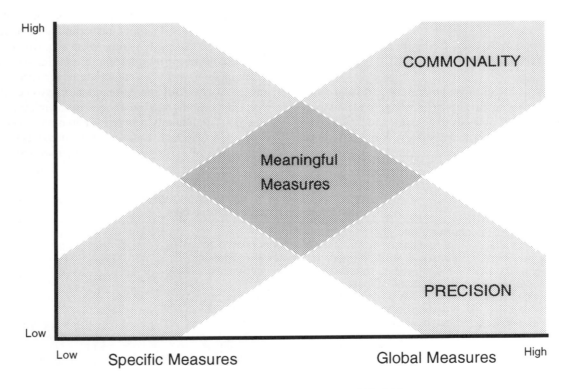

FIG. 1. Precision and commonality in cross-cultural quality of life assessment as a function of the abstraction level of a construct. The *shaded area* indicates the target range in formulating cross-cultural items.

achieving acceptable commonality at the expense of some precision.

The question is not how to reach optimal psychometric sophistication but how criteria of psychometrics and feasibility can be suitably combined. In the early years of quality of life research in oncology no cancer-specific instruments were available; lengthy, comprehensive generic and psychiatric scales were used. Although not cancer specific and therefore likely to be less sensitive, this approach fully met the standards of ''classical'' test theory; from this theoretical point of view, comprehensive scales are generally regarded as more reliable and valid than shorter ones. Practical experience gained from applying quality of life measures in cancer clinical trials, however, has made clear that feasibility issues, such as acceptability of the instruments, respondent burden, and the costs of data collection and processing, are of major importance in this setting. Consequently, shorter, cancer-specific instruments have been developed. They measure only selected concepts and include fewer items (16,17). This attention toward feasibility is particularly relevant for international trials.

In comparing treatments the key measurement issue is whether an instrument is responsive to clinically important changes even if these changes are small (18). For equally responsive measures, however, a measure with small variance will detect a smaller clinical change than will a measure with large variance. Statistically significant changes in measures may be too small to be clinically relevant. On the other hand, in certain situations the clinically relevant differences may be finer than those easily detectable. Therefore, sample size considerations may influence the selection of the measurement approach. Given that international cancer clinical trials include hundreds or even thousands of patients, differences in outcome may be detected even by relatively rough measures. Hence, considering cost-effectiveness (e.g., psychometric performance, feasibility issues and costs), measurement approaches differ in a large-scale trial compared with a small-scale or an intermediate-sized one.

The power of a measure to detect a clinically important difference may vary across languages and cultures. This may be due to methodological shortcomings (e.g., poor translation or scaling in particular language versions). Alternatively, such variations may reflect cultural differences in the perception and weighting of disease and treatment sequelae, such as a tendency to stoic self-control or exasperated emotional expression in particular cultures. It is unsafe to assume *a priori* that a measure's sensitivity as well as specificity is robust cross-culturally, even if the measure is linguistically adapted across these cultures. In addition to the standard reliability and validity criteria, we recommend investigating the *culture-specific responsiveness* of the applied measures and not just interpreting international quality of life data overall. Criteria concerning how to estimate a quality of life measure's responsiveness have been discussed elsewhere (19,20).

How Can This Measurement Standard be Met Cross-Culturally?

There are basically two options. Investigators may develop a new quality of life measure and thereby include the cultures to be investigated in all steps of the instrument development, from initial conceptualization to clinical validation and establishment of norms. This strategy offers a solid ground for an approach with high cross-cultural validity focusing even on subtle cultural differences in the perception of quality of life domains. However, this approach is extremely demanding in both time and economic resources. A model for such a strategy and measurement development has been presented by the World Health Organization (WHO) (21). The WHO Quality of Life (WHOQOL) instrument is a generic measure designed for multiple clinical and research functions.

One quality of life instrument specifically developed for international cancer clinical trials is the QLQ-C30 questionnaire created by the European Organization for Research and Treatment of Cancer (EORTC) (22). Issues particularly relevant for subgroups of patients are assessed by supplementary cancer site–specific modules (23). The QLQ-C30 has been developed and field-tested in a collaborative effort across Western European countries, Canada, Australia, and Japan. The result is an instrument particularly well suited for international trials.

An alternative to the specific development of instruments for the international setting is to transpose a measure previously developed in a single culture to other cultures. The inventory of both generic and cancer-specific quality of life instruments with a reasonable basis of validation data at least in one culture has been considerably widened in the last several years. The vast majority of these instruments have been developed in Anglo-Saxon cultures and might provide the starting point for selecting and adapting measures corresponding to the particular end points of the trial. Overall, this option is more efficient and economical than developing a new instrument.

Transposing a quality of life measure to other languages or cultures is a subtle multistep process. In regard to questionnaire adaptation several distinct conceptual and linguistic types of equivalence and the more formal issue of scalar equivalence need to be considered (14,15,24). Guidelines and recommendations for cross-cultural adaptation have been established (14,23–25).

Guillemin et al. (24) have suggested a standard approach and explored the quality of cross-cultural adaptation among 17 health-related quality of life measures. Their findings indicate that this phase of instrument development is often neither openly described nor appropriately carried out. There are particular caveats to consider both in instrument development and application. For example, if a questionnaire is originally developed in English in the U.S., immigrants, who may know English sufficiently well to answer the questionnaire in this language may still refer to their native culture in estimating the subjective impact of disease and treatment-related sequelae.

Despite careful conceptual and linguistic adaptation, the weighting of content of items may vary across cultures. Items pertaining to the emotional and social experience are particularly sensitive to this problem (7,26). For example, in a comparison of weightings given to the items of the Nottingham Health Profile (NHP) (27), a generic instrument from England, a high agreement was found between Swedish and English samples (patients and healthy individuals) (26). However, there were a few discrepancies; for example, "I wake up feeling depressed" was viewed with much greater seriousness by the English and "I've forgotten what it is like to enjoy myself" was ranked as more severe by the Swedes. In such cases the items need to be recalibrated to achieve scalar equivalence. A measure has scalar equivalence if it can be demonstrated that the construct is measured on the same metric.

Scalar equivalence is important for any scaling procedure and its measurement criteria, such as ranking of preferences, estimating utilities, or aggregating items to (summary) scale scores. It is the most difficult to achieve. It is also difficult to achieve in those measures that are developed on the assumption of a linear fit between item and scale scores (i.e., equal item weights). To develop weights in an adapted version, the same method should be applied as in the original version. These methods include the basic psychometric techniques in scale development and validation, for example, factor analysis for dimensionality, testing against external criteria, or expert ratings for face validity. There is no absolute test of equivalence for any instrument. Therefore, multiple complementary strategies have to be used, each dealing with one or two types of equivalence. Hui and Triandis (15) present a comprehensive methodological framework for assessing the different types of equivalence. It is also helpful to use a common reference scale for all cultures involved, such as the EORTC QLQ-C30 (22).

The NHP (27) has been adapted to various European countries by the European Group for Health Measurement and Quality of Life Assessment (25). A finding in adapting the French version suggests that the variation in item weights within a country among different sociodemographic groups may be comparable to or even exceed the variation across countries (28); the most discordance was found in the physical mobility domain. Socioeconomic factors are of special concern. If these findings are confirmed the comparative interpretation of quality of life outcomes in international cancer clinical trials will become even more difficult, since sociodemographic factors of patients randomized are likely to vary among institutions both within a country and across countries or language groups, respectively.

The question of whether the treatment differences indicated by a quality of life measure are important to the patient's own perception of his or her quality of life is especially relevant in international trials. Values and preferences may not just be different among cultural groups and individuals but also change within individuals over time and across different situations (e.g., progress of disease). One strategy for the trade-off between measurement precision and cross-cultural commonality is to complementarily assess measures on different levels of abstraction among the cultures involved and investigate their relationship and their responsiveness to different clinical situations.

In the International Quality of Life Assessment project, the Medical Outcomes Study Short Form Health Survey (SF-36) (29), a generic instrument developed in the U.S., is being adapted to various American, European, and Asian cultures, and population norms for each country involved are being generated (30). It is expected that the normed scales and indices will eventually allow comparisons of the relative benefits of different treatments in various diseases across countries.

The question of relevance of population norms for quality of life end points in international cancer clinical trials needs further attention. From a methodological point of view it may shed new light on a clinical phenomenon described since the beginning of quality of life research in oncology. There is some evidence that patients, in contrast to physicians, are not evaluating their current well-being and health status in reference to previous health, but in the process of becoming and staying ill are "reframing" their reference points (i.e., adopting the point of view of a sick person) (31). This reframing possibly explains why patients with cancer or other chronic diseases, when tested with standard psychometric tests, such as for psychological distress (32), show scores in the same range or even better, than samples of healthy individuals. It is not known whether this process varies among cultures.

Achieving cross-cultural equivalence is probably less complex in single-item compared with multi-item scales. Especially in the linear analog self-assessment (LASA) format, where only the two poles of a 10-cm line are labeled with words describing the two extremes of the item content, calibration may be simpler. From a practical point of view this approach responds to the need for a flexible as well as specific instrument. It is adaptable to questions where no appropriate measures are available. In addition, single-item scales are attractive in regard to respondent burden. However, the tendency toward simplicity may result in measurement instruments that are too insensitive to reflect key differences (33). Only by psychometric testing can this pitfall be avoided.

Single-item scales have shown satisfying concurrent validity in many studies in cancer patients, particularly in the LASA format (34). Still, sound multi-item scales that include stable, consistently discriminating factors are theoretically expected to have a higher reliability and validity compared with single-item scales. Hence, in the setting of a clinical trial, larger variances not explained by the treatment intervention might well be found for scores from single-item scales. However, in international cancer clinical trials, which often include large numbers of patients, some loss in precision may not be very relevant (35).

Based on these considerations and on previous studies in metastatic breast cancer (36,37), the International Breast Cancer Study Group (IBCSG) has developed and implemented global indicators of components of quality of life in the LASA format for large international trials in which comprehensive scales are less feasible (4). In global estimations and judgments, the score reflects a patient's subjective, intuitive choice and weighting of different aspects, summarized in a single response. From this point of view, global judgments are an alternative to the predefined weighting system of multi-item scales for cross-cultural comparisons (38). Specific disease and treatment-related symptoms can also be assessed and their changing impact on the global measures can be examined in different cultures, over time, and across different situations (e.g., on/off treatment).

In summary, in developing and adapting quality of life measures for international cancer clinical trials at present there are more questions than answers. No recommendations can be given about numerical standards of cross-cultural equivalence to be achieved in the setting of a cancer clinical trial. More data are needed to validly estimate cultural effects on patient ratings of health-related quality of life measures or to draw any final conclusion about the relevance of this phenomenon for cancer treatment comparisons. Estimating minimal clinically relevant changes has been neglected in most measures and studies, even within a single culture or nation. Cross-cultural head-to-head comparisons of potential measures might make a substantial contribution to instrument development. The conceptual and methodological issues summarized in Table 1 are mainly based on theoretical assumptions and need to be confirmed by clinical trial data. This is the main challenge for the future.

Including Sociodemographic Data

In international cancer clinical trials it is helpful to compare the sociodemographic characteristics of patients in the trial with both the national and international populations to estimate to what extent the sample reflects the population. In addition, sociodemographic factors are associated with general health. Socioeconomic factors, in particular, are major predictors of mortality (39,40). They have been shown to predict cancer survival (41,42), yet in cancer clinical trials this information has rarely been assessed. Demographic characteristics are also often related to patients' quality of life. Therefore, it is important to collect this information and to examine its relationship with both quality of life and biomedical outcomes.

As in quality of life assessment, however, trade-offs must be made between the ideal of obtaining comprehensive sociodemographic information and the feasibility of collecting these data. For example, because of the diversity of school systems a detailed standard international assessment for education or occupation is generally not feasible. In addition to the core demographic data (age, gender, race, marital status, employment status) and depending upon the specific cultures involved and upon the objectives of the trial, we recommend that at least one indicator of socioeconomic status, such as educational level, be assessed.

Data Collection and Management

Compliance with patient-rated quality of life questionnaires has been a key issue in the development of quality of life measures in cancer clinical trials (43–46). Whereas a comprehensive quality of life approach may be feasible within a multicenter trial conducted within a single country, an international setting adds complexity to logistics and monitoring and therefore sets further limitations.

There is a general agreement that the conventional methods for data collection and management developed in the 1960s for multicenter cancer clinical trials need to be modified for quality of life assessment. Much of the information required for biomedical assessment can be obtained retrospectively from the hospital's medical records. Quality of life data, however, must be assessed directly from the patient at predefined time points. Staff and patients must make additional effort in order to get an acceptable compliance rate and data quality. Several approaches have been suggested, including interviewing patients by telephone (47), mailing questionnaires, restricting quality of life assessment to selected, specially equipped centers only, and developing a quality of life approach that is simple enough to be easily integrated into clinical routine. Specific recommendations for international trials cannot be given because issues of study design, specific end points, and economic resources need to be considered in each trial. The various approaches may have an impact not just on compliance but also on nonresponse bias, data quality, and patient-rated scores (48).

In analogy to the two models for measuring quality of life proposed by Guyatt et al. (49), the various ways of data collection can be subsumed in two basic approaches. The "Rolls-Royce" approach is for investigators with substantial resources who are interested in a comprehensive quality of life assessment. In this approach all institutions participating in the clinical trial also participate in the quality of life assessment. In each institution, sufficient research staff with no other conflicting duties is available for all steps of data collection and local data management. This approach results in excellent compliance and data quality; it is often utilized in small studies. The "Volkswagen" approach is for investigators with limited resources who are tailoring the quality of life assessment to the specific end points of the trial. This approach also often includes all institutions participating in the trial but the different steps of data collection and local data management are carried out by members of the local staff who work on non–quality of life aspects of the study. Therefore, special measures for good compliance and data quality are necessary. Large-scale international cancer clinical trials are usually conducted using this approach. Hence, a quality of life instrument proposed for use in international trials has to be feasible within these limitations.

The most common approach to assessing quality of life in large-scale trials is to integrate questionnaires into the *clinical routine* at selected time points during patient treatment and follow-up. Practical guidelines are summarized in Table 2. Many of these also apply to trials within a single country, but they are especially important within a large-scale international trial.

The key problem in an international trial is that the logistics for managing patient care differ widely among institutions. Given a "Volkswagen" approach, the central data management staff must design procedures that are flexible enough to meet specific local needs. It is essential to have one person in each local institution who is responsible for coordination of quality of life assessment and for communication both within the local institution and with the central

data managers and study coordinator. Because accrual and follow-up in these trials takes many years, changes in local staff are likely to occur. Therefore, ongoing quality monitoring and supervision are critical.

As shown in cancer trials conducted both on a national (46) and an international level (4), good compliance with repeated quality of life assessments is possible with this approach but requires special effort. Issues affecting compliance in an international setting are much the same as those in a national setting, but are more complex due to the differences in local logistics, treatment policies, resources, and patient populations (e.g., socioeconomic and cultural factors). In our experience, the primary reasons for poor compliance are local administrative problems, especially forgetting to present the questionnaire to the patient.

On the patients' side poor compliance is not only due to the demand of repeatedly filling in questionnaires, but also to how the questionnaire is presented to the patient. Appropriate instruction needs to be given, including the purpose of the study, and misunderstandings have to be clarified (50). A similar experience has been described in regard to patients' withdrawal from cytotoxic treatment. Such decisions are

TABLE 2. *Practical guidelines for the implementation of quality of life assessment in large-scale international cancer clinical trials*

Study design and protocol development
  Quality of life assessment as an integral part of the trial, not optional; objectives, methods, and guidelines explicitly stated in the protocol
  Consultation with all study participants during protocol development, including with patients in pilot phase
Central data management
  Central study coordinator with regular, ongoing contact with responsible local coordinators; individualized feedback complementing regular standardized feedback across all institutions
  At the time of randomization, notification of all required assessment dates to the local data managers
  Completed quality of life questionnaire required as eligibility criterion for randomization (46); if not feasible, remind the physician at randomization to have the patient fill in the baseline questionnaire
  Joint organization of management of quality of life data and biomedical data
  Promotion of exchange of experience across institutions by group meetings
  Training of the local data managers concerning goals and methodology of the study and of the need for a standardized data collection setting
  Feedback to institutions about evolution of the study (compliance, preliminary results) on a regular basis (group meetings, newsletter)
Institution
  Support by the head of the department by providing time and space for quality of life assessments
  Avoiding patient selection for quality of life assessment (e.g., by socioeconomic status, or exclusion of randomized patients from a distant satellite clinic)
  One responsible person for local coordination of data collection and management who is fluent in the language in which the study is being conducted
Local data management
  Information to the patient about goals of the study and need for completion of the questionnaire
  Assistance to the patient in questionnaire completion (as much as necessary, as little as possible)
  Clarification of misunderstandings (e.g., questionnaire not a psychodiagnostic tool, or a substitute for physician-patient interview)
  Explanation of reasons for repetitive assessments and motivation of the patient
Questionnaire (self-rating)
  Simple self-explanatory instructions
  Short enough to be filled in within routine clinical visit
  Cross-culturally adapted formulation of instruction and items
  Uniform response format (as far as possible)

Modified from ref. 45.

related not only to actual toxicity and tumor symptoms but also to how the treatment is presented to the patient (51). Poorly educated patients may have difficulties understanding questionnaires and may need special assistance (43).

The willingness to fill out forms and questionnaires generally varies between cultures. Whereas in some cultures it has become routine, in others it may be perceived as an invasion of privacy. Correspondingly, some quality of life domains are more difficult to assess in some cultures than in others; sexuality and body image are examples. In our experience, discomfort with a particular domain may also be a problem for nurses and physicians, who may hesitate to present these questions to patients. Asking patients for sociodemographic data has also been found to be a sensitive issue for both patients and medical staff in some cultures. Cross-cultural pilot testing is essential in order to prove feasibility and to determine how these issues might be handled. To avoid misunderstandings and biases, quality of life assessment procedures must be standardized as much as possible.

In summary, feasibility issues are crucial in applying quality of life principles in cancer clinical trials internationally. Clinical hypothesis testing and its methodological requirements may clearly conflict with practical limitations of an international setting. A group experienced in the logistics of data collection in multi-center trials and methods tailored to the specific setting of an international trial is necessary.

Standardizing Data Collection

An acceptable compliance rate is usually considered a sufficient measure for data quality, assuming that questionnaires received at the office for central data management have been filled in in the local institutions according to the rules and guidelines stated in the study protocol. This may be a valid assumption in local and regional trials, where the setting of data collection can relatively easily be standardized and monitored, and where funding may be available for specifically trained research staff (i.e., ''Rolls-Royce'' approach).

Given a ''Volkswagen'' approach in international trials, there may be local modifications or violations of the standards specified in the protocol that are cumbersome to monitor and control for. A typical example is that on a busy oncology ward the interaction between the patient and the primary physician can influence a patient's answers to the questionnaire (50); for example, a discussion of anticipated health problems before a patient fills in the questionnaire may influence the patient's responses.

In our experience, two institutional issues need special emphasis in studying quality of life end points internationally: timing of assessments and conflicting overlap with local research studies and supportive care interventions.

Exact *timing* of quality of life assessment is very im-

portant, as the timing may have an impact on patient self-estimation. This is especially true for the timing in relation to the intervention being studied. In scheduling chemo- and radiotherapy a certain flexibility is usually provided by the study protocol. For practical reasons, the quality of life assessment is linked to clinical treatment or follow-up visits. Because of this, time constraints of medical staff are a serious problem and may cause imprecise timing. This is especially true for the baseline quality of life assessment, which is frequently done either on the first day of chemotherapy or a few days before. At this time many clinical and laboratory examinations must be completed, the institution must obtain the patient's informed consent, and in most trials the patient must be randomized. As described for breast cancer patients receiving adjuvant chemotherapy, variation in baseline timing of quality of life assessment can have a substantial influence on patient self-estimation (52). It is reasonable to assume that timing of assessments following baseline also affect the quality of life scores in trials where acute and subacute side effects of a toxic regimen are being investigated.

Variations in timing of quality of life assessment may be linked to variations in timing of treatment. Not only medical factors (e.g., toxicity, comorbidity), but also institutional factors, patient characteristics, and staff's attitude may play a role, and are therefore of particular concern in an international setting. In the international breast cancer trial cited above, time from definitive surgery to start of chemotherapy was shorter for premenopausal than for postmenopausal patients; also, among postmenopausal patients, chemotherapy started later than endocrine therapy. The median time for definitive surgery to adjuvant therapy varied considerably from institution to institution, but the timing pattern for the three above-mentioned subgroups was similar within each institution (52). Oncologists probably have more concern about recovery from surgery for older than for younger patients and for patients receiving toxic chemotherapy than for those receiving endocrine therapy. The question of timing effects on patient self-estimation of quality of life measures needs further systematic investigation.

Overlap with local studies or supportive care interventions are also likely in international trials and may influence patient-rated quality of life measures. This is specially relevant for behavioral interventions focused on the subjective tolerance of chemo- or radiotherapy. Also, psychosocial support programs may be standard in some institutions, or in some countries but not in others. A detailed assessment of antiemetic treatment and local antiemetic trials is desirable but may not be feasible in all centers participating in a large-scale trial. Responses to quality of life questions exploring nausea and vomiting may then be systematically different at those institutions performing the more detailed investigation. Institutional variation in ancillary quality of life investigations, interventions, and data collection procedures should be documented.

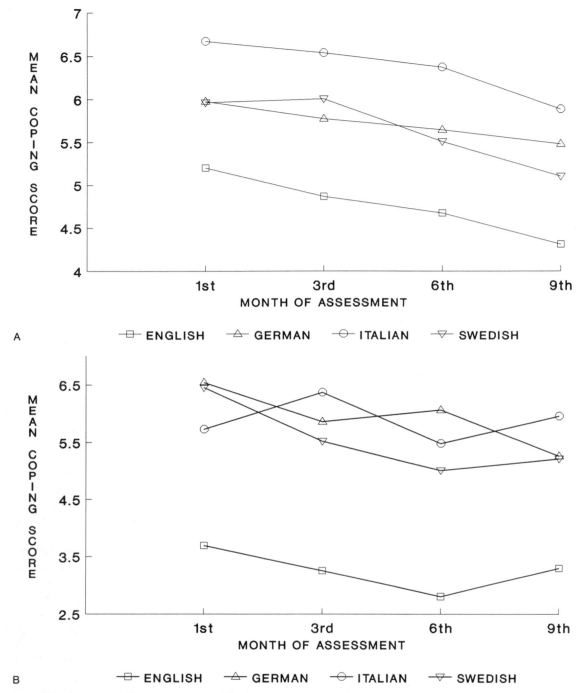

FIG. 2. Mean of the square roots of scores for the PACIS (coping) scale according to language for 154 premenopausal (**A**) and 111 postmenopausal (**B**) patients. Squared scores range from 0 to 10, with a higher score indicating more effort to cope. (From ref. 4, with permission.)

Statistical Considerations

In an international setting the measurement of quality of life across cultures must be as equivalent as possible. The measures must be examined in regard to internal reliability and validity; for multi-item scales, this examination must include weights applied to the individual items. The multidimensionality of the construct of quality of life adds to the difficulty of achieving reliability and validity cross-culturally.

Cultural factors can influence quality of life measures in two ways (53). First, they may affect the *pattern* of relationship among measures. For example, although pain is expected to correlate positively with functional disability, in one culture the two measures may show a linear relationship and in another a nonlinear one. Such pattern effects are less likely with a carefully developed instrument, but their possible presence should still be investigated by intracultural analyses. A consistent relationship among conceptually related domains across language or other cultural subgroups is an indication of cross-cultural construct validity. Second, the patterns of the relationships among the measures can be the same among cultures, but the average magnitude of the responses may differ among cultures. This kind of *position* effect may reflect methodological shortcomings, as well as cultural differences, institutional factors (e.g., differences in antiemetic treatment), or random variation.

The effect of cultural differences may be greater than the impact of treatment modalities. In an analysis of serial quality of life data in patients with operable breast cancer randomized into two IBCSG trials of adjuvant therapy, language was the factor that explained most of the variance (4). The language and time effects within four language groups and across the first 9 months of adjuvant treatment (chemotherapy, endocrine therapy, or combination) are displayed in Fig. 2, which shows as an example the mean values of a single-item indicator for perceived adjustment (54). For both pre- and postmenopausal patients there is a general decline in scores over time, indicating that over time less effort is required to cope with the disease. The responses of the patients to the English scale are consistently lower than for other languages for both pre- and postmenopausal patients, and the Italian scale yields responses that are higher for the premenopausal group. The pattern of scores across time is similar throughout, illustrating the absence of a language by time interaction. Thus, in these trials, analyses of quality of life changes over time can be based upon data pooled across language.

Cultural effects can be adjusted for by stratifying the quality of life analysis according to language or cultural group. In this way, the treatment comparisons are performed within strata and the results are combined across strata to obtain an overall treatment effect measure. In cases where it can be demonstrated that the treatment effect is the same within each language/culture, simply adjusting the analysis by including an effect for language/culture in the statistical model will often be sufficient.

Missing data is a major problem in international trials of quality of life. Although some data may be assumed to be missing randomly, as, for example, because of an occasional oversight by research staff, frequently data are missing on a nonrandom basis. For example, data may be available preferentially from those patients with relatively good quality of life or from those who are satisfied with their physician and treatment. Strategies for handling missing data in the analysis of longitudinal measures have been developed and are discussed elsewhere (see chapter by Fairclough and Gelber). In an international trial, the reasons for missing

data may be culturally dependent. As part of the analysis, the subset of cases with quality of life data should be compared with the subset without in regard to biomedical and sociodemographic variables, both overall and within each cultural group. Nonresponse bias in follow-up can be estimated in comparing the baseline scores of compliant and noncompliant patients. Compliance rates and data quality also need to be compared cross-culturally.

LIMITATIONS AND OPPORTUNITIES OF AN INTERNATIONAL SETTING

Interpreting Quality of Life Data and Applying the Results in Clinical Decision Making

Several potential biases need to be considered when interpreting international quality of life data. First, the clinical relevance of quality of life differences among the compared treatments may be interpreted from a particular culture's point of view (i.e., "ethnocentric" interpretation). For example, in a trial comparing in- and outpatient treatments, an outcome difference in impairment of social activities and family life would be judged differently in cultures with a strong family identification and a rich familial network (e.g., Mediterranean cultures) compared with more individualistic cultures where personal responsibility has a higher value and family life is focused on the nuclear family (e.g., U.S. Caucasians).

Uncritically interpreting quality of life findings across cultures may introduce a further bias in applying results of clinical trials in individual decision making. Not just the relative importance of the multiple domains of "quality" of survival, but also the importance of "quantity" of survival may differ among cultures. Therefore, the factors that influence treatment choice may differ, too. This applies to both patients and physicians. In addition to fairly objective biomedical features, nonmedical factors are known to influence medical decisions; for example, in a population-based study of patients with non–small cell lung cancer in two rural U.S. states, choice of treatment was found to vary according to social and economic factors (55). Including cross-cultural quality of life data adds complexity to this problem.

Specific cultural biases in patient selection within cultural groups may confound trial results, leading to the incorrect conclusion of cultural differences in quality of life (i.e., "ecological fallacy"). If differences in quality of life among culture groups are found, institutional factors and patient characteristics need to be considered before concluding that there are "true" cultural differences in the perception of disease and treatment. For example, in some countries patients with a higher socioeconomic status are more likely to participate in cancer clinical trials, whereas in other countries they are less likely to participate.

Given the current state of cross-cultural research in psycho-oncology, quality of life data in international cancer clinical trials have to be interpreted with caution. More information is needed about the perception and understanding of cancer and its treatment in various cultures. International cancer clinical trials offer an ideal testing ground to investigate whether or not the quality of life results of a clinical trial can be generalized across cultures.

In-Depth Parallel Studies within Subgroups

To further understand the clinical relevance of the quality of life measures applied in an international trial from a culture-specific point of view, subgroups of patients can be investigated in more depth in selected centers. For example, generic or culture-specific instruments can be administered along with the trial instrument within one country (presupposing no interfering effects). This strategy may also provide complementary information for interpreting cross-cultural differences.

In a comparative investigation of a single-item indicator for perceived adjustment in a subset of patients enrolled in IBCSG adjuvant breast cancer trials, we found quite different patterns of specific disease and treatment-related problems experienced and coping strategies used by Italian Swiss as compared to German Swiss patients (54). This resulted in an effect by language/culture interaction on the mean values of the global indicator stable over time (Fig. 2). For example, Italian Swiss patients showed a greater tendency to express emotional problems than German Swiss patients. Furthermore, the impact of biomedical and sociodemographic data varied. For example, in German Swiss patients, nodal status had a strong impact on perceived adjustment, whereas no association was found in Italian Swiss patients. Similarly, education had a strong impact in Italian Swiss patients only. Such culture or institution-related differences do not preclude treatment comparisons across cultures, provided that a measure with sufficient commonality and precision is used that captures the multiple factors on a single dimension (see Fig. 1).

Introducing an Epidemiological Perspective

Bio-psycho-social interactions, such as biomedical predictors of psychosocial adjustment, or, conversely, coping and social support as predictors of survival, are usually studied in small cohorts where psychosocial variables can be assessed comprehensively, but where there is considerable heterogeneity in biomedical factors. In contrast, in an international cancer clinical trial, it is not feasible to do a comprehensive assessment of quality of life and socioeconomic status. However, the large biomedically homogeneous sample and well-documented follow-up offer an excellent opportunity for generating epidemiological hypotheses.

CONCLUSIONS

Quality of life can be assessed in international cancer clinical trials, provided the analysis is conducted by a group experienced in the logistics of data collection in multicenter trials and that uses methods that are tailored to the specific question and setting of an international trial. To be applicable within clinical routine, the measurement approach has to be simple, focusing on the end points of the trial. In our experience this should generally involve patient-rated questionnaires. Development of measures that are equivalent cross-culturally requires attention to conceptual, linguistic, and scaling issues. Standardization of data collection, especially timing, compliance, and data quality, requires special efforts. Cultural factors are expected to have an effect on patients' perception of their disease and treatment and therefore need to be considered in data analysis and interpretation of results.

ACKNOWLEDGMENTS

The authors wish to thank the principal investigators, data managers, and biostatisticians of the International Breast Cancer Study Group (IBCSG), especially Harriet Peterson, M.S., and Heidi Gusset, R.N., B.S.N., for many stimulating contributions to the issues discussed in this review. We are grateful to Hanneke de Haes, Ph.D., for her critical and helpful comments. Without enthusiastic cooperation across disciplines, national borders, and cultures, studying quality of life in international cancer clinical trials would not be possible.

REFERENCES

1. Souhami R. Large-scale studies. In: Williams CJ, ed. *Introducing new treatments for cancer. Practical, ethical and legal problems.* Chichester: John Wiley, 1992:173–187.
2. Harris JR, Lippman ME, Veronesi U, Willett W. Breast cancer (third of three parts). *N Engl J Med* 1992;327:473–480.
3. Goldhirsch A, Gelber RD, Simes RJ, Glasziou P, Coates AS, for the Ludwig Breast Cancer Study Group. Costs and benefits of adjuvant therapy in breast cancer: a quality-adjusted survival analysis. *J Clin Oncol* 1989;7:36–44.
4. Hürny C, Bernhard J, Gelber RD, et al, for the International Breast Cancer Study Group. Quality of life measures for patients receiving adjuvant therapy for breast cancer: an international trial. *Eur J Cancer* 1992;28:118–124.
5. Trill M Die, Holland J. Cross-cultural differences in the care of patients with cancer. *Gen Hosp Psychiatry* 1993;15:21–30.
6. Cleeland CS, Ladinsky JL, Serlin RC, Thuy NC. Multidimensional measurement of cancer pain: comparisons of US and Vietnamese patients. *J Pain Sympt Manag* 1988;3:23–27.
7. Patrick DL, Sittampalam Y, Somerville SM, Carter WB, Bergner M. A cross-cultural comparison of health status values. *Am J Public Health* 1985;75:1402–1407.
8. Maslow AH. *Motivation and personality.* New York: Harper & Row, 1954.
9. Hofstede G. The cultural relativity of the quality of life concept. *Acad Manage Rev* 1984;9:389–398.
10. Hofstede G. *Culture's consequences: international differences in work-related values.* Beverly Hills: Sage, 1980.

11. Campos SS, Johnson TM. Cultural considerations. In: Spilker B, ed. *Quality of life assessments in clinical trials.* New York: Raven Press, 1990:163–170.

12. Aaronson NK, Bullinger M, Ahmedzai SA. A modular approach to quality-of-life assessment in cancer clinical trials. *Recent Results Cancer Res* 1988;111:231–247.

13. Guyatt GH, Jaeschke R. Measurement in clinical trials: choosing the appropriate approach. In: Spilker B, ed. *Quality of life assessments in clinical trials.* New York: Raven Press, 1990:37–46.

14. Anderson GF, Alonso J, Kohn LT, Black C. Analyzing health outcomes through international comparisons. *Med Care* 1994;32:526–534.

15. Hui CH, Triandis HC. Measurement in cross-cultural psychology. *J Cross-Cult Psychol* 1985;16:131–152.

16. Knippenberg FCE van, Haes JCJM de. Variance and dissent. Measuring the quality of life of cancer patients: psychometric properties of instruments. *J Clin Epidemiol* 1988;41:1043–1053.

17. Donovan K, Sanson-Fisher RW, Redman S. Measuring quality of life in cancer patients. *J Clin Oncol* 1989;7:959–968.

18. Jaeschke R, Guyatt GH. How to develop and validate a new quality of life instrument. In: Spilker B, ed. *Quality of life assessments in clinical trials.* New York: Raven Press, 1990:47–57.

19. Deyo RA, Diehr P, Patrick DL. Reproducibility and responsiveness of health status measures. Statistics and strategies for evaluation. *Controlled Clin Trials* 1991;12(suppl):142–158.

20. Lydick E, Epstein RS. Interpretation of quality of life changes. *Qual Life Res* 1993;2:221–226.

21. WHOQOL Group. Study protocol for the World Health Organization project to develop a quality of life assessment instrument (WHOQOL). *Qual Life Res* 1993;2:153–159.

22. Aaronson NK, Ahmedzai S, Bergman B, et al. The European Organization for Research and Treatment of Cancer QLQ-C30: a quality-of-life instrument for use in international clinical trials in oncology. *J Natl Cancer Inst* 1993;85:365–376.

23. Sprangers MAG, Cull A, Bjordal K, Groenvold M, Aaronson NK, for the EORTC Study Group on Quality of Life. The European Organization for Research and Treatment of Cancer approach to quality of life assessment: guidelines for developing questionnaire modules. *Qual Life Res* 1993;2:287–295.

24. Guillemin F, Bombardier C, Beaton D. Cross-cultural adaptation of health-related quality of life measures: literature review and proposed guidelines. *J Clin Epidemiol* 1993;46:1417–1432.

25. Hunt SM, Alonso J, Bucquet D, Niero M, Wiklund I, McKenna S. Cross-cultural adaptation of health measures. *Health Policy* 1991;19:33–44.

26. Hunt SM, Wiklund I. Cross-cultural variation in the weighting of health statements: a comparison of English and Swedish valuations. *Health Policy* 1987;8:227–235.

27. Hunt SM, McEven J, McKenna SP. The Nottingham Health Profile: subjective health status and medical consultations. *Soc Sci Med* 1981;15A:221–229.

28. Bucquet D, Condon S, Ritchie K. The French version of the Nottingham Health Profile. A comparison of items weights with those of the source version. *Soc Sci Med* 1990;30:829–835.

29. Ware JE Jr, Sherbourne C. The MOS 36-item Short-Form Health Survey (SF-36). I. Conceptual framework and item selection. *Med Care* 1992;30:473–483.

30. Aaronson NK, Acquadro C, Alonso J, et al. International quality of life assessment (IQOLA) project. *Qual Life Res* 1992;1:349–351.

31. Breetvelt IS, van Dam FS. Underreporting by cancer patients: the case of response-shift. *Soc Sci Med* 1991;32:981–987.

32. Cassileth BR, Lusk EJ, Brown LL, Cross PA. Psychosocial status of cancer patients and next of kin: normative data from the profile of mood states. *J Psychosoc Oncol* 1985;3:99–105.

33. Maguire P. Psychosocial well-being in testicular cancer patients. *Eur J Cancer* 1992;28A:722.

34. Butow P, Coates A, Dunn S, Bernhard J, Hürny C. On the receiving end IV: validation of quality of life indicators. *Ann Oncol* 1991;2:597–603.

35. Hürny C, Bernhard J, Coates A, et al, for the International Breast Cancer Study Group. Responsiveness of a single-item indicator versus a multi-item scale: assessment of emotional well-being in an international adjuvant breast cancer trial. Submitted.

36. Coates A, Gebski V, Bishop J, et al., for the Australian-New Zealand Breast Cancer Trials Group. Improving the quality of life during chemotherapy for advanced breast cancer. A comparison of intermittent and continuous treatment strategies. *N Engl J Med* 1987;317:1490–1495.

37. Coates A, Gebski V, Signorini D, et al., for the Australian New Zealand Breast Cancer Trials Group. Prognostic value of quality-of-life scores during chemotherapy for advanced breast cancer. *J Clin Oncol* 1992;10:1833–1838.

38. Sartorius N. Cross-cultural comparisons of data about quality of life: a sample of issues. In: Aaronson NK, Beckmann J, eds. *The quality of life of cancer patients.* New York: Raven Press, 1987:19–24.

39. Wilkinson RG. Income distribution and life expectancy. *Br Med J* 1992;304:165–168.

40. Pappas G, Queen S, Hadden W, Fisher G. The increasing disparity in mortality between socioeconomic groups in the United States, 1960 and 1986. *N Engl J Med* 1993;329:103–109.

41. Vagerö D, Persson G. Cancer survival and social class in Sweden. *J Epidemiol Community Health* 1987;41:204–209.

42. Cella DF, Orav EJ, Kornblith AB, et al., for the Cancer and Leukemia Group B. Socioeconomic status and cancer survival. *J Clin Oncol* 1991;9:1500–1509.

43. Ganz P, Haskell C, Figlin R, et al. Estimating the quality of life in a clinical trial of patients with metastatic lung cancer using the Karnofsky performance status and the Functional Living Index-Cancer. *Cancer* 1988;61:849–856.

44. Yancik R, Edwards BK, Yates JW. Assessing the quality of life of cancer patients: practical issues in study implementation. *J Psychosoc Oncol* 1989;7:59–74.

45. Hürny C, Bernhard J, Joss R, et al., for the Swiss Group for Clinical Cancer Research (SAKK). Feasibility of quality of life assessment in a randomized phase III trial of small cell lung cancer—a lesson from the real world. *Ann Oncol* 1992;3:825–831.

46. Sadura A, Pater J, Osoba D, et al. Quality-of-life assessment: patient compliance with questionnaire completion. *J Natl Cancer Inst* 1992;84:1023–1026.

47. Kornblith A, Anderson J, Cella D, et al. Quality of life assessment of Hodgkin's disease survivors: a model for cooperative clinical trials. *Oncology* 1990;4:93–101.

48. McHorney CA, Kosinski M, Ware JE Jr. Comparisons of the costs and quality of norms for the SF-36 health survey collected by mail versus telephone interview: results from a national survey. *Med Care* 1994;32:551–567.

49. Guyatt GH, Bombardier C, Tugwell PX. Measuring disease specific quality of life in clinical trials. *Can Med Assoc J* 1986;134:889–895.

50. Bernhard J, Gusset H, Hürny C. Quality of life assessment in cancer clinical trials: an intervention by itself? *Support Cancer Care* 1995;3:66–71.

51. Richardson JL, Marks G, Levine A. The influence of symptoms of disease and side effects of treatment on compliance with cancer therapy. *J Clin Oncol* 1988;6:1746–1752.

52. Hürny C, Bernhard J, Coates A, et al., for the International Breast Cancer Study Group. Timing of baseline quality of life assessment in an international adjuvant breast cancer trial: its effect on patient self-estimation. *Ann Oncol* 1994;5:65–74.

53. Leung K, Bond MH. On the empirical identification of dimensions for cross-cultural comparisons. *J Cross-Cult Psychol* 1989;20:133–151.

54. Hürny C, Bernhard J, Bacchi M, et al., for the Swiss Group for Clinical Cancer Research (SAKK) and the International Breast Cancer Study Group (IBCSG). The perceived adjustment to chronic illness scale (PACIS): a global indicator of coping for operable breast cancer patients in clinical trials. *Support Care Cancer* 1993;1:200–208.

55. Greenberg E, Chute C, Stukel T, et al. Social and economic factors in the choice of lung cancer treatment: a population-based study in two rural states. *N Engl J Med* 1988;318:612–617.

Quality of Life and Pharmacoeconomics in Clinical Trials, Second Edition, edited by B. Spilker.
Lippincott-Raven Publishers, Philadelphia © 1996.

CHAPTER 73

Cross-Cultural Instrument Equating: Current Research and Future Directions

David F. Cella, Stephen R. Lloyd, and Benjamin D. Wright

INTRODUCTION

The subjective, multidimensional concept that is shaped by, but not entirely dependent upon, the effects of disease and treatment, has come to be called quality of life, or health-related quality of life (QOL). QOL evaluation differs from classical toxicity ratings in two important ways: (a) It incorporates more aspects of function (e.g., mood, affect, social well-being) than those that have typically been attributed to treatment, and (b) it focuses on the patient's perspective (1). We offer the following definition: health-related QOL refers to the effect that a medical condition or treatment has upon one's actual or perceived physical, mental, and social well-being.

There is considerable and growing interest in evaluating the QOL of people who present themselves for medical care. Because QOL is subjective (1), its evaluation must be drawn from the patient's perspective. Questionnaires to assess QOL have evolved out of this necessity. Most of these questionnaires have been developed in the English language. Given

the limited availability of QOL assessment methods that are sensitive to the needs of linguistically, culturally, and educationally diverse patients (1–7), many such patients are excluded from current QOL evaluations in clinical trials. As a result, we know very little about the impact of diseases and their treatments upon people from diverse backgrounds. We have had to compensate for this by assuming that the QOL responses of literate, English-speaking patients are representative of patients with low-literacy skills and those who speak other languages. This assumption must be tested, using materials that have been carefully prepared so as to maintain both consistent meaning of measurement and respect for diversity across groups.

CULTURE, LANGUAGE, AND LITERACY

Culture influences health behavior and perceptions by shaping explanations of sickness, social position, and meaning of life (8–11). In any multicultural context, people with medical conditions possess attributes that create barriers to standard QOL evaluation, such as different language and low literacy. When an instrument developed in English with primarily Anglo-European patients is adapted to other languages or cultures, it is important to produce a culturally equivalent instrument. This is best understood not as an effort to make different groups of people look the same, but

D. F. Cella: Department of Psychology and Social Sciences, Rush Medical College, Chicago, Illinois 60637.

S. R. Lloyd: Department of Psychology and Social Sciences, Rush-Presbyterian-St. Luke's Medical Center, Chicago, Illinois 60612.

B. D. Wright: Departments of Education and Psychology, MESA Psychometric Laboratory, University of Chicago, Chicago, Illinois 60612.

to ensure that different groups of people are evaluated without significant bias.

Low-literacy patients require interviewer assistance when completing QOL forms, so it becomes important to justify the use of interview assistance with these patients by demonstrating its comparability to self-administered form completion. Because the poor of the United States, for example, are disproportionately represented by black non-Hispanics and Hispanics (12), the special needs and perspectives of these groups extend beyond language, culture, and literacy into issues of poverty (8–11,13). For example, while perception of well-being is embedded in culture, it also passes through a filter of social status and personal resources. We are therefore compelled to attempt to disentangle these interrelated effects by evaluating social status as a variable related to language and culture. Proper adaptation and cross-cultural validation of an existing and uniculturally validated QOL instrument enables one to include a more diverse (and therefore representative) collection of patients entered into multicenter clinical trials. The availability of valid and responsive QOL measurement for such a diverse group of patients helps provide useful information to clinicians when choosing (along with their patients) from among treatment protocols or options. Community-based treatment decision making would then be informed by more accurate, representative QOL outcome data.

EQUATING INSTRUMENTS

Equivalence of an instrument in different languages and cultures may be demonstrated across five dimensions: content, semantic, technical, criterion, and conceptual (9,14–18). Flaherty and colleagues (9) present a taxonomy of these five dimensions of equivalence, which are summarized in Table 1.

Methodological Contributions to Equivalence

Regarding semantic and content equivalency, it is desirable to obtain a QOL instrument with the following characteristics: (a) written in grammatically correct, simple language; (b) containing vocabulary in common usage across all reference groups; (c) translated items retaining the *meaning* of the original instrument; (d) conveying the same *intent* as the original instrument; and (e) content remaining culturally relevant. Semantic and content equivalency are best established using extensive input from representative groups of bilingual and bicultural experts as well as patients themselves. Technical equivalence refers to the likelihood that a measure adapted for application with culturally (or linguistically) diverse patient groups achieves the same measurement effect across those groups. This can be enhanced by standardizing administration across interviewers and sites, as well as by directly comparing measurement results across diverse groups. The internal structure and psychometric characteris-

TABLE 1. *Types of cross-cultural equivalence of instruments*

Type of equivalence	Definition
Content	The *content* of each item is *relevant* to the phenomenon of each culture
Semantic	The *meaning* of each item is the same in each culture after translation into the language and idiom of each culture
Technical	The *method* of assessment (e.g., paper-and-pencil, interview) is comparable in each culture with respect to the data that it yields
Criterion	The *interpretation* of the measurement of the variable remains the same when compared with the norm for each culture studied
Conceptual	The instrument is measuring the same *theoretical construct* in each culture

Adapted from ref. 9, with permission.

tics of instruments may change when instruments are translated and used across different cultures (11,19). This will most likely occur when the instrument does not first establish cultural (semantic, content, and technical) equivalence (9,11,14,15,20). Thus, it is very important to carry out cross-cultural and cross linguistic instrument adaptation to promote maximum equivalency. This can be accomplished by using a panel of expert bilingual/bicultural advisors for review. Technical equivalence can be established by standardizing administration across interviewers and sites, and comparing interview-generated data to that collected from self-administration.

Statistical Contributions to Equivalence

Some types of equivalence are typically demonstrated using statistical data analysis. For example, it is desirable that the interpretation of measured QOL is similar and anchored to comparable intracultural norms (*criterion equivalence*). It is also important to ensure that the instrument is measuring the same theoretical construct in each culture (*conceptual equivalence*).

Statistical test equating is a common psychometric problem. Two general approaches exist: those driven by traditional test theory (21–23), and those driven by item response (latent trait) theory (17,18,24–26). Traditional approaches have not provided satisfactory solutions to detecting biased items and equating tests (24). For example, the usual test of association between measures used to evaluate equivalence has been the correlation coefficient. But, the correlation coefficient depends on the variability in the sample relative to the measurement error. Thus, its magnitude depends on the choice of subjects. Using, instead, a sample-free item response theory method for equating measures and removing item bias and a series of psychometric analyses and intergroup comparisons, one can examine the equivalence of QOL measurement across cultures, languages, and literacy.

QOL test equating across cultural groups *within* language is also important. Many of the same concerns about cultural meaning and relevance of questioning can be applied to African Americans compared with European (white) Americans. While both groups speak native English, their cultural values and mores vary considerably. For example, DiClemente el al. (27) found that black and Hispanic adolescents held different myths, misconceptions, and levels of perceived risk about HIV/AIDS. Social networks are more important and useful to African Americans, particularly women, thereby providing important sources of information and support (8). Cultural differences in attitudes toward such practices as euthanasia and organ donation have been documented. Specifically, black non-Hispanics are less favorable toward euthanasia (28,29) and less likely to donate organs (30), compared to other cultural groups. Most previous cross-cultural research has viewed cultural sensitivity in rather narrow ways, focusing on language alone or limited contextual factors. Others have extended this to include cultural dynamics (8,31,32), acculturation (11), and biculturalism (33,34). Black non-Hispanic patient responses to QOL items can be influenced not only by African-American values, including the strong role of church and family support networks, but also by the African principles of unity, self-determination, collective community responsibility, cooperation, purpose, creativity, and faith (8,13). Similarly, Hispanic QOL responses can be influenced by Hispanic cultural values of allocentrism (emphasis on the needs of the ''in-group'') (35), simpatia (need for smooth social relationships), familialism, power distance (respect for social power), and differences in conceptions of personal space, gender role, and time orientation (11).

CULTURE-FAIR VERSUS CULTURE-FREE

The meaning of QOL is deeply embedded in culture. Aspects of QOL such as role performance, emotional well-being, social well-being, and even physical well-being, are evaluated by people in the context of their cultural script, or understanding of underlying cultural rules and structure. To expect any measure of QOL to be free of cultural influence, or ''culture-free,'' is fundamentally unrealistic. However, we work toward constructing measures based on common cores of items that are not culture-biased and not more attractive (or repulsive) to one group over another. Developing item equivalence across cultures does *not* imply that measures will show equivalent QOL levels across different groups of people. Indeed, it may be that levels of QOL differ across cultural or linguistic groups. This is an empirical question that should be addressed as such without making prior assumptions. ''Equivalence'' in this context refers to the absence of item bias. It is more important to demonstrate

that a scale is unbiased when it is applied to different groups of people than it is to show that there are no significant differences across these groups on the attribute that the scale measures. It may be, for example, that the QOL of Spanish-speaking patients is lower than that of English-speaking patients. We would want a measure than can detect, not mask, that difference if it exists. But we would also want some evidence that the detection of that difference is not based upon items that are systematically and unfairly biased in favor of English-speaking patients.

In addition to language and culture, there is the issue of literacy. It is desirable to justify paraprofessional interview assessment of QOL as an equivalent (or at least equivalent with correction) form of QOL data collection. The demands of cost-efficiency in multicenter clinical trials precludes the administration of a QOL interview to all patients. Self-administered questionnaire is thus the method of choice. However, this carries the risk of excluding or at least confusing low-literacy patients who cannot complete the form. And this is no small problem. In Puerto Rico, two thirds of the population is medically indigent (36), and their median educational level is eighth grade, suggesting that low literacy is prevalent in that population. Similar figures are likely in developing nations and underserved urban and rural areas of developed nations.

Self versus Interviewer Administration

Because low-literacy patients require interviewer administration, and because most high-literacy patients in clinical trials will, for reasons of convenience and cost, be asked to self-administer, it is important to evaluate the comparability of self and interviewer administration.

This requires a three- (rather than two) facet psychometric analysis, in which not only patients and QOL items (the usual two facets) are specified and measured, but also a third facet in which interviewers themselves are also specified and measured for their influence on the response levels of the patients they help. When an interviewer participates in a QOL rating, then the measure of the patient being helped must be corrected for the bias introduced by the influence of the interviewer (37).

These three-facet analyses address the issue of *technical equivalence* by examining whether different methods of obtaining self-report data can be adjusted to produce comparable measures. There have been many studies outside the QOL field that have empirically examined the question of whether data collected by interview are significantly different than data collected by self-administration. Generally, studies that compare interview-administered data to self-administered data find little difference in the responses given (38–42). When differences *are* found, they favor the interview technique because, when done well, it is less susceptible to inaccuracies, inconsistencies, and missing data (2,3,43). It is likely, therefore, that the quality of self-administered QOL data could be improved were data collectors on site trained to help patients with their QOL forms and to check for completeness before ending assessment.

Interviewer Selection

The conclusions drawn from QOL studies have significant implications for the interpretation of outcomes of medical treatments. Patients must therefore be helped to feel as comfortable as possible, maximizing the likelihood that they will provide useful data. For this it is important that interviewers be perceived as members of a similar culture to whatever extent is possible, to set patients at ease, and to facilitate removal of status barriers between examiner and respondent.

TRANSLATION TECHNIQUES

There are many translation services and techniques available (14,15,44–46). These include one-way translation, translation by committee, iterative double (back) translation (with or without decentering), and simultaneous forward/single back translation (with or without decentering). One-way translation entails simply asking a bilingual individual to translate the original version into the target language. This usually results in a translation that corresponds to the denotative rather than connotative meaning of the original (11). This approach is quite limited insofar as there is no check on the single translator, often resulting in statistical nonequivalence (47). Translation by committee involves commissioning two independent translators, then having them meet to resolve differences and generate a consensus document, or having a third objective translator choose the better version. This technique is less costly than the forward-backward-forward translation techniques, but is vulnerable to the fact that translators may share a common worldview that similarly distorts both translations, and that translators may be hesitant to criticize one another in a committee setting, resulting in premature closure on differences that need resolving. In its simplest form, the double (back) translation method employs two independent translators in sequence, with the first translation from the source to the target language and then back into the same language. Comparisons are then made of the two versions in the source language, to identify inconsistencies and loss or change of meaning. These inconsistencies are then resolved by the researcher, preferably in conjunction with a bilingual expert in linguistics, by returning to the translators for discussion.

This method, while among the best available, has some limitations. First, similar to the committee approach, it is susceptible to the possibility that translators share a common worldview that could lead one to back-translate a close match to the original, even where the idea is not properly portrayed in the source language. Therefore, in our work we have added expert advisory input from as many different cultural backgrounds as represented within the target language. We have also employed two independent back-translators who are not only bilingual but also bicultural. Finally, we prefer whenever possible to reiterate the backward-forward sequence after having had a chance to pilot the current forward-backward-forward document with up to 50 patients, further ensuring semantic and content equivalence. All of this together maximizes the likelihood that statistical equivalence, which can be tested with clinical trial data, will be demonstrated across language versions. The decentering technique allows for modification of the language of the original (source) version of the instrument when going through the iterative translation process. Although decentering is desirable in the ideal, it becomes increasingly difficult to justify as an instrument builds a data base using the original (source) wording.

A fourth translation technique, simultaneous forward/single backward translation, is very much like the third with one key difference: in the double-back iterative approach, there is only one new document created at any given time, either the first forward, first backward, or second forward translation. In some cases and of necessity, second backward and third forward versions might evolve. In the simultaneous forward/single backward approach, two simultaneous forward translations are created by independent translation teams. The two forward translations are then reconciled into a third forward translation, which is then subjected to back-translation. The reconciled forward translation and back-translation are then submitted to expert bilingual and bicultural advisors for comment and specific assistance with deriving a final forward translation. This method requires the handling of more documents simultaneously than the double-back approach, but tends in our experience to produce a more reliable translation.

Pilot Testing for Relevance

Using the best final forward translation, items can be subjected to pilot testing with patients whose native tongue is that of the target (translated) document. Patients provide their viewpoint on each item in terms of its perceived relevance or importance to their QOL. This can be done using a Likert scale of relevance (e.g., 1, little or no relevance to QOL; 2, somewhat relevant to QOL; 3, very relevant to QOL; 4, extremely relevant to QOL). Patients' interpretations of even the above simple four-category rating scale, and their understanding of the meanings of ''relevant'' and ''relevance'' must be studied carefully for functional equivalence both within and across patient groups. It is not only the QOL items that must be equated but also the labels and use of the QOL rating scale by which patient responses are collected and recorded. Patients should also be encouraged to identify items that are missing for them and could be included (48–50). This addresses the *content equivalence* of the target and source documents.

Expert Advisory Committee Review

After completing the translation and pilot testing, a final review of item description and content can be made by a committee of expert advisors. Committee members are asked to consider the summarized input from the initial pilot study interviews. They are also provided with summary scores for each of the QOL domains as measured by the instrument, and with a histogram plot of frequency with which each item was raised as problematic, expressed as a percentage of all patients. The specific nature of the patients' difficulty with each item can be appended for reference. Committee members are asked to focus specifically on any items that were considered problematic by more than 20% of patients. Each member can also systematically rate each item for QOL construct relevance on a four-point Likert scale, as above. To ensure content equivalency, expert advisory committee members should also be asked if there are any items *not* covered by the items that have specific cultural relevance and should therefore be included.

Linguist's Final Revision

It is useful to include the input of a linguist during the later stage of the translation process. Using input from the expert advisors, summarized input from pilot patients, and all forward and back-translated documents, the linguist can synthesize the translations and manage any lingering discrepancies.

EVALUATING STATISTICAL EQUIVALENCE

Analyzing for statistical equivalence of measurement is a two-step process. The first step is at the measurement level, where the purpose is to determine whether a given rating scale works in the same manner with different groups of people. This step is crucial when one is interested in detecting systematic measurement bias and a particular rating scale is used with different groups of people (e.g., Hispanic vs. black non-Hispanic vs. white non-Hispanic culture; Spanish vs. English language; high vs. low literacy) or administered in different ways (e.g., self vs. interviewer). Then the extent to which each QOL item with which the rating scale is used performs similarly across different reference groups is of critical interest when determining which of the QOL items can be used to provide an unbiased basis for comparing groups. We are seeking assurance that any detected group difference (as analyzed in the analysis step) is not based upon items that are systematically biased in favor of one of the groups. We need rating scale categories and QOL items that match across groups on both category step and item "difficulty" (52). The measurement step of equivalence construction and testing provides that reassurance.

The second step after establishing and evaluating equivalence is the analysis level, in which we evaluate scale mea-

sure differences across reference groups and test conditions to determine what real differences exist.

Measurement Step

When, as in cross-cultural equating, one is attempting to equate two forms of the same test, and the same form of a test with different groups (presumed to have comparable distributions) the traditional raw score techniques have proven problematic in several ways. These problems are traceable primarily to the nonlinearity of all raw scores. For equating QOL measures, therefore, we turn to other methods of modern psychometrics.

Item Analysis

Andrich (53) has extended the Rasch (26) model for ordinal data while incorporating subject (patient) effects (54). The Rasch model is a particular specification for the relations among parameters that can be deduced from the requirements for additive conjoint measurement and for Fisherian sufficient statistics. The Rasch model is particularly easy to work with because parameter estimation problems are considerably fewer than those associated with more general item response theory models (24). The simplest form of the Rasch model (18,26,53,55) uses two parameters: β_i to mark patient i's "ability" to achieve a high score (i.e., high QOL) and δ_j to mark item j's "difficulty." The linear quantity that is modeled is the difference between patient ability and item difficulty, $\beta_i - \delta_j$. This Rasch (26) logistic model for the probability of a "correct" response is

$$\text{Prob}\{x_{ij} : \beta_i \, \delta_j\} = P_{ijx} = \frac{\exp\,[x_{ij}(\beta_i - \delta_j)]}{1 + \exp\,[x_{ij}(\beta_i - \delta_j)]}, \quad \text{for } x = 0,1$$

where x is a binomial variable equal to 1 when the response is "correct," and 0 otherwise. This model for handling dichotomous data has been expanded by Andrich (53) for items with more than two ordered categories (e.g., Likert scaling), and by Masters (56) for items with partial credit scoring. Andrich's model for rating scales, which is appropriate for most QOL equating, breaks the item difficulty parameter into two components: the location or scale value of the item on the underlying variable, and the location of each response category step relative to the item location (17). Computer programs, e.g., BIGSTEPS (57) and FACETS (58) are commercially available to conduct Rasch model rating scale analyses and produce the necessary plots. The unique property of this model is that the person abilities and item difficulties can be estimated independently of one another by means of conditional maximum likelihood. The sample data matrix exhibits the patient QOL raw scores as row marginals and the QOL item raw scores as column marginals. The patient QOL raw scores can be used to remove the influence of their abilities from the estimation of the item difficulties (δ_j), resulting in a sample-free item calibration. Similarly, the item raw scores can be used to remove the influence of item difficulty from the estimation of patient ability (β_i), resulting in test-free patient measurement. Thus, the QOL patient and QOL item raw scores are sufficient for estimating patient QOL measures and QOL item calibrations. These parameters can be estimated (one for each patient, one for each item, and one for each step in the QOL response categories) by means of the following Rasch logit (log odds) model for a linear relationship between patient ability β_i, QOL item difficulty δ_j and rating step difficulty τ_k:

$$\log \frac{P_{ijk}}{P_{ijk-1}} = \beta_i - \delta_j - \tau_k$$

Having a way to determine item difficulty independently of the sample or its subgroups enables us to detect and diagnose item bias. The most important indicator of item bias is not whether the item systematically differentiates relevant subgroups in the same way that most other items do, but whether it does so in an unmodeled (i.e., unpredicted) way that differs from the way other items function. Unmodeled idiosyncratic differences reflect *differential interaction* between some items and some persons, which in turn confuses interpretation of results. Items that differentiate groups in unexpected ways can be identified as biased and investigated as to their content to determine the likely sources of that bias. This process can be done for each comparison across language, culture, literacy, or any variable whose different levels are being equated. To illustrate, the technique will be described for a Spanish-to-English language comparison. For this comparison, different versions of the same test (Spanish and English) must be administered to different groups, so it requires a modified equivalent groups design.

1. Items are first preexamined by the expert advisors, at least two professional translators, and a linguist, to evaluate and modify any that are expected to be biased either in favor of Spanish- or English-speaking people. The result of these revisions is that in their current (tested) form, none of the items is expected to be biased toward either of the groups.
2. After all patients have been tested, calibrations of each test scale are done separately for Spanish- and English-speaking patients (17,18). Because QOL is expected to be multidimensional and the Rasch model constructs the best single dimension that the data provided can support, emphasis is placed upon subscale comparisons rather than total or global score comparisons in these calibrations.
3. The calibrated item difficulties from the separate analysis of each sample for each subscale and the total score are centered and plotted against each other, with Spanish on the y-axis and English on the x-axis.
4. An identity line is drawn through the origin of each plot with a slope of 1.

5. Statistical control (95% confidence interval) lines are drawn around the identity lines to guide interpretation, and the plots are examined to see if any items fall outside the control lines, thereby reflecting *possible* bias (17,18,59). The area between the dotted lines in Fig. 1 depicts the "identity region," or the area around the identity line that depicts acceptable item deviation (59).
6. Items identified as possibly biased are reviewed, plot by plot, to obtain direction on interpreting the plots and determining the most useful disposition of the item, given its content and context.
7. Within each bivariate plot, items that fall outside the 95% statistical control lines but must be kept for construct reasons are entered into the data set as "doubled items" for the Spanish-English comparison. In essence this entails creating *two* items out of one, with missing data coded on Spanish-speaking patients for the English version, and on English-speaking patients for the Spanish version. Instead of occupying one field in the data set, the doubled items each occupy two fields: one for the Spanish patients and one for the English patients. These items when anchored by the calibrations of the common core items that have been found to retain their relative spacing across groups can then be used in the construction of quantitatively sound Spanish-to-English comparisons.

This process is repeated for each of the planned comparisons. The end product of these analyses and plots is a set of unbiased subsets of QOL items that, based upon previous experience with similar Rasch model scaling, may well include the majority of the original items. These unbiased subsets of items can then be used in the next step of testing for measure differences: the analysis step. In addition to informing us of item equivalence (lack of bias), the Rasch technique of psychometric item analysis provides two distinctly advantageous features: (a) measures on a linear (i.e., interval) scale, and (b) a per person measure standard error and response pattern validity fit statistics. All of these features form a solid basis from which to compare reference groups in the analysis step.

Analysis Step

Equivalence across levels of the explanatory variables (e.g., culture, language), meaning commensurable measures have been successfully established, can be tested using a variety of multivariate techniques. One hypothesis entering into these analyses should be that the QOL items will be predominantly unbiased. Therefore, one would expect that QOL measure comparisons across patient groups will vary according to noncultural explanatory variables (e.g., performance status, prognosis), but not according to language, culture, literacy, or mode of administration. This amounts to testing an hypothesis of no measurement differences across levels of culture, language, literacy, and administration method.

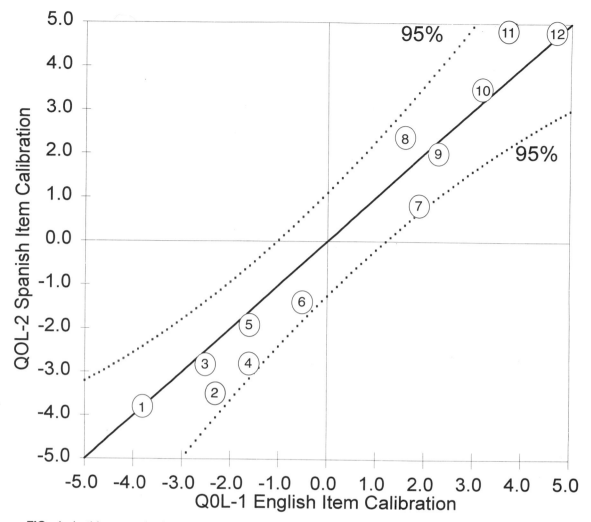

FIG. 1. In this example, items 1–12 are plotted according to calibrated "difficulty." The fact that they all fall within the 95% statistical control lines (*dotted*) indicates absence of bias.

LISREL Analysis

LISREL modeling is used in social science research to analyze complex constructs such as health-related quality of life (60–63). A basic premise of the LISREL approach is that we are interested in studying abstract concepts that are not directly measurable. These concepts, implied by the QOL items, are referred to as *latent variables.* What the researcher does possess are observed or *manifest variables* that are assumed to reflect the underlying constructs. LISREL allows the investigator to specify relations between unobserved and observed, or latent and manifest, variables. It is essentially a confirmatory factor analysis strategy that enables one to determine how well the measured variables (QOL indicators) are generated by the latent variables (underlying factors or scales). Once QOL interval measures have been established, one can review the consequences of the Rasch modeling with a series of LISREL analyses. In

so doing, one can take into account Rasch measurement error and validate the QOL measure across subsamples of patients. The Rasch measures should be used rather than the raw scores, because one is assured that they are interval data, complete and precise (i.e., with the necessary standard errors of measurement).

Multivariate Statistical Analysis

Because of their desirable properties as described above, logit measures produced by the Rasch model analyses can be used as the units of analysis. Standard bivariate statistical tests including analysis of variance and *t*-tests can be used to assess the bivariate relationships of QOL responses to cultural and linguistic variables under study. However, these analyses alone may not allow the investigators to sort out the relative influence of each of the cultural variables nor their combined explanatory power.

The null hypothesis underlying these analyses is that noncultural explanatory variables (e.g., performance status, socioeconomic status, gender, age) are the only significant predictors of variability in QOL scores. If additional main and/or interaction effects are detected, this would lead one to reject the null hypothesis and offer alternative explanations. For example, it may be that the English and Spanish versions of the instrument work in the same way (i.e., are the same in terms of item calibration and difficulty), but nevertheless show differences between Spanish- and English-speaking patients. This would suggest that the instrument is detecting a "true" difference between the two groups rather than one based upon bias in the instrument itself. In other words, the finding of significant differences in these analyses, although not predicted, does not reflect a problem of measurement, but rather an unexpected difference among some of the patient strata that requires further exploration. It remains to be determined whether other culture-fair items should be added at that time, with that determination made largely based upon review of the extent of item bias found in the Rasch model analysis. Generally speaking, no, or limited, bias would suggest no need for additional items, whereas moderate to extensive item bias (e.g., over 30% of items) would argue for addition of more unbiased items (64).

APPLICATION TO CLINICAL TRIALS

The applicability of the measurement approach described in this chapter must be tested in clinical trials. Clinical trials organizations should focus on standardization of methods of administration, timing of measurement, training of support staff, and quality control of data collection.

Even rather small differences in administration technique, if consistent, can result in systematic assessment bias. It is therefore important to ensure standard administration of any QOL instrument. In the Eastern Cooperative Oncology Group, for example, a QOL orientation and training video has been produced as a companion to ongoing training and quality assurance for data managers. Semiannual booster sessions at each group meeting also help to keep awareness high and data quality at its maximum. Administration methodology is presented in writing, by example during data manager training, and by handing out the companion videotape on test administration. Quality control checks on the data collection procedures and on the actual data collected are done by the study coordinator who tracks all patients entered into any of the QOL studies. Emphasis is on completeness rather than content of the data.

On-site personnel should be advised during training that interviewer assistance is particularly important to obtain complete data from patients with special language needs and compromised literacy and performance status. For this reason, and because it tends to provide better-quality data (3,42,43), institutional study interviewers should be instructed in methods to assist patients in completing the self-report forms in the packet without biasing their responses.

CONCLUSIONS

Most of today's clinical trials in medicine take place in a multicultural, multilingual context. Quality of life, an important end point in many of these trials, can only be measured by asking patients themselves. This creates the need for multilingual assessment of quality of life with multicultural validity. This chapter summarized current methods of translation and test equating that offer directions for future research.

REFERENCES

1. Cella DF. Quality of life: the concept. *J Palliat Care* 1992;8(3):8–13.
2. Cella DF, Tulsky DS. Measuring quality of life today: methodological aspects. *Oncology* 1990;4(5):29–38.
3. Nayfield SG, Hailey BJ, McCabe M. *Quality of life assessment in cancer clinical trials: report of the Workshop on Quality of Life Research in Cancer Clinical Trials, July 16–17, 1990.* Washington, DC: US Department of Health and Human Services, 1991.
4. Barofsky I, Sugarbaker P. Cancer. In: Spilker B, ed. *Quality of life assessment in clinical trials.* New York: Raven Press. 1990:419–439.
5. Aaronson NK, Beckman J. *The quality of life of cancer patients.* Monograph Series of the European Organization for Research on Treatment of Cancer (EORTC), vol 17. New York: Raven Press, 1987.
6. Fayers PM, Jones DR. Measuring and analysing quality of life in cancer clinical trials: a review. *Stat Med* 1983;2:429–446.
7. Osoba D, ed. *Effect of cancer on quality of life.* Boca Raton, FL: CRC Press, 1991.
8. Brisbane FL, Womble M. *Working with African Americans: the professional's handbook.* Chicago, IL: HRDI International Press, 1992.
9. Flaherty JA, Gaviria FM, Pathak D, Mitchell T, Winthrob R, Richman JA, Birz S. Developing instruments for cross-cultural psychiatry research. *J Nerv Ment Dis* 1988;176(5):257–263.
10. Kleinman A, Eisenberf L, Good B. Culture, illness and care: clinical lessons from antropologic and cross-cultural research. *Ann Intern Med* 1978;88:251–258.
11. Marin G, Marin BVO. *Research with Hispanic populations.* Applied Social Research Methods Series, vol 23. Newberry Park, CA: Sage, 1991.
12. US Department of Health and Human Services. *Health status of minorities and low income groups.* DHHS Pub (HRSA) HRS-P-DV 85-1. Washington, DC: US Government Printing Office, 1985.
13. Billingsley A. *Black families in white America.* Englewood Cliffs, NJ: Prentice Hall, 1968.
14. Flaherty JA. Appropriate and inappropriate research methodologies for Hispanic mental health. In: Gaviria M, ed. *Health and behavior: research agenda for Hispanics.* Chicago: University of Illinois Press, 1987.
15. Bravo M, Canino GJ, Rubio-Stipee M, Woodbury-Farina M. A cross cultural adaptation of a psychiatric epidemiologic instrument: the Diagnostic Interview Schedule's adaptation in Puerto Rico. *Cult Med Psychiatry* 1991;15:1–18.
16. Woodcock RW. *Examiner's manual: Woodcock Language Proficiency Battery–Revised.* Allen, TX: DLM, 1991.
17. Wright B, Masters J. *Rating scale analysis.* Chicago: Mesa Press, 1982.
18. Wright B, Stone M. *Best test design.* Chicago: Mesa Press, 1979.
19. Deyo RA. Pitfalls in measuring health status of Mexican Americans: comparative validity of the English and Spanish Sickness Impact Profile. *Am J Public Health* 1984;74(6):569.
20. Canino GJ, Bird HR, Shrout PE, Rubio-Stipee M, Bravo M, Martinez R, Sesman M, Guzman A, Guevara LU, Costas H. The Spanish Diagnostic Interview Schedule. Reliability and concordance with clinical diagnoses in Puerto Rico. *Arch Gen Psychiatry* 1987;44:720–726.

21. Angoff WH. Scales, norms and equivalent scores. In: Thorndike RL, ed. *Educational measurement,* 2nd ed. Washington, DC: American Council on Education, 1971.
22. Gullickson H. *Theory of mental tests.* New York: Wiley, 1950.
23. Holland PW, Rubin DR, eds. *Test equating.* New York: Academic Press, 1982.
24. Hambleton RK, Swaminathan H. *Item response theory: principles and applications.* Boston, MA: Kluwer-Nijhoff, 1985.
25. Lord FM, Novick MR. *Statistical theories of mental test scores.* Reading, MA: Addison-Wesley, 1968.
26. Rasch G. *Probabilistic models for some intelligence and attainment tests.* Copenhagen: Danish Institute for Educational Research, 1960. (Reprinted by the University of Chicago Press, 1980, with a Foreword and Afterword by Benjamin D. Wright. Reprinted again by the MESA Press, University of Chicago, 1992.
27. DiClemente RJ, Boyer CB, Morales ES. Minorities and AIDS: knowledge, attitudes and misconceptions among Black and Latino adolescents. *Am J Public Health* 1988;78(1):55–57.
28. Jorgenson DE, Neubecker RC. Euthanasia: a national survey of attitudes toward voluntary termination of life. *Omega* 1981;11(4):281–291.
29. Rao VVP, Staten F, Rao VN. Racial differences toward euthanasia. *Euthanasia Rev* 1988;2(4):260–267.
30. Davidson MN, Devney P. Attitudinal barriers to organ donation among black Americans. *Transplant Proc* 1991;23(5):2531–2532.
31. de la Cancela V. Minority AIDS prevention: moving beyond cultural perspectives towards sociopolitical empowerment. *AIDS Educ Prevent* 1989;1(2):141–153:
32. Singer M. Confronting the AIDS epidemic among IV drug users: does ethnic culture matter? *AIDS Educ Prevent* 1991;3(3):258–283.
33. La Fromboise TD, Rowe W. Skills training for bicultural competence: rationale and application. *J Consult Clin Psychol* 1983;30:589–595.
34. Oetting ER, Beauvais F. Orthogonal cultural identification theory: the cultural identification of minority adolescents. *Int J Addict* 1990–91;25(5A,6A):655–685.
35. Marin G, Triandis HC. Allocentrism as an important characteristic of the behavior of Latin Americans and Hispanics. In: Diaz-Guerrero R, ed. *Cross-cultural and national studies in social psychology.* Amsterdam: Elsevier 1985:85–104.
36. Burgos R. *Los retos de la Decada del '90. Perspectivas Economicas de la Industria de la salud.* San Juan, Puerto Rico: Departamento de Salud, Consejo General de Salud.
37. Linacre JM. *An extension of the Rasch model to multi-faceted situations.* Chicago: University of Chicago, 1987.
38. Hochstim JR. A critical comparison of three strategies of collecting data from households. *J Am Stat Assoc* 1967;62:976–989.
39. Walker AH, Restuccia JD. Obtaining information on patient satisfaction with hospital care: mail versus telephone. *Health Serv Res* 1984;19(3):83–96.
40. Warner JL, Berman JJ, Weyant JM, Ciarlo JA. Assessing mental health program effectiveness: a comparison of three client follow-up methods. *Eval Rev* 1983;7:635–659.
41. Dillman DA. *Mail and telephone surveys: the total design method.* New York: John Wiley, 1978.
42. Locander W, Sudman S, Bradburn N. An investigation of interview method, threat and response distortion. *J Am Stat Assoc* 1976;71:269–274.
43. Anderson JP, Bush JW, Berry CC. Classifying function for health outcome and quality-of-life evaluation. *Med Care* 1986;24:454–469.
44. Brislin R. Back-translation for cross-cultural research. *J Cross Cultural Psychol* 1970;1:185–216.
45. Hui C, Triandis HC. Measurement in cross-cultural psychology: a review and comparison of strategies. *Cross Cultural Psychol* 1985;16:131–150.
46. Aaronson NK, Acquadro C, Alonso J, et al. International quality of life assessment (IQOLA) project. *Qual Life Res* 1992;1:349–351.
47. Berkanovic E. The effects of inadequate language translation on Hispanics' responses to health surveys. *Am J Public Health* 1980;70:1273–1276.
48. Cella DF, Tulsky DS, Gray G, et al. The Functional Assessment of Cancer Therapy (FACT) Scale: development and validation of the general measure. *J Clin Oncol* 1993;11(3):570–579.
49. Tulsky DS, Cella DF, Sarafian B, et al. Development and validation of the Functional Assessment of Cancer Treatment (FACT-G). *Proceedings of the International Congress of Psychosocial Oncology.* Beaune, France, October 12–14, 1992:99.
50. Cella DF. Manual for the Functional Assessment of Cancer Therapy (FACT) Scales, version 3. Chicago, IL: Rush-Presbyterian-St. Luke's Medical Center, 1994.
51. Lord FM. A theory of test scores. *Psychometric Monograph* 1952:7.
52. Angoff WH. Use of difficulty and discrimination indices for detecting item bias. In: Berk RA, ed. *Handbook of methods for detecting test bias.* Baltimore, MD: Johns Hopkins University, 1982.
53. Andrich D. A rating formulation for ordered response categories. *Psychometrika* 1978;43:561–573.
54. Agresti A. *Categorical data analysis.* New York: John Wiley, 1990:399–401.
55. Masters JN. *A Rasch model for rating scales.* Unpublished doctoral dissertation. Chicago: University of Chicago, 1980.
56. Masters GN. A Rasch model for partial credit scoring. *Psychometrika* 1982;47:149–174.
57. Wright BD, Linacre JM. *BIGSTEPS: Rasch analysis/computer program.* Chicago: MESA Press, 1992.
58. Linacre JM, Wright BD. *FACETS: many-faceted Rasch analysis.* Chicago: MESA Press, 1992.
59. Wright B, Stone M. Identifying item bias: measurement. Primer No. 9. Wilmington, DE: JASTAK, 1991.
60. Bentler PM. Multivariate analysis with latent variables: causal modeling. *Annu Rev Psychol* 1980;31:419–456.
61. Bentler PM. Latent variable structural models for separating specific from general effects. In: Seechrist L, Perrin E, Bunker J, eds. *Research methodology: strengthening causal interpretations of nonexperimental data.* Washington, DC: HHS/PHS, Agency for Health Care Policy and Research, May 1990:61–83.
62. Joreskog KG, Sorbom D. *LISREL VI users' guide.* Mooresville, IN: Scientific Software, 1984.
63. Pedhazur EJ. *Multiple regression in behavioral research,* 2nd ed. New York: Holt, Rinehart and Winston, 1982:636–681.
64. Wright B, Stone M. Quality control plots for evaluating co-relations: measurement primer no. 26. Wilmington, DE: JASTAK, 1992.

Quality of Life and Pharmacoeconomics in Clinical Trials, Second Edition, edited by B. Spilker.
Lippincott-Raven Publishers, Philadelphia © 1996.

CHAPTER 74

Applications of Health Status Assessment to Health Policy

Donald L. Patrick and Pennifer Erickson

INTRODUCTION: HEALTH POLICY AS COSTS AND OUTCOMES

Over the past century, advances in public health and medicine, along with social, economic, and environmental progress, have improved the health of the public in most Western nations. In the United States, life expectancy has increased almost 30 years on average. Monumental gains have been made in identifying both the leading causes of death, disease, and disability and the means to prevent or treat them. Yet many major health problems remain unresolved. Among others, heart disease, stroke, emphysema, arthritis, back pain, cancer, sexually transmitted diseases, accidental injuries, addictive disorders, and violence continue to threaten the public's health. Providing access to health services, improving quality of care, and reducing inequalities in health outcomes remain major challenges to health and social policy.

Society's main response to these problems continues to be increased investment in health care, including preventive, caring, and curing interventions. We will spend $1 trillion in 1994 ($4,000 per person) in the United States on medical care (1). Rapid advances in technology, increased use of more intensive modes of therapy and diagnosis, and an aging population all contribute to this increase in expenditures. At the present time, the United States spends nearly three times

more on health care than most other Western nations. Yet the health-related quality of life of people in the United States when measured in terms of life expectancy and other health indicators is no higher than that for residents of Western Europe or Japan, where health expenditures are considerably lower.

As a nation, Americans look to health policy to help decide how to make health expenditures reap more benefits. Increasingly decision makers, providers, patients, and the public ask that every additional expenditure be justified according to expected outcomes. Health decision making has never been more important, whether to reduce inefficiency, eliminate ineffective medical procedures, increase competition, improve quality, change reimbursement formulas, or ration services.

To a large extent, the United States shapes its health policy by the way in which resources are distributed to competing programs based on anticipated benefits, even though most health policy decisions have not been made using an explicit set of economic and sociopolitical criteria (2). The measurement of anticipated benefits associated with health care is the application of health status assessment to which this chapter is addressed. Other chapters in this section address specific examples of health status assessment in the development and evaluation of health policy alternatives. This chapter introduces the logic of using estimates of costs and benefits of different health care interventions in deciding which alternatives to fund. Sometimes this information is derived from clinical trials, and hence, the importance of including this introduction in this volume. Where possible, examples

D. L. Patrick: Department of Health Services, University of Washington, Seattle, Washington 98195.
P. Erickson: Clearinghouse on Health Indexes, OAEHP, National Center for Health Statistics, Hyattsville, Maryland 20782.

from clinical trials and from studies of prevention effectiveness, one of the major concerns of health policy analysts, are used. Our objectives are, first, to suggest how health status can be used to develop and evaluate health policy in general, and, second, to illustrate how health status assessments from clinical trials can be used in cost and outcomes tables [quality-adjusted life year (QALY) gained league tables] for evaluating medical effectiveness and allocating resources.

Given society's unwillingness to accept increased spending on health care, health decisions are increasingly being made with some estimate of the costs and benefits of each alternative. For example, heart disease, cancer, and strokes are the leading causes of death, but the actual precipitating causes are tobacco, unhealthful diet and activity patterns, alcohol, infections, chemicals, and other preventable factors (3). However, information for making such cost-benefit comparisons is not always available. Thus, discussion and debate center on assumptions, estimates, or other information about the relationship between costs and outcomes. Such assumptions are particularly important when information is presented as cost per quality-adjusted life year gained, or as used in this chapter, cost per year of healthy life gained.

HEALTH STATUS AS THE OUTCOME

We advocate the use of health and quality of life outcomes to measure the benefits of health expenditures and to assess the structure and process of health care delivery. We focus on health-related quality of life as the most relevant and comprehensive outcome measure for comparing costs. Health-related quality of life is defined as the value assigned to duration of life as modified by impairments, functional states, perceptions, and social opportunities that are influenced by disease, injury, treatment, or policy (2). Because health-related quality of life incorporates social values, life expectancy, and a comprehensive description of health, it addresses the trade-off between how long people live and how well they live. Health-related quality of life can be used as an indicator of both the process of care and the structure of health care delivery.

EVALUATING PROCESS AND OUTCOME

Increases in health care spending, attention to the quality of health care, and concern about access to health care have focused attention on the assessment of outcomes in relation to both the inputs and processes of health care delivery. Candidate processes of care and structural elements of the health care system can be briefly outlined as the following examples of policy alternatives:

- Increasing access to health care with the evaluation of the impact of increasing access on health outcomes.
- Assessing need for health care by evaluating health status of different population groups and particular target popula-

tions such as minority groups, rural areas, persons with particular health problems to reduce inequalities in health.
- Targeting prevention activities toward the problems of heart disease, stroke, fatal and nonfatal occupational injuries, motor vehicle–related injuries, low birthweight, and gunshot wounds.
- Providing consumers with information and guidelines about self-management of health to reduce demand for health services.
- Evaluating the quality of care delivered by particular providers or with different systems of delivery using health status outcomes, often known as outcomes management.
- Improving management and increasing efficiency through using managed care providers, reducing the number of physicians, using intermediate-level practitioners, and related approaches.
- Increasing competition among providers through disseminating statistics on costs, quality, and outcomes, or soliciting competitive bids among providers.
- Regulating hospital costs by reducing admissions and average lengths of stay, and by controlling provider payment through price-control programs, diagnosis-related groups, and other means of shifting costs outside the hospital. Many reimbursement studies are in this category.
- Reducing health care capacity through curtailing growth in investments and requiring certificates of need.
- Evaluating medical practices, producing practice guidelines, and limiting reimbursement to those procedures and practices that show evidence of effectiveness.
- Rationing services by defining a basic benefits package and denying health care to persons who cannot afford to pay for services not in the benefit package or limiting availability even to those who can pay for it.

Many of these policy initiatives concern the supply side of health care spending. Improving management, increasing competition, regulating hospital costs and provider payment, and reducing health care capacity are strategies for changing inputs to the health care system. Although potentially effective in the short term, these supply-side solutions are unlikely to have long-term effects on expenditure growth.

Innovations in management, for example, may reduce spending when first introduced, but have little effect on growth rates in the long term. Savings achieved through reductions in hospital admissions and lengths of stay were significant in the 1980s. If further drops in inpatient days are accompanied by increases in ambulatory care including home health care, savings are likely to decline and total costs can be expected to rise (4). Other measures need to be applied if hospital cost containment is to be sustained.

Regulation of provider payment has shown considerable promise in curtailing health care spending. Vigorous monitoring of provider payment is necessary, however, to prevent changes in diagnostic practices, charging, and other unintended consequences of regulation. The savings accrued from regulating provider payment, i.e., limiting increases or reducing reimbursement, may be considerably reduced because of the costs in administering the regulatory program.

The final two strategies for controlling health care spending in the above list—medical effectiveness evaluations and rationing—are based on outputs of the health care system rather than inputs. Medical effectiveness evaluations concern the distribution of resources to competing interventions, usually on the basis of benefit. Interventions may be evaluated only on the basis of effectiveness, defined as health status outcomes, without formal comparisons with expenditures. Evaluations of health programs, clinical interventions, and regulatory practices are examples. The major goals of effectiveness evaluations are (a) to establish the magnitude of effect, if any; (b) to disseminate the results of the evaluation often or through practice guidelines; and (c) to eliminate ineffective interventions through changes in practice or administrative behavior, such as changes in benefits or reimbursement formula. Eventually a reallocation of resources to more effective procedures is the goal of these activities.

Rationing refers to the distribution of resources to services or individuals according to various sets of rules. On the one hand, these rules may be explicit, such as the eligibility criteria that exclude persons from benefits and services. An example that affects many people in the United States is the use of the federal poverty level to determine eligibility for state-provided health care to people with low income through the Medicaid program. On the other hand, rules may be implicit, such as inequality in the rates of coronary artery bypass grafting between elderly white and African-American patients who receive such treatment under the Medicare program. Nationally, the sex- and age-adjusted bypass grafting rate in 1986 was 27.1 per 10,000 for whites, but only 7.6 for blacks (5). The goal of both evaluation and rationing is the reallocation of resources to more effective procedures to not only control costs but also maintain or improve health outcomes.

Outcomes may also be related formally to costs. Outcomes or benefits may be gains in life expectancy, years of healthy life, or illnesses and injuries averted after prevention or treatment. Costs include the expenditures incurred in the provision of services or goods for treatment or prevention and medical care as well as loss of productivity. As discussed below, analysts conduct cost-benefit, cost-effectiveness, and cost-utility analyses of health interventions to compare health outcomes and health care costs. The cost and outcome of different interventions for a single condition may be compared, e.g., back surgery compared with medical treatment for treatment of back pain. Alternatively, multiple interventions may be included within one costs and outcomes analytic framework, e.g., coronary artery bypass graft surgery and heart transplantation within an entire array of heart disease treatments. The results of these analyses can then be used as guidelines for distributing resources to interventions with a lower ratio of costs to outcomes. These methods play a central role in the health resource allocation strategy

developed by Patrick and Erickson (2) and described briefly below.

HEALTH RESOURCE ALLOCATION STRATEGY

Medical-effectiveness evaluations and rationing share an emphasis on and rediscovery of health care outcomes within the context of expended resources. Among the benefits expected to result from increased spending on health care resources are improved health status and quality of life. Depending on the level of expected benefits, the investment of resources may be constrained for some health interventions and expanded for others. Allocation decisions usually identify the constraints within which the total amount of resources available are distributed to meet the demands of those eligible to consume them. The process of distributing available resources to eligible consumers according to a defined set of criteria is political. Choices in health care are made not by the data, but rather by decision makers who evaluate criteria based on the data.

Table 1 contains the eight steps of the health resource allocation strategy. This strategy makes explicit the trade-offs among different states of health and quality of life to estimate whether a population is better or worse off with competing interventions. These trade-offs are built on the basic notion that health state preferences reflect the perceived value assigned to how long we live and how well we live. Alternative methods for assigning preferences to health states are identified to provide the means for making these trade-offs between quantity and quality.

Quantity of health is the expected duration of survival or life expectancy of a population, as influenced by mortality and health status. Expected duration of life depends on prognosis or course of illness and wellness across time. Assigning preferences to health states permits different domains of health-related quality of life to be combined with prognosis into a single index called *years of healthy life*. Years of healthy life can be calculated by adjusting the expected duration of survival by the point-in-time estimate of health-related quality of life (6).

In implementing the health resource allocation strategy, the analyst should estimate all costs attributed to each of the alternative courses of action, including out-of-pocket expenses and psychic costs incurred by recipients of health care services. Health costs and health-related quality of life outcomes are compared for each alternative by calculating the ratio of costs per-year-of-healthy-life gained for each alternative course of action. These ratios are ranked from low to high within the budget constraint included in the ranking. Ratios that are less than the budget constraint are recommended as cost effective. Not all cost-ineffective interventions remain unfunded and not all cost-effective alternatives are funded. As stated earlier, the decisions are political, and the rankings are merely a guide for discussion and debate against the wishes of the many stakeholders and vested

TABLE 1. *Eight steps in the health resource allocation strategy*

1. Specify the health decision by
   Describing the sociocultural and health services context of the decision
   Identifying alternative courses of action under consideration
   Identifying stakeholders
   Defining stakeholder values for outcomes of alternatives
   Recognizing the assumptions used in the socioeconomic evaluation
   Specifying the budgetary constraints to be considered
2. Classify health outcomes as health states by
   Identifying relevant concepts, domains, and indicators of health-related quality of life
   Listing the hypothesized relationships among concepts, domains, and indicators
   Selecting combination of domains to be included in the health state classification
3. Assign values to health states by
   Identifying population of judges to assign preferences
   Sampling health states to be assigned preference weights
   Selecting a method of preference measurement
   Collecting preference judgments and assigning preference weights to health states
4. Measure health-related quality of life of target population using primary data collection or secondary analysis to
   Classify individuals in target population into health states
   Assign a preference weight to the health state of each individual
   Average scores of all individuals to obtain a point-in-time estimate of the target population's health-related quality of life
5. Estimate prognosis and years of healthy life by
   Calculating expected duration of survival (life expectancy) of target population
   Calculating years of healthy life by adjusting duration of survival by the point-in-time estimate or observed differences in health-related quality of life
6. Estimate direct and indirect health care costs by
   Identifying all organizing and operational costs attributed to each of the alternative courses of action
   Specifying out-of-pocket expenses and productivity losses incurred by the recipients of each alternative
7. Rank costs and outcomes of health care alternatives by
   Calculating the ratio of costs per year of healthy life gained for each alternative course of action
   Ranking the ratios from low to high with the budget constraint included in this ranking
   Identifying ratios that are less than the budget constraint as cost-effective
8. Revise rankings of costs and outcomes by
   Reviewing rank order of each alternative course of action with stakeholders in the decision
   Adjusting the rank order based on stakeholder challenges and community consensus on the values and goals of health care
   Recommending the revised rank order to political decision makers

Adapted from ref. 2.

interest parties. The remainder of this chapter considers how the rankings of health care costs and outcomes are made (step 7 of Table 1).

COST-BENEFIT, COST-EFFECTIVENESS, AND COST-UTILITY ANALYSES

Rankings of costs and outcomes from various health interventions, including prevention activities, medical and surgical treatments, and rehabilitation programs, are usually based on one of three forms of economic analysis: cost-benefit analysis, cost-effectiveness analysis, and cost-utility analysis. Cost-benefit analysis is derived from economic theory and involves comparing both costs and outcomes in terms of monetary units. Expected costs attributed to an intervention are subtracted from the associated benefits to form an expression of net benefits. If the net benefit is positive, then the generally accepted decision rule is to fund the intervention. Cost-benefit analysis has not been widely used in health policy making because of the difficulty of using

monetary units (dollars) to value life. Although willingness-to-pay, human capital, and revealed-preference methodologies have proved useful for assigning monetary value to human life in selected studies, conceptual and practical concerns have prevented any single method from becoming widely accepted (7,8).

Cost-effectiveness analysis compares costs and health outcomes without explicitly assigning values to human life. Rather, outcomes are expressed in any one of a number of natural, or biologically meaningful, units, including life years saved, number of disability days saved, and number of cases averted (9,10). When health outcomes are measured in different units in different studies, cost-effectiveness analysis cannot be used to compare costs and outcomes across different interventions. Thus, the lack of commensurate units of measurement can limit the use of cost-effectiveness analysis in policy applications.

As a result of the difficulties with applying and interpreting results from both cost-benefit and cost-effectiveness analyses, cost-utility analysis is becoming the recommended method for ranking costs and outcomes. Cost-utility analysis not only overcomes the difficulty of using monetary units (dollars) as required by cost-benefit analysis but also overcomes the limitation of diverse units of measurement by using a standard measure of health outcome, regardless of health intervention, namely years of healthy life or quality-adjusted life years. Broadly defined, a year of healthy life is duration of life discounted by some fraction between 0 and 1 that estimates quality of life during one year. For example, a person whose health prevents him or her from working for one year may have a quality-of-life score of 0.65; this person is said to have 0.65 years of healthy life for the year. Alternatively, the person is considered as being fully functional about two-thirds of the year. The concept of years of healthy life can be expanded to cover more than one year and more than one person. For example, if the duration of life is 10 years and the quality-adjustment factor is 0.65, then a person is said to have 6.5 years of healthy life over the interval. Alternatively, ten people living one year each with an average quality of life score of 0.65 are also said to have 6.5 years of healthy life in the aggregate.

In evaluating health interventions, the quality-adjustment factor may include concepts of physical, mental, and social function as well as impairments and disadvantages (2). The specific concepts and domains that are included in a health outcome measure depend, to a large extent, on the purpose for which a measure is developed. Table 2 summarizes the main concepts in nine standardized generic approaches for collecting information that can be used to estimate years of healthy life: Disability Distress Ratio Scale; EuroQol; Fifteen-Dimension Scale; Health Utilities Index Mark I, Mark II, and Mark III; Index of Health-Related Quality of Life; Interim Years of Healthy Life; and the Quality of Well-Being Scale.

Concepts are combined to form health states that represent operational definitions of health. For example, one health state that is used in the Interim Years of Healthy Life measure developed by the National Center for Health Statistics is being in very good health and limited in major activity. When measures include more concepts, such as the Index of Health-Related Quality of Life, the health states are more comprehensive. Regardless of their complexity, mutually exclusive health states that described health-related quality of life are arrayed along a continuum that ranges from optimal to minimal health. The order in which health states are placed along this continuum depends on the value or utility that individuals or society place on each state.

Definitions of health status and placement on the continuum are by no means "value free" activities in and for themselves. Many measures systematically assign lower values to states of increasing disability. Although movements between states may be equally valued regardless of the level of disability reflected in the state, dysfunction and disability remain negatively valued. Assigning negative values to disability may have social consensus; nevertheless, this is discriminating when applied to populations of disabled people, many of whom enjoy a high quality of life. Thus, it is important to be able to decompose the measures and their weighing schemes for hidden assumptions and biases.

TABLE 2. *Principal concepts of health-related quality of life contained in existent instruments for assessing years of healthy life*

Concept	Disability distress ratio	EuroQol	15D	Health Utility Index Mark I	Health Utility Index Mark II	Health Utility Index Mark III	Index of Health-Related QOL	HP2000 Years of Healthy Life	Quality of Well-Being Scale
Health perceptions			**					**	
Social function									
Social relations	**			**			**		**
Usual social role	**			**			**		
Intimacy/sexual							**		
Function									
Communication/speech		**			**				
Mental function									
Cognitive function			**		**	**	**		
Emotional function		**		**		**			
Mood/feelings					**		**		
Physical function									
Mobility	**	**	**	**	**	**	**		**
Physical activity	**			**				**	**
Self-care		**	**			**	**		
Impairment									
Sensory function/loss			**		**	**	**		
Symptoms/impairments	**	**		**	**	**	**		**

VALUE APPROACHES TO HEALTH STATUS MEASUREMENT

The nine generic systems in Table 2 elicit preferences for health states primarily through the use of one of three methods: the standard gamble technique; the time trade-off technique; or category scaling methods, including the feeling thermometer and the rating scale. Each of these methods is briefly discussed below. For more detailed information about the methods and their applications see other chapters in this volume or Patrick and Erickson (2). The standard gamble technique has been referred to by many economists as the "gold standard" or "classical method" of measuring utilities because it stems directly from expected utility theory (11–13; Torrance GW, personal communication). In addition, the standard gamble technique can be used to elicit information about utility for states that are perceived as being worse than death as well as for acute, or temporary, health states (14). To assist respondents in assigning utility scores to these choices, investigators have developed visual aids such as a probability wheel and a chance board (15,16). Although the standard gamble technique's tie to expected utility theory makes it the method of choice from a theoretical perspective, investigators and respondents often indicate that the method is confusing and burdensome. For example, in a study of stroke patients, Wolfson et al. (17) found that respondents had difficulties understanding what was expected of them and sometimes resisted the notion of gambling with one's health.

The time trade-off technique was developed to provide a more user-friendly variant of the standard gamble (18). A visual aid, called the time trade-off board, has been developed to assist respondents (15). The time trade-off and standard gamble techniques have been found to give similar but not identical results (17); utilities were generally higher when assessed by the standard gamble than by the time trade-off technique. Gafni and colleagues (12) suggest that since the time trade-off technique is not directly related to a behavioral theory, it is impossible to interpret discrepancies between utilities determined by time trade-off technique and those that are obtained by different methods.

The third method, category scaling, or the method of equal-appearing intervals arising from psychophysics, requires that a person rate states along a continuum that has clearly specified end points, such as perfect health or most desirable and death or least desirable. The method of category rating was first used for collecting information about utilities for health in the development of the Quality of Well-Being Scale (19). Subsequently, Torrance and colleagues (20) used a rating scale to develop social utilities in their evaluation of the neonatal intensive care units. Although not without respondent burden, category scaling has been found to be acceptable to a wide variety of respondents (19–21, 57).

In collecting information on preferences, an investigator may decide to ask respondents to supply information about the values they place on different health states at the same time they are asked about their current health status. This approach is most frequently used in clinical studies. Information on utilities that is obtained in this way is study dependent and usually condition specific. Neither the utilities themselves nor the study results can be easily generalized to broader population groups and treatment experiences, although the estimates may be compared across studies.

To avoid these problems of external validity, investigators often design a study in which data on preferences are collected independently of the survey in which health state information is collected. Preferences that are independent of an individual's health condition and the study context may or may not reflect society's values for health. This assumption is made, however. The independent approach has been most frequently used with instruments that have been created specifically for use in policy analysis (22–24).

Another alternative for arriving at a set of health state preferences is the approach that was used for developing the Healthy People 2000 Years of Healthy Life measure. Time and other resources available for developing this measure required that preferences be developed from existing data (25). The first step was to use survey data to determine scores between 0.0 and 1.0 for health perceptions and activity limitation that would maximize the correlation between these two concepts. The state of being limited in self-care activities and being in excellent health was linked to a similar state in the Health Utility Index Mark I in order to obtain a standard gamble–based utility for this health state. With this information, a multiattribute utility function was developed to assign a utility to each of 30 possible health states. This approach to determining utilities might be used in other applications as long as the results are interpreted cautiously and compared with directly measured preferences using the same definitions and health states when used for costs and outcomes comparisons.

The calculation of a year of healthy life combines the preference that an individual places on a state of health to "quality adjust" duration of life. Information about duration of life is generally available when conducting a longitudinal observational study. In the absence of cohort data, life expectancy information can be used (25).

DECISION-ANALYTIC APPROACHES TO HEALTH STATUS MEASUREMENT

An alternative to using a specific instrument and collecting data from target populations is that of decision analysis, another approach that has been adopted for use in evaluating outcomes associated with different health interventions (26,27). This technique is based on traditions and methods stemming from operations research and game theory to form an analytic structure for arriving at decisions under conditions of uncertainty. Early applications of decision analysis in the fields of medicine and health care focused on clinical problems (28). More recently, applications of decision analysis have broadened to include public policy issues such as the role of alternative exercise interventions in preventing heart disease (29). Often, data used in decision-analytic approaches are derived from clinical trials that provide the probabilities of outcome associated with the different intervention in the decision analysis.

Like cost-utility analysis, decision analysis involves assigning a score to the relative value of a health outcome, otherwise known as a utility or preference for a given health state. These utilities are incorporated into a "decision tree" that describes all of the possible outcomes associated with a health condition and its treatment. At the point of each decision, or node, a probability is assigned to the likelihood of a particular outcome occurring. The expected outcome along any given limb of the decision tree is the sum of the utilities associated with the outcomes weighted by the probabilities of their occurrence (28).

Unlike cost-utility analysis, however, utilities used in decision analysis are most commonly based on personal judgments supplied by a small group of clinicians. For example, in identifying the preferred treatment for chronic nonvalvular atrial fibrillation among persons 70 to 75 years of age, Naglie and Detsky (30) derived utilities based on the opinions of three clinicians. Such utilities reflect the experience and values of the judges rather than that of a wider group of persons or society in general. Thus, the gain in health benefit calculated from utilities based on clinician judgment may be biased when compared with the gain based on utilities collected from patients with a specific disease or disability or members of the general population, regardless of their health condition.

This brief discussion about sources of information on preferences for various health states introduces broader notions and concerns associated with the perspective from which the evaluation of costs and outcomes is taken. For example, in designing a costs and outcomes assessment as part of a clinical trial, a pharmaceutical company may be interested in assessing gains that accrue to an individual and his or her immediate social network. When approving the same medicine for licensure, however, a government regulatory agency may want an analysis that considers all costs and outcomes to society regardless of who benefits (23).

In the context of cost-utility analysis, Weinstein and Stason (31) recommend that analysts take the societal perspective when compiling data to be used for analysis. Taking this view means that health outcomes as well as costs are measured across all members of society. Thus, the data are comprehensive and broadly applicable. To form a measure of health outcome that is representative of the population, researchers start from the position that health-related quality of life data are collected from an individual (14,22). Information from individuals is then averaged to estimate the level of health for a society.

For public policy, the appropriate view is that of society, that is, the effect that an intervention will have on the social welfare of everyone in the society. A societal perspective includes all medical and nonmedical costs as well as personal indirect costs regardless of who pays. The intervention may be targeted to a single group, although the benefits accrued may be to all persons in society, or more often a pool of persons insured. For example, if comprehensive human immunodeficiency virus (HIV) counseling, testing, referral, and partner notification services cause just one of five individuals who learn they are HIV-positive to adjust their behavior and prevent at least one more new HIV infection, the benefits are 20 times the cost (32). This societal view also incorporates a broad range of costs and health outcomes as well as the ethical, social, and legal impacts of the intervention allowing the decision maker to choose among alternative, competing programs (33).

Analyses using more restrictive perspectives on cost are limited to drawing conclusions within the organizational context bounded by the choice of the cost data. For example, health insurers may try to determine the costs accruing to their companies. When interpreting the results of special studies, one should be clear about the objectives and the perspective taken as both limit the inferences that can be drawn from the results, especially with regard to generalizing the results to society at large (34).

RANKING COSTS AND OUTCOMES

Recent health care reform debates were shaped by the assumption of scarce resources and increasing demands for these resources, not only by the health sector but also by other sectors of the economy, such as education and criminal justice. In this environment, issues of cost containment, access to care, and health insurance coverage all suggest that policy makers will need a well-defined allocation strategy to avoid policies that have adverse consequences on the nation's level of health. In allocating resources to health care, Williams (35) argues that interventions should be ranked so that those that cost less per year of healthy life gained are given priority over those costing more. This strategy is attractive because it allows policy makers to provide the highest level of health with a given budget constraint, which is often determined politically. Mathematically this health maximization problem can be set up as one of constrained optimization with society's health in the objective function and the budgetary information in the constraint.

Using years of healthy life addresses the problem of interpersonal comparisons when aggregating utilities for making statements about social welfare. Although preference measurement is used in constructing a measure of years of healthy life, the result is a set of health-related quality of life scores that represents the relative importance that individuals place on health rather than on the utility that individuals gain from health. With preference scaling of health states, the health-related quality of life scores are invariant across all people in the same state. That is, all people in the same health state are assigned the same score. This feature of health scores based on preference measurement differs from the standard use of the concept of utility in which people in the same state might be expected to have different levels of utility (36–39). Thus, aggregating individual health status scores to maximize society's level of health is not considered to be the same as making interpersonal comparisons of utility.

Gafni and colleagues criticize the health maximization approach because it fails to include utility maximization and thus is not subject to the standard efficiency conditions of microeconomic theory. To overcome this limitation of years of healthy life for use in cost-utility analysis, these investigators have proposed the use of the healthy year equivalent for measuring health (39). The healthy year equivalent (HYE) makes no assumption about the form of the individual's utility function, whereas the year of healthy life model assumes that all individuals have utility functions of the same form. In addition to the nonrestrictive assumption about the form of the utility function, the developers of the healthy year equivalent cite its consistency with the efficiency criterion of economic theory as another advantage of using healthy year equivalents rather than years of healthy life for quantifying health outcomes.

The healthy year equivalent is a relatively new approach to assessing health for use in costs and outcomes analysis. This approach has been criticized as being overly complicated to use and as confusing the concept that is being measured with the method of measurement (40). Others have taken issue with the basic premise that healthy year equivalents are more representative of consumer preferences than are years of healthy life (41). These criticisms and the lack of a standard method for assessing outcome that can be readily applied has resulted in relatively few applications of the healthy year equivalent for policy making to date. Instead, numerous rankings of interventions are available in which years of healthy life have been used to measure health outcomes.

As an example of the ranking of costs and outcomes, comparisons of interventions using cost-utility analysis are shown in Table 3 for a selected set of interventions. Interventions are ranked in ascending order according to the ratio of costs and outcomes. Such tables are referred to as "league" tables (42,43). Each ratio indicates the cost of the intervention per-year-of-healthy-life gained from the intervention. Interventions with lower ratios are estimated to produce an additional year of healthy life at a lower cost than interventions with higher ratios. Thus, based on a cost-effectiveness criterion alone, interventions with lower ratios that fall within the allowable budget are recommended for funding than are those with higher ratios that exceed the budget constraint.

Ideally, these league tables should be constructed using costs and outcomes information collected from a common source, including population at risk, survey methodology, preference measurement, and consistent assumptions about the relevant costs and health states included. Since no such data source exists, cost-utility ratios based on a variety of sources are frequently compiled into league tables using different methods, assumptions, and analytic techniques. The effect of these methodological differences is often analyzed

TABLE 3. *Estimated cost per year of healthy life gained using the Health Utilities Index*

Intervention (reference)	Reported cost/YHL gained in U.S. dollars (year)	Adjusted cost/YHL gained in U.S. dollars (1991)
Postpartum anti-D (53)	<$0 (1977)	<$0
Antepartum treatment of primiparae and multiparae (average) (54)	$1,223 (1983)	$2,150
Neonatal intensive care of low-birth-weight infants, 1000–1499 g (55)	$2,800 (1978)	$8,000
Neonatal intensive care of very-low-birth-weight infants, 500–999 g (55)	$19,600 (1978)	$56,100
Continuous ambulatory peritoneal dialysis (56)	$35,100 (1980)	$82,900
Hospital hemodialysis (56)	$40,200 (1980)	$94,900

Adapted from ref. 2.
Method of adjustment:
$$C/YHL_{1991} = (MCPI_{1991}/MCPI_{py}) \times C/YHL_{py}$$
where
C/YHL_{1991} = adjusted cost/YHL gained in 1991
$MCPI_{1991}$ = Medical Care Price Index for 1991
$MCPI_{py}$ = Medical Care Price Index for previous year
C/YHL_{py} = Cost/YHL gained for previous year
For example, for antepartum treatment the adjusted ratio has been calculated as follows:
$C/YHL_{1991} = MCPI_{1991} / MCPI_{1983} \times C/YHL_{1983} = 177/100.6 \times \$1,223 = \$2,152$
Note: MCPI data are from *Statistical Abstracts 1992.*

using sensitivity analyses within individual studies. The validity of accompanying costs and outcomes using different methods, however, is largely unknown.

Also in the ideal, the ranking of costs and outcomes ratios should be done using marginal estimates of both costs and health outcomes to permit policy makers to deal with allocation decisions that address not only whether an intervention should be funded but also those decisions that consider the extent, intensity, or how much of a particular intervention should be funded. In practice, marginal data are rarely available and analysts make do with information about average costs and outcomes. In a review of 21 interventions that had been evaluated using cost-utility analysis, Drummond and colleagues (43) found only one that was based on marginal analysis; 19 were based on average values and for one the information about how costs and outcomes were estimated was not ascertainable. Use of average rather than marginal estimates, especially for comparing interventions in a league table, may mislead policy makers. In a classic example of the impact of using average rather than marginal data, Neuhauser and Lewicki (44) showed that among the recommended six screening tests for colonic cancer, the marginal cost could be as much as 20,000 times higher than the average cost. Decisions based on average, rather than marginal, values may underestimate the impact that implementation of an intervention might have on the overall cost.

Another issue that needs to be borne in mind when interpreting the ranking of costs and outcomes is the stochastic nature of the cost-effectiveness ratio. When costs and outcomes data are collected as part of a clinical trial or health survey, then the estimates are usually subject to both sampling and nonsampling error. In such cases, it may be possible to estimate a standard error for the ratio so that confidence intervals can be applied (45,46). For ratios that are close to the threshold that separates the cost-effective from the cost-ineffective ratios, confidence intervals can be used to indicate the position of the interventions associated with these ratios relative to the budget constraint.

For example, suppose that the threshold had been set at $15,000 and a deterministic ratio of $16,500 had been obtained for coronary artery bypass graft surgery. From this ratio, the intervention would appear to be cost-ineffective. If, however, information were available so that confidence intervals could be placed about this ratio, we might see that the cost per year of healthy life gained ranged from $14,500 to $18,500. Since the lower range is below the threshold value, the surgery might be considered cost-effective and thus included in the set of affordable interventions for the given budget constraint.

In addition to stochastic elements, estimates of costs and outcomes may be biased by the nature of the data collection, editing, and analysis processes. For example, study designers may allow information on quality of life to be supplied by a surrogate who responds for the actual study participant. Although the use of such proxy respondents may have the advantage of convenience and minimize problems of missing information, the data may be biased. For example, elderly wives may perceive their husbands to be in a lower health status than their spouses would rate their own health.

The use of selected populations or treatment centers from clinical trial data is another limitation of the league tables that have been published to date. Selection may be defined in terms of the type of patient, e.g., healthier, better educated, more compliant. For example, in a cost-utility analysis that was conducted as part of a clinical trial of arthritis therapy, patients were excluded from the study if they were over 65 years of age, had severe arthritis or serious concomitant disease, had been previously treated with antineoplastic agents, had recently been treated with selected arthritis or other medications, or had elevated status in a number of laboratory tests (47). Yet data from the National Health Interview Survey indicate that almost one-half of the cases of arthritis reported in 1990 occurred among persons 65 years of age and older (48). Thus, treatment comparisons in this clinical study were made on a relatively young, probably healthy, subset of the noninstitutionalized U.S. population that has arthritis.

Another selection bias may be based on the application of a given intervention at a specialized treatment center, e.g., a neonatal intensive care unit in a teaching hospital. In the case of special treatment centers, both the costs and outcomes may be higher so that it is not easy to predict the direction of the bias. Data from local areas that can be characterized by different practice patterns represent another type of selection that might introduce bias into league tables that are compiled from different data sources (49,50).

In summary, care must be exercised in interpreting the information in composite league tables that rank interventions using different methods for estimating costs and outcomes. These differences may mean that the ratios are not comparable even though they all reflect the cost per-year-of-healthy-life gained (49).

The information contained in Table 3 is derived using the Health Utility Index and thus incorporates a common definition of health states, comparable methods of preference measurement, and other comparable analytic techniques. Although appearing clear and easy to interpret, this display of costs and outcomes information obscures many assumptions and methodological issues that underlie the estimation of both costs and outcomes for each intervention. For example, these estimated ratios are sensitive to the selection of patients, cost of tests or treatments, and the intensity of the interventions as valuated. Furthermore, new tests and treatments are constantly under development and existing treatments are refined, particularly when they have been recently developed. Rapid advances in technology should also be considered. Nevertheless, rankings like that shown in Table 3 provide an ordering of magnitude useful for the discussion of interventions ''at the margin'' of an acceptable ratio within the budget constraints or far outside of it.

These criticisms of league tables suggest that if the purpose of cost-utility analysis, when done as a part of a clinical study, is to assist policy makers contain costs and at the same time maintain or increase the level of health, then one approach is for the same methods for assessing health care costs and outcomes to be applied systematically to all interventions, as was attempted in the Oregon Medicaid waiver experiment (51). At the present time, due in part to the lack of consensus on concepts and methods of measurement, the development of a metric for converting costs and outcomes into a common rubric is a more promising approach to producing information on costs and outcomes comparisons that can be used across a wide array of health interventions. Toward this end, researchers have called for the adoption of a set of standards that might include the following topics: methods for estimating direct and indirect health care costs, techniques for valuing health outcomes, and recommended ranges for discount rates (23,33,52).

CONCLUSIONS: FROM TECHNICAL PROCESS TO DECISION

It cannot be overemphasized that the ranking of health care alternatives according to cost per year of healthy life gained is a technical procedure. Judgments of worth are not made by technical data; they necessarily use the prevailing cultural, political, and ethical values of the community. All stakeholders in the health decisions should be involved, and rankings must be reviewed by stakeholders and adjusted to reflect the fullest possible range of community values before decision makers, the final arbitrators, assign priorities and allocate resources. This sociopolitical process is essential and desirable in applying the Health Resource Allocation Strategy to health decisions that affect all members of the community equally or unequally.

No one likes to be denied a service or benefit that he or she considers desirable or effective. Likewise, there is hardly an intervention that is not effective for some person in some place and at some level of health. Nevertheless, choices in health care have to be and will be made, often using informal variants of cost-benefit or cost-effectiveness analysis and without attention to a sociopolitical process whereby costs and outcomes and the technical data can be debated. Rankings of costs and outcomes take some of the "smoke and mirrors" out of the decision process, even though critics charge that the quality of science in costs and outcomes comparisons does not meet acceptable standards. Debate over the ranking and its elements of input reveals the larger clash between goals and stakeholders in the health care system.

Health-related quality of life data from clinical trials, epidemiologic studies, and decision analyses increasingly will inform the debate on health policy alternatives. Many of these data will not, however, be placed in an allocation framework such as that presented in this chapter. For example, within preventive interventions alone, community-based

activities, clinical preventive services, and socioeconomic policies compete with benefits, costs, and savings.

Outcomes research will provide more and more data for the meta-analytic approach to decision making, the context for health status in health policy. The quality of outcomes information must improve to meet the demand of decision makers in an efficient and effective manner sensitive to the values and lives of different stakeholders. Choices will be made, informed or uninformed by data and the input of the community. As health status measurement develops, we anticipate it will inform the decision makers and continue to fuel the debate over what alternatives to fund or not fund.

REFERENCES

1. Burner SF, Waldo DR, McKasick D. National health expenditures projections through 2030. *Health Care Finan Rev* 1993;14:1–29.
2. Patrick DL, Erickson P. *Health status and health policy: allocating resources to health care.* New York: Oxford University Press, 1993.
3. McGinnis JM, Foege WH. Actual causes of death in the United States. *JAMA* 1993;270:2207–2212.
4. Schwartz WB, Mendelson DN. Hospital cost containment in the 1980s: hard lessons learned and prospects for the 1990s. *N Engl J Med* 1991;324(15):1037–1042.
5. Goldberg KC, Hartz AJ, Jacobsen SJ, Krakauer H, Rimm AA. Racial and community factors influencing coronary artery bypass graft surgery rates for all 1986 Medicare patients. *JAMA* 1992;267:1473–1477.
6. Erickson P, Wilson RW, Shannon I. *Years of healthy life. Statistical note.* Hyattsville, MD: National Center for Health Statistics, 1995.
7. Sirken MG. Error effects of survey questionnaires on the public's assessments of health risks. *Am J Public Health* 1986;76(4):367–368.
8. Thompson MS, Read JL, Liang M. Willingness-to-pay concepts for societal decisions in health. In: Kane RL, Kane RA, eds. *Values and long-term care.* Lexington, MA: Lexington Books, 1982:103–125.
9. Oster G, Huse DM, Delea TE, Colditz GA. Cost-effectiveness of nicotine gum as an adjunct to physician's advice against cigarette smoking. *JAMA* 1986;256(10):1315–1318.
10. Simpson N. Effects of isotretinoin on the quality of life of patients with acne. *Pharmacoeconomics* 1994;6(2):108–113.
11. von Neuman J, Morgenstern O. *Theory of games and economic behavior.* Princeton, NJ: Princeton University Press, 1994.
12. Gafni A, Birch S, Mehrez A. Economics, health and health economics: HYEs versus QALYs. *J Health Econ* 1993;11:325–339.
13. Gyldmark M, Morrison GC. Re-appraising the use of contingent valuation: a reply. *Health Econ* 1993;2:363–365.
14. Torrance GW. The measurement of health state utilities for economic appraisal. *J Health Econ* 1986;5(1):1–30.
15. Furlong W, Feeny D, Torrance GW, Barr R, Horsman J. *Guide to design and development of health-state utility instrumentation.* (CHEPA working paper series 90-9). Hamilton, Ontario: McMaster University, 1990.
16. Torrance GW. Social preferences for health states: a empirical evaluation of three measurement techniques. *Socio-Econ Plan Sci* 1976;10:129–136.
17. Wolfson AD, Sinclair AJ, Bambardier C, McGeer A. Preference measurements for functional status in stroke patients: interrater and intertechnique comparison. In: Kane RL, Kane RA, eds. *Values and long-term care.* Lexington, MA: Lexington Books, 1982:191–214.
18. Torrance GW, Thomas WH, Sackett DI. A utility maximization model for evaluation of health care programs. *Health Serv Res* 1972;7(2):118–133.
19. Patrick DL, Bush JW, Chen MM. Towards an operational definition of health. *J Health Soc Behav* 1973;14(1):6–23.
20. Torrance GW. Multiattribute utility theory as a method of measuring social preferences for health states in long-term care. In: Kane RL, Kane RA, eds. *Values and long-term care.* 1982:127–156.
21. Carter WB, Bobbitt RA, Bergner M, Gilson BS. Validation of an

interval scaling: the Sickness Impact Profile. *Health Serv Res* 1976;11(4): 516–528.

22. Funshel S, Bush JW. A Health-Status Index and its application to health-services outcomes. *Operations Res* 1970;18(6):1021–1066.

23. Drummond MF, Stoddart GL, Torrance GW. *Methods for the economic evaluation of health care programmes.* New York: Oxford University Press, 1987.

24. Ontario Ministry of Health. An overview of the survey content of the Ontario Health Survey. *Ontario Health Survey Bull* 1990;February.

25. Erickson P, Wilson RW. A short term for "quality-adjusted life years." *Am J Public Health* 1994;84(5):866.

26. Raiffa H. *Decision analysis: introductory lectures on choices under uncertainty.* Reading, MA: Addison-Wesley, 1968.

27. Weinstein MC, Fineberg, HV, Elstein AS, et al. *Clinical decision analysis.* Philadelphia, PA: WB Saunders, 1980.

28. Pauker SG, Kassirer JP. Medical progress: decision analysis. *N Engl J Med* 1987;316(5):250–258.

29. Hatziandreu EI, Koplan JP, Weinstein MC, Caspersen CJ, Warner KE. A cost-effectiveness analysis of exercise as a health promotion activity. *Am J Public Health* 1988;78(11):1417–1421.

30. Naglie IG, Detsky AS. Treatment of chronic nonvalvular atrial fibrillation in the elderly: a decision analysis. *Med Decis Making* 1992;12(4): 239–249.

31. Weinstein MC, Stason WB. Foundations of cost-effectiveness analysis for health and medical practices. *N Engl Med J* 1977;296(13):716–721.

32. Holgrave DR, Valdiserre NO. Virus counseling, testing, referral and partner notification series: a cost-benefit analysis. *Intern Med* 1993;153:1225–1230.

33. Luce BR, Elixhauser A. *Standards for socioeconomic evaluation of health care products and services.* New York: Springer-Verlag, 1990.

34. Russell LB. *Is prevention better than cure?* Washington, DC: Brookings Institution, 1986.

35. Williams A. Economics of coronary artery bypass grafting. *Br Med J* 1985;291(6491):326–329.

36. Wagstaff A. QALYs and the equity-efficiency trade-off. *J Health Econ* 1991;10:21–41.

37. Torrance GW, Feeny D. Utilities and quality-adjusted life years. *Int J Technol Assess Health Care* 1989;5:559–578.

38. Loomes G, McKenzie L. The use of QALYs in health care decision making. *Soc Sci Med* 1989;28(4):299–308.

39. Mehrez A, Gafni A. Quality-adjusted life years, utility theory, and healthy-years equivalent. *Med Decis Making* 1989;9(2):142–149.

40. Buckingham K. A note in HYE (Health Years Equivalent). *J Health Econ* 1993;11:301–309.

41. Culyer AJ, Wagstaff A. QALYs and HYEs. *J Health Econ* 1993;11:311–323.

42. Mason J, Drummond MF, Torrance GW, George LK. Some guidelines on the use of cost effectiveness league tables. *Br Med J* 1993; 306(6877):570–572.

43. Drummond MF, Torrance GW, Mason J. Cost-effectiveness league tables: more harm than good? *Soc Sci Med* 1993;37(1):33–40.

44. Neuhauser D, Lewicki AM. What do we gain from the sixth stool guaiac? *N Engl J Med* 1975;293(5):226–228.

45. Drummond M, O'Brien B. Clinical importance, statistical significance and the assessment of economic and quality-of-life outcomes. *Health Econ* 1993;2:205–212.

46. O'Brien BJ, Drummond MF, Labelle RJ, et al. In search of power and significance: issues in the design and analysis of stochastic cost-effectiveness studies in health care. *Med Care* 1994;32(2):150–163.

47. Bombardier C, Ware J, Russell IJ, Larson M, Chalmers A, Read JL. Auranofin therapy and quality of life in patients with rheumatoid arthritis: results of a multicenter trial. *Am J Med* 1986;81(4):565–578.

48. Benson V, Marano M. *Current estimates from the National Health Interview Survey, 1992. Vital and Health Statistics,* vol 10(189). Hyattsville, MD: National Center for Health Statistics, 1994.

49. Gerard K, Mooney G. QALY league tables: handle with care. *J Health Econ* 1993;2:59–64.

50. Wennberg J, Gittlesohn A. Small area variations in health care delivery. *Science* 1973;182:1102–1108.

51. U.S. Congress, Office of Technology Assessment. *Evaluation of the Oregon medicaid proposal.* (OTA-H-531). Washington, DC: U.S. Government Printing Office, 1992.

52. Gold M. *Cost-effectiveness panel on clinical preventive services.* Washington, DC: Department of Health and Human Services, 1993.

53. Torrance GW, Zipursky A. Cost-effectiveness analysis of treatment with anti-D. Rh Prevention Conference, McMaster University, Hamilton, Ontario, 1977.

54. Torrance GW, Zipursky A. Cost-effectiveness of antepartum prevention of Rh immunization. *Clin Perinatol* 1984;11(2):267–281.

55. Boyle MG, Torrance HW, Sinclair JC, et al. Economic evaluation of neonatal intensive care of very-low-birth-weight infants. *N Engl J Med* 1983;308(22):1045–1057.

56. Churchill DN, Morgan J, Torrance GW. Quality of life in end-stage renal disease. *Peritoneal Dialysis Bull* 1984;Jan–Mar:20–23.

57. EuroQol Group. EuroQol—a new facility for the measurement of health-related quality of life. *Health Policy* 1990;16:199–208.

Quality of Life and Pharmacoeconomics in Clinical Trials, Second Edition, edited by B. Spilker.
Lippincott-Raven Publishers, Philadelphia © 1996.

CHAPTER 75

Ethical and Medical Basis of Health Care Rationing

Stefan Björk

INTRODUCTION

What fundamental values ought to rule rationing and priority setting in health care? Is it proper to accept any criteria other than ethical or medical ones? If other criteria are thought to be acceptable, what kind of guidelines do they apply, and what are the implications—economic and otherwise—of applying them? If we accept only ethical and medical criteria, is there a clear-cut dividing line between an ethical criterion and a medical one? Accepting ethical criteria does not mean that we can content ourselves with presenting *one* completed solution; the recommended solution is necessarily determined by its underlying ethical theory or approach. Clearly, then, a number of crucial questions have to be asked and answered if we are to feel confident that the health services are sound and provide us with the care and cure we expect from them. To illuminate the basic problems of health care rationing, this chapter discusses the general causes of a changing health care field, the goals of health service according to different specification, and the criteria and basis for rationing.

S. Björk: The Swedish Institute for Health Economics, S-220 02 Lund, Sweden.

A CHANGING HEALTH CARE FIELD

Health care is currently undergoing radical changes in many countries throughout the world. Surveys among the general public (each averaging 1,000 respondents) performed from 1988 to 1990 showed that a majority of the people in Australia, Italy, Japan, the United States, France, the United Kingdom, and Sweden wanted a totally different health care system, or maintained that extensive changes were necessary in the health care system (1). Whenever major changes are taking place, it is especially important to be explicit about the nature of the basic criteria for assigning priorities and allocating available resources. Otherwise, the relevant decisions will be made in a haphazard manner in which prejudices are likely to prevail. In some of the countries, concerned officials have published reports on rationing and priorities, including discussions of ethical and other bases and practical recommendations, e.g., in Oregon in the U.S., New Zealand, Norway, the Netherlands, and Sweden (2–6). The changes are not only of an organizational and financial nature, they also affect the ethical foundations on which publicly funded health care rests. The most apparent effects of these changes in health care pertain to the content of health services and to access to health care for the general public. Content is modified along with increased medical knowledge and changes in available resources; the increas-

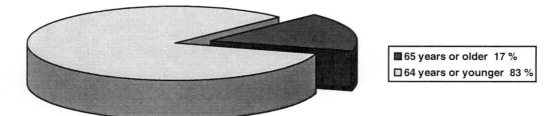

FIG. 1. The number of individuals 65 years of age and older of the total Swedish population. Percent.

ing limitations in access to health care are due to the relatively limited health care resources.

A number of new medical technologies (often expensive ones) are now used in a number of different areas. The applied new technologies are medically more efficient, and can often be used for a wider range of diagnoses than the technologies they are replacing. As a result, more individuals can be treated for a wider range of injuries and diseases. However, this leads to an increase in costs and demand, as well as to an increase in the average life span. The higher average age in the population entails a change in the panorama of disease; disorders typically associated with the elderly are becoming statistically more common. The impediments to providing health care for many diseases are no longer due to our lack of adequate and appropriate therapies but rather to the lack of funds.

AGE: NEEDS AND EFFECT ON HEALTH CARE

Rationing by health policy planners may affect groups in the society differently. The aged may be particularly affected. In Sweden, people aged 65 years and over represent 17% of the population (Fig. 1), but 47% of the total health care expenditure is devoted to them (Fig. 2). Twenty-three percent of the total health care expenditure is spent on individuals aged 80 and over (Fig. 3), even though they represent only 3.5% of the total population (Fig. 4) (7). The future outlook for Sweden and many other industrialized countries is that the number of elderly will increase, as will the demand for health care (8). This raises a number of crucial questions that are essential for health policy planners to consider.

The aged suffer more ill-health and therefore require more health care. Is there a fixed correlation between age and the proportion of need? Is there a fixed correlation between the severity of a disease and the magnitude of the need for treatment? Is the need greater the more diseases an individual has, or is the need greater if the individual rarely suffers ill-health? Are needs the sole criterion for health care rationing? Is it reasonable to consider the medical effect of a treatment, too? Normally, the medical effect will be better with young individuals than with old ones. Does considering the medical effect imply discrimination against the elderly? As old individuals are more likely than young ones to suffer from chronic diseases, the balance between young and old also implies a balance between cure and care; what ought to be the proper balance? These questions can be summarized as follows:

1. Does an older individual in general have a greater health care need than a young individual?
2. Is there a fixed correlation between how often an individual has a disease and the severity of a disease on the one hand, and how great the need is on the other hand?
3. Should the medical effect of an intervention always be considered?

One utiliarian avenue of argument is as follows. The more individuals we can cure, the more individuals will (one hopes) work and pay taxes, thus funding the health services. This argument suggests that it is better to concentrate resources in health care on technologies that aim at cure for the young than to concentrate resources on caring for and treating the old (e.g., nursing homes); this, the argument goes, duly entails more resources to health care and better chances of treating more individuals in the future. The objec-

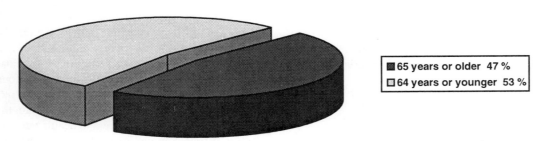

FIG. 2. Health care expenditures for individuals 65 years of age and older. Percent.

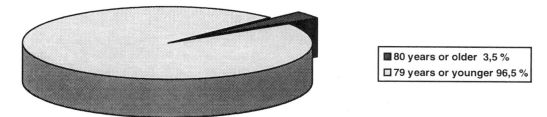

FIG. 3. Health care expenditures for individuals 80 years of age and older in Sweden. Percent.

tion to this argument is that it does not help those who demand access to health care today. It is not self-evident that the needs of individuals who suffer from a disease today are of less concern than future individuals with the disease, who will have better therapeutic options. Yet another objection is that a need for care may very well be greater than a need for cure.

The basis of rationing of health care can be either needs (9) or medical effectiveness (10), or both. The question of how to deal with age groups and the relation between cure and care is affected by the position one takes. In addition, individuals with different social situations may be differently affected (e.g., parents versus nonparents). The therapeutic effect plus cost of a treatment is a possible criterion for rationing health care. Sometimes it is argued that economic considerations are essential to rationing. However, the Oregon project shows that such considerations are not sound. The reason is that considering only costs and consequences leads to a high level of medical intervention "if it is cheap and has a long-term benefit" as Mason and Julnes (11) puts it, implying that no chronic states or caring activities are suitable for economic considerations. Nevertheless, economical considerations are important in view of the fact that resources are limited, and we want to obtain as much health care as possible for the available resources. However, this does not mean that these considerations ought to be, or even can be, part of the basic values applied in health care rationing; furthermore, economic considerations do not help us avoid the problem of rationing. We can delay rationing problems by increasing cost-effectiveness, but we cannot avoid them (12).

As a consequence of the relative scarcity of resources, the demographic changes, and the increasing medical knowledge, the prerequisites for health care services are different now compared with what they were a mere 10 years ago, and the need for establishing priorities is becoming more and more urgent. As the demographic trend continues toward an older population, one of the crucial problems that decision makers have to solve is how to decide what respective proportions should be allocated to disorders primarily affecting young people versus typically old age diseases and injuries. How are these decisions to be made? Ought they to be made on strictly a medical basis, or on an ethical basis, or on some other basis—an economic one, for instance? Should we follow the recommendation of Callahan and colleagues: "The highest future goal of medicine for the elderly should be a reduction in morbidity and disability and not an explicit effort to reduce mortality or increase average life expectancy" (13). This decision should be guided by the overall aim of publicly funded health care, and the decisive task is not only to specify that aim, but to develop appropriate guidelines for implementing it. The guidelines should be sufficiently explicit but still allow for different practical solutions. Practical consequences are what ultimately matters to the general public, and those consequences have to be experienced as just and sound by the general public. However, different bases, e.g., medical, ethical, and economical, allow for different solutions, which is why it is important to clarify what bases are accepted and applied. It is essential for those decisions to be understandable to the general public. Being, ultimately, the financers of health care, they are entitled to know what they are paying for.

FIG. 4. The number of individuals 80 years of age and older of the total Swedish population. Percent.

THE AIM OF THE HEALTH SERVICES

To understand the aim of health care, it is necessary to know what is meant by "health." The World Health Organization (WHO) definition—"Health is a state of complete physical, mental, and social well-being and not merely the absence of disease or infirmity"—may be the most frequently used definition, and perhaps the most criticized one as well. Culyer et al. (14) maintain that the WHO definition of health has led to an "inflation in needs," and they argue that it is not realistic. The problem inherent in this definition is that almost nothing is excluded; anything that has to do with the physical, psychological, and social life of an individual is by definition part of that individual's health. The application of this definition entails an ever-increasing "market" for those involved with the health services. In general this means that physicians and nurses are supposed to deal with anything from bodily injuries to mental and emotional suffering. With this definition much more is expected of health care professionals than with a more limited definition of health. However, some commentators hold that the WHO definition has merit in that it describes the many dimensions of health (6). And almost two-thirds of a random sample of individuals engaged in the health care profession in Sweden prefer the WHO definition to a more narrow definition, i.e., that health is the absence of disease or infirmity (15). For the purpose of this chapter it is not possible to explore the broad, holistic approach to health. The holistic approach to which the WHO definition of health may apply has been elaborated and presented by Nordenfelt (16).

One way of rationing and prioritizing the delivery of health care is to modify the definition of health. A more restricted definition (e.g., health is the absence of disease or infirmity) than that of the WHO would alter the content of health care. In this sense it is possible to talk about "rationing by definition." Applying such definition means that the physicians would return to medicine, which would have the largest effect in primary care and the least in clinical medicine. Critics would then say that physicians were heartless medical engineers. If, on the other hand, physicians were to accept the WHO definition, then they would be regarded as medical imperialists, extending the purview of medicine (17).

Distributive Justice

The aim of publicly financed health care is to offer good care on a fair basis to the general public. This means that distributive justice, fairness or equity, and the Hippocratic oath are emphasized—it is all a matter of doing what is best for the patients and avoiding anything that might bring harm to them. The values reflected in the Hippocratic as well as in other medical oaths reflect fundamental ethical values. To offer good care with high quality, medical knowledge is necessary. Good care and equal access for the general public

are the explicit objectives of health care in, for instance, the Netherlands, New Zealand, Norway, and Sweden (3–6). The overall aim of the Swedish health services, for example, is stated in the second section of the Health Care Act: "The goal of the health care sector is good health and care on equal terms for the entire population" (18). In the United States, the fairness of the Oregon plan (original and later version) has been discussed (19). Questions of distributive justice play a crucial part in health care objectives in several countries, which suggests that such considerations are important in health care rationing.

The ethical discussion of health care during the last few decades dealt extensively with the question of what is, or should be, the proper notion of justice. Even though no consensus is, or will ever be, attained, the discussion makes it clear that ethical considerations are central to the formulation of aims in health care. It is almost axiomatical that a welfare program, such as public health care, should be assessed according to its ability to promote justice (20). The crucial question, then, is whether it matters what definition of justice we apply. The answer to that question is that it certainly does. The system would be differently designed if we used a libertarian (21) definition of justice rather than an egalitarian one (22). However, as we proceed to the next step, we find that the same concept of justice is likely to be differently interpreted. For instance, Swensson (10) argues that Rawls' egalitarian definition of justice as "fairness," applied to intensive care units, leads to a ranking of patients based on available prognostic data. With reference to the notion of fairness, Moss and Siegler (23) contend that patients who developed end-stage liver failure through no fault of their own should have higher priority than those whose end-stage liver failure resulted from alcoholism. They maintain that it is fair to consider matters of lifestyle as a cause of disease, and Swensson holds that it is fair to consider the expected effect of a treatment as a criterion for rationing. These interpretations are not contradictory, but they focus on different aspects of health care. It might not be appropriate to apply the same definition in all countries. Pauly (24) states that the definition of equity applied in the U.S. would not be accepted in Canada (24). There are a number of different definitions of justice, equity, and fairness in addition to Rawls' (22) egalitarian and Nozick's (21) libertarian definitions that are not discussed in this chapter (25–27).

Equity and Efficiency

The amount of resources distributed to health care determines its volume; the definition of health determines the inclusion criteria for health services offered to the general public; and the aim of health care determines the rationing of these services, the concept of justice being essential. Sometimes it is argued that it is sufficient to make health care more efficient in order to avoid rationing dilemmas. But in a survey in Norway, physicians said that the severity of disease, the rule of rescue, and the ideal of equality were more fundamental than the goal of producing health efficiently (28). Making health care more efficient is not a solution to the rationing dilemma. What it suggests is that we should do what we do most efficiently, not that we should do what we consider right. The aim of health care prescribes *what* to do, and the rationale of efficiency shows us *how* to do it the best way. Efficiency is a mean, not an end (20), which is why it cannot be part of the aim of health care. Good health is the objective. This means that economic considerations, in terms of efficiency (i.e., accepted as an economically detectable effect according to economic theory) are subordinated to the values expressed in the overall aim of the health services. Economic considerations are certainly not redundant; on the contrary, they strongly influence the allocation of resources between curing activities. Besides, it has rightly been maintained that it is unethical not to use available resources efficiently (29–31).

There are ethically sound reasons for striving to attain as much knowledge as possible on how the health care system works, such as by providing economic assessments of the efficiency of different technologies. It is important to determine the answers to some critical methodological questions: What economic method is used? How does it work, and is it generally accepted among economists? What about the quality-adjusted life years (QALY) method? Warren (32), for instance, argues that this method does not meet the needs of elderly patients, and Hadorn (33) warns us that the application of this method may result in general discrimination. Williams (34) argues that the alternatives to QALY are even worse, because they have never been soundly expressed, suggesting that they are implicit and impossible to assess from the point of view of equity. (Williams suggests further readings and provides a defense of the QALY method.)

Do the available economic methods fit all medical therapies? Medical interventions that cure are often appropriate for economic assessments, but hardly caring activities. The lack of relevant data causes problems for economic assessments (35). It is possible to make economic assessments of the effects of those medical therapies where relevant data are available; but to what extent can we apply the same method in assessing, for instance, mental or chronic disease, where the benefits are described in terms of good nursing care and quality of life? Whether it is possible, from an economic point of view, to assess the latter dimensions remains a controversial issue, and it is obviously easier to determine the effects of a heart transplant than it is to pinpoint the effect of psychotherapy.

RATIONING

From a democratic point of view, it is important that health care rationing be explicit. To increase the public's confidence in health care, people need to know how their tax dollars are being used. Explicit rationing is also necessary in order to find out how the overall objective of health care is interpreted and how well it is achieved (36). By tradition, rationing has been implicit and often expressed in terms of medical needs (5,37); in the UK, the tradition of implicit rationing is still considered to be strong (37). If explicit rationing is not practiced, there is a risk that the weak patients, those who are the least troublesome, those who demand the most expensive treatments, those whose lifestyle is dubious, and those who have no production value are excluded. As Lyttkens (38) puts it, we might be justified in asking if obfuscation is an implicit policy objective, implying that it is not. Consequently the insistence on transparency (39) and explicit rationing in the health services is morally sound.

Priority Setting

The words *ration* and *priority* are sometimes used in a muddled way. The difference between the two words is that priority entails only internal ranking, whereas rationing entails also the implementation of assigned priorities. Webster's dictionary expresses the distinction as follows: to prioritize is to place in an order of priority, and a ration is an amount that one permits oneself or that one is permitted. Another way of specifying the concept of rationing is to say that it involves discussing the allocation of resources on an emotional level (40). As Chadwick (41) states, the term *rationing* has acquired a bad image, while the term *priority* has been thought preferable. The explanation is that rationing has a negative emotional value, while priority has a positive emotional value. The fact that resources are limited implies that we have to ration among those services that possess the lowest degree of priority. As was claimed above, the bases for assigning priorities and rationing ought to be of an ethical and medical nature, and economic assessments should be part of the information package of services supplied by health care. Such packages should also include information on the total effect of different treatments, described in terms of cure as well as care—that is, nursing care and quality of life.

Process

The need of health care, the medical effect of a treatment, and the cost and all relevant consequences of nontreatment and treatment ought to be considered in health care rationing. Here is a list of the steps in the rationing process:

1. rank the needs of health care,
2. estimate present and future needs of health care,
3. calculate the costs of health care for each need,
4. specify the medical efficacy of different treatments for each need,
5. calculate the effectiveness of different treatments,
6. specify the valid level of quality,

7. ration on the basis of the above steps and according to the budget.

The steps need not be performed in this order. The ranking of needs involves several steps such as defining health care need (see below), assessing the access of different patient categories to health care, and the implications of the outcome in terms of fairness. It also entails determining whether there is a specific relationship between the characteristics of a patient category and the seriousness of a need for health care. One criticism of the Oregon project was that it did not consider individual needs (42). Different individuals may experience a disease differently and suffer differently from it, which means that they will have different needs in this sense, even though they are in the same state of health. When the rationing guidelines are composed, this fact should be considered. Each step involves a number of considerations; there are other ways of specifying the different steps involved [see for example Patrick and Erickson (43)]. However, the main steps are the ranking of needs, the determining of what is medically possible, and the specifying of costs.

Medical Basis

What is a medical criterion that may be used as a basis for rationing? Rationing on a medical basis means rationing according to expected medical results. In practice, the actions taken by physicians are also guided by ethical considerations expressed in the Hippocratic oath (doing what is best for the patient and avoiding doing any harm). However, rationing strictly according to medical criteria amounts to considering the medical efficacy of a treatment only.

Applying a strict definition of medical benefit (i.e., clinically measured or observed), a Swedish study of a small number of county-council politicians showed that the medical basis for rationing was, on the whole, considered to be the most important one compared with ethical and economical factors (44). A public health decision stands a better chance of being accepted by the general public if it is supported in terms of medical needs and medical benefits (medically positive effects of a medical intervention) than if other needs or benefits are adduced (e.g., economic or ethical). It is easier to gain acceptance for not providing an intervention for medical reasons, than to say that the intervention is not cost-effective. Consequently, it is important to keep these distinctions separate. It might be tempting to disguise other criteria for rationing as medical criteria. However, medical criteria are not above the community in which they are applied and must be accountable to that community; thus, it is essential to call everything by its proper name (5). Medical knowledge is the professional content of health care, so medical criteria are necessary for rationing.

It is clear that the medical basis of health care rationing is a necessary element; the question is what part ethical and other criteria ought to play in the rationing process. Nowadays, it is not unusual to advocate that a physician should consider economical aspects in relation to each patient in addition to purely clinical aspects (15,45,46).

Nonmedical Basis

Traditional medical ethics is concerned with a number of different situations where it seems sound to consider other criteria besides medical ones in cases of rationing. The cases discussed are often hypothetical ones. Frequently discussed criteria include lifestyle (smoking, alcohol intake, bad eating habits, high-risk sports), social situation (parents versus nonparents), age, and employment situation. Surveys show that partial or even total application of such factors as criteria for rationing is accepted by a majority (15,45). Jecker (47) has issued a warning regarding gender inequalities. As there are more women among the elderly in the U.S., there is risk of disproportionalities in funding between the sexes if age-based rationing is applied. The disproportion according to gender may be even more emphasized between diseases funded and diseases not funded.

Empirical surveys show that lifestyle is to a great extent accepted as a criterion for rationing among individuals engaged in health care (15,44,48). The same is true for age, social situation, and employment situation (Table 1). Thus nonmedical criteria seem to be widely accepted as grounds for rationing in health care; for instance, almost three out of four people argue that alcohol intake is a valid criterion (Table 1). The ultimate aim of introducing nonmedical criteria is the long-term modification of people's behavior. There is also a hope that the demand—and maybe the need—for health care would decrease. Whether this would actually occur is an empirical issue. It has been claimed that the fact that individuals actually embrace certain values, e.g., that parenthood is socially more worthy than not being a parent, is a reason to consider social worth as a possible basis for rationing (49). This argument takes a democratic approach. Still it can be claimed, rightly, that the fact that individuals hold a specific position in itself is not a reason to promote it as a norm. There are at least two reasons for not doing so. First, it is against a fundamental principle of social policy that all individuals have same value. All human beings have an equal right to health. This principle can be phrased in many ways and is represented in the Swedish constitution as well as in the WHO's declaration of human rights. Second, using a social value as a criterion for rationing might reflect prejudices and other unreflected positions held by individuals. The consequences a position leads to must be considered, and more information and discussion is needed to avoid ill-founded positions. If a position is going to be promoted to be a norm, strong and explicit arguments are needed. Acceptance of a social value as a criterion may lead to criticism from other vantage points as well, such as from the slippery-slope argument and the rule of rescue.

TABLE 1. *The acceptance of different criteria for rationing in health care, found among different groups engaged in the health services (15): percent*

	Politicians		Administrators		Physicians	
	Agree wholly or partly	Do not agree	Agree wholly or partly	Do not agree	Agree wholly or partly	Do not agree
Age	71	22	75	21	89	5
Parenthood	51	35	49	39	47	37
Risk of premature retirement	49	48	50	44	57	34
Lifestyle						
Smoking	73	25	70	29	52	44
Drinking	74	23	70	28	66	29
Bad eating habits	73	23	72	26	61	35

Slippery-Slope Argument and Rule of Rescue

According to the slippery-slope argument, once a deviation from a basic rule has been accepted, more and better arguments are required to prevent further deviation. In the end, even prejudices are likely to be accepted as criteria. In a sense, the slippery-slope argument is a preservatory argument, putting the burden of proof on those who want to accomplish changes. On the other hand, it stops prejudices from being part of (explicit) rationing. The slippery-slope argument holds that changing criteria pertaining to, for instance, rationing in health care is a very delicate matter, and one should be careful when deciding what criteria to accept for rationing, as prejudices might be disguised as alternative criteria.

The rule of rescue says that saving life is the most fundamental aim of the medical profession, suggesting that individuals whose lives are threatened by injury or disease have the greatest needs. Rule of rescue is one argument against relying exclusively on economic assessments of medical outcomes (50). It maintains that individuals have a strong proclivity for rescuing endangered life, even when it would be more cost-effective to do something else with the available resources. The rule has been used to back up arguments against the method used in constructing the first Oregon priority setting list (51). Meulen and colleagues (13) explicitly argue against this rule applied to the elderly. Nevertheless, it has had virtually axiomatic status in the medical tradition for many years.

The need for transparency in decisions on rationing has been articulated, with a view to preventing prejudices from slipping into the criteria underlying decisions (39). The rule of rescue is a normative argument, presenting an ethical norm. The slippery-slope argument and the claim for transparency are more concerned with what the rationing process *ought* to look like.

A criterion does not possess one value only—a favorable or an unfavorable one. In some cases, or at some levels, the value of a criterion might be the opposite of its value in another case. Age is one example. Empirical data show that age in the individual case is taken to be an unfavorable criterion, but on an aggregated level it turns out to be a favorable one (15). In the individual case, the young individual is preferred to the old one; but when decisions are made regarding the reallocation of resources between different spheres of activities (e.g., care of the elderly, preventive care, *in vitro* fertilization, fetal monitoring, care of sufferers from senile dementia), old age constitutes grounds for extended resource allocation.

Another type of dualism involves the motive for accepting the risk that people might lose their jobs as a criterion. An economic and utilitarian argument is that it is best for public welfare if individuals who are productive are given priority over others. If individuals in the risk zone are given priority, more of them will go back to work. This engenders more tax money, which, so the argument runs, leads to extended resources for the health services. Another way of arguing in favor of accepting this criterion is to say that individuals at risk of losing their jobs have a greater need for health care than those who are not in that position. The consequences of not being prioritized are more serious for them, as the loss of employment entails negative psychological as well as social consequences. Some might argue against this, saying that these needs are not primary medically relevant. The counterargument is that the consequences are secondarily medically relevant, and that that is sufficient.

It is not as yet clear what parts nonmedical criteria play in the process of rationing.

ETHICAL CONSIDERATIONS

Ethics constitutes an inquiry into the fundamental principles and basic concepts that guide human actions and thoughts. Two qualities are the mark of an ethical approach: to explicate underlying assumptions for positions held, and to be empathic toward others. One basic distinction between different ethical theories is provided by the communitarian-autonomy distinction. Who is the justified decision maker for an individual, the individual him- or herself or somebody else? And what is most important, the origin of resources (how is possession justified), or the distribution of available resources? This distinction plays an important role in the debate between libertarianism and egalitarianism as well as in the discussion of the concept of distributive justice. But in respect to health care rationing, it is more interesting to discuss distribution than origin.

From the individual's point of view, the ultimate inducement that an individual has for leading his or her life determines what ethical theory he or she will accept. What is considered to be the meaning of life is the ultimate motive. It is rarely the case that individuals have an (explicit) ethical theory guiding their lives; moreover, they do not usually believe that it is possible to create an ethical theory. There are different strategies for explicating rules for leading an ethically good life. One approach is to say that there is no such thing as a universal ethical principle, and that every case is special and must be solved according to its very specific characteristics [see Warnke (52) and Clarke and Simpson (53) for a discussion]. For quite a long time, the Anglo-Saxon tradition amounted to discussing consequentialism (utilitarianism being the most debated version) versus deontology. This discussion can be summarized as: should we stick to a rule for how to lead our lives, or should we calculate the optimal consequences before deciding what action to perform or suppress? Yet another approach consists of the application of ethical principles, such as the principle of autonomy, justice, nonmaleficence, and beneficence (25).

In acute situations in health care, there is no time to discuss the likely consequences of nontreatment and of different treatments. In such cases a rule of thumb is needed. Such rules should be based on previous discussions and reviews of probable consequences. On the policy level, there is time to discuss the consequences of different decisions on rationing, which does not necessarily lead to the construction of rules of thumb on this level. Nevertheless, it might help to find a consensus on some of the basic ethical values that should govern rationing in health care.

Equity

There are different ways of handling the problem of rationing in health care, and there is no simple solution. In the context of rationing, the ethical discussion on distributive justice and equity may be fruitful. Several principles of equity have been discussed in the relevant literature. The following are the most frequent ones (25):

1. To each person an equal share.
2. To each person according to need.
3. To each person according to effort.
4. To each person according to contribution.
5. To each person according to merit.
6. To each person according to free-market exchanges.

Some ethical theories accept all six principles, even though it is more common for a smaller number to be accepted. The principles also apply to different fields; health care usually focuses on needs, while jobs and promotions are awarded according to contribution and merit. What is interesting in respect of rationing in the health services is to concentrate on equity or justice as needs (medical or others) and consequences (medical and other effects of a medical intervention, such as the effect on the public welfare), as these standpoints occur most frequently in the debate and are the most interesting ones. Focusing on needs originates from the deontological ethical tradition, whereas concentrating on medical effects originates in a consequentialistic ethical tradition. However, we cannot envisage an orthodox application of the theories in the field of health care; we are merely concerned with loose connections between them and everyday practice.

Health Care Need

Specifying the concept of equity to be applied in health care rationing as "to each person according to need" means that it becomes important what specification of a need we employ, and in particular health care need. Liss (54) presents some definitions: the ill-health notion (a need for medical care exists when there are some deficiencies in health), the normative notion (a need for health care exists when an assessor believes that health care ought to be provided), and the supply notion (the capacity to benefit from a medical intervention determines when a need is at hand). According to the supply notion it is not possible to need help if there is no help. This definition is common among economists (55). However, there are at least two strong arguments against the definition. The first illustrates that this definition is counterintuitive; suppose we are stuck in the desert without water. Would it then not be reasonable to say that we still do have a need for water? Furthermore, does it make sense to say that John died from thirst in the desert, although he did not have any need for water? The other argument is that with this definition no research and development can be motivated by a need. The supply notion is static and nondynamic: and even those who defend this definition, Cuyler and Wagstaff (56) seem to abandon this definition stating that, "We . . . admit of the possibility of unmet need" (p. 6). So the supply notion of need seems to have too many weaknesses. However, this does not mean that capacity to benefit is unimportant. It is important, but has to be kept out of the definition of a need in order to make it meaningful to talk about unmet needs and to motivate medical research and development from a need perspective.

Yet another specification is suggested by Liss (54). Need is instrumental, and the thing that is needed is that which is necessary for achieving a certain goal, and health is the goal of health care needs. In this sense, a health care need is understood as the medical interventions necessary for attaining health. Some needs are more urgent than others, e.g., emergency care versus other care. One difficulty with needs consists in grading the size of the difference between two or more needs. To rank needs we require a norm. Liss suggests seven ways to rank needs (55). In this context the distinction between needs and wants is often presented.

Needs have to do with what is necessary, as decided by the medical profession; wants involve that which individuals wish to happen. However, the Dutch committee on choices in health care seems to adopt another view and discuss three approaches: the individual, the professional, and the community (5). Different approaches give different determinations of need. From the individual's perspective it is the individual's goals that are central; it is the objectively determined biomedical limitations that determine the need from the professional's point of view; and from the community perspective it is the inability to participate in society that determines a need. The rank order between the three levels is that the community level is above the other two levels. The practical implication is the same as if the distinction between need and want is maintained.

Public Welfare

Apart from need, as specified above, it is sometimes maintained that the consequences to the general public ought to be a criterion for rationing, which might be taken as a special form of utilitarianism. Furthermore, satisfying a need for health care, interpreted as above, is sometimes in conflict with that which yields the best consequences for the general public, and one might have to choose between them. The negative aspect of using increased public welfare as the primary criterion for rationing is that it will ultimately lead to a health care designed for the wealthy and healthy, and the poor and unwell will be shut out. The reason is that it then is acceptable to consider aspects that affect the outcome in terms of welfare, for instance lifestyle and the productivity of a person. Explicitly accepted criteria like these would also have adverse effects on the physician-patient relationship. The patient's confidence in the physician's decision could be shaken. The consistent application of the pubic welfare as the ultimate criterion for rationing would entail absurd consequences; it would, for instance, not be worthwhile to treat extremely old or severely chronically ill individuals, and the health services would only take care of individuals who were basically healthy and important to society.

What is good for the public welfare ought not be considered a criterion for rationing in health care. The consequences would be highly unsound and unjust. The basic foundation of the health services, the willingness to care for the infirm without first checking to see whether they have any money, would then be undermined. From an ethical point of view, it is always of fundamental importance to consider the equity perspective, especially in the case of health care.

The main issues where rationing in the health services is concerned are (a) stating what the relevant needs are, (b) deciding if and how they can be satisfied, and (c) weighting the needs. As resources are limited, we also need to know the costs of different medical interventions. However, we cannot let the effectiveness of an intervention determine the weighting of needs or choices between possible interventions. If we were to follow this line, we would choose those we could cure before those in chronic states, giving priority to interventions with a good and inexpensive effect, e.g., curing thumb-sucking before treating cancer. Designing a health care system according to such criteria cannot be considered to be sound.

However, the marginal contribution—in terms of effectiveness—to health of the available resources ought to be considered. Consequently, up to a point the need itself and what is medically possible to do about it form the sole criterion for rationing. After that, costs and marginal effects ought to be considered, for ethical reasons. However, it is important in this context to focus on the degree of detection. It is much easier to determine the effect of a cataract operation than that of psychoanalysis. Still, a patient's need for psychoanalysis might be much greater than another patient's need for a cataract operation. Caring for a chronic sufferer might also satisfy a greater need than performing, for instance, the cataract operation for another patient. Value for money, hence, must not be interpreted as detectable and explicit. This is often the case, though, and that is why the marginal contribution cannot be a basic criterion for rationing.

It is ethically decreeded to strive for gaining as much health as possible from the available resources. Need and medical effects are the bases for all rationing decisions where costs and marginal consequences (marginal utility) are subordinated.

CONCLUSIONS

If we use the WHO definition of health and interpret equity as giving to each individual according to his or her need, an objective of health care would then consist in ensuring, for each individual, the interventions necessary to meet all of his or her medical needs (e.g., nursing care, home care). Rationing would be necessary and would be based on the severity of the needs. On the one hand, this would imply a grading of needs according to a norm; on the other, the possibility of satisfying a need must be taken into consideration. The latter means, according to the WHO definition of health, that the difference between cure and care activities has to be assessed, and the marginal effects according to costs involved may be considered for cure activities, too. In short this means that medical criteria are necessary to use in health care rationing, as are ethically explicit views on distributive justice or equity. In addition, efforts to attain economic effectiveness are ethically motivated for medical interventions that cure, but for caring activities this is not the case. Consequently, there is no such thing as a direct correlation between needs and costs. The suggestion put forward by Callahan and colleagues with regard to the elderly, to the effect that we should aim for a reduction in morbidity and disability and not strive to reduce mortality and increase average life expectancy, is sound and just if we are prepared to make an addition to the specification of a health care need, namely that health or health-related need is a dynamic concept with a correlation to age. One specification is to concentrate resources for the elderly to caring activities and to give priority to other groups in acute and high technological interventions (15). This entails an acceptance of the notion that there is a natural life span.

In this chapter I have argued that professional medical knowledge is necessary for rationing in the health care, as is an ethical basis. Ethics serves as the basic norm determining the objective of health care (*what* to do) and medical knowledge tells us what can be done and what can not be done. Standardized methods, like the economic methods, are always inconclusive. This does not mean that they are redundant, but that they can only contribute additional information to the process of rationing, and only for interventions that cure, not for activities that care. Together with medical knowledge, information about cost and economical consequences, guide us in *how* to fulfill the objective of the health care in the best way. In the rationing process there will always be room for intuition and new knowledge. But then it is important to be heedful of prejudices disguised as medical or ethical criteria for rationing. To avoid prejudices, decisions on rationing need to be transparent. Rationing on the basis of what seems to be good for the public welfare is not sound and just. What ought to be the basis for rationing is need, and health care need ought not be defined so that it includes capacity to benefit. The answer to the initial question in this chapter is: No, it is not acceptable to rely on any other criteria than medical and ethical ones for health care rationing. And moreover only some ethical criteria are sound. The severity of the health care need ought to be the basis for health care rationing, and what is good for the public welfare as well as prejudices, lifestyle, and social value ought not to be an acceptable norm to rank needs.

REFERENCES

1. Blendon RJ, Leitman R, Morrison I, Donelan K. Satisfaction with health systems in ten nations. *Health Affairs* 1990;Summer:185–192.
2. Oregon Health Services Commission. *Prioritization of health services.* Oregon Department of Human Resources, Salem, 1991.
3. Core Services Committee. *The best of health 2.* Wellington: The National Advisory Committee on Core Health and Disability Support Services, 1993.
4. NOU. *Retningslinjer for prioriteringer innen norsk helsetjeneste (Guidelines for setting priorities in the norwegian health services).* Universitetsforlaget A/S, Sosialdepartementet 1987;23.
5. Government Committee. *Choices in health care.* Ministry of Welfare, Health and Cultural Affairs, The Netherlands, 1992.
6. SOU. *Vårdens Svåra Val. (The difficult choices in the health care).* Stockholm: Socialdepartementet 1995:5.
7. Ohlsson R. *Sjukvårdskostnader och demografisk struktur. (Health care costs and demographic structure).* Stockholm: IHE, 1990.
8. Gerdtham UG, Jönsson B. Heath care expenditures in Sweden—an international comparison. *Health Policy* 1991;19:211–228.
9. Edhag O, Norberg KA. De medicinska behoven måste få styra sjukvårdens prioriteringar. (The medical needs must govern the settings of priorities in the health care). *Läkartidningen* 1992;89:1577–1579.
10. Swensson MD. Scarcity in the intensive care unit: principles of justice for rationing ICU beds. *Am J Med* 1992;5:551–555.
11. Mason T, Julnes T. Oregon's list is a deadly prescription. *Health Week* 1990;May 21:18.
12. Have, HAMJ ten. Choosing core health services in the Netherlands. *Health Care Anal* 1993; :43–47.
13. Meulen R ter, Topinková E, Callahan D. What do we owe the elderly? Allocating social and health care resources. *Hasting Center Report*, no. 2. March-April 1994, special supplement.
14. Culyer AJ, Evans RG, Graf von der Schulenburg J-M, van de Ven WPMM, Weisbrod BA. *Svensk sjukvård—bäst i världen? (Swedish health care—best in the world?).* Stockholm: SNS Förlag, 1992.
15. Björk S, Rosén P. *Värden i Vården. (Values in the health care).* Stockholm: Landstingsförbundet, 1994.
16. Nordenfelt L. *On the nature of health.* Dordrecht: Reidel, Philosophy & Medicine No. 26, 1987.
17. Hjort FP. Prioritering fra filosofi til praksis. (Setting priorities from philosophy to praxis). *Socialmedicinsk tidskrift* 1992;6–7:318–326.
18. Sahlin L. *Hälso-och Sjukvårdslagen, med kommentarer (The Health Care Act, with comments).* Stockholm: Statens nämnd för utgivande av förvaltningsrättsliga publikationer, 1991.
19. Daniels N. Is the Oregon rationing plan fair? *JAMA* 1991;17:2232–2235.
20. Le Grand J. Equity versus efficiency: the elusive trade-off. *Ethics* 1990;100:554–568.
21. Nozick R. *Anarchy, state, utopia.* New York: Basic Books, 1974.
22. Rawls J. *A theory of justice.* Cambridge, MA: Harvard University Press, 1971.
23. Moss AH, Siegler M. Should alcoholics compete equally for liver transplantation? *JAMA* 1991;10:1295–1298.
24. Pauly MV. Fairness and feasibility in national health care systems. *Health Econ* 1992;1:93–103.
25. Beauchamp TL, Childress JF. *Principles of biomedical ethics,* 3rd ed. New York: Oxford University Press, 1989.
26. Daniels N. *Just health care.* Cambridge: Cambridge University Press, 1985.
27. Engelhart HT. Right to health care. In: *The foundation of bioethics.* Oxford: Oxford University Press, 1986.
28. Fredriksen S, Arnesen T. Er Helsevesenets viktigeste oppgave a produsere helse? (Is the main goal of the health care services to produce health?). *Tidsskr Nor Laegeforen* 1993;27:3375–3377.
29. Maynard A. Prioritising health care—dreams and reality. In: Malek M, ed. *Setting priorities in health care.* Chichester: John Wiley, 1994:1–18.
30. Williams A. The role of health economics in clinical decision-making: is it ethical? *Respir Med* 1991;85(suppl B):3–5.
31. Culyer T. The morality of efficiency in health care—some uncomfortable implications. *Health Econ* 1992;1:7–18.
32. Warren JM. Rationing health care resources. Is the quality-adjusted life-year a helpful guide? *Can Fam Physician* 1994;40:123–128.
33. Hadorn DC. The problem of discrimination in health care priority setting. *JAMA* 1992;11:1454–1459.
34. Williams A. *Economics, QALYs and medical ethics—a health economist's perspective.* Discussion paper 121. York: The University of York, 1994.
35. Jönsson B. Vi måste ha bättre kunskaper! (We must have better knowledge!) In: Arvidsson G, ed. *Prioritering i sjukvården etik och ekonomi.* Stockholm: SNS Förlag, 1993.
36. Björk S. Omedvetna eller medvetna prioriteringar. (Unconscious or conscious rationing). In: *Prioriteringar och etik inom vården: Västerbottens läns landsting.* 1991.
37. Redmayne S, Klein R, Day P. *Sharing our resources—purchasing and priority setting in the NHS.* NAHAT research paper no. 11. Bath: University of Bath, 1993.
38. Lyttkens CH. Access, need equity and priorities in health care. In: Philiphs C, Westerhäll L, eds. *Patients' rights: informed consent, access and equality.* Stockholm: Nerenius & Santérus Förlag, 1994:155–169.
39. Normand C. Making priority setting a priority. In: Malek M, ed. *Setting priorities in health care.* Chichester: John Wiley, 1994:327–332.
40. Klein R. Dimensions of rationing: who should do what? *Br Med J* 1993;307:309–311.

41. Chadwick R. Fairness is at issue. *Br Med J* 1994;308:907.
42. Grannemann TW. Priority setting: a sensible approach to medicaid policy? *Inquiry* 1991;28:300–305.
43. Patrick DL, Erickson P. *Health status and health policy—quality of life in health care evaluation and resource allocation.* New York: Oxford University Press, 1993.
44. Björk S, Rosén P. *Prioriteringar i sjukvården—en empirisk studie av sjukvårds politikers syn på resursfördelningen. (Priorities in the health care—an empirical study of county council politicians view of resource allocation).* Lund: IHE Working paper. 1993:1, 1993.
45. Björk S, Rosén P. Setting health care priorities in Sweden: the politician's point of view. *Health Policy* 1993;26:141–154.
46. Durbin M. Bone marrow transplantation: economic, ethical, and social issues. *Pediatrics* 1988;5:774–783.
47. Jecker NS. Age-based rationing and women. *JAMA* 1991;21:3012–3015.
48. Björk S, Rosén P. *Perspektiv på sjukvård i förändring. (Perspectives on a changing health care).* Lund: IHE Workingpaper, 1994.
49. Williams A. Ethics and efficiency in the provision of health care. In: Bell JM, Mendus S, eds. *Philosophy and medical welfare.* Cambridge: Adlard, 1988.
50. Jonsen A. Bentham in a box: technology assessment and health care allocation. *Law Med Health Care* 1986;14:172–174.
51. Hadorn DC. Setting health care priorities in Oregon, cost effectiveness meets the rule of rescue. *JAMA* 1991;17:2218–2225.
52. Warnke G. *Justice and interpretation.* Oxford: Polity Press and Basil Blackwell, 1992.
53. Clarke SG, Simpson E, eds. *Anti-theory in ethics and moral conservatism.* New York: State University of New York Press, 1989.
54. Liss PE. *Health care need.* Averbury: Athenaeum Press, Newcastle upon Tyne, 1993.
55. Culyer AJ. Need, values and health status measurement. In: Culyer AJ, Wright KG, eds. *Economic aspects of health services.* London: Martin Robertson, 1978.
56. Culyer AJ, Wagstaff A. *Need, equality and social justice.* Discussion paper 90. Toronto: York University, Centre for Health Economics, 1991.

Quality of Life and Pharmacoeconomics in Clinical Trials, Second Edition, edited by B. Spilker.
Lippincott-Raven Publishers, Philadelphia © 1996.

CHAPTER 76

Using Decision-Analysis Approaches to Integrate QOL and Cost Data in Drug Therapy Selection

William F. McGhan

INTRODUCTION

Health care costs in the United States are now moving through the level of $1 trillion per year. About 7% of these expenditures, or about $70 billion, are for prescription and nonprescription drugs. Although drugs are considered by many to be a very cost-effective part of care, total health expenditures now consume over 12% of the gross national product of the United States, and this percentage is larger for the U.S. than for other industrialized nations. Cost containment and cost effectiveness have become important concepts in health care, and efforts are being made to reduce unnecessary costs in all facets of care. Group purchasing, contract bidding, prescribing protocols, and strict drug formularies are some of the mechanisms that health insurers and managed care plans are implementing to control their costs (1).

Decision support systems are a new, evolving group of tools that have grown out of decision theory into practical spreadsheet calculations and computer programs and now arriving at a level of analysis that would have been impossible for most pharmaceutical purchasers only a few short years ago. These decision tools developed from business and economics. Many of the computer-based tools are supported by a body of knowledge that has been dubbed "decision theory." This theory leads us to a set of quantitative techniques for handling uncertain aspects of any decision environment. These techniques are based on a group of

related constructs that seek to describe or prescribe how individuals or groups of people choose a course of action when faced with several alternatives and a variable amount of knowledge about the determinants of the outcomes of those alternatives (2–4).

DECISION ANALYSIS

Weinstein and Fineberg (5) define decision analysis as "a systematic approach to decision making under conditions of uncertainty." Decision analysis is an approach that is explicit, quantitative, and prescriptive.

It is explicit in that it forces the decision maker to separate the logical structure into its component parts so they can be analyzed individually then recombined systematically to suggest a decision. It is quantitative in that the decision maker is compelled to be precise about values placed on outcomes. Finally, it is prescriptive in that it aids in deciding what a person should do under a given set of circumstances. The basic steps in decision analysis include identifying and bounding the decision problem, structuring the decision problem over time, characterizing the information needed to fill in the structure, and then choosing the preferred course of action.

Decision trees, as illustrated in Fig. 1, may be considered to be the most familiar framework for decision analyses. The mathematics along a "branch" in decision trees can be converted to rows in a spreadsheet (Table 1) (6–8). There are other, theory related, alternative mechanisms (in addition to the traditional decision trees) that are being utilized and published in the health care literature. One popular alternative approach is multiattribute utility theory (MAUT). MAUT

W. F. McGhan: Institute for Pharmaceutical Economics; Department of Pharmacy Practice and Administration, Philadelphia College of Pharmacy and Science, Philadelphia, Pennsylvania 19104.

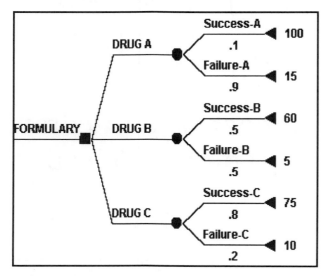

FIG. 1. Decision tree based on data from Table 1.

is a procedure for identifying, characterizing, and comparing the variables that may affect a decision. MAUT has been used for years to analyze managerial and policy decisions and it is now being seen in health care publications. In his paper on decision making for selecting calcium-channel blockers, Schumacher (9) elaborates on a ten-step process:

1. Determine the viewpoint of the decision makers.
2. Identify the decision alternative.
3. Identify the attributes to be evaluated.
4. Identify the factors used to evaluate the attributes.
5. Establish a utility scale to evaluate each attribute (e.g., 0–100).
6. Transform the values from each factor to scores on the utility scale.
7. Determine the relative weight of each attribute and factor.
8. Calculate the total utility score for each decision alternative.
9. Determine which alternative has the greatest utility score.
10. Perform a sensitivity analysis.

Cano and Fujita (10), in their article on using decision analysis for formulary evaluation of third-generation cephalosporins, have warned that drug class reviews without the benefit of the systematization of decision support are at greater risk for subjectivity, hastiness, and emotional and often ill-advised decision making (even in the face of well-established pharmacy and therapeutics committees). Their article presents a multi-tiered decision-analysis approach that includes the following:

1. Identify and establish boundaries of the decision problem
   a. Select drugs for formulary review
   b. Establish evaluation criteria
   c. Collect data (clinical and financial)
2. Structure the decision problem
   a. Assign weights to the evaluation criteria
   b. Agree to select the two top-ranking agents
3. Characterize the information needed to fill in the cells
   a. Record drug-specific data necessary for evaluation
   b. Quantitate each drug's ranking score per criterion and in total
4. Choose the preferred course of action
   a. Apply sensitivity analysis to the data
   b. Recommend formulary inclusion based on total evaluation scores

COMBINING COSTS AND QUALITY OF LIFE

An important part of model building is the listing of key attributes or factors to be compared in the model. The following factors are generally recognized as important in drug therapy evaluations (1):

1. Costs
   A. Direct costs
      a. Acquisition cost of drug
      b. Administration cost
      c. Monitoring cost
      d. Laboratory cost
   B. Indirect costs
      a. Days lost from work for patient
      b. Productivity lost due to premature death

TABLE 1. *Example of expected utility calculations often seen in decision tree analysis*

	Outcome	Utility (U)	Probability (P)	Expected utility (U × P)	Total expected utility	Rank
Drug A	Success	100	0.1	10		
	Fail	15	0.9	13.5	23.5	Third
Drug B	Success	60	0.5	30		
	Fail	5	0.5	2.5	32.5	Second
Drug C	Success	75	0.8	60		
	Fail	10	0.2	2	62	First

Note: The drug with the highest expected utility is the preferred therapy. See Fig. 1 for a display of these data in a decision tree format.

2. Outcomes
   A. Drug cure rate (efficacy rate at controlling symptoms)
   B. Compliance
   C. Adverse reaction rates
   D. Quality of life scores
   E. Years of life gained

The effort required of formulary committees or group purchasing committees to engage in formal decision analysis can often be quite daunting. With the advent of the computer and its ability to help organize information however, well-documented computer programs are beginning to facilitate these important decisions.

There have now been developed by various organizations and firms decision support software packages that are being utilized to evaluate drugs for inclusion on major drug formularies. Some of these software packages have been developed so that individuals can take portable computers into the field and incorporate the concerns of the drug purchaser or prescriber into the decision analysis for various drug products.

When developing computerized decision support software the following steps are considered:

Step 1: Analysis of decision support approaches. A technical comparison should be conducted of the capabilities and general characteristics of various software approaches. Options might include spreadsheets, decision trees, and multiattribute models. The technical assessment of software includes its cost, reliability and dependability, copyright and copy considerations, and user friendliness.

Step 2: Development of model parameters. Based on input from decision makers and experts, variables, attributes, and weights should be established for the model construction.

Step 3: Collection and input of effectiveness, quality of life, and economic data. This phase involves collection of clinical and economic data from the literature or from clinical trials. These data eventually allow comparison of the various drugs and therapy alternatives. The data relate to the cost of treatments, quality of life, and other clinical outcomes.

Step 4: Field testing and training. Field testing and validation of any decision software is an important step. Training can also assist the software developers with feedback for determining improvements in ease of use, preferences, and performance characteristics. Feedback during ongoing use of the software is crucial to facilitating success of the system.

Step 5: Monitoring and updates. The program developers should continue to monitor the success of the system with ongoing feedback from the decision makers in the field. The developers of the decision support systems should continue to monitor the clinical and economic literature and periodically update the computer program.

BASIC EXAMPLES

Table 1 provides a simple example of the calculations of expected utilities that are involved in decision tree analysis (2). The decision tree with these numbers is presented in Fig. 1. In this example, quality of life and cost data would have to be incorporated into the utility score (U). The utility score would be ascertained from experts, practitioners, and/or patients. If desirable and possible, the utility score could in fact be developed as "net benefits" in dollars (benefits minus costs) of one therapy over another.

Expanding, for the sake of example, on the concepts of cost-utility analysis and multiattributes, Table 2 provides columns for both cost and expected utility. This is an example in which cost is separated from the utility or effectiveness score.

To emphasize the health economic aspects of these analyses, Table 3 reminds us that we should be sure to include many different cost items (beyond drug acquisition costs) in calculating all of the direct and indirect costs as listed earlier in this chapter. Table 4 provides a simple illustration of how one might use a multiattribute approach and expert input to generate total scores (in this case a success index) based on quality of life scores and level of adverse drug reactions. In Table 2, we generated a cost-utility ratio. A similar mathematical ratio could be developed from these two key sets of numbers in Tables 3 and 4. But as a different way to display the data, it is common to summarize the cost and success index from Tables 3 and 4 in graph form (Fig. 2), thus allowing the decision maker to visualize both cost and outcome parameters, which can be lost in a simple ratio. These are all basic examples of some of the approaches that are being used in decision support software. All decision systems should be tested and evaluated to determine if they ultimately produce high quality and cost-effective patient outcomes.

TABLE 2. *Example of cost-utility analysis*

	Total cost ($)	Expected utility	Cost-utility ratio (dollars per utile)	Rank
Drug A	$40	20.8	1.92	Third
Drug B	$50	27.5	1.82	Second
Drug C	$75	52	1.44	First

Note: The drug with the lowest cost per utile would be the preferred therapy.

TABLE 3. *Example of cost considerations in economic study*

Alternatives	Direct costs ($)	Indirect costs ($)	Total costs ($)
Drug V	20	90	110
Drug W	30	75	105
Drug X	25	80	105
Drug Y	45	70	115
Drug Z	40	85	125

TABLE 4. *Example of quality of life scores and (ADR) considerations combined through a multiattribute approach*

Alternatives	QOL score[a] (%)	Absence of ADR[b] (%)	Success index (%)
Drug V	84	91	75
Drug W	84	70	59
Drug X	95	89	84
Drug Y	95	78	73
Drug Z	95	89	84

[a]QOL Score as a percent of maximum possible score.
[b]In this example the absence of ADR is calculated as 100% minus the total percent of ADRs.
Note: These numbers are generally developed through review of the literature and input of expert panel. In this example, success index is calculated by multiplying QOL percent score by absence of ADR score. ADR, adverse drug reactions.

CONCLUSIONS

No matter how powerful a computer and its program might be, it is obvious that the emphasis must be on effective decisions that generate good patient outcomes. These decision support systems should help to add more rational decision tools for decision makers or prescribers who in the past may have made their determinations impulsively and irrationally and clouded with personal biases and personal heuristics that often lead to inappropriate patient care.

In this age of growing cost-containment concerns, individual bias and impulsive judgments are becoming riskier methods of operation. There is a growing requirement to justify each clinical judgment and base the justification on cost effectiveness and treatment efficacy. Decision support systems are bringing a new methodology to drug therapy. The adoption of robust and valid decision systems can help with financial decisions and interactions between buyers and sellers of health care services. Although it may seem from this chapter that drug decision software would be based on postmarketing data, some researchers have been involved in planning and collecting information to build these analytical models during clinical trials prior to drug approval. The intent here is to have a decision support system available when the drug is approved for marketing.

Decision makers are moving from more subjectively based heuristics to more formal means of ascertaining patient specific and institutional concerns into more quantifiable

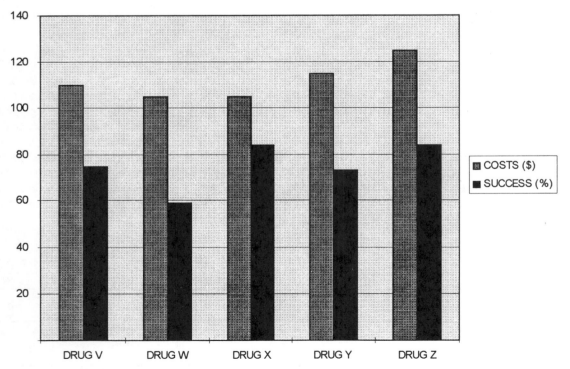

FIG. 2. Comparison of costs ($) versus success (%): sample data.

utility values. Utility values are not easy to estimate. There are no easy methods of estimating the utility value of pain, suffering, or inconvenience. There is disagreement on who determines utility values, but there is a growing emphasis on patients' involvement in decision making that will directly affect their own outcomes.

In the long-run analysis, it is expected that we will make continual progress toward narrowing down the uncertainties in patient care. A computer chip manufacturer may like to boast that its production methods have led to a quality control outcome that results in .9972 perfect components being produced with each run. Its system is technology controlled. In health care decisions, we have yet to adopt this level of tolerance, but cost containment issues and outcomes management may one day require that drug therapy and drug formularies achieve a similar kind of perfection with regard to the intended therapeutic outcome of drug regimens. This trend alone should give the impulsive decision maker pause to reconsider any reluctance to use decision support systems.

In these days of fiscal restraint and cost control, decision support systems with cost included can prove an invaluable tool for the managerial and clinical practitioner. If some of the principles of cost-effective clinical decision making would permeate the cognitive processes of health practitioners, a less costly style of health care might result.

Decision support systems are potentially effective methods for more objectively making decisions based on the probable ranges of outcomes and costs. Health care practitioners, both clinical and managerial, should find these tools useful alternatives in coping with decision-making situations brought on by diagnosis-related groups and other forms of fiscal restraint.

These tools are important additions to the health practitioner's repertoire of decision-making skills. Any health care practitioner or manager who desires to make important improvement for the health care team should continue to explore these techniques for evaluating drug therapy and patient care.

REFERENCES

1. Bootman JL, Townsend R, McGhan WF. *Principles of pharmacoeconomics.* Cincinnati: Harvey Whitney, 1991.
2. Einarson TR, McGhan WF, Bootman JL. Decision analysis applied to pharmacy practice. *Am J Hosp Pharm* 1985;42:364–371.
3. Sox HC Jr. Decision analysis: a basic clinical skill? (Editorial). *N Engl J Med* 1987;316:271–272.
4. Crane VS. Developing a rational basis for cost-effective antibiotic selection in a community hospital: use of the decision analysis method. *Adv Ther* 1987;4:137–144.
5. Weinstein MC, Fineberg HV. *Clinical decision analysis.* Philadelphia: WB Saunders, 1980.
6. Barr JT, Schumacher GE. Decision analysis. In: Bootman JL, Townsend R, McGhan WF, eds. *Principles of pharmacoeconomics.* Cincinnati: Harvey Whitney, 1991.
7. Schumacher GE, Barr JT. Applying decision analysis in therapeutic drug monitoring: using decision trees to interpret serum theophylline levels. *Clin Pharm* 1986;5:325–333.
8. Barr JT, Schumacher GE. Applying decision analysis in therapeutic drug monitoring: using receiver-operating characteristic curves in comparative evaluations. *Clin Pharm* 1986;5:239–246.
9. Schumacher GE. Multiattribute evaluation in formulary decision making as applied to calcium-channel blocker. *Am J Hosp Pharm* 1991; 48:301–308.
10. Cano SB, Fujita NK. Formulary evaluation of third-generation cephalosporins using decision analysis. *Am J Hosp Pharm* 1988;45:566–569.

SUGGESTED READINGS

Eraker SA, Polister P. How decisions are reached: physician and patient. *Ann Intern Med* 1982;97:262–268.

Eraker SA, Sox HC. Assessment of patients' preferences for therapeutic outcomes. *Med Decis Making* 1981;1:29–39.

Gagnon JP, Osterhaus JT. Proposed drug cost effectiveness methodology. *Drug Intell Clin Pharm* 1987;21:211–215.

Kassirer JP, Moskowitz AJ, Law J, et al. Decision analysis: a progress report. *Ann Intern Med* 1987;106:275–291.

Kresel JJ, Hutchings HC, MacKay DN, et al. Application of decision analysis to drug selection for formulary addition. *Hosp Form* 1987;22: 658–676.

Martin CM, Douglas AK. Getting ''value for money'': measuring the quality and outcome of general practice care. *Med J Aust* 1993;159: 253–256.

Plante DA, Kassirer JP, Zarin DA, et al. Clinical decision consultation service. *Am J Med* 1986;80:1169–1176.

Witte KW, Eck TA, Vogel DP. Decision analysis applied to the purchase of frozen premixed intravenous admixtures. *Am J Hosp Pharm* 1985;42: 835–839.

Quality of Life and Pharmacoeconomics in Clinical Trials, Second Edition, edited by B. Spilker.
Lippincott-Raven Publishers, Philadelphia © 1996.

CHAPTER 77

Outcomes Research and Quality of Care

Donald M. Steinwachs, Albert W. Wu, and Kathleen A. Cagney

INTRODUCTION

The goal of health care is to protect, promote, and maintain the health status of people. Traditional measures of our success include increases in life expectancy, reductions in disease-specific mortality (e.g., coronary artery disease), and improvements in clinical indicators (e.g., the proportion of hypertensives with adequate blood pressure control). All of these are relevant, yet they are not totally satisfactory. For those who survive, there is a need to know how well the person functions in all aspects of life affected by health. Until recently, we have rarely had information available to address this concern. Even now, we are only beginning to collect information on patient outcomes of care in terms of functional (health) status and satisfaction (1).

As we have come to more fully appreciate that what people value is their health status, rather than their disease status, the demand for policy-relevant information regarding the impact of new technologies and health programs on health status has grown substantially. This can be seen in the 1989 Congressional legislation creating the Agency for Health Care Policy and Research (AHCPR) and its Center for Medical Effectiveness Research. The agency is mandated to undertake research on the effectiveness of medical care in terms of its impact on patient outcomes, including health

status and quality of life. Also, the Food and Drug Administration (FDA) encourages the collection of quality of life effects of experimental drugs before final FDA approval. Similar actions have been taken by European drug regulatory agencies.

The debate around health care reform provided further evidence of an evolution in thinking toward perceived need for new metrics by which to judge health care effectiveness. National attention has focused on "report cards" that would compare patient outcomes and costs across different health plans. All of this suggests a new vision of the future in which the value of health care services is measured from the patient's perspective in terms of how services make a difference in day-to-day living, complementing traditional metrics based on disease status and mortality.

The role and likely contribution of health status information in health policy are discussed in this chapter. Specific areas to be considered include:

1. policy-relevant information on the effectiveness of medical care and methods to improve it,
2. information to inform consumers (patients) regarding choices and their likely impact on outcomes, and
3. information relevant for policy makers facing issues involving insurance coverage, benefit design, provider organization, and payment reform.

It is clear that no single source of information alone will shape the future of health care. However, shifts in perspectives and values can significantly refocus policy objectives.

    D. M. Steinwachs, A. W. Wu, and K. A. Cagney: Health Services Research and Development Center, Johns Hopkins University, Baltimore, Maryland 21205.

Giving greater weight to the patient's perspective and values may lead us toward a system that puts increased emphasis on treatments and technologies that improve people's lives, with less emphasis on extending life that lacks substantial quality for the individual.

CONCEPTUAL MODEL: LINKING HEALTH STATUS AND HEALTH CARE SERVICES

Health status incorporates measures of the physical, mental, and social functioning of individuals. The determinants of health status are broadly conceived to include environmental, genetic, behavioral, and biological influences. To the extent these factors lead to decrements in health status, they may translate into needs for care. Health services are designed to meet needs for care and to contribute toward improvements in health status, and/or the prevention of future decrements. It is notable that not all health services are directed at needs for care that result from changes in health status. Preventive services are prescribed to prevent risks to future health.

A critical question is how we measure the success of health policy. One answer is that successful health policies lead to the provision of services to meet needs for care, and ultimately, these services have an impact on the population's health. This perspective gives priority to the provision of services that can meet those needs and that will have a positive impact on health status (2).

There are generic and disease-specific measures of health status. This discussion will focus on generic measures as typified by the SF-36 (3), Sickness Impact Profile (4), and the Quality of Well-Being Scale (5). However, there are numerous disease-specific measures that focus on functional status for specific diagnoses. The disease-specific measures may be more useful in the translation of health status decrements into needs for services than generic measures. In medical effectiveness research, both generic and disease-specific measures of functional status are generally used to measure patient outcomes.

In summary, health status can be conceptualized as a starting point for defining health care needs. These needs are translated by health professionals into specific disease and syndrome categories that may be expected to benefit from treatment and preventive services. Ultimately, changes in health status become a measure of the patient's outcomes and a metric against which to assess effectiveness of treatment.

EFFECTIVENESS: MEASURING AND IMPROVING HEALTH CARE

Medical effectiveness researchers strive to explain how well diagnostic, treatment, and preventive services work in day-to-day practice. Sometimes effectiveness research is confused with efficacy studies in which the impact of services (e.g., new drug) is tested under ideal conditions. Ideal conditions may differ from actual practice in many ways. Under ideal conditions, highly motivated and compliant patients are chosen for the study, patients get the treatment for free, and patients with complicating conditions are excluded. In actual practice, patients may have varying levels of motivation and have to pay something. The sickest patients generally suffer from multiple conditions. The goal of effectiveness research is to provide the information needed by policy makers, administrators, providers, and patients to improve the provision of medical care. Patient outcomes studies funded by AHCPR, as well as those being conducted under other auspices, are beginning to provide insights into the range of opportunities that exist to improve the effectiveness of existing health care services.

Factors Affecting the Level of Effectiveness

The provision of medical care involves a complex process that can fail to function optimally for many reasons. To understand how to begin to set priorities for improving the effectiveness of health care, we will need to identify specific factors that detract from providing effective care and their relative importance. This assessment will vary by health problem, as well as by patient and provider circumstances. However, the categories of relevant factors are likely to remain relatively constant. These will be described and illustrated.

Access to Care

In the recent report from the Institute of Medicine, access to care was defined as "the timely receipt of appropriate care" (6). If access is poor, the receipt of care is delayed as in the case of late diagnosis of treatable cancers and the resulting increase in mortality. Access is an issue in which the consumer, system of care, and financing arrangements interact to determine if the need for care is recognized by the person or system, if care is sought, and, when sought, if it is received. We know many populations have poor access to care, but even populations that are well served frequently fail to meet the definition for optimal access.

Appropriate Diagnosis and Treatment

There is no central data source on the frequency with which appropriate diagnosis and treatment occurs. Research studies have found substantial differences between actual prevalence and rates of diagnosis for some conditions, and between accepted standards of practice and what is actually received (7). However, it is difficult to extrapolate from these studies to estimate the overall state of practice.

One example that illustrates both of the problems of adequate diagnosis and treatment is depression. Despite the existence of efficacious treatments for depression, studies have shown that approximately half of the individuals with major depression are not diagnosed by their providers (8). Among those diagnosed and treated, 39% of patients used inappropriately low doses of antidepressants. In the Medical Outcomes Study it was found that when measuring the outcomes of care for those not diagnosed versus those diagnosed and undertreated, and those diagnosed and appropriately treated, the outcomes varied significantly. Those appropriately treated had the best outcomes, those not diagnosed the worst, and those diagnosed but not adequately treated experienced intermediate outcomes (9–11). Clearly, the effectiveness of depression treatment could be improved.

Patient Adherence to Treatment

Providers sometimes challenge effectiveness studies as discounting the contribution of patient noncompliance. Indeed, the literature is replete with studies that show medication compliance to be about 50%. How can this be changed? A range of studies examining in detail the processes of care may provide some suggestions. Hall and colleagues (12) have found that the provider's communication style affects patient satisfaction with care and adherence to treatment and follow-up recommendations. Simple interventions to remind patients about appointments have been found to be effective (13). Possibly, a critical issue concerns how responsibility is shared between patient and provider for assuring ongoing management of conditions. Sharing arrangements would be expected to vary by patient preferences, personal capacity to self-manage care, and extent of informal caregiving support.

Resources

Consistently, research has shown that there are large differences in effectiveness of services by socioeconomic status. In part, these differences reflect availability of resources including financial, educational, social support, and others. The ability to obtain care, manage the requirements of treatment, and to achieve good outcomes are linked to resources. Some of these translate into risk factors for disease and injury including poor nutrition, inadequate housing, and adverse environmental risks.

PATIENT OUTCOMES OF CARE: ASSESSING EFFECTIVENESS

Assessing effectiveness of care among treated patients is the usual approach for judging treatment effectiveness and in making comparisons between providers. There are now a range of private and publicly funded outcomes measurement activities being undertaken.

One set of initiatives in outcomes measurement are sponsored by the Health Outcomes Institute, which makes data collection instruments publicly available to assess patient outcomes of common conditions (e.g., asthma, cataract surgery, depression, hip fracture surgery). In work we have done with the Managed Health Care Association interest group on Outcomes Management Systems, we have been testing the feasibility and utility of these methods for capturing information on patient outcomes (14). The findings are that in most managed care organizations (MCO) it is feasible to sample patients based on disease (particularly for chronic diseases) and obtain completed patient questionnaires including information on health status, treatment, knowledge, and satisfaction at two or more points in time. The questionnaire is designed to provide information to link patient health status and disease status outcomes to treatment, to answer questions such as:

- Is treatment by a specialist or a primary care physician equivalent in outcomes and satisfaction among patients with comparable severity of illness?
- Does treatment meet accepted standards of practice (guidelines) and what impact does not meeting treatment guidelines have on patient outcomes?
- Are patients adequately prepared to manage the treatment requirements of their disease (health problem) and what difference in outcomes are there between those who can self-manage and those who cannot?

The next step will be to evaluate the utility of answers to these questions in terms of identifying opportunities for improving the quality of care and patient outcomes. Although one can be optimistic, the translation of knowledge into changes in practice continues to be an uncertain process.

POPULATION-BASED HEALTH STATUS: OBSERVED VERSUS EXPECTED HEALTH STATUS

The ultimate measure of health care effectiveness is in the achievement of maximum health status in the population or community. This may differ from medical effectiveness measured at the patient level, in part because some individuals fail to obtain appropriate health care services on a timely basis. One concern has been that we may focus too many resources on high-technology acute care and too little on ambulatory and primary health care. Consider a hospital that provides high-quality inpatient acute care but less adequate primary care to the community. It provides excellent care for an acute problem (e.g., stroke), but does less well in treating an important predisposing condition (e.g., hypertension). Better treatment of the hypertension would reduce the number of strokes and improve the health status of the community. Unfortunately, we have tended to reward hospitals for their acute care capabilities rather than their primary care functions. Similarly, the rewards for specialists are generally greater than for primary care physicians who are more likely to diagnose and manage conditions such as hypertension.

Instead of grading hospitals or MCOs for the health status of their patients, a different approach would be to grade a hospital for the health of the community it served, or an MCO for the health of all of its covered lives. This is easier to accomplish when an organization is responsible for a clearly defined population of patients, particularly as the sole source of care, and when panels of patients are stable over time. Under these circumstances the attribution of community (population) health status to specific providers is clearer.

The choice of health indicators by which to assess effectiveness is a key decision. Care should be taken in choosing a limited set that gives attention to the full range of health care (mental health, medical, surgical, preventive) and to the range of health providers. In addition, priority should be given to conditions that contribute most to premature mortality and excess morbidity in the population, and those for which there is prior evidence of inadequate or poor quality of care.

Prognostic and risk models now being developed for disease outcomes, will need to be developed for functional status outcomes (15). Using these, it would be possible to calculate expected health status for a population, and to follow that population over time to determine how expected outcomes compare to those actually observed. The difference between expected and observed outcomes could be thought of as the difference between the potential efficacy of the system, and its current effectiveness, and would provide a population-based measure of the quality of care being delivered.

INFORMATION FOR CONSUMERS (PATIENTS)

One of the objectives of AHCPR is to provide information useful to patients in making choices among alternative treatments. As mentioned above, the health care reform debate stimulated discussion regarding making choices between health care plans and providers, not just specific treatments. How useful is outcomes information in making such choices?

Research by Kasper et al. (16) suggests that interactive videos can be developed to share with patients the expected consequences for health outcomes based on what is known regarding alternative treatments. One program has been developed for patients facing prostate surgery, comparing watchful waiting to immediate surgery. Preliminary evidence suggests that use of the shared decision-making programs results in a shift away from surgical treatment. The practice guidelines published by AHCPR include a consumer version of this guideline. As yet, little is known regarding how useful this is and to what extent it affects patient decision making.

In the long-term it is reasonable to expect that the more educated and informed the public is regarding the risks and benefits (outcomes) of medical care, the better will be their decisions. This may or may not change current rates of treatment, but is likely to increase satisfaction with outcomes due to a better understanding of outcomes, both good and poor, and the impact these can have on the person's day-to-day life.

HEALTH POLICY AND ACCOUNTABILITY

The orientation toward patient outcomes information as a central element in judging the performance of health care providers can be extended to evaluating policies related to health care systems. The historical basis for this is clear. Specially funded initiatives at federal and state levels have responded to higher than average rates of infant mortality, cancer deaths, and other major causes of mortality. As information on health status outcomes beyond mortality becomes more readily available, how will this information influence policy decisions? Recent examples of efforts to use this type of information suggest possible answers.

Insurance Coverage Decisions: Oregon's Experience

In 1990, the state of Oregon attempted to use outcome measures as a tool for prioritizing conditions and treatments to be covered under Medicaid. By applying a cost/utility formula to a list of 2,000 medical conditions, it was hoped that the Medicaid program could eliminate coverage of non-beneficial treatments and expand its base, thereby offering the greatest benefit to the greatest number of people.

Oregon approached this decision-making process with the use of the General Health Policy Model (17). This model expressed benefits and side effects of any health care service in terms of equivalent values of completely well years of life. By dividing the cost of the program by the well-years added, an estimate of the cost/utility of the program could be calculated. This cost/utility ratio could then be used to compare the relative value of different services, since all treatment-condition pairs had a common metric. The focus of this model departed from those with a traditional emphasis on the progression of a single disease, since these have often neglected the side effects introduced by treatment. Hence, by incorporating benefits, side effects, and the relative importance of each, a comprehensive view of net treatment benefits could be obtained (18).

When the ranking from the above formula was completed, however, many felt uncomfortable with the result. The ranking of several condition-treatment pairs seemed counterintuitive (that treatments for thumb-sucking and acute headaches ranked higher than treatments for AIDS is an often cited example). Subjective reordering of the list by Oregon Health Services Commissioners was then employed, along with the three other levels of human judgment used in the model (community values assessed in town meetings, medical judgment of treatment efficacy, and ratings of the desirability of health states) to determine the final ranking. When the application was submitted to the Department of Health and Human Services (DHHS) in 1992, it was rejected based on distrust of the health state ratings. They believed that the Oregon preference survey on quality of life "quantified stereotypic assumptions about persons with disability" (18). A revised application that eliminated the quality of life component was approved by DHHS in 1993.

However, Kaplan (19) has demonstrated that of the four levels of judgment used, the health state ratings had the greatest evidence of reliability and validity. Kaplan points out that the most replicable part of the model was omitted from the proposal since the health state ratings were the only component that was obtained using a systematic methodology.

Public Accountability: Report Cards

Public awareness of the limits of medical knowledge, variability in practice, and the occurrence of malpractice have all served to increase perceived needs for better accountability mechanisms. Public accountability for quality is maintained by each state through control of licensure of health care professionals and the accreditation of health care facilities. This system is successful in assuring that professionals have received training for practice and that facilities meet at least minimum standards. This system is not designed to assure that all health professionals practice using the latest medical knowledge; indeed, there are major disagreements among some of the health professions regarding what is desirable and appropriate treatment for specific conditions.

A range of ideas has emerged that could provide better information by which to judge the performance of the health care system, health plans, and individual providers. These include implementation of report cards with cost and quality of care (outcomes) information, expanded development of practice guidelines with public information regarding provider adherence, improved quality monitoring systems that share performance information with providers and the public, and wider implementation of outcomes management methods. Much of this information will have little value to the average person, although it may make it possible to publish local consumer reports on hospitals and managed care organizations. It should have substantial value for regulators and for the professions to assure the public that the highest standards of health care practice are being promoted and actions are being taken to correct substandard performance.

CONCLUSIONS

Health policy debates regarding the role of high-cost technology, policy decisions to cover or not cover specific procedures, and professional and public perceptions of the appropriate role of the patient in decision making are all likely to change as better and more comprehensive information on outcomes of care become available.

The effects are likely to be highly varied. Better information will empower the patient to be a partner with the physician or other health professional in making decisions regarding treatment, rehabilitation, and care at the end of life. Better information will sharpen debates regarding who should pay (insurer or patient) when treatment does not lengthen life or only marginally improves the quality of life, or when the prognosis is that neither is likely to occur (e.g., intensive care at the end of life). The role of new and emerging diagnostic and treatment methodologies will no doubt be subject to equally intense debates regarding benefits and risks. Thus, the hope is that health status information will provide a basis for more informed health policy. As discussed, it should serve to enhance our capacity to monitor the quality of care and to strengthen mechanisms for assuring a high level of public accountability for the quality of care being provided.

The complexity and urgency of the challenge to develop useful information to inform public is nowhere clearer than in health care today. The emerging field of patient outcomes studies is beginning to provide information that appears to have great potential for clarifying what we know about the benefits and risks of health care services. The translation of this information into policy recommendations will be highly complex and may not always lead to the desired end—better health for all Americans at a more affordable cost. It will certainly take us farther than we have been able to go before in measuring the value received for the health care resources expended.

REFERENCES

1. Ware JE, Gander B, and the IQOLA Project Group. The SF-36 health survey: development and use in mental health research and the IQOLA project. *Int J Ment Health* 1994;23(2):49–73.
2. Steinwachs DM. Application of health status assessment measures in policy research. *Med Care Suppl* 1989;27(3):S12–S26.
3. Ware JE, Sherbourne CD. The MOS 36-item short form health survey (SF-36): I. Conceptual framework and item selection. *Med Care* 1992;20:473–483.
4. Bergner M, Bobbitt RA, Carter WB, Gilson BS. The sickness impact profile: development and final revision of a health status measure. *Med Care* 1981;19:787–805.
5. Kaplan RM, Anderson JP. The quality of well-being scale: rationale for a single quality of life index. In: Walker SR and Rosser RM, eds. *Quality of life assessment and application.* Lancaster, England: MTP Press, 1988:51–78.
6. Millman M, ed. Report of a study by a committee of the Institute of Medicine, Division of Health Care Services. Access to health care in America. National Academy Press, February 1993.
7. Chassin MR. Improving quality of care with practice guidelines. *Front Health Serv Manage* 1993;10:40–44.
8. Shapiro S, Skinner EA, Kramer M, Steinwachs DM, Regier DA. Measuring need for mental health services in a general population. *Med Care* 1985;23:1033–1043.
9. Wells KB, Hays RD, Burnham A, et al. Detection of depressive disorder for patients receiving prepaid or fee-for-service care: results from the Medical Outcomes Study. *JAMA* 1989;262:3298.
10. German PS, Shapiro S, Skinner EA, et al. Detection and management of mental health problems of older patients by primary care providers. *JAMA* 1987;257:489.

11. Wells KB, Katon W, Rogers B, Camp P. Use of minor tranquilizers and antidepressant medications by depressed outpatients: results from the medical outcomes study. *Am J Psychiatry* 1994;151:694–700.
12. Hall JA, Roter DL, Katz NR. Meta-analysis of correlates of provider behavior in medical encounters. *Med Care* 1988;26(7):657–675.
13. Steinwachs DM. Measuring provider continuity in ambulatory care: an assessment of alternative approaches. *Med Care* 1979;17(6):551–565.
14. Steinwachs DM, Wu AW, Skinner EA. How will outcomes management work? *Health Aff* 1994;13:153–162.
15. Wu AW, Damiano AM, Lynn J, et al. Predicting future functional status for seriously ill hospitalized adults: the SUPPORT prognostic model. *Ann Intern Med* 1995;122:342–350.
16. Kasper JF, Mulley AG, Wennberg JE. Developing shared decision making programs to improve the quality of health care. *QRB* 1992; :183–190.
17. Kaplan RM, Anderson JP. A general health policy model: update and applications. *Health Serv Res* 1988;23:203–235.
18. Kaplan RM. Value judgment in the Oregon Medicaid Experiment. *Med Care* 1994;32(10):975–988.
19. Kaplan RM, ed. *The Hippocratic predicament: affordability, access, and accountability in American medicine.* San Diego, CA: Academic Press, 1993.
20. Bergner M. Measurements of health status. *Med Care* 1985;23:696–704.

APPENDIX: DEFINITIONS OF TERMS

Outcomes research is a comprehensive approach to determining the effects of medical care using a variety of data sources and measurement methods. Outcomes research includes the rigorous determination of what works in medical care and what does not, and how different providers compare with regard to their results on patient outcomes. In outcomes research, a distinction is made between efficacy and effectiveness. **Efficacy** refers to how a treatment works in ideal circumstances, when delivered to selected patients by providers most skilled at providing it. **Effectiveness** refers to how a treatment works under ordinary conditions by the average practitioner for the typical patient.

Quality of care can be defined as the difference between efficacy and effectiveness that can be attributed to care providers. According to Donabedian's widely accepted model of quality of care, it is necessary to assess the "structure, process, and outcomes" of care.

Structure refers to stable elements that form the basis of the health system, such as the type of facility, administrative organization, and provider qualifications.

Process refers to what happens in the medical interaction and includes the technical and interpersonal skills of the physician and other providers. Process measures compare care delivered with relevant standards.

Outcomes are the measurable events and observations that are presumed to occur in part due to the structure and process of medical care.

Health status as defined by Bergner (20) includes at least five dimensions: (a) genetic and inherited characteristics; (b) biochemical, physiologic, and anatomic condition, including impairment of these systems, disease, signs, and symptoms; (c) **functional status,** which includes performance of the usual activities of life, such as self-care, physical activities, and work; (d) mental condition, which includes positive and negative feelings; and (e) health potential, including longevity and prognosis.

Quality of life encompasses a person's assessment of all aspects of their experience. Some important dimensions are distant from medical concern (e.g., achievement and spiritual fulfillment).

Appropriateness studies establish standard indications against which the use of a particular medical intervention is judged. Methods to produce indications involve careful analysis of what is known and the use of expert physicians to fill in gaps in knowledge and come to consensus about indications. Appropriateness studies can inform guidelines to help the practicing physician decide under what circumstances a procedure should or should not be done.

Quality of Life and Pharmacoeconomics in Clinical Trials, Second Edition, edited by B. Spilker.
Lippincott-Raven Publishers, Philadelphia © 1996.

CHAPTER 78

Health Policy Implications of Using Quality of Life Measures in the Economic Evaluation of Health Care

Alan H. Williams

INTRODUCTION

It is a forbidding task to contribute to a book with over 100 chapters when yours is far down in the batting order. At that stage the reader is at best likely to be somewhat bemused, and at worst utterly jaded. Moreover, your illustrious precursors may have left you with very little new to say. All you can hope to do is to give the kaleidoscope a good shake and hope that the now-familiar material looks markedly different simply through rearrangement and refocusing. This is the limit of my ambition in this chapter, but it is nonetheless an important ambition, because health policy (broadly interpreted) is the most important potential field of application for quality of life measures, and economic evaluation is the most powerful analytical approach within which to deploy them.

Before I attempt to substantiate that claim I need to define more clearly my chosen realm of discourse. To do this I shall first narrow the range of health policy substantially, and then go on to be more specific about the kind of health care system I am thinking about. I will then highlight the inevitability of decentralization, the cyclical nature of policy making, and the ubiquity of policy makers. Then I can tackle the central question, which is how economic evaluation (with

A. H. Williams: Centre for Health Economics, University of York, York YO1 5DD, England.

a strong quality of life component) might bear on their various decisions.

I also have to distinguish the use of quality of life measures for evaluative purposes from their use for predictive or diagnostic purposes. Monitoring changes in a patient's quality of life (e.g., levels of pain and/or disability) may be an important guide to the clinical severity of the condition and thereby serve both as a guide to appropriate treatment and as a predictor of the likely future course of the condition. For such purposes the "weights" used for the measure will essentially be probabilities, designed to enable a clinician to assign a patient with more or less confidence to a particular category for treatment or prognosis purposes. There is no necessary correlation between such weights and the "values" attached by patients or others to that particular health state. In what follows I shall be solely concerned with the use of quality of life measures for evaluative purposes, and it is important that this be borne in mind. It is equally important to bear in mind that a quality of life measure designed for diagnostic or predictive purposes may not be appropriate for evaluative purposes (1).

HEALTH POLICY OR HEALTH CARE POLICY?

There is a natural tendency in the context of pharmacoeconomics to assume that "health policy" means "health care policy," whereas in fact it is a much broader concept. It includes attempts to persuade people to change their lifestyle (e.g., to give up smoking, change their diet, take more exercise), it includes the use of regulatory and fiscal measures to improve safety in the home, in the workplace, on the roads, and in public transport, and it even includes concerns over environmental pollution at local and global levels. In each of these cases quality of life issues and economic issues mingle inescapably, as do distributional issues, both between different groups of people here and now, and between different generations through time. Each of these health policy issues warrants a book of its own, but since the subject of *this* book is pharmacoeconomics and clinical trials, I will restrict myself here to the narrower domain of *public policy with respect to health care,* which is still too broad to handle in any great depth in the space available.

HEALTH CARE SYSTEMS

There are two broad ideological streams out of which health care systems have developed (in a sometimes rather haphazard and incoherent way). These might be called the "libertarian" and the "egalitarian" (2). The libertarian ideology tends to favor markets and financial incentives as the key mechanism for ensuring the appropriate provision of health care, and to leave this largely in the hands of private organizations. The egalitarian ideology focuses attention upon "needs," doubts the capacity of markets to respond to these very sensitively, and therefore favors public provision of one kind or another. For the private market-oriented system, it is techniques of financial appraisal that are the appropriate analytical tools for optimization purposes, and quality of life issues are not likely to be important, except for marketing purposes (3). For the public health care system, the key issues requiring clarification are the definition of "need" and a clear articulation of what it is that is to be equalized between different claimants. If it turns out that "need" is related in any way to "capacity to benefit" (4), it is *economic* appraisal techniques that are appropriate for optimization purposes. Financial appraisal compares revenues and expenditures (money outlays) in order to determine what is profitable. Economic appraisal compares benefits and costs (real sacrifices, whether associated with financial transactions or not) in order to determine what is beneficial. And the concept of benefit, in the context of health care, incorporates both changes in life expectancy and changes in quality of life. In this context, a concern for quality of life becomes a central, rather than an incidental, focus of interest (5). In what follows, therefore, I shall assume that the health care system that we are considering has among its objectives the maximization of the health of the community it serves, subject to some real resource constraints. And "health" is taken to embrace both life expectancy and quality of life, suitably weighted. The health care system may also be pursuing equity concerns, in which case the analytical task becomes more difficult, and the structure of the economic appraisal more complex, but that is incidental to my main theme in this chapter and has been discussed elsewhere (6,7).

DECENTRALIZATION

It is important to acknowledge from the outset that all health care systems have to operate in a decentralized manner. Fundamentally this is because of information overload. There is no way that anyone away from the clinical encounter between practitioner and patient can handle all the information that those two parties have. Key elements within it can be filtered out and reviewed elsewhere, and the art of effective delegation lies in selecting that key information and processing it promptly and effectively. And the same considerations apply in the reverse direction. There is no way that the individual practitioner can handle all the information that management has about overall patterns of work, resource deployment, future budgetary prospects, and so on, for the whole organization. Again, key information can be made available that is regarded as of special relevance in the clinical situation, but that is all. The fact that everyone has incomplete information, and everyone has some scope for discretionary behavior, means that health policy is effectively made at all levels in the health care system. Whether health policy is internally consistent depends on how this discretion is exercised. This in turn depends on each policy maker's motivation (Is it the same as that of the organization?), the incentive structure facing each policy maker (Does it lead to the behavior that the organizational objectives require?), and the capacity of each policy maker to formulate and act upon such system-required policies (Is the necessary knowledge there when it is needed?). This capacity depends on the competence of the person, and upon the information available to her or him at the time. Such a decentralized system will only behave optimally when each decision maker is put in a position where both the costs and the benefits of each decision are properly taken into account when a decision is made.

I know of no health care system that has achieved this ideal, and many of the problems facing health care systems all over the world have this weakness as their root cause. Practitioners are more concerned with benefits than with costs, managers are more concerned with work done rather than outcome, financial controllers are more concerned with keeping people within budgets rather than making them more efficient, and so on. To the extent that economic appraisal techniques are able to incorporate appropriate measures of input, throughput, and output, they should be applicable at all levels and help to overcome at least some of the deficiencies of current institutional arrangements. Doctors need to take costs into account in a systematic way, managers need to look beyond workload to effectiveness (including effects on patients' quality of life), and finance directors need to adapt budgeting and accounting practices to promote resource optimization in a cost-effectiveness sense. Economic appraisal, in the form of cost-utility analysis, has an important integrating role to play between these competing perspectives.

THE POLICY-MAKING CYCLE

It is important to recognize that irrevocable one-off policy decisions are rare. Usually, the adoption of a policy is followed by some monitoring of its effects, some audit of the behavior of those responsible for carrying it out, and some periodic reevaluation of the policy to see whether it needs changing. In the financial field this cycle typically follows a rigid annual timetable, but in clinical and managerial contexts it is far more variable (and sometimes nonexistent!). This variability has both favorable and unfavorable effects upon the scope of economic appraisal. The favorable effect is that the time constraints for results may be more flexible and more conducive to good quality analysis. The unfavorable effect is that the time is never quite ripe. As with the assessment of new technologies, during the development phase it is too early because things are still in a state of flux, and then the technology becomes so widely diffused and so firmly embodied in current practice that it is too late to conduct anything other than a postmortem! The optimal timing of health policy reviews (and the choice of topic and terms of reference) is a major unresolved problem in itself, and it requires more systematic thought if the full potential of economic appraisal techniques is to be realized.

KEY LEVELS OF POLICY MAKING

Because of the inescapably decentralized nature of health care provision, there are many policy makers in the system, many of whom hardly recognize themselves as playing that role. Any noncapricious decision to acquire resources, or to use them in a particular way, is a policy decision, whether that resource is an extra hour of overtime for some member of staff, the decision to replace a dressing, change a drug regime, move a patient, change an allowance, reorganize a scheduling system, or whatever. We must not think of health policy as being only about grand issues such as whether to reform a whole health care system, or close a hospital, or change the way doctors are paid. Policy making is extremely pervasive, and most of it is "unwitting," in the sense that it is undertaken without recognizing its essential features, which are always a comparison of some (selected) costs and some (selected) benefits. The role of economic appraisal in that context is to make such comparisons more explicit, more systematic, and more appropriate.

The scope for doing this is tremendous (and far greater than our current capacities, so some prioritization will eventually be needed). Picking out a few policy choices when the effect on the quality of life of patients should be a key variable, the following list springs readily to mind:

1. Is it better to use "disposables" or "reusables" in some specified context?
2. What is the best diagnostic strategy, given certain presenting characteristics?
3. To which patients should a particular treatment be offered?
4. How intensively or for how long should a particular treatment be offered to a particular kind of patient?
5. Which therapeutic tasks are best done by which people?
6. How many doctors/nurses/dentists and other health professionals do we need?
7. Which patients/treatments are more appropriately dealt with in primary rather than secondary care?
8. What is the appropriate role of intensive care in a hospital system?
9. What is the best location for a hospital or health center?
10. How do different methods of financing (or regulating) health care affect the level and pattern of health care and thereby the health of patients?
11. What kinds of health care should be in a "basic package" and what should be "optional extras"?
12. To which health projects should an international aid agency give priority?

The answer to all these questions is that it depends on the costs and benefits associated with each of the relevant policy options. But that begs many interesting and important issues about which costs and which benefits should be taken into account in each case. This is the subject that will be my central concern in what follows, concentrating on the role of quality of life measures, and the implications for their structure and broad content. To do this it will be advantageous to distinguish some key levels of policy making and treat them one by one. The levels in question will be

1. Clinical
2. Practice
3. Provider organization
4. Purchasing organization

By "clinical" policy is meant how decisions are made about how best to treat[1] a particular patient presenting with particular characteristics. By "practice" policy is meant how a clinician (or group of clinicians practising together) decides which sort of patients the practice will be organized to treat and what resources the practice will seek to deploy in order to do so. By "provider organization" is meant something larger than a practice, for instance a whole hospital, which will be made up of many separate practices or specialties. By "purchaser organization" is meant any organization financing the provision of health care on behalf of patients (for instance, an insurance company, a governmental agency, or an international agency like the World Bank). In specific circumstances a more complex classification of policy makers may be needed, but this will be sufficiently complex for my immediate purpose.

CLINICAL DECISION MAKING

If a clinician is seen as a perfect agent for the patient, then clinical policies will simply be designed to maximize the health of each patient individually. If part of the costs of treatment fall on the patient or on the patient's family, then this objective should be modified so as to balance the costs to the patient against the benefits to the patient. In either case, the values of the patient (and the patient's family) will be paramount, and any quality of life measure should reflect this. This implies that no standard set of weights can be employed, because each person will have different concerns, and will weigh alternatives differently. The task of the clinician is to describe as accurately as possible the consequences of each alternative course of action in terms of life expectancy and quality of life, and leave the patient to choose according to her or his own (private) set of values. So the role of quality of life measures in this context is to provide a descriptive system, cast in terms that lay people can understand, which encompasses any dimension of health-related quality of life that is likely to be affected by any of the alternatives on offer. It points to the need for a quality of life measure that is a quite complex descriptive profile, possibly hierarchical, but without any prespecified weights or scoring system. And the role of clinical trials is to ensure that such descriptive material is generated so that clinicians can share it with their patients rather than relying entirely on their own clinical experience. An economic appraisal tailor-made for this situation would consider only costs (financial and other, such as informal care) to patients and their families, and only health benefits to them. It would need to be a private calculation made according to the particular values of each patient/family. It is not feasible.

But this is a very restricted and unrealistic scenario. It is restricted because it excludes from the decision-making process the views of other parties who have a legitimate interest in it, and it is unrealistic because clinicians are not perfect agents; they have interests of their own. Clinicians are likely to be influenced in their policies by the demands different alternatives make on their own time and energy, and by the effects on their own income and/or professional advancement. In other words, to understand the foundations of their clinical policies we will need a broader form of economic analysis than that indicated above, which will include costs and benefits to the clinician. Since clinicians typically feel coy about admitting that they are not perfect agents, such analyses are likely to be conducted without their cooperation in an attempt to infer the extent to which they do depart from what they claim to be their pure agency role.[2]

One of the costs to the clinician may well be the time required to enter into elaborate descriptions of possible outcomes from possible courses of action that the clinician thinks are unlikely to be very beneficial for a particular patient, and then of having to elicit the valuations of patients for these various scenarios, in a context in which the relevant issues are very unfamiliar (and emotionally disturbing) to the patient and the patient's family. So there will be a tendency to simplify the procedure somewhat, and especially to substitute the clinician's own values for those of the patient (possibly justified by claiming that they are derived from the typical values expressed by patients in the past). This is what recourse to clinical experience is all about, and it shifts the focus of economic appraisal from the values of individual patients to the values of individual clinicians. As regards quality of life measures, it implies that each clinician is likely to have a favorite measure, chosen because it happens to reflect one's own set of values. In the extreme, these measures will not be standard ones at all, but some idiosyncratic system tailored to the particular beliefs and concerns of that clinician. If such a measure is explicit and systematic, it could be used in an economic appraisal, but the results would not be generalizable.

The other weakness of the "clinician as perfect agent" scenario is that there are other people with a legitimate interest in the clinical encounter besides the doctor and the patient. This interest arises because the patient is not paying the full cost of the encounter and its consequences, and those that are paying the rest have a right to have their views taken into account, too. Moreover, at each point in time there will be some limitation upon the resources available for treatment. This limit may simply be financial, or it may be a real resource constraint in terms of system capacity (the availability of beds, operating theatres, doctors, drugs, etc.). These constraints mean that every decision to treat one person is a decision to deny the resources so used to some other person who might have benefited from them. The views of this other person then also need to be taken into account. Typically we do not know who this particular individual will be, but only that he or she will be one of a class of people who might benefit from a particular kind of treatment if it were offered to them. So we have two other parties to bring into the calculus—those who are sacrificing money and those who are sacrificing health improvements (with some possible overlap between the two). What this implies for the appropriate quality of life measure is that it needs to reflect the values of this wider group, a matter more conveniently considered in relation to the next level of policy making.

PRACTICE POLICY

A clinical practice may be quite specialized (e.g., concerned only with cardiac surgery) or quite general (e.g., in primary care). If it has a fixed budget, and the problem is how best to spend that budget on, say, patients with a particular condition, then a quality of life measure specific to that condition will be all that is required, provided that it reflects the values of all the people with that condition, whether they actually become patients or not. The quality of life measure may be a profile or an index, but the applicability of a profile will be severely limited if different patients get different sorts of gains from treatment (e.g., some get pain relief but little improvement in functional capacity, while for others the opposite is the case). In such a situation it will be necessary to weigh the one kind of change against the other to determine which is on balance is best. At a policy level this means establishing some *group* value, which will reflect individual values but may not be identical with those of any specific individual. This may create problems where the optimal treatment depends on people's values (e.g., whether they are more concerned with pain relief than with improved functional capacity) so they may need to be divided into subgroups accordingly with a different quality of life indicator used for each. But how is the practice going to decide the distribution of practice resources between the two groups?

This brings us into the realm of the more general practice, where a fixed budget has to be distributed between rival claimants who suffer from different conditions and/or require different treatments. Condition-specific or treatment-specific quality of life measures will no longer be of any use, whether of the profile variety or of the index variety, because they will not be comparing like with like or using a common valuation framework. In this situation a generic measure will be required, one that encompasses a wide enough range of health-related quality of life characteristics to pick up any effect that is likely to be important to any of the people who suffer from any of the conditions covered by the practice. And such a measure will not function well for this purpose unless it generates a single index score that reflects the values of all those ''at risk'' (i.e., all patients or potential patients). This group may well be so diverse as to be indistinguishable from a random sample of the general public. Thus the appropriate health-related quality of life measure in this case would be a generic measure yielding a single index value based on the values of the general public.

PROVIDER ORGANIZATIONS

The distinction between a broad-ranging clinical practice and a provider organization is so blurred that I will treat it as seamless rather than as a sharp dichotomy. In general, a practical difference is likely to be that a provider organization (e.g., a hospital) will be allocating resources internally between clinical practices (e.g., specialists), so it may be from the provider organization that a practice gets the ''fixed'' budget assumed in the preceding section. The problem facing the provider organization is how to divide its budget between its constituent clinical practices, and this brings us back to the problem discussed in the preceding paragraph. It will now be even more likely that the only appropriate reference group as a source for value weights in a generic health-related quality of life measure will be the general public.

But there is a possible complication here, because the provider organization may be serving many different and distinct clienteles. For instance, it may have a contractual obligation to provide one particular group of services for one population, a different one for another, and both to a third. If they all have the same set of values regarding health-related quality of life, this diversity will cause no additional problems. But if their values differ, we shall need a generic quality of life measure that describes the various dimensions in the same way, but can have different values plugged into it according to the population to be served.[3]

PURCHASING ORGANIZATIONS

This leads us naturally into our final level of health care policymaking, that concerned with purchasing decisions. Here it is necessary to distinguish between those organizations in which the group of people for whom health care is being purchased is the same group of people as are meeting the costs, and those organizations that are purchasing health care for one group, which is being paid for by another group (although possibly with some overlap between the two). In the first case purchasing decisions should be guided by the values of those for whom care is being purchased, so again what is needed is a generic health-related quality of life measure that incorporates their values and generates a single index so that priority-setting policies can be established across very diverse activities. In the second case there may well be tension between the values of those for whom care is being purchased and those who are paying for it. It would be useful in this case to have a generic quality of life measure that could incorporate each set of values in turn to test which decisions were sensitive to any differences in values, and which robust. Then the sensitive ones could be discussed more fully to see whether some agreement might be reached, which might turn out to be no more than a clear statement of whose values are to count in such circumstances.

This distinction between beneficiaries and cost bearers is usually not as stark as it has been presented here. It is more common for the two roles to be played simultaneously by each individual. When we are patients we bring one set of values to bear, but as taxpayers we typically adopt a more restrictive stance. We may agree with the policies, but do not wish them to be applied to us! I think this is less of a problem for heath-related quality of life measurement itself, but much more of a problem for economic evaluation in general, recognizing that such an evaluation is increasingly likely to incorporate such measures. It is best seen as bearing on the cost side of the evaluation. When we are patients, cost should be no object (especially if it is mainly borne by others). When we are taxpayers we are painfully aware of the sacrifices that have to be made in other aspects of our quality of life if we devote too much of our money to health care. Unfortunately, in the present state of quality of life measurement we cannot make these broader comparisons in a systematic way, so the discussion currently remains at a rather informal level. But we should not lose sight of the fact that alongside health-related quality of life there is also education-related quality of life, personal security–related quality of life, and so on.

CONCLUSIONS

The essence of the above discussion is set out in Table 1. It will be seen that three characteristics of health-related quality of life measures have been highlighted—whether specific or generic, whether profiles or indexes, and where the weights come from.

Because policy is made at many different levels in the health care system, by many different people, serving many different clienteles, there is a role for many different types of health-related quality of life measures. However, they are not all equally appropriate in each particular circumstance, and my stress has been upon whose values they express. There is a regrettable tendency to derive scoring systems (within profiles as well as within indexes) from statistical data that have no explicit valuations in them at all. Even a ranking from better to worse implies such a valuation, and it is too frequently made on the basis of a professional judgment about severity, which owes more to biomedical criteria than to patient preferences. In an evaluative context

this has to stop. At the very least such judgments need to be systematically tested against the values of patients and/ or the general public. But it would be better if scoring systems in measures intended to be used to judge whether someone had improved or worsened were derived *ab initio* from such values.

This chapter also discussed the tension between specific and generic measures of health-related quality of life. Such is the complexity of the financing arrangements in most health care systems today that it can now never be the case that all the costs are borne by a particular patient or even by the particular group of patients for whom a disease-specific or treatment-specific measure is intended. This points to the need always to use a (preference-based) generic measure alongside any specific measure, if it is likely that the data will ever be used to determine policy at any level whatsoever. There is no longer such a thing as a doctor-patient encounter that has no impact on the interests of other parties.

The measurement of health-related quality of life has properly become a central concern of those responsible for health care policy at all levels, and we are still in the early stages of development from a methodological viewpoint, and still at a minimal level of systematic application from an empirical standpoint. The establishment of orthodoxy or standardization at this delicate stage would doubtless be counterproductive in the long run, despite its attractions in the short run to those who understandably feel overwhelmed, and somewhat bemused, by the proliferation of such diverse approaches to this important task. But what is perhaps called for at this stage is careful thought about the properties required for the performance of different tasks, and the matching of measures to tasks. I have concentrated on the evaluative task, which is a crucial one at all levels. If my analysis is correct, then the conclusion must be that there are very few health-related quality of life measures in existence at present that are suited to the evaluative task, and still fewer that have been specifically designed for it. If one is interested in evaluation, as a simple diagnostic test when looking at any health-related quality of life measure, one must ask these two questions:

1. Whose values does its scoring system reflect?
2. For what policy issue would those values be the appropriate ones?

In most cases it will be difficult to answer the first question. And for the surviving cases, one may well find their scope surprisingly limited. We still have a long way to go.

TABLE 1. *Health-related quality of life measures by type and appropriate policy context*

Policy context	Appropriate type of measure
Clinical	
Perfect agency	Disease-specific descriptive profile with no scoring system
Imperfect agency	Disease-specific descriptive profile with weights reflecting clinician's opinions
Practice	
Narrowly restricted budget	Disease-specific profile or index with weights reflecting values of specific clientele
Broadly restricted budget	Generic profile or index with weights reflecting values of patients and potential patients
Provider	
With a specific clientele	Generic profile or index with weights reflecting values of the population served
With a variety of clienteles	Generic profile or index capable of incorporating a variety of values
Purchaser	
Serving and financed by same population	Generic index with weights reflecting the values of the population served
Serving one population but financed by a different one	Generic index capable of incorporating a variety of values

REFERENCES

1. Williams A. *Health Econ* 1992;1:255–258.
2. Williams A. Review article. Priority setting in public and private health care: a guide through the ideological jungle. *J Health Econ* 1988;7: 173–183.
3. Drummond MF. *Economic evaluation of pharmaceuticals: science or marketing?* Discussion paper 91. Toronto: University of York, Centre for Health Economics, 1991.

4. Williams A. Need as a demand concept (with special reference to health). In: Culyer AJ, ed. *Economic policies and social goals.* London: Martin Robertson, 1974.

5. Williams A. Priority setting in a needs-based system. In: Gelijns AC, ed. *Technology and health care in an era of limits.* Washington, DC: National Academy Press, 1992:79–95.

6. Williams A. Economics, society and health care ethics. In: Gillon R, ed. *Principles of health care ethics.* New York: Wiley, 1994:829–842.

7. Williams A. *Economics, QALYs and medical ethics.* Discussion paper 121. Toronto: University of York, Centre for Health Economics, 1994.

ENDNOTES

1. By "treatment" is meant any activity that is part of the therapeutic process, so it would include rescue and transportation, diagnosis, information-giving, reassurance, counseling, remedial and rehabilitative activities, as well as medical and nursing activities.

2. The literature on "supplier induced demand" is an example of this kind of enterprise.

3. This is what the EUROQOL measure aims to do (see Chapter 22).

Quality of Life and Pharmacoeconomics in Clinical Trials, Second Edition, edited by B. Spilker.
Lippincott-Raven Publishers, Philadelphia © 1996.

CHAPTER 79

Rules for Evaluating Medical Technologies

David M. Eddy

INTRODUCTION

Before we launch a new medical technology, we would like to show that it satisfies four criteria:

- It improves the health outcomes patients care about—pain, death, anxiety, disfigurement, disability.
- Its benefits outweigh its harms.
- Its health effects are worth its costs.
- And, if resources are limited, it deserves priority over other technologies.

To apply any of these criteria we need to estimate the magnitude of the technology's benefits and harms. We want to gather this information as accurately, quickly, and inexpensively as possible to speed the use of technologies that have these properties and direct our energy away from technologies that do not.

There are many ways to estimate a technology's benefits and harms. They range from simply asking experts (pure clinical judgment) to conducting multiple randomized controlled trials, with anecdotes, clinical series, data bases, nonrandomized controlled trials, and case-control studies in between. The choice of a method has great influence on the cost of the evaluation, the duration of time required for the evaluation, the accuracy of the information gained, the complexity of administering the evaluation, and the ease of defending the subsequent decisions.

D. M. Eddy: Southern California Kaiser Permanente, Walnut Center, Pasadena, California 91188.

This chapter was reproduced from *Modern Methods of Clinical Investigation* 1990:117–134, with permission of the National Academy of Sciences and the National Academy Press.

The problem before us is to determine which set of methods delivers information of sufficiently high quality to draw conclusions with confidence, at the lowest cost in time and money.

CURRENT EVALUATIVE METHODS

Currently, very different methods are used to evaluate different types of medical technologies. There are some amazing inconsistencies. In some settings, we insist on direct evidence that compares the effects of the technology against suitable controls, using multiple randomized controlled trials in a variety of settings. In other settings, we do not require any direct comparison of the technology and a control, or any explicit comparison of the technology's benefits versus its harms or costs.

A good example of the first strategy is the evaluation required by the Food and Drug Administration for approval of drugs. I will never forget my first exposure to a new drug application. It described more than a dozen randomized controlled trials involving about 2,000 patients. It filled a room; consisted of 65,000 pages, which, if stood in a pile, would reach 49.5 feet; cost more than $10 million; required four years to complete; and needed a truck to haul it to Washington. At the other end of the spectrum is the evaluation of medical and surgical procedures. For most, there are no randomized controlled trials at all.

There are even inconsistencies within these categories. For example, we can insist that a pharmaceutical company produce the finest evidence that a drug alters some intermediate outcome (e.g., intraocular pressure), but require no controlled evidence at all that changing the intermediate outcome improves the outcome of real interest to patients (e.g., loss of visual field or blindness). We can require dozens of randomized controlled trials to demonstrate that a drug is effective for a particular indication, and leave it to pure clinical judgment to determine its effectiveness for other indications.

These inconsistencies have tremendous implications for the quality of care, the cost of research, and the time required to get effective innovations into widespread use. Consider just the implications for costs. If we demanded at least two randomized controlled trials for every innovation, research costs would be increased by billions of dollars a year. If we were to accept clinical judgment for every innovation, we could save billions of dollars that we now spend on randomized controlled trials, and speed the introduction of new technologies by years.

Given these inconsistencies and their implications, it is worthwhile to ask what information we are really trying to gather with our system for evaluating medical technologies. That might help us determine the best way to gather it.

WHAT ARE WE TRYING TO LEARN?

We need two things to make decisions about a technology. First, we must estimate the approximate magnitude of its benefits and harms. Second, we must determine the range of uncertainty about the estimates. These two points are so

crucial to an understanding of the different methods for evaluating technologies that they are worth discussion.

Suppose the outcome of interest is the probability of dying after a heart attack and the technology is a thrombolytic agent. Suppose an experiment has been conducted with 400 patients randomly allocated to receive either the treatment (200 patients) or a placebo (200 patients). Finally, suppose that during the follow-up period, 20 patients in the placebo group died of heart attacks, while 10 patients in the treated group died. Thus, without treatment, the chance of dying of a heart attack is 20 in 200 or 10%; with treatment, the chance of dying of a heart attack is 10 in 200, or 5%. The magnitude of the effect of treatment is a 5% decrease in the chance of dying of a heart attack (10% − 5% = 5%). This effect is shown as the large arrow in Fig. 1.

For a variety of reasons (e.g., sample size), there is uncertainty about an estimate of this type. This uncertainty can be displayed in terms of confidence intervals or probability distributions. For this particular example, the 95% confidence intervals for the estimated effect of the technology range from 0.2% to −10.2%. These are indicated by the smaller arrows on the graph. The range of uncertainty can also be displayed as a probability distribution for the effect of the technology; it is shown as the solid line. (The height of the distribution at any point reflects the probability that the true reduction in mortality is near that point. Thus, the most likely value for the reduction in mortality is the value under the highest point of the distribution, 5%.)

Both the estimated magnitude of the technology and the range of uncertainty are important. For example, it makes

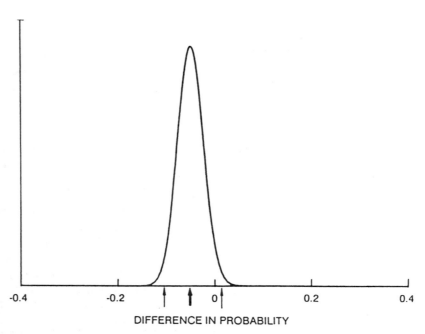

FIG. 1. Results of randomized controlled clinical trial of hypothetical treatment for heart attacks. Best estimates of the effect (*large arrow*), 95% confidence limits (*small arrows*), and probability distribution of the effect (*solid line*).

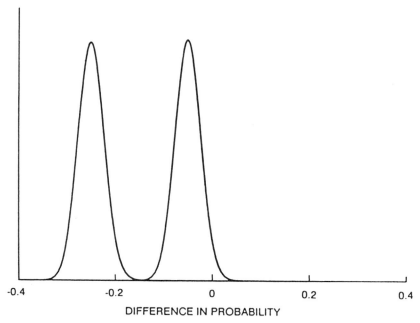

FIG. 2. Probability distributions of effects of two hypothetical treatments for heart attacks. Treatment A (best estimate of effect is −0.05), treatment B (best estimate of effect is −0.25).

a big difference whether the technology reduces the chance of dying of a heart attack by 5% or by 25% (Fig. 2). It also makes a big difference whether the range of uncertainty is ±5.2% or ±8.3% (Fig. 3). To people who interpret statistical significance rigidly, there is even a big difference between a range of uncertainty of ±5.2% and ±4.9% (Fig. 4).

QUALITY OF INFORMATION IN DIFFERENT DESIGNS: FACE VALUE

All methods for evaluating a technology, from the lowly pure clinical judgment to the lofty randomized controlled trial, provide information on the magnitude of effect and

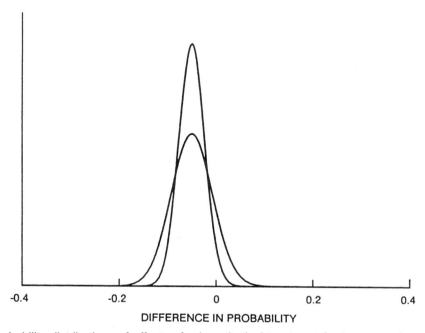

FIG. 3. Probability distributions of effects of a hypothetical treatment for heart attacks as estimated from two randomized controlled clinical trials. Trial A (narrow range of uncertainty), trial B (wider range of uncertainty).

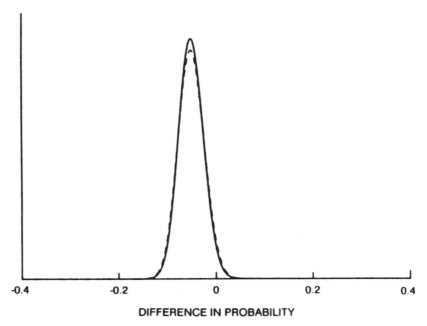

FIG. 4. Probability distributions of effects of a hypothetical treatment for heart attacks as estimated from two randomized controlled clinical trials. Trial A statistically significant (*solid line*), trial B not statistically significant (*dashed line*).

the range of uncertainty. Furthermore, for the empirical methods, if it were reasonable to take each method at face value (i.e., if it were possible to assume that there were no biases to internal or external validity), then all the designs, case for case, would be almost equally good at estimating the magnitude and range of uncertainty of an outcome. Stated another way, if all the results could be taken at face value, randomized controlled trials, case for case, would not provide any more precise or certain information than designs that are considered less rigorous, such as nonrandomized controlled trials, case-control studies, comparisons of clinical series, or analyses of data bases.

Consider, for example, two studies of breast cancer screening in women over age 50. One was a randomized controlled trial of approximately 100,000 women (58,148 women in the group offered screening and 41,104 women in the control group) (1). After 7 years of follow-up, there were 71 breast cancer deaths in the group offered screening and 76 breast cancer deaths in the control group. The other was a case-control study in which 54 cases (women who had died of breast cancer) were matched three to one with 162 controls (women who had not died of breast cancer) (2). Retrospective analysis of screening histories found that 11 of the 54 cases had been screened, compared with 73 of the 162 controls. The probability distributions for the percent reduction in mortality implied by these two studies, taken at face value, are shown in Fig. 5. The degree of certainty (as indicated by the variance or width of the distribution) is just as high for the case-control study as for the randomized controlled trial. The main determinant of the variance of the estimate

is not the total number of people involved in the study (100,000 women in the randomized controlled trial versus 216 in the case-control study), but the number of outcomes of interest that occurred (in this case, breast cancer deaths). The variances in the two studies are similar largely because there were almost as many outcomes in the case-control study (54) as in either group of the randomized controlled trial (71 and 76, respectively).

Thus, if we take the two studies at face value, it is clear that they provide virtually the same information. The difference between the studies is logistics. The randomized controlled trial involved recruiting and randomizing 100,000 people, screening about half of them, and following everyone for more than a decade. The logistics of the case-control study, on the other hand, were much simpler and less expensive. It required identifying only 54 women who died of breast cancer (the cases), 162 women matched by year of birth who have not died of breast cancer (the controls), and retrospective ascertainment of which women had been screened. The study collapses down to about 200 women and can be done in six months.

Similar stories can be told about the other designs. Provided the number of cases with the outcome of interest are similar, the degree of certainty in the face value estimates of all the designs will be similar. But the logistics can be vastly different. To push the example to the extreme, if there were a data base that had the pertinent records, the logistics would be as simple as doing the computer runs.

So, if the quality of the information gained by different designs is essentially the same, but the logistics, costs, and

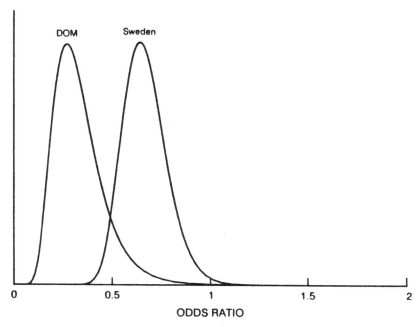

FIG. 5. Probability distributions of two controlled clinical trials of breast cancer screening taken at face value. Swedish prospective RCT; DOM retrospective case-control study.

time required are very different, the choice of the best design should be quite simple: pick the fastest and least expensive. What is wrong with this picture?

BIASES

The problem, of course, is with the assumption made at the beginning of the story. There we postulated that it was reasonable to take each design at face value—that is, to assume that there were no biases. In fact, there are biases that affect all evaluative methods. Furthermore, the effects of biases determine the rules for evaluating technologies. To solve the problem of choosing the best evaluative methodologies, we need some background on biases.

It is convenient to separate biases into two types. Biases to internal validity affect the accuracy of the results of the study as an estimate of the effect of the technology in the setting in which a study was conducted (e.g., the specific technology, specific patient indications, and so forth). Biases to external validity affect the applicability of the results to other settings (where the techniques, patient indications, and other factors might be different).

Examples of biases to internal validity include patient selection bias, crossover, errors in measurement of outcomes, and errors in ascertainment of exposure to the technology. Patient selection bias exists when patients in the two groups to be compared (e.g., the control and treated groups of a controlled trial) differ in ways that could affect the outcome of interest. When such differences exist, a differ-

ence in outcomes could be due at least in part to inherent differences in the patients, not to the technology. Crossover occurs either when patients in the group offered the technology do not receive it (sometimes called "dilution") or when patients in the control group get the technology (sometimes called "contamination"). Errors in measurement of outcomes can affect a study's results if the technique used to measure outcomes (e.g., claims data, patient interviews, urine tests, blood samples) do not accurately measure the true outcome. Patients can be misclassified as having had the outcome of interest (e.g., death from breast cancer) when in fact they did not, and vice versa. Errors in ascertainment of exposure to the technology can have an effect similar to crossover. A crucial step in a retrospective study is to determine who got the technology of interest and who did not. These measurements frequently rely on old records and fallible memories. Any errors affect the results.

An example of bias to external validity is the existence of differences between the people studied in the experiment and the people about whom you want to draw conclusions (sometimes called a "population bias"). For example, they might be older or sicker. Another example occurs when the technology used in the experiment differs from the technology of interest, because of differences in technique, equipment, provider skill, or changes in the technology since the experiment was performed. This is sometimes called "intensity bias."

Different evaluative methods are vulnerable to different biases. At the risk of gross oversimplification, Table 1 illustrates the vulnerabilities of different designs to biases. A

TABLE 1. *Susceptibility of various designs to biases*

| Design | Internal validity | | | | External validity | |
	Patient selection	Crossover	Error in measurement of outcomes	Error in ascertainment of exposure	Population	Technology
RCT	0	+ +	+	0	+ +	+ +
nonRCT	+	+	+	0	+	+
CCS	+ +	0	+	+ + +	0	+
Comparison of clinical series	+ + +	0	+	0	+	+
Data bases	+ +	0	+ +	+ +	0	+

0 implies minimal vulnerability to a bias.
+ + + implies high vulnerability to a bias.
RCT, randomized controlled trials; CCS, case-control studies.

zero implies that the bias is either nonexistent or likely to be negligible; three plus signs indicate that the bias is likely to be present and to have an important effect on the observed outcome. Methodologists can debate my choices, and there are innumerable conditions and subtle issues that will prevent agreement from ever being reached; the point is not to produce a definitive table of biases, but to convey the general message that all the designs are affected by biases, and the patterns are different for different designs.

For example, a major strength of the randomized controlled trial is that it is virtually free of patient selection biases. Indeed, that is the very purpose of randomization. In contrast, nonrandomized controlled trials, case-control studies, and data bases are all subject to patient selection biases. On the other hand, randomized controlled trials are more affected by crossover than the other four designs. All studies are potentially affected by errors in measurement of outcomes, with data bases more vulnerable than most because they are limited to whatever data elements were originally chosen by the designers. Case-control studies are especially vulnerable to misspecification of exposure to the technology, because of their retrospective nature. Data bases can be subject to the same problem, depending on the accuracy with which the data elements were coded.

With respect to external validity, randomized controlled trials are sensitive to population biases, because the recruitment process and admission criteria often result in a narrowly defined set of patient indications. Randomized controlled trials are also vulnerable to concerns that the intensity and quality of care might be different in research settings than in actual practice. The distinction between the "efficacy" of a technology (in research settings) and the "effectiveness" of a technology (in routine practice) reflects this concern. Thus, the results of a trial might not be widely applicable to other patient indications or less controlled settings. Data bases and case-control studies, on the other hand, tend to draw from "real" populations. All designs are susceptible to changes in the technology, but in different ways. Because they are prospective, randomized controlled trials and nonrandomized controlled trials are vulnerable to future

changes. Because they are retrospective, case-control studies and retrospective analyses of data bases are vulnerable to differences between the present and the past.

Now that we admit that biases are present and potentially important, our problem becomes much more complicated. We can no longer choose the simplest, quickest, and least expensive design. Now the choice must take potential biases into account.

HEURISTICS

It is easy to imagine that this new problem is extremely complicated. In fact, it can be argued that it exceeds the capacity of the unaided human mind. What, then, do we do? After all, this is a real problem that we have been facing for decades.

In response to the complexity of the problem, we have developed a set of mental simplifications, or heuristics, that convert what would be a very complicated set of judgments into a series of rather simple "yes" and "no" questions. The first and most important heuristic deals with the biases. Typically, we simplify our approach to biases by sorting them into two categories. For each design and each bias, we either declare that bias to be acceptable, take the study at face value, and ignore the bias from that point on; or we declare the bias to be unacceptable, and ignore the study from that point on. This said, it is important to understand that different people can have very different ideas about what constitutes an "acceptable" bias. Someone who believes in only the most rigorous randomized controlled trials (what we might call a "strict constructionist") might say the potential biases of data bases (or case-control studies, or nonrandomized controlled trials) are too great to accept. On the other hand, a clinical expert might be quite content to take anecdotes and clinical series at face value.

The next heuristic deals with the difficulty of estimating the magnitude of an effect (e.g., the magnitude of the reduction in mortality achieved by breast cancer screening). That can be quite complex, especially if there are multiple studies with different designs and different results. A much simpler approach is to determine if there is any effect at all, without worrying about its actual magnitude. In practice, we calculate the probability that the study would indicate there is an effect when in fact there is not—the statistical significance of the study. If the result is statistically significant, we feel good, even if the actual magnitude of the effect is very small, or if we have not even estimated the actual magnitude.

The third heuristic deals with the difficult balance between the possibility of rejecting a technology that in fact is effective, versus accepting a technology that in fact is not effective. The most visible heuristic is to declare a technology effective when the *p*-value—the chance of accepting an ineffective technology—falls below 5%. This heuristic can be applied without ever calculating the chance of the first type of error (rejecting an effective technology). The mesmerizing power of this statistic can be surprising. For years, the *p*-value of another study that examined breast cancer screening for women younger than age 50 hovered just above the magic threshold of 5%. When some authors found a different way to calculate the statistics that pushed the *p*-value below .05 (3), the National Cancer Institute issued a press release that made national news. This behavior is especially touching because almost half the women in the "screened group" did not receive all the scheduled examinations—a bias that overwhelms the meaning of the *p*-value. But there are other heuristics. Toward the other extreme is the common sentiment among practitioners that unless a technology has been proven not to be effective, it should be considered effective. The point is not that the heuristics are applied uniformly, simply that they are applied widely. The last set of heuristics is the most sweeping. To deal with the complex issues raised by costs and limited resources, we simply ignore costs and limits on resources.

Our main concern is with the first heuristic, in which some biases are declared acceptable and others are not. Consider the implications of different points of view. To insist on seeing randomized controlled trial "proof" of effectiveness before approving a technology, and to not allow case-control studies, nonrandomized controlled trials, analysis of data bases, or comparisons of clinical series (call this the "strict constructionist approach") is essentially saying that a patient selection bias is not acceptable (Table 1). However, whenever a randomized controlled trial is taken at face value—for example, the results are analyzed by "intent to treat" without adjusting for crossover—the implication is that crossover, errors in measurement of outcomes, and biases to external validity are either acceptable or somebody else's problems. Ironically, leaving it to decision makers to deal with biases to external validity implies an acceptance of clinical judgment as the preferred method to adjust for those biases.

Now consider the implied set of beliefs at the other end of the spectrum. Those willing to make decisions on the basis of anecdotes and clinical series (let us call them "loose constructionists") are saying either that all the biases that affect those sources of evidence are acceptable, or that it is

possible and appropriate to adjust for them subjectively. For example, anyone who draws a conclusion about alternative technologies by comparing separate clinical series of the technologies is either accepting patient section bias and a wide variety of other confounding factors or claiming an ability to adjust for them mentally.

To summarize the main points about biases: Every design is affected by biases. Different designs are affected differently by different biases. And there is no way to escape subjective judgments in dealing with biases. The last point is especially important for what follows. Current evaluative methods rely on subjective judgments for such questions as which technologies require empirical evidence (e.g., drugs, devices, clinical procedures), what types of evidence are acceptable, which outcomes must be demonstrated empirically, when intermediate outcomes are acceptable, which intermediate outcomes to use, which patient indications require empirical evidence, how to extend results to other patient indications, which biases are acceptable, an acceptable α-level for determining statistical significance, and so forth. We can imagine that everything is purely objective, but subjective judgments are all around us. The question is not *whether* we allow the use of subjective judgments, but *how* we use them. Should they be implicit and informal, with every man for himself, or explicit, formal, organized, and open to review?

OPTIONS

Now let us return to the problem of choosing the best evaluative strategy. There are three main options:

1. accept the status quo with its inconsistencies and wide variations in degrees of rigor used by various approaches;
2. determine which of the current approaches is the most desirable, and move the other approaches toward that end of the spectrum; for example, we could make the strict constructionist approach more loose or the loose constructionist approach more strict; or,
3. develop a new approach that combines the two extremes.

To decide the merits of these three options, it is necessary to return to the objective. It is to speed the acceptance and diffusion of technologies that are worth the costs and deserve priority, and to restrain technologies for which these conditions do not hold. The status quo (option #1) is highly variable in achieving this objective. We suspect that the strict approach is too slow; too expensive; discards some information from designs that, although not "perfect," are at least useful; and inhibits or at least retards the introduction of some effective technologies. On the other hand, we suspect the loose approach is too subjective, too inaccurate, too arbitrary, and too hidden. It provides no information on the magnitudes of the outcomes; the conclusions can depend more on which experts you happen to choose than the merits of the technology; there is no trial, making it impossible to examine the logic of the judgments; and it appears to accept too many technologies that are in fact not effective. Furthermore, the basis for deciding which technologies need which types of evaluations seems arbitrary. Is there really any reason to believe there is something inherent about drugs versus procedures that makes multiple randomized controlled trials necessary for drugs, but clinical series and clinical judgment best for procedures? It is difficult to argue that the status quo is the appropriate choice.

This has implications for the second option, picking one of the extremes and moving everything in that direction. If we believe the strict approach is too rigid, we do not want to move everything in that direction. Would we really want to require 49.5 feet of documentation on every technology, every indication? Similarly, if we believe the loose approach is too loose, we should not trade in the virtues of rigor for it.

The third option is to draw on the strengths of both. This approach, dare we call it the ''flexible but firm'' approach, might proceed with the following steps:

1. Drop any preconceived conclusions about which experimental designs are acceptable or not, and which types of subjective judgments are acceptable or not.
2. Gather whatever empirical evidence exists, from any design. If a group is in the process of designing a new study to determine the effectiveness of a technology, it is free to explore and submit any designs it chooses.
3. For each study, identify the potential biases.
4. Estimate the magnitudes of each bias (including, when appropriate, the range of uncertainty about the estimates).

At this point we reach the main fork in the road. Traditionally, anyone evaluating evidence would make a judgment at this point about whether the biases are acceptable. If they are deemed unacceptable, the study, and all the information in it, is discarded. If the biases are considered acceptable, the study is admitted and from that time on the biases are assumed to be unimportant. Thus, the traditional choice is whether to take the study at *no* value, or to take it at *face* value.

The flexible but firm approach would take a middle course. It would use formal methods to adjust the results of the studies for biases, and use the adjusted results to make decisions about the merits of the technology. For example, if a randomized controlled trial has crossover, the traditional approach would analyze the data by ''intent to treat,'' which is tantamount to ignoring the bias. The flexible but firm approach would not take the trial at face value but would estimate the proportions of people who crossed over, and adjust for the bias accordingly. If it is thought that patients who crossed over might not be representative of their group (e.g., they might be at higher risk of the outcome), that belief would be quantified and incorporated in the adjustment. Other biases could be addressed in similar fashion. Thus, the remaining steps for the flexible but firm approach are

5. Adjust the results of the studies for biases.
6. Use the adjusted results as the best information available for decisions.

The hallmark of the flexible but firm approach is that it uses formal techniques (e.g., statistical models of biases) to incorporate focused subjective judgments (not global clinical impressions) to adjust (not simply accept or reject) results of studies to achieve the best combination of evidence and judgment. The philosophy behind it is that ''one size doesn't fit all.'' The validity of a particular design depends on the question being asked, the disease, the technology, the results, and the suspected biases, among other things. It is not an immutable property of the design.

AN EXAMPLE

Let us return to the two studies of breast cancer screening in women older than age 50. Suppose we are interested in the effectiveness of breast cancer screening in women age 50 to 64 with a combination of breast physical examinations and mammography delivered every 2 years (call this the circumstances of interest). The randomized controlled trial is affected by several biases. The main bias to internal validity is that about 20% of the group offered screening did not receive it (dilution), and about 5% of the control group received screening outside the trial (contamination). Potential biases to external validity are (a) the randomized controlled trial involved only mammography (not breast physical examination and mammography), (b) screening was delivered every 3 years (not 2), and (c) the setting was a randomized controlled trial (not ''usual care'').

Adjusting for these biases requires estimating the magnitude of each bias. Suppose we estimate that dilution and contamination occurred in the percentages reported (20% and 5%, respectively), that the lack of breast physical examination and the longer frequency caused the observed results to understate the effectiveness of the combination of breast physical examination and mammography by about 40% (with a 95% confidence range of 30% to 50%) (4–7), and that the setting of the trial was natural enough not to affect external validity. Adjustment for these assumptions delivers the estimated effect of breast cancer screening in the circumstances of interest shown in Fig. 6. The randomized controlled trial taken at face value is included in the figure for comparison (dashed line).

The other study was a case-control study. The main biases to which it is subject are patient selection bias and errors of ascertainment of exposure to screening. The external validity of the study is high because it involved a combination of breast physical examination and mammography delivered every 2 years in women age 50 to 64 under natural conditions.

The investigators have provided information indicating that when screening was offered, those who chose not to get screened appeared to have an inherently worse prognosis after a cancer was detected (8). Suppose we believe the relative risk of breast cancer death in the women who declined screening, compared with those who accepted screening, was 1.4. Suppose also we believe that the methods for

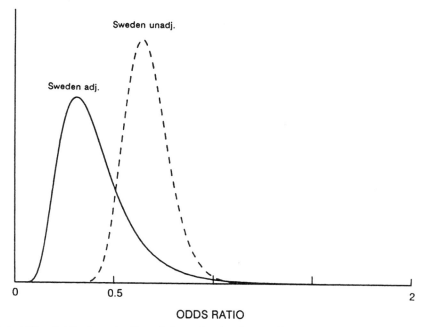

FIG. 6. Probability distributions for Swedish randomized controlled clinical trial taken at face value and adjusted for biases. Face value represented by *dashed line*, value adjusted for biases (see text) by *solid line*.

ascertaining who got screened in the 7 years prior to the analysis (e.g., chart review, records of screening centers, patient recall, and family recall) were subject to the following error rates:

P("not screened" | screened, cancer)	15%
P("not screened" | screened, no cancer)	5%
P("screened" | not screened, cancer)	5%
P("screened" | not screened, no cancer)	8%

Under this set of beliefs, the probability distribution for the effectiveness of breast cancer screening in the circumstances of interest is shown in Fig. 7, which includes for comparison the study's results taken at face value, and the two distributions derived from the randomized controlled trial.

This example could be made richer by incorporating uncertainty about any of the estimates of biases, by considering other potential biases that might affect the studies, by introducing and adjusting five other controlled studies of breast cancer screening for this age group (9–13), and by synthesizing the results of all the studies into a single probability distribution.

It is important to understand that the estimation of biases should not be taken lightly. Ideally, bias estimates should be based on empirical evidence (e.g., data on potential biases should be collected during the conduction of a study) and impartial panels should review the assumptions. This example is intended to demonstrate a method, not promote particular numbers. The concept is that it is possible to improve on the current approach, in which data are either accepted at face value, rejected, or adjusted implicitly by pure subjective judgment. It is also important to understand that formal methods of adjusting for biases cannot and should not make every piece of evidence look good. For some studies, by the time adjustments have been made, with honest descriptions of the ranges of uncertainty, there will be virtually nothing left. The distributions will be virtually flat, providing no information about the effect of the technology.

Many people will be uncomfortable with this example. Discomfort caused by disagreement with the specific adjustments is open for discussion. A panel might be appointed to determine the most reasonable assumptions, and the implications of a range of assumptions can be explored. If the discomfort is due to the attempt to incorporate any judgments at all in the interpretation of an experiment, remember the alternatives. If no explicit adjustments are made, the options are either to accept the study at face value (which violates our belief that it is biased), to reject it outright (which violates our belief that it contains some usable information), or to make the adjustments silently (which is more prone to error and closed to review). If the discomfort is simply because the approach is different, let it sink in for a while.

I can already hear the complaints. From the rigorous side: "What a disaster! Admit the value of subjective judgments?! Tamper with the integrity of a randomized controlled trial by 'adjusting' it?! We've spent decades trying to make the evaluative process completely rigorous and clean—you're undoing decades of hard-fought rigor." From the other side: "Do you realize how much more work this would involve? You want us to wait for experimental evidence and actually

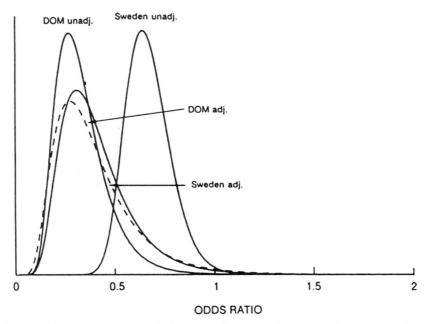

FIG. 7. Probability distributions for Swedish randomized controlled clinical trial taken at face value and adjusted for biases (see text) and for DOM case-control study taken at face value and adjusted for biases (see text). Face value represented by *dashed line,* value adjusted for biases (see text) by *solid line.*

describe and defend our beliefs? Don't you realize that medicine is an art, not a science?''

The facts are that even in the strictest forums, subjective judgments already are an integral part of the interpretation of evidence, that the results of experiments already are adjusted, and that the choice of ''accept at face value'' versus ''reject'' is the grossest form of adjustment. The current system is not rigorous and clean; it is inconsistent and arbitrary. Remember that under the current system, about three-fourths of technologies go unevaluated by *any* formal means. At the same time, evaluative problems are too complex to be left to judgment alone. Subjective judgments should be used only after all the evidence has been exhausted, they should be highly focused, and they should be integrated with empirical evidence by formal methods.

IMPLICATIONS FOR DECISION MAKERS

The flexible but firm approach will modify the amount of work needed to collect and interpret evidence. For the people who produce the evidence, adoption of a new approach could either decrease or increase the research burden, depending on the current standard that must be met. Compared with the rigorous approach, it should be faster and simpler to gather evidence, because a wider variety of designs can be chosen from, and most of the new options are logistically simpler than the randomized controlled trial. But compared with the loose approach, the proposed approach will require considerably more research, more work to esti-

mate the magnitudes of biases, and more work to perform the adjustments.

The flexible but firm approach will generally make life more difficult for the people who interpret the evidence to make decisions, regardless of whether the current approach is rigorous or subjective. The reason is that in both cases the proposed approach eliminates the ''take it or leave it'' heuristic that so simplifies the interpretation of biases. It also eliminates use of the *p*-value to determine when the evidence is sufficient and whether the technology is appropriate (Fig. 4). The proposed approach replaces these heuristics with a requirement for explicit identification, estimation, and incorporation of biases. This requires more work, more documentation, and more exposure to criticism.

CONCLUSIONS

There is no doubt that a change in the evaluative techniques currently used by groups such as the Food and Drug Administration or by clinicians would require major changes in the way we think about medical practices and in the types of evidence required to make decisions. There is also little doubt that we can extract more understanding from existing information, can gather sufficient evidence to make at least some decisions faster and less expensively, and can eliminate or at least narrow the glaring inconsistencies that now exist. The flexible but firm approach would allow us to cut back a bit on the strictness with which some technologies are evaluated, and put more energy into increasing the rigor with which other technologies are evaluated.

REFERENCES

1. Tabar L, Fagerberg CJG, Gad A, et al. Reduction in mortality from breast cancer after mass screening with mammography. *Lancet* 1985;1:829–832.
2. Collette HJA, Rombach JJ, Day NE, DeWaard F. Evaluation of screening for breast cancer in a non-randomised study (The DOM Project) by means of a case-control study. *Lancet* 1984;1:1224–1226.
3. Chu KC, Smart CR, Tarone RE. Analysis of breast cancer mortality and stage distribution by age for the health insurance plan clinical trial. *J Natl Cancer Inst* 1988;80:1125–1132.
4. Eddy DM. *Screening for cancer: theory, analysis and design.* Englewood Cliffs, NJ: Prentice-Hall, 1980.
5. Bailar JC III. Mammography: a contrary view. *Ann Intern Med* 1976;84:77–84.
6. Shapiro S. Evidence on screening for breast cancer from a randomized trial. *Cancer* 1977;39:2772–2782.
7. Shwartz M. An analysis of the benefits of serial screening for breast cancer based upon a mathematical model of the disease. *Cancer* 1978;51:1550–1564.
8. DeWaard F, Collette HJA, Rombach JJ, Collette C. Breast cancer screening, with particular reference to the concept of "high risk" groups. *Breast Cancer Res Treat* 1988;11:125–132.
9. Shapiro S, Venet W, Strax P, et al. Current results of the breast cancer screening randomized trial: The Health Insurance Plan (HIP) of Greater New York Study. In: *Screening for breast cancer.* Toronto: Sam Huber, 1988:chapter 6.
10. Verbeek ALM, Hendriks JHCL, Holland R, et al. Mammographic screening and breast cancer mortality: age-specific effects in Nijmegen Project, 1975–1982. *Lancet* 1985;1:865–866.
11. Palli D, DelTurco MR, Buiatti E, et al. A case-control study of the efficacy of a non-randomized breast cancer screening program in Florence (Italy). *Int J Cancer* 1986;38:501–504.
12. U.K. Trial of Early Detection of Breast Cancer Group. First results on mortality reduction in the U.K. trial of early detection of breast cancer. *Lancet* 1988;2:411–416.
13. Andersson I, Aspegren K, Janzon L, et al. Mammographic screening and mortality from breast cancer: The Malmo Mammographic Screening Trial. *Br Med J* 1988;297:943–948.

Quality of Life and Pharmacoeconomics in Clinical Trials, Second Edition, edited by B. Spilker.
Lippincott-Raven Publishers, Philadelphia © 1996.

CHAPTER 80

International Price Comparisons

Patricia M. Danzon

ISSUES AND OVERVIEW

International comparisons of pharmaceutical prices are increasingly being used by governments around the world as a criterion for setting reimbursement under social insurance programs. Comparisons with prices in other countries are routinely used in Canada, Italy, and France. In the United States, President Clinton's Health Security Act proposed to consider prices in over 20 other countries in determining the ''reasonableness'' of prices charged under the proposed new Medicare outpatient drug benefit. More generally, comparisons of pharmaceutical prices in Canada and the United Kingdom (1–3) have been used to support proposals for government regulation of pharmaceutical prices in the U.S.

Comparing drug prices internationally poses formidable measurement problems, because the range of medicines available differs across countries; each product may have many different dosage forms, strengths, and pack sizes, and the same compound may be used for different therapeutic purposes in different countries. Moreover, prices can be measured at the level of the manufacturer, the wholesaler, or the consumer, with quite different results and different implications. Resolving these issues requires judgment by the analyst as to the most appropriate methods for the particular context and question at issue. There is no single ''gold

P. M. Danzon: Department of Health Care Systems and Insurance and Risk Management, The Wharton School, University of Pennsylvania, Philadelphia, Pennsylvania 19104.

standard'' methodology for international price comparisons that is best for all purposes, and none is perfect.

The use of international price comparisons as a criterion in regulating domestic price levels rests on two hidden assumptions—that prices would be too high in the absence of regulation and that prices should be the same across countries. Yet there are many reasons why prices differ in practice and, from a policy perspective, there is no compelling reason for requiring uniform prices across countries.

This chapter discusses some of these methodological issues in making international price comparisons for pharmaceuticals, and illustrates the results of alternative choices. Reasons for price differences are discussed.

PURPOSES OF INTERNATIONAL PRICE COMPARISONS

International price comparisons are used for two primary purposes: (a) Prices of individual medicines in different countries are used as a benchmark for regulating prices for new products under public insurance programs, and (b) The cost of a broader market basket of medicines is used as a measure of the effect of alternative regulatory regimes on the cost of pharmaceuticals. The rate of inflation of pharmaceutical prices has also been used (4). The focus is usually on prices at the manufacturer level. Prices at the consumer level reflect, in addition to manufacturer prices, the wholesale and distribution margins. In countries where these margins are also regulated, regulation of manufacturer prices implies regulation of final prices to consumers.

MEASUREMENT ISSUES

Ideally, the comparison should be made for identical products or baskets of products. In practice, this is often not feasible because the products available in one country may not be available in the other country or may only be available in different forms and strengths, possibly with different therapeutic indications, reflecting differences in medical norms, consumer preferences, and regulatory systems. The analyst must make judgments about how best to adjust for these noncomparabilities. There is a fundamental trade-off: if strict comparability is required along all possible dimensions (chemical composition, manufacturer, dosage form, strength, pack size) the sample of drugs that can be included in the comparison will be a very small and nonrepresentative subset of the range of medicines that is available to consumers in each country. In general, a rough measure of the right construct for a representative sample is likely to be preferable to an accurate measure of the wrong construct for an unrepresentative sample. Note, however, that even with information on all medicines used in each country, it is not possible to construct a price index that is fully representative for either country, because medicines that are available in only one country cannot be included in the index.

Sample

The issue of sample selection arises when the objective of the analysis is to compare the cost of a broad-based basket of drugs as a proxy for the cost of medicines to consumers (as affected by ex-manufacturer prices). Ideally, the sample should be selected randomly, or with probability weighting, where the weights reflect frequency of use. In practice, the information necessary for random or stratified sampling is often not available. Prior studies have typically selected a subset of the leading products in one or more countries, as measured by number of scripts. The potential for bias that results from focusing on leading products is more severe the narrower is the definition of a "product." A narrow definition would be a specific dosage form of a specific manufacturer's product, for example, Pfizer's Procardia XL in tablet form at a particular strength. A broad definition would be the molecule nifedipine. Sample selection based on leading products should, at a minimum, sample from leading products in both countries under comparison.

Generics

A major issue in sample selection is whether and how to include generic versions of originator compounds. The extent of generic penetration differs across countries. There is very little use of generics in the price-regulated countries such as France and Italy. However, generics account for over one-third of the market in the U.S. and this is expected to grow as a large number of leading compounds go off-patent in the next 5 years and pharmacy benefit managers increasingly adopt generic substitution programs. Germany, the U.K., and Canada also aggressively encourage generic substitution through their reimbursement systems. Since generics often offer consumers a lower cost alternative to the branded product, the exclusion of generics can lead to serious bias. Since generics are usually manufactured by different local companies in each country, prices of generics must be compared without regard to manufacturer.

Over-the-Counter Medicines

A second form of inexpensive alternative for off-patent compounds is the over-the-counter (OTC) form, which does not require a doctor's prescription. OTC forms may be imperfect substitutes for the Rx form, because OTCs are often weaker strengths in order to be safe under self-medication. Nevertheless, for many common conditions OTCs offer an inexpensive form of drug therapy that should be reflected in a representative measure of the overall cost of pharmaceuticals from the consumer's perspective.

Matching Criteria

Ideally, prices should be compared for products that are identical in all relevant respects in the different countries—same active ingredient, same manufacturer, same brand name, same dosage form, strength, and pack size. However if such strict comparability is required, the sample is necessarily confined to a very small and nonrepresentative subset of the medicines available in each country.

The requirement of same manufacturer and brand name may be appropriate in a comparison of launch prices for a specific new compound, although from an economic or policy perspective there is no presumption that launch prices should necessarily be the same in different countries.

However, when the purpose of the study is to compare the cost of medicines to consumers in different countries, the requirement of matching manufacturer or brand is counterproductive. This requirement has the effect of limiting the comparison to compounds sold internationally by subsidiaries of multinational companies. It automatically excludes originator products that are globalized by out-licensing to one or more local manufacturers in each country. It also excludes generics, which are typically manufactured by local companies rather than multinational companies. Such exclusions are inappropriate. In particular, the exclusion of generics tends to bias upward the estimate of prices in countries where generics have a large market share as a low-cost substitute for branded products.

For consumer-focused comparisons, a simple alternative strategy to comparing prices for products matched on molecule, manufacturer, and strength is to compare the price of the molecule, computed as the volume-weighted average of prices charged by all manufacturers of the compound, including originator, licensees, and generic manufacturers. Implicitly, this assumes that generics are perfect substitutes for the originator brand. If generics are not viewed as perfect substitutes, then more subtle weighting schemes can be used (5).

Price and Volume Measures

There are several possible units of quantity, each with a corresponding measures of price—the pack, the pill or capsule, dose, daily dose, course of therapy, or gram of active ingredient. None of these provides a uniform unit of measurement in all countries, since even the definition of a normal course of therapy can differ cross-nationally, reflecting local medical norms.

The practical choices are often between price per pack, price per standard unit, or price per gram of active ingredient. A standard unit is defined as one tablet, one capsule, 5 ml of a liquid, and so on, and is a rough proxy for a dose. Using price per standard unit or per gram permits aggregation over all dosage forms, strengths, and packsizes. Price per pack, averaged over pack sizes, leads to systematic biases because the size mix of packs differs systematically across countries. In particular, some countries permit distribution in very large packs to pharmacists who then split the packs for retail distribution. Other countries that do not permit pharmacists to split packs have much smaller average pack size, which tends to mean higher price per pill, since price per pill is typically lower in larger packs. Confining the comparison to packs that are available in both countries restricts the sample to pack sizes that may not be typical in either country under comparison.

Since a standard unit is a rough measure of a dose, it is preferred for comparisons that include a number of different compounds. Price per gram of active ingredient may be useful for comparing prices for a single compound. However, for comparisons of market baskets of compounds, measures based on price per gram are very sensitive to the sample, because of great differences across compounds in the grams of active ingredient required for a standard dose.

Weighting of Market Baskets

An accurate cross-national comparison of the cost of medicines to consumers requires weighting the prices of different products to reflect their relative importance in overall expenditures. However, when the relative importance of different medicines differs considerably across countries, there is no unique optimal weighting scheme. The analyst should choose the weights most appropriate to the context and question at issue.

For example, if the question is, What would be the cost of medicines to U.S. consumers if they faced U.K. prices? then current U.S. consumption patterns should be used as weights, assuming that U.S. doctors and consumers would be unlikely to switch to U.K. consumption patterns, even if faced with U.K. prices, at least in the short run.

However, the evidence suggests that consumption in each country does tend to move toward products that are relatively inexpensive in that country. This negative association between price and volume is reinforced in countries such as France, where regulators tend to impose larger price cuts on high-volume products. Thus to the extent that volume does adjust toward lower-priced products over time, comparisons of prices in the U.K. relative to the U.S. that use U.S. weights may overstate the long run cost of medicines to U.S. consumers if they faced U.K. prices.

The literature on price measurement has developed several standard price indexes, each of which reflects different assumptions and results in a different measures of cross-country price differences (6). In the context of a bilateral international price comparison, we can define a Laspeyres index as an index that weights each price by the volume of the home or base country. The Paasche index uses the foreign-country weights. The Fisher index is the geometric mean of the Laspeyres and Paasche indexes.

If there are strong country-specific preferences and medical norms for pharmaceuticals, such that demand is relatively unresponsive to price, then the Laspeyres index that uses domestic consumption patterns may be the most appropriate. A desirable property of the Fisher index is transitivity, that is, the measure of price difference is independent of the country used as base, after inversion. This is not true of the more common Laspeyres and Paasche indexes, which yield very different measures of price difference, depending on which country is treated as the base. A disadvantage of the Fisher index is that it implies that consumption patterns would be identical if both countries faced the same prices.

EXAMPLES OF DIFFERENT PRICE INDEXES

To illustrate the effects of some of these factors on international price comparisons, Table 1 reports price indexes for Canada and Japan relative to the U.S. for single-molecule cardiovascular products, using alternative sample and matching criteria, pricing units, and weights. The indexes are based on IMS data for all cardiovascular medicines sold through outpatient pharmacies, for the year ending September 1992. IMS America is a market research company, based in Plymouth Meeting, Pennsylvania, that collects data on many aspects of pharmaceutical marketing.

On the left half of Table 1, products are matched if they have the same active ingredient and either the same manufac-

TABLE 1. *Price indexes for single molecule cardiovasculars, 1992*

Index	Matched by IPN		Matched by Mol/ATC	
	Canada	Japan	Canada	Japan
Laspeyres (kg)	1.062	2.789	1.166	1.191
Laspeyres (SU)	0.969	0.713	0.954	0.740
Paasche (kg)	1.046	0.987	1.016	0.868
Paasche (SU)	0.973	0.555	0.908	0.620
Fisher (kg)	1.054	1.659	1.088	1.017
Fisher (SU)	0.971	0.629	0.931	0.677
Unweighted (kg)	1.009	1.157	2.166	3.728
Unweighted (SU)	0.948	0.498	1.627	0.877
N	68.000	33.000	52.000	59.000

From ref. 7.
IPN, international product name; kg, kilogram; Mol/ATC, molecule/anatomical therapeutic category; SU, standard unit.

turer or same brand name, as designated by the IMS international product name (IPN). Imposing these conditions for matching drugs eliminates from the sample originator products that are sold under license, hence by different manufacturers in different countries, and most generics. The exception is that some unbranded generics are included, because IMS assigns the molecule name as the IPN for generics that are unbranded or with unknown manufacturer.

On the right half of Table 1, the product is defined by molecule and 4-digit anatomical therapeutic category (Mol/ATC), regardless of manufacturer or brand name. The price for a multisource molecule is the weighted average price over all manufacturers of that compound for a particular 4-digit therapeutic category. If different packs of a molecule are designated for different therapeutic categories, they are treated as distinct products, since different therapeutic objectives may require specific dosage forms or strengths and market conditions may differ.

Price indexes are reported using both price per standard unit (SU) and price per kilogram of active ingredient (kg). In each case, the Laspeyres indexes use U.S. volumes as weights and the Paasche indexes use foreign weights. The Fisher indexes are the geometric mean of the Laspeyres and Paasche indexes. The mean of the unweighted price relatives (ratios) are also reported, to illustrate the effects of omitting weighting. This is not a recommended form of price comparison, since the results can differ in sign as well as magnitude, depending on which country's price is in the denominator of the ratios. N is the number of observations—IPNs or Mol/ATCs in the index. All indexes measure the foreign price relative to the U.S. price. Values less than 1 imply lower prices abroad than in the U.S. and values greater than 1 imply lower prices in the U.S.

Several conclusions emerge from these comparisons. First, of the 354 IPNs in the cardiovascular category in the U.S., only 68 (19%) are available in Canada and 33 (9%) in Japan. The number of matching products would be smaller if we required the same molecule and same manufacturer, since the IPN match includes some unbranded generics. Requiring that the products also match on dosage form and

strength would further reduce the number of matching products that can be included in the indexes.

When products with the same molecule and therapeutic category (Mol/ATC) are treated as equivalent, regardless of manufacturer or brand, over half of the sample can be matched; of the 105 molecules available in the U.S., 52 are also available in Canada and 59 in Japan. Nevertheless, almost half of the molecules remain excluded from the indexes, even with this less restrictive definition of comparable products. This comparison between indexes based on IPN match and Mol/ATC match illustrates the trade-off between strict comparability of products compared and the size and market share of the sample that can be included in the comparison. It also illustrates the limited coverage of any index, even using a broad definition of product. Because the Mol/ATC indexes are more representative, remaining comments are based on these indexes.

These indexes illustrate the sensitivity of conclusions to the measure of price and to the weights used. Comparing Canada with the U.S., and using U.S. weights, Canada is 16.6% more expensive based on price per kilogram but 4.6% less expensive based on price per standard unit. Using Canadian weights, Canada appears only 1.6% more expensive than the U.S. based on price per kilogram and 9.2% cheaper based on price per standard unit.

Comparing Japan to the U.S. and using U.S. weights, Japan is 19.1% more expensive based on price per kilo, and 26% cheaper based on price per standard unit. However, using Japanese weights, Japan is 23.2% cheaper based on price per kilo, and 38% cheaper based on price per standard unit.

A persistent feature of international price comparisons is that each country appears relatively less expensive in an index based on its own consumption patterns (Laspeyres indexes) than with foreign weights (Paasche indexes). This reflects the tendency noted earlier, for each country to consume relatively more of the medicines that are relatively inexpensive in that country.

For these cardiovascular products, both Japan and, to a lesser extent, Canada appear more costly relative to the U.S.

when prices are compared per kilogram of active ingredient than per standard unit. This implies that in both countries strength per dose is on average lower than in the U.S. Note that this statement applies on average over all cardiovascular medicines, but not necessarily for any particular medicine.

REASONS FOR PRICE DIFFERENCES

These indexes have illustrated that measures of international price differences are very sensitive to several methodological choices that the analyst must make: the definition of a product, sample selection, matching criteria, weighting procedure, and unit of measure for price and volume.

However, even if we could identify a large, random sample of completely standardized, matching products—each an identical pack size, form, and strength of a specific compound of a particular manufacturer—prices could differ cross-nationally for other reasons related to currency conversion, economic factors, and regulation.

Currency Conversion

To illustrate the effect of currency fluctuations, consider a product that was launched at the same price in Germany and the U.S. in 1982. Assume that over the decade 1982 to 1992 prices remained unchanged in each country's own currency. Nevertheless, because the dollar declined against the German mark over this period, the German product would appear more expensive in 1992 if converted at 1992 exchange rates. To measure the true change in relative price to consumers, we must convert the 1992 price in marks to dollars at 1982 exchange rates. However, if we are interested in revenues from the perspective of a U.S. manufacturer, then the current exchange rate is the relevant measure, even if it provides an inaccurate measure of the change over time in the local currency price within the foreign country.

Costs and Demand

Economic factors that affect costs and market conditions may differ across countries and hence contribute to international price differences. These factors include costs and delays in obtaining regulatory approval; costs of manufacturing, promotion, distribution, and taxes; effective economic life, including volumes and post-patent generic penetration; availability of complements and substitutes; and other determinants of demand. Although some of these costs are fixed costs rather than per unit variable costs, on average a company must cover these fixed costs in order to stay in business. Thus on average prices must be higher in countries with higher fixed costs, other things being equal.

Moreover, several of these factors undergo change over time, and this can dramatically affect international price comparisons at different points in time. For example, the recent growth of managed pharmacy benefit programs in the U.S. has made the market more price competitive. Thus international price comparisons based on data several years old may misrepresent the current situation. A further implication of the growth of managed care is the growth of discounting. This has been extended through regulation to Medicaid and other government programs. Consequently for the U.S. (and for any other country where discounting is common), list prices are an increasingly inaccurate measure of transactions prices, and indexes based on list prices misrepresent the true situation.

Regulation

In most countries other than the U.S., prices for pharmaceuticals are regulated either directly or indirectly. France and Italy regulate prices directly, based on such factors as costs, therapeutic merit, international comparisons, and internal comparisons with existing products. Germany, the Netherlands, Denmark, and New Zealand operate reference price systems of reimbursement. Products are grouped based on generic or therapeutic substitutability. Reimbursement for all products in the group is limited to the median or minimum price of products in the group. If a manufacturer's price, after adding wholesale and retail margins, exceeds the reference price, the excess is charged to the patient. This creates strong incentives for manufacturers to price at the reference price. In the U.S., Medicaid programs in several states have operated a similar system of "maximum allowable charge" for generic substitutes, and a similar system has been proposed for a new Medicare outpatient drug benefit, if enacted.

As of 1993, roughly half of the market in Germany was covered by reference pricing and extensions are planned to over 70%. Extending reference pricing system beyond generic substitutes entails judgment as to what products should be considered therapeutically equivalent, although chemically different. Controversy over this issue has slowed the implementation of phase II and phase III of the German system. These decisions require trade-offs between cost control for social insurance programs, access for patients, and incentives for innovation.

In Japan, medicines are dispensed by doctors and hospitals. The government regulates reimbursement prices. Manufacturers compete by offering discounts to physicians and hospitals, who profit from the margin between the ex-wholesaler price and the reimbursement price. Every 2 years the government surveys the wholesaler prices and revises the reimbursement price downward if the margin between reimbursement and weighted average wholesaler price exceeds some margin (currently 13%). Thus in Japan prices decline over the life of a product. This creates strong incentives to introduce new products, since even marginal extensions of existing products may command a higher price. International price comparisons involving Japan can consequently be very sensitive to the average age of the products included.

POLICY CONSIDERATIONS

The use of international price comparisons for regulatory benchmarking implicitly assumes that prices should be the same in different countries. However, this presumption has no basis in economics. On the contrary, economic theory concludes that uniform pricing is often undesirable in situations where several consumer groups benefit from a common resource, but different consumers differ in their true valuations of this resource.

This theory of pricing in the presence of joint costs is highly relevant to the pharmaceutical industry. The cost structure of new pharmaceuticals is characterized by an unusually large proportion of joint costs, that is, costs that cannot rationally be allocated to specific consumers or particular dosage forms and strengths. The major component of joint costs is research and development (R&D); in addition, some costs of manufacturing, promotion, and other overhead are common to different products or different countries served by the same product.

The pitfall of joint costs is that every purchaser has an incentive to attempt to pay only their marginal costs, leaving others to pay the joint costs. Moreover, manufacturers would rationally be willing to sell as long as price covers marginal cost, even if that is only a fraction of fully allocated average cost. Yet if everyone free-rides and pays only their marginal costs, revenues overall will be insufficient to cover the common costs. In the long run, the supply of new medicines that require costly R&D will dry up.

One approach to recouping the joint costs would be to require all users to pay a pro rata share, which would imply paying the same price if variable costs were uniform. However, economic theory indicates that this solution leads to a suboptimal investment in products with common costs and suboptimal consumption of these products, once developed.

A preferable approach, if it were practical, would be to charge all users their true ''willingness to pay'' for new therapies. Unfortunately, true willingness to pay is very hard to measure. Actual demand for medicines is distorted by insurance and by government controls in countries with social insurance systems. Nevertheless, casual evidence suggests that willingness to pay for new medical therapies, either medicines or other devices and procedures, varies greatly across countries. To the extent that this is true, those who place a higher value on the added safety, convenience or chance of cure that comes with newer therapies will be the greatest losers if they refuse to pay more than a pro rata share of joint costs.

The use of international price comparisons for setting prices for pharmaceuticals tends to force a convergence of prices across all markets included in the comparison. If prices rise in previously low-priced markets, some consumers in these markets will forgo more costly medicines, although they would have been willing to cover their marginal costs and possibly contribute some amount to the common costs. If prices fall in previously high-priced markets, these consumers gain in the short run. But in the long run they will also be worse off, as the decline in global revenues adversely affects the incentive and ability of companies to invest in innovative R&D. If the pace of innovation declines, those consumers who in fact place the highest value on new technologies will suffer the greatest loss.

CONCLUSIONS

Despite the fact that international price comparisons for pharmaceuticals often involve faulty methodology, are based on inappropriate assumptions, and tend to support mistaken policy conclusions, the demand for such comparisons is increasing. The analyst undertaking such studies should, at minimum, take care to point out the potential biases that may result from his or her sample selection and other methodological choices. Sensitivity analysis can be used to illustrate effects of particular choices. Finally, warnings about the limited usefulness of such studies for policy purposes are essential.

REFERENCES

1. U.S. General Accounting Office. *Prescription drugs: companies typically charge more in the United States than in Canada.* Washington, DC: GAO/HRD-92-110, Sept. 20, 1992.
2. U.S. General Accounting Office. *Prescription drugs: companies typically charge more in the United States than in the United Kingdom.* Washington, DC: GAO/HEHS-94-29, Jan. 12, 1994.
3. Association Belge des Consommateurs. Statement for the United States Senate Special Committee on Aging, Nov. 16, 1989.
4. U.S. General Accounting Office. *Prescription drugs: spending controls in four European countries.* Washington, DC: GAO/HEHS-94-30, May 17, 1994.
5. Griliches Z, Cockburn I. Generics and new goods in pharmaceutical price indexes. Paper presented at the American Enterprise Institute Conference on Competitive Strategies in the Pharmaceutical Industry, Washington, D.C. October 27, 1993.
6. Diewert WE. The economic theory of index numbers: a survey. In: Deaton A, ed. *Essays in the theory and measurement of consumer behavior in honor of Sir Richard Stone.* London: Cambridge University Press; 1981:163–233.
7. Danzon PM, Kim J. 1995 International Price Comparisons for Pharmaceuticals. Philadelphia: University of Pennsylvania, The Wharton School, Working Paper.

Quality of Life and Pharmacoeconomics in Clinical
Trials, Second Edition, edited by B. Spilker.
Lippincott-Raven Publishers, Philadelphia © 1996.

CHAPTER 81

Roles of Government Agencies in Support and Application of Quality of Life Research

Susan G. Nayfield

INTRODUCTION

Over the past decade, as the public has become more involved in making decisions about health care, a new focus has developed on the impact of preventive and therapeutic interventions on the quality of daily life. This is in addition to the more traditional focus on the ability of therapeutic interventions to change biological end points and to prolong life.

In response, clinicians, health service managers, and policy makers increasingly look beyond physiologic outcomes to consider the effect of the health care process on the general health and well-being of patients and populations. The concept of quality of life (QOL) as the functional effect of an illness and its consequent therapy on a patient, as perceived by the patient, has become a major consideration at levels of health care ranging from individual instances of patient–physician decision making, through studies of efficacy and effectiveness of interventions, to policy decisions regarding health resources.

As the goal of medical care expands to include maximizing quality of life, it becomes obvious that decisions must be based on accurate and reliable information about this health care outcome. The potential for federal agencies, particularly of the National Institutes of Health (NIH), to foster

research in quality of life and other health care outcomes is presented in this chapter. Examples of clinical issues in breast cancer risk, diagnosis, and treatment are used to highlight areas in which QOL research has made major contributions to current practices, as well as areas of current and future research for which QOL questions are integral components of study objectives.

GOVERNMENT SUPPORT FOR QOL RESEARCH

Research can be defined as the "systematic search or intensive study directed towards fuller scientific knowledge or understanding" (1). In "basic research," the primary motivation is the pursuit of knowledge for its own sake, with no specific application necessarily foreseen other than long-term potential for fundamental results. "Applied research," directed toward the practical application of knowledge or understanding, includes clinical trials designed to evaluate the efficacy of new therapeutic and prevention interventions. The paradigm of translating basic research findings into clinical applications is particularly relevant to the developing field of QOL research.

Developmental and Methodologic Research

The need for basic research to explore and understand constructs contributing to quality of life, and thus to enhance the development of valid and reliable assessment methods,

S. G. Nayfield: Division of Cancer Prevention and Control, National Cancer Institute, National Institutes of Health, Bethesda, Maryland 20892.

has been emphasized in earlier chapters. For cancer, with the psychosocial and survival implications of its diagnosis, understanding how the disease and its diagnosis interact with individual attitudes toward illness, sense of independence, and life expectations is of major importance. Basic research in these areas of QOL is particularly relevant because it provides the scientific and methodologic foundations for subsequent clinical applications. These applications pervade the natural history of a disease process, extending from the period before development of disease, through risk assessment and notification, prevention, early detection, and treatment.

The NIH Revitalization Act of 1993 establishes that women and members of minority groups and their subpopulations must be included in all NIH-supported biomedical and behavioral research projects involving human subjects, unless inclusion is inappropriate to the health of the subjects or the purpose of the research (2). For clinical studies that include quality of life end points, this requirement for cultural sensitivity raises specific methodologic issues. To measure QOL outcomes across a culturally diverse study population, an investigator must use an assessment method that is culturally "transparent," i.e., one based only on constructs shared by participants from different backgrounds or, alternatively, an instrument that has been translated, adapted, and validated for each subgroup to incorporate language and concepts unique to its cultural identity.

Implementation of the NIH Revitalization Act stresses the need not only for culturally sensitive methods to assess quality of life, but also for an understanding of how measures taken in one cultural background relate or compare to those made in another. Basic research exploring the relationship between quality of life and culture and developing culturally sensitive assessment tools is critical to support minority participation in medical research.

QOL Considerations in Health Promotion and Disease Prevention

The subtle but important role of QOL in health promotion and disease prevention is gaining recognition as health care emphasis shifts further toward these areas. In the prevention setting, as in the context of treatment, clinically beneficial effects, adverse reactions, and other factors (e.g., convenience and costs) filter through personal values and beliefs to influence quality of life (3). For individuals without disease, the expected impact of a prevention regimen on QOL will contribute to the decision to begin the intervention and the actual impact on QOL will be a major determinant of long-term adherence/compliance. Thus QOL end points should be carefully considered in the design and planning phases of studies in all phases of health promotion and disease prevention.

Knowledge of personal risk of a disease such as breast cancer may motivate women toward appropriate screening behaviors. However, the heightened awareness associated with risk notification can have potentially untoward consequences on quality of life, particularly in the domains of psychological well-being and social interactions (4). Among some women at "high risk" of breast cancer, the anxiety related to perceived susceptibility has been shown to interfere with adherence to mammography guidelines (5) and to lead to avoidance of clinical breast examination and breast self-examination (6). The inclusion of outcome variables within specific QOL domains in these studies has enhanced our understanding of how risk assessment and notification influence quality of life and subsequent screening behaviors. As genetic technology advances to allow DNA-based testing for breast cancer susceptibility, QOL considerations will play an increasing role in decisions about prevention, including the decision to undergo genetic risk assessment (7).

The ongoing Breast Cancer Prevention Trial (BCPT), sponsored by the National Cancer Institute, is a randomized, placebo-controlled clinical trial testing the efficacy of the drug tamoxifen in preventing breast cancer among women at increased risk of the disease. Additional health benefits from tamoxifen include lowering of blood lipids and stabilizing postmenopausal bone loss. Potential side effects include vasomotor and gynecologic symptoms attributable to the drug in 10% to 20% of women receiving it (8). Assessment of quality of life among women participating in a large clinical trial of adjuvant tamoxifen following surgery for early stage breast cancer revealed that patients receiving tamoxifen reported feeling less feminine and having less sexual desire significantly less often than did patients randomized to placebo, despite a significantly increased frequency of hot flashes (9). QOL assessment has been included in the routine follow-up evaluation of all participants in the BCPT to monitor participants for subtle side effects and to enhance the investigators' understanding of how they influence compliance. The selection of QOL instruments used in the Postmenopausal Estrogen/Progestin Interventions (PEPI) Trial evaluating the effects of various hormone replacement therapies (HRTs) on cardiovascular disease risk factors (10) will permit comparison of QOL effects of tamoxifen to those of common HRT regimen and thus broaden perspectives on QOL aspects of women's health issues.

QOL Assessment in Treatment Clinical Trials

The concept of quality of life as an important part of medical decision making has been most readily adopted in the treatment setting. In 1985, the United States Food and Drug Administration recognized benefit to quality of life, as well as improved survival, as a basis for approval of new anticancer drugs (11). QOL considerations have been accepted as especially important in cancer treatment decision making when different treatments give similar medical outcomes but have different toxicities, or when one treatment yields a better outcome but has more severe toxicities (12).

Increasingly, quality of life end points are included as outcome measures in clinical research evaluating new medications or technologies, in addition to the traditional end points of disease response, survival, and toxicities.

A major advance in the management of primary operable breast cancer has been the demonstration in randomized clinical trials that disease-free survival and overall survival for patients treated with lumpectomy followed by radiation therapy are no different from those for patients treated with mastectomy (13,14). Because of psychiatric morbidity associated with mastectomy for many women, lumpectomy with radiation therapy has been viewed as preferable because it preserves the breast (15). Indeed, a prospective study of participants in a randomized clinical trial documented greater anxiety, more sexual problems, and greater dissatisfaction with body image among patients randomized to have mastectomy compared to those assigned to breast-conserving therapy (16). For situations in which women are given a choice of surgical treatment, few differences in QOL, performance status, or adaptation have been identified between women who elect breast-conserving therapy and those who choose mastectomy, although the former may require more psychosocial support because of the added burden of radiation therapy (17). Thus, for many women with early stage breast cancer, the choice of initial treatment is based on considerations of factors relevant to QOL domains, and their decisions have been enhanced by information from carefully conducted QOL research.

The role of high-dose chemotherapy with autologous bone marrow transplantation (HDC/ABMT) as therapy for patients with metastatic breast cancer is currently one of the most controversial issues in cancer medicine. While Phase I and II clinical trials have, in general, shown higher response rates for these regimen compared to conventional chemotherapy, whether these findings translate into meaningful health benefits is unknown (18,19). For example, statistical modeling based on data from Phase I/II studies predicts an improvement in 5-year survival from 4.3% for conventional chemotherapy to 15.8% for HDC/ABMT (20). However, the mortality from HDC/ABMT may be as high as 12% compared to 1% for conventional chemotherapy, and morbidity is similarly increased for the more intensive treatment.

Phase III clinical trials are currently under way to compare the use of HDC/ABMT in patients with metastatic breast cancer responding to conventional-dose chemotherapy to conventional-dose therapy alone, and similar studies are evaluating the efficacy of these regimen for patients with early stage breast cancer who are at high risk of the development of metastatic disease. It is crucial that outcome variables for these studies include measures of quality of life and subtle treatment-related morbidity as well as the usual end points of toxicity and survival, so that reliable information on costs and benefits can guide patients, physicians, and policy makers in decisions regarding this new technology.

Technology Transfer from Research Setting to Community Practice

The transfer of efficacious medical interventions from the research setting into clinical practice, resulting in improved health outcomes in community practice, is the ultimate goal of most clinical research. The advances in the management of breast cancer through this process of technology transfer are reflected in both improved survival and decreased morbidity (21) with associated improvement in quality of life.

In 1983, the National Cancer Institute (NCI) implemented the Community Clinical Oncology Program (CCOP) to enhance the adoption of state-of-the-art oncology practice by community physicians (22). In this program, community oncologists are linked to large cooperative clinical trials groups and actively participate in their clinical research protocols for cancer treatment and prevention. Currently, CCOP oncology practices contribute about one-third of all patients entered into NCI-sponsored clinical trials. The QOL research in cancer prevention and treatment supported through the CCOP adds a special dimension to the results of clinical trials because it reflects the impact on quality of life on interventions delivered in the community setting.

Differences between the medical efficacy of an intervention in expert hands and its effectiveness in customary community practice are relevant to its impact on broader measures of health, including quality of life, as well as to variations in technology transfer to community practice. The Agency for Health Care Policy and Research's Medical Treatment Effectiveness Program supports research to evaluate the effectiveness and cost-effectiveness of alternative clinical interventions in the community setting (23). The program's goal of improving health outcomes is based on measuring outcomes directly in terms of death, disability, and quality of life, rather than measuring the structure or process of health care. Research funded under this initiative includes prospective collection of primary outcome data by Patient Outcome Research Teams (PORTs), with emphasis on not only the outcome variables but also on the social and cultural context of illness and health care (24). Current PORT projects evaluate interventions for the prevention, diagnosis, treatment, and long-term management of common clinical conditions, including breast cancer.

One aspect of technology transfer relevant to current medical care is the level of intervention required to produce desired medical and QOL outcomes. For breast cancer care in the research setting, patients with early stage disease undergo regular surveillance after initial treatment to detect recurrent disease at its earliest appearance and thus to establish the clinical end point of disease-free survival. This follow-up approach has frequently been adopted in community practice, based on the assumption that further therapy at earliest recurrence may confer an overall survival advantage. Despite wide variations in the complexity and costs of routine follow-up programs, only recently has the effectiveness of intensive follow-up been challenged (25). Randomized controlled clinical trials of intensive follow-up management with regularly scheduled laboratory tests and imaging studies compared to routine follow-up with only clinically indicated studies have confirmed no benefit to overall survival associated with the intensive regimen (26,27). Quality of life end points of emotional well-being, body image, social functioning, symptoms, and satisfaction did not differ significantly between intensive and routine follow-up groups in the second study, supporting conservative follow-up without compromise to survival or quality of life.

Policy Development and Evaluation

The Consensus Development Program of the NIH was launched in 1977 to promote communication from the research community to practicing physicians and the public. Consensus development panels, including research scientists, physicians, consumers, and others, review current scientific knowledge and research results in an effort to reach general agreement on whether a given medical technology—a device, drug, or medical or surgical procedure—is safe and effective. The conclusions and recommendations of the consensus panel are widely publicized and are often regarded as practice guidelines or standards of care.

The Consensus Development Program has emphasized QOL considerations in conference planning and consensus statement development, particularly those addressing issues in breast cancer treatment. The 1985 Consensus Development Conference on Adjuvant Chemotherapy for Breast Cancer acknowledged the goal of adjuvant therapy to improve survival significantly while maintaining quality of life, acknowledging that potential benefits should be balanced against side effects, including psychological, social, and economic costs (28). The Conference's treatment recommendations for subgroups of breast cancer patients in whom survival advantages were small or uncertain emphasized the importance of QOL factors in therapy decisions. The 1990 Consensus Development Conference on Early Stage Breast Cancer recognized breast conservation treatment as appropriate therapy and urged consideration of psychosocial factors in decisions regarding primary surgery (15); for patients with node-negative disease, the Conference urged that decisions concerning adjuvant therapy include considerations of its impact on quality of life. Ongoing research is evaluating the effect of these guidelines on physicians' practice patterns and subsequent patient outcomes of quality of life and health status.

Quality of life research also plays an important role in developing public policy regarding health care and in evaluating policy implementation as a public health intervention. For example, the importance of choice in breast cancer treatment to a patient's subsequent quality of life (15) has oriented state legislatures toward ensuring that patients receive complete information about treatment options. To date, 18 states have enacted legislation addressing physician disclo-

sure of treatment alternatives to breast cancer patients (29). Although individual state statutes vary in scope and responsibility placed on the physician, many mandate the development or distribution, or both, of printed summaries describing alternatives in surgical and adjuvant therapy.

The consequences of this legislation on physician practice and patient outcome have not yet been systematically evaluated. Research on decision-making styles among breast cancer patients suggests that, for many women, information about technical aspects or risks of therapy may disrupt, rather than enhance, the decision-making process (30). Thus quality of life and health status outcomes are of primary concern in assessing the public health impact of this legislation.

CONCLUSIONS

Accurate and reliable information about the impact of a medical intervention on quality of life is an important factor in health care decision making. Federal agencies such as the NIH are in a unique position to foster basic QOL research, to promote incorporation of quality of life and other nontraditional health care outcomes into federally funded applied research programs, and to include QOL considerations in policy development and evaluation.

This opportunity extends beyond the specific examples included in this chapter. While QOL issues arise frequently (and, often, publicly) in decisions regarding cancer treatment options, these considerations are equally applicable to basic and clinical research in many other diseases and chronic conditions. They are also relevant throughout the natural history of a disease process, in preventive interventions as well as in diagnostic and treatment issues, and in technology transfer of research findings into community-based clinical practice.

As medical technology becomes even more sophisticated (e.g., gene therapy) and medical issues more complex (e.g., testing for genetic risk factors), the opportunity—and necessity—for including QOL end points to complement traditional clinical outcomes become more relevant to the goals of federally sponsored programs.

ACKNOWLEDGMENTS

The author acknowledges the assistance of Katy L. Benjamin and Dr. Susan Czajkowski, whose perspectives have been important in the development of this topic.

REFERENCES

1. NIH Manual. Section 1820, p 2; release 2/22/85.
2. Section 492B, Public Law 103-43.
3. Spilker B. Introduction. In: Spilker B, ed. *Quality of life assessment in clinical trials.* New York: Raven Press, 1990:7.

4. Lerman C, Rimer BK, Engstrom P. Cancer risk notification: psychosocial and ethical implications. *J Clin Oncol* 1991;9:1275–1282.
5. Lerman C, Daly M, Sands C, et al. Mammography adherence and psychological distress among women at risk for breast cancer. *J Natl Cancer Inst* 1993;85:1074–1080.
6. Kash KM, Holland JC, Halper MS, et al. Psychological distress and surveillance behaviors of women with a family history of breast cancer. *J Natl Cancer Inst* 1992;84:24–30.
7. Lerman C, Daly M, Masny A, et al. Attitudes about genetic testing for breast–ovarian cancer susceptibility. *J Clin Oncol* 1994;12:843–850.
8. Nayfield SG, Karp JE, Ford LG, et al. Potential role of tamoxifen in prevention of breast cancer. *J Natl Cancer Inst* 1991;83:1450–1459.
9. Breast Cancer Prevention Trial Protocol P-1: A Clinical Trial to Determine the Worth of Tamoxifen for Preventing Breast Cancer. National Surgical Adjuvant Breast and Bowel Project, 1992:2.6.
10. PEPI Investigators. The Postmenopausal Estrogen/Progestins Intervention Trial: rationale, design, and conduct. *Control Clin Trials,* in press.
11. Johnson JR, Temple R. Food and Drug Administration requirements for approval of new anticancer drugs. *Cancer Treat Rep* 1985;69:1155–1157.
12. Selby P, Robertson B. Measurement of quality of life in patients with cancer. *Cancer Surv* 1987;6:521–543.
13. Veronesi U, Saccozzi R, Del Vecchio M, et al. Comparing radical mastectomy with quadrantectomy, axillary dissection, and radiotherapy in patients with small cancers of the breast. *N Engl J Med* 1981;305:6–11.
14. Fisher B, Bauer M, Margolese R, et al. Five-year results of a randomized clinical trial comparing total mastectomy and segmental mastectomy with or without radiation in the treatment of breast cancer. *N Engl J Med* 1985;312:665–673.
15. Early stage breast cancer: consensus statement. NIH Consensus Development Conference, June 18–21, 1990. *Cancer Treat Res* 1992;60:383–393.
16. Schain WS, Findlay P, d'Angelo T, et al. A prospective psychosocial assessment of breast cancer patients receiving mastectomy or radiation therapy in a randomized clinical trial. *Proc ASCO* 1985;4:248.
17. Ganz PA, Schag AC, Lee JJ, et al. Breast conservation versus mastectomy. Is there a difference in psychological adjustment or quality of life in the year after surgery? *Cancer* 1992;69:1729–1738.
18. Eddy DM. High-dose chemotherapy with autologous bone marrow transplantation for the treatment of metastatic breast cancer. *J Clin Oncol* 1992;10:657–670.
19. Davidson NE. Out of the courtroom and into the clinic. *J Clin Oncol* 1992;10:517–519.
20. Triozzi PL. Autologous bone marrow and peripheral blood progenitor transplant for breast cancer. *Lancet* 1994;344:418–419.
21. Wood WC. Progress from clinical trials on breast cancer. *Cancer* 1994;74:2606–2609.
22. Cobau CD. Clinical trials in the community. *Cancer* 1994;74:2694–2700.
23. Salive ME, Mayfield JA, Weissman NW. Patient outcome research teams and the Agency for Health Care Policy and Research. *Health Serv Res* 1990;25:697–708.
24. Agency for Health Care Policy and Research. Medical Treatment Effectiveness Research: PORT-II. AHCPR Grant Announcement. Rockville, MD: Department of Health and Human Services, Public Health Service, August 1993.
25. Tomiak E, Piccart M. Routine follow-up of patients after primary therapy for early breast cancer: changing concepts and challenges for the future. *Ann Oncol* 1993;4:199–204.
26. Rosselli Del Turco M, Palli D, Cariddi A, et al. Intensive diagnostic follow-up after treatment of primary breast cancer: a randomized trial. *JAMA* 1994;271:1593–1597.
27. GIVIO Investigators. Impact of follow-up testing on survival and quality of life in breast cancer patients. A multicenter randomized controlled trial. *JAMA* 1994;271:1587–1592.
28. Adjuvant chemotherapy for breast cancer. NIH Consensus Development Conference, September 9–11, 1985. *Cancer Treat Res* 1992;60:375–382.
29. Nayfield SG, Bongiovanni GC, Alciati MH, et al. Statutory requirements for disclosure of breast cancer treatment alternatives. *J Natl Cancer Inst* 1994;86:1202–1208.
30. Pierce PF. Deciding on breast cancer treatment: a description of decision behavior. *Nurs Res* 1993;42:22–28.

Quality of Life and Pharmacoeconomics in Clinical Trials, Second Edition, edited by B. Spilker.
Lippincott-Raven Publishers, Philadelphia © 1996.

CHAPTER 82

Measuring Health-Related Quality of Life in Pediatric Populations: Conceptual Issues

Peter L. Rosenbaum and Saroj Saigal

INTRODUCTION

Kyle was born at 25 weeks gestation, weighing only 760 g. He had a prolonged and rocky course of neonatal intensive care and developed retinopathy of prematurity causing blindness of his right eye and moderate impairment of his left. At age 16 he wears glasses to correct myopia, but is in good health, attends an age-appropriate grade in high school, and gets along well with friends. Both he and his parents rate his quality of life (QOL) as excellent.

Andrea's perinatal course was similar to Kyle's, but with a very different outcome. At age 12 she has severe quadriplegic cerebral palsy, is profoundly cognitively impaired, wears eyeglasses for myopia secondary to retinopathy of prematurity, and is completely dependent for all activities of daily living. We are unable to assess Andrea's perceptions of her own quality of life. "Objective" valuation would suggest that her quality of life is very poor. Her parents cherish and care wonderfully for her and refuse to place a value on her health status.

These two vignettes illustrate several of the issues and challenges implicit in measuring children's health-related quality of life (HRQL). What domains of children's function should be considered to determine HRQL—and how are these chosen? From whose perspectives should valuations of HRQL be made: those of parents, children, professionals,

or the general community? Why should we want to measure HRQL? How does this notion enrich our understanding of health status or of our efforts to assess the impact of impaired health? In what way are quality of life measures different from the assessments of functional status that are typically used to evaluate the outcomes of treatments? To answer these questions, it may be helpful to consider several ways of thinking about health and function beyond the traditional medical model.

Taylor (1) proposed a paradigm of disease–illness–predicament to capture different dimensions of the biopsychosocial phenomena of health impairments. In this model, *disease* refers to the actual pathology that can be seen to accompany (and usually cause) the condition experienced by the patient as *illness* with symptoms and clinical signs. The *predicament* involves the idiosyncratic impacts of the disease processes as they create illnesses in individuals, each person undergoing a unique experience of the *illness* caused by that *disease*.

Health-related quality of life can be used to *describe* aspects of the impact of disease or illness in individuals. In this sense HRQL offers a perspective *complementary* to the biomedical considerations of disease and illness. This perspective incorporates, but goes beyond, the specific functional assessments that are the traditional focus of the medical clinician. As we shall try to illustrate, this is important because clinicians and others may measure and thus put values on states of ill health differently from those who actually live with them. Decisions are being made increasingly about the allocation of resources for individuals with diseases or for programs to groups of such individuals. It is

P. L. Rosenbaum and S. Saigal: Department of Pediatrics, McMaster University/Chedoke-McMaster Hospitals, Hamilton Ontario L8N 3Z5, Canada.

therefore very important to understand the personal experience and impact of illnesses and disorders, as well as to describe the standard biological and functional morbidities usually reported when considering diseases.

To illustrate the point, consider cerebral palsy from the perspective of the World Health Organization's concepts of impairment, disability, and handicap (2). Cerebral palsy refers to a group of conditions in which there is abnormality in the development of movement and postural control due to a nonprogressive "impairment" (2) of the developing central nervous system. By definition, these conditions cause permanently disordered movement of parts or all of the body. The functional manifestations include, at a minimum, gross motor "disability" (2). However, to the extent that individuals with these conditions can attend school or work, have friends, pursue leisure activities of their choice, and live a full life, they are not necessarily "handicapped" (2). In other words, the self-assessed HRQL of people with cerebral palsy might be good despite significant degrees of physical disability. Furthermore, people with equal degrees of functional limitation might vary considerably on measures of HRQL. In this sense HRQL conveys different (and additional) information from that offered by, for example, measures of motor function.

In addition to the descriptive or discriminative (3) value of accounts of HRQL, quality of life assessments can be used to *evaluate* the impact of individual treatments or programs of services to populations. Thus, for example, one might wish to evaluate the impact, on a group of adolescents with cerebral palsy, of a community-based sports and recreation program designed to promote socialization and increase community participation. Standard biomedical or functional evaluations of these teens before and after the program might detect differences in fitness or perhaps range of motion of major limb joints. A well-designed HRQL measure, however, might detect changes in the overall social–emotional well-being of these youth in a way that provides different and useful information about their experience of life and about the impact of the program. Note, however, that even if the biomedical or functional dimensions did not change on standardized measures, other factors of importance to the adolescents, assessed by an HRQL measure, might improve and validate the usefulness of the program. Like any measurement tool, it is important to have evidence of the psychometric (measurement) properties of an HRQL instrument and to know in particular that the measure(s) can detect change over time when change actually occurs.

A third potential use of measures of HRQL is to *predict* the future status of people with an illness or condition. To pursue once again the example of cerebral palsy, it might be the case that aspects of HRQL in preadolescent children could be much better predictors of social–emotional adaptation in adolescence than any of a variety of standard biomedical or functional considerations, such as severity of motor impairment, intellectual capacity, or indices of fitness. If HRQL captures an individual's adaptation to their medical problems, such a measure may provide information that

has long-term implications quite different from the usual assessments of function, all of which have their own very real importance for descriptions of health status, planning of treatments, and the evaluation of those interventions.

One might argue in addition that well-validated predictive measures of HRQL would be particularly useful in the field of child health, where future planning for developing children is a prominent consideration for parents as well as for health, educational, and other professionals. Work to be described in this chapter suggests that predictive measures of HRQL in children will increasingly provide perspectives that have been lacking to date and that will inform our thinking and planning in child health.

ISSUES IN DEVELOPING QOL MEASURES FOR CHILDREN

Several unique issues bear consideration when discussing the assessment of HRQL in children. Each relates in one way or another to age, cognitive capacity, and the changing nature of children throughout the developing years to late adolescence, or to the problem of whose perspectives to use in assessing HRQL. Clinicians and researchers interested in assessing HRQL in children need to understand these challenges before beginning to use or develop measures for the pediatric population.

What Dimensions of Function Should Be Assessed?

The first important issue involves the problem of which aspects or dimensions of function to include (or ignore) in assessing children's HRQL. Among the dilemmas this question raises is the problem of deciding from an adult perspective what constitutes "quality of life" in children, whose life experiences and daily activities differ substantially from those of adults. Furthermore, adult observers may vary in their perspectives, depending on whether they are parents, caregivers, policy makers, or community citizens. We shall return to this point later.

As an example, in a study of the quality of life of children and youth who had undergone surgical repair of high imperforate anus, Ditesheim and Templeton (4) evaluated children's school attendance, social relations, and physical capabilities and limitations, using a parent-completed questionnaire. The findings on this assessment were contrasted to scores on a previously described fecal continence (FC) measure also developed by these investigators. It is not clear from the report how the items of the QOL measure were chosen, whether patient or parental input was sought, or whether reliability of parental responses on the measure was assessed. The discussion raises interesting points about the validity of the QOL measure. The authors report their *a priori* expectation that "each child's QOL score would be the same as his FC score when measured quantitatively" (p. 585). This was frequently not the case and prompted discussion about "environmental influences that affected QOL in each age group" (p. 585).

One conclusion to be drawn from this work is that individuals' assumptions about what constitutes quality of life can lead investigators to consider features of children's daily life that may or may not be important to the children or their families or provide a valid reflection of the children's life experience.

Herndon et al. (5) took a different approach to assessing quality of life in children after extensive third-degree thermal injury. What they report, however, is a broad array of separate medical, physical, functional, and psychological outcomes, without aggregation into an HRQL-style measure. While there is little doubt, on the face of it, that the various factors considered by these investigators are relevant sequelae of severe burns, and that each would be expected to influence children's short- and long-term quality of life, this approach does not enable investigators to evaluate the *interactions* of these many features on the overall quality of life of children.

The major limitation of most of the available measures of health status, well-being, and utility-based quality of life for the general population of children is that they are all largely based on the conceptualizations of their investigator. Recognizing the lack of explicit social value-based scales, Cadman et al. (6) generated an adult and child social value, preference, and utility-based definition of quality of life for children. Starting with 16 attributes of health and function measured in the Ontario Child Health Study (7), these investigators measured the relative importance of each of these attributes to children's overall quality of life as judged by a general population sample of parents and their children in grades 6 through 8 (ages 11 to 13 years), using previously developed preference and utility measurement scaling methods (8). Six attributes met criteria for inclusion in the multiattribute definition of children's quality of life: sensory and communication ability, happiness, self-care ability, freedom from moderate to severe chronic pain or discomfort, learning and school ability, and physical ability (6). These dimensions were subsequently incorporated by Feeny et al. (9) into a multiattribute health status classification measure called the Health Utilities Index-Mark II (HUI-Mark II) that has been used to study the long-term health status of survivors of childhood leukemia (10–12), brain tumors (13), and extremely low-birthweight infants requiring neonatal intensive care (14).

Briefly, the HUI-Mark II includes seven attributes—sensation, mobility, emotion, cognition, self-care, pain, and fertility—considered most important by parents and children (9) (Table 1). Each attribute has three to five defined levels, ranging from normal function to severe dysfunction. The comprehensive health status of any child, at any particular time, can be described by a seven-element vector (X1, X2, ... and X7) in which Xi represents the level of the attribute i (1 to 3, 1 to 4, or 1 to 5, depending on the number of levels defined for attribute i). To date, the HUI-Mark II system has been demonstrated to have the capability to discriminate

among populations of children surviving "high-risk" versus "standard-risk" acute lymphoblastic leukemia (11), and between populations of extremely low-birthweight (ELBW) school-age children and matched term controls (14). Barr et al. (15) present an overview of this approach to measuring HRQL.

Developmental Change

A second challenge in assessing HRQL in children concerns age, development, and the capabilities of children. In a study to determine the attributes comprising well-being or quality of life in young handicapped children, Cadman and Goldsmith (16) found that an index applicable to 3-yr-old children could not be applied to those 5 yr of age. In the functional status measurement of the RAND Health Insurance Study, there were separate scales for children aged 0 to 4 years and those aged 5 to 13 years (17). No attempt was made to assess mental or social health in children under 5 years in that study (17).

Despite the face validity of the HUI-Mark II (Table 1), it is obvious that allowances must be made "for age" in several attributes when classifying a child's multiattribute health status. Furthermore, there may be a lower age limit for the applicability of this system as described in Table 1. Attempts by our group to apply this classification system retrospectively to prospectively collected data on 3-yr-old ex-premature children have been only partially successful to date. This reflects the difficulty of translating the system as written (for school-age children and youth) to the cognitive, behavioral and functional characteristics of 3-yr-olds. In particular, the attributes of cognition and self-care require reformulation to capture appropriately the range of activities of preschoolers in a manner analogous to, and concordant with, the existing system.

Work is currently under way to create a new HUI-PS, modeled on the present system, as a means of capturing HRQL in preschoolers. If it is possible to develop age-appropriate versions of HUI across the age range from 3 years to adolescence, the system could then be used to track HRQL in individuals and populations such as ELBW infants as they develop. Furthermore, if there were a reasonable degree of consistency and stability of HRQL from an early age (e.g., in the long-term development of ex-premature infants), it would be possible to use measures of HRQL early in life to "predict" late outcome. Much of our knowledge about "long-term" outcome in many populations of children with chronic health and developmental problems is relatively out of date when published, because of changes in the natural history and/or management of these conditions (18).

Whose Perspectives Are Important?

Whose perspectives on children's quality of life are important? This perplexing issue constitutes a third dilemma in

TABLE 1. *Multiattribute Health Status Classification System*

Attribute	Level	Description
Sensation	1	Ability to see, hear, and speak normally for age
	2	Requires equipment to see or hear or speak
	3	Sees, hears, or speaks with limitations even with equipment
	4	Blind, deaf, or mute
Mobility	1	Ability to walk, bend, lift, jump, and run normally for age
	2	Walks, bends, lifts, jumps, or runs with some limitations, but does not require help
	3	Requires mechanical equipment (e.g., canes, crutches, braces, or wheelchair) to walk or get around independently
	4	Requires the help of another person to walk or get around and requires mechanical equipment as well
	5	Unable to control or use arms and legs
Emotion	1	Generally happy and free from worry
	2	Occasionally fretful, angry, irritable, anxious, depressed, or suffering night terrors
	3	Often fretful, angry, irritable, anxious, depressed, or suffering night terrors
	4	Almost always fretful, angry, irritable, anxious, depressed
	5	Extremely fretful, angry, irritable, or depressed usually requiring hospitalization or psychiatric institutional care
Cognition	1	Learns and remembers school work normally for age
	2	Learns and remembers school work more slowly than classmates, as judged by parents and/or teachers
	3	Learns and remembers very slowly and usually requires special educational assistance
	4	Unable to learn and remember
Self-care	1	Eats, bathes, dresses, and uses the toilet normally for age
	2	Eats, bathes, dresses, or uses the toilet independently, but with difficulty
	3	Requires mechanical equipment to eat, bathe, dress, or use the toilet independently
	4	Requires the help of another person to eat, bathe, dress, or use the toilet
Pain	1	Free of pain and discomfort
	2	Occasional pain; discomfort relieved by nonprescription drugs or self-control activity without disruption of normal activities
	3	Frequent pain; discomfort relieved by oral medicines with the occasional disruption of normal activities
	4	Frequent pain; frequent disruption of normal activities; discomfort requires prescription narcotics for relief
	5	Severe pain. Pain not relieved by drugs and constantly disrupts normal activities
Fertility	1	Ability to have children with a fertile spouse
	2	Difficulty in having children with a fertile spouse
	3	Unable to have children with a fertile spouse

From Feeny et al. (9).

trying to understand HRQL in childhood. Here, as elsewhere, several issues contribute to the problem. In studies such as those of Ditesheim et al. (4) and Herndon et al. (5), health professionals wished to evaluate the long-term outcome of the children to whom they had provided care. Their interests reflected a legitimate concern about the late impact of interventions for complex disorders that affect children's lives forever. Whether the findings from these studies are concordant with, or different from, the perspectives and values of the parents of these children, or of the children themselves, is unclear in these reports. In addition, if different groups of health professionals value and assess different functional attributes, it is difficult to compare or aggregate findings from one enquiry to another.

Some efforts have been made to explore consistency and variation across observers in measuring HRQL. In a study of response comparability regarding measures of patients' health and functional status, Magaziner et al. (19) interviewed elderly patients with hip fractures and selected proxy caregivers about the patients' functional and health status before fractures. These investigators reported that agreement ranged widely from very poor to good and discussed a number of factors that might explain these often divergent findings. While considering the possibility that attention to the structure of measures might improve response comparability, these workers also recognize that the impact of the patients' disabilities on proxy respondents probably represents an important influence on the way those respondents view and report on the HRQL of "patients."

Barr et al. (13) described interesting variations in perspectives on children's HRQL. They applied the HUI-Mark II multiattribute system to a small population of child survivors of brain tumors and found differences among physicians, nurses, and parents in their judgments of children's multiattribute health status. The general tendency was for both nurses and parents to report more morbidity than was reported by physicians. Comparisons between nurses and parents showed that parents perceived greater morbidity in their children than did nurses. These observations are similar to those of Churchill et al. (20), who examined visual analog scale value scores for actual health status of 123 adults with end-stage renal disease. In general, patients tended to value their own health condition more highly than did nurses or physicians.

Another important illustration of differences in perspective across observers is the work of Cadman and colleagues (21), who found large differences between health professionals and parents of children with long-term impairments when they explored relative values concerning several dimensions of quality of life for young neurodevelopmentally disabled children. The perspectives of parents, the general adult public, and professionals working with such children and their families were examined. No differences were found between parents and the general population, but professionals differed considerably in their definition of well-being. Specifically, clinicians valued children's mood and behavior, and child and family function, substantially higher than did parents, who in turn placed a higher premium on the importance of mobility and self-care for children with disabilities. Points of agreement included the importance of prognosis, communication, and cognition.

In addition to the problem of parent–professional differences in judgments of children's HRQL, it is important to remember that parental reports represent a proxy response about their children's function. Although parents are clearly the most knowledgeable source of information about their children, some attributes in a multiattribute health status measure are more difficult to observe than others; and although parents know directly whether a child needs glasses to see well or requires help with mobility, their judgments about emotion or pain are based on their interpretation of their child's behavior, and thus provide indirect accounts of HRQL. Furthermore, because children's behavior may vary according to the setting (e.g., home or school) (22), parents' reports may be valid but incomplete accounts of children's status.

In a series of studies currently being conducted by Saigal, Feeny, and Rosenbaum and co-workers (23–27), the issue of perspectives in HRQL is being explored in several ways. The population under study is a cohort of ELBW adolescents, a demographically matched comparison group, and the parents of these teenagers. In addition to the comparison of parent and youth self-reports of health status, it has been possible to examine how youth evaluate their health status when asked specifically about "you," in contrast to their evaluation of an "objective" scenario that describes their *own* multiattribute health status as if it were another person. Some of the results currently available are preliminary, but the findings certainly add new information—and raise new questions—about the assessment of HRQL.

Briefly, we have followed a geographically defined regional cohort of ELBW children prospectively from birth into their teenage years. At age 8 yr, we compared the HRQL of 156 ELBW children with a control group of 145 children born at term (28). The study used the utility equation employed by Torrance et al. (29), which was applied to the multiattribute health state descriptions of the children (14). Mean HRQL scores were 0.82 ± 0.21 for ELBW children and 0.95 ± 0.07 for controls ($p < .0001$). The ELBW group also had greater variability and a higher proportion with scores in the lower range. These utility scores were derived from a general population perspective and are therefore not specifically representative of preferences from the perspective of these particular parents and children.

In the studies of these children as adolescents, we have measured health status by direct personal interviews independently with the children and their parents (23), using two preference measurement instruments (feeling thermometer and chance board) (15). We elicited preferences for their "own" or "own child's" health state, as well as for four hypothetical health states common to preterm children. Comparison of the multiattribute health status of teens as reported by teen–parent dyads showed remarkable consistency between teens and parents. Differences were observed mainly in cognition, where teens tended to describe themselves at a higher level of function than did their parents; and in sensation, where teens identified more problems compared with parent reports. However, comparison of the HRQL scores assigned by teens and parents revealed interesting results (24). Both groups of teens tended to rate themselves and the hypothetical health states lower than parental ratings. It appears that teens' HRQL ratings were more consistent with each other than with their parents, suggesting a "developmental" influence on how adolescents evaluate their health status. These data have implications when parents act as proxy respondents for rating their children's quality of life.

When should children's self-reports be sought, and how should they be interpreted? The answer to these questions is unclear, and the issues require further study. In part, the answer reflects both developmental considerations about the capacity of children to comprehend the cognitive tasks involved in the assessment of HRQL, and the purpose of the inquiry. We have been able to demonstrate that teenage ex-premature children can indeed describe their health status and that they report a higher frequency and more complex and severe limitations compared to controls (25). However, preference measurement techniques suggest that ELBW children do not perceive themselves to be very different from controls (26). Apparently, despite their disabilities, ELBW children appear to place a relatively high valuation of their own health. A particularly interesting (unpublished) illustration of this point is the comparison of youth evaluations of their own HRQL (when explicitly evaluating themselves) and their evaluation of a scenario describing their personal multiattribute health status as if it were someone else. ELBW adolescents rated their own HRQL substantially higher than that of the scenario about themselves (89.3 vs 82.6, t = 3.49, $p = 0.001$). The control group adolescents rated themselves and the scenario quite similarly, although here there was a nonsignificantly higher rating for self than for the scenario (91.2 vs 88.8, t = 1.65, $p = 0.103$). These findings may be, in part, a function of a broader range of impairments in the ELBW adolescents, leaving more room for variation than in the control group. However, other comparisons in adult studies between evaluations of subjective and "objective" scenarios of what is apparently the same situation lead to similar findings, with the valuation of the "personal" health state usually higher than that of the scenario (W. Furlong, *personal communication*).

Although the perspectives of children in evaluating their health status and HRQL are extremely important, innovative, and relevant, the very children for whom we would most like to obtain direct measures are often unable to participate because of severe disabilities. Under these circumstances, the perspectives of parents are valuable in enabling us to assess every child in population-based studies. In our studies, we have been able to demonstrate that although parents of ELBW children report a greater burden of disability in their children than do parents of control children, these differences are not fully reflected in the HRQL scores assigned by parents of ELBW children (27). Their children's mean HRQL scores were 0.91 ± 0.20, despite the fact that approximately one-fourth of children had neurosensory impairments! Thus, although both ELBW teens and the parents rated their HRQL fairly high, ELBW parents were more "generous" than their children in assigning HRQL ratings. These data have implications when involving parents in making medical decisions in the neonatal intensive care unit. Overall, however, it is important to observe that adolescents are usually able to offer "reasonable" responses to questions about health status and about their valuations of scenarios, and they should be given the opportunity to speak for themselves. Furthermore, while there may be a degree of distortion in parental responses about their children's health status and HRQL, parents represent an excellent source of information about their children's HRQL.

CONCLUSIONS

What have we learned about measuring health-related QOL in children? Recent work suggests that standardized,

scientifically credible generic multiattribute health status measures can provide useful descriptive and discriminative information about populations of children with various health and developmental problems. These observations in turn can be used to compute a standardized cardinal utility (ranging from 0.0 [death] to 1.0 [perfect health]) that provides a summary of the "value" of that particular aggregation of functional attributes. Some of the problems previously described as being associated with evaluation of HRQL in children (30) have been at least partially addressed.

For the clinician or researcher who wishes to assess HRQL in children, however, many unresolved challenges remain. First, as illustrated by the data and examples from our work with ELBW and control adolescents, observer perspective remains an important variable regarding exactly what is reported and how it is valued. This is true with respect to parent–child variations in reported HRQL. It is illustrated even more dramatically in the differences between teens' judgments of their own HRQL when overtly referring to themselves and in their apparently objective valuation of a scenario prepared for each adolescent individually (during a standardized interview) based on their own reports of their multiattribute functional status. These latter observations suggest that, despite the elaborately developed and standardized ways of measuring HRQL, there are still some important differences between "objective" and "subjective" valuations of the "same" status. The extent to which these findings are a function of the ages of the respondents is unclear.

Second, we still do not have a good idea of the developmental or intellectual capabilities required to complete the HUI-Mark II classification tasks. While one would expect ordinary preadolescents to be able to report their own subjectively experienced multiattribute health status, they would likely have more difficulty assigning relative values to scenario descriptions of children with different degrees and combinations of functional limitations. The challenge of making "standard gambles" on a chance board seems to be considerably greater, and much more work is required to understand when and how well these intellectually demanding tasks can be done by children. And there is the added likelihood that the relative values and importance of various functional states might be quite different to children or adolescents than to adults, simply as a function of different life experiences. All these issues remain to be studied and clarified.

Third, much work is needed to understand the "clinical" meaning of differences in HRQL scores or of changes in scores over time in response to changes in health status. While some information appears to be emerging on these issues in the field of adult HRQL (D. Feeny, *personal communication*), further experience is required with clinical measurement systems like the ones described in this essay in order to know how to interpret HRQL scores in childhood.

There are tremendous advantages to the use of standard approaches to measurement of HRQL in childhood. If we can agree on ways of assessing HRQL, and apply consistent systems to the outcomes of populations of children with various conditions, we may begin to be able to compare the well-being of children across time, space, and disorders. We may then have some common language with which to discuss the impact of conditions on children, to assess the value (or costs) of interventions, and to recognize changing patterns of outcome over time in a way that is currently often very difficult. It is only through collaborative efforts that these goals may eventually be reached.

ACKNOWLEDGMENTS

We acknowledge the considerable help and support of our colleagues Dr. David Feeny, Mr. Bill Furlong, and Dr. Ronald Barr for sharing their advice, perspectives and experience in the measurement of HRQL in children.

REFERENCES

1. Taylor DC. The components of sickness: diseases, illnesses and predicaments. In: Apley J, Ounsted C, eds. *One child.* London: Heinemann, 1982:1–13.
2. *International classification of impairments, disabilities and handicaps.* Geneva: World Health Organization, 1980.
3. Guyatt GH, Kirschner B, Jaeschke R. Measuring health status: what are the necessary measurement properties. *J Clin Epidemiol* 1992;45:1341–1345.
4. Ditesheim JA, Templeton JM Jr. Short term vs. long term quality of life in children following repair of high imperforate anus. *J Pediatr Surg* 1987;22:581–587.
5. Herndon DN, LeMaster J, Beard S, et al. The quality of life after major thermal injury in children: an analysis of 12 survivors with greater than or equal to 80% total body, 70% third-degree burns. *J Trauma* 1986;26:609–619.
6. Cadman D, Goldsmith C, Torrance GW. *A methodology for a utility-based health status index for Ontario children.* Final report to the Ontario Ministry of Health. Hamilton: McMaster University, 1986.
7. Boyle M, Offord D, Hoffman H, et al. Ontario child health study: methodology. *Arch Gen Psychiatry* 1987;44:826–831.
8. Torrance GW. Social preferences for health states: an empirical evaluation of three measurement techniques. *Socio-econ Plan Sci* 1976;10:129–136.
9. Feeny D, Furlong W, Barr RD, Torrance GW, Rosenbaum P, Weitzman S. A comprehensive multi-attribute system for classifying the health status of survivors of childhood cancer. *J Clin Oncol* 1992;10:923–928.
10. Feeny D, Leiper A, Barr RD, et al. The comprehensive assessment of health status in survivors of childhood cancer: application to high risk acute lymphoblastic leukemia. *Br J Cancer* 1993;67:1047–1052.
11. Barr RD, Furlong W, Dawson S, et al. An assessment of global health status in survivors of acute lymphoblastic leukemia in childhood. *Am J Pediatr Hematol Oncol* 1993;15:284–290.
12. Billson AL, Walker DA. Assessment of health status in survivors of cancer. *Arch Dis Child* 1994;70:200–204.
13. Barr RD, Pai MKR, Weitzman S, et al. A multi-attribute approach to health status measurement and clinical management—illustrated by an application to brain tumors in childhood. *Int J Oncol* 1994;4:639–648.
14. Saigal S, Rosenbaum P, Stoskopf B, et al. Comprehensive assessment of the health status of extremely low birth weight children at eight years of age: comparison with a reference group. *J Pediatr* 1994;125:411–417.
15. Barr RD, Feeny D, Furlong W, Weitzman S, Torrance GW. A preference-based approach to health-related quality of life for children with cancer. *Int J Pediatr Hematol Oncol* 1995, in press.
16. Cadman D, Goldsmith C. Construction of social value or utility-based health indices: usefulness of factorial experimental design plans. *J Chronic Dis* 1986;39:643–651.
17. Eisen M, Donald C, Ware JE, Brook R. *Conceptualization and Measurement of Health for Children in the Health Insurance Study.* Publication R-2313-HEW. Santa Monica, CA: Rand Corp., 1980.
18. Saigal S, Rosenbaum P, Hattersley B, Milner R. Decreased disability rate among 3-year-old survivors weighing 501 to 1000 grams at birth and born to residents of a geographically defined region from 1981 to 1984 compared with 1977 to 1980. *J Pediatr* 1989;114:839–846.
19. Magaziner J, Simonsick EM, Kashner TM, Hebel JR. Patient-proxy response comparability on measures of patient health status and functional status. *J Clin Epidemiol* 1988;41:1065–1074.
20. Churchill DN, Torrance GW, Taylor DW, et al. Measurement of quality of life in end-stage renal disease: the time trade-off approach. *Clin Invest Med* 1987;10(1):14–20.
21. Cadman D, Goldsmith C, Bashim P. Values, preferences, and decisions in the care of children with developmental disabilities. *J Dev Behav Pediatr* 1984;5:60–64.
22. Achenbach TM, McConaughy SH, Howell CT. Child/adolescent behavioral and emotional problems: implications of cross-informant correlations for situational specificity. *Psychol Bull* 1987;101:213–232.
23. Saigal S, Rosenbaum PL, Feeny DH, Furlong WJ. Comparison of the perception of health status within premature and control teen/parent dyads. *Pediatr Res* 1995;37(4):271A.
24. Saigal S, Furlong WJ, Rosenbaum PL, Feeny DH. Do teens differ from parents in rating health-related quality of life?: a study of premature and control teen/parent dyads. *Pediatr Res* 1995;37:271A.
25. Saigal S, Rosenbaum PL, Furlong WJ, Feeny DH, Burrows, E. Self-assessment of their own health status by extremely low birthweight and control teenagers using a multi-attribute health status classification system. *Pediatr Res* 1995;37(4):271A.
26. Saigal S, Feeny DH, Furlong WJ, Rosenbaum PL, Burrows, E. How premature teens perceive their own health-related quality of life: comparison with controls. *Pediatr Res* 1995;37:271A.
27. Saigal S, Furlong WJ, Feeny DH, Rosenbaum PL. Parents' perceptions of the health-related quality of life of teenage extremely low birthweight and control children. *Pediatr Res* 1995;37:40A.
28. Saigal S, Feeny D, Furlong W, Rosenbaum P, Burrows E, Torrance G. Comparison of the health-related quality of life of extremely low birth weight children and a reference group of children at age eight years. *J Pediatr* 1994;125:418–425.
29. Torrance GW, Zhang Y, Feeny DH, Furlong W, Barr RD. Multi-attribute preference functions for a comprehensive health status classification system. Working Paper 92-18, Centre for Health Economics and Policy Analysis. Hamilton: McMaster University, 1992.
30. Rosenbaum P, Cadman D, Kirpalani H. Pediatrics: assessing quality of life. In: Spilker B, ed. *Quality of life assessments in clinical trials.* New York: Raven Press, 1990:205–214.

Quality of Life and Pharmacoeconomics in Clinical Trials, Second Edition, edited by B. Spilker.
Lippincott-Raven Publishers, Philadelphia © 1996.

CHAPTER 83

Measuring Health Outcomes in Pediatric Populations: Issues in Psychometrics and Application

Jeanne M. Landgraf and Linda N. Abetz

That which we are, we are—
  One equal temper of heroic hearts,
  Made weak by time and fate, but strong in will
  To strive, to seek, to find, and not to yield
  A. L. Tennyson
  Ulysses

INTRODUCTION

The present time finds us at an important crossroad in the child health assessment field. Despite important gains in the development and availability of preventive health therapies, such as immunizations and vaccines, and an increase in the number of low birth weight survivors (1,2), the overall health of U.S. children has recently received a mediocre rating (3). In addition, the absence of standardized measurement strategies and comprehensive generic health assessment instruments that capture both psychosocial and physical health, irrespective of child age, gender, culture, or medical condition, has been cited as a fundamental roadblock in the attempt to quantify and understand the prevalence, severity, and

daily impact of childhood chronic illness in terms that are socially meaningful (4–6). The current demand for well-validated, yet practical, health outcomes questionnaires for children and youth spreads beyond epidemiologic studies to diverse applications, such as community-based studies and clinical trials to different health care settings, including hospitals, managed care organizations, and home care. In fact, the breadth of this demand is visible both geographically and in the diversity of conditions to be assessed. Most regions within the United States, the countries of Australia, Canada, Malta, Mexico, and at least seven nations in Western Europe are investigating the health outcomes of children. Target conditions include asthma, attention deficit hyperactivity disorder, cancer, cerebral palsy, clubfoot, epilepsy, growth hormone deficiency, human immunodeficiency virus/acquired immune deficiency syndrome (HIV/AIDS), hearing impairment, low stature, scoliosis, and renal failure.

To meet the growing demand for child health assessment tools, practitioners often construct their own questionnaires

    J. M. Landgraf and L. N. Abetz: Child Health Assessment Project, The Health Institute, New England Medical Center, Boston, Massachusetts 02111.

or adapt adult forms without basing their instrument development on sound principles of measurement science. Questionnaire development is an iterative process, however, that demands scientific rigor beyond a single application. The general purpose of this chapter is to enumerate and discuss scientific standards for evaluating and using child health assessment outcome questionnaires (often referred to as health-related quality of life) and to identify instruments that have been specifically developed and validated for pediatric populations.

EVALUATION STANDARDS

Evaluation criteria are organized under two broad headings labeled "psychometric properties" and "application issues." The most useful measures will be those that demonstrate excellent psychometric properties, but are also easy to employ and interpret across multiple applications. For example, a measure that meets the appropriate scientific standards for reliability and validity, but requires a trained interviewer and more than 45 minutes to complete, would not meet objective standards of use in an applied clinical setting.

Psychometric Properties

Reliability and validity are the two fundamental cornerstones of measurement theory. In pediatric populations, it is essential to evaluate an instrument's psychometric integrity within age, gender, and ethnic subgroups. Although these extensive evaluations may appear more cumbersome in pediatric populations, one could argue that these psychometric issues are also important in adult assessment research, as discussed later in the chapter.

Reliability

An instrument (i.e., questionnaire) is reliable to the extent that the results it yields are consistent across multiple administrations. Reliability is assessed by estimating how much the variation in a person's score for a given health dimension is "truthful" or "real" relative to chance or random occurrence (7). Reliability can be estimated by examining the stability of responses from one point of administration to another. Most often, reliability is reported in terms of a Cronbach's α-coefficient which ranges from 0 to 1.0 (8). This number is a proportion that indicates how much the measurement is reliable. Acceptable standards differ depending on the purpose of the comparison. For example, a coefficient of > .90 is recommended for analysis at the individual patient level (7). Most experts agree, however, that coefficients ranging from .50 to .70 are sufficient for group-level analyses (7,9). Reliability of a set of items (referred to as a scale) is determined, in part, by the number of items and their homogeneity. It is possible, therefore, to achieve a relatively high coefficient using a large pool of items. Consequently, reliability alone is an insufficient standard for establishing the integrity of pediatric health assessment questionnaires. Furthermore, evidence suggests that children's understanding of health is determined in part by their cognitive and emotional development, thereby affecting the overall reliability of self-reported health outcomes (10–12).

Validity

Validity is the handmaiden of reliability and provides evidence of a questionnaire's ability to measure the construct(s) it was specifically designed to target. Although validity can be assessed in a number of complementary ways (7), three common methods are used in the evaluation of adult health assessment questionnaires—content, construct, criterion (13). Briefly, content validity asks the questions, "Are the items and response choices adequate?" and "Do they measure what is claimed?" Construct validity seeks to provide more empirical evidence to this basic query by asking whether the hypothesized set of questions used to operationalize a given health construct (e.g., physical functioning) inadvertently elicits information about other independent constructs (e.g., self-esteem). Criterion validity asks whether health assessment scores are systematically related to an objective criterion. For example, in a recent study, the empirical relationship between self-reported health outcomes in adolescents with end-stage renal failure and clinical data, such as interdialytic weight gain, blood urea nitrogen levels, predialysis blood pressure, and serum phosphate and calcium levels, was examined (14).

Evaluating the validity of a child instrument is an ongoing process as new information about the meaning and interpretation of the data it yields in previously unexplored conditions, settings, and populations become known. In addition to establishing the validity of individual health concepts, the overall theoretical model or framework of a pediatric health assessment questionnaire should be empirically supported. Evidence in this regard (or lack thereof) should be carefully considered when deliberating the potential use and adoption of any instrument.

Naturally, as pediatric health assessment questionnaires become more refined and usable, scholarly debate about other important psychometric attributes will emerge. Pediatric health assessment efforts are best served by keeping apprised of related methodologic advances and integrating them into a broader research agenda. For example, in the adult health measurement arena, recent dialogues have emerged about a previously undefined attribute of validity—responsiveness to change (15,16). Responsiveness is the ability of a measure to capture hypothesized or expected change. This attribute of validity will be most relevant for studies involving multiple administrations of health assessment questionnaires. Potential applications in pediatric populations include randomized clinical trials and projects designed to assess the long-term impact of health education (intervention) programs, such as effective asthma management.

Application Issues

Application is defined as "the act of putting to use" (17). Historically, and with good reason, there is a tacit assumption that widespread dissemination of a questionnaire is unadvisable until sufficient data are known about its reliability and validity. Often, data used to evaluate the instrument are collected during a process of application that is carefully defined and controlled. On the surface, such practices seem well-grounded and logical, but they also raise several key questions. If questionnaire development is an iterative process, how does one define the term "sufficient" data? At what critical point is an instrument "usable"? If the test experiences do not mirror real-world application, is the questionnaire truly "usable"? It is important to evaluate the feasibility of pediatric assessment instruments in "true to life" settings. For example, can a parent with an ill child complete an instrument in a busy pediatrician's office?

Despite good intention to the contrary, both developers and users fail to recognize that application is an integral and dynamic part of the scientific process. Thus, development of health assessment questionnaires must not only be guided by scientific standards, but also by issues that are tangible and pragmatic (e.g., What if the primary caregiver is a young teen or not the biologic parent? What if the respondent is a child? How long does it take to complete? What level of reading comprehension is required? What if the respondent is not a native English speaker?). To achieve standards of science in concert with standards of application requires not only a paradigm shift, but an active willingness on the part of developers and potential users to collaborate much earlier in the measurement process.

To be truly well grounded, a child development perspective needs to be incorporated into the construction, validation, and adoption of pediatric health assessment tools. Developmentalists appreciate that childhood is culturally distinct from adulthood. Adapting standardized adult tools for use with pediatric populations is a strategy that fails to recognize the importance and implication of this fundamental premise. Pediatric health assessment tools must reflect the full extent of the cultural uniqueness of childhood across its different developmental thresholds. Thus, central to issues concerning an instrument's application and use are important questions about its relevance or applicability. Scientifically, the term is referred to as content validity and is based on "rational appeal" (7). As more and more members of the lay research community respond to the health outcomes directive, they will be forced to consider carefully the avocation of a pediatric assessment tool. Given the dearth of well-validated child instruments, it is imperative that an appropriate exposition of content validity or "relevance" criteria be provided so as to better inform their evaluation

and decision-making process. To be applicable, an outcomes instrument must apply to children at both the macro level (i.e., in the concepts to be measured) and at the micro level (i.e., in the items used to operationalize a given health concept).

Relevance at the Macro Level

The following general questions may be useful guides to consider when evaluating whether a health outcomes instrument is conceptually relevant for a specific pediatric population:

Considering the age of your target sample, are the concepts contained in the instrument developmentally appropriate?
Does the questionnaire capture both the psychosocial as well as the physical dimension of health?
Is each concept measured comprehensively? Are both positive (i.e., well-being) and negative (i.e., limitations) ends of the conceptual spectrum being measured? For example, is physical functioning measured by items that vary in gradation of strenuousness or degree of difficulty? Are different aspects of general mental health captured, such as positive affect, depression, and anxiety?
Are there conceptual gaps? For example, mental health is composed of both external and internal states. Generally, external states are measured by asking a respondent to rate the frequency of behaviors observed for the target child. Internal states reflect attributes of positive affect, anxiety, or depression. For children and especially adolescents, self-esteem is also an important indicator of mental well-being. However, most adult health assessment questionnaires rely on items that tap only internal states such as positive affect, anxiety, or depression. In general, due to the absence of these and other important health concepts, such as family relationships, adult tools are generally not conceptually applicable to pediatric populations.

Relevance at the Micro Level

At the item level, relevance can be guided by noting whether examples and activities are germane to children in general. Obviously, a questionnaire that asks about driving or playing golf is not suitable for a pediatric population. Relevance can be further determined by examining the applicability of items and concepts across three fundamental characteristics of the target child population—gender, age, and culture (racial, ethnic, and socioeconomic).

Gender

It is commonly accepted that boys and girls develop and mature physically and psychosocially along different time trajectories. Given this fundamental premise, evaluating the applicability of individual items and sets of items to each gender seems warranted. Whenever possible, gender neutral examples should be used. However, language is inherently biased, reflecting the nuances and preferences of a culture that are not always obvious to the writer. Given this bias, a more objective criterion would be to test empirically the suitability of items and item sets across gender groups, thereby providing evidence of their "neutrality." Information about the convergent and discriminant validity of items (i.e., the strength of their hypothesized linear relationship with the underlying concepts being measured and the significance of their disassociation with other unrelated items in the questionnaire) and other psychometric information (e.g., the percentage of children achieving perfect scores and lowest possible scores) would be advantageous. For example, a physical functioning scale that targets gender-specific sports or household jobs may inadvertently skew responses, resulting in more favorable ratings for one sex relative to the other.

Age

The primary milestones of children as they mature from infancy through middle childhood, adolescence, and late adolescence have been carefully documented in the developmental literature (18,19). Investigators in the child health assessment field have been sensitive to the conceptual and methodologic challenge this presents (20,21). For example, in addition to attending school and engaging in activities with friends, the "role" of mid-adolescent children (ages 14 to 16) often includes having a paying job. Appropriately, queries about limitations in activities need to capture the full multidimensionality of "role" expectations. However, items about work would not apply to children just a few years younger, for example, early adolescent children (11 to 13 years). (Although one could effectively argue that babysitting and having a paper route represent "work" roles.) Thus, applicability at both the item level and concept level needs to be demonstrated empirically across developmentally appropriate age groups. Unfortunately, as noted in the 1991 OTA report (5), investigators use different age cutoffs, further confounding the complexity of assessing and understanding the health of children and adolescents.

Culture

The emerging ethnic, racial, and socioeconomic diversity of children in the United States (22) warrants careful consideration in both the construction and validation of pediatric health assessment tools and in determining their "applicability." For example, items used to operationalize self-esteem, such as body image, academic achievement, or ability to make friends, may be perceived differently across cultures, indirectly affecting overall scores for this concept and confounding results across groups of children with different ethnic backgrounds. Similarly, items used to assess physical functioning traditionally target activities common to children of white middle class status (e.g., riding a bike). As mentioned previously, pediatric instrument developers should be held accountable to provide empirical evidence of an instrument's applicability across ethnically and socioeconomically diverse groups of children.

Using equivalent forms and analytic methods, it is possible to evaluate the linguistic and conceptual relevance (i.e., applicability) of health questionnaires in co-cultures within the United States and abroad (23–26). The optimal strategy, however, is to integrate information and experiences from these cultural and international studies before a questionnaire is standardized in its parent country (27). During a recent visit with Swedish colleagues, we learned that a widely accepted American instrument for adults underwent appropriate translation using an acceptable methodology, but the resulting questionnaire was "useless." Despite cultural similarities between adults in the United States and Sweden, the source questionnaire contained many idiomatic expressions that were culturally irrelevant for Swedes.

In summary, given the current state of the art for pediatric instruments, routine, empirical testing to determine the applicability of instruments to both boys and girls of different ages and cultural backgrounds is strongly recommended. This strategy will ultimately lead to more objective, robust, and universally applicable methods for assessing health outcomes in children.

FIVE CRITICAL ISSUES FOR STUDY DESIGN

Once it has been determined that concepts and corresponding items are appropriate across gender, age, ethnicity, and socioeconomic status of the target child population, a cadre of related application issues needs to be considered. Since these issues may significantly impact study design and the data collection process, appropriate resolution should be guided by both practicality and the best scientific standards available. Often however, these two guiding principles are viewed as incompatible, hindering efforts to achieve a mutually satisfying balance between them.

Given the absence of well-validated measurement strategies and tools for pediatric populations, achieving an appropriate balance between science and application is pivotal at this time. Lessons learned from real-life application experiences could greatly advance our understanding of fundamental measurement issues regarding trade-offs in using proxy-respondents versus children to report on pediatric health status. Certainly, with regard to children and adolescents, the issues of application are complex, and often the challenges they present raise new questions. Thus, each new application becomes an exploration of key issues and concerns that can be integrated into a scientifically rich data base. Based on our own experience and the challenges presented by a diverse group of instrument users, five of the most common, yet critical, questions related to application of assessment instruments in pediatric populations are identified and discussed.

Who Is the Most Appropriate Respondent?

Selection of the primary respondent needs to be deliberately and carefully considered. To best evaluate responses to health questions and perceived changes in a child's health, it is essential that a single respondent be identified for the duration of the data collection period. Biologic relationship to the target child may not always be the best determinant. In some cultures, extended family members (i.e., grandparents, aunts, or uncles) assume primary responsibility for providing care to a child and may be the most knowledgeable respondent. Even if a biologic parent is identified as the primary respondent, differences in assessments due to parental gender can be expected. For example, early evidence suggests that relative to maternal reports, fathers will rate children as having fewer behavioral or psychiatric problems (28–30). In general, because most studies inadvertently target maternal respondents, potential differences in measurement properties based on parent gender, as well as differences in perceived health status, are relatively unexplored. Although no differences were found by race in the psychometric properties of the SF-36 Health Survey (31), differences by gender and race were found for the CES-D in adults (32). These discrepant findings for distinct measures of health in adults underscore the need for complementary and routine evaluation efforts within the child health measurement field.

In some situations, children themselves may be the "optimal" reporter. For example, in a proposed AIDS trial of children 5 to 9 years of age, identifying the primary caregiver was difficult because the child was never brought to the clinic by the same person. Mailing out health forms or conducting phone interviews with the primary caregiver was not possible because many of these children came from disadvantaged backgrounds and their caregivers moved frequently and were not accessible by phone.

It has been suggested in the literature that children as young as 5 years of age can provide empirically reliable reports on concrete concepts such as pain and over-the-counter medication use (33–35). A more conservative estimate of 9 or 10 years of age is recommended for subjective concepts such as behavior (36,37) or self-esteem (38,39). According to previous literature, children's self-assessments of psychosocial health will differ from those of their parents (40–42). More recent investigations yield findings that contradict these earlier reports and suggest that relatively high agreement can be obtained between maternal reporters and their children for some concepts (43–47). High agreement, however, should not suggest that report from one source is identical to that of another. The real question remains, "Is valuable information lost by focusing exclusively on the use of proxy-reporters to obtain standardized information about

the health and well-being of the pediatric population?" If the goal of measurement is to develop useful methods to better understand the perceived health and well-being of children and to provide information that may effect meaningful change with regard to their clinical care, further study in this area seems warranted.

What Is the Optimal Mode of Administration?

There is no definitive answer to this fundamental question. Not all questionnaires are designed to be self-administered; some require the use of a trained interviewer. From a measurement perspective, it is imperative to use the prescribed mode of administration for which an instrument has been validated. Often, though, mode of administration is determined by cost or other issues specific to a given study, clinical trial, or the condition to be assessed. Few investigators have assessed response effects (e.g., response rates, data quality, psychometric properties) to different modes of administration for a particular instrument. However, a recent study in the adult health assessment field indicates that fundamental tradeoffs must be considered in the evaluation and selection of appropriate survey methodologies (48). Similar investigations need to be incorporated in the measurement agenda for the pediatric health assessment field.

Will the Respondent Be Able to Comprehend and/or Read the Instrument?

Although instrument developers will provide information about the suitability of a form for a given age range, its readability is not generally addressed. However, it is an important component and one that directly impacts the usability of a tool with disadvantaged populations or ethnically diverse groups whose native language is not American English. It is also important to remember that verbal proficiency is not synonymous with literate (i.e., reading) ability.

Although readability generally refers to paper and pencil instruments, it is an equally salient issue for interview-administered questionnaires. The overall readability of an instrument is determined by assessing the difficulty of several factors including the use of active or passive voice, syntactical complexity, the number of words per sentence, the number of syllables per sentence, and paragraph length (49–51). Currently, word processing software programs will calculate the reading and comprehension level of a questionnaire. However, as suggested, providing detailed information about the readability of instruments across groups differing in culture, ethnicity, and sociodemographic status is not currently a standardized practice.

Readability of a pediatric questionnaire may also be influenced by factors such as print size, clarity of instructions and layout. Often these issues are addressed by the developer prior to the standardization of an instrument. However, problems may not surface until the form is applied across diverse settings and conditions. It is therefore advisable to ask a small representative sample of potential respondents, including children, to complete the questionnaire prior to implementing data collection on a large scale. If properly conducted, the feasibility test should reveal problems with difficult items, phrases, or general layout of the instrument. Interview-administered questionnaires for children and caregivers should also be subjected to appropriate field-test conditions.

Is the Instrument Length Appropriate?

An instrument must be sufficiently long to be scientifically robust, yet short enough to meet the practical demands of real-world application. Achieving an appropriate balance between minimizing respondent burden and including sufficient number of items so as to detect meaningful differences is especially problematic with pediatric populations. If sample sizes are large, sufficient precision may be obtained with very coarse measures (7). Conversely, to achieve sufficient item variance with a small sample of subjects would require the use of a graduated response continuum and a large number of items. Pediatric studies require measurement systems that are appropriate for small sample sizes. Despite the prevalence of chronic childhood conditions (4), the pool of pediatric patients for a specified health problem is relatively small (compared with adults). Preliminary evidence suggests, however, that it is possible to achieve a significant reduction in respondent burden with minimal loss of precision in discriminating across and within different child chronic condition groups (43,44).

What Is a Meaningful Difference?

To be truly useful, a questionnaire and the items or item sets it contains must be sensitive enough to detect differences in health outcomes that are not only statistically significant, but clinically and socially meaningful as well. The Medical Outcomes Study (52,53) was an important watershed for significant advances in adult health measurement in this area. As yet, however, there are insufficient data to truly understand the relative impact of score differences for diverse pediatric populations, including traditional chronic medical conditions (e.g., asthma) and ''new'' morbidities (4,21), such as developmental, behavioral, and learning disorders. As the burgeoning interest in pediatric health assessment continues to grow, research in this area should result in the accumulation of evidence that will be of significant benefit to both practitioners and measurement experts.

IDENTIFICATION OF GENERIC PEDIATRIC HEALTH ASSESSMENT INSTRUMENTS

The secondary objective of this chapter was to identify potential instruments for measuring generic health-related outcomes in children (birth through 18 yr of age) and to provide a brief summary of corresponding psychometric findings. Disease-specific instruments were beyond the immediate scope of interest and were excluded from our review. An extensive psychological and medical literature search was conducted using key phrases, such as quality of life, health status indicators, generic health surveys, health outcomes, outcomes assessment, and activities of daily living. The plethora of individual concept-specific measures identified in the literature—cognitive development (54,55); motor development/physical functioning (56–58); temperament (59); emotional and behavioral problems (36,37,60–63); social activities (64); general health perceptions/vulnerability (65,66); morbidity/mortality rates (67–69); and risk factors (67)—underscores the need for standardization both in the conceptualization and in the operationalization of health-related outcomes for children and youth.

The search did yield, however, the identification of several questionnaires that were comprehensive (i.e., captured both physical and psychosocial health) and generic (applicable to children irrespective of age, gender, ethnicity, or medical condition) and for which published psychometric information was available. The instruments and related projects include the Child Health and Illness Profile (70), Dartmouth COOP Charts for Children and Adolescents (71,72), Functional Status II (73,74), The Health Institute's Child Health Assessment Project (14,43,44,75), Health Insurance Experiment/RAND (76,77), National Health Interview Survey (4,78), Ontario Child Health Study (79), and the Quality of Well-Being Scale (80). The latter instrument was not specifically designed for pediatric populations but is included because information about its adaptability to children has been noted in the literature and in conversations with colleagues.

It is not possible to provide an in-depth review of the generic instruments and their related projects in the space allotted. Therefore, information about the content of each instrument and an overview of their general purpose, target age range, respondent, mode of administration, number of items, and psychometric results are summarized in Tables 1 and 2, respectively.

The variability of descriptor information about the instruments and the general absence of data regarding their applicability to diverse settings, conditions, socioeconomic groups, and cultures underscores the need for greater collaboration between measurement experts and health care constituents and reveals the complexity and challenges that characterize the field. The current length of most questionnaires is prohibitive; short forms are needed to reduce respondent burden and to make patient-based health assessment instru-

TABLE 1. *Content of generic health assessment instruments for children*

Content	CHIP	COOP	FSII-R	THI/CHAP 5+ Parent	THI/CHAP 5+ Self	THI/CHAP 0–5 Parent	HIE 5+	HIE 0–4	NHIS	OCHS	QWB
Conditions/symptoms											
Conditions	✓			✓	✓	✓	✓	✓	✓	✓	
Symptoms	✓			✓	✓	✓	✓	✓		✓	✓
Illness specific symptoms			✓						✓	✓	
Functioning											
Cognitive (school)	✓	✓								✓	
Family	✓	✓		✓	✓	✓				✓	
General			✓	✓	✓	✓			✓		
Number of sick days	✓										
Physical/mobility	✓	✓	✓	✓	✓	✓	✓	✓	✓	✓	✓
Role	✓			✓	✓		✓	✓		✓	✓
Social	✓	✓	✓	✓	✓		✓			✓	✓
Mental Health											
Behavior	✓	✓	✓	✓	✓	✓	✓		✓	✓	
Energy		✓									
Mental health	✓	✓		✓	✓					✓	
Self-esteem	✓	✓		✓	✓						
Temperament						✓					
Parent											
General health				✓		✓	✓	✓		✓	
Impact on parent				✓		✓	✓	✓			
Mental health				✓		✓	✓	✓			
Other											
Coping	✓										
General health perceptions	✓	✓		✓	✓	✓	✓	✓	✓		
Growth and development							✓	✓			
Pain	✓	✓		✓	✓	✓					
Risk behaviors	✓	✓								✓	
Social support		✓								✓	

CHIP, Child Health and Illness Profile (70); COOP, Dartmouth COOP Project (71,72); FSII-R, Functional Status II-R (73,74); THI/CHAP, The Health Institute/Child Health Assessment Project (14,43,44,75); HIE, Rand Health Insurance Experiment (76,77); NHIS, National Health Interview Survey (4,78); OCHS, Ontario Child Health Study (79); QWB, Quality of Well-Being Scale (80).

ments more attractive to providers, payers, and consumers. Comprehensive instruments that measure health-related outcomes of infants and toddlers are also needed. Relatively few instruments were designed for parallel reporting between caregivers and children themselves, thereby compromising our potential to understand the trade-offs in this area. Finally, most caregiver completed instruments do not provide for a self-report of their own health (in addition to that of the target child), further circumscribing our appreciation of the relationship between self-perceived health and proxy-reported health.

CONCLUSIONS

The work reported herein, although not exhaustive, does represent an advance for the field of pediatric health assessment in general. Certainly, further validation and refinement of existing measures are needed. To design instruments that are scientifically robust, yet practical and easy to administer, score, and interpret, will require timely implementation of state-of-the-art measurement theory in conjunction with welcomed input from clinicians and researchers with real-world experience. It is hoped that decisions at this important cross-

TABLE 2. *Overview of generic health assessment instruments for children*

Instrument/ project	Purpose	Age range (yr)	Respondent	Mode of administration	No. of items	Reliability	Validity[a]
Child Health & Illness Profile (70)	Assess physical & mental health	11–17	Youth	Self administered survey	153	α: .42–.93 Test-retest: r = .53–.87	Content, criterion, construct, discriminant, validity (70)
Dartmouth COOP Project (71,72)	Inquiry into functioning & health-related quality of life	8–12 13–18	Child Youth	Self administered picture & word charts	Child: 9 Youth: 14	Test-retest: Child: r = .31–.72 Youth: r = .57–.85 α: .60–.94	Concurrent validity (71,72)
Functional Status II-R (73,74)	Assess general & specific health factors	0–16	Parent	Structured interview	Long: 43[b] Short: 14	α: All > = .80	Discriminant, construct, concurrent validity (73,74)
The Health Institute Child Health Assessment Project (14,43,44,75)	Assess physical & psychosocial functioning	5–15 0–5 10–15	Parent Parent Youth	Self administered questionnaire	Parent: 5+: 107[c] 0–5: 135[b,c] Youth: 106[c]	Parent: 5+α: .70–.98 0–5α: .68–.91 Youthα: .62–.91	Discriminant construct, concurrent, criterion validity (14,43,44,75)
The RAND Health Insurance Experiment (76,77)	Assess physical & mental functional disability	0–4 5–13	Parent Parent	Self administered questionnaire	0–4: 157 5+: 122	0–4α: .53–.77 5+α: .57–.87	Content, construct, concurrent validity (76,77)
National Health Interview Survey (4,78)	Epidemiologic	0–18	Parent	Structured telephone interview	65	Not reported (4,78)	Not reported (4,78)
Ontario Child Health Study (79)	Determine prevalence of emotional & behavioral disorders	4–16 12–16	Parent Youth	Interviewer & self administered questionnaire	Parent: 304 Youth: 169	Disorder checklist Test-retest: r = .86 α: .80	Utility-based validity (79)
Quality of Well-Being Scale (80)	Determine applicability to pediatric oncology patients	4–18	Parent	Structured face-to-face interview	# of items not reported; takes 15 min to complete	Inter-rater reliability: .70–1.0 α: All > = .92	Concurrent validity (80)

[a]Strategies for establishing the validity of instruments are varied and complex; there is not sufficient space to describe adequately. Thus, the reader is referred to the literature as noted.

[b]Number of items is age dependent.

[c]Psychometric evaluations of short forms are currently under way; number of items in short forms ranges from 25 to 50.

road will be guided by a collective commitment "to strive, to seek, to find, and not to yield."

ACKNOWLEDGMENTS

This research was supported by The Health Institute, New England Medical Center. The authors wish to express their appreciation to Susan D. Keller, Ph.D., and Martha S. Bayliss, M.Sc., for their valuable comments on the manuscript, and to John E. Ware, Ph.D., for his helpful insights during scholarly discussions.

REFERENCES

1. Wegman ME. The annual summary of vital statistics—1993. *Pediatrics* 1994;94:792–803.
2. Paneth N. Tiny babies—enormous cost. *Birth* 1992;19:154–155.
3. Williams CL. *Child health report card 1993.* New York: American Health Foundation, 1994.
4. Newacheck PW, Taylor WR. Childhood chronic illness: prevalence, severity, and impact. *Am J Public Health* 1992;82:364–371.
5. Office of Technology Assessment. *Adolescent health.* Vol I: *Summary and policy options.* Washington, DC: US Government Printing Office, April 1991.
6. American Medical Association. *Profiles of adolescent health series.* Vol I: *America's adolescents: how healthy are they?,* Chicago, IL: American Medical Association, 1990.
7. Nunnally JC, Bernstein IH. *Psychometric theory.* 3rd ed. New York: McGraw-Hill, 1994.

8. Cronbach LJ. Coefficient alpha and the internal structure of tests. *Psychometrika* 1951;16:297–334.

9. Helmsteader GC. *Principles of Psychological Measurement.* New York: Appleton-Century-Crofts, 1964.

10. Bibace R, Walsh ME. Development of children's concepts of illness. *Pediatrics* 1980;66:912–917.

11. Maddux JE, Roberts MC, Sledden EA, Wright L. Developmental issues in child health psychology. *Am Psychol* 1986;41:25–34.

12. Perrin EC, Gerrity PS. There's a demon in your belly: children's understanding of illness. *Pediatrics* 1981;67:841–849.

13. Bungay KM, Ware JE Jr. *Measuring and monitoring health-related quality of life.* Kalamazoo, MI: Upjohn, 1993.

14. Kurtin PS, Landgraf JL, Abetz L. Patient-based health status measurements in pediatric dialysis: expanding the assessment of outcome. *Am J Kidney Dis* 1994;24:376–382.

15. Guyatt G, Walter S, Norman G. Measuring change over time: assessing the usefulness of evaluation instruments. *J Chronic Dis* 1994;40:171–178.

16. Hays RD, Hadorn D. Responsiveness to change: an aspect of validity, not a separate dimension. *Qual Life Res* 1992;1:73–75.

17. *Webster's Ninth new collegiate dictionary.* Springfield, MA: Merriam-Webster, 1990.

18. Meisels SJ, Shonkoff JP, eds. *Handbook of early childhood intervention.* Cambridge, MA: Cambridge University Press, 1992.

19. Feldman SS, Elliott GR. *At the Threshold—The Developing Adolescent.* Cambridge, MA: Harvard University Press, 1990.

20. Starfield B. Child health status and outcome of care: a commentary on measuring the impact of medical care in children. *J Chronic Dis* 1987;40:109S–115S.

21. Rosenbaum P, Cadman D, Kirplani H. In: Spilker B, ed. *Quality of Life Assessment in Clinical Trials.* New York: Raven Press, 1990:205–215.

22. Lewit EG, Baker LG. Race and ethnicity changes for children. In: Behrman R, ed. *The future of children: critical health issues for children and youth.* Vol 3. Los Angeles: The Center for the Future of Children, the David and Lucile Packard Foundation, 1994:134–144.

23. Brislin RW. Back-translation for cross-cultural research. *J Cross-Cultural Res* 1970;1:185–216.

24. Bracken BA, Barona A. State of the art procedures for translating, validating, and using psychoeducational tests in cross-cultural assessment. *School Psychol Int* 1991;12:119–132.

25. Hui CH, Triandis HC. Measurement in cross-cultural psychology. *J Cross-Cultural Psychol* 1985;16:131–152.

26. Hunt SM, Alonso J, Bucquet D, Niero M, Wilkund I, McKenna S. Cross-cultural adaption of health measures. *Health Policy* 1991;19:33–44.

27. EuroQol Group. EuroQOL: a new facility for the measurement of health-related quality of life. *Health Policy* 1990;16:199–208.

28. Jensen PS, Traylor J, Xenakis SN, et al. Child psychopathology rating scales and interrater agreement. I. parents' gender and psychiatric symptoms. *J Am Acad Child Adolesc Psychiatry* 1988;27:442–450.

29. Reynolds WM, Anderson G, Bartell N. Measuring depression in children: a multimethod assessment investigation. *J Abnorm Child Psychol* 1985;13:513–526.

30. Rothbart MK, Maccoby EE. Parent's differential reactions to sons and daughters. *J Pres Soc Psychol* 1966;4:237–243.

31. Johnson PA, Goldman L, Orav EJ, Garcia T, Pearson SD, Lee TH. Comparison of the Medical Outcomes Study Short-Form 36-Item Health Survey in black patients and white patients with acute chest pain. *Med Care* 1995;33:145–160.

32. Callahan CM, Wolinsky FD. The effect of gender and race on the measurement properties of the CES-D in older adults. *Med Care* 1994;32:341–356.

33. Tyler DC, Ahn Tu JD, Chapman CR. Toward validation of pain measurement tools for children: a pilot study. *Pain* 1993;52:301–309.

34. Adesman AR, Walco GA. Validation of the Charleston Pediatric Pain Pictures in school-age children. *J Clin Child Psychol* 1993;21:10–13.

35. Bush PJ, Davidson FR. Medicine and drugs: what do children think? *Health Educ Q* 1982;9:113–128.

36. Achenbach TM, Edelbrock CS. The child behavior profile. I. Boys aged 6–11. *J Consult Clin Psychol* 1978;46:478–488.

37. Achenbach TM, Edelbrock CS. The child behavior profile. II. Boys aged 12–16 and girls aged 6–11 and 12–16. *J Consult Clin Psychol* 1979;47:223–233.

38. Piers EV. *Revised manual Piers-Harris children's self-concepts scale.* Los Angeles: Western Psychological Services, 1985.

39. Harter S. The perceived competence scale for children. *Child Dev* 1982;53:87–97.

40. Herjanic B, Herjanic M, Brown R, et al. Are children reliable reporters? *J Abnorm Child Psychol* 1975;3:41–48.

41. Reich W, Herjanic B, Welner Z, et al. Development of a structured psychiatric interview for children. *J Abnorm Child Psychol* 1982;10:325–326.

42. Herjanic B, Reich W. Development of a structured psychiatric interview for children. *J Abnorm Child Psychol* 1982;10:307–324.

43. Landgraf JM, Ware JE Jr, Schor E, Davies AR, R-Roh K. Health profiles in children with psychiatric and other medical conditions. Paper presented at Ninth World Congress of Psychiatry, Rio de Janiero, Brasil, June 6–12, 1993.

44. Landgraf JM, Ware JE Jr, Schor E, Davies AR, R-Roh K. Comparison of health status profiles for children with medical conditions: preliminary psychometric and clinical results from the Children's Health and Quality of Life Project. Paper presented at the Tenth Annual Meeting of the Association for Health Services Research, Washington, DC, June 27–29, 1993.

45. Kazdin AE, French NH, Unis AS, et al. Assessment of childhood depression: correspondence of child and parent ratings. *J Am Acad Child Psychiatry* 1983;2:157–164.

46. Canning EH, Hanser SB, Sahde KA, et al. Mental disorders in chronically ill children: parent–child discrepancy and physician identification. *Pediatrics* 1992;90:692–696.

47. Weissman MM, Wickramaratre P, Warner V, et al. Assessing psychiatric disorders in children. *Arch Gen Psychiatry* 1987;44:747–753.

48. McHorney CA, Kosinski M, Ware JE Jr. Comparisons of the costs and quality of norms for the SF-36 Health Survey collected by mail versus telephone interview: results from a national survey. *Med Care* 1994;6:551–567.

49. Fry E. Fry's readability graph: clarifications, validation, and extension to level 17. *J Reading* 1977;Dec:242–252.

50. Privette G, David S. Reliability and readability of a questionnaire: peak performance and peak experience. *Psycholog Rep* 1986;58:491–494.

51. Lapp D, Flood J. *Teaching reading to every child.* New York: Macmillan, 1978.

52. Stewart AL, Ware JE Jr. *Measuring functional status and well-being: the Medical Outcomes Study approach.* Durham, NC: Duke University Press, 1992.

53. Stewart AL, Greenfield S, Hays RD, et al. Functional status and well-being of patients with chronic conditions: results from the Medical Outcomes Study. *JAMA* 1989;262:907–913.

54. Bayley N. Manual for the Bayley scales of infant development. New York: The Psychological Corporation, 1969.

55. Thorndike RL, Hagen EP, Sattler JM. *The Stanford–Binet intelligence scale.* 4th ed. Chicago: Riverside Publishing Co., 1986.

56. Haley SM, Coster WJ, Ludlow LH, et al. *Pediatric Evaluation of Disability Inventory: development, standardization and administration manual.* Boston: New England Medical Center, 1992.

57. Lansky LL, List MA, Lansky SB, Cohen ME, Sinks LF. Toward the development of a play performance scale for children (PPSC). *Cancer* 1985;56:1837–1840.

58. Singh G, Balu HA, Fries JF, Goldsmith DP. Measurement of health status in children with juvenile rheumatoid arthritis. *Arthritis Rheum* 1994;37:1761–1769.

59. Carey W. A simplified method for measuring infant temperament. *J Pediatr* 1970;77:188–194.

60. Achenbach TM, Edelbrock C, Howell C. Empirically based assessment of the behavioral/emotional problems of 2 and 3 year old children. *J Abnorm Child Psychol* 1987;15:629–650.

61. Jellinek MS, Murphy JM, Robinson J, et al. Pediatric symptom checklist: screening school-age children for psychosocial dysfunction. *J Pediatr* 1988;112:201–209.

62. Walker DK, Stein REK, Perrin EC, Jessop DJ. Assessing psychosocial adjustment of children with chronic illnesses: a review of the technical properties of Pars III. *Dev Behav Pediatr* 1990;11:116–121.

63. Fombonne E, Achard S. The vineland adaptive behavior scale in a sample of normal French children: a research note. *J Child Psychol Psychiatry* 1993;34:1051–1058.

64. Dubow E, Tisak J, Causey D, Hryshko A, Reid G. A two-year longitudinal study of stressful life events, and social problem-solving skills:

contributions to children's behavioral and academic adjustment. *Child Dev* 1991;62:583–599.

65. McCormick MD, Altreya BH, Bernbaum JC, Charney EB. Preliminary observations on maternal rating of health of children: data from three subspecialty clinics. *J Clin Epidemiol* 1988;41:323–329.

66. Perrin E, West P, Culley B. Is my child normal yet? Correlates of vulnerability. *Pediatrics* 1989;83:355–363.

67. Fink R. Issues and problems in measuring children's health status in community health research. *Soc Sci Med* 1989;29:715–719.

68. Nahata M. Status of child health worldwide. *Ann Pharmacother* 1992;26:559–561.

69. Wolfe B, van der Gaag J, Perlman M. A new health status index for children. In: van der Gaag J, Perlman M, eds. *Health, economics and health economics.* Amsterdam: North-Holland, 1981:283–304.

70. Starfield B, Reiley A, Green B, Ensminger M, Ryan S, et al. The adolescent child health and illness profile: a population-based measure of health. *Med Care* 1995;33(5):553–566.

71. Baribeau P, Berger D, Jette A, Kairys S, Keller A, Landgraf J, Wasson G, Wasson J. Coop functional health status charts for children and adults: a system to measure functional health status in physicians' offices. Final Report to the Henry J. Kaiser Family and the W.T. Grant Foundations. Dartmouth Medical School. Hanover, NH: Dartmouth COOP Project, Department of Community and Family Medicine, Dartmouth Medical School, 1991.

72. Wasson JH, Kairys SW, Nelson EC, Kalishman N, Baribeau P. A short survey for assessing health and social problems of adolescents. *Fam Pract* 1994;38:489–494.

73. Stein REK, Jessop DJ. Functional status II(R): a measure of child health status. *Med Care* 1990;28:1041–1055.

74. Lewis CC, Pantell RH, Keickhefer GM. Assessment of children's health status. Field test of new approaches. *Med Care* 1989;27:S54–S65.

75. Landgraf JM, Abetz L. The Infant/Toddler Quality of Life Questionnaire: conceptual framework, logic, content, and preliminary psychometric results. Final Report to Schering-Plough Laboratories and Health Technology Associates. Boston: New England Medical Center, 1994.

76. Eisen M, Donald C, Ware JE, Brook R. *Conceptualization and measurement of health for children in the health insurance study.* Publication R-2313-HEW. Santa Monica, CA: Rand Corporation, 1980.

77. Eisen M, Ware JE, Donald C. Measuring components of children's health status. *Med Care* 1979;17:902–921.

78. National Health Interview Survey. Current Estimates from the National Health Interview Survey. NHIS Child Health Supplement 1988.

79. Boyle MH, Offord DR, Hofmann HG, et al. Ontario child health study. I. Methodology. *Arch Gen Psychiatry* 1987;44:826–831.

80. Mulhern RK, Horowitz ME, Ochs J, Friedman AG, Armstrong FD, Copeland D, Kun LE. Assessment of quality of life among pediatric patients with cancer, psychological assessment. *J Consult Clin Psychol* 1989;1:130–138.

Quality of Life and Pharmacoeconomics in Clinical Trials, Second Edition, edited by B. Spilker.
Lippincott-Raven Publishers, Philadelphia © 1996.

CHAPTER 84

Geriatrics: Perspective on Quality of Life and Care for Older People

T. Franklin Williams

INTRODUCTION

The later years of people's lives bring into sharper focus essential features of quality of life (QOL) and their interrelations with quality of care, which are actually important throughout life. Gerontology and geriatrics have much to contribute to understanding the entire life span. Factors that in earlier years of life at first seem to be optional become critical in old age for the maintenance of a person's integrity, independence, and autonomy; they become life-or-death matters, both figuratively and literally. What are these important elements of quality of life and care, how do they interrelate, and how may we approach more adequate recognition and assessment of them and response to them?

As background for considering these questions, we need an accurate picture of what old age is really like. Fortunately the results of much recent research, as well as increasingly common experiences of all of us with the rapidly increasing numbers of old and very old people, provide much clearer details about old age than were available until very recently. This picture may be summarized as follows, with regard to older, and especially very old, people, who

1. show great individual differences, greater than any other age; and

2. may maintain extraordinarily stable physical, mental, personality, and social characteristics; but
3. are likely to acquire disabilities in any or all of these realms, which may or may not be remediable;
4. may continue to contribute to the life and well-being of themselves, their families, and society;
5. are likely at times to need some or much care by others; and
6. such needs typically occur in clusters of events.

It is clear, first, that there are immense individual differences among older people, more than at any earlier age, in virtually all types of characteristics—physical, mental, psychological, health, and socioeconomic. Thus, when we consider what quality of life means to an older person and what features of quality of care may contribute to that quality of life, we *must* arrive at highly individualized conclusions. This principle is recommended for all ages, but it may not be so essential in some aspects of earlier life as it is in the lives of older people, as noted below.

Second, we now know that many older persons may continue to be remarkably healthy and functional in all or most ways into very late years. Contrary to pervasive earlier views of inevitable decline in physical and mental functions, changes in personality, and losses of social involvement, much recent research has established the stability of all these aspects for many persons into their 80s or beyond—for at least some, even beyond 100 years. Even in organ systems in which there are age-related changes, if good lifestyle

T. F. Williams: Monroe Community Hospital, University of Rochester, Rochester, New York 14620.

practices are present and in the absence of overt disease, there is sufficient adaptability and reserve function for most activities (1,2). This knowledge helps define the challenges for maintenance of quality of life.

Third, we also know that chronic disabling conditions become progressively more common as persons age, and impinge on reserves and threaten loss of functional independence (1,3). It is also clear that we can do more to restore or compensate for much of this functional loss, through rehabilitative measures (including physical and occupational therapy), prostheses (e.g., eyeglasses and other aids to vision, hearing aids, canes, walkers) and environmental modifications such as specially designed kitchen work spaces, modified controls for driving automobiles, and chairlifts for stairs.

Fourth, contrary to the common view that most older people are burdens on society, we now know that most older persons continue to contribute in personal, informal, and formal ways to their own maintenance and to their families and communities (4). Common examples include daily care of grandchildren, while the middle generation is engaged in paid work, maintenance of their own residence, and a great variety of volunteer community activities.

Fifth, many older persons at various stages of their later lives do need fluctuating amounts of help from, and care by, others, most of which is provided by family members but also by formal care services. Among persons ages 85 and older—the most rapidly growing portion of our population—40% are disabled to the degree of needing daily help (5). A major challenge here is to focus on respecting the older person's individuality and autonomy.

Sixth, when conditions or events that threaten loss of quality of life (e.g., diseases, injuries, and social losses), occur in older people, they typically occur in multiples and against a background of already limited reserves. This is why any single new threat that might appear to be of only limited importance for a younger person is likely to pose a critical problem for an older person. This is also why it is necessary to approach the maintenance of quality of life for older persons with comprehensive consideration of the multiple factors present—physical, psychological, social, economic, spiritual—and the interrelatedness of quality of life and quality of care.

Finally, as background for discussing specific aspects of quality of life and quality of care, an overriding goal and concern of older people for their own quality of life is that they maintain (or regain) as much personal independence as possible. This refers to each of the domains of quality of life. It is the personal autonomy and the freedom to make choices and to live one's own life according to one's own decisions, both small and large, that means most. The maintenance of identity is the chief task of very old persons (6), but we should also keep in mind that what is good for older persons is good for all ages.

Against such a background, let us first consider characteristics of quality of life that older persons may determine or influence for themselves and how these may be assessed or measured. Then what is required to provide high-quality care to support the desired quality of life will be examined.

QUALITY OF LIFE CHARACTERISTICS DETERMINED OR INFLUENCED BY OLDER PERSONS THEMSELVES

Lifestyle Factors

It is clear from numerous studies that a prudent diet, regular exercise (physical and mental), no smoking, only modest amounts of (or no) alcohol, and adequate sleep are all important for maintaining good health and independence into later years. Regular physical and mental activities, in particular, have been neglected in the past and their benefits have been recently well documented. Regular physical activity has been shown to be as beneficial in older as in younger persons for increasing or maintaining aerobic capacity and muscle mass and strength, minimizing bone less, and improving blood lipids and glucose tolerance (7–10). Although not specifically studied in older persons, it can be assumed that the beneficial effects on mood produced by physical activity applies in older as well as in younger persons also. Recent studies have also shown that the active use of cognitive functions contributes to their maintenance or improvement in older persons (11,12).

Methods for assessing and measuring these factors exist in epidemiologic and demographic studies, such as the Alameda County studies, as well as studies conducted by the National Center for Health Statistics, the National Institute on Aging, and the Bureau of the Census. A bibliographic summary of aging-related statistical studies is available from the National Institute on Aging.

Screening and Early Detection of Potential Problems

Despite the need for more studies of the benefits of some screening efforts in relation to their costs, there is reasonable consensus on the value of certain procedures that can lead to early detection and effective prevention or treatment of potentially disabling conditions, thus contributing to quality of life maintenance. Professional groups in Canada and the United States have addressed this issue, including its application to older persons (13–16). A recent review and consensus on recommendations, prepared by an expert committee for the United Seniors Health Cooperative, encompass these screening procedures at various specified intervals: blood pressure; occult blood in stool; digital rectal examination; breast examination and mammography; pelvic examination with Papanicolaou test; vision; hearing; blood lipids; hematocrit; urinalysis; thyroid function; vaccination for influenza, *Pneumococcus,* and tetanus; and specific attention at physical examinations to skin, oral health, and feet (17). A diary recording the completion of these tests is recommended for each older person.

PSYCHOLOGICAL, SOCIAL, AND ECONOMIC FACTORS AFFECTING QUALITY OF LIFE

The quality of life of older persons is clearly influenced by psychological, social, and economic factors in the same way that younger persons are influenced, for the most part. At the same time there are features of special importance in the lives of older people that may be highlighted here. In the psychological realm, longitudinal studies establish the remarkable constancy or stability of basic personality characteristics, as seen for example in the studies of McCrae and Costa (18), against which any changes in behaviors or symptoms can appear as signals for further inquiry. Concern about any suspected loss of cognitive function is very frequent among older persons and also deserves explicit attention. The satisfaction of continuing to contribute to others is important to most older persons and should be a part of psychosocial assessment.

In the social realm, contrary to some earlier views, it is clear that most older people maintain as close ties to their families and social networks as they had in earlier life (19). Here again, individual variation is important, and longitudinal information is critical in assessing the meaning of current social relationships and activities to the quality of life of a specific older person.

In the economic aspects of their lives, older persons usually have little or no opportunity to add to their fixed retirement income and are concerned first about security and second about unanticipated costs, especially in health care.

All these realms are important to the quality of life wherever an older person may be, and in whatever state of health of disability: in her/his lifelong home, retirement community, or nursing home, with or without disabilities. They should be part of an assessment of quality of life in any setting.

CHARACTERISTIC NEEDS FOR, AND PROVISION OF, QUALITY CARE AFFECTING QUALITY OF LIFE IN OLDER PERSONS

Disabling conditions, physical or mental, in older persons are clearly common threats to maintenance of the independence that is a key to their quality of life. Not only are affected persons at risk of losing some control over their own lives but they also face the depressing sense of being a "burden" to family members or others, as well as upsetting financial costs. Elsewhere in this volume (chapter 14–16), measures of physical and mental functioning in general, and in certain disease conditions in particular, are addressed. Here the most common disabling conditions for older, and especially very old (age 85+), persons may be noted: dementia, loss of mobility (due to arthritis, stroke, peripheral vascular disease, and hip fractures—usually associated with osteoporosis, loss of vision, loss of hearing, depression, and

urinary incontinence. Assessment measures for all these features exist but could also use further refinement.

The impact of any of these conditions on the maintenance of independence and quality of life is influenced by the lifestyle factors referred to earlier as well as by the strength and stability of the family and other social and economic resources. It is obvious that all these factors must be examined simultaneously when assessing their impact on quality of care and quality of life.

What Is High-Quality Care?

In the face of threats to independence posed by disabling conditions in older persons as well as the large private and public burdens of care and the associated costs, there is an understandable widespread interest in the types, quantity, and quality of care involved and in its costs. Concerning quality of care, it can be observed that virtually all the attention has been on documenting and eliminating *poor* or unacceptable care, that is, to aim through assessment and interventions to accomplish *minimum* levels of quality of care. These goals are certainly desirable, but they fall short of seeking or achieving *high*-quality care, the care each of us would like for ourselves or our older relatives or friends. Anything less than high-quality care will fall short of helping achieve a high quality of life for those needing care.

High-quality care for older persons can be defined as "care that is desired by the informed patient or client (and family); is based on the sound judgment of the professionals involved, from scientific studies and/or experience; and is agreed upon and carried out in a relationship of mutual trust and respect" (20). Others have given essentially the same definition (21,22). This general definition would apply to care for persons of any age, but let us consider specific features of its application to older persons needing care.

As already emphasized, the older person's highest priority will usually be to regain as much independence as possible; thus the emphasis in the approach to care should be fundamentally *rehabilitative*. A comprehensive rehabilitation philosophy and approach should infuse virtually all care for disabled older persons, in acute as well as in chronic care settings, using the skills of a variety of professionals. Also important is an informed patient and family, so that care plans (which are likely to involve chronic or long-term activities) are mutually understood and agreed upon (23). Fortunately, there are good sources of information for the public about most common problems affecting older persons, including help from many support groups such as those concerned with Alzheimer's disease, arthritis, diabetes, osteoporosis, or strokes. Professionals also have a responsibility to provide adequate information.

Second, in carrying out their part in achieving high quality of care for disabled older persons, the involved professionals must start with the recognition, emphasized earlier, that multiple complex problems (medical, functional, and psychosocial) are almost always present simultaneously; thus, a *comprehensive, multidisciplinary assessment* and development of a comprehensive care plan are essential first steps in achieving high-quality care. This necessity has been stressed in the recent Consensus Development Conference on this topic at the National Institutes of Health (24,25). A major focus of the care plan should be on rehabilitative potential and efforts. Sound judgment based on up-to-date knowledge of the scientific literature relevant to the patient's conditions is also an obvious necessity.

The third component of high-quality care, namely that the care be conducted in a relationship of mutual respect and agreement (26), is often the weakest link: the fundamental individuality and right to autonomy of the disabled person is not respected. There is much evidence of caregivers—family members as well as professionals—talking about the affected person rather than with her or him, making decisions about and for that person rather than with her or him. This problem is perhaps most obvious in many nursing home settings in which the person is "institutionalized", i.e., fitted into the routines of the institution, rather than *individualizing* the care to the preferences as well as the needs of the older person. That truly individualized approaches can be achieved is illustrated in some nursing homes in Scandinavia and elsewhere, as well as a few in this country (27).

Assessing and Accomplishing High-Quality Care

Little attention has been paid to developing methods for assessing high-quality care in older persons, and perhaps even less to steps taken to achieve it. It appears feasible that measures for documenting the components of high-quality care described above can be developed and used. For example, the patient's preferences for daily living routines can be determined and documented, and the performance of caregivers can be assessed against them. The extent of the patient's understanding of the disease conditions present and of the options for treatment can be noted, as well as the professionals' responses. Specific efforts in rehabilitative therapy can be noted, as well as response. A consensus panel has identified specific disease conditions for which high-quality care can make a real difference in outcome, as well as types of services that may be most important in improving quality of care (28).

To accomplish such care, we need to expand the numbers and then take full advantage of the new generation of physicians and other professionals in the health and human services fields who are specially trained in gerontology and geriatrics. Physicians in internal medicine and family medicine are obtaining certification of special competence in geriatrics, and special competency certification in geropsychiatry is now available. Similar special competencies are developing in other professions. It should be a matter of policy that all care organizations, such as hospitals, nursing homes, group practices, and retirement communities, have a team of such specially prepared professionals as part of

their staffs, called upon to give leadership in the care of older persons with disabilities or other complex problems.

Furthermore, it is suggested that more responsibility be given to chiefs of services, the directors of caring organizations, for ensuring that high-quality care, not just meeting minimal standards, is accomplished. This is essentially a personal responsibility for the person in charge to exercise throughout the staff and operations. They should be accountable to an informed board, including representatives of patients and their families, as well as professionals. In essence this is the structure by which we have nominally organized our caring systems, but boards typically have given most attention to capital, financial, and management features, and too little attention to ensuring that the key staff leaders are in turn assuring high-quality care.

CONCLUSIONS

We should establish ambitious, but nevertheless attainable, individualized goals of high-quality care for older persons in need of such care, and also establish the expectation that our professionals are going to be prepared for, and supervised in providing, such a level of care that any of us would be pleased to receive it.

REFERENCES

1. Williams TF. Current status of biomedical and behavioral research in aging. In: Andreopoulos S, Hogness JR, eds. *Health care for an aging society.* New York: Churchill Livingstone, 1989:123–137.
2. Williams TF. Aging versus disease: which changes seen with age are the result of "biological aging"? *Generations* 1992; XVI:21–25.
3. National Center for Health Statistics. Data on older Americans: United States, 1992. Centers for Disease Control and Prevention/National Center for Health Statistics, Series 3, Number 27.
4. Kahn RL. Productive behavior: assessment, determinants, and effects. *J Am Geriatr Soc* 1983;31:750–757.
5. *Americans Needing Help to Function at Home.* Public Health Service Advance Data No. 92. DHHS Publication No. 83-1250. Washington, DC: U.S. Department of Health and Human Services, 1983.
6. Lieberman MH, Tobin SS. *The experience of old age: stress, coping and survival.* New York: Basic Books, 1983.
7. Seals DR, Hagberg JM, Hurley BF, et al. Endurance training in older men and women. I. Cardiovascular responses to exercise. *J Appl Physiol* 1984;57:1024–1029.
8. Seals DR, Hagberg JM, Hurley BF, et al. Effects of endurance training on glucose tolerance and plasma lipid levels in older men and women. *JAMA* 1984;252:645–649.
9. Dalsky GP, Stocke KS, Ehsani AA, et al. Weight-bearing exercise training and lumbar bone mineral content in postmenopausal women. *Ann Intern Med* 1988;108:824–828.
10. Fiatarone MA, Marks EC, Ryan ND, Meredith CN, Lipsitz LA, Evans WJ. High-intensity strength training in nonagenarians: effects in skeletal muscle. *JAMA* 1990;263:3029.
11. Baltes PB, Lindenberger U. On the range of cognitive plasticity in old age as a function of experience: 15 years of intervention research. *Behav Ther* 1988;19:283–300.
12. Rodin J. Aging and health: effects of the sense of control. *Science* 1986;233:1271–1276.
13. Canadian Task Force on the Periodic Health Examination. The periodic health examination. 2. 1985 update. *Can Med Assoc J* 1986;134:724–727.
14. Medical Practice Committee, American College of Physicians. Periodic health examination: a guide for designing individualized health care in the asymptomatic patient. *Ann Intern Med* 1981;95:729–732.

15. Council on Scientific Affairs. Medical evaluation of healthy persons. *JAMA* 1983;249:1626–1633.

16. Institute of Medicine, National Academy of Sciences. *The second fifty years: prompting health and preventing disability.* Washington, DC: National Academy Press, 1990.

17. United Seniors Expert Panel. *Taking charge of your health.* Special Report. Washington, DC: United Seniors Health Cooperative, 1988.

18. McCrae RR, Costa PT Jr. *Emerging lives, enduring dispositions: personality in adulthood.* Boston: Little, Brown, 1984.

19. Shanas E. Social myth as hypothesis: the case for the family relations of older people. *Gerontologist* 1979;19:3–9.

20. Williams TF. Quality of care for older people: challenges for research and teaching. Los Angeles: Kesten Memorial Lecture, Andrus Gerontology Center, 1988.

21. Lohr KN, Yordy KD, Thier SO. Current issues in quality of care assessment *Health Aff (Millwood)* 1988;7:5–18.

22. Council on Medical Service. Quality of care. *JAMA* 1986;256:1032–1034.

23. Davies AR, Ware JE Jr. Involving consumers in quality of care assessment. *Health Aff (Millwood)* 1988:7:33–48.

24. National Institutes of Health Consensus Development Conference Statement. Geriatric assessment methods for clinical decision-making. *J Am Geriatr Soc* 1988;36:342–347.

25. Solomon DH. Geriatric assessment: methods for clinical decision-making. *JAMA* 1988;259:2450–2452.

26. Steffen GE. Quality medical care: a definition. *JAMA* 1988;260:56–61.

27. Williams CC. The experience of long term care in the future. *J Gerontol Social Work* 1989;14:3–18.

28. Fink A, Siu A, Brock RH, et al. Assuring the quality of health care for older persons: an expert panel's priorities. *JAMA* 1987;258:1905–1908.

Quality of Life and Pharmacoeconomics in Clinical Trials, Second Edition, edited by B. Spilker.
Lippincott-Raven Publishers, Philadelphia © 1996.

CHAPTER 85

Frail Older Patients: Creating Standards of Care

Marsha D. Fretwell

INTRODUCTION

In the preceding chapter, Williams (1) described some pertinent characteristics of older persons as background for developing and applying measures of quality to the experience of older individuals in our acute and long-term care systems. This chapter focuses on two of these characteristics: (a) the multiplicity of factors (physical, mental, emotional, social, and economic) that interact in a complex fashion at any point in time in an older person's life; and (b) the resulting enhancement of interindividual variation among older individuals of a given chronological age. Based on these attributes, the argument is made that *personal preferences and individualized care plans are intrinsic to the definition of quality of life (QOL) and care in this group.* This requirement of individualized clinical therapies and care is then related to the research methodology used in the creation of standards of care and the evaluation of the effectiveness and efficiency of our medical and social interventions. The role of an individual's physical, cognitive, and emotional functions as pivotal outcomes in the evaluation of both quality of life and care is highlighted. The need for studies using outcome measures that are adequately sensitive and specific is discussed. The chapter concludes with the description of a systematic approach for the collection and integration of patient information and the creation of patient care plans

that allow individualization of the therapies within a standard set of domains.

COMPLEXITY AND INDIVIDUAL VARIATION

As humans age, there is a continuous interaction of environmental and genetic factors that accentuates the uniqueness of each person. Individuals of the same chronologic age may differ considerably in such physiologic or biologic functions as vital capacity, cardiac output, creatinine clearance, and visual accommodation (2). These wide biological differences in individuals of a given chronologic age significantly reduce the usefulness of age as a single criterion for triaging services or categorizing patients within population-based studies. Additionally, within one individual, age-related changes in one organ system are not necessarily predictive of similar changes in other organ systems.

In any given individual, the aging process may be better viewed as the ongoing interaction of biological processes, surrounding social forces, idiosyncratic health behaviors, and life-style stresses. This complex interactive process is superimposed on the underlying asynchronous physical, cognitive, and emotional development curves (3). Over time, in susceptible individuals, losses in the physical, mental, social, and economic spheres of life become more frequent and require continuous adaptation. How well an individual adapts to change becomes a central factor determining both the length and quality of one's life (4). As one becomes frail and more dependent on the care of others, and particularly if

M. D. Fretwell: The Senior Wellness Clinic, Wilmington, North Carolina 28405.

this care is in the setting of an institution, the determinants of the quality of one's life begin to merge with those of the quality of one's care. Eventually, the burden of irreversible changes is so great and the capacity of the individual to respond to environmental stress is so limited that a simple pulmonary pneumonia, even if diagnosed and treated appropriately, may be the patient's final illness.

PERSONAL PREFERENCE AND INDIVIDUALIZED STANDARDS OF CARE

Acute and long-term care of frail older individuals highlights the shift in focus of our health care system. Health care has changed from treating a single disease underlying an illness to managing the individual's entire burden of disease and disability over a sustained period of time (5). The outcome of any illness is usually more dependent on various attributes of the host, positive or negative, than the absolute virulence of the infective organism or the progressive nature of the disease. Assisting each individual to achieve and maintain his or her optimal physical, cognitive, and emotional function for that point in life becomes the overriding goal of care. A critical role for physicians is to provide accurate prognostic information for an individual, i.e., telling patients where they are on their life's course at any given point in time. This enables patients to participate appropriately in decision making about their care.

The inherent complexity of frail older persons offers a significant challenge in diagnosis and prognosis not only for physicians, but also for administrators and regulators who are attempting to establish standards of care. A large number of interacting variables influence health outcomes following a single episode of illness in these elderly patients with multiple chronic diseases and functional disabilities. The information base for diagnosis must be large and the treatments multidimensional to achieve an optimal outcome. Generalizations about treatment are unproductive, and may be counterproductive, if one condition greatly influence treatment of another. Additionally, many functional problems of the elderly such as incontinence and immobility have multiple underlying etiologies (6). Failure to identify and treat all underlying etiologies may lead to a persistence of the functional problem despite appropriate treatment of one of the etiologies.

Even if all the information from the multiple domains influencing health outcomes is collected and considered for accuracy of diagnosis and prognosis, the patient's values about the planned treatment could override and determine the actual outcome (1). For instance, the person's attitude about feeding tubes is a major determinant of outcome in instances where malnutrition is the central problem. If a competent frail older person refuses the placement of a feeding tube when it represents the only mechanism for refeeding and survival, he or she has chosen this to be the final illness. If the prognosis for this episode of illness is constructed on

the medical illness and functional status of the individual without consideration of personal preference for treatment, the predicted outcome could be very different from the actual outcome. If appropriate application of the standard treatment for medical disease is the only measure of quality, this person has received poor care. If allowing individual autonomy in the decisions that affect him is a measure, then this person has received the highest quality of care.

For frail older persons, the standards established for their health care have a fundamental impact on their quality of life. This concept, taken with the complexity and individual variation among individuals, supports the regular inclusion of personal preference and individualized care plans in our definition of high-quality health care.

THE PROBLEM: INDIVIDUAL PATIENTS AND GENERIC STANDARDS

Clinicians have always been challenged by the translation of data obtained from the basic sciences and population-based studies into information that is relevant and useful for decision making with individual patients (7). Clinical investigations and pharmacological studies that exclude very old individuals on multiple medications or those with multiple chronic illnesses have limited application in the care of frail and/or chronically ill older persons. Research utilizing the methodologies of clinical epidemiology may provide data that support the treatment of certain problems. Often, however, the study results summarize the causal factors without identifying the appropriate patients for clinicians to treat (8). Additionally, this approach to study design has focused on asking questions that are amenable to answering with currently available research methodology. These questions may not always be relevant to the clinician caring for individual patients. This tension between a clinician's concern for the individual patient and the use of aggregate data methodology to extend knowledge is a critical feature of our considerations in creating standards of care for frail older persons (9).

"Standard" is one of several words, such as criterion, gauge, measure, test, and yardstick, that refer to sets of rules or principles by which we evaluate the quality of something. "Standard" itself implies an objective, impartial set of rules that have actually been defined in advance and are usually derived from aggregates of individual information in scientific studies. Once the standard is established, the item that is under scrutiny is usually evaluated in a yes–no comparison with the standard (10). In discussions of the standards used to measure the quality of care, Donabedian's original framework—structure, process, and outcome—is usually applied (11). Currently, much of the attention in the pursuit of quality is focused on assessment of patient outcomes (12). The mechanisms for establishing standards for patient outcomes are most often based on analyses of large aggregates of patient data and use implicit criteria such as "preventable death'' and ``avoidable hospitalization'' (13). These criteria are applied retrospectively to completed episodes of care and may therefore be a source of anxiety to clinicians, rather than a source of learning. Although there is a growing sophistication in the description of an individual's risk factors and outcomes, we are at the very beginning of understanding how patient preference, i.e., the creation of standards that are partial to individual patients, might be included in the evaluation of quality of care.

FUNCTIONAL MEASURES: ISSUES RELATING TO STANDARDS OF CARE

Explicit measures of appropriate care to date have included the benefits, risks, and costs of care. Benefits usually include increased life expectancy, pain relief, reduced anxiety, and improved functional outcomes. Risks include morbidity, decline in functional outcomes, mortality, and psychological distress. *As our population under care ages, the gold standard of care, survival at all costs, is slowly being replaced by relevant measures of physical, cognitive, and emotional function.* Their widespread inclusion in both studies of the quality of life and the quality of care confirms their importance as valid measures of human activity. Function as a focus of care has been elaborated by investigators such as Karnofsky (14), Katz et al. (15), and Lawton and Brody (16) in response to the needs of patients undergoing restorative care of chronic arthritis and treatment of cancer, acute cerebrovascular accidents, and fractures of the hip. Measures of human function range from a cell membrane's pumping sodium to an individual's ability to file her income tax. This chapter focuses on those cognitive and physical functions of frail older persons that are necessary for living independently.

Basic functional measures, such as the Katz Index of Activities of Daily Living, have been appropriately applied (a) to predict patient outcomes, (b) to measure the effectiveness of restorative interventions, and (c) to orient the medical care of frail older individuals toward issues relevant to their independence and dignity (17). Other indexes of functional disability, such as Barthel's Index (18) and the Older Americans Research and Service Instrument (19), may also be helpful for higher levels of function. Additional scales such as Spitzer's Quality of Life Scale (20), which includes both the basic and higher levels of human function, may be needed. The choice of a particular scale is determined by an understanding of the norm of activities for a group of individuals at a certain point in the natural history of their life and illness. When evaluating the impact of different therapies for a specific illness, quality of life and care scales must focus on the expected change in functional activities in order to be adequately sensitive. For instance, surgeries that affect only the upper body or extremities in otherwise functionally intact individuals, require evaluation instruments that focus on upper extremity functions.

The Katz Index was developed within the context of specific neurological and structural impairments but has been successfully applied to measure change in function in large aggregates of older individuals, regardless of the different etiological factors underlying that change. When used as an outcome measure in acute and long-term care, the activities of daily living score behaves as an integrated summary of multiple physical and cognitive etiological variables and is therefore an accurate and concise source of information for making a statement of prognosis.

If an individual's change in function after treatment is used as an indicator of the quality of care he receives, we need additional baseline information to predict accurately the best possible trajectory of functional change for that person. If our predictors are appropriate, the comparison of the actual functional outcome following a given treatment with the predicted one offers one measure of the quality of treatment. Using the change in a functional outcome measure in this manner requires that we not only know the overall degree of functional impairment at baseline but also have an understanding of (a) the specific contribution of certain diagnoses, medications, and malnutrition to the functional impairment; (b) the potential for change or reversibility of each of the diagnoses and functional impairments driving the summary Katz score; and (c) the length of time and the change over time of the various functional states.

The best example of this concept is given by examination of the changes in cognitive function that occur in the acute care hospital. In acutely ill older patients, the risk of acute confusional states appears to be about 25% or higher (21), especially for those patients with chronically impaired cognition. Once a patient becomes delirious, the risk of losing other functions (e.g., continence, mobility) is greater, and, of equal importance, the probability of regaining either continence or mobility is minimal until the confusional state is reversed. Therefore, the prevention or early detection and treatment of delirium is a critical marker for quality in acute hospital care.

If, in examining cognitive function change in a patient during a hospital stay, the only measure used is a summary scale combining the changes of acute (reversible) and chronic (irreversible) confusion, one has a measure of the degree of confusion, but no understanding of its etiology. On the other hand, if a measure is constructed which distinguishes those with acute and reversible changes in cognitive function from those with chronic irreversible impairment, the diagnostic and prognostic accuracy of the measure will be enhanced. Accurate prognosis provides the basis for appropriate expectations and allows evaluation of whether accurate diagnosis and appropriate treatment has occurred for an individual patient.

Once we understand the nature and degree of a patient's dysfunction, there are other issues that affect patient outcomes. These include the availability of treatment, the risk-to-benefit ratio of treatment, and the patient's personal preference for treatment. These factors must be included in prognosis statements to achieve the most accurate trajectory of functional change. Additionally, as individuals reach the final phase of their lives, small changes in function that may be imperceptible by current measures can have a strong influence on their quality of life (22). For instance, individuals considered completely dependent, as assessed by the Katz Index of Activities of Daily Living are no longer able to feed themselves. What are the measures that will help us determine the quality of care and therefore the quality of life for these individuals? For one individual, supporting continued independence in feeding by providing finger foods is the correct approach; for another, hand feeding by a caretaker is better. Unfortunately, in our current approach to care, we are just beginning to be sensitive to the functional decline associated with natural death and to provide resources that allow it to happen in the setting most conducive to meeting individual needs.

CREATING STANDARDS FOR FRAIL OLDER PERSONS

The goal of health care is to assist each individual to maintain and improve her or his ability to function independently in her or his everyday life. As one ages and approaches the last phase of life, this goal remains the same, but the level of functioning may be different. Given the degree of variation among persons of the same chronologic age, and given the potential complexity of the burden of disease and disability that may occur in the very old or very frail, personal preferences and individualized care plans become central to the definition of high-quality care. There appears to be a fundamental conflict involved in our task. Standards, by definition, cannot be individualized; they are impartial rules, based on the average. Yet older persons, physicians, and caring families routinely acknowledge the tremendous need for an individualized approach to care.

How can individualized care plans and the resulting patient outcomes be evaluated? How can a standard of care for frail or very old persons be defined and measured?

This section describes one approach to creating patient care plans that preserves the individualization of therapies and personal preferences of the patient but accomplishes this within the framework of a standardized functional health status assessment, the Care and Resource Evaluation Tool (the CARE Tool).

Care and Resource Evaluation Tool

The CARE Tool is organized into 11 standard domains or areas of concern: Diagnoses, Pain, Shortness of Breath, Medications, Nutrition, Urination, Defecation, Cognition, Emotion, Mobility, and Self-care (Table 1). These same domains or areas of concern also form the framework of the individualized care plan (Table 2). These domains were developed from a need to standardize the patient care plans and subsequent interventions in a randomized controlled trial designed to test the effectiveness of interdisciplinary geriatric assessment in acute care (23). In this study, the standardized care plan format was applied to 200 patients over the age of 75 yr who were entering the hospital for the treatment of acute medical and surgical diseases. The standardized care plan format made it possible to categorize every diagnosis and patient problem and the subsequent recommendations of the treatment team into one of the 11 domains or areas of concern. Table 3 shows the categories and some of the problems identified under these areas of concern.

On the CARE Tool, the functional health status in each of these domains is measured on a scale of 1 to 6, with 1 representing the highest level of health or function and 6 representing the lowest. In this approach to creating and achieving a high standard of care for frail older patients, the CARE Tool performs several functions. First, it provides the clinician with a comprehensive yet rapid baseline or screening assessment of the older patient's current health and function. It extends the assessment beyond the traditional medical model to encompass both the biopsychosocial model proposed by Engel (24) and the functional model, proposed by Katz (17). Once completed by the clinician or a team of clinicians, it provides a quantitative baseline assessment of the older individual that can be used to identify the particular areas of concern for an individual patient, estimate his or her clinical prognosis, and predict subsequent utilization of acute care and long-term care services. After the assessment is complete and appropriate therapies have been discussed with the patient and adjusted for their personal preference, the CARE Tool may then be used to select realistic health and functional goals that might be achieved through the recommended therapies. Thus it is possible to frame the individual therapies for each person within a standard set of functional health measures, whose scores can be aggregated for quantitative analysis.

The Individualized Care Plan

For each diagnosis and for each of the ten other areas listed in Table 2, the patient is assessed and all problems are identified. Reversible ones are first identified (Table 2, column 1) and recommendations consistent with the standard of medical practice are listed (see Table 2, column 2). Irreversible problems, especially those that influence the overall prognosis, are also noted. In column 3, the patient's preference about the standard recommendations are noted. For instance, if the diagnosis is colon carcinoma, the standard of medical practice is surgery; if the patient is competent and chooses to refuse surgery, this is noted. Column 4 then contains the actual recommendations, i.e., those standard practices modified by the patient preference. Patient preferences are elicited for all recommendations in each of the

TABLE 1. Care Tool-Provider Assessment

PATIENT: _____   SSN: _____   DATE: _____

AREAS OF CONCERN	1	2	3	4	5	6
# OF DIAGNOSIS	0-1	2	3	4	5	≥6
PAIN	None	Intermittent. NoRx	Intermittent, requires Rx.	Constant, controlled with Rx.	Limits ADLs	Constant, uncontrollable.
SHORTNESS OF BREATH	None	With vigorous exercise	Carrying moderate load or walking up steep hill	Going upstairs, carrying a light load on a level	Limits ADLs	Oxygen required
NUMBER OF MEDICATIONS	None	1-2	3-4	5-6	3-6 with history of adverse reactions	>6
NUTRITION (ALBUMIN AND BODY WEIGHT)	No problem	3.5, or >1-10 lbs over/under normal weight	3.5, or >1-15 lbs over/under normal weight	3.49-3.1, or >20 lbs over/under normal weight	3.0-2.5, or >25 lbs over/under normal weight	<=2.9, or 30+ lbs over/under normal weight
URINATION	Intact	Symptoms of frequency or urgency	Aware; Occasional accidents/Nocturia >2 times	Aware; Daily accidents	Unaware; Daily accidents	Catheter
DEFECATION	Q 3 day, no clinical symptoms	Q 3 day with history of diarrhea or constipation	Q 3 day with symptoms of diarrhea or constipation	> Q 3 day or using laxative regularly	Aware; Impacted or incontinent	Unaware; Impacted or incontinent
COGNITION	Intact 3/3	Mild short-term memory loss 2/3	Moderate short-term memory loss 1/3	Severe short-term memory loss 0/3	Acute confusional state; Hallucinations	Unresponsive
EMOTION	Intact	History of anxiety/depression	Symptoms of anxiety	Symptoms of depression	Vegetative symptoms; Sleep, appetite and energy disorder	Psychotic; Hallucinations
MOBILITY	Intact & regularly exercising	Intact; Driving car or using public transportation	Does not drive; but independent and ambulatory in community; Can use public transportation	Independent ambulation in home only; &/or walker or cane	Requires 1 person assist	Requires 2 person assist
SELF CARE	Independent	Requires assistance with shopping, transportation	Requires assistance with shopping, meal prep, housekeeping	Requires assistance with bathing, dressing	Requires assistance with toileting	Requires assistance with feeding

[Functional assessment form based on research conducted by Marsha D. Fretwell, M.D.]

TABLE 2. *Individualized care plan*

Areas of concern (problems listed below)	Score from CARE tool	Standard medical practice	Patient preference for treatment	Actual recommendations	Predicted score from CARE tool
Diagnoses 1. 2.					
Pain 1.					
SOB 1.					
Medication 1.					
Nutrition 1.					
Urination 1.					
Defecation 1.					
Cognition 1.					
Emotion 1.					
Mobility 1.					
Self-care 1.					

diagnoses and the ten other areas: Medications (patient may refuse chemotherapy or antidepressants), Nutrition (patient may refuse a feeding gastrostomy tube), Urination (patient may refuse a Foley catheter), Cognition, Emotion, Mobility (patient may refuse to go to rehabilitation), and Self-care (patient may refuse to go to day care). The actual recommendations (column 4) include only those treatments and therapies that the patient (or the patient and the family) finds acceptable. Presumably, with this degree of input, the recommendations will be appropriate and compliance will be high.

If we create an individualized care plan for a hypothetical patient who has fallen, fractured her femur and undergone a surgical repair, we would proceed as follows. Before creating the care plan, the clinician completes the Care Tool and places the scores on the care plan (column 2, Table 4). In this particular example, we see that the patient has developed an acute confusional state (row 8, Cognition, Table 4) after surgery, so most of the assessment information is taken from her bedside nurse or from her chart. Next, for each diagnosis and for each of the ten other areas listed in Table 4, the patient is assessed and all problems are identified and placed on the care plan (column 1, Table 4). Recommendations consistent with the standard of medical practice are listed (column 3, Table 4) and reconciled with the patient's prefer-

ences, if they are known. In this patient, finding this information may involve discussions with other providers, the dietitian, for instance or with the family. The actual recommendations (column 5, Table 4) include only those treatments and therapies that the patient (or the patient and family) finds acceptable. In our current scenario, the central problem is under Cognition: an acute confusional state, which gives the patient a CARE Tool assessment score of (5) for cognitive function. The provisional and actual recommendation is to replace the patient's intermittent narcotic pain medication with "round-the-clock" acetaminophen or Tylenol. The "goal" of this therapeutic maneuver is to improve the patient's cognitive function, which is captured by predicting that her Cognition CARE Tool assessment score following treatment will be lower, for instance, a score of 2, which would indicate a return to her baseline (from previous assessment or family input) mild short-term memory impairment. Outcome goals for each of the remaining domains are focused on restoring and/or maintaining our frail older patient at an optimal level of physical, cognitive, and emotional function. Despite the adherence of this care planning process to these 11 functional health domains and the use of a standard set of global baseline and outcome assessments to establish the goals of care, within

TABLE 3. Problems identified by areas of concern in acutely ill older patients receiving interdisciplinary team assessments and care[a]

Areas of concern	Example of problem	Patients N	%
Diagnosis	Sensory impairment	24	13
Medications	Adverse drug reaction	25	14
Nutrition	Protein malnutrition	43	23
Urination	Urinary incontinence	21	11
Defecation	Bowel incontinence	11	6
Cognition	Cognitive impairment	58	32
Emotion	Depression	48	26
Mobility	Falls	9	5
Self-care	Require assist with toileting	29	16

[a]N = 185.

each domain and global goal, the recommendations can be individualized and made consistent with the personal preferences of the patient.

Setting Standards of Care for Frail Older Persons

The above process of developing an individualized care plan can be accomplished by either an independent practitioner or, in the event of high risk or particularly complex patients, an interdisciplinary team. In the setting of a Geriatric Assessment Unit, this approach has demonstrated value and proven benefits to health care outcomes (25). Among the benefits are better diagnostic accuracy and treatment planning, more appropriate placement decisions with fewer referrals to nursing homes, improved functional and mental status of the patient, prolonged survival of the patient, and lower overall use of costly institutional care services (26,27).

Assessing Quality of Care at the Practice or Institutional Level

This process of creating individualized care plans may be transformed into a system for assessing the quality of care at the physician practice or institutional level. Optimally, the application of the CARE Tool for completing baseline assessments and setting patient outcome goals in a physician's practice or institutional setting would be within a larger electronic patient information system.

The CARE Tool is currently being used by primary care physicians as part of the Aging 2000 study, a project funded by the Hartford Foundation and currently under way

throughout the state of Rhode Island (28). In this project, primary care physicians complete the CARE Tool and individualized care plans annually in their more vigorous older patients and quarterly or as a change in status requires it in their frailer patients.

In patients requiring hospitalization, the optimal period for completing assessments, creating individualized care plans, and setting patient goals or predicted outcomes is within the first 72 hr after admission. At other points in time (e.g., discharge or set intervals within prolonged hospitalizations), new assessments of each domain are made and compared with these outcomes predicted at admission. Based on this feedback, each individualized care plan is modified and "new" outcomes are established. This process is also repeated at predetermined intervals following discharge.

In any site where health care is provided, this process offers a prospective approach to setting standards and evaluating quality, allows outcome goals to be individualized, and provides timely feedback that may be incorporated into continuing education as well as quality assurance programs. This process does not replace existing quality improvement programs for evaluating the structure and process of medical care. Rather, it extends them by acknowledging the complexity of treating diseases and managing illness in frail older people. If we are to use outcome measures as a means of evaluating the quality of care or life for frail older people, the predicted outcomes against which the actual outcome is compared must be accurate or appropriate for the individual.

By systematizing the patient assessment and cueing the clinician to organize assessment data into a standard patient care plan, this process promotes accurate predictions about patient outcomes. By routinely providing feedback in the form of actual patient outcomes for each of the diagnoses and the ten other domains discussed above, the complexity of each patient's natural history is clarified, and learning is promoted. Including clinicians in the process of setting goals for their patients will improve their ability to make prognosis statements. Including the patient's preferences about treatment and comparing them to a statement of standard treatment not only ensures an individualization of care, but may improve compliance. Additionally, the process clarifies issues about patient competency and documents the reasons for variation from standard medical practice.

At the institutional level, the use of standard assessments to establish the current status of the individual in each diagnosis and the other ten domains and standard assessments for predicted outcomes, allows data from multiple individual patients to be aggregated. Institutional practice standards for improving or maintaining nutritional status, patient mobility, and cognitive and emotional function may be set. Charts may be flagged for review based on a negative differential between the predicted and actual outcomes.

For more complex patients or for patients known to be at high risk of a poor outcome (e.g., a prolonged length of

TABLE 4. *Individualized care plan completed for hypothetical patient*

Areas of concern (problems listed below)	Score from CARE Tool	Standard medical practice	Patient preference for treatment	Actual recommendations	Predicted score from CARE Tool
Diagnoses 1. Hip fracture 2. CHF	2	Surgical repair	Surgical repair	Surgical repair	2
Pain 1. Postoperative	3	Narcotic PRN	No preference	Tylenol around the clock	3
SOB 1. Inactive	3	Avoid CHF		Monitor status	3
Medication 1. Narcotic 2. Lasix 3. Laxative		1. D/C 2. Continue 3. Continue		1. Tylenol 2. Continue 3. Continue	3
Nutrition 1. Low albumin	4	Nutritional suppl.	Sustacal	Sustacal	3
Urination 1. Foley	6	Foley	Bedside commode	Bedside commode	4
Defecation 1. Constipation	4	Laxative	No laxative	Improve mobility	2
Cognition 1. Acute confusion	5	Evaluate etiology	Clear mentation	D/C narcotic	2
Emotion 1. Anxiety	3	Medicate	No more medication	Orient and reassure	2
Mobility 1. Impaired	6	Uncoop; no PT	Mobility go home	Resume PT	4
Self-care	5	Uncoop; no OT/PT	Go home	OT/PT	3

stay; being placed in a nursing home for the first time or an unaccountable death), a team care and management system can be used. High-risk patients are identified at admission and receive functional assessments from their primary nurse and an interdisciplinary team conference that includes the physician and other traditionally utilized hospital staff, i.e., dietitian, pharmacist, physical therapist, and social worker. More recently nontraditional staff from Risk Management and Utilization Review have been included, which allows early and complete integration of the clinical, functional, and financial elements of contemporary hospital care. The interdisciplinary team structure is optimal for providing the necessary subspecialty expertise, professional self-scrutiny, and emotional support for the difficult task of creating appropriate standards for care of those patients who are dying (29) or those for whom no direct knowledge of personal preference is available.

CONCLUSIONS

This process of setting and achieving individualized standards of care by evaluating the relationship between predicted and actual outcomes is derived from the theory underlying W. Edward Demming's and other's work on Japanese and American industry over the last 30 yr (30). Identified recently in the *New England Journal of Medicine* as "The

Theory of Continuous Improvement" (31), it focuses on a prospective and educational approach to quality, rather than a retrospective and punitive one. Most importantly, by first addressing the uniqueness and need for personal preference in each older person with a serious illness and then involving the clinician in a self-evaluative approach to the highest quality of care, this process preserves the traditional structure of the patient–clinician relationship.

REFERENCES

1. Williams TF. The future of aging. John Stanley Soulter Lecture. *Arch Phys Med Rehabil* 1987;68:335–338.
2. Gilcrist BA, Rowe JW. The biology of aging. In: Rowe JW, Besdine RW, eds. *Health and disease in old age*. 1st ed. Boston: Little Brown, 1982:15–25.
3. Costa PT, McCrae RR. Concepts of functional or biological age: a critical review. In: Andres R, Bierman EL, Hazzard WR, eds. *Principles of geriatric medicine*. New York: McGraw-Hill, 1985:30–37.
4. Rowe JW, Kahn RI. Human aging: usual and successful. *Science* 1987;237:143–149.
5. Fried LP, Bush TL. Morbidity as a focus of preventive health care in the elderly. *Epidemiol Rev* 1988;10:48–64.
6. Judd HL. Prevention of osteoporosis. In: Solomon DH, moderator. New issues in geriatric care. *Ann Intern Med* 1988;108:718–732.
7. Andres R. Normal aging versus disease in the elderly. In: Andres R, Bierman EL, Hazzard WR, eds. *Principles in geriatric medicine*. New York: McGraw-Hill, 1985:30–37.
8. Malenka DJ, Baron JA. Cholesterol and coronary heart disease: the importance of patient-specific attributable risk. *Arch Intern Med* 1988;148:2247–2252.

9. Murphy EA. Commentary: public and private hypotheses. *J Clin Epidemiol* 1989;1:79–84.
10. Hayakawa SH. *Choosing the right word.* New York: Perennial Library, Harper & Row, 1968:584.
11. Donabedian A. Evaluating the quality of medical care. *Milbank Q* 1966;44:166–203.
12. Knaus WA, Nash DB. Editorial: predicting and evaluating patient outcomes. *Ann Intern Med* 1988;7:521–522.
13. Dubois RW, Brook RH. Preventable deaths: who, how often, and why? *Ann Intern Med* 1988;109:582–589.
14. Karnofsky DA, Burcheneal JH. The clinical evaluation of chemotherapeutic agents in cancer. In: Macleod CM, ed. *Evaluation of chemotherapeutic agents.* New York: Columbia University Press. 1949:191–208.
15. Katz S, Vignos PJ, Moskowitz RJ, Thompson HM, Suec KH. Comprehensive outpatient care in rheumatoid arthritis. *JAMA* 1968;206:1249–1254.
16. Lawton MP, Brody EM. Assessment of older people: self-maintaining and instrumental activities of daily living. *Gerontologist* 1969;9:179–186.
17. Katz S. Assessing self-maintenance activities of daily living, mobility and instrumental activities of daily living. *J Am Geriatr Soc* 1983;37:721–727.
18. Mahoney FI, Barthel DW. Functional evaluation: the Barthel Index. *Md S Med J* 1965;14:61–65.
19. Fillenbaum GG. *Multidimensional Functional Assessment: the Oars Methodology.* 2nd ed. Durham, N.C.: Duke University, The Center for the Study of Aging and Human Development, 1978.
20. Spitzer WO, Dobson AH, Hall J, et al. Measuring quality of life in cancer patients: a concise QL-index for use by physicians. *J Chronic Dis* 1981;34:585–597.
21. Lipowski ZJ. Delirium in the elderly patient. In: Desforges JF, ed. *Medical intelligence, current concepts: geriatrics. N Engl J Med* 1989;320:578–581.
22. Feinstein AR, Josephy BR, Wells CK. Scientific and clinical problems in indexes of functional disability. *Ann Intern Med* 1986;105:413–420.
23. Fretwell MD, Raymond PM, McGarvey S, Owens N, Silliman RA, Mor V. The Senior Care Study: a controlled trial of a consultant/unit based geriatric assessment program in acute care. *J Am Geriatr Soc* 1990;38:1073–1081.
24. Engel GL. The clinical application of the biopsychosocial model. *Am J Psychol* 1980;137:535–544.
25. Rubenstein LZ, Josephson KR, Wieland GD, et al. Effectiveness of a geriatric evaluation unit. A randomized clinical trial. *N Engl J Med* 1984;311:1664–1670.
26. Epstein AM, Hall JA, Besdine R, et al. The emergence of geriatric assessment units. The "new technology of geriatrics." *Ann Intern Med* 1987;106:299–303.
27. Stuck AE, Siu AL, Wieland GD, Adams J, Rubenstein LZ. Comprehensive geriatric assessment: a meta-analysis of controlled trials. *Lancet* 1993;342:1032–1036.
28. *Aging 2000: care integration project.* New York: The Hartford Foundation, 1994.
29. Carlson RW, Devich L, Frank RR. Development of a comprehensive supportive care team for the hopelessly ill on a university hospital medical service. *JAMA* 1988;259:378–383.
30. Deming WE. *Quality, productivity, and competitive position.* Cambridge, MA: Massachusetts Institute of Technology, Center for Advanced Engineering Study, 1982.
31. Berwick, DM. Continuous improvement as an ideal in health care. Sounding Board. *N Engl J Med* 1989;320:53–56.

Quality of Life and Pharmacoeconomics in Clinical Trials, Second Edition, edited by B. Spilker.
Lippincott-Raven Publishers, Philadelphia © 1996.

CHAPTER 86

Measuring Health-Related Quality of Life in Older and Demented Populations

Anita L. Stewart, Cathy D. Sherbourne, and Meryl Brod

INTRODUCTION

Older Adults

As a group, individuals over the age of 65 are extremely heterogeneous with respect to their health and quality of life (QOL), more dissimilar than similar. Whereas most younger populations tend to be very healthy on average, with relatively little variation, older populations often include many who have remained healthy and many whose health has become quite poor. Thus, although increasing age is associated with *average* losses in health, there is substantial variability within older age groups (1). Data on the physical functioning scores of a general population illustrate this phenomenon; although average scores declined across age groups, the variability increased (2). A similar pattern was observed for general health perceptions (2). Thus, many

older adults continue to experience a healthy and functional life. For example, Jette and Branch (3) found that a great majority of older adults in the Framingham Disability Study were able to perform a variety of physical functions without help and without difficulty, even in the age category 75 to 84 years.

This pattern of declining average health but increasing variability is not apparent in some of the more subjective components of health-related quality of life, such as psychological well-being. In the same general population survey, McHorney and colleagues (2) found that average scores on psychological well-being remained approximately the same across age groups, as did the variability. In a longitudinal study of patients being treated for various chronic conditions, psychological well-being improved with age (4). Thus, the extent of the diversity may depend on the domain of quality of life being addressed.

It naturally follows in observing this increased variation among older adults in physical health that at least some of the decline that was once considered inevitable is now considered mutable. Not only can factors such as health behaviors and preventive care impact on subsequent health, but evidence is accumulating that health-related quality of life can improve as well as deteriorate among older adults (5–7). For example, some of the cognitive loss that has been

A. L. Stewart: Department of Social and Behavioral Science, University of California, San Francisco; Institute for Health and Aging, San Francisco, California 94143.
C. D. Sherbourne: RAND Health Sciences Program, Santa Monica, California 90407.
M. Brod: Department of Medicine, Center for Clinical and Aging Services Research, UCSF/Mount Zion Center on Aging, San Francisco, California 94118.

considered part of aging may be due to extrinsic factors such as nutritional or educational differences and thus may be reversible (8).

Another factor that distinguishes older adults from younger ones is the increased complexity of health problems faced by older persons when they are ill (9). Older adults are more likely than younger adults to have comorbid chronic conditions and are more likely to be at risk of having poor outcomes as a result of any one condition and its treatment (9). In addition, the outcomes of care for a particular condition may depend on the nature of other conditions and their treatments.

Dementia

Dementia is a syndrome of losses in cognitive function characterized by memory loss for recent events but eventually affecting other cognitive functions, including language and perception (10,11). As these cognitive functions progressively deteriorate, the ability to perform complex tasks of daily living become increasingly difficult. Persons with dementia may thus have significant impairment in their social, occupational, self-care, cognitive, and communicative abilities (12,13). Some exhibit significant disturbing behaviors, such as aggression, noisiness, abusiveness, and wandering (14). Because of their cognitive dysfunction, persons with dementia have a loss of insight and capacity for self-observation and tend to forget recent experiences and feelings (15,16). Thus, they may be unaware of various symptoms or deny them if queried. The extensive nature of the problems associated with dementia significantly affects these individuals' quality of life, as well as their ability to respond directly to questions about their quality of life.

There are many causes of dementia, but senile dementia of the Alzheimer's type is the most common, accounting for nearly two thirds of dementing conditions. The second most common form of dementia is multiinfarct dementia, but dementia has several other causes, including Parkinson's disease, alcohol abuse, drug toxicity, brain tumors, and depression (10). The prevalence of dementia increases dramatically with age; about one-half of all nursing home residents have some form of cognitive impairment (14,17).

As with aging in general, however, it is important when referring to persons with dementia to distinguish the various stages of dementia. Persons in earlier stages of dementia have more insight and comprehension than those in later stages. Furthermore, there are differences in the areas in which dementia affects individuals (e.g., verbal, spatial), especially in the early stages. Some individuals are able to function independently to some extent, as indicated by findings that some proportion of those who are demented live alone (13). Although the functional decline of persons with dementia is very certain, there is considerable variation, even within stages (18). For example, Winogrond and Fisk (19) observed that even when cognitive functioning declined, some patients continued to exhibit appropriate behavior.

Thus, both the conceptualization of quality of life and the approaches to its measurement depend on the stage and the nature of the dementia, as well as a variety of other factors, such as comorbid illness.

Finally, although persons with dementia may have lost many of their cognitive functions, we agree with Whitehouse and Rabins (20) that intact cognition is not necessary for happiness and that emotional well-being can result from a variety of sources such as relationships, activity, and human touch, all of which are experienced by persons with dementia. Thus, quality of life is an extremely salient concept for persons who may be losing their ability to function as a whole person in society.

Overview

This chapter discusses conceptual issues that should be considered when assessing the quality of life of older persons in general and specific issues that pertain to persons with dementia. We do not focus on issues pertaining to individuals living in institutional settings, but mention them briefly. We then review methodological considerations, including special psychometric issues, data quality, issues pertaining to proxy reports (when to use proxies, the nature of proxy reports), and issues in choosing specific instruments for assessing quality of life in older populations. Numerous measures are available to assess quality of life in older adults, but these are not reviewed here. For persons with dementia, fewer measures are available, and we have attempted to review the special issues of assessment for these persons and refer the reader to measures that we are aware of. We then discuss some practical issues for investigators, including the tolerance of older populations for burden and redundancy, format and design of the questionnaire, and the number of response choices. A few additional issues are noted with respect to persons with dementia.

CONCEPTUALIZATION OF HEALTH-RELATED QOL

Older Adults

Quality of life has been defined in Chapters 2 and 3 (*this volume*). Briefly, quality of life is a broad multidimensional concept that can cover many different aspects of people's lives. Health-related quality of life focuses on those domains that are more closely related to health and that can be improved or harmed by medical interventions. These include domains of physical functioning, ability to perform a broad variety of other activities (including work, housework, community activities), psychological distress and well-being, self-esteem, sense of control, social functioning, pain, fatigue and energy, sleep, family functioning, and sexual functioning (21–25).

Are conceptualizations of quality of life that are appropriate for younger populations appropriate for older persons as well? Most conceptual frameworks of quality of life (or health-related quality of life) probably include all domains that are relevant to older adults. Older adults, just as younger adults, consider these same aspects of quality of life to be relevant and important. However, the relative importance of each domain may differ in older adults compared with the importance that younger persons may attribute to the domains. Furthermore, definitions of the domains may differ slightly for older persons because of their changing roles and living situations. For example, role functioning may need to be defined in terms of roles other than work to be more appropriate. Finally, the precise way in which each domain is defined may vary for older adults, especially those who are less healthy, in order to reflect the increased variability found in older populations. For example, physical functioning may need to be defined in terms of more basic functions such as getting in and out of a chair or climbing a few steps to be appropriate for an older population.

It is important to make a conceptual distinction between physical functioning and self-care and self-maintenance activities when assessing older adults. Many studies and measurement approaches define physical functioning in terms of various physical activities (walking, bending) as well as self-care (dressing, bathing) and self-maintenance (shopping, laundry) activities. Because of the importance of variations in ability to perform self-care activities among frail and demented persons, it is important to define these more precisely than to simply include them as one of several physical activities. There is a need to distinguish physical activities per se from more complex activities, such as shopping, doing errands, and doing laundry, because the ability to perform complex activities is dependent on not only the physical movements involved, but on environmental factors and an individual's cognitive abilities as well. For example, the ability to shop depends on people's physical abilities and on the distance and nature of transportation to the store. Thus, although it is important to know whether people are having difficulty with these activities, this difficulty only partially reflects physical functioning.

In defining limitations in usual activities (e.g., role functioning), one would likely focus less on problems with work and more on problems with a broader variety of daily activities, such as volunteering, social activities, caregiving, and recreational activities. Similarly, although family functioning and sexual functioning remain important areas to include in an overall conceptual framework, the assessment approaches need to take into account the fact that many older adults have lost their spouses and may live alone or in congregate living situations.

When the target population includes persons who are institutionalized, functional status needs to be defined in ways that are more appropriate to the daily life of this setting and take into consideration the fact that this group is the most frail and impaired. Thus, within institutionalized populations, there may be additional refinements needed in defining

some of the domains of quality of life, related to what Brody (26) has called the "iatrogenic diseases of institutional life," factors such as depersonalization, social distance from family and friends, inflexibility of routines and menus, and lack of identity. Others who work in institutional settings focus on quality of life as the assessment of the subjective importance and perceived availability of autonomy (i.e., control over and ability to take part in meaningful activities), security (physical safety and comfort), and interpersonal relations (27). Defining functioning in terms of the ability to shop and do errands or perform household chores is inappropriate, as is conceptualizing physical functioning in terms of the ability to perform heavy or vigorous activities. In addition, the concept of quality of life within an institutionalized setting may need to be broadened to focus on such concepts as privacy or a sense of control.

Persons with Dementia

Are there components of health-related quality of life that are unique to persons with dementia? Or are the frameworks typically used appropriate for demented persons as well? Because of the significant impairments in occupational and self-care abilities, most health assessments of persons with dementia (aside from the assessment of the dementia itself) focus on functional status (ability to care for themselves independently) and symptoms (wandering, agitation) (28). Depression is an important problem among those with dementia, hence is typically included as part of the assessment of their status (29). Sleep disorders have been identified as a particular problem of persons with Alzheimer's disease (14). Few investigators have attempted to assess other more subjective aspects of quality of life such as psychological well-being, self-esteem, sense of control, or overall life satisfaction of those with dementia, presumably because cognitively impaired individuals are less able to articulate these aspects of their lives. Although depression is often assessed, it is usually assessed in terms of whether the person has a depressive disorder rather than in terms of subjective well-being. Thus, it is important to determine whether the conceptual frameworks that are typically used in studies of older adults would apply in those with dementia. Brod and Stewart (30) developed a conceptual framework appropriate for persons with dementia based on the literature as well as focus groups of health care professionals caring for individuals with dementia, caregivers, and persons with early-stage dementia. Although many of the areas of relevance are identical to those in general quality of life frameworks, some additional areas were identified that may be especially relevant to dementia patients, such as a sense of aesthetics (e.g., ability to enjoy nature, being outdoors, and music) and participation in various enjoyable activities. In addition, these investigators found that definitions of some concepts need to be expanded or refined to be appropriate to those with dementia. For example, self-esteem needs to include concepts of embarrassment and self-consciousness as well as feelings of being valued and useful, and psychological well-being concepts need to include feelings of frustration.

METHODOLOGICAL CONSIDERATIONS

As with all survey research, data quality problems vary as a function of the education, cultural background, language, motivation, cognitive status, sensory limitations, ability to communicate, and physical and mental health of respondents. Because older persons on average have more sensory deficits, memory and attention difficulties, and physical limitations, and may be less educated than younger persons, it is more likely that data quality problems will occur in older age groups. However, the important point is that it is not age per se that accounts for data quality problems, but the presence of these other factors.

Data Quality in Studies of Older Adults

Measures of health-related quality of life in older adults should meet standard psychometric criteria of variability, reliability, validity, and sensitivity, which are well described elsewhere (31–36). However, there are some special considerations when working with older adults and cognitively impaired persons. Instead of relying on prior evidence of the psychometric adequacy of measures, in studies of older adults it is important to re-evaluate the psychometric features of the measures in the population being studied to assure their adequacy for that particular population.

Reliability

Reliability is the extent to which scores are free of random error, that is, are reproducible, repeatable, and consistent. Internal-consistency reliability tends to diminish with age, although often not by much (37). For example, Sherbourne and Meredith (37) reported the internal-consistency reliability for a variety of Medical Outcomes Study (MOS) measures for several age groups and found few differences; in the cases in which the older groups had poorer reliability, it was still >0.70. However, it should be noted that the MOS panel was selected, in part, based on the completeness of patient data up to that point; thus, these reliability results may be somewhat inflated relative to other patient samples. Greater attention to reliability of measurement in older adult studies is needed. Virtually nothing is known about the reliability of different kinds of measures in cognitively impaired persons when data are collected directly from them by self-report. Some studies suggest that proxy ratings of observable behaviors (e.g., wandering, agitation, incontinence, and memory loss) can be collected reliably. For example, the Functional Dementia Scale, which quantifies the severity of disabilities in the areas of activities of daily living, orientation, and affect has been shown to have high

levels of internal-consistency reliability (>0.83) with more moderate agreement between raters (ranging from 48% to 75% on the 20 items) (38). Similarly, a behaviorally based rating scale developed by Loewenstein et al. (28) found high interrater reliability (>0.93) for scales designed to measure time orientation, communication skills, financial skills, identification of road signs, shopping, eating, and dressing subskills in persons with dementia. When using performance-based measures of various functional abilities, Mahurin et al. (12) found test–retest reliabilities of 0.81 for the total score.

Validity

Validity refers to the extent to which a measure or instrument actually assesses what it is intended to assess. Establishing the validity of a measure is an ongoing process, one that involves the acquisition of evidence about the meaning and interpretation of the measure from a variety of studies and settings. The validation of any measure for one purpose does not support its validity for another purpose or necessarily its use in other populations or settings. Thus, measures that have been considered valid when used in younger populations should be validated again in older populations.

One validity issue that may be especially relevant in quality of life studies of older adults is that of socially desirable or "rosy" response bias (39). These are tendencies of respondents to provide responses either to appear favorably (e.g., active, functional, nondepressed) or well-satisfied even if they are not. The latter is more likely to occur when questions are asked in general ways (e.g., overall life satisfaction) as opposed to being more specific (e.g., satisfaction with level of energy). Thus, care should be taken to develop instruments for older adults that minimize the possibility of socially desirable responding. One method is to vary the direction of item wording so that high scores do not always have the same meaning (e.g., use balanced scales).

Sensitivity to Change

When quality of life measures are to be used to monitor change over time, it is essential to know whether the measure selected is responsive to clinically important changes (40–42). The responsiveness (or sensitivity) of measures to change may be especially important in studies of older populations because of the tendency to use short-form or single-item measures to reduce respondent burden. These short-form measures may have less precision to detect change. In one study of older adults, restricted activity days measures were somewhat more responsive to known changes in health than were measures of physical functioning, self-rated health, or positive affect, although each of the measures was sensitive in certain tests (43). In a study of older persons entering a residential care facility, Siu et al. (44) found that the physical functioning scale from the MOS 20-item short-form survey was more sensitive to decrements in physical performance (performance-based tests of gait, balance, 50 foot walk) than the COOP physical function chart, the Katz Activities of Daily Living Scale, and the Lawton–Brody Instrumental Activities of Daily Living Scale. None of the measures was sensitive to improvement in performance-based physical function.

Other General Data Quality Issues

Although data quality problems may be more likely to occur in older age groups, it is important to understand the *magnitude* of the problems—i.e., whether they are of sufficient magnitude to seriously affect one's ability to use the data. Using data from a personal interview, Colsher and Wallace (45) evaluated the percent of ''don't know'' responses, inconsistent responses, and item refusals in a sample of 3,097 persons aged 65 and older (mean age = 78 years). Results suggested that the effects of age are complex and that data quality depended on multiple factors including physical health and functioning, cognitive problems, affective status, and item content. For example, inconsistent responses were predicted by depressive symptoms, memory problems, mental status, and physical functioning, but not by age (45). Even in cases in which there was a relationship between data quality and age, the magnitude of the problem was not serious. For example, the range of ''don't know'' responses in the oldest age group studied (85+ years) was 0.4% to 5.9% at baseline (median of four types of health concepts studied) and ranged from 0.1% to 2.1% at follow-up.

Missing data, however, are strongly correlated with older age and reduced health (43,46). McHorney et al. (47) found that missing data occurred more frequently among those who were older, minorities, and those who were socioeconomically disadvantaged. The extent of missing data, even in older age groups, varies by health measure (37,46), suggesting that some missing data may be due to the difficult nature or inappropriate context of certain questions. Thus, missing data can serve as a clue that the measures may need to be modified to be clearer and less ambiguous to older respondents or to reflect more accurately their life condition (e.g., living alone with no sexual partner). However, because of the increased prevalence of missing data in older and sicker populations, studies of older adults need to develop appropriate methods for handling the missing data to maintain the internal and external validity of study findings. Some of the options for estimating missing data include use of the sample mean, use of the person mean, regression estimates based on other available data, and other imputation methods (48,49).

Methods of Instrument Administration

Several methods of administration are available—self-administration, self-report using a personal or telephone interview, proxy report, subjective ratings by trained observers (including clinicians), and performance-based testing. Performance-based assessments are those in which individuals actually perform specific physical, self-care, or cognitive tasks (e.g., walk a certain distance, put on a shirt, count backward from some number) and are assigned scores by trained observers according to a standardized scoring scheme. Selection of an appropriate method of administration that will provide data of the highest quality for the particular population being studied requires an understanding of the advantages and comparability of each.

Each of the different methods of data collection has advantages for different populations. Self-administration is the least expensive and offers respondents the most privacy. However, it can be problematic for those with vision, reading, language, or cognitive problems as evidenced by the increased missing data when self-administration is used (2,50). Thus, use of self-administration may require extensive follow-up of missing and inconsistent responses. Personal and telephone interviews may be a viable alternative. Although they are more time-consuming than self-administration, both in terms of staff and respondent burden, the savings of time needed to follow up on missing data and nonreturned self-administered forms may somewhat offset these costs. Although hearing impairments are prevalent in the elderly, only 5% of persons over age 65 reported having difficulty using a telephone (51). However, telephone interviews may be more stressful for those with hearing problems (52) and may take longer and thus be more taxing. When personal interviews are used, the use of response cards with response choices written out have proven helpful (53).

For measures of physical functioning, cognitive functioning, and self-care and self-maintenance activities, performance-based measures allow assessment of those who are moderately or severely cognitively impaired as well as those who have other problems (e.g., vision, hearing) precluding self-report. Advantages of performance-based assessments are that they can be used to test persons with language or communication problems and they are less influenced by culture and education than self-report measures (54). Disadvantages include their cost and time, the need for special equipment, special training of examiners, and the fact that they tend to assess individuals outside their own familiar environment which may result in atypical scores (55,56).

One approach that is used in many studies is to use mixed modes of data collection, combining the advantages of different modes to obtain the highest response rate and the best data quality (57). Using mixed-mode approaches requires an understanding of the equivalence of the various methods of data collection (e.g., interview vs. self-administration) in terms of reported data (57). The optimal mixed mode is one that combines telephone and face-to-face interviews because of the general demonstrated equivalence of these two methods (58). Another option is to begin with self-administration and provide help for those who have difficulty with this response mode. For example, McHorney et al. (2) found that a mailed questionnaire followed by telephone interview yielded the best overall response rate in a general population, although they did not specifically report these findings for older adults. Less is known about the equivalence of self-administration and personal interview (59), although they were equivalent in a needs assessment study (50). There is some evidence that self-administration is associated with poorer ratings of health status and greater reports of chronic conditions, suggesting that self-administration may yield more accurate (less socially desirable) information than face-to-face administration (2). The equivalence of different methods may vary depending on the content of the questions (60).

In studies of dementia patients, especially when focusing on more affective dimensions of quality of life, the use of *multiple modes* of data collection may be useful, in order to converge on a valid score for a demented person (14). For example, Teresi et al. (14) suggest that one could obtain data on emotional well-being from a nurse, from direct observation, and from the demented person directly (in the case of mild or moderate dementia).

Proxies vs. Self-Report

When to Use Proxies

For dementia patients and for older persons with functional disabilities, proxies must often be used to obtain reliable and valid data. However, it is important to determine at what point a proxy report is essential to obtain adequate data quality.

Can self-report ever be used for persons with dementia? It is widely assumed that self-reports are not valid in patients with dementia. Although proxy reports may be necessary for those in advanced stages of dementia, it is probable that those in early and possibly middle stages could answer a limited set of questions for themselves. For example, although individuals with severe dementia self-reported few memory problems, those with mild and moderate dementia reported memory complaints corresponding to the severity of the dementia (61). In developing a caregiver-rated quality of life instrument, DeJong et al. (62) interviewed caregivers but reported that the dementia patients themselves often contributed their perceptions during the interviews. Others have also shown that early-stage dementia patients can participate in support groups, report feelings, and express concerns regarding their disease (63–65). Additionally, an early-stage dementia patient has written of her experiences with the disease (66). Studies are badly needed to determine the extent to which self-reports can be accurately obtained directly from persons at different stages of dementia.

The challenge in determining how persons with dementia are feeling is perhaps to first learn how to find ways to enable them to express their feelings. As noted by Rodin (67), "discovering the person within the dementia is compa-rable to learning the language and patterns of a foreign culture." For example, some demented persons can read but do not comprehend (68). It is possible that by better understanding ways in which persons with dementia communicate, assessments can be tailored to these ways.

The Nature of Proxy Reports

Several factors affect the ability of proxies to provide accurate reports, including the relationship of the proxy to the person being evaluated, the nature of the questions (objective vs. subjective), the affective status of the proxy, and the cognitive and affective status of the person being evaluated (15,69). Despite this, the nature of the bias when using proxies appears to be reasonably consistent across studies. In one study, proxies overestimated patient disability in the area of instrumental activities relative to patients but were somewhat similar to the patients in ratings of self-care activities (69). Agreement was greater when proxies lived with the patient. Rubenstein and colleagues (70) found that ratings of functioning in instrumental activities of daily living by patients, nurses, and family members differed; patients rated their functioning the best and family members rated their functioning the worst. In another study, ratings of several functional tasks were made by patients, family members, and physicians. Compared with performance-based measures of function, patients were more accurate in rating their own level of functioning than were family members or physicians (71). Results of all these studies suggest that some bias is undoubtedly introduced by using proxy responses, and the magnitude and nature of the bias depends on a variety of factors.

Kiyak et al. (15) found that the discrepancies between self-report and reports by a family member were large for those with Alzheimer's disease but not different for a normal comparison group on measures of activities of daily living and instrumental activities of daily living. Patients with Alzheimer's disease reported consistently higher scores (more functional) on all measures than did their family member. The investigators interpreted this as either a lack of insight among demented patients, or that caregivers are overestimating limitations due to the burden they themselves are experiencing. This is an important distinction to evaluate. However, the Alzheimer's patients did report declines in functioning over time, suggesting that they were aware of some decline. Winogrond and Fisk (19) note that families may exaggerate a patient's dysfunction because they are comparing the person to his or her previously high level of functioning.

Most of the studies cited above focus on the ability of proxies to rate somewhat objective facets of the person's life such as their functioning or behavior. Less is known about the ability of proxies to rate more subjective information such as feelings of well-being and depression, although more subjective questions are harder for proxies to report accurately than more objective ones (54). Teri and Truax (29) found that caregivers were able to rate the depression of dementia patients accurately, even when they were depressed themselves. Teri and Wagner (72) tested the concordance of three sources of information on depression, based on the Hamilton Rating Scale for Depression. They found that caregivers and clinicians both viewed patients as more depressed than patients viewed themselves. In another study, proxies reported lower emotional health and satisfaction on the part of older subjects than did the older subjects themselves, but reported similar levels of overall health, functional status (body care and movement, mobility, ambulation, home management), and social activity (73). However, the nature of the discrepancies varied depending on the overall health of the subjects and on the amount of time the proxy spent each week helping the subject. Those proxies who spent more time with the respondent per week tended to rate the subject's functioning as poorer than the subject did.

ISSUES IN CHOOSING SPECIFIC INSTRUMENTS AND APPROACHES FOR ASSESSING QUALITY OF LIFE

Older Populations

The most important concern when selecting instruments relevant to older adults is the nature of the population being studied and the possible variation in that population. Studies of frail older adults will face less sample heterogeneity than studies of older adults with hypertension, many of whom are functioning well. The more heterogeneous the sample, the more difficult it is to select a single instrument that will take into account the full range of functioning likely to be exhibited by the sample.

Potential floor or ceiling effects are the greatest problem to be dealt with in selecting measures that are appropriate. For example, if a large proportion of the sample has the lowest possible score on a particular measure or scores near the lower end of the scale, further change in that direction cannot be detected. This problem can be minimized by selecting measures appropriate to the specific population under study and by pilot testing potential measures in a sample similar to the one to be included. For example, measures of ability to perform self-care and self-maintenance activities (e.g., bathe, cook, shop) in a relatively active nonfrail older population would tend to have ceiling effects (most would receive the best possible score). Similarly, if measures developed for use in healthier populations are applied in a frail population, many individuals will likely score at the worst possible end of the scale, decreasing one's ability to detect meaningful differences among individuals. Floor and ceiling effects vary depending on the particular measure. For example, floor effects were most pronounced in a measure of role limitations due to physical health than in a measure of physical functioning in older age groups (74).

Several key multidimensional instruments are available that are appropriate for use in older populations, each providing a set of multi-item measures of a variety of quality of life domains. Many of these are reviewed in Section III (*this volume*). However, other multidimensional measures not addressed in section III of this book that would be useful in older adult populations include the MOS Functioning and Well-Being Profile (75), the Functional Status Questionnaire (76), the Duke UNC Health Profile (77), the Older Americans Resources and Services (OARS) Multidimensional Functional Assessment Questionnaire (MFAQ) (78), the Multilevel Assessment Instrument (79), and the Rand Health Insurance Experiment measures (80). Multidimensional overall quality of life indexes designed for older adults are also available such as the Life Satisfaction Index (81), and the Philadelphia Geriatric Center Morale Scale (82,83).

Reviews of many of these comprehensive profiles and of single measures that focus on older adults are available. The most inclusive is that of Kane and Kane (84), but others are available as well (85–88). Other reviews are also available that do not specifically focus on older adults, but that review measures appropriate for older adults, including one by McDowell and Newell (89), as well as by Wilkin et al. (90). For example, McDowell and Newell review various measures of activities of daily living and instrumental activities of daily living.

Because many depressive symptoms scales include a number of somatic items (appetite loss, sleep problems), there is concern that use of these scales to measure depressive symptoms in older adults (who have more of these somatic symptoms) may be less valid (91). Thus, the use of measures that do not contain the somatic symptoms may be more appropriate for older adults. For example, the Geriatric Depression Scale (GDS) (92) was developed to be applicable to those with physical health problems by not including somatic items, and was designed to provide a simple yes/no format to be easy for older persons to complete.

When selecting standard instruments that contain a profile of health-related quality of life measures such as the Sickness Impact Profile, the SF-36, or the Functional Status Index that have been developed for chronically ill persons in general, it is possible to select out those subscales that are not appropriate for certain older populations. For example, Krenz et al. (93) omitted the work subscale from the SIP when administering the SIP to patients referred for possible dementia. However, there are probably only a few settings in which this decision might be appropriate since many older adults continue to work well into their seventh decade.

Demented Populations

Although demented patients may be able to respond directly for themselves in early stages, they will eventually lose this ability as their disease progresses. If self-report by the patients themselves is not to be used, the choice must be made as to whether to use proxy reports of the patient's status or to conduct direct performance-based tests. If a study is intended to last over a period of time in which progression of the dementia is likely to occur, it is important to begin these proxy or performance-based assessments at the outset to be able to monitor change over time using the same method. Furthermore, because the validity of the proxy report varies depending on who the proxy is, it would be helpful to use the same proxy over time.

General profiles of health-related quality of life developed for general populations or those with chronic illness (described above) may be appropriate for application in demented populations if they are completed by proxies, although these measures may miss some important concepts and may not focus on the particular aspects of functioning that are of special relevance. For example, the Sickness Impact Profile was administered by trained interviewers to a sample of patients with Alzheimer's-type dementia and to their family members regarding the patients (93). These investigators concluded that it was valid when completed by family members (proxies) for the subjects (93) but not when subjects were directly assessed.

There are some instruments designed specifically to assess general functioning in demented populations. These were designed to account for the special problems in functioning that demented patients face. Some are designed to be completed by caregivers such as an instrument by DeJong et al. (62) that assesses mobility, self-care, participation in household and leisure activities, and social functioning. A performance-based measure is available that assesses various functional capacities of dementia patients such as their telephone skills, ability to prepare a letter to mail, taking a telephone message, identifying and counting currency, shopping skills, and dressing and grooming skills (28). This measure has good interrater and test–retest reliability as well as convergent and discriminant validity. Another performance-based instrument has been developed by Mahurin et al. (12), the Structured Assessment of Independent Living Skills (SAILS). This instrument assesses motor skills, eating, dressing, expressive language, receptive language, time and orientation, money-related skills, instrumental activities, and social interaction. The subscales all discriminated between dementia patients and normal controls and some evidence of the reliability of the total score was presented. There is an excellent review of measures and measurement issues pertaining to dementia patients in institutional settings by Teresi and colleagues (14).

We know of no multidimensional instruments that tap a broad range of domains of quality of life, including subjective components, in dementia patients. Brink (94) found that the Geriatric Depression Scale was valid for dementia patients with mild or moderate dementia, but not for those with severe dementia. However, Burke et al. (95) found that the Geriatric Depression Scale was not valid when applied to a sample of patients with mild dementia of the Alzheimer's type. A measure of participation in activities that are enjoyable, the Pleasant Events Schedule, was designed for use in assisting those caring for demented persons in planning activities (96). Although not developed as a quality of life instrument, it could be adapted for use in evaluating extent of participation in enjoyed activities.

PRACTICAL ISSUES AND POINTERS FOR THE INVESTIGATOR

Older Populations

Although methods used in younger populations may apply as well in older populations, modifications may need to be made if the older population being studied is more frail. Four of these modifications are discussed below.

Tolerance for Length/Burden

There appears to be variation in the extent to which older subjects consider completion of interviews and surveys as burdensome. Some investigators have found that many older adults enjoy interviews and even wish to prolong the interview (57), although this may not apply to self-administered questionnaires. However, respondent burden may be a considerable problem for the oldest-old and those with multiple health problems. Because many older adults are not accustomed to elaborate paper and pencil tests, a long self-administered survey may seem tedious. If questionnaires must be long, respondents should be encouraged to complete them a little at a time (e.g., early and late in the day). Similarly, telephone interviews can be conducted in more than one phase (39), although this is likely to result in increased rates of noncompletion of the second part (57). No more than 1 or 2 weeks should elapse between the two evaluations. Use of pretesting in the population being studied can help determine the acceptable burden.

Tolerance for Redundancy

Most commonly used measures of health utilize multi-item Likert scales (because of their many advantages in terms of reliability, validity, sensitivity, ability to derive scores for persons with missing data, and tendency to minimize acquiescent response bias). One problem with such scales is that they tend to ask a series of similar questions. Anecdotally, older individuals seem to be less tolerant of being asked a series of similar items, a belief confirmed by Wallace et al. (97), who report that redundant questions are considered demeaning and irritating by older adults. They suggest that efforts be made to develop abbreviated forms of some of the more commonly used scales. They further note that high internal consistency of multi-item scales is to an extent due to consistency bias—a tendency to respond to similar items in consistent ways, regardless of actual content, suggesting that many scales could be shortened without compromising their validity.

Format and Design of Self-Administered Questionnaires

The formatting of the questions and the questionnaires both need to take into account the special needs of less advantaged segments of the older adult population. Guidelines for formatting are available (98,99). Guidelines generally recommend simplicity of presentation, i.e., keeping questions short, using simple familiar words, avoiding compound sentences, and avoiding double negatives (98). To the extent that recognition memory can be used rather than recall memory, data quality will be improved. For example, rather than ask respondents to write in the number of days or recall precise events, it is preferable to provide a set of predetermined categories and require only that the respondent select the most appropriate category. In designing response choices, it is important to be aware that the options provide a context which in part determines the responses elicited from participants in the study (100,101).

Questionnaires need to be readable by those who have vision problems. Allowing sufficient space on the page helps prevent confusion due to crowding of questions, reducing the chance that questions will be missed. Selection of background colors that are light so that the highest possible contrast is obtained facilitates this, as does use of a large print size (font size 14 is preferred by many older adults). For interviews and surveys of older adults who may have numerous health problems to report, it is helpful to organize the questions to enable respondents to respond positively at the end (98).

Number of Response Choices

The optimal number of response choices is an issue in general research methodology, but is more controversial in studies of older adults. Some believe that in very old subgroups, dichotomous response choices are best. Hence the popularity of the Geriatric Depression Scale, which consists of statements to which respondents answer yes or no (92). However, others have found that dichotomous items were disliked by most respondents because the restriction to two choices makes it difficult to adequately respond (39).

In one study of older respondents' preferences for different formats, 5-point scales were best liked and had the best distributions (39). There is evidence that for many domains, the reliability of measurement plateaus around five response options (102). Some have found that responses to 5-point items closely approximate more continuous response data (103,104). However, in a study of different types of response formats for evaluative items in a sample of older adults, items with 10 response choices tended to yield the best data quality whereas items with only four response choices yielded the worst (105).

Persons with Dementia

Although the field has not advanced to the point that it is clear at what stage a patient with dementia can answer for themselves regarding their quality of life, it is clear that it is a possibility for at least some patients. Thus, we encourage the use of existing measures in these patients, taking into account the issues discussed above.

Because patients with dementia have a shortened attention span, and because they may tire easily and be susceptible to anxiety during assessments (19), direct assessments may need to be truncated (e.g., 10 to 15 minutes at most). We recommend that face-to-face interviews be used exclusively, to facilitate their motivation to complete the interview. If self-administration is used, patients may forget the instructions or get stuck and may need to be remotivated to complete the survey. The use of questions that are short and clear and that use very simple response scales may be necessary, such as yes–no scales. If more complex scales are needed, response trees can be used in which further discrimination is made after each yes-no response. For example, if the person answers "yes" to feeling happy, one can then ask if they feel a little bit happy or very happy. The use of visual cues might facilitate their response, although this remains to be tested. That is, if the person finds it difficult to answer questions, they might be able to point to the appropriate response on a chart. It is possible that the COOP charts with their added pictures might be helpful (106,107). Similarly, the faces scale published by Andrews and Withey (108) to assess overall life satisfaction includes a series of simple faces with different expressions.

The use of recognition rather than recall memory may facilitate assessment. That is, providing patients with a few response choices from which to choose rather than asking them to recall an answer should yield better quality data. Questions that contain a time frame may need to be modified to a very short time frame. Because patients lose their memory for the recent past, questions framed in the present or distant past may be more accurately answered. Thus, instead of asking how they felt over the past several weeks, one might ask how they are feeling today or recently. Patients may need to be tested in rooms and settings in which they feel comfortable and safe, to minimize problems from occurring (19). However, it is recommended that they be interviewed in privacy without their family members present to minimize bias.

FUTURE RESEARCH

Because of the considerable measurement error and bias that appears to be introduced by the use of proxies, additional research is needed for a better understanding of the nature of the error (69). Pragmatically, Magaziner et al. (69) note that because of the necessity to use proxy reports in many trials, they should continue to be used, but their use should be reported and evaluated.

Because of the limited research that directly assesses health-related quality of life in demented patients (most studies use proxy ratings), efforts are needed to determine the extent to which early and perhaps middle stage dementia patients can directly provide information regarding their own health-related quality of life. Thus, it is a question for future research to determine under what conditions and stage of dementia patients are capable of providing reliable and valid information about their health and quality of life. In addition, efforts are needed to improve assessment methods for persons with communication difficulties, so that we can find potential ways for them to express how they feel.

As existing measures of quality of life are used in studies of older persons and those with dementia, it is imperative that their reliability and validity be assessed and reported, to facilitate the continued refinement of those instruments with poor psychometric characteristics and encourage continued use of those that perform well. We recommend that quality of life studies in older patients routinely incorporate at least some methodological analyses, so that progress can be made toward this goal. If every study or clinical trial included one basic methodological question (validity test of a particular measure in relation to another measure or to clinical status), considerable advances could be made in our knowledge of the adequacy of measures in these special populations.

Although many promising measures of health-related quality of life have been published, there continues to be a need for comprehensive conceptual frameworks that appropriately tap domains of relevance to persons with dementia. The focus has been on functional aspects of their lives, thus, there is a need to expand the conceptualization and measurement into the more subjective aspects of their lives. These instruments need to address the issues of those in early stages of dementia. Because of the communication and cognitive deficits of this population, these approaches will require innovative methods for determining how these individuals feel.

CONCLUSIONS

To conclude, we believe that quality of life assessment in older populations should be approached in much the same way that it is in younger populations, with appropriate attention to the issues raised above. Further, studies of the health and quality of life of older persons have been underway for decades, thus there is a wealth of information and history to draw on. Studies of the quality of life of dementia patients, on the other hand, are rare, and emphasize behavioral domains rather than subjective well-being. Thus, efforts to determine how to assess these other important domains in persons with dementia are a priority. As more studies of the quality of life of all older persons are conducted, we hope that results of such studies will lead to improvements in quality of life outcomes for older persons in a variety of settings.

ACKNOWLEDGMENTS

Segments of this chapter have been published elsewhere (22,109). The authors gratefully acknowledge the helpful comments of Susan Kay Lang, MBA, OTR.

REFERENCES

1. Rowe JW, Kahn RL. Human aging: usual and successful. *Science* 1987;237:143–149.
2. McHorney CA, Kosinski M, Ware JE. Comparisons of the costs and quality of norms for the SF-36 health survey collected by mail versus telephone interview: results from a national survey. *Med Care* 1994;32:551–567.
3. Jette AM, Branch LG. The Framingham Disability Study. II. Physical disability among the aging. *Am J Public Health* 1981;71:1211–1216.
4. Cassileth BR, Lusk EJ, Strouse TB, et al. Psychosocial status in chronic illness: a comparative analysis of six diagnostic groups. *N Engl J Med* 1984;311:506–511.
5. Schaie KW, Willis SL. Can decline in adult intellectual functioning be reversed? *Dev Psychol* 1986;22:223–232.
6. Manton KG. A longitudinal study of functional change and mortality in the United States. *J Gerontol Soc Sci* 1988;43:S153–S161.
7. Kaplan GA, Strawbridge WJ, Camacho T, et al. Factors associated with change in physical functioning in the elderly: a six-year prospective study. *J Aging Health* 1993;5:140–153.
8. Schaie KW. The course of adult intellectual development. *Am Psychol* 1994;49:304–313.
9. Fried LP, Wallace RB. The complexity of chronic illness in the elderly: from clinic to community. In: Wallace RB, Woolson RF, eds. *The epidemiologic study of the elderly.* New York: Oxford University Press, 1992:10.
10. Larson EB, Kukull WA, Katzman RL. Cognitive impairment: dementia and Alzheimer's disease. *Annu Rev Public Health* 1992;13:431–439.
11. Whitehouse PJ. Dementia: the medical perspective. In: Binstock RH, Post SG, Whitehouse PJ, eds. *Dementia and aging.* Baltimore: Johns Hopkins University Press, 1992:21.
12. Mahurin RK, DeBettignies BH, Pirozzolo FJ. Structured assessment of independent living skills: preliminary report of performance measures of functional abilities in dementia. *J Gerontol Psychol Sci* 1991;46:P58–P66.
13. Webber PA, Fox P, Burnette D. Living alone with Alzheimer's disease: effects on health and social service utilization patterns. *Gerontologist* 1994;34:8–14.
14. Teresi J, Lawton P, Ory M, et al. Measurement issues in chronic care populations: dementia special care. *Alzheimer Dis Assoc Disord* 1994;8(Suppl):S144–S183.
15. Kiyak HA, Teri L, Borson S. Physical and functional health assessment in normal aging and in Alzheimer's disease: self-reports vs family reports. *Gerontologist* 1994;34:324–330.
16. Anderson SW, Tranel D. Awareness of disease states following cerebral infarction, dementia, and head trauma: standardized assessment. *Clin Neuropsychol* 1989;3:327–339.
17. National Institute on Aging. *Progress report on Alzheimer's disease 1992.* NIH Publication No. 92-3409.
18. Teri L, Hughes JP, Larson EB. Cognitive deterioration in Alzheimer's disease: behavioral and health factors. *J Gerontol Psychol Sci* 1990;45:P58–P63.

19. Winogrond IR, Fisk AA. Alzheimer's disease: assessment of functional status. *J Am Gerontol Soc* 1983;31:780–785.
20. Whitehouse PJ, Rabins PV. Quality of life and dementia. *Alzheimer Dis Assoc Disord* 1992;6:135–137.
21. Aaronson NK, Bullinger M, Ahmedgar S. A modular approach to quality of life assessment in cancer clinical trials. *Recent Results Cancer Res* 1988;111:231–249.
22. Stewart AL, King AC. Conceptualizing and measuring quality of life in older populations. In: Abeles RP, Gift HC, Ory MG, eds. *Aging and quality of life.* New York: Springer, 1994:27.
23. Stewart AL. A framework of health concepts. In: Stewart AL, Ware JE Jr, eds. *Measuring functioning and well-being: the Medical Outcomes Study approach.* Durham, NC: Duke University Press, 1992:12.
24. Ware JE Jr, Sherbourne CD. The MOS 36-Item Short-Form Health Survey (SF-36). I. Conceptual Framework and Item Selection. *Med Care* 1992;30:473–483.
25. Bergner M. Measurement of health status. *Med Care* 1985;23:696–704.
26. Brody E. A million procrustean beds. *Gerontologist* 1973;13:430–435.
27. Lind D. *Quality of life assessment: a profile of resident satisfaction.* Washington, DC: American Association of Homes for the Aging, 1980.
28. Loewenstein DA, Amigo E, Duara R, et al. A new scale for the assessment of functional status in Alzheimer's disease and related disorders. *J Gerontol Psychol Sci* 1989;44:P114–121.
29. Teri L, Truax P. Assessment of depression in dementia patients: association of caregiver mood with dementia ratings. *Gerontologist* 1994;34:231–234.
30. Brod M, Stewart AL. Quality of life of persons with dementia: a theoretical framework. *Gerontologist* 1994;34:47.
31. Nunnally JC. *Psychometric theory.* 2nd ed. New York: McGraw-Hill, 1978.
32. Stewart AL, Hays RD, Ware JE Jr. Methods of validating health measures. In: Stewart AL, Ware JE Jr, eds. *Measuring functioning and well-being: the Medical Outcomes Study approach.* Durham, NC: Duke University Press, 1992:309.
33. Stewart AL, Hays RD, Ware JE Jr. Methods of constructing health measures. In: Stewart AL, Ware JE Jr, eds. *Measuring functioning and well-being: the Medical Outcomes Study approach.* Durham, NC: Duke University Press, 1992:67.
34. Edwards AL. *Techniques of attitude scale construction.* New York: Appleton-Century-Crofts, 1957.
35. DeVellis RF. *Scale development.* Vol. 26. Newbury Park: Sage, 1991.
36. Ware JE. Standards for validating health measures: definition and content. *J Chronic Dis* 1987;40:473–480.
37. Sherbourne CD, Meredith LS. Quality of self-report data: a comparison of older and younger chronically ill patients. *J Gerontol* 1992;47:S204–211.
38. Moore JT, Bobula JA, Short TB, et al. A functional dementia scale. *J Fam Pract* 1983;16:499–503.
39. Carp FM. Maximizing data quality in community studies of older people. In: Lawton MP, Herzog AR, eds. *Special research methods for gerontology.* Amityville, NY: Baywood, 1989:93.
40. Guyatt GH, Deyo RA, Charlson M, et al. Responsiveness and validity in health status measurement: a clarification. *J Clin Epidemiol* 1989;42:403–408.
41. Deyo RA, Diehr P, Patrick DL. Reproducibility and responsiveness of health status measures. *Controlled Clin Trials* 1991;12(Suppl):142S–158S.
42. Tugwell P, Bombardier C, Bell M, et al. Current quality-of-life research challenges in arthritis relevant to the issue of clinical significance. *Controlled Clin Trials* 1991;12:217S–225S.
43. Wagner EH, LaCroix AZ, Grothaus LC, et al. Responsiveness of health status measures to change among older adults. *J Am Gerontol Soc* 1993;41:241–248.
44. Siu AL, Ouslander JG, Osterweil D, et al. Change in self-reported functioning in older persons entering a residential care facility. *J Clin Epidemiol* 1993;46:1093–1102.
45. Colsher PL, Wallace RB. Data quality and age: health and psychobehavioral correlates of item nonresponse and inconsistent responses. *J Gerontol* 1989;44:P45–52.
46. Scholes D, LaCroix AZ, Wagner EH, et al. Tracking progress towards national health objectives in the elderly: what do restricted activity days signify? *Am J Public Health* 1991;81:485–488.
47. McHorney CA, Ware JE, Lu R, et al. The MOS 36-item Short-Form Health Survey (SF-36): III. Tests of data quality, scaling assumptions, and reliability across diverse patient groups. *Med Care* 1994;32:40–66.
48. Little RJA, Rubin DB. *Statistical analysis with missing data.* New York: Wiley, 1987.
49. Raymond MR. Missing data in evaluation research. *Eval Health Profs* 1986;9:395–420.
50. Leinbach RM. Alternatives to the face-to-face interview for collecting gerontological needs assessment data. *Gerontologist* 1982;22:78–82.
51. Dawson D, Hendershot G, Fulton J. NCHS Advance Data, Vital and Health Statistics of the NCHS, No. 133, June 10.
52. Herzog AR, Rodgers WL, Kulka RA. Interviewing older adults: a comparison of telephone and face-to-face modalities. *Public Opin Q* 1983;47:405–418.
53. Kutner NG, Ory MG, Baker DI, et al. Measuring the quality of life of the elderly in health promotion intervention clinical trials. *Public Health Rep* 1992;107:530–539.
54. Zimmerman SI, Magaziner J. Methodological issues in measuring the functional status of cognitively impaired nursing home residents: the use of proxies and performance-based measures. *Alzheimer Dis Assoc Disord* 1994;8(suppl):S281–290.
55. Guralnik JM, Branch LG, Cummings SR, et al. Physical performance measures in aging research. *J Gerontol* 1989;44:M141–146.
56. Guralnik JM, LaCroix AZ. Assessing physical function in older populations. In: Wallace RB, Woolson RF, eds. *The epidemiologic study of the elderly.* New York: Oxford University Press, 1992:159.
57. Rodgers WL, Herzog AR. Collecting data about the oldest old: problems and procedures. In: Suzman RM, Willis DP, Manton KG, eds. *The oldest old.* New York: Oxford University Press, 1992:135.
58. Herzog AR, Rodgers WL. Interviewing older adults: mode comparison using data from a face-to-face survey and a telephone resurvey. *Public Opin Q* 1988;52:84–99.
59. Herzog AR, Kulka RA. Telephone and mail surveys with older populations: a methodological overview. In: Lawton MP, Herzog AR, eds. *Special research methods for gerontology.* Amityville, NY: Baywood, 1989:63.
60. Rodgers WL, Herzog AR. Interviewing older adults: the accuracy of factual information. *J Gerontol* 1987;42:387–394.
61. Grut M, Jorm AF, Fratiglioni L, et al. Memory complaints of elderly people in a population survey: variation according to dementia stage and depression. *J Am Gerontol Soc* 1993;41:1295–1300.
62. DeJong R, Osterlund OW, Roy GW. Measurement of quality-of-life changes in patients with Alzheimer's disease. *Clin Ther* 1989;11:545–554.
63. David P. Effectiveness of group work with the cognitively impaired older adult. *Am J Alzheimers Care Relat Disord Res* 1991:10–16.
64. Yale R. *A guide to facilitating support groups for newly diagnosed Alzheimer's patients.* Palo Alto, CA: Alzheimer's Association, Greater San Francisco Bay Area, 1991.
65. Foley JM. The experience of being demented. In: Binstock RH, Post SG, Whitehouse PJ, eds. *Dementia and aging.* Baltimore: Johns Hopkins University Press, 1992:30.
66. McGowin DF. *Living in the labyrinth: a personal journey through the maze of Alzheimer's.* San Francisco: Elder Books, 1993.
67. Rodin MB. An anthropology of dementia. *Center Aging* 1993;9:1–2.
68. Sloane PD, Mathew LJ. An assessment and care planning strategy for nursing home residents with dementia. *Gerontologist* 1991;31:128–131.
69. Magaziner J, Simonsick EM, Kashner TM, et al. Patient–proxy response comparability on measures of patient health and functional status. *J Clin Epidemiol* 1988;41:1065–1074.
70. Rubenstein LZ, Schairer C, Wieland GD, et al. Systematic biases in functional status assessment of elderly adults: effects of different data sources. *J Gerontol* 1984;39:686–691.
71. Elam JT, Beaver T, El Derwi D, et al. Comparison of sources of functional report with observed functional ability of frail older persons. *Gerontologist* 1989;29(suppl):308A.
72. Teri L, Wagner AW. Assessment of depression in patients with Alzheimer's disease: concordance among informants. *Psychol Aging* 1991;6:280–285.
73. Epstein AM, Hall JA, Tognetti J, et al. Using proxies to evaluate

quality of life: can they provide valid information about patients' health status and satisfaction with medical care? *Med Care* 1989;27(suppl):S91–98.

74. Ware JE, Snow KK, Kosinski M, et al. *SF-36 Health Survey: manual and interpretation guide.* Boston: The Health Institute, New England Medical Center, 1993.

75. Stewart AL, Sherbourne CD, Hays RD, et al. Summary and discussion of MOS measures. In: Stewart AL, Ware JE Jr, eds. *Measuring functioning and well-being: the Medical Outcomes Study approach.* Durham, NC: Duke University Press, 1992:345.

76. Jette AM, Davies AR, Cleary PD, et al. The Functional Status Questionnaire. *J Gen Intern Med* 1986;1:143–149.

77. Parkerson GR, Gehlbach SH, Wagner EH, et al. The Duke-UNC Health Profile: an adult health status instrument for primary care. *Med Care* 1981;19:806–828.

78. George LK, Fillenbaum GG. OARS methodology: a decade of experience in geriatric assessment. *J Am Gerontol Soc* 1985;33:607–615.

79. Lawton MP, Moss M, Fulcomer M, et al. A research and service oriented Multilevel Assessment Instrument. *J Gerontol* 1982;37: 91–99.

80. Brook RH, Ware JE, Davies-Avery A, et al. Overview of adult health status measures fielded in Rand's Health Insurance Study. *Med Care* 1979;17(suppl).

81. Neugarten BL, Havighurst RJ, Tobin SS. The measurement of life satisfaction. *J Gerontol* 1961;16:134–143.

82. Lawton MP. The Philadelphia Geriatric Center Morale Scale: a revision. *J Gerontol* 1975;30:85–89.

83. Liang J, Bollen KA. The structure of the Philadelphia Geriatric Center Morale Scale: a reinterpretation. *J Gerontol* 1983;30:77–84.

84. Kane RA, Kane RL. *Assessing the elderly: a practical guide to measurement.* Lexington, MA: Lexington Books, 1981.

85. George LK, Bearon LB. *Quality of life in older persons: meaning and measurement.* New York: Human Sciences Press, 1980.

86. Applegate WB, Blass JP, Williams TF. Instruments for the functional assessment of older patients. *N Engl J Med* 1990;322:1207–1214.

87. Wiener JM, Hanley RJ, Clark R, et al. Measuring the activities of daily living: comparisons across national surveys. *J Gerontol* 1990;45:S229–237.

88. Arnold SB. The measurement of quality of life in the frail elderly. In: Birren JE, Lubben JE, Rowe JC, et al, eds. *The concept and measurement of quality of life in the frail elderly.* San Diego: Academic Press, 1991:50.

89. McDowell IY, Newell C. *Measuring health: a guide to rating scales and questionnaires.* New York: Oxford University Press, 1987.

90. Wilkin D, Hallam L, Doggett MA. *Measures of Need and Outcome for Primary Health Care.* Oxford: Oxford University Press, 1992.

91. Kessler RC, Foster C, Webster PS, et al. The relationship between age and depressive symptoms in two national surveys. *Psychol Aging* 1992;7:119–126.

92. Yesavage JA, Brink TL, Rose TL, et al. Development and validation of a geriatric depression screening scale: a preliminary report. *J Psychiatr Res* 1983;17:37–49.

93. Krenz C, Larson EB, Buchner DM, et al. Characterizing patient dysfunction in Alzheimer's-type dementia. *Med Care* 1988;26:453–461.

94. Brink TL. Limitations of the GDS in cases of pseudodementia. *Clin Gerontol* 1984;2:60–61.

95. Burke WJ, Houston MJ, Boust SJ, et al. Use of the Geriatric Depression Scale in dementia of the Alzheimer's type. *J Am Gerontol Soc* 1989;37:856–860.

96. Teri L, Logsdon RG. Identifying pleasant activities for Alzheimer's disease patients: the Pleasant Events Schedule-AD. *Gerontologist* 1991;31:124–127.

97. Wallace RB, Kohout FJ, Colsher PL. Observations on interview surveys of the oldest old. In: Suzman RM, Willis DP, Manton KG, eds. *The oldest old.* New York: Oxford University Press, 1992:123.

98. Kohout FJ. The pragmatics of survey field work among the elderly. In: Wallace RB, Woolson RF, eds. *The epidemiologic study of the elderly.* New York: Oxford University Press, 1992:91.

99. Aday LA. *Designing and conducting health surveys: a comprehensive guide.* San Francisco: Jossey-Bass, 1991.

100. Schwarz N, Hippler H. Response alternatives: the impact of their choice and presentation order. In: Biemer P, Groves R, Mathiowetz N, et al, eds. *Measurement errors in surveys.* New York: Wiley, 1991:41.

101. Schwarz N, Hippler H, Deutsch B, et al. Response scales: effects of category range on reported behavior and comparative judgments. *Public Opin Q* 1985;49:388–395.

102. Cicchetti DV, Showalter D, Tyrer PJ. The effect of number of rating scale categories on levels of interrater reliability: a Monte Carlo investigation. *Appl Psychol Measurement* 1985;9:31–36.

103. Bollen KA, Barb KH. Pearson's R and coarsely categorized measures. *Am Sociol Rev* 1981;46:232–239.

104. Johnson DR, Creech JC. Ordinal measures in multiple indicator models: a simulation study of categorization error. *Am Sociol Rev* 1983; 48:398–407.

105. Rodgers WL, Herzog AR, Andrews FM. Interviewing older adults: validity of self-reports of satisfaction. *Psychol Aging* 1988;3:264–272.

106. Nelson EC, Landgraf JM, Hays RD, et al. The functional status of patients: how can it be measured in physicians' offices? *Med Care* 1990;28:1111–1126.

107. Nelson EC, Landgraf JM, Hays RD, et al. The COOP Function Charts: a system to measure patient function in physicians' offices. In: WONCA Classification Committee, ed. *Functional status measurement in primary care.* New York: Springer-Verlag, 1990:97.

108. Andrews FM, Withey SB. *Social indicators of well-being.* New York: Plenum Press, 1976.

109. Stewart AL, Hays RD. Conceptual, measurement, and analytic issues in assessing health in older adults in older populations. In: Hickey T, Speers MA, eds. *Public health and aging.* Baltimore: The Johns Hopkins University Press, in press.

Quality of Life and Pharmacoeconomics in Clinical Trials, Second Edition, edited by B. Spilker.
Lippincott-Raven Publishers, Philadelphia © 1996.

CHAPTER 87

Substance Abuse Disorders

David S. Metzger, Richard F. Davis, and Charles P. O'Brien

INTRODUCTION

Quality of life (QOL) assessments attempt to measure the well-being of individuals. Although various definitions of quality of life can be found in the literature, each incorporates a similar set of domains differing primarily in their degree of specificity (1,2). These domains include physical health and somatic concerns, psychological adjustment, economic and occupational issues, familial functioning, and social integration. In many clinical settings, the psychological, economic, familial, and social (i.e., nonmedical) aspects of patient functioning are either neglected or understated in diagnostic assessment and treatment planning and generally are not considered an integral part of the disease process. However, in the diagnosis and treatment of individuals dependent on alcohol and other substances, these quality of life problems define common areas of difficulty and are often central to the prognosis of treatment. In fact, individuals diagnosed with substance use disorders are often first identified as a result of such problems.

Substance dependence, as distinguished from *substance abuse,* is a complex disorder, and quality of life assessments among substance-dependent individuals present challenges that may not arise in the study of other patient populations. Patient heterogeneity, diagnostic insensitivity, etiological uncertainty, and chronicity are all characteristic of this disor-

der, and each has an impact on the content and process of measurement. This chapter reviews these issues briefly, beginning with a description of the current diagnostic criteria for substance dependence and substance abuse and concluding with the presentation of a set of measures having demonstrated value in assessing these patient populations.

DIAGNOSTIC CRITERIA FOR SUBSTANCE USE DISORDERS

To gain an overview of the nature of substance use disorders, their common symptoms, and their relationship to quality of life, it is appropriate to begin with a review of the criteria used to make the diagnoses of substance dependence and substance abuse. This review also provides a basis for examining the close relationship between substance use disorders and functional difficulty in the areas commonly used to define quality of life.

Substance Dependence

Seven criteria for dependence on a psychoactive substance are presented in the fourth edition of the *Diagnostic and Statistical Manual of Mental Disorders* (DSM-IV) (3). The diagnosis of substance dependence is based on the presence of three or more of the these criteria at any time in the same 12-month period. Obviously, individuals differ with regard to the severity of their dependence, as reflected in the number of criteria that are met. Although the symptoms of depen-

D. S. Metzger, R. F. Davis, and C. P. O'Brien: Center for Studies of Addiction, University of Pennsylvania/Department of Veterans Affairs Medical Center, Philadelphia, Pennsylvania 19104.

dence are similar across various categories of substances, for certain classes some symptoms are less salient, and in a few instances not all symptoms apply. In general, however, the seven symptoms can be grouped into three common areas: (1) development of tolerance or withdrawal, (2) loss of control over timing and amount consumed, and (3) interference with completion of occupational and social obligations.

The development of tolerance or of withdrawal-related symptoms presents important indicators of dependence. Tolerance is characterized by either (a) the need to use markedly increased quantities of the substance in order to achieve intoxication or the desired effect, or (b) markedly diminished effect with continued use of the same amount of the substance. Withdrawal symptoms often appear when intake of the substance is stopped. The intensity of withdrawal symptoms varies significantly among individuals and substances. Furthermore, symptoms of tolerance and withdrawal may develop when certain other types of medication are taken for legitimate medical reasons. Thus, tolerance and/or withdrawal alone do not imply abuse or dependence (i.e., addiction). (The DSM-IV provides separate criteria sets for withdrawal for most classes of substances.)

Although in some cases symptoms of withdrawal can be severe and include delirium, severe depression, tachycardia, nausea, fatigue, and insomnia, for many patients withdrawal symptoms can be managed safely and effectively on an outpatient basis (4). A final criterion of dependence is the use of the same (or a closely related) substance, in order to ward off the unpleasant feelings of withdrawal. As the physical symptoms of withdrawal appear, the dependent individual becomes increasingly uncomfortable. The uncomfortable feelings of withdrawal often act as cues for the initiation of further substance seeking, thus maintaining the dependence.

With regard to the criteria related to an individual's loss of control, a common characteristic of dependence is the persistent desire or unsuccessful attempts to regulate the use of the substance. This is characterized by frequent attempts and failures to eliminate or reduce consumption. A second control-related symptom is when substances are consumed more frequently and in larger quantities or over a longer period than intended. A third related symptom is the increasing amount of time devoted to activities necessary for the acquisition, preparation, administration, and recovery from the effects of the substance.

Dependence is also characterized by its interference with the completion of important obligations. This would include intoxication or withdrawal symptoms when important work, school, or family tasks need to be completed. Work might be missed or assignments neglected. The social interference caused by substance use may also appear as a withdrawal or reduction of involvement in important social, familial, or work activities due to the use of substances or to withdrawal from their effects. Dependence is also characterized by the continued use of substances known to have caused or exacerbated a chronic or recurrent social, psychological, or physical disorder. Thus, the substance-dependent individual will of-

ten present to the clinician with an extensive history of incidents in which substance use resulted in or contributed to social and occupational difficulty. Yet in spite of this history, the patient continues to use the substance. Dependent individuals often have an inability to recognize the extent to which their substance use has interfered with their functioning.

Substance Abuse

Unlike the criteria for substance dependence, two diagnostic criteria for substance abuse do not include tolerance, withdrawal, or a pattern of compulsive use. Instead, the criteria for substance abuse include only the harmful consequences of repeated use. The symptoms of substance abuse are principally related to the third common area of symptoms described for substance dependence, i.e., interference with the completion of occupational and social obligations. The essential feature of substance abuse is a maladaptive pattern of substance use leading to clinically significant impairment or distress indicated by one or more symptoms occurring within a 12-month period.

Symptoms defining the first of two diagnostic criteria for substance abuse include recurrent substance use resulting in a failure to fulfill major role obligations at work, school, or home; recurrent substance use in situations in which it is physically hazardous; recurrent substance-related legal problems; and continued substance use despite having persistent or recurrent social or interpersonal problems caused or exacerbated by the effects of the substance. The second criterion for substance abuse is simply that symptoms have never met the criteria for substance dependence for the class of substance under consideration (3).

The aforementioned symptoms or symptom clusters represent the behavioral characteristics that form the basis of the diagnoses of substance dependence and substance abuse. They are presented here to provide a definitional foundation for understanding substance use disorders and their intimate relationship to quality of life concerns. Together, the criteria reflect the extent to which substance dependence and substance abuse interact with the physical, psychological, and social functioning of an individual. Each is linked either directly, as in the case of occupational interference, or indirectly, as with control issues, to the individual's quality of life. In fact, these quality of life problems are so often associated with substance use disorders that they have frequently been viewed as being caused solely by the dependence or abuse (5). This widely held belief has resulted in a somewhat narrow interpretation of substance use disorders and their treatment. Finally, although not specifically addressed here as a distinct measurement issue, it is also important to note that, given the high prevalence of human immunodeficiency virus (HIV) infection among intravenous drug users, acquired immunodeficiency syndrome (AIDS), and its associated complications will have long-lasting impact on the quality of life of this subgroup of the substance-dependent populations.

RELATIONSHIP BETWEEN QUALITY OF LIFE AND SUBSTANCE USE DISORDERS

It is commonly conceived that substance abuse and dependence develop in an incremental and progressive manner. As the use of substances increases, a person's social and productive involvements become less stable and at greater risk of disruption and dissolution. Under this progressive paradigm, the cause of an individual's problems is seen as the direct result of the increasing substance use. Greater amounts of time are devoted to thoughts of the substance, its procurement, and its use. As a consequence of this increased substance use and related behavior, the attention devoted to family and personal relationships, work, and health diminishes, leading to profound problems in an individual's life and in the lives of family and friends.

Given this progressive disease model of dependence and the problems associated with increased use, treatment and measurement have frequently centered around the quantity and frequency of continued substance use. Specifically, treatment has focused on abstinence and measurement on quantity and frequency of use. It is reasoned that because the problems of a substance-dependent individual are the result of substance use, these problems will dissipate as the use of the substance diminishes. It is therefore reasonable to expect that improvements in these "collateral" areas of functioning will be observed when the abuse is brought under control. However, several reports (6,7) have provided evidence that calls into question the validity of this model of dependence, which causally links dependent individual's occupational, psychological, and social problems to their substance use. These investigations have found that improvements in these related problem areas do not always occur when substance use ceases. Many patients who stop using substances continue to experience problems in other areas of functioning. These findings would suggest that individuals may not experience far-reaching changes in their quality of life as a result of the elimination of their substance use.

This issue has important implications in the design of clinical interventions and the measurement of their success. In light of the independence of these problem areas, it is important that the criteria selected for use in clinical trials be tied to the dependence- or abuse-related problems of the individual. For example, it is appropriate that employment be a goal of treatment and criterion for success for patient's who have lost a job as a result of substance use. However, for an individual who entered treatment with a history of chronic unemployment, the application of employment as a goal of treatment is less valid. Interventions should be directed at the full range of problems experienced by the patient, and not merely focused on his or her substance use. Substance use disorders cannot be diagnosed and treated solely on the basis of quantity and frequency of use. This is not meant to minimize the importance of treating and monitoring patient's continued substance use. The elimination of continued substance use may be necessary to produce improvements in the patient's quality of life, but it is not always sufficient.

MEASUREMENT ISSUES IN SUBSTANCE USE DISORDERS

In spite of the known relationship between substance abuse and dependence and a broad range of functional difficulties, the quality of life of substance abusers has rarely been measured as a distinct construct. This is particularly true of methods that have asked patients to report their perceived quality of life in its various component parts. In fact, the literature contains only one report that uses subjective assessments of the substance-dependent patient's quality of life (8). Not surprisingly, this study found that patients entering treatment reported extremely low ratings of their health, work, housing, and social relationships. Only slight and nonsignificant gains during the 3- and 6-month follow-up periods were observed. Subjective assessments of well-being may be of limited value in the absence of more objective indicators of functioning.

As stated earlier, diagnostic and evaluative criteria have typically been centered around assessing quantity and frequency of substance use. Less intensive effort has focused on the assessment of health and psychological problems, employment, family, and legal problems. These are the common problem areas of substance-dependent individuals, and improvements in these areas of functioning are often expectations of treatment. The measurement of these variables among abusing and dependent patients presents challenges that should be considered in the design of clinical investigations. These include the problems of available data sources, delayed diagnosis, and the timing of assessments.

There is no litmus test for substance abuse or dependence. Unlike many other conditions, no laboratory tests exist that can alone confirm the diagnosis of abuse or dependence. Although specific diagnostic criteria are provided—and there is good interrater reliability using DSM-IV criteria—much of the information on which these criteria rely is only available from the reports of patients, their families, or others closely involved with the individual. By the time patients reach treatment, they may be unavailable or unwilling to provide information. Consequently, patient self-report is the primary, and often the only, source of information available to make a diagnosis and set treatment goals. Self-reports of substance-dependent patients have been shown to be valid and reliable (9–11), but investigations must be designed and conducted with an awareness of the limited data sources and a sensitivity to the issues involved in conducting clinical interviews with patients and their family members.

The substance-abusing or substance-dependent patient is often first identified to the clinician as a result of disruptions or deteriorations in quality of life. Frequently, individuals are identified as substance dependent as a result of incidents that take place on the job or in the community. Patients are sometimes identified due to accidents, injuries, or illnesses caused by their abuse. Police contact such as an arrest for driving under the influence has become a common first public indicator of abuse. The loss of income or depleted savings is also common among substance-dependent individuals. These are all examples of the types of incidents that motivate individuals to seek treatment after what are often long histories of use. Rarely do patients present to the clinician with a concern that they may be developing symptoms of dependence. As a consequence of this delay in making a diagnosis, serious occupational, social, psychological, and physical problems typically predate the diagnosis of substance abuse or dependence. This may be one of the most important features of substance use disorders distinguishing them from many other medical conditions—the patient's quality of life is most at risk prior to diagnosis and treatment involvement. This has implications for the measurement process. Any assessment at the point of entry into a treatment episode is likely to define the nadir of a cycle and caution must be used in interpreting such measures as a baseline of pretreatment functioning. Assessments with substance abusers will therefore differ from other patient groups who are struggling to maintain their pretreatment quality of life which is often at greatest risk following diagnosis.

Substance dependence is accurately viewed as a chronic disorder, characterized by periods of abstinence followed by relapse to substance use. This must also be considered in the timing and the frequency of assessments. Patients often respond quickly to interventions, showing rapid improvement over their pretreatment patterns of use. Patients begin to feel better and are more able to control their use. This success often proves to be short-lived once the patient is exposed to the environmental and emotional cues that have been intimately linked to the dependence. Frequently, the stress produced by unemployment or family problems is cited as a factor in the return to substance use. The chronic nature of dependence requires that regular follow-up assessments be incorporated into the design of investigations.

QUALITY OF LIFE INSTRUMENTS

Considering the preceding discussion, it should be expected that substance-abusing and substance-dependent populations will demonstrate difficulties in diverse functional areas, and this may be the most important consideration in selecting quality of life instruments. Clinical investigators must be prepared to screen for the presence of these problems, assess their severity, and monitor their status over time. The necessity for such a broad-based approach to assessment limits the range of available instruments. The instruments recommended here are those that have demonstrated value in measuring quality of life domains, and each relies on self-report. These instruments may also be administered at follow-up assessment points. Each of these instruments has been used extensively with substance-abusing and substance-dependent patients. Four instruments are presented here: the Addiction Severity Index (5th edition), the Beck Depression Inventory, the Symptom Checklist-90-R, and the Brief Symptom Inventory. The Addiction Severity Index provides the clinician and researcher with coverage on a range of quality of life issues. The Beck Depression Inventory, the Symptom Checklist-90-R, and the Brief Symptom Inventory are suggested as instruments to measure the psychological dimensions of well-being in a direct and valid manner. When used in conjunction with the Addiction Severity Index, the Beck Depression Inventory, the Symptom Checklist-90-R, or the Brief Symptom Inventory provides the investigator with a well-rounded assessment package incorporating subjective and objective indicators of well-being in a complete range of functional areas.

Addiction Severity Index

The Addiction Severity Index (5th ed) is perhaps the most widely used assessment tool in the field of substance abuse treatment and research. The Addiction Severity Index is a structured clinical interview which combines objective and subjective data to produce ratings of problem severity in seven functional areas: medical, employment and support, drug use, alcohol use, legal status, family/social relationships and psychological status. The Addiction Severity Index was developed to assess "the multiple problems seen in alcohol and drug dependent persons" (12). Its comprehensive coverage of relevant areas of functioning, its incorporation of both objective and subjective information, its widespread use and citation in the published literature, and its performance characteristics with regard to validity and reliability make it the most appropriate tool available for quality of life assessments among abusing and dependent populations.

Owing to many changes in the field of substance abuse treatment since the Addiction Severity Index was originally developed in 1980, and to improve the general utility and contemporary value of the instrument, the Index has been updated and a significantly more detailed and comprehensive user's manual added. The 5th edition of the Addiction Severity Index contains new items in existing sections to assess route of drug administration; additional illegal activities; emotional, physical, and sexual abuse; quality of the recovery environment; and history of close personal relationships. It is important to note that *no changes were made in the composite scoring* to maintain comparability with previous editions (13).

The Addiction Severity Index is designed to be administered in a personal interview, which takes approximately 50 min to 1 hr to complete. The administration time will vary somewhat, depending on the capacity of the patient to respond clearly and concisely to each item. The interview format alleviates problems caused by poor reading levels of some patients and allows the opportunity to probe responses for clarification and confirm that the respondent adequately understands the question being asked.

Completion time will also depend on the interviewer's familiarity with the structure and content of the Addiction Severity Index. In this regard, it is important that the Index be administered by an individual who has an adequate knowledge of the instrument and practice in its administration. A number of items require awareness of methods and interpretations not clearly obvious from the form itself. The available training materials are a unique strength of the Index. These include a set of instructional videotapes, a detailed manual, and a scoring guide. The videotapes provide an orientation to the instrument and a sample interview. It is not appropriate to use the Addiction Severity Index without reviewing these materials.

Two types of quantitative scores are produced by the Addiction Severity Index in each of the seven problem areas: severity ratings and composite scores. Severity ratings are subjective assessments made by the interviewer describing the degree to which the patient is currently experiencing difficulty and consequently her or his need for additional treatment. Severity scores range from 0, meaning no real problem/additional treatment not necessary, to 9, meaning a life-threatening problem/additional treatment essential. The severity ratings are based on the responses to questions in each particular area and are meant to reflect the amount, duration, and intensity of the symptoms. Specific guidelines are provided to interviewers to help them arrive at a valid and reliable score.

Composite scores are computed from the responses to specific items contained in the Addiction Severity Index. As with severity ratings, the composite scores are produced for each of the seven problem areas. They were developed primarily to provide a numerical basis for determining change and treatment outcome and as such are more appropriate for statistical analyses. The composite scores and severity ratings have been assessed with regard to their validity and reliability (12–15). Severity ratings and composite scores have demonstrated high levels of interrater, test–retest, and concurrent reliability.

Aside from the severity ratings and composite scores produced by the Index, the completion of an Addiction Severity Index interview provides a rich clinical picture of the patient and a sound basis for treatment planning. The questions provide an opportunity to probe and elicit clinically relevant information from the patient. It is this dual clinical/research function that has made the Addiction Severity Index a valuable tool in the field of substance abuse treatment and research.

The Addiction Severity Index has limitations. It has been used most widely with individuals entering substance abuse treatment. Scant performance data are available for the Index

when it is used to measure non-substance abuse problems in general psychiatric or medical populations. It is difficult to predict the costs to validity and reliability of the instrument when used with other patient populations. Although not necessarily a limitation, the fact that the Addiction Severity Index is administered in a 50-minute to 1-hour personal interview conducted by a trained technician may restrict its application.

Beck Depression Inventory

Depression is an important construct in the comprehensive assessment of substance abuse and dependence and may be considered a good global indicator of perceived quality of life. The Beck Depression Inventory is a 21-item questionnaire that is most frequently self-administered, but it can also be completed as part of a clinical interview. If self-administered, a sixth grade reading level is suggested. It is widely used and often cited in the professional literature, and the scale has been shown to validly and reliably assess depression in many patient groups including substance abusers (16). The form is designed to be self-administered and can be completed by most individuals in 5 to 10 minutes. Individuals are presented with 21 sets of statements about their behaviors and cognitions. Each set contains four statements from which respondents must choose one that best describes themselves. Each statement within a set is numbered from 0 to 3, indicating increasing severity. The sum of the values of the selected statements forms the individual's depression score. The score range is therefore 0 to 63. Since its development (17), the Beck Depression Inventory has appeared in several different versions. A shorter 13-item form is available but is not recommended here because of the possibility that the shorter form may assess only one cognitive dimension of depression (16).

The items included in the scale were selected based on the basis of the systematic consolidation of symptoms of depression identified through clinical observation. These items include mood, pessimism, sense of failure, lack of satisfaction, guilt feelings, sense of being punished, self-dislike, self-accusation, suicidal wishes, crying, irritability, social withdrawal, indecisiveness, distortion of body image, work inhibition, sleep disturbance, fatigue, loss of appetite, weight loss, somatic preoccupation, and loss of libido.

Symptom Checklist-90-R

The Symptom Checklist-90-R is a self-administered questionnaire that asks patients to rate the degree to which they have been troubled over the preceding week by common symptoms of psychological distress. It is suggested as a useful tool in quality of life studies because of the importance of this symptom domain in understanding the substance abuser's response to treatment. Psychiatric severity has been shown to be the best predictor of response to treatment, and the Symptom Checklist-90-R provides a more fine-grained assessment of this symptom dimension than is available using the Addiction Severity Index alone. The scale has been widely used since its introduction and has demonstrated its value in clinical investigations, its coverage of the content area, and its acceptability to substance-abusing and substance-dependent populations.

In addition to an overall general symptom score, the 90 items form subscales that yield scores on nine-symptom constructs. These constructs include somatization, obsessive-compulsiveness, interpersonal sensitivity, psychoticism, anxiety, depression, hostility, phobic anxiety, and paranoid ideation.

The Symptom Checklist-90-R has its origins in the 77-item Hopkins Symptom Checklist (18,19) developed as an outcome measure for use in psychotherapy research. This early version of the scale formed the basis of the Symptom Checklist-90, which underwent revision to become the Symptom Checklist-90-R. The psychometric properties of the scale have been examined, and both internal consistency and test–retest reliability coefficients were quite good for each of the subscales, averaging about .85 (20). The Symptom Checklist-90 has also been shown to correlate highly with the Minnesota Multiphasic Personality Inventory (MMPI) (21), the Hamilton Depression Rating Scale, and the Social Adjustment Scale (22,23).

The scale is self-administered and takes approximately 15 minutes to complete. The items can be read to individuals who have difficulty reading. The manual states that the scale can be used with individuals as young as 13 years of age, with the assistance of a technician. The Symptom Checklist-90-R is appropriate for use with psychiatric and medical patients, with the obvious exception of individuals who are acutely psychotic. The Symptom Checklist-90-R has been widely used with alcoholic and substance-abusing populations and is sensitive to the changes produced by psychoactive substances. The scale does not appear to be sensitive to practice effects resulting from repeated administrations and can be used in studies requiring follow-up assessments.

Brief Symptom Inventory

The Brief Symptom Inventory is a self-report, 53-item instrument providing point-in-time psychological symptom status. It is a condensed version of the Symptom Checklist-90-R. The Brief Symptom Inventory correlates very highly with the Symptom Checklist-90 across all dimensions (24), confirming that the instrument is a valid measure of the symptom constructs of the Symptom Checklist-90. One published report (25) investigated whether the Brief Symptom Inventory had sufficient discriminative validity to distinguish between groups with various levels of substance abuse, between those having fewer or more quality of life areas affected, and between primary clients and their significant

others. The results of the study indicated that the Brief Symptom Inventory does have value in making such discriminations. One advantage to its use is the minimization of professional time in the intake and evaluation process.

Although the Brief Symptom Inventory focuses only on the identified patient, other factors, such as family, social network, and other quality of life domains, remain important considerations for comprehensive treatment. In spite of its narrow focus on the individual patient, however, the Brief Symptom Inventory appears to have more than sufficient validity to recommend its use with substance-using populations. Used in conjunction with the Addiction Severity Index, the Brief Symptom Inventory provides the clinician/researcher with a well-rounded assessment package in a complete range of functional areas.

CONCLUSIONS

These four scales provide the clinical researcher with a set of tools having demonstrated value in the comprehensive assessment of quality of life difficulties among individuals diagnosed with substance use disorders. Ongoing research and development with regard to both new instrumentation and methodologies is clearly needed. Of particular importance is the development of new instruments or the revision of existing tools to respond to the changing substances of abuse and dependence and issues associated with their use. For example, all the scales presented here were developed prior to the widespread use of cocaine and its more virulent form, crack. It is likely that dependent patterns of use develop more rapidly among cocaine users. However, the measurement implications of these issues remain to be empirically examined. Similarly, the increasing importance of the role of substance use in the transmission of HIV is not adequately addressed by current instrumentation. The risk of HIV infection has begun to impact not only on substance preference, but on the method of use and the social integration of substance users as well (26). Changes in substance preference and routes of administration, for example, will likely affect quality of life measurement in substance-using populations.

Continued research is also warranted in the development of valid and reliable scales for use in the assessment of adolescents, although work in this area is currently under way. None of the instruments presented has been validated with this growing patient population. Another important area in need of investigation is the impact on data quality of the method of questioning substance-dependent individuals. No recent assessments of the validity of data collected through personal interview as compared with similar information collected through self-administered questionnaires have been performed. Patients may be more accurate in their reports of sensitive information when questioned using the more impersonal questionnaire approach. The degree of disclosure obtained through differing methods may also be a function of demographic and cultural variables. Given the substantial efficiency achieved through the use of this method, it is important to assess its validity.

The important role of quality of life issues in the identification and treatment of substance use disorders demands that ongoing effort be devoted to the refinement and development of measurement tools and methods. In learning more about the relationship between quality of life problems and substance use, we will expand our understanding of abuse and dependence, their casual mechanisms, and their effective treatment.

REFERENCES

1. Flanagan JC. Measurement of quality of life: current state of the art. *Arch Phys Med Rehabil* 1982;63:56–59.
2. Andrews FM, Withey SB. *Social Indicators of Well-being: Americans' Perceptions of Life Quality.* New York: Plenum Press, 1976.
3. American Psychiatric Association. *Diagnostic and Statistical Manual of Mental Disorders.* 4th ed. Washington, DC: American Psychiatric Association, 1987.
4. Hayashida MD, Alterman AI, McLellan AT, et al. Comparative effectiveness and costs of inpatient and outpatient detoxification of patients with mild to moderate alcohol withdrawal syndrome. *N Engl J Med* 1989;320:358–365.
5. Levine HG. The discovery of addiction. *J Stud Alcohol* 1978;39:41–53.
6. Rounsaville BJ, Kosten TR, Kleber HD. The antecedents and benefits of achieving abstinence in opioid addicts: a 2.5-year follow-up study. *Am J Drug Alcohol Abuse* 1987;13:213–229.
7. McLellan AT, Luborsky L, Woody GE, O'Brien CP, Kron R. Are the "addiction-related" problems of substance abusers really related? *J Nerv Ment Dis* 1981;169:232–239.
8. Irwin PH. Quality of life assessment and drug abuse treatment program evaluation. *Eval Prog Plan* 1981;4:123–130.
9. Amsel Z, Mandell W, Matthais L, et al. Reliability and validity of self-reported illegal activities and drug use collected from narcotic addicts. *Int J Addict* 1976;11:325–336.
10. Bale RN. The validity and reliability of self report data from heroin addicts: mailed questionnaires compared to face to face interviews. *Int J Addict* 1979;14:993–1000.
11. Pompi KF. The reliability of biographical information obtained from court stipulated clients newly admitted to treatment. *Am J Drug Alcohol Abuse* 1979;6:79–95.
12. McLellan AT, Luborsky L, Woody GE, O'Brien CP. An improved diagnostic evaluation instrument for substance abuse patients: the Addiction Severity Index. *J Nerv Ment Dis* 1980;168:26–33.
13. McLellan AT, Kushner H, Metzger D, et al. The fifth edition of the Addiction Severity Index. *J Subst Abuse Treat* 1992;9:199–213.
14. Kosten TR, Rounsaville BJ, Kleber HD. Concurrent validity of the Addiction Severity Index. *J Nerv Ment Dis* 1983;171:606–610.
15. McLellan AT, Luborsky L, Cacciola J, et al. New data from the Addiction Severity Index: reliability and validity in three centers. *J Nerv Ment Dis* 1985;173:412–423.
16. Beck AT, Steer RA, Garbin MG. Psychometric properties of the Beck Depression Inventory: twenty-five years of evaluation. *Clin Psychol Rev* 1988;8:77–100.
17. Beck AT, Ward CH, Mendelson M, et al. An inventory for measuring depression. *Arch Gen Psychiatry* 1961;4:561–571.
18. Derogatis LR, Lipman RS, Covi L, Rickels K. Factorial invariance of symptom dimensions in anxious and depressed neuroses. *Arch Gen Psychiatry* 1972;27:659–665.
19. Derogatis LR, Lipman RS, Rickels K, Uhlenhuth EH, Covi L. The Hopkins Symptom Checklist (HSCL): a self report symptom inventory. *Behav Sci* 1974;19:1–15.
20. Derogatis LR. *SCL-90 revised version manual—I.* Baltimore: Clinical Psychometrics Research Unit, Johns Hopkins University School of Medicine, 1983.
21. Derogatis LR, Rickels K, Rock AF. The SCL-90 and the MMPI: a step in the validation of a new self report scale. *Br J Psychiatry* 1976;128:280–289.
22. Weissman MM, Sholomskas D, Pottenger M, et al. Assessing depressive symptoms in five psychiatric populations: a validation study. *Am J Epidemiol* 1977;106:203–214.
23. Weissman MM, Pursoff BA, Thompson WD, et al. Social adjustment by self report in a community sample and in psychiatric outpatients. *J Nerv Ment Dis* 1978;166:317–326.
24. Derogatis LR. *The SCL-90 manual—I: scoring, administration and procedures for the SCL-90.* Baltimore: Clinical Psychometric Research, 1977.
25. Royse D, Drude K. Screening drug abuse clients with the Brief Symptom Inventory. *Int J Addict* 1984;19(8):849–857.
26. Des Jarlais DC, Friedman SR, Sotheran JL, et al. Continuity and change within an HIV epidemic. *JAMA* 1994;271:121–127.

Quality of Life and Pharmacoeconomics in Clinical Trials, Second Edition, edited by B. Spilker.
Lippincott-Raven Publishers, Philadelphia © 1996.

CHAPTER 88

Rehabilitation: Issues in Functional Assessment

Ralph R. Turner

INTRODUCTION

Historically, the need for functional status assessment in rehabilitation emerged from clinical practice as the emphasis shifted from a medically based health concept to a psychosocial model. The individual rather than the organ became the unit of analysis and active pathology was evaluated indirectly through its effect on functioning of the individual (1).

Now firmly established, the functional perspective has continued to grow, requiring more refined and methodologically sound assessment techniques. As the health care reform movement continues to impact all sectors of the health care delivery system, opportunities have been found to cross-fertilize assessment research development and applied activities. One source has been in the health services research arena, where health status assessment has been identified as a key component in outcomes research.

While much of the earlier functional scale development work had not benefited either from long-standing psychometric methodology or from new advances in health status assessment, the conditions for creating change were in place when the issues were discussed earlier (2) and beginning to exert their influence. The purpose of this chapter is to provide an overview of measurement principles for functional assessment in rehabilitation in light of recent advances in health

status assessment in health services research. The goal is to provide the reader with an applied framework from which to make informed choices about integrating work from two fields that share substantial common ground.

CONCEPTUAL FRAMEWORK FOR FUNCTIONAL AND HEALTH STATUS ASSESSMENT

As with impairment, disability, and handicap, so too have the terms "functional status," "functional limitations," and "functional assessment" often been interchanged. Early usage of functional limitation stemmed from a predominantly medical focus on impairment (3). Jette (1) suggested that functional assessment needs to operate from the perspective of the individual as the unit of analysis and "pathology, as represented by various physical manifestations or symptoms, (should be) evaluated through its effect on functioning of the individual." Jette's subdivision of functioning within rehabilitation includes physical, mental, emotional, and social performance. Brown et al. (4) described an integrated model of functional assessment and rehabilitation outcomes, which included as individual level variables demographic, structural, and basic functioning, cognitive and psychological functioning, knowledge, and applied functioning.

These broader views of rehabilitation fit closely with the health status assessment approach. Schipper and Levitt (5) have defined quality of life as a pattern of function, measured

R. R. Turner: Department of Health Economics, Johnson and Johnson, Inc., Raritan, New Jersey 08869.

over time, that incorporates physical ability, psychological well-being, and social interactions. This view is consistent with those prepared by Wenger et al. (6) as well as Patrick and Erickson (7), who view health-related quality of life as, "the value assigned to duration of life as modified by the impairment, functional states, perception, and social opportunities that are influenced by disease, injuries, treatment, or policy." In all of these, there is common agreement that measuring performance within these domains through functional assessment provides a comprehensive picture of the interaction between the individual and the environment at the disability and handicap levels. When viewed as an extension of earlier work that focused primarily on physical limitations at the impairment level, a matrix emerges which organizes levels of limitation (i.e., impairment, disability, and handicap) and content domains that can be used to clarify assessment goals. The conceptual framework proposed by Stineman and Granger (8), which synthesized and expanded the work of Nagi (9,10) and Wood (11), describes the production of three classes of data which are necessary to implement successful rehabilitation intervention (Fig. 1).

Concepts are organized across three levels: organ, person, and society. Within each, the prevailing results, directly or indirectly, in either impairment, disability, or handicap. Anatomical, physiological, or psychological defects determine impairment or organic dysfunction. Performance defects within the physical and social environment contribute to disability or difficulty with tasks. And environmental or societal defects influenced by social norms and policy create handicaps or social disadvantage. The unifying concept here is that each of these represents limitations in function, whether in using skills, performing activities, or fulfilling

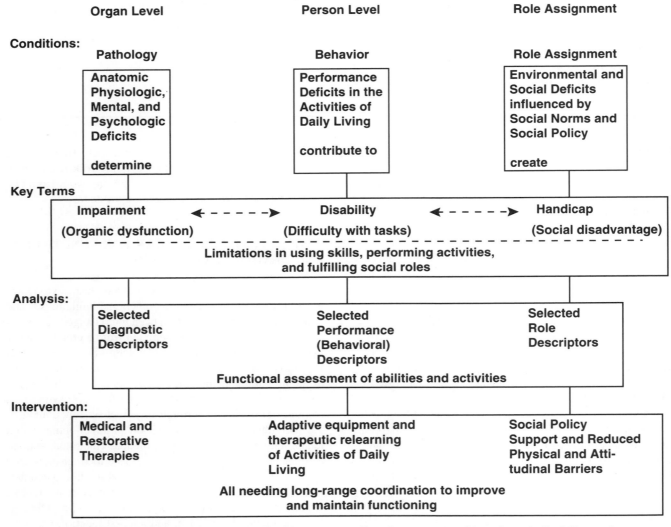

FIG. 1. Integrative model for rehabilitation concepts. *Top,* the concepts of impairment, disability, and handicap are related across organ, person, and societal levels. *Bottom,* the role of functional assessment in producing three classes of data are presented leading to rehabilitation intervention. (From Granger, ref. 16, with permission.)

social roles. Although analysis of these functional limitations has a different focus, depending on the level of interest, at the core is the need for outcomes to be conceptualized and defined in measurable terms.

Health status assessment plays a key role in outcomes research and health care reform in a variety of health care delivery systems. Growing from large scale research programs like the Health Insurance Experiment (HIE) (12) and the Medical Outcomes Study (MOS) (13), these programs produced much of the seminal work in health status assessment and resulted in general agreement among researchers on the components of a conceptual framework which organizes much of the current research activities.

Patrick and Erickson (7,14) have synthesized much of this conceptual work. The core concepts in their model include (a) opportunity (disadvantage because of health; capacity for health); (b) health perception (self-ratings and satisfaction); (c) functional status (social, psychological, and physical function); (d) impairment (symptoms, signs, and physiological evidence); and (e) death and duration of life. While a number of these terms are similar to those used in Granger's model, there are important differences (15). Functional status, physical function, psychological function, and social function all involve content similar to that used by Granger's model and others (3,16). The greatest difficulty involves similar terminology with meanings different from that employed by the World Health Organization (WHO) (11). Impairment includes both the WHO concepts of loss or abnormality of psychologic, physiologic, or anatomic structures or function and morbidity (symptoms, signs, and physiologic evidence). The advantage comes from the incorporation of health-related quality of life (HRQL), which focuses on the impact of illness, disease, injury and therapeutic intervention on usual activities.

Functional Assessment Measurement in Rehabilitation

Functional assessment in rehabilitation settings has not always benefited from sound measurement technology. Kelman and Willner (17) cited problems in outcome definition, standardization of methods, and technical quality of the measures in 1962. Keith (18) and Frey (3), and even more recently Barer (19), found that while progress has been made, there was scope for additional improvement. Too many scales were developed for institution-specific use with little regard for either previous work or psychometric techniques.

Genuine progress has been made in addressing the critical issues of conceptual models, terminology, and standardization (20,21). As trends in health status assessment from outcomes research involving chronic disease management, elderly long-term care, and rehabilitation begin to converge, new and different resources are being brought to bear. Measurement is moving from situation and institution-specific scale development to broader-based, coordinated, interdisciplinary work. The earlier call by Ellwood (22) for the development of a national "outcome management information system" with quality of life assessment at its core has resulted in an extensive applied research program by the Agency for Health Care Policy and Research [AHCPR] Patient Outcome Research Team (PORT) projects. Many of these, for example, the Stroke and Knee-Replacement PORTs, have direct relevance for rehabilitation. Large-scale program evaluation projects involving functional assessment have been implemented in rehabilitation settings as well. Perhaps the best example is the Uniform Data System for Medical Rehabilitation (UDS) (23), which includes the Functional Independence Measure (FIM) as an integral component.

ASSESSMENT SELECTION CRITERIA

For those responsible for making assessment decisions, sound theoretical and practical advice and guidance have been offered. Especially important contributions have been made by Feinstein (24), McDowell and Newell (25), Patrick and Erickson (7), and Spilker (26). Earlier, Brown et al. (4) presented an integrative model that linked functional assessment and outcome measurement. In each of these practical guides there are a series of criteria that serve as tools to be used to select an assessment approach. The approach presented here differs in degree and emphasis rather than in fundamental concepts. All these recent guides have a great deal in common and the reader is encouraged to pursue them as a means of expanding the scope of this chapter.

Clarification of Purpose

The first step in selecting a functional assessment scale is to ask, "What is the question?" Although seemingly obvious and intuitive, this basic process of identifying and clarifying the measurement objectives is often either inadequately addressed or, more seriously, overlooked altogether. Yet the admittedly difficult process of clarifying, in measurable terms, what the intended outcomes are is often enlightening and greatly facilitates the assessment process.

Matching the user's intentions, once they have been clearly stated, with those of the scale developer is an essential second step. The criteria used in the scale development process may differ substantially from the user's purpose. Scales with evidence that supports one purpose may not serve well when applied to a different task. Kirshner and Guyatt (27) present a useful taxonomy that classifies assessment scales into discriminative, predictive, and evaluative categories. Each type of scale addresses substantially different objectives. Discriminative scales are designed to separate patients (or clients or subjects) into discrete classes that can be defined according to specific diagnostic criteria. Predictive scales serve a similar role. However, here patients are classified into groups against a known criterion, or "gold standard." Evaluative scales differ markedly from the other two since they are intended to reflect clinically important change when it occurs. Each type of scale has a useful role to play in rehabilitation but mismatching the types may result in incorrect assessment information. All too often discriminative scales are used to assess change in function following rehabilitation intervention. Although change may have occurred, the scale may be insensitive to it, resulting in incorrect conclusions.

The criteria for developing each type of scale differ at nearly every step in the test development process. Figure 2 summarizes these differences. Although much of the functional assessment scale development literature does not yet reflect this level of technical sophistication (18), the user should become familiar with the underlying assumptions. Key questions such as, ''Do I want to group patients according to their current functional ability?'' or ''Do I want to classify clients according to prognosis for successful vocational placement?'' or ''Am I interested in determining how much functional change occurs as a result of my rehabilitation treatment program?'' all reflect this basic distinction, help clarify objectives, and set a much clearer course for instrument selection. This distinction in type of measurement adds a third dimension to the conceptual framework which now permits functional assessment to be incorporated into a measurement model that synthesizes the clarification needed in the basic terminology, the domains of interest necessary for a comprehensive assessment of functions and quality of life, and the purposes for which the scale was developed.

A three-dimensional model is presented in Fig. 3 that is based, in part, on the assessment proposal by Frey (3). Along one axis are the areas of assessment—impairment, disability, and handicap. Much of the early functional assessment work focused on the impairment level but it is now clear that changing models have expanded the scope to disability, with preliminary attention being paid to the handicap level. Along the second axis are the domains of assessment that are generally accepted as relevant for rehabilitation outcomes as well as in health status assessment. Along the third axis are the types of measurement classified by Kirshner and Guyatt.

This model can be used to guide the questions the user needs to ask at the onset of the assessment task: What is the appropriate unit of analysis? How many, and which content domains are relevant? What is my assessment goal? Answers to these questions should help identify a preliminary set of instruments, which can then be examined more closely for evidence of psychometric quality and practical application.

MAJOR ISSUES IN SCALE DEVELOPMENT

	DISCRIMINATIVE CRITERIA	PREDICTIVE CRITERIA	EVALUATIVE CRITERIA
ITEM SELECTION:	– Tap important components of the domain – Universal applicability to respondents – Stability over time	– Statistical association with criterion measure	– Tap areas related to change in health status – Responsiveness to clinically significant change
ITEM SCALING:	– Short response sets which facilitate uniform interpretation	– Response sets which maximize correlations with the criterion measure	– Response sets with sufficient gradations to register change
ITEM REDUCTION:	– Internal scaling or consistency – Comprehensiveness and reduction of random error vs. respondent burden	– Power to predict vs. respondent burden	– Responsiveness vs. respondent burden
RELIABILITY:	– Large and stable intersubject variation: correlation between replicate measures	– Stable inter and intrasubject variation: chance corrected agreement between replicate measures	– Stable intrasubject variation insignificant variation between replicate measures
VALIDITY:	– Cross-sectional construct validity: relationship between index and external measures at a single point in time	– Criterion validity: agreement with criterion measure	– Longitudinal construct validity: relationship between changes in index and external measures over time
RESPONSIVENESS:	– Not relevant	– Not relevant	– Power of the test to detect a clinically important difference

FIG. 2. Summary of issues in functional assessment measurement. From Kirshner and Guyatt, ref. 18, with permission.

Psychometric Properties

Once the central question and purpose are clarified, the user's task is to balance psychometric quality with practical considerations. Both issues have been discussed in recent health assessment and functional assessment publications. Excellent summaries of this theoretical basis for measurement are provided by McDowell and Newell (25) and Feinstein (24), with more technical discussions found in Nunnally (28), Thorndike (29), and Torgerson (30). What follows here is an overview of the key issues and suggested guidelines.

Reliability

All measurement involves some degree of error. Although such error cannot be eliminated, the degree to which it is minimized reflects the extent to which the score can be considered stable and reproducible (28). Ware (31) suggested a standard where reliability coefficients above .90 are required for making comparisons between individuals, whereas between-group comparisons require coefficients in the .50 to .70 range. However, most of the scale development literature suggests .70 as a benchmark standard.

Three types of reliability are typically employed in functional assessment scale development, depending on the type and purpose of the measure. Test–retest reproducibility refers to the stability of a score derived from serial administration of a measure by the same rater. Timing is one of the key factors to consider when judging the evidence for this type of reliability. Enough time has to elapse to minimize the effects of memory, yet too much time may allow the phenomenon under study to change significantly. Profes-

sional judgment and experience are required to determine whether the reliability assessment design is adequate. For example, the effects of arthritis fluctuate, creating difficulty for the assessment of reliability, whereas aspects of spinal cord injury are remarkably stable (1). While Pearson correlation coefficients are usually reported, the intraclass correlation coefficient for reliability (32) may be preferred, as it accounts for variability between different test occasions and among respondents.

A second factor is related to the type of scale that is developed. Kirshner and Guyatt (27) suggest that the nature of the reliability data ought to differ across the three types of scales. A useful discriminative index must demonstrate large and stable between-subject variation. So must predictive scales, but with an additional requirement there should not be any systematic change in subject scores over time. Evaluative indices, however, which should evidence small within-subject variation in stable subjects are large change in scores when functional status improves or deteriorates. This analysis has rarely been reported in the functional assessment literature, but it is presented here to illustrate the importance of the compatibility between scale construction and use and to encourage rehabilitation researchers to include such information.

When scores are obtained from measures administered and scored by different raters, interrater or interobserver reliability is assessed. The interrater reliability coefficient is generally determined from correlations between different raters' judgments. The interobserver correlation (κ) or Kendall's index of concordance (W) are typically used where responses of more than two raters are being compared (14). In rehabilitation settings in which staff teams are often used to generate client-level information, good interrater reliability is an essential quality to be considered in scale selection.

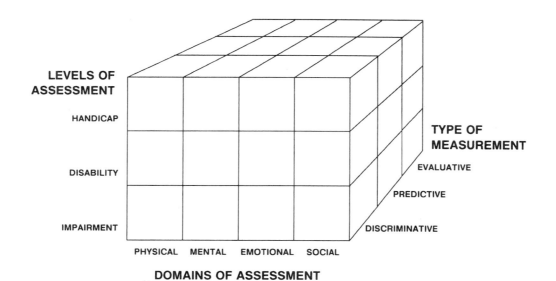

FIG. 3. A three-dimensional model for functional assessment.

Internal consistency assesses the extent to which different items within a particular scale are measuring the same content or characteristic. Several formulas are available for estimating the correlations between all possible pairs of items, e.g., Kuder–Richardson and Cronbach's α-coefficient. Internal consistency is particularly important in judging whether the items being grouped together measure a unified underlying domain. If the coefficient does not meet the proposed .70 criterion, the resulting scale score may be too unreliable to accurately detect the presence of the construct (e.g., pain), or to detect change following rehabilitation intervention.

Validity

Reliability is a necessary but insufficient condition for validity. Additional evidence is needed to indicate whether a scale is measuring what it purports to measure. There are several types of validity, and a basic understanding of the role they play in adding evidence of a measure's value is necessary for making informed decisions about test selection. Feinstein (24) offers practical guidance for evaluating validity. A more extensive discussion can be found in Brinberg and Kidder (33).

Most programmatic attempts to establish validity begin with content validity. This refers to how adequately the sampling of questions reflects the aims of the index, as specified in the conceptual definition of its scope (14). Content validity is rarely tested statistically owing, in large part, to the absence of a standard which can be measured. Rather, expert opinion is sought and systematically gathered within a well-specified conceptual framework. The main difficulty does not lie in using a consensus but rather with getting a suitable group of authorities (24). In rehabilitation this issue is compounded by substantially different models and world views. Emphasis on impairment or disability creates concern about content validity among users since the distinction directly reflects the differences between the medical and psychosocial models (35). When selecting scales, all of the user groups should be consulted concerning agreement on the models and, subsequently, whether there is sufficient support for content validity within that model.

Criterion validity proceeds when an established measure, or "gold standard" exists against which the new measure can be compared. Both the established and the new measure are administered simultaneously, and the results are compared with an appropriate correlation techniques. Criterion validity appears to be most relevant for functional assessment at the impairment level. For example, several well-established clinical procedures exist for the diagnosis of organ pathology. Functional scales that are intended to be easier and less expensive to administer than these have a useful role to play in the screening process.

For most functional assessment scales, as for most health status assessment scales, no gold standard exists. Evidence

for construct validity must be gathered, but no single procedure provides definitive proof (25). Rather, correlations must be shown to be in the hypothesized direction and of the expected magnitude provided by the authors. Of course, constructs themselves vary in the degree of consensus and supporting evidence they possess. Often, advanced analytical methods such as factor and cluster analysis can be used to provide empirical support for the constructs.

A serious shortcoming for most functional assessment scales is the lack of sound evidence for validity. Validation research is difficult in rehabilitation because of the levels of differences in viewpoint and changes in conceptualization that have been discussed here. Consequently, the user should make an effort to review the case for validity that the developer presents. McDowell and Newell (25) provide assistance. First, it needs to be understood that the magnitude of the validity coefficient is constrained by the reliability of both the proposed and the standard measure (technically, the product of the square root of each reliability coefficient). Reported validities need to approach this upper bound, rather than perfection, as a key criterion. Second, it may be useful to translate correlation coefficients into a more useful concept. The basic assumption is that the functional assessment measure is being used to predict some criterion. The purpose of validity is to estimate how much the accuracy of the prediction is improved based on knowing the score on the measurement. A simple approach is to square the correlation coefficient. If a health measure correlates .70 with a criterion, it will provide about a 50% reduction in error compared with guessing. The key point here is that correlation coefficients of .50 or lower begin to lose their predictive value rapidly. More elaborate approaches can be found in Helmstadt (36). More generally, the validation approach taken by scale developers needs to be examined. Validation programs should systematically state and test clear hypotheses, attempt to disprove hypotheses that the scales measure something other than the stated purpose, and employ a variety of validation approaches (25).

Responsiveness

Responsiveness, precision, and sensitivity represent a third consideration for scale selection. Responsiveness refers to the power of a scale to detect clinically important change when it occurs (27) and is similar in concept to precision, which refers to the degree of change in the phenomenon that can be detected. By contrast, sensitivity traditionally refers to positivity in the presence of disease (1).

As shown in Fig. 2, responsiveness is an issue only for evaluative indices. In clinical trials, scales are needed that can detect often small but clinically significant differences. While different across different disease levels, such change may be operationalized as that magnitude which alters prognosis, therapy, or intensity of follow-up (1). In rehabilitation, change is often the key outcome indicator (4), yet many functional assessment scales were not designed to detect meaningful change.

Practical Considerations

The success of systematic functional assessment depends directly on the match between the assessment purpose, the rehabilitation setting, and the characteristics of the scale. These practical issues were discussed by Brown et al. (4), who identified two broad dimensions of functional assessment scales. Brown et al. argued that relevance (i.e., the match between the content and structure of the scale and the user's information needs) is the essential first practical consideration. Obviously if the data are seen as irrelevant to the problem, psychometric quality will not matter; the information will be ignored. Further, the information must be produced feasibly. This analysis of the resource limitations and constraints has been further refined by Ware (31).

With the exception of respondent burden, the issues involved in determining the acceptability of an instrument are rarely reported in the literature or in the users' manuals which accompany the scale. Yet issues such as whether the scale was used successfully in a similar setting and the nature of missing or incomplete data have direct implications for the relevance and feasibility of the information.

Respondent burden is one practical consideration that does receive attention. A key question is how long the scale takes to administer. The majority of patients can complete four standardized items per minute, according to Ware's research (31), with longer time needed for more disabled or disadvantaged respondents. Administrative time is certainly important, but it is not the only respondent burden of concern. Attention needs to be directed toward psychological stress as well. The issues here involve the difficulty or complexity of an interview or questionnaire, and the content. Sensitivity to client needs within the assessment process is an especially important consideration in rehabilitation (37).

Mode of administration is a second component of practical consideration, and can range from time-consuming and fairly resource intensive direct observation through generally less costly and more easily managed self-administered questionnaires. Each type has advantages and disadvantages that need to be reviewed against the central objectives of the study. Tracking changes in the effectiveness of interpersonal skill training for mildly mentally retarded workers may well require direct observation by trained technicians, for example, whereas pain management and mobility in arthritic patients may be accurately assessed with a self-administered questionnaire.

The final two considerations involve length/administration time and the need for special training or equipment. The time to complete the assessment is important, but so too is the time necessary to prepare for the administration and to deal with the assessment data following the administration. Once completed, one must ask how much "massag-

ing'' is needed to transform the responses into usable data. Open-ended questions, for example, yield rich and unique information but are resource-intensive to convert to usable data. Other assessment approaches require special training and equipment. These can represent substantial investment of resources, and trade-offs with data quality need to be considered.

It is not being argued that short, self-administered assessments are the best approach. Rather, users are encouraged to keep the objectives of the assessment in sharp focus and to make informed decisions about the trade-offs associated with producing data necessary to meet those objectives. With this in mind, one final point needs to be made. Time and resources invested in pilot studies often yield tremendous benefit. Good estimates of response burden, issues of administrative complexity, and "bench-testing" of data reduction and analytic procedures are all possible with brief, well-planned pilot studies involving a similar set of respondents.

Scale Development Example: Functional Independence Measure

The application of these psychometric techniques and standards to functional assessment in rehabilitation can be found in literature describing the development of the FIM.

Faced with a need to produce uniform, high-quality data for client and administrative management, program evaluation, and clinical epidemiological research regarding disabilities, a joint Task Force of the American Congress of Rehabilitation Medicine and the American Academy of Physical Medicine and Rehabilitation designed a patient data set and an assessment instrument for universal use among medical rehabilitation facilities. The Uniform Data System consists of patient information that is collected from facilities which subscribe to the data management service and is organized into thirteen impairment groups. Patient demographic characteristics, diagnosis, impairment group membership, length of hospital inpatient stay, and hospital discharges are included. At the heart of the system is the FIM (23,34).

The FIM was designed to be simple and practical enough for general adoption by several types of medical rehabilitation facilities but with enough discriminatory power to permit its use as an outcomes measure for administrative management and program evaluation (34). The scale consists of 18 ordinal items covering self-care, sphincter control, mobility, locomotion, communication, and social cognition. Each item is rated by therapists according to a seven-level scale of disability, ranging from total assist (1) to complete independence (7).

Evidence for Reliability

Because the FIM is used across several different settings, acceptable interrater reliability was an essential component. Hamilton et al. (38) report good levels for both intraclass correlation coefficients and weighted κ (39). The total FIM score intraclass coefficient of 263 inpatients assessed by pairs of clinicians at 21 hospitals was .97, FIM subscore correlations ranged from .93 to .96, and FIM item scores had an average κ value of .71. These results were supported by Chau et al. (40) in France. Raters (52 educators, 26 physiotherapists, and 12 occupational therapists) completed FIMs for 198 children and adolescent rehabilitation patients. Weighted κ exceeded .70 for all subscales except memory (.63). Internal consistency was assessed by Cronbach α for the FIM and its subscales (41). The coefficients were nearly all high (α <.90 for admission and discharge total scores) with only the two-item locomotion below the usual standard (α = .63).

Scaling Method

The FIM was originally intended to produce a single total score to be used to produce a "cost efficiency index," yielded by dividing the difference between admission and discharge total FIM scores by the length of stay or cost. However, concern has been raised about combining items representing multidimensional abilities into a single score, and about the indeterminate distances between hierarchical functional assessment scale categories (42,43). Substantial work addressing these issues for the FIM though Rasch analysis has been reported (44,45). Rasch analysis is a statistical technique for constructing interval measures from ordinal data. Simultaneous measurement of subjects and items from person–item interactions are produced. The Rasch scaling units are logits, log-odds units, which are usually transformed to a 1 to 100 interval scale for convenience (45) and are thus candidates for standard parametric analysis.

Using the UDS data base, Rasch analysis of the FIM for a sample of 27,669 patients revealed two dimensions rather than one—motor and cognition. Examination of the relationship between the FIM raw scores and FIM measures identified cut-off scores for low (35) and high (60) independence to produce performance profiles across the individual items for use by rehabilitation facilities (45). By having established consistent motor and cognitive components across thirteen impairment groups, the FIM provides a linear measure where scoring is not dependent on local data. Then discharge expectancies can be based on these scaling results providing a basis for program evaluation (46).

Evidence for Validity

Considerable evidence for construct validity has been gathered for the FIM. Hypotheses that the FIM should decrease with increasing age and comorbidity, and vary with patient discharge destination were supported. Evidence for specific impairment types was somewhat less compelling (41). The FIM was found to be the best predictor among several functional scales of the burden of care necessary for

multiple sclerosis patients (47), and stroke patients (48). In related work with Model Systems, the FIM was found to be reasonably suited for use among traumatic brain injured patients, especially inpatient settings (49).

The FIM development literature provides a useful example for understanding how the various psychometric procedures discussed in this section are employed to produce a useful scale. Although originally intended to produce a single score, subsequent innovating work using Rasch analysis produced an important change in direction which has had a direct influence on other functional assessment scale development projects (43,49,50).

FUNCTIONAL ASSESSMENT INSTRUMENTS IN REHABILITATION

An important resource is McDowell and Newell's *Measuring health: a guide to rating scales and questionnaires* (25), which takes a broader view of health assessment than just rehabilitation. However, this book proceeds from the World Health Organization (WHO) definition of impairment, disability, and handicap, and the authors use that framework to review functional disability and handicap measures, along with others that are relevant to rehabilitation and provide a bridge between functional and health status assessment. Scales are compared in a particularly useful summary chart that includes numerical characteristics, number of items, applications, administrative mode, an assessment of current usage, and assessment of both the thoroughness and results of reliability and validity testing. Furthermore, each scale is summarized according to a standard format that describes the purpose, conceptual basis, description, exhibits, reliability and validity, alternative forms, reference standards, commentary availability, and references.

In addition, several review articles and relevant volumes have been published that form a solid foundation of conceptual and technical issues for critically examining functional assessment in rehabilitation: see Brown et al. (4), Granger and Gresham (51), Halpern and Fuhrer (52), Spilker et al. (53,54), Wallace (55), Gresham and Labi (56), Keith (18), and Feeny et al. (57).

Examples of Functional Assessment Scales

This section summarizes five scales that reflect different components of the three-dimensional functional assessment model. All have well-documented psychometric quality and together they have been used in a variety of studies with large numbers of rehabilitation patients and clients. These scales were selected as examples, in part, because of their diversity. The intent is to demonstrate that careful consideration of the assessment objectives and guidelines discussed previously should result in functional assessment scales demonstrating variety in content and format. It is not the intent of this section to recommend these as priority scales that should be given first consideration. Since each of these examples has well-documented reliability and validity evidence, those aspects of the guidelines are not presented here.

General Rehabilitation

Vocational

User objective: To obtain a low burden and comprehensive overview of the client's functional limitations and strengths that are relevant for vocational rehabilitation.

Scale example: Functional Assessment Inventory (FAI) (Crew and Athelstan, refs. 58,59).

Functional assessment model:

Levels: disability, handicap
Areas: physical, mental, emotional, social
Type: discriminative (possible evaluative)

Purpose: To provide a summary of a rehabilitation client's functional limitations and strengths based on existing case file, interview, and counselor knowledge and information.

Description: The Functional Assessment Inventory is a rating scale containing 30 four-point limitation ratings and a ten-item strength checklist. The rating items are operationally defined in behavioral terms with levels of limitation corresponding to none, mild, moderate, or severe. The inventory is completed by the rehabilitation counselor using information from medical and other relevant records, interviews, and observations.

Practical issues: The Functional Assessment Inventory is relatively short, requiring 5 to 10 minutes to complete by a knowledgeable counselor. Training is not required but is preferred to insure interobserver and test/re-test reliability.

Scoring and use: The Functional Assessment Inventory produces an overview of functional limitations that are relevant for vocational rehabilitation outcomes based on existing information. No new diagnostic information is produced by this inventory. Both a total numerical score and seven subscale scores are produced from ordinal ratings. The subscales result from factor analysis and evidence for responsiveness (i.e., change in response to services) has been reported. The Functional Assessment Inventory can provide information for problem identification, eligibility determinations, information organizations, goal setting, and service planning within the vocational rehabilitation setting.

Medical

User objective: To obtain a broad-based and comprehensive description of inpatient functioning in medical rehabilitation settings.

Scale example: Functional Independence Measure (FIM) (Keith et al., 34).

Functional assessment model:

Levels: disability
Areas: physical, mental,
Type: discriminative, evaluative

Purpose: To measure degree of disability, which is relevant during inpatient medical rehabilitation.

Description: The FIM uses 18 items in which a patient's degree of disability and burden of care are apparent. Each item is rated according to a seven-level classification (Total Assist to Complete Independence).

Practical issues: The FIM is rated by therapists and other care providers first at admission and again at discharge from the rehabilitation facility. The FIM requires about 60 minutes of training and 10 minutes to complete.

Scoring and use: The FIM scoring system is intended to measure Motor and Cognitive function at admission to and discharge from the rehabilitation facility. While the therapists ratings are ordinal, interval scores bases on Rasch analysis provide profiles for comparative data regarding program management and evaluation. The FIM provides information through the Uniform Data System that can be used for program evaluation and outcomes research information (cost data are included) as well as client tracking.

Specific Rehabilitation

Physical Disability

User objective: To describe the functional limitation in activities of daily living of patients with primarily physical disabilities.

Scale example: Rapid Disability Rating Scale (RDRS) Linn and Linn, ref. 60).

Functional assessment model:

Levels: Impairment, disability
Areas: physical (one-item overview of mental and emotional)
Type: discriminative

Purpose: The Rapid Disability Rating Scale was designed to summarize the physical capacity of elderly chronic hospitalized and community-based patients.

Description: The Rapid Disability Rating Scale is an 18-item, four-point rating scale designed to be completed by an expert who is knowledgeable of the patient. The rating scales for each question range from None (completely independent or normal behavior) to Total (person cannot, will not, or may not [because of medical restriction] perform the behavior). The scale is composed of three parts. One describes assistance with activities of daily living (e.g., eating, bathing, grooming); the second describes the degree of disability (e.g., communication, diet, incontinence); and the third consists of three general questions about confusion, uncooperativeness, and depression.

Practical issues: The Rapid Disability Rating Scale can be completed in less than 5 minutes when rated by an expert knowledgeable of the patient. No special training is required.

Scoring and use: The items are weighted equally in calculating an overall score which ranges from 18 to 72. The items may be combined according to the parts of the scale. The ratings have been used successfully to classify patients according to level of disability. Community dwelling individuals average about 21, hospitalized patients average about 32, and nursing home patients average about 36.

Psychiatric Disability

User objectives: To assess the functional adjustment of chronically mentally ill to community living.

Scale example: Social Adjustment Scale (SAS) (Weissman and Gothwell, ref. 61).

Functional assessment model:

Levels: disability
Areas: emotional, social
Type: discriminative, evaluative

Purpose: To assess patient functioning, generally and interpersonally, and patient satisfaction in six instrumental role areas.

Description: There are two versions of the Social Adjustment Scale, an interview form and a self-report version, both of which contain 42 items. Each covers functioning in work, social-leisure activities, relationship with extended family, and marital roles as spouse, parent, and member of family unit.

Scoring and use: Two scoring methods are used: a mean score for each section and an overall score. The focus on social adjustment provides a framework for designing a rehabilitation treatment program.

Health Assessment Applied to Rehabilitation

User objective: To obtain comprehensive functional information that can be used for program planning, health surveys, and patient progress.

Scale example: Sickness Impact Profile (SIP) (Bergner et al., ref. 62).

Functional assessment model:

Levels: disability
Areas: physical, emotional, social
Type: discriminative

Purpose: To provide a behaviorally based measurement of perceived health status that reflects ''universal patterns'' of limitations that may be affected by sickness or disease, regardless of specific conditions, treatments, individual characteristics, or prognosis.

Description: The Sickness Impact Profile consists of 136 statements in 12 categories. Each item describes a change

in behavior and specifies the extent of limitation (e.g., I stay away from home only for brief periods of time). Respondents check (self-report) or indicate (interview) only the items that describe them on a given day.

Practical issues: As a self-administered scale, the Sickness Impact Profile requires 20 to 30 minutes. The interview version may take longer and is recommended for more impaired respondents.

Scoring and use: The Sickness Impact Profile is one of the few interval scales available in health assessment. Scores are calculated using item weights that indicate relative severity of each statement. The weights are derived from equal-appearing scaling procedures and permit the production of a total score and scale score with interval properties.

Because the Sickness Impact Profile has undergone extensive validation and normative testing, it permits direct comparison across a variety of groups within rehabilitation settings, and between clients and other disabled or nondisabled groups.

FUNCTIONAL ASSESSMENT IN REHABILITATION SETTINGS

There are three main activities in rehabilitation for which functional assessment information can be gainfully used: client management, program evaluation, and research. In client management settings, functional information can provide useful information at each of the critical decision points. In medical rehabilitation settings, the focus is on the individual patient and the information is used to assess initial status, design treatment plans, monitor programs, evaluate the patient's status at the end of treatment to determine whether treatment goals have been achieved, and communicate results (35,63).

In vocational rehabilitation, client management issues are similar and functional assessment has an important role to play. At screening, functional assessment information can be used to assess current levels of functioning and predict probability of a successful rehabilitation, although current rehabilitation outcome measures need further refinement (64). A second important application is at the diagnostic level. Often, batteries of time-consuming (and costly) tests are ordered regardless of the particular needs of the client or counselor. Functional information can be used to organize existing information and target specific areas where additional in-depth information is needed using, for example, the Functional Assessment Inventory. Or, functional assessment information can provide an initial diagnosis based on new information as is the case with the Preliminary Diagnostic Questionnaire (65).

Once specific client problems have been identified and described functionally, specific services targeted toward those functional limitations can be planned and implemented. During the course of service delivery, progress toward intermediate goals can be tracked as change in functional status and, at case closure, rehabilitation outcomes can be recorded as change in functional problem area as well as enhancements (e.g., cognitive skills) as a result of service delivery.

The second major purpose of functional information is in program evaluation (63). Evaluation activities can be grouped into four classes: program planning and development, program monitoring, impact assessment, and cost-outcome comparison (66). For each of these, functional assessment information can be applied for specific evaluation tasks such as identifying appropriate target populations (the severely disabled, for example), determining if service delivery has produced an improvement, or if there has been a change in status which can be attributed to the intervention, and determining whether those outcomes were delivered economically. This latter point has received a great deal of attention in rehabilitation settings and the role of functional information is becoming more prominent (67).

The third application of functional assessment information is in *research*. A prime example is the use of functional data as descriptors in epidemiological and clinical research. The addition of functional status descriptors to the traditionally collected mortality and clinically diagnosed morbidity data provides an integrative component not only for rehabilitation, but for health care in general (22,68). Furthermore, it is through research that the models and concepts discussed earlier have become increasingly clarified. Through the process of identifying terms, research methodologists have been obligated to define more precisely what variables should be included in functional assessment (68).

Technical Considerations

When using functional assessment scales, there are a number of technical considerations that influence the analysis and interpretation of functional information across each of the assessment applications.

Scaling methods are used to translate the descriptive items in the measure into numerical estimates of functional level (28–30). The most adequate numerical scale possible is the most desirable, but constructing such scales is complex, and respondent burden often increases (25,30).

The application of Rasch analysis to functional assessment represents an important technical advance in functional assessment. The developers of the FIM have made extensive use of this technique (34,41,44,45) as has the Patient Evaluation and Conference System (PECS) (42,43). The method has also been applied in comparative analyses for traumatic head injury (49) and pain (50). In all of these, the problem of using widely accepted qualitative descriptors (e.g., "mild," "moderate," "severe") in ordinal scales to produce psychometrically sound interval scales has been solved.

In most cases, the instrument requires the combination of scale items into composite measures or scales. A number of key assumptions underlie this procedure and the user should try to ascertain the degree to which they are met in the scales being considered (69,70):

1. Each item contributes to the pool of information about the construct.
2. The method of combination is consistent with the relationships among the items.
3. All items are scored in the same direction.
4. All items measure the construct in approximately the same units (or they have been standardized and weighted).
5. The resulting measure (or construct) has a meaningful interpretation.

These approaches to weighting the components have been used but most of the functional assessment work to date has relied simply on investigator-defined scores. The scale developer assigns higher scores to items that reflect, in the developer's opinion, a higher level of functioning. Problems arise with the assumption of social consensus and when respondents rate combinations of attributes (14). Some advanced methods are available, but they are rarely used in functional assessment scales in rehabilitation. A variety of category scaling methods, for example, the equal-appearing index, can be used to produce interval scales, although criticism has been leveled at the use of fixed categories. Magnitude estimation techniques are used for producing ratio scales that are rare in health assessment in general and functional assessment in particular (25).

CONCLUSIONS

Functional assessment in rehabilitation is now tied firmly both to the process of rehabilitation and to program management and evaluation. As accountability for patient and program outcome becomes increasingly important across the health care delivery system generally, outcomes research based on patient functioning will play an ever more central role.

Scales are being developed from a conceptual framework that accurately reflects the distinction among impaired, disability, and handicap, and incorporates the multidimensional array of functional areas relevant for rehabilitation and health-related quality of life. Furthermore, the field is now benefiting from the application of the best technology and highest standards available. As measurement progress proceeds in both rehabilitation and health status assessment, opportunities for synergy increase.

The conditions for this linkage are in place. Both disabled and nondisabled persons are living longer and require more long-term care. Also, acute diseases are giving way to chronic conditions in developed countries. Health care resource planning in general is beginning to reflect the convergence of these factors. In rehabilitation, effective management of client services, program evaluation, and research all require accurate and useful information. Functional assessment, produced from conceptually and technically sound measures, is a valuable source of much of that information.

REFERENCES

1. Jette AM. Concepts of health and methodological issues in functional assessment. In: Granger CV, Gresham GE, eds. *Functional assessment in rehabilitation medicine*. Baltimore: Williams & Wilkins, 1984.
2. Turner RR. Rehabilitation. In: Spilker B, ed. *Quality of life assessments in clinical trials*. New York: Raven Press, 1990.
3. Frey WD. Functional assessment in the '80's: a conceptual enigma, a technical challenge. In: Halpern AS, Fuhrer MJ, eds. *Functional assessment in rehabilitation*. Baltimore: Paul H. Brookes, 1984:1–10.
4. Brown M, Gordon W, Diller L. Functional assessment and outcome measurement: an integrated review. In: Pan EL, Backer TE, Vash CL, eds. *Annual review of rehabilitation*. Vol 3. New York: Springer, 1983: 93–120.
5. Schipper H, Levitt M. Measuring quality of life: risks and benefits. *Cancer Treat Rep* 1985;69:1115–1122.
6. Wenger NK, Mattson ME, Furberg CD, Elinson J, eds. *Assessment of quality of life in clinical trials of cardiovascular therapies*. New York: LeJacq, 1984.
7. Patrick DL, Erickson P. *Health status and health policy: quality of life in health care evaluation and resource allocation*. New York: Oxford University Press, 1993.
8. Stineman MG, Granger CV. Outcome studies and analysis: principles of rehabilitation that influence outcome analysis. In: Felsenthal G, Garrison SJ, Steinberg FU, eds. *Rehabilitation of the aging and elderly patient*. Baltimore: Williams & Wilkins, 1994.
9. Nagi SZ. *Disability and rehabilitation*. Columbus: Ohio State University Press, 1969.
10. Nagi SZ. Some conceptual issues in disability and rehabilitation. In: Sussman MB, ed. *Sociology and rehabilitation*. Columbus: Ohio State University Press, 1965.
11. Wood PHN. Classification of impairment and handicap. Document WHO/ICDP/REV-CONF/75.15. Geneva: World Health Organization, 1975.
12. Stewart AL, Ware JE, Brook RH. Construction and scoring of aggregate functional state measures. Vol I. Santa Monica, CA: RAND, 1982.
13. Stewart AL, Ware SE, eds. *Measuring functioning and well-being: the Medical Outcomes Study approach*. Durham, NC: Duke University Press, 1992.
14. Patrick DL, Erickson PE. Assessing health-related quality of life for clinical decision making. Walker SR, Rosen RM, eds. *Quality of life: assessment and application*. Lancaster, PA: MTP Press, 1988.
15. Keith RA. Functional status and health status. *Arch Phys Med Rehabil* 1994;75:478–483.
16. Granger CV. A conceptual model for functional assessment. In: Granger CV, Gresham GE, eds. *Functional assessment in rehabilitation medicine*. Baltimore: Williams & Wilkins, 1984.
17. Kelman HR, Willner A. Problems in measurement and evaluation of rehabilitation. *Arch Phys Med Rehabil* 1962;43:172–181.
18. Keith RA. Functional assessment measures in medical rehabilitation: current status. *Arch Phys Med Rehabil* 1984;65:74–78.
19. Barer D. Assessment in rehabilitation. *Rev Clin Gerontol* 1983;3:169–186.
20. Task Force on Standards for Measurement in Physical Therapy. Standards for tests and measurements in physical therapy practice. *Phys Ther* 1991;71:589–622.
21. Johnston MV, Keith RA, Hinderer SR. Measurement standards for interdisciplinary medical rehabilitation. *Arch Phys Med Rehabil* 1992;73(suppl):51–52.
22. Ellwood PM. Outcome management: a technology of patient experience. *N Engl J Med* 1988;318:1551–1556.
23. Hamilton DD, Granger CV, Sherwin FS, et al. A uniform national data system for medical rehabilitation. In: MJ Fuhrer, ed. *Rehabilitation outcomes: analysis and measurement*. Baltimore: Paul H. Brookes Co., 1987:135.
24. Feinstein AR. *Clinimetrics*. New Haven: Yale University Press, 1987.
25. McDowell I, Newell C. *Measuring health: a guide to rating scales and questionnaires*. New York: Oxford University Press, 1987.
26. Spilker B, ed. *Quality of life assessments in clinical trials*. New York: Raven Press, 1990.
27. Kirshner B, Guyatt G. A methodological framework for assessing health indices. *J Chronic Dis* 1985;38:27–36.
28. Nunnally JC. *Psychometric theory*. 2nd ed. New York: McGraw-Hill, 1978.
29. Thorndike RL. *Applied psychometrics*. Boston: Houghton-Mifflin, 1982.
30. Torgerson GS. *Theory and methods of scaling*. New York: Wiley, 1978.
31. Ware JE. Methodological considerations in selection of health status assessment procedures. In: Wenger NK, Mattson ME, Furberg CD, et al., eds. *Assessment of quality of life in clinical trials of cardiovascular therapies*. New York: LeJacq, 1984.
32. Winer B. *Statistical principles in experimental design*. 2nd ed. New York: McGraw-Hill, 1971.
33. Brinberg D, Kidder LH. *Forms of validity in research*. San Francisco: Jossey-Bass, 1982.
34. Keith RA, Granger CV, Hamilton BB, Sherwin FS. The Functional Independence Measure: a new tool for rehabilitation. In: Eisenberg MG, Grzeskiak RE, eds. *Advances in clinical rehabilitation*. New York: Springer-Verlag, 1987:6–18.
35. Alexander J, Fuhrer M. Functional assessment of physical impairment. In: Halpern AS, Fuhrer MS, eds. *Functional assessment in rehabilitation*. Baltimore: Paul H. Brookes, 1984:45–60.
36. Helmstadt GC. *Principles of psychological measurement*. London: Methuen, 1966.
37. Vash CL. Evaluation from the client's point of view. In: Halpern AS, Fuhrer MJ, eds. *Functional assessment in rehabilitation*. Baltimore: Paul H. Brookes, 1984:253–268.
38. Hamilton BB, Laughlin JA, Granger CV, et al. Inter-rater agreement of the seven level Functional Independence Measure (FIM). *Arch Phys Med Rehabil* 1991;72:572.
39. Fleiss JL. *Statistical methods for rates and proportions*. 2nd ed. New York: Wiley, 1981.
40. Chau N, Daler S, Andrew J, Patris A. Inter-rater agreement of two functional independence scales: the Functional Independence Measure (FIM) and a subjective uniform continuous scale. *Disabil Rehabil* 1994;16:63–71.
41. Dodds TA, Martin DP, Stolov WC, Deyo RA. A validation of the Functional Independence Measure and its performance among rehabilitation inpatients. *Arch Phys Rehabil* 1993;74:531–536.
42. Silverstein B, Kilgore KM, Fisher WP, et al. Applying psychometric criteria to functional assessment in medical rehabilitation. I. Exploring unidimensionality. *Arch Phys Med Rehabil* 1991;72:631–637.
43. Silverstein B, Fisher WP, Kilgore KM, et al. Applying psychometric criteria for functional assessment in medical rehabilitation. V. Defining internal measures. *Arch Phys Med Rehabil* 1992;73:507–518.
44. Linacre JM, Heinemann AW, Wright BO, et al. The functional independence measure as a measure of disability. Research report 91-01. Chicago: Rehabilitation Services Evaluation Unit, Rehabilitation Institute of Chicago, 1991.
45. Granger CV, Hamilton BB, Linacre JM, et al. Performance profiles of the functional independence measure. *Am J Phys Med Rehabil* 1993;72:84–89.
46. Heinemann AW, Linacre JM, Wright DB, et al. Relationships between impairment and physical disability as measured by the Functional Independence Measure. *Arch Phys Med Rehabil* 1993;74:566–573.
47. Granger CV, Cotter AC, Hamilton BB, et al. Functional assessment scales: a study of persons with multiple sclerosis. *Arch Phys Med Rehabil* 1990;71:870–875.
48. Granger CV, Cotter AC, Hamilton BB, et al. Functional assessment scales: a study of persons after stroke. *Arch Phys Med Rehabil* 1993;74:133–138.
49. Hall KM, Hamilton BB, Gordon WA, et al. Characteristics and comparisons of functional assessment indices: Disability Rating Scale, Functional Independence Measure and Functional Assessment Measure. *J Head Trauma Rehabil* 1993;8:60–74.
50. McArthur DL, Cohen MJ, Schandler SL. Rasch analysis of functional assessment scales: an example using pain behaviors. *Arch Phys Med Rehabil* 1991;71:296–304.

51. Granger CV, Gresham GE. *Functional assessment in rehabilitation medicine.* Baltimore: Williams & Wilkins, 1984.
52. Halpern AS, Fuhrer MJ. *Functional assessment in rehabilitation.* Baltimore: Paul H. Brookes, 1984.
53. Spilker B, Molinek FR, Johnston KA, et al. Quality of life bibliography and indexes. *Med Care* 1990;28(suppl):D51–577.
54. Spilker B, Simpson RL, Tison HH. Quality of life bibliography and indexes: 1991 update. *J Clin Res Pharmacoepidemiol* 1991;6:205–266.
55. Wallace CJ. Functional assessment in rehabilitation. *Schizophr Bull* 1986;12:604–624.
56. Gersham GL, Labi ML. Functional assessment instruments currently available for documenting outcomes in rehabilitation medicine. In: Granger CF, Gresham GE, eds. *Functional assessment in rehabilitation medicine.* Baltimore: Williams & Wilkins, 1984.
57. Feeny D, Guyatt G, Patrick D. Proceedings of the international conference on the measurement of quality of life as an outcome in clinical trials. *Controlled Clin Trials* 1991;12(suppl):795–745.
58. Crew NM, Athelstan GT. Functional assessment in vocational rehabilitation: a systematic approach to diagnosis and goal setting. *Arch Phys Rehabil* 1981;62:299–305.
59. Turner RR. Functional assessment in vocational rehabilitation: validation, extension, and applications. Final Report. National Institute of Handicapped Research. Grant G008300163. October 1987.
60. Linn MW, Linn DS. The Rapid Disability Rating Scale-2. *J Am Geriatr Soc* 1982;30:378–382.
61. Weissman MM, Gothwell S. Assessment of social adjustment by patient self-report. *Arch Gen Psychiatry* 1976;33:1111–1115.
62. Bergner M, Bobbitt RA, Carter WB, Gilson BS. The Sickness Impact Profile: development and final revision of a health status measure. *Med Care* 1981;19:787–805.
63. Keith RA. Functional assessment in program evaluation for rehabilitation medicine. In: Granger CV, Gresha GL, eds. *Functional assessment in rehabilitation medicine.* Baltimore: Williams & Wilkins, 1984.
64. Backer TE. New directions in rehabilitation outcomes measurement. In: Pan EL, Backer TE, Vash CL, eds. *Annual review of rehabilitation.* Vol 1. New York: Springer, 1980:193–230.
65. Moriarity JB. Preliminary diagnostic questionnaire: PDQ. Dunbar: West Virginia Rehabilitation Research and Training Center, 1981.
66. Rossi PH, Freeman HC, Wright SR. *Evaluation: a systematic approach.* Beverly Hills, CA: Sage, 1979.
67. Berkowitz M. Benefit-cost analysis in rehabilitation. In: Granger CF, Gresham GE, eds. *Functional assessment in rehabilitation medicine.* Baltimore: Williams & Wilkins, 1984.
68. Labi ML, Gresham GE. Some research applications of functional assessment instruments used in rehabilitation medicine. In: Granger CV, Gresham GE, eds. *Functional assessment in rehabilitation medicine.* Baltimore: Williams & Wilkins, 1984.
69. Fisher WP. Measurement-related problems in functional assessment. *Am J Occup Ther* 1993;47:331–338.
70. Ware JE, Brook RH, Davis-Avery A, Williams KN, Stewart AL. Conceptualization and measurement of health for adults in the health insurance study. Vol I. *Model of health and methodology.* Santa Monica, CA: RAND Corporation, 1980 (R-1987-HEW).

Quality of Life and Pharmacoeconomics in Clinical Trials, Second Edition, edited by B. Spilker.
Lippincott-Raven Publishers, Philadelphia © 1996.

CHAPTER 89

Defining Quality of Life in Chronic Pain

Victor C. Lee and John C. Rowlingson

INTRODUCTION

Pain, in spite of being a common and fundamental human experience, is a complex and elusive phenomenon. The efforts of physicians, neurophysiologists, and behavioral psychologists, approaching the problem of pain from many perspectives, have given us tools for understanding this phenomenon, although many questions remain unanswered. The English word *pain* has its roots in the Latin *poena* and the Greek *poine,* both of which signify penalty, or punishment. In a biological sense, pain serves a protective role in guarding the organism from injury. The definition of pain proposed by the International Association for the Study of Pain reflects this association between pain and injury: "an unpleasant sensory and emotional experience associated with actual or potential tissue damage, or described in terms of such damage" (1). When the presence of pain no longer serves a useful protective role, and persists in spite of efforts to alleviate it, the pain itself becomes a problem. And when pain persists for months and years in spite of efforts to diagnose and treat the causes of this pain, the problem becomes one of chronic pain, the focus of this chapter.

V. C. Lee and J. C. Rowlingson: Department of Anesthesiology, University of Virginia Health Sciences Center, Charlottesville, Virginia 22908.

Chronic pain is experienced in a very diverse cross section of patients. Some examples of such patients would include those suffering from chronic musculoskeletal complaints such as fibromyalgia, spinal disorders (frequently involving failed back surgery), or joint disorders (degenerative or rheumatoid arthritis, temporomandibular joint dysfunction); patients presenting with neuropathic pain syndromes such as postherpetic neuralgia, tic douloureux, causalgia, phantom-limb pain, brachial plexus avulsion, and diabetic neuropathy; and other sufferers of chronic painful disorders such as refractory headaches and chronic abdominopelvic pain syndromes of known etiology (e.g., chronic pancreatitis) or unknown etiology. It is not always possible to apply a precise medical diagnosis, however, and the causes of chronic pain remain poorly understood by most of the medical community.

Chronic pain, however real to the patient, often cannot be understood according to the usual conventions of symptomatology and pathophysiology. Often there is no "objective" evidence of tissue injury, or if an injury occurred it has long since passed the usual time course for healing and symptom resolution. Furthermore, the usual clinical markers of ongoing disease (physical examinations, radiological and laboratory tests), are frequently unrevealing and inadequate for understanding the causes of the pain. These patients have often received what is judged to be an appropriate course

TABLE 1. *Features of the chronic pain syndrome*

1. Compared to other patients, the chronic pain patient is less likely to have objective findings and less likely to have a satisfactory diagnosis.
2. Pain is likely to be attributed to a specific event, such as a work-related injury or motor vehicle accident, and litigation is quite common.
3. These patients are likely to report a greater level of pain compared to other patients, and have a greater likelihood of experiencing psychological disturbances such as depression, social withdrawal, substance abuse, and diminished appetite, energy, and libido.
4. They are more likely to fail conservative treatment and are poor surgical candidates as well.
5. They consume a disproportionate share of medical and compensation costs and are frequent and inappropriate users of the health care system.
6. These patients are less likely to return to work, particularly if the period of unemployment has exceeded six months.

Based on Crook and Tunks (2).

of medical or surgical workup and treatment, but the patient is inexplicably left with persistent pain. The pain may often be out of proportion to what is considered a "normal" response, and frequently it is the patient alone who is convinced of the "reality" of his or her pain. Faced with a condition that cannot be satisfactorily diagnosed and for which little or no relief can be found, unable to function in his or her normal day-to-day existence because of preoccupation with that pain and its unanswered questions, the patient with chronic pain is beset with dissatisfaction and a deteriorating quality of life. A recognizable pattern of clinical features emerges, resulting in such descriptions as the "chronic pain syndrome" (2), presented in Table 1.

Given the poor understanding of most chronic pain states, much of pain therapy remains empirical, non-standardized, and in many cases inadequate. Notwithstanding, practitioners in the health care arena still need to find meaningful ways of characterizing pain severity and its impact upon quality of life, and to assess critically the seemingly limited clinical approaches presently employed for managing chronic pain in terms of efficacy and cost. The increasing cost-consciousness of medical practice obligates the players in that arena to utilize methods of outcome monitoring in order to maintain and improve the standards of pain management practice. This will assure the optimal utilization of health care resources while also providing the maximum benefit to patients. These concerns lie at the heart of quality of life studies in chronic pain.

QUANTIFYING PAIN: UNIDIMENSIONAL VS. MULTIDIMENSIONAL ASSESSMENT TOOLS

Pain is often characterized as a sensory experience, and is quantified in terms of the intensity of that sensation, often invoking unidimensional intensity measures of the type described below. On the other hand, there are characteristics of the pain experience which go beyond the sensation itself. These characteristics have to do with the emotional, or affective, attributes of the pain as well as the cognitive, or evalative, attributes of the pain. Multidimensional pain inventories, of the type detailed below are frequently utilized to provide a more complete characterization of the pain experience than is possible with a undimensional scale alone. Since pain is a subjective experience, all pain quantification techniques are necessarily self-reported measures of pain. Specific methods are used in quantifying the subjective experience of pain. Table 2 presents a summary of these instruments.

Unidimensional Scoring of Pain Intensity

Unidimensional measures of pain intensity are commonly employed in studies of clinical and experimental pain and the effects of analgesic interventions. Such instruments are typified by the numerical rating scale and the visual analog scale. The numerical rating scale typically ranges from 0 to 10 or 0 to 100, and the patient selects a number that reflects the intensity of his or her pain. The visual analog scale is a 10-cm line representing a linear spectrum of pain intensity, the opposite ends of which are labelled with such descriptions as "no pain" and "worst possible pain" (Fig. 1). The patient is asked to make a mark at a point along the 10-cm line that represents the intensity of his or her pain on this scale (3). In addition to the numerical and visual analog scales, there are verbal descriptor rating scales (3), also referred to as adjectival or categorical scales, which contain descriptive words (e.g., none, little, mild, moderate, severe) and function as unidimensional pain rating scales. Meaningful use of such pain intensity scales requires a cognitive understanding of the linear or the categorical representation of pain intensity. Hence there may be problems in applying these methods to certain individuals with poorly developed numerical, graphic, or verbal skills. The validity and reliability of the visual analog scale have been questioned by some

TABLE 2. *Instruments used to quantify pain*[a]

Unidimensional scoring of pain intensity
  Numerical rating scale (3)
  Visual analog scale (VAS) (3)
  Verbal rating scales (VRS) (3)
Multidimensional pain assessment instruments
  McGill Pain Questionnaire (MPQ) (8)
  Dartmouth Pain Questionnaire (11)
  West Haven–Yale Multidimensional Pain Inventory (WHYMPI, or MPI) (12)
  Brief Pain Inventory (BPI) (14)
  Memorial Pain Assessment Card (17)
Spatiotemporal characterization of pain
  Pain drawing
  Pain diary

[a]Numbers in parentheses are reference numbers.

No Pain ———————————————— Worst Pain

FIG. 1. The 10-cm visual analog scale.

(4,5), but endorsed by others (6). On the whole these scales continue to be widely used in clinical pain studies and are sensitive to treatment effects. The 101-point numerical scale (equivalent to the visual analog scale when millimeter designations are used) appears to possess the greatest sensitivity to treatment effects, given the number of categorical choices possible (7), although the human ability to actually discriminate 101 discrete levels of pain intensity is debatable. Additionally, the range of pain intensities represented by one individual's 0 to 100 scale may not be quite the same as another's 0 to 100 scale, since the ''worst possible pain'' may signify something quite different from one individual to another. Hence, studies employing self-controlled measurements (or within-subjects designs) and assurance of adequate statistical power are desirable. One final note: there is an implicit assumption in all these measures that pain intensity is a bounded linear function, and the statistical methods currently used embrace this assumption. While this concept is debatable, the great volume of literature published to date appears to have allowed this assumption to prevail.

Multidimensional Assessment of Pain

As mentioned previously, there are inadequacies with unidimensional measures of pain, given the complex attributes of pain that go beyond the sensory experience per se. In recognition of the multidimensional nature of pain, Melzack created the McGill Pain Questionnaire (MPQ) (8) from a list of 102 adjectives which characterize pain with regard to its sensory, affective, and evaluative attributes (Table 3). The relative value of each descriptor is ranked on a categorical scale. The sensory properties of pain are characterized by such adjectives as ''lancinating,'' ''throbbing,'' ''wrenching,'' and ''burning.'' The affective properties of pain are characterized by such adjectives as ''sickening,'' ''frightful,'' and ''wretched.'' The evaluative aspect of pain correlates with pain intensity, but additionally reflects the patient's level of tolerance of the pain experience and includes such descriptors as ''distressing,'' ''troublesome,'' and ''unbearable.'' The inventory is considerably dependent upon English language skills (not surprising, since the original 102 terms were derived from a survey administered to academic and professional people [9]), and this may pose an obstacle to the use of this instrument in certain patients. A short-form MPQ, employing only 15 descriptors in conjunction with a four-point severity scale, has been developed which appears to demonstrate treatment sensitivity comparable to that of the original, and may reduce some of the language skill requirements inherent in the original (10). Translations of instruments such as the MPQ into languages besides English are often seen in the literature, but is difficult

TABLE 3. McGill Pain Questionnaire descriptors

Sensory adjectives
  Temporal: flickering, quivering, pulsing, throbbing, beating, pounding
  Spatial: jumping, flashing, shooting
  Punctate pressure: pricking, boring, drilling, stabbing, lancinating
  Incisive pressure: sharp, cutting, lacerating
  Constrictive: pinching, pressing, gnawing, cramping, crushing
  Traction pressure: tugging, pulling, wrenching
  Thermal: hot, burning, scalding, searing; cool, cold, freezing
  Brightness: tingling, itchy, smarting, stinging
  Dullness: dull, sore, hurting, aching, heavy
  Miscellaneous: tender, taut, rasping, splitting
Affective adjectives
  Tension: tiring, exhausting
  Autonomic: sickening, suffocating
  Fear: fearful, frightful, terrifying
  Punishment: punishing, gruelling, cruel, vicious, killing
  Miscellaneous: wretched, blinding
Evaluative adjectives
  Annoying, troublesome, miserable, intense, unbearable, mild, discomforting, distressing, horrible, excruciating

Adapted from Melzack (8).

to cross-validate such instruments, since it is difficult to convey subtleties inherent in each individual language, not to mention the cultures from which they derive.

The relationship between pain and day-to-day functioning is addressed in a number of related multidimensional pain assessment questionnaires. The Dartmouth Pain Questionnaire (11) was developed specifically as an adjunct to the MPQ. It additionally addresses impaired function and should be coadministered with the MPQ to be useful. The West Haven–Yale Multidimensional Pain Inventory (12) (WHYMPI, or MPI) uses 52 items derived from a cognitive–behavioral construct, which address the relationship of pain and suffering to psychosocial interaction and daily activities. The MPI is considered relatively brief to administer and has demonstrated reliability and validity (13). The Brief Pain Inventory (BPI) (14) was developed as a tool for assessing quality of life in conjunction with cancer pain. This shortened form of the original Wisconsin Brief Pain Questionnaire (15) overcomes some of the shortcomings of the original instrument. It has particular validity in the cancer pain population but has demonstrated value in arthritis patients as well (16). The Brief Pain Inventory includes items concerning pain severity, functional interference, medication use and efficacy, and pain beliefs. While there may be concerns about administering follow-up questionnaires that are overly cumbersome, many of the above inventories can be completed in a 5- to 15-minute period (20). One multidimensional inventory is especially brief, taking literally seconds to complete. This is the Memorial Pain Assessment Card, a tool which has been used in quality of life studies concerning cancer patients. It consists of three linear analog scales (Pain

Scale, Relief Scale, Mood Scale) and a set of categorical adjectives describing pain intensity, and appears to be correlated with other more detailed pain and mood inventories (17). For patients experiencing a great deal of morbidity and who may have difficulty with lengthy assessments, an assessment tool requiring little time to complete presents a distinct advantage.

Additional Factors Associated with the Pain Experience

The spatial and the temporal characteristics of pain sensation are important dimensions of the pain experience. The spatial characteristics of pain are often represented in the so-called "pain drawing," a two-dimensional somatographic representation of the human body. A pain drawing is often included in pain questionnaires (Fig. 2), as a means of characterizing the location, radiation, and size of the painful region(s). The patient is asked to shade in the portion of the diagram corresponding to the distribution of his or her somatic pain, and include a numeric quantifier of pain intensity. Documentation of the spread or the regression of pain is accomplished by use of the pain drawing. The total body area involved in pain, as well as unusual or bizarre somatographic representations (e.g., pain migration, pain coming from outside the body) may bear special significance to the clinician and investigator.

The temporal element of pain sensation may be assessed by the use of a "pain diary," a patient-maintained written log of personal daily experiences that is capable of reflecting the day-to-day and even hour-to-hour changes in pain intensity and quality. The time course of waxing and waning pain, as well as the influence of external factors, time of day, or analgesic intervention may be documented. In clinical situations involving chronic recurring episodes of pain (e.g., as in chronic pancreatitis), the frequency of these pain episodes is as important to monitor as the intensity of pain. Use of a pain diary increases the validity of the sampling of self-reported pain intensity, and it is recognized that multiple sampling of pain scores, as opposed to infrequently obtained random pain scores, improves the reliability and validity of average pain estimates (18). An adequate representation of baseline pain is essential in assuring that the naturally occurring cyclical upswings and downswings in pain intensity, by virtue of serendipity, are not mistakenly interpreted as treatment effects. The concept that a serendipitous improvement in pain may be falsely identified as a treatment "success" is referred to as regression to the mean (19).

The circumstances under which pain occurs can be an important qualifier of the severity of pain. It is important to recognize that pain intensity is not a constant, but can vary with activities as well as perturbations in the physical and social environment. Characterization of activity-dependent pain is important in the assessment of chronic pain (e.g., what activities are inhibited because of the pain? is pain provoked by work? by recreation?). The limitations of pain upon activity are an essential component of a functional capacity evaluation, a tool often used in attempting to quantify residual work capacity. A pain diary may serve as a useful means of documenting circumstance-dependent and

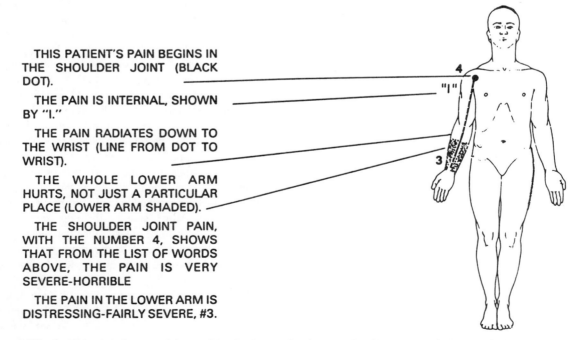

THIS PATIENT'S PAIN BEGINS IN THE SHOULDER JOINT (BLACK DOT).

THE PAIN IS INTERNAL, SHOWN BY "I."

THE PAIN RADIATES DOWN TO THE WRIST (LINE FROM DOT TO WRIST).

THE WHOLE LOWER ARM HURTS, NOT JUST A PARTICULAR PLACE (LOWER ARM SHADED).

THE SHOULDER JOINT PAIN, WITH THE NUMBER 4, SHOWS THAT FROM THE LIST OF WORDS ABOVE, THE PAIN IS VERY SEVERE-HORRIBLE

THE PAIN IN THE LOWER ARM IS DISTRESSING-FAIRLY SEVERE, #3.

FIG. 2. Pain drawing used for patient intake evaluations at the University of Virginia Pain Management Center.

activity-related pain intensity, which have a bearing on quality of life.

Pain intensity is often measured in an indirect fashion by analysis of analgesic requirement, particularly postsurgical pain. Such an analysis equates analgesic consumption with intensity of pain and assumes that patients will both demand and receive pain medication until a certain level of pain relief is experienced, that a certain consistently reproducible lowering of pain is achieved in all patients receiving similar doses of medication, and that there is some common end point of satisfaction that is reached by all patients. Such assumptions, needless to say, may prove dangerously false when subjected to more careful scrutiny. More properly considered, medication usage is a complex behavioral phenomenon, and behavioral measures of pain often fail to correlate with pain intensity (20). Notwithstanding, utilization of medication remains an important measure of life quality in studies of chronic pain, regardless of its correlation with actual pain intensity. Medication use can be recorded in a pain diary, which is a means of documenting analgesic use as well as compliance with medications and even the experience of medication side effects, all of which are important quality of care and quality of life indices.

INSTRUMENTS USED TO ASSESS PSYCHOLOGICAL FUNCTION IN CHRONIC PAIN PATIENTS

The use of instruments for the assessment of global psychological functioning in patients with chronic pain constitutes an enormous quantity of the literature of chronic pain. Such instruments have been variously used to categorize patients, to compare populations, to monitor progress of therapy, and to predict successful response to therapy. These assessment tools may be broadly grouped into the following categories: assessment of personality, assessment of affect, assessment of coping, and assessment of pain beliefs. The role of such psychological instruments is not all that well established in clinical studies of quality of life, but some of the major instruments are included in this discussion for completeness. It does seem intuitively obvious that certain traits measured by these instruments (e.g., depression, coping ability) are intimately related to quality of life and that studies of life quality should possess some means of evaluating such characteristics. Examples of psychological instruments employed in pain studies are discussed here and are listed in Table 4.

Assessment of Personality and Global Psychological Function

The Minnesota Multiphasic Personality Inventory (MMPI) bears the arguable distinction of being the most extensively investigated psychometric tool in the field of chronic pain. It was developed as a means of assessing

TABLE 4. *Instruments used to assess psychological dysfunction in chronic pain patients[a]*

Assessment of personality and global psychological function
Minnesota Multiphasic Personality Inventory (MMPI, MMPI-2) (21,29)
Symptom Checklist-90R (SCL-90R) (33)
Millon Health Behavioral Inventory (MBHI) (36)
Illness Behavior Questionnaire (IBQ) (39)
Assessment of affect
Beck Depression Inventory (BDI) (40)
Zung Self-Rating Depression Scale (41)
Spielberger State-Trait Anxiety Scale (STAI) (42)
Profile of Mood States (POMS) (43)
Assessment of coping
Coping Strategies Questionnaire (CSQ) (46)
Ways of Coping Questionnaire (WOC) (48)
Assessment of beliefs
Survey of Pain Beliefs (SOPA) (50)
Pain Information and Beliefs Questionnaire (PIBQ) (51)
Arthritis Self Efficacy Questionnaire (ASEQ) (52)

[a]Numbers in parentheses are reference numbers.

psychological disturbance by the use of a 566-item, true–false questionnaire from which ten clinical scales and three validity scales are derived (21). Some interesting findings have been reported in the chronic pain population. Sternbach and associates (22) reported affective and behavioral differences in chronic pain vs. acute pain patients, and the presence of litigation correlated with a potentiation of psychoneurotic features in comparison with patients not involved in such litigation. Interestingly, they concluded that the MMPI did not differ in patients with "positive" physical findings as compared to patients with "negative" physical findings. The MMPI has not proved a means of discriminating "organic" from "psychogenic" pain (22,23). As a prognosticator of favorable or unfavorable response of chronic pain patients to treatment, some of the surgical literature supports the use of the MMPI for predicting response to surgical interventions in chronic low back pain, such as lumbar disc surgery (24) and chemonucleolysis (25), although response to multidisciplinary pain management (26,27) is not well predicted by MMPI scores. The difference may lie in the way that "favorable" outcome is measured. Return to work appears to correlate with MMPI scores, and the need for vocational rehabilitation may also be predicted on the basis of this (28).

Both the original MMPI and its newer revised version, the MMPI-2 (29) depend on normative populations for interpretation of results, and herein lie some of the problems. Neither the original nor the updated instrument employ an appropriate normative population upon which to make meaningful conclusions about individual chronic pain patients (30) and the endorsement of questionnaire items relating to somatic symptoms, which is common in the chronic pain patient population, tends to distort the interpretation of the individual's psyche when compared to a nonmedical population (31,32). The cumbersome nature of such a lengthy questionnaire as the MMPI may limit the convenience of its use as a routine clinical tool and may potentially alienate patients (due to its overt psychoanalytical nature), diminishing their cooperativeness in a comprehensive pain program.

The Symptom Checklist-90R (SCL-90R) is a 90-item questionnaire also used to characterize psychological disturbance. From it are derived nine clinical scales and three global scales of disturbance (33). Its relative brevity represents an advantage over the MMPI, although its lack of validity scales has been cited as a potential weakness (34). Its normalization is based on the psychiatric patient population, and the appropriateness of this normative population has been questioned, particularly in view of the different ways in which distress is reported in pain patients when compared to psychiatric patients (35). There is little information to confirm the ability of the SCL-90R to predict a successful outcome of pain management therapy (30).

The Millon Behavioral Health Inventory (MBHI), developed to evaluate psychological functioning in medical patients, uses 150 true–false questions from which twenty subscales are derived that measure the patient's style of relating to health care provider, degree of stress, and illness responses (36). Since it is normalized to the medical patient population, some of the problems of misinterpretation of self-reported physical symptoms inherent in the MMPI are overcome. Its relative brevity compared with the MMPI is also an advantage. Its reliability and validity have been established by the author, but unfortunately its ability to predict a successful outcome of behavioral and multidisciplinary pain programs is limited (37,38).

The Illness Behavioral Questionnaire (39) uses 62 true–false items from which seven scales are derived that measure abnormal illness behavior, a type of patient behavior having to do with symptom expression associated with a paucity of physical findings and illness role-playing. Generally speaking, patients with a psychosomatic predilection score higher on the Illness Behavioral Questionnaire, but the reliability and validity of this instrument have been questioned (30).

Assessment of Affect

A number of instruments are used specifically for the assessment of mood and affect. The Beck Depression Inventory is a 21-item questionnaire that assesses severity of depression (40). Some of the somatic symptoms and vegetative symptoms, common in chronic pain and cancer pain, may be overly interpreted as reflecting clinical depression (30). The Zung Self-Rating Depression Scale is another commonly used instrument employing 20 self-rated items for assessing clinical depression (41), although reliability and validity are not incontrovertibly established for chronic pain. The Spielberger State-Trait Anxiety Inventory uses 20 self-rated items to assess anxiety (42). Another commonly en-

countered instrument for assessing dysphoric mood is the Profile of Mood States (43), which consists of 65 items in its original form and 11 items in a subsequently shortened version (44). The Profile of Mood States as well as the preceding mood state and depression inventories are very commonly used in studies of cancer pain, where mood dysphoria is highly relevant to quality of life.

Assessment of Coping

The use of coping strategies represents a positive adaptation to chronic pain (45) and includes such methods as distraction from the pain experience by maintaining activity and using positive coping statements. In spite of its seeming relevance to life quality, and in spite of its apparent promise as a cognitive behavioral pain management strategy, there are few psychological assessment instruments which deal directly with coping. The field is largely represented by two such instruments. The Coping Strategies Questionnaire (46) uses 50 self-report items to assess the presence of adaptive and maladaptive coping strategies. Although promising, there remain some theoretical problems with this instrument involving factor analysis and defining meaningful dimensions of coping (47). The Ways of Coping questionnaire uses 55 self-report items to assess a number of cognitive strategies for dealing with stress (48). This tool was originally developed to assess a broadly-based medical population, but has been subsequently modified to include chronic pain-relevant items (49). In spite of its application as a research tool in understanding patient beliefs and coping, its clinical value has not been well-established (47).

Assessment of Beliefs

The direct relationship of beliefs about the nature of pain to life quality is unclear. However, there is interest in assessing pain beliefs as a means of interpreting patient satisfaction and predicting successful outcome of pain therapy and rehabilitation. As such, this particular area of psychometric analysis may play a role in medical decision-making and shepherding of medical care resources if it can be determined who seems most likely to benefit from currently existing pain treatments. The Survey of Pain Attitudes (50), Pain Information and Beliefs Questionnaire (51), and the Arthritis Self Efficacy Questionnaire (52) are representative instruments in this field, although a number of others are described (47). It is beyond the scope of this discussion to elaborate upon the subtleties of the use of these instruments. The incorporation of pain belief instruments into quality of life studies has not been well established, but it does seem reasonable to consider that as predictors of outcome such instruments may indeed assist in the medical decision-making process and hence impact on quality and standards of care. As discussed later, pretreatment beliefs may exert an enormous influence on the degree of satisfaction expressed by patients undergoing chronic pain treatment, and this is an important concept to appreciate when satisfaction data are being analyzed.

MEASURES OF ACTIVITY AND FUNCTIONING

Perhaps one of the most relevant quality of life measures to monitor in patients, whether they are suffering from cancer pain or chronic nonmalignant musculoskeletal pain, is the level of activity and functioning. It is not the intention of this discussion to present the various methods by which physical strength and range of motion are assessed, since such data are more applicable to individual patients (e.g., for setting goals, monitoring progress of therapy, and determining work limitations), rather than to populations of patients. Standards for evaluating functional capacity and residual functional capacity are poorly defined and not universally agreed upon. Additionally, functional ability correlates poorly with pain perception. For example, Mayer and colleagues attempted to define objective physical function-derived measures in the evaluation of low back pain patients undergoing rehabilitation (53) using physical measurements in eight categories: 1) range of motion, 2) cardiovascular fitness and muscle endurance, 3) gait speed, 4) timed simulation of daily activities, 5) static lifting, 6) lifting under load, 7) isometric and isokinetic dynamic trunk strength, and 8) global effort rating. The return to work rate after completion of the rehabilitation program was quite commendable in the Mayer study (82%), but there was little correlation with pain relief; i.e., the investigators found it possible to achieve functional rehabilitation without significant improvement in pain (53). It is unclear how applicable such measures are to other groups of chronic pain patients, or how increased work capacity alone without reduction in pain would translate into an appreciably improved quality of life (since pain interference with leisure and other nonwork activities is not addressed when only task-related physical measurements are used).

By contrast, as a means of documenting participation in day-to-day activities common to wide cross sections of the patient population, a number of self-report measures assessing health-related function have been devised as a means of quantifying day-to-day functioning and the impact of pain and illness upon that functioning, without the use of objective physical measurements. These instruments are quite extensively used in quality of life outcome studies relating to chronic pain as well as cancer pain (Table 5).

The Short Form Health Survey (SF-36) (54) was developed in conjunction with the Medical Outcomes Study (MOS) and is a 36-item self-report or interview-driven inventory that assesses a) health-related limitations in physical activities, b) limitations in social activities due to physical or emotional problems, c) role activity limitations due to

TABLE 5. *Measures of activity and functioning*[a]

Medical Outcomes Study Short Form Health Survey (SF-36) (54)
Sickness Impact Profile (SIP) (57)
Roland–Morris Disability Questionnaire (58)
Chronic Illness Problem Inventory (CIPI) (60)
Pain Disability Index (PDI) (61)
Karnofsky Performance Status Scale (62)
Oswestry Low Back Pain Disability Questionnaire (63)
Chronic Pain Grade (64)
Nottingham Health Profile (65)
Medical Outcomes Survey-Pain Index (MOS-PI) (66)

[a]Numbers in parentheses are reference numbers.

physical problems, d) somatic pain, e) psychological stress and well-being, f) role-activity limitations due to emotional problems, g) energy and fatigue, and h) general health perceptions. Validation and reliability data have been provided for the SF-36 (55,56), and its relatively short format promotes convenience of administration.

Another commonly used instrument for assessing activity and function is the Sickness Impact Profile (57), originally developed as a robust instrument capable of sensitivity sufficient to detect health status changes over time and within groups (13). There are 136 items administered by questionnaire or interview (taking 20 to 30 minutes), which cover a range of categories dealing with social interactions, movement, home activities, recreation, and others. Each of the 12 scales can be separately administered without apparently compromising the construct validity (13). A prominent adaptation of the SIP creates a disability-focused checklist from 24 items of the Sickness Impact Profile. This adaptation has been termed the Roland–Morris Disability Questionnaire (58). It has been found to compare favorably in performance with the original SIP in the assessment of chronic back pain, with the exception of having less sensitivity for psychosocial function and more sensitivity for physical function (59), and is considerably easier to administer than the original Sickness Impact Profile, owing to its brevity.

Some additional instruments capable of quantifying functional activity should be noted here: The Chronic Illness Problem Inventory (60), the Pain Disability Index (61), the Karnofsky Performance Status Scale (62), the Oswestry Low Back Pain Disability Questionnaire (63), the Chronic Pain Grade (64), and the Nottingham Health Profile (65). Additionally, there is the relatively brief Medical Outcomes Survey-Pain Index (MOS-PI) (66) of which 8 of its 12 items are taken from the Wisconsin Brief Pain Questionnaire (15). This is not an exhaustive listing of medical self-report function and activity inventories, and others appear in the literature. Selection of an appropriate functional status instrument would need to take into account the population being studied, the severity of incapacity, and the relevant outcomes that are being investigated. A discussion of functional measures appropriate to studies of low back pain is included later in this chapter.

ASSESSMENT OF SATISFACTION

The concept of patient satisfaction is an evolving one in the present atmosphere of health care reform. The interest in patient satisfaction data clearly has implications concerning consumerism and the medical marketplace, as well as the issue of improving quality of care. The field is certainly a controversial one, and various aspects of this controversy have been discussed by Miaskowski (67). These include issues concerning whether patient satisfaction has anything at all to do with actual quality of medical care, if consumers possess adequate qualifications to make judgments about medical care, how much perceptions of quality are molded by the personal appeal of the care provider and by the "quantity" of what is delivered to the consumer (i.e., numerous and repetitive tests that create the illusion of good medical care), and whether it is appropriate to allow medical practice to be somehow molded by popular opinion. On the other hand, it is also pointed out that it is relatively easy and cost-effective to obtain patient satisfaction data (compared with the difficulty and expense of medical record reviews, for example) and that unique information is obtained which is not available from any other source (67). It is difficult to imagine how to assess quality of life without some kind of self-reporting of satisfaction. Indeed, satisfaction assessment tools will probably become increasingly common as this field develops. Some examples are provided here.

Satisfaction may be defined for any aspect of care, as will be illustrated in this discussion. The most basic level of satisfaction reporting in studies of pain involve pain relief scores. A pain relief score is defined as a self-reported percentage estimate of pain relief in response to an analgesic intervention (20). Alternatively, a visual analog score for pain relief may be utilized, as illustrated by the Memorial Pain Assessment Card (17). In the situation of acute pain, this may be linked to administration of an analgesic drug. In cancer patients, pain relief estimates are an invaluable means of judging adequacy of an analgesic medication regimen, and supplement the actual pain scores. In chronic pain, relief scores may be linked to individual treatments or to overall response to a pain management program. It is not clear whether relief scores need to be proportionate in magnitude to changes in the actual pain score to be valid. This is because these two concepts (pain intensity and pain relief) may not be derived from the same cognitive and evaluative processes—therefore, they are not necessarily correlated numerically (J. D. Haddox, *personal communication* 1987).

In addition to pain relief, there are other dimensions of satisfaction which may be assessed in the situation of chronic pain. Deyo and Diehl (68) devised a patient satisfaction checklist consisting of nine items dealing primarily with the quality of interpersonal relationships with care providers, including adequacy of information and education. The primary conclusion drawn from this study was that satisfaction largely hinged upon whether the patient felt that his care provider had given an adequate enough explanation of the etiology of the back problem.

The satisfaction assessment instrument devised by Ware et al. (69) includes three dimensions which assess art of care (e.g., interpersonal characteristics, courteousness, caring attitude), technical quality (e.g., knowledge, skill, experience), and efficacy (perception of effectiveness of care). Linn and Greenfield (70) applied this satisfaction instrument in a study of arthritis, cardiology, and endocrinology patients suffering from chronic medical conditions and found that the satisfaction measures were in fact influenced by perceived health, view of life, and social circumstances (i.e., a pre-existing belief system).

Hazard et al. (71) devised a simple satisfaction assessment instrument consisting of a 0 to 10 global satisfaction score to rate the outcome of treatment for back pain. A conclusion of this particular study was that satisfaction had little to do with improvements in VAS, physical function, or Oswestry disability scores (63) over the treatment period but was weakly correlated with pain and disability at the time of the follow-up questionnaire (5-year follow-up). The authors suggest that pretreatment expectations may influence satisfaction, echoing views espoused by Shutty et al. (72) and Miaskowski (67). The influence of pretreatment beliefs upon treatment satisfaction is a recurrent theme, and may point to the necessity of evaluating patient beliefs and expectations about the nature and treatment of pain in order to draw any meaningful conclusions about patient satisfaction.

CALCULATING THE COSTS

The costs of chronic pain must be considered not only from the perspective of the medical costs incurred by the health care system, but from the perspective of the costs to the patient in terms of quality of life. Neither can be done simply, but this discussion outlines some of the work that has been described in the literature.

Costs of medical care derived from worker's compensation and from Social Security Disability can be used to illustrate the economic impact of chronic pain on our health care system. The Worker's Compensation Board of New York State paid more than $.5 billion in 1982 for 121,082 claims that had been closed that year, with more than $40 million of that sum paid for 1,595 back injury claims (medical and hospitalization costs are not included in these figures) (73). Similarly, the Quebec Worker's Compensation Board paid $21 million in medical costs and $129 million in salary compensation for 45,858 claims relating to spinal disorders (74). Extrapolation of such figures leads to staggering estimates of the national costs for chronic pain and injury. Bonica's estimate of the 1980 costs for low back pain alone in the United States was $23.2 billion, a composite estimate of direct medical costs, lost earnings and services, and mortality (75). The amount of lost work time is not trivial. When back pain is considered along with other chronically painful conditions such as cancer pain, headache pain, cardiovascular pain, orofacial pain, visceral pain, and neuralgic pain, Bonica's 1980 estimates projected that more than 50 million Americans experience varying periods of disability due to chronic pain, resulting in more than 700 million lost workdays. On the other hand, Harris and associates (76), in the 1985 Nuprin Pain Report, reported the estimated number of lost workdays from back pain alone to be 1.3 billion person-days, with joint pain (1.0 billion person-days) and headache (0.6 billion person-days) following closely behind (77).

The financial costs of chronic pain cannot be known precisely, since the contribution of the pain itself can only be estimated. In general, such calculations take into consideration medical costs, costs of lost workdays and services, costs of supporting disability, and administrative costs. For reasons that go beyond the scope of this discussion, medical costs are subject to many variables, including individual practice styles and method of reimbursement (e.g., fee for service vs. contracted care). Interpretation of any estimated medical costs should take into account exactly how those costs were figured. Costs of lost workdays may represent an idealized situation that assumes the perpetual existence of a given job (which fails to consider that such jobs may come or go, depending on the economic situation) and continuing productivity of an individual (which fails to take into account a possibly unmotivated individual who may have been fired for other reasons). And so, interpretation of estimates of lost workdays should similarly be viewed critically. Estimates of the costs of disability also vary depending on the disability-granting agency and how that agency calculates the dollar value of disability. For example, the Social Security Administration allows pain as the basis for disability if it is supported by medical findings, and if the pain produces physical or mental impairments (77). Benefits are granted only if the individual is found to be unable to pursue *any* gainful employment. The Veteran's Administration does not generally consider pain as an independently disabling condition. Rather, to the extent that pain accompanies well-documented pathophysiology, disability will be figured on the basis of those limitations attributable to that pathologic condition. Pain in excess of this is not factored into the disability determination, which differs somewhat from the Social Security Administration guidelines (77). As with the Social Security Administration, the individual is denied benefits if he is capable of lower-paying work. State Workers' Compensation laws tend to vary from state to state, but in general also require supporting medical findings in addition to the complaint of pain. Unlike the federal programs, Workers' Compensation generally makes benefits available when the individual is no longer able to do his or her usual job or is unable to find alternative employment commensurate with prior training and income level (77) and will not deny benefits if the individual is capable of lower-paying work. The actual calculation of the benefit may vary from state to state. Private insurance companies will provide disability benefits in accordance with the contractual agreement with its client, and this will vary from policy to policy. As before, pain is allowed as a disabling condition to the extent that its presence is supported by medical findings (77).

The costs of chronic pain to the patient, in terms of decrement in quality of life, have only been rudimentarily addressed. Perhaps the prototypical example of attaching value to life quality is the concept of the Quality-Adjusted Life Year (QALY), which is also discussed elsewhere in this book. Kaplan (78) has applied this concept to assessing life quality in cancer patients, by attaching hypothetical values to a variety of factors involving physical and social functioning as well as symptoms including nausea, insomnia, and pain, based on a Quality of Well-Being (QWB) model. Values are derived from surveys of the general population that indicate desirability and undesirability of certain clinical states. By application of mathematical weighting and conversion factors to express outcomes in common measurement units, health outcomes may be represented in terms of equivalent numbers of well years of life, and costs per QALY units can be calculated in order to guide health care choices. For example, the value of pain reduction from an interventional pain-relieving treatment can be weighed against the co-morbidity of the procedure itself (loss of mobility, nausea, incontinence).

Because the QALY concept is based on models of health, it is only as good as the model on which it is based. Controversies abound, as would naturally be expected. Besides the obvious concerns about the ethics of rationing health care resources, there are controversies in the weighting and valuation of the various health characteristics. The use of surveys essentially amounts to applying majority rule (assuming that public feeling has been adequately sampled) to determine which conditions and symptoms are more or less desirable than others. The choices of one individual (e.g., which may be influenced by gender, culture, ethnicity) may have little to do with the survey results, and yet the status of his or her health characteristics will be judged against these standards. Technical problems have been cited with the QALY concept, such as failure to account for duration of symptoms in addition to magnitude of symptoms, failure to provide age-adjusted valuations of symptoms and impairments, the assumption that all individuals would concur with a "constant proportional time trade-off" of remaining of years of life in return for some increment of improvement in health status irrespective of the absolute duration of those years, and the risk of generating concerns of discrimination against groups of individuals who are denied a certain intervention in favor of providing some other form of intervention to another group on the bases of QALYs (79,80). Although some of these concerns may possibly be addressed by changing the models on which QALYs are calculated, there is still the dilemma of applying a value system to an individual who may feel and value things very differently. For example, most will agree that the pain of labor in childbirth is quite extreme. Yet, men may not share the same appreciation of this as women, and this may have political implications upon the policy-setting process in determining whether epidural analgesia should be made available to all women. Or, consider that a terminal cancer patient may achieve similar levels of analgesia with a relatively inexpensive oral opioid or a relatively expensive intraspinal opioid delivery system, and yet he prefers the latter because there is much less sedation and he can remain more interactive with his family. Is the positive gain in his QALYs enough to justify the cost of the intraspinal delivery system? Such questions are not easily answered, and it will require continuing appraisal and reappraisal for QALYs to achieve widespread validity and acceptance.

Lastly, the concept that positive outcomes are associated with increased life quality has spawned the concept that reimbursement of medical services should be driven by outcomes (81). One of the perceived flaws in our present medical system is the unchecked financial rewards offered to providers for performing increasingly complex procedures upon patients, regardless of whether or not a positive outcome is produced. The patient may be made better or made worse by the procedure, but the fee is paid regardless, and therefore the physician is encouraged to offer more and more procedures. The benefit is not proportionate to the costs of care, because there is no restriction on the amount of care that is given. Under an outcomes-driven reimbursement system the financial incentive to perform multiple procedures on patients, regardless of whether or not they benefit the patient, is removed. Reimbursement is maximized if the outcome is favorable, and minimized if the outcome is not favorable. Expensive procedures would be discouraged if there was minimal likelihood of their producing a positive increment in health quality. The "currency" of health quality and the value of health quality under such a system would undoubtly be determined by some form of QALY unit. If the system by which QALYs are calculated is to be reasonable and fair to all who are affected by this system (not only the patient, but the payor and the provider will all have a stake in this system), each participant in such a system must become involved with the process of creating this system.

APPLICATION OF OUTCOME MEASURES

The use of outcome measures in studies of chronic pain is continually evolving. The multiplicity of instruments which are used in outcome assessments in the chronic pain field probably emphasizes the fact that no single idealized measure has been found. Instruments need to be selected on the basis of the particular condition being studied, the population affected by the condition, and the interventions being investigated. If low back pain is taken as a prototypical chronic pain problem, the approaches to assessing outcomes

and quality of life in therapy for low back pain can illustrate the strategies which have been used, keeping in mind that the approaches to studying low back pain may not be as applicable to other chronic pain problems (e.g., headaches) and that low back pain itself may represent a heterogeneous collection of disorders. Nevertheless, the population represented by chronic low back pain is of interest because of the economic impact of this disorder (see Calculating the Costs).

Suggested parameters (82,83) to monitor with the low back pain patient would include standard medical data (history, physical examination, and diagnostic studies), pain and symptom questionnaires (e.g., the MPQ [8,10], or the BIP [16]), indicators of function (mobility, employment, social, and leisure activities), self-reported functional questionnaires (e.g., the SIP [57], the SF-36 [56], or the Roland–Morris Disability Questionnaire [58]), and a satisfaction questionnaire. Although self-report functional assessment instruments are often not considered to represent "hard data" on par with physical examination and laboratory measures, it has been pointed out that there is less variability for the self-report instruments than with physical exam parameters and interpretations of diagnostic studies (83). The SIP, Roland–Morris, and Oswestry questionnaires seem to have particular validity and reliability when applied to the chronic back pain population (84).

CONCLUSIONS

Because of increasing emphasis on outcomes analysis in medicine as a yardstick for judging the value of medical treatments, chronic pain therapy must turn to increasingly sophisticated methods of demonstrating the impact of pain management in terms of outcome produced. Evaluation of quality of life in the situation of chronic pain is an evolving field, and the methods for assessing pain management outcomes are only beginning to establish themselves.

Assessment of life quality in chronic pain begins with an assessment of the pain itself. Being a wholly subjective phenomenon, techniques of self-reporting of pain are essential tools in defining the characteristics of pain. Unidimensional measures of pain intensity, such as the verbal description, numerical, and visual analog scales, are commonly used. Multidimensional pain assessments, such as the MPQ, the Multidimensional Pain Inventory and the BPI increase the ability to define the more subtle characteristics of the pain experience such as the affective dimension. Pain drawings and pain diaries help establish the spatiotemporal aspects of the pain.

A number of global measures of psychological functioning have been applied to pain studies, such as the MMPI, the Symptom Checklist-90R, the Illness Behavior Questionnaire, and the Beck Depression Inventory. Although their role in quality of life studies has not been fully established, it would seem that certain dimensions which these instruments are capable of assessing, such as depression, pain beliefs, and coping ability, would play a role in characterizing quality of life and assessing outcomes. However, caution must be used in interpreting any instrument lacking normative data specific to the chronic pain population.

Measures of physical and social functioning, in the form of self-report questionnaires such as the MOS SF-36, the SIP, and the Roland–Morris Disability Questionnaire, are very commonly used as indicators of function. Function is probably the single most important factor to assess in quality of life studies of chronic pain.

Measures of satisfaction appear to be desirable in quality of life studies, although these instruments have not yet fully established themselves. One of the key confounding factors in interpretation of satisfaction data is that satisfaction may have more to do with the patient's pre-existing beliefs and expectations than with the actual treatment outcome.

The costs of chronic pain can be considered twofold. First, the cost to society in terms of lost workdays and services and the costs of administering medical care. Secondly, there are the costs to the patient in terms of a compromised life style and reduction in quality of life. There is no universally accepted method of calculating these costs, and it is important to understand the methods used by authors of studies in order to derive any meaning from them. Estimating the cost of life quality ultimately necessitates the creation of a valuation system such as that embraced by the QALY concept. As this type of valuation system evolves, such calculations may have a considerable impact on the practice and reimbursement of medical services.

The incorporation of quality of life measures into studies of chronic pain is becoming increasingly common, as it needs to be in the current climate of health care reform. Use of such measures will ultimately promote an outcomes-driven paradigm of administering health care, including chronic pain therapy. Such a system would influence decisions to use or withhold treatments. Because all who are involved—the patient, the provider, and the payor—have a stake in this system, involvement in the process of shaping this system is crucial for everybody.

ACKNOWLEDGMENTS

The author gratefully acknowledges the advice and support of Douglas E. DeGood, Ph.D, and J. Alexander Dale, Ph.D.

REFERENCES

1. Merskey H, Bogduk N, eds. IASP Task Force on Taxonomy. *Description of chronic pain syndromes and definition of pain terms.* 2nd ed. Seattle: IASP Press, 1994:210.
2. Crook J, Tunks E. Defining the "chronic pain syndrome": an epidemiological method. In: Fields HL, Dubner R, Cervero F, eds. *Advances in pain research and therapy.* Vol 9. New York: Raven Press, 1985: 871–877.
3. Jensen MP, Karoly P. Self-report scales and procedures for assessing pain in adults. In: Turk DC, Melzack M, eds. *Handbook of Pain Assessment.* New York: Guilford Press, 1992:35–151.
4. Huskisson EC. Visual analog scales. In: Melzack R, ed. *Pain management and assessment.* New York: Raven Press, 1983:33–37.
5. Carlsson AM. Assessment of chronic pain. I. Aspects of the reliability and validity of the visual analog scale. *Pain* 1983;16:87–101.
6. Ohnhaus EE, Adler R. Methodological problems in the measurement of pain: a comparison between the verbal rating scale and the visual analog scale. *Pain* 1975;1:379–384.
7. Jensen MP, Karoly P, Braver S. The measurement of clinical pain intensity: a comparison of six methods. *Pain* 1986;27:117–126.
8. Melzack R. The McGill Pain Questionnaire: major properties and scoring methods. *Pain* 1975;1:277–299.
9. Melzack R, Torgerson WS. On the language of pain. *Anesthesiology* 1971;34:50–59.
10. Melzack R. The short-form McGill Pain Questionnaire. *Pain* 1987;30: 191–197.
11. Corson JA, Schneider MJ. The Dartmouth Pain Questionnaire: an adjunct to the McGill Pain Questionnaire. *Pain* 1984;19:59–69.
12. Kerns RD, Turk DC, Rudy TE. The West Haven–Yale Multidimensional Pain Inventory (WHYMPI). *Pain* 1985;23:345–356.
13. Kerns RD, Jacob MC. Assessment of the psychosocial context of the experience of chronic pain. In: Turk DC, Melzack R, eds. *Handbook of pain assessment.* New York: Guilford Press, 1992:235–253.
14. Cleeland CS. Pain assessment in cancer. In: Osoba D, ed. *Effect of cancer on quality of life.* Boca Raton, FL: CRC Press, 1991:293–305.
15. Daut RL, Cleeland CS. The prevalence and severity of pain in cancer. *Cancer* 1982;50:1913–1918.
16. Daut RL, Cleeland CS, Flanery RC. Development of the Wisconsin Brief Pain Questionnaire to assess pain in cancer and other disease. *Pain* 1983;17:197–210.
17. Fishman B, Pasternak S, Wallenstein SL, Houde RW, Holland JC, Foley KM. The Memorial Pain Assessment Card. A valid instrument for evaluation of cancer pain. *Cancer* 1987;60:1151–1158.
18. Jensen MP, McFarland CA. Increasing the validity of pain intensity measurement in chronic pain patients. *Pain* 1993;55:195–203.
19. Von Korff M. Epidemiological and survey methods: chronic pain assessment. In: Turk DC, Melzack M, eds. *Handbook of pain assessment.* New York: Guilford Press, 1992:391–408.
20. Chapman CR, Syrjala KL. Measurement of pain. In: Bonica JJ, Loeser JD, Chapman CR, Fordyce WE, eds. *The management of pain.* 2nd ed. Philadelphia: Lea & Febiger, 1990:580–594.
21. Hathaway SR, McKinley JC. *Manual for the Minnesota Multiphasic Personality Inventory.* New York: Psychological Corporation, 1951, 1967, 1983.
22. Sternbach RA, Wolf SR, Murphy RW, Akeson WH. Traits of pain patients: the low-back "loser." *Psychosomatics* 1973;14:226–229.
23. Rook JC, Pesch RN, Keeler EC. Chronic pain and the questionable use of the Minnesota Multiphasic Personality Inventory. *Arch Phys Med Rehabil* 1981;62:373–376.
24. Pondaag W, Oostdam EMM. Predicting the outcome of lumbar disc surgery by means of preoperative psychological testing. In: Bonica JJ, Liebeskind JC, Albe-Fessard DG, eds. *Advances in pain research and therapy.* Vol 3. New York: Raven Press 1979:713–717.
25. Wiltse LL, Rocchio PD. Preoperative psychological tests as predictors of success of chemonucleolysis in the treatment of the low-back syndrome. *J Bone Joint Surg* 1975;57A:478–483.
26. Moore JE, Armentrout DP, Parker JC, Kivlahan DR. Empirically derived pain-patient MMPI subgroups: prediction of treatment outcome. *J Behav Med* 1986;9:51–63.
27. Cummings C, Evanski PM, Debendetti MJ, Anderson EE, Waugh TR. Use of the MMPI to predict outcome of treatment for chronic pain. In: Bonica JJ, Liebeskind JC, Albe-Fessard DG, eds. *Advances in pain research and therapy.* New York: Raven Press, 1979:667–670.
28. Hammonds W, Brena SF. Pain classification and vocational evaluation in chronic pain states. In: Melzack R, ed. *Pain management and assessment.* New York: Raven Press, 1983:197–203.
29. Hathaway SR, McKinley JC, Butcher JN, Dahlstrom WG, Graham JR, Tellegen A, Kaemmer B. *Minnesota Multiphasic Personality Inventory-2: manual for administration.* Minneapolis: University of Minnesota Press, 1989.
30. Bradley LA, Haile JM, Jaworski TM. Assessment of psychological status using interviews and self-report instruments. In: Turk DC, Mel-

zack M, eds. *Handbook of pain assessment.* New York: Guilford Press, 1992:193–213.

31. Pincus T, Callahan LF, Bradley LA, Vaughan WK, Wolfe F. Elevated MMPI scores for hypochondriasis, depression, and hysteria in patients with rheumatoid arthritis reflect disease rather than psychological status. *Arthritis Rheum* 1986;29:1456–1466.

32. Moore JE, McFall ME, Kivlahan DR, Capestany F. Risk of misinterpretation of MMPI schizophrenia scale elevations in chronic pain patients. *Pain* 1988;32:207–213.

33. Derogatis LR. *The SCL-90R: Administration, scoring and procedures manual.* Baltimore: Clinical Psychometrics Research Unit, Johns Hopkins University, 1977.

34. Jamison RN, Rock DL, Parris WCV. Empirically derived Symptom Checklist-90 subgroups of chronic pain patients: a cluster analysis. *J Behav Med* 1988;11:147–158.

35. Buckelew SP, DeGood DE, Schwartz DP, Kerler RM. Cognitive and somatic item response patterns of pain patients, psychiatric patients, and hospital employees. *J Clin Psychol* 1986;42:852–860.

36. Green CJ, Millon T, Meagher RB Jr. The MBHI: its utilization in assessment and management of the coronary bypass surgery patient. *Psychother Psychosomat* 1983;39:112–121.

37. Gatchel RJ, Deckel AW, Weinberg N, Smith JE. The utility of the Millon Behavioral Health Inventory in the study of chronic headaches. *Headache* 1985;25:49–54.

38. Gatchel RJ, Mayer TG, Capra P, Barnett J, Diamond P. Millon Behavioral Health Inventory: its utility in predicting physical function in patients with low back pain. *Arch Phys Med Rehabil* 1986;67:878–882.

39. Pilowsky I, Spence ND. Patterns of illness behavior in patients with intractable pain. *J Psychosom Res* 1975;19:279–287.

40. Beck AT, Ward CH, Mendelson M, Mock J, Erbaugh J. An inventory for measuring depression. *Arch Gen Psychiatry* 1961;4:561–571.

41. Zung WWK. A self-rating depression scale. *Arch Gen Psychiatry* 1965;12:63–70.

42. Spielberger CD, Gorsuch RL, Lushene RE. *Manual for the state-trait anxiety inventory.* Palo Alto, CA: Consulting Psychologists Press, 1970.

43. McNair DM, Lorr M, Droppleman LF. *EITS manual for the profile of mood states.* San Diego: Educational and Industrial Testing Service, 1971.

44. Cella DF, Jacobson PB, Orav EJ, Holland JC, Silberfarb PM, Rafla S. A brief POMS measure of distress for cancer patients. *J Chronic Dis* 1987;40:939–942.

45. Jensen MP, Karoly P. Control beliefs, coping efforts, and adjustment to chronic pain. *J Consult Clin Psychol* 1991;50:431–438.

46. Rosenstiel AK, Keefe FJ. The use of coping strategies in low-back patients: relationship to patient characteristics and current adjustment. *Pain* 1983;17:33–44.

47. DeGood DE, Shutty MS. Assessment of pain beliefs, coping, and self-efficacy. In: Turk DC, Melzack M, eds. *Handbook of pain assessment.* New York: Guilford Press, 1992:214–234.

48. Folkman S, Lazarus RS. An analysis of coping in a middle-aged community sample. *J Health Social Behav* 1980;21:219–239.

49. Turner JA, Clancy S, Vitaliano PP. Relationships of stress, appraisal and coping, to chronic low back pain. *Behav Res Ther* 1987;25:281–288.

50. Jensen MP, Karoly P, Huger R. The development and preliminary validation of an instrument to assess patients' attitudes toward pain. *J Psychosom Res* 1987;31:393–400.

51. Schwartz DP, DeGood DE, Shutty MS. Direct assessment of beliefs and attitudes of chronic pain patients. *Arch Phys Med Rehabil* 1985;66:806–809.

52. Lorig K, Chastain RL, Ung E, Shoor S, Holman HR. Development and evaluation of a scale to measure perceived self-efficacy in people with arthritis. *Arthritis Rheum* 1989;32:37–44.

53. Mayer TG, Gatchel RJ, Kishino N, Keeley J, Mayer H, Capra P, Mooney V. A prospective short-term study of chronic pain patients utilizing novel objective functional measurement. *Pain* 1986;25:53–68.

54. Ware JE, Sherbourne CD. The MOS 36-item Short-Form Health Survey [SF-36]. *Med Care* 1992;30:473–483.

55. McHorney CA, Ware JE Jr, Raczek AE. The MOS 36-item Short-Form Health Survey (SF-36): II. Psychometric and clinical tests of validity in measuring physical and mental health constructs. *Med Care* 1993;31:247–263.

56. McHorney CA, Ware JE Jr, Sherbourne CD. The MOS 36-item Short-Form Health Survey (SF-36). Tests of data quality, scaling assumptions, and reliability across diverse patient groups. *Med Care* 1994;32:40–66.

57. Bergner M, Bobbitt RA, Carter WB, Gilson BS. The Sickness Impact Profile: development and final revision of a health status measure. *Med Care* 1981;19:787–805.

58. Roland M, Morris R. A study of the natural history of back pain. Part I. Development of a reliable and sensitive measure of disability in low-back pain. *Spine* 1983;8:141–144.

59. Deyo RA. Comparative validity of the sickness impact profile and shorter scales for functional assessment in low-back pain. *Spine* 1986;11:951–954.

60. Kames LD, Naliboff BD, Heinrich RL, Schag CC. The Chronic Illness Problem Inventory: problem-oriented psychosocial assessment of patients with chronic illness. *Int J Psychiatr Med* 1984;14:65–75.

61. Pollard CA. Preliminary validity study of the Pain Disability Index. *Percept Motor Skills* 1984;59:974.

62. Karnofsky DA, Abelman WH, Craver LF, Burchenal JH. The use of the nitrogen mustards in the palliative treatment of carcinoma. *Cancer* 1948;1:634–656.

63. Fairbank JC, Couper J, Davies JB, O'Brien JP. The Oswestry low back pain disability questionnaire. *Physiotherapy* 1980;66:271–273.

64. Von Korff M, Ormel J, Keefe FJ, Dworkin SF. Grading the severity of chronic pain. *Pain* 1992;50:133–149.

65. Kind P, Carr-Hill R. The Nottingham Health Profile: a useful tool for epidemiologists? *Soc Sci Med* 1987;25:905–910.

66. Sherbourne CD. Pain measures. In: Steward AL, Ware JE, eds. *Measuring functioning and well-being: the Medical Outcomes Study approach.* Durham, NC: Duke University Press, 1993:220–234.

67. Miaskowski C. Pain management: quality assurance and changing practice. In: Gebhart GF, Hammond DL, Jensen TS, eds. *Proceedings of the Seventh World Congress on Pain, progress in pain research and management.* Vol. 2. Seattle: IASP Press, 1994:75–96.

68. Deyo RA, Diehl AK. Patient satisfaction with medical care for low-back pain. *Spine* 1986;11:28–30.

69. Ware JE Jr, Davies-Avery A, Stewart AL. The measurement and meaning of patient satisfaction. *Health Med Care Serv Rev* 1978;1:2.

70. Linn LS, Greenfield S. Patient suffering and patient satisfaction among the chronically ill. *Med Care* 1982;20:425–431.

71. Hazard RG, Haugh LD, Green PA, Jones PL. Chronic low back pain, the relationship between patient satisfaction and pain, impairment, and disability outcomes. *Spine* 1994;19:881–887.

72. Shutty MS Jr, DeGood DE, Tuttle DH. Chronic pain patient's beliefs about their pain and treatment outcomes. *Arch Phys Med Rehabil* 1990;71:128–132.

73. Haddad GH. Analysis of 2932 worker's compensation back injury cases, the impact on cost to the system. *Spine* 1987;12:765–769.

74. Spitzer WO, Leblanc FE, Dupuis M. Scientific approach to the assessment and management of acitivity-related spinal disorders. *Spine* 1987;12(suppl 1):S9–S59.

75. Bonica JJ. The nature of the problem. In: Carron H, McLaughlin RE, eds. *Management of low back pain.* Boston: J Wright, PSG, 1982:1–15.

76. Louis Harris and Associates. *Nuprin Pain Report.* New York, 1985.

77. Osterweis M, Kleinman A, Mechanic D, eds. Institute of Medicine Committee on Pain, Disability, and Chronic Illness Behavior. *Pain and disability. Clinical, behavioral, and public policy perspectives.* Washington, DC: National Academy Press, 1987.

78. Kaplan RM. Quality of life assessment for cost/utility studies in cancer. *Cancer Treat Rev* 1993;10(suppl A):85–96.

79. Cubbon J. The principle of QALY maximisation as the basis for allocating health care resources. *J Med Ethics* 1991;17:181–184.

80. Loomis G, McKenzie L. The use of QALYs in health care decision making. *Soc Sci Med* 1989;28:299–308.

81. Kaplan RM. The Ziggy theorem: toward an outcomes-focused health psychology. *Health Psychol* 1994;13:451–460.

82. Williams RC. Toward a set of reliable and valid measures for chronic pain assessment and outcome research. *Pain* 1988;35:239–251.

83. Deyo RA, Andersson G, Bombardier C, Cherkin DC, Keller RB, Lee CK, Liang MH, Lipscomb B, Shekelle P, Spratt KF, Weinstein JN. Outcome measures for studying patients with low back pain. *Spine* 1994;19:2032S–2036S.

84. Hoffman RM, Turner JA, Cherkin DC, Deyo RA, Herron LD. Therapeutic trials for low back pain. *Spine* 1994;19:2068S–2075S.

Quality of Life and Pharmacoeconomics in Clinical Trials, Second Edition, edited by B. Spilker.
Lippincott-Raven Publishers, Philadelphia © 1996.

CHAPTER 90

Quality of Life after Coronary Revascularization Procedures

Carol E. Cornell, James M. Raczynski, and Albert Oberman

INTRODUCTION

Coronary artery bypass grafting (CABG) and percutaneous transluminal coronary angioplasty (PTCA) are the most frequently performed coronary revascularization procedures (1,2); the use of these interventions continues to increase concurrent with improvements in techniques and technology (3). Despite technological advances, however, accumulated evidence suggests that coronary revascularization procedures significantly improve survival for only selected subgroups of patients relative to medical therapies (4–9). Owing in part to the limited survival benefit resulting from coronary revascularization procedures for many types of patients (10), assessment of changes in quality of life is an increasingly important outcome for studies of patients receiving these procedures. Quality of life has received some attention

among patients undergoing coronary revascularization and a variety of other cardiovascular procedures, including cardiac transplants (11,12), valvular surgeries (13,14), and other types of open heart procedures (15). Although the rationale for these costly and complex procedures largely depends on improvements in quality of life, these outcomes have not received the attention they deserve.

This chapter reviews studies of quality of life after coronary revascularization since 1989 when the previous edition was completed (16). We focus on the studies of quality of life after CABG and PTCA since the quality of life issues for patients undergoing these procedures are similar. Cardiac transplant studies are not reviewed because of the unique psychosocial issues involved in organ transplantation. Studies of other procedures are not reviewed because of a relative lack of quality of life data. Our review includes only those studies containing data for at least 100 CABG and/or PTCA patients and excludes editorials, articles not written in English, and reports not explicitly dealing with quality of life.

Several limitations should be kept in mind. First, the technologies used in coronary revascularization are evolving

C. E. Cornell, J. M. Raczynski, and A. Oberman: Division of Preventive Medicine, Department of Medicine, University of Alabama at Birmingham, Birmingham, Alabama 35205.

rapidly, so comparisons of treatments made today may not always be applicable to new techniques. Second, the outcome varies, in part, on clinical characteristics of the anatomic lesion; patient characteristics, such as age and gender; and the skill of the individual interventionist. Therefore, it is important to examine quality of life separately for age, gender, and ethnic groups, as well as for various clinical characteristics of the disease. Third, the time since intervention is important, as reocclusion often occurs early, even within the first 6 months, particularly after PTCA (17). Moreover, the data suggest a decline in CABG postoperative quality of life improvements after 10 years, at least in comparison to medically treated patients (18,19). Thus, short-term outcomes should be distinguished from long-term outcomes, and longer-term follow-up of patients is desirable. Fourth, relatively little is known about quality of life changes in the general population over long periods. So, the inclusion of nonpatient comparison groups may be important. Finally, a number of studies reviewed here were not conducted in the United States. Some aspects of quality of life, such as return to work, depend greatly on social and economic factors (20–22). This issue must be considered carefully for data collected in countries with systems that differ from those in the United States.

ASSESSMENT OF QUALITY OF LIFE AFTER CABG AND PTCA

No specific measures have been developed for assessing the quality of life of patients with coronary heart disease (CHD), as has been discussed by others (23,24). Yet, standardized instruments are available for assessing quality of life in general, and these may be used in the assessment of CABG and PTCA patients. Detailed discussions of measurement issues and of instruments for assessing quality of life can be found elsewhere in this volume, particularly in Sections II and III on quality of life scales and measures. Some measurement considerations are discussed here, and the major domains that should be addressed with patients undergoing coronary revascularization procedures are outlined.

For CABG and PTCA patients, quality of life measures should be obtained before and then periodically after revascularization. Ideally, baseline preoperative measures should be collected before perioperative emotional responses confound measures such as well-being, emotional responses, and even performance on cognitive tests. Historical objective baseline data such as work status and absenteeism may be useful, but objective premorbid data for other quality of life dimensions are often not available. In addressing changes in quality of life after CABG and PTCA, the major domains of importance include psychological functioning, social interactions, functional capacity, and economic measures.

PSYCHOLOGICAL FUNCTIONING

Two major dimensions of psychological well-being among patients after coronary revascularization have been examined in the literature—emotional and neuropsychological. These studies are summarized in Table 1, but studies examining only neurological changes alone are not included.

Emotional Measures

Global Indices

Studies assessing global emotional functioning and satisfaction with CABG surgery have shown favorable changes relative to preoperative assessments. Caine et al. (25) reported at 1 year post-CABG that 91% of patients rated their conditions as "completely better" or "definitely improved," and 70% rated their overall quality of life as higher relative to presurgery. Langeluddecke et al. (26) supported this finding of benefit at 6 and 12 months following CABG surgery. Engblom and colleagues (27) reported that most patients expected CABG surgery to improve their abilities to engage in hobbies and in sexual and physical activities. At 12 months after surgery, 65% of the 194 patients available for follow-up described their surgical outcome as meeting their expectations. While this study did not examine the benefit of counseling, these findings highlight the importance of preoperative counseling to caution patients that not all functioning may return to levels enjoyed prior to CHD onset. Such counseling may help patients develop more realistic expectations and facilitate recovery and adjustment after revascularization.

Studies of PTCA patients have similarly shown improvement in global indices of satisfaction and psychological functioning following the procedure. McKenna et al. (28) examined patients before and at 6 to 8 weeks and 6 to 12 months following PTCA. Total scores for life satisfaction and general health improved at 6 to 8 weeks compared with pre-PTCA levels, and these changes were maintained at 6 to 12 months. Fifty-two percent of patients described the procedure as having a very beneficial effect on their health and well-being, 28% reported moderate or slight benefit, 8% were unsure, and 12% noted no benefit at all. All patients in the last group had had initially unsuccessful PTCA or required later CABG, underscoring the degree to which perceived benefit and satisfaction relate to outcome and subsequent disease progression.

Specific Emotional Measures

Most studies examining depression and anxiety have indicated emotional improvement following both CABG and PTCA. Engblom and colleagues (27) assessed depression prior to CABG and at 2 and 8 months postsurgery. Depres-

TABLE 1. *Psychological aspects of quality of life*

Study/Reference	Population	Measures	Duration of follow-up	Results
Guadagnoli et al. (1992) (28)	268 (169 <65 yr; 99 ≥65 yr) consecutive CABG pts at 4 hospitals	Standardized mental health inventory (121)	6 mo	Older patients (pts) reported higher level of mental health functioning than younger pts in unadjusted and adjusted analyses
Allen et al. (1990) (30)	Consecutive groups of 106 CABG pts (mean age, 55) 64 PTCA pts (mean age, 53)	Standardized mental health measures (121)	1 yr	Both groups improved in mental health scores over 1 yr with a trend for CABG pts to improve >PTCA pts ($p = .08$)
Langeluddecke et al. (1989) (26)	117 CABG pts (mean age, 56) admitted to 2 Australian hospitals	Standardized adjustment to illness scale (PAIS[a]; 122); CESD[b] (123); STAI[c] (124)	1 yr	Improvement in global psychosocial functioning, depression, and anxiety; 69% reported satisfaction with surgical outcome
Caine et al. (1991) (25)	100 male CABG pts (<60 yr old, mean age, 51) at a British hospital	Supplemented Nottingham Health Profile (125)	1 yr	Most pts described conditions (91%) and overall quality of life (70%) as improved; overall improvements in emotional reactions
Engblom et al. (1992) (27)	201 male CABG pts (<65 yr, mean age, 54) at Finnish hospital, randomized to rehabilitation or hospital Tx control	Interview and custom-designed questionnaire; BDI[d] (126)	1 yr	65% of pts reported outcome in line with expectations; depression improved in pts in rehabilitation group
McIntyre et al. (1990) (31)	250 older CABG pts (70–86 yr, mean age, 74.2)	Self-report	>1 mo	6% depressed and 3.3% had neurological deficits at follow-up
McKenna et al. (1992) (29)	102 PTCA pts (mean age, 56) with no prior PTCA or CABG at several Australian hospitals	General Health Questionnaire (127) and custom life satisfaction ratings	1 yr	Improvement in total life satisfaction, general health scores, and anxiety; 52% described procedure as very beneficial; 28% noted slight or moderate benefit
Blumenthal et al. (1991) (47)	39 consecutive pts (mean age, 59.2) for CABG (n=20), PTCA (n=8), or valve replacement (n=11)	Sternberg memory search task (128), Digit Symbol and Digit Span of WAIS[e] (129), Trail Making Test, Part B (130)	Acute hospital-ization period	On Digit Symbol, decline for valve and CABG pts, no change for PTCA pts; on Sternberg memory task, marginally significant ($p<.08$) increased reaction time for valve and CABG pts, and decreased reaction time for PTCA pts

[a]Psychological Adjustment to Illness Scale.
[b]Center for Epidemiologic Studies-Depression Scale.
[c]State-Trait Anxiety Inventory.
[d]Beck Depression Inventory.
[e]Wechsler Adult Intelligence Scale.

sion decreased in patients in a rehabilitation program at 8 months post-CABG compared with both preoperative and 2-month postoperative levels. In another study, older patients reported a higher level of mental health functioning 6 months after hospital discharge than younger patients in analyses adjusted for clinical and demographic characteristics. Across age groups, patients who functioned better before surgery, who had less severe comorbid disease, and who were married reported better functioning after surgery (28).

Fewer data exist for PTCA patients, but similar postprocedure improvement has been noted. McKenna et al. (29)

reported specific improvement in General Health Questionnaire anxiety scores from pre-PTCA to 6 to 8 weeks post-PTCA, results that were maintained at 6- to 12-month follow-up. In a nonrandomized comparison, both PTCA and CABG groups significantly improved in mental health functioning over 1-, 6-, and 12-month follow-up periods, but CABG patients tended to improve more than PTCA patients ($p = .08$) (30).

As noted for global measures of psychological functioning, some studies have reported preoperative impairment in specific measures of mood compared with levels in the general population. Langeluddecke et al. (26) found that prior to CABG, average depression and anxiety scores were higher in the patient group than reported in the general population. Despite improvements, depression scores remained slightly higher than reported for the general population up to 12 months after surgery; suggesting that normal psychological functioning may not always be restored.

Other studies concur that mood impairments persist for some patients, despite overall improvements in emotional responses with CABG and PTCA. McIntyre and colleagues (31) assessed 70- to 86-year-old CABG patients and reported that 15 of the 241 surviving patients were depressed at least 1 month after surgery. Caine et al. (25) observed significant improvements at 3 months post-CABG in emotional reactions. However, irritability and concentration difficulties were still reported by 6% and 7% of patients at 3 and 12 months, respectively. Higher levels of depression and anxiety may have prognostic importance for patients with CHD (32–38). Clinical trials are now planned to evaluate the efficacy of aggressive psychotherapeutic treatment of affective disorders in producing morbidity and mortality benefits.

Neuropsychological Measures

Common types of neurological sequelae following CABG are subtle, cognitive deficits that usually resolve over a period of months (39). However, some patients suffer major neurologic complications, such as stroke, and continue to exhibit cognitive deficits (40–43). Neurological deficits are less common after CABG than following intracardiac surgeries, such as valve replacement, but this situation may change as more older patients and those with more advanced disease undergo CABG (39). Although many studies mention neurological deficit in a few patients as an operative complication (44), only a few studies have conducted formal neuropsychological testing (45,46). None of these studies meets our inclusion criteria in terms of sample size. However, we include one study that provides some preliminary information about neuropsychological aspects of quality of life following both CABG and PTCA.

Blumenthal et al. (47) used a battery of neuropsychological measures to assess cognitive functioning 1 day prior to surgery, and again prior to hospital discharge, in 39 patients following CABG, PTCA, or cardiac valve repair. Cognitive performance on the Digit Symbol subtest of the Wechsler Adult Intelligence Scale was unaffected in PTCA patients, but significant postprocedure impairment was found for patients undergoing cardiac valve repair and CABG, with valve surgery patients exhibiting the greatest deficits. A trend (p < .08) was also observed for longer reaction times for both CABG and valve surgery patients, with CABG patients outperforming those undergoing cardiac valve repair. By contrast, PTCA patients had decreased reaction times following the procedure, suggesting better functioning. These data

agree with earlier studies (48), indicating that cognitive performance may decline following CABG, although not to the extent observed after valve repairs. The differences between CABG and PTCA most likely relate to the use of general versus local anesthesia, the need for circulatory support during CABG, and the prolonged recovery after an operative procedure (47).

Summary

Changes in emotional functioning and satisfaction following CABG and PTCA are generally favorable relative to preoperative assessments. However, revascularization procedures alone do not return all patients to a level of emotional functioning comparable to those without CHD. Limited and nonrandomized comparisons of emotional changes between CABG and PTCA patients indicate that the emotional benefits are not universal and CABG patients may benefit more than PTCA patients, although these findings should be viewed as highly preliminary. Limited data also suggested a particular emotional benefit for older patients and for those who were functioning better before surgery, who had less severe comorbid disease, and who were married (28). Recent studies suggest a strong association between depression in CHD patients and the risk of future cardiac events. Thus, psychological counseling for depression may be indicated for patients who do not otherwise improve. Preoperative counseling may also be beneficial to promote more realistic recovery expectations and facilitate recovery and adjustment after revascularization.

The finding that CABG affects neuropsychological functioning, at least in the short-term, while PTCA does not (47) also has implications for preoperative counseling with CABG patients and their families. Although some predictors of neuropsychological sequelae, such as older age, have been identified, additional research is still needed to identify those at risk for these complications.

SOCIAL INTERACTION

Improved social interaction with family members and others has been cited as evidence of recovering quality of life following cardiovascular procedures. In addition to its role as an index of improvement, social support appears to be an important predictor of physiologic outcome. In the Beta-Blocker Heart Attack Trial, social isolation in combination with a high level of stress increased the risk of death fourfold (49). Other studies have similarly implicated social factors in recovery from a cardiac event (49–57). The effect of myocardial revascularization on social interactions thus has implications beyond quality of life. Studies that have examined social interaction measures of quality of life among CABG and PTCA patients are summarized in Table 2.

TABLE 2. *Social interaction aspects of quality of life*

Study/Reference	Population	Measures	Duration of follow-up	Results
Guadagnoli et al. (1992) (28)	268 (169 <65 yr; 99 ≥65 yr) consecutive CABG pts at 4 hospitals	3-item social activity scale (131)	6 mo	High level of social functioning among all pts; no difference in social functioning between younger and older pts
Allen et al. (1990) (30)	Consecutive groups of 106 CABG pts (mean age, 55) and 64 PTCA pts (mean age, 53)	Standardized social functioning measure (121)	1 yr	At baseline and at 1 mo, PTCA pts reported higher functioning in social functioning than CABG pts; by 6 mo, both groups reported comparable social functioning; by 1 yr, CABG pts reported better social functioning than PTCA pts
Langeluddecke et al. (1989) (26)	117 CABG pts (mean age, 56) at 2 Australian hospitals	Standardized adjustment to illness scale (122); Pleasant Events Schedule (132)	1 yr	67% reported increased family involvement; 65% reported increased involvement in overall social activities
Caine et al. (1991) (25)	100 male CABG pts (<60 yr; mean age, 51) at a British hospital	Supplemented Nottingham Health Profile (125)	1 yr	Decreased no. of pts reported health-related problems in home relationships and holidays; improvements in social isolation and health-related problems with social activities; 69% increase in pts reporting no restrictions on social activities
Allen et al. (1990) (58)	125 consecutive male CABG pts ≤65 yr	Standardized functional status questionnaire (121) and pt interviews	6 mo	Improvements in social and leisure activity scores 6 mo post-CABG, but 13% continued to experience difficulties
Engblom et al. (1992) (27)	201 male CABG pts (<65 yr; mean age, 54) at Finnish hospital	Interview and custom-designed questionnaire	1 yr	Decreased social activities for pts not in rehabilitation 6 mo post-CABG, but increase to preoperative levels at 1 yr
McKenna et al. (1992) (29)	102 initial PTCA pts (mean age, 56) with no prior PTCA or CABG at several Australian hospitals	General health questionnaire (127) and custom life satisfaction ratings	1 yr	Mean return to social and leisure activities of 14 days; improvements in social dysfunction and satisfaction with social and leisure activities at 6–8 wk post-PTCA, and maintained at 6–12 mo

CABG, coronary artery bypass grafting; PTCA, percutaneous transluminal coronary angioplasty; pts, patients.

Familial Interactions

Studies of familial interaction have generally reported improvement or no change following CABG surgery. Caine et al. (25) found fewer CABG patients reporting health-related problems in home relationships and holidays after their surgeries than at the preoperative assessment. In another study, most CABG patients reported no preoperative change or decreased family activities resulting from their illness (26). At 12 months postsurgery, 67% reported increased family involvement, but a small proportion (5%) of patients reported a significant decline in familial social activities. In terms of extended family involvement, patients reported low impairment levels prior to surgery and no change following

surgery. No studies have reported specifically on familial interactions following PTCA.

Nonfamilial Social Interactions

Studies assessing nonfamilial social interactions are more plentiful than those assessing familial interactions; findings generally support improvements in social functioning with CABG and PTCA. Langeluddecke et al. (26) reported increased social involvement among 65% of their patients after surgery with only 5% noting a decline in social involvement at 12 months post-CABG. Similarly, Guadagnoli et al. (28) noted that increased levels of social functioning were reported among both younger (<65 years) and older (≥65 years) patients at 6 months post-CABG. Caine et al. (25) observed significant pre–post-improvements in social isolation at 3 months post-CABG, and a 69% increase in the number of patients reporting no restrictions in social activities. In this study, physical mobility, pain, and overall quality of life prior to surgery predicted postoperative social functioning at 3 months. Social activities at one year were similarly associated with lower preoperative physical mobility scores and quality of life ratings, including work status. Despite these positive findings, 7% of patients complained that they were ''treated like an invalid'' by others for as long as 12 months after surgery.

Despite overall improvement, some patients continue to experience impairments in social functioning following CABG. Allen et al. (58) found that 13% of their sample of patients continued to experience difficulties in social and leisure activities at 6 months post-CABG, despite significant decreases in numbers of patients reporting impairment in this area. Six-month social and leisure functioning was best predicted by self-efficacy for returning to social and leisure activities at 1 month post-CABG and by postoperative treadmill results.

Evaluating the effects of PTCA on social functioning, McKenna and colleagues (29) reported improvements from pre-PTCA scores in social dysfunction and in satisfaction with social and leisure activities, with sustained improvement at the 6- to 12-month assessment. Mean time between PTCA and full return to social and leisure activities in this study was only 14 days. In a single comparison of social functioning among CABG and PTCA patients, PTCA patients reported better social functioning than CABG patients at 1 month after the procedure (30). By 6 months, however, both groups of patients reported comparable levels of social functioning; and by one year, CABG patients actually reported better social functioning than PTCA patients.

Summary

Social functioning apparently improves following both CABG surgery and PTCA. One study suggested a short-term advantage of PTCA over CABG at 1 month after the procedure; but by 6 months, this difference had disappeared, and CABG patients actually reported better social functioning than PTCA patients (30). Despite overall improvement, a small proportion of patients who undergo CABG surgery appear to worsen in their social functioning, an effect that is likely to exist among PTCA patients as well. This detrimental effect of CABG surgery on social functioning may exist in as many as 13% of patients who continue to experience difficulties in social and leisure activities 6 months after CABG (58). Identification of patients at risk of sustained impairment in social functioning may be predicted by self-efficacy for returning to social and leisure activities soon after CABG and by exercise performance (58), possibly

allowing for specialized interventions among high-risk patients to improve social functioning. Given the demonstrated association between social isolation and CHD morbidity and mortality, aggressive strategies for improving social functioning should be explored.

SYMPTOMATIC RELIEF AND FUNCTIONAL CAPACITY

Symptomatic relief and functional capacity have been examined from a general perspective and from the ability to engage in particular activities. Studies that have examined functional capacity measures as part of quality of life among CABG and PTCA patients after surgery are summarized in Table 3. Studies that have only examined changes in functional capacity through changes in self-reported symptoms or medical testing are not included.

Symptomatic Relief and General Functional Capacity

Angina, related symptoms, and the use of antianginal medications are indices most commonly used to infer quality of life in the medical and surgical literature. All clinical trials of CABG outcome have reported relief of angina in younger individuals (25–27,59) and older CABG patients (31,60–63). Abilities to engage in physical and other activities and level of exertion at which symptoms are experienced also increases relative to preoperative levels (25,59,63). Perceived quality of life and perceived benefit and satisfaction with surgery appear related to this symptom improvement (60,61).

Despite marked improvements in angina and other symptoms associated with increased myocardial perfusion following surgery, significant numbers of patients continue to report symptoms directly and indirectly related to CHD or to the CABG. For example, Caine et al. (25) found that 28% and 26% of patients continued to report fatigue, weight gain, muscle stiffness, and chest or leg pain at 3 and 12 months post-CABG, respectively. In the long term, recurrence of angina is also common. Sergeant and colleagues (64) reported a return of angina in 37% of 5,880 patients at 15 years after their first CABG surgery. Angina prevalence decreased to a low at 4 years, then increased steadily over the 15-year follow-up period. An early peak in angina related to surgical procedures, such as incomplete revascularization; while later angina related to gender, cardiovascular disease risk factors, and severity of initial angina, all of which may be associated with accelerated disease progression.

For those studies evaluating PTCA, a majority have similarly reported improvements in self-reported angina and less use of antianginal medications. This demonstrated symptom improvement with PTCA occurred among all ages, including patients younger than age 40 (65), middle-aged patients (29,59,66) and those 80 years of age and older (67).

TABLE 3. *Functional capacity and symptom relief*

Study/Reference	Population	Measures	Duration of follow-up	Results
Guadagnoli et al. (1992) (28)	268 consecutive CABG pts (169 <65 yr; 99 ≥65 yr) at 4 hospitals	Cardiac-related symptoms and Specific Activities Scale	6 mo	No difference between older and younger pts; exertional dyspnea and peripheral edema in 19–25% of pts; most pts reported high functional level with activities needing ≥7 metabolic equivalents
Allen et al. (1990) (30)	Consecutive groups of 106 CABG pts (mean age, 55) and 64 PTCA pts (mean age, 53)	Standardized physical functional status measure (121)	1 yr	At baseline and 1 mo, PTCA pts reported higher functioning and activities of daily living than did CABG pts; by 6 mo and 1 yr, physical functional status was comparable between groups
Smith et al. (1991) (61)	109 CABG pts (≥75 yr)	Self-report	11–68 mo (mean, 33 mo)	Of 78 surviving pts, 93% were NYHA class I or II; 89% reported leading active lives
Johnston et al. (1989) (63)	111 CABG pts (>65 yr; mean age, 69) and 548 younger pts (mean age, 54) at a Glasgow hospital	Interview or physician questionnaire	Mean, 19.8 mo	77% of older pts angina-free; 16% reported symptom improvement; 64% decreased use of antianginal medications; 85/93 "improved" older pts were "fully active and independent"
Tsai et al. (1991) (68)	112 consecutive CABG pts (≥80 yr)	Pt questionnaire	Mean, 7.5 mo	73% of survivors reported improved general health; 13% reported no change; 14% noted worsened health; from pre-CABG, 40% reported moderate to higher activity, 26% sedentary, 34% restricted in activity; 68% reported exercising and 78% reported less shortness of breath during exercise
Allen et al. (1990) (58)	125 consecutive male CABG pts ≤65 yr	Standardized functional status questionnaire (121) and pt interviews	6 mo	At 6 mo post-CABG, 45% of pts reported no change or decreased activity levels, 40% reported difficulties with or refraining from vigorous activity, 13% continued to experience difficulties in activities of daily living
Langeluddecke et al. (1989) (26)	117 CABG pts (mean age, 56) at 2 Australian hospitals	Standardized adjustment to illness scale (122)	1 yr	Improvements in angina and ability to perform home duties at 6 mo; 43% reported improvements in vocational functioning at 12 mo; improvements in quality of marital relationship, sexual interest, and activity at 1 yr; continued impairment for some pts
McIntyre et al. (1990) (31)	250 older CABG pts (70–86 yr; mean age, 74.2)	Self-report	≥ 1 mo	None of elderly pts reported recurrence of angina in the short term
Engblom et al. (1992) (27)	201 male CABG pts (<65 yr; mean age, 54) at Finnish hospital	Interview and custom-designed questionnaire	1 yr	44.5% improved to CCS class I or II; increased leisure activities for pts in rehabilitation at 6 and 12 mo; 45% reported satisfaction with sexual activity; 9.5% reported improvement, but 40% reported deterioration in sexual functioning at 1 yr

TABLE 3. *Continued.*

Study/Reference	Population	Measures	Duration of follow-up	Results
Kallis et al. (1993) (69)	254 CABG, valve replacement, or other cardiac surgery pts (>70 yr)	University of York questionnaire (133–135)	mean, 19 mo	Decreased disability and distress for 60% and 67% of pts; no change for 34% and 30%; deterioration among 6% and 3%, respectively
Caine et al. (1991) (25)	100 male CABG pts (<60 yr; mean, 51) at a British hospital	Supplemented Nottingham Health Profile (125)	1 yr	Decreased angina and shortness of breath; improved exertional level before symptoms; improved occupational activities, physical mobility, pain, sleep, and energy at 3 mo; 63% and 77% increases for household and recreational activities, respectively; decreases in no. of problems in sexual functioning
Little et al. (1993) (67)	110 PTCA pts (≥80 yr)	Questionnaire and telephone interviews; correspondence with physician	6–48 mo (mean, 18.1)	88% of survivors would have procedure again and >90% reported appreciated prolonged life, freedom from chest pain, improved quality of life, return to activities, enjoyment of recreation and travel; 66% able to live alone, 55% able to drive, 38% able to care for spouse; mean ratings of 8.9 for recovery of health, 8.3 for quality of life, 8.0 for life satisfaction on 10-pt scales
McKenna et al. (1992) (29)	102 PTCA pts (mean age, 56) with no prior PTCA or CABG at several Australian hospitals	General Health Questionnaire (127) and life satisfaction ratings	1 yr	Improvement at 6–8 wk in work satisfaction and exercise test duation, maintained at 6–12 mo; improvement at 6–12 mo in no. of pts exercising regularly

CABG, coronary artery bypass surgery; PTCA, percutaneous transluminal coronary angioplasty; CCS, Canadian Cardiovascular Society; NYHA, New York Heart Association; pts, patients.

Perceived change in general health and physical functioning has also been examined. Tsai et al. (68) found that 73% of surviving patients over the age of 80 reported improvements in general health relative to presurgery, while 13% reported no change, and only 14% reported worsened health at a mean of 7.5 months post-CABG. Others have similarly reported high functional levels after CABG even among older patients (28,63,69).

One study assessing general functional capacity following PTCA found that both male and female older patients had a median post-PTCA convalescence period of 1 week, after which they returned to "full normal activity" (67). Eighty-eight percent of long-term surviving patients reported that they would have the procedure again, and more than 90% reported "appreciated" benefit from PTCA in terms of "prolonged life," "freedom from chest pain," and "improved quality of life." Subjects also reported high ratings of recovery of health, quality of life, and life satisfaction.

Specific Measures of Functional Ability

Earlier studies of vocational, avocational, and sexual functioning tended to rely on self-report recall rather than on more objective indices of functional capacity in specific settings (16). More recent studies have used standardized measures instead of or in addition to patient self-report.

Vocational Measures

Studies assessing vocational functioning following CABG and PTCA have shown improvement relative to preprocedure assessment. Caine et al. (25) observed significant improvement at 3 months post-CABG in occupational activities. Similarly, McKenna and colleagues (29) reported specific improvement from pre- to 6 to 8 weeks post-PTCA in work satisfaction scores, with changes maintained at 6 to

12 month follow-up. Langeluddecke et al. (26) reported significant improvement in work performance 6 and 12 months after CABG surgery on PAIS (Psychological Adjustment to Illness Scale [1]) vocational scores relative to preoperative impaired levels. Overall, as noted for other quality of life indices, preoperative vocational functioning may be impaired secondary to CHD and, while postoperative improvements occur, they do not necessarily indicate a return to pre-illness levels.

Avocational Measures

Improvements after CABG have been noted for physical mobility, pain, sleep, energy, and hobbies (25), and for home maintenance and household activities (25,26) up to 12 months after surgery. Despite these overall improvements, most patients continue to be limited in activities requiring vigorous exercise or heavy labor. Caine et al. (25) reported that 26 to 28% of patients were unable to engage in activities requiring heavy manual labor over 12 months after surgery. Allen and colleagues (58) reported that 13% of their post-CABG patients continued to experience difficulties in activities of daily living. At 6 months post-CABG, 45% noted no change or a decrease in overall activity compared with preoperative levels, and 45% reported continuing difficulties or refraining altogether from engaging in moderately vigorous physical activity. Of patients over 80 years of age assessed at a mean of 7.5 months post-CABG, 40% reported moderate to higher levels of activity than before surgery, while 26% were sedentary, and 34% restricted their activity (68).

One study found that unrestricted postoperative home life was predicted by preoperative functional capacity, including working and experiencing less shortness of breath prior to surgery, waiting time for surgery, and higher overall preoperative quality of life (25). Another found that physical functional status at 6 months was best predicted by self-efficacy to perform daily living activities at time of hospital discharge in a manner similar to that seen in post-myocardial infarction patients (58). The latter finding suggests that addressing patients' self-confidence to resume normal activities following cardiovascular surgery may be important in promoting recovery (58).

Overall improvements have similarly been noted following PTCA in nonwork activities. More than 90% of surviving older patients reported that PTCA had allowed them to "return to former activities" and "enhanced their ability" to enjoy recreation and travel. Sixty-six percent of these patients reported that they were capable of living alone, 55% were able to drive, and 38% felt able to care for a spouse (67). These changes in activities correspond to other reports of improved exercise capacity up to 12 months after PTCA (29).

A comparison of CABG and PTCA patients (30) found that PTCA patients reported significantly better functioning

and activities of daily living than did CABG patients at baseline and one month after their procedures. However, by 6 months and through the 1 year of follow-up, functional capacity was comparable between the two groups. These findings suggest that while avocational functioning may improve more rapidly following PTCA than CABG, there are minimal, if any, long-term differences between the two revascularization procedures.

Sexual Measures

A few studies have assessed changes in sexual measures after CABG, but none has specifically addressed this area of functioning following PTCA. Sexual functioning shows overall impairment prior to CABG and improvement for some patients following surgery, but many patients continue to experience impaired sexual functioning. Langeluddecke et al. (26) found diminished sexual interest and activity prior to CABG, with improvements in sexual interest and activities and in quality of marital relationships in most patients 12 months after surgery. However, 33% of patients continued to experience CHD-related impairment at 12 months post-CABG. PAIS sexual functioning scores showed similar impairment prior to surgery and slight, but significant, improvement at 6 months. These findings concur with other reports that 26–28% of patients continued to report sexual limitations up to 12 months after surgery (25). In a Finnish study, Engblom et al. (27) found that a surprisingly high 90.5% of patients reported diminished sexual activity prior to CABG. At 12 months post-CABG, only 9.5% of patients reported improved sexual functioning, while 40% reported deterioration in sexual functioning. Patients who reported diminished sexual functioning prior to CABG were less satisfied with their postoperative sex life and more frequently reported a worsening of sexual functioning that those without preoperative sexual impairment.

Sexual functioning is related to a number of variables, including emotional and psychological factors; and may be determined, in part, by concern on the part of a spouse over placing undue stress on the patient. Thus, many factors, some only peripherally related to CHD, influence patients' sexual activity. Coronary revascularization may help mitigate some of these factors, but others are likely to remain, resulting in modest improvements in sexual functioning for some patients and little change for many.

Summary

All clinical trials of CABG outcome have reported improvement in angina, regardless of patients' ages. Concurrent with this decrease in angina, CABG patients demonstrate overall improvement in physical and other activities and in level of exertion at which symptoms are experienced. Improvements have also been found in perceptions of change in quality of life, benefit and satisfaction with surgery, and improvement in general health, changes that appear related to symptom improvement. Despite marked improvements in angina and other symptoms, significant numbers of patients continue to report symptoms directly and indirectly related to CHD or to CABG, and recurrence of angina is not uncommon.

Symptom changes following PTCA have been less often examined than with CABG, but improvements in self-reported angina and use of antianginal medications have been noted. Postprocedure improvements in specific areas of functioning generally appear related to preoperative functioning in occupational, home life, and sexual activities. Physical functional status also appears to be predicted by self-efficacy to perform daily living activities at hospital discharge. Thus, addressing patients' self-confidence in their abilities to resume normal activities following revascularization may promote recovery. While PTCA may offer more short-term improvement in functional parameters compared with CABG, this differential advantage appears to diminish over time (30).

ECONOMIC MEASURES

Economic factors have generally been viewed from two perspectives—return to work and cost-effectiveness. Return to work has often been a focus of quality of life assessment among coronary revascularization patients, not only as a result of the ease of collecting this measure and as an indicator of economic factors, but as an indirect measure of functional capacity as well. Cost-effectiveness analyses have also been undertaken to examine the benefits of procedures. Since most of the costs are borne by third-party payers, these analyses generally reveal the cost-effectiveness of the surgery from a societal perspective. Studies that have addressed economic factors in the quality of life of CABG and PTCA patients are summarized in Table 4.

Return to Work

Most studies examining employment rates following CABG surgery find improvement relative to preoperative levels (26,70). Not surprisingly, those who were employed postoperatively have been found to be younger than those who had been granted a disability pension and were not working (70). Return to work has been reported as declining with repeat CABG from a rate of 61.2% with the first surgery to only 14% after the second surgery (71). Although employment rates improve following surgery, they generally do not return to pre-illness levels, and a worsening of financial status has been reported by a significant number of patients (25). Moreover, many patients who do return to work return to lighter types of work or reduced hours (25). Predictors of return to work have included physical and functional

status prior to surgery, such as preoperative employment, shortness of breath, physical mobility, and length of time waiting for surgery (25).

Return to work rates following PTCA also show the benefit of this procedure. McKenna et al. (29) reported that only 24% of working patients were employed at a "desired level" prior to PTCA, while 78% were working at their previous level at 6 to 8 weeks post-PTCA. The mean time between PTCA and return to work was 22 days. Among younger (mean age, 34 years) patients, 76% employed prior to PTCA returned to the same job held previously, 17% changed jobs or returned to part-time work, and only 7% did not return to work (65).

Several studies have compared return to work rates following CABG and PTCA. In one study, the proportion of patients employed remained at about 70% for both CABG and PTCA patients across the 1 year follow-up, except for a transient decrease in employed CABG patients for the first 6 months after surgery (30). Another study (72) found comparable pre-treatment employment rates and post-treatment increases in employment for CABG and PTCA patients. For those without angina, however, PTCA patients (73%) were more likely than CABG patients (55%) to be working at 6- to 18-month follow-up (72). The finding that PTCA patients are more likely than CABG patients to resume employment may be due more to patient-specific disease factors rather than to differences in the two procedures. Mark et al. (73) reported that when demographic, clinical, and functional status factors were taken into account, there were no significant differences in numbers of working PTCA, CABG, and medically treated patients at 1 year. Thus, while PTCA patients may return to work earlier than CABG patients, PTCA does not preserve employment more effectively than CABG when other factors are controlled (73).

Cost-Effectiveness Analyses

Cost-effectiveness has been evaluated from data on hospital and patient-reported costs of surgery and length of hospital stay. One study reported a median postoperative cost for CABG of $12,912 (74). For patients aged 75 and older, an average total hospital cost of $27,183 has been reported (61). Not surprisingly, repeated surgery is more expensive than first-time surgery by a factor of 1.8 after correcting for inflation (71).

Length of hospital stay has been well studied as a proxy for costs in samples of CABG patients and appears to vary across studies from a mean total hospital stay of 9.9 days among 30- to 80-year-old CABG survivors (75), to a mean of 21.3 hospital days for patients aged 75 years and older (61) and a mean postoperative hospital stay of 12 days among 70- to 86-year-old patients (31). Variability across studies in length of hospital stay appears related to age and, even among older patients, to complications, particularly the

TABLE 4. *Economic aspects of quality of life*

Study/Reference	Population	Measures	Duration of follow-up	Results
Dougenis et al. (1992) (71)	1,363 pts for 1st-time CABG; 49 (42 males; 5 females; mean age, 54) pts for repeat CABG	Financial status; return to work	Mean, 3.7 yr; range, 10–108 mo	61.2% returned to work after 1st surgery; 14% returned to work after repeat surgery; among 15 consecutive 1st-time and 5 2nd-time CABG pts, correcting for inflation, repeat surgery was 1.8 times more expensive than 1st-time surgery
McGee et al. (1993) (72)	Consecutive groups of 112 CABG and 119 PTCA pts in Ireland (mean age, 56)	Return to work	6–18 mo	Pretreatment employment rates comparable between groups (41% and 38% for CABG and PTCA pts, respectively); post-Tx rates increased comparably between groups (59% and 68%, respectively); for pts without angina, PTCA pts were more likely to return to work (73% vs 55% PTCA and CABG pts, respectively)
Allen et al. (1990) (30)	Consecutive groups of 106 CABG (mean age, 55) and 64 PTCA pts (mean age, 53)	Return to work	1 yr	For both groups, employment remained at about 70% across follow-up, except for a small decrease in CABG pts up to 6 mo after surgery
Lundbom et al. (1992) (70)	250 CABG pts (224 males; 26 females; mean age, 58) in Norway	Return to work	Median follow-up of 32 mo (range, 19–52 mo)	Preoperative employment of 25.6% increased to 38.8% postoperatively; age was significantly associated with postoperative employment
Caine et al. (1991) (25)	100 male CABG pts (<60 yr; mean age, 51) in Britain	Return to work, financial status	1 yr	At 3 mo and 1 yr post-CABG, 43% and 73% had returned to work; of those not working, 48% intended to return to work; lighter work activities and/or fewer work hours reported by some pts; negative financial impact of CHD both pre- and post-CABG reported by pts
Langeluddecke et al. (1989) (26)	117 CABG pts (mean age, 56) in Australia	Return to work	1 yr	10% increase in retired pt, with 55% of these anticipating retirement preoperatively; slight decrease in full- or part-time employed, but almost 1/2 of unemployment due to CHD preoperatively returned to work postoperatively
Mark et al. (1992) (73)	1252 pts (<65 yr; mean, 54) n=449 with CABG; n=312 with PTCA; n=491 with medical therapy	Return to work	1 yr	At 1 yr, 84% of PTCA, 79% of CABG, and 76% of medical pts working, but difference not significant when other factors controlled; crossover was 9% from PTCA to CABG and 4% from CABG to PTCA
Smith et al. (1991) (61)	109 CABG pts (≥75 yr)	Hospital costs, length of hospital stay	11–68 mo (mean, 33)	Hospital stays ranged from 3 to 157 days (mean 21.3) with average hospital cost of $27,183
McIntyre et al. (1990) (31)	250 CABG pts (70–86 yr old)	Length of hospital stay	≥1 mo	Mean postoperative hospital stay, 12 days
Saw (1990) (75)	370 CABG pts (30–80 yr old) in Singapore	Length of hospital stay	Limited to acute hospitalization	Mean total hospital stay, 9.9 days; length of stay related to major medical complications
Buffet et al. (1994) (65)	140 PTCA pts (<40 yr; mean, 34) in France	Return to work	1–12 yr (mean, 6)	76% employed prior to PTCA returned to same job; 17% changed jobs or returned to work part-time; 9% did not return to work

TABLE 4. *Continued.*

Study/Reference	Population	Measures	Duration of follow-up	Results
McKenna et al. (1992) (29)	102 PTCA pts	Return to work	1 yr	24% employed at "desired level" pre-PTCA; of these, 78% working at previous level at 6–8 wk post-PTCA; mean time between PTCA and return to work, 22 days
Forman et al. (1992) (76)	907 PTCA pts (>60 yr)	Length of hospital stay	Limited to acute hospitalization	Total hospital stays averaged: 9 days for 60–69 yr olds; 11 days for 70–79 yr olds; 18 days for >80 yr olds; post-PTCA stays for 3 age groups averaged 5, 7, and 11 days, respectively

CABG, coronary artery bypass grafting; CHD, coronary heart disease; PTCA, percutaneous transluminal angioplasty.

increased incidence of cerebrovascular accident and other medical problems in older patients following CABG (62,75).

One study has assessed length of hospital stay following PTCA for different age classifications of older patients (76). Total hospital stays averaged 9 days for the 60- to 69-year-old patients, 11 days for the 70- to 79-year-old group, and 18 days for the over-80 age group. Post-PTCA hospitalization similarly averaged 5, 7, and 11 days, respectively. These data further emphasize the increased cost of coronary revascularization for older patients.

Summary

Studies of return to work following both CABG and PTCA have demonstrated improvements relative to preoperative assessment; but employment rates do not return to pre-CHD levels, and many patients return part-time or to lighter work activities. Not surprisingly, return to work is higher for younger than for older patients and following initial surgery than after a subsequent procedure. Although return to work does provide a useful index of improved functional capacity, this should not be viewed as synonymous with improved quality of life, as some patients may view return to work as a negative outcome (22). Certainly, patients with attractive retirement options may choose not to return to work if circumstances permit and view this as a satisfactory situation. Thus, employment status should be supplemented with other measures of quality of life that take into account patients' subjective perceptions of outcome after CABG and PTCA.

Increased costs of coronary revascularization appear to be associated with older age, repeat procedures, and medical/surgical complications. As medical and surgical techniques improve, decreases may be expected in medical/surgical complications and perhaps in need for repeat procedures. Such technological advances should increase the cost-effectiveness of revascularization procedures for patients of all ages.

SPECIAL POPULATIONS

Older Persons

Advances in coronary revascularization techniques together with our aging population have resulted in increasing numbers of older patients being referred for CABG (77). At some hospitals, this increase has been dramatic with a reported increase in octogenarians receiving CABG surgery from 1% in 1981 to 8% in 1989 (68).

Although older patients have more medical and surgical complications following revascularization procedures, these patients typically demonstrate improvement in quality of life. In general, outcomes for older and younger patients after CABG appear comparable in terms of cardiac-related symptoms, functional capacity, social functioning (28), and other quality of life indices (62,63), after adjustment for clinical and demographic characteristics (28). Self-reported overall benefits also appear favorable when older patients are asked about general health and level of activity (60,61,68). One study even reported higher levels of mental health functioning after CABG among older persons than among younger patients (28).

Although studies are fewer than for CABG, outcomes following PTCA are similarly favorable. Older patients who undergo PTCA generally report decreased symptoms, return to former activities, and "appreciated" benefit from PTCA in terms of "prolonged life," "freedom from chest pain," and "improved quality of life" (67).

Older persons may show quality of life impairments after coronary revascularization in cognitive functioning. Higher rates of cerebrovascular accident and surgical complications among older patients have been documented (62,78) and these may be associated with persisting neuropsychological impairments. For example, McIntyre et al. (31) reported that 3.3% of 70- to 86-year-old patients demonstrated neurological deficits at 30 days or more following CABG. Higher rates of surgical complications may also increase economic costs for older patients. Studies have reported hospital stays of up to twice as long for patients over age 80 years as compared with those aged 60 to 69 years (76) and corresponding higher surgery costs for older persons (62). Little et al. (67) emphasize the importance of considering quality of life benefits for very aged patients in clinical decision making, as no revascularization procedure is expected to produce significant increases in life expectancy for these individuals.

Women

Quality of life benefits may be equally important in making clinical decisions for women, as rates of surgical mortality, incomplete revascularization, early and late graft occlusion, and recurrent angina have been found to be more common among women than men (79,80). Unfortunately, most studies have not reported gender comparisons in quality of life following coronary revascularization. Some studies have included only male patients in their samples, while others have included women but have not reported gender differences.

In one study that did examine gender differences, Little et al. (67) reported similar clinical outcomes for PTCA in octogenarian women and men. Both male and female patients reported a median period of convalescence of 1 week, after which they returned to "full normal activity," and men and women did not differ in use of antianginal medications. However, older women appeared to suffer more quality of life impairment than older men. Specifically, women reported being less able to conduct activities of independent living, such as driving and living alone, and being somewhat less satisfied with their quality of life. In addition, women had lower ratings than men for recovery of health, quality of life, and life satisfaction. Little and colleagues (67) speculated that these gender differences in quality of life were not related to medical outcomes, as gender groups were comparable for clinical outcomes, such as PTCA success and long-term survival. However, gender differences have been reported for morbidity outcomes, such as recurrence of anginal symptoms (64). These types of subtle morbidity differences may account for somewhat poorer quality of life outcomes among women.

SUMMARY OF QUALITY OF LIFE AMONG CABG AND PTCA SURGERY PATIENTS

Overall, the quality of life of post-CABG patients appears to improve from perioperative and even preoperative levels. PTCA patients show comparable improvements in quality of life, except that their improvement is more rapid than with CABG, since they lack the requisite surgical recovery time. Conversely, CABG patients may suffer an initial decrement in their quality of life as they recover from surgery,

but quality of life eventually appears to improve to levels comparable to outcomes seen with PTCA patients. Studies of quality of life following both PTCA and CABG generally remain poorly controlled for type of treatment and, with the exception of return to work and functional parameters, are observational rather than randomized. Long-term follow-up studies of quality of life among CABG patients compared to medically treated patients suggest that differences between the groups appear to diminish at 10 years, due in part to the return of symptoms in surgical patients, but also to the number of CABG surgeries conducted in the previously treated medical patients (18,19). While very long-term follow-up studies of PTCA patients have not yet been reported, it is likely that the benefits of PTCA will also decrease over time as the disease progresses and restenosis occurs.

METHODS OF IMPROVING QUALITY OF LIFE

Methods used to improve quality of life following coronary revascularization include exercise rehabilitation programs, behavioral interventions, social support, patient education, and comprehensive programs that combine several of these strategies. Earlier studies suggested that supervised exercise rehabilitation programs for CABG patients improved work capacity (81,82), work status, anginal complaints, and ratings of well-being and quality of life (83,84), and stimulated beneficial psychosocial changes among participants (85,86). Exercise rehabilitation and even testing alone can assist patients in overcoming perceptions of disability (87), dispelling fears associated with physical exertion, encouraging participation in new activities (88–90) and strengthening feelings of well-being, self-esteem, and self-confidence (85). Behavioral interventions alone or in combination with other interventions can also favorably impact on prognosis in post-myocardial infarction patients (91–94). Behavioral interventions initiated prior to surgery may facilitate adjustment and foster realistic patient expectations about postoperative quality of life (95–97). Interventions conducted both pre- and post-surgery may assist patients in developing adaptive coping strategies and decrease anxiety and depression, which in turn should enhance return to work (98,99) and recovery from surgery (100), and may affect subsequent morbidity and mortality (101–104).

The importance of adequate social support from medical personnel, family and friends, coworkers, and/or other cardiac patients should not be underestimated; because social isolation and inadequate social support have been related to increased mortality and morbidity following myocardial infarction (52–57). Social support from physicians and other health care providers who work closely with patients and family members to facilitate recovery and return to work appears to be highly important (105). Attitudes expressed by physicians and employers, as well as preparation of patients and their families psychologically for the rehabilitation period, may enhance convalescence (85,106). Group support, in the form of coronary clubs or other peer or therapist-facilitated groups, may also be beneficial in promoting quality of life improvements. The importance of social support is emphasized by findings that even among married CABG patients, those with spouses who visited frequently recovered more quickly from surgery and required less pain medication than patients whose spouses visited less frequently (107).

Patient education is perhaps the minimal level of intervention needed to foster realistic expectations and facilitate postoperative adjustment. Cardiac patients report that they receive adequate education and preparation regarding return to activities, but not about emotional reactions to surgery and effects on social functioning (108). Health care providers need to address issues directly concerning recovery and return to work (109) but should go further and encourage patients to ask questions and discuss areas about which they might be concerned, raising issues about emotional reactions in particular (108). This may benefit patients in reducing their anxiety and depression and improving their quality of life (85,110). A recent study (111) demonstrates the modest benefits that may result from educational programs. The program was offered by nurses in a randomized, controlled design implemented in two hospitals. The intervention consisted of (a) a slide-tape presentation addressing anxiety, depression, problem solving, and sources of potential conflict with family members; (b) a one-to-one counseling session allowing individualization of the program; and (c) six telephone contacts during the eight weeks after hospital discharge to provide support, reinforce the educational message, and promote high self-efficacy expectations for performing activities. While no benefits were seen for mood ratings and quality of life indicators, modest benefits were found in patients' self-confidence to engage in activities following surgery.

Comprehensive programs may benefit patients' quality of life more than limited approaches. A preliminary study suggests the benefits of a combined rehabilitation, psychological, and social support intervention in improving the quality of life of CABG patients after surgery (112). Significantly greater improvements in psychosocial quality of life variables have also been reported with a combined educational and counseling program than with education or counseling alone (90). The benefits of a comprehensive rehabilitation program have recently been examined by Perk and colleagues (113), who compared 49 post-CABG patients with 98 doubly matched control patients receiving standard care. The rehabilitation program consisted of follow-up at a coronary clinic, repeated health education, and outpatient physical training, beginning 6 weeks after surgery. Over the first year after surgery, fewer rehabilitation patients were admitted to the hospital and less often. Fewer of the rehabilitation patients were using anxiolytics; and over a mean follow-up period of 38 months, rehabilitation patients rated their work capacity as higher than controls.

A recent Finnish study (27) reported a more modest benefit of combined rehabilitation programs, but suggested that participation in a comprehensive rehabilitation program could speed improvement in avocational functioning for male CABG patients. Patients were randomly assigned to either a rehabilitation group or a hospital treatment control condition. The rehabilitation program began 2 to 3 weeks prior to surgery and included informational, exercise, dietary, and psychological components. No significant differences between the rehabilitation and hospital groups were found in patient expectations, cardiac symptoms, satisfaction with sexual functioning, or hospital admissions. However, rehabilitation patients reported participating in more domestic hobbies and hobbies requiring physical activity compared with control participants at 12 months postsurgery.

Summary

Supervised exercise rehabilitation programs are clearly beneficial in improving quality of life for CABG patients. Emerging data also suggest benefits of behavioral interventions alone or in combination with other interventions in post-myocardial infarction patients. Increasing evidence suggests that behavioral interventions, particularly when combined with other forms of rehabilitative treatment, will have beneficial effects on quality of life, and possibly even morbidity and mortality outcomes. These interventions might most appropriately be initiated prior to medical procedures to promote realistic patient expectations about adjustment and facilitate development of adaptive coping strategies. While results appear to support the efficacy of behavioral interventions in improving quality of life outcomes for cardiovascular patients, a need exists for randomized, controlled studies to examine treatment benefits and refine treatment approaches.

Several different levels of intervention might currently be considered by clinicians. At a minimum, health care providers should address issues of recovery and return to work (109) and actively encourage patients to ask questions and discuss their concerns, particularly in emotional areas (108). Structured educational programs may also be developed to ensure that relevant aspects of patients' adjustment are addressed (111). Finally, more comprehensive programs involving rehabilitation, psychological, and social support components might be considered. Importantly, quality of life benefits appear to be associated directly with the level of intervention (113).

CONCLUSIONS

CABG surgery increases the survival rate for some types of patients, particularly those with left main coronary artery disease and those with three-vessel disease and left ventricular dysfunction (114–118). For patients with less severe disease, PTCA may offer similar survival benefits, but initial findings are not dramatic (119). Even among patients for whom there is a prolongation of life, but especially among those for whom the survival benefit is questionable, issues of quality of life are paramount. The effects of CABG and PTCA on specific dimensions of quality of life have been subjectively summarized in Table 5. Pluses indicate a positive change in a particular quality of life dimension, while minuses suggest negative effects of surgery on the variable. Most patients benefit from CABG for at least 5 years, with beneficial effects appearing to diminish prior to 10 years after operation. Most patients also benefit from PTCA, probably to an extent comparable to that of CABG with successful PTCA outcome. The benefit may be more immediately apparent with PTCA, as the effects of recovery from surgery are less of an issue.

Overall, it is difficult to determine the net gain in quality of life with both CABG and PTCA for several reasons. Foremost is the lack of controlled, randomized investigations examining quality of life changes. The few controlled studies are particularly difficult to interpret due to the large numbers of patients who cross over treatments, the lack of a comprehensive quality of life assessment battery, and grouping of patients together without consideration for age, disease severity, and gender subgroups. With PTCA becoming in-

creasingly common, more studies comparing quality of life following PTCA and CABG need to be conducted.

It is clear with CABG surgery and is probably also the case with PTCA, that preprocedure functioning substantially influences postprocedure outcome. The return to work literature clearly demonstrates the adverse effects of sustained periods of disability upon this dimension of quality of life; patients who undergo longer periods of disability are less likely to return to work. While return to work is influenced by many factors, social learning theory (120) suggests that learning the disability role mediates in part the effect of length of disability upon employment and other measures of quality of life. Surgery and relief from symptoms alone cannot be expected to overcome this learning effect. Quality of life after CABG might be improved by minimizing periods of disability. Current data indicate that most medically treated patients will eventually cross over to surgical treatment. Earlier CABG may have implications for improved quality of life unless otherwise indicated. However, patients who require repeat revascularization obviously endure some of the highest financial costs and potentially the greatest adverse effects on quality of life. The answer to this dilemma appears to lie in determining the optimal time for surgical intervention both medically and in terms of quality of life.

Other research needs exist as well. Analysis of quality of life among patient subgroups needs to be undertaken based on age, gender, ethnicity, and severity of disease. More comprehensive approaches to understanding predictors of quality of life changes for patients need to be undertaken so that more effective surgical decision rules are determined. An extremely important area for research is that of developing and evaluating methods to promote quality of life among cardiovascular patients.

Despite the paucity of randomized, controlled studies, both PTCA and CABG appear to improve the functional capacity and overall quality of life of patients with coronary artery disease. The current issue with quality of life among PTCA and CABG patients is not one of whether improvement is seen, but rather how to maximize and maintain improvement, shifting the focus from longitudinal to treatment outcome research. We assert that comprehensive intervention programs that include behavioral components are likely to produce optimal quality of life outcomes after coronary revascularization.

TABLE 5. *Subjective estimates of CABG surgery on quality of life dimensions*[a,b]

Dimension	Effect of CABG surgery	Effect of PTCA
Psychological	+	+
Anxiety	+	+
Depression	+	+
Neuropsychological	− −	+
Social interactions	+ +	+ +
Family	+	?
Nonfamilial	+ +	+ + +
Symptom relief and functional capacity	+ + +	+ + +
General functioning and symptom relief	+ + +	+ + +
Vocational functioning	+	+
Avocational functioning	+	+ +
Sexual functioning	+	?
Economic	−	0
Return to work	+	+
Cost-effectiveness	+	+ +
Individual economic impact	− −	−

[a]Estimates of change are relative to preprocedure, but not necessarily to pre-illness, levels of functioning.

[b]Number of pluses on scale indicates degree of beneficial effect; number of minuses indicates degree of negative effect; 0, no effect; ?, insufficient data.

REFERENCES

1. *1988 heart facts.* Dallas: American Heart Association, 1988.
2. *1992 heart and stroke facts.* Dallas: American Heart Association, 1992.
3. Chiriboga DE, Yarzebski J, Golberg R, Chen Z, Gurwitz J, Gore J, Alpert J, Dalen J. A community-wide perspective of gender differences and temporal trends in the use of diagnostic and revascularization procedures for acute myocardial infarction. *Am J Cardiol* 1993;71:268–273.
4. CASS Principal Investigator and their Associates. Coronary artery

surgery study CASS: a randomized trial of coronary bypass surgery. Survival data. *Circulation* 1983;68:939–950.

5. European Coronary Study Group. Long-term results of prospective randomized study of coronary artery bypass surgery in stable angina pectoris. *Lancet* 1982;2:1173–1180.

6. Hemenway D, Sherman H, Mudge GH, et al. Comparative costs versus symptomatic and employment benefits of medical and surgical treatment of stable angina pectoris. *Med Care* 1985;23:133–141.

7. Varnauskas E, and the European Coronary Surgery Study Group. Twelve-year follow-up of survival in the randomized European Coronary Surgery Study. *N Engl J Med* 1988;319:332–337.

8. Alderman EL, Bourassa MG, Cohen LS, Davis KB, Kaiser GG, Killip T, Mock MB, Pettinger M, Robertson TL, for the CASS investigators. Ten-year follow-up of surgical and myocardial infarction in the randomized coronary artery surgery study. *Circulation* 1990;82:1629–1646.

9. Peduzzi P, Detre K, Murphy ML, Thomsen J, Hultgren H, Takaro T, and the Veterans Administration Coronary Artery Bypass Cooperative Study Group. Ten-year incidence of myocardial infarction and prognosis after infarction. *Circulation* 1991;83:747–755.

10. Jollis JG, Jackman JD Jr, Dean LS. Percutaneous transluminal coronary angioplasty in the elderly: Results, indications, and approach. In: Roubin GS, Califf RM, O'Neill WW, Phillips HR III, Stack RS, eds. *Interventional cardiovascular medicine.* New York: Churchill Livingstone, 1994:343–353.

11. Wallwork J, Caine N. A comparison of the quality of life of cardiac transplant patients and coronary artery bypass graft patients before and after surgery. *Qual Life Cardiovasc Care* 1985;1:317–331.

12. Baldwin JC, Stinson EB. Quality of life after cardiac transplantation. *Qual Life Cardiovasc Care* 1985;1:332–335.

13. Jenkins CD, Stanton BA, Savageau JA, et al. Coronary artery bypass surgery: physical, psychological, social, and economic outcomes six months later. *JAMA* 1983;250:782–788.

14. Magni G, Unger HP, Valfre C, et al. Psychosocial outcome one year after heart surgery: a prospective study. *Arch Intern Med* 1987;147:473–477.

15. Neil CA. Quality of life issues in the adult with congenital heart disease. *Qual Life Cardiovasc Care* 1987;3:5–14.

16. Raczynski JM, Oberman A. Cardiovascular surgery patients. In: Spilker B, ed. *Quality of life assessments in clinical trials.* New York: Raven Press, 1990:295–332.

17. Califf RM, Ohman EM, Frid DJ, Fortin DF, Mark DB, Hlatky MA, Herndon JE II, Bengston JR. Restenosis: the clinical issues. In Topol EJ, ed. *Intervention cardiology.* Philadelphia: WB Saunders, 1989.

18. Peduzzi P, Hultgren H, Thomsen J, et al. Ten-year effect of medical and surgical therapy on quality of life: Veterans Administration Cooperative Study of coronary artery surgery. *Am J Cardiol* 1987;59:1017–1023.

19. Rogers WJ, Coggin CJ, Gersh BJ, et al. Ten year followup of quality of life in patients randomized to medicine vs CABG: Coronary Artery Surgery Study (CASS). *Circulation* 1988;78(suppl II);II-258.

20. Oberman A, Finklea JF. Return to work after coronary artery bypass grafting. *Ann Thorac Surg* 1982;34:353–355.

21. Mayou R. The psychiatric and social consequences of coronary artery surgery. *J Psychosom Res* 1986;30:255–271.

22. Mayou R. Quality of life in cardiovascular disease. *Psychother Psychosom* 1990;54:99–109.

23. Oberman A, Mattson ME, Alderman E, et al. Report of the working group: coronary artery bypass graft surgery. In: Wenger NK, Mattson ME, Furberg CD, Elinson J, eds. *Assessment of quality of life in clinical trials of cardiovascular therapies.* New York: LeJacq, 1984:311–314.

24. Wenger NK, Mattson ME, Furberg CD, et al. Assessment of quality of life in clinical trials of cardiovascular therapies. *Am J Cardiol* 1984;54:908–913.

25. Caine N, Harrison SCW, Sharples LD, Wallwork J. Prospective study of quality of life before and after coronary artery bypass grafting. *BMJ* 1991;302:511–517.

26. Langeluddecke P, Fulcher G, Baird D, Hughes C, Tennant C. A prospective evaluation of the Psychosocial effects of coronary artery bypass surgery. *J Psychosom Res* 1989;33:37–45.

27. Engblom E, Hämäläinen H, Lind J, Mattlar CE, Ollila S, Kallio V, Inberg M, Knuts LR. Quality of life during rehabilitation after coronary artery bypass surgery. *Qual Life Res* 1992;1:167–175.

28. Guadagnoli E, Ayanian JZ, Cleary PD. Comparison of patient-reported outcomes after elective coronary artery bypass grafting in patients aged ≥ and <65 years. *Am J Cardiol* 1992;70:60–64.

29. McKenna KT, McEniery PT, Maas F, Aroney CN, Bett JHN, Cameron J, Garrahy P, Hold G, Hossack KF, Murphy AL. Clinical results and quality of life after percutaneous transluminal coronary angioplasty: a preliminary report. *Cathet Cardiovasc Diagn* 1992;27:89–94.

30. Allen JK, Fitzgerald ST, Swank RT, Becker DM. Functional status after coronary artery bypass grafting and percutaneous transluminal coronary angioplasty. *Am J Cardiol* 1990;65:921–925.

31. McIntyre AB, Ballenger JF, King AT. Coronary artery bypass surgery in the elderly. *J SC Med Assoc* 1990;86:435–439.

32. Frasure-Smith N, Lesperance F, Talajic M. Depression following myocardial infarction: impact on 6-month survival. *JAMA* 1993;270:1819–1825.

33. Ahern DK, Gorkin L, Anderson JL, Tierney C, Hallstrom A, Ewart C, for the Cardiac Arrhythmia Pilot Study (CAPS) Investigators. *Behavioral variables and mortality or cardiac arrest in the CAPS.* Presented at the annual meeting of the American Heart Association, New Orleans, Nov 1989.

34. Kennedy GJ, Hofer MA, Chen D. Significance of depression and cognitive impairment in patients undergoing programmed stimulation of cardiac arrhythmias. *Psychosom Med* 1987;49:410–421.

35. Silverstone PH. Depression increases mortality and morbidity in acute life-threatening medical illness. *J Psychosom Res* 1990;34:651–657.

36. Carney RM, Rich MW, Freedland KE, Saini J, teVelde A, Simeone C, Clark K. Major depressive disorder predicts cardiac events in patients with coronary artery disease. *Psychosom Med* 1988;50:627–633.

37. Sloan R, Bigger J Jr. Biobehavioral factors in Cardiac Arrhythmia Pilot Study (CAPS): review and examination. *Circulation* 1991(suppl II);83:II-52–II-57.

38. Ladwig KH, Kiesert M, Konig J, Breithardt G, Borggrefe M. Affective disorders and survival after acute myocardial infarction: results from the post-infarction late potential study. *Eur Heart J* 1991;12:959–964.

39. Nussmeier NA. Neuropsychiatric complications of cardiac surgery. *J Cardiothorac Vasc Anesth* 1994;8(suppl 1):13–18.

40. Savageau JA, Stanton BA, Jenkins CD, Frater RWM. Neuropsychological dysfunction following elective cardiac operation: a six-month reassessment. *J Thorac Cardiovasc Surg* 1982;84:595–600.

41. Sakakibara Y, Shihara H, Terada Y, et al. Central nervous system damage following surgery using cardiopulmonary bypass: a retrospective analysis of 1386 cases. *Jpn J Surg* 1991;21:25–31.

42. Tuman KJ, McCarthy RJ, Najafi H, et al. Differential effects of advanced age on neurologic and cardiac risks of coronary artery operations. *J Thorac Cardiovasc Surg* 1992;104:1510–1517.

43. Greeley WJ, Ungerleider RM. Assessing the effect of cardiopulmonary bypass on the brain. *Ann Thorac Surg* 1991;52:417–419.

44. Kuroda Y, Uchimoto R, Kaieda R, et al. Central nervous system complications after cardiac surgery: a comparison between coronary artery bypass grafting and valve surgery. *Anesth Analg* 1993;76:222–227.

45. Bashein G, Townes BD, Nessly ML, Bledsoe SW, Hornbein TF, Davis KB, Goldstein DE, Coppel DB. A randomized study of carbon dioxide management during hypothermic cardiopulmonary bypass. *Anesthesiology* 1990;72:7–15.

46. Townes BD, Bashein G, Hornbein TF, et al. Neurobehavioral outcomes in cardiac operations: a prospective controlled study. *J Thorac Cardiovasc Surg* 1989;98:774–782.

47. Blumenthal JA, Madden DJ, Burker EJ, Croughwell N, Schniebolk S, Smith R, White WD, Hlatky M, Reves JG. A preliminary study of the effects of cardiac procedures on cognitive performance. *Int J Psychosom* 1991;38:13–16.

48. Robinson M, Blumenthal JA, Burker EJ, Hlatky M, Reves JG. Coronary artery bypass grafting and cognitive function: a review. *J Cardiopul Rehabil* 1990;10:180–189.

49. Ruberman W, Weinblatt E, Golberg JD, Chaudhary BS. Psychosocial influences on mortality after myocardial infarction. *N Engl J Med* 1984;311:552–559.

50. Berkman LF, Syme SL. Social networks, host resistance, and mortality: a nine year follow up study of Alameda County residents. *Am J Epidemiol* 1979;109:186–204.

51. Berkman L, Breslow L. *Health and ways of living: findings from the Alameda County study.* New York: Oxford University Press, 1983.

52. House JS, Robbins C, Metzner HC. The association of social relationships and activities with mortality: perspective evidence from the Tecumseh community health study. *Am J Epidemiol* 1982;116:123–140.

53. Schoenbach VJ, Kaplan BH, Freman L, Kleinbaum DG. Social ties and mortality in Evans County, Georgia. *Am J Epidemiol* 1986;123:577–591.

54. Case RB, Moss AJ, Case N, McDermott M, Eberly S. Living alone after myocardial infarction: impact on prognosis. *JAMA* 1992;267:515–519.

55. Williams RB, Barefoot JC, Califf RM. Prognostic importance of social and economic resources among medically treated patients with angiographically documented coronary artery disease. *JAMA* 1992;267:520–524.

56. Ruberman W. Psychosocial influence on patients with coronary heart disease. *JAMA* 1992;267:559–560.

57. Fiebach NH, Viscoli CM, Horwitz RI. Differences between women and men in survival after myocardial infarction: biology or methodology? *JAMA* 1990;263:1092–1096.

58. Allen JK, Becker DM, Swank RT. Factors related to functional status after coronary artery bypass surgery. *Heart Lung* 1990;19:337–343.

59. Vacek JL, Rosamond TL, Stites HW, Rowe SK, Robuck W, Dittmeier G, Beauchamp GD. Comparison of percutaneous transluminal coronary angioplasty versus coronary artery bypass grafting for multivessel coronary artery disease. *Am J Cardiol* 1992;69:592–597.

60. Huysmans HA, Van Ark E. Predictors of perioperative mortality, morbidity and late quality of life in coronary bypass surgery. *Eur Heart J* 1989;10(suppl H):10–12.

61. Smith JM, Rath R, Feldman DJ, et al. Coronary artery bypass grafting in the elderly: changing trends and results. *J Cardiovasc Surg* 1991;33:468–471.

62. Albes JM, Schistek R, Baier R, et al. Early and late results following coronary bypass surgery beyond the age of 75 years. *Thorac Cardiovasc Surg* 1991;39:289–293.

63. Johnston FA, Spyt T, Reece I, Hillis WS, Dunn FG. CABG in the Elderly: the Glasgow experience. *Gerontology* 1989;35:165–170.

64. Sergeant P, Lesaffre E, Flameng W, Suy R, Blackstone E. The return of clinically evident ischemia after coronary artery bypass grafting. *European Journal of Cardiothoracic Surgery* 1991;5:447–457.

65. Buffet P, Colasante B, Feldmann L, Danchin N, Juilliere Y, Anconina J, Cuilliere M, Cherrier F. Long-term follow-up after coronary angioplasty in patients younger than 40 years of age. *American Heart Journal* 1994;127(3):509–513.

66. Rupprecht HJ, Brennecke R, Kottmeyer M, Bernhard G, Erbel R, Pop T, Meyer J. Short- and long-term outcome after PTCA in patients with stable and unstable angina. *Eur Heart J* 1990;11:964–973.

67. Little T, Milner MR, Lee K, et al. Late outcome and quality of life following percutaneous transluminal coronary angioplasty in octogenarians. *Cathet Cardiovasc Diagn* 1993;29:261–266.

68. Tsai TP, Nessin S, Kass RM, et al. Morbidity and mortality after coronary artery bypass in octogenarians. *Ann Thorac Surg* 1991;51:983–986.

69. Kallis P, Unsworth-White J, Munsch C, Gallivan S, Smith EEJ, Parker DJ, Pepper JR, Treasure T. Disability and distress following cardiac surgery in patients over 70 years of age. *Eur J Cardiothorac Surg* 1993;7:306–312.

70. Lundbom J, Myhre HO, Ystgaard B, Bolz KD, Hammervold R, Levang OW. Factors influencing return to work after aortocoronary bypass surgery. *Scand J Thorac Cardiovasc Surg* 1992;26:187–192.

71. Dougenis D, Naik S, Brown AH. Is repeated coronary surgery for recurrent angina cost effective? *Eur Heart J* 1992;13:9–14.

72. McGee HM, Graham T, Crowe B, Horgan JH. Return to work following coronary artery bypass surgery or percutaneous transluminal coronary angioplasty. *Eur Heart J* 1993;14:623–628.

73. Mark DB, Lam LC, Lee KL, Clapp-Channing NE, Williams RB, Pryor DB, Califf RM, Hlatky MA. Identification of patients with coronary disease at high risk for loss of employment. A prospective validation study. *Circulation* 1992;86:1485–1494.

74. Smith LR, Milano CA, Molter BS, Elbeery JR, Sabiston DC, Smith PK. Preoperative determinants of postoperative costs associated with coronary artery bypass graft surgery. *Circulation* 1994;90:II-124–II-128.

75. Saw HS. Coronary artery bypass surgery in the elderly. *Ann Acad Med* 1990;19:45–50.

76. Forman DE, Berman AD, McCabe CH, Baim DS, Wei JY. PTCA in the elderly: the "young-old" versus the "old-old." *J Am Gerontol Soc* 1992;40:19–22.

77. Edmunds LH, Stephenson LW, Edie RN, et al. Open-heart surgery in octogenarians. *N Engl J Med* 1988;319:131–135.

78. Roberts A, Woodhall DD, Conti CR, et al. Mortality, morbidity, and cost-accounting related to coronary artery bypass graft surgery in the elderly. *Ann Thorac Surg* 1985;39:426–432.

79. Becker RC, Corrao JM, Alpert JS. Coronary artery bypass surgery in women. *Clin Cardiol* 1988;11:443–448.

80. Weintraub WS, Wenger NK, Jones EL, Carver JM, Guyton RA. Changing clinical characteristics of coronary surgery patients: differences between men and women. *Circulation* 1993;88(2):79–86.

81. Hartung GH, Rangel R. Exercise training in post-myocardial infarction patients: comparison of results with high risk coronary and post-bypass patients. *Arch Phys Med Rehabil* 1981;62:147–150.

82. Waites TF, Watt EW, Fletcher GF. Comparative functional and physiologic status of active and dropout coronary bypass patients from a rehabilitation program. *Am J Cardiol* 1983;51:1087–1090.

83. Russell RO, Wayne JB, Oberman A, et al. Return to work after treatment for coronary artery disease: role of the physician. *Prim Cardiol* 1981;7(5):12–23.

84. Ben-Ari E, Kellerman JJ, Fisman E, et al. Benefits of long-term physical training in patients after coronary artery bypass grafting—a 58-month follow-up and comparison with a nontrained group. *J Cardiopulm Rehabil* 1986;6:165.

85. Oberman A. Rehabilitation of patients with coronary artery disease. In: Braunwald E, ed. *Heart disease: a textbook of cardiovascular medicine.* 3rd ed. Philadelphia: WB Saunders, 1987:1395.

86. Stevens R, Hanson P. Comparison of supervised and unsupervised exercise training after coronary bypass surgery. *Am J Cardiol* 1984;53:1524–1528.

87. Wenger NK. The coronary patient: psychosocial, societal, and vocational aspects of recovery. *Qual Life Cardiovasc Care* 1988;4:86–94.

88. Prosser G, Carson P, Phillips R. Exercise after myocardial infarction: long-term rehabilitation effects. *J Psychosom Res* 1985;29:535.

89. Fontana AF, Kerns RD, Rosenberg RL, et al. Exercise training for cardiac patients: adherence, fitness, and benefits. *J Cardiopulm Rehabil* 1986;6:4.

90. Ott C, Bergner M. The effect of rehabilitation after myocardial infarction on quality of life. *Qual Life Cardiovasc Care* 1985;1:176.

91. Oldenberg B, Perkins RJ, Andrews G. Controlled trial of psychological intervention in myocardial infarction. *J Consult Clin Psychol* 1985;53:852.

92. Ornish D, Scherwitz LW, Doody RS, et al. Effects of stress management training and dietary changes in treating ischemic heart disease. *JAMA* 1983;249:54.

93. Friedman M, Thoresen CE, Gill JJ, et al. Alteration of type A behavior and reduction in cardiac recurrences in postmyocardial infarction patients. *Am Heart J* 1984;108:237.

94. Thoresen CE, Friedman M, Powell LH, et al. Altering type A behavior pattern in postmyocardial infarction patients. *J Cardiopulm Rehabil* 1985;5:258.

95. Folks DG, Blake DJ, Fleece L, et al. Quality of life six months after coronary artery bypass surgery: a preliminary report. *South Med J* 1986;79:397–399.

96. Mayou R, Bryant B. Quality of life after coronary artery surgery. *Q J Med* 1987;62:239–248.

97. Reitan RM. *Manual for administration of neuropsychological test batteries for adults and children.* Indianapolis: RM Reitan, 1969.

98. Dupuis G, Perrault J, Kennedy E, et al. Delay in return to work after coronary artery bypass surgery: a biobehavioral analysis. *Circulation* 1988;78(suppl II):II-227.

99. Hlatky MA, Haney T, Barefoot JC, Califf RM, Mark DB, Williams RB. Medical psychological and social correlates of work disability among men with coronary artery disease. *Am J Cardiol* 1986;58:911–915.

100. Radley A, Green R. Styles of adjustment to coronary graft surgery. *Soc Sci Med* 1985;20:461–472.

101. Magni G, Unger HP, Valfre C, et al. Psychosocial outcome one year after heart surgery: a prospective study. *Arch Intern Med* 1987;147:473–477.

102. Frasure-Smith N, Lesperance F, Talajic M. Depression following

myocardial infarction: impact on 6-month survival. *JAMA* 1993;270:1819–1825.

103. Ahern DK, Gorkin L, Anderson JL, Tierney C, Hallstrom A, Ewart C, for the Cardiac Arrhythmia Pilot Study (CAPS) Investigators. *Behavioral variables and mortality or cardiac arrest in the CAPS.* Presented at the annual meeting of the American Heart Association, New Orleans, Nov 1989.

104. Sloan R, Bigger J Jr. Biobehavioral factors in Cardiac Arrhythmia Pilot Study (CAPS): review and examination. *Circulation* 1991;83(suppl II):II-52–II-57.

105. Oberman A, Finklea JF. Return to work after coronary artery bypass grafting. *Ann Thorac Surg* 1982;34:353–355.

106. Liddle HV, Jensen R, Clayton PD. The rehabilitation of coronary surgical patients. *Ann Thorac Surg* 1982;34:374–382.

107. Kulik JA, Mahler HIM. Social support and recovery from surgery. *Health Psychol* 1989;8:221–238.

108. Stanton BA, Jenkins CD, Savageau JA, et al. Perceived adequacy of patient education and fears and adjustments after cardiac surgery. *Heart Lung* 1984;13:525–531.

109. Walter PJ, Amsel BJ. Return to work after coronary artery bypass graft surgery: the role of the primary care physician. *Qual Life Cardiovasc Care* 1987;3:31–35.

110. Tesar GE, Hackett TP. Psychologic management of the hospitalized cardiac patient. *J Cardiopulm Rehabil* 1985;5:219.

111. Gilliss CL, Gortner SR, Hauck WW, Shinn JA, Sparacino PA, Tompkins C. A randomized clinical trial of nursing care for recovery from cardiac surgery. *Heart Lung* 1993;22:125–133.

112. Boulay FM, David PP, Bourassa MG. Strategies for improving the work status of patients after coronary artery bypass surgery. *Circulation* 1982;66(suppl III):III-43–III-49.

113. Perk J, Bedback B, Engvall J. Effects of cardiac rehabilitation after coronary artery bypass grafting on readmissions, return to work, and physical fitness. *Scand J Soc Med* 1990;18:45–51.

114. The Veterans Administration Coronary Artery Bypass Surgery Cooperative Study Group. Eleven-year survival in the Veterans Administration randomized trial of coronary bypass surgery for stable angina. *N Engl J Med* 1984;311:1333–1339.

115. European Coronary Artery Surgery Study Group. Long-term results of prospective randomized study of coronary artery bypass surgery in stable angina pectoris. *Lancet* 1982;2:1173–1180.

116. Passamani E, Davis KB, Gillespie MJ, et al. A randomized trial of coronary artery bypass surgery: survival of patients with a low ejection function. *N Engl J Med* 1985;312:1665–1671.

117. Scott SM, Luchi RJ, Deupree RH, et al. Veterans Administration Cooperative Study for treatment of patients with unstable angina. *Circulation* 1988;78(suppl 1):I-113–I-121.

118. Takaro R, Hultgren HN, Lipton MJ, et al. The VA cooperative randomized study of surgery for coronary occlusive disease. II. Subgroup with significant left main lesions. *Circulation* 1976;54(suppl III):III-107–III-117.

119. Mark DB, Nelson CL, Califf RM, Harrell FE, Lee KL, Jones RH, Fortin DF, Stack RS, Glower DD, Smith LR, DeLong ER, Smith PK, Reves JG, Jollis JG, Tcheng JE, Muhlbaier LH, Lowe JE, Phillips HR, Pryor DB. Continuing evolution of therapy for coronary artery disease. Initial results from the era of coronary angioplasty. *Circulation* 1994;89:2015–2025.

120. Bandura A. *Social learning theory.* Englewood Cliffs, NJ: Prentice-Hall, 1977.

121. Jette AM, Davies AR, Cleary PD, Calkins DR, Rubenstein LV, Fink A, Kosecoff J, Young RT, Brook RH, Delbano T. The functional status questionnaire: reliability and validity when used in primary care. *J Gen Intern Med* 1986;1:143–149.

122. Derogatis LR, Lopez MC. The psychological adjustment to illness scale (PAIS & PAIS-SR) administration, scoring and procedures manual—I. Baltimore: Johns Hopkins University School of Medicine, 1983.

123. Radloff L. The CES-D scale: a self report depression scale for research in the general population. *Annu Psychol Meas* 1977;3:315–401.

124. Speilberger CD, Gorusch RL, Lushene R, Vagg PR, Jacobs GA. Manual for the state trait anxiety inventory (Form Y). Palo Alto, CA: Consulting Psychologist Press, 1983.

125. McEwen J. The Nottingham health profile: a measure of perceived health. In: Teeling-Smith G, ed. *Measuring the social benefits of medicine.* London: Office of Health Education, 1985:75–84.

126. Beck AT, Ward CH, Mendelson M, Mock JE, Erbaugh JK. An inventory for measuring depression. *Arch Gen Psychiatry* 1961;4:561–571.

127. Goldenberg D. *Manual of the general health questionnaire.* Manchester: Nfer-Nelson, 1978.

128. Sternberg S. Memory scanning: mental processes revealed by reaction-time experiments. *Am Sci* 1969;57:421–457.

129. Wechsler D. *The measurement of adult intelligence.* 3rd ed. Baltimore: Williams & Wilkins, 1944.

130. Reitan RM. Validity of the trail making test as an indication of organic brain damage. *Percept Motor Skills* 1958;8:271–276.

131. Stewart AL, Hays RD, Ware JE. The MOS short-form general health survey: reliability and validity in a patient population. *Med Care* 1988;26:724–735.

132. MacPhillamy DJ, Lewinsohn PM. The pleasant events schedule: studies on reliability, validity and scale intercorrelation. *J Consult Clin Psychol* 1983;50:363–380.

133. Coast J. Reprocessing data to form QALYs. *BMJ* 1992;305:87–90.

134. Gudex C, Kind P. *The QALY toolkit.* University of York: Centre for Health Economics, Discussion Paper 1988;38:1–36.

135. Rosser RM, Watts VC. Measurement of hospital output. *Int J Epidemiol* 1972;1:361–368.

Quality of Life and Pharmacoeconomics in Clinical Trials, Second Edition, edited by B. Spilker.
Lippincott-Raven Publishers, Philadelphia © 1996.

CHAPTER 91

Cardiovascular Disorders

Nanette K. Wenger, Michelle J. Naughton, and Curt D. Furberg

INTRODUCTION

The contemporary practice of cardiology deals predominantly with the care of patients with chronic illness. The goal of therapy for a chronic illness is generally not to cure the disease, but rather to alleviate its symptoms, improve the patient's functional capabilities, and retard the progression of the underlying disease. Thus, an evaluative component that addresses the way in which a patient's life is affected by the illness and its care, in addition to the traditional measures of morbidity and mortality, appears warranted. Spitzer has termed this the assessment of "clinically relevant human attributes" (1). This chapter provides a rationale for the inclusion of health-related quality of life (HRQL) in studies assessing cardiovascular disorders, an overview of HRQL, and finally issues surrounding the assessment of HRQL in various cardiovascular conditions.

RATIONALE FOR HEALTH-RELATED QOL STUDIES IN CARDIOVASCULAR DISORDERS

The rationale for HRQL studies varies with different subsets of patients with cardiovascular disease. For example, in

N. K. Wenger: Emory University School of Medicine, Grady Memorial Hospital, Atlanta, Georgia 30303.
M. J. Naughton and C. D. Furberg: Department of Public Health Sciences, Bowman Gray School of Medicine, Wake Forest University, Winston-Salem, North Carolina 27157.

patients with advanced congestive cardiac failure, morbidity and mortality are perhaps insensitive measures for comparing outcomes because this is a highly symptomatic disorder with a generally poor prognosis. The goals of therapy, the relief of symptoms with a resultant comfort of the patient for the remaining duration of life, and the maintenance of a limited functional capacity are more likely to be influenced by treatment and can be ascertained by the assessment of HRQL attributes.

Very different considerations apply when preventive therapies are instituted for cardiovascular disorders, typically in asymptomatic individuals. Examples of these therapies include those for mild systemic arterial hypertension, asymptomatic hypercholesterolemia, and asymptomatic ventricular dysfunction. These disorders are characterized by an excellent prognosis and very low incidence of complications, at least in the short term, and often a relatively low rate of individual complications, even over months to years. In these situations, morbidity and mortality data are not typically helpful for characterizing treatment outcomes. However, because most therapies for these conditions may produce symptoms in an otherwise symptomless individual, it is important to address those features that may adversely alter the individual's functional status and sense of well-being.

Considerations differ further when an intervention for a serious and often life-threatening illness may entail manifestations of drug toxicity and resultant morbidity. An example is the use of most antiarrhythmic drugs designed to control potentially life-threatening arrhythmias. To determine the appropriate role of these interventions, it is necessary to compare the patient's quality of life under standard care and the potential for urgent intermittent hospitalizations for life-threatening problems with the possibly reduced mortality, but likely toxicity associated with an otherwise effective control of the arrhythmia.

A final category of problems involves acute life-threatening illnesses, the prototype of which is myocardial infarction, for which invasive and high-risk interventions, acute thrombolysis and acute angioplasty, to name a few, have the dual goals of improving short-term survival and limiting morbidity, despite the potential discomforts and high risk of complications in the short term.

BACKGROUND

Overview of HRQL

Over the years, several definitions of HRQL have been proposed. These have ranged from very broad perspectives, reminiscent of the early definitions of quality of life, to narrower definitions more specific to HRQL (2). We have proposed the following definition for this chapter:

Health-related quality of life concerns those attributes valued by patients, including their resultant comfort or sense of well-being; the extent to which they are able to maintain reasonable physical, emotional, and intellectual function; and the degree to which they retain their ability to participate in valued activities within the family, in the workplace, and in the community (3).

This definition explicitly emphasizes the multidimensional aspects of HRQL, and that both functional status and perceptions regarding valued activities are critical to assess. Although there has been some debate on the definition of HRQL, a recent conference involving an international group of HRQL investigators reached agreement on the fundamental dimensions essential to any HRQL assessment (4). These primary dimensions include: physical functioning, psychological functioning, social functioning and role activities, and the individuals' overall life satisfaction and perceptions of their health status. Other commonly assessed dimensions of HRQL include cognitive or neuropsychological functioning, personal productivity, and intimacy and sexual functioning. Measures of sleep disturbance, pain, and other symptoms are often used as well. The specific dimensions included in a particular study will vary with the study population, the type and severity of the condition or illness, and, in the case of clinical trials, the intervention being assessed.

Types of HRQL Measures

Measures of HRQL can be classified as either generic or condition specific. Generic measures are designed to assess HRQL in a broad range of populations and health states. In general, generic measures are multidimensional and usually address at least the domains of physical, social, and emotional functioning; perceived health status; and life satisfaction. Examples of such measures include the Sickness Impact Profile (5), the Rand-36 Health Status Profile (6), and the Quality of Well-being Scale (7).

The examination of a variety of dimensions of a patient's life are of value in identifying both unanticipated benefits and side effects of therapy. Generic measures that encompass the major areas of HRQL can identify those aspects that are affected by the condition and its management. It is obvious, however, that the benefits of a therapy can be overestimated if adverse or unwanted effects are not considered. Thus, a weakness of generic instruments is that they may fail to examine detailed aspects of treatment adequately for specific symptoms or functions related to a disease.

By contrast, condition-specific HRQL measures are designed for use in specific populations (i.e., elderly, ethnic groups) or health conditions/diseases. In terms of cardiovascular disorders, the New York Heart Association functional classification can be used to assess limitations of a person's ability to perform physical activity (8). The Specific Activity Scale, also a measure of the ability to perform physical activity, is thought by some to be more precise (9), and correlates well with measured maximal oxygen uptake at graded exercise testing (10). Chest pain in patients with coronary heart disease can be classified by the Rose chest pain questionnaire (11) or the Canadian Cardiovascular Society measure of severity (12). Several indices are available for the measurement of dyspnea, and are particularly useful in patients with heart failure (13,14).

A problem with condition-specific measures is that many domains of interest, even in a specific illness, vary with the stage or severity of that illness, the medical therapy employed, the age of the patient, and any comorbidity. For example, persons with congestive heart failure may be more concerned with maintaining a reasonable degree of physical functioning so that they can complete some daily activities and interact with friends and family. Different dimensions of HRQL, however, may be of interest to the coronary patient with stable angina pectoris as compared with one who has acute myocardial infarction or who is undergoing coronary angioplasty or coronary bypass surgery.

Another major problem of condition-specific measures is that they do not easily permit comparison of HRQL outcomes between populations with different conditions, a feasible comparison when generic HRQL measures are employed. The difficulty in assessing particular health conditions further reflects the complex relationships among the HRQL dimensions. For example, increasing severity of physical symptoms and resultant decrease in physical capacities may cause depression or other emotional dysfunction. On the other hand, depression or emotional dysfunction may lead to limitations of physical function. Although specific aspects related to the illness are addressed in greater detail when condition-specific measures are used, the total scope of HRQL attributes must be assessed as well. These include general well-being; physical, cognitive, emotional functioning; social participation; and the like. This is why many investigators also use generic HRQL instruments or subscales in the same study to supplement the information obtained from a condition-specific measure.

Patient–Family Interrelationships and Perceptions

The effects of an illness or disability and its treatment often extend beyond the patient. Therefore, it is often advisable to address the impact of the condition on the family and/or close friends, in addition to the patient. Family members' reactions to the patient's condition, and the degree of emotional and tangible support they provide, have been shown to influence a patient's emotional well-being and compliance with medical therapy, as well as his or her morbidity and mortality (15). In addition, an ill family member may have differing impacts of the HRQL of family members (e.g., fear of the patient dying or being disabled, caregiver strain), which may in turn have an effect on the patient.

The perceptions of the patients and their families regarding the condition will reflect their personal value systems and judgments regarding what constitutes well-being, life satisfaction, and health status. Often there is lack of congruence between the patients' and families' perceptions of the impact of the condition and its therapy. It is important to distinguish perceptions of health status from actual health. Individuals who are ill, and who perceive themselves as such, may after a period of adjustment reset their expectations and adapt to their life situation, and thus possess a positive sense of well-being. Other persons with the same condition, however, may become gradually more dissatisfied with their life situation, and rate their overall quality of life as poor. It is interesting to note that perceived health ratings are strongly and independently associated with an increased risk of morbidity and mortality (16–18). In other words, individuals' health perceptions are important predictors of health outcomes, independent of their clinical health status.

Expectations (both the patient's and the family's) also constitute important determinants of satisfaction with the outcome of therapy. In many chronic and progressive illnesses, with time, as symptoms become increasingly severe and activities become more stringently restricted, patient expectations are likely to lessen as to the degree of improvement that can be obtained. As new therapies improve the outlook for both morbidity and mortality, it is important to assess patients' perceptions of their health status, as well as their expectations of treatment benefits.

Return to Work as a Component of Quality of Life

In the past, many cardiovascular studies were characterized by an inordinate and probably disproportionate focus on return to work as a measure of HRQL, so much so that in a number of reports, work appears to have been used almost as a surrogate for quality of life. Whereas return to work may be an important component of life quality for many patients, return to work measures only one aspect of HRQL and does not, even for that dimension, address such components as job satisfaction, job performance, opportunities for advancement, and the adequacy of income.

In many populations, particularly the severely impaired, the elderly, and women who may have only been in the paid work force intermittently, return to remunerative work is not a reasonable goal of most interventions. Furthermore, there is abundant evidence that many other nonmedical (non-intervention-related) aspects predominantly influence return to work, including pre-illness employment history, patient and family preferences, the job category and skill level, the level of unemployment in the community, financial status, and the employer's and the patient's perceptions of limitations. Indeed, in a number of studies, the patient's pre-intervention expectation of the ability to return to work was the most important determinant of employment outcome. In many return-to-work studies, perception of health status, rather than actual health status, and perception of ability to work, rather than objective measures of functional capability, often proved the overwhelming determinant.

More recent studies assessing HRQL have broadened the concept of work to include a range of productive activities, both paid and unpaid. Such measures include volunteer and community activities, household tasks and caregiving activities, as well as paid employment. These instruments provide a more comprehensive view of the individual's functional status, with respect to productive activities, than focusing solely on return to work.

HRQL DATA AND COST-EFFECTIVENESS

Increasingly, HRQL data are being used to determine the cost-effectiveness of medical therapies. These data are valuable in evaluating the benefits obtained from a particular intervention versus the resources required to obtain the desired treatment effect. Information regarding the positive and negative effects of interventions on individual's HRQL is an important component of these analyses. Please see Chapter 76, 78, 111–127 for more information about the incorporation of HRQL data into cost-effectiveness analyses.

HRQL ASSESSMENT IN CARDIOVASCULAR DISORDERS

Systemic Arterial Hypertension

The management of patients with asymptomatic or minimally symptomatic mild to moderate systemic arterial hypertension is used as a prototype of an asymptomatic cardiovascular illness that requires long-term therapy, whether it be an alteration of lifestyle and/or pharmacotherapy. In these instances, therapies are not designed for immediate benefit, but for the lifelong prevention of late complications, and thus are preventive interventions predominantly. Comparable concerns will be encountered in the management of patients with asymptomatic hypercholesterolemia (19) and in the treatment of asymptomatic ventricular dysfunction (as discussed in association with congestive heart failure).

The management of these conditions is far different than for the therapy of severe uncontrolled accelerated hypertension. In these situations, the short-term, life-threatening consequences of cerebrovascular accident, heart failure, myocardial infarction, and renal failure, among others, take precedence over any short-term impact on quality of life. Thus, the assessment of HRQL in these circumstances will have a different focus than an evaluation of therapies in asymptomatic or mild to moderately severe hypertensive persons.

Both behavioral and pharmacologic interventions for patients with mild asymptomatic hypertension have provided the greatest longitudinal experience in assessing aspects of HRQL as outcome measures (20–25). The prognosis for these patients, based on the traditional biomedical measures of morbidity and mortality, is very favorable (at least in the short term, e.g., 4 or 5 years), such that the traditional outcomes typically will not discriminate among therapies, nor will they identify the positive and negative impacts of each intervention on quality of life. Because these patients are essentially asymptomatic, evaluations of both behavioral and pharmacologic therapies must involve a comprehensive assessment of HRQL, including emotional well-being, physical functioning, social roles and activities, symptoms, and health perceptions. Health perceptions are also of clinical importance, because long-term adherence to the recommended interventions, if effective, will undoubtedly influence outcome. Perceptions of the seriousness of the problem and of the importance and value of the therapy on the part of patients (and family members) will influence compliance with recommended treatments.

An additional problem, documented in the area of hypertension, relates to the "labeling effect," which is an alteration in an individual's sense of well-being, general activity level, and work attendance based solely on the knowledge that hypertension is present, even prior to the initiation of therapy. These responses have been shown to occur whether or not hypertension was subsequently determined to be present (26–29). In a randomized clinical trial, however, this effect can be controlled as there is no reason to expect that persons more susceptible to the labeling effect would be clustered in one treatment group as compared with another. The randomization process, if performed correctly, would distribute these individuals throughout the treatment and control conditions.

Behavioral interventions, such as substantial changes in lifestyle including dietary modification to effect weight reduction and decrease sodium intake, increased activity level (exercise), smoking cessation, and moderation in alcohol use, will also influence participants' HRQL (21,24,27). Fur-

thermore, since there are now a number of categories of antihypertensive medications available that can effect a comparable reduction in blood pressure, presumably with comparable long-term health benefits, HRQL data will be an important determinant in analyses evaluating the relative effectiveness of various agents (23,30–37), and cost–benefit of different therapies (38,39). In addition, the impact of diverse interventions on HRQL must be examined because adherence to a medication will be substantially influenced by whether the therapy interferes with the individual's desired lifestyle (40).

Among the issues examined in a number of clinical trials comparing categories of antihypertensive drugs are the effect of the therapy on alertness (22), cognitive functioning (20,35,41), sleep disturbance (23,31,42), sexual functioning (22,42–44), physical symptoms (20,22,33,35,36), perceived well-being (20,33,45), psychological functioning (20,22–23,31,33,35,46), perceived health (23), activity levels (33–35), and social roles (20,22). These features must be combined with the consideration of medication-taking problems (particularly the dose frequency), the cost, the requirements for medical tests for the surveillance of therapy, and for office visits for surveillance of care (47,48). Because these patients are asymptomatic, therapy does not have the potential to improve their functional status and sense of well-being but can only cause new symptoms, decrease their ability to function, and ultimately result in poorer adherence to therapy if the unwanted effects are substantial.

A number of adverse effects of selected antihypertensive agents have been identified. These include depression (31), lack of emotional control (23), sleep disturbance (23,31), impaired cognitive functioning (27,41), mood alterations, and sexual dysfunction (42–44). Considerable research, conducted during the past decade, compared the relative merits of various pharmacotherapies, such that more information is available to assist clinicians in tailoring drug choices to the individual patient. Although research is now conducted on elderly patients (49–51), women (52,53), and minority populations (54), more information is needed. Greater attention must be paid by investigators to the use of standardized and validated instruments in clinical trials, particularly with select populations and cultural groups.

HEART FAILURE

Patients with heart failure represent the other extreme of the spectrum of cardiovascular illness. Characteristically, these patients are chronically and progressively ill, are severely symptomatic, are usually receiving multiple medications, have concomitant restrictions of dietary intake and of activity, and are elderly. More important, however, is that even with recent improvements in therapy and in short-term survival (55–58), their overall prognosis remains poor. Therefore, the major goal of therapy for patients with this problem is to reduce or limit symptoms and improve their comfort level for the remaining duration of life, as well as maintain their current level of physical functioning. Because the physical capacity of these individuals is borderline, the maintenance of independence is often precarious and may be adversely impacted by any unwanted effect of therapy. It is this outcome, maintenance of autonomy and independent living, that is a primary focus of HRQL research in heart failure.

Because many components of HRQL may be influenced by an intervention for heart failure, the use of multidimensional assessment instruments is recommended (59). Among the domains to be considered are the effect of therapy on the ability to ambulate and to perform self-care; to continue home management and household tasks; to get adequate sleep and rest; to engage in pleasurable activities such as hobbies, recreational activities, and sexual activity; to perform social roles with family and friends; to retain a sense of control and self-reliance; to retain intellectual and cognitive function; to use health resources; and to retain aspects of emotional stability that involve expectations, positive affect, life satisfaction, and reasonable optimism about the future.

Another important aspect to assess is the expectations of the patients regarding the outcome of their illness, and particularly the outcome of therapy. With the demonstration in recent years that newer forms of pharmacotherapy can improve survival as well as improve symptoms and functional capacity (55–58), it will be important to determine whether patients' expectations of subjective improvement are met.

The New York Heart Association functional classification, often used to define whether "usual" activities can be performed without resultant symptoms, may be misleading, in that "usual" activities at the time of intervention may be significantly less than those typically undertaken months or years previously (60). The Specific Activity Scale (9) although perhaps overcoming some of these problems, appears able only to detect sizable improvements in functional capacity. The New York functional classification is similarly insensitive to change. Other indices are available for the clinical assessment of dyspnea, defining the magnitude of effort needed for its precipitation (13,14). In a review of HRQL measures in heart failure, the Minnesota Living with Heart Failure Questionnaire was identified as the only condition-specific measure to address a wide range of HRQL impairments, and also show responsiveness to change in the context of double-blind, multicenter, pharmaceutical clinical trials (61).

Because cerebral blood flow may change with alterations in cardiac output and peripheral vascular resistance, it appears prudent to assess the finer and more detailed aspects of cognitive function, including attention, concentration, memory, learning ability, and recall, among others, as has been done in some studies of antihypertensive medications (62). Preliminary data from patients with dilated cardiomyopathy referred for cardiac transplantation showed a high incidence of moderate to severe verbal cognitive deficits

and deficits of higher cortical function at baseline evaluation (63). Even subtle deficits may have a major impact on adherence to medical regimens, psychological adjustment, and HRQL (64). The Studies of Left Ventricular Dysfunction measured cognitive functioning with Vocabulary, the Digit Span Test, and the Trails Making A and B Tests (65). The results of these tests varied by the New York Heart Association classifications. No differences were found among classes in the area of Vocabulary or in the more complex attention, motor-tracking task, Trails Making B. Differences in the attention-concentration task, Digit Span, and the relatively less complex Trails Making A task were found, however, in class I as opposed to classes II to III.

Among the data derived from clinical studies of heart failure is the information that exercise capacity correlates poorly with left ventricular ejection fraction (65,66). Despite the fact that left ventricular ejection fraction is a good predictor of survival, many patients with a very poor ejection fraction have a reasonable exercise capacity (66–68). Exercise capacity, however, does not reliably predict survival. In other patients, it is the pace at which an activity is performed that is a significant determinant of exercise tolerance (69). Similarly, the symptomatic status of patients with heart failure correlates poorly with indices of ventricular function (67,68), but little is known about the relationship between the objectively determined physical work capacity and features of quality of life. This lack of consistency among exercise capacity, hemodynamic changes, symptoms, prognosis, and quality of life attributes is problematic in the assessment of outcomes of therapeutic interventions for heart failure. Improvement in physiologic parameters, without comparable improvement in functional status and in the quality of life characteristics deemed important by the patient, probably should not be termed a favorable outcome (67).

In the SOLVD trial, the other end of the spectrum of heart failure was also addressed, i.e., asymptomatic left ventricular dysfunction. As noted above, this aspect is more akin to asymptomatic systemic arterial hypertension than it is to severe and symptomatic congestive cardiac failure. Because of the generally unfavorable prognosis once heart failure becomes clinically manifest, the question has appropriately been raised as to the potential benefit of pharmacotherapy in the asymptomatic stage of ventricular dysfunction. Results from the SOLVD trial indicated that chronic angiotensin-converting enzyme inhibitor treatment slowed or reserved left ventricular dilation in patients with asymptomatic LV systolic dysfunction (70). Compared with symptomatic patients, asymptomatic patients were shown to manifest a slower rate of spontaneous left ventricular dilation and less reduction in left ventricular volumes by the use of enalapril.

As a result of the asymptomatic versus symptomatic expression of heart failure, a condition-specific measure cannot reasonably be considered for "heart failure" as a general problem. In the asymptomatic stage of ventricular dysfunction, a therapy has only the potential, at least in the short term, to produce symptoms and adversely affect perceptions of health status and well-being. Therefore, a range of dimensions of HRQL should be considered, and a generic or global measure seems most appropriate. Certainly physical and emotional functioning should be measured, as well as interpersonal relationships, sexual adjustment, leisure activity, and work function. In this asymptomatic population, indices of physical work capacity or dyspnea will not differentiate among outcomes.

A recent review of HRQL ascertainment in heart failure provides information on the reliability, validity and responsiveness of HRQL instruments to changes in clinical status (61). Currently, both generic and condition-specific measures are used in clinical trials of heart failure. Additional data have to be collected, however, to validate and determine changes in instrument scores that correspond to small, medium, and large changes in HRQL and clinical status (61).

CORONARY ATHEROSCLEROTIC HEART DISEASE—ANGINA PECTORIS AND MYOCARDIAL INFARCTION

Very different HRQL domains are of concern for stable ambulatory patients with angina pectoris than for patients with an acute and unexpected serious illness, such as acute myocardial infarction. Still other features are applicable for the same coronary patients undergoing coronary angioplasty or coronary bypass surgery.

For the patient with stable angina pectoris, the major concerns relate to physical functioning, symptoms, emotional well-being, personal productivity/occupation, social roles and activities, with attention to the requirements for follow-up medical care. Because this is a prominently symptomatic illness, the degree to which the intervention ameliorates function-limiting symptoms is often an important outcome measure. In this regard, disease-specific measures may be of value, particularly those that address chest pain, the major symptom of coronary heart disease. The Rose Questionnaire (11) and the Canadian Cardiovascular Society classification (12) are frequently used instruments. The impact on function can be measured by the New York Heart Association classification, although the features of "usual" activity as a precipitant of symptoms present the problems previously cited (9), probably accounting for the less than satisfactory correlation of the New York Heart Association classification with exercise capacity. The Specific Activity Scale is purported to overcome some of these problems but cannot measure small degrees of change; it does, however, correlate well with measured maximal oxygen uptake at exercise testing (10). In the Veterans Administration Cooperative Study of Coronary Artery Bypass Surgery for stable angina pectoris, an angina scoring system combined the severity of angina and a medication score (71). An instrument developed by Olsson and colleagues (72) is described as combining features of both the New York Heart classification and survival data. A recent study indicated that contemporary outpatients with angina are frequently women and elderly with high rates of rest, illness, and mental stress-related angina (73). These data suggest the need for the development of reliable instruments to measure nonphysical stress-related angina and its relationship to HRQL.

Generic HRQL instruments are also used to assess the range of life domains affected by angina pectoris. The Sickness Impact Profile and the Nottingham Health Profile have been able to detect treatment effects in patients with angina (74), and the Psychological General Well-Being Index has been used to measure general positive and negative affective states (75). Supplementing an angina- or heart disease-specific measure with a generic HRQL instrument will provide valuable information about the effect of the condition and its treatment on an individual's HRQL.

The management of chronic, stable angina pectoris is an area in which several categories of effective therapeutic options are available for reduction of myocardial ischemia and the attendant relief of chest pain. Therefore, the choice among surgical and drug therapies—nitrate drugs, calcium blocking drugs, and β-blocking drugs—is often dependent on their impact on HRQL, as well as on the patient's comorbid conditions (76–78).

The setting of acute myocardial infarction poses far different HRQL issues; these differ in the intensive care setting and during the remainder of the hospital stay, as well as postdischarge from the hospital. Previously in the traditional intensive care setting, primary concerns included the degree of discomfort, the ability to achieve sleep and rest, and the impact on responsiveness, alertness, emotional state, and orientation. Although these remain important, the acute invasive interventions, such as acute coronary thrombolysis and acute coronary angioplasty, must be examined for their impact on a range of HRQL dimensions, in addition to the traditional measures of morbidity and mortality. There should be particular emphasis on physical, emotional, and cognitive functioning. With this acute, unanticipated, yet life-threatening illness, the need for patients to make immediate decisions and choices among potentially equal, but often high-risk therapies, must be addressed.

Following transfer from the intensive care setting and during the remainder of the hospital stay, the primary HRQL areas of concern for measurement include the effects of the intervention on mobility, symptoms, emotional well-being, cognitive and intellectual function, and interactions with family and friends. After discharge from the hospital, the additional concerns of performance of usual activities and social roles, personal productivity/work, sleep dysfunction and sexual functioning become important, and the impact of the illness on HRQL may vary by the age and gender of the patient (79–81). The effect of various pharmacotherapies on patients' HRQL following a myocardial infarction are also important to assess (82–84).

In recent years it has been determined that there are a number of clinical settings and arteriographic characteristics for which both coronary angioplasty and coronary bypass surgery are reasonable therapeutic options. The comparison of these two interventions is between the early intensive perioperative morbidity related to surgery and the potential late angioplasty failure with the attendant fear, anxiety, and subsequent acute symptoms. Studies have been conducted to assess the impact of such procedures on patients' HRQL (85,86), and investigators are beginning to assess the special treatment concerns of elderly individuals (87–89).

An additional area of intensive investigation is the impact on subtle features of neuropsychological functioning by the cardiopulmonary bypass procedure needed for coronary bypass surgery. Comparing coronary angioplasty with coronary bypass surgery is an ideal setting in which to examine, by a variety of tests of neuropsychological functioning, whether there is an impact on neurologic deficits, memory, motor coordination, recognition, and reasoning, among others from cardiopulmonary bypass (90).

ARRHYTHMIAS

Primarily in association with coronary atherosclerotic heart disease, but also in the setting of cardiomyopathy of varied causes, there has been major concern with life-threatening ventricular arrhythmias. The anti-arrhythmic therapies entail considerable risk of drug toxicity and morbidity, in addition to their impact on various aspects of life quality. Although the drugs are typically administered on an ambulatory basis, there is a need for frequent tests and office visits for surveillance. The impact on HRQL of this aspect of care must be considered, in addition to the actual issues of medication taking and adherence.

A number of drugs have been studied, initially in the Cardiac Arrhythmia Pilot Study and subsequently in the Cardiac Arrhythmia Suppression Trial, to determine the morbidity and mortality impact of a variety of newer anti-arrhythmic compounds. The effect of rehabilitation on the HRQL and incidence of ventricular arrhythmias in patients after myocardial infarction has also been investigated (91). Results from the Cardiac Arrhythmia Suppression Trial study of antiarrhythmic medications indicated that patients with heart failure and previous myocardial infarction, as well as those with angina and dyspnea, had a worse HRQL in terms of symptoms, emotional well-being, and physical and social functioning than those not experiencing these symptoms (92).

CONCLUSIONS

In a number of investigations of coronary heart disease-related conditions, the satisfaction of patients with the outcomes of their medical care reflected preponderantly HRQL issues, or essentially those attributes valued by patients. In order to ascertain the full impact of an intervention, these attributes, as well as the traditional measures of morbidity and mortality, must be examined. The information gained from these investigations is important clinically in that data obtained from these studies can assist clinicians in tailoring treatments to meet an individual patient's preferences and values. Further work is needed in determining the clinical significance of scores obtained on HRQL instruments and in reformatting information so that the pivotal items can be assessed readily during a brief clinical encounter, such as an office visit.

REFERENCES

1. Spitzer WO. Keynote Address: State of science 1986: Quality of life and functional status as target variables for research. *J Chronic Dis* 1987;40:465–471.
2. Stewart A. Conceptual and methodological issues in defining quality of life: state of the art. *Prog Cardiovasc Nurs* 1992;7:3–11.
3. Wenger NK, Furberg CD. Cardiovascular disorders. In: Spilker B, ed. *Quality of life assessment in clinical trials.* New York: Raven Press, 1990:335–345.
4. Berzon R, Hays RD, Shumaker SA. International use, application, and performance of health-related quality of life instruments. *Qual Life Res* 1993;2:236–368.
5. Bergner M, Bobbitt RA, Carter WB, et al. The Sickness Impact Profile: development and final revision of a health status measure. *Med Care* 1981;19:787–805.
6. Hays RD, Sherbourne CD, Mazel RM. The Rand 36-Item Health Status Survey 1.0. *Health Econ* 1993;2:217–227.
7. Bush JW. General health policy model/quality of well-being (QWB) scale. In: Wenger NK, Mattson ME, Furberg CD, et al., eds. *Quality of life in clinical trials of cardiovascular therapies.* New York: LeJacq, 1984:189–199.
8. Harvey RM, Doyle EF, Ellis K, et al. Major changes made by the Criteria Committee of the New York Heart Association. *Circulation* 1974;49:390.
9. Goldman L, Hashimoto B, Cook EF, et al. Comparative reproducibility and validity of systems for assessing cardiovascular functional class: advantages of a new Specific Activity Scale. *Circulation* 1981;64:1227–1234.
10. Lee TH, Shammash JB, Ribeiro JP, et al. Estimation of maximum oxygen uptake from clinical data: performance of the Specific Activity Scale. *Am Heart J* 1988;115:203–204.
11. Rose GA, Blackburn H. *Cardiovascular survey methods.* Geneva: World Health Organization 1986;56:1–188.
12. CASS Principal Investigators and their Associates. Coronary artery surgery study (CASS). A randomized trial of coronary artery bypass surgery. Quality of life in patients randomly assigned to treatment groups. *Circulation* 1983;68:951–960.
13. Foxman B, Lohr KN, Brook RH, et al. *Conceptualization and measurement of physiological health in adults, v. congestive heart failure.* Santa Monica, CA: Rand Corp., September 1982.
14. Mahler DA, Weinberg DM, Wells CK, et al. The measurement of dyspnoea. Content, interobserver agreement and physiologic correlates of two new clinical indexes. *Chest* 1984;85:751–758.
15. Shumaker SA, Hill RD. Gender differences in social support and physical health. *Health Psychol* 1991;10:102–111.
16. LaRue A, Bank L, Jarvik L, et al. Health in old age: how do physicians' rating and self-ratings compare? *J Gerontol* 1979;34:687–691.
17. Kaplan GA, Camacho TC. Perceived health and mortality: a nine year follow-up of the human population laboratory cohort. *Am J Epidemiol* 1983;117:292–295.
18. Mossey JM, Shapiro E. Self-rated health: a predictor of mortality among the elderly. *Am J Public Health* 1982;72:800–808.
19. Lefebvre RC, Hursey KG, Carleton RA. Labeling of participants in high blood pressure screening programs. Implications for blood cholesterol screenings. *Arch Intern Med* 1988;148:1993–1997.
20. Croog SH, Elias MF, Colton T, et al. Effects of antihypertensive medications on quality of life in elderly hypertensive women. *Am J Hypertens* 1994;7(4 Pt 1):329–339.

21. Dubbert PM, Martin JE, Cushman WC, et al. Endurance exercise in mild hypertension: effects on blood pressure and associated metabolic and quality of life variables. *J Hum Hypertens* 1994;8:265–272.

22. Omvik P, Thaulow E, Herland OB, et al. Double-blind, parallel, comparative study on quality of life during treatment with amlodipine or enalapril in mild or moderate hypertensive patients: a multicentre study. *J Hypertens* 1993;11:103–113.

23. Testa MA, Anderson RB, Nackley JF, Hollenberg NK. Quality of life and antihypertensive therapy in men. A comparison of captopril with enalapril. The Quality-of-Life Hypertension Study Group. *N Engl J Med* 1993;328:907–913.

24. Wassertheil-Smoller S, Oberman A, Blaufox MD, Davis B, Langford H. The Trial of Antihypertensive Interventions and Management (TAIM) Study. Final results with regard to blood pressure, cardiovascular risk, and quality of life. *Am J Hypertens* 1992;5:37–44.

25. Steiner SS, Friedhoff AJ, Wilson BL, Wecker JR, Santo JP. Antihypertensive therapy and quality of life: a comparison of atenolol, captopril, enalapril and propranolol. *J Hum Hypertens* 1990;4:217–225.

26. Johnston ME, Gibson ES, Terry CW, et al. Effects of labeling on income, work, and social function among hypertensive employees. *J Chronic Dis* 1984;37:417–423.

27. Macdonald LA, Sackett DL, Haynes RB, et al. Hypertension: the effects of labeling on behavior. *Qual Life Cardiovasc Care* 1985;1:129–139.

28. Polk BF, Harlan LC, Cooper SP, et al. Disability days associated with detection and treatment in a hypertension control program. *Am J Epidemiol* 1984;119:44–53.

29. Haynes RB, Sackett DL, Taylor DW, et al. Increased absenteeism from work after detection and labeling of hypertensive patients. *N Engl J Med* 1977;296:732–739.

30. Omvik P, Thaulow E, Herland OB, et al. A long-term, double-blind, comparative study on quality of life during treatment with amlodipine or enalapril in mild or moderate hypertensive patients: a multicentre study. *Br J Clin Pract* 1994;73:23–30.

31. Amir M, Cristal N, Bar-on D, Loidl A. Does the combination of ACE inhibitor and calcium antagonist control hypertension and improve quality of life? The Lomir-MCT-IL study experience. *Blood Pressure* 1994;1(suppl):40–42.

32. Cruikshank JM, McAinsh J. Beta blockers and quality of life. *Br J Clin Pract* 1992;46:34–38.

33. Palmer AJ, Fletcher AE, Rudge PJ, et al. Quality of life in hypertensives treated with atenolol or captopril: a double-blind crossover trial. *J Hypertens* 1992;10:1409–1416.

34. Fletcher AE, Battersby C, Adnitt P, et al. Quality of life on antihypertensive therapy: a double-blind trial comparing quality of life on pinacidil and nifedipine in combination with a thiazide diuretic. European Pinacidil Study Group. *J Cardiovasc Pharmacol* 1992;20:108–114.

35. Fletcher A, Bulpitt C. Quality of life in the treatment of hypertension. The effect of calcium antagonists. *Drugs* 1992;1(44 suppl):135–140.

36. Dahlof C, Dimenas E, Kendall M, Wiklund I. Quality of life in cardiovascular diseases. Emphasis on beta-blocker treatment. *Circulation* 1991;86(suppl 6S):VII08–VIII8.

37. Herlitz H. ACE-inhibitors and quality of life. *Scand J Prim Health Care* 1990;1S:85–88.

38. Wiklund I. Quality of life and cost-effectiveness in the treatment of hypertension. *J Clin Pharm Ther* 1994;19:81–87.

39. Gafni A. Measuring the adverse effects of unnecessary hypertension drug therapy: QALYs vs. HYE. *Clin Invest Med* 1991;14:266–270.

40. Turner RR. Role of quality of life in hypertension therapy: implications for patient compliance. *Cardiology* 1992;80S(1):11–22.

41. McCorvey E Jr, Wright JT Jr, Culbert JP, et al. Effect of hydrochlorothiazide, enalapril, and propranolol on quality of life and cognitive and motor function in hypertensive patients. *Clin Pharm* 1993;12:300–305.

42. Dahlof C. Quality of life/subjective symptoms during beta-blocker treatment. *Scand J Prim Health Care* 1990;1S:73–80.

43. Wassertheil-Smoller S, Blaufox MD, Oberman A, et al. Effect of antihypertensives on sexual function and quality of life: the TAIM Study. *Ann Intern Med* 1991;114:613–620.

44. Chang SW, Fine R, Siegel D, et al. The impact of diuretic therapy on reported sexual function. *Arch Intern Med* 1991;151:2402–2408.

45. Dahlof C. Well-being (quality of life) in connection with hypertensive treatment. *Clin Cardiol* 1991;14:97–103.

46. Muller A, Montoya P, Schandry R, Hartl L. Changes in physical symptoms, blood pressure and quality of life over 30 days. *Behav Res Ther* 1994;32:593–603.

47. Croog SH, Levine S, Testa M, et al. The effects of antihypertensive therapy on quality of life. *N Engl J Med* 1986;314:1657–1664.

48. Jachuck SJ, Brierly H, Jachuck S, et al. The effect of hypotensive drugs on quality of life. *J R Coll Gen Pract* 1982;32:103–105.

49. Applegate WB, Pressel S, Wittes J, et al. Impact of the treatment of isolated systolic hypertension on behavioral variables. Results from the systolic hypertension in the elderly program. *Arch Intern Med* 1994;154:2154–2160.

50. James MA, Potter JF. The effect of antihypertensive treatment of the quality of later years. *Drugs Aging* 1993;3:26–39.

51. Fletcher A, Bulpitt C. Quality of life and antihypertensive drugs in the elderly. *Aging* 1992;4:115–123.

52. Robbins MA, Elias MF, Croog SH, Colton T. Unmedicated blood pressure levels and quality of life in elderly hypertensive women. *Psychosom Med* 1994;56:251–259.

53. Applegate WB, Phillips HL, Schnaper H, et al. A randomized controlled trial of the effects of three antihypertensive agents on blood pressure control and quality of life in older women. *Arch Intern Med* 1991;151:1817–1823.

54. Croog SH, Kong BW, Levine S, et al. Hypertensive black men and women. Quality of life and effects of antihypertensive medications. Black Hypertension Quality of Life Multicenter Trial Group. *Arch Intern Med* 1990;150:1733–1741.

55. Cohn JN, Archibald DG, Ziesche S, et al. Effect of vasodilator therapy on mortality in chronic congestive heart failure. Results of a Veterans Administration Cooperative Study. *N Engl J Med* 1986;314:1547–1552.

56. The CONSENSUS Trial Study Group. Effects of enalapril on mortality in severe congestive heart failure. Results of the Cooperative North Scandinavian Enalapril Survival Study (CONSENSUS). *N Engl J Med* 1987;316:1429–1435.

57. Packer M. Prolonging life in patients with congestive heart failure: the next frontier. *Circulation* 1987;75(suppl IV):1–3.

58. SOLVD Investigators. Effect of enalapril on survival in patients with reduced left ventricular ejection fractions and congestive heart failure. *N Engl J Med* 1991;325:293–302.

59. Jessup M, Brozena S. Assessment of quality of life in patients with chronic congestive heart failure. *Qual Life Cardiovasc Care* 1988;4:53–57.

60. Goldman L, Cook EF, Mitchell N, et al. Pitfalls in the serial assessment of cardiac functional status. How a reduction in "ordinary" activity may reduce the apparent degree of cardiac compromise and give a misleading impression of improvement. *J Chronic Dis* 1982;35:763–771.

61. Guyatt GH. Measurement of health-related quality of life in heart failure. *J Am Coll Cardiol* 1993;22(4 suppl A):185A–191A.

62. Rajagopalan B, Raine AEG, Cooper R, et al. Changes in cerebral blood flow in patients with severe congestive cardiac failure before and after captopril treatment. *Am J Med* 1984;76(suppl 5B):86–90.

63. Petrucci RJ, Jessup M, Cavarocchi J, et al. Cognitive function in patients with symptomatic dilated cardiomyopathy before and after cardiac transplantation. *Transplant Proc* 1988;20:810 (abstract).

64. Farmer ME. Cognitive deficits related to major organ failure: the potential role of neuropsychological testing. *Neuropsychol Rev* 1994;4:117–160.

65. Gorkin L, Norvell NK, Rosen RC, et al. Assessment of quality of life as observed from the baseline data of the Studies of Left Ventricular Dysfunction (SOLVD) Trial Quality-of-Life Substudy. *Am J Cardiol* 1993;71:1069–1073.

66. Smith RF, Johnson G, Ziesche S, et al. Functional capacity in heart failure. Comparison of methods for assessment and their relation to other indexes of heart failure. The V-HeFT VA Cooperative Studies Group. *Circulation* 1993;87(6S):VI88–VI93.

67. Guyatt GH. Methodologic problems in clinical trials in heart failure. *J Chronic Dis* 1985;38:353–363.

68. Franciosa JA. Epidemiologic patterns, clinical evaluation, and long-term prognosis in chronic congestive heart failure. *Am J Med* 1986;80(suppl. 2B):14–21.

69. Feinstein AR, Joseph BR, Wells CK. Scientific and clinical problems in indexes of functional disability. *Ann Intern Med* 1986;81:641–664.

70. Konstam MA, Kronenberg MW, Rousseau MF, et al. Effects of the angiotensin converting enzyme inhibitor enalapril on the long-term progression of left ventricular dilatation in patients with asymptomatic systolic dysfunction. *Circulation* 1993;88:2277–2283.

71. Peduzzi P, Hultgren H. Angina scoring method in the Veterans Administration Randomized Study of Bypass Surgery. *Am J Epidemiol* 1985;122:477–484.

72. Olsson G, Lubsen J, van Es GA, et al. Quality of life after myocardial infarction: effect of long-term metoprolol on mortality and morbidity. *BMJ* 1986;292:1491–1493.

73. Pepine CJ, Abrams J, Marks RG, Morris JJ, Scheidt SS, Handberg E. Characteristics of a contemporary population with angina pectoris. TIDES Investigators. *Am J Cardiol* 1994;74:226–231.

74. Visser MC, Fletcher AE, Parr G, Simpson A, Bulpitt CJ. A comparison of three quality of life instruments in subjects with angina pectoris: the Sickness Impact Profile, the Nottingham Health Profile, and the Quality of Well-Being Scale. *J Clin Epidemiol* 1994;47:157–163.

75. Wiklund I, Comerford MB, Dimenas E. The relationship between exercise tolerance and quality of life in angina pectoris. *Clin Cardiol* 1991;14:204–208.

76. Bulpitt CJ, Fletcher AE. Quality of life and the heart: evaluation of therapeutic alternatives. *Br J Clin Pract* 1994;73:18–22.

77. Blake P, Berry SC, Readman A, Ratcliffe M, Godley M. A comparison of epanolol and nifedipine in stable angina patients: results of a multicentre trial. *Cardiology* 1991;79:249–255.

78. Rupprecht HJ, Brennecke R, Kottmeyer M, Bernhard G, Erbel R, Pop T, Meyer J. Short- and long-term outcome after PTCA in patients with stable and unstable angina. *Eur Heart J* 1990;11:964–973.

79. Wiklund I, Herlitz J, Johansson S, Bengtson A, Karlson BW, Persson NG. Subjective symptoms and well-being differ in women and men after myocardial infarction. *Eur Heart J* 1993;14:1315–1319.

80. Conn VS, Taylor SG, Abele PB. Myocardial infarction survivors: age and gender differences in physical health, psychosocial state and regimen adherence. *J Adv Nurs* 1991;16:1026–1034.

81. Conn VS, Taylor SG, Wiman P. Anxiety, depression, quality of life, and self-care among survivors of myocardial infarction. *Issues Ment Health Nurs* 1991;12:321–331.

82. Gorkin L, Follick MJ, Geltman E, et al. Quality of life among patients post-myocardial infarction at baseline in the Survival and Ventricular Enlargement (SAVE) Trial. *Qual Life Res* 1994;3:111–119.

83. Rawles J, Light J. Loss of quality adjusted days as a trial endpoint: effect of early thrombolytic treatment in suspected myocardial infarction. Grampion Region Early Anistreplase Trial (GREAT). *J Epidemiol Comm Health* 1993;47:377–381.

84. Just H, Drexler H, Taylor SH, Siegrist J, Schulgen G, Schumacher M. Captopril versus digoxin in patients with coronary artery disease and mild heart failure. A prospective, double-blind, placebo-controlled multicenter study. The CADS Study Group. *Herz* 1993;1S:436–443.

85. Buffet P, Colasate B, Feldmann L, et al. Long-term follow-up after coronary angioplasty in patients younger than 40 years of age. *Am Heart J* 1994;127:509–513.

86. Bliley AV, Ferrans CE. Quality of life after coronary angioplasty. *Heart Lung* 1993;22:193–199.

87. Salley RK, Robinson MC. Ischemic heart disease in the elderly: the role of coronary angioplasty and coronary artery bypass grafting. *South Med J* 1993;86:2S15–2S22.

88. Krumholz HM, Forman DE, Kuntz RE, Baim DS, Wei JY. Coronary revascularization after myocardial infarction in the very elderly: outcomes and long-term follow-up. *Ann Intern Med* 1993;119:1084–1090.

89. Little T, Milner MR, Lee K, Constantine J, Pichard AD, Lindsay J Jr. Late outcome and quality of life following percutaneous transluminal coronary angioplasty in octogenarians. *Cathet Cardiovasc Diagn* 1993;29:261–266.

90. Shaw PJ, Bates D, Cartlidge NEF, et al. Neurologica and neuropsychologic morbidity following major surgery: comparisons of coronary artery bypass and peripheral vascular surgery. *Stroke* 1987;18:700–707.

91. Hertzeanu HL, Shemesh J, Aron LA, et al. Ventricular arrhythmias in rehabilitated and non-rehabilitated post-myocardial infarction patients with left ventricular dysfunction. *Am J Cardiol* 1993;71:24–27.

92. Wiklund I, Gorkin L, Pawitan Y, et al. Methods for assessing quality of life in the cardiac arrhythmia suppression trial (CAST). *Qual Life Res* 1992;1:187–201.

Quality of Life and Pharmacoeconomics in Clinical Trials, Second Edition, edited by B. Spilker.
Lippincott-Raven Publishers, Philadelphia © 1996.

CHAPTER 92

Hypertension

Ingela K. Wiklund

INTRODUCTION

The goals of treatment have changed from a traditional curative aim to the prevention and control of disease, for example, as concerns the treatment of hypertension. Quality of life (QOL) issues are now receiving a good deal of attention because they introduce a broader range of outcomes, and a considerable number of studies have been carried out in the field of cardiovascular diseases and cancer, since they are the major causes of mortality and morbidity (1,2).

In clinical trials of pharmaceutical products, quality of life is being used increasingly as a therapeutic end point (1). These studies could be especially important when treating hypertension, a disease that is not associated with severe symptoms or disability. Quality of life studies may assist the industry in the regulatory approval process by supporting the primary efficacy outcome. Although the Food and Drug Administration (FDA) does not currently require quality of life data to be provided during the drug approval process, data on drug effects on quality of life are included as a secondary end point in virtually all new drug applications submitted to the FDA (3,4). In clinical practice, information on quality of life outcomes given to physicians and health

care managers may facilitate decision making about alternative drug therapy (5). Similarly, the gains of treatment with regard to quality of life, in addition to the possibility of months or years of added survival, are particularly appealing to hypertensive patients, because treatment is typically initiated at an early age, is lifelong, and may induce side effects.

Quality of life outcomes are also being used in questions concerning the pricing of, and reimbursement for, new pharmaceutical entities (6). Quality of life data added to the efficacy and safety data may enhance the profile of one product by showing its advantages over another and may also help justify its market price. Quality of life advantages have long been used as an important marketing tool, for instance, as regards antihypertensive drugs, which are typically in heavy competition.

Among the many requirements of an ideal antihypertensive drug is that it is cost-effective to the society by reducing morbidity and mortality in diseases followed by hypertension. In this situation, quality of life measures can be used as independent indicators of health outcomes for cost-effectiveness analysis, or they can be combined with survival to produce quality-adjusted life-years for cost–utility analysis (7). Costs are also a key issue for many patients and may influence compliance, as suggested by the results of a study in which patients with uncontrolled blood pressure tended to have a lower income than that of subjects whose blood pressure was well controlled (8).

I. K. Wiklund: Department of Behavioural Medicine, Astra Hassel AB, S-431 83 MOLNDAL, Sweden; and Department of Public Health and Primary Health Care, University of Bergen, N-5009 Bergen, Norway.

WHY QUALITY OF LIFE IN HYPERTENSION?

High blood pressure is common in all industrialized countries today. During the past two decades, the number of patients aware of their condition has increased dramatically. The percentage of patients taking medication to control their condition has increased substantially (9). Characteristic of hypertension is that it is generally considered an asymptomatic condition, and with a very low incidence of events and/or complications, at least in the short-term perspective. In a long-term perspective, however, morbidity and complications thereof, and mortality, play a much more significant role. High blood pressure is established as a powerful risk factor for total ischemic heart disease and cerebrovascular mortality in both sexes, especially in middle-aged men and in the elderly (9–12). In hypertension, therapies are designed not for the immediate benefit they provide, but for the lifelong prevention of late complications. The results of the Swedish Trial in Old Patients with Hypertension (STOP-Hypertension) (13), Systolic Hypertension in the Elderly Program (SHEP) (14), and European Working Party on High Blood Pressure in the Elderly (EWPHE) (15) and many other trials have clearly demonstrated that lowering an elevated blood pressure significantly reduces the incidence of strokes and myocardial infarctions and improves prognosis by reducing mortality. From this perspective, it has been argued that surrogate end points, such as quality of life, or glucose tolerance, may provide an unsound, and often incorrect, basis for determining the management of hypertension (16).

A major challenge in the management of hypertension is to achieve as high a compliance rate as possible in order to guarantee a successful long-term blood pressure-lowering therapy and improved prognosis. The long-term survival of treated hypertensive patients has been demonstrated to be dependent on the degree of compliance; therefore, noncompliance represents a serious problem (17). Degree of compliance is clearly related to how efficacious the blood pressure control has been, as shown in a study in which the blood pressure response was better in fully compliant patients than in noncompliant patients (18). Because hypertensive patients are essentially asymptomatic, quality of life measures should be included primarily to ensure that therapy does not compromise quality of life. Even though the development of new, safe, effective, and well-tolerated pharmaceutical entities has accelerated in recent years, most drugs used in the treatment of hypertension may induce subtle adverse effects that affect the quality of life. Therefore, the evaluation of antihypertensive therapy requires a more complete understanding of the impact of treatment. From the patient's perspective, the effects of treatment on quality of life will determine whether that patient will continue with treatment.

But poor compliance is not only a result of drug-induced symptoms, since symptoms, unrelated to medication occurring during therapy, have also been shown to reduce compliance dramatically (18). Similarly, other factors, such as number of tablets, a poor doctor–patient relationship, and long waiting hours, have an adverse impact on compliance (19). In fact, the major problem of treating hypertension is that treatment in most cases does not make much of a difference because it does not provide symptom relief, whereas the major goal of treatment is long term—to change the natural history of the disease. With such a long-term goal, the patient's motivation to comply with the prescribed regimen is likely to diminish with time. It is therefore important to reiterate that the rationale for monitoring quality of life during antihypertensive therapy is to ensure that potential side effects do not interfere with the quality of life, as this leads to poor compliance.

FACTORS CONFOUNDING QUALITY OF LIFE REPORTING IN HYPERTENSION

Even though hypertension is usually considered an asymptomatic condition, high blood pressure in itself may be associated with a number of symptoms, such as headache on waking, blurred vision, nocturia and unsteadiness (20), dizziness (21), sexual problems (22), and cognitive impairment (23,24). These symptoms, which are similar to those described in conjunction with antihypertensive drug therapy, are also commonly reported in untreated hypertensive patients (20,25). In a screening for hypertension among healthy volunteers, untreated hypertensive subjects with a diastolic blood pressure above 95 mmHg reported significantly more emotional distress and sleeping problems than borderline hypertensives and normotensives (26). Another study showed that when patients with mild hypertension included in a randomized trial were compared with normotensive subjects, the latter group enjoyed a better quality of life than did the hypertensive patients, both before and after treatment (27). Similarly, it has been shown that patients whose blood pressure is well controlled have a better quality of life than those with uncontrolled blood pressure (28).

Another important finding, highlighted in several studies, suggests that impaired cognitive, sensory, and psychomotor functions observed in untreated hypertensive patients (23,29) were almost completely normalized after antihypertensive therapy (30,31). In the Trial of Antihypertensive Interventions and Management (TAIM), blood pressure reduction resulted in improvement with regard to sleep disturbances, physical complaints, and satisfaction with health and with sex, and this improvement was interpreted by the investigators to be related to the blood pressure reduction per se (32). Recent results from another study similarly suggest that effective blood pressure control has beneficial effects on mental and emotional functions, including quality of sleep (33). Altogether, these data suggest that untreated high blood pressure may be associated with symptoms and that antihypertensive treatment has a favorable impact on quality of life.

Many side effect symptoms are as frequently reported during placebo treatment as on active therapy. This was already noted in the Medical Research Council trial (34). In another study, 80% of the hypertensive patients complained of fatigue before treatment, i.e., when receiving no medication, compared with 71% after placebo treatment (35). In the Treatment of Mild Hypertension Study, placebo-treated patients reported an even higher incidence of side effect symptoms than those given any of the active treatment regimens (36). Furthermore, symptoms often attributed to high blood pressure or to its treatment are commonly reported in a general population (37–39). Moreover, problems, such as sexual dysfunction, are also a frequent adjunct to the use of other drugs, such as antidepressants (40).

A further confounding factor in relation to symptom reporting and high blood pressure is "the labeling effect," i.e., being given a diagnosis of hypertension. A diagnosis of hypertension may actually give rise to symptoms and decrease the general well-being because the patient becomes more involved with personal health, including an increased awareness of bodily symptoms. Some studies have even noted a rise in absenteeism from work after hypertension has been diagnosed (41,42).

Hence, all symptoms reported by hypertensive patients are not necessarily caused by antihypertensive drug therapy. Randomly selected hypertensive and normotensive patients often present with a wide variety of symptoms (20,43). It is therefore important to have a symptom score at baseline, as was indeed indicated by the results of an evaluation by the Australian National Blood Pressure Study (44). Many clinicians fail to estimate the frequency of symptoms before drug therapy is initiated, thus obscuring the possibility of distinguishing symptoms that are drug induced from those that are generally present or related to the disease.

WHAT IS QUALITY OF LIFE IN HYPERTENSION?

Certainly, antihypertensive therapy may elicit unwanted side effects that compromise the patient's quality of life. It is important to go beyond the well-known pharmacological class-specific side effects, however. Since quality of life is a concept that refers to a multitude of subjective experiences important to people's lives, side effects, whether derived from standardized symptom complaint lists filled in by the patient, spontaneous reports, or active questioning, cannot be regarded as equivalent to quality of life. Moreover, discrepant estimates may be obtained in formal scales as opposed to clinical inquiry (45,46).

In hypertension, there seems to be general agreement that relevant aspects of quality of life to evaluate during antihypertensive drug therapy include well-being and symptomatic complaints (47). Anxiety, depression, lack of vitality, sleep disturbance, and sexual dysfunction are often studied because they are believed to be associated with antihypertensive therapy or with elevated blood pressure. Changes in alertness, memory, and intellectual functioning must also be explored, particularly in the elderly, in whom a slight deterioration may result in loss of independence.

MEASUREMENT ISSUES

By definition, quality of life information stems from the patient. The best and easiest way to obtain information about how patients feel and function, and how they respond to treatment, is to ask them. In fact, the agreement between physician-based and subjectively derived quality of life outcomes has been shown to be virtually nonexistent (48), or at best modest (49). Clinicians often express concern about burdening or upsetting their patients with quality of life assessments. Rather, most patients welcome the opportunity to report how their disease and treatment are affecting them (50).

In clinical trials, the use of standard well-documented, self-administered questionnaires represents an attractive, efficient, and cost-effective solution (51–57). Standard questionnaires provide reproducible data and a uniform procedure of administration and scoring can be followed (53,55). A disadvantage is that certain groups may be excluded, such as those who cannot read and write, which may introduce selection bias. By contrast, patients recruited to clinical trials inevitably represent a select group. Another problem is that the use of self-administered questionnaires involves the possibility of losing certain values. Careful quality control of the questionnaires can minimize this. What about interviews? An advantage is that most patients can be assessed and that completeness of data is ensured. The disadvantages are of greater concern, however. Interviewers have to be trained, bias may be introduced relating to the interviewer's age, gender, or race, and the scoring is subject to interpretation bias. For example, active questioning by the clinician was found to demonstrate fewer sexual problems than the confidential questionnaires used in the study (58). Similarly, bias may also be introduced when the physician is involved in the quality of life assessment as a result of personal expectations. This was actually demonstrated by a trial in which, though not part of the protocol, some physicians performed the quality of life assessment (59). Patients were either treated with a centrally acting drug or with an angiotension-converting enzyme (ACE) inhibitor. The patient questionnaires showed no differences between the treatment groups at baseline. After 3 months, however, the patients reported improvement irrespective of treatment. By contrast, the physicians, who were not blinded, reported deterioration in almost all quality of life measures on the centrally acting drug and improvement on the angiotension-converting enzyme inhibitor (59). Therefore, in most multicenter clinical trials, the use of standard questionnaires has become the most common way of assessing quality of life.

Quality of Life Questionnaires

Generic and disease-specific questionnaires represent two different types of measures for the assessment of quality of life. While generic measures were designed primarily for descriptive purposes, to delineate as comprehensively as possible the full impact of a disease or its symptoms, specific measures have been developed to monitor the response to treatment in a particular condition (60,61). The generic measures are applicable to a wide range of populations, whereas the specific measures, by definition, are confined to addressing the problems of selected patient groups. The main advantage of the generic measures is their broad coverage, and the fact that they allow comparisons of different patient populations or across studies (51). A disadvantage is that, in addition to being lengthy and time-consuming to complete, they may not address topics of particular relevance for a given disease. Evidence suggests that they are less responsive to treatment-induced changes than to specific measures (60–62). Although generic measures do have uses, in clinical trials they do not, by and large, have the same range, sensitivity, and flexibility to deal with the specific problems as disease-specific measures. In hypertension, responsiveness is a key issue because the differences between drugs are generally very small. A commonly used approach to the evaluation of quality of life in clinical trials in hypertension is to use a battery of questionnaires addressing specific, as well as more general, aspects (63–66).

Irrespective of whether a generic or disease-specific measure is employed, the use of standard scales ensures that their psychometric properties are well established (67). Carefully designed, controlled, and validated questionnaires represent a powerful tool for evaluating differences between treatment effects on quality of life. Despite the availability of a number of well-established quality of life instruments, many investigators still insist on developing their own methods. Many of these ad hoc measures have unknown psychometric characteristics and do not permit comparison of studies. The FDA has been reported to be particularly concerned about the quality of scales designed for use in specific clinical trials of drug therapy, because they may be poorly constructed and often lack psychometric documentation (5,68). It is, therefore, wisest to confine the assessments to the use of established measures, which provide a better basis for comparisons with previously reported study results (52,66).

Quality of Life Questionnaires in Hypertension

An approach to the evaluation of quality of life in hypertension would be to address the areas in which the patients' quality of life has been compromised owing to unwanted side effects. Several specific measures have been developed for use in antihypertensive drug trials. One of the earliest was the Symptom Complaint Rate, which has 30 symptoms and side effects (69), later modified to contain two additional symptoms, and with five graded response options instead of the yes/no alternatives of the original version (70). The Minor Symptom Evaluation (MSE) Profile has 24 items and uses bipolar analogue scales to assess primarily CNS-related side-effect symptoms (71). Some of the symptoms combine into three dimensions, i.e., vitality, sleep, and contentment. The Subjective Symptom Assessment (SSA) Profile includes 42 of the most frequently reported side-effect symptoms in conjunction with antihypertensive drug therapy, including placebo, and has six dimensions depicting cardiac symptoms, dizziness, gastrointestinal symptoms, peripheral/circulatory symptoms, sex life, and emotional distress (72). The response format is based on Visual Analogue scales. Visual Analogue scales also form the basis of the Aspect scale, which apart from 34 side-effect symptoms covers mood in terms of hedonic tone, relaxation and activity (73). Typical features of all these scales are that they focus primarily on symptoms that are recognized side effects to antihypertensive therapies (69,71–73). A recently described specific scale also involves aspects associated with dysfunctions such as sleep disturbances, sexual dysfunction, or depression (27).

Comparatively few studies have employed generic health profiles to address quality of life in antihypertensive drug trials, most likely because they carry redundant questions and are likely to be subjected to typical floor effects, and are less responsive to the small changes involved in antihypertensive drug trials (74). For the assessment of positive well-being as well as of negative affects, mood scales are available. One commonly used scale is the Psychological General Well-being (PGWB) index, in which patients rate each of the 22 questions on a six-point scale (75). Apart from providing an overall score, the PGWB index gives specific information about anxiety, depression, vitality, self-control, health and well-being. The Profile of Mood States, which addresses aspects of mood using 65 positive and negative adjectives on a five-point scale, combined into dimensions such as anxiety, depression, anger, confusion, vitality, and fatigue (76), has also been employed frequently. By contrast, psychiatric rating scales such as the General Health Questionnaire (77) or the Symptom Rating Test (78), which tap psychiatric morbidity in terms of anxiety, depression, somatic complaints, cognitive problems, and hostility, focus exclusively on negative symptoms and distress. The same applies to other depression scales, or anxiety inventories, which focus entirely on a variety of problems within the respective domains of anxiety and depressed mood (79). Taking into consideration that the general well-being of hypertensive subjects is similar to that of a healthy population, floor effects are likely to be present. This means that the scale will only be able to register deterioration, not improvement. This may be the reason why some investigators have chosen to address the relationship between depression and, for instance, β-blockers, on the basis of increased concomitant use of antidepressant (80,81). One problem with prescription studies is that the indication for treatment may have varied with the drugs used; i.e., it is not guaranteed that the prescriptions concerned hypertensive patients only. Another objection is that the diagnosis of depression on the basis of prescription data only is unreliable.

The Health Status Index (HSI) is a measure of activity and perceived well-being derived from responses to questions on work, absence due to sickness, and interference with lifestyle caused by treatment (82). The HSI provides a global score ranging from 0 at death to 100 at perfect health, which makes it particularly useful for cost–benefit and cost-effectiveness analysis. Additionally, specific measures of dysfunction in terms of sleep disturbances (83), sexual problems (84), physical function (85), social interaction (86), and life satisfaction (87) are commonly included in the batteries employed in most of the recently performed large-scale multicenter clinical studies. Table 1 lists questionnaires and their use in some trials on quality of life in hypertension (63–71,73,75–79,82–84,88–101). Typically, the scales used in international multicenter trials have been translated and back-translated according to international principles (88,102).

In contrast to self-assessment quality of life questionnaires, the methods used to assess behavioral and neuropsychological functions are based on objective laboratory assessments. They require a trained person to administer them. Behavioral performance tests represent objective measures that reflect cognitive ability (i.e., memory, concentration, and intellectual functioning, as well as specific responses denoting alertness, reaction time, and perceptual speed) and are measured using techniques such as the critical flicker fusion test, the trail-making test, and reaction time, to mention a few. Behavioral performance tests and methods for the evaluation of neuropsychological functions have been extensively reviewed elsewhere (103,104).

GENERAL METHODOLOGICAL ISSUES

The same methodological standards required for other variables in the protocol should also apply to quality of life

TABLE 1. *Summary of commonly used questionnaires for the assessment of quality of life in hypertension*

Questionnaire/Reference	Comment	Study reference
Well-Being		
The Psychological General Well-Being (PGWB) Index (75)	The PGWB index and the POMS tap both positive and negative effects, while the GHQ and the SRT are oriented toward discriminating psychiatric cases from healthy individuals.	58,63,88,89–92
The Profile and Mood State (POMS) (76)		65,88,93
The General Health Questionnaire (GHQ) (77)		94,110
The Symptom Rating Scale (SRT) (79)		94–97
Symptoms		
Health Status Index (HSI) (82)	The HSI gives a global score, which makes it useful for cost–benefit and cost-effectiveness analyses.	65,88,93,95–97
Sexual function		
The Sexual Symptom Distress Index (84)	The most reliable techniques for diagnosing erectile problems, i.e., measurements of penile tumescence or rigidity during sleep or erotic arousal, are rarely employed in clinical trials.	36,63,90
Sleep disturbance		
The Sleep Dysfunction Scale (83)	For more reliable measurements, self-reports could be supplemented with EEG recordings.	63
Side effects		
Complaint rate (69,70)	It is, in our opinion, important to supplement spontaneous reporting and active questioning with standard self-administered symptom checklists for a uniform and more sensitive evaluation of subtle symptoms.	88,93,95–97
Minor Symptom Evaluation (MSE) Profile (71)		98–100
Subjective Symptom-Assessment (SSA) Profile (72)		46
Aspect Scale (73)		101
Cognitive function		
Standardized behavioral performance tests of memory, concentration, alertness, perception and psychomotor capacity.	Evaluation of cognitive and neuropsychological function cannot be based on subjective symptom reports alone, but must be confirmed by using adequately standardized tests performed in the laboratory setting.	63,89,90,103,104

assessments. Previously, many studies evaluating aspects of quality of life in hypertension used open, single-blind study designs and undocumented ad hoc methods for the evaluation of Quality of Life; this also represents a concern to the FDA (68). The duration of the follow-up has been short, and the number of subjects has been comparatively small (105). Randomized double-blind controlled clinical trials using a control group are required. The specific subjective features of quality of life assessments mean that the design of trials using quality of life as an end point must be carefully considered. Among factors of crucial importance are the duration of the follow-up period, because it is related to placebo effects and to side effects (51,55,106).

Placebo-Control Group

More results from studies comparing placebo and active therapy are required to clarify whether symptoms are related to high blood pressure or to its treatment, and whether side effect symptoms are important enough to interfere with aspects of quality of life. Provided the patients are carefully monitored during the study period, there are no important ethical concerns against withholding active treatment from hypertensive patients for limited periods of time. Since placebo treatment is quite effective, in particular in the short-term perspective, this needs to be taken into account when deciding the duration of the follow-up period.

Duration of the Follow-up Period

While pharmacological effects might be distinguished almost immediately, it generally takes a much longer time before the patients themselves perceive the full benefits of treatment in terms of improved well-being and ability to enjoy day-to-day activities. Similarly, negative effects will occur during the first few weeks, whereas important differences may not appear until 6 months later (107). Usually, a period of at least 3 months, and preferably 6 months, is recommended in clinical trials of chronic disease (106). Unless a sufficiently long follow-up period is allowed, the results may indicate no clear distinction between two different treatments despite the fact that differences do exist (107).

Frequency of Assessments

In most cases, it is sufficient with one assessment at randomization, and one at the end of the trial, provided care is taken to ensure that all patients who discontinue the trial prematurely fill in a final set of the quality of life questionnaires at the time of discontinuation (4,66). Whether the quality of life assessments should be repeated during the course of the trial depends on whether one wants to explore how soon changes can be observed, and if they are transient or not. Repeated measurements could be used to clarify if, and when, patients become adapted to side effects. Typically, trial results seem to be reported in terms of changes from baseline to end of treatment, leaving the intermediate results unreported, even if quality of life has been measured as often as twice in one day once a week during a 10-week period (101), or every month (63). It is desirable to report some information on the results of repeated measurements during a trial. Moreover, factors such as multiplicity problems and the risk of overburdening patients should be balanced against how often assessments should be repeated.

Sample Size Estimates

Many quality of life studies have lacked the sensitivity and power to identify treatment effects. Since it is part of the nature of well-being and subjective perceptions that they should vary considerably, the sample sizes required for quality of life data may be larger than for the clinical variables. Sample size calculations using data from previous quality of life studies should be performed prior to the start of the study in the same way as is standard for all clinical efficacy outcomes. If the expected differences between treatments are small, even larger samples must be included. For example, in studies evaluating the effect of drug therapy on quality of life in hypertension, sample sizes exceeding 200 patients per treatment group are generally needed.

Stratification

Even though gender differences have a great impact on the frequency of symptomatic complaints and perceived quality of life, the influence of gender is rarely investigated or subjected to control. Women report a higher incidence of symptoms and rate quality of life lower than men in the general population do (37,108). Similarly, female infarction patients generally have a worse score than that of men, with regard to subjective symptoms and well-being (109). For many reasons, a group of men is more likely to be relatively homogeneous than is a group of women (107). The few studies that have reported significant differences between antihypertensive drugs in relation to quality of life included only men (63,64). In fact, the inclusion of only male patients may well account for these results. Unless gender is stratified for, larger patient samples may be required. In trials involving a comparatively small number of subjects, stratification for gender should be mandatory. Greater emphasis on age and other characteristics that possibly influence the results should be made in the future. Age effects will potentially combine with gender effects to confound results. In the elderly, concomitant diseases are common and will influence the application of quality of life measurements. Quality of life estimates with regard to life satisfaction and treatment outcomes in the elderly are likely to differ from those made in a younger population, both as a function of chronic disease, advancing age, and different expectations. All these issues need to be taken into account when using quality of life as an end point in clinical trials of elderly hypertensives. An age range must be defined or stratification for age performed, as behavioral changes may differ in middle-aged and elderly populations (107).

Administration of Questionnaires

Standardized information explaining the relevance and purpose of the quality of life assessment should be provided, and full confidentiality should always be promised (55). In order to facilitate quality control and to ensure that the questionnaires are completed by patients, questionnaires should be administered at the clinic. A standardized procedure for the administration of the questionnaires is essential, as the quality of life measures may be particularly vulnerable to the influence of closer contact with the investigative staff.

The patient must be allowed to sit in peace and quiet and answer the questions before the physical examination, and before the blood pressure recording, in order to avoid bias, as the results could influence the response to the questionnaires. One could doubt, however, whether such a procedure could be adhered to when more than 100 centers are involved.

Other Factors to Consider

Care must be taken to ensure good compliance when quality of life assessments are being made, and this is often best achieved by making this assessment a mandatory part of the protocol (57). A simple design, a nondemanding form of data collection, and a comparatively short and simple set of quality of life questionnaires are facilitating factors. Training of staff and monitoring, in particular during the early phase of the trial, are always essential.

TABLE 2. *General methodological aspects*

Factors	Remarks
Randomized, double-blind design	Randomized, double-blind design is mandatory in clinical trials studying hypertension.
Sample size Appropriate power calculations must be performed, in particular when the quantifiable differences between drugs are very small, which is usually the case in antihypertensive drug trials.	Large sample sizes are generally required in order to derive valid conclusions. The sensitivity of the scale must be known.
Control A control group, using a relevant competitor drug/drugs is necessary. Consider a placebo control group as well.	A placebo control group may facilitate interpretation of results.
Design A parallel group design is always safe.	Despite obvious advantages of a crossover design in terms of power, the risks of carryover effects should be taken into account.
Duration of follow-up A minimum of 12 weeks is required, preferably 24 weeks.	Sufficient follow-up is necessary in order to allow for adaptation to side effects, and for the full treatment effect to be distinguished.
Stratification Gender is a confounding variable.	It may be advantageous to stratify for gender.
Number of investigators Should not be too large in relation to the patient sample.	A minimum number of patients per investigator is desirable to reduce variability of results (and thus increase the power of the study). At least ten, preferably twenty or more, patients per investigator usually increases the quality of life data.
Dosage It is important to compare drugs at equipotent dosages, and effects.	Effects on well-being should be related to effects on blood pressure. One should be careful not to describe side effects elicited by large doses of drugs in nonresponding (or poorly responding) patients, as this is not a clinically relevant situation.

In hypertension studies, differences in results from comparisons of the same drugs may reflect many confounding influences such as study population, dose or drug formulation. It is important to compare equipotent and commonly used doses. If several doses are used, an analysis of the dose-response relationship with respect to quality of life should be made. Similarly, the preparation of the compound may be of importance. Such is the case with slow-release formulations, which induce fewer side effects because of an even plasma concentration.

ANALYSIS AND INTERPRETATION OF QUALITY OF LIFE DATA

Since quality of life measures are multiple, it is essential to state clearly in advance what the primary quality of life outcomes are. Subsidiary measures can then be used to elaborate the findings, and the clinical efficacy outcomes to confirm them. Unless this is done, statistical multiplicity problems are bound to ensue (53,66). However, problems related to multiplicity are rarely addressed. On the contrary, differences at the interdrug level, as well as changes from baseline for each drug, are commonly analysed for individual items (63,89,110). This is particularly tempting when the differences are small or nonexistent (111). Multiplicity problems may also ensue when side effects derived from spontaneous reports, active questioning, and a standardized symptom questionnaire are employed in parallel, and subsequently analyzed at the single item level within the framework of the same trial (101). The statistical power is reduced with multiple significance testing, due to the increased risk of encountering "chance findings" when many analyses are performed. Univariate statistical techniques to analyze the multiple measures that follow with quality of life assessments need to be considered.

Although small differential effects on quality of life have been observed in many studies, few attempts have been made to appreciate the clinical significance of these findings. A direct comparison of treatment results can be obtained irrespective of the measure used by computing either confidence interval or effect sizes, or both (66,112). A change amounting to 5% seems reasonable and may be compatible with what is considered relevant to the clinical effect variables. Smaller score changes should therefore be interpreted with caution (113,114). Some general methodological aspects are summarized in Table 2.

CONCLUSIONS

Quality of life assessments during antihypertensive drug therapy have been receiving increasing attention during the past decade. It is important to know whether patients experience negative effects on quality of life because, apart from the discomfort evoked, side effects may reduce compliance. Hypertensive patients do not seem to be quite as asymptom-atic as generally assumed. On the contrary, the growing bulk of evidence suggests that high blood pressure gives rise to symptoms and that treatment of high blood pressure per se may instead be associated with reductions in subtle symptoms and impairment of neuropsychological functions. Similarly, other results have indicated that active therapy is better than placebo.

Even though an adverse impact on quality of life is a serious problem to the individual patient, because it may limit compliance and thereby the efficacy of treatment, one should remember that quality of life is only one aspect of antihypertensive treatment. If the treatment scenario is broadened to include mortality and morbidity as well, i.e., to achieve a reduction in cardiovascular risk factors, the aim with regard to quality of life is that quality of life be maintained. The new guidelines on the management of mild hypertension issued in the United States highlight the danger of relaxing the concern for risk reduction and costs in favor of surrogate end points, although these may carry great significance in the individual patient.

Assessments of the effects of antihypertensive drugs should be made in controlled clinical trials using well-validated questionnaires that have the ability to detect symptomatic side effects of therapy, and their potential impact on well-being and other relevant aspects of quality of life in hypertension. A range of standard international questionnaires is available for the assessment of specific as well as general aspects of distress and dysfunction that may be related to the treatment of hypertension. It is not sufficient to have selected the appropriate methods to assess quality of life. In the future greater attention must be devoted to a range of general methodological issues as well.

REFERENCES

1. Wenger NK. Assessment of quality of life: a medical imperative. *Cardiovasc Drug Ther* 1988;1:553–558.
2. Kaplan RM. Health-related quality of life in cardiovascular disease. *J Consult Clin Psychol* 1988;56:382–392.
3. Coons SJ, Kaplan RM. Assessing health-related quality of life: application to drug therapy. *Clin Ther* 1992;14:850–858.
4. Smith ND. Quality of life studies from the perspective of an FDA reviewing statistician. *Drug Infect J* 1993;27:617–623.
5. Revicki DA, Rothman M, Luce B. Health-related quality of life assessments and the pharmaceutical industry. *PharmacoEconomics* 1992;1:394–408.
6. Henry D. Economic analysis as an aid to subsidization decisions: the development of Australian guidelines for pharmaceuticals. *PharmacoEconomics* 1992;1:54–67.
7. Drummond M, Coyle D. Assessing the economic value of antihypertensive medicines. *J Hum Hypertens* 1992;6:495–501.
8. Shulman NB, Martinez B, Brogan D, Carr AA, Miles CG. Financial cost as an obstacle to hypertensive therapy. *Am J Public Health* 1986;76:1105–1108.
9. The Fifth Report on the Joint National Committee on Detection, Evaluation, and Treatment of High Blood Pressure. *Arch Intern Med* 1993;153:154–183.
10. Lapidus L. Ischaemic heart disease, stroke, and total mortality in women—results from a prospective study in Gothenburg, Sweden. *Acta Med Scand* 1985;705(suppl):1–42.
11. Rutan GH, Kuller LH, Neaton JD, Wenthworth DN, McDonald RH, Smith WM. Mortality associated with diastolic hypertension and iso-

lated systolic hypertension among men screened for the Multiple Risk Factor Intervention Trial. *Circulation* 1988;77:504–514.

12. Dyer AR, Stamler J, Shekelle RB, et al. Pulse pressure—III: prognostic significance in four Chicago epidemiologic studies. *J Chronic Dis* 1982;35:283–294.

13. Dahlöf B, Lindholm LH, Hansson L, Scherstén B, Ekbom T, Wester PO. Morbidity and mortality in the Swedish Trial in Old Patients with Hypertension (STOP-Hypertension). *Lancet* 1991;338:1281–1285.

14. SHEP Cooperative Research Group. Prevention of stroke by antihypertensive drug treatment in older persons with isolated systolic hypertension. Final results of the Systolic Hypertension in the Elderly Program (SHEP). *JAMA* 1991;265:3255–3264.

15. Amery A, Birkenhäger W, Brixko P, et al. Mortality and morbidity results from the European Working Party on High Blood Pressure in the Elderly trial. *Lancet* 1985;15:1349–1354.

16. Anon. New trials in older hypertensives. *Lancet* 1991;338:1299–1300.

17. Perry HM Jr, Camel GH. Survival of treated hypertensive patients as a function of compliance and control. *J Hypertens* 1984;2(suppl 3):S197–199.

18. Luscher TF, Vetter H, Siegenthaler W, Vetter W. Compliance in hypertension: facts and concepts. *J Hypertens* 1985,3(suppl 1):S3–9.

19. Schaub AF, Steiner A, Vetter W. Compliance to treatment. *Clin Exp Hypertens* 1993;15:1121–1130.

20. Bulpitt CJ, Dollery CT, Carne S. Change in symptoms of hypertensive patients after referral to hospital clinic. *Br Heart J* 1976;38:121–128.

21. Weiss NS. Relation of high blood pressure to headache, epistaxis, and selected other symptoms. The United States Health Examination Survey of Adults. *N Engl J Med* 1972;287:632–633.

22. Bansal S. Sexual dysfunction in hypertensive men. A critical review of the literature. *Hypertension* 1988;12:1–10.

23. Shapiro AP, Miller RE, King HE, Gincherau EH, Fitzgibbon K. Behavioural consequences of mild hypertension. *Hypertension* 1982; 4:355–360.

24. Vanderploeg RD. Relationship between systolic and diastolic blood pressure and cognitive functioning in hypertensive subjects: an extension of previous findings. *Arch Clin Neuropsychol* 1987;2:101–109.

25. Siegrist J, Matschinger H, Motz W. Untreated hypertensives and their quality of life. *J Hypertens* 1987;5(suppl 1):S15–20.

26. Dimenäs ES, Wiklund IK, Dahlöf CG, Lindvall KG, Olofsson BK, De Faire UH. Differences in the subjective well-being and symptoms of normotensives, borderline hypertensives and hypertensives. *J Hypertens* 1989;7:885–890.

27. Bar-On D, Amir M. Reexamining the quality of life of hypertensive patient. A new self-structured measure. *Am J Hypertens* 1993;6: 62S–66S.

28. Perry HM, Brown RD, Herman TS, Meyer JH, Norton JM, Thurm RH. Improved quality of life with good blood pressure control: a comparison of captopril, propranolol, and methyldopa. Abstracts from the International Symposium on ACE Inhibition, London, 1989, February 14–17: Abs F071.

29. Elias MF, Robbins MA, Schultz NR Jr, Streeten DH, Elias PK. Clinical significance of cognitive performance by hypertensive patients. *Hypertension* 1987;9:192–197.

30. Miller RE, Shapiro AP, King HE, Gincherau EH, Hosutt JA. Effect of antihypertensive treatment in the behavioural consequences of elevated blood pressure. *Hypertension* 1984;6:202–208.

31. Streufert S, DePadova A, McGlynn T, Piasecki M, Pogash R. Effects of betablockade with metoprolol on simple and complex task performance. *Health Psychol* 1989;8:143–158.

32. Wassertheil-Smoller S, Oberman A, Blaufox MD, Davis B, Langford H. The Trial of Antihypertensive Interventions and Management (TAIM) study. Final results with regard to blood pressure, cardiovascular risks, and quality of life. *Am J Hypertens* 1992;5:37–44.

33. Amir M, Cristal N, Bar-On D, Loidl A. Does the combination of ACE inhibitor and calcium antagonist control hypertension and improve quality of life? *Blood Press* 1994;3(suppl):40–42.

34. Adverse reactions to bendrofluazide and propranolol for the treatment of mild hypertension: report of Medical Research Council Working Party on mild to moderate hypertension. *Lancet* 1981;2:539–543.

35. Schoenberger J, Croog S, Sudilovsky A, Levine S, Banne R. Self-reported side effects from antihypertensive drugs: a clinical trial. *Am J Hypertens* 1990;3:123–132.

36. The Treatment of Mild Hypertension Study: a randomized, placebo-controlled trial of nutritional-hygienic regimen along with various drug monotherapies. *Arch Intern Med* 1991;151:1413–1423.

37. Tibblin G, Bengtsson C, Furunes B, Lapidus L. Symptoms by age and sex. The population studies of men and women in Gothenburg, Sweden. *Scand J Prim Health Care* 1990;8:9–17.

38. Kullman S, Svärdsudd K. Differences in perceived symptoms/quality of life in untreated hypertensive and normotensive men. *Scand J Prim Health Care* 1990;(suppl 1):47–53.

39. Reidenberg MM, Lowenthal DT. Adverse nondrug reactions. *N Engl J Med* 1968;279:678–679.

40. Harrison WM, Stewart J, Ehrhardt AA, et al. A controlled study of the effects of antidepressants on sexual function. *Psychopharmacol Bull* 1985;21:85–88.

41. Haynes RB, Sackett DL, Taylor DW, Gibson ES, Johnson AL. Increased absenteeism from work after detection and labelling of hypertensive patients. *N Engl J Med* 1978;299:741–744.

42. Mann AH. Hypertension: psychological aspects and diagnostic impact in a clinical trial. *Psychol Med* 1984(suppl 5):1–35.

43. Curb JD, Borhani NO, Blaszkowski TP, Zimbaldi N, Fotiu S, Williams W. Patient-perceived side effects to antihypertensive drugs. *Am J Prev Med* 1985;1:36–40.

44. Bauer GE, Baker J, Hunyor SN, Marshall P. Side-effects of antihypertensive treatment: a placebo-controlled study. *Clin Sci Mol Med* 1978;4(suppl):341S–344S.

45. Dimsdale JE. Reflections on the impact of antihypertensive medications on mood, sedation and neuropsychological functioning. *Arch Intern Med* 1992;152:35–39.

46. Wallander AM, Dimenäs E, Svärdsudd K, Wiklund I. Evaluation of three methods of symptom reporting in a clinical trial of felodipine. *Eur J Clin Pharmacol* 1991;41:187–196.

47. Bulpitt CJ, Fletcher AE. Quality of life evaluation of antihypertensive drugs. *PharmacoEconomics* 1992;1:95–102.

48. Jachuck SJ, Brierley H, Jachuck S, Willcox PM. The effect of hypertensive drugs on the quality of life. *J R Coll Gen Pract* 1982;32: 103–105.

49. Slevin ML, Plant H, Lynch D, Drinkwater J, Gregory WM. Who should measure quality of life, the doctor or the patient? *Br J Cancer* 1988;57:109–112.

50. Fallowfield LJ, Baum M, Maguire GP. Do psychological studies upset patients? *J R Soc Med* 1987;80:59.

51. Wiklund I, Dimenaes E, Wahl M. Factors of importance when evaluating quality of life in clinical trials. *Controlled Clin Trials* 1990;11: 169–179.

52. MacKeigan LD, Pathak DS. Overview of health-related quality of life measures. *Am J Hosp Pharm* 1992;49:2236–2245.

53. Cox DR, Fitzpatrick R, Fletcher AE, Gore SM, Spiegelhalter DJ, Jones DR. Quality of life assessment: can we keep it simple? *J R Stat Soc A* 1992;155:353–393.

54. Fitzpatrick R, Fletcher A, Gore S, Jones D, Spiegelhalter D, Cox D. Quality of life measures in health care. I. Applications and issues in assessment. *BMJ* 1992;305:1074–1077.

55. Fletcher AE. Measurement of quality of life in clinical trials of therapy. *Recent Results Cancer Res* 1988;111:216–230.

56. Aaronson NK. Quality of life assessments in clinical trials: methodological issues. *Controlled Clin Trials* 1989;10:195S–208S.

57. Aaronson NK. Assessing the quality of life in patients in cancer clinical trials: common problems and common sense solutions. *Eur J Cancer* 1992;28A:1304–1307.

58. Chang SW, Fine R, Siegel D, et al. The impact of diuretic therapy on reported sexual function. *Arch Intern Med* 1991;151:2402–2408.

59. Fletcher AE, Hunt BM, Bulpitt CJ. Evaluation of quality of life in clinical trials of cardiovascular disease. *J Chronic Dis* 1987;40: 557–569.

60. Guyatt G, Veldhuyzen Van Zanten SJ, Feeny DH, Patrick DL. Measuring quality of life in clinical trials: a taxonomy and review. *Can Med Assoc J* 1989;140:1441–1448.

61. Patrick DL, Deyo RA. Generic and disease-specific measures in assessing health status and quality of life. *Med Care* 1989;27:217–232.

62. Fitzpatrick R, Ziebland S, Jenkinson C, Mowat A, Mowat A. Importance of sensitivity to change as a criterion for selecting health status measures. *Qual Health Care* 1992;1:89–93.

63. Croog SH, Levine S, Testa MA, et al. The effects of antihypertensive therapy on the quality of life. *N Engl J Med* 1986;314:1657–1664.

64. Testa MA, Anderson RB, Nackley JF, Hollenberg NK. Quality of

life and antihypertensive therapy in men. *N Engl J Med* 1993;328:907–913.

65. Palmer AJ, Fletcher AE, Rudge PJ, Andrews CD, Callaghan TS, Bulpitt CJ. Quality of life in hypertensives treated with atenolol or captopril: a double blind crossover trial. *J Hypertens* 1992;10:1409–1416.

66. Fletcher A, Gore S, Jones D, Fitzpatrick R, Spiegelhalter D, Cox D. Quality of life measures in health care II: design analysis and interpretation. *BMJ* 1992;305:1145–1148.

67. Kirshner B, Guyatt G. A methodological framework for assessing health indices. *J Chronic Dis* 1985;38:27–36.

68. Anon. Quality of life ad claims should not be based on open-label "seeding" studies; FDA has continuing "concerns" about quality of life claims in general. *FDC Rep* 1991;January 21:15–16.

69. Bulpitt CJ, Dollery CT, Carne S. A symptom questionnaire for hypertensive patients. *J Chronic Dis* 1974;27:309–323.

70. Bulpitt CJ, Fletcher AE. Measurement of quality of life in hypertension: a practical approach. *Br J Clin Pharmacol* 1990;30:353–364.

71. Dahlöf C, Dimenäs E, Olofsson B. Documentation of an instrument for assessment of subjective CNS-related symptoms during cardiovascular pharmacotherapy. *Cardiovasc Drug Ther* 1989;3:919–927.

72. Dimenäs E, Dahlöf C, Olofsson B, Wiklund I. An instrument for quantifying subjective symptoms among untreated and treated hypertensives: development and documentation. *J Clin Res Pharmacoepidemiol* 1990;4:205–217.

73. Jern S. Questionnaire for the assessment of symptoms and psychological effects in cardiovascular therapy (the ASPECT scale). *Scand J Prim Health Care* 1990;1:(suppl) 31–32.

74. Weir MR, Josselson J, Ekelund L-G, et al. Nicardipine as antihypertensive monotherapy: positive effects on quality of life. *J Hum Hypertens* 1991;5:205–213.

75. Dupuy HJ. The psychological general well-being (PGWB) index. In: Wenger NK, Mattson ME, Furberg CF, Elinson J, eds. *Assessment of quality of life in clinical trials of cardiovascular therapies.* New York: LeJacq, 1984:170–183.

76. McNair DM, Lorr M, Doppleman LF. *Manual of the profile of mood states.* San Diego, CA: San Diego Educational and Industrial Testing Service, 1971.

77. Goldberg D. *The detection of psychiatric illness by questionnaire.* Oxford: Oxford University Press, 1972.

78. Kellner R, Sheffield BF. A self-rating scale of distress. *Psychol Med* 1973;3:88–100.

79. Derogatis LR, Lipman RS, Covi L. SCL-90: an outpatient psychiatric rating scale—preliminary report. *Psychopharmacol Bull* 1973;9:13–28.

80. Avorn J, Everitt DE, Weiss S. Increased anti-depressant use in patients prescribed beta-blockers. *JAMA* 1986;255:357–360.

81. Thiessen BQ, Wallace SM, Blackburn JL, Wilson TW, Bergman U. Increased prescribing of antidepressants: subsequent to beta-blocker therapy. *Arch Intern Med* 1990;150:2286–2290.

82. Fanshel S, Bush JW. A health status index and its application to health service outcomes. *Oper Res* 1970;18:1021–1066.

83. Jenkins CD, Stanton B-A, Savageau JA, Denlinger P, Klein MD. Coronary artery bypass surgery: physical, psychological, social, and economic outcomes six months later. *JAMA* 1983;250:782–788.

84. Hogan MJ, Wallin JD, Bauer RM. Antihypertensive therapy and male sexual dysfunction. *Psychosomatics* 1980;21:234–237.

85. Hypertension Detection and Follow-up Program, DHVD, National Heart, Lung, and Blood Institute, NIH, Besthesda, MD. The effect of treatment on mortality in "mild" hypertension: results of the hypertension detection and follow-up program. *N Engl J Med* 1982;307:976–980.

86. Croog SH, Levine S. *After a heart attack: social and psychological factors eight years later.* New York: Human Science Press, 1982.

87. The Rand Corporation, Santa Monica, CA.

88. Fletcher AE, Bulpitt CJ, Chase DM, et al. Quality of life with three antihypertensive treatments: cilazapril, atenolol, nifedipine. *Hypertension* 1992;19:499–507.

89. Steiner SS, Friedhoff AJ, Wilson BL, Wecker JR, Santo JP. Antihypertensive therapy and quality of life: a comparison of atenolol, captopril, enalapril and propranolol. *J Hum Hypertens* 1990;4:217–225.

90. Croog SH, Kong BW, Levine S, Weir MR, Baume RM, Saunders E. Hypertensive black men and women. Quality of life and effects of antihypertensive medications. *Arch Intern Med* 1990;150:1733–1741.

91. Applegate WB, Phillips HL, Schnaper H, et al. A randomized controlled trial of the effects of three antihypertensive agents on blood pressure control and quality of life in older women. *Arch Intern Med* 1991;151:1817–1823.

92. Omvik P, Thaulow E, Herland OB, Eide I, Midha R, Turner RR. Double-blind, parallel, comparative study on quality of life during treatment with amlodipine or enalapril in mild or moderate hypertensive patients: a multicentre study. *J Hypertens* 1993;11:103–113.

93. Zachariah PK, Brobyn R, Kann J, et al. Comparison of quality of life on nitrendipine and propranolol. *J Cardiovasc Pharmacol* 1988;12:(suppl 4)S29–35.

94. Herrick AL, Waller PC, Berkin KE, et al. Comparison of enalapril and atenolol in mild to moderate hypertension. *Am J Med* 1989;86:421–426.

95. Fletcher AE, Chester PC, Hawkins CM, Latham AN, Pike LA, Bulpitt CJ. The effects of verapamil and propranolol on quality of life in hypertension. *J Hum Hypertens* 1989;3:125–130.

96. Hill JF, Bulpitt CJ, Fletcher AE. Angiotension converting enzyme inhibitors and quality of life: the European trial. *J Hypertens* 1985;3(suppl 2):S91–94.

97. Palmer A, Fletcher A, Hamilton G, Muriss S, Bulpitt C. A comparison of verapamil and nifedipine on quality of life. *Br J Clin Pharmacol* 1990;30:365–370.

98. Dimenäs E, Östergren J, Lindvall K, Dahlöf C, Westergren G, de Faire U. Comparison of CNS-related subjective symptoms in hypertensive patients treated with either a new controlled release (CR/ZOK) formulation of metoprolol or atenolol. *J Clin Pharmacol* 1990;30 (suppl):S82–90.

99. Dimenäs E, Dahlöf C, Olofsson B, Wiklund I. CNS-related subjective symptoms during treatment with beta-adrenoceptor antagonists (atenolol, metoprolol): two double-blind placebo controlled studies. *Br J Clin Pharmacol* 1989;28:527–534.

100. Dahlöf C, Dimenäs E, Kendall M, Wiklund I. Quality of life in cardiovascular diseases. Emphasis on β-blocker treatment. *Circulation* 1984(suppl VI):VI-108–118.

101. Os I, Bratland B, Dahlöf B, Gisholt K, et al. Lisinopril or nifedipine in essential hypertension? A Norwegian multicenter study on efficacy, tolerability and quality of life in 828 patients. *J Hypertens* 1991;9:1097–1104.

102. Guillemin F, Bombardier C, Beaton D. Cross-cultural adaptation of health-related quality of life measures: literature review and proposed guidelines. *J Clin Epidemiol* 1993;46:1417–1432.

103. Turkkan JS. Behavioral performance effects of antihypertensive drugs: human and animal studies. *Neurosci Biobehav Rev* 1988;12:111–122.

104. Dimsdale JE, Newton RP, Joist T. Neuropsychological side effects of beta-blockers. *Arch Intern Med* 1989;149:514–525.

105. Hjemdahl P, Wiklund IK. Quality of life on antihypertensive drug therapy: scientific end-point or marketing exercise? *J Hypertens* 1992;10:1437–1446.

106. Bulpitt CJ, Fletcher AE. Measurement of quality of life in angina. *J Hypertens* 1987;5(suppl):S41–45.

107. Hollenberg NK, Testa M, Williams GH. Quality of life as a therapeutic end-point: an analysis of therapeutic trials in hypertension. *Drug Safety* 1991;6:83–93.

108. Domecq C, Naranjo CA, Ruiz I, Busto U. Sex-related variations in the frequency and characteristics of adverse drug reactions. *Int J Clin Pharmacol Ther Toxicol* 1980;18:362–366.

109. Wiklund I, Herlitz J, Johansson S, Bengtson A, Karlsson BW, Persson NG. Subjective symptoms and well-being differ in women and men after myocardial infarction. *Eur Heart J* 1993;14:1315–1319.

110. Fletcher AE, Bulpitt CJ, Hawkins CM, et al. Quality of life on antihypertensive therapy: a randomized double-blind controlled trial of captopril and atenolol. *J Hypertens* 1990;8:463–466.

111. Frimodt-Moeller J, Loldrup Poulsen D, Kornerup HJ, Bech P. Quality of life, side effects and efficacy of lisinopril compared with metoprolol in patients with mild to moderate essential hypertension. *J Hum Hypertens* 1991;5:215–221.

112. Lydick E, Epstein RS. Interpretation of quality of life changes. *Qual Life Res* 1993;2:221–226.

113. Testa MA. Interpreting quality of life clinical trial data for use in the clinical practice of antihypertensive therapy. *J Hypertens* 1987;5 (suppl 1):S9–13.

114. Jaeschke R, Guyatt GH, Keller J, Singer J. Interpreting changes in quality of life score in N of 1 randomized trials. *Controlled Clin Trials* 1991;12:(4 suppl) 226S–233S.

Quality of Life and Pharmacoeconomics in Clinical Trials, Second Edition, edited by B. Spilker.
Lippincott-Raven Publishers, Philadelphia © 1996.

CHAPTER 93

Neurologic Illness

Robert S. Wilson, Christopher G. Goetz, and Glenn T. Stebbins

INTRODUCTION

Quality of life studies have particular relevance in neurology. The brain, spinal cord, and peripheral nerves control neurologic function for the entire body, and damage to these organs can have highly specific or widespread consequences. Neurologic measures must accommodate implicitly the gamut of possible anatomic involvements, sensory and motor dysfunction, and cognitive impairment of both mild and severe intensity. For example, some neurologic conditions will produce highly focal abnormalities, such as a weak hand, involuntary eye closure, or isolated facial pain. Other degenerative conditions affect function throughout the body and may involve all neurologic spheres. By contrast, diffuse encephalopathies may cause few motor or sensory problems but cause cognitive and emotional abnormalities that devastate quality of life. Pharmacologic treatment of some disorders may succeed in alleviating signs and symptoms of neurologic illness, but at the cost of side effects that adversely affect quality of life. In short, the diverse manifestations of neurologic disorders and the agents used to treat these disorders underscore the importance of quality of life to any consideration of neurologic disorders or their treatment.

The heterogeneous manifestations of neurologic illnesses have made it difficult to apply a simple or single set of quality of life measures to all disorders. Age and level of cognitive dysfunction, in particular, are critical considerations in the selection, adaptation, or construction of various scales. However, in some domains of quality of life, such

as physical function, the behaviors of interest are relatively finite, hence the feasibility of the use of more general and psychometrically established scales. This chapter is organized into two sections. The first section discusses four dimensions of quality of life: physical, financial, social, and psychological. Within each of these domains, available measures and pertinent considerations are addressed. The second section considers specific neurologic applications of these measures.

QUALITY OF LIFE MEASURES

Physical Function

The impact of illness on the ability to perform activities of daily living has long been recognized as an important and practical matter in the management of neurologic patients. As a result, a range of scales has been developed. Two problems in this proliferating area exist, however. First, some scales do not exclusively focus on physical disability, so social and cognitive dysfunction contaminate activities of daily living scores. These scales lack construct validity and can create dilemmas for the neurologic rater when different functions deteriorate at different rates. For example, the Schwab and England Scale (1), currently used in Parkinson's disease, and the Shoulson-Fahn Scale (2), used in Huntington's disease, require that the examiner consider simultaneously multiple sources of physical and nonphysical disability, in order to arrive at a single measure of functional capacity. Such unidimensional ratings of multidimensional behavior are inherently limited and, although convenient,

R. S. Wilson, C. G. Goetz, and G. T. Stebbins: Department of Neurological Sciences, Rush University, Rush-Presbyterian–St. Luke's Medical Center, Chicago, Illinois 60612.

lack the capacity to determine changes in discrete areas of neurologic dysfunction. Second, the scales are often restricted to only one disease or disease type, precluding comparisons across the broad spectrum of neurologic illnesses. Historically, some of the more widely used scales were constructed with a single disease in mind or have evolved into a relatively exclusive applicability to one type of disease. For example, the Northwestern University Disability Scale has been used repeatedly to measure the activities of daily living function in Parkinson's disease and has not been widely applied to other disorders (3). Nevertheless, because it rates six functional domains—walking, dressing, feeding, hygiene, speech, and eating—which are reasonably representative of the activities of daily living domain, the scale is potentially applicable to a far wider range of neurologic disorders.

In fact, the number of physical activities of daily living is finite, and the range of neurologic competence in such activities can be specified. Within the domain of physical function, use of the same scale in different disorders may therefore be entirely feasible. Perhaps the most widely used other-report measures of activities of daily living in neurology are those developed by Lawton and Brody (4), Katz et al. (5), and Mahoney and Barthel (6). Lawton and Brody's Physical Self-Maintenance Scale, for example, identifies six areas of rudimentary physical activity: eating, dressing, bathing, toileting, walking, and hygiene. Each function is scored on a five-point behaviorally anchored interval scale. The scale was originally developed to evaluate disability among the elderly, hence is particularly appropriate for such varied neurologic disorders as cerebrovascular accident, Alzheimer's disease, and Parkinson's disease. The Physical Self-Maintenance Scale is often used in conjunction with the Instrumental Activities of Daily Living Scale devised by Lawton and Brody (4), which assesses more cognitively mediated activities critical to independent living. Items address activities such as shopping, use of transportation and telephone, and handling finances. Used in conjunction, the Physical Self-Maintenance Scale and Instrumental Activities of Daily Living Scale are unique and provide comprehensive psychometrically sound measurements of two specific subdomains of activities of daily living. The scale developed by Katz et al. (5) is an ordinal measure of six activities of daily living functions that are presumed lost and regained sequentially. The Barthel Index (6) is perhaps the most widely used activities of daily living scale. There are 11 items, and scoring is on an interval system that is helpful for statistical analyses. The items are rationally weighted such that mobility and continence contribute disproportionately to the total score. Scales developed by Nagi (7) and by Rosow and Breslau (8) have proved helpful in community studies. A useful supplement to other report measures of the physical capacity to carry out daily living activities is provided by direct measurement of physical functioning. Such an approach is especially helpful when a reliable informant is unavailable. A carefully specified and well-validated set of direct physical performance measures was developed by Guralnik and colleagues for use with the elderly (9,10). These measures focus heavily on lower extremity function. A range of approaches to measuring manual dexterity, speed, and strength are described by Lezak (11).

Psychological Function

Psychological function is critical to any concept of quality of life, particularly in patients with neurologic disease. Both cognitive and affective functioning have been assessed with a wide variety of measures. Arguably, the most disabling aspect of neurologic illness is cognitive dysfunction. Damage to the cerebral cortex, basal ganglia, thalamus, limbic system, or adjacent structures can dramatically compromise diverse intellectual functions. These effects can be seen with focal pathology, resulting in various forms of amnesia, aphasia, and cognitive disorganization. Alternatively, diffuse encephalopathies seen with degenerative disorders such as Alzheimer's disease or Huntington's disease may produce global cognitive deterioration, generally referred to as dementia.

Review of measures of specific cognitive functions is beyond the scope of this chapter. The interested reader may refer to Lezak (11) and Heilman and Valenstein (12). A number of psychometrically adequate dementia screening measures are available (e.g., refs. 13–15). In selecting any psychological performance measure, however, it is critical that the difficulty level of the scale be appropriate for the population of interest.

As an alternative or supplement to direct measurement of cognitive functioning, the investigator may select rating scales. Scales have been developed that make use of the patient, a significant other, a trained clinician, or some combination of these raters. For example, the Brief Cognitive Rating Scale (16) and the Global Deterioration Scale (17) require the clinician to rate either a single or multiple dimensions of cognition. The Katz Adjustment Scale (18) and the Sickness Impact Profile (19) allow for rating by either the patient or significant other. In assessing cognitive decline, ratings by a significant other or clinician, or both, are preferable to the patient's rating.

In the authors' opinion, some direct performance measure should also be included in a cognitive assessment of quality of life. Although subjective evaluations of cognitive functioning have a place in quality of life assessment, these evaluations can be influenced by extraneous factors (e.g., depression). Use of objective measures provides a means of evaluating the validity of the subjective ratings.

Affective changes are the second area of psychological investigation. Such changes are common in neurologic disease and are potentially disabling, particularly if they remain unrecognized. Such affective alterations may be the direct result of the neurologic lesion; when damage to the frontal lobes or limbic system occurs, a range of disordered emotional behavior, including disinhibition, depression or hypo-manic episodes, or hallucinations, may result and affect quality of life. In such instances, patients may show few or no cognitive changes. In other instances, when affective changes do not occur as part of the neurologic lesion, emotional reactions to neurologic disability still can dramatically alter quality of life. Depressive reactions frequently develop as a secondary result of new disability or chronic illness. In some conditions, like Parkinson's disease, it may be especially difficult to separate the direct emotional effects of the disease from the reactive components. Regardless of the source, depression of at least a mild degree is common with diffuse encephalopathies like Parkinson's disease and Huntington's disease (20).

Measurement of affect within the context of quality of life has not always focused on clinical dimensions of emotional behavior like depression or anxiety. Rather, constructs such as life satisfaction and psychological well-being are commonly employed. A range of instruments are available for measurement of these or similar constructs (21–25). To a certain extent, the proliferation of such measures is an index of the elusiveness of concepts such as life satisfaction. In fact, no "gold standards" exist in this domain, and it may not be reasonable to expect a single measure to be equally applicable in all situations. Since the sources of life satisfaction change as patients age (26), selection of such measures requires adaptation of tools to the target population.

Economic Function

The financial impact of neurological disease has received significant attention in public health studies but much less in clinical neurologic assessments. A number of measures have been developed, and issues of concern have been raised. Among the latter is the issue of how economic function should be measured: objectively versus subjectively, and directly versus indirectly. Objective measures of the economic impact of disease might include days of work missed, hospital days or outpatient visits to health care professionals, and medication. These direct costs can be supplemented by indirect costs such as residential alterations necessitated by the disease and days of work missed by family members providing care to the patient. Alternatively, the evaluations may focus on the perceived economic impact of the illness. Thus, on the Multidimensional Functional Assessment Questionnaire (22), ratings of directly relevant medical costs supplement the subjective impact on finances of the illness. On the Sickness Impact Profile (19), a multidimensional and psychometrically sound measure of quality of life, the Work and Home Management scales measure the extent to which the patient is able to perform occupational and household duties, respectively. Disability in these domains has clear financial implications, although no direct estimate of this cost is provided in the scale. The choice of measurement approaches in the economic domain is complex and depends

on the purposes to be accomplished. In a cost–benefit analysis of a specific neurologic treatment, for example, direct estimates of cost are preferable. From a broader perspective in which economics is one of several domains being evaluated, measures of perceived financial burden may suffice.

The economic impact of a given disease will, of course, largely relate to the patient's economic status before the disease began. Two patients may have similar cerebrovascular accidents and require the same nursing care at home. The wealthy patient will engage a daily nurse with little economic impact, whereas the same care for the poorer patient may have far-reaching economic consequences. Premorbid financial status is not typically considered in objective measurement of economic impact but may implicitly influence ratings of perceived financial burden.

Social Function

Evaluation of the quality and quantity of an individual's social interaction is the fourth area of quality of life measurement. In practice, most measures have tended to focus on social networks, access to community services, and recreational activities. The impact of neurologic disease on the patient's social network has not been well studied, since in many cases the social changes are a mere consequence of the three other domains already discussed. However, many scales are available (19,22,27) and could reasonably be incorporated into neurologic evaluations.

The usual approach to assessing social networks begins with the patient or an informant identifying a set of key individuals in the patient's life. Each is rated along several dimensions. Thus, in the Philadelphia Geriatric Scale (27), the extent to which each individual provides emotional support, encouragement, companionship, and advice is rated. In other inventories, the focus is on more objective variables, such as the proximity of these key individuals and their frequency of contact with the patient. In either case, the intent is to determine whether the patient's social world has contracted as a result of illness.

On the Social Interaction subscale of the Sickness Impact Profile, the same construct is assessed less tediously through a series of questions requiring only a yes/no response. It is noteworthy that on the Sickness Impact Profile, the Social Interaction scale is part of the psychosocial factor; the other scales that define this factor (e.g., Communication, Emotional Behavior) are clearly psychological, rather than social, in nature. In fact, the lack of attention to social interaction in neurologic disease may reflect the fact that such effects are indirect. That is, the social impact of neurologic diseases may be mediated by the physical and psychological sequelae. In this regard, it is noteworthy that adverse effects on social networks have been studied more in persons responsible for the care of neurologic patients, those with Alzheimer's disease in particular, than in patients themselves (28,29).

NEUROLOGIC APPLICATIONS OF QUALITY OF LIFE MEASUREMENT

The heterogeneity of the manifestations of neurologic illnesses has resulted in diverse approaches to measuring quality of life. In this section, examples of the application of quality of life measurement to neurologic disorders are presented.

Dementia

With the aging of the population in the United States and other industrialized nations, concern about Alzheimer's disease and other dementing illnesses affecting elderly persons has grown. Epidemiologic studies suggest that approximately 10% of those over the age of 65 have Alzheimer's disease; prevalence is estimated to be nearly 50% in those over the age of 85 (30). Although many conditions are capable of causing global cognitive impairment in older persons, Alzheimer's disease or cerebrovascular disease, or a combination, are thought to be the primary causes of dementia in this age range.

Dementia, or global cognitive impairment, poses an obstacle to quality of life measurement, as the patient's subjective report cannot safely be assumed to be valid. Indeed, awareness of cognitive (31) and affective (32–34) symptoms in Alzheimer's disease and in other neurologic conditions (35) has been demonstrated to be deficient. These findings should not be surprising since an inability to form an enduring record of recent experiences is the most prominent feature of Alzheimer's disease, even in its early stages.

A variety of methods are available for measurement of the dimensions of the quality of life construct reviewed earlier in this chapter (e.g., physical function). That is, by relying on direct measures of performance and the report of proxy respondents, level of function in physical, psychological, economic, and social domains can be assessed. Missing from these assessments is the subjective viewpoint of the patient, however, so that what is being measured might be more accurately called health status than quality of life. The idea of quality of life has been quite useful in assessing those who provide care for persons with dementia.

Evaluation of Treatment

The multidimensionality of the quality of life construct makes it particularly appropriate for evaluations of different therapeutic approaches. For example, quality of life measures have been used to describe the outcome of epilepsy surgery (36), radiation therapy for brain tumor (37), *Botulinum* toxin for spasmodic torticollis (38), and adrenal medullary transplant surgery for Parkinson's disease (39). The latter two examples are considered below in more detail for illustrative purposes.

Although pharmacological treatment of Parkinson's disease has proved effective, disease progression and chronic medication side effects limit therapeutic efforts. Recently, adrenal medullary autografts to caudate nucleus have been used in severely impaired Parkinson's disease patients who no longer respond adequately to dopaminergic replacement therapy. The procedure involves a caudate nucleus biopsy and placement of the patient's adrenal medullary cells onto the biopsy site in contact with the ventricular cerebrospinal fluid. Proposed mechanisms for the amelioration of Parkinson's disease by this graft have included enhanced dopamine production by the adrenal medulla cells and possibly the transfer or synthesis of trophic growth factors in the brain.

Among five men and two women studied by Stebbins et al. (39), mean age at surgery was 50.3 years, mean age of Parkinson's disease onset was 38.7 years, mean Parkinson's disease duration was 11.6 years, and mean duration of levodopa treatment was 11.0 years. Before surgery, all patients had severe Parkinson's disease and had serious balance problems or could not stand alone during part of the day. All suffered severe fluctuations in their motor response, spending a mean 39.3% of the waking day "off" and 60.7% "on."

The scales chosen to study motor efficacy in this protocol were the Unified Parkinson's Disease Rating Scale (40), the Hoehn and Yahr stage (41), and the Schwab and England Scale (1). The Unified Parkinson's Disease Rating Scale was selected because it provided objective measurements of Parkinsonian motor problems and had subscales that assessed subjective complaints by the patient and activities of daily living. The Hoehn and Yahr rating provided a global measure of parkinsonism and the Schwab and England Scale provided a global measure of functional independence. In addition, neuropsychological performance tests were administered to assess changes in cognitive and affective function. Finally, the Sickness Impact Profile (19) was selected to measure quality of life. The Sickness Impact Profile is among the most comprehensive and psychometrically sound measures of quality of life; 12 internally consistent subscales yield two summary factor scores. The items are readily observable behaviors and are scored on the basis of an interview with either the patient or a proxy respondent. The latter option is particularly important in evaluating neurologic patients who may be cognitively impaired.

Of the original seven patients, one patient expired due to causes unrelated to the surgery. The six remaining patients reported improvements in selective aspects of quality of life, including sleep and rest, social isolation, and ambulation at one year after surgery. These improvements in quality of life were significantly correlated with improved motor functioning as assessed by the Schwab-England Activities of Daily Living scale, and duration of medication effect. By 2 years after surgery, Stebbins et al. (39) found that the improvements in quality of life seen at 1 year after surgery disappeared. This loss of improvement paralleled declines in motor functioning, activities of daily living, and duration of medication effects. The decline in functioning at 2 years after surgery was thought to be due to progression of the disease or to loss of the implant efficacy, or both.

Another example of assessing the effect of treatment for neurological disorders on quality of life is a study by Stebbins et al. (38). These investigators studied the effects of a treatment for spasmodic torticollis on quality of life as measured by the Sickness Impact Profile. Spasmodic torticollis is a form of dystonia that results in the maintenance of an abnormal posture of the neck. These patients are often unable to see directly ahead without compensating by twisting their torsos. Currently, the standard treatment for this disorder involves the injection of small doses of *Botulinum* toxin into the affected muscles. This effectively denervates the muscle, allowing the patient to maintain a more normal neck posture. In the untreated state, the disability associated with spasmodic torticollis includes neck muscle hypertrophy, pain, social embarrassment, and psychological distress.

In this study, the Sickness Impact Profile was administered to spasmodic torticollis patients before and 4 weeks after injection of *Botulinum* toxin. Selective improvements were found for the following quality of life domains: emotional behavior, physical self-care, ability to engage in homemaking activities, social isolation, ambulation, and communication. In addition, the composite measure of overall psychological functioning improved. These improvements were consistent with improvements in neck posture as assessed by the patient and the treating physician (38).

CONCLUSIONS

The incorporation of quality of life measures in neurologic evaluations of disease or treatment is an increasing practice. Scales are now available that can provide assessment of specific facets of quality of life relevant to patients with neurologic disease. Although disease-specific scales are sometimes a necessity, they tend to be less psychometrically established and do not permit comparisons across disease categories. In the final analysis, however, the choice of scales for a given study will depend on the research objectives. Wider extension of quality of life studies to caregivers and families may demonstrate a more complete assessment of the impact of neurological disease and putative therapies.

In the coming decade, one major focus of pharmacologic research in neurology will be the improvement in drug delivery systems. Documenting objective improvement from one formulation to another can be difficult, however, as the drug is the same in both instances. Quality of life measures may prove particularly applicable in measuring the impact of these new formulations. As an example, levodopa was developed during the 1960s as a treatment for Parkinson's disease. It still remains the mainstay of therapy, although its delivery has been altered by more modern pharmacologic manipulations. The addition of carbidopa to levodopa facilitates delivery to the central nervous system. More recently, a long-acting protein-bound formulation has been developed to decrease the frequent dosing schedule that is so often necessary with this drug.

In spite of these innovations, the drug itself remains levodopa, and objective measures of improvement from one formulation to another are difficult to establish. Nevertheless, incorporation of quality of life measures into the assessments would likely document the impact of fewer side effects with the levodopa–carbidopa combination and the enhanced independence that patients feel when they switch from the short-acting to the long-acting form. These assessments may offer an improved means of monitoring new or more subtle therapies in the future.

REFERENCES

1. Schwab RS, England AC. Projection technique for evaluating surgery in Parkinson's disease. In: Gillingham FJ, Donaldson MC, eds. *Third symposium on Parkinson's disease.* Edinburgh: Churchill Livingstone, 1969:152–157.
2. Shoulson I, Fahn S. Huntington's disease: clinical care and evaluation. *Neurology* 1979;29:1–3.
3. Koller WC. *Handbook of Parkinson's disease.* New York: Dekker, 1987:482–488.
4. Lawton MP, Brody EM. Assessment of older people: self-maintaining and instrumental activities of daily living. *Gerontologist* 1969;9:179–186.
5. Katz S, Ford AB, Moskowitz RW. Studies of illness in the aged: the index of ADL, a standardized measure of biological and psychosocial function. *JAMA* 1963;185:914–919.
6. Mahoney FJ, Barthel DW. Functional evaluation: the Barthel Index. *Md Med J* 1965;14:61–65.
7. Nagi SZ. An epidemiology of disability among adults in the United States. *Millbank Mem Fund Q* 1976;54:439–468.
8. Rosow I, Breslau N. A Guttman health scale for the aged. *J Gerontol* 1966;21:556–559.
9. Guralnik JM, Branch LG, Cummings SR, Curbe JD. Physical performance measures in aging research. *J Gerontol Med Sci* 1989;44:M141–M146.
10. Guralnik JM, Simonsick EM, Ferrucci L, Glynn RJ, Berkman LF, Blazer DG, Shcerr PA, Wallace RB. A short physical performance battery assessing lower extremity function: association with self-reported disability and prediction of mortality and nursing home admission. *J Gerontol Med Sci* 1994;49:M85–M94.
11. Lezak M. *Neurological assessment.* New York: Oxford University Press, 1983.
12. Heilman KM, Valenstein E. *Clinical neuropsychology.* New York: Oxford University Press, 1979.
13. Folstein MF, Folstein SE, McHugh PR. Mini-Mental State. A practical guide for grading the cognitive state of patients for the clinician. *J Psychiatr Res* 1975;12:189–198.
14. Mattis S. Mental status examination for organic mental syndrome in the elderly patient. In Bellak L, Karasu T, eds. *Geriatric psychiatry.* New York: Grune & Stratton, 1976.
15. Mohs RC, Rosen WG, Greenwald BS, Davis KL. Neuropathologically validated scales for Alzheimer's disease. In: Crook T, Ferris S, Bartus R, eds. *Assessment in geriatric psychiatry.* New Canaan, CT: Mark Powley Associates, 1983:37–45.
16. Reisberg B, Schneck MK, Ferris SH, Schwartz GE, de Leon MJ. The Brief Cognitive Rating Scale (BCRS): findings in primary degenerative dementia (PDD). *Psychopharmacol Bull* 1983;19:47–50.
17. Reisberg B, Ferris SH, de Leon MJ, Crook T. The Global Deterioration Scale (GDS): an instrument for the assessment of primary degenerative dementia (PDD). *Am J Psychiatry* 1982;139:1136–1139.
18. Katz MM, Lyerly SB. Methods for measuring adjustment and social

behavior in the community. 1. Rationale, description, discriminative validity and scale development. *Psychol Rep* 1963(suppl 4-V13);13: 503–535.

19. Bergner M, Bobbitt RA, Carter WB, Gilson BS. The Sickness Impact Profile: development and final revision of a health status measure. *Med Care* 1981;19:787–805.

20. Cummings JL, Benson DF. *Dementia: a clinical approach.* Boston: Butterworths, 1983.

21. Anderson JP, Bush JW, Berry CC. Classifying function for health outcome and quality-of-life evaluation. *Med Care* 1986;24:454–469.

22. Duke University Center for the Study of Aging. *Multidimensional functional assessment. The OARS methodology.* 2nd ed. Durham, NC: Duke University Press, 1978.

23. George LK, Bearon LB. *Quality of life in older persons.* New York: Human Sciences Press, 1980.

24. Lawton MP. The varieties of well-being. *Exp Aging Res* 1983;7:65–72.

25. Neugarten BL, Havighurst RJ, Tobin S. The measurement of life satisfaction. *J Gerontol* 1961;16:134–143.

26. Neugarten BL. Personality and aging. In: Birren JE, Schaie KW, eds. *Handbook of the psychology of aging.* New York: Van Nostrand–Reinhold, 1977.

27. Lawton MP, Moss M, Fulcomer M, Kleban MH. A research and service oriented multilevel assessment instrument. *J Gerontol* 1982;37:91–99.

28. Cantor MA. Strain among caregivers: a study of the experience in the United States. *Gerontologist* 1983;23:597–604.

29. Rabins RV, Mace NL, Lucas MJ. The impact of dementia in the family. *JAMA* 1982;248:333–335.

30. Evans DA, Funkenstein HH, Albert MS, Scherr PA, Cook NR, Chown MJ, Hebert LE, Hennekens CH, Taylor JO. Prevalence of Alzheimer's disease in a community population of older persons—higher than previously reported. *JAMA* 1989;262:2551–2556.

31. McGlynn SM, Kaszniak AW. When metacognition fails: impaired awareness of deficit in Alzheimer's disease. *J Cognit Neurosci* 1991;3: 183–189.

32. Burke WJ, Houston MJ, Boust SJ, Roccaforte WH. Use of the Geriatric Depression Scale in dementia of the Alzheimer type. *J Am Geriatr Soc* 1989;37:856–860.

33. Mackenzie TB, Robiner WN, Knopman DS. Differences between patient and family assessments of depression in Alzheimer's disease. *Am J Psychiatry* 1989;146:1174–1178.

34. Gilley DW, Wilson RS, Fleischman DA, Harrison DW, Goetz CG, Tanner CM. Impact of Alzheimer's-type dementia and information source on the assessment of depression. *Psychologic Assess* 1995; 7:42–48.

35. McGlynn SM, Schacter DL. Unawareness of deficits in neuropsychological syndromes. *J Clin Exp Neuropsychol* 1989;11:143–205.

36. Vickrey BG, Hays RD, Brook RH, Engel J, Rausch R. Validation of a quality of life measure in epilepsy surgery patients. *Neurology* 1991; 41:403.

37. Taphoorn MJB, Heimans JJ, Schiphorst AK, Snoek FJ, Lindeboom J, Wolbers JG, Karim ABMF. Quality of life in long-term survivors of biopsy-proven low-grade glioma treated with and without radiotherapy and in long-term survivors of low-grade hematological malignancies. *Ann Neurol* 1992;34:314.

38. Stebbins GT, Comella CL, Buchman A. Changes in quality of life following BOTOX injection for spasmodic torticollis. *Movement Disord* 1992;7:135.

39. Stebbins GT, Gilley DW, Goetz CG, Tanner CM, Wilson RS, Comella CL, Klawans HL. Quality of life in Parkinson's disease patients at two years following adrenal-medulla/caudate implant. *Neurology* 1991;41: 398.

40. Fahn S, Elton RL. Unified Parkinson's Disease Rating Scale. In: Fahn S, et al., eds. *Recent developments in Parkinson's disease.* Vol. II. Florham Park, NJ: Macmillan Healthcare, 1987:153–163.

41. Hoehn MM, Yahr MD. Parkinsonism: onset, progression, and mortality. *Neurology* 1967;17:427–442.

Quality of Life and Pharmacoeconomics in Clinical Trials, Second Edition, edited by B. Spilker.
Lippincott-Raven Publishers, Philadelphia © 1996.

CHAPTER 94

Quality of Life Assessment for People with Epilepsy

Joyce A. Cramer

INTRODUCTION

More than two million Americans have epilepsy, with 125,000 new cases identified annually (1). Patients face a range of health-related quality of life problems after diagnosis, whether or not seizures are well controlled. Epilepsy is a diverse disorder expressed physically as a tendency to have recurrent seizures. The diagnosis is made after possible metabolic events or structural lesions are ruled out as causes. The two major types of epilepsies are generalized (where both sides of the brain are involved simultaneously) and partial (where seizures originate in one or more specific locations in the brain). Several types of seizures can occur within each type of epilepsy. Generalized seizures, including absence ("petit mal") and myoclonic seizures (spells of brief muscle jerks), can progress to generalized tonic–clonic seizures ("grand mal"). Both absence and myclonic seizures are common in children. Partial epilepsies include simple partial seizures (where consciousness is not impaired), com-

plex partial seizures (where consciousness is impaired), and generalized tonic clonic seizures. Simple and complex partial seizures can have a variety of manifestations, ranging from a brief tingling sensation or muscle activity (arm or leg movements), to altered consciousness, automatic or repetitive activity (e.g., unbuttoning clothing, lip-smacking), or unintelligible utterances. Partial seizures beginning in one small area of the brain can spread, causing increasing impairments, including tonic–clonic seizures.

TREATMENT AND PROGNOSIS

Treatment with antiepileptic drugs usually is instituted after the diagnosis of epilepsy is made. Unfortunately, most adults with partial epilepsy continue to have simple partial, complex partial, or secondarily generalized tonic–clonic seizures, despite treatment with antiepileptic drugs. Two controlled prospective studies of adults with newly treated epilepsy showed that the cumulative proportion of patients remaining free of complex partial seizures for 2 years after initiating treatment was only 22% (2,3). An open population study, consisting mostly of children with primary general-

J. A. Cramer: Yale University School of Medicine, New Haven, Health Services Research (116A), VA Medical Center, West Haven, Connecticut 06516.

ized epilepsy, found relapse in more than one-half of patients during 2 years of follow-up (4). The possibility of recurrent seizures is a silent but ever-present component of daily life for most patients who carry the diagnosis of epilepsy.

Although some patients enter a period of remission while treated, careful withdrawal of medication in selected patients resulted in 41% relapsing within 2 years (5). Because of the high risk of recurrence following discontinuation of antiepileptic drugs, many physicians counsel adult patients to continue therapy chronically (6). The risk of a breakthrough seizure during medication taper often necessitates driving restrictions for several months. Nonetheless, attempts to withdraw medication from children often are warranted to avoid risks of adverse effects from medications. Some patients with medication-refractory seizures can become seizure free after surgical resection of the portion of brain tissue from which seizures are generated. Nonetheless, even successful epilepsy surgery does not guarantee remediation of underlying health-related quality of life issues.

SPECIAL ISSUES FOR PEOPLE WITH EPILEPSY

Epilepsy Is a Chronic Burden

The diagnosis of epilepsy indicates a chronic disorder, often requiring lifelong treatment. The impact of seizures and treatment with antiepileptic drugs can linger even after long-term remission is achieved. Jacoby (7) described epilepsy as "both a medical diagnosis and a social label." The stigma and underlying worry about epilepsy should be considered even in long-term follow-up of patients with few or no recent seizures. In a Veterans Administration (VA) epilepsy study, adult patients (90% male) who discontinued treatment were mostly young men (under 25 years) with no previous medical disorder. They were assumed to be denying the diagnosis of epilepsy and need to take medication to control seizures by stopping treatment (8). The burden of the diagnosis, with possible restrictions on driving and working, was removed by denying the diagnosis and refusing care. Many of these patients were later seen for reevaluation at the time of subsequent seizures, when some accepted the diagnosis and need for treatment. However, issues of compliance with medication, restrictions on drinking alcohol, requirements for special driver's license approval and reporting of epilepsy on job and insurance applications may encumber patients forever. Epilepsy differs from almost all other medical disorders because of these legal restrictions and requirements. Thus, evaluation of epilepsy-related quality of life requires special attention to social burdens.

Physical Issues

Most people with epilepsy lead normal lives, punctuated by the possibility of a seizure occurring with no warning.

Seizures do increase the risk of bone fracture, burns, and drowning, as well as unexplained death (9). Medications that are taken daily to reduce seizure threshold in the brain carry the potential burden of adverse physical effects (e.g., sedation, nausea, double vision, tremor) and mental effects (e.g., cognitive, memory impairments), some of which could be subtle but chronic (2,3). Quality of life measures show impairment in people who have systemic or neurological adverse effects (10,11).

Psychological Issues

Anxiety about the occurrence of seizures is a common concern, not only because of the suddenness of events, but also because of the possibility of negative sequelae. Fear of exposure before friends and work colleagues plays a part in self-imposed social restrictions for some patients. The actual or perceived sense of dependency can be fostered by parents of children and by spouses and families of adult patients. Children with epilepsy had twice as many referrals for mental health services (12% vs. 23%) as the local population of children (12). Hermann et al. (13) described the more frequent manifestations of psychological problems associated with epilepsy. Depression is the most frequently reported issue, both immediately after the diagnosis and over the long term. Studies are needed to determine the contributions of the diagnosis, seizure activity, and medications. Several new antiepileptic drugs appear to have few cognitive effects, less sedation, and little impact on mood, compared to older medications (e.g., phenobarbital, phenytoin), but more experience is needed to verify these impressions.

Social Issues

Seizure onset at a young age often limits social opportunities (14,15). Adolescents can be cruel in their shunning and demeaning of a peer with a physical, mental, or social deficiency. Some schools bar children from extracurricular athletic and gym classes. Parents of friends have been known not to allow children with epilepsy in their homes, for fear of liability. High rates of social disabilities in children with epilepsy are reflected by a threefold higher use of special education services (12% vs. 35%), low employment after completing their education (16% vs. 30%), and high incidence of inadvertent teenage pregnancy (13%) (12). Growing up in such a stigmatized atmosphere limits opportunities for socialization. As young adults, possibilities for marriage are limited both by opportunities and anxieties about dependency on parents, ability to support a family, child-bearing, and child-raising capabilities. Some patients fear dropping a baby, while others worry that their children will inherit epilepsy. This problem is compounded by diminished fertility in men and women, related to use of some antiepileptic drugs and possibly by the effects of epilepsy on the brain (16). Overall lack of self-esteem is expressed by many patients who feel that no one would want to marry them (7).

Employment, Driving and Legal Issues

Many U.S. insurers refuse to cover people with epilepsy, or limit coverage for life and health insurance. Employers frequently restrict the types of jobs that can be performed by people with epilepsy (e.g., no work with power equipment) to avoid harm in case of a seizure while working. In the past (before enactment of the Americans with Disabilities Act in 1993), questions about a history of seizures often appeared on employment applications, leading to refusal to employ the person. If the applicant did not honestly answer such questions, the employment could be terminated if epilepsy was later revealed. Patients were frequently told to avoid high stress positions or "settle" for a less demanding job, thereby limiting possibilities for advancement. Camfield et al. (12) reported that 30% of epilepsy patients ages 18 to 24 were unemployed, compared to 14 to 17% of the local population. Underemployment is a common concern, particularly for those who have experienced a seizure at work or whose employers know of the diagnosis. Examples range from an architect working as a draftsman to a truck driver working as a stockroom clerk. The Epilepsy Foundation of America (Landover, MD) advocates to assist people with epilepsy with employment-related problems. The 1993 Americans with Disabilities Act identified epilepsy as a disorder for which special protection must be ensured. Employers no longer may ask questions about medical history prior to offering employment, but work responsibilities can be limited as necessary, on the basis of capabilities. Currently employed persons who develop epilepsy cannot be discharged solely because of the diagnosis. The law requires the employer to accommodate to people with disabilities (e.g., with special equipment, protective devices). People with epilepsy should divulge this information after hiring, to allow the employer to adjust the position as necessary to people's needs.

Epilepsy is an unusual medical diagnosis in that legislation specifically restrains driving privileges (17). Some municipalities require physicians to report the diagnosis of epilepsy to the Department of Motor Vehicles, which might affect the physician–patient relationship (17). The patient's license to drive might be withdrawn until the physician provides documentation that the patient has been seizure free for a specified period (3 to 12 months). Some states require the seizure-free period to occur without medication, while others allow the remission period to be medicated. Automobile liability insurance is available, usually in special "assigned risk" plans, but often at high cost and with limited coverage (17). A consensus statement prepared by the American Academy of Neurology, American Epilepsy Society, and Epilepsy Foundation of America (18) puts forth suggestions for reasonable licensing legislation based on medical criteria. The need for this statement exemplifies the importance of driving privileges for people with epilepsy, and the restrictiveness of much of the current legislation.

DEVELOPMENT OF QUALITY OF LIFE INSTRUMENTS FOR EPILEPSY

Traditional long-term clinical approaches to care for epilepsy patients revolve around adjustment of medication based on type, severity, and frequency of seizures and adverse effects (19). Recognizing the limits of medication to manage or control this episodic disorder, neurologists need to be able to care for the patient as an entity, including physical, psychological, social, educational, vocational, and other life domains. Historically, formal neuropsychological testing has been used to define functional brain deficits with some attention to mood. The Minnesota Multiphasic Personality Inventory (MMPI) was often used to assess personality issues. In 1980, Dodrill et al. (20) used a neuropsychological approach in the development of the Washington Psycho-Social Inventory (WPSI) in the style of the MMPI. The WPSI is a self-report profile measure encompassing health-related quality of life (QOL) dimensions as well as other constructs. A decade later, Chaplin et al. (21) asked epilepsy patients in England to describe problems related to having epilepsy. Most patient concerns related to their adjustment to seizures. This survey was refined into a list of 14 social issues pertinent to epilepsy.

Well-Being Scale

Collings (22) formulated an overall well-being scale including six subscales: self-esteem, life fulfillment, social difficulty, physical symptoms, worries, affect-balance. Testing in 392 patients with active epilepsy showed lower well-being on all scales than a nonepilepsy control group. The visibility of severe seizures and frequency of seizures were directly related to well-being. Self-image (perception of self) and epilepsy were most predictive of overall well-being. Other important variables included few seizures, mild seizures, recent diagnosis, confidence in the diagnosis, and employment.

Evolution of the Liverpool Quality of Life Battery

A battery of quality of life assessments for people with epilepsy (the Liverpool battery), has been developed and modified by a consortium in England. Initially using eight scales, including a newly developed seizure severity scale with perception/control and ictal/postictal components (23), Baker et al. (24) reported that the battery detected differences in quality of life for patients receiving a new antiepileptic drug during a clinical trial. Jacoby et al. (25) used a series of five standard questionnaires [Nottingham Health Profile (26), Scale of Positive Affect (27), Self-esteem Scale (28), Mastery Scale (29), Stigma Scale (30)] to assess people who had infrequent seizures or had been seizure-free for many years, and who had stopped taking antiepileptic drugs. As expected, those with well-controlled seizures had few problems, but recurrence of seizures was associated with negative responses. Patients who were not having seizures continued to report a perception of the stigma of epilepsy.

Of the 100 patients with severe epilepsy who completed an early version of the Liverpool QOL Battery, 33% were anxious, 15% were depressed, 50% had low self-esteem, 84% had low perceived internal control, and 31% were unhappy (31). Few patients had problems with social function or dissatisfaction with housing, but 21% were dissatisfied with their work situation. Psychological variables were the most important predictors of one another. Seizure severity significantly predicated anxiety, low self-esteem, and locus of control problems. Seizure frequency contributed little to variance of any psychological variable. Smith et al. (32) concluded that epilepsy, irrespective of seizure frequency, may be a major determinant of psychosocial problems. Thus, contrary to typical use of seizure frequency as the major end point to evaluate antiepileptic drugs, it may not be the sole measure of efficacy without consideration of psychosocial problems.

A revised version of the Liverpool QOL Battery (Table 1) was evaluated in 79 patients with severe epilepsy (24). Of the two scales for seizure severity, only the ictal subscale differentiated between seizure types. In this group, the incidence of depression was 6% and anxiety was 25%. Comparing the two treatment groups (drug vs. placebo), they defined sensitivity to change as difference between mean scale scores for each group (32). Significant differences were seen for the ictal seizure subscale (patient and carer reports), happiness scale, and the mastery scale. New scales have been added to the original Liverpool battery (Table 1). The Impact of Epilepsy Scale measures several aspects of daily life, including relationships with spouse/partner, other close family members, and friends; social activities; work; health; feelings about self; plans and ambitions for the future (33). A Life Fulfillment Scale allows patients to consider the difference between their actual and desired circumstances (34). The approach of this group is to select appropriate measures to develop batteries tailored to assist in answering specific clinical questions. Thus, not all measures will be used repeatedly in every study.

Jacoby (35) explored the concept that people with epilepsy feel stigmatized by the diagnosis, while making a distinction between *felt* and *enacted* stigma (36). She administered a stigma scale to 564 epilepsy patients who were participating in a clinical trial of medication withdrawal, covering issues about whether other people were uncomfortable with them, treated them as inferior, or preferred to avoid them (30). Interestingly, only 14% expressed any sense of stigma, 12% considered their epilepsy a serious illness, and 8% worried a lot about their epilepsy. A significant relationship was seen between reports of stigma and poor scores for self esteem, mastery, energy, emotional reaction, and social isolation, as well as description of epilepsy as a serious illness. Similarly, those who reported a stigma felt that epilepsy diminished work opportunities, affected their work, and were treated unfairly at work. These issues describe enacted stigma on the part of the employers. Jacoby (35) describes these processes as contributing to the ''undesired differentness in epilepsy.''

TABLE 1. *Liverpool assessment battery*

Scale	No. of items
Liverpool Seizure Severity scale	
Perception of control	8
Ictal/Postictal effects	11
Nottingham Health Profile[a]	38
SEALS Activities of Daily Living[a]	19
Social Problems Questionnaire[a]	33
Hospital Anxiety and Depression scale	14
Affect Balance scale	10
Profile of Mood States[a]	36
Rosenberg Self-Esteem scale	10
Liverpool Mastery scale	7
Stigma scale[b]	—
Life Fulfillment scale[b]	—
Impact of Epilepsy scale[b]	—
Adverse Effects[b]	—

From Baker et al. (24).
Additional information may be obtained from Dr. Baker at the Department of Neurosciences, Walton Hospital, Rice Lane, Liverpool L9 1AE, UK.
[a]Deleted from later versions.
[b]Added to later versions.

Quality of Life Assessment Schedule

Kendrick and Trimble (37) hypothesized that quality of life could be improved either by increasing actual abilities or decreasing expectations, and that people judge their current quality of life in relation to past experiences and other people. The Quality of Life Assessment Schedule (QOLAS), based on a repertory grid technique, was used in extensive interviews with 50 residents of the Chalfont Centre for Epilepsy (UK). Patients were asked to identify specific issues important to their lives in the domains of physical functioning, cognition, emotion, social functioning, economic/work status. A Construct Importance Scale was developed in which patients identified at least ten issues important to themselves. The issues were divided into areas of physical functioning, cognitive abilities emotional status, social functioning, and economic/employment status. Patients rated their problems during follow-up. A global score discriminated between patients who had experienced significant life events from those reporting no such events. Analyses by gender showed little difference between women and men with epilepsy in their perception of quality of life (38). The profiles showed differences between actual (NOW) and desired (LIKE) status as perceived by the individual. This labor-intensive interview method for assessment of quality of life is not feasible for large populations, but works well for hospital settings where extended time periods for interviews are available, such as during evaluation for epilepsy surgery. The novel method focuses on an individual's beliefs and expectations in a flexible, systematic approach to health-related quality of life (39).

Epilepsy Surgery Inventory

The Epilepsy Surgery Inventory (ESI-55) was developed to assess the health-related quality of life outcomes of patients who undergo surgical treatment of intractable epilepsy (40). Development of this measure used the method of combining a generic core measure, the RAND 36-Item Health Survey 1.0 (SF-36) (41,42), with a 19-item supplement. Supplemental items tapped into areas of particular importance to individuals who undergo epilepsy surgery, such as cognitive function, role limitations due to memory problems, and epilepsy-specific health perceptions. The supplement also included two items on overall quality of life. The ESI-55 contains 11 multi-item scales (Table 2). Three composite scores (mental health, physical health, and role limitations/cognitive) and an overall ESI-55 score can be derived by weighting and summing individual scale scores.

Assessments were based on data from a survey of 224 consecutive patients at a Los Angeles center who were evaluated for resective brain surgery to treat intractable epilepsy. Patients who became seizure free after surgery had signifi-

cantly better scores than patients having continued seizures with altered consciousness on all 11 scales of the ESI-55, while patients with simple partial seizures (no alteration of consciousness) scored in-between. The health perceptions scale discriminated the most strongly between this classification of patients by degree of postoperative seizure control (40).

Development of the Quality of Life in Epilepsy (QOLIE) Instruments

The method used to develop the ESI-55 was replicated in the development of an expanded quality of life measure for the large proportion of patients with epilepsy whose seizures are controlled or for those who have low-to-moderate seizure frequency (not severe epilepsy that might be treated with surgery). The RAND 36-Item Health Survey 1.0 (41) was used as a generic core with additional general items (pictorial chart developed for the Dartmouth COOP (43) and an overall quality of life item from the Faces Scale (44). Supplementary items were relevant to adults with epilepsy. A test instrument was administered to 304 adults in the United States whose seizure frequency ranged from none, low, moderate, or high during the past year, according to specific guidelines. A patient-designated proxy also completed an identical questionnaire, except that questions were rephrased to elicit the proxy's assessment of the patient's health-related quality of life.

The final measure, the Quality of Life in Epilepsy (QOLIE-89) Inventory, contains 86 items grouped into 17 multi-item scales and three single items (10) (Table 3). Factor analysis of the 17 scales revealed four HRQL dimensions: (1) epilepsy-targeted, (2) cognitive, (3) mental health, and (4) physical health. Patients also completed a battery of neuropsychological tests (45) and were evaluated for systemic and neurologic effects of medications using a modification of the adverse effect scales developed for the Veterans Affairs Epilepsy Cooperative Studies (46). Like the ESI-55, an overall score and four composite scores can be calculated by weighting and summing individual scale scores. Two shorter instruments also have been developed, containing subsets of items in the QOLIE-89. The QOLIE-31 has 31 items grouped into seven multi-item scales and the QOLIE-10 contains ten single items (Table 3).

Evaluation of the relationship between the QOLIE-89 and a battery of neuropsychological tests showed that the largest correlations were observed between the Profile of Mood States and the QOLIE-89 (47). In another analysis, health care utilization tended to be inversely correlated with QOLIE-89 scores, whereas education and employment were directly correlated with higher (better) scores. Examination of the relationship between QOLIE-89 scores and epilepsy severity revealed that patients having no seizures in the preceding year scored significantly higher (better) than did patients with high frequency seizures on the overall score, on

TABLE 2. *ESI-55 scales*

Scale	No. of items
Health perception	9
Energy/fatigue	4
Overall QOL	2
Social function	2
Emotional well-being	5
Cognitive functioning	5
Physical functioning	10
Pain	2
Role limitation	
Emotional	5
Physical	5
Memory	5
Change in health	1

From Vikrey et al. (40).

Permission to use the ESI-55 and scoring manual may be obtained by writing to RAND, 1700 Main Street, PO Box 2138, Santa Monica, CA 90407-2138 (Attention: Contracts and Grant Services). Additional information may be obtained from Dr. Vickrey at that address.

TABLE 3. *QOLIE-89[a] and QOLIE-31[b] scales and number of items in each scale[c]*

Scale	No. of items
Health perceptions	6
Seizure worry*	5
Physical function	10
Role limitation–physical	5
Role limitation–emotional	5
Pain	2
Overall quality of life*	2
Emotional well-being*	5
Energy/fatigue*	4
Attention/concentration*	9
Memory	6
Language	5
Medication effects*	3
Social function, work, driving*	11
Social support	4
Social isolation	2
Health discouragement	2
Sexual function[d]	1
Change in health	1
Overall health*,[d]	1

From Devinsky et al. (10).

[a]The QOLIE-89 contains 17 scales with 87 field-tested questions.

[b]The shorter QOLIE-31 includes items from the seven scales marked with an asterisk.

[c]The QOLIE-10 contains one or more questions from each of the seven QOLIE-31 scales.

[d]Two additional items were added after validation studies.

Permission to use the QOLIE-89 or QOLIE-31 and scoring manuals may be obtained by writing to: RAND, 1700 Main Street, PO Box 2138, Santa Monica, CA 90407-2138 (Attention: Contracts and Grant Services). Permission to use the QOLIE-10 may be obtained from Professional Postgraduate Services (400 Plaza Drive, Secaucus, NJ 07094). Additional information may be obtained from J. Cramer, VA Medical Center, Health Services Research (116A), 950 Campbell Avenue, West Haven, CT 06156.

three of four composite scores, and on eight of 17 individual scales (seizure worry, health discouragement, work/driving/social function, attention/concentration, role limitations—emotional, social isolation, energy/fatigue, and health perceptions). The epilepsy-targeted composite score and its component scales discriminated the most highly across epilepsy severity groups (10). Both the seizure-free and low seizure frequency groups reported significantly better status on the epilepsy-targeted factor than did groups with moderate or high seizure frequency (Fig. 1). Overall scores for systemic and neurological toxicity showed negative correlations with all four factors and the overall score. In general, agreement between patients' and proxies' reports of the patients' health-related quality of life was good, particular for less subjective scales that assess functioning (48). These findings suggest differences among seizure frequency groups.

Health-Related Quality of Life Questionnaire for People with Epilepsy

A group of investigators from the United States and England collaborated in the formation of a quality of life assessment battery that combines epilepsy specific features of the Liverpool battery with additional items, and includes the Medical Outcomes Survey SF-36 Health Study—UK Version (42). Wagner et al. (11) described the development of a battery to assess general and epilepsy-specific issues that assess the impact of seizures and medications on health-related quality of life. The 171-item developmental questionnaire, completed by 136 epilepsy patients in the United Kingdom, included 31 previously validated and newly developed scales: (1) the MOS SF-36 Health Survey–United Kingdom Version as a measure of general health, (2) additional generic health measures, (3) items specific to the impact of epilepsy and antiepileptic drug therapy, and (4) items measuring symptom occurrence and impact (Table 4). A patient-completed symptom checklist was used to measure the frequency and impact of symptoms commonly related to the use of antiepileptic drugs, excluding symptoms that were covered in separate scales. In addition, open-ended questions were included to identify problems not covered in the scales. Some scales were modified to enhance epilepsy specificity (29,49,50). Patients were grouped according to seizure frequency into four groups: seizure free for at least the past 6 months, seizure free for 3 to 6 months, seizure free for 1 week to 3 months, or having had seizures during the past week.

The six epilepsy-specific scales (mastery, impact, experience, worry, agitation, and distress) were among the best discriminators between seizure groups. Almost all the scales showed significant differences between patients who were seizure free for more than 6 months and patients with recent seizures, demonstrating the ability of the scales to differentiate between groups. Both seizure-free patients and those with recent seizures scored lower (worse), particularly on the generic scales, when they reported symptoms on the checklist. Specific symptoms showing best correlations with low scale scores were unsteadiness, hand tremor, slow reaction, headache, and upset stomach.

General Health-Related QOL Assessment by SF-36

Wagner et al. (51) evaluated general health-related quality of life in 148 people with epilepsy using the MOS SF-36 Health Survey (42). Scores were compared with those of a nonepilepsy, well population from the National Survey of Functional Health Status (52), matched for sociodemographic variables. The epilepsy patients had significantly lower scores in six of eight domains. Only physical functioning and bodily pain scale scores were not different. Patients who had at least one seizure during the week before the

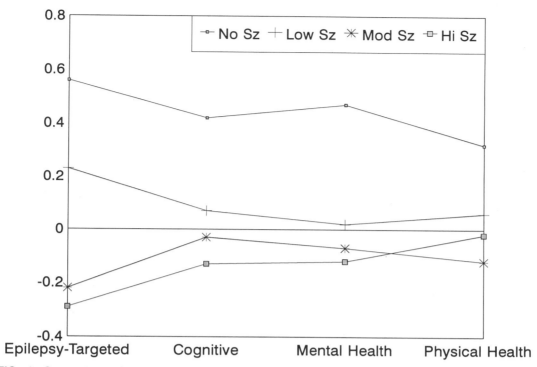

FIG. 1. Comparison of T scores on the four QOLIE-89 factors showing differences among seizure frequency groups. The seizure-free group scored significantly higher (*p* < .05) than all other groups on cognitive, mental health, and physical health factors. Both seizure-free and low seizure frequency groups scored significantly higher than other groups on epilepsy-targeted issues. The high seizure group scored significantly lower than all other groups on cognitive issues. The moderate seizure group was significantly better than low and high groups, but worse than the seizure-free group for physical health issues. Data from Devinsky et al. (10).

TABLE 4. *Health-related quality of life questionnaire for people with epilepsy (HQLQ-E)*

Domains	No. of items
General health-related quality of life	
SF-36 (UK version)	36
Additional general health-related quality of life	
Mental Health	17
Overall QOL	1
Cognition	13
Epilepsy specific quality of life scales	
Mastery	6
Impact	8
Experience	13
Worry	9
Agitation	2
Distress	2
Seizure severity	
Percept	8
Ictal	12
Symptoms	16
Open-ended questions	2

From Wagner et al. (11).

[a]The HQLQ-E contains 31 multi-item scales and 171 items. Additional information may be obtained from Dr. Wagner at The New England Medical Center, The Health Institute, 750 Washington Street, Boston, MA 02111.

assessment (31%) had significantly lower scores than those of patients who were seizure free for more than 1 year (27%). Systemic and neurologic effect assessment (46), controlling for the impact of time since the last seizure, showed that patients with adverse effects (76%) had worse health status in five domains than that of patients without adverse effects (53).

Vickrey et al. (54) compared quality of life scores of postoperative epilepsy surgery patients with different degrees of seizure control to reports of patients with hypertension, diabetes, heart disease, or depressive symptoms from the Medical Outcomes Study (55). These comparisons were made possible because all patients completed the RAND 36-Item Health Survey (41) and an overall quality of life Dartmouth COOP chart (43). Findings were that completely seizure-free epilepsy patients (i.e., those who were "cured" of their epilepsy) reported better quality of life than did the MOS patients on almost all comparisons. By contrast, the postsurgical patients having persistence of seizures with loss of consciousness scored lower (worse) than MOS patients with hypertension, diabetes, and heart disease on overall quality of life and on emotional well-being, but better than MOS patients with depressive symptoms on these measures.

These two studies add to information about the value of both versions of the SF-36 in comparisons among disease and well populations.

ASSESSMENTS OF ADOLESCENTS AND CHILDREN

Just as normal ranges for laboratory tests must be adjusted for age, quality of life instruments must also be revised to address issues specific to the age group. Adolescents with epilepsy have special concerns about the feasibility of driving and dating that differ from the perspective of adults. One approach to assessment of children is to interview the parent/caregiver, albeit recognizing that the responses might not reflect what is important to the child. Another issue of concern in families is the impact of a sibling's epilepsy on the other children.

Austin et al. (14) have described correlates of behavior problems in children. Measures included the Child Behavior Checklist (56), the Family Inventory of Life Events (57), and the Family Inventory of Resources for Management (57), in addition to demographic and seizure variables. Studying 127 children (aged 8 to 12 years) and their mothers with self-report questionnaires, interviews, and medical records, these investigators found five variables that related to behavior problems: female gender, family stress, family mastery, extended family social support, and seizure frequency.

Comparing children with epilepsy to children with asthma, Austin et al. (58) found more compromises in psychological, social, and school domains in the epilepsy group. The children (aged 8 to 12 years) were evaluated for school attendance, adverse effects of medications, episodes of illness, and Child Behavior Checklist by interviews with mothers. Teachers also rated the Child Behavior Checklist. The children completed the Piers–Harris Children's Self-Concept Scale (59), Child Attitude Toward Illness Scale (CATIS) (60), and the family Apgar scales (61). The magnitude of differences between the two types of illness and other findings suggests that some other factor is related to poor quality of life for children with epilepsy. Other reports suggest an association with low neurologic function (62). Additional studies are needed to define aspects of quality of life for children and adolescents with epilepsy.

USE OF QUALITY OF LIFE MEASURES IN EPILEPSY CLINICAL TRIALS

Although several groups have developed approaches to measuring quality of life for people with epilepsy, few data are available demonstrating their sensitivity to change. Several clinical trials now underway will provide the populations and interventions (new medications) to assess the value of the various instruments. Unfortunately, it is doubtful that any of the current medication trials have adequate power to detect small, short-term changes in quality of life, making it likely that the instruments might be declared insensitive.

At this early stage of quality of life research in epilepsy, caution is needed in interpretation of results, particularly for individual scales. These initial studies will provide information about the amount of change in individual scales and total scores that represents a clinically important difference (63). In addition, information is not available about how frequently to repeat quality of life measures, and when. The timing of the initial assessment should not occur during the excitement of enrolling in a clinical trial or initiating a presurgical evaluation. Taking the time for a second administration during a baseline period before an intervention might be important to demonstrate the lack of difference between the first and second exposure.

Medication Trials

The typical clinical trial of an investigational antiepilepsy medication added to standard medications does not usually produce dramatic clinical changes. Thus, large changes in quality of life end points should not be expected. Most trials are relatively brief (3 to 6 months of blinded follow-up), further reducing the likelihood of finding major changes. Patients who are followed long-term while taking open-label medication often have other changes in therapy that complicate further interpretation of drug effect, as does partial compliance with medications (64).

When valproate was introduced for control of absence, myoclonic, and primary generalized tonic–clonic seizures, many patients experienced remarkable improvements in several functional areas. In a retrospective survey of 60 patients followed for 2 to 13 years after initiation of valproate, Mattson et al. (65) reported that 79% achieved seizure control, 87% were employed (plus 8% still in school), several with a significant improvement in occupational status. The frequency of patients with a motor vehicle license increased from 21% to 78%, with an additional five patients eligible but not electing to obtain a license. Cognitive functioning and mood state also were significantly improved after conversion to valproate monotherapy (66). Although no formal quality of life instrument was used for evaluation, changing medication made a significant impact on many aspects of quality of life. The use of an instrument designed to tap domains important for epilepsy patients could reveal similar changes after introduction of a new medication or other alteration in regimen.

Jacoby et al. (25) investigated the impact of medication withdrawal compared to continuation of treatment in patients who had no seizures for the previous 2 years. Patients who relapsed while taking medications did less well than those who relapsed after discontinuation of medication, probably because of disappointment that they would remain seizure-free. They also concluded that continuing to take medications implies persistence of epilepsy, whether or not seizures are controlled. Patients whose medication was discontinued and who remained free of seizures were able to shed the stigma of the diagnosis. These findings are similar to clinical impressions noted when patients became seizure-free after changing to valproate monotherapy, even though they remained on medication. Many patients forgot how frequently and how severe and debilitating their tonic–clonic seizures had been, after 1 year of good control (65).

Surgical Studies

Another major avenue for quality of life assessment is the impact of epilepsy surgery, which can be curative for some patients. Early evaluation of quality of life before the special attention and stresses of the presurgical evaluation is important to define the patient in a "usual" state. Follow-up assessment should not be attempted too soon after surgery, but might profitably be repeated over several years postoperatively to evaluate changes over time. Survey research has shown that a surgical success does not always equate with a social recovery. Augustine et al. (67) found that most patients who did not work before surgery were unable to work after successful surgery. Many patients who worked before surgery, despite frequent seizures, resumed work. Some patients who returned to work noted an improved level of work function. Seizure control was only one of many factors related to occupational adjustment.

The ESI-55 was sensitive to differences between patients whose surgery rendered them seizure-free and those with continued seizures (40). The 44 patients who became seizure free scored significantly higher than the 55 patients whose seizures continued, with intermediate scores to patients who continued to have mild seizures (without altered consciousness). The implications of these findings include not only prognostic information for patients but also data on the social cost–benefit for this expensive procedure.

CROSS-CULTURAL ADAPTATION

All the currently available scales originated in the United States and the United Kingdom, requiring cross-cultural adaptation before being used elsewhere. Guyatt (68) noted that adaptations to other languages and cultures requires more than a translation of terms and experiences. Less emphasis should be given to the perfection of translation and more focus on the opportunity to improve on the original instrument, or add items that are pertinent to the cultural group. Nonetheless, the luxury of creating an instrument better tailored to the individual country often is subjugated to the need for uniformity of data collection in all participating countries during multinational clinical trials. This is particularly important for epilepsy because of the different cultural perspectives and regulations pertaining to driving, work limitation, access to medical care, special educational and vocational training, and disability status among countries (68).

CONCLUSIONS

Faced with a high probability of seizure recurrence at some time, or of infrequent but never fully controlled seizures (however mild), most adults with epilepsy bear the burden of the diagnosis chronically. Quality of life questionnaires could be useful in epilepsy clinical trials and medical practice, allowing patients to express their concerns about a variety of issues affected by the diagnosis, seizures, and medication. Several newly developed instruments need evaluation over the next few years to determine their suitability for use in clinical trials and in clinical experience.

ACKNOWLEDGMENTS

Helpful comments and supplementary material provided by Drs. Gus Baker, Orrin Devinsky, Ann Jacoby, Barbara Vickrey, and Anita Wagner are greatly appreciated.

REFERENCES

1. National Institutes of Health Consensus Conference, Surgery for Epilepsy. *JAMA* 1990;264:729.
2. Mattson RH, Cramer JA, Collins JF, et al. Comparison of carbamazepine, phenobarbital, phenytoin and primidone in partial and secondarily generalized tonic clonic seizures. *N Engl J Med* 1985;313:145–151.
3. Mattson RH, Cramer JA, Collins JF, and the Department of Veterans Affairs Epilepsy Cooperative Study No. 264 Group. A comparison of valproate with carbamazepine for the treatment of partial seizures and secondarily generalized tonic-clonic seizures in adults. *N Engl J Med* 1992;327:765–771.
4. Beghi E, Tognoni G. Prognosis of epilepsy in newly referred patients: a multicenter prospective study. *Epilepsia* 1988;29:236–243.
5. Chadwick D, for the Medical Research Council Antiepileptic Drug Withdrawal Study Group. Randomized study of antiepileptic drug withdrawal in patients in remission. *Lancet* 1991;337:1175–1180.
6. Berg AT, Shinnar S. Relapse following discontinuation of antiepileptic drugs: a meta-analysis. *Neurology* 1994;44:601–608.
7. Jacoby A. Epilepsy and the quality of everyday life: findings from a study of people with well-controlled epilepsy. *Soc Sci Med* 1992;34:657–666.
8. Cramer JA, Collins JF, Mattson RH. Can categorization of patient background problems be used to determine early termination in a clinical trial? *Controlled Clin Trials* 1988;9:47–63.
9. Hauser WA, Hesdorffer DC. *Epilepsy: frequency, causes, and consequences.* New York: Demos Press, 1990:1–378.
10. Devinsky O, Vickrey BG, Cramer JA, Perrine K, Hermann B, Meador K, Hays RD. Development of the quality of life in epilepsy (QOLIE) inventory. *Epilepsia* 1995 (in press).
11. Wagner AK, Keller SD, Kosinski M, Baker GA, Jacoby A, Hsu MA, Chadwick DW, Ware JE. Advances in methods for assessing the impact of epilepsy and antiepileptic drug therapy on patients' health-related quality of life. *Qual Life Res* 1995;4:115–134.
12. Camfield C, Camfield P, Smith B, Gordon K, Dooley J. Biologic factors as predictors of social outcome of epilepsy in intellectually normal children: a population-based study. *J Pediatr* 1993;122:869–873.
13. Hermann BP, Whitman S. Behavioral and personality correlates of epilepsy: a review, methodological critique, and conceptual model. *Psychol Bull* 1984;95:451–497.
14. Austin JK, Risinger MW, Beckett LA. Correlates of behavior problems in children with epilepsy. *Epilepsia* 1992;33:1115–1122.
15. Freeman JM, Vining EPG, Pillas DJ. *Seizures and epilepsy in childhood: a guide for parents.* Baltimore: John Hopkins University Press, 1990.

16. Cramer JA, Jones EE. Reproductive function in epilepsy. *Epilepsia* 1991;32(suppl 6):S19–26.
17. Krumholz A. Driving and epilepsy: a historical perspective and review of current regulations. *Epilepsia* 1994;35:668–674.
18. American Academy of Neurology, American Epilepsy Society, Epilepsy Foundation of America. Consensus statements, sample statutory provisions, and model regulations regarding driver licensing and epilepsy. *Epilepsia* 1994;35:696–705.
19. Cramer JA. Quality of life for people with epilepsy. In: Devinsky O, ed. *Neurologic clinics: Epilepsy II: Special Issues.* New York: WB Saunders, 1994;12:1–13.
20. Dodrill CB, Batzel LW, Queisser HR, Temkin NR. An objective method for the assessment of psychological and social problems among epileptics. *Epilepsia* 1980;21:123–135.
21. Chaplin JE, Yepez R, Shorvon S, Floyd M. A quantitative approach to measuring the social effects of epilepsy. *Neuroepidemiology* 1990;9:151–158.
22. Collings JA. Psychosocial well-being and epilepsy: an empirical study. *Epilepsia* 1990;31:418–426.
23. Baker GA, Smith DF, Dewey M, Morrow J, Crawford PM, Chadwick DW. The development of a seizure severity scale as an outcome measure in epilepsy. *Epilepsy Res* 1991;8:245–251.
24. Baker GA, Smith DF, Dewey M, Jacoby A, Chadwick DW. The initial development of a health-related quality of life model as an outcome measure in epilepsy. *Epilepsy Res* 1993;16:65–81.
25. Jacoby A, Johnson A, Chadwick DM, on behalf of the Medical Research Council Antiepileptic Drug Withdrawal Group. Psychosocial outcomes of antiepileptic drug discontinuation. *Epilepsia* 1992;33:1123–1131.
26. Hunt S, McKewan J, McKenna SP. *The Nottingham Health Profile: user's manual.* 1981.
27. Bradburn NM. *The structure of psychological well-being.* Chicago: Aldine, 1969.
28. Rosenberg M. *Society and the adolescent self-image.* Princeton, NJ: Princeton University Press, 1965.
29. Pearlin L, Schooler C. The structure of coping. *J Health Soc Behav* 1978;19:2–21.
30. Hyman MD. The stigma of stroke. *Geriatrics* 1971;5:132–141.
31. Smith DF, Baker GA, Dewey M, Jacoby A, Chadwick DW. Seizure frequency, patient-perceived seizure severity and the psychosocial consequences of intractable epilepsy. *Epilepsy Res* 1991;9:231–241.
32. Smith DF, Baker GA, Davies G, et al. Outcomes of add-on treatment with lamotrigine in partial epilepsy. *Epilepsia* 1993;34:312–322.
33. Jacoby A, Baker GA, Smith DF, Dewey M, Chadwick DW. Measuring the impact of epilepsy: the development of a novel scale. *Epilepsy Res* 1993;16:83–88.
34. Baker GA, Jacoby A, Smith DF, Dewey ME, Chadwick DW. The development of a novel scale to assess life fulfillment as part of the further refinement of a quality of life model for epilepsy. *Epilepsia* 1994;35:591–596.
35. Jacoby A. Felt versus enacted stigma: a concept revisited. Evidence from a study of people with epilepsy in remission. *Soc Sci Med* 1994;38:269–274.
36. Scambler G, Hopkins A. Being epileptic: coming to terms with stigma. *Sociol Health Illness* 1986;8:26–43.
37. Kendrick AM, Trimble MR. Patient-perceived quality of life: what is important to the patients with epilepsy? *Seizure* 1992;1(suppl A):1–10.
38. McGuire-Kendrick AM. Quality of life in women with epilepsy. In: Trimble MR, ed. *Women and Epilepsy.* London: Wiley, 1991: 13–30.
39. Kendrick AM, Trimble MR. Repertory grid in the assessment of quality of life in patients with epilepsy: the quality of life assessment schedule. In: Trimble MR, Dodson WE, eds. *Epilepsy and quality of life.* New York: Raven Press, 1994:151–163.
40. Vickrey BG, Hays RD, Graber J, Rausch R, Engel J, Brook RH. A health-related quality of life instrument for patients evaluated for epilepsy surgery. *Med Care* 1992;30:299–319.
41. Hays RD, Sherbourne C, Mazel E,. The RAND 36-item health survey 1.0 *Health Econ* 1993;2:217–227.
42. Ware JE, Sherbourne CD. A 36-item Short Form Health Survey (SF-36). I. Conceptual framework and item selection. *Med Care* 1992;30:473–483.
43. Nelson EC, Landgraf JM, Hays RD, Wasson JH, Kirk JW. The functional status of patients: how can it be measured in physician's offices? *Med Care* 1990;28:1111–1126.
44. Andrews FM, Withey SB. *Social indicators of well-being. Americans' perception of life quality.* New York: Plenum Press, 1976.
45. Perrine K. A new quality of life inventory for epilepsy patients: interim results. *Epilepsia* 1993;34(suppl 4):S28–33.
46. Cramer JA, Smith DB, Mattson RH, Delgado-Escueta AV, and the VA Epilepsy Cooperative Study #118 Group. A method of quantification for the evaluation of antiepileptic drug therapy. *Neurology* 1983; 33(suppl 1):26–37.
47. Perrine K, Devinsky O, Meador KJ, Hermann BP, Cramer JA, Hays RD, Vickrey BG. The relationship of neuropsychological functioning to quality of life in epilepsy. *Arch Neurol* 1995 (in press).
48. Hays RD, Vickrey BG, Hermann B, Cramer JA, Spritzer K, Perrine K, Meador K, Devinsky O. Agreement between self- and proxy-reports of health-related quality of life in epilepsy patients. *Qual Life Res* 1995;4:159–168.
49. Stewart AL, Greenfield S, Hays RD, et al. Functional status and well-being of patients with chronic conditions: results from the Medical Outcomes Study. *JAMA* 1989;262:907–911.
50. Ware JE, Johnston SA, Davies-Avery A, Brook R. *Conceptualization and measurement of health for adults in the Health Insurance Study, Vol III: Mental health.* Publication No. R-1987/3-HEW. Santa Monica, CA: RAND, 1979.
51. Wagner AK, Bungay KM, Bromfield EB, Ehrenberg BL. Health-related quality of life of adult persons with epilepsy as compared with health-related quality of life of well persons. *Epilepsia* 1993;34(suppl 6):5.
52. Thalji L, Haggerty CC, Rubin R, Berckmans TR, Parker BL. *1990 National survey of functional health status: final report.* Chicago: National Opinion Research Center, 1991.
53. Wagner AK, Bungay KM, Bromfield E, Ehrenberg BL. Relationship of health-related quality of life to seizure control and antiepileptic drug side effects. *Epilepsia* 1994;35(Suppl 8):56.
54. Vickrey BG, Hays RD, Rausch R, Sutherling WW, Engel JP, Brook RH. Quality of life of epilepsy surgery patients as compared to outpatients with hypertension, diabetes, heart disease, and/or depressive symptoms. *Epilepsia* 1994;35:597–607.
55. Tarlov AR, Ware JE, Greenfield S, et al. The Medical Outcomes Study: an application of methods for monitoring the results of medical care. *JAMA* 1989;262:925–930.
56. Aschenbach TM, Edelbrock C. *Manual for the child behavior checklist and revised child behavior profile.* Burlington, VT: University of Vermont Department of Psychiatry, 1983.
57. McCubben HI, Thompson AI, eds. *Family assessment inventories for research and practice.* Family stress coping and health project. Madison: University of Wisconsin, 1987.
58. Austin JK, Smith MS, Risinger MW, McNelis AM. Childhood epilepsy and asthma: comparison of quality of life. *Epilepsia* 1994;35:608–615.
59. Piers EV. *Piers–Harris Children's Self-Concept Scale.* Revised manual. Los Angeles: Western Psychological Services, 1984.
60. Austin JK, Huberty TJ. Development of the Child Attitude Toward Illness Scale. *J Pediatr Psychol* 1993;18:467–480.
61. Austin JK, Huberty TJ. Revision of the family APGAR for use with 8-year-olds. *Fam Syst Med* 1989;7:323–327.
62. Hermann BP. Quality of life in epilepsy. *J Epilepsy* 1981;5:153–165.
63. Juniper EF, Guyatt GH, Willan A, Griffith LE. Determining a minimal important change in a disease-specific quality of life questionnaire. *J Clin Epidemiol* 1994;47:81–87.
64. Cramer JA. Compliance and quality of life. In: MR Trimble, WE Dodson, eds. *Epilepsy and quality of life.* New York: Raven Press, 1994:49–63.
65. Mattson RH, Prevey ML, Cramer JA, Novelly RA, Swick CT. Lifestyle changes in epilepsy patients following treatment with valproate. *Proc R Soc Med Symp Ser* 1989;152:275–280.
66. Prevey ML, Mattson RH, Cramer JA. Improvement in cognitive functioning and mood state after conversion to valproate monotherapy. *Neurology* 1989;39:1640–1641.
67. Augustine EA, Novelly RA, Mattson RH, Glaser GH, Williamson PD, Spencer DD, Spencer SS. Occupational adjustment following neurosurgical treatment of epilepsy. *Ann Neurol* 1984;15:68–72.
68. Guyatt GH. The philosophy of health-related quality of life translation. *Qual Life Res* 1994;2:461–465.

Quality of Life and Pharmacoeconomics in Clinical Trials, Second Edition, edited by B. Spilker.
Lippincott-Raven Publishers, Philadelphia © 1996.

CHAPTER 95

Severe Mental Illness in the Community

Anthony F. Lehman and Barbara J. Burns

INTRODUCTION

Within the field of psychiatric research, the principal focus of quality of life (QOL) assessment has been on the severely mentally ill, persons suffering from such long-term and disabling illnesses as schizophrenia, chronic depression, manic-depressive illness, and severe personality disorders. The reason for this focus lies in the pervasive effects that these psychiatric disorders can have on individuals' lives, limiting their range of life experiences, and perhaps rendering general population measures of quality of life insensitive to the issues faced by this disabled population. Conversely, for persons with nondisabling mental health problems, such as short-term depression and anxiety reactions, instruments available to assess quality of life in the general population are probably adequate. These are not addressed in this chapter. Therefore, the chapter summarizes measures available to assess the quality of life of persons with severe mental illnesses.

Further explanation of the predominant disease model for these disorders will clarify the reason that quality of life assessments may be of particular relevance in this population. Although the pathophysiologies of these various disorders are not yet well understood and undoubtedly differ from each other, all are currently conceptualized in terms of a "stress-vulnerability" model (1). That is, persons so afflicted have a biological vulnerability to developing characteristic symptoms of the disease (e.g., hallucinations and delusions in schizophrenia; anhedonia, suicidal ideation, dysphoria in depression; hyperactivity, flight of ideas, hypersexuality in mania), and stress tends to activate this vulnerability to produce symptoms. This conceptualization has led researchers to take interest in the patient's psychological and social contexts as sources of stress. Quality of life indicators of social well-being (functioning and environmental resources) and psychological well-being (life satisfaction, self-esteem, morale) may therefore capture important aspects of the person's life that relate to stress and in turn to illness course and outcome.

AVAILABLE TESTS

This section summarizes the characteristics of seven available measures for assessing quality of life in the severely mentally ill. For each instrument the following information is provided: name of instrument, key reference(s), original purpose, patients studied, type of instrument, number of items, length of administration, summary content, psychometric properties, method of data analysis, and availability of comparative data.

A. F. Lehman: Department of Psychiatry, University of Maryland, Baltimore, Maryland 21201.
B. J. Burns: Department of Psychiatry, Duke University, Durham, North Carolina 27701.

Satisfaction with Life Domains Scale

Key reference: Baker and Intagliata (1982) (2)

Purpose: To evaluate the impact of the community support program in New York State on the quality of life of chronically mentally ill patients

Patients studied: Chronically mentally ill outpatients, age 18–86, in two community support programs, N = 118

Type of instrument: Self-report scale administered by interview

Number of items: 15

Length of administration: "brief," probably less than 10 minutes

Summary of content:

A. *Physical functioning:* None

B. *Social functioning:* None

C. *Economic functioning:* None

D. *Psychological functioning:* Individual items—Satisfaction with housing, neighborhood, food to eat, clothing, health, people lived with, friends, family, relations with other people, work/day programming, spare time, fun, services and facilities in area, economic situation, place lived in now compared to state hospital, total life satisfaction score

Psychometric properties: Total score correlates 0.64 with Bradburn Affect Balance Scale (3); total score correlates 0.29 with Global Assessment Scale (4)

Data analysis: Data are reported as item score frequencies and means (7-interval scale)

Comparative data: The frequencies and means on these items can be compared with item scores in a national QOL survey of the general population (5)

Oregon Quality of Life Questionnaire

Key reference: Bigelow et al. (1982, 1991) (6,7)

Purpose: To assess quality of life outcomes for evaluating community mental health service delivery

Patients studied:

A. Sample of patients at intake to community mental health programs in Oregon, N = 874 (includes chronically mentally ill, drug abusers, alcoholics, and general psychiatric patients)

B. Sample of community mental health program patients at follow-up (later in treatment), N = 380

C. Nonpatient community sample, N = 100

Type of instrument: Self-report questionnaire and semistructured interview versions

Number of items: 263 (self-report version); 146 (semistructured interview version)

Length of administration: 45 minutes

Summary of content:

A. *Physical functioning:* Meaningful use of leisure time

B. *Economic functioning:* Work at home, employability, work on the job, school

C. *Social functioning:* Independence, friend role, close friend role, spouse role, parent role, social support

D. *Psychological functioning:* Psychological distress, well-being, tolerance of stress

E. *Other:* Negative consequences—alcohol

Negative consequences—drugs

Psychometric properties:

Internal consistency reliability: 0.17–0.89 (median = 0.65)

Discriminant validity: differences detected as predicted across the three samples studied

Test–retest reliabilities (interval not specified): 0.37–0.64 (median = 0.50)

Sensitivity: Detected treatment effects of service system changes across time and sites

Data analysis: Analyses of variance comparing three cohorts.

Comparative data: Available on the three cohorts studied

Standardized Social Schedule

Key reference: Clare and Cairns (1978) (8)

Purpose: To assess the nature and extent of social maladjustment and dysfunction in chronic neurotic patients attending their family doctors.

Patients studied:

A. Nonpsychiatric patients with "adverse" social circumstances, N = 48

B. Chronic neurotic outpatients, N = 221

C. Women with premenstrual complaints, N = 104

Type of interview: Semistructured interview with patient (and key informant, if available) by trained interviewer; ratings by interviewer and subject

Number of items: Varies from 17 to 48, depending on version

Length of administration: Not given

Summary of content: Scales include material conditions, social management, satisfaction and housing, occupation/social role, economical, leisure/social activities, family and domestic relations, marital

A. *Physical functioning:* Extent of leisure activities

B. *Economic functioning:* Housing conditions, occupational stability, family income

C. *Social functioning:* Household care; housekeeping, quality of relations with workmates, neighbors and family; marital relationship quality; extent of social activities

D. *Psychological functioning:* Satisfaction with housing, work, income, leisure, social relationships, family relationships, parental role, marriage

E. *Other:* Residential stability; opportunities for leisure and social activities, interaction with neighbors, interactions with relatives

Psychometric properties: Interrater K_W on items range from 0.55 to 0.94 (median = 0.76); factor structure *not* stable across populations; differentiated as predicted across populations studied

Data analysis: Data presented mainly as frequencies of persons scoring in the maladaptive range on various items across populations

Comparative data: Compared three populations studied according to percent of each group functioning in the maladaptive range

Comment: Emphasizes "maladaptation"

Quality of Life Scale

Key reference: Heinrichs et al. (1984) (9)

Purpose: To assess deficit syndrome in patients with schizophrenia

Patients studied: Outpatients with schizophrenia, N = 111 (described as not applicable to inpatients)

Type of instrument: Semistructured interview by trained clinician

Number of items: 21

Length of administration: 45 minutes

Summary of content: Scale scoring—Intrapsychic Foundations, Interpersonal Relations, Instrumental Role, Total Score
  A. *Physical functioning:* Commonplace activities
  B. *Economic functioning:* Occupational role, work functioning, work level, possession of commonplace objects
  C. *Social functioning:* Interpersonal relations (household, friends, acquaintances, social activity, social network, social initiative, social withdrawal, sociosexual functioning)
  D. *Psychological functioning:* Sense of purpose, motivation, curiosity, anhedonia, aimless inactivity, empathy, emotional interaction, work satisfaction

Psychometric properties: Interrater reliabilities on conjointly conducted interviews range from 0.84 to 0.97 on summary scales; individual item intraclass correlations range from 0.5 to 0.9; confirmatory factor analysis conducted; validity not assessed

Comparative data: None

Data analysis: Reports mean scores for individual items

Quality of Life Interview

Key references: Lehman et al. (1982, 1986), Lehman (1988) (10–12)

Purpose: To assess QOL of persons with severe mental illness living in board and care homes, hospital, and other supervised settings

Patients studied:
  A. Severely mentally ill in Los Angeles board and care homes (N = 278)
  B. Inpatients of a state mental hospital (N = 99)
  C. Severely mentally ill in supervised community residences (N = 92)

Type of instrument: Structured interview by trained lay interviewers

Number of items: 143

Length of administration: 45 minutes

Summary of content:
  A. *Physical functioning:* Number of leisure activities
  B. *Economic functioning:* Current employment status, total monthly financial support, monthly spending money
  C. *Social functioning:* Frequency of family contacts, frequency of social contacts, frequency of religious activities, legal problems and victimization
  D. *Psychological functioning:* General perceived health status, general life satisfaction, satisfaction with living situation, family relations, social relations, leisure, work, religious activities, finances, safety, and health
  E. *Other:* Medical and psychiatric care during the past year

Psychometric properties: Internal consistency reliabilities range: life satisfaction scales: 0.79–0.88 (median = 0.85); objective quality of life scales: 0.44–0.82 (median = 0.68); reliabilities replicated on two severely mentally ill populations

Test–retest reliabilities (1 week): life satisfaction scales: 0.41–0.95 (median = 0.72); objective quality of life scales: 0.29–0.98 (median = 0.65)

Construct and predictive validity assessed as good by confirmatory factor analysis and multivariate model prediction

Data analysis: Between group comparisons (inpatient vs. outpatient; severely mentally ill vs. general population and disadvantaged subgroups in the general population); multivariate predictive model of general well-being

Comparative data: General population norms on life satisfaction (5); norms for inpatient vs. outpatient severely mentally ill

Quality of Life Self-Assessment Inventory

Key reference: Skantze (1993) (13)

Purpose: To provide information about which aspects of quality of life are particularly important to patients and natural raters to assist in therapeutic planning

Patients studied: Outpatients with chronic schizophrenia, N = 66

Type of instrument: Self-report inventory completed by patient, followed by a semistructured interview with a clinician to confirm patient's ratings of satisfaction and dissatisfaction and to discuss implications for treatment planning

Number of items: 100

Length of administration: 10 minutes for patient to complete self-rated inventory, plus 40–50 minutes for semistructured interview

Summary of content: Scoring: For all areas, ratings are "satisfactory" or "unsatisfactory"

  A. *Physical functioning:* Physical health
  B. *Economic functioning:* Finances
  C. *Social functioning:* Household and self-care, contacts, dependence, work, and leisure
  D. *Psychological functioning:* Knowledge and education, inner experiences, mental health
  E. *Other:* Housing, housing environment, community services, religion

Psychometric properties: 7- to 10-day test–retest correlation for overall scale = 0.88

Data analysis: Scores computed for 14 domain scales listed above plus overall scale

Comparative data: Comparative data from university students

Community Adjustment Form

Key reference: Stein and Test (1980) (14)

Purpose: To assess life satisfaction and other quality of life outcomes in a randomized study of an experimental system of community-based care for the severely mentally ill versus standard care

Patients studied: Patients seeking admission to a state hospital (50% schizophrenia), N = 130

Type of instrument: Semistructured self-report interview; type of interviewer not specified (probably nonclinical)

Number of items: 140 (approximate)

Length of administration: Not indicated (estimate 45 minutes)

Summary of content:

  A. *Physical functioning:* Leisure activity scale (same as Lehman Quality of Life Interview)
  B. *Economic functioning:* Quality of living situation; employment history and status; income sources and amounts; free lodging and/or meals
  C. *Social functioning:* Contact with friends, family contact, legal problems
  D. *Psychological:* 21-item life satisfaction scale, self-esteem scale
  E. *Other:* Medical care, agency utilization

Psychometric properties: None reported

Data analysis: Repeated measures comparing two treatment groups; most scales appear sensitive to differentiate the two treatment groups over time

Comparative data: Results replicated in Australian study (15) (except for no between-group differences found in life satisfaction in the Australian study)

Lancaster Quality of Life Profile

Key reference: Oliver (1991–1992) (16)

Purpose: To assess the impact of community care programs serving persons with severe mental illnesses under mandate from the British government

Patients studied: Patients with chronic mental illness in a variety of community settings in the United Kingdom and in Colorado

Type of instrument: Structured interview by trained lay interviewer

Number of items: 100

Length of administration: 1 hour

Summary of content:

  A. *Physical functioning:* Health
  B. *Economic functioning:* Finances
  C. *Social functioning:* Work/education, leisure/participation, social relations, family relations
  D. *Psychological:* Satisfaction with—work/education, leisure/participation, religion, finances, living situation, legal and safety, family relations, social relations, and health
  E. *Other:* Living situation, legal and safety, religion

Psychometric properties: Test–retest reliabilities for life satisfaction scales range from 0.49 to 0.78; internal consistency reliabilities for these scales range from 0.84 to 0.86. Content, construct, and criterion validities assessed as adequate

Comparative data: Results reported on samples from the United Kingdom and Colorado; many of the scales are derived from the Lehman Quality of Life Interview (see above)

CHOOSING A MEASURE

The choice of a measure must rest with the investigator's particular purpose and needs. Several of the measures presented provide comprehensive assessments of quality of life and have been reasonably well assessed from a psychometric standpoint. These include the Oregon Quality of Life Questionnaire, the Lehman Quality of Life Interview, the Heinrichs–Carpenter Quality of Life Scale, the Lancaster Quality of Life Profile, and the Quality of Life Self-Assessment Inventory. All cover similar domains of quality of life functioning and have acceptable psychometric properties. They have been used with typical samples of severely mentally ill patients in the United States or Europe, which included high percentages of psychotic patients. These instruments require approximately 45–60 min to administer. Our experience has been that most investigators either do not want to devote this length of time to quality of life assessment or want to include other items not contained in these instruments. Therefore many probably administer subsections of these longer instruments, supplemented by additional items from other sources. If this approach is taken, we strongly recommend that at least the original subscales be kept intact. The major argument for using the complete instruments is that each was developed with a comprehensive quality of life model in mind.

Some general comments and caveats are warranted for the investigator seeking a quality of life measure for the severely mentally ill, whether one of those described above or some other. First, a major problem with using normative quality of life measures in this population is that floor effects are frequently encountered in social and economic functioning. Therefore, for these two areas of quality of life functioning, special attention must be paid to instrument sensitivity. Such floor effects are not typically a problem with the severely mentally ill in the quality of life areas of physical functioning and psychological functioning (life satisfaction). Second, significant numbers of these patients have problems with task perseverance and comprehension. Therefore, pencil-and-paper questionnaires are generally not advised. Note that all the instruments discussed here use face-to-face interviews. Finally, psychopathology affects patients' ratings of their quality of life. In the only study of this phenomenon, anxiety and depression had significant effects on patients' perceived life satisfaction (17). Therefore, quality of life assessments of these patients should be accompanied by a concomitant assessment of psychopathologic symptoms to reduce the confounding effects of psychiatric syndromes on quality of life assessments.

USING A MEASURE

There are essentially three situations in which investigators have used a quality of life measure in studies of the severely mentally ill: (a) to assess patients' current quality of life to establish a baseline or to compare samples cross-sectionally; (b) to monitor the mediating effects of changes in quality of life on core clinical outcomes, for example, symptom levels and relapse; and (c) to assess quality of life as a primary longitudinal outcome of research interventions. To our knowledge there have been no studies of the utility of quality of life assessments for prescribing interventions, although the Quality of Life Self-Assessment Inventory (QLS-100) is used clinically for this purpose.

STATISTICAL CONSIDERATIONS

The types of statistical analyses used for each of the measures included in this chapter have been briefly summarized in the sections above. For the most part, the data have been analyzed to detect between-group differences, using standard univariate or multivariate techniques. Typically, data are reported as scale scores or item means or frequencies. All these measures generate multiple quality of life indicators, which increases the risk of type I errors in analyses due to multiple comparisons. Such potential errors should be taken into account using such techniques as multivariate analysis of variance for multiple dependent variables or Bonferroni's correction.

DATA INTERPRETATION AND EXTRAPOLATION

Because of the newness of this field in psychiatric research, it is not possible to make specific recommendations about the interpretation of quality of life data. Conceptually,

quality of life is seen as related to, but distinct from such clinical syndromes as depression and anxiety. Perhaps, the most important point about interpretation that can be made at present is the need to distinguish psychological quality of life, for example, life satisfaction or morale, from clinical symptomatology, particularly depression. We know that measures of psychological quality of life functioning are clearly affected by clinical symptomatology (17). However, at least conceptually, life satisfaction and its quality of life equivalents are to be distinguished from clinical syndromes. This distinction has particular relevance with regard to implications for interventions. That is, one might attempt to effect various changes in a patient's environment to improve housing, financial, or work dissatisfaction, whereas one might prescribe a clinical intervention, such as an antidepressant, to alleviate symptoms of depression. Certainly we can foresee the development of an interactive model between quality of life and clinical symptomatology, but at the very least we can say that to interpret quality of life data adequately from psychiatrically impaired populations, one needs to assess both quality of life and clinical syndromes.

For some of the measures described above, there are published norms for different samples of patients, thus allowing some comparisons of new patient samples with these samples. For the life satisfaction measures in the Lehman Quality of Life Interview and Satisfaction with Life Domains Scale, there are also national normative data because these measures were based heavily upon prior work assessing general quality of life in the United States (5).

AREAS FOR FUTURE IMPROVEMENT

In order to advance quality of life assessment for severely mentally ill persons to the point that more scientifically and clinically meaningful applications can be achieved, there are several areas of needed work. First, for each potential use of a quality of life measure, care must be taken to be clear that the constructs measured by the instrument reflect those variables of interest in a particular study. The existing literature is characterized by conceptually clear but disparate models of quality of life as well as by overly broad and vague definitions of the phrase "quality of life." Definitions include life satisfaction, illness-related "deficit states," multidimensional models of well-being, and ill-defined notions that are appealing but vague. A commonly agreed upon definition of quality of life seems desirable, but may not be practical, given its multiple intents. Second, there needs to be some agreement about how to measure quality of life. This will allow us to begin to accumulate comparable data across studies and populations. Third, we need to compare quality of life data from psychiatrically impaired populations with those from other nonpsychiatric groups, particularly the physically disabled and the general population to establish some normative perspective. Fourth, we need a better understanding about how quality of life varies naturally over time in psychiatric populations, the predictive validity of quality of life measures for subsequent illness course and outcome, and the sensitivity of quality of life measures for detecting treatment effects among these patients, who may at best experience very modest improvements. Finally there is a need for basic conceptual work to develop better models for integrating quality of life data into a general model of outcome for persons with severe mental illnesses.

CONCLUSIONS

The eventual role that quality of life assessment will play in the development and evaluation of policies and programs for the severely mentally ill remains to be seen. The concept of quality of life, both in planning and evaluation, fits current trends in thinking about the needs of these patients. Instruments, including those presented here, now exist to evaluate their quality of life, although we may expect continued evolution of these measures as more mental health evaluators attempt to assess quality of life. At this juncture, some form of quality of life assessments are being employed in several longitudinal studies of treatment services for the severely mentally ill. As these studies reach fruition, we will have a better idea of the value of quality of life assessments in planning for our severely mentally ill citizens.

REFERENCES

1. Spring B, Zubin J. Vulnerability to schizophrenic episodes and their prevention in adults. In: Albee GW, Joffe JM, eds. *Primary prevention in psycho-pathology: the issues.* Hanover, NH: University Press of New England, 1977:254–284.
2. Baker F, Intagliata J. Quality of life in the evaluation of community support systems. *Eval Program Plann* 1982;5:69–79.
3. Bradburn NM. *The structure of psychological well-being.* Chicago, Aldine, 1969.
4. Endicott J, Spitzer R, Fleiss J, Cohen J. The global assessment scale: a procedure for measuring overall severity of psychiatric disturbance. *Arch Gen Psychiatry* 1976;33:766–771.
5. Andrews FM, Withey SB. *Social indicators of well-being.* New York: Plenum Press, 1976.
6. Bigelow DA, Brodsky G, Steward L, Olson M. The concept and measurement of quality of life as a dependent variable in evaluation of mental health services. In: Stahler GJ, Tash WR, eds. *Innovative approaches to mental health evaluation.* San Diego: Academic Press, 1982:345–366.
7. Bigelow DA, McFarland BH, Olson MM. Quality of life of community mental health clients: validating a measure. *Community Ment Health J* 1991;27:125–133.
8. Clare AW, Cairns VE. Design, development and use of a standardized interview to assess social maladjustment and dysfunction in community samples. *Psychol Med* 1978;8:589–604.
9. Heinrichs DW, Hanlon TE, Carpenter WT. The quality of life scale: an instrument for rating the schizophrenic deficit syndrome. *Schizophren Bull* 1984;10:388–398.
10. Lehman AF, Ward NC, Linn LS. Chronic mental patients: the quality of life issue. *Am J Psychiatry* 1982;10:1271–1276.
11. Lehman AF, Possidente S, Hawker F. The quality of life of chronic mental patients in a state hospital and community residences. *Hosp Community Psychiatry* 1986;37:901–907.
12. Lehman AF. A quality of life interview for the chronically mentally ill. *Eval Program Plann* 1988;11:51–62.
13. Skantze K. *Defining subjective quality of life goals in schizophrenia: the Quality of Life Self-Assessment Inventory, QLS-100, a new approach to successful alliance and service development.* Goteborg, Sweden: Department of Psychiatry, Sahlgrenska Hospital, University of Gothenburg, 1993.
14. Stein LI, Test MA. Alternative to mental hospital treatment. I. Conceptual model, treatment program and clinical evaluation. *Arch Gen Psychiatry* 1980;37:392–397.
15. Hoult J, Reynolds J. Schizophrenia: a comparative trial of community oriented and hospital oriented psychiatric care. *Acta Psychiatr Scand* 1984;69:359–372.
16. Oliver JPJ. The social aftercare directive: development of a quality of life profile for use in community services for the mentally ill. *Social Work Social Sci Rev* 1991–1992;3:4–45.
17. Lehman AF. The effects of psychiatric symptoms on quality of life assessments among the chronic mentally ill. *Eval Program Plann* 1983;6:143–151.
18. Lehman AF. The well-being of chronic mental patients: assessing their quality of life. *Arch Gen Psychiatry* 1983;40:369–373.

Quality of Life and Pharmacoeconomics in Clinical Trials, Second Edition, edited by B. Spilker.
Lippincott-Raven Publishers, Philadelphia © 1996.

CHAPTER 96

Inflammatory Bowel Disease

Douglas A. Drossman

INTRODUCTION

The term *inflammatory bowel disease* describes two common medical disorders afflicting up to 500,000 persons in this country. Ulcerative colitis, a disease of the colon, presents with rectal bleeding, diarrhea, and pain. Crohn's disease can affect most of the gastrointestinal tract and presents with abdominal pain, diarrhea, vomiting, fever, infection, and weight loss with nutritional disturbances. The health care costs for inflammatory bowel disease patients are considerable: more is spent for the inpatient care of a patient with inflammatory bowel disease than for gallbladder surgery, appendectomy, or peptic ulcer disease (1).

There is growing scientific recognition in gastroenterology that biological data are insufficient to explain a patient's health status, and additional information relating to quality of life and psychosocial factors must be obtained to better understand and care for patients with these disorders (2,3). This is particularly true for inflammatory bowel disease, as research and treatment must be directed toward helping patients psychosocially adapt to a chronic, unpredictable disorder with varying degrees of clinical impairment.

Traditionally, the evaluation and treatment of inflammatory bowel disease have been based on the degree of disease activity and its complications. These are relatively crude measures of health status, because most patients—even with mild disease activity—may experience major effects on their quality of life. Existing measures of disease activity are not sensitive enough to assess the full impact of the disorder; standardized assessments of health-related quality of life (HRQL) are being developed to improve our ability to gather these data and implement more effective treatment. This chapter discusses some of the unique features related to studying HRQL in IBD and reviews existing studies on HRQL with this patient population.

FEATURES UNIQUE TO HRQL RESEARCH IN IBD

IBD Is a Heterogeneous Condition

Traditionally, ulcerative colitis and Crohn's disease have been studied together, yet these are different medical conditions that may require separate evaluation of HRQL. For example, Crohn's disease consists of three anatomic subgroups: ileitis, involving the small intestine; colitis, involving the large intestine; and ileocolitis. Patients within each group behave differently in terms of clinical presentation, symptom characteristics, complications, morbidity, and psychological impact. Patients with Crohn's colitis are likely to be troubled with diarrhea and bleeding, those with ileitis experience postprandial abdominal pain, and those with ileo-

D. A. Drossman: Department of Medicine and Psychiatry, Division of Digestive Diseases, University of North Carolina, Chapel Hill, North Carolina 27599.

colitis are also more likely to have fistulous disease of the perianal area. Similarly, patients with ulcerative colitis experience variable effects from the disease, depending on the anatomic extent of the disease and its severity, from rectal urgency to diarrhea and bleeding. Patients with ulcerative colitis also tend to have better HRQL than do patients with Crohn's disease, possibly related to less severe disease severity (3) and the fact that this condition can be "cured" by colectomy.

An additional problem is that indices of disease activity have been developed using patient groups with more severe disease activity. Therefore, the measures of inflammation or disease complications (e.g., degree of bleeding, or an abdominal mass), which contribute to the scoring systems derived from referral centers, may not apply to patients in other settings with lesser degrees of inflammation ("ceiling" effect). Furthermore, subgroups of patients with inflammatory bowel disease have certain complications (e.g., perianal fistulas) not factored into the original indices but that still have considerable physical and psychosocial impact. Only recently has a separate index been developed for patients with perianal disease, and it was confirmed that the Crohn's Disease Activity Index (CDAI) was not sufficient to assess health status in this population (4).

These examples highlight the limitations of using "standard" disease activity or HRQL measures in a population with marked clinical heterogeneity. Further studies of sufficient numbers of patients with different clinical conditions are needed for an adequate determination of the type and degree of impairments that are unique for each subpopulation of IBD.

Disease Activity Assessment Is Insufficient to Assess HRQL

The traditional method for evaluating IBD has been through clinical parameters, including symptoms, and findings in the physical examination, blood studies, x-rays, and, most recently, endoscopy. Primarily for research purposes, these assessment tools have led to the development of quantitative indices of disease activity (2). While it may be assumed that these measures correlate with HRQL, this is not always true. The indices reviewed here were designed to quantify the biological activity of the disease or the physician's assessment of this activity. While some include symptoms, little attention was paid in their development to global health perceptions or physical and psychosocial function.

Crohn's Disease

The most commonly used index of disease activity is the CDAI, developed by Best et al. (5) in 1976. This index was used in the National Cooperative Crohn's Disease Study to provide both a uniform set of clinical parameters for evaluation and as a quantitative measure of treatment effect in response to prednisone or sulfasalazine. Regression analysis of 18 variables from 1,897 visits of 112 patients yielded eight weighted variables (abdominal pain, bowel habits, general well-being, use of antidiarrheal agents, complications, wasting, abdominal mass, and hemoglobin) that correlated with the physician's subjective impression of disease activity based on a four-point Likert scale (very well, fair to good, poor, very poor). The index correlated with the physician's opinion (r = .7), but a relation between the patient's global sense of well-being and the index was not assessed.

Other investigators have modified the CDAI or used different variables to assess disease activity. The Harvey–Bradshaw Index (6) was designed to simplify the CDAI for clinical use. Using five clinical features (abdominal pain, bowel habits, well-being, complications, and abdominal mass), these authors prospectively compared their index with the CDAI in 112 patients and found that the Harvey–Bradshaw Index correlated very highly (r = .93) with the CDAI.

In 1984, as part of the International Organization for the Study of Inflammatory Bowel Disease, Myren et al. (7) formulated a ten-item binary (present or absent) scoring system. To provide more flexibility in scoring, Wright et al. (8) developed a similar index, but scored items 0 to 3 (absent to severe). In the belief that subjective complaints are unreliable, Van Hees et al. (9) used the physical examination and laboratory studies to create a more "objective" index of activity. The index correlated well (r = .95) with the physician's assessment, but not as well with the CDAI (r = .67), which also included the patient's subjective symptoms. By contrast, Sandler et al. (10) identified three subjective symptoms not requiring physician assessment (stool frequency, abdominal pain, and sense of well-being) that correlated well (r = .87) with the CDAI, and this permitted the assessment of disease activity through survey methods.

Ulcerative Colitis

The first attempts to assess disease activity in ulcerative colitis began with the initial description in 1912 of the radiological characteristics of ulcerative colitis using barium enema examination. Physicians were then able to consider the anatomic extent of the condition as well as the degree of inflammation by sigmoidoscopy. The first classification system for ulcerative colitis was described in 1954 by Truelove and Witts (11). These investigators characterized mild, moderate, or severe disease activity on the basis of equal weighting of six factors: diarrhea, fever, tachycardia, anemia, erythrocyte sedimentation rate (ESR), and physical examination. This disease activity measure has been widely used in ulcerative colitis research because it is easy to use and accurately portrays the physician's clinical assessment of activity. Some problems with this scale (12) include its limited sensitivity by recognizing only three degrees of severity (mild, moderate, severe), and the fact that patients don't always fit into one of the assigned categories. While the scale reflects clinicians' opinions of disease activity, it does not predict expected short-term prognosis in response to treatment or the need for surgery (13). The Truelove and Witts index, or a slightly modified version (14), are the most widely used indices of disease activity for ulcerative colitis.

All these indices were derived directly or indirectly from biological measures, a few symptoms, or the physician's impression of disease activity, rather than from the patient's perception of illness. In fact, efforts were made to reduce subjective data, as they were considered less reliable than "objective" findings. But not surprisingly, we know that clinicians rely heavily on patients' subjective reports to make "objective" diagnostic decisions and plan treatment. Therefore, it would be logical to develop (HRQL) measures to capture the patient's experience of the illness for clinical assessment and to determine treatment effect, and none of these measures can fulfill that task.

Methodological Concerns

The variation in illness severity between ambulatory clinics and referral centers (15), and the fact that clinical subgroups of IBD have different symptom patterns, make it unlikely that a representative IBD population can be acquired for standardization of a single HRQL measure (16). Furthermore, previous studies to evaluate HRQL in IBD have been methodologically limited because (a) healthy or medical comparison groups were not used, (b) studies were done by retrospective analyses, (c) nonstandardized instruments and unskilled interviewers were used to obtain the data, and (d) insensitive outcome factors (e.g., ability to work) were used as measures of HRQL. Only during the past few years has appropriate attention been paid to the development of standardized instruments. What follows is a summary of the development of instruments and findings related to HRQL in IBD.

ASSESSMENT OF QUALITY OF LIFE IN INFLAMMATORY BOWEL DISEASE

Early Retrospective Studies Using Nonstandardized Measures

The earliest quality of life assessments in inflammatory bowel disease were designed to only a portion of studies describing prognosis or to evaluate surgical outcome. Generally, the authors used global assessments rather than standardized scales (Table 1). For example, Bergman and Krause (17) examined the clinical course of 186 Crohn's disease patients treated between 1956 and 1968 and rated patients' general health or quality of life as I (good general health), II (reduced ability to work), or III (unable to work). After 10 years' observation, 87% of patients (no comparison group) were rated as quality of life I, 9% quality of life II, and 4% quality of life III. It was concluded that Crohn's disease

patients had a good quality of life outcome. Gazzard et al. (18) interviewed 85 outpatients with Crohn's disease and administered the Eysenck Personality Inventory (EPI) and a questionnaire about knowledge of disease, work status, marriage and sexual life, financial problems, and worries. They found that most patients live useful optimistic lives and that the patient's premorbid personality is the most important determinant of one's health prospects. Hendriksen and Binder (19) interviewed 122 patients with ulcerative colitis to obtain data on their family, as well as their social, emotional, and professional lives, and concluded that ulcerative colitis patients adapted well to their condition and suffered few social or professional disabilities (as measured by marital status, the frequency of family or sexual problems, leisure activities, physical and earning capacity, the incidence of mental disorders, and the intake of alcohol and other drugs). Sorensen et al. (20) interviewed 106 patients with Crohn's disease regarding family, social, and professional conditions and found that patients reported little effect on family/social problems or physical activity, but that exacerbations of the disease strained personal/professional relations. An equal percentage of patients and controls were married and had children, and there were no differences in social and physical activity. Crohn's disease patients had a slightly higher socioeconomic level, and 65% were employed (versus 64% of controls). Only 3% of Crohn's disease patients were on disability, and both patients and controls had less than 11 sick days annually. Finally, Meyers et al. (21) used a psychosocial survey to assess interpersonal relations, school/job performance, recreational activity, sexuality, and body image in 51 patients 5 to 10 years after their first elective surgery for Crohn's disease. Following surgery, patients noted long-term improvement in the five psychosocial areas as well as physical symptoms and perceived the operation as having provided long-term improvement in their quality of life.

In recent years, investigators have begun to address quality of life issues in ulcerative colitis and Crohn's disease by applying existing standardized measures or developing new ones specific for these disorders. Both general and disease-specific measures of quality of life yield important information.

"Global" Measure

The simplest measure of HRQL employs a "global" question in which the patient incorporates the multiple domains of HRQL in a single response. The CDAI used diary cards to assess general well-being ("generally well, slightly below par, poor, very poor, terrible") (5). Although this item was scored by physicians, Sandler et al. (10) showed that, along with stool frequency and abdominal pain, the self-assessment of general well-being correlated highly with the CDAI itself.

In a national survey of persons with IBD belonging to the Crohn's and Colitis Foundation of America (CCFA)

TABLE 1. *Quality of life assessment in inflammatory bowel disease: retrospective data*

Study/disease	No. of patients entered	Quality of life measure	Results and comments
Bergman and Krause, CD (17)	186	Quality of life 10.5 yr after surgery I. Good health II. Reduced ability to work III. Unable to work	I. 87% II. 9.1% III. 3.6%
Gazzard et al., CD (18)	85	Morbid Anxiety Index (MAI) Eysenck Personality Questionnaire (EPQ) Questionnaire including knowledge of disease, work record, married and sexual life, financial problems Disease activity (clinical and biochemical features)	1. Males tended to be more introverted/neurotic. 2. 74 pts felt well or perfectly well, 11 pts felt poor; only 5 pts gave up work because of disease. 3. Little change in married/family life: 9 thought marriage worse, 19 felt mariage improved, half noted less frequent intercourse. 4. The premorbid personality is the most accurate determinant of outcome.
Hendriksen and Binder, UC (19)	122	Questionnaire of professional, emotional, and family conditions Age- and sex-matched acute illness patient controls	1. No significant differences in severe family problems (16% pts, 12% controls), frequency of sexual problems (12% vs. 11%), previous treatment for mental disorders (13% vs. 17%), social/physical activities, or absence from work. 2. More IBD pts with higher socioeconomic status and education (university degrees) 12% pts vs. 2% controls, $p < .05$), and fewer unskilled workers (23% vs. 35%).
Sorensen et al., CD (20)	106	Personal interview concerning professional conditions, family relations, sex life, living conditions, use of EtOH/tobacco/drugs, and diet. Score kept for social activity (frequent participation, cultural, sports, courses, frequent contact with friends, travel), physical activity. Age- and sex-matched controls.	1. Family/social: equal numbers married (67% vs. 71%), and had regular sexual activity (72% vs. 73%). 2. Previous psychiatric assistance in 10% pts, 8% controls. 3. No differences in social or physical activity scores. 4. No differences in percent employed, amount of sick leave. 5. Life insurance: 25% CD pts vs. 36% controls. 6. CD pts reported reduced capacity for work (23%) and reduced leisure activities (21%).
Meyers et al., CD (21)	53	Psychosocial survey recording overall satisfaction, physical symptoms, relationships, school, and employment, recreation, sexuality, body image, influence of ileostomy, recurrences.	1. 92% believed first surgery helpful. 2. Patients less symptomatic (18% vs. 48% preop). 3. Improved relations with friends and family (improvement 19% vs. 62% preop). 4. Fewer school/employment difficulties (14% vs. 71%). 5. Improved body image (10% vs. 37%).

CD, Crohn's disease; UC, ulcerative colitis; pts, patients.

(22), the response to the question "How would you rate your general well-being" on a five-point scale (1 = terrible; 2 = poor; 3 = fair; 4 = good; 5 = very good) indicated that this population generally felt well (ulcerative colitis patients scored 4.6 ± 0.04 S.E. and Crohn's disease patients 4.5 ± 0.02 SE). Well-being scores were understandably lower for a clinical sample of patients seen by gastroenterologists (ulcerative colitis, 2.5 ± 1.1, CD = 1.8 ± 0.9) (23). This global measure of general well-being was also found to be a strong predictor of physician visits for patients with IBD (22). While providing useful information on general health status, single item scores are limited because they yield no information about the factors determining the patient's response.

General (Generic) Measures

General or generic measures assess HRQL independent of the specific features of the disease (24). The advantages are that they can identify several realms of dysfunction, allow comparison between different groups, and many have been extensively validated (25). The disadvantages are that they may be insensitive to changes related to a specific disease (bowel function, abdominal pain). Two basic types of generic measures are used in IBD assessment (26,27).

Health Profiles

Health profiles incorporate several domains or dimensions of the patient's experience and behavior, such as physical or psychosocial functioning, or perceptions of disease impact. One example of a standardized health profile used in IBD is the Sickness Impact Profile (SIP), a measure of functional status (28). The self-administered, 136-item SIP assesses patient perceptions of performance in 12 areas of activity related to activities of daily living. The categories may be grouped into an overall score, a physical dimensional score (A = ambulation, M = mobility, BCM = body care and movement), a psychosocial dimensional score (SI = social interaction, AB = alertness behavior, EB = emotional behavior, C = communication), and several independent scores (SR = sleep and rest, E = eating, W = work, HM = home management, RP = recreation and pastimes). The test has good convergent and discriminant validity and has been validated by clinician assessments of patient health status, by scores from other functional assessment instruments, and by independent comparison with objective measure of dysfunction among patients with other medical disorders. It has test retest reliability of .92 and an internal consistency of .94.

Using the SIP, Drossman et al. (23) first characterized the functional status in 150 IBD patients (63 ulcerative colitis, 87 Crohn's disease). The results (Table 2) indicated (1) IBD patients exhibited moderate functional impairment when compared to an HMO comparison group, and this impairment existed more in the social/psychological realm than in the physical dimensions; (2) Crohn's disease patients reported more dysfunction than those with ulcerative colitis, (3) hospitalized patients showed much higher scores than

ambulatory patients (SIP overall score 28 vs 8); and (3) functional status more than disease activity is closely correlated with other ratings of health status. The SIP showed moderate to good correlation (Table 3) with other health status measures: patient's and physician's global assessment of health, and health care utilization. In comparison, the physician's rating of disease activity correlated poorly with both measures and with functional status (Table 3).

In a later study of a nonclinical sample of 997 persons with IBD (22) belonging to the CCFA, the authors noted several other findings. First, despite a number of symptoms and complications related to IBD, the health status of this population, when evaluating daily function (SIP), psychological distress (SCL-90), health care use, and coping style (Ways of Coping-R) was generally good. Psychological distress scores were only slightly elevated above the general population mean (T-score for ulcerative colitis, 54; for Crohn's disease, 56). Daily functional status (SIP) was generally good, and similar to the clinical patient study (23), impairment occurred more in psychological (SIP Psychological 7.4) and social (e.g., SIP Recreation 13.4, SIP Home Management 7.0) than physical functioning (SIP Physical 2.8). Second, similar to the clinical study (23), members with Crohn's disease had significantly greater psychosocial difficulties (e.g., SIP Psychological 8.1, SCL-90 Overall 55.7) and health care use (2.7 MD visits/6 months) than those with ulcerative colitis (6.1, 53.7, 2.3, respectively). However, further analysis indicated that the greater psychosocial difficulties of the Crohn's disease group were related to them having greater disease severity. Third, the CCFA members coped with disease-related stress predomi-

TABLE 2. *Mean Sickness Impact Profile scores: ulcerative colitis and Crohn's disease outpatients*

Scale	CD	UC	HMO comparison group
Overall	8.64	5.21	3.8
Physical	4.89	3.19	2.0
Psychosocial	10.25	5.60	4.0
Emotional behavior	15.7	7.72	3.6
Sleep and rest	17.46	9.12	7.0
Social interaction	11.76	6.84	5.3

Adapted from Drossman et al. (23).
UC, ulcerative colitis; CD, Crohn's disease; HMO, health maintenance organization.

TABLE 3. *Sickness Impact Profile: correlational data*

	Ulcerative colitis		Crohn's disease	
	R	p<	R	p<
Overall SIP with:				
Patient's health rating	0.35	0.009	0.51	0.0001
Physician's health rating	0.33	0.01	0.37	0.0007
Physician visits	[0.36	0.13]	0.41	0.001
Hospitalizations	0.32	0.02	0.40	0.0002
Surgeries	[−0.01	0.94]	0.28	0.07
Disease activity with				
Overall SIP score	0.29	0.03	[0.10	0.42]
Patient's health rating	[0.20	0.16]	0.24	0.04
Physician's health rating	0.37	0.005	0.39	0.0003
Physician visits	[0.05	0.71]	0.37	0.002
Hospitalization	[0.12	0.39]	[0.11	0.33]
Surgeries	[0.12	0.48]	[0.05	0.76]

Adapted from Drossman et al. (23).
SIP, Sickness Impact Profile.
[ ] = Not statistically significant.

nantly through social support, keeping feelings of distress from interfering with activities, and by problem solving and positive reappraisal. These "problem-based" coping strategies are considered adaptive in buffering psychosocial distress (29); this hypothesis was supported by further analysis. Finally, regression analyses indicated that psychologic distress and functional status were strong predictors of physician visits, while disease activity measures were not significant predictors. However, in predicting numbers of hospitalizations and operations, the disease-related measures (e.g., symptom severity, steroid dosage, weight loss) were strong predictors.

Utility Measures

Utility measures are applications of techniques derived from clinical decision making that can be used to determine patient preferences to a type of treatment. One example, the Time Trade-off Technique (TTOT) (30), evaluates the patient's perception of existing health compared to death. A score ranging from 0.0 (equal to death) to 1.0 (full health) is obtained by having the patient choose between (1) living in the present state of health with all its physical and psychosocial limitations, or (2) a shorter life span but in perfect health. For example, two 30-year-old patients with Crohn's disease might be expected to live until 75 (based on actuarial tables). The patient who is in fair health may feel well enough to trade only 5 years of life (and live until age 70) in full health. This person would have a utility score of 70/75 = 0.93. In comparison, the other patient who experiences very poor health may be willing to trade off 30 years of life (and live until age 45) in full health, and the utility score would be 45/75 = 0.60.

For IBD, the change in a utility score can be used to determine patient preferences to a treatment. McLeod et al. (31) used two utility measures, the Time Trade-off (TTOT) and the Direct Questioning of Objectives (DQO), to answer whether colectomy for ulcerative colitis leads to improvement in HRQL and whether there is a differential effect among the three surgical procedures: conventional ileostomy, Kock pouch, and Ileal pouch-anal anastomosis. The authors studied 20 patients prior to colectomy and again 1 year postoperatively. The mean utility scores for the TTOT increased from 0.58 ± 0.34 to 0.98 ± 0.07 after surgery, and similarly, the DQO increased from 0.38 ± 0.27 to 0.88 ± 0.19 ($p < 0.05$). In a second study, the authors compared the utility scores for patients who had colectomy and these three surgeries at least 1 year previously. The TTOT and DQO scores for the three groups were not significantly different (ranging from 0.95 to 0.97 for TTOT and from 0.86 to 0.89 for DQO), suggesting that the choice of surgery is irrelevant at least one year later.

Like other single-item measures, the utility score does not provide information on the domains within which improvement or deterioration occurs. Therefore, this type of measure is frequently administered with standardized health profile measures.

Disease-Specific Measures

Compared to the described generic measures, disease-specific instruments evaluate the special states and concerns of patients having a particular disease. Generally, they are more responsive to clinical changes that occur over time (32), and the questions relate closely to areas routinely evaluated by physicians. For example, a disease-specific measure for Crohn's disease might have questions relating to bowel habit, abdominal pain, and sexual functioning, while one for rheumatoid arthritis might assess hand strength and mobility. This makes disease-specific measures particularly useful for clinical trials, but they are unable to discriminate between patients having different disease conditions.

Table 4 lists the features of the HRQL instruments developed for IBD. All scales have content validity; i.e., the items adequately represent the domains under study. Most scales (IBDQ, Cleveland Clinic Scale, RFIPC, UC/CD Health Status Scales) have concurrent validity, in which the scores correlated with other validated HRQL instruments. Finally, some scales (IBDQ, Cleveland Clinic Scale, UC/CD Health Status Scales) have construct validity where the hypotheses used to develop the instrument are tested and confirmed against patient group characteristics or other health status measures.

Inflammatory Bowel Disease Questionnaire

The Inflammatory Bowel Disease Questionnaire (IBDQ) was devised to assess the results of clinical trials in IBD (33,34). The instrument examines four domains that are important to patients' lives: bowel symptoms, systemic symptoms, and emotional and social function, and is relatively short and simple to complete. Items were selected from literature review, other questionnaires, and responses from clinicians caring for IBD patients. Ninety-seven subjects with inflammatory bowel disease were given the 30-item questionnaire, and the results (Table 5) indicate that primary bowel symptoms, systemic symptoms, and altered emotional function were common. Functional and social impairment were less frequent. Apart from primary bowel complaints, patients seldom volunteered other facets of quality of life impairment, and this was particularly true for impairment of emotional function. Moreover, although many patients noted troublesome symptoms, the majority of inflammatory bowel disease patients did not report major disruption in their work or personal lives.

Recently, a validation of the IBDQ was undertaken among 305 patients as a part of a randomized multicenter treatment trial of cyclosporine versus placebo (35). The IBDQ scales were significantly correlated with the CDAI (r = 0.67;

TABLE 4. *Specific health status instruments for IBD*

Name	Scales	Comments
Inflammatory Bowel Disease Questionnaire (IBDQ) (24) 32-item Likert Scale Interview format	Bowel Symptoms, Systemic Symptoms, Social Function, Emotional Function	Well standardized; designed for clinical trials; developed on "sick" patients—GI referrals and inpatients
Modified IBDQ (36) 36-item Likert Scale Self-administered	Bowel Symptoms, Systemic Symptoms, Social Function, Emotional Function, Functional Impairment	Derived from IBDQ; developed on "well" patients—local chapter of NFIC
Cleveland Clinic IBD Questionnaire (37) 47-item Likert Scale Interview format	Functional/Economic, Social/Recreational, Affect/Life in general, Medical/Symptoms	Correlates with SIP; developed on UC/CD surgical/nonsurgical groups; quality of life index distinguishes groups
Rating Form of IBD Patient Concerns (RFIPC) (39) 25-item Visual Analog Scale Self-administered	Impact of Disease, Sexual Intimacy, Complications, Body Stigma	Correlates with SIP and SCL-90; developed on "well" patients—CCFA national sample
UC/CD Health Status Scales (41) 9 or 10-item Likert Scale Physician/patient scoring	Ulcerative colitis, Crohn's Disease	Standardized to health care use, function, psychological distress in CCFA national sample; designed to discriminate mild/severe illness and predict outcome; better predictor than CDAI

TABLE 5. *Inflammatory bowel disease symptom questionnaire, spontaneous versus elicited response*[a,b]

Dimension and item	No. of spontaneous responses (%)	Mean[c] importance	No. of elicited responses (%)	Mean importance
Bowel symptoms				
Frequent bowel movements	78 (86.7)	4.3	12 (13.3)	3.6
Loose bowel movements	53 (74.6)	4.0	18 (25.4)	4.4
Abdominal cramps	43 (53.8)	4.0	37 (46.2)	3.5
Pain in the abdomen	45 (69.2)	4.3	20 (30.8)	3.3
Systemic symptoms				
Fatigue	43 (48.9)	4.3	45 (51.1)	3.7
Overall feeling unwell	6 (7.2)	4.0	77 (92.8)	3.7
Feeling worn out	12 (14.6)	3.6	70 (85.4)	3.8
Emotional function				
Frustrated	34 (44.7)	4.0	42 (55.3)	3.6
Depressed	37 (50)	3.8	37 (50)	3.1
Worried about surgery	2 (3.4)	4.5	56 (96.6)	3.7
Social impairment				
Avoiding events where washrooms not close at hand	7 (12.5)	4.0	49 (87.5)	3.1
Canceling social engagements	7 (14)	3.9	43 (86)	3.5
Functional impairment				
Inability to attend work/school regularly	15 (41.7)	4.0	21 (58.3)	3.9

[a]A total of 97 subjects were asked to list all physical, emotional, and social problems experienced as a result of inflammatory bowel disease. When the subjects had no more "spontaneous" items to volunteer, they were asked to identify any additional items from the problem pool that represented problems for them ("elicited" responses).

[b]Adapted from Mitchell et al. (33).

[c]Subjects rated the mean importance of each item on a 5-point Likert scale from "not very important" to "extremely important."

$p < 0.0001$) and found to be both reliable and responsive to changes in measures of disease activity.

The generalizability of the IBDQ may be limited by the fact that the patient population standardizing the instrument was selected by convenience, and certain subgroups of patients, namely those with ileostomy or proctitis, were excluded from analysis and scale development. Therefore, the instrument may not be responsive to ileostomy patients who have significant impairment in social or psychologic function due to body image concerns or to patients with perianal disease who often restrict social or sexual activities because of perianal pain or discharge or psychologic concerns (4). The lack of a comparison group limits knowledge as to the degree of impairment reflected by the scores, but this can be obtained in future studies that also evaluate patients with functional bowel disorders or other chronic conditions. Finally, many items may be intercorrelated. For example, in the systemic symptom category, fatigue, feeling unwell, and feeling worn out are conceptually similar, and they may reflect certain emotional states, like depression. Nevertheless, the IBDQ remains one of the only fully standardized disease-specific measures for Crohn's disease, and it is likely to be useful for most patients studied with this condition.

Modified IBDQ

A modified IBDQ (36) was tested in a sample of patients having milder disease. While not fully standardized (the IBD data were only compared to a normal control group), the use of many of the same questions as the IBDQ provides some concurrent validity.

Cleveland Clinic Questionnaire

The Cleveland Clinic questionnaire (37) focused on assessing activities of daily living rather than medical symptoms. The interview-directed questionnaire contained 47 items covering four domains: functional/economic, social/recreational, affect/life, and medical/symptoms. The items were selected from clinical experience and literature review, and showed good test–retest reliability over a 2-week period. The questionnaire had construct validity based on items that correlated with the SIP. From the 47 questions, a quality of life index was constructed by condensing the questionnaire to include only those 18 items that significantly differentiated between the four patient groups.

Using this questionnaire on 164 ambulatory patients (94 ulcerative colitis, 70 Crohn's disease) from a registry at the Cleveland Clinic, the authors found that patients with Crohn's disease had poorer HRQL than those with ulcerative colitis. In addition, patients with surgical histories reported poorer HRQL than those with no history. Using a cutoff score of 60, the proportion in each group with poor HRQL (<60) were: ulcerative colitis–no surgery 4.7%, ulcerative colitis–surgery 15.7%, Crohn's disease–no surgery 15.0%,

and Crohn's disease–surgery 30%. It is unclear why ulcerative colitis–surgery patients did so poorly, since presumably they would be "cured" by colectomy. However, since the study was undertaken at a major medical center, there may be a preferential selection of patients who develop surgical complications.

Even though this questionnaire was designed to be disease specific, a recent study showed it to have discriminative capability, much like a generic instrument. Using a slightly modified version of the Cleveland Clinic scale, Rudick et al. (38) reported that patients with multiple sclerosis and rheumatoid arthritis had poorer HRQL than the IBD group.

Rating Form of IBD Patient Concerns

The Rating Form of IBD Patient Concerns (RFIPC) (39) is a specialized questionnaire that rates the most important worries and concerns of patients with IBD. Its development was based on the premise that specific worries and concerns may affect the patient's adjustment to the illness or satisfaction with treatment, and possibly the clinician's educational approach and choice of treatment. For example, in planning for a total colectomy, an adolescent who is worried about social stigmatization by an external ostomy is likely to prefer and do better with an ileoanal procedure, whereas an older patient more settled in his life may be more concerned with urgency, diarrhea, and anal leakage, and may prefer a standard Brooke ileostomy.

Twenty-one items were first identified from videotaped interviews of IBD patients. The items were then tested on a sample of 150 IBD patients (63 ulcerative colitis, 87 Crohn's disease) (23) who were asked: "Because of your condition, how concerned are you with . . . ?" The items were rated by patients from 0 to 100 (0 = not at all; 100 = a great deal) on a visual analog scale and then tested on a sample of 150 IBD patients (63 ulcerative colitis, 87 Crohn's disease) (23), where an additional four fill-in items were obtained. The revised questionnaire of 25 items was then standardized on 997 persons with IBD belonging to the Crohn's and Colitis Foundation of America (39). Using these data, factor analyses identified four clinically relevant indices: (1) impact of disease (e.g., being a burden on others, loss of energy, loss of bowel control), (2) sexual intimacy (e.g., intimacy, loss of sexual drive, ability to perform sexually), (3) complications of disease (e.g., developing cancer, having surgery, dying early), and (4) body stigma (e.g., producing unpleasant odors, feeling dirty or smelly).

Table 6 displays the identified worries and concerns, their mean severity, on a 0–100 scale, and the comparative rankings between ulcerative colitis and Crohn's disease. The most intense concerns related to the uncertain future of the disease, the effects of medication, energy level, surgery (and having an ostomy bag), being a burden on others, loss of bowel control, and developing cancer. There were clinically consistent disease-related differences: those with Crohn's

TABLE 6. *IBD concerns: ranking and comparison of ulcerative colitis and Crohn's disease*[a,b]

	All (N = 991)		UC (N = 320)		CD (N = 671)		
	Mean	SD	Mean	Rank	Mean	Rank	p
Uncertain nature of my disease	58.6	31.2	54.3	4	60.6	1	—
Effects of medication	56.3	34.3	54.7	3	57.0	3	0.3256
Energy level	55.4	33.7	48.9	6	58.5	2	—
Having surgery	52.9	33.1	50.8	5	54.0	4	1471
Having an ostomy bag	52.1	36.9	55.6	1	50.5	5	0430
Being a burden on others	47.8	33.0	42.6	8	50.3	6	—
Loss of bowel control	46.1	34.1	47.7	7	45.3	8	0.2916
Developing cancer	45.4	33.1	55.5	2	40.6	12	—
Ability to achieve full potential	43.8	33.3	38.6	9	46.2	7	—
Producing unpleasant odors	41.7	34.6	37.4	12	43.9	9	—
Feelings about my body	40.4	32.7	38.1	10	41.5	11	0.1220
Pain or suffering	39.5	28.5	34.3	14	42.0	10	—
Feeling out of control	38.0	32.6	37.7	11	38.2	13	0.8295
Attractiveness	35.8	32.0	32.1	16	37.6	14	0.0126
Having access to quality medical care	34.5	35.2	33.2	15	35.1	15	0.4334
Dying early	33.5	30.5	36.9	13	31.8	20	0.0176
Intimacy	32.2	32.6	31.2	17	32.6	17	0.5302
Loss of sexual drive	31.6	32.9	30.5	18	32.1	19	0.4836
Feeling alone	31.0	31.5	28.3	19	32.3	18	0.0654
Financial difficulties	30.3	30.2	25.5	21	32.8	16	—
Ability to perform sexually	27.6	31.0	26.2	20	28.3	22	0.3294
Passing the disease to others	27.1	33.3	22.5	23	29.4	21	—
Feeling "dirty" or "smelly"	26.1	30.3	24.6	22	26.8	23	0.2786
Being treated as different	21.6	27.2	19.7	24	22.5	24	0.1341
Ability to have children	18.1	28.9	18.7	25	18.0	25	0.7294
Score:	38.7	20.4	37.0		39.6		0.0676

From Drossman et al. (39).
[a]Significant difference (*p* < .002), adjusting for multiple comparisons (45).
[b]RFIPC scores range from 0 = "not at all," to 100 = "a great deal."

disease were more concerned with their energy level, being a burden on others, achieving their full potential, experiencing pain or suffering, financial costs, and passing on the disease to others. Those with ulcerative colitis were more concerned with developing cancer.

A potential limitation of the RFIPC is that it was not designed to assess health status independently in terms of symptoms or functional status. However, studies show it to be significantly correlated with self-reports of well-being and health, psychological distress (SCL-90), and daily function (SIP and SF-36) (39,40). In clinical practice, the RFIPC may be used to identify a patient's personal areas of concern which can then be addressed through education or counseling. In research, the individual items, the averaged total score (Sumscore) or the subscale scores for the four clinically relevant indices can be used to assess responsiveness to counseling or education interventions.

UC/CD Health Status Scales

Based on the formulation that health status and health outcome is determined by both disease-related and psychosocial factors (2) the UC/CD Health Status Scales (41) were created. The authors first identified symptoms and other clinical items that discriminated active from inactive disease, then performed factor analyses to reduce these items to clusters sharing common symptom relationships, and finally developed weighted indices for both disease conditions by using regression analyses that predicted a composite measure of health status that included health care use, daily function (SIP) and psychological distress (SCL-90). The final symptom items in the scales were stronger predictors of the outcome measure than the Crohn's Disease Activity Index (5). The ulcerative colitis and Crohn's disease scales explained 17% and 21% more of the variance of this health status measure. Prospective validation is needed to confirm the potential role of this instrument for assessing prognosis and treatment response.

Studies of Postcolectomy Patients with Ulcerative Colitis

A somewhat specialized situation involves HRQL assessment of patients with ulcerative colitis who have undergone colectomy. As previously discussed, studies employing utility measures indicate that patients undergoing this operation, regardless of the type of operation, have improved scores (31,42). In another study (43) of more than 1,000 ulcerative colitis colectomy patients involving three types of operations (conventional ileostomy, Kock pouch, ileoanal anastomosis), the authors evaluated whether these procedures had differential effects on HRQL. Using retrospective data from postcolectomy patients, the authors developed an HRQL questionnaire to evaluate restrictions (restricted, no change or improved) related to social activity, sports, housework, recreation, family relationships, sexual activity, and travel. They found that patients with ileal pouch-anal anastomoses had fewer restrictions in sports and sexual activities than those with Kock pouches ($p < 0.05$), whereas those with Kock pouches in turn had fewer restrictions in these activities, but more restrictions in travel than those with Brooke ileostomies ($p < 0.05$). All other categories were similar between groups. While the findings of this study are consistent with clinical expectations, the measures used were not standardized, and therefore will require further confirmation.

In another study comparing IBD patient worries and concerns (RFIPC) between CCFA members having ostomies to those without ostomies, the authors found that those with ostomies had fewer concerns about cancer, surgery and having an ostomy. Furthermore, they did not report more body-image concerns (sexuality, intimacy, attractiveness) (44). Finally, another study evaluated HRQL in postcolectomy ulcerative colitis patients using the SIP, SF-36, and a TTOT. When compared to a healthy reference population, HRQL was found to be excellent by all three measures, and the scale scores were strongly intercorrelated (42). These studies support the notion that quality of life is improved in response to colectomy for ulcerative colitis and that the presence of an ostomy does not worsen disease-related concerns.

CONCLUSIONS

Health-related quality of life is an important component of research and clinical evaluation in various medical conditions. During the past several years, the number of HRQL studies in IBD has increased markedly. Using both generic and disease-specific measures, the findings indicate that most patients with IBD experience good HRQL. A summary of the results in IBD are indicated in Table 7 (24).

For the future, additional studies will be needed to further characterize HRQL in IBD in several ways: (1) to establish group norms for existing generic and disease-specific measures in patients with IBD, (2) to determine whether disease-related differences (ulcerative colitis versus Crohn's disease and clinical subgroups) exist, (3) to determine how complications unrelated to disease activity (incontinence, strictures, obstruction, pain, and physical deformity) affect quality of life, (4) to use HRQL measures in interventional trials as a more sensitive measure of treatment effect, and (5) to implement prospective studies to determine the predictive effect of various HRQL measures on clinical outcome.

TABLE 7. *Summary of HRQL findings in IBD using standardized measures*

1. For most ambulatory patients, HRQL is generally good (22,23,33,37).
2. Functional impairment is greater in the psychological and social than are physical dimensions (22,23,36).
3. Patients with Crohn's disease have greater impairment of HRQL than is found in those with ulcerative colitis (see #4) (22,23,37).
4. There is a strong relationship between disease severity and HRQL impairment (22,37). This explains the poorer HRQL in CD.
5. Disease-related worries and concerns are associated with psychological distress and poor function (39); reduction in these concerns via education/counseling may improve HRQL.
6. For the CCFA population, impaired HRQL is successfully mediated through problem-based coping strategies (e.g., social support, problem solving, positive reappraisal) (22).
7. Quality of life measures such as functional status and disease-related concerns correlate better with well-being than does the physician's rating of disease activity (23). Similarly, quality of life measures are stronger predictors of health care visits than is disease activity (22,23).
8. Patients with Crohn's disease who have had surgery report poorer HRQL than those who have not (37). This may relate to postsurgical Crohn's disease patients having more severe disease.
9. For ulcerative colitis, colectomy regardless of surgical repair, is associated with improved HRQL (31,43,46), reduced worries about disease and no worsening of body image concerns (44).

REFERENCES

1. Drossman DA. Psychosocial aspects of ulcerative colitis and Crohn's disease. In: Kirsner JB, Shorter RG, eds. *Inflammatory bowel disease.* Philadelphia: Lea & Febiger, 1988:209–226.
2. Garrett JW, Drossman DA. Health status in inflammatory bowel disease: biological and behavioral considerations. *Gastroenterology* 1990;99:90–96.
3. Drossman DA. Psychosocial factors in ulcerative colitis and Crohn's disease. In: Kirsner JB, Shorter RG, eds. *Inflammatory bowel disease.* Philadelphia: Lea & Febiger, 1995:492–512.
4. Irvine EJ. Usual therapy improves perianal Crohn's Disease as measured by a new disease activity index. *J Clin Gastroenterol* 1995; 20:27–32.
5. Best WR, Becktel JM, Singleton JW, Kern FJ. Development of a Crohn's disease activity index. National Cooperative Crohn's disease study. *Gastroenterology* 1976;70:439–444.
6. Harvey RF, Bradshaw JM. A simple index of Crohn's disease activity. *Lancet* 1980;1:514.
7. Myren J, Bouchier IAD, Watkinson G, Softley A, Clamp SE, DeDombal FT. The O.M.G.E. multinational inflammatory bowel disease survey 1976–1982: a further report on 2,657 cases. *Scand J Gastroenterol* 1984;95(Suppl):1–27.
8. Wright JP, Marks IN, Parfitt A. A simple clinical index of Crohn's disease activity: the Cape Town Index. *S Afr Med J* 1985;68:502–503.
9. Van Hees P, Van Elteren PH, Van Lier HJJ, Van Tongeren JHM. An index of inflammatory activity in patients with Crohn's disease. *Gut* 1980;21:279–286.
10. Sandler RS, Jordon MC, Kupper LL. Development of a Crohn's index for survey research. *J Clin Epidemiol* 1988;41:451–458.
11. Truelove SC, Witts LJ. Cortisone in ulcerative colitis, preliminary report on a therapeutic trial. *BMJ* 1954;2:375–378.
12. Singleton JW. Clinical activity assessment in inflammatory bowel disease. *Dig Dis Sci* 1987;32:42s–45s.
13. DeDombal FT. Measuring and quantifying the status of patients with inflammatory bowel disease. In: DeDombal FT, Myren J, Bouchier

IAD, Watkinson G, eds. *Inflammatory bowel disease: some international data and reflections.* New York: Oxford University, 1986:267–285.

14. Singleton JW. Medical management of acute colitis. In: Westbrook DL, Tan KG, Bijuen AB, eds. *Present management of ulcerative and Crohn's colitis.* Breda: Medical World, 1982:103–108.

15. Drossman DA. Psychosocial aspects of inflammatory bowel disease. *Stress Med* 1986;2:119–128.

16. Mendeloff AI, Calkins BM. The epidemiology of idiopathic inflammatory bowel disease. In: Kirsner JB, Shorter RG, eds. *Inflammatory bowel disease.* Philadelphia: Lea & Febiger, 1988:1–35.

17. Bergman L, Krause U. Crohn's Disease: A long-term study of the clinical course in 186 patients. *Scand J Gastroenterol* 1977;12:937–944.

18. Gazzard BG, Price HL, Libby GW, Dawson AM. The social toll of Crohn's disease. *BMJ* 1978;2:1117–1119.

19. Hendriksen C, Binder V. Social prognosis in patients with ulcerative colitis. *BMJ* 1980;281:581–583.

20. Sorensen VZ, Olsen BG, Binder V. Life prospects and quality of life in patients with Crohn's disease. *Gut* 1987;28:382–385.

21. Meyers S, Walfish JS, Sachar DB, Greenstein AJ, Hill AG, Janowitz HD. Quality of life after surgery for Crohn's disease: a psychological survey. *Gastroenterology* 1980;78:1–6.

22. Drossman DA, Leserman J, Mitchell CM, Li Z, Zagami EA, Patrick DL. Health status and health care use in persons with inflammatory bowel disease: a national sample. *Dig Dis Sci* 1991;36:1746–1755.

23. Drossman DA, Patrick DL, Mitchell CM, Zagami EA, Appelbaum MI. Health related quality of life in inflammatory bowel disease: functional status and patient worries and concerns. *Dig Dis Sci* 1989;34:1379–1386.

24. Drossman DA. Quality of life in IBD: methods and findings. In: Rachmilewitz D, ed. *Falk Symposium #72: inflammatory bowel diseases—1994.* Dordrecht: Kluwer Academic Publishers, 1994:105–116.

25. Patrick DL, Erickson P. What constitutes quality of life? Concepts and dimensions. *Clin Nutr* 1988;7:53–63.

26. Patrick DL, Deyo RA. Generic and disease-specific measures in assessing health status and quality of life. *Med Care* 1989;27:S217–S232.

27. Guyatt GH, Feeny DH, Patrick DL. Measuring health-related quality of life. *Ann Intern Med* 1993;118:622–629.

28. Bergner M, Bobbitt RA, Carter WB. The Sickness Impact Profile: development and final revision of a health status measure. *Med Care* 1981;19:787–805.

29. Lazarus RS, Folkman S. *Stress, appraisal and coping.* New York: Springer, 1984.

30. Torrance GW, Thomas WH, Sackett DL. A utility maximization model for evaluation of health care program. *Health Serv Res* 1972;7:118–133.

31. McLeod RS, Churchill DN, Lock AM, Vanderburgh S, Cohen Z. Quality of life of patients with ulcerative colitis preoperatively and postoperatively. *Gastroenterology* 1991;101:1307–1313.

32. Guyatt GH, Walter S, Norman G. Measuring change over time: assessing the usefulness of evaluative instruments. *J Chronic Dis* 1987;40:171–178.

33. Mitchell A, Guyatt G, Singer J, Irvine EJ, Goodacre R, Tompkins C, Williams N, Wagner F. Quality of life in patients with inflammatory bowel disease. *J Clin Gastroenterol* 1988;10:306–310.

34. Guyatt G, Mitchell A, Irvine EJ, Singer J, Williams N, Goodacre R, Tompkins C. A new measure of health status for clinical trials in inflammatory bowel disease. *Gastroenterology* 1989;96:804–810.

35. Irvine EJ, Feagan B, Rochon J, Archambault A, Fedorak RN, Groll A, Kinnear D, Saibil F, McDonald JWD. Quality of life: a valid and reliable measure of therapeutic efficacy in the treatment of inflammatory bowel disease. *Gastroenterology* 1994;106:287–296.

36. Love JR, Irvine EJ, Fedorak RN. Quality of life in inflammatory bowel disease. *J Clin Gastroenterol* 1992;14:15–19.

37. Farmer RG, Easley KA, Farmer JM. Quality of life assessment by patients with inflammatory bowel disease. *Cleve Clin J Med* 1992;59:35–42.

38. Rudick RA, Miller D, Clough JD, Gragg LA, Farmer RG. Quality of life in multiple sclerosis: comparison with inflammatory bowel disease and rheumatoid arthritis. *Arch Neurol* 1992;49:1237–1242.

39. Drossman DA, Leserman J, Li Z, Mitchell CM, Zagami EA, Patrick DL. The rating form of IBD patient concerns: a new measure of health status. *Psychosomat Med* 1991;53:701–712.

40. Shearin M, Provenzale D, Tillinger W, Phillips B, Sherman R, Bollinger R, Koruda M, Drossman DA. Post-colectomy health status measurements in patients with a history of ulcerative colitis. *Am J Gastroenterol* 1994;89:1714 (abstract).

41. Drossman DA, Li Z, Leserman J, Patrick DL. Ulcerative colitis and Crohn's disease health status scales for research and clinical practice. *J Clin Gastroenterol* 1992;15:104–112.

42. Shearin M, Tillinger W, Phillips B, Provenzale D, Bollinger R, Koruda M, Drossman DA. Postcolectomy health status and quality of life in patients with a history of ulcerative colitis. *Gastroenterology* 1994;106:A27 (abstract).

43. Kohler LW, Pemberton JH, Zinsmeister AR, Kelly KA. Quality of life after proctocolectomy. A comparison of Brooke ileostomy, Kock pouch, and ileal pouch-anal anastomosis. *Gastroenterology* 1991;101:679–684.

44. Drossman DA, Mitchell CM, Appelbaum MI, Patrick DL, Zagami EA. Do IBD ostomates do better? A study of symptoms and health-related quality of life. *Gastroenterology* 1989;96:A130 (abstract).

45. Cupples LA, Heeren T, Schatzkin A, Colton T. Multiple testing of hypotheses in comparing two groups. *Ann Intern Med* 1984;100:122–129.

46. Tjandra JJ, Fazio VW, Church JM, Oakley JR, Milsom JW, Lavery IC. Similar functional results after restorative proctocolectomy in patients with familial adenomatous polyposis and mucosal ulcerative colitis: life quality and psychological morbidity with an ileostomy. *Am J Surg* 1993;165:322–325.

Quality of Life and Pharmacoeconomics in Clinical Trials, Second Edition, edited by B. Spilker. Lippincott-Raven Publishers, Philadelphia © 1996.

CHAPTER 97

Quality of Life Assessment in Gastrointestinal Surgery

Robin S. McLeod

INTRODUCTION

The traditional outcome measures for assessing surgical procedures have been morbidity and mortality. In the early part of this century, these were appropriate, since most gastrointestinal operations were associated with high complication and operative mortality rates. For instance, the operative mortality was 32% among the first 61 patients in whom Miles performed an abdominoperineal resection. As late as the 1950s, the operative mortality rate for this procedure approached 10% (1,2). Similarly high rates were reported for gastrectomy, the Whipple procedure, and anterior resection. Thus, the decision to adopt an operative technique was largely based on whether it resulted in a lower operative mortality and, in some instances, improved long-term survival.

Postoperative quality of life has been considered only sporadically in the surgical literature since the turn of the century. It has tended to be of secondary concern, with greater emphasis placed on the mortality rate and operative complications. The recent interest in quality of life probably reflects the changing patterns of surgical diseases and the evolution of surgical procedures. In the early part of this century, surgery was often reserved for patients who suffered from fatal conditions or where there was little else to offer.

Thus, survival was of utmost importance in assessing the success of the operation. With improvements in anaesthetic and surgical techniques, the discovery of antibiotics, and advances in nutrition and other supportive measures, both mortality and morbidity have been significantly reduced. For most gastrointestinal surgical procedures the operative mortality is less than 1%. Thus, mortality is of limited use as an outcome measure to discriminate between two surgical techniques or compare a surgical technique with medical therapy. As a consequence of the improved results, the indications for surgery have also changed. Surgery is no longer limited to patients where there is no other option. Rather, for many gastrointestinal procedures, the most frequent indication for surgery is failure of medical therapy. In these patients, objective assessments such as radiological, endoscopic, or pathological findings are of secondary importance in evaluating the success of the procedure. Instead, the success of the operation is determined by whether the patient is cured of his or her symptoms and hence his or her quality of life is improved.

Other outcome measures have been used to evaluate surgical procedures including the assessment of functional results. For instance, stool frequency for operations on the bowel and the presence or absence of dumping symptoms for gastric surgery have frequently been reported. In assessing patients with reflux esophagitis, objective evidence may be obtained using manometry, barium studies and esophagoscopy. However, since the indication for surgery in most patients is the persistence of intractable symptoms, the patient's symptoms

R. S. McLeod: Departments of Surgery and Preventive Medicine and Biostatistics, University of Toronto, Clinical Epidemiology Unit, Samuel Lunenfeld Research Institute, Mount Sinai Hospital, Toronto, Ontario M5G 1X5, Canada.

and overall satisfaction with the operation would appear to be the more appropriate measures to assess postoperative outcome.

"Softer" measures in the domain of quality of life (e.g., ability to work and participate in sports) have been considered less frequently. However, it is likely that the need to assess operations in terms of their effect on overall health will become more and more important. Newer operations are being developed for the express purpose of improving quality of life without any improvement in survival rates or decrease in morbidity. The developments in the field of reconstructive surgery for ulcerative colitis is a good example. Recognizing the difficulty some patients had in adjusting to a conventional Brooke ileostomy, the Kock continent ileostomy and later, ileal reservoir and ileoanal anastomosis were developed. Since the complication rate following both of these procedures tends to be higher than following total proctocolectomy and ileostomy, it is imperative that the patient's quality of life is indeed improved. Thus, tools to quantitatively evaluate and compare the three operations are required. Highly selective vagotomy and strictureplasty in Crohn's disease are other examples of newer operations that must be evaluated against the standard operations to determine their role.

Similarly, the introduction of laparoscopy has had a major effect on the field of gastrointestinal surgery in the past few years. While these procedures appear to cause less pain and result in lower analgesia requirements, it is uncertain whether they result in improved outcome including quality of life. They must be evaluated against the more traditional open approach to determine their role in the modern surgical armamentarium, especially because they are costly to the health care system.

Finally, as knowledge of and interest in medicine by lay people increases, patients are also participating more, not only in the decision of when to operate but also in which operation to have. In order to provide them with information on which to base their decisions, it may be necessary to evaluate quality of life. Patients are naturally reluctant to undergo surgery if the negative impact of surgery is greater than the effects of the disease and side effects of medical therapy. In evaluating surgical procedures, long-term outcome may be as or more important to the patient than the complication rate in making his decision. This was borne out in a survey of patients with continent ileostomies, in which we found that 94% of patients stated they would rather have revisionary surgery, should complications occur, rather than have a conventional ileostomy re-established. This included one patient who had already had six operations because of complications associated with the continent ileostomy (3).

Despite the recognized need for measuring quality of life, validated instruments to measure it are lacking in most areas of gastrointestinal surgery. Most studies assessing quality of life have been qualitative in nature. Often questionnaires containing a variety of items covering physical, and possibly social and psychological function have been administered to patients. The obvious limitation of this approach is that a quantitative assessment which considers all aspects of health is not obtained. Thus, one cannot compare different procedures nor the preoperative with the postoperative status of patients. Statistical testing cannot be performed.

Because of this lack, this chapter is not devoted to a discussion of the various instruments available for measuring quality of life as in the other chapters. Instead, it will summarize work that has been done in measuring quality of life following gastrointestinal surgery and discuss areas where future efforts might be directed.

AREAS IN WHICH QUALITY OF LIFE ASSESSMENTS ARE APPROPRIATE

While quality of life has become a more important issue, not all conditions require quality of life assessments. In procedures such as appendectomy, where patients are cured of the illness for which they underwent surgery and do not experience side effects related to the operation, quality of life assessments are unnecessary.

Table 1 lists some conditions which are appropriately evaluated with quality of life measures. These conditions have been divided into three general categories. The first category includes gastrointestinal diseases for which the major indication for surgery is failure of medical management or intractable symptoms. It could be argued that portal hypertension does not fit into this category, because the major indication for surgery is bleeding. However, because hepatic encephalopathy is commonly present preoperatively and is a major concern when performing surgery, quality of life is a very important issue in assessing surgery for this condition. The second category is cancer surgery. Although survival remains the most important outcome measure for assessing surgery for primary cancers, quality of life is an important consideration in operating on patients for palliation. It is also of major concern if the surgery is mutilating (e.g., pelvic exenteration). Finally, the third category is transplantation surgery. Quality of life has aroused considerable interest because of the economic impact of transplantation surgery.

TABLE 1. *Conditions in which quality of life measures are appropriate*

Gastrointestinal diseases in which the major indication for surgery is persistent symptoms
Reflux esophagitis
Peptic ulcer
Crohn's disease
Ulcerative colitis
Portal hypertension
Chronic pancreatitis
Cancer surgery
Palliative cancer surgery
"Mutilating" surgery
Transplantation surgery

The status of quality of life measurements as they pertain to these areas is discussed in the following sections. Once again, it must be emphasized that quality of life assessment is, for the most part, in its infancy within this field so there are relatively few specific instruments for measuring quality of life in any of these areas.

GENERAL ASSESSMENT OF GASTROINTESTINAL SURGERY

Eyspach and colleagues have developed a 36-item index that was designed to be used to assess outcome in all gastrointestinal disorders (4). It is self-administered. The items include those assessing upper and lower gastrointestinal symptoms. In addition, items cover physical, psychological, sexual, and social domains. Scores may range from 0 to 144 with higher scores indicating improved well-being.

This instrument was tested for reliability in a cohort of 50 individuals. The intraclass correlation coefficient was 0.92. Validity was assessed by comparing results with those from the Affect Balance Scale and Spitzer's Quality of Life Index.

The investigators used this index to assess outcome in 194 patients who underwent laparoscopic cholecystectomy and found the index to be responsive. Our group has used it to assess outcome in patients who had undergone a Whipple procedure (5). However, although this measure may be useful to assess outcome in gastrointestinal diseases, further studies to assess its responsiveness in individual conditions are required. Its value, however, appears to be that it may be used to assess all gastrointestinal procedures so it is not operation or disease specific.

ANTIREFLUX SURGERY

The Gastroesophageal Reflux Disease Activity Index (GRACI) was developed as an outcome measure for the Veterans Affairs Gastroesophageal Reflux Disease Study (6,7). This was a randomized controlled trial comparing medical to surgical therapy for gastroesophageal reflux. The GRACI consists of four items: the percentage of each day that a patient has heartburn, the general severity of esophagitis for the day, the number of episodes of odynophagia, and the number of episodes of coughing or wheezing. The results of these symptoms are weighted and aggregated with scores ranging from 0 to 100%.

This instrument was developed by collecting data on 12 symptoms in a pilot study of 145 patients. Multiple regression analysis was then used to estimate which group of symptoms correlated best with physicians' assessments of reflux disease activity. Subsequently, in the trial, the mean GRACI scores and findings on esophagoscopy and level of patient satisfaction (measured on a Likert scale) were found to correlate.

The value of this index is that it is the first and only outcome measure developed to assess outcome for antireflux surgery trials. Its limitations are that it measures functional status only without assessing the psychological or social domains. It has not been tested for reliability and has only had limited testing for validity. Further use in clinical trials may help to determine its usefulness as an outcome measure in assessing antireflux therapy.

GASTRIC SURGERY

Gastric surgery was one of the first areas of surgery in which postoperative quality of life came under scrutiny. Although bleeding and perforation are sometimes indications for surgery in peptic ulcer disease, most often the indication is persistence of intractable symptoms. Side effects such as dumping symptoms are not uncommon postoperatively. Thus, surgery can be a trade-off of intractable ulcer symptoms for other symptoms of varying severity related to the operation. At one time, gastric surgery was one of the most common procedures performed by the abdominal surgeon, so it is not surprising that there was considerable interest in the assessment of postoperative results.

Approximately 40 years ago, the Visick scale was devised to evaluate postoperative results following gastrectomy (8). Using this scale, an overall rating, on a scale of one to four, is assigned to each patient (Table 2). It is not ''operation specific'' so it can be used to compare the various surgical procedures performed for peptic ulcer disease. Indeed, it has been used as one of the major outcome measures in several clinical trials evaluating peptic ulcer surgery (9–13).

There are several limitations to this scale. First, it is an extremely subjective assessment of the result. Second, although patients are interviewed to elicit symptoms and their

TABLE 2. *Modified Visick scale for assessing peptic ulcer surgery*

Category	Definition
I Excellent	Absolutely no symptoms; perfect result
II Very good	Patient considers result perfect, but interrogation elicits mild occasional symptoms easily controlled by minor adjustment to diet
III Satisfactory	Mild or moderate symptoms not controlled by care, causing some discomfort, but patient and surgeon satisfied with result; symptoms do not interfere seriously with life or work
IV Unsatisfactory	Moderate or severe symptoms or complications that interfere considerably with work or enjoyment of life; patient or doctor dissatisfied with result; includes all cases with proven recurrent ulcer and those submitted to further operation, even though the latter may have been followed by considerable symptomatic improvement

satisfaction with the procedure, ultimately the interviewer rates the result. The interviewer's assessment may not correlate with that of the patient especially if the surgeon who performed the operation is also the person interviewing the patient. Hall and colleagues (14) found this to be true when both the surgeon and patient were asked to grade the result. When interobserver reliability was tested, agreement on the overall Visick gradings was low, although there was high agreement on whether symptoms were present and the severity of them. Test retest reliability and validity have not been formally tested. Despite these limitations, the Visick Scale continues to be used in the assessment of peptic ulcer surgery probably because it has been used for many years and surgeons are familiar with it. However, a new instrument is probably needed if one contemplates undertaking future trials evaluating peptic ulcer surgery.

Two recent instruments have been developed to assess medical therapy for peptic ulcer disease. Neither have been tested in surgical patients. Korman developed an index based on the McMaster Inflammatory Bowel Disease Questionnaire (15,16). There were six questions related to ulcer pain, seven related to emotional function, and four related to social function. Although reliability and validity testing were not performed, the items appeared to be sensitive to change. Dimenas and colleagues developed the Gastrointestinal Symptom Rating Scale (GSRS), which was also developed to assess the results of medical management of peptic ulcer disease (17–19).

Troidl and coworkers (20) have developed an instrument to measure outcome following gastrectomy for gastric carcinoma. This instrument contains both disease specific variables as well as those relating to overall physical and social function. The total scores assigned to the patient can range from 0 to 14. This instrument has been tested against a modification of the Visick Scale and the Spitzer Index of Quality of Life and found to be better at discriminating patients than either of the other two. The literature does not clearly state whether the instrument has been tested for reliability.

ULCERATIVE COLITIS

There has been ongoing interest in quality of life in this area since the development of the Kock continent ileostomy and the ileal reservoir and ileoanal anastomosis procedure. These procedures were developed to improve quality of life in patients requiring surgery for ulcerative colitis. Multiple articles in the literature assess the quality of life of patients with conventional ileostomies, ileorectal anastomosis, Kock continent ileostomies, and ileal reservoirs (3,21–29). In all of these, results of patient surveys were reported. Various items covering physical function, psychological well-being and social function were assessed, as were subjective global perceptions.

The major limitation of all these studies is that quality of life was not measured quantitatively. Thus, the value of this information is limited in that it is virtually impossible to compare the quality of life achieved by patients with a conventional ileostomy to that of patients with a continent ileostomy or ileal reservoir. Additionally, the preoperative status cannot be compared with the postoperative status. There are, however, no instruments available that have been developed specifically to measure quality of life of ileostomates.

Our group has used two different techniques which provide a global assessment of the patient's health status: the time trade-off technique (TTOT) and the direct questioning of objectives (DQO) (30,31). These techniques are used to assign a utility to the patient's perceived quality of life. It is assumed that patients implicitly incorporate the physical, emotional, and social aspects of health in the estimation of utility or perceived quality of life. Utilities may range from 0, signifying death, to 1, signifying normal health.

In the TTOT, each patient is presented with a choice between two hypothetical options. The first is to continue in the patient's present health state, with its physical, emotional, and social limitations for a lifetime (t) determined by actuarial data. The subject is told that there will be no change in the health state except for the normal aging process. The alternative choice is a shorter time (x) in a state of full health except for the normal aging process. The interviewer then adjusts x until a point of ambivalence is reached. The value x/t is the utility for the health state for the individual.

The direct questioning of objectives was developed by Detsky et al. for assessing quality of life in patients on home parenteral nutrition. In performing this, three life objectives that are chosen by and important to the patient are elicited. A category scaling is used to derive "importance" weights on a scale of 0–10 for each objective. A category scaling is then used to measure, on a scale of 0–1.0, the patient's ability to achieve objective in his present status. Quality of life is estimated as a weighted average of the patient's ability to achieve his or her objectives, with the weights determined by the "importance" values.

These instruments were used in two situations: the quality of life of patients with a conventional ileostomy, Kock continent ileostomy, or ileal reservoir was compared by studying 93 patients who had one of these procedures at least 1 year previously (32). In addition, 20 patients were studied preoperatively to assess their quality of life with ulcerative colitis and compare it with their quality of life 12 months postoperatively. Several standard psychological tests were administered; assessments by the patient, surgeon, and family members were ascertained to test the construct validity of the instruments in this patient population. Our results indicated that postoperatively, patients had a high quality of life, irrespective of the procedure, with mean utilities of >.90. Quality of life was significantly higher in patients postoperatively than preoperatively. In addition, the instruments were able to detect differences in quality of life according to disease activity and according to whether the procedure was considered a "success" or a "failure" by the surgeon.

In this study, both instruments were highly acceptable to patients and easy to use by the interviewer after only a brief training period. The average time to administer both the time trade-off technique and the direct questioning of objectives was less than 15 minutes. Quantitative assessments considering all aspects of health were obtained. Results were amenable to statistical testing. Although both instruments were able to detect changes between the preoperative and postoperative states of patients, they may be insensitive to detecting smaller changes in health status.

CROHN'S DISEASE

The National Cooperative Crohn's Disease Study group developed the Crohn's Disease Activity Index (CDAI) during the 1970s to measure disease activity (33). This group recognized that Crohn's disease is a chronic illness characterized by spontaneous exacerbations and that changes in symptoms and signs may not be accompanied by changes in objective measures such as radiological or endoscopic findings. Subsequently, other instruments have been developed by other groups, many of them modeled after or modifications of the CDAI (34–37). A major component of each is the assessment of bowel function. Other symptoms and signs as well as certain laboratory measures are incorporated into them. Well-being is considered in some; otherwise, all items refer only to physical function. Reliability and validity have been variably assessed.

These instruments have not been used to evaluate surgical treatment. Further validation of them is necessary in this patient population since some of the attributes may not be pertinent in postsurgical patients. For instance, because patients have had a bowel resection, stool frequency may not correlate with disease activity in the postsurgical patient. For patients with ileostomies, stool frequency is an irrelevant item. However, such instruments would potentially be useful in comparing medical to surgical therapies or where there is residual disease (e.g., stricture plasty) after surgery.

Irvine and colleagues (16) have developed an instrument for measuring the subjective health status of patients with inflammatory bowel disease. Unlike the other instruments, this instrument includes items related to patients' subjective evaluation of their functional status. It contains attributes pertaining to four aspects of their lives: symptoms directly related to primary bowel disturbance, systemic symptoms, emotional status, and social function. No physical signs or laboratory values are included. It was developed for measuring outcome in clinical trials of patients with either ulcerative colitis or Crohn's disease. This instrument was initially validated on a cohort of 61 outpatient volunteers, most of whom having mild disease. Subsequently, it has been used as a

secondary outcome measure in a multicenter trial assessing drug therapy in Crohn's disease and found to be responsive to change (38). The results also correlated with those of the Crohn's disease Activity Index and Harvey Bradshaw Index. This instrument has not been used to evaluate surgical results, nor has it been used in a clinical trial of ulcerative colitis patients.

There are two indexes which have been developed to evaluate outcome in perianal Crohn's disease. Allan and colleagues developed a seven-item instrument with each item scored on a linear analogue scale of 0–10 (39). Twenty-five patients with perianal Crohn's disease were studied before and after treatment, and the index was found to be sensitive to change. It also discriminated between patients with perianal Crohn's disease and normal volunteers. However, reliability was not tested, nor was it validated further. Irvine and colleagues developed a similar index known as the Perianal Disease Activity Index (PDAI) (40). It consists of four items: discharge, induration, pain, and activity level. Each item is scored on a 5-point scale (0–4). In 16 patients, mean PDAI was significantly improved following treatment. These investigators have validated it against the CDAI, Harvey Bradshaw Index, and physician and patient global assessments. There were strong correlations between the PDAI and physician and patient global assessments but poor correlations with the CDAI and Harvey Bradshaw Index, suggesting it may be more sensitive to change in perianal activity. Again, these instruments hold promise but further evaluation is necessary.

Other than these instruments, no instruments are available that have been developed specifically for measuring quality of life of Crohn's disease patients postoperatively. It has been assessed with patient surveys and also in one report, using the time trade-off technique and direct questioning of objectives (41–43). Tillinger and colleagues assessed 12 patients before and 3 and 6 months after surgery. CDAI and the Rating Form of IBD Patient Worries and Concerns were also assessed. There was significant improvement in quality of life postoperatively using these instruments.

PANCREATIC SURGERY

Unfortunately, most patients with cancer of the pancreas present late and are not candidates for resective surgery. For those who do have limited disease, plus patients with periampullary tumors, the Whipple procedure is usually performed. This procedure is a major operation entailing resection of the duodenum, head of the pancreas distal bile duct, and often the distal stomach. There has been concern that following surgery patients have poor gastrointestinal function and a poor quality of life. Our group performed a cross-sectional study using the time trade-off technique (TTOT), direct questioning of objectives (DQO), and the Gastrointestinal Quality of Life Index (GIQLI) to assess outcome in this group of patients compared with a group of patients who had cholecystectomies (5). Quality of life was uniformly high using all three instruments. As a result, one could not comment on the discriminative validity of these instruments.

For those patients who have a noncurative lesion, there are a variety of treatment options including resection, surgical bypass procedures, and endoscopic stenting. Little work has been done in assessing quality of life in this cohort of patients. This is an area in which more work is required because quality of life is of importance as palliation is the goal.

LIVER TRANSPLANTATION

Quality of life is a major issue in assessing outcome following liver transplantation. In this area, most studies have been qualitative in nature, with results derived from questionnaires (44,45).

Recently, Paul and colleagues (46) have developed an instrument to assess quality of life in patients with end-stage liver disease before and after liver transplantation. The questionnaire is self-administered and has been tested for reliability and validity.

CANCER SURGERY

Quality of life measurements are as important in the evaluation of surgery in cancer patients as they are in evaluating medical therapy. Although there are no instruments which have been developed specifically for use in surgical oncology, instruments such as the Spitzer Quality of Life Index, Karnofsky Scale, and Eastern Cooperative Oncology Group Performance Scale have been used frequently (47–49). These instruments are not discussed further here, as they are discussed in other chapters.

CONCLUSIONS

It is well recognized that quality of life is an important consideration in performing surgery for gastrointestinal diseases. However, to date, most attempts at measuring it have been relatively unsophisticated and much work is needed to measure quality of life quantitatively. In this chapter, an attempt was made to outline areas where quality of life assessments are needed and to review the literature on work performed to date.

Future efforts should be directed toward developing instruments that measure quality of life in patients undergoing gastrointestinal surgery. Surgeons have been criticized for not evaluating surgical procedures critically in controlled clinical trials. To a large extent, this criticism is valid. However, in order to perform clinical trials, appropriate outcome measures must be chosen. Thus, the need for instruments to measure quality of life is apparent. Disease-specific or operation-specific instruments appear to be required. Mea-

sures of general health, for the most part, tend to be insensitive to measuring changes in postoperative health or in comparing different procedures. Prior to developing an instrument, its purpose should be explicitly stated because the items included will vary accordingly. For instruments used to compare the preoperative and the postoperative status, items must be chosen that are important and relevant to the patient both before and after surgery. In those situations, in which this may not be possible, instruments that measure the global health status of patients may be more appropriate.

REFERENCES

1. Miles WE. A method of performing abdominoperineal excision for carcinoma of the rectum and of the terminal portion of the pelvic colon. *Lancet* 1908;2:1812.
2. Gabriel WB. Discussion on major surgery in carcinoma of the rectum, with or without colostomy, excluding the anal canal and including the rectosigmoid. *Proc R Soc Med* 1957;50:1041.
3. McLeod RS, Fazio VW. Quality of life with the continent ileostomy. *World J Surg* 1984;8:90–95.
4. Eyspach E, Williams JI, Wood-Dauphinee S, Ure BM, Schmulling C, Neugebauer E, Troidl H. The gastrointestinal quality of life index (GIQLI) development and validation of a new instrument. *Chirurgia* 1993;64:264–274.
5. McLeod RS, Taylor BR, O'Connor BI, Greenberg GR, Jeejeebhoy KN, Royall D, Langer B. Quality of life, nutritional status, and gastrointestinal hormone profile following the Whipple Procedure. *Am J Surg* 1995;169:179–185.
6. Spechler SJ. Comparison of medical and surgical therapy for complicated gastroesophageal reflux disease in veterans. *N Engl J Med* 1992;326:786–792.
7. Spechler SJ, Williford WO, Krol WF, VA Cooperative Study Group #277. Development and validation of a Gastroesophageal Reflux Disease Activity Index (GRACI). *Gastroenterology* 1990;98:A130.
8. Visick AH. A study of the failures after gastrectomy. *Ann R Coll Surg Engl* 1948;3:266–284.
9. Goligher JC, de Dombal FT, Duthie HL, Latchmore AJC. Five-to-eight-year results of Leeds/York controlled trial of elective surgery for duodenal ulcer. *BMJ* 1968;1:781–787.
10. Jordan PH. A prospective study of parietal cell vagotomy and selective vagotomy-antrectomy for treatment of duodenal ulcer. *Ann Surg* 1976;183:619–627.
11. Stoddard CJ, Vassilakis JS, Duthie HL. Highly selective vagotomy or truncal vagotomy and pyloroplasty for chronic duodenal ulceration: a randomized, prospective clinical study. *Br J Surg* 1978;65:793–796.
12. Dorricott NJ, McNeish AR, Alexander-Williams J, et al. Prospective randomized multicentre trial of proximal gastric vagotomy or truncal vagotomy and antrectomy for chronic duodenal ulcer: interim results. *Br J Surg* 1978;65:152–154.
13. Christiansen J, Jensen HE, Poul EP, Bardram L, Henriksen FW. Prospective controlled vagotomy trial for duodenal ulcer. Primary results, sequelae, acid secretion, and recurrence rates two to five years after operation. *Ann Surg* 1981;193:49–56.
14. Hall R, Horrocks JC, Clamp SE, de Dombal FT. Observer variation in results of surgery for peptic ulceration. *Br J Med* 1976;1:814–816.
15. Korman MG. Quality of life in duodenal ulcer. *Scand J Gastroenterol* 1993;28(suppl)199:28–31.
16. Guyatt GI, Mitchell A, Irvine EJ, Singer J, Williams N, Goodacre R, Tompkins C. A new measure of health status for clinical trials in inflammatory bowel disease. *Gastroenterology* 1989;96:804–810.
17. Dimenas E, Glise H, Hallerback B, et al. Quality of life in patients with upper gastrointestinal symptoms. An improved evaluation of treatment regimens? *Scand J Gastroenterol* 1993;28:681–687.
18. Glise H. Quality of life assessments in patients with peptic ulcer treatment and follow-up. *Scand J Gastroenterol* 1993;199:34–39.
19. Dimenas E. Methodological aspects of evaluation of quality of life in upper gastrointestinal diseases. *Scand J Gastroenterol* 1993;28(Suppl)199:18–21.

20. Troidl H, Kusche J, Vestweber KH, Eypasch E, Koeppen L, Bouillon B. Quality of life: an important endpoint both in surgical practice and research. *J Chron Dis* 1987;40:523–528.

21. Jagelman DG, Lewis CB, Rowe-Jones DC. Ileorectal anastomosis: appreciation by patients. *BMJ* 1969;1:756–757.

22. Oakley JR, Jagelman DG, Fazio VW, Lavery IC, Weakley FL, Easley K, Farmer RG. Complications and quality of life after ileorectal anastomosis for ulcerative colitis. *Am J Surg* 1985;149:23–30.

23. Roy PH, Sauer WG, Beahrs OH, Farrow GM. Experience with ileostomies. Evaluation of long-term rehabilitation in 497 patients. *Am J Surg* 1970;119:77–86.

24. Morowitz DA, Kirsner JB. Ileostomy in ulcerative colitis. A questionnaire study of 1,803 patients. *Am J Surg* 1981;141:370–375.

25. McLeod RS, Lavery IC, Leatherman JR, Maryland PA, Fazio VW, Jagelman DG, Weakley FW. Factors affecting quality of life with a conventional ileostomy. *World J Surg* 1986;10:474–480.

26. McLeod RS, Lavery IC, Leatherman JR, Maryland PA, Fazio VW, Jagelman DG, Weakley FW. Patient evaluation of the conventional ileostomy. *Dis Colon Rectum* 1985;28:152–154.

27. Kock NG, Darle N, Kewenter J, Myrvold H, Philipson B. The quality of life after proctocolectomy and ileostomy. A study of patients with conventional ileostomies converted to continent ileostomies. *Dis Colon Rectum* 1974;17:287–292.

28. Nilsson LO, Kock NG, Kylberg F, Myrvold HE, Palselius I. Sexual adjustment in ileostomy patients before and after conversion to continent ileostomy. *Dis Colon Rectum* 1981;24:287–290.

29. Pezim ME, Nicholls RJ. Quality of life after restorative proctocolectomy with pelvic ileal reservoir. *Br J Surg* 1985;72:31–33.

30. Torrance GW, Thomas WH, Sackett DL. A utility maximization model for evaluation of health care programs. *Health Serv Res* 1972;7:118–133.

31. Detsky AS, McLaughlin JR, Abrams HB, L'Abbe KA, Whitwell J, Bombardier C, Jeejeebhoy KN. Quality of life of patients on long-term total parenteral nutrition at home. *J Gen Intern Med* 1986;1:26–33.

32. McLeod RS, Cohen Z, Churchill DN, Lock AM, Isbister S. Measurement of quality of life of patients with ulcerative colitis undergoing surgery. *Gastroenterology* 1991;101:1307–1313.

33. Best WR, Becktel JM, Singleton JW, Kern F Jr. Development of a Crohn's disease activity index. National Cooperative Crohn's Disease Study. *Gastroenterology* 1976;70:439–444.

34. Myren J, Bouchier AID, Watkinson G, Softley A, Clamp SE, de Dombal FT. The O.M.G.E. Multinational Inflammatory Bowel Disease Survey 1976–1982. A further report on 2,657 cases. *Scand J Gastroenterol* 1982;19(Suppl 95):1–27.

35. de Dombal FT, Softley A. IOIBD Report No. 1: observer variation in calculating indices of severity and activity in Crohn's disease. *Gut* 1987;28:474–481.

36. Harvey RF, Bradshaw JM. A simple index of Crohn's disease activity. *Lancet* 1980;1:514.

37. Van Hees PAM, Van Elteren PH, Van Lier HJJ, Van Tongeren JHM. An index of inflammatory activity in patients with Crohn's disease. *Gut* 1980;21:279–286.

38. Irvine EJ, Feagan B, Rochon J, Archambault A, Fedorak RN, Groll A, Kinnear D, Saibil F, McDonald JD. Quality of life: a valid and reliable measure of therapeutic efficacy in the treatment of inflammatory bowel disease. *Gastroenterology* 1994;106:287–296.

39. Allan A, Linares L, Sponer HA, Alexander-Williams J. Clinical index to quantitate symptoms of perianal Crohn's disease. *Dis Colon Rectum* 1992;35:656–661.

40. Irvine EJ, Stoskopf B, Donnelly M. A disease activity index for patients with perianal Crohn's disease. *Gastroenterology* 1990;98:A177.

41. Meyers S, Walfish JS, Sachar DB, Greenstein AJ, Hill AG, Janowitz HD. Quality of life after surgery for Crohn's disease: a psychological survey. *Gastroenterology* 1980;78:1–6.

42. Lindhagen T, Ekelund G, Lenadoer L, Hildell J, Lindstrom C, Wenckert A. Pre- and post-operative complications in Crohn's disease with special reference to duration of preoperative disease history. *Scand J Gastroenterol* 1984;19:194–203.

43. Tillinger W, Moser G, Genser D, Lochs H. Quality of life of patients with Crohn's disease: effect of surgery. *Gastroenterology* 1994;106:A1052.

44. Tarter RE, Van Thiel DH, Hegedus AM, Schade RR, Gavaler JS, Starzl TE. Neuropsychiatric status after liver transplantation. *J Lab Clin Med* 1984;103:776–782.

45. Tarter RE, Erb S, Biller PA, Switala J, Van Thiel DH. The quality of life following liver transplantation: a preliminary report. *Gastroenterol Clin North Am* 1988;17:207–217.

46. Paul A, Greig PD, Williams JI. (Personal Communication).

47. Spitzer WO, Dobson AJ, Hall J, et al. Measuring the quality of life of cancer patients. A concise QL-index for use by physicians. *J Chron Dis* 1981;34:585–597.

48. Karnofsky DA, Burchenal JH. The clinical evaluation of chemotherapeutic agents in cancer. In: McLeod CM, ed. *Evaluation of chemotherapeutic agents*. New York: Columbia University Press, 1949:191–205.

49. Kalser MH, Barkin J, MacIntyre JM. Pancreatic cancer—assessment of prognosis by clinical presentation. *Cancer* 1985;56:397–402.

Quality of Life and Pharmacoeconomics in Clinical Trials, Second Edition, edited by B. Spilker.
Lippincott-Raven Publishers, Philadelphia © 1996.

CHAPTER 98

Measuring Disease-Specific Quality of Life in Men With Benign Prostatic Hyperplasia

Harry A. Guess

INTRODUCTION

This chapter reviews available instruments to measure symptoms of benign prostatic hyperplasia (BPH) and the effect of these symptoms on several domains of quality of life. We first present enough medical background to make the rest of the chapter accessible to interested readers with little or no knowledge of BPH. Next, we review published measurement instruments that have been used in clinical trials or epidemiologic studies. Although some results of recent studies are mentioned, the focus is on the measurement process itself, rather than on study results.

MEDICAL BACKGROUND

Pathological Process

Benign prostatic hyperplasia is a disease of men characterized histologically by the formation of nonmalignant prostatic nodules and clinically by signs and symptoms of urinary obstruction caused by the abnormal growth (1). Autopsy studies suggest that pathological evidence of BPH is present

H. A. Guess: Department of Epidemiology, CB 7400, University of North Carolina, Chapel Hill, North Carolina 27599; Merck Research Laboratories, Blue Bell, Pennsylvania 19422.

in nearly half of men in their fifties and nearly all men over 80 years of age (2). The BPH nodules occur mainly in the region of the prostate adjacent to the urethra, so that considerable obstruction may result from a relatively small amount of extra growth. Alternatively, considerable prostatic enlargement due to BPH sometimes occurs in the absence of much obstruction (3). The ill-defined term *prostatism* refers to the symptom complex characteristic of BPH. The course of the disease is quite variable in individual patients. No combination of symptoms is diagnostic of BPH and prostate size is only weakly correlated with symptoms. Nonetheless, symptoms related to BPH are present in the majority of men 60 years of age and older (3) and account for most of the morbidity attributable to the disease (4).

Symptoms and Their Effects on Patients

Because of urinary outflow obstruction caused by BPH, men with BPH often need to push or strain to begin urination. This may be quite painful. As the obstruction progresses, the pressure necessary for complete bladder emptying may exceed that which can be supplied by one contraction of the bladder detrusor muscle. This results in the symptom of involuntary starting and stopping of the stream during urination (diuria). Eventually, the amount of force required to empty the bladder exceeds the detrusor capacity altogether, and progressive decompensation begins, with incomplete bladder emptying (residual urine), presenting symptomatically as a sensation of incomplete emptying. As the residual urine volume increases, the amount of new urine produced before the sensation to void is perceived again becomes progressively smaller. This leads to difficulty in postponing urination and to increasingly frequent urination, both during the day and night (nocturia). These symptoms often interfere with sleep, make it difficult for patients to perform normal work or social activities, and can lead to social embarrassment. Another common symptom is that of dribbling upon completion of urination. This is always inconvenient, often leads to wet underwear, and sometimes leads to the embarrassment of wet outer clothes.

Further possible complications of the outflow obstruction and residual urine include urinary tract infections and formation of bladder stones. Reflux of urine into the ureters can also occur, causing hydronephrosis and sometimes pyelonephritis with permanent renal damage. Finally, acute and very painful episodes of complete urinary retention may develop, necessitating emergency surgical intervention. While aspects of the natural history of BPH can be described in qualitative terms, quantitative epidemiologic information on the course of these events is lacking. In particular it is not clear how often specific complications might be expected to occur, with what prognostic factors, in what sequence, with what timing, and with what effect on the patients' daily lives.

Treatment Options and Practice Guidelines

For many years BPH was treated almost exclusively by surgical resection of the obstructing tissue. More recently a variety of different treatment options have been introduced. Current surgical treatments include transurethral prostatectomy (TURP), transurethral prostatic incision, laser prostatectomy, hyperthermia, and prostatic stents. Medical treatments for symptomatic BPH include use of α-antagonists to relieve neuromuscular components of BPH and five α-reductase inhibitors to shrink the prostate. BPH accounts for an estimated 1.7 million physician office visits and more than 300,000 prostatectomies annually in the United States, making surgery for BPH the second most common major operation for men age 65 and older (1,4). Most of these prostatectomies are performed for relief of symptoms and improvement of quality of life, rather than for absolute indications related to complications (4).

The large number of prostatectomies for BPH is accompanied by a high rate of small geographic area variability in age-adjusted rates of prostatectomy for BPH. Within the United States, these rates can vary by a factor of 3 among local hospital service areas (5,6). Variation in age-adjusted rates between and within European countries is also substantial (7). Efforts to explain this high variability motivated research to develop a decision-analytic model based on probabilities derived from the medical literature and from analyses of medical claims data bases (8). The decision that maximized quality-adjusted-life-months was particularly sensitive to how much symptoms bothered patients and interfered with their lives. The investigators concluded that new methods were needed to permit patients to evaluate decision about prostatectomy based on their own preferences and results of a decision analysis to their case. As an outgrowth of this work, there has been an increased emphasis on assessment of symptoms and quality of life in men with BPH.

In a clinical practice guideline for the diagnosis and treatment of BPH issued by the Agency for Health Care Policy and Research (AHCPR), lack of understanding of the natural history of BPH was identified as a reason for controversy about who, when, and how to treat and for the substantial variation in treatment patterns that has been found both among small areas in the United States and within and among European countries (9, page 1). The guideline recommended that symptoms of BPH be taken into account in making treatment recommendations and that the symptom assessment be made using a standard symptom questionnaire known as the American Urological Association Symptoms Index (AUASI) (4). The guideline also pointed out that in diagnosing BPH, other known causes of voiding dysfunction should be identified prior to reviewing treatment options with the patient.

INSTRUMENTS FOR BPH SYMPTOMS AND BPH-SPECIFIC QUALITY OF LIFE

Why BPH-Specific Instruments Are Needed

It is evident from the discussion above that symptoms can affect the lives of patients in a variety of ways, including interference with daily activities, increased inconvenience caused by the need to urinate frequently, embarrassment from frequent urination, discomfort and embarrassment from wet clothes, worries about complications, lack of sleep, and painful urination. Furthermore, men differ in the extent to which symptoms of BPH affect their daily lives and in their willingness to undergo the inconvenience, cost, and risks of treatment (8). While generic health status measures, such as the SF-36 (10) can provide a useful overall assessment of functional status in a number of different domains, such measures do not provide sufficient detail to characterize the particular ways in which urinary symptoms affect patients and the ways in which different treatments affect different aspects of the disease process. Some treatments may be more effective on the so-called irritative symptoms (e.g., frequent urination, nocturia), while others may be more effective against the symptoms directly related to the obstruction (e.g., difficulty in starting urination, sensation of incomplete emptying). Surgical treatments offer potentially quicker relief, but with perhaps some increased risk of complications. For all these reasons, it is desirable to have BPH-specific instruments that can characterize how symptoms affect patients' lives.

This situation is similar to that which prevails in many other diseases, such as rheumatoid arthritis, where specialized health status measures have proved useful, as a supplement to generic measures, in characterizing effects of interventions (11). The value of BPH-specific health status measures is that these measures provide greater ability to characterize treatment effects on social, psychological, and physical functioning of patients with BPH than is provided by generic health status measures. In the sections below we will review several important BPH-specific health status measures and explain how these may be used in clinical trials, epidemiologic studies, and clinical practice.

It is important for readers to realize that the order in which questionnaires are introduced in this chapter is *not* the same as the chronological order in which they were developed. Instead of tracing the historical development of these questionnaires in chronological order, relating each to the ones that preceded it, we have chosen first to review the most widely used questionnaires and then to discuss earlier questionnaires in relation to these. The symptom questionnaire that has gained the widest acceptance in the United States is the American Urological Association Symptom Index (AUASI), which was first published in 1992 (4). The developers of the AUASI have also developed and validated a brief disease-specific quality-of-life questionnaire, the BPH Impact Index (12), which we have chosen to discuss along with the AUASI, since it is designed to be used together with the AUASI. To illustrate problems in questionnaire translation, we then discuss development, pilot testing, and the use of the French version of the AUASI (13–17). Next, we discuss an earlier BPH symptom and quality of life questionnaire, which was developed and validated for use in community-based epidemiologic studies (18). Although this was developed prior to availability of the AUASI, it permits computation of AUASI scores and it shows how the AUASI relates to several BPH-specific quality-of-life domains. We briefly review the development, validation, and interpretation of the BPH symptom questionnaire used in Phase III clinical trials of finasteride in the treatment of BPH (19,20), which were started in 1988. The main point of mentioning this work in the present chapter is to show how results from community-based studies can be used to help calibrate a symptom score, by relating the raw scores to population percentiles. Finally, some other BPH symptom and quality of life questionnaires are briefly mentioned (30–34).

American Urological Association Symptom Index (AUASI) and BPH Impact Index

The AUASI was developed by a multidisciplinary group of urologists and health services researchers appointed by the American Urological Association (AUA), which is the medical specialty society for urology in the United States (4). The work was undertaken with the recognition that none of the previously published symptom measures was believed to be completely satisfactory. The goal was to develop

a short, practical, self-administered, clinically sensible index with excellent psychometric properties to capture the severity of urinary symptoms related to BPH as it is diagnosed and treated in the course of usual urological care throughout the United States (4).

The AUASI includes seven symptoms: (1) needing to push or strain to begin urination, (2) weak urinary stream, (3) stopping and starting during urination, (4) sensation of incomplete bladder emptying, (5) needing to urinate again within two hours after finishing urination, (6) difficulty in postponing urination, and (7) having to get up several times during the night to urinate (4). The frequency of each of these symptoms over the past month is scored on a six-point scale ranging from "not at all" (0) to "always" (5). The score range for the scale formed by summing the responses of the seven questions is 0–35. Scores in the range of 0–7 are designated as "mild symptoms," those in the range 8–19, as "moderate symptoms," and those in the range 20–35 as "severe symptoms." These ranges were established based on how bothersome the symptoms were to the patients. Men with scores of 7 or less commonly rated urination as not at all bothersome. Using the cut-off limit of 7 or less gave a sensitivity of 79% and a specificity of 83 percent for distinguishing BPH patients from a control population. The BPH patients were drawn from urologists' offices. The control patients, drawn from a general medical clinic, were men between the ages of 18 and 55 years of age, who were not being seen for either prostate or urinary complaints and, who, when asked, denied any prostate or urinary problems.

The same authors have developed a three-question BPH Impact Index to measure how BPH affects quality of life (12). The questions ask how much a prostate condition causes worry about health, limits daily activities, and causes discomfort. In a prospective study of 546 patients, this measure was evaluated along with the AUASI and two general quality of life measures. The BPH Impact Index was found to be more sensitive to differences in symptoms than were the general measures. However, the authors identified the low internal consistency of this index (Cronbach's $\alpha = 0.65$, as measured in one population of BPH patients) as a potential weakness. On the other hand, one might also regard this relatively low level of internal consistency as an expected—and not a detrimental—consequence of having a rather parsimonious domain with just three questions, each of which addresses a separate aspect of the impact of BPH on quality of life.

International Prostate Symptom Score: American and French Versions and French Studies of BPH-Specific Quality of Life

At the Second International Consultation on BPH, held in Paris in June 1993, the same questions and response options as are used in the AUASI were adopted as the International Prostate Symptom Score (I-PSS) (13). The

Committee on Symptom Evaluation of the Second International Consultation on BPH recommended that the I-PSS be used for symptom evaluation, "as one factor in a multifactorial treatment strategy of BPH."

A French language version of the I-PSS was developed by Sagnier and colleagues (14,15) using a three-step process. The first step involved translation by a professional translator, followed by a review of the translation by an eight-person panel, which included a urologist, a general practitioner, questionnaire survey professional, and epidemiologists. This panel, most of whose members were French but were also fluent in English, met several times and proposed linguistic changes to achieve optimal clarity of each question. The second step involved review of a working version of the questionnaire to a group of 30 professional interviewers in a one-day session, which included presentation and review of the questionnaire, debriefing, and feedback from the group of interviewers. This resulted in additional editorial changes and changes in the response scale.

The third step involved a pilot study on one hundred French men aged 65–80 years, randomly selected from the general population. The questionnaire was administered at home in face-to-face interviews conducted by 20 professional interviewers. These interviews involved a qualitative assessment of the clarity of the questions and response scale. For each respondent, a log of difficulties with the questionnaire was produced and the interviewers were asked to rate the interviewee's understanding of each question on a scale of 0–3. The definitive French version of the I-PSS was finalized at the completion of the piloting process. The actual French questionnaire and an English summary of major differences between it and the American English original were published as part of the Proceedings of the Second International Consultation on BPH (15). A more detailed description of the methodology was published in French (14).

The Committee on Symptom Evaluation of the Second International Consultation endorsed the French version of the I-PSS and recommended that translation of the I-PSS into other languages could be performed using either the French version or the original American English version as the starting point (13). The French version was subsequently used in a nationwide survey of urological symptoms and quality of life in French men, using probability sampling methods to ensure an epidemiologically valid nationally representative sample (16,17). This is the first nationwide urological symptom survey ever conducted in any country. The quality of life questionnaire for this French survey was developed based in part on American instruments, especially that developed by Epstein and colleagues (18). However, the French instrument was intended to reflect the French cultural environment rather than to be simply a translation of American instruments. Thus, for example, the French instrument (14,15) asked about BPH-specific interference with dining with family and friends, while the American instrument (18) did not.

The discussion of the development of the French version of the I-PSS and the French BPH-specific quality of life questions makes it clear that translation problems should be considered from the very beginning when developing a questionnaire that will be used internationally. Two questions that appear equally acceptable in one language may represent very different levels of difficulty in achieving cultural equivalence when translated into another language. Some idioms translate poorly and translations can produce shifts in meaning with unintended consequences. Ambiguous phrases in the language of origin of a questionnaire may require choosing one of several more precise phrases in another language. This makes it important to understand the intent of the developers of the original instrument when developing translations. Finally, cultural differences in medical practice can pose problems that have nothing to do with the language itself.

Olmsted County Community-Based Study

Questionnaire Development and Validation

Epstein and colleagues (18) developed, validated, and published a new instrument for measuring BPH-specific symptoms and BPH-specific health-related quality of life. This work was undertaken as part of the preparation for the Olmsted County Study of Urinary Symptoms and Health Status Among Men (OCS), where the questionnaire has been used. To generate items for the questionnaire, a literature search of prior questionnaires was first made. Next, interviews were held both with urologists and with BPH patients presenting for treatment at Mayo Clinic, to identify areas considered important to patients and to clinicians, and to devise questions that covered these areas.

Content validity was assured by the item generation process described above. Construct validity was assessed by several methods, described in the publication (18), and discriminant validity was assessed by comparing the scores of men with BPH for whom surgery was recommended to the scores of men with BPH for whom surgery was not recommended and by comparing scores of men with and without BPH. Responsiveness to surgical treatment was assessed by administering the questionnaire to 23 men with BPH just prior to and 12–18 weeks after transurethral prostatectomy (TURP). Domains which demonstrated statistically significant responsiveness to TURP were (1) symptom frequency, (2) symptom bother, (3) BPH-specific interference in daily activities, (4) worries and concerns, and (5) the depression sub-scale of the Psychological General Well-Being scale (PGWB).

The one totally new area of the questionnaire is the BPH-specific interference with daily activities. This scale was constructed from the responses in interviews of patients with BPH. The scales is based on seven questions that ask about the extent to which urinary symptoms interfere with: (1)

drinking fluids before traveling, (2) drinking fluids before going to bed, (3) driving for 2 hours without stopping, (4) getting enough sleep at night, (5) going to places that have no toilet, (6) playing outdoor sports such as golf, and (7) going to movies, shows, or church. Each question is scored from 0 (none of the time) to 4 (all the time). Thus, a composite score describing the extent of interference with living activities can be calculated by adding the responses, with possible scores ranging from 0 to 28.

The final published questionnaire included 49 questions divided into the following six domains: (1) symptom frequency, (2) amount of bother associated with each symptom, (3) psychological general well-being, (4) BPH-specific interference in daily activities, (5) worries and concerns about urinary function and prostate cancer, and (6) sexual satisfaction. The final questionnaire used in the Olmsted County Study supplemented the above questionnaire with questions on demographics, personal medical history, family medical history, fluid intake, alcohol intake, smoking, health insurance status, and health-care-seeking behavior.

Questionnaire Use in Community-Based Epidemiologic Studies

The Epstein questionnaire has been used in community-based epidemiologic studies of urinary symptoms and health-care-seeking behavior in Olmsted County, Minnesota (3,21–23), Scotland (24–28), and Japan (29). Girman and colleagues (23) found that men with moderate to severe voiding symptoms reported, on average, four to six times the degree of bother and interference with daily activities and twice the level of worry of men with mild symptoms. A higher percentage of men with moderate to severe symptoms (26 percent to 33 percent) than mild symptoms (less than 8 percent) reported limiting intake of fluids before bedtime or difficulty in driving for two hours without stopping. This study also confirmed the original clinic-based studies (4) in which an AUASI of 8 or more was found to differentiate men with and without some degree of bother due to urinary symptoms. Figure 1 (23) presents age-adjusted mean scores for urinary symptom bother, interference with living activities, worries and concerns about urinary symptoms, psychological general well-being, and sexual satisfaction for each of the three levels of symptoms defined by the AUASI. In Figure 1, the scores were divided by the range for each domain so as to achieve a scale of 0–1 for compatibility and graphic clarity. It is evident that there is a progressive detrimental effect on each of these domains with increasing levels of urinary symptoms.

In comparing levels of symptoms and interference with daily living activities between Scottish and American men, using this questionnaire, it was found that Minnesota men reported urinary symptoms that were more frequent, more

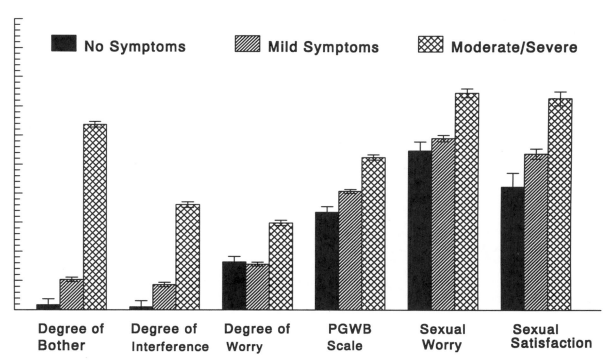

FIG. 1. Quality of life measures in relation to urinary symptoms among men in the Olmsted County Study of Urinary Symptoms and Health Status Among Men. The graph shows the age-adjusted mean quality of life measures among men with no symptoms (AUASI = 0), mild symptoms (AUASI 1–7), and moderate to severe symptoms (AUASI 8 and higher). The quality of life domain scores were divided by their range so as to place all scales on a common standard of 0–1. From Girman et al. (23).

bothersome, and interfered more with living activities than did Scottish men of comparable age (28). Nonetheless, within each AUASI symptoms score category, the extent to which urinary symptoms interfered with living activities was essentially the same (Fig. 2) (28). The authors concluded that although there appear to be important differences in urinary symptom prevalence between Scottish and American men, the AUASI provides a consistent measure of the extent to which urinary symptoms interfere with living activities in both populations. These results lend further support to use of the AUASI in symptom evaluation of men with BPH.

Merck Phase III Clinical Trial Symptom Questionnaire

BPH-Symptom Score

Phase III clinical trials of the five α-reductase inhibitor finasteride were started in late 1988, at which time the AUASI had not yet been developed. To measure symptoms in these trials, a questionnaire was developed based both on earlier BPH symptom questionnaires by Boyarsky, et al. (30), Madsen and Iversen (31), and the Maine Medical Assessment Program (32) and on recommendations by outside consultants. A validation study of the Phase III questionnaire was subsequently published by Bolognese and colleagues (19). The Merck Phase III symptom questionnaire included nine questions scored on a five-point scale, yielding a symptom score with a range of 0–36. Scores based on this questionnaire are used in the publication of the study results (20).

Interpretation of Treatment Effects

One of the difficulties in interpreting clinical trial results based on changes in any symptom score such as the above is understanding the meaning of the score changes resulting from treatment. One way to approach this would be to express changes in terms of the percentage change on a scale of 0–36. A problem with this approach is that it depends on the theoretical range of the score, even though few if any patients ever achieve a score even close to the theoretical maximum. In the finasteride clinical trials, less than 5% of patients had symptom scores above 18. Hence the top half of the scale was devoted to measuring differing degrees of severity in the five percent of the patients with the worst scores. Most of the patients had scores in a relatively narrow middle range of scores.

Another approach to characterizing the symptom score changes is to use community-based data to establish the percentile distribution of the symptom scores and then to translate the score changes into changes in the percentile scores. This is the approach used to communicate results of standardized educational tests, where the percentile scores are more meaningful than raw scores. Also, a similar, but much more comprehensive approach has been taken with the SF-36 (10), where national age- and gender-specific norms have been obtained, as well as norms applicable to many chronic conditions. We applied this approach to the finasteride clinical trials, using data from the Olmsted County Study discussed above. Figure 3 (21) shows the percentile distribution of Merck Phase III symptom scores in a randomly selected community-based sample of 1,314 healthy men aged 50–79 with no history of prostate surgery, prostate cancer, or other conditions known to affect voiding function (3,21,22). These scores, based on a 5-point scale, were computed from the Olmsted County Study questionnaire by using the Phase III questions and collapsing the 7-point scale in the Olmsted County Study questionnaire, i.e., the Epstein questionnaire (18), to the 5-point scale in the Phase III questionnaire. Also shown on the same graph are pretreatment and posttreatment scores from (a) the clinical trials, and (b) from a separate study of 23 patients who completed symptom questionnaires just before and approximately 12 to 18 weeks after undergoing transurethral prostatectomy (TURP) for BPH (18).

Treatment with finasteride for 36 or 48 months reduced symptoms from about the 84th community percentile to the 59th community percentile, while treatment with TURP reduced symptoms from the 97th community percentile to

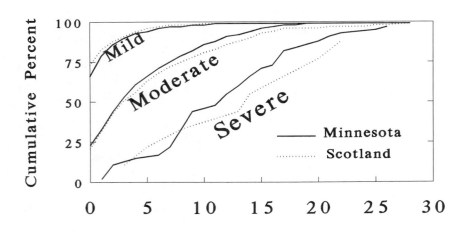

FIG. 2. Relationship between AUASI and interference with living activity among men in Minnesota and in Scotland. For each of the two geographic locations, the cumulative percentile distribution of the living activity scores, as defined in the text and in [18], is plotted separately for men with AUASI in the range of mild (AUASI 0–7), moderate (AUASI 8–19), and severe (AUASI 20–35). From Guess et al. (28).

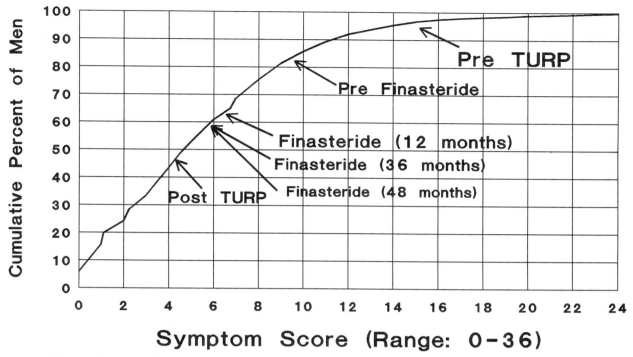

FIG. 3. Percentile distribution of Merck symptom scores in a randomly selected, community-based sample of 1,314 men aged 50–79 years with no history of prostate surgery, prostate cancer, or other conditions known to affect voiding function. Also shown in the pretreatment and posttreatment mean scores for men in the North American Phase III Clinical Trial of PROSCAR (finasteride, MSD) in the treatment of BPH and the presurgery and postsurgery mean scores of 23 men who were treated with transurethral prostatectomy for BPH at Mayo Clinic. From Guess et al. (21).

the 49th community percentile. This comparison is likely to be more understandable to clinicians and patients than simply describing the finasteride results as having reduced mean symptom scores by 3.8 points on a scale of 0–36. The latter statement lacks any population context. Also it is difficult to judge the clinical significance of the changes without any knowledge of score distributions. Also, merely describing the changes as 3.8 points on a scale of 0–36 would not have distinguished between the above results and a score change from 30 to 26.2 points, which would have left starting and ending scores above the 99th population percentile.

Two important conclusions may be derived from these considerations. The first is that expressing changes in terms of population percentiles can help both patients and clinicians interpret treatment effects. The second is that population-based data can be helpful in symptom scale development and evaluation. In the latter regard, it is worth noting that not only the Merck symptom score but also the AUASI may be better adapted to evaluating symptoms among patients with moderate to severe symptoms than among patients with mild symptoms. About one-half of the AUASI is devoted to characterizing varying degrees of severity in the 5% of the community men with the most severe symptoms. This suggests that both the Merck Phase III symptom score and AUASI may be somewhat better suited to following changes over time in urinary symptoms among men with

BPH having moderate to severe symptoms than among men with BPH having only mild symptoms.

Other Quality of Life Questionnaires Used in Studies of BPH

Several other BPH-specific health-related quality-of-life questionnaires have been developed, validated, and used in clinical studies of men with BPH within the past several years. Lukacs et al. (33) developed and validated a BPH-specific quality of life measure consisting of 20 questions scored on visual analog scales and covering four domains relating to physical, mental, social, and global effects of BPH. This was subsequently used in an open-label, uncontrolled study of the α_1-blocker, alfuzosin (33). In addition, the criterion validity of a general quality of life measure, the Nottingham Health Profile, was studied by comparing questionnaire responses to other patient-reported measures before and after transurethral prostatectomy in 388 men with BPH (34).

CONCLUSIONS

Symptoms of benign prostatic hyperplasia are well characterized by the AUASI (4). With increasing severity of symptoms there is an increasing effect on living activities, worries and concerns, and psychological general well-being (17,23). This has been demonstrated independently in the United States (3,23), Scotland (24–28), and France (16,17). The relationship between symptoms and living activities is highly consistent between populations with very different symptom prevalences (28). Normative data from community-based studies can be useful in providing a translation of raw symptom scores into population percentile scores so as to help make clinical trial results more understandable (21). BPH-specific quality of life instruments can add to the information provided by generic instruments and symptom scores. All three types of measures (symptom scores, generic quality of life measures, and disease-specific quality of life measures) serve useful and distinct purposes in helping to characterize both the effects of BPH on patients' lives and how these effects are modified by medical and surgical interventions.

REFERENCES

1. Guess HA. Benign prostatic hyperplasia antecedents and natural history. *Epidemiol Rev* 1992;14:131–153.
2. Berry SJ, Coffey DS, Walsh PC, Ewing LL. The development of human benign prostatic hyperplasia with age. *J Urol* 1984;132:474–479.
3. Chute CG, Panser LA, Girman CJ, Oesterling JE, Guess HA, Lieber MM. The prevalence of prostatism: a population-based survey of urinary symptoms. *J Urol* 1993;150:85–89.
4. Barry MJ, Fowler FJ, O'Leary MP, Bruskewitz RC, Holtgrewe HL, Mebust WK, Cockett ATK, and the Measurement Committee of the American Urological Association. The American Urological Association symptom index for benign prostatic hyperplasia. *J Urol* 1992; 148:1549–1557.
5. Barnes BA, O'Brien E, Comstock C, D'Arpa DG, Donahue CL. Report on variation in rates of utilization of surgical services in the commonwealth of Massachusetts. *JAMA* 1985;254:371–375.
6. Wennberg JE, Mulley AG Jr, Hanley D, Timothy RP, Fowler FJ Jr, Roos NP, Barry MJ, McPherson K, Greenberg ER, Soule D. An assessment of prostatectomy for benign urinary tract obstruction. Geographic variations and the evaluation of medical care outcomes. *JAMA* 1988;259:3027–3030.
7. McPherson K, Wennberg JE, Hovind OB, Clifford P. Small-area variations in the use of common surgical procedures: an international comparison of New England, England, and Norway. *N Engl J Med* 1982; 307:1310–1314.
8. Barry MJ, Mulley AG Jr, Fowler FJ, Wennberg JW. Watchful waiting vs immediate transurethral resection for symptomatic prostatism. The importance of patients' preferences. *JAMA* 1988;259:3010–3017.
9. McConnell JD, Barry MJ, Bruskewitz RC, Bueschen AJ, Denton SE, Holtgrewe HL, Lange JL, McClennan BL, Mebust WK, Reilly NJ, Roberts RG, Sacks SA, Wasson JH. *Benign prostatic hyperplasia: diagnosis and treatment. Clinical Practice Guideline.* Number 8, AHCPR Publication No. 94-0582. Rockville, MD: Agency for Health Care Policy and Research, Public Health Service, U.S. Department of Health and Human Services. February, 1994.
10. Ware JE Jr. *SF-36 Health survey manual and interpretation guide.* Boston: The Health Institute, New England Medical Center. 1994.
11. Patrick DL, Erickson P. *Health status and health policy-allocating resources to health care.* New York: Oxford University Press, 1993: 138–139.
12. Fowler FJ Jr, Barry MJ. Quality of life assessment for evaluating benign prostatic hyperplasia treatments. An example of using a condition-specific index. *Eur Urol* 1993;24(Suppl 1):24–27.
13. Mebust WK, Bosch R, Donovan J, Okada K, O'Leary MA, Villers A, Ackerman R, Batista JE, Boyle P, Denis L, Leplege A. Symptom evaluation, quality of life, and sexuality. In: Cockett ATK, Khoury S, Aso Y, Chatelain C, Denis L, Griffiths K, Murphy G, eds. *Proceedings of the second international consultation on benign prostatic hyperplasia, Paris June 27–30, 1993.* 1993:131–143.
14. Sagnier PP, Macfarlane G, Richard F, Botto H, Teillac P, Boyle P. Adaptation et validation en langue francaise du score international des symptômes de l'hypertrophie bénigne de la prostate. *Prog Urol* 1994; 4:532–540.
15. Sagnier PP, Macfarlane G, Richard F, Botto H, Teillac P, Boyle P. Adaptation and cultural validation in French language of the international prostate symptom score and quality of life assessment. In: Cockett ATK, Khoury S, Aso Y, Chatelain C, Denis L, Griffiths K, Murphy G, eds. *Proceedings of the second international consultation on benign prostatic hyperplasia. Paris June 27–30, 1993.* 1993:144–147.
16. Sagnier PP, Macfarlane G, Richard F, Botto H, Teillac P, Boyle P. Results of an epidemiological survey employing a modified American Urological Association Index for benign prostatic hyperplasia in France. *J Urol* 1994;151:1266–1270.
17. Sagnier PP, Macfarlane G, Teillac P, Botto H, Richard F, Boyle P. Impact of symptoms of prostatism on bothersomeness and quality of life of men in the French community. *J Urol* 1995;153:669.
18. Epstein RS, Deverka PA, Chute CG, Panser L, Oesterling JE, Leiber MM, Schwartz S, Patrick D. Validation of a new quality of life questionnaire for benign prostatic hyperplasia. *J Clin Epidemiol* 1992;45: 1431–1445.
19. Bolognese JA, Kozloff RC, Kunitz SC, Grino PB, Patrick DL, Stoner E. Validation of a symptoms questionnaire for benign prostatic hyperplasia. *Prostate* 1992;21:247–254.
20. Gormley GJ, Stoner E, Bruskewitz RC, Imperato-McGinley J, Walsh PC, McConnell JD, Andriole GL, Geller J, Bracken BR, Tenover JS, Vaughan ED, Pappas F, Taylor A, Binkowitz B, Ng J, for the Finasteride Study Group. The effect of finasteride in men with benign prostatic hyperplasia. *N Engl J Med* 1992;327:1185–1191.
21. Guess HA, Jacobsen SJ, Girman CJ, Oesterling JE, Chute CG, Panser LA, Lieber MM. The role of community-based longitudinal studies in evaluating treatment effects—example: benign prostatic hyperplasia. *Med Care* 1995;33.
22. Jacobsen SJ, Guess HA, Panser L, Girman CJ, Chute CG, Oesterling E, Lieber MM. A population-based study of health care-seeking behavior for treatment of urinary symptoms, *Arch Fam Med* 1993;2:729–735.
23. Girman CJ, Epstein RS, Jacobsen SJ, Guess HA, Panser LA, Oesterling JE, Lieber MM. Natural history of prostatism: impact of urinary symptoms on quality of life in 2,115 randomly selected community men. *Urology* 1994;44:825.
24. Garraway WM, Collins GN, Lee RJ. High prevalence of benign prostatic hypertrophy in the community. *Lancet* 1991;338:469–471.
25. Garraway W, McKelvie G, Rogers A, Hehir M. Benign prostatic hypertrophy influences on daily living in middle-aged and elderly men. *Urology* 1992;161–164.
26. Garraway WM, Armstrong C, Auld S, King D, Simpson RJ. Follow-up of a cohort of men with untreated benign prostatic hyperplasia. *Eur Urol* 1993;24:313–318.
27. Tsang KK, Garraway WM. Impact of benign prostatic hyperplasia on general well-being of men. *Prostate* 1993;23:1–7.
28. Guess HA, Chute CG, Garraway WM, Johnson CL, Panser LA, Lee RJ, McKelvie GB, Oesterling JE, Lieber MM. Similar level of urologic symptoms have similar impact in Scottish and American men—though Scots report less symptoms. *J Urol* 1993;150:1701–1705.
29. Tsukamoto T, Kumamoto Y, Masumori N, Miyake H, Rhodes T, Girman CJ, Guess HA, Jacobsen SJ, Lieber MM. Prevalence of prostatism in Japanese men in a population-based study with comparison to a similar American study *J Urol* (in press).
30. Boyarsky S, Jones G, Paulson DF, Prout GR Jr. A new look at bladder neck obstruction by the Food and Drug Administration regulators: Guidelines for investigation of benign prostatic hypertrophy. *Trans Am Assoc Genitourin Surg* 1977;68:29.
31. Madsen PO, Iversen P. A point system for selecting operative candidates. In: Hinman F, ed. *Benign prostatic hypertrophy.* New York: Springer-Verlag, 1983:763–765.
32. Fowler FJ Jr, Wennberg JE, Timothy RP, Barry MJ, Mulley AG Jr, Hanley D. Symptom status and quality of life following prostatectomy. *JAMA* 1988;259:3018–3022.
33. Lukacs B, McCarthy C, Grange JC. Long-term quality of life in patients with benign prostatic hypertrophy: preliminary results of a cohort survey of 7,093 patients treated with an alpha-1-adrenergic blocker, alfuzosin. QOL BPH Study Group in General Practice. *Eur Urol* 1993; 24(suppl 1):34–40.
34. Doll HA, Black NA, Flood AB, McPherson K. Criterion validation of the Nottingham Health Profile: patient views of surgery for benign prostatic hypertrophy. *Soc Sci Med* 1993;37:115–122.

Quality of Life and Pharmacoeconomics in Clinical Trials, Second Edition, edited by B. Spilker.
Lippincott-Raven Publishers, Philadelphia © 1996.

CHAPTER **99**

Determining Quality of Life in the Renal Replacement Therapies

Atara Kaplan De-Nour and Andrew L. Brickman

INTRODUCTION

End-stage renal disease is the terminal and final phase of several very different conditions. Some of the diseases that lead to end-stage renal disease are hereditary and can be localized only to the kidney (e.g., polycystic disease) or can affect many systems including the kidney (e.g., familial Mediterranean fever). In contrast, other diseases that cause end-stage renal disease are not hereditary. Some affect only the kidney (e.g., glomerulonephritis and pyelonephritis), whereas in other cases the disease process preceding end-stage renal disease is varied, and patients go through different stages of disease and comorbidity. Common to all is the nonfunctioning of kidneys which, if renal replacement therapy is not initiated, will ultimately proceed to uremia and death.

It is now some 30 years since the renal replacement therapies have graduated from experimental medicine to accepted modalities of treatment of end-stage renal disease. In the early years, there were few dialysis facilities, and these were greatly limited in the number of patients that could be dialyzed. Medical centers had committees, comprised of physicians and other medical staff, clergy, patient representatives and other lay representatives. The purpose of these

committees was to select who would receive the life-sustaining treatment. Different selection procedures were used including, value to society and "first come first served." In addition, the likelihood that the patient would adjust to treatment and participate in rehabilitation was considered. Ultimately, these early committees evaluated the potential dialysis patient's medical condition in light of their potential for achieving mental and social well-being: in end-stage renal disease, they were the first to grapple with defining and assessing quality of life.

Over the last three decades, resources and facilities have been greatly expanded. Each year about 50–60 new patients per million population will require renal replacement therapy. The availability of renal replacement therapy, however, differs greatly in various countries, from under 50 to more than 250 per million population. As a result, the almost unlimited availability of renal replacement therapy has greatly increased the number of patients maintained by these procedures. For example, the prevalence of end-stage renal disease treatment is more than 700 per million in Japan, more than 600 in the United States and more than 500 per million in Germany. Associated with these numbers are staggering medical costs, in a time of increasing awareness of limited medical resources. For example, the average per patient cost in 1990 of renal replacement therapy in the United States is $36,600, with estimated Medicare expenditures for the end-stage renal disease program totalling more than $5 billion (1). These huge differences are caused mostly by financial considerations. The differences between countries, however, are not only in the number of patients on renal

A. K. De-Nour: Department of Psychiatry, Hadassah University Hospital, Jerusalem, Israel.
A. L. Brickman: Department of Psychiatry (D-79), University of Miami School of Medicine, Miami, Florida 33136.

replacement therapy, but also in the relative proportions of the different modes of treatment.

Unfortunately, the promised of a life-sustaining treatment has not been entirely met. Notwithstanding the great progress in the medical and technical aspects of renal replacement therapy, survival leaves a lot to be desired: 5-year survival in the United States is only 40%, in Europe it is 48%, and in Japan it reaches 54% (these numbers are adjusted for age and diabetes on which these countries differ). Furthermore, many end-stage renal disease patients often have had extensive comorbidity, severe limitations in ability to work, and restricted possibilities for social interaction. Understandably, the societies supporting this expensive and sometimes heroic effort began to ask the simple question: what is the quality of life of a patient receiving renal replacement therapy? Is this something we should be supporting?

As the options for renal replacement therapy increased, not only were differences emerging in the relative costs associated with these therapies, but also in the associated quality of life. Hemodialysis was the first widely available renal replacement therapy and in most countries it is still the most common. Hemodialysis requires being hooked up to a machine 9 hr/week and following a strict diet (low sodium, low proteins, and greatly restricted fluid intake). It is mostly done in hospitals or centers and is supervised by professional staff. Patients on hemodialysis most often have severe sexual problems and sooner or later will have severe bone problems. Home hemodialysis gives more freedom and allows them to compensate more easily for food binges, but it imposes a burden on their helper. Recently, human recombinant erythropoietin has been developed to address dialysis-related anemia. In the United States, a major justification for coverage under the end-stage renal disease Medicare program was enhanced quality of life. Another form of dialysis is peritoneal dialysis. Intermittent peritoneal dialysis is carried out in the hospital or at home with the patient tethered to a machine for 12 hours; continuous ambulatory peritoneal dialysis is gaining popularity in most countries and allows greater freedom. Continuous ambulatory peritoneal dialysis relieves the patient from being hooked to a machine and from most of the dietary restrictions, but it imposes a grave danger of infection and peritonitis. Although, initially, hemodialysis was the only therapeutic option, experimental renal transplantation was being attempted as early as the late 1950s with identical twins. More complex immunosuppressant steroid therapies extend kidney graft compatibility. However, it was not until the introduction of the immunosuppressant cyclosporine that modern era kidney transplantation began (2). Thus today, the third mode of renal replacement therapy is transplantation, usually from a cadaver donor and less commonly from a living related donor. Kidney transplantation is the preferred renal replacement therapy for children, and is only limited in availability by the number of donor kidneys. Transplantation restores the patient's freedom and relieves the dietary restrictions but imposes the side effects of steroids and the fear of rejection.

One finds a very different array of services in different countries. For example, in England, about 44% of patients are on chronic peritoneal treatment, while in Japan, only about 4% and worldwide, 17%. Similarly, the rate per million population of kidney transplantation is 44 in Sweden, 33 in the United States, and less than one in Japan. It is unclear why these differences exist beyond financial considerations or differences in attitudes about organ donation. When we have a new patient what do we recommend? Which modality of renal replacement therapy is the best? Thus research has concentrated on quality of life (QOL) in the various modalities available for the treatment of end-stage renal disease. The present chapter therefore will try to summarize the available knowledge about QOL in the renal replacement therapies and try to suggest what can be done to increase knowledge in this area.

To a certain extent, end-stage renal disease is a unique situation in medicine. We are dealing with a fairly large patient population, more than 100,000 in the countries that are members of the European Dialysis and Transplant Association, who would have been dead but for renal replacement therapy and who may yet survive for many years. All factors that determine or modify patients' quality of life can be studied in end-stage renal disease and its different therapies. Indeed, machine-dependent life and replaced organ-dependent life caught the interest of the behavioral scientists from their beginnings in the early 1960s. By now there are hundreds of articles as well as a number of books on various aspects of quality of life of patients with end-stage renal disease. One would think that we know all there is to know about the quality of life of patients in the different modes of renal replacement therapy. The fact is, however, that we know little about the quality of life of end-stage renal disease patients.

The World Health Organization stated, "Health is a state of complete physical, mental and social well-being and not merely the absence of diseases and infirmity" (WHO). Therefore, when we speak of quality of life we should actually assess to what extent complete physical, mental, and social well-being has been achieved. However, most studies of end-stage renal disease patients and renal replacement therapy have not addressed all three facets of quality of life. Furthermore, different researchers have used different definitions of quality of life, and therefore very different measures can be found. To make the issue even more complicated, the symptoms of uremia are very similar to the symptoms of depression and medication (e.g., steroids, antihypertensive drugs) and can have massive psychological effects. Furthermore, physical, mental, and social well-being are strongly interrelated and it is often difficult to discover the directionality: i.e., does physical condition influence emotional condition or the other way around?

Many hundreds of papers have been written about the quality of life of end-stage renal disease patients and recent extensive reviews have summarized much of this literature (3–6). Therefore the present chapter will not review and summarize even the recent literature. We will try to address three issues:

1. Problems in quality of life (QOL) research in End Stage Renal Disease (ESRD) patients
2. Relative advantages and disadvantages of the various renal replacement therapies in terms of QOL
3. Suggested future research

PROBLEMS IN QOL RESEARCH IN END-STAGE RENAL DISEASE

Three factors have handicapped and plagued QOL research in renal replacement therapy: definition of QOL, case mix or population studied, and measurement instruments.

Definition of Quality of Life

This book is dedicated to QOL, as well as to its definition. Nonetheless, it is important to clarify the definition of QOL as it applies to end-stage renal disease. Although, there is general agreement that QOL does not simply equal happiness, there appears to be little further agreement. For example, according to Alexander and Williams (7), "The fundamental basis of QOL involves continuously functioning reciprocal interaction between the patient and his environment and encompasses such crucial areas as interrelations, physical well being, social activities, personal development, recreation and economic circumstances." This is a broad definition. However, we do not really expect "personal development" in severe medical illness. Stout and Auer (8) (#6 Gokal) divided the definition into objective measures (mobility, physical performance, employment) and subjective measures (ability to lead a satisfactory social life and ability to have appropriate sexual and affectionate relationships with family and friends). The "employment" part of this definition is problematic. Employment depends not only on the individual but also the social policy and rate of unemployment in the society.

Investigators in the field define QOL somewhat differently. For example, Roberta Simmons (9) speaks of three dimensions of QOL: the physical dimension, which includes health perception, health satisfaction, difficulties in daily activities; the emotional dimension, which includes self-esteem, happiness and life satisfaction; and the social dimension, which includes vocational rehabilitation, sexual adjustment, marital and family adjustment. In contrast, Sensky (6) simply says that, "Quality of life is a highly complex concept with no agreed operational definition." We cannot but agree with that statement.

Some investigators have differentiated between 'objective' and "subjective" QOL. Actually, these terms are used quite differently. One usage refers to objective/subjective *methods* of evaluation. In other words, the patient's assessment is regarded as subjective. Conversely, the assessment

is objective when done by the physician or other members of the treatment team. Ample evidence throws doubt on the "objectiveness" of the physician as a rater of QOL. However, possible bias of the medical team is beyond the scope of this chapter. Another division of QOL into objective and subjective constructs is by *dimension* of QOL: what the patient does (works, walks up the stairs, washes with or without help) is regarded as "objective." What the patient feels (thinks or perceives) is regarded as "subjective."

Is QOL, then, an objective construct, or only subjective? For example, is the objective limitation in daily activity what decreases QOL or is it how much one minds these limitations? For some, limitations in motility could be extremely distressing while for others it would not be so. The problem of objective and subjective constructs in QOL was clearly demonstrated in Borgel's (10) study of nearly 500 dialysis patients with diabetes compared to 120 diabetic patients with functional kidneys. He found, as could have been expected, that the dialysis patients were greatly restricted in their activities of daily life (the objective measure in his study). Dialysis patients with diabetes also reported, subjectively, more pain and more fatigue than the non-dialysis diabetic patients. However, contrary to what would be expected, there were no differences in patients' assessment of "care burden" nor in their global assessment of QOL. In trying to explain the lack of difference in QOL of dialysis and non-dialysis patients the authors concluded, "We suggest that chronic illness could progressively modify the reference used by the patient for scaling his/her global quality of life."

Thus, Borgel et al. have introduced, without elaborating, an intriguing concept that QOL is an ongoing process. The patient's assessment of it is influenced by his or her reference, such as by what is "remembered" of the previous medical condition. This issue of possible effects of past medical condition on present assessment of QOL will be addressed later. Yet, there are different explanations to the unexpected finding of patients on dialysis reporting better QOL than those not yet on dialysis. For example, Harris et al. (11) also reported unexpected results in the same direction. Patients with chronic renal failure, but still not needing dialysis, had much lower QOL (as measured by the Sickness Impact Profile) than patients on dialysis. The authors suggested an explanation that is very interesting though different from the one just mentioned; patients with highest Sickness Impact Profile scores (those doing worst) die before they reach dialysis.

Case Mix

If we are not sure what QOL is, there is no doubt that some factors influence it greatly. Case mix is important in all QOL studies and even more so in end-stage renal disease which is the terminal condition of very different diseases and disease processes. Diabetes should be the first factor considered because there is general agreement that the QOL of diabetic patients is far lower than that of other groups of patients. In some studies diabetic patients compose approximately one-fourth of the sample. In other studies they are completely excluded because of their special and severe problems. Other co-morbidity can also influence QOL, e.g., neurological and cardiac problems. Earlier studies of QOL often did not provide information, nor control for, co-morbidity. The change is not only due to increased sophistication in QOL studies, but to inclusion of sicker patients with multiple medical problems, who in the past would have been rejected. Most recent studies do provide information about co-morbidity, and some try to develop an "illness index." For example, Julius et al. (12) used a 14-item inventory of chronic conditions and diseases, excluding the primary cause for end-stage renal disease and giving each condition an equivalent weight. Some have even developed a specific severity index for end-stage renal disease (13), which so far has not received much attention.

Although less complete than the effects of co-morbidity, there is also agreement about other factors influencing QOL. For example, gender effects have been reported with women doing less well after (12) and before renal replacement therapy (11). Others, however, found little difference between the genders but significantly lower QOL in older patients (14). Other factors mentioned as influencing QOL of end-stage renal disease include education, with higher education equaling better QOL; income, where patients with higher income do better, as well as race, with whites doing less well than blacks. Indeed, race must be a powerful influence because whites in the United States have higher education and income relative to blacks but still have reported lower QOL. Case mix relative to co-morbidity and sociodemographic background becomes extremely important when studying and comparing QOL in the different modalities of treatment: more men than women are on home hemodialysis and more men than women get transplanted. Whites receive transplants more than blacks and older patients receive transplants much less than younger patients. Therefore, at least some of the cross-sectional studies (and most studies are of a cross-sectional design) have tried to control statistically for differences in case mix (12,14–16).

Other possible factors that potentially influence QOL have received only scant attention, for example, the effect of time in renal replacement therapy on QOL. One of the few recent papers with some data about this (16) reported that dialysis time before transplantation does not affect QOL after transplant. But what about the effects of time in the same modality? Is QOL the same in the first, fifth, and tenth year? There is similarly little information about the possible influence of previous treatments on QOL. There is complete disagreement about failed transplants, i.e., the QOL of patients who return from transplantation to other modes of dialysis. While some (16) report they do significantly less well than patients in that mode who have not been trans-

planted, others (17) report they do as well as other patients on dialysis. There is a dearth of information on prerenal replacement therapy psychosocial adjustment, personality and coping. There is not even information on prerenal replacement therapy psychiatric morbidity. Certainly, these factors have the potential to influence QOL and should be included in "controlling" case mix.

To repeat and to stress, the issue of case mix is due to the fact that renal replacement therapy placement is not accidental. In other words, but for one study in which patients were randomized between hemodialysis and intermittent peritoneal dialysis (which is a rare modality of treatment), we could find no randomized studies of modality of treatment—hemodialysis, continuous ambulatory peritoneal dialysis, or transplantation. Furthermore, the process of why or how a treatment decision is made is not given. One can infer the patient's background influences this placement—there are usually more men in home hemodialysis (because their wives are ready caregivers?) and more men than women get cadaver transplants. There are more blacks in center dialysis and they are transplanted less than whites. Why? Most importantly, we have not found a study which reported that patients had input into their modality of treatment and how this exclusion from the decision process about treatment influenced their future QOL. Therefore, to compare QOL of end-stage renal disease patients in different modalities of treatment, there needs to be statistical control of at least the obvious factors—sex, age, race, education, diabetes, and co-morbidity.

Instruments

The single greatest problem that has handicapped severity research in QOL of end-stage renal disease patients is that of instrumentation. It is difficult to find half a dozen studies that have used the same instruments. Two recent reports also included information about measures used in earlier studies (18,14). As briefly described above, there is some disagreement about what should be measured and even more disagreement about how it should be measured.

Measures used can be divided into three basic types:

1. General measures have been developed to study community samples, i.e., basically healthy people. The obvious advantage of these measures is that they enable comparison of QOL of patients to the general population.
2. Generic measures have been developed to study aspects of sick people's behavior/adjustment/quality of life. The advantage of this group of measures is that they make it possible to compare different patient populations.
3. Specific measures have been developed, or sometimes just composed, for studying the specific problems of a specific group of patients, in the present case end-stage renal disease. These measures could be more sensitive. However, these specific measures prevent comparison

with other patient populations. Furthermore, some of the specific measures have been well validated whereas others have not.

These is no way to summarize all the information gathered by these three methods. Furthermore, the following brief review does not try to present the "best" studies and merely aims at bringing some representative examples.

General Measures

The most commonly used general measures are those of Campbell et al. (19). For emotional well-being; Index of well-being (9 items) with its components of Index of general affect (8 items) and Overall Life Satisfaction. These measures were used by such investigators as Evans (20), Deniston et al. (14), Simmons et al. (16), and Barrett et al (21). Using these measures, great differences were found in the emotional well-being of end-stage renal disease patients by modality of renal replacement therapy with center hemodialysis doing worst and transplanted patients doing best. Actually, transplanted patients had higher emotional well-being than the well American population. Sensky (22) criticized these scales for not having been validated for end-stage renal disease populations and for correlating highly with depression. Kurtin and Nissenson (4) also questioned the high happiness of transplanted patients and suggested that it might be related to steroid high and/or to a patient comparing his or her condition to prior life on dialysis. Regardless, this finding of transplanted patients being happier than the American norm was not found on any other measure.

Generic Measures

Many generic measures have been used. Unfortunately, few researchers have used the same generic measures. Following are some of the more frequently used measures in recent studies.

Karnofsky's performance scale (23) of physical activity has been often used (20,21,24,25). Although some regard the scale as a drawback when administered to the medical staff, others regard it as an "objective" measure of physical condition. Nevertheless, on this scale, transplanted patients were found to do better than dialysis patients, erythropoietin improved the score of dialysis patients, and the Karnofsky score on entry to dialysis was found to predict 2-year mortality.

Activities in daily living was another measure often used and regarded as an "objective" measure. However, different researchers have used different activities of daily living scales. For example, Parfrey et al. (25), Barrett et al. (21), as well as McClellan et al. (24) used Spitzer et al. (26). Borgel et al. (10) used the Barthel Index (27) and Julius et al. (12) used a modification of Katz Index. At the same time, Deniston et al. (14) used an Activities of Daily Living (ADL) Index unique to this study. Thus, there seems to be agreement that activities in daily life are an important part of quality of life. There is however no agreement which instrument should be used. All the above-mentioned indices are short ones and all represent the concept that what a patient *does* or *can do* is an important component of QOL.

A fairly recent measure—Medical Outcomes Study 36-Item Short Form Health Survey (SF-36) (28)—has been used in dialysis patients (29). One advantage of this measure is that there are norms for American healthy population as well as American general population. The questionnaire covers both physical and mental dimensions.

The Sickness Impact Profile (30) has been used quite often as either the whole 136-item questionnaire (providing 12 domains, a total score, and physical and psychosocial subscales) or as only the physical subscale. To give just some examples, patients with chronic renal failure had much higher (worse) scores than patients on center hemodialysis (11). Transplanted patients had lowest (best) scores with home hemodialysis next; continuous ambulatory peritoneal dialysis and center hemodialysis had highest scores (15). However, when case mix was controlled (by multiple regression) the superiority of transplantation over the other renal replacement therapy decreased substantially. Julius et al. (12) used only the 45-item physical Sickness Impact Profile and found it highly correlated with activities of daily living. Laupacis et al. (31) used it in their randomized study of erythropoietin and found an improvement in the Physical Sickness Impact Profile scores, but not in the scores of the Psychosocial Sickness Impact Profile. Deniston et al. (14) also used the Sickness Impact Profile and showed the strong correlation of the physical Sickness Impact Profile with activities of daily living and of the psychosocial Sickness Impact Profile with well-being and affect indices. Thus, one can certainly join Dew and Simmon's (32) assessment of this measure as sensitive to quality of life as well as to changes in QOL. It has the advantage of having been used in many diseases, as well as in the general population. The length of this questionnaire is the only major drawback.

Ferrans and Powers (18) developed a quality of life index to measure QOL both in healthy and sick people using also dialysis patients. We have not however found studies using this index in end-stage renal disease.

Specific Measures

Quite a few specific measures have been developed or used. Parfrey (25) developed and validated a health questionnaire specific for end-stage renal disease which examines physical as well as psychosocial well-being. The authors suggested that it could be useful in comparing the various renal replacement therapies, but it seems that their suggestion has not been accepted. A disease-specific questionnaire developed and validated by Laupacis et al. (31)—the Kidney Disease Questionnaire (KDQ)—has also not been used by other groups. Some have developed and validated a specific measure because of cultural reasons, i.e., feeling that translation of measures into another language and into another culture could be inappropriate (33). The trouble, however, with so-called specific questionnaires is that often they are not developed and tested measures but a collection of items that seem to have face validity (34). The use of such measures prevents comparing the specific studied group to other end-stage renal disease studies.

QOL IN THE RENAL REPLACEMENT THERAPIES

Two significant questions are addressed in this section. First, is there a difference in QOL of patients by modality of treatment and, second, is the progress in renal replacement therapy accompanied by improvement in QOL? Each of these questions is addressed separately, although the issues described above, definition of QOL, case-mix and measurement problems prevent clear-cut answers.

Modalities of Renal Replacement Therapy and QOL

To repeat, there are no randomized studies. Furthermore, most studies are of cross-sectional design and the comparison groups differ greatly (case mix). Yet, overall, the QOL of transplanted patients is superior to that of patients on dialysis. This opinion is strongly supported by studies of Evans et al. (17) and Simmons et al. (16). Yet, when case mix was carefully controlled in a study that used a well-validated measure (Sickness Impact Profile), the superiority of transplantation became only minimal (15). In a study of a small group of male transplant patients compared with a matched group of hemodialysis patients, we failed to find any difference in QOL measures (35). Muthny and Koch (36) reported on one of the few prospective studies and reported (on their measures) a clear advantage of QOL of transplanted patients, although this did not affect employment. Parfrey et al. (25) presented results that highlight the importance of what measures are used. He followed up a small group from dialysis to a year after transplantation and found a significant deterioration in QOL on his measure and a significant improvement on Campbell's indices.

Thus it seems there is still not sufficient data to recommend transplantation whole heartedly. Excluding medical indications and ignoring financial indications it can be argued that the patient's wish should be the determining factor. Patients should be given the fullest information about advantages and disadvantages of dialysis and transplantation. We even suggest that patients who do well on dialysis in terms of medical condition, compliance, and QOL should be encouraged to remain on dialysis. Patients should never get the message that transplantation is the solution of all problems. The available data does not support this contention.

Furthermore, patients might do better on transplantation if their expectations were more realistic.

Even less is known about comparative QOL in the two major methods of dialysis: center hemodialysis and continuous ambulatory peritoneal dialysis. This question was addressed most thoroughly by Simmons et al. (16), although they compared a large population on continuous ambulatory peritoneal dialysis to a small population of center hemodialysis patients. In the initial analysis, the superiority of continuous ambulatory peritoneal dialysis over hemodialysis was clear. However, when background characteristics and disease history variables were controlled, the advantage of continuous ambulatory peritoneal dialysis nearly disappeared. Julius et al. (12) also compared the renal replacement therapy modalities. His center hemodialysis group and continuous ambulatory peritoneal dialysis group were different in terms of background, medical history, and comorbidity. Once these factors were controlled, no significant difference was found in the QOL of these two groups. Therefore, no clear superiority has been demonstrated in the QOL of center hemodialysis and continuous ambulatory peritoneal dialysis. Possibly, if pre-end-stage renal disease personality traits were used to formulate an indication for placement on dialysis, more differences might have been apparent. For example, continuous ambulatory peritoneal dialysis could be better and easier for people who value highly independence, freedom of movement, or for whom restrictions and compliance (fluids restriction) are difficult.

Progress in Renal Replacement Therapy and QOL

The renal replacement therapies are continuing to change and improve. It is impossible to review the impact of all these changes on QOL. Yet, two changes are particularly salient. Cyclosporine has had a profound effect on posttransplantation treatment. However not many studies have evaluated the impact of cyclosporine on QOL of transplanted patients. Evans (20) found no significant differences between patients on cyclosporine and on conventional posttransplant immunosuppression treatment. By contrast, Simmons and Abress (9) reported on a randomized cyclosporine study that showed clear advantages in QOL of the cyclosporine group.

Erythropoietin was introduced with much excitement and with expectations. So much so that even toward the end of 1993 Kurtin and Nissenson wrote, "Finally, any study completed before the availability of recombinant erythropoietin must be questioned because of the numerous and significant improvements both in subjective and objective quality of life after the introduction of this drug." Many papers were written in recent years on this subject making a complete review impossible in this limited space. We therefore, concentrate only on three reports: Evans (20) and Levin et al. (29), which both studied large populations, and Laupacis et al. (31), who reported on a smaller, but randomized, sample using measures with recognized reliability and validity.

Evans's patients were initially in very poor medical condition with Karnofsky scores under 30. Before erythropoietin, 30% of patients had normal Karnofsky scores. By contrast, after erythropoietin, nearly 50% had normal scores. In addition, happiness (mostly Campbell indices) also improved. On many of these indices they scored better than the American general population. Their ability to work however remained as poor as before. Evan used a different QOL measure: the SF-36. On this measure too, at baseline, the patients were much worse than the U.S. general population. Their improvement with erythropoietin was made especially on the subscale of Vitality. Laupacis's patients improved especially in the physical dimensions of the specific questionnaire developed by him and much less on the psychological dimensions of this questionnaire. They improved significantly on the physical Sickness Impact Profile, but not on the psychosocial Sickness Impact Profile, and also not on the Time Trade-Off. Most correlations between the increase in hemoglobin and the psychological measures were on the whole significant, but low. Thus the data about the effects of erythropoietin on QOL are unclear. It seems that there is certainly improvement in patient physical well-being. Physical well-being is an important dimension of QOL; the fact that it is not followed by an increase in the rate of employment should not be troublesome. It is less clear how much improvement occurs in patients' psychological well-being. An additional possibility is that it might be a question of time. Levin's follow-up was 1 year and Laupacis's only 6 months. It is possible that physical well-being improves with little lag after improvement of anemia, but psychological well-being improves later.

These data emphasize one additional point. No doubt comorbidity and biochemistry have a great influence on QOL in terms of physical and psychosocial well-being. However, other factors are as important in emotional well-being, and to a lesser extent physical well-being. Therefore we should not expect major improvement in QOL by improving only the medical aspects of renal replacement therapy.

CONCLUSIONS AND SUGGESTED FUTURE RESEARCH

Hundreds of papers, as well as a substantial number of books, have been written about the quality of life of end-stage renal disease (ESRD). It is therefore reasonable to question whether the area has been exhaustively explored, implying that further research is a waste of effort, time, and money. To our regret, this is not the case. Two facts stand out clearly. First, quality of life of end-stage renal disease patients (not to mention that of their families, who were completely excluded from the present discussion) is quite poor and leaves much to be desired. Second, we still do not have a convincing answer to the question: which of the renal replacement therapies is better in terms of QOL?

We need to know more if we wish to improve the QOL of end-stage renal disease patients, if we want to know what renal replacement therapy to recommend for which patients. Even if we give up on improving QOL, we will be forced into clearer answers by medical economics. For example, Evans (37) reported that end-stage renal disease makes up about 0.35% of the Medicare population and accounts for 3.7% of its expenditure. Should these huge sums of money be spent for a 5-year survival of less than 40%, and that at poor quality of life? And should we increase costs further by prescribing erythropoietin that improves the physical condition but not real functioning and doubtfully adds to emotional well-being? Ultimately, measures need to reflect utility and quality-adjusted life-years of the various renal replacement therapies.

The time of cross-sectional studies is over. Cross-sectional studies are not only old fashioned but clash with what we regard as basic in QOL. QOL is not a stable, static condition, but an ever-fluctuating one. Certainly it changes with medical condition.

However, we suggest that even when medical condition is stable there is change in the perception of QOL—the patient constantly compares his or her present QOL to memory of past QOL. If medical condition is stable, a gradual improvement in assessment of QOL can be seen. When medical condition improves the patient can "overshoot" and regard his QOL as better even then that of the general population. A further issue is that medical condition is objective. All other factors should be subjective, that is, how the patient feels about them. Last but not least is the question of sample size. In some areas of medicine, large-scale multicenter international studies continue to be carried out, including outcome measures of QOL. For some unknown reason, this has not been done in end-stage renal disease.

Thus, we suggest a multicenter international study, carried out by nephrologists and behavioral scientists to gather data before patients go on renal replacement therapy. The initial examination should include, in addition to the medical data, assessment of personality (coping) and support system as well as QOL measures. In follow-up, we suggest that special attention be paid to how the patient was placed on renal replacement therapy, what were the indications for it, and what was the patient's input into this decision. Finally, quality of life measures should include both generic and validated specific measures. They should be short enough to be read-ministered during a few years' follow-up. Once such a study is done, it will be possible to prescribe QOL indications for the various renal replacement therapies as well as plan rational intervention for improving QOL in end-stage renal disease.

REFERENCES

1. USRDS 1993 Annual Data Report: Prevalence and cost of ESRD therapy. *Am J Kidney Dis* 1993;22:22–29.

2. Murray JE. Human organ transplantation: background and consequences. *Science* 1992;256:1411–1415.
3. Gokal R. Quality of life in patients undergoing renal replacement therapy. *Kidney Int* 1993;40:23S–27S.
4. Kurtin P, Nissenson AR. Variation in end-stage renal disease patient outcomes: what we know, what should we know, and how do we find it out? *J Am Soc Nephrol* 1993;3:1738–1747.
5. Levenson JL, Glocheski S. Psychological factors affecting end-stage renal disease: a review. *Psychosomatics* 1991;32(4):382–389.
6. Sensky T. Psychosomatic aspects of end-stage renal failure. *Psychother Psychosom* 1993;59:56–68.
7. Alexander JL, Willems EP. Quality of life: some measurement requirements. *Arch Phys Med Rehabil* 1981;62:261–265.
8. Stout J, Auer J. Rehabilitation and quality of life on CAPD. In: Gokal R, ed. *Continuous ambulatory peritoneal dialysis*. Edinburgh: Churchill Livingstone, 1986:327–348.
9. Simmons RG, Abress L. Quality-of-life issues for end-stage renal disease patients. *Am J Kidney Dis* 1990;15(3):201–208.
10. Borgel F, Benhamou PY, Zmirou D, Balducci F, Halimi S, Cordonnier D. Assessment of handicap in chronic dialysis diabetic patients (uremidiab section study). *Scand J Rehabil Med* 1992;24:203–208.
11. Harris LE, Luft FC, Rudy DW, Tierney WM. Clinical correlates of functional status in patients with chronic renal insufficiency. *Am J Kidney Dis* 1993;21:161–166.
12. Julius M, Hawthorne VM, Carpentier-Alting P, Kneisley J, Wolfe R, Port FK. Independence in activities of daily living for end-stage renal disease patients: biomedical and demographic correlates. *Am J Kidney Dis* 1989;13:61–69.
13. Craven J, Littlefield C, Rodin G, Murray M. The endstage renal disease severity index (ESRD-SI). *Psychol Med* 1991;21:237–243.
14. Deniston OL, Carpentier-Alting P, Kneisley J, Hawthorne VM, Port FK. Assessment of quality of life in end-stage renal disease. *Health Serv Res* 1989;24:555–578.
15. Hart LG, Evans RW. The functional status of ESRD patients as measured by the sickness impact profile. *J Chron Dis* 1987;40(suppl 1):117S—130S.
16. Simmons RG, Anderson CR, Abress LK. Quality of life and rehabilitation differences among four end-stage renal disease therapy groups. *Scand J Urol Nephrol Suppl* 1990;131:7–22.
17. Evans RW, Manninen DL, Garrison LP Jr, et al. The quality of life of patients with end-stage renal disease. *N Engl J Med* 1985;312:553–559.
18. Ferrans CE, Powers MJ. Quality of life index: development and psychometric properties. *ANS* 1985;8(1):15–24.
19. Campbell A, Converse PE, Rodger WL. *The quality of American life*. New York: Russell Sage Foundation, 1976.
20. Evans RW. Recombinant human erythropoietin and the quality of life of end-stage renal disease patients: a comparative analysis. *Am J Kidney Dis* 1991;18(4):62–70.
21. Barrett BJ, Vavasour HM, Major A, Parfrey PS. Clinical and psychological correlates of somatic symptoms in patients on dialysis. *Nephron* 1990;55(1):10–15.
22. Sensky T. Measurement of the quality of life in end-stage renal failure. *N Engl J Med* 1988;319:1353.
23. Karnofsky DA, Burchenal JH. In: McLeod CM, ed. *Evaluation of chemotherapeutic agents*. New York: Columbia University Press, 1949:191.
24. McClellan WM, Anson C, Birkeli K, Tuttle E. Functional status and quality of life: predictors of early mortality among patients entering treatment for end-stage renal disease. *J Clin Epidemiol* 1991;44:83–89.
25. Parfrey PS, Vavasour H, Bullock M, Harnett JD, Gault MH. Development of a health questionnaire specific for end-stage renal disease. *Nephron* 1989;52:20–28.
26. Spitzer WO, Dobson AJ, Hall J, et al. Measuring the quality of life of cancer patients: a concise quality of life for use by physicians. *J Chron Dis* 1981;34:585–597.
27. Mahoney FI, Barthel DW. Functional evaluation: the Barthel index. *Md Med J* 1965;14:61–65.
28. Stewart AL, Greenfield S, Hayes RD, et al. Functional status and well being of patients with chronic conditions: results of the medical outcomes study. *JAMA* 1989;262:907–913.
29. Levin NW, Lazarus JM, Nissenson AR. Maximizing patient benefits with erythropoietin alfa therapy. National cooperative rHu erythropoietin study in patients with chronic renal failure—an interim report. *Am J Kidney Dis* 1993;22(suppl 1):3S–12S.
30. Bergner M, Bobbit RA, Carter WB, Gilson BS. The sickness impact profile: development and final revision of a health status measure. *Med Care* 1981;19(8):787–805.
31. Laupacis A, Wong C, Churchill D, and the Canadian erythropoietin study group. The use of generic and specific quality-of-life measures in hemodialysis patients treated with erythropoietin. *Controlled Clin Trials* 1991;12:168S–179S.
32. Dew MA, Simmons RG. The advantage of multiple measures of quality of life. *Scand J Urol Nephrol Suppl* 1990;131:23–30.
33. Park H, Bang WR, Kim SJ, Kim ST, Lee JS, Kim S, Han JS. Quality of life of ESRD patients: development of tool and comparison between transplant and dialysis patients. *Transplant Proc* 1992;24(4):1435–1437.
34. Gorlen T, Ekeberg O, Abdelnoor M, Enger E, Aarseth HP. Quality of life after kidney transplantation. A 10–22 years follow-up. *Scand J Urol Nephrol* 1993;27:89–92.
35. Sayag R, Kaplan de Nour A, Shapira Z, Kahan E, Boner G. Comparison of psychosocial adjustment of male nondiabetic kidney transplant and hospital hemodialysis patients. *Nephron* 1990;54(3):214–218.
36. Muthny FA, Koch U. Quality of life of patients with end-stage renal failure. *Contrib Nephrol* 1991;89:265–273.
37. Evans RW. Quality of life assessment and the treatment of end-stage renal disease. *Transplant Rev* 1990;4(1):28–51.

Quality of Life and Pharmacoeconomics in Clinical Trials, Second Edition, edited by B. Spilker.
Lippincott-Raven Publishers, Philadelphia © 1996.

CHAPTER 100

Quality of Life in Chronic Obstructive Pulmonary Disease

A. John McSweeny and Karen T. Labuhn

INTRODUCTION

Chronic obstructive pulmonary disease (COPD) represents one of the debilitating diseases of adult life. Edelman and colleagues (1) have defined COPD as "a process characterized by the presence of chronic bronchitis or emphysema that may lead to the development of airways obstruction." Although there is some disagreement among pulmonologists as to the precise definition of COPD, the term has enjoyed common use in the medical literature for approximately 25 years, and almost all pulmonologists would agree that the cardinal feature of COPD is expiratory airflow obstruction (2). The primary clinical signs of COPD include chronic cough, chronic expectoration, shortness of breath during physical exertion, and reduction in expiratory airflow as measured by spirometry. In addition, inflammatory damage to lung airways and alveoli are observed during autopsy (3). The major subtypes of COPD, chronic bronchitis and emphysema, while representing somewhat distinct syndromes, often exist concomitantly and both conditions result in subnormal amounts of gas exchange in the lungs and decreased arterial oxygen tension, a condition termed hypox-

emia. Chronic bronchitis is an inflammatory disease of the airways that is associated with airway narrowing, increased secretion of glandular fluids, and chronic cough, whereas emphysema is a destructive disease characterized by the breakdown of alveolar walls, permanent enlargement of alveolar spaces, and loss of elastic recoil of lung tissue (3).

Chronic obstructive pulmonary disease is relatively common. Estimates from the 1989 National Health Interview Survey show that about 12 million Americans have chronic bronchitis and about 2 million have emphysema (4). In 1985, the age-adjusted prevalence rates for COPD were 110:1,000 for males and 119:1,000 for females (5). Prevalence rates for men rose only slightly from 1979 to 1985, whereas those for women increased by more than one third (5). The age-adjusted death rate for COPD rose 71% from 1966 to 1986, during which time the death rate from all causes declined by 22% (6). During the late 1980s, COPD was the fifth leading cause of all deaths in the United States (4,7). It also was the underlying cause for 3.6% of all deaths in the United States and a contributory factor in an additional 4.3% of deaths (5).

The three known risk factors for developing COPD are cigarette smoking, severe hereditary α_1-antitrypsin deficiency, and exposure to occupational and environmental dusts and gases. Of these three, cigarette smoking is the most important risk for individuals living in developed countries (8). Current estimates suggest that cigarette smoking accounts for 80%

A. J. McSweeny: Department of Psychiatry, Medical College of Ohio, Toledo, Ohio 43699.
K. T. Labuhn: College of Nursing, Wayne State University, Detroit, Michigan 48202.

to 90% of the risk of developing COPD in the United States (9). COPD mortality reflects primarily the effects of historical smoking patterns among birth cohorts now reaching advanced age (10).

Several studies have demonstrated a link between genetically determined deficiency of α_1-antitrypsin and emphysema. However, α_1-antitrypsin deficiency is estimated to account for less than 10% of the risk of COPD in North America. Occupational exposures to dusts, fumes, and gases contribute to the development of chronic bronchitis, and for smokers, these exposures increase their risk of COPD (8). The fact that many smokers do not develop any pulmonary disability can be at least partially explained by variations in smoking patterns and environmental exposures. Individual smokers' body defense mechanisms also play an important role in determining whether they develop COPD (3). Current investigations are in progress to clarify the complex interactions between cigarette smoking, environmental risks, and defense factors in COPD pathology (3,8).

The physical effects of COPD and hypoxemia are well known and include decreased cardiac efficiency, decreased ability to engage in sustained physical activity, adverse changes in blood chemistry, and chronic shortness of breath (2,11). More recent studies indicate that COPD is associated with cerebral dysfunction as well (12,13).

COPD is not reversible and cannot be "cured." However, it can be managed using a combination of approaches. Make (14) suggests that the primary goals of COPD management should be (1) reduction of airflow obstruction, (2) prevention or treatment of complications associated with the disease, and (3) improvement of quality of life. Bronchodilator medications are used to help keep airways open and antibiotics are used to treat or prevent infection (11). Corticosteroid therapy, α_1-protease inhibitor replacement therapy, and mucolytic therapy (designed to manage sticky sputum) have proved helpful in selected patients (11). Pulmonary rehabilitation programs, which include patient and family education, breathing training, and systematic exercise, help the patient learn how to cope with the effects of the disease, as well as how to maximize function (14–18). Finally, supplemental oxygen use can be helpful in returning arterial oxygen levels and blood chemistry closer to normal (11,14,19,20).

The preceding represents only a cursory overview of the pathophysiology, etiology, epidemiology, and treatment of COPD. Interested readers are strongly encouraged to consult other sources. Excellent introductions may be found in Cugell (2) and Niewoehner (11), while a more comprehensive treatment is available in Petty (21).

MEASURING HEALTH-RELATED QUALITY OF LIFE IN COPD

General Measures

Psychometricians interested in medical research recently have developed several instruments designed specifically to measure health-related quality of life (HRQL) or similar concepts and that may be used with a variety of medical conditions. Several of these "general" measures are reviewed in some detail by McSweeny and Creer (22) as well as in chapters elsewhere in this volume. The Sickness Impact Profile (SIP) (23) and the Quality of Well-Being Scale (QWB) (24) have been used in several studies of COPD and have established validity for this population (22,25,26). Accordingly, they may deserve particular consideration when assessment of HRQL is planned with COPD patients. In addition, because they are not disease specific, they may also be used to make comparisons among populations of patients.

COPD-Specific Measures

Disease-specific measures can be designed to include items particular to the condition being studied as well as omit items that are not particular to the condition. This permits brevity and maximizes the probability that the instrument will be sensitive to the effects of treatment.

A few COPD-specific quality of life measures are available. The best known and most completely described is the Chronic Respiratory Disease Questionnaire (CRDQ) developed by Guyatt and colleagues (27). The CRDQ contains 20 questions and covers four dimensions of functioning: dyspnea (shortness of breath), fatigue, emotional function, and mastery or "a feeling of control over the disease" (28). The CRDQ is administered to the patient by a trained interviewer and requires approximately 20 minutes to complete. In the initial evaluation, Guyatt and colleagues (27) found that the instrument was reliable and sensitive to the effects of bronchodilator or steroid treatment, as well as a rehabilitation program. In addition, changes in the CRDQ were moderately but significantly related to changes in pulmonary function variables, exercise capability and clinician or self-improvement ratings. Subsequent studies (28–32) have produced similar evidence for the validity of the CDRQ. Since this instrument includes physical symptoms related to the COPD disease process, it may be particularly useful for periodic clinical evaluations of patients' adjustment.

The St. George's Respiratory Questionnaire (33–35) is a 76-item questionnaire that measures three dimensions: (a) symptoms (associated with pulmonary disease), (b) activities (which are likely to be limited by dyspnea), and (c) impacts (social and psychological functioning). Studies conducted by Jones and colleagues indicate that the test correlates to a respectable degree with two measures of general HRQL—the SIP and the QWB—and appears to be more sensitive than either of the other two instruments to changes in the level of disease severity, especially in cases of mild to moderately severe respiratory disease (33). It has also demonstrated test–retest reliability (35).

Maillé and colleagues have developed the Quality of Life Questionnaire for Respiratory Illness, which is intended for use with asthma as well as with COPD (36,37). Fifty-five items were chosen for the questionnaire from a pool of 221 accordingly to whether COPD or asthma patients indicated that an item applied to their recent experience. The items are grouped into seven subscales: (a) breathing problems; (b) physical problems; (c) emotions; (d) situations triggering or enhancing breathing problems; (e) daily and domestic activities; (f) social activities, relationships, and sexuality; and (g) general activities. Split-half reliabilities for the subscales varied from 0.68 to 0.89, and the scales demonstrated moderate and significant correlations with several measures of severity of illness, including degree of dyspnea. A major limitation of the instrument is that it is only available in Dutch and French versions. However, efforts to translate it into North American English are planned (Kaptein AA, *personal communication,* 1994).

Other COPD-specific instruments, which are documented to varying degrees, include a longer questionnaire by Guyatt and colleagues (38), as well as questionnaires by Cox et al. (39), Dardes et al. (40), Hanson (41), Kinsman et al. (42), and Moody et al. (43,44).

REVIEW OF CURRENT FINDINGS

Emotional Disturbances Associated with COPD

Depression

By far the most commonly reported emotional consequence associated with COPD is depression. Depressive symptoms, including pessimism, self-dislike, and feelings of sadness, have been reported in virtually every study of the psychological aspects of COPD as well as in reviews of the literature (45–51).

Although initial findings came from studies in North America, highly similar results have emerged from more recent studies in the United Kingdom and Italy (33,40,52, 53). In some cases, the consistency across studies reflects the fact that the Minnesota Multiphasic Personality Inventory (MMPI) (54) was used as the measure of depression, which contains several items concerned with somatic symptoms. However, depression has been noted to be the predominant emotional difficulty in studies that have used instruments other than the MMPI, including those that have used the perspective of a relative (25,33,38,39,43,44,52–60).

Depression appears to be a relatively common problem among COPD patients. Agle and Baum (61) reported ''significant'' depression in 74% of their patients, whereas both Light et al. (51) and McSweeny et al. (25) reported that 42% of their patients were primarily depressed. McSweeny et al. noted that an additional 7% had symptoms of depression combined with other psychiatric symptoms. Toshima et al. (59) and Yellowlees (62) reported a lower rate of depression in COPD—16%. The differences between the studies might reflect differences in patient samples and measurement methods, but the basic finding that COPD patients are a high risk for depression is consistent.

Undoubtedly, depression is common in many chronic dis-

eases. Friedman and Booth-Kewly (63) performed a meta-analysis of 101 studies concerned with the psychological aspects of various chronic diseases and found that depression was the most commonly reported psychological symptom. However, in their recent review, Kaplan et al. (46) note that COPD patients are more likely to experience depression than patients with most other chronic diseases.

Opinions vary as to the causes of depression in COPD. Most investigators have focused on the psychosocial consequences of COPD such as the loss of pleasurable activities, economic hardship, and difficulties in coping (45,47,52,64, 65). Others have suggested that physiological factors, including the hypoxygenation of the limbic system and related brain mechanisms, might also be relevant factors (25,66). Labuhn (67) tested the relative importance of a variety of psychosocial, medical, and physiological factors in the development of depression in a group of 303 COPD patients using multivariate casual-modeling methods known as path analysis. The results of this study suggest that although physiological factors did play an important role in the development of depression, the depression that COPD patients experience is largely a reaction to their situation. This study is described in more detail later.

More recently, Toshima et al. (58) found that level of depression in COPD patients was significantly correlated with measures of functional status, including activities of daily living, exercise endurance, perceptions of self-efficacy, and social support. Correlations between depression and physiologic measures, such as blood gases, were not generally significant. Toshima et al. also interpreted their data as supporting the functional or situational explanation of depression in COPD.

Other Emotional Disturbances

A variety of other emotional disturbances have been reported in addition to depression. These include anxiety, irritability, hysterical disorders, somatic preoccupation, dependency, and aggressive behavior (25,38,42,47,48,50,52,53, 57,59,61,62,68–72).

The findings of anxiety and somatic preoccupation appear to be fairly reliable across studies. Anxiety, in particular, is observed in almost all studies of COPD, irrespective of whether the MMPI is employed. It is not difficult to imagine that anxiety and concern about one's bodily condition would be a common occurrence in COPD. As was the case with depression, the rates of anxiety disorders vary considerably from study to study. Agle and Baum (61), for example, reported disabling anxiety in 96% of their patients, while Yellowlees (62) reported that 34% of their patients suffered from excessive anxiety. At the lower end of the spectrum, Karajgi et al. (72) reported that 16% of their COPD patients had an anxiety disorder, whereas Light et al. (51) reported a rate of only 2%. McSweeny et al. (25) reported somatic preoccupation in 8.7% of their patients in contrast to 0% in the demographically matched control group.

Findings of hysterical disorders, suspiciousness, and aggressive behavior have been less reliable. Although some of the earlier studies reported hysterical tendencies (69), later studies have not consistently confirmed these results. McSweeny et al. (25) found that 2.7% of their COPD patients exhibited primarily hysterical symptoms, compared with 1.5% of the older healthy individuals. In addition, the MMPI hysteria scale, often used as the criterion of hysterical complaints, contains a high number of somatic symptoms.

McSweeny et al. (25) also failed to find unusual degrees of suspiciousness or anger, although relatives of the patients did report a moderately high degree of oppositional behavior. The lack of overt hostility is consistent with the clinical picture of the "emotional straightjacket" described by Dudley et al. (73). On the basis of Dudley's (74) classic studies of the psychophysiology of breathing, Dudley et al. (73) suggested that the COPD patient learns to avoid the expression of strong emotions, including anger, to prevent the excessive oxygen uptake that occurs in conjunction with physiological arousal. This relationship between dyspnea and emotional status was also observed by Burns and Howell (69), who found that "disproportionately breathless" COPD patients had higher rates of emotional distress than the remaining COPD patients. In addition, the dyspnea improved with the resolution of emotional disturbance.

Social Role Functioning and Activities of Daily Living

General Activities

The performance of basic social roles and activities of daily living (ADL) is often used as a standard for the impact of a disease entity on quality of life. Although early studies of COPD and quality of life concentrated on emotional functioning, several recent studies in North America, the United Kingdom, and Europe have described the impact of COPD on social role functioning and ADL in some detail.

A relatively early study was conducted by Barstow (64). She reported that "major changes" were evident in the "style of living" manifested by the COPD patients in her study. These included alterations in bathing, grooming, dressing, eating, sleeping, and mobility. She noticed, for example, that "the mode of dress was altered in favor of less restrictive clothing that was easily slipped on and off." Food intake was decreased by many of the patients because an overdistended stomach would interfere with diaphragmatic breathing. Sleep/rest difficulties received particular attention in Barstow's report. Disruptions of sleep because of cough, dyspnea, or restlessness were common. In addition, Barstow reported some sleep changes that were apparently related to endogenous depression.

The availability of the SIP during the late 1970s led to a series of studies of the effects of chronic illness with that instrument. Four such studies had been completed during the last decade. The first, conducted by McSweeny et al.

(25), demonstrated a broad range of disturbances in sleep and rest and activities of daily living. In all categories of the SIP except one, COPD patients reported a much higher percentage of impairment than did control subjects. The only category not affected differentially was employment, presumably because the COPD and control groups both contained many elderly retired persons. The areas of functioning found most severely affected were home management and sleep/rest. Eating and communication, on the other hand, seemed to be only moderately affected by the disease (Fig. 1). Additional results from the Katz Adjustment Scale-Form R (KAS-R;66), which represented the viewpoint of relatives, indicated that relatives regarded the patient's social role functioning as deficient; they expected less of the patients but still felt dissatisfied with the patients' performance of socially expected activities.

Prigatano et al. (57) also used the SIP and KAS-R with COPD patients who had mild hypoxemia. Their findings were quite similar to those obtained by McSweeny et al. with severe hypoxemic patients, although, as might be expected, the degree of impairment was proportionately less. One interesting exception was that Prigatano and colleagues did find significant differences in employment status between COPD patients and controls. This appears to be because the control subjects in the study conducted by Prigatano et al. were much more likely to be employed than those in that of McSweeny et al. (25). This, in turn, is the result of a greater proportion of persons younger than 65 among the patients and controls in the Prigatano et al. study. In summary, employment status is more likely to be a significant issue for younger patients than for older patients and may be affected even in those who have small reductions in the availability of oxygenated blood.

A third U.S. study with the SIP was conducted by Bergner et al. (75), with three groups of COPD outpatients receiving home or office care. These patients, accordingly, would be less ill than those in the McSweeny et al. study, and was the case with the Prigatano et al. study, they were less impaired although the overall level of impairment was still much higher than expected relative to norms.

Williams and Bury (52,53) studied 92 outpatients with COPD who, on average, were similar in severity of airways impairment and socioeconomic status to the patients in the study by Prigatano et al. (57). Williams and Bury used a version of the SIP modified for use by British patients. Despite the differences in wording and the location of study (England versus the United States), the results were virtually identical to those of Prigatano et al. and differed from those of McSweeny et al. only in terms of degree of impairment.

A second British team, Jones et al. (33), studied 160 outpatients who were slightly less impaired overall than the Williams and Bury and Prigatano et al. samples in terms of lung function. Unlike Williams and Bury, Jones et al. used the standard SIP. The overall level of impairment was considerably lower than in the previous studies, although for the most part the pattern of impairment was similar. Interest-

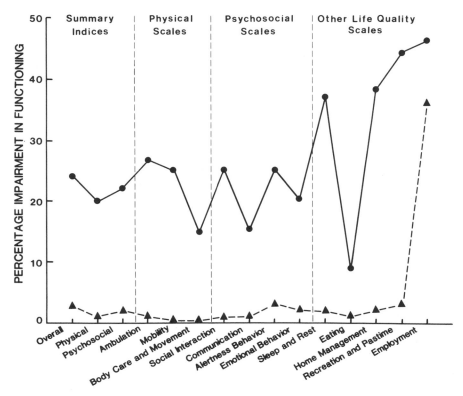

FIG. 1. Mean sickness impact profiles for patients with chronic obstructive pulmonary disease (COPD) and control subjects. Patients with COPD are significantly (*p* <0.001) more impaired on all scales except employment using paired *t*-tests (N = 66). NOTT, nocturnal oxygen therapy trial. Adapted from McSweeny et al. (25). (© American Medical Association. Reprinted with permission.)

ingly, employment was not greatly impaired in the Jones et al. study, and it is worth noting that the patients were closer in age to those in the McSweeny et al. sample, which tends to confirm the point made earlier about the relationship of age to the significance of employment. Another interesting finding from Jones et al. was a correlation between quality of life as measured by the SIP and walking distance that was significantly higher than the correlation between spirometric (lung function) indices and walking distance.

Recent studies of COPD using the SIP also have been conducted in Holland and Sweden (76,77). The Dutch study is particularly interesting because patients at a relatively early stage of the disease were included. As might be expected, the SIP for these patients are much more similar to those for normal elderly than the profiles from most of the other studies with the SIP. Still, significant differences between the patients and normal elderly were found for the three summary indices (Overall, Physical, and Psychosocial) as well as for the specific indices of Communication, Emotional Behavior, Sleep/Rest, Eating, Home Management, and Employment. Consistent with other studies, the authors found little relationship between SIP scores and lung-function parameters.

Not all recent studies of COPD and quality of life have employed the SIP, of course. Other studies have employed

the Nottingham Health Profile (78–80), the CRDQ (27–32), the QWB (26,55,59,81) or alternative methods of assessing general life functioning (38–40, 42–44) and have produced comparable results. A survey of 130 COPD patients by Hanson (41) deserves some particular attention. Her questionnaire included 40 items assessing 11 areas, including several aspects of social role functioning and activities of daily living, such as employment, self-care, home/personal business, marriage, care of grandchildren, and dependency on others. Hanson's results were consistent with those from the SIP-based studies in that she found a general negative effect of COPD across the different categories in her survey. One interesting aspect of her study is that her questionnaire was bipolar, that is, it allowed respondents to indicate a positive impact of COPD on different aspects of life as well as a negative impact. In fact, a few individuals did report positive effects, ranging from 28% for care of grandchildren to 40% for marriage. Qualitative studies with in-depth interviews to obtain more information about interpersonal aspects of illness-related retirement and caregiving might shed more light on these findings.

The samples in the studies described above were predominantly male. This is related to the fact that until recently, smoking was a predominantly male activity. Sexton and Monro (82) have provided a specific investigation of female

COPD patients. Seventy-two women with diagnosed COPD and 40 demographically similar women who had no chronic illness were compared on their perceived health status, problems of daily living, amount of subjective stress, and life satisfaction. The questionnaire used for this study included demographic and illness-related questions as well as adapted versions of the Subjective Stress Scale (83) and the Life Satisfaction Index (84), which Sexton and Munro (85) had tested in an earlier study of COPD spouses' quality of life. In comparison with their health controls, the female COPD patients were found to have lower perceived health status, more subjective stress, and less life satisfaction. They also reported more problems in daily living. Major problems included shortness of breath and fatigue, loneliness and depression, and restricted household and social activities.

Sexual Functioning

One topic not assessed in detail in most of the previously described studies was that of sexual functioning. Other investigators, however, have paid more attention to this important aspect of life quality. In one of the earlier studies on the topic, Kass et al. (86) reported that 19% of their male COPD patients were impotent. More recent studies have suggested even higher rates of sexual dysfunction among men. Fletcher and Martin (87), for example, reported that 30% of their COPD patients were impotent and that an additional 5% had ceased intercourse because of dyspnea. Frequency of intercourse for the remaining 65% of their patients fell to 16% of predisease levels.

Sexton and Munro's (85) study of the impact of COPD on the spouse's life also provides evidence of sexual dysfunction associated with the disease. These investigators compared the subjective experiences of 45 wives of male COPD patients with those of 30 age-matched women whose husbands had no chronic illness. The patient's wives reported significantly fewer marital relations than did the comparison wives. It was found that 54% of the COPD wives no longer engaged in sexual relations, and 48% of these wives, versus 15% of the controls, stated that they had no desire for sexual relations. The wives of the COPD patients also gave significantly lower ratings on their own health status, and this may account for their lack of sexual interest. Health differences between these two groups of age-matched wives could also be due to stressors related to living with a COPD patient, however. The COPD wives reported many difficulties with sleeping due to their husbands' breathing problems. They also had taken on many extra responsibilities and had given up many of their own social activities because of their husbands' illnesses.

Only limited data exist concerning sexual functioning in female COPD patients, although it is probably safe to assume that the factors that affect sexual functioning in men affect sexual functioning in women as well. One self-report study concerning sexual functioning in a mixed sex (62% men,

38% women) sample that does exist is the previously described one by Hanson (41). She found that among the 11 life areas assessed in her study, sexual functioning was the area most consistently rated as being negatively affected by COPD. Thus, Hanson's results are consistent with the more objective findings from Fletcher and Martin (87) and Kass et al. (86) and also suggest that COPD presents problems for sexual functioning for women as well as for men. Unfortunately, Hanson did not report results separately for men and women, and we are still left in some doubt. Clearly, the sexuality of female COPD patients is a neglected area in need of further research.

One controversy in the area of sexuality and COPD concerns whether the problems observed are largely secondary to a past history of marital and sexual difficulties or to the relatively immediate physical effects of the disease. Kass et al. (86) reported on a sample of 90 men and 10 women and concluded that the sexual problems associated with COPD patients were *not* primarily due to the effects of the disease. Rather, such problems were the results of lifelong patterns of behavior. The presence of a wife who was angered by the level of support required by her husband was also mentioned as a common problem in the maintenance of good sexual functioning. The authors provided five case histories (all were of men) to illustrate their conclusions.

In contrast to the report by Kass et al. are the more recent findings of Fletcher and Martin (87). Fletcher and Martin carefully assessed erectile dysfunction in relation to cardiopulmonary, hormonal, and neurovascular dysfunction. They concluded:

> Data from this study suggest that sexual dysfunction and erectile impotence can accompany COPD in the absence of other known causes of sexual problems. Furthermore, sexual dysfunction tended to be worse in those subjects with more severe pulmonary function impairment as assessed by pulmonary function tests, blood gases, and exercise tests [p. 420].

Fletcher and Martin did note that several of their subjects who were impotent by nocturnal penile tumescence had high scores on some MMPI scales, but only one of their 20 subjects had clearly psychogenic impotence. In the remainder COPD was responsible for both sexual dysfunction and emotional disturbance independently or at least some of the psychological distress was secondary to sexual failure brought on by COPD.

In summary, COPD has a documented negative effect on sexual functioning in men and probably in women as well. Although psychosocial factors play an important role in sexual functioning, the sexual dysfunction associated with COPD is closely linked with cardiopulmonary dysfunction and hypoxemia.

Hobbies and Recreational Activities

The effect of COPD on activities that bring enjoyment to one's life has been the object of several recent studies.

McSweeny et al. (25) noted that their patients with COPD reported severe restrictions in recreation and other leisure time activities. The SIP results suggested a reduction of 40% to 50% in pleasurable activities—certainly an important aspect of life quality. Indeed, the category of Recreation and Pastimes showed the greatest level of impairment relative to the other categories on the SIP when compared with the control group. The results from the KAS-R indicated the relatives also recognized decrements in the free-time activities of the patients.

Studies by Bergner et al. (75), Jones et al. (33), Prigatano et al. (57), Schrier et al. (76), Ström et al. (77), and Williams and Bury (52,53) produced results quite similar to those of McSweeny et al., with the exception that the effects were less severe. A reduction of 15% to 40% in pleasurable activities was seen in the mildly hypoxemic patients on the SIP. This was, again, the most impaired category on this test in three of the studies (33,57,77) and the second most impaired category in a fourth (52,53). In addition, KAS-R-results from Prigatano et al. indicated that the relatives were aware of the problem.

That there is a significant loss of pleasurable activities in COPD is relevant to theories of depression that suggest that the loss of reinforcers is a major contributory factor in the development of depression (88). Therefore, it is possible that helping COPD patients to maintain old hobbies and to develop new ones might ameliorate the negative impact of COPD on emotional status.

FACTORS AFFECTING LIFE QUALITY IN COPD

Demographic Factors

The studies described previously have indicated considerable variability in the quality of life of patients with COPD. Accordingly, factors that might modify the impact of COPD on quality of life have been a topic of interest to researchers.

Guyatt et al. (89), McSweeny et al. (25), Prigatano et al. (57), and Williams and Bury (52,53) examined quality of life as measured by the SIP in relation to several demographic variables. Age was found to contribute significantly, in a negative fashion, to quality of life in the McSweeny et al. and Williams and Bury samples, but not in the Prigatano et al. group. Guyatt et al. found that older patients reported fewer emotional problems than younger patients. While this finding is not consistent with the other studies of COPD, it does agree with the results of a study involving patients with several other chronic diseases (90). The reasons for the discrepant findings concerning the relationship of age to quality of life remain unclear.

McSweeny et al., Prigatano et al., and Williams and Bury have also reported significant effects for socioeconomic status and education on quality of life in COPD patients. Generally, better educated and more affluent patients fared better than those with lesser education and more limited resources.

Economic security has been found to be related to life satisfaction in several other studies. In a study of 163 COPD patients and their spouses, Young (91) found that patients' monetary savings and health insurance, as well as their personal resources (positive illness perceptions, knowledge of the illness, regimen compliance, and religion) predicted better adaptation. The female COPD patients in Sexton and Munro's (82) study identified financial concerns as one of their major problems. Similarly, the COPD wives in Sexton and Munro's (85) earlier study had greater life satisfaction if they were satisfied with the amount of money that was available.

Psychological and Behavioral Factors

Psychological Assets and Social Support Resources

A number of investigators have studied COPD patients' psychosocial assets and social support resources in relating to quality of life. Sandhu (51) defines psychosocial assets as "those individual characteristics and social supports that allow coping with or modifying one's environment." After reviewing the chronic illness literature, he concluded that psychosocial assets seem to "play a major, perhaps central, role in the patient's ability to cope adaptively." Sandhu noted that high assets correlate with positive outcome in medical treatment, whereas low assets typically are associated with a variety of poor outcomes, including increased morbidity and mortality.

Investigations among asthma and COPD patients indicate that patients who have stronger psychosocial assets require less medication and adapt to life changes more readily (92), respond more positively to group therapy (93), are less likely to be depressed (58) and have less dyspnea, better regimen compliance, and longer survival time (47). It is important to recognize that the concept of psychosocial assets includes psychological characteristics of the patient, such as emotional stability and coping style, as well as the amount of support the person receives from external sources. Thus, while COPD patients' psychosocial assets do predict outcomes relevant to quality of life, it is unclear how much of the impact is related to the patients' internal psychological resources and how much is related to external social supports.

Recently, investigators have used more precise measures of external support. They also have attempted to study social support in relation to other factors which influence quality of life. Jensen (94) studied the impact of social support and various risk factors in COPD patients' symptom management. He found that social support and life stress predicted the number of hospitalizations better than did the patient's demographic characteristics, the severity of the illness, or previous hospitalizations. Labuhn (67) found that married COPD patients demonstrated better exercise tolerance than was displayed by single, widowed, or divorced patients, even controlling for age, disease severity, and neuropsychological functioning. Marriage did not have a significant influence on patients' depressed mood states, but it indirectly contributed to patients' physical and psychosocial functioning through its impact on their exercise capacity.

Additional studies provide evidence concerning personal social supports and COPD patients' quality of life. Barstow (64) conducted home interviews with COPD patients to assess their problems and coping strategies. The patients in this study identified the presence of a supportive spouse as the most important factor for successful coping. Sexton and Munro (82) had similar findings in their study of female COPD patients; 95% of married patients identified their husbands as important sources of support. The husbands provided instrumental support by helping out with various household activities, treatments, and other things needed. About one-half of women with COPD talked their problems over with their husbands. They also turned to friends, relatives, and children for emotional support.

In the study by Young (91), the availability of community resources was not directly related to patients' self-adaptation, but it did have a significant impact on the adaptation of the patients' spouses. Only 20% of Young's COPD patients reported that they received assistance from persons other than their spouses, children, and parents, and this may account for the greater importance of community support for the spouses. About two-thirds of the COPD spouses in Sexton and Munro's (86) study reported that they relied on their sons and daughters for help; 46% of these wives identified the physician as an important source of support; 37% also relied on friends, and 34% relied on neighbors.

In another study, of 126 COPD patients, Anderson (95) used causal modeling techniques to examine the relative contributions of selected demographic, physical, and psychosocial factors to self-reported quality of life. Life quality in this study was measured with a 16-item version of the Quality of Life Scale originally developed by Flanagan (96) and adapted by Burckhardt et al. (97) for chronic illness situations. The instrument taps six domains of life quality: physical and material well-being; relations with other people; social, community, and civic activities; personal development and fulfillment; recreation; and independence. Anderson (95) found that, among COPD patients, age, disease severity, and functional status were significant determinants of their self-reported life quality. Three psychosocial variables—depression, self-esteem, and perceived social support—had a direct impact on quality of life. These variables also mediated (or buffered) the impact of the disease-related variables on the patients' quality of life.

Findings from the above studies have suggested that most COPD patients rely heavily on their immediate families for support, while family members may rely on each other and on professional and community resources. It is important to consider the implications of these findings for patients who live alone as well as the quality of life of COPD patients' families. Additional investigations are needed to examine COPD family's social support needs in more detail, and to evaluate the effectiveness of interventions directed toward mobilizing supports.

Kaplan and colleagues (46) reviewed data from other studies of social support and chronic disease which provide additional evidence for the importance of this variable in understanding the variability in the effects of COPD on quality of life.

Family Functioning

COPD, like most chronic illnesses, has a negative impact on the family's functioning and quality of life as well as the identified patients' quality of life. The preceding section discussed some of the problems experienced by spouses of COPD patients. The manner in which family members interact with each other in attempting to deal with the illness influences the patient's adjustment of life quality. The family's response also can influence the course of the illness, as well as the happiness of the family unit itself (98).

Bruhn (99) points out that chronic illness is more likely to be disintegrative than integrative for families. As duties and responsibilities are taken away from the ill person and are assumed by another, the ill person experiences a sense of loss, while the other family member is over-burdened. Sexton and Munro's studies (82,85) indicate that this is the case in many COPD families. About one-third of these investigators' female COPD patients said they felt lonely and depressed, despite the support given by their husbands and families. The major problems of COPD patients' wives were being worried over their husband's physical condition and his negative attitudes and irritability, and coping with the loss of their own freedom. Less than one-third of the COPD patients' wives said they shared problems with their husbands. Most were afraid that this would cause their husbands to have an attack of breathlessness.

COPD patients and their family members often have different perceptions about the patients' capabilities and the problems posed by the illness. Guyatt et al. (27,89) had 36 pairs of COPD patients and their significant others complete identical questionnaires about problems posed by the illness. The COPD questionnaire included 108 items related to dyspnea, mastery, fatigue, sleep disturbance, emotional problems, social problems, and cognitive function. The patients identified more of the items as problematic than did their significant others, but the significant other attached greater importance to the problems they identified. Only 17 items were identified as problematic by equal numbers of patients and significant others, and correlations between the patients' and relatives' total scores were moderate in strength.

In studies conducted by Guyatt et al., the severity of COPD patients' airflow limitation was not significantly related to their identified problems. These investigators emphasize the importance of physicians asking patients and their families about their views of illness-related problems, rather than relying on physical disease indicators. This appears to be good advice, because if COPD patients and their family members do not share their perceptions of these problems, it will be difficult for them to find mutually acceptable solutions. Differing views and expectations can contribute to the COPD patients' isolation and depression, as well as to the spouses' subjective stress. A potential scenario is that the COPD patient and spouse may achieve a kind of shared life style that limits the quality of life for both (85).

In general, research on family caregiving suggests that clinicians need to be very sensitive to the needs of spouse caregivers, particularly when the caregiver is elderly. While home care often is preferred by patients, spouses, and other family members, the caregiving role can be very demanding and place much physical, emotional, and financial strain on the caregiver (100,101). Spouse caregivers typically are middle-aged or elderly, and most have at least one chronic illness (102). They may be at risk for exacerbations of their own illness if they do not receive adequate support for the caregiving role. In addition, up to one-third of spouse caregivers are employed (103), and therefore need to juggle caregiving responsibilities and work outside the home. Even if caregiver spouses do not experience acute physical health problems, they may break down under the emotional strain of caregiving. The burdens of caregiving in the home are becoming more recognized, and support services (e.g., respite programs, spouse support groups, and printed self-help materials are becoming more available in communities and health care settings. Crossman et al. (102), Eisdorfer and Cohen (104), Lubkin (101), and Mace and Babins (105) review resources options.

Coping Strategies

The specific coping strategies used by COPD patients to deal with the illness also affect their quality of life. Both cognitive and behavioral coping strategies are important. Fagerhaugh (106) discusses "routing" as a basic behavioral strategy that COPD patients can use to conserve energy while carrying out their daily activities. Routing includes planning the number and types of activities needed; making judgments about when to delete, postpone, or condense activities; and anticipating obstacles and planning solutions. Halcomb (107) emphasizes the changes in lifestyle that are necessary in order for COPD patients to improve their physical and mental well-being. Patients need guidance in learning how to mobilize support resources and deal with family and marital problems, as well as how to prevent and manage disease symptoms. Effective intervention should give the patient a sense of control over the environment. Stollenwerk (108) also recommends assessing the spiritual resources of COPD patients for their potential as a coping resource. In a study of self-care practices among COPD patients, she found that patients' values and spiritual beliefs affected their decisions regarding self-care, as well as their attitudes and emotional stability. Stollenwerk encourages professionals to become better aware of patients' values in order to assist individual patients to achieve their own goals.

Self-efficacy and Mastery

Kaplan and colleagues (46) have suggested that the concept of self-efficacy, originally described by Bandura (109), is important in understanding a patient's ability to cope adequately with the effects of COPD and to benefit from pulmonary rehabilitation programs. In addition, Toshima et al. (59) reported that a rehabilitation program improved self-efficacy expectations for walking more effectively than a simple education program with COPD patients. In a more recent study by Toshima et al. (60), self-efficacy for walking was not improved by rehabilitation, nor was it related to QWB scores or depression as measured by the CES-D (110), although it was related to exercise capability.

Moody et al. (44) assessed the personality variable of Mastery, as described by Guyatt and Berman and colleagues (27), in a sample of 45 COPD patients and reported a significant correlation with general quality of life as measured by a scale developed by Spitzer et al. (111). Given the similarity of the concepts of Mastery and Self-Efficacy, the finding from Moody and her colleagues would appear to support the hypotheses of Kaplan and his colleagues. However, the importance of self-efficacy in the quality of life of COPD patients requires additional verification.

Smoking

Cigarette smoking has serious implications for COPD patients' quality of life. Continued smoking contributes to the physical disease process and exacerbates the patients' respiratory symptoms (8,11). When persons with COPD quit smoking or substantially reduce their smoking rates, the decline in lung function is much less rapid, and in some cases returns to that associated with normal aging (112–114). In comparison with current smokers, ex-smokers have less sputum production, fewer chest infections, easier breathing, and greater tolerance for physical activities (112,114). As a result, they may experience themselves to be physically healthier and more comfortable than do current smokers (115). COPD ex-smokers also are more capable of performing physical and psychosocial activities associated with everyday living, and may be more emotionally adjusted (57).

Most persons with diagnosed COPD are aware that smoking contributes to their lung disease, and they report that they have been advised to quit smoking (116). Most of these persons also say that they want to quit smoking, but they have little confidence in their ability to quit. In the study by Pederson et al. (116), 75% of the current smokers stated that they wanted to quit smoking, but only 20% were certain they would quit within 6 months. In a review of the literature on physician advice to quit smoking, Pederson (117) found quitting rates of 20% to 56% for COPD patients. Other investigators have found that from two-thirds to three-fourths of patients in respiratory rehabilitation programs eventually quit smoking (118). However, Mausner (119) found that most persons with COPD make multiple attempts to quit smoking before achieving success.

Labuhn et al. (120) interviewed 136 COPD patients about their experiences with quitting smoking and found results similar to those of Mausner (119). Both ex-smokers and current smokers reported multiple relapses. The most frequently used methods to quit smoking were ''cold turkey'' and gradual cutting down. Few individuals used self-help materials, received counseling on quitting strategies, or participated in smoking cessation programs. Most of the patients were not aware of the available resources for smoking cessation, and 50% of the current smokers requested that information be sent to them. Future studies on COPD patients' smoking cessation attempts also need to address the role of emotional arousal during the quitting process (116), as well as issues of self-efficacy known to affect one's ability to change one's behavior (115).

Treatment and Rehabilitation

Effects on Quality of Life

The findings concerning the effects of treatment and rehabilitation on quality of life in COPD is mixed. Several controlled and uncontrolled studies have reported improvements in quality of life as a response to pulmonary rehabilitation (30,121–124) or oxygen therapy (40). Other studies have either provided negative results or have been inconclusive (8,29,125,126). The best that can be said at present is that rehabilitation and oxygen treatment appear to have a positive effect on quality of life in many cases and that further research is necessary to determine what aspects of rehabilitation and treatment are most likely to produce benefits in terms of quality of life.

Physiologic Factors

Physiological factors related to the COPD disease process account for some of the limitations in life quality. There is ample evidence that respiratory functioning itself has a significant impact on patients' functioning. When bronchodilators are prescribed for symptomatic relief of breathing problems, temporary improvements in patients' functional capacity and emotional states often are seen (122). Oxygen treatment may also result in improved functioning for some, although not all, patients (125–127).

Several investigators have examined the relationship of exercise capability, pulmonary function variables, and other measures of the efficiency of the cardiopulmonary system to quality of life (25,33,52,53,56,57,60,76). The relationship between traditional spirometric variables or blood gases and quality of life has been found to be statistically significant in most of the studies, but quite weak and probably of limited clinical significance. Although Light et al. (51) present contradictory data, the relationship between exercise capability and quality of life was quite robust across the studies noted in the preceding sentences. This would suggest that the ability to engage in physical activity is an important determinant in one's quality of life. Data from an evaluation of a rehabilitation program by Toshima and colleagues (58) also support the relationship between exercise capability and depression. Those patients whose emotional status improved also showed improvement in terms of treadmill performance.

Neuropsychological and Related Factors

Neuropsychological Effects of COPD

Several studies conducted during the past 25 years have clearly established that patients with moderate to severe COPD suffer deficits in brain function, as reflected in standardized neuropsychological measures (12,13,128–131). Perhaps the most comprehensive study on the neuropsychological effects of hypoxemia in COPD was conducted by Grant and colleagues (12). They studied 302 patients with mild to severe hypoxemic COPD in addition to 99 healthy control subjects matched on the basis of sociodemographic variables. An expanded version of the Halstead Reitan Neuropsychological Test Battery (HRNTB) (132) was employed to assess quality of brain function. The HRNTB is the most widely used set of measures in North America used to evaluate cognitive, memory, perceptuomotor, and related skills known to be sensitive to brain function. Univariate statistical tests were significant across almost all measures, indicating neuropsychological deficit, when patients were compared with control subjects.

In order to enhance the meaningfulness of the findings, subjects were divided on the basis of blood gas studies into normal, mild hypoxemia, moderate hypoxemia, and severe hypoxemia groups. Blind clinical ratings were made by three experienced neuropsychologists of performance in seven functional areas in addition to a global rating. The results are displayed in Figure 2. These data indicate that neuropsychological functioning is sensitive in general to the effects of hypoxemia and that the overall severity of the effects are related to the severity hypoxemia. However, a closer inspection of Figure 2 also reveals that all neuropsychological functions are not equally sensitive to the effects of hypoxemia. Mild hypoxemia has no significant effect on simple sensory skills, and even severe hypoxemia produces only mild deficits in the typical case. By contrast, even mild hypoxemia results in marked deficits in abstraction/flexibility with additional hypoxemia resulting in even more disability. Other ability areas demonstrate intermediate patterns of response to hypoxemia. The findings of Grant et al. (12) have implications for quality of life. If we assume that different aspects of quality of life depend on different skills, it follows that

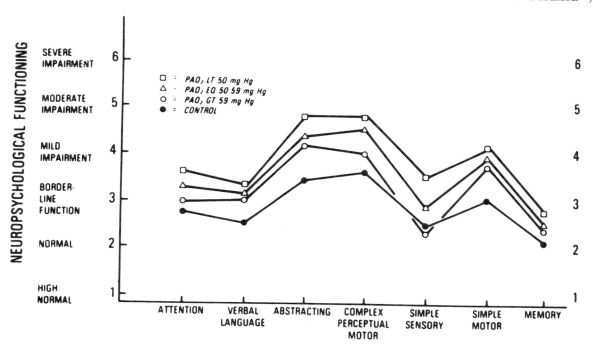

FIG. 2. Neuropsychological performance of COPD patients at three levels of hypoxemia and age-matched controls. (Adapted from Grant et al. (12). Reprinted with permission.)

certain areas of life functioning will be more or less affected by different degrees of hypoxemia.

Relationship of Neuropsychologic Status to Quality of Life in COPD

Relatively simple analyses of the relationship between neuropsychological functioning and quality of life were conducted by McSweeny et al. (25) and Prigatano et al. (57). McSweeny and co-workers found moderate but significant correlations between neuropsychological summary measures and Quality of Life as measured by the Sickness Impact Profile Total Score (23). Similarly, clinician ratings of neuropsychological impairment were found to make a significant contribution to a multiple regression analysis also incorporating measures of age, socioeconomic status, and severity of COPD as predictors with SIP Total Score as the dependent variable. The results of this analysis led McSweeny et al. (25) to suggest the heuristic model shown in Figure 3, which relates COPD, neuropsychological functioning and other variables affecting quality of life.

Prigatano and colleagues (57) also found a significant relationship between neuropsychological functioning and quality of life using the same summary indices as McSweeny et al. However, the relationship was less robust and neuropsychological functioning did not contribute significantly to a multiple regression analysis predicting life quality. On the other hand, Prigatano and colleagues did find more robust relationships between quality of life and measures of emotional status.

McSweeny and colleagues (133) took advantage of the availability of the combined data set described above in the discussion of the neuropsychological studies of Grant et al. (12), to study the interrelationships between neuropsychological functioning and quality of life. Analyses using simple correlations, canonical correlations, and multiple regression techniques indicated that neuropsychological measures do predict quality of life. Neuropsychological status was more consistently related to activities of daily living and performance of basic social roles than to emotional functioning. Complex, multifunctional neuropsychological tasks were found to be the best overall predictors of life functioning whereas more specific neuropsychological tests served as better predictors of specific life functions. A test of language served as the best predictor of communication skills, for example. Additional analyses indicated that the variance contributed by the neuropsychological tests to the life quality indices was typically significant and separate from the variance accounted for by age and education.

Labuhn (67) sought to investigate the interrelationships between life quality and other aspects of functioning in more detail with the data provided by Grant et al. (12). Specifically, she attempted to develop and test a multivariate model for explaining depression in COPD using path analysis (134). The model represented an attempt to integrate the various biological, psychological, and sociological explanations of depressed mood as applied to COPD patients. The path model

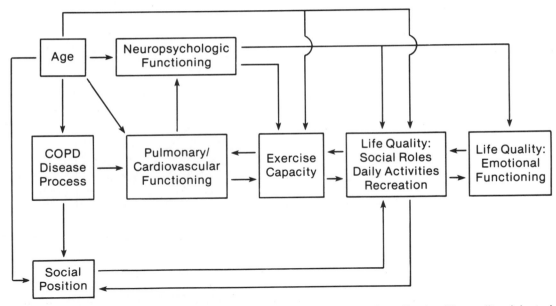

FIG. 3. Heuristic model for interrelation of COPD and other variables affecting life quality. Adapted from McSweeney et al. (25). (© American Medical Association. Reprinted with permission.)

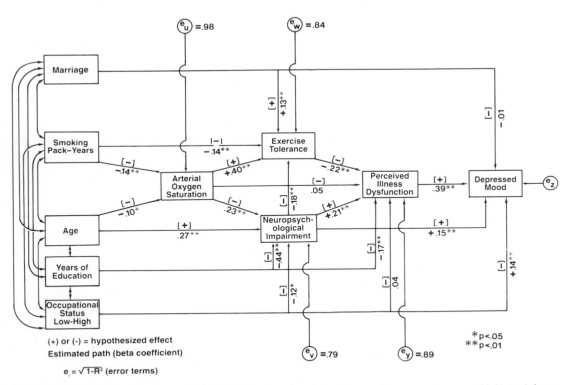

FIG. 4. Path model for depressed mood in chronic obstructive pulmonary disease. (Adapted from LaBuhn (67).)

(Fig. 4) included five sociodemographic variables and five clinical or disease-related variables. According to the model, one variable—perceived illness dysfunction (self-reported physical and psychosocial deficits as measured by the SIP)—directly impacts on mood, with more dysfunctional patients having higher levels of depressed mood (POMS depression/dejection). Five variables—smoking, age, education, exercise tolerance and arterial oxygen saturation—indirectly influence depressed mood through their effects on other variables in the model. Three variables—neuropsychological impairment (Average Impairment Rating), occupational status, and marital status—were hypothesized to have both direct and indirect effects on depressed mood.

Figure 4 and Table 1 show the standardized regression coefficients for linkages in the hypothesized model. Table 1 also includes a summary of the direct, indirect, and total effects of each predictor variable on depressed mood. Findings from this study indicate that perceived illness dysfunction, which reflects patients' difficulties in carrying out their daily physical and psychosocial activities, makes the largest contribution to depressed mood. Neuropsychological impairment directly contributes to depressed mood; it also has a negative impact on exercise tolerance, physical functioning, and psychosocial functioning. Neuropsychological impairment also serves as an important intervening variable between depressed mood and disease severity (as measured by oxygen saturation), education, and age. Exercise tolerance only has a small effect on depressed mood, but it also contributes to quality of life by influencing patients' physical and psychosocial functioning. Oxygen saturation has no direct effect on quality of life measures, but it indirectly affects life quality by its influence on patients' exercise tolerance and neuropsychological functioning.

Additional analyses from Labuhn's study suggests that the relative contribution of predictor variables to COPD patients' life quality may change as the disease progresses.

TABLE 1. *Direct, indirect, and total effects of predictors on the NOTT and IPPB patients' depressed mood scores*

Predictor variable effect	Direct effect	Indirect effect	Total
Perceived illness dysfunction	+0.39	0.0000	+0.3900
Neuropsychological impairment	+0.15	+0.0973	+0.2473
Exercise tolerance	0.00	−0.0858	−0.0858
Arterial oxygen saturation	0.00	−0.1007	−0.1007
Occupational status (low–high)	+0.14	−0.0453	+0.0947
Education (low–high)	0.00	−0.0751	−0.0751
Age	0.00	+0.0834	+0.0834
Smoking pack-years	0.00	+0.0274	+0.0274
Marriage	−0.01	−0.0112	−0.0212

Adapted from Labuhn (67).

For instance, psychosocial factors appear to be more important in explaining depressed mood when patients have mild to moderately severe disease, but physiological and neuropsychological factors are more predictive of depressed mood for patients with advanced disease. Overall, quality of life is never a simple function of disease severity. A wide range of adjustment is seen at all stages of the disease.

CONCLUSIONS

The investigations reviewed in the preceding sections underline the importance of psychological factors in the experience of COPD and of the patient's ability to cope with life and to benefit from rehabilitation and treatment. Thus, it would seem axiomatic that psychological variables should be included as outcome variables in most patients and as predictor or moderator variables in some patients, when medical and rehabilitative interventions for COPD are evaluated. In addition, psychological factors may also be useful in explaining some aspects of respiration in COPD that cannot be otherwise explained (69,74,135). Future research should include formal evaluations of psychological interventions for COPD patients that are aimed at ameliorating the psychological consequences of COPD as well as at improving the process and outcome of treatment and rehabilitation programs.

Clinical Implications

Clinicians who care regularly for patients with COPD will not be surprised that researchers have found that many of their patients are unhappy, anxious, obstreperous, and unable to manage social transactions appropriate to their age and socioeconomic situation. Perhaps, the more important finding, however, is that life quality is not simply a function of the patient's cardiopulmonary pathophysiology. Rather, the ability of the COPD patient to cope is influenced by age, social position, coping skills, family support, neuropsychological status, and other factors. Thus, the older and more disadvantaged patient is likely to have more social impairment and subjective distress. At the same time, changes in mental abilities may make the patient less able to understand treatment and less cooperative and flexible in seeking alternative sources of satisfaction.

Current research leads to the prediction that the patient with the poorest life quality would be the least likely to respond to traditional intervention because of the COPD-associated features of advanced age, low social position, and depressed cognitive set, and neuropsychological deficit. This prediction is borne out by one study by Pattison et al. (93) that attempted to use insight-oriented group psychotherapy with COPD patients. Several persons in this program became openly hostile to the implication that they might have a ''psychological problem''; others showed little or no benefit. I. Grant (*personal communication*, 1988) suggests that a

cognitive behavioral-oriented therapy should be more efficacious with COPD patients than insight-oriented therapy. In
addition, Rosser et al. (136) obtained encouraging results
with individual psychotherapy. In general, however, the utility of psychotherapy with COPD patients requires additional investigation.

A more fruitful approach might be to integrate psychosocial supports into a multimodal pulmonary rehabilitation
program, a suggestion also made by Dudley et al. (137).
Psychological interventions that are part of standard patient
education and rehabilitation programs are less obtrusive,
more acceptable to patients, and have greater potential for
success than does traditional psychotherapy. For example,
a program devised by the American Lung Association of
West Virginia (138) includes both didactic lectures concerning the psychosocial effects of COPD and how to cope with
them and structured group exercises for patients with COPD
and their families. This program puts a particular emphasis
on "depersonalizing" the emotional effects of COPD by
attributing them to the disease process and teaching patients
how to maximize access to activities that would yield psychological reinforcement. This program has also been adopted
for use with patient support groups.

The psychosocial management of the COPD patient has
received brief treatment in this chapter. For further suggestions, the reader is advised to consult Dudley et al. (137,
139,140), Grant and Timms (141), Kaplan et al. (46),
McSweeny and Grant (142), and Sandhu (50).

ACKNOWLEDGMENTS

The authors acknowledge the contributions of colleagues
who helped develop many of the concepts presented in this
chapter: Thomas L. Creer, Robert M. Kaplan, Igor Grant,
Robert K. Heaton, and Kenneth M. Adams.

REFERENCES

1. Edelman NH, Kaplan RM, Buist AS, et al. Chronic obstructive pulmonary disease. *Chest* 1992;102(suppl):243S–256S.
2. Cugell DW. COPD: a brief introduction for behavioral scientists. In:
McSweeny AJ, Grant I, eds. *Chronic obstructive pulmonary disease:
a behavioral perspective.* New York: Marcel Dekker, 1988:1–18.
3. Nadel JA. General principles and diagnostic approach. In: Murray
JS, Nadel JA, eds. *Textbook of respiratory medicine.* 2nd ed. Vol 2.
Philadelphia: WB Saunders, 1994:1245–1258.
4. Adams PF, Benson V. *Current estimates from the National Health
Interview Survey, 1989.* National Center for Health Statistics. Vital
Health Statistics, 1990, 10:96.
5. Feinlieb M, Rosenberg HM, Collins JG, et al. Trends in COPD morbidity and mortality in the United States. *Am Rev Respir Dis* 1989;
140:S9–S18.
6. Higgins MW, Thom T. Incidence, prevalence, and mortality: intra-
and intercountry differences. In: Hensley MJ, Saunders, NA, eds.
Clinical epidemiology of chronic obstructive pulmonary disease. New
York: Marcel Dekker, 1989:23–44.
7. Center for Disease Control. Mortality patterns—United States 1987.
MMWR 1990;39:12.
8. Buist AB, Vollmer WM. Smoking and other risk factors. In: Murray
JF, Nadel JA, eds. *Textbook of respiratory medicine.* 2nd ed. Vol 2.
Philadelphia: WB Saunders, 1994:1259–1287.
9. US Surgeon General. *The health consequences of smoking: chronic
pulmonary lung disease.* Publ No. 84-50205, Washington, DC: US
Department of Health and Human Resources, 1984.
10. Snider GL, Faling JSI. Chronic bronchitis and emphysema. In: Murray
JF, Nadel JA, eds. *Textbook of respiratory medicine.* 2nd ed. Vol. 2
Philadelphia: WB Saunders, 1994:1331–1397.
11. Niewoehner D. Clinical aspects of chronic obstructive pulmonary
disease. In: Baum GL, Wolinsky EL, eds. *Textbook of pulmonary
diseases.* 5th ed. Vol. 2. Boston: Little, Brown & Co. 1994:995–1027.
12. Grant I, Prigatano GP, Heaton RK, et al. Progressive neuropsychological impairment in relation to hypoxemia in chronic obstructive pulmonary disease. *Arch Gen Psychiatry* 1987;44:999–1006.
13. Prigatano GP, Grant I. Neuropsychological correlates of COPD. In:
McSweeny AJ, Grant I, eds. *Chronic obstructive pulmonary disease:
a behavioral perspective.* New York: Marcel Dekker, 1988:39–57.
14. Make B. COPD: management and rehabilitation. *Am Fam Physician* 1991;43:1315–1324.
15. Casaburi R, Petty TL. *Principles and practice of pulmonary rehabilitation.* Philadelphia: WB Saunders, 1993.
16. Haas F, Axen K, Salazar-Schicchi J, et al. Pulmonary rehabilitation.
In: Baum GL, Wolinsky EL, eds. *Textbook of pulmonary diseases.*
5th ed. Vol. 2. Boston: Little, Brown & Co. 1994:1215–1244.
17. Ries AL. Position paper of the American Association of Cardiovascular and Pulmonary Rehabilitation: scientific basis of pulmonary rehabilitation. *J Cardiopulm Rehabil* 1990;10:418–441.
18. Ries AL. Pulmonary rehabilitation: rationale, components, and results.
J Cardiopulm Rehabil 1991;11:23–28.
19. Petty TL. Medical management of COPD. In: McSweeny AJ, Grant I,
eds. *Chronic obstructive pulmonary disease: a behavioral perspective.*
New York: Marcel Dekker, 1988:87–103.
20. Petty TL. Long-term outpatient oxygen therapy. In: Petty TL, ed.
Chronic obstructive pulmonary disease. 2nd ed. Revised and expanded. New York: Marcel Dekker, 1985:375–388.
21. Petty TL. *Chronic obstructive pulmonary disease.* 2nd ed. Revised
and expanded. New York: Marcel Dekker, 1985.
22. McSweeny AJ, Creer TL. Health-related quality of life assessment
in medical care. In: Bone RC, ed. *Disease-a-Month.* St. Louis: CV
Mosby, 1995;16:1–72.
23. Bergner M, Bobbitt RA, Carter W, et al. The Sickness Impact Profile:
development and final revision of a health status measure. *Med
Care* 1981;12:787–805.
24. Kaplan RM, Bush JW, Berry CC. Health status. Types of validity
and the index of well-being. *Health Serv Res* 1976;11:478–507.
25. McSweeny AJ, Grant I, Heaton RK, et al. Life quality of patients
with chronic obstructive pulmonary disease. *Arch Intern Med* 1982;
142:473–478.
26. Kaplan RM, Atkins CJ, Timms R. Validity of a quality of well-being
scale as an outcome measure in chronic obstructive pulmonary disease.
J Chron Dis 1984;37:85–95.
27. Guyatt GH, Berman LB, Townsend M, et al. A measure of quality
of life for clinical trials in chronic lung disease. *Thorax* 1987;42:773–
778.
28. Cottrell JJ, Paul C, Ferson S. Quality of life measures in COPD
patients: how do they compare? *Am Rev Respir Dis* 1992;145(suppl):
A767.
29. Elliott MW, Simonds AK, Caroll MP, et al. Domiciliary nocturnal
nasal intermittent positive pressure ventilation in hypercapnic respiratory failure due to chronic obstructive lung disease: effects on sleep
and quality of life. *Thorax* 1992;47:342–348.
30. Goldstein RS, Gort EH, Brown DL, et al. A controlled trial of respiratory rehabilitation. *Am Rev Respir Dis* 1992;145(suppl):A767.
31. Guyatt GH, Townsend M, Keller JL, Singer J. Should study subjects
see their previous responses? Data from a randomized control trial.
J Clin Epidemiol 1989;42:913–920.
32. Jaeschke R, Singer J, Guyatt GH. Measurement of health status:
Ascertaining the minimal clinically important difference. *Controlled
Clin Trials* 1989;10:407–415.
33. Jones PW, Baveystock CM, Littlejohns P. Relationships between
general health measured with the Sickness Impact Profile and respiratory symptoms, physiological measures, and mood in patients with
chronic airflow limitation. *Am Rev Respir Dis* 1989;140:1538–1543.

34. Jones PW, Quirk FH, Baveystock CM. The St. George's Respiratory Questionnaire. *Respir Med* 1991;85(suppl B):25–31.

35. Jones PW, Quirk FH, Baveystock CM, et al. A self-completed measure of health status for chronic airflow limitation. *Am Rev Respir Dis* 1992;145:1321–1327.

36. Maillé AR, Koning CJM, Kaptein AA. Developing a quality of life questionnaire for patients with respiratory illness. *Qual Life Newsl* 1993;6:5.

37. Maillé AR, Kaptein AA, Koning CJM, et al. Developing a quality of life questionnaire for patients with respiratory illness. *Monaldi Arch Chest Dis* 1994;49:76–78.

38. Guyatt GH, Townsend M, Berman LB, et al. Quality of life in patients with chronic airflow obstruction. *Br J Dis Chest* 1987;81:45–54.

39. Cox NJM, Hendricks JCM, Dijkhuizen R, et al. Usefulness of a medicopsychological questionnaire for lung patients. *Int J Rehabil Res* 1991;14:267–272.

40. Dardes N, Chiappini MG, Moscatelli B, et al. Quality of life of COPD patients treated by long-term oxygen. *Lung* 1990;168(suppl):789–793.

41. Hanson EI. Effects of chronic lung disease on life in general and sexuality: perceptions of adult patients. *Heart Lung* 1982;11:435–441.

42. Kinsman RA, Yaroush RA, Fernandez E, et al. Symptoms and experiences in chronic bronchitis and emphysema. *Chest* 1983;83:755–761.

43. Moody L, McCormick K, Williams A. Disease and symptom severity, functional status, and quality of life in chronic bronchitis and emphysema. *J Behav Med* 1990;13:297–306.

44. Moody L, McCormick K, Williams A. Psychophysiologic correlates of quality of life in chronic bronchitis and emphysema. *West J Nurs Res* 1991;13:337–352.

45. Williams SJ. Chronic respiratory illness and disability: a critical review of the psychosocial literature. *Soc Sci Med* 1989;28:791–803.

46. Kaplan RM, Eakin EG, Ries A. Psychosocial issues in the rehabilitation of patients with chronic obstructive pulmonary disease. In: Casaburi R, Petty TL, eds. *Principles and practice of pulmonary rehabilitation.* Philadelphia: WB Saunders, 1993:351–365.

47. Dudley DL, Glaser EM, Jorgenson BN, et al. Psychosocial concomitants to rehabilitation in chronic obstructive pulmonary disease. Part I. Psychosocial and psychological considerations. *Chest* 1980;77:413–420.

48. Greenberg GD, Ryan JJ, Bourlier PE. Psychological and neuropsychological aspects of COPD. *Psychosomatics* 1985;26:29–33.

49. McSweeny AJ. Quality of life in relation to COPD. In: McSweeny AJ, Grant I, eds. *Chronic obstructive pulmonary disease: a behavioral perspective.* New York: Marcel Dekker, 1988:59–95.

50. Sandhu HS. Psychosocial issues in chronic obstructive pulmonary disease. *Clin Chest Med* 1986;7:629–642.

51. Light RW, Merrill EJ, Despars JA, et al. Prevalence of depression and anxiety in patients with COPD: relationship to functional capacity. *Chest* 1985;87:35–38.

52. Williams SJ, Bury MR. "Breathtaking": the consequences of chronic respiratory disorder. *Int Disab Stud* 1989;11:114–120.

53. Williams SJ, Bury MR. Impairment, disability and handicap in chronic respiratory illness. *Soc Sci Med* 1989;29:609–616.

54. Dahlstrom WG, Welsh GS, Dahlstrom LE. *An MMPI handbook.* Rev. ed. Minneapolis: University of Minnesota, 1972.

55. Eakin EG, Sassi-Dambron D, Kaplan RM, et al. Clinical trial of rehabilitation in chronic obstructive pulmonary disease. *J Cardiopulm Rehabil* 1992;12:105–110.

56. Niederman MS, Clemente PH, Fein AM, et al. Benefits of a multidisciplinary pulmonary rehabilitation program: improvements are independent of lung function. *Chest* 1991;99:798–804.

57. Prigatano GP, Wright EC, Levin D. Quality of life and its predictors in patients with mild hypoxemia and chronic obstructive pulmonary disease. *Arch Intern Med* 1984;144:1613–1619.

58. Toshima MT, Blumberg E, Ries AL, et al. Does rehabilitation reduce depression in patients with chronic obstructive pulmonary disease? *J Cardiopulm Rehabil* 1992;12:261–269.

59. Toshima MT, Kaplan RM, Ries AL. Experimental evaluation of rehabilitation in chronic obstructive pulmonary disease: short-term effects on exercise endurance and health status. *Health Psychol* 1990;9:237–252.

60. Toshima MT, Kaplan RM, Ries AL. Self-efficacy expectations in chronic obstructive pulmonary disease rehabilitation. In: Schwarzer

R, ed. *Self-efficacy: thought control of action.* Washington, DC: Hemisphere, 1992:325–354.

61. Agle DP, Baum GL. Psychosocial aspects of chronic obstructive pulmonary disease. *Med Clin North Am* 1977;61:749–758.

62. Yellowlees PM. The treatment of psychiatric disorders in patients with chronic airways obstruction. *Med J Aust* 1987;147:349–352.

63. Friedman HS, Booth-Kewley S. The "disease-prone personality": a meta-analytic view of the construct. *Am Psychol* 1987;42:539–555.

64. Barstow RE. Coping with emphysema. *Nurs Clin North Am* 1974;9:137–145.

65. Post L, Collins C. The poorly coping COPD patient: a psychotherapeutic perspective. *J Psychiatry Med* 1981;82;11:173–182.

66. Katz IR. Is there a hypoxic affective syndrome? *Psychosomatics* 1980;23:846–853.

67. Labuhn KT. An analysis of self-reported depressed mood in chronic obstructive pulmonary disease. Doctoral dissertation, University of Michigan, 1984. *Diss Abs Int* 1984;45:524B.

68. Agle DP, Baum GL, Chester EH, et al. Multidiscipline treatment of chronic pulmonary insufficiency. 1. Psychologic aspects of rehabilitation. *Psychosom Med* 1973;35:41–49.

69. Burns BH, Howell JBL. Disproportionately severe breathlessness in chronic bronchitis. *Q J Med* 1969;38:277–294.

70. Gift AG, Plaut SM, Jacox A. Psychologic and physiologic factors related to dyspnea in subjects with chronic obstructive pulmonary disease. *Heart Lung* 1986;15:595–601.

71. Hodgkin JE. Prognosis in chronic obstructive pulmonary disease. *Clin Chest Med* 1990;11:555–569.

72. Karajgi B, Rifkin A, Doddi S, et al. The prevalence of anxiety disorders in patients with chronic obstructive pulmonary disease. *Am J Psychiatry* 1990;147:200–201.

73. Dudley DL, Wermuth C, Hague W. Psychosocial aspects of care in the chronic obstructive pulmonary disease patient. *Heart Lung* 1973;2:289–303.

74. Dudley DL. *Psychophysiology of respiration in health and disease.* New York: Appleton-Century-Crofts, 1969.

75. Bergner M, Hudson LD, Conrad DA, et al. The cost and efficiency of home care for patients with chronic lung disease. *Med Care* 1988;26:566–579.

76. Schrier AC, Dekker FW, Kaptein AA, et al. Quality of life in elderly patients with chronic nonspecific lung disease seen in family practice. *Chest* 1990;98:894–899.

77. Ström K, Boe J, Herala M, et al. Assessment of two oxygen treatment alternatives in the home. *Int J Technol Assess Health Care* 1990;6:489–497.

78. Alonso J, Antó JM, González M, et al. Measurement of general health status of non-oxygen-dependent chronic obstructive pulmonary disease patients. *Med Care* 1992;30(suppl):MS125–MS134.

79. Dompeling E, Van Grunsven PM, Molema J, et al. Early detection of patients with fast progressive asthma or chronic bronchitis in general practice. *Scand J Prim Health Care* 1992;10:143–150.

80. van Schayck CP, Rutten-van Mölken MPMH, van Doorslaer EKA, et al. Two-year bronchodilator treatment in patients with mild airflow obstruction: contradictory effects on lung function and quality of life. *Chest* 1992;102:184–1391.

81. Anderson JP, Kaplan RM, Berry CG, et al. Interday reliability of function assessment for a health-status measure: the Quality of Well-Being Scale. *Med Care* 1989;27:1076–1083.

82. Sexton DL, Monro BH. Living with a chronic illness: the experience of women with chronic obstructive pulmonary disease (COPD). *West J Nurs Res* 1988;10:26–44.

83. Chapman JM, Reeder LG, Massey FJ. The relationship of stress, tranquilizers and serum cholesterol levels in a sample population under study for coronary heart disease. *Am J Epidemiol* 1966;83:537–547.

84. Neugarten B, Havinghurst R, Tobin S. The measurement of life satisfaction. *J Gerontol* 1961;16:134–143.

85. Sexton DL, Monro BH. Impact of a husband's chronic illness (COPD) on the spouse's life. *Res Nurs Health* 1985;8:83–90.

86. Kass I, Updegraff K, Muffly RB. Sex in chronic obstructive pulmonary disease. *Med Aspects Hum Sex* 1972;6:33–42.

87. Fletcher EC, Martin RJ. Sexual dysfunction and erectile impotence in chronic obstructive pulmonary disease. *Chest* 1982;81:413–421.

88. Costello CG. Depression: loss of reinforcers or loss of reinforcer effectiveness? *Behav Ther* 1972;2:240–247.

89. Guyatt GH, Townsend M, Berman LB, et al. Quality of life in patients with chronic airflow obstruction. *Br J Dis Chest* 1987;81:45–54.

90. Casselith BR, Luck EJ, Strouse TB, et al. Psychosocial status in chronic illness: a comparative analysis of six diagnostic groups. *N Engl J Med* 1984;311:506–511.

91. Young RF. Marital adaptation and response in chronic illness: the case of COPD. Doctoral dissertation, Wayne State University, 1981. *Diss Abs Int* 1982;42:4947A.

92. De Araujo G, Van Arsdel PP, Holmes TH, et al. Life change, coping ability and chronic intrinsic asthma. *J Psychosom Res* 1973;17: 359–363.

93. Pattison EM, Rhodes RJ, Dudley DL. Response to groups treatment in patients with severe chronic lung disease. *Int J Group Psychother* 1971;21:214–255.

94. Jensen PS. Risk protective factors, and supportive interventions in chronic airway obstruction. *Arch Gen Psychiatry* 1983;40:1203–1207.

95. Anderson KL. *Quality of life in chronic obstructive pulmonary disease.* Dissertation completed at Oregon Health Sciences University School of Nursing, May 1993.

96. Flanagan JC. A research approach to improving our quality of life. *Am Psychol* 1978;33:138–147.

97. Burckhardt CS, Woods SL, Schultz AA, et al. Quality of life of adults with chronic illness: a psychometric study. *Res Nurs Health* 1989; 12:347–354.

98. Litman TJ. The family as a basic unit in health and medical care: a social behavioral overview. *Soc Sci Med* 1974;8:495–519.

99. Bruhn J. Effects of chronic illness on the family. *J Fam Pract* 1977; 4:1057–1060.

100. Archbold P, Stewart B. *Family caregiving across the life span.* Paper presented at the International Nursing Research Congress, American Nurses Association Council of Nurse Researchers. Washington, DC: October 1987.

101. Lubkin I. The family caregiver. In: Lubkin I, ed. *Chronic illness: impact and interventions.* 2nd ed. Boston: Jones & Bartlett, 1990: 200–217.

102. Crossman L, London C, Barry C. Older women caring for disabled spouses: a model for supportive services. *Gerontologist* 1981;21;5: 464–470.

103. Soldo B, Myllyluoma J. Caregivers who live with dependent elderly. *Gerontologist* 1983;23:605–611.

104. Eisdorfer C, Cohen D. Management of the patient and family coping with dementing illness. *J Fam Pract* 1983;12:831–837.

105. Mace NL, Babins PV. *The 36-hour day.* Baltimore: Johns Hopkins University Press, 1981.

106. Fagerhaugh S. Getting around with emphysema. In: Strauss AL, ed. *Chronic illness and quality of life.* St. Louis: CV Mosby, 1975:99–107.

107. Halcomb R. Promoting self-help in pulmonary patient education. *Respir Ther* 1984;14:49–54.

108. Stollenwerk R. An emphysema client: self care. *Home Healthcare Nurse* 1985;3:36–40.

109. Bandura A. Self-efficacy: toward a unifying theory of behavioral change. *Psychol Rev* 1977;84:191–215.

110. Radloff LS. The CES-D Scale: a self-report depression scale for research in the general population. *Appl Psychol Measure* 1977;1:385.

111. Spitzer WO, Dobson JH, Chesterman E, et al. Measuring the quality of life of cancer patients. *J Chron Dis* 1981;34:585–597.

112. Fletcher C, Peto R, Tinker C, et al. *The natural history of chronic bronchitis and emphysema.* Oxford: Oxford University Press, 1976.

113. Hughes JA, Hutchinson D, Bellang DE, et al. The influence of cigarette smoking and its withdrawal on the annual change in lung function in pulmonary emphysema. *Q J Med* 1982;51:115–124.

114. Petty TL. Pulmonary medicine. *JAMA* 1985;254:2271–2273.

115. Devins GM, Edwards PJ. Self-efficacy and smoking reduction in chronic obstructive pulmonary disease. *Behav Res Ther* 1988;26:127–135.

116. Pederson LL, Wanklin JM, Baskerville JC. The role of health beliefs in compliance with physician advice to quit smoking. *Soc Sci Med* 1984;19:573–580.

117. Pederson LL. Compliance with physician advice to quit smoking: a review of the literature. *Prev Med* 1982;11:71–84.

118. Dudley DL, Aickin M, Martin CV. Cigarette smoking in a chest clinic population—psychophysiologic variables. *J Psychosom Res* 1977;21: 367–375.

119. Mausner JS. Cigarette smoking among patients with respiratory disease. *Am Rev Respir Dis* 1970;102:704–713.

120. Labuhn LT, Lewis C, Koon K, et al. Smoking cessation experiences of chronic lung disease patients living in rural and urban areas of Virginia. *J Rural Health* 1993;9:305–313.

121. Atkins CJ, Kaplan RM, Timms RM, et al. Behavioral exercise programs in the management of chronic obstructive pulmonary disease. *J Consult Clin Psychol* 1984;52:591–603.

122. Guyatt GH, Berman LB, Townsend M. Long-term outcome after respiratory rehabilitation. *Can Med Assoc J* 1987;137:1089–1095.

123. Kaplan RM, Atkins CJ. Behavioral interventions for patients with COPD. In: McSweeny AJ, Grant I, eds. *Chronic obstructive pulmonary disease: a behavioral perspective.* New York: Marcel Dekker, 1988:123–162.

124. Make B, Glenn K, Iklé D, et al. Pulmonary rehabilitation improves the quality of life of patients with chronic obstructive pulmonary disease (COPD). *Am Rev Respir Dis* 1992;145(suppl):A767.

125. Heaton RK, Grant I, McSweeny AJ, et al. Psychologic effects of continuous and nocturnal oxygen therapy. *Arch Intern Med* 1983:143: 1941–1947.

126. Heaton RK. Psychological effects of oxygen therapy for COPD. In: McSweeny AJ, Grant I, eds. *Chronic obstructive pulmonary disease: a behavioral perspective.* New York: Marcel Dekker, 1988:105–121.

127. Petty TL. Home oxygen in advanced chronic obstructive pulmonary disease. *Med Clin North Am* 1981;65:615–627.

128. Krop HD, Block AJ, Cohen E. Neuropsychologic effects of continuous oxygen therapy in chronic obstructive pulmonary disease. *Chest* 1973;64:317–322.

129. Prigatano GP, Parsons OA, Wright EC, et al. Neuropsychological test performance in mildly hypoxemic patients with chronic obstructive pulmonary disease. *J Consult Clin Psychol* 1983;51:108–116.

130. Rourke SB, Grant I, Heaton RK. Neurocognitive aspects of chronic obstructive pulmonary disease. In: Casaburi R, Petty TL, eds. *Principles and practice of pulmonary rehabilitation.* Philadelphia: WB Saunders, 1993:79–91.

131. McSweeny AJ, Labuhn KT. The relationship of neuropsychological functioning to health-related quality of life in systemic medical disease: the example of chronic obstructive pulmonary disease. In: Grant I, Adams KM, eds. *Neuropsychological assessment in neuropsychiatry.* Vol. 2. New York: Oxford University Press, (in press).

132. Reitan RM, Wolfson D. *The Halstead-Reitan Neuropsychological Test Battery: theory and clinical interpretation.* Tucson: Neuropsychology Press, 1985.

133. McSweeny AJ, Grant I, Heaton RK, et al. Relationship of neuropsychological status to everyday functioning in healthy and chronically ill persons. *J Clin Exp Neuropsychol* 1985;7:281–291.

134. Asher HB. *Casual modeling.* Beverly Hills, CA: Sage, 1976.

135. Clark RJH, Cochrane GM. Effect of personality on alveolar ventilation in patients with chronic airways obstruction. *BMJ* 1970;1:273–275.

136. Rosser R, Danford J, Heslop A. Breathlessness and psychiatric morbidity in chronic bronchitis and emphysema: a study of psychotherapeutic management. *Psychol Med* 1983;13:93–110.

137. Dudley DL, Glasser EM, Jorgenson BN, et al. Psychosocial concomitants in chronic obstructive pulmonary disease. Part II. Psychosocial treatment. *Chest* 1980;77:544–551.

138. Carlson J, Hoy R, McSweeny AJ, et al. *Your guide to better breathing: instructor's manual.* Charleston, WV: American Lung Association of West Virginia, 1981.

139. Dudley DL, Sitzman J. Psychobiological evaluation and treatment of COPD. In: McSweeny AJ, Grant I, eds. *Chronic obstructive pulmonary disease: a behavioral perspective.* New York: Dekker, 1988: 183–235.

140. Dudley DL, Glaser EM, Jorgenson BN, et al. Psychosocial concomitants to rehabilitation in chronic obstructive pulmonary disease. Part III. Dealing with psychiatric disease. *Chest* 1980;77:667–684.

141. Grant I, Timms RM. Psychiatric disturbances in chronic obstructive pulmonary disease. In: Bondow RA, Moses KM, eds. *Manual of clinical problems in chronic obstructive pulmonary disease.* Boston: Little, Brown, 1985.

142. McSweeny AJ, Grant I. *Chronic obstructive pulmonary disease: a behavioral perspective.* New York: Marcel Dekker, 1988.

Quality of Life and Pharmacoeconomics in Clinical Trials, Second Edition, edited by B. Spilker.
Lippincott-Raven Publishers, Philadelphia © 1996.

CHAPTER 101

Asthma and Allergy

Elizabeth F. Juniper and Gordon H. Guyatt

INTRODUCTION

Until fairly recently, health-related quality of life (HRQL) was rarely incorporated into asthma and allergy clinical studies at least in part because of the absence of disease-specific instruments. The demand for such instruments was limited by the assumption that conventional clinical outcomes provided an accurate reflection of how patients are feeling and how they are able to function physically, socially, and emotionally in their day-to-day lives. Several recent studies have challenged this assumption by showing that correlations between conventional indices of clinical severity and quality of life are only modest (1–4). Clinicians and investigators can no longer be confident that if there are improvements in the conventional indices of clinical severity that the patient has benefited or that no improvement in conventional mea-

sures means that the patient has not improved (4). The recent development of scientifically sound HRQL instruments for asthma and rhinoconjunctivitis which have strong measurement properties allows easy and quick assessment of quality of life in clinical trials, surveys, and clinical practice. A number of other nonrespiratory conditions of allergic origin remain, including disorders of the skin and gastrointestinal tract, in which little HRQL research has been done.

HRQL research in asthma and rhinoconjunctivitis has highlighted the areas of impairment that patients experience. Adults with asthma are not only troubled by the symptoms themselves, such as shortness of breath, wheeze, and cough, they also are troubled by limitation of daily activities (occupational, social, and physical), sleep impairment, emotional problems such as anxiety and frustration, and problems associated with exposure to atmospheric stimuli such as cigarette smoke (5–8). The burden of illness for children with asthma is similar. However, children also experience important HRQL impairments because of their inability to integrate fully with their peers (9–12).

The impact of rhinoconjunctivitis (hayfever) is frequently underestimated by clinicians (13). However, a survey using

E. F. Juniper: Department of Clinical Epidemiology and Biostatistics, McMaster University Faculty of Health Sciences, Hamilton, Ontario L8N 3Z5, Canada.

G. H. Guyatt: Departments of Clinical Epidemiology and Biostatistics and Medicine, McMaster University Faculty of Health Sciences, Hamilton, Ontario L8N 3Z5, Canada.

a generic HRQL instrument, the SF-36, showed that the actual degree of HRQL impairment in these patients can be quite severe (14). Not only are the patients troubled by their nasal and eye symptoms, they are also bothered by fatigue, headaches, lack of sleep, poor concentration, impairment and limitation in their normal daily activities and emotional problems such as frustration and embarrassment (15).

GENERIC INSTRUMENTS

A strength of generic instruments, including health profiles and utility measures, is that they permit comparison of impairment of HRQL across different conditions. They are unlikely, however, to fully capture all areas of specific interest. For instance, the Sickness Impact Profile (SIP) tends to focus on basic activities of daily living (e.g., feeding, dressing), which are not impaired in most asthma and allergy patients (1,16). In addition, health profiles may not be responsive to small but important changes when used in clinical trials (2). Preliminary work suggests that the SF-36 may have satisfactory properties as a discriminative instrument in asthma with moderate cross-sectional correlations (r = 0.30–0.50) with clinical asthma severity scores in 5 of the 9 domains of the SF-36 and with FEV1 % predicted in 3 of the 9 domains (17). Similar properties were found for rhinoconjunctivitis (14).

DISEASE-SPECIFIC INSTRUMENTS

Recognition that the generic instruments are often insufficiently responsive to changes or differences in HRQL that are important to patients has led to the development of disease-specific instruments for both asthma and rhinoconjunctivitis. A number of instruments claim to measure HRQL but focus exclusively on symptom and physical activity limitations that clinicians consider important and do not incorporate the functional impairments that are important to patients. We have restricted our review to those instruments that measure all aspects important to the patient and for which there are published reports of development methods and measurement properties. Currently, ten disease-specific HRQL instruments are applicable to patients with asthma and three for rhinoconjunctivitis. We summarize the instruments and the performance characteristics that investigators may need to take into consideration when selecting an instrument.

ASTHMA-SPECIFIC QUALITY OF LIFE INSTRUMENTS

Asthma Quality of Life Questionnaire (Juniper)

The Asthma Quality of Life Questionnaire (1,5) is a 32-item questionnaire for adults with asthma. The items, iden-

tified by asthma patients as being important, are in four domains: symptoms, emotions, exposure to environmental stimuli, and activity limitation. Patients respond to each item on a 7-point scale. Five of the 11 items in the activity limitation domain are self-identified by patients. The instrument is in both interviewer and self-administered format and takes approximately 10 minutes to complete at the first visit and 5 minutes at follow-up.

There have been two studies in which the measurement properties of the Asthma Quality of Life Questionnaire have been evaluated, the first was a formal validation study (1), and the second was part of clinical study of patients seen in an emergency department for asthma exacerbations (3).

The first (1) was an 8-week single-cohort study of 39 adults with asthma. Asthma quality of life, symptoms, asthma medication use, airway hyperresponsiveness, and generic HRQL (SIP and a shortened form of the Rand General Health Survey) were evaluated at baseline, 4 and 8 weeks. Patients with inadequately controlled asthma were offered additional inhaled steroids. Using global rating of change questionnaires, patient health status was classified as having remained stable or having changed for each time period (baseline–4 weeks and 4–8 weeks). In patients who remained stable, the instrument demonstrated good reliability both for overall quality of life and for individual domains with intraclass correlation coefficients ranging from 0.89 to 0.94. Responsiveness was demonstrated by the instrument's ability to detect change in overall quality of life and all domains in those patients who changed ($p < 0.001$) and in being able to differentiate between those who changed and those who remained stable ($p < 0.001$). Longitudinal and cross-sectional correlations between asthma quality of life and both conventional clinical asthma measures and generic HRQL were close to predictions made before the analysis. In the longitudinal correlations, changes in asthma quality of life were highly correlated (r > 0.5) with changes in clinical asthma control, and generic quality of life as measured by the Rand, moderately correlated (r = 0.35–0.5) with peak flow rates and medication use and weakly correlated (r = 0.20–0.35) with FEV1 % predicted, airway responsiveness and the SIP. In the cross-sectional correlations, asthma quality of life was highly correlated with clinical asthma control and the Rand, moderately correlated with the SIP but not correlated with FEV1 % predicted, peak flow rates, or airway responsiveness.

In the second study (3), 43 adults were treated for asthma exacerbations in the emergency department and re-evaluated after 7–10 days. Asthma quality of life, spirometry, and generic HRQL (SIP) were assessed at each visit. As in the first study, global rating of change questionnaires were used to determine whether patients changed their health status. In the stable patients, the intraclass correlation coefficient for overall quality of life and for each of the domains ranged from 0.90 to 0.96. Responsiveness was clearly demonstrated by significant changes in all domains of asthma quality of life. In cross-sectional correlations, asthma quality of life correlated well with the SIP (r = 0.49) and asthma symptoms (r = 0.74), but not so well with the FEV1 % predicted (r = 0.27). In the longitudinal correlations, change in asthma quality of life correlated well with global rating of change (r = 0.78) and moderately with change in FEV1 (r = 0.43). Changes in the SIP were not reported.

Using global rating of change questionnaires (18), the clinical interpretability of the Asthma Quality of Life Questionnaire was determined. Both studies showed that a change in score of 0.5, both for overall quality of life and for the individual domains, represents a minimal important difference. The minimal important difference is defined as the smallest difference in score in the domain of interest that patients perceive as beneficial and would mandate, in the absence of troublesome side effects or excessive cost, a change in the patient's management (19). It was also shown that a change in quality of life score of approximately 1.0 represents a moderate change and a change in score greater than 2.0 represents a large change in HRQL. Using the responsiveness index derived from the minimal important difference and the pooled within-subject standard deviation, clinical study sample sizes have been calculated for various alpha and beta error rates (1). For example, a parallel group design clinical trial with the alpha error rate (two-sided) set at 0.05 and the β error rate at 0.1, requires a sample size of 35 patients per group.

Asthma Quality of Life Questionnaire (Marks)

The AQLQ (2,6), designed for adults with asthma, is a self-administered questionnaire containing 20 items in four domains: breathlessness and physical restrictions, mood disturbance, social disruption, and concerns for health. Patients rate each item on a 5-point scale. The investigators selected items using both importance as rated by patients and psychometric techniques. The questionnaire takes approximately 5 minutes to complete.

The instrument has been thoroughly tested for both discriminative and evaluative properties. Test–retest reliability was assessed in 58 patients with stable asthma and resulted in an intraclass correlation coefficient of 0.80. Cross-sectional construct validity was evaluated in a survey of 87 patients. Asthma quality of life showed moderate correlation with the amount of medication used (r = 0.38) but no correlations with both FEV1 % predicted (r = −0.20) and airway responsiveness (r = −0.16). Evaluative properties were examined in a cohort of 44 adults with asthma followed for 3–4 months. In the 19 subjects who improved according to clinical criteria, the instrument was able to measure changes in quality of life and show that these changes were greater than those observed in stable patients (p = 0.007). In the longitudinal correlations, asthma quality of life was moderately correlated with asthma symptoms (r = 0.37) and airway hyperresponsiveness (r = 0.38), but not with peak flow variability (r = 0.12) or the SIP (r = 0.18).

Living with Asthma Questionnaire (Hyland)

The Living with Asthma Questionnaire (7,20) is a 68-item instrument with 11 domains: social/leisure, sport, holidays, sleep, work, colds, morbidity, effects on others, medication use, sex, and dysphoric states and attitudes. Items, identified from patient focus group discussions, were selected for the questionnaire using psychometric techniques and factor analysis. Unlike the Juniper (1) and Marks (6) instruments, impairments experienced as a direct result of asthma symptoms are not included. Responses are given using a 3-point scale, suggesting that it may have acceptable discriminative properties but be less responsive to within-patient changes.

The test–retest of the instrument was evaluated in two postal surveys separated by 2 months; 95 responses were obtained and showed a correlation coefficient (r) = 0.95. For cross-sectional construct validity, the Living with Asthma questionnaire was highly correlated with the SIP (r = 0.66, n = 76), moderately with steroid prescribing (r = 0.35, n = 40), and moderately with peak flow rates (r = 0.44, n = 40). There has been no formal study of the evaluative properties of the instrument but it has been used in a 425 patient double-blind placebo-controlled clinical trial of salmeterol, a very efficacious long-acting β-agonist (21). Although there were highly significant differences in peak flow rates between salmeterol and placebo (p = 0.0001), only 63% of patients on salmeterol showed improvement in quality of life compared to 46% on placebo. Although this difference reached significance (p <0.05), the results suggest that the 3-point response options may limit the responsiveness of the instrument.

St. George's Respiratory Questionnaire (Jones)

The St. George's Respiratory Questionnaire (22) is self-administered and is applicable to adult patients with both reversible and fixed airway obstruction. It contains 76 items in three domains: symptoms, activity, and impacts (on daily life). The methods used for the development have not yet been published and so the criteria for item selection are unclear.

The questionnaire, when presented to 40 patients with asthma on two occasions, spaced 2 weeks apart, showed an intraclass correlation coefficient of 0.91. In a cross-sectional study of 141 patients with long-standing airflow limitation, the activity domain correlated with the 6 minute walk test (r = −0.35), the MRC dyspnea grade (r = 0.50) and the SIP (r = 0.39), but not with the FEV1 (r = 0.01). Similar correlations were found for the impacts domain but the symptom domain did not correlate with any of the clinical or generic HRQL measures.

In 133 patients with chronic airflow limitation followed for one year, there was very little change in clinical status and so from this study it is difficult to judge the evaluative properties of the instrument. However, in a 719-asthma patient randomized placebo-controlled trial of nedocromil, only the impacts domain of the questionnaire showed a difference between nedocromil and placebo (p <0.05) (23). With a large sample size and a treatment of established therapeutic benefit, this suggests that the questionnaire may not be very responsive to small but important changes in quality of life.

Life Activities Questionnaire for Adult Asthma (Creer)

This instrument for adults (8) with asthma has 70 items in seven domains (physical activities, work activities, outdoor activities, emotions and emotional behavior, home care, eating and drinking activities, and miscellaneous). Items were selected on the basis of frequency of experience by patients. Responses are given on a 5-point scale and the questionnaire is self-administered. The instrument shows high internal consistency with a Cronbach's α of 0.96–0.97. Measurement properties necessary for confident use as either a discriminative or evaluative instrument have not been published.

Respiratory Illness Quality of Life Questionnaire (Maille) (24)

This questionnaire has 55 items in 7 domains (breathing problems, physical problems, emotions, situations triggering or enhancing breathing problems, daily and domestic activities, social activities, relationships and sexuality, general activities) and is applicable to patients with COPD or asthma. Cross-sectional correlations between the domains and clinical indices of disease severity ($r = 0.14 - 0.59$) suggest that the instrument may have acceptable discriminative properties but reliability has not been reported and neither have the measurement properties necessary for use in clinical trials.

Asthma Bother Profile (Hyland) (25)

The 22 items in this self-administered questionnaire were selected from 5 earlier asthma and COPD quality of life instruments (1,2,20,22,26) to measure the psychological impact of asthma. The measurement properties of this instrument have not yet been published.

Comparison of Quality of Life Instruments in Adults with Asthma

In a 6-week, double-blind, randomized comparison of salmeterol and salbutamol, Rutten van Molken (27) and her colleagues compared the measurement properties of the Asthma Quality of Life Questionnaire (1), the Living with Asthma Questionnaire (20), the SIP (28), the Standard Gamble (29) and the Feeling Thermometer (29). The results showed that both the Asthma Quality of Life Questionnaire and the Living with Asthma Questionnaire have good discriminative properties and that of the two the Asthma Quality of Life is more responsive and has better longitudinal validity. Of the generic instruments, the SIP has acceptable discriminative properties. The Feeling Thermometer is responsive but has poor construct validity making it questionable what it is measuring. The Standard Gamble has poor measurement properties for both evaluation and discrimination.

Summary of Adult Asthma Quality of Life Instruments

Data available suggest that the first four adult instruments (1,6,20,22) have measurement properties that enable them to be used satisfactorily for discriminative purposes but only the first two by Juniper et al. (1) and Marks et al. (6) have been shown to have good responsiveness and longitudinal construct validity, properties that are essential for use in clinical trials. The additional advantage of the Juniper questionnaire is that the interpretability of the data has been addressed.

Pediatric Asthma Quality of Life Questionnaire

This questionnaire (30) has been designed for children with asthma, aged 7–17 years. It has 23 items in three domains: symptoms, activity limitation, and emotional function; three of the activity items are self-identified by the patient. Items were selected on the basis of their importance to the children themselves. It is both self- and interviewer-administered with 7-point response options and takes approximately 10 minutes to complete. Patients experience no difficulty understanding the questions or the response options. In a 52-patient validation study, the questionnaire has shown good measurement properties and validity as both an evaluative and discriminative instrument. In patients who are stable, it has very acceptable reliability with an intraclass correlation coefficient of 0.84. It has also shown good responsiveness in being able to detect changes in patients whose health state changed ($p < 0.001$) and being able to differentiate between stable and unstable patients ($p < 0.0001$). Correlations between the instrument and both conventional clinical asthma measures and generic HRQL were close to predicted for both longitudinal and cross-sectional validation. For the longitudinal correlations, asthma quality of life was highly correlated ($r > 0.5$) with generic quality of life (Feeling Thermometer), moderately correlated ($r = 0.35–0.5$) with peak flow rates and beta agonist use, weakly correlated ($r = 0.20–0.35$) with clinical asthma control and not correlated with FEV1 % predicted. For the cross-sectional correlations, asthma quality of life was highly correlated with clinical asthma control and β-agonist use, moderately correlated with the Feeling Thermometer, weakly correlated with peak flow rates, and not correlated with

FEV1 % predicted. The clinical interpretation of changes in score is very similar to that found for the Asthma Quality of Life Questionnaire (1), namely, a change in score of approximately 0.5 represents a minimal important difference.

Life Activities Questionnaire for Childhood Asthma (Creer) (31)

This 71-item questionnaire focuses on activity limitations and, with a Cronbach's α of 0.97, may have some redundancies. Test-retest yielded a Pearson correlation coefficient of 0.76. Other measurement properties have not yet been published.

Childhood Asthma Questionnaires (French) (32)

Three separate questionnaires have been developed for children aged 4–7 years (CAQA), 8–11 years (CAQB) and 12–16 years (CAQC). Reliability has been reported for each (CAQA: ICC = 0.59–0.63, CAQB: ICC = 0.72–0.75 and CAQC: ICC = 0.68–0.84). However, no differences were observed between asthmatic and non-asthmatic children in the quality of life domain. Lack of ability to differentiate between these children suggests that the instrument may have poor discriminative properties. Cross-sectional correlations with other indices of asthma are not provided. Data are not yet available on responsiveness and longitudinal validity.

RHINOCONJUNCTIVITIS-SPECIFIC QUALITY OF LIFE INSTRUMENTS

Rhinoconjunctivitis Quality of Life Questionnaire

This questionnaire (15) has been designed for use in adult patients with both seasonal and perennial atopic and also nonatopic rhinoconjunctivitis. There are 28 items, selected on the basis of their importance to patients, in seven domains: sleep, nonrhinoconjunctivitis symptoms, activity limitations, nasal symptoms, eye symptoms, practical problems, and emotional function. 7-point response options are used and the instrument may be interviewer or self-administered.

The measurement properties of the instrument were evaluated in a clinical trial comparing regular versus "when needed" use of beclomethasone nasal spray for the treatment of seasonal allergic rhinitis (33). The instrument has good reliability with an intraclass correlation coefficient of 0.86 and has shown excellent responsiveness being able to show clinically important differences between the two active treatment regimens. Evidence of its longitudinal validity has been strengthened by its successful use in a number of clinical studies (4,34,35), but its cross-sectional construct validity has not yet been evaluated.

Adolescent Rhinoconjunctivitis Quality of Life Questionnaire

Although very similar to the adult questionnaire, the 25 items in this instrument (36) were selected because they are important to adolescents (12–17 years). These younger patients do not experience so much trouble with sleeping as adults but the rhinoconjunctivitis has a much larger impact on ability to function in role activities (school). There are six domains—practical problems, nonhayfever symptoms, nasal symptoms, eye symptoms, activity limitations, and emotional problems—and 7-point response options are used. The instrument was tested in a clinical trial in which fluticasone nasal spray and loratadine were compared during the ragweed pollen season (36). Medications were started when patients were symptomatic and during the 4 weeks of treatment they showed highly significant improvements in all domains of rhinoconjunctivitis quality of life ($p < 0.0001$). The instrument also showed good responsiveness in being able to detect significant differences between the two treatments for all domains except activity limitations and eye symptoms. Correlations between rhinoconjunctivitis quality of life and conventional diary symptoms were moderate (r = 0.35–0.5) and very close to predicted for all domains. Reliability and cross-sectional correlations have not yet been evaluated.

Rhinitis Quality of Life Questionnaire

This questionnaire (37) was derived from the adult Rhinoconjunctivitis Quality of Life Questionnaire by removing all items that relate specifically to eye symptoms. The instrument was evaluated in a clinical trial comparing budesonide nasal spray administered as an aerosol and as a powder in perennial rhinitis. Patients were symptomatic at the start of the study and showed highly significant improvements in all domains of rhinitis quality of life during the 6 weeks of treatment ($p < 0.008$), but neither the quality of life instrument nor conventional clinical outcomes was able to detect any difference between the two treatments. The longitudinal correlations between each of the domains and diary nasal symptoms were high (r = 0.63–0.78). The discriminative properties of this instrument have not yet been evaluated.

CONCLUSIONS

Disease-specific quality of life questionnaires are now available for asthma that have good measurement properties for both discriminative and evaluative use. Others, for rhinoconjunctivitis, have good evaluative properties. Health-related quality of life assessment should be included in all relevant clinical studies to ensure that the aspect of the condition that is most important to the patient is captured.

REFERENCES

1. Juniper EF, Guyatt GH, Ferrie PJ, Griffith LE. Measuring quality of life in asthma. *Am Rev Respir Dis* 1993;147:832–838.
2. Marks GB, Dunn SM, Woolcock AJ. An evaluation of an asthma quality of life questionnaire as a measure of change in adults with asthma. *J Clin Epidemiol* 1993;46:1103–1111.
3. Rowe BH, Oxman AD. Performance of an asthma quality of life questionnaire in an outpatient setting. *Am Rev Respir Dis* 1993;148: 675–681.
4. Juniper EF, Guyatt GH, Ferrie PJ, King DR. Sodium cromoglycate eye drops: regular versus "as needed" use in the treatment of seasonal allergic conjunctivitis. *J Allergy Clin Immunol* 1994;94:36–43.
5. Juniper EF, Guyatt GH, Epstein RS, Ferrie PJ, Jaeschke R, Hiller TK. Evaluation of impairment of health-related quality of life in asthma: development of a questionnaire for use in clinical trials. *Thorax* 1992;47:76–83.
6. Marks GB, Dunn SM, Woolcock AJ. A scale for the measurement of quality of life in adults with asthma. *J Clin Epidemiol* 1992;45: 461–472.
7. Hyland ME, Finnis S, Irvine SH. A scale for assessing quality of life in adult asthma sufferers. *J Psychomat Res* 1991;35:99–110.
8. Creer TL, Wigal JK, Kotses H, McConnaughy K, Winder JA. A life activities questionnaire for adult asthma. *J Asthma* 1992;29:393–399.
9. Townsend M, Feeny DH, Guyatt GH, Seip AE, Dolovich J. Evaluation of the burden of illness for pediatric asthmatic patients and their parents. *Ann Allergy* 1991;67:403–408.
10. Christie MJ, French D, Sowden A, West A. Development of child-centred disease-specific questionnaires for living with asthma. *Psychosomat Med* 1993;55:541–548.
11. Nocon A. Social and emotional impact of childhood asthma. *Arch Dis Child* 1991;66:458–460.
12. Usherwood TP, Scrimgeour A, Barber JH. Questionnaire to measure perceived symptoms and disability in asthma. *Arch Dis Child* 1990; 65:779–781.
13. International Rhinitis Management Working Group. International consensus report on the diagnosis and management of rhinitis. *Allergy* 1994;19(suppl):1–34.
14. Bousquet J, Bullinger M, Fayol C, Marquis P, Valentin B, Burtin B. Assessment of quality of life in chronic allergic rhinitis using the SF-36 questionnaire. *J Allerg Clin Immunol* 1994;94:182–188.
15. Juniper EF, Guyatt GH. Development and testing of a new measure of health status for clinical trials in rhinoconjunctivitis. *Clin Exp Allergy* 1991;21:77–83.
16. Jones PW, Baveystock CM, Littlejohn P. Relationships between general health measured with the sickness impact profile and respiratory symptoms, physiological measures and mood in patients with chronic airflow limitation. *Am Rev Respir Dis* 1989;140:1538–1543.
17. Bousquet J, Knani J, Dhivert H, Richard A, Chicoye A, Ware JE, Michel FB. Quality of life in asthma. 1. Internal consistency and validity of the SF-36 questionnaire. *Am J Respir Crit Care Med* 1994;149: 371–375.
18. Juniper EF, Guyatt GH, Willan A, Griffith LE. Determining a minimal important change in a disease-specific quality of life questionnaire. *J Clin Epidemiol* 1994;47:81–87.
19. Jaeschke R, Singer J, Guyatt GH. Measurement of health status: ascertaining the minimal clinically important difference. *Controlled Clin Trials* 1989;10:407–415.
20. Hyland ME. The living with asthma questionnaire. *Respir Med* 1991; 85:13–16.
21. Palmer JBD, Hyland ME. Salmeterol in clinical practice: comparator and safety studies, quality of life studies. *Eur Respir Rev* 1991;1:301–303.
22. Jones PW, Quirk FH, Baveystock CM, Littlejohns P. A self-complete measure of health status for chronic airflow limitation. *Am Rev Respir Dis* 1992;145:1321–1327.
23. Maille AR, Kaptein AA, Konig CJM, Zwinderman AH. Developing a quality of life questionnaire for patients with respiratory illness. *Monaldi Arch Chest Dis* 1994;49:76–78.
24. Hyland ME, Ley A, Fisher DW, Woodward V. Measurement of psychological distress in asthma and asthma management programs. *Br J Clin Psychol* 1995 (in press).
25. Guyatt GH, Berman LB, Townsend M, Puglsey SO, Chamber LW. A measure of quality of life for clinical trials in chronic lung disease. *Thorax* 1987;42:773–778.
26. Rutten-van Molken MPMH, Clusters F, van Doorslaer EKA, Jansen CCM, Heurman L, Maesen FVP, Smeets JJ, Bommer AM, Raaijmakers JAM. Comparison of performance of four instruments in evaluating the effects of salmeterol on asthma quality of life. *Eur Respir J* 1995;8:888–898.
27. Bergner M, Bobbitt RA, Carter WB, Gilson BS. The sickness impact profile; development and final revision of a health status measure. *Med care* 1981;19:787–805.
28. Torrance GW. Measurement of health status utilities for economic appraisal. *Health Econom* 1986;5:1–30.
29. Jones PW. Nedocromil sodium quality of life study group. Quality of life, symptoms and pulmonary function in asthma: long-term treatment with nedocromil sodium examined in a controlled multicentre trial. *Eur Respir J* 1994;7:55–62.
30. Juniper EF, Guyatt GH, Feeny DH, Ferrie PJ, Griffith LE, Townsend M. Measuring quality of life in children with asthma. *J. Allergy Clin Immunol* 1995;95:226.
31. Creer TL, Wigal JK, Kotses H, Hatala JC, McConnaughty K, Winder JA. A life activities questionnaire for childhood asthma. *A Asthma* 1993;30:467–473.
32. French DJ, Christie MJ, Sowden AJ. The reproducibility of the childhood asthma questionnaires: measures of quality of life for children with asthma aged 4–16 years. *Qual Life Res* 1994;3:213–224.
33. Juniper EF, Vivieros M, O'Byrne PM, Guyatt GH. Aqueous beclomethasone dipropionate nasal spray: regular versus "as required" use in the treatment of seasonal allergic rhinitis. *J Allergy Clin Immunol* 1990;86:3–6.
34. Juniper EF, Willms DG, Guyatt GH, Ferrie PJ. Aqueous beclomethasone dipropionate nasal spray in the treatment of seasonal (ragweed) rhinitis. *Can Med Assoc J* 1992;147:887–892.
35. Juniper EF, Guyatt GH, Archer B, Ferrie PJ. Aqueous beclomethasone dipropionate in the treatment of ragweed pollen-induced rhinitis: further exploration of "as needed" use. *J Allergy Clin Immunol* 1993;92: 66–72.
36. Juniper EF, Guyatt GH, Dolovich J. Assessment of quality of life in adolescents with allergic rhinoconjunctivitis: development and testing of a questionnaire for clinical trials. *J Allergy Clin Immunol* 1994; 93:413–423.
37. Juniper EF, Guyatt GH, Andersson B, Ferrie PJ. Comparison of powder and aerosolized budesonide in perennial rhinitis: validation of rhinitis quality of life questionnaire. *Ann Allergy* 1993;70:225–230.

Quality of Life and Pharmacoeconomics in Clinical Trials, Second Edition, edited by B. Spilker.
Lippincott-Raven Publishers, Philadelphia © 1996.

CHAPTER 102

Diabetes Mellitus

Richard S. Beaser, Sharon B. Garbus, and Alan M. Jacobson

INTRODUCTION

Physicians have historically been dedicated to improving the patient's well-being (1,2) and quality of life (3); these challenges are viewed by many health care professionals as an integral part of disease management. Although there are various descriptions of "quality of life," most contain several common elements that relate to the patients' subjective perception of well-being: physical status and functioning, emotional/psychological status, social functioning, and disease- or treatment-related symptoms (4). When viewed within this framework, diabetes represents a classic example of a chronic condition where maximizing quality of life must reflect and balance the individual patients' needs and desires with the imperatives of disease management. Establishing this balance is a major challenge in caring for people with diabetes. The primary objectives of diabetes care are managing symptoms and maintaining function, avoiding acute and chronic complications, and maximizing quality of life (5). When managing patients with diabetes, clinical decisions usually do not pertain to critical life and death issues; therefore, the prescribed medications are used primarily to im-

prove quality of life rather than to acutely save lives (4). Treatments used to maintain long-term glucose control often impact on the patient's lifestyle and require changes in habits and routines (6). However, improved glucose control promotes good health and can provide an enhanced quality of life that would not have occurred had lifestyle compromises not been made. Thus, the psychological impact of diabetes reflects the condition's potential for disability on the one hand, and the complexity of the therapeutic regimen on the other. This impact should be addressed by clinicians to design treatment programs that will optimize psychological well-being as well as medical health.

In the United States, 80% of available health care resources are allocated to patients with chronic diseases such as diabetes (7,8), with management typically focused on prevention and treatment. In today's cost containment health care environment, patients and third-party payors play an important role in medical decision-making, with economic consequences increasingly influencing these decisions (9). To optimize clinical decision-making, however, the immediate and long-term economic impact needs to be balanced against the short-term and long-term effects on quality of life. Thus, in addition to the traditionally measured parameters of safety and efficacy in clinical trials, the importance of obtaining health-related quality of life outcome data for

R. S. Beaser, S. B. Garbus, and A. M. Jacobson: Joslin Diabetes Center, Boston, Massachusetts 02215.

therapeutic regimens is increasing as providers strive to optimize treatments and allocate resources (7,10,11). In no disease are these issues more relevant than diabetes mellitus.

DIABETES MELLITUS

Diabetes mellitus affects approximately 13 million people in the United States; it is estimated that up to half of this population may not be diagnosed (12). The two most common clinical types of diabetes are type I, insulin-dependent diabetes mellitus (IDDM), and type II, non-insulin-dependent diabetes mellitus (NIDDM) (13). While these two types of diabetes produce the elevation of blood glucose levels, they differ in postulated pathophysiology, clinical presentation, treatment approach, and impact on quality of life.

Type I Diabetes

Most cases of type I diabetes are caused by the autoimmune destruction of the insulin-producing pancreatic β cells (14). The β-cell destruction may occur subclinically over the years. However, the clinical presentation, particularly in younger patients, includes rapid development of the "classical" symptoms of diabetes—polyuria, polydypsia, polyphagia, weight loss, and, occasionally, ketoacidosis. With subnormal insulin production, glucose cannot be used as the primary energy source and blood glucose levels increase. Replacement insulin injection therapy is required to restore normal metabolic balance, hence the name "insulin-dependent diabetes" (15).

The Diabetes Control and Complications Trial (DCCT) demonstrated that intensive diabetes therapies can greatly reduce the risk of developing some diabetic complications (16). Many physicians currently prescribe therapy that uses multidose insulin regimens that run the spectrum from simple to complex. With added treatment regimen complexity, the patient needs to perform additional self-care activities such as self-monitoring of blood glucose. Careful attention to diet and exercise is necessary, although more flexibility in these parameters is acceptable by using compensatory adjustments of insulin doses.

Conventional insulin regimens include the standard "split-mix" program, using two fairly stable daily doses of combinations of regular plus intermediate-acting (NPH or Lente) insulins. Expansion of these programs to three daily insulin injections, with daily variations of some insulin doses, constitutes "intensified conventional" therapy (15). True intensive diabetes therapies consist of three daily doses of regular insulin that can be adjusted according to self-blood glucose test results along with consideration of food consumption, activity, and timing. With intensive therapy, multiple daily injections or subcutaneous insulin infusion pumps may be used (15,17).

The goal of all these treatments is to use exogenous insulin to restore the insulin action to be as close to the natural metabolic patterns as possible. Yet, compared to the body's own exquisitely sensitive control mechanisms, these exogenous replacement schemes are relatively crude and often lead to overdosing or underdosing of insulin and resulting hypoglycemia or hyperglycemia. Many patients feel that they are living on a "tightrope"—balancing between "too high and too low." When severe, these aberrations in normal glucose patterns can interfere with daily living, quality of life and, perhaps, have long-term ill-effects. Thus, treatment of type I diabetes requires a careful balance among the factors affecting glucose control: food consumption, activity, and insulin. This complex regimen requires precise timing, self-monitoring of blood glucose, and frequent visits to the health care team, all scheduled among the activities of daily living.

Type II Diabetes

Type II diabetes most commonly occurs because of a state of insulin resistance that cannot be overcome by a relative insufficiency of insulin production. When people develop insulin resistance, their own insulin is less effective in triggering the influx of energy-providing glucose into cells. To overcome this resistance, many patients develop the compensatory action of producing above-normal amounts of insulin, referred to as hyperinsulinemia. Yet, whatever the level of insulin, when it is insufficient to overcome the insulin resistance, type II diabetes occurs. Over time, many patients also develop a reduction in pancreatic insulin-producing capacity, resulting in below-normal insulin production.

Insulin resistance, which may or may not be accompanied by type II diabetes, has been associated with other conditions—hypertension and hyperlipidemia—risk factors for macrovascular diseases, including coronary artery, cerebrovascular, and peripheral vascular occlusive diseases. Many people with type II diabetes, and, in particular, those with the above conditions, are often obese, further impacting on their health and quality of life. Therefore, much of the management of type II diabetes goes beyond just glucose control and addresses reduction of these risk factors.

The initial treatment of type II diabetes is diet and exercise—measures that can also provide benefits to the other associated medical conditions. However, lifestyle changes are often required that can be extremely difficult for patients with well-entrenched habits to accomplish. Behavior modification techniques are enhanced when the patient perceives that these lifestyle changes will improve their diabetes control as well as their quality of life, perhaps by improving appearance, overall health, energy level, or self-esteem.

If diet and exercise do not adequately control type II diabetes, oral hypoglycemic agent therapy is added. Oral agents increase pancreatic sensitivity to rising glucose levels leading to increased insulin production. These agents also sensitize the peripheral cells to insulin action, thus reducing insulin resistance. If the maximum dosage of an oral agent is not sufficient to control the glucose levels, insulin therapy may be necessary. These patients, referred to as "insulin requiring" type II patients, may be producing some endogenous insulin, but are still considered to have NIDDM, as they do not physiologically lack insulin production capacity.

Complications of Diabetes

The reason to treat patients with type I and type II diabetes dynamically, and to attempt to restore blood glucose levels to normal, is to avoid the acute and chronic complications of hyperglycemia and the signs and symptoms that they can cause. Although the amelioration of the acute symptoms requires only crude balancing of the glucose levels, close to normal glucose patterns throughout the day and night are needed to reduce the long-term complications of diabetes in people with both type I and type II diabetes (16).

The previously mentioned macrovascular complications (hypertension, hyperlipidemia, coronary artery, cerebrovascular and peripheral vascular disease) and microvascular complications of diabetes can affect many organ systems. Microvascular disease damages smaller blood vessels, particularly in the eyes and kidneys. This can cause diabetic retinopathy and visual loss, or diabetic nephropathy, possibly leading to kidney failure, with dialysis or transplantation becoming necessary for survival. Neuropathy due to diabetes damages the nerves. Sensory neuropathies, often directly related to poor glucose control, can cause discomfort and eventually lead to sensory loss. Sensory neuropathies and/or peripheral vascular disease can lead to severe foot infections and ulcers, often with the resultant need for vascular bypass or even amputations. Motor neuropathies resulting in muscle wasting can limit physical abilities and, in severe forms, can be debilitating. Neuropathies of the autonomic nervous system can lead to orthostatic hypotension, male impotence or retrograde ejaculation, cardiac arrhythmias, digestive problems, or dysfunctional sweating. Thus, the assessment of the treatment and disease process of diabetes on the patient's quality of life involves both the potential threat and realities of coping with complications, as well as the impact of the self-care regimen.

QUALITY OF LIFE RESEARCH IN DIABETES MELLITUS

Psychosocial Factors That Impact on Quality of Life Measures

The importance of psychosocial factors can be viewed from dual perspectives: a patient's psychosocial status before the diagnosis of diabetes can affect how he or she deals with the disease and the recommended treatments, and the diagnosis and prescribed treatment regimen can have a profound psychosocial impact on the patient (18). Therefore,

merely measuring posttherapeutic intervention psychosocial responses without gauging preintervention status will not provide all the information needed to properly assess the impact of a treatment modality. Preintervention status has a significant impact on adherence to the prescribed regimen; compliance is one of the most difficult aspects of diabetes management (6,19) and a critical component in conducting clinical trials.

Health-related quality of life perceptions for people with diabetes cannot be separated from the complex diabetes treatment regimen that includes dietary behavior, exercise, medication, glucose monitoring, and safety and preventive measures (20). Patients frequently feel that their lives are negatively affected due to diabetes, partly because of the necessity to integrate and coordinate the various components of the treatment regimen into normal life activities (21).

The correlation of quality of life satisfaction with improvements in the level of diabetes care and patient adherence to treatment has been well reported in the literature (22,23) and supports the validity of including quality of life measurements in clinical trials of diabetes therapy. Mayou et al. (24) conducted a trial in 57 IDDM patients and 121 NIDDM patients attending outpatient clinics. The NIDDM group was randomly allocated to diet, tablet or ultralente insulin therapy. The results for the NIDDM group showed little disruption to their lives, but 27% of this group reported considerable loss of enjoyment and reduction in social life and previously pursued leisure activities, possibly due to reported fatigue. Patients in the IDDM group, for the most part, did not reduce activities. The reported diminished quality of life in this group reflected the need to plan regular meals and the desire to fit diabetes management around everyday activities. These findings, however, were not related to age of onset of diabetes, age at the time of the study or duration of illness.

Similarly, Anderson et al. (25) revised a Diabetes Attitude Scale, originally designed to measure the attitudes of health care professionals, to also include the perceptions of people with diabetes. Most patients felt that diabetes detracted from quality of life, while agreeing that maintaining good blood glucose control could positively impact on developing complications. However, depending on which component of the treatment plan fits more comfortably into their framework of self-acceptance, patients may selectively follow one aspect while disavowing others. Therefore, in clinical trials adherence assessments for these patients must be multifactorial, capturing and separately gauging the impact of each component of the treatment regimen.

A classic example of variable acceptance of treatment regimens is a patient's agreement to use, and subsequent acceptance of and compliance with, insulin treatment regimens (26,27). Anxiety about successfully performing self-injection techniques, loss of personal freedom, and even fear of consequences on employment have been reported obstacles to insulin use (28). Patients may view the need for insulin as a signal of loss of self-control—the beginning of life's terminal decline—whereas for others, it is the key to restoring good health.

Psychosocial factors including stress may have a direct "psychosomatic" effect on metabolic control (29) either directly or through their influence on compliance behaviors. Disease awareness, adaptive tolerance, and cooperation are emotional responses that significantly influence how successful a patient may be in trying to undertake the tasks necessary to restore metabolic control (30). Individual differences in personality, coping skills, social support systems, and health beliefs can also influence ultimate adaptation to diabetes and treatment components (31).

Using a generic model developed and validated by one of the investigators, Hanestad et al. (32) surveyed 247 persons with IDDM to determine to what degree metabolic control was associated with self-assessed quality of life. Patients were divided into two groups, poorly regulated and well regulated, depending on glycosylated hemoglobulin levels measured during a regularly scheduled clinic visit. No association was found between the objective physical state as reflected by blood glucose control, and self-assessed satisfaction with life. The only statistically significant differences between the two groups were sociability and loneliness; well-regulated persons felt less sociable and more lonely than poorly regulated persons. Likewise, in a randomized trial evaluating the effect of an educational program on metabolic control and quality of life for IDDM patients by deWeerdt et al. (33), no significant effect of this intervention was reported.

The age of patients with diabetes spans from early childhood to old age, with each stage bringing different therapeutic and perception of quality of life challenges to the health care provider and researcher. In children and adolescents, sequelae of the disease include diminished cognitive functioning, school performance, and self-esteem, and behavioral problems. Overall adjustments can pose challenges in implementing insulin treatment and the diabetic regimen (34). Family support and behaviors are particularly important in helping or hindering a child or adolescent comply with a diabetes treatment regimen (35), and even family structure has been shown to influence compliance with the treatment program (36,37).

In the elderly, the impact of diabetes on physical, emotional, cognitive, and social function is quite pronounced (38), suggesting that a clinical approach to managing these patients should include quality of life assessments, along with traditional clinical evaluations. As the disease progresses, risk increases for neurobehavioral disorders, psychiatric disturbances including depression and anxiety disorders, and eating disorders (29). The effect of diabetic complications and the resultant risk of adverse drug experiences compound all the psychosocial factors that impact on quality of life for these patients (38).

The onset of complications in all patients with diabetes brings additional concerns and challenges. Psychosocial differences exist among patients with diabetes complications according to both the number and type of complications present. Researchers have demonstrated that quality of life was significantly related to the presence of diabetic complications, when compared to patients with no complications (39–41). Rodin (42) used the Sickness Impact Profile (SIP) to study illness-related functional impairment in 158 adults with IDDM. The sample included 22 patients with end-stage renal disease (ESRD) on dialysis. Patients with both IDDM and ESRD were considerably more disabled than those without this complication, demonstrating that when assessing quality of life in patients with diabetes, results may be misleading unless the extent and severity of diabetes complications are considered. In this trial, as in others (39–41), the absence of serious medical complications was associated with only relatively mild functional impairment. Careful consideration and assessment of the age-specific effects of treatments, complications, and psychosocial factors on the patient's perceptions of quality of life are crucial if the impact of diabetic therapeutic interventions is to be determined. The many psychosocial factors associated with the diabetes disease process and treatment regimen suggest that appropriate patient screening and validated quality-of-life measurement instruments are crucial for the study data to provide statistical significance and clinical relevance.

MEASURING QUALITY OF LIFE IN PATIENTS WITH DIABETES MELLITUS

Generic Versus Disease-Specific Measures

Despite the body of literature on the impact of psychosocial factors in patients with diabetes, only recently have clinical studies included quality of life assessments (43). The initial methodological issue is whether to use a disease-specific or generic instrument, or a combination to study the diabetic factors (duration, complications, and complexity of treatment) and nondiabetic factors (co-morbidity, demography, and socioeconomic status). Properties of the ideal measures would include the ability to monitor the effects of treatment and self-management on quality of life as an adjunct to clinical measures of success such as blood glucose levels or the presence of diabetes complications (44).

Generic measures are most useful for cross-illness comparisons of treatments and illnesses, although these measures may be less sensitive to changes in patient functional capacity than illness-specific measures (45–47). Various combinations of separate generic and specific measures, modified generic measures, disease-specific supplements, and batteries can be used depending on the study objectives, methodological concerns and practical considerations (48). In studies of patients with diabetes, the usefulness of generic measures varies depending on the stage and type of illness. However, illness-specific measures can assess subtle distinctions as well as problems inherent in the disease and treatment process (34). In a recent trial, Jacobson et al. (47) examined the perception of quality of life of 240 patients with type I and type II diabetes and compared the psychometric properties of a generic measure, the Medical Outcome Study Health Survey—SF-36, and a disease-specific measure, the Diabetes Quality of Life Measure (DQOL). The authors concluded that although the DQOL was more sensitive to lifestyle issues and concerns of younger patients and the SF-36 provided more information on functional health status, the measures could be useful in combination in quality of life studies in patients with type I and type II diabetes. Like other studies (39,40,42), results showed that quality of life decreased in relation to an increase in complications.

Parkerson et al. (49) compared the health-related quality of life of adult IDDM patients using a disease-specific instrument, the DQOL, and two generic instruments, the Duke Health Profile (DUKE) and the General Health Perceptions Questionnaire. They reported that the generic measures provided as much or more information on these patients. Of interest was the suggestion of the authors that the use of generic measurements to identify nondiabetic problems that might respond to intervention could enhance the effect of the diabetes-specific therapy.

Nerenz et al. (50) established an Outcomes Management data base to provide an ongoing assessment of health status in patients with type I and type II diabetes to obtain information on quality of life from the patient's perspective, as well as from clinical predictor variables. A combination of instruments provided information for the data base: the patient self-reported health status using the SF-36; physician ratings of patients' health status along the major dimensions of the SF-36; a set of diabetes-specific health status items, demographic information, and a set of clinical variables known collectively as the Diabetes Technology of Patient Experience (TyPE) scale Form 2.2. Information was obtained either by mail or in person in a clinic setting and used for assessment and intervention of clinical outcomes. For example, the finding that the physician's rating of the general health status of the patient was significantly higher than the patient's rating focused the health care professionals on quality of life issues.

In a study comparing three measures of health status in 284 patients with diabetes in an outpatient population, Bardsley et al. (44) used the Nottingham Health Profile (NHP), four categories of an anglicized version of the Sickness Impact Profile (the Functional Limitations Profile (FLP), and a scale of Positive Well-being (PWB). The PWB scale was independent of physical disability, but the NHP and the FLP provided a useful assessment of general health in diabetes with a bias in identifying the minority of patients with more severe health problems. The authors reported that the NHP and FLP, and possibly the PWB, were insensitive to the subtle changes in well-being associated with managing metabolic disturbances and did not appropriately assess the impact of diabetes on the disruption of lifestyle.

A few studies have evaluated quality of life in patients with diabetes in the context of other chronic medical conditions. Stewart et al. (51) in the Medical Outcome Study (MOS), reported that patients with diabetes were not differentiated by type of illness, duration, or level of complications, although subjects with multiple conditions showed greater decrements in functioning and well-being than those with only one condition. Another psychiatric community study by Wells et al. (52) found that rates of depression in patients with diabetes were higher than the nondiabetic sample.

Diabetes Quality of Life Measure: A Diabetes-Specific Quality of Life Instrument

The DQOL (53) is a diabetes-specific quality of life measure originally constructed for the previously discussed DCCT (16). The DCCT was a multicenter controlled, randomized clinical trial of 1,441 patients with IDDM that evaluated the effects of two different diabetes treatment regimens on the appearance and progression of early microvascular and neuropathic complications. Patients were randomly assigned to standard diabetes treatment or an experimental treatment regimen requiring extensive patient reeducation that included diet and exercise regimens, self-monitoring of blood glucose four times a day, and three or more daily injections of insulin or the use of an insulin pump.

Although the DQOL was constructed to assess quality of life outcomes concerning the patient-perceived personal burden of participating in the DCCT study, the intent of the researchers was to design an instrument with applicability to a wider range of diabetic patients. The reliability and validity study of the DQOL for the DCCT (53) demonstrates that the instrument is broadly applicable to diverse groups of diabetic patients in clinical settings and in trials of new diabetes treatments. The DQOL study was conducted in a group of conventionally treated patients with similar characteristics to the DCCT group in age, duration of diabetes, and level of early vascular complications.

The DQOL is an easily administered multiple-choice assessment instrument, applicable to patients using different methods of diabetes management. It has four primary scales with 46 core items designed to measure the patient's personal perceptions of diabetes care and treatment: satisfaction with treatment, impact of treatment, worry about the future effects of diabetes, and worry about social/vocational issues (see Appendix). There is also a single overall well-being scale derived from national surveys of quality of well-being. A 16-item scale that assesses schooling, experience, and family relationships for patients living with their parents can provide relevant information in adolescent populations.

Responses to questions are made with a five-point Likert scale. Satisfaction is rated from 1 (very satisfied) to 5 (very dissatisfied). Impact and worry scales are rated from 1 (no impact or never worried) to 5 (always affected or always worried). The single item assessing general quality of life is rated on a four-point scale, to maintain continuity with past use. The DQOL is scored based on the approach of the

Medical Outcome Survey (54) with each scale, and the total rated with 0 representing the lowest possible quality of life and 100 representing the highest possible quality of life. The DQOL was initially validated against measures of psychiatric symptoms, perceived well-being, and adjustment to illness.

The DCCT Research Group that developed and validated the DQOL expected that other studies using the instrument would help provide additional understanding of the psychometric properties of the measure. Lloyd et al. (39) further validated the scale and confirmed diminished quality of life for people having multiple complications of diabetes. Most recently, the trial by Jacobson et al. (47) previously discussed provided validation of the DQOL in combination with the Medical Outcome Survey. Ingersoll and Marreo (55) conducted a study on 74 children and adolescents to adapt the DQOL for specific use in youths, as many of the items on the original scale were of limited relevance to the lives of this younger patient population.

Responsive evaluative measures can detect important and subtle changes in health-related quality of life over time (46); two longitudinal studies demonstrated the ability of the DQOL to detect sensitivity to change. Nathan et al. (56) studied patients with diabetes who had developed end-stage renal disease, and subsequently received a kidney transplant or a combined pancreas/kidney transplant. The investigators reported that patients who had received the combined kidney/pancreas transplant and were relieved from the daily self-care activities of diabetes showed a distinct improvement in quality of life as measured by the DQOL total score and all subscales. In another study, Selam et al. (57) used the DQOL to compare the quality of life of patients who received either implantable insulin pump therapy or injectable insulin therapy. Unlike the study by Nathan et al., these patients experienced only a modest change in lifestyle plus improvement in hypoglycemic frequency. This resulted in a smaller improvement in quality of life detected only in the satisfaction subscale of the DQOL; and showed the ability of the instrument to detect subtle changes.

Guidelines for Selecting Quality of Life Instruments for Clinical Trials in Patients with Diabetes

Measurement of health-related quality of life when evaluating therapeutic interventions requires the selection of reliable and validated measures that are sensitive to the effects of change (58,59). In designing clinical trials in patients with diabetes, quality of life assessment should be included as an integral component of the protocol, since the study end points chosen will influence the questions asked and the frequency of assessments. A general approach to the selection of a measurement strategy should start with a careful assessment of the patient sample in light of the research issues, patient characteristics, and length of the trial. In a short drug trial, a tool that asks for an assessment of quality of life during the past month must be sensitive enough to measure the drug effect (2).

The quality of life assessment package can therefore be thought of as having three components:

A generic measure that may allow for comparison to other illness groups
An illness-oriented measure, which may be more sensitive to change for a particular illness such as diabetes
Questions and questionnaires that are selected to address specific study elements

In each instance, the patient sample under evaluation and study specifics should guide the measure selection. The SIP (60) is overall a useful generic measure, but one that is unlikely to be useful in a young, otherwise healthy sample. If the study population has specific complications or problems that can influence quality of life, then illness-specific and problem-specific measurements should be added. For example, if treatment is directed toward painful neuropathy, then, in addition to diabetes-specific measures, it would be critical to incorporate pain indices as well.

The previously discussed diabetes treatment regimen can significantly affect lifestyle or produce debilitating side-effects. Treatment of diabetes-related complications such as renal disease or hypertension can result in special considerations and burdens to the patient. Therefore, if it is anticipated that the study treatment will produce specific side effects, this will influence quality of life instrument selection. For instance, in a trial with an antihypertensive agent that may effect mood changes, the protocol should include an assessment on emotional well-being. Finally, many clinical trials in patients with diabetes involve changes in the self-treatment regimen that may have complex or subtle effects on a patient's lifestyle. In the DCCT study, patients randomized to the intensive treatment group were required to increase the frequency of self-testing and number of insulin injections, and pay particular attention to food consumption and activity levels. Measuring the impact of diabetes on quality of life in this study mandated an assessment beyond metabolic control to address the effect of other specific lifestyle-related considerations.

In summary, selecting quality of life instruments for patients with diabetes is determined by the specific characteristics of the patients to be studied and the research questions to be addressed. A package that includes previously validated generic and condition-specific measures can be augmented by special questions or questionnaires that address study-specific research issues.

CONCLUSIONS

The medical management of diabetes must transcend controlling blood glucose levels and reflect the individualized needs of the patient, considering all the medical, psychosocial, and perceived quality of life factors that influence the disease process. There is growing recognition by health care professionals that in some chronic illnesses like diabetes, when it is not possible to cure the disease, quality of life may be one of the most important health outcomes to consider in assessing treatment efficacy (4,45,61,62). Assessment of quality of life in clinical trials of patients with diabetes will be affected by the duration and severity of the disease, age of the patient, expected benefits and adverse effects of treatment, necessary lifestyle changes, presence of complications, level of health care, patient support system, and degree of compliance to the prescribed treatment regimen. Because of the complexity of the treatment regimen, confounding psychosocial factors, and the high possibility of co-morbidity, the reliability, validity, and specificity of the scales are of paramount importance in selecting instruments to effectively evaluate the response to therapy. It is clear that clinical trials to evaluate the safety and efficacy of a diabetes treatment regimen must consider the impact of that treatment on the patient's quality of life as well.

APPENDIX: DIABETES QUALITY OF LIFE QUESTIONNAIRE (53)

Satisfaction

1. How satisfied are you with the amount of time it takes to manage your diabetes?
2. How satisfied are you with the amount of time you spend getting checkups?
3. How satisfied are you with the time it takes to determine your sugar level?
4. How satisfied are you with your current treatment?
5. How satisfied are you with the flexibility you have in your diet?
6. How satisfied are you with the burden your diabetes is placing on your family?
7. How satisfied are you with your knowledge about your diabetes?
8. How satisfied are you with your sleep?
9. How satisfied are you with your social relationships and friendships?
10. How satisfied are you with your sex life?
11. How satisfied are you with your work, school, and household activities?
12. How satisfied are you with the appearance of your body?
13. How satisfied are you with the time you spend exercising?
14. How satisfied are you with your leisure time?
15. How satisfied are you with life in general?

Impact

1. How often do you feel pain associated with the treatment for your diabetes?
2. How often are you embarrassed by having to deal with your diabetes in public?
3. How often do you have low blood sugar?
4. How often do you feel physically ill?
5. How often does your diabetes interfere with your family life?
6. How often do you have a bad night's sleep?
7. How often do you find your diabetes limiting your social relationships and friendships?
8. How often do you feel good about yourself?
9. How often do you feel restricted by your diet?
10. How often does your diabetes interfere with your sex life?
11. How often does your diabetes keep you from driving a car or using a machine (eg, a typewriter)?
12. How often does your diabetes interfere with your exercising?
13. How often do you miss work, school, or household duties because of your diabetes?
14. How often do you find yourself explaining what it means to have diabetes?
15. How often do you find that your diabetes interrupts your leisure-time activities?
16. How often do you tell others about your diabetes?
17. How often are you teased because you have diabetes?
18. How often do you feel that because of your diabetes you go to the bathroom more than others?
19. How often do you find that you eat something you shouldn't rather than tell someone that you have diabetes?
20. How often do you hide from others the fact that you are having an insulin reaction?

Worry: Social/Vocational

1. How often do you worry about whether you will get married?
2. How often do you worry about whether you will have children?
3. How often do you worry about whether you will not get a job you want?
4. How often do you worry about whether you will be denied insurance?
5. How often do you worry about whether you will be able to complete your education?
6. How often do you worry about whether you will miss work?
7. How often do you worry about whether you will be able to take a vacation or a trip?

Worry: Diabetes-Related

1. How often do you worry about whether you will pass out?
2. How often do you worry that your body looks different because you have diabetes?
3. How often do you worry that you will get complications from your diabetes?
4. How often do you worry about whether someone will not go out with you because you have diabetes?

REFERENCES

1. Wiklund I, Lindvall K, Swedberg KI. Assessment of quality of life in clinical trials. *Acta Med Scand* 1986;220:1–3.
2. Ganz PA. Methods of assessing the effect of drug therapy on quality of life. *Drug Safety* 1990;5(4):233–242.
3. Freed MM. Quality of life: the physician's dilemma. *Arch Phys Med Rehabil* 1984;65:109–111.
4. Coons SJ, Kaplan RM. Assessing health-related quality of life: application to drug therapy. *Clin Ther* 1992;14:850–858.
5. Krall LP, Beaser RS. *Joslin Diabetes Manual. 12th Edition.* Malvern, PA: Lea & Febiger; 1989.
6. Glasgow RE. Compliance to diabetes regimens. Conceptualization, complexity, and determinants. In: Cramer JA, Spilker B, eds. *Patient compliance in medical practice and clinical trials.* New York: Raven Press, 1991:209–244.
7. Jonsson B. Assessment of quality of life in chronic diseases. *Acta Paediatr Scand (suppl)* 1987;337:164–169.
8. Revicki DA. Health-related quality of life in the evaluation of medical therapy for chronic illness. *J Fam Pract* 1989;29:377–380.
9. Revicki DA. Quality of life research and the health care industry. *J Res Pharm Econ* 1990;2(1):41–53.
10. Birch-Johnson K. The economics of screening for microalbuminuria in patients with insulin-dependent diabetes mellitus. *PharmacoEconomics* 1994;5(5):357–360.
11. Eiser C, Tooke JE. Quality of life evaluation in diabetes. *PharmacoEconomics* 1993;4(2):85–91.
12. American Diabetes Association, 1993 Vital Statistics.
13. Bennett PH. Definition, diagnosis, and classification of diabetes mellitus and impaired glucose tolerance. In: Kahn CR, Weir GC, eds. *Joslin's diabetes mellitus.* 13th ed. Philadelphia: Lea & Febiger, 1994:193–200.
14. Eisenbarth GS, Ziegler AG, Colman PA. Pathogenesis of insulin-dependent (Type I) diabetes mellitus. In: Kahn CR, Weir GC, eds. *Joslin's diabetes mellitus.* 13th ed. Philadelphia: Lea & Febiger, 1994:216–239.
15. Beaser RS. *Outsmarting diabetes. A dynamic approach for reducing the effects of insulin-dependent diabetes.* Minneapolis, MN: Chronimed Publishing, 1994.
16. The Diabetes Control and Complications Trial Research Group. The effect of intensive treatment of diabetes on the development and progression of long-term complications in insulin-dependent diabetes mellitus. *N Engl J Med* 1993;329:977–986.
17. Hirsch IB, Farkas-Hirsch R, Skyler JS. Intensive insulin therapy for type I diabetes mellitus. *Diabetes Care* 1990;13:1265–1283.
18. Dunning PL, Petrie R. Exploring the psychosocial aspects of diabetes: the yellow ball. *Diabetes Educ* 1994;20(1):64–65.
19. Cerkoney KAP, Hart LK. The relationship between the health belief model and compliance of persons with diabetes mellitus. *Diabetes Care* 1980;3:594–598.
20. Hanestad BR. Self-reported quality of life and the effect of different clinical and demographic characteristics in people with type I diabetes. *Diabetes Res Clin Pract* 1993;19:139–149.
21. Hanestad BR, Albrektsen G. Quality of life, perceived difficulties in adherence to a diabetes regimen, and blood glucose control. *Diabetic Med* 1991;8:759–764.
22. Wikby A, Hornquist JO, Andersson P. Background, quality of life and metabolic control in patients with insulin-dependent diabetes mellitus. *Diabetes Res Clin Pract* 1991;13:53–62.
23. Eiser C, Flynn M, Green E, et al. Quality of life in young adults with type I diabetes in relation to demographic and disease variables. *Diabetic Med* 1992;9:375–378.
24. Mayou R, Bryant B, Turner R. Quality of life in non-insulin-dependent diabetes and a comparison with insulin-dependent diabetes. *J Psychosomat Res* 1990;34(1):1–11.
25. Anderson RM, Donnelly MB, Dedrick RF. Measuring the attitudes of patients towards diabetes and its treatment. *Patient Educ Counsel* 1990;16:231–245.
26. Bashoff EC, Beaser RS. Insulin therapy: patients' perceptions and design of insulin regimens. *Postgrad Med* 1995;97:86–96.
27. Wolf FM, Jacober SJ, Wolf LL, et al. Quality of life activities associated with adherence to insulin infusion pump therapy in the treatment of insulin-dependent diabetes mellitus. *J Clin Epidemiol* 1989; 42(12):1129–1136.

28. Wilkinson G. The influence of psychiatric, psychological and social factors on the control of insulin-dependent diabetes mellitus. *J Psychosomat Res* 1987;31:277–286.
29. Jacobson AM, Hauser ST, Anderson BJ, Polonsky W. Psychosocial aspects of diabetes. In: Kahn CR, Weir G, eds. *Joslin's diabetes mellitus.* 13th ed. Philadelphia: Lea & Febiger, 1994:431–450.
30. Szabo-Kallai K, Gyimesi A, Ivanyi J. Role of emotional factors in diabetes. *Acta Diabetol* 1990;27:23–29.
31. Lundman B, Norberg A. Coping strategies in people with insulin-dependent diabetes mellitus. *Diabetes Educ* 1993;19:198–204.
32. Hanestad BR, Hornquist JO, Albrektsen G. Self-assessed quality of life and metabolic control in persons with insulin-dependent diabetes mellitus (IDDM). *Scand J Soc Med* 1991;19(1):57–65.
33. deWeerdt I, Visser AP, Kok GJ, et al. Randomized controlled multicentre evaluation of an education programme for insulin-treated diabetic patients: effects on metabolic control, quality of life, and costs of therapy. *Diabetic Med* 1991;8:338–345.
34. Jacobson AM, de Groot M, Samson J. Quality of life research in patients with diabetes mellitus. In: Dimsdale JE, Baum A, eds. *Underlying perspectives on behavioral medicine.* Hillsdale, NJ: Lawrence Erlbaum Associates, 1994:241–262.
35. McKelvey J, Waller DA, North AJ, et al. Reliability and validity of the Diabetes Family Behavior Scale (DFBS). *Diabetes Educ* 1993; 19:125–132.
36. Jacobson AM, Hauser S, Lavori P, et al. Adherence among children and adolescents with IDDM over a four-year longitudinal follow up. I. The influence of patient coping and adjustment. *J Pediatr Psychiatry* 1990;15:511–526.
37. Edelstein J, Linn MW. The influence of the family on control of diabetes. *Soc Sci Med* 1985;21:541–544.
38. O'Connor PJ, Jacobson AM. Functional status measurement in elderly diabetic patients. *Clin Geriatr Med* 1990;6:865–882.
39. Lloyd CE, Matthews KA, Wing RR, Orchard TJ. Psychosocial factors and complications of IDDM. The Pittsburgh epidemiology of diabetes complications study. VIII. *Diabetes Care* 1992;15:166–172.
40. Gafvels C, Lithner F, Borjeson B. Living with diabetes: Relationship to gender, duration and complications. A survey in northern Sweden. *Diabetic Med* 1993;10:768–773.
41. Testa MA, Simonson DC. Measuring quality of life in hypertensive patients with diabetes. *Postgrad Med J* 1988;64(suppl 3):50–58.
42. Rodin G. Quality of life in adults with insulin-dependent diabetes mellitus. *Psychother Psychosom* 1990;54:132–139.
43. Jaeschke R, Guyatt GH, Cook D. Quality of life instruments in the evaluation of new drugs. *PharmacoEconomics* 1992;2:84–94.
44. Bardsley MJ, Astell S, McCallum A, Home PD. The performance of three measures of health status in an outpatient diabetes population. *Diabetic Med* 1993;10:619–626.
45. Guyatt GH, Bombardier C, Tugwell PX. Measuring disease-specific quality of life in clinical trials. *Can Med Assoc J* 1986;134:889–895.
46. Guyatt GH, Feeny DH, Patrick DL. Measuring health-related quality of life. *Ann Intern Med* 1993;118:622–629.
47. Jacobson AM, de Groot M, Samson JA. The evaluation of two measures of quality of life in patients with type I and type II diabetes. *Diabetes Care* 1994;17:267–274.
48. Patrick DL, Deyo RA. Generic and disease-specific measures in assessing health status and quality of life. *Med Care* 1989;27(3 suppl): S217–S232.
49. Parkerson GR, Connis RT, Broadhead WE, et al. Disease-specific versus generic measurement of health-related quality of life in insulin-dependent diabetic patients. *Med Care* 1993;31:629–639.
50. Nerenz DR, Repasky DP, Whitehouse FW, Kahkonen DM. Ongoing assessment of health status in patients with diabetes mellitus. *Med Care* 1992;30(5 suppl):MS112–123.
51. Stewart AL, Greenfield S, Hays RD, et al. Functional status and well-being of patients with chronic conditions. *JAMA* 1989;262:907–913.
52. Wells KB, Golding JM, Burnam MA. Psychiatric disorder in a sample of the general population with and without chronic medical conditions. *Am J Psychol* 1988;145:976–981.
53. The DCCT Research Group. Reliability and validity of a Diabetes Quality of Life Measure (DQOL) for the Diabetes Control and Complications Trial (DCCT). *Diabetes Care* 1988;11(9):725–732.
54. Ware JE, Sherbourne CD. The MOS 36-item short-form health survey (SF-36). I. Conceptual framework and item selection. *Med Care* 1992; 30:473–481.

55. Ingersoll GM, Marrero DG. A modified quality-of-life measure for youths: psychometric properties. *Diabetes Educ* 1991;17:114–118.

56. Nathan DM, Fogel H, Norman D, et al. Long-term metabolic and quality of life results with pancreatic/renal transplantation in insulin-dependent diabetes mellitus. *Transplantation* 1991;52:85–91.

57. Selam JL, Micossi P, Dunn FL. Clinical trial of programmable implantable insulin pump for Type I diabetes. *Diabetes Care* 1992;15:877–884.

58. Guyatt GH, Veldhuyzen Van Zanten SJO. Measuring quality of life in clinical trials: a taxonomy and review. *Can Med Assoc J* 1989;140:1441–1448.

59. Fletcher AE, Bulpitt CJ. Measurement of quality of life in clinical trials of therapy. *Cardiology* 1988;75(suppl 1):41–52.

60. Bergner M, Bobbitt RA, Carter WB, Gilson B. The Sickness Impact Profile: development and final revision of a health status measure. *Med Care* 1981;19(8):787–805.

61. Deyo RA. Measuring functional outcomes in therapeutic trials for chronic disease. *Control Clin Trial* 1984;5:223–240.

62. Buxton MJ, Drummond MF. Quality of life measurement in the development of medicines. *Pharm J* 1990;244:260–262.

Quality of Life and Pharmacoeconomics in Clinical Trials, Second Edition, edited by B. Spilker.
Lippincott-Raven Publishers, Philadelphia © 1996.

CHAPTER 103

Cancer: Psychosocial Aspects

Ivan Barofsky

INTRODUCTION

The research literature on psychosocial aspects of cancer has grown significantly since the advent of the Cancer Rehabilitation Program of the National Cancer Institute (1). Evidence for this growth includes at least two journals dedicated exclusively to publishing psychosocial oncology studies (e.g., *The Journal of Psychosocial Oncology* and *Psychooncology*), as well as some recently published books (2,3). Interest in the assessment of the quality of life (QOL) of the cancer patient has also experienced growth although not necessarily as rapidly as other disease areas (Goodyear, [104]). In addition, a number of publications have adequately summarized the available cancer-specific quality of life assessments instruments (4–6). Included among them is the author's chapter on cancer in the first edition of this book (4). This chapter takes an entirely different approach.

What has not been discussed in sufficient detail is the relationship between psychosocial issues and quality of life assessment for the cancer patient. The simple assumption that they are one and the same runs the risk of conceptual and empirical confusion. Clarifying the relationship between these two research areas is one of the objectives of this paper. In addition, this chapter focuses on the use of a quality of life assessment in clinical decision making, particularly when to start and stop cancer treatment. Starting and stopping treatment are natural markers that can have a profound qualitative impact on a person, yet it is a research area that has remained outside the mainstream of psychosocial research. The major reason for this may be that the field of clinical

decision making evolved from a different intellectual tradition, economics, and therefore its methods and data may appear disjointed with psychosocial studies. This chapter will provide a bridging framework so that the relationship between these two areas of research will be more obvious.

Quality of life assessments can be used as an outcome measure of the current state of a person, independent of treatment, as the direct consequence of the decision to start or stop a treatment, but also prospectively as a *predictor of outcome*. Most past quality of life assessment research of the cancer patient consists of cross-sectional studies using convenience samples (4). More recently, there has been an increase in the number of studies that have included quality of life assessments in cancer clinical trials (4). Some of these studies have focused on tracing the direct impact of cancer and its treatment on quality of life (4). This last type of quality of life research has been particularly useful, as it provides a method for optimizing the qualitative consequences of a treatment regimen. Each of these applications of a quality of life assessment requires that the respondent participate in a cognitive task, which may consist of generating a rating, selecting a multiple-choice item, writing an answer to an open-ended question, and so on. Common to all these cognitive tasks is the person's reliance on memories of past events and experiences. The applications of quality of life assessments differ, however, in that in one this information is used to project about events in the future, while in another the person reflects about the consequences of events that have already taken place. It is sometimes possible to find items reflecting several types of cognitive tasks, as well as several referents in the same questionnaire. This type of assessment instrument reflects the fact that a person may want to know what the treatment has done to his or her quality of life, but also what may happen in the future as a result of this treatment.

I. Barofsky: Department of Psychiatry and Behavioral Sciences, The Johns Hopkins University School of Medicine, Baltimore, Maryland 21224

Consider the situation in which patients are to decide to start or stop treatment. Here they may reflect on what has already happened to them, what is currently true for them, and what may happen in the future as part of the decision-making process. For example, patients may feel fine when they are asked to self-examine a breast or testicle, or to have a screening or physical examination. Similarly, patients may be coping well with their treatment and its consequences and be asked to stop treatment. In either case, patients are being asked to experience change, changes that may lead to quality of life consequences. Delay, avoidance, and noncompliance with screening or treatment recommendations would then be seen as behavioral responses reflecting the patients' reluctance to change their state—in effect, an effort by patients to sustain their quality of life as they know it.

In addition to resistance to change, the information on which patients have to base change is often ambiguous. As a result, patients may need to consider the available information, use this information to predict their quality of life, and decide whether this is a quality of life they desire. This type of contemplative task may occur when a person is deciding to initiate adjuvant therapy, resume therapy after a recurrence, deciding to have prophylactic mastectomy, opt for unconventional therapy, and so on. Although the information on disease progression and diagnostic tests (7) may be ambiguous, what is also true is that a person has to translate this information into individualized probability statements. Thus, what we know about the risk of failing to decide to start treatment is stated in probability terms, and it is the patient's task to translate this information into individual risks and preferences. Efforts at rationalizing this process have resulted in the development of the field of clinical decision analysis (see the section Measuring Anticipated QOL Outcomes).

Stopping treatment also occurs under a number of different circumstances, each of which may include a prediction of or current assessment of quality of life. For example, a patient or a clinician may anticipate quality of life change before deciding that the patient has had a sufficient chemotherapy dose, rather than wait until an actual adverse event occurs. Much chemotherapy is administered with the philosophy that more is better. Dose escalation is assumed to lead to adequate cell kill, but it may also reflect the fact that biological markers are not available to decide that a therapeutic objective has been reached. Currently, toxic responses (e.g., impaired liver function, thrombocytopenia) are used as criteria to stop dose escalation. To the extent that there is an overlap between toxicity and quality of life measures, quality of life measures may be involved in the decision to stop therapy. When has a patient exhausted therapy? Does this ever occur? Does the use of quality of life criteria become more relevant as a criterion to stop treatment when a patient enters the terminal phase of life? Thus, there are a variety of circumstances that evoke predictive, cross-sectional or treatment-linked quality of life assessments when deciding to stop treatment.

PSYCHOSOCIAL ISSUES AND QUALITY OF LIFE ASSESSMENT

Figure 1 represents an attempt to piece together a number of clinically relevant stages in the natural history of cancer diagnosis and treatment. As a person progresses through these stages, the contribution of activities associated with the stage increasingly determine the quality of life of the person. For example, a person may anticipate that by engaging in health behaviors, such as self-monitoring, symptoms may be recognized, diagnosed, and treated that will affect quality of life. By contrast, quality of life may be directly diminished as a result of treatment, independent of the person's expectations. A person may experience the predicted adverse quality of life consequences as a request to give up old habits, such as smoking, or to have a diagnostic test, and so on. For each example, the person may make an effort to sustain quality of life, however unhealthy. Overcoming this resistance and understanding how to initiate health behaviors has been the focus of Prochaska and DiClemente's (8) research. These investigators describe a process that includes a precontemplative, contemplative, determinated, active, and maintenance stage. Each of these stages can be visualized as steps people go through to open their quality of life to change. By contrast, treatments can produce direct quality of life changes, such as when chemotherapy modifies a patient's endocrine status, resulting in diminished interest in intimacy, or affects their neuromuscular functioning resulting in impairments in activities of daily living, and so on.

The importance of different measures of quality of life change (predictive, cross-sectional, or treatment-related) plus the tendency of people to preserve their quality of life (9) are also key to understanding the relationship between psychosocial and quality of life measurement. In general, there is increasing consensus that a quality of life assessment is an outcome measure (10) that reflects a person's subjective reports of their performance and accomplishments, and their preference for these states. When strictly applied, this definition helps order the relative role of a variety of psychosocial and quality of life measures. For example, it is not uncommon to find that a measure of depression or anxiety is considered a quality of life measure. According to the above definition, this would only be true if the person perceived that their affective state affected their behavior or functions. In this scheme, depression, anxiety, and even pain act as modifiers of functional quality of life outcomes, and not necessarily as measures of a person's qualitative state. In addition, many of the common psychosocial measures, such as attribution, coping, denial, and helplessness, reflect *processes* that may have qualitative consequences. What is sometimes confusing to investigators is the fact that these same process variables can imply a quality of life change without, necessarily, mandating it. As a result, some investigators consider studies of psychosocial aspects of cancer as measures of quality of life when they are best considered the study of processes that may or may not lead to a change in

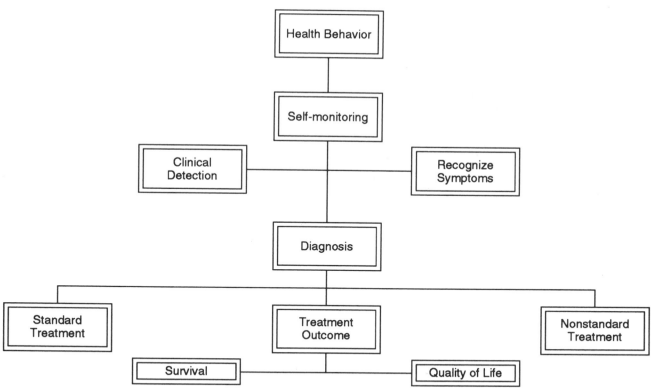

FIG. 1. One aspect of health behavior self-monitoring can lead to either the clinical detection of symptoms and/or by the person recognizing the significance of symptoms. This information can then be used to diagnose and treat a person. Treatment may be standard or nonstandard. The outcome of this treatment has an impact on survival or quality of life of the person.

a quality of life outcome. The situation is further complicated because depression or anxiety questionnaires may contain items that refer both to process and to outcome. Failure to distinguish between process and outcome within assessment instruments and in the design of the assessment tasks themselves is an important one and could account for some of the unexpected results found in recent applications of quality of life assessments (see the section, Lumpectomy Versus Modified Mastectomy).

The difference between psychosocial and quality of life measures can be conceptualized in a model. Figure 2 shows that changes in psychosocial variables and quality of life measures will follow a standard dose-response function as disease severity increases. It also predicts that at the same level of disease, severity quality of life measures are less likely to change than psychosocial measures. Also illustrated is the *coping index* (analogous to the therapeutic index), defined as the difference between the two functions at the midpoint of each function. What the coping index demonstrates is the extent to which psychosocial variables can forestall adverse changes in quality of life. Thus, as the adaptive capacity of an individual becomes less effective, as measured by the reduced probability of psychosocial vari-

ables (e.g., facilitating coping, denial, and effective attribution), the probability of an adverse quality of life impact increases. Events that may alter the cancer patient's adaptive capacity include disease recurrence and domestic events. Figure 2 also provides an opportunity to define *suffering*. Suffering would be operationally defined as the point at which such psychosocial activities as attribution, coping, or denial do not prevent changes in quality of life (as measured by changes in the various domains of quality of life). Graphically, this would occur when the two functions overlap. This can occur in at least two ways: first, when the coping index is minimal, resulting in the overlap of both functions; and second, when at a specific level of disease severity, psychosocial factors do not contribute to the continued preservation of quality of life.

So far a distinction has been made between process (psychosocial measures) and outcome (quality of life measures) measures and the fact that outcome measures can reflect predictive, cross-sectional, or treatment-related changes. The purpose of making these distinctions is to help organize and interpret the available research literature, as well as increase the analytical potential available when doing a quality of life assessment of the cancer patient.

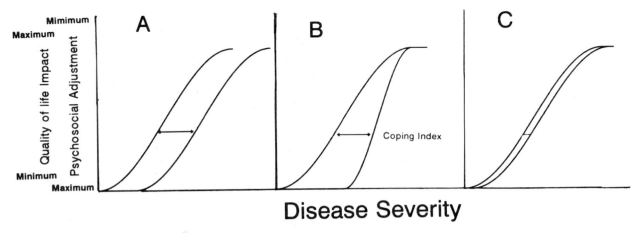

FIG. 2. Plotted in this figure are three models of the relationship between psychosocial adjustment and quality of life impact. The basic relationship depicted is that as disease severity increases, the capacity of an individual to adapt psychosocially decreases and the quality of life impact of the disease increases. Also implied in each panel is the fact that the quality of life impact (righthand function) will be delayed relative to psychosocial change. **(A)** Parallel relationship with the distance between functions, at the midpoint of adjustment or impact, as reflecting the coping index. **(B,C)** Suffering—when the ability of a person to adjust psychosocially provides no advantage to the person. **(B)** This occurs at the point of minimal psychosocial adjustment and maximum quality of life impact. **(C)** Situation in which there is minimal coping advantage, so that little of the person's life can be protected from the adverse consequences of increases in disease severity.

THE MEANINGFULNESS OF A QUALITY OF LIFE ASSESSMENT

The difference between psychosocial issues and quality of life assessments has become part of the ongoing debate on how best to capture the meaning of quality of life in the assessment process (11). For example, creating a quality of life assessment by combining measures of coping, affective change, with functional status may appear to generate a more comprehensive, meaningful or valid picture of quality of life but also runs the risk of diluting the analytic potential of any study that uses such an assessment. It clearly limits establishing causal relationships, since tautological situations are too often created, such as when variables may be either independent or dependent variables. Depression is a good example of a measure that is often used, sometimes in the same study, as a predictor variable in a regression equation or as an independent variable to be associated with some functional outcome.

Costain and colleagues (12) addressed some of these issues when they compared two quality of life assessments that they administered to a group of cancer patients. These investigators selected two assessment instruments that differed in terms of the conceptual model implicit in the design of the assessments, one reflecting a function-based and the other a meaning-based quality of life assessment. The two assessments were found to generate different pictures of the cancer patients they were studying. The two assessment instruments that Costain et al. (12) compared differed in the wording, response format, and proportion of items dealing with different quality of life dimensions. Their study makes the point that the way a quality of life assessment is constructed will determine the type and usefulness of the information generated. They are also aware of the fact that questionnaires can be designed for different purposes. What is less clear is whether these investigators recognize that, in pursuit of a "meaningful" quality of life assessment, they have achieved adequate description, but in so doing limited the analytic potential of a study.

In addition, enriched or "meaningful" quality of life assessments do not necessarily provide information that clinicians can use to modify, or even design, their treatment regimens. If integration of quality of life measures into clinical practice is the objective of the assessment task, a specific approach is mandated involving clearly linking aspects of the treatment process with anticipated qualitative outcomes. Most often this involves assessing functions or other operationally definable outcome measures.

Two basic methods are used to integrate a quality of life assessment into the clinical decision-making process, in general, and to decide to start or stop treatment, in particular (4). The first method integrates the assessment task into the treatment development process itself. It is essentially a treatment optimization process designed to minimize the potential for adverse quality of life outcomes and ease the decision-making process. The history of the development of treatment for soft tissue sarcoma (4) is an example of this approach. The second approach involves a two-step process whereby a treatment is assessed and then modified as a result of what is learned from the initial assessment.

This approach, which is far more common than the first, is also the approach most likely to be affected by the conceptual model underlying the assessment instrument (e.g., does the instrument consist of outcome only or both process and outcome measures?).

If the function-based model offers greater analytic potential and clinical value, can it still approximate a "meaningful" description of quality of life? This chapter uses a model of quality of life assessment (10,13) that includes measures of function and a description of a person's preferences for being in a particular functional state. This two-step approach was first suggested by Bush (14), who recognized that the data generated by a quality of life assessment have the potential of being confounded by the failure to distinguish between process and outcome variables and predictive, cross-sectional, and treatment-related measures. Bush suggested separating the two elements to ensure that the description of a person's health states be as unbiased as possible and that estimates of preferences for being in a particular health state be population based. By using the population's preferences for outcome he could ensure the generality of any resultant inference, and apply his results to policy decisions. In addition, Barofsky (13) stated that Bush, knowingly or not, has captured in his model one of the several elements (see Barofsky [14]) of the cognitive process that a person would ordinarily use when generating a global quality of life assessment. Ware (15) takes an alternative approach that relies on the World Health Organization (WHO) definition of health, to provide a conceptual foundation for the quality of life assessment and psychometric characterization to establish the reliability and validity of the assessment.

PREDICTIVE QUALITY OF LIFE ASSESSMENT

Conceptualizing quality of life assessments as based on a common cognitive process that may have different referents (current or in the future) is important because it provides a context for organizing an otherwise diverse set of research within a common framework. This is also true within types of quality of life assessments. Thus, studies of worry (16), utility or preference measures (17), and prospective decision-making systems based on retrospectively generated quality of life data (18) all have a common cognitive and future reference.

Lerman et al. (19) illustrate the value of worry by cancer patients as an outcome measure, but it also confirms the distinction previously made between psychosocial and quality of life measures. Lerman and colleagues were studying the psychological impact of receiving the results of breast cancer screening mammograms on the intentions of women to engage in breast self-examination and receive clinical breast examinations and follow-up mammograms. The patient's initial mammograms were classified as either normal or as having a low or high level of suspicion of abnormality. They asked whether the person was worried (a predictive measure) about having breast cancer, whether her mood (a process measure) or functioning (an outcome measure) would be affected as a result of this worrying, and whether she was anxious about getting a mammogram. Their data illustrate that as a person's worries shift from developing a disease to the impact of the disease on mood and functioning, the percentage of persons affected decreases (19). These workers also found that the frequency of breast self-examination or intentions to have a mammogram did not vary as a function of the degree of abnormalities revealed in the mammogram. This study was of interest because it confirmed the prediction made in Figure 2 that the proportion of persons who report an impact on their mood would be higher than the proportion who reported an adverse impact of this information on their functioning. The implication of these data was that a number of persons whose mood was affected by the outcome of the mammogram were able to cope and not have the information affect their ability to function. Inspection of the scale demonstrates that items are included that describe a person's worries about both the process (psychosocial adjustment) and outcome (quality of life) of cancer and its treatment.

By asking her patients about worry, Lerman and colleagues (19) focus attention on a cognitive process which can also be used as an index of predictive quality of life change. Worry has been defined as "a chain of thoughts and images, negatively affect-laden and relatively uncontrollable. The worry process represents an attempt to engage in mental problem solving on an issue whose outcome is uncertain but contains the possibility of one or more negative outcomes" (20). Anxiety is the primary emotional correlate of worry. Studies of cancer patients suggest that 30% to 40% of oncology patients report moderate to high levels of anxiety (21). In a study involving three oncology centers, Lerman et al. (22) report that worries about developing breast cancer, in otherwise healthy women, are more likely to affect functioning in young and older than middle-aged women.

Stefanek et al. (16) report the development of a worry scale that is specific for the cancer patient. Although their 30-item scale has been subjected to a limited amount of psychometric evaluation they were able to show that those patients who were classified as a worrier (those who were "somewhat or very worried") were 14 times more likely to have low social support, six times more likely to be a male, but only 1.14 times more likely to have had a prior cancer treatment. Inspection of the scale shows that items are included that describe a person's worries about both the process (psychosocial adjustment) and outcome (quality of life) of cancer and its treatment.

Questions dealing with worry can be found as individual items in many psychosocial assessments of the cancer patient (23–25). Often these items are folded into generalized measures of distress or appraisal of threat, masking attempts to trace the impact of worry. Still the literature is clear on the importance of worry and related measures as predictors of psychosocial adjustment and quality of life outcome (26).

Clinical decision analysis is a rapidly expanding field of study that has evolved out of economics and psychology (27). Discussion analysis includes a set of methods that can be used to determine the relative risks and benefits of choices, particularly when choosing between alternative treatments. It also permits individualized treatment choices. It is finding increasing application in decision analysis involving the cancer patient (28). It has been applied to the study of such choices as whether the patient should have a laryngectomy or irradiation for laryngeal cancer (29), adjuvant therapy for node-negative breast cancer patients (30), and even a mastectomy or breast conservation operation (31). The key component of a clinical decision analysis is the generation of quantitative estimates of preferences, or utilities, which can then be used to characterize the choice the person has to make. These estimates involve the application of formalized methodologies, including the standard gamble, time trade-off, or visual analog scales. A typical study involves the patient considering their preference for two alternatives, each of which represents some future treatment/disease outcome. When the time trade-off methodology is used, for example, a person is asked to choose between two health states that differ in duration prior to death. Thus, the patient may have to decide whether he or she prefers living a shorter healthy life or a longer but more symptomatic life. The actual duration of the life is varied until time periods are found when the person is neutral in their preferences. The fact that the participant in this study is continually asked to project their preference to the future makes the time trade-off and other utility methodologies analogous to the measurement of worry. In both cases, the person is being asked to anticipate an outcome.

Verhoef and colleagues (31) illustrate the application of clinical decision making to selecting breast-conserving surgery or a mastectomy. These investigators used currently available data on the mortality risk, local recurrence rate, proportion of operable relapses, and other factors and a Markov modeling process to determine the fate of patients receiving breast-conserving surgery or mastectomy. They define five states and calculated transitional probabilities to be each of these states. What they found overall was that their model predicted that mastectomy patients would live an average of 20.92 years, while patients who received breast-conserving surgery would live 21.31 years. Thus, the breast-conserving patients would live 0.39 years longer. On the other hand, breast-conserving patients who were at risk of recurrence had a lower life expectancy (20.54 years). Verhoef and colleagues also calculated the benefit in terms of quality-adjusted life years (QALYs) for breast-conserving treatment and found that a reduced benefit for younger women. Apparently, there is an optimal age range for breast-conserving treatment, and patients at each extreme are at a disadvantage.

Most of the data gathered from clinical decision-making studies are gathered from persons who are not patients. The reason for not using patients as subjects is that they often have already been treated, so that to be asked to decide between treatments, one of which they experienced and the other they did not, would likely bias their responses. In addition, it might be considered unethical to ask persons to consider treatment options that will not be available to them. An alternative approach involves the use of data gathered from patients who have experienced a disease and its treatment and use this information to inform new patients what they can expect to experience, depending on their decisions. Using data from the Ludwig Breast Cancer Cooperative group, Gelber and colleagues (18,32) clinical trials evaluating alternative chemotherapy regimens generated just such a methodology. The approach the authors took was to measure the time that a person did not experience toxicity. The Q-TWIST (quality-adjusted time without symptoms of disease and subjective toxic effects of treatment) methodology (32) provide a basis for the individual patient to state their preferences and get some estimate of what they can expect for outcome as a function of treatment decision. The relevance of probability states based on group data and applied to individual patients remains an empirical issue, but clearly the Q-TWIST methodology represents one approach to the problem of formalizing predictive quality of life assessments.

LUMPECTOMY VERSUS MODIFIED MASTECTOMY: A CONTROVERSY REVISITED

One of the objectives of quality of life assessments is to provide a qualitative basis for resolving clinical or treatment dilemmas. Thus, it has been particularly disappointing to investigators to note that the available studies comparing lumpectomy and mastectomy for early-stage breast cancer have failed to establish major quality of life differences between treatments (33). Approximately 21 studies have been reported to date, involving a range of patient groups, assessment instruments, and so on, providing a diverse but large data set to consider. Table 1 summarizes some of the characteristics of 19 studies (34–54; one investigator reported the same data set three times but over three different time periods). Most of these studies have accrued patients consecutively and consist of either retrospective or longitudinal designs. Treatment assignment was mostly by the patients choosing their treatment with randomization being the exception. Fifteen of the 19 studies used standardized psychosocial assessments, and 13 studies used psychosocial assessment instruments developed for the specific study. Only five studies used either standardized ($N = 2$) or clinically derived ($N = 3$) quality of life assessment instruments. Occasionally there were studies that taped a limited number of quality of life domains (e.g., sexual activity), but these were not included because it was clear from the paper that the measure was being used as an index of psychosocial

TABLE 1. *Summary of characteristics of studies comparing psychosocial adjustment and quality of life assessment of early breast cancer patients receiving a breast-conserving procedure or mastectomy*

Study/year/ref.	Sampling procedure	Study design	Treatment assignment[a]	Assessment and instruments[b]	Study objective[c]
Sanger and Reznikoff (1981) (34)	Matched controls	Retrospective	Choice/no choice	SPA	Psychosocial adjustment
Schain et al. (1983) (35)	Matched controls	Retrospective	Randomization	CDPA	Psychosocial adjustment, OACP
Beckmann et al. (1983) (36)	Matched controls	Retrospective	Choice/no choice	CDPA	Psychosocial adjustment
Ashcroft et al. (1985) (37)	Consecutive	Longitudinal	Choice/choice or no choice	SPA	Psychosocial adjustment
Bartelink et al. (1985) (38)	Consecutive	Retrospective	Not reported	CDPA, TOA	Psychosocial adjustment, OACP
Steinberg et al. (1985) (39)	Matched controls	Retrospective	Choice or no choice/not reported	SPA, CDPA, CDQA	Psychosocial adjustment, QOLA
Taylor et al. (1985) (40)	Consecutive	Retrospective	Not reported	SPA, CDPA, SQA	Psychosocial adjustment, QOLA
Baider et al. (1986) (41)	Matched controls	Retrospective	Choice/not reported	SPA	Psychosocial adjustment
de Haes et al. (1986) (42)	Consecutive	Longitudinal	Randomization/ randomization	SPA, CDQA	Psychosocial adjustment, QOLA
Fallowfield et al. (1986) (43)	Consecutive	Retrospective	Choice or randomization/ choice or randomization	SPA, CDPA	Psychosocial adjustment
Ganz et al. (1987) (44)	Consecutive	Retrospective	Not reported	SPA, CDPA, CDQA	Psychosocial adjustment, QOLA
Lasry et al. (1987) (45)	Consecutive	Retrospective	Randomization/ randomization	SPA, CDPA	Psychosocial adjustment
Kemeny et al. (1988) (46)	Consecutive	Longitudinal	Randomization/ randomization	SPA, CDPA	Psychosocial adjustment
Levy et al. (1989) (47)	Consecutive	Longitudinal	Choice or randomization/ choice or randomization	SPA	Psychosocial adjustment
Maunsell et al. (1989) (48)	Consecutive	Longitudinal	Not reported	SPA, CDPA	Psychosocial adjustment
Meyer and Aspegren (1989) (49)	Consecutive	Retrospective	Choice/choice	CDPA	Psychosocial adjustment
Wolberg et al. (1989) (50)	Consecutive	Longitudinal	Choice/choice or no choice	SPA	Psychosocial adjustment
Pozo et al. (1992) (51)	Consecutive	Longitudinal	Choice/choice or no choice	SPA, CDPA, SQA	Psychosocial adjustment, QOLA
Omne-Ponten et al. (1994) (52)	Consecutive	Longitudinal	Choice/choice	SPA	Psychosocial adjustment

Adapted from Table 2 in Kiebert et al. (33).

[a]Treatment assignments (choice, no choice, or no report) for breast-conserving therapy/mastectomy.

[b]Assessment instruments were classified as including either standardized psychosocial assessments (SPA), clinically developed psychosocial assessment (CDPA), standardized quality of life assessments (SQA), clinically developed quality of life assessments (CDQA), or treatment outcome assessments (TOA). Clinically developed tools were often extracted from standardized assessments.

[c]Study objectives were classified as assessing psychosocial adjustment, quality of life (QOLA), or outcomes attributable to clinical procedures (e.g., surgery/chemotherapy, or irradiation; OACP).

adjustment. What was also clear from the table is that all the reported studies had assessment of the psychosocial adjustment of the patient as their primary function and that quality of life assessment was the focus of only five studies. Two studies assessed outcomes attributable to clinical procedures.

In their original study, which summarized most of the same data in Table 1, Kiebert et al. (33) indicate that in most instances there was no difference in psychosocial adjustment as a function of surgical procedure for early breast cancer. The major exception to this statement was their observation that there was a fairly consistent disturbance in body image and sexuality in the mastectomy patients between studies, but not for the breast-conserving patient. Reframed from the context of the current discussion, what this means is that all the investigators reporting studies were interested in determining whether women differed in the process whereby they responded to their breast surgery, and only a few of them were concerned about the outcome as a result of type of surgery. The conclusion that there was no difference in process might imply that there will be no difference in outcome; however, considering the quality and nature of the reported studies in Table 1, this may not be an appropriate conclusion: (a) because quality of life studies tend to cover a broader range of social and economic issues than psychosocial assessments, thus, the fact that surgery patients might not differ in self-esteem does not mean they will not differ in terms of total income, the extent they travel, their concern about crime, and so on; and (b) because not one of the reported 19 studies used what would today be called a standardized generic quality of life assessment (55). Most often the quality of life assessment was confined to a few global visual analog scales. Only one study included a cancer-specific quality of life assessment (44). In addition, quality of life studies can provide information on the preferences people have for the state they are in (14). None of the 19 studies listed in Table 1 provided these types of data. The assumption in all these studies is that if one of the surgery groups was different from the other, that one group would be better off than the other. Usually, the person determining what is "better" is the investigator, yet this is information that can be garnered directly from the patient by studying their preferences. A second set of reasons has to do with the quality of the data in Table 1. All the studies in Table 1 are based on convenience samples and usually small-sized convenience samples. In addition, there was no consistency between studies in terms of the types of psychosocial assessments used. Thus, conceptually and empirically there does not seem to be any justification, at this point, to conclude that there is no difference in the quality of life outcome as a function of type of breast cancer surgery.

Do the studies summarized in Table 1 provide any additional support for the model illustrated in Figure 2? Most studies were not designed to tap the analytic distinction expressed in Figure 2; however, Steinberg et al. (39) found that emotional distress accounted for 64% of the variance of the items included in their questionnaires, while life pattern changes accounted for 23%. The CORES, the questionnaire included in the study conducted by Ganz et al. (44), includes items that could easily support the distinction between psychosocial adjustment and functional status, but the distinction was not included as part of the analysis of their data. The study by Kemeny et al. (46) shows that, in general, disturbances in emotional and sexual activities and body image were greater than disturbances in activities, but this was observed over a limited range and represented mild change. The study by Omne-Ponten et al. (54) also provides support (see Table 2) for the distinction, but the number of patients involved was very small ($N = 5$ for each group).

CONCLUSIONS

This brief review of an ever-growing dynamic aspect of quality of life research—studies of the quality of life of the cancer patient—has focused on some of its accomplishments, but also on its conceptual and empirical limitations. This review permits the following conclusions:

1. Investigators need to differentiate studies of psychosocial adjustment and quality of life research—not only because each has come from overlapping but different traditions, but also because the failure to see the differences in measurement objectives undercuts the value of each. Thus, the study of the process whereby a patient responds to cancer and its treatment is critical—just not the same as measuring just its outcome.

2. The writings of Fadin and LePlege (11), and others, have focused attention on the need for meaningful quality of life assessments. What remains controversial is how this can be achieved.

3. Distinguishing the type of quality of life assessment (cross-sectional, treatment-dependent, and predictive) is important, since they represent very different references (present, intervention-related, future). The notion that a common cognitive model with different references can account for several different methods of assessing quality of life makes it possible to integrate a diverse set of data within a common framework.

4. Finally, applying quality of life research under less than optimal conceptual and empirical conditions can lead to dilution of its potential contribution to clinical decision making, as was seen from the current review of the qualitative consequences of surgery for early-stage breast cancer.

REFERENCES

1. Barofsky I. The status of psychosocial research and rehabilitation of the cancer patient. *Semin Oncol Nursing* 1992;8:190–201.
2. Holland JC, Rowland JH. *Handbook of psychoncology: psychological care of the patient with cancer.* New York: Oxford, 1989.

3. Watson M, ed. *Cancer patient care: psychological treatment methods.* Leicester: BPS Books, 1991.

4. Barofsky I, Sugarbaker PH. Cancer. In: Spilker B, ed. *Quality of life assessments in clinical trials.* New York: Raven, 1990:419–439.

5. Cella DF, Tulsky DS. Measuring quality of life today: methodological aspects. *Oncology* 1991;4:29–38 (appendix pp. 209–232).

6. Osoba D, ed. *Effect of cancer on quality of life.* Boca Raton, Florida: CRC Press, 1991.

7. Elmore JG, Wells CK, Lee CH, Howard DH, Feinstein AR. Variability in radiologists' interpretations of mammograms. *N Engl J Med* 1994; 331:1493–1499.

8. Prochaska JO, DiClemente CC. Status and processes of self-change of smoking towards an integrative model of change. *J Consult Clin Psychol* 1983;15:390–395.

9. Costa PT, McCrae RR, Zonderman AB. Environmental and dispositional influences on well-being: longitudinal follow-up of an American national sample. *Br J Psychol* 1987;78:299–306.

10. Patrick DL, Erickson P. *Health status and health policy: allocating resources to health care.* New York: Oxford University Press, 1993.

11. Fadin R, LePlege A. Assessing quality of life: moral implications for clinical practice. *Med Care* 1992;30(suppl 5):166–175.

12. Costain K, Hewison J, Howes M. Comparison of a function-based model and a meaning-based model of quality of life in oncology: multi-dimensionality examined. *J Psychosoc Oncol* 1993;11:17–37.

13. Barofsky I. Conceptual model of quality of life assessment and clinical judgment. In: Zittoun R, ed. *Quality of life of cancer patients: a review.* Lassay-les-Chateaux, France, 1992:7–15.

14. Bush JW. Relative preferences versus relative frequencies in health-related quality of life evaluation. In: Wenger NK, Mattson ME, Furberg CD, Elinson J, eds. *Assessment of quality of life in clinical trials of cardiovascular therapies.* New York: LeJacq, 1984:118–139.

15. Ware JE. Methodological considerations in the selection of health status assessment procedures. In: Wenger NK, Mattson ME, Furberg CD, Elinson J, eds. *Assessment of quality of life in clinical trials of cardiovascular therapies.* New York: LeJacq, 1984:87–111.

16. Stefanek ME, Shaw A, DeGeorge D, Tsottles N. Illness-related worry among cancer patients: prevalence, severity, and content. *Cancer Invest* 1989;7:365–371.

17. Llewellyn-Thomas HA, Thiel EC, McGreal MJ. Cancer patients' evaluations of their current health status on influence of expectations, comparisons, actual health status, and mood. *Med Decis Making* 1992; 12:115–122.

18. Gelber RD, Goldhirsch A. A new endpoint for the assessment of adjuvant therapy in postmenopausal women with operable breast cancer. *J Clin Oncol* 1986;4:1172–1779.

19. Lerman C, Trock B, Rimer BK, Jepson C, Brody D, Boyce A. Psychological side-effects of breast cancer screening. *Health Psychol* 1991; 10:259–267.

20. Borkovec TD, Robinson E, Pruzinsky T, Depree JA. Preliminary exploration of worry: some characteristics and processes. *Behav Res Ther* 1983;21:9–16.

21. Stefanek ME, Derogatis LP, Shaw A. Psychological distress among oncology patients: prevalence and severity as measured with the Brief Symptom Inventory. *Psychosomatics* 1987;28:530–539.

22. Lerman C, Kash K, Stefanek ME. Younger women at increased risk for breast cancer: perceived risk, psychological well-being, and surveillance behavior. *Monogr J Nat Cancer Inst* 1994;16:171–176.

23. Ferris LE, Shamian J, Tudiver F. The Toronto Breast Self-Examination Instrument (TBSEI): its development, reliability, and validity data. *J Clin Epidemiol* 1991;44:1309–1317.

24. Frank-Stromborg M. Reaction to the diagnosis of cancer questionnaire: development and psychometric evaluation. *Nurs Res* 1989;38:364–369.

25. Trotta P. Breast self-examination: factors influencing compliance. *Oncol Nurs Forum* 1980;7:13–17.

26. Vinokur AD, Threatt BA, Vinokur-Kaplan D, Satariano WA. The process of recovery from breast cancer for younger and older patients: changes during the first year. *Cancer* 1990;65:1242–1254.

27. Weinstein MC, Fineberg HV. *Clinical Decision Analysis.* Philadelphia: WB Saunders, 1980.

28. Llewellyn-Thomas HA, Sutherland HJ, Ciampi A, Ethezadi-Amioli J, Boyd NF, Till JE. Assessment of values in laryngeal cancer: liability of measurement methods. *J Chron Dis* 1984;37:283–291.

29. Stalpers LJA. *Clinical decision-making in oncology with special reference to patients with cancer of the head and neck.* Thesis, Katholieke Universiteit Nijmegen, 1991.

30. Hillner VE, Smith TJ. Efficacy and cost-effectiveness of adjuvant chemotherapy in women with node-negative breast cancer. A decision analysis model. *N Engl J Med* 1991;324:160–168.

31. Verhoef LCG, Stalpers LJA, Verbeek ALM, Wobbes T, van Daal WAJ. Breast-conserving treatment or mastectomy in early breast cancer: a clinical decision analysis with special reference to risk of local recurrence. *Eur J Cancer* 1991;27:1132–1137.

32. Goldhirsch A, Gelber RD, Simes RJ, Glasziou P, Coates AS, for the Ludwig Breast Cancer Study Group. Costs and benefits of adjuvant therapy in breast cancer: a quality-adjusted survival analysis. *J Clin Oncol* 1989;7:36–44.

33. Kiebert GM, de Haes JCJM, van de Velde CJH. The impact of breast-conserving treatment and mastectomy on the quality of life of early stage breast cancer patients: a review. *J Clin Oncol* 1991;9:1059–1070.

34. Sanger CK, Reznikoff M. A comparison of the psychological effects of breast-saving procedures with the modified radical mastectomy. *Cancer* 1981;48:2341–2346.

35. Schain W, Edwards BK, Gorrell CR, de Moss EB, Lippman ME, Gerber LH, Lichter AS. Psychological and physical outcomes of primary breast cancer therapy: mastectomy vs excisional biopsy and radiation. *Breast Cancer Res Treat* 1983;3:377–382.

36. Beckmann J, Johansen L, Richardt C, Blichert-Toft M. Psychological reactions in younger women operated on for breast cancer. *Dan Med Bull* 1983;30(suppl 2):10–13.

37. Ashcroft JJ, Leinster SJ, Slade PD. Breast cancer-patient choice of treatments: preliminary communication. *J R Soc Med* 1985;78: 43–46.

38. Bartelink H, van Dam F, van Dongen J. Psychological effects of breast-conserving therapy in comparison with radical mastectomy. *Int J Radiat Oncol Biol Phys* 1985;11:381–385.

39. Steinberg MD, Juliano MA, Wise L. Psychological outcome of lumpectomy versus mastectomy in the treatment of breast cancer. *Am J Psychol* 1985;142:34–39.

40. Taylor SE, Lichtman RR, Wood JV, Bluming AZ, Dosik GM, Leibowitz RL. Illness-related and treatment-related factors in psychological adjustment to breast cancer. *Cancer* 1985;55:2506–2513.

41. Baider L, Rizel S, Kaplan De-Nour A. Comparison of couples' adjustment to lumpectomy and mastectomy. *Gen Hosp Psychiatry* 1986;8: 251–257.

42. de Haes JCJM, van Oostrom MA, Welvaart K. The effect of radical and conserving surgery on the quality of life of early breast cancer patients. *Eur J Surg Oncol* 1986;12:337–342.

43. Fallowfield LJ, Baum M, Maguire GP. The effects of breast conservation on psychological morbidity associated with diagnosis and treatment of early breast cancer. *BMJ* 1986;293:1331–1334.

44. Ganz PA, Shag CC, Polinsky ML, Heinrich RL, Flack VF. Rehabilitation needs in breast cancer: the first month after primary therapy. *Breast Cancer Res Treat* 1987;10:243–253.

45. Lasry J-CM, Margolese RG, Poisson R, Shibata H, Fleischer D, Lafleur D, Legault S, Taillefer S. Depression and body image following mastectomy and lumpectomy. *J Chron Dis* 1987;40:529–534.

46. Kemeny MM, Wellisch DK, Schain WS. Psychological outcome in a randomized surgical trial for treatment of primary breast cancer. *Cancer* 1988;62:1231–1237.

47. Levy SM, Herberman RB, Lee JK, Lippman ME, D'Angelo T. Breast conservation vs mastectomy: distress sequela as a function of choice. *J Clin Oncol* 1989;7:367–375.

48. Maunsell E, Brisson J, Deschenes L. Psychological distress after initial treatment for breast cancer: a comparison of partial and total mastectomy. *J Clin Epidemiol* 1989;42:765–771.

49. Meyer L, Aspegren K. Long-term psychological sequela of mastectomy and breast conserving treatment for breast cancer. *Acta Oncol* 1989; 28:13–18.

50. Wolberg WH, Romsaas EP, Tanner MA, Malec JF. Psychosexual adaptation to breast cancer surgery. *Cancer* 1989;63:1645–1655.

51. Pozo C, Carver CV, Noriega V, Harris SD, Robinson DS, Ketcham AS, Legaspi A, Moffat FL, Clark KC. Effects of mastectomy vs lumpectomy on emotional adjustment to cancer: a prospective study of the first year post-surgery. *J Clin Oncol* 1992;10:1292–1298.

52. Omne-Ponten M, Holmberg L, Sjoden PO. Psychosocial adjustment

among women with breast cancer stages 1 and 2: six-year follow-up of consecutive patients. *J Clin Oncol* 1994;12:1778–1782.

53. Holmberg L, Omne-Ponten M, Burns T, Adami HO, Bergstrom M. Psychological adjustment after mastectomy and breast conserving treatment. *Cancer* 1989;64:969–974.

54. Omne-Ponten M, Holmberg L, Burns T, Adami HO, Bergstrom MR. Determinants of the psychosocial outcome after operation for breast cancer: results of a prospective comparative interview study following mastectomy and breast conservatism. *Eur J Cancer* 1992;28:1062–1067.

55. Bergner M, Bobbitt RA, Kressel S, Pollard WE, Gilson BS, Morris JR. The Sickness Profile: conceptual foundations and methodology for the development of a health status measure. *Int J Health Serv* 1976; 6:393–415.

Quality of Life and Pharmacoeconomics in Clinical Trials, Second Edition, edited by B. Spilker.
Lippincott-Raven Publishers, Philadelphia © 1996.

CHAPTER 104

Incorporating Quality of Life Assessment into Clinical Cancer Trials

Michael D. E. Goodyear and Michael A. Fraumeni

The mind is its own place and in itself
Can make a heav'n of hell, a hell of heav'n (1)

INTRODUCTION

Traditionally, outcomes in clinical cancer research have relied on either response rates or survival (classically 5-year survival) (2). Although there has always been some tacit acknowledgment that life may have dimensions of both quantity and quality, the implicit assumption has been that once a patient dies, the quality of life is essentially zero, the lower limit on any of the scales. However, if formal assessments of the quality of life have taught us anything, they have demonstrated that from a patient's perspective there exist health states *worse* than death (3,4).

Two important themes in clinical research have contributed to the rapid proliferation of quality of life assessment in clinical trials. On the one hand, from a perspective of society and third party payer, an increasingly technology intense medical practice combined with shrinking resources has led to more intense scrutiny of the relevance of outcomes and more demanding criteria for the adoption of new therapeutic strategies (5). Not totally unrelated, but from a consumer perspective, has been a revolt against paternalism in

medicine, which is all too commonly seen as obsessed with technology at the expense of human happiness.

In response to these forces, there is an increasing awareness among health care professionals that "the ultimate goal of all health care endeavours is the restoration or preservation of health-related quality of life" (6). There is no particular reason to believe that oncologists are any less aware of the global dimensions of the goals of medical care than their colleagues in other disciplines. These appear to have been first enumerated sometime in the middle ages—*Guerir quelquefois, soulager souvent, consoler toujours* ("to cure sometimes, to relieve often, to comfort always") (7)—and appear to enshrine at least the concept of a dimension of quality in life.

HISTORICAL CONSIDERATIONS

Barofsky (8) provided a general history of the evolution of the quality of life concept. Roberts proposed a theoretical graph of "general health" ("the degree of happiness and comfort which the patient enjoys") against time as early as 1934 (9), and a similar approach was described by Carlens in 1970 (10), using the term "quality of survival," as described by Feinstein and Spitz (11) the previous year. While the term "quality of life" had followed the concept from political (12,13) and sociological (14) usage, to assess well-being at a population level, into the general medical literature during the 1960s (15), it appeared somewhat later in oncol-

M. D. E. Goodyear and M. A. Fraumeni: Hamilton Regional Cancer Centre, McMaster University, Hamilton, Ontario L8V 5C2, Canada.

ogy, but by 1975 had warranted a review (16), an editorial (17), and a commentary (18). Recently, there has been an increasing trend toward the use of the term "health-related quality-of-life" (19–23) to emphasize the application of quality of life research in health care, given its many other uses. A number of authors (24–26) have described the growth of the literature in this area, using terms such as "explosive".

A MEDLINE search was conducted, listing articles indexed with the MeSH term "Quality of Life" as a descriptor in the database for the period 1966–1993, without language restriction. The search was then repeated using the pre-explodable term "neoplasms" pre-exploded (Table 1, Fig. 1). These figures need to be interpreted with some caution. Quality of life became a minor descriptor in 1975–1976, and a major descriptor in 1977. Therefore, articles published prior to 1975, and abstracted by this key word, only appear because they were abstracted after 1974, and therefore the apparent sharp rise seen in 1975 is an artifact of the indexing process. Although there appears to be a steep rise in publications in 1989, and a faster rate of growth since then, a logarithmic transformation fits the data between 1975 and 1993 better than a linear function. The present doubling time is about 3 years (27). Early data for 1994 suggest that the

trend depicted here is continuing. Articles dealing with cancer consistently occupied about 22% of the total quality of life literature. Roberts (25) found that reference to the elderly population were the commonest, followed by cancer, healthy individuals and cardiovascular disease. Strain (28) and Osoba (27,29), among others, have reviewed the early phase of this literature evolution, drawing attention to the progression from a dominance of social and behavioral science papers dealing with the general concept of health status, to clinician investigators reporting the application of quality of life methods. There has also been an evolution from simple questionnaires developed on an intuitive basis to tools based on sound methodologically psychometric and econometric principles. Fortunately, there has also been a discernible trend to replace longer original questionnaires with shortened forms, without critical loss of information (30–32).

All 17 articles from the first 3 years in which quality of life was indexed (1973–1975) were retrieved and reviewed. Most were descriptive of patient's symptoms following treatment, dealing with rehabilitation, or merely acknowledged the concept of the bidimensionality of survival, or used the phrases "quality of life" or "quality (of) survival." For instance, Handley (33) stated that "Quantity of life is only half the equation. In my view quality is as important, if not

TABLE 1. *Number of published articles containing "quality of life" as a key word, and together with neoplasms in Medline 1966–1993[a]*

Year	Total quality of life		Quality of life and neoplasms		
	N	Cumulative	N	Percentage	Cumulative
1969	1	1	0		
1970	2	3	0		
1971	0	3	0		
1972	3	6	0		
1973	5	11	1	20	1
1974	8	19	1	13	2
1975	98	117	15	15	17
1976	166	283	16	10	33
1977	142	425	19	13	52
1978	195	620	32	16	84
1979	229	849	51	22	135
1980	207	1,056	49	24	184
1981	228	1,284	41	18	225
1982	270	1,554	58	21	283
1983	273	1,827	59	22	342
1984	284	2,111	59	21	401
1985	331	2,442	72	22	473
1986	407	2,849	88	22	561
1987	483	3,332	90	19	651
1988	490	3,822	114	23	765
1989	789	4,611	194	25	959
1990	902	5,513	213	24	1,172
1991	926	6,439	207	22	1,379
1992	1,096	7,535	256	23	1,635
1993	1,238	8,773	277	22	1,912
Total:	8,773		1,912	22	

[a]Percentages are the proportion of quality of life articles dealing with neoplasia. Cumulative totals to date are given for each category.

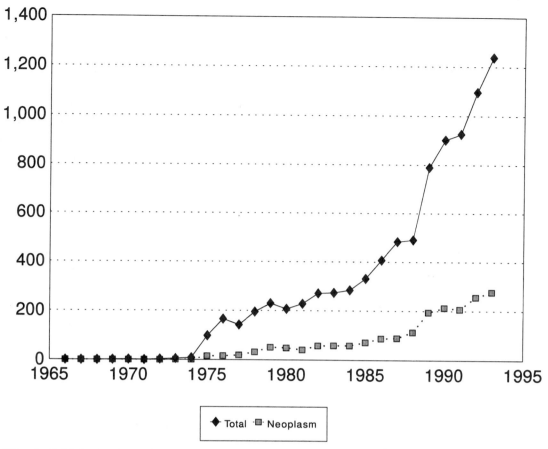

FIG. 1. Published articles per year containing "quality of life" as a descriptor, and containing both "quality of life" and a reference to neoplasms. Diamonds represent the total quality of life literature, and squares the literature dealing with cancer.

more important, than quantity." Three investigators attempted some form of quantification. Laing et al. (34) classified lung cancer patients as "good or excellent" or "other" at each visit, and tabulated the length of time patients spent in the former state. Pennington and Milton (35) used a similar approach for patients with intracerebral metastatic melanoma, classifying status as "acceptable" or "other," and adjusting survival for the time spent in the acceptable category (Q months). Burge et al. (36) refined this further by developing a scale of 0–5 for the best quality of life attained in survivors of acute myeloid leukemia. In each case, the health status was assessed by the health care provider, rather than the consumer. The next phase, which saw the application of quantitative psychometric methods to the assessment of quality of life in cancer patients, followed the pioneering work of Priestman and Baum (36a) in the United Kingdom, in the following year, who used linear analog self-assessment to assess patients being treated for advanced breast cancer. This work is also important in marking a departure from health-care provider to consumer assessment of health status. From these evolved the contemporary era using more complex instruments, derived from patient input, based on sound

psychometric principles, addressing several dimensions of human activity and feeling, and subjected to formal evaluation.

Even since the first edition of this book in 1990 (37), there has been a rapid upsurge of interest in quality of life assessment in general, together with its application in oncology, with close to a thousand additional publications. Most cooperative groups, in both adult (38–43) and pediatric (44) oncology, now have quality of life committees. Since 1992 there has been a journal (*Quality of Life Research*) devoted to quality of life issues, and an international society has been formed (45). There are textbooks devoted to quality of life assessment in cancer (46,47), and the World Health Organization has maintained a Collaborating Centre for Quality of Life Studies in Cancer in Winnipeg since 1989 (Schipper H: *personal communication*). The American Society of Clinical Oncology has indexed Quality of Life in its annual proceedings since 1985, and standard oncology texts are starting to cover the subject (21). There are also a number of recent comprehensive overviews of quality of life in cancer available (23,38,46–58). The literature dealing specifically with pediatric oncology is smaller, but also growing

(44,59–69), and poses special problems. General issues dealing with both problems of quality of life in the young, the elderly, and the frail have been dealt with elsewhere in this work.

Despite this apparent emergence from the arcane to the clinical arena, the bulk of the effort expanded to date has been on theoretical aspects and the development of tools (questionnaires), rather than routine clinical application, and the number of specific clinical interventions that have been developed with quality of life assessment, as the primary end points remain very few indeed. The utility (a term whose use needs to be somewhat circumspect because it also has another very specific meaning within the economics based quality of life literature, as discussed below) of such assessments tends to be predominantly in trials of equivalence, revealing a conceptual evolution from simple toxicity assessment. Far more challenging conceptually are trials resulting in different outcomes in longevity or objective tumor dimensions, where the question becomes more one of asking the price of such a presumed advance.

Although frequently considered as a toxicity scale with added dimensions of psychosocial nature (70,71), quality of life assessment in cancer has another conceptual ancestor in the construct referred to as performance status by oncologists (72). As such, the assessment of functional status has a respectable history virtually as old as chemotherapy itself, reflecting a new thinking about the meaning of health during the postwar era (73–75). Although the original 1948 Karnofsky scale (76) has proved a useful tool (77), as has the similar but simpler Zubrod (ECOG) (78,79) scale, the major limitation has been their unidimensionality, being essentially a quantification of activity levels. Whether either of these approaches actually achieves a true integration of the sum total of the multiple impacts of disease, treatment and changes in social milieu, which the cancer patient encounters, is questionable. The advantages of the performance scales is their conceptual simplicity and ease of assessment, although considerable problems can arise with interpretation. Recently several investigators have suggested that quality of life assessments may be more powerful determinants of prognosis than performance status (72,80–84). If this observation has more widespread validity, initial quality of life status will need to be controlled for in clinical trials, as a source of patient heterogeneity.

Barr et al. (44) and others (72,85) have argued that quality of life assessment should not only be included in all cancer clinical trials but should also be a routine tool for the management of patients.

Considering that multidimensional measures were first reported in a clinical cancer trial by Priestman and Baum in 1976 (85a), it is reasonable to ask whether the practicing oncologist can now take a well-documented questionnaire, use it to measure outcomes, and understand the results that he or she may obtain. The answer to this question depends on a lot of things, perhaps the most important of which is one which lies at the heart of all scientific inquiry—"what

is the exact question being asked?" Perhaps this quandary is best expressed by saying that although everybody knows what they mean by the quality of life, it is not a definable entity with universal interpretation (85, 86–88), and there are many ways of looking at it, none of which capture the richness of the human experience in its entirety (89).

MEASURES OF THE QUALITY OF LIFE

Recognition of the need to describe heterogeneity in, and perturbations of, the state of human health and happiness led to the need to measure or quantify this construct in a meaningful (valid) and reproducible (reliable) form. If one were to attempt a classification scheme of quality of life measures that have been adopted in clinical cancer research, and to display this in a hierarchical form, it might look like Table 2. Given the number of tools available in each category, the clinician is faced with a bewildering choice. The situation is further complicated by the apparent dichotomy between two philosophical approaches to quality of life assessment, derived from different disciplines. Most of the measures utilized in oncology practice to date, particularly in clinical trials, have been derived from psychological testing models, and are hence known as psychometric. Economists, on the other hand, have approached quality of life assessment more from economic theory and decision-making, using cost-benefit analysis. Their measures are based on the per-

TABLE 2. *Hierarchical classification of quality of life measures adopted in clinical cancer trials*

Population-derived measures
   Medical Outcome Study Short Form—MOS SF (30,90–93)
   Quality of Well-Being Scale[a] (94–98)
   Multi-attribute Health Status[a] (4,44,66–69)
Health-related measures
   Sickness Impact Profile (99,100)
Psychological instruments
   Beck Depression Scale (101)
   Profile of Moods Scale (102–104)
Activity scales for cancer patients
   Karnofsky Scale (76,77,106–108)
   Zubrod (ECOG) Scale (78,79)
Multidimensional scales for cancer patients
   Cancer Rehabilitation Evaluation System (31,109,110)
   European Organization for Research and Treatment of
     Cancer Quality-of-Life Questionnaire (108,111–118)
   Functional Assessment of Cancer Therapy Scales (119)
   Functional Living Index-Cancer (107,120,121)
   Multidimensional Quality of Life Scale (19,122,123)
   Quality of Life Index (124,125)
   Rotterdam Symptom Check List (126–128)
Instruments derived for specific cancers
   Breast Cancer Linear Analogue Self Assessment
     (32,129–131)
Instruments derived for specific clinical cancer contexts
   Breast Cancer Chemotherapy Questionnaire (113,132)
   Head and Neck Radiotherapy Questionnaire (133)

[a]Utility-based measures.

ceived relative worth of different health states, preference for which can be quantified between 0 and 1, as a utility. Examples of the latter approach are the Quality of Well-Being Scale (94–98), the Multi-Attribute Health-Status Classification System (4,44,66–69), Q-TWiST (quality of life adjusted time without symptoms and toxicity) (134–139), the standard gamble (66,140,141), and the time trade-off (141–143). Neither approach alone is wholly satisfactory, and a meaningful integration remains one of the challenges for the future (21).

All too often in determining exactly what tools are appropriate in the clinical context in question, investigators have concluded that none met their needs, hence the continual appearance of new scales developed for specific contexts. At one end of the scale, generic questionnaires measuring functioning and well-being (90) may prove too insensitive (144,145) to detect change in the specific setting chosen, while at the other end very context-specific questionnaires, such as the Head and Neck Radiotherapy Questionnaire (133), may depend so heavily on specific toxicities as to limit their generalizability. The generic measures certainly have the advantage of enabling comparisons between populations (and hence meta-analyses) and are more likely to have been repeatedly validated in differing contexts. On the other hand, such measures may lack the ability to answer specific context-sensitive questions about the impact of specified interventions on the subjects and therefore need to be combined with a more ad hoc measure. Indeed, the use of multiple measures is not uncommon, although this reflects some of the current uncertainty about the appropriate measures to incorporate, and carries a penalty in terms of feasibility and compliance.

One compromise solution is that adopted by the European Organization for Research on Treatment of Cancer (EORTC), among others (129), which has developed a general core module (112,112a,114,115,117) together with specific modules for use in individual disease sites (112,112a,118,118a). A similar approach is being taken with the Functional Assessment of Cancer Therapy Scales (119).

A number of investigators (50,51,146,147) have listed a variety of measures that meet minimal criteria for use in patients with cancer. Osoba (147) argues that the key properties are quantifiability, being based on a multidimensional construct, having a scientific basis (including psychometric evaluation with a high degree of reliability and validity) and demonstrated feasibility. He also states a preference for measures incorporating both a core or global component, as well as items that are contextually specific. To this list one might add demonstrated utility in the methodological context in which the measure is being applied—can it answer the question being asked? A partial list of measures that more or less meet these criteria appears in Table 3. A number of comparative reviews and descriptions of these measures have been previously published (21,26,37,51,146). The actual instruments (with the exception of the Breast Cancer Linear Analogue Self Assessment and the Multi-attribute

TABLE 3. *Examples of quality of life instruments for use in cancer that meet minimal criteria.*

Breast Cancer Chemotherapy Questionnaire—BCQ (113,132)
Cancer Rehabilitation Evaluation Systems—CARES (31,109,110)
European Organization for Research and Treatment of Cancer Quality-of-Life Questionnaire–EORTC QLQ (108,111–118)
Functional Assessment of Cancer Therapy Scales—FACT (119)
Functional Living Index Cancer—FLIC (107,120,121)
Linear Analogue Self-Assessment (32,129–131)
Medical Outcome Study Short Form—MOS SF (30,90–93)
Multidimensional Quality of Life Scale (19,122,123)
Quality of Life Index—QL-Index (124,125)
Rotterdam Symptom Check List (126–128)

Health-Status Classification System) were published as an appendix to a special issue of the journal *Oncology*, in 1990 (53).

INCORPORATING QUALITY OF LIFE MEASURES INTO CLINICAL CANCER TRIALS

Several investigators have commented on the conceptual barriers to the incorporation of quality of life measures into clinical trials (49,148). These include the very disparate approaches of clinicians and behavioral scientists to research issues, compounded by unfamiliarity with the complexity of psychometric jargon (149). Furthermore, much of the early work was at a descriptive level, and instruments were developed in a context of distinguishing between groups (discriminative properties), rather than the key property required in a clinical trial: the repeated measurement of longitudinal change in an individual or group (evaluative properties) (144,145,150).

If quality of life assessment is going to achieve a maturity as an outcome measure in clinical trials, it must be subject to at least the same degree of evaluation as the more traditional clinical and laboratory measures, including assessment of sensitivity, specificity, accuracy, predictive value, and likelihood ratios (150). In selecting outcome measures, such properties will be important in determining their ultimate usefulness, as will their relative cost, invasiveness and morbidity when compared to more traditional tests and procedures.

The array of measures that have been used in cancer is alarmingly large. Barofsky and Sugarbaker (37) reviewed eight measures in the first edition of this book in 1990. Grant et al. (26) reviewed 14 and Cella and Tulsky (51), in the same year, listed 24 measures that have had general usage. Many of these are described and reviewed in detail elsewhere in this text. It is important to first appreciate that while, to the individual health provider or consumer the concept of quality of life, whether formalized or not, is likely to be an integral unidimensional construct, the consensus (51) is that this unidimensional concept can be deconstructed into a multidimensional array. While many published measures, including the performance scales of activity already mentioned, fall into the general concept of quality of life, as understood by the expansion of traditional concepts of response, survival and toxicity to incorporate the functioning of the whole individual, they do not meet the accepted meaning of quality of life assessment (51) on their own, and contemporary quality of life literature tends to be restricted to true multidimensional measures. Since multidimensionality is a continuum, and the boundaries of dimensions may overlap, Cella and Tulsky (51) suggest a three-dimension minimum for a free-standing quality of life measure, and that dimensions be preferably defined by factor analysis. This is not to deny a role for single-issue scales or even global uniscales (151), as long as they are not considered a simpler substitute. While a global uniscale may be a simple and useful summary index, it prevents any understanding of the nature of change. Similarly specific measures of outcomes of interest, such as neuropsychological studies (59, 152,153), may be valid and important end points in certain contexts, but should not be confused with the more global concept.

In addition to disease-specific measures, there are now available a wide variety of symptom-specific or problem-specific measures including anorexia (154), depression (155, 156), general mood distress (102), nausea (157,158), vomiting (159), sexual dysfunction (160–163), symptom distress (164–166), pain (167–172), and treatment satisfaction (173).

In considering the choice of a measure or measures, the investigator's concerns will fall into three broad areas. In the first group are the theoretical properties of the measure under consideration. The evaluation of these psychometric properties are considered elsewhere in this work, but clearly the choice must be tailored carefully to the question at hand (and not vice versa). The second group of considerations are more practical ones dealing with the resources available, whereas the third group deals with the demonstrated usefulness of the measure within the proposed clinical context. This will include the degree of generalizability of the findings.

It is important to understand that although there may be a number of published guidelines for the incorporation of quality of life assessments (51,146,148,174,175), there are no gold standards (174,176), and probably never will be, given the multiplicity of clinical contexts and research questions under consideration. However one potential danger with the current diversity of measures is that of having to interpret clinical trials in which the use of different measures within the trial leads to apparently conflicting results. This leads to urgent consideration of the translatability of measures of quality of life derived from varying instruments.

Nevertheless, there is a discernible trend toward a convergence of approach for a general measure of quality of life, with the most commonly used measures being that of the EORTC in Europe and Canada and the FACT (119) as used in the trials of the Eastern Cooperative Oncology Group and the Radiation Therapy Oncology Group (43). Both instruments are discussed in more detail elsewhere. As Cella and Tulsky have pointed out (51), in the absence of commonly recognized instruments with proven utility, the tendency is to overburden patients and staff as a protection against missing something important. Ironically the result may be that even more is missed because of low accrual and poor compliance.

The rapid proliferation of Quality of Life Committees within the cooperative oncology groups is rapidly leading to a situation in which some measure of quality of life considerations is included in outcome assessments as a matter of course in much the same way that toxicity might be (Cella D, *personal communication*). Therefore, the conceptual barriers may be moving more toward those of interpretation rather than of implementation (177). The increasing dominance of the clinical oncology literature by the cooperative groups, and by intergroup studies in particular, is likely to lead to increasing convergence of the measures adopted, since there are many advantages to the use of a standard measure or measure within a group.

WHAT HAS QUALITY OF LIFE ASSESSMENT IN ONCOLOGY ACHIEVED?

Osoba (23) recently reviewed the literature to summarize the findings from the incorporation of quality of life research into oncological practice. A multidimensionality in the quality of life construct has been emphasized throughout. There is now a body of literature, both in the methodological development area, as well as the applied context, in which uni- and multidimensional instruments have been directly compared (108). In general, the simpler instruments correlate better with specific domains of their multidimensional counterparts than with the overall scores, implying that the latter underrepresent the complex impact of the burden of illness and treatment. Nevertheless, there are also examples where only very specific dimensions of the perceived quality of life are perturbed by an intervention without this being reflected in the global quality of life score, at least to the degree that our current methods are sufficiently sensitive to detect this. This illustrates the importance of examining the individual domains as well as global scores, and suggests there may be a place for context-specific instruments in addition to global measurements, where the question being asked is also very specific.

While the question of the relative validity of observer-rated quality of life versus subject-rated estimates can be arguably considered to be somewhat philosophical, it is important to realize that the available research is congruent with the intuitive observation that the two are not very well correlated, and indeed are likely to be measuring different things. To his credit, Milton (1) recognized this incongruity of perceptions based on the external circumstances, and the state of well-being, more than 300 years ago. The state of mind depending as much on inner resources as opposed to the external forces applied, just as stress, whether an engineering or psychological concept, reflects the *effects* of force on material, not just the force applied (178). Patients with moderate to severe cognitive disability or psychological distress form the extreme range of this disparity. Although arguably from the viewpoint of preserving autonomy and minimizing paternalism, the individual's pursuit of health and happiness is of paramount importance, society is still entitled to ask questions about health status outcomes from a societal perspective in evaluating medical interventions in a world of finite resources. Thus, in specific contexts either or both approaches may be valid.

Clearly no degree of methodological rigor will compensate for the problems of feasibility and compliance. Indeed the goal of maximizing autonomy may be compromised by inflicting excessively burdensome evaluation. Reports of achieved compliance vary widely (113,179,180), reflecting contexts, instruments used, and selection. Reported results of compliance may be over-estimates, since some studies make completion of quality of life assessment a selection criteria (113). However, such techniques are an accepted way of ensuring a high efficiency in clinical trials by maximizing compliance and do not necessarily invalidate the findings. On the other hand, variation in compliance is unlikely to be a random source of error (181), limiting generalizability. Lower compliance rates may be acceptable within the context of methodological development of instruments, where the evaluation is likely to be more complex but are more problematic when the tools are applied in the evaluation of other interventions.

Preliminary data suggest that quality of life assessments may be fulfilling one of the reasons for their development, namely estimating the trade-offs inherent in noncurative interventions, between the impacts of disease and treatment (85,182,183). Such an approach may eventually lead to valuable information regarding the optimum duration of treatment, and be an aid to starting and stopping treatment. This approach is incorporated into a current EORTC—NCIC trial of the value of treatment of asymptomatic metastatic gastrointestinal cancer.

Prospective use of quality of life assessment has led to new insights on how treatments disrupt living and how specific symptoms affect other functions (159), whereas baseline quality of life assessment may be the most useful predictors of outcome, and tolerance of treatment (116).

CHALLENGES

In such a relatively new and rapidly evolving field, the perceived challenges are necessarily multiple, complex, and even at times overwhelming. Among the problems that will need to be addressed will be finding ways to effectively and meaningfully integrate the two dimensions of cancer survival, its longevity and its quality. Other problems are the specific clinical contexts of the extremes of life (57) and the compromised patient (Barofsky I, *personal communication*), including the question of how to estimate the quality of life in longitudinal series when a patient becomes too ill to complete the standard instruments (180,184,185).

A new challenge just starting to achieve increasing attention is the integration of quality of life assessments together with economic analysis (5,141,186), into a broader outcomes context. Building this approach into clinical trials design is in its infancy at present (Cella D, *personal communication*).

CONCLUSIONS

Both patients and oncology services have come to a recognition, born of seeming lack of progress, that the outcome of cancer treatments must incorporate a trade-off of the effects of intervention against any change in either current symptomatology or future longevity by assessing both the dimensions of quality and quantity of the resultant life. Combined with threads from areas of intellectual endeavor as diverse as political science, economics, sociology, and ecology, this impetus has resulted in a dramatic increase in activity related to the development and more recently the application of methods of measuring health status in cancer patients. While some progress has been made toward expressing health status as a global quantity incorporating the resultant effects of many forces on a patient's life at a particular time point, it is less clear how alterations in the integral resultant life with its dual dimensions can be combined in a single measure in evaluation of those interventions. Ironically this concept, which was one of the first proposed in describing how interventions might impact in ways other than purely in terms of survival, remains one of the most difficult to incorporate conceptually. Roberts (9) originally perceived an approach analogous to the pharmacodynamic concepts of the area under a curve, without appreciating the application of varying utilities (187) to different health states. A more recent approach to this dilemma is that of Q-TWiST (quality of life-adjusted time without symptoms and toxicity) (134–139), a utility-based refinement of the concept of quality-adjusted life years (187–189).

There seems good evidence that at least some quality of life assessments have important prognostic ability. It is hoped that there is a slowing down in the development of new measures, as opposed to the adaptation of current measures to specific circumstances, and the accumulation of more experience with these measures in a variety of contexts. Just as toxicity measures incorporated into current trials need to reflect the nature of the clinical context, the specific interventions, and the question being asked, so judicious use of quality of life measures will need to evaluate the context and may require multiple measures under some circumstances. This makes it all the more important to have measures which are feasible and minimally invasive.

Equally important will be the demand in a finite resource system for the rigorous evaluation of the incorporation of quality of life assessment into clinical trials (190). To this end there is an urgent need to define at least context-specific gold standards against which new candidate measures must be compared.

As did John Milton (1608–1674) in *Paradise Lost* (1), oncologists have had to shift their frame of reference from a predominantly objective one derived from the perspective of modern molecular medicine, to a more holistic subjective framework, albeit based firmly on scientific underpinnings. They have grasped this opportunely, just as the system in which they work has placed them into unfamiliar partnerships with those whom they treat, to usher in a new era of decision making.

ACKNOWLEDGMENTS

We are grateful to Dr. Monica Grantham, Department of Palliative Care, Henderson General Hospital, Hamilton, Ontario, for assistance with historical sources, and to Dr. David Osoba, Communities Oncology Programme, British Columbia Cancer Agency, Vancouver, British Columbia, for continued inspiration over the years.

REFERENCES

1. Milton J. *Paradise Lost.* 1667;1:254.
2. O'Young J, McPeek B. Quality of life variables in surgical trials. *J Chron Dis* 1987;40:513–522.
3. Torrance GW. Health states worse than death. In: van Eimeren W, Engelbrecht R, Flagle CD, eds. *Third international conference on system science in health care.* Berlin: Springer, 1984:1085–1089.
4. Torrance GW, Zhang Y, Feeny DH, Furlong WJ, Barr RD. Multiattribute preference functions for a comprehensive health status classification system. McMaster University Centre for Health Economics and Policy Analysis Working Paper 92-118, September 1992.
5. Reynolds T. Quality of life adds a human dimension to studies on treatment cost-effectiveness *J Natl Cancer Inst* 1994;86:661–662.
6. Osoba D. The evolving role of health-related quality-of-life assessment in oncology. Why measure quality of life? *Oncol Advisor* 1993;1(4):7–8.
7. Strauss MB, ed. *Familiar medical quotations.* Boston: Little, Brown, 1968.
8. Barofsky I. Quality of life assessment. Evolution of the concept. In: Ventafrida V, Yancik R, van Dam FSAM, Tamburini M, eds. *Quality of life assessment and cancer treatment.* Amsterdam: Elsevier, 1986: 11–18.
9. Roberts F. The radiation treatment of neoplasms, VI. *Br J Radiol* 1934;7:151–155.
10. Carlens E, Dahlström G, Nōu E. Comparative measurements of quality of survival of lung cancer patients after diagnosis. *Scand J Respir Dis* 1970;51:268–275.
11. Feinstein AR, Spitz H. The epidemiology of cancer therapy. I. Clinical problems of statistical surveys. *Arch Intern Med* 1969;123:171–186.
12. Report of the President's Commission of National Goals. *Goals for Americans.* Englewood Cliffs: Prentice-Hall, 1960.
13. Anonymous spokesperson for the Great Society (1964). In: Campbell A, ed. *The sense of well-being in America. Recent patterns and trends.* New York: McGraw-Hill, 1981:4.
14. Campbell A. *The sense of well-being in America. Recent patterns and trends.* New York: McGraw-Hill, 1981.
15. Elkington JR. Medicine and the quality of life. *Ann Intern Med* 1966;64:711–714.
16. Luce JK, Dawson JJ. Quality of life. *Semin Oncol* 1975;2:323–327.
17. Editorial. Quality of life. *J Pract Nurs* 1975;25:13.
18. Patterson WB. The quality of survival in response to treatment. *JAMA* 1975;233:280–281.
19. Padilla GV, Mishel MH, Grant MM. Uncertainty, appraisal and quality of life. *Qual Life Res* 1992;1:155–165.
20. Staquet M, Aaronson NK, Ahmedzai S, et al. Health-related quality of life research. *Qual Life Res* 1992;1:3.
21. Cella DF. Quality of life as an outcome of cancer treatment. In: Groenwald SL, Frogge MH, Goodman M, Yarbro CH, eds. *Cancer nursing, principles and practice,* 3rd ed. Boston: Jones and Bartlett, 1993:197–207.
22. Guyatt GH, Feeny DH, Patrick DL. Measuring health-related quality of life. *Ann Intern Med* 1993;118:622–629.
23. Osoba D. Lessons learned from measuring health-related quality of life in oncology. *J Clin Oncol* 1994;12:608–616.
24. Joyce CRB. In: *Medicines and Risk/Benefit Decisions.* Lancaster: MTP, 1986.
25. Roberts G. A study of the literature on clinical aspects of quality of life. MSc thesis, City University 1988 Explosion of interest in quality of life. *Centre Med Res News* 1988;6(2):6.
26. Grant M, Padilla GV, Ferrell BR, Rhiner M. Assessment of quality of life with a single instrument. *Semin Oncol Nurs* 1990;6:260–270.
27. Osoba D. The evolving role of health-related quality-of-life assessment in oncology. The early years. *Oncol Advisor* 1993;1(1):3–4.
28. Strain JJ. The evolution of quality of life evaluations in cancer therapy. *Oncology* 1990;4(5):22–27.
29. Osoba D. The evolving role of health-related quality-of-life assessment in oncology. The modern era. *Oncol Advisor* 1993;1(2):1–4.
30. Stewart AL, Hays RD, Ware JE. The MOS short-form general health survey. Reliability and validity in a patient population. *Med Care* 1988;26:724–735.
31. Schag CAC, Ganz PA, Heinrich RL. Cancer Rehabilitation Evaluation System–Short Form (CARES-SF). A cancer specific rehabilitation and quality of life instrument. *Cancer* 1991;68:1406–1413.
32. Bliss JM, Selby PJ, Robertson B, Powles TJ. A method for assessing the quality of life of cancer patients. Replication of the factor structure. *Br J Cancer* 1992;65:961–966.
33. Handley RS. Carcinoma of the breast. *Ann R Coll Surg Engl* 1975;57:59–66.
34. Laing AH, Berry RJ, Newman CR, Peto J. Treatment of inoperable carcinoma of bronchus. *Lancet* 1975;2:1161–1164.
35. Pennington DG, Milton GW. Cerebral metastasis from melanoma. *Aust NZ J Surg* 1975;45:405–409.
36. Burge PS, Prankerd TAJ, Richards JDM, Sare M, Thompson DS, Wright P. Quality and quantity of survival in acute myeloid leukaemia. *Lancet* 1975;2:621–624.
36a. Priestman TJ, Baum M. Evaluation of quality of life in patients receiving treatment for advanced breast cancer. *Lancet* 1976;1: 899–901.
37. Barofsky I, Sugarbaker PH. Cancer. In: Spilker B, ed. *Quality of life assessments in clinical trials.* New York: Raven, 1990:419–439.
38. Moinpour CM, Feigl P, Metch B, Hayden KA, Meyskens FL, Crowley J. Quality of life end points in cancer clinical trials. Review and recommendations. *J Natl Cancer Inst* 1989;81:485–495.
39. Moinpour CM, Hayden KA, Thompson IM, Feigl P, Metch B. Quality of life assessment in Southwest Oncoloy Group Trials. *Oncology* 1990;4(5):79–84,89.
40. Skeel RT. Quality of life assessment in cancer clinical trials—it's time to catch up. *J Natl Cancer Inst* 1989;81:472–473.
41. Ganz PA, Moinpour CM, Cella DF, Fetting JH. Quality-of-life assessment in cancer clinical trials. A status report. *J Natl Cancer Inst* 1992;84:994–995.
42. Osoba D. The Quality of Life Committee of the Clinical Trials Group of the National Cancer Institute of Canada. Organization and functions. *Qual Life Res* 1992;1:211–218.
43. Scott CB, Stetz J, Bruner DW, Wasserman TH. Radiation Therapy Oncology Group quality of life assessment: design, analysis, and data management issues. *Qual Life Res* 1994;3:199–206.
44. Barr RD, Pai MK, Weitzman S, Feeny D, Furlong W, Rosenbaum

P, Torrance GW. A multi-attribute approach to health status measurement and clinical management—illustrated by an application to brain tumours in childhood. *Int J Oncol* 1994;4:639–648.

45. Proceedings of the inaugural meeting of the International Health-related Quality of Life Society, 3–4 February 1994, Brussels, Belgium. *Qual Life Res* 1994;3:39–103.

46. Aaronson NK, Beckmann J, eds. *The quality of life of cancer patients.* New York: Raven, 1987.

47. Osoba D, ed. *Effect of cancer on quality of life.* Boca Raton, FL: CRC, 1991.

48. Milder JW, ed. Proceedings of the American Cancer Society's Working Conference on Methodology in Behavioral and Psychosocial Cancer Research, St. Petersburg, Florida, April 21–23, 1983. *Cancer* 1984;53(10)(Suppl):2217–2384.

49. Aaronson NK. Quality of life assessment in clinical trials. Methodological issues. *Controlled Clin Trials* 1989;10:195S–208S.

50. Donovan K, Sanson-Fisher RW, Redman S. Measuring quality of life in cancer patients. *J Clin Oncol* 1989;7:959–968.

51. Cella DF, Tulsky DS. Measuring quality of life today. Methodological aspects. *Oncology* 1990;4(5):29–38,69.

52. Muthny FA, Koch U, Stump S. Quality of life in oncology patients. *Psychother Psychosom* 1990;54:145–160.

53. Tchekmedyian NS, Cella DF, eds. Quality of life in current oncology practice and research. Proceedings of an international symposium. Long Beach, California. *Oncology* 1990;4(5):21–208 (special issue).

54. Varicchio CG, Ferrans CE. Quality of life assessment in clinical practice. *Semin Oncol Nurs* 1990;6(4):247–311.

55. Stevens J, ed. Proceedings of the American Cancer Society's Second Workshop on Methodology in Behavioral and Psychosocial Cancer Research, Santa Monica, California, December 5–8, 1989. *Cancer* 1991;67(3)(suppl):765–867.

56. Nayfield SG, Ganz PA, Moinpour CM, Cella DF, Hailey BJ. Report from a National Cancer Institute (USA) workshop on quality of life assessment in cancer clinical trials. *Qual Life Res* 1992;1:203–210.

57. Tchekmedyian NS, Cella DF, Mooradian AD. Care of the older cancer patient. Clinical and quality of life issues. *Oncology* 1992;6(2)(suppl):1–160 (special issue).

58. Skeel RT. Quality of life dimensions that are most important to cancer patients. *Oncology* 1993;7(12):55–70.

59. Rowland JH, Glidewell OJ, Sibley RF, et al. Effects of different forms of central nervous system prophylaxis on neuropsychologic function in childhood leukemia. *J Clin Oncol* 1984;2:1327–1335.

60. Brouwers P. Neuropsychological abilities of long-term survivors of childhood leukemia. In: Aaronson NK, Beckmann J, eds. *The quality of life of cancer patients.* New York: Raven, 1987:153–165.

61. Kamphuis RP. The concept of quality of life in pediatric oncology. In: Aaronson NK, Beckmann J, eds. *The quality of life of cancer patients.* New York: Raven, 1987:141–151.

62. Last BF, van Veldheuzen AMH. Psychosocial research in childhood cancer. In: Aaronson NK, Beckmann J, eds. *The quality of life of cancer patients.* New York: Raven, 1987:127–134.

63. Mann JR. Psychosocial aspects of leukemia and other cancers during childhood. In: Aaronson NK, Beckmann J, eds. *The quality of life of cancer patients.* New York: Raven, 1987:135–139.

64. Hinds PS. Quality of life in children and adolescents with cancer. *Semin Oncol Nurs* 1990;6:285–291.

65. Hinds P, Scholes S, Gattuso J, Riggins M, Heffner B. Adaptation to illness in adolescents with cancer. *J Assoc Pediatr Oncol Nurs* 1990;7:64–65.

66. Feeny D, Barr RD, Furlong W, Torrance GW, Weitzman S. Quality of life of the treatment process in pediatric oncology. An approach to measurement. In: Osoba D, ed. *Effect of cancer on quality of life.* Boca Raton, FL: CRC, 1991:73–88.

67. Feeny D, Furlong W, Barr RD, Torrance GW, Rosenbaum P, Weitzman S. A comprehensive multiattribute system for classifying the health status of survivors of childhood cancer. *J Clin Oncol* 1992; 10:923–928.

68. Barr RD, Furlong W, Dawson S, et al. An assessment of global health status in survivors of acute lymphoblastic leukemia in childhood. *Am J Pediatr Hematol Oncol* 1993;15:284–290.

69. Feeny D, Leiper A, Barr RD, Furlong W, Torrance GW, Rosenbaum P. The comprehensive assessment of health status in survivors of childhood cancer. Application to high-risk acute lymphoblastic leukaemia. *Br J Cancer* 1993;67:1047–1052.

70. Vieti TJ. Evaluation of toxicity. Clinical issues. *Can Treat Rep* 1980; 64:457–461.

71. Leventhal BG, Wittes RE. Treatment toxicity and quality of life. In: *Research methods in clinical oncology.* New York: Raven, 1988: 23–40.

72. Weeks J. Quality of life assessment. Performance status upstaged? *J Clin Oncol* 1992;10:1827–1829.

73. World Health Organization. Constitution of the World Health Organization. *WHO Chron* 1947;1:29–43.

74. World Health Organization. Measurement of levels of health. Report of a study group. *WHO Tech Rep Ser* 1957;No. 137:3–29.

75. World Health Organization. The uses of epidemiology in the study of the elderly. Report of a WHO-scientific group on the epidemiology of aging. *WHO Tech Rep Ser* 1984;No. 706:3–84.

76. Karnofsky DA, Abelmann WH, Craver LF, Burchenal JH. The use of the nitrogen mustards in the palliative treatment of carcinoma. With particular reference to bronchogenic carcinoma. *Cancer* 1948; 1:634–656.

77. Mor V, Laliberte L, Morris JN, Wiemann M. The Karnofsky Performance Status Scale. An examination of its reliability and validity in a research setting. *Cancer* 1984;53:2002–2007.

78. Zubrod CG, Schneiderman M, Frei E, et al. Appraisal of methods for the study of chemotherapy of cancer in man. Comparative therapeutic trial of nitrogen mustard and triethylene thiophosphoramide. *J Chron Dis* 1960;11:7–33.

79. Oken MM, Creech RH, Tormey DC, et al. Toxicity and response criteria of the Eastern Cooperative Oncology Group. *Am J Clin Oncol* 1982;5:649–655.

80. Kaasa S, Mastekaasa A, Lund E. Prognostic factors for patients with inoperable non-small cell lung cancer, limited disease. The importance of patients' subjective experience of disease and psychosocial well-being. *Radiother Oncol* 1989;15:235–242.

81. Ganz P, Lee JJ, Siau J. Quality of life assessment. An independent prognostic variable for survival in lung cancer. *Cancer* 1991;67: 3131–3135.

82. Ruckdeschel JC, Piantadosi S. Quality of life assessment in lung surgery for bronchogenic carcinoma. *Theor Surg* 1991;6:201–205.

83. Coates A, Gebski V, Signorini D, et al. Prognostic value of quality-of-life scores during chemotherapy for advanced breast cancer. *J Clin Oncol* 1992;10:1833–1838.

84. Seidman AD, Lepore J, Yao T-J, et al. Prognostic value of baseline quality of life assessment in patients receiving taxol + GCSF for refractory metastatic breast cancer. *Proc Am Soc Clin Oncol* 1994; 13:434(abstract 1493).

85. Slevin ML. Quality of life. Philosophical question or clinical reality. *BMJ* 1992;305:466–469.

85a.Priestman TJ, Baum M. Evaluation of quality of life in patients receiving treatment for advanced breast cancer. *Lancet* 1976;1i:899–901.

86. Campbell A, Converse PE, Rodgers WL. *The quality of American life. Perceptions, evaluations, and satisfactions.* New York: Sage, 1976.

87. Feinstein AR. Clinimetric perspectives. *J Chron Dis* 1987;40: 635–640.

88. Shurlock B. The quality of life. Do we really know what we mean? *Med Post* 1988;24(February 2):10.

89. Aaronson NK, cited in Vanchieri C. Patients' quality of life under study in Europe. *J Natl Cancer Inst* 1993;85:12–13.

90. Stewart AL, Ware JE, eds. *Measuring functioning and well-being.* Durham, NC: Duke University Press, 1992.

91. Ware JE, Sherbourne CD. The MOS 36-item short-form health survey (SF-36). I. Conceptual framework and item selection. *Med Care* 1992;30:473–483.

92. McHorney CA, Ware JE, Raczek AE. The MOS 36-item short-form health survey (SF-36). II. Psychometric and clinical tests of validity in measuring physical and medical constructs. *Med Care* 1993;31: 247–263.

93. McHorney CA, Ware JE, Lu JFR, Sherbourne CD. The MOS 36-item short-form health survey (SF-36). III. Tests of data quality, scaling assumptions, and reliability across diverse patient groups. *Med Care* 1994;32:40–66.

94. Patrick DL, Bush JW, Chen MM. Methods for measuring levels of well-being for a health status index. *Health Serv Res* 1973;8:228–245.

95. Kaplan RM, Bush JW, Berry CC. Health status. Types of validity and the index of well being. *Health Serv Res* 1976;11:478–507.

96. Anderson JP, Bush JW, Berry CC. Classifying function for health outcome and quality-of-life evaluation. *Med Care* 1986;24:454–470.

97. Kaplan RM, Anderson JP. A general health policy model. Update and applications. *Health Serv Res* 1988;23:203–236.

98. Anderson JP, Kaplan RM, Berry CC, Bush JW, Rumbaut RG. Interday reliability of function assessment for a health status measure. The quality of well-being scale. *Med Care* 1989;27:1076–1083.

99. Bergner M, Bobbitt RA, Pollard WE, Martin DP, Gilson BS. Sickness Impact Profile. Validation of a health status measure. *Med Care* 1976;14:57–67.

100. Bergner M, Bobbitt RA, Carter WB, Gilson BS. The Sickness Impact Profile. Development and final revision of a health status measure. *Med Care* 1981;19:787–805.

101. Beck AT. *Depression, Clinical, experimental, and theoretical aspects.* New York: Hoeber, 1967.

102. McNair DM, Lorr M, Droppleman LF. *EITS manual for the profile of mood states.* San Diego: Educational and Industrial Testing Service, 1971.

103. Cella DF, Jacobsen PB, Orav EJ, Holland JC, Silberfab PM, Rafla S. A brief POMS measure of distress for cancer patients. *J Chron Dis* 1987;40:939–942.

104. Cella DF, Orofiamma B, Holland JC, et al. The relationship of psychological distress, extent of disease, and performance status in patients with lung cancer. *Cancer* 1987;60:1661–1667.

105. Hutchinson TA, Boyd NF, Feinstein AR. Scientific problems in clinical scales, as demonstrated in the Karnofsky index of performance status. *J Chron Dis* 1979;32:661–666.

106. Schag CC, Heinrich RL, Ganz PA. Karnofsky performance status revisited. Reliability, validity, and guidelines. *J Clin Oncol* 1984;2:187–193.

107. Ganz PA, Haskell CM, Figlin RA, la Soto N, Siau J. Estimating the quality of life in a clinical trial of patients with metastatic lung cancer using the Karnofsky performance status and the functional living index—cancer. *Cancer* 1988;61:849–856.

108. Schaafsma J, Osoba D. The Karnofsky performance status scale re-examined. A cross-validation with the EORTC-C30. *Qual Life Res* 1994;3:413–424.

109. Schag CAC, Heinrich RL. Development of a comprehensive quality of life measurement tool: CARES. *Oncology* 1990;4(5):135–138,147.

110. Ganz PA, Schag CAC, Lee JJ, Sim M-S. The CARES. A generic measure of health-related quality of life for patients with cancer. *Qual Life Res* 1992;1:19–29.

111. Aaronson NK, Ahmedzai S, Bullinger M, et al. The EORTC core quality-of-life questionnaire. Interim results of an international field study. In: Osoba D, ed. *Effect of cancer on quality of life.* Boca Raton, FL: CRC, 1991:185–203.

112. Bjordal K, Kaasa S. Psychometric validation of the EORTC core quality of life questionnaire, 30-item version and a diagnosis-specific module for head and neck cancer patients. *Acta Oncol* 1992;31:311–321.

112a. Bjordal K, Ahlner-Elmqvist M, Tollesson E, et al. Development of a European Organization for Research and Treatment of Cancer (EORTC) questionnaire module to be used in quality of life assessments in head and neck cancer patients. *Acta Oncol* 1994;33:879–885.

113. Sadura A, Pater J, Osoba D, Levine M, Palmer M, Bennett K. Quality-of-life assessment. Patient compliance with questionnaire completion. *J Natl Cancer Inst* 1992;84:1023–1026.

114. Aaronson NK, Ahmedzai S, Bergman B, et al. The European Organization for Research and Treatment of Cancer QLQ-C30. A quality-of-life instrument for use in international clinical trials in oncology. *J Natl Cancer Inst* 1993;85:365–376.

115. Niezgoda HE, Pater JL. A validation study of the domains of the core EORTC quality of life questionnaire. *Qual Life Res* 1993;2:319–325.

116. Osoba D, Zee B, Sadura A, Pater J, Quirt I. Measurement of quality of life in an adjuvant trial of gamma interferon versus levamisole in malignant melanoma. In: Salmon SE, ed. *Adjuvant therapy of cancer.* Vol VII. Philadelphia: JB Lippincott, 1993:412–416.

117. Osoba D, Zee B, Pater J, Warr D, Kaizer L, Latreille J. Psychometric properties and responsiveness of the EORTC Quality of Life Questionnaire (QLQ-C30) in patients with breast, ovarian and lung cancer. *Qual Life Res* 1994;3:353–364.

118. Sprangers MAG, Cull A, Bjordal K, Groenvold M, Aaronson NK. The European Organization for Research and Treatment of Cancer

119. Cella DF, Tulsky DS, Gray G, et al. The functional assessment of cancer therapy scale. Development and validation of the general measure. *J Clin Oncol* 1993;11:570–579.

120. Schipper H, Clinch J, McMurray A, Levitt M. Measuring the quality of life of cancer patients. The Functional Living Index—Cancer. Development and validation. *J Clin Oncol* 1984;2:472–483.

121. Morrow GR, Lindke J, Black P. Measurement of quality of life in patients. Psychometric analyses of the Functional Living Index—Cancer (FLIC). *Qual Life Res* 1992;1:287–296.

122. Presant CA, Klahr C, Hogan L. Evaluating quality-of-life in oncology patients. Pilot observations. *Oncol Nurs For* 1981;8:26–30.

123. Padilla GV, Presant C, Grant MM, Metter G, Lipsett J, Heide F. Quality of life index for patients with cancer. *Res Nursing Health* 1983;6:117–126.

124. Spitzer WO, Dobson AJ, Hall J, et al. Measuring the quality of life of cancer patients. A concise QL-index for use by physicians. *J Chron Dis* 1981;34:585–597.

125. Wood-Dauphinee S, Williams JI. The Spitzer quality-of-life index. Its performance as a measure. In: Osoba D, ed. *Effect of cancer on quality of life.* Boca Raton, FL: CRC, 1991:169–184.

126. De Haes JCJM, Welvaart K. Quality of life after breast cancer surgery. *J Surg Oncol* 1985;28:123–125.

127. De Haes JCJM, Raatgever JW, van der Burg MEL, Hamersma E, Neijt JP. Evaluation of the quality of life of patients with advanced ovarian cancer treated with combination chemotherapy. In: Aaronson NK, Beckmann J, eds. *The quality of life of cancer patients.* New York: Raven, 1987:215–226.

128. Watson M, Law M, Maguire GP, Robertson B, Greer S, Bliss JM, Ibbotson T. Further development of a quality of life measure for cancer patients. The Rotterdam Symptom Checklist (revised). *Psychoncology* 1992;1:35–44.

129. Selby PJ, Chapman J-AW, Etazadi-Amoli J, Dalley D, Boyd NF. The development of a method for assessing the quality of life of cancer patients. *Br J Cancer* 1984;50:13–22.

130. Bell DR, Tannock IF, Boyd NF. Quality of life measurement in breast cancer patients. *Br J Cancer* 1985;51:577–580.

131. Boyd NF, Selby PJ, Sutherland JH, Hogg S. Measurement of the clinical status of patients with breast cancer. Evidence for the validity of self assessment with linear analogue scales. *J Clin Epidemiol* 1988;41:243–250.

132. Levine MN, Guyatt GH, Gent M, et al. Quality of life in stage II breast cancer. An instrument for clinical trials. *J Clin Oncol* 1988;6:1798–1810.

133. Browman GP, Levine MN, Hodson DI, et al. The head and neck radiotherapy questionnaire. A morbidity/quality-of-life instrument for clinical trials of radiation therapy in locally advanced head and neck cancer. *J Clin Oncol* 1993;11:863–872.

134. Gelber RD, Goldhirsch A. A new endpoint for the assessment of adjuvant therapy in postmenopausal women with operable breast cancer. *J Clin Oncol* 1986;4:1772–1779.

135. Gelber RD, Gelman RS, Goldhirsch A. A quality-of-life oriented endpoint for comparing therapies. *Biometrics* 1989;45:781–795.

136. Goldhirsch A, Gelber RD, Simes RJ, Glasziou P, Coates AS. Costs and benefits of adjuvant therapy in breast cancer. A quality-adjusted survival analysis. *J Clin Oncol* 1989;7:36–44.

137. Glasziou PP, Simes RJ, Gelber RD. Quality adjusted survival analysis. *Stat Med* 1990;9:1259–1276.

138. Gelber RD, Goldhirsch A. Quality-adjusted survival analysis. *J Clin Oncol* 1991;9:526.

139. Till JE, De Haes JCJM. Quality-adjusted survival analysis. *J Clin Oncol* 1991;9:525–526.

140. Utility analysis. Clinical decisions involving many possible outcomes. In: Weinstein MC, Fineberg HV, et al., eds. *Clinical decision analysis.* Philadelphia: WB Saunders, 1980:184–227.

141. Goodwin PJ. Economic evaluations of cancer care. Incorporating quality of life issues. In: Osoba D, ed. *Effect of cancer on quality of life.* Boca Raton, FL: CRC, 1991:125–136.

142. Torrance GW, Thomas WH, Sackett DL. A utility maximization model for evaluation of health care programs. *Health Serv Res* 1972;7:118–133.

143. Torrance GW. Measurement of health state utilities for economic appraisal. A review. *J Health Econ* 1986;5:1–30.

144. Kirshner B, Guyatt G. A methodological framework for assessing health indices. *J Chron Dis* 1985;38:27–36.
145. Guyatt G, Walter S, Norman G. Measuring change over time. Assessing the usefulness of evaluative instruments. *J Chron Dis* 1987; 40:171–178.
146. Osoba D, Aaronson NK, Till JE. A practical guide for selecting quality-of-life measures in clinical trials and practice. In: Osoba D, ed. *Effect of cancer on quality of life*. Boca Raton, FL: CRC, 1991:89–104.
147. Osoba D. The evolving role of health-related quality-of-life assessment in oncology. A brief review of selected multidimensional questionnaires. *Oncol Advisor* 1994;2(2):3–4.
148. Gotay CC, Korn EL, McCabe MS, Moore TD, Cheson BD. Building quality of life assessment into cancer treatment studies. *Oncology* 1992;6(6):25–28, 30–37.
149. Mor V, Guadagnoli E. Quality of life measurement. A psychometric tower of Babel. *J Clin Epidemiol* 1988;11:1055–1058.
150. Deyo RA, Centor RM. Assessing the responsiveness of functional scales to clinical change. An analogy to diagnostic test performance. *J Chron Dis* 1986;39:897–906.
151. Gough IR, Furnival CM, Schilder L, Grove W. Assessment of the quality of life of patients with advanced cancer. *Eur J Cancer Clin Oncol* 1983;19:1161–1165.
152. Crossen JR, Garwood D, Glatstein E, Neuwelt EA. Neurobehavioral sequelae of cranial irradiation in adults. A review of radiation-induced encephalopathy. *J Clin Oncol* 1994;12:627–642.
153. Meyers CA, Weitzner M, Byrne K, Valentine A, Champlin RE, Przepiorka D. Evaluation of the neurobehavioral functioning of patients before, during, and after bone marrow transplantation. *J Clin Oncol* 1994;12:820–826.
154. Tchekmedyian NS, Hickman M, Siau J, Greco A, Aisner J. Treatment of cancer anorexia with megestrol acetate. Impact on quality of life. *Oncology* 1990;4(5):185–192, 194.
155. Endicott J. Measurement of depression in patients with cancer. *Cancer* 1984;53(suppl):2243–2249.
156. Smith GR, Witt AS, Golding JM. The relationship of function-specific mental health measures to psychiatric diagnoses. *Controlled Clin Trials* 1991;12:180S–188S.
157. Morrow GR. The assessment of nausea and vomiting. Past problems, current issues, and suggestions for future research. *Cancer* 1984; 53(suppl):2267–2280.
158. Wilan AR, Warr D, Pater JL, Levitt M, Erlichman C, Osoba D. Methodological issues in anti-emetic studies. In: Osoba D, ed. *Effect of cancer on quality of life*. Boca Raton, FL: CRC, 1991:229–249.
159. Lindley CM, Hirsch JD, O'Neill CV, Transau MC, Gilbert CS. Quality of life consequences of chemotherapy-induced emesis. *Qual Life Res* 1992;1:331–340.
160. Andersen BL. Sexual functioning morbidity among cancer survivors. Current status and future research directions. *Cancer* 1985;55: 1835–1842.
161. Greenberg DB. The measurement of sexual dysfunction in cancer patients. *Cancer* 1984;53(suppl):2281–2286.
162. Lasry J-C M. Women's sexuality following breast cancer. In: Osoba D, ed. *Effect of cancer on quality of life*. Boca Raton, FL: CRC, 1991:215–227.
163. Pozo C, Carver CS, Noriega V, et al. Effects of mastectomy versus lumpectomy on emotional adjustment to breast cancer. A prospective study of the first year postsurgery. *J Clin Oncol* 1992;10:1292–1298.
164. McCorkle R, Young K. Development of a symptom distress scale. *Cancer Nurs* 1978;1:373–378.
165. McCorkle R, Quint-Benoliel J. Symptom distress, current concerns and mood disturbance after diagnosis of life-threatening disease. *Soc Sci Med* 1983;17:431–438.
166. McCorkle R. The measurement of symptom distress. *Semin Oncol Nurs* 1987;3:248–256.
167. Ahles TA, Blanchard EB, Ruckdeschel JC. The multidimensional nature of cancer-related pain. *Pain* 1983;17:277–288.
168. Beyer JE, Wells N. Assessment of cancer pain in children. In: Patt RB, ed. *Cancer pain*. Philadelphia: JB Lippincott, 1993:57–84.
169. Cleeland CS. Pain assessment in cancer. In: Osoba D, ed. *Effect of cancer on quality of life*. Boca Raton, FL: CRC, 1991:293–305.
170. Melzack R. The McGill pain questionnaire. Major properties and scoring methods. *Pain* 1975;1:277–299.
171. Portenoy RK. Pain and quality of life. Theoretical aspects. In: Osoba D, ed. *Effect of cancer on quality of life*. Boca Raton, FL: CRC, 1991:279–292.
172. Rowlingson JC, Hamill RJ, Patt RB. Comprehensive assessment of the patient with cancer pain. In: Patt RB, ed. *Cancer pain*. Philadelphia: JB Lippincott, 1993:23–39.
173. Ware JE, Snyder MK, Wright WR, Davies AR. Defining and measuring patient satisfaction with medical care. *Eval Prog Plann* 1983; 6:247–263.
174. Aaronson NK. Quality of life research in cancer clinical trials. A need for common rules and language. *Oncology* 1990;4(5):59–66,70.
175. Schipper H. Guidelines and caveats for quality of life measurement in clinical practice and research. *Oncology* 1990;4(5):51–57,70.
176. Priestman TJ. Evaluation of quality of life in women with breast cancer. In: Aaronson NK, Beckman JH, eds. *The quality of life of cancer patients*. New York: Raven, 1987:193–200.
177. Lydick E, Epstein RS. Interpretation of quality of life changes. *Qual Life Res* 1993;2:221–226.
178. Goodyear M. The psychoendocrinology of sleep disturbance. Studies in the use of questionnaires to elicit subjective accounts of sleeping patterns, and their interrelations with adrenocortical function, personality profiles and symptomatology. BSc thesis, Department of Surgery, Monash University, 1971.
179. Hürny C, Bernhard J, Joss R, et al. Feasibility of quality of life assessment in a randomised phase III trial of small cell lung cancer. A lesson from the real world. *Ann Oncol* 1992;3:825–831.
180. Hopwood P, Stephens RJ, Machin D. Approaches to the analysis of quality of life data. Experiences gained from a Medical Research Council Lung Cancer Working Party palliative chemotherapy trial. *Qual Life Res* 1994;3:339–352.
181. Brorsson B, Ifver J, Hays RD. The Swedish health-related quality of life survey. *Qual Life Res* 1993;2:33–45.
182. Baum M, Priestman T, West RR, Jones EM. A comparison of subjective responses in a trial comparing endocrine with cytotoxic treatment in advanced carcinoma of the breast. In: Mouridsen HT, Palshof T, eds. *Breast cancer. Experimental and clinical aspects*. Oxford: Pergamon, 1980:223–226.
183. Coates A, Gebski V, Bishop JF, et al. Improving the quality of life during chemotherapy for advanced breast cancer. A comparison of intermittent and continuous treatment strategies. *N Engl J Med* 1987; 317:1490–1495.
184. Zwinderman AH. Statistical analysis of longitudinal quality of life data with missing measurements. *Qual Life Res* 1992;1:219–224.
185. Morris J, Coyle D. Quality of life questionnaires in cancer clinical trials. Imputing missing values. *Psycho-oncology* 1994;3:215–222.
186. Smith TJ, Hillner BE, Desch CE. Efficacy and cost-effectiveness of cancer treatment. Rational allocation of resources based on decision analysis. *J Natl Cancer Inst* 1993; :1460–1474.
187. Mehrez A, Gafni A. Quality-adjusted life-years, utility theory, and healthy-years equivalents. *Med Decis Making* 1989;9:142–149.
188. Carr-Hill RA, Morris J. Current practice in obtaining the "Q" in QALYs. A cautionary note. *BMJ* 1991;303:699–701.
189. Nord E. An alternative to QALYs. The saved young life equivalent. *BMJ* 1992;305:875–877.
190. Feeny D, Guyatt G, Tugwell P, eds. *Health care technology*. Effectiveness, efficiency and public policy. Montréal: Institute for Research on Public Policy, 1986.

Quality of Life and Pharmacoeconomics in Clinical Trials, Second Edition, edited by B. Spilker.
Lippincott-Raven Publishers, Philadelphia © 1996.

CHAPTER 105

Quality of Life in Bone Marrow Transplant

Betty R. Ferrell, Marcia M. Grant, and Marie B. Whedon

INTRODUCTION

The population of bone marrow transplant (BMT) survivors can, in many ways, serve as a model for quality of life (QOL) research. This population depicts an advance in medical technology which has prolonged life for many cancer patients, yet in the process has created significant impact on all dimensions of quality of life. Patients undergoing bone marrow transplant have already faced a life-threatening illness and have often endured years of previous aggressive treatment (1).

Bone marrow transplant is a procedure that involves all aspects of the illness experience. Patients often endure a phase of intensive care during the actual transplantation, experience an initial year of acute symptoms and close monitoring, and then face a future that may vary from virtual cure and normalcy or one of chronic graft-versus-host disease (cGVHD), recurrent disease, and even death. Regardless of the course of illness, the procedure of bone marrow transplantation is certain to impact all dimensions of quality of life for both patient and family members.

As a medical advance which is increasing in use, and yet also one of considerable expense, the topic of bone marrow transplantation is also a model case for exploration of health policy applications of the QOL concept. This chapter discusses the issues and factors related to QOL in bone marrow transplant, reviews literature in this area, and discusses issues related to QOL measurement and other research issues.

ISSUES AND FACTORS RELATED TO QOL IN BONE MARROW TRANSPLANT

Based on previous QOL research and surveys of a sample of 119 long-term bone marrow transplant survivors, Ferrell and colleagues proposed a model of the impact of bone marrow transplant on patient's QOL (2,3). The quality of life/bone marrow transplant model (Fig. 1) depicts the impact of transplant and survivorship on four domains, including physical well-being, psychological well-being, social well-being, and spiritual well-being. This model depicts separate domains of QOL yet, as with other areas of QOL research, it is evident that there are significant interrelationships between domains. A disruption in one domain may influence other domains and QOL in general.

For instance, fatigue is a symptom recognized under physical well-being but may also affect the ability to resume family roles (social well-being) and coping style (psychological well-being). Viewing effects of bone marrow transplant from a broader QOL perspective provides the health care provider with an appreciation of the need for a comprehensive assessment of the survivor's QOL and rehabilitation needs. Previous literature related to QOL in bone marrow transplant will be reviewed using these domains as an organizing framework.

B. R. Ferrell and M. M. Grant: Department of Nursing Research and Education, City of Hope National Medical Center, Duarte, California 91010.

M. B. Whedon: Dartmouth Hitchcock Medical Center, Lebanon, New Hampshire 03756.

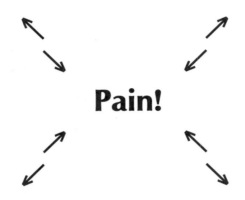

**Physical Well Being &
Symptoms**

Functional Ability
Strength / Fatigue
Sleep & Rest
Nausea
Appetite
Constipation

Psychological Well Being

Anxiety
Depression
Enjoyment / Leisure
Pain Distress
Happiness
Fear
Cognition / Attention

Pain!

Social Well Being

Caregiver Burden
Roles and Relationships
Affection / Sexual Function
Appearance

Spiritual Well Being

Suffering
Meaning of Pain
Religiosity
Transcendence

FIG. 1. Published articles per year containing "Quality of Life" as a descriptor and containing both "Quality of Life" and a reference to neoplasms. Diamonds represent the total quality of life literature, and squares the literature dealing with cancer.

Physical Well-Being

Long-term effects of bone marrow transplant, also known as delayed or late complications, are defined as phenomenon that result from bone marrow transplantation and occur or continue longer than 100 days after bone marrow transplant (4–8). The time between 100 days and 1 year is unique from other cancer groups and from the subsequent years of bone marrow transplant survivorship. It is marked by many physical effects and frequent checkups and is more accurately viewed as a continuation of acute posttreatment recovery. During this first year, the patient's status may change dramatically with regard to all QOL domains. Beyond the first year, many of the effects of bone marrow transplant will resolve, yet some may continue as chronic health problems.

Physiological long-term effects can be considered in the domain of physical well-being. This aspect of post bone marrow transplant quality of life after bone marrow transplant is objectively recorded by many transplant centers and is the most extensively described in the literature. A growing body of literature has provided in-depth insight into the undesirable physiological effects that may occur after marrow transplantation (9–14).

Physiological effects can be categorized by etiology. The impact on physical well-being is caused either from the transplant (e.g., cGVHD), from the effects of chemotherapy, radiation therapy, and/or immunosuppressive agents (including secondary malignancies) or from the original disease (primarily relapse).

Long-term effects are caused by graft-versus-host disease (GVHD) and its treatment. These patients unfortunately develop several physiological effects that will remain chronic symptoms. GVHD occurs exclusively in allogeneic marrow recipients and more frequently in recipients with less well-matched donors. The incidence is 33% in patients with matched sibling donors, 49% in those with nonidentical family member donors, and 64% in recipients of unrelated donors. Furthermore, the greater the degree of mismatch, the earlier in the period after bone marrow transplant cGVHD is likely to occur (day 133 in recipients of unrelated marrow versus day 201 in recipients of related marrow). It rarely occurs after day 500. The overall probability of occurrence is 42% to 46% in those survivors over age 20 versus approximately 13% in patients less than 9 years (8).

Total body irradiation is recognized as the aspect of treatment that has the most extensive long-term morbidity. As a result, attempts have been made to eliminate it, when possible, from bone marrow transplant preparative treatment regimens. Most notable effects include endocrine dysfunction (growth, thyroid, and reproductive effects) (7,8), visual changes (cataracts) (5,7), cognitive dysfunction (15), and second cancers (14).

Patterns of physiological effects can be expected to change as treatment and GVHD regimens change. Some effects may increase in frequency, others may decrease, and some new unanticipated effects may be recognized. For instance, before immunosuppressive treatment of cGVHD, the incidence of severe, generalized scleroderma and respiratory insufficiency occurred in 50% of transplant survivors. Now the problem is observed in only 5% to 10% of survivors (10). Results from long-term studies have prompted changes in doses and schedules of total body irradiation in hopes of reducing such complications as second malignancies (14) and cognitive dysfunction (15).

As a group of cancer patients, the bone marrow transplant population does represent one of significant disruption in physical well-being. As summarized in Table 1, these physiological effects affect many organ systems and also are chronic health problems. These physical symptoms are also obviously linked to quality of life as they impact function and resumption of normal social and work-related activities.

Psychological Well-Being

Several investigators have studied the bone marrow transplant population as a model group for evaluating psychological response to aggressive treatment and as an exploration of cancer survivorship. Researchers have described the psychological responses of adults (16–19) and children (20).

Psychological well-being encompasses the areas of regaining normalcy, anxiety, depression, fear of recurrence, and coping with survival (2). The first attempts to understand post-transplant QOL focused primarily on psychological effects (21) and adjustment. Wolcott and colleagues studied 17 allogeneic survivors (median 42 months after post-bone marrow transplant and found that between 15% to 25% reported significant emotional distress, low self-esteem, and less than optimal life satisfaction (22). Several investigators have applied standard measures of psychological well-being (i.e., the Profile of Mood States, Psychological Adjustment to Illness Scale) used in other cancer populations to compare this unique group of cancer survivors.

Most investigators have reported positive results with regard to psychological well-being. Most of the studies have described the bone marrow transplant patients as "glad to be alive" or to have a "second chance" at life, especially because most have exhausted other treatment options before they had a bone marrow transplant (7,17). Despite evidence of adverse effects from bone marrow transplant such as severe symptoms or extreme social disruption, many survivors report an unexpectedly high QOL. It may be that survivors are influenced by their feelings of indebtedness to their health care providers or that their sense of simply "being alive" overshadows other aspects of QOL.

Social Well-Being

Social well-being encompasses issues of relationships, family, intimacy, work, and social reintegration. Of these, work or vocational issues and personal relationships/intimacy issues have been the major focus of the social concerns domain of QOL to date. The relationship between QOL and role function or ability to return to one's former type of employment was described by Baker and colleagues (23). Life satisfaction was positively related to retention of pre-bone marrow transplant role status, especially for men. Others report that 50% to 74% of previously employed patients return to former jobs or new full-time employment (24–26).

Sexuality and reproductive issues have often been discussed within the physical domain as issues of fertility and physical effects of treatment. Investigators have also explored the social dimensions of intimacy and sexuality. Many patients who had bone marrow transplant report difficulty in resuming relationships, whereas others reported improved relationships (27). Some researchers have explored disruption in sexual function related to the transplant or other cancer treatments such as the radiation therapy (27–29). In general, bone marrow transplant survivors have reported a heightened appreciation for their family and other personal relationships (2,26,30). A major void exists in the literature with regard to the family members of the bone marrow transplant patient. There is an absence of family caregiver

TABLE 1. *Post-BMT physical effects in adults that occur or remain after 1 year*

Long-term effect	Incidence (%)	Comments	Reference
Chronic GVHD effects	33–64	Lower incidence in matched, higher incidence in unrelated	8,9
Skin	79	Lichenoid and scleroderma	7,8,13
Liver	73	Occasional progression to biliary cirrhosis	9,7,8,13
Oral	72–80	Oral sicca may lead to dental decay; oral sensitivity common	9,8,13
Ophthalmic	38–47	Sicca, grittiness, discomfort, photophobia	6,8,9,13
Intestinal	16	Diarrhea, steatorrhea	6,8,9,13,37
Myofacial	11	Myositis, polyarthritis, limited range of motion	6–8,13
Pulmonary	11	Obstructive defects, bronchiolitis obliterans	8,9,13
Esophageal	6	Strictures	8,9,13
GI/nutritional	28	Weight loss	
	18	Xerostomia	
	8	Anorexia	36
Other		Myasthenia gravis, autoimmune thrombocytopenia, vaginal sicca	9
Non-GVHD effects			
Pulmonary			
Restrictive disease	7–20		5,9,11
Obstructive airway	5–10		5,9,11
Genitourinary			
Reproductive		Some normal pregnancies have resulted in women, and fathered by men post-BMT sterility	5,6,7,9,37
Men	90–100		
Women	90–100	Sterility, ovarian failure, no menses, early menopause	
Bladder	Reported	Bladder shrinkage, s/p. Hemorrhagic cystitis	9
Renal			
Radiation nephritis	Reported		7,9
Renal insufficiency	20	Begins 1 yr or later	7,12
Neurological			
Visual/cataracts	19–75	Lowest incidence with chemotherapy only, highest with single-dose TBI, also from steroid therapy	7,9
Neuropsychological	Reported	Memory, attention, concentration difficulties, slowed cognitive processing	9,15,38
Thyroid function	15–65	Hypothyroidism usually due to TBI, reduced incidence in fractionated dose	5,7,9
Aseptic necrosis of the bone	10	Due to high-dose corticosteroid treatment for acute GVHD	7,9

From Whedon and Ferrell (43).
S/P, status post; TBI, total body irradiation.
[a]Only reviews and recently reported primary sources that update the comprehensive previously published reviews are listed.

outcomes or of including family members as subjects in QOL research related to bone marrow transplant.

Haberman and colleagues have made important contributions to understanding QOL in bone marrow transplant through their exploration of "Demands of Recovery." An initial study by these investigators described how 125 adult survivors of bone marrow transplant (6–18.4 years posttransplant) perceived the quality of their lives. This research has used qualitative research methods to conduct interviews of bone marrow transplant survivors in order to define the true demands of bone marrow transplant survivorship. This initial qualitative approach led to later development of a quantita-

tive instrument, the "Demands of Illness" inventory, which has been used extensively by Haberman and others in QOL research (31).

Spiritual Well-Being

The spiritual domain is the least well delineated in QOL studies in general and certainly within the bone marrow transplant population. This focus was first defined by Ferrell and colleagues as a separate area in their earlier QOL studies and later applied to the bone marrow transplant population (2). Responses by bone marrow transplant survivors to interviews regarding QOL included the themes of "Spirituality Increased" and "Increased Appreciation of Life." Thirty-three responses from the 119 subjects specifically addressed issues such as global spirituality (inner strength, conviction, and life goals), religiousness (faith in God, trust, indebtedness to God), and life appreciation (overall priorities, valued relationships). Additional responses under the theme of being healthy often referred to "spiritual health" (2,3).

Survivors frequently express an altered life goal or altered life meaning, but its effect on the nature of overall survival is unclear. A distinct change is often reflected in the degree of indebtedness of the survivor toward the physicians, nurses, donors, society, and health care system. This burden can be increased by the phenomenon of "survivor guilt," that is, experiencing some remorse in being alive, while knowing patients who did not survive.

Two additional studies have used qualitative approaches in studying the impact of transplant and both have identified spiritual issues. Ersek's study used a grounded theory approach to elicit the experiences of hoping in 10 men and 10 women who had undergone bone marrow transplant (32). Most subjects had allogeneic transplants and were interviewed during the pre-admission period, between days 9–12 posttransplant, and again during days 25–28 posttransplant. Two major categories were used to describe the process by which the subjects described their experiences. The first category, "Dealing With It," included the process of confronting the negative possibilities that were part of the treatment experience. The other category, "Keeping It in Its Place," was defined as the process by which the subjects controlled or limited their response to the disease and therapy. These opposing categories allowed the individual to maintain hope. By using both strategies, individuals were able to transcend each strategy and continue to hope.

The second recent qualitative study was conducted by Steeves, and focused on the quest for meaning in bone marrow transplant survivors (33). Six male patients were followed, two who endured long hospitalization and died after 65 and 67 days, two who also never left the hospital but died within 2 weeks of transplant, and a third pair who were survivors and who left the hospital after 30 days and were interviewed as outpatients up to 100 days posttransplant. All patients underwent allogeneic transplant with a family member being the donor. Analysis was done on the extensive interview data using hermeneutic analysis. This analysis is especially valuable in examining interview data related to meaning. Results were extensive, and can be partially described in ways that patients used to continue to understand the meanings of their lives as they went through the toxic treatment experience. Two different ways were identified: they renegotiated their social position in a new situation, and they tried to reach an understanding of their experiences as a whole (32,33).

METHODOLOGICAL CONSIDERATIONS

The research summarized above demonstrates the unique dimensions of QOL for bone marrow transplant survivors. Because transplant impacts all dimensions of QOL, measurement of the QOL construct in the bone marrow transplant population must be multidimensional and sensitive to the experiences of this population (34).

Table 2 includes a summary of the major themes identified in the study by Ferrell and Grant and colleagues in their initial efforts to define QOL for bone marrow transplant survivors (2,3). The distinctive features of QOL for this group of cancer patients provides direction for methodological and measurement issues in QOL research.

TABLE 2. *QOL for BMT survivors*

Summary of themes
  Being healthy (physical, mental, and spiritual)
  Having a heightened appreciation for life
  Having family and relationships
  Being normal
  Being satisfied and fulfilled with life
  Being able to work/Financial success
  Being independent
  Being alive
  Having self-esteem, self-respect

How has BMT affected QOL?
  A second chance was given
  The opportunity to improve my QOL was given
  Appreciation for life and relationships increased
  Numerous side effects occurred
  Spirituality increased
  Strength and stamina is decreased
  Work/Activities are limited
  Infertility resulted
  Fear of relapse is present

What makes QOL better?
  Having good health (physical, mental, spiritual)
  Having family and friends
  Being alive/having appreciation for life
  Having a positive attitude/peace of mind
  Having a job/money/finances
  Having goals/being productive

What makes QOL worse?
  Experiencing physical losses
  Losing relationships
  Having unfulfilled goals
  Being financially distressed (money, job)

What could physicians or nurses do to improve QOL?
  Be accessible
  Reinforce current education
  Increase patient participation in decision making
  Provide support groups
  Discover a cure

From Ferrell et al. (2).

TABLE 3. *QOL studies in BMT*

Investigators	Total no./type of patients	Median age at survey (range, yr)	Median time (months) post-BMT (range)	Measures	Major outcomes/findings

Wolcott et al. (22)	26 allo
	
	13 leuk
	13 NM
		27.9
		(17–51)
			42
			(18–89)
				Global
				  Self-assessment of current health
				Physical well-being
				  Health status assessment
				Psychological well-being
				  Profile of Mood States
				  Simmons Self-Esteem
				
				Social well-being
				  Weissman Social Adjustment Scale (SAS-SR)
				Spiritual well-being
				  Life satisfaction
					Positively associated with time since BMT
					
					25% reported ongoing medical problems
					
					15–25% reported significant emotional distress and low self-esteem; not associated with time since BMT
					
					15–25% reported less than optimal life satisfaction

Hengeveld et al. (28)	17 allo
	
	16 leuk
	1 NM
		28
		(18–44)
			34
			(12–60)
				Global
				  Interview regarding information and preparation, support, coping behaviors, family reactions
				Physical well-being
				  Karnofsky (observed)
				Psychological well-being
				  Beck Depression Inventory
				  Symptom Checklist 90
				Social well-being
				  Employment status
				Spiritual well-being
				  Not measured
					Subjects felt ill-prepared for post-BMT emotional and sexual problems
					
					50–100% reported sexuality and fertility problems
					
					Occupational disability

Reference	Sample	Age mean (range)		Domains	Results
Andrykowski et al. (1)	23 allo 18 leuk 5 NM	34.4 (19–49)	26.2 (3–52)	Global Other comments: Pre-BMT expectations-34% said they were worse off post-BMT than they expected pre-BMT. Compared FLIC scores with cancer patients undergoing therapy. A follow-up longitudinal assessment of the above subjects {Andrykowski et al. (22)} demonstrated 50% unemployed for health reasons, and psychological function did not improve with passage of time. Physical well-being Functional Living Index Cancer (FLIC)-Total Combined Function Psychological well-being Profile of Mood States FLIC-emotional Social well-being FLIC-social Spiritual well-being Not measured	Younger age < 30 at BMT associated with less fatigue, improved physical function Younger age < 30 at BMT associated with better psychological function
Andrykowski et al. (42) (longitudinal assessment)	Same as above				
Andrykowski et al. (24)	29 allo 26 leuk 3 NM	34.4 (18–51)	51 (12–90)	Global	QOL about the same as renal transplant patients Age during BMT, education, TBI were good predictors of QOL Sex, cGVHD, prior disease did not predict QOL

TABLE 3. Continued.

Investigators	Total no./type of patients	Median age at survey (range, yr)	Median time (months) post-BMT (range)	Measures	Major outcomes/findings
	(5/29 partial match) (compared with 29 renal transplant patients)			Physical well-being Sleep, energy, appetite scale Symptom Experience Report (SER) Perceived Health Questionnaire (PHQ) FLIC Psychological well-being Profile of Mood States	Older age associated with poor physiological function, 69% reported decreased energy compared with pre-BMT Perceived poorer health than others their age Greater mood disturbance than other groups. More difficult to predict than physical or functional state Greater disturbance than coronary bypass patients
				Psychological Adjustment to Illness Scale (PAIS) Social well-being PAIS subscales Sickness Impact Profile (SIP) Employment Spiritual well-being Not measured Global	Higher education levels associated with less illness-related dysfunction and higher QOL (higher FLIC) 38% not employed for health reasons
Wingard et al. (25)	135 96 allo 32 auto 7 syn 109 leuk/lymph 26 NM	31 (18–53)	37 (6–149)	Not measured Physical well-being Health Perception Scale Health Statement Karnofsky Scale (physician and patient report) Pain Scale Clinically significant illness (physician rated) Psychological well-being Not measured Social well-being Social Function Scale Employment/school attendance Job discrimination Insurance discrimination Spiritual well-being Not measured	93% Karnofsky >80; 70/79 patients matched physicians on their ratings 70% reported 0–mild pain 33% rated to have clinically significant illness 51% FT; 14% PT; 32% UE 70% reported job discrimination 39% reported trouble getting insurance

Reference	N	Age		QOL dimension	Results
Altmaier et al. (27)	12	29.4 (17–41)	32.8 (25–41)	Global	Compared with chemotherapy patients; the study concluded that objectively, QOL in BMT was lower than chemotherapy group; however, BMT group did not report lower function
				Physical well-being Physical concerns/symptoms Mobility Self-care Karnofsky Scale	60% had 1 or more episodes of pneumonia; 75% rated self "healthy" 75% able to care for self; 83% had 90 on Karnofsky Scale
				Psychological well-being Degree of stress Anxiety/depression-interviewer rated	Low distress
				Social well-being Relationship changes	20% reported improved relationships 33% reported worsened relationships (over sexual issues) 25% reported difficulties in sexual function 58% reported FT; 16% PT; 25% UE
				Sexual function Employment Spiritual well-being Not measured	
Belec (30)	24 23 allo 1 auto 16 leuk 4 lymph 4 NM (5/23 partial match)	32.7 (20–50)	23 (12–38)	Global Quality of Life Index (QLI) of Ferrans and Powers Further qualitative data gathered by an 11-item semi-structured interview (content analysis)	91.6% had score in upper range QOL perceptions not affected by passage of time
				Physical well-being QLI-health/functioning	Number of physical problems associated with low health subscale; 50% had fatigue and lack of energy since BMT; 75% continued to worry about health
				Psychological well-being QLI-psychological/spiritual Social well-being QLI-socioeconomic; family	All family scores in upper end of range indicating a high positive influence of family on patient-reported QOL
				Spiritual well-being QLI-psychological/spiritual	90% responded that the BMT experience led to reassessment of priorities and values

TABLE 3. *Continued.*

Investigators	Total no./ type of patients	Median age at survey (range, yr)	Median time (months) post-BMT (range)	Measures	Major outcomes/findings
Ferrell et al. (2,3) (Qualitative)	119 allo 60 leuk 35 lymph 24 NM	34.7 (18–57)	48 (3–288)	Global Qualitative 6-item open-ended questionnaire (City of Hope BMT-QOLS) e.g., How do you think that BMT has affected your QOL? Reported responses listed under specific domains. BMT-QOL (quantitative tool)	Responses grouped by themes and reported here under domains
Grant et al. (39) (Reliability and validity reported on BMT-QOL tool developed based on interviews with above patients)	BMT-QOL tool administered to above, plus 60 additional patients			Physical well-being City of Hope BMT-QOLS	Numerous side effects (e.g., weight loss, visual changes, cardiac, persistent alopecia) Decreased strength and stamina Being healthy (physical, mental, spiritual) Being independent
				BMT-QOL Psychological well-being City of Hope BMT-QOLS BMT-QOL Social well-being City of Hope BMT-QOLS	Being healthy (physical, mental, spiritual) Being normal Work and activities are limited Being able to work, financial success Having family/relationships
				BMT-QOL Spiritual well-being City of Hope BMT-QOLS	Spirituality increased Increased appreciation of life Being healthy (physical, mental, spiritual)

1024

Reference	N	Age (yr)	Time of assessment	Domains/measures	Findings
Chao et al. (29)	58 auto 47 lymph 11 leuk	36 (19–53)	12 months (QOL also measured at day 90, 180, 270)	Global Global scale (0–10) Physical well-being Karnofsky (BMT questionnaire with items in each domain) Weight Appetite Sleep Colds Medicines Psychological well-being Body image Social well-being Employment Sexual satisfaction Spiritual well-being Not measured	8.9 at 1 year Median 100% (60–100% range) Fatigue, peripheral neuropathy, balance problems noted Did not improve with time-36% dissatisfied with sexual function
Haberman (26) Haberman et al. (31) (qualitative data reported)	125 allo 12 syn 2 auto	38 (26–62) 32 (19–50)	121 (6–221)	Global Themes reported from the Long-Term Recovery Open-Ended Questionnaire (10 items), e.g., What has the experience of reestablishing your daily life and recovering from transplant been like for you? What things have been the most difficult for you to deal with since the transplant? Physical well-being Psychological well-being Social well-being Spiritual well-being	Responses grouped by themes and reported here under domains Dealing with physical complications Reestablishing life was difficult Reestablishing life was easy/smooth Achieving a new normalcy Recovery is dynamic process of adaptation Life is not different Life is slower paced Social adjustment by family, friends, peers Returning to work/financial concerns Dealing with relationship changes Dealing with social changes A new valuing of life/a changed perspective of time

TABLE 3. *Continued.*

Investigators	Total no./ type of patients	Median age at survey (range, yr)	Median time (months) post-BMT (range)	Measures	Major outcomes/findings
Bush et al. (40) (quantitative measure of above subjects)	125 111 allo 12 syn 2 auto			Global EORTC QLQ-C30 Physical well-being EORTC QLQ-C30 BMT-Specific Symptom Module Ware Health Perceptions Questionnaire Psychological well-being EORTC QLQ-C30 Demands of BMT Recovery Inventory Profile of Mood States Social well-being EORTC QLQ-C30 Demands of BMT Recovery Inventory Spiritual well-being	(Data not available prepublication)
Schmidt et al. (41)	162 allo 136 leuk 4 lymph 22 NM/other	60 (12–156)		Global City of Hope/Stanford Long-Term BMT Survivor Index–Items listed under each domain QOL rating (1–10) Physical well-being Karnofsy (physician rated), weight, appetite, sleep, sex, colds, appearance, medicines, cataracts, cGVHD, diarrhea, skin, bleeding, fever, mouth sores Psychological well-being Physical/emotional support needs Social well-being Marital status Employment status Spiritual well-being Not measured	Median rating = 9 31% reported cGVHD 19% reported frequent colds 8% reported skin changes 39% reported cataract development 94% reported normal appetite 98% reported normal appearance 69% reported sexual activity similar to pre-BMT 74% employed

From Whedon and Ferrell (43).
allo, allogeneic; auto, autologous; EORTC, European Organization for Research on Treatment of Cancer; FT, full-time; leuk, leukemia; lymph, lymphoma; NM, nonmalignant; PT, part-time; syn, syngeneic; UE, unemployed.

Instruments Used in Quality of Life and Bone Marrow Transplant Research

Table 3 summarizes studies that have explored QOL specifically in bone marrow transplant survivors (43). This summary demonstrates a variety of methodological approaches which have combined standard measures with disease specific measures of QOL. It is encouraging to note that many investigators have attempted to use self report measures and to isolate the experiences unique to bone marrow transplant and to include multiple domains.

Practical Issues

The nature of the bone marrow transplant trajectory ranging from acute and often critical illness to long-term survival creates many challenges for investigators. Bone marrow transplant undoubtedly exemplifies the multidimensional nature of QOL with great diversity within the domains over time (44).

One area of important consideration is the need to use longitudinal evaluation in the design of future therapeutic trials when evaluating different pretreatments or conditioning regimens within transplant (i.e., chemotherapy alone versus combined radiation/chemotherapy regimens). There is a need to begin evaluation of QOL prior to transplant as well, and to continue QOL evaluation much longer than in previous studies in order to better understand the long term needs of this group.

A final note on research of bone marrow transplant survivors is the unusually high rates of participation that have been observed (between 86% to 100%) in bone marrow transplant–quality of life studies (25,27–29). Although this is a positive effect for researchers, it may be evidence of the spiritual domain effect of ''wanting to give back'' and ''owing a debt of gratitude'' to their health care providers who offered them a chance at cure. Bone marrow transplant researchers should be sensitive in their approach to survivors who may sacrifice autonomy in their sense of indebtedness.

Future Research

Many areas of future research have been identified to continue to build our knowledge of QOL in bone marrow transplant. Winer and Sutton (35) identified specific needs for future research to include (a) identification of subjects who do not usually respond to QOL surveys and who may represent those with poorer QOL outcomes of bone marrow transplant; (b) QOL issues in the immediate pre- and post-transplant phase, or the more acute stage; (c) comparisons between types of bone marrow transplant such as the autologous and allogeneic groups; (d) prospective studies such that data are obtained on subjects who may die during the course of treatment rather than only from the survivors; and

(e) studies designed to evaluate interventions designed to improve QOL in bone marrow transplant.

Future research should continue to refine instruments which reflect the needs of bone marrow transplant patients across the domains of physical, psychological, social and spiritual well-being. Research should include the bone marrow transplant donors as well as family members.

CONCLUSIONS

Bone marrow transplant is recognized as a major advance over the previous years and one with significant potential for the future. As a treatment created to extend quantity of life in individuals who otherwise are often considered destined for advancing or terminal illness, bone marrow transplant has resulted in many issues related to quality of life. QOL evaluation must capture the dimensions of transplant and survivorship and provide direction for improved care for patients and their families.

REFERENCES

1. Andrykowski MA, Henslee PJ, Farrall GF. Physical and psychosocial functioning of adult survivors of allogenic bone marrow transplant. *Bone Marrow Transplant* 1989;4:75–81.
2. Ferrell BR, Grant M, Schmidt GM, et al. The meaning of quality of life for bone marrow transplant survivors. Part 1. The impact of bone marrow transplantation on quality of life. *Cancer Nurs* 1992;15: 153–160.
3. Ferrell B, Grant M, Schmidt GM, Rhiner M, Whitehead C, Fonbuena P, Forman SJ. The meaning of quality of life for bone marrow transplant survivors. Part 2. Improving quality of life for bone marrow transplant survivors. *Cancer Nurs* 1992;15:247–253.
4. Deeg JH, Storb R, Thomas DE. Bone marrow transplantation: a review of delayed complications. *Br J Haematol* 1984;57:185–208.
5. Deeg HJ. Delayed complications and long-term effects after bone marrow transplantation. *Hematol Oncol Clin North Am* 1990;4:641–657.
6. Nims JW, Strom S. Late complications of bone marrow transplant recipients: nursing care issues. *Semin Oncol Nurs* 1988;4:47–54.
7. Kolb HJ, Bender-Gotze C. Late complications after allogenic bone marrow transplantation for leukemia. *Bone Marrow Transplant* 1990; 6:61–72.
8. Sullivan KM, Agura E, Anasetti C, et al. Chronic graft-versus-host disease and other late complications of bone marrow transplantation. *Semin Hematol* 1991;28:250–259.
9. Deeg HJ. Delayed complications of marrow transplantation: results of 1988–1990. *Ann Intern Med* 1992;116:505–512.
10. Sullivan KM, Mori M, Sanders J, et al. Late complications of allogeneic and autologous marrow transplantation. *Bone Marrow Transplant* 1992; 10:127–134.
11. Nims JW. Survivorship and rehabilitation. In: Whedon MN, ed. *Bone marrow transplantation: principles, practice, and nursing insights.* Boston: Jones and Bartlett, 1991:333–345.
12. Lawton CA, Cohen EP, Barber-Derus SW, et al. Late renal dysfunction in adult survivors of bone marrow transplantation. *Cancer* 1991;67: 2795–2800.
13. Buchsel P. Bone marrow transplantation. In: Groenwalk SL, Frogge MH, Goodman M, Yarbro CH, eds. *Cancer nursing. Principles and practice.* Boston: Jones and Bartlett, 1991:320–330.
14. Kolb HJ, Guenther W, Duell T, et al. Cancer after bone marrow transplantation. *Bone Marrow Transplant* 1992;10:135–138.
15. Andrykowski MA, Altmaier EM, Barnett RL, et al. Cognitive dysfunction in adult survivors of allogeneic marrow transplantation: relationship to dose of total body irradiation. *Bone Marrow Transplant* 1990;6:267–276.

16. Wolcott DL, Fawzy FI, Wellisch DK. Psychiatric aspects of bone marrow transplant: a review and current issues. *Psychiatric Med* 1987; 4:299–317.

17. Folsom T, Popkin M. Current and future perspectives on psychiatric involvement in bone marrow transplantation. *Psychiatric Med* 1987; 4:319–328.

18. Brown HN, Kelly MJ. Stages of bone marrow transplantation: a psychiatric perspective. *Psychosom Med* 1976;38:439–446.

19. Gaston-Johansson F, Franco T, Zimmerman L. Pain and psychological distress in patients undergoing autologous bone marrow transplantation. *Oncol Nurs Forum* 1992;19(1):41–48.

20. Gardner CG, August CS, Githens J. Psychological issues in bone marrow transplantation. *Pediatrics* 1977;60:625–631.

21. Haberman MR. Psychosocial aspects of bone marrow transplantation. *Semin Oncol Nurs* 1988;4:55–59.

22. Wolcott DL, Wellisch DK, Fawzy FI, et al. Adaptation of adult bone marrow transplant recipient long-term survivors. *Transplantation* 1986; 41:478–483.

23. Baker F, Curbow B, Wingard JR. Role retention and quality of life of bone marrow transplant survivors. *Soc Sci Med* 1991;32:697–704.

24. Andrykowski MA, Altmaier EM, Barnett RL, et al. The quality of life in adult survivors of allogeneic bone marrow transplantation. Correlates and comparison with matched renal transplant recipients. *Transplantation* 1990;50:399–406.

25. Wingard JR, Curbow B, Baker F, Piantadosi S. Health, functional status, and employment of adult survivors of bone marrow transplantation. *Ann Intern Med* 1991;144:113–118.

26. Haberman M. Quality of life issues for bone marrow transplantation survivors. In: *Proceedings of the bone marrow transplant symposia at the seventh international conference on cancer nursing.* Middlesex, England, Scutari, 1992:22–24.

27. Altmaier EM, Gingrich RD, Fyfe MA. Two-year adjustment of bone marrow transplant survivors. *Bone Marrow Transplant* 1991;7: 311–316.

28. Hengeveld MW, Houtman RB, Zwaan FE. Psychological aspects of bone marrow transplantation: a retrospective study of 17 long-term survivors. *Bone Marrow Transplant* 1988;3:69–75.

29. Chao NJ, Tierney DK, Bloom JR, et al. Dynamic assessment of quality of life after autologous bone marrow transplantation. *Blood* 1990;80: 825–830.

30. Belec RH. Quality of life: perceptions of long-term survivors of bone marrow transplantation. *Oncol Nurs Forum* 1992;19:31–37.

31. Haberman M, Bush N, Young K, Sullivan KM. Quality of life of adult long-term survivors of bone marrow transplantation: a qualitative analysis of narrative data. *Oncol Nurs Forum* 1993;20:1545–1553.

32. Ersek M. The process of maintaining hope in adults undergoing bone marrow transplantation for leukemia. *Oncol Nurs Forum* 1992;19: 883–889.

33. Steeves RH. Patients who have undergone bone marrow transplantation: their quest for meaning. *Oncol Nurs Forum* 1992;19:899–905.

34. Corcoran-Buchsel P. Long-term complications of allogeneic bone marrow transplantation: nursing implications. *Oncol Nurs Forum* 1986; 13:61–70.

35. Winer EP, Sutton LM. Quality of life after bone marrow transplantation. *Oncology* 1994;8(1):19–31.

36. Lenssen P, Sherry ME, Cheney CL, et al. Prevalence of nutrition-related problems among long-term survivors of allogeneic marrow transplantation. *J Am Diet Assoc* 1990;90:835–842.

37. Shiobara S, Nakao S, Yamaguchi M, et al. Complete recovery of sperm production following bone marrow transplantation for leukemia. *Bone Marrow Transplant* 1992;10:313–314.

38. Andrykowski MA, Schmitt FA, Gregg ME, et al. Neuropsychologic impairment in adult bone marrow transplant candidates. *Cancer* 1992; 70:2288–2297.

39. Grant M, Ferrell BR, Schmidt GM, et al. Measurement of quality of life in bone marrow transplantation survivors. *Qual Life Res* 1992; 1:375–384.

40. Bush N, Haberman M, Donaldson CL, et al. Quality of life of 25 adults surviving 6–18 years after bone marrow transplantation. *Social Science Med* March 1995;40(4):479–490.

41. Schmidt GM, Niland JC, Forman SJ, et al. Extended follow-up in 212 long-term allogeneic bone marrow transplant survivors: addressing issues of quality of life. *Transplantation* 1993;55:551–557.

42. Andrykowski MA, Henslee PJ, Barnett RL. Longitudinal assessment of psychosocial functioning of adult survivors of allogeneic bone marrow transplantation. *Bone Marrow Transplant* 1989;4:505–509.

43. Whedon M, Ferrell BR. Quality of life in adult bone marrow transplant patients: beyond the first year. *Semin Oncol Nurs* 1994;10(1):42–57.

44. Whedon MB, ed. *Bone marrow transplantation: principles, practice, and nursing insights.* Boston: Jones and Bartlett, 1991.

Quality of Life and Pharmacoeconomics in Clinical Trials, Second Edition, edited by B. Spilker.
Lippincott-Raven Publishers, Philadelphia © 1996.

CHAPTER 106

Chronic Rheumatic Disorders

Elizabeth W. Karlson, Jeffrey N. Katz, and Matthew H. Liang

INTRODUCTION

More than 100 diverse rheumatic disorders (1) bound together by musculoskeletal complaints result in disability, and reduce quality of life. With few exceptions, their cause is unknown, and primary prevention and cure are not possible. Most forms of arthritis do not shorten life span. For practical purposes, it is useful to think of five common patterns of rheumatic disability: rheumatoid, osteoarthritis, spondylitis, and systemic rheumatic disease and soft tissue disease disabilities.

Rheumatoid disability (rheumatoid arthritis, seronegative polyarthritis, juvenile arthritis, psoriatic arthritis, Reiter's syndrome) results from conditions with polyarticular involvement such as rheumatoid arthritis and juvenile rheumatoid arthritis. Rheumatoid arthritis is the most common chronic inflammatory disease leading to disability. Rheumatoid disability is characterized by multiple joint involvement, chronicity, variable symptoms of disability, and occasional systemic symptoms such as fatigue, fever, and weight loss.

Features of rheumatoid disability are influenced by the person's age and social role. In children, polyarthritis affects biological, psychological, and social growth and development. It may interfere with the attainment of educational and career goals, and the acquisition of skills required for a job and family life. In adolescence it may interfere with

emancipation from parents, interacting with peers, self-esteem, and body image.

Polyarthritis affects the critical issues of early adulthood, which include separation from parents and home, training, career choice, achieving economic independence, peer relationships, and finding a mate. In middle age, polyarthritis may affect career development, raising a family, family relationships, or return to work when children are grown. Polyarthritis in older persons accentuates the aging process and accelerates physical dependency. The deformities associated with chronic arthritis contribute to psychosocial disability and physical limitation.

Osteoarthritis disability, with its involvement of the small joints of the hand or of the weight-bearing joints of the lower extremity and back, is characterized by onset in middle or old age, lack of systemic symptoms, and mono- or pauci-articular involvement.

Osteoarthritis disability unfolds slowly, paralleling the aging process; thus its psychosocial impact is not as prominent as rheumatoid disability. Indeed, many individuals (and physicians) assume that musculoskeletal symptoms from osteoarthritis are an inevitable part of aging. In the oldest old, it is the most common form of chronic arthritis and a major reason for dependence and being homebound.

Spondylitis disability (e.g., ankylosing spondylitis, spondylitis associated with psoriasis, inflammatory bowel disease, juvenile arthritis, Reiter's syndrome, etc.) is characterized by stiffness or restrictive movement of the spine, with occasional involvement of the peripheral joints, most commonly the shoulder, hip, or knee. The disability is characterized by male predominance, onset in young and middle-age adults, and by the episodic nature of the peripheral arthritis.

E. W. Karlson, J. N. Katz, and M. H. Liang: Departments of Rheumatology/Immunology and Medicine, Harvard Medical School, Brigham and Women's Hospital, Robert B. Brigham Multipurpose Arthritis and Musculoskeletal Diseases Center, Boston, Massachusetts 02115.

Spondylitis disability is generally compatible with good function except severe cases of spinal involvement or when it involves peripheral joints, in which case it can affect mobility. Usually physical mobility and independence are maintained. Spondylitis in young adult males may affect self-esteem, body image, leisure activities, and peer relationships, particularly in the exercise and physique-conscious milieu of our society.

Systemic rheumatic disease disability is illustrated by the functional problems from systemic rheumatic diseases such as systemic lupus erythematosus, scleroderma, Sjögren's syndrome or disease, polymyositis, vasculitis, and some patients with rheumatoid arthritis. Except for the latter, arthralgias are more common than arthritis and much of the disability is due to other organ involvement such as lung or heart, or from constitutional symptoms such as fatigue and decreased endurance. These disabilities affect work capacity and socialization. Self-esteem and body image may be impaired by medications such as steroids which produce Cushingoid features and facial hair in high doses or the disease process itself (e.g., tight skin and contractures of the joint seen in scleroderma). Additional problems include the sense of stigmatization and victimization from having a rare disease, and the fear of relapse or death.

Soft tissue disorder disability is characterized by regional pain as in tendinitis, regional pain and paresthesias as in nerve entrapment or generalized pain associated with fatigue as in fibromyalgia. These conditions have high prevalence. Regional syndromes may be work related and there is a risk of chronic disability and interference with both work and recreational activities.

Rheumatic disorders, therefore, vary in their clinical expression, yet each has a major effect on function and the medical management is directed toward preserving and restoring function. In 1949 the American Rheumatism Association Functional Classes were developed (2). Since then, hundreds of ad hoc, nonstandardized, loosely defined assessments of activities of daily living have been used by clinicians. In 1977, attempts to assess health status or quality of life by questionnaires expanded tremendously. A wealth of descriptive literature exists on the psychometrics of these instruments, and their application to clinical trials is commonplace. It is our goal to review the work done in measuring function and health status in the rheumatic and musculoskeletal diseases, some conceptual limitations to their use, and future research directions.

DEFINITIONS

The terms used in describing the impact of arthritis on the individual can be defined as follows. *Impairment* is demonstrable anatomic loss or damage, a physiologic state. Examples include a limited range of motion or a number of inflamed joints. An impairment may or may not cause functional

limitations. For instance, a patient with a loss of 10° of elbow extension without other joint impairment usually will not have problems dressing or feeding. *Disability* is the functional limitation caused by an impairment that interferes with what a patient needs or wants to do. Physical *function* is the complex integrated physical ability dependent on physical integrity of the joints and an intact neuromotor system to perform tasks needed for activities of daily living, that is to care for oneself, to play, to work, and so forth. When the activities of daily living concept is extended beyond essential activities in the home and community, the term instrumental activities of daily living is used. These include using a telephone, shopping for groceries, etc. The lack of ability to do instrumental activities of daily living suggests a need for special services. *Health status* or *quality of life,* an ephemeral concept, embodies the dimensions of physical, social, and emotional function. *Functional status* is a subset of health status that refers specifically to physical functioning.

Function is a complex phenomenon. Disability for an individual arises when there is a discrepancy between ability and need, when one's capabilities are not sufficient for independence. This is dependent on whether there is an actual or perceived need for a specific function, a patient's expectations, his/her motivation, and the support system. Function changes over the course of people's development in terms of what they are capable of doing and what they wish or need to do. In children and adolescents, rapid change and maturation of cognitive, behavioral, emotional, and psychological function are the rule, whereas in adult life, those capacities are stable but life circumstances are changing.

HEALTH STATUS AND QUALITY OF LIFE MEASUREMENT

The instruments for measuring health status or quality of life (Table 1) cover a variety of dimensions of health, including physical, social, and emotional functioning. Some instruments are general health status measures that have been applied to rheumatic disorders (4–6). Others are measures developed for rheumatic diseases, particularly rheumatoid arthritis, the most prevalent chronic polyarthritis (7–14). Measures of function emphasizing those affected by arthritis of the spine are available (15,16). Only one instrument assesses patient priorities (12). Only one assesses patient satisfaction with their functional level (10). Even with these gaps, a diverse literature demonstrates the potential of health status measurement both in clinical work and as a research tool. General health status measures are useful in health policy research when comparisons are made across diseases regarding outcome or cost effectiveness for the purposes of resource utilization. Disease-specific instruments assess within-subject change in health status over time and are useful for measuring clinically important changes in response to treatments (17).

TABLE 1. *Quality of life and health status measures in systemic rheumatic disease: selected examples*

General
  Sickness Impact Profile (SIP) (4)
  Quality of Well-Being (QWB) (6)
  McMaster Health Index Questionnaire (MHIQ) (7)

Arthritis specific
  Arthritis Impact Measurement Scales (AIMS) (8)
  Health Assessment Questionnaire (HAQ) (9)
  Functional Status Index (FSI) (11)
  MACTAR Questionnaire (12)
  Lee Functional Status Instrument (13)
  Toronto Functional Capacity Questionnaire (14)

These newer instruments are as reliable as traditional measures of improvement in clinical status, such as traditional measures used in rheumatic diseases (based on anthropometric approaches or laboratory tests such as 25-yard walk time or erythrocyte sedimentation rate). Health status instruments are interchangeable in their ability to measure major clinically significant improvement, but have varying ability to demonstrate changes in subdimensions such as social and global function (18–20). Other studies indicate that measures of function or health status predict mortality and correlate with utilization of health services (21,22). A simple functional questionnaire is an economic and efficient technique for case finding and has been applied in developing countries for diagnosis of community burden (23).

General Measures

The Sickness Impact Profile (SIP) contains 136 items on patient status (4). Questions are answered true or false. Scores for items use predetermined weights based on rater panel estimates of relative severity of the dysfunction. Three of the categories (ambulation, body care, and mobility) may be aggregated into a physical dimension; and four categories (emotional behavior, social interaction, alertness behavior, and communication) may be aggregated into a psychosocial dimension. Five categories are independent (work, sleep and rest, eating, home management, and recreation and pastimes). The Sickness Impact Profile is available in a self-administered form or can be administered in an interview. It requires up to 30 minutes to complete as an interview. Some investigators have eliminated two to three of the least relevant subscales to decrease the respondent's burden (24,25). It has been validated in a number of disorders, including arthritis. A total score is computed by summing categories and then standardizing to a percentage of the maximum. The instrument may accurately reflect change for groups of arthritis patients but appears to be relatively insensitive to changes in individual patients (26).

The Quality of Well-Being (QWB) (5) and its earlier version the Index of Well-Being (6) evaluate mobility, physi-

cal activity, and social activity. An interviewer determines what the patient did and did not do because of illness during the last 6 days. Scoring for particular levels of function is based on preference weights derived from normals and has been validated in rheumatoid arthritis patients (5). The interview requires a trained assessor, and takes 20 minutes to complete. The instrument has been validated, but may not be as sensitive as other measures to changes seen in patient status during a clinical trial in rheumatoid arthritis (19). Major limitations are the complexity of the instrument and the requirement for a specially trained interviewer. In Oregon, the QWB has been used in a major public policy debate to prioritize health services covered by Medicare.

The McMaster Health Index Questionnaire measures the quality of life in patients with rheumatoid disease (7). It measures physical function in physical activities, self-care activities, mobility, communication, and global physical activity. A social index combines general well-being, work performance, material welfare, support and participation with friends and family, and global social function. The emotional index measures feelings about personal relationships, self-esteem, thoughts concerning the future, critical life events, and global emotional function. It contains 59 items, is self-administered, and takes about 15 to 20 minutes to complete.

Arthritis-Specific Measures

The Arthritis Impact Measurement Scales (AIMS), a health status or quality of life instrument developed for rheumatoid arthritis, has 48 multiple-choice questions with nine subscales measuring physical, social, and mental health status (8). The possible range of scores on each subscale is 0 to 10; subscale results are averaged to obtain a total score. The scale is self-administered and takes 15 to 20 minutes to complete, and has been used in a number of studies on rheumatic disease. The AIMS2 is a revised and expanded version of the AIMS that takes approximately 20 minutes to complete. It has a standardized format, three new scales measuring arm function, work, and support from family and friends, and a problem attribution section with yes/no questions. Its reliability and internal validity have been demonstrated in a cross-sectional study, but its sensitivity to change has not been tested (27). The AIMS has also been adapted for use in the elderly as the GERI-AIMS, designed to discriminate between arthritis-specific and general functional impairment (28). Although reliable and valid, the GERI-AIMS has not been widely used.

The Health Assessment Questionnaire (HAQ) (9), a self-administered instrument, exists in two formats, a short form that requires 3 minutes to complete, and a longer version requiring 20 minutes. The short form is composed of 24 questions on activities of daily living and mobility. The answers to the short form yield a summated index between 0 and 3 on a continuous scale. The questionnaire is a validated instrument that has been used in a clinical trial of rheumatoid arthritis (19), and was incorporated into the 2nd National Health and Nutrition Examination Study. It is a predictor of health services utilization (21). The longer version adds additional questions relating to pain, global severity, income, job change, cost of medical care, and side effects of therapy.

The Functional Status Index (FSI) measures dependence, pain, and difficulty experienced in the performance of 18 activities of daily living grouped under 5 headings: mobility, hand activities, personal care, home chores, and interpersonal activities (11). Each activity is rated between 0 and 4 on each dimension. Studies on patients with rheumatoid arthritis show validity and a high degree of interobserver reliability. In self-assessed format, it takes 10 to 20 minutes to complete.

The McMaster Toronto Arthritis Patient Preference Disability Questionnaire (MACTAR) was developed for use in clinical trials in rheumatoid arthritis (12). Using a semi-structured interview, patients are asked to designate key functional activities based on their own preferences, and the five activities that rank highest are evaluated. At the end of a study period patients are asked if their ability to perform the ranked activities has improved, worsened, or stayed the same. This technique may be more sensitive to small changes when compared with conventional standardized questionnaires. The problems in evaluating each patient in a different way are formidable, and this approach requires further investigation.

The Toronto Functional Capacity Questionnaire assesses function in personal care, upper extremity activities, mobility, work, and leisure activities (14). The instrument is administered by an interviewer and requires approximately 10 minutes to complete. Weighting of responses is based on preferences derived from panels of occupational and physical therapists and rheumatologists. Reliability and validity have been demonstrated. The instrument has been shown to be sensitive to change in clinical trials (12).

Short Forms

One disadvantage of the instruments described above is their length; most require at least 15 to 20 minutes to complete. This becomes burdensome if general health status is measured along with disease-specific measures in a study and may be a problem in daily practice. Shorter measures have been developed that appear to retain the desirable psychometric properties of the longer instruments (Table 2).

Several short generic health status measures are available. The 36-item short form, SF-36, was derived from a larger battery of questions administered in the Medical Outcomes Study (29). The SF-36 has 36 multiple choice questions aggregated into eight subscales: physical function, social support, role function, pain, mental health, emotional problems, vitality and general health. It can be self-administered or administered by a trained interviewer. In studies of total

TABLE 2. *Short forms*

General
  SF-36 (29)
  Functional Status Questionnaire (FSQ) (30)
  Nottingham Health Profile (32)

Arthritis specific
  Convery Polyarticular Disability Index (33)
  Modified Health Assessment Questionnaire (MHAQ) (10)
  Shortened version of the Arthritis Impact Measurement Scale (36)

hip replacement and arthroscopic meniscectomy we find it easily understood by patients and sensitive to improvement following surgery. Its sensitivity to change and validity for use in rheumatoid arthritis has not been demonstrated.

The Functional Status Questionnaire (FSQ) was developed to measure health status quickly in the outpatient general medicine setting (30). The FSQ has 34 items with subscales for physical, psychological and social/role function and requires 10 to 20 minutes to complete. This instrument is reliable, valid and sensitive to clinical change following total hip replacement (31).

The Nottingham Health Profile (NHP) and its earlier version the Nottingham Health Index (NHI) are intended to give a brief measure of perceived physical, social and emotional health (32). The NHP is similar to the SIP, except that the NHP asks about feelings and emotional states directly, rather than by changes in behavior, and emphasizes the respondent's subjective assessment of his or her health. The NHP contains 38 items encompassing six dimensions: energy, pain, physical mobility, emotional reactions, sleep and social isolation and takes under 10 minutes to complete. It has been validated for use in rheumatoid arthritis where the pain and mobility scales were correlated with clinical measures of disease activity. It was shown to correlate highly with the AIMS in the pain, physical mobility, and depression/anxiety subscales.

The Modified Health Assessment Questionnaire (MHAQ) is an arthritis-specific short form of proven reliability, validity, sensitivity to clinical change and prognostic utility (10). The MHAQ evaluates physical function through questions derived from the HAQ and adds new scales for change in function, satisfaction and pain in the performance of each of these activities. It can be completed in less than 5 minutes. While the MHAQ was not responsive to the beneficial effect of methotrexate in RA in one large study (34), it has been demonstrated to predict important outcomes such as morbidity, mortality and costs (35,36).

The 48-item AIMS has been reduced to a short form with 18 items by selecting two items with highest internal consistency and correlation with the total scale score from each of the nine AIMS subscales (37). The reliability, validity and sensitivity of this measure in clinical research have not been tested adequately to date.

Short health status forms offer the promise of decreasing respondent burden in clinical research and integrating health status measurement into clinical practice. The SF-36 has become the dominant instrument used in outcome measurement and research on diverse medical and surgical conditions. The SF-36 has few items relevant to upper extremity function and therefore should be supplemented with disease-specific questions for use in rheumatoid arthritis. Although shorter instruments are desirable, sensitivity is probably greater for the longer instruments.

LIMITATION OF QUALITY OF LIFE MEASURES

Selecting the measures for use in a clinical trial is like making a bet; it is an attempt to anticipate and measure the multiple dimensions of health and the consequences of therapies prescribed. To some degree the instruments listed are interchangeable but as discussed above, the dimensions covered by each instrument vary and have differential sensitivity to change. Sensitivity is the ability of an instrument to detect any change and instruments have been compared in this property by a number of statistical techniques. Responsiveness, the ability to measure a clinically important or meaningful change has had comparatively much less study.

When studied, multidimensional instruments or subscales of these instruments have floors or ceilings in their capacity to detect change, and this relates to the subject's baseline score and the number of items or gradations of change that address one end or the other of the continuum of function observed (38).

Nearly all of the instruments have been developed and tested in adults with rheumatoid arthritis and, as such, the experience with other arthritis conditions is somewhat limited. The HAQ and AIMS have been used in osteoarthritis and total joint replacement (31,39). The reliability and validity in the very young or very old has not been demonstrated. The AIMS, for instance, must be used with care in children (40). Instruments developed in one setting need modification when used in another culture (41).

Not all costs and benefits of interventions are measurable or predictable. We spend a great deal of energy deciding what items should be included in a questionnaire, but we cannot anticipate the complete consequences of an intervention in the short or long run. There are many examples in the rheumatic diseases to illustrate that outcomes require continued assessment. Corticosteroids for rheumatoid arthritis improved patients' sense of well-being and reduced synovitis dramatically, but it was not until a decade after the introduction of steroids that patients suffered considerable morbidity and mortality from excess steroid therapy. Quality of life in patients treated with steroids shows major improvement in the first few months of therapy. However, the instruments we have might not capture the disfiguring effects of steroids which distress so many patients, nor the disability from steroid-induced fractures.

Function is relative. Psychometrically sound instruments assume that function can be measured in all patients with the same instrument. However, patients' function is relative to their age, sex, motivation, social supports, priorities, and goals, and to their needs for daily living, work, and recreation. Because function is relative, a small change in an individual's function may make a lot of difference. The small change may be totally adequate for the person's needs, yet not meet statistical norms. Investigators have developed preference weighted measures to better capture patient priorities but whether the greater resources required to administer these measures results in sufficiently improved validity or responsiveness remains largely unexplored.

Covering a range of functional activities in a comprehensive questionnaire provides breadth at the sacrifice of depth. The measurement of specific functions in questionnaires is too crude for monitoring patients. For example, function of the carpal metacarpal joint may be assessed by a question on difficulty with fastening buttons or doing zippers. The hand surgeon needs to measure and detect more subtle change that might be more appropriately derived from measurement of grip and pinch strength and standardized dexterity measures. Self-reported symptoms and function do not necessarily correlate with objective impairments (42,43), underscoring the need to use both types of measures.

Questionnaires cannot make a specific etiologic diagnosis or replace a clinical evaluation of the subtle, interrelated components of function such as motivation, neuromuscular competency, cognitive ability, joint integrity, availability of environmental modifications and social supports, and the like. Also, self-reported function can be unreliable and can overestimate or underreport observed performance (23,44). Even with reliable responses, the information is too general to be useful in the individual patient. For example, in a patient with difficulty walking, the problem may be due to motivation, pain (structural or inflammatory or both), muscle strength, impairment of the nervous system, instability of the joint, and more.

Another limitation of health status questionnaires is the unresolved issue of whether each item should be weighted equally. From a clinical perspective, not all activities of daily living are equal for a patient, and the technology of deriving weights leaves the clinician dissatisfied.

Willingness-to-pay as a method for eliciting preferences in rheumatic disease, in our experience, has had response rates of less than 50% (45,46). We feel this is because patients cannot understand the task, are hostile to the type of question, or have little idea of how much is spent on specific health care items. On the other hand, a modified time-trade-off was administered effectively by telephone to an older group with hip arthritis (47).

The preferences of a group may not be those of the individual. Inasmuch as function is relative, so are values placed on it. The preferences expressed by healthy, reasonable individuals are not those of the sick and the anxious. Educational status and age also influence patient preferences (47). Preferences of the sick and anxious do not remain constant during the vicissitudes of rheumatic illnesses which are characterized by chronicity and an unpredictable waxing and waning course. Values change with time, and experiences of illness or personal circumstances change because people learn, adjust, or accommodate over the course of illness. No system for patient preference measurement takes into account this dynamic state.

The analysis of patient preference in decision making fails to address the "confusion" and sense of crisis which is part of the illness experience. Whereas some patients see their illness experience as an area in which they can and should exert control of their fate, many do not wish to take responsibility for determining their "fate" by expressing preference.

SELECTION OF APPROPRIATE MEASURES FOR CLINICAL STUDIES

The goal of medical care is to do no harm, to relieve pain and suffering, and to improve and maintain one's physical, social, and emotional function. Thus, any evaluation of an intervention, whether it is medication, surgery, or a program with elements of these, should examine if these goals are achieved and to what extent. Some interventions relieve symptoms and improve function promptly, whereas others may take time or require that a patient be rehabilitated from some stable level of function. In the same light, known and unknown negative effects can occur immediately or as a delayed or cumulative consequence. For a medical intervention designed to treat a root cause or primary mechanism of joint destruction, such as synovitis, one should see evidence of improved inflammation. To the degree that psychosocial dysfunction results from the rheumatic condition, one would expect improvement of these parameters. However, prolonged psychological symptoms or innate traits are not likely to be helped by attention to synovitis alone. In fact, a discrepancy between one's perceived function and objective signs of disease is often a clue that there is something else going on that needs attention.

General health status measures are preferred to arthritis-specific ones for questions of health policy in which decision makers must allocate resources to different conditions. The use of such scales in a clinical trial can help the investigator relate the findings to other diseases and the policy maker to understand the trade-offs in resource allocation. The use of a general health status measure may not capture the specific outcomes seen in a disorder. The best approach is to examine each item to determine if there is sufficient coverage of all relevant dimensions for a specific disorder, if these items are sufficiently scaled to spread out individuals on a continuum, and if the items are possibly symptoms seen as part of the disease complex. On this latter point, depression and inability to get going in the morning are frequently seen in inflammatory arthritis such as rheumatoid arthritis; this cannot be considered a specifically psychoaffective symptom. There is temptation to take a scale from a general measure to be used in a specific study. Authors of instruments recoil at the thought and would argue from a psychometric point of view that disaggregating the scale will not insure reliability or validity. This is particularly true if the index results in one score; omitting a subscale will not allow one to compute the score.

Arthritis-specific scales usually provide better coverage of dimensions of health thought to be important in a particular condition. The advantage of using an arthritis-specific scale is that clinicians may have a better sense of what changes on the scale mean, and they may have been used in other studies for comparison. All health status measures measure a broad number of variables but not in any great depth. A glance at the nine-volume *Mental Measurements Yearbook* shows countless scales for any psychoaffective symptom, all of which have been tested for reliability and validity. Unfortunately, sophisticated scales to measure any specific psychological trait or symptom may be too long for application in a clinical trial where a host of independent variables are being measured.

In selecting measures for clinical trials in rheumatic conditions, specifically inflammatory arthritis, one needs to have a detailed clinical understanding of the range of benefits and adverse reactions that might be expected, and to get the best measure for each of the positive and negative attributes of the intervention. Traditional anthropometric measures should be supplemented by measures of physical function and health status. The battery should include a general health status measure if the results are to be used in health policy. If available, a disease-specific health status measure such as the Arthritis Impact Measurement Scale, the Modified Health Assessment Questionnaire, or the Health Assessment Questionnaire should also be used. The evaluation should include some measure of whether patients are satisfied with their state and global evaluations of whether they experience a change, the importance of the change to them, and whether the treatment was worth it considering all the positive effects on disease and negative effects, and the effort required for monitoring the drug or following the recommendations of the prescription.

Indirect and direct costs should be evaluated after efficacy has been determined. The most expensive portion of health care is hospitalization or institution-based care followed by diagnostic tests, radiographs, drugs, and so on. Health care costs paid for by insurance or out-of-pocket are poorly remembered and there should be validation against objective data. Hospital costs should include information on length of stay and cost based on some relative value scale rather than charges that are idiosyncratic and variable from region to region. Hospitalization rates and length of stay are biased by recent changes in health financing and may not reflect clinical necessity.

We have used and compared the Sickness Impact Profile, Index of Well-Being, Functional Status Index, Arthritis Impact Measurement Scale, and Modified Health Assessment Questionnaire in a variety of descriptive and evaluative studies. In addition, using joint replacement surgery as a model, we have studied the performance and relative measurement sensitivity of these instruments (20). All the instruments correlated highly with one another and demonstrated change. We found that of the five instruments, the Functional Status Index had the most missing data. The Arthritis Impact Measurement Scale, Functional Status Index, and Sickness Impact Profile were equally efficient in detecting improvement in mobility, but the Health Assessment Questionnaire and Index of Well-Being were about a half as efficient as the other three instruments. For pain evaluation, the Arthritis Impact Measurement Scale was more sensitive than the Health Assessment Questionnaire. The Index of Well-Being and Sickness Impact Profile do not have a pain subscale. With regard to social function the Sickness Impact Profile, Index of Well-Being, and Health Assessment Questionnaire were more sensitive than the Arthritis Impact Measurement Scale. For global function the Sickness Impact Profile, Arthritis Impact Measurement Scale, and Index of Well-Being were more efficient than the Functional Status Index or Health Assessment Questionnaire. We also studied relative sensitivity to change, or responsiveness of one long health status measure, the AIMS and 4 short health status measures, the SF-36, FSQ, MHAQ and shortened AIMS. The short measures were as sensitive to change in the global dimension as the SIP and all but the shortened AIMS were sensitive to change in the physical dimension (31).

From a practical point of view the Index of Well-Being is an arduous questionnaire to administer, somewhat counterintuitive and artificial for patients, and requires resources to train interviewers. However, it has the advantage of being a ratio scale with a true zero point (which is not terribly relevant in rheumatic diseases, in general), thus making it the best instrument for calculating quality-adjusted life-years, a prerequisite for cost-benefit studies. In a controlled drug trial in rheumatoid arthritis, it displayed the smallest change of the techniques used to measure change (19). The omission of pain as a dimension makes it less desirable as a single instrument in rheumatic disorders since pain is a central concern for patients (48,49).

The Sickness Impact Profile is much easier to understand by patients, is self-administered, and has been used in numerous rheumatic disorders. It results in one score. It has dichotomous response categories which are less responsive than multi-item responses. It contains questions related to continence and communication which are not relevant to rheumatic disorders.

The Functional Status Index enables a patient to disaggregate their function along three dimensions of dependence, pain, and difficulty experienced. This is not always understood or possible for patients. In elderly patients, there was poor compliance and response rates with this question (50). We found the same in a study of patients undergoing total joint arthroplasty (20).

The Arthritis Impact Measurement Scale is convenient to use and of the arthritis scales is probably the most widely used next to the Modified Health Assessment Questionnaire or Health Assessment Questionnaire in published studies. The latest version, AIMS2 is improved still. The Modified Health Assessment Questionnaire is convenient and assesses patient satisfaction with their level of functioning. The SF-36 and FSQ are easy for patients to complete, take less time than longer measures, are highly responsive to change and sensitive to disability in OA and TJR (31,51).

Because there are no perfect measures of function or health status, careful consideration of likely outcomes and which instruments provide the best coverage is necessary. Multiple measures and serial assessment of outcome using different approaches, such as combining questionnaires with open-ended interviews about the same outcome, may be necessary when the sensitivity of an instrument is unknown. No instrument will help a weak study design. Thus, blinded evaluation, randomization, and definition of ''meaningful'' effect are essential.

FUTURE DIRECTIONS

Questionnaires quantitatively measure physical function and health status in rheumatic disease patients. Their limitations are inherent to their form and attempt to circumscribe a boundless and sometimes amorphous dimension of impact on the average patient. Development of such instrumentation has gone as far as it can except perhaps for developing specific items for different types of rheumatic disease disability. Evaluating patient priorities and their satisfaction with their state provides additional areas for future research, but we are nearly there. Evaluating the techniques of assessing sensitivity and developing a coherent conceptual framework and methods for evaluating responsiveness or clinical importance of a change score should be a major priority if we are to bring instruments that are of great research utility into normal clinical practice. Ultimately, if patient care and outcome are to be improved, attention to function must be incorporated in the daily practice, and tools for its screening, follow-up, and diagnosis need to be developed. It is likely that these will come from improved understanding of epidemiology of function in the rheumatic diseases, the natural course of functional decline, and if, in fact, there are critical points at which intervention might make a difference.

To know a functional problem exists is only the start, and physicians at all levels need to have improved understanding of where and what can be done to improve function. Recent attempts to more equitably reimburse physicians for cognitive work will certainly create some incentive for this. Trials of the impact of functional status data on clinicians' decision making have been disappointing (52–54), indicating that much work remains to be done before this technology of functional status assessment is successfully transferred to the clinic. McVey performed a randomized controlled trial (RCT) of multiple health status instruments in conjunction with a geriatric consultation team who performed a multidimensional evaluation and made specific recommendations and was unable to show significant improvements in functional status between cases and controls (52). Rubenstein conducted an RCT of the FSQ with an educational intervention directed at internists (53). Although most physicians considered the functional status evaluation useful, there were no changes in functional status in either the cases or controls. Kazis studied the use of the AIMS and the HAQ when provided to rheumatologists during routine office visits in patients with stable rheumatoid arthritis (54). Health status information had no effect on either the process or the outcome of care. The reason for lack of improvement in functional status in these studies may have been the stability of disease in subjects and the timing of when the information was provided. In fact, most control subjects had little change in functional status over the course of the studies.

CONCLUSIONS

Increasingly, policy makers are looking to health status measurement as a way to assess the quality of care delivered by individual physicians or institutions. Mortality rates are too insensitive and likely reflect case-mix rather than physician or institution performance. Health status measures are reliable, valid, and may be more sensitive to differences. Validity, however, is a property specific to a particular characteristic an instrument is designed to measure. Health status measures demonstrate patient improvement in studies of the clinical efficacy of total joint replacement surgery and of certain medications. None of the measures, however, have been shown to be valid indicators of physician or institution performance. There is considerable anxiety among clinicians regarding the use of health status measures as indicators of quality; we advocate added study of this critical issue.

Even if changes in health status correlate with an independent assessment of the quality of care, careful interpretation is required. Much of the dysfunction identified in health status measures (e.g., social function) involves a complex interaction between disease process and the environment. How broad is the physicians' mandate to intervene in these spheres, and how accountable are physicians or institutions for reversing these impairments?

We feel that the most valuable aspect of health status measures is their ability to capture the human condition. It is acknowledged that social and emotional function, and the interplay between impairment and needs, are critical to patients. At issue, among other things, is whether physicians can be held accountable for problems that stem from diverse causes, for problems resulting from innate personality characteristics, or for reckless health behavior such as excess alcohol or smoking.

Many aspects of health status, function, and preferences will not surrender to multivariate techniques. Improved patient evaluation must become more quantitative, but functional and health status questionnaires, provide the vocabulary without the richness, the nuance. Statistics are normative and the emphasis is on similarities; patient care emphasizes differences. Psychometric approaches alone are not miscible with individual patient care, but the interaction between the two domains is a necessary and desirable goal for all we seek to accomplish with clinical investigation.

ACKNOWLEDGMENTS

We gratefully acknowledge the expert assistance of Jacqueline Mazzie and Mary Scamman, in the preparation of this manuscript.

REFERENCES

1. Classification of the rheumatic diseases. In: Schumacher HR, ed. *Primer on the rheumatic diseases*. Atlanta: Arthritis Foundation, 1993: 81–83.
2. Steinbrocker O, Traeger CH, Battman RC. Therapeutic criteria in rheumatoid arthritis. *JAMA* 1949;140:659–662.
3. Liang MH, Jette AM. Measuring functional ability in chronic arthritis: a critical review. *Arthritis Rheum* 1981;24:80–86.
4. Bergner M, Bobbitt RA, Pollard WE, Martin DP, Gilson BS. The Sickness Impact Profile: validation of a health status measure. *Med Care* 1976;14:57–67.
5. Balaban DJ, Sagi PC, Goldfarb NI, Nettler S. Weights for scoring the quality of well-being (QWB) instrument among rheumatoid arthritis: a comparison to general population weights. *Med Care* 1986;24: 973–980.
6. Kaplan RM, Bush JW, Berry CC. Health status: types of validity for an index of well-being. *Health Serv Res* 1976;11:478–507.
7. Chambers LW, MacDonald LA, Tugwell P, et al. The McMaster Health Index Questionnaire as a measure of quality of life for patients with rheumatoid disease. *J Rheumatol* 1982;9:780–784.
8. Meenan RF, Gertman PM, Mason JH. Measuring health status in arthritis: the Arthritis Impact Measurement Scales. *Arthritis Rheum* 1980;23:146–152.
9. Fries JF, Spitz P, Kraines RG, Holman HR. Measurement of patient outcome in arthritis. *Arthritis Rheum* 1980;23:137–145.
10. Pincus T, Summey JA, Soraci SA Jr, Wallston KA, Hummon NP. Assessment of patient satisfaction in activities of daily living using a modified Stanford Health Assessment Questionnaire. *Arthritis Rheum* 1983;26:1346–1353.
11. Jette AM. Functional Status Index: reliability of a chronic disease evaluation instrument. *Arch Phys Med Rehabil* 1980;61:395–401.
12. Tugwell P, Bombardier C, Buchanon WW, Goldsmith CH, Grace E. The MACTAR Questionnaire—an individualized functional priority approach for assessing improvement in physical disability in clinical trials in rheumatoid arthritis. *J Rheumatol* 1987;14:446–451.
13. Lee P, Jasani MK, Dick WC, Buchanan WW. Evaluation of a functional index in rheumatoid arthritis. *Scand J Rheumatol* 1973;2:71–77.
14. Helewa A, Goldsmith CH, Smyth HA. Independent measurement of functional capacity in rheumatoid arthritis. *J Rheumatol* 1982;9:794–797.
15. Dougados M, Gueguen A, Nakache J-P, Nguyen M, Mery C, Amor B. Evaluation of a functional index and an articular index in ankylosing spondylitis. *J Rheumatol* 1988;15:302–307.

16. Daltroy LH, Larson MG, Roberts WN, Liang MH. A modification of the Health Assessment Questionnaire for the spondyloarthropathies. [published erratum appears in *J Rheumatol* 1991;18(2):305]. *J Rheumatol* 1990;17(7):946–950.

17. Patrick DL, Deyo RA. Generic and disease-specific measures in assessing health status and quality of life. *Med Care* 1989;27(suppl 3):S217–S232.

18. Meenan RF, Anderson JJ, Kazis LE, Egger MJ, Altz-Smith M, Samuelson CO Jr, Willkens RF, Solsky MA, Haynes SP, Blocka KL, Weinstein A, Guttadauria M, Kaplan SB, Klippel J. Outcome assessment in clinical trials: evidence for the sensitivity of a health status measure. *Arthritis Rheum* 1984;27:1344–1352.

19. Bombardier C, Ware J, Russell IJ, Larson M, Chalmers A, Read JL, the Auranofin Cooperating Group. Auranofin therapy and quality of life in patients with rheumatoid arthritis: results of a multicenter trial. *Am J Med* 1986;81:565–578.

20. Liang MH, Larson MG, Cullen KE, Schwartz JA. Comparative measurement efficiency and sensitivity of five health status instruments for arthritis research. *Arthritis Rheum* 1985;28:542–547.

21. McNevitt MC, Yelin EH, Henke CJ, Epstein WV. Risk factors for hospitalization and surgery for rheumatoid arthritis: implications for capitated medical payments. *Ann Intern Med* 1986;105:421–428.

22. Mitchell DM, Spitz PW, Young DY, et al. Survival, prognosis, and causes of death in rheumatoid arthritis. *Arthritis Rheum* 1986;29:706–714.

23. Liang MH, Phillips E, Scamman M, Lurye CS, Keith A, Cohen L, Taylor G. Evaluation of a pilot program for rheumatic disability in an urban community. *Arthritis Rheum* 1981;24:937–943.

24. Liang MH, Katz JN, Phillips C, Sledge C, Cats-Baril W. The AAOS total hip arthroplasty outcome form: results of a nominal group process. *J Bone Joint Surg* 1991;73A:639–46.

25. Deyo RA, Walsh NE, Martin DC, Schoenfeld LS, Ramamurthy S. A controlled trial of transcutaneous electrical nerve stimulation (TENS) and exercise for chronic low back pain. *N Engl J Med* 1990;322:1627–1634.

26. Deyo RA, Inui TS. Towards clinical applications of health status measures: sensitivity of scales to clinically important changes. *Health Serv Res* 1984;19:275–289.

27. Meenan RF, Mason JH, Anderson JJ, Guccione AA, Kazis LE. AIMS2. *Arthritis Rheum* 1992;35(1):1–10.

28. Hughes SL, Edelman P, Chang RW, Singer RH, Shuette P. The GERI-AIMS. *Arthritis Rheum* 1991;34:856–866.

29. Ware JE Jr, Sherbourne CD. The MOS 36-item short-form health survey (SF-36). A conceptual framework and item selection. *Med Care* 1992;30(6):473–483.

30. Jette AM, Davies AR, Cleary PD, et al. The Functional Status Questionnaire: reliability and validity when used in primary care. *J Gen Intern Med* 1986;1:143–149.

31. Katz JN, Larson MG, Phillips CB, Fossel AH, Liang MH. Comparative measurement sensitivity of short and longer health status measures. *Med Care* 1992;30:917–25.

32. Fitzpatrick R, Ziebland S, Jenkinson C, Mowat A, Mowat A. A generic health status instrument in the assessment of rheumatoid arthritis. *Br J Rheum* 1992;31:87–90.

33. Convery FR, Minteer MA, Amiel D, Connett KL. Polyarticular disability: a functional assessment. *Arch Phys Med Rehabil* 1977;58:494–499.

34. Weinblatt ME, Kaplan H, Germain BF, Merriman RC, Solomon SD, Wall B, Anderson L, Block S, Irby R, Wolfe F, et al. Low dose methotrexate compared with auranofin in adult rheumatoid arthritis. A thirty-six week, double-blind trial. *Arthritis Rheum* 1990;33:330–338.

35. Pincus T, Callahan LF, Sale WG, Brooks AL, Payne LE, Vaughn WK. Severe functional declines, work disability, and increased mortality in seventy-five rheumatoid arthritis patients studied over nine years. *Arthritis Rheum* 1984;27:864–872.

36. Pincus T, Brooks RH, Callahan LF. Prediction of long-term mortality in patients with rheumatoid arthritis according to simple questionnaire and joint count measures. *Ann Intern Med* 1994;120:26–34.

37. Wallston KA, Brown GK, Stein MJ, Dobbins CJ. Comparing the short and long versions of the Arthritis Impact Measurement Scales. *J Rheumatol* 1989;16:1105–1109.

38. Stucki G, Daltroy LH, Katz JN, Johannesson M, Liang MH. Interpretation of change scores in ordinal clinical states and health status measures (submitted).

39. Bradley JD, Brandt KD, Katz BP, Kalasinski LA, Ryan SI. Comparison of an antiinflammatory dose of ibuprofen, an analgesic dose of ibuprofen, and acetaminophen in the treatment of patients with osteoarthritis of the knee. *N Engl J Med* 1991;325:87–91.

40. Coulton CJ, Zborowsky E, Lipton J, et al. Assessment of the reliability and validity of the Arthritis Impact Measurement Scales for children with juvenile arthritis. *Arthritis Rheum* 1987;30:819–824.

41. Kirwan JR, Reeback JS. Stanford Health Assessment Questionnaire modified to assess disability in British patients with rheumatoid arthritis. *Br J Rheum* 1986;25:206–209.

42. Katz JN, Larsen MG, Sabra A, Krarup C, Stirrat CR, Sethi R, Eaton HM, Fossel AH, Liang MH. Carpal tunnel syndrome: diagnostic utility of the history and physical examination findings. *Ann Intern Med* 1990;17:1495–1998.

43. Davis MA, Ettinger WH, Neuhaus JM, Barclay JD, Segal MR. Correlates of knee pain among US adults with and without radiographic knee osteoarthritis. *J Rheumatol* 1992;19:1943–1949.

44. Spiegel JS, Hirshfield MS, Spiegel TM. Evaluating self-care activities: comparison of a self-reported questionnaire with an occupational therapist interview. *Br J Rheumatol* 1985;24:357–361.

45. Thompson MS, Read JL, Liang MH. Willingness-to-pay concepts for societal diseases in health. In: Kane RL, Kane RA, eds. *Values and long term care.* Lexington, MA: DC Heath, 1982:103–105.

46. Thompson MS, Read JL, Liang MH. Feasibility of willingness-to-pay measurement in chronic arthritis. *Med Decis Making* 1981;4:195–215.

47. Katz JN, Phillips CB, Fossel AH, Liang MH. Stability and responsiveness of utility measures. *Med Care* 1994;32:183–188.

48. Kazis LE, Meenan RF, Anderson JJ. Pain in the rheumatic diseases: investigation of a key health status component. *Arthritis Rheum* 1983;26:1017–1022.

49. Liang MH, Rogers M, Larson M, et al. The psychosocial impact of systemic lupus erythematosus and rheumatoid arthritis. *Arthritis Rheum* 1984;27:13–19.

50. Liang MH, Partridge AJ, Larson MG, Gall V, Taylor JE, Master R, Feltin M, Taylor J. Evaluation of comprehensive rehabilitation services for elderly homebound patients with arthritis and orthopedic disability. *Arthritis Rheum* 1984;27:258–266.

51. Katz JN, Wright EA, Guadagnoli E, Liang MH, Karlson EW, Cleary PH. Differences between men and women undergoing orthopedic surgery for osteoarthritis. *Arthritis Rheum* 1994;37:687–694.

52. Mcvey LJ, Becker PM, Saltz CG, Feussner JR, Cohen JH. Effect of a geriatric consultation on functional status of elderly hospitalized patients, a randomized, controlled trial. *Ann Intern Med* 1989;110:79–84.

53. Rubenstein LV, Calkins DR, Young RT, et al. Improving patient function: a randomized trial of functional disability screening. *Ann Intern Med* 1989;111:836–842.

54. Kazis LE, Callahan LF, Meenan RF, Pincus T. Health status reports in the care of patients with rheumatoid arthritis. *J Clin Epidemiol* 1990;43:1243–1253.

Quality of Life and Pharmacoeconomics in Clinical Trials, Second Edition, edited by B. Spilker.
Lippincott-Raven Publishers, Philadelphia © 1996.

CHAPTER 107

Quality of Life in Orthopedics

James G. Wright

INTRODUCTION

Orthopedic surgeons in clinical medicine and research are confronted with a broad range of questions related to the diagnoses, prognoses, and treatment of orthopedic disease The issue which most frequently confronts the individual orthopedic surgeon, however, is does a particular surgical treatment benefit patients. Evaluation of orthopedic treatments require the determination of an outcome (1). Comparison of the outcomes between two different treatments (or between a treatment and no treatment) are used to make inferences about treatment effectiveness (1).

Orthopedic surgical treatments can have one or more of the following aims: to preserve life, to treat symptoms or complaints (usually pain and functional disability), to restore function, or to prevent future functional decline. Because relatively few orthopedic diseases, with the exception of orthopedic oncology, are life-threatening, the most common expectation of orthopedic treatments is that they either treat complaints, such as patients with osteoarthritis prior to joint arthroplasty, or restore function, such as patients with loss of function due to a fracture. A few orthopedic treatments, principally in pediatric orthopedics, are intended to prevent future decline in function where patients present with no complaints and have normal function, but treatment is aimed at preventing future, often long-term, decline. For example, children with hip subluxation will have no complaints until middle age but surgical treatment in childhood

is directed towards preventing the "premature" development of osteoarthritis.

This chapter will discuss the outcomes which can be used to evaluate orthopedic patients and focus specifically on quality-of-life measures in orthopedics. The chapter will begin with a general discussion of the different types of outcome measurements available in orthopedics, discuss their relative advantages and disadvantages, and finally, provide specific examples of quality-of-life measures that may be applicable to orthopedic surgery.

OUTCOME MEASURES IN ORTHOPEDICS

Although nonclinical outcomes, such as cost and length of hospital stay, may be of interest to hospital administrators, third-party payers, and health policymakers, for surgeons and patients, clinical outcomes are usually much more relevant. Clinical outcomes include mortality, morbidity, and functional outcomes. As previously discussed, mortality is an infrequent outcome of most surgical procedures except in orthopedic oncology. Even in orthopedic oncology, however, quality-of-life issues are becoming increasingly prominent, such as comparing the quality of life of patients receiving amputation and limb salvage procedures. Morbidity and complications of surgical procedures are a relatively infrequent outcome of the orthopedic surgery. Thus, orthopedic surgeons have focused primarily on the functional outcomes of their surgical procedures as being most relevant to patients and surgeons.

Functional outcomes can be measured using objective or subjective measurements. Objective measurements include

J. G. Wright: Division of Orthopaedic Surgery and Clinical Epidemiology Unit, Hospital for Sick Children, University of Toronto, Toronto, Ontario M5G 1X8, Canada.

physiologic measures (joint motion or muscle strength) or capacity measures (gait analysis or timed 50 foot walking distance). Objective measures have several advantages including immediate relevance to the surgeon and the assumption of reliability—despite this assumption, objective measurements are not necessarily reliable (2). The major concern with objective measurements, however, is that they may bear little relevance to the reasons for performing the surgery and patients' expectations of surgery (2). Although objective outcomes are important and should be measured, the evaluation of most surgical treatments should be based upon the intended purpose of the orthopedic treatment, which is usually directed towards subjective outcomes, such as relief of complaints or restoration of function.

Scales that could be used to evaluate the subjective functional outcomes of orthopedic procedures, discussed more extensively elsewhere in this book, include disease-specific (or condition-specific) measures, generic health-status measures, and quality-of-life measures (3). Generic health-status and quality-of-life measures are intended to have a broad perspective and measure all aspects of health which, in addition to pain and function, include mental, emotional, and social function (3).

Generic health-status measures have not been developed specifically for orthopedic applications but scales, such as the Sickness Impact Profile (SIP) and the Short Form (SF-36), have been used to evaluate the outcome of orthopedic procedures (4–11). In contrast, disease-specific measures (referring both to the content of the scale and to the attribution of the complaints to a specific condition) evaluate the specific aspects of the disease which are the focus of the intervention. The primary advantage of disease-specific scales is that they tend to focus on those aspects of the disease that are most relevant to patients and clinicians (3,12). Most disease-specific scales in orthopedics concentrate on pain and physical function, which for orthopedic patients is the major determinant of their quality of life. The remainder of this chapter will focus on the use of these scales in orthopedics.

ISSUES FOR QOL MEASUREMENTS IN ORTHOPEDICS

The orthopedic literature contains an innumerable number of indices and rating scales, all with the intention of evaluating disease-specific function; usually focusing on pain and function. These scales commonly concentrate on a single joint, a single orthopedic procedure, or on a specific disease or clustering of diseases. Despite the extensive number of scales that have been described, many do not meet the standards for scales set in other aspects of this text (12–16). First, the intended purpose of the scale, the problems with prior scales, and how the described scale intends to improve on previous scales is often not articulated. Second, surgeons have seldom stated the domains that they wish to measure

with their scale. Third, despite the extensive experience of the expert clinicians who developed the scales, seldom have these scales included the input of patients or been developed with formal methods of item generation and reduction. This ad hoc manner of scale development has resulted in many scales purporting to measure the same phenomenon but with different content and different (and arbitrary) symptom weighting. Thus, patients may receive dramatically different ratings dependent on which rating scale is used (17,18). Fourth, many of the scales are constructed in ways which make them difficult to use. For example, walking distances may be quantitated in 0–1,4–6, and > 10 blocks without a clear idea of how to rate a patient who walks seven blocks. Fifth, the scales often create a summary score by combining patient symptoms and disabilities with measures of impairment, such as range of motion and joint stability. Finally, few if any of these scales have undergone rigorous testing for reliability, validity, and responsiveness.

SPECIFIC EXAMPLES OF QOL MEASURES IN ORTHOPEDICS

Specific outcome measures that could be used to evaluate orthopedic patients are discussed in the sections that follow. Each section, grouped according to anatomic region, begins with scales recommended by the relevant specialty society. Additional measures for each anatomic region will be discussed and were chosen because they are feasible (completable in less than 15–20 minutes), self-administered, have been developed with a formal process of item generation and reduction, and have documented evidence of their reliability and validity. Because there have been relatively few head-to-head comparisons of these measures, the relative superiority of these measures is uncertain.

Lower Extremity Measures

Hip and Knee Arthritis

Hip and knee surgery for patients with arthritic joints is a major proportion of orthopedic surgery. Many different outcome measures, called "hip or knee rating scales," have been constructed by experienced surgeons to quantify patients' complaints in evaluating severity of dysfunction from joint disease. The scales all have a similar format, in which patients receive a rated score on several subscales for specified aspects of pain and disability. Each specified complaint is graded for severity. Each symptom has an arbitrary point score assigned by the surgeon(s) who originally developed the scale. When the scores are summed for each complaint on each subscale, the total score indicates the degree of joint dysfunction. Change in patients' status, when calculated from the difference in scores before and after joint replacement, is the measure outcome. Because no scale has demonstrated clear superiority, a confusing array of scales are available and comparisons between trials is extremely difficult (19–21). For example, at least 36 scales can be used to evaluate knee arthroplasty (22).

In an attempt to create some conformity, the Knee and Hip Societies have developed standardized evaluation systems. The Knee Society standardized rating scheme is intended to evaluate patients undergoing knee arthroplasty. The clinical rating system was developed using an informal consensus process among a group of clinicians from the Knee Society (23). The knee rating system combines pain, stability, and range of motion together (with deductions for flexion contracture, extension lag and misalignment) as a "knee assessment" score and walking distance and stair-climbing together (with deductions for mobility aids) as a "patient function" score. Although the scale was developed by "consensus", a complete description of the methods of development are lacking and patients were not included in the development of the scale. Furthermore, the reliability and validity of this rating system is unknown.

A formal nominal group process of clinicians was used to develop the "Total Hip Arthroplasty Outcome Evaluation Form." The evaluation system has been endorsed by the Hip Society, the American Academy of Orthopedic Surgeons, and the Societe Internationale de Chirurgie Orthopedique et de Traumatologie (SICOT) (24,25). The evaluation form considers pain, work activity, activities of daily living, gait, satisfaction and expectations of the patient undergoing hip arthroplasty. The form also provides separate guidelines for the physical examination, complications, and radiographic evaluation. The form, however, did not involve patients in the development, nor does it provide details of how to aggregate the responses to provide a summary score. Furthermore, the reliability and validity of this evaluation system are unknown.

The Western Ontario and McMaster University Osteoarthritis (WOMAC) index is a scale based on interviews with patients with lower extremity arthritis. Although it was not developed specifically to measure the outcome after surgical procedures, such as joint arthroplasty, the scale was derived from out-patients with osteoarthritis of the hip and/or knee (26–30), a group similar to patients receiving hip and knee arthroplasty. The final scale, based on a consensus of the 100 patients, includes 5 pain items, 2 stiffness items, and 17 physical function items, which all receive equal weighting and are summed together as three subscales to obtain the final scores (28). The scale, which is self-administered, has been shown to have a Cronbach's alpha and test-retest reliability of approximately 0.80 (27). Construct validity has been demonstrated by correlation with 4 measures of disease severity; joint tenderness, Lequesne index, Bradburn index, and the McMaster Health Index Questionnaire (30). Responsiveness was demonstrated in a randomized controlled trial of nonsteroidal antiinflammatory drugs (NSAIDs) in the treatment of osteoarthritis (30).

Three additional scales, called patient-specific scales, have been developed which focus on complaints of individual patients receiving hip arthroplasty. Patient-specific scales may be particularly important if individual patients vary in either the spectrum of complaint or the importance of their symptoms (31). For example, before hip arthroplasty, a patient may complain of significant difficulty climbing stairs and value relief of that complaint above all else, whereas another patient may have only mild difficulty climbing stairs or attach no importance to the relief of stair climbing difficulty.

The McMaster-Toronto Arthritis Patient Function Preference Questionnaire (MACTAR) is a patient-specific scale. Patients list and rank their individual symptoms in the order that they would most prefer to have them improved by treatment (32–34). Patients are rated only on their four most important symptoms before and after therapy. The MACTAR demonstrated superior responsiveness when compared with the Lee Functional index, McMaster Health Index Questionnaire, joint count, joint swelling, joint tenderness/pain, joint circumference, morning stiffness, severity of pain, overall assessment, and physician assessment of disease activity in a randomized placebo-controlled trial of methotrexate in rheumatoid arthritis. In a second approach, patients prior to total hip arthroplasty rated their "five areas of life most important to their overall quality-of-life" using a vertical visual analog scale (35). The patients also rated the quality of life of 30 hypothetical cases to determine relative weights for their self-rated quality of life. The ratings with weights are summed together to derive an individual global quality-of-life score. The test-retest correlation of the global quality-of-life scores was 0.88. The third approach, called the Patient-specific Index (PASI), evaluates all important symptoms mentioned by patients and uses patient's individual ratings of importance to generate weights for the complaints (31). Patients rate separately the severity and importance of their individual complaints which are combined together to generate a patient-specific score. The reliability and validity of the PASI has not yet been documented. The disadvantages of all the patient-specific scales is that they all require interviewer administration and their superiority over other scales, such as the WOMAC, is unproven.

Knee: Sports Injury

The International Knee Documentation Committee has developed an evaluation system for patients with knee ligament injuries (36). The form rates patients' activity level and symptoms (pain, swelling, giving way) but also includes range of motion, joint stability, crepitus, joint space narrowing on radiographs, and a functional (one-leg hop) test in a summary score. The methods used to develop this scale are not reported and the reliability and validity of this scale is unknown.

Another scale, based on interviews with patients, has been developed to assess quality-of-life in patients receiving anterior cruciate ligament reconstruction surgery. The scale, which is self-administered, was developed after interviews with 100 patients. Patients use visual analogue scales to rate 34 items grouped into domains of symptoms and physical complaints, work-related concerns, recreational activities, lifestyle and emotional aspects (37). The instrument is currently completing reliability, validity, and responsiveness testing (Mohtadi, N, *personal communications*).

Foot and Ankle

The American Orthopedic Foot and Ankle Society (AOFAS) has developed an assessment instrument which provides separate subscales for the ankle/hind foot, midfoot, forefoot score (metatarophalangeal level) and forefoot score (toe level). The clinical rating system was developed by informal consensus of a committee of the AOFAS and intended for a wide variety of clinical situations, such as "arthrodesis, arthroplasty, and ligament reconstruction." The indices consider pain, function, and walking distance but also incorporate joint motion, gait abnormality, and alignment into the total score (38). The reliability and validity of these scales are unknown.

A scale, called the foot function index, was designed to measure "the impact of foot pathology on function in terms of pain, difficulty and activity restriction." Although the scale may be relevant to many foot disorders, the scale was evaluated only on patients with rheumatoid arthritis (39). The 23-item scale is self-administered and grouped into three subscales of pain—disability, and activity limitation (including walking, climbing stairs, and getting up from chairs)—but also provides an overall summary score. Patients rate each of the 23 items, using visual analog scales. Test–retest reliability scores for total and subscales scores ranged from 0.69 to 0.87 and internal consistency ranged from 0.73 to 0.96. Construct validity was determined using factor analysis and demonstrating correlation with joint counts and 50 feet walking time.

UPPER EXTREMITY MEASURES

The Association of Shoulder and Elbow Surgeons (ASES) has developed a standardized assessment form based on the informal consensus of a group of surgeons from the ASES. The standardized form evaluates patients' pain, medication, instability, and 10 activities, including dressing, self-care, reaching, throwing, working, and sports. The form includes guidelines for a separate physician assessment of range of motion, strength, instability, and other physical examination signs (40). The reliability and validity of the form are unknown.

A specific questionnaire has been developed to assess the severity of symptoms and functional status of patients with carpal tunnel syndrome (41). The self-administered 19-item question evaluates pain, other symptoms, and 11 functional activities including writing, dressing, self-care, and meal preparation. The test-retest correlation was 0.91–0.93, and internal consistency was 0.89–0.91. The validity was demonstrated by correlation with two-point discrimination and monofilament testing. Although this scale describes many symptoms and disabilities relevant for patients with upper extremity disorders, its usefulness in diseases other than carpal tunnel syndrome is unknown.

The Arthritis Impact Measurement Scale (AIMS-2) was developed to "evaluate health status in patients with rheumatoid disease" (42,43). The AIMS-2 evaluated patients both with rheumatoid and osteoarthritis. The 78-item questionnaire is divided into twelve subscales; mobility level, walking and bending, hand and finger function, arm function, self-care, household tasks, social activities, support from family and friends, arthritis pain, work, level of tension, and mood. The internal consistency of the subscales was 0.72–0.91 and test–retest reliability was 0.78–0.94. Validity was determined by correlation of the AIMS-2 with patients' overall ratings of health status and was able to discriminate between different disease groups, sex, age, and subjects' educational level. The scale, which is self-administered, is reported to take approximately 20 minutes to complete and was acceptable to the majority of respondents. Although the scale is intended primarily for the arthritic population, many of the subscales measure functional abilities of the upper extremity.

Spine Measures

The North American Spine Society has developed a scale to evaluate "patient-centered" pain and functional outcome of patients with spinal disorders. The self-administered questionnaire requires approximately 20 minutes to complete and focuses on pain and functional limitations, such as dressing, walking, sitting, recreation, work, and sex life. The test–retest intraclass correlations of the scales were 0.85–0.99, with Cronbach's α of 0.71–0.93 and demonstrated strong correlation with portions of the SF-36 (44).

The St. Thomas Disability Questionnaire (or Roland and Morris scale) is a modification of the Sickness Impact Profile (45). The scale focuses on those issues from the SIP relevant to the spine, and the symptoms and disabilities are attributed to the spine. The instrument is self-administered with 24 yes/no questions focusing on symptoms and functional disabilities, such as walking, stairs, sitting, dressing, standing, and work. A second part of the questionnaire requires patients to rate their pain using a "thermometer" (modified) visual analogue scale. The test–retest correlation was 0.9 and construct validity was determined by correlation with physical assessment of gait or sitting abnormalities and limitation in range of motion.

Pediatric Measures

Measurement of quality-of-life in children is complicated by decisions of who should respond to the questionnaire (child, parent, or caregiver), whether children can validly respond to questionnaires, and the effects of development on childrens' function (46).

The Pediatric Evaluation of Disability Inventory (PEDI) focuses on children with chronic illnesses 0.5–7 years of age. The scale is completed by the parent and focuses on domains of self-care, mobility, and social function. The subscales have κ values of 0.67–0.80 and were able to discriminate between normal and disabled children (47–51). The scale, however, requires a structured parent interview or clinician observation.

The Juvenile Arthritis Functional Assessment Form (JA-FAR) was developed to evaluate children aged 7–18 with rheumatoid arthritis. This 23-item scale, which is self-administered, can be completed by parents or children and evaluates both upper and lower extremity function (52,53). The internal consistency was 0.85. The scale was also able to discriminate between normal and control patients and correlated with the Steinbrook classification and the number of involved joints.

The Rand scale is designed to measure the health status of children less than 13 years old. The Rand scale evaluates all aspects of childrens' function with five subscales of mental health, social health, general health perceptions, developmental milestones, and physical function. The physical activity subscale includes role–activity limitations, self-care–mobility–function, and total functional limitations. The scale is intended for moderately or mildly disabled children. The five subscales have high internal reliabilities (Cronbach alpha ≥ 0.50) and acceptable indexes of construct validity (54,55).

CONCLUSIONS

Pain, functional disabilities, and other aspects of quality of life should be used, in addition to more traditional orthopedic measurements, to evaluate orthopedic surgery. Scales developed by talking to patients, using rigorous methods of item generation and reduction, that have documented reliability and validity, are available and should be used to evaluate the quality of life of orthopedic patients.

REFERENCES

1. Feinstein AR. *Clinical epidemiology: the architecture of clinical research.* Philadelphia: WB Saunders, 1985.
2. Wright JG, Feinstein AR. Improving the reliability of orthopaedic measurements. *J Bone Joint Surg* 1992;74B:287–291.
3. Patrick DL, Deyo RA. Generic and disease-specific measures in assessing health status and quality of life. *Med Care* 1989;27:S217–S232.
4. Bombardier C, Melfi CA, Paul J, Green R, Hawker G, Wright J, Coyte P. Comparison of a generic and disease-specific measure of pain and physical function after knee replacement surgery. *Med Care* 1995;33:AS131–144.
5. Kantz ME, Harris WJ, Levitsky K, Ware JE, Davies AR. Methods for assessing condition-specific and generic functional status outcomes after total knee replacement. *Med Care* 1992;30:240–250.
6. Katz JN, Larson MG, Phillips CB, Fossel AH, Liang MH. Comparative measurement sensitivity of short and longer health status instruments. *Med Care* 1992;30:917–925.
7. Liang MH, Larson MG, Cullen KE, Schwartz JA. Comparative measurement efficiency and sensitivity of five health status instruments for arthritis research. *Arthritis Rheum* 1985;28:542–547.
8. McHorney CA, Ware JE, Raczek AE. The MOS 36-item short-form health survey (SF-36): II. Psychometric and clinical tests of validity in measuring physical and mental health constructs. *Med Care* 1993;31:247–263.
9. McHorney CA, Ware JE, Rogers W, Raczek AE, Lu JFR. The validity and relative precision of MOS short- and long-form health status scales and Dartmouth COOP charts. *Med Care* 1992;30:MS253–MS265.
10. Stewart AL, Hays RD, Ware JE. Communication: The MOS short-form and general health survey: reliability and validity in a patient population. *Med Care* 1988;26:724–735.
11. Ware JE, Sherbourne CD. The MOS 36-item short-form health survey. *Med Care* 1992;30:473–483.
12. Wiklund I, Karlberg J. Evaluation of quality of life in clinical trials. Selecting quality-of-life measures. *Controlled Clin Trials* 1991;12:204S–216S.
13. Feinstein AR. *Clinimetrics.* New Haven: Yale University Press, 1987.
14. Feinstein AR, Josephy BR, Wells CK. Scientific and clinical problems in indexes of functional disability. *Ann Intern Med* 1986;105:413–420.
15. Streiner DL, Norman GR. *Health measurement scales: a practical guide to their development and use.* Oxford: Oxford University Press, 1989.
16. Wright JG, Feinstein AR. A comparative contrast of clinimetric and psychometric methods for constructing indexes and rating scales. *J Clin Epidemiol* 1992;45:1201–1218.
17. Anderson G. Hip assessment: a comparison of nine different methods. *J Bone Joint Surg* 1972;54-B:621–625.
18. Callaghan JJ, Dysart SH, Savory CF, Hopkinson WJ. Assessing the results of hip replacement: a comparison of five different rating systems. *J Bone Joint Surg* 1990;72B:1008–1009.
19. Galante J. Editorial. The need for a standardized system for revaluating the results of total hip surgery. *J Bone Joint Surg* 1985;67A:511–512.
20. Galante J. Evaluation of results of total hip replacement editorial. *J Bone Joint Surg* 1990;72A:159–160.
21. Gartland JJ. Orthopaedic clinical research. Deficiencies in experimental design and determinations of outcome. *J Bone Joint Surg* 1988;70A:1357.
22. Drake BG, Callahan CM, Dittus RS, Wright JG. Global rating systems used in assessing knee arthroplasty outcomes. *J Arthroplasty* 1994;9(4):409–417.
23. Insall JN, Dorr LD, Scott RD, Scott WN. Rationale of the Knee Society clinical rating system. *Clin Orthop* 1989;248:13–14.
24. Johnston RC, Fitzgerald RH, Harris WH, Poss R, Muller ME, Sledge CB. Clinical and radiographic evaluation of total hip replacement. A standard system of terminology for reporting results. *J Bone Joint Surg* 1990;72A:161–168.
25. Liang MH, Katz JN, Phillips C, Sledge C, Cats-Baril W. The American Academy of Orthopaedic Surgeons Task Force on Outcome Studies. The total hip arthroplasty outcome evaluation form of the American Academy of Orthopaedic Surgeons. *J Bone Joint Surg* 1991;73A:639–646.
26. Bellamy N. Critical review of clinical assessments techniques for rheumatoid arthritis trials: new developments. *Scand J Rheumatol* 1989;80(suppl):3–16.
27. Bellamy N. Pain assessment in osteoarthritis: experience with the WOMAC osteoarthritis index. *Semin Arthritis Rheumatol* 1989;18:14–17.
28. Bellamy N, Buchanan W. A preliminary evaluation of the dimensionality and clinical importance of pain and disability in osteoarthritis of the hip and knee. *Clin Rheumatol* 1986;5:231–241.
29. Bellamy N, Buchanan W, Goldsmith CH, Campbell J, Duku E. Signal measurement strategies: are they feasible and do they offer any advantage in outcome measurement in osteoarthritis? *Arthritis Rheumatol* 1990;33:739–745.
30. Bellamy N, Buchanan W, Goldsmith C, Campbell J, Stitt L. Validation Study of WOMAC: a health status instrument for measuring clinically important patient relevant outcomes to anti-rheumatic drug therapy in patients with osteoarthritis of the hip or knee. *J Rheumatol* 1988;15:1833–1840.
31. Wright J, Rudicel S, Feinstein A. Asking patients what they want. *J Bone Joint Surg* 1994;76B:229–230.
32. Tugwell P, Bombardier C, Buchanan WW, Goldsmith CH, Grace E, Hanna B. The MACTAR patient preference disability questionnaire—an individualized functional priority approach for assessing improve-

ment in physical disability in clinical trials in rheumatoid arthritis. *J Rheumatol* 1987;14:446–451.

33. Tugwell P, Bombardier C, Buchanan W, Goldsmith C, Grace E, Bennett K, Williams H, Egger M, Alarcon G, et al. Impact on quality of life assessed by traditional standard-item and individualized patient preference health status questionnaires. *Arch Intern Med* 1990;150: 59–62.

34. Tugwell P, Bombardier C, Bell M, Bennett K, Bensen W, Grace E, Hart L, Goldsmith C. Current quality of life research challenges in arthritis relevant to the issue of clinical significance. *Controlled Clin Trials* 1991;12:271S–225S.

35. O'Boyle CA, McGee H, Hickey A, O'Malley K, Joyce CRB. Individual quality of life in patients undergoing hip replacement. *Lancet* 1992;339:1088–1091.

36. Pynsent PB, Fairbank JCT, Carr A. *Outcome measures in orthopaedics.* Oxford: Butterworth–Heinemann, 1993:242–243.

37. Mohtadi NG. Quality of life assessment as an outcome in anterior cruciate ligament reconstructive surgery. In: Jackson DW, Arnoczky SP, Frank CB, Simon TM, Woo SLY, eds. *The anterior cruciate ligament current and future concepts.* New York: Raven, 1993:439–444.

38. Kitaoka HB, Alexander IJ, Adelar RS, Nunley JA, Myerson MS, Sanders M. Clinical rating system for ankle–hindfoot, midfoot, hallux, and lesser toes. *Foot Ankle Int* 1994;15:349–353.

39. Budiman-Mak E, Conrad KJ, Roach KE. The foot function index: a measure of foot pain and disability. *Clin Epidemiol* 1991;44:561–570.

40. Richards RR, An KN, Blgliani LU, Freldman RJ, Gartsman GM, Gristina AG, Iannotti JP, Mow VC, Sidles JA, Zuckerman JD. A standardized method for the assessment of shoulder function. Research Committee. *Am Shoulder Elbow Surg* (submitted).

41. Levine DW, Simmons BP, Koris MJ, Daltroy LH, Hohl GG, Fossel AH, Katz JN. A self-administered questionnaire for the assessment of severity of symptoms and functional status in carpal tunnel syndrome. *J Bone Joint Surg* 1993;75A:1585–1592.

42. Meenan RF, Mason JH, Anderson JJ, Guccione AA, Kazis LE. AIMS2: the content and properties of a revised and expanded arthritis impact measurement scales health status questionnaire. *Arthritis Rheum* 1992;35(1):1–10.

43. Potts MK, Brandt KD. Evidence of the validity of the arthritis impact measurement scales. *Arthritis Rheum* 1987;30(1):93–96.

44. Daltroy LH, Cats-Baril WL, Katz JN, Fossel AH, Liang MH. North American Spine Society back pain questionnaire reliability and validity study. (Submitted).

45. Roland M, Morris R. 1982 Volvo Award in Clinical Science. A study of the natural history of back pain. Part I. Development of a reliable and sensitive measure of disability in low-back pain. *Spine* 1983; 8:141–144.

46. Young NL, Wright JG. Measuring paediatric physical function. *J Pediatr Orthop* 1995;15:244–253.

47. Feldman AB, Haley SM, Coryell J. Concurrent and construct validity of the pediatric evaluation of disability inventory. *Phys Ther* 1990;70: 602–610.

48. Gans BM, Haley SM, Hallenborg SC, Mann N, Inacio CA, Faas RM. Description and interobserver reliability of the Tufts assessment of motor performance. *Am J Phys Med Rehabil* 1988;67:202–210.

49. Haley SM, Coster WJ, Faas RM. A content validity study of the pediatric evaluation of disability inventory. *Pediatr Phys Ther* 1991;3: 177–184.

50. Haley SM, Ludlow LH. Application of the hierarchical scales of the Tufts assessment of motor performance for school-aged children and adults with disabilities. *Phys Ther* 1992;72:191–206.

51. Haley SM, Ludlow LH, Gans BM, Faas RM, Inacio CA. Tufts assessment of motor performance: an empirical approach to identifying motor performance categories. *Arch Phys Med Rehabil* 1991;72:359–366.

52. Lovell DJ, Howe S, Shear E, Hartner S, McGirr G, Schulte M, Levinson J. Development of a disability measurement tool for juvenile rheumatoid arthritis. The Juvenile Arthritis Functional Assessment Scale. *Arthritis and Rheum* 1989;32:1390–1395.

53. Howe S, Levinson J, Shear E, Hartner S, McGirr G, Schulte M, Lovell D. Development of a disability measurement tool for juvenile rheumatoid arthritis. The juvenile arthritis functional assessment report for children and their parents. *Arthritis Rheum* 1991;34:873–879.

54. Eisen M, Ware JE, Donal CA, Brook RH. Measuring components of children's health status. *Med Care* 1979;17:902–921.

55. Eisen M, Donald CA, Ware JE Jr, Brook RH. Conceptualization and measurement of health in children in the health insurance study. *Rand* 1980:R2313-HEW.

Quality of Life and Pharmacoeconomics in Clinical Trials, Second Edition, edited by B. Spilker.
Lippincott-Raven Publishers, Philadelphia © 1996.

CHAPTER 108

Measurement of Visual Functioning and Health-Related Quality of Life in Eye Disease and Cataract Surgery

Carol M. Mangione, Paul P. Lee, and Ron D. Hays

INTRODUCTION

The goal of ophthalmic practice is to enhance, restore, or preserve vision. From the visually impaired person's perspective, eyesight is important not only because it is a sensory function, but because it enables one to perform a range of desired or necessary physical and cognitive activities essential for independent living and well-being. Whereas physicians and clinical researchers are most interested in understanding the underlying mechanisms and structures that allow persons to see and in the effect of various eye diseases on such structures and processes, patients want to see because vision makes participation in a wide range of activities possible and influences overall physical functioning and emotional well-being (1–6). Many clinical researchers have demonstrated that loss of vision carries significant

economic and psychological costs for individuals and for society (7,8). Additionally, others have demonstrated that diminished visual acuity is associated with decreased performance of instrumental activities of daily living, poorer cognitive abilities, and ultimately poorer health-related quality of life (9–14).

Recently, there has been increasing recognition of the importance of assessing a broad array of outcomes such as physical function, social function, and overall health, in addition to the standard clinical end points when evaluating medical interventions or technologies (15,16). But, except for a small number of studies designed to assess outcome after cataract extraction, measurement of visual functioning and health-related quality of life has rarely been incorporated into ophthalmologic research. Measurement of self-reported visual functioning and health-related quality of life in vision research may capture positive or negative attributes of an intervention that are not reflected in observed changes in clinical end points such as visual acuity. Additionally, visual loss is one of the leading causes of disability with aging (17). Therefore, a better understanding of the positive impact of vision-preserving therapies on health-related quality of life and specifically patient's capacity for independent living may preserve resource allocation for these therapies. Finally,

C. M. Mangione and R. D. Hays: Division of General Medicine and Health Services Research, Department of Medicine, University of California at Los Angeles Medical School, Los Angeles, California 90095; RAND–Health Sciences Program, Santa Monica, California 90407.
    P. P. Lee: Doheny Eye Institute at University of Southern California Medical School; RAND–Health Sciences Program, Santa Monica, California 90407.

collection of self-reported visual functioning and health-related quality of life permits comparisons across vision-specific and other medical conditions and technologies. These comparisons and the cumulative knowledge of health status will establish the relative burden of different conditions and the relative merits of interventions or therapies on a comparable metric.

THREE VISION-TARGETED MEASURES

The optimal approach to measuring health-related quality of life is to include a generic core measure, such as the SF-36/RAND 36-Item Health Survey 1.0 (18,19), and supplement it with vision-targeted items (20,21). The generic core makes it possible to compare persons with eye disease to the general population (22) and to those with other chronic conditions. Because the vision-targeted measures assess the specific symptoms or areas of disability that are of greatest clinical interest and concern to persons with the condition, they are more likely to be sensitive to clinically relevant differences, including changes over time.

It is useful to place self-report measures of visual functioning in the context of other vision-targeted tools that are available to the clinical investigator. Methods for measuring visual functioning can be classified by the degree and type of patient participation required to complete the assessment. The first group of measures are the physical measures, such as lens or retinal photographs. These require cooperation but little participation from the subject. Thus, a strength of physical measures is the limited opportunity for subjects to introduce bias into data collection. However, errors may be introduced by limitations in the measurement equipment and the investigator may introduce bias in the grading of the data collected. Investigator bias can be minimized by employing independent, masked graders of the data. Physical measures are quite useful for assessing the progression of early, pre-symptomatic stages of eye diseases. The biggest limitation of these measures is the lack of information describing the clinical or functional implications of abnormal physical findings. For example, many of the retinal photographic abnormalities associated with the diagnosis of macular degeneration are also observed to a lesser degree in the normal aging eye (23).

The second group of measures are the performance-based measures, such as Snellen visual acuity, measurement of visual fields, and many of the newer technologies for assessing visual functioning, such as contrast sensitivity or glare testing. These tools are principally designed for clinical practice but have been used frequently as research end points (24). Many performance-based measures have the advantage of being widely accepted as valid end points by researchers and practicing ophthalmologists. Additionally, changes in measures such as visual acuity have intuitive and accepted functional implications in the ophthalmologic community. These measures are effort dependent and require a cooperative and cognitively intact participant. Sources of random and systematic (bias) error in performance-based measures include the subject, the equipment, and the operator who conducts and interprets the test. Despite the potential for error, few data have been published describing the reliability of many performance-based measures, such as those designed to measure glare disability or automated measures of contrast sensitivity. The potentially greatest limitation of performance-based measures is that many aspects of visual functioning, such as visual difficulties with specific lighting or weather conditions, are not captured.

The third group of measures are self-reports of visual functioning (25–28). Most self-assessments are questionnaires that assess the patient's perception of visual disability or limitations in the performance of visual activities. These measures are useful for evaluating medical technologies designed to preserve or improve aspects of visual functioning that are not readily measured by physical or performance-based measures. For example, one may be interested in describing the functional impact of a low vision services program. The persons eligible for these services may be legally blind, and it is unlikely that provision of low-vision services will change the participants' measured visual acuity. At the same time, it is probable that low vision services improve patients' abilities to perform vision-dependent activities such as reading or walking outdoors. If the investigator only measures a performance-based measure, such as visual acuity, it is unlikely that he or she will demonstrate benefit from a low vision intervention. However, the patients' functional capacity may be greatly enhanced by the treatment. The low to moderate correlations (0.2 to 0.4) between performance-based measures such as visual acuity and self-report measures of visual functioning indicates that these two types of measures capture different aspects of visual function (3,10, 26,28,29).

A strength of self-report measures is that they provide the patients' perspective on the impact of progressive ocular conditions or treatments on capacity for independent visual functioning, and they are likely to reflect these types of treatment effects. For some interventions or treatments, patients' perception of changes in visual functioning may be the most relevant end point. Additionally, vision-targeted questionnaires specifically tailored to the content area of interest may enhance the investigator's ability to detect small but potentially important within-subject change at two or more points in time in two or more treatment arms.

All questionnaires are dependent on cooperative and cognitively able participants, and are limited by respondent bias and/or placebo effects. This limitation is particularly relevant for the interpretation of reports of benefit or harm from observational studies of vision preserving or sight restoring therapies. For example, many investigators have measured pre- and post-operative visual functioning among subjects who have had cataract extraction and intraocular lens implantation (3, 30–33). Most of these investigations do not include a comparable, nonsurgical control group. The lack of a control group may inflate the observed benefit because, in general, subjects who have undergone surgery tend to be highly motivated to perceive benefit from the treatment, and therefore, may be biased toward reporting improvements (34). Although self-report measures may be especially susceptible to placebo effects, the recorded changes on performance-based measures such as visual acuity may also be influenced by the ophthalmologist's and patient's desire to observe improvement after a surgical procedure. Questionnaire data are also limited by potential confounding from other chronic ocular or medical conditions. Both potential limitations can be addressed by either including a comparable control group, or by randomizing participants to the intervention of interest versus alternative treatments, which will balance confounding characteristics in both groups under study. In general, randomization greatly increases the probability that the marginal benefit or harm attributable to the treatment of interest will be observable. Finally, because of limitations in feasible length and investigator's biases about the areas of greatest importance for participants, self-report measures that omit aspects of visual functioning and well-being regarded as important by subjects will not be valid indicators of their health-related quality of life.

SUMMARY OF PUBLISHED SELF-REPORT MEASURES FOR THE ASSESSMENT OF VISUAL FUNCTIONING

There are a number of questionnaires designed for the assessment of visual functioning. However, while occasionally used for the assessment of persons with other eye diseases, most of these were specifically constructed for use among patients with cataracts. One of the earliest of these measures is the Visual Function Index developed by Bernth-Petersen (35). The Visual Function Index evaluates eleven vision-specific tasks that most of the subsequent scales in the literature and currently under development include such as reading, distance vision, and watching television. Additionally, this survey includes items that address mobility limitations due to visual loss. One summary score is generated for the measure using weights from a statistical multivariate method called appropriate scoring developed by Fisher (36). The Visual Function Index has not been widely used in clinical studies or in the care of ophthalmology patients in the United States.

As part of a study of outcomes after cataract extraction and intraocular lens implantation in 1992, Mangione et al. (26) developed a survey entitled the Activities of Daily Vision Scale. This questionnaire allows the participant to rate their difficulty with 20 common visual activities that were identified in open-ended interviews with elderly persons with bilateral cataracts. The Activities of Daily Vision Scale was found to have high internal consistency (Cronbach $\alpha = 0.94$) and high test–retest reliability (Spearman's r = 0.87) when administered to subjects twice, 48 hours apart. Recently,

prospective longitudinal changes in ADVS scores have been published for patients before and after cataract extraction (33).

The newest vision-targeted survey in the literature is the VF-14 (28). The VF-14 was developed for use in a national study of outcomes after cataract extraction (32). The VF-14 consists of 14 items that assess many of the visual activities included in the Visual Function Index and the Activities of Daily Vision Scale. The VF-14 has the advantage of being shorter than the 20-item Activities of Daily Vision Scale, yet it has very high reliability (Cronbach's $\alpha = 0.85$). Prospectively collected longitudinal change scores have also been published for the VF-14 (32). Although when used to assess outcome after cataract extraction a ceiling effect was present for both the VF-14 and the Activities of Daily Vision Scale, on average both measures demonstrated a statistically significant 16 percent improvement in visual functioning after cataract extraction.

The Visual Activity Questionnaire developed by Sloane et al. (27) is the only published visual functioning questionnaire not designed specifically for the evaluation of persons with cataracts. This questionnaire has strong face validity because the goal of the item selection strategy was to target areas of visual functioning previously identified to be affected by the normal aging process. Because of this orientation, the Visual Activity Questionnaire covers aspects of visual functioning that are not comprehensively represented in other questionnaires such as difficulty with activities that pertain to visual search, color discrimination, and use of the peripheral visual fields This survey consists of 33 items and also has high internal consistency (Cronbach $\alpha > 0.82$ for all subscales) (27).

Many investigators have recognized the importance of including the patients' perceptions of visual functioning when studying other eye diseases. However, the majority of these investigations have used vision-targeted questions with unknown psychometric properties. The questions asked were usually derived from clinical experience. Therefore, except for the Visual Activity Questionnaire, there is an absence of reliable and valid tools for the measurement of the central outcome of interest to most patients, i.e., visual functioning, for almost every major eye condition except cataract.

To address the absence of a vision-targeted questionnaire with known psychometric properties that could be used for persons with eye diseases other than cataract, the National Eye Institute has sponsored a research program to develop such a questionnaire that will cover the areas of functioning and well-being identified as important by persons having one of five major eye diseases. This National Eye Institute sponsored questionnaire is the first measure of visual functioning to derive items from a formal, multi-condition focus group process. Items were derived from a content analysis of the transcripts from 25 focus groups that consisted of 8–10 patients with the same chronic eye condition. The conditions represented in the focus groups include senile cataract, age-related macular degeneration, glaucoma, diabetic retinopathy, and CMV retinitis (37). Pilot tests of the draft instrument are currently underway. Except for one study which used patient interviews, every other scale published to date has derived items from the medical literature or the experience of providers of care.

USE OF VISION-TARGETED AND GENERIC MEASURES OF HEALTH-RELATED QUALITY OF LIFE IN OPHTHALMOLOGIC (NONCATARACT) OBSERVATIONAL STUDIES

Previous studies of persons with eye disease other than cataracts have used questions designed to evaluate the functional impact of a narrowly defined condition or treatment and derived from common symptoms associated with the condition of interest. In general, these studies used ad hoc measures and failed to provide documentation for the reliability and validity of these measures. These descriptions of visual disability or functional difficulties attributed to vision are limited to reports of visual function after enucleation for ocular melanoma (38) or visual limitations after laser treatments for diabetic retinopathy (39) or have emphasized specific tasks, such as face recognition in macular degeneration and other retinal disorders (40–42).

Many of the early investigations that incorporated self-reported visual functioning also reported tests of association between the responses to questions and measured Snellen visual acuity (39). For example, Russell et al. in their study of persons with diabetic retinopathy, found significant correlations between difficulties with work performance and measured visual acuity in the better eye (Pearson's r = 0.64, $p < 0.05$). These investigators also found that many of the visual problems reported most frequently by persons undergoing laser treatment for diabetic retinopathy were not significantly correlated with measured visual acuity. In general, reports of correlations between responses to vision-targeted questions and measured visual acuity have been in the 0.2–0.6 range in multiple studies.

VISION-TARGETED AND GENERIC MEASURES OF HEALTH-RELATED QUALITY OF LIFE IN OBSERVATIONAL STUDIES OF CATARACT EXTRACTION

Despite the widely recognized central role of functional disability for determining whether cataract surgery is indicated (43–45), until recently, the use of self-assessment measures to estimate visual functioning or generic health-related quality of life before surgery has been a rare event. The earliest work on visual function after cataract extraction was conducted in the pre-intraocular lens era by Bernth-Petersen (3). Bernth-Petersen interviewed consecutive patients with the Visual Function Index before and one year after cataract extraction. Patients were also asked about satisfaction with the outcome of cataract surgery and had pre- and postopera-

tive measurements of visual acuity. At 1 year after surgery, significant improvements in reading capacity, distance vision, television watching, and other activities were noted. This was the first study to compare the effect of other eye diseases on outcome after cataract surgery and to document that those with macular degeneration had poorer visual functioning than those without other eye diseases.

In the first prospective study of visual functioning after cataract surgery in the intraocular lens implantation era, Applegate et al. measured outcome with multiple vision-specific and generic instruments. In this study, mean visual acuity improved in the treated eye, but 13% of the patients had no improvement or deterioration in visual acuity after the surgery. On a 5-point self-rating scale of two vision-dependent activities (reading and driving), subjects improved by an average of only 0.2 points ($p < 0.05$) postoperatively, and they did not improve at all on the Activities of Daily Living Scale in the Functional Assessment Inventory (46). Even though there was mean improvement in measured acuity, lack of improvement in the Activities of Daily Living portion of the Functional Assessment Inventory may have been because most of the participants were totally independent prior to cataract extraction, and therefore could not improve on the scale.

Since 1992, three additional observational studies of outcome after cataract extraction have used a design that is similar to Applegate et al. but have included standardized questionnaires designed to assess vision-targeted functioning and generic health-related quality of life (31–33). Except for the study by Brenner et al. (31), these studies have used published questionnaires with previously estimated reliability and validity for measurement of generic health-related quality of life before and after surgery. The two studies that used previously published questionnaires (32,33) failed to demonstrate improvements in generic health-related quality of life after cataract extraction, confirming the earlier findings from Applegate et al.

Using a variety of questions designed to estimate visual functioning, all three of these studies have demonstrated a similar proportion of patients with improvements in vision-targeted measures after cataract extraction. Among patients without other eye diseases, Javitt et al. (29) reported that 75% and 92% improved in self-reported visual function after surgery. The percentage improved depended on whether the patients had cataract extraction in their first, second, or both eyes during the follow-up period. A second multicenter study found that 89% of patients reported improvements on the VF-14 after cataract extraction and lens implantation (32). Even though ADVS and VF-14 cover similar content area, only 77% of the patients in Mangione et al.'s study of outcomes after cataract surgery had positive change on the ADVS (33). The proportion classified as improvers in the ADVS study may have been lower because of greater ocular comorbidity in this group of patients. All of these investigations have classified any positive change on a questionnaire as improvement without accounting for random variation in the scales. Of course, this approach results in overestimation of true improvement.

In addition to reporting improvements in visual functioning after surgery, each of these studies also reported on changes in generic health-related quality of life after surgery. Brenner et al. reported a positive correlation between questions that assess visual function and improvements in mental health, current life satisfaction, and selected aspects of social functioning that the investigators felt may be mediated by sight (23). To capture changes in health-related quality of life, Steinberg et al. administered the Sickness Impact Profile (SIP), a multidimensional survey designed to measure the behavioral impact of illness (47). Although 89% of participants had improvements in their vision-targeted VF-14 scores, only 67% had SIP change scores greater than zero, and the mean decline in SIP scores (-2.1 ± 5.7) for the cohort after surgery was not significant. However, by reporting nonsignificant positive changes as "percent improved" the investigators are overestimating the magnitude of improvements after surgery.

Mangione et al. (33) used the SF-36 (18) to capture changes in health-related quality of life after cataract extraction. Despite improvements in vision-targeted Activities of Daily Vision scores, except for physical functioning which improved at three months after surgery, the remainder of the SF-36 sub-scales were either unchanged or worse. It is likely that the SF-36 physical functioning was most sensitive to the impact of cataract extraction because the majority of the items in this sub-scale are vision dependent. However, when compared with patients in whom ADVS scores were unchanged at one year after surgery, patients with average improvement in ADVS scores had 10% to 59% less decline across all SF-36 dimensions except for role limitations due to emotional problems, where the association between the sub-scale and the vision-targeted questions was not significant. The findings from all three of these studies suggest that although the benefit from cataract extraction and intraocular lens implantation does not translate into average improvements in generic health status, those with the greatest improvements in visual functional status had smaller observed declines in generic health status.

VISION-TARGETED AND GENERIC MEASURES OF HEALTH-RELATED QUALITY OF LIFE IN VISION-SPECIFIC CLINICAL TRIALS

To date, the vast majority of clinical trials designed to study the efficacy of treatments for eye diseases or disabilities have used widely accepted clinical end points such as visual acuity (24) or progression of visual field defects (48). A recent trial examining the efficacy of foscarnet versus ganciclovir for the treatment of cytomegalovirus (CMV) retinitis used both visual acuity and mortality as primary end points (49). The strength of these end points lie in their known reproducibility (24) and face validity. But, these measures

are limited by the lack of knowledge about the functional and health-related quality of life implications of small, but potentially relevant changes, such as a two line change in Snellen visual acuity. Additionally, traditional measures of visual function and vision-targeted questionnaires are unlikely to capture medication or surgical treatment side effects or their influence on health-related quality of life. For this reason, in clinical studies it is particularly important to also incorporate standardized symptom scales when possible. The influence of treatment benefits and side effects on health-related quality of life becomes critically important when more than one treatment administered in a clinical trial is found to be efficacious for preventing the primary end point of interest such as blindness. This situation occurred in the CMV retinitis trial referenced above.

The recently published National Eye Institute's 5 year research agenda emphasizes the importance of measuring both vision-targeted and generic health-related quality of life in vision research (50). In response to this, many recently initiated clinical trials in the vision sciences have included self-report measures designed to assess patients' perceptions of visual functioning and health-related quality of life. For example, two ongoing National Eye Institute sponsored clinical trials, the Ocular Hypertension Treatment Study and the Collaborative Initial Glaucoma Treatment Study, have incorporated measures of health-related quality of life, the SF-36 (18) and the Sickness Impact Profile (47), respectively, as secondary end points during the long-term follow-up phase of the trials (51). Additionally, an ongoing clinical trial designed to prospectively compare the long-term outcomes of treatment for ocular melanoma has recently incorporated both a vision-targeted measure of functioning (Activities of Daily Vision Scale) and a generic measure of health-related quality of life (SF-36) as secondary end points for the trial (52).

Recent empiric work suggests that self-reports of visual functioning, generic health-related quality of life (SF-36 and SIP), and traditional physician measures of patient function (e.g., Snellen acuity) tap into different dimensions of vision (29–33). The correlation between visual acuity and visual functioning, for example, are on the order of 0.3 and 0.45. Visual functioning, in turn, correlates at a similar level with overall health status. However, visual acuity either does not, or only very weakly, correlates (<0.12) with specific general health status measures or scale components of such measures. Very little empirical research describes the relationship between visual symptoms and other dimensions of health. Thus, it is apparent that at least these four, if not more, dimensions should be measured to fully understand the outcomes of eye conditions and interventions.

CONCLUSIONS

In summary, empirical data support that the three types of measures of visual functioning (physical, performance-based, and self-report) describe different aspects of visual functioning. Additionally, the lack of correlation between vision-targeted questionnaires and generic measures of health-related quality of life support that these measures are capturing different aspects of health-related quality of life. Therefore, the optimal approach to measuring health-related quality of life in vision research is to include a standardized generic core measure, such as the SF-36, and supplement it with vision-targeted scales that assess functioning and symptoms. Currently available questionnaires designed for the assessment of visual functioning are limited because most are designed for persons with cataracts, and there are minimal data describing their performance characteristics when applied to persons with other eye diseases. Additionally, there are few surveys with estimated reliability and validity that assess symptoms from eye diseases and there is an absence of vision-targeted measures that incorporate the subject's preference for visual states. Currently, there is interest in incorporating assessments of health-related quality of life into clinical quality of care systems (16), but this process will require further development and evaluation of self-report tools before these can be fully integrated into practice settings.

ACKNOWLEDGMENTS

Dr. Mangione is supported by a Clinical Investigator Award 1K08-AG00605, National Institute on Aging, National Institutes of Health. Additionally, preparation of this article was supported in part by the National Eye Institute, National Institutes of Health, and by RAND from its internal funds.

REFERENCES

1. Kosnik W, Winslow L, Kline D, Rasinki K, Sekuler R. Vision changes in daily life throughout adulthood. *J Gerontol Psychol Sci* 1988;43: 63–70.
2. Kline DW, Kline T, Fozard JL, Kosnik W, Schieber F, Sekuler R. Vision, aging, and driving: the problems of older drivers. *J Gerontol Psychol Sci* 1992;47:27–34.
3. Bernth-Petersen P. The effectiveness of cataract surgery, a retrospective study. *Acta Ophthalmol (Copenh)* 1981;59:50.
4. Lundstrom M, Fregell G, Sjoblom. Vision related daily life problems in patients waiting for cataract extraction. *Br J Ophthalmol* 1994; 78:608–611.
5. Lee PP, Kington R, Lillard L. The impact visual problems on health status. *Ophthalmology* 1993;100(suppl):130.
6. Lee PP, Hays R, Spritzer K. The functional impact of blurred vision on health status. *Invest Ophthal Vis Sci* 1993;34:790 (abstract).
7. Chiang YP, Bassie LB, Javitt JC. Federal budgetary cost of blindness. *Millbank Q* 1992;70;319–340.
8. Scott RA. *The making of blind men.* New York: Russell Sage Foundation, 1969.
9. Marx MS, Werner P, Cohen-Mansfield J, Feldman R. The relationship between low vision and performance of activities of daily living in nursing home residents. *J Am Geriatr Soc* 1994;40:1018–1020.
10. Scott IU, Schein OD, West S, Bandeen-Roche K, Enger C, Folstein MF. Functional status and quality of life measurement among ophthalmic patients. *Arch Ophthalmol* 1994;112:329–335.
11. Carabellese C, Appolonio I, Rozzini R, Bianchetti A, Frisoni GB, Frattola L, Trabucchi M. Sensory impairment and quality of life in a community elderly population. *J Am Geriatr Soc* 1993;41:401–407.
12. Tinetti ME, Speechley M, Ginter SF. Risk factors for falls among elderly persons living in the community. *N Engl J Med* 1988;319: 1701–1707.
13. Glynn RJ, Seddon JM, Krug JH, et al. Falls in elderly patients with glaucoma. *Arch Ophthalmol* 1991;109:205–210.
14. Uhlmann RF, Larson EB, Koepsell TD, Rees TS, Duckert LG. Visual impairment and cognitive dysfunction in Alzheimer's disease. *J Gen Intern Med* 1991;6:126.
15. Lee PP, Javitt JC. Measuring the benefit and value of services. *Arch Ophthalmol* 1994;112:32.
16. Lee PP, Schachat AP. Evaluating quality of care in the new health care environment. *Arch Ophthalmol* 1995:149–152.
17. Nelson KA. Visual impairment among elderly Americans: statistics in transition. *J Vis Impair Blind* 1987;81:331–334.
18. Ware JE, Sherbourne CD. The MOS 36-item short-form health survey (SF-36). I. Conceptual framework and item selection. *Med Care* 1992; 30:473–483.
19. Hays RD, Sherbourne CD, Mazel RM. The RAND 36-item Health Survey 1.0. *Health Econ* 1993;2:217–227.
20. Guyatt GH, Bombardier C, Tugwell PX. Measuring disease-specific quality of life in clinical trials. *Can Med Assoc J* 1986;134:889–895.
21. Patrick DL, Deyo RA. Generic and disease-specific measures in assessing health status and quality of life. *Med Care* 1989;27:S217.
22. Ware JE. Measuring patients views: the optimum outcome measure. *BMJ* 1993;306:1426–1430.
23. Sarks SH, Sarks JP. Age-related macular degeneration: atrophic form. In: Schachat AP, Murphy RP, Patz AP, eds. *Retina*. Vol. 2, St Louis: CV Mosby, 1989:152–155.
24. Ferris FL, Kassoff A, Bresnick GH, Bailey I. New visual acuity charts for clinical research. *Am J Ophthamol* 1982;94:91–96.
25. Bernth-Petersen P. Visual functioning in cataract patients—methods for measuring and results. *Acta Ophthalmol (Copenh)* 1981;59:198–205.
26. Mangione CM, Phillips RS, Seddon JM, et al. Development of the "Activities of Daily Vision Scale": a measure of visual functional status. *Med Care* 1992;30:1111–1126.
27. Sloane ME, Ball K, Owsley C, et al. The visual activities questionnaire: developing an instrument for assessing problems in everyday visual tasks. *Tech Dig Noninvasive Assess Vis Sys* 1992;1:26–29.
28. Steinberg EP, Tielsch JM, Schein OD, et al. The VF-14 an index of functional impairment in patients with cataract. *Arch Ophthalmol* 1994; 112:630–638.
29. Javitt JC, Brenner MH, Curbow B, et al. Outcomes of cataract surgery improvement in visual acuity and subjective visual function after surgery in the first, second, and both eyes. *Arch Ophthalmol* 1993;111: 686–691.
30. Applegate WB, Miller ST, Elam JT, Freeman JM, Wood TO, Gettlefinger TC. Impact of cataract surgery with lens implantation on vision and physical function in elderly patients. *JAMA* 1987;257:1064.
31. Brenner MH, Curbow B, Javitt JC, et al. Vision change and quality of life in the elderly, response to cataract surgery and treatment of other chronic ocular conditions. *Arch Ophthalmol* 1993;111:680–685.
32. Steinberg EP, Tielsch JM, Schein OD, et al. National study of cataract surgery outcomes, variation in 4-month postoperative outcomes as reflected in multiple outcome measures. *Ophthalmology* 1994;101: 1131–1141.
33. Mangione CM, Phillips RS, Lawrence MG, et al. Improved visual function and attenuation of age-related declines in health-related quality of life after cataract extraction. *Arch Ophthalmol* 1994;112:1419–1425.
34. Dimond EG, Kittle CF, Crockett JE. Comparison of internal mammary artery ligation and sham operation for angina pectoris. *Am J Cardiol* 1960;5:483–486.
35. Bernth-Petersen P. Cataract surgery outcome assessments and epidemiologic aspects. *Acta Ophthalmol (Copenh)* 1985;63:s174.
36. Fisher RA. Statistical methods for research workers. Edinburgh: Oliver and Boyd, 1936.
37. Mangione CM, Lee PP, Berry SH, Hays RD, Janz NK, Klein R, Owsley C. Development of a questionnaire for the assessment of visual function. *Invest Ophthalmol Vis Sci* 1995;36:1962A.
38. Edwards MG, Schuchat NP. Impact of Enucleation for Choroidal Melanoma on the Performance of Vision-Dependent Activities. *Arch Ophthalmol* 1991;109:519–521.

39. Russell PW, Sekuler R, Fetkenhour C. Visual functioning after pan-retinal photocoagulation: a survey. *Diabetes Care* 1985;8:57–60.

40. Ebert EM, Fine AM, Markowitz J, et al. Functional vision in patients with neovascular maculopathy and poor visual activity. *Arch Ophthalmol* 1986:104;1009–1012.

41. Fine SL, The MPS Group. Early detection of extrafoveal neovascular membranes by daily central field evaluation. *Ophthalmology* 1985:92;603–609.

42. Alexander MF, Maguire MG, Lietman JM, et al. Assessment of visual function in patients with age-related macular degeneration of low visual acuity. *Arch Ophthalmol* 1988:106;1543–1547.

43. Agency for Health Care Policy and Research. Cataract in adults: management of functional impairment. AHCPR Publications No. 93-0542, March 1993.

44. American Academy of Ophthalmology. *Cataract in the otherwise health adult eye.* San Francisco: American Academy of Ophthalmology, 1989.

45. McIntyre DJ. *Guidelines for cataract practice.* Bellevue, WA: McIntyre Eye Clinic and Surgical Center, 1993.

46. *Multidimensional functional assessment: the OARS methodology.* 2nd ed. Durham, NC: Duke University Press, 1978.

47. Bergner M, Bobbitt RA, Carter WB, et al. The Sickness Impact Profile: development and final revision of a health status measure. *Med Care* 1981;19:787–805.

48. Esterman B. Functional scoring of the binocular field. *Ophthalmology* 1982;89:1226–1234.

49. SOCA Research Group. Mortality in patients with the acquired immunodeficiency syndrome treated with either foscarnet or ganciclovir for cytomegalovirus retinitis. *N Engl J Med* 1992;326:213–220.

50. National Advisory Eye Council. *Vision research—a national plan: 1994–1998.* NIH Publication No. 93-3186, Bethesda: National Institutes of Health, 1993.

51. Janz NK, Wren PA, Lichter PR, et al. Assessing quality of life in the Collaborative Initial Glaucoma Treatment Study (CIGTS). Abstract presentation, American Academy of Ophthalmology Meeting, San Francisco, California 1994.

52. Collaborative Ocular Melanoma Study Group. Design and methods of a clinical trial for a rare condition: The collaborative ocular melanoma study group. COMS report 3. *Controlled Clin Trials* 1993;14:362–369.

Quality of Life and Pharmacoeconomics in Clinical Trials, Second Edition, edited by B. Spilker.
Lippincott-Raven Publishers, Philadelphia © 1996.

CHAPTER 109

AIDS

A. David Paltiel and Aaron A. Stinnett

INTRODUCTION

Considerations of quality of life and pharmacoeconomics are particularly salient in the context of acquired immunodeficiency syndrome (AIDS). Human immunodeficiency virus (HIV) illness is distinguished from most other diseases both by the special character of the patient population and by the unprecedented social crisis occasioned by the epidemic. The uniqueness of the situation and the emergence of influential patient advocacy groups have contributed to the evolution of a view that, in matters affecting people with HIV, traditional methods of evaluation may be inadequate. An opportunity exists to apply innovative approaches to quality of life assessment and pharmacoeconomic analysis and to speed new technologies to market. This chapter surveys the principles of evaluation analysis as they pertain to AIDS and discusses some unresolved issues in the context of HIV clinical care.

BACKGROUND

Distinctive features of HIV illness and the AIDS patient population lend a special flavor and a particular urgency to

issues of quality of life assessment and pharmacoeconomic analysis. In this section, we explore some of these unique characteristics and discuss their implications with regard to clinical trial design and the evaluation of new technologies.

Youth

Perhaps the most striking feature of the AIDS patient population, taken as a whole, is its relative youth. In November, 1993, the Centers for Disease Control and Prevention reported that HIV infection had become the leading cause of death among men aged 25–44 and the fourth leading cause of death among women in that age group (1). Were it not for their HIV infection, many patients might be expected to live long and unusually fruitful lives. Even when the infection is present, patients with asymptomatic HIV illness can maintain stable and productive physical, emotional, social, and vocational lives for 15 years or more.

Marginalization

A second distinguishing feature of the HIV patient population is that a disproportionate number belong to marginalized communities, many of which are not afforded the same rights and opportunities as others in society: gay men, intravenous drug users, commercial sex workers, prisoners, and the home-

A. D. Paltiel and A. A. Stinnett: Department of Health Policy and Management, Harvard School of Public Health, Boston, Massachusetts 02115.

less. It is not uncommon for the members of populations outside of society's mainstream to develop separate, alternative (sometimes labeled *counter-cultural*) value structures. Distinctive perceptions of reality and preference evolve in marginalized communities; traditional instruments to measure quality of life and therapeutic efficacy may not, therefore, be calibrated to these populations' standards of good, bad, desirable, and undesirable.

Sophistication and Activism

People with AIDS constitute an unusually informed, well organized, and visible patient population (2). Coalitions of patients and advocates—drawn primarily but not exclusively from the gay community—have succeeded in mounting a sustained attack on the traditional paternalism and risk-aversion of the drug regulation and clinical experimentation process. Activists have put regulators, scientists, and manufacturers on the defensive, forcing decisions to be made under the bright lights of the political process and shifting the premise of clinical trial investigation from a strictly scientific focus to a more consumer-centered orientation (3). Motivated as much by their need for access to care as by their sense of altruism, people with AIDS look upon participation in clinical trials less as a burden and more as an avenue to treatment. At the same time, however, these sophisticated consumers remain largely distrustful of the institutions that organize trials (the government, universities, the pharmaceuticals industry, and the medical establishment). As a result, it is not unusual to find that AIDS trials suffer from an uncommon degree of crossover and attrition (4). All of this complicates the evaluation process and strengthens the case for a more refined, AIDS-specific yardstick of both the quality and the efficacy of care.

Quantity Versus Quality Trade-offs

HIV infection is rapidly evolving into a chronic condition. Increasingly, the primary clinical concern of patents is not so much to cure their illness as it is to alleviate symptoms and to maintain, for as long as possible, the highest attainable degree of personal independence—in short, they seek to enhance their functional health status in the presence of infection. Traditional measures of clinical outcome that focus narrowly on survival may not be relevant to this patient group; what is required is a metric that captures the quality of life, functional capacity, and productivity criteria that are the center of concern for people with HIV. The search for such a measure is complicated by the paucity of satisfactory therapies for HIV illness. This forces decision makers to confront the sad fact that incremental extensions of life expectancy may only be obtainable at the price of a dramatic deterioration in quality of life. Consider, for example, the detrimental impact that antiretroviral side effects may have

on a patient's overall sense of well-being (5). In some instances, HIV-related medicines offer no survival benefit at all; such is the case, for example, with topical treatments for Kaposi's sarcoma, which improve comfort and enhance body image but do nothing to prolong life (6). Increasingly, the differences between alternative medicines are more likely to lie in their respective impacts on quality of life than in their effects on survival. As quality of life considerations begin to play a larger role in differentiating one course of therapy from another, analysts must expect to observe a far greater degree of variation in patient preferences from one individual to the next. To illustrate, consider the use of ganciclovir and foscarnet in the treatment of *Cytomegalovirus* infection: patients must receive these therapies intravenously, requiring a lifetime commitment to medical care several times a week (7). For some patients, the preservation of vision may be sufficient incentive to endure such a regimen; for others, it may not. Inclusion of quality-of-life considerations in the assessment of clinical outcomes can improve the sensitivity of decision making and its impact on what matters to the patient over the use of raw survival figures alone.

Absence of a Satisfactory End Point

Further complicating matters, there does not yet exist a universally accepted end point for HIV and AIDS clinical trials. Because of the long interval between the moment of HIV infection and the emergence of AIDS-defining symptoms, the standard clinical end points (mortality, survival time, symptom-free survival) are not usually practical. HIV trials often focus on intermediate measures of disease progression such as the CD4 lymphocyte count, p24 antigen titer, or some other laboratory-based surrogate marker. These, however, have been criticized as poor predictors of clinical impact, prognosis, and experience-based patient well-being (8,9).

This unique set of circumstances—a young and sophisticated but marginalized population suffering from a chronic illness for which no life-prolonging therapies have convincingly been shown to exist—conspire to create a heightened sense of urgency and a need to expedite and tailor-fit the process by which new medical technologies are developed, evaluated, approved, and brought to market. The special nature of AIDS has not gone unnoticed at the Food and Drug Administration (FDA). Indeed, much of the progress made over the last ten years in revising the rules governing the approval and regulation of new drugs has been achieved in the realm of HIV illness and, most particularly, antiretroviral therapies (10–12). Groundbreaking developments include new rules that permit the sale of unapproved investigational new drugs to treat serious or immediately life-threatening illnesses; widening of the definition of drugs eligible for expedited review; broader use of surrogate markers; relaxation of requirements governing the importation of small quantities of unapproved drugs from foreign sources for use on an individual basis; and implementation of ''Phase IV'' postmarketing studies (13–16).

The special nature of AIDS also calls for new thinking in the field of quality of life and pharmacoeconomic evaluation. The purpose of the next section is to explore the theoretical underpinnings of such research.

OBJECTIVES AND FOUNDATIONS

Consider the following statement of purpose:

HIV-related quality of life assessment and pharmocoeconomic evaluation seek to assist decision makers in choosing from among competing alternatives in situations of uncertainty and limited resources.

Evaluation aims to promote better decision making. In the particular context of HIV therapies, the goal is to inform choices by identifying those medicines that produce the greatest attainable reduction in HIV- and AIDS-related mortality and morbidity given constraints both on our understanding of the costs and benefits and on the resources that can be devoted to this purpose. Research in HIV-related quality of life assessment and pharmacoeconomics aims to produce timely, descriptively accurate, and relevant information regarding such decisions. It is the systematic identification of the beliefs and preferences that underpin decisions. It is a method of holding expert opinion and assumptions up to public scrutiny so that they can be understood, evaluated, criticized, modified, and refined by all interested parties. A quantitative, analytic toolkit is employed to achieve this end: the vocabulary of probability theory makes precise the many fuzzy terms (e.g., probably, very much, most of the time, or a reasonable amount) that so often insulate expert opinion from serious public scrutiny; utility and health-related quality of life assessment instruments are employed to assign consistent, analytic meaning to values, choices and preferences; a rigorously defined structure specifies critical trade-offs, thus isolating points of contention and illuminating areas of agreement; and sensitivity analysis is performed to examine the robustness of decisions to changes in underlying assumptions. In short, the goal of HIV-related evaluation is emphatically not to supplant the patient, the physician, the expert, the regulator, or the politician as the ultimate decision maker; nor is it to trivialize the pivotal role played by intangible issues and the ''gut feel'' in most real-world policy debates. Rather, it is to inform the decision making process using quantitative methods to explore the beliefs and values that lie at the heart of all difficult HIV care choices.

Implicit in the statement of purpose presented above are a number of fundamental assumptions regarding the market for health care that are rarely made explicit in analyses of medical technologies and that merit special scrutiny in the context of HIV illness and AIDS-related clinical care. Among

the most basic of these economic principles is the idea that human wants are unlimited, while the resources available to satisfy these wants are scarce. The first part of this statement (sometimes referred to as the *principle of nonsatiation*) might, at first blush, appear to be obvious; there are, however, some cases in which more is not necessarily better, and in which human wants for a particular good can indeed be satisfied. While it is the exception to the rule in most economic situations, the existence of a ''saturation point'' may be fairly common in the market for HIV care where there is a limit to how much treatment and therapy some patients can endure. Thus, maximizing an externally determined objective function (e.g., survival) may not always be appropriate.

A second principle, following directly from the first, is the inevitability of choice. While demand for some goods may be finite, it is generally held to be true that not all wants can be satisfied. Resource limitations constrain consumers, forcing them to make choices about how scarce assets will be allocated among competing options. For any alternative that is selected, another alternative must be forgone. At the heart of economic analysis is the idea of opportunity costs: the value of activities precluded by a particular action or choice. From the standpoint of economic efficiency, the wisdom of investing in a particular program of treatment or research cannot be considered in isolation; rather, it should be measured in the context of alternate uses for those resources, both within the realm of AIDS policy and in other sectors of society.

The inevitability of choice does not in itself signal a need for formal economic evaluation and regulation. In what economists refer to as a ''perfectly competitive'' market, the invisible forces of supply and demand can be relied upon to allocate resources efficiently with no need for external fine-tuning. In the market for health care, however, economists have identified various sources of market failure that prevent this optimal outcome (17). One example is the presence of moral hazard, a situation in which the individual making a decision about whether or not to consume a good (e.g., a medical treatment) does not pay the full price of that good. Privately insured patients receiving the benefits of a therapy, for example, generally pay only a fraction of the cost, the remainder being borne by their insurance company and fellow policyholders. Because the individual's decision does not take into account the full societal cost of the treatment, moral hazard can lead to overuse of services (18,19). A second source of market failure is the presence of externalities, situations in which one person does not fully take into account the consequences of his or her actions on the well-being of others. Externalities are an important consideration in the context of infectious diseases like AIDS, where one person's decision of whether or not to adopt preventive measures can affect the risks of infection population-wide.

In the presence of market failures, external intervention may be necessary to assure the efficient allocation of scarce resources. The methods of pharmacoeconomics, cost-effectiveness analysis, and cost–benefit analysis are rooted in the simple principle of rational allocation of costs and benefits. This tenet holds that decisions should be made on the basis of a careful comparison of marginal costs and marginal benefits—that is, the net benefits conferred for each additional unit of resources spent.

The preceding discussion provides only a cursory survey of the principles and assumptions that underpin the theory of economic evaluation. Decision makers should explore these themes further, to draw their own conclusions as to the appropriateness of these arguments as an intellectual justification for the use of economic evaluation as an aid to decision making in medical care, public health, and AIDS policy (20). The remainder of this chapter is built on these foundations, and focuses on their practical and theoretical implications for the evaluation of interventions related to HIV illness and AIDS.

ANALYTICAL DESIGN ISSUES

The foundations introduced in the previous section raise as many issues as they resolve. Many of their essential elements remain the subject of debate and controversy when applied to the design of HIV-related evaluations. Who, for example, is the appropriate decision maker? What are the competing alternatives to which a new technology should be compared? Which costs are germane to the analysis and how can they be evaluated? What is a suitable measure of health outcome and how can it be expressed?

The Decision Maker

The first step in an evaluation is to determine the appropriate perspective for the analysis. This can be a thorny exercise, since nearly every player in the health policy arena has a stake in HIV- and AIDS-related resource allocation decisions. Among the interested parties are prudent purchasers (including HMO formulary committees, insurance companies, government health financing agencies, and self-insured employers) seeking value for money; patients who are increasingly involved—both financially and intellectually—in their own clinical care decisions; pharmaceutical manufacturers seeking to inform internal research and development decisions, pricing policies, and marketing efforts; government regulators charged with the licensing of new technologies; and society, which seeks the greatest improvement in overall well-being for resources consumed. More often than not, a health intervention serves to redistribute costs and benefits among these stakeholders. For example, an HMO's decision to include an expensive new antiretroviral therapy in its formulary benefits the manufacturer and the patient but may impose additional burdens (in the form of higher premiums) on the majority of health plan members and their

employers. Depending on whose perspective is adopted, assessments of a therapy's appropriateness and cost-effectiveness may diverge.

Most AIDS-related cost-effectiveness analyses found in the scholarly literature adopt the societal perspective, from which all costs and benefits are taken into account regardless of whom they affect. It often makes sense, however, to consider a decision from multiple viewpoints. In the case of a new AIDS therapy, for example, an analysis performed from the societal perspective might be reconsidered both from the viewpoint of a local walk-in clinic and from the perspective of the manufacturer; the walk-in clinic's assessment of net costs will likely be smaller than the societal valuation due to the availability of federal and state subsidies; in contrast, the manufacturer may treat many of society's perceived costs as revenue items. By considering this single decision from multiple perspectives, it becomes possible to identify both expected gainers and potential losers. This information can help elucidate competing stakeholders' incentives, identify likely areas of conflict, and suggest strategies for outreach or coalition building in the policy process. Moreover, by bringing the tradeoffs among the affected parties into sharper focus, the adoption of multiple perspectives can provide valuable information for decision makers concerned with issues of equity.

Comparators

The economic consequences of a particular action only have meaning in light of the alternative activities precluded. From an economic point of view, the costs associated with the introduction of a new HIV therapy must be considered relative to some comparator intervention forgone. In general, the incremental impact of a new technology should be assessed with respect to the best option currently available or to the most widely accepted alternative. For many AIDS-related therapies, however, the task of choosing an appropriate comparator is easier said than done. The reasons are many. First, there often fails to exist any treatment that might serve as a basis for comparison. Consider, for example, ACTG 204, a trial examining the effectiveness of valaciclovir prophylaxis in preventing the complications of cytomegalovirus in AIDS patients with CD4 counts below $100/mm^3$ (21). In the absence of any satisfactory alternative, an economic evaluation of valaciclovir might have to employ the "do-nothing" strategy as its only realistic comparator. Second, even in instances where an alternative course of action exists, rapid flux in what is considered "the best available alternative" can complicate the analysis and bias any estimates of the efficacy of the new technology. In the case of prophylaxis against *Pneumocystis carinii* pneumonia (PCP), for example, efficacy has been demonstrated for a variety of medicines, including trimethoprim-sulfamethoxazole (22–24), dapsone (25–27), and aerosolized pentamidine

(28,29). Randomized controlled trials have been undertaken to compare them, both to each other and to newer regimens including atovaquone, primaquine/clindamycin, and higher dose aerosolized pentamidine (30–32). While these studies promise to determine the most effective agent and dosage regimen for PCP prophylaxis, care must be taken to choose a truly appropriate alternative medicine and to ensure that an evaluation based on an outdated comparator is not employed to exaggerate the efficacy of a new technology.

Costs

The net costs of a new therapy represent the change in resource consumption resulting from the selection of that intervention over the relevant comparison program. Costs can be categorized as direct, indirect, or intangible. While there is general consensus that all relevant direct and indirect costs should be captured in an analysis, the inclusion of intangible costs is more controversial.

In theory, the direct cost estimate should include all resource consumption wholly attributable to the delivery of the therapy in question. Examples of direct costs include not only the costs of administering the treatment, but also the costs of any other medicines or tests made necessary or unnecessary by its administration, as well as the costs of any additional inpatient hospital bed days and professional fees. In practice, however, determining the total direct costs associated with an HIV/AIDS treatment can be tricky (33–37). In addition to the common difficulties of isolating social resource costs from billing charges (38) and of incorporating the time value of money and health (39,40), additional complications arise as a result of the special character of HIV illness and the AIDS epidemic. In evaluating therapies that extend the asymptomatic state following HIV infection, for example, it may be important to include any net expected direct costs associated with changes in infection rates that are attributable to the treatment. These are referred to as external costs. The presence of an effective drug may both reduce the infectivity of the infected person and extend the period of time for which that person remains active and infectious (41). The same drug may also lead to an increase in the rate of voluntary HIV testing and to a reduced incentive for uninfected individuals to avoid high-risk behavior (42, 43). Depending on the magnitude of these changes, such a treatment may produce either an increase or a decrease in the spread of HIV and its associated direct costs (44). Another direct cost that may be relevant but not obvious relates to the nature of opportunistic infections in AIDS patients. As improved prophylaxis and treatment enable patients to live longer with more advanced immune dysfunction, previously rare opportunistic infections (e.g., *Mycobacterium avium* complex infection and cytomegalovirus infection) are becoming more common. To the extent that increases in such competing risks can be modeled, it is important for an

analysis to include the long-run expected direct costs and consequences of prolonged survival.

Some published estimates of the direct costs of AIDS can be found in the scholarly literature (45–49). Others may be obtained from publicly available datasets such as the AIDS Cost and Service Utilization Survey (ACSUS) (50). This AHCPR-sponsored, multisite, longitudinal survey of AIDS patients examined a variety of issues related to cost of AIDS care, utility and access. The survey included nearly 2,100 patients at 26 sites in 10 U.S. cities. The ACSUS patient population has notable diversity with respect to regions, service delivery systems, incidence rates and distributions of patients by source of payment, exposure category, and stage of illness (51). A follow-up to ACSUS currently being conducted by the RAND Corporation (the HIV Costs and Services Utilization Study or HCSUS) will employ a probability sampling mechanism and will attempt to capture a broader spectrum of provider types.

Indirect costs measure the impact of an intervention on the productivity of patients, family members, and others. While there is general agreement that indirect costs should be included in an evaluation, consensus has not been reached on how best to capture and report them. In some analyses, lost productivity is measured in monetary terms and treated as a component of resource costs; in other studies, it is incorporated into patients' estimates of their quality of life or well-being. Either treatment of indirect costs can be justified but care must be taken to avoid double counting; in other words, indirect costs must not be treated simultaneously as a resource cost and as a component of quality-adjusted health outcome. Given the unusual youth and productivity of many people with HIV and AIDS, the indirect societal costs of the epidemic are substantial; however, the special nature and heterogeneity of the at-risk population complicate efforts to estimate those costs. For example, it is not clear how society should value either the indirect economic costs attributable to the loss of an HIV-positive IV drug user who stole to support his habit or the forgone illegal income of prostitutes.

Finally, the importance and relevance of the psychic or intangible costs of AIDS cannot be overstated. As a practical matter, however, they defy estimation. A thorough accounting of the costs of AIDS ought to capture the very real costs of fear of infection, altruistic concern for those touched by the epidemic, despair and pain over the loss of loved ones, and stress suffered by family, friends, and—if not reflected in quality-adjusted health outcome measures—patients. Nevertheless, the realities of the policy process force analysts to deal with that which can be made tangible and to perform an objective, credible comparison of the consequences of dollars spent on one program over another. Often, the analyst is best advised to present the tangible costs as fairly and explicitly as possible, leaving it to the informed judgment of society to weigh them against the less readily quantifiable aspects of the problem.

Outcome Measures

Ideally, measures of health effectiveness should reflect all relevant changes in both morbidity and mortality resulting from an intervention. In practice, multiple outcome measures may be of interest in an HIV-related evaluation. These can include changes in clinical markers (e.g., CD4 count), symptom-free survival, overall length of life, and quality-adjusted length of life. In cases in which a medicine is thought to produce changes in viral load and infectivity, it may also prove necessary to consider any changes in the number of secondary infections produced (or averted) and the downstream epidemiological consequences. To reflect the composite impact of survival, well-being, toxicity, and side effects, analysts have developed special measures that are sensitive to both the quality and the quantity of life. These scales provide us with a standard currency with which to compare different health outcomes. One popular measure employed to represent net health effectiveness is the quality-adjusted life-year (or QALY) (52–55). QALY methods assign each possible health state a numerical weight between 0 (representing a health state equivalent to death) and 1 (denoting perfect health); quality-adjusted life expectancy is obtained by multiplying each health state's quality weight by the duration of time spent in that health state and then summing.

Methods of comparative evaluation of health states can be traced to two distinct schools of thought: the psychometric perspective and economics/decision theory (56–58). The psychometric approach is most commonly employed in situations where the purpose of the exercise is descriptive. Examples include work in health services research, outcomes research, and clinical epidemiology. The psychometric method involves the distillation of a large number of quality-of-life-influencing variables down to a smaller number of health status scales. The result is a description of a health state as a profile of scores on a handful of independent dimensions, representing the domains of health. Health status measurement instruments collect information regarding patient perceptions and preferences over such dimensions as mobility, physical activity, pain, disability, cognitive deficits, emotional well-being, life satisfaction, and social function. Numeric scores are assigned to patient assessments on each dimension. There is typically a clear ordering of levels of function within each domain. Generally, however, the scores carry only ordinal meaning; in other words, different scores on a particular scale tell us something about how a decision maker ranks alternatives, but they connote nothing with regard to that person's relative strength of preference between alternatives. Values on each scale are usually summed, sometimes with weights attached to reflect the relative importance of dimensions. While this procedure introduces a welcome degree of flexibility, it is unclear how the weighting factors should be determined. Moreover, in cases where individually determined weights are applied across populations (e.g., when the analysis is performed from a societal perspective), there is an implicit assumption that all individuals share the same mean preference for one health outcome over another.

Health status instruments that emerge from the psychometric school of thought can adopt either a generic or a disease-specific perspective (59). Generic (or global) quality of life assessment instruments use standardized questions that can be applied across a broad spectrum of diseases, therapies, and population subclasses. Some of the best understood and most comprehensive assessment instruments fit in this category, including: the Nottingham Health Profile (60), the Quality of Well-Being Scale (61), the Sickness Impact Profile (62), the Medical Outcomes Study (MOS) (63–65), the Katz Activities of Daily Living Index (66), the Duke–UNC Health Profile (67), the Karnofsky Performance Status Score (68), the Health Assessment Questionnaire (69), the Quality of Life Index (70), the Functional Status Questionnaire (71), and others (72–76).

Although they are easily applied to interdisease and interpatient comparisons, generic health measures cannot isolate determinants of quality of life that may be unique either to a particular illness or to a specific segment of the patient population. Disease-specific instruments are designed to address this weakness by providing greater content validity and improved sensitivity to disease particulars (e.g., natural history, patient demography, and therapeutic intervention). Many well-known generic quality of life assessment instruments have been adapted for particular use in patients with HIV illness. These include the Medical Outcomes Study (77–79), the Sickness Impact Profile and the Symptom Distress Scale (80), Spitzer's Quality of Life Index (81), the Karnofsky Performance Status scale (82), and the Quality of Well-Being Scale (83,84). In some cases, existing instruments have been combined into a comprehensive new index for HIV patients (85). New HIV-specific scales include: the HIV Patient-Reported Status and Experience Scale (HIV-PARSE) (86,87), the AIDS Health Assessment Questionnaire (AIDS-HAQ) (88), the HIV Overview of Problems Evaluation System (HOPES) (89), and others (90–99).

Whether they adopt a generic or a disease-specific perspective, psychometric health state indices are designed for descriptive purposes and are difficult to apply in the context of resource allocation and choice (100,101). In contrast, economic/decision theoretic instruments are specifically intended for use in decision making situations where a preference between competing alternatives must be obtained, even in the face of limited, imperfect information. Decision theoretic quality of life assessment tools seek to assign to each health state a holistic, value-based numerical score—commonly referred to as a utility—whose cardinal value embodies the decision maker's strength of preference. This approach is grounded in the economic theory of choice under uncertainty (102). A variety of well-established and documented techniques exists to elicit utilities including the standard gamble (also known as the basic reference lottery ticket) and the time-trade-off method (103–105). The standard gamble measures the decision maker's preference between an immediate, ensured outcome and an uncertain prospect that simultaneously offers both the chance of a better result and the risk of a worse one. The probabilities of better and worse outcomes are varied until indifference between the certain and the risky prospects is achieved. The time-trade-off seeks to identify the amount of current life expectancy in a particular health state that the decision maker would be willing to give up in exchange for a shorter length of life in perfect health.

One important area of ongoing research aims to bridge the gap that exists between the psychometric health status indices and the economic/decision-analytic methods of utility elicitation. Work in this field seeks to develop quality of life measures that use health-state classification systems to estimate utilities. Patients are asked to answer questions about their health status along a number of dimensions, such as functional capacity, emotional well-being, pain, and sensory function. The answers are combined into a single metric which (assuming certain restrictions to be true with regard to personal preferences under uncertainty) can be interpreted as cardinal utilities; structural parameter estimates necessary for these calculations can be obtained by surveying a representative sample from the population of interest. The best-known example of this approach is the Health Utilities Index, developed by Torrance and colleagues (106).

A utility elicitation instrument that has received recent attention and application is the EuroQol (107). This is a generic model that generates a single index value for each health state. It has been employed to examine quality of life in HIV patients receiving erythropoietin for anemia and prophylactic rifabutin (108,109). Another instrument that has been applied to patients with HIV is the Quality-Adjusted Time Without Symptoms and Toxicity (Q-TWiST) (110). Originally developed to evaluate adjuvant therapies for breast cancer, the Q-TWiST method measures time spent in symptom-free health states without disease progression for patients with HIV. It has been applied to the evaluation of quality of life in patients receiving zidovudine therapy (5,111) and in HIV-infected psychiatric outpatients (112).

Only a handful of HIV-related evaluation studies have employed economic utilities to measure quality of life. This can be explained, in part, by the difficulties of administering the standard gamble, the time-trade-off, and other measurement instruments in a clinical setting. It may also be due to the poor correlations that have been shown to exist between utility measures and the better-understood psychometric indices described above (56). Nevertheless, as the focus of future clinical investigations and evaluations shifts more and more toward questions of resource allocation, cost-containment, and decision making, these methods are likely to see wider application.

CHOICE OF ASSESSMENT INSTRUMENT

A broad selection of instruments is available for the elicitation of quality of life in patients with HIV illness. There is no absolute answer to the question of which method is best; indeed, when funds permit the use of a variety of scales, there is rich additional information to be obtained from comparing the results of multiple, complementary indices. This section outlines a few considerations that may be helpful to investigators in choosing from among the many available alternatives.

What Is the Research Objective?

Considerations of quality of life enter into all manner of HIV-related evaluations, spanning the range from purely descriptive studies of "what is" to more normative assessments of "what ought to be." In choosing one health status instrument over another, investigators should consider the positioning of their research question with respect to that continuum.

Research that focuses predominantly on descriptive issues (including studies of clinical practice, patient monitoring surveys, and population-wide epidemiological investigations) may be well served by one of the widely used psychometric measures. Health status indices can be helpful in characterizing changes in perceived quality of life resulting from a particular intervention. The more popular scales are well understood, rigorously documented, and conveniently standardized. They have been extensively tested on a variety of patient populations and have, in many instances, been adapted for particular use in HIV-infected populations.

Researchers concerned more with normative issues (including comparative treatment evaluations, cost-effectiveness studies, resource allocation questions, and appraisals of societal priority setting) may wish to consider a quality of life assessment instrument that adheres to a stricter set of rules regarding preference and choice. Utility-based approaches to the construction of QALYs have a number of properties that commend them for use when making decisions about the efficient allocation of limited health care resources. Measures of utility can be interpreted as having cardinal meaning (i.e., their results reflect differences in strength or intensity of preference). This cardinality lends interpretability to cost-effectiveness ratios constructed using utility-based outcome measures. In addition, the axioms of choice and preferences on which utility measures are based constitute a defensible framework for rational decision making that has considerable normative appeal to many people (102,113). Because they focus on individual choice, economic/decision-theoretical measures permit the analyst to capture the preferences of the particular population under study, rather them imposing a single, externally-determined weighting scheme on all affected people.

How Constrained Are the Resources?

The choice of a quality of life assessment instrument is often limited by considerations of time, money and expertise. In the clinical trial setting, for example, the decision of whether or not to include a "quality component" in the investigation often boils down to such issues as implementation cost, brevity of the elicitation process, ease of self-administration, and required degree of interviewer training. Some HIV-related quality of life assessment instruments have been adapted for express use in such resource-constrained settings (87,90).

The adoption of a brief, self-administered assessment instrument over a more detailed, comprehensive measure involves a delicate trade-off: the time and money savings are offset by reduced reliability, diminished internal consistency, and loss of precision. Wu and Rubin (99) have argued that in the case of investigations that focus on individual monitoring and decision making, this may be an unacceptable price to pay; on the other hand, the trade-off may be justifiable in screening and detection situations (where sensitivity is more critical than specificity) or in the case of large group comparisons.

How Diverse Is the Population?

Clinical investigations of the efficacy of HIV therapies grow increasingly more diverse with respect to both the demography and the geography of the study population. This increased diversity forces investigators to confront the critical role played by language, culture, and standard of living in shaping perceptions of health-related quality of life. Researchers whose investigations cross linguistic, socioeconomic, or international boundaries should consider the adoption of quality of life assessment instruments that have been carefully translated and tested to ensure consistency of meaning, reliability, and validity. For study populations that span linguistic groups, a small number of scales have been carefully translated, primarily for use in western European settings (114–116). Less has been achieved in adapting scales either to a broader range of languages or to the diversity of cultural and socioeconomic groups represented by the HIV patient population.

How Unique Is the Population?

As the inventory presented above suggests, there has been a veritable epidemic in recent years of health-related quality of life assessment scales and indices. It would appear to have become fashionable for investigators to assert that existing scales are not specific enough to detect clinically relevant changes in the particular population they wish to study. This may or may not be true; what is apparent, however, is that the assertion is rarely verified before the work of developing another index begins (117). Moreover, expansion of the number of assessment scales complicates the work of comparing illnesses, therapies, populations, and studies. Given the recent proliferation of both general and disease-specific indices, researchers should consider the likely incremental value of yet one more instrument.

CONCLUSIONS

Questions of HIV-related resource allocation and clinical decision making present policymakers with a tangled web of epidemiological, economic, psychological, and statistical considerations. Emerging technologies in the fields of pharmacoeconomics and quality of life assessment can contribute to the unraveling of that web by bringing the trade-offs involved in policy decisions into sharper focus. At the same time, however, it bears repeating that policy evaluations are a means of informing—and not replacing—decision makers. The choices that must be made with regard to HIV- and AIDS-related resource allocation will require a degree of compassion and an ethical foundation that cannot be supplied by economic theory or mathematical models.

REFERENCES

1. Centers for Disease Control and Prevention. *National seroprevalence surveys.* HIV/NCID/11-93/036. Washington, DC: U.S. Government Printing Office, 1992.
2. Dunbar MM. Shaking up the status quo: how AIDS activists have challenged drug development and approval procedures. *Food Drug Cosmetic Law J* 1991;46:673–706.
3. Edgar H, Rothman DJ. New rules for new drugs: the challenge of AIDS to the regulatory process. *Milbank Q* 1990;68(suppl 1):111–142.
4. Byar DP, Schoenfeld DA, Green SB, et al. Design considerations for AIDS trials. *N Engl J Med* 1990;323:343–1347.
5. Lenderking WR, Gelber RD, Cotton DJ, et al. Evaluation of the quality of life associated with zidovudine treatment in asymptomatic human immunodeficiency virus infection. *N Engl J Med* 1994;330:738–743.
6. Northfelt DW, Kah JO, Volberding PA. Treatment of Kaposi's sarcoma. *Haematol Oncol Clin North Am* 1991;5:297–309.
7. Merigan TC, Resta S. Cytomegalovirus: where have we been and where are we going? *Rev Infect Dis* 1990;12:S811–S819.
8. Cohen J. Searching for markers on the AIDS trail. *Science* 1992;258:388–390.
9. Lagakos S, Hoth DF. Surrogate markers in AIDS: where are we? Where are we going? *Ann Intern Med* 1992;116:599–601.
10. Gladwell M. Beyond HIV: the legacies of health activism. *Washington Post,* Oct 15, 1992:A29.
11. Cooper EC. Changes in normal drug approval process in response to the AIDS crisis. *Food Drug Cosmetic Law J* 1990;45:329–338.
12. Edgar H, Rothman DJ. New rules for new drugs: the challenge of AIDS to the regulatory process. *Milbank Q* 1990;68(suppl 1):111–142.
13. Kessler DA. The regulation of investigational drugs. *N Engl J Med* 1989;320:281–288.
14. Burlington DB. Statutory and regulatory framework for drug approval. *J Acquir Immune Defic Syndr* 1990;3(suppl 2):S4–S9.
15. Siegel JE, Roberts MJ. Reforming FDA policy: lessons from the AIDS experience. *Regulation* 1991;14:71–77.
16. Merigan TC. You can teach an old dog new tricks: how AIDS trials are pioneering new strategies. *N Engl J Med* 1990;323:1341–1343.
17. Phelps CE. *Health economics.* New York: Harper-Collins, 1992.
18. Arrow KJ. Uncertainty and the welfare economics of medical care. *Am Econ Rev* 1963;53:941–973.

19. Pauly MV. The economics of moral hazard: comment. *Am Econ Rev* 1968;58:531–537.
20. Mishan EJ. *Cost-benefit analysis*. New York: Praeger, 1976.
21. AIDS Clinical Trial Group (ACTG) Protocol 204. A randomized, double-blind trial of valciclovir prophylaxis for opportunistic cytomegalovirus end-organ disease in HIV-infected patients with advanced HIV infection. 1993.
22. Fischl MA, Dickinson GM, La Voie L. Safety and efficacy of sulfamethoxazole and trimethoprim chemoprophylaxis for *Pneumocystis carinii* pneumonia in AIDS. *JAMA* 1988;259:1185–1189.
23. Ruskin J, LaRiviere M. Low-dose co-trimoxazole for prevention of *Pneumocystis carinii* pneumonia in human immunodeficiency virus. *Lancet* 1991;337:468–471.
24. Wormser GP, Horowitz HW, Duncanson FP, et al. Low-dose intermittent trimethoprim-sulfamethoxazole for prevention of *Pneumocystis carinii* pneumonia in patients with human immunodeficiency virus infection. *Arch Intern Med* 1991;151:688–692.
25. Hughes WT, Kennedy W, Dugdale M, et al. Prevention of *Pneumocystis carinii* pneumonia in AIDS patients with weekly dapsone (letter). *Lancet* 1990;336:1066.
26. Metroka CE, Jacobus D, Lewis N. Successful chemoprophylaxis for pneumocystis with dapsone or bactrum. *Presented at the fifth international conference on AIDS,* June 4–9, 1989, Montreal, Canada.
27. Torres RA, Palermo S, Gregory G, et al. Prophylaxis for *Pneumocystis carinii* pneumonia (PCP) with aerosol pentamidine (AP) or oral dapsone (OD) in patients with AIDS or severe ARC. *Presented at the fifth international conference on AIDS.* June 4–9, 1989, Montreal, Canada.
28. Leoung GS, Feigal DW, Montgomery AB. Aerosolized pentamidine for prophylaxis against *Pneumocystis carinii* pneumonia. *N Engl J Med* 1990;323:769–775.
29. Hirschel B, Lazzarin A, Chopard P, et al. A controlled study of inhaled pentamidine for primary prevention of *Pneumocystis carinii* pneumonia. *N Engl J Med* 1991;324:1079–1083.
30. Hughes W, Leoung G, Kramer F, et al. Comparison of Atovaquone (566C80) with trimethoprim-sulfamethoxazole to treat *Pneumocystis carinii* pneumonia in patients with AIDS. *N Engl J Med* 1993;328:1521–1527.
31. Hardy W, Feinberg J, Finkelstein D, et al. A controlled trial of trimethoprim-sulfamethoxazole or aerosolized pentamidine for secondary prophylaxis of *Pneumocystis carinii* pneumonia in patients with the acquired immune deficiency syndrome. *N Engl J Med* 1992;327:1842–1848.
32. Schneider M, Hoepelman A, Karel J, et al. A controlled trial of aerosolized pentamidine or trimethoprim-sulfamethoxazole as primary prophylaxis against *Pneumocystis carinii* pneumonia in patients with HIV infection. *N Engl J Med* 1992;327:1836–1841.
33. Drummond M, Davies L. Treating AIDS: the economic issues. *Health Policy* 1988;10:1.
34. Hay JW. Econometric issues in modeling the costs of AIDS. *Health Policy* 1989;11:125.
35. Knickman J, et al. Protocol 3, comparisons of the cost effectiveness of alternative models for organizing services for persons with AIDS. National Center for Health Services Research and Health Care Technology Assessment, Rockville, MD 1989 Supplement.
36. Pascal A. Conceptual issues in assessing the economic effects of the HIV epidemic. *Health Policy* 1989;11:105.
37. Scitovsky AA, Cline MW, Abrams DI. Effects of the use of AZT on the medical care costs of persons with AIDS in the first 12 months. *J Acquir Immune Defic Syndr* 1990;3:904.
38. Finkler SA. The distinction between cost and charges. *Ann Intern Med* 1982;96:102–109.
39. Cropper ML, Portney PR. Discounting and the evaluation of lifesaving programs. *J Risk Uncertainty* 1990;3:369–379.
40. Keeler EB, Cretin S. Discounting of life-saving and other nonmonetary effects. *Manage Sci* 1983;29:300–306.
41. Anderson RM, Gupta S, Ray RM. Potential of community-wide chemotherapy or immunotherapy to control the spread of HIV-1. *Nature* 1995;350:356–359.
42. Philipson TJ, Posner RA. *Private choices and public health: the AIDS epidemic in an economic perspective.* Cambridge, MA: Harvard University Press, 1983.
43. Philipson TJ, Posner RA, Wright JH. *Why AIDS prevention programs don't work. Issues in Science and Technology* Spring:1994;10:33–35.
44. Paltiel AD, Kaplan EH. Modeling zidovudine therapy: a cost-effectiveness analysis. *J Acquir Immune Defic Syndr* 1991;4:795–804.
45. Hellinger FJ. The lifetime costs of treating a person with HIV. *JAMA* 1993;270:474–479.
46. Bennett CL, Civitanic M, Pascal A. The costs of AIDS in Los Angeles. *J Acquir Immune Defic Syndr* 1991;4:197–203.
47. Bennett CL, Pascal A, Civitanic M, et al. Medical care costs of intravenous drug users with AIDS in Brooklyn. *J Acquir Immune Defic Synd* 1992;5:1–6.
48. Lee PR, Durbin M, Kahn JG. Cost of HIV and AIDS for privately insured persons in California, 1985–1990. Institute for Health Policy Studies, University of California, San Francisco. Final Report submitted to the Health Resources and Services Administration, US Public Health Service, Contract no. 282-88-0018 (1991).
49. Scitovsky AA, Rice DP. Estimates of the direct and indirect costs of acquired immunodeficiency syndrome in the United States, 1985, 1986, and 1991. *Public Health Rep* 1987;102:5–17.
50. Special section on the AIDS cost and service utilization survey (ACSUS). *Health Services Res* 1994;29:523–581.
51. Berk ML, Maffeo C, Schur CL. Research Design and Analysis Objectives. AIDS Cost and Services Utilization Survey (ACSUS) Reports, No. 1. AHCPR Pub. No. 93-0019. Rockville, MD: Agency for Health Care Policy and Research, 1993.
52. Torrance GW, Feeny D. Utilities and quality-adjusted life years. *Int J Technol Assess Health Care* 1989;5:559–575.
53. Torrance GW. Utility approach to measuring health related quality of life. *J Health Econ* 1986;5:1–30.
54. Sox HC, Blatt MA, Higgins MC, et al. *Medical decision making.* Boston: Butterworths, 1988:216–220.
55. Owens DK, Sox HC. Medical decision making: probabilistic medical reasoning. In: Shortliffe EH, Perreault LE, Fagan LM, Wiederhold G, eds. *Medical informatics: computer applications in medicine.* Reading, MA: Addison-Wesley, 1990:70–116.
56. Tsevat J. Methods for assessing health-related quality of life in HIV-infected patients. *Psychol Health* 1994;9:19–30.
57. Wu AW, Lamping DL. Assessment of quality of life in HIV disease. *AIDS* 1994;8:S349–359.
58. Patrick DL, Erickson P. *Health status and health policy: quality of life in health care evaluation and resource allocation.* New York: Oxford University Press, 1992.
59. Patrick DL, Deyo RA. Generic and disease-specific measures in assessing health status and quality of life. *Med Care* 1989;27:S217–S232.
60. Hunt SM, McKenna SP, McEwen J, Williams J, Papp E. The Nottingham Health Profile: subjective health status and medical consultations. *Soc Sci Med* 1981;15A:221–230.
61. Kaplan RM, Anderson JP. The quality of well-being scale: rationale for single quality of life index. In: Walker CS, ed. *Quality of life: assessment and application.* London: MTP Press, 1988:51–77.
62. Bergner M, Bobbitt RA, Carter WB, Gilson BS. The Sickness Impact Profile: development and final revision of a health status measure. *Med Care* 1981;19:787–805.
63. Ware JE Jr, Sherbourne CD. The MOS 36-item short-form health survey (SF-36):1. Conceptual framework and item selection. *Med Care* 1992;30:473–483.
64. McHorney CA, Ware JE Jr, Raczek AE. The MOS 36-item Short-Form Health Survey (SF-36):II. Psychometric and clinical tests of validity in measuring physical and mental health constructs. *Med Care* 1993;31:247–263.
65. Stewart AL, Ware JE, eds. *Measuring functioning and well-being: the Medical Outcomes Study Approach.* Durham, NC: Duke University, 1992.
66. Katz S, Ford AB, Moskowitz RW, Jackson BA, Jaffe MW. Studies of illness in the aged: the index of ADL: a standardized measure of biological and psychosocial function. *JAMA* 1963;185:914–919.
67. Parkerson GR, Gehlbach SH, Wagner EH, James SA, Clapp NE, Muhlbaier LH. The Duke-UNC Health Profile: an adult health status instrument for primary care. *Med Care* 1981;19:806–828.
68. Karnofsky DA, Abelmann WH, Craver LF, Burchenal JH. The use of nitrogen mustards in the palliative treatment of carcinoma. *Cancer* 1948;1:634–656.
69. Fries JF, Spitz PW, Young DY. The dimensions of health outcomes: the Health Assessment Questionnaire, disability, and pain scales. *J Rheumatol* 1982;9:789–793.

70. Spitzer WO, Dobson AJ, Hall J, et al. Measuring the quality of life and cancer patients: a concise QL-index for use by physicians. *J Chronic Dis* 1981;34:585–597.

71. Jette AM. Functional status instrument: reliability of a chronic disease evaluation instrument. *Arch Phys Med Rehabil* 1980;61:395–401.

72. Nelson EC, Berwick DM. The measurement of health status in clinical practice. *Med Care* 1989;27:S77–S90.

73. Spilker B, Molinek FR Jr, Johnston KA, Simpson RL Jr, Tilson HH. Quality of life bibliography and indexes. *Med Care* 1990;28:DS1–DS77.

74. Bergner M, Rothman ML. Health status measures: an overview and guide for selection. *Annu Rev Public Health* 1987;8:191–210.

75. Kaplan RM. Quality of life measurement. In: Karoly P, ed. *Measurement strategies in health psychology*. New York: Wiley-Interscience, 1985:115–146.

76. Walker SR, Rosser RM. *Quality of life: assessment and applications.* London: Ciba Foundation, 1988.

77. Wachtel T, Piette J, Mor V, Stein M, Fleishman J, Carpenter C. Quality of life in persons with human immunodeficiency virus infection: measurement by the medical outcomes study instrument. *Ann Intern Med* 1992;116:129–137.

78. Burgess A, Dayer M, Catalan J, Hawkins D, Gazzard B. The reliability and validity of two HIV-specific health-related quality-of-life measures: a preliminary analysis. *AIDS* 1993;7:1001–1008.

79. Lubeck DP, Fries JF. Changes in quality of life among persons with HIV infection. *Qual Life Res* 1992;1:359–366.

80. Ragsdale D, Morrow JR. Quality of life as a function of HIV classification. *Nurs Res* 1990;39:355–359.

81. Williams JBW, Rabkin JG. The concurrent validity of terms in the quality of life index in a cohort of HIV-positive and HIV-negative gay men. *Controlled Clin Trials* 1991;12(suppl 4):129S–141S.

82. Dournon E, Rozenbaum W, Michon C, et al. Effects of zidovudine in 365 consecutive patients with AIDS or AIDS-related complex. *Lancet* 1988;2:1297–1302.

83. Wu AW, Mathews WC, Brysk LT, et al. Quality of life in a placebo-controlled trial of zidovudine in patients with AIDS and AIDS-related complex. *J Acquir Immune Defic Syndr* 1990;3:683–690.

84. Kaplan RM, Anderson JP, Wu AW, Mathews WC, Kozin F, Orenstein D. The quality of well-being scale: applications in AIDS, cystic fibrosis, and arthritis. *Med Care* 1989;27:S27–S43.

85. Cleary PD, Fowler FJ, Weissman J, et al. Health-related quality of life in persons with acquired immune deficiency syndrome. *Med Care* 1993;31:569–580.

86. Berry SH, Bozzett SA, Hays RD, et al. Measuring patient-reported health status and experience in advanced HIV disease: the HIV-PARSE survey instrument. Santa Monica: RAND, 1994.

87. Bozzette SA, Hays RD, Berry SH, Kanouse DE. A perceived health index for use in patients with advanced HIV disease: derivation, reliability, and validity. *Med Care* 1994;32:716–731.

88. Lubeck DP, Fries JF. Changes in quality of life among persons with HIV infection. *Qual Life Res* 1992;1:359–366.

89. Ganz PA, Schag CAC, Kahn B, Peterson L. Assessing the quality of life of HIV infected persons: clinical and descriptive information from studies with the HOPES. *Psychol Health* 1994;9:93–110.

90. Wu AW, Rubin HR, Mathews WC, et al. A health status questionnaire using 30 items from the medical outcomes study. Preliminary validation in persons with early HIV infection. *Med Care* 1991;29:786–798.

91. Wu AW, Rubin HR, Mathews WC, et al. Functional status and well-being in a placebo controlled trial of zidovudine in early symptomatic HIV infection. *J Acquir Immune Defic Syndr* 1993;6:452–458.

92. Gelber RD, Lenderking WR, Cotton DJ, et al. Quality-of-life evaluation in a clinical trial of zidovudine therapy in patients with mildly symptomatic HIV infection. *Ann Intern Med* 1992;116:961–966.

93. Kaplan RM, Anderson JP, Wu AW, et al. The quality of well-being scale. Applications in AIDS, cystic fibrosis, and arthritis. *Med Care* 1989;27:S27–S43.

94. Lubeck DP, Fries JF. Changes in quality of life among persons with HIV infection. *Qual Life Res* 1992;1:359–366.

95. Testa MA, Lenderking WR. Measuring health-related quality of life in ACTG 175 (forthcoming).

96. Hays RD, Shapiro MF. An overview of generic health related quality of life measures for HIV research. *Qual Life Res* 1992;1:91–98.

97. Rapkin BD, Smith MY. Assessment of functional status in persons with HIV infection. *Phys Med Rehabil* 1993;7(Suppl):S43–S71.

98. Burgess A, Catalan J. Health-related quality of life in HIV infection. *Int Rev Psychiatry* 1991;3:357–364.

99. Wu AW, Rubin HR. Measuring health status and quality of life in HIV and AIDS. *Psychol Health* 1992;6:251–264.

100. Tandon PK. Applications of global statistics in analyzing quality of life data. *Stat Med* 1990;9:819.

101. Bozzette SA, Duan N, Berry S, Kanouse DE. Analytic difficulties in applying quality of life outcomes to clinical trials of therapy for HIV disease. Presented at *Symposium on quality of life methodology at quality of life and HIV infection: the biopsychosocial dimension*, Amsterdam, July 1992. *Psychol Health* 1994;9:143–156.

102. Von Neumann J, Morgenstern O. *Theory of games and economic behavior*. New York: Wiley, 1953.

103. Raiffa H. *Decision analysis: introductory lectures on choices under uncertainty*. Reading, MA: Addison-Wesley, 1968.

104. Weinstein MC, Fineberg HV, Elstein AS, et al. *Clinical decision analysis*. Philadelphia: WB Saunders, 1980.

105. Torrance GW. Utility approach to measuring health-related quality of life. *J Chronic Dis* 1987;40:593–600.

106. Torrance GW, Boyle MH, Horwood SP. Application of multi-attribute utility theory to measure social preferences for health states. *Oper Res* 1982;30:1043–1069.

107. The EuroQol Group. EuroQol—a new facility for the measurement of health-related quality of life. *Health Policy* 1990;16:199–208.

108. Revicki DA, Brown RE, Henry DH, et al. Recombinant human erythropoietin and health-related quality of life of AIDS patients with anemia. *J Acquir Immune Defic Syndr* 1994;7:474–484.

109. Revicki DA, Simpson KN, Wu AW, et al. Quality of life in rifabutin prophylaxis for *Mycobacterium avium* complex in people with AIDS (abstract). *Qual Life Res* 1994;3:44.

110. Gelber RD, Goldhirsch A, Cavelli F. Quality-of-life-adjusted evaluation of adjuvant therapies for operable breast cancer. The international breast cancer study group. *Ann Intern Med* 1991;114:621–628.

111. Gelber RD, Lenderking WR, Cotton DJ, et al. Quality-of-life evaluation in a clinical trial of zidovudine therapy in patients with mildly symptomatic HIV infection. *Ann Intern Med* 1992;116:961–966.

112. Lenderking WR, Worth JL, Beckett MD. Quality of life assessment in HIV-infected psychiatric outpatients: perceived health, functional status, symptoms, and preferences for cardiopulmonary resuscitation. *Psychol Health* 1994;9:51–64.

113. Pliskin JS, Shepard DS, Weinstein MC. Utility functions for life years and health status. *Oper Res* 1980;28:206–224.

114. Gilson BS, Erikson D, Chavez CT, et al. A Chicano version of the Sickness Impact Profile (SIP). *Culture Med Psychiatry* 1980;4:137–150.

115. Bucquet D, Condon S, Ritchie K. The French version of the Nottingham Health Profile: a comparison of the item weights with those of the source version. *Soc Sci Med* 1990;30:829–835.

116. Alonso J, Anto JM, Moreno C. Spanish version of the Nottingham Health Profile: translation and preliminary validity. *Am J Public Health* 1990;80:704–708.

117. Drummond MF, Davies L. Economic analysis alongside clinical trials: revisiting the methological issues. *Int J Technol Assess Health Care*. 1991;7:561–573.

Quality of Life and Pharmacoeconomics in Clinical Trials, Second Edition, edited by B. Spilker.
Lippincott-Raven Publishers, Philadelphia © 1996.

CHAPTER 110

Nutrition and Quality of Life Measurement

Carol E. Smith and Susan V. M. Kleinbeck

INTRODUCTION

The benefits of good nutritional status are lauded by health professionals; guidelines to ensure nutritional status are published by schools, state and federal agencies, and health care organizations. Yet empirical evidence exhibiting positive improvement in quality of life (QOL) outcome measures as a consequence of nutritional intervention remains difficult to demonstrate (1–4). This chapter provides evidence the association of QOL and nutritional status can be gleaned in clinical trials. This chapter also (a) clarifies the concept quality of life as it relates to nutritional status in health or disease, (b) evaluates the use of a generic and/or a specific quality of life instrument, and (c) specifies measures that reflect oral, enteral, and/or parenteral nutrition status of the population of interest (5,6). This chapter explores these issues based on a review of the literature and published empirical studies.

CONCEPTUALIZING QOL AS A MULTIDIMENSIONAL CONSTRUCT

In the past, QOL was either undefined or conceptualized from a rather narrow perspective of a professional specialty (7–10). Most investigators agree that QOL is a multidimen-

C. E. Smith and S. V. M. Kleinbeck: University of Kansas School of Nursing, Kansas City, Kansas 66160.

sional concept divided broadly into a minimum of four dimensions: physical, functional, mental, and social (11,12). Padilla's QOL Index (13) is a scale with five domains—psychological, physical, symptoms–side effects, nutrition, and social/financial—designed to measure QOL in cancer patients. The nutrition domain addresses the patient's ability to eat, taste changes, worry about weight, and eating as a pleasure. However, Cella (11) warns that these subdivisions or domains may not fit neatly under one of the major dimensions of QOL. Rather, subdivisions like nutrition may straddle more than one dimension, such as appetite and the ability to derive pleasure during eating occurring in two domains: physical and nutrition (14).

DEFINITIONS

The early definitions and measures of QOL include utility analyses (15), which reported ratings of quality-adjusted life-years (QALYs), calculated as the number of years of additional survival associated with the improved health state (16–18). Cost utility analysis has been used extensively to justify the expenditure for nutritional treatments to government policymakers (19). However, this approach includes no information relative to activities of daily living and energy to carry out desired life roles (e.g., mother, employee, and/ or student), nor does the approach relate health status to QOL (20,21).

Health-Related Quality of Life

Health-Related quality of life (HRQL) is a circumscribed measure that is narrower in scope than the more general quality of life term and reflects the quality of daily living perceived by an individual with acute illness or chronic disease (22). Definitions of HRQL may reflect an individual's satisfaction with their state of physical, mental, and social well-being (9,23). It is critical to measure the value a person places on functional ability in relation to what is seen as possible or ideal, because a person's behavior is based on such comparisons (24).

Value-Related Quality of Life

In this chapter, the term QOL refers to health-related quality and is defined as a person's sense of well-being relative to their values in five general areas of life—health, functional ability, family, socioeconomics, psychologic status, and spiritual condition. Value-related QOL definitions also should be defined broadly to include patient and family measures of productive social, economic, spiritual, or other areas of life (25). People judge their well-being and quality of life relative to their life goals or the values they hold (26–30). As Gill and Feinstein (31) point out in their recent review of 75 QOL articles, incorporating patients' values and preferences is what distinguishes QOL from other health measures. The primary advantage of the definition presented here is the ability to compare QOL across groups without eliminating individuals' differing sets of values and goals (e.g., culture, socioeconomics, or functional status).

The importance of measuring individuals' values in estimating QOL is captured by Ferrans and Powers (27) in their Quality of Life Index (QLI). On this index, subjects first rate the importance of response items related to four areas of life (health and function, socioeconomics, family, and psychological/spiritual status) on a five-point Likert-type scale. Those same items then are rated by the subject according to the degree of satisfaction the individual has with each item. The two ratings are compared, resulting in a value-weighted QOL calculation. The QLI score represents a perception of four dimensions of quality with an appreciation of the individual's preferences in life. This unique feature allows for a multidimensional assessment of quality of life that distinctively measures an appreciation of each person's preferences in life that still can be compared to others. Thus, this index brings a unique contribution to the study of QOL.

Using the QLI of Ferrans and Powers, Smith (7) found that patients (N = 116) dependent on total parenteral nutrition (TPN) have scores comparable to those reported for hemodialysis (32–34) and liver transplant patients (35) but higher than cancer patients who were experiencing pain (36). When individual scores in the four areas were reviewed, clear distinctions between patients were seen. For example, some patients had indicated great importance but little satisfaction with family life. These distinctions allow for measurements of QOL that potentially could identify the interactions between the treatment being tested in the clinical trial and each person's values. The non-ill family members of the TPN patients in Smith's study (7) had scores similar to those of healthy college students but were a standard deviation above the patients' scores. These results indicate sensitivity of the instrument to lack of physical illness and to degree of severity (e.g., pain).

Nutrition-Related Quality of Life

Evidence for the importance of nutrition-related QOL comes from research with patients who are dependent on nutritional support for health and, in some cases, survival. Ladefoged measured the QOL in 13 total parenteral nutrition (TPN) patients and judged the extent of physical distress, psychological symptoms, social and leisure restrictions, acceptance of parenteral therapy, and overall satisfaction with life (very satisfied to not satisfied) (37). In broadening the measures of QOL, Burns (a clinical nurse specialist) and colleagues reported their results of a three-year study of 63 HTPN patients (38). Mortality was low (5%), and 78% of the patients returned to a normal lifestyle; however, 73% required repeated hospitalization, mainly for suspected sepsis. As commentary indicated, the lack of consideration of social rehabilitation (having enough energy to be involved in social and employment activities) were significant limitations of these studies.

Relationship between QOL and Nutrition: Functional Status

Nearly all measures of QOL, whether generic or disease specific, include health and functional status measures. Health (both physical and mental states) is undergirded by nutritional status. Functional status, defined as the energy to carry out everyday activities, is positively related to nutritional status, in that energy in the form of carbohydrates and glucose that supply the muscle, neuron, and organ cells with substrates for cellular function are required to carry out everyday activities. For example, neural synapses in both the brain and muscle tissue require balanced fluids and electrolytes; the ability of the immune system to produce mast cells, antibodies, and leukocytes are dependent on protein stores; and organ tissue development and repair are contingent upon the presence of essential amino acids (39). Recently, even the nonessential amino acids have been associated with functional ability, as measured by perceived levels of vigor (40). Functional status, described by a person's ability to maintain daily activities and roles, reflects nutritional status alterations. Instruments to obtain patients' perceptions of everyday functioning quantify individuals for comparison to others with similar illnesses or treatments and also allow for self-comparison over time. For evaluating results of TPN therapy, the national data base uses an ordinal descriptive scale (ranging from minimal to complete) to rate each subject's function in normal age-related activities (e.g., able to complete school work, sustain employment, or manage household tasks) (41). This rating scale allows for distinguishing successful social and physical rehabilitation to TPN (42).

The nutritional status measures selected for use in a clinical trial must be specific to the topic of interest or represent a component of nutrition appropriate to the variables under study. A measure of self-perceived and investigator-rated functional status also should be obtained (43–46). Whether blood laboratory values or the more global self-rated level of energy to carry out everyday activities is used, the measure must represent the component of nutrition appropriate to the variables under study. Functional ability (e.g., level of energy to carry out everyday activities) is greatly influenced by a person's nutritional status. Thus, each person's perceived function and, if possible, blood laboratory measures of nutrition should be considered in all clinical trials (47). The strength of the association between nutrition and QOL is clearly dependent on the specificity of the nutritional measure selected.

QOL INSTRUMENTS

There are three basic approaches to QOL measurement. One is through the use of generic instruments which provide a summary of health-related QOL, another focuses on a specific group or condition (48–51), and the third combines attributes of both the generic and specific measures. Table 1 delineates the broad scope of the generic measures as compared to the specific measures that target a particular group and measure all aspects of that group's HRQL.

HRQL is influenced by health habits, knowledge, and attitudes, as well as the availability of health care services, social networks, and economic resources of the individual. Furthermore, family, community, and cultural elements influence each of these factors. Therefore, measures of the effectiveness of nutritional and functional treatments to improve QOL entail more than a sample of blood or the recording of dietary intake. Investigators must also incorporate social and public health treatments in clinical trials (52).

Community-level measures related to nutrition might be generated by addressing concepts similar to those associated with individual QOL. For example, physical fitness and function levels would be higher in "healthy" communities that provide jogging/walking/bicycling paths or opportunities to exercise during work hours. Social function would be influenced by providing public transportation for disadvantaged persons, leisure time, or employment opportunities. Low-fat menus in restaurants would enable people to select healthy foods. Changes can also occur at the organizational level. Grocery stores might provide low-fat, low-sodium

TABLE 1. *Distinguishing attributes of QOL instruments*

Generic QOL	Specific QOL
Broadly applicable across different diseases, medical treatments, and demographic/cultural groups	Measures characteristics of a group (specific disease, special population, certain function, given condition)
Useful for distinguishing between-subject differences at a point in time (e.g., policy studies)	Used to assess within-subject changes in health status over two or more points in time (e.g., clinical trials)
Capable of classifying populations into specific states (e.g., better or worse QOL)	Required to detect small changes in scores between experimental and control groups (how much QOL has changed)
Responses are solicited across several domains	Instrument focus is specific to the area of interest, "due to my cancer..."
Examples: The Sickness Impact Profile (SIP), Euroqual, Medical Outcomes Study (MOS)	*Examples:* Quality of Life Index for Cancer (QLI-Ca), Inflammatory Bowel Disease Questionnaire

convenience foods, or employers could install new exercise facilities. In addition, social policy changes could provide what, in essence, constitutes nutritious quality of life in a community by providing vending machines available with healthy snack foods. Certainly in this cost-conscious era, health care is viewed as more than an extenuation of life. In reality, the health dimension represents the services, medications, dietary regimens, and treatments that ameliorate disease and, more importantly, add to people's ability to function in their chosen, everyday life roles (53).

Selecting a Measure

Although there are QOL measures with strong psychometric properties (criterion/construct validity), no gold standard currently exists (48). Therefore, the investigator will need to evaluate several instruments critically before selecting one for a nutrition study (49,54). Selection criteria should include (a) empirical evidence that the instrument can distinguish minimal patient status changes in the area of interest over time or across treatments, (b) compatibility with the investigator's concept of QOL and the posed research questions, (c) an acceptable psychometric history, (d) whether patients will consider the items relevant (face validity), and (e) ease of administration for staff and patients (1,48,49).

Because QOL has been included only recently in nutrition studies, a suitable instrument that incorporates all variables of interest may be difficult to locate. One approach is to select a standardized QOL measure and add the illness/treatment-specific variables. Notice in Table 3 how Ovesen, Hannibal, and Mortesen used a known QOL measure and substituted items regarding appetite and how good the food

TABLE 2. *Standard references for nutrition status measurement and science*

Year	Author	Title	Publication/Publisher
1976	BR Bistrian, GL Blackburn, J Vitale, D Chochran, J Naylor	"Prevalence of malnutrition in general medical patients"	*Journal of the American Medical Association*, Vol. 235, No. 15, pp. 1567–1570.
1979	MH Seltzer, JA Bastidas, DN Cooper, P Engler, B Slocum, HS Fletcher	"Instant nutritional assessment"	*Journal of Parenteral and Enteral Nutrition*, Vol. 3, No. 3, pp. 157–159.
1984	JP Baker, AS Detsky, DE Wesson, SL Wolman, S Stewart, J Whitewell	"Nutritional assessment: a comparison of clinical judgment and objective measures"	*Medical Association Journal*, Vol. 130, No. 2, pp. 180–181.
1984	AM Boza, HM Shizgal	"The Harris Benedict equation reevaluated: Resting energy requirements and the body cell mass"	*American Journal of Clinical Nutrition*, Vol. 40, pp. 168–182.
1984	AS Detsky, JP Baker, RA Mendelson, SL Wolman, DE Wesson, KN Jeejeebhoy	"Evaluating the accuracy of nutritional assessment techniques applied to hospitalized patients: methodologies and comparisons"	*Journal of Parenteral and Enteral Nutrition*, Vol. 8, No. 2, pp. 153–159.
1984	KN Jeejeebhoy	"Objective measurements of nutritional deficit [editorial]"	*Journal of Parenteral and Enteral Nutrition*, Vol. 8, No. 1, pp. 1–2.
1984	RT Ottow, HA Bruining, J Jeekel	"Clinical judgment versus delayed hypersensitivity skin testing for the prediction of postoperative sepsis and mortality"	*Surgery, Gynecology, and Obstetrics*, Vol. 159, No. 5, pp. 475–477.
1984	I Warnold, K Lundholm	"Clinical significances of preoperative nutritional status in 215 noncancer patients"	*Annals of Surgery*, Vol. 199, No. 3, pp. 299–305.
1986	BR Bistrian	"Some practical and theoretic concepts in the nutritional assessment of the cancer patient"	*Cancer*, Vol. 8 (Suppl), pp. 1863–1866.
1986	RA Pettigrew, GL Hill	"Indicators of surgical risk and clinical judgment"	*British Journal of Surgery*, Vol. 73, No. 1, pp. 47–51.
1987	AS Detsky, JR McLaughlin, JP Baker, N Johnston, S Whittaker, RA Mendelson, KN Jeejeebhoy	"What is subjective global assessment of nutritional status?"	*Journal of Parenteral and Enteral Nutrition*, Vol. 11, No. 1, pp. 8–13.

1987	WO Spitzer	"State of science 1986: Quality of life and functional status as target variables for research"	Journal of Chronic Disease, Vol. 40, No. 6, pp. 465–471.
1988	HL Greene, KM Hambidge, R Schanler, RC Tsang	"Guidelines for the use of vitamins, trace elements, calcium, magnesium, and phosphorus in infants and children receiving total parenteral nutrition: report on the Subcommittee on Pediatric Parenteral Nutrient Requirements from the Committee on Clinical Practice Issues of the American Society for Clinical Nutrition"	American Journal of Clinical Nutrition, Vol. 48, pp. 1324–1342.
1988	DL Patrick, P Erickson	"What constitutes quality of life? Concepts and dimensions"	Clinical Nutrition, Vol. 7, No. 2, pp. 53–63.
1988	JJ Pomposelli, EA Flores, BR Bistrian	"Role of biochemical mediators in clinical nutrition and surgical metabolism"	Journal of Parenteral and Enteral Nutrition, Vol. 12, pp. 212–218.
1990	ST Fry	"Ethical Issues in Total Parenteral Nutrition"	In B Pillar, Project Director & S Perry, Program Director, "Evaluating Total Parenteral Nutrition: Final Report and Core Statement of the Technology Assessment and Practice Guidelines Forum" [symposium]. Nutrition, Vol. 6, No. 4, pp. 329–332.
1990	JR Saffle, CM Larson, J Sullivan	"A randomized trial of indirect calorimetry-based feedings in thermal injury"	Journal of Trauma, Vol. 30, No. 7, pp. 776–783.
1991	DF Cella	"Functional status and quality of life. Current views on measurement and intervention"	In Functional status and quality of life in persons with cancer, pp. 1–12. American Cancer Society.
1992	DF Cella	"Overcoming difficulties in demonstrating health outcome benefits"	Journal of Parenteral and Enteral Nutrition, Vol. 6 (Suppl 6), pp. 106S–111S.
1992	AL Steward, JE Ware (eds)	Measuring function and well-being	Duke University Press
1993	EP Shronts	"Basic concepts of immunology and its application to clinical nutrition"	Nutrition in Clinical Practice, Vol. 8, No. 4, pp. 177–183.
1994	RF Kushner, EA Ayello, PL Beyer, A Skipper, CE Van Wey III, EA Young, LB Balogun	"National Coordinating Committee clinical indicators of nutrition care"	Journal of the American Dietetic Association, Vol. 94, No. 10, pp. 1168–1177.
1994	ME Shils, JA Olson, M Shike	Modern nutrition in health and disease (8th ed., Vol. 1)	Lea & Febiger

TABLE 3. *Relationship between quality of life and nutrition: reported clinical findings*

Authors/design and sample	Quality of life measure	Nutrition measure			Intervention	Results
		Anthropometric	Diet	Serum		
Keithley, Zeller, Szeluga, Urganski (2) Comparative descriptive design; AIDS (N = 33) and non-AIDS (N = 7)	Quality of Life Index (QLI for Cancer, Ferrans and Powers) 35 items of satisfaction/importance of health and functioning, social/economic status, psychological/spiritual, family	Height Weight Triceps skin fold Midarm circumference	Four food diaries (4 days each) for self-report; included portions and brand names. *Analysis* Computer program: "Nutritionist III"	Albumin *Immune tests:* White blood cell with differential T-helper cells	9 mo observation; no diet instruction or intervention	QLI not significantly different across HIV+ groups; no report of HIV− subjects, perhaps because cancer version used; no relationship between QLI subscales or total scores and nutrition measures Protein and calories (% basal energy expenditure) were adequate. Inadequate (<RDA) intake of vitamins and minerals Anthropometric measure within normal limits except triceps skin fold (which was not significant) Serum albumin different in Gp4 (sickest and N = 1); could be liver function or hydration; T-helper cells number not related to albumin level Conclusion: Although there was a downward trend in protein and calorie, there was no relationship between QLI and nutrition; homosexual/bisexual males often left the family subscale unanswered; need QLI for this subgroup
N = 40 homosexual and bisexual males; HIV+ subjects divided into four groups using modified Walter Reed AIDS staging criteria: Gp1 = 9 Gp2 = 13 Gp3 = 9 Gp4 = 2 HIV− subjects: Gp5 = 7						
Ollenschlaeger, Thomas, Konkol, Diehl, Roth (77) Randomized Prospective Control Clinical Trial: Treatment Group (Gp1) N = 13; Control Group (Gp2) N = 16	Weekly by Gp1 only. 16-item investigator developed subjective well-being analog (0–10) during chemotherapy Items characterized typical complaints of leukemia pa-	Daily weight quantified by percentage of Broca weight (definition of nutritional status)	Dietician record of food intake. kcal/kg^{-1} IBW, median of daily intake	None	All: Free choice from menu of 1–2g protein, 30–50 kcal/kg^{-1} body weight Gp1: Daily dietician counseling, nutrition education, motivation,	Factor 1 = 16-item quality of life analog scale factored (3) and labeled as weakness/malaise (50% variance) Factor 2 = Psychological distress (11.7% of variance) Factor 3 = Side effects of regimen (7.7% variance) Correlation (p = <0.01) of: Weight loss to factor 1; r = 0.40 Energy intake to factor 1; r = −0.24 Energy intake to factor 3; r = −0.40

Sample	Measures	Intervention	Results
N = 29; Hospitalized, with acute leukemia during chemotherapy (median 10 weeks). Criteria: Weight loss >5% in the last three months or <90% of Ideal Body Weight (IBW)	tients under treatment	medication information Gp2: Free menu only	Quality of hospital diet to factor 3; r = −0.50 End of 10 wk regime: Gp1 = 68.8% regained weight Gp2 = 31.3% regained weight Conclusion: Quality of life and nutritional behavior are related
Ovesen, Allingstrup, Hannibal, Mortensen, Hansen (3) Prospective randomized clinical trial; stratified by primary disease, weight loss (±5%), performance status N = 105, with life expectancy of >3 months: Treatment Group (Gp1) N = 57 (74% female); Control Gp (Gp2) N = 48 (79% female) Diagnosis: Breast, ovarian, or lung cancer; about 20:40:40 ratio	1. QL-Index (Spitzer) × 3 (before chemotherapy cycle, and first diet visit; support of family item on QL-Index was replaced with item about appetite and pleasure of eating) 2. Global analog 100 mm: "How good is your quality of life?" (extremely poor to extremely excellent) Six times: 1. Weight 2. Mean values of 3 measures of triceps, biceps, subscapular, and suprailiac skin fold used to calculate body density 3. Fat-free mass (FFM) calculated from above 4. Arm circumference and triceps skin fold used to calculate midarm muscle area Three-consecutive-day self-report diet diary × 6 over 5 months.	None Gp1 = Individualized oral nutrition counseling by dietitian twice a month for 5 months Gp2 = Nutrition support at discretion of MD (usual treatment)	Although increases in Gp1 were present, changes from initial measurement of anthropometric measures were limited but not significant; only significant change was in triceps skin fold (possibly type 1 error from multiple comparisons) Energy intake and protein intake all significantly different from initial testing for Grp1 only; no difference in Grp2 (note: No change in weight) After 6 cycles, 63% of Gp1 responded to chemotherapy compared to 46% in Gp2 (p = 0.11); no difference in survival rates QL index increased significantly at the end of chemotherapy for both groups; probable cause of increased QL index scores was amount of tumor regression, rather than nutrition Global analog unchanged pre/post Conclusion: Small increase in weight (Gp1) not reflected in improvement to quality of life

TABLE 3. *Continued.*

Authors/design and sample	Quality of life measure	Nutrition measure				Intervention	Results
		Anthropometric	Diet	Serum			

Authors/design and sample	Quality of life measure	Anthropometric	Diet	Serum	Intervention	Results
Ovesen, Hannibal, Mortensen (55) Posthoc comparative descriptive N = 104; 22–77 yr with breast (19), ovarian (47), or lung (38) cancer with near-normal physical performance function condition. Gp1 < 5% weight loss Gp2 > 5% weight loss	General Health Questionnaire (GHQ): 30-item psychosocial health test QL-Index (Spitzer): family support replaced with appetite and food tastes good item Linear analog (100 mm); "How good is the quality of your life?" Answered at home once before chemotherapy	Group identification: Habitual weight (self-report) minus present weight 1. Weight 2. Mean values of 3 measures of triceps, biceps, subscapular, and suprailiac skin fold used to calculate body density 3. Fat-free mass (FFM) calculated from above 4. Arm circumference and triceps skin fold used to calculate midarm muscle area	3-consecutive-day self-report diary before first chemotherapy	Albumin	Observation	GHQ (psychologic/social health) Factor Analysis (high inner correlations): Factor 1 = Social functioning Factor 2 = Depression/anxiety Factor 3 = Outlook/happiness Factor 4 = Insomnia GHQ correlation were significant with: QL index; r = 0.56 Global analog; r = −0.49 Energy intake/kg FFM; r = −0.30 Protein intake/kg FFM; r = −0.38 Not significant with weight loss No correlation reported for albumin QL-Index to weight loss; r = 0.42 p <001. QL index not different between subjects with extensive and localized disease; no significant difference between groups on energy and protein expressed as FFM Conclusion: GHQ and QL in patients losing weight is lower (QL index has strong physical domain)

1070

Study	Design/Sample	Quality of Life Measure	Other Measures	Dietary Measures	Biochemical Measures	Procedure	Results/Conclusion
Rogers, Donahoe, & Costantino (60) Randomized clinical trial N = 27: Treatment Group (Gp1) N = 15; Control Group (Gp2) N = 12; all with chronic obstructive pulmonary disease and <90% ideal body weight (IBW) Exclusions: 1. No exacerbation of obstructive disease within last eight weeks 2. Any disease that affects weight		Sickness Impact Profile at 2 month pretesting	Height Weight Triceps skin fold Midarm circumference Energy 1. Resting energy expenditure (O_2 intake on awakening) 2. Exercise test: 12-min walking distance 3. Muscle test: ventilatory and handgrip (average of both hands) 4. Dyspnea analog (100 mm) No dysp = 0 5. Dyspnea oxygen cost analog (has activities of daily living along line)	Diet history in home with meal observation. During hospital: Nutrition analysis program "Food Processor II" (food weight before and after by dietitian) At home: 3-day diet diary/month according to prescribed trained method; mailed monthly	Albumin, total protein, total lymphocyte count, transferrin, retinol binding protein and prealbumin 24-hr urine: nitrogen creatine	All: 3 weeks of pretesting; 1 wk of hospitalization following randomization; repeat testing at week 4 and month 4 Gp1: Counseling (Symptom management, meal plan) and supplement (>1.7 × resting energy expenditure) for 4 weeks; repeat testing at wk 4 and discharge; 1 home visit before month 4 test Gp2: Discharged to home, free choice of diet, readmitted for week 4 test	No significant differences in SIP scores between groups at pretesting or at 4 months posttreatment (generic scale) Gp1 increased in weight (2.4 kg) over control which had a 0.5-kg loss ($p = 0.04$). Gp1 exercise, handgrip, and ventilatory function improved, but not significantly. No relationship reported between biochemical markers and quality of life Triceps and midarm measures increased but not significantly Conclusion: Nutrition improved muscle function and exercise performance (Functional Status); nutrition is only minimally related to SIP measure; dyspnea improved non-significantly with nutrition intervention; most improvement in hospital; cannot get same improvement at home

tasted for the family support items (55). Variables that nutritionists may want to include are the symptoms of weight loss/gain, anorexia, and weakness, as well as satisfaction with eating, mood, pain, or social interaction (1). However, because single-item instruments (e.g., How good is the quality of life?) and single-concept ratings (e.g., pain or mood scales) do not recognize the multidimensional aspect of QOL, investigators are cautioned not to limit their instrument selection to a single dimension.

NUTRITIONAL MEASURES

Normative height and weight age-related life insurance tables and growth and development curves for children have been the standard measures for nutritional status for decades (56–58). Table 2 lists the standard references that can be used to select nutrition measures and/or evaluate nutritional aspects of clinical trials. More recently, serum elements and self-report diaries of food intake or function have served as convenient clinical measures of nutrition (Table 3). The use of simple blood laboratory measures (e.g., glucose tolerance) or anthropological measures (e.g., triceps skin fold) either ignore the complexity of the construct of nutritional status or are too complex (e.g., percentage of body fat estimated using the water submersion technique) to be carried out reliably (59). As Table 3 illustrates, measures specific to the population render more significant results than traditional nutritional testing alone (60).

Clinical Assessment

Evaluation of subjects' baseline nutritional status by experienced clinicians is essential to the interpretation of clinical trial results (61). The Subjective Global Assessment (SGA), a clinical observation measure based on history and physical data, is a structured method of estimating a subject's nutritional state (62,63). The SGA serves as a data collection form of nutritional history (height and weight change, dietary intake, gastrointestinal symptoms of >2 weeks, functional capacity, and metabolic demand of primary diagnosis) and the presence of abnormal physical characteristics (muscle wasting, edema, ascites, mucosal lesions, cutaneous lesions, and hair change). At the close of the assessment, the clinician is directed to declare whether the individual is (a) well nourished, (b) moderately (or suspected of being) malnourished, or (c) malnourished. The interrater reliability for the SGA rankings was 91% (100 out of 109 case agreement), which is 78% beyond agreement percentages that could be expected by chance alone ($\kappa = 0.784$) (63). The ordinal rankings of the SGA are predictive of individuals likely to develop nutritionally mediated complications of disease (64). The data suggest that it is better to rely on a combination of historical, physical, and functional measures, rather than depending on anthropometric indicators and laboratory tests alone. Indeed, the superiority of clinical judgment has been confirmed by Ottow et al. (65), who demonstrated that clinical judgment was superior to measurement of delayed hypersensitivity in predicting postoperative infection, and by Pettigrew and Hill (66), who reported the SGA identified the risk of complications as effectively as the best plasma protein indicators.

Energy Intake and Expenditures

Clinical trials designed to test the effectiveness of nutritional intervention compare two levels (e.g., treatment versus control) of oral intake (see Table 3) or compare one mode (e.g., enteral versus parenteral) of intake with another (67). Measurement of the effect of nutritional energy intake may be by self-report, direct observation, serum laboratory testing, anthropologic measurements, or any combination of the four methods. Energy expenditures can be calculated by indirect calorie expenditure (calorimetry). Calculation of calorimetry of subjects may be by standardized formula or by portable computerized machine; however, the convenience of a simple formula may be misleading. In a sample of stressed patients, the energy demands increase and decrease and will vary with age (68). Using a formula to estimate the resting energy expenditure for research purposes may introduce some degree of measurement error due to individual differences. Indirect calorimetry based on a ratio of ventilatory oxygen to carbon dioxide (V_{O_2}/V_{CO_2}) measured at the bedside is a more accurate measure of resting energy expenditure. The difficulty with testing energy expenditure with the computerized machine is the expense of each measurement. In studies involving subjects at extremes of age during the convalescence from a complex illness, the investigator will need to weigh the expense of the indirect computerized calorimetry against the need to demonstrate small but significant changes in energy consumption.

Self-Report and Observation Methods

Unfortunately, observation of oral intake generally requires confinement of the subject in a nutritional research center or hospital to control and document actual calories consumed. Although costly and cumbersome to implement, observation of oral intake provides more accurate information than self-report and more clearly illustrates the positive relationship between nutrition and quality of life (60). When data are gathered solely by self-report, the potential of measurement error diluting the treatment effect is high. Subjects may forget to record information and rely on memory to complete the data collection form at a later time, or the 3-day food diary may be done during days when the patient is the most compliant (known as the *Hawthorne effect*). The expense of hospitalization for data collection solely by direct observation is prohibitive; however, a combination of the two techniques may be reasonable. For example, Rogers and colleagues (60) collected a diet history in the home with observation of meal preparation at the beginning of the study, scheduled a home visit during the second and fourth months of the study, and still required the usual 3-day food diary on a monthly basis. Self-reported data can also be strengthened by repeated measurements over time and collection of information during both weekdays and weekends. Requiring brand names of food products in addition to measured portions in the diet diary will increase further the accuracy of the nutritional analysis of data (2).

Serum Laboratory Testing

Creatinine index, lymphocyte counts, total lymphocyte counts (white blood cells multiplied by lymphocyte $\times$ 100), binding protein, and albumin concentration have all been related to nutritional status (60–71). Using randomized, controlled blinded design with TPN subjects at Brigham and Women's Hospital, researchers concluded that well-being, that is, vigor-inertia on the Profile of Mood States (POMS) (72), from baseline correlated with biological blood nitrogen levels and functional status (self-reported survey of fatigue, vigor, depression) (40). This was one of the first nutrition intervention studies demonstrating a relationship between improvement in patients' self-reported functional status and other clinical measures (improved nitrogen balance, early discharge from the hospital, and fewer episodes of infection). The physician and dietitian authors of the study concluded that vigor reports may prove useful and inexpensive when evaluating the nutritional status of patients. Furthermore, nutritional support using glutamine supplements have resulted in reduced toxicity and sustained function for patients undergoing chemotherapy (73).

Matarese and colleagues reported at an American Dietetic Association Research conference about extensive laboratory and anthropological assessments of hospitalized patients (N = 3,086) and use of nutrition status measures as predictors of mortality risk within 2 weeks of the nutrition measures (74). Univariant analysis revealed age, percent of weight change, albumin levels, transferrin, total lymphocyte count, delayed hypersensitivity skin tests, the prognostic nutrition index score ($p < 0.001$), and triceps skin fold ($p = 0.004$) were variables predictive of death within two weeks. The negative predictive value (0.97) of the logistic regression model was much higher than the positive predictive value (0.145), and the maximum sensitivity and specificity were relatively high (69% and 70%, respectively). While these data suggest that the multiple objective measures are predictive of survival, no measure of the quality of life of the survivor was obtained.

Anthropometric Measures

As Table 3 illustrates, anthropometric measures of nutrition do not consistently reflect change in status of postexperimental treatment. The discussion section of a research report will often indicate that the anthropometric data for the treatment group were "improved, but not significantly" (3,60). The difficulty in achieving a significant change may be related to the sensitivity of the measures (63). Mechanical bioelectrical impedance analysis and laboratory controlled determinations may result in anthropometric changes that occur beyond that which is possible by chance (2).

Normative base values of height, weight, skin fold by age, race, and sex for populations in a variety of nations are available in a two-volume reference by Sails et al. (64). This compilation describes the "state of the science" information in minute detail useful to nutritional inquiry.

Functional Status

The coding scheme designed to standardize energy costs required to perform activities of daily living has been tested and published by public health and sports medicine investigators (75). The compendium of physical activities lists a five-digit code that classifies activities of daily living, leisure and recreation, occupation, and rest and its intensity as the ratio of work metabolic rate to resting metabolic rate (METs). The intensity assigned to activities in the compendium were determined by selecting a mean energy expenditure value for each of the 19 major types of activity.

The advantage to the researcher of this compendium is that a system to measure energy expended for most activities a subject might describe (along with a computer input code) is readily available. In QOL studies, the total amount of energy expended over a day or week could translate into functional status. Higher-energy activities indicate higher functional status; lower energy expenditure activities represent lower functional status. Instrumentation to collect the activity level should include the type, duration, and intended purpose of the activity performed.

Socioeconomic Variables

The economic limitations of some people's resources may inhibit their purchase of nutritious food. The availability of socioeconomic resources (e.g., transportation, money, cooking and refrigeration facilities, access to fresh produce) are related to nutritional status; measures of these variables should be posed as QOL indicators (76).

CONCLUSIONS

Opportunities and challenges abound as investigators strive to measure the positive effect of nutritional intervention on the quality of peoples' lives. We recommend consideration of the following during the development of clinical trials, including measures of nutritional status:

Recognize QOL as a multidimensional construct that is influenced by individuals' values and goals.

Include a functional status self-report that measures everyday activities.

Measure individual activity levels to render an estimation of daily energy use.

Incorporate population-specific QOL variables with standardized instruments having acceptable psychometric properties.

Examine a variety of socioeconomic indicators capable of assessing QOL in the family and community (e.g., income available for food, mode of transportation to the grocery store).

ACKNOWLEDGMENTS

Research cited herein was supported by NIH NINR grant K07NR00020, Carol E. Smith, RN, PhD, Principal Investigator. Jan Hudnall is acknowledged for her superb editorial assistance.

REFERENCES

1. Cella DF. Overcoming difficulties in demonstrating health outcome benefits. *JPEN* 1992;16(suppl 6):106S–111S.
2. Keithley JK, Zeller JM, Szeluga DJ, Urbanski PA. Nutritional alterations in persons with HIV infections. *Image J Nurs Schol* 1992;24: 183–189.
3. Ovesen L, Allingstrup L, Hannibal J, Mortensen EL, Hansen OP. Effect of dietary counseling on food intake, body weight, response rate, survival, and quality of life in cancer patients undergoing chemotherapy: a prospective, randomized study. *J Clin Oncol* 1993;11: 2043–2049.
4. Wilson DM. Long-term tube feeding practices and involvement of nurses in tube feeding decisions. *Can J Aging* 1991;10:333–334.
5. Aaronson NK. Quality of life in research in cancer clinical trials: a need for common rules and language. *Oncology* 1990;4(5):59–66.
6. Goodinson SM, Singleton J. Quality of life: a critical review of current concepts, measures, and their clinical implications. *Int J Nurs Stud* 1989;26(4):327–341.
7. Smith CE. Quality of life in long-term total parenteral nutrition patients and their family caregivers. *JPEN* 1993;17:501–506.
8. Katz S. The science of quality of life [editorial]. *J Chronic Dis* 1987; 40(6):459–463.
9. Zahn L. Quality of life: conceptual and measurement issues. *J Adv Nurs* 1992;17:795–800.
10. Schipper H, Clinch J, Powell V. Definitions and conceptual issues. In: Spilker B, ed. *Quality of life assessment in clinical trials.* New York: Raven Press, 1990:11–24.
11. Cella DF. Functional status and quality of life: Current views on measurement and intervention. In: *Functional status and quality of life in persons with cancer.* Atlanta, Ga: American Cancer Society 1991: 1–12.
12. Spilker B. Introduction. In Spilker B, ed. *Quality of life assessments in clinical trials.* New York: Raven Press, 1990:3–9.
13. Padilla GV. Validity of health-related quality of life subscales. *Prog Cardiovasc Nurs* 1992;7(1):13–20.
14. Padilla GV, Grant MM. Quality of life as a cancer nursing outcome variable. *Adv Nurs Sci* 1985;8(1):45–60.
15. Torrance GW. Toward a utility theory foundation for health status index models. *Health Serv Res* 1976;11(4):349–369.
16. Torrance GW. Utility approach to measuring health-related quality of life. *J Chronic Dis* 1987;40(6):593–603.
17. Torrance GW, Boyle MH, Horwood SP. Application of multi-attribute utility theory to measure social preferences for health states. *Oper Res* 1982;30:1043–1069.
18. Patrick DL, Erickson P. *Health status and health policy: quality of life in health care evaluation and resource allocation.* New York: Oxford University Press, 1993.
19. Detsky AS, McLaughlin JR, Abrams HB, Whittaker JS, Whitewell J, L'Abbe K, Jeejeebhoy KN. A cost-utility analysis of the home parenteral nutrition program at Toronto General Hospital: 1970–1982. *JPEN* 1986;10:49–57.
20. Gilmore A. Sanctity of life versus quality of life—the continuing debate. *Can Med Assoc J* 1984;130:180–181.
21. Kuhse H, Singer P. The quality/quantity-of-life distinction and its moral importance for nurses. *Int J of Nurs Stud* 1989;26:203–212.
22. Patrick DL, Erickson P. What constitutes quality of life? Concepts and dimensions. *Clin Nutr* 1988;7(2):53–63.
23. Ferrans C, Powers M. Quality of life index: development and psychometric properties. *Adv Nurs Sci* 1985;8(1):15–24.
24. Cella DF, Cherin EA. Quality of life during and after cancer treatment. *Compr Ther* 1988;14:69–75.
25. Benner P. Quality of life: A phenomenological perspective on explanation, prediction, and understanding in nursing science. *Adv Nurs Sci* 1985;8(1):1–14.
26. CDCP surveys Americans on quality of life perceptions. *Psychiatr News* 1994;29:7,21.
27. Ferrans CE, Powers MJ. Psychometric assessment of the Quality of Life Index. *Res Nurs Health* 1992;15(1):29–38.
28. Ferrans CE. Quality of life: conceptual issues. *Semin Oncol Nurs* 1990;6:248–254.
29. Padilla GV, Ferrell B, Grant MM, Rhiner M. Defining the content domain of quality of life for cancer patients with pain. *Cancer Nurs* 1990;13(2):108–115.
30. Spitzer WO. State of science 1986: quality of life and functional status as target variables for research. *J Chronic Dis* 1987;40:465–471.
31. Gill TM, Feinstein AR. A critical appraisal of the quality of quality of life measurements. *JAMA* 1994;272:619–626.
32. Bihl MA, Ferrans CE, Powers MJ. Comparison stressors and quality of life of dialysis patients. *ANNA J* 1988;15(1):27–37.
33. Evans RW, Manninen DL, Garrison LP Jr, Hart LG, Blagg CR, Gutman RA, Hull AR, Lowrie EG. The quality of life of patients with end-stage renal disease. *N Engl J Med* 1985;312:553–559.
34. Ferrans CE, Powers MJ, Kasch CR. Satisfaction with health care of hemodialysis patients. *Res Nurs Health* 1987;10:367–374.
35. Hicks FD, Larson JL, Ferrans CE. Quality of life after liver transplant. *Res Nurs Health* 1992;15(2):111–119.
36. Chibnall JT, Tait RC. The quality of life scale: a preliminary study with chronic pain patients. *Psychol Health* 1990;4:283–292.
37. Ladefoged K. Quality of life in patients on permanent home parenteral nutrition. *JPEN* 1981;5(2):132–137.
38. Burnes J, O'Keefe SJ, Fleming CR, Devine RM, Berkner S, Herrick L. Home parenteral nutrition—a 3-year analysis of clinical and laboratory monitoring. *JPEN* 1992;16(4):327–332.
39. Kaufman M. *Nutrition in public health: a handbook for developing programs and services.* Gaithersburg, MD: Aspen, 1990.
40. Young LS, Bye R, Scheltinga M, Ziegler TR, Jacobs DO, Wilmore DW. Patients receiving glutamine-supplemented intravenous feedings report an improvement in mood. *JPEN* 1993;17:422–427.
41. Howard L, Heaphey L, Fleming CR, Lininger L, Steiger E. Four years of North American Registry home parenteral nutrition outcome data and their implications for patient management. *JPEN* 1991;15:384–393.
42. Oley Foundation. *North American home parenteral and enteral nutrition patient registry: Annual report with outcome profiles.* Albany, NY: Author, 1993.
43. Baker CA. Postoperative patients' psychological well-being: Implications for discharge preparation. In: Funk SG, Tornquist EM, Champagne MT, Copp LA, Wiese RA, eds. *Key aspects of recovery: Improving nutrition, rest, and mobility.* New York: Springer, 1990:181–197.
44. Blackburn GL, Thornton PA. Nutritional assessment of the hospitalized patient. *Med Clin N Am* 1979;63:1103–1115.
45. Schipper H, Clinch J, McMurray A, Levitt M. Measuring the quality of life of cancer patients: the Functional Living Index—Cancer: Development and validation. *J Clin Oncol* 1984;2:472–483.
46. Rosenberg IH, Miller JW. Nutritional factors in physical and cognitive functions of elderly people. *Am J Clin Nutr* 1992;55(suppl 6):1237S–1243S.

47. Summers S. Nutritional assessment of surgical patients. In: Summers S, Ebbert DW, eds. *Ambulatory surgical nursing: a nursing diagnosis approach.* Philadelphia: JB Lippincott 1992:257–274.

48. Guyatt GH, Feeny DH, Patrick DL. Measuring health-related quality of life. *Ann Intern Med* 1993;118:622–629.

49. Guyatt GH, Veldhuyzen-Van Zanten SJ, Feeny DH, Patrick DL. Measuring quality of life in clinical trials: a taxonomy and review. *Can Med Assoc J* 1989;140:1441–1448.

50. Drossman DA, Patrick DL, Mitchell CM, Zagami EA, Appelbaum MI. Health-related quality of life in inflammatory bowel disease. Functional status and patient worries and concerns. *Dig Dis Sci* 1989;34:1379–1386.

51. Ferrans CE. Development of a Quality of Life Index for patients with cancer. *Oncol Nurs Forum* 1990;17(suppl 3):15–21.

52. Quality of life as a new public health measure. *MMWR* 1994;43:375–380.

53. Loveland-Cherry CJ, Youngblut JM, Leidy NW. A psychometric analysis of the Family Environment Scale. *Nurs Res* 1989;38:262–266.

54. Aaronson NK. Quality of life assessment in clinical trials: methodologic issues. *Controlled Clin Trials* 1989;10(suppl 4):195S–208S.

55. Ovesen L, Hannibal J, Mortesen EL. The interrelationship of weight loss, dietary intake, and quality of life in ambulatory patients with cancer of the lung, breast, and ovary. *Nutr Cancer* 1993;19:159–167.

56. Davies DP. Growth for "small-for-dates" babies. *Early Hum Dev* 1981;5(1):95–105.

57. Jeejeebhoy KN. Objective measurements of nutritional deficit [editorial]. *JPEN* 1984;8(1):1–2.

58. Seltzer MH, Bastidas JA, Cooper DN, Engler P, Slocum B, Fletcher HS. Instant nutritional assessment. *JPEN* 1979;3:157–159.

59. Steward AL, Ware JE, eds. *Measuring functioning and well-being.* Durham, NC: Duke University Press, 1992.

60. Rogers RM, Donahoe M, Costantino J. Physiologic effects of oral supplemental feeding in malnourished patients with chronic obstructive pulmonary disease. A randomized control study. *Am Rev Respir Dis* 1992;146:1511–1517.

61. Warnold I, Lundholm K. Clinical significances of peroperative nutritional status in 215 noncancer patients. *Ann Surg* 1984;199:299–305.

62. Detsky AS, McLaughlin JR, Baker JP, Johnston N, Whittaker S, Mendelson RA, Jeejeebhoy KN. What is subjective global assessment of nutritional status? *JPEN* 1987;11(1):8–13.

63. Detsky AS, Baker JP, Mendelson RA, Wolman SL, Wesson DE, Jeejeebhoy KN. Evaluating the accuracy of nutritional assessment techniques applied to hospitalized patients: methodology and comparisons. *JPEN* 1984;8(2):153–159.

64. Shils ME, Olson JA, Shike M. *Modern nutrition in health and disease.* 8th ed. Vol. 1. Philadelphia: Lea & Febiger, 1994.

65. Ottow RT, Bruining HA, Jeekel J. Clinical judgment versus delayed hypersensitivity skin testing for the prediction of postoperative sepsis and mortality. *Surg Gynecol Obstet* 1984;159(5):475–477.

66. Pettigrew RA, Hill GL, Indicators of surgical risk and clinical judgment. *Br J Surg* 1986;73(1):47–51.

67. Moore FA, Feliciano DV, Andrassy RJ, McArdle AH, Booth FV. Early enteral feeding, compared with parenteral, reduces postoperative septic complications. The results of a meta-analysis. *Ann Surg* 1992;216:172–183.

68. Saffle JR, Larson CM, Sullivan J. A randomized trial of indirect calorimetry-based feedings in thermal injury. *J Trauma* 1990;30:776–783.

69. Baker JP, Detsky AS, Wesson DE, Wolman SL, Stewart S, Whitewell J. Nutritional assessment: a comparison of clinical judgement and objective measures. *N Engl J Med* 1982;306:969–972.

70. Kushner RF, Ayello EA, Beyer PL, Skipper A, Van Way CE III, Young EA, Balogun LB. National Coordinating Committee clinical indicators of nutrition care. *J Am Diet Assoc* 1994;94:1168–1177.

71. Shronts EP. Basic concepts of immunology and its application to clinical nutrition. *Nutr Clin Pract* 1993;8:177–183.

72. McNair DM, Lorr M, Droppleman LF. *Manual for the profile of mood states.* San Diego: EdITS/Educational and Industrial Testing Service, 1992.

73. Klimberg VS, Nwokedi E, Hutchins LF, Pappas AA, Lang NP, Broadwater JR, Read RC, Westbrook KC. Glutamine facilitates chemotherapy while reducing toxicity. *JPEN* 1992;16(suppl 6):83S–87S.

74. Matarese LE, Deers MA, Curtas S, Steiger E. Nutrition assessment and the development of a mortality risk index (abstract). In: *Proceedings of the 1992 Annual Research Meeting of the American Dietetic Association.*

75. Ainsworth BE, Haskell WL, Leon AS, Jacobs DR Jr, Montoye HJ, Sallis JF, Paffenbarger RS Jr. Compendium of physical activities: classification of energy costs of human physical activities. *Med Sci Sports Exerc* 1993;25(1):71–80.

76. Toner HM, Morris JD. A social-psychological perspective of dietary quality in later adulthood. *J Nutr Elder* 1992;11(4):35–53.

77. Ollenschlager WT, Thomas W, Konkol KV, Diehl E, Roth E. Nutritional behavior and quality of life during oncological polychemotherapy. Results of a prospective study on the efficacy of oral nutrition therapy in patients with acute leukaemia. *Eur J Clin Invest* 1992;22:546–553.

Quality of Life and Pharmacoeconomics in Clinical Trials, Second Edition, edited by B. Spilker.
Lippincott-Raven Publishers, Philadelphia © 1996.

CHAPTER 111

Relationship of Pharmacoeconomics and Health-Related Quality of Life

Dennis A. Revicki

INTRODUCTION

Changing health care systems in the United States and other developed countries, as well as increasing expenditures for health care services, have placed an emphasis on performing economic evaluations of new medicines. These studies are directed at demonstrating value in terms of health outcomes of the expenditures associated with adopting the new medical treatment into the health care system. The medical outcomes (effectiveness) movement has further encouraged the assessment of new and existing medical treatments (1). Measures of health-related quality of life (HRQL) are increasingly viewed as important outcomes of medical and surgical interventions (2–4). The purpose of this chapter is to explicate the relationship between HRQL outcomes and pharmacoeconomic evaluations of new medical therapies. It will attempt to show the linkage between evaluations of HRQL and economic studies of pharmaceuticals.

Eisenberg (5) points out that the primary pharmacoeconomic problem results from the tension between providing all medical services that are technically feasible or that patients desire and somehow financing these services with limited resources. This tension between the desire for the

newest medical technology and paying for health care services requires industry and providers to conduct studies to show that the new medical technologies are worthwhile expenditures of health care resources. HRQL outcomes represent one of a continuum of medical outcomes that can be used to measure the impact of pharmaceutical interventions on health. Without information on patient outcomes, decisions about new medical treatments may be made based only on economic considerations.

The comprehensive evaluation of pharmaceuticals requires evidence of safety and clinical efficacy, as well as evidence of its impact on patient functioning and well-being and health care costs (6). Physicians, health administrators, government and private insurers, and patients and their families want to know the effect of medical treatments on HRQL. Judicious use of limited health care resources requires that medical technologies be adopted and used that provide real improvements in health outcomes at some acceptable cost.

Pharmacoeconomic evaluations are designed to compare the medical costs and health outcomes associated with a new medical therapy to the costs and outcomes of the existing alternative medical treatment (7,8). The comparative medical treatment often is another pharmaceutical, but can be a surgical treatment or other health care intervention. To complete a pharmacoeconomic study, both the medical costs and health outcomes need to be specified and collected and then analyzed to determine the cost-effectiveness of the new drug treatment compared to the alternative treatment.

   D. A. Revicki: Health Outcomes Research, Medical Technology Assessment Program, Arlington, Virginia 22201; Department of Health Policy and Administration, School of Public Health, University of North Carolina at Chapel Hill, Chapel Hill, North Carolina 27599.

HEALTH OUTCOMES

<table>
<tr><td></td><td></td><td>+</td><td>-</td></tr>
<tr><td>MEDICAL</td><td>+</td><td>A</td><td>B</td></tr>
<tr><td>COSTS</td><td></td><td></td><td></td></tr>
<tr><td></td><td>-</td><td>C</td><td>D</td></tr>
</table>

FIG. 1. Possible findings of pharmacoeconomic evaluation. From Ellwood (1). Comparisons of health outcomes and medical costs are from the perspective of the new medical technology. A positive sign (+) indicates the findings are supportive of the new technology and a negative sign (−) indicates the findings are not supportive of the new medical technology.

Figure 1 illustrates a simplification of the possible outcomes of a pharmacoeconomic study comparing a new pharmaceutical treatment to an alternative treatment. The comparison assumes that health-related outcomes are measured with relevant and psychometrically sound indicators and there was comprehensive assessment of health service utilization and costs. Quadrants B and D suggest that the new treatment may be harmful and cost more (Quadrant B) or result in decreases in health outcomes, but at lower cost. The most positive finding is demonstrated in Quadrant C. In this situation, the new drug treatment results in improved health outcomes at a lower cost compared to the alternative treatment. These findings represent the truly breakthrough therapies that have significant health benefits and are successful in lowering health care costs. In reality, many new medical treatments provide only an incremental increase in health outcomes at some additional expenditure in medical costs (Quadrant A). Therefore, in this situation a value judgment is necessary about the increase in health outcomes is worth the added health care costs (5,7–9).

Not shown are the situations in which the two treatments are equivalent in medical costs or health outcomes. Where health outcomes are comparable, the economic evaluation reduces to a comparison of medical costs (e.g., cost-minimization analysis). When medical costs are equal, differences are compared in clinical and HRQL outcomes. The interpretation of health-related outcomes may be complicated in cases in which clinical outcomes (e.g., blood pressure) are not different and where the profile of HRQL outcomes does not clearly support one treatment or show a mix of positive and negative findings.

This comprehensive pharmaceutical evaluation incorporates measures of clinical efficacy, impact on HRQL, and economic components. Indicators of clinical efficacy and safety are necessary to demonstrate that the drug treatment is not toxic and effects the biochemical or physiological systems it is intended to impact. Measures of HRQL demonstrate how application of the medication and disease affects health status, everyday activities and functioning, and well-being. Finally, the health economic measures quantify how application of the treatment impacts on the use of health care resources and the costs associated with the use of these services.

EVALUATION OF HEALTH-RELATED QUALITY OF LIFE OUTCOMES

Two main approaches have been used to evaluate health-related outcomes in pharmacoeconomic studies, psychometric health status and utility/preference measures. The health status measures can be further subdivided into generic and specific measures (2,3,10,11). Both approaches have advantages and disadvantages, and their proponents have not demonstrated any clear superiority for the evaluation of medicines (3). There are trade-offs in their application in pharmacoeconomic studies and no single measure can be recommended for all studies.

Psychometric Health Status Measures

The psychometric health status measures provide comprehensive, multidimensional assessment of relevant HRQL dimensions and the generic measures can be used across populations, diseases, and medical treatments to measure HRQL. For example, the Medical Outcomes Study short-form 36 (SF-36) contains eight scales (12,13) and physical and mental health summary scores can be constructed from SF-36 scales (14). The Sickness Impact Profile (SIP) (15,16) contains 12 scales and two summary scores, physical and psychosocial, and a total score. Many of the generic health status measures have demonstrated reliability and validity, discrimination ability, and responsiveness to clinically meaningful changes. Many of the health status measures are sensitive to the occurrence of clinical symptoms (17,18) or relatively small differences between medicines (19). They can, therefore, be usefully employed in studies to measure the combined impact of treatment (both effectiveness and adverse effects) and disease on health outcomes.

More recent research effort in HRQL is in developing and validating specific measures (10). Disease-specific measures are believed to be more sensitive to treatment effects. However, despite the greater face validity of disease-specific scales, the literature does not uniformly support their greater responsiveness. Clinicians are sometimes uncertain about the responsiveness of health status measures to small, clinically meaningful changes and have difficulty translating changes in scores (20). However, a number of health status scales have demonstrated ability to discriminate between groups (14) and clinical responsiveness (18–20). The recommended approach is to incorporate both generic and specific instruments to comprehensively assess HRQL in randomized clinical trials of new medical therapies.

Utility/Preference Measures

The utility measures represent the strength of a person's preference for different health outcomes or conditions under conditions of uncertainty (21–23). Preferences are the values persons assign to health states when uncertainty is not a condition of measurement. Utilities, or preferences, are quantified on a scale from 1 (anchored as perfect health or the best possible health state) to 0 (anchored as death or the worst possible health state). A number of techniques have been used to assign preferences directly or indirectly, including categorical rating scales, standard gamble, time trade-off, and multiattribute indexes. Both hypothetical and current health states can be rated using preference measures. The utility measures are compatible with economic evaluations, and there is evidence supporting reliability of these scores, but few validity data (24). There is some controversy about the definition of utilities/preferences and the methods used to elicit these scores.

Utility scores can be combined with survival data to calculate quality-adjusted life years (QALYs), which are useful indicators of outcome for cost-effectiveness analysis (or cost-utility analysis). Although utilities have clear advantages for pharmacoeconomic evaluations, especially those based on clinical decision analysis and modeling, there are some concerns. Utility scores vary by the structure and content of health state descriptions, how outcomes are framed, and different scaling methods (25,26). There is a concern about the level of respondent understanding, the cognitive complexity of the measurement task, and various population and contextual effects (25,27). Utility scores may not be sensitive to subtle clinical effects (18,28,29).

Multiattribute Utility Measures

Multiattribute utility measures have been developed that represent hybrids of the psychometric and utility-based measures. The Quality of Well-Being Scale (30–32) and the Health Utility Index (33,34) use multidimensional health indexes and different scaling methods to calculate preference scores. However, there are differences in the way utility/preference scores are obtained by the Quality of Well-Being Scale and Health Utilities Index. The Quality of Well-Being Scale obtains information about multidimensional health states and then use separate utility weights from population surveys to combine them. The Health Utility Index requires subjects to rate their own health state on a series of questions and then uses a multiattribute status classification to assign utility scores. The multiattribute approach may be easier to incorporate into clinical studies, although to date the Quality of Well-Being Scale has been included in several clinical trials (31,32), and the Health Utilities Index has also been used in clinical trials (34). Other more recently developed scales, such as the EuroQOL (35), may also have applications in clinical trials and pharmacoeconomic studies. Brazier and colleagues (28) are attempting to derive a multiattribute utility index on the basis of selected SF-36 dimensions. However, the validity, clinical responsiveness, and practical characteristics of these measures in prospective pharmacoeconomic studies need to be demonstrated.

Relationship between Health Status and Utility/Preference Measures

Research has demonstrated that psychometric health status and utility/preference scores are at best only moderately correlated (25,36–38). A recent review of studies on the relationship between utility and health status measures found that they shared only 18% to 25% of variance in standard gamble utilities and 25% to 43% variance in time trade-off utilities (36). Health status and utility/preferences scales measure different components of health outcomes. A person's current HRQL may only partially account for his or her preferences for their current health state. It is uncertain whether this weak correlation is due to poor respondent understanding of the utility measurement task and the cognitive complexity of the utility assessment scales. Health status and utility scales assess different aspects of HRQL and are not interchangeable in pharmacoeconomic evaluations. It is clear that a person's preference for their current health condition is not interchangeable with ratings of their functioning and well-being.

INTEGRATING HEALTH-RELATED QUALITY OF LIFE IN PHARMACOECONOMIC STUDIES

Utility-based HRQL outcomes are an integral part of pharmacoeconomic evaluations (3,6). Early work by Fanshel and Bush (39) and Weinstein and Stason (40) suggested that quality of life is an inherent part of cost-effectiveness analysis and must be introduced into economic evaluations of health care interventions. Around the same time, Torrance (41) examined different methods for eliciting social preferences for health states. The health outcome of a medicine equals the years of life saved adjusted by the quality of life gained due to decreases in morbidity minus the quality of life lost due to the adverse effects of treatment (40). Quality-adjusted life-years represent years of life weighted in some way for the effects of treatment and disease progression on HRQL. Most often, utility or preference scores supply the weights for this adjustment. Utility-based and psychometrically based HRQL outcomes represent suitable measures for evaluating the positive and negative impact of both illness and treatment in pharmacoeconomic studies. In general, psychometrically based HRQL measures assess the outcomes of medications more comprehensively, although utility-based measures are more easily integrated into cost-effectiveness analyses.

Theoretically, it is possible to include different HRQL measures as indicators of outcome in cost-effectiveness analysis; this has proved difficult in practice. For example, the Hamilton Depression Rating Scale and the SF-36 could be used to evaluate the health outcomes of two different antidepressants. Changes in the resultant profile of scores can be compared by treatment. If the medical costs are lower and the depression and HRQL outcomes all show that the new antidepressant is superior to the comparison antidepressant, there is no problem for the pharmacoeconomic evaluation. The comparison is still positive when there is no difference in costs, but superiority in depression or HRQL outcomes.

However, when the new treatment has higher medical costs and improved HRQL outcomes, comparison is complicated by the number of scales (8 in the case of the SF-36). The analyst could calculate 8 separate incremental cost-effectiveness ratios, but potentially conflicting ratios makes interpretation difficult. The use of the new physical and mental health summary scores based on the SF-36 (14,42) simplifies this problem somewhat, but still may lead to conflicting outcomes. For example, how does the analyst resolve improvements in mental health outcomes against decreases in physical function?

In cost-utility analysis, the outcomes of medical treatment are expressed as QALYs (22,43,44). QALYs integrate mortality and morbidity to express health status in terms of equivalents of well-years of life. Although QALYs are useful denominators for cost-effectiveness ratios, QALYs differ depending on the methods used to develop weights (or utilities/preferences) for adjusting years of life for impact on HRQL (23). The application of utility assessments in pharmacoeconomic studies has raised concerns about how comparable QALYs are across studies and different methods for generating preferences (45,46).

ISSUES RELATED TO HEALTH-RELATED QUALITY OF LIFE IN PHARMACOECONOMIC EVALUATIONS

The world is a multivariate place. The outcomes of pharmaceutical interventions are multiple and it is most informative to provide information on the profile of HRQL and other outcomes of medical treatment. Multiple outcomes give comprehensive and complete information on the impact of new treatments on patient functioning and well-being. Although it is sometimes difficult for clinicians and health policy makers to integrate multivariate outcomes, global summary scores fail to disclose the exact differences between treatment alternatives. Summary indicators, such as utility scores and QALYs, can easily be incorporated into cost-effectiveness analyses. These indicators may hide outcomes that may be important to patients or to clinicians. For example, a new antiretroviral improves survival for persons with human immunodeficiency virus (HIV) disease, but it also causes nausea in 40% and decrements in energy and psychological distress in 30% of treated patients. A QALY will represent this nausea and impact on energy and psychological distress by adjusting this increased survival by some weight. However, the survival gain may overwhelm the decrement in HRQL, leading clinicians to believe that the treatment is a good choice for all patients with HIV. Without complete information on the impact of the therapy, physicians may be unable to target the treatment to those most likely to benefit or be unaware of negative effects that may offset potentially positive outcomes.

A problem associated with incorporating all but the simplest utility/preference measures in prospective pharmacoeconomic evaluations rest in their measurement complexity. Although utility assessment has been introduced into several clinical trials (31,47–50), the practice is not widespread. Time trade-off and standard gamble methods require visual props and interview administration by trained research personnel. Even then it is uncertain whether the respondents actually understand and make ratings as intended by the investigators. The Health Utilities Index, EuroQOL, and other utility indexes classify persons into multidimensional health states on the basis of responses to a series of questions. It may be easier to incorporate these types of measures into clinical trials, but little information is available about the responsiveness and validity of the utility indexes.

One major advantage of incorporating QALYs into the pharmacoeconomic evaluations of new medicines is the comparison of cost per QALY gained findings for the new treatment to established, adopted therapies in league tables. This comparison can provide some insight into the relative cost-effectiveness of the new treatment and may assist in resource allocation decisions. League tables are suspect, and not all QALYs (or costs) may be comparable (45,46). A QALY in one pharmacoeconomic study may not be comparable to a QALY in another study, because of different methods for estimating health state utilities. Other factors that impact on the comparability of QALYs and costs between studies include the discount rates used on costs and benefits, the range and type of costs, the choice of a treatment alternative, modeling assumptions, treatment of uncertainty, and quality of the medical outcome data (46). Until there is more agreement on the content and consistency in the reporting of cost per QALY ratios in descriptive tables, they represent at best crude indicators relative rankings of medical technologies. Care should be exercised when interpreting the findings in league tables.

The weak association between utility/preference measures and health status measures and the lack of responsiveness of utilities is troublesome for pharmacoeconomic studies. Unless there are dramatic changes in patient outcomes, such as the impact of knee replacement surgery, many clinically meaningful changes resulting from medical interventions may be missed, or at least undervalued, using utility/preference scales. Proponents of utility measures counter that differences that cannot be perceived by human judges may be too small to be clinically significant. Utilities are used increasingly to generate QALYs as measures of effectiveness in economic evaluations. The use of potentially insensitive measures in cost-effectiveness analysis may lead to inaccurate decisions about the impact of new medicines on health-related outcomes. The health status measures do have substantial evidence for responsiveness to clinically meaningful changes in patient outcomes so there remains the possibility of conflicting findings.

After determining safety and clinical efficacy, there is a need to determine the impact of the pharmaceutical therapy on patient functioning and well-being. Both psychometrically based health status measures—generic and disease-specific—and utility or preference-based measures are needed for a comprehensive evaluation of health outcomes. The application of multiple outcome measures raises the possibility of conflicting health outcomes when evaluating a specific medical treatment. However, in practice, well-designed studies with sound hypotheses and measures and adequate statistical power most often find evidence of significant positive effects or nonsignificant differences. It makes no sense to conduct a HRQL study if there are no or little clinical differences, either in terms of primary efficacy outcomes or adverse effects, between the new and existing alternative treatments. Why develop and test a new treatment with no advantages over existing treatments for a specific disease? If there is evidence of some important clinical difference between the new and alternative, approved medical therapies, it is likely that this difference will translate into some impact on patient functioning and well-being. Unexpected negative or positive effects on HRQL can occur and are possible in pharmacoeconomic evaluations.

There are always trade-offs between different outcomes of interest to clinicians and patients, unless the new treatment is truly a breakthrough product. It is better to be aware of the profile of clinical and HRQL outcomes. This will allow physicians and patients to make intelligent, informed choices about medical therapies.

CONCLUSIONS

HRQL outcomes are important and necessary components to defining ''effectiveness'' in cost-effectiveness analyses.

More widespread requirements to demonstrate effectiveness of new medicines and cost-effectiveness will necessitate integrating HRQL into pharmacoeconomic evaluations. Pharmacoeconomic studies need to include measures of clinical outcomes and generic and specific health status, and collect data on the use and costs of health care services. When the new pharmaceutical therapy is expected to result in improved health benefits and somewhat higher medical costs, one of the utility/preference measures should be included to construct summary indicators of health outcome, such as the QALY. Given the current state of health status measurement technology, no single instrument or measurement approach can be used for every pharmacoeconomic evaluation. Selection of HRQL measures depend on the objectives of the evaluation, the targeted disease and population, psychometric characteristics, practical issues, such as respondent burden, and available resources (2,3,51).

Additional research is needed to improve health status and utility measurement. For example, is it possible to construct preference-weighted health status scores from existing generic health status measures and can these new measures be usefully employed in pharmacoeconomic studies? The QALY concept, although not without its critics and problems, seems to offer a possible summary indicator of health outcome for cost-effectiveness analyses. There is continued disagreement about how to develop weights for calculating QALYs (23) and comparing cost-utility analyses and QALYs from different studies is problematic (45,46).

Future research needs to examine the responsiveness of health status measures and needs to translate changes in scores in clinically meaningful ways. The level of respondent understanding and cognitive complexity of utility/preference assessment techniques needs to be studied. If utilities and the QALYs constructed from these utilities represent useful ways to define outcomes in pharmacoeconomic evaluations, their validity needs to be demonstrated. The measurement characteristics of utility/preference measures need to be further studied; method variation needs to be separated from individual preference variation. We also need improvements in ways to elicit preferences from patients and members of the general population. Finally, continued research should be encouraged on merging the measurement approaches of psychometrics and utility assessment. It needs to be determined whether the utility methods for enumerating scales and for combining different components of health can be applied to psychometric health status measures. Multiattribute utility techniques may prove most feasible for constructing preference-weighted health status measures with the strengths of psychometric scales and application in economic analysis of utility scales.

The combination of generic and/or specific health status measures with utility measures provides for comprehensive evaluation of the impact of treatments on patient functioning and well-being and allows for outcome measures that can be easily incorporated into economic evaluations. Utility and health status measures result in different yet related and complementary assessments of health outcomes. Complete information on the treatment's impact on patient outcomes is available for interested clinicians, patients and health care decision makers to make informed decisions about regulatory approval and pricing and prescribing treatments. HRQL assessments put the ''outcome'' in medical outcome studies and the ''effectiveness'' in cost-effectiveness analyses as part of comprehensive pharmacoeconomic evaluations. The failure to measure HRQL may result in decisions based only on safety and clinical efficacy and economic considerations. Patient assessments of the outcomes in pharmacoeconomic studies are important for evaluating new medicines. Combining health status and preference measures with economic outcomes provides more comprehensive information on the impact of medical treatments on patient and societal outcomes.

REFERENCES

1. Ellwood P. Outcomes management: a technology of patient experience. *N Engl J Med* 1988;318:1549–1556.
2. Patrick DL, Erickson P. *Health status and health policy: allocating resources to health care.* New York: Oxford University Press, 1992: 1–478.
3. Revicki DA. Health care technology assessment and health-related quality of life. In: Banta HD, Luce BR, eds. *Health care technology and its assessment: an international perspective.* New York: Oxford University Press, 1993:114–131.
4. Ware JE Jr. The use of health status and quality of life measures in outcomes and effectiveness research. Prepared for the National Agenda Setting Conference on Outcomes and Effectiveness Research, Agency for Health Care Policy and Research, Alexandria, VA, April 1991.
5. Eisenberg JM. Clinical economics: a guide to economic analysis of clinical practices. *JAMA* 1989;262:2879–2886.
6. Revicki DA, Rothman M, Luce BR. Health-related quality of life assessment and the pharmaceutical industry. *Pharmacoeconomics* 1992; 1:394–408.
7. Drummond MF, Stoddart GL, Torrance GW. *Methods for the economic evaluation of health care programmes.* New York: Oxford University Press, 1987:1–182.
8. Banta HD, Luce BR. *Health care technology and its assessment: an international perspective.* New York: Oxford University Press, 1993: 1–352.
9. Laupacis A, Feeny DH, Detsky AS, Tugwell PX. How attractive does a new technology have to be to warrant adoption and utilization? Tentative guidelines for using clinical and economic evaluations. *Can Med Assoc J* 1992;146:473–481.
10. Patrick DL, Deyo R. Generic and disease-specific measures in assessing health status and quality of life. *Med Care* 1989;27:S217–S232.
11. Guyatt GH, Feeny DH, Patrick DL. Measuring health-related quality of life. *Ann Intern Med* 1993;118:622–629.
12. Ware JE Jr, Sherbourne CD. The MOS 36-item short-form health survey (SF-36): conceptual framework and item selection. *Med Care* 1992;30:473–483.
13. Ware JE Jr. MOS, MOS-36 short form health survey. In: Spilker B, ed. *Quality of life and pharmacoeconomics in clinical trials.* New York: Raven Press 1995;34:337–346.
14. Ware JE Jr, Bayliss MS, Kosinski M, et al. Comparisons of methods for the scoring and statistical analysis of the SF-36 health profile and summary measures. *Med Care* 1995;33:AS264–279.
15. Bergner M, Bobbit RA, Carter WB, Gilson BS. The Sickness Impact Profile: development and final revision of a health status measure. *Med Care* 1981;19:787–805.
16. Damiano A. Sickness impact profile. In: Spilker B, ed. *Quality of life and pharmacoeconomics in clinical trials.* New York: Raven Press, 1995;35:347–354.
17. Revicki DA, Allen H, Bungay K, Williams GH, Weinstein MC. Responsiveness and calibration of the general well-being adjustment scale in patients with hypertension. *J Clin Epidemiol* 1994;47:1333–1342.
18. Revicki DA, Wu AW, Murray M. Change in clinical status, health status and health utility outcomes in HIV-infected patients. *Med Care* 1995;33:AS173–182.
19. Testa MA, Anderson RB, Nackley JF, et al. Quality of life and antihypertensive therapy in men: a comparison of captopril and enalapril. *N Engl J Med* 1993;328:907–913.
20. Deyo R, Patrick DL. Barriers to the use of health status measures in clinical investigation, patient care, and policy research. *Med Care* 1989; 27:S254–S268.
21. Torrance GW. Measurement of health state utilities for economic appraisal: a review. *J Health Econ* 1986;5:1–30.
22. Torrance GW, Feeny DH. Utilities and quality-adjusted life years. *Int J Tech Assess Health Care* 1989;5:559–575.
23. Kaplan RM, Feeny DH, Revicki DA. Methods for assessing relative importance in preference based outcome measures. *Qual Life Res* 1993; 2:467–475.
24. Froberg D, Kane R. Methodology for measuring health-state preferences. II. scaling methods. *J Clin Epidemiol* 1989;42:459–471.
25. Revicki DA. Relationship between health utility and psychometric health status measures. *Med Care* 1992;30:MS274–MS282.
26. Mulley A. Assessing patient's utilities: can the ends justify the means? *Med Care* 1989;27:S269–S281.
27. Froberg D, Kane R. Methodology for measuring health-state preferences. III. Population and context effects. *J Clin Epidemiol* 1989;42: 585–592.
28. Brazier J. The short-form 36 (SF-36) health survey and its use in pharmacoeconomic evaluation. *Pharmacoeconomics* 1995;7:403–415.
29. Katz JN, Phillips CB, Fossel AH, Liang MH. Stability and responsiveness of utility measures. *Med Care* 1994;32:183–188.
30. Kaplan RM, Bush J. Health-related quality of life measurement for evaluation research and policy. *Health Psychol* 1982;1:61–80.
31. Kaplan RM, Anderson J, Wu AW, et al. The quality of well-being scale: applications in AIDS, cystic fibrosis, and arthritis. *Med Care* 1989;27:S27–S43.
32. Kaplan RM, Anderson JP. The general health policy model: an integrated perspective. In: Spilker B, ed. *Quality of life and pharmacoeconomics in clinical trials.* New York: Raven Press 1995;32:309–322.
33. Torrance GW, Zhang Y, Feeny D, et al. *Multi-attribute preference functions for a comprehensive health status classification system.* Paper 92-18. Hamilton, Ontario: McMaster University, 1992.
34. Feeny DH, Torrance GW, Furlong WJ. Health utilities index (HUI). In: Spilker B, ed. *Quality of life and pharmacoeconomics in clinical trials.* New York: Raven Press, 1995;26:239–252.
35. Kind P. The EuroQOL instrument: an index of health-related quality of life. In: Spilker B, ed. *Quality of life and pharmacoeconomics in clinical trials.* New York: Raven Press, 1995;22:191–202.
36. Revicki DA, Kaplan RM. Relationship between psychometric and utility-based approaches to the measurement of health-related quality of life. *Qual Life Res* 1993;2:477–487.
37. Tsevat J, Goldman L, Lamas GA, et al. Functional status versus utilities in survivors of myocardial infarction. *Med Care* 1991;29:1153–1159.
38. Fryback DG, Dasbach EJ, Klein R, et al. Health assessments by SF-36, quality of well-being index and time-tradeoffs: predicting one measure from another. *Med Decision Making* 1992;12:348.
39. Fanshel S, Bush J. A health-status index and its applications to health-services research. *Operations Res* 1970;18:1021–1066.
40. Weinstein MC, Stason WB. Foundations of cost-effectiveness analysis for health and medical practices. *N Engl J Med* 1977;296:716–721.
41. Torrance GW. Social preferences for health states. An empirical evaluation of three measurement techniques. *Socio-Economic Plan Sci* 1976; 10:129–136.
42. McHorney CA, Ware JE Jr, Raczek AK. The MOS 36-item short-form health survey (SF-36): II psychometric and clinical tests of validity in measuring physical and mental health constructs. *Med Care* 1994; 31:247–263.
43. Kamlet M. *The comparative benefits modeling project. A framework for cost-utility analysis of government health care programs.* Washington, DC: US Department of Health and Human Services, Public Health Service, 1992.
44. Kaplan RM. Utility assessment for estimating quality-adjusted life years. In: Sloan F, ed. *Cost-effectiveness of pharmaceuticals.* New York: Cambridge Press, 1994.
45. Drummond MF, Torrance GW, Mason JM. Cost-effectiveness league tables: more harm than good? *Soc Sci Med* 1993;37:33–40.

46. Mason JM. Cost-per-QALY league tables: their role in pharmacoeconomic analysis. *Pharmacoeconomics* 1994;5:472–481.
47. Feeny DH, Torrance GW. Incorporating utility-based quality of life assessment measures in clinical trials. *Med Care* 1989;27:S190–S204.
48. Bombardier C, Ware J, Russell I, et al. Auranofin therapy and quality of life in patients with rheumatoid arthritis: results of a multicenter trial. *Am J Med* 1986;81:565–578.
49. Canadian Erythropoietin Study Group. Association between recombinant human erythropoietin and quality of life and exercise capacity of patients receiving haemodialysis. *BMJ* 1990;300:573–578.
50. Wu AW, Mathews WC, Brysk LT, et al. Quality of life in a placebo-controlled trial of zidovudine in patients with AIDS and AIDS-related complex. *J Acquir Immun Def Synd* 1990;3:683–690.
51. Bergner M, Rothman M. Health status measures: an overview and guide for selection. *Annu Rev Public Health* 1987;8:191–210.

Quality of Life and Pharmacoeconomics in Clinical Trials, Second Edition, edited by B. Spilker.
Lippincott-Raven Publishers, Philadelphia © 1996.

CHAPTER 112

Designing and Conducting Cost-Benefit Analyses

Magnus Johannesson and Milton C. Weinstein

INTRODUCTION

In cost-benefit analysis both costs and benefits are measured in monetary terms. Unlike cost-effectiveness analysis in which the ratio of costs to effects must be compared with an external standard to judge the desirability of a health program, cost-benefit analysis permits a direct comparison of benefits and costs in the same units (1). The challenge, however, is to measure health benefits in monetary units.

According to economic theory, the consequences of a program should be measured as the *willingness to pay* of the individuals who bear the consequences. These consequences may include benefits such as increased probabilities of survival or improved quality of life, and they may include offsetting adverse effects such as side effects, complications, and inconvenience of treatment. Therefore, the major additional requirement in the design of cost-benefit as compared with cost-effectiveness studies in the health field is a method for measuring willingness to pay for the net consequences of health programs.

HUMAN CAPITAL

Until recently, most cost-benefit studies in the health field used the human capital method to value health improvements

(2,3). The human capital method values life saving and health improvements in terms of the amount of additional economic productivity associated with improved health, as measured by earnings in the labor force and as the decreased health care costs. As a result of theoretical work done mostly in the 1960s and 1970s, however, the human capital approach has been discredited by economists because it does not measure the value that individuals place on their own health and survival (4,5). Instead, principles of social choice theory imply that the value of health improvements should be based on individuals' own willingness to pay for these improvements. These values can in turn be based either on revealed preferences in markets or by direct elicitations known as contingent valuations.

REVEALED PREFERENCES

One approach to measuring the willingness to pay for health consequences is to observe decisions that individuals actually make concerning health risks, thereby inferring their willingness to trade money for these consequences. This approach is usually referred to as the revealed preference approach. One market that lends itself to the study of revealed preference is the labor market, where wage premiums are offered to induce workers to accept more risky jobs (6,7). Other sources of revealed preference data include consumer choices to purchase safety, such as the decision whether to use automobile safety belts (8), whether to purchase smoke-detectors (9), and whether to undertake steps to reduce indoor radon exposures (10).

It is often difficult to apply the revealed preference approach for health care programs because health care services

M. Johannesson: Centre for Health Economics, Stockholm School of Economics, Box 6501, S-113 83 Stockholm, Sweden.
M. C. Weinstein: Department of Health Policy and Management, Harvard School of Public Health, Boston, Massachusetts 02115.

are usually not purchased directly on a market. An alternative method, instead of assessing willingness to pay for programs holistically, is to assess willingness to pay for the consequences themselves, such as changes in mortality probabilities, changes in health status, or gains in quality-adjusted life expectancy. In this approach, the health outcomes of programs are estimated, and willingness to pay is assessed for these units of health outcome, based on decisions that may not directly concern the health program of interest. Thus, for example, the willingness to pay for a hypertension treatment program could be estimated by revealed preferences from labor market studies in which health effects comparable in magnitude to those of the hypertension program are valued. One disadvantage of decoupling the valuation of consequences from the program context is that the context effects may be important: studies have for instance shown that the importance attached to health risks depends on numerous attributes of the source of those risks and not just their magnitude (11,12). Nevertheless, if evidence from actual decision-making behavior is desired, it may be necessary to extrapolate from one context of health risk reduction to another.

CONTINGENT VALUATION

The chief alternative to using revealed preference to estimate the willingness to pay of individuals for improved health consequences is to use surveys to investigate the expressed willingness to pay of individuals. This method, known as the contingent valuation method, was developed in environmental economics to estimate the value of environmental changes such as cleaner air and the preservation of a recreational area (13,14). The development of the contingent valuation method in environmental economics has led, in turn, to increased interest in the application of cost-benefit analysis to medical care. Although one of the earliest applications of contingent valuation was applied to the value of mobile coronary care units (15), only a small number of applications have appeared in the medical field, e.g., on the willingness to pay for hypertension treatment (16,17).

Because the issues concerning the estimation of the costs of health programs are the same for both cost-effectiveness and cost-benefit analysis, we will concentrate on the role of contingent valuation in the valuation of health consequences in cost-benefit analysis.

First, we devote two sections to the principal alternative designs of contingent valuation questionnaires: open-ended contingent valuation questions and binary (yes/no) contingent valuation questions. Different forms of potential bias in a contingent valuation study are then discussed. After that we devote a section to the recommendations of the NOAA (National Oceanic and Atmospheric Administration) contingent valuation panel and the NOAA proposed regulations for the measurement of nonuse values of the environment. These recommendations are germane to the evaluation of

health care programs because they reflect current opinion regarding the role of contingent valuation in research. We conclude with some observations on the role of contingent valuation in clinical research.

OPEN-ENDED CONTINGENT VALUATION QUESTIONS

Contingent valuation questions can be classified as either open-ended or binary valuation questions. In open-ended valuation questions, the researcher tries to measure the maximum willingness to pay of each respondent, and in binary valuation questions the respondent accepts or rejects only one price (bid) level for the good.

The following is an example of an open-ended contingent valuation question (16):

This question concerns how you personally value your treatment against high blood pressure. Because the treatment against high blood pressure claims a lot of health care resources, a possible development is that patients in the future will have to pay a larger proportion of the treatment cost, in the form of higher user fees. Assume that this will be the case and that user fees are raised. At present, a patient treated for high blood pressure pays on average SEK (Swedish crowns) 350 a year in user fees for drugs and physician visits. How much is the highest amount you would be prepared to pay per year in the form of user fees for your current treatment?

. . . . **SEK per year**

Interviews (face-to-face or on the telephone) or mail questionnaires can be used for eliciting willingness to pay with open-ended questions. It is possible to ask the respondent directly for the maximum willingness to pay in an open-ended question, but usually aids are used to make it easier for the respondent to answer. It has been found to be difficult to get respondents to state a maximum willingness to pay directly, leading to problems of nonresponse.

One aid that is used in interviews is the so-called bidding game, introduced by Randall et al. (18). A bidding game resembles an auction. A first bid is made to the respondent, who accepts or rejects, and then the bid is raised or lowered depending on the answer. The process goes on until the respondent's maximum willingness to pay is reached.

Payment cards can also be used to display a range of willingness-to-pay values from which the respondent may choose. It should be mentioned that it is possible to use bidding-game or payment card type of questions also in mail questionnaires, using a multiple-choice format.

The major problem with the bidding game method is that it involves the risk of starting-point bias (see the discussion about different forms of bias below), which means that the respondent's stated willingness to pay is influenced by the first bid offered. This phenomenon is related to the anchoring and adjustment heuristic in behavioral decision theory (19).

Payment cards can lead to similar problems because the multiple choices offered may affect the selection made.

BINARY CONTINGENT VALUATION QUESTIONS

Problems with starting point bias in contingent valuation studies have led researchers to start experimenting with using binary valuation questions. In a binary contingent valuation question, the respondent is asked to accept or reject a single bid, which they would have to pay in exchange for a program or some improvement in health status.

The following is an example of a binary contingent valuation question (16):

This question concerns how you personally value your treatment against high blood pressure. Since the treatment against high blood pressure claims a lot of health care resources a possible development is that patients in the future will have to pay a larger proportion of the treatment cost, in the form of higher user fees. Assume that this will be the case and that user fees are raised. At present a patient treated for high blood pressure pays on average SEK 350 a year in user fees for drugs and physician visits. Would you choose to continue your current treatment against high blood pres-

sure, if the user fees for the treatment were raised to SEK 2,000 per year?

☐ **YES**
☐ **NO**

A respondent who accepts the bid in a binary contingent valuation question is assumed to have a maximum willingness to pay in excess of the bid, whereas a respondent who rejects the bid is assumed to have a maximum willingness to pay less than the bid. The population of respondents is stratified into subsamples, each offered a different bid. By analyzing the various subsamples, it is possible to calculate the proportion of respondents who are willing to pay each bid (price). This is illustrated in Figure 1. The curve represented in Figure 1 can be interpreted as an aggregate demand curve for the program or health improvement. The study design that uses binary contingent valuation questions is sometimes referred to as the referendum approach because the question in some cases can be phrased as a vote on a referendum.

Binary valuation questions were first used in the classic study by Bishop and Heberlein (20) concerning the value of goose-hunting permits, and this is now the most com-

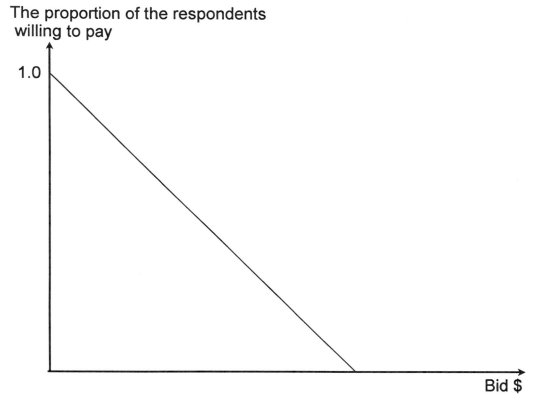

FIG. 1. The proportion of the respondents willing to pay as a function of the bid (price) in a contingent valuation study.

monly used elicitation technique. An advantage of this approach is that it resembles a market situation for the respondent because individuals are used to decide whether to buy or not to buy a good at a specific price. The binary approach also avoids the problem of starting point bias because the individual is only given one bid.

The disadvantage of the binary approach is that the information received from each respondent is substantially less than in the case of open-ended questions. With a binary question, the only information received from each respondent is whether the willingness to pay is greater or smaller than the bid. To estimate the mean willingness to pay based on binary contingent valuation data, the relationship between the bid and the proportion of respondents who are willing to pay the bid has to be estimated, i.e., the curve in Figure 1 has to be estimated. The mean willingness to pay in the population is the area below the curve, and the median willingness to pay is the price where the proportion of acceptance is 0.5, i.e., the price at which 50% would answer yes and 50% would answer no to the contingent valuation question.

To estimate the relationship between the proportion that are willing to pay and the bid, either regression analysis or nonparametric methods can be used. The regression technique most commonly used to analyze binary contingent valuation data is logistic regression (21,22), in which the bid is the focal explanatory variable, possibly along with covariates.

Because the mean willingness to pay based on binary contingent valuation questions can be sensitive to the choice of the functional relationship between the bid and the proportion that are willing to pay (21,23–25), it can also be useful to estimate the mean willingness to pay using a nonparametric method (25). The nonparametric method was developed by Kriström (25), and it is a simple way of estimating the mean willingness to pay. To estimate the demand curve, the proportion of yes answers at each bid level is used. If the proportion of yes answers increases between any two bid levels, the proportions are pooled between the two data points to ensure a nonincreasing function. The process of pooling is iterated across bid levels until a nonincreasing proportion of yes answers is achieved. Linear interpolation between the nonincreasing proportions is then used to construct the curve.

The disadvantage of the nonparametric approach is that it is not possible to calculate the effect of different explanatory variables on willingness to pay, e.g., to test if the willingness to pay is related to income or to the perceived health benefit of the program. In practice, it is therefore useful to use both the nonparametric method and logistic regression to analyze data from a binary contingent valuation study.

The general recommendation in the literature is currently to use binary rather than open-ended contingent valuation questions because binary questions more closely reflect real decisions made by the respondents on the market and because open-ended questions suffer from starting-point bias

(if bidding games or payment cards are used) or nonresponse (if maximum willingness to pay is assessed directly). In studies that have compared binary and open-ended contingent valuation questions, the mean willingness to pay has been higher with the binary approach (14,25–29). Because open-ended and binary contingent valuation questions have not yet been calibrated against real decisions, it is impossible to conclude for sure that binary contingent valuation questions are more valid than open-ended contingent valuation questions. In contingent valuation studies of health care programs, however, it seems most appropriate to use the binary approach until further evidence is available that may change that recommendation. To clearly resolve the issue, studies are needed where responses to both types of questions are compared with real money transactions.

The survey instrument in a contingent valuation study is of the utmost importance. When constructing the instrument, a number of sources of potential bias are important to bear in mind. In the next section, we will review these biases based on the bias typology developed by Mitchell and Carson (14).

POTENTIAL BIAS IN A CONTINGENT VALUATION STUDY

According to the bias typology of Mitchell and Carson (14), the sources of potential bias in a contingent valuation study can be divided into five main areas: incentives to misrepresent responses, implied value cues, scenario misspecification, sample design and execution biases, and inference biases. The first three areas concern the design of the contingent valuation instrument, whereas the other two areas concern more general issues relating to the sampled population and to the way the results are used. We will focus mainly on the design issues here.

Incentives to misrepresent responses produce two types of bias: strategic bias and compliance bias. Strategic bias means that respondents feel it is in their self-interest to state a lower or higher amount than their true value. The well-known free-rider problem in economics is an example of strategic behavior. Here, individuals try to avoid paying for public goods by understating their true willingness to pay, because they know they cannot be excluded from consuming these goods once they have been provided. Strategic bias can produce both overstatements and understatements of the true value. For example, if the respondents think that the provision of the good is dependent on the stated valuation of the good but that their actual level of payment for the good will be independent of the value given, there is an incentive to exaggerate the valuation. If, on the other hand, respondents believe that the provision of the good is independent of the value given but that the level of payment is dependent on their stated valuation, then there is an incentive to understate the valuation. Empirical studies have failed, however, to clearly demonstrate that strategic bias exists to a large extent (28–33).

The most well-known type of compliance bias is interviewer bias. Interviewer bias, a pervasive phenomenon in survey research, means that respondents overstate or understate their true valuation to please the interviewer. Sponsor bias is another form of compliance bias, indicating that respondents give valuations that differ from their true valuations to comply with the presumed sponsor of the investigation.

Implied value cues are a form of anchoring bias. Implied value cues include starting-point bias, range bias, relational bias, importance bias, and position bias. Implied value cues exist when some information contained in the contingent valuation instrument implies a certain value for the good.

Starting-point bias is present when the respondent's valuation is affected by some suggested willingness-to-pay amount that is given in the question. The standard case is that the respondent is affected by the first bid in a bidding game. Because starting point bias has been shown to be an important problem in contingent valuation studies using bidding games, this approach is seldom used at present (28, 34–36).

Range bias is similar to starting-point bias, except that instead of a single starting point, there is a range of potential willingness-to-pay amounts that is introduced by the survey instrument and which affects the value given by the respondent. So-called payment cards are the typical example where the respondent can choose one amount from a range of values.

Relational bias means that the description of the good being valued presents information about its relationship to other goods, thereby influencing the amount given by the respondent. Importance bias can arise if the valuation instrument suggests to the respondent that the good being valued is particularly important and valuable. This may lead respondents to exaggerate their true valuation. Position bias is induced if the ordering of questions suggests to the respondent some value of the good that influences the valuation.

Scenario misspecification occurs when the respondent does not respond to the correct contingent scenario, usually because the contingent valuation question is formulated incorrectly. This group of biases can be divided into theoretical misspecification bias, amenity misspecification bias, and context misspecification bias.

Theoretical misspecification occurs if the scenario represents an incorrectly specified consequence of the policy change being valued. Amenity misspecification occurs when the good being valued by the respondent differs from the one intended by the researcher, possibly because the respondent misunderstands the question. The respondent might be induced, for example, to express an attitude or belief instead of a valuation for the good if the question is perceived in a symbolic way. Another possibility is that the respondent values a different quantity or quality of the good than that intended by the researcher.

Context misspecification bias is also a case of misunderstanding the question, but in this case it is not the good but the context of the market that is perceived in a way that differs from what was intended. An example of a context attribute that can be perceived in a manner not intended by the researcher is the payment vehicle (i.e., the way that it is stated that the respondent will pay for the good, such as through an increased tax or a direct user charge). Context misspecification bias is also present if the order of the questions affects the valuation or if respondents give a "reasonable" valuation instead of their greatest willingness to pay.

Sample design and execution biases are mainly statistical problems. This type of bias arises, for example, if the population surveyed does not correspond to the population to whom the benefits will accrue. Nonresponse will also bias estimates of willingness to pay if respondents' willingness to pay is not the same as the unmeasured willingness to pay of nonrespondents.

The last group of biases is inference bias. Inference bias can arise if preferences have changed from the time of the contingent valuation survey to the time the results are used for decision making. Another, and more insidious, form of inference bias may occur if the analyst adds together the willingness to pay for each of a number of different goods to evaluate a policy package but these goods were valued independently of each other. Goods evaluated independently cannot in theory be added to get the total willingness to pay for the goods (37), because the acquisition of a complementary or substitute good will affect the willingness to pay for other goods and because of income effects caused by payments for other goods.

The bias typology of Mitchell and Carson (14) differs from that used by previous researchers (13). Information bias and hypothetical bias are, for instance, not included in the typology by Mitchell and Carson (14). What used to be called "information bias" (13) cannot truly be termed a bias, because the answer to a question in a contingent valuation study is contingent on the information given. If the information changes, the good that is valued changes.

Another putative bias results from the hypothetical nature of contingent valuation questions. However, Mitchell and Carson (14) have argued that the hypothetical nature of the situation in a contingent valuation study can increase the variance in the answers but that there is no evidence from contingent valuation studies that the estimates are biased in any systematic way.

In the last few years, some evidence has surfaced, however, that the willingness to pay amounts, based on hypothetical contingent valuation studies, are higher than the willingness to pay amounts based on actual decisions (38,39). Unless this bias can be explained by other forms of bias, such as strategic bias, hypothetical bias should be reintroduced as a systematic bias in contingent valuation studies.

Carson (40) has listed five conditions for a valid contingent valuation scenario. These conditions should not be viewed as sufficient to guarantee the validity of a contingent valuation scenario, but they may be useful to think about in the design of a contingent valuation study. The criteria are that the scenario be: theoretically accurate, policy-relevant, understandable by the respondent as intended, plausible to the respondent, and meaningful to the respondent. Perhaps, the most important feature of these criteria is that they illustrate the importance of a plausible and meaningful scenario to enhance validity. The first two criteria can be fulfilled through correctly specifying the problem, and the other three can be satisfied by careful pilot testing of the instrument.

THE NOAA PANEL REPORT AND THE NOAA PROPOSED REGULATIONS

There has been a major controversy regarding the use of the contingent valuation method to measure so-called "existence values" in environmental economics. Existence values are values of environmental resources not directly related to any use of the resources. The premise is that people are willing to pay to preserve a wilderness area even though they never expect to visit the area. Existence values can be viewed as a form of altruism, and the issue is thus similar to the question of how to measure the willingness-to-pay of individuals for health programs that affect others.

After the Exxon-Valdez oil spill in Alaska, the state of Alaska contracted with several practitioners of contingent valuation to assess the loss-of-existence values due to the oil spill. The intent was to use these values as part of the damage assessment in court. Exxon, in response, retained a group of economists to make the case that the contingent valuation method could not be used to assess existence values. A fierce debate followed between these groups of economists.

Following this debate, the responsible government agency for damage assessments in connection with oil spills, the National Oceanic and Atmospheric Administration (NOAA), appointed a panel of economic experts to evaluate the use of the contingent valuation method in determining existence values. This panel was co-chaired by Professor Kenneth Arrow of Stanford and Professor Robert Solow of MIT, both Nobel laureates. Because of their relevance to the use of contingent valuation in clinical studies, we review the report of this panel (38) and the proposed regulations from NOAA for natural resource damage assessments (39).

The NOAA panel report (38) identified a number of problems with the contingent valuation method, but at the same time stated that the contingent valuation method seemed to yield some useful information. One of the problems raised by the panel was based on the indications that hypothetical willingness to pay exceeds real willingness to pay. It was stated, however, that this overestimation may be systematic, so that willingness to pay based on contingent valuation studies can be adjusted for this bias.

Another problem raised by the panel is the evidence that contingent valuations tend to be insensitive to the size of the program. For example, in some studies the willingness to pay to clean up one lake in an area might be almost as great as the willingness to pay to clean up all lakes in an area (41). In the health context, an example might be similar willingness to pay for risk reductions of widely differing magnitude, e.g., 1% or 10%. This problem is sometimes also referred to as "embedding."

A related problem raised by the panel was the so-called "warm-glow" effect. Some critics of the contingent valuation method have argued that what individuals express in contingent valuation studies are not so much valuations of environmental changes as expressions of willingness to donate to charities (41). A contingent valuation response would then express some kind of general approval of the environmental program rather than a valuation. This could be an explanation for that the willingness to pay does not vary with the size of the program. The invariance of willingness to pay with program size and the "warm-glow" effect might also be interpreted as examples of scenario misspecification; that is, the respondent answers some other question than that intended by the researcher.

A further problem in contingent valuation studies discussed by the panel is the absence of a meaningful budget constraint as perceived by the respondent. The problem is that individuals may answer contingent valuation questions without thinking about where the money would come from; that is, what alternative consumption that they would reduce. The panel criticizes contingent valuation studies for not reminding respondents that they would have to reduce some other spending to pay for the good in question.

The panel also proposes a number of guidelines for contingent valuation studies. They recommend the use of the binary referendum approach for eliciting willingness to pay in surveys, rather than the use of open-ended questions. Furthermore, they recommend the use of interviews in contingent valuation studies rather than mail surveys. Face-to-face interviews are the preferred approach, but telephone interviews may also be acceptable in some cases. They also propose that a budget constraint should be imposed on the respondents by reminding them of alternative spending possibilities and making it clear that the payment will reduce the consumption of other goods.

Another recommendation of the panel was that respondents should be given the option of not responding to a contingent valuation question. Specifically, a "no answer" or "don't know" option should be added to the binary contingent valuation question so that individuals are not forced to state a "yes" or a "no" response.

It was also recommended that the answers to the valuation question be followed up with a question about the reason for the response. The follow-up question could serve as a way to sort out the responses that reflect true valuations of the good from protest bids and other types of answers. The panel also recommends what they call a conservative design of contingent valuation studies. This means that when there is ambiguity about some aspect of the survey or the analysis of the data, the option that will tend to underestimate willingness to pay should be chosen.

After the report of the NOAA panel on contingent valuation, NOAA issued a set of proposed regulations concerning the use of contingent valuation studies as a basis for natural resource damage assessment (39). This document stated that contingent valuation studies can be used to value existence values for damage assessment as long as the contingent valuation studies follow the standards in the proposed regulations.

The standards in the proposed regulations rely heavily on the report of the expert panel. The regulations recommend the use of face-to-face interviews and the use of the binary referendum contingent valuation format. They also require that the response rate be at least 70% in a contingent valuation study to be considered valid. Contingent valuation studies are required to demonstrate sensitivity to the size of the program by using different subsamples of respondents.

The regulations also state that the willingness to pay from a contingent valuation study should be reduced by 50%, as a conservative correction for the property that hypothetical willingness to pay seem to exceed real willingness to pay.

Many of the issues raised in connection with the NOAA panel report and the proposed regulations are of interest for cost-benefit analysis of health programs. It is a reasonable requirement that the study demonstrates willingness to pay increases with the size of the program or of a health effect such as the size of a risk reduction. The recommendation to reinforce the budget constraint by reminding individuals that the payment has to be taken from their own disposable income also seems useful, as do the queries into reasons for different types of responses as a means of screening for invalid responses.

Perhaps, the most important need in contingent valuation research at the present time, however, is for studies to compare hypothetical payments with real money payments. Even if hypothetical willingness to pay overestimates real willingness to pay, there may be a systematic relationship, so that real willingness to pay can be predicted based on hypothetical willingness to pay. It is important that such studies be carried out in relation to health goods, because it is possible that the validity of the contingent valuation method differs for different types of goods. It may also be easier to find cases where real payments can be compared with hypothetical payments in the health area than in the environmental area owing to the private goods nature of many health services.

CONTINGENT VALUATION AND CLINICAL RESEARCH

If a clinical trial is used as a basis for a cost-benefit analysis, there are two different ways to use the contingent valuation method. The contingent valuation method could be incorporated directly in a clinical trial that compares two or more alternative treatments to investigate the willingness to pay for the treatments in the different groups. One test of validity could then be carried out by testing if the willingness to pay increases with the size of the health effects. This assumes that the size of the health effects can somehow be measured. If, for example, an experimental treatment reduces the risk of some event, one could measure the perceived risk reduction of the patients and test whether the willingness to pay increases with the perceived risk reduction. For treatments that improve quality of life it may be possible to correlate improvements in quality of life with willingness to pay. If the number of QALYs gained are estimated in the trial for the different treatments, it could also be tested whether willingness to pay increases with the number of QALYs gained. An advantage of using the contingent valuation method within a clinical trial is that it should be possible to achieve a high response rate.

Alternatively, the results of the clinical trial could be used to describe the health consequences of different treatments, and then these health improvements could be valued using the contingent valuation method in either a general population sample or a sample of patients with the disease under study. By valuing the size of the health improvement in different subsamples, it can be tested if willingness to pay increases with the size of the health improvement.

It should be noted that cost-benefit analysis and cost-effectiveness analysis should not necessarily be viewed as mutually exclusive approaches to economic evaluation. To use cost-effectiveness analysis for decision making, the willingness to pay per effectiveness unit (e.g., life years or QALYs gained) has to be determined. The contingent valuation method (or revealed preference studies) could then be used to estimate the willingness to pay per unit of effectiveness in order to provide an external standard for cost-effectiveness ratios.

It is also important to remember that the contingent valuation method should be regarded still as an experimental method. Much more basic research remains to be done to test the validity of the method before it can be used with any confidence in decision making about the allocation of resources in medical care. Many of the research issues concerning the collection of preference data through surveys are also common to the measurement of quality of life and the measurement of quality weights to construct QALYs. One lesson from environmental economics is also that to collect high quality data through contingent valuation will neither be inexpensive nor trivial and in the health care field it seems important to move beyond the pilot test type of studies carried out thus far into more rigorously designed contingent valuation studies.

ACKNOWLEDGMENTS

Dr. Johannesson was supported by the National Corporation of Swedish Pharmacies and the Harvard Center for

Risk Analysis. Dr. Weinstein was supported in part by grants R01-HS06258 and P01-HS06341 from the Agency for Health Care Policy and Research, U.S. Public Health Service.

REFERENCES

1. Boadway RW, Bruce N. *Welfare economics.* Oxford: Blackwell, 1984.
2. Weisbrod B. *Economics of public health: measuring the impact of diseases.* Philadelphia: University of Pennsylvania Press, 1961.
3. Rice D. Estimating the cost of illness. *Am J Public Health* 1967;57: 424–440.
4. Schelling TC. The life you save may be your own. In: Chase SB, ed. *Problems in public expenditures analysis.* Washington D.C.: Brookings Institution, 1968.
5. Mishan EJ. Evaluation of life and limb: a theoretical approach. *J Pol Econ* 1971;79:687–705.
6. Thaler R, Rosen S. The value of saving a life: evidence from the market. In: Terleckyj NE, ed. *Household production and consumption.* Cambridge, MA: NBER, 1976.
7. Viscusi WK. Labor market valuations of life and limb: empirical estimates and policy implications. *Public Policy* 1978;26:359–386.
8. Blomquist G. Value of life saving: implications of consumption activity. *J Pol Econ* 1979;87:540–558.
9. Dardis R. The value of a life: new evidence from the marketplace. *Am Econ Rev* 1980;70:1077–1082.
10. Akerman J, Johnson FR, Bergman L. Paying for safety: voluntary reduction of residential radon risks. *Land Econ* 1991;67:435–446.
11. Starr C. Social benefit versus technological risk. *Science* 1969;165: 1232–1238.
12. Fischhoff B, Slovic P, Lichtenstein S, Read S, Combs B. How safe is safe enough? a psychometric study of attitudes towards risks and benefits. *Pol Sci* 1978;9:127–152.
13. Cummings RG, Brookshire DS, Schulze WD, eds. *Valuing environmental goods.* New Jersey: Rowman and Allanheld, 1986.
14. Mitchell RC, Carson RT. Using surveys to value public goods: the contingent valuation method. Washington D.C.: Resources for the Future, 1989.
15. Acton JP. Evaluating public programs to save lives: the case of heart attacks. Santa Monica: The Rand Corporation, RAND Report R-950-RC, 1973.
16. Johannesson M, Jönsson B, Borgquist L. Willingness to pay for antihypertensive therapy: results of a Swedish pilot study. *J Health Econ* 1991;10:461–474.
17. Johannesson M, Johansson P-O, Kriström B, Gerdtham U-G. Willingness to pay for antihypertensive therapy: further results. *J Health Econ* 1993;12:95–108.
18. Randall A, Ives BC, Eastman C. Bidding games for valuation of aesthetic environmental improvements. *J Environ Econ Man* 1974;1:132–149.
19. Kahneman D, Slovic P, Tversky A. *Judgement under uncertainty: heuristics and biases.* Cambridge: Cambridge University Press, 1982.
20. Bishop RC, Heberlein JA. Measuring values of extra market goods: are indirect measures biased? *Am J Agric Econ* 1979;61:926–930.
21. Hanemann MW. Welfare evaluations in contingent valuation experiments with discrete responses. *Am J Agric Econ* 1984;66:332–341.
22. Cameron TA. A new paradigm for valuing non-market goods using referendum data: maximum likelihood estimation by censored logistic regression. *J Environ Econ Man* 1988;13:255–268.
23. Boyle KJ, Bishop RC. Welfare measurements using contingent valuation: a comparison of techniques. *Am J Agric Econ* 1988;70:21–28.
24. Bowker JM, Stoll JR. Use of dichotomous choice nonmarket methods to value the whooping crane resource. *Am J Agric Econ* 1988;70:372–381.
25. Kriström B. A non-parametric approach to the estimation of welfare measures in discrete response valuation studies. *Land Econ* 1990;66: 135–139.
26. Sellar CJ, Chavas JP, Stoll JR. Validation of empirical measures of welfare change: a comparison of nonmarket techniques. *Land Econ* 1985;61:156–175.
27. Kriström B. Discrete and continuous valuation questions; do they give different answers? Swedish University of Agricultural Sciences in Umeå, Department of Forest Economics, Working paper 90, 1989.
28. Rowe RD, D'Arge RC, Brookshire DS. An experiment on the economic value of visibility. *J Environ Econ Man* 1980;7:1–19.
29. Bohm P. Estimating demand for public goods: an experiment. *Eur Econ Rev* 1972;3:111–130.
30. Scherr BA, Babb EM. Pricing public goods: an experiment with two proposed pricing systems. *Public Choice* 1975;23:35–48.
31. Brookshire DS, Ives BC, Schulze WD. The valuation of aesthetic preferences. *J Environ Econ Man* 1976;3:325–346.
32. Smith VL. The principle of unanimity and voluntary consent in social choice. *J Pol Econ* 1977;85:1125–1139.
33. Milon JW. Contingent valuation experiments for strategic behavior. *J Environ Econ Man* 1989;17:293–308.
34. Brookshire DS, Randall A, Stoll JR. Valuing increments and decrements of natural resource service flows. *Am J Agric Econ* 1980;62: 478–488.
35. Thayer MA. Contingent valuation techniques for assessing environmental impacts: further evidence. *J Environ Econ Man* 1981;8:27–44.
36. Boyle KJ, Bishop RC, Welsh MP. Starting point bias in contingent valuation bidding games. *Land Econ* 1985;61:188–194.
37. Johansson P-O. *The economic theory and measurement of environmental benefits.* Cambridge: Cambridge University Press, 1987.
38. National Oceanic and Atmospheric Administration. Report of the NOAA panel on contingent valuation. Federal Register 1993;58;4602–4614.
39. National Oceanic and Atmospheric Administration. Oil pollution act of 1990: proposed regulations for natural resource damage assessment. Mimeography, 1993.
40. Carson RT. Constructed markets. In: Braden JB, Kolstad CD, eds. *Measuring the demand for environmental quality.* Amsterdam: Elsevier/North Holland, 1991.
41. Hausman JA. *Contingent valuation: a critical assessment.* Amsterdam: Elsevier/North Holland, 1993.

Quality of Life and Pharmacoeconomics in Clinical Trials, Second Edition, edited by B. Spilker.
Lippincott-Raven Publishers, Philadelphia © 1996.

CHAPTER 113

Designing and Conducting Cost-Minimization and Cost-Effectiveness Analyses

Brian E. Rittenhouse

There's no economy in going to bed early to spare candles
if the result is twins.
Chinese Proverb (1)

INTRODUCTION

While methods of economic analysis of medical technology
(particularly pharmaceuticals) must continue to develop to
meet the challenges of both marketplace and, often enough
in some countries, regulatory authorities, significant strides
have already been made over what once passed for economic
analysis in this field. Not that long ago—and still in some
circles—economics consisted of a search for inexpensive
pharmaceuticals where "inexpensive" was defined solely
with reference to acquisition cost. A significant development
occurred when it was recognized that daily treatment cost
was a more meaningful concept than, for example, cost per
capsule, and, for some, methods development halted after
this advance.

Doubtless, in some cases, using pharmaceutical daily
treatment cost as the basis for economic "analysis" may
not induce significant error—at least in terms of the use/no
use decision for the product, though the quantitative answers
to real economic questions about cost and value implications
are wholly eluded. However, basing decisions solely on
daily treatment cost may lead one to the false economizing

illustrated by the opening quotation. Downstream events,
not the least of which is some measure of outcome, must
be considered if economic analysis is to be honestly brought
to bear on an issue. Other downstream issues relating to costs
must also be considered, for example, the use of concomitant
medications, monitoring of blood levels, hospitalizations,
physician visits, etc. A simple look at daily treatment cost
will lead to proper economic decisions only fortuitously.
Pronouncing on the "cost-effectiveness" of a product evaluated only in this way is certainly a sloppy use of the term
even in cases where the (qualitative) result would be the same
(e.g., use the product) had economics been used properly.

The task of economic evaluation is an increasingly important one. Economic evaluations are not mere academic
exercises; they are now and will continue to be used to
justify if not determine decisions on the everyday practice
of medicine (e.g., formulary listing). Accuracy and attention
to detail are of crucial importance. "Cost-effective" is probably one of the most misused descriptors in both medical
literature and the layperson vernacular. Doubilet et al. (2)
surveyed the literature in 1986 noting the frequent misuse
of the term. To some, this presents a significant problem
since the term has a very specific definition that actually
excludes much of what those who use the term inaccurately
mean when they use it. Others consider this semantic discussion tantamount to the proverbial "tempest in a teapot" and
would rather get on with substantive issues. To a degree
both parties are right. However, the definitional point is such
a simple one to make (and follow) that to continue to err in
this matter seems almost unforgivable. One may interpret
the misuse of the terms as a (perhaps imperfect) signal of

B. E. Rittenhouse: Division of Pharmaceutical Policy and Evaluative Sciences, School of Pharmacy, University of North Carolina
at Chapel Hill, Chapel Hill, North Carolina 27599.

a lack of familiarity with both the basics and the nuances in the economic evaluation literature. This field is frequently more complex than it initially appears to be. Approaching the subject casually is to be avoided. Perhaps Alexander Pope (3) said it best: "A little Learning is a dang'rous thing."

This chapter first defines the methods of cost-minimization analysis (CMA) and cost-effectiveness analysis (CEA); this is followed by a discussion of the common and unique characteristics of each method. Finally, the particularly unique interpretive issues in decision making and statistics that pertain to CEA are addressed. The theoretical justification of CEA is beyond the scope of this chapter. In fact, it may be beyond the scope of much more than this chapter as Garber and Phelps (4) have argued that the technique has little, if any, formal justification in the economic literature. Nonetheless, it is widely used. As the discussion herein implies, even within the informal justification framework, the technique is frequently misused.

DEFINING CMA AND CEA

Cost-minimization analyses (CMA) and Cost-Effectiveness Analyses (CEA) are analytical methods in the pharmacoeconomic armamentarium. They accompany Cost-Utility Analysis (CUA) and Cost-Benefit Analysis (CBA) in being designed to pronounce on the optimality of various types of interventions in an economic context. Often the list of analytical methods also includes Quality of Life analysis (QOL) and Cost-of-Illness (COI) studies. These latter methods do not explicitly consider the optimality of an intervention, but serve to measure its impact on either outcome or cost alone. The primary differentiating factor between the two methods addressed in this chapter and CBA and CUA (as alternative methods) lies in the way intervention effects are treated. In CUA and CBA effects are explicitly valued in either "utility" or monetary terms. In CMA and CEA effects are not valued (5).

It must be emphasized that both CMA and CEA can only indicate relative superiority. They answer questions such as "Which is better?" or "What does it cost to bring about a certain effect?" from an economic point of view. They do not claim that what is better is necessarily worth doing. Thus, treatment A may be economically superior in producing an outcome compared to treatment B, but it may still cost so much to produce such a marginally valuable effect that its use remains unappealing. CBA is the only method that is generally suited to pronouncements on anything but relative worth in that it explicitly states whether benefits exceed costs. If so, the project is worth pursuing (although others may be even more worthwhile).

In CMA, effects are placed in a completely subordinate position and more or less wholly ignored except to show (or, more frequently, assume) equivalence in effect between interventions. The CMA task then is limited to assessing costs of the alternatives. Since effects are the same, the

decision as to optimal intervention is based on cost alone. The cheapest intervention is deemed (relatively) optimal, barring any other relevant noneconomic considerations (e.g., ethical arguments). This is the simplest of all methods of economic evaluation, though its simple definition belies the potential for error. To the extent that the assumption of equal effect is flawed, the analysis makes an incorrect cost comparison of two different things. Furthermore, as we shall see, costing issues are not always clear; here too one may oversimplify.

Treatments whose effects are identical are not particularly common. In practice, this method is little used (more accurately, when it is used, it is often used improperly or often enough referred to as CEA). Part of the confusion relates to a misconception of what economics is all about (6). Economics is as much about the attributes of what is purchased as it is about its costs. Critics of economic evaluation techniques, as well as some analysts, who would never overlook this in making their own consumer choices, often appear to do so in their professional work. Ignoring differential effects and concentrating exclusively on costs will not lead to optimal decisions.

CEA is a more common technique than CMA. Using CEA requires not that effects be identical, but that they be comparable in terms of some "natural unit" of effect, such as cases detected, number of lives saved, or years of life saved. Once effects are reduced to these common natural units, the cost of achieving them can be compared. This method shares the costing difficulties of CMA and introduces the added dimension of differential effect, making it at the same time both more useful and more difficult to implement. Clearly this is a much more useful method as it permits comparisons among highly diverse interventions. Thus, two treatments might save lives with different probabilities and costs; however, both treatments can be described by their cost per (statistical) life year saved, making them comparable in terms of the costs of achieving that outcome.

A purported strength of CEA (and CMA) is the ability to evaluate intermediate outcomes. CBA and CUA are typically considered to be somewhat limited by the need for information on final outcomes (that which is to be valued in the analysis) in order to use the studies (5,7). In spirit the techniques are in fact not limited to final outcomes, as one may certainly value intermediate outcomes by linking them to likely final outcomes. In fact, the linkages to final outcomes are not always clear and this can introduce additional error into the evaluation process (see Chapter 126, this volume).

A drawback of CEA is that all effects are assumed to be valued identically. This is a potential problem for two reasons. Firstly, some effects that may be equal in terms of effects expressed in "natural units," may differ markedly in quality associated with the effect (hence the development of CUA from CEA). Second, natural units are assumed to be all equivalent in another sense. One year of life saved for each of 20 people is assumed to be equivalent to 20 (discounted) years of life for one person. [Issues of discounting of costs and effects are addressed in Drummond (5).] Ethics aside, it is simply not clear that people value even their own lives this way. Even within an individual, it is not clear that two (discounted) years of life are perceived as twice as valuable as one. CEA treats life years as if they were equally valuable (excepting for the application of a time discount rate). CUA attempts to take the valuations of one of these factors into account (quality), though it has been criticized with respect to its success (8).

A further drawback of CEA is that health care interventions are rarely so similar so as to be measurable in terms of a single effect. For example, Edelson et al. (9) found captopril to rank poorly as compared to other angiotensin-converting enzyme (ACE) inhibitors from a cost-effectiveness standpoint when the effect measure was projected mortality. However, Croog et al. (10) found captopril to be superior in terms of blood pressure control and health-related quality of life. Multiple effects cannot typically be incorporated in CEA. Drummond et al. (5) suggested using CEA when one of the following conditions apply: "(a) that there is one, unambiguous objective of the intervention(s) and therefore a clear dimension along which effectiveness can be assessed; or (b) that there are many objectives, but that the alternative interventions are thought to achieve these to the same extent."

COMMON ISSUES

Costing Caveats

Costing seems to be a straightforward issue. This discussion approaches the issue of cost in two ways. First the costs that need to be considered and how they need to be considered will be presented. These issues pertain to both CMA and CEA. Then the additional importance of differential effect for costing in CEA will be addressed. The interesting way in which cost interacts with effect in decision making based on CEA is described in the following section.

Let us posit two interventions for the same indication and potentially for the same patient. Treatment A costs $1000 and B costs $1100. They achieve exactly the same effect—saving a life with probability equal to one (with the same adverse event profile). What possible justification might one have for using B? None apparently. However, if the costs are incurred by different parties in differing proportions there may be significant conflict over the appropriate treatment. Consider the patient with no pharmaceutical benefit in his or her insurance scheme. If the costs of A are predominantly pharmaceutical and the costs of B primarily in nonpharmaceutical areas covered by insurance, the patient may well prefer B, the more expensive treatment (the insurance company preferring the opposite). This issue of the analytical perspective of the analysis is quite important. An analysis done from the two perspectives discussed above (patient and insurer) would not yield the same answer (nei-

ther quantitatively nor perhaps qualitatively) as one done from a total cost point of view (often called the societal point of view).

Related to analytical perspective is the issue of defining costs. The perspective of a third party payer on the relevant costs are whatever the payer must pay (i.e., the charges for various services provided). However, other perspectives may identify wholly different costs of providing these same services. An obvious case was discussed earlier. To the patient with full insurance, the monetary costs of these services are viewed as zero. Many economic analyses purport to be done from the perspective of society. This would (or should) imply that all "true economic costs" of procedures (rarely, if ever, equal to the charges assessed for them) are tallied as input into the analysis. The societal perspective does not distinguish between payers as being patients or insurers; rather, it would attempt to determine the true total cost of a particular service. Internal analyses for providers might take a similar approach to certain cost issues—identify the true cost of supplying a service in order to determine internal benefits of reducing or expanding use of the service. the term "true cost" here refers to an economic concept generally foreign to noneconomists—that of "opportunity cost" (11,12). Every action has a potential opportunity cost. A nurse who spends time making a bed in a hospital does not use that particular time in any other way. The opportunity cost of making the bed is the sacrifice of the next most valuable thing he or she could have been doing with that time. If the nurse would do nothing if this time were not spent making beds, the opportunity cost of that activity is zero.

It has been claimed that freeing time in small quantities (by removing the need for making beds as an example) does not in fact save resources since, unless fewer nurses can be hired by such freeing up of time, no resources are saved. This is misleading. Freeing a nurse's time allows the same nurse to pursue another activity on the schedule, providing that much more output from the same staff as before. The bed-making time is valued by the value of the service that the nurse would perform that was previously not done because of insufficient time available. If, in fact, the nurse would do nothing if such time were freed, then the true cost of the making of the bed would be zero. Note that nothing has been said about the nurse's salary or benefit rate, but (under the highly restrictive assumption of doing nothing as the relevant alternative for time spent making a bed) we have assigned a true cost (zero) to the activity. This is obviously independent of charges for such activity. However, under the assumption of zero true cost, stopping the activity would imply no extra benefit supplied to the hospital, just as (presumably) starting it added no cost (under the somewhat restrictive assumption that "doing nothing" is the only alternative activity). In this sense we can see that opportunity costs bear little resemblance to nurses' salaries or actual charges for services. It works the other way as well. For example, an unpaid volunteer in a hospital charges nothing for providing services; however, the opportunity cost of the volunteer time can be positive and, in fact, generally will be positive. It is probably clear that valuing services at their true costs is quite difficult. Moreover, such valuation may be highly specific to particular facilities with certain staffing arrangements, workloads and case mixes. Any valuation specific to a particular setting is less transferable elsewhere. This is also true of charges that tend to reflect many things specific to their settings that have nothing to do with the costs of services provided. The proverbial ten dollar aspirin tablet from the hospital pharmacy would be an example. Thrown in with some idea of true cost of activities are overhead costs, costs associated with unpaid bills, and other costs. The hospital is typically not concerned with true costs, but with average costs, and ensuring that service incomes are covering their average costs and contributing to overhead. Individual ways of accounting for various overhead expenses and departments can influence the charge that is calculated (5,11,12). Charges must be calculated in such a way so that institutions remain profitable, and it is certainly true that, for example, many hospital services could not be profitable without "overhead" equipment and personnel. However, the addition of some particular activity may not imply any additional overhead expenditure. If this is so, including an overhead component in true costs is inaccurate, as these overhead costs are incurred independent of the added activity.

In many pharmaceutical analyses, true costs are wholly ignored. If the analysis is being done from the perspective of an organization interested only in charges, this is appropriate, though Drummond et al. (5) suggest that any analysis should also present the perspective of society, requiring an estimate of true costs. In other cases, analysts err by such oversight either out of ignorance or simply to expedite the analysis. This may have significant effects on an analysis. Eisenberg and Kitz (13) used several measures of cost (and charge) in their study of early discharge antibiotic treatment for osteomyelitis. Of particular importance was the number used to represent the cost/charge of hospitalization. Estimated "cost" savings varied between $509 and $22,232 for the program depending on the "cost" estimate used. The estimate used for true costs led to the $509 figure. This estimate came from the New Jersey Diagnosis-Related Groups (DRGs), which break down hospitalization into a variable cost component, thus approximating true costs of the service.

Having mentioned the importance of these costing issues, I will subsequently ignore them here as they do not solely apply to CEA/CMA. From hereon, we assume that any cost analysis has been done from the correct perspective and has been done correctly. Other cost issues have not been discussed here due to space limitations. Chief among these in importance is probably that of adjusting costs for differential timing—discounting. This topic is covered adequately elsewhere; interested readers are referred to other sources (5,7).

In CMA, the analytical task should be clear now. The decision from the point of view of the perspective chosen is clear. Treatment A is the cheaper alternative and achieves the same effect. It is preferred. If the analysis were a CEA, matters become a little more complicated. Now we have the potential for A and B to have different effects and different costs. This seemingly small difference has important ramifications in two areas:

1. If treatments have different effects, they are likely to have different costs that will be linked to the different effects. These will differ from costs in CMA, and the nature of such costs should be discussed.
2. The joint importance of cost and effect imply that decision-making rules are somewhat more complex than in CMA where costs alone are used to determine optimal decisions.

Before pursuing these topics, which are relevant to CEA, brief mention is made of some concerns about measuring effects that are common to both CMA and CEA.

Elusive Effects

Measuring effects is crucial for CEA (and CBA and CUA). The typical effect measure in pharmacoeconomics is taken from a randomized, controlled trial of one or more pharmaceuticals. In the case where placebo is the comparison in the trial, an economic evaluator is faced with a difficult problem, in that placebos are not in fact given in practice and the data from such a comparison will not (unless there is a complete absence of a placebo effect) reflect the effects to be expected under "no treatment." Clearly, if "no treatment" is not a relevant alternative, the placebo comparison helps even less. For a CEA that relies on data solely from a trial, the placebo comparison is of little value. More reasonable is an active comparator—not just any active comparator, but a market-relevant one. This too may mean many things to many people. In short, the comparator should be that which is most relevant to whomever the study is being used to influence. Based on formal economic evaluation guidelines for the Australian government reimbursement authority, the relevant comparator is the most widely used alternative in Australia (14). In the latest version of the Canadian guidelines, the relevant comparator is "both existing practice and minimal practice," each of which is defined in the guidelines. It is therein further emphasized that "all other reasonable alternative therapies should be at least discussed" (15). That decided, there remains a crucial issue that is very difficult to overcome—the randomized, controlled trial framework is generally a biased study design for making economic (or other) inferences about the population of most relevance—those who will in practice be given the drug. Detailed discussion of this point is beyond the scope of this chapter. Very briefly, however, the randomized, controlled trial recruitment patterns, and protocol-driven treatment, among other influences, will tend to lessen the real world relevance of randomized, controlled trial-based studies. This precaution should always be kept in mind when basing effect measures on randomized, controlled trial results (8,16). (See Chapter 126, this volume, for further discussion of this point.)

NEW ASPECTS OF COSTS AND EFFECTS IN CEA

With CMA, the issue reduces to finding the cheapest treatment since the outcomes are identical. In CEA issues become more complex. The lack of a requirement for identical effects implies a twofold increase in complexity. One may compare completely different treatments for different indications to determine which should receive priority in cases of restricted funding availability. In such a case, not only are treatment effects going to differ, but so will baseline effects (and costs) and therefore incremental treatment effects (and costs). Baseline effects and costs are those associated with current treatments or existing programs for a given indication. A new treatment must be evaluated in terms of its effects and costs over and above the treatment already supplied. Thus, in CEA, both baseline and treatment effects will generally differ between treatments, making an analyst's job more difficult. When the comparison treatments are for the same indication and are analyzed incrementally from the same baseline, some of this complexity is reduced; however, the issue of incremental analysis remains. This issue is addressed further in the next section.

Once different treatment effects are admitted for consideration, the possibility exists for more complicated cost implications of treatments. For example, if treatments succeed at different rates, treatment failure costs may be relevant. To the extent that such failures imply further costs (e.g., treating the failure event itself, discontinuing the treatment, initiating new treatments, monitoring the blood levels associated with new treatments), differential failure rates will imply additional costs that may further differentiate the total costs of treatment.

The measure of effect may be straightforward (e.g., lives saved) or can be somewhat innovative. Sculpher and Buxton (17) used episode-free days as a measure of effect in asthma treatment. Such a measure allows for the combination of efficacy and safety end points into a single effect measure (days with neither adverse events nor efficacy problems). CEA requires a single measure of effect. It appears unlikely, however, that a day with adverse events is valued equally to a day without treatment efficacy. Therefore, such innovative "constructed" unidimensional effects may be questionable until the assumptions used are shown to be reasonable. When an intervention has more than one important dimension of effect, either some innovative way of combining effects must be developed or a method suited to multidimensional effects (e.g., CUA or CBA) must be used.

DECISION MAKING WITH CEA

CEA results are presented in ratio form: the cost per unit of effect. Thus a cost of $100,000 to save 20 (discounted) years of life implies a $5,000 cost per life year saved. Sometimes results are presented in units of effect per dollar cost, driving home the opportunity cost in effects of dollars spent (18). Interestingly, Eddy (19) attributes part of the counterintuitive nature of initial rankings in Oregon's adventure with priority setting in health care to a misunderstanding based on the use of cost-effectiveness ratios as opposed to the alternative of effectiveness-cost ratios. The numbers used to compute the ratio are the same, but the intuition of the reciprocal measures is quite different. This ratio presentation may also obscure some interesting information since a cost-effectiveness ratio of $5,000 per life year saved can reflect both an investment that saves a single year of life at the cost of $5,000, as well as that which saves 20 discounted life years at a cost of $100,000 (and many other combinations that result in the same ratio). While these two cases have identical cost-effectiveness ratios, what is being accomplished in each case is quite different. It may be important to acknowledge this, rather than bury the difference in a cost-effectiveness ratio. The interaction between cost and effect (even once they are properly defined) is potentially confusing. It can become even more confusing once quality considerations enter the analysis in CUA or other variants of economic evaluation (20).

How can these ratios be used to facilitate proper decision making? First, the issue of an average cost-effectiveness ratio which is generally what is meant by a "cost-effectiveness ratio" must be discussed. One may imagine that a particular intervention achieves a cost-effectiveness ratio that appears to be well within either an available budget or within society's willingness to pay for such effects. Thus, we may have a new therapy (B) that has a cost-effectiveness ratio of $5,000 per life year saved. Let us say for now that this represents one life year saved and the cost of the treatment is $5,000. This ratio would appear to be quite reasonable compared to other interventions that society endorses, but it would be inappropriate to investigate the treatment in isolation from alternatives. If it is the only available treatment, then the above cost effectiveness ratio may be appropriate. However, if alternatives exist, then the $5,000 figure may be irrelevant for good economic decision making (but falsely appealing).

If, for example, some current treatment (A) for the same indication exists that saves one life year at a cost of $3,000, our new treatment suddenly does not look very good, despite its apparently appealing cost-effectiveness ratio when examined in isolation. This example allows us to focus on the appropriate issue which is not cost-effectiveness ratios, but incremental cost-effectiveness ratios. A proper analysis would not provide a stand-alone cost-effectiveness ratio, but would incorporate the knowledge and implications of treatment that

TABLE 1. *Summary of costs and effects of treatments used in example calculations*

	Treatments					
	A	A'	B	B'	B"	B'''
Costs	$3,000	$6,000	$5,000	$5,500	$4,500	$2,000
Effects	1 LY	2 LY	1 LY	1.1 LY	.9 LY	1.7 LY
Average cost-effectiveness ratios	$3,000/LY	$3,000/LY	$5,000/LY	$5,000/LY	$5,000/LY	$1,176/LY

already exists. The relevant issue is what the new treatment provides in addition to the old treatment (and what additional costs it imposes). This is not meant to imply that it is used with the old treatment. Rather, summing up effects and costs under scenario 1 with treatment A and scenario 2 with treatment B, each alone, then subtracting, yields the incremental costs and incremental effects of altering the treatment program of A in favor of B. If the above example data are correct, the relevant incremental cost-effectiveness ratio is in fact infinitely high, as no incremental effect is provided (since the number of life years saved is identical), but an incremental cost is incurred.

In spirit, the same incremental approach may be applied to CMA and a decision made as to whether the cheapest treatment provides sufficient value to be adopted. In this particular case, because the effects are identical, the CMA rule of choosing the cheapest intervention (provided that it supplies effects deemed to be ''worth it''), and the CEA rule of evaluating the value of incremental effects against their incremental costs would lead to the same conclusion, since the infinite cost-effectiveness ratio is rather clearly unattractive. The above example was fairly straightforward, but incremental analysis can be quite useful and produce surprising results, sometimes indicating potential dangers in casual intuition and appeal to average cost-effectiveness ratios. Continuing the example (see Table 1), suppose intervention A has been used and that intervention A' becomes available, providing two (discounted) years of life saved at a cost of $6,000. Both treatments have the same cost-effectiveness ratios ($3,000/LY); however, rather clearly (if we do not succumb to the deceptive influences of identical cost-effectiveness ratios), one is unlikely to be indifferent between these two interventions. For a $3,000 incremental cost ($6,000–$3,000), one may obtain an additional life year (2-1) by using A'. In this case, the incremental cost effectiveness ratio is identical to the average. Moreover, if the initial intervention (A) was worth doing, then so is A', since the $3,000 to save a life year was ''shown'' to be ''worth it'' by virtue of the initial intervention (costing $3,000/LY) being done in the first place. If it is worth $3,000 to save a year of life by using intervention A, then it is worth it to spend an additional $3,000 to save an additional life year by other means (in this case by using A'). Suppose now that instead of A' we consider intervention B' that provides 1.1 years of life saved at a cost of $5,500 ($5,000/LY). Clearly

the original intervention (A) has a lower cost effectiveness ratio ($3,000/LY). It appears to be ''cost-effective.'' Is it superior? The answer to the question is found in incremental analysis. The new intervention (B') both costs more and produces greater positive effect than A. These incremental costs and effects must be examined before the relative cost-effectiveness of the choices can be determined. By using the new treatment instead of the existing one, we will spend $2500 more ($5,500–$3,000) and achieve .1 additional life years saved (1.1–1). The incremental cost-effectiveness ratio is thus $25,000 per additional life year saved. By many measures, $25,000 is a reasonable price for a year of life and would be deemed ''worth it.'' Thus, we have what may appear to be a counterintuitive result that the treatment with the higher cost-effectiveness ratio is preferred to that with a lower ratio. This example shows both the deceptive nature of average cost-effectiveness ratios and the power of incremental analysis.

If the new treatment (say B") had instead been slightly less effective (e.g. .9 years) and slightly less costly (e.g., $4,500) (but with the same cost-effectiveness ratio as in the example given ($5,000/LY), its average cost-effectiveness ratio is markedly misleading since it shows an apparently reasonable figure, whereas the incremental cost-effectiveness ratio (with increased cost ($4,500–$3,000) and decreased effect (0.9–1) compared to treatment A) would in fact be negative (-$15,000/LY). Negative incremental cost effectiveness ratios can be either very good or very bad, depending on the source of the negativity. The above example shows positive incremental costs and negative incremental benefits (a bad case). A negative incremental cost effectiveness ratio is also a result of negative incremental costs and positive incremental effects—a good case as it costs less to achieve more. Black (21) notes that negative incremental cost effectiveness ratios should not be assessed. The more common case is one in which both costs and effects are greater with a new treatment. In this case, the incremental cost-effectiveness ratio will be positive and further evaluation is necessary, as we still do not know much about desirability without a specific ratio to assess. The point is that we must now evaluate whether the additional effect produced by the new program is worth the additional cost required to bring it about.

We can trace the source of the false appeal of average cost effectiveness ratios to the fact that they (implicitly) assume that current costs and effects are both zero (i.e., that nothing is currently being done and that there are no costs or effects). However, even without treatment, not all cases of a severe disease will, for example, die. Also, even in the absence of a specific treatment alternative, costs are rarely zero. To base a cost-effectiveness analysis on the (implicit) assumption that costs and effects are zero may be improper and can lead one to supposing that an intervention with an average cost-effectiveness ratio of $5,000/life-year is a worthwhile investment, when, in fact, it may not be at all. Whether current treatment is no treatment or some active alternative, incremental analysis is essential for optimizing decision making from an economic point of view. On the off chance that someone now considers all ambiguity relating to CEA to be cleared up, another complication is introduced. We saw that intervention B′ may be superior to A despite its worse (average) cost-effectiveness ratio. Incremental analysis shows its incremental effects to be potentially worth its incremental costs. Let us say that we do pronounce the costs "worth it" and therefore deem B′ superior to A.

Suppose now that there is a budget limitation of $11,000 and that both treatments are usable in multiple cases with identical costs and effects as described above. The previous discussion assumed that we were considering alternative interventions for one patient. Here we expand the discussion to consider multiple patients. For $11,000, one may supply three patients each an additional one year of life by using treatment A (or a total of three years of life—with $2,000 left over). Alternatively, one may use the new treatment and provide two patients with 1.1 additional years of life (for a total of 2.2 years and no surplus of funds left over). The new treatment (the one shown above to be superior—or "worth it" over the existing treatment) provides less total years of life saved for fewer people at a greater cost and is clearly inferior in this scenario (ignoring discounting issues). This example indicates some of the complex interactions possible in CEA. For further discussions of using CEA under budget restrictions, see Drummond et al. (5) and Cantor (22).

GRAPHIC REPRESENTATIONS OF COST-EFFECTIVENESS RATIOS

The above discussion may be usefully supplemented by graphical depictions. Both Drummond et al. (5) and Eisenberg (23) have used diagrams to indicate these concepts. A similar diagram is shown in Figure 1.

Point B in Figure 1 represents the cost and effect of the new treatment for the example discussed above; the slope from the origin to point B is 1/5, representing the ratio 1 to $5(000), the effect to cost ratio, which is the reciprocal of the cost-effectiveness ratio. The point itself (by assumption) represents one life saved and $5,000 spent. The slope of the line from the origin is equal to the effectiveness-cost ratio. (If the line were extended to be twice as long, the effects and costs would each be multiplied by two, indicating two

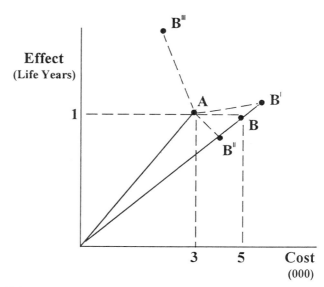

FIG. 1. Illustration of effectiveness–cost ratios of a new treatment B (various versions) versus that of an established treatment A.

lives saved with $10,000, but with the same effectiveness-cost ratio.) Point A represents the existing treatment (with a slope of 1/3 representing its effectiveness-cost ratio). Note that (by construction) A provides the same absolute level of effect (one life year) for less cost than the new treatment, B. The choice is clear. As before, the incremental cost-effectiveness ratio for B is infinite (the incremental effectiveness-cost ratio is zero).

The ratio form of presentation can be deceptive. Note that the 1:5(000) ratio does not necessarily imply that the treatment only saves one life year for $5,000 but that this is the average result per $5,000 expenditure. This 1:5 ratio can represent many different costs and effects that, when combined, yield the 1:5 relationship. Points B and B′ in Figure 1 both imply the same average effectiveness-cost ratio. However, B′ represents a different (increased) level of effect (e.g., 1.1 life years) and cost (e.g., $5,500) in order to have the same average effectiveness-cost ratio as B. This additional effect is very important in allowing B′ to be potentially a good program where B is clearly not, although their average effectiveness-cost ratios are identical. What is of crucial importance to cost-effectiveness discussions is whether the added benefit is worth the added cost. The average cost-effectiveness ratio indicated by the line from the graph's origin to point A represents an incremental cost-effectiveness ratio in which the alternative has zero effect and zero cost (the origin on the graph). If that describes the relevant alternative, the average cost-effectiveness ratio is equal to the incremental cost-effectiveness ratio and no interpretive problem exists. One must merely value the incremental effect produced and compare that value to the incremental cost of producing it to determine if A should be used. Generally, neither existing treatments nor "no-treatment" alternatives have both zero costs and zero effects.

If now we contemplate introducing treatment B with A as the relevant alternative, using the average cost-effectiveness ratio (forgetting about A) to evaluate B or B′ can lead one seriously astray. The average effectiveness-cost ratio is represented by the line from the origin to point B and should be irrelevant once it is determined that A is the relevant alternative treatment. The relevant ratio is represented by the slope of the line connecting points A and B or B′, and represents the incremental effectiveness-cost ratio. As stated above, this situation requires evaluation of whether the incremental effect is worth the incremental cost. If budget exists to reach B′, and if B′ is deemed "worth its cost" (as compared to A alone), B′ should be done and A discontinued. The incremental ratio for B (compared to A) is infinite and would be represented by a horizontal line from A to B. If instead, B actually cost more than A and had less effect (e.g., B″), the incremental ratio (and the slope connecting the points) would be negative, in this case indicating incremental increased costs and decreased effect. This case was mentioned earlier. While the average cost-effectiveness ratio of B″ is not unattractive, it is irrelevant. B‴ represents the other case where a negative incremental cost effectiveness ratio results but the new treatment should be adopted. Note that the three points, B, B′, and B″ have the same average cost effectiveness ratios, but very different incremental cost effectiveness ratios. It is the incremental ratio that provides the essential information.

What about the case where two new treatments (C and D) vie for the market? The incremental ratios versus A may both be appealing (and may be greater or less than their average cost effectiveness ratios which are irrelevant). It is interesting to note that comparing the incremental ratios AC and AD may mislead (Fig. 2). C looks superior, since its incremental cost-effectiveness ratio versus A is better than that of D versus A. However, note that if C were chosen, the incremental cost-effectiveness ratio of D over C would still be positive, so that if budget were available, and the incremental effects of D were deemed to be "worth" its increased costs over C, D should be chosen. This is true despite its worst average cost effectiveness ratio among A, C and D as a group). If D′ were the alternative, it should not be chosen over C. D′ is clearly inferior to C (based on incremental cost-effectiveness ratios) if budget is available. However, if budget were an issue and one could not afford C, D′ may be worth its cost as it supplies (at a cost) positive incremental effect over A. Drummond et al. (5) provide a good discussion of decision making in the presence of a budget constraint and various assumptions regarding an equity constraint for treating all patients in the same way or being able to "discriminate" with treatments. The latter case is superior from a purely economic viewpoint as in the presence of a budget constraint, it allows for the provision of more health (at the population level) for the same expenditure level. Equity considerations may lead one to reject the pure economic approach in such a case.

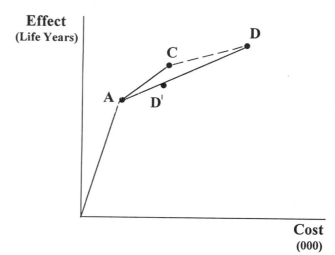

FIG. 2. Comparison of three new candidate treatments (C, D, and D′) using effectiveness–cost ratios.

Most of these examples have assumed that the interventions were for individuals as opposed to groups or populations. If we switch our orientation to groups, the possibility of simply repeating intervention A for a different person arises (repeating A in an individual may generally not make sense). Returning to the example, repeating A instead of moving to a new treatment, B″″, will be the preferred alternative if, by repeating A, the same level of costs and effects may be produced in a second individual (Fig. 3). Thus for any individual patient, the choice is between A and B″″, but for a group, the choice may be A for an individual, followed by its duplication in other members of the patient group. In Figure 3, this would imply an extension of the line OA from the origin to double its length (if effects and costs are identical for the second individual). The duplication of A (to A′) implies a greater effect for the same cost as B″″. Clearly, the incremental cost effectiveness ratio (AA′) is superior to AB″″. Thus, if individuals for whom A will work effectively remain unserved, duplicating A is superior to using treatment B″″.

However, after some point in the duplication of A for different people, the costs will probably rise or the effects will fall (or both). This is a basic economic concept. Effects will eventually fall as one has applied the therapy to all individuals of high risk, for example, and one begins to move into a different risk group (24). With a reduction in a priori risk, there will likely be a reduction in risk modification due to treatment—a reduced effect. Costs too will tend to rise if only those of case identification. Note that with the declining potential for benefit, but a presumably roughly equal risk of adverse events (another type of cost) that accompanies the increased provision of services to those less and less likely to benefit, comes a decreasing ability to obtain a net gain by using the treatment in any given patient. Some cases walk through the doors of a treatment clinic. As those

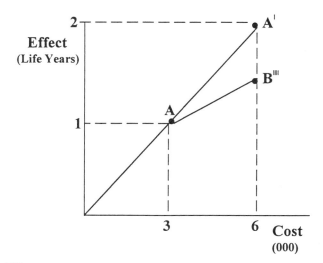

FIG. 3. Comparison of the effectiveness–cost ratios with treatment B when duplicating intervention A is possible.

cases are treated, further application of the treatment requires more and more sophisticated case finding, perhaps through educational/marketing campaigns or active screening programs. In any case, costs are likely not to decrease unless the technology has a significant learning curve that has not yet been climbed.

At some point, duplicating A will be unable to be accomplished with the same costs and/or effects as initially seen. Using it in different groups may imply a lower incremental cost-effectiveness than that associated with using B''''. (B may present less risk of adverse events so that it is less affected by the decline in net benefit hypothetically attributed to A above.) That is, it may eventually make more sense economically to stop searching for new candidates for treatment A and go on to supplying treatment B'''' to all patients in this indication area (at least those in the original risk group whose cost-effectiveness ratios correspond to those in Fig. 1).

The implications of evaluating new treatments inappropriately only in high-risk or low-risk groups (or where it is easy or difficult to identify cases) is potentially quite important as either the new treatment or the old (or both) may be evaluated in inappropriate risk groups. All cost-effectiveness ratios may be affected, leading one to perhaps incorrectly deem a new intervention to not be cost-effective when it is or to be cost-effective when it is not. Drummond et al. (26) make a similar point in cautioning that the relevant alternative to a new treatment must be itself worthwhile (i.e., it is truly a relevant alternative as opposed to merely an available one). Showing a new treatment to be incrementally cost-effective compared to one that is not good itself is a useless (or duplicitous) exercise.

Thus, we can now see that for all treatments whose effectiveness-cost ratios are indicated in Figures 1 to 3, it is important that the levels of service (and the recipients of

treatment) be defined properly; otherwise measures of cost and effect and incremental ratios may be based on inefficient applications of the technology.

STATISTICAL ISSUES AND CEA

Those in the business of efficacy determination are sometimes confused by the apparent lack of statistical hypothesis testing or confidence interval estimation in pharmacoeconomic studies. In pharmacoeconomics the potential variation in results of studies is typically captured in sensitivity analyses where parameters (e.g., efficacy rates) are varied to determine the sensitivity of the results to such variation (26). However, sensitivity analysis leaves much to be desired in terms of its being arbitrary in scope and interpretation and practically limited in its ability to indicate effects of simultaneous variation in more than a few underlying parameters (27). Next to the apparently more highly developed statistical methods used in comparing clinical end points, economic analysts of CEA data appear to be somewhat lacking in statistical sophistication. However, the statistical issues inherent in CEA make conventional statistical analysis sometimes inappropriate and at other times highly complicated relative to, for example, conventional comparisons of means in an analysis of treatment efficacy (28).

The crux of the statistical issue relates to the frequent "nonsampled" nature of much of the data (particularly cost data) in CEA. Economic data are often point estimates with no sampling variation. In the absence of such variation, conventional hypothesis testing or confidence interval estimation is not possible. Senn (29) and Rittenhouse and O'Brien (see Chapter 126, this volume) address another sense in which these data (including health outcomes) are "nonsampled" in that they do not represent random sampling from a population of great interest to pharmacoeconomists and medical care decision makers. The population of interest to decision makers is that which will eventually receive the evaluated products. The accuracy of any inferences from the "sample" to these other groups must be questioned. The method of recruitment in trials which often form the basis for economic evaluations certainly does not conform to standard notions of sampling in statistics. With the advent of economic data acquisition as part of clinical trials used to assess treatments in CEA (30) has come a greater ability to at least measure sampling variation (although it does not solve the problem of the sample not being drawn from a population of ultimate interest). These data put economic data more or less on par with clinical data in the ability to analyze them more conventionally. O'Brien et al. (28) suggest several possibilities for building statistical testing and confidence interval estimation into CEA. The methods are more complex than those typically used in clinical outcomes analysis primarily because of the ratio presentation of results of CEA and the probable lack of independence between the constituent numerator and denominator. These investigators suggest an urgent need for empirical work on testing their suggestions.

CONCLUSIONS

The above discussion largely avoided the details of what determines that a product (via its incremental cost-effectiveness ratio) is "worth" its cost. Economic evaluations should estimate an incremental cost-effectiveness ratio and judge the treatment to be "worth it" by comparing it to other interventions that cost more in bringing about a similar incremental effect. Economic analysis still frequently uses average cost-effectiveness ratios (though calling them simply, "cost-effectiveness ratios"), ignoring the necessity of using incremental analysis in defiance of all methodological discussions in the literature. Formal considerations of whether interventions are worthwhile are often done with so-called "league tables," which rank interventions by, say, cost per life year saved. Implicitly such league tables assume that all analyses they include are done (a) correctly, and (b) with comparable methods (since method variability can lead to variability in results). Formal league tables (much less their informal counterparts) rarely conform to these requirements. Consequently, any comparisons may be off-target in pronouncing on the "worth it?" question (25,31).

The above discussion of CEA decision making is interesting in light of the preference for CEA (and CUA) in pharmacoeconomics over the more traditional tool (in economics) of CBA. Discomfort over the necessity in CBA of placing monetary values on, for example, the value of life or its quality led to the adoption of CEA by most evaluators of medical technology. However, Phelps and Mushlin (32) have indicated that, while analysts may be able to skirt the issue of valuing life monetarily by using CEA (or CUA), ultimate decision makers do not have this luxury. As the discussion of "worth it" above implies, someone eventually must decide whether $100,000 per life is "worth it" relative to other uses of such funds (not necessarily just those allocated to health care) (6). At the point at which such a decision is made, decision makers have implicitly valued life monetarily by their choice. The fact that the analyst escapes without confronting this task probably does much to explain the relative popularity of the CEA method.

The CEA method is very popular. Adams (33) found that 76.5% of economic analyses associated with clinical trials were CEA. Given the limited accuracy of examining only one dimension of outcomes, one might question whether the tool is being applied appropriately (even ignoring the potential misuse of league tables in the implementation phase as described above). These practical criticisms aside, some researchers have questioned the ability of even methodologically sound CEA to assist in the optimal allocation of resources (its implicit if not explicit goal). Garber and Phelps (34) have noted that CEA appears to be without justification in "first principles" of economic analysis. Birch and Gafni (31) have provided a more directed criticism of CEA (and CUA) as being generally inconsistent with the welfare economic theory that it (at least implicitly) purports to adhere to.

While Birch and Gafni (31) do not suggest a complete lack of usefulness of CEA (or CUA), they do suggest limiting the use (or at least the welfare claims about results based on the use) of these methods and moving to a "higher level" of analysis—cost-benefit analysis. As Phelps and Mushlin (32) have pointed out, CEA applications cannot avoid (at least implicit) monetary valuations, so the age-old defense of CEA over CBA with respect to this aspect is based on false notions. Recent evidence suggests that the field of economic evaluation in health care is becoming more accepting of CBA (35). This may be less a reflection of its superior methodological claims than the fact that more economists are making themselves heard in this field. In contrast, perhaps, to the popular image of what economists do, many are trained in and attempt to practice a notion of societal improvement based on optimal planning (which sometimes means no planning—letting the market work when it can). While economists do not always "get it right," they are at least trained in the proper tasks and methods to get it right and are aware of the numerous pitfalls strewn about the policy arena into which many of the unaware will plunge. It may be of great value to have more of them "on board" in the coming years of continuing methods development and practice of economic evaluation in health care. It is clear that the demand for economic evaluation in health care is great. In our rush to satisfy that demand, let us be sure to give these health care needs the merit they deserve and not skimp on proper attention to detail in the pursuit of what we casually think looks right. We would all do well to recall another of Pope's epigrams: "Fools rush in where Angels fear to tread" (3).

REFERENCES

1. Himmelstein DU, Woolhandler S, Bor DH. Will cost effectiveness analysis worsen the cost effectiveness of health care? *Int J Health Serv* 1988;18:1–9.
2. Doubilet P, Weinstein MC, McNeil BJ. Use and misuse of the term "cost effective" in medicine. *N Engl J Med* 1986;314:253–256.
3. Pope A. An essay on criticism. In: Tilloston G, Fussell P, Waingrow M, eds. *Eighteenth century English literature.* New York: Harcourt, Brace & World, 1969:1711.
4. Garber AM, Phelps CE. *Economic foundations of cost-effectiveness analysis.* Stanford, CA: National Bureau of Economic Research, June 1993.
5. Drummond MF, Stoddart GL, Torrance GW. *Methods for the economic evaluation of health care programmes.* New York: Oxford University Press, 1987.
6. Rittenhouse B. Economic incentives and disincentives for efficient prescribing. *PharmacoEconomics* 1994;6:222–232.
7. Luce BR, Elixhauser A. *Standards for the socioeconomic evaluation of health care services.* New York: Springer-Verlag, 1990.
8. Gafni A, Birch S. Equity considerations in utility-based measures of health outcomes in economic appraisal: an adjustment algorithm. *J Health Econ* 1991;10:329–342.
9. Edelson JT, Tosteson AN, Sax P. Cost-effectiveness of misoprostol for prophylaxis against nonsteroidal anti-inflammatory drug-induced gastrointestinal tract bleeding (see comments). *JAMA* 1990;264:41–47.

10. Croog SH, Levine S, Testa MA, et al. The effects of anti-hypertensive therapy on the quality of life. *N Engl J Med* 1986;314:1657–1664.

11. Finkler SA. Cost finding for high-technology, high-cost services: current practice and a possible alternative. *Health Care Manage Rev* 1980;5(3):17–29.

12. Finkler SA. The distinction between cost and charges. *Ann Intern Med* 1982;96:102–109.

13. Eisenberg JM, Kitz DS. Savings from outpatient antibiotic therapy for osteomyelitis. *JAMA* 1986;225:1584–1588.

14. Drummond MF. Basing prescription drug payment on economic analysis: the case of Australia. *Health Affairs* 1992;11:191–196.

15. Canadian Coordinating Office for Health Technology Assessment. Guidelines for economic evaluation of pharmaceuticals, 1st edition. Ottowa Canada: CCOHTA, 1994.

16. Rittenhouse B. Another deficit problem: the deficit of relevant information when clinical trials are the basis for pharmacoeconomic research. *J Res Pharm Econ* 1996;7(3) (in press).

17. Sculpher MJ, Buxton MJ. The episode-free day as a composite measure of effectiveness. *PharmacoEconomics* 1993;4:345–352.

18. Russell L. Opportunity costs in modern medicine. *Health Affairs* 1992; 11:167–169.

19. Eddy DM. Oregon's methods: did cost-effectiveness analysis fail? *JAMA* 1991;266:2135–2141.

20. Rittenhouse B. Potential inconsistencies between cost-effectiveness and cost-utility analyses: an upstairs/downstairs socioeconomic distinction. *Int J Technol Assess Health Care* 1995;11(2):365–376.

21. Black WC. The CE plane: a graphic representation of cost-effectiveness. *Med Decis Making* 1990;12:212–214.

22. Cantor S. Cost-effectiveness analysis, extended dominance, and ethics: a quantitative assessment. *Med Decis Making* 1994;14:259–265.

23. Eisenberg JM. Clinical economics: a guide to the economic analysis of clinical practices. *JAMA* 1989;262:2879–2886.

24. Goldman L, Sia ST, Cook EF, Rutherford JD, Weinstein MC. Cost and effectiveness of routine therapy with long-term beta-adrenergic antagonists after acute myocardial infarction. *N Engl J Med* 1988;319: 152–157.

25. Drummond MF, Torrance GW, Mason J. Cost-effectiveness league tables: more harm than good? *Soc Sci Med* 1993;37(1):33–40.

26. Weinstein MC, Stason WB. Foundations of cost-effectiveness analysis for health and medical practices. *N Engl J Med* 1977;296:716–721.

27. O'Brien BJ, Drummond MF, Labele RJ, Willan A. In search of power and significance: issues in the design and analysis of stochastic cost-effectiveness studies in health care. *Med Care* 1994;32:150–163.

28. O'Brien BJ, Drummond MF. Statistical versus quantitative significance in the socioeconomic evaluation of medicines. *PharmacoEconomics* 1994;5:389–398.

29. Senn SJ. Clinical trials and epidemiology. *J Clin Epidemiol* 1990;43: 628–632.

30. Drummond MF, Davies L. Economic analysis alongside clinical trials. *Int J Technol Assess Health Care* 1991;7:561–573.

31. Birch S, Gafni A. Cost effectiveness/utility analyses: do current decision rules lead us to where we want to be? *J Health Econ* 1992;11: 279–296.

32. Phelps C, Mushlin A. On the near equivalence of cost-effectiveness and cost-benefit analysis. *Int J Technol Assess Health Care* 1991;7:12–21.

33. Adams ME, McCall NT, Gray DT, Orza MJ, Chalmers TC. Economic analysis in randomized control trials. *Med Care* 1992;30:231–243.

34. Garber AM, Phelps CE. *Economic foundations of cost-effectiveness analysis*. Stanford, CA: National Bureau of Economic Research, 1993.

35. Johannesson M, Jonsson B. Economic evaluation in health care: is there a role for cost-benefit analysis? *Health Policy* 1991;17:1–23.

Quality of Life and Pharmacoeconomics in Clinical Trials, Second Edition, edited by B. Spilker.
Lippincott-Raven Publishers, Philadelphia © 1996.

CHAPTER 114

Designing and Conducting Cost-Utility Analyses

George W. Torrance

INTRODUCTION

Cost-utility analyses are a particular form of economic evaluation in which the outcomes are expressed in quality-adjusted life years (QALY) gained, and the quality-adjustment weights come from utilities (1). In this definition, the term *utility* is used in its broad sense referring to any cardinal measure of preference, not just in its narrow sense referring to von Neumann–Morgenstern utility (2). Cost-utility analyses are in fact just a special form of cost-effectiveness analysis, and all the requirements and considerations for cost-effectiveness analysis apply equally to cost-utility analysis.

The potential advantage of cost-utility analysis is three-fold. First, the QALY is an absolutely general measure of health outcome that simultaneously captures changes in both mortality and morbidity, and is applicable to all diseases and conditions. Thus, it provides a common metric for comparing programs of all types. Second, cost-utility analysis incorporates the preferences of individuals for the outcomes. Clearly, any approach that wishes to be responsive to individuals must incorporate their preferences. Third, when the preferences are measured using von Neumann–Morgenstern utilities, cost-utility analysis has the added advantage that

the measured preferences are precisely interpretable. They are cardinal measures of preference by individuals, on an interval scale with two predefined anchor points, based on the dominant normative paradigm of decision making under uncertainty, von Neumann–Morgenstern utility theory (2).

Terminology in the field of economic evaluation is not uniform. Readers will find studies labeled cost-utility analysis that are not, and studies not labeled cost-utility analysis that are. For example, some investigators label their studies as a cost-utility analysis whenever they use QALYs, even if the weights are undocumented or not based on cardinal preferences (3). Others never use the label cost-utility analysis, and categorize such studies in the more general category of cost-effectiveness analyses (3–5). Thus, readers need to beware, and check for themselves to determine whether QALYs are being used and, if so, the source of the QALY weights.

Because it enables comparability across studies of all diseases and conditions, cost-utility analysis is an important analytic technique for economic evaluation in general, and for clinical trials in particular. For example, the Canadian national guidelines for the economic evaluation of pharmaceuticals (6) encourage the use of cost-utility analysis or cost-benefit analysis because they permit broad comparisons. However, the fundamental measurement techniques to implement cost-utility analysis, the determination of preference scores, is better developed than the comparable techniques to implement cost-benefit analysis, willingness to pay

G. W. Torrance: Department of Clinical Epidemiology and Biostatistics, Centre for Health Economics and Policy Analysis, Department of Management Science, McMaster University, Hamilton, Ontario L8N 3Z5, Canada.

measurements. Thus, cost-utility analysis should be strongly considered whenever an economic evaluation is considered in connection with a clinical trial.

STUDY DESIGN

Most aspects of the overall study design are not unique to a cost-utility analysis, and thus, are dealt with only briefly in this chapter.

Comparator and Incremental Analysis

The appropriate comparator for an economic evaluation may differ from that for a clinical trial of safety and efficacy. Ideally, in an economic evaluation a new drug or treatment should be compared to all feasible alternative treatments, at all levels of intensity (dosage or other variations in aggressiveness of treatment), to determine the most cost-effective treatment for the disorder. If such data were available, it could be analyzed using the incremental cost-effectiveness algorithm to determine the appropriate recommendation (4,7).

In practice, such a comprehensive study is normally impractical, and studies are restricted to one, or at most a few comparators. The primary comparator should be the dominant existing treatment that the new treatment would replace. If there is no single dominant existing treatment, the study may require several comparators. Moreover, if the dominant existing treatment is relatively costly and ineffective, such that it may not itself be cost-effective, the new treatment should also be compared against a low cost, effective treatment, if one exists (6).

In designing a cost-utility analysis as part of a clinical trial the researcher must determine that the comparator in the trial is appropriate and sufficient for an economic evaluation. The addition of a cost-utility component to a trial may require that additional arms be added to the trial to accommodate additional comparators.

Prospective Versus Retrospective

Cost-utility analyses can be undertaken prospectively as part of a clinical trial, or retrospectively after the trial is completed. The prospective approach is superior because the required data can be identified in advance and collected carefully during the trial. In the retrospective approach, it is all too common to find after the trial is completed that important relevant data was not collected and is no longer available. Then estimates or modelling based on expert judgment or secondary data sources is often used in lieu of primary data; this is clearly an inferior approach. The discussion in this chapter is geared to the use of cost-utility analyses prospectively in clinical trials.

Primary Outcomes

Intermediate outcomes, such as blood pressure, cholesterol levels, serum creatinine levels, and the like, are unsuitable for cost-utility analyses. Final outcomes in terms of health-related quality of life (HRQL) and quantity of life (mortality) are required. These relevant outcomes may occur both in the short term and in the long term. Examples of short term relevant outcomes are the impacts on HRQL of the treatment process; for example, drug side effects, side effects of chemotherapy and radiation, and pain and suffering associated with corrective surgery. Examples of long term relevant outcomes are mortality and long term HRQL.

Because many clinical trials are designed with short term intermediate outcomes as the primary outcome measure, they must be augmented, and possibly extended, to accommodate a cost-utility analysis. Augmentation is required to capture cost and HRQL data on an ongoing basis. Extension is required to capture the relevant long term outcomes, or at least to gather sufficient data to provide a sound basis for modelling the remaining impact of the treatment.

The question addressed by a cost-utility analysis in a clinical trial is whether or not it is appropriate to initiate the treatment alternative under study. Accordingly, the analysis should use an intent to treat strategy; that is, all outcomes should be assigned to the treatment arm to which the patient was originally randomized, whether or not that treatment on the patient was maintained.

Sample Size

At the moment there are no well-established procedures for determining the appropriate sample size for an economic evaluation. Two different approaches are possible: hypothesis testing and estimation.

In the hypothesis testing approach, the sample size would be determined for the economic question in the same way that it is handled for the clinical question. This would require the researcher to specify policy significant differences in the costs and QALYs, to estimate variances for costs and QALYs, and to select acceptable error rates for type I and type II errors—and there is no reason that the conventional rates of 5% and 10%, respectively, should apply. Although research is underway, procedures to implement the hypothesis testing approach have not yet been developed (8,9).

In the estimation approach, the cost-utility ratio is treated as the variable of interest, and methods are developed to estimate the confidence interval around this ratio, given a particular sample size. Then, depending upon the magnitude of the ratio and the confidence interval, statements can be made about the probability that the true ratio lies above or below certain policy significant threshold levels (10). The problem with this approach is that it requires one to know the final cost-utility ratio in order to determine an appropriate sample size.

Finally, there would be a potential ethical problem if the sample size required for economic purposes exceeded that required for clinical purposes. Would it be ethical to continue to randomize patients beyond the point where the clinical answer was known, just to gather better economic data? Given all these problems and uncertainties, the current advice to researchers adding a cost-utility component to a clinical trial is to maximize the precision in the final cost-utility ratio by using all the sample size available in the clinical trial, but not to add to the sample size.

Viewpoint

All approaches to economic evaluation, including cost-utility analysis, can be undertaken from a number of different viewpoints or perspectives. The most comprehensive viewpoint is that of society, in which all costs and benefits are identified and counted in the analysis regardless of who incurs the costs or who receives the benefits. This broad societal viewpoint is generally regarded as the appropriate primary viewpoint for economic evaluations (6,11).

Although the societal viewpoint is relevant for overall resource allocation decisions, it may not be relevant to particular individuals or organizations making decisions about participating in, providing, or paying for a specific treatment. Accordingly, one or more of the following additional viewpoints can be included in a study, if deemed relevant: (a) patient and family; the costs, in both finances and time, that fall on the patient and family, and the value of the outcomes as seen by the patient and family, (b) health care provider organizations; the costs imposed on various types of hospitals, health maintenance organizations (HMOs), or other providers, (c) third-party payers and governments at all levels; the costs that fall on governments or organizations that fund various health services; and (d) business; the costs and benefits to an employer because of changes in health-related activities of employees.

COSTS

It is useful to think of costing as consisting of three steps: identification, measurement, and valuation. Identification is the task of identifying in advance all the types of costs that will need to be gathered for the analysis. Measurement consists of capturing data on quantities of resources used. Valuation places a price, actually a cost, on them.

Identification

Identification of relevant costs takes place during the planning stages of the study. In a clinical trial, an important principle is that costs are only relevant if they differ between the arms of the trial. The problem is that it is hard to know in advance whether certain seemingly unrelated costs may

somehow, in fact, be related to the intervention and may differ between arms of the trial. If the data is not gathered, you will never know for sure. Thus, trial design is a compromise between the desire to gather all resource utilization no matter how seemingly unrelated to the treatment under study, and the desire to be efficient and reduce the burden on investigators and patients by not gathering large amounts of irrelevant information. A common compromise is to gather all major events (deaths, hospitalizations) regardless of cause, and all other events that can possibly be attributed to the disease under study or to the treatment.

Measurement

Measurement takes place during the trial, and consists of recording resource utilization, not in dollars but in quantities of specific resources used. For example, physician visits by specialty and type of visit; laboratory tests by type of test; drugs by dosage and quantity; hospitalizations by days of stay in different types of wards, major procedures received, tests performed, and so forth; and lost work time by hours or days.

There are a number of advantages to gathering utilization, rather than costs, at this step. First, true costs are often not available, and will have to be determined in a separate study. For example, this is generally true in hospitals in the United States, where charges are readily available, but costs are not, and the difference may be quite significant (12). Second, the results of the study can be more readily generalized beyond the specific jurisdiction and organizations in which the study was conducted. Other jurisdictions, even other countries, can determine if the utilization patterns would be the same in their area or if not, what changes should be made, and then can cost out the utilizations using more relevant local costs. Third, because trials are usually ongoing over a number of years, it is much easier to cost all items in constant dollars of a particular year using this strategy.

Gathering these resource utilization data is not easy. In general, comprehensive linkable data systems do not exist, or are not readily accessible, to enable the automatic gathering of these kinds of data on patients in a trial. Trial centers will be aware of resource utilizations associated with treatments initiated in their center, but not necessarily of other care provided elsewhere. The only person who knows of all the care received and all the costs incurred by patient and family in the trial is the patient and family themselves. The challenge is to find out about the cost item from the patient or family, and, in general, to go to the source to get the actual data on resource utilization. This requires strategies to encourage patients to record relevant items as they occur on an ongoing basis. Such strategies include patient diaries, telephone reminders, patient incentives, and the development of a strong feeling of ownership and responsibility in the patients. Once the patient has identified the item, the research staff at the participating center can track down the actual details of the utilization and record the data on the Case Report Form.

Valuation

Valuation consists of determining an appropriate unit cost in dollars for the items measured above. The appropriate unit cost will depend upon the viewpoint. For example, for the societal viewpoint, the appropriate cost would be the average cost for this item across all of society. For other viewpoints, it would be the average cost of the item from that particular viewpoint. Note that in the more narrow secondary viewpoints many items have a zero cost. High-quality unit costs are not universally and readily available for all types of items. In a clinical trial this valuation step often involves a separate study to determine unit costs for the items. For example, it may involve a careful costing analysis of representative hospitals, using state-of-the-art cost accounting techniques (13).

QUALITY-ADJUSTED LIFE-YEARS

One of the key features of a cost-utility analysis is its use of the QALY concept. Results of cost-utility studies are reported in terms of cost per QALY gained.

Concept

The idea of QALYs can be traced to the pioneering work of Herbert Klarman and colleagues on chronic renal failure published in 1968 (14). They noted that the quality of life with a kidney transplant was better than that with dialysis, and estimated the difference at 25%. The cost per life year gained by the different treatment options was calculated with and without this quality adjustment. Although they did not use the term *quality-adjusted life year,* the concept was identical.

The advantage of the QALY as a measure of health output is that it can simultaneously capture gains from reduced morbidity (quality gains) and reduced mortality (quantity gains), and integrate these into a single measure. A simple example is displayed in Figure 1. Without the intervention the individual's health-related quality of life would deteriorate according to the lower path and they would die at time Death 1. With the intervention they would deteriorate more slowly, would live longer, and would die at time Death 2. The area between the two paths is the QALY gained by the intervention. For instruction purposes the area can be divided into two parts, A and B, as shown. Then, part A is the amount of QALY gained due to quality improvements (i.e., the quality gain during time that the person would have otherwise been alive anyhow), and part B is the amount of QALY gained due to quantity improvements (i.e., the amount of life extension, but factored by the quality of that life extension).

Much more complicated cases can be handled. The paths may cross each other. For example, many cancer treatments cause a QALY loss in the short term in order to achieve a QALY gain in the longer term. The paths may be identical for a long time after the intervention and only diverge in the distant future. An example of this pattern could be a hypertension drug that is well tolerated and has no side effects but eventually averts serious cardiovascular events.

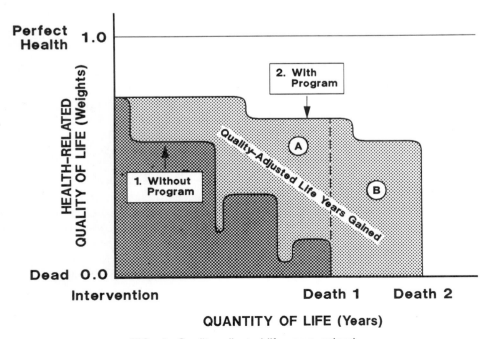

FIG. 1. Quality-adjusted life-years gained.

Quality Weights

To satisfy the QALY concept the quality weights must be (a) measured on an interval scale, (b) anchored on perfect health and death, and (c) based on preferences. An interval scale is a particular type of cardinal scale in which ratios of intervals have meaning, but ratios of scale quantities do not. A well-known example of an interval scale is temperature, for example, °F or °C. The interval scale property means that it is correct to state that the gain in temperature in going from 40°F to 80°F is twice as much as the gain in going from 40°F to 60°F, but it is incorrect to state that 80°F is twice as hot as 40°F. The former statement holds true whether the temperature is measured in °F or °C, while the latter does not. Another way to think of the interval scale property is that an increase in scale value from 0.1 to 0.2 must have the same meaning as an increase from 0.8 to 0.9. This is required in the case of QALYs because these two increases would lead to the same QALY gained and will be treated as equivalent in the QALY model.

An interval scale has the property that any two points on the scale can be given any arbitrary quantities, and the rest of the values are determined relative to these two "anchor" points. In temperature scales the two anchor points are the freezing and boiling points of water. To determine the °F scale these are set at 32 and 212; to determine the °C scale they are set at 0 and 100.

The scale of QALY weights may contain many points, but two points that must be on the scale are perfect health and death. These two are required because they will both occur in programs being evaluated with the QALY model, and weights will be required for them. Because these two must always be on the scale, and because they are well-specified and understood, they have been selected to be the two anchor points for the scale of QALY weights. To specify the scale, these two points can be given any two arbitrary values, as long as perfect health is given to the larger value. Two particularly convenient values to select are 0.0 for dead and 1.0 for perfect health, and this is the conventional scale for QALY weights.

The QALY weights should be based on preferences. The QALY approach is used to quantify the health output of programs and to identify, at least implicitly, programs that produce better outcomes from those that do not. In this context better is operationalized as outcomes that are more preferred or more desirable. Of course, QALY weights could be based on other factors such as the impact of the health state on earnings, the impact of the health state on health care utilization, or the prevalence of the health state in the population, or on psychometric scaling techniques, but none of these approaches is appropriate for identifying better or more desirable outcomes and discriminating these from those that are worse or less desirable.

A variety of preference-based measurement techniques can be, and have been, used to determine QALY weights; however, we prefer the use of von Neumann–Morgenstern utilities, for reasons discussed in the section on Utilities.

In summary, QALY weights should be preferences, preferably von Neumann–Morgenstern utilities, measured on an interval scale anchored with a score of 0.0 for death and 1.0 for perfect health.

Calculation of QALYs

Conceptually, the QALY calculation is very straightforward. Referring to Figure 1, the QALYs gained is the area under path 2 less the area under path 1. The area under each path is simply the sum of the quality weights for the various health states on the path each multiplied by the duration of the health state in years or fractions of years. This is the QALYs gained without discounting.

Because individuals and society prefer gains of all types, including health gains, to occur earlier rather than later, future amounts are multiplied by a discount factor to adjust for this time preference. Several recent guidelines in North America have recommended that the discount rate be 5% per year (6,11). The technique of discounting is described in detail elsewhere (1) but consists essentially of taking amounts that will occur in the future and moving them year by year back to the present by reducing the amount each year by 5% of the remaining amount. This discounting applies to QALYs that will be gained in the future.

Alternatives to QALYs

The QALY concept is not without controversy. For a sample of the debate, see references 15–26, and associated comments and rebuttals. The critics range from those who argue that the QALY approach is needlessly complex and should be replaced by simpler disaggregated measures (20) to those who claim that the QALY approach is overly simplistic and should be replaced by more complex methods allegedly theoretically superior (22,27). Several alternatives to QALYs have been suggested, and two are described briefly below.

Healthy year equivalents have been suggested as an alternative to QALYs (22,27). These would be calculated by measuring the utility for each possible health path of changing health states and converting this utility through a second measurement into its healthy year equivalents. One major problem with this approach is its practicality. In most real problems the number of measurements required would be enormous because the number of different possible health paths that could be taken would be exceedingly large. Moreover, each measurement would be cognitively very demanding because it would require the respondent to assess an entire complex path in one holistic judgment.

Saved young life equivalents has also been suggested as a replacement for QALYs (28). The idea would be to determine the equivalency between the health output of the program under study and a standard measure defined as the saving of one young healthy life. That is, the program under study would be judged to be equivalent to a certain number of saved young lives. All programs would be measured in terms of their equivalent saved young lives, and this would be the common metric of program output replacing the QALY.

Both potential alternatives to the QALY are still at the early stages of being debated and investigated. In the meantime the conventional QALY remains the dominant approach.

UTILITIES

The term *utility* has been around for several centuries, has been used by a variety of disciplines, and has a number of related but different meanings (29–31). Thus, it creates a significant potential for confusion and for people to talk past each other. In a broad way the term has always been synonymous with preference; the more preferable an outcome, the more utility associated with it. The differences arise when approaches are developed to define the concept more precisely and to measure it.

Measured preferences may be ordinal or cardinal. For ordinal preferences outcomes are simply rank ordered from most preferred to least preferred. For cardinal preferences, a number must be attached to the outcome that in some sense represents the strength of preference for the outcome relative to the others. These numbers should be measured such that they fall on an interval scale, in two senses. First, in terms of measurement theory, the scale is an interval scale like °F in the sense that it has no natural zero, and therefore is unique only up to a positive linear transformation, and not to a positive multiplicative transformation. Second, in terms of the individual's preferences, the scale must have the equal interval property in the sense that the interval from 0.1 to 0.2 has the same meaning to the individual as the interval from 0.8 to 0.9 (32).

Direct Measurement of Preferences

As discussed earlier, the QALY model requires weights that represent preferences measured on an interval scale, anchored to death = 0.0 and perfect health = 1.0. There are three popular methods for the direct measurement of such preferences: visual analog scale, time trade-off, and standard gamble. For details of the measurement instruments see Chapters 12 and 27 (*this volume*).

In the decision science literature a distinction is made between preferences that are measured under conditions of certainty, like the visual analog scale and the time trade-off, and those that are measured under conditions of uncertainty, like the standard gamble. The former are called "values," while the latter are called "utilities" (33). More precisely, the latter should be called von Neumann Morgenstern utilities to link them to their theoretical foundation in von Neumann–Morgenstern expected utility theory (2) and to differentiate them from the broad definition of utilities discussed above. However, this labelling distinction is honored more

in the breach than the practice. Thus, readers should beware whenever the term utility is used and should determine whether the writer is describing von Neumann–Morgenstern utilities, values, or ordinal utilities/values.

Von Neumann–Morgenstern utility theory is the dominant normative paradigm for decision making under uncertainty. That is, it is considered the best theory for how decisions under uncertainty ought to be made, in order to be both consistent with the fundamental axioms of the theory and internally coherent. The strength of the system comes from the fact that the fundamental axioms are compellingly simple and logical, and appear to represent desirable properties of good decision making under conditions of uncertainty. The paradigm has survived decades of attack, and still remains the leading paradigm for decision making under uncertainty (34).

Quality weights for QALY calculations can be based on values (measured with visual analog scaling or time trade-off) or on von Neumann–Morgenstern utilities (measured with standard gamble). However, von Neumann–Morgenstern utilities are more attractive as quality weights for QALY calculations for a number of reasons. First, von Neumann–Morgenstern is the appropriate paradigm for decision making under uncertainty, that is, decisions that involve uncertainties and risk, and this clearly applies to decisions regarding health care interventions. Second, von Neumann–Morgenstern utilities are based on a sound theoretical foundation, and this, in turn, provides three advantages. The utilities are precisely interpretable. The utilities are also useful for clinical decision analysis at the patient level, and the development of clinical guidelines, and thus their use can help integrate the two levels of decision making: bedside and policy. Finally, with additional assumptions, the QALY model using von Neumann Morgenstern utilities can be linked to welfare economics, which is considered by most economists to be the proper basis for societal resource allocation decisions (35).

Indirect Measurement of Preferences

The direct measurement of preferences using instruments like visual analog scaling, time trade-off, and standard gamble is complex and time-consuming (e.g., see Chapter 27, *this volume*). An alternative is to determine the preference scores for health states indirectly by using one of the multiattribute systems developed for that purpose (36,37). At the moment there are two fully developed systems, and one under development. The two fully developed systems are the Quality of Well-Being (see Chapter 32, *this volume* and the Health Utilities Index (see Chapter 36, *this volume*). The one under development is the EuroQol (38,39) and Chapter 22, *this volume*.

One of the distinctions among these systems is the type of preference score provided. The Quality of Well-Being was scored using category scaling, which provides values, not von Neumann–Morgenstern utilities. EuroQol does not yet have a published scoring formula, but the measurements have used visual analog scaling, and more recently time trade-off. Thus, a scoring formula based on their work to date would provide value scores. The first version of the Health Utilities Index (Mark I) was value scored using visual analog scaling and time trade-off (1). The second version (Mark II) has been scored two ways; value scores from visual analog scaling and utility scores from standard gambles (see Ch. XX, *this volume*). The third version (Mark III) will also be scored two ways, value and utility. Thus, the Health Utilities Index is the only system that provides the preferred scores for QALY weights, that is, von Neumann–Morgenstern utilities.

CONCLUSIONS

Cost-utility analyses are an appropriate and highly desirable form of economic evaluation for use with clinical trials. In the trial design, consideration must be given to the comparator treatment or treatments, the length of follow-up, the outcomes measured, and the sample size in order to accommodate a cost-utility analysis. The analysis should use an intent to treat strategy, and the primary viewpoint of the analysis should be societal. Relevant resource utilization should be gathered prospectively during the trial, and costed later based on appropriate standard costs if available, or on special costing studies. Incremental outcomes should be converted into QALYs gained using preference-based quality weights that are measured on an interval scale anchored on perfect health and death. Von Neumann–Morgenstern utilities are the most appropriate type of preferences for use as quality weights; these may be measured directly using the standard gamble instrument or determined indirectly using the health utility index system.

REFERENCES

1. Drummond MF, Stoddart GL, Torrance GW. *Methods for the economic evaluation of health care programmes.* Oxford: Oxford University Press, 1987.
2. von Neumann J, Morgenstern O. *Theory of games and economic behaviour.* Princeton, NJ: Princeton University Press, 1944.
3. Weinstein MC. Principles of cost-effective resource allocation in health care organizations. *Int J Tech Assmt in Hlth Care* 1990;6:93–103.
4. Gerard K. Cost-utility in practice: a policy maker's guide to the state of the art. *Health Policy* 1992;21:249–279.
5. Nord E. Toward quality assurance in QALY calculations. *Int J Tech Assmt in Hlth Care* 1993;9(1):37–45.
6. Canadian Coordinating Office for Health Technology Assessment. Guidelines for economic evaluation of pharmaceuticals: Canada. 1st Ed. Ottawa: CCOHTA, 1994.
7. Torrance GW, Thomas WH, Sackett DL. A utility maximization model for evaluation of health care programs. *Health Serv Res* 1972;7:118–133.
8. Drummond MF, O'Brien BJ. Clinical importance, statistical significance and the assessment of economic and quality-of-life outcomes. *Health Econ* 1993;2:205–212.
9. O'Brien BJ, Drummond MF, Labelle RJ, et al. In search of power

10. Willan AR, O'Brien BJ. Cost-effectiveness ratios in clinical trials: from deterministic to stochastic models. *1994 Proceedings of the Biopharmaceutical Section.* Alexandria, Virginia: The American Statistical Association, *American Statistical Association,* 1994:19–28.
11. U.S. Department of Health and Human Services, Public Health Service, Centres for Disease Control and Prevention. *A practical guide to prevention effectiveness: decisions and economic analyses.* Atlanta: Center for Disease Control and Prevention, 1994.
12. Finkler SA. The distinction between cost and charges. *Ann Intern Med* 1982;96:102–109.
13. Horngren CT, Foster G, Datar SM. *Cost accounting: a managerial emphasis.* 8th ed. Englewood Cliffs, NJ: Prentice-Hall, 1994.
14. Klarman HE, Francis J, Rosenthal GD. Cost-effectiveness analysis applied to the treatment of chronic renal disease. *Med Care* 1968;6(1):48–54.
15. Donaldson C, Atkinson A, Bond J, et al. Should QALYs be programme-specific? *J Health Econ* 1988;7:239–257.
16. Weinstein MC. A QALY is a QALY is a QALY—or is it? *J Health Econ* 1988;7:289–290.
17. Loomes G, McKenzie L. The use of QALYs in health care decision making. *Soc Sci Med* 1989;28:299–308.
18. Mehrez A, Gafni A. Quality-adjusted life years, utility theory, and healthy-years equivalents. *Med Decis Making* 1989;9:142–149.
19. Carr-Hill RA. Allocating resources to health care: is the QALY (quality adjusted life year) a technical solution to a political problem? *Int J Health Serv Res* 1991;21:351–363.
20. Cox DR, Fitzpatrick R, Fletcher AE, et al. Quality-of-life assessment: can we keep it simple? *J R Stat Soc A* 1992;155,pt 3:353–393.
21. Gafni A, Birch S. Economics, health and health economics: HYEs versus QALYs. *J Health Econ* 1993;11:325–339.
22. Mehrez A, Gafni A. Healthy-years equivalents versus quality-adjusted life years: in pursuit of progress. *Med Decis Making* 1993;13:287–292.
23. Culyer AJ, Wagstaff A. QALYs versus HYEs. *J Health Econ* 1993;11:311–323.
24. Fryback DG. QALYs, HYEs, and the loss of innocence (editorial). *Med Decis Making* 1993;13:271–272.
25. Johannesson M, Pliskin JS, Weinstein MC. Are healthy-years equivalents: an improvement over quality-adjusted life years? *Med Decis Making* 1993;13:281–286.
26. Broome J. Qalys. *J Publ Econ* 1993;50:149–167.
27. Mehrez A, Gafni A. Quality-adjusted life years, utility theory, and healthy-years equivalents. *Med Decis Making* 1989;9:142–149.
28. Nord E. An alternative to QALYs: the saved young life equivalent (SAVE). *BMJ* 1992;305:875–877.
29. Cooper R, Rappoport P. Were the ordinalists wrong about welfare economics? *J Econ Lit* 1984;22:507–530.
30. Miyamoto JM. Generic utility theory: measurement foundations and applications in multiattribute utility theory. *J Math Psychol* 1988;32:357–404.
31. Sen A. Utility—ideas and terminology. *Econ Phil* 1991;7:277–283.
32. Bossert W. On intra- and interpersonal utility comparisons. *Soc Choice Welfare* 1991;8:207–219.
33. Keeney RL, Raiffa H. *Decisions with multiple objectives: preferences and value tradeoffs.* New York: John Wiley & Sons, 1976.
34. Edwards W. Toward the demise of economic man and woman: bottom lines from Santa Cruz. In: W. Edwards (ed.), *Utility theories: measurements and applications.* Boston: Kluwer Academic Publishers, 1992:253–267.
35. Garber AM, Phelps CE. Economic foundations of cost-effective analysis. NBER Working Paper No. 4164. Cambridge, MA: National Bureau of Economic Research, 1992.
36. Feeny D, Furlong W, Boyle M, et al. Multi-attribute health status classification systems: health utilities index. *PharmacoEconomics* 1995; 7(6):503–520.
37. Torrance GW, Furlong W, Feeny D, et al. Multi-attribute preference functions: health utilities index. *PharmacoEconomics* 1995 (in press).
38. EuroQol Group: EuroQol—a new facility for the measurement of health-related quality of life. *Health Policy* 1990;16:199–208.
39. Essink-Bot ML, Stouthard ME, Bonsel GJ. Generalizability of valuations on health states collected with the EuroQol questionnaire. *Health Econ* 1993;2:237–246.

and significance: issues in the design and analysis of stochastic cost-effectiveness studies in health care. *Med Care* 1994;2:150–163.

Quality of Life and Pharmacoeconomics in Clinical Trials, Second Edition, edited by B. Spilker.
Lippincott-Raven Publishers, Philadelphia © 1996.

CHAPTER 115

Practical Aspects of Designing and Conducting Pharmacoeconomic Studies

Andrew M. Baker

INTRODUCTION

Economic evaluation continues to gain importance in health care generally and in regard to the adoption of pharmaceutical products specifically. Growth in the level of health economics research activity undertaken by the pharmaceutical industry is evident in terms of staff expansion, number of projects conducted, and number of studies published (1–3). Several factors have put pressure on all industrialized nations, most of which finance and deliver care for their citizens, to make decisions regarding the allocation of increasingly limited resources. These factors include the proliferation of new and expensive health care technologies, the shift from treatment of acute to chronic diseases, and an aging population increasing the demand for care. In the United States, a trend toward prospective capitated payment for the delivery of health care has produced similar incentives to contain health care spending. The result has been rationing of care. Such rationing is explicit in most countries through limitations on access to care, resulting in waiting periods for some services. In the United States, which places a lower premium on equity in access, rationing is implicit in the form of a large uninsured or inadequately insured

population. It is within this context that public and private organizations paying for and delivering health care have demanded manufacturers of pharmaceutical technologies to demonstrate the expected marginal benefits and costs over existing therapies.

Application of outcomes or pharmacoeconomic research can provide a number of benefits for manufacturers, payers, providers, and consumers of health care. For example, pharmaceutical companies develop models to assess the socioeconomic value; hence, the commercial viability, of drugs in development. Manufacturers also conduct comparative studies in order to encourage the inclusion of their products on formularies and in clinical practice guidelines, and to assist in obtaining optimal pricing (the uses of economic evaluation by pharmaceutical companies is the subject of a separate chapter in this book). Payers, such as government authorities and insurance companies, as well as providers, such as hospitals and managed care organizations, are using pharmacoeconomic research results to determine coverage, aid in formulary decisions, set reimbursement rates, and develop practice guidelines. In addition, patients face copayment schemes that encourage them to seek value for money spent.

Clearly, analyses must be carried out according to the well-established principles of health economics if they are to contribute to decision making (4–10). This chapter offers the perspective of a pharmaceutical industry outcomes researcher and focuses primarily on some of the practical

A. M. Baker: Outcomes Research, U.S. Pharmaceuticals Group, Pfizer Inc, New York, New York 10017.

aspects of planning and implementing pharmacoeconomic studies.

PHARMACOECONOMIC RESEARCH THROUGHOUT PRODUCT LIFE

Most pharmaceutical product managers appreciate the role of health economics in supporting marketing. Many also have a general sense of the resource requirements in terms of personnel, time, and cost. Few, however, are familiar with the specific activities that should be pursued in order to document and convey the value of their products.

Pharmacoeconomic studies can be undertaken in a variety of ways and at various times throughout the product life cycle. Initial models can be used in early development to begin defining the socioeconomic profile for a product based on assumptions regarding the possible clinical attributes, as well as epidemiologic, medical, and cost data for the disease and its treatment. Such viability analyses, which may begin as early as Phase I, can continue during Phase II as new information regarding the clinical profile becomes available and a range of potentially sustainable prices is established. Phase II is also an appropriate stage at which to begin identifying health economic information needs, environmental issues surrounding the pricing and marketing of the compound, and desired messages. At this point it is important for the pharmacoeconomics practitioner to help develop realistic company expectations regarding the potential for conferring net cost savings through use of the product. The outcomes research plan can be developed during Phase II. It may include an assessment of the environment; key assumptions regarding clinical benefit, pricing, and reimbursement; activities to be pursued; potential messages; and pharmacoeconomic research strategy. The planned research may include feasibility studies, economic models, cost-of-care analyses, incorporation of economic and quality of life measurement into Phase III trials, and postmarketing studies. A clear delineation of responsibilities, assignments, budgets and timelines should also be included. Following submission of clinical data for the purpose of regulatory approval, outcomes research trials that might more closely approximate actual clinical practice can be undertaken. Country-specific and setting-specific studies can also be conducted. These studies might use pooled clinical data and local or institutional epidemiological data, cost data and practice patterns. It may also be more feasible to base sample size calculations for prospective outcomes trials on socioeconomic end points in the postmarketing phase. Significant human and financial resources are required to conduct studies at multiple sites with large numbers of patients.

ASSESSING THE ENVIRONMENT

A thorough assessment of the economic environment into which a product will be launched provides the context within which messages about the disease and the product's role in its treatment can be developed. Ideally, one would want to identify the current and anticipated major customers, their potential use and level of sophistication with socioeconomic data, the costs associated with the disease and the agent's therapeutic class, the financial incentives under which these customers operate, and the processes in place for submission of health economic data. Two key elements of the environmental assessment—selection of relevant comparators and of targeted audiences—are discussed in greater detail below.

Identification of the most relevant alternative therapies can be viewed as part of the environmental assessment. Selection of a comparator for clinical trials is typically based on the information required for regulatory purposes. This is often placebo, except where ethics or guidelines require active comparators, such as in trials of antiinfectives. The pharmacoeconomic researcher is interested in demonstrating the value of a product vis-à-vis its most relevant therapeutic alternatives. Determining this comparator is often made more complex, as common clinical practice may vary across countries and practice settings. Inclusion of all relevant comparators is rarely either desirable or feasible, but consideration should ensure that the comparison will be meaningful to the target audience. In some cases, a government authority or payer will dictate the comparator, requesting that it be the least expensive or the market leader. For example, guidelines being adopted in Canada call for comparisons with both existing practice, defined as either the single most prevalent clinical practice, as well as with minimum practice, defined as the lowest cost, but still efficacious, comparator (11). Additionally, Australia's guidelines call for the comparator to be the most common therapy (12).

It is necessary to determine the relevant audiences for the pharmacoeconomic evaluation in order for the information to be meaningful to various decision makers. Possible perspectives for an economic analysis include those of government registration authorities, public health officials, formulary committees, and pharmacy or employee benefit managers. Often market research is conducted to identify the payers relevant to a given therapy. Knowing the emphasis that each of these payers places on economic data in decision making will help guide investments in conducting economic analyses. It is also critical to understand the economic incentives at work in the financing and delivery of care. For example, physicians may be under contract with a managed care organization that rewards them for containing pharmaceutical costs. Hospitals, which are increasingly accepting contracts to deliver care on a capitated basis, have incentives to reduce lengths of stay. Thus, administrators might be receptive to information demonstrating shorter stays through use of a therapy with a higher acquisition cost than existing agents. The societal perspective would consider all relevant audiences, including for example, the cost to employers of work absences associated with a disease. Technically, this approach may seem simpler, as it may exclude any attempt to attribute costs to particular stakeholders. It also may represent the

TABLE 1. *Framework for developing economic positioning*

Comparative treatment strategy	Clinical advantage of Product X versus comparative treatment	Expected health care resource offset (likelihood of offset)	Audience for which health economic advantage is beneficial
Currently available IV therapies	Oral administration	Less nurse time for IV administration (high) Shorter length of stay (moderate)	Hospital Third-party payer if lower reimbursement negotiated Patient

most theoretically pure approach as it considers all costs (as well as outcomes) involved in delivering care. From a practical standpoint, however, no decision makers, including government authorities in countries with nationalized health care, are responsible for all costs; therefore, it may not be a relevant perspective from which to determine coverage or reimbursement for particular therapies.

DEVELOPING ECONOMIC POSITIONING

Marketers have traditionally developed a positioning strategy for their product based on its clinical attributes, such as its efficacy, safety, formulation, and dosing. For purposes of pharmacoeconomics, it is necessary to convert these clinical dimensions into economic messages or hypotheses. Economic hypotheses can be formulated by considering four pieces of information: (a) the treatment strategy against which the product will be compared, (b) the clinical advantage of the product against this alternative, (c) the health care resources that may be offset by demonstrating this clinical advantage (along with an estimate of the likelihood of such an offset), and (d) the audience for whom this economic message will be meaningful.

The application of such a framework is illustrated in Table 1. Assume that Product X is an oral formulation antibiotic being developed to treat an infection in severely ill hospitalized patients for whom only intravenous (IV) treatments currently exist. From the hospital's perspective, economic savings could be achieved by reducing or possibly eliminating the need for IV administration. This would be relevant if the hospital were reimbursed on a capitated per-patient basis. By contrast, third-party payors might benefit if a lower reimbursement could be negotiated with the hospital.

PLANNING A PHARMACOECONOMIC STUDY

Defining the Research Question

One of the initial tasks in planning an evaluation is to translate these socioeconomic messages into specific research questions. Drummond et al. (7) suggest that a well-defined research question should include the alternatives to be compared and the perspective of the evaluation. It may

also be useful to specify the time frame for the analysis and in broad terms what is being measured. An example of a well-defined pharmacoeconomic research question is "What will be the additional costs and benefits to a managed care organization over the course of one year by using Product X instead of Product Y in the treatment of Disease A?" Once potential health economic messages and corresponding research questions are identified based on a hypothesized advantage of the product over a relevant comparator from the perspective of a particular payer, it is useful to prioritize the contribution that generating data demonstrating each message might make to meeting the commercial objectives for the product. As resources available for conducting such studies are limited, the anticipated gain from research must justify required investments. In order to make informed decisions, however, it is necessary to consider the types of study designs which may be pursued to generate data supportive of the economic positioning.

Alternative Research Approaches

Economic evaluation study designs can be grouped into a number of broad categories (1). Prospective evaluations are usually either "piggy-back" studies, in which economic analysis is grafted onto a clinical protocol, or stand-alone outcomes trials, in which the study is designed specifically to assess cost-effectiveness or quality of life.

Retrospective designs typically fall into two categories. Economic analysis of an existing clinical trial is often pursued when it is found that patients taking the agent of interest experienced some clinical advantage, such as fewer hospitalizations or drug-related adverse events. Economic evaluations of large data bases, such as payer claims data sets, have been quite common in the United States due to their availability (13). This approach generally compares cohorts and involves careful statistical control of possible confounding variables, such as age, gender, disease severity, and comorbidities. Other sources of medical care resource use information include data bases of the National Center for Health Statistics, industry associations, such as the American Hospital Association, Medicaid, state hospital discharge data, and managed care organizations. These data bases can also be used to estimate health care service costs to apply in pharmacoeconomic evaluations. No one source exists to measure all types of costs; thus, the researcher must make trade-offs in terms of completeness, timeliness, cost of access, quality, and representativeness.

The use of claims data for economic evaluations offers several advantages. First, claims data provide a real-world view of treatment, unaffected by issues of small sample size, strict inclusion criteria, and protocol-influenced costs. Also, these studies are typically less expensive to undertake than a prospective trial. Since longitudinal data are available, the effect of a therapy over time can be observed. Claims data contain records of large numbers of patients, enabling the researcher to assess the likelihood that rare events will occur and to extrapolate the results of an economic evaluation to a broader population. Several managed care organizations have systems that integrate pharmacy data and other medical service by diagnosis code, presenting interesting research opportunities. Data on filled, rather than merely written, prescriptions can offer insight into therapy compliance.

Limitations also exist regarding the use of claims data. The quality, validity, and reliability of such data are often unknown, and assessing these properties can be a major undertaking. It may be difficult to account for selection bias in terms of particular types of patients receiving certain interventions (14). Furthermore, claims data are just that—records of billed charges—and may be inaccurate because in some settings incentives exist for providers to maximize reimbursement by miscoding. These records also do not contain information on the indirect costs due to lost productivity. Missing data may bias results in ways that are not obvious. Perhaps most importantly, retrospective analyses cannot be conducted until a product has been on the market long enough for data to accumulate; therefore, results are not available early in the product life cycle.

Another common design is the simulation model. The two primary types of modeling approaches are the decision-analytic model and the epidemiologically based model. The former is used to assess clinical decisions involving present disease, while the latter is used to estimate the impact of decisions on health promotion or disease prevention. A fundamental tool of pharmacoeconomic modeling is the decision tree. Weinstein and Fineberg (15) identify three structural components to a decision tree: alternative actions, events following the actions, and outcomes. A decision tree framework can be applied to assess the relative costs and benefits of alternative therapeutic strategies (16).

Another option is to combine the above approaches. Often, for example, data from a prospective economic analysis are sufficient to make therapy selection decisions for a patient with characteristics similar to those studied in a trial, but a model is needed to extrapolate the likely impact of such a decision on a subpopulation or within the context of a specific clinical setting. As the topics of using large data bases for retrospective studies and designing decision-analytic models are addressed elsewhere in this book, the primary

focus here is to discuss the practical aspects of planning and undertaking prospective pharmacoeconomic studies.

Prospective Economic Analysis

How a prospective economic evaluation will be designed is influenced by a variety of factors, including (1) the reason for undertaking the evaluation, (2) the need to adhere to regulatory requirements for conducting trials, such as those addressing safety within particular therapeutic areas; (c) the availability of data; (d) the availability of resources, such as time, expertise, and money; (e) access to an evaluable population; (f) the planned use of the study results; and (g) the relevant time period for analysis—generally, a longer period of evaluation will be more relevant for health care decision makers.

Double-blind randomized controlled trials are considered the best method of determining the true impact of a health care intervention. Randomization distributes potential confounders to the groups by chance and results in clinical studies having quite high internal validity, that is, the degree to which the study results are true for the cohort evaluated. The trade-off comes when we try to extrapolate the trial results beyond the actual study population. For decision makers using the results of health economic analyses, external validity is very important. As a result, controlled trials are not always the ideal design for economic evaluations.

In order to understand the limitations of conducting prospective economic evaluations, it is useful to consider the factors that threaten the potential generalizability of randomized clinical trials (17,18). First, the exclusion criteria in trials usually result in evaluation of an unrepresentative group of patients. Second, many studies are conducted in teaching hospitals or sites with strong academic influence that do not usually represent the majority of practice. Perhaps most importantly, many protocols stipulate more frequent utilization of resources, such as laboratory tests or length of hospitalization, so that the cost of treatment would not be comparable to that expected in actual clinical practice. In addition, the closer monitoring of patients may reveal health problems or asymptomatic adverse events which would not have been identified under non-trial circumstances and lead to a higher cost of treatment. Also, researchers usually make little attempt to follow patients who discontinue medications for various reasons.

A number of practical challenges are presented when attempting to incorporate economic evaluation into clinical trials (19). First, the research effort is made more complicated. In many cases, it will be difficult to resolve the issue of study-mandated resource utilization. Generalizing the results of the study to broader marketing targets may be difficult. Also, there may be some reluctance both from the clinical research team and from their investigators to adding the economic component into the trial.

Nonetheless, a number of significant advantages exist to incorporating economic analysis into clinical trials. One advantage is that internal validity will not be challenged, as randomization should minimize selection bias. Certainly obtaining health economic data simultaneous to obtaining clinical data presents marketing staff with access to useful information in a timely manner. There are also efficiencies in terms of human and financial resources. Consequently, the number of clinical trials including economic analysis has increased in recent years (20). As this field has matured, the key methodological aspects of incorporating economic evaluation into clinical trials have been addressed by pharmacoeconomic researchers (1,21–25). The practical application of these research methods is discussed here.

It is important to identify when it is appropriate to incorporate economic evaluation into clinical trials. First, and perhaps most importantly, clinical trials should be reviewed with an eye toward generating data that support the identified health economic messages. Factors likely to influence selection of trials in which to incorporate economic evaluation include the study objective, target population, design, sample size, evaluation period, and perhaps most importantly, the planned comparator. Many clinical studies address issues of safety and effectiveness through inclusion of a placebo control. This means that the most relevant clinical alternatives are not always compared in the same trial. Generally speaking, Phase III research provides the most valuable opportunities to include economic evaluation in clinical studies. Although late Phase III and postmarketing studies are more likely to include relevant comparators, there is a trade-off in the timeliness of obtaining data. Once studies are selected, the clinical case report forms can be reviewed to determine what resource utilization, if any, may be planned for collection, and supplementary data collection instruments can be designed.

A number of additional practical issues warrant consideration. First, sample size in economic evaluations piggy-backed on Phase III clinical trials is usually determined by sample size requirements for the primary study end point. But since greater variation may be seen in economic data than in clinical data, the marginal impact of a drug may have to be quite large to show statistically significant differences from the control therapy. For example, a relatively small number of high cost hospitalizations can disproportionately affect both the mean total cost and associated variance. These issues are currently receiving attention by researchers (26–28). One suggestion has been to base sample size estimates more on improving the accuracy of the economic data and less on the necessary magnitude for a cost-effectiveness outcome (28). The reporting of best- and worst-case scenarios has also been recommended, although this may tend to understate or overstate cost-effectiveness as the likelihood of a number of variables moving in the same direction simultaneously may be remote. A variety of methods for assessing the external validity and generalizability of economic study results are currently being explored by the research community and may ultimately be used in conjunction with one another. It may become even more important, therefore, to consider the development of simulation models that can apply economic results to specific settings of care.

Owing to the perceived burden of adding economic data collection, the clinical research team may be reluctant to mandate that all patients participate. Investigators may prefer that the economic data collection be optional for the patient. This raises a number of selection bias issues and should be avoided, since the evaluation would involve outcome data based on the complete sample and the economic data based on a potentially biased subset (25).

Determining what economic data to collect should receive careful attention. Cost-of-care studies or caregiver interviews can be conducted during Phase II in order to identify the resources consumed in treating the disease under study. Although theoretically appealing, collection of all resource utilization by patients may pose practical difficulties. One suggestion has been to collect data on what are believed to be the most significant resource items and then evaluate the implications of this approach by collecting complete resource use for a sample of patients in the trial (29). In designing resource utilization data collection forms, minimizing the number of open-text fields will reduce the work necessary to cost such resources later.

It is often more practical to collect physical units of resources consumed by the patient, such as the number of outpatient and emergency department visits and the number and length of hospitalizations, as opposed to monetary costs or charges, unless it is an institution-specific evaluation. The analyst can then apply local or institutional costs so that evaluations will be relevant to particular audiences and viewed from multiple perspectives. For international application of study results, the analyst can work with local economists who assist in costing resources appropriately. Fee schedules, claims data bases, published studies, and surveys can be used to develop lists of relevant costs for medical resources.

Economic theory defines the cost of a resource as the benefit foregone, or opportunity lost, by not using it in its best alternative use, and distinguishes between economic costs and financial, or accounting, costs (30). Because cost information is accumulated and accounted for at the department level, rather than the patient level at many health care institutions, accounting costs may not be assigned to the department in which consumption took place. Charges, which are based in part on financial costs, may therefore differ significantly from economic costs (9,31). In order to assess efficiency accurately, economic evaluations should use ''true'' costs, and not charges. Pragmatically, however, charges may be acceptable when comparative, as opposed to absolute, costing is required. In addition, from the perspective of particular stakeholders, such as third-party payers, charges are indeed the value of interest.

Perhaps one of the most daunting challenges relates to the fact that some resources, such as lab tests, may be incurred solely for the primary efficacy research question posed in the trial. This is particularly difficult in pre-approval studies, where a "usual care" arm may not be appropriate. Ways to address this issue include making assumptions about what tests or other interventions would be anticipated in actual practice or minimizing, to the extent possible, protocol-mandated utilization. This must be done without compromising efficacy measurement or adequate monitoring of drug safety.

Traditional clinical trials are typically conducted just long enough to measure a particular efficacy outcome. Health care decision makers, however, are generally interested in the longer-term economic implications of various interventions. Longer-term costs and outcomes can sometimes be modeled based on epidemiological data. In some therapeutic areas, such as prevention of diabetic complications, where clinical researchers must rely on intermediate end points to demonstrate efficacy, models will inevitably have to be developed to predict the economic implications of treatment.

Randomized controlled trials often exclude from efficacy analysis discontinuations or dropouts due to lack of efficacy, side effects, or complications. From an economic perspective, it is relevant to assess what happens to these patients. Such extended follow-up of dropouts raises regulatory concerns regarding reporting of safety data. An approach that can be considered for handling this conflict is the use of a formal substudy protocol.

While clinical trials present the analyst with a number of methodological and practical challenges, many can be addressed reasonably well. In addition, incorporating economic analysis into Phase III trials provides opportunities to obtain useful data early in the product's life.

An alternative to piggy-backing economic evaluation into planned clinical trials is to undertake an outcomes-specific prospective study, which may enable the analyst to circumvent many of the methodological and practical problems of incorporating economic evaluation into planned trials. Banta and Luce (1) have identified several advantages and disadvantages to this approach. For example, external validity may be increased by designing the study to more closely reflect actual practice. Also, power calculations can be based on economic end points. In addition, investigators may be more likely to accept the goals of the study, since it is presented as an outcomes trial. A number of practical drawbacks are associated with this approach, however. The project will be more expensive as an entire trial needs to be conducted. A study that includes usual care treatment strategies may only be possible once the product is launched due to regulatory requirements, and the data would not be as timely. Finally, relaxing inclusion criteria to simulate "real-world" practice may allow potential confounding variables to threaten internal validity.

FEASIBILITY ASSESSMENT

The wisdom of pursuing a particular research approach can be determined systematically through conduct of a feasibility study. The two primary objectives of a feasibility assessment are to determine the likelihood of demonstrating the medical resource offset identified in the health economic messages and to identify the design elements required to generate data supportive of this message. The first of these objectives can be addressed by developing a basic decision-analytic model representing the relevant clinical pathways associated with management of the disease in question. The model can help test the key assumptions that would underlie a potential pharmacoeconomic evaluation. Such a model should include probabilities and costs associated with various treatment options and possible sequelae. It is more important at this stage to be comfortable with the range of estimates for each parameter in the model than to have precision in the parameters' base case values. Practice patterns, however, may differ significantly based on such factors as geography (e.g., country, region, urban versus rural), setting of care (e.g., academic versus community institution, managed care organization versus fee-for-service practice), and type of caregiver (e.g., physician versus nurse practitioner, primary care clinician versus specialist). In well-defined disease areas, many of the data for the model may be available in the literature. This can be supplemented with information obtained from surveys of caregivers. It is critically important to make sure that the time period of disease treatment and the economic perspective selected for analysis are consistent for all pathways throughout the model. The model can be used throughout the planning process as values of key variables are updated. Refinement of the research question is a natural consequence of the modeling exercise.

The second objective of a feasibility assessment is to determine how a study capable of persuasively demonstrating the hypothesized socioeconomic advantage would be designed. For example, a power calculation can be conducted to determine the sample size needed to demonstrate a significant difference from the comparator. Many of the resource requirements for the potential study, such as time, personnel, and perhaps most importantly expense, will be driven by the proposed sample size. Other resources, such as necessary data and analytical skills, can also be forecast through the feasibility assessment. Pharmacoeconomic planners and company management can then make a more informed decision regarding whether a proposed study could be undertaken within practical constraints.

IMPLEMENTATION ISSUES

For a number of reasons, much of the health economic research sponsored by the pharmaceutical industry is carried out with the assistance of experts from academic institutions and private consulting firms. In some countries, governmental authorities wish to see studies performed by local experts. There may also be thought leaders in particular fields who lend credibility with decision makers. And in many pharmaceutical companies, the perceived need for health economic research currently outweighs the ability of this functional area to meet this demand. Selection of lead investigators is as important to the success of pharmacoeconomic studies as it is for clinical trials. Identification of program needs will enable the project coordinator to match investigators to these needs. The relative importance to the project of expertise and practical experience in areas such as modeling, economics, epidemiology, quality-of-life research, and clinical trial design should be weighed. Of course, a consultant's reputation, ability to meet deadlines, and service fees are also key considerations. Finally, to assume that an organization can outsource all pharmacoeconomic activities without a thorough understanding of the intricacies of the fundamental aspects of the project is a serious error.

Identification of pharmacoeconomic research sites plays a key role in the success of projects. Increasingly, managed care organizations are becoming involved in such research, recognizing the benefits it can confer, such as generating data for use in making formulary decisions and developing clinical practice guidelines (32,33). Prior research experience and appropriate staff may be among the most important factors. In addition to the principal investigator, the qualifications of supportive personnel, such as study coordinators, clinical pharmacists, nurses, and other staff that may be directly involved with a research protocol should be considered. Aspects of a managed care organization that should be assessed include an appropriate patient population, continuity of patient membership, access to an institutional review board, and useful information systems. If medical records are a part of the research, consider their ease of access, level of integration of pharmacy and other medical resource use, and inclusion of information on disease severity, comorbidities, concomitant medications, costs and charges.

The earlier the need to incorporate economic parameters into a clinical trial is recognized, the greater the likelihood of obtaining high-quality data. Until the practice of planning and conducting health economic studies becomes routine for an organization, however, opportunities for capturing such data will be identified at various points during the conduct of clinical trials. The point at which the need to incorporate economic evaluation is recognized can also determine the research approach taken. Boyer and Pathak (34) compared three approaches to incorporating pharmacoeconomic research into clinical trials—independent, addendum, and integrated. These investigators suggest that the least desirable approach is the independent approach, in which the pharmacoeconomic protocol and data collection instruments are completely separated from the clinical trial. In this case, the clinical research team and investigators may view this aspect of the research as optional or supplementary, threaten-

ing to increase the length or cost of the study. Presenting the economic component as independent to the efficacy objectives of the trial may compromise the completeness and accuracy of economic data collection, although the research team may be most willing to accept this approach. In addition, if the economic data collection must continue beyond the duration of the trial's clinical data collection (to be more relevant for policy decision makers), it may be advantageous to have a separate substudy protocol. The addendum approach offers a minor improvement in that the pharmacoeconomic protocol and data collection forms, although remaining separate from their clinical counterparts, are introduced together with the clinical documents as a package. The integrated approach includes the pharmacoeconomic data as primary end points in the trial, by explicitly stating so in the protocol and including the relevant data forms in the casebook. As with the clinical data, the pharmacoeconomic protocol should clearly state who is to complete the data collection instrument, as well as what specifically is being measured; when, where, and how frequently it should be administered; and how the data should be submitted for processing.

Just as quality-of-life survey instruments need to be evaluated for their psychometric properties, it is similarly important that the resource utilization data collection instrument, whether it is a paper-based case report form, patient diary, or interviewer administered questionnaire, be sufficiently "pretested." Typically this can be done by comparing reported resource utilization to actual utilization based on chart review of a subsample of patients. Although this is an easy task to omit, if a pretest is not conducted, the risk of encountering problems in data collection is considerable.

Pharmacoeconomic data measurement represents a novel dimension of conducting trials for many investigators as well as the clinical research team. Convening an investigators' meeting is a common way to identify potential problems with a protocol and with data collection and reporting processes, in addition to generating enthusiasm for the research. If the clinical research team is in agreement, it is quite useful to discuss the importance of the pharmacoeconomic elements of the study at the investigators' meeting as well. To the extent possible, the pharmacoeconomic dimensions should be described as an integrated aspect of the study. If incorporation of the outcomes components of the study occurred late in the planning process, it is still useful to present a broad overview of the importance of collecting economic data and the general approach to be taken during the study to the investigators.

The pharmacoeconomic analyst should work with the clinical trial data manager to review data base development and to define data specifications. The economic analysis plan should be designed before data collection instruments are finalized. Collecting data that will not be used will waste time and money. In addition, provisions must be incorporated into the computerized data analysis program, to account for missing or censored data.

LOGISTICAL AND ORGANIZATIONAL CHALLENGES

A number of organizational and procedural issues can influence the success of efforts to carry out pharmacoeconomic studies. Historically, the medical and marketing divisions of pharmaceutical companies did not interact to a significant extent, perhaps rooted in a mutual distrust of motives. The medical division relied on knowledge of the products to design prospective studies with little input from marketing, while marketing depended on clinical trial results to position and promote its products without an opportunity to comment on protocol design. In order to develop health economic strategies successfully, many interdisciplinary activities must take place and organizational barriers need to disappear.

Also, a conflict exists between the need to take a worldwide approach to clinical programs for each product, while ensuring that the results of pharmacoeconomic evaluations will be relevant to specific customers and geographic markets. This is obviously difficult as medical practice patterns can vary significantly, limiting the applicability of data. This conflict between the requirement for a worldwide data base and the need to be responsive to local marketing needs can sometimes be addressed through development of market-specific health economic models.

Throughout this process, timing is critical. The sooner the need to incorporate economic evaluation into a clinical trial is identified, the higher the likelihood that the appropriate multidisciplinary input required for success can be provided. Lines of communication should be established at the beginning of the process so that questions can be raised and resolved expeditiously. Project teams should meet regularly to review progress or problems. It is perhaps equally important to inform staff outside the research team of the likelihood of being able to demonstrate a favorable outcome. Managing expectations can also establish internal credibility for the health economics practitioners. Pharmacoeconomics represents another tool through which an organization can demonstrate the value of a product; it does not represent a panacea for the marketing challenges of the day.

CONCLUSIONS

Market forces and public policies continue to increase the competitiveness of the health care industry. A wide array of stakeholders are demanding that research-based pharmaceutical companies demonstrate the relative costs and benefits associated with the use of their products. Many of the theoretical dimensions of conducting health economic evaluations of pharmaceuticals have been addressed by the research community. This chapter highlights some of the pragmatic aspects of designing and conducting pharmacoeconomic studies from the perspective of an industry-based researcher. If companies are to be successful in these activities, they must educate internal audiences regarding the value and limitations of pharmacoeconomics, select products for analyses carefully, incorporate health economic planning early in the development of compounds, adhere to principles of sound economic evaluation, assess realistically the resources necessary for high quality research, and determine the contribution their research has made to decision making. As calls for standards and guidelines in this rapidly evolving science increase, it will be critical to assess their implications both on innovation in the field and on the ability of pharmaceutical companies to comply from a practical perspective with such recommendations.

REFERENCES

1. Banta HD, Luce BR. *Health care technology and its assessment: an international perspective.* New York: Oxford University Press, 1993.
2. Winter S. The pharmaceutical industry's response to cost-containment initiatives. *PharmacoResources* 1994;11:3–4.
3. Zitter M, Sanker A. Outcomes research and your marketing plan. *Product Management Today* April 1994:12–15.
4. Weinstein MC. Economic assessments of medical practices and technologies. *Med Decis Making* 1981;1:309–330.
5. Dao T. Cost-benefit and cost-effectiveness analysis of drug therapy. *Am J Hosp Pharm* 1985;42:791–802.
6. Guyatt G, Drummond M, Feeny D, et al. Guidelines for the clinical and economic evaluation of health care technologies. *Soc Sci Med* 1986;22:393–408.
7. Drummond MF, Stoddart GL, Torrance GW. *Methods for the economic evaluation of health care programmes.* New York: Oxford University Press, 1987.
8. Eisenberg JM. Clinical economics: a guide to the economic analysis of clinical practices. *JAMA* 1989;262:2879–2886.
9. Luce BR, Elixhauser A. *Standards for the socioeconomic evaluation of health care products and services.* Berlin: Springer-Verlag, 1990.
10. Bootman JL, Townsend RJ, McGhan WF. *Principles of pharmacoeconomics.* Cincinnati: Harvey Whitney, 1991.
11. Canadian Coordinating Office for Health Technology Assessment. *Guidelines for economic evaluation of pharmaceuticals: Canada,* 1st ed. November 1994.
12. Commonwealth of Australia. *Guidelines for the pharmaceutical industry on preparation of submissions to the Pharmaceutical Benefits Advisory Committee: including submissions involving economic analyses.* Canberra: Department of Health, Housing and Community Services, 1992.
13. Gable CB, Friedman RF, Holzer SS, Baum K. Pharmacoepidemiological studies in automated claims databases: methodological issues. *J Res Pharm Econ* 1992;4(4):53–68.
14. Baum K, Muggeo L, Gable CB, Friedman RF, Holzer SS. Incorporating severity of illness measures into retrospective claims-based cost-effectiveness analyses. *J Res Pharm Econ* 1993;5(1):59–68.
15. Weinstein MC, Fineberg HV. *Clinical decision analysis.* Philadelphia: WB Saunders, 1980.
16. Bentkover JD, Baker AM, Kaplan H. Nabumetone in elderly patients with osteoarthritis: economic benefits versus ibuprofen alone or ibuprofen plus misoprostol. *PharmacoEconomics* 1994;5:335–342.
17. Sackett DL. Bias in analytic research. *J Chronic Dis* 1979;32:51–63.
18. Spilker B. *Guide to clinical trials.* New York: Raven Press, 1991.
19. Baker AM. Piggy-back economic evaluations: opportunities and challenges. *Health Econ Selected Rev* 1994;3(4):1–2.
20. Adams ME, McCall NY, Gray DT, Orza MJ, Chalmers TC. Economic analysis in randomized control trials. *Med Care* 1992;30:231–243.
21. Drummond MF, Stoddart GL. Economic analysis and clinical trials. *Controlled Clin Trials* 1984;5:115–128.
22. Drummond MF, Smith GT, Wells N. *Economic evaluation in the development of medicines.* London: Office of Health Economics, 1988.
23. Bootman JL, Larson LN, McGhan WF, Townsend RJ. Pharmacoeconomic reserch and clinical trials: concepts and issues. *Ann Pharmacother* 1989;23:693–697.

24. Drummond MF, Davies L. Economic analysis alongside clinical trials: revisiting the methodological issues. *Int J Technol Assess Health Care* 1991;7(4):561–573.

25. Eisenberg JM, Schulman KA, Glick HA, Koffer H. Pharmacoeconomics: economic evaluation of pharmaceuticals. In: Strom B, ed. *Pharmacoepidemiology,* 2nd Ed. Chichester, England: John Wiley & Sons, 1994.

26. Drummond M, O'Brien B. Clinical importance, statistical significance and the assessment of economic and quality-of-life outcomes. *Health Econ* 1993;2:205–212.

27. O'Brien BJ, Drummond MF. Statistical versus quantitative significance in the socioeconomic evaluation of medicines. *PharmacoEconomics* 1994;5:389–398.

28. O'Brien BJ, Drummond MF, Labelle RJ, Willan A. In search of power and significance: issues in the design and analysis of stochastic cost-effectiveness studies in health care. *Med Care* 1994;32(2):150–163.

29. Glick HA. *The economic assessment of Phase III clinical trials: some issues in the measurement of resource utilization,* unpublished manuscript, 1994.

30. Lipsey RG, Steiner PO, Purvis DD. *Economics,* 7th Ed. New York: Harper & Row, 1984.

31. Finkler SA. The distinction between costs and charges. *Ann Intern Med* 1982;96:102–109.

32. Fifer S. Conducting outcomes research: how can HMOs get started? *Pharm Therap* 1991;16:1011–1013.

33. Clouse J. Pharmacoeconomics: a managed care perspective. *Top Hosp Pharm Manage* 1994;13(4):54–59.

34. Boyer JG, Pathak DS. Establishing value through pharmacoeconomics: the emerging third objective in clinical trials. *Top Hosp Pharm Manage* 1994;13(4):1–10.

Quality of Life and Pharmacoeconomics in Clinical Trials, Second Edition, edited by B. Spilker. Lippincott-Raven Publishers, Philadelphia © 1996.

CHAPTER 116

Developing Guidelines for Pharmacoeconomic Trials

Bert Spilker

INTRODUCTION

The field of pharmacoeconomics is exploding, and its impact at the national as well as patient level has never been more important. Yet, much of the data obtained from pharmacoeconomic trials are seriously flawed or biased, and the process of designing these trials requires consensus in setting criteria (i.e., guidelines). Pharmacoeconomic trials are a subset of Phase I to IV and all other clinical trials. This chapter reviews important biases in pharmacoeconomic trials and describes how they are introduced in the trial's design. An approach to reduce these biases is suggested.

Pharmacoeconomic trials provide extremely important data that assist formulary committees, physicians and other health care professionals, regulatory authorities, health policy experts, and pharmaceutical companies in decision making. Data are obtained through prospective trials or by retrospective analyses, although it is generally accepted that prospective trials provide more accurate and reliable data than retrospective studies.

All clinical trials are subject to numerous biases at any stage—from creating the trial design to interpreting the results. Most of these biases can affect the data. Biases enter a trial because of something that was done or not done—but should have been. These sins of commission and omission may involve failure to include all relevant information necessary to address adequately the objectives of the protocol. The sins of commission include inappropriately choosing or evaluating parameters.

HOW BIASES ARE INTRODUCED INTO PHARMACOECONOMIC TRIALS

When an individual or group in a pharmaceutical company designs and implements a pharmacoeconomic trial, he or she often approaches this task in a totally different manner than would be used in other clinical trials. With traditional clinical trials, there are established methods and approaches for choosing the objectives, design, parameters, methods, and measurements used (1). Even though the author of a clinical protocol may believe he or she knows the outcome of a trial before it starts, the use of standardized approaches and the need to follow Good Clinical Practices standards assures all parties that the trial was designed and conducted according to rigorous scientific principles. Any questions about specific aspects of a trial can be answered by an audit, conducted either during or after the trial. There is, of course, a small degree of flexibility in most clinical trials (and a great degree of flexibility in a few), whereby the author may consciously try to influence the trial's results to favor his or her test medicine, hypothesis, or desired outcome. This

B. Spilker: Orphan Medical, Inc. Minnetonka, Minnesota 55305.

could involve carefully choosing the time post-dose to assess certain effects, failing to measure long-term effects of the comparator medicine, or by similar approaches. Many, if not most, of these practices will be obvious to astute readers of the clinical trial report or evaluation.

On the other hand, it is remarkably easy for the author of a pharmacoeconomic protocol to abuse the scientific process. The most egregious example is where the author starts with the answer he or she wants and then works backward to determine the trial design, parameters, methods, and measures needed to demonstrate that effect. The protocol is then written to accomplish that purpose. For example, the group involved in creating the protocol asks themselves how their product can be shown to be more cost-effective than another. Even if a clinical trial design is already written—as it often is for trials where pharmacoeconomic evaluations are intended to be superimposed on an existing protocol—authors also may work backwards. In that situation, however, there are usually more constraints on the trial designs and parameters than if the pharmacoeconomic trial is designed de novo (i.e., from the beginning).

Evaluation of Costs

The techniques used to evaluate costs in pharmacoeconomic trials are usually the same for cost-benefit, cost-effectiveness, cost-utility, and cost-minimization methods. Bias may be readily introduced in the evaluation of costs if only some of the direct or indirect costs are measured (Tables 1 and 2). If an investigator measures all direct and indirect costs, the results could be presented in a straightforward table. Alternatively, a list of all direct and indirect costs could be explained in the discussion of methods, with a summary of the totals included under results. If the reader does not know what specific categories of costs were measured, and only totals are given, the implication could be drawn that the missing values would have influenced the data and were intentionally omitted. This is not solely a theoretical issue. In reading reports of many pharmacoeconomic trials, it is often impossible to determine which specific costs were measured.

Even expressing the wholesale cost of a medicine itself may be biased. For example, the cost of a medicine may be given for a single pill, a single dose (e.g., two pills), the total daily dose (e.g., two pills three times a day), the total cost per episode (e.g., 7 days), cost per milligram, cost per package, or the total cost per month. All medicines compared must use the same types of costs (e.g., wholesale cost, retail cost). A medicine claimed to be cheaper or more expensive than another may clearly be so on one scale (e.g., per dose) but not another (e.g., per day) (Table 3).

Costs of a medicine in one setting (e.g., hospital) may differ significantly from another (e.g., clinic, community pharmacy, another hospital) because of different discounts offered by the manufacturer or distributor. Articles must

TABLE 1. *Selected direct costs that may be measured in pharmacoeconomic trials[a]*

1. Cost of the medicine (whether based on wholesale prices to the pharmacy or retail prices to the patient must be specified)[b]
2. Cost of the pharmacy and nurses' time to prepare the medicine
3. Cost of any equipment and supplies (e.g., syringes, tubing, vials) needed to administer the medicine
4. Cost of actually administering the medicine (e.g., nurses' time)
5. Cost of monitoring the patient on the day the medicine is given, as well as prior to that day (e.g., laboratory costs, professional charges)
6. Cost of monitoring the patient after the medicine is given
7. Cost of concomitant medicines or other treatments that must be given with the medicine (e.g., potassium supplements for a diuretic)
8. Cost of the clinic visit(s) for the occasion(s) when the medicine is given; costs may be calculated for one visit, one episode, or a fixed time, such as one year
9. Cost of hospitalization stays (e.g., room and board) per year or on another basis
10. Cost of all health professionals, support personnel, administrators, and any volunteers
11. Cost of continuing on a chronic medicine for the patient's lifetime
12. Cost of switching a patient from their existing treatment to a new treatment
13. Costs of diagnosing and treating anticipated adverse events

[a]Other items to add to this list could be chosen for relevant situations (e.g., cost to diagnose a patient). Not all items on this list will be relevant for a specific product or trial.

[b]The complexities of measuring this apparently straightforward cost are discussed in the text. Consistency must be used in comparing different treatments in terms of assessing actual costs to a group (e.g., hospital) versus charges (i.e., to the patient or their insurance company).

TABLE 2. *Selected indirect costs that may be measured in pharmacoeconomic trials*

1. Transportation to and from the clinic, hospital, or other place relating to the treatment·
2. Food, hotel, parking costs, and other necessary expenses for patients and those who accompany them
3. Baby-sitting, child care costs, or costs for care of a parent
4. Other ancillary medical treatments and medicines recommended as a result of taking the primary medicine (e.g., the need for follow-up care, which may involve rehabilitation, physical, or mental therapies)[a]
5. Wages lost because of the disease or treatment, including adverse reactions
6. Costs of re-treating patients who fail to respond to treatment
7. Costs of treating unexpected complications
8. Counseling required because of psychosocial problems, the inability to work, or for other reasons
9. Other consequences of treating patients
10. Overhead for the facilities used

[a]This category is often viewed as a direct cost of the therapy. Whichever classification is used, it must be considered.

TABLE 3. *Six alternatives for comparing costs*[a]

Cost	Medicine A	Medicine B	Medicine C
Per tablet[c]	*$1.00*[b]	$1.50	$2.00
Per dose	2 tablets make up one dose and cost $2.00	1 tablet costs *$1.50*	1 tablet costs $2.00
Per day	Medicine taken twice a day and costs $4.00	Medicine taken three times a day and costs $4.50	Medicine taken once a day and costs *$2.00*
Per course of therapy	Duration of 10 days costs $40	Duration of 10 days costs $45	Duration of 7 days costs *$14*
Per package	20 tablets per box costs *$20*	30 tablets per box costs $45	12 tablets per box costs $24
Per milligram	50 mg–$.02 per mg	150 mg–*$.01 per mg*	5 mg–$.40 per mg

Modified with permission of Raven Press from Spilker (2).

[a]Other ways to express the costs of the medicine include monitoring cost, cost of professional visits and services, and costs of hospitalization. Alternative or additional ways to express costs relate to costs saved or a comparison of costs with other treatments for the same problem.

[b]The least expensive medicine for each description is underlined, illustrating that each medicine *could* be described as the least expensive, depending on how the data are presented.

[c]Cost could be expressed per milliliter of solution or per unit of therapy (e.g., capsule, suppository, patch).

specify the cost per unit of product to enable other groups to extrapolate results from a study to their own situation. The ratio of costs to benefits is readily affected by the cost of a product and this will change, not only from setting to setting, but also within any one setting over a period of years.

It is also desirable to describe (when possible) how changes in cost will affect the cost-to-benefit ratio. Major changes in cost may or may not have a significant effect on the cost-to-benefit ratio, especially in comparison to another treatment.

If the direct costs of the medicine can be improperly manipulated or biased, other direct (and indirect) costs probably are also subject to "creative" measurement and presentation. A fair way to compare costs of chronically used medicines is on a per month or year basis. On the other hand, antibiotic costs for acute treatments are best compared on a per-episode basis. Obtaining costs for investigational medicines is impossible in most cases because they are not priced.

Evaluation of Efficacy or Effectiveness

Measures of effectiveness can be readily tailored to achieve a desired result by carefully selecting (1) the time period for evaluation (e.g., only the first week, month, or year after treatment is started), (2) the health care providers whose time involved in the treatment is assessed (e.g., physicians, nurses, physical therapists), (3) the location and type of service (e.g., clinic, hospital), and (4) the test instruments, laboratories, procedures used. There are cases when numerous tests and scales are used to measure quality of life, but only those that yield positive results are reported. Data from tests that show no difference or a beneficial effect for the alternative treatment are sometimes not reported. Similar situations could occur in clinical trials where only results of selective tests are reported.

It is generally easier to evaluate whether a pharmacoeconomic trial has introduced bias in the measurement of costs than in the measurement of efficacy or effectiveness. Several of the basic categories of efficacy in a clinical trial or effectiveness in clinical practice conditions that are vulnerable to manipulation in a pharmacoeconomic study are listed in Table 4. Some of the parameters measured in trials assessing a medicine's efficacy do not directly relate to an observable clinical benefit (e.g., apparent pharmacokinetic advantages in metabolism or elimination that are clinically nonapparent). The measure of effectiveness or utility (Table 5) is subject to an even greater degree of bias. An experienced pharmacoeconomist can (if desired) almost always show any medicine to be more cost-effective than any other.

Does this mean that pharmacoeconomists are biased scientists, clinicians, or economists? Absolutely not! Rather, it means that a set of appropriate rules and principles must be established that underlie the discipline and practice of pharmacoeconomics, and level the playing field for all groups conducting trials.

TABLE 4. *Efficacy categories that may be manipulated in a pharmacoeconomic trial*

1. Parameters chosen to measure a disease, symptom, or clinical sign (e.g., swelling of legs or shortness of breath to assess patients with congestive heart failure)
2. Methods used to measure the parameter (e.g., assessing leg swelling by using a tape measure, a scale of 1 to 4, or pain on walking)
3. Instruments used and how they are applied (e.g., just before medicine is taken, at bedtime, 20 minutes after medicine, one hour after medicine)
4. Analysis of the data
5. Interpretation of the data
6. Extrapolation of the data
7. Other categories (e.g., patient compliance, comfort, and convenience of treatment)

TABLE 5. *Selected efficacy categories usually measured in a pharmacoeconomic trial*

1. Time spent in hospital per year or other time period
2. Cost of hospitalizations per year or other time period
3. Number of physician, emergency room, or clinic visits per year or other time period
4. Number or times per year that ancillary treatment is required
5. Improvements of one or more clinical symptoms in severity, duration, or qualitative nature
6. Improvements of one or more clinical signs in intensity, duration, frequency, or qualitative nature
7. Improvements of one or more laboratory measures of a biological sample (e.g., blood, urine)
8. Improvement of one or more physical laboratory parameters (e.g., EEG, EKG, pulmonary function tests)
9. Improvement of a patient's quality of life
10. Subjective improvement reported by the patient, family, or others
11. Number of episodes or exacerbations per year
12. Changes in the natural history of the disease
13. Survival
14. Time spent by the physician and other health professionals per year
15. Number of days of work lost per year due to the disease

EXAMPLES OF HOW BIAS MAY BE INADVERTENTLY INTRODUCED INTO PHARMACOECONOMIC TRIALS

Bias is commonly introduced into clinical or pharmacoeconomic trials by conducting them in an artificial environment. For example, clinical trials conducted in a clinic or hospital setting yield data that are extrapolated to the "real" world of medical practice in physicians' offices. The same principle applies when costs obtained in an artificial environment are extrapolated to the real world.

The costs for a new medicine or treatment measured in a clinical trial would almost certainly differ from those in actual medical practice. For example, even if the physician and staff time charges are included in a trial comparing two treatments, in actual practice it might not be necessary for patients to go to a tertiary care facility where significant charges for professional staff time would occur. The intensity of patient monitoring is usually greater in a tertiary care facility than in a primary care practice; and, the time spent by staff during a trial and the number of tests conducted are usually far greater than during routine care. Another example of differences between settings is when two products are available from a primary care provider, but one requires more clinic visits per year than another (e.g., when one requires more frequent monitoring of liver function than the other). This difference might not be assessed in a hospital setting. Most of the laboratory and other tests run in a clinical trial are not conducted in the real world of medical practice. Also, the question of which setting and what type of patient to consider as the model of the real world is important because many medicines are used in a variety of settings but to different degrees.

Another bias sometimes inadvertently introduced into a pharmacoeconomic trial involves data obtained for one group of patients being extrapolated to another group. For example, a product that is more cost-effective than another for severely ill patients may be more expensive for mildly ill patients. A new, more expensive treatment may decrease the hospitalization time for severely ill patients and thus save money. By contrast, mildly ill patients do not need to be hospitalized and would be paying for a more expensive medicine.

In addition to severity of disease, almost any patient or disease characteristic may be the basis of introducing bias into a pharmacoeconomic evaluation. Chapter 83 of *Guide to Clinical Trials* (1) presents many hundreds of examples where bias may enter one or another aspect of a clinical trial, and many of these factors could also introduce bias into a pharmacoeconomic trial.

Whenever an overqualified person performs a service (e.g., a physician making the bed in a hospital), the task should be valued and the cost measured as if the appropriate person were doing it. The same principle applies for extrapolating data from countries in which relatively underqualified professionals perform services that would not be medically, ethically, or legally acceptable in another country. Although these practices generally reflect cultural or other differences, they could represent attempts to make one (or more) treatments appear more or less expensive than they truly are.

A final example of how bias may be inadvertently introduced is for an author of a report to inappropriately mix the levels on which the trial is being conducted, interpreted, and extrapolated. The levels referred to are single patient, trial patients, groups of patients with a specific disease, and all patients with that disease. For example, a clinical trial conducted in a carefully selected group of patients may be interpreted as if they were representative of the entire population of patients with a specific disease. Similarly, a trial conducted at an institutional level cannot always be extrapolated to either a specific patient or another type of institution (e.g., tertiary care hospital to health maintenance organization).

Many other pharmacoeconomic measurements conducted in a clinical trial could differ markedly from values obtained in clinical practice. As a result, the reader (or writer) of a report, as well as the designer of a pharmacoeconomic evaluation, should evaluate carefully how the data are going to be used, as well as how to obtain the most objective data to answer major questions. These precautions reduce the risk that major health decisions will be made from biased or inappropriately extrapolated data.

RESPONSES BY PHARMACEUTICAL AND OTHER HEALTH-RELATED COMPANIES

Adequate standards are needed for designing, conducting, and interpreting pharmacoeconomic trials. Pharmaceutical and other health-related companies should strive to raise the rigor of current practices. Trials should be approached in a logical, objective, and scientifically disinterested way. This reduces the risks to both the investigator and the medicine developer. A company cannot afford to develop medicines based on false data, misleading interpretations, inappropriate analyses, or the subjective desires of senior managers for a medicine "to work." The same thinking, attitudes, and also the same consequences do not currently exist for pharmacoeconomic trials.

Unfortunately, pharmacoeconomic trials are not currently conducted under universally accepted, structured guidelines. In fact the market pressures predominate to act in scientifically inappropriate ways. Some companies make outrageous claims of economic superiority of their medicine that can not be substantiated by a dispassionate and objective view of the data. Government agencies are rightfully attempting to monitor advertising claims and promotional practices. But, the design of pharmacoeconomic trials has not been challenged, and companies feel compelled to design trials that "objectively" prove the economic superiority of their own medicine. The *New England Journal of Medicine* has recognized this problem (4) and has taken reasonable steps to protect the journal's standards. It would be a positive step if other journals followed their lead.

Many people appear to believe that incorporating appropriate statistical input and considerations into a clinical trial's design and data analysis is adequate to reduce or eliminate bias in pharmacoeconomic trials. Statistical input into clinical trial design is primarily in the area of number and type of groups, number of patients per group, tests to use in the analysis of results, and other related concepts. Statistical input does not generally influence the type of backward planning of a protocol's objectives and choice of parameters and methods that this paper discusses. Therefore, statistical input, no matter how erudite and correct, cannot be counted on to have a major role in eliminating the biases discussed.

Industry representatives tend to rationalize their current investigational procedures. A few of the commonly heard industry claims are listed below.

Because of the pressures from marketing and other groups within pharmaceutical companies, it is difficult for health economists and their staff to act in a totally objective manner. If the staff act objectively and the pharmacoeconomic data obtained are not what the marketing groups and senior managers desire, it is certain that the results will not be presented to any group. Moreover, advancement opportunities for responsible staff are likely to diminish, and it is possible that their jobs may be placed in jeopardy. No company wants to spend money on pharmacoeconomic trials where the outcomes go against their product. Within the bounds of acceptable practices, the company always wants to increase the chance of a positive (or at least a useful) result for marketing.

Pressures placed on company staff are often transferred to vendors or contractors hired to design and run the trials. They also work backward in most cases to find the parameters, methods, and measures that show the results their clients want. If the vendors insist on designing and conducting more objective trials, they may not be rehired. Ironically, adhering to high standards of design may adversely affect the vendor's reputation. Several highly reputable vendors have told me they attempt to educate their clients about the benefits of adhering to high standards, but are usually told to use the (biased) approach of ensuring that the data "turn out as expected."

It must be stressed that no one involved in these practices believes he or she is acting unethically in any way. They are doing exactly what all other industry professionals do. The author is *not* accusing anyone of unethical behavior, although establishing guidelines and improving standards will increase the ethical foundation of pharmacoeconomic trials.

SHOULD THE CURRENT SITUATION BE CHANGED?

Why should anyone associated with the pharmaceutical industry or a clinical research organization wish to change

Commonly made statements that support poor scientific practices and standards	Appropriate responses that support high scientific practices and standards
1. Everybody designs pharmacoeconomic trials by working backward.	*True*—But of course this does not mean it is correct or even in the company's best interest to design trials that way.
2. There are no rules or practice standards for pharmacoeconomic trials that are being followed by most groups.	*True*—But of course this does not mean that practice standards should not be created.
3. There are no standard methods to use for designing pharmacoeconomic trials.	*False*—The three major methods[a] plus a few minor ones are well developed and are standard methods.
4. The methods used in pharmacoeconomic trials are not validated.	*False*—The methods used in most trials are well validated (3). Some people confuse pharmacoeconomic methods with quality of life methods where the validation of most methods is not good.
5. Why shouldn't we choose the parameters we want to measure, since those are the ones we know will show an important difference between treatments.	–There is a certain logic in this reply. The most appropriate retort is presented in the rest of this article and in the conclusion, focusing on the consequences of not establishing practice standards.

[a]Cost-benefit, cost-effectiveness, and cost-utility methods.

this situation? There are a number of answers, ranging from the ethical (because the current approach is inherently unscientific and biased) to the more practical (because it is counterproductive for the industry not to change).

To understand why the current approach will not benefit the industry in the long term, we must ask how data are being used and what the consequences are of not changing the current approach. Data on pharmacoeconomics are being used (a) to consider products for inclusion on formularies by various committees, (b) to obtain appropriate pricing by those regulatory authorities or other groups that establish or help to establish prices, (c) to inform physicians about prescribing products, and (d) to convince the public and legislators of the value of modern medicines, among other purposes. Many important groups are targeted to receive pharmacoeconomic data; the validity of the data as judged by these groups has important consequences for the industry.

Clearly, the inherently flawed approach to acquiring data cannot be continually ignored by the groups reviewing those data. People are already asking probing questions. The usual response from company economists is that the target groups are comparing apples and oranges; and, that if two (or 22) companies each show that their medicine is cost effective, it is because different methods, parameters, and measures were used. This is precisely the point! Everyone who judges pharmacoeconomic data should want to have a better way of knowing that the economic aspects of different medicines or treatments can be compared fairly and directly. If the current situation continues, the credibility of industry-generated pharmacoeconomic data will undoubtedly be called into question. After that, it is a short step for formulary committees or other groups who receive data to question the value of all data they receive and to discount or even dismiss its value in helping them make economic decisions.

If this occurs, the recipients of pharmacoeconomic data, be it formulary committee or regulatory agency, may impose its own guidelines in terms of measures, parameters, and methods on those groups submitting data and insist that every company follow their guidelines, regardless of how costly or inappropriate they might be. Of course, there are other approaches that the recipient group could take to address the problem—and none of these approaches is likely to please pharmaceutical companies. Some pharmacoeconomic models now allow the recipient institutions to conduct their own sensitivity analyses of the data.

HISTORICAL EXAMPLES IN WHICH IMPLEMENTATION OF STANDARDS REDUCED BIAS

The standards of clinical medicine are higher today than at anytime in the past, and more and more medical practices and decisions are based on results of clinical trials. In fact, clinical trials may be said to have "come of age." Spilker

(5) discusses the criteria by which a discipline can be said to "come of age" and then discusses why clinical trials meet these criteria. A good example is the development of internationally accepted Good Clinical Practice Standards, which more correctly should be called Good Clinical Trial Practice Standards. These guidelines have had a great influence on improving the reliability of clinical trials, and they are a result of many years of hard work by many people and organizations.

As another example of improved standards, 30 years ago it was common in clinical trials to measure numerous efficacy parameters and then to determine which one or ones were statistically significant. If a positive effect was found, the trial's outcome was labeled positive and the results published. This approach allowed the investigator to determine—after a trial was completed—what parameters were most important and what constituted a positive result. Data dredging by analyzing subsets and looking for positive results was common. Bias could easily be introduced and influence a trial's outcome. Fortunately, this approach is no longer acceptable. Now, the primary parameters used to define efficacy and to indicate a positive result must be defined before the trial begins.

Three decades ago, a clinician would give all the data from a completed trial to a statistician. The statistician would then choose the tests to use to analyze the data. This approach opens the trial analyses to bias, and it is currently not used in most clinical trials sponsored by the pharmaceutical industry. Statisticians choose their tests to use in advance of the trial's initiation and often are asked to analyze the groups data in terms of Treatment A and Treatment B, prior to breaking the blind.

Many people jokingly say a statistician can prove anything, and the statistics reported in many newspapers and magazines reinforce this notion. However, the accepted rules of Good Statistical Practice (as part of Good Clinical Practice) establish guidelines, and statistical practices can be readily audited to assure adherence. While honest differences often exist among statisticians about which tests to use and many statistical decisions are not black and white, high standards will ensure prescribers (and users) of new medicines that the FDA and most other regulatory authorities have carefully assessed the statistical aspects of every new medicine's application. Journals also are alert to identify inappropriate statistical analyses, although not all journals currently conduct specific statistical reviews of manuscripts. However, this practice should be followed routinely, thereby allowing editors to reject manuscripts that lack appropriate statistical analyses and presentations.

ESTABLISHING STANDARDS FOR PHARMACOECONOMIC TRIALS

It is clear that no single pharmacoeconomic methodology (cost-effectiveness, cost utility, cost-benefit) will be suitable for evaluating new medicines or treatments in all situations. Appropriate parameters for each pharmacoeconomic trial must be identified on a case-by-case basis. Nonetheless, there are a number of principles that should be discussed to establish practice standards. A consensus document would be a valuable first step. Among the guidelines to be discussed are the following:

1. All direct and indirect costs of a treatment must be measured in a pharmacoeconomic trial, unless there are specific reasons not to do so and these are clearly stated. Evaluating only certain costs is unacceptable because bias can result. All costs should be explicitly stated in publications and reports or by reference to an accepted list.

2. Intangible costs such as grief, pain, anxiety, depression, loss of companionship, are not to be measured directly in pharmacoeconomic trials, even though these costs are often quite important in legal cases and from other perspectives (e.g., ethical). These emotions are often experienced by the family, friends, and coworkers of the patient in addition to the patient himself or herself. Circumstances may be established when it is relevant to measure these costs in pharmacoeconomic trials. These factors are often either directly or indirectly included in most evaluations of quality of life, which in itself is an important efficacy measure. Intangible costs are not generally assigned a financial value in an analysis of costs.

3. Cost-benefit methods are rarely, if ever, relevant for pharmaceutical companies to use when evaluating the pharmacoeconomics of a single medicine or treatment. This method, however, is valid and has other important uses (e.g., for academic studies, for allocating national resources among various diseases for treatment or research).

4. There is no single method (e.g., cost-utility or cost-effectiveness) that is preferable to use in all pharmacoeconomic studies.

5. If data are obtained in an artificial environment as is true for most clinical trials, then their relevance for actual clinical practice environments should be discussed in detail when interpreting results.

6. Wherever relevant, every effort should be made to conduct randomized, controlled, prospective studies and all studies should be as rigorously controlled as is possible.

7. Pharmacoeconomic trial protocols, either add-ons to clinical trials or as independent trials should be reviewed prior to conduct, whenever possible, by at least one experienced economist, an experienced clinical trialist, and by a statistician. It may also be relevant to discuss the trial protocol with one or more members of the target group that will eventually review the results.

8. It is not always mandatory to measure the most important efficacy parameters when designing a cost-effectiveness assessment. The most important parameter could be too difficult to measure, take too much time to evaluate, or be too expensive to evaluate. In addition, an adequate surrogate marker may be readily available. For example, in most diseases efficacy or effectiveness can be measured with a number of parameters including clinical symptoms, clinical signs, laboratory parameters, laboratory tests, physician or other health professional assessments (including subjective evaluations), and patient-based measures (including subjective evaluations), not to mention economic assessments of efficacy (e.g., days at work). The basis on which the choice is made is critical. This issue requires further discussion to determine what standards are appropriate.

9. It is often counterproductive to conduct pharmacoeconomic trials early in a medicine's development when the most appropriate dosages and means of using the medicine are incompletely known. This practice can lead to the collection of incorrect data that may lead to inappropriate conclusions. An early trial on erythropoietin reported that it cost £126,290 to achieve a quality of life-adjusted year, whereas a later trial found the value was £20,022 (6).

10. A logical series of steps to design and conduct a pharmacoeconomic trial should be discussed and recommended. [One such proposal is given in Chapter 42 of *Guide to Clinical Trials* (1).]

Other principles and standards will undoubtedly emerge from discussions among the participants who create these guidelines. The best group or groups to organize and convene this type of meeting would be a regulatory authority, a trade association of the industry, a national academy of sciences, and/or another independent organization that would not represent a single company, academic institution, or vested interest.

The outcome of these meetings would undoubtedly raise the scientific standards and credibility of pharmacoeconomic trials. If a national meeting were held first, an international meeting could follow at an appropriate time. Some of the additional questions that an international group might also address are (a) on what basis can pharmacoeconomic data be pooled from multiple countries? (b) on what basis can pharmacoeconomic data be extrapolated from one country to another? (c) what is the impact of price differences among countries? and (d) what is the impact of differences in medical practice, health care systems, and reimbursement systems on obtaining and interpreting pharmacoeconomic data? Other chapters in this book address some of these issues.

One alternative to the meeting approach is for peer pressure and general consensus to gradually force people to adhere to the most appropriate guidelines and standards. This approach is often effective, particularly when adopted by grant-making groups and journal editors, although it is likely to take more time than a consensus meeting to achieve the goal.

CONCLUSIONS

Given the great number of reasons to reduce biases in the design and conduct of pharmacoeconomic trials, it is concluded that establishing guidelines for pharmacoeconomic trials will provide a major benefit to all people who use these data and ultimately to all patients. Fortunately, this goal can be achieved through national and international cooperation among academic, regulatory authority, and industry personnel.

ACKNOWLEDGMENTS

The author thanks Dr. William McGhan, Dr. Brian Rittenhouse, Dr. John Schoenfelder, and Dr. Stephen Schondelmeyer for reading the manuscript and making valuable suggestions.

REFERENCES

1. Spilker B. *Guide to clinical trials,* Raven Press, New York. 1991
2. Spilker B. *Multinational pharmaceutical companies: principles and practices.* 2nd Ed. Raven Press, New York, 1994.
3. Drummond MF, Stoddart GL, Torrance GW. *Methods for economic evaluation of health care programmes.* Oxford University Press, Oxford, 1987.
4. Kassirer JP, Angell M. The "journal's" policy on cost-effectiveness analyses. *N Engl J Med* 1994;331:669–670.
5. Spilker B. Clinical trials come of age. *Drug News Perspect* 1993;6: 224–228.
6. Risks of Early Cost-benefit Conclusions. *SCRIP* No. 1876, November 26, 1993, p. 27.

Quality of Life and Pharmacoeconomics in Clinical Trials, Second Edition, edited by B. Spilker.
Lippincott-Raven Publishers, Philadelphia © 1996.

CHAPTER 117

Users of Pharmacoeconomic Data

Alan L. Hillman and Joseph A. Leveque

INTRODUCTION

In 1970, Alvin Toffler (1) described a world of "Future Shock," in which advances in technology outpaced society's ability to cope with them. The many resultant problems included ethical, economic, and social challenges about how to allocate the benefits of this brave new world of high technology. Now, nearly 25 years later, the health care industry has begun to respond to this challenge with the new science of economic analysis. Although this field can help answer allocation decisions among all different types of technology, this chapter focuses on pharmacoeconomics—the way in which users of pharmaceuticals can implement economic analysis to determine efficient applications of new drugs.

If the United States is ever to achieve the elusive dual objectives of universal coverage and cost containment, insurers, providers, patients, regulators, and manufacturers all must become more facile with the science of collecting and applying sophisticated health outcome information, such as pharmacoeconomics. Just so much "fat" can be cut out of the system. Once this is achieved, proactive resource allocation decisions must be made to favor investments in

A. L. Hillman: Center for Health Policy, Leonard Davis Institute of Health Economics; Division of General Internal Medicine, School of Medicine; Health Care Systems Department, The Wharton School, University of Pennsylvania, Philadelphia, Pennsylvania 19104.
J. A. Leveque: Scientia, Inc., San Francisco, California 94002.

medical interventions with efficient, long-term health care benefits (2). Some of these resource use decisions will ultimately save money; others will enhance benefits achieved. Either way, pharmacoeconomics will play a prominent role in formulating cost and outcome data so that decision makers may allocate the health care dollar wisely.

PHARMACOECONOMICS AND THE EVOLVING U.S. HEALTH CARE SYSTEM

Until recently, health care financing in the United States centered around a retrospective fee-for-service—or transaction-based—system, wherein third-party insurers insulated patients and providers from the cost impact of their decisions. Now, we are rapidly evolving to a system of risk sharing among insurer, patient, and providers that seeks to control and slow the rate of health care expenditures while ensuring appropriate care (3).

As a result, the health care system has been undergoing a reorganization from solo providers into horizontal and vertical networks of hospitals, physician groups, home health care agencies, and other ancillary facilities. It is hoped that integrated systems will provide an efficient structure for building and monitoring the quality of care, foster streamlined operations, and improve expense control (3).

An important tool necessary to compete in, and meet the challenges of, such an integrated, competitive, cost-conscious health care marketplace will be the ability to measure, monitor, and control both clinical and economic outcomes of care. Many of the tools necessary to collect and manage these data are just now maturing, with pharmacoeconomic analysis being the most advanced field in the outcomes world. Accurate pharmacoeconomic analyses will play a pivotal role in the allocation of pharmaceutical budgets within integrated health care systems. Pharmaceutical manufacturers will need to prove the economic efficiency of their products (along with safety and efficacy) to their marketplace of Pharmacy and Therapeutics Committees and Clinical Guidelines Committees. In turn, these insurers will need to convince *their* marketplace of employers and government agencies that their covered portfolio of drugs, devices, and procedures is both cost competitive and invested in technologies that will benefit the employer (as well as the patient). For example, a drug that costs more than comparators may be worthwhile to formulary decision makers, if employers see the additional value it offers (e.g., earlier return to work, fewer missed days of work, or improved productivity).

DIFFERENT PERSPECTIVES OF USERS OF PHARMACOECONOMIC DATA

Third-party payers, regulators, providers and patients, and medical product manufacturers have different perspectives about, and uses for, pharmacoeconomic data. Insurers (and government regulators) focus on how to meet their coverage obligations to large pools of beneficiaries in an efficient fashion to keep premiums competitive. Sometimes, they face the dilemma of knowing what works in ideal situations, such as Food and Drug Administration (FDA) approval of safety and efficacy, without knowing what works best in actual, clinical practice. Pharmacoeconomic analyses help quantify both effectiveness—does the intervention work in actual, clinical practice?—and efficiency—is the outcome derived from using the intervention worth the value of resources consumed to achieve it? (4). Decision makers may use this information to determine the interventions to add to their covered benefits package and the price this constellation of benefits will command in the marketplace.

While third-party payers can use pharmacoeconomics to guide coverage and reimbursement decisions, providers' and patients' perspectives about economic information are quite different. On the one hand, providers and patients must focus on appropriateness (using only what works best) and execution (doing well only what works best) (4). On the other hand, provider (and patient) concerns are influenced by the way they are compensated (or the way they pay). Under the traditional system of fee-for-service indemnification, charges are passed almost invisibly through a third party, creating little incentive to control costs. Managed care places providers at different levels of financial risk by making them and patients accountable for economic, clinical, as well as outcomes of care (3). Providers that have access to pharmacoeconomic data can limit their risk exposure, advance quality, and contain costs. Risk is shared

among insurer, provider and patient in many different ways, to varying extents, and with variable effect, depending on concomitant organizational characteristics (3).

Some argue that providers and patients should not use pharmacoeconomic data to make individual clinical decisions at the bedside (so-called "bedside rationing"). Rather, they believe that the proper role for use of pharmacoeconomic data by providers (and patients) is to facilitate their impact on formulary and guidelines committees. In other words, it is acceptable for providers and consumers to make recommendations about cost-effective practices for statistical populations of enrollees in specific clinical circumstances, but not individual patients, for whom they must do what is appropriate and best (within the rules and coverage policies of their organization).

Outside the United States, pharmaceutical companies use pharmacoeconomics to make registration and pricing decisions. In the United States, manufacturers use pharmacoeconomics to price products, to determine and market their value relative to other interventions, and to compete for spots on closed formularies. Manufacturers are incorporating pharmacoeconomic methods into their clinical trials to meet the information needs of these audiences.

Manufacturers are, appropriately, beginning to include pharmacoeconomics earlier in the research and development (R&D) process to facilitate "go/no-go" decisions in their research process. Modelling the necessary break-even pricing may help decision makers in manufacturing companies to determine whether to continue to invest in development of a new pharmaceutical, especially if it is not going to be a "breakthrough" agent. Therefore, one use of pharmacoeconomic data is to help determine whether to halt the development process if a pharmaceutical does not perform to economic or clinical expectations. (Indeed, the most common mistake made by pharmaceutical companies is not considering the economic performance of a new pharmaceutical early enough by performing rigorous economic analyses.) Finally, manufacturers are currently struggling with the best placement of pharmacoeconomic units within their companies, a decision that must be based on the culture and organization of each company. One factor preventing pharmaceutical manufacturers from fully integrating such analyses into their R&D process is the marketing paradox that exists in the United States. That is, whereas the market demands information on how pharmaceuticals behave in actual clinical practice, the FDA will not allow manufacturers to promote their product unless two well-controlled, clinical trials exist for economic data (similar to their requirements for clinical approval). The FDA continues to actively evaluate this requirement.

TYPES OF PHARMACOECONOMIC APPROACHES

Pharmacoeconomic analyses may contain (a) different types of costs and benefits (e.g., direct costs, indirect costs, and intangible costs); (b) different types of perspectives as discussed above; and (c) different types of analyses such as cost identification, cost benefit, and cost-effectiveness. In addition, the analyses must include discounting, sensitivity analyses, and a report of incremental as well as total and average results. These and other details of how to perform an economic analysis are discussed elsewhere in this book. However, since the three basic approaches to collecting pharmacoeconomic data—prospective trials, retrospective designs, and simulation models—have direct relevance to the way pharmacoeconomic data are used, we will explore the strengths and limitations of each briefly here.

Until recently, pharmacoeconomic studies generally were performed using retrospective approaches or simulations. In a retrospective approach, a pharmacoeconomic analysis uses clinical (and sometimes economic) data produced by one or more clinical trials. This approach requires various assumptions, which invariably leave the analysis open to criticism. Similarly, simulations depend almost entirely on assumptions. A simulation is a "what if" approach to the economic impact of a drug, often using the opinions of experts in a spreadsheet model.

Although these approaches have merits (e.g., simulation models will always be used for medical situations in which the outcome cannot be determined for many years after the intervention takes place), it is clear that the state-of-the-art pharmacoeconomic analysis is a prospective study, planned and executed concomitantly with the clinical evaluation of the pharmaceutical. Just as an economic analysis is only as strong as the underlying clinical research, prospectively collected economic data will always produce stronger science than other approaches.

One disadvantage of prospective trials, however, is that phase III studies often involve highly protocol-driven medical care, which does not reflect actual clinical practice because of the careful selection and follow-up of patients and the tests and procedures mandated to document safety and efficacy. Thus, when an economic analysis is done in conjunction with a Phase III trial, it is sometimes necessary to "adjust" the results to better reflect actual clinical practice. However, in Phase III-B or Phase IV studies, in which proving safety and efficacy is not an issue, the pharmacoeconomic evaluations are often performed in a fashion that reflects actual clinical practice much more closely.

Therefore, while it is generally useful to begin pharmacoeconomic evaluation of new pharmaceuticals early, in order to gain some idea of their economic and/or quality of life benefits (and to better plan subsequent "actual practice" studies), the most powerful pharmacoeconomic data generally comes from carefully designed Phase III-B or Phase IV studies.

Another consideration for users of pharmacoeconomic data is the need to avoid the use of intermediate outcomes, which may not reflect actual economic or quality of life outcomes accurately. For example, just because a new drug for multiple sclerosis may reduce plaques seen on magnetic resonance imaging (MRI), this may not translate into long-term improvements in quality of life. Conversely, even if

such a drug had a reduced relapse rate in the short term, longer-term follow-up might show higher relapse rates, worse quality of life, and hence, less impressive cost-effectiveness. Thus, the timing, patient population, duration, perspective, and power of the study to show a difference must be carefully considered by users of the data.

Current state-of-the-art pharmacoeconomic analyses are incremental prospective, "usual-care" cost-effectiveness studies that include all relevant direct medical costs and relevant end points. Comparators should be clinically relevant to managed care buyers and their markets (i.e., employers). Indirect costs and benefits generally are not valued in dollar terms but, rather, are counted as units unto themselves. (Leaving these units in non-dollar terms is what makes this approach a cost-effectiveness analysis, rather than a cost-benefit analysis, in which outcomes would be translated into dollar terms as well.) Hence, results are reported, for example, as incremental cost per quality-adjusted-year-of-life saved or quality-adjusted-day-of-work-loss avoided.

Any economic analysis will be better than no economic analysis in the future worldwide marketplace. That is, compounds introduced without an assessment of the pharmacoeconomic component will be assumed to have a negative such impact, since the development process will be assumed by purchasers to "weed out" those compounds with a negative pharmacoeconomic profile. Even if the economic analysis of a new drug shows only equivalence to comparators, then, at least, manufacturers will have a "foot in the door"—i.e., to offer a good drug along with other value-added services and/or product discounts. On the other hand, if the new agent proves to be cost-effective and/or cost saving, then its marketing would be greatly enhanced.

WHEN SHOULD PHARMACOECONOMIC ASSESSMENTS BE CONDUCTED?

Not all interventions require pharmacoeconomics evaluations. Figure 1 provides a useful matrix for assisting with this decision. In contrast to other industries in which technology tends to become less expensive with time, medical advances usually provide marginal improvement in outcome with an increase in cost. Incremental cost-effectiveness assessments should always be undertaken when net costs and benefits run in the same direction. Intervention with net negative costs (i.e., cost savings) and net positive effectiveness as compared with a baseline intervention should always be selected, and one should abandon interventions that have net positive costs but net negative effects (5).

Pharmacoeconomic assessments can be used to help ration—i.e., provide information on the equitable allocation of scarce resources. The decreasing marginal utility theory developed by the Austrian School of Economics in the late nineteenth century describes the idea of decreasing return for an additional unit increase in spending (6). This theory is also the fundamental construct underlying pharma-

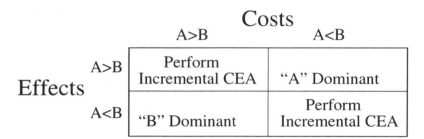

FIG. 1. Priority matrix for determining the need for pharmacoeconomic analysis of two competing products: A and B.

coeconomics—medical interventions must be assessed to determine their benefit or health effect as a function of cost.

In Figure 2, the part of the curve labeled A represents proven applications with demonstrated safety, efficacy, effectiveness, and efficiency, for example, immunizations and the treatment of common infections with antibiotics. Part B of the curve represents marginally less effective treatments, for example, bone marrow transplants for some cancers. Part C of the curve represents treatments that increase costs without affecting health, for example, using a third generation cephalosporin when a first generation one is more appropriate. Part D represents treatments that increase costs but decrease health care quality, for example, using antibiotics to treat viral infections (7). Treatments on parts C and D of the curve represent health care resources that are wasted on one patient and cannot be used to improve the health of another patient. In turn, these reductions in efficiency increase cost for society (8), without underlying improvements (and possibly even decrements) in quality of care.

How, then, can pharmacoeconomics be used to allocate resources to both effective and efficient interventions? Pharmacoeconomic assessments should be used to rank interventions in increasing order of cost to effectiveness. Funds can be expended on the most cost-effective treatments first,

going down the list of options until all funds are exhausted. Consider the hypothetical example represented in Table 1.

A provider organization is considering interventions A, B, C, and D for addition to its benefits package and must decide how to efficiently allocate its limited budget for new programs. Interventions A, B, and C are costly, but all have incremental benefit by producing increased expected quality-adjusted survival for the entire enrollment. Intervention D saves money but reduces quality-adjusted survival. If the plan has only $100,000 available for new interventions, how should it allocate these resources?

First, the health plan could exhaust its available funds by purchasing only A and B, providing 350 quality-adjusted life-years (QALYs) to the population. The additional purchase of D would save $20,000, but decreases total QALYs by 20, diminishing the net overall benefit to 330. Thus, the best option would be for the decision maker to "purchase" all four new interventions. The $20,000 saving from intervention D allows purchase of intervention C, increasing total QALYs by 30. By implementing all four new interventions (and not just A and B) benefits can be optimized (360 QALYs) for the entire population (9).

Users of pharmacoeconomic data must understand that the mathematical results of pharmacoeconomic calculations alone are insufficient to make allocation decisions. Instead, a decision maker's budget, intuition, the number and percentage of a population affected by a particular illness, and the timing of the intervention's effects must be considered with the average, incremental, and total cost results of pharmacoeconomic evaluations. In the aforementioned example, it would be inappropriate for a decision maker to buy intervention A (even though it has the highest cost-effectiveness) if no one in the decision maker's population was expected to contract the ailment treated by intervention A. Thus, users of the

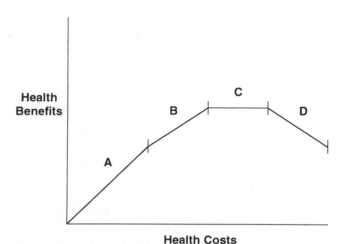

FIG. 2. Theory of decreasing marginal value as applied to health care.

TABLE 1. Incremental cost-effectiveness of four hypothetical interventions

Intervention	Incremental costs ($)	Incremental utility (QALY)	Incremental cost/ Incremental utility (cost per QALY)
A	50,000	250	$200
B	50,000	100	$500
C	20,000	30	$667
D	(20,000)	(20)	$1,000

pharmacoeconomic data must recognize that pharmacoeconomic analyses are a tool to assist decision making, rather than an answer unto themselves.

EXAMPLES OF PHARMACOECONOMICS IN CLINICAL CASE MANAGEMENT

Case management is the process of prospectively monitoring health care resource utilization, quality of care, and patient outcomes (10). It is standard in managed care. Pharmacoeconomics can assist case management by identifying optimal treatments. Until now, case management has relied on simple acquisition cost analyses. The unfortunate drawback of such an approach is that it sometimes leads to the use of lower priced interventions without consideration for long term costs and health effects.

For example, in any given year more than eight million cases of urinary tract infection (UTI) are reported in the United States. Most of these infections affect women between the ages of 15 and 45, resulting in direct medical care costs of $1 billion and countless days of lost work. Uncomplicated UTIs are treated in the ambulatory setting with oral antibiotics. If left untreated or if patients fail therapy, life-threatening and costly complications such as pyelonephritis (kidney infection) or sepsis (bloodstream infection) can occur. Table 2 presents a simple hypothetical cost analysis designed to determine the least expensive treatment for UTI.

Often Drug A is initially chosen over Drug B, because Drug A is one-half as expensive as Drug B. However, this analysis of acquisition costs is not a true cost-effectiveness analysis, which would transcend the acquisition price of the drug and assess the value of higher success rates, better compliance (due to shorter treatment duration and less frequent daily administration), decreased complication rates, enhanced worker productivity, and improved quality of life. These parameters can only be understood through a comprehensive economic analysis that considers *total* streams of costs and benefits.

For example, at 99%, Drug B has a better overall success rate than Drug A (88%), due to superior efficacy, better compliance, and fewer side effects such as vaginitis and skin rashes. Therefore, as shown in Figure 3, a comprehensive cost-benefit analysis, including all the long-term costs and benefits of each drug, shows that Drug B is a better

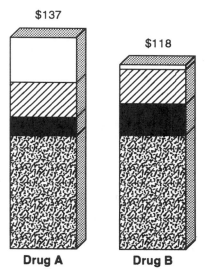

FIG. 3. More comprehensive hypothetical cost-benefit analysis of two drugs to treat urinary tract infection.

TOTAL COSTS ($)

	Drug A	Drug B
☐ Complications/Failures	30	3
▨ Laboratory	22	22
■ Medications	10	20
▨ Physicians	73	73
	$135	**$118**

buy than Drug A. Unfortunately, the short-sighted focus of American corporations on quarterly earnings, rather than long-term performance, often forces users of a pharmacoeconomic data to base their decisions on an analysis of acquisition costs (Fig. 2), rather than true pharmacoeconomic results (Fig. 3). A similar problem occurs when health system pharmacies are considered cost centers, rather than units that contribute to the entire health system budget. In this way, medicines that may increase the pharmacy budget but reduce the overall cost of care to the health system can be overlooked because pharmacy directors are focused on their own bottom line, rather than what is best for the health system as a whole.

A more comprehensive economic analysis might include the following considerations. Before treatment is initiated, most patients will seek medical attention in a doctor's office or an emergency room. Laboratory tests are then ordered (e.g., urinalysis, urine culture) and interpreted, followed by choice of either Drug A or B. The only difference in resource utilization for a typical patient thus far is the cost of medication dispensed.

Differences arise after the initial treatment period. Drug A fails to achieve a cure in 12% of patients, creating the

TABLE 2. *Simple hypothetical cost analysis of antibiotics used to treat urinary tract infection*

Drug	Cost/pill ($)	Dosing	Recommended duration of treatment (days)	Total cost of therapy ($)
A	0.25	qid	10	10
B	2.00	bid	5	20

need for additional physician visits, laboratory tests, and medications. Serious cases of failure may result in hospitalization for administration of intravenous antibiotics. Other complications and side effects result in additional treatment costs, extended absenteeism, and prolonged pain and suffering.

This simple example demonstrates that an investment of $10 in Drug B results in long-term net savings of $17 per patient. In addition, the benefits of Drug B's superior efficacy (higher success rate) and tolerability (lower complication rate) results in nonmonetary improvements in quality of life and reduced absenteeism. These nonmonetary improvements could be converted into monetary equivalents to further show the benefit of Drug B over Drug A (i.e., as a cost-benefit analysis), or they could be quantified and displayed as a cost per nonmonetary benefit achieved (e.g., cost per day-of-work-loss avoided) in a cost-effectiveness analysis.

Another simple hypothetical example compares pharmaceutical to nonpharmaceutical interventions. Consider the treatment of benign prostatic hypertrophy (BPH). In the United States more than 28 million men with BPH are receiving a variety of treatments, including surgery or medications, or both. The current "definitive" treatment is transurethral resection of the prostate (TURP), an invasive surgical procedure. More than 400,000 TURPs were performed in 1993 and, although highly effective in relieving the symptoms of bladder outlet obstruction, the procedure is associated with some morbidity and a low risk of mortality (11) (Fig. 4).

During the past few years, alternatives to TURP have been introduced, including less invasive transurethral surgical approaches using lasers or microwaves. In addition, noninvasive treatment with medication is becoming increasingly popular with and without surgical intervention. Finally, observation or "watchful waiting" is always a consideration.

TURP is an inpatient procedure requiring general anesthesia and a 3- to 5-day hospital stay. It is associated with some perioperative complications (e.g., infection and hemorrhage) that prolong hospitalization and increase costs. In addition, there may be postoperative complications such as incontinence and impotence, which incur additional costs and reduce patient's quality of life. TURP has proved 80% effective in relieving bladder outlet obstruction and achieving patient satisfaction.

Consider a hypothetical new noninvasive treatment (NNIT) performed in the outpatient setting without general anesthesia. It causes less perioperative and postoperative complications than occur with TURP. The procedure is, however, only 60% to 70% effective in relieving the symptoms of BPH. With additional treatments, symptom relief increases to 76%.

Whereas medicines are the least invasive treatment for BPH, they are also less effective than either of the surgical procedures. Thus, although the initial cost data reported in Figure 4 support the use of drugs as first-line treatment for BPH (drugs produce the most efficient outcome in the first

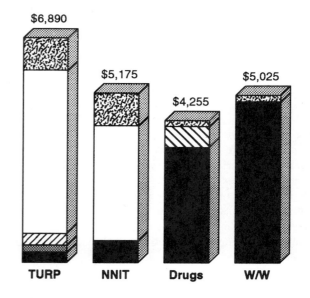

Service	TURP	NNIT	Drugs	W/W
Physician	$1,000	$1,000	$180	$200
Hospital/Clinic	5,000	3,500	0	0
Perioperative Complications	360	35	0	0
Postoperative Complications	210	0	0	0
Medications	0	0	630	0
Additional Treatments	320	640	3,445	4,825
Total	**$6,890**	**$5,175**	**$4,255**	**$5,025**

FIG. 4. Hypothetical cost identification of treatment for benign prostate hypertrophy.

year of treatment), this analysis omits two important aspects of treatment. First, it does not incorporate the health benefit of patient satisfaction, which is the primary end point of care. Second, whereas surgery is for most patients a definitive treatment, drugs require treatment for life. Figure 5 incorporates these issues into the hypothetical analysis.

When satisfaction is used as the determinant of effectiveness, rather than cost (see Sections III–IV, *this volume*), drugs are still less expensive than NNIT, but the overall measure of difference in value between the two interventions decreases substantially. Furthermore, when outcomes beyond 1 year are assessed, the hypothetical NNIT becomes more cost-effective. These examples highlight the importance of conducting pharmacoeconomic assessments that are comprehensive; they must include all relevant costs along

Treatment	Direct Costs	Satisfaction Initial	Satisfaction Year 1	Cost per Sat. Patient
– – TURP	$6,890	80%	88%	$7,830
--- NNIT	$5,175	70%	76%	$6,810
— Drugs	$4,255	50%	65%	$6,545
— W/W	$5,025	30%	62%	$8,105

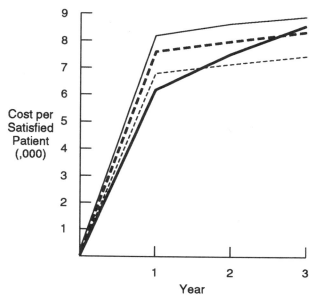

FIG. 5. Hypothetical cost-effectiveness analysis of benign prostate hypertrophy treatment.

an appropriate period of follow-up. (The difference between monetary and nonmonetary outcomes such as improvements in quality of life and functional status are discussed in detail elsewhere in Chapter 114.)

OTHER PRACTICAL APPLICATIONS OF PHARMACOECONOMICS

Users of pharmacoeconomic data may also apply this information in two other related areas: decision support and cost containment.

Decision Support

Practice Guidelines

Health planners in both the private and public sectors are becoming increasingly interested in the development of clinical practice guidelines, especially for the treatment of common diseases. Differences in certain medical care patterns across countries, regions, states, cities, groups, and individual providers, independent of factors that could account for this variability (e.g., severity of illness) are several-fold (12). Given this variability, specialty societies have spent considerable time and money bringing together consensus panels to summarize and disseminate practice guidelines, with the goal of reducing unnecessary and poor quality care. Unfortunately, to date, these guidelines have not included pharmacoeconomic data (13).

Practice guidelines represent an attempt to balance the processes and costs of medical interventions, improve quality and value, optimize efficiency, and reduce waste (12). Practice guidelines can facilitate economic analysis by assessing and measuring the output of the health care system (13). In turn, pharmacoeconomics can facilitate the development of practice guidelines by determining the types and quantity of resources utilized to achieve optimal outcomes of care. Thus, an effective practice guideline steers physicians and patients toward the treatment(s) most likely to yield the highest level of patient satisfaction for the least amount of resources expended, that is, to maximize value.

Step Protocols

Step protocols establish a rank order in which products may be used to treat a particular indication. Unlike practice guidelines, step protocols are usually involuntary. In most cases, the use of lower cost drugs is required for primary therapy (e.g., generic substitution). If these drugs fail or result in a treatment-limiting side effect, utilization of other more expensive products is allowed.

In the UTI example, pharmacoeconomic analysis could determine the drug most cost-effective for first line therapy. In this assessment, Drug B achieves the optimal clinical outcome up to a premium of $17 per patient.

Cost Containment

Provider Risk Sharing

In health care, financial risk sharing takes the form of capitated reimbursement and various other mechanisms through which providers are encouraged toward efficient care (14–17). In the capitation arrangement, the provider of a service or product receives a predetermined "prospective" amount of compensation to deliver a predetermined set of covered services. Reliable pharmacoeconomic data allows providers and insurers to include medicines in the capitated services, thus magnifying the incentive to prescribe drugs efficiently.

Beneficiary Cost Shifting

Similarly, costs can be shifted to beneficiaries to facilitate prudent buying on their part. Tiered co-pays are common, for example, co-pays for generic drugs generally are lower than copays for brand name medications. This arrangement still allows choice but steers consumers toward lower-cost medicines. Tiered co-pays also may be used to promote formulary use (versus prescribing drugs not on the formulary) and mail service, by decreasing co-pays for items obtained from these sources. Specific deductibles for drug benefits are another common form of beneficiary cost shifting. Pharmacoeconomic analysis can help determine the medicines to which beneficiaries should be steered to ensure appropriate and prudent utilization of resources.

Usage Restrictions

Usage restrictions exclude certain classes of drugs or specific products from coverage, limit coverage to specific diagnoses, and/or limit the duration of coverage for certain therapies. Limiting coverage to specific diagnoses helps control experimental or off-label uses of drugs or medical devices. Most frequently, limited coverage is enforced by subjecting off-label use of pharmaceuticals to pre-authorization programs, for example, wherein a pharmacist must call the physician to confirm the patient's diagnosis and prescription before dispensing the drug.

Pharmacoeconomic data can be used to influence usage restrictions. For example, until recently, drugs and devices used to prevent pregnancy generally had not been included in benefits packages. Moreover, recent advances, including hormonal implants and injections have proven to be both highly effective and costly. Nonetheless, contraceptive failure results in unplanned pregnancy with end points such as premature termination, term delivery, or preterm delivery. While preterm delivery is associated with the highest direct medical costs, by far, these outcomes all are associated with indirect expenditures and extreme intangible social costs. Quantifying the costs of unplanned pregnancy using economic analysis, even in ballpark terms demonstrates the value of preventing unplanned pregnancy. Such research then provides policy makers with incentives to lift restrictions on the utilization of these products, and in some cases encourage their use.

Cost Containment and Decision Support

Formularies

A formulary is a list of all drugs reimbursed under a pharmacy benefit plan. A formulary may be open or closed. An open formulary allows payment for drugs not formally listed. Open formularies offer incentives to use certain pharmaceuticals through physician education and differential co-payment. Patients deciding to accept a physician's suggestion of a nonformulary drug may pay an additional amount, either a fixed additional fee or a percentage of the drug's price. More importantly, use of nonclosed formulary drugs

usually results in full patient responsibility for the price of the agent at the pharmacy. Pharmacoeconomic assessments should serve as a basis for making formulary decisions.

Preferred Product Programs

Preferred product programs (PPP) are used to obtain rebates from manufacturers. Rebates are given in return for listing of a drug on the formulary and perhaps conferring preferential status over drugs within the same therapeutic class. Typically, rebates offered by manufacturers increase as utilization or market share of the contracted drug increases.

Pharmacoeconomics allows drug manufacturers to quantify the value of their products and determine what price the market will bear. In this case, the "market" is access to the PPP list. Pharmacoeconomic data allow manufacturers to negotiate higher prices (or build anticipated rebates into their prices) and providers to negotiate lower ones.

CONCLUSIONS

There are myriad ways in which health decision makers—insurers, regulators, manufacturers, providers, and patients—can use pharmacoeconomic data to improve the efficient allocation of health care resources. As society attempts to catch up with the successes of its research and development and technology infrastructure, new scientific approaches such as pharmacoeconomics must be used to help rationalize the allocation of our scarce resources.

Pharmacoeconomics is a new science continually being improved and refined by those who produce the data and those who use it. Nonetheless, it will always remain a decision aid, not a tool to make decisions by itself. Users of pharmacoeconomic data may implement it in clinical case management, as well as decision support and cost containment. The common challenge to all users is to design and implement pharmacoeconomic analyses that are comprehensive, timely, unbiased and focused on all the relevant cost and benefits from their perspective, whenever they occur (18).

REFERENCES

1. Toffler A. *Future shock.* New York. Random House, 1970.
2. Donabedian A. The quality of care: how can it be assessed? *JAMA* 1988;260:1743–1748.
3. Brown A. *Report on the evolution of health care.* Baltimore: Alex Brown and Sons, 1993.
4. Leveque J. Consumption-based taxation: an alternative approach to health care reform. *SGIM News* 1993;5(16):3.
5. Eisenberg JM. Clinical economics: a guide to the economic analysis of clinical practices. *JAMA* 1989;262:879–886.
6. Eatwell J, Milgate M, Newman P, eds. *The new pelgrave: a dictionary of economics.* Vol 3. Stockton Press, 1987:320–322.
7. Hochla PKO, Tuason VB. The pharmacy and therapeutics committee: cost containment considerations. *Arch Intern Med* 1992;152:1173–1175.

8. James BC. Improving quality can reduce costs. *AMA Qual Assur Rev* 1989;1(1):4.
9. Granata AV. Strengthening quality of care in the era of health reform: cost-utility optimization model to establish a framework for adjusting practice guideline recommendations. Master's thesis, University of Pennsylvania, 1994.
10. Cohen D. Introducing quality into cost-effectiveness. *Qual Assur Health Care* 1990;2:313–319.
11. *Medicare cost report.* (Data on file) Washington, DC: Health Care Financing Administration, 1992.
12. James B. Implementing clinical practice guidelines through clinical quality improvement. *Front Health Serv Manag* 1991;19(1):3–31.
13. Koepke M, Cronin C, Lazar A. How insurers, purchasers, and employers view their need for guidelines: report of Washington business group on Health-AHCPR focus groups. *Qual Rev Bull* 1992; :480–482.
14. Hillman AL. Financial incentives for physicians in HMOs: is there a conflict of interest? *N Engl J Med* 1987;317:1743–1748.
15. Hillman AL, Pauly MV, Kerstein J. How do financial incentives affect physicians' clinical decisions and the financial performance of health maintenance organizations? *N Engl J Med* 1989;321:86–92.
16. Hillman AL. Managing the physician: rules versus incentives. *Health Affairs* 1991;10:138–146.
17. Hillman AL, Welch WP, Pauly MV. Contractual arrangements between HMOs and primary care physicians: three-tiered HMOs and risk pools. *Med Care* 1992;30:136–148.
18. Hillman, et al. and The Task Force on Principles for Health Care Technology. Economic analysis of health care technology. A report on principles. *Ann Intern Med* 1995;122:60–69.

Quality of Life and Pharmacoeconomics in Clinical Trials, Second Edition, edited by B. Spilker.
Lippincott-Raven Publishers, Philadelphia © 1996.

CHAPTER 118

Use of Pharmacoeconomic Data by Regulatory Authorities

Paul P. Glasziou and Andrew S. Mitchell

INTRODUCTION

Governments worldwide have responded in a variety of ways to raising health care budgets. Some have attempted to limit a range of available services and therapeutic goods, some have tried to regulate the prices paid for these goods and services, and some have tried to increase competition. Pharmaceuticals, which already have very strict regulations in development and licensing, have been a particular target, not only because of their rising costs, but also because of the greater ease in their regulation. One state Medicaid program in the United States moved to limit the number of medications available per month. Others have tried to limit or eliminate drugs perceived as expensive.

Many of these restraints have been implemented solely on the basis of cost, without considering the consequent benefits. Given that resources will always be limited, a potentially better strategy is to consider the value for money of pharmaceuticals and medical procedures (1). Expensive pharmaceuticals or medical procedures that also provide large benefits and perhaps decreased downstream costs may provide a better use of health care expenditure than less expensive items with minimal benefit.This principle of selecting pharmaceuticals for subsidy on the basis of their value for money has been recently introduced in both Australia (1) and Canada (2).

This chapter examines the history, process, and content of the Australian *Guidelines* and also compares the Australian approach with developments elsewhere in the world.

DEVELOPMENT OF THE AUSTRALIAN GUIDELINES

The Pharmaceutical Benefits Scheme (PBS) in Australia provides access to many community prescribed drugs at the cost of a small copayment to the patient. This government subsidy accounts for more than 90% of total community prescription drug costs of more than $2 billion. Most marketed drugs do not obtain widespread use until they are listed under the PBS. The decision on which drugs to list is made by the Minister for Health acting on the recommendations made by the Pharmaceutical Benefits Advisory Committee (PBAC), which meets four times per year.

In late 1987, an amendment to the National Health Act of 1953 (which defines the operation of the PBS) required that the PBAC will consider, when recommending a drug to be subsidized, "the effectiveness and cost of therapy involving the use of the drug, preparation or class, including by comparing the effectiveness and cost of that therapy with that of alternative therapies." Since then, a number of changes in the listing process have been introduced to permit implementation of this policy (3). A report was commissioned to provide the general approach to, and rationale for, techniques for the economic analysis of pharmaceutical products (4). A specific set of draft *Guidelines* was released in August 1990; companies were encouraged to consider presenting an economic analysis in each submission to the

P. P. Glasziou: Department of Social and Preventive Medicine, Medical School, Herston, Qld 4006, Australia.

A. S. Mitchell: Pharmaceutical Evaluation Section, Canberra, ACT 2601, Australia.

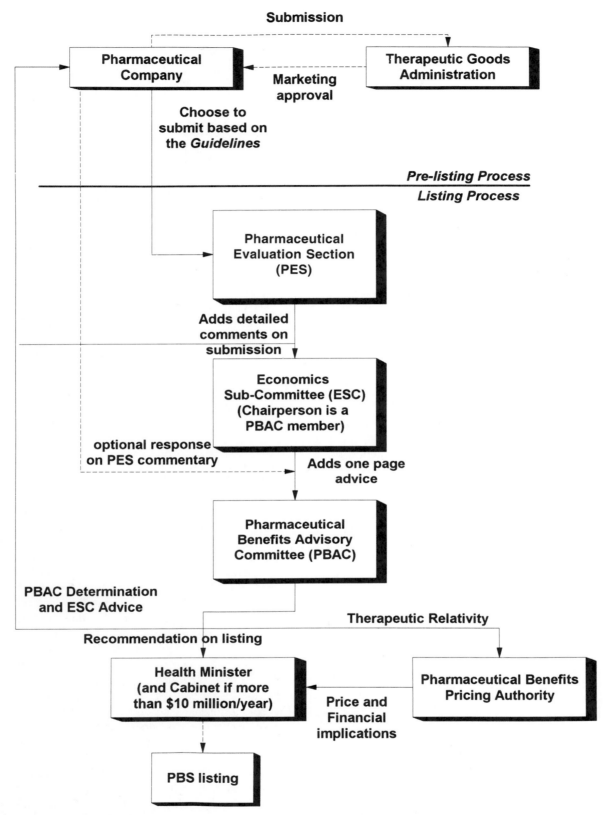

FIG. 1. Process for considering submissions for Pharmaceutical Benefits Scheme listing.

PBAC, but this was not mandatory. Over a period of 18 months, comments, criticism, and experience were gained with the draft *Guidelines* and they were subsequently redrafted (5). In parallel with this a *Manual of Resource Items and Their Associated Costs* (6) was developed to ease the burden on companies doing economic analyses. This provided appropriate costs to use for most pharmaceuticals and health services. As from January 1993, an economic analysis became mandatory for all new applications for listing of pharmaceutical products on the Schedule of Pharmaceutical Benefits.

Australian Listing Process

The process for considering a submission for PBS listing in Australia is illustrated in Figure 1. The Therapeutic Goods Administration is responsible for approving the marketing of a drug in Australia, including the particular indications, doses, and product information. Safety, efficacy, and quality are considered in making this decision. Having attained marketing approval, a company may now choose to apply to the PBAC for listing on the Pharmaceutical Benefits Scheme within the approved indications and doses. At this stage the *comparative* effectiveness, costs, and relative value for money become important.

Submissions for listing of new drugs or for substantial changes to current listings of current drugs (e.g., to add an indication or change a restriction) are made to the PBAC. These submissions must now provide information on both the medical aspects and the cost-effectiveness as detailed in the *Guidelines*. The submissions require data and analysis in seven areas: (a) pharmacologic data, (b) outcomes of therapy, (c) assessment of outcomes, (d) results of clinical

1. **Type of analysis:** *Data submissions should indicate at this stage the type of economic study that is being put forward. There are four main categories.*

   (a) cost-minimisation; (b) cost-effectiveness; (c) cost-utility; and (d) cost-benefit.

   Please state which type of study you have conducted.

2. **Population used in the economic analysis:** *What population have you used as a basis for the calculation of costs and outcomes?*

3. **Time horizons:** *What time horizons have you used in the calculations and why?*

4. **Quantification of outcomes over time:** *Quantify the outcomes of the alternative therapies described in Section 5 in the population described in Section 6.2 for the time period(s) in which they are expected to occur.*

5. **Direct medical costs:** *For the population described in Section 6.2, estimate the net direct medical costs involved in the alternative therapies in the time periods in which they are expected to occur.*

6. **Direct non-medical costs:** *Are there any changes in direct non-medical costs you think should be included in the analysis? If so, estimate these for each time period following the procedure outlined in Section 6.5.*

7. **Calculation of present value of net costs and outcomes:** *Please calculate the present value of net costs and outcomes.*

8. **Summary data:** *Please provide a cost per unit outcome of the proposed drug and alternative treatment regimen(s).*

9. **Marginal analyses:** *Where relevant please provide the marginal cost of achieving each additional unit of benefit with the proposed drug.*

10. **Sensitivity analyses:** *On what basis were the sensitivity analyses performed?*

FIG. 2. Data required for economic appraisal of submissions for new Pharmaceutical Benefits Scheme listings *(from Section 6 of the Guidelines).*

studies, (e) economic basis of the submission, (f) estimated use of the drug, and (g) financial implications to the PBS.

It is the task of the Pharmaceutical Evaluation Section (PES), which currently has a full-time staff of four evaluators, to first assess these submissions in detail. This involves checking the submissions for compliance with the *Guidelines,* accuracy of the calculations and the models and if necessary, completeness of the literature review. The PES then prepares a written commentary which is forwarded alongside the submission to the Economics Sub-Committee for expert and independent review. This committee consists of up to nine members with a specification that at least three members should have (a) experience and training in health economics, (b) experience in clinical trials analysis, meta-analysis and use of statistical models and decision analysis, and (c) membership of the PBAC. An observer from the Australian Pharmaceutical Manufacturers Association also attends the meeting, as part of a policy of transparency to industry.

The main brief of the Economics Sub-Committee is to review and interpret the economic analysis submitted, and advise on their quality, validity, and relevance. The committee meets four times per year, reviewing approximately 22 submissions. Concise advice is passed on to the parent committee, the PBAC, regarding the cost-effectiveness analysis. The PBAC uses this information when considering whether to recommend to the Health Minister that the listing should be made and, if so, for which indications and whether there should be any restrictions. The PBAC also advises the Pharmaceutical Benefits Pricing Authority (PBPA) on whether a therapeutic relativity exists between the new drug and other listed drugs. This therapeutic relativity extends beyond therapeutic equivalence (which, like other reference pricing systems, mandates that pricing equivalence be negotiated with the company) to include advice on therapeutic superiority (for which a price premium can be negotiated). If no therapeutic relativity can be set, the PBPA applies other criteria to the price negotiation (usually the costs of supply plus a profit margin).

When deciding whether to declare that the drug be listed on the PBS, the Health Minister considers the recommendations of the PBAC on the listing of each drug, the price negotiated following PBPA deliberations and the PBPA's estimate of the financial implications of the listing. If the financial implications are likely to exceed $10 million/year, the Cabinet is also consulted in the decision.

The entire process of PES assessment, Economics Sub-Committee review and PBAC consideration exists within a tight schedule. The PBAC (which also considers a large amount of other matters) clears its agenda at each meeting. The meetings are thirteen weeks apart (to accommodate four meetings each year) so, allowing for 2 weeks to process the results of the previous meeting, evaluation of submissions occurs over eleven weeks. This is broken down into 7 weeks for the PES commentaries, 1½ weeks for the Economics Sub-Committee members to review their agendas, 1½ weeks for the Sub-Committee advice to be prepared and ratified, and 1 week for PBAC members to review the Sub-Committee advice (having received their agendas 2 weeks earlier).

The introduction of the cost-effectiveness requirements and the move toward evidence-based decision making has had the effect of increasing the transparency of this process to the sponsor companies. Written feedback is now provided within 15 working days of the PBAC meeting on Economics Subcommittee advice and ratified PBAC deliberations. During 1995, companies will start to receive the PES commentaries and the PBAC Secretariat's submissions before the PBAC meeting with the opportunity to provide a brief response for PBAC consideration.

CONTENT OF THE GUIDELINES

The questions asked for the economic analysis by the *Guidelines* are presented in Figure 2. Three types of economic analyses are permitted: (a) cost-minimization, (b) cost-effectiveness, and (c) cost-utility analysis. Cost-benefit analyses are not encouraged.

Cost-minimization is used when the new drug is considered equivalent to one already listed, but for which the same or a lower price is sought. Clinical evidence of the dose equivalence is required to support such an application, but the economics thereafter are straightforward.

Cost-effectiveness is the most commonly used form of analysis. Here the new drug must demonstrate a clinical advantage. This clinical advantage then needs to be quantified in order to enable a judgment about whether the cost per unit outcome achieved is acceptable.

In a cost-utility analysis, the clinical advantage is expressed as quality-adjusted life-years (QALYs—a pseudo-utility) or as utility units. It is recognized that the techniques for doing this are currently extremely varied and no standard has been set. Very few such analyses have been submitted thus far, though several have submitted analyses reporting costs per life-year saved.

In estimating costs, the analysis should include not only the cost of the intervention and its comparison intervention, but also the other associated medical costs of use—other drugs, medical services, hospital services, diagnostic and investigational services, and community-based services—for both the new and comparison drugs. Direct nonmedical costs such as day care and physiotherapy may also be included. Indirect costs, that is, worker productivity losses due to illness, are more contentious. If these are to be included in an analysis, there must be a presentation of the results both with and without the indirect costs included. In addition, the standards of evidence for indirect costs are the same as those for any other study outcome, and thus there is a preference for a randomized trial evidence of changes in indirect costs.

EXPERIENCE WITH THE GUIDELINES

The first 2 years of experience with the *Guidelines* working in practice has been reasonably smooth. Both the Economics Sub-Committee and the PBAC have felt that the economic analyses have helped shed light on many of the listing decisions being made. As might be expected in such a unique venture, this experience has also uncovered several problem areas and the *Guidelines* are currently being revised. However, most of this revision will consist of clarifications and rearrangement, rather than a reworking of the basic principles, which have worked quite well in practice.

A total of 133 economic evaluations have been submitted for new drugs or to support requests to change current listings since the beginning of 1991. This includes 32 evaluations during the nonmandatory period of 1991 and 1992 (another 30 submissions for which an economic evaluation could have been provided were also received in these two years, so are not included in the total above). There was a slight increase to 35 evaluations during the first mandatory year of 1993, and an even bigger increase to 66 evaluations in 1994 (which reflects the processing of a backlog of marketing approvals for new drugs by the Therapeutic Goods Administration). Table 1 provides a breakdown of the type of analysis submitted.

The following sections describe some of the more important problems that have been encountered either by companies preparing submissions or by the Economics Sub-Committee reviewing submissions.

1. *Choice of Comparator:* Cost-effectiveness looks at the incremental advantage of a new therapy, and hence the choice of comparison therapy is vital. The *Guidelines* state that it should be ''the therapy which most prescribers would replace in practice.'' The therapy may be a nondrug therapy. The choice clearly requires some judgment about what is going to happen after the listing is made. This is usually based on data concerning current usage of the potential comparators, as well as some expert judgment. A particular problem here is whether a new, but advantageous, member of an established class of drugs will replace other members of the same class or a different class, e.g., will a better alpha-1 blocker for hypertension replace other alpha-1 blockers or ACE inhibitors? Current practice is to consider that usu-

ally new class members, if adopted, will replace older class members.

There are alternative choices of comparator, such as, the cheapest alternative therapy, the most effective therapy, the most cost-effective therapy, or no therapy (which would give the average rather than the incremental cost-effectiveness). The *Guidelines* choice is recognized as being a moving target, in that prescribing practice can change rapidly. However, all alternatives are subject to this problem. From a theoretical standpoint, none of these alternatives will always be ''correct.'' However, the *Guidelines* choice is a reasonable and pragmatic solution to this problem.

Finally, the process has highlighted the need for comparative, rather than placebo-controlled, trials when there is an established therapy. Without this, judgments about the comparative clinical effects and costs are difficult. The only alternative is to compare the size of effect seen in placebo controlled trials of the two competing agents. However, such indirect comparisons are problematic because of differing populations, measures, study design, and other factors, and head-to-head comparisons are preferable when available. It has been suggested that such governmental support of such trials is often more cost-effective than reliance on the indirect evidence (7).

2. *Levels of Evidence:* The *Guidelines* suggest that, if clinical trial evidence is available, it is to be preferred. An appendix provides an explicit hierarchy of levels of evidence: from randomized controlled trials (highest) to expert opinion (lowest). Within each of these categories, some guidance is given on quality, such as a preference for the use of intention-to-treat for clinical trials, and the use of more than one expert opinion.

As trials are rarely conducted with a cost-effective analysis in mind, most economic analyses will usually need to put together several pieces of data into an overall economic model. Many of the criticisms of the submissions to date have been because of flawed evidence used for a vital component of the economic model. For example, claims might be made in reduction of outpatient utilization because of diminished severity of disease, but estimates are based on expert opinion, rather than on results seen within a randomized trial. If the overall cost-effectiveness is highly sensitive to the precise value of this shaky estimate, this raises concern over the true cost-effectiveness.

3. *Meta-analysis:* A related issue is the identification, choice, and synthesis of appropriate pieces of information used in the economic model. It would be desirable to apply here the standard methods of meta-analysis be applied here: all the potentially relevant studies are identified, and the best quality is then used. If there are several good-quality studies, it would be appropriate to meta-analyze these. However, standard methods do not currently exist for incorporating meta-analytic results into a cost-effectiveness analysis, although some preliminary guidelines have been given (8). A number of technical issues in relation to combining esti-

TABLE 1. *Types of economic analysis submitted to the PBAC*

Type of analysis	N	%
Cost-minimization	37	28
Cost-effectiveness	59	44
Cost-utility	2	2
Qualitative	34	26

mates of effect have also arisen and are being incorporated into the revision of the *Guidelines* (e.g., the choice of fixed effects or random effects models).

4. *Estimating the Size of the Benefit:* Clinical trials currently emphasize tests of statistical significance and estimation of the *relative* effect (relative risk, relative hazard ratio, proportional reduction), whereas an absolute benefit is required for the economic analysis. This requires a definition of a patient oriented outcome or set of clinically meaningful outcomes and a calculation of the absolute difference in these attributable to the new therapy. This often raises difficulties for companies trying to translate the results of Phase III trials conducted for other reasons into an estimate of the size of the benefit. Even when this can be achieved, there is still the problem of interpreting the results. What is the social value of a 5% improvement in lung function, of preventing one fit per year, or of a night's sleep undisturbed by asthma? Most studies have not included quality of life data, and, as stated earlier, few analyses are presented as cost-utility analyses. Nevertheless, some value assessment must be made.

5. *Cost-Effectiveness Threshold:* Whereas the *Guidelines* encourage the use of a cost-utility analysis, no threshold has been stated. Laupacis et al. (9) and an early version of the Ontario Guidelines suggested that less than $20,000 per QALY was acceptable, and $20,000 to $100,000 per QALY was a "gray zone." However, these limits have been dropped. Thus while Australian decisions have been informed by the cost per QALY, no particular threshold has been stated. However, with time and the accumulation of reject/accept decisions, companies may begin to infer a (nonexistent) threshold.

Developments in Other Countries

The province of Ontario in Canada is the only other jurisdiction currently requiring and using cost-effectiveness analysis for pharmaceutical listing decisions (2). The two sets of guidelines are more similar than they are different: both involve a detailed prescription for a clearly documented incremental cost-effectiveness analysis from a societal per-

spective, preferably based on controlled trial evidence. One procedural difference is that the Australian process occurs in two stages (ESC and PBAC), whereas Ontario uses a single committee. Some other differences are listed in Table 2.

Many European countries already encourage, but do not require, submission of economic analyses when pricing is considered (10). However, the lack of a national formulary means that most countries could not easily implement something similar to the Australian system. However, this can and has occurred at the level of hospital and insurance plans. In the United States, cost-effectiveness analyses are used by some HMOs and sporadically by other large health insurance companies, such as Blue Cross–Blue Shield.

CONCLUSIONS

The Australian approach has been a ground-breaking experiment in which many governmental agencies have shown interest. However, it has posed a number of difficulties for both companies and government, including the need to refine the *Guidelines* and the costs to both parties of supplying and appraising the economic information. In this context, it is interesting to compare this with the process in Oregon (11), which has attempted a "revolutionary" approach to using information on cost-effectiveness for all aspects of medical care. By contrast, the Australian approach has been limited (to pharmaceuticals) and is evolutionary, in that attention is focused primarily on new listings or alterations to listings. This has made the process both politically acceptable and logistically feasible.

REFERENCES

1. Henry D. Economic analysis as an aid to subsidisation decisions: the development of Australian guidelines for pharmaceuticals. *PharmacoEconomics* 1992;1:54–67.
2. Province of Ontario. *Ontario guidelines for economic analysis of pharmaceutical products.* Toronto: Ontario Ministry of Health 1994: 1–15.
3. Aristides M, Mitchell A. Applying the Australian Guidelines for reimbursement of pharmaceuticals. *PharmacoEconomics* 1994;3:196–201.

TABLE 2. *Some differences between the Australian and Ontario guidelines*

Guideline	Australia	Ontario
Comparator	"Most likely to be replaced"	"Least expensive" and "most commonly used"
Viewpoint	Societal, with direct costs; indirect cost permitted in secondary analysis	Societal, with direct and indirect costs disaggregated
Utility/QALYs	Permitted	Strongly encouraged
Presentation	One of (a) cost-minimization, (b) cost-effectiveness, or (c) cost-utility	Staged presentation of (a) cost-comparison, (b) cost-consequence, (c) cost-effectiveness, (d) cost-utility, and (e) cost-benefit
Analysts	No specification	Declaration of source of funding and (preferably) description of contract

4. Commonwealth of Australia. *Background document on the use of economic analysis as a basis for inclusion of pharmaceutical products on the Pharmaceutical Benefits Scheme.* Canberra: Australian Government Publishing Service 1993:1–58.
5. Commonwealth of Australia. *Guidelines for the pharmaceutical industry on preparation of submissions to the Pharmaceutical Benefits Advisory Committee: including submissions involving economic analyses.* Canberra: Australian Government Publishing Service 1992:1–28.
6. Commonwealth of Australia. *Manual of resource items and their associated costs.* Canberra: Australian Government Publishing Service 1992:1–24.
7. Glasziou PP. Support for trials of promising medications through the Pharmaceutical Benefits Scheme. *Med J Aust* 1995;162:2–6.
8. Simes RJ, Glasziou PP. Meta-analysis and quality of evidence in the economic evaluation of drug trials. *PharmacoEconomics* 1992;1:282–292.
9. Laupacis A, Feeny D, Detsky AS, Tugwell PX. How attractive does a new technology have to be to warrant adoption and utilization? Tentative guidelines for using clinical and economic evaluation. *Can Med Assoc J* 1992;146:473–481.
10. Drummond M. Value-for-money assessments in Australia and beyond. *Spectrum* 1994;55-1–55-13.
11. Welch H, Larson E. Dealing with limited resources: the Oregon decision to curtail funding for organ transplantation. *N Engl J Med* 1988;319:171–173.

Quality of Life and Pharmacoeconomics in Clinical Trials, Second Edition, edited by B. Spilker.
Lippincott-Raven Publishers, Philadelphia © 1996.

CHAPTER 119

Use of Pharmacoeconomic Data by Pharmaceutical Companies

Brian Lovatt

INTRODUCTION

Pharmacoeconomic data are finding use not only within the pharmaceuticals industry, but as part of the industry's communication with its customers as well. Today, very few of the major pharmaceuticals companies operate without an established pharmacoeconomic internal unit or a dedicated team of people charged with the responsibility of undertaking or managing the economic evaluation of their new or established medicines. However, there is no uniformity in the approaches taken by these companies in the way they integrate health economics within their organizations or in their utilization of pharmacoeconomic data.

INTERNAL USE OF PHARMACOECONOMICS

It is difficult to generalize on the approaches companies are taking in this area because not all companies are at the same stage of competency; some companies are obviously becoming very experienced in the application of health economics, having successfully integrated pharmacoeconomics into their product development process. However, many more companies are carrying out health economic studies on an individual product or even on an individual clinical trial-by-trial basis. What is clear is that all these companies

B. Lovatt: Business Economics, The Wellcome Foundation Ltd., Beckenham, Kent BR3 3BS, England.

understand that economic evaluation is now becoming a critical part of the development of new medicines. The more experienced companies are also using health economics and business economics in an integrated way to maximize the return on the now significant investment required to take compounds through all the different stages of development to the market and beyond. Research and development costs are significant, according to some authorities, if you take into account the costs associated with failed programs the cost may be more than $350 million today for each new chemical entity.

Companies are therefore looking to experienced health economists to help ensure that they "customer focus" their development programs to ensure that they commercialize products from the time they enter economic evaluation, thereby positively influencing the time to market and the overall return during the life of the product. This will help generate the funds necessary for future research programs.

Many major companies have employed these specialist pharmaceuticals economists giving them a competitive advantage in the new environment.

The work they undertake can be divided into the following sections:

1. Selection of appropriate compounds for economic evaluation
2. Collection of appropriate data during the product's development for inclusion in pricing and reimbursement submissions

3. Provision of comparative assessments that are personalized for major customers
4. Continued pharmacoeconomic support of marketed medicines by evaluation versus new comparators or treatment alternatives, both drug and nondrug

Each of these areas of application is creating new challenges to the culture, management structure, and internal organization of research-based pharmaceuticals companies.

USE OF PHARMACOECONOMICS DURING EARLY DEVELOPMENT

One of the important goals of senior management in the industry at this time is to improve, as much as possible, the current attrition rate of products during development, along with ensuring that the compounds that do survive the ever increasing safety hurdles have an acceptable commercial profile. One critical way of ensuring success is to be certain that the new compounds satisfy "real" medical needs. To answer the questions of both the marketing and clinical teams, it is necessary to carry out sophisticated research within the purchaser, provider, and prescriber segments and directly with the patients. This research will address the relative value that each of these "customers" places on current therapies, the "in development" treatments (both drug and nondrug), and will assess such factors as commercial potential and market size.

SELECTION OF APPROPRIATE COMPOUNDS FOR DEVELOPMENT

To deliver one molecule to the marketplace, it may be necessary to screen up to 10,000 agents in the laboratory; even then, seven or eight out of ten new products will fail to return the capital invested. Improvement in the ratio of the number of compounds appropriate to move from the research to the development phase, or the development stage to the market, is therefore an important goal in ensuring the future success of the industry.

Pharmacoeconomic methodology adds value at the research stage or early development stage by profiling the disease along with appropriate patient segmentation and alternative uses of the molecule. A clear understanding of the target product profile can therefore be discussed with the clinicians, even during early research programs.

PHARMACOECONOMIC DATA CAPTURE AND ANALYSIS

The data sets that result from pharmacoeconomic research are both large and extremely complex, requiring both expert staff and fairly sophisticated computer systems to handle them. Without these resources it will be difficult to be confi-

dent that appropriate review of all the information can be undertaken, and that appropriate recommendations will be produced. When you consider that the research effort required in pharmacoeconomic studies may be spread across some six to eight countries, sometimes even more, the potential complexities multiply. The study may also cover two or more potential indications for the product, and review several competitive medicines, or treatments. It is not surprising therefore that considerable difficulties often exist in the collection of data. In almost all, if not all, projects it is this lack of data that has created the requirement to employ sophisticated computer programs. Indeed, these programs are (in addition to their operator's skill) acknowledged to be producing competitive advantage for their sponsors. It is worth noting that another major difficulty caused by this complexity is the time factor. It can take up to 6 to 8 months to complete the essential data capture, if all markets are running the data capture program in parallel. Analysis will take an additional 6 to 7 weeks. This time factor may not pose a problem if the company knows that it will be working in a particular therapeutic area.

When potential in-license candidates are being assessed, both the lack of data and the time required to carry out any external research produce extremely difficult issues.

HEALTH ECONOMICS AND DRUG DEVELOPMENT

Drug development has become considerably more complex over the past 15 years, requiring sophisticated project management. The increased complexity and extensive data capture burden necessary to satisfy current regulatory requirements has resulted in increased development times with associated increase in costs and reduction in the period of patent protection once the product is launched. Companies have responded to these issues in various ways, resulting in improved efficiency of the development process and reducing the time to launch. These initiatives are obviously valuable, but they should also incorporate the dimension of commercial viability.

Data sets that contain sufficient information on safety to obtain a license may not necessarily increase understanding of the *comparative* safety and efficacy relative to the treatment alternatives that the customers in the major market or markets see as important. Issues such as the indication, formulation, dosage, target patient population, and study comparators are all key determinants of the acceptance of a product once launched and can be changed sometimes. However, they also represent the key to determinants of a trial program's resource requirements and time. Balance is important and a pragmatic approach needs to be taken free of any of the understandable biases. The requirement in some markets is to have available objective data on the resource impact of new agents prior to launch, for the purpose of price setting (as in France) or for the purpose of agreeing on reimbursement (as in Australia). Because of the requirement in several major markets to submit a dossier that contains an economic evaluation either with, or shortly after, the submission of the regulatory package, this means that the data needs to be collected during the early regulatory phase.

USE OF PHARMACOECONOMIC DATA IN MARKETING

Molecules that are technologically elegant are no longer guaranteed success in the current cost-constrained marketplace. To ensure some success, a product profile must be capable of offering "visible" benefits, that is, benefits that are both clinically significant and perceived to be value for money. Agents that deliver this combination of "value in use" are now critical for commercial success. For some time now the payers or providers in some major markets have sought objective information on the resource impact of important new medicines, prior to listing them on formularies, agreeing on a premium price, or reimbursing them at an appropriate level. The industry is concerned because they have observed that some valuable products have suffered limited use due to a lack of data or to a shortage of appropriately experienced staff, at the purchaser's or provider's end. It is still not unusual to find that some of the larger health care providers are satisfied to make comparisons between the newer products and the older or established agents using the acquisition price alone, with some comparison of the safety and efficacy profiles. This type of evaluation in the absence of appropriate outcomes data cannot identify the most cost-effective alternative and therefore misleads. It is still common to find that, even in institutions that are aware of the value of pharmacoeconomics, they will still invest a great deal of time and money in the construction of comprehensive formularies utilizing simple comparisons of acquisition prices when comparative assessment of outcome are unavailable. Pharmacoeconomics, when employed during the development of medicines, permits objective assessments of all the costs and consequences that are likely to be seen when the product is used. This helps the company address the questions of price and positioning and helps ensure that the reviewers in various institutions take the total cost and benefits of the product into account. With limited resources and unlimited demand, health care providers need to demonstrate that they are maximizing care and, in the case of medicines, pharmacoeconomics has brought them the necessary tools. However, it is the pharmaceuticals industry that is investing significantly in pharmacoeconomic research for several obvious reasons.

Designing studies that can satisfy the needs of more than one or two of the key customers is often extremely difficult because of the design requirements when undertaking multi-

national regulatory trials. Disparate medical practice, both across and within countries, is very difficult to address in any multicountry study and can cause significant problems of interpretation of effect. This variability is normally controlled for in the protocol. However, if the customers need to understand the impact of the new treatment on their patient population any movement away from the customers' normal or usual care will potentially reduce the value of the study conclusion in guiding their decision making.

ADDRESSING THE NEEDS OF MAJOR CUSTOMERS

Within the early product development program it is becoming essential to ensure that your product will demonstrate value within the major customer's areas of focus when used for the target indication. Often it is the way that these different customers have reacted to the need to manage their health care costs, particularly the way they are controlling access to the drug budget, that will ultimately determine the manner in which companies can communicate the benefits of new agents. Therefore, it is important to monitor continuously the needs and organization of major customers. When carrying out a customer needs assessment, it should be acknowledged that the appropriate customers are often different for different treatments, and sometimes will be different from one health care setting to another.

PHARMACOECONOMIC GUIDELINES

Initiatives such as the Australian pharmaceutical benefits authority request for submission of an economic evaluation to support reimbursement. The Canadian (Ontario) guidelines for formulary listing and the UK guideline for the economic evaluation of medicines are all early examples of the regulation of pharmacoeconomics. However, many experts from within the industry have concerns based primarily on the lack of consistency among these guidelines, making it extremely difficult to design a multinational study. Other concerns focus on the lack of flexibility in methodological approach. All these guidelines clearly affect the volume and type of data needed from the population studied in any one market.

Prioritization is crucial. The trial design acceptable to each of the regulatory bodies needs to be reviewed, along with issues such as the choice of comparator and the proposed launch sequence. In the end, both the total number of customers and the data needs that can be addressed during any development program require assessment on the basis of the available time and resources. However, it may be possible to negotiate slightly different designs with the regulators, especially if good clinical practice may be adversely affected, or if ethical committees would object to or may not like the design of the data capture proposed.

THE NEED TO PLAN EARLY

Factors such as the time scale on dossier preparation for pricing and reimbursement need to be considered, especially as this can affect launch timing. All these issues point to the necessity for all companies to ensure that very early in the planning stages of a drug's development they undertake sufficient research to ensure that they accommodate the needs of major customers. Otherwise they risk delays in the reimbursement of their products or even the need to carry out additional clinical trials.

Pharmacoeconomic groups within companies can also contribute to the understanding of the current and future economic and social impact of diseases and their treatment. This information can help to better focus an important part of the research program.

CONCLUSIONS

Future success in pharmaceuticals research will require significantly more information than ever before. However, at this time both the quantity and quality of data available are often very limited. The only solution to improve success at this stage is to invite the researchers and experts representing the company's development, production, regulatory, marketing, and other units, to review each development candidate objectively, not only from the traditional producer perspective but, to take a clearly market oriented or customer-focused view. The pharmaceutical health economist is often best placed to represent the market's (customer's) needs in this type of forum. For this reason, it is no surprise to see that specialist health economic units within companies are now developing large data bases and can draw on knowledge gained from what is often considerable interaction with providers, payers, advisers, prescribers, and patient groups.

In the end, the decision to take a product into development will not be made on the above criteria alone; multiple factors need to be considered, e.g., technical and marketing capability, current development pipeline, future therapeutic focus, product base, portfolio fit, and a myriad of other factors.

Quality of Life and Pharmacoeconomics in Clinical Trials, Second Edition, edited by B. Spilker.
Lippincott-Raven Publishers, Philadelphia © 1996.

CHAPTER 120

Uses of Pharmacoeconomic Data by Policy Makers and Pharmaceutical Benefit Managers

Stephen W. Schondelmeyer

INTRODUCTION

Health care program managers are faced with achieving efficient use of limited resources to provide effective health care. Pharmacoeconomic data on pharmaceutical use may be quite useful to health care program managers. There are, however, many potential pitfalls in the use of such data. First, drug use must be understood within the context of the overall health care program framework. Definitions of terms and the units of analysis for tracking pharmaceutical use must be clearly known. Identifying reliable sources of pharmacoeconomic data and efficient information systems is important. The incentives for health care system management (e.g., competition versus regulation) will affect how allocations of limited resources are made. Cost-impact indicators should be carefully chosen and the cost impact on all parties affected (e.g., physicians, pharmacists, patients, hospitals, and pharmaceuticals companies) should be considered. Interventions in the health care delivery process can be targeted at many levels, but such interventions must be targeted at the source of a problem rather than at the symptoms. If the implications of pharmacoeconomic data are realized and appropriately acted on, the true value of drug therapy can be achieved. The real value of drug therapy is determined only by the degree to which a given patient's health care improves.

Health benefit program managers, whether in the public or in the private sector, have a difficult job. Although our health care needs and the therapies and technologies to meet them are expanding, we have limited resources as a society. Prioritization of how we spend our health care dollars will become increasingly necessary, and the use of pharmacoeconomic data will be an important part of the process by

S. W. Schondelmeyer: PRIME Institute, College of Pharmacy, University of Minnesota, Minneapolis, Minnesota 55455.

which we choose our priorities. Managers of health benefit programs can easily become myopic—focusing on managing budgets rather than on managing effective patient care. Health care benefit plans, however, will be judged by, and held accountable for, delivering appropriate health care outcomes, ensuring an acceptable quality of care, providing patient satisfaction, and ensuring efficient use of resources. Efficient resource use will become increasingly critical, that is, delivering the most health care outcomes with the limited resources available. Successful health care providers and producers (including pharmaceuticals manufacturers) will understand and facilitate efficient resource use.

Health Care Delivery Program Framework

Before describing the pitfalls in the use of pharmacoeconomic data, several basic principles important to the appropriate use of such data are described. First, one should examine the use of pharmaceuticals within the context of the broader health care program in which pharmaceuticals will be used. The health care program environment surrounding the use of pharmaceuticals must be understood before pharmacoeconomic data can be used. Particularly important is an understanding of the level of need for health care products and services and the amount of financial resources available to meet that need.

Any health care program can be viewed from the broad program framework shown in Figure 1. This framework may be briefly explained by describing how it applies to

pharmaceuticals. When a person has a health need and the financial resources (private or public) to pay for health care services, health care is sought. This need and the financial resources become inputs to the program, which are then used to pay for the services of physicians and pharmacists and for products such as prescription drugs. These personnel perform certain activities (i.e., physician diagnoses the problem; pharmacist dispenses the medication and counsels the patient on how to use the medication), which produces an output (physician visits, prescriptions). Ultimately, though, the effectiveness of the health program depends on the degree to which the outputs produce desired outcomes. An appropriate outcome is one that results in an improvement of the patient's health care status.

Total Drug Expenditures

A second consideration is understanding the sources of change in health care program expenditures. Total health care expenditures will be the sum of expenditures for all types of products and services that are covered, plus program administrative costs. Total expenditures may include the cost for hospital visits, physician visits, clinical laboratory procedures, emergency department visits, pharmaceuticals, and other health care services. For each type of product or service, such as pharmaceuticals, one can further break down the factors contributing to the expenditure level. The equation presented in Figure 2 indicates factors that will influence total drug expenditures in a health care program Table 1.

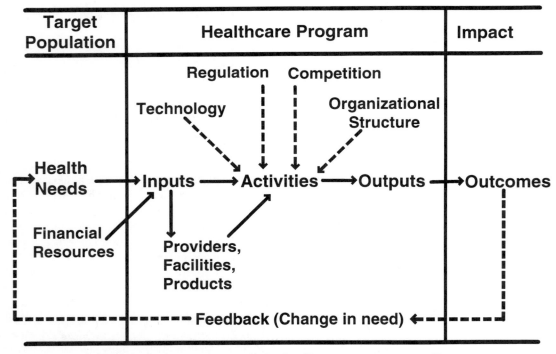

FIG. 1. Framework for examining health care program expenditures.

TABLE 1. *Factors that contribute to total drug expenditures*

Total drug expenditures =			
[population ×	intensity ×	efficiency] +	administrative costs
No. of persons covered	Prescriptions/person/year	Cost/prescription	Administrative programs

Type of persons
  Age and gender mix
  Income levels
  Disease types and
    incidence
	Days therapy/Rx
	Type of Rx
	Cost-sharing
	  (e.g., copay/Rx)
		Product price
		Inflation rate
		Pharmacy fee
			Electronic claims
			  processing
			Utilization review
			Formulary with P&T
			  committee

When attempting to manage total drug expenditures, it is important to determine the role of each of these factors and to target any cost management programs only at the source of the problem. Also, one should realize that changes in the drug expenditures may influence total health care expenditures, particularly if the drug therapy results in avoiding other, more costly health care services. Management of health care expenditures should not be done by a "line item budget mentality," but should result instead from an understanding of the factors influencing such expenditures and from an examination of the impact such changes will have on the health care outcome of program recipients. Proper program management should identify both the source, and effect, of expenditure changes, targeting any cost management solutions only at the source of the problem.

Definitions and Comparisons

It is critical to know the definition of terms being used and use only factors that are comparable and appropriate for the conclusion being made. This point can be illustrated by reviewing the role of drugs and health care in the broader society. In the United States, for example, the Health Care Financing Administration (HCFA) reports that drugs account for about 7.8% of the national health expenditures. This percentage is often quoted in the literature as representing the total expenditure on prescription drugs in the United States. Actually, the number reported as "drugs and other medical sundries" in the United States, and in many other countries, includes only outpatient medications—both prescription and over-the-counter—while pharmaceuticals used in hospitals, physicians' offices, other institutional settings, public health programs, and the military are accounted for in their respective portions of the national health expenditures. After accounting for pharmaceuticals from all settings, such medications account for nearly 10% of U.S. health expenditures.

Comparisons Among Countries

One can easily make mistakes when comparing national health expenditures across countries. Consider the hypothetical country, Country X, listed in Table 2 in comparison with the United States. Country X spends 12% of its national health expenditures on outpatient pharmaceuticals and, after accounting for pharmaceuticals in other settings, drugs represent 15% of national health expenditures. It would be tempting, but erroneous, to conclude from comparing these percentages (10% in the United States vs. 15% in Country X), that Country X spends more on pharmaceuticals than the United States. Why is this misleading? The United States could be spending more or Country X could be spending less on other health care services. To put this in proper perspective the expenditures on drugs can be viewed as a proportion of each nation's gross domestic product (GDP). National health expenditures represent 14% of the U.S. gross domestic product and pharmaceuticals, at 10% of national health expenditures, consume 1.4% of the gross domestic product. Therefore, the United States actually spends a larger share of its gross domestic product on pharmaceuticals than does Country X (1.4% vs. 0.9%).

Units of Analysis for Drug Use

Pharmacoeconomic studies of drug use require some means of operationalizing what one means by "drug use." First, one must decide which "drugs" are of interest, that is, those that are available on prescription only, those that

TABLE 2. *Drug and national health expenditures in relation to gross domestic product in the United States and theoretical country X*

Economic indicator[a]	United States (%)	Country X (%)
Outpatient drugs (% of NHE)	7.8	12.0
Drugs, all settings (% of NHE)	10.0	15.0
NHE expenditures (% of GDP)	14.0	6.0
Drugs, all settings (% of GDP)	1.4	0.9

[a]NHE, national health expenditures; GDP, gross domestic product.

are available over-the-counter, or both. Also, one must determine whether drugs in outpatient settings, inpatient settings, physicians' offices, other settings, or some combination of these settings, are of interest. In comparing drug utilization or expenditures across countries, differences in how drugs are classified (i.e., prescription or over-the-counter) must be considered.

Drug expenditures per capita are reported by most countries and are often compared across countries. Comparison of drug expenditures across countries needs to be adjusted to account for differences in currency or for differences in purchasing power parity across countries, depending on the objective of the comparison. Once these adjustments have been made and drug expenditures among countries are converted to equivalent units, one can determine which country spends the most per capita on drugs. As noted in Figure 2, "drug expenditures" are a function of several factors, including intensity (prescriptions/person/year) and efficiency (cost/prescription). In other words, expenditures are a function of both volume of use and price.

Suppose a comparison of two countries shows that one country spends twice as much as another country on outpatient prescription drugs. No conclusion can be drawn with respect to differences in drug use without adjusting for differences in drug price levels in the two countries. If the drug price levels in these two countries are found to be similar, it can be concluded that the utilization rate of the two countries differs by a factor of 2:1. However, if the drug price levels are found to be twice as high in the country with higher drug expenditures, it would have to be concluded that the actual drug utilization rate is similar, even though the drug expenditure rates differ substantially. The point is that a difference in drug expenditures is not an accurate indicator of differences in drug utilization, unless the differences in prices are considered.

Drug Utilization

Another concern in comparing drug utilization is the level in the drug use process at which one collects data on drug utilization. Drug utilization may be defined as—and data may be collected on—the number of medications prescribed, the number of prescriptions dispensed, or the number of medication units (e.g., tablets or capsules) actually consumed. These are all related, but not necessarily identical concepts. A person may be given a prescription by a physician, yet not have it filled, for a variety of reasons. The medical problem may have been resolved before the prescription was filled; the medication may have been too expensive and the patient could not afford it; or the patient may have thought that the medication was not effective or not needed. Medications may be dispensed and not actually used by the patient. The medical problem may have been resolved before the person actually used any, or all, of the medication; the medication may have been so expensive that

the patient decided to use only one-half as much as prescribed trying to stretch the medication; or the patient may have decided that the medication was not effective, not needed, or was causing an adverse effect. One should always know which level of drug use data has been collected and that comparisons of drug use are being made with data collected in a similar manner and at similar levels in the drug use process.

The unit of analysis employed to measure drug use is another point at which utilization data may be misinterpreted. Drug use may be measured in dosage units (e.g., tablets or capsules), weight (milligrams or kilograms), prescriptions, or days of therapy. While each of these units of analysis has appropriate uses, they may each be misused. Drug utilization of a population is usually expressed in number of prescriptions per person per time period (e.g., month or year), largely because medications are dispensed as prescriptions and are paid for under insurance schemes as prescriptions. Most computerized drug data bases use prescriptions as the principal unit of analysis. Prescriptions may not, however, give an accurate indication of differences in the level of drug use among patients. *Days of therapy*, if available, appears to be a more stable unit of measure than any of the other units of analysis for comparing drug use. A day of therapy is a common concept, regardless of the patient, drug, drug strength, disease, insurance scheme, or country. To illustrate how utilization levels will vary depending upon the 'unit of analysis' chosen, the drug use of four hypothetical patients is described in Table 3. Differences in drug utilization found by several alternative units of analysis will be compared with the difference in utilization represented by days of therapy/year. If we choose to compare units/year (I), patients Q, X, and Y used six times as many units/year (720 vs. 120) as patient Z, even though these patients used only three times as many days therapy/year (J, 360 vs. 120). Comparison based on weight of the drug's active ingredient per day (G) would suggest that patients Q and X used twice as many milligrams per day (300 mg vs. 150 mg) as patient Z and 7.5 times as many milligrams (300 mg vs. 40 mg) as patient Y. Prescriptions per year as the utilization measure indicates that patients Q and Y used three times as many prescriptions (H, 12 vs. 4) as patients X and Z. In terms of days therapy/year, however, patients Q, X, and Y each used the same number of days therapy/year (360 days), and patient Z used only one-third as many days therapy/year (120 days). Interestingly, patients Q and X used the same number of days therapy/year (360 days), even though patient Q used three times as many prescriptions (12 vs. 4).

With these basic principles outlined, common pitfalls related to the use of pharmacoeconomic data by drug therapy decision makers are reviewed in the remainder of this chapter. The topics addressed include

(1) Information sources and systems
(2) Incentives to use pharmacoeconomic data
(3) Indicators of pharmacoeconomic effect
(4) Interventions based on pharmacoeconomic findings

TABLE 3. *Various units of analysis for measuring the drug utilization of four hypothetical patients*

A	B	C	D	E	F	G	H	I	J
Patient	Drug	mg/unit	Units/days	Days/ prescription	Units/ prescription (D × E)	mg/day (C × D)	Prescriptions/ yr (360/F)	Units/yr (F × H)	Days therapy/yr (E × H)
Q	Zantac	150	2	30	60	300	12	720	360
X	Zantac	150	2	90	180	300	4	720	360
Y	Pepcid	20	2	30	60	40	12	720	360
Z	Zantac	150	1	30	30	150	4	120	120

(5) Implications for appropriate use of pharmacoeconomic data

INFORMATION SOURCES AND SYSTEMS

Pharmacoeconomic data can come from a variety of sources, such as clinical trials, medical records audits, claims payment data bases, or specifically designed pharmacoeconomic studies. These data sources vary widely in quality and in terms of comprehensiveness with respect to types of data one may need for a pharmacoeconomic study. Claims data bases usually offer computerized access to retrospective data from large groups of patients. Although these data bases may be useful in conducting pharmacoeconomic studies, the data bases have a number of limitations, including lack of clinical indicators and outcomes, other data inadequacies, inability to integrate drug data with other data bases, and limitations on data access and use.

Claims Versus Clinical Data Bases

Claims data bases often do not include diagnosis, let alone clinical information such as the blood pressure of a hypertensive or the blood glucose of a diabetic. To compensate for this shortcoming, some have used the medications one is taking as an implicit indicator of the patient's diagnosis. For certain drug therapies, this may be straightforward (e.g., insulin use usually implies that one is a diabetic) but, for other drug therapies this is difficult, if not impossible. What diagnosis would one assign to a patient taking a β-blocker or a diuretic? On the other hand, clinical records are not always accurate or complete either, and they are not often computerized. Evaluations of physicians' records have shown that prescribed drugs are not always listed and, when they are, the information is often incomplete. The medical record may mention the drug name, but not have the strength, dosage form, directions, or duration of therapy.

Data Inadequacies

Claims data bases may be inadequate for other reasons. For example, an attempt to determine all drugs received by a given patient may be hampered by the fact that they may not be in the claims data base. Typically, the claims data base will only have those prescriptions that were paid for by the health care program. Prescription drugs not covered by the program, such as those that cost less than the program's copay amount (e.g., $5.00), those that are not on the formulary or drug list, and those that are nonprescription medications, may not be in the data base. These inadequacies must be accounted for when conducting pharmacoeconomic studies. Also, if one wants to know which drugs are actually being used by a given patient, the claims data base cannot usually answer that question. The claims data base can indicate which drugs were dispensed to a given patient, but whether the patient used the medication and how he or she used it cannot be determined from the claims payment record.

Data Integration

Data bases from health care programs have other limitations. Prescription claims data bases are among the largest data bases that a health care program has to manage, since prescriptions account for one-third to one-half of all health-related claims in most programs. Typically, health care programs have their medical and hospital claims records on one system, administering their prescription program in a totally separate claims-processing system. Few programs can link the prescription data with other patient or health-related data. Even if such a link can theoretically be made, it is no easy task for most health care programs to get the data processing staff, and the computer access time, to match up prescription and other health care records. In the future, these integrated data bases will become increasingly important.

Data Access and Analysis

A health care program has certain confidentiality obligations with respect to patient-specific data. For a pharmaceuticals company to use such a data base, the data must be blinded as to patient-specific identifiers, or the research must be done by the health care program or academic researchers. Claims data bases of health care programs have considerable value for managing the health benefit and for producers, such as pharmaceuticals manufacturers, selling products to the program. Managers of health care programs who learn to integrate their health-related data bases and to use them to manage the care of their patients effectively will be able to use their resources more efficiently.

INCENTIVES

What incentive do various organizations have to look at pharmacoeconomic data? Managers of health care systems may use pharmacoeconomic data to help them make decisions consistent with their institution's overall purpose. In the United States, most of health care systems are privately run by companies that have to deliver a profit to their shareholders. Therefore, the incentive for being in business and the factors that will drive their drug therapy decisions will be a combination of: profit, patient care, and efficient use of resources. Health care companies in the United States are not necessarily out to line their pockets with money, but in some cases there are conflicting interests among profits, efficient resource use, and effective patient care. Other health care delivery organizations may be nonprofit (public or private) institutions that do not have the same stockholder and profit motives. Effectiveness of either type of organization, for-profit or not-for-profit, will be greatly influenced by the degree of competition and regulation in the market, short-term versus long-term considerations, and the means for allocating limited resources.

Competition Versus Regulation

Competition holds that a fair and equitable price for products and services will be achieved in the marketplace. This approach assumes that many sellers will compete for the business of many buyers when the buyers have complete information on price and quality. Also assumed is that sellers have low barriers to entry and that the products or services are interchangeable or have close substitutes readily available. When these conditions are not met, competition does not work normally. Often regulation is implemented to correct for the market anomalies or distortions. Regulation may be used to improve either the equity (distribution of rights) or efficiency (distribution of resources) within a society. The market for pharmaceuticals will probably never be a truly competitive market, because the ultimate result of buyer dissatisfaction is the decision not to buy the product. This decision is very different for necessity items such as pharmaceuticals in comparison with normal commodities such as a color television. Suppose you were in the market for a color television and had picked one out to buy, but before you got back to the store to make the purchase the price went up 25%. As a consumer you would have several alternatives: (1) buy a different, lower-cost brand of color television; (2) decide that the color television is still worth the price even after the 25% increase; or (3) decide that the price is too high and express your dissatisfaction by deciding not to buy the color television. Now, imagine that you are a well-maintained epileptic patient and that the drug company raises the price of your medication 25% in 1 year (as one company recently did). As the patient, you do not have the opportunity to buy a different, lower-cost brand of medication (unless generic substitution is allowed) for this particular drug). You may decide that the medication is still worth the price, but you may not have enough money to pay for the medication. Even if you decided that the drug price is too high and that it is not worth the higher price, it would not be rational for you to stop taking the medication as an expression of price dissatisfaction. Life without a color television is a very different choice from life without epileptic medication.

Most European countries have health care, including pharmaceuticals; this is guaranteed for the majority of their citizens. Governments subsidize the cost of health care, which serves to distort the normal competitive market because the patient does not have to pay the full cost of health care. The patient delegates decision making to health care providers, and the health care providers are not usually held responsible for the cost of that health care. These conditions may lead to excessive prices and to overutilization, resulting in increased drug expenditure. In exchange for this broad-based government-subsidized health care, European governments have imposed regulation on their health care and pharmaceuticals markets. The governments of nearly all industrialized nations, except the United States, regulate some combination of price, profits, and utilization of pharmaceuticals. Regulatory mechanisms have been used to correct the market's inefficiency and to make the market function more like a competitive market. Governments should search for the minimum amount of regulation necessary to correct the market distortions and then let the market function.

Short- Versus Long-Term Considerations

The use of pharmacoeconomic data by decision makers to determine whether a given pharmaceutical will be covered may lead to different decisions, depending on whether one takes a short-term or a long-term view of the impact. The drug coverage decisions of health maintenance organizations (HMOs) in the United States provide an example of this pitfall. Most health maintenance organizations have found that their patient population moves away or changes health plans every $2\frac{1}{2}$ to 3 years. As some patients leave the plan, other new patients may enter the plan. When faced with deciding whether the HMO will cover a drug therapy that has a long-term, chronic impact (i.e., cholesterol-lowering agents), the HMO managers may decide not to cover these drugs because they know that many of their patients will leave their system before the drug's effect would be fully realized. Who's interest is being served by this decision? Drug companies with therapies that have a long-term impact (greater than 2 to 3 years) may be at a disadvantage when marketing to HMOs that have a short-sighted view of the long-term effects of drug therapy.

Affordability Equals Accessibility

In health care systems in which the government does not guarantee a minimum level of access to health care services, the lack of affordability of products and services becomes a barrier to access. This is the case in the United States, where more than 30 million people do not have health insurance, yet their income is too high to qualify them for the indigent care program known as Medicaid. Affordability is a concept that is a measure of a person's ability to pay for something in relation to the cost of that product for that person. This concept is influenced by the resources available to an individual, by the level of need for health care products or services, by the level of need for other products and services (i.e., housing, food, utilities), and by the price of all products and services needed.

Assessing affordability does not necessarily require a judgment about the appropriateness of the price for a given product, although that question is often raised when a product becomes unaffordable to many. Pharmacoeconomic studies may indicate when a drug product is unaffordable by a significant number of persons in a society. Such a finding does not necessarily mean that the drug product is overpriced. For similar reasons, one cannot conclude that a drug product is appropriately priced simply because most people can afford it. Affordability can be changed either by changes in the price of the drug or by providing coverage under private or public insurance schemes. Affordability then becomes framed within the context of ability of the insurance scheme to pay for needed products and services.

Cost-effectiveness Does Not Equal Affordability

Many people have the perception that any drug that can be shown to be cost-effective will automatically be covered by a health insurance scheme. Demonstration of cost-effectiveness for a drug therapy or other health care technology does not necessarily mean that the therapy or technology is affordable. First, almost any drug can be shown to be cost-effective compared to something. If nothing else, a drug will probably be cost-effective in comparison to placebo. Drug therapy decision makers expect cost-effectiveness comparisons for a new drug to be conducted against the leading drugs in a therapeutic category, rather than placebo or "old drug" A. Even if a new drug is shown to be cost-effective against the leading therapy in its category, it is not necessarily affordable.

One might argue that if a drug therapy is cost-effective, the payer—whether an individual or a health plan—cannot afford *not* to cover the drug therapy. This would be true if the payer did not have any resource constraints. Most

payers—whether individuals, private health plans, or government health plans—do not have unlimited resources, however. Therefore, the demonstration of cost-effectiveness does not necessarily ensure that drug therapy is affordable or that it will be paid for or covered.

An illustration of this principle can be drawn from the automobile industry. The Mercedes automobile has been demonstrated to be one of the most cost-effective auto purchases one can make in the United States. Because of the high resale value of a Mercedes over time, this car appears to be a wise investment. If this is true, why don't more Americans drive a Mercedes? Not necessarily because they have made a more cost-effective automobile purchase, but because many Americans have limited resources that do not permit them to make such a purchase, even if they wanted to do so. In the same way, both individuals and health plans have limited resources to spend on health care. These purchasers will consider cost-effectiveness studies in prioritizing their purchases, but they are sure to run out of resources before they run out of cost-effective drugs and technologies that could be purchased. Not all cost-effective drugs and technologies are affordable, because of limited resources.

Allocation of Limited Resources

Both society and the individuals within a society have limited resources. How will these limited resources be allocated within the health care system? The ideal situation would be a health care system that allows us to maximize benefits to the individual and at the same time to maximize benefits to society. Sometimes these two goals work together, but many times they do not. Access to pharmaceuticals will be affected by the criteria used to make decisions about allocating resources. Numerous allocation rules could be used:

Ability to pay
First come first served or sequential (until resources run out)
Equal access
Equal care for equal need
Equal expenditures or resource use
Patient want or preference or need
Maximum benefit for those with minimum resources
Maximize benefit to society
Maximize benefit to the individual

None of the above allocation rules is necessarily the one correct method. The appropriateness of an allocation rule will depend on the society and its cultural values. Allocation rules may also vary by type of health care decision; that is, life-threatening drug therapies may be allocated by a different method than symptomatic drug therapies. Most health care systems use a combination of allocation rules. Certainly, although all health care systems ration resources, but the allocation of resources in most systems is rather implicit and rarely talked about. As a society we must become much more explicit about how we allocate limited health care resources. The decision-making processes of health care systems, in general, and of individual health care providers must become much more transparent to all parties involved, including patient, provider, and payer. We must gain a better understanding of the nature and extent of conflicts that arise in this allocation process. Our health care systems must also become much more explicit about how these conflicts will be resolved. This problem will become even more acute as the level of health care need continues to grow, while individual and societal resources remain limited.

INDICATORS

Pharmacoeconomic studies typically use some form of cost indicator as a means to compare drug therapies. First, several common cost impact indicators are discussed. Next, their role in drug therapy decision making is described. Cost impact can be examined from many perspectives, so one must determine "cost impact for whom?"

Cost-Impact Indicators

A number of cost-impact indicators have been used to evaluate differences among alternative drug therapies. Common cost-impact indicators include cost acquisition, cost efficiency, and cost-effectiveness indicators (Fig. 2). These indicators can be described by making reference to the health care program framework. Cost acquisition indicators measure cost per input (i.e., cost per tablet or cost per capsule). Cost efficiency indicators are cost per output (i.e., cost per prescription). The third indicator is cost-effectiveness, which is determined by measuring the cost per outcome. For example, the cost-effectiveness of a drug for an acute illness would be the cost per resolved episode. For a chronic illness, the cost-effectiveness would be cost per year for properly maintained disease.

Cost per input is rarely a good economic indicator for comparing drug therapy. Use of this indicator should be limited to comparisons of generic substitutes shown to have equivalent bioavailability. Similarly, cost per output can easily be misleading. Paying the lowest possible cost for prescription dispensing can result in favoring pharmacists with increased workloads who do not take time to counsel their patients or to carefully review prescription orders. One U.S. study showed that about 1.9% of all outpatient prescriptions would have caused significant harm to the patient if the pharmacist had not intervened and contacted the physician for a change in the prescription. Pharmacists that filled higher numbers of prescriptions per hour found a smaller proportion of problems. In other words, paying too little as a dispensing fee to pharmacists may result in harm to patients and in increasing other health care costs.

Cost per outcome (i.e., cost-effectiveness) is one of the most useful cost impact indicators. The question to be answered here is: How much does it cost for all related health

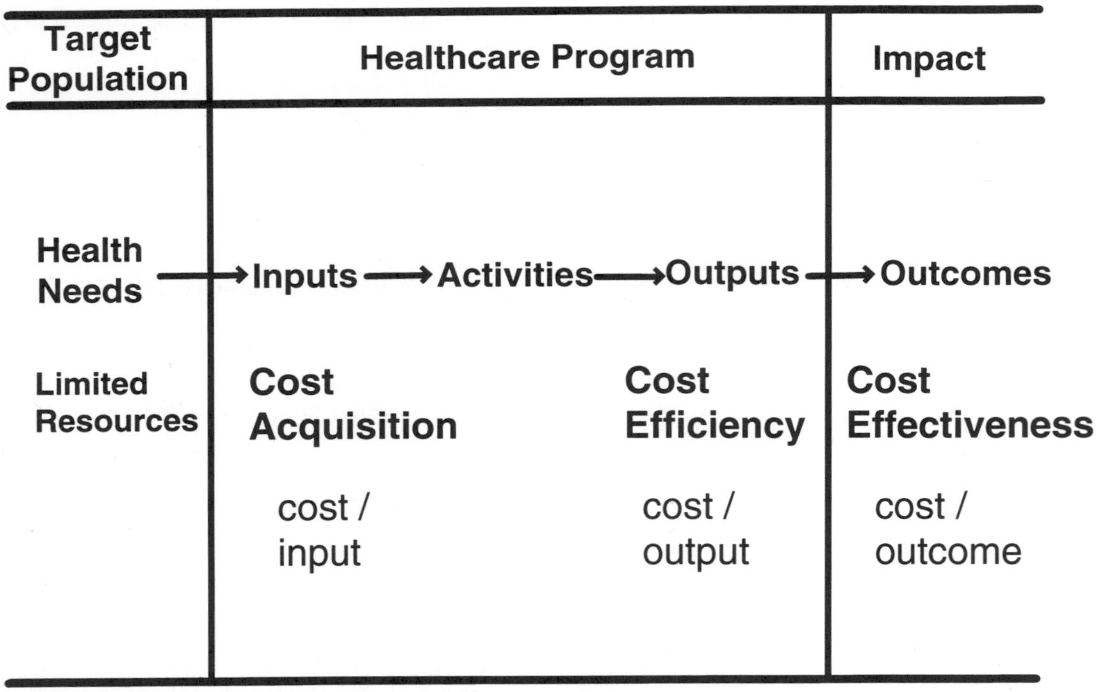

FIG. 2. Cost-impact indicators within the health care program framework.

care services to improve the patient's health care outcome? This indicator involves comparing drug therapies on the basis of the total cost of care per outcome over an appropriate period. For acute diseases, this may be a few days to a month, while for chronic diseases this may be several months to a year, or even over a lifetime. Cost-benefit analysis is another type of cost impact study that reduces both the cost and the benefits to economic terms. Direct and indirect costs are usually included in cost-benefit studies.

Since most managed care organizations in the United States find it difficult to link their pharmacy data base with hospital and physician data bases, it is difficult for them to conduct cost-effectiveness studies using their computerized data bases. Many managed care organizations, however, realize the potential value of linking these data bases and they are building the linkages to accomplish a comprehensive data base system. Such a development has particular significance for pharmaceuticals companies, because it may inform the managed care organization more about the effectiveness and safety of a newly launched drug than is known by the drug company itself.

In the United States, a drug company will have experience with a few thousand patients at the time their drug is approved for marketing. Within 1 year after a drug is marketed, the large HMO systems (those with 1 to 15 million enrollees) in the United States may have actual clinical experience with the drug in tens of thousands, if not hundreds of thousands, of patients. The HMO can capture these extremely timely and valuable postmarketing surveillance data and use these data to compare the relative impact of new drug A versus new drug B or other leading drugs on the market. Today, most comparative studies among drugs done for the regulatory agencies are new drug A versus placebo or versus the "old dog" original product in the therapeutic class. Whereas these regulatory comparisons are of some use, the ability of managed care organizations to compare the leading drugs in a therapeutic class, using their own patients and data base systems, will ultimately have far more influence on their decision making.

Role of Pharmacoeconomic Studies

Pharmacoeconomic studies must not be used simply as a marketing ploy. If a company uses cost-effectiveness claims or other pharmacoeconomic claims in medical communications, it is essential that quality control studies be conducted to back up any such claims. Quality control studies are those conducted by credible researchers using well-documented methods. If companies do not do this, they run the risk of tarnishing the value of cost-impact studies in the eyes of decision makers. Cost-impact studies will need to be adapted to each relevant setting and they will not be easily transferable across countries or health care settings. That is, if you have a drug which is shown to be cost-effective in the hospital, a health maintenance organization would surely

question the relevance of this study to cost-effective drug therapy in the outpatient environment. Or, a cost-effectiveness study in the British National Health Service may not be applicable to a managed care organization in the United States.

An explicit statement of cost factors should always be made; that is, the price of the drug and other major cost factors should be stated. With the wide variance in drug prices across practice settings and across countries, this factor alone makes it difficult to transfer results to other settings. Also, one must remember that the price is a major factor in determining the cost-effectiveness of a drug. Raising or lowering the price of the drug in relation to other costs for patient care can change the drug's cost-effectiveness without any change in the drug's known safety or effectiveness.

Cost Impact for Whom?

Who's bottom line is to be considered when conducting a pharmacoeconomic study on a drug therapy?—society's, consumers' (e.g., individual patients or groups of patients with specific diseases), providers' (e.g., physicians, pharmacists, or hospitals), producers' (i.e., drug manufacturer's), the health delivery scheme (e.g., a national health program or a managed care organization), or all of the above. How are conflicts to be resolved? How do health care providers make a decision when societal and individual interests are in conflict?

A cost-benefit or cost-effectiveness study may have different results when adding up the costs and benefits from different perspectives. While most cost-impact studies ultimately attempt to examine the impact on society as a whole, one must keep in mind the impact on health of individual patients. The cost impact on others in the system can also influence their decision making and behaviors. For example, drug therapy that replaces a particular surgical procedure may provide an overall savings to the health care system, but surgeons are not likely to favor the treatment if it means fewer procedures and less income. Consequently, to understand the total impact on the market, the perspective of each party in the process must be considered. The cost impact on all parties is important to consider when performing and analyzing economic studies of drug therapy.

INTERVENTIONS

Once a health care program has compared drug therapy alternatives using pharmacoeconomic studies, and other information, and determined the appropriate role of specific drug therapy, how does it ensure that these drug therapies will be used as intended? Several avenues for influencing drug use are available, including limits on drug coverage; limits on drug payments; or interventions targeted at changing the behavior of physicians, pharmacists, or patients. One must be careful at this point to define clearly the objective for a given intervention and to target such interventions at the source of the defined problem. At the same time, the ultimate objective of the health care system must be kept in mind. The goal of a health care system is not managing budgets; rather, it is improving patient health care outcomes while efficiently using resources.

Again, we must be reminded that drug expenditures are a function of price and volume. Controlling drug prices is easier than controlling utilization, but it is not necessarily better health care program management. Although attempts at managing drug expenditures are focused on drug prices, we must not forget that ensuring appropriate utilization of drugs is also essential to drug expenditure management. Inappropriate overuse should be discouraged and underuse of needed therapy corrected. Both can be costly in monetary and in patient health care outcome.

Limit Coverage

Many managed care plans in the United States, and most national health plans in other countries, do not cover all marketed drugs. A list of covered drugs may be developed or, conversely, a list of drugs excluded from coverage may be prepared. Certain drugs that have a high potential for adverse effects, misuse, abuse, or a high cost may be placed on restricted status requiring prior authorization from the health plan before coverage is approved. Whether intended or not, just the "hassle factor" of having the extra step of obtaining prior approval for a drug by giving a justification for its use will decrease substantially the use of a drug product.

Other attempts at limiting drug expenditures have focused on controlling the number of prescriptions a person can obtain, regardless of the level of need. Several Medicaid programs in the United States have used this approach, but evaluation of the effects of this cost management strategy suggests that expenditures for other health care services increase when necessary therapy is not available due to an arbitrary cap on prescription benefits. Limitations on drug therapy coverage should always take into account differences in patient need.

Coverage of drugs may be limited in another way. The managers of a health care plan may decide that if lower-cost, generic equivalent drug products are available, the plan will only cover the cost of the generic unless the originator brand is determined to be "medically necessary" by the patient's physician. In other health care programs, it may be determined that certain drugs are therapeutically equivalent and that they may be interchanged according to a protocol established by participating physicians and pharmacists. In these cases, the program may select one or a few single-source, patient-protected drugs within a therapeutic category for coverage. Or the program managers may ask drug companies with competing products to provide competitive bids so that the plan can select the lowest-cost therapeutic equivalent drug products for coverage.

Limit Payment

Payment limits for drugs may be established in a variety of ways. The health care plan may negotiate or set drug prices, limit inflation in drug prices, or demand discounts or rebates. Specific drug payments may be limited by establishing a maximum allowable cost or a reference price for a given drug product or a therapeutic category of drugs. When faced with cost management pressure, program administrators can easily fall into the line-item budget mentality. This approach can lead to cutting payment for the drugs line-item in the budget without consideration of the effect that such a cut will have on other expenditures such as hospitalizations, emergency room or urgent care visits, physician office visits, or other services. Before a specific cut is undertaken, the plan administrator should anticipate how this change will affect the behavior of physicians, pharmacists, and patients.

Health care program managers must be careful to distinguish who will bear the brunt of payment limits. In the United States, Medicaid programs had experienced ever-growing drug expenditures and administrators attempted to limit the growth in these expenditures by limiting reimbursement to pharmacists. Despite cuts in pharmacists' payments over time, the growth in drug expenditures failed to abate, and pharmacists' margins continued to decline. Finally, it was realized that most of the growth in expenditures in the Medicaid program was coming from increases in drug product prices at the manufacturer level. The U.S. Congress passed the Medicaid drug rebate program, which targeted the cost containment effort at manufacturer prices.

Physician Interventions

Physician prescribing behaviors have a significant influence on drug program expenditures. Physician prescribing indicators can be established and monitored to determine which physicians are complying with established protocols and formularies and which are not. One must be careful, though, in judging or penalizing high prescribers without careful examination. High prescribers may be viewed as overprescribers, but this is not always the case. Adjustments need to be made for such factors as physician specialty, patient age and gender mix, diagnosis and severity of illness mix. The percentage of a physician's prescriptions that are for single-source brands versus generically available drug products can be monitored and will have a significant impact on drug expenditure.

Physicians can be provided comparative performance feedback on the measures being tracked. This feedback should indicate a given physician's performance level in relation to both the norm and any program targets. Some health care plans have begun to give physicians a drug expenditure target or budget. If the drug budget across all patients for that physician is exceeded, the physician bears part of the financial risk or burden. If physician-prescribing patterns are found to be abnormal or unreasonable, the physician can be given feedback in comparison to the performance of peers. Physicians who are high prescribers may be selected out for more careful review. Not all high prescribers are overprescribers. Adjustments should be made for several factors, including physician specialty, patient age and gender mix, disease and severity of illness mix. Often simply informing a physician that his or her prescribing does not meet the expected standards set by peers will produce a change in behavior. If the behavior is not satisfactorily changed over time, the physician may be discontinued as a program participant.

Pharmacist Interventions

Pharmacists in the United States are able to select lower-cost generic equivalent drug products. Many health care plans encourage or insist that lower-cost generic products be used when possible. Nearly 40% of outpatient prescriptions in the United States are for generic medications. The range of savings from use of generic medications in the United States is from 20% to more than 80% of the brand name price. Pharmacists also end up being the drug policemen for most insurance schemes with respect to formulary compliance, generic dispensing, correcting prescribing errors, screening for drug interactions, and drug utilization review. Payments to pharmacists for solving drug-related problems, even if a prescription is not dispensed, are made by some insurance schemes in the United States and Canada.

Patient Interventions

Patient drug use behaviors are influenced by the cost of access to medications. In many countries nearly all prescriptions are covered under a government-sponsored health care plan. This is not the case in the United States, where nearly one-half of all outpatient prescriptions are paid for, out-of-pocket, by the consumer and another 35% are paid for by private insurance schemes. Fixed dollar copayments (e.g., $5.00 per prescription) are used by some insurance plans to influence patient demand for prescriptions. Other plans use percentage co-insurance (e.g., 20% of the prescription cost) or deductibles (e.g., $500 per year—an amount that must be paid by the consumer in a given year before the plan will cover prescription costs. Patients are sometimes given an incentive to use generic medications, such as lower copayments, or none at all, if the patient accepts the generic rather than the brand name product.

CONCLUSIONS

Several implications can be drawn from the pitfalls in use of pharmacoeconomic data. These implications can best be summarized by the axiom: "If you don't know where you are going, you are not likely to get there." Cost management actions of health care programs should be monitored broadly, targeted at the source of the problem, and made transparent to those affected. Although limited resources will mean that some cost-effective drug therapies will not necessarily be affordable, the health care system should be designed so that the true value of those drug therapies that are covered will be fully realized.

Monitor Impact Broadly

The economic impact of pharmaceuticals should be monitored from a broad perspective. To determine the full pharmacoeconomic impact of pharmaceuticals, their effect on patient health status should be monitored from a broad perspective. Whereas managing the amount spent directly on pharmaceuticals is important, the greatest impact of pharmaceuticals on cost management may be from reductions in other more costly health care services. The relationship between appropriate pharmaceutical use and total health care costs is essential to understanding the true value of pharmaceuticals in cost management.

Target Solutions to Source of Problem

Solutions to cost management problems must be targeted at the source of the problem. While the impact of pharmaceuticals is to be monitored broadly, any solutions must be carefully targeted at the source of the problem. We must realize that the effect of drug therapy is not necessarily on the drug expenditure budget. Many health care programs attempt to manage total health expenditures by focusing on each line item of their budget, such as drugs, physician services, hospital care, and other such expenditures. If, after considering the impact of pharmaceuticals on total health expenditures, program managers determine that cost management of pharmaceuticals is appropriate, the solutions should be carefully targeted at the source of the problem.

We must identify what is causing the problem with respect to drug expenditures. How many patients are covered? Is their drug use appropriate? How much does the drug cost from the manufacturer? What are the administrative costs? Is patient cost-sharing necessary or appropriately designed? The specific problem may be related to any one, or a combination, of these factors. It is far easier to control price than to control utilization, but utilization is more often the source of the problem than price per se. If a large number of patients are using drugs inappropriately, not only are the drug expenditures wasted, but other health care costs may be unnecessarily increased as well. If price or profit controls are not properly implemented, total health care expenditures may not decrease at all. For example, an overutilization or an overpricing problem may need to be targeted at just a few specific drug therapy categories, rather than at all therapeutic categories. Also, health care managers must consider the alternative actions, and their related costs, which are likely to be taken by physicians, pharmacists, patients, and others when a specific cost management program is implemented.

Make Decisions Transparent

Cost management decisions in health care should be transparent. Many cost management plans are adopted by health care programs that are never understood by those who are targeted. Consequently, the intended effect of the cost management program is not achieved, and in some cases the outcome may be the opposite of what was intended. Health care programs should explain the intent of their cost management actions, so that physicians, pharmacists, patients, and drug companies can know how the action is expected to influence both health care expenditures and patient health outcomes. This transparency of decisions also means that health care providers and producers, including pharmaceuticals manufacturers, will have to make their decisions more transparent as well. Manufacturers will need to justify both promotional activities and pricing practices in relation to total health care costs and outcomes.

Not All Cost-effective Therapies Are Affordable

Not all cost-effective therapies and technologies are affordable. Even though a therapy or technology may be cost-effective, it may not be affordable because of limited resources at either individual or societal levels. Health care programs must make choices even among cost-effective therapies to keep expenditures within the limited resources available for health care. Cost-effective therapies for one health care purpose will have to compete with cost-effective therapies for another purpose. This competition for health care resources will become more intense as all health care costs become a larger part of the gross domestic product in a given country. Physicians, hospitals, pharmacists, drug companies, long-term care facilities, and other health care providers and producers will compete for limited health care resources.

Value of Drug Therapy

The real value of drug therapy is determined only by the degree to which a patient's health care outcome improves. The value of a pharmaceutical is not determined by the amount of research and development conducted by the drug company, nor by the price the drug company charges or by the price the pharmacist charges or the health plan allows; rather, the real value is determined only by the degree to which a given patient's health care improves. A specific drug may have certain inherent properties, such as safety and effectiveness, but these properties are not sufficient to ensure that the drug will improve a patient's health care outcome. In addition to being safe and effective, a drug must be appropriately prescribed, efficiently distributed, and correctly used. If the health care system is designed in such a way that neither the physician nor the pharmacist ensures that the patient knows how to use the medication correctly, the true value of an otherwise safe and effective drug is not likely to be realized. The value of drug therapy can only be realized when drugs are appropriately prescribed and when physicians and pharmacists counsel patients on why and how to use their medication correctly. Ensuring appropriate drug use should be as important to a pharmaceuticals company, and to the health care program, as is determining the safety and effectiveness of a drug.

Quality of Life and Pharmacoeconomics in Clinical Trials, Second Edition, edited by B. Spilker.
Lippincott-Raven Publishers, Philadelphia © 1996.

CHAPTER 121

Use and Opportunities for Administrative Data Bases in Pharmacoeconomic Research

John E. Paul and Hugh H. Tilson

INTRODUCTION

The use of administrative data bases in health services research received a tremendous boost through the establishment of the medical effectiveness/patient outcomes research team (PORT) program supported by the Agency for Health Care Policy and Research (AHCPR) (1,2). Outcomes research in the health care field can be defined as analysis that attempts to explain or describe the results of any type of medical treatment or intervention. Types of outcomes commonly examined in medical effectiveness research include, among others, mortality, morbidity, costs, length of stay, quality of care, and patient satisfaction. Many of these outcomes can be elucidated by retrospective examination of administrative data, i.e., data collected and archived primarily for management, versus research, purposes. All the AHCPR-funded PORTs have included components that use administrative data to examine outcomes. Important applications have included (a) natural history of disease and impact of illness studies, including assessments of rates and trends over large and small geographic areas; (b) examination of costs, access, treatment, and utilization issues relating to procedures and medical regimens, including pharmaceuticals; (c) study of adverse events requiring large populations (i.e., for rare but important reactions), and long-term follow-up (i.e., for late side effects); (d) as an adjunct to clinical

trials and to study effectiveness of therapies under "real-world" situations; and (e) as potential sampling frames for subsequent primary data collection (3). Applications in pharmacoeconomic research for administrative data analyses range across the spectrum, from preclinical drug development, where natural history/impact of illness studies are needed, through postmarketing support, where comparative "real-world" effectiveness/outcome/safety studies and modeling of different therapies are possible.

This chapter provides (a) an overview of the types of existing administrative data bases appropriate for outcomes and pharmacoeconomics research; (b) advantages, disadvantages, and other concerns related to using administrative data bases; (c) methodological and analytical issues and approaches; and (d) an example of the use of administrative data in pharmacoeconomic research.

TYPES OF ADMINISTRATIVE DATA BASES

In general, an administrative data base is any collection of information recorded in a uniform manner and used for ongoing program operation or assessment. Within administrative data bases, a "record" or "observation" may refer to the demographics of a particular patient, or may refer to a hospitalization or other health care encounter, such as an office visit, laboratory test, or a prescription. Different administrative data bases also focus on health care providers, the health care "marketplace," or any of several other units of interest. Usually, information for these data bases is collected over a span of time and is regularly updated. Data are gathered for a variety of purposes, commonly related to

J. E. Paul: Clinical Analytical Services, Disease Management Division, Glaxo Wellcome, Inc., Research Triangle Park, North Carolina 27709.

H. H. Tilson: Epidemiology, Surveillance, and Policy Research, Glaxo Wellcome, Inc., Research Triangle Park, North Carolina 27709.

health care resource use, and submitted for the purpose of reimbursement, such as in fee-for-service Medicaid, or used for business management, such as in managed-care situations. Administrative data bases can focus on specific patient populations, such as enrollees in a health management organization (HMO), or on more general populations, such as

aged Medicare Part A recipients, which can in turn serve as proxies (e.g., for all U.S. residents or for those over the age of 65) (3).

Large administrative data bases useful for pharmacoeconomic research can be broadly grouped into three types: (1) service/utilization data; (2) provider/institutional data; and

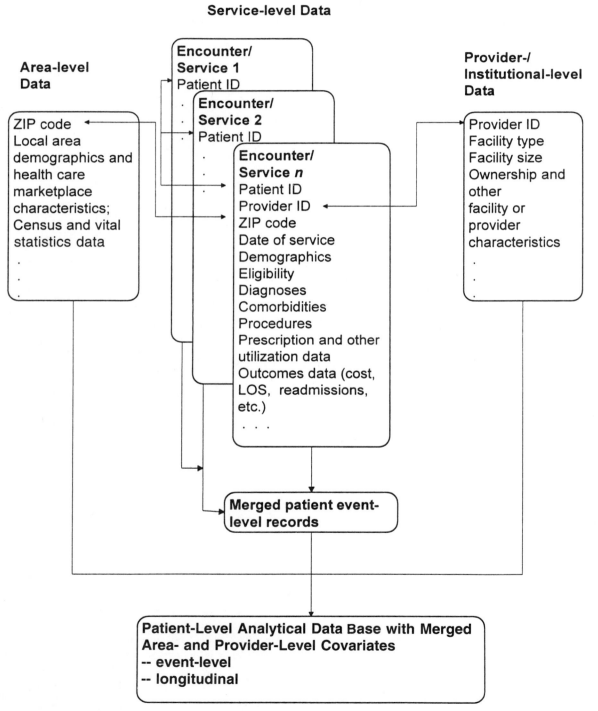

FIG. 1. Relationships and linkages among three main types of administrative data bases.

(3) area-level socioeconomic/health care marketplace data. Although these data bases may have different units of analysis, they can often be linked by a common variable in order to create an analytical data base focused on the particular research question, and gathering necessary analytical covariates from several sources that might be missing from a single source. The power of administrative data base research is fully realized only when such linkages are accomplished (2). Figure 1 provides a schematic view of the interrelationship of the three types of administrative data bases. Note that the primary administrative data of interest are usually the patient service-level data, linked within and across episodes by a unique patient identifier, and with provider data and area-level data by provider identifiers and patient ZIP code of residence. The goal is to produce a patient-level analytical data base that builds health care events out of discrete service-level data and merges in useful data from other sources. Furthermore, longitudinal patient-level data bases can be built from events linked over time for systems, such as Medicare, in which patient enrollment is consistent. Longitudinal data bases, such as those possible with some of the Canadian provincial systems, provide some of the best opportunities for outcomes research.

In addition to population-based administrative data, there are many specialized large data bases which are of potential use in pharmacoeconomics. These other data bases include disease registries, epidemiologic cohort data bases, health survey data, and some large clinical trial data bases. Linkage of these data bases with administrative data bases, while often desirable and potentially informative, can be highly problematic as a result of logistical and confidentiality considerations; moreover, the populations represented by these specialized data bases are usually highly selected and nonrepresentative of populations as a whole. It is important initially to establish the expected role and value of each data base proposed for linkage and avoid unnecessary work and possibly misleading information.

Table 1 provides examples of administrative and other large data bases within this classification system. The largest amount of administrative data research to date has focused on service/utilization statistics within publicly funded systems, in particular Medicare. Since administrative data are normally collected at the service level, care must be taken in the definition and construction of episodes or events from discrete encounters and services. State-level Medicaid data research is of particular interest for pharmacoeconomic applications because state Medicaid programs are required to provide coverage of prescription drugs. Finally, as managed care spreads and becomes increasingly sophisticated, research applications with proprietary data, such as that from insurance companies, HMOs, and pharmacy benefits managers (PBMs), are becoming more common and feasible.

Individual patient experience data are often initially linked to explore the basic exposure-outcome question. Subsequent linkage to provider data, in particular hospital data from the American Hospital Association Annual Survey, allows

TABLE 1. *Examples of administrative data bases, by category*

I. Service/Utilization Data
  A. Federal-level data
    1. HCFA Medicare Statistical System
    2. Medicaid data (federal-level)
    3. Department of Veterans Affairs data
    4. Department of Defense data (including CHAMPUS)
  B. State-/provincial-level data
    1. Medicaid Management Information System data
    2. State hospital discharge data systems
    3. Provincial health plans/prescription drug plans (e.g., Saskatchewan, Manitoba)
  C. Private/proprietary data bases
    1. Blue Cross–Blue Shield data; data bases from other insurers
    2. Hospital system and HMO data bases
    3. Pharmacy Benefit Manager (PBM) data bases
    4. Hospital discharge data bases and proprietary data (e.g., CPHA)
    5. Automated medical record datasets (e.g., Regenstrief, GPRD)
II. Provider/Institutional Data
  A. Medicare provider of service data
  B. American Hospital Association Annual Survey data
  C. American Medical Association Master File data
III. Area-level Sociodemographic Data
  A. Health resource and manpower data (e.g., area resource file)
  B. Vital and health statistics data bases (e.g., census; National Death Index)
IV. Clinical/epidemiologic/health survey data bases
  A. Disease registries (e.g., cancer, end-stage renal disease)
  B. Epidemiologic data bases (e.g., Framingham Study, Manitoba Provincial Health Database)
  C. Health survey data (e.g., National Health Interview Survey)

inclusion of covariates useful in multivariate analysis and economic modeling, such as facility size, teaching status/medical school affiliation, services, and ownership (e.g., for-profit/not-for-profit). Physician provider data can provide information on specialty and years since medical school graduation. Area-level data from census or vital statistics, or from compiled data bases such as the Area Resource File of the Department of Health and Human Services, can provide equally important explanatory variables such as availability of providers, demographics of the derivative population, and "denominator" data for the calculation of rates.

ADVANTAGES, DISADVANTAGES, APPLICATIONS, AND CAVEATS

There are several immediate and obvious advantages to the use of administrative data bases in health services and pharmacoeconomic research. First, because they are already in place, administrative data bases offer the ability to address matters of policy concern in a timely and cost-effective manner. Although interim conclusions may have to be validated with longer-term studies (e.g., clinical trials or more traditional epidemiologic studies), the short-term responsiveness of these data sources is a major strength. Administrative data bases also provide large numbers of records and broad patient coverage, including both standard and nonstandard treatment. The sizes and coverage offered through administrative data bases are often much greater than could be realized in a much more costly primary data collection effort. Administrative data bases can have good external validity, although it is critical to understand fully the population represented by the data base (4,5). Fundamental to large data base research is an understanding of the realities behind the data base, often possible only by rigorous investigation and validation, including consulting sources and medical record abstraction.

Researchers in a variety of health-related fields, including pharmacoeconomics, are taking advantage of these already collected data to help answer important research questions. Quam et al. (6) demonstrated the cost-effectiveness and reliability of medical and pharmacy claims data for epidemiologic research by comparing claims data with medical record data and patient surveys. Ray et al. (7) have shown the use of Medicaid data in Tennessee to detect drug utilization patterns as part of a program to encourage more cost-effective prescribing. Jick (8,9) demonstrated the ability to use linked data from managed care settings in the United States and new automated medical records in the U.K. to evaluate associations between prescription drug use and clinical outcomes. Finally, AHCPR is currently supporting a number of medical effectiveness studies under the "Outcomes of Pharmaceutical Therapy" program, which is using state Medicaid data, HMO data, and registry data, both with and without accompanying primary data collection.

Even though many potential opportunities have been shown, researchers must also address potential problems. Principal among the problems is that which is inherent in all population-based, nonexperimental approaches: nonrandom selection of patients, with resulting unknown potential biases. This problem may be addressed through careful and cautious use of the data base and presentation of results. It is also possible to validate conclusions reached through large data base analyses by using more robust experimental approaches. Hlatky et al. (10) showed that clinical trial data can be processed through models built with administrative data. The extent to which predicted values from the resultant models correspond to actual clinical trial outcomes becomes the basis for assessing the validity of the administrative data model.

From a quality standpoint, Hui et al. (11) note that data bases developed for purposes other than research may have few or no edit checks performed on them and may also contain incomplete data. Although stratification and statistical adjustment can help, serious biases can occur as a result of missing data. Moreover, data validity (e.g., edit checks) may have to be addressed through selective (i.e., statistical) accessing of primary records.

Logistical and data management issues with regard to administrative data bases can be substantial. One important issue is that of confidentiality and access. These data bases usually contain personal identifiers or other means for establishing personal identification. These data bases may also contain sensitive proprietary information. Since individual patient permission is usually not part of large data base research, protocols regarding the use of the data and provisions for protection of confidentiality are essential. Low-cost and highly effective methods to ensure confidentiality, such as encrypted identification numbers and suppression of cells with low numbers of cases, have become standard practice. The use of administrative data bases also avoids ethical issues about randomization to potentially nonefficacious therapies (including placebo) and avoids the artificiality introduced by primary data collection. Administrative data base research spares the patient from direct intrusion and may offer the only feasible way to extend our knowledge in some areas.

Another concern that must be addressed when using administrative data bases is consistency over time. For example, changes in variable coding and editing standards can make analyses that cover a certain time period difficult. In some cases, such as for Medicare, files are kept "open" for several years. Corrections, additions, and edits 2 or 3 years after the original information was collected can be made. Thus, reanalyses on the same data base can yield different results from one point to another. Examples of changes in coding standards include changing versions of the International Classification of Diseases (ICD), and from ICD-9 procedure codes to CPT-4 procedure codes. Moreover, the definition of a case may also change, as has happened in the case of human immunodeficiency virus (HIV) disease. Changes in coding incentives (and therefore information that gets chosen for coding) due to changes in reimbursement methodologies (e.g., for Diagnosis-Related Groups [DRGs]) can also make comparisons over time problematic. Accuracy of coding itself is also a concern (12).

Other potential coding problems include those of "laterality" (i.e., left versus right), and of identifying primary versus subsequent procedures. Thus, it can be problematic within current ICD-9-CM coding schemes to know whether it was the right or left knee, hip, eye, and so forth, that was operated on, and whether the procedure was an initial operation or a subsequent operation attributable to failure of the first one. Imputation techniques based on other data in the data bases have been devised (13); in cases in which this is not possible it may be necessary to go back and review medical records. Romano et al. (14) demonstrate an alternative approach assessing diagnostic coding within administrative data bases and report that risk models developed from administrative data may be biased because of selective underreporting. Finally, "rule-out" or "suspected" diagnoses are occasionally included on the administrative record. To the extent these are considered as "confirmed" diagnoses, incorrect conclusions may be reached.

Within pharmacoeconomic research, problems can occur in establishing the indication for the use of a particular drug, since both on- and off-label use is frequent within a population, and use for multiple indications is also possible. Careful examination of diagnoses and comorbidities on the current record (and previous as well as subsequent records, if possible) can often provide confidence in including or excluding the case from consideration.

There are also important analytical and statistical issues to consider when using administrative data bases. Among the most important is an understanding of the coverage of the data base, i.e., inclusion or exclusion criteria for cases, events, or variables (15), and the completeness of the data base for the population, both within a record and across an individual's records. Lack of familiarity with the data base can easily lead to improper generalization if it turns out that the coverage and completeness are not fully understood (4).

TABLE 2. *Example of use of administrative data for pharmacoeconomic research*

Overview: Focus groups of oncologists and infectious disease specialists indicated that prophylactic use of antiviral agents in immunosuppressed cancer patients may be less than optimal, resulting in unnecessary morbidity and costs of care for these patients. The incidence of infections in actual-practice situations, and the consequences of herpes infections in these patients in terms of resource consumption, are unknown. A retrospective study based on administrative data was undertaken to elucidate these questions.

Purpose: (a) To determine the cost and outcomes associated with hospitalizations in which herpesvirus infections are indicated as primary or secondary diagnoses; (b) to determine the level of use, and costs and outcomes associated with, antiviral therapy during hospitalization of immunosuppressed leukemia/lymphoma cancer patients.

Data bases used: A commercially available, multiyear, hospital discharge data base, with expanded data on pharmaceutical use during the hospitalization was selected for this study. The data base contains more than 1 million discharges over the 27-month period of interest. Data were merged from other commercial data bases, e.g., the American Hospital Association Annual Survey, and from publicly available data bases, such as the Medicare Cost Reports (hospital-specific) and the Area Resource File.

Methods: A detailed initial data request was prepared in cooperation with the commercial vendor. The data request specified inclusion and exclusion criteria for the diagnosis codes used to select a record. The vendor produced preliminary tables from which the final selection strategy was developed. Records were selected from 142 hospitals in the nationwide data base, representing 14,406 hospitalizations in which primary or secondary diagnoses of herpesvirus infections were present and 44,703 hospitalizations in which there were primary or secondary diagnoses of leukemia or lymphoma; 1,141 hospitalizations had both herpes and leukemia/lymphoma diagnoses. The frequency of these discharge diagnoses within the entire data base was compared with results from the National Discharge Survey, a statistically representative sample of all hospitalizations in the United States, to test the representativeness of the data base.

Analysis files were built separately for herpes hospitalizations and for leukemia/lymphoma hospitalizations. Hospital-specific and area covariates were merged from linked files. Antiviral use was characterized by (a) type of antiviral, (b) timing within the hospitalization ("early" versus "late") and (c) mode of administration—intravenous oral versus "step-down" (IV-to-oral switch during hospitalization). Outcomes included total and drug charges (converted to costs through use of the Medicare hospital-specific cost-to-charge ratios), length of stay, and discharge destination. Severity was accounted for by the number of comorbidities as reflected in secondary diagnoses. Both descriptive tables and multivariate models were constructed.

Preliminary results: Preliminary results indicate a lower-than-expected use of antiviral agents in both primary diagnosis herpes hospitalizations and in hospitalizations for leukemia/lymphoma, consistent with the opinions of the initial focus groups. Preliminary multivariate analyses indicate that lower total costs and shorted hospitalization length of stay are associated with herpes hospitalizations in which early aggressive treatment with antiviral agents has been used. Final results from the analysis are pending and will be published in the literature.

Cautions and caveats: Potential drawbacks and concerns regarding the study should be recognized, including the facts that (a) the sample was a convenience sample, not randomly selected, (b) there are nonrandomly missing data for certain variables within the data base, and (c) measurement of severity and thus case mix adjustment is very difficult with administrative data alone. To address this last concern, the study proposes a follow-up chart review of a sample of cases from the data base in order to test the validity of the severity-adjustment procedures. Note, however, that the intention of this study was not to demonstrate the safety and efficacy of antiviral agents in these situations, something that would clearly require a clinical trial to accomplish. The intention was to investigate actual practice effectiveness of this treatment, and the associated short-term outcomes of that treatment, in response to specific clinical questions. The administrative data approach and study results have so far proved to be a rich source of information from a very large number of cases. Important patient outcomes information has resulted, which will be further tested and evaluated through medical chart review or perhaps other primary data collection efforts, including clinical trials.

The fact that many of the administrative data bases have to do with reimbursement is a potential strength for pharmacoeconomic research. These data bases, however, are generally organized around payment line items, such as physician, pharmacy, and hospital charges, that require construction of "episodes of care" by linkage of service-level records, as previously shown in Figure 1. Mitchell et al. (16) describe critical analytical issues faced by the PORTs in administrative data base analysis, and approaches related to (a) identification of index cases or patient cohorts; (b) defining the length of the episode; (c) measuring outcomes; and (d) identifying adverse events and associated sequelae.

Because of the large number of records in administrative data bases, caution must be used in interpreting and reporting statistical results. As the number of records used in an analysis increases, the standard errors of estimates will diminish. This leads to a higher likelihood of statistical significance (i.e., smaller p-values). In other words, a small difference between two values is likely to be a statistically significant difference. It is up to clinicians and other experts associated with the study, however, to determine whether the difference is "clinically significant." Furthermore, large administrative data bases provide the opportunity for large numbers of multiple comparisons. The risk of meaningless chance association is substantial if "data dredging" or "fishing expeditions" are undertaken. It is therefore essential for the validity and credibility of the research that the research questions and the methodologic and statistical approach be established a priori.

It is also important to get current clinical input with regard to codes, since conventions for coding may vary from one data base to another, based on function, and reimbursement incentives related to coding may change over time. Coding of comorbid conditions, functional status, and severity of illness also represent potentially critical information gaps in the use of administrative data bases. For pharmacoeconomic research, inadequate linkages may exist between pharmacy and patient medical data, or services and episodes may be defined differently, requiring great care in producing the merged analytical file.

Finally, there may be subtle and/or complex characteristics of the data bases, and unwritten or non-updated documentation. Lack of familiarity with file designs and/or survey sampling designs can lead to erroneous conclusions. It is important to have an early working relationship with people who are familiar with the structure of the data base, so that the "oral" as well as written documentation may be accessed, and not-so-obvious as well as obvious pitfalls avoided. All these analytical and statistical issues are made more complex when multiple administrative data bases are combined or linked.

Table 2 details an application of administrative data, in this case expanded hospital discharge data linked to area- and provider-level files, to answer pharmacoeconomic questions on the use and outcomes associated with antiviral agents in herpes and/or immunosuppressed cancer patient hospitalizations.

CONCLUSIONS

Administrative data base analysis is becoming a vital component of pharmacoeconomic research. Rather than being valued for what it can offer, it is often criticized, however, for not offering the methodological rigor of randomized clinical trials (17). Only in recent years, however, have computer capabilities and data base quality caught up enough to permit the development of methods allowing the pharmacoeconomist to use such data with confidence. Because of this, there is currently little standardization in the approaches researchers have taken with administrative data bases. "Validation protocols," defined as careful documentation of all steps in constructing analysis files from the source data bases, would allow both replication of results as well as research audits. Furthermore, the validation of a statistically representative sample of records against primary sources may be necessary. Although administrative data bases allow great opportunity for data exploration and hypothesis generation, research protocols need to be explicit about the questions the administrative data base research is expected to address. Administrative data should be seen as only one of several important sources of information for outcomes research; however, the GAO (18) notes that administrative data bases can serve as a highly cost-effective adjunct to information from other primary sources, including randomized controlled clinical trials. "Cross-design synthesis," as described in the 1992 GAO Report, offers an approach to medical effectiveness research in which the complementary strengths and weaknesses of randomized clinical trials and large data base analyses can be exploited in a cost-effective manner.

The use of pre-existing administrative data bases in the assessment of health care technologies, resource use, and patient outcomes will probably become increasingly prevalent due to favorable cost, timeliness, and ease-of-access issues. Uses in the area of pharmacoeconomic research are just developing but have great promise with the increasing sophistication and coverage/linkage potential of data bases at all levels—provider, insurer, and government. The increasingly greater use of computer support for health care administration under managed care also makes it highly likely that these data bases will be harnessed. The potentially great influence this research may have, however, and the wide-ranging nature of conclusions make it critical that the use of this methodology be done carefully and that analyses be subject to strict research designs.

REFERENCES

1. Roper WL, Winkenwerder W, Hackbarth CM, Krakauer H. Effectiveness in health care: an initiative to evaluate and improve medical practice. *N Engl J Med* 1988;319:1197–1202.

2. Agency for Health Care Policy and Research (AHCPR). Report to Congress: the feasibility of linking research-related data bases to federal and non-federal medical administrative data bases. Publ. no. 91-0003. Rockville, MD: Agency for Health Care Policy and Research, 1991.
3. Paul JE, Melfi CA, Smith TK, Freund DA, Katz BP, Coyte PC, Hawker GA. Linking primary and secondary data for outcomes research: methodology of the Total Knee Replacement Patient Outcomes Research Team. 1994 in "Proceedings of the Sixth Conference on Health Survey Methods." National Center for Health Statistics, Rockville, MD, 1995 (forthcoming).
4. Fisher ES, Baron JA, Malenka DJ, Barrett J, Bubolz TA. Overcoming potential pitfalls in the use of Medicare data for epidemiologic research. *Am J Public Health* 1990;80:1487–1490.
5. Paul JE, Weis KA, Epstein RA. Databases for variations research. *Med Care* 1993;31(suppl):YS96–YS102.
6. Quam L, Ellis L, Venus P, Clouse J, Taylor CG, Leatherman S. Using claims data for epidemiologic research: the concordance of claims-based criteria with the medical record and patient survey for identifying a hypertensive population. *Med Care* 1993;31:498–507.
7. Ray WA, Griffin MR, Baugh DK. Mortality following hip fracture before and after implementation of the prospective payment system. *Arch Intern Med* 1990;150:2109–2114.
8. Jick H. Use of automated data bases to study drug effects after marketing. *Pharmacotherapy* 1985;5:278–279.
9. Jick H. The Boston collaborative drug surveillance program and the Puget Sound health maintenance organization. *Drug Inform J* 1985;19:237–242.
10. Hlatky MA, Califf RM, Harrell FE, Lee KL, Mark DB, Pryor DB. Comparison of predictions based on observational data with the results of randomized controlled clinical trials of coronary artery bypass surgery. *J Am Coll Cardiol* 1988;11:237–245.
11. Hui SL, McDonald CJ, Katz BP, eds. Methods of using large data bases in health care research: problems and promises. *Proceedings of the third biennial Regenstrief conference. Stat Med* 1991;10:505.
12. Fisher ES, Whaley FS, Krushat WM, Malenka DJ, Fleming C, Baron JA, Hsia DC. The accuracy of Medicare's hospital claims data: progress, but problems remain. *Am J Public Health* 1992;82:243–248.
13. Heck DA, Melfi CA, Kalasinski LA, Katz BP, Arthur D. Predicting the probability of reoperation during the two years following knee replacement surgery. Indiana University, 1994.
14. Romano PS, Ross LL, Luft HS, et al. A comparison of administrative versus clinical data: coronary artery bypass surgery as an example. *J Clin Epidemiol* 1994;47:249–260.
15. Cherkin DC, Deyo RA, Volinn E, Loeser JD. Use of the international classification of diseases (ICD-9-CM) to identify hospitalizations for mechanical low back problems in administrative data bases. *Spine* 1992;17:817–825.
16. Mitchell JB, Bubolz T, Paul JE, Pashos CL, Escarce JJ, Muhlbaier LH, et al. Using Medicare claims for outcomes research. *Med Care* 1994;32(suppl):7.
17. Anderson C. Measuring what works in health care. *Science* 1994;263:1080–1082.
18. General Accounting Office (GAO). Cross design synthesis: a new strategy for medical effectiveness research. Publ. no. GAO/PEMD-92-18. Washington, DC: U.S. General Accounting Office, 1992.

Suggested Readings

Connell FA, Diehr P, Hart LG. The use of large data bases in health care studies. *Annu Rev Public Health* 1987;8:51–74.

DeFriese, GH. The secondary data bases of health services research: need for a national inventory. *Health Serv Res* 1991;25:829–830.
Department of Veterans Affairs, Houston HSR&D Program. *Data base sources for research in quality of care and utilization of health services.* Report no. TR-92-01. Houston, TX: Veterans Affairs Medical Center, 1992.
Deyo RA, Cherkin DC, Ciol MA. Adapting a clinical comorbidity index for use with ICD-9-CM administrative data bases. *J Clin Epidemiol* 1992;45:613–619.
Dor A. Holahan J. Urban–rural differences in Medicare physician expenditures. *Inquiry* 1990;27:3107–318.
Epstein M. Uses of state level hospital discharge data bases. *J Am Health Inf Manage Assoc* 1992;63:32.
Fleming C, Fisher ES, Chang C-H, Bubolz TA, Malenka DJ. Studying outcomes and hospital utilization in the elderly: the advantages of a merged data base for Medicare and Veterans Affairs hospitals. *Med Care* 1992;30:377–399.
Grady ML, Schwartz HA, eds. *Medical effectiveness research data methods: summary report.* Publ. no. 92-0056 Rockville, MD: Agency for Health Care Policy and Research, 1992.
Green J, Wintfeld N. How accurate are hospital discharge data for evaluating effectiveness of care? *Med Care* 1993;31:719–731.
Hand R, Sener S, Imperato J, Chmiel JS, Sylvester JA, Fremgen A. Hospital variables associated with quality of care for breast cancer patients. *JAMA* 1991;266:3429–3432.
Klingman D, Pine PL, Simon J. Outcomes of surgery under Medicaid. *Health Care Financ Rev* 1990;11:1–16.
Krieger N. Overcoming the absence of socioeconomic data in medical records: validation and application of a census-based methodology. *Am J Public Health* 1992;82:703–710.
Lubitz, J. "Linking HCFA data with data from external sources." In: *Proceedings of 1989 HCFA data users conference.* Baltimore: U.S. Department of Health and Human Services, Health Care Financing Administration, Bureau of Data Management and Strategy, 1989.
Lurie N. Administrative data and outcomes research. *Med Care* 1990;28:867–869.
Potosky AL, Riley GF, Lubitz JD, Mentnech RM, Kessler LG. Potential for cancer related health services research using a linked Medicare-tumor registry data base. *Med Care* 1993;31:732–748.
Ray WA, Griffin MR. Use of Medicaid data for pharmacoepidemiology. *Am J Epidemiol* 1989;129:837–849.
Roos NP, Roos LL, Mossey J, Havens B. Using administrative data to predict important health outcomes: entry to hospital, nursing home, and death. *Med Care* 1988;26:221–239.
Wadja A, Roos LL. Simplifying record linkage: software and strategy. *Comput Biol Med* 1991;117:239.
Warren JL, Babish JD, Nicholson G. *Use and linking of Medicare data bases to create episode of care files.* Working paper: Epidemiology Branch, Division of Beneficiary Studies, Office of Research, and the Health Standards and Quality Bureau. Baltimore: Health Care Financing Administration, 1989.
Whittle J, Steinberg EP, Anderson GF, Herbert R. Accuracy of Medicare claims data for estimation of cancer incidence and resection rates among elderly Americans. *Med Care* 1991;29:1126–1236.
Whittle J. An appraisal of the role of claims and discharge abstract data bases in medical technology assessment. In: Identifying Health Technologies That Work. OTA-H-608. Washington, D.C.: U.S. Government Printing Office, September 1994.

Quality of Life and Pharmacoeconomics in Clinical Trials, Second Edition, edited by B. Spilker.
Lippincott-Raven Publishers, Philadelphia © 1996.

CHAPTER 122

Problems in Undertaking Pharmacoeconomic Assessments in Phase III Clinical Trials: The Case of Colony-Stimulating Factors

Michael F. Drummond, Joseph Menzin, and Gerry Oster

ECONOMIC EVALUATION OF PHARMACEUTICALS

The Growing Need for Economic Evaluation

Increased pressures on health care budgets have made it important not only to demonstrate the safety and efficacy of new drugs but also to show that they give value for money. This is particularly true for recombinant drugs, such as lenograstim, which may be perceived to be costly.

Economic data can assist in discussions about reimbursement (public subsidy) and support price negotiations in jurisdictions where such data are required. Indeed, in come countries (most notably Australia and some provinces of Canada), provision of economic data is now mandatory, and the government has established guidelines for economic studies (1,2). In many European countries, submission of economic data is encouraged, although not yet officially required (3).

Challenges in the Design of Lenograstim Economic Evaluations

Three randomized clinical trials were recently conducted, two of which examined the role of lenograstim in correcting

neutropenia in patients receiving treatment for inflammatory breast cancer (4) and non-Hodgkin's lymphoma (5) respectively, while the third examined whether use of lenograstim would permit intensification of the dose of cytotoxic chemotherapy in patients with small cell lung cancer (6). An overview of these clinical trials is presented in Table 1.

To explore the economic effects of lenograstim therapy, a program of pharmacoeconomic studies was designed and implemented in conjunction with these clinical trials. Two teams of pharmacoeconomics experts—one from Germany and the other from Italy—were assigned joint responsibility for evaluating lenograstim in the inflammatory breast cancer trial. French and UK teams were assigned the task of evaluating lenograstim in the non-Hodgkin's lymphoma and small cell lung cancer trials, respectively.

In these evaluations, it was hypothesized that the efficacy of lenograstim in shortening the duration of neutropenia would result in reduced costs for treating infections, which could be substantial if the patient required hospitalization. In addition, if the duration of neutropenia is reduced, delays in chemotherapy may be less likely, and there is a greater chance that the planned dose intensity of chemotherapy can be maintained. This may result in therapeutic benefits in tumor response and survival. Indeed, in the small cell lung cancer trial, the objective was to intensify the dose by shortening the periods between chemotherapy cycles, as this was thought to improve the chances of survival. However, documenting these potential benefits of therapy posed several challenges.

M. F. Drummond: Centre for Health Economics, University of York, Heslington, York Y01 5DD, England.

J. Menzin and G. Oster: Policy Analysis Inc., Brookline, Massachusetts 02146.

TABLE 1. *Overview of lenograstim clinical trials included in the pharmacoeconomics program*

Trial	Design	No. of patients	Countries (no. of centers)	Chemotherapy	Lenograstim regimen	Clinical outcomes
Inflammatory breast cancer (4)	Randomized double-blind, placebo control	120	France (10)	Four 21-day cycles with fluorouracil, epirubicin and cyclophosphamide	5 μg/kg/day on days 6–16 of cycle	Correction of neutropenia Incidence of infection Tumor response
Non-Hodgkin's lymphoma (5)	Randomized, double-blind, placebo control	162	France (13) Belgium (1)	Four 14-day cycles with cyclophosphamide, vindesine, bleomycin, methylprednisolone, and doxorubicin or mitoxantrone	5 μg/kg/day on days 6–13 of cycle	Correction of neutropenia Incidence of infection Chemotherapy dose intensity Delay in treatment Tumor response
Small cell lung cancer (6)	Randomized open-label, untreated control	65	UK (1)	Six 28-day cycles with vincristine, ifostamide, carboplatin and etoposide	5 μg/kg/day on days 4–26 of cycle	Chemotherapy dose intensity Incidence of infection Survival Correction of neutropenia

[a]Treatment terminated 2 days before the next cycle of chemotherapy if neutrophil level ≥1.0 × 10^9/L, or if patient is free of infection.

Atypical Settings

It is often suggested that the setting for most phase III clinical trials is atypical of normal clinical practice. That is, trials are often performed at specialist centers by highly committed investigators using the latest equipment and in a selected subset of the patient population, who may comply better with therapy. Consequently, it can be difficult to generalize from the clinical results obtained in such trials, which are often more optimistic than those obtained in regular practice. There may be an even greater impact on the economic data, particularly if clinical practice is different at specialist centers, or if a substantial amount of resource use is mandated by the trial protocol, which may require additional clinical visits or investigations to be performed.

In the lenograstim clinical trials considered here, protocol-driven costs and benefits were not considered a significant problem, since the trial protocols were fairly "naturalistic" and investigators were allowed to treat patients as they would in routine clinical practice. However, it is possible that the closer monitoring of patients in these trials may have led to some very severe cases of neutropenia being averted and/or infections being treated more quickly. If anything, this would bias the economic results *against* lenograstim, since it would cause the cost of neutropenia to be underestimated.

The small cell lung cancer trial was carried out in a single specialist center in the United Kingdom (Manchester). Specialist centers may differ from others in terms of both the procedures followed and the unit costs (prices) of resources. The latter deviation from normal costs can be adjusted for in an economic study by pricing resources not at the level observed in the center concerned, but at a level more representative of the health care system generally. For example, it would be possible to use national salary rates in costing

medical and nursing time, and the most widely available formulation in costing antibiotic regimens. The other potential difference in practice patterns is much more difficult to adjust for without systematically studying the differences between centers.

An additional issue, affecting the German and Italian studies of lenograstim in patients with breast cancer, is that the clinical trial on which these studies were based was undertaken in France. It has been found elsewhere that differences in clinical practice exist between countries (7), and it might therefore be argued that resource use in the trial in France may not be typical of that in Germany or Italy. Thus, an alternative to a "trial-based" analysis (i.e., pricing quantities of resources consumed in the trial in France using German and Italian unit costs) would be to undertake a "practice-adjusted" analysis based on clinical practice observed in the countries concerned. This would involve the use of modeling approaches to make adjustments to the quantities of resources observed, as well as the prices.

While such an approach has a number of advantages, it is not clear what adjustments should be made to the resource use observed in a trial. At least the data collected in trials are assembled according to an agreed protocol, and the process is fairly transparent. When making practice adjustments, the analyst may be open to accusations of bias where these favor the drug of interest, or where legitimate explanations cannot be given. Certainly, the reader of such a study would like to see evidence that clinical practice does vary from setting to setting, and that such deviations are important enough to warrant adjustments. Panels of clinical experts (clinical delphi panels), while acceptable in the past for advising on practice variations (8), may be less acceptable in the future.

A further consequence of departing from trial-based resource use data is that the link between clinical results and economic cost is lessened; that is, the clinical results observed in a trial are dependent on the clinical practices used. Is it right to infer that the same clinical results would be observed with a slightly different resource mix? Where trial-based economic data are available, departures from their use for the primary economic analysis need to be fully justified.

Finally, it may be that the protocol for using the drug of interest may vary between the clinical trial and routine practice. This was an issue in economic evaluations of lenograstim, since the protocol mandated the use of lenograstim with every cycle of chemotherapy, whereas in practice it is likely that clinicians may use recombinant granulocyte colony-stimulating factor (rG-CSF) more selectively, for those patients determined to be at greatest risk of neutropenia. However, similar arguments to those given above apply. That is, how strong is the evidence that regular clinical practice differs from that in the trial and, if so, where is the evidence that the clinical results obtained in the trial would also be obtained with a different rG-CSF regimen? Analysts *should* therefore be cautious about making adjustments to resource use data collected alongside clinical trials. Issues relating to the economic impact of lenograstim in regular clinical practice are discussed further in the preceding article by Oster and colleagues (9).

Use of Proximal End Points

The primary purpose of phase III clinical trials is to establish the efficacy of new drugs. Therefore, it is not surprising that many clinical trials fail to capture all of the end points relevant to economic evaluation. In the case of the three lengrastim clinical trials, we were fortunate that major elements of resource utilization were recorded, because it was recognized at an early stage that economic issues surrounding the use of the drug would be important.

However, even though key resource items may be recorded, economic evaluations can still pose challenges because such recording may not necessarily match the availability of unit cost data. This problem is compounded when economic evaluations need to be performed in different countries, since the sophistication and scope of health service accounting systems varies greatly from place to place. This is an important consideration when designing resource data collection systems, as there is little point in collecting detailed data on resource quantities if unit costs for these are unavailable.

In countries with insurance-based health care systems, more data are usually available on fees and payments, such as hospital charges. The main issue here concerns whether charges reflect true costs. In countries with national health services, charge data are not so widely available. Here, the challenge is to estimate unit costs from general budgetary data.

Another challenge is that although many clinical trials measure parameters related to efficacy, these may not be

ideal for purposes of economic evaluation. For example, in economic evaluations it is desirable to assess clinical end points that have some meaning to the patient, such as length and/or quality of life. However, in phase III clinical trials, it is often considered sufficient to assess short-term biological markers such as serum levels and disease progression. The acceptability of short term markers varies from one clinical field to another. For example, in the field of hypertension, there is widespread acceptance that control of blood pressure is a reliable predictor of long term outcome (i.e., avoidance of fatal and nonfatal strokes). There is less agreement, however, that control of serum cholesterol has a favorable impact on overall mortality (10).

Only one of the three clinical trials of lenograstim included measurement of mortality. Instead, the main clinical end points in the trials were the duration of neutropenia, the rates of documented infection, chemotherapy delay and tumor response and, in two of the trials, the dose intensity of chemotherapy.

For these reasons, trial-based economic evaluations would have to be restricted to cost-minimization analyses, the hypothesis being that lenograstim would reduce the rate of infection, and thereby health care costs. Depending on the level of cost reduction, this may or may not be enough to offset the cost of lenograstim therapy. In situations in which overall cost reduction is achieved, such a study design is satisfactory. However, where the use of lenograstim adds to the overall cost, the obvious question to ask is: Does the benefit justify the increased cost?

In the trial in patients with small cell lung cancer, where information on survival was collected along with supporting data on the dose intensity of chemotherapy, it would be possible to undertake a cost-effectiveness analysis based on the trial itself. However, the only measures of clinical outcome in the other two trials related to infection control (which presumably affects quality of life, as well as cost) and chemotherapy delay (which may affect tumor response and survival). In principle, it would be possible to make inferences about long-term outcomes based on these short-term measures by modelling the impact of dose intensification on survival. However, this would require a number of assumptions that may undermine confidence in the economic evaluation as a whole.

The focus on cost minimization would introduce another complication. While lenograstim would be likely to reduce the costs of treating infections, it may also allow more chemotherapy to be given, at increased cost. Therefore, in a simple cost-minimization analysis, lenograstim would be "penalized" for achieving its clinical objective of enabling the full course of chemotherapy to be given on schedule. This problem could be overcome by separately identifying the chemotherapy costs and focusing the analysis on the "excess" costs of infection-related care. Whereas many economists would have concerns about departing from a consideration of all relevant costs, this approach offers the advantage that neither the benefits nor the costs of chemotherapy enter into the analysis. In situations in which the beneficial effects of chemotherapy on survival or quality of life can be considered in a cost-effectiveness or cost-utility analysis, it would clearly be inappropriate to exclude costs of this treatment.

Inappropriate Follow-up

Drummond and Davis (8) point out that many clinical trials employ only short-term follow-up. Often this is because of the cost of performing long-term trials. However, even in the case of short-term trials of prophylactic antibiotic therapy, patients are often withdrawn from the trial when they have an infection. From the viewpoint of economic evaluation, this is often the point at which patients become interesting, as significant costs may be incurred in treating the infection concerned.

In the three trials of lenograstim, patients were not withdrawn merely because they developed an infection, although a number were lost to follow-up. The reasons for dropout varied among the studies, but included chemotherapy toxicity and death. Clinical trials can be analyzed in terms of either intent-to-treat or evaluable cohorts (i.e., those patients who complete the full course of therapy). For pure efficacy assessments, it is often informative to consider as a subgroup those patients receiving ideal therapy.

However, the appropriate perspective for economic evaluation is unambiguously intent to treat, since economic assessments need to relate to practice in the real world, not practice under ideal conditions. Therefore, if the focus of a given clinical trial is the assessment of efficacy, it may be necessary to undertake further data collection for those patients who drop out of the study. At the very least, it is necessary to establish that those patients dropping out do not incur significant health care costs during the relevant follow-up period. Since drugs have side effects, as well as therapeutic benefits, the costs for patients dropping out may be significant. For example, a study of clozapine therapy for schizophrenia (11) was criticized for ignoring dropouts, since a serious side effect of the drug concerned was agranulocytosis. By excluding dropouts, the costs of treating agranulocy-

tosis were excluded, as were those for increased hospitalizations (12). On the other hand, the relative lack of expensive side effects may sometimes provide a strong argument in favor of a new drug, so follow-up of dropouts may support the economic case for the drug concerned.

The extent of the challenge in following up dropouts is related to the time horizon for the clinical or economic study. Typically in economic evaluations, a defined follow-up period is set, and all treatment groups are studied for the same period of time. In the lenograstim economic studies, the choice of follow-up period was not straightforward. Most chemotherapy regimens involve a number of cycles with intervening periods in which the patient recovers before the next administration of therapy. Lenograstim is intended to be given with each cycle (Fig. 1). The inflammatory breast cancer trial involved four cycles over a planned duration of 84 days, while the non-Hodgkin's lymphoma trial involved four cycles scheduled over 56 days.

One approach would be to consider the cycle of chemotherapy to be the relevant time horizon. This was the approach adopted by Crawford et al. (13) in a clinical report of nonglycosylated rG-CSF (filgrastim), which also included measurement of some resource items such as days of hospitalization. This approach is flawed, however, in that it fails to consider costs and consequences for those patients who do not complete the full course of therapy in their original treatment group. This occurred often in the study by Crawford et al., since patients who experienced infection were withdrawn from the trial and given open-label rG-CSF.

The alternative would be to define a fixed time horizon corresponding to the full course of chemotherapy. However, this is not straightforward, particularly in a situation in which patients in one treatment group may experience more treatment delays than those in the other. This was considered likely in the case of lenograstim, as one of the presumed advantages of rG-CSF is that, by reducing the rate of febrile neutropenia, it may enable more patients to complete their chemotherapy as scheduled. The dilemma is illustrated in Figure 2. Let us suppose that the full course of chemotherapy involves four cycles given over 84 days (as in the inflammatory breast cancer trial) and that, because of higher rates of neutropenia, there are more chemotherapy delays in the

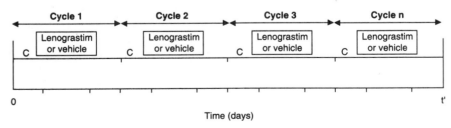

FIG. 1. Standard design of lenograstim clinical trials. t′ is the minimum time required to complete n cycles of chemotherapy; a prolonged recovery period (up to 2 weeks per cycle for persistent toxicity or 3 weeks for severe infection) could delay initiation of subsequent cycles. C, chemotherapy.

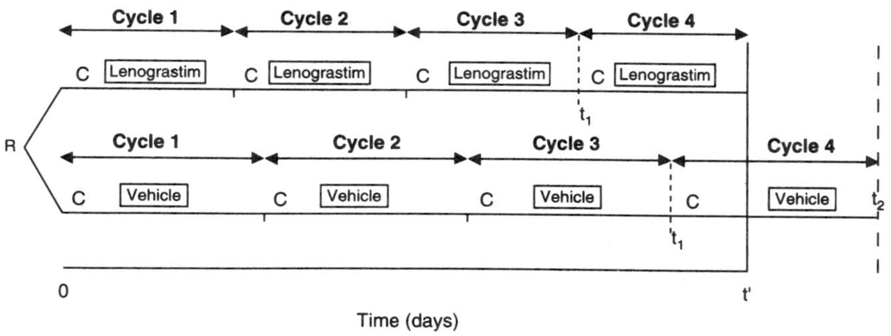

FIG. 2. Choice of time horizons in economic evaluations of lenograstim. This example pertains to the expected results from a trial of a therapy requiring four cycles, as in the breast cancer and non-Hodgkin's lymphoma trials. C, chemotherapy.

group receiving vehicle. There are a number of competing time horizons for an economic study.

One possibility would be to consider only the first three cycles of chemotherapy, since these are completed by patients in both groups. Therefore, at least in terms of therapy given, there would be some notion of equivalence. However, the problem with this approach, using a time horizon (t_1), is that the length of follow-up would differ between groups. Thus, the time period over which patients could potentially incur costs is shorter for the lenograstim group. It could be argued that this introduces bias in favor of lenograstim.

An alternative approach would be to set a time horizon far into the future (t_2), by which time all patients would have completed the full course of chemotherapy. This would have the benefit of being the same for both groups. However, t_2 may be some distance in the future and some patients in the vehicle group may *never* complete the full course of therapy. Also, the further we look into the future, the greater the chance that the costs incurred bear no relation to the disease of interest or its treatment. A long time horizon also imposes significant demands in terms of additional data collection.

Still another approach would be again to use the same time horizon for each group, but to base this on the original scheduled course of treatment (84 days). This introduces a conservative bias because the lenograstim group is likely to incur greater costs of chemotherapy in the 84 days. Nevertheless, this approach has the advantage that the time horizon is based on the original treatment plan and the delays incurred by patients in the vehicle group may have associated costs in the treatment of infections.

The three issues mentioned above represented the major methodological challenges in the economic evaluations of lenograstim. It should be recognized that the challenges are interrelated. For example, the decisions made about the time horizon for the economic studies relate to the quantity of available economic data. Also, the issue of the choice of time horizon becomes more important when data on final outcomes (i.e., survival) are not available.

Statistical Testing

Finally, it is worth mentioning that trial-based economic evaluations raise new challenges relating to the statistical analysis of results. In the past, most economic evaluations have treated cost data as being *deterministic* (i.e., without variance). That is, a point estimate is typically presented. However, where economic data are gathered alongside clinical trials, these can be viewed as being *stochastic* (i.e., having a mean and variance). Since it is customary to perform statistical tests in order to assess whether differences in clinical outcomes of a given size truly exist, the question arises as to whether cost data should be analyzed in a similar way (14,15).

The first problem is that, for economic data, it is difficult to specify what a quantitatively important difference would be. In the design of clinical trials, it is customary to specify the magnitude of the improvement in outcome that would be worthwhile. In the case of economic outcomes, is this difference $1, $1000, or a given percentage of total costs? Also, the relevant difference in cost is itself related to the degree of clinical improvement obtained. After all, economic evaluation seeks to assess whether a given increase in resource use and costs is justified in terms of the benefits achieved.

Therefore, it is unclear whether statistical tests should be performed separately on costs and outcomes, or on cost-effectiveness ratios per se. Even within a cost-minimization framework where the only relevant difference is that of cost, it is unclear whether tests should be performed on differences in physical quantities of resources, or on financial amounts (i.e., costs).

Financial amounts may incorporate variability in both physical quantities of resource use as well as the unit costs of those resources. For these reasons, the variance in total cost may be quite large, and it is unlikely that a study designed to assess efficacy would have sufficient statistical power to show a difference in total cost at conventional levels of statistical significance. Therefore, it would be necessary to assess statistical power before deciding whether statistical tests should be performed at all and, if so, whether they should be performed on resource quantities or costs.

A further complication arises from the fact that many of the resource use variables, such as days of antibiotic therapy and days in hospital, are nonnormally distributed. This would suggest that nonparametric tests should be applied and that medians, rather than means, should be reported. However, for economic analyses the mean is the more relevant measure, as it is important to reflect in the cost calculations those few patients who consume a disproportionate level of resources. Therefore, it was decided to report means, but to assess for statistically significant differences in resource utilization by employing nonparametric tests. (The p-values reported relate therefore to the Wilcoxon test.)

Finally, the standard method of allowing for uncertainty in economic evaluations is to undertake a sensitivity analysis, in which the assumptions about the value of key parameters are varied in order to test the robustness of study results. Therefore, if data are being treated as being stochastic in a trial-based economic evaluation, is there still a role for sensitivity analysis? There may still be a role, because some of the price data could be deterministic. It might be instructive to re-work the analysis applying price data from different settings, comparing one country with another or tertiary care centers with general hospitals.

CONCLUSIONS

The methodological challenges posed by the lenograstim economic evaluations were significant. After discussion of the points outlined above, a single approach was agreed on for all three economic evaluations. The essential elements of these evaluations were as follows:

Economic analyses would be trial-based, using data on resource use collected during the clinical studies

The primary form of economic evaluation would be cost identification, including all costs but separately identifying chemotherapy costs and 'excess' (i.e., infection-related) treatment costs

Economic analyses would be based on an intent-to-treat perspective, with efforts being made to track costs for patients who dropped out of the trials.

The period of follow-up would be the same for both the lenograstim and vehicle groups, and would be set at the minimum time to complete the required number of cycles of chemotherapy (i.e., t_1 in Fig. 2).

Tests of statistical significance would be performed only on a few major elements of resource use that were thought to be important determinants of overall cost, with confidence intervals reported only for total costs.

Overall, the three economic evaluations discussed in other articles in this supplement adhered to this approach, although specific features of each clinical trial led to minor adaptations in methodology. These are discussed in each case.

REFERENCES

1. Anonymous. *Guidelines for the submission of data to the Pharmaceutical Benefits Advisory Committee (PBAC) including economic analysis.* Commonwealth of Australia, Canberra: 1992.
2. Drummond MF. Cost-effectiveness guidelines for reimbursement of pharmaceuticals: is economic evaluation ready for its enhanced status? *Health Econ* 1992;1:85–92.
3. Drummond MF, Rutten FFH, Brenna A, et al. Economic evaluation of pharmaceuticals: a European perspective. *Pharmacoeconomics* 1993; 4:173–186.
4. Chevallier B, Chollet P, Merrouche Y, et al. Glycosylated rHuG-CSF (lenograstim) prevents morbidity from FEC-HD chemotherapy in inflammatory breast cancer (IBC). *Proc Am Soc Clin Oncol* 1993; 12:137.
5. Gisselbrecht C, Lepage E, Haioun C, et al. Lenograstim (glycosylated recombinant human G-CSF) supported chemotherapy optimization in aggressive nonHodgkin's lymphoma (NHL). *Proc Am Soc Clin Oncol* 1993;12:363.
6. Woll PS, Hodgketts H, Lomax L, et al. Use of rHuG-CSF (lenograstim) to dose intensity in small cell lung cancer (SCLC): a randomized study. *Eur J Cancer* 1993;29A(suppl 6):S154.
7. Drummond MF, Bloom BS, Carrin G, et al. Issues in the cross-national assessment of health technology. *Int J Technol Assess Health Care* 1992;8:671–682.
8. Davies LM, Drummond MF. Assessment of costs and benefits of drug therapy for treatment resistant schizophrenia in the United Kingdom. *Br J Psychiatry* 1993;162:38–42.
9. Oster G, Menzin J, Richard D, Chabernaud V. Overview of the lenograstim pharmacoeconomics programme. *Pharmacoeconomics* 1994;6:9–17.
10. Muldoon MF, Manuck SB, Matthews KA. Lowering cholesterol concentrations and mortality: a quantitative review of primary prevention trials. *BMJ* 1990;301:309–314.
11. Revicki D, Luce B, Weschler JM, et al. Cost-effectiveness of clozapine for treatment-resistant schizophrenic patients. *Hosp Community Psychiatry* 1990;41:850–854.
12. Frank RG. Clozapine's cost-benefits. Correspondence. *Hosp Community Psychiatry* 1991:42–92.
13. Crawford J, Ozer H, Stoller R, et al. Reduction by granulocyte colony–stimulating factor of fever and neutropenia induced by chemotherapy in patients with small-cell lung cancer. *N Engl J Med* 1991;325:164–170.
14. O'Brien B, Drummond MF, Labelle R, et al. In search of power and significance: issues in the design and analysis of stochastic economic appraisals. *Med Care* 1994;32:150–163.
15. Drummond MF, O'Brien B. Clinical importance, statistical significance and the assessment of economic and quality-of-life outcomes. *Health Econ* 1993;2:205–212.

Quality of Life and Pharmacoeconomics in Clinical Trials, Second Edition, edited by B. Spilker.
Lippincott-Raven Publishers, Philadelphia © 1996.

CHAPTER 123

Comparing Pharmacoeconomic Data from Different Clinical Trials

Flemming Ørnskov and Bengt G. Jönsson

INTRODUCTION

Pharmacoeconomic research increasingly involves the conduct of economic analyses alongside clinical trials. In these studies, data on resource utilization are collected alongside the clinical trial, and monetary value is assigned at a later stage. The inclusion of economic data collection in clinical trials adds to the aggregate costs of the trial and provides potential benefits by implementing the results into clinical practice. There are other advantages of clinical trials with embedded economic evaluations in addition to those that help doctors and patients decide about individual treatment. One such advantage is to provide data to assist decision makers to allocate resources and to distinguish appropriate and desirable variations in practice from those that are neither (1).

An important question is whether there is any evidence of the impact of these studies and their results on health care policy and decision making. Disappointingly enough, according to a recent analysis of 66 studies involving economic appraisal of health care technologies, it appeared that these studies have a relatively low impact on actual health care policy and decision making (2). However, the same could be said for most clinical trials. Hence, before adding an economic evaluation to a clinical trial, the important issue to consider is whether the additional costs outweigh the additional benefits obtained by including this evaluation. One possible argument is that the costs of the clinical trial may be trivial in comparison with the costs of applying the interventions in practice, in particular if they lead to inefficient allocation of scarce health care resources (3).

The purpose of this chapter is to review issues in comparing and assessing pharmacoeconomic results from multiple trials in which the economic evaluation has been either the main objective of the trial, which is rare, or embedded in (be that alongside or as a post hoc data analysis to) the clinical trial. The latter is by far the most frequent. To illustrate some of our main points, we have also included a case study relating to antiarrhythmic drug therapy.

CONDUCTING A LITERATURE REVIEW OF ECONOMIC EVALUATION OF DRUG THERAPY

The first step in any comparative analysis of cost-effectiveness studies is to identify systematically the published and available unpublished papers to be included in the review, to examine eligibility of the data for inclusion, and to abstract data for analysis. One may even suspect, though we can present no proof, that publication and reference biases may present a bigger challenge when dealing with

F. Ørnskov: Department of Outcomes Research, Merck & Co., Whitehouse Station, New Jersey 08889.

B.G. Jönsson: Centre for Health Economics, Stockholm School of Economics, Stockholm, Sweden.

economic evaluations as compared to clinical evaluations. This may increase the importance of including unpublished studies, however controversial this may be (4).

A good review of cost-effectiveness literature, like any systematic review, should be based on an intimate personal knowledge of the field, the participants, the problems that arise, and the reputation of involved institutions and individual scientists. Hence, the review should ideally be undertaken by someone with an extensive experience with research in the particular field. A knowledge of formal literature review techniques is a necessary complement to this experience but cannot replace it.

Each paper should be evaluated for two key points. First, the validity of the clinical data on which the economic evaluation is based. Second, whether the economic evaluation is based on results concerning a risk factor (e.g., bone mineral density in osteoporosis intervention trials as a surrogate for fracture end point or cholesterol reduction as a surrogate for reduction in cardiac mortality or whether the analysis is based on data in *real* outcomes or events, such as stroke instead of blood pressure.

Having reviewed individual papers, it is important to assess whether the results from different trials using the same surrogate end points correlate both among themselves and, more importantly, with results from event outcomes studies that may be available. This provides no final proof but gives an indication of the validity of the use of surrogate measures. In addition to the results obtained in a systematic review and meta-analysis, another issue of primary importance, yet somewhat overlooked, is the resource collection method used.

It is clear that the validity of the results of statistical analysis comparing results from several studies depends on the validity of the underlying data (5). The indexing terms available for searching Medline for cost-effectiveness studies remain unsatisfactory. A mechanism is needed to register known studies, preferably by tagging Medline entries retrospectively and incorporating trials published in journals not indexed by Medline into the system. Exactly the same issue is important in identifying relevant studies for systematic review of clinical trials.

Subjective judgment is necessary in carrying out a structured comparison of results from several individual cost-effectiveness studies, as is the case for meta-analysis, despite the much acclaimed attempt to use various rules to achieve objectivity in reviewing scientific data (6). These judgments will determine which studies are both relevant and methodologically sound enough to be included, as well as how to handle the outcomes and statistical implications of heterogeneity in these studies. This will also avoid speculative interpretations, leading to a better understanding of the relevance of certain outcomes and economic results.

Although we undoubtedly need more well-conducted and methodologically innovative pharmacoeconomic analyses, either alongside clinical trials or as separate studies, we cannot

afford to disregard the knowledge to be learned from structured aggregation of knowledge from already published studies. One of the problems of conflicting results could be succumbing to pessimism regarding the value of pharmacoeconomic analyses as such. What is called for is more moderation in using the results from such trials, perhaps without embracing conclusions of a study until other studies support them (7). This cautious attitude is of particular importance from a health policy perspective, as the final objective is to encourage physicians and other clinical decision makers to use these results to guide the cost-effective use of pharmaceuticals (8).

DIFFERENT APPROACHES TO ECONOMIC EVALUATION OF DRUG TREATMENT

When comparing economic evaluations on the basis of clinical data, a distinction can be made between clinical and economic issues. Typically, analysis of efficacy data from a randomized clinical trial begins with a null hypothesis, i.e., that there is no difference between treatment and control. The null hypothesis is tested against a one- or two-tailed alternative (the treatment is more effective, or the treatment is more or less effective than the control) (9). Different clinical effectiveness measures can be used, but comparability when including different clinical studies in economic evaluations is limited to interventions aimed at the same clinical result. For example, studies in hypertension can relate costs to blood pressure reduction, reduction in events, reduction in mortality, life-years gained, and quality-adjusted life-years (QALY) gained. Hence, one may have to limit the studies included in a systematic review. In a review of economic evaluation of hypertension treatment, Jönsson and Johannesson (10) only included studies that reported the results in terms of cost per QALY.

The key economic issue is the choice of effectiveness and outcome measures. In addition to the generation of relevant economic hypotheses, the credibility of economic appraisals involving pharmaceuticals depends on a number of methodological variables such as selection of relevant economic evaluation technique, study design, data collection, and data analysis. There are a number of approaches to economic evaluation of drug treatment: (a) an economic evaluation conducted alongside a clinical trial and based on a (separate) protocol; (b) a retrospective economic analysis based on outcomes data from a clinical trial; and (c) a prospective study with a primary economic hypothesis.

In the first case, a separate protocol may have been developed either with or without a specific statistical analysis plan. Many of these protocols are of poor quality and with no specific hypothesis allowing for "fishing expeditions" for statistically significant results, once the trial has been completed. Even more problematic is the fact that the chief investigators, often independent of the sponsor, may have only been exposed to a summary data analysis plan, or in some cases only the case report forms, for the economic evaluation substudy. This may occur out of a perceived lack of interest for economic studies on the part of the investigators and/or lower priority given to these substudies by the sponsor.

Indeed, there may be an understandable sponsor resistance to encumber pivotal safety and efficacy trials with economic evaluations because they may lead to soliciting additional adverse experiences, such as through recording unscheduled physician visits during the trial, that have no causal link to the drug under investigation, but more to the nature of questioning. This may have a profound negative impact on the sponsor when reported, as required, to regulatory agencies and could be seen as an argument for not including those aspects in Phase III, and perhaps even Phase IV clinical trials.

In the second case, which is more usual, the analysis is done retrospectively on and was not an integral part of the clinical trial. The advantage of this approach is that the economic evaluation does not interfere with the clinical trial. By contrast, relevant resource or outcomes data may not be collected, rendering the economic evaluation less useful or even impossible to conduct. This is less likely to happen in the third type of study, in which the sole purpose of the study is to investigate differences in costs or cost-effectiveness. This type of study design is rare.

For the two first approaches to economic evaluation, the resource utilization efforts are frequently followed by independent unit cost studies, often international, if it is a multicenter trial. This is comparable to opening a Pandora's box of problems relating to the handling of standard costs and valuing opportunity costs. The problem becomes most evident when it is necessary to aggregate resource quantities from different international sites in a multicenter trial and add unit costs to them. In these instances, issues such as differences in patient management (e.g., variances in length of hospital stay for the same diagnosis) take on major significance and may jeopardize the economic evaluation. Also, policy makers may be less interested in cost-effectiveness results based on aggregate as opposed to country-specific data.

Standardization of how effectiveness is reported is clearly a necessity for increased comparability in the future. Canadian guidelines for economic evaluation already advocate cost-utility and cost-benefit analysis, primarily due to the greater opportunities for comparability (11). The economic data are often reported in a summary fashion and in a separate manuscript, usually written by someone with health economic training in conjunction with one or several coauthors from the original clinical publication. Several analyses of current practice in the economic evaluation of pharmaceuticals suggest that some standards are required, as many analyses are of poor quality (12,13).

In addition, the level of agreement on aspects of economic evaluation methodology differs from one aspect to another (14,15). In principle, most health economists agree that economic evaluations should compare relevant alternatives in a realistic setting. By contrast, there is still considerable debate about the handling of statistical issues like uncertainty and approaches to sensitivity analysis (16,17). Given the rapid developments in pharmacoeconomic methodology, it is probably preferable that voluntary guidelines for the purpose of maintaining methodological standards seek to specify attainable standards to which everyone should aspire, but allow analysts to improve on these if they wish.

ASSIGNING COSTS TO RESOURCE USE

Several problems occur in evaluating medical resources collected in clinical trials mainly due to a lack of standardization (18). Methods for assigning monetary value to medical resource units have not been standardized, and no agreement exists as to the best way of doing so, whether this implies using local or nationally representative cost figures. One has to decide which type of data to use (e.g., claims data, national survey data, administrative data, or market research data), and whether to use costs or charges when valuing medical resources (15).

The choice of either using costs or charges ultimately depends on the perspective of the analysis. If the perspective is the payer it is straightforward. However, in a social cost-benefit analysis, all relevant resources must be included and valued. Although one, in theory, should use marginal instead of average costs, marginal costs are rarely available. It is also controversial whether sensitivity analysis is sufficient to account for price variations and to measure the impact of varying the discount rate.

Studies also differ in the way resources are valued. Although most researchers agree on the principle of valuing resources according to the opportunity cost (i.e., their value in best alternative use), they differ in the principles used to define these values. One way to achieve comparability is to have a set of defined standard costs. The Australian guidelines include such a list. However, this approach has both pros and cons. Another issue is the definition of the costs included in the analysis. For example, some cost-effectiveness analyses include costs in added years of life (23), while others ignore these costs (24). Some studies include indirect costs, whereas others exclude these costs.

It is preferable for costs to be presented in a disaggregated form, so that cost-effectiveness ratios can be calculated in a way that they are comparable. It is also important to realize whether the cost data have been collected and valued within the clinical trial or outside the trial. The most common procedure is to collect resource use within the trial and to use prices from sources outside the trial; this has practical appeal, but there are several problems. The factor combination used is a consequence of the relative prices. A special problem occurs when you have international multicenter studies where both clinical prices and both absolute and relative prices differ between centers.

FRAMEWORK FOR A SYSTEMATIC REVIEW OF PHARMACOECONOMIC DATA

In order to get started with a systematic review of pharmacoeconomic data in a particular therapeutic area, we have outlined a simple approach in Table 1. A distinction is first made between clinical data originating from one single trial and data from meta-analysis from different trials. A meta-analysis has the advantage of contributing more data but also has inherited complexities (*vide infra*). One practical example of possible problems with meta-analysis is the debate around selective serotonin reuptake inhibitors versus tricyclic antidepressants in the treatment of depression. Much of the debate about the cost-effectiveness of these drugs has centered around the fact that different meta-analyses give different results, possibly induced by significantly different dropout rates (19–21).

If a study is based on a single clinical trial, there is the advantage of a direct link between costs and effects. One must distinguish between two different types of studies. The first type of study is one in which economic evaluation was decided on in advance. The second type, the most common, is the study in which the economic evaluation has been undertaken after completion of the clinical trial. However, it still uses some resource data collected in the trial, but no formal protocol for the economic evaluation was decided on before the clinical study was completed and the data analyzed. A third type of study is one in which the sole purpose of the study is to investigate differences in costs or cost-effectiveness (this is rare). However, most studies have a primary clinical purpose, and the economic evaluation is added on (22).

Meta-analysis rules out the subjective factors outlined above. It can be done by simply feeding the published results to a computer and coming up with an effect size. The computer avoids the bias of the subjective approach but simply adds the biases of the authors of the original articles. The chief problem when comparing economic evaluations regarding the same drug treatment indication (e.g., hypertension) is that there is no single established methodology, and there is a lack of conformity between different studies. One way of limiting the number and scope of studies in a systematic review is to include only those studies that use life-years gained (or QALY) as an outcome measure (11). This approach is not without problems, for example, when such terms as *fraction of benefit* (the fraction of the expected risk reduction achieved through treatment) are introduced (23).

Several sources of "noise"—heterogeneity—can be identified when performing a systematic review of economic evaluations in a given disease area. Some examples are outlined in Table 2.

A review involving statistical compilation of data may prove that despite the fact that the studies lack methodological uniformity, it may be possible to see trends such as greater effectiveness of treatment in certain sub-populations (e.g., particular age groups). It is important to know whether the analysis was done prospectively or retrospectively. It is also important to identify the populations used in the different trials to evaluate whether they are comparable.

Other discrepancies may arise as a result of differences in time and location of the studies. Some of this variation can be resolved by the process of discounting, but different discount rates may be applied. In addition, some studies may only include direct costs, while others also take indirect costs into consideration. It is also important to realize that the cost-effectiveness ratio may depend on age, e.g., the cost-effectiveness of hypertension treatment improves with patient age for both men and women (24).

There are several important times when investigators involved in a clinical trial are required to perform some judgment about what size of effect is clinically important. First, when they have to decide the sample size, when a trial is designed. Second, when upon completion of the trial they are reviewing the observed difference in efficacy. To determine the sample size when a trial is designed, a threshold must be set for a minimum clinically important difference, this judgment being combined with other judgments on acceptable risks of type I and II errors, often set by convention, and estimates of variability in the outcome of interest. There appears to be no a priori definition of the minimum clinically important difference.

Methodologies for the generation of clinical data are relatively well developed, whereas important methodological issues for pharmacoeconomics remain subject to discussion. Consequently, the key objective is to increase the methodological rigor of economic evaluations. In comparing results from different studies covering the same pharmaceutical products, it is important not only to review the validity of the economic evaluation but also the quality of the clinical data on which the economic evaluation is based. This is

TABLE 1. *Different approaches to economic evaluation of drug treatment*

	Single trial		Meta-analysis of several trials
	Prospective (Economic evaluation)	Retrospective	
Reduction in risk factor			
Reduction in risk			

TABLE 2. *Possible sources of heterogeneity in economic evaluations*

Populations studied
  Entirely different populations
  Different subgroups (age, sex, etc.)
  From different geographical locations
Different time periods assessed
  Length of follow-up
  Intermittent/continuous data registration
Perspective of analysis (e.g., payer versus social)
Use of different or differential discount rates
Inclusion of only direct or both direct and indirect costs

particularly an issue when the economic evaluation has been conducted alongside a clinical trial, leading to the expectation of the same standards of measurements and statistical analysis, as are typically applied to clinical data (25,26).

CLINICAL VERSUS ECONOMIC OUTCOMES: WHAT IS A SIGNIFICANT DIFFERENCE?

It is important to consider the selection of treatment alternatives, in particular if the study involves international comparisons. The problem is that many published studies involving economic evaluations either compare data obtained to no treatment or treatments that will produce large differences but may not represent relevant alternatives. The reality is that economic evaluations are often conducted based on randomized, clinical trials that will produce only moderate differences in outcomes, despite the fact that these differences may be potentially very important to patients (27). Individually, most of these trials are too small to assess any economic differences reliably. There are two ways to overcome this problem: (a) conducting large, yet expensive prospective randomized trials; or (b) meta-analysis of completed trials. However, meta-analysis of completed, published, and perhaps even unpublished studies, have many problems that will lead to additional problems in any attempt to conduct economic evaluations retrospectively.

In terms of relevance, a difference in outcome should be of sufficient magnitude to influence the physician's attitude to switch from one drug to another. A frequently applied strategy is to increase the delta to reduce the sample size and cost, leading to delta ultimately being a compromise in the face of competing objectives (28). Consequently, one could argue that before constructing an incremental cost-effectiveness ratio, the differences in both numerator (cost) and denominator (effect) must have been shown to be statistically significant. Therefore, cost-effectiveness essentially becomes embedded in at least two statistical hypotheses concerning differences in costs and effects. Ideally, the magnitude of difference in effectiveness should be not only statistically, but clinically relevant as well. One may also use different type I errors for costs and effects. Finally, the issue is whether it would be possible to construct a confi-

dence interval for an incremental cost-effectiveness ratio, and eventually how this might be used in the interpretation of cost-effectiveness data.

Inferences concerning relative value for money is often made from league tables, which provide rankings of interventions in terms of cost-effectiveness with little indication of the uncertainty around estimates. A standardized confidence interval would be a useful addition when comparing estimates in league tables to determine where differences really exist and where they were probably attributable to chance alone. League tables offer only part of the basis for interpreting cost-effectiveness ratios from completed studies. An alternative approach is to set a threshold in terms of value for money prior to the study. The weakness of this approach is not in the statistics but in the arbitrary thresholds being imposed as indicators of relative value. However, these quantitative thresholds are no more arbitrary than those used in clinical trials.

Standardization of instruments to measure both clinical and economic factors is a crucial next step in the evolution of useful research-based information. An example is thrombolytic therapy (e.g., streptokinase and tissue plasminogen activator) after myocardial infarction. The literature shows that far more effort has been put into designing and conducting large clinical trials than in identifying which outcomes, other than death, should be measured and how different outcomes may be valued to measure overall benefit (29). A comparison of effectiveness must therefore include both costs and outcomes, in particular if, as is the case for streptokinase and tissue plasminogen activator, costs differ substantially and measurable differences in benefits are deemed small (30). However, the literature contains few studies of cost-effectiveness, and those that have been reported show little consistency in methods, costs measured, discounting of future costs and benefits, or how costs are related to outcomes.

EXAMPLES OF ECONOMIC EVALUATION OF MEDICAL THERAPY

One of the simpler ways to conduct an economic evaluation of drug therapy is to calculate cost per life-year saved. Two such studies have used modeling techniques applied retrospectively to trial results and produced different answers, at least partly because different perspectives were used. One estimated the direct cost per life-year saved for a moderate infarct as $171,000 (1987 prices) for intravenous streptokinase and $158,000 for intravenous tissue plasminogen activator (31). A similar study—one limited to Medicare costs—calculated a direct cost per life saved of $52,700 for streptokinase and $56,900 for tissue plasminogen activator (32). An alternative and valid technique would be to calculate cost per added life-year. None of these studies incorporates quality of life measures. Such studies are rare and vary in the instruments used to measure quality of life. Retrospective studies of intracoronary streptokinase have estimated direct costs for each additional QALY on the basis of survival at 1 and 3 years, respectively, from $3,300 to $4,000 (1993 prices), using data from the same clinical trial (at 1 and 3 years of follow-up) (33,34). One such study of tissue plasminogen activator estimated a cost per QALY saved of $1,000 (1993 prices), including indirect costs (35).

Another example is hormone replacement therapy for osteoporosis. Although several studies have consistently found a relationship between the use of hormone replacement therapy and risk of hip fracture, none of the existing studies of this relationship are a randomized prospective clinical trial (36). The limitations of such observational studies as definitive evidence of a causal relationship between an intervention and a clinical outcome are well known. Support for the proposition that hormone replacement therapy reduces hip fracture incidence comes from a number of clinical trials in postmenopausal women that have shown a statistically significant reduction in the incidence of osteoporosis-related fractures, other than hip fractures, in users of hormone replacement therapy (37,38). However, there are issues related to duration of therapy and compliance, in particular as hormone replacement therapy probably has to be continued for a decade to have an effect, leaving little direct evidence on which to build a quantitative estimate of such effect. Hence, any systematic review of economic evaluation of osteoporosis prevention and treatment, not only covering hormone replacement therapy but also other relevant treatment alternatives, such as bisphosphonates, calcitonin, fluoride, and calcium, runs into the problem of lack of reliable and valid data to base the cost-effectiveness analyses on. This precludes clear-cut conclusions about the cost-effectiveness of osteoporosis prevention and treatment (39).

An additional obstacle to meaningful comparisons of results from different economic trials is the case in which the potential benefits and risks of therapy have not been clearly delineated, despite a large number of clinical trials. One such example is antiarrhythmic therapy. This becomes even more complicated if one has to include a comparison with a nondrug intervention such as implantable cardioverter-defibrillators in the treatment of ventricular arrhythmia and the prevention of sudden cardiac death. This also provides a good case study for comparing data from different clinical studies that have involved economic evaluations.

CLINICAL IMPORTANCE OF PHARMACOECONOMIC DATA—THE CASE OF ANTIARRHYTHMIC THERAPY

In 1991, important new data in antiarrhythmic therapy were obtained by the Cardiac Arrhythmia Suppression Trial (CAST), in which patients convalescing from myocardial infarction who had asymptomatic ventricular ectopic beats that were suppressed by encainide and flecainide were randomly assigned to long-term therapy or placebo (40). The mortality rate in the patients receiving either drug was two to three times higher than that in patients receiving placebo (41). A likely explanation for the increase in mortality was an increase in fatal arrhythmias caused by antiarrhythmic drug therapy (41).

The result of this trial led physicians to call into question the assumption that drug-induced suppression of this particular arrhythmia was desirable (41). Adding to this trend was the fact that apart from CAST II no other trials with a similar design for other antiarrhythmic drugs have ever been conducted. For patients at very high risk of recurrent ventricular tachycardia or fibrillation (e.g., those resuscitated after cardiac arrest), an implantable cardioverter-defibrillator is an option (42). The results of CAST, combined with the positive reports of retrospective research on health outcomes of implantable cardioverter-defibrillator patients, and the approval by Medicare to reimburse implantation of cardioverter-defibrillators caused many cardiologists to embrace them quickly for patients at risk of sudden cardiac death (43). However, the value of implanted devices has never been demonstrated in randomized trials, and several studies suggest that their effect on long-term survival (beyond 5 years) may be small (44,45).

Approximately two thirds of patients receiving implanted cardioverter-defibrillators are also prescribed antiarrhythmic drugs (46). The antiarrhythmic drug and cardioverter-defibrillator work in a complementary manner. The drug tries to preclude arrhythmias, and the cardioverter-defibrillator suppresses them if they do start, making patient selection for implantation of a cardioverter-defibrillator difficult. The survival rate of patients with implantable cardioverter-defibrillators in Table 3 ranges from 89% to 95% after 1 year, approximately 84% at 2 years, ranges from 65% to 82% after three years, and is about 74% after 5 years. The large ranges of the survival rates are most likely due to the incomparability of the methods used by various researchers to collect the data.

It should be noted that estimates from recent research provide more conservative survival rates than the earlier research. This is most likely because earlier research design did not control for concomitant drug therapy, demographics, case mix, and indicators of severity such as ejection fraction

TABLE 3. *Cumulative survival rate of patients with implantable cardioverter-defibrillators*

First author/ref/yr	1 yr (%)	2 yr (%)	3 yr (%)	5 yr (%)
Kelly (47) (1988)	95			
Winkle (48) (1989)	92	84	82	74
Newman (49) (1992)	89		65	
Uther (50) (1992)	89	84		
Fogoros (51) (1990)[a]				67
Axtell (52) (1991)[a]		60		
Uther (50) (1992)[a]	70	54		

[a]Among low ejection fraction patients (<40%).

between the treatment and the control groups. The perioperative mortality ranges from 2% to 8%, depending on how it is defined and measured (53). Researchers have estimated that implanted cardioverter-defibrillators improve survival by 8 to 21 months (54). This statistic raises the obvious question: at what cost are these improvements in survival being made? Several cost-effectiveness studies have tried to answer this question. Table 4 highlights the published results of the four major cost-effectiveness studies conducted on patients with implanted cardioverter-defibrillators.

Kuppermann et al. (55) used a Markov state transition model to estimate the net cost-effectiveness of a defibrillator, when used in a high-risk patient. They calculated a cost-effectiveness ratio of $17,100 per life-year saved, and with sensitivity analysis of influential factors, they were confident that the true value lay between $15,000 and $25,000. Larsen et al. (56) estimated the marginal cost-effectiveness ratio for implanted cardioverter-defibrillators versus amiodarone therapy to be $29,200 per life-year saved. If technological improvements result in an extended average battery life, they estimated that the marginal cost-effectiveness could decrease to $21,800 to $13,800.

O'Brien et al. (57) calculated the total mortality adjusted and discounted cost of implantable cardioverter-defibrillators over 20 years to be £28,400 compared with £2,300 for amiodarone. Their cost-effectiveness ratios ranged from £8,200 to £15,400 ($16,500 to $31,000) per life-year gained, which is very similar to the estimates found by Larsen et al. (56). The estimates noted by Anderson and Camm (58) of £22,400 to £57,000 ($33,500 to $85,500) are somewhat higher than those of the other researchers. However, their sensitivity analysis showed that these figures may decrease substantially due to medical and technical advances, such as the use of transvenous implantation, increased battery life, and improved diagnostic methods to identify high-risk patients.

A cost of $20,000 to $40,000 per life-year saved compares favorably to estimates such as $20,000 to $100,000 for hypertension, depending on the patient population (59). However, it is controversial whether earlier or more widespread implantation of cardioverter-defibrillators in high-risk patients may lead to some cost offsets and improved cost-effectiveness figures due to a reduction in diagnostic testing and average length of hospitalization, as proponents are advocating (60). The obvious danger of reducing diagnostic testing is that it may lead to implantation of cardioverter-defibrillators into patients for whom less expensive drug treatment would have been sufficient. A number of researchers question the validity of some of these findings, contending that some of the retrospective studies may have analyzed noncomparable cardiac populations, perhaps due to changes in patient selection criteria or variance in therapeutic strategies. However, although high-risk patients can be identified, implantation of cardioverter-defibrillators is not known to reduce the risk (61,62). It is possible that cardioverter-defibrillators may only change the mode of death in some high-risk patients from arrhythmic to nonarrhythmic. The only way to measure the true efficacy of cardioverter-defibrillators is by randomized clinical trials (63).

Concomitant antiarrhythmic drug therapy was given to patients with cardioverter-defibrillators in many of the previous studies. The favorable outcomes of these patients were therefore due not only to the cardioverter-defibrillators but also to efficacious drugs such as amiodarone. Total arrhythmia-related death rate or even total cardiac death rate calculated in previous studies are inappropriate end points due to the difficulty of precise classification of the cause of death and susceptibility to investigator bias. Therefore, the appropriate end point to measure is total mortality. The trade-off of accounting for the misclassification problem by including unrelated deaths is that it will result in underestimation of benefits of a therapy in absolute terms. However, in sufficiently large, controlled studies, the incidence of such unrelated deaths should be nearly the same for each treatment arm, such that the relative benefits of the therapies are not affected.

Although qualitative research has been done to understand quality of life concerns that patients with cardioverter-defibrillators have, no attempt has been made to incorporate these concerns quantitatively into the cost-effectiveness models. If an antiarrhythmic drug has a favorable side effect profile, by including quality of life utility values into calculating cost-effectiveness ratios, it is quite possible that the marginal cost-effectiveness of cardioverter-defibrillators and drug as concomitant therapy is minimal when compared to cardioverter-defibrillators alone. Also, the marginal cost-effectiveness of cardioverter-defibrillators when compared to drug could be much more expensive than the $20,000 to $40,000 per life-year saved value derived by earlier research when evaluated in this manner.

TABLE 4. *Cost-effectiveness of implantable cardioverter-defibrillators*

First author/ref/yr	Therapies compared	CE ratio (per life-year saved)
Kuppermann (55) (1990)	ICD[a] vs. CDT	$17,100 (15,000–25,000)
Larsen (56) (1992)	ICD[a] vs. amiodarone vs. CDT	$29,200 (13,800–21,800)[b]
O'Brien (57) (1992)	ICD[a] or amiodarone	£8,200–15,400 (~$12,800–24,000)
Anderson (58) (1993)	ICD[a] vs. amiodarone	£22,400–57,000 (~$34,900–88,900)

CE, cost-effectiveness; CDT, conventional drug therapy; ICD, implantable cardioverter-defibrillator.
[a]Second-generation ICD.
[b]Expressed in 1989 U.S. dollars.

The clinical impact of these devices will be predicated by not only absolute survival benefits, but also by their relative advantages over alternative therapies in terms of survival, safety, morbidity, quality of life, and cost. Their impact on public health will depend on the effectiveness of screening methods for identification of population likely to benefit from primary prevention. Risk stratification algorithms are now being tested in several ongoing clinical trials. The economic impact on health care budgets of the cardioverter-defibrillators will largely be determined by the future cost of the devices, hospital costs associated with the therapy, and accurate patient population selection. This brief review of the literature has identified many flaws in previous clinical research of implantable cardioverter-defibrillators and antiarrhythmic agents used to treat recurrent ventricular tachycardia or fibrillation (64,65), leading to a nearly insurmountable challenge in terms of conducting a systematic review of the economic aspects of treatment. Ongoing assessment and randomized clinical trials are essential to the continual development of this therapy and its diffusion into health care systems (66,67). It is hoped that clinical trials now under way will help define the relative risks and benefits of implantable cardioverter-defibrillators, amiodarone, sotalol, and newer drugs in preventing sudden death. The validity of future economic evaluations depends on such trials.

CONCLUSIONS

The policy goal of embedding economic evaluations in clinical trials should be that decision making will lead not only to evidence-based medicine, but also to better and more efficient allocation of health care resources (68). One way of distinguishing between clinical and economic trials is that clinical trials often have a well-defined clinical question to address, whereas the *real* objective of economic evaluations is to guide the allocation of scarce resources. This may sometimes lead to subsequent criticism of an economic evaluation stating that the underlying clinical studies do not adequately represent clinical reality. One reason for that may be that the policy implications of the results first become evident when an economic evaluation for purposes of simplicity extracts the main clinical outcomes and develops the consequences for resource allocation.

Clinical trials serve a specific and particular objective (e.g., measures safety and efficacy) that may render them less than ideal as a vehicle for an economic trial. Placebo, often used in clinical trials as a "relevant" comparator, may be of no or poor value as a comparator in an economic trial. Furthermore, many clinical trials measure only intermediate outcomes making the ultimate impact on the health of the patients a matter of educated guesswork in the economic evaluation. In such cases, economic evaluations often leave themselves open to criticism which may be reinforced if the underlying clinical study later comes under attack for poor methodology (69) or the results are simply rendered obsolete by later trials.

When trying to test an economic hypothesis, one should ideally design the study mainly for that purpose and perform power calculations accordingly. However, a trade-off is often made between the clinical and economic evaluation. For an economic evaluation, a naturalistic trial (i.e., a design mirroring actual, hopefully rational, clinical practice as closely as possible) is preferable. On the contrary, most clinical trials have a very narrow objective leading to a design that at best reflects ideal (i.e., "scientific") clinical medicine. Hence, clinical objectives often take priority over economic evaluations, something which may be acceptable and relevant in phase III trials, but much less so in phase IV trials.

Evidence-based clinical economics should emphasize the need for rigorous evaluations of the published literature and the consequences for treatment recommendations and allocation of resources between different treatment alternatives. It will also be important to focus on ways to improve the reporting of pharmacoeconomic studies. This should include not only more informative abstracts, providing the reader with a series of relevant headings pertaining to the design, conduct, and analysis of both cost and effectiveness of a study. The next step will be to develop a structured reporting that will provide sufficiently detailed information about the design, conduct, and analysis of the study for the reader to have confidence in the results (70). Particularly when modeling is involved, it is important to provide this information to ensure that the results provide a valid, unbiased estimate of the "truth."

Concerns over the validity of privately funded health service research in this area is not in itself a criteria for inclusion or noninclusion of results in a systematic review. Some of the distortions of the scientific process ascribed to private sector can also occur in research funded by the public sector (e.g., in terms of dependence on potential founders). More important is to agree on the fact that private sector research in this area should be subject to the same scientific and professional norms that govern scientific research (71).

ACKNOWLEDGMENTS

The authors express their thanks to Mr. Santanu Datta, doctoral student in Health Services Research at the University of North Carolina at Chapel Hill, School of Public Health, for helping review the extensive literature on antiarrhythmic therapy in general and implantable cardioverter-defibrillators in particular during his 1994 summer internship at Merck & Co., and Ms. Gillian M. Cannon, Senior Director, Department of Outcomes Research, Merck & Co., Inc., for thorough review and helpful suggestions. The opinions expressed are those of the authors, not of the institutions they are affiliated with.

REFERENCES

1. Delamonthe T. Using outcomes research in clinical practice. *BMJ* 1994;308:1583–1584.
2. Davies L, Coyle D, Drummond M, and the EC Network on the Methodology of Economic Appraisal of Health Technology. Current status of economic appraisal of health technology in the European community. Report of the network. *Soc Sci Med* 1994;38:1601–1607.
3. Fletcher RH. The costs of clinical trials. *JAMA* 1989;262:1842.
4. Oxman AD, Cook DJ, Guyatt GH, et al. Users' guide to the medical literature. VI. How to use an overview. *JAMA* 1994;272:1367–1371.
5. Dickersin K, Scherer R, Lefebvre C. Identifying relevant studies for systematic reviews. *BMJ* 1994;309:1286–1291.
6. Thompson SG. Why sources of heterogeneity in meta-analysis should be investigated. *BMJ* 1994;309:1351–1355.
7. Angel M, Kassirer J. Clinical research—what should the public believe? *N Engl J Med* 1994;331:189–190.
8. Shulkin DJ. Enhancing the role of physicians in the cost-effective use of pharmaceuticals. *Hosp Form* 1994:262–273.
9. Soutre EJ, Qing W, Hardens M. Methodological approaches to pharmaco-economics. *Fundam Clin Pharmacol* 1994;8:101–107.
10. Johannesson M, Jönsson B. A review of cost-effectiveness analyses of hypertension treatment. *PharmacoEconomics* 1992;1:250–264.
11. Canadian Office for Health Technology Assessment. *Guidelines for economic evaluation of pharmaceuticals: Canada.* 1st Ed. November 1994. Ottawa, Ontario, Canada.
12. Udvarhelyi IS, Colditz GA, Arti Rai AB, et al. Cost-effectiveness and cost-benefit analyses in the medical literature: are the methods being used correctly? *Ann Intern Med* 1992;116:238–244.
13. Gerard K. Cost-utility in practice: a policy maker's guide to the state of art. *Health Policy* 1992;21:249–279.
14. Wells N. Economic evaluation of drugs: a UK pharmaceutical perspective. *PharmacoEconomics* 1992;1:14–19.
15. Drummond MF. Guidelines for pharmacoeconomic studies. The ways forward. *PharmacoEconomics* 1994;6:493–499.
16. O'Brien B, Drummond MF, Labelle R. In search of power and significance: issues in the design and analysis of stochastic economic appraisals. *Med Care* 1994;32:150–163.
17. Briggs AH, Sculpher MJ, Buxton MJ. Uncertainty in the economic evaluation of healthier technologies: the role of sensitivity analysis. *Health Econ* 1994;3:95–104.
18. Copley-Merriman C, Lair TJL. Valuation of medical resource units collected in health economic studies. *Clin Ther* 1994;16:553–568.
19. Jönsson B. Economic evaluation and clinical uncertainty: response to Freemantle and Maynard. *Health Econ* 1994;3:305–307.
20. Dunbar GC, Cohn JB, Fabre LF, Feighner JP, et al. A comparison of paroxetine, imipramine and placebo in depressed outpatients. *Br J Psychiatry* 1991;159:394–398.
21. Song F, Freemantle N, Sheldon TA, House A, et al. Selective reuptake inhibitors: meta-analysis of efficacy and acceptability. *BMJ* 1993;306:683–687.
22. Levin L-Å, Jönsson B. Cost-effectiveness of thrombolysis: a randomized study of intravenous rt-PA in suspected myocardial infarction. *Eur Heart J* 1992;13:2–8.
23. Weinstein MC, Stason WB. Allocation of resources to manage hypertension. *N Engl J Med* 1977;296:732–739.
24. Johannesson M. The impact of age on the cost-effectiveness of hypertension treatment: an analysis of randomized drug trials. *Med Decis Making* 1994;14:236–244.
25. Adams ME, McCall NT, Gray DT, et al. Economic analysis in randomized clinical trials. *Med Care* 1992;30:231–243.
26. Drummond MF, Davies LM. Economic analysis alongside clinical trials: revisiting the methodological issues. *Int J Technol Assess Health Care* 1991;7:561–573.
27. Clarke MJ, Stewart LA. Obtaining data from randomized controlled trials: how much do we need for reliable and informative meta-analyses? *BMJ* 1994;300:1007–1010.
28. O'Brien BJ, Drummond MF. Statistical versus quantitative significance in the socioeconomic evaluation of medicines. *PharmacoEconomics* 1994;5:389–398.
29. Szczepura A. Finding a way through the cost and benefit maze. *BMJ* 1994;309:1314–1315.
30. McMurray J, Rankin A. Recent advances in cardiology. I. Treatment of myocardial infarction, unstable angina, and angina pectoris. *BMJ* 1994;309:1343–1350.
31. Laffel GL, Fineberg HV, Braunwald E. A cost effectiveness model for coronary thrombolysis/reperfusion therapy. *J Am Coll Cardiol* 1987;10;79–90B.
32. Steinberg EP, Topol EJ, Sakin JW, et al. Cost and procedure implications of thrombolytic therapy for acute myocardial infarction. *J Am Coll Cardiol* 1988;12:58–68A.
33. Vermeer P, Simoons ML, De Zwaar C, et al. Cost benefit analysis of early thrombolytic treatment with intracoronary streptokinase. Twelve months follow up report of the randomized multicenter trial conducted by the Interuniversity Cardiology Institute of the Netherlands. *Br Heart J* 188;59:527–534.
34. Simoons ML, Vos J, Martens LL. Cost-utility analysis of thrombolytic therapy. *Eur Heart J* 1991;12:694–699.
35. Levin L-Å. Thyrombolytics in acute myocardial infarction as a case study. In: Warren KS, Mosteller F, eds. *Doing more good than harm: the evaluation of health care interventions. Ann NY Acad Sci* 1993;703:63–73.
36. Naess'en T, Persson I, Adami HO, et al. Hormone replacement therapy and the risk for first hip fracture. *Ann Intern Med* 1990;113:95–103.
37. Riggs BL, Seaman E, Hodgson SF, et al. Effect of the fluoride/calcium regimen on vertebral fracture occurrence in postmenopausal osteoporosis. *N Engl J Med* 1982;306:446–450.
38. Lufkin EG, Wahner HW, O'Fallon WM, et al. Treatment of postmenopausal osteoporosis with transdermal estrogen. *Ann Intern Med* 1992;117:1–9.
39. Johannesson M, Jönsson B. Economic evaluation of osteoporosis prevention. *Health Policy* 1993;24:103–124.
40. Echt DS, Liebson PR, Mitchell LB, et al. Mortality and morbidity in patients receiving encainide, flecainide, or placebo. *N Engl J Med* 1991;324:781–788.
41. Roden DM. Risks and benefits of antiarrhythmic therapy. *N Engl J Med* 1994;331:785–791.
42. Saksena S. Survival of implantable cardioverter-defibrillator recipients: can the iceberg remain submerged? *Circulation* 1992;85:1616–1618. (Erratum, *Circulation* 1992;86:1347.)
43. Singh BN. Do antiarrhythmic drugs work? Some reflections on the implications of the cardiac arrhythmia suppression trial. *Clin Cardiol* 1990;13:725–728.
44. Kim SG, Fisher JD, Choue CW, et al. Influence of left ventricular function on outcome of patients with implantable defibrillators. *Circulation* 1992;85:1304–1310.
45. Newman D, Sauve MJ, Herre J, et al. Survival after implantation of the cardioverter defibrillator. *Am J Cardiol* 1992;69:899–903.
46. Dorian P, Newman D. The implantable defibrillator and antiarrhythmic drugs—competitive and complementary treatment for severe ventricular arrhythmia. *Clin Cardiol* 1993;16:827–830.
47. Kelly PA, Cannom DS, Hasan G, et al. The automatic implantable cardioverter defibrillator: efficacy, complications and survival in patients with malignant ventricular arrhythmias. *J Am Coll Cardiol* 1988;11:1278–1286.
48. Winkle RA, Mead RH, Ruder MA, et al. Long-term outcomes with the automatic implantable cardioverter-defibrillator. *J Am Coll Cardiol* 1989;13:1353–1361.
49. Newman D, Sauve MJ, Herre J, et al. Survival after implantation of the cardioverter defibrillator. *Am J Cardiol* 1992;69:899–903.
50. Uther JF. The automatic implantable defibrillator is the most realistic and cost-effective way of preventing sudden cardiac death. *Aust NZ J Med* 1992;22 (suppl 5):636–638.
51. Fogoros RN, Elson JJ, Bonnet CA, et al. Efficacy of the automatic implantable cardioverter-defibrillator in prolonging survival in patients with severe underlying cardiac disease. *J Am Coll Cardiol* 1990;16:381–386.
52. Axtell K, Tchou P, Akhtar M. Survival in patients with depressed left ventricular function treated by implantable cardioverter defibrillator. *PACE* 1991;14(pt II):291–296.
53. Kim SG. Implantable defibrillator therapy. Does it really prolong life? How can we prove it? *Am J Cardiol* 1993;71:1213–1218.
54. Newman D, Herre J, Sauve MJ, et al. The automatic implantable cardioverter defibrillator and patient survival: a case control study. *J Am Coll Cardiol* 1989;13:65A.

55. Kuppermann M, Luce BR, McGovern B, et al. An analysis of the cost effectiveness of the implantable defibrillator. *Circulation* 1990;81: 91–100.

56. Larsen GC, Manolis AS, Sonnenberg FA, et al. Cost-effectiveness of the implantable cardioverter-defibrillator: effect of improved battery life and comparison with amiodarone therapy. *J Am Coll Cardiol* 1992;19:1323–1334.

57. O'Brien BJ, Buxton MJ, Rushby JA. Cost effectiveness of the implantable cardioverter defibrillator: a preliminary analysis. *Br Heart J* 1992;68:241–245.

58. Anderson MH, Camm AJ. Implications for present and future applications of the implantable cardioverter-defibrillator resulting from the use of a simple model of cost efficacy. *Br Heart J* 1993;69:83–92.

59. Dorian P, Newman D. The implantable defibrillator and anti-arrhythmic drugs—competitive and complementary treatment for severe ventricular arrhythmia. *Clin Cardiol* 1993;16:827–830.

60. O'Donoghue S, Platia EV, Robinson SB, Mispireta L. Automatic implantable cardioverter-defibrillator: is early implantation cost effective? *J Am Coll Cardiol* 1990;16:1258–1263.

61. Saksena S, Camm AJ. Implantable defibrillators for prevention of sudden death: technology at a medical and economic crossroad. *Circulation* 1992;85:2316–2321.

62. Connolly SJ, Yusuf S. Evaluation of the implantable cardioverter defibrillator in survivors of cardiac arrest: the need for randomized trials. *Am J Cardiol* 1992;69:959–962.

63. Greene HL. Antiarrhythmic drugs versus implantable defibrillators: the need for a randomized controlled study. *Am Heart J* 1993;127: 1171–1178.

64. Kim SG, Fischer JD, Furman S, et al. Benefits of implantable defibrillators are overestimated by sudden death rates and better represented by the total arrhythmia death rate. *J Am Coll Cardiol* 1991;17:1587–1592.

65. Cannom DS. A critical appraisal of indications for the implantable cardioverter defibrillator (ICD). *Clin Cardiol* 1992;15:369–372.

66. Saksena S. The impact of implantable cardioverter defibrillator therapy on health care systems. *Am Heart J* 1994;127(4 pt 2):1193–1200.

67. de Lissovoy G, Guarnieri T. Cost-effectiveness of the implantable cardioverter-defibrillator. *Prog Cardiovasc Dis* 1993;36:209–213.

68. Guyatt GH, Rennie D. Users' guide to the medical literature. *JAMA* 1993;270:2096–2097.

69. Johannesson M, Wikstrand J, Jönsson B, Berglund G, Tuomilehto J. Cost-effectiveness of antihypertensive treatment. Metoprolol versus thiazide diuretics. *PharmacoEconomics* 1993;3(1):36–44.

70. The Standards of Reporting Trials Group. A proposal for structured reporting of randomized controlled trials. *JAMA* 1994;272(24):1926–1931.

71. Kallich JD, Hays RD. The benefits and pitfalls of health services research funded by proprietary firms. *Qual Life Res* 1994;3:231–233.

Quality of Life and Pharmacoeconomics in Clinical Trials, Second Edition, edited by B. Spilker.
Lippincott-Raven Publishers, Philadelphia © 1996.

CHAPTER **124**

A Bayesian Approach to the Economic Evaluation of Health Care Technologies

David A. Jones

INTRODUCTION

In recent years, there has been a rapid increase in the availability of economic data at the patient level, particularly data captured alongside clinical trials. For these types of data, a stochastic rather than a deterministic approach to data analysis is appropriate. Consequently, there has been a growing interest by pharmacoeconomists in conventional statistical inference, such as hypothesis testing and confidence intervals. Whether such techniques have a meaningful interpretation when applied to pharmacoeconomic data is in itself a major topic for debate. However, one wonders whether it is too premature to debate these issues when a more fundamental question is still left unanswered. This question concerns the wisdom of pursuing the conventional approach when other possible approaches have not been fully explored. One of these alternative approaches is to use Bayes methodology. This paper investigates the hypothesis that Bayesian methods may be better suited to the needs of pharmacoeconomics than conventional statistical methods.

The conventional approach to statistical inference (more commonly referred to as the classical or frequentist approach) usually involves hypothesis testing and confidence interval estimation. However, the classical approach has many limitations. These limitations have made interpretation

of study results difficult and confusing even to statisticians. Classical statisticians have for many years been trying to find solutions to these inherent difficulties but without satisfactory success. A ''solution'' has sometimes been found by trying to interpret classical statistics in a Bayesian way. In many cases, this has been equivalent to giving the right answer to the right question, but using the wrong method to achieve it. Furthermore, classical methods invariably provide answers to the wrong questions and thus fail to answer the real questions that matter to the researcher. Some of these limitations, many of which are insurmountable within the classical framework, are discussed in a later section.

Despite these limitations, the classical approach is now regarded as the gold standard for many areas of scientific research. In fact, many medical journals will reject studies that have not been classically designed (i.e., using power and sample size calculations) or where the data have not been analyzed using classical statistical techniques (e.g., confidence intervals, p-values). However, even when the studies themselves are acceptable, much useful and informative data is often ignored or lost simply because those unforgiving p-values (the hallmark of the frequentist) are considered too big. Medical journals are the first target for many pharmacoeconomic studies, particularly those based on data generated from a randomized controlled clinical trial. The result is considerable pressure on pharmacoeconomists to adopt the classical approach to the analysis of pharmacoeconomic data despite the limitations of the methodology.

D. A. Jones: Department of Strategic Health Economics, Glaxo Wellcome PLC, Beckenham, Kent BR3 3BS, England.

Bayes theorem is not a new concept in economic evaluation. In fact, Bayesian theory underpins a lot of the pharmacoeconomic modeling, but this has not been fully understood or developed by pharmacoeconomists. This chapter demonstrates that by treating pharmacoeconomic data as a collection of random variables, a far more powerful and sophisticated application of Bayes theorem becomes possible. Not only is the Bayes approach not new to economic evaluation, it is also a perfectly natural extension of the classical approach. This will become evident in the following discussion.

What follows is a brief, simplified excursion through the theory underpinning the Bayesian approach. Every opportunity is taken to compare and contrast with the classical approach and to show how the methodology can be applied to pharmacoeconomics.

CLASSICAL STATISTICAL INFERENCE

The use of hypothesis testing for making statistical inferences about an unknown parameter(s) is now fairly commonplace in the sciences today. The results of the hypothesis test is usually presented as a table of summary statistics comprising a measure of central location (e.g., the mean and/or median), a measure of spread (e.g., the standard deviation and/or the standard error), and a probability interval (e.g., a 95% confidence interval on the statistic(s) of interest); p-values are also often computed. These p-values have the objective of informing the researcher as to whether the hypothesis can be reasonably rejected. This is classical statistical inference. However, despite its popularity, there are drawbacks to this approach which can be remedied by Bayesian methods. One of these drawbacks can be illustrated by the following example, adapted from an example by Iverson, 1984 (Ref. 1).

Suppose we want to study whether a particular patient group using a new medication would require fewer than 2 days in hospital where 2 days is considered the average length of stay, using current therapy. Suppose the statistical null hypothesis is that the probability equals 0.5 that a randomly chosen patient requires fewer than 2 days in hospital on a particular medication. Assume that a random sample of 10 patients are recruited and a two-sided test is carried out. If the null hypothesis is true, the binomial distribution can be used to find that the probability of the sample containing 0 patients with <2 days hospitalization (and 10 patients with ≥2 days hospitalization) equals 1/1024. Similarly, the probability of 1 patient with <2 days hospitalization (and 9 patients with ≥2 days hospitalization) equals 10/1,024, the probability of 9 patients with <2 days hospitalization (and 1 patient with ≥2 days hospitalization) equals 10/1,024, and the probability that all 10 patients requires <2 days hospitalization equals 1/1,024. If we reject the null hypothesis for 0, 1, 9, or 10 patients with <2 days, the significance level of the test equals the sum of these probabilities, 22/1024 = 0.02.

The 10 patients are now recruited, and suppose there are 9 patients with hospitalization <2 days. The result falls in the rejection region for this test; we can therefore report that the null hypothesis is rejected with a 0.02 significance level. However, this significance level consists partly of the probability of the observed sample data and partly of the probability of data that were not observed. In this example, the significance level also contains the probabilities for 0, 1, or 10 patients with hospitalization <2 days. Consequently, in classical statistics, the probabilities of data that did not occur in the sample are also used as evidence against the null hypothesis. This would appear to be a very odd way of interpreting the results of a study.

The reason for this difficulty stems from the way that probabilities are defined in classical statistics. Classical probabilities tell us what will happen in the long run if we were to draw a large number of samples. For instance, in the above example, if the null hypothesis was true, 2% of the samples would fall into the rejection region and thus lead to a false rejection of the hypothesis. However, in this example, only one sample was drawn. Trying to interpret significance levels on the basis of a single sample is difficult.

Similar problems arise with trying to interpret confidence intervals. Classical theory states that, in the long run, with data from many samples and therefore many confidence intervals, a proportion of the intervals will contain the true parameter while the other intervals will not. Using various assumptions, one can then calculate the probabilities of various events happening in the long run if the null hypothesis was true. However, it is difficult to know how to handle these probabilities once the results from the one (and only) sample are known. All we know is that the single known confidence interval either contains the true parameter or it does not, but we have no basis for claiming that one or the other event is true.

BAYESIAN STATISTICAL INFERENCE

Bayes uses a prior belief about a hypothesis and then modifies this in the light of new data in order to arrive at a posterior belief. Classical statistical methods usually take an assumed relationship between data and the unknown parameters and then tries to find a single numerical estimate for the unknown parameters together with an interval of uncertainty (usually 95%). It then often tests (yes or no), whether the true value is equal to some hypothesized value.

Bayesian statistical methods does not consist of a set of procedures (estimates, tests, confidence intervals) for each new type of problem encountered. The Bayesian approach deals with uncertainty by treating data collection as an ongoing process whereby current beliefs are modified in the light of new information. In this way, the uncertainty about the parameter values is reduced but is never completely removed. In other words, statistics is not seen as an obscure science far removed from everyday experience. It is viewed simply as a formal way of learning from experience, starting from an initial uncertainty about the parameter and modifying that uncertainty in the light of new evidence.

If we accept this approach, two questions need to be answered. First, how can one appropriately represent prior beliefs and secondly, how can one update current beliefs when new data are obtained. In answer to the first question, if useful inferences are to be made, beliefs about unknowns should be represented as probabilities. Questions about unknown parameters can then always be answered in terms of statements about relative odds or risks. These quantities are then directly relevant for decision making. The answer to the second question is more technical but can be simply explained. There are essentially three components that comprise Bayes' theorem:

1. *Model of how the data relate to the unknown parameters:* This is called the likelihood function. This tells us how likely are the data to arise, given some specific values of the unknown parameters.
2. *Prior beliefs about the unknown parameters before seeing the data:* This is called the *prior probability density*. This tells us how much belief one can attach to these specified values of the unknown parameters before observing the data.
3. *Posterior beliefs after seeing the data:* This is called the posterior probability density. This tells us how much belief one can attach to these specified values of the unknown parameters after observing the data.

According to Bayes' theorem, the following relationship between the components is true.

$$\text{Prob(parameters/data)} = \frac{\text{Prob(data/parameters)}}{\text{Prob(data)}} \times \text{Prob(parameters)}$$

which can be simply stated as:

Posterior beliefs = standardized likelihood × prior belief

The formula works in a very simple and logical way. Values of the unknown parameters that give rise to large values of the standardized likelihood lead to higher posterior beliefs than do values of the unknown parameters, which give rise to small values of the standardized likelihood. Thus, we increase our beliefs in parameter values that are highly compatible with the data we have observed; and we correspondingly decrease our beliefs in parameter values that are unlikely to have resulted in the data actually observed.

When further related data are obtained, the current posterior becomes the new prior. In other words, the Prob(parameters/previous data), are updated via Bayes' theorem to give Prob(parameters/previous and new data). This can be repeated as each piece of new data comes in so that we are continually "learning from experience."

STRENGTHS AND WEAKNESSES OF BAYESIAN METHODS

Bayesian Weaknesses

Bayes theorem comprises three components: a prior probability distribution, the likelihood probabilities, and the posterior distribution of the parameter(s). However, problems can arise in finding both the prior distribution and the likelihood probabilities. Some methods for expressing the prior knowledge as a probability distribution are described in a subsequent section. Difficulties can also arise in manipulating Bayes' theorem in order to find the posterior distribution.

The issues of sensitivity (or robustness) concern both Bayesian as well as classical statistics. For instance, in Bayesian statistics, the sensitivity of the resulting posterior distribution to deviations from the assumed prior and likelihood distribution needs to be investigated. If there is significant sensitivity, we need to investigate ways of using other probability distributions. However, whereas classical statistics is limited in its choice of usable distributions, Bayesian methods can handle a wide variety of general probability distributions.

Finding a posterior distribution can be made much easier if we can identify a conjugate prior distribution. A conjugate prior distribution is a distribution that when combined with the distribution of the data leads to a conveniently simple posterior distribution. Using conjugate prior distributions, Bayes' theorem easily produces posterior distributions. However, with more complicated prior distributions, one may have to go back to first principles and use the theorem to derive the posterior distribution. For instance, it is possible to end up with integrals that have to be handled with numerical methods. However, modern numerical methods and modern computers can greatly simplify these calculations.

Bayesian Strengths

Statistical inference, particularly hypothesis testing, has been dominated by classical statistics. The approach is now almost routinely used in clinical research and is rapidly being adopted by researchers analyzing pharmacoeconomic data from clinical trials. However, the Bayesian approach to statistical inference has certain strengths that should make it the method of choice for the analysis of pharmacoeconomic data, and for certain other areas of scientific research as well.

One of the main strengths of Bayesian statistics is that it can handle problems that cannot be easily handled by classical methods. For instance, when two sets of observations come from populations where the variances are unequal, there is no exact classical solution as to how to test the hypothesis that the two population means are equal. This is likely to be a common occurrence in pharmacoeconomic data since in most cases it would be very unreasonable to assume equal variances. Furthermore, it can be shown that even small differences in variances can lead to significant adjustments to the posterior distribution. However, Bayesian statistics does offer a solution to the problem of comparing two means with unequal variances (Box and Tiao, 1973) (Ref. 2).

Classical statistics claim that prior beliefs should be replaced by the sample data, once they become available. In other words, everything we currently know about an unknown parameter is contained entirely within the observed sample data. This would appear to be an unlikely scenario and, in fact, can lead to complications in interpretation as shown in the following example, adapted from an example by Iverson, 1984 (Ref. 1).

A null hypothesis states that 30% of a population of patients would show a reduction in overall treatment costs as a result of using a new drug. However, in a random sample of N = 10 patients, it was found that only one person showed a reduction in overall treatment costs. Using the classical approach, a binomial distribution with N = 10 and $p = 0.3$, gives a p-value = 0.15—usually not small enough to be considered statistically significant. The classical interpretation of this result is that if we drew many samples of ten from this population of patients, then 15% of these samples would have either 0 or one patient showing a reduction in overall treatment costs, assuming the null hypothesis is true.

The intention in the above example was to sample ten patients and find out how many patients showed a reduction in overall treatment costs. However, suppose the intention was to sample patients until one found a patient that showed a reduction in overall treatment costs and then to stop sampling. In this situation, the sample size is a random variable. In another sample with one patient showing a reduction in costs, we might have had to sample 7 or 11 patients or some other number before stopping. The observed data in our original sample is N = 10, and the more extreme data would have been 11 or 12 or anything larger. In this situation (from the negative binomial distribution), $p = 0.05$, which is borderline significant with a one-sided test. The classical interpretation of this probability is that if we draw many samples containing exactly one person in favor, then 5% of these samples would have 10 or more observations, assuming the null hypothesis is true. The p-value in this case is therefore three times smaller than the previous p-value, despite the fact that the observed data is the same. The only difference is that in the first case the intention was to take 10 patients and count how many showed a reduction in overall treatment costs, while in the second case the intention was to keep on sampling until one patient was found to show a reduction in overall costs.

Further complications can arise with classical statistics; if there was no prior plan to sample 10 patients, one just ended up with 10 patients, one of whom showed reduced overall treatment costs. It just happened that those were the data when the sampling stopped. In this case classical statistics has nothing to offer for the analysis of these data since no formal model can be used and no analysis is possible.

Thus, in classical statistics, very different conclusions can arise from the analysis of the same data and sometimes conclusions cannot be made at all. However, Bayesian inference does not care whether the data collected stopped after 10 observations, after the first patient to show a reduction in overall costs, or for some other reason. All that matters are the data. In Bayesian analysis, the information in the data consists of 1 patient showing a reduction in costs and 9 patients who don't, and this information is expressed mathematically in the likelihood function $(p)^1(1-p)^9$ for this example. The likelihood function is combined with the prior distribution, and if the prior is a β distribution, we know that the posterior distribution is also the beta distribution no matter why the data collection was stopped.

There are also a number of other reasons why the Bayesian approach should be favored over the classical approach. For instance, many times we do have prior information, making it possible to use informative prior distributions. With informative prior distributions we get posterior distributions that are more peaked and with smaller variances. This means we can assess the unknown parameters with more precision and therefore get shorter Bayesian probability intervals for the parameters than we do with noninformative prior distribution. The obvious example of this use of prior information is in forecasting studies, where prior information is usually available from data collected over an earlier period.

Bayesian statistics has also the advantage of being far easier to understand (although not necessarily easier to apply). Concepts from classical statistics such as significance level, power of a test, sampling distribution, and confidence interval have been difficult to understand. Bayesian inference, with its more general notion of uncertainty, delivers conclusions that are much easier to interpret and much easier to understand.

The Bayesian approach is also far more natural than the classical approach because it is more closely associated with the research process itself than is classical inference. The research problem starts with an initial uncertainty about 1 or more parameters, data are collected in order to increase our information about the parameters, and in light of the new information, the initial uncertainty has been reduced. This is exactly the approach adopted by Bayesians. It begins with a prior distribution of the parameters, calculates the probability of the data given various parameter values, and then combines the prior distribution with the data probabilities using Bayes' theorem, to produce a posterior distribution of the parameters. Bayesian inference uses the concept of probability to express uncertainty about the unknown parameters. By contrast, classical inference calculates the probability of the observed data. However, this is logically flawed, since there is no uncertainty attached to the observed data; it is already known.

PRIOR BELIEFS

One of the most difficult aspects of implementing the Bayes' approach is that of eliciting the prior beliefs about a parameter(s). Bayesian analysis requires a prior distribution for the unknown parameter. Even if we are truly ignorant about the parameter, we still need to specify a prior distribution in order to apply Bayes' theorem. In choosing a prior distribution, we can distinguish between an informative and noninformative prior distribution. A noninformative prior distribution can be described as the weakest form of prior opinion about the parameter being studied. In most cases, the rectangular distribution is used as a noninformative prior distribution. In this way, total ignorance is expressed by the idea that all values of the parameters are equally likely over the relevant range of values. The use of noninformative prior distributions, such as the rectangular distribution, can lead to results that correspond numerically to those obtained from classical statistics. However, interpretation of the results is widely different, as described in an earlier section.

Research is cumulative. One of the main strengths of Bayesian over classical inference is that it permits the use of knowledge from earlier research in the analysis of results from new research. This implies that we should seek out prior knowledge and express such knowledge in informative prior distributions as part of the research. The argument against the rectangular prior distribution (and noninformative prior distributions in general) is that there is always some available prior probabilistic knowledge, which should be made explicitly expressed in an informative prior distribution.

A prior distribution expresses the prior belief of a population parameter before any new data are available. Information about parameters is typically limited and can vary from one person to the next. Prior distributions are therefore largely subjective, meaning that different people analyzing the same problem could well have different prior distributions that may produce different posterior distributions. However, Bayesian inference is not alone in having subjective choices affect the analysis. In classical testing, one analyst may reject the null hypothesis and another analyst may accept the same null hypothesis when analyzing the same data set. This may be because they have chosen different significance levels for determining rejection or acceptance of a null hypothesis and this choice is subjective. Bayesian inference is subjective in a different way. If two people have different opinions about something, even the same limited empirical facts will modify these opinions differently. If the prior distributions are very informative and the new information in the data is limited, the posterior distributions will necessarily differ. However, the individual posterior distributions will be brought closer together than the individual prior distributions because of the common data.

ELICITING PRIOR BELIEFS IN PHARMACOECONOMIC STUDIES

Considerable care and thought need to go into the process of eliciting prior beliefs. There are no set rules for eliciting priors as a person's prior information is very much dependent on the nature of the problem and also dependent on their personal knowledge. Moreover, we all may have different beliefs about the same situation. Consequently, a careful structuring of expert opinion via a consensus conference, a Delphi panel (a form of structured consensus making), or a survey of practitioners, may be necessary when the medical literature does not suffice. Possible techniques for eliciting expert opinion include the following:

1. Suppose one is interested in eliciting prior beliefs from a panel of experts concerning the possible reduction in hospital stay arising from the use of a new treatment. One could rank the events (such as the event that the new treatment reduces hospital stay by 0, 1, 2, 3, 4, 5, or greater than 5 days) according to their prior probabilities of occurrence perhaps using a visual analogue scale extending from 0 (= impossible) to 1 (= certain).
2. Suppose one is interested in whether or not a new therapy will reduce overall treatment costs by more than X dollars (event A say). Let $p = P(A)$ is the degree of belief that event A will occur. Suppose you are offered a choice between the following two options:

   Option 1. Receive a million dollars (pounds sterling, marks, yen) if Event A occurs but nothing if it does not;
   Option 2. Enter a lottery in which you receive a million dollars (pounds sterling, marks, yen) with probability p, but you receive nothing with probability $1-p$.

   If you are indifferent between options 1 and 2, your degree of belief in Event A is p. In practice, one would vary p until indifference is achieved. One would then choose another event B, which may be the event that the new treatment will reduce overall costs by more than $(X+1)$ dollars, and so on.
3. For eliciting prior information about the mean of a normal distribution such as the average drug costs for a particular disease arising from the use of a new medication, one could ask direct questions, such as What are the most likely and unlikely values?, What are the 25% and 75% quantiles?, and Can you sketch your beliefs?

Fitting Prior Distributions to Pharmacoeconomic Data

Fitting prior distributions to the responses to the above questions may not be easy. However, even fairly vague knowledge can be represented by a probability distribution.

For instance, suppose the pharmacoeconomist is interested in estimating the proportion of patients that would show a reduction in overall hospital costs as a result of a new treatment. Eliciting prior expert opinion might suggest that the proportion is almost certainly less than 0.5, that it is quite likely to be between 0.2 and 0.4, and that one would be surprised if the proportion were less than 0.2 or greater than 0.4. One could sketch a probability distribution that reflects these vague beliefs by specifying that most of the probability is between 0.1 and 0.5, and perhaps two-thirds of the probability is between 0.2 and 0.4.

The prior distribution should reflect as accurately as possible the prior information about the parameter. At the same time, it should also be easy as possible to work with. However, these two requirements may be in conflict.

EXAMPLES

The following simple examples illustrate the Bayesian approach to statistical inference. The calculations and plots were produced by the software program 'First Bayes' developed by Professor Anthony O'Hagan, Nottingham University, England.

Example 1:

Empirical data on the number of days in hospital are collected for two groups of patients: one group treated with the standard drug and the other treated with a new drug. We wish to compare the number of days spent in hospital between the two treatment groups; 10 patients in each treatment group are sampled.

Standard drug: 38, 39, 37, 33, 19, 28, 60, 38, 29, 37
New drug: 14, 19, 52, 23, 16, 20, 17, 38, 2, 21

Assume independent normal samples with a common variance.

1. *First assume a weak prior (a rectangular distribution):* The posterior means are 35.8 days and 22.2 days for the standard drug and the new drug, respectively. The 90% highest density intervals, which are defined as the shortest 90% intervals, are (29.7, 41.9) and (14.2, 30.2), respectively. As these intervals only slightly overlap, this would suggest that the new drug is likely to lead to less time spent in hospital than the current standard drug. However, we can confirm this properly by working out the posterior distribution for the difference in the treatment means. This distribution gives a difference in means of 13.6 and variance 33.77. The probability that it is less than zero is 0.0116, so it is very probably positive. Alternatively, a Bayesian test of equality of the two drugs gives the test probability of 0.023 (twice the previous probability, as this is essentially a two-sided test). These results are identical to the classical results because the prior belief is weak. The 90% HDI for the variance is from 79.6 to 256.7. The probability that it is less than 79.6 is 0.013, whereas the probability that it exceeds 256.7 is 0.087. This differs quite markedly from the classical equal-tailed confidence interval which for a 90% interval is (93.5, 287.8), which is 10% wider.

2. *Now assume that we have an informative prior about the number of days spent in hospital:* For instance, suppose our prior beliefs about the difference between the treatment groups can be represented by a prior probability distribution N (0, 15.09). Then the posterior distribution has mean difference of 9.07. The 90% HDI is (2.10, 16.04) with probability that the difference is less than zero being 0.017. A Bayesian test of equality of the two

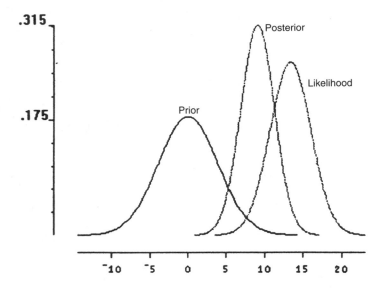

FIG. 1. An informative prior.

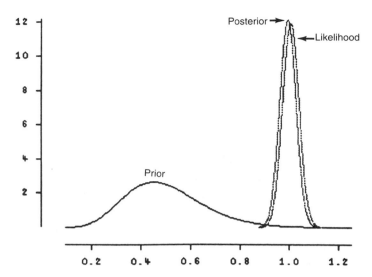

FIG. 2. A weak prior.

drugs gives the test probability of 0.034. This would still suggest that the new drug leads to a reduction in days spent in hospital but the evidence is less strong with the informative prior compared with the noninformative prior. A triplot of the prior, likelihood, and posterior distributions is shown in Fig. 1.

Example 2:

A new treatment is expected to reduce the number of specialist visits. A sample of 900 patients who had received the treatment reported the following number of visits to see a specialist during the course of their illness:

Number of specialist visits:	0	1	2	3	4	5	6
Frequency:	327	340	160	53	16	3	1

Assume the number of specialist visits follows a Poisson model.

1. *Assume a fairly weak prior, which is γ (20,10):* The posterior mean is then 0.99 with a 90% HDI of (0.94, 1.05). This is only slightly less than the mean from the likelihood distribution (i.e., the data without the prior), as shown in Fig. 2. Thus the weak prior had very little effect on the mean obtained from the data; consequently, the Bayes mean is almost identical to the classical mean.

2. *However, assume a more informative prior, which is γ (500, 350):* The posterior mean is now 0.90 with a 90% HDI of (0.85, 0.94). The posterior mean is now noticeably less than the classical mean as shown in Fig. 3.

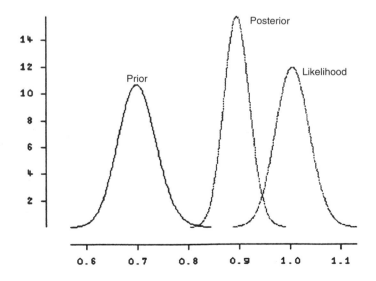

FIG. 3. An informative prior.

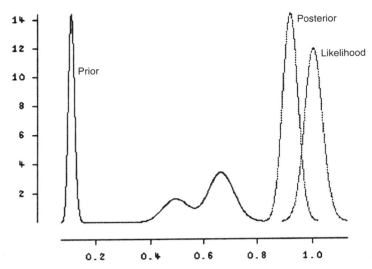

FIG. 4. A complex informative prior.

3. *One can also assume more complex priors such as a linear combination of* γ. Suppose the following distribution provides the best fit to opinions expressed by a sample of experts:

$$[0.2 \times \gamma(200, 100)] + [0.4 \times \gamma(300, 200)] + [0.4 \times \gamma(900, 100)]$$

This gives a posterior mean of 0.92 with a 90% HDI of (0.87, 0.97). This is again a fairly informative prior that has a noticeable effect on the likelihood as shown in Fig. 4.

CONCLUSIONS

If a new approach is to be routinely adopted, it has to be made easy to apply as well as easy to understand. Bayes is far easier to understand than classical statistics, and many of the computational difficulties that have previously held back its full development have been largely overcome. The natural evolution of statistics will ensure that the Bayes approach will be the standard for most areas of scientific research within a few years. It is in the interests of pharmacoeconomists, particularly those involved with the economic evaluation of medicines, to lead this break with tradition otherwise the development of the science could be seriously delayed.

Pharmacoeconomists have been handed a pair of poorly fitting shoes by way of classical statistics. When the shoes don't fit, pharmacoeconomists and their data are blamed for having poorly fitting feet. The pharmacoeconomist is then compelled to choose or modify the study to suit the methods when it is actually more appropriate for a pharmacoeconomist to choose the methods to suit the study. The pharmacoeconomist should try to find the methods that appropriately fit the nature of their discipline. The Bayes philosophy is simple and natural. It fits comfortably into the scientists' way of thinking and carrying out research. Pharmacoeconomists now need to make those concepts explicit and then to be consistent and thorough in their application.

REFERENCES

1. Iverson GR. *Bayesian statistical inference.* Newbury Park, CA: Sage Publications, 1984.
2. Box GEP, Tiao GC. *Bayesian inference in statistical analysis.* Reading, MA: Addison-Wesley, 1973.

Suggested Readings

1. Barnett V. *Comparative statistical inference.* 2nd ed. New York: Wiley, 1982.
2. Bayes, TR. An essay towards solving a problem in the doctrine of chances. Philosophical Transactions of the Royal Society, London, 1973;53:370–418.
3. De Finetti B. *Theory of probability: a critical introductory treatment.* 2 vols. New York: Wiley, 1974–1975.
4. DeGroot MH. *Optimal statistical decisions.* New York: McGraw-Hill, 1970.
5. Gelfand AE, Smith AFM. London: Wiley (in press).
6. Gilks W, Richardson S, Spiegelhalter D. *Practical Monte Carlo Markov Chains.* London: Chapman and Hall (in press).
7. Jeffreys HS. *Theory of probability.* 3rd ed. Oxford: University Press, 1951.
8. Lindley DV. *Introduction to probability and statistics from a Bayesian viewpoint.* Cambridge: University Press, 1965.
9. Lindley DV. *Making decisions.* 2nd ed. London: Wiley, 1985.
10. O'Hagan A. *Probability: methods and measurements.* London: Chapman and Hall, 1988.
11. O'Hagan A. *Kendall's advanced theory of statistics.* vol. 2B. *Bayesian Inference.* London: Edward Arnold (in press).
12. Smith JQ. *Decision analysis: a Bayesian approach.* London: Chapman and Hall, 1988.
13. Stuart A, Ord JK. *Kendall's advanced theory of statistics. vol. 2: Classical inference and relationships,* 5th ed. London: Edward Arnold, 1991.

Quality of Life and Pharmacoeconomics in Clinical Trials, Second Edition, edited by B. Spilker. Lippincott-Raven Publishers, Philadelphia © 1996.

CHAPTER 125

Using Decision Analysis to Conduct Pharmacoeconomic Studies

Judith T. Barr and Gerald E. Schumacher

INTRODUCTION

We face decisions every day of our lives. Whether they are as mundane as deciding what to have for dinner or as complex as the choice of an antibiotic for a patient with a life-threatening infection, most decisions share four common elements—choice, consequences, probabilities, and outcomes.

First, decisions involve choices between more than one possible choice, option, or strategy. Decisions can range from dichotomous "yes/no" selections to situations where a range of possible alternatives must be considered. For example, when selecting the antibiotic for the patient with a life-threatening infection, based on patient information and other prior information, we may narrow our options to three or four possible choices that we will further consider.

Second, each choice leads to a sequence of possible consequences or events which occur over time following the decision. Identifying consequences requires a series of "if/then" questions. For example, if you select one of the antibiotics, what will happen? Will the antibiotic produce an adverse event, or will it not? If it does produce the adverse event,

is it severe enough to discontinue the antibiotic? If the antibiotic is continued, will it or will it not resolve the infection?

Third, there is uncertainty as to which of the consequences will occur. If we were 100% certain that there was an antibiotic that had no adverse effects, cured all infections, and was of reasonable cost, it would be the obvious antibiotic choice and we would not be faced with a decision. But most clinical decisions do not come with such certainty. Instead we are forced to implicitly incorporate into our decision-making process our own probability estimates concerning how often the various consequences will happen.

Finally, for all decisions, we select some type of outcome measurement to judge the relative success of each of our decision options. In the antibiotic example we could use single dimensional outcome measures such as infection cure rate, survival rate, or cost of treatment to evaluate which of the antibiotic options is more effective than the others. Or we could combine cost with some unit of effectiveness or utility to generate a two-dimensional outcome measure, such as a cost per unit of effectiveness or cost per utility unit.

We make these kinds of decisions every day. Using our intuitive processes, we either rapidly make the choice or more thoughtfully, but generally implicitly, try to juggle the elements of the decision—the choices, consequences, probabilities, and outcomes—and make our selection. But

    J. T. Barr and G. E. Schumacher: Bouvé College of Pharmacy and Health Sciences, Northeastern University-105-DK, Boston, Massachusetts 02115.

there are methods to guide us in improving our decision-making processes and to make decisions based on an explicit and orderly examination of the factors involved in the decision. Decision analysis is one of these methods.

In the following sections, we will review the foundations of decision analysis, develop the steps in the decision analytic process, and summarize how investigators have used decision analysis to structure decisions involving pharmaceutical products. We will conclude by presenting a case to illustrate the factors that should be considered when applying a decision analytic approach to pharmacoeconomic studies.

WHAT IS DECISION ANALYSIS?

Decision analysis provides an orderly, analytical approach to assist the decision maker in identifying the preferred course of action from among competing alternatives. It is *explicit*—it forces you to structure the decision you face as well as identify the consequences of the possible decision outcomes; it is *quantitative*—it forces you to assign numbers to probability estimates and outcome valuations; and it is *prescriptive*—the analysis identifies the route to take to maximize the expected value of the decision as you have specified the structure of the decision, its probabilities, and its outcome values.

The early origins of decision analysis can be found in the work of Ramsey and his operational theory of action based on the combination of probabilities and utilities (1). This and the economic and game theory work of Von Neumann and Morgenstern (2) laid the foundation for the fields of operations research and systems analysis. During World War II, the Allies used these formal analytical techniques to analyze military problems involving allocation of scarce resources. Decision analysis, cost-effectiveness analysis, cost-benefit analysis, and other techniques evolved from these early efforts. Raiffa (3) popularized the use of decision analysis in the business world, early leaders such as Ledley and Lusted (4,5) introduced it into the medical community, and by the early 1970s, decision analysis had reached the medical literature (6–8).

The Society for Medical Decision Making was established in 1977 and publishes a quarterly journal, *Medical Decision Making;* clinical decision consultation services have been established to provide assistance with complex patient-specific decisions (9); and the American Association of Medical Colleges has recommended the inclusion of clinical decision analysis in the undergraduate medical curriculum (10). In a comprehensive 1987 review article that classified difficult clinical problems into 13 types of decisions, Kassirer et al. (11) identified nearly 200 studies in which investigators had applied decision analysis to a wide range of medical and surgical conditions.

The field continued to grow and in 1994, in preparation for this chapter, we identified 81 articles in which investigators had used decision analysis to determine the optimal choice in a decision involving one or more pharmaceutical products (12–92). While we will refer to some of these studies in later sections, we summarize their key features in Tables 1 and 2.

TABLE 1. *Taxonomy of decision analyses involving pharmaceutical products*[a]

Type of decision	Abbreviations	Example (reference)
Choosing among treatments	Choose/Rx	For cadaveric kidney transplantation, should steroids be combined with cyclosporine or azathioprine? (12)
		What is the most cost-effective regimen for the antimicrobial treatment of serious infection? (13)
Choosing between treatment and no treatment	Rx/NoRx	Should streptokinase be used in elderly patients with suspected acute myocardial infarction? (14)
		Should the elderly receive chemotherapy for node-negative breast cancer? (15)
Determining routine interventions	Routine	How can the probability of a return visit be incorporated into the decision to treat, not treat, or culture patients with pharyngitis? (16)
		What should be the approach to diagnose and treat carcinoma of unknown primary origin? (17)
Preventing disease	Prev/Dis	Should children universally be vaccinated against hepatitis B? (18)
		Should a 56-year-old man bitten by an opossum receive rabies prophylaxis? (19)
Preventing complications of established disease	Prev/Comp	Should patients with mitral valve prolapse receive predental antibiotics? (20)
		Should prophylaxis be used to prevent deep-vein thrombosis in major orthopedic surgery? (21)
Interpreting therapeutic drug monitoring (TDM) test results	Interp/Test	How can you incorporate patient-specific estimates of toxicity in the interpretation of TDM results? (22)
		How can you incorporate test performance characteristics in the interpretation of TDM results? (23)
Defining context in which a TDM test is useful	Test/Context	At what probability of toxicity does performing a TDM test provide useful information? (24)

Adopted from Kassirer et al. (9).

TABLE 2. *Clinical applications of decision analysis involving medications*

Medication class	First author (reference)	Clinical condition	Taxonomy[a]	Method	Evaluation type; metric
Anesthesia	Sun (25)	Dental	Choose/Rx	Tree	Utility maximization
Angiotensin-converting enzyme inhibitor	Paul (26)	Cong heart failure	Choose/Rx	Markov	CEA[b]; years of life saved
Antibiotic	Bor (27)	Valve prolapse	Prev/Comp	Numerical	Effectiveness; fewest deaths
	Callahan (28)	Otitis media	Choose/Rx	Tree	CA[c]; drug costs
	Carlson (29)	Dysuria	Choose/Rx	Tree	CA, effectiveness; days of morbidity averted
	Centor (16)	Pharyngitis	Routine	Tree	Effectiveness; cure
	Clemens (20)	Dental/mitral valve	Prev/Comp	Tree	CEA; prevented case, yr of life
	Hillner (30)	Pharyngitis	Routine	Numerical	Effectiveness; well days
	Holloway (31)	Serious infections	Choose/Rx	Numerical	CEA, nephrotoxicity averted
	Jorgensen (32)	Otitis media	Choose/Rx	Tree	Cost analysis; cost of treatment
	Kresel (33)	Serious infections	Choose/Rx	Tree	Cost analysis; cost of treatment
	Magid (34)	Lyme disease	Prev/Dis	Tree	CEA; complications prevented
	Paladino (35)	Serious infections	Choose/Rx	Tree	CA; institutional costs
	Paladino (36)	Nosocomial pneumo	Choose/Rx	Tree	CA; institutional costs
	Plante (37)	Endocarditis	Choose/Rx	Tree	Utility maximization
	Reves (38)	Travelers' diarrhea	Prev/Dis	Tree	CA; medical + loss day
	Shapiro (39)	Hysterectomy	Prev/Dis	Tree	CA; infection costs
	Stamm (40)	Urinary tract infection	Prev/Dis	Tree	CA; clinic costs
	Stern (41)	Papulopustular acne	Choose/Rx	Tree	CEA; morbidity + side effects averted
	Tsevat (42)	Artificial joints	Prev/Dis	Tree	CU[d]; QALY[e]
	Tsevat (43)	Sickle cell + penicillin	Prev/Comp	Tree	CEA; life saved
	Washington (44)	Gonorrhea	Choose/Rx	Tree	CA, effectiveness; averted PID ectopic pregnancy, infertility
	Weinstein (13)	Serious infection	Choose/Rx	Tree	CEA; life expectancy gained
	Weiss (45)	Otitis media	Choose/Rx	Tree	CA; Medical cost + lost work
Anticoagulant	Pauker (46)	Heart disease	Prev/comp	Tree	CU; QALY
Antidepressant	Jönsson (47)	Depression	Choose/Rx	Tree	CEA; success treated patient
Antiemetic	Buxton (48)	Cancer	Choose/Rx	Tree	CA; cost of episode of care
	Zbozek (49)	Cancer	Choose/Rx	Tree	CU; QALY
Antifungal	Gottlieb (50)	Lymphoma	Rx/No Rx	Tree	Utility maximization
Antimalarial	Sudre (51)	Malaria	Choose/Rx	Tree	CEA; deaths prevented, cure
Antiplatelet	Oster (52)	Stroke	Prev/Dis	Tree	Cost utility; QALY
Antitubercular	Koplan (53)	Tuberculosis	Prev/Dis	Tree	CEA; case averted
	Rose (54)	Diabetes with positive skin test	Prev/Comp	Markov	Effectiveness, life expectancy
	Taylor (55)	Positive skin tests	Prev/Dis	Tree	Benefit, TB cases averted Risks; hepatitis cases caused
Antiviral	Barza (56)	Herpes encephalitis	Rx/No Rx	Tree	Effectiveness, p of survival
	McCarthy (57)	HIV	Rx/No Rx	Markov	CEA; life year gained
	Oddone (58)	HIV	Rx/No Rx	Markov	CEA; life without AIDS
Calcium channel blocker	Gonzalez (59)	Atrial fibrillation	Choose/Rx	Tree	Effectiveness, Composite score
Chemotherapy	Desch (15)	Node-neg breast CA	Rx/No Rx	Markov	Cost utility; QALY
	Djulbegovic (60)	Large-cell lymphoma	Choose/Rx	Markov	Effectiveness; QALY maximize
	Hillner (61)	Node-neg breast CA	Rx/No Rx	Markov	CU; QALY
	Hillner (62)	Stage 4 breast CA	Rx/No Rx	Markov	CEA + CU; life-year, QALY
	Hillner (63)	Early breast cancer	Choose/Rx	Markov	CU; QALY
	Levine (17)	Ca of known origin	Routine	Tree	CEA; survival at 1 yr
	Rutherford (64)	Hodgkin's	Choose/Rx	Tree	Effectiveness; disease-free life extension in 5 yr
	Smith (65)	Early breast cancer	Choose/Rx	Markov	CEA; additional life
Contrast media	Barrett (66)	Cardiac catheterization	Choose/Rx	Tree	CU; QALY
	Calvo (67)	Urography	Choose/Rx	Tree	CEA; toxicity and severe adverse effects prevented

TABLE 2. *Continued.*

Medication class	First author (reference)	Clinical condition	Taxonomy[a]	Method	Evaluation type; metric
Granulocyte colony-stimulating factor	Lyman (68)	Small lung cell CA	Rx/No Rx	Tree	Cost analysis; cost of stay
H₂ antagonist	Hillman (69)	GERD	Choose/Rx	Tree	CEA; symptom-free month
	Oster (70)	Acid-peptic disorder	Rx/No Rx	Markov	Effectiveness; relief
	Read (71)	Dyspepsia	Routine	Tree	CEA; mortality, weeks of pain
Hormone replacement	Hillner (72)	Osteoporosis	Prev/Dis	Markov	Effectiveness; QALY
	Tosteson (73)	Osteoporosis	Prev/Dis	Markov	CU; QALY
	Zubialde (74)	Postmenopause	Rx/No Rx	Markov	Effectiveness; life-years
Immune globulin	Klassen (75)	Kawasaki	Choose/Rx	Tree	CA + effectiveness; coronary artery dilation/aneurysm prevented
	Weeks (76)	Leukemia	Prev/Comp	Numerical	CU; QALY
Immunosuppressant	Cuchural (77)	Transplant + melanoma	Rx/No Rx	Tree	Utility maximization; QALY
	Simon (12)	Kidney transplant	Choose/Rx	Markov	CEA; life-year
Monoclonal antibody	Chalfin (78)	Gram-neg sepsis	Choose/Rx	Tree	CEA; survivor
Prostaglandin	Edelson (79)	NSAID GI bleeding in rheumatoid arthritis	Prev/Comp	Tree	CEA; years of life saved
	Gabriel (80)	Osteoarthritis + NSAID[f]	Prev/Comp	Tree	CEA; GI event averted
	Gabriel (81)	RA using NSAIDs	Prev/Comp	Tree	CU; quality-adjusted life days
	Hillman (69)	GERD	Choose/Rx	Tree	CEA; symptom-free month
	Knill-Jones (82)	Arthritis + NSAID	Prev/Comp	Tree	CA; cost savings per patient
Therapeutically monitored drugs					
Digoxin	Eraker (83)	Cardiac	Interp/Test	Numerical	Diagnostic accuracy
Theophylline	Schumacher (22)	Pulmonary	Interp/Test	Tree	Utility maximization
Multiple	Schumacher (84)	Possible toxicity	Interp/Test	Numerical	Diagnostic accuracy
	Schumacher (23)	Possible toxicity	Interp/Test	Numerical	Diagnostic accuracy
	Schumacher (24)	Possible toxicity	Test/Cont	Tree	Utility maximization
Thrombolytic	Krumholz (14)	Suspected AMI	Rx/No Rx	Numerical	CEA; life-years saved
	Midgette (85)	AMI	Choose/Rx	Tree	CEA; life saved
	O'Meara (86)	Deep-vein thrombosis	Choose/Rx	Numerical	Utility maximization; QALY
	Oster (21)	Deep-vein thrombosis in orthopedic surgery	Prev/Comp	Tree	CA, effectiveness; number of deep-vein thrombosis, deaths, pulmonary emboli
	Oster (87)	Thromboembolism in general surgery	Prev/Comp	Tree	CEA; additional year of life saved
Vaccine	Bloom (88)	Hepatitis B	Prev/Dis	Tree	CEA; years of life saved
	Cantor (19)	Rabies	Prev/Dis	Tree	CU; QALY
	Grabenstein (89)	Influenza	Prev/Dis	Tree	Cost-benefit analysis
	Koplan (90)	Pertussis	Prev/Dis	Tree	Cost-benefit analysis benefit; complications prevented risk; permanent disability, death
	Krahn (18)	Hepatitis B	Prev/Dis	Markov	CEA; extra year of life
	Nettleman (91)	Tuberculosis	Prev/Dis	Numerical	CA, effectiveness; life-years gained, active TB prevented
	Oddone (92)	Hepatitis B	Prev/Dis	Tree	CEA; case prevented, life-year saved, per life

[a]See Table 1.
[b]Cost-effectiveness analysis.
[c]Cost analysis.
[d]Cost utility.
[e]Quality-adjusted life-years.
[f]Nonsteroidal antiinflammatory drug.

We modified Kassirer's taxonomy of thirteen types of clinical decision analyses (11) to create a unique taxonomy of decision analyses that include some type of decision involving pharmaceutical products. Table 1 displays this taxonomy, seven types of pharmaceutical decisions, and examples of each type of decision. Thirty-one of the 81 decision analyses involving pharmaceutical products examining "Choosing among drug treatments"; 12, "Choosing between drug treatment and no treatment"; 4, "Determining a routine intervention for common conditions"; 18, "Preventing disease"; 11, "Preventing complications of an established disease"; 4, "Interpreting therapeutic drug monitoring (TDM) test results"; and 1, "Defining the context in which a TDM test is valuable."

Table 2 summarizes each of the 81 decision analyses: medication class studied, author, clinical condition for which the medications were considered, taxonomy or type of decision question asked, decision analytic method (see the section Identify and Bound the Decision), type of economic or effectiveness evaluation, and the metric(s) used as the unit(s) of outcome measurement. Investigators performed 22 analyses involving antibiotics, eight examining chemotherapy issues, seven involving vaccination policy, five each examining prostaglandin and thrombolytic agents, and smaller numbers of studies in such areas as postmenopausal hormone replacement and antiemetic therapy.

Not only have investigators applied decision analysis to a wide range of pharmaceutical questions, they also have used different methods of economic and/or effectiveness evaluation to answer those questions. Sixty-one of the studies incorporated some type of economic evaluation into the decision analysis. Twenty-nine of the studies used cost-effectiveness analysis, while 12 examined costs only, and five did not link the measured effectiveness with the calculated costs to yield a cost-effectiveness ratio. Thirteen analyses combined costs with utilities for a cost-utility analysis and two studies used cost-benefit analysis. Fifteen investigators considered only effectiveness without linking effectiveness to costs and nine used utility maximization. We have included these latter, noneconomic articles in this review because they also provide insight into the factors which should be considered when applying decision analysis to pharmaceutical decisions.

As described in the following sections, the steps of the decision analytic approach create a structured, but flexible, template upon which different types of pharmacoeconomic studies can be organized.

STEPS AND METHODOLOGIC CONSIDERATIONS IN THE DECISION ANALYTIC PROCESS

Decision analysis involves six major steps. We first present the steps and then discuss methodologic issues related to each step in the process.

1. Identify the decision, including the selection of the decision options to be studied. Bound the timeframe of the decision and determine from which perspective the decision is to be made.
2. Structure the decision and the consequences of each decision option over time.
3. Assess the probability that each consequence will occur.
4. Determine the value of each outcome (e.g., in dollars, quality-adjusted life years saved, utilities).
5. Select the option with the highest expected outcome.
6. Determine the robustness of the decision by conducting a sensitivity analysis and varying the values of probabilities and outcomes over a range of likely values.

Without such a structured process, decisions involving multiple factors are often flawed when the decision maker implicitly attempts to juggle and combine important elements (93). Errors occur because it is difficult to intuitively combine complex information, generate revised probabilities, and give proportional weight to events of differing importance which occur at differing times (94,95). Decision analysis provides the structure to identify these factors explicitly and to combine the various sources of information quantitatively to identify the decision option that offers the best chance for the desired outcome.

But decision analysis is more than a systematic approach to solving problems under conditions of uncertainty. It creates a fundamental change in the way in which one approaches a decision. The use of decision analysis engenders an attitude towards the problem or decision—to think more analytically; to force the consideration of consequences of actions; to recognize explicitly that uncertainty is present, to estimate the degree of uncertainty, and to assess **your** attitude towards risk; and to determine which are the relevant outcome measures and to value **your** preferences for the alternative outcomes.

The definitions and conventions of clinical decision analysis presented by Weinstein and Fineberg (96) are used throughout the chapter. We also have incorporated the recommendations of the Inter-PORT Decision Modeling work group (97), composed of a team of decision analytic experts representing each of the Patient Outcome Research Teams (PORTs), and sponsored by the Agency for Health Care Policy and Research.

Identify and Bound the Decision

You set the ground rules for the decision in this step. What is the decision and what options will be considered? Who will be the decision maker and whose/what perspective will be considered? What patient population is to be studied? Over what time horizon will the consequences be analyzed? Which decision model will be used? What unit(s) of outcome measurement(s) will be included in the decision? The answers to these questions are necessary to properly frame the analysis, structure the decision, and collect the appropriate data.

What Is the Decision and What Options Will Be Considered?

Depending on the scope of the decision, the decision model may require a large or small number of decision options. If the goal of the analysis is to determine the best treatment strategy for a condition, then all reasonable treatment options should be included. However, only two or three options may be needed when a more limited question is considered.

The Inter-PORT Decision Modeling work group recommends that the decision options include extreme strategies to represent the range of possibilities from passivity to aggressiveness in clinical treatment (97). The incorporation of a "no treatment" option is particularly useful in providing baseline information for marginal cost-effectiveness studies and other economic analyses of alternative treatment strategies. With "no treatment" as an embedded part of the decision, the outcomes of the least costly treatment option can be compared to those of a strategy of doing nothing. When the "no treatment" option is omitted, an artificial situation is created in which all the costs and benefits are attributed to the least costly alternative, rather than differentiating between the portion associated with the "do-nothing" strategy and with the marginal change associated with the least costly alternative.

Most decision analyses involving pharmaceutical products compared only two or three treatment alternatives. However some studies, such as the prevention of venous thromboembolism after general surgery (87) and of deep-vein thrombosis in major orthopedic surgery (21) included a range of seven possible strategies from "do nothing" to combination interventions. While investigators routinely included the "do nothing" strategy in analyses involving prevention of disease and complications, they did not incorporate the "do nothing" option in most decisions examining the choice among competing treatment alternatives. Given the long history of intervention in many of these clinical conditions, the omission of the "do nothing" option may be due to the lack of cost and outcome data related to the natural course of these conditions.

Who Will Be the Decision Maker and Whose/What Perspective Will Be Considered?

This question is asked primarily to determine from whose or what perspective the analysis is to be conducted. Although it can be argued that to achieve maximal societal good all allocative decisions should be made from a societal perspective, patients, providers, departments, and institutions frequently make decisions based on their unique perspective. Is the decision analysis being performed to determine the preferred course of care for an individual patient care decision, to determine the composition of a managed care formulary, or to determine national health policy? Is it from the point of view of the pharmacy department, the hospital, an insurance company, a health maintenance organization, a corporation, or society? The identification of the decision maker and the perspective of the decision determines such downstream factors as the time frame, costs, and outcomes to be considered.

A variety of decision perspectives were used in the 81 decision analytic articles examining pharmaceutical products. For example, investigators included the perspective of an individual patient (19,30,37,50,61,77,86), pharmacy department (28), an institution (35,36,78), unspecified third-party payers (6,18,20,31,66,69,73), Medicare (12,89), health maintenance organizations (42,85), provincial governments of Canada (17,80), and society (12,15,18,19,26,27,39,52, 57,65,66,70,75,76,81,82,92). Two Canadian studies, one evaluating contrast media for diagnostic catherization (66) and the other determining universal vaccination for newborns against hepatitis B (18), performed the analyses from both a societal and third party payor perspective to permit generalizability to Canadian and American audiences. However, nearly half of the authors failed to identify the perspective of their analyses.

What Patient Population Is to Be Studied?

Given that disease severity and rates of medication effectiveness and adverse events can vary across populations, the decision maker must determine not only the perspective of the study, but also the patient population to be studied. Is the analysis to structure a decision related to an individual patient; to selected patient subpopulations based on such variables as gender, age, or disease severity; or to all patients with a clinical condition?

Several of the decision analyses examined therapeutic actions related to a specific patient situation: should a 56-year-old overweight man bitten by an opossum receive postexposure rabies prophylaxis? (19), what antibiotic should be used in a patient with suspected enterococcal endocarditis with penicillin allergy? (37), should amphotericin be administered to a patient with hematologic malignancy and suspected disseminated Candidiasis (50)?, and should immunosuppression be continued in a transplant patient with malignant melanoma? (77). While useful as examples of how a complex patient problem can be approached, these clinical cases can serve as more than a case study if the author details the degree of generalizability of conclusions to other patients and/or conducts a sensitivity analysis (see the section Sensitivity Analysis) to vary the specific patient characteristics to those more representative of a broader population.

The question of whether different conclusions will be reached for different subpopulations can be examined either directly or indirectly. In the direct approach, investigators determine that there may be too much variation within the patient population and it is necessary to perform different analyses for each relevant patient subpopulation. In the indirect approach, the conclusions of a general population analysis are then challenged by varying the underlying assumptions of the model to reflect the differing characteristics of patient subpopulations.

The direct approach can more accurately model the impact of the subpopulation on the consequences, probabilities, and outcomes of the decision. Examples of subpopulation analyses include a cost-effectiveness analysis of thrombolytic therapy with streptokinase for acute myocardial infarction with the analysis limited to patients 75 years or older (14); cost-effectiveness analyses of misoprostol for prophylaxis against nonsteroidal antiinflammatory drug-induced gastrointestinal tract bleeding in four populations—all users, users 60 years and over, users with rheumatoid arthritis, and users with a proven history of gastrointestinal bleed (79); and two economic analyses of strategies for the use of high- versus low-osmolality contrast media in a population of low-risk and a separate population of high-risk patients (66,67).

Over What Time Period Will the Analysis Apply?

Selection of the time horizon for the analysis places bounds on the period of time over which the decision and its consequences are to be studied. The selection of that time period is dependent on the nature of the clinical question and the medication class considered; the period of time required to achieve therapeutic effectiveness, detect adverse events, and resolve medication sequelae; the perspective of the decision maker; and the availability of data to support the analysis. Depending on the clinical question, the time horizon for the evaluation can be selected to incorporate only the immediate near-term effects or extended to also include the more comprehensive assessment of the long-term sequelae and consequences of the medication decision. Both natural units (days, weeks, months, years) and functional units (episode of illness, remainder of life) of time can be considered.

Two medication classes can be used to illustrate the link between the time course of the clinical condition and the appropriate time frame of the decision—antibiotics and chemotherapeutic agents. Given that the purpose of an antibiotic generally is to cure a short-term infection, most investigators who used decision analysis to identify the optimal antibiotic selection restricted the analysis either to a specific number of days (30–32,38) or to the "episode of care," an unspecified period of time needed to achieve cure (16,28,29,33,37, 42,45). Some investigators conducted the analyses from multiple time periods. For example, because the major cost consideration in a decision analysis to compare the cost-

effectiveness of antimicrobial agents used for treatment or prophylaxis of travelers' diarrhea was the cost associated with a day of incapacitation due to illness, the investigators performed the analysis on travels of three different durations—3, 7, and 14 day trips.

Two antibiotic studies had variations on the "episode of care" period of time. Performing an analysis from an institutional perspective, Paladino and Fell (36) limited their pharmacoeconomic evaluation of treatment of serious infections to only "antibiotic length of stay." Weinstein et al. (13), also evaluating antibiotic treatment of serious infection, extended the "episode of care" period to incorporate sequelae of antibiotic treatment which could have clinical and economic implications beyond the period of antibiotic treatment. Overall, 18% of the antibiotic studies did not identify the time horizon of the analysis, thus limiting cross-study comparisons due to potential variation in time-dependent costs and effects.

Alternatively, longer time periods are needed to evaluate interventions designed to suppress future events and extend life. Consistent with the nature of the clinical course of most cancers, analyses involving chemotherapeutic agents examined the consequences of the treatment decisions over longer time periods. In four cost-utility analyses, Hillner and colleagues (61,63), Desch et al. (15), and Smith and Hillner (65) modeled the costs and effects of chemotherapy and other treatment regimens for the remainder of the patient's life in individuals with early breast cancer. In other chemotherapy studies, 5-year time periods were used for stage 4 breast cancer (62) and Hodgkin's disease (64), while survival was assessed after one year in a pharmacoeconomic study of the cost-effectiveness of chemotherapy for the treatment of cancers of known origins (17).

Decision analytic studies, built on data available from clinical trials, are limited to the time period of the clinical trial. For example, a pharmacoeconomic assessment of alternative treatments for persistent gastroesophageal reflux disease "was limited to a 7-month period to reflect the specific time frame of the published controlled trials, which generally used a 4- or 8-month treatment period followed by 6 months of follow-up" (69). If a randomized clinical trial is of sufficient duration to detect both the efficacy of the medication as well as the associated adverse events, the time period should be adequate and the trial's data suitable for inclusion into an evaluation.

Overall, 19% of the decision analyses involving pharmaceutical products did not include the time horizon of the study.

What Decision Model Will Be Used?

Depending on the time frame of the events being modeled and the complexity of the interaction of various consequences of each decision option, three possible decision models can be considered: a decision tree, a Markov model, and a simulation model.

The decision tree model graphically structures and follows the progress of a patient or patient population from the choice of decisions through a defined period of time. It is best used to structure decisions when any event subsequent to the decision usually happens only once and at some prespecified time, and the patient is not at continuous risk for the condition or sequelae to reoccur. If an event does recur, it must be inserted as a branch within the decision tree. The decision tree model is limited if the event of interest does not always happen at the same time, and different values or preferences are associated with the event occurring at different times (e.g., death in 1 year versus 10 years). The differential timing of the event cannot be built into the model but must be reflected in the utility of the outcome. As shown in Table 2, 69% of the decision analyses involving pharmaceutical products used the decision tree model.

A Markov model should be considered when patients fluctuate among a finite number of clinical states over time, when events can reoccur because patients remain exposed to risk, and when the timing of the transition between health states is uncertain but affects the utility of the state. In this model, the prognosis of a disease is viewed as a set of transitions between a set of health states during the time horizon of the decision. The period of time is divided into equal increments of time or cycles. During each cycle, the patient may make a transition from one clinical state of a given utility to another state with a different utility. While the transitions cannot be predicted definitely, their probabilities can be estimated. The length of time spent in each state and the associated utility of the state are combined to determine the expected value for each decision option (98,99).

Sixteen of the decision analyses involving pharmaceutical products were based on Markov models (12,15,18,26,54,57, 58,60–63,65,70,72–74). These primarily involved clinical decisions associated with patients transitioning among multiple health states over extended time horizons. Cancer therapy (15,60–63,65), hormone replacement (72–74), and treatment of patients testing positive for the human immunodeficiency virus (57,58) are examples of clinical conditions examined using the Markov model.

Simulation models are used to structure decisions affected by complex interrelationships among the component factors within the model. Epidemics and other conditions in which the actions and interactions of some individual will affect others are good candidates for simulation modeling (97). We did not identify any simulations involving pharmaceutical products.

In ten studies, the investigators indicated that a decision analysis or decision analytic approach was used in the evaluation, but did not include a decision tree or indicate which decision model was used. We identify these articles in Table 2 by indicating that the method was ''numerical'' in that it

followed the explicit, quantitative approach but did not specify the type of decision analytic modeling performed.

What Are the Decision Criteria?

When selecting outcome measures or decision criteria, not only must investigators determine the metric to capture the effects of the interventions, they also must consider the degree to which they wish the analysis to be comparable to other studies. If costs and disease-specific outcome measures are selected, the results may be limited to comparison of resource allocation only within the treatment options for the specific clinical condition. And if a new outcome measure is developed, unless other more recognized measures are also included, the study may not be comparable to any other analysis. On the other hand, if an investigator wishes to assess patient preferences or to compare the relative resource utilization of the considered interventions to similar disease or other intervention programs, then utilities can be determined or estimated and a cost-utility analysis performed.

Table 2 lists the evaluation type of each of the 81 articles and the metric selected as its decision criteria. Seventy-five percent of the articles included cost as a decision criteria. Of these 47% were cost-effectiveness studies; 28%, cost analyses; 21%, cost-utility; and 3%, cost-benefit. All cost-utility studies determined some quality adjusted period of time (quality adjusted life years or quality adjusted days) thus permitting broad cross-study comparisons. However, the cost-effectiveness studies used a variety of both general and disease-specific outcome measures such as years of life saved. While a metric such as ''years of life saved'' will permit cross-study comparison (14,18,25,26,57,65,79,87,92), more disease-linked measures such as ''gastrointestinal event averted'' (81), ''life without AIDS'' (58) will restrict comparisons to studies of similar conditions.

One particular study demonstrates the importance of the decision maker determining the type of outcome variables which are to be included in the analysis, and if more than one, which is of the greatest value. Read et al. (71) used decision analysis to answer the question: which of four options is the best treatment for dyspepsia? The analysis did not reveal one best approach because the preferred option depended on which outcome measure was most valued by the decision maker. If mortality was to be minimized, the upper gastrointestinal series prior to selection of therapy yielded higher survival. However, if weeks of pain was to be minimized, ulcer therapy begun immediately would provide the most pain-free days. On the other hand, if the direct costs were to be minimized, symptomatic therapy could be implemented with the lowest costs. Overall, there was no one best option, because the option with the highest expected outcome depended on the different values of the different decision makers.

Answers to these five questions establish the foundation on which the decision analysis is performed. For example, unless the decision perspective, patient population, and time frame of the study are clearly specified, the analyst will not know whether or not data from a 2-month general population study conducted from a societal perspective are of value to the clinical question and patient population being considered. Without a priori establishing the bounds and characteristics of the analysis, investigators are likely to create conflicts within their models when data from different perspectives, different time horizons, or different patient populations are inappropriately combined during the analytic process.

Structure the Decision and Its Consequences Over Time

This is one of the most powerful features of decision analysis. Using the decision tree model, the decision maker is forced to explicitly structure the situation, thus changing the unexamined, intuitive process into one in which the thought process is clearly articulated. Laying out the tree prods the decision maker to identify the relationships that exist between the decision options and the consequences of selecting each of the alternative options. The tree becomes a tool to assist in thinking through a decision, as well as to assist in communications among individuals and departments working on the same analysis. With a decision tree, co-workers can identify where they agree or disagree in the considered alternatives and consequences, suggest additional consequences that must be included in the tree, or recommend that a branch be trimmed.

A decision tree begins with a choice node (a small square) with branches indicating the considered options originating from the choice node and structured to the right. The choice node indicates that the decision maker has the ability to choose among the options or branches originating from that node. The structure of the tree continues to the right as the consequences of each action are identified and added. These consequences are structured chronologically over time by asking a series of "if, then" questions. For example, if the decision maker chooses Option A, what will happen? If the decision maker cannot control the occurrence of the next event, and a possibility exists that any one of several things will happen if Option A is chosen, a choice node (a small circle) is inserted in the Option A branch followed by the possible events which may occur. A choice node indicates that there is uncertainty about what will happen next.

To conduct a comprehensive pharmacoeconomic study, the decision maker must structure the decision tree to include both the effectiveness and adverse events of the medication. At a minimum, this ensures that both the cost of the medication, as well as the induced costs associated with adverse events, are included in the analysis.

Figure 1 presents a simplified tree of a decision between two fictional antihypertensive agents—Hyperzap and Hyper-

fiz. For this simplified model, the "do-nothing" and empirical therapy options are not included. The choice node between the remaining two options (node 1) is on the left side of the tree and indicates that a decision is to be made between the two branch options that originate from the choice node. Next, the consequences of each option are structured chronologically from left to right. We have determined that the effectiveness of both of these medications proceeds their potential adverse events. Therefore, employing the line of "if, then" questioning, if Hyperzap is chosen, will it or will it not be effective? These two possibilities originate from the second node—a chance node, indicating what happens at this point is uncertain. If more detail about the degree of effectiveness is to be considered, the tree can be "bushed out" to include high, medium, and low effectiveness as well as the possibility of no effect.

Next, a second set of "if, then" questions are asked: If Hyperzap is/is not effective, will it/will it not be associated with adverse events? Node 4 indicates that if Hyperzap is effective, it may or may not produce adverse events. Although not included in the structure of this tree, to generate sufficient detail for the pharmacoeconomic analysis, a further series of "if/then" questions should ask: If adverse events are present, then what type of events? Depending on the perspective of the decision maker, the type of patient population, and the time horizon of the decision, additional consequences may be modeled and further detail may be added to the tree.

Decision models are prone to errors of both logic and structure (97). Common errors identified by the Inter-PORT Decision Modeling work group include

1. *Conditioning of action on unobservable states:* This frequently occurs when the results of diagnostic tests are incorporated into the decision tree. Investigators assume that a positive test indicates that the patient has a condition without appreciating that most diagnostic tests are associated with some degree of classification error. They then incorporate into their decision, or condition their decision upon, faulty information which does not represent the unobserved true status of the patient. Test results must be interpreted based on the estimate of the underlying prevalence of disease. The explicit consideration of test performance characteristics and diagnostic uncertainty has been incorporated into a pharmacoeconomic teaching case (100).
2. *Violations of symmetry:* All options must model prognosis the same way. For example, consider a tree where one option structures different levels of severity with associated different utilities and the other options do not model the prognosis the same way. If the underlying distribution among the different levels of severity changes, the expected value of the first option will change, but not those of the other options because their

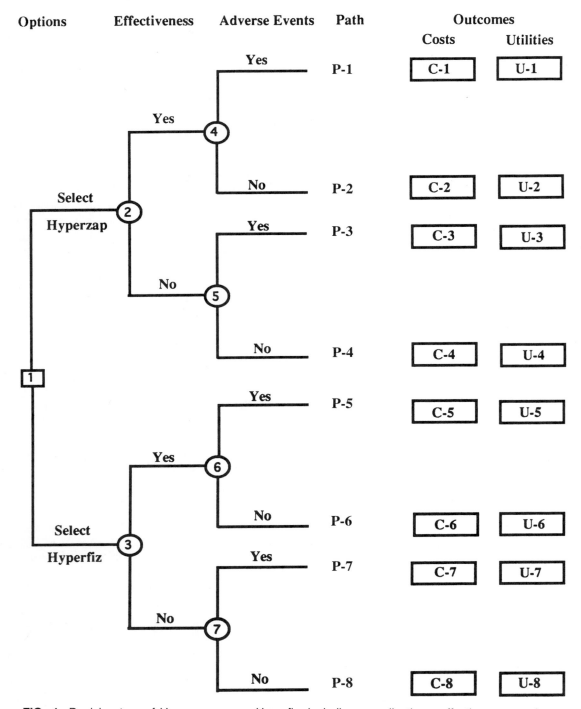

FIG. 1. Decision tree of Hyperzap versus Hyperfiz, including complications, effectiveness, and outcomes of decision options.

branch structure failed to indicate that there was a difference in the severity of the condition.

3. *Failure to apply consistent bias:* When constructing a decision analytic model, it is frequently necessary to make simplifying assumptions which may introduce biases. The InterPORT group recommends that all biases

should go against the strategy which proves to be optimal according to the model so that relaxing them will not affect the decision. If the decision tree includes biases which apply in opposite directions, it is impossible to say how the simplifying assumptions affect the results of the analysis.

A computer program, based on these and other rules of model construction, has been developed to critique the structure of decision trees automatically. Bunyon, the computer program developed by Wellman et al. (101), can automatically identify many common errors based on purely structural characteristics without the need for knowledge of the subject content. While not a comprehensive critique of all steps within the decision analytic process, Bunyon is an important contribution in improving the structure of decision analysis.

Additional insight can be gained about the construction of decision trees by examining the 61 decision analytic articles which employed decision trees to assess pharmaceutical products. These articles are indicated in Table 2 by the designation "tree" under the Method column.

Assess Probabilities

The decision maker must estimate the probability that each of the consequences at each chance node will occur. That means that in the simplified decision tree in Figure 1, probabilities must be determined for each consequence originating from chance nodes 2 to 7. The sum of the probabilities of all consequences originating from each chance node must sum to 1.0; therefore, it is essential that all possible consequences be identified at each chance node. Because there is a 100% certainty that something will happen at each chance node, nodes with probabilities totaling less than 1.0 have not identified all possibilities, or probabilities have been estimated incorrectly.

A large, randomized control trial providing information on the options being considered would provide an ideal data base to determine probabilities. However, those are rarely found in the clinical literature. Instead the investigator must obtain probability estimates from limited clinical trial information, meta-analyses, expert opinion, or other clinicians.

These sources are flawed. Clinical trials may be of insufficient size to detect rare events. This leads to distortions in the model, especially when a rare event occurs and is associated with great cost. Expert or peer estimates could be considered, but psychologists say that we are poor estimators of probabilities (102). We tend to overestimate the occurrence of rare events and underestimate the frequency with which common events happen. And experts, basing their estimates on their atypical and more seriously ill patient population, also overestimate the frequency of the uncommon.

When using clinical trial information for probability estimates, investigators must be careful to match the source of the estimates with the population being studied. If the decision analysis is comparing the costs and effects of two medications in a population of 75 years and older adults, the selection of a general population-based data source for the estimation of clinical effectiveness and adverse events would not be appropriate. The same caution should be raised with the combination of trial results for meta-analysis. Trial results should be combined only if they are based on similar patient populations.

The investigators conducting pharmacoeconomic studies based on decision analysis used a variety of methods to obtain probability estimates. Seven performed meta-analysis (13,15,65,74,81,85,86), and another eight used Delphi or a modified Delphi techniques to incorporate the estimates of from five to 154 experts (20,27,38,41,47,51,53,88). While some could base their estimates on large clinical trial data bases (12,14,15,26,58,71,75,76), others relied on clinical trials that may be too small to detect rare but costly events (39,48). Registries (52,66,82), clinic records (32), population studies (52,54,55,73,90), and unpublished trials (14,35) were also used as sources for probability estimates.

As more clinical decisions are based on the cost and consequences of effective, rather efficacious, therapeutic interventions, it is essential that the collection of this type of probabilistic patient outcome information become routine practice. An accurate pharmacoeconomic assessment is not possible unless costs can be linked to the probabilities of clinical consequences of the interventions, and that those probabilities be determined in routine practice. Until pharmacoepidemiologic data from Phase 4 trials are available to determine these probabilities, probability estimates based on efficacy trials, meta-analyses of efficacy trials, and Delphi techniques involving expert opinions will serve as our best approximations.

Value Outcomes

Just like any other type of pharmacoeconomic analysis, decision analysis requires that the economic costs and other outcome valuations be determined for the different treatment options. However, what makes decision analysis different from the other approaches is that decision analysis provides a clear, explicit structure that outlines discrete paths of events—a decision path—which needs to be valued. A decision path originates from the initial choice nodes on the left and proceeds to the right as the consequences of the initial decision are detailed and the tree is developed. For our simplified case, eight decision paths are identified and are labeled P-1, P-2, P-3, and so on, in Figure 1.

Now with the decision being structured and probabilities assigned to the uncertain events, the investigator must determine the value of each of the decision paths. For economic outcomes, this involves summing the costs associated with the events which happen in each path. For example, in our simplified Hyperzap versus Hyperfiz example, which are the costs associated with treating patients who follow each of the eight paths? In Path #1, the individual receives Hyperzap, the medication is effective, but the patient has an adverse event. With a tree which more fully specifies the types of adverse events, accurate cost estimates can be determined for each of the paths in the decision tree; these values are entered at the right of each of the decision paths, C-1, C-2, C-3, and so on.

In these decision-analytic studies involving pharmaceutical products, investigators used a variety of definitions and methods to estimate costs. Definitions ranged from a limited view of costs based solely on the cost of the antibiotic to the pharmacy (28) to a societal definition of costs to include all direct costs regardless of the source of payment (73). Sources of cost data included labor costs estimated by industrial engineering studies (13), medical resources estimated by the "author's best judgment and subjected to extensive sensitivity analyses" (76), a cost-accounting software package used during a clinical trial (43), a step-down allocation (incorporating indirect costs and cost-to-charge ratios) of revenue-producing cost centers to determine unit costs of hospital resources (26), estimates from DRG weights (12, 73), Medicare data for terminal cancer care (65), Red Book prices for medications (35), and Delphi and investigator estimates (38).

Valuations for noneconomic decision criteria also are necessary. If the study is a cost-utility analysis, utilities must be determined for each of the paths (103). Through time trade-off and standard reference gamble techniques, patients can be directly questioned about the utility they associate with or preferences they have for each of the clinical paths. However, only one of the 13 cost-utility analyses included patient-generated utilities, these from 57 patients with rheumatoid arthritis (81). In the other cost-utility analyses, investigators (15,42,46,52,63,66), previously published expert opinion (73), oncology staff (61,76), oncology and nursing focus groups (62), Torrance and Feeney utility values (49), and faculty, residents, and medical students (19) provided the estimates of patient preference. The degree to which these individuals can empathically and accurately value the selected outcome—utility estimates of patient preferences for different disease states—must be determined.

One of the noneconomic decision analyses highlights this issue. O'Meara et al. (86) conducted a decision analysis to determine whether streptokinase plus heparin or heparin alone was the preferred option for patient with deep-vein thrombosis. The analysis was conducted from the perspective of the patient, was modeled for the remainder of the patient's life, and used quality-adjusted life-years as the outcome measure. Sixteen patients who had deep-vein thrombosis and 20 who had not experienced the condition provided utility estimates using the standard reference gamble technique. All patients valued avoiding an early death as more important than preventing an outcome that affects quality of life. This patient-based decision analysis identified heparin alone as the preferred option, while current treatment recommendations, based on professional judgment, recommend combination therapy.

Valuation for other noneconomic measures are based on expert opinion, clinical trials, literature reports, structured patient interviews, National Health Interview Survey, and Medicare data.

Choose the Preferred Course of Action—Calculate the Expected Value for the Economic and Noneconomic Outcome of Each Decision Option or Strategy?

How does one combine the various decision options, probability estimates, and outcome valuations to choose the preferred course of action? How does one "solve" a decision tree?

First, it is necessary to break the decision tree into its component parts and analyze smaller sections. This is done in reverse order of the tree's development by starting from the right and working back to the initial decision or choice node on the left. The process is called "averaging out and folding back," since each path's outcome value is weighted by its probability of occurrence (averaging out) working from right to left, from outcomes to options (folding back). The weighted value at the chance node is called an "expected value" because it is the expected, but not certain, value based on probabilistic estimates that events of different valuations will occur.

At each chance node, outcome values are combined with, and weighted by, their respective probability of occurring. This yields an expected value at each chance node. If the decision analysis has only one choice node, the averaging out and folding back process continues until the expected values are determined for the options originating from the original choice node. If there are one or other choice nodes embedded in the analysis, at each embedded choice node, the option with the highest expected value is selected, and this value is carried to the left to the next chance node.

From the identification of the decision options, the time frame, the decision criteria, and the objectives of the decision maker; through the structuring of the decision and the identification of all consequences; to probability estimation and outcome valuation; the clinical question now has had an explicit, structured, analytic, and quantitative assessment with a preferred action course identified.

Sensitivity Analysis

Sensitivity analysis is the last step in the decision analytic process. The purpose of this last step is to challenge the robustness of the analytic conclusions by varying the estimated values of the probabilities and outcomes. Although the probability and outcome values which were incorporated into the model were the average or best estimates, a wide range of reasonable values would have been possible for most studies.

If available, confidence intervals of the variables serve as a convenient range over which the probability and outcome estimates can be varied. Each time a new value is substituted for the base case estimate, the expected value of the option is recalculated. If one decision option has the highest expected value throughout the likely range of a probability or outcome value, the decision is said to be robust and not sensitive to that factor. Most of the decision analyses involving pharmaceutical products used one-, two-, or three-way sensitivity analysis during which one, two, or three values are varied simultaneously.

If the preferred option does change as one of the values is varied, threshold analysis can be used to determine the value at which the decision changes from one option to another. For example, Centor and Witherspoon (16) varied the frequency with which an individual would return for a follow-up of a sore throat and changed treatment strategies based on the probability of patient follow-up. Buxton and O'Brien (48) used threshold analysis to calculate a price at which ondansetron therapy would be equal in costs to other treatment alternatives.

Monte Carlo simulations (104) can be performed when more than two of the base case values are to be varied simultaneously. In Monte Carlo simulation, the base case estimates of all probability and outcome values are simultaneously varied across their probability distributions so that the uncertainties in all values are collectively considered. For each run of the model, a value for each variable included in the Monte Carlo simulation is randomly selected from within its distribution, and the expected values of each option are recalculated. This random assignment of values from within the distribution to all probability and outcome estimates is repeated a specified number of runs. Only four decision analyses involving pharmaceutical products examined the robustness of their conclusions by the use of Monte Carlo simulations (49,68,78,81).

CASE STUDY—MIGRAINE THERAPY

We now present an individual case study of a patient with migraine. The decision analysis will be conducted from the perspective of the patient, will be limited to the first 48 hours after a migraine begins, and will use the decision tree model. The patient is the decision maker and has selected personal costs and utilities as the outcome measures. As the case is presented, consider how the analysis might differ if, rather than the individual patient, a pharmacy benefit program, an indemnity insurance company, a managed organization, a group of employers, or society was the decision maker and the analysis was to apply to a population of patients who had less than three migraines per month? Also consider an expanded time frame. What if the decision maker decided to examine the implications of this decision over a 1-year period and selected a Markov model because the risk of migraine is continuous?

A.B. is a 40-year-old woman who has a long history of migraine dating back to entering high school. There is no clear pattern to the frequency of her attacks. Some months she has three to four episodes. Other months she has only one. Occasionally, she has even gone through a month without an attack. There is no precipitating event—onset of menses often provokes an episode in many women—that brings on her migraines.

When the migraine strikes, she usually takes oral promethazine for nausea and an oral ergotamine preparation as a vasoconstrictor to reduce the pain. This has been effective two-thirds of the time. But some of the adverse reactions accompanying the ergot have often been troubling to her. When the pain is particularly stubborn and intense, she has occasionally gone to the emergency department for an injection of an ergotamine derivative and/or an injectable narcotic such as meperidine.

During the past year she once tried sumatriptan in her physician's office, a relatively new injectable preparation that shares some of the actions of the ergot derivatives, but may be more effective with less accompanying adverse effects. It was effective for her and, except for some discomfort at the injection site, there were no other adversities. There is an autoinjector device available for self-administration of the drug, but she thinks that she would be uneasy using it during an attack.

Now she has been told by her physician about an intranasal narcotic-like derivative, butorphanol, which is very effective in aborting the pain and has a sedative potential that enhances recovery. Transnasal butorphanol may be self-administered easily and safely by metered-dose aerosol at any time. While the frequency of adverse effects is similar to ergotamine and sumatriptan, butorphanol may have an abuse potential which could make some patients wary.

A.B.'s situation is similar to many migraine patients. She is not a typical candidate for prophylactic (preventive) treatment because she does not regularly exceed two episodes per month, nor does she fail to regularly get relief from abortive treatment, or have predictable events associated with the onset of attacks. For years she has sought relief by using well-known antiemetic and vasoconstrictor preparations that have been effective more often than not; had some adverse effects not uncommonly associated with usage, but side effects she understood; and a cost, at least for the treatment itself (not including follow-up expenses when treatment fails), that was relatively inexpensive compared to the newer modalities. She is receptive to potentially more effective agents such as injectable sumatriptan or transnasal butorphanol. But each brings with it a new set of disconcerting considerations and each treatment is much more expensive (higher co-payment) than routine use of her traditional regimen.

The decision tree in Figure 2 is constructed from the perspective of the patient. As mentioned earlier, the perspective could be that of a third-party payer or society as a whole, but the structure of the tree would be altered somewhat. In its present form, the tree provides a structure for the decision

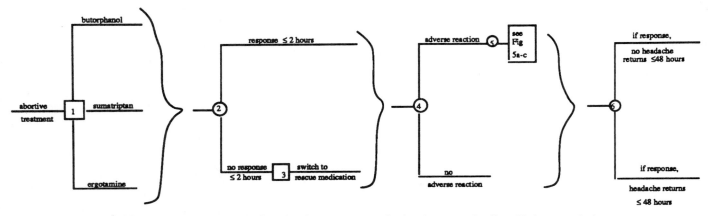

FIG. 2. Decision analysis for abortive treatment of migraine over the first 48–hour period.

analysis of the three alternative interventions discussed above for the abortive treatment of migraine, using the first 48 hours after onset of the attack as the time frame.

Structuring the Tree

1. Given that the patient has no contraindications to the use of the alternatives, the tree begins with the selection of a drug regimen at node 1, a choice node.
2. After taking the drug, 2 hours is chosen as the interval for characterizing response in this analysis at node 2 (a chance node), as this seems realistic, and data are available from various studies so the patient either responds or does not in this time. Of course, what constitutes response must be determined prior to the analysis and it is possible, if data are available, to set a shorter or longer period of time for determining response.
3. If the patient responds, then node 4, a chance node, depicts whether adverse effects from the drug do or do not occur. The most commonly encountered adverse reactions for each drug are shown in chance nodes 5a to c in Figs. 3 to 5.
4. Whether the patient experiences adverse reactions from the drug or not, if a therapeutic response did occur at

node 2, the patient's headache may or may not return within an arbitrarily set interval of 48 hours, as described at node 6.
5. Back at node 2, if no response to the regimen occurs within 2 hours, a decision is made, as noted at node 3 (a choice node), to switch to a rescue medication. Although a number of options exist, common ones include taking an additional dose (more than the recommended regimen) of the original drug, more likely a switch to one of the alternative regimens not selected, or a narcotic analgesic. For simplicity, the rescue is assumed to be effective whereas, in reality, a chance node showing response or not should be appended, similar to node 2 for the original regimen. In addition, if a narcotic is selected, no adverse reactions are shown similar to those for the primary drugs in Figs. 3 to 5. And, if the rescue medication differs from the primary regimen, a more comprehensive tree would take the cumulative adverse reactions for both regimens into account.

Estimating Probabilities and Measuring Outcomes

To solve the decision analysis in Figure 2, three types of information must be obtained to perform a cost-utility analysis:

1. For each possible consequence (branch) resulting from nodes 2 and 4-6 in Figs. 2–5, the probability associated with the occurrence of each consequence must be estimated. The combined probability of all consequences originating from a chance node must sum to 1.0 (or 100%). While it is theoretically possible to do a series of "N of 1" trials to determine the probability of effective therapy, of adverse reaction, and of symptom return, it is not practical. Probability estimates from literature reports of patients with similar clinical symptoms would be an appropriate proxies. Sensitivity analysis could examine the effect of varying these estimates on the overall selection decision.

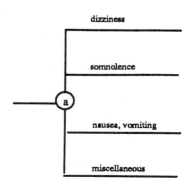

FIG. 3. Butorphanol, adverse reactions.

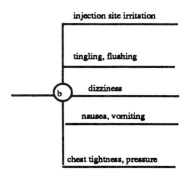

FIG. 4. Sumatriptan, adverse reactions.

2. The decision maker (the patient) has specified this to be a cost-utility analysis with costs defined as personal costs. Therefore, all personal costs (drug acquisition, lost income due to incapacitation, and other associated expenses) for each of the decision paths must be calculated.

3. Similarly, the patient's utility for each of the paths must also be determined using time trade-off or standard reference gamble. One example of a path is selecting butorphanol, responding in ≤2 hours, with no adverse reactions from the drug, and no return of headache. Another example is: selecting sumatriptan, responding in ≤2 hours, experiencing irritation at the injection site and nausea, and a headache that returns in ≤48 hours. Obviously, for this decision analysis, it is very unlikely that A.B. would consider any of the decision paths as being perfect health (utility of 1.0) or death (utility of 0). So for each path in this tree, A.B. assigns an individual utility value that is less than 1 but greater than 0 and represents her relative preferences for the different clinical outcomes. If the analysis were from the perspective of a managed care group and involved a cohort of patients, population-based utility values for each clinical path would need to be determined.

When all data are in place, the analysis concludes with (a) the "averaging out and folding back" of the outcome

valuations of each path by their probability of occurring, and (b) a sensitivity analysis in which the values of important variables are varied across a range of possible values.

A number of alternative trees and decision analyses could be applied to migraine treatment. We focused above on the patient perspective, for abortive treatment, over a 48-hour period.

1. An alternative analysis could focus on a longer time frame than 48 hours. This would be an important consideration for regimens with adverse effects that may take longer than two days to appear (e.g., abuse potential resulting from the narcotic derivative, butorphanol). Also, a Markov model should be considered for the longer time period because the risk of migraine remains, and it is likely to recur.
2. Another analysis could compare preventive to abortive treatment. This may be useful for patients like A.B. above who are not clear candidates for preventive regimens.
3. The perspective of the decision maker structures the tree and its analysis. A managed care health plan may likely be more concerned about the cost-effectiveness than the cost-utility of alternative regimens, with costs restricted to those incurred by the plan. A societal perspective may be concerned about cost-effectiveness and/or cost-benefit, defining costs more broadly as those incurred by the health care provider, patient, and society in general.
4. Even changing the dosage forms will affect the analyses. Costs, response rates, and adverse reaction rates may vary in changing routes of administration.

Although presenting only a portion of the complete decision analysis that would be necessary to determine A.B.'s preferred course of therapy, this case illustrates a number of the considerations which must be incorporated into a decision analysis. This decision tree provides the graphic structure for communication between patient and clinician as well as other members of the clinical team. And it can be modified to structure the decision from different perspectives (a pharmacy benefit manager, managed care organization, or employer perspective); consider different options; revise the probabilities based on the new population of interest; and value the outcomes of each path, again based on the new population of interest.

DECISION ANALYTIC COMPUTER SUPPORT

Decision support systems provide the computational power to conduct complex analyses of problems with multiple consequences, probability estimates, and outcome valuations. All prompt the analyst to identify the decision options, to structure the consequences of the decision options, to place chance nodes and probability estimates, and to assign values to outcomes. Most also provide support for sensitivity analyses, Monte Carlo simulations, and Markov computations. While three systems were originally developed for medi-

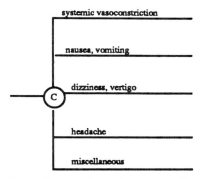

FIG. 5. Ergotamine, adverse reactions.

cal application—D-Maker, CE Tree (105), and SMLTREE (106)—others were designed for a generic audience and can be adapted for clinical applications—Aborist: Decision Tree Software (Texas Instruments, Dallas, TX) (107), DPL (108), Supertree (Strategic Decisions Group, Menlo Park, CA), and Data 2.5 (TreeAge Software, Inc., PO Box 990207, Boston, MA 02199, 617-536-2128). Data 2.5 is available for Macintosh computers. All others, as well as Data™ 2.6, are available in MS-DOS or Windows versions.

To enable novices to construct decision trees automatically, Sonnenberg et al. (109) developed MIDAS, a system that frames questions and encodes the answers as well as guides the actual construction of a tree following decision rules of syntax, and so on. And to assist in the interpretation of the results of the analysis, Langlotz and colleagues (110) have developed a system for generating computer-based explanations of decision-theoretic advice.

CONCLUSIONS

Pharmacoeconomic evaluations would be strengthened by the use of fully developed and specified decision analytic models. The explicit processes of decision analysis provides the template upon which all forms of pharmacoeconomic evaluations—cost efficiency, cost-effectiveness, cost utility, and cost-benefit studies—can be more carefully and comprehensively organized and conducted. From the framing of the question, to identifying the options, perspective, and time frame for the analysis; identifying and structuring the sequence of events and consequences that may follow when an option is chosen; estimating the probabilities that these events and consequences will occur; valuing the outcomes for each chosen option in both economic and noneconomic units; and finally determining the option with the highest expected value or outcome for the decision maker—all are explicit steps that assist the decision maker to incorporate all factors affecting the decision, its consequences, and outcomes. Given that institutional constraints and limited financial resources will continue to influence health care allocations, decision analysis provides a method by which we can improve our position within this new health care market.

REFERENCES

1. Ramsey FP. Truth and probability. In: Kyberg HE, Smokler HE, eds. *Studies in subjective probability*. New York: John Wiley & Sons, 1964.
2. Von Newmann J, Morgenstern. *Theory of games and economic behavior*. 2nd ed. Princeton, NJ: Princeton University Press; 1947.
3. Raiffa H. *Decision analysis: introductory lectures under uncertainty*. Reading, MA: Addison-Wesley, 1968.
4. Ledley RS, Lusted LB. Reasoning foundations of medical diagnosis. *Science* 1959;130:9–21.
5. Lusted LB. *Introduction to medical decision making*. Springfield, IL: Charles C Thomas, 1968.
6. Lusted LB. Decision-making studies in patient management. *N Engl J Med* 1971;284:416–424.
7. McNeil BJ, Keeler E, Adelstein SJ. Primer on certain elements of medical decision making. *N Engl J Med* 1975;293:221–215.
8. Kassirer JP. The principles of clinical decision making: an introduction to decision analysis. *Yale J Biol Med* 1976;49:149–164.
9. Kassirer JP, Moskowitz AJ, Lau J, Pauker SG. Decision analysis: a progress report. *Ann Intern Med* 1987;106:275–291.
10. Plante DA, Kassirer JP, Zarin DA, Pauker SG. Clinical decision consultation service. *Am J Med* 1986;80:1169–1176.
11. *Physicians in the twenty-first century: The GPEP report*. Washington, DC: Association of American Medical Colleges, 1984.
12. Simon DG. A cost-effectiveness analysis of cyclosporine in cadaveric kidney transplantation. *Med Decis Making* 1986;6:199–207.
13. Weinstein MC, Read JL, MacKay DN, Kresel JJ, Ashley H, Halvorsen KT, Hutchings HC. Cost-effective choice of antimicrobial therapy for serious infections. *J Gen Intern Med* 1986;1:351–363.
14. Krumholz HM, Pasternak RC, Weinstein MC, Friesinger GC, et al. Cost effectiveness of thrombolytic therapy with streptokinase in elderly patients with suspected acute myocardial infarction. *N Engl J Med* 1992;327:7–13.
15. Desch CE, Hillner BE, Smith TJ, et al. Should the elderly receive chemotherapy for node-negative breast cancer? A cost-effectiveness analysis examining total and active life-expectancy outcomes. *J Clin Oncol* 1993;11:77–782.
16. Centor RM, Witherspoon JM. Treating sore throats in the emergency room: the importance of follow-up in decision making. *Med Decis Making* 1982;2:463–469.
17. Levine MN, Drummond MF, Labelle RJ. Cost-effectiveness in the diagnosis and treatment of carcinoma of unknown primary origin. *Can Med Assoc J* 1985;133:977–987.
18. Krahn M, Detsky AS. Should Canada and the United States universally vaccinate infants against hepatitis B? *Med Decis Making* 1993;13:4–20.
19. Cantor SB, Clover RD, Thompson RF. A decision-analytic approach to postexposure rabies prophylaxis. *Am J Public Health* 1994;84:114–1148.
20. Clemens JD, Ransohoff DF. A quantitative assessment of pre-dental antibiotic prophylaxis for patients with mitral-valve prolapse. *J Chronic Dis* 1984;37:531–544.
21. Oster G, Tuden RL, Colditz GA. Cost-effectiveness analysis of prophylaxis against deep-vein thrombosis in major orthopedic surgery. *JAMA* 1987;257:203–208.
22. Schumacher GE, Barr JT. Applying decision analysis in therapeutic drug monitoring: Using decision trees to interpret serum theophylline concentrations. *Clin Pharm* 1986;5:325–333.
23. Schumacher GE, Barr JT. Using population-based serum drug concentration cutoff values to predict toxicity: test performance and limitations compared with Bayesian interpretation. *Clin Pharm* 1990;9:788–796.
24. Schumacher GE, Barr JT. Bayesian and threshold probabilities in therapeutic drug monitoring: when can serum drug concentrations alter clinical decisions? *Am J Hosp Pharm* 1994;51:321–327.
25. Sun S. Choice of anaesthesia in dental operations. *Med Inform* 1991;16:15–24.
26. Paul SD, Kuntz KM, Eagle KA, Weinstein MC. Costs and effectiveness of angiotensin converting enzyme inhibition in patients with congestive heart failure. *Arch Intern Med* 1994;154:1143–1149.
27. Bor DH, Himmelstein DU. Endocarditis prophylaxis for patient with mitral valve prolapse: a quantitative analysis. *Am J Med* 1984;76:711–717.
28. Callahan CW. Cost effectiveness of antibiotic therapy for otitis media in a military pediatric clinic. *Pediatr Infect Dis J* 1988;7:622–625.
29. Carlson KJ, Mulley AG. Management of acute dysuria: a decision-analysis model of alternative strategies. *Ann Intern Med* 1985;102:244–249.
30. Hillner BE, Centor RM. What a difference a day makes: a decision analysis of adult streptococcal pharyngitis. *J Gen Intern Med* 1987;2:242–248.
31. Holloway JJ, Smith CR, Moore RD, Feroli R, Lietman PS. Comparative cost effectiveness of gentamicin and tobramycin. *Ann Intern Med* 1984;101:764–769.
32. Jorgenson GM, Erramouspe J. Cost-effectiveness of selected management options for acute otitis media in ambulatory clinic patients. *Consult Pharm* 1991;6:241–245.
33. Kresel JJ, Hutchings HC, MacKay DN, et al. Application of decision

analysis to drug selection for formulary addition. *Hosp Formul* 1987;22:658–676.

34. Magrid D, Schwartz B, Craft J, Schwartz JS. Prevention of lyme disease after tick bites: a cost-effectiveness analysis. *N Engl J Med* 1992;327:534–541.

35. Paladino JA. Cost-effectiveness comparison of cefepime and ceftazidime using decision analysis. *PharmacoEconomics* 1994;5:505–512.

36. Paladino JA, Fell RE. Pharmacoeconomic analysis of cefmenoxime dual individualization in the treatment of nosocomial pneumonia. *Ann Pharmacother* 1994;28:384–389.

37. Plante DA, Pauker SG. Enterococcal endocarditis and penicillin allergy: which drug for the bug? *Med Decis Making* 1983;3:81–109.

38. Reves RR, Johnson PC, Ericsson CD, DuPont HL. A cost-effectiveness comparison of the use of antimicrobial agents for treatment or prophylaxis of traveler's diarrhea. *Arch Intern Med* 1989;148:2421–2427.

39. Shapiro M, Schoenbaum SC, Tager IB, Munoz A, Polk BF. Benefit-cost analysis of antimicrobial prophylaxis in abdominal and vaginal hysterectomy. *JAMA* 1983;249:1290–1294.

40. Stamm WE, McKevitt M, Counts GW, et al. Is antimicrobial prophylaxis of urinary tract infections cost effective? *Ann Intern Med* 1981;94:251–255.

41. Stern RS, Pass TM, Komaroff AL. Topical versus systemic agent treatment for papulopustular acne: a cost-effectiveness analysis. *Arch Dermatol* 1984;120:1571–1578.

42. Tsevat J, Durand-Zaleski I, Pauker SG. Cost-effectiveness of antibiotic prophylaxis for dental procedures in patients with artificial joints. *Am J Public Health* 1989;79:739–743.

43. Tsevat J, Wong JB, Pauker SG, Steinberg MH. Neonatal screening for sickle cell disease: a cost-effectiveness analysis. *J Pediatr* 1991;118:546–554.

44. Washington AE, Browner WS, Korenbrot CC. Cost-effectiveness of combined treatment for endocervical gonorrhea: considering co-infection with *Chlamydia trachomatis*. *JAMA* 1987;257:2056–2060.

45. Weiss JC, Melman ST. Cost effectiveness in the choice of antibiotics for the initial treatment of otitis media in children: a decision analysis approach. *Pediatr Infect Dis* 1988;7:23–26.

46. Pauker SG, Eckman MH, Levine HJ. A decision analytic view of anticoagulant prophylaxis for thromboembolism in heart disease. *Chest* 1989;95(suppl):161S–169S.

47. Jönsson B, Bebbington PE. What cost depression? The cost of depression and the cost-effectiveness of pharmacological treatment. *Br J Psychiatry* 1994;164:665–673.

48. Buxton MJ, O'Brien BJ. Economic evaluation of ondansetron: preliminary analysis using clinical trial data prior to price setting. *Br J Cancer* 1992;66(suppl 19):S64–S67.

49. Zbrozek AS, Cantor SB, Cardenas MP, Hill DP. Pharmacoeconomic analysis of ondansetron versus metoclopramide for cisplatin-induced nausea and vomiting. *Am J Hosp Pharm* 1994;51:1555–1563.

50. Gottlieb JE, Pauker SG. Whether or not to administer amphotericin to an immunosuppressed patient with hematologic malignancy and undiagnosed fever. *Med Decis Making* 1981;1:75–93.

51. Sudre P, Breman JG, McFarland D, Koplan JP. Treatment of chloroquine-resistant malaria in African children: a cost-effectiveness analysis. *Int J Epidemiol* 1992;21:146–154.

52. Oster G, Huse DM, Lacey MJ, Epstein AM. Cost-effectiveness of ticlopidine in preventing stroke in high-risk patients. *Stroke* 1994;25:1149–1156.

53. Koplan JP, Farer LS. Choice of preventive treatment for isoniazid-resistant tuberculous infection. *JAMA* 1980;244:2736–2740.

54. Rose DN, Silver AL, Schechter CB. Tuberculosis chemoprophylaxis for diabetics: are the benefits of isoniazid worth the risk. *Mt Sinai J Med* 1985;52:253–258.

55. Taylor WC, Aronson MD, Delbanco TL. Should young adults with a positive tuberculin test take isoniazid? *Ann Intern Med* 1981;94:808–813.

56. Barza M, Pauker SG. The decision to biopsy, treat, or wait in suspected herpes encephalitis. *Ann Intern Med* 1980;92:641–649.

57. McCarthy BD, Wong JB, Muñoz A, Sonnenberg FA. Who should be screened for HIV infections: a cost-effectiveness analysis. *Arch Intern Med* 1993;153:1107–1116.

58. Oddone EZ, Cowper P, Hamilton JD, et al. Cost effectiveness analysis of early zidovudine treatment of HIV infected patients. *Br Med J* 1993;307:1322–1325.

59. Gonzalez ER, Ornato JP, Lawson CL. Clinical decision analysis modeling: short-term control of ventricular response rate in atrial fibrillation or atrial flutter—digoxin versus diltiazem. *Pharmacotherapy* 1994;14:446–451.

60. Djulbegovic B, Hollenberg J, Woodcock TM, Herzig R. Comparison of different treatment strategies for diffuse large-cell lymphomas: a decision analysis. *Med Decis Making* 1991;11:1–8.

61. Hillner BE, Smith TJ. Efficacy and cost effectiveness of adjuvant chemotherapy in women with node-negative breast cancer. *N Engl J Med* 1991;324:160–168.

62. Hillner BE, Smith TJ, Desch CE. Efficacy and cost-effectiveness of autologous bone marrow transplantation in metastatic breast cancer. *JAMA* 1992;267:2055–2061.

63. Hillner BE, Smith TJ, Desch CE. Assessing the cost effectiveness of adjuvant therapies in early breast cancer using a decision analysis model. *Breast Cancer Res Treat* 1993;25:97–105.

64. Rutherford CJ, DesForges JF, Barnett AI, et al. The decision between single- and combined-modality therapy for Hodgkin's disease. *Am J Med* 1982;72:63–70.

65. Smith TJ, Hillner BE. The efficacy and cost-effectiveness of adjuvant therapy of early breast cancer in premenopausal women. *J Clin Oncol* 1993;11:771–776.

66. Barrett BJ, Papfrey PS, Foley RN, et al. An economic analysis for the use of contrast media for diagnostic cardiac catherization. *Med Decis Making* 1994;14:325–335.

67. Calvo MV, Pilar del Val M, Mar Alvarez M, Dominguez-Gil A. Decision analysis applied to assess cost-effectiveness of low-osmolality contrast medium for intravenous urography. *Am J Hosp Pharm* 1992;49:577–584.

68. Lyman GH, Lyman CG, Sanderson RA, et al. Decision analysis of hematopoietic growth factor use in patients receiving cancer chemotherapy. *J Natl Cancer Inst* 1993;85:488–493.

69. Hillman AL, Bloom BS, Fendrick AM, Schwartz JS. Cost and quality effects of alternative treatments for persistent gastroesophageal reflux disease. *Arch Intern Med* 1992;152:1467–1472.

70. Oster G, Huse DM, Delea TE, Colditz GA, Richter JM. The risks and benefits of an Rx-to -OTC switch: the case of over-the-counter H2-blockers. *Med Care* 1990;28:834–852.

71. Read L, Pass TM, Komaroff AL. Diagnosis and treatment of dyspepsia: a cost-effectiveness analysis. *Med Decis Making* 1982;2:415–438.

72. Hillner BE, Hollenberg JP, Pauker SG. Postmenopausal estrogens in prevention of osteoporosis: benefit virtually without risk if cardiovascular effects are considered. *Am J Med* 1986;80:1115–1127.

73. Tosteson ANA, Rosenthal DI, Melton LJ, Weinstein MC. Cost effectiveness of screening perimenopausal white women for osteoporosis: bone densitometry and hormone replacement therapy. *Ann Intern Med* 1990;113:594–603.

74. Zubialde JP, Lawler F, Clemenson N. Estimated gains in life expectancy with use of postmenopausal estrogen therapy: a decision analysis. *J Fam Pract* 1993;36:271–280.

75. Klassen TP, Rowe PC, Gafni A. Economic evaluation of intravenous immune globulin therapy for Kawasaki syndrome. *J Pediatr* 1993;122:538–542.

76. Weeks JC, Tierney MR, Weinstein MC. Cost effectiveness of prophylactic intravenous immune globulin in chronic lymphocytic leukemia. *N Engl J Med* 1991;325:81–86.

77. Cucharel GJ, Levey AS, Pauker SG. Kidney failure or cancer: should immunosuppression be continued in a transplant patient with malignant melanoma? *Med Decis Making* 1984;4:83.

78. Chalfin DB, Blair Holbein ME, Fein AM, Carlon GC. Cost-effectiveness of monoclonal antibodies to gram-negative endotoain in the treatment of gram-negative sepsis in ICU patients. *JAMA* 1993;269:249–254.

79. Edelson JT, Tosteson ANA, Sax P. Cost-effectiveness of misoprostol for prophylaxis against nonsteroidal anti-inflammatory drug-induced gastrointestinal tract bleeding. *JAMA* 1990;264:41–47.

80. Gabriel SE, Jaakkimainen RL, Bombardier C. The cost-effectiveness of misoprostol for nonsteroidal antiinflammatory drug-associated adverse gastrointestinal events. *Arthritis Rheum* 1993;36:447–459.

81. Gabriel SE, Campion ME, O'Fallon WM. A cost-utility analysis of misoprostol prophylaxis for rheumatoid arthritis patients receiving nonsteroidal antiinflammatory drugs. *Arthritis Rheum* 1994;37:333–341.

82. Knill-Jones R, Drummond M, Kohli H, Davies L. Economic evaluation of gastric ulcer prophylaxis in patients with arthritis receiving non-steroidal anti-inflammatory drugs. *Postgrad Med J* 1990;66:639–648.

83. Eraker SA, Sasse L. The serum digoxin test and digoxin toxicity: a Bayesian approach to decision making. *Circulation* 1981;64:409–420.

84. Schumacher JT, Barr JT. Making serum drug levels more meaningful. *Ther Drug Monit* 1989;11:580–584.

85. Midgette AS, Wong JB, Beshansky JR, et al. Cost-effectiveness of streptokinase for acute myocardial infarction: a combined meta-analysis and decision analysis of the effects of infarct location and of likelihood of infarction. *Med Decis Making* 1994;14:108–117.

86. O'Meara JJ, McNutt RA, Evans AT, Moore SW, Downs SM. A decision analysis of streptokinase plus heparin as compared with heparin alone for deep-vein thrombosis. *N Engl J Med* 1994;330:1864–1869.

87. Oster G, Tuden RL, Colditz GA. Prevention of venous thromboembolism after general surgery: cost-effectiveness analysis of alternative approaches to prophylaxis. *Am J Med* 1987;82:889–899.

88. Bloom BS, Hillman AL, Fendrick AM, Schwartz JS. A reappraisal of hepatitis B virus vaccination strategies using cost-effectiveness analysis. *Ann Intern Med* 1993;118:298–306.

89. Grabenstein JD, Hartzema AG, Guess HA, et al. Community pharmacists as immunization advocates: cost-effectiveness of a cue to influenza vaccination. *Med Care* 1992;30:503–513.

90. Koplan JP, Schoenbaum SC, Weinstein MC, Fraser DW. Pertussis vaccine—an analysis of benefits, risks and costs. *N Engl J Med* 1979;301:906–911.

91. Nettleman MD. Use of BCG vaccine in shelters for the homeless: a decision analysis. *Chest* 1993;103:1087–1090.

92. Oddone EZ, Cowper PA, Hamilton JD, Feussner JR. A cost-effectiveness analysis of hepatitis B vaccine in predialysis patients. *Health Serv Res* 1993;28:97–121.

93. Kassirer JP, Kopelman RI. Cognitive errors in diagnosis: instantiation, classification, and consequences. *Am J Med* 1989;86:433–441.

94. Berwick DM, Fineberg HV, Weinstein MC. When physicians meet numbers. *Am J Med* 1981;71:991–998.

95. Moskowitz AJ, Kuipers BJ, Kassirer JP. Dealing with uncertainty, risks, and tradeoffs in clinical decision: a cognitive science approach. *Ann Intern Med* 1988;108:435–449.

96. Weinstein MC, Fineberg HV, eds. *Clinical decision analysis.* Philadelphia: WB Saunders, 1980.

97. Sonnenberg FA, Roberts MS, Tsevat J, et al. Toward a peer review process for medical decision analysis models. *Med Care* 1994;32:JS52–S64.

98. Beck JR, Pauker SG. The Markov process in medical prognosis. *Med Decis Making* 1983;3:419.

99. Sonnenberg FA, Beck JR. Markov models in medical decision making: a practical guide. *Med Decis Making* 1993;13:322–338.

100. Barr JT, Schumacher GE. Decision analysis and pharmacoeconomic evaluations. In: Bootman JL, McGhan W, Townsman R, eds. *Pharmacoeconomics.* Cincinnati: Harvey Whitney Books, 1991:112–133.

101. Wellman MP, Eckman MH, Fleming C, et al. Automated critiquing of medical decision trees. *Med Decis Making* 1989;9:272–284.

102. Tversky A, Kahneman D. Judgment under uncertainty; heuristics and biases. *Science* 1974;185:1124–1131.

103. Torrance GW, Feeny D. Utilities and quality-adjusted life years. *Int J Technol Assess Health Care* 1989;5:559–575.

104. Doubilet P, Begg CB, Weinstein MC, et al. Probabilistic sensitivity analysis using Monte Carlo simulation. *Med Decis Making* 1985;5:157–177.

105. Pass TM, Goldstein LG. CE Tree: a computerized aid for cost-effectiveness analysis. In: Hefferman HG, ed. *Proceedings of the fifth symposium on computer applications in medical care.* Washington, DC, IEEE Computer Society, 1981:219–221.

106. Hollenberg J. *SMLTREE: the all purpose decision tree builder.* Boston: Pratt Medical, 1985.

107. Franke DW, Hall CR. *Arborist: decision tree software.* Dallas, TX: Texas Instruments, 1984.

108. DPL: *Standard Version User Guide.* Belmont: Duxbury Press, 1994.

109. Sonnenberg FA, Hagerty CG, Kulikowski CA. An architecture for knowledge based construction of decision models. *Med Decis Making* 1994;14:27–39.

110. Langlotz CP, Shortliffe EH, Fagan LM. A methodology for generating computer-based explanations of decision-theoretic advice. *Med Decis Making* 1988;8:290–303.

Quality of Life and Pharmacoeconomics in Clinical Trials, Second Edition, edited by B. Spilker.
Lippincott-Raven Publishers, Philadelphia © 1996.

CHAPTER **126**

Threats to the Validity of Pharmacoeconomic Analyses Based on Clinical Trial Data

Brian E. Rittenhouse and Bernie J. O'Brien

INTRODUCTION

Pharmacoeconomic methods continue to evolve because of pressures from various sources to scrutinize both costs and consequences of providing medical care. A debate has recently been sparked between those who engage in "outcomes research," using predominantly observational and other nonexperimental methods, and the traditional "hard core" medical researchers, who have a predilection for experimental design in the form of the randomized, controlled trial. Some of the latter group have assailed "outcomes research" as lacking in "scientific validity" (1). Although we acknowledge the imperfect nature of "outcomes research" methods, we offer a critique of randomized, controlled trial-derived data in their use in economic evaluations (particularly in premarketing pharmaceutical trials). Specifically, we question the validity of inferences based on such data to the world of clinical practice. It is this practice-based world that is of primary interest to those engaged in pharmacoeconomics. To date, the literature has been relatively silent on this topic (2).

Rather than joining either of the two warring parties in this debate, we choose a middle course of compromise. Our basic premise is that there exist potential threats to the validity of all research methods, including randomized, controlled trials. Such threats imply a potential bias in all methods. Our conclusion is that informative and practical research (which surely is what pharmacoeconomics attempts to be) requires a melding of methods. Our suggestion for such efforts appeals to notions of building models of treatment choice which are conglomerates of data from various sources, acknowledging that no single source can provide that which is necessary for fulfilling the pharmacoeconomics task.

This chapter reviews the ongoing debate between outcomes researchers and clinical trialists, focusing on the distinction between threats to internal and external validity. We examine seven threats to the validity of pharmacoeconomic studies based on randomized, controlled trials, giving examples from the literature and concluding with suggestions for future research directions for pharmacoeconomics that combine aspects of both experimental and observational design.

PHARMACOECONOMICS METHODS

Edmund Pelligrino has said that "Investigators seem to have settled for what is measurable instead of measuring

B. E. Rittenhouse: Division of Pharmaceutical Policy and Evaluative Sciences, School of Pharmacy, University of North Carolina at Chapel Hill, Chapel Hill, North Carolina 27599.
B. J. O'Brien: Department of Clinical Epidemiology and Biostatistics, McMaster University and the Centre for Evaluation of Medicines, St. Joseph's Hospital, Hamilton, Ontario L8N 4A6, Canada.

what they would really like to know'' (3). This rather pragmatic approach to difficult research questions is widespread in both of the research camps we describe herein. Indeed, compromises in methodological approaches permeate research in all fields. What is it that we in pharmacoeconomics would really like to know? Keeping this question in mind during the following discussion of methods debates surrounding pharmacoeconomics will assist in sorting out a position to take on these debates. Pharmacoeconomics should attempt to evaluate the question of not whether a new treatment *could* be, say, cost-effective, but whether it is, in fact, likely to be so. This practical orientation, we believe, defines the field and dictates the challenges we present below.

Methods of pharmacoeconomic analysis have evolved considerably in the relatively brief history of the field. What we would really like to know has not changed. What we consider measuring has. Early discussion of the acquisition cost of pharmaceuticals was quickly replaced by conjectures (based on somewhat casual support from data) regarding possible downstream cost savings consequent to product use. As dissatisfaction with casual conjectures as a foundation for pharmacoeconomics mounted, an ''obvious solution'' appeared. The randomized controlled trial is the centerpiece of product testing and marketing regulatory approval. The economic analyst could rely on the randomized, controlled trial for ''hard'' data for the same reason that the randomized, controlled trial was institutionalized for indicating efficacy—strength of research design. If the possibility of selection bias is important for assessing efficacy, it is clearly also important for assessing, for example, cost-effectiveness. Since economic evaluations meld clinical with economic implications, economic analysts must be aware of threats to validity of outcomes results as much as clinical researchers are. For these reasons (plus its ready availability), the randomized, controlled trial has become the workhorse of pharmacoeconomics (4,5).

In (seemingly) another world, the Agency for Health Care Policy and Research (AHCPR) has recently spent a considerable sum—$200 million, according to Sheldon (1)—in evaluating alternative treatments in terms of both traditional clinical outcomes as well as nontraditional economic and quality of life outcomes. Much of this effort has been in the form of Patient Outcomes Research Teams (PORTs) specific to various indication areas. The PORTs often rely on literature review and so-called ''observational'' data (as distinguished from experimental, e.g., randomized, controlled trial, data), based on analyses of data bases from hospitals, insurance companies and Medicare (1). The genesis of much of the recent methods debate can be traced to reactions to these studies.

THE DEBATE ON METHODS

Recent criticisms of ''outcomes research,'' generally defined so as to exclude the randomized, controlled trial, have emphasized the inferential problems associated with meth-

ods in observational epidemiology. These problems have been acknowledged by experts in epidemiology for years (6), although their conclusions are somewhat less pessimistic than those of some recent critics. Perhaps chief among the problems is the possibility of selection bias—that allocation of patients to treatments is influenced by patient or disease attributes (e.g., severity). Such selection can obviously interfere with the assignment of responsibility for outcome to the treatments. Randomization, at least in theory, solves this problem.

The randomized, controlled trial would appear to be a ''gold standard'' method. However, we believe, following McPherson (7), that there is a danger, to paraphrase Voltaire, of ''the best becoming the enemy of the good.'' In a comment that was directed at case-control studies, but that could be equally applied to the entire field of observational epidemiology, Senn (8) has stated that ''the fact that such studies seem difficult to justify when judged by the standards of clinical trials is not sufficient to condemn them. We do not call geology malformed because it is not physics.'' Far from being a malformed science, nonexperimental studies sometimes offer advantages in terms of cost, timeliness, appropriate design and ethics (6,9–11).

One researcher disposed to claiming disciplinary reign is Richard Peto, who has provided perhaps the most caustic criticism of nonexperimental methods to date in stating that major investment in outcomes research ''is worse than just destroying the money because it gives the illusion of information'' (12). Such extreme views only serve to polarize views on the nature of valid methods of inquiry. What is often overlooked by those favoring the exclusive use of randomized, controlled trial methods is the distinction between internal and external validity.

INTERNAL VERSUS EXTERNAL VALIDITY

The term *validity* is used rather casually by many researchers. To others, such as Hennekens and Buring (6), it has a specific meaning that corresponds to what we, following Cook and Campbell (13), will call internal validity. This is a very specific notion of whether we can confidently make statements about treatment cause and effect in the sample of patients studied, what Senn (8) has called ''proof within the trial.'' If there is less control over the environment, particularly over the allocation of treatments to patients, the link from cause to effect is weakened. One of the great virtues of randomization is its ability to equally distribute (in theory) both known and unknown potential confounding influences to all treatment arms. The controlled environment of the randomized, controlled trial further implies limitations to other influences on patients during the course of treatment. The inferential basis from cause to effect is quite strong for the population studied, under the conditions of the study. While practical difficulties may limit its use sometimes, the randomized, controlled trial is the unassailable gold standard for such a comparison.

TABLE 1. *Confidence levels in validity of study types*

Study type	Externally valid?	Internally valid?
Randomized, controlled trial	Low confidence	High confidence
Data base	High confidence	Low confidence

Based on Eddy (10) and GAO (11).

The evaluation and experimental design literature has long recognized threats to a second type of validity—external validity (13). In health care, Kleinbaum et al. (14) also bifurcate the concept of validity into internal and external dimensions. This dual notion is common though exact definitions differ (11,15). What is universal among those using the term external validity is the attribute of generalizability to populations not represented in the study. Hennekens and Buring (6) use the term *validity* synonymously with internal validity and use *generalizability* to capture the concept of external validity. They specifically emphasize that while one can have (in our terms) internal validity without external validity, one cannot have the reverse. Both types of validity are necessary to make confident inferences about treatment effect in populations of interest. It must be emphasized that internal validity, while possible without external validity, is not highly useful in pharmacoeconomics (and perhaps elsewhere). Given the frequently stringent selection criteria often used in premarketing pharmaceutical trials, external validity may be a significant problem. Although external validity in the absence of internal validity is somewhat meaningless, much of value can be learned from studies whose internal validity is less than perfect. Table 1 summarizes randomized, controlled trials and data base analyses from perspectives of their internal and external validity. The high confidence in the external validity for data bases must be considered in light of the accompanying low confidence in internal validity and, correspondingly, the high confidence in the internal validity of the randomized, controlled trial must be weighted against the low confidence in its external validity. Other methods in observational epidemiology tend to fit in the table in between the extremes offered by data bases and randomized, controlled trials (10).

Having laid the conceptual ground to support our case that two types of validity must be addressed in any pharmacoeconomic effort, we now itemize some specific concerns that may significantly threaten the external validity of economic analyses based on randomized, controlled trials.

SEVEN THREATS TO THE VALIDITY OF RANDOMIZED, CONTROLLED TRIAL-BASED PHARMACOECONOMICS

Although the high degree of internal validity associated with the randomized, controlled trial design is desirable for making causal treatment-outcome inferences about efficacy,

we have suggested that the randomized, controlled trial design often suffers from poor external validity (i.e., generalizability to real-world clinical practice). This weakens its basis for estimating parameters on effectiveness and cost that are relevant to policy discussions on resource allocation. In this section we discuss, with examples, seven general threats to the validity of pharmacoeconomic studies that are based, retrospectively or prospectively, on randomized, controlled trial data.

Choice of Comparison Therapy

A fundamental threat to the validity of any pharmacoeconomic study exists when the comparison therapy is not the most relevant for the policy question being addressed. A comparison that may be relevant for testing safety and efficacy, such as placebo, is unlikely to be the most relevant comparison for an economic study of the new drug. If the relevant economic question is to assess whether the added population health benefits are worth the added cost, a relevant comparison is the most widely used current therapy for the disease in question. For example, in assessing the cost-effectiveness of the new antiemetic drug, ondansetron, Buxton and O'Brien (16) made comparison (using published trials) against a widely used and effective existing therapy—metroclopromide (17). Earlier trials (18,19) comparing against placebo (i.e., proxy for no therapy) were not a relevant comparison for the incremental economic question. Even if no treatment is the relevant alternative, placebo controls are unlikely to represent a no-treatment alternative adequately. This follows from the very arguments that support their inclusion in trials. If there is a placebo effect, the no-treatment alternative will not be adequately proxied by placebo. Despite potential ethical (20) and economic arguments against the use of placebo, the U.S. Food and Drug Administration regulatory rules encourage a continued use of such comparisons. Using existing therapy as the comparison does not restrict the study to comparison only against other drugs. For example, the economic case in favor of introducing cimetidine for duodenal ulcer was based on comparison against the costly and risky alternative for many patients, which was surgery (21), even though the product licensing trials were against placebo. Similarly, in evaluating a new medical device such as an implantable defibrillator for patients at risk of fatal cardiac arrhythmias as relevant clinical and economic comparison is drug therapy with amiodarone (22).

In situations in which the relevant comparison is an existing drug therapy, the existing clinical trials may have used an active drug comparison that is not the most relevant. For example, the approval of the first low-molecular-weight heparin (enoxaparin) in Canada for prophylaxis against deep-vein thrombosis (DVT) following orthopedic surgery was based on trial comparisons against standard heparin. Although the cost-effectiveness of enoxaparin versus heparin was studied (23), the authors questioned whether this was the most relevant economic comparison because survey evidence in the United States and Canada suggested that warfarin was the most widely used drug in this indication (24). Unfortunately, in building the revised economic analysis comparing enoxaparin and warfarin (25), there was a weaker inferential base for efficacy because no head-to-head trials of these drugs had been published. It is noteworthy that the Australian guidelines for conducting economic evaluations for submission to the Pharmaceutical Benefits Advisory Committee (for decisions on formulary listing) require a comparison against the most widely used alternative in Australia (26). Recent Canadian guidelines for the economic evaluation of pharmaceuticals emphasize both a) treatment likely to be replaced and b) minimal treatment.

Gold Standard Measurement of Outcomes

A common problem facing the economist wishing to use clinical trial data for making inferences about cost-effectiveness is that trials often employ measurements for outcomes that are more detailed, invasive or frequent than is customary in usual care. For example, in comparing alternative acid suppressant drugs, the outcome of duodenal ulcer recurrence is usually determined in clinical trials by endoscopy of all patients at fixed follow-up times (28). Outside of a trial, the management of such patients would be based largely on symptoms. Therefore, for the economic analysis to be externally valid, it must reflect the fact that some persons without symptoms will have ulcer recurrence—although silent—and some persons with symptoms may not have ulcer recurrence. The use of rates of recurrence based on endoscopy will misrepresent the reality of clinical practice and bias the pharmacoeconomic results.

Another example is the diagnosis of DVT in clinical trials of low-molecular-weight heparin. The gold standard measurement in such studies is venography—an invasive, relatively expensive, often painful test involving injection of contrast media. However, if in regular practice venography is not universally and routinely used to test for DVT, how useful is this knowledge of the "truth" for economic evaluation? In a study of enoxaparin, O'Brien et al. (25) used the true rates of DVT (treatment and control) as the prior probabilities of disease in a decision analytic model that incorporated the conditional likelihood and costs of these DVT, detected by a routine diagnostic algorithm based on clinical signs and symptoms and ultrasound. Such a model includes the costs and outcomes of errors in diagnosis, that will happen in routine practice but were not part of the trial, because the physician will not generally use costly and invasive tests as first-line therapy. Rather, such testing is used typically to confirm suspicions based on clinical symptoms. Modeling techniques may be used to predict resource use based on counterfactuals—what would have happened clinically had the atypical test not been used? Those clinical events would then drive further testing in clinical practice, contributing to resource use (29). Such "adjustments" to

efficacy data are necessary to make data externally valid for economic inferences, but they also require some ex-trial data input, for example, on the sensitivity and specificity of clinical diagnosis and ultrasound.

Intermediate Versus Final Health Outcomes

In clinical trials of diseases where event rates are small, such as reduction of cardiovascular risk factors or cases of DVT, it has become customary to study and report intermediate biomedical markers as outcomes because sample sizes to test differences in final outcome such as mortality are often prohibitive (29). Trials of cholesterol-lowering drugs are a good example in which the outcome is the measured change in total blood cholesterol or some subfraction (30). For economic analysis to inform resource allocation, we are interested in what impact such changes will have on final health outcomes, such as mortality and morbidity. This often results in attempts to use existing epidemiologic data (e.g., cohort studies such as Framingham) to construct models that can predict changes in final outcomes (e.g., deaths and myocardial infarctions) from changes in risk factors (31). Canadian guidelines on pharmacoeconomic study design are clear that intermediate outcomes must, by some means, be translated into final health outcomes (27). The overall validity of the economic study therefore depends crucially upon the way in which the relationship between intermediate and final outcomes has been quantified. For example, the early cost-effectiveness model of tissue plasminogen activator (TPA) in acute myocardial infarction by Laffel et al. (32) was based on mortality projections of early trial data on the intermediate outcome of arterial patency by angiography. Subsequent trials with mortality as the measured outcome have yielded far more conservative estimates of the mortality benefits of this drug.

Inadequate Patient Follow-up

A particular problem with the retrospective use of clinical trial data is where patient follow-up and data collection terminate abruptly when the patient experiences one of the outcome "events" of interest. From the perspective of the economic analyst, this can be frustrating because much of the cost associated with the new therapy may be incurred in the treatment of such events. Many examples can be found in cardiovascular drug therapy where events such as stroke or MI are recorded but with no indication of the health care resources used to manage the cases. This is familiar terrain for the health economist who must now devise some method (e.g., expert panel, practice audit, insurance claims data base) to estimate what resources are typically used in such circumstances.

In addition to missing data on resource use, the randomized, controlled trial may be based on frequency of, or time to, first event only. In many diseases, the relevant time horizon for the economic evaluation might be longer so as to capture the recurrence of a disease or problem associated with therapy. Examples include long-term drug management for duodenal ulcer and coronary restenosis following procedures such as coronary angioplasty. It has been common in economic studies of such diseases to use statistical models (e.g., Markov processes) as a means of estimating disease recurrence, and associated costs, based on existing knowledge of time-to-first event. For an example relating to glyceryl trinitrate patches in infusion failure, see O'Brien et al. (33).

The problem of inadequate follow-up is a characteristic *fait accompli* of using existing trial data to attempt to address a question for which they were not collected. In principle, the economist's life is made easier by including economic questions at the design stage of the randomized, controlled trial, but this raises other questions of whether observed costs and outcomes are "driven" by the research protocol.

Protocol-Driven Costs and Outcomes

A problem with basing cost estimates on data gathered as part of a trial is the extent to which one is capturing resource use associated with the trial per se (i.e., costs of doing research) rather than the costs of providing the therapy. These so-called protocol-driven costs can arise in a number of different ways. For example, to preserve blinding in their comparison of oral gold (auranofin) versus placebo, Thompson et al. (34) required regular blood tests for patients randomized to placebo. In the analysis, they excluded these costs from the placebo control group. But while this exclusion of a cost is a "fix" for the immediate problem, there may be some more subtle cost and outcome consequences of the mandated visit for blood tests in the placebo group. For example, there may be an "ascertainment bias" in that physicians have an opportunity to more closely observe the control group than would be the case in the real world; problems may get picked up quicker in the trial setting merely because the placebo patients were coming into the clinic for 'sham' blood tests. Hence there may be both outcome and cost consequences which should be adjusted for generalizability to a real-world setting.

Another central feature of clinical trials is the emphasis of conforming to the rules mandated by the protocol, i.e., compliance by investigators and patients. Great efforts (e.g., patient diaries, investigator prompting) are typically made in the conduct of a clinical trial to ensure that patients properly consume their prescribed medications and that physicians prescribe such drugs according to protocol. In fact, blinding will cause dosing frequency differences to be subsumed. To the extent that such patients do not comply as well with the prescribed therapy in practice, true effects may be a dilution of those originally observed in the clinical trial. For example, the Lipid Research Clinics Coronary Primary Prevention Trial (35) demonstrated a clear association be-

tween compliance with the study drug (cholestyramine for cholesterol lowering) and outcomes. One must take care in attributing outcome to greater compliance as there are other effects that may confound the apparent compliance effect (36). Nonetheless, if treatment does have an effect, it is clear that compliance at some level must influence the level of that effect.

Observed treatment effect will most likely be diluted when the drug is being prescribed outside the strictures of a trial. More importantly, perhaps, is that compliance differences between treatments in a trial may either underestimate or overestimate those to be expected in practice, since whatever causes differences in compliance (e.g., dosing schedules) will not generally be equally distributed between treatment arms, either within or outside of a trial. Because differences are relevant for economic analyses and compliance differences in turn may lead to efficacy and safety differences, this potential for bias may be very important.

Geographical Transferability of Trial Evidence

Pharmacoeconomic evidence gathered in one country does not always extrapolate well to other countries. As demonstrated by Drummond et al. (37), using the example of misoprostol in reducing NSAID-induced gastrointestinal problems, this portability issue owes much to differences in practice patterns and resource prices between different health care systems. In the Drummond study, even though the price of misoprostol was higher in the United States (compared to the United Kingdom, France, and Belgium), the cost-effectiveness was best in the United States because the cost of managing gastrointestinal problems was higher in the United States due mainly to higher surgeon fees.

An issue that has received less attention is the extent to which the basic epidemiology (i.e., safety and efficacy parameters) from a randomized, controlled trial done in one country can be applied to another country for purposes of estimating cost-effectiveness. Consider, for example, the U.S.-based EPIC trial (38), which compared a new monoclonal antibody (c7E3) against placebo for reducing the risk of abrupt reocclusion following coronary angioplasty. The primary study end point was a composite of death, nonfatal myocardial infarction, unplanned surgical revascularization, unplanned repeat coronary angioplasty, unplanned implantation of a coronary stent, or insertion of an intra-aortic balloon pump for refractory ischemia. Bolus and infusion of c7E3 showed a 35% relative risk reduction against placebo in this composite outcome (12.8% vs. 8.3%, $p = 0.008$). Suppose that one now wanted to use these U.S. trial data to make some inference about the cost-effectiveness of the new drug in another country (e.g., Canada). Can these data be used?

The simplistic route is to take these trial data and attempt to apply Canadian cost data (collected from some nontrial source) for procedures avoided such as coronary angioplasty (PTCA) and coronary artery bypass graft (CABG). A difficulty with this is that the trial protocol did not mandate how these complications should be managed and so U.S. investigators had discretion about whether to use PTCA or CABG or some other intervention. The composite trial end point is therefore a mixture of biological end points (death, non-fatal MI) and health care utilization end points (PTCA, CABG, stents). The utilization-based outcomes will be influenced, inter alia, by availability of resources and reimbursement of procedures within the institution and health care system. Hence, to the extent that trial end points embody country-specific practice patterns and health care utilizations, they may restrict their transferability to other settings.

Selected Patient and Provider Populations

To increase the ratio of statistical signal to noise when estimating a treatment effect, it makes sense to restrict the population for study to those individuals most likely to respond to the new drug. The price of increasing this aspect of internal validity is reduced external validity in that the generalizability of results to populations not studied comes into question. For example, how reasonable is it to presume that the results of cholesterol-lowering trials done predominantly in middle-aged males can be used to justify cholesterol-lowering therapy in the elderly and children (30)? Economics can offer no solution to this problem, but it brings it into sharp focus because cost-effectiveness inferences about a new drug should not be universal—"this drug is cost-effective"—but conditional on factors such as age, sex and disease risk status of the defined patient group.

There are some interesting issues for economic evaluation concerning how persons recruited into trials may be atypical of the disease population from which they were sampled. For example, in measuring patient preferences (utilities) for alternative outcomes using the standard gamble (39), the persons in the trial have already displayed some preference for risk taking by agreeing to be randomized to therapy. That such person's risk-based preferences elicited through the standard gamble may not represent those of the patients who refused the "risky" randomization would not be surprising. An interesting point raised by McPherson (7) is that a randomized trial may actually underestimate a treatment effect, because in the 'real world' patients will choose which therapy they want, and there is some limited evidence to suggest synergy between patient choice and therapeutic outcome. There is also evidence that patients agreeing to be randomized tend to be healthier than the general disease population. This aspect of the sampling done in randomized, controlled trial recruitment would appear to invalidate statistical inference to the general population as "the patients are not a random sample of any useful population to which we might wish to generalize results, nor could they ever be, since by definition of being involved in a trial they have all given consent" (8).

Finally, the health care providers (investigators) in clinical trials will typically be overrepresented by academic physicians, the greater knowledge and skill of whom may tend to lead to an overestimate of the treatment effect that will be realized once the drug is used in the wider community of practitioners. If, for example, diagnostic abilities or inclusion criteria for a trial differ from those in practice, patient populations may differ substantially from those who will eventually receive the treatments with detrimental effects or external validity. Rittenhouse (40) showed the potentially significant biases of trial-based analysis of highly selected populations by comparing the diagnostic abilities observed in the trial with extra-trial data on diagnostic abilities of physicians in a practice environment for the same indication. To some extent, the advent of the large sample cardiovascular randomized trials (e.g., ISIS, GUSTO) will broaden the inferential base of the data with respect to providers, mitigating such problems. However, the potential benefits from these large trials will not generally be available in premarketing environments.

NEW DIRECTIONS

Early experience with pharmacoeconomics relied on retrospective looks at trial data which were never intended to be used for economic purposes. Unavoidably, these pharmacoeconomic analyses relied on modeling techniques to speculate on the economic implications of certain efficacy or safety end points. Data bases were examined, expert opinion solicited or literature surveyed (informally or formally via meta-analytic methods). This information was combined with retrospective analyses of trial data, typically in a decision analytic model. More recently, we have seen the development of prospective trial designs that explicitly incorporate economic data collection. An extreme interpretation might be that the need for modeling has passed, or will, as soon as retrospective pharmacoeconomics ceases to be practiced. Our arguments in this chapter suggest that this would be incorrect.

Although theoretically some of the problems with the randomized, controlled trial can be limited by design, practical difficulties may preclude many such remedies. For example, FDA-mandated placebo controls restrict the latitude of researchers at least for pivotal trials designed for use in U.S. product registration. Other problems with randomized, controlled trials are more inherent with the design. If we can agree that our ultimate interest, at least for pharmacoeconomics, is in some scientifically based notion of both external validity and internal validity, it is clear that no stand-alone method will provide high levels of assurance for both. We have shown that reliance on randomized, controlled trials, even those prospectively designed to include economic variables, will not provide all necessary information for pharmacoeconomics.

Our critique of the randomized, controlled trial, as used in economic evaluations, and examples of attempts at "correcting" for bias suggests that models can improve upon the basic randomized, controlled trial stand-alone study; however, two problems remain. The first is whether such models will be accepted by health care practitioners, insurers or regulatory bodies. The randomized, controlled trial has become such a sacred cow to many that "correcting" its results may appear to be quite inappropriate. Moreover, those concerned with the potential for bias in pharmacoeconomics research (41) may balk at giving license to modelers to adjust randomized, controlled trial-based data. Although we believe that models can provide helpful and timely assistance to the pharmacoeconomist (and other technology assessors), given the lack of methodological standards in the field, the market implications of results, and the susceptibility to a modeling equivalent of "data mining," much care needs to be taken in interpreting and evaluating these studies.

The other problem with our suggestions is related to the first. Even with careful, well-documented and transparent methods in modeling that are accepted by "the customer," there will remain the suspicion that one will only truly know the real world implications of new treatments once they are actually *in* the real world. The timing needs of both pharmaceutical manufacturers as well as users of their products require that technology assessment be accomplished rapidly. The tasks of disseminating valuable products and restricting poor ones both require timely assessment. This fact requires a different approach than might be the case were assessment purely an academic venture. If the time were available (and the cost of waiting more limited) deferring economic assessment to a postmarketing stage might be preferable. At this point, prospective cohort studies might be designed (perhaps even randomized ones in more "naturalistic" settings). While acknowledging the potential value of naturalistic experimental with fewer controls over them, one must question what the contribution really is. With either observational studies or randomized, controlled trials, the potential biases are well known and in some cases measurable and correctable. Naturalistic experiments are potentially confusing hybrids with as yet unknown characteristics concerning the extent of threats to both internal and external validity. More research in this area may be helpful.

In addition to interpretive difficulties, in the pre-marketing environment, the combination of randomized, controlled trials with modeling is the only option available—"naturalistic" settings will not be permitted. In the post-marketing environment, new potential for pharmacoeconomics modeling exists to explore whether the premarketing study claims have been fulfilled. Additional evidence based on observational epidemiology may be very useful in answering questions about the real world implications of using technologies previously evaluated only through randomized, controlled trial and/or modeling studies. Revisiting pharmacoeconomics once post-marketing data are available may be an ideal

way to confirm or question earlier randomized, controlled trial-based results. French governmental authorities have negotiated agreements with firms to incorporate evidence from postmarketing studies in decision making (42,43) so that "real conditions of use" can be examined. This acceptance and revisitation of the issue once additional data are available may be a good procedure to follow for pharmacoeconomics rather than delaying marketing or pricing reimbursement decisions with protracted negotiations based on questioning of the reality of randomized, controlled trial-based results. A more innovative idea has come from Thaler (44) and Hofstee (45) who have in another context suggested that researchers engage in reputational bets on ultimate outcomes of their predictions. One might modestly propose that a similar construct be applied to pharmacoeconomics that is based on randomized, controlled trial data, or, in fact, on pharmacoeconomics in general.

Numerous investigators (10,11,15,46,47) have indicated the value of bringing observational epidemiology to bear on pharmacoeconomics issues. Eddy (10) has emphasized the possible time and cost savings from observational epidemiology methods. Droitcour et al. (47) and the General Accounting Office (11) have supplied a comprehensive argument for combining studies of complementary designs, implying that all designs have strengths that may be exploited for technology assessment. Eddy et al. (15) have argued similarly that formal methods of meta-analysis may be used to combine results from different study designs to eliminate biases. In a test of a combination of modeling and observational data versus randomized, controlled trials, Hlatky et al. (48) indicated a high degree of substitutability. The efforts at modeling in health care are developing rapidly and are exploiting the earlier efforts in other fields (11,47). However, all these suggestions to incorporate observational epidemiology into health care evaluations require data that are only likely to be available after the product has been marketed. Timing considerations may continue to prevent the full incorporation of observational methods in economic evaluations until marketing has occurred. At that point, such evidence can be included to further assist in modeling efforts.

CONCLUSIONS

The acknowledgment of potential bias in randomized, controlled trials (i.e., threats to external validity) used for pharmacoeconomics purposes is slowly occurring (2). The major point of this discussion is that while evidence of effect must be present, and such evidence may need to come from randomized, controlled trials, there is still much value added to be gained by supplementary modeling based on other sources of data. This modeling has always been a necessity in pharmacoeconomics models that retrospectively cull through trial data and piece together economic implications. It will still be necessary if prospective trials incorporate economic data acquisition, as they are doing increasingly. Furthermore, even in postmarketing environments, modeling based upon randomized, controlled trials and PORT-type studies will be valuable. Such evidence will be able to provide more accurate information for input into models than the more conjectural ancillary data available at the premarketing stage of modeling. Formulary listing based on early premarketing models may be usefully revisited several years later to determine if earlier results are borne out in practice. This research needs to appeal to a multiplicity of study designs and requires a dedication to interdisciplinary research and a willingness to modify what has become standard protocol to incorporate new methods. With luck and perseverance, this field can avoid the general prophecy of Max Planck: ''A new scientific truth does not triumph by convincing its opponents and making them see the light, but rather because its opponents eventually die, and a new generation grows up with it'' (49).

REFERENCES

1. Sheldon TA. Please bypass the PORT. *BMJ* 1994;309:142–143.
2. Rittenhouse B. Another deficit problem: the deficit of relevant information when clinical trials are the basis for pharmacoeconomic research. *J Res Pharm Econ* 1996;7(3) (in press).
3. Meinert CL, Tonascia S. *Clinical trials: design, conduct, and analysis.* New York: Oxford University Press, 1986:119.
4. Drummond MF, Davies L. Economic analysis alongside clinical trials: revisiting the methodological issues. *Int J Technol Assess Health Care* 1991;7:561–573.
5. Adams ME, McCall NT, Gray DT, Orza MJ, Chalmers TC. Economic analysis in randomized control trials. *Med Care* 1992;30:231–243.
6. Hennekens CH, Buring JE. *Epidemiology in medicine.* Boston: Little, Brown, 1987.
7. McPherson K. The best and the enemy of the good: randomized controlled trials, uncertainty, and assessing the role of patient choice in medical decision making. *J Epidemiol Community Health* 1994;48: 6–15.
8. Senn SJ. Clinical trials and epidemiology. *J Clin Epidemiol* 1990; 43:628–632.
9. Rubin DB. Estimating causal effects of treatments in randomized and nonrandomized studies. *J Educ Psychol* 1974;66:688–701.
10. Eddy DM. Should we change the rules for evaluating medical technologies? In: Gelijns AC, ed. *Modern methods of clinical investigation.* Washington, DC: National Academy Press, 1990:117–134.
11. U.S. General Accounting Office. *Cross-design synthesis: a new strategy for medical effectiveness research.* U.S. GAO/PEMD-92-18, March 1992.
12. Anderson C. Measuring what works in health care. *Science* 1994;263: 1080–1082.
13. Cook TD, Campbell DT. *Quasi-experimentation: design and analysis issues for field settings.* Boston: Houghton Mifflin, 1979.
14. Kleinbaum DG, Kupper LL, Morganstern H. *Epidemiologic research: principles and quantitative methods.* New York: Van Nostrand–Reinhold, 1982:187.
15. Eddy DM, Hasselblad V, Shachter R. *Meta-analysis by the confidence profile method: the statistical synthesis of evidence.* San Diego: Academic Press, 1992.
16. Buxton MJ, O'Brien BJ. Economic evaluation of ondansetron: preliminary analysis using trial data prior to price setting. *Br J Cancer* 1992; 66(suppl XIX):564–567.
17. Rusthoven J, O'Brien BJ, Rocchi A. Ondansetron versus metoclopramide in the prevention of chemotherapy-induced emesis and nausea: a meta-analysis. *Int J Oncol* 1992;1:443–450.
18. Beck TM, Ciociola AA, Jones SE, et al. Efficacy of oral ondansetron in the prevention of emesis in outpatients receiving cyclophosphamide-based chemotherapy. *Annals Intern Med* 1993;118:407–413.
19. Cubeddu LX, Hoffmann IS, Fuenmayor NT, Finn AL. Efficacy of ondansetron (GR 38032F) and the role of serotonin in cisplatin-induced nausea and vomiting. *N Engl J Med* 1990;332:810–816.
20. Rothman KJ, Michels KB. The continuing unethical use of placebo controls. *N Engl J Med* 1994;331:394–398.
21. Culyer AJ, Maynard AK. Cost-effectiveness of duodenal ulcer treatment. *Soc Sci Med* 1981;15c:3–11.
22. O'Brien BJ, Buxton M, Rushby JA. Cost-effectiveness of the implantable cardioverter defibrillator: a preliminary analysis. *Br Heart J* 1992;68:241–245.
23. Anderson DR, O'Brien BJ, Levine MN, Roberts R, Wells PS, Hirsh J. Efficacy and cost-effectiveness of low molecular weight heparin versus standard heparin in the prevention of deep vein thrombosis following total hip replacement arthroplasty. *Ann Intern Med* 1993; 119:1105–1112.
24. Paiment GD, Wessinger SJ, Harris WH. Survey of prophylaxis against venous thromboembolism in adults undergoing hip surgery. *Clin Orthop* 1987;223:188–193.
25. O'Brien BJ, Anderson D, Goeree R. Cost-effectiveness of enoxaparin versus warfarin prophylaxis against deep vein thrombosis after total hip replacement. *Can Med Assoc J* 1994;150:1083–1172.
26. Drummond MF. Basing prescription drug payment on economic analysis: the case of Australia. *Health Affairs* 1992;11:191–196.
27. CCOHTA (1994) Canadian Coordinating Office for Health Technology Assessment. *Guidelines for the Economic Evaluation of Pharmaceuticals: Canada,* 1st ed. Ottawa: CCOHTA, November 1994.
28. Walt RP, Hunt RH, Misiewicz JJ, et al. Comparison of ranitidine and cimetidine maintenance treatment of duodenal ulcer. *Scand J Gastroenterol* 1984;19:1045–1047.
29. Rittenhouse BE. Removing protocol-induced effects from clinical trials to generate practice-relevant results in economic evaluations. (Submitted)
30. O'Brien BJ. *Cholesterol and coronary heart disease: consensus or controversy?* London: Office of Health Economics, 1991.
31. Edelson JT, Weinstein MC, Tosteson ANA, et al. Long-term cost-effectiveness of various initial monotherapies for mild to moderate hypertension. *JAMA* 1990;263:407–413.
32. Laffel GL, Fineberg HV, Braunwald E. A cost-effectiveness model for thrombosis/reperfusion therapy. *J Am Coll Cardiol* 1987;10 (suppl B):79B–90B.
33. O'Brien BJ, Buxton MJ, Khawaja HT. An economic evaluation of transdermal glyceryl trinitrate in the prevention of intravenous infusion failure. *J Clin Epidemiol* 1990;43:757–763.
34. Thompson MS, Read JL, Hutchings HC, Harris ED. The cost-effectiveness of aurofarin: results of a randomized clinical trial. *J Rheumatol* 1989;15:35–42.
35. Lipid Research Clinics Program. The lipid research clinics coronary primary prevention trial results. I. Reductions in the incidence of coronary heart disease. *JAMA* 1984;251:351–364.
36. Hennekens CH, Buring JE. Methodologic considerations in the design and conduct of randomized trials: the U.S. physicians' health study. *Controlled Clin Trials* 1989;10:142S–150S.
37. Drummond MF, Bloom BS, Carrin G, et al. Issues in the cross-national assessment of health technology. *Int J Technol Assess Health Care* 1992;8:671–682.
38. EPIC Investigators. Use of monoclonal antibody directed against the platelet glycoprotein lib/IIIa receptor in high-risk coronary angioplasty. *N Engl J Med* 1994;330:956–961.
39. Torrance GW. Measurement of health state utilities for economic appraisal: a review. *J Health Econ* 1986;5:1–30.
40. Rittenhouse BE. The relevance of searching for effects under a clinical trial lamp post: a key issue. *Med Decis Making* (in press).
41. Hillman AL, Eisenberg JM, Pauly MV, Bloom BS, Glick H, Kinosian B, Schwartz JS. Avoiding bias in the conduct and reporting of cost-effectiveness research sponsored by pharmaceutical companies. *N Engl J Med* 1991;324:1362–1365.
42. Anonymous. Imigran's French approval. *Scrip* 1992;1759:23.
43. Anonymous. Imigran's pricing in France. *Scrip* 1992;1761:4.
44. Thaler RH. The psychology and economics conference handbook: comments on Simon, on Einhorn and Hogarth, and on Tversky and Kahneman. In: Hogarth RM, Reder MW, eds. *Rational choice: the contrast between economics and psychology.* Chicago: University of Chicago Press, 1986:95–100.
45. Hofstee WKB. Methodological decision rules as research policies: a

betting reconstruction of empirical research. *Acta Psychol (Amst)* 1984;56:93–109.

46. Chrischilles E. The contribution of epidemiology to pharmacoeconomic research. *Drug Infect J* 1992;26:219–229.

47. Droitcour J, Silberman G, Chelimsky E. Cross-design synthesis. *Int J Technol Assess Health Care* 1993;9:440–449.

48. Hlatky MA, Califf RM, Harrell FE, Lee KL, Mark DB, Pryor DB. Comparison of predictions based on observational data with the results of randomized controlled clinical trials of coronary artery bypass surgery. *J Am Coll Cardiol* 1988;11:237–245.

49. Meinert CL, Tonascia S. *Clinical trials: design, conduct, and analysis.* New York: Oxford University Press, 1986:15.

Quality of Life and Pharmacoeconomics in Clinical Trials, Second Edition, edited by B. Spilker.
Lippincott-Raven Publishers, Philadelphia © 1996.

CHAPTER 127

The Future of Pharmacoeconomics

Michael F. Drummond

INTRODUCTION

Predicting the future is notoriously difficult, with the only certainty being that the prediction is going to be wrong. Anyone discussing the future of pharmacoeconomics five years ago would probably not have predicted that the exponential rise in the number of studies would continue, that there would be at least one major international journal (Eisenberg, 1992) (1), and that at least two jurisdictions would have made the provision of economic data mandatory prior to reimbursement (public subsidy) of new medicines (2,3).

However, undeterred by this likely lack of success, I make a few predictions below. These emanate from trends that can already be observed and are organized in the following manner: the future in the methodology of studies, the future in the conduct of studies, and the future in applications and uses of pharmacoeconomics studies.

METHODOLOGY OF STUDIES

In the published literature, I expect to observe a major trend away from modeling studies, incorporating data and assumptions from many sources, toward trial-based studies. Where modeling studies are performed, they are likely to incorporate clinical data from major published meta-analyses or overviews of the effectiveness of particular medicines.

The major driving force behind this change is the need for increased credibility in pharmacoeconomics studies (*vide supra*). Whereas economists themselves are comfortable with models, and often use them in very innovative ways, there is a growing sense of frustration among those from other disciplines, including the major audiences for published studies.

This frustration has arisen because in medicine and pharmaceutical sciences there is much more emphasis on the measurement of outcome, usually within the context of a controlled study. Thus, the data fall where the data fall. By contrast, in a modeling study the analyst can manipulate the data and make assumptions, providing the methods are made explicit. There is a sense in which one can obtain any desired result, depending upon the model and the assumptions used.

Of course, the distinction drawn here between modeling studies and trial-based studies is a little artificial. Some modelling studies draw heavily on data from randomized controlled trials. Some trial-based studies incorporate an element of modeling, either to adapt what was found in the trial to other settings or to project costs and outcomes beyond the period observed in the trial. However, even where modeling is used as an adjunct, the study user is likely to expect the "within-trial" result to be reported and increased emphasis is likely to be placed on what was found, rather than what was assumed.

The demand for trial-based pharmacoeconomic studies is likely to become most apparent in situations in which measurement is considered feasible, that is, where the clinical effect of the medicine concerned can be observed within a reasonable amount of time, or where the impact on resource use of superior efficacy or a better side effect profile can be assessed during a clinical trial. The estimation of these parameters through physician Delphi panels (3a) is likely to be regarded as less convincing in the future.

This leaves those problematic situations where the true clinical effect of a medicine can only be observed as the result of a large, long-term, clinical trial, e.g., the impact of lowering cholesterol on overall mortality, or the impact of hormone replacement therapy on fractures in postmenopausal women. Here, I still expect a resistance from some

M. F. Drummond: Centre for Health Economics, University of York, Heslington, York YO1 5DD, England.

quarters to modeling studies, and I have no obvious solution for the analyst, other than to keep refining the models as new data become available. Also, it seems somewhat unfair to take economists to task for modeling in these situations, since they are usually only trying to predict the likely outcome of the use of drugs that have already been licensed for the indications concerned.

Another likely trend is that the clinical trials themselves will become more naturalistic; that is, they will be undertaken in settings that more closely reflect regular clinical practice. This change would probably have come about in any case, but it has certainly also been driven by the increased interest in pharmacoeconomics, where data closely reflecting the real world are required for the assessment of cost-effectiveness.

The trend toward naturalistic studies poses methodological challenges for those conducting trials and may be somewhat curtailed during Phase IIIA, where placebo comparisons are more common to assess safety and efficacy and where close monitoring of patients is required. However, there appear to be fewer obstacles in Phase IIIB or Phase IV, and many pharmaceutical companies are realizing that, pharmacoeconomics aside, such trials have greater credibility with clinical practitioners.

The trend toward trial-based studies is already posing new challenges to economists, and in one or two areas I expect to see more discussion and debate in the future. One such area is the statistical analysis of economic data (4,5), where analysts have only just begun to grapple with sample size calculations for pharmacoeconomic studies and the analysis of differences in cost-effectiveness ratios. I expect that widely accepted methods will be established within the next 5 years.

Another area that is beginning to tax the minds of economists is the analysis of economic data from multinational trials. Whereas it is customary to pool the clinical data from such trials, this may be less legitimate for the economic data, where a number of factors (not controlled for in the trial protocol) may influence resource use and cost (6). (These include such factors as relative price levels and the availability of health care resources.)

Even where pooling of resource use data is acceptable, can these data then merely be priced in a range of currencies? Where pooling is *not* appropriate, should data from individual countries be used, as it is likely that small sample sizes will prevent statistically significant differences being shown? Also, if individual country resource data are used, should these be combined, in a cost-effectiveness ratio, with the individual country effectiveness data or with the overall trial result? The latter would be consistent with the reporting of the clinical data, but may be inappropriate if it was thought that the different resource inputs in different locations did influence clinical outcome.

There are no right or wrong answers to some of these questions, but over the next few years I expect widely accepted protocols for the analysis of multicountry data to emerge. Such protocols are likely to be embodied in the analysis plan for the economic study in order to minimize the chances of bias arising from selective analysis of the economic data at a later stage.

Apart from the general methodological issues arising from a trend toward trial-based studies, the other main area of methods development is likely to be in aspects of economic benefit measurement. There is already a sizeable literature on the measurement of indirect costs and benefits (7), on alternative methods of health state preference valuation (8,9) and on the assessment of willingness-to-pay for improved health (10).

Whereas I expect these issues to continue to preoccupy economists, my prediction is that debates about which is the "best" benefit measure are unlikely to be high on the agenda of the users of pharmacoeconomic data. For example, I suspect that they will be unlikely to accept estimates of willingness-to-pay as the only measure of benefit, even if this is to be preferred theoretically. They are much more likely to require data on a range of economic benefit measures, including descriptive data on physical effects and quality of life, and to come to their own judgment on the relative weights to be assigned to one outcome compared with another.

I also expect to see more discussion of the potential for standardization of economic evaluation methods. Several papers have already reviewed the extent of agreement or disagreement on aspects of methodology (11,12). Also, the various government and nongovernment guidelines for economic studies (*vide supra*) embody elements of methodological standards. It is already possible to detect key areas of consensus, for example on the appropriate perspective (viewpoint) for studies and on the choice of comparator. If, as I suspect, economic studies are to become more important in the future, more agreement on methodological standards will be of benefit both to the users of economic data and to those within industry and academia who generate them.

Finally, while trial-based studies are likely to become increasingly prominent in the published literature, activity in modelling will not necessarily subside. I expect that much more of such work will be internal to pharmaceutical companies themselves, exploring issues such as "what would be the likely economic impact of this medicine if the expected clinical effects are observed in future clinical trials?" Or, "what would be the likely economic benefits of investing resources in the development of a more convenient route of administration of a particular medicine?" Therefore, economic analyses, focused mainly on modeling, are likely to play a greater role in medicine development and commercial decisions.

CONDUCT OF STUDIES

As pharmacoeconomics has grown in importance, much more attention has been focused on the credibility of studies in the public domain. The use of acceptable methods is one component of this, but in the United States in particular a growing emphasis has been placed on issues of conduct, including the declaration of financial interests and the nature of the contractual relationship between the researcher and the sponsoring company (13).

The issues of credibility need to be addressed if pharmacoeconomics is to have any future, and it is therefore likely that both researchers and the sponsors of studies will ultimately realize that some regulation of the process is beneficial to both parties, as well as to the users of studies. Therefore, the question is one of how far such controls should go. The *New England Journal of Medicine* (14) has recently introduced restrictions on the publication of pharmacoeconomic studies. Studies will have to be conducted by individuals with no financial links with the research sponsor (if this is a pharmaceutical company) or any of its competitors, and the funding for the study will have to be to a nonprofit organization, such as a university or hospital.

Whether other journals impose the same restrictions remains to be seen, but it is likely that many journals will take a greater interest in the financial links between researchers and sponsors, and the nature of the contract for the research. In the future I expect that the minimum requirements of most journals will include a declaration of interests and evidence of a contract giving rights to publication. In general, I expect the future conduct of pharmacoeconomic studies to mirror that of clinical studies. That is a protocol and an analysis plan will be specified up front. This will obviously become easier when there is more standardization of economic evaluation methodology.

It is much harder to predict the likely role of company personnel in pharmacoeconomic studies in the future. In clinical research company personnel are often coauthors of papers, if their contribution to study design and analysis warrants this. The alternative scenario for pharmacoeconomics is that, because of the concerns about bias expressed by the *New England Journal of Medicine* and other parties, the vast majority of studies will be undertaken by independent researchers having an "arms-length" relationship with the company. Thus the role for company personnel would be a facilitating one, with no expectation of authorship on papers.

Therefore, under this scenario, company personnel are likely to play a much more important role in undertaking internal modeling studies, in commissioning work from outside experts, and in preparing company submissions in those jurisdictions in which the provision of pharmacoeconomics data is mandatory. Authorship on published papers for company personnel would therefore likely be restricted to nonproduct-related issues, such as general methodological developments, and to situations in which they could not possibly have influenced the outcome of the study. My guess is that the scenario outlined above is likely to be realized, because of the concerns about potential bias in economic studies, as compared with clinical studies. However, this would be regrettable, because an ideal world research contributions would be recognized irrespective of the researcher's affiliation. It is therefore incumbent on those working in pharmacoeconomics to develop procedures that minimize actual and perceived bias.

APPLICATIONS AND USES OF PHARMACOECONOMICS

The most obvious change over the past 5 years has been the development of formal requirements for economic data in a number of jurisdictions. However, a much more fundamental and lasting change is the growing recognition, on the part of health care decision makers at all levels, that value for money criteria are important.

Therefore, whereas we might expect that a few more jurisdictions will make the provision of economic data mandatory, the greatest expansion in the use of pharmacoeconomics is likely to be in the communication by pharmaceutical companies of economic data to their customers. This is not to say that there will not be a growth in guidelines for pharmacoeconomics studies. On the contrary, in countries where there is no formal requirement for the submission of economic data, methodological or ethical guidelines assume considerable importance if reliable data are to be generated (15).

The recent voluntary guidelines in the United Kingdom (16) and the report of the University of Pennsylvania Task Force in the United States (A.L. Hillman, *personal communication*, 1994) suggest that this might be the case, as neither of these countries currently mandates the provision of economic data. In countries such as the United States and the United Kingdom, where there is no central pricing or reimbursement procedure for pharmaceuticals, pharmacoeconomic data have the greatest potential use in formulary decisions, at the level of the hospital or health maintenance organization (HMO), or in influencing individual prescribers. Here partnerships are already emerging between industry and major providers (e.g., HMOs in the United States) in undertaking joint research projects (17). The objective of this research is often to assess whether the adoption of a new drug *does* lead to more cost-effective health care provision in a practical setting. I expect to see a growth in such studies over the next 5 years, in Phase III as well as Phase IV.

At the same time, jurisdictions with a formal requirement for the provision of economic data are likely to review their procedures. (Indeed, this is already happening in Australia.) One component of such a review will be to assess whether the methodological guidelines laid down have proved workable in practice. That is, have companies been able to comply with the guidelines in undertaking studies, and have official committees been able to appraise company submissions adequately?

However, a much more important aspect of the review of formal requirements relates to their overall objectives and to whether these are being met. It is important to make a distinction between the objective of cost containment and that of value for money. It has been argued that formal guidelines for the provision of pharmacoeconomic data may not be a very efficient form of cost containment (15). In addition, the increased transparency implicit in such a process may be as much a constraint on government as it is on industry. This is already proving to be the case in Australia, where it has now been agreed that companies will have access to the assessments, by government officials, of their submissions.

In the long run, the only sustainable objective of formal economic data requirements is to secure better value for money. Hence the assessment of their worth has to be in terms of whether reimbursement or pricing committees make better decisions (i.e., those leading to more cost-effective health care provision) than in the absence of such data. In practice, this may be difficult to show one way or the other.

Another likely change in the requirements for formal submission of economic data relates to the timing of such submissions. In Australia and Ontario, the main focus is currently on provision of data once a new drug has marketing authorization. The same is true for submissions to pricing committees in some European countries.

However, there is a growing recognition that economic data provided at product launch are at best preliminary, since much of the clinical data may relate to efficacy rather than effectiveness and there is little experience with the use of the drug in regular clinical practice. Therefore, in the future there may be a trend toward revisiting the economic issues after a drug has been on the market for 3 to 4 years, although the terms and conditions for such a re-evaluation are unclear.

This relates back to the earlier discussion about modeling versus trial-based studies. It may be that, at the time of launch, evidence based on models drawing on efficacy data may be acceptable. Whereas for the review 4 years after launch, more measurements of actual impacts on cost and outcomes may be required.

CONCLUSIONS

This chapter has attempted to make some predictions for the future of pharmacoeconomics, focusing on the next 5 years. The following arguments have been made:

1. *The main trend in the development of methods:* This trend is likely to be toward the measurement of economic parameters alongside clinical trials and to lead to more naturalistic trials and to developments in the statistical analysis of economic data.
2. *The main trend in the conduct of studies:* This trend will be toward the development of ethical codes that will have, as their main purpose, maintenance or improvement of the credibility of pharmacoeconomic studies. Such a trend is inevitable because, in the long run, it is in the interests not only of the users of studies but also researchers and sponsors;
3. *The main trend in the application and use of studies:* This trend will not be toward the growth of formal requirements, such as in Australia, but toward a more widespread interest in economic data at all levels in the health care system. Therefore, there will be a number of potential audiences

for pharmacoeconomic data. The main role for guidelines for the provision of data will be in the establishment of standards for the methodology and conduct of studies. There will also be a move toward greater harmonization in the standards of analysis required by different jurisdictions. But, on the other hand, I could be wrong.

ACKNOWLEDGMENTS

I am grateful to Linda Davies for comments on an earlier draft and to Vanessa Windass for secretarial assistance. All the predictions are my own responsibility.

REFERENCES

1. Eisenberg JM. Why a journal or pharmacoeconomics? *Pharmacoeconomics* 1992;1(1):2–4.
2. Commonwealth of Australia. *Guidelines for the pharmaceutical industry on preparation of submissions to the Pharmaceutical Benefits Advisory Committee.* Canberra: Australian Government Publishing Service, 1992.
3. Ministry of Health (Ontario). *Ontario guidelines for economic analysis of pharmaceutical products.* Toronto: Ministry of Health, 1994.
3a. Davies LM, Drummond MF. Assessment of costs and benefits of drug therapy for treatment resistant schizophrenia in the United Kingdom. *Br J Psychiatry* 1993;162:38–42.
4. O'Brien B, Drummond MF, Labelle R, Willan A. In search of power and significance: issues in the design and analysis of stochastic economic appraisals. *Med Care* 1994;32:150–163.
5. Van Hout BA, Al MJ, Gordon GS, Rutten FFH. Costs, effects and cost-effectiveness ratios alongside a clinical trial. *J Health Econ* 1994;3:309–319.
6. Drummond MF, Bloom BS, Carrin G, et al. Issues in the cross-national assessment of health technology. *Int J Technol Assess Health Care* 1992;8:671–682.
7. Koopmanschap MA, Rutten FFH. Indirect costs in economic studies: confronting the confusion. *PharmacoEconomics* 1993;4:446–454.
8. Mehrez A, Gafni A. Healthy years equivalents versus quality-adjusted life-years: in pursuit of progress. *Med Decis Making* 1993;13:287–292.
9. Johannesson M, Pliskin JS, Weinstein MC. Are healthy years equivalents an improvement over quality-adjusted life-years? *Med Decision Making* 1993;13:281–286.
10. Johannesson M, Jönsson B. Economic evaluation in health care: is there a role for cost-benefit analysis? *Health Policy* 1991;17:1–23.
11. Drummond MF, Brandt A, Luce B, et al. Standardizing economic evaluations in health care: practice, problems and potential. *Int J Technol Assess Health Care* 1993;9:26–36.
12. Luce BR, Simpson K. *Methods of cost-effectiveness analysis: areas of consensus and debate.* Washington, DC: Battelle (MEDTAP) Research Center, 1992.
13. Hillman AL, Eisenberg JM, Pauly MV, et al. Avoiding bias in the conduct and reporting of cost-effectiveness research sponsored by pharmaceutical companies. *N Engl J Med* 1991;324:1362–1365.
14. Kassirer JP, Angell M. The Journal's policy on cost-effectiveness analyses (editorial). *N Engl J Med* 1994;331:669–670.
15. Drummond MF. Guidelines for pharmacoeconomic studies: the ways forward. *PharmacoEconomics* 1994 (in press.)
16. Department of Health (UK) and the Association of the British Pharmaceutical Industry. *Pharmaceutical Industry and Department of Health Guidelines for the Economic Analysis of Medicines.* London: Department of Health, 1994.
17. Oster G, Borok GM, Menzin J, Heyse JF, Epstein RS, et al. A randomized trial to assess effectiveness and costs in clinical practice: rationale and design of the Cholesterol Reduction Intervention Study (CRIS). *Controlled Clin Trials* 1994;14:235–250.
18. Drummond MF. The emerging government requirement for economic evaluation of pharmaceuticals. *PharmacoEconomics* 1994;6(suppl 1):42–50.

Subject Index

Subject Index

Instruments Index

Instruments of Quality of Life Index